The
MAXWELL
LEADERSHIP
BIBLE

THIS BIBLE BELONGS TO

GIVEN BY

DATE

OCCASION

The
MAXWELL
LEADERSHIP
BIBLE

The
MAXWELL
LEADERSHIP
BIBLE

NKJV
NEW
KING
JAMES
VERSION™

John C. Maxwell
Executive Editor

THOMAS NELSON BIBLES

A Division of Thomas Nelson, Inc.
www.ThomasNelson.com

CONTENTS

THE OLD TESTAMENT

THE NEW TESTAMENT

INTRODUCTION

Where do most people go to learn leadership? The answer to that question today is that they search many places. Some examine the world of politics. Others seek models in the entertainment industry. Many look to the world of business. Most people seem to look to successful CEOs, management consultants, and theoreticians with Ph.D.s to learn about leadership.

But the truth is, the best source of leadership teaching today is the same as it has been for thousands of years. If you want to learn leadership, go to the greatest Book on leadership ever written—the Bible.

You are holding in your hands a tool that has the potential to change your life and the course of your development as a spiritual leader. It is a Bible that draws out the leadership principles that have been woven into it by the One who invented leadership. Who could possibly teach us more about leadership than God Himself?

With so many different Bibles to choose from on the shelves of bookstores today, why would anyone take the time and energy to create a Leadership Bible?

The Crying Need of the Church Today Is Leadership

The most critical problem facing the church today is the leadership vacuum that grew during the Twentieth Century. Church expert and statistician George Barna asserts, "Leadership remains one of the glaring needs of the church. People are often willing to follow God's vision, but too frequently they have no exposure to either vision or true leadership." Just a few years ago, Barna penned some sobering conclusions based on his research: "After fifteen years of digging into the world around me, I have reached several conclusions regarding the future of the Christian church in America. The central conclusion is that the American church is dying due to lack of strong leadership. In this time of unprecedented opportunity and plentiful resources, the church is actually losing influence. The primary reason is the lack of leadership. . . . Nothing is more important than leadership."

Christ left His church on earth to do work that has an eternal impact. If the local church isn't well led, then the bride of Christ suffers, and she will not be able fulfill her mission for this generation.

God Himself Calls Us to Leadership

God is the Ultimate Leader, and He calls every believer to lead others. God could have arranged His creation any number of ways. He chose to create human beings who possess spirits and the capacity to relate to Him and follow Him, yet who are not forced to do so. When mankind fell into sin, God could have easily executed a plan of redemption that did not include sinful people in the process. But He has called us to participate and to lead others as we follow Him. He makes that clear from the beginning: "Let Us make man in Our image, according to Our likeness; let them have dominion . . ." (Gen. 1:26).

I wholeheartedly believe that everything rises and falls on leadership. By that I mean that, more than anything else, the leadership of any group or organization will determine its success or failure. You can see the impact of leadership frequently in the Bible. In ancient Israel, when God's people had a good king, all was well with the nation. When they had a bad king, things went poorly for everyone. That's why Scripture teaches that without a vision people perish (see Prov. 29:18).

The call to leadership is a consistent pattern in the Bible. When God decided to raise up a nation of His own, He didn't call upon the masses. He called out one leader—Abraham. When He wanted to deliver His people out of Egypt, He didn't guide them as a group. He raised up a leader to do it—Moses. When it came time for the people to cross into the Promised Land, they followed one man—Joshua. Every time God desires to do something great, He calls a leader to step forward. Today He still calls leaders to step forward for every great work.

Believers Often Misunderstand the True Nature of Leadership

Somewhere along the way, countless Christians became convinced that if they were going to follow Christ, they must become sheepish, quiet, and withdrawn. The problem is that they have confused meekness with weakness. As Christians we recognize our own weaknesses, but that is when God's strength is perfected in us (see 2 Cor. 12:9). What God desires is that we display a broken boldness.

A follower of God should be a leader of people. That's more than just being "boss" or having a leadership position. And it certainly doesn't mean being pushy or in control. Jesus taught that it means serving others (see Matt. 20:25–28). While there is a gift of leadership (according to Romans 12:8), you need not possess that gift to exert your influence in a Christlike way. Leadership is influence—nothing more, nothing less. If you are being salt and light as Jesus commanded, then you have begun to obey God's call to leadership.

All Believers Can Further Their Potential with Leadership

One of the most important leadership lessons I teach—it's the first law in The 21 Irrefutable Laws of Leadership—is the Law of the Lid, which states, "Leadership ability determines a person's level of effectiveness." That is key when working with others. Greater than resources, talent, money, or intelligence, leadership makes the difference when it comes to making an impact. Consequently, my goal in creating this Leadership Bible is to enable you to raise the "lid" on your own effectiveness. I want you to reach your potential in Christ! To become more Christlike, you need to think and act more like a leader. You must become a person of influence.

Good Leadership Is the Best Means for Leaving a Lasting Legacy

We live in an age of tolerance, where protecting feelings is more highly valued than proclaiming the truth. People look with suspicion upon anyone who desires to influence others to embrace their beliefs. I want to encourage you to buck popular opinion. As Thomas Jefferson proclaimed, "In matters of fashion, swim with the current. In matters of conscience, stand like a rock."

I want to challenge you to become a dedicated student of leadership—if you aren't already one. Becoming a good leader may not guarantee that you will be able to leave a spiritual legacy for future generations, but it certainly provides you the greatest opportunity to do so.

The Law of Legacy states, "True success is measured by succession." A legacy that does not include people has no eternal value. That is why leadership is critical. Make it your aim to practice transformational leadership, where people's lives are changed from the inside out. That kind of leadership is based on character, conviction, and Christlikeness. In other words, transformational leadership follows the pattern laid down in Scripture.

The need of the hour is great. That is why I have dedicated my life to teaching leadership in the church. And I will continue to do so until God calls me home. My hope is that this Leadership Bible will be of great value and assistance to you. In addition to God's Word, which is more precious than riches, it contains leadership truths, principles, and examples which I have drawn from the Scriptures and attempted to make accessible through case studies, profiles, outlines, and lessons. Study from it, use it in your prayer times, teach from it, and use it as a reference tool as you face leadership challenges at home, in the marketplace, and at church.

My prayer is that you will be transformed by spending time with the men and women God has used as leaders to change the world for millennia. And if you are transformed as a leader, then you won't be able to keep from influencing your world.

Dr. John C. Maxwell

GOD HAS ALREADY CALLED *YOU* TO LEAD!

Leadership is for everyone! How can I make such a bold claim? Because every person who accepts Christ is called to influence others. Everyone. Leadership is not just for a select few.

Years ago in his book *Spiritual Leadership,* J. Oswald Sanders gave the best definition of leadership I've ever read. He simply stated, "Leadership is influence." I have embraced that definition and taught it to thousands and thousands over the years. If you are a follower of Christ, then you recognize that you are called to influence others. Jesus said it this way: "You are the salt of the earth. . . . You are the light of the world. . . . Let your light so shine before men, that they may see your good works and glorify your Father in heaven" (Matt. 5:13–16).

It doesn't matter if you are a CEO or a stay-at-home mom; if you call yourself a Christian, then you are called to influence others. That's why it's important for you to learn to become a better leader—whether you are the parent in a family, the pastor of a church, the president of a company, or a potential leader for the next generation.

The problem is that, if you are like most people, you may not wake up in the morning, look in the mirror and say, "Now, there's a godly, effective leader if I ever saw one." Today most people don't believe they can make a positive impact on the world they live in. Even most pastors feel this way. In 1997 the Barna Research Group reported that 95 percent of American pastors said they don't believe they have the spiritual gift of leadership. Nor do they feel they have been adequately prepared for the task of leadership.

The truth is that few people are naturals when it comes to leading others. But everyone has potential. I believe you can become a better leader, regardless of your age, gender, marital status, or profession.

Sociologists say that even introverted people will influence an average of 10,000 people in their lifetime. Just think about that! Someone who's not even trying to lead others will impact many. Just think about what one person can do if he or she is intentional about leading—as Jesus directed us to be. What kind of impact potential has God put inside of you?

I want you to see yourself as a leader. I want you to learn from the best leaders who ever lived—the men and women in the Bible. No matter how strong or weak your leadership is—whether you are a "4" or a "9"—I want you to improve and reach your leadership potential for the glory of God.

Your friend,

John C. Maxwell

PREFACE

Purpose

In the preface to the 1611 edition, the translators of the Authorized Version, known popularly as the King James Bible, state that it was not their purpose "to make a new translation . . . but to make a good one better." Indebted to the earlier work of William Tyndale and others, they saw their best contribution to consist in revising and enhancing the excellence of the English versions which had sprung from the Reformation of the sixteenth century. In harmony with the purpose of the King James scholars, the translators and editors of the present work have not pursued a goal of innovation. They have perceived the Holy Bible, New King James Version, as a continuation of the labors of the earlier translators, thus unlocking for today's readers the spiritual treasures found especially in the Authorized Version of the Holy Scriptures.

A Living Legacy

For nearly four hundred years, and throughout several revisions of its English form, the King James Bible has been deeply revered among the English-speaking peoples of the world. The precision of translation for which it is historically renowned, and its majesty of style, have enabled that monumental version of the word of God to become the mainspring of the religion, language, and legal foundations of our civilization.

Although the Elizabethan period and our own era share in zeal for technical advance, the former period was more aggressively devoted to classical learning. Along with this awakened concern for the classics came a flourishing companion interest in the Scriptures, an interest that was enlivened by the conviction that the manuscripts were providentially handed down and were a trustworthy record of the inspired Word of God. The King James translators were committed to producing an English Bible that would be a precise translation, and by no means a paraphrase or a broadly approximate rendering. On the one hand, the scholars were almost as familiar with the original languages of the Bible as with their native English. On the other hand, their reverence for the divine Author and His Word assured a translation of the Scriptures in which only a principle of utmost accuracy could be accepted.

In 1786 Catholic scholar Alexander Geddes said of the King James Bible, "If accuracy and strictest attention to the letter of the text be supposed to constitute an excellent version, this is of all versions the most excellent." George Bernard Shaw became a literary legend in our century because of his severe and often humorous criticisms of our most cherished values. Surprisingly, however, Shaw pays the following tribute to the scholars commissioned by King James: "The translation was extraordinarily well done because to the translators what they were translating was not merely a curious collection of ancient books written by different authors in different stages of culture, but the Word of God divinely revealed through His chosen and expressly inspired scribes. In this conviction they carried out their work with boundless reverence and care and achieved a beautifully artistic result." History agrees with these estimates. Therefore, while seeking to unveil the excellent *form* of the traditional English Bible, special care has also been taken in the present edition to preserve the work of *precision* which is the legacy of the 1611 translators.

Complete Equivalence in Translation

Where new translation has been necessary in the New King James Version, the most complete representation of the original has been rendered by considering the history of usage and etymology of words in their contexts. This principle of complete equivalence seeks to preserve *all* of the information in the text, while presenting it in good literary form. Dynamic equivalence, a recent procedure in Bible translation, commonly results in paraphrasing where a more literal rendering is needed to reflect a specific and vital sense. For example, complete equivalence truly renders the original text in expressions such as "lifted her voice and wept" (Gen. 21:16); "I gave you cleanness of teeth" (Amos 4:6); "Jesus met them, saying, 'Rejoice!' " (Matt. 28:9); and " 'Woman, what does your concern have to do with Me?' " (John 2:4). Complete equivalence translates fully, in order to provide an English text that is both accurate and readable.

In keeping with the principle of complete equivalence, it is the policy to translate interjections which are commonly omitted in modern language renderings of the Bible. As an example, the interjection *behold,* in the older King James editions, continues to have a place in English usage, especially in dramatically calling attention to a spectacular scene, or an event of profound importance such as the Immanuel prophecy of Isaiah 7:14. Consequently, *behold* is retained for these occasions in the present edition. However, the Hebrew and Greek originals for this word can be translated variously, depending on the circumstances in the passage. Therefore, in addition to *behold,* words such as *indeed, look, see,* and *surely* are also rendered to convey the appropriate sense suggested by the context in each case.

In faithfulness to God and to our readers, it was deemed appropriate that all participating scholars sign a statement affirming their belief in the verbal and plenary inspiration of Scripture, and in the inerrancy of the original autographs.

Devotional Quality

The King James scholars readily appreciated the intrinsic beauty of divine revelation. They accordingly disciplined their talents to render well-chosen English words of their time, as well as a graceful, often musical arrangement of language, which has stirred the hearts of Bible readers through the years. The translators, the committees, and the editors of the present edition, while sensitive to the late-twentieth-century English idiom, and while adhering faithfully to the Hebrew, Aramaic, and Greek texts, have sought to maintain those lyrical and devotional qualities that are so highly regarded in the Authorized Version. This devotional quality is especially apparent in the poetic and prophetic books, although even the relatively plain style of the Gospels and Epistles cannot strictly be likened, as sometimes suggested, to modern newspaper style. The Koine Greek of the New Testament is influenced by the Hebrew background of the writers, for whom even the gospel narratives were not merely flat utterance, but often song in various degrees of rhythm.

The Style

Students of the Bible applaud the timeless devotional character of our historic Bible. Yet it is also universally understood that our language, like all living languages, has undergone profound change since 1611. Subsequent revisions of the King James Bible have sought to keep abreast of changes in English speech. The present work is a further step toward this objective. Where obsolescence and other reading difficulties exist, present-day vocabulary, punctuation, and grammar have been carefully integrated. Words representing ancient objects, such as *chariot* and *phylactery,* have no modern substitutes and are therefore retained.

A special feature of the New King James Version is its conformity to the thought flow of the 1611 Bible. The reader discovers that the sequence and selection of words, phrases, and clauses of the new edition, while much clearer, are so close to the traditional that there is remarkable ease in listening to the reading of either edition while following with the other.

In the discipline of translating biblical and other ancient languages, a standard method of transliteration, that is, the English spelling of untranslated words, such as names of persons and places, has never

been commonly adopted. In keeping with the design of the present work, the King James spelling of untranslated words is retained, although made uniform throughout. For example, instead of the spellings *Isaiah* and *Elijah* in the Old Testament, and *Esaias* and *Elias* in the New Testament, *Isaiah* and *Elijah* now appear in both Testaments.

King James doctrinal and theological terms, for example, *propitiation, justification,* and *sanctification,* are generally familiar to English-speaking peoples. Such terms have been retained except where the original language indicates need for a more precise translation.

Readers of the Authorized Version will immediately be struck by the absence of several pronouns: *thee, thou,* and *ye* are replaced by the simple *you,* while *your* and *yours* are substituted for *thy* and *thine* as applicable. *Thee, thou, thy* and *thine* were once forms of address to express a special relationship to human as well as divine persons. These pronouns are no longer part of our language. However, reverence for God in the present work is preserved by capitalizing pronouns, including *You, Your,* and *Yours,* which refer to Him. Additionally, capitalization of these pronouns benefits the reader by clearly distinguishing divine and human persons referred to in a passage. Without such capitalization the distinction is often obscure, because the antecedent of a pronoun is not always clear in the English translation.

In addition to the pronoun usages of the seventeenth century, the *-eth* and *-est* verb endings, so familiar in the earlier King James editions, are now obsolete. Unless a speaker is schooled in these verb endings, there is common difficulty in selecting the correct form to be used with a given subject of the verb in vocal prayer. That is, should we use *love, loveth,* or *lovest? do, doeth, doest,* or *dost? have, hath,* or *hast?* Because these forms are obsolete, contemporary English usage has been substituted for the previous verb endings.

In older editions of the King James Version, the frequency of the connective *and* far exceeded the limits of present English usage. Also, biblical linguists agree that the Hebrew and Greek original words for this conjunction may commonly be translated otherwise, depending on the immediate context. Therefore, instead of *and,* alternatives such as *also, but, however, now, so, then,* and *thus* are accordingly rendered in the present edition, when the original language permits.

The real character of the Authorized Version does not reside in its archaic pronouns or verbs or other grammatical forms of the seventeenth century, but rather in the care taken by its scholars to impart the letter and spirit of the original text in a majestic and reverent style.

The Format

The format of the New King James Version is designed to enhance the vividness and devotional quality of the Holy Scriptures:

- Subject headings assist the reader to identify topics and transitions in the biblical content.
- Words or phrases in *italics* indicate expressions in the original language which require clarification by additional English words, as also done throughout the history of the King James Bible.
- *Oblique type* in the New Testament indicates a quotation from the Old Testament.
- Verse numbers in **bold type** indicate the beginning of a paragraph.
- Prose is divided into paragraphs to indicate the structure of thought.
- Poetry is structured as contemporary verse to reflect the poetic form and beauty of the passage in the original language.
- The covenant name of God was usually translated from the Hebrew as "LORD" or "GOD" (using capital letters as shown) in the King James Old Testament. This tradition is maintained. In the present edition the name is so capitalized whenever the covenant name is quoted in the New Testament from a passage in the Old Testament.

The Old Testament Text

The Hebrew Bible has come down to us through the scrupulous care of ancient scribes who copied the original text in successive generations. By the sixth century A.D. the scribes were succeeded by a group known as the Masoretes, who continued to preserve the sacred Scriptures for another five hundred years in a form known as the Masoretic Text. Babylonia, Palestine, and Tiberias were the main centers of Masoretic activity; but by the tenth century A.D. the Masoretes of Tiberias, led by the family of ben Asher, gained the ascendancy. Through subsequent editions, the ben Asher text became in the twelfth century the only recognized form of the Hebrew Scriptures.

Daniel Bomberg printed the first Rabbinic Bible in 1516–17; that work was followed in 1524–25 by a second edition prepared by Jacob ben Chayyim and also published by Bomberg. The text of ben Chayyim was adopted in most subsequent Hebrew Bibles, including those used by the King James translators. The ben Chayyim text was also used for the first two editions of Rudolph Kittel's *Biblia Hebraica* of 1906 and 1912. In 1937 Paul Kahle published a third edition of *Biblia Hebraica*. This edition was based on the oldest dated manuscript of the ben Asher text, the Leningrad Manuscript B19a (A.D. 1008), which Kahle regarded as superior to that used by ben Chayyim.

For the New King James Version the text used was the 1967/1977 Stuttgart edition of the *Biblia Hebraica*, with frequent comparisons being made with the Bomberg edition of 1524–25. The Septuagint (Greek) Version of the Old Testament and the Latin Vulgate also were consulted. In addition to referring to a variety of ancient versions of the Hebrew Scriptures, the New King James Version draws on the resources of relevant manuscripts from the Dead Sea caves. In the few places where the Hebrew was so obscure that the 1611 King James was compelled to follow one of the versions, but where information is now available to resolve the problems, the New King James Version follows the Hebrew text. Significant variations are recorded in the center reference column.

The New Testament Text

There is more manuscript support for the New Testament than for any other body of ancient literature. Over five thousand Greek, eight thousand Latin, and many more manuscripts in other languages attest the integrity of the New Testament. There is only one basic New Testament used by Protestants, Roman Catholics, and Orthodox, by conservatives and liberals. Minor variations in hand copying have appeared through the centuries, before mechanical printing began about A.D. 1450.

Some variations exist in the spelling of Greek words, in word order, and in similar details. These ordinarily do not show up in translation and do not affect the sense of the text in any way.

Other manuscript differences such as omission or inclusion of a word or a clause, and two paragraphs in the Gospels, should not overshadow the overwhelming degree of *agreement* which exists among the ancient records. Bible readers may be assured that the most important differences in English New Testaments of today are due, not to manuscript divergence, but to the way in which translators view the task of translation: How literally should the text be rendered? How does the translator view the matter of biblical inspiration? Does the translator adopt a paraphrase when a literal rendering would be quite clear and more to the point? The New King James Version follows the historic precedent of the Authorized Version in maintaining a literal approach to translation, except where the idiom of the original language cannot be translated directly into our tongue.

The King James New Testament was based on the traditional text of the Greek-speaking churches, first published in 1516, and later called the Textus Receptus or Received Text. Although based on the relatively few available manuscripts, these were representative of many more which existed at the time but only became known later. In the late nineteenth century, B. Westcott and F. Hort taught that this text had been officially edited by the fourth-century church, but a total lack of historical evidence for this event has forced a revision of the theory. It is now widely held that the Byzantine Text that largely supports the Textus Receptus has as much right as the Alexandrian or any other tradition to be weighed in determining the text of the New Testament. Those readings in the Textus Receptus which have weak support are indicated in the center reference column as being opposed by both Critical and Majority Texts (see "Center-Column Notes").

Since the 1880s most contemporary translations of the New Testament have relied upon a relatively few manuscripts discovered chiefly in the late nineteenth and early twentieth centuries. Such translations depend primarily on two manuscripts, Codex Vaticanus and Codex Sinaiticus, because of their greater age. The Greek text obtained by using these sources and the related papyri (our most ancient manuscripts) is known as the Alexandrian Text. However, some scholars have grounds for doubting the faithfulness of Vaticanus and Sinaiticus, since they often disagree with one another, and Sinaiticus exhibits excessive omission.

A third viewpoint of New Testament scholarship holds that the best text is based on the consensus of the majority of existing Greek manuscripts. This text is called the Majority Text. Most of these manuscripts are in substantial agreement. Even though many are late, and none is earlier than the fifth century, usually their readings are verified by papyri, ancient versions, quotations from the early church fathers, or a combination of these. The Majority Text is similar to the Textus Receptus, but it corrects those readings which have little or no support in the Greek manuscript tradition.

Today, scholars agree that the science of New Testament textual criticism is in a state of flux. Very few scholars still favor the Textus Receptus as such, and then often for its historical prestige as the text of Luther, Calvin, Tyndale, and the King James Version. For about a century most have followed a Critical Text (so called because it is edited according to specific principles of textual criticism) which depends heavily upon the Alexandrian type of text. More recently many have abandoned this Critical Text (which is quite similar to the one edited by Westcott and Hort) for one that is more eclectic. Finally, a small but growing number of scholars prefer the Majority Text, which is close to the traditional text except in the Revelation.

In light of these facts, and also because the New King James Version is the fifth revision of a historic document translated from specific Greek texts, the editors decided to retain the traditional text in the body of the New Testament and to indicate major Critical and Majority Text variant readings in the center reference column. Although these variations are duly indicated in the center-column notes of the present edition, it is most important to emphasize that fully eighty-five percent of the New Testament text is the same in the Textus Receptus, the Alexandrian Text, and the Majority Text.

Footnotes

Significant explanatory notes, alternate translations, and cross-references, as well as New Testament citations of Old Testament passages, are supplied in the footnotes.

Important textual variants in the Old Testament are identified in a standard form.

The textual notes in the present edition of the New Testament make no evaluation of readings, but do clearly indicate the manuscript sources of preadings. They objectively present the facts without such tendentious remarks as "the best manuscripts omit" or "the most reliable manuscripts read." Such notes are value judgments that differ according to varying viewpoints on the text. By giving a clearly defined set of variants the New King James Version benefits readers of all textual persuasions.

Where significant variations occur in the New Testament Greek manuscripts, textual notes are classified as follows:

1. NU-Text

These variations from the traditional text generally represent the Alexandrian or Egyptian type of text described previously in "The New Testament Text." They are found in the Critical Text published in the twenty-seventh edition of the Nestle-Aland Greek New Testament (N) and in the United Bible Societies' fourth edition (U), hence the acronym, "NU-Text."

2. M-Text

This symbol indicates points of variation in the Majority Text from the traditional text, as also previously discussed in "The New Testament Text." It should be noted that M stands for whatever reading is printed in the published *Greek New Testament According to the Majority Text,* whether supported by overwhelming, strong, or only a divided majority textual tradition.

The textual notes reflect the scholarship of the past 150 years and will assist the reader to observe the variations between the different manuscript traditions of the New Testament. Such information is generally not available in English translations of the New Testament.

THE
OLD TESTAMENT

GENESIS
It All Begins with God—the Ultimate Leader

SUMMARY

Genesis, the book of beginnings, overflows with leadership lessons. It profiles some of the greatest leaders in the Bible—but everything begins with God, the Ultimate Leader. After creating the universe and the planet on which we live, He handed leadership of the earth over to humankind (1:26).

You and I were created to lead and to rule. Sin marred our ability to lead, however, and Genesis introduces the story of God's plan to redeem sinfully independent people from the bondage of following their fallen nature. Isn't most of history the story of conflict among people trying to lead and rule one another, independent from God's direction? That's why Genesis often gives accounts of men and women trying to sort out whether to lead or follow, obey or rebel, serve God or live for themselves.

Because God designed people to lead—to "have dominion over" the earth (1:26, 28)—we know that we possess a ruling capacity. But as sinful beings, we tend to go our own way instead of following God's leadership.

Genesis 6 tells us that humankind became so wicked and self-serving that God determined to start over. God flooded the earth, sparing the family of only one man, Noah. After the Flood the earth began to repopulate itself, and people learned to cooperate with one another—but still they failed to follow God. The Tower of Babel (11:1–9) provides a major symbol of humankind's arrogance. The people had a clear vision and strong leadership, but they rebelled against God. That is why God confused their speech and inaugurated a new leadership plan for them. He divided the people into language groups, then later chose one of those groups—the Hebrews—as His very own, to set an example for others.

God's leadership of the Hebrews began just before His eternal covenant with Abram (later renamed Abraham) and continued with the patriarchs: Isaac, Jacob, and Joseph. The leadership lessons they learned fill the final 38 chapters of Genesis. God intended not only for them to remain pure for Him, but also to lead other nations back to God by modeling a lifestyle that would entice followers.

God's Role in Genesis

God wanted His creation to begin well. He communicated His vision for the world to Adam, to Noah, to Abraham, then to Isaac and Jacob. Like all good leaders, God took initiative. Yet He never forced His leadership on anyone. Each time His people failed, He laid out His plan, then selected those He would invite to take appropriate action. He relentlessly pursued His plan of redeeming men and women from their failures, even as He maintained a relationship with them.

Leaders in Genesis

Adam, Noah, Abraham, Isaac, Jacob, Joseph, Potiphar, Pharaoh

Other People of Influence in Genesis

Eve, the builders of the Tower of Babel, Sarah, Lot, Rebekah, Laban, Esau, Potiphar's wife

Lessons in Leadership

- God created humankind to lead and rule, but only within the context of His leadership.
- Leaders must learn to adjust their plans while holding tenaciously to the vision.
- Everyone leads and follows someone.
- No one can lead well without following well.
- Individuals must see the benefits of the vision before they will commit to it.
- To win trust, leaders must exhibit both character and competence.

LEADERSHIP HIGHLIGHTS IN GENESIS

The History of Creation

1 In the beginning God created the heavens and the earth. ²The earth was without form, and void; and darkness *was*ᵃ on the face of the deep. And the Spirit of God was hovering over the face of the waters.

³Then God said, "Let there be light"; and there was light. ⁴And God saw the light, that *it was* good; and God divided the light from the darkness. ⁵God called the light Day, and the darkness He called Night. So the evening and the morning were the first day.

⁶Then God said, "Let there be a firmament in the midst of the waters, and let it divide the waters from the waters." ⁷Thus God made the firmament, and divided the waters which *were* under the firmament from the waters which *were* above the firmament; and it was so. ⁸And God called the firmament Heaven. So the evening and the morning were the second day.

⁹Then God said, "Let the waters under the heavens be gathered together into one place, and let the dry *land* appear"; and it was so. ¹⁰And God called the dry *land* Earth, and the gathering together of the waters He called Seas. And God saw that *it was* good.

¹¹Then God said, "Let the earth bring forth grass, the herb *that* yields seed, *and* the fruit tree *that* yields fruit according to its kind, whose seed *is* in itself, on the earth"; and it was so. ¹²And the earth brought forth grass, the herb *that* yields seed according to its kind, and the tree *that* yields fruit, whose seed *is* in itself according to its kind. And God saw that *it was* good. ¹³So the evening and the morning were the third day.

¹⁴Then God said, "Let there be lights in the firmament of the heavens to divide the day from the night; and let them be for signs and seasons, and for days and years; ¹⁵and let them be for lights in the firmament of the heavens to give light on the earth"; and it was so. ¹⁶Then God made two great lights: the greater light to rule the day, and the lesser light to rule the night. *He made* the stars also. ¹⁷God set them in the firmament of the heavens to give light on the earth, ¹⁸and to rule over the day and over the night, and to divide the light from the darkness. And God saw that *it was* good. ¹⁹So the evening and the morning were the fourth day.

²⁰Then God said, "Let the waters abound with an abundance of living creatures, and let birds fly above the earth across the face of the firmament of the heavens." ²¹So God created great sea creatures and every living thing that moves, with which the waters abounded, according to their kind, and every winged bird according to its kind. And God saw that *it was* good. ²²And God blessed them, saying, "Be fruitful and multiply, and fill the waters in the seas, and let birds multiply on the earth." ²³So the evening and the morning were the fifth day.

²⁴Then God said, "Let the earth bring forth the living creature according to its kind: cattle and creeping thing and beast of the earth, *each* according to its kind"; and it was so. ²⁵And God made the beast of the earth according to its kind, cattle according to its kind, and everything that creeps on the earth according to its kind. And God saw that *it was* good.

²⁶Then God said, "Let Us make man in Our image, according to Our likeness; let them have dominion over the fish of the sea, over the birds of the air, and over the cattle, over allᵃ the earth and over every creeping thing that creeps on the

---

Creation:
The Ultimate Leader
Initiates
(Genesis 1:1—2:25)

H ave you ever recognized God as the Ultimate Leader? Not only did He create the universe, redeem humankind, innovate with entrepreneurial energy, and act as a maverick—He also leads.

Although God could have ruled and redeemed planet earth on His own, He chose to include mortals in His plans. Think about it! He could have limited His creation to animals of instinct—but He didn't. He created human beings with a will of their own, men and women who must choose to follow His leadership according to His plan. God always brings others with Him.

As the Ultimate Leader, God always initiates. He initiated the creation of the universe. He initiated the birth of our species. And He initiated the redemption process, extending Himself to us so that we might be saved.

As you read the Scripture, watch how often God demonstrates His magnificent leadership. Truly, He is the Ultimate Leader!

1:2 ᵃWords in italic type have been added for clarity. They are not found in the original Hebrew or Aramaic. **1:26** ᵃSyriac reads *all the wild animals of.*

earth." [27]So God created man in His *own* image; in the image of God He created him; male and female He created them. [28]Then God blessed them, and God said to them, "Be fruitful and multiply; fill the earth and subdue it; have dominion over the fish of the sea, over the birds of the air, and over every living thing that moves on the earth." [29]And God said, "See, I have given you every herb *that* yields seed which *is* on the face of all the earth, and every tree whose fruit yields seed; to you it shall be for food. [30]Also, to every beast of the earth, to every bird of the air, and to everything that creeps on the earth, in which *there is* life, *I have given* every green herb for food"; and it was so. [31]Then God saw everything that He had made, and indeed *it was* very good. So the evening and the morning were the sixth day.

2 Thus the heavens and the earth, and all the host of them, were finished. [2]And on the seventh day God ended His work which He had done, and He rested on the seventh day from all His work which He had done. [3]Then God blessed the seventh day and sanctified it, because in it He rested from all His work which God had created and made.

[4]This *is* the history[a] of the heavens and the earth when they were created, in the day that the LORD God made the earth and the heavens, [5]before any plant of the field was in the earth and

before any herb of the field had grown. For the LORD God had not caused it to rain on the earth, and *there was* no man to till the ground; [6]but a mist went up from the earth and watered the whole face of the ground.

[7]And the LORD God formed man *of* the dust of the ground, and breathed into his nostrils the breath of life; and man became a living being.

Life in God's Garden

[8]The LORD God planted a garden eastward in Eden, and there He put the man whom He had formed. [9]And out of the ground the LORD God made every tree grow that is pleasant to the sight and good for food. The tree of life *was* also in the midst of the garden, and the tree of the knowledge of good and evil.

[10]Now a river went out of Eden to water the garden, and from there it parted and became four riverheads. [11]The name of the first *is* Pishon; it *is* the one which skirts the whole land of Havilah, where *there is* gold. [12]And the gold of that land *is* good. Bdellium and the onyx stone *are* there. [13]The name of the second river *is* Gihon; it *is* the one which goes around the whole land of Cush. [14]The name of the third river *is* Hiddekel;[a] it *is*

2:4 [a]Hebrew *toledoth,* literally *generations* **2:14** [a]Or *Tigris*

Born to Lead!
(Genesis 1:26–31)

Y ou and I were born to lead. Take a look at five observations based on Genesis 1:26–31 that suggest our God-given leadership potential:

1. **Being made in God's image means we were created to lead (v. 26).** After God says, "Let Us make man in Our image," He says, "Let them have dominion. . . ." One way we reflect God's image is by leading.

2. **God commanded both male and female to have dominion (v. 27).** Both men and women have been given the ability and authority to lead. Leadership is not gender specific.

3. **We are to rule over the earth, but not necessarily over each other (v. 28).** We were not directed to rule each other, but over the earth's creatures. History is largely the story of how men and women have perverted their God-given roles by trying to rule each other.

4. **All of us are to serve one another in the areas of our gifting and purpose (vv. 29, 30).** God created everything for a purpose. Our *general* purpose is to lead, but each of us should ask God, "Lord, what's my *specific* purpose?"

5. **Each person's leadership is best exercised in his or her area of giftedness (v. 31).** When we discover our gifts, we will naturally lead in those areas where we are most productive, intuitive, comfortable, influential, and satisfied.

COMMUNICATION

Adam Failed to Connect with Eve

(Genesis 2:15–17; 3:1–6)

In Genesis 3 we see a leader who failed in an area crucial to all leaders: communication. By failing to communicate effectively with his wife, Adam botched his role as the first spiritual leader of the human race.

God clearly told Adam that a certain tree was off limits. "Of every tree of the garden you may freely eat," God told him, "but of the tree of the knowledge of good and evil you shall not eat, for in the day that you eat of it you shall surely die" (Gen. 2:16, 17). At the time Adam received this command, Eve was not present; according to Genesis 2, she had not yet been created. Consequently, it was up to Adam to pass along what God had said.

So why didn't Adam clearly communicate God's instructions to Eve? Why the breakdown in the line of communication? Certainly Eve did not completely understand what would happen if she ate the forbidden fruit. Consider her muddled response to the serpent: "God has said, 'You shall not eat it, nor shall you touch it, lest you die' " (Gen. 3:3). Eve added the phrases, "nor shall you touch it," and "lest you die." God never said any such thing. So where did she get her faulty information?

Maybe the "telephone game" can give us a clue. Have you ever played it? Everyone sits in a circle. One person whispers a message into the ear of an adjacent player, who whispers the words to the next person, and so it continues down the line. When the last person to play whispers the phrase into the ear of the one who began the game, a great distortion in the message is often revealed.

Five Reasons for Adam's Faulty Communication

Adam's communication to Eve went similarly astray. His message broke down for five basic reasons:

1. He ignored some details in the message he was supposed to communicate.
2. He allowed Eve's voice to influence him more than God's voice.
3. He failed to hold himself accountable for his communication.
4. He forgot what God had said about the consequences of disobedience.
5. He did not take responsibility for the results of his faulty communication.

Let's learn from Adam's mistake. You may be a good speaker—but are you a good communicator? Do you pay close attention to what God tells you? Do you give appropriate attention to detail? When you lead, do you make sure your audience gets the message? And do you take responsibility for what God has entrusted to you?

For a positive example of communication, see p. 333.

the one which goes toward the east of Assyria. The fourth river *is* the Euphrates.

[15]Then the LORD God took the man and put him in the garden of Eden to tend and keep it. [16]And the LORD God commanded the man, saying, "Of every tree of the garden you may freely eat; [17]but of the tree of the knowledge of good and evil you shall not eat, for in the day that you eat of it you shall surely die."

[18]And the LORD God said, "*It is* not good that man should be alone; I will make him a helper comparable to him." [19]Out of the ground the LORD God formed every beast of the field and every bird of the air, and brought *them* to Adam to see what he would call them. And whatever Adam called each living creature, that *was* its name. [20]So Adam gave names to all cattle, to the birds of the air, and to every beast of the field. But for Adam there was not found a helper comparable to him.

[21]And the LORD God caused a deep sleep to fall on Adam, and he slept; and He took one of his ribs, and closed up the flesh in its place. [22]Then the rib which the LORD God had taken from man He made into a woman, and He brought her to the man.

[23]And Adam said:

"This *is* now bone of my bones
And flesh of my flesh;
She shall be called Woman,
Because she was taken out of Man."

[24]Therefore a man shall leave his father and mother and be joined to his wife, and they shall become one flesh.

[25]And they were both naked, the man and his wife, and were not ashamed.

The Temptation and Fall of Man

3 Now the serpent was more cunning than any beast of the field which the LORD God had made. And he said to the woman, "Has God indeed said, 'You shall not eat of every tree of the garden'?"

[2]And the woman said to the serpent, "We may eat the fruit of the trees of the garden; [3]but of the fruit of the tree which *is* in the midst of the garden, God has said, 'You shall not eat it, nor shall you touch it, lest you die.'"

[4]Then the serpent said to the woman, "You will not surely die. [5]For God knows that in the day you eat of it your eyes will be opened, and you will be like God, knowing good and evil."

[6]So when the woman saw that the tree *was* good for food, that it *was* pleasant to the eyes,

---

The Law of E. F. Hutton: Eve Speaks
(Genesis 3:4–6)

Remember the old TV commercial? "When E. F. Hutton talks, people listen." Regardless of their titles, real leaders influence others. The story of Eve demonstrates the impact of *negative* influence. Although God commissioned Adam as her spiritual leader, Eve usurped the role of influencer. Adam followed his wife rather than God, and together they led humankind into sin.

---

and a tree desirable to make *one* wise, she took of its fruit and ate. She also gave to her husband with her, and he ate. [7]Then the eyes of both of them were opened, and they knew that they *were* naked; and they sewed fig leaves together and made themselves coverings.

[8]And they heard the sound of the LORD God walking in the garden in the cool of the day, and Adam and his wife hid themselves from the presence of the LORD God among the trees of the garden.

[9]Then the LORD God called to Adam and said to him, "Where *are* you?"

[10]So he said, "I heard Your voice in the garden, and I was afraid because I was naked; and I hid myself."

[11]And He said, "Who told you that you *were* naked? Have you eaten from the tree of which I commanded you that you should not eat?"

[12]Then the man said, "The woman whom You gave *to be* with me, she gave me of the tree, and I ate."

[13]And the LORD God said to the woman, "What *is* this you have done?"

The woman said, "The serpent deceived me, and I ate."

[14]So the LORD God said to the serpent:

"Because you have done this,
You *are* cursed more than all cattle,
And more than every beast of the field;
On your belly you shall go,
And you shall eat dust
All the days of your life.
[15] And I will put enmity
Between you and the woman,
And between your seed and her Seed;
He shall bruise your head,
And you shall bruise His heel."

¹⁶To the woman He said:

"I will greatly multiply your sorrow and
    your conception;
In pain you shall bring forth children;
Your desire *shall be* for your husband,
And he shall rule over you."

¹⁷Then to Adam He said, "Because you have
heeded the voice of your wife, and have eaten
from the tree of which I commanded you, saying, 'You shall not eat of it':

"Cursed *is* the ground for your sake;
In toil you shall eat *of* it
All the days of your life.
¹⁸ Both thorns and thistles it shall bring forth
    for you,
And you shall eat the herb of the field.
¹⁹ In the sweat of your face you shall eat
    bread
Till you return to the ground,
For out of it you were taken;
For dust you *are,*
And to dust you shall return."

²⁰And Adam called his wife's name Eve, because she was the mother of all living.

²¹Also for Adam and his wife the Lord God
made tunics of skin, and clothed them.
²²Then the Lord God said, "Behold, the man
has become like one of Us, to know good and
evil. And now, lest he put out his hand and take
also of the tree of life, and eat, and live forever"— ²³therefore the Lord God sent him out
of the garden of Eden to till the ground from
which he was taken. ²⁴So He drove out the man;
and He placed cherubim at the east of the garden of Eden, and a flaming sword which turned
every way, to guard the way to the tree of life.

Cain Murders Abel

4 Now Adam knew Eve his wife, and she
conceived and bore Cain, and said, "I have
acquired a man from the Lord." ²Then
she bore again, this time his brother Abel. Now
Abel was a keeper of sheep, but Cain was a tiller
of the ground. ³And in the process of time it
came to pass that Cain brought an offering of
the fruit of the ground to the Lord. ⁴Abel also
brought of the firstborn of his flock and of
their fat. And the Lord respected Abel and
his offering, ⁵but He did not respect Cain and
his offering. And Cain was very angry, and his
countenance fell.

⁶So the Lord said to Cain, "Why are you

PROFILE IN LEADERSHIP

ADAM

FIRST LEADER TO DROP THE BALL
(Genesis 3:6–19)

At the moment he received God's mandate to rule over the earth, Adam became the first spiritual leader in human history. Initially, this meant overseeing the garden and providing direction to his family. Adam was to be a good
steward over his resources and relationships. Unfortunately, he failed on both
counts.

When Eve brought the forbidden fruit to Adam, he mismanaged God's creation by eating it. Adam also mismanaged his wife by remaining passive when
he should have taken a stand, thus allowing both Eve and himself to fall
morally. When God confronted him with his sin, he blamed others: "The *woman*
whom *You* gave to be with me, she gave me of the tree, and I ate" (Gen. 3:12,
emphasis added).

Spiritual leadership isn't complex; it simply requires a willingness to take
responsibility. Sadly, many spiritual leaders continue to duplicate Adam's mistake by shirking their responsibilities at home, in the neighborhood, on the job,
and in the church. They forget that while Adam's failure started at home, in
just a short time it damaged all his relationships, spoiled the beautiful place he
lived, and ultimately devastated the entire world. And the whole mess can be
traced back to one spineless refusal to lead.

angry? And why has your countenance fallen? [7]If you do well, will you not be accepted? And if you do not do well, sin lies at the door. And its desire *is* for you, but you should rule over it."

[8]Now Cain talked with Abel his brother;[a] and it came to pass, when they were in the field, that Cain rose up against Abel his brother and killed him.

[9]Then the LORD said to Cain, "Where *is* Abel your brother?"

He said, "I do not know. *Am* I my brother's keeper?"

[10]And He said, "What have you done? The voice of your brother's blood cries out to Me from the ground. [11]So now you *are* cursed from the earth, which has opened its mouth to receive your brother's blood from your hand. [12]When you till the ground, it shall no longer yield its strength to you. A fugitive and a vagabond you shall be on the earth."

[13]And Cain said to the LORD, "My punishment *is* greater than I can bear! [14]Surely You have driven me out this day from the face of the ground; I shall be hidden from Your face; I shall be a fugitive and a vagabond on the earth, and it will happen *that* anyone who finds me will kill me."

[15]And the LORD said to him, "Therefore,[a] whoever kills Cain, vengeance shall be taken on him sevenfold." And the LORD set a mark on Cain, lest anyone finding him should kill him.

The Family of Cain

[16]Then Cain went out from the presence of the LORD and dwelt in the land of Nod on the east of Eden. [17]And Cain knew his wife, and she conceived and bore Enoch. And he built a city, and called the name of the city after the name of his son—Enoch. [18]To Enoch was born Irad; and Irad begot Mehujael, and Mehujael begot Methushael, and Methushael begot Lamech.

[19]Then Lamech took for himself two wives: the name of one *was* Adah, and the name of the second *was* Zillah. [20]And Adah bore Jabal. He was the father of those who dwell in tents and have livestock. [21]His brother's name *was* Jubal. He was the father of all those who play the harp and flute. [22]And as for Zillah, she also bore Tubal-Cain, an instructor of every craftsman in bronze and iron. And the sister of Tubal-Cain *was* Naamah.

[23]Then Lamech said to his wives:

4:8 [a]Samaritan Pentateuch, Septuagint, Syriac, and Vulgate add *"Let us go out to the field."*
4:15 [a]Following Masoretic Text and Targum; Septuagint, Syriac, and Vulgate read *Not so.*

EVE — A LEADER WHO LEARNED FROM FAILURE
(Genesis 4:1—5:5)

PROFILE IN LEADERSHIP

God created Eve to fill an unmet need in Adam's otherwise perfect world. She entered a land free of pain, heartache, and sin, but her fluctuating emotions made obedience a struggle. Eventually she influenced Adam to join her in sin. Their choice to follow Satan rather than God brought devastating consequences that continue to plague us even today.

Eve exchanged a life without pain for a hostile and even brutal environment. Yet her subsequent life demonstrated an ability to recover from failure and move forward. She restored her relationship with God, and when her firstborn child arrived, she acknowledged her dependence on God. While Scripture does not comment on her parenting skills, it does indicate that Cain developed a resentful and jealous spirit. As a result, Eve became the first mother to endure the heartache of a murdered child.

Eve did not use her pain as an excuse to reject God or question Him, as she had in the garden. Nor did she allow a root of bitterness to spring up. When God gave her Seth, she expressed gratitude for this new life. Ultimately, Eve came to represent a strong leader willing to accept the consequences of her choices and learn from her mistakes.

"Adah and Zillah, hear my voice;
Wives of Lamech, listen to my speech!
For I have killed a man for wounding me,
Even a young man for hurting me.
24 If Cain shall be avenged sevenfold,
Then Lamech seventy-sevenfold."

A New Son

25 And Adam knew his wife again, and she bore a son and named him Seth, "For God has appointed another seed for me instead of Abel, whom Cain killed." 26 And as for Seth, to him also a son was born; and he named him Enosh.[a] Then *men* began to call on the name of the LORD.

The Family of Adam

5 This is the book of the genealogy of Adam. In the day that God created man, He made him in the likeness of God. 2 He created them male and female, and blessed them and called them Mankind in the day they were created. 3 And Adam lived one hundred and thirty years, and begot *a son* in his own likeness, after his image, and named him Seth. 4 After he begot Seth, the days of Adam were eight hundred years; and he had sons and daughters. 5 So all the days that Adam lived were nine hundred and thirty years; and he died.

6 Seth lived one hundred and five years, and begot Enosh. 7 After he begot Enosh, Seth lived eight hundred and seven years, and had sons and daughters. 8 So all the days of Seth were nine hundred and twelve years; and he died.

9 Enosh lived ninety years, and begot Cainan.[a] 10 After he begot Cainan, Enosh lived eight hundred and fifteen years, and had sons and daughters. 11 So all the days of Enosh were nine hundred and five years; and he died.

12 Cainan lived seventy years, and begot Mahalalel. 13 After he begot Mahalalel, Cainan lived eight hundred and forty years, and had sons and daughters. 14 So all the days of Cainan were nine hundred and ten years; and he died.

15 Mahalalel lived sixty-five years, and begot Jared. 16 After he begot Jared, Mahalalel lived eight hundred and thirty years, and had sons and daughters. 17 So all the days of Mahalalel were eight hundred and ninety-five years; and he died.

18 Jared lived one hundred and sixty-two years, and begot Enoch. 19 After he begot Enoch, Jared lived eight hundred years, and had sons and daughters. 20 So all the days of Jared were nine hundred and sixty-two years; and he died.

21 Enoch lived sixty-five years, and begot Methuselah. 22 After he begot Methuselah, Enoch walked with God three hundred years, and had sons and daughters. 23 So all the days of Enoch were three hundred and sixty-five years. 24 And Enoch walked with God; and he *was* not, for God took him.

25 Methuselah lived one hundred and eighty-seven years, and begot Lamech. 26 After he begot Lamech, Methuselah lived seven hundred and eighty-two years, and had sons and daughters. 27 So all the days of Methuselah were nine hundred and sixty-nine years; and he died.

28 Lamech lived one hundred and eighty-two years, and had a son. 29 And he called his name Noah, saying, "This *one* will comfort us concerning our work and the toil of our hands, because of the ground which the LORD has cursed." 30 After he begot Noah, Lamech lived five hundred and ninety-five years, and had sons and daughters. 31 So all the days of Lamech were seven hundred and seventy-seven years; and he died.

32 And Noah was five hundred years old, and Noah begot Shem, Ham, and Japheth.

The Wickedness and Judgment of Man

6 Now it came to pass, when men began to multiply on the face of the earth, and daughters were born to them, 2 that the sons of God saw the daughters of men, that they *were* beautiful; and they took wives for themselves of all whom they chose.

3 And the LORD said, "My Spirit shall not strive[a] with man forever, for he *is* indeed flesh; yet his days shall be one hundred and twenty years." 4 There were giants on the earth in those days, and also afterward, when the sons of God came in to the daughters of men and they bore *children* to them. Those *were* the mighty men who *were* of old, men of renown.

5 Then the LORD[a] saw that the wickedness of man *was* great in the earth, and *that* every intent of the thoughts of his heart *was* only evil continually. 6 And the LORD was sorry that He had made man on the earth, and He was grieved in His heart. 7 So the LORD said, "I will destroy man whom I have created from the face of the earth, both man and beast, creeping thing and birds of the air, for I am sorry that I have made them." 8 But Noah found grace in the eyes of the LORD.

4:26 [a]Greek *Enos* 5:9 [a]Hebrew *Qenan*
6:3 [a]Septuagint, Syriac, Targum, and Vulgate read *abide.* 6:5 [a]Following Masoretic Text and Targum; Vulgate reads *God;* Septuagint reads LORD *God.*

Noah Pleases God

⁹This is the genealogy of Noah. Noah was a just man, perfect in his generations. Noah walked with God. ¹⁰And Noah begot three sons: Shem, Ham, and Japheth.

¹¹The earth also was corrupt before God, and the earth was filled with violence. ¹²So God looked upon the earth, and indeed it was corrupt; for all flesh had corrupted their way on the earth.

The Ark Prepared

¹³And God said to Noah, "The end of all flesh has come before Me, for the earth is filled with violence through them; and behold, I will destroy them with the earth. ¹⁴Make yourself an ark of gopherwood; make rooms in the ark, and cover it inside and outside with pitch. ¹⁵And this is how you shall make it: The length of the ark *shall be* three hundred cubits, its width fifty cubits, and its height thirty cubits. ¹⁶You shall make a window for the ark, and you shall finish it to a cubit from above; and set the door of the ark in its side. You shall make it *with* lower, second, and third *decks.* ¹⁷And behold, I Myself am bringing floodwaters on the earth, to destroy from under heaven all flesh in which *is* the breath of life; everything that *is* on the earth shall die. ¹⁸But I will establish My covenant with you; and you shall go into the ark—you, your sons, your wife, and your sons' wives with you. ¹⁹And of every living thing of all flesh you shall bring two of every *sort* into the ark, to keep *them* alive with you; they shall be male and female. ²⁰Of the birds after their kind, of animals after their kind, and of every creeping thing of the earth after its kind, two of every *kind* will come to you to keep *them* alive. ²¹And you shall take for yourself of all food that is eaten, and you shall gather *it* to yourself; and it shall be food for you and for them."

²²Thus Noah did; according to all that God commanded him, so he did.

The Great Flood

7 Then the LORD said to Noah, "Come into the ark, you and all your household, because I have seen *that* you *are* righteous before Me in this generation. ²You shall take with you seven each of every clean animal, a male and his female; two each of animals that *are* unclean, a male and his female; ³also seven each of birds of the air, male and female, to keep the species alive on the face of all the earth. ⁴For after seven more days I will cause it to rain on the earth forty days and forty nights, and I will destroy from the face of the earth all living things that I have made."

[5]And Noah did according to all that the LORD commanded him. [6]Noah *was* six hundred years old when the floodwaters were on the earth.

[7]So Noah, with his sons, his wife, and his sons' wives, went into the ark because of the waters of the flood. [8]Of clean animals, of animals that *are* unclean, of birds, and of everything that creeps on the earth, [9]two by two they went into the ark to Noah, male and female, as God had commanded Noah. [10]And it came to pass after seven days that the waters of the flood were on the earth. [11]In the six hundredth year of Noah's life, in the second month, the seventeenth day of the month, on that day all the fountains of the great deep were broken up, and the windows of heaven were opened. [12]And the rain was on the earth forty days and forty nights.

[13]On the very same day Noah and Noah's sons, Shem, Ham, and Japheth, and Noah's wife and the three wives of his sons with them, entered the ark— [14]they and every beast after its kind, all cattle after their kind, every creeping thing that creeps on the earth after its kind, and every bird after its kind, every bird of every sort. [15]And they went into the ark to Noah, two by two, of all flesh in which *is* the breath of life. [16]So those that entered, male and female of all flesh, went in as God had commanded him; and the LORD shut him in.

[17]Now the flood was on the earth forty days. The waters increased and lifted up the ark, and it rose high above the earth. [18]The waters prevailed and greatly increased on the earth, and the ark moved about on the surface of the waters. [19]And the waters prevailed exceedingly on the earth, and all the high hills under the whole heaven were covered. [20]The waters prevailed fifteen cubits upward, and the mountains were covered. [21]And all flesh died that moved on the earth: birds and cattle and beasts and every creeping thing that creeps on the earth, and every man. [22]All in whose nostrils *was* the breath of the spirit[a] of life, all that *was* on the dry *land,* died. [23]So He destroyed all living things which were on the face of the ground: both man and cattle, creeping thing and bird of the air. They were destroyed from the earth. Only Noah and those who *were* with him in the ark remained *alive.* [24]And the waters prevailed on the earth one hundred and fifty days.

Noah's Deliverance

8 Then God remembered Noah, and every living thing, and all the animals that *were* with him in the ark. And God made a wind to pass over the earth, and the waters subsided. [2]The fountains of the deep and the win-

The Law of Sacrifice: God and Noah
(Genesis 6:17, 18; 8:21, 22)

Some of the saddest words in Scripture occur in Genesis 6:6: "And the LORD was sorry that He had made man on the earth, and He was grieved in His heart." It saddened God that every human being except for Noah's immediate family would have to be destroyed. He loved the men and women whom He had created to be like Him, those who were to rule the earth and reflect His glory.

God determined to start again, even without a guarantee that the survivors and their descendants would do a better job of following Him. God made a covenant with Noah, giving up His right to ever again flood the earth to cleanse it of sinful humanity. Noah gave up everything he had accumulated in his long life in order to start over. *Sacrifice always precedes success.* They had to give up to go up.

dows of heaven were also stopped, and the rain from heaven was restrained. [3]And the waters receded continually from the earth. At the end of the hundred and fifty days the waters decreased. [4]Then the ark rested in the seventh month, the seventeenth day of the month, on the mountains of Ararat. [5]And the waters decreased continually until the tenth month. In the tenth *month,* on the first *day* of the month, the tops of the mountains were seen.

[6]So it came to pass, at the end of forty days, that Noah opened the window of the ark which he had made. [7]Then he sent out a raven, which kept going to and fro until the waters had dried up from the earth. [8]He also sent out from himself a dove, to see if the waters had receded from the face of the ground. [9]But the dove found no resting place for the sole of her foot, and she returned into the ark to him, for the waters *were* on the face of the whole earth. So he put out his hand and took her, and drew her into the ark to himself. [10]And he waited yet another seven days, and again he sent the dove out from the ark. [11]Then the dove came to him in the evening, and behold, a freshly plucked olive leaf *was* in her mouth; and Noah knew

7:22 [a]Septuagint and Vulgate omit *of the spirit.*

that the waters had receded from the earth. [12]So he waited yet another seven days and sent out the dove, which did not return again to him anymore.

[13]And it came to pass in the six hundred and first year, in the first *month,* the first *day* of the month, that the waters were dried up from the earth; and Noah removed the covering of the ark and looked, and indeed the surface of the ground was dry. [14]And in the second month, on the twenty-seventh day of the month, the earth was dried.

[15]Then God spoke to Noah, saying, [16]"Go out of the ark, you and your wife, and your sons and your sons' wives with you. [17]Bring out with you every living thing of all flesh that *is* with you: birds and cattle and every creeping thing that creeps on the earth, so that they may abound on the earth, and be fruitful and multiply on the earth." [18]So Noah went out, and his sons and his wife and his sons' wives with him. [19]Every animal, every creeping thing, every bird, *and* whatever creeps on the earth, according to their families, went out of the ark.

God's Covenant with Creation

[20]Then Noah built an altar to the LORD, and took of every clean animal and of every clean bird, and offered burnt offerings on the altar. [21]And the LORD smelled a soothing aroma. Then the LORD said in His heart, "I will never again curse the ground for man's sake, although the imagination of man's heart *is* evil from his youth; nor will I again destroy every living thing as I have done.

[22] "While the earth remains,
Seedtime and harvest,
Cold and heat,
Winter and summer,
And day and night
Shall not cease."

9 So God blessed Noah and his sons, and said to them: "Be fruitful and multiply, and fill the earth.[a] [2]And the fear of you and the dread of you shall be on every beast of the earth, on every bird of the air, on all that move *on* the earth, and on all the fish of the sea. They are given into your hand. [3]Every moving thing that lives shall be food for you. I have given you all things, even as the green herbs. [4]But you shall not eat flesh with its life, *that is,* its blood. [5]Surely for your lifeblood I will demand *a reckoning;* from the hand of every beast I will require it, and from the hand of man.

From the hand of every man's brother I will require the life of man.

[6] "Whoever sheds man's blood,
By man his blood shall be shed;
For in the image of God
He made man.
[7] And as for you, be fruitful and multiply;
Bring forth abundantly in the earth
And multiply in it."

[8]Then God spoke to Noah and to his sons with him, saying: [9]"And as for Me, behold, I establish My covenant with you and with your descendants[a] after you, [10]and with every living creature that *is* with you: the birds, the cattle, and every beast of the earth with you, of all that go out of the ark, every beast of the earth. [11]Thus I establish My covenant with you: Never again shall all flesh be cut off by the waters of the flood; never again shall there be a flood to destroy the earth."

[12]And God said: "This *is* the sign of the covenant which I make between Me and you, and every living creature that *is* with you, for perpetual generations: [13]I set My rainbow in the cloud, and it shall be for the sign of the covenant between Me and the earth. [14]It shall be, when I bring a cloud over the earth, that the rainbow shall be seen in the cloud; [15]and I will remember My covenant which *is* between Me and you and every living creature of all flesh; the waters shall never again become a flood to destroy all flesh. [16]The rainbow shall be in the cloud, and I will look on it to remember the everlasting covenant between God and every living creature of all flesh that *is* on the earth." [17]And God said to Noah, "This *is* the sign of the covenant which I have established between Me and all flesh that *is* on the earth."

Noah and His Sons

[18]Now the sons of Noah who went out of the ark were Shem, Ham, and Japheth. And Ham *was* the father of Canaan. [19]These three *were* the sons of Noah, and from these the whole earth was populated.

[20]And Noah began *to be* a farmer, and he planted a vineyard. [21]Then he drank of the wine and was drunk, and became uncovered in his tent. [22]And Ham, the father of Canaan, saw the nakedness of his father, and told his two brothers outside. [23]But Shem and Japheth took a garment, laid *it* on both their shoulders, and went backward

9:1 [a]Compare Genesis 1:28 **9:9** [a]Literally *seed*

and covered the nakedness of their father. Their faces *were* turned away, and they did not see their father's nakedness.

[24]So Noah awoke from his wine, and knew what his younger son had done to him. [25]Then he said:

> "Cursed *be* Canaan;
> A servant of servants
> He shall be to his brethren."

[26]And he said:

> "Blessed *be* the LORD,
> The God of Shem,
> And may Canaan be his servant.
> [27] May God enlarge Japheth,
> And may he dwell in the tents of Shem;
> And may Canaan be his servant."

[28]And Noah lived after the flood three hundred and fifty years. [29]So all the days of Noah were nine hundred and fifty years; and he died.

Nations Descended from Noah

10 Now this *is* the genealogy of the sons of Noah: Shem, Ham, and Japheth. And sons were born to them after the flood.

[2]The sons of Japheth *were* Gomer, Magog, Madai, Javan, Tubal, Meshech, and Tiras. [3]The sons of Gomer *were* Ashkenaz, Riphath,[a] and Togarmah. [4]The sons of Javan *were* Elishah, Tarshish, Kittim, and Dodanim.[a] [5]From these the coastland *peoples* of the Gentiles were separated into their lands, everyone according to his language, according to their families, into their nations.

[6]The sons of Ham *were* Cush, Mizraim, Put,[a] and Canaan. [7]The sons of Cush *were* Seba, Havilah, Sabtah, Raamah, and Sabtechah; and the sons of Raamah *were* Sheba and Dedan.

[8]Cush begot Nimrod; he began to be a mighty one on the earth. [9]He was a mighty hunter before the LORD; therefore it is said, "Like Nimrod the mighty hunter before the LORD." [10]And the beginning of his kingdom was Babel, Erech, Accad, and Calneh, in the land of Shinar. [11]From that land he went to Assyria and built Nineveh, Rehoboth Ir, Calah, [12]and Resen between Nineveh and Calah (that *is* the principal city).

[13]Mizraim begot Ludim, Anamim, Lehabim, Naphtuhim, [14]Pathrusim, and Casluhim (from whom came the Philistines and Caphtorim). [15]Canaan begot Sidon his firstborn, and Heth;

[16]the Jebusite, the Amorite, and the Girgashite; [17]the Hivite, the Arkite, and the Sinite; [18]the Arvadite, the Zemarite, and the Hamathite. Afterward the families of the Canaanites were dispersed. [19]And the border of the Canaanites was from Sidon as you go toward Gerar, as far as Gaza; then as you go toward Sodom, Gomorrah, Admah, and Zeboiim, as far as Lasha. [20]These *were* the sons of Ham, according to their families, according to their languages, in their lands *and* in their nations.

[21]And *children* were born also to Shem, the father of all the children of Eber, the brother of Japheth the elder. [22]The sons of Shem *were* Elam, Asshur, Arphaxad, Lud, and Aram. [23]The sons of Aram *were* Uz, Hul, Gether, and Mash.[a] [24]Arphaxad begot Salah,[a] and Salah begot Eber. [25]To Eber were born two sons: the name of one *was* Peleg, for in his days the earth was divided; and his brother's name *was* Joktan. [26]Joktan begot Almodad, Sheleph, Hazarmaveth, Jerah, [27]Hadoram, Uzal, Diklah, [28]Obal,[a] Abimael, Sheba, [29]Ophir, Havilah, and Jobab. All these *were* the sons of Joktan. [30]And their dwelling place was from Mesha as you go toward Sephar, the mountain of the east. [31]These *were* the sons of Shem, according to their families, according to their languages, in their lands, according to their nations.

[32]These *were* the families of the sons of Noah, according to their generations, in their nations; and from these the nations were divided on the earth after the flood.

The Tower of Babel

11 Now the whole earth had one language and one speech. [2]And it came to pass, as they journeyed from the east, that they found a plain in the land of Shinar, and they dwelt there. [3]Then they said to one another, "Come, let us make bricks and bake *them* thoroughly." They had brick for stone, and they had asphalt for mortar. [4]And they said, "Come, let us build ourselves a city, and a tower whose top *is* in the heavens; let us make a name for ourselves, lest we be scattered abroad over the face of the whole earth."

10:3 [a]Spelled *Diphath* in 1 Chronicles 1:6
10:4 [a]Spelled *Rodanim* in Samaritan Pentateuch and 1 Chronicles 1:7 **10:6** [a]Or *Phut* **10:23** [a]Called *Meshech* in Septuagint and 1 Chronicles 1:17
10:24 [a]Following Masoretic Text, Vulgate, and Targum; Septuagint reads *Arphaxad begot Cainan, and Cainan begot Salah* (compare Luke 3:35, 36).
10:28 [a]Spelled *Ebal* in 1 Chronicles 1:22

The Law of the Big Mo: The Tower of Babel

(Genesis 11:4)

Momentum is a leader's best friend. Unity of vision, language, and effort among the people of Babel provided tremendous momentum. Unfortunately, they used the Big Mo to go their own direction. As a result, God halted their momentum by confusing their language and scattering them to the four winds.

⁵But the LORD came down to see the city and the tower which the sons of men had built. ⁶And the LORD said, "Indeed the people *are* one and they all have one language, and this is what they begin to do; now nothing that they propose to do will be withheld from them. ⁷Come, let Us go down and there confuse their language, that they may not understand one another's speech." ⁸So the LORD scattered them abroad from there over the face of all the earth, and they ceased building the city. ⁹Therefore its name is called Babel, because there the LORD confused the language of all the earth; and from there the LORD scattered them abroad over the face of all the earth.

Shem's Descendants

¹⁰This *is* the genealogy of Shem: Shem *was* one hundred years old, and begot Arphaxad two years after the flood. ¹¹After he begot Arphaxad, Shem lived five hundred years, and begot sons and daughters.

¹²Arphaxad lived thirty-five years, and begot Salah. ¹³After he begot Salah, Arphaxad lived four hundred and three years, and begot sons and daughters.

¹⁴Salah lived thirty years, and begot Eber. ¹⁵After he begot Eber, Salah lived four hundred and three years, and begot sons and daughters.

¹⁶Eber lived thirty-four years, and begot Peleg. ¹⁷After he begot Peleg, Eber lived four hundred and thirty years, and begot sons and daughters.

¹⁸Peleg lived thirty years, and begot Reu. ¹⁹After he begot Reu, Peleg lived two hundred and nine years, and begot sons and daughters.

²⁰Reu lived thirty-two years, and begot Serug. ²¹After he begot Serug, Reu lived two hundred and seven years, and begot sons and daughters.

²²Serug lived thirty years, and begot Nahor. ²³After he begot Nahor, Serug lived two hundred years, and begot sons and daughters.

²⁴Nahor lived twenty-nine years, and begot Terah. ²⁵After he begot Terah, Nahor lived one hundred and nineteen years, and begot sons and daughters.

²⁶Now Terah lived seventy years, and begot Abram, Nahor, and Haran.

Terah's Descendants

²⁷This *is* the genealogy of Terah: Terah begot Abram, Nahor, and Haran. Haran begot Lot. ²⁸And Haran died before his father Terah in his native land, in Ur of the Chaldeans. ²⁹Then Abram and Nahor took wives: the name of Abram's wife *was* Sarai, and the name of Nahor's wife, Milcah, the daughter of Haran the father of Milcah and the father of Iscah. ³⁰But Sarai was barren; she had no child.

³¹And Terah took his son Abram and his grandson Lot, the son of Haran, and his daughter-in-law Sarai, his son Abram's wife, and they went out with them from Ur of the Chaldeans to go to the land of Canaan; and they came to Haran and dwelt there. ³²So the days of Terah were two hundred and five years, and Terah died in Haran.

Promises to Abram

12 Now the LORD had said to Abram:

"Get out of your country,
From your family
And from your father's house,
To a land that I will show you.
² I will make you a great nation;
I will bless you
And make your name great;
And you shall be a blessing.
³ I will bless those who bless you,
And I will curse him who curses you;
And in you all the families of the earth
shall be blessed."

⁴So Abram departed as the LORD had spoken to him, and Lot went with him. And Abram *was* seventy-five years old when he departed from Haran. ⁵Then Abram took Sarai his wife and Lot his brother's son, and all their possessions that they had gathered, and the people whom they had acquired in Haran, and they departed to go to the land of Canaan. So they came to the land of Canaan. ⁶Abram passed through the land to the place of Shechem, as far as the terebinth tree

The Law of Connection: God and Abram

(Genesis 12:1–7)

A t first glance, the incident at the Tower of Babel looks like an angry God bent on punishing the people for disobedience. But it was much more than that; actually, God was implementing a plan called "divide and conquer." In Genesis 11, the Lord divided the people into many language groups. In Genesis 12, He chose one of those groups and made a covenant with one of their members. God spoke to Abram and promised to bless him, and through him to bless the entire human race. Because of that covenant, Abram became the father of the Hebrew nation.

It's important to observe how God proposed His plan. He told Abram that He would bless him, along with his cattle, land, family, and name. God spoke to Abram heart to heart, revealing to him the blessings he would enjoy through the covenant. And Abram was no dummy: He took God up on the proposed deal.

While Abram might have chosen to obey God simply because He is God, the Lord made the effort to connect with Abram first. He touched Abram's heart before asking for his hand.

of Moreh.[a] And the Canaanites *were* then in the land.

[7]Then the LORD appeared to Abram and said, "To your descendants I will give this land." And there he built an altar to the LORD, who had appeared to him. [8]And he moved from there to the mountain east of Bethel, and he pitched his tent *with* Bethel on the west and Ai on the east; there he built an altar to the LORD and called on the name of the LORD. [9]So Abram journeyed, going on still toward the South.[a]

Abram in Egypt

[10]Now there was a famine in the land, and Abram went down to Egypt to dwell there, for the famine *was* severe in the land. [11]And it came to pass, when he was close to entering Egypt, that he said to Sarai his wife, "Indeed I know that you *are* a woman of beautiful countenance. [12]Therefore it will happen, when the Egyptians see you, that they will say, 'This *is* his wife'; and they will kill me, but they will let you live.

[13]Please say you *are* my sister, that it may be well with me for your sake, and that I[a] may live because of you."

[14]So it was, when Abram came into Egypt, that the Egyptians saw the woman, that she *was* very beautiful. [15]The princes of Pharaoh also saw her and commended her to Pharaoh. And the woman was taken to Pharaoh's house. [16]He treated Abram well for her sake. He had sheep, oxen, male donkeys, male and female servants, female donkeys, and camels.

[17]But the LORD plagued Pharaoh and his house with great plagues because of Sarai, Abram's wife. [18]And Pharaoh called Abram and said, "What *is* this you have done to me? Why did you not tell me that she *was* your wife? [19]Why did you say, 'She *is* my sister'? I might have taken her as my wife. Now therefore, here is your wife; take *her* and go your way." [20]So Pharaoh commanded *his* men concerning him; and they sent him away, with his wife and all that he had.

Abram Inherits Canaan

13 Then Abram went up from Egypt, he and his wife and all that he had, and Lot with him, to the South.[a] [2]Abram *was* very rich in livestock, in silver, and in gold. [3]And he went on his journey from the South as far as Bethel, to the place where his tent had been at the beginning, between Bethel and Ai, [4]to the place of the altar which he had made there at first. And there Abram called on the name of the LORD.

[5]Lot also, who went with Abram, had flocks and herds and tents. [6]Now the land was not able to support them, that they might dwell together, for their possessions were so great that they could not dwell together. [7]And there was strife between the herdsmen of Abram's livestock and the herdsmen of Lot's livestock. The Canaanites and the Perizzites then dwelt in the land.

[8]So Abram said to Lot, "Please let there be no strife between you and me, and between my herdsmen and your herdsmen; for we *are* brethren. [9]*Is* not the whole land before you? Please separate from me. If *you* take the left, then I will go to the right; or, if *you* go to the right, then I will go to the left."

[10]And Lot lifted his eyes and saw all the plain of Jordan, that it *was* well watered everywhere (before the LORD destroyed Sodom and Gomorrah) like the garden of the LORD, like the land of Egypt as you go toward Zoar. [11]Then Lot chose for

---

12:6 [a]Hebrew *Alon Moreh* **12:9** [a]Hebrew *Negev*
12:13 [a]Literally *my soul* **13:1** [a]Hebrew *Negev*

21 QUALITIES

VISION

Abraham Seizes What He Sees
(Genesis 12:1—22:4)

While followers may obsess on the challenges immediately before them, leaders see the future from a distance. They dream dreams not only about what can happen now, but also about what could happen in the next year, the next decade, even the next generation.

When God told Abraham to leave the comfort of his home in Haran, his relatives, and everything familiar, so that he might start fresh in another land (Gen. 12), Abraham caught a vision. God gave Abraham the hope of fathering a great nation; in fact, God said he would become the father of many nations! Abraham felt compelled to follow this great vision, even when he had nothing else to rely on.

Lessons from Abraham on Vision

By observing Abraham in Genesis 12—22, we can learn the criteria for a God-given vision. A vision must:

1. Begin with God's priorities (Gen. 12:1, 2). God initiated the vision, not Abraham. When leaders start with God's vision, they can more easily maintain direction and keep their motives pure.

2. Connect with the leader's identity (Gen. 15:2–4). The vision Abraham received fit him and Sarah exactly; it matched the needs and desires of this barren couple. Even better, its fulfillment would serve others.

3. Include others (Gen. 12:2, 3). A vision from God always involves and blesses others. The Lord told Abraham he would be blessed in order to bless many nations, which is precisely what happened through the birth of Christ many generations later.

4. Be bigger than the leader (Gen. 17:1–8). While Abraham wanted to father an heir, God wanted him to father *nations*. That hope went far beyond Abraham's wildest dreams (and his own capabilities). Such a huge vision would take more than a lifetime to fulfill.

5. Connect with the leader's deepest convictions (Gen. 18:9–12). The vision that captured Abraham's heart mirrored his strongest values, including his desire for family and land.

6. Be tangible and easily communicated (Gen. 15:5). God gave Abraham a tangible picture of the vision: Look at the sands on the shore, He said, and at the stars in the sky. These objects served as visual aids to help Abraham embrace and fulfill the vision.

7. Have eternal value (Gen. 17:19, 20). Abraham's vision went far beyond his life on earth and included more than wealth and fame. His vision would affect the eternal destiny of millions.

For a negative example of vision, see p. 31.

himself all the plain of Jordan, and Lot journeyed east. And they separated from each other. ¹²Abram dwelt in the land of Canaan, and Lot dwelt in the cities of the plain and pitched *his* tent even as far as Sodom. ¹³But the men of Sodom *were* exceedingly wicked and sinful against the LORD.

¹⁴And the LORD said to Abram, after Lot had separated from him: "Lift your eyes now and look from the place where you are—northward, southward, eastward, and westward; ¹⁵for all the land which you see I give to you and your descendants[a] forever. ¹⁶And I will make your descendants as the dust of the earth; so that if a man could number the dust of the earth, *then* your descendants also could be numbered. ¹⁷Arise, walk in the land through its length and its width, for I give it to you."

¹⁸Then Abram moved *his* tent, and went and dwelt by the terebinth trees of Mamre,[a] which *are* in Hebron, and built an altar there to the LORD.

Lot's Captivity and Rescue

14 And it came to pass in the days of Amraphel king of Shinar, Arioch king of Ellasar, Chedorlaomer king of Elam, and Tidal king of nations,[a] ²*that* they made war with Bera king of Sodom, Birsha king of Gomorrah, Shinab king of Admah, Shemeber king of Zeboiim, and the king of Bela (that is, Zoar). ³All these joined together in the Valley of Siddim (that is, the Salt Sea). ⁴Twelve years they served Chedorlaomer, and in the thirteenth year they rebelled.

⁵In the fourteenth year Chedorlaomer and the kings that *were* with him came and attacked the Rephaim in Ashteroth Karnaim, the Zuzim in Ham, the Emim in Shaveh Kiriathaim, ⁶and the Horites in their mountain of Seir, as far as El Paran, which *is* by the wilderness. ⁷Then they turned back and came to En Mishpat (that *is,* Kadesh), and attacked all the country of the Amalekites, and also the Amorites who dwelt in Hazezon Tamar.

⁸And the king of Sodom, the king of Gomorrah, the king of Admah, the king of Zeboiim, and the king of Bela (that *is,* Zoar) went out and joined together in battle in the Valley of Siddim ⁹against Chedorlaomer king of Elam, Tidal king of nations,[a] Amraphel king of

13:15 ᵃLiterally *seed,* and so throughout the book
13:18 ᵃHebrew *Alon Mamre* 14:1 ᵃHebrew *goyim*
14:9 ᵃHebrew *goyim*

ABRAHAM
A LEADER WHO WENT THE DISTANCE
(Genesis 12:1—25:11)

PROFILE IN LEADERSHIP

When Jews in New Testament days spoke of their heritage and spiritual legacy, they claimed Abraham as their father (John 8:33, 39). Why did they give him the title "father," a term of respect synonymous with leadership? Because Abraham went the distance.

Genesis 11:31 tells us that Abraham's father, Terah, set out for Canaan from Ur of the Chaldeans long before Abraham made a similar trip. But for some reason, Terah stopped in Haran and never continued his journey. Did Terah receive an original call from God to move to the Promised Land . . . but neglect to follow through? We'll never know.

We do know that Abraham never made such a mistake. Although he made other leadership errors, Abraham always seemed to follow through on his commitments. When God called him to depart to an unknown land, he went the distance. When enemies abducted Lot and his goods, Abraham pursued the kidnappers and subdued them (Gen. 14:14–16). When commanded to circumcise the males of his household, Abraham did it "that very same day" (17:23). And when God asked Abraham to take his beloved son, Isaac, to Mount Moriah and sacrifice him there, Abraham followed through to the last detail. Only a last-second angelic intervention spared the young man's life (22:1–19). No wonder that God, the Ultimate Leader, called Abraham "My friend" (Is. 41:8)!

Shinar, and Arioch king of Ellasar—four kings against five. [10]Now the Valley of Siddim *was full of* asphalt pits; and the kings of Sodom and Gomorrah fled; *some* fell there, and the remainder fled to the mountains. [11]Then they took all the goods of Sodom and Gomorrah, and all their provisions, and went their way. [12]They also took Lot, Abram's brother's son who dwelt in Sodom, and his goods, and departed.

[13]Then one who had escaped came and told Abram the Hebrew, for he dwelt by the terebinth trees of Mamre[a] the Amorite, brother of Eshcol and brother of Aner; and they *were* allies with Abram. [14]Now when Abram heard that his brother was taken captive, he armed his three hundred and eighteen trained *servants* who were born in his own house, and went in pursuit as far as Dan. [15]He divided his forces against them by night, and he and his servants attacked them and pursued them as far as Hobah, which *is* north of Damascus. [16]So he brought back all the goods, and also brought back his brother Lot and his goods, as well as the women and the people.

[17]And the king of Sodom went out to meet him at the Valley of Shaveh (that *is,* the King's Valley), after his return from the defeat of Chedorlaomer and the kings who *were* with him.

Abram and Melchizedek

[18]Then Melchizedek king of Salem brought out bread and wine; he *was* the priest of God Most High. [19]And he blessed him and said:

"Blessed be Abram of God Most High,
    Possessor of heaven and earth;
[20]   And blessed be God Most High,
    Who has delivered your enemies into your
        hand."

And he gave him a tithe of all.

[21]Now the king of Sodom said to Abram, "Give me the persons, and take the goods for yourself."

[22]But Abram said to the king of Sodom, "I have raised my hand to the LORD, God Most High, the Possessor of heaven and earth, [23]that I *will take* nothing, from a thread to a sandal strap, and that I will not take anything that *is* yours, lest you should say, 'I have made Abram rich'— [24]except only what the young men have eaten, and the portion of the men who went with me: Aner, Eshcol, and Mamre; let them take their portion."

God's Covenant with Abram

15 After these things the word of the LORD came to Abram in a vision, saying, "Do not be afraid, Abram. I *am* your shield, your exceedingly great reward."

[2]But Abram said, "Lord GOD, what will You give me, seeing I go childless, and the heir of my house *is* Eliezer of Damascus?" [3]Then Abram said, "Look, You have given me no offspring; indeed one born in my house is my heir!"

[4]And behold, the word of the LORD *came* to him, saying, "This one shall not be your heir, but one who will come from your own body shall be your heir." [5]Then He brought him outside and said, "Look now toward heaven, and count the stars if you are able to number them." And He said to him, "So shall your descendants be."

[6]And he believed in the LORD, and He accounted it to him for righteousness.

[7]Then He said to him, "I *am* the LORD, who brought you out of Ur of the Chaldeans, to give you this land to inherit it."

[8]And he said, "Lord GOD, how shall I know that I will inherit it?"

[9]So He said to him, "Bring Me a three-year-old heifer, a three-year-old female goat, a three-year-old ram, a turtledove, and a young pigeon." [10]Then he brought all these to Him and cut them in two, down the middle, and placed each piece opposite the other; but he did not cut the birds in two. [11]And when the vultures came down on the carcasses, Abram drove them away.

[12]Now when the sun was going down, a deep sleep fell upon Abram; and behold, horror *and* great darkness fell upon him. [13]Then He said to Abram: "Know certainly that your descendants will be strangers in a land *that is* not theirs, and will serve them, and they will afflict them four hundred years. [14]And also the nation whom they serve I will judge; afterward they shall come out with great possessions. [15]Now as for you, you shall go to your fathers in peace; you shall be buried at a good old age. [16]But in the fourth generation they shall return here, for the iniquity of the Amorites *is* not yet complete."

[17]And it came to pass, when the sun went down and it was dark, that behold, there appeared a smoking oven and a burning torch that passed between those pieces. [18]On the same day the LORD made a covenant with Abram, saying:

"To your descendants I have given this land, from the river of Egypt to the great river, the

---

14:13 [a]Hebrew *Alon Mamre*

River Euphrates— [19]the Kenites, the Kenezzites, the Kadmonites, [20]the Hittites, the Perizzites, the Rephaim, [21]the Amorites, the Canaanites, the Girgashites, and the Jebusites."

Hagar and Ishmael

16 Now Sarai, Abram's wife, had borne him no *children*. And she had an Egyptian maidservant whose name was Hagar. [2]So Sarai said to Abram, "See now, the LORD has restrained me from bearing *children*. Please, go in to my maid; perhaps I shall obtain children by her." And Abram heeded the voice of Sarai. [3]Then Sarai, Abram's wife, took Hagar her maid, the Egyptian, and gave her to her husband Abram to be his wife, after Abram had dwelt ten years in the land of Canaan. [4]So he went in to Hagar, and she conceived. And when she saw that she had conceived, her mistress became despised in her eyes.

[5]Then Sarai said to Abram, "My wrong *be* upon you! I gave my maid into your embrace; and when she saw that she had conceived, I became despised in her eyes. The LORD judge between you and me."

[6]So Abram said to Sarai, "Indeed your maid *is* in your hand; do to her as you please." And when Sarai dealt harshly with her, she fled from her presence.

[7]Now the Angel of the LORD found her by a spring of water in the wilderness, by the spring on the way to Shur. [8]And He said, "Hagar, Sarai's maid, where have you come from, and where are you going?"

She said, "I am fleeing from the presence of my mistress Sarai."

[9]The Angel of the LORD said to her, "Return to your mistress, and submit yourself under her hand." [10]Then the Angel of the LORD said to her, "I will multiply your descendants exceedingly, so that they shall not be counted for multitude." [11]And the Angel of the LORD said to her:

> "Behold, you *are* with child,
> And you shall bear a son.
> You shall call his name Ishmael,
> Because the LORD has heard your
>   affliction.
> [12] He shall be a wild man;
> His hand *shall be* against every man,
> And every man's hand against him.
> And he shall dwell in the presence of all
>   his brethren."

[13]Then she called the name of the LORD who spoke to her, You-Are-the-God-Who-Sees; for she said, "Have I also here seen Him who sees me?" [14]Therefore the well was called Beer Lahai Roi;[a] observe, *it is* between Kadesh and Bered.

[15]So Hagar bore Abram a son; and Abram named his son, whom Hagar bore, Ishmael. [16]Abram *was* eighty-six years old when Hagar bore Ishmael to Abram.

The Sign of the Covenant

17 When Abram was ninety-nine years old, the LORD appeared to Abram and said to him, "I *am* Almighty God; walk before Me and be blameless. [2]And I will make My covenant between Me and you, and will multiply you exceedingly." [3]Then Abram fell on his face, and God talked with him, saying: "'As for Me, behold, My covenant is with you, and you shall be a father of many nations. [5]No longer shall your name be called Abram, but your name shall be Abraham; for I have made you a father of many nations. [6]I will make you exceedingly fruitful; and I will make nations of you, and kings shall come from you. [7]And I will establish My covenant between Me and you and your descendants after you in their generations, for an everlasting covenant, to be God to you and your descendants after you. [8]Also I give to you and your descendants after you the land in which you are a stranger, all the land of Canaan, as an everlasting possession; and I will be their God."

[9]And God said to Abraham: "As for you, you shall keep My covenant, you and your descendants after you throughout their generations. [10]This *is* My covenant which you shall keep, between Me and you and your descendants after you: Every male child among you shall be circumcised; [11]and you shall be circumcised in the flesh of your foreskins, and it shall be a sign of the covenant between Me and you. [12]He who is eight days old among you shall be circumcised, every male child in your generations, he who is born in your house or bought with money from any foreigner who is not your descendant. [13]He who is born in your house and he who is bought with your money must be circumcised, and My covenant shall be in your flesh for an everlasting covenant. [14]And the uncircumcised male child, who is not circumcised in the flesh of his foreskin, that person shall be cut off from his people; he has broken My covenant."

[15]Then God said to Abraham, "As for Sarai your wife, you shall not call her name Sarai, but

---

16:14 [a]Literally *Well of the One Who Lives and Sees Me*

21 QUALITIES

PROBLEM SOLVING

Sarah Does God's Will Her Way

(Genesis 16:1–16)

Those who master problem solving—one of the 21 Indispensable Qualities of a Leader—find that it's one of the fastest ways to gain leadership in any group. Anyone who can solve problems will never lack influence.

But the influence gained isn't always positive.

Consider the case of Sarah. God told her husband, Abraham, that his offspring would grow as numerous as the sands of the seashore and the stars in the sky. But there was a problem: Sarah was barren and past the age of childbearing. As the years passed, God's promise didn't appear any closer to fulfillment.

Sarah faced a problem and felt compelled to solve it. Lacking the patience to trust God to keep His promise, Sarah looked to her own methods. After waiting more than a decade for a son, she felt she had waited long enough and unwisely attempted to fulfill God's will in her way, through an Egyptian servant named Hagar.

Sarah's solution, however, gave her no peace. When Hagar became pregnant by Abraham and bore a son named Ishmael, Sarah despised both Hagar and her newborn son. Hagar had done what she was asked, but satisfaction eluded Sarah.

Control Freak!

The true problem facing Sarah was not a need for offspring, but her own impatience. Sarah wanted *control*—something that has afflicted many leaders throughout history. Instead of trusting God, Sarah tried to make the promise come true by using her own methods and according to her own timetable. She depended upon her own strength when she should have leaned on Almighty God. She illustrates what happens when an insecure leader tries to work independently of God. Insecure leaders:

1. Believe God is inattentive, absent, or even against them.
2. Allow their circumstances to determine their understanding of God's character.
3. See life through a perspective of scarcity rather than abundance.
4. Become self-seeking and manipulative.
5. Feel intimidated and deal with others through intimidation.
6. Resent the success of others and angrily turn on them.
7. Think that if one person succeeds, someone else must lose.
8. Blame others for their dilemmas.
9. See themselves as martyrs.
10. Conclude that attempts at control seem more logical than trusting God.

Do you identify with Sarah? Do you struggle with a desire to control problems rather than doing things God's way? If so, ask God to reveal how He would have you deal with your problems in a way that honors Him.

For a positive example of problem solving, see p. 1493.

Sarah *shall be* her name. [16]And I will bless her and also give you a son by her; then I will bless her, and she shall be *a mother of* nations; kings of peoples shall be from her."

[17]Then Abraham fell on his face and laughed, and said in his heart, "Shall *a child* be born to a man who is one hundred years old? And shall Sarah, who is ninety years old, bear *a child?*" [18]And Abraham said to God, "Oh, that Ishmael might live before You!"

[19]Then God said: "No, Sarah your wife shall bear you a son, and you shall call his name Isaac; I will establish My covenant with him for an everlasting covenant, *and* with his descendants after him. [20]And as for Ishmael, I have heard you. Behold, I have blessed him, and will make him fruitful, and will multiply him exceedingly. He shall beget twelve princes, and I will make him a great nation. [21]But My covenant I will establish with Isaac, whom Sarah shall bear to you at this set time next year." [22]Then He finished talking with him, and God went up from Abraham.

[23]So Abraham took Ishmael his son, all who were born in his house and all who were bought with his money, every male among the men of Abraham's house, and circumcised the flesh of their foreskins that very same day, as God had said to him. [24]Abraham *was* ninety-nine years old when he was circumcised in the flesh of his foreskin. [25]And Ishmael his son *was* thirteen years old when he was circumcised in the flesh of his foreskin. [26]That very same day Abraham was circumcised, and his son Ishmael; [27]and all the men of his house, born in the house or bought with money from a foreigner, were circumcised with him.

The Son of Promise

18 Then the LORD appeared to him by the terebinth trees of Mamre,[a] as he was sitting in the tent door in the heat of the day. [2]So he lifted his eyes and looked, and behold, three men were standing by him; and when he saw *them,* he ran from the tent door to meet them, and bowed himself to the ground, [3]and said, "My Lord, if I have now found favor in Your sight, do not pass on by Your servant. [4]Please let a little water be brought, and wash your feet, and rest yourselves under the tree. [5]And I will bring a morsel of bread, that you may refresh your hearts. After that you may pass by, inasmuch as you have come to your servant."

They said, "Do as you have said."

[6]So Abraham hurried into the tent to Sarah and said, "Quickly, make ready three measures of fine meal; knead *it* and make cakes." [7]And Abra-

ham ran to the herd, took a tender and good calf, gave *it* to a young man, and he hastened to prepare it. [8]So he took butter and milk and the calf which he had prepared, and set *it* before them; and he stood by them under the tree as they ate.

[9]Then they said to him, "Where *is* Sarah your wife?"

So he said, "Here, in the tent."

[10]And He said, "I will certainly return to you according to the time of life, and behold, Sarah your wife shall have a son."

(Sarah was listening in the tent door which *was* behind him.) [11]Now Abraham and Sarah were old, well advanced in age; *and* Sarah had passed the age of childbearing.[a] [12]Therefore Sarah laughed within herself, saying, "After I have grown old, shall I have pleasure, my lord being old also?"

[13]And the LORD said to Abraham, "Why did Sarah laugh, saying, 'Shall I surely bear *a child,* since I am old?' [14]Is anything too hard for the LORD? At the appointed time I will return to you, according to the time of life, and Sarah shall have a son."

[15]But Sarah denied *it,* saying, "I did not laugh," for she was afraid.

And He said, "No, but you did laugh!"

Abraham Intercedes for Sodom

[16]Then the men rose from there and looked toward Sodom, and Abraham went with them to send them on the way. [17]And the LORD said, "Shall I hide from Abraham what I am doing, [18]since Abraham shall surely become a great and mighty nation, and all the nations of the earth shall be blessed in him? [19]For I have known him, in order that he may command his children and his household after him, that they keep the way of the LORD, to do righteousness and justice, that the LORD may bring to Abraham what He has spoken to him." [20]And the LORD said, "Because the outcry against Sodom and Gomorrah is great, and because their sin is very grave, [21]I will go down now and see whether they have done altogether according to the outcry against it that has come to Me; and if not, I will know."

[22]Then the men turned away from there and went toward Sodom, but Abraham still stood before the LORD. [23]And Abraham came near and said, "Would You also destroy the righteous with the wicked? [24]Suppose there were fifty righteous within the city; would You also destroy the place

---

18:1 [a]Hebrew *Alon Mamre* **18:11** [a]Literally *the manner of women had ceased to be with Sarah*

and not spare *it* for the fifty righteous that were in it? ²⁵Far be it from You to do such a thing as this, to slay the righteous with the wicked, so that the righteous should be as the wicked; far be it from You! Shall not the Judge of all the earth do right?"

²⁶So the LORD said, "If I find in Sodom fifty righteous within the city, then I will spare all the place for their sakes."

²⁷Then Abraham answered and said, "Indeed now, I who *am but* dust and ashes have taken it upon myself to speak to the Lord: ²⁸Suppose there were five less than the fifty righteous; would You destroy all of the city for *lack of* five?"

So He said, "If I find there forty-five, I will not destroy *it*."

²⁹And he spoke to Him yet again and said, "Suppose there should be forty found there?"

So He said, "I will not do *it* for the sake of forty."

³⁰Then he said, "Let not the Lord be angry, and I will speak: Suppose thirty should be found there?"

So He said, "I will not do *it* if I find thirty there."

³¹And he said, "Indeed now, I have taken it upon myself to speak to the Lord: Suppose twenty should be found there?"

So He said, "I will not destroy *it* for the sake of twenty."

³²Then he said, "Let not the Lord be angry, and I will speak but once more: Suppose ten should be found there?"

And He said, "I will not destroy *it* for the sake of ten." ³³So the LORD went His way as soon as He had finished speaking with Abraham; and Abraham returned to his place.

Sodom's Depravity

19 Now the two angels came to Sodom in the evening, and Lot was sitting in the gate of Sodom. When Lot saw *them,* he rose to meet them, and he bowed himself with his face toward the ground. ²And he said, "Here now, my lords, please turn in to your servant's house and spend the night, and wash your feet; then you may rise early and go on your way."

And they said, "No, but we will spend the night in the open square."

³But he insisted strongly; so they turned in to him and entered his house. Then he made them a feast, and baked unleavened bread, and they ate.

⁴Now before they lay down, the men of the city, the men of Sodom, both old and young, all the people from every quarter, surrounded the

---

SARAH

GOD HAD THE LAST LAUGH
(Genesis 18:9–15; 21:1–7)

PROFILE IN LEADERSHIP

God saw Sarah's laughter and He knew what she was thinking.

The elderly woman heard the Lord tell her husband, the even older Abraham, that within a year she would bear him a son. *How could this be?* she wondered. To her ears it sounded implausible, preposterous. How could an 89-year-old woman and a 99-year-old man have a child? *Wishing a thing does not make it so,* she may have thought.

Sarah doubted because she looked at her circumstances and not at the God who keeps His promises. The revelation just seemed too good to be true—so she laughed. Not out loud. And not enough so that anyone but God would notice (Gen. 18:12). She laughed quietly, in unbelief and impatience, not uproariously, in faith and celebration.

Yet God noticed, and God would have the last laugh. He challenged Sarah's unbelief with a sharp, "Is anything too hard for the LORD?" (18:14).

The Bible tells us that a year after Sarah's moment of unbelief and impatience, God brought her another kind of laughter, the kind that accompanies the joy of a promise kept—the only kind of promise God makes.

Impatient leaders need to learn what Sarah discovered that day: God always keeps His promises, but in His timing and in His way.

house. [5]And they called to Lot and said to him, "Where are the men who came to you tonight? Bring them out to us that we may know them *carnally*."

[6]So Lot went out to them through the doorway, shut the door behind him, [7]and said, "Please, my brethren, do not do so wickedly! [8]See now, I have two daughters who have not known a man; please, let me bring them out to you, and you may do to them as you wish; only do nothing to these men, since this is the reason they have come under the shadow of my roof."

[9]And they said, "Stand back!" Then they said, "This one came in to stay *here*, and he keeps acting as a judge; now we will deal worse with you than with them." So they pressed hard against the man Lot, and came near to break down the door. [10]But the men reached out their hands and pulled Lot into the house with them, and shut the door. [11]And they struck the men who *were* at the doorway of the house with blindness, both small and great, so that they became weary *trying* to find the door.

Sodom and Gomorrah Destroyed

[12]Then the men said to Lot, "Have you anyone else here? Son-in-law, your sons, your daughters, and whomever you have in the city— take *them* out of this place! [13]For we will destroy this place, because the outcry against them has grown great before the face of the LORD, and the LORD has sent us to destroy it."

[14]So Lot went out and spoke to his sons-in-law, who had married his daughters, and said, "Get up, get out of this place; for the LORD will destroy this city!" But to his sons-in-law he seemed to be joking.

[15]When the morning dawned, the angels urged Lot to hurry, saying, "Arise, take your wife and your two daughters who are here, lest you be consumed in the punishment of the city." [16]And while he lingered, the men took hold of his hand, his wife's hand, and the hands of his two daughters, the LORD being merciful to him, and they brought him out and set him outside the city. [17]So it came to pass, when they had brought them outside, that he[a] said, "Escape for your life! Do not look behind you nor stay anywhere in the plain. Escape to the mountains, lest you be destroyed."

[18]Then Lot said to them, "Please, no, my lords! [19]Indeed now, your servant has found favor in your sight, and you have increased your mercy which you have shown me by saving my life; but I cannot escape to the mountains, lest some evil overtake me and I die. [20]See now, this city *is* near

enough to flee to, and it *is* a little one; please let me escape there (*is* it not a little one?) and my soul shall live."

[21]And he said to him, "See, I have favored you concerning this thing also, in that I will not overthrow this city for which you have spoken. [22]Hurry, escape there. For I cannot do anything until you arrive there."

Therefore the name of the city was called Zoar.

[23]The sun had risen upon the earth when Lot entered Zoar. [24]Then the LORD rained brimstone and fire on Sodom and Gomorrah, from the LORD out of the heavens. [25]So He overthrew those cities, all the plain, all the inhabitants of the cities, and what grew on the ground. [26]But his wife looked back behind him, and she became a pillar of salt.

[27]And Abraham went early in the morning to the place where he had stood before the LORD. [28]Then he looked toward Sodom and Gomorrah, and toward all the land of the plain; and he saw, and behold, the smoke of the land which went up like the smoke of a furnace. [29]And it came to pass, when God destroyed the cities of the plain, that God remembered Abraham, and sent Lot out of the midst of the overthrow, when He overthrew the cities in which Lot had dwelt.

The Descendants of Lot

[30]Then Lot went up out of Zoar and dwelt in the mountains, and his two daughters were with him; for he was afraid to dwell in Zoar. And he and his two daughters dwelt in a cave. [31]Now the firstborn said to the younger, "Our father *is* old, and *there is* no man on the earth to come in to us as is the custom of all the earth. [32]Come, let us make our father drink wine, and we will lie with him, that we may preserve the lineage of our father." [33]So they made their father drink wine that night. And the firstborn went in and lay with her father, and he did not know when she lay down or when she arose.

[34]It happened on the next day that the firstborn said to the younger, "Indeed I lay with my father last night; let us make him drink wine tonight also, and you go in *and* lie with him, that we may preserve the lineage of our father." [35]Then they made their father drink wine that night also. And the younger arose and lay with him, and he did not know when she lay down or when she arose.

[36]Thus both the daughters of Lot were with child by their father. [37]The firstborn bore a son

---

19:17 [a]Septuagint, Syriac, and Vulgate read *they*.

and called his name Moab; he *is* the father of the Moabites to this day. ³⁸And the younger, she also bore a son and called his name Ben-Ammi; he *is* the father of the people of Ammon to this day.

Abraham and Abimelech

20 And Abraham journeyed from there to the South, and dwelt between Kadesh and Shur, and stayed in Gerar. ²Now Abraham said of Sarah his wife, "She *is* my sister." And Abimelech king of Gerar sent and took Sarah.

³But God came to Abimelech in a dream by night, and said to him, "Indeed you *are* a dead man because of the woman whom you have taken, for she *is* a man's wife."

⁴But Abimelech had not come near her; and he said, "Lord, will You slay a righteous nation also? ⁵Did he not say to me, 'She *is* my sister'? And she, even she herself said, 'He *is* my brother.' In the integrity of my heart and innocence of my hands I have done this."

⁶And God said to him in a dream, "Yes, I know that you did this in the integrity of your heart. For I also withheld you from sinning against Me; therefore I did not let you touch her. ⁷Now therefore, restore the man's wife; for he *is* a prophet, and he will pray for you and you shall live. But if you do not restore *her,* know that you shall surely die, you and all who *are* yours."

⁸So Abimelech rose early in the morning, called all his servants, and told all these things in their hearing; and the men were very much afraid. ⁹And Abimelech called Abraham and said to him, "What have you done to us? How have I offended you, that you have brought on me and on my kingdom a great sin? You have done deeds to me that ought not to be done." ¹⁰Then Abimelech said to Abraham, "What did you have in view, that you have done this thing?"

¹¹And Abraham said, "Because I thought, surely the fear of God *is* not in this place; and they will kill me on account of my wife. ¹²But indeed *she is* truly my sister. She *is* the daughter of my father, but not the daughter of my mother; and she became my wife. ¹³And it came to pass, when God caused me to wander from my father's house, that I said to her, 'This *is* your kindness that you should do for me: in every place, wherever we go, say of me, "He *is* my brother." ' "

¹⁴Then Abimelech took sheep, oxen, and male and female servants, and gave *them* to Abraham; and he restored Sarah his wife to him. ¹⁵And Abimelech said, "See, my land *is* before

you; dwell where it pleases you." ¹⁶Then to Sarah he said, "Behold, I have given your brother a thousand *pieces* of silver; indeed this vindicates youᵃ before all who *are* with you and before everybody." Thus she was rebuked.

¹⁷So Abraham prayed to God; and God healed Abimelech, his wife, and his female servants. Then they bore *children;* ¹⁸for the LORD had closed up all the wombs of the house of Abimelech because of Sarah, Abraham's wife.

Isaac Is Born

21 And the LORD visited Sarah as He had said, and the LORD did for Sarah as He had spoken. ²For Sarah conceived and bore Abraham a son in his old age, at the set time of which God had spoken to him. ³And Abraham called the name of his son who was born to him—whom Sarah bore to him—Isaac. ⁴Then Abraham circumcised his son Isaac when he was eight days old, as God had commanded him. ⁵Now Abraham was one hundred years old when his son Isaac was born to him. ⁶And Sarah said, "God has made me laugh, *and* all who hear will laugh with me." ⁷She also said, "Who would have said to Abraham that Sarah would nurse children? For I have borne *him* a son in his old age."

Hagar and Ishmael Depart

⁸So the child grew and was weaned. And Abraham made a great feast on the same day that Isaac was weaned.

⁹And Sarah saw the son of Hagar the Egyptian, whom she had borne to Abraham, scoffing. ¹⁰Therefore she said to Abraham, "Cast out this bondwoman and her son; for the son of this bondwoman shall not be heir with my son, *namely* with Isaac." ¹¹And the matter was very displeasing in Abraham's sight because of his son.

¹²But God said to Abraham, "Do not let it be displeasing in your sight because of the lad or because of your bondwoman. Whatever Sarah has said to you, listen to her voice; for in Isaac your seed shall be called. ¹³Yet I will also make a nation of the son of the bondwoman, because he *is* your seed."

¹⁴So Abraham rose early in the morning, and took bread and a skin of water; and putting *it* on her shoulder, he gave *it* and the boy to Hagar, and sent her away. Then she departed and wandered in the Wilderness of Beersheba. ¹⁵And the water in the skin was used up, and she

20:16 ᵃLiterally *it is a covering of the eyes for you*

placed the boy under one of the shrubs. [16]Then she went and sat down across from *him* at a distance of about a bowshot; for she said to herself, "Let me not see the death of the boy." So she sat opposite *him,* and lifted her voice and wept.

[17]And God heard the voice of the lad. Then the angel of God called to Hagar out of heaven, and said to her, "What ails you, Hagar? Fear not, for God has heard the voice of the lad where he *is.* [18]Arise, lift up the lad and hold him with your hand, for I will make him a great nation."

[19]Then God opened her eyes, and she saw a well of water. And she went and filled the skin with water, and gave the lad a drink. [20]So God was with the lad; and he grew and dwelt in the wilderness, and became an archer. [21]He dwelt in the Wilderness of Paran; and his mother took a wife for him from the land of Egypt.

A Covenant with Abimelech

[22]And it came to pass at that time that Abimelech and Phichol, the commander of his army, spoke to Abraham, saying, "God *is* with you in all that you do. [23]Now therefore, swear to me by God that you will not deal falsely with me, with my offspring, or with my posterity; but that according to the kindness that I have done to you, you will do to me and to the land in which you have dwelt."

[24]And Abraham said, "I will swear."

[25]Then Abraham rebuked Abimelech because of a well of water which Abimelech's servants had seized. [26]And Abimelech said, "I do not know who has done this thing; you did not tell me, nor had I heard *of it* until today." [27]So Abraham took sheep and oxen and gave them to Abimelech, and the two of them made a covenant. [28]And Abraham set seven ewe lambs of the flock by themselves.

[29]Then Abimelech asked Abraham, "What *is the meaning of* these seven ewe lambs which you have set by themselves?"

[30]And he said, "You will take *these* seven ewe lambs from my hand, that they may be my witness that I have dug this well." [31]Therefore he called that place Beersheba,[a] because the two of them swore an oath there.

[32]Thus they made a covenant at Beersheba. So Abimelech rose with Phichol, the commander of his army, and they returned to the land of the Philistines. [33]Then *Abraham* planted a tamarisk tree in Beersheba, and there called on the name of the LORD, the Everlasting God. [34]And Abraham stayed in the land of the Philistines many days.

Abraham's Faith Confirmed

22 Now it came to pass after these things that God tested Abraham, and said to him, "Abraham!"

And he said, "Here I am."

[2]Then He said, "Take now your son, your only *son* Isaac, whom you love, and go to the land of Moriah, and offer him there as a burnt offering on one of the mountains of which I shall tell you."

[3]So Abraham rose early in the morning and saddled his donkey, and took two of his young men with him, and Isaac his son; and he split the wood for the burnt offering, and arose and went to the place of which God had told him. [4]Then on the third day Abraham lifted his eyes and saw the place afar off. [5]And Abraham said to his young men, "Stay here with the donkey; the lad[a] and I will go yonder and worship, and we will come back to you."

[6]So Abraham took the wood of the burnt offering and laid *it* on Isaac his son; and he took the fire in his hand, and a knife, and the two of them went together. [7]But Isaac spoke to Abraham his father and said, "My father!"

And he said, "Here I am, my son."

Then he said, "Look, the fire and the wood, but where *is* the lamb for a burnt offering?"

[8]And Abraham said, "My son, God will provide for Himself the lamb for a burnt offering." So the two of them went together.

[9]Then they came to the place of which God had told him. And Abraham built an altar there and placed the wood in order; and he bound Isaac his son and laid him on the altar, upon the wood. [10]And Abraham stretched out his hand and took the knife to slay his son.

[11]But the Angel of the LORD called to him from heaven and said, "Abraham, Abraham!"

So he said, "Here I am."

[12]And He said, "Do not lay your hand on the lad, or do anything to him; for now I know that you fear God, since you have not withheld your son, your only *son,* from Me."

[13]Then Abraham lifted his eyes and looked, and there behind *him was* a ram caught in a thicket by its horns. So Abraham went and took the ram, and offered it up for a burnt offering instead of his son. [14]And Abraham called the name of the place, The-LORD-Will-Provide;[a] as it is said *to* this day, "In the Mount of the LORD it shall be provided."

21:31 [a]Literally *Well of the Oath* or *Well of the Seven*
22:5 [a]Or *young man* **22:14** [a]Hebrew *YHWH Yireh*

The Law of Sacrifice: Abraham Pays a Price

(Genesis 22:1–18)

Did you know that God provides tests as measures of progress and as proving grounds for every person He calls to lead? Genesis 22 begins with a divine test. God calls Abraham to climb Mount Moriah and sacrifice his beloved son. If Abraham would resolve to give up Isaac, God knew he would be willing to do anything asked of him—and therefore would be a perfect candidate to become the father of the Hebrew people.

Leadership tests differ from one another, but all have a few things in common:

1. **Leaders get tested at each stage of growth.**
2. **The leaders goal is to pass the test.**
3. **Testing always precedes promotion.**
4. **Self-promotion or promotion by others can never replace divine promotion.**
5. **Promotion requires sacrifice.**

While Abraham's trial foreshadowed what God intended to do with His only begotten Son thousands of years later, it also provided a leadership test.

[15]Then the Angel of the LORD called to Abraham a second time out of heaven, [16]and said: "By Myself I have sworn, says the LORD, because you have done this thing, and have not withheld your son, your only *son*— [17]blessing I will bless you, and multiplying I will multiply your descendants as the stars of the heaven and as the sand which *is* on the seashore; and your descendants shall possess the gate of their enemies. [18]In your seed all the nations of the earth shall be blessed, because you have obeyed My voice." [19]So Abraham returned to his young men, and they rose and went together to Beersheba; and Abraham dwelt at Beersheba.

The Family of Nahor

[20]Now it came to pass after these things that it was told Abraham, saying, "Indeed Milcah also has borne children to your brother Nahor: [21]Huz his firstborn, Buz his brother, Kemuel the father of Aram, [22]Chesed, Hazo, Pildash, Jidlaph, and Bethuel." [23]And Bethuel begot Rebekah.[a] These eight Milcah bore to Nahor, Abraham's brother. [24]His concubine, whose name was Reumah, also bore Tebah, Gaham, Thahash, and Maachah.

Sarah's Death and Burial

23 Sarah lived one hundred and twenty-seven years; *these were* the years of the life of Sarah. [2]So Sarah died in Kirjath Arba (that *is,* Hebron) in the land of Canaan, and Abraham came to mourn for Sarah and to weep for her.

[3]Then Abraham stood up from before his dead, and spoke to the sons of Heth, saying, [4]"I *am* a foreigner and a visitor among you. Give me property for a burial place among you, that I may bury my dead out of my sight."

[5]And the sons of Heth answered Abraham, saying to him, [6]"Hear us, my lord: You *are* a mighty prince among us; bury your dead in the choicest of our burial places. None of us will withhold from you his burial place, that you may bury your dead."

[7]Then Abraham stood up and bowed himself to the people of the land, the sons of Heth. [8]And he spoke with them, saying, "If it is your wish that I bury my dead out of my sight, hear me, and meet with Ephron the son of Zohar for me, [9]that he may give me the cave of Machpelah which he has, which *is* at the end of his field. Let him give it to me at the full price, as property for a burial place among you."

[10]Now Ephron dwelt among the sons of Heth; and Ephron the Hittite answered Abraham in the presence of the sons of Heth, all who entered at the gate of his city, saying, [11]"No, my lord, hear me: I give you the field and the cave that *is* in it; I give it to you in the presence of the sons of my people. I give it to you. Bury your dead!"

[12]Then Abraham bowed himself down before the people of the land; [13]and he spoke to Ephron in the hearing of the people of the land, saying, "If you *will give it,* please hear me. I will give you money for the field; take *it* from me and I will bury my dead there."

[14]And Ephron answered Abraham, saying to him, [15]"My lord, listen to me; the land *is worth* four hundred shekels of silver. What *is* that between you and me? So bury your dead." [16]And Abraham listened to Ephron; and Abraham weighed out the silver for Ephron which he had named in the hearing of the sons of Heth, four hundred shekels of silver, currency of the merchants.

22:23 [a]Spelled *Rebecca* in Romans 9:10

[17]So the field of Ephron which *was* in Machpelah, which *was* before Mamre, the field and the cave which *was* in it, and all the trees that *were* in the field, which *were* within all the surrounding borders, were deeded [18]to Abraham as a possession in the presence of the sons of Heth, before all who went in at the gate of his city.

[19]And after this, Abraham buried Sarah his wife in the cave of the field of Machpelah, before Mamre (that *is,* Hebron) in the land of Canaan. [20]So the field and the cave that *is* in it were deeded to Abraham by the sons of Heth as property for a burial place.

A Bride for Isaac

24 Now Abraham was old, well advanced in age; and the LORD had blessed Abraham in all things. [2]So Abraham said to the oldest servant of his house, who ruled over all that he had, "Please, put your hand under my thigh, [3]and I will make you swear by the LORD, the God of heaven and the God of the earth, that you will not take a wife for my son from the daughters of the Canaanites, among whom I dwell; [4]but you shall go to my country and to my family, and take a wife for my son Isaac."

[5]And the servant said to him, "Perhaps the woman will not be willing to follow me to this land. Must I take your son back to the land from which you came?"

[6]But Abraham said to him, "Beware that you do not take my son back there. [7]The LORD God of heaven, who took me from my father's house and from the land of my family, and who spoke to me and swore to me, saying, 'To your descendants[a] I give this land,' He will send His angel before you, and you shall take a wife for my son from there. [8]And if the woman is not willing to follow you, then you will be released from this oath; only do not take my son back there." [9]So the servant put his hand under the thigh of Abraham his master, and swore to him concerning this matter.

[10]Then the servant took ten of his master's camels and departed, for all his master's goods *were in* his hand. And he arose and went to Mesopotamia, to the city of Nahor. [11]And he made his camels kneel down outside the city by a well of water at evening time, the time when women go out to draw *water.* [12]Then he said, "O LORD God of my master Abraham, please give me success this day, and show kindness to my master Abraham. [13]Behold, *here* I stand by the well of water, and the daughters of the men of the city are coming out to draw water. [14]Now let

it be that the young woman to whom I say, 'Please let down your pitcher that I may drink,' and she says, 'Drink, and I will also give your camels a drink'—*let* her *be the one* You have appointed for Your servant Isaac. And by this I will know that You have shown kindness to my master."

[15]And it happened, before he had finished speaking, that behold, Rebekah, who was born to Bethuel, son of Milcah, the wife of Nahor, Abraham's brother, came out with her pitcher on her shoulder. [16]Now the young woman *was* very beautiful to behold, a virgin; no man had known her. And she went down to the well, filled her pitcher, and came up. [17]And the servant ran to meet her and said, "Please let me drink a little water from your pitcher."

[18]So she said, "Drink, my lord." Then she quickly let her pitcher down to her hand, and gave him a drink. [19]And when she had finished giving him a drink, she said, "I will draw *water* for your camels also, until they have finished drinking." [20]Then she quickly emptied her pitcher into the trough, ran back to the well to draw *water,* and drew for all his camels. [21]And the man, wondering at her, remained silent so as to know whether the LORD had made his journey prosperous or not.

[22]So it was, when the camels had finished drinking, that the man took a golden nose ring weighing half a shekel, and two bracelets for her wrists weighing ten *shekels* of gold, [23]and said, "Whose daughter *are* you? Tell me, please, is there room *in* your father's house for us to lodge?"

[24]So she said to him, "I *am* the daughter of Bethuel, Milcah's son, whom she bore to Nahor." [25]Moreover she said to him, "We have both straw and feed enough, and room to lodge."

[26]Then the man bowed down his head and worshiped the LORD. [27]And he said, "Blessed *be* the LORD God of my master Abraham, who has not forsaken His mercy and His truth toward my master. As for me, being on the way, the LORD led me to the house of my master's brethren." [28]So the young woman ran and told her mother's household these things.

[29]Now Rebekah had a brother whose name *was* Laban, and Laban ran out to the man by the well. [30]So it came to pass, when he saw the nose ring, and the bracelets on his sister's wrists, and when he heard the words of his sister Rebekah, saying, "Thus the man spoke to me," that he

---

24:7 [a]Literally *seed*

went to the man. And there he stood by the camels at the well. ³¹And he said, "Come in, O blessed of the LORD! Why do you stand outside? For I have prepared the house, and a place for the camels."

³²Then the man came to the house. And he unloaded the camels, and provided straw and feed for the camels, and water to wash his feet and the feet of the men who *were* with him. ³³*Food* was set before him to eat, but he said, "I will not eat until I have told about my errand."

And he said, "Speak on."

³⁴So he said, "I *am* Abraham's servant. ³⁵The LORD has blessed my master greatly, and he has become great; and He has given him flocks and herds, silver and gold, male and female servants, and camels and donkeys. ³⁶And Sarah my master's wife bore a son to my master when she was old; and to him he has given all that he has. ³⁷Now my master made me swear, saying, 'You shall not take a wife for my son from the daughters of the Canaanites, in whose land I dwell; ³⁸but you shall go to my father's house and to my family, and take a wife for my son.' ³⁹And I said to my master, 'Perhaps the woman will not follow me.' ⁴⁰But he said to me, 'The LORD, before whom I walk, will send His angel with you and prosper your way; and you shall take a wife for my son from my family and from my father's house. ⁴¹You will be clear from this oath when you arrive among my family; for if they will not give *her* to you, then you will be released from my oath.'

⁴²"And this day I came to the well and said, 'O LORD God of my master Abraham, if You will now prosper the way in which I go, ⁴³behold, I stand by the well of water; and it shall come to pass that when the virgin comes out to draw *water,* and I say to her, "Please give me a little water from your pitcher to drink," ⁴⁴and she says to me, "Drink, and I will draw for your camels also,"—*let* her *be* the woman whom the LORD has appointed for my master's son.'

⁴⁵"But before I had finished speaking in my heart, there was Rebekah, coming out with her pitcher on her shoulder; and she went down to the well and drew *water.* And I said to her, 'Please let me drink.' ⁴⁶And she made haste and let her pitcher down from her *shoulder,* and said, 'Drink, and I will give your camels a drink also.' So I drank, and she gave the camels a drink also. ⁴⁷Then I asked her, and said, 'Whose daughter *are* you?' And she said, 'The daughter of Bethuel, Nahor's son, whom Milcah bore to him.' So I put the nose ring on her nose and the bracelets on her wrists. ⁴⁸And I bowed my head and wor-shiped the LORD, and blessed the LORD God of my master Abraham, who had led me in the way of truth to take the daughter of my master's brother for his son. ⁴⁹Now if you will deal kindly and truly with my master, tell me. And if not, tell me, that I may turn to the right hand or to the left."

⁵⁰Then Laban and Bethuel answered and said, "The thing comes from the LORD; we cannot speak to you either bad or good. ⁵¹Here *is* Rebekah before you; take *her* and go, and let her be your master's son's wife, as the LORD has spoken."

⁵²And it came to pass, when Abraham's servant heard their words, that he worshiped the LORD, *bowing himself* to the earth. ⁵³Then the servant brought out jewelry of silver, jewelry of gold, and clothing, and gave *them* to Rebekah. He also gave precious things to her brother and to her mother.

⁵⁴And he and the men who *were* with him ate and drank and stayed all night. Then they arose in the morning, and he said, "Send me away to my master."

⁵⁵But her brother and her mother said, "Let the young woman stay with us *a few* days, at least ten; after that she may go."

⁵⁶And he said to them, "Do not hinder me, since the LORD has prospered my way; send me away so that I may go to my master."

⁵⁷So they said, "We will call the young woman and ask her personally." ⁵⁸Then they called Rebekah and said to her, "Will you go with this man?"

And she said, "I will go."

⁵⁹So they sent away Rebekah their sister and her nurse, and Abraham's servant and his men. ⁶⁰And they blessed Rebekah and said to her:

"Our sister, *may* you *become*
The mother of thousands of ten thousands;
And may your descendants possess
The gates of those who hate them."

⁶¹Then Rebekah and her maids arose, and they rode on the camels and followed the man. So the servant took Rebekah and departed.

⁶²Now Isaac came from the way of Beer Lahai Roi, for he dwelt in the South. ⁶³And Isaac went out to meditate in the field in the evening; and he lifted his eyes and looked, and there, the camels *were* coming. ⁶⁴Then Rebekah lifted her eyes, and when she saw Isaac she dismounted from her camel; ⁶⁵for she had said to the servant, "Who *is* this man walking in the field to meet us?"

The servant said, "It *is* my master." So she took a veil and covered herself.

[66]And the servant told Isaac all the things that he had done. [67]Then Isaac brought her into his mother Sarah's tent; and he took Rebekah and she became his wife, and he loved her. So Isaac was comforted after his mother's *death*.

Abraham and Keturah

25 Abraham again took a wife, and her name *was* Keturah. [2]And she bore him Zimran, Jokshan, Medan, Midian, Ishbak, and Shuah. [3]Jokshan begot Sheba and Dedan. And the sons of Dedan were Asshurim, Letushim, and Leummim. [4]And the sons of Midian *were* Ephah, Epher, Hanoch, Abidah, and Eldaah. All these *were* the children of Keturah.

[5]And Abraham gave all that he had to Isaac. [6]But Abraham gave gifts to the sons of the concubines which Abraham had; and while he was still living he sent them eastward, away from Isaac his son, to the country of the east.

Abraham's Death and Burial

[7]This *is* the sum of the years of Abraham's life which he lived: one hundred and seventy-five years. [8]Then Abraham breathed his last and died in a good old age, an old man and full *of years,* and was gathered to his people. [9]And his sons Isaac and Ishmael buried him in the cave of Machpelah, which *is* before Mamre, in the field of Ephron the son of Zohar the Hittite, [10]the field which Abraham purchased from the sons of Heth. There Abraham was buried, and Sarah his wife. [11]And it came to pass, after the death of Abraham, that God blessed his son Isaac. And Isaac dwelt at Beer Lahai Roi.

The Families of Ishmael and Isaac

[12]Now this *is* the genealogy of Ishmael, Abraham's son, whom Hagar the Egyptian, Sarah's maidservant, bore to Abraham. [13]And these *were* the names of the sons of Ishmael, by their names, according to their generations: The firstborn of Ishmael, Nebajoth; then Kedar, Adbeel, Mibsam, [14]Mishma, Dumah, Massa, [15]Hadar,[a] Tema, Jetur, Naphish, and Kedemah. [16]These *were* the sons of Ishmael and these *were* their names, by their towns and their settlements, twelve princes according to their nations. [17]These *were* the years of the life of Ishmael: one hundred and thirty-seven

---

25:15 [a]Masoretic Text reads *Hadad*.

PROFILE IN LEADERSHIP

JACOB

A LEADER MADE USABLE THROUGH BROKENNESS
(Genesis 25:26—32:32)

Natural leaders have it easy, right? Not always. Even leaders gifted with tremendous natural leadership can have a very difficult time, especially with issues of character.

That was true for Jacob. From the very beginning he wielded great influence. No matter what he did or where he went, he stirred things up. He captured the heart of his mother and the birthright of his brother, turning Isaac's household upside down. He had a similar impact on the household of Laban. Over time, his leadership created great prosperity. And it was his sons who founded the twelve tribes of the Hebrew nation.

Wealthy, strong, influential, and blessed with a large family, Jacob seemed to have everything. But a leader who goes his own way and seeks to benefit only himself cannot be an effective instrument in God's hands. God had to break Jacob to make him useful. In the breaking process, Jacob—the deceiving "heel-catcher"—became Israel, a "prince with God" who purposed to serve God rather than himself.

Natural leaders often need to be broken. Consider your natural ability to lead a gift from God, but your character a gift to present back to God. Remember: Every time you stand up under the weight of adversity, you are being prepared, as Jacob was, to better serve God and lead people.

years; and he breathed his last and died, and was gathered to his people. [18](They dwelt from Havilah as far as Shur, which *is* east of Egypt as you go toward Assyria.) He died in the presence of all his brethren.

[19]This *is* the genealogy of Isaac, Abraham's son. Abraham begot Isaac. [20]Isaac was forty years old when he took Rebekah as wife, the daughter of Bethuel the Syrian of Padan Aram, the sister of Laban the Syrian. [21]Now Isaac pleaded with the LORD for his wife, because she *was* barren; and the LORD granted his plea, and Rebekah his wife conceived. [22]But the children struggled together within her; and she said, "If *all is* well, why *am* I like this?" So she went to inquire of the LORD.

[23]And the LORD said to her:

"Two nations *are* in your womb,
Two peoples shall be separated from your
    body;
One people shall be stronger than the
    other,
And the older shall serve the younger."

[24]So when her days were fulfilled *for her* to give birth, indeed *there were* twins in her womb. [25]And the first came out red. *He was* like a hairy garment all over; so they called his name Esau.[a] [26]Afterward his brother came out, and his hand took hold of Esau's heel; so his name was called Jacob.[a] Isaac *was* sixty years old when she bore them.

[27]So the boys grew. And Esau was a skillful hunter, a man of the field; but Jacob was a mild man, dwelling in tents. [28]And Isaac loved Esau because he ate *of his* game, but Rebekah loved Jacob.

Esau Sells His Birthright

[29]Now Jacob cooked a stew; and Esau came in from the field, and he *was* weary. [30]And Esau said to Jacob, "Please feed me with that same red *stew,* for I *am* weary." Therefore his name was called Edom.[a]

[31]But Jacob said, "Sell me your birthright as of this day."

[32]And Esau said, "Look, I *am* about to die; so what *is* this birthright to me?"

[33]Then Jacob said, "Swear to me as of this day."

So he swore to him, and sold his birthright to Jacob. [34]And Jacob gave Esau bread and stew of lentils; then he ate and drank, arose, and went his way. Thus Esau despised *his* birthright.

Influence: Jacob Cons Esau, Rebekah Deceives Isaac

(Genesis 25:29–34; 27:1–30)

Influence can be both positive and negative. The Bible tells us that Jacob "influenced" the birthright away from his brother Esau, the oldest son. A little later, Rebekah helped Jacob to "influence" the best blessing out of his father, a boon intended for his brother. It took *influence* to bring both events to pass. A person can wield influence in many ways. Consider seven such methods, beginning with the worst:

1. **Force:** the use of physical strength to influence others.
2. **Intimidation:** bullying others verbally or emotionally to get them to act against their will.
3. **Manipulation:** coercing others to act, sometimes against their will.
4. **Exchange:** giving something in order to receive from others (I scratch your back; you scratch mine).
5. **Persuasion:** the use of verbal skills to move someone to action.
6. **Motivation:** energizing others so that they want to act.
7. **Honor:** communicating esteem to others by serving them, thus inspiring them to act.

Isaac and Abimelech

26 There was a famine in the land, besides the first famine that was in the days of Abraham. And Isaac went to Abimelech king of the Philistines, in Gerar.

[2]Then the LORD appeared to him and said: "Do not go down to Egypt; live in the land of which I shall tell you. [3]Dwell in this land, and I will be with you and bless you; for to you and your descendants I give all these lands, and I will perform the oath which I swore to Abraham your father. [4]And I will make your descendants

25:25 [a]Literally *Hairy* 25:26 [a]Literally *Supplanter*
25:30 [a]Literally *Red*

21 QUALITIES

VISION

Esau Fails to See the Big Picture
(Genesis 25:29–34; 32:3–23; 33:1–20)

In Esau the Bible paints a powerful picture of a leader without vision. While the eyes of some folks may be larger than their stomachs, in this case the problem was exactly the opposite.

Isaac and Rebekah's firstborn son, Esau, loved the great outdoors from very early in life. He became a skillful hunter, growing strong and resourceful and as rugged as they come. But he lived so completely in the present, depending solely on his own strength and resources, that he repeatedly failed to clearly see the future.

Esau succumbed to the kind of temptations that still entice leaders today. Take a look at six characteristics of Esau's nearsightedness and see whether any of them might trouble you:

1. Esau focused solely on the here and now, convinced that tomorrow never comes.
2. Esau relied on his natural gifts and on his birth order rather than on God's plan.
3. Esau's shortsightedness prompted him to give up the ultimate to get the immediate (a single meal).
4. Esau, favored by his father, may have thought that Isaac's love would bail him out of any poor decision he might make.
5. Esau's limited vision caused him to marry a Hittite, a choice which grieved his parents.
6. Esau's clouded vision blinded him from the deception of his brother Jacob.

In a legacy symbolic of his life, Esau's descendants became the enemies of Israel. Whenever you see the word *Edom* or read of Israel's clashes with the Edomites in Scripture, think of Esau, for it is through him that these persistent opponents of Israel came into existence. The animosity between these two ancient peoples can be seen even in the Psalms: "Remember, O LORD, against the sons of Edom the day of Jerusalem, who said, 'Raze it, raze it, to its very foundation!' " (Ps. 137:7).

Today we remember Esau as a self-centered man with faulty vision. Hebrews 12:15, 16 tells us to examine ourselves, "lest there be any fornicator or profane person like Esau, who for one morsel of food sold his birthright."

And yet God extends His grace! Before Esau died, he showed that he had matured. Genesis 32; 33 describe a fearful meeting between Esau and his estranged brother. When the pair finally meet after years of separation, Esau embraces the deceiver Jacob and forgives him on the spot. Could it be that before he closed his eyes for the last time, Esau finally saw with clear vision? Perhaps. But imagine what *might have been* had he developed that vision sooner!

For a positive example of vision, see p. 16.

multiply as the stars of heaven; I will give to your descendants all these lands; and in your seed all the nations of the earth shall be blessed; [5]because Abraham obeyed My voice and kept My charge, My commandments, My statutes, and My laws."

[6]So Isaac dwelt in Gerar. [7]And the men of the place asked about his wife. And he said, "She *is* my sister"; for he was afraid to say, "*She is my* wife," *because he thought,* "lest the men of the place kill me for Rebekah, because she *is* beautiful to behold." [8]Now it came to pass, when he had been there a long time, that Abimelech king of the Philistines looked through a window, and saw, and there was Isaac, showing endearment to Rebekah his wife. [9]Then Abimelech called Isaac and said, "Quite obviously she *is* your wife; so how could you say, 'She *is* my sister'?"

Isaac said to him, "Because I said, 'Lest I die on account of her.'"

[10]And Abimelech said, "What *is* this you have done to us? One of the people might soon have lain with your wife, and you would have brought guilt on us." [11]So Abimelech charged all *his* people, saying, "He who touches this man or his wife shall surely be put to death."

[12]Then Isaac sowed in that land, and reaped in the same year a hundredfold; and the LORD blessed him. [13]The man began to prosper, and continued prospering until he became very prosperous; [14]for he had possessions of flocks and possessions of herds and a great number of servants. So the Philistines envied him. [15]Now the Philistines had stopped up all the wells which his father's servants had dug in the days of Abraham his father, and they had filled them with earth. [16]And Abimelech said to Isaac, "Go away from us, for you are much mightier than we."

[17]Then Isaac departed from there and pitched his tent in the Valley of Gerar, and dwelt there. [18]And Isaac dug again the wells of water which they had dug in the days of Abraham his father, for the Philistines had stopped them up after the death of Abraham. He called them by the names which his father had called them.

[19]Also Isaac's servants dug in the valley, and found a well of running water there. [20]But the herdsmen of Gerar quarreled with Isaac's herdsmen, saying, "The water *is* ours." So he called the name of the well Esek,[a] because they quarreled with him. [21]Then they dug another well, and they quarreled over that *one* also. So he called its name Sitnah.[a] [22]And he moved from there and dug another well, and they did not quarrel over it. So he called its name Rehoboth,[a] because he said, "For now the LORD has made room for us, and we shall be fruitful in the land."

[23]Then he went up from there to Beersheba. [24]And the LORD appeared to him the same night and said, "I *am* the God of your father Abraham; do not fear, for I *am* with you. I will bless you and multiply your descendants for My servant Abraham's sake." [25]So he built an altar there and called on the name of the LORD, and he pitched his tent there; and there Isaac's servants dug a well.

[26]Then Abimelech came to him from Gerar with Ahuzzath, one of his friends, and Phichol the commander of his army. [27]And Isaac said to them, "Why have you come to me, since you hate me and have sent me away from you?"

[28]But they said, "We have certainly seen that the LORD is with you. So we said, 'Let there now be an oath between us, between you and us; and let us make a covenant with you, [29]that you will do us no harm, since we have not touched you, and since we have done nothing to you but good and have sent you away in peace. You *are* now the blessed of the LORD.'"

[30]So he made them a feast, and they ate and drank. [31]Then they arose early in the morning and swore an oath with one another; and Isaac sent them away, and they departed from him in peace.

[32]It came to pass the same day that Isaac's servants came and told him about the well which they had dug, and said to him, "We have found water." [33]So he called it Shebah.[a] Therefore the name of the city *is* Beersheba[b] to this day.

[34]When Esau was forty years old, he took as wives Judith the daughter of Beeri the Hittite, and Basemath the daughter of Elon the Hittite. [35]And they were a grief of mind to Isaac and Rebekah.

Isaac Blesses Jacob

27 Now it came to pass, when Isaac was old and his eyes were so dim that he could not see, that he called Esau his older son and said to him, "My son."

And he answered him, "Here I am."

[2]Then he said, "Behold now, I am old. I do not know the day of my death. [3]Now therefore, please take your weapons, your quiver and your bow, and go out to the field and hunt game for me. [4]And make me savory food, such as I love, and bring *it* to me that I may eat, that my soul may bless you before I die."

26:20 [a]Literally *Quarrel* 26:21 [a]Literally *Enmity* 26:22 [a]Literally *Spaciousness* 26:33 [a]Literally *Oath* or *Seven* [b]Literally *Well of the Oath* or *Well of the Seven*

⁵Now Rebekah was listening when Isaac spoke to Esau his son. And Esau went to the field to hunt game and to bring *it.* ⁶So Rebekah spoke to Jacob her son, saying, "Indeed I heard your father speak to Esau your brother, saying, ⁷'Bring me game and make savory food for me, that I may eat it and bless you in the presence of the LORD before my death.' ⁸Now therefore, my son, obey my voice according to what I command you. ⁹Go now to the flock and bring me from there two choice kids of the goats, and I will make savory food from them for your father, such as he loves. ¹⁰Then you shall take *it* to your father, that he may eat *it,* and that he may bless you before his death."

¹¹And Jacob said to Rebekah his mother, "Look, Esau my brother *is* a hairy man, and I *am* a smooth-*skinned* man. ¹²Perhaps my father will feel me, and I shall seem to be a deceiver to him; and I shall bring a curse on myself and not a blessing."

¹³But his mother said to him, "*Let* your curse *be* on me, my son; only obey my voice, and go, get *them* for me." ¹⁴And he went and got *them* and brought *them* to his mother, and his mother made savory food, such as his father loved. ¹⁵Then Rebekah took the choice clothes of her elder son Esau, which *were* with her in the house, and put them on Jacob her younger son. ¹⁶And she put the skins of the kids of the goats on his hands and on the smooth part of his neck. ¹⁷Then she gave the savory food and the bread, which she had prepared, into the hand of her son Jacob.

¹⁸So he went to his father and said, "My father."

And he said, "Here I am. Who *are* you, my son?"

¹⁹Jacob said to his father, "I *am* Esau your firstborn; I have done just as you told me; please arise, sit and eat of my game, that your soul may bless me."

²⁰But Isaac said to his son, "How *is* it that you have found *it* so quickly, my son?"

And he said, "Because the LORD your God brought *it* to me."

²¹Isaac said to Jacob, "Please come near, that I may feel you, my son, whether you *are* really my son Esau or not." ²²So Jacob went near to Isaac his father, and he felt him and said, "The voice *is* Jacob's voice, but the hands *are* the hands of Esau." ²³And he did not recognize him, because his hands were hairy like his brother Esau's hands; so he blessed him.

²⁴Then he said, "*Are* you really my son Esau?"

He said, "I *am.*"

²⁵He said, "Bring *it* near to me, and I will eat of my son's game, so that my soul may bless you." So he brought *it* near to him, and he ate; and he brought him wine, and he drank. ²⁶Then his father Isaac said to him, "Come near now and kiss me, my son." ²⁷And he came near and kissed him; and he smelled the smell of his clothing, and blessed him and said:

> "Surely, the smell of my son
> *Is* like the smell of a field
> Which the LORD has blessed.
> ²⁸ Therefore may God give you
> Of the dew of heaven,
> Of the fatness of the earth,
> And plenty of grain and wine.
> ²⁹ Let peoples serve you,
> And nations bow down to you.
> Be master over your brethren,
> And let your mother's sons bow down to you.
> Cursed *be* everyone who curses you,
> And blessed *be* those who bless you!"

Esau's Lost Hope

³⁰Now it happened, as soon as Isaac had finished blessing Jacob, and Jacob had scarcely gone out from the presence of Isaac his father, that Esau his brother came in from his hunting. ³¹He also had made savory food, and brought it to his father, and said to his father, "Let my father arise and eat of his son's game, that your soul may bless me."

³²And his father Isaac said to him, "Who *are* you?"

So he said, "I *am* your son, your firstborn, Esau."

³³Then Isaac trembled exceedingly, and said, "Who? Where *is* the one who hunted game and brought *it* to me? I ate all *of it* before you came, and I have blessed him—*and* indeed he shall be blessed."

³⁴When Esau heard the words of his father, he cried with an exceedingly great and bitter cry, and said to his father, "Bless me—me also, O my father!"

³⁵But he said, "Your brother came with deceit and has taken away your blessing."

³⁶And *Esau* said, "Is he not rightly named Jacob? For he has supplanted me these two times. He took away my birthright, and now look, he has taken away my blessing!" And he said, "Have you not reserved a blessing for me?"

³⁷Then Isaac answered and said to Esau, "Indeed I have made him your master, and all his brethren I have given to him as servants; with

grain and wine I have sustained him. What shall I do now for you, my son?"

³⁸And Esau said to his father, "Have you only one blessing, my father? Bless me—me also, O my father!" And Esau lifted up his voice and wept.

³⁹Then Isaac his father answered and said to him:

"Behold, your dwelling shall be of the fatness of the earth,
And of the dew of heaven from above.
⁴⁰ By your sword you shall live,
And you shall serve your brother;
And it shall come to pass, when you become restless,
That you shall break his yoke from your neck."

Jacob Escapes from Esau

⁴¹So Esau hated Jacob because of the blessing with which his father blessed him, and Esau said in his heart, "The days of mourning for my father are at hand; then I will kill my brother Jacob."

⁴²And the words of Esau her older son were told to Rebekah. So she sent and called Jacob her younger son, and said to him, "Surely your brother Esau comforts himself concerning you *by intending* to kill you. ⁴³Now therefore, my son, obey my voice: arise, flee to my brother Laban in Haran. ⁴⁴And stay with him a few days, until your brother's fury turns away, ⁴⁵until your brother's anger turns away from you, and he forgets what you have done to him; then I will send and bring you from there. Why should I be bereaved also of you both in one day?"

⁴⁶And Rebekah said to Isaac, "I am weary of my life because of the daughters of Heth; if Jacob takes a wife of the daughters of Heth, like these *who are* the daughters of the land, what good will my life be to me?"

28 Then Isaac called Jacob and blessed him, and charged him, and said to him: "You shall not take a wife from the daughters of Canaan. ²Arise, go to Padan Aram, to the house of Bethuel your mother's father; and take yourself a wife from there of the daughters of Laban your mother's brother.

³ "May God Almighty bless you,
And make you fruitful and multiply you,
That you may be an assembly of peoples;
⁴ And give you the blessing of Abraham,
To you and your descendants with you,
That you may inherit the land

In which you are a stranger,
Which God gave to Abraham."

⁵So Isaac sent Jacob away, and he went to Padan Aram, to Laban the son of Bethuel the Syrian, the brother of Rebekah, the mother of Jacob and Esau.

Esau Marries Mahalath

⁶Esau saw that Isaac had blessed Jacob and sent him away to Padan Aram to take himself a wife from there, *and that* as he blessed him he gave him a charge, saying, "You shall not take a wife from the daughters of Canaan," ⁷and that Jacob had obeyed his father and his mother and had gone to Padan Aram. ⁸Also Esau saw that the daughters of Canaan did not please his father Isaac. ⁹So Esau went to Ishmael and took Mahalath the daughter of Ishmael, Abraham's son, the sister of Nebajoth, to be his wife in addition to the wives he had.

Jacob's Vow at Bethel

¹⁰Now Jacob went out from Beersheba and went toward Haran. ¹¹So he came to a certain place and stayed there all night, because the sun had set. And he took one of the stones of that place and put it at his head, and he lay down in that place to sleep. ¹²Then he dreamed, and behold, a ladder *was* set up on the earth, and its top reached to heaven; and there the angels of God were ascending and descending on it.

¹³And behold, the LORD stood above it and said: "I *am* the LORD God of Abraham your father and the God of Isaac; the land on which you lie I will give to you and your descendants. ¹⁴Also your descendants shall be as the dust of the earth; you shall spread abroad to the west and the east, to the north and the south; and in you and in your seed all the families of the earth shall be blessed. ¹⁵Behold, I *am* with you and will keep you wherever you go, and will bring you back to this land; for I will not leave you until I have done what I have spoken to you."

¹⁶Then Jacob awoke from his sleep and said, "Surely the LORD is in this place, and I did not know *it.*" ¹⁷And he was afraid and said, "How awesome *is* this place! This *is* none other than the house of God, and this *is* the gate of heaven!"

¹⁸Then Jacob rose early in the morning, and took the stone that he had put at his head, set it up as a pillar, and poured oil on top of it. ¹⁹And he called the name of that place Bethel;ᵃ but the

---

28:19 ᵃLiterally *House of God*

name of that city had been Luz previously. [20]Then Jacob made a vow, saying, "If God will be with me, and keep me in this way that I am going, and give me bread to eat and clothing to put on, [21]so that I come back to my father's house in peace, then the LORD shall be my God. [22]And this stone which I have set as a pillar shall be God's house, and of all that You give me I will surely give a tenth to You."

Jacob Meets Rachel

29 So Jacob went on his journey and came to the land of the people of the East. [2]And he looked, and saw a well in the field; and behold, there *were* three flocks of sheep lying by it; for out of that well they watered the flocks. A large stone *was* on the well's mouth. [3]Now all the flocks would be gathered there; and they would roll the stone from the well's mouth, water the sheep, and put the stone back in its place on the well's mouth.

[4]And Jacob said to them, "My brethren, where *are* you from?"

And they said, "We *are* from Haran."

[5]Then he said to them, "Do you know Laban the son of Nahor?"

And they said, "We know him."

[6]So he said to them, "Is he well?"

And they said, "*He is* well. And look, his daughter Rachel is coming with the sheep."

[7]Then he said, "Look, *it is* still high day; *it is* not time for the cattle to be gathered together. Water the sheep, and go and feed *them*."

[8]But they said, "We cannot until all the flocks are gathered together, and they have rolled the stone from the well's mouth; then we water the sheep."

[9]Now while he was still speaking with them, Rachel came with her father's sheep, for she was a shepherdess. [10]And it came to pass, when Jacob saw Rachel the daughter of Laban his mother's brother, and the sheep of Laban his mother's brother, that Jacob went near and rolled the stone from the well's mouth, and watered the flock of Laban his mother's brother. [11]Then Jacob kissed Rachel, and lifted up his voice and wept. [12]And Jacob told Rachel that he *was* her father's relative and that he *was* Rebekah's son. So she ran and told her father.

[13]Then it came to pass, when Laban heard the report about Jacob his sister's son, that he ran to meet him, and embraced him and kissed him, and brought him to his house. So he told Laban all these things. [14]And Laban said to him, "Surely you *are* my bone and my flesh." And he stayed with him for a month.

Jacob Marries Leah and Rachel

[15]Then Laban said to Jacob, "Because you *are* my relative, should you therefore serve me for nothing? Tell me, what *should* your wages *be?*" [16]Now Laban had two daughters: the name of the elder *was* Leah, and the name of the younger *was* Rachel. [17]Leah's eyes *were* delicate, but Rachel was beautiful of form and appearance.

[18]Now Jacob loved Rachel; so he said, "I will serve you seven years for Rachel your younger daughter."

[19]And Laban said, "*It is* better that I give her to you than that I should give her to another man. Stay with me." [20]So Jacob served seven years for Rachel, and they seemed *only* a few days to him because of the love he had for her.

Jacob, Rachel, and the Law of Victory
(Genesis 29:16–30)

"Leaders find a way for the team to win," states the Law of Victory. That means good leaders are whatever-it-takes people. They are the "go to" guys and gals who always find a way to achieve their goals. Such a description certainly fits Jacob, the stubborn young man who fell in love with Rachel.

After requiring Jacob to work seven years for his younger daughter's hand in marriage, Laban substituted his older daughter, Leah—and Jacob didn't discover the deception until the morning after his wedding night. Some men would have battled Laban. Others might have simply walked away. Jacob fumed, but he didn't give up. He loved Rachel so deeply that he did what he had to do; he worked another seven years to get her. Jacob practiced the Law of Victory as a leader who did whatever it took to reach his goal.

[21]Then Jacob said to Laban, "Give *me* my wife, for my days are fulfilled, that I may go in to her." [22]And Laban gathered together all the men of the place and made a feast. [23]Now it came to pass in the evening, that he took Leah his daughter and brought her to Jacob; and he went in to her. [24]And Laban gave his maid Zilpah to his daughter Leah *as* a maid. [25]So it came to pass in the morning, that behold, it *was* Leah. And he said to Laban, "What is this you have done to

me? Was it not for Rachel that I served you? Why then have you deceived me?"

26And Laban said, "It must not be done so in our country, to give the younger before the first-born. 27Fulfill her week, and we will give you this one also for the service which you will serve with me still another seven years."

28Then Jacob did so and fulfilled her week. So he gave him his daughter Rachel as wife also. 29And Laban gave his maid Bilhah to his daughter Rachel as a maid. 30Then *Jacob* also went in to Rachel, and he also loved Rachel more than Leah. And he served with Laban still another seven years.

The Children of Jacob

31When the LORD saw that Leah *was* unloved, He opened her womb; but Rachel *was* barren. 32So Leah conceived and bore a son, and she called his name Reuben;a for she said, "The LORD has surely looked on my affliction. Now therefore, my husband will love me." 33Then she conceived again and bore a son, and said, "Because the LORD has heard that I *am* unloved, He has therefore given me this *son* also." And she called his name Simeon.a 34She conceived again and bore a son, and said, "Now this time my husband will become attached to me, because I have borne him three sons." Therefore his name was called Levi.a 35And she conceived again and bore a son, and said, "Now I will praise the LORD." Therefore she called his name Judah.a Then she stopped bearing.

30 Now when Rachel saw that she bore Jacob no children, Rachel envied her sister, and said to Jacob, "Give me children, or else I die!"

2And Jacob's anger was aroused against Rachel, and he said, "*Am* I in the place of God, who has withheld from you the fruit of the womb?"

3So she said, "Here is my maid Bilhah; go in to her, and she will bear *a child* on my knees, that I also may have children by her." 4Then she gave him Bilhah her maid as wife, and Jacob went in to her. 5And Bilhah conceived and bore Jacob a son. 6Then Rachel said, "God has judged my case; and He has also heard my voice and given me a son." Therefore she called his name Dan.a 7And Rachel's maid Bilhah conceived again and bore Jacob a second son. 8Then Rachel said, "With great wrestlings I have wrestled with my sister, *and* indeed I have prevailed." So she called his name Naphtali.a

9When Leah saw that she had stopped bearing, she took Zilpah her maid and gave her to Jacob as wife. 10And Leah's maid Zilpah bore Jacob

a son. 11Then Leah said, "A troop comes!"a So she called his name Gad.b 12And Leah's maid Zilpah bore Jacob a second son. 13Then Leah said, "I am happy, for the daughters will call me blessed." So she called his name Asher.a

14Now Reuben went in the days of wheat harvest and found mandrakes in the field, and brought them to his mother Leah. Then Rachel said to Leah, "Please give me *some* of your son's mandrakes."

15But she said to her, "*Is it* a small matter that you have taken away my husband? Would you take away my son's mandrakes also?"

And Rachel said, "Therefore he will lie with you tonight for your son's mandrakes."

16When Jacob came out of the field in the evening, Leah went out to meet him and said, "You must come in to me, for I have surely hired you with my son's mandrakes." And he lay with her that night.

17And God listened to Leah, and she conceived and bore Jacob a fifth son. 18Leah said, "God has given me my wages, because I have given my maid to my husband." So she called his name Issachar.a 19Then Leah conceived again and bore Jacob a sixth son. 20And Leah said, "God has endowed me *with* a good endowment; now my husband will dwell with me, because I have borne him six sons." So she called his name Zebulun.a 21Afterward she bore a daughter, and called her name Dinah.

22Then God remembered Rachel, and God listened to her and opened her womb. 23And she conceived and bore a son, and said, "God has taken away my reproach." 24So she called his name Joseph,a and said, "The LORD shall add to me another son."

Jacob's Agreement with Laban

25And it came to pass, when Rachel had borne Joseph, that Jacob said to Laban, "Send me away, that I may go to my own place and to my country. 26Give *me* my wives and my children for whom I have served you, and let me go; for you know my service which I have done for you."

27And Laban said to him, "Please *stay,* if I have found favor in your eyes, *for* I have learned by

---

29:32 aLiterally *See, a Son* 29:33 aLiterally *Heard* 29:34 aLiterally *Attached* 29:35 aLiterally *Praise* 30:6 aLiterally *Judge* 30:8 aLiterally *My Wrestling* 30:11 aFollowing Qere, Syriac, and Targum; Kethib, Septuagint, and Vulgate read *in fortune.* bLiterally *Troop* or *Fortune* 30:13 aLiterally *Happy* 30:18 aLiterally *Wages* 30:20 aLiterally *Dwelling* 30:24 aLiterally *He Will Add* experience that the LORD has blessed me for your sake." ²⁸Then he said, "Name me your wages, and I will give it."

²⁹So Jacob said to him, "You know how I have served you and how your livestock has been with me. ³⁰For what you had before I came was little, and it has increased to a great amount; the LORD has blessed you since my coming. And now, when shall I also provide for my own house?"

³¹So he said, "What shall I give you?"

And Jacob said, "You shall not give me anything. If you will do this thing for me, I will again feed and keep your flocks: ³²Let me pass through all your flock today, removing from there all the speckled and spotted sheep, and all the brown ones among the lambs, and the spotted and speckled among the goats; and these shall be my wages. ³³So my righteousness will answer for me in time to come, when the subject of my wages comes before you: every one that is not speckled and spotted among the goats, and brown among the lambs, will be considered stolen, if it is with me."

³⁴And Laban said, "Oh, that it were according to your word!" ³⁵So he removed that day the male goats that were speckled and spotted, all the female goats that were speckled and spotted, every one that had some white in it, and all the brown ones among the lambs, and gave them into the hand of his sons. ³⁶Then he put three days' journey between himself and Jacob, and Jacob fed the rest of Laban's flocks.

³⁷Now Jacob took for himself rods of green poplar and of the almond and chestnut trees, peeled white strips in them, and exposed the white which was in the rods. ³⁸And the rods which he had peeled, he set before the flocks in the gutters, in the watering troughs where the flocks came to drink, so that they should conceive when they came to drink. ³⁹So the flocks conceived before the rods, and the flocks brought forth streaked, speckled, and spotted. ⁴⁰Then Jacob separated the lambs, and made the flocks face toward the streaked and all the brown in the flock of Laban; but he put his own flocks by themselves and did not put them with Laban's flock.

⁴¹And it came to pass, whenever the stronger livestock conceived, that Jacob placed the rods before the eyes of the livestock in the gutters, that they might conceive among the rods. ⁴²But when the flocks were feeble, he did not put them in; so the feebler were Laban's and the stronger Jacob's. ⁴³Thus the man became exceedingly prosperous, and had large flocks, female and male servants, and camels and donkeys.

Jacob Flees from Laban

31 Now Jacob heard the words of Laban's sons, saying, "Jacob has taken away all that was our father's, and from what was our father's he has acquired all this wealth." ²And Jacob saw the countenance of Laban, and indeed it was not favorable toward him as before. ³Then the LORD said to Jacob, "Return to the land of your fathers and to your family, and I will be with you."

⁴So Jacob sent and called Rachel and Leah to the field, to his flock, ⁵and said to them, "I see your father's countenance, that it is not favorable toward me as before; but the God of my father has been with me. ⁶And you know that with all my might I have served your father. ⁷Yet your father has deceived me and changed my wages ten times, but God did not allow him to hurt me. ⁸If he said thus: 'The speckled shall be your wages,' then all the flocks bore speckled. And if he said thus: 'The streaked shall be your wages,' then all the flocks bore streaked. ⁹So God has taken away the livestock of your father and given them to me.

¹⁰"And it happened, at the time when the flocks conceived, that I lifted my eyes and saw in a dream, and behold, the rams which leaped upon the flocks were streaked, speckled, and gray-spotted. ¹¹Then the Angel of God spoke to me in a dream, saying, 'Jacob.' And I said, 'Here I am.' ¹²And He said, 'Lift your eyes now and see, all the rams which leap on the flocks are streaked, speckled, and gray-spotted; for I have seen all that Laban is doing to you. ¹³I am the God of Bethel, where you anointed the pillar and where you made a vow to Me. Now arise, get out of this land, and return to the land of your family.'"

¹⁴Then Rachel and Leah answered and said to him, "Is there still any portion or inheritance for us in our father's house? ¹⁵Are we not considered strangers by him? For he has sold us, and also completely consumed our money. ¹⁶For all these riches which God has taken from our father are really ours and our children's; now then, whatever God has said to you, do it."

¹⁷Then Jacob rose and set his sons and his wives on camels. ¹⁸And he carried away all his livestock and all his possessions which he had gained, his acquired livestock which he had gained in Padan Aram, to go to his father Isaac in the land of Canaan. ¹⁹Now Laban had gone to shear his sheep, and Rachel had stolen the household idols that were her father's. ²⁰And Jacob stole away, unknown to Laban the Syrian, in that he did not tell him that he intended to flee.

²¹So he fled with all that he had. He arose and crossed the river, and headed toward the mountains of Gilead.

Laban Pursues Jacob

²²And Laban was told on the third day that Jacob had fled. ²³Then he took his brethren with him and pursued him for seven days' journey, and he overtook him in the mountains of Gilead. ²⁴But God had come to Laban the Syrian in a dream by night, and said to him, "Be careful that you speak to Jacob neither good nor bad."

²⁵So Laban overtook Jacob. Now Jacob had pitched his tent in the mountains, and Laban with his brethren pitched in the mountains of Gilead.

²⁶And Laban said to Jacob: "What have you done, that you have stolen away unknown to me, and carried away my daughters like captives *taken* with the sword? ²⁷Why did you flee away secretly, and steal away from me, and not tell me; for I might have sent you away with joy and songs, with timbrel and harp? ²⁸And you did not allow me to kiss my sons and my daughters. Now you have done foolishly *in* so doing. ²⁹It is in my power to do you harm, but the God of your father spoke to me last night, saying, 'Be careful that you speak to Jacob neither good nor bad.' ³⁰And now you have surely gone because you greatly long for your father's house, *but* why did you steal my gods?"

³¹Then Jacob answered and said to Laban, "Because I was afraid, for I said, 'Perhaps you would take your daughters from me by force.' ³²With whomever you find your gods, do not let him live. In the presence of our brethren, identify what I have of yours and take *it* with you." For Jacob did not know that Rachel had stolen them.

³³And Laban went into Jacob's tent, into Leah's tent, and into the two maids' tents, but he did not find *them*. Then he went out of Leah's tent and entered Rachel's tent. ³⁴Now Rachel had taken the household idols, put them in the camel's saddle, and sat on them. And Laban searched all about the tent but did not find *them*. ³⁵And she said to her father, "Let it not displease my lord that I cannot rise before you, for the manner of women *is* with me." And he searched but did not find the household idols.

³⁶Then Jacob was angry and rebuked Laban, and Jacob answered and said to Laban: "What *is* my trespass? What *is* my sin, that you have so hotly pursued me? ³⁷Although you have searched all my things, what part of your household things have you found? Set *it* here before my brethren and your brethren, that they may judge between us both! ³⁸These twenty years I *have been* with you; your ewes and your female goats have not miscarried their young, and I have not eaten the rams of your flock. ³⁹That which was torn *by beasts* I did not bring to you; I bore the loss of it. You required it from my hand, *whether* stolen by day or stolen by night. ⁴⁰*There* I was! In the day the drought consumed me, and the frost by night, and my sleep departed from my eyes. ⁴¹Thus I have been in your house twenty years; I served you fourteen years for your two daughters, and six years for your flock, and you have changed my wages ten times. ⁴²Unless the God of my father, the God of Abraham and the Fear of Isaac, had been with me, surely now you would have sent me away empty-handed. God has seen my affliction and the labor of my hands, and rebuked *you* last night."

Laban's Covenant with Jacob

⁴³And Laban answered and said to Jacob, "*These* daughters *are* my daughters, and *these* children *are* my children, and *this* flock *is* my flock; all that you see *is* mine. But what can I do this day to these my daughters or to their children whom they have borne? ⁴⁴Now therefore, come, let us make a covenant, you and I, and let it be a witness between you and me."

⁴⁵So Jacob took a stone and set it up *as* a pillar. ⁴⁶Then Jacob said to his brethren, "Gather stones." And they took stones and made a heap, and they ate there on the heap. ⁴⁷Laban called it Jegar Sahadutha,ᵃ but Jacob called it Galeed.ᵇ ⁴⁸And Laban said, "This heap *is* a witness between you and me this day." Therefore its name was called Galeed, ⁴⁹also Mizpah,ᵃ because he said, "May the LORD watch between you and me when we are absent one from another. ⁵⁰If you afflict my daughters, or if you take *other* wives besides my daughters, *although* no man *is* with us—see, God *is* witness between you and me!"

⁵¹Then Laban said to Jacob, "Here is this heap and here is *this* pillar, which I have placed between you and me. ⁵²This heap *is* a witness, and *this* pillar *is* a witness, that I will not pass beyond this heap to you, and you will not pass beyond this heap and this pillar to me, for harm. ⁵³The God of Abraham, the God of Nahor, and the God of their father judge between us." And Jacob swore by the Fear of his father Isaac. ⁵⁴Then Jacob offered a sacrifice on the mountain,

---

31:47 ᵃLiterally, in Aramaic, *Heap of Witness*
ᵇLiterally, in Hebrew, *Heap of Witness*
31:49 ᵃLiterally *Watch*

and called his brethren to eat bread. And they ate bread and stayed all night on the mountain. [55]And early in the morning Laban arose, and kissed his sons and daughters and blessed them. Then Laban departed and returned to his place.

Esau Comes to Meet Jacob

32 So Jacob went on his way, and the angels of God met him. [2]When Jacob saw them, he said, "This *is* God's camp." And he called the name of that place Mahanaim.[a]

[3]Then Jacob sent messengers before him to Esau his brother in the land of Seir, the country of Edom. [4]And he commanded them, saying, "Speak thus to my lord Esau, 'Thus your servant Jacob says: "I have dwelt with Laban and stayed there until now. [5]I have oxen, donkeys, flocks, and male and female servants; and I have sent to tell my lord, that I may find favor in your sight."'"

[6]Then the messengers returned to Jacob, saying, "We came to your brother Esau, and he also is coming to meet you, and four hundred men *are* with him." [7]So Jacob was greatly afraid and distressed; and he divided the people that *were* with him, and the flocks and herds and camels, into two companies. [8]And he said, "If Esau comes to the one company and attacks it, then the other company which is left will escape."

[9]Then Jacob said, "O God of my father Abraham and God of my father Isaac, the LORD who said to me, 'Return to your country and to your family, and I will deal well with you': [10]I am not worthy of the least of all the mercies and of all the truth which You have shown Your servant; for I crossed over this Jordan with my staff, and now I have become two companies. [11]Deliver me, I pray, from the hand of my brother, from the hand of Esau; for I fear him, lest he come and attack me *and* the mother with the children. [12]For You said, 'I will surely treat you well, and make your descendants as the sand of the sea, which cannot be numbered for multitude.'"

[13]So he lodged there that same night, and took what came to his hand as a present for Esau his brother: [14]two hundred female goats and twenty male goats, two hundred ewes and twenty rams, [15]thirty milk camels with their colts, forty cows and ten bulls, twenty female donkeys and ten foals. [16]Then he delivered *them* to the hand of his servants, every drove by itself, and said to his servants, "Pass over before me, and put some distance between successive droves." [17]And he commanded the first one, saying, "When Esau my brother meets you and asks you, saying, 'To whom do you belong, and where are you going?

Jacob: Breaking Before Blessing
(Genesis 32:24–32)

Jacob turned a crucial corner the night he wrestled the Angel of God. He broke physically when the Angel dislocated his hip, but he also broke emotionally—he told the truth about his name and character. From that moment on, Jacob began to fulfill his God-ordained destiny.

All leaders, like Jacob, must "wrestle" with God in order to receive His blessing. God blessed Jacob because:

1. **Jacob was alone with God (v. 24).** All distractions had been removed.
2. **Jacob was hungry for God (v. 26).** He desperately wanted to receive what God had for him.
3. **Jacob was broken by God (vv. 25–28).** He allowed God to break him and change him.
4. **Jacob was honest with God (v. 27).** He stopped pretending in order to let God work in his life.

Have you "prevailed" with God in this way? Leaders cannot do anything of significance in the kingdom of God until they humble themselves before God and seek His face. You must be broken in order to be blessed!

Whose *are* these in front of you?' [18]then you shall say, 'They *are* your servant Jacob's. It *is* a present sent to my lord Esau; and behold, he also *is* behind us.'" [19]So he commanded the second, the third, and all who followed the droves, saying, "In this manner you shall speak to Esau when you find him; [20]and also say, 'Behold, your servant Jacob *is* behind us.'" For he said, "I will appease him with the present that goes before me, and afterward I will see his face; perhaps he will accept me." [21]So the present went on over before him, but he himself lodged that night in the camp.

Wrestling with God

[22]And he arose that night and took his two wives, his two female servants, and his eleven sons, and crossed over the ford of Jabbok. [23]He

32:2 [a]Literally *Double Camp*

took them, sent them over the brook, and sent over what he had. [24]Then Jacob was left alone; and a Man wrestled with him until the breaking of day. [25]Now when He saw that He did not prevail against him, He touched the socket of his hip; and the socket of Jacob's hip was out of joint as He wrestled with him. [26]And He said, "Let Me go, for the day breaks."

But he said, "I will not let You go unless You bless me!"

[27]So He said to him, "What *is* your name?"

He said, "Jacob."

[28]And He said, "Your name shall no longer be called Jacob, but Israel;[a] for you have struggled with God and with men, and have prevailed."

[29]Then Jacob asked, saying, "Tell *me* Your name, I pray."

And He said, "Why *is* it *that* you ask about My name?" And He blessed him there.

[30]So Jacob called the name of the place Peniel:[a] "For I have seen God face to face, and my life is preserved." [31]Just as he crossed over Penuel[a] the sun rose on him, and he limped on his hip. [32]Therefore to this day the children of Israel do not eat the muscle that shrank, which *is* on the hip socket, because He touched the socket of Jacob's hip in the muscle that shrank.

Jacob and Esau Meet

33 Now Jacob lifted his eyes and looked, and there, Esau was coming, and with him were four hundred men. So he divided the children among Leah, Rachel, and the two maidservants. [2]And he put the maidservants and their children in front, Leah and her children behind, and Rachel and Joseph last. [3]Then he crossed over before them and bowed himself to the ground seven times, until he came near to his brother.

Commitment: Esau Releases Jacob

(Genesis 33:1–4)

After years of estrangement, Jacob and Esau finally met. The reunion terrified Jacob, for Esau had threatened to kill him (Gen. 27:41). Yet Esau ran to his brother, embraced him, and wept—forgiving Jacob for everything. In the end, Esau's commitment to his brother overwhelmed his thirst for revenge.

---

[4]But Esau ran to meet him, and embraced him, and fell on his neck and kissed him, and they wept. [5]And he lifted his eyes and saw the women and children, and said, "Who *are* these with you?"

So he said, "The children whom God has graciously given your servant." [6]Then the maidservants came near, they and their children, and bowed down. [7]And Leah also came near with her children, and they bowed down. Afterward Joseph and Rachel came near, and they bowed down.

[8]Then Esau said, "What *do* you *mean by* all this company which I met?"

And he said, "*These are* to find favor in the sight of my lord."

[9]But Esau said, "I have enough, my brother; keep what you have for yourself."

[10]And Jacob said, "No, please, if I have now found favor in your sight, then receive my present from my hand, inasmuch as I have seen your face as though I had seen the face of God, and you were pleased with me. [11]Please, take my blessing that is brought to you, because God has dealt graciously with me, and because I have enough." So he urged him, and he took *it*.

[12]Then Esau said, "Let us take our journey; let us go, and I will go before you."

[13]But Jacob said to him, "My lord knows that the children *are* weak, and the flocks and herds which are nursing *are* with me. And if the men should drive them hard one day, all the flock will die. [14]Please let my lord go on ahead before his servant. I will lead on slowly at a pace which the livestock that go before me, and the children, are able to endure, until I come to my lord in Seir."

[15]And Esau said, "Now let me leave with you *some* of the people who *are* with me."

But he said, "What need is there? Let me find favor in the sight of my lord." [16]So Esau returned that day on his way to Seir. [17]And Jacob journeyed to Succoth, built himself a house, and made booths for his livestock. Therefore the name of the place is called Succoth.[a]

Jacob Comes to Canaan

[18]Then Jacob came safely to the city of Shechem, which *is* in the land of Canaan, when he came from Padan Aram; and he pitched his tent before the city. [19]And he bought the parcel of land, where he had pitched his tent, from the children of Hamor, Shechem's father, for one

---

32:28 [a]Literally *Prince with God* **32:30** [a]Literally *Face of God* **32:31** [a]Same as *Peniel,* verse 30 **33:17** [a]Literally *Booths*

hundred pieces of money. [20]Then he erected an altar there and called it El Elohe Israel.[a]

The Dinah Incident

34 Now Dinah the daughter of Leah, whom she had borne to Jacob, went out to see the daughters of the land. [2]And when Shechem the son of Hamor the Hivite, prince of the country, saw her, he took her and lay with her, and violated her. [3]His soul was strongly attracted to Dinah the daughter of Jacob, and he loved the young woman and spoke kindly to the young woman. [4]So Shechem spoke to his father Hamor, saying, "Get me this young woman as a wife."

[5]And Jacob heard that he had defiled Dinah his daughter. Now his sons were with his livestock in the field; so Jacob held his peace until they came. [6]Then Hamor the father of Shechem went out to Jacob to speak with him. [7]And the sons of Jacob came in from the field when they heard it; and the men were grieved and very angry, because he had done a disgraceful thing in Israel by lying with Jacob's daughter, a thing which ought not to be done. [8]But Hamor spoke with them, saying, "The soul of my son Shechem longs for your daughter. Please give her to him as a wife. [9]And make marriages with us; give your daughters to us, and take our daughters to yourselves. [10]So you shall dwell with us, and the land shall be before you. Dwell and trade in it, and acquire possessions for yourselves in it."

[11]Then Shechem said to her father and her brothers, "Let me find favor in your eyes, and whatever you say to me I will give. [12]Ask me ever so much dowry and gift, and I will give according to what you say to me; but give me the young woman as a wife."

[13]But the sons of Jacob answered Shechem and Hamor his father, and spoke deceitfully, because he had defiled Dinah their sister. [14]And they said to them, "We cannot do this thing, to give our sister to one who is uncircumcised, for that would be a reproach to us. [15]But on this condition we will consent to you: If you will become as we are, if every male of you is circumcised, [16]then we will give our daughters to you, and we will take your daughters to us; and we will dwell with you, and we will become one people. [17]But if you will not heed us and be circumcised, then we will take our daughter and be gone."

[18]And their words pleased Hamor and Shechem, Hamor's son. [19]So the young man did not delay to do the thing, because he delighted in Jacob's daughter. He was more honorable than all the household of his father.

[20]And Hamor and Shechem his son came to the gate of their city, and spoke with the men of their city, saying: [21]"These men are at peace with us. Therefore let them dwell in the land and trade in it. For indeed the land is large enough for them. Let us take their daughters to us as wives, and let us give them our daughters. [22]Only on this condition will the men consent to dwell with us, to be one people: if every male among us is circumcised as they are circumcised. [23]Will not their livestock, their property, and every animal of theirs be ours? Only let us consent to them, and they will dwell with us." [24]And all who went out of the gate of his city heeded Hamor and Shechem his son; every male was circumcised, all who went out of the gate of his city.

[25]Now it came to pass on the third day, when they were in pain, that two of the sons of Jacob, Simeon and Levi, Dinah's brothers, each took his sword and came boldly upon the city and killed all the males. [26]And they killed Hamor and Shechem his son with the edge of the sword, and took Dinah from Shechem's house, and went out. [27]The sons of Jacob came upon the slain, and plundered the city, because their sister had been defiled. [28]They took their sheep, their oxen, and their donkeys, what was in the city and what was in the field, [29]and all their wealth. All their little ones and their wives they took captive; and they plundered even all that was in the houses.

[30]Then Jacob said to Simeon and Levi, "You have troubled me by making me obnoxious among the inhabitants of the land, among the Canaanites and the Perizzites; and since I am few in number, they will gather themselves together against me and kill me. I shall be destroyed, my household and I."

[31]But they said, "Should he treat our sister like a harlot?"

Jacob's Return to Bethel

35 Then God said to Jacob, "Arise, go up to Bethel and dwell there; and make an altar there to God, who appeared to you when you fled from the face of Esau your brother."

[2]And Jacob said to his household and to all who were with him, "Put away the foreign gods that are among you, purify yourselves, and change your garments. [3]Then let us arise and go up to Bethel; and I will make an altar there to God, who answered me in the day of my distress and has been with me in the way which I have

---

33:20 [a]Literally God, the God of Israel

gone." [4]So they gave Jacob all the foreign gods which *were* in their hands, and the earrings which *were* in their ears; and Jacob hid them under the terebinth tree which *was* by Shechem. [5]And they journeyed, and the terror of God was upon the cities that *were* all around them, and they did not pursue the sons of Jacob. [6]So Jacob came to Luz (that *is,* Bethel), which *is* in the land of Canaan, he and all the people who *were* with him. [7]And he built an altar there and called the place El Bethel,[a] because there God appeared to him when he fled from the face of his brother.

[8]Now Deborah, Rebekah's nurse, died, and she was buried below Bethel under the terebinth tree. So the name of it was called Allon Bachuth.[a]

[9]Then God appeared to Jacob again, when he came from Padan Aram, and blessed him. [10]And God said to him, "Your name *is* Jacob; your name shall not be called Jacob anymore, but Israel shall be your name." So He called his name Israel. [11]Also God said to him: "I *am* God Almighty. Be fruitful and multiply; a nation and a company of nations shall proceed from you, and kings shall come from your body. [12]The land which I gave Abraham and Isaac I give to you; and to your descendants after you I give this land." [13]Then God went up from him in the place where He talked with him. [14]So Jacob set up a pillar in the place where He talked with him, a pillar of stone; and he poured a drink offering on it, and he poured oil on it. [15]And Jacob called the name of the place where God spoke with him, Bethel.

Death of Rachel

[16]Then they journeyed from Bethel. And when there was but a little distance to go to Ephrath, Rachel labored *in childbirth,* and she had hard labor. [17]Now it came to pass, when she was in hard labor, that the midwife said to her, "Do not fear; you will have this son also." [18]And so it was, as her soul was departing (for she died), that she called his name Ben-Oni;[a] but his father called him Benjamin.[b] [19]So Rachel died and was buried on the way to Ephrath (that *is,* Bethlehem). [20]And Jacob set a pillar on her grave, which *is* the pillar of Rachel's grave to this day.

[21]Then Israel journeyed and pitched his tent beyond the tower of Eder. [22]And it happened, when Israel dwelt in that land, that Reuben went and lay with Bilhah his father's concubine; and Israel heard *about it.*

Jacob's Twelve Sons

Now the sons of Jacob were twelve: [23]the sons of Leah *were* Reuben, Jacob's firstborn, and Simeon, Levi, Judah, Issachar, and Zebulun; [24]the sons of Rachel *were* Joseph and Benjamin; [25]the sons of Bilhah, Rachel's maidservant, *were* Dan and Naphtali; [26]and the sons of Zilpah, Leah's maidservant, *were* Gad and Asher. These *were* the sons of Jacob who were born to him in Padan Aram.

Death of Isaac

[27]Then Jacob came to his father Isaac at Mamre, or Kirjath Arba[a] (that *is,* Hebron), where Abraham and Isaac had dwelt. [28]Now the days of Isaac were one hundred and eighty years. [29]So Isaac breathed his last and died, and was gathered to his people, *being* old and full of days. And his sons Esau and Jacob buried him.

The Family of Esau

36 Now this *is* the genealogy of Esau, who is Edom. [2]Esau took his wives from the daughters of Canaan: Adah the daughter of Elon the Hittite; Aholibamah the daughter of Anah, the daughter of Zibeon the Hivite; [3]and Basemath, Ishmael's daughter, sister of Nebajoth. [4]Now Adah bore Eliphaz to Esau, and Basemath bore Reuel. [5]And Aholibamah bore Jeush, Jaalam, and Korah. These *were* the sons of Esau who were born to him in the land of Canaan.

[6]Then Esau took his wives, his sons, his daughters, and all the persons of his household, his cattle and all his animals, and all his goods which he had gained in the land of Canaan, and went to a country away from the presence of his brother Jacob. [7]For their possessions were too great for them to dwell together, and the land where they were strangers could not support them because of their livestock. [8]So Esau dwelt in Mount Seir. Esau *is* Edom.

[9]And this *is* the genealogy of Esau the father of the Edomites in Mount Seir. [10]These *were* the names of Esau's sons: Eliphaz the son of Adah the wife of Esau, and Reuel the son of Basemath the wife of Esau. [11]And the sons of Eliphaz were Teman, Omar, Zepho,[a] Gatam, and Kenaz. [12]Now Timna was the concubine of Eliphaz, Esau's son, and she bore Amalek to Eliphaz. These *were* the sons of Adah, Esau's wife. [13]These *were* the sons of Reuel: Nahath, Zerah, Shammah, and Mizzah. These were the sons of Basemath, Esau's wife.

35:7 [a]Literally *God of the House of God*
35:8 [a]Literally *Terebinth of Weeping* **35:18** [a]Literally *Son of My Sorrow* [b]Literally *Son of the Right Hand*
35:27 [a]Literally *Town of Arba* **36:11** [a]Spelled *Zephi* in 1 Chronicles 1:36

[14]These were the sons of Aholibamah, Esau's wife, the daughter of Anah, the daughter of Zibeon. And she bore to Esau: Jeush, Jaalam, and Korah.

The Chiefs of Edom

[15]These *were* the chiefs of the sons of Esau. The sons of Eliphaz, the firstborn *son* of Esau, were Chief Teman, Chief Omar, Chief Zepho, Chief Kenaz, [16]Chief Korah,[a] Chief Gatam, *and* Chief Amalek. These *were* the chiefs of Eliphaz in the land of Edom. They *were* the sons of Adah.

[17]These *were* the sons of Reuel, Esau's son: Chief Nahath, Chief Zerah, Chief Shammah, and Chief Mizzah. These *were* the chiefs of Reuel in the land of Edom. These *were* the sons of Basemath, Esau's wife.

[18]And these *were* the sons of Aholibamah, Esau's wife: Chief Jeush, Chief Jaalam, and Chief Korah. These *were* the chiefs *who descended* from Aholibamah, Esau's wife, the daughter of Anah. [19]These *were* the sons of Esau, who is Edom, and these *were* their chiefs.

The Sons of Seir

[20]These *were* the sons of Seir the Horite who inhabited the land: Lotan, Shobal, Zibeon, Anah, [21]Dishon, Ezer, and Dishan. These *were* the chiefs of the Horites, the sons of Seir, in the land of Edom.

[22]And the sons of Lotan were Hori and Hemam.[a] Lotan's sister *was* Timna.

[23]These *were* the sons of Shobal: Alvan,[a] Manahath, Ebal, Shepho,[b] and Onam.

[24]These *were* the sons of Zibeon: both Ajah and Anah. This *was the* Anah who found the water[a] in the wilderness as he pastured the donkeys of his father Zibeon. [25]These *were* the children of Anah: Dishon and Aholibamah the daughter of Anah.

[26]These *were* the sons of Dishon:[a] Hemdan,[b] Eshban, Ithran, and Cheran. [27]These *were* the sons of Ezer: Bilhan, Zaavan, and Akan.[a] [28]These *were* the sons of Dishan: Uz and Aran.

[29]These *were* the chiefs of the Horites: Chief Lotan, Chief Shobal, Chief Zibeon, Chief Anah, [30]Chief Dishon, Chief Ezer, and Chief Dishan. These *were* the chiefs of the Horites, according to their chiefs in the land of Seir.

The Kings of Edom

[31]Now these *were* the kings who reigned in the land of Edom before any king reigned over the children of Israel: [32]Bela the son of Beor reigned in Edom, and the name of his city *was* Dinhabah. [33]And when Bela died, Jobab the son of Zerah of Bozrah reigned in his place. [34]When Jobab died, Husham of the land of the Temanites reigned in his place. [35]And when Husham died, Hadad the son of Bedad, who attacked Midian in the field of Moab, reigned in his place. And the name of his city *was* Avith. [36]When Hadad died, Samlah of Masrekah reigned in his place. [37]And when Samlah died, Saul of Rehoboth-*by*-the-River reigned in his place. [38]When Saul died, Baal-Hanan the son of Achbor reigned in his place. [39]And when Baal-Hanan the son of Achbor died, Hadar[a] reigned in his place; and the name of his city *was* Pau.[b] His wife's name *was* Mehetabel, the daughter of Matred, the daughter of Mezahab.

The Chiefs of Esau

[40]And these *were* the names of the chiefs of Esau, according to their families and their places, by their names: Chief Timnah, Chief Alvah,[a] Chief Jetheth, [41]Chief Aholibamah, Chief Elah, Chief Pinon, [42]Chief Kenaz, Chief Teman, Chief Mibzar, [43]Chief Magdiel, and Chief Iram. These *were* the chiefs of Edom, according to their dwelling places in the land of their possession. Esau *was* the father of the Edomites.

Joseph Dreams of Greatness

37 Now Jacob dwelt in the land where his father was a stranger, in the land of Canaan. [2]This *is* the history of Jacob.

Joseph, *being* seventeen years old, was feeding the flock with his brothers. And the lad *was* with the sons of Bilhah and the sons of Zilpah, his father's wives; and Joseph brought a bad report of them to his father.

[3]Now Israel loved Joseph more than all his children, because he *was* the son of his old age. Also he made him a tunic of *many* colors. [4]But when his brothers saw that their father loved him more than all his brothers, they hated him and could not speak peaceably to him.

36:16 [a]Samaritan Pentateuch omits *Chief Korah.*
36:22 [a]Spelled *Homam* in 1 Chronicles 1:39
36:23 [a]Spelled *Alian* in 1 Chronicles 1:40 [b]Spelled *Shephi* in 1 Chronicles 1:40 36:24 [a]Following Masoretic Text and Vulgate (*hot springs*); Septuagint reads *Jamin;* Targum reads *mighty men;* Talmud interprets as *mules.* 36:26 [a]Hebrew *Dishan* [b]Spelled *Hamran* in 1 Chronicles 1:41 36:27 [a]Spelled *Jaakan* in 1 Chronicles 1:42 36:39 [a]Spelled *Hadad* in Samaritan Pentateuch, Syriac, and 1 Chronicles 1:50 [b]Spelled *Pai* in 1 Chronicles 1:50 36:40 [a]Spelled *Aliah* in 1 Chronicles 1:51

JOSEPH AND THE LAW OF PROCESS

Leadership Develops Daily, Not in a Day
(Genesis 37:1—50:22)

Becoming a leader is a lot like investing in the stock market. If you hope to make a fortune in a day, you're doomed. It's what you do day by day, over the long haul, that matters most. If you continually develop your leadership, letting your "assets" compound over time, the inevitable result is growth.

Although some individuals have greater natural gifts than others, nearly all the skills of leadership can be learned and improved. But that process doesn't happen overnight. Leadership has so many facets: respect, experience, emotional strength, people skills, discipline, vision, momentum, timing—the list goes on. That's why leaders require so much seasoning to be effective.

The good news is that you can grow in your ability to lead. Regardless of your starting point, you can improve.

Joseph was a cocky kid, too arrogant for his own good. He didn't think it enough to be the favorite of his father, the child who received special treatment, the son of Jacob's old age. Joseph had to rub it in.

When God gave Joseph a dream revealing that he would one day lead his family—not only his 11 brothers, but also his parents—Joseph thoughtlessly told everyone about it. Twice. His father rebuked him. His brothers wanted revenge.

And they got it.

Early in his life, Joseph didn't know how to skillfully work with others. He lacked experience, wisdom, and humility—three qualities gained only with the passage of time. Joseph's life illustrates the Law of Process. Observe how time and experience contributed to the development of Joseph's leadership skills:

PHASE ONE: I don't know what I don't know.

Everyone starts out in a state of ignorance. That's where Joseph began. He didn't understand the dynamics of his family. Either he couldn't imagine how his brothers might react when he described his dream, or he didn't care. The Scripture says his brothers already hated him; when he described his dream, they hated him even more. Joseph did and said things without understanding the interpersonal issues involved. His ignorance cost him more than two decades of alienation from his family.

PHASE TWO: I know what I don't know.

It took a life-changing incident to capture Joseph's attention and start him on the road to change. Thrust into slavery in Egypt, he began to learn what he didn't know. He came to understand that leadership is difficult and carries a huge weight of responsibility. Over the years, Joseph suffered betrayal and learned hard lessons in human nature, relationships, and leadership. The process molded his character, granting him both patience and humility. Eventually he recognized God as his source of blessing and power.

PHASE THREE: I know and grow and it starts to show.

Leaders who show great skill when opportunities arise, shine only because they've paid the price of preparation. When Pharaoh finally called Joseph, the young man performed with excellence and great wisdom. He didn't succeed because he suddenly got good at age 30; he succeeded because he paid the price for 13 years. Joseph's hard-won wisdom and discernment got him promoted to second in command of what was then the most powerful nation on earth.

PHASE FOUR: I simply go because of what I know.

During seven years of plenty, Joseph executed his leadership plan with great skill. He filled the cities of Egypt with grain and prepared the country for a famine. But one can see how far his leadership had grown only by observing what he did during the lean years that followed. While he focused on feeding the people of Egypt, the strength of his leadership allowed him to feed the people of other lands as well. In the process, he brought untold money, livestock, and land into his master's possession. He also fulfilled the prophecy of his teenage dreams.

Every effective leader needs time to develop, but time alone cannot make someone an effective leader. Some individuals never discover the Law of Process, never work at growth, and therefore remain at Phase One their entire lives.

Fortunately for the children of Israel, Joseph did not stop at the first stage. He grew in his journey from the pit to the palace. Yet nearly 23 years passed before he reunited with his brothers and saw his own vision fulfilled. At the end, Joseph realized that God had directed the process of his development as a leader, and that he had been groomed for a much greater purpose than he ever imagined as a cocky teenager.

By the time his father died, Joseph had learned to see things from God's perspective. When his brothers feared for their lives, Joseph calmed their nerves by saying, "Do not be afraid, for am I in the place of God? But as for you, you meant evil against me; but God meant it for good, in order to bring it about as it is this day, to save many people alive" (Gen. 50:19, 20).

At last Joseph could trace God's hand over all the years of his life. And he understood the Lord's long-term plan for His people, a plan Joseph helped fulfill by growing into the leader God desired him to be.

The Law of Intuition: Joseph Takes Effective Action in a Crisis

(Genesis 37:5–36; 39:1—41:16)

Problems never paralyze great leaders; they know that solutions usually exist. The Scripture shows that Joseph accomplished much because he enjoyed:

1. **A significant vision from God (37:5, 6, 9–11).** As a youth, Joseph knew God had something special in mind for him.

2. **A vital relationship with God (39:2, 21, 23).** Scripture says that "the LORD was with" Joseph.

3. **A strong character developed through difficulties (39:7, 8).** With each new trial, Joseph grew stronger.

4. **Practical experience gained through life (39:22).** Joseph grew in ability and experience when he took charge of the prison.

5. **A special giftedness from God (41:15, 16).** Joseph's ability to interpret dreams enabled him to make a difference in many lives.

6. **A unique blessing from God (39:3–5).** Four times the Bible expresses God's blessing of Joseph with some version of, "whatever he did, the LORD made it prosper" (Gen. 39:2, 3, 21, 23).

⁵Now Joseph had a dream, and he told *it* to his brothers; and they hated him even more. ⁶So he said to them, "Please hear this dream which I have dreamed: ⁷There we were, binding sheaves in the field. Then behold, my sheaf arose and also stood upright; and indeed your sheaves stood all around and bowed down to my sheaf."

⁸And his brothers said to him, "Shall you indeed reign over us? Or shall you indeed have dominion over us?" So they hated him even more for his dreams and for his words.

⁹Then he dreamed still another dream and told it to his brothers, and said, "Look, I have dreamed another dream. And this time, the sun, the moon, and the eleven stars bowed down to me."

¹⁰So he told *it* to his father and his brothers; and his father rebuked him and said to him,

"What *is* this dream that you have dreamed? Shall your mother and I and your brothers indeed come to bow down to the earth before you?" ¹¹And his brothers envied him, but his father kept the matter *in mind*.

Joseph Sold by His Brothers

¹²Then his brothers went to feed their father's flock in Shechem. ¹³And Israel said to Joseph, "Are not your brothers feeding *the flock* in Shechem? Come, I will send you to them."

So he said to him, "Here I am."

¹⁴Then he said to him, "Please go and see if it is well with your brothers and well with the flocks, and bring back word to me." So he sent him out of the Valley of Hebron, and he went to Shechem.

¹⁵Now a certain man found him, and there he was, wandering in the field. And the man asked him, saying, "What are you seeking?"

¹⁶So he said, "I am seeking my brothers. Please tell me where they are feeding *their flocks*."

¹⁷And the man said, "They have departed from here, for I heard them say, 'Let us go to Dothan.'" So Joseph went after his brothers and found them in Dothan.

¹⁸Now when they saw him afar off, even before he came near them, they conspired against him to kill him. ¹⁹Then they said to one another, "Look, this dreamer is coming! ²⁰Come therefore, let us now kill him and cast him into some pit; and we shall say, 'Some wild beast has devoured him.' We shall see what will become of his dreams!"

²¹But Reuben heard *it,* and he delivered him out of their hands, and said, "Let us not kill him." ²²And Reuben said to them, "Shed no blood, *but* cast him into this pit which *is* in the wilderness, and do not lay a hand on him"—that he might deliver him out of their hands, and bring him back to his father.

²³So it came to pass, when Joseph had come to his brothers, that they stripped Joseph *of* his tunic, the tunic of *many* colors that *was* on him. ²⁴Then they took him and cast him into a pit. And the pit *was* empty; *there was* no water in it.

²⁵And they sat down to eat a meal. Then they lifted their eyes and looked, and there was a company of Ishmaelites, coming from Gilead with their camels, bearing spices, balm, and myrrh, on their way to carry *them* down to Egypt. ²⁶So Judah said to his brothers, "What profit *is there* if we kill our brother and conceal his blood? ²⁷Come and let us sell him to the Ishmaelites, and let not our hand be upon him, for he *is* our brother *and* our flesh." And his brothers listened. ²⁸Then Midian-

ite traders passed by; so *the brothers* pulled Joseph up and lifted him out of the pit, and sold him to the Ishmaelites for twenty *shekels* of silver. And they took Joseph to Egypt.

²⁹Then Reuben returned to the pit, and indeed Joseph *was* not in the pit; and he tore his clothes. ³⁰And he returned to his brothers and said, "The lad *is* no *more;* and I, where shall I go?"

³¹So they took Joseph's tunic, killed a kid of the goats, and dipped the tunic in the blood. ³²Then they sent the tunic of *many* colors, and they brought *it* to their father and said, "We have found this. Do you know whether it *is* your son's tunic or not?"

³³And he recognized it and said, "*It is* my son's tunic. A wild beast has devoured him. Without doubt Joseph is torn to pieces." ³⁴Then Jacob tore his clothes, put sackcloth on his waist, and mourned for his son many days. ³⁵And all his sons and all his daughters arose to comfort him; but he refused to be comforted, and he said, "For I shall go down into the grave to my son in mourning." Thus his father wept for him.

³⁶Now the Midianites[a] had sold him in Egypt to Potiphar, an officer of Pharaoh *and* captain of the guard.

Judah and Tamar

38 It came to pass at that time that Judah departed from his brothers, and visited a certain Adullamite whose name *was* Hirah. ²And Judah saw there a daughter of a certain Canaanite whose name *was* Shua, and he married her and went in to her. ³So she conceived and bore a son, and he called his name Er. ⁴She conceived again and bore a son, and she called his name Onan. ⁵And she conceived yet again and bore a son, and called his name Shelah. He was at Chezib when she bore him.

⁶Then Judah took a wife for Er his firstborn, and her name *was* Tamar. ⁷But Er, Judah's firstborn, was wicked in the sight of the LORD, and the LORD killed him. ⁸And Judah said to Onan, "Go in to your brother's wife and marry her, and raise up an heir to your brother." ⁹But Onan knew that the heir would not be his; and it came to pass, when he went in to his brother's wife, that he emitted on the ground, lest he should give an heir to his brother. ¹⁰And the thing which he did displeased the LORD; therefore He killed him also.

¹¹Then Judah said to Tamar his daughter-in-law, "Remain a widow in your father's house till my son Shelah is grown." For he said, "Lest he also die like his brothers." And Tamar went and dwelt in her father's house.

¹²Now in the process of time the daughter of Shua, Judah's wife, died; and Judah was comforted, and went up to his sheepshearers at Timnah, he and his friend Hirah the Adullamite. ¹³And it was told Tamar, saying, "Look, your father-in-law is going up to Timnah to shear his sheep." ¹⁴So she took off her widow's garments, covered *herself* with a veil and wrapped herself, and sat in an open place which *was* on the way to Timnah; for she saw that Shelah was grown, and she was not given to him as a wife. ¹⁵When Judah saw her, he thought she *was* a harlot, because she had covered her face. ¹⁶Then he turned to her by the way, and said, "Please let me come in to you"; for he did not know that she *was* his daughter-in-law.

So she said, "What will you give me, that you may come in to me?"

¹⁷And he said, "I will send a young goat from the flock."

So she said, "Will you give *me* a pledge till you send *it?*"

¹⁸Then he said, "What pledge shall I give you?"

So she said, "Your signet and cord, and your staff that *is* in your hand." Then he gave *them* to her, and went in to her, and she conceived by him. ¹⁹So she arose and went away, and laid aside her veil and put on the garments of her widowhood.

²⁰And Judah sent the young goat by the hand of his friend the Adullamite, to receive *his* pledge from the woman's hand, but he did not find her. ²¹Then he asked the men of that place, saying, "Where is the harlot who *was* openly by the roadside?"

And they said, "There was no harlot in this *place.*"

²²So he returned to Judah and said, "I cannot find her. Also, the men of the place said there was no harlot in this *place.*"

²³Then Judah said, "Let her take *them* for herself, lest we be shamed; for I sent this young goat and you have not found her."

²⁴And it came to pass, about three months after, that Judah was told, saying, "Tamar your daughter-in-law has played the harlot; furthermore she *is* with child by harlotry."

So Judah said, "Bring her out and let her be burned!"

²⁵When she *was* brought out, she sent to her father-in-law, saying, "By the man to whom

---

37:36 [a]Masoretic Text reads *Medanites.*

these belong, I *am* with child." And she said, "Please determine whose these *are*—the signet and cord, and staff."

[26]So Judah acknowledged *them* and said, "She has been more righteous than I, because I did not give her to Shelah my son." And he never knew her again.

[27]Now it came to pass, at the time for giving birth, that behold, twins *were* in her womb. [28]And so it was, when she was giving birth, that *the one* put out *his* hand; and the midwife took a scarlet *thread* and bound it on his hand, saying, "This one came out first." [29]Then it happened, as he drew back his hand, that his brother came out unexpectedly; and she said, "How did you break through? *This* breach *be* upon you!" Therefore his name was called Perez.[a] [30]Afterward his brother came out who had the scarlet *thread* on his hand. And his name was called Zerah.

Joseph a Slave in Egypt

39 Now Joseph had been taken down to Egypt. And Potiphar, an officer of Pharaoh, captain of the guard, an Egyptian, bought him from the Ishmaelites who had taken him down there. [2]The LORD was with Joseph, and he was a successful man; and he was in the house of his master the Egyptian. [3]And his master saw that the LORD *was* with him and that the LORD made all he did to prosper in his hand. [4]So Joseph found favor in his sight, and served him. Then he made him overseer of his house, and all *that* he had he put under his authority. [5]So it was, from the time *that* he had made him overseer of his house and all that he had, that the LORD blessed the Egyptian's house for Joseph's sake; and the blessing of the LORD was on all that he had in the house and in the field. [6]Thus he left all that he had in Joseph's hand, and he did not know what he had except for the bread which he ate.

Now Joseph was handsome in form and appearance.

[7]And it came to pass after these things that his master's wife cast longing eyes on Joseph, and she said, "Lie with me."

[8]But he refused and said to his master's wife, "Look, my master does not know what *is* with me in the house, and he has committed all that he has to my hand. [9]*There is* no one greater in this house than I, nor has he kept back anything from me but you, because you *are* his wife. How then can I do this great wickedness, and sin against God?"

[10]So it was, as she spoke to Joseph day by day, that he did not heed her, to lie with her *or* to be with her.

[11]But it happened about this time, when Joseph went into the house to do his work, and none of the men of the house *was* inside, [12]that she caught him by his garment, saying, "Lie with me." But he left his garment in her hand, and fled and ran outside. [13]And so it was, when she saw that he had left his garment in her hand and fled outside, [14]that she called to the men of her house and spoke to them, saying, "See, he has brought in to us a Hebrew to mock us. He came in to me to lie with me, and I cried out with a loud voice. [15]And it happened, when he heard that I lifted my voice and cried out, that he left his garment with me, and fled and went outside."

[16]So she kept his garment with her until his master came home. [17]Then she spoke to him with words like these, saying, "The Hebrew servant whom you brought to us came in to me to mock me; [18]so it happened, as I lifted my voice and cried out, that he left his garment with me and fled outside."

[19]So it was, when his master heard the words which his wife spoke to him, saying, "Your servant did to me after this manner," that his anger was aroused. [20]Then Joseph's master took him and put him into the prison, a place where the king's prisoners *were* confined. And he was there in the prison. [21]But the LORD was with Joseph and showed him mercy, and He gave him favor in the sight of the keeper of the prison. [22]And the keeper of the prison committed to Joseph's hand all the prisoners who *were* in the prison; whatever they did there, it was his doing. [23]The keeper of the prison did not look into anything *that was* under *Joseph's* authority,[a] because the LORD was with him; and whatever he did, the LORD made *it* prosper.

The Prisoners' Dreams

40 It came to pass after these things *that* the butler and the baker of the king of Egypt offended their lord, the king of Egypt. [2]And Pharaoh was angry with his two officers, the chief butler and the chief baker. [3]So he put them in custody in the house of the captain of the guard, in the prison, the place where Joseph *was* confined. [4]And the captain of the guard charged Joseph with them, and he served them; so they were in custody for a while. [5]Then the butler and the baker of the king of Egypt, who *were* confined in the prison, had a dream, both of them, each man's dream in one night *and* each man's dream with its *own* inter-

---

38:29 [a]Literally *Breach* or *Breakthrough*
39:23 [a]Literally *his hand*

The Law of Solid Ground: Joseph Earns Trust

(Genesis 39:1—41:16)

The Bible describes some dark and difficult times in Joseph's life. But it also reveals that every time he faced adversity, he used it to develop himself personally and to build trust with others. As a result, Joseph made one comeback after another and proved himself trustworthy as a leader.

Consider a few of the ways he earned trust along the way:

Adversity	Comeback
1. Sold into Egyptian slavery	1. Developed competence and organization in the palace
2. Framed as an adulterer	2. Used his ability to discern dreams and solve problems
3. Forgotten in prison	3. Displayed the wisdom to interpret Pharaoh's dream
4. Endured seven years of famine	4. Prepared to save the country and bring Pharaoh great wealth
5. Faced the return of his treacherous brothers	5. Showed patience and integrity in dealing with others

The Law of Solid Ground teaches that leadership operates on the basis of trust. How did Joseph gain trust following his bouts with adversity? He won it through regularly displaying competence and character in his connections with others. He was able to follow each setback with a comeback because he practiced the Law of Solid Ground.

pretation. ⁶And Joseph came in to them in the morning and looked at them, and saw that they *were* sad. ⁷So he asked Pharaoh's officers who *were* with him in the custody of his lord's house, saying, "Why do you look *so* sad today?"

⁸And they said to him, "We each have had a dream, and *there is* no interpreter of it."

So Joseph said to them, "Do not interpretations belong to God? Tell *them* to me, please."

⁹Then the chief butler told his dream to Joseph, and said to him, "Behold, in my dream a vine *was* before me, ¹⁰and in the vine *were* three branches; it *was* as though it budded, its blossoms shot forth, and its clusters brought forth ripe grapes. ¹¹Then Pharaoh's cup *was* in my hand; and I took the grapes and pressed them into Pharaoh's cup, and placed the cup in Pharaoh's hand."

¹²And Joseph said to him, "This *is* the interpretation of it: The three branches *are* three days. ¹³Now within three days Pharaoh will lift up your head and restore you to your place, and you will put Pharaoh's cup in his hand according to the former manner, when you were his butler. ¹⁴But remember me when it is well with you, and

please show kindness to me; make mention of me to Pharaoh, and get me out of this house. ¹⁵For indeed I was stolen away from the land of the Hebrews; and also I have done nothing here that they should put me into the dungeon."

¹⁶When the chief baker saw that the interpretation was good, he said to Joseph, "I also *was* in my dream, and there *were* three white baskets on my head. ¹⁷In the uppermost basket *were* all kinds of baked goods for Pharaoh, and the birds ate them out of the basket on my head."

¹⁸So Joseph answered and said, "This *is* the interpretation of it: The three baskets *are* three days. ¹⁹Within three days Pharaoh will lift off your head from you and hang you on a tree; and the birds will eat your flesh from you."

²⁰Now it came to pass on the third day, *which was* Pharaoh's birthday, that he made a feast for all his servants; and he lifted up the head of the chief butler and of the chief baker among his servants. ²¹Then he restored the chief butler to his butlership again, and he placed the cup in Pharaoh's hand. ²²But he hanged the chief baker, as Joseph had interpreted to them. ²³Yet the chief butler did not remember Joseph, but forgot him.

Pharaoh's Dreams

41 Then it came to pass, at the end of two full years, that Pharaoh had a dream; and behold, he stood by the river. ²Suddenly there came up out of the river seven cows, fine looking and fat; and they fed in the meadow. ³Then behold, seven other cows came up after them out of the river, ugly and gaunt, and stood by the *other* cows on the bank of the river. ⁴And the ugly and gaunt cows ate up the seven fine looking and fat cows. So Pharaoh awoke. ⁵He slept and dreamed a second time; and suddenly seven heads of grain came up on one stalk, plump and good. ⁶Then behold, seven thin heads, blighted by the east wind, sprang up after them. ⁷And the seven thin heads devoured the seven plump and full heads. So Pharaoh awoke, and indeed, *it was* a dream. ⁸Now it came to pass in the morning that his spirit was troubled, and he sent and called for all the magicians of Egypt and all its wise men. And Pharaoh told them his dreams, but *there was* no one who could interpret them for Pharaoh.

⁹Then the chief butler spoke to Pharaoh, saying: "I remember my faults this day. ¹⁰When Pharaoh was angry with his servants, and put me in custody in the house of the captain of the guard, *both* me and the chief baker, ¹¹we each had a dream in one night, he and I. Each of us dreamed according to the interpretation of his *own* dream. ¹²Now there *was* a young Hebrew man with us there, a servant of the captain of the guard. And we told him, and he interpreted our dreams for us; to each man he interpreted according to his *own* dream. ¹³And it came to pass, just as he interpreted for us, so it happened. He restored me to my office, and he hanged him."

¹⁴Then Pharaoh sent and called Joseph, and they brought him quickly out of the dungeon; and he shaved, changed his clothing, and came to Pharaoh. ¹⁵And Pharaoh said to Joseph, "I have had a dream, and *there is* no one who can interpret it. But I have heard it said of you *that* you can understand a dream, to interpret it."

¹⁶So Joseph answered Pharaoh, saying, "*It is* not in me; God will give Pharaoh an answer of peace."

¹⁷Then Pharaoh said to Joseph: "Behold, in my dream I stood on the bank of the river. ¹⁸Suddenly seven cows came up out of the river, fine looking and fat; and they fed in the meadow. ¹⁹Then behold, seven other cows came up after them, poor and very ugly and gaunt, such ugliness as I have never seen in all the land

---

PHARAOH — LEADING WITH HUMILITY
(Genesis 41:1–55)

PROFILE *in* **LEADERSHIP**

The Pharaoh who ruled Egypt at the time of Joseph showed remarkable wisdom and insight, as well as a heart receptive to truth. God strategically positioned this humble man as king over Egypt at a crucial time in world history.

When nightmares awakened Pharaoh, he recognized something odd was happening. As a strong leader he acknowledged his sense of unease, but as a humble leader he enlisted the advice of others. He summoned Joseph, who successfully interpreted his dreams.

Do you think Pharaoh knew his kingdom hung in the balance as he carefully processed the message God had given him? It took great wisdom and humility to designate Joseph as the point person and to give him the authority and resources necessary to survive the coming calamity. But he did it. And the people followed his leadership, carefully storing up grain during seven prophesied years of plenty. When the predicted hard times arrived, Pharaoh once more deferred to Joseph. The king of Egypt put himself and his people into the capable hands of this foreigner.

Had this Pharaoh been arrogant or intimidated by Joseph, millions would have starved. Instead, Pharaoh listened carefully, empowered Joseph to act—and in so doing, insured his own legacy as an effective leader.

of Egypt. [20]And the gaunt and ugly cows ate up the first seven, the fat cows. [21]When they had eaten them up, no one would have known that they had eaten them, for they *were* just as ugly as at the beginning. So I awoke. [22]Also I saw in my dream, and suddenly seven heads came up on one stalk, full and good. [23]Then behold, seven heads, withered, thin, *and* blighted by the east wind, sprang up after them. [24]And the thin heads devoured the seven good heads. So I told *this* to the magicians, but *there was* no one who could explain *it* to me."

[25]Then Joseph said to Pharaoh, "The dreams of Pharaoh *are* one; God has shown Pharaoh what He *is* about to do: [26]The seven good cows *are* seven years, and the seven good heads *are* seven years; the dreams *are* one. [27]And the seven thin and ugly cows which came up after them *are* seven years, and the seven empty heads blighted by the east wind are seven years of famine. [28]This *is* the thing which I have spoken to Pharaoh. God has shown Pharaoh what He *is* about to do. [29]Indeed seven years of great plenty will come throughout all the land of Egypt; [30]but after them seven years of famine will arise, and all the plenty will be forgotten in the land of Egypt; and the famine will deplete the land. [31]So the plenty will not be known in the land because of the famine following, for it *will be* very severe. [32]And the dream was repeated to Pharaoh twice because the thing *is* established by God, and God will shortly bring it to pass.

[33]"Now therefore, let Pharaoh select a discerning and wise man, and set him over the land of Egypt. [34]Let Pharaoh do *this*, and let him appoint officers over the land, to collect one-fifth *of the produce* of the land of Egypt in the seven plentiful years. [35]And let them gather all the food of those good years that are coming, and store up grain under the authority of Pharaoh, and let them keep food in the cities. [36]Then that food shall be as a reserve for the land for the seven years of famine which shall be in the land of Egypt, that the land may not perish during the famine."

Joseph's Rise to Power

[37]So the advice was good in the eyes of Pharaoh and in the eyes of all his servants. [38]And Pharaoh said to his servants, "Can we find *such a one* as this, a man in whom *is* the Spirit of God?"

[39]Then Pharaoh said to Joseph, "Inasmuch as God has shown you all this, *there is* no one as discerning and wise as you. [40]You shall be over my house, and all my people shall be ruled according to your word; only in regard to the throne will I be greater than you." [41]And Pharaoh said to Joseph, "See, I have set you over all the land of Egypt."

[42]Then Pharaoh took his signet ring off his hand and put it on Joseph's hand; and he clothed him in garments of fine linen and put a gold chain around his neck. [43]And he had him ride in the second chariot which he had; and they cried out before him, "Bow the knee!" So he set him over all the land of Egypt. [44]Pharaoh also said to Joseph, "I *am* Pharaoh, and without your consent no man may lift his hand or foot in all the land of Egypt." [45]And Pharaoh called Joseph's name Zaphnath-Paaneah. And he gave him as a wife Asenath, the daughter of Poti-Pherah priest of On. So Joseph went out over *all* the land of Egypt.

[46]Joseph was thirty years old when he stood before Pharaoh king of Egypt. And Joseph went out from the presence of Pharaoh, and went throughout all the land of Egypt. [47]Now in the seven plentiful years the ground brought forth abundantly. [48]So he gathered up all the food of the seven years which were in the land of Egypt, and laid up the food in the cities; he laid up in every city the food of the fields which surrounded them. [49]Joseph gathered very much grain, as the sand of the sea, until he stopped counting, for *it was* immeasurable.

[50]And to Joseph were born two sons before the years of famine came, whom Asenath, the daughter of Poti-Pherah priest of On, bore to him. [51]Joseph called the name of the firstborn Manasseh:[a] "For God has made me forget all my toil and all my father's house." [52]And the name of the second he called Ephraim:[a] "For God has caused me to be fruitful in the land of my affliction."

[53]Then the seven years of plenty which were in the land of Egypt ended, [54]and the seven years of famine began to come, as Joseph had said. The famine was in all lands, but in all the land of Egypt there was bread. [55]So when all the land of Egypt was famished, the people cried to Pharaoh for bread. Then Pharaoh said to all the Egyptians, "Go to Joseph; whatever he says to you, do." [56]The famine was over all the face of the earth, and Joseph opened all the storehouses[a] and sold to the Egyptians. And the famine became severe in the land of Egypt. [57]So all countries came to Joseph in Egypt to buy *grain*, because the famine was severe in all lands.

41:51 [a]Literally *Making Forgetful* **41:52** [a]Literally *Fruitfulness* **41:56** [a]Literally *all that was in them*

Joseph's Brothers Go to Egypt

42 When Jacob saw that there was grain in Egypt, Jacob said to his sons, "Why do you look at one another?" ²And he said, "Indeed I have heard that there is grain in Egypt; go down to that place and buy for us there, that we may live and not die."

³So Joseph's ten brothers went down to buy grain in Egypt. ⁴But Jacob did not send Joseph's brother Benjamin with his brothers, for he said, "Lest some calamity befall him." ⁵And the sons of Israel went to buy *grain* among those who journeyed, for the famine was in the land of Canaan.

⁶Now Joseph *was* governor over the land; and it was he who sold to all the people of the land. And Joseph's brothers came and bowed down before him with *their* faces to the earth. ⁷Joseph saw his brothers and recognized them, but he acted as a stranger to them and spoke roughly to them. Then he said to them, "Where do you come from?"

And they said, "From the land of Canaan to buy food."

⁸So Joseph recognized his brothers, but they did not recognize him. ⁹Then Joseph remembered the dreams which he had dreamed about them, and said to them, "You *are* spies! You have come to see the nakedness of the land!"

¹⁰And they said to him, "No, my lord, but your servants have come to buy food. ¹¹We *are* all one man's sons; we *are* honest *men;* your servants are not spies."

¹²But he said to them, "No, but you have come to see the nakedness of the land."

¹³And they said, "Your servants *are* twelve brothers, the sons of one man in the land of Canaan; and in fact, the youngest *is* with our father today, and one *is* no more."

¹⁴But Joseph said to them, "It *is* as I spoke to you, saying, 'You *are* spies!' ¹⁵In this *manner* you shall be tested: By the life of Pharaoh, you shall not leave this place unless your youngest brother comes here. ¹⁶Send one of you, and let him bring your brother; and you shall be kept in prison, that your words may be tested to see whether *there is* any truth in you; or else, by the life of Pharaoh, surely you *are* spies!" ¹⁷So he put them all together in prison three days.

¹⁸Then Joseph said to them the third day, "Do this and live, *for* I fear God: ¹⁹If you *are* honest *men,* let one of your brothers be confined to your prison house; but you, go and carry grain for the famine of your houses. ²⁰And bring your youngest brother to me; so your words will be verified, and you shall not die."

And they did so. ²¹Then they said to one another, "We *are* truly guilty concerning our brother, for we saw the anguish of his soul when he pleaded with us, and we would not hear; therefore this distress has come upon us."

²²And Reuben answered them, saying, "Did I not speak to you, saying, 'Do not sin against the boy'; and you would not listen? Therefore behold, his blood is now required of us." ²³But they did not know that Joseph understood *them,* for he spoke to them through an interpreter. ²⁴And he turned himself away from them and wept. Then he returned to them again, and talked with them. And he took Simeon from them and bound him before their eyes.

The Brothers Return to Canaan

²⁵Then Joseph gave a command to fill their sacks with grain, to restore every man's money to his sack, and to give them provisions for the journey. Thus he did for them. ²⁶So they loaded their donkeys with the grain and departed from there. ²⁷But as one *of them* opened his sack to give his donkey feed at the encampment, he saw his money; and there it was, in the mouth of his sack. ²⁸So he said to his brothers, "My money has been restored, and there it is, in my sack!" Then their hearts failed *them* and they were afraid, saying to one another, "What *is* this *that* God has done to us?"

²⁹Then they went to Jacob their father in the land of Canaan and told him all that had happened to them, saying: ³⁰"The man *who is* lord of the land spoke roughly to us, and took us for spies of the country. ³¹But we said to him, 'We *are* honest *men;* we are not spies. ³²We *are* twelve brothers, sons of our father; one *is* no *more,* and the youngest *is* with our father this day in the land of Canaan.' ³³Then the man, the lord of the country, said to us, 'By this I will know that you *are* honest *men:* Leave one of your brothers *here* with me, take *food for* the famine of your households, and be gone. ³⁴And bring your youngest brother to me; so I shall know that you *are* not spies, but *that* you *are* honest *men.* I will grant your brother to you, and you may trade in the land.'"

³⁵Then it happened as they emptied their sacks, that surprisingly each man's bundle of money *was* in his sack; and when they and their father saw the bundles of money, they were afraid. ³⁶And Jacob their father said to them, "You have bereaved me: Joseph is no *more,* Simeon is no *more,* and you want to take Benjamin. All these things are against me."

³⁷Then Reuben spoke to his father, saying,

"Kill my two sons if I do not bring him *back* to you; put him in my hands, and I will bring him back to you."

³⁸But he said, "My son shall not go down with you, for his brother is dead, and he is left alone. If any calamity should befall him along the way in which you go, then you would bring down my gray hair with sorrow to the grave."

Joseph's Brothers Return with Benjamin

43 Now the famine *was* severe in the land. ²And it came to pass, when they had eaten up the grain which they had brought from Egypt, that their father said to them, "Go back, buy us a little food."

³But Judah spoke to him, saying, "The man solemnly warned us, saying, 'You shall not see my face unless your brother *is* with you.' ⁴If you send our brother with us, we will go down and buy you food. ⁵But if you will not send *him,* we will not go down; for the man said to us, 'You shall not see my face unless your brother *is* with you.'"

⁶And Israel said, "Why did you deal *so* wrongfully with me *as* to tell the man whether you had still *another* brother?"

⁷But they said, "The man asked us pointedly about ourselves and our family, saying, '*Is* your father still alive? Have you *another* brother?' And we told him according to these words. Could we possibly have known that he would say, 'Bring your brother down'?"

⁸Then Judah said to Israel his father, "Send the lad with me, and we will arise and go, that we may live and not die, both we and you *and* also our little ones. ⁹I myself will be surety for him; from my hand you shall require him. If I do not bring him *back* to you and set him before you, then let me bear the blame forever. ¹⁰For if we had not lingered, surely by now we would have returned this second time."

¹¹And their father Israel said to them, "If *it must be* so, then do this: Take some of the best fruits of the land in your vessels and carry down a present for the man—a little balm and a little honey, spices and myrrh, pistachio nuts and almonds. ¹²Take double money in your hand, and take back in your hand the money that was returned in the mouth of your sacks; perhaps it was an oversight. ¹³Take your brother also, and arise, go back to the man. ¹⁴And may God Almighty give you mercy before the man, that he may release your other brother and Benjamin. If I am bereaved, I am bereaved!"

¹⁵So the men took that present and Benja-

min, and they took double money in their hand, and arose and went down to Egypt; and they stood before Joseph. ¹⁶When Joseph saw Benjamin with them, he said to the steward of his house, "Take *these* men to my home, and slaughter an animal and make ready; for *these* men will dine with me at noon." ¹⁷Then the man did as Joseph ordered, and the man brought the men into Joseph's house.

¹⁸Now the men were afraid because they were brought into Joseph's house; and they said, "*It is* because of the money, which was returned in our sacks the first time, that we are brought in, so that he may make a case against us and seize us, to take us as slaves with our donkeys."

¹⁹When they drew near to the steward of Joseph's house, they talked with him at the door of the house, ²⁰and said, "O sir, we indeed came down the first time to buy food; ²¹but it happened, when we came to the encampment, that we opened our sacks, and there, *each* man's money *was* in the mouth of his sack, our money in full weight; so we have brought it back in our hand. ²²And we have brought down other money in our hands to buy food. We do not know who put our money in our sacks."

²³But he said, "Peace *be* with you, do not be afraid. Your God and the God of your father has given you treasure in your sacks; I had your money." Then he brought Simeon out to them.

²⁴So the man brought the men into Joseph's house and gave *them* water, and they washed their feet; and he gave their donkeys feed. ²⁵Then they made the present ready for Joseph's coming at noon, for they heard that they would eat bread there.

²⁶And when Joseph came home, they brought him the present which *was* in their hand into the house, and bowed down before him to the earth. ²⁷Then he asked them about *their* well-being, and said, "*Is* your father well, the old man of whom you spoke? *Is* he still alive?"

²⁸And they answered, "Your servant our father *is* in good health; he *is* still alive." And they bowed their heads down and prostrated themselves.

²⁹Then he lifted his eyes and saw his brother Benjamin, his mother's son, and said, "*Is* this your younger brother of whom you spoke to me?" And he said, "God be gracious to you, my son." ³⁰Now his heart yearned for his brother; so Joseph made haste and sought *somewhere* to weep. And he went into *his* chamber and wept there. ³¹Then he washed his face and came out; and he restrained himself, and said, "Serve the bread."

³²So they set him a place by himself, and

them by themselves, and the Egyptians who ate with him by themselves; because the Egyptians could not eat food with the Hebrews, for that *is* an abomination to the Egyptians. ³³And they sat before him, the firstborn according to his birthright and the youngest according to his youth; and the men looked in astonishment at one another. ³⁴Then he took servings to them from before him, but Benjamin's serving was five times as much as any of theirs. So they drank and were merry with him.

Joseph's Cup

44 And he commanded the steward of his house, saying, "Fill the men's sacks with food, as much as they can carry, and put each man's money in the mouth of his sack. ²Also put my cup, the silver cup, in the mouth of the sack of the youngest, and his grain money." So he did according to the word that Joseph had spoken. ³As soon as the morning dawned, the men were sent away, they and their donkeys. ⁴When they had gone out of the city, *and* were not *yet* far off, Joseph said to his steward, "Get up, follow the men; and when you overtake them, say to them, 'Why have you repaid evil for good? ⁵*Is* not this *the one* from which my lord drinks, and with which he indeed practices divination? You have done evil in so doing.'"

⁶So he overtook them, and he spoke to them these same words. ⁷And they said to him, "Why does my lord say these words? Far be it from us that your servants should do such a thing. ⁸Look, we brought back to you from the land of Canaan the money which we found in the mouth of our sacks. How then could we steal silver or gold from your lord's house? ⁹With whomever of your servants it is found, let him die, and we also will be my lord's slaves."

¹⁰And he said, "Now also *let* it *be* according to your words; he with whom it is found shall be my slave, and you shall be blameless." ¹¹Then each man speedily let down his sack to the ground, and each opened his sack. ¹²So he searched. He began with the oldest and left off with the youngest; and the cup was found in Benjamin's sack. ¹³Then they tore their clothes, and each man loaded his donkey and returned to the city.

¹⁴So Judah and his brothers came to Joseph's house, and he *was* still there; and they fell before him on the ground. ¹⁵And Joseph said to them, "What deed *is* this you have done? Did you not know that such a man as I can certainly practice divination?"

¹⁶Then Judah said, "What shall we say to my lord? What shall we speak? Or how shall we clear ourselves? God has found out the iniquity of your servants; here we are, my lord's slaves, both we and *he* also with whom the cup was found."

¹⁷But he said, "Far be it from me that I should do so; the man in whose hand the cup was found, he shall be my slave. And as for you, go up in peace to your father."

Judah Intercedes for Benjamin

¹⁸Then Judah came near to him and said: "O my lord, please let your servant speak a word in my lord's hearing, and do not let your anger burn against your servant; for you *are* even like Pharaoh. ¹⁹My lord asked his servants, saying, 'Have you a father or a brother?' ²⁰And we said to my lord, 'We have a father, an old man, and a child of *his* old age, *who is* young; his brother is dead, and he alone is left of his mother's children, and his father loves him.' ²¹Then you said to your servants, 'Bring him down to me, that I may set my eyes on him.' ²²And we said to my lord, 'The lad cannot leave his father, for *if* he should leave his father, *his father* would die.' ²³But you said to your servants, 'Unless your youngest brother comes down with you, you shall see my face no more.'

²⁴"So it was, when we went up to your servant my father, that we told him the words of my lord. ²⁵And our father said, 'Go back *and* buy us a little food.' ²⁶But we said, 'We cannot go down; if our youngest brother is with us, then we will go down; for we may not see the man's face unless our youngest brother *is* with us.' ²⁷Then your servant my father said to us, 'You know that my wife bore me two sons; ²⁸and the one went out from me, and I said, "Surely he is torn to pieces"; and I have not seen him since. ²⁹But if you take this one also from me, and calamity befalls him, you shall bring down my gray hair with sorrow to the grave.'

³⁰"Now therefore, when I come to your servant my father, and the lad *is* not with us, since his life is bound up in the lad's life, ³¹it will happen, when he sees that the lad *is* not *with us,* that he will die. So your servants will bring down the gray hair of your servant our father with sorrow to the grave. ³²For your servant became surety for the lad to my father, saying, 'If I do not bring him *back* to you, then I shall bear the blame before my father forever.' ³³Now therefore, please let your servant remain instead of the lad as a slave to my lord, and let the lad go up with his brothers. ³⁴For how shall I go up to my father if the lad *is* not with me, lest perhaps I see the evil that would come upon my father?"

Joseph Revealed to His Brothers

45 Then Joseph could not restrain himself before all those who stood by him, and he cried out, "Make everyone go out from me!" So no one stood with him while Joseph made himself known to his brothers. [2]And he wept aloud, and the Egyptians and the house of Pharaoh heard *it*.

[3]Then Joseph said to his brothers, "I *am* Joseph; does my father still live?" But his brothers could not answer him, for they were dismayed in his presence. [4]And Joseph said to his brothers, "Please come near to me." So they came near. Then he said: "I *am* Joseph your brother, whom you sold into Egypt. [5]But now, do not therefore be grieved or angry with yourselves because you sold me here; for God sent me before you to preserve life. [6]For these two years the famine *has been* in the land, and *there are* still five years in which *there will be* neither plowing nor harvesting. [7]And God sent me before you to preserve a posterity for you in the earth, and to save your lives by a great deliverance. [8]So now *it was* not you *who* sent me here, but God; and He has made me a father to Pharaoh, and lord of all his house, and a ruler throughout all the land of Egypt.

[9]"Hurry and go up to my father, and say to him, 'Thus says your son Joseph: "God has made me lord of all Egypt; come down to me, do not tarry. [10]You shall dwell in the land of Goshen, and you shall be near to me, you and your children, your children's children, your flocks and your herds, and all that you have. [11]There I will provide for you, lest you and your household, and all that you have, come to poverty; for *there are* still five years of famine."'

[12]"And behold, your eyes and the eyes of my brother Benjamin see that *it is* my mouth that speaks to you. [13]So you shall tell my father of all my glory in Egypt, and of all that you have seen; and you shall hurry and bring my father down here."

[14]Then he fell on his brother Benjamin's neck and wept, and Benjamin wept on his neck. [15]Moreover he kissed all his brothers and wept over them, and after that his brothers talked with him.

[16]Now the report of it was heard in Pharaoh's house, saying, "Joseph's brothers have come." So it pleased Pharaoh and his servants well. [17]And Pharaoh said to Joseph, "Say to your brothers, 'Do this: Load your animals and depart; go to the land of Canaan. [18]Bring your father and your households and come to me; I will give you the best of the land of Egypt, and you will eat the fat of the land. [19]Now you are commanded—do this: Take carts out of the land of Egypt for your little ones and your wives; bring your father and come. [20]Also do not be concerned about your goods, for the best of all the land of Egypt *is* yours.'"

[21]Then the sons of Israel did so; and Joseph gave them carts, according to the command of Pharaoh, and he gave them provisions for the journey. [22]He gave to all of them, to each man, changes of garments; but to Benjamin he gave three hundred *pieces* of silver and five changes of garments. [23]And he sent to his father these *things:* ten donkeys loaded with the good things of Egypt, and ten female donkeys loaded with grain, bread, and food for his father for the journey. [24]So he sent his brothers away, and they departed; and he said to them, "See that you do not become troubled along the way."

The Law of Empowerment: Joseph and His Brothers

(Genesis 45:4–7)

When Joseph's brothers realized that the one they had betrayed could now do with them what he pleased, they feared payback time had arrived. Instead of retaliating, however, Joseph blessed them and empowered them to complete the task that had brought them to Egypt: to secure food for their families. A careful reading of Genesis 45:4–7 reveals the qualities that made Joseph such an empowering leader:

1. **A strong sense of security.** "Please come near to me" (v. 4).
2. **A strong sense of identity.** "I am Joseph your brother" (v. 4).
3. **A strong sense of empathy.** "Do not therefore be grieved or angry with yourselves" (v. 4).
4. **A strong sense of purpose.** "For God sent me before you to preserve life" (v. 5).
5. **A strong sense of perspective.** "There are still five years in which there will be neither plowing nor harvesting. And God sent me before you to preserve a posterity for you in the earth" (vv. 6, 7).

²⁵Then they went up out of Egypt, and came to the land of Canaan to Jacob their father. ²⁶And they told him, saying, "Joseph *is* still alive, and he *is* governor over all the land of Egypt." And Jacob's heart stood still, because he did not believe them. ²⁷But when they told him all the words which Joseph had said to them, and when he saw the carts which Joseph had sent to carry him, the spirit of Jacob their father revived. ²⁸Then Israel said, "*It is* enough. Joseph my son *is* still alive. I will go and see him before I die."

Jacob's Journey to Egypt

46 So Israel took his journey with all that he had, and came to Beersheba, and offered sacrifices to the God of his father Isaac. ²Then God spoke to Israel in the visions of the night, and said, "Jacob, Jacob!"

And he said, "Here I am."

³So He said, "I *am* God, the God of your father; do not fear to go down to Egypt, for I will make of you a great nation there. ⁴I will go down with you to Egypt, and I will also surely bring you up *again;* and Joseph will put his hand on your eyes."

⁵Then Jacob arose from Beersheba; and the sons of Israel carried their father Jacob, their little ones, and their wives, in the carts which Pharaoh had sent to carry him. ⁶So they took their livestock and their goods, which they had acquired in the land of Canaan, and went to Egypt, Jacob and all his descendants with him. ⁷His sons and his sons' sons, his daughters and his sons' daughters, and all his descendants he brought with him to Egypt.

⁸Now these *were* the names of the children of Israel, Jacob and his sons, who went to Egypt: Reuben *was* Jacob's firstborn. ⁹The sons of Reuben *were* Hanoch, Pallu, Hezron, and Carmi. ¹⁰The sons of Simeon *were* Jemuel,[a] Jamin, Ohad, Jachin,[b] Zohar,[c] and Shaul, the son of a Canaanite woman. ¹¹The sons of Levi *were* Gershon, Kohath, and Merari. ¹²The sons of Judah *were* Er, Onan, Shelah, Perez, and Zerah (but Er and Onan died in the land of Canaan). The sons of Perez were Hezron and Hamul. ¹³The sons of Issachar *were* Tola, Puvah,[a] Job,[b] and Shimron. ¹⁴The sons of Zebulun *were* Sered, Elon, and Jahleel. ¹⁵These *were* the sons of Leah, whom she bore to Jacob in Padan Aram, with his daughter Dinah. All the persons, his sons and his daughters, *were* thirty-three.

¹⁶The sons of Gad *were* Ziphion,[a] Haggi, Shuni, Ezbon,[b] Eri, Arodi,[c] and Areli. ¹⁷The sons of Asher *were* Jimnah, Ishuah, Isui, Beriah, and Serah, their sister. And the sons of Beriah *were*

Heber and Malchiel. ¹⁸These *were* the sons of Zilpah, whom Laban gave to Leah his daughter; and these she bore to Jacob: sixteen persons.

¹⁹The sons of Rachel, Jacob's wife, *were* Joseph and Benjamin. ²⁰And to Joseph in the land of Egypt were born Manasseh and Ephraim, whom Asenath, the daughter of Poti-Pherah priest of On, bore to him. ²¹The sons of Benjamin *were* Belah, Becher, Ashbel, Gera, Naaman, Ehi, Rosh, Muppim, Huppim,[a] and Ard. ²²These *were* the sons of Rachel, who were born to Jacob: fourteen persons in all.

²³The son of Dan *was* Hushim.[a] ²⁴The sons of Naphtali *were* Jahzeel,[a] Guni, Jezer, and Shillem.[b] ²⁵These *were* the sons of Bilhah, whom Laban gave to Rachel his daughter, and she bore these to Jacob: seven persons in all.

²⁶All the persons who went with Jacob to Egypt, who came from his body, besides Jacob's sons' wives, *were* sixty-six persons in all. ²⁷And the sons of Joseph who were born to him in Egypt *were* two persons. All the persons of the house of Jacob who went to Egypt were seventy.

Jacob Settles in Goshen

²⁸Then he sent Judah before him to Joseph, to point out before him *the way* to Goshen. And they came to the land of Goshen. ²⁹So Joseph made ready his chariot and went up to Goshen to meet his father Israel; and he presented himself to him, and fell on his neck and wept on his neck a good while.

³⁰And Israel said to Joseph, "Now let me die, since I have seen your face, because you *are* still alive."

³¹Then Joseph said to his brothers and to his father's household, "I will go up and tell Pharaoh, and say to him, 'My brothers and those of my father's house, who *were* in the land of Canaan, have come to me. ³²And the men *are* shepherds, for their occupation has been to feed livestock; and they have brought their flocks, their herds, and all that they have.' ³³So it shall be, when Pharaoh calls you and says, 'What is your

---

46:10 [a]Spelled *Nemuel* in 1 Chronicles 4:24   [b]Called *Jarib* in 1 Chronicles 4:24   [c]Called *Zerah* in 1 Chronicles 4:24   **46:13** [a]Spelled *Puah* in 1 Chronicles 7:1   [b]Same as *Jashub* in Numbers 26:24 and 1 Chronicles 7:1   **46:16** [a]Spelled *Zephon* in Samaritan Pentateuch, Septuagint, and Numbers 26:15   [b]Called *Ozni* in Numbers 26:16   [c]Spelled *Arod* in Numbers 26:17   **46:21** [a]Called *Hupham* in Numbers 26:39   **46:23** [a]Called *Shuham* in Numbers 26:42   **46:24** [a]Spelled *Jahziel* in 1 Chronicles 7:13   [b]Spelled *Shallum* in 1 Chronicles 7:13

occupation?' ³⁴that you shall say, 'Your servants' occupation has been with livestock from our youth even till now, both we *and* also our fathers,' that you may dwell in the land of Goshen; for every shepherd *is* an abomination to the Egyptians."

47 Then Joseph went and told Pharaoh, and said, "My father and my brothers, their flocks and their herds and all that they possess, have come from the land of Canaan; and indeed they *are* in the land of Goshen." ²And he took five men from among his brothers and presented them to Pharaoh. ³Then Pharaoh said to his brothers, "What *is* your occupation?"

And they said to Pharaoh, "Your servants *are* shepherds, both we *and* also our fathers." ⁴And they said to Pharaoh, "We have come to dwell in the land, because your servants have no pasture for their flocks, for the famine *is* severe in the land of Canaan. Now therefore, please let your servants dwell in the land of Goshen."

⁵Then Pharaoh spoke to Joseph, saying, "Your father and your brothers have come to you. ⁶The land of Egypt *is* before you. Have your father and brothers dwell in the best of the land; let them dwell in the land of Goshen. And if you know *any* competent men among them, then make them chief herdsmen over my livestock."

⁷Then Joseph brought in his father Jacob and set him before Pharaoh; and Jacob blessed Pharaoh. ⁸Pharaoh said to Jacob, "How old *are* you?"

⁹And Jacob said to Pharaoh, "The days of the years of my pilgrimage *are* one hundred and thirty years; few and evil have been the days of the years of my life, and they have not attained to the days of the years of the life of my fathers in the days of their pilgrimage." ¹⁰So Jacob blessed Pharaoh, and went out from before Pharaoh.

¹¹And Joseph situated his father and his brothers, and gave them a possession in the land of Egypt, in the best of the land, in the land of Rameses, as Pharaoh had commanded. ¹²Then Joseph provided his father, his brothers, and all his father's household with bread, according to the number in *their* families.

Joseph Deals with the Famine

¹³Now *there was* no bread in all the land; for the famine *was* very severe, so that the land of Egypt and the land of Canaan languished because of the famine. ¹⁴And Joseph gathered up all the money that was found in the land of Egypt and in the land of Canaan, for the grain which they bought; and Joseph brought the money into Pharaoh's house.

¹⁵So when the money failed in the land of Egypt and in the land of Canaan, all the Egyptians came to Joseph and said, "Give us bread, for why should we die in your presence? For the money has failed."

¹⁶Then Joseph said, "Give your livestock, and I will give you *bread* for your livestock, if the money is gone." ¹⁷So they brought their livestock to Joseph, and Joseph gave them bread *in exchange* for the horses, the flocks, the cattle of the herds, and for the donkeys. Thus he fed them with bread *in exchange* for all their livestock that year.

¹⁸When that year had ended, they came to him the next year and said to him, "We will not hide from my lord that our money is gone; my lord also has our herds of livestock. There is nothing left in the sight of my lord but our bodies and our lands. ¹⁹Why should we die before your eyes, both we and our land? Buy us and our land for bread, and we and our land will be servants of Pharaoh; give *us* seed, that we may live and not die, that the land may not be desolate."

²⁰Then Joseph bought all the land of Egypt for Pharaoh; for every man of the Egyptians sold his field, because the famine was severe upon them. So the land became Pharaoh's. ²¹And as for the people, he moved them into the cities,ᵃ from *one* end of the borders of Egypt to the *other* end. ²²Only the land of the priests he did not buy; for the priests had rations *allotted to them* by Pharaoh, and they ate their rations which Pharaoh gave them; therefore they did not sell their lands.

²³Then Joseph said to the people, "Indeed I have bought you and your land this day for Pharaoh. Look, *here is* seed for you, and you shall sow the land. ²⁴And it shall come to pass in the harvest that you shall give one-fifth to Pharaoh. Four-fifths shall be your own, as seed for the field and for your food, for those of your households and as food for your little ones."

²⁵So they said, "You have saved our lives; let us find favor in the sight of my lord, and we will be Pharaoh's servants." ²⁶And Joseph made it a law over the land of Egypt to this day, *that* Pharaoh should have one-fifth, except for the land of the priests only, *which* did not become Pharaoh's.

47:21 ᵃFollowing Masoretic Text and Targum; Samaritan Pentateuch, Septuagint, and Vulgate read *made the people virtual slaves.*

Joseph's Vow to Jacob

²⁷So Israel dwelt in the land of Egypt, in the country of Goshen; and they had possessions there and grew and multiplied exceedingly. ²⁸And Jacob lived in the land of Egypt seventeen years. So the length of Jacob's life was one hundred and forty-seven years. ²⁹When the time drew near that Israel must die, he called his son Joseph and said to him, "Now if I have found favor in your sight, please put your hand under my thigh, and deal kindly and truly with me. Please do not bury me in Egypt, ³⁰but let me lie with my fathers; you shall carry me out of Egypt and bury me in their burial place."

And he said, "I will do as you have said."

³¹Then he said, "Swear to me." And he swore to him. So Israel bowed himself on the head of the bed.

Jacob Blesses Joseph's Sons

48 Now it came to pass after these things that Joseph was told, "Indeed your father *is* sick"; and he took with him his two sons, Manasseh and Ephraim. ²And Jacob was told, "Look, your son Joseph is coming to you"; and Israel strengthened himself and sat up on the bed. ³Then Jacob said to Joseph: "God Almighty appeared to me at Luz in the land of Canaan and blessed me, ⁴and said to me, 'Behold, I will make you fruitful and multiply you, and I will make of you a multitude of people, and give this land to your descendants after you *as* an everlasting possession.' ⁵And now your two sons, Ephraim and Manasseh, who were born to you in the land of Egypt before I came to you in Egypt, *are* mine; as Reuben and Simeon, they shall be mine. ⁶Your offspring whom you beget after them shall be yours; they will be called by the name of their brothers in their inheritance. ⁷But as for me, when I came from Padan, Rachel died beside me in the land of Canaan on the way, when *there was* but a little distance to go to Ephrath; and I buried her there on the way to Ephrath (that is, Bethlehem)."

⁸Then Israel saw Joseph's sons, and said, "Who *are* these?"

⁹Joseph said to his father, "They *are* my sons, whom God has given me in this *place*."

And he said, "Please bring them to me, and I will bless them." ¹⁰Now the eyes of Israel were dim with age, *so that* he could not see. Then Joseph brought them near him, and he kissed them and embraced them. ¹¹And Israel said to Joseph, "I had not thought to see your face; but in fact, God has also shown me your offspring!"

¹²So Joseph brought them from beside his knees, and he bowed down with his face to the earth. ¹³And Joseph took them both, Ephraim with his right hand toward Israel's left hand, and Manasseh with his left hand toward Israel's right hand, and brought *them* near him. ¹⁴Then Israel stretched out his right hand and laid *it* on Ephraim's head, who *was* the younger, and his left hand on Manasseh's head, guiding his hands knowingly, for Manasseh *was* the firstborn. ¹⁵And he blessed Joseph, and said:

"God, before whom my fathers Abraham
   and Isaac walked,
The God who has fed me all my life long
   to this day,
¹⁶ The Angel who has redeemed me from all
   evil,
Bless the lads;
Let my name be named upon them,
And the name of my fathers Abraham and
   Isaac;
And let them grow into a multitude in the
   midst of the earth."

¹⁷Now when Joseph saw that his father laid his right hand on the head of Ephraim, it displeased him; so he took hold of his father's hand to remove it from Ephraim's head to Manasseh's head. ¹⁸And Joseph said to his father, "Not so, my father, for this *one is* the firstborn; put your right hand on his head."

¹⁹But his father refused and said, "I know, my son, I know. He also shall become a people, and he also shall be great; but truly his younger brother shall be greater than he, and his descendants shall become a multitude of nations." ²⁰So he blessed them that day, saying, "By you Israel will bless, saying, 'May God make you as Ephraim and as Manasseh!' " And thus he set Ephraim before Manasseh.

²¹Then Israel said to Joseph, "Behold, I am dying, but God will be with you and bring you back to the land of your fathers. ²²Moreover I have given to you one portion above your brothers, which I took from the hand of the Amorite with my sword and my bow."

Jacob's Last Words to His Sons

49 And Jacob called his sons and said, "Gather together, that I may tell you what shall befall you in the last days:

² "Gather together and hear, you sons of
   Jacob,
And listen to Israel your father.

3 "Reuben, you are my firstborn,
My might and the beginning of my
strength,
The excellency of dignity and the
excellency of power.
4 Unstable as water, you shall not excel,
Because you went up to your father's bed;
Then you defiled *it*—
He went up to my couch.

5 "Simeon and Levi *are* brothers;
Instruments of cruelty *are in* their dwelling
place.
6 Let not my soul enter their council;
Let not my honor be united to their
assembly;
For in their anger they slew a man,
And in their self-will they hamstrung an ox.
7 Cursed *be* their anger, for *it is* fierce;
And their wrath, for it is cruel!
I will divide them in Jacob
And scatter them in Israel.

8 "Judah, you *are he* whom your brothers shall
praise;
Your hand *shall be* on the neck of your
enemies;
Your father's children shall bow down
before you.
9 Judah *is* a lion's whelp;
From the prey, my son, you have gone up.
He bows down, he lies down as a lion;
And as a lion, who shall rouse him?
10 The scepter shall not depart from Judah,
Nor a lawgiver from between his feet,
Until Shiloh comes;
And to Him *shall be* the obedience of the
people.
11 Binding his donkey to the vine,
And his donkey's colt to the choice vine,
He washed his garments in wine,
And his clothes in the blood of grapes.
12 His eyes *are* darker than wine,
And his teeth whiter than milk.

13 "Zebulun shall dwell by the haven of the
sea;
He *shall become* a haven for ships,
And his border shall adjoin Sidon.

14 "Issachar is a strong donkey,
Lying down between two burdens;
15 He saw that rest *was* good,
And that the land *was* pleasant;
He bowed his shoulder to bear *a burden,*
And became a band of slaves.

16 "Dan shall judge his people
As one of the tribes of Israel.
17 Dan shall be a serpent by the way,
A viper by the path,
That bites the horse's heels
So that its rider shall fall backward.
18 I have waited for your salvation, O LORD!

19 "Gad, a troop shall tramp upon him,
But he shall triumph at last.

20 "Bread from Asher *shall be* rich,
And he shall yield royal dainties.

21 "Naphtali *is* a deer let loose;
He uses beautiful words.

22 "Joseph *is* a fruitful bough,
A fruitful bough by a well;
His branches run over the wall.
23 The archers have bitterly grieved him,
Shot *at him* and hated him.
24 But his bow remained in strength,
And the arms of his hands were made
strong
By the hands of the Mighty *God* of Jacob
(From there *is* the Shepherd, the Stone of
Israel),
25 By the God of your father who will help
you,
And by the Almighty who will bless you
With blessings of heaven above,
Blessings of the deep that lies beneath,
Blessings of the breasts and of the womb.
26 The blessings of your father
Have excelled the blessings of my
ancestors,
Up to the utmost bound of the everlasting
hills.
They shall be on the head of Joseph,
And on the crown of the head of him
who was separate from his brothers.

27 "Benjamin is a ravenous wolf;
In the morning he shall devour the prey,
And at night he shall divide the spoil."

28All these *are* the twelve tribes of Israel, and
this *is* what their father spoke to them. And he
blessed them; he blessed each one according to
his own blessing.

Jacob's Death and Burial

29Then he charged them and said to them: "I
am to be gathered to my people; bury me with
my fathers in the cave that *is* in the field of

Ephron the Hittite, [30]in the cave that *is* in the field of Machpelah, which *is* before Mamre in the land of Canaan, which Abraham bought with the field of Ephron the Hittite as a possession for a burial place. [31]There they buried Abraham and Sarah his wife, there they buried Isaac and Rebekah his wife, and there I buried Leah. [32]The field and the cave that *is* there *were* purchased from the sons of Heth." [33]And when Jacob had finished commanding his sons, he drew his feet up into the bed and breathed his last, and was gathered to his people.

50 Then Joseph fell on his father's face and wept over him, and kissed him. [2]And Joseph commanded his servants the physicians to embalm his father. So the physicians embalmed Israel. [3]Forty days were required for him, for such are the days required for those who are embalmed; and the Egyptians mourned for him seventy days.

[4]Now when the days of his mourning were past, Joseph spoke to the household of Pharaoh, saying, "If now I have found favor in your eyes, please speak in the hearing of Pharaoh, saying, [5]'My father made me swear, saying, "Behold, I am dying; in my grave which I dug for myself in the land of Canaan, there you shall bury me."

Now therefore, please let me go up and bury my father, and I will come back.'"

[6]And Pharaoh said, "Go up and bury your father, as he made you swear."

[7]So Joseph went up to bury his father; and with him went up all the servants of Pharaoh, the elders of his house, and all the elders of the land of Egypt, [8]as well as all the house of Joseph, his brothers, and his father's house. Only their little ones, their flocks, and their herds they left in the land of Goshen. [9]And there went up with him both chariots and horsemen, and it was a very great gathering.

[10]Then they came to the threshing floor of Atad, which *is* beyond the Jordan, and they mourned there with a great and very solemn lamentation. He observed seven days of mourning for his father. [11]And when the inhabitants of the land, the Canaanites, saw the mourning at the threshing floor of Atad, they said, "This *is* a deep mourning of the Egyptians." Therefore its name was called Abel Mizraim,[a] which *is* beyond the Jordan.

[12]So his sons did for him just as he had commanded them. [13]For his sons carried him to the

---

50:11 [a]Literally *Mourning of Egypt*

How Character Breeds Perspective

(Genesis 50:15–21)

Joseph puts his entire life in perspective in the final chapter of Genesis. During the height of a terrible famine, his brothers humbly come before him and bow down, just as he had predicted decades earlier. But instead of using his enormous power to punish them, he said, "You meant evil against me, but God meant it for good, in order to bring it about as it is this day, to save many people alive" (Gen. 50:20).

How does one develop such a godly (and rare) perspective? What enabled Joseph to refrain from exacting the kind of vengeance most of us would be tempted to dish out in similar circumstances? One word: character. Because Joseph had spent years in God's character-building course, he could maintain a proper perspective and use his power to bless his brothers rather than curse them.

How a leader deals with the circumstances of life tells you many things about his character. Crisis doesn't necessarily make character, but it certainly does reveal it. Adversity is a crossroads that makes a person choose one of two paths: character or compromise. Every time he chooses character, he becomes stronger, even if that choice brings negative consequences (remember why Joseph ended up in prison?). The development of character is at the heart of our development as leaders.

If you want God's perspective on life, then make sure to develop your character. It's the only way, as Joseph reminds us.

land of Canaan, and buried him in the cave of the field of Machpelah, before Mamre, which Abraham bought with the field from Ephron the Hittite as property for a burial place. [14]And after he had buried his father, Joseph returned to Egypt, he and his brothers and all who went up with him to bury his father.

Joseph Reassures His Brothers

[15]When Joseph's brothers saw that their father was dead, they said, "Perhaps Joseph will hate us, and may actually repay us for all the evil which we did to him." [16]So they sent *messengers* to Joseph, saying, "Before your father died he commanded, saying, [17]"Thus you shall say to Joseph: "I beg you, please forgive the trespass of your brothers and their sin; for they did evil to you."' Now, please, forgive the trespass of the servants of the God of your father." And Joseph wept when they spoke to him.

[18]Then his brothers also went and fell down before his face, and they said, "Behold, we *are* your servants."

[19]Joseph said to them, "Do not be afraid, for *am* I in the place of God? [20]But as for you, you meant evil against me; *but* God meant it for good, in order to bring it about as *it is* this day, to save many people alive. [21]Now therefore, do not be afraid; I will provide for you and your little ones." And he comforted them and spoke kindly to them.

Death of Joseph

[22]So Joseph dwelt in Egypt, he and his father's household. And Joseph lived one hundred and ten years. [23]Joseph saw Ephraim's children to the third *generation*. The children of Machir, the son of Manasseh, were also brought up on Joseph's knees.

[24]And Joseph said to his brethren, "I am dying; but God will surely visit you, and bring you out of this land to the land of which He swore to Abraham, to Isaac, and to Jacob." [25]Then Joseph took an oath from the children of Israel, saying, "God will surely visit you, and you shall carry up my bones from here." [26]So Joseph died, *being* one hundred and ten years old; and they embalmed him, and he was put in a coffin in Egypt.

EXODUS
Examples of Leadership Abound

SUMMARY

Examples of leadership abound in Exodus, beginning with the Lord Himself. Once God established a people for His own and they pledged to follow Him, He proceeded to the next stage of leadership necessary for building them into a people whose hearts beat to the same rhythm as His own.

Consider the process: God led His people through generations of slavery in Egypt and made them into a great nation. He led Moses into the wilderness to prepare and develop him as a leader. The Lord took 80 years to ready Moses for the task of guiding God's new nation out of Egypt, across the desert, and into the Promised Land. Over time, the Israelites became not just a handful of families, but a massive, ethnic population—large enough to frighten even the Egyptians. Moses became the first political leader of a full-fledged, Israelite nation.

In the beginning, national success looked to be just around the corner. The Hebrews had an educated leader, Moses; they had a plan; they enjoyed great organization; they had received a vision, clearly stated by God and reiterated by Moses; and they had agreed to a sharply defined goal. Nothing could derail them, right?

Wrong.

The Israelites soon lost sight of the vision. When Moses took too long to receive the "constitution" for their nation (the Ten Commandments), they fashioned a golden calf and began to worship it. When the journey grew long and uncomfortable, they began to whine, then grumble, then complain. More than once, they nearly revolted against Moses' leadership. A two-week trip through the desert ultimately took more than four decades!

The Book of Exodus records how God's people failed to cooperate, doubted the vision, disobeyed the rules, worshiped material things, forgot their goals, and soured on their leader—all of which delayed their dream by 40 years. Not only did the people doubt Moses' leadership, they also doubted God's. We can learn a great deal from the accounts in Exodus.

God's Role in Exodus

You'd have to be blind to miss God's leadership in this book. He is there all the time, talking face to face with Moses and mentoring him to be the CEO of Israel.

God dispenses multitudes of signs and wonders to give everyone plenty of reasons to follow, trust, and obey. He directs the nation's path through the desert, across the Red Sea, and during the 40 years of wandering, visually reminding His people of His presence and power through a cloud by day and a pillar of fire by night.

Yet it never seems to be enough for the people of Israel. They continue to doubt, delay, and defy Moses—a huge disappointment for one of the greatest leaders of all time.

Leaders in Exodus

Moses, Aaron, Pharaoh, Joshua

Other People of Influence in Exodus

Midwives, Miriam, Jochebed, Pharaoh's magicians, Jethro

Lessons in Leadership

- Leaders need time and experience to grow and prepare for leadership.

- Leading means planning: plan your work and work your plan.

- Leaders should never try to do everything all alone.

- Leaders must be prepared for things to go awry.

- Leaders must continually remind themselves and others of past successes.

- Leaders must repeatedly cast the vision.

LEADERSHIP

HIGHLIGHTS IN EXODUS

Israel's Suffering in Egypt

1 Now these *are* the names of the children of Israel who came to Egypt; each man and his household came with Jacob: [2]Reuben, Simeon, Levi, and Judah; [3]Issachar, Zebulun, and Benjamin; [4]Dan, Naphtali, Gad, and Asher. [5]All those who were descendants[a] of Jacob were seventy[b] persons (for Joseph was in Egypt *already*). [6]And Joseph died, all his brothers, and all that generation. [7]But the children of Israel were fruitful and increased abundantly, multiplied and grew exceedingly mighty; and the land was filled with them.

[8]Now there arose a new king over Egypt, who did not know Joseph. [9]And he said to his people, "Look, the people of the children of Israel *are* more and mightier than we; [10]come, let us deal shrewdly with them, lest they multiply, and it happen, in the event of war, that they also join our enemies and fight against us, and *so* go up out of the land." [11]Therefore they set taskmasters over them to afflict them with their burdens. And they built for Pharaoh supply cities, Pithom and Raamses. [12]But the more they afflicted them, the more they multiplied and grew. And they were in dread of the children of Israel. [13]So the Egyptians made the children of Israel serve with rigor. [14]And they made their lives bitter with hard bondage—in mortar, in brick, and in all manner of service in the field. All their service in which they made them serve *was* with rigor.

[15]Then the king of Egypt spoke to the Hebrew midwives, of whom the name of one *was* Shiphrah and the name of the other Puah; [16]and he said, "When you do the duties of a midwife for the Hebrew women, and see *them* on the birthstools, if it *is* a son, then you shall kill him; but if it *is* a daughter, then she shall live." [17]But the midwives feared God, and did not do as the king of Egypt commanded them, but saved the male children alive. [18]So the king of Egypt called for the midwives and said to them, "Why have you done this thing, and saved the male children alive?"

[19]And the midwives said to Pharaoh, "Because the Hebrew women *are* not like the Egyptian women; for they *are* lively and give birth before the midwives come to them."

[20]Therefore God dealt well with the midwives, and the people multiplied and grew very mighty. [21]And so it was, because the midwives feared God, that He provided households for them.

1:5 [a]Literally *who came from the loins of* [b]Dead Sea Scrolls and Septuagint read *seventy-five* (compare Acts 7:14).

Pharaoh Violates the Laws of Connection and Empowerment

(Exodus 1:8–22)

The first chapter of Exodus introduces us to a man with great power, but little character or wisdom. The leader of the most powerful nation of the ancient world, this pharaoh had little in common with the confident ruler who led Egypt during Joseph's day. He constantly worried that others might usurp his power, felt his security threatened, and consequently sabotaged his own leadership. Notice how he responded to the challenges he faced (along with what he should have done).

Threat	Pharaoh's Response	Right Response
Jewish population size	Oppress and force labor	Position them well
Jewish babies born	Kill all the males	Equip them to lead
Jewish complaints	Drive them harder as slaves	Lighten their loads
Racial conflict	Ruthlessly dominate them	Build relationships

The Law of Empowerment teaches that only secure leaders give power to others. The emotional deficits of this pharaoh prevented him from empowering others. He felt threatened by the gifts, clout, or growing numbers of others. Consumed by damage control, he failed to benefit everyone by brokering the available talents and resources. In the end, he destroyed his nation, his army, and his own rule.

²²So Pharaoh commanded all his people, saying, "Every son who is born[a] you shall cast into the river, and every daughter you shall save alive."

Moses Is Born

2 And a man of the house of Levi went and took *as wife* a daughter of Levi. ²So the woman conceived and bore a son. And when she saw that he *was* a beautiful *child,* she hid him three months. ³But when she could no longer hide him, she took an ark of bulrushes for him, daubed it with asphalt and pitch, put the child in it, and laid *it* in the reeds by the river's bank. ⁴And his sister stood afar off, to know what would be done to him.

⁵Then the daughter of Pharaoh came down to bathe at the river. And her maidens walked along the riverside; and when she saw the ark among the reeds, she sent her maid to get it. ⁶And when she opened *it,* she saw the child, and behold, the baby wept. So she had compassion on him, and said, "This is one of the Hebrews' children."

⁷Then his sister said to Pharaoh's daughter, "Shall I go and call a nurse for you from the Hebrew women, that she may nurse the child for you?"

⁸And Pharaoh's daughter said to her, "Go." So the maiden went and called the child's mother. ⁹Then Pharaoh's daughter said to her, "Take this child away and nurse him for me, and I will give *you* your wages." So the woman took the child and nursed him. ¹⁰And the child grew, and she brought him to Pharaoh's daughter, and he became her son. So she called his name Moses,[a] saying, "Because I drew him out of the water."

Moses Flees to Midian

¹¹Now it came to pass in those days, when Moses was grown, that he went out to his brethren and looked at their burdens. And he saw an Egyptian beating a Hebrew, one of his brethren. ¹²So he looked this way and that way, and when he saw no one, he killed the Egyptian and hid him in the sand. ¹³And when he went out the second day, behold, two Hebrew men were fighting, and he said to the one who did the wrong, "Why are you striking your companion?"

¹⁴Then he said, "Who made you a prince and a judge over us? Do you intend to kill me as you killed the Egyptian?"

1:22 [a]Samaritan Pentateuch, Septuagint, and Targum add *to the Hebrews.* **2:10** [a]Literally *Drawn Out*

HEBREW MIDWIVES

PEOPLE OF INFLUENCE
(Exodus 1:15–20)

PROFILE IN LEADERSHIP

W ho changes the course of history? Kings? Potentates? Generals? The wealthy? Sure. But more often than not, it's men and women with no power and little social standing who most significantly reshape this world.

When the king of Egypt grew worried about the exploding numbers of Hebrew slaves, he summoned two midwives, Shiphrah and Puah, and instructed them to murder all Hebrew male newborns. But these midwives feared God and refused to obey such a wicked command. Despite the king's threats, they would not buckle under and continued to deliver healthy male Hebrews. Although they had no way of knowing it, their risky decision helped to spare the life of Moses, Israel's God-ordained deliverer.

In civil disobedience, Shiphrah and Puah risked their lives to protect the children God had placed in their care. Their bravery prompted God to show them kindness by blessing them with families of their own. No doubt their children and grandchildren took part in the great exodus from Egypt.

At a strategic juncture in history, these Hebrew midwives—politically powerless, socially despised, economically disadvantaged—defied the ruler of Egypt to obey the God they feared. Their perilous choice to do the right thing protected the line of Abraham through which the Messiah would come, thus fulfilling God's plan for not only the Hebrews, but for all mankind.

The Law of Process: Moses and the Test of Time

(Exodus 2:1—4:31)

How did God prepare Moses to be His man to lead the Hebrews out of Egyptian bondage? He prepared him not in a day, but over time; not through an event, but with a process. Of course, others before Moses waited years for God to fulfill His leadership development process:

- Noah—waited 120 years before the predicted rains arrived.
- Abraham—waited 25 years for a promised son.
- Joseph—waited 14 years in prison for a crime he didn't commit.
- Job—waited perhaps a lifetime, 60–70 years, for God's justice.

God prepares leaders in a Crock-Pot, not in a microwave oven. More important than the awaited goal is the work God does in us while we wait. Waiting deepens and matures us, levels our perspective, and broadens our understanding. Tests of time determine whether we can endure seasons of seemingly unfruitful preparation, and indicate whether we can recognize and seize the opportunities that come our way.

So Moses feared and said, "Surely this thing is known!" [15]When Pharaoh heard of this matter, he sought to kill Moses. But Moses fled from the face of Pharaoh and dwelt in the land of Midian; and he sat down by a well.

[16]Now the priest of Midian had seven daughters. And they came and drew water, and they filled the troughs to water their father's flock. [17]Then the shepherds came and drove them away; but Moses stood up and helped them, and watered their flock.

[18]When they came to Reuel their father, he said, "How *is it that* you have come so soon today?"

[19]And they said, "An Egyptian delivered us from the hand of the shepherds, and he also drew enough water for us and watered the flock."

[20]So he said to his daughters, "And where *is* he? Why *is it that* you have left the man? Call him, that he may eat bread."

[21]Then Moses was content to live with the man, and he gave Zipporah his daughter to Moses. [22]And she bore *him* a son. He called his name Gershom,[a] for he said, "I have been a stranger in a foreign land."

[23]Now it happened in the process of time that the king of Egypt died. Then the children of Israel groaned because of the bondage, and they cried out; and their cry came up to God because of the bondage. [24]So God heard their groaning, and God remembered His covenant with Abraham, with Isaac, and with Jacob. [25]And God looked upon the children of Israel, and God acknowledged *them.*

Moses at the Burning Bush

3 Now Moses was tending the flock of Jethro his father-in-law, the priest of Midian. And he led the flock to the back of the desert, and came to Horeb, the mountain of God. [2]And the Angel of the LORD appeared to him in a flame of fire from the midst of a bush. So he looked, and behold, the bush was burning with fire, but the bush *was* not consumed. [3]Then Moses said, "I will now turn aside and see this great sight, why the bush does not burn."

[4]So when the LORD saw that he turned aside to look, God called to him from the midst of the bush and said, "Moses, Moses!"

And he said, "Here I am."

[5]Then He said, "Do not draw near this place. Take your sandals off your feet, for the place where you stand *is* holy ground." [6]Moreover He said, "I *am* the God of your father—the God of Abraham, the God of Isaac, and the God of Jacob." And Moses hid his face, for he was afraid to look upon God.

[7]And the LORD said: "I have surely seen the oppression of My people who *are* in Egypt, and have heard their cry because of their taskmasters, for I know their sorrows. [8]So I have come down to deliver them out of the hand of the Egyptians, and to bring them up from that land to a good and large land, to a land flowing with milk and honey, to the place of the Canaanites and the Hittites and the Amorites and the Perizzites and the Hivites and the Jebusites. [9]Now therefore, behold, the cry of the children of Israel has come to Me, and I have also seen the oppression with which the Egyptians oppress them. [10]Come now, therefore, and I will send you to Pharaoh that you may bring My people, the children of Israel, out of Egypt."

2:22 [a]Literally *Stranger There*

When God Chooses a Leader

(Exodus 2:11—4:20)

Moses provides a wonderful case study on how God calls a leader out of a crowd to perform an assignment.

1. **God gives the leader an emotional investment in the work.**
   Moses "bought into" the idea of freeing the Hebrews from bondage even before God called him to the task.

2. **God affirms the leader through others.**
   When Moses told Jethro about his encounter at the burning bush, his father-in-law affirmed him.

3. **God gives the leader mentors.**
   Moses asked for and received help from Jethro, Aaron, and others.

4. **God builds on the leader's strengths, experiences, and background.**
   God used everything in Moses' background to help him fulfill his calling: the fine education he received in Egypt; his knowledge of Pharaoh; his understanding of Egypt; and his time in the wilderness.

5. **God often refines the leader's character in obscurity.**
   Moses received a 40-year "seminary education" in the desert.

6. **God instills in the leader the value of hard work.**
   Moses may not have worked much in the Egyptian palace, but he learned its worth in the desert!

7. **God sustains that leader with a powerful vision.**
   Moses caught the vision of the Promised Land long before the Hebrew slaves did.

8. **God brings others alongside the leader to compensate for their weaknesses.**
   Moses enjoyed the help of Aaron as spokesman, Joshua as general, and Hur as battle supporter.

---

[11]But Moses said to God, "Who *am* I that I should go to Pharaoh, and that I should bring the children of Israel out of Egypt?"

[12]So He said, "I will certainly be with you. And this *shall be* a sign to you that I have sent you: When you have brought the people out of Egypt, you shall serve God on this mountain."

[13]Then Moses said to God, "Indeed, *when* I come to the children of Israel and say to them, 'The God of your fathers has sent me to you,' and they say to me, 'What *is* His name?' what shall I say to them?"

[14]And God said to Moses, "I AM WHO I AM." And He said, "Thus you shall say to the children of Israel, 'I AM has sent me to you.'"

[15]Moreover God said to Moses, "Thus you shall say to the children of Israel: 'The LORD God of your fathers, the God of Abraham, the God of Isaac, and the God of Jacob, has sent me to you. This *is* My name forever, and this *is* My memorial to all generations.' [16]Go and gather the elders of Israel together, and say to them, 'The LORD God of your fathers, the God of Abraham, of Isaac, and of Jacob, appeared to me, saying, "I have surely visited you and *seen* what is done to you in Egypt; [17]and I have said I will bring you up out of the affliction of Egypt to the land of the Canaanites and the Hittites and the Amorites and the Perizzites and the Hivites and the Jebusites, to a land flowing with milk and honey."'

[18]Then they will heed your voice; and you shall come, you and the elders of Israel, to the king of Egypt; and you shall say to him, 'The LORD God of the Hebrews has met with us; and now, please, let us go three days' journey into the wilderness, that we may sacrifice to the LORD our God.'

[19]But I am sure that the king of Egypt will not let you go, no, not even by a mighty hand. [20]So I will stretch out My hand and strike Egypt with all My wonders which I will do in its midst; and after that he will let you go. [21]And I will give this people favor in the sight of the Egyptians; and it shall be, when you go, that you shall not go empty-handed. [22]But every woman shall ask of her neighbor, namely, of her who dwells near her house, articles of silver, articles of gold, and

Moses' Life Mission and His Five Big Excuses

(Exodus 3:11—4:14)

Most of us can list excuses why we don't lead effectively, just as Moses did. When God called him, he instantly thought of five reasons why he couldn't lead.

Excuse One: Who Am I? (3:11).
Moses struggled with his identity. He just didn't feel qualified; he thought God had picked the wrong leader.
God's response: It doesn't matter who you are. I am with you (3:12).

Excuse Two: Who Are You? (3:13).
Moses felt a lack of intimacy. He didn't know God well enough to describe Him to the people and lacked convictions concerning his relationship with God.
God's response: I AM WHO I AM. I AM ever present. I AM everything you need (3:14).

Excuse Three: What if they don't listen? (4:1).
Moses felt intimidated. He worried about the people's reaction to him.
God's response: When I'm finished, they'll listen (4:2–9).

Excuse Four: I've never been a good speaker (4:10).
Moses fretted about his inadequacies. Who would listen to him if he couldn't even speak well?
God's response: Guess who made your mouth? (4:11, 12).

Excuse Five: I know you can find someone else (4:13).
Moses felt inferior. He compared himself to others—even his brother—and decided that he came up short.
God's response: OK, I will let Aaron go with you . . . but I'm still calling *you* to go (4:14).

---

clothing; and you shall put *them* on your sons and on your daughters. So you shall plunder the Egyptians."

Miraculous Signs for Pharaoh

4 Then Moses answered and said, "But suppose they will not believe me or listen to my voice; suppose they say, 'The LORD has not appeared to you.'"

²So the LORD said to him, "What *is* that in your hand?"

He said, "A rod."

³And He said, "Cast it on the ground." So he cast it on the ground, and it became a serpent; and Moses fled from it. ⁴Then the LORD said to Moses, "Reach out your hand and take *it* by the tail" (and he reached out his hand and caught it, and it became a rod in his hand), ⁵"that they may believe that the LORD God of their fathers, the God of Abraham, the God of Isaac, and the God of Jacob, has appeared to you."

⁶Furthermore the LORD said to him, "Now put your hand in your bosom." And he put his hand in his bosom, and when he took it out, behold, his hand *was* leprous, like snow. ⁷And He said, "Put your hand in your bosom again." So he put his hand in his bosom again, and drew it out of his bosom, and behold, it was restored like his *other* flesh. ⁸"Then it will be, if they do not believe you, nor heed the message of the first sign, that they may believe the message of the latter sign. ⁹And it shall be, if they do not believe even these two signs, or listen to your voice, that you shall take water from the river[a] and pour *it* on the dry *land*. The water which you take from the river will become blood on the dry *land*."

¹⁰Then Moses said to the LORD, "O my Lord, I *am* not eloquent, neither before nor since You have spoken to Your servant; but I *am* slow of speech and slow of tongue."

¹¹So the LORD said to him, "Who has made man's mouth? Or who makes the mute, the deaf, the seeing, or the blind? *Have* not I, the LORD? ¹²Now therefore, go, and I will be with your mouth and teach you what you shall say."

¹³But he said, "O my Lord, please send by the hand of whomever *else* You may send."

¹⁴So the anger of the LORD was kindled against Moses, and He said: "Is not Aaron the Levite your brother? I know that he can speak

---

4:9 [a]That is, the Nile

well. And look, he is also coming out to meet you. When he sees you, he will be glad in his heart. [15]Now you shall speak to him and put the words in his mouth. And I will be with your mouth and with his mouth, and I will teach you what you shall do. [16]So he shall be your spokesman to the people. And he himself shall be as a mouth for you, and you shall be to him as God. [17]And you shall take this rod in your hand, with which you shall do the signs."

Moses Goes to Egypt

[18]So Moses went and returned to Jethro his father-in-law, and said to him, "Please let me go and return to my brethren who *are* in Egypt, and see whether they are still alive."

And Jethro said to Moses, "Go in peace."

Major Barriers to Successful Planning

(Exodus 4:21)

When Moses finally agreed to fulfill his divine assignment, he heard some unsettling news: God would harden Pharaoh's heart. The plan would work, but not right away.

Good leaders develop plans, but they also expect to make adjustments along the way. Rarely does any plan succeed without a bump or a glitch.

---

[19]Now the LORD said to Moses in Midian, "Go, return to Egypt; for all the men who sought your life are dead." [20]Then Moses took his wife and his sons and set them on a donkey, and he returned to the land of Egypt. And Moses took the rod of God in his hand.

[21]And the LORD said to Moses, "When you go back to Egypt, see that you do all those wonders before Pharaoh which I have put in your hand. But I will harden his heart, so that he will not let the people go. [22]Then you shall say to Pharaoh, 'Thus says the LORD: "Israel *is* My son, My firstborn. [23]So I say to you, let My son go that he may serve Me. But if you refuse to let him go, indeed I will kill your son, your firstborn."'"

[24]And it came to pass on the way, at the encampment, that the LORD met him and sought to kill him. [25]Then Zipporah took a sharp stone and cut off the foreskin of her son and cast *it* at Moses'[a] feet, and said, "Surely you *are* a husband of blood to me!" [26]So He let him go. Then she said, "*You are* a husband of blood!"—because of the circumcision.

[27]And the LORD said to Aaron, "Go into the wilderness to meet Moses." So he went and met him on the mountain of God, and kissed him. [28]So Moses told Aaron all the words of the LORD who had sent him, and all the signs which He had commanded him. [29]Then Moses and Aaron went and gathered together all the elders of the children of Israel. [30]And Aaron spoke all the words which the LORD had spoken to Moses. Then he did the signs in the sight of the people. [31]So the people believed; and when they heard that the LORD had visited the children of Israel and that He had looked on their affliction, then they bowed their heads and worshiped.

First Encounter with Pharaoh

5 Afterward Moses and Aaron went in and told Pharaoh, "Thus says the LORD God of Israel: 'Let My people go, that they may hold a feast to Me in the wilderness.'"

4:25 [a]Literally *his*

The Law of Navigation: Plan Ahead

(Exodus 5:1)

No question about it, Moses had a major challenge on his hands. Not only did he have to convince everyone—including Pharaoh—to let him lead the Hebrew slaves out of Egypt, but he had to plan the whole process. To mobilize his countrymen he first had to organize them. That required shrewd planning.

For more than 25 years the following acronym has helped leaders to think through their plans whenever a major challenge or opportunity approaches:

P—Predetermine your course of action.
L—Lay out your goals.
A—Adjust your priorities.
N—Notify key personnel.
A—Allow time for acceptance.
H—Head into action.
E—Expect problems.
A—Always point to your successes.
D—Daily review your progress.

MOSES AND THE LAW OF SACRIFICE

A Leader Must Give Up to Go Up
(Exodus 3:1—4:13)

Many leaders want to climb the corporate ladder, hoping that freedom and power wait at the top. They don't realize that leadership really requires sacrifice.

Leaders who want to rise must do more than take an occasional cut in pay; they have to give up their rights. That's true of every leader regardless of profession. Talk to any leader, and you will find he has made repeated sacrifices. The higher that leader has climbed, the greater the sacrifices he usually has made. Effective leaders sacrifice much that is good in order to dedicate themselves to what is best.

Leadership demands constant sacrifice. It is an ongoing process, not a one-time payment. The circumstances may change from person to person, but the principle doesn't: Leadership means sacrifice.

What price are you willing to pay to become a more effective leader? Many leaders keep so busy pursuing their vision and rallying their people that they give it little thought. But leadership always requires sacrifice; no one achieves success without it.

How was Moses able to give up so much and make such great sacrifices without growing bitter or resentful toward God? And what made him willing to return to Egypt as God's servant after he had enjoyed the best the country had to offer? A quick look at Moses' life shows how God molded him into an effective leader.

1. Moses was alone with God.

Had Moses stayed in Egypt, would he have listened when God called him? Who knows? But Moses' exile in Midian gave him 40 years of reflection time. When God finally appeared to him in the burning bush, Moses had grown quiet enough to hear God's voice.

Leaders in our day take too little time to get alone with God. Most seem continually on the go and rarely quiet themselves. If that description fits you, change your habits and set aside some time to be alone with God. Don't force God to send you to the desert to get your attention.

2. Moses was honest with God.

By the time Moses met God at the burning bush, no trace remained of the cockiness characteristic of his life in Egypt. He knew his weakness. When God told Moses that he would bring the people out of Egypt, the chastened man replied, "Who am I that I should go to Pharaoh, and that I should bring the children of Israel out of Egypt?" (Ex. 3:11). Only as an older man, humble before God, could Moses be of any use to God.

The Lord can use you, too, if you will look at yourself honestly, admit your weaknesses, and humble yourself before God.

3. Moses was hungry for God.

What does it take to make someone *really* hungry for God? It's different for each of us. Some desire to know God even from childhood. A personal tragedy may realign the priorities of others. And some *never* turn to God. For Moses, it took four decades in the wilderness.

Could Moses have given up all hope of doing something worthwhile with his life before God finally spoke to him? Probably so. A person can't be staunchly self-reliant and hungry for God at the same time.

4. Moses was broken by God.

God did not force Himself or His will on Moses. God waited for Moses to willingly come to Him: "When the LORD saw that he turned aside to look, God called to him from the midst of the bush and said, 'Moses, Moses!' " (Ex. 3:4). Once Moses had turned to God, he could be broken.

Brokenness involves two things: removing inappropriate pride and self-reliance and building healthy God-reliance. God tamed Moses' self-reliance and pride in the desert, but to create trust He had to break the man's fears. Moses dealt with different kinds of fear in his encounter with God:

- **Fears concerning himself.** Moses doubted his own value (Ex. 3:11). God responded by assuring Moses of his purpose.
- **Fears concerning God.** Moses feared who God might be. He wanted to know His name and character (Ex. 3:13). God responded by overwhelming Moses with His presence.
- **Fears concerning others.** Moses then worried about how God's people would respond (Ex. 4:1)—hadn't they already rejected him? God responded by demonstrating His power and commitment.
- **Fears concerning his ability.** Moses doubted himself—both his speech (Ex. 4:10) and ability (4:13). God responded by providing him with a partner, his brother Aaron.

With his willfulness broken, his fears overcome, and his purpose reaffirmed, Moses finally placed himself in the hands of God.

Life is filled with trade-offs—but you can trade up only if you have something to sacrifice. Moses had to sacrifice his status and his material possessions to get prepared for his life purpose. And then to fulfill it, again he had to sacrifice. The second time he relinquished the security and safety of obscurity in the desert to return to his boyhood home.

If you desire to lead—if you hope to find and fulfill the purpose for which God created you—then you must have something to give. Keep growing and building your personal assets and hold lightly the things God gives you. And remember: You may need to sacrifice them at any time to answer His call.

²And Pharaoh said, "Who *is* the LORD, that I should obey His voice to let Israel go? I do not know the LORD, nor will I let Israel go."

³So they said, "The God of the Hebrews has met with us. Please, let us go three days' journey into the desert and sacrifice to the LORD our God, lest He fall upon us with pestilence or with the sword."

⁴Then the king of Egypt said to them, "Moses and Aaron, why do you take the people from their work? Get *back* to your labor." ⁵And Pharaoh said, "Look, the people of the land *are* many now, and you make them rest from their labor!"

⁶So the same day Pharaoh commanded the taskmasters of the people and their officers, saying, ⁷"You shall no longer give the people straw to make brick as before. Let them go and gather straw for themselves. ⁸And you shall lay on them the quota of bricks which they made before. You shall not reduce it. For they are idle; therefore they cry out, saying, 'Let us go *and* sacrifice to our God.' ⁹Let more work be laid on the men, that they may labor in it, and let them not regard false words."

¹⁰And the taskmasters of the people and their officers went out and spoke to the people, saying, "Thus says Pharaoh: 'I will not give you straw. ¹¹Go, get yourselves straw where you can find it; yet none of your work will be reduced.'" ¹²So the people were scattered abroad throughout all the land of Egypt to gather stubble instead of straw. ¹³And the taskmasters forced *them* to hurry, saying, "Fulfill your work, *your* daily quota, as when there was straw." ¹⁴Also the officers of the children of Israel, whom Pharaoh's taskmasters had set over them, were beaten *and* were asked, "Why have you not fulfilled your task in making brick both yesterday and today, as before?"

¹⁵Then the officers of the children of Israel came and cried out to Pharaoh, saying, "Why are you dealing thus with your servants? ¹⁶There is no straw given to your servants, and they say to us, 'Make brick!' And indeed your servants *are* beaten, but the fault *is* in your *own* people."

¹⁷But he said, "You *are* idle! Idle! Therefore you say, 'Let us go *and* sacrifice to the LORD.' ¹⁸Therefore go now *and* work; for no straw shall be given you, yet you shall deliver the quota of bricks." ¹⁹And the officers of the children of Israel saw *that* they *were* in trouble after it was said, "You shall not reduce *any* bricks from your daily quota."

²⁰Then, as they came out from Pharaoh, they met Moses and Aaron who stood there to meet them. ²¹And they said to them, "Let the LORD look on you and judge, because you have made us abhorrent in the sight of Pharaoh and in the sight of his servants, to put a sword in their hand to kill us."

Israel's Deliverance Assured

²²So Moses returned to the LORD and said, "Lord, why have You brought trouble on this people? Why *is* it You have sent me? ²³For since I came to Pharaoh to speak in Your name, he has done evil to this people; neither have You delivered Your people at all."

6 Then the LORD said to Moses, "Now you shall see what I will do to Pharaoh. For with a strong hand he will let them go, and with a strong hand he will drive them out of his land."

²And God spoke to Moses and said to him: "I *am* the LORD. ³I appeared to Abraham, to Isaac, and to Jacob, as God Almighty, but *by* My name LORD[a] I was not known to them. ⁴I have also established My covenant with them, to give them the land of Canaan, the land of their pilgrimage, in which they were strangers. ⁵And I have also heard the groaning of the children of Israel whom the Egyptians keep in bondage, and I have remembered My covenant. ⁶Therefore say to the children of Israel: 'I *am* the LORD; I will bring you out from under the burdens of the Egyptians, I will rescue you from their bondage, and I will redeem you with an outstretched arm and with great judgments. ⁷I will take you as My people, and I will be your God. Then you shall know that I *am* the LORD your God who brings you out from under the burdens of the Egyptians. ⁸And I will bring you into the land which I swore to give to Abraham, Isaac, and Jacob; and I will give it to you *as* a heritage: I *am* the LORD.'" ⁹So Moses spoke thus to the children of Israel; but they did not heed Moses, because of anguish of spirit and cruel bondage.

¹⁰And the LORD spoke to Moses, saying, ¹¹"Go in, tell Pharaoh king of Egypt to let the children of Israel go out of his land."

¹²And Moses spoke before the LORD, saying, "The children of Israel have not heeded me. How then shall Pharaoh heed me, for I *am* of uncircumcised lips?"

¹³Then the LORD spoke to Moses and Aaron, and gave them a command for the children of Israel and for Pharaoh king of Egypt, to bring the children of Israel out of the land of Egypt.

6:3 ᵃHebrew *YHWH,* traditionally *Jehovah*

The Leader's Motivation and Personal Vision

(Exodus 6:2, 3)

God knew that Moses needed to be motivated if he were to pull off the task given to him. Exodus 6 recounts how God rekindled his vision of freeing the people from slavery. God revealed Himself in a new way, giving Moses His personal name, Yahweh (vv. 2, 3)—something he never did with Abraham, Isaac, or Jacob. God motivated Moses through a very personal vision.

Leaders can indeed learn from each other, but when it comes to fulfilling a vision, we all need a personal encounter with God and a personal vision that matches who we are. Leaders need a vision that is . . .

1. *Personal* to who they are (it is owned by the leader).
2. *Practical* for when they live (it meets a relevant need).
3. *Possible* for what they have (it matches their gifts).
4. *Parallel* to who they are (it compliments their passion and personality).
5. *Portable* for where they go (it can move with them).
6. *Powerful* for how they live (it stretches them to accomplish more than they could on their own).
7. *Profitable* for what they do (it gets results).
8. *Pleasurable* for who they are (it brings fulfillment and satisfaction).
9. *Purposeful* for why they live (it fulfills their God-given mission).
10. *Providential* for where they are heading (it provides a God-sized destiny).

The Family of Moses and Aaron

[14]These *are* the heads of their fathers' houses: The sons of Reuben, the firstborn of Israel, *were* Hanoch, Pallu, Hezron, and Carmi. These are the families of Reuben. [15]And the sons of Simeon *were* Jemuel,[a] Jamin, Ohad, Jachin, Zohar, and Shaul the son of a Canaanite woman. These *are* the families of Simeon. [16]These *are* the names of the sons of Levi according to their generations: Gershon, Kohath, and Merari. And the years of the life of Levi *were* one hundred and thirty-seven. [17]The sons of Gershon *were* Libni and Shimi according to their families. [18]And the sons of Kohath *were* Amram, Izhar, Hebron, and Uzziel. And the years of the life of Kohath *were* one hundred and thirty-three. [19]The sons of Merari *were* Mahli and Mushi. These *are* the families of Levi according to their generations.

[20]Now Amram took for himself Jochebed, his father's sister, as wife; and she bore him Aaron and Moses. And the years of the life of Amram *were* one hundred and thirty-seven. [21]The sons of Izhar *were* Korah, Nepheg, and Zichri. [22]And the sons of Uzziel *were* Mishael, Elzaphan, and Zithri. [23]Aaron took to himself Elisheba, daughter of Amminadab, sister of Nahshon, as wife; and she bore him Nadab, Abihu, Eleazar, and Ithamar. [24]And the sons of Korah *were* Assir, Elkanah, and Abiasaph. These are the families of the Korahites. [25]Eleazar, Aaron's son, took for himself one of the daughters of Putiel as wife; and she bore him Phinehas. These *are* the heads of the fathers' houses of the Levites according to their families.

[26]These *are the same* Aaron and Moses to whom the LORD said, "Bring out the children of Israel from the land of Egypt according to their armies." [27]These *are* the ones who spoke to Pharaoh king of Egypt, to bring out the children of Israel from Egypt. These *are the same* Moses and Aaron.

Aaron Is Moses' Spokesman

[28]And it came to pass, on the day the LORD spoke to Moses in the land of Egypt, [29]that the LORD spoke to Moses, saying, "I *am* the LORD. Speak to Pharaoh king of Egypt all that I say to you."

[30]But Moses said before the LORD, "Behold, I *am* of uncircumcised lips, and how shall Pharaoh heed me?"

7 So the LORD said to Moses: "See, I have made you *as* God to Pharaoh, and Aaron your brother shall be your prophet. [2]You shall speak all that I command you. And Aaron your brother shall tell Pharaoh to send the chil-

---

6:15 [a]Spelled *Nemuel* in Numbers 26:12

The Law of the Inner Circle: Moses Needed Aaron

(Exodus 6:26—7:20)

Who wouldn't tremble at receiving a call like the one given to Moses? He quaked at the daunting task before him, and so would we. Such a challenge would require every ounce of courage we could muster.

From the very beginning, Moses' feelings of inadequacy prompted him to build an "inner circle" of close supporters. His brother Aaron quickly became a critical member of his team, and over time Moses assembled a unit that both shared his vision and complemented his weaknesses. Through the years Moses added to this inner circle, each time including individuals who possessed different gifts but the same vision as he.

How about you? Who sits in your inner circle? Do they share your vision? Do they have complementary gifts, useful where you need them most—or does that idea threaten you? Find yourself some Aarons, Jethros, and Joshuas, or you won't be able to accomplish all that God has for you.

dren of Israel out of his land. ³And I will harden Pharaoh's heart, and multiply My signs and My wonders in the land of Egypt. ⁴But Pharaoh will not heed you, so that I may lay My hand on Egypt and bring My armies *and* My people, the children of Israel, out of the land of Egypt by great judgments. ⁵And the Egyptians shall know that I *am* the LORD, when I stretch out My hand on Egypt and bring out the children of Israel from among them."

⁶Then Moses and Aaron did *so;* just as the LORD commanded them, so they did. ⁷And Moses *was* eighty years old and Aaron eighty-three years old when they spoke to Pharaoh.

Aaron's Miraculous Rod

⁸Then the LORD spoke to Moses and Aaron, saying, ⁹"When Pharaoh speaks to you, saying, 'Show a miracle for yourselves,' then you shall say to Aaron, 'Take your rod and cast *it* before Pharaoh, *and* let it become a serpent.'" ¹⁰So Moses and Aaron went in to Pharaoh, and they did

so, just as the LORD commanded. And Aaron cast down his rod before Pharaoh and before his servants, and it became a serpent. ¹¹But Pharaoh also called the wise men and the sorcerers; so the magicians of Egypt, they also did in like manner with their enchantments. ¹²For every man threw down his rod, and they became serpents. But Aaron's rod swallowed up their rods. ¹³And Pharaoh's heart grew hard, and he did not heed them, as the LORD had said.

The First Plague: Waters Become Blood

¹⁴So the LORD said to Moses: "Pharaoh's heart *is* hard; he refuses to let the people go. ¹⁵Go to Pharaoh in the morning, when he goes out to the water, and you shall stand by the river's bank to meet him; and the rod which was turned to a serpent you shall take in your hand. ¹⁶And you shall say to him, 'The LORD God of the Hebrews has sent me to you, saying, "Let My people go, that they may serve Me in the wilderness"'; but indeed, until now you would not hear! ¹⁷Thus says the LORD: "By this you shall know that I *am* the LORD. Behold, I will strike the waters which *are* in the river with the rod that *is* in my hand, and they shall be turned to blood. ¹⁸And the fish that *are* in the river shall die, the river shall stink, and the Egyptians will loathe to drink the water of the river."'"

¹⁹Then the LORD spoke to Moses, "Say to Aaron, 'Take your rod and stretch out your hand over the waters of Egypt, over their streams, over their rivers, over their ponds, and over all their pools of water, that they may become blood. And there shall be blood throughout all the land of Egypt, both in *buckets of* wood and *pitchers of* stone.'" ²⁰And Moses and Aaron did so, just as the LORD commanded. So he lifted up the rod and struck the waters that *were* in the river, in the sight of Pharaoh and in the sight of his servants. And all the waters that *were* in the river were turned to blood. ²¹The fish that *were* in the river died, the river stank, and the Egyptians could not drink the water of the river. So there was blood throughout all the land of Egypt.

²²Then the magicians of Egypt did so with their enchantments; and Pharaoh's heart grew hard, and he did not heed them, as the LORD had said. ²³And Pharaoh turned and went into his house. Neither was his heart moved by this. ²⁴So all the Egyptians dug all around the river for water to drink, because they could not drink the water of the river. ²⁵And seven days passed after the LORD had struck the river.

Moses: The Plagues and the Law of Victory

(Exodus 7:2—11:3)

How can anyone think that Moses relished confronting Pharaoh with the plagues? While he obeyed God and warned Pharaoh of each coming judgment, he asked God to send them only to accomplish his goal. We see no pride or arrogance in him; he certainly did not summon the plagues to draw attention to himself. Moses simply called down God's judgment until Pharaoh broke and released the Hebrews.

The Law of Victory teaches that leaders find a way for the team to win. In this case, several plagues were required to convince Pharaoh to let God's people go. And how can we describe Moses' attitude during those plagues? What enabled him to win the victory he sought?

1. He was *patient* (7:2, 3).
2. He was *consistent* (7:4–7).
3. He was *discerning* (8:10, 11).
4. He was *prayerful* (8:12).
5. He was *tenacious* (11:1).
6. He was *credible* (11:3).

The Second Plague: Frogs

8 And the LORD spoke to Moses, "Go to Pharaoh and say to him, 'Thus says the LORD: "Let My people go, that they may serve Me. ²But if you refuse to let *them* go, behold, I will smite all your territory with frogs. ³So the river shall bring forth frogs abundantly, which shall go up and come into your house, into your bedroom, on your bed, into the houses of your servants, on your people, into your ovens, and into your kneading bowls. ⁴And the frogs shall come up on you, on your people, and on all your servants."'"

⁵Then the LORD spoke to Moses, "Say to Aaron, 'Stretch out your hand with your rod over the streams, over the rivers, and over the ponds, and cause frogs to come up on the land of Egypt.'" ⁶So Aaron stretched out his hand over the waters of Egypt, and the frogs came up and covered the land of Egypt. ⁷And the magicians did so with their enchantments, and brought up frogs on the land of Egypt.

⁸Then Pharaoh called for Moses and Aaron, and said, "Entreat the LORD that He may take away the frogs from me and from my people; and I will let the people go, that they may sacrifice to the LORD."

⁹And Moses said to Pharaoh, "Accept the honor of saying when I shall intercede for you, for your servants, and for your people, to destroy the frogs from you and your houses, *that* they may remain in the river only."

¹⁰So he said, "Tomorrow." And he said, "*Let it be* according to your word, that you may know that *there is* no one like the LORD our God. ¹¹And the frogs shall depart from you, from your houses, from your servants, and from your people. They shall remain in the river only."

¹²Then Moses and Aaron went out from Pharaoh. And Moses cried out to the LORD concerning the frogs which He had brought against Pharaoh. ¹³So the LORD did according to the word of Moses. And the frogs died out of the houses, out of the courtyards, and out of the fields. ¹⁴They gathered them together in heaps, and the land stank. ¹⁵But when Pharaoh saw that there was relief, he hardened his heart and did not heed them, as the LORD had said.

The Third Plague: Lice

¹⁶So the LORD said to Moses, "Say to Aaron, 'Stretch out your rod, and strike the dust of the land, so that it may become lice throughout all the land of Egypt.'" ¹⁷And they did so. For Aaron stretched out his hand with his rod and struck the dust of the earth, and it became lice on man and beast. All the dust of the land became lice throughout all the land of Egypt. ¹⁸Now the magicians so worked with their enchantments to bring forth lice, but they could not. So there were lice on man and beast. ¹⁹Then the magicians said to Pharaoh, "This *is* the finger of God." But Pharaoh's heart grew hard, and he did not heed them, just as the LORD had said.

The Fourth Plague: Flies

²⁰And the LORD said to Moses, "Rise early in the morning and stand before Pharaoh as he comes out to the water. Then say to him, 'Thus says the LORD: "Let My people go, that they may serve Me. ²¹Or else, if you will not let My people go, behold, I will send swarms *of flies* on you and your servants, on your people and into your houses. The houses of the Egyptians shall be full of swarms *of flies,* and also the ground on which they *stand.* ²²And in that day I will set apart the land of Goshen, in which My people dwell, that no swarms *of flies* shall be there, in order that you may know that I *am* the LORD in the midst of

the land. [23]I will make a difference[a] between My people and your people. Tomorrow this sign shall be."'" [24]And the LORD did so. Thick swarms *of flies* came into the house of Pharaoh, *into his* servants' houses, and into all the land of Egypt. The land was corrupted because of the swarms *of flies.*

[25]Then Pharaoh called for Moses and Aaron, and said, "Go, sacrifice to your God in the land."

[26]And Moses said, "It is not right to do so, for we would be sacrificing the abomination of the Egyptians to the LORD our God. If we sacrifice the abomination of the Egyptians before their eyes, then will they not stone us? [27]We will go three days' journey into the wilderness and sacrifice to the LORD our God as He will command us."

[28]So Pharaoh said, "I will let you go, that you may sacrifice to the LORD your God in the wilderness; only you shall not go very far away. Intercede for me."

[29]Then Moses said, "Indeed I am going out from you, and I will entreat the LORD, that the swarms *of flies* may depart tomorrow from Pharaoh, from his servants, and from his people. But let Pharaoh not deal deceitfully anymore in not letting the people go to sacrifice to the LORD."

[30]So Moses went out from Pharaoh and entreated the LORD. [31]And the LORD did according to the word of Moses; He removed the swarms *of flies* from Pharaoh, from his servants, and from his people. Not one remained. [32]But Pharaoh hardened his heart at this time also; neither would he let the people go.

The Fifth Plague: Livestock Diseased

9 Then the LORD said to Moses, "Go in to Pharaoh and tell him, 'Thus says the LORD God of the Hebrews: "Let My people go, that they may serve Me. [2]For if you refuse to let *them* go, and still hold them, [3]behold, the hand of the LORD will be on your cattle in the field, on the horses, on the donkeys, on the camels, on the oxen, and on the sheep—a very severe pestilence. [4]And the LORD will make a difference between the livestock of Israel and the livestock of Egypt. So nothing shall die of all *that* belongs to the children of Israel."'" [5]Then the LORD appointed a set time, saying, "Tomorrow the LORD will do this thing in the land."

[6]So the LORD did this thing on the next day, and all the livestock of Egypt died; but of the livestock of the children of Israel, not one died. [7]Then Pharaoh sent, and indeed, not even one of the livestock of the Israelites was dead. But the heart of Pharaoh became hard, and he did not let the people go.

The Sixth Plague: Boils

[8]So the LORD said to Moses and Aaron, "Take for yourselves handfuls of ashes from a furnace, and let Moses scatter it toward the heavens in the sight of Pharaoh. [9]And it will become fine dust in all the land of Egypt, and it will cause boils that break out in sores on man and beast throughout all the land of Egypt." [10]Then they took ashes from the furnace and stood before Pharaoh, and Moses scattered *them* toward heaven. And *they* caused boils that break out in sores on man and beast. [11]And the magicians could not stand before Moses because of the boils, for the boils were on the magicians and on all the Egyptians. [12]But the LORD hardened the heart of Pharaoh; and he did not heed them, just as the LORD had spoken to Moses.

The Seventh Plague: Hail

[13]Then the LORD said to Moses, "Rise early in the morning and stand before Pharaoh, and say to him, 'Thus says the LORD God of the Hebrews: "Let My people go, that they may serve Me, [14]for at this time I will send all My plagues to your very heart, and on your servants and on your people, that you may know that *there is* none like Me in all the earth. [15]Now if I had stretched out My hand and struck you and your people with pestilence, then you would have been cut off from the earth. [16]But indeed for this *purpose* I have raised you up, that I may show My power *in* you, and that My name may be declared in all the earth. [17]As yet you exalt yourself against My people in that you will not let them go. [18]Behold, tomorrow about this time I will cause very heavy hail to rain down, such as has not been in Egypt since its founding until now. [19]Therefore send now *and* gather your livestock and all that you have in the field, for the hail shall come down on every man and every animal which is found in the field and is not brought home; and they shall die."'"

[20]He who feared the word of the LORD among the servants of Pharaoh made his servants and his livestock flee to the houses. [21]But he who did not regard the word of the LORD left his servants and his livestock in the field.

[22]Then the LORD said to Moses, "Stretch out your hand toward heaven, that there may be hail in all the land of Egypt—on man, on beast, and

---

8:23 [a]Literally *set a ransom* (compare Exodus 9:4 and 11:7)

on every herb of the field, throughout the land of Egypt." ²³And Moses stretched out his rod toward heaven; and the LORD sent thunder and hail, and fire darted to the ground. And the LORD rained hail on the land of Egypt. ²⁴So there was hail, and fire mingled with the hail, so very heavy that there was none like it in all the land of Egypt since it became a nation. ²⁵And the hail struck throughout the whole land of Egypt, all that *was* in the field, both man and beast; and the hail struck every herb of the field and broke every tree of the field. ²⁶Only in the land of Goshen, where the children of Israel *were,* there was no hail.

²⁷And Pharaoh sent and called for Moses and Aaron, and said to them, "I have sinned this time. The LORD *is* righteous, and my people and I *are* wicked. ²⁸Entreat the LORD, that there may be no *more* mighty thundering and hail, for *it is* enough. I will let you go, and you shall stay no longer."

²⁹So Moses said to him, "As soon as I have gone out of the city, I will spread out my hands to the LORD; the thunder will cease, and there will be no more hail, that you may know that the earth *is* the LORD's. ³⁰But as for you and your servants, I know that you will not yet fear the LORD God."

³¹Now the flax and the barley were struck, for the barley *was* in the head and the flax *was* in bud. ³²But the wheat and the spelt were not struck, for they *are* late crops.

³³So Moses went out of the city from Pharaoh and spread out his hands to the LORD; then the thunder and the hail ceased, and the rain was not poured on the earth. ³⁴And when Pharaoh saw that the rain, the hail, and the thunder had ceased, he sinned yet more; and he hardened his heart, he and his servants. ³⁵So the heart of Pharaoh was hard; neither would he let the children of Israel go, as the LORD had spoken by Moses.

The Eighth Plague: Locusts

10 Now the LORD said to Moses, "Go in to Pharaoh; for I have hardened his heart and the hearts of his servants, that I may show these signs of Mine before him, ²and that you may tell in the hearing of your son and your son's son the mighty things I have done in Egypt, and My signs which I have done among them, that you may know that I *am* the LORD."

³So Moses and Aaron came in to Pharaoh and said to him, "Thus says the LORD God of the

---

PHARAOH

ATTITUDE: MY WAY OR THE HIGHWAY
(Exodus 10:1–29)

PROFILE *IN LEADERSHIP*

Does the greatness of a nation automatically make its ruler great? Pharaoh seemed to think so. Not only did Pharaoh rule with absolute power, he also displayed absolute arrogance. He thought of himself as a god and demanded that others see him the same way.

How ironic that the wealth of a nation, along with its power, came into Pharaoh's possession through the hand of the Lord's servant, Joseph (Gen. 47). But years passed, and when another servant of God approached another man sitting on the throne of Egypt, an ugly confrontation erupted. Pharaoh reveals his arrogant character through his defiant response to Moses' request that he let the people go into the wilderness to worship their God: "Who is the LORD, that I should obey His voice to let Israel go? I do not know the LORD, nor will I let Israel go" (Ex. 5:2).

Pharaoh's pride led to arrogance, and his arrogance to rigidity. In time, his heart became stone-cold and hard. He could have written a song, "My Way or the Highway." Of course, the Israelites chose the highway and headed for the Promised Land, leaving Egypt with their pockets stuffed with Egyptian gold. And Pharaoh's way led his army straight to the bottom of the sea.

Hebrews: 'How long will you refuse to humble yourself before Me? Let My people go, that they may serve Me. ⁴Or else, if you refuse to let My people go, behold, tomorrow I will bring locusts into your territory. ⁵And they shall cover the face of the earth, so that no one will be able to see the earth; and they shall eat the residue of what is left, which remains to you from the hail, and they shall eat every tree which grows up for you out of the field. ⁶They shall fill your houses, the houses of all your servants, and the houses of all the Egyptians—which neither your fathers nor your fathers' fathers have seen, since the day that they were on the earth to this day.'" And he turned and went out from Pharaoh.

⁷Then Pharaoh's servants said to him, "How long shall this man be a snare to us? Let the men go, that they may serve the LORD their God. Do you not yet know that Egypt is destroyed?"

⁸So Moses and Aaron were brought again to Pharaoh, and he said to them, "Go, serve the LORD your God. Who are the ones that are going?"

⁹And Moses said, "We will go with our young and our old; with our sons and our daughters, with our flocks and our herds we will go, for we must hold a feast to the LORD."

¹⁰Then he said to them, "The LORD had better be with you when I let you and your little ones go! Beware, for evil is ahead of you. ¹¹Not so! Go now, you who are men, and serve the LORD, for that is what you desired." And they were driven out from Pharaoh's presence.

¹²Then the LORD said to Moses, "Stretch out your hand over the land of Egypt for the locusts, that they may come upon the land of Egypt, and eat every herb of the land—all that the hail has left." ¹³So Moses stretched out his rod over the land of Egypt, and the LORD brought an east wind on the land all that day and all that night. When it was morning, the east wind brought the locusts. ¹⁴And the locusts went up over all the land of Egypt and rested on all the territory of Egypt. They were very severe; previously there had been no such locusts as they, nor shall there be such after them. ¹⁵For they covered the face of the whole earth, so that the land was darkened; and they ate every herb of the land and all the fruit of the trees which the hail had left. So there remained nothing green on the trees or on the plants of the field throughout all the land of Egypt.

¹⁶Then Pharaoh called for Moses and Aaron in haste, and said, "I have sinned against the LORD your God and against you. ¹⁷Now therefore, please forgive my sin only this once, and en-treat the LORD your God, that He may take away from me this death only." ¹⁸So he went out from Pharaoh and entreated the LORD. ¹⁹And the LORD turned a very strong west wind, which took the locusts away and blew them into the Red Sea. There remained not one locust in all the territory of Egypt. ²⁰But the LORD hardened Pharaoh's heart, and he did not let the children of Israel go.

The Ninth Plague: Darkness

²¹Then the LORD said to Moses, "Stretch out your hand toward heaven, that there may be darkness over the land of Egypt, darkness which may even be felt." ²²So Moses stretched out his hand toward heaven, and there was thick darkness in all the land of Egypt three days. ²³They did not see one another; nor did anyone rise from his place for three days. But all the children of Israel had light in their dwellings.

²⁴Then Pharaoh called to Moses and said, "Go, serve the LORD; only let your flocks and your herds be kept back. Let your little ones also go with you."

²⁵But Moses said, "You must also give us sacrifices and burnt offerings, that we may sacrifice to the LORD our God. ²⁶Our livestock also shall go with us; not a hoof shall be left behind. For we must take some of them to serve the LORD our God, and even we do not know with what we must serve the LORD until we arrive there."

²⁷But the LORD hardened Pharaoh's heart, and he would not let them go. ²⁸Then Pharaoh said to him, "Get away from me! Take heed to yourself and see my face no more! For in the day you see my face you shall die!"

²⁹So Moses said, "You have spoken well. I will never see your face again."

Death of the Firstborn Announced

11 And the LORD said to Moses, "I will bring one more plague on Pharaoh and on Egypt. Afterward he will let you go from here. When he lets you go, he will surely drive you out of here altogether. ²Speak now in the hearing of the people, and let every man ask from his neighbor and every woman from her neighbor, articles of silver and articles of gold." ³And the LORD gave the people favor in the sight of the Egyptians. Moreover the man Moses was very great in the land of Egypt, in the sight of Pharaoh's servants and in the sight of the people.

⁴Then Moses said, "Thus says the LORD: 'About midnight I will go out into the midst of Egypt; ⁵and all the firstborn in the land of Egypt

shall die, from the firstborn of Pharaoh who sits on his throne, even to the firstborn of the female servant who *is* behind the handmill, and all the firstborn of the animals. ⁶Then there shall be a great cry throughout all the land of Egypt, such as was not like it *before,* nor shall be like it again. ⁷But against none of the children of Israel shall a dog move its tongue, against man or beast, that you may know that the LORD does make a difference between the Egyptians and Israel.' ⁸And all these your servants shall come down to me and bow down to me, saying, 'Get out, and all the people who follow you!' After that I will go out." Then he went out from Pharaoh in great anger.

⁹But the LORD said to Moses, "Pharaoh will not heed you, so that My wonders may be multiplied in the land of Egypt." ¹⁰So Moses and Aaron did all these wonders before Pharaoh; and the LORD hardened Pharaoh's heart, and he did not let the children of Israel go out of his land.

The Passover Instituted

12 Now the LORD spoke to Moses and Aaron in the land of Egypt, saying, ²"This month *shall be* your beginning of months; it *shall be* the first month of the year to you. ³Speak to all the congregation of Israel,

saying: 'On the tenth of this month every man shall take for himself a lamb, according to the house of *his* father, a lamb for a household. ⁴And if the household is too small for the lamb, let him and his neighbor next to his house take *it* according to the number of the persons; according to each man's need you shall make your count for the lamb. ⁵Your lamb shall be without blemish, a male of the first year. You may take *it* from the sheep or from the goats. ⁶Now you shall keep it until the fourteenth day of the same month. Then the whole assembly of the congregation of Israel shall kill it at twilight. ⁷And they shall take *some* of the blood and put *it* on the two doorposts and on the lintel of the houses where they eat it. ⁸Then they shall eat the flesh on that night; roasted in fire, with unleavened bread *and* with bitter *herbs* they shall eat it. ⁹Do not eat it raw, nor boiled at all with water, but roasted in fire—its head with its legs and its entrails. ¹⁰You shall let none of it remain until morning, and what remains of it until morning you shall burn with fire. ¹¹And thus you shall eat it: *with* a belt on your waist, your sandals on your feet, and your staff in your hand. So you shall eat it in haste. It *is* the LORD's Passover.

¹²'For I will pass through the land of Egypt on that night, and will strike all the firstborn in

---

MOSES   THE UNEXPECTED LEADER
(Exodus 11:3)

PROFILE IN LEADERSHIP

What words come to mind when you think of great leaders? It's doubtful that "meek" appears at the top of your list—yet that is the precise word God chose to describe Moses. Numbers 12:3 declares that "the man Moses was very humble, more than all men who were on the face of the earth."

Moses had reasons to be humble. He certainly wasn't a natural leader. Nothing in Scripture indicates he attracted or led anyone during the first 80 years of his life. Although he was "learned in all the wisdom of the Egyptians, and was mighty in words and deeds" (Acts 7:22), we have no record of significant accomplishment during his first 40 years. So far as we know, his first attempt at exerting his influence to help the people resulted in the murder of an Egyptian and his flight from the country. The next 40 years Moses spent in exile in the desert of Midian, a time so uneventful that Scripture sums it up in three verses (Ex. 2:21–23).

You don't have to be a "natural" to become a great leader; you simply need a heart for God and a teachable spirit. Most of the great leaders in Scripture were made, not born. Happily for us, God is still making them today. Could you be one?

A Leader's Communication: God Instructs His People

(Exodus 12:3–23)

Without the ability to communicate, a leader travels alone. No one will catch your vision unless you first transfer a picture of it into his or her heart. That's what God did when He clearly explained to the Hebrew families how they could spare the lives of their firstborn sons.

the land of Egypt, both man and beast; and against all the gods of Egypt I will execute judgment: I *am* the LORD. [13]Now the blood shall be a sign for you on the houses where you *are*. And when I see the blood, I will pass over you; and the plague shall not be on you to destroy *you* when I strike the land of Egypt.

[14]"So this day shall be to you a memorial; and you shall keep it as a feast to the LORD throughout your generations. You shall keep it as a feast by an everlasting ordinance. [15]Seven days you shall eat unleavened bread. On the first day you shall remove leaven from your houses. For whoever eats leavened bread from the first day until the seventh day, that person shall be cut off from Israel. [16]On the first day *there shall be* a holy convocation, and on the seventh day there shall be a holy convocation for you. No manner of work shall be done on them; but *that* which everyone must eat—that only may be prepared by you. [17]So you shall observe *the Feast of* Unleavened Bread, for on this same day I will have brought your armies out of the land of Egypt. Therefore you shall observe this day throughout your generations as an everlasting ordinance. [18]In the first *month,* on the fourteenth day of the month at evening, you shall eat unleavened bread, until the twenty-first day of the month at evening. [19]For seven days no leaven shall be found in your houses, since whoever eats what is leavened, that same person shall be cut off from the congregation of Israel, whether *he is* a stranger or a native of the land. [20]You shall eat nothing leavened; in all your dwellings you shall eat unleavened bread.'"

[21]Then Moses called for all the elders of Israel and said to them, "Pick out and take lambs for yourselves according to your families, and kill the Passover *lamb.* [22]And you shall take a bunch of hyssop, dip *it* in the blood that *is* in the basin, and strike the lintel and the two doorposts with the blood that *is* in the basin. And none of you shall go out of the door of his house until morning. [23]For the LORD will pass through to strike the Egyptians; and when He sees the blood on the lintel and on the two doorposts, the LORD will pass over the door and not allow the destroyer to come into your houses to strike *you.* [24]And you shall observe this thing as an ordinance for you and your sons forever. [25]It will come to pass when you come to the land which the LORD will give you, just as He promised, that you shall keep this service. [26]And it shall be, when your children say to you, 'What do you mean by this service?' [27]that you shall say, 'It *is* the Passover sacrifice of the LORD, who passed over the houses of the children of Israel in Egypt when He struck the Egyptians and delivered our households.'" So the people bowed their heads and worshiped. [28]Then the children of Israel went away and did *so;* just as the LORD had commanded Moses and Aaron, so they did.

The Tenth Plague: Death of the Firstborn

[29]And it came to pass at midnight that the LORD struck all the firstborn in the land of Egypt, from the firstborn of Pharaoh who sat on his throne to the firstborn of the captive who *was* in the dungeon, and all the firstborn of livestock. [30]So Pharaoh rose in the night, he, all his servants, and all the Egyptians; and there was a great cry in Egypt, for *there was* not a house where *there was* not one dead.

The Exodus

[31]Then he called for Moses and Aaron by night, and said, "Rise, go out from among my people, both you and the children of Israel. And go, serve the LORD as you have said. [32]Also take your flocks and your herds, as you have said, and be gone; and bless me also."

[33]And the Egyptians urged the people, that they might send them out of the land in haste. For they said, "We *shall* all *be* dead." [34]So the people took their dough before it was leavened, having their kneading bowls bound up in their clothes on their shoulders. [35]Now the children of Israel had done according to the word of Moses, and they had asked from the Egyptians articles of silver, articles of gold, and clothing. [36]And the LORD had given the people favor in the sight of the Egyptians, so that they granted them *what they requested.* Thus they plundered the Egyptians.

Equipping: God Used Aaron to Equip Moses During the Plagues

(Exodus 5:1—12:37)

By sending ten plagues on the people of Egypt, God accomplished many objectives at once. Not only did He secure the release of the Hebrews, He also taught the Egyptians lessons about Him. Each plague spoke symbolically to the Egyptian people, establishing beyond doubt that the God of Israel was THE God. And through the plagues God also taught Moses lessons on leadership.

Because Moses resisted a return to Egypt when God called him at the burning bush (Ex. 3; 4), God allowed his brother, Aaron, to accompany him. God used Aaron to equip Moses during the plagues:

- *The First Five Plagues:* Aaron used God's staff while Moses watched.
- *The Sixth Plague:* Aaron and Moses worked together to summon the plague of boils.
- *The Last Four Plagues:* Moses worked alone as Aaron watched.

From then on, Moses took the lead in everything. How often does God use willing associates to prepare His chosen leaders for success!

[37]Then the children of Israel journeyed from Rameses to Succoth, about six hundred thousand men on foot, besides children. [38]A mixed multitude went up with them also, and flocks and herds—a great deal of livestock. [39]And they baked unleavened cakes of the dough which they had brought out of Egypt; for it was not leavened, because they were driven out of Egypt and could not wait, nor had they prepared provisions for themselves.

[40]Now the sojourn of the children of Israel who lived in Egypt[a] *was* four hundred and thirty years. [41]And it came to pass at the end of the four hundred and thirty years—on that very same day—it came to pass that all the armies of the LORD went out from the land of Egypt. [42]It *is* a night of solemn observance to the LORD for bringing them out of the land of Egypt. This *is* that night of the LORD, a solemn observance for all the children of Israel throughout their generations.

Passover Regulations

[43]And the LORD said to Moses and Aaron, "This *is* the ordinance of the Passover: No foreigner shall eat it. [44]But every man's servant who is bought for money, when you have circumcised him, then he may eat it. [45]A sojourner and a hired servant shall not eat it. [46]In one house it shall be eaten; you shall not carry any of the flesh outside the house, nor shall you break one of its bones. [47]All the congregation of Israel shall keep it. [48]And when a stranger dwells with you *and wants* to keep the Passover to the LORD, let all his males be circumcised, and then let him come near and keep it; and he shall be as a native of the land. For no uncircumcised person shall eat it. [49]One law shall be for the native-born and for the stranger who dwells among you."

[50]Thus all the children of Israel did; as the LORD commanded Moses and Aaron, so they did. [51]And it came to pass, on that very same day, that the LORD brought the children of Israel out of the land of Egypt according to their armies.

The Firstborn Consecrated

13 Then the LORD spoke to Moses, saying, [2]"Consecrate to Me all the firstborn, whatever opens the womb among the children of Israel, *both* of man and beast; it is Mine."

The Feast of Unleavened Bread

[3]And Moses said to the people: "Remember this day in which you went out of Egypt, out of the house of bondage; for by strength of hand the LORD brought you out of this *place.* No leavened bread shall be eaten. [4]On this day you are going out, in the month Abib. [5]And it shall be, when the LORD brings you into the land of the Canaanites and the Hittites and the Amorites and the Hivites and the Jebusites, which He swore to your fathers to give you, a land flowing with milk and honey, that you shall keep this service in this month. [6]Seven days you shall eat unleavened bread, and on the seventh day *there shall be* a feast to the LORD. [7]Unleavened bread shall be eaten seven days. And no leavened bread shall be seen among you, nor shall leaven be seen among you in all your quarters. [8]And you shall tell your son in that day, saying, '*This is done* because of what the LORD did for me when I

12:40 [a]Samaritan Pentateuch and Septuagint read *Egypt and Canaan.*

came up from Egypt.' ⁹It shall be as a sign to you on your hand and as a memorial between your eyes, that the LORD's law may be in your mouth; for with a strong hand the LORD has brought you out of Egypt. ¹⁰You shall therefore keep this ordinance in its season from year to year.

The Law of the Firstborn

¹¹"And it shall be, when the LORD brings you into the land of the Canaanites, as He swore to you and your fathers, and gives it to you, ¹²that you shall set apart to the LORD all that open the womb, that is, every firstborn that comes from an animal which you have; the males *shall be* the LORD's. ¹³But every firstborn of a donkey you shall redeem with a lamb; and if you will not redeem *it,* then you shall break its neck. And all the firstborn of man among your sons you shall redeem. ¹⁴So it shall be, when your son asks you in time to come, saying, 'What *is* this?' that you shall say to him, 'By strength of hand the LORD brought us out of Egypt, out of the house of bondage. ¹⁵And it came to pass, when Pharaoh was stubborn about letting us go, that the LORD killed all the firstborn in the land of Egypt, both the firstborn of man and the firstborn of beast. Therefore I sacrifice to the LORD all males that open the womb, but all the firstborn of my sons I redeem.' ¹⁶It shall be as a sign on your hand and as frontlets between your eyes, for by strength of hand the LORD brought us out of Egypt."

The Wilderness Way

¹⁷Then it came to pass, when Pharaoh had let the people go, that God did not lead them *by* way of the land of the Philistines, although that *was* near; for God said, "Lest perhaps the people change their minds when they see war, and return to Egypt." ¹⁸So God led the people around *by* way of the wilderness of the Red Sea. And the children of Israel went up in orderly ranks out of the land of Egypt.

¹⁹And Moses took the bones of Joseph with him, for he had placed the children of Israel under solemn oath, saying, "God will surely visit you, and you shall carry up my bones from here with you."ᵃ

²⁰So they took their journey from Succoth and camped in Etham at the edge of the wilderness. ²¹And the LORD went before them by day in a pillar of cloud to lead the way, and by night in a pillar of fire to give them light, so as to go by day and night. ²²He did not take away the pillar of cloud by day or the pillar of fire by night *from* before the people.

God's Tangible Leadership: The Pillar and the Cloud

(Exodus 13:21)

God's use of cloud and fire taught Israel to expect dynamic divine leadership. He would provide more than a set of rules; when His pillar of fire halted, they were to stop. When it moved, they were to follow. In a similar way, leadership today must be both definitive and dynamic.

The Red Sea Crossing

14 Now the LORD spoke to Moses, saying: ²"Speak to the children of Israel, that they turn and camp before Pi Hahiroth, between Migdol and the sea, opposite Baal Zephon; you shall camp before it by the sea. ³For Pharaoh will say of the children of Israel, 'They *are* bewildered by the land; the wilderness has closed them in.' ⁴Then I will harden Pharaoh's heart, so that he will pursue them; and I will gain honor over Pharaoh and over all his army, that the Egyptians may know that I *am* the LORD." And they did so.

⁵Now it was told the king of Egypt that the people had fled, and the heart of Pharaoh and his servants was turned against the people; and they said, "Why have we done this, that we have let Israel go from serving us?" ⁶So he made ready his chariot and took his people with him. ⁷Also, he took six hundred choice chariots, and all the chariots of Egypt with captains over every one of them. ⁸And the LORD hardened the heart of Pharaoh king of Egypt, and he pursued the children of Israel; and the children of Israel went out with boldness. ⁹So the Egyptians pursued them, all the horses *and* chariots of Pharaoh, his horsemen and his army, and overtook them camping by the sea beside Pi Hahiroth, before Baal Zephon.

¹⁰And when Pharaoh drew near, the children of Israel lifted their eyes, and behold, the Egyptians marched after them. So they were very afraid, and the children of Israel cried out to the LORD. ¹¹Then they said to Moses, "Because *there were* no graves in Egypt, have you taken us away

13:19 ᵃGenesis 50:25

The Law of Buy-In: Moses Gains Credibility
(Exodus 14:1–28)

The approach of the Egyptian army terrified the Israelites, and they placed heavy pressure on Moses to handle this crisis. Moses didn't panic, since he had seen the power of God's handiwork. Instead, he exuded both poise and peace, winning for himself great credibility as a leader. Through one incident he became the nation's "go to" leader. Note what gave him credibility:

1. **He projected calm instead of craziness.**
   "And Moses said to the people, 'Do not be afraid. Stand still, and see the salvation of the LORD, which He will accomplish for you today' " (Ex. 14:13).
2. **He projected confidence instead of cowardice.**
   "For the Egyptians whom you see today, you shall see again no more forever" (Ex. 14:13).
3. **He projected clarity instead of confusion.**
   "And the LORD said to Moses, 'Why do you cry to Me? Tell the children of Israel to go forward' " (Ex. 14:15).
4. **He projected competence instead of clumsiness.**
   "Then Moses stretched out his hand over the sea; and the LORD caused the sea to go back by a strong east wind all that night, and made the sea into dry land, and the waters were divided. So the children of Israel went into the midst of the sea on the dry ground, and the waters were a wall to them on their right hand and on their left" (Ex. 14:21, 22).

to die in the wilderness? Why have you so dealt with us, to bring us up out of Egypt? ¹²*Is this not the word that we told you in Egypt, saying, 'Let us alone that we may serve the Egyptians'? For it would have been* better for us to serve the Egyptians than that we should die in the wilderness."

¹³And Moses said to the people, "Do not be afraid. Stand still, and see the salvation of the LORD, which He will accomplish for you today. For the Egyptians whom you see today, you shall see again no more forever. ¹⁴The LORD will fight for you, and you shall hold your peace."

¹⁵And the LORD said to Moses, "Why do you cry to Me? Tell the children of Israel to go forward. ¹⁶But lift up your rod, and stretch out your hand over the sea and divide it. And the children of Israel shall go on dry *ground* through the midst of the sea. ¹⁷And I indeed will harden the hearts of the Egyptians, and they shall follow them. So I will gain honor over Pharaoh and over all his army, his chariots, and his horsemen. ¹⁸Then the Egyptians shall know that I *am* the LORD, when I have gained honor for Myself over Pharaoh, his chariots, and his horsemen."

¹⁹And the Angel of God, who went before the camp of Israel, moved and went behind them; and the pillar of cloud went from before them and stood behind them. ²⁰So it came between the camp of the Egyptians and the camp of Israel. Thus it was a cloud and darkness *to the one,* and it

gave light by night *to the other,* so that the one did not come near the other all that night.

²¹Then Moses stretched out his hand over the sea; and the LORD caused the sea to go *back* by a strong east wind all that night, and made the sea into dry *land,* and the waters were divided. ²²So the children of Israel went into the midst of the sea on the dry *ground,* and the waters *were* a wall to them on their right hand and on their left. ²³And the Egyptians pursued and went after them into the midst of the sea, all Pharaoh's horses, his chariots, and his horsemen.

²⁴Now it came to pass, in the morning watch, that the LORD looked down upon the army of the Egyptians through the pillar of fire and cloud, and He troubled the army of the Egyptians. ²⁵And He took off ᵃ their chariot wheels, so that they drove them with difficulty; and the Egyptians said, "Let us flee from the face of Israel, for the LORD fights for them against the Egyptians."

²⁶Then the LORD said to Moses, "Stretch out your hand over the sea, that the waters may come back upon the Egyptians, on their chariots, and on their horsemen." ²⁷And Moses stretched out his hand over the sea; and when the morning appeared, the sea returned to its full depth, while

14:25 ᵃSamaritan Pentateuch, Septuagint, and Syriac read *bound.*

the Egyptians were fleeing into it. So the LORD overthrew the Egyptians in the midst of the sea. [28]Then the waters returned and covered the chariots, the horsemen, *and* all the army of Pharaoh that came into the sea after them. Not so much as one of them remained. [29]But the children of Israel had walked on dry *land* in the midst of the sea, and the waters *were* a wall to them on their right hand and on their left.

[30]So the LORD saved Israel that day out of the hand of the Egyptians, and Israel saw the Egyptians dead on the seashore. [31]Thus Israel saw the great work which the LORD had done in Egypt; so the people feared the LORD, and believed the LORD and His servant Moses.

The Song of Moses

15 Then Moses and the children of Israel sang this song to the LORD, and spoke, saying:

"I will sing to the LORD,
For He has triumphed gloriously!
The horse and its rider
He has thrown into the sea!
[2] The LORD *is* my strength and song,
And He has become my salvation;
He *is* my God, and I will praise Him;
My father's God, and I will exalt Him.
[3] The LORD *is* a man of war;
The LORD *is* His name.
[4] Pharaoh's chariots and his army He has
cast into the sea;
His chosen captains also are drowned in
the Red Sea.
[5] The depths have covered them;
They sank to the bottom like a stone.

[6] "Your right hand, O LORD, has become
glorious in power;
Your right hand, O LORD, has dashed the
enemy in pieces.
[7] And in the greatness of Your excellence
You have overthrown those who rose
against You;
You sent forth Your wrath;
It consumed them like stubble.
[8] And with the blast of Your nostrils
The waters were gathered together;
The floods stood upright like a heap;
The depths congealed in the heart of the
sea.
[9] The enemy said, 'I will pursue,
I will overtake,
I will divide the spoil;
My desire shall be satisfied on them.

I will draw my sword,
My hand shall destroy them.'
[10] You blew with Your wind,
The sea covered them;
They sank like lead in the mighty waters.

[11] "Who *is* like You, O LORD, among the gods?
Who *is* like You, glorious in holiness,
Fearful in praises, doing wonders?
[12] You stretched out Your right hand;
The earth swallowed them.
[13] You in Your mercy have led forth
The people whom You have redeemed;
You have guided *them* in Your strength
To Your holy habitation.

[14] "The people will hear *and* be afraid;
Sorrow will take hold of the inhabitants of
Philistia.
[15] Then the chiefs of Edom will be
dismayed;
The mighty men of Moab,
Trembling will take hold of them;
All the inhabitants of Canaan will melt
away.
[16] Fear and dread will fall on them;
By the greatness of Your arm
They will be *as* still as a stone,
Till Your people pass over, O LORD,
Till the people pass over
Whom You have purchased.
[17] You will bring them in and plant them
In the mountain of Your inheritance,
In the place, O LORD, *which* You have made
For Your own dwelling,
The sanctuary, O LORD, *which* Your hands
have established.

[18] "The LORD shall reign forever and ever."

The Law of Victory: The Celebration!
(Exodus 15:1–21)

Leaders know the importance of identifying, celebrating, and remembering victories. After escaping Egypt, Moses led the people of Israel in a song of celebration. The Lord drowned the Egyptian army in the Red Sea, ensuring that Israel would never again have to run from Pharaoh. Celebration is often the reward for victory.

¹⁹For the horses of Pharaoh went with his chariots and his horsemen into the sea, and the LORD brought back the waters of the sea upon them. But the children of Israel went on dry *land* in the midst of the sea.

The Song of Miriam

²⁰Then Miriam the prophetess, the sister of Aaron, took the timbrel in her hand; and all the women went out after her with timbrels and with dances. ²¹And Miriam answered them:

"Sing to the LORD,
For He has triumphed gloriously!
The horse and its rider
He has thrown into the sea!"

Bitter Waters Made Sweet

²²So Moses brought Israel from the Red Sea; then they went out into the Wilderness of Shur. And they went three days in the wilderness and found no water. ²³Now when they came to Marah, they could not drink the waters of Marah, for they *were* bitter. Therefore the name of it was called Marah.ᵃ ²⁴And the people complained against Moses, saying, "What shall we drink?" ²⁵So he cried out to the LORD, and the LORD showed him a tree. When he cast *it* into the waters, the waters were made sweet.

There He made a statute and an ordinance for them, and there He tested them, ²⁶and said, "If you diligently heed the voice of the LORD your God and do what is right in His sight, give ear to His commandments and keep all His statutes, I will put none of the diseases on you which I have brought on the Egyptians. For I *am* the LORD who heals you."

²⁷Then they came to Elim, where there *were* twelve wells of water and seventy palm trees; so they camped there by the waters.

Bread from Heaven

16 And they journeyed from Elim, and all the congregation of the children of Israel came to the Wilderness of Sin, which is between Elim and Sinai, on the fifteenth day of the second month after they departed from the land of Egypt. ²Then the whole congregation of the children of Israel complained against Moses and Aaron in the wilderness. ³And the children of Israel said to them, "Oh, that we had died by the hand of the LORD in the land of Egypt, when we sat by the pots of meat *and* when we ate bread to the full! For you have brought us out into this wilderness to kill this whole assembly with hunger."

⁴Then the LORD said to Moses, "Behold, I will rain bread from heaven for you. And the people shall go out and gather a certain quota every day, that I may test them, whether they will walk in My law or not. ⁵And it shall be on the sixth day that they shall prepare what they bring in, and it shall be twice as much as they gather daily."

⁶Then Moses and Aaron said to all the children of Israel, "At evening you shall know that the LORD has brought you out of the land of Egypt. ⁷And in the morning you shall see the glory of the LORD; for He hears your complaints against the LORD. But what *are* we, that you complain against us?" ⁸Also Moses said, "*This shall be seen* when the LORD gives you meat to eat in the evening, and in the morning bread to the full; for the LORD hears your complaints which you make against Him. And what *are* we? Your complaints *are* not against us but against the LORD."

⁹Then Moses spoke to Aaron, "Say to all the congregation of the children of Israel, 'Come near before the LORD, for He has heard your complaints.'" ¹⁰Now it came to pass, as Aaron spoke to the whole congregation of the children of Israel, that they looked toward the wilderness, and behold, the glory of the LORD appeared in the cloud.

¹¹And the LORD spoke to Moses, saying, ¹²"I have heard the complaints of the children of Israel. Speak to them, saying, 'At twilight you shall eat meat, and in the morning you shall be filled with bread. And you shall know that I *am* the LORD your God.'"

¹³So it was that quails came up at evening and covered the camp, and in the morning the dew lay all around the camp. ¹⁴And when the layer of dew lifted, there, on the surface of the wilderness, was a small round substance, *as* fine as frost on the ground. ¹⁵So when the children of Israel saw *it,* they said to one another, "What is it?" For they did not know what it *was.*

And Moses said to them, "This *is* the bread which the LORD has given you to eat. ¹⁶This is the thing which the LORD has commanded: 'Let every man gather it according to each one's need, one omer for each person, *according to the* number of persons; let every man take for *those* who *are* in his tent.'"

¹⁷Then the children of Israel did so and gathered, some more, some less. ¹⁸So when they measured *it* by omers, he who gathered much had nothing left over, and he who gathered little had no lack. Every man had gathered according to each one's need. ¹⁹And Moses said, "Let no

---

15:23 ªLiterally *Bitter*

one leave any of it till morning." [20]Notwithstanding they did not heed Moses. But some of them left part of it until morning, and it bred worms and stank. And Moses was angry with them. [21]So they gathered it every morning, every man according to his need. And when the sun became hot, it melted.

[22]And so it was, on the sixth day, *that* they gathered twice as much bread, two omers for each one. And all the rulers of the congregation came and told Moses. [23]Then he said to them, "This *is what* the LORD has said: 'Tomorrow *is* a Sabbath rest, a holy Sabbath to the LORD. Bake what you will bake *today,* and boil what you will boil; and lay up for yourselves all that remains, to be kept until morning.'" [24]So they laid it up till morning, as Moses commanded; and it did not stink, nor were there any worms in it. [25]Then Moses said, "Eat that today, for today *is* a Sabbath to the LORD; today you will not find it in the field. [26]Six days you shall gather it, but on the seventh day, the Sabbath, there will be none."

[27]Now it happened *that some* of the people went out on the seventh day to gather, but they found none. [28]And the LORD said to Moses, "How long do you refuse to keep My commandments and My laws? [29]See! For the LORD has given you the Sabbath; therefore He gives you on the sixth day bread for two days. Let every man remain in his place; let no man go out of his place on the seventh day." [30]So the people rested on the seventh day.

[31]And the house of Israel called its name Manna.[a] And it *was* like white coriander seed, and the taste of it *was* like wafers *made* with honey.

[32]Then Moses said, "This *is* the thing which the LORD has commanded: 'Fill an omer with it, to be kept for your generations, that they may see the bread with which I fed you in the wilderness, when I brought you out of the land of Egypt.'" [33]And Moses said to Aaron, "Take a pot and put an omer of manna in it, and lay it up before the LORD, to be kept for your generations." [34]As the LORD commanded Moses, so Aaron laid it up before the Testimony, to be kept. [35]And the children of Israel ate manna forty years, until they came to an inhabited land; they ate manna until they came to the border of the land of Canaan. [36]Now an omer *is* one-tenth of an ephah.

Water from the Rock

17 Then all the congregation of the children of Israel set out on their journey from the Wilderness of Sin, according to the commandment of the LORD, and camped in Rephidim; but *there was* no water

for the people to drink. [2]Therefore the people contended with Moses, and said, "Give us water, that we may drink."

So Moses said to them, "Why do you contend with me? Why do you tempt the LORD?"

[3]And the people thirsted there for water, and the people complained against Moses, and said, "Why *is* it you have brought us up out of Egypt, to kill us and our children and our livestock with thirst?"

The Rod of God

(Exodus 17:3–7)

God's people received an important lesson on authority when they learned to trust God for provision. Time and again the Lord provided what they needed, thus demonstrating His right to lead them.

Moses learned to depend on God as the ultimate authority. One of the keys to Moses' greatness is the statement: "Moses cried out to the LORD" (Ex. 17:4). Leaders earn their authority; few individuals just give it to someone. God earned the trust of His people and "earned" His authority through several means:

1. *Production:* He made a way for His people to cross the Red Sea safely.
2. *Protection:* He eliminated the Egyptian army in the Red Sea.
3. *Provision:* He provided manna and quail for the people to eat.
4. *Problem Solving:* He produced water from a rock.

---

[4]So Moses cried out to the LORD, saying, "What shall I do with this people? They are almost ready to stone me!"

[5]And the LORD said to Moses, "Go on before the people, and take with you some of the elders of Israel. Also take in your hand your rod with which you struck the river, and go. [6]Behold, I will stand before you there on the rock in Horeb; and you shall strike the rock, and water will come out of it, that the people may drink."

And Moses did so in the sight of the elders of Israel. [7]So he called the name of the place

---

16:31 [a]Literally *What?* (compare Exodus 16:15)

Massah[a] and Meribah,[b] because of the contention of the children of Israel, and because they tempted the LORD, saying, "Is the LORD among us or not?"

Victory over the Amalekites

[8]Now Amalek came and fought with Israel in Rephidim. [9]And Moses said to Joshua, "Choose us some men and go out, fight with Amalek. Tomorrow I will stand on the top of the hill with the rod of God in my hand." [10]So Joshua did as Moses said to him, and fought with Amalek. And Moses, Aaron, and Hur went up to the top of the hill. [11]And so it was, when Moses held up his hand, that Israel prevailed; and when he let down his hand, Amalek prevailed. [12]But Moses' hands *became* heavy; so they took a stone and put *it* under him, and he sat on it. And Aaron and Hur supported his hands, one on one side, and the other on the other side; and his hands were steady until the going down of the sun. [13]So Joshua defeated Amalek and his people with the edge of the sword.

The Law of the Inner Circle: Moses Needed Help

(Exodus 17:8–13)

No leader can thrive without teammates, as the life of Moses illustrates. As Joshua and his troops fought the Amalekites, Moses held God's staff in his hands, assisted by Aaron and Hur, members of his inner circle. No leader should ever take the journey—or the credit—by himself.

---

[14]Then the LORD said to Moses, "Write this *for* a memorial in the book and recount *it* in the hearing of Joshua, that I will utterly blot out the remembrance of Amalek from under heaven." [15]And Moses built an altar and called its name, The-LORD-Is-My-Banner;[a] [16]for he said, "Because the LORD has sworn: the LORD *will have* war with Amalek from generation to generation."

Jethro's Advice

18 And Jethro, the priest of Midian, Moses' father-in-law, heard of all that God had done for Moses and for Israel His people—that the LORD had brought Israel out of Egypt. [2]Then Jethro, Moses' father-

in-law, took Zipporah, Moses' wife, after he had sent her back, [3]with her two sons, of whom the name of one *was* Gershom (for he said, "I have been a stranger in a foreign land")[a] [4]and the name of the other *was* Eliezer[a] (for *he said,* "The God of my father *was* my help, and delivered me from the sword of Pharaoh"); [5]and Jethro, Moses' father-in-law, came with his sons and his wife to Moses in the wilderness, where he was encamped at the mountain of God. [6]Now he had said to Moses, "I, your father-in-law Jethro, am coming to you with your wife and her two sons with her."

[7]So Moses went out to meet his father-in-law, bowed down, and kissed him. And they asked each other about *their* well-being, and they went into the tent. [8]And Moses told his father-in-law all that the LORD had done to Pharaoh and to the Egyptians for Israel's sake, all the hardship that had come upon them on the way, and *how* the LORD had delivered them. [9]Then Jethro rejoiced for all the good which the LORD had done for Israel, whom He had delivered out of the hand of the Egyptians. [10]And Jethro said, "Blessed *be* the LORD, who has delivered you out of the hand of the Egyptians and out of the hand of Pharaoh, *and* who has delivered the people from under the hand of the Egyptians. [11]Now I know that the LORD *is* greater than all the gods; for in the very thing in which they behaved proudly, *He was* above them." [12]Then Jethro, Moses' father-in-law, took[a] a burnt offering and *other* sacrifices *to offer* to God. And Aaron came with all the elders of Israel to eat bread with Moses' father-in-law before God.

[13]And so it was, on the next day, that Moses sat to judge the people; and the people stood before Moses from morning until evening. [14]So when Moses' father-in-law saw all that he did for the people, he said, "What *is* this thing that you are doing for the people? Why do you alone sit, and all the people stand before you from morning until evening?"

[15]And Moses said to his father-in-law, "Because the people come to me to inquire of God. [16]When they have a difficulty, they come to me, and I judge between one and another; and I make known the statutes of God and His laws."

[17]So Moses' father-in-law said to him, "The thing that you do *is* not good. [18]Both you and

---

17:7 [a]Literally *Tempted* [b]Literally *Contention*
17:15 [a]Hebrew *YHWH Nissi* **18:3** [a]Compare
Exodus 2:22 **18:4** [a]Literally *My God Is Help*
18:12 [a]Following Masoretic Text and Septuagint;
Syriac, Targum, and Vulgate read *offered.*

JETHRO AND THE LAW OF INTUITION

Leaders Evaluate Everything with a Leadership Bias
(Exodus 18:1–24)

Leadership intuition often separates the greatest leaders from the merely good ones. Some people are born with great leadership intuition; others have to work hard to develop and hone it. But however it evolves, the result is a combination of natural ability and learned skills. This informed intuition makes crucial issues jump out at the leader, enabling him or her to get a handle on intangible factors, understand them, and work with them to accomplish leadership goals.

Successful leaders see every situation in terms of available resources: money, raw materials, technology, and, most important, people. Intuitive leaders can sense what's happening among their people and almost instantly know their hopes, fears, and concerns. Leaders also have the ability to step back from what's happening and see not only where they and their people have gone, but also where they are headed—as if they can smell change in the wind.

■   ■   ■

Everyone has some kind of intuition, especially in his or her area of natural giftedness. If your gift is mercy, then you can sense when someone needs comfort, and you know how to give it. If service is your gift, you instinctively know when and how to help those in need. And if you are naturally gifted at leadership, then you see everything with a leadership bias.

Moses was a good leader, not a natural one. When he met with Jethro, he hadn't led Israel for long (the Hebrew nation had just left Egypt). But over those long years in the desert, Moses' leadership improved—and so did his intuition.

Jethro, on the other hand, appears to be a natural. How do we know that? Because he looked at a situation unlike anything he had ever seen—leading more than a *million* disgruntled, displaced ex-slaves—and knew exactly how to handle it. That's intuition in action. Who he *was* determined what he *saw*. Jethro, the leader, saw everything with a leadership bias.

Of all the laws of leadership, the Law of Intuition is the most difficult to teach. Reading provides the best analogy for understanding intuition. Intuitive leaders "read" their people.

Jethro, the Reading Leader
Let's consider how Jethro handled Moses' situation. Like all intuitive leaders, Jethro read:

1. Situations
An intuitive leader can quickly size up a situation. Jethro watched Moses in action for a day and immediately reacted. Jethro didn't have to hire a consultant, form a

committee, or do extensive research. He instantly saw a leadership problem. All leaders may not settle on a solution as quickly as Jethro did, but when they rely on their intuition, they rapidly sense that a situation needs their attention.

2. Trends

An intuitive leader sees what's happening in the present and understands where an organization is headed. Jethro could see Moses heading for trouble. He told his son-in-law, "Both you and these people who are with you will surely wear yourselves out. For this thing is too much for you; you are not able to perform it by yourself" (Ex. 18:18).

Maybe Moses settled disputes effectively; maybe not. But even if he were able to get by with doing everything, he could never sustain it. As the population grew, his situation would worsen. Jethro knew that disaster lay ahead if Moses didn't change.

3. Resources

Intuitive leaders know how to resource their vision. They don't take anything for granted, and they maximize whatever is at hand to achieve their goals. Jethro identified Israel's greatest assets: Moses' heart, God's favor, and the people. He directed Moses to seek God's counsel, to teach the people God's laws, and to empower the people to share the burden. Jethro's plan utilized everything of value the people possessed.

4. People

Skill with people is perhaps the greatest ability of an intuitive leader. Some can understand what it takes to lead; others can actually do it. Jethro understood people and leadership well enough to know how to empower Moses' leadership, even though he had no personal experience with those who had just escaped Egypt. Jethro knew leadership had to be based on ability, not position, and he instinctively understood that the right people were present to lead thousands, hundreds, fifties, and tens. They just had to be put into place.

5. Himself

An intuitive leader reads himself. He understands his strengths, his weaknesses, and his individual calling. Jethro not only read and understood Moses' leadership problem; he realized he was not the man for the job. So he read and evaluated Moses' leadership ability and planned accordingly.

Look at any leader with sharp intuition, and you will see an ability to read a leadership situation. When Nehemiah looked at the wall in Jerusalem, he knew what to do. When Joseph understood Pharaoh's dream, he knew how to prepare for the famine. Intuition, whether natural or developed intentionally, helps a *good* leader to become a *great* leader.

The Law of Reproduction:
The Day Moses Became a Leader

(Exodus 18:19–26)

Something revolutionary happened after Jethro confronted Moses over his leadership methods: Moses moved from merely ministering, to leading. Instead of doing all the judging himself, he released other leaders to join him and lead according to their gifts.

At this point the government of Israel grew exponentially. How? Moses had reproduced himself. In order to do so, he had to change both his way of thinking and his way of working. Moses made seven changes to become a leader:

1. He became a man of prayer (v. 19).
2. He committed himself to communication (v. 20).
3. He laid out the vision (v. 20).
4. He developed a plan (v. 20).
5. He selected and trained the leaders (v. 21).
6. He released them to do the work (v. 22).
7. He did only what they could not do (v. 22).

What happened when Moses changed? God supplied strength for Moses and peace for the people (Ex. 18:23).

these people who *are* with you will surely wear yourselves out. For this thing *is* too much for you; you are not able to perform it by yourself. ¹⁹Listen now to my voice; I will give you counsel, and God will be with you: Stand before God for the people, so that you may bring the difficulties to God. ²⁰And you shall teach them the statutes and the laws, and show them the way in which they must walk and the work they must do. ²¹Moreover you shall select from all the people able men, such as fear God, men of truth, hating covetousness; and place *such* over them *to be* rulers of thousands, rulers of hundreds, rulers of fifties, and rulers of tens. ²²And let them judge the people at all times. Then it will be *that* every great matter they shall bring to you, but every small matter they themselves shall judge. So it will be easier for you, for they will bear *the burden* with you. ²³If you do this thing, and God *so* commands you, then you will be able to endure, and all this people will also go to their place in peace."

²⁴So Moses heeded the voice of his father-in-law and did all that he had said. ²⁵And Moses chose able men out of all Israel, and made them heads over the people: rulers of thousands, rulers of hundreds, rulers of fifties, and rulers of tens. ²⁶So they judged the people at all times; the hard cases they brought to Moses, but they judged every small case themselves.

²⁷Then Moses let his father-in-law depart, and he went his way to his own land.

Israel at Mount Sinai

19 In the third month after the children of Israel had gone out of the land of Egypt, on the same day, they came *to* the Wilderness of Sinai. ²For they had departed from Rephidim, had come *to* the Wilderness of Sinai, and camped in the wilderness. So Israel camped there before the mountain.

³And Moses went up to God, and the LORD called to him from the mountain, saying, "Thus you shall say to the house of Jacob, and tell the children of Israel: ⁴'You have seen what I did to the Egyptians, and *how* I bore you on eagles' wings and brought you to Myself. ⁵Now therefore, if you will indeed obey My voice and keep My covenant, then you shall be a special treasure to Me above all people; for all the earth *is* Mine. ⁶And you shall be to Me a kingdom of priests and a holy nation.' These *are* the words which you shall speak to the children of Israel."

⁷So Moses came and called for the elders of the people, and laid before them all these words which the LORD commanded him. ⁸Then all the people answered together and said, "All that the LORD has spoken we will do." So Moses brought back the words of the people to the LORD. ⁹And the LORD said to Moses, "Behold, I come to you

The Law of Connection: God's Covenant, God's Rules

(Exodus 19:3–13)

Have you ever noticed how God introduced the Ten Commandments? Before He spoke His laws to the people in Exodus 20, He took time to remind them of three vital truths:

1. The love He had for them
2. The victories He'd won for them
3. The future He planned for them

God spoke about how He intended to bless Israel as His children, and He warned them of the boundaries to keep—how to survive His fiery presence on Mount Sinai. Only then did He give them His commandments to obey. Do you see the genius of the sequence?

Leaders touch a heart before they ask for a hand. Before God demanded His people keep His rules, He reminded them of His relationship and blessings. That gave them all the incentive they needed to follow through on their commitment!

in the thick cloud, that the people may hear when I speak with you, and believe you forever."

So Moses told the words of the people to the LORD.

¹⁰Then the LORD said to Moses, "Go to the people and consecrate them today and tomorrow, and let them wash their clothes. ¹¹And let them be ready for the third day. For on the third day the LORD will come down upon Mount Sinai in the sight of all the people. ¹²You shall set bounds for the people all around, saying, 'Take heed to yourselves *that* you do *not* go up to the mountain or touch its base. Whoever touches the mountain shall surely be put to death. ¹³Not a hand shall touch him, but he shall surely be stoned or shot *with an arrow;* whether man or beast, he shall not live.' When the trumpet sounds long, they shall come near the mountain."

¹⁴So Moses went down from the mountain to the people and sanctified the people, and they washed their clothes. ¹⁵And he said to the people, "Be ready for the third day; do not come near *your* wives."

¹⁶Then it came to pass on the third day, in the morning, that there were thunderings and lightnings, and a thick cloud on the mountain; and the sound of the trumpet was very loud, so that all the people who *were* in the camp trembled. ¹⁷And Moses brought the people out of the camp to meet with God, and they stood at the foot of the mountain. ¹⁸Now Mount Sinai *was* completely in smoke, because the LORD descended upon it in fire. Its smoke ascended like the smoke of a furnace, and the whole mountainᵃ quaked greatly. ¹⁹And when the blast of the trumpet sounded long and became louder and louder, Moses spoke, and God answered him by voice. ²⁰Then the LORD came down upon Mount Sinai, on the top of the mountain. And the LORD called Moses to the top of the mountain, and Moses went up.

²¹And the LORD said to Moses, "Go down and warn the people, lest they break through to gaze at the LORD, and many of them perish. ²²Also let the priests who come near the LORD consecrate themselves, lest the LORD break out against them."

²³But Moses said to the LORD, "The people cannot come up to Mount Sinai; for You warned us, saying, 'Set bounds around the mountain and consecrate it.'"

²⁴Then the LORD said to him, "Away! Get down and then come up, you and Aaron with you. But do not let the priests and the people break through to come up to the LORD, lest He break out against them." ²⁵So Moses went down to the people and spoke to them.

The Ten Commandments

20 And God spoke all these words, saying:

² "I *am* the LORD your God, who brought you out of the land of Egypt, out of the house of bondage.

³ "You shall have no other gods before Me.

⁴ "You shall not make for yourself a carved image—any likeness *of anything* that *is* in heaven above, or that *is* in the earth beneath, or that *is* in the water under the earth; ⁵you shall not bow down to them nor serve them. For I, the LORD your God, *am* a jealous God, visiting the iniquity of the fathers upon the children to the third and fourth *generations* of those who hate Me, ⁶but showing mercy to thousands, to those who love Me and keep My commandments.

19:18 ᵃSeptuagint reads *all the people.*

7 "You shall not take the name of the LORD your God in vain, for the LORD will not hold *him* guiltless who takes His name in vain.

8 "Remember the Sabbath day, to keep it holy. 9Six days you shall labor and do all your work, 10but the seventh day *is* the Sabbath of the LORD your God. *In it* you shall do no work: you, nor your son, nor your daughter, nor your male servant, nor your female servant, nor your cattle, nor your stranger who *is* within your gates. 11For *in* six days the LORD made the heavens and the earth, the sea, and all that *is* in them, and rested the seventh day. Therefore the LORD blessed the Sabbath day and hallowed it.

12 "Honor your father and your mother, that your days may be long upon the land which the LORD your God is giving you.

13 "You shall not murder.

14 "You shall not commit adultery.

15 "You shall not steal.

16 "You shall not bear false witness against your neighbor.

17 "You shall not covet your neighbor's house; you shall not covet your neighbor's wife, nor his male servant, nor his female servant, nor his ox, nor his donkey, nor anything that *is* your neighbor's."

The People Afraid of God's Presence

18Now all the people witnessed the thunderings, the lightning flashes, the sound of the trumpet, and the mountain smoking; and when the people saw *it,* they trembled and stood afar off. 19Then they said to Moses, "You speak with us, and we will hear; but let not God speak with us, lest we die."

20And Moses said to the people, "Do not fear; for God has come to test you, and that His fear may be before you, so that you may not sin." 21So the people stood afar off, but Moses drew near the thick darkness where God *was.*

The Law of the Altar

22Then the LORD said to Moses, "Thus you shall say to the children of Israel: 'You have seen that I have talked with you from heaven. 23You shall not make *anything to be* with Me—gods of silver or gods of gold you shall not make for yourselves. 24An altar of earth you shall make for Me, and you shall sacrifice on it your burnt offerings and your peace offerings, your sheep and your oxen. In every place where I record My name I will come to you, and I will bless you. 25And if you make Me an altar of stone, you shall not build it of hewn stone; for if you use your tool on it, you have profaned it. 26Nor shall you go up by steps to My altar, that your nakedness may not be exposed on it.'

The Law Concerning Servants

21 "Now these *are* the judgments which you shall set before them: 2If you buy a Hebrew servant, he shall serve six years; and in the seventh he shall go out free and pay nothing. 3If he comes in by himself, he shall go out by himself; if he *comes in* married, then his wife shall go out with him. 4If his master has given him a wife, and she has borne him sons or daughters, the wife and her children shall be her master's, and he shall go out by himself. 5But if the servant plainly says, 'I love my master, my wife, and my children; I will not go out free,' 6then his master shall bring him to the judges. He shall also bring him to the door, or to the doorpost, and his master shall pierce his ear with an awl; and he shall serve him forever.

7"And if a man sells his daughter to be a female slave, she shall not go out as the male slaves do. 8If she does not please her master, who has betrothed her to himself, then he shall let her be redeemed. He shall have no right to sell her to a foreign people, since he has dealt deceitfully with her. 9And if he has betrothed her to his son, he shall deal with her according to the custom of daughters. 10If he takes another *wife,* he shall not diminish her food, her clothing, and her marriage rights. 11And if he does not do these three for her, then she shall go out free, without *paying* money.

The Law Concerning Violence

12"He who strikes a man so that he dies shall surely be put to death. 13However, if he did not lie in wait, but God delivered *him* into his hand, then I will appoint for you a place where he may flee.

14"But if a man acts with premeditation against his neighbor, to kill him by treachery, you shall take him from My altar, that he may die.

15"And he who strikes his father or his mother shall surely be put to death.

16"He who kidnaps a man and sells him, or if he is found in his hand, shall surely be put to death.

17"And he who curses his father or his mother shall surely be put to death.

18"If men contend with each other, and one strikes the other with a stone or with *his* fist, and he does not die but is confined to *his* bed, 19if he rises again and walks about outside with his staff, then he who struck *him* shall be acquitted. He shall only pay *for* the loss of his time, and shall provide *for him* to be thoroughly healed.

20"And if a man beats his male or female servant with a rod, so that he dies under his hand, he shall surely be punished. 21Notwithstanding, if he remains alive a day or two, he shall not be punished; for he *is* his property.

22"If men fight, and hurt a woman with child, so that she gives birth prematurely, yet no harm follows, he shall surely be punished accordingly as the woman's husband imposes on him; and he shall pay as the judges *determine*. 23But if *any* harm follows, then you shall give life for life, 24eye for eye, tooth for tooth, hand for hand, foot for foot, 25burn for burn, wound for wound, stripe for stripe.

26"If a man strikes the eye of his male or female servant, and destroys it, he shall let him go free for the sake of his eye. 27And if he knocks out the tooth of his male or female servant, he shall let him go free for the sake of his tooth.

Animal Control Laws

28"If an ox gores a man or a woman to death, then the ox shall surely be stoned, and its flesh shall not be eaten; but the owner of the ox *shall be* acquitted. 29But if the ox tended to thrust with its horn in times past, and it has been made known to his owner, and he has not kept it confined, so that it has killed a man or a woman, the ox shall be stoned and its owner also shall be put to death. 30If there is imposed on him a sum of money, then he shall pay to redeem his life, whatever is imposed on him. 31Whether it has gored a son or gored a daughter, according to this judgment it shall be done to him. 32If the ox gores a male or female servant, he shall give to their master thirty shekels of silver, and the ox shall be stoned.

33"And if a man opens a pit, or if a man digs a pit and does not cover it, and an ox or a donkey falls in it, 34the owner of the pit shall make *it* good; he shall give money to their owner, but the dead *animal* shall be his.

35"If one man's ox hurts another's, so that it dies, then they shall sell the live ox and divide the money from it; and the dead *ox* they shall also divide. 36Or if it was known that the ox tended to thrust in time past, and its owner has not kept it confined, he shall surely pay ox for ox, and the dead animal shall be his own.

Responsibility for Property

22 "If a man steals an ox or a sheep, and slaughters it or sells it, he shall restore five oxen for an ox and four sheep for a sheep. 2If the thief is found breaking in, and he is struck so that he dies, *there shall be* no guilt for his bloodshed. 3If the sun has risen on him, *there shall be* guilt for his bloodshed. He should make full restitution; if he has nothing, then he shall be sold for his theft. 4If the theft is certainly found alive in his hand, whether it is an ox or donkey or sheep, he shall restore double.

5"If a man causes a field or vineyard to be grazed, and lets loose his animal, and it feeds in another man's field, he shall make restitution from the best of his own field and the best of his own vineyard.

6"If fire breaks out and catches in thorns, so that stacked grain, standing grain, or the field is consumed, he who kindled the fire shall surely make restitution.

7"If a man delivers to his neighbor money or articles to keep, and it is stolen out of the man's house, if the thief is found, he shall pay double. 8If the thief is not found, then the master of the house shall be brought to the judges *to see* whether he has put his hand into his neighbor's goods.

9"For any kind of trespass, *whether it concerns* an ox, a donkey, a sheep, or clothing, *or* for any kind of lost thing which *another* claims to be his, the cause of both parties shall come before the judges; *and* whomever the judges condemn shall pay double to his neighbor. 10If a man delivers to his neighbor a donkey, an ox, a sheep, or any animal to keep, and it dies, is hurt, or driven away, no one seeing it, 11then an oath of the LORD shall be between them both, that he has not put his hand into his neighbor's goods; and the owner of it shall accept *that,* and he shall not make *it* good. 12But if, in fact, it is stolen from him, he shall make restitution to the owner of it. 13If it is torn to pieces *by a beast, then* he shall bring it as evidence, *and* he shall not make good what was torn.

14"And if a man borrows *anything* from his neighbor, and it becomes injured or dies, the owner of it not *being* with it, he shall surely make *it* good. 15If its owner *was* with it, he shall not make *it* good; if it *was* hired, it came for its hire.

Moral and Ceremonial Principles

16"If a man entices a virgin who is not betrothed, and lies with her, he shall surely pay the bride-price for her *to be* his wife. 17If her father utterly refuses to give her to him, he shall pay money according to the bride-price of virgins.

¹⁸"You shall not permit a sorceress to live.
¹⁹"Whoever lies with an animal shall surely be put to death.
²⁰"He who sacrifices to *any* god, except to the LORD only, he shall be utterly destroyed.
²¹"You shall neither mistreat a stranger nor oppress him, for you were strangers in the land of Egypt.
²²"You shall not afflict any widow or fatherless child. ²³If you afflict them in any way, *and* they cry at all to Me, I will surely hear their cry; ²⁴and My wrath will become hot, and I will kill you with the sword; your wives shall be widows, and your children fatherless.
²⁵"If you lend money to *any of* My people *who are* poor among you, you shall not be like a moneylender to him; you shall not charge him interest. ²⁶If you ever take your neighbor's garment as a pledge, you shall return it to him before the sun goes down. ²⁷For that *is* his only covering, it *is* his garment for his skin. What will he sleep in? And it will be that when he cries to Me, I will hear, for I *am* gracious.
²⁸"You shall not revile God, nor curse a ruler of your people.
²⁹"You shall not delay *to offer* the first of your ripe produce and your juices. The firstborn of your sons you shall give to Me. ³⁰Likewise you shall do with your oxen *and* your sheep. It shall be with its mother seven days; on the eighth day you shall give it to Me.
³¹"And you shall be holy men to Me: you shall not eat meat torn *by beasts* in the field; you shall throw it to the dogs.

Justice for All

23 "You shall not circulate a false report. Do not put your hand with the wicked to be an unrighteous witness. ²You shall not follow a crowd to do evil; nor shall you testify in a dispute so as to turn aside after many to pervert *justice*. ³You shall not show partiality to a poor man in his dispute.
⁴"If you meet your enemy's ox or his donkey going astray, you shall surely bring it back to him again. ⁵If you see the donkey of one who hates you lying under its burden, and you would refrain from helping it, you shall surely help him with it.
⁶"You shall not pervert the judgment of your poor in his dispute. ⁷Keep yourself far from a false matter; do not kill the innocent and righteous. For I will not justify the wicked. ⁸And you shall take no bribe, for a bribe blinds the discerning and perverts the words of the righteous.
⁹"Also you shall not oppress a stranger, for you know the heart of a stranger, because you were strangers in the land of Egypt.

The Law of Sabbaths

¹⁰"Six years you shall sow your land and gather in its produce, ¹¹but the seventh *year* you shall let it rest and lie fallow, that the poor of your people may eat; and what they leave, the beasts of the field may eat. In like manner you shall do with your vineyard *and* your olive grove. ¹²Six days you shall do your work, and on the seventh day you shall rest, that your ox and your donkey may rest, and the son of your female servant and the stranger may be refreshed.
¹³"And in all that I have said to you, be circumspect and make no mention of the name of other gods, nor let it be heard from your mouth.

Three Annual Feasts

¹⁴"Three times you shall keep a feast to Me in the year: ¹⁵You shall keep the Feast of Unleavened Bread (you shall eat unleavened bread seven days, as I commanded you, at the time appointed in the month of Abib, for in it you came out of Egypt; none shall appear before Me empty); ¹⁶and the Feast of Harvest, the firstfruits of your labors which you have sown in the field; and the Feast of Ingathering at the end of the year, when you have gathered in *the fruit of* your labors from the field.
¹⁷"Three times in the year all your males shall appear before the Lord GOD.ᵃ
¹⁸"You shall not offer the blood of My sacrifice with leavened bread; nor shall the fat of My sacrifice remain until morning. ¹⁹The first of the firstfruits of your land you shall bring into the house of the LORD your God. You shall not boil a young goat in its mother's milk.

The Angel and the Promises

²⁰"Behold, I send an Angel before you to keep you in the way and to bring you into the place which I have prepared. ²¹Beware of Him and obey His voice; do not provoke Him, for He will not pardon your transgressions; for My name *is* in Him. ²²But if you indeed obey His voice and do all that I speak, then I will be an enemy to your enemies and an adversary to your adversaries. ²³For My Angel will go before you and bring you in to the Amorites and the Hittites and the Perizzites and the Canaanites and the Hivites and the Jebusites; and I will cut them off. ²⁴You shall not bow down to their gods, nor serve them, nor do according to their works; but

---

23:17 ᵃHebrew *YHWH*, usually translated LORD

you shall utterly overthrow them and completely break down their *sacred* pillars.

[25]"So you shall serve the LORD your God, and He will bless your bread and your water. And I will take sickness away from the midst of you. [26]No one shall suffer miscarriage or be barren in your land; I will fulfill the number of your days.

[27]"I will send My fear before you, I will cause confusion among all the people to whom you come, and will make all your enemies turn *their* backs to you. [28]And I will send hornets before you, which shall drive out the Hivite, the Canaanite, and the Hittite from before you. [29]I will not drive them out from before you in one year, lest the land become desolate and the beasts of the field become too numerous for you. [30]Little by little I will drive them out from before you, until you have increased, and you inherit the land. [31]And I will set your bounds from the Red Sea to the sea, Philistia, and from the desert to the River.[a] For I will deliver the inhabitants of the land into your hand, and you shall drive them out before you. [32]You shall make no covenant with them, nor with their gods. [33]They shall not dwell in your land, lest they make you sin against Me. For *if* you serve their gods, it will surely be a snare to you."

Israel Affirms the Covenant

24 Now He said to Moses, "Come up to the LORD, you and Aaron, Nadab and Abihu, and seventy of the elders of Israel, and worship from afar. [2]And Moses alone shall come near the LORD, but they shall not come near; nor shall the people go up with him."

[3]So Moses came and told the people all the words of the LORD and all the judgments. And all the people answered with one voice and said, "All the words which the LORD has said we will do." [4]And Moses wrote all the words of the LORD. And he rose early in the morning, and built an altar at the foot of the mountain, and twelve pillars according to the twelve tribes of Israel. [5]Then he sent young men of the children of Israel, who offered burnt offerings and sacrificed peace offerings of oxen to the LORD. [6]And Moses took half the blood and put *it* in basins, and half the blood he sprinkled on the altar. [7]Then he took the Book of the Covenant and read in the hearing of the people. And they said, "All that the LORD has said we will do, and be obedient." [8]And Moses took the blood, sprinkled *it* on the people, and said, "This is the blood of the covenant which the LORD has made with you according to all these words."

On the Mountain with God

[9]Then Moses went up, also Aaron, Nadab, and Abihu, and seventy of the elders of Israel, [10]and they saw the God of Israel. And *there was* under His feet as it were a paved work of sapphire stone, and it was like the very heavens in *its* clarity. [11]But on the nobles of the children of Israel He did not lay His hand. So they saw God, and they ate and drank.

[12]Then the LORD said to Moses, "Come up to Me on the mountain and be there; and I will give you tablets of stone, and the law and commandments which I have written, that you may teach them."

[13]So Moses arose with his assistant Joshua, and Moses went up to the mountain of God. [14]And he said to the elders, "Wait here for us until we come back to you. Indeed, Aaron and Hur *are* with you. If any man has a difficulty, let him go to them." [15]Then Moses went up into the mountain, and a cloud covered the mountain.

[16]Now the glory of the LORD rested on Mount Sinai, and the cloud covered it six days. And on the seventh day He called to Moses out of the midst of the cloud. [17]The sight of the glory of the LORD *was* like a consuming fire on the top of the mountain in the eyes of the children of Israel. [18]So Moses went into the midst of the cloud and went up into the mountain. And Moses was on the mountain forty days and forty nights.

Offerings for the Sanctuary

25 Then the LORD spoke to Moses, saying: [2]"Speak to the children of Israel, that they bring Me an offering. From everyone who gives it willingly with his heart you shall take My offering. [3]And this *is* the offering which you shall take from them: gold, silver, and bronze; [4]blue, purple, and scarlet *thread,* fine linen, and goats' *hair;* [5]ram skins dyed red, badger skins, and acacia wood; [6]oil for the light, and spices for the anointing oil and for the sweet incense; [7]onyx stones, and stones to be set in the ephod and in the breastplate. [8]And let them make Me a sanctuary, that I may dwell among them. [9]According to all that I show you, *that is,* the pattern of the tabernacle and the pattern of all its furnishings, just so you shall make *it.*

The Ark of the Testimony

[10]"And they shall make an ark of acacia wood; two and a half cubits *shall be* its length, a cubit and a half its width, and a cubit and a half

---

23:31 [a]Hebrew *Nahar,* the Euphrates

The Law of Buy-In: Leading Change

(Exodus 24:1–7)

It was a watershed day for everyone—a whole new life had begun! The Israelites got off to a fresh start when they affirmed the covenant God had offered them.

To make it work, however, they discovered they would have to change their lifestyles and shift their paradigms—and that would take shrewd leadership. Sometimes (as in the desert) the majority even wanted to return to Egypt!

Peter Drucker helps us to learn from Moses about how to lead people into change, even in the wilderness:

Lessons from the Wilderness

1. *Magnify the plagues.*

   To make Pharaoh release God's people, Moses called down the plagues, and he didn't stop until the old system gave way. At this stage, problems are your friend. Don't solve them; they convince people that they need to let go of the old way.

2. *Mark the ending.*

   What a symbolic and memorable "boundary event" Moses had in the crossing of the Red Sea! After his people walked through the waters on dry land, there was no turning back.

3. *Deal with the "murmuring."*

   Don't be surprised when some lose confidence in your leadership somewhere between where they came from and where they're going. Moses heard things like, *Does our leader know the way? We've never done it this way before! What was so bad about Egypt?* In times of transition, look for opportunities to show concern for how your people feel; interact with the strugglers.

4. *Give people access to decision makers.*

   Thanks to Jethro, Moses appointed a new cadre of leaders to narrow the gap between the people and the decision makers. As a result, the people felt more connected.

5. *Capitalize on the creative opportunity of the wilderness.*

   It was in the wilderness, not the Promised Land, that a big innovation took place: God handed down the Ten Commandments. Some of your biggest breakthroughs will also take place in the wilderness.

6. *Resist the urge to rush ahead.*

   It often seems that little happens in the wilderness, but great transformation takes place there. Don't jeopardize it by hurrying ahead or removing the pain of giving birth to a new vision. Let God do His work.

7. *Understand that "wilderness leadership" is special.*

   Moses did not enter the Promised Land. His kind of leadership fit the transition time, where things seemed confusing and fluid. The nation needed Joshua to enter Canaan, because he led the military, and because a settled life required new skills. Movements and organizations don't always need a new leader, but they do require a new style of leadership once the transition is complete.

its height. ¹¹And you shall overlay it with pure gold, inside and out you shall overlay it, and shall make on it a molding of gold all around. ¹²You shall cast four rings of gold for it, and put *them* in its four corners; two rings *shall be* on one side, and two rings on the other side. ¹³And you shall make poles *of* acacia wood, and overlay them with gold. ¹⁴You shall put the poles into the rings on the sides of the ark, that the ark may be carried by them. ¹⁵The poles shall be in the rings of the ark; they shall not be taken from it. ¹⁶And you shall put into the ark the Testimony which I will give you.

¹⁷"You shall make a mercy seat of pure gold; two and a half cubits *shall be* its length and a cubit and a half its width. ¹⁸And you shall make

two cherubim of gold; of hammered work you shall make them at the two ends of the mercy seat. [19]Make one cherub at one end, and the other cherub at the other end; you shall make the cherubim at the two ends of it *of one piece* with the mercy seat. [20]And the cherubim shall stretch out *their* wings above, covering the mercy seat with their wings, and they shall face one another; the faces of the cherubim *shall be* toward the mercy seat. [21]You shall put the mercy seat on top of the ark, and in the ark you shall put the Testimony that I will give you. [22]And there I will meet with you, and I will speak with you from above the mercy seat, from between the two cherubim which *are* on the ark of the Testimony, about everything which I will give you in commandment to the children of Israel.

The Table for the Showbread

[23]"You shall also make a table of acacia wood; two cubits *shall be* its length, a cubit its width, and a cubit and a half its height. [24]And you shall overlay it with pure gold, and make a molding of gold all around. [25]You shall make for it a frame of a handbreadth all around, and you shall make a gold molding for the frame all around. [26]And you shall make for it four rings of gold, and put the rings on the four corners that *are* at its four legs. [27]The rings shall be close to the frame, as holders for the poles to bear the table. [28]And you shall make the poles of acacia wood, and overlay them with gold, that the table may be carried with them. [29]You shall make its dishes, its pans, its pitchers, and its bowls for pouring. You shall make them of pure gold. [30]And you shall set the showbread on the table before Me always.

The Gold Lampstand

[31]"You shall also make a lampstand of pure gold; the lampstand shall be of hammered work. Its shaft, its branches, its bowls, its *ornamental* knobs, and flowers shall be *of one piece.* [32]And six branches shall come out of its sides: three branches of the lampstand out of one side, and three branches of the lampstand out of the other side. [33]Three bowls *shall be* made like almond *blossoms* on one branch, *with* an *ornamental* knob and a flower, and three bowls made like almond *blossoms* on the other branch, *with* an *ornamental* knob and a flower—and so for the six branches that come out of the lampstand. [34]On the lampstand itself four bowls *shall be* made like almond *blossoms, each with* its *ornamental* knob and flower. [35]And *there shall be* a knob under the *first* two branches of the same, a knob under the *second* two branches of the same, and a knob

under the *third* two branches of the same, according to the six branches that extend from the lampstand. [36]Their knobs and their branches *shall be of one piece;* all of it *shall be* one hammered piece of pure gold. [37]You shall make seven lamps for it, and they shall arrange its lamps so that they give light in front of it. [38]And its wick-trimmers and their trays *shall be* of pure gold. [39]It shall be made of a talent of pure gold, with all these utensils. [40]And see to it that you make *them* according to the pattern which was shown you on the mountain.

The Tabernacle

26 "Moreover you shall make the tabernacle *with* ten curtains *of* fine woven linen and blue, purple, and scarlet *thread;* with artistic designs of cherubim you shall weave them. [2]The length of each curtain *shall be* twenty-eight cubits, and the width of each curtain four cubits. And every one of the curtains shall have the same measurements. [3]Five curtains shall be coupled to one another, and *the other* five curtains *shall be* coupled to one another. [4]And you shall make loops of blue *yarn* on the edge of the curtain on the selvedge of *one* set, and likewise you shall do on the outer edge of *the other* curtain of the second set. [5]Fifty loops you shall make in the one curtain, and fifty loops you shall make on the edge of the curtain that *is* on the end of the second set, that the loops may be clasped to one another. [6]And you shall make fifty clasps of gold, and couple the curtains together with the clasps, so that it may be one tabernacle. [7]"You shall also make curtains of goats' *hair,* to be a tent over the tabernacle. You shall make eleven curtains. [8]The length of each curtain *shall be* thirty cubits, and the width of each curtain four cubits; and the eleven curtains shall all have the same measurements. [9]And you shall couple five curtains by themselves and six curtains by themselves, and you shall double over the sixth curtain at the forefront of the tent. [10]You shall make fifty loops on the edge of the curtain that is outermost in *one* set, and fifty loops on the edge of the curtain of the second set. [11]And you shall make fifty bronze clasps, put the clasps into the loops, and couple the tent together, that it may be one. [12]The remnant that remains of the curtains of the tent, the half curtain that remains, shall hang over the back of the tabernacle. [13]And a cubit on one side and a cubit on the other side, of what remains of the length of the curtains of the tent, shall hang over the sides of the tabernacle, on this side and on that side, to cover it. [14]"You shall also make a covering of ram skins

dyed red for the tent, and a covering of badger skins above that.

¹⁵"And for the tabernacle you shall make the boards of acacia wood, standing upright. ¹⁶Ten cubits *shall be* the length of a board, and a cubit and a half *shall be* the width of each board. ¹⁷Two tenons *shall be* in each board for binding one to another. Thus you shall make for all the boards of the tabernacle. ¹⁸And you shall make the boards for the tabernacle, twenty boards for the south side. ¹⁹You shall make forty sockets of silver under the twenty boards: two sockets under each of the boards for its two tenons. ²⁰And for the second side of the tabernacle, the north side, *there shall be* twenty boards ²¹and their forty sockets of silver: two sockets under each of the boards. ²²For the far side of the tabernacle, westward, you shall make six boards. ²³And you shall also make two boards for the two back corners of the tabernacle. ²⁴They shall be coupled together at the bottom and they shall be coupled together at the top by one ring. Thus it shall be for both of them. They shall be for the two corners. ²⁵So there shall be eight boards with their sockets of silver—sixteen sockets—two sockets under each of the boards.

²⁶"And you shall make bars of acacia wood: five for the boards on one side of the tabernacle, ²⁷five bars for the boards on the other side of the tabernacle, and five bars for the boards of the side of the tabernacle, for the far side westward. ²⁸The middle bar shall pass through the midst of the boards from end to end. ²⁹You shall overlay the boards with gold, make their rings of gold *as* holders for the bars, and overlay the bars with gold. ³⁰And you shall raise up the tabernacle according to its pattern which you were shown on the mountain.

³¹"You shall make a veil woven of blue, purple, and scarlet *thread,* and fine woven linen. It shall be woven with an artistic design of cherubim. ³²You shall hang it upon the four pillars of acacia *wood* overlaid with gold. Their hooks *shall be* gold, upon four sockets of silver. ³³And you shall hang the veil from the clasps. Then you shall bring the ark of the Testimony in there, behind the veil. The veil shall be a divider for you between the holy *place* and the Most Holy. ³⁴You shall put the mercy seat upon the ark of the Testimony in the Most Holy. ³⁵You shall set the table outside the veil, and the lampstand across from the table on the side of the tabernacle toward the south; and you shall put the table on the north side.

³⁶"You shall make a screen for the door of the tabernacle, *woven of* blue, purple, and scarlet *thread,* and fine woven linen, made by a weaver. ³⁷And you shall make for the screen five pillars of acacia *wood,* and overlay them with gold; their hooks *shall be* gold, and you shall cast five sockets of bronze for them.

The Altar of Burnt Offering

27 "You shall make an altar of acacia wood, five cubits long and five cubits wide—the altar shall be square—and its height *shall be* three cubits. ²You shall make its horns on its four corners; its horns shall be of one piece with it. And you shall overlay it with bronze. ³Also you shall make its pans to receive its ashes, and its shovels and its basins and its forks and its firepans; you shall make all its utensils of bronze. ⁴You shall make a grate for it, a network of bronze; and on the network you shall make four bronze rings at its four corners. ⁵You shall put it under the rim of the altar beneath, that the network may be midway up the altar. ⁶And you shall make poles for the altar, poles of acacia wood, and overlay them with bronze. ⁷The poles shall be put in the rings, and the poles shall be on the two sides of the altar to bear it. ⁸You shall make it hollow with boards; as it was shown you on the mountain, so shall they make *it.*

The Court of the Tabernacle

⁹"You shall also make the court of the tabernacle. For the south side *there shall be* hangings for the court *made of* fine woven linen, one hundred cubits long for one side. ¹⁰And its twenty pillars and their twenty sockets *shall be* bronze. The hooks of the pillars and their bands *shall be* silver. ¹¹Likewise along the length of the north side *there shall be* hangings one hundred *cubits* long, with its twenty pillars and their twenty sockets of bronze, and the hooks of the pillars and their bands of silver.

¹²"And along the width of the court on the west side *shall be* hangings of fifty cubits, with their ten pillars and their ten sockets. ¹³The width of the court on the east side *shall be* fifty cubits. ¹⁴The hangings on *one side of the gate shall be* fifteen cubits, *with* their three pillars and their three sockets. ¹⁵And on the other side *shall be* hangings of fifteen *cubits, with* their three pillars and their three sockets.

¹⁶"For the gate of the court *there shall be* a screen twenty cubits long, *woven of* blue, purple, and scarlet *thread,* and fine woven linen, made by a weaver. It *shall have* four pillars and four sockets. ¹⁷All the pillars around the court shall have bands of silver; their hooks *shall be* of silver and their sockets of bronze. ¹⁸The length of the court

shall be one hundred cubits, the width fifty throughout, and the height five cubits, made of fine woven linen, and its sockets of bronze. ¹⁹All the utensils of the tabernacle for all its service, all its pegs, and all the pegs of the court, shall be of bronze.

The Care of the Lampstand

²⁰"And you shall command the children of Israel that they bring you pure oil of pressed olives for the light, to cause the lamp to burn continually. ²¹In the tabernacle of meeting, outside the veil which is before the Testimony, Aaron and his sons shall tend it from evening until morning before the LORD. It shall be a statute forever to their generations on behalf of the children of Israel.

Garments for the Priesthood

28 "Now take Aaron your brother, and his sons with him, from among the children of Israel, that he may minister to Me as priest, Aaron and Aaron's sons: Nadab, Abihu, Eleazar, and Ithamar. ²And you shall make holy garments for Aaron your brother, for glory and for beauty. ³So you shall speak to all who are gifted artisans, whom I have filled with the spirit of wisdom, that they may make Aaron's garments, to consecrate him, that he may minister to Me as priest. ⁴And these are the garments which they shall make: a breastplate, an ephod,ᵃ a robe, a skillfully woven tunic, a turban, and a sash. So they shall make holy garments for Aaron your brother and his sons, that he may minister to Me as priest.

The Ephod

⁵"They shall take the gold, blue, purple, and scarlet thread, and the fine linen, ⁶and they shall make the ephod of gold, blue, purple, and scarlet thread, and fine woven linen, artistically worked. ⁷It shall have two shoulder straps joined at its two edges, and so it shall be joined together. ⁸And the intricately woven band of the ephod, which is on it, shall be of the same workmanship, made of gold, blue, purple, and scarlet thread, and fine woven linen.

⁹"Then you shall take two onyx stones and engrave on them the names of the sons of Israel: ¹⁰six of their names on one stone and six names on the other stone, in order of their birth. ¹¹With the work of an engraver in stone, like the engravings of a signet, you shall engrave the two stones with the names of the sons of Israel. You shall set them in settings of gold. ¹²And you shall put the two stones on the shoulders of the ephod

as memorial stones for the sons of Israel. So Aaron shall bear their names before the LORD on his two shoulders as a memorial. ¹³You shall also make settings of gold, ¹⁴and you shall make two chains of pure gold like braided cords, and fasten the braided chains to the settings.

The Breastplate

¹⁵"You shall make the breastplate of judgment. Artistically woven according to the workmanship of the ephod you shall make it: of gold, blue, purple, and scarlet thread, and fine woven linen, you shall make it. ¹⁶It shall be doubled into a square: a span shall be its length, and a span shall be its width. ¹⁷And you shall put settings of stones in it, four rows of stones: The first row shall be a sardius, a topaz, and an emerald; this shall be the first row; ¹⁸the second row shall be a turquoise, a sapphire, and a diamond; ¹⁹the third row, a jacinth, an agate, and an amethyst; ²⁰and the fourth row, a beryl, an onyx, and a jasper. They shall be set in gold settings. ²¹And the stones shall have the names of the sons of Israel, twelve according to their names, like the engravings of a signet, each one with its own name; they shall be according to the twelve tribes.

²²"You shall make chains for the breastplate at the end, like braided cords of pure gold. ²³And you shall make two rings of gold for the breastplate, and put the two rings on the two ends of the breastplate. ²⁴Then you shall put the two braided chains of gold in the two rings which are on the ends of the breastplate; ²⁵and the other two ends of the two braided chains you shall fasten to the two settings, and put them on the shoulder straps of the ephod in the front.

²⁶"You shall make two rings of gold, and put them on the two ends of the breastplate, on the edge of it, which is on the inner side of the ephod. ²⁷And two other rings of gold you shall make, and put them on the two shoulder straps, underneath the ephod toward its front, right at the seam above the intricately woven band of the ephod. ²⁸They shall bind the breastplate by means of its rings to the rings of the ephod, using a blue cord, so that it is above the intricately woven band of the ephod, and so that the breastplate does not come loose from the ephod.

²⁹"So Aaron shall bear the names of the sons of Israel on the breastplate of judgment over his heart, when he goes into the holy place, as a memorial before the LORD continually. ³⁰And you shall put in the breastplate of judgment the Urim

---

28:4 ᵃThat is, an ornamented vest

and the Thummim,[a] and they shall be over Aaron's heart when he goes in before the LORD. So Aaron shall bear the judgment of the children of Israel over his heart before the LORD continually.

Other Priestly Garments

31"You shall make the robe of the ephod all of blue. 32There shall be an opening for his head in the middle of it; it shall have a woven binding all around its opening, like the opening in a coat of mail, so that it does not tear. 33And upon its hem you shall make pomegranates of blue, purple, and scarlet, all around its hem, and bells of gold between them all around: 34a golden bell and a pomegranate, a golden bell and a pomegranate, upon the hem of the robe all around. 35And it shall be upon Aaron when he ministers, and its sound will be heard when he goes into the holy *place* before the LORD and when he comes out, that he may not die.

36"You shall also make a plate of pure gold and engrave on it, *like* the engraving of a signet:

HOLINESS TO THE LORD.

37And you shall put it on a blue cord, that it may be on the turban; it shall be on the front of the turban. 38So it shall be on Aaron's forehead, that Aaron may bear the iniquity of the holy things which the children of Israel hallow in all their holy gifts; and it shall always be on his forehead, that they may be accepted before the LORD.

39"You shall skillfully weave the tunic of fine linen *thread,* you shall make the turban of fine linen, and you shall make the sash of woven work. 40"For Aaron's sons you shall make tunics, and you shall make sashes for them. And you shall make hats for them, for glory and beauty. 41So you shall put them on Aaron your brother and on his sons with him. You shall anoint them, consecrate them, and sanctify them, that they may minister to Me as priests. 42And you shall make for them linen trousers to cover their nakedness; they shall reach from the waist to the thighs. 43They shall be on Aaron and on his sons when they come into the tabernacle of meeting, or when they come near the altar to minister in the holy *place,* that they do not incur iniquity and die. *It shall be* a statute forever to him and his descendants after him.

Aaron and His Sons Consecrated

29 "And this is what you shall do to them to hallow them for ministering to Me as priests: Take one young bull and two rams without blemish, 2and unleavened bread, unleavened cakes mixed with oil, and un-leavened wafers anointed with oil (you shall make them of wheat flour). 3You shall put them in one basket and bring them in the basket, with the bull and the two rams.

4"And Aaron and his sons you shall bring to the door of the tabernacle of meeting, and you shall wash them with water. 5Then you shall take the garments, put the tunic on Aaron, and the robe of the ephod, the ephod, and the breastplate, and gird him with the intricately woven band of the ephod. 6You shall put the turban on his head, and put the holy crown on the turban. 7And you shall take the anointing oil, pour *it* on his head, and anoint him. 8Then you shall bring his sons and put tunics on them. 9And you shall gird them with sashes, Aaron and his sons, and put the hats on them. The priesthood shall be theirs for a perpetual statute. So you shall consecrate Aaron and his sons.

10"You shall also have the bull brought before the tabernacle of meeting, and Aaron and his sons shall put their hands on the head of the bull. 11Then you shall kill the bull before the LORD, *by* the door of the tabernacle of meeting. 12You shall take *some* of the blood of the bull and put *it* on the horns of the altar with your finger, and pour all the blood beside the base of the altar. 13And you shall take all the fat that covers the entrails, the fatty lobe *attached* to the liver, and the two kidneys and the fat that *is* on them, and burn *them* on the altar. 14But the flesh of the bull, with its skin and its offal, you shall burn with fire outside the camp. It *is* a sin offering.

15"You shall also take one ram, and Aaron and his sons shall put their hands on the head of the ram; 16and you shall kill the ram, and you shall take its blood and sprinkle *it* all around on the altar. 17Then you shall cut the ram in pieces, wash its entrails and its legs, and put *them* with its pieces and with its head. 18And you shall burn the whole ram on the altar. It *is* a burnt offering to the LORD; it *is* a sweet aroma, an offering made by fire to the LORD.

19"You shall also take the other ram, and Aaron and his sons shall put their hands on the head of the ram. 20Then you shall kill the ram, and take some of its blood and put *it* on the tip of the right ear of Aaron and on the tip of the right ear of his sons, on the thumb of their right hand and on the big toe of their right foot, and sprinkle the blood all around on the altar. 21And you shall take some of the blood that is on the

---

28:30 [a]Literally *the Lights and the Perfections* (compare Leviticus 8:8)

altar, and some of the anointing oil, and sprinkle *it* on Aaron and on his garments, on his sons and on the garments of his sons with him; and he and his garments shall be hallowed, and his sons and his sons' garments with him.

²²"Also you shall take the fat of the ram, the fat tail, the fat that covers the entrails, the fatty lobe *attached to* the liver, the two kidneys and the fat on them, the right thigh (for it *is* a ram of consecration), ²³one loaf of bread, one cake *made with* oil, and one wafer from the basket of the unleavened bread that *is* before the LORD; ²⁴and you shall put all these in the hands of Aaron and in the hands of his sons, and you shall wave them *as* a wave offering before the LORD. ²⁵You shall receive them back from their hands and burn *them* on the altar as a burnt offering, as a sweet aroma before the LORD. It *is* an offering made by fire to the LORD.

²⁶"Then you shall take the breast of the ram of Aaron's consecration and wave it *as* a wave offering before the LORD; and it shall be your portion. ²⁷And from the ram of the consecration you shall consecrate the breast of the wave offering which is waved, and the thigh of the heave offering which is raised, of *that* which *is* for Aaron and of *that* which is for his sons. ²⁸It shall be from the children of Israel *for* Aaron and his sons by a statute forever. For it is a heave offering; it shall be a heave offering from the children of Israel from the sacrifices of their peace offerings, *that is,* their heave offering to the LORD.

²⁹"And the holy garments of Aaron shall be his sons' after him, to be anointed in them and to be consecrated in them. ³⁰That son who becomes priest in his place shall put them on for seven days, when he enters the tabernacle of meeting to minister in the holy *place.*

³¹"And you shall take the ram of the consecration and boil its flesh in the holy place. ³²Then Aaron and his sons shall eat the flesh of the ram, and the bread that *is* in the basket, *by* the door of the tabernacle of meeting. ³³They shall eat those things with which the atonement was made, to consecrate *and* to sanctify them; but an outsider shall not eat *them,* because they *are* holy. ³⁴And if any of the flesh of the consecration offerings, or of the bread, remains until the morning, then you shall burn the remainder with fire. It shall not be eaten, because it *is* holy.

³⁵"Thus you shall do to Aaron and his sons, according to all that I have commanded you. Seven days you shall consecrate them. ³⁶And you shall offer a bull every day *as* a sin offering for atonement. You shall cleanse the altar when you make atonement for it, and you shall anoint it to

sanctify it. ³⁷Seven days you shall make atonement for the altar and sanctify it. And the altar shall be most holy. Whatever touches the altar must be holy.ᵃ

The Daily Offerings

³⁸"Now this *is* what you shall offer on the altar: two lambs of the first year, day by day continually. ³⁹One lamb you shall offer in the morning, and the other lamb you shall offer at twilight. ⁴⁰With the one lamb shall be one-tenth *of an ephah* of flour mixed with one-fourth of a hin of pressed oil, and one-fourth of a hin of wine *as* a drink offering. ⁴¹And the other lamb you shall offer at twilight; and you shall offer with it the grain offering and the drink offering, as in the morning, for a sweet aroma, an offering made by fire to the LORD. ⁴²*This shall be* a continual burnt offering throughout your generations *at* the door of the tabernacle of meeting before the LORD, where I will meet you to speak with you. ⁴³And there I will meet with the children of Israel, and *the tabernacle* shall be sanctified by My glory. ⁴⁴So I will consecrate the tabernacle of meeting and the altar. I will also consecrate both Aaron and his sons to minister to Me as priests. ⁴⁵I will dwell among the children of Israel and will be their God. ⁴⁶And they shall know that I *am* the LORD their God, who brought them up out of the land of Egypt, that I may dwell among them. I *am* the LORD their God.

The Altar of Incense

30 "You shall make an altar to burn incense on; you shall make it of acacia wood. ²A cubit *shall be* its length and a cubit its width—it shall be square—and two cubits *shall be* its height. Its horns *shall be* of one piece with it. ³And you shall overlay its top, its sides all around, and its horns with pure gold; and you shall make for it a molding of gold all around. ⁴Two gold rings you shall make for it, under the molding on both its sides. You shall place *them* on its two sides, and they will be holders for the poles with which to bear it. ⁵You shall make the poles of acacia wood, and overlay them with gold. ⁶And you shall put it before the veil that *is* before the ark of the Testimony, before the mercy seat that *is* over the Testimony, where I will meet with you.

⁷"Aaron shall burn on it sweet incense every morning; when he tends the lamps, he shall burn incense on it. ⁸And when Aaron lights the lamps

---

29:37 ᵃCompare Numbers 4:15 and Haggai 2:11–13

at twilight, he shall burn incense on it, a perpetual incense before the LORD throughout your generations. [9]You shall not offer strange incense on it, or a burnt offering, or a grain offering; nor shall you pour a drink offering on it. [10]And Aaron shall make atonement upon its horns once a year with the blood of the sin offering of atonement; once a year he shall make atonement upon it throughout your generations. It *is* most holy to the LORD."

The Ransom Money

[11]Then the LORD spoke to Moses, saying: [12]"When you take the census of the children of Israel for their number, then every man shall give a ransom for himself to the LORD, when you number them, that there may be no plague among them when *you* number them. [13]This is what everyone among those who are numbered shall give: half a shekel according to the shekel of the sanctuary (a shekel *is* twenty gerahs). The half-shekel *shall be* an offering to the LORD. [14]Everyone included among those who are numbered, from twenty years old and above, shall give an offering to the LORD. [15]The rich shall not give more and the poor shall not give less than half a shekel, when *you* give an offering to the LORD, to make atonement for yourselves. [16]And you shall take the atonement money of the children of Israel, and shall appoint it for the service of the tabernacle of meeting, that it may be a memorial for the children of Israel before the LORD, to make atonement for yourselves."

The Bronze Laver

[17]Then the LORD spoke to Moses, saying: [18]"You shall also make a laver of bronze, with its base also of bronze, for washing. You shall put it between the tabernacle of meeting and the altar. And you shall put water in it, [19]for Aaron and his sons shall wash their hands and their feet in water from it. [20]When they go into the tabernacle of meeting, or when they come near the altar to minister, to burn an offering made by fire to the LORD, they shall wash with water, lest they die. [21]So they shall wash their hands and their feet, lest they die. And it shall be a statute forever to them—to him and his descendants throughout their generations."

The Holy Anointing Oil

[22]Moreover the LORD spoke to Moses, saying: [23]"Also take for yourself quality spices—five hundred *shekels* of liquid myrrh, half as much sweet-smelling cinnamon (two hundred and fifty *shekels*), two hundred and fifty *shekels* of sweet-smelling cane, [24]five hundred *shekels* of cassia, according to the shekel of the sanctuary, and a hin of olive oil. [25]And you shall make from these a holy anointing oil, an ointment compounded according to the art of the perfumer. It shall be a holy anointing oil. [26]With it you shall anoint the tabernacle of meeting and the ark of the Testimony; [27]the table and all its utensils, the lampstand and its utensils, and the altar of incense; [28]the altar of burnt offering with all its utensils, and the laver and its base. [29]You shall consecrate them, that they may be most holy; whatever touches them must be holy.[a] [30]And you shall anoint Aaron and his sons, and consecrate them, that *they* may minister to Me as priests.

[31]"And you shall speak to the children of Israel, saying: 'This shall be a holy anointing oil to Me throughout your generations. [32]It shall not be poured on man's flesh; nor shall you make *any other* like it, according to its composition. It *is* holy, *and* it shall be holy to you. [33]Whoever compounds *any* like it, or whoever puts *any* of it on an outsider, shall be cut off from his people.'"

The Incense

[34]And the LORD said to Moses: "Take sweet spices, stacte and onycha and galbanum, and pure frankincense with *these* sweet spices; there shall be equal amounts of each. [35]You shall make of these an incense, a compound according to the art of the perfumer, salted, pure, *and* holy. [36]And you shall beat *some* of it very fine, and put some of it before the Testimony in the tabernacle of meeting where I will meet with you. It shall be most holy to you. [37]But *as for* the incense which you shall make, you shall not make any for yourselves, according to its composition. It shall be to you holy for the LORD. [38]Whoever makes *any* like it, to smell it, he shall be cut off from his people."

Artisans for Building the Tabernacle

31 Then the LORD spoke to Moses, saying: [2]"See, I have called by name Bezalel the son of Uri, the son of Hur, of the tribe of Judah. [3]And I have filled him with the Spirit of God, in wisdom, in understanding, in knowledge, and in all *manner of* workmanship, [4]to design artistic works, to work in gold, in silver, in bronze, [5]in cutting jewels for setting, in carving wood, and to work in all *manner of* workmanship.

[6]"And I, indeed I, have appointed with him

30:29 [a]Compare Numbers 4:15 and Haggai 2:11–13

Aholiab the son of Ahisamach, of the tribe of Dan; and I have put wisdom in the hearts of all the gifted artisans, that they may make all that I have commanded you: ⁷the tabernacle of meeting, the ark of the Testimony and the mercy seat that *is* on it, and all the furniture of the tabernacle— ⁸the table and its utensils, the pure *gold* lampstand with all its utensils, the altar of incense, ⁹the altar of burnt offering with all its utensils, and the laver and its base— ¹⁰the garments of ministry,ᵃ the holy garments for Aaron the priest and the garments of his sons, to minister as priests, ¹¹and the anointing oil and sweet incense for the holy *place*. According to all that I have commanded you they shall do."

The Sabbath Law

¹²And the LORD spoke to Moses, saying, ¹³"Speak also to the children of Israel, saying: 'Surely My Sabbaths you shall keep, for it *is* a sign between Me and you throughout your generations, that *you* may know that I *am* the LORD who sanctifies you. ¹⁴You shall keep the Sabbath, therefore, for *it is* holy to you. Everyone who profanes it shall surely be put to death; for whoever does *any* work on it, that person shall be cut off from among his people. ¹⁵Work shall be done for six days, but the seventh *is* the Sabbath of rest, holy to the LORD. Whoever does *any* work on the Sabbath day, he shall surely be put to death. ¹⁶Therefore the children of Israel shall keep the Sabbath, to observe the Sabbath throughout their generations *as* a perpetual covenant. ¹⁷It *is* a sign between Me and the children of Israel forever; for *in* six days the LORD made the heavens and the earth, and on the seventh day He rested and was refreshed.'"

¹⁸And when He had made an end of speaking with him on Mount Sinai, He gave Moses two tablets of the Testimony, tablets of stone, written with the finger of God.

The Gold Calf

32 Now when the people saw that Moses delayed coming down from the mountain, the people gathered together to Aaron, and said to him, "Come, make us gods that shall go before us; for *as for* this Moses, the man who brought us up out of the land of Egypt, we do not know what has become of him."

²And Aaron said to them, "Break off the golden earrings which *are* in the ears of your wives, your sons, and your daughters, and bring *them* to me." ³So all the people broke off the golden earrings which *were* in their ears, and

---

The Law of Respect: Aaron Replaces Moses

(Exodus 32:1–6)

While Moses spoke with God on the mountain, the Israelites began to wonder just where their leader had gone. It didn't take them long to look for a new leader, at least for a season. As they gathered around Aaron to request his help in making a golden calf, they violated the first of the Ten Commandments they were about to receive.

Although Aaron's convictions lagged seriously behind those of Moses, the people begged him to take charge. Why? Probably because of the Law of Respect. Once Moses pulled his disappearing act, the people looked for the next strongest leader to take over. They did so because:

1. People are like sheep without a shepherd. They always need a leader; Jesus said so (Mark 6:34).
2. People focus on immediate felt needs. They struggle with delayed gratification.
3. People suffer memory failure. They always ask: What's the leader done for me lately?
4. People are insecure. They begin to worry without abundant signs of hope.

---

brought *them* to Aaron. ⁴And he received *the* gold from their hand, and he fashioned it with an engraving tool, and made a molded calf.

Then they said, "This *is* your god, O Israel, that brought you out of the land of Egypt!"

⁵So when Aaron saw *it,* he built an altar before it. And Aaron made a proclamation and said, "Tomorrow *is* a feast to the LORD." ⁶Then they rose early on the next day, offered burnt offerings, and brought peace offerings; and the people sat down to eat and drink, and rose up to play.

⁷And the LORD said to Moses, "Go, get down! For your people whom you brought out of the land of Egypt have corrupted *themselves.* ⁸They have turned aside quickly out of the way which I commanded them. They have made themselves a molded calf, and worshiped it and sacrificed to it, and said, 'This *is* your god, O

31:10 ᵃOr *woven garments*

Israel, that brought you out of the land of Egypt!'"⁹And the LORD said to Moses, "I have seen this people, and indeed it *is* a stiff-necked people! ¹⁰Now therefore, let Me alone, that My wrath may burn hot against them and I may consume them. And I will make of you a great nation."

¹¹Then Moses pleaded with the LORD his God, and said: "LORD, why does Your wrath burn hot against Your people whom You have brought out of the land of Egypt with great power and with a mighty hand? ¹²Why should the Egyptians speak, and say, 'He brought them out to harm them, to kill them in the mountains, and to consume them from the face of the earth'? Turn from Your fierce wrath, and relent from this harm to Your people. ¹³Remember Abraham, Isaac, and Israel, Your servants, to whom You swore by Your own self, and said to them, 'I will multiply your descendants as the stars of heaven; and all this land that I have spoken of I give to your descendants, and they shall inherit *it* forever.'"ᵃ ¹⁴So the LORD relented from the harm which He said He would do to His people.

¹⁵And Moses turned and went down from the mountain, and the two tablets of the Testimony *were* in his hand. The tablets *were* written on both sides; on the one *side* and on the other they were written. ¹⁶Now the tablets *were* the work of God, and the writing *was* the writing of God engraved on the tablets.

¹⁷And when Joshua heard the noise of the people as they shouted, he said to Moses, "*There is* a noise of war in the camp."

¹⁸But he said:

"*It is* not the noise of the shout of victory,
Nor the noise of the cry of defeat,
But the sound of singing I hear."

¹⁹So it was, as soon as he came near the camp, that he saw the calf *and* the dancing. So Moses' anger became hot, and he cast the tablets out of his hands and broke them at the foot of the mountain. ²⁰Then he took the calf which they had made, burned *it* in the fire, and ground *it* to powder; and he scattered *it* on the water and made the children of Israel drink *it*. ²¹And Moses said to Aaron, "What did this people do to you that you have brought *so* great a sin upon them?"

²²So Aaron said, "Do not let the anger of my lord become hot. You know the people, that they *are* set on evil. ²³For they said to me, 'Make us gods that shall go before us; *as for* this Moses, the

man who brought us out of the land of Egypt, we do not know what has become of him.' ²⁴And I said to them, 'Whoever has any gold, let them break *it* off.' So they gave *it* to me, and I cast it into the fire, and this calf came out."

²⁵Now when Moses saw that the people *were* unrestrained (for Aaron had not restrained them, to *their* shame among their enemies), ²⁶then Moses stood in the entrance of the camp, and said, "Whoever *is* on the LORD's side—*come* to me!" And all the sons of Levi gathered themselves together to him. ²⁷And he said to them, "Thus says the LORD God of Israel: 'Let every man put his sword on his side, and go in and out from entrance to entrance throughout the camp, and let every man kill his brother, every man his companion, and every man his neighbor.'" ²⁸So the sons of Levi did according to the word of Moses. And about three thousand men of the people fell that day. ²⁹Then Moses said, "Consecrate yourselves today to the LORD, that He may bestow on you a blessing this day, for every man has opposed his son and his brother."

³⁰Now it came to pass on the next day that Moses said to the people, "You have committed a great sin. So now I will go up to the LORD; perhaps I can make atonement for your sin." ³¹Then Moses returned to the LORD and said, "Oh, these people have committed a great sin, and have made for themselves a god of gold! ³²Yet now, if You will forgive their sin—but if not, I pray, blot me out of Your book which You have written."

³³And the LORD said to Moses, "Whoever has sinned against Me, I will blot him out of My book. ³⁴Now therefore, go, lead the people to *the place* of which I have spoken to you. Behold, My Angel shall go before you. Nevertheless, in the day when I visit for punishment, I will visit punishment upon them for their sin."

³⁵So the LORD plagued the people because of what they did with the calf which Aaron made.

The Command to Leave Sinai

33 Then the LORD said to Moses, "Depart *and* go up from here, you and the people whom you have brought out of the land of Egypt, to the land of which I swore to Abraham, Isaac, and Jacob, saying, 'To your descendants I will give it.' ²And I will send *My* Angel before you, and I will drive out the Canaanite and the Amorite and the Hittite and the Perizzite and the Hivite and the Jebusite. ³*Go up* to a land flowing with milk and honey; for I

32:13 ᵃGenesis 13:15 and 22:17

Moses Sets the Example: Intimacy with God

(Exodus 33:7–11)

Modeling provides the basis of all true leadership. Leaders must set the example for their followers. The number one management principle in the world is this: *People do what people see.*

Moses demonstrated this truth. The people watched him as he spent time with God, interceding for them in intimate, personal communion—and it changed them more than any sermon could have. If you want to enjoy an intimate relationship with God, as Moses did, you must practice what he did:

1. *Separate yourself regularly (33:7).*
   You must come apart from the crowd. The key phrase is: *outside the camp.*
2. *Seek God with all your heart (33:7).*
   You must pursue truth over popularity. The key phrase is: *sought the LORD.*
3. *Be watched by the public (33:8).*
   You must be willing to take a risk, even though it feels intimidating to be watched and scrutinized. The key phrase is: *watched Moses.*
4. *Learn to listen and obey God's voice (33:9).*
   You must practice the patience of silence and submission. The key phrase is: *The LORD talked with Moses.*
5. *Enter covenant partnership with God (33:10, 11).*
   You must be faithful and committed, just as Moses was a trustworthy partner with God. The key phrase is: *The LORD spoke to Moses face to face, as a man speaks to his friend.*

will not go up in your midst, lest I consume you on the way, for you *are* a stiff-necked people."

⁴And when the people heard this bad news, they mourned, and no one put on his ornaments. ⁵For the LORD had said to Moses, "Say to the children of Israel, 'You *are* a stiff-necked people. I could come up into your midst in one moment and consume you. Now therefore, take off your ornaments, that I may know what to do to you.'" ⁶So the children of Israel stripped themselves of their ornaments by Mount Horeb.

Moses Meets with the LORD

⁷Moses took his tent and pitched it outside the camp, far from the camp, and called it the tabernacle of meeting. And it came to pass *that* everyone who sought the LORD went out to the tabernacle of meeting which *was* outside the camp. ⁸So it was, whenever Moses went out to the tabernacle, *that* all the people rose, and each man stood *at* his tent door and watched Moses until he had gone into the tabernacle. ⁹And it came to pass, when Moses entered the tabernacle, that the pillar of cloud descended and stood *at* the door of the tabernacle, and *the* LORD talked with Moses. ¹⁰All the people saw the pillar of cloud standing *at* the tabernacle door, and all

the people rose and worshiped, each man *in* his tent door. ¹¹So the LORD spoke to Moses face to face, as a man speaks to his friend. And he would return to the camp, but his servant Joshua the son of Nun, a young man, did not depart from the tabernacle.

The Promise of God's Presence

¹²Then Moses said to the LORD, "See, You say to me, 'Bring up this people.' But You have not let me know whom You will send with me. Yet You have said, 'I know you by name, and you have also found grace in My sight.' ¹³Now therefore, I pray, if I have found grace in Your sight, show me now Your way, that I may know You and that I may find grace in Your sight. And consider that this nation *is* Your people."

¹⁴And He said, "My Presence will go *with you,* and I will give you rest."

¹⁵Then he said to Him, "If Your Presence does not go *with us,* do not bring us up from here. ¹⁶For how then will it be known that Your people and I have found grace in Your sight, except You go with us? So we shall be separate, Your people and I, from all the people who *are* upon the face of the earth."

¹⁷So the LORD said to Moses, "I will also do

this thing that you have spoken; for you have found grace in My sight, and I know you by name."

[18]And he said, "Please, show me Your glory."

[19]Then He said, "I will make all My goodness pass before you, and I will proclaim the name of the LORD before you. I will be gracious to whom I will be gracious, and I will have compassion on whom I will have compassion." [20]But He said, "You cannot see My face; for no man shall see Me, and live." [21]And the LORD said, "Here is a place by Me, and you shall stand on the rock. [22]So it shall be, while My glory passes by, that I will put you in the cleft of the rock, and will cover you with My hand while I pass by. [23]Then I will take away My hand, and you shall see My back; but My face shall not be seen."

Moses Makes New Tablets

34

And the LORD said to Moses, "Cut two tablets of stone like the first *ones,* and I will write on *these* tablets the words that were on the first tablets which you broke. [2]So be ready in the morning, and come up in the morning to Mount Sinai, and present yourself to Me there on the top of the mountain. [3]And no man shall come up with you, and let no man be seen throughout all the mountain; let neither flocks nor herds feed before that mountain."

[4]So he cut two tablets of stone like the first *ones.* Then Moses rose early in the morning and went up Mount Sinai, as the LORD had commanded him; and he took in his hand the two tablets of stone.

[5]Now the LORD descended in the cloud and stood with him there, and proclaimed the name of the LORD. [6]And the LORD passed before him and proclaimed, "The LORD, the LORD God, merciful and gracious, longsuffering, and abounding in goodness and truth, [7]keeping mercy for thousands, forgiving iniquity and transgression and sin, by no means clearing *the guilty,* visiting the iniquity of the fathers upon the children and the children's children to the third and the fourth generation."

[8]So Moses made haste and bowed his head toward the earth, and worshiped. [9]Then he said, "If now I have found grace in Your sight, O Lord, let my Lord, I pray, go among us, even though we *are* a stiff-necked people; and pardon our iniquity and our sin, and take us as Your inheritance."

The Covenant Renewed

[10]And He said: "Behold, I make a covenant. Before all your people I will do marvels such as

---

Moses Leads from His Divine Anointing

(Exodus 34:5–7)

After Moses shattered the first set of stone commandments, the Lord directed him to chisel out some replacements. When he brought down the new set, his face shone with the glory of God. The nature and character of God had begun to rub off on Moses. The glory took such tangible form that he had to wear a veil over his face. The Israelites sensed both God's presence in Moses' leadership and a divine anointing to lead.

Do others describe your leadership as "anointed"? What does it mean to be anointed? Here's one way to break it down. Anointed leadership is characterized by:

1. *Charisma*
   The anointed enjoy a sense of giftedness that comes from God. It seems magnetic.
2. *Character*
   People see God's nature in your leadership. They trust you.
3. *Competence*
   You have the ability to get the job done. Your leadership produces results.
4. *Conviction*
   Your leadership has backbone. You always stand for what is right.

---

have not been done in all the earth, nor in any nation; and all the people among whom you *are* shall see the work of the LORD. For it *is* an awesome thing that I will do with you. [11]Observe what I command you this day. Behold, I am driving out from before you the Amorite and the Canaanite and the Hittite and the Perizzite and the Hivite and the Jebusite. [12]Take heed to yourself, lest you make a covenant with the inhabitants of the land where you are going, lest it be a snare in your midst. [13]But you shall destroy their altars, break their *sacred* pillars, and cut down their wooden images [14](for you shall worship no other god, for the LORD, whose name *is* Jealous, *is* a jealous God), [15]lest you make a covenant with the inhabitants of the land, and they play the harlot with their gods and make sacrifice to their gods, and *one of them* invites you and you eat of his sacrifice, [16]and you take of his daughters for your sons, and his daughters play the harlot with their gods and make your sons play the harlot with their gods.

[17]"You shall make no molded gods for yourselves.

[18]"The Feast of Unleavened Bread you shall keep. Seven days you shall eat unleavened bread, as I commanded you, in the appointed time of the month of Abib; for in the month of Abib you came out from Egypt.

[19]"All that open the womb *are* Mine, and every male firstborn among your livestock, *whether* ox or sheep. [20]But the firstborn of a donkey you shall redeem with a lamb. And if you will not redeem *him,* then you shall break his neck. All the firstborn of your sons you shall redeem.

"And none shall appear before Me empty-handed.

[21]"Six days you shall work, but on the seventh day you shall rest; in plowing time and in harvest you shall rest.

[22]"And you shall observe the Feast of Weeks, of the firstfruits of wheat harvest, and the Feast of Ingathering at the year's end.

[23]"Three times in the year all your men shall appear before the Lord, the LORD God of Israel. [24]For I will cast out the nations before you and enlarge your borders; neither will any man covet your land when you go up to appear before the LORD your God three times in the year.

[25]"You shall not offer the blood of My sacrifice with leaven, nor shall the sacrifice of the Feast of the Passover be left until morning.

[26]"The first of the firstfruits of your land you shall bring to the house of the LORD your God. You shall not boil a young goat in its mother's milk."

[27]Then the LORD said to Moses, "Write these words, for according to the tenor of these words I have made a covenant with you and with Israel." [28]So he was there with the LORD forty days and forty nights; he neither ate bread nor drank water. And He wrote on the tablets the words of the covenant, the Ten Commandments.[a]

The Shining Face of Moses

[29]Now it was so, when Moses came down from Mount Sinai (and the two tablets of the Testimony *were* in Moses' hand when he came down from the mountain), that Moses did not know that the skin of his face shone while he talked with Him. [30]So when Aaron and all the children of Israel saw Moses, behold, the skin of his face shone, and they were afraid to come near him. [31]Then Moses called to them, and Aaron

and all the rulers of the congregation returned to him; and Moses talked with them. [32]Afterward all the children of Israel came near, and he gave them as commandments all that the LORD had spoken with him on Mount Sinai. [33]And when Moses had finished speaking with them, he put a veil on his face. [34]But whenever Moses went in before the LORD to speak with Him, he would take the veil off until he came out; and he would come out and speak to the children of Israel whatever he had been commanded. [35]And whenever the children of Israel saw the face of Moses, that the skin of Moses' face shone, then Moses would put the veil on his face again, until he went in to speak with Him.

Sabbath Regulations

35 Then Moses gathered all the congregation of the children of Israel together, and said to them, "These *are* the words which the LORD has commanded *you* to do: [2]Work shall be done for six days, but the seventh day shall be a holy day for you, a Sabbath of rest to the LORD. Whoever does any work on it shall be put to death. [3]You shall kindle no fire throughout your dwellings on the Sabbath day."

Offerings for the Tabernacle

[4]And Moses spoke to all the congregation of the children of Israel, saying, "This *is* the thing which the LORD commanded, saying: [5]'Take from among you an offering to the LORD. Whoever *is* of a willing heart, let him bring it as an offering to the LORD: gold, silver, and bronze; [6]blue, purple, and scarlet *thread,* fine linen, and goats' *hair;* [7]ram skins dyed red, badger skins, and acacia wood; [8]oil for the light, and spices for the anointing oil and for the sweet incense; [9]onyx stones, and stones to be set in the ephod and in the breastplate.

Articles of the Tabernacle

[10]"All *who are* gifted artisans among you shall come and make all that the LORD has commanded: [11]the tabernacle, its tent, its covering, its clasps, its boards, its bars, its pillars, and its sockets; [12]the ark and its poles, *with* the mercy seat, and the veil of the covering; [13]the table and its poles, all its utensils, and the showbread; [14]also the lampstand for the light, its utensils, its lamps, and the oil for the light; [15]the incense altar, its poles, the anointing oil, the sweet incense, and the screen for the door at the entrance of the tabernacle; [16]the altar of burnt offering with its bronze

34:28 [a]Literally *Ten Words*

grating, its poles, all its utensils, *and* the laver and its base; [17]the hangings of the court, its pillars, their sockets, and the screen for the gate of the court; [18]the pegs of the tabernacle, the pegs of the court, and their cords; [19]the garments of ministry,[a] for ministering in the holy *place*—the holy garments for Aaron the priest and the garments of his sons, to minister as priests.'"

The Tabernacle Offerings Presented

[20]And all the congregation of the children of Israel departed from the presence of Moses. [21]Then everyone came whose heart was stirred, and everyone whose spirit was willing, *and* they brought the LORD's offering for the work of the tabernacle of meeting, for all its service, and for the holy garments. [22]They came, both men and women, as many as had a willing heart, *and* brought earrings and nose rings, rings and necklaces, all jewelry of gold, that is, every man who *made* an offering of gold to the LORD. [23]And every man, with whom was found blue, purple, and scarlet *thread*, fine linen, goats' *hair,* red skins of rams, and badger skins, brought *them.* [24]Everyone who offered an offering of silver or bronze brought the LORD's offering. And everyone with whom was found acacia wood for any work of the service, brought *it.* [25]All the women *who were* gifted artisans spun yarn with their hands, and brought what they had spun, of blue, purple, *and* scarlet, and fine linen. [26]And all the women whose hearts stirred with wisdom spun yarn of goats' *hair.* [27]The rulers brought onyx stones, and the stones to be set in the ephod and in the breastplate, [28]and spices and oil for the light, for the anointing oil, and for the sweet incense. [29]The children of Israel brought a freewill offering to the LORD, all the men and women whose hearts were willing to bring *material* for all kinds of work which the LORD, by the hand of Moses, had commanded to be done.

The Artisans Called by God

[30]And Moses said to the children of Israel, "See, the LORD has called by name Bezalel the son of Uri, the son of Hur, of the tribe of Judah; [31]and He has filled him with the Spirit of God, in wisdom and understanding, in knowledge and all manner of workmanship, [32]to design artistic works, to work in gold and silver and bronze, [33]in cutting jewels for setting, in carving wood, and to work in all manner of artistic workmanship.

[34]"And He has put in his heart the ability to teach, *in* him and Aholiab the son of Ahisamach, of the tribe of Dan. [35]He has filled them with skill to do all manner of work of the engraver

and the designer and the tapestry maker, in blue, purple, and scarlet *thread,* and fine linen, and of the weaver—those who do every work and those who design artistic works.

36 "And Bezalel and Aholiab, and every gifted artisan in whom the LORD has put wisdom and understanding, to know how to do all manner of work for the service of the sanctuary, shall do according to all that the LORD has commanded."

The People Give More than Enough

[2]Then Moses called Bezalel and Aholiab, and every gifted artisan in whose heart the LORD had put wisdom, everyone whose heart was stirred, to come and do the work. [3]And they received from Moses all the offering which the children of Israel had brought for the work of the service of making the sanctuary. So they continued bringing to him freewill offerings every morning. [4]Then all the craftsmen who were doing all the work of the sanctuary came, each from the work he was doing, [5]and they spoke to Moses, saying, "The people bring much more than enough for the service of the work which the LORD commanded *us* to do."

[6]So Moses gave a commandment, and they caused it to be proclaimed throughout the camp, saying, "Let neither man nor woman do any more work for the offering of the sanctuary." And the people were restrained from bringing, [7]for the material they had was sufficient for all the work to be done—indeed too much.

Building the Tabernacle

[8]Then all the gifted artisans among them who worked on the tabernacle made ten curtains woven of fine linen, and of blue, purple, and scarlet *thread; with* artistic designs of cherubim they made them. [9]The length of each curtain *was* twenty-eight cubits, and the width of each curtain four cubits; the curtains *were* all the same size. [10]And he coupled five curtains to one another, and *the other* five curtains he coupled to one another. [11]He made loops of blue *yarn* on the edge of the curtain on the selvedge of one set; likewise he did on the outer edge of *the other* curtain of the second set. [12]Fifty loops he made on one curtain, and fifty loops he made on the edge of the curtain on the end of the second set; the loops held one *curtain* to another. [13]And he made fifty clasps of gold, and coupled the curtains to one another with the clasps, that it might be one tabernacle.

35:19 [a]Or *woven garments*

[14]He made curtains of goats' *hair* for the tent over the tabernacle; he made eleven curtains. [15]The length of each curtain *was* thirty cubits, and the width of each curtain four cubits; the eleven curtains *were* the same size. [16]He coupled five curtains by themselves and six curtains by themselves. [17]And he made fifty loops on the edge of the curtain that is outermost in one set, and fifty loops he made on the edge of the curtain of the second set. [18]He also made fifty bronze clasps to couple the tent together, that it might be one. [19]Then he made a covering for the tent of ram skins dyed red, and a covering of badger skins above *that.*

[20]For the tabernacle he made boards of acacia wood, standing upright. [21]The length of each board *was* ten cubits, and the width of each board a cubit and a half. [22]Each board had two tenons for binding one to another. Thus he made for all the boards of the tabernacle. [23]And he made boards for the tabernacle, twenty boards for the south side. [24]Forty sockets of silver he made to go under the twenty boards: two sockets under each of the boards for its two tenons. [25]And for the other side of the tabernacle, the north side, he made twenty boards [26]and their forty sockets of silver: two sockets under each of the boards. [27]For the west side of the tabernacle he made six boards. [28]He also made two boards for the two back corners of the tabernacle. [29]And they were coupled at the bottom and coupled together at the top by one ring. Thus he made both of them for the two corners. [30]So there were eight boards and their sockets—sixteen sockets of silver—two sockets under each of the boards.

[31]And he made bars of acacia wood: five for the boards on one side of the tabernacle, [32]five bars for the boards on the other side of the tabernacle, and five bars for the boards of the tabernacle on the far side westward. [33]And he made the middle bar to pass through the boards from one end to the other. [34]He overlaid the boards with gold, made their rings of gold *to be* holders for the bars, and overlaid the bars with gold.

[35]And he made a veil of blue, purple, and scarlet *thread,* and fine woven linen; it was worked *with* an artistic design of cherubim. [36]He made for it four pillars of acacia *wood,* and overlaid them with gold, with their hooks of gold; and he cast four sockets of silver for them.

[37]He also made a screen for the tabernacle door, of blue, purple, and scarlet *thread,* and fine woven linen, made by a weaver, [38]and its five pillars with their hooks. And he overlaid their capitals and their rings with gold, but their five sockets *were* bronze.

Making the Ark of the Testimony

37Then Bezalel made the ark of acacia wood; two and a half cubits *was* its length, a cubit and a half its width, and a cubit and a half its height. [2]He overlaid it with pure gold inside and outside, and made a molding of gold all around it. [3]And he cast for it four rings of gold *to be set* in its four corners: two rings on one side, and two rings on the other side of it. [4]He made poles of acacia wood, and overlaid them with gold. [5]And he put the poles into the rings at the sides of the ark, to bear the ark. [6]He also made the mercy seat of pure gold; two and a half cubits *was* its length and a cubit and a half its width. [7]He made two cherubim of beaten gold; he made them of one piece at the two ends of the mercy seat: [8]one cherub at one end on this side, and the other cherub at the *other* end on that side. He made the cherubim at the two ends *of one piece* with the mercy seat. [9]The cherubim spread out *their* wings above, *and* covered the mercy seat with their wings. They faced one another; the faces of the cherubim were toward the mercy seat.

Making the Table for the Showbread

[10]He made the table of acacia wood; two cubits *was* its length, a cubit its width, and a cubit and a half its height. [11]And he overlaid it with pure gold, and made a molding of gold all around it. [12]Also he made a frame of a handbreadth all around it, and made a molding of gold for the frame all around it. [13]And he cast for it four rings of gold, and put the rings on the four corners that *were* at its four legs. [14]The rings were close to the frame, as holders for the poles to bear the table. [15]And he made the poles of acacia wood to bear the table, and overlaid them with gold. [16]He made of pure gold the utensils which were on the table: its dishes, its cups, its bowls, and its pitchers for pouring.

Making the Gold Lampstand

[17]He also made the lampstand of pure gold; of hammered work he made the lampstand. Its shaft, its branches, its bowls, its *ornamental* knobs, and its flowers were of the same piece. [18]And six branches came out of its sides: three branches of the lampstand out of one side, and three branches of the lampstand out of the other side. [19]There were three bowls made like almond *blossoms* on one branch, with an *ornamental* knob and a flower, and three bowls made like almond *blossoms* on the other branch, with an *ornamental* knob and a flower—and so for the six branches coming out of the lampstand. [20]And on the

lampstand itself *were* four bowls made like almond *blossoms, each with* its *ornamental* knob and
flower. [21]*There was* a knob under the *first* two
branches of the same, a knob under the *second*
two branches of the same, and a knob under the
third two branches of the same, according to the
six branches extending from it. [22]Their knobs and
their branches were of one piece; all of it *was* one
hammered piece of pure gold. [23]And he made its
seven lamps, its wick-trimmers, and its trays of
pure gold. [24]Of a talent of pure gold he made it,
with all its utensils.

Making the Altar of Incense

[25]He made the incense altar of acacia wood.
Its length *was* a cubit and its width a cubit—*it
was* square—and two cubits *was* its height. Its
horns were *of one piece* with it. [26]And he overlaid
it with pure gold: its top, its sides all around, and
its horns. He also made for it a molding of gold
all around it. [27]He made two rings of gold for it
under its molding, by its two corners on both
sides, as holders for the poles with which to bear
it. [28]And he made the poles of acacia wood, and
overlaid them with gold.

Making the Anointing Oil and the Incense

[29]He also made the holy anointing oil and the
pure incense of sweet spices, according to the
work of the perfumer.

Making the Altar of Burnt Offering

38 He made the altar of burnt offering
of acacia wood; five cubits *was* its
length and five cubits its width—*it
was* square—and its height *was* three cubits. [2]He
made its horns on its four corners; the horns
were *of one piece* with it. And he overlaid it with
bronze. [3]He made all the utensils for the altar: the
pans, the shovels, the basins, the forks, and the
firepans; all its utensils he made of bronze. [4]And
he made a grate of bronze network for the altar,
under its rim, midway from the bottom. [5]He cast
four rings for the four corners of the bronze
grating, *as* holders for the poles. [6]And he made
the poles of acacia wood, and overlaid them with
bronze. [7]Then he put the poles into the rings on
the sides of the altar, with which to bear it. He
made the altar hollow with boards.

Making the Bronze Laver

[8]He made the laver of bronze and its base of
bronze, from the bronze mirrors of the serving
women who assembled at the door of the tabernacle of meeting.

Making the Court of the Tabernacle

[9]Then he made the court on the south side;
the hangings of the court *were of* fine woven
linen, one hundred cubits long. [10]There *were*
twenty pillars for them, with twenty bronze
sockets. The hooks of the pillars and their bands
were silver. [11]On the north side *the hangings were*
one hundred cubits *long,* with twenty pillars and
their twenty bronze sockets. The hooks of the
pillars and their bands *were* silver. [12]And on the
west side *there were* hangings of fifty cubits, with
ten pillars and their ten sockets. The hooks of the
pillars and their bands *were* silver. [13]For the east
side *the hangings were* fifty cubits. [14]The hangings
of one side *of the gate were* fifteen cubits *long, with*
their three pillars and their three sockets, [15]and
the same for the other side of the court gate; on
this side and that *were* hangings of fifteen cubits,
with their three pillars and their three sockets.
[16]All the hangings of the court all around *were of*
fine woven linen. [17]The sockets for the pillars
were bronze, the hooks of the pillars and their
bands *were* silver, and the overlay of their capitals
was silver; and all the pillars of the court had
bands of silver. [18]The screen for the gate of the
court *was* woven of blue, purple, and scarlet
thread, and of fine woven linen. The length *was*
twenty cubits, and the height along its width *was*
five cubits, corresponding to the hangings of the
court. [19]And *there were* four pillars *with* their four
sockets of bronze; their hooks *were* silver, and the
overlay of their capitals and their bands *was* silver. [20]All the pegs of the tabernacle, and of the
court all around, *were* bronze.

Materials of the Tabernacle

[21]This is the inventory of the tabernacle, the
tabernacle of the Testimony, which was counted
according to the commandment of Moses, for
the service of the Levites, by the hand of
Ithamar, son of Aaron the priest.
[22]Bezalel the son of Uri, the son of Hur, of
the tribe of Judah, made all that the LORD had
commanded Moses. [23]And with him *was* Aholiab
the son of Ahisamach, of the tribe of Dan, an engraver and designer, a weaver of blue, purple, and
scarlet *thread,* and of fine linen.
[24]All the gold that was used in all the work of
the holy *place,* that is, the gold of the offering,
was twenty-nine talents and seven hundred and
thirty shekels, according to the shekel of the
sanctuary. [25]And the silver from those who were
numbered of the congregation *was* one hundred
talents and one thousand seven hundred and
seventy-five shekels, according to the shekel of
the sanctuary: [26]a bekah for each man (*that is,* half

a shekel, according to the shekel of the sanctuary), for everyone included in the numbering from twenty years old and above, for six hundred and three thousand, five hundred and fifty *men.* [27]And from the hundred talents of silver were cast the sockets of the sanctuary and the bases of the veil: one hundred sockets from the hundred talents, one talent for each socket. [28]Then from the one thousand seven hundred and seventy-five *shekels* he made hooks for the pillars, overlaid their capitals, and made bands for them.

[29]The offering of bronze *was* seventy talents and two thousand four hundred shekels. [30]And with it he made the sockets for the door of the tabernacle of meeting, the bronze altar, the bronze grating for it, and all the utensils for the altar, [31]the sockets for the court all around, the bases for the court gate, all the pegs for the tabernacle, and all the pegs for the court all around.

Making the Garments of the Priesthood

39 Of the blue, purple, and scarlet *thread* they made garments of ministry,[a] for ministering in the holy *place,* and made the holy garments for Aaron, as the LORD had commanded Moses.

Making the Ephod

[2]He made the ephod of gold, blue, purple, and scarlet *thread,* and of fine woven linen. [3]And they beat the gold into thin sheets and cut *it into* threads, to work *it in* *with* the blue, purple, and scarlet *thread,* and the fine linen, *into* artistic designs. [4]They made shoulder straps for it to couple *it* together; it was coupled together at its two edges. [5]And the intricately woven band of his ephod that *was* on it *was* of the same workmanship, *woven of* gold, blue, purple, and scarlet *thread,* and of fine woven linen, as the LORD had commanded Moses.

[6]And they set onyx stones, enclosed in settings of gold; they were engraved, as signets are engraved, with the names of the sons of Israel. [7]He put them on the shoulders of the ephod *as* memorial stones for the sons of Israel, as the LORD had commanded Moses.

Making the Breastplate

[8]And he made the breastplate, artistically woven like the workmanship of the ephod, of gold, blue, purple, and scarlet *thread,* and of fine woven linen. [9]They made the breastplate square by doubling it; a span *was* its length and a span its width when doubled. [10]And they set in it four rows of stones: a row with a sardius, a topaz, and an emerald was the first row; [11]the second row, a

turquoise, a sapphire, and a diamond; [12]the third row, a jacinth, an agate, and an amethyst; [13]the fourth row, a beryl, an onyx, and a jasper. *They were* enclosed in settings of gold in their mountings. [14]*There were* twelve stones according to the names of the sons of Israel: according to their names, *engraved like* a signet, each one with its own name according to the twelve tribes. [15]And they made chains for the breastplate at the ends, like braided cords of pure gold. [16]They also made two settings of gold and two gold rings, and put the two rings on the two ends of the breastplate. [17]And they put the two braided *chains* of gold in the two rings on the ends of the breastplate. [18]The two ends of the two braided *chains* they fastened in the two settings, and put them on the shoulder straps of the ephod in the front. [19]And they made two rings of gold and put *them* on the two ends of the breastplate, on the edge of it, which *was* on the inward side of the ephod. [20]They made two *other* gold rings and put them on the two shoulder straps, underneath the ephod toward its front, right at the seam above the intricately woven band of the ephod. [21]And they bound the breastplate by means of its rings to the rings of the ephod with a blue cord, so that it would be above the intricately woven band of the ephod, and that the breastplate would not come loose from the ephod, as the LORD had commanded Moses.

Making the Other Priestly Garments

[22]He made the robe of the ephod of woven work, all of blue. [23]And *there was* an opening in the middle of the robe, like the opening in a coat of mail, *with* a woven binding all around the opening, so that it would not tear. [24]They made on the hem of the robe pomegranates of blue, purple, and scarlet, and of fine woven *linen.* [25]And they made bells of pure gold, and put the bells between the pomegranates on the hem of the robe all around between the pomegranates: [26]a bell and a pomegranate, a bell and a pomegranate, all around the hem of the robe to minister in, as the LORD had commanded Moses.

[27]They made tunics, artistically woven of fine linen, for Aaron and his sons, [28]a turban of fine linen, exquisite hats of fine linen, short trousers of fine woven linen, [29]and a sash of fine woven linen with blue, purple, and scarlet *thread,* made by a weaver, as the LORD had commanded Moses.

39:1 [a]Or *woven garments*

[30]Then they made the plate of the holy crown of pure gold, and wrote on it an inscription *like* the engraving of a signet:

HOLINESS TO THE LORD.

[31]And they tied to it a blue cord, to fasten *it* above on the turban, as the LORD had commanded Moses.

The Work Completed

[32]Thus all the work of the tabernacle of the tent of meeting was finished. And the children of Israel did according to all that the LORD had commanded Moses; so they did. [33]And they brought the tabernacle to Moses, the tent and all its furnishings: its clasps, its boards, its bars, its pillars, and its sockets; [34]the covering of ram skins dyed red, the covering of badger skins, and the veil of the covering; [35]the ark of the Testimony with its poles, and the mercy seat; [36]the table, all its utensils, and the showbread; [37]the pure *gold* lampstand with its lamps (the lamps set in order), all its utensils, and the oil for light; [38]the gold altar, the anointing oil, and the sweet incense; the screen for the tabernacle door; [39]the bronze altar, its grate of bronze, its poles, and all its utensils; the laver with its base; [40]the hangings of the court, its pillars and its sockets, the screen for the court gate, its cords, and its pegs; all the utensils for the service of the tabernacle, for the tent of meeting; [41]and the garments of ministry,[a] to minister in the holy *place:* the holy garments for Aaron the priest, and his sons' garments, to minister as priests.

[42]According to all that the LORD had commanded Moses, so the children of Israel did all the work. [43]Then Moses looked over all the work, and indeed they had done it; as the LORD had commanded, just so they had done it. And Moses blessed them.

The Tabernacle Erected and Arranged

40 Then the LORD spoke to Moses, saying: [2]"On the first day of the first month you shall set up the tabernacle of the tent of meeting. [3]You shall put in it the ark of the Testimony, and partition off the ark with the veil. [4]You shall bring in the table and arrange the things that are to be set in order on it; and you shall bring in the lampstand and light its lamps. [5]You shall also set the altar of gold for the incense before the ark of the Testimony, and put up the screen for the door of the tabernacle. [6]Then you shall set the altar of the burnt offering before the door of the tabernacle of the tent of meeting. [7]And you shall set the laver between the tabernacle of meeting and the altar, and put water in it. [8]You shall set up the court all around, and hang up the screen at the court gate.

[9]"And you shall take the anointing oil, and anoint the tabernacle and all that *is* in it; and you shall hallow it and all its utensils, and it shall be holy. [10]You shall anoint the altar of the burnt offering and all its utensils, and consecrate the altar. The altar shall be most holy. [11]And you shall anoint the laver and its base, and consecrate it.

[12]"Then you shall bring Aaron and his sons to the door of the tabernacle of meeting and wash them with water. [13]You shall put the holy garments on Aaron, and anoint him and consecrate him, that he may minister to Me as priest. [14]And you shall bring his sons and clothe them with tunics. [15]You shall anoint them, as you anointed their father, that they may minister to Me as priests; for their anointing shall surely be an everlasting priesthood throughout their generations."

[16]Thus Moses did; according to all that the LORD had commanded him, so he did.

[17]And it came to pass in the first month of the second year, on the first *day* of the month, *that* the tabernacle was raised up. [18]So Moses raised up the tabernacle, fastened its sockets, set up its boards, put in its bars, and raised up its pillars. [19]And he spread out the tent over the tabernacle and put the covering of the tent on top of it, as the LORD had commanded Moses. [20]He took the Testimony and put *it* into the ark, inserted the poles through the rings of the ark, and put the mercy seat on top of the ark. [21]And he brought the ark into the tabernacle, hung up the veil of the covering, and partitioned off the ark of the Testimony, as the LORD had commanded Moses.

[22]He put the table in the tabernacle of meeting, on the north side of the tabernacle, outside the veil; [23]and he set the bread in order upon it before the LORD, as the LORD had commanded Moses. [24]He put the lampstand in the tabernacle of meeting, across from the table, on the south side of the tabernacle; [25]and he lit the lamps before the LORD, as the LORD had commanded Moses. [26]He put the gold altar in the tabernacle of meeting in front of the veil; [27]and he burned sweet incense on it, as the LORD had commanded Moses. [28]He hung up the screen *at* the door of the tabernacle. [29]And he put the altar of burnt offering *before* the door

---

39:41 [a]Or *woven garments*

of the tabernacle of the tent of meeting, and offered upon it the burnt offering and the grain offering, as the LORD had commanded Moses. ³⁰He set the laver between the tabernacle of meeting and the altar, and put water there for washing; ³¹and Moses, Aaron, and his sons would wash their hands and their feet *with water* from it. ³²Whenever they went into the tabernacle of meeting, and when they came near the altar, they washed, as the LORD had commanded Moses. ³³And he raised up the court all around the tabernacle and the altar, and hung up the screen of the court gate. So Moses finished the work.

The Cloud and the Glory

³⁴Then the cloud covered the tabernacle of meeting, and the glory of the LORD filled the tabernacle. ³⁵And Moses was not able to enter the tabernacle of meeting, because the cloud rested above it, and the glory of the LORD filled the tabernacle. ³⁶Whenever the cloud was taken up from above the tabernacle, the children of Israel would go onward in all their journeys. ³⁷But if the cloud was not taken up, then they did not journey till the day that it was taken up. ³⁸For the cloud of the LORD *was* above the tabernacle by day, and fire was over it by night, in the sight of all the house of Israel, throughout all their journeys.

LEVITICUS
God Establishes a Pattern of Life

SUMMARY

In Leviticus God establishes a pattern of life for both His leaders and His people. The book reminds us that leading means being an example—living a life worth imitating. It teaches us that God requires more than lip service to the cause. Our lives should reflect high values and a high standard for living visible to everyone.

Leviticus describes the beginning of a new era for the Israelites—something like what happens when a C.E.O. establishes the policies and procedures for a brand-new organization. The Jewish nation has just gotten off the ground, like a church plant or a new business. All the employees need a system to help them get things done. They need a management-approved track to run on, which is exactly what God lays out.

The first 16 chapters teach us how to approach God, while the last 11 chapters teach us how to relate with Him and each other. The book also lists blessings for obedience and consequences for disobedience.

With the ground rules in place, the nation can now move from an entrepreneurial phase to an established phase. Organizational structure enables this huge group of people called the Israelites to evolve from a *meandering crowd* into a *meaningful community*.

Scores of books have been written on the difference between leading and managing; the two functions are distinctly different. Managers may not always be leaders, but leaders must be able to manage what has begun until people and systems emerge to enable the operation to run smoothly.

God's Role in Leviticus

Once again, God takes initiative and begins laying out the rules for approaching Him. Because God is holy, Israel's relationship with Yahweh could not be treated flippantly. God leads Moses and the people through the most intricate details of their relationship—from the offerings they were to offer, to the laws surrounding moral purity, to how to implement the required sacrifices. God is holy, therefore His people are to be holy.

Leadership is not some isolated category in our life. We cannot separate our lifestyle from our leadership, or vice versa. God's mega-message in this book to leaders is this: Character does count. Our personal life tremendously impacts our public leadership.

Leaders in Leviticus

Moses, Aaron, Nadab, Abihu, Ithamar

Other People of Influence in Leviticus

Eleazar

Lessons in Leadership

- Leaders must first be good followers.

- Character counts—inward purity impacts outward profession.

- Leadership must be driven by values, not public opinion.

- God disciplines careless disobedience and blesses careful faithfulness.

LEADERSHIP HIGHLIGHTS IN LEVITICUS

The Burnt Offering

1 Now the LORD called to Moses, and spoke to him from the tabernacle of meeting, saying, [2]"Speak to the children of Israel, and say to them: 'When any one of you brings an offering to the LORD, you shall bring your offering of the livestock—of the herd and of the flock.

[3]"If his offering *is* a burnt sacrifice of the herd, let him offer a male without blemish; he shall offer it of his own free will at the door of the tabernacle of meeting before the LORD. [4]Then he shall put his hand on the head of the burnt offering, and it will be accepted on his behalf to make atonement for him. [5]He shall kill the bull before the LORD; and the priests, Aaron's sons, shall bring the blood and sprinkle the blood all around on the altar that *is by* the door of the tabernacle of meeting. [6]And he shall skin the burnt offering and cut it into its pieces. [7]The sons of Aaron the priest shall put fire on the altar, and lay the wood in order on the fire. [8]Then the priests, Aaron's sons, shall lay the parts, the head, and the fat in order on the wood that *is* on the fire upon the altar; [9]but he shall wash its entrails and its legs with water. And the priest shall burn all on the altar as a burnt sacrifice, an offering made by fire, a sweet aroma to the LORD.

[10]"If his offering *is* of the flocks—of the sheep or of the goats—as a burnt sacrifice, he shall bring a male without blemish. [11]He shall kill it on the north side of the altar before the LORD; and the priests, Aaron's sons, shall sprinkle its blood all around on the altar. [12]And he shall cut it into its pieces, with its head and its fat; and the priest shall lay them in order on the wood that *is* on the fire upon the altar; [13]but he shall wash the entrails and the legs with water. Then the priest shall bring *it* all and burn *it* on the altar; it *is* a burnt sacrifice, an offering made by fire, a sweet aroma to the LORD.

[14]"And if the burnt sacrifice of his offering to the LORD *is* of birds, then he shall bring his offering of turtledoves or young pigeons. [15]The priest shall bring it to the altar, wring off its head, and burn *it* on the altar; its blood shall be drained out at the side of the altar. [16]And he shall remove its crop with its feathers and cast it beside the altar on the east side, into the place for ashes. [17]Then he shall split it at its wings, *but* shall not divide *it* completely; and the priest shall burn it on the altar, on the wood that *is* on the fire. It

---

The Law of Sacrifice: We Must Give Up to Get It Right

(Leviticus 1:1—6:30)

Have you ever stopped to think that the "laws of sacrifice" in the Book of Leviticus illustrate the leadership principle we call the Law of Sacrifice? God lays out specific instructions regarding how His people are to offer sacrifices acceptable to Him. He makes it abundantly clear that they must give up certain things in order to get right with Him—and getting right with Him is crucial in light of the big picture.

Cain and Abel made the first offerings recorded in the Bible. The early leaders of the Old Testament made sacrifices to God wherever they settled. Abraham, Isaac, and Jacob built sacrificial altars. Noah offered sacrifices of thanksgiving after the Flood. What did all these sacrifices mean, and how can a leader today apply the purposes of these sacrifices?

Offerings	Meaning	Leader's Application
Burnt Offering	Purging of sinful acts by the worshipper	A leader must pursue moral purity.
Grain Offering	Giving the best from a person's property	A leader must offer excellent effort and service.
Peace Offering	Expressed praise to God and fellowship with others	A leader must commit to prioritize relationships.
Sin (Guilt) Offering	To atone for sin when restitution was impossible	A leader must request forgiveness when wrong.
Trespass Offering	Made for unintentional or lesser offenses	A leader must desire to maintain communication/momentum.

Planning: The Sacrifices Were Plans to Solve Problems
(Leviticus 1:1—6:30)

The fastest way to gain leadership is to solve problems. When Adam and Eve first sinned, it was God who initiated a plan for animal sacrifices to atone for sin. God saw the problem and God solved it. The levitical directions for sacrifices were simply plans to solve sure-to-occur problems. Consider the biblical importance of planning:

1. God did it.
   "Did you not hear long ago how I made it, from ancient times that I formed it? Now I have brought it to pass" (Is. 37:26).

2. Noah did it.
   Noah received explicit instructions to build the ark. He finished its construction in 120 years, exactly as God told him. And the well-built ship withstood months of flooding.

3. Nehemiah did it.
   Nehemiah developed long-range plans to rebuild the wall of Jerusalem. He visualized the project, then planned for its construction. Israelites completed the work in 52 days.

4. David did it.
   David made long-range plans to build the temple. God did not allow him to build it, but David did all the planning and secured the construction materials to get the job done.

5. Jesus told parables about it.
   Jesus often spoke about the necessity of planning (Matt. 7:24–27; Luke 14:28–32; 16:1–8).

How well do you plan? Remember, tomorrow's production begins with today's preparation.

---

is a burnt sacrifice, an offering made by fire, a sweet aroma to the LORD.

The Grain Offering

2 ¹When anyone offers a grain offering to the LORD, his offering shall be *of* fine flour. And he shall pour oil on it, and put frankincense on it. ²He shall bring it to Aaron's sons, the priests, one of whom shall take from it his handful of fine flour and oil with all the frankincense. And the priest shall burn *it as* a memorial on the altar, an offering made by fire, a sweet aroma to the LORD. ³The rest of the grain offering *shall be* Aaron's and his sons'. *It is* most holy of the offerings to the LORD made by fire.

⁴"And if you bring as an offering a grain offering baked in the oven, *it shall be* unleavened cakes of fine flour mixed with oil, or unleavened wafers anointed with oil. ⁵But if your offering *is* a grain offering *baked* in a pan, *it shall be of* fine flour, unleavened, mixed with oil. ⁶You shall break it in pieces and pour oil on it; it *is* a grain offering.

⁷"If your offering *is* a grain offering *baked* in a covered pan, it shall be made *of* fine flour with oil. ⁸You shall bring the grain offering that is made of these things to the LORD. And when it

is presented to the priest, he shall bring it to the altar. ⁹Then the priest shall take from the grain offering a memorial portion, and burn *it* on the altar. *It is* an offering made by fire, a sweet aroma to the LORD. ¹⁰And what is left of the grain offering *shall be* Aaron's and his sons'. *It is* most holy of the offerings to the LORD made by fire.

¹¹"No grain offering which you bring to the LORD shall be made with leaven, for you shall burn no leaven nor any honey in any offering to the LORD made by fire. ¹²As for the offering of the firstfruits, you shall offer them to the LORD, but they shall not be burned on the altar for a sweet aroma. ¹³And every offering of your grain offering you shall season with salt; you shall not allow the salt of the covenant of your God to be lacking from your grain offering. With all your offerings you shall offer salt.

¹⁴"If you offer a grain offering of your firstfruits to the LORD, you shall offer for the grain offering of your firstfruits green heads of grain roasted on the fire, grain beaten from full heads. ¹⁵And you shall put oil on it, and lay frankincense on it. It *is* a grain offering. ¹⁶Then the priest shall burn the memorial portion: *part* of its beaten grain and *part* of its oil, with all the frankincense, as an offering made by fire to the LORD.

The Peace Offering

3 'When his offering *is* a sacrifice of a peace offering, if he offers *it* of the herd, whether male or female, he shall offer it without blemish before the LORD. [2]And he shall lay his hand on the head of his offering, and kill it *at* the door of the tabernacle of meeting; and Aaron's sons, the priests, shall sprinkle the blood all around on the altar. [3]Then he shall offer from the sacrifice of the peace offering an offering made by fire to the LORD. The fat that covers the entrails and all the fat that *is* on the entrails, [4]the two kidneys and the fat that *is* on them by the flanks, and the fatty lobe *attached* to the liver above the kidneys, he shall remove; [5]and Aaron's sons shall burn it on the altar upon the burnt sacrifice, which *is* on the wood that *is* on the fire, *as* an offering made by fire, a sweet aroma to the LORD.

[6]'If his offering as a sacrifice of a peace offering to the LORD *is* of the flock, *whether* male or female, he shall offer it without blemish. [7]If he offers a lamb as his offering, then he shall offer it before the LORD. [8]And he shall lay his hand on the head of his offering, and kill it before the tabernacle of meeting; and Aaron's sons shall sprinkle its blood all around on the altar.

[9]Then he shall offer from the sacrifice of the peace offering, as an offering made by fire to the LORD, its fat *and* the whole fat tail which he shall remove close to the backbone. And the fat that covers the entrails and all the fat that *is* on the entrails, [10]the two kidneys and the fat that *is* on them by the flanks, and the fatty lobe *attached* to the liver above the kidneys, he shall remove; [11]and the priest shall burn *them* on the altar *as* food, an offering made by fire to the LORD.

[12]'And if his offering *is* a goat, then he shall offer it before the LORD. [13]He shall lay his hand on its head and kill it before the tabernacle of meeting; and the sons of Aaron shall sprinkle its blood all around on the altar. [14]Then he shall offer from it his offering, as an offering made by fire to the LORD. The fat that covers the entrails and all the fat that *is* on the entrails, [15]the two kidneys and the fat that *is* on them by the flanks, and the fatty lobe *attached* to the liver above the kidneys, he shall remove; [16]and the priest shall burn them on the altar *as* food, an offering made by fire for a sweet aroma; all the fat *is* the LORD's.

[17]'*This shall be* a perpetual statute throughout your generations in all your dwellings: you shall eat neither fat nor blood.' "

The Sin Offering

4 Now the LORD spoke to Moses, saying, [2]"Speak to the children of Israel, saying: 'If a person sins unintentionally against any of the commandments of the LORD *in anything* which ought not to be done, and does any of them, [3]if the anointed priest sins, bringing guilt on the people, then let him offer to the LORD for his sin which he has sinned a young bull without blemish as a sin offering. [4]He shall bring the bull to the door of the tabernacle of meeting before the LORD, lay his hand on the bull's head, and kill the bull before the LORD. [5]Then the anointed priest shall take some of the bull's blood and bring it to the tabernacle of meeting. [6]The priest shall dip his finger in the blood and sprinkle some of the blood seven times before the LORD, in front of the veil of the sanctuary. [7]And the priest shall put some of the blood on the horns of the altar of sweet incense before the LORD, which is in the tabernacle of meeting; and he shall pour the remaining blood of the bull at the base of the altar of the burnt offering, which is at the door of the tabernacle of meeting. [8]He shall take from it all the fat of the bull as the sin offering. The fat that covers the entrails and all the fat which *is* on the entrails, [9]the two kidneys and the fat that *is* on them by the flanks, and the fatty lobe *attached* to the liver above the kidneys, he shall remove, [10]as it was taken from the bull of the sacrifice of the peace offering; and the priest shall burn them on the altar of the burnt offering. [11]But the bull's hide and all its flesh, with its head and legs, its entrails and offal— [12]the whole bull he shall carry outside the camp to a clean place, where the ashes are poured out, and burn it on wood with fire; where the ashes are poured out it shall be burned.

[13]'Now if the whole congregation of Israel sins unintentionally, and the thing is hidden from the eyes of the assembly, and they have done *something against* any of the commandments of the LORD *in anything* which should not be done, and are guilty; [14]when the sin which they have committed becomes known, then the assembly shall offer a young bull for the sin, and bring it before the tabernacle of meeting. [15]And the elders of the congregation shall lay their hands on the head of the bull before the LORD. Then the bull shall be killed before the LORD. [16]The anointed priest shall bring some of the bull's blood to the tabernacle of meeting. [17]Then the priest shall dip his finger in the blood and sprinkle *it* seven times before the LORD, in front of the veil. [18]And he shall put *some* of the blood on

the horns of the altar which *is* before the LORD, which *is* in the tabernacle of meeting; and he shall pour the remaining blood at the base of the altar of burnt offering, which is at the door of the tabernacle of meeting. ¹⁹He shall take all the fat from it and burn *it* on the altar. ²⁰And he shall do with the bull as he did with the bull as a sin offering; thus he shall do with it. So the priest shall make atonement for them, and it shall be forgiven them. ²¹Then he shall carry the bull outside the camp, and burn it as he burned the first bull. It *is* a sin offering for the assembly.

²²'When a ruler has sinned, and done *something* unintentionally *against* any of the commandments of the LORD his God *in anything* which should not be done, and is guilty, ²³or if his sin which he has committed comes to his knowledge, he shall bring as his offering a kid of the goats, a male without blemish. ²⁴And he shall lay his hand on the head of the goat, and kill it at the place where they kill the burnt offering before the LORD. It *is* a sin offering. ²⁵The priest shall take some of the blood of the sin offering with his finger, put *it* on the horns of the altar of burnt offering, and pour its blood at the base of the altar of burnt offering. ²⁶And he shall burn all its fat on the altar, like the fat of the sacrifice of the peace offering. So the priest shall make atonement for him concerning his sin, and it shall be forgiven him.

²⁷'If anyone of the common people sins unintentionally by doing *something against* any of the commandments of the LORD *in anything* which ought not to be done, and is guilty, ²⁸or if his sin which he has committed comes to his knowledge, then he shall bring as his offering a kid of the goats, a female without blemish, for his sin which he has committed. ²⁹And he shall lay his hand on the head of the sin offering, and kill the sin offering at the place of the burnt offering. ³⁰Then the priest shall take *some* of its blood with his finger, put *it* on the horns of the altar of burnt offering, and pour all *the remaining* blood at the base of the altar. ³¹He shall remove all its fat, as fat is removed from the sacrifice of the peace offering; and the priest shall burn it on the altar for a sweet aroma to the LORD. So the priest shall make atonement for him, and it shall be forgiven him.

³²'If he brings a lamb as his sin offering, he shall bring a female without blemish. ³³Then he shall lay his hand on the head of the sin offering, and kill it as a sin offering at the place where they kill the burnt offering. ³⁴The priest shall take *some* of the blood of the sin offering with his finger, put *it* on the horns of the altar of burnt of-

fering, and pour all *the remaining* blood at the base of the altar. ³⁵He shall remove all its fat, as the fat of the lamb is removed from the sacrifice of the peace offering. Then the priest shall burn it on the altar, according to the offerings made by fire to the LORD. So the priest shall make atonement for his sin that he has committed, and it shall be forgiven him.

The Trespass Offering

5 'If a person sins in hearing the utterance of an oath, and *is* a witness, whether he has seen or known *of the matter*—if he does not tell *it,* he bears guilt.

²'Or if a person touches any unclean thing, whether *it is* the carcass of an unclean beast, or the carcass of unclean livestock, or the carcass of unclean creeping things, and he is unaware of it, he also shall be unclean and guilty. ³Or if he touches human uncleanness—whatever uncleanness with which a man may be defiled, and he is unaware of it—when he realizes *it,* then he shall be guilty.

⁴'Or if a person swears, speaking thoughtlessly with *his* lips to do evil or to do good, whatever *it is* that a man may pronounce by an oath, and he is unaware of it—when he realizes *it,* then he shall be guilty in any of these *matters.*

⁵'And it shall be, when he is guilty in any of these *matters,* that he shall confess that he has sinned in that *thing;* ⁶and he shall bring his trespass offering to the LORD for his sin which he has committed, a female from the flock, a lamb or a kid of the goats as a sin offering. So the priest shall make atonement for him concerning his sin.

⁷'If he is not able to bring a lamb, then he shall bring to the LORD, for his trespass which he has committed, two turtledoves or two young pigeons: one as a sin offering and the other as a burnt offering. ⁸And he shall bring them to the priest, who shall offer *that* which *is* for the sin offering first, and wring off its head from its neck, but shall not divide *it* completely. ⁹Then he shall sprinkle *some* of the blood of the sin offering on the side of the altar, and the rest of the blood shall be drained out at the base of the altar. It *is* a sin offering. ¹⁰And he shall offer the second *as* a burnt offering according to the prescribed manner. So the priest shall make atonement on his behalf for his sin which he has committed, and it shall be forgiven him.

¹¹'But if he is not able to bring two turtledoves or two young pigeons, then he who sinned shall bring for his offering one-tenth of an ephah of fine flour as a sin offering. He shall put no oil

on it, nor shall he put frankincense on it, for it *is* a sin offering. [12]Then he shall bring it to the priest, and the priest shall take his handful of it as a memorial portion, and burn *it* on the altar according to the offerings made by fire to the LORD. It *is* a sin offering. [13]The priest shall make atonement for him, for his sin that he has committed in any of these matters; and it shall be forgiven him. *The rest* shall be the priest's as a grain offering.'"

Offerings with Restitution

[14]Then the LORD spoke to Moses, saying: [15]"If a person commits a trespass, and sins unintentionally in regard to the holy things of the LORD, then he shall bring to the LORD as his trespass offering a ram without blemish from the flocks, with your valuation in shekels of silver according to the shekel of the sanctuary, as a trespass offering. [16]And he shall make restitution for the harm that he has done in regard to the holy thing, and shall add one-fifth to it and give it to the priest. So the priest shall make atonement for him with the ram of the trespass offering, and it shall be forgiven him.

[17]"If a person sins, and commits any of these things which are forbidden to be done by the commandments of the LORD, though he does not know *it,* yet he is guilty and shall bear his iniquity. [18]And he shall bring to the priest a ram without blemish from the flock, with your valuation, as a trespass offering. So the priest shall make atonement for him regarding his ignorance in which he erred and did not know *it,* and it shall be forgiven him. [19]It is a trespass offering; he has certainly trespassed against the LORD."

6 And the LORD spoke to Moses, saying: [2]"If a person sins and commits a trespass against the LORD by lying to his neighbor about what was delivered to him for safekeeping, or about a pledge, or about a robbery, or if he has extorted from his neighbor, [3]or if he has found what was lost and lies concerning it, and swears falsely—in any one of these things that a man may do in which he sins: [4]then it shall be, because he has sinned and is guilty, that he shall restore what he has stolen, or the thing which he has extorted, or what was delivered to him for safekeeping, or the lost thing which he found, [5]or all that about which he has sworn falsely. He shall restore its full value, add one-fifth more to it, *and* give it to whomever it belongs, on the day of his trespass offering. [6]And he shall bring his trespass offering to the LORD, a ram without blemish from the flock, with your valuation, as a trespass offering, to the priest. [7]So the priest shall make

---

Modeling Leadership: Israel to Be an Example
(Leviticus 6:1—10:20)

"**E**xample is not the main thing influencing others," said Albert Schweitzer. "It is the only thing."

Leviticus 6—10 gives detailed instructions about how leaders are to implement sacrifices, how they are to be publicly ordained, and how they are to live a life of total obedience. Why all the fuss? Because example is the most important tool a leader possesses. People do what people see. Note a few of the areas God's priests and leaders were to model:

1. Moral and ethical lifestyle
2. Proper appearance
3. Pure conscience
4. Excellence in fulfilling duties
5. Healthy relationships and restitution
6. Establishing proper priorities
7. Maintaining regulations and guidelines
8. Initiating forgiveness and atonement

Once Israel's leaders had established model lifestyles, God called the entire nation to set an example for the rest of the world. The Hebrews were to model godly behavior for other nations!

---

atonement for him before the LORD, and he shall be forgiven for any one of these things that he may have done in which he trespasses."

The Law of the Burnt Offering

[8]Then the LORD spoke to Moses, saying, [9]"Command Aaron and his sons, saying, 'This *is* the law of the burnt offering: The burnt offering *shall be* on the hearth upon the altar all night until morning, and the fire of the altar shall be kept burning on it. [10]And the priest shall put on his linen garment, and his linen trousers he shall put on his body, and take up the ashes of the burnt offering which the fire has consumed on the altar, and he shall put them beside the altar. [11]Then he shall take off his garments, put on other garments, and carry the ashes outside the camp to a clean place. [12]And the fire on the altar shall be kept burning on it; it shall not be put out. And the priest shall burn wood on it every

morning, and lay the burnt offering in order on it; and he shall burn on it the fat of the peace offerings. [13]A fire shall always be burning on the altar; it shall never go out.

The Law of the Grain Offering

[14]"This *is* the law of the grain offering: The sons of Aaron shall offer it on the altar before the LORD. [15]He shall take from it his handful of the fine flour of the grain offering, with its oil, and all the frankincense which *is* on the grain offering, and shall burn *it* on the altar *for* a sweet aroma, as a memorial to the LORD. [16]And the remainder of it Aaron and his sons shall eat; with unleavened bread it shall be eaten in a holy place; in the court of the tabernacle of meeting they shall eat it. [17]It shall not be baked with leaven. I have given it *as* their portion of My offerings made by fire; it *is* most holy, like the sin offering and the trespass offering. [18]All the males among the children of Aaron may eat it. *It shall be* a statute forever in your generations concerning the offerings made by fire to the LORD. Everyone who touches them must be holy.' "[a]

[19]And the LORD spoke to Moses, saying, [20]"This *is* the offering of Aaron and his sons, which they shall offer to the LORD, *beginning* on the day when he is anointed: one-tenth of an ephah of fine flour as a daily grain offering, half of it in the morning and half of it at night. [21]It shall be made in a pan with oil. *When it is* mixed, you shall bring it in. The baked pieces of the grain offering you shall offer *for* a sweet aroma to the LORD. [22]The priest from among his sons, who is anointed in his place, shall offer it. *It is* a statute forever to the LORD. It shall be wholly burned. [23]For every grain offering for the priest shall be wholly burned. It shall not be eaten."

The Law of the Sin Offering

[24]Also the LORD spoke to Moses, saying, [25]"Speak to Aaron and to his sons, saying, 'This *is* the law of the sin offering: In the place where the burnt offering is killed, the sin offering shall be killed before the LORD. It *is* most holy. [26]The priest who offers it for sin shall eat it. In a holy place it shall be eaten, in the court of the tabernacle of meeting. [27]Everyone who touches its flesh must be holy.[a] And when its blood is sprinkled on any garment, you shall wash that on which it was sprinkled, in a holy place. [28]But the earthen vessel in which it is boiled shall be broken. And if it is boiled in a bronze pot, it shall be both scoured and rinsed in water. [29]All the males among the priests may eat it. It *is* most holy. [30]But no sin offering from which *any* of the blood is

brought into the tabernacle of meeting, to make atonement in the holy *place*,[a] shall be eaten. It shall be burned in the fire.

The Law of the Trespass Offering

7 'Likewise this *is* the law of the trespass offering (it *is* most holy): [2]In the place where they kill the burnt offering they shall kill the trespass offering. And its blood he shall sprinkle all around on the altar. [3]And he shall offer from it all its fat. The fat tail and the fat that covers the entrails, [4]the two kidneys and the fat that *is* on them by the flanks, and the fatty lobe *attached* to the liver above the kidneys, he shall remove; [5]and the priest shall burn them on the altar *as* an offering made by fire to the LORD. It *is* a trespass offering. [6]Every male among the priests may eat it. It shall be eaten in a holy place. It *is* most holy. [7]The trespass offering *is* like the sin offering; *there is* one law for them both: the priest who makes atonement with it shall have *it*. [8]And the priest who offers anyone's burnt offering, that priest shall have for himself the skin of the burnt offering which he has offered. [9]Also every grain offering that is baked in the oven and all that is prepared in the covered pan, or in a pan, shall be the priest's who offers it. [10]Every grain offering, *whether* mixed with oil or dry, shall belong to all the sons of Aaron, to one *as much* as the other.

The Law of Peace Offerings

[11]"This *is* the law of the sacrifice of peace offerings which he shall offer to the LORD: [12]If he offers it for a thanksgiving, then he shall offer, with the sacrifice of thanksgiving, unleavened cakes mixed with oil, unleavened wafers anointed with oil, or cakes of blended flour mixed with oil. [13]Besides the cakes, *as* his offering he shall offer leavened bread with the sacrifice of thanksgiving of his peace offering. [14]And from it he shall offer one cake from each offering *as* a heave offering to the LORD. It shall belong to the priest who sprinkles the blood of the peace offering.

[15]"The flesh of the sacrifice of his peace offering for thanksgiving shall be eaten the same day it is offered. He shall not leave any of it until morning. [16]But if the sacrifice of his offering *is* a vow or a voluntary offering, it shall be eaten the same day that he offers his sacrifice; but on the next day the remainder of it also may be eaten;

6:18 [a]Compare Numbers 4:15 and Haggai 2:11–13
6:27 [a]Compare Numbers 4:15 and Haggai 2:11–13
6:30 [a]The Most Holy Place when capitalized

[17]the remainder of the flesh of the sacrifice on the third day must be burned with fire. [18]And if *any* of the flesh of the sacrifice of his peace offering is eaten at all on the third day, it shall not be accepted, nor shall it be imputed to him; it shall be an abomination *to* him who offers it, and the person who eats of it shall bear guilt.

[19]"The flesh that touches any unclean thing shall not be eaten. It shall be burned with fire. And as for the *clean* flesh, all who are clean may eat of it. [20]But the person who eats the flesh of the sacrifice of the peace offering that *belongs* to the LORD, while he is unclean, that person shall be cut off from his people. [21]Moreover the person who touches any unclean thing, *such as* human uncleanness, *an* unclean animal, or any abominable unclean thing,[a] and who eats the flesh of the sacrifice of the peace offering that *belongs* to the LORD, that person shall be cut off from his people.'"

Fat and Blood May Not Be Eaten

[22]And the LORD spoke to Moses, saying, [23]"Speak to the children of Israel, saying: 'You shall not eat any fat, of ox or sheep or goat. [24]And the fat of an animal that dies *naturally,* and the fat of what is torn by wild beasts, may be used in any other way; but you shall by no means eat it. [25]For whoever eats the fat of the animal of which men offer an offering made by fire to the LORD, the person who eats *it* shall be cut off from his people. [26]Moreover you shall not eat any blood in any of your dwellings, *whether* of bird or beast. [27]Whoever eats any blood, that person shall be cut off from his people.'"

The Portion of Aaron and His Sons

[28]Then the LORD spoke to Moses, saying, [29]"Speak to the children of Israel, saying: 'He who offers the sacrifice of his peace offering to the LORD shall bring his offering to the LORD from the sacrifice of his peace offering. [30]His own hands shall bring the offerings made by fire to the LORD. The fat with the breast he shall bring, that the breast may be waved *as* a wave offering before the LORD. [31]And the priest shall burn the fat on the altar, but the breast shall be Aaron's and his sons'. [32]Also the right thigh you shall give to the priest *as* a heave offering from the sacrifices of your peace offerings. [33]He

---

7:21 [a]Following Masoretic Text, Septuagint, and Vulgate; Samaritan Pentateuch, Syriac, and Targum read *swarming thing* (compare 5:2).

PROFILE IN LEADERSHIP

AARON

THE COST AND EXPECTATION OF LEADERSHIP
(Leviticus 7:33–35)

Aaron, like many leaders throughout history, received a divine calling. God chose Aaron and his sons to serve as Israel's priests and charged them with carrying out rituals and sacrifices on behalf of all Israelites. Scripture gives meticulous detail to their ordination and calling. Their conduct was to be beyond reproach—and God made it crystal clear that failure to uphold His established guidelines would result in death.

Numerous accounts in the Book of Leviticus demonstrate the high cost and expectation that goes with a holy calling to leadership positions. As the high priest, Aaron was the only one authorized to enter the Most Holy Place and appear before the very presence of God. The Lord set Aaron apart for his holy work.

Despite his high calling, Aaron struggled with his authority and later caved in to the depraved wishes of the people. He failed at a crucial juncture and led Israel in a pagan worship service, an abomination that led to the deaths of many Israelites. Aaron had been set apart for God's service, but he chose to live and lead otherwise.

The failure of a leader usually results in consequences far more grave than the fall of a non-leader. On the day Aaron failed, "about three thousand men of the people fell [died]" (Ex. 32:28). When leaders fail, followers pay the price.

among the sons of Aaron, who offers the blood of the peace offering and the fat, shall have the right thigh for *his* part. ³⁴For the breast of the wave offering and the thigh of the heave offering I have taken from the children of Israel, from the sacrifices of their peace offerings, and I have given them to Aaron the priest and to his sons from the children of Israel by a statute forever.' "

³⁵This *is* the consecrated portion for Aaron and his sons, from the offerings made by fire to the LORD, on the day when *Moses* presented them to minister to the LORD as priests. ³⁶The LORD commanded this to be given to them by the children of Israel, on the day that He anointed them, *by* a statute forever throughout their generations.

³⁷This *is* the law of the burnt offering, the grain offering, the sin offering, the trespass offering, the consecrations, and the sacrifice of the peace offering, ³⁸which the LORD commanded Moses on Mount Sinai, on the day when He commanded the children of Israel to offer their offerings to the LORD in the Wilderness of Sinai.

Aaron and His Sons Consecrated

8And the LORD spoke to Moses, saying: ²"Take Aaron and his sons with him, and the garments, the anointing oil, a bull as the sin offering, two rams, and a basket of unleavened bread; ³and gather all the congregation together at the door of the tabernacle of meeting."

⁴So Moses did as the LORD commanded him. And the congregation was gathered together at the door of the tabernacle of meeting. ⁵And Moses said to the congregation, "This *is* what the LORD commanded to be done."

⁶Then Moses brought Aaron and his sons and washed them with water. ⁷And he put the tunic on him, girded him with the sash, clothed him with the robe, and put the ephod on him; and he girded him with the intricately woven band of the ephod, and with it tied *the ephod* on him. ⁸Then he put the breastplate on him, and he put the Urim and the Thummim[a] in the breastplate. ⁹And he put the turban on his head. Also on the turban, on its front, he put the golden plate, the holy crown, as the LORD had commanded Moses.

¹⁰Also Moses took the anointing oil, and anointed the tabernacle and all that *was* in it, and consecrated them. ¹¹He sprinkled some of it on the altar seven times, anointed the altar and all its utensils, and the laver and its base, to consecrate them. ¹²And he poured some of the anointing oil on Aaron's head and anointed him, to consecrate him.

¹³Then Moses brought Aaron's sons and put tunics on them, girded them with sashes, and put hats on them, as the LORD had commanded Moses.

¹⁴And he brought the bull for the sin offering. Then Aaron and his sons laid their hands on the head of the bull for the sin offering, ¹⁵and Moses killed *it*. Then he took the blood, and put *some* on the horns of the altar all around with his finger, and purified the altar. And he poured the blood at the base of the altar, and consecrated it, to make atonement for it. ¹⁶Then he took all the fat that *was* on the entrails, the fatty lobe *attached to* the liver, and the two kidneys with their fat, and Moses burned *them* on the altar. ¹⁷But the bull, its hide, its flesh, and its offal, he burned with fire outside the camp, as the LORD had commanded Moses.

¹⁸Then he brought the ram as the burnt offering. And Aaron and his sons laid their hands on the head of the ram, ¹⁹and Moses killed *it*. Then he sprinkled the blood all around on the altar. ²⁰And he cut the ram into pieces; and Moses burned the head, the pieces, and the fat. ²¹Then he washed the entrails and the legs in water. And Moses burned the whole ram on the altar. It *was* a burnt sacrifice for a sweet aroma, an offering made by fire to the LORD, as the LORD had commanded Moses.

²²And he brought the second ram, the ram of consecration. Then Aaron and his sons laid their hands on the head of the ram, ²³and Moses killed *it*. Also he took *some* of its blood and put it on the tip of Aaron's right ear, on the thumb of his right hand, and on the big toe of his right foot. ²⁴Then he brought Aaron's sons. And Moses put *some* of the blood on the tips of their right ears, on the thumbs of their right hands, and on the big toes of their right feet. And Moses sprinkled the blood all around on the altar. ²⁵Then he took the fat and the fat tail, all the fat that *was* on the entrails, the fatty lobe *attached to* the liver, the two kidneys and their fat, and the right thigh; ²⁶and from the basket of unleavened bread that was before the LORD he took one unleavened cake, a cake of bread *anointed with* oil, and one wafer, and put *them* on the fat and on the right thigh; ²⁷and he put all *these* in Aaron's hands and in his sons' hands, and waved them *as* a wave offering before the LORD. ²⁸Then Moses took them from their hands and burned *them* on the altar, on the burnt offering. They *were* consecration offerings for a sweet aroma. That *was* an offering made by

8:8 [a]Literally *the Lights and the Perfections* (compare Exodus 28:30)

Aaron: God's Call, People's Confirmation

(Leviticus 8:1–36)

Aaron receives his ordination to the priesthood in Leviticus 8. By that time the people already recognized him as a leader, but now God gives him his divine calling. The Lord instructs Aaron to wear certain garments and accessories as an outward symbol of an inward call.

For the godly leader, the call of God becomes a personal foundation for ministry, a point of revelation. One dare not enter a spiritual position without a divine calling. God's call is the first step for anyone who desires a spiritual leadership position.

The Call

Every call has two components: inward and outward. God's hand on the person provides the inward component. Through it the person recognizes that he or she is supposed to occupy a leadership position. And the outward component? This comes when others confirm that God's hand does indeed rest on the person. Only God anoints a person to lead and minister; at best, organizations merely recognize and agree with His anointing. A spiritual leader's authority comes from God, not men.

The word "authorize" is derived from a Latin word which means "to increase or to grow." Frank Damazio reminds us that the word "authorize" suggests the spiritual meanings of: a builder of spiritual buildings; a creator of spiritual families; a doer of spiritual deeds; an author of spiritual writings; a teacher of spiritual knowledge; a spiritual advisor of actions; a promoter of spiritual plans; a supporter of spiritual laws; a spiritual leader in public life; a model of spiritual conduct; a spiritual guardian of women and minors; and a champion of other's spiritual welfare.

Your Response

A few signs often accompany God's call of a person into vocational ministry. Romans 1:14–16 suggests some of these signs:

1. "I am eager" (a sense of passion and urgency about reaching people)
2. "I am obligated" (a feeling that one cannot do anything else vocationally)
3. "I am not ashamed" (a conviction to do what others may think illogical)

The Ordination

The word "ordain" comes from a Latin word that means to "set in order, to arrange, appoint or regulate." To ordain someone means to officially appoint that person to an office and to regulate his or her ministry activities. True ordination does not precede ministry; it follows it. Only after a person exercises obvious spiritual influence, enabled by the Holy Spirit, is that individual ready to be ordained by humans. God calls, and the people confirm the call through ordination.

---

fire to the LORD. [29]And Moses took the breast and waved it *as* a wave offering before the LORD. It was Moses' part of the ram of consecration, as the LORD had commanded Moses.

[30]Then Moses took some of the anointing oil and some of the blood which *was* on the altar, and sprinkled *it* on Aaron, on his garments, on his sons, and on the garments of his sons with him; and he consecrated Aaron, his garments, his sons, and the garments of his sons with him.

[31]And Moses said to Aaron and his sons, "Boil the flesh *at* the door of the tabernacle of meeting, and eat it there with the bread that *is* in the basket of consecration offerings, as I commanded, saying, 'Aaron and his sons shall eat it.' [32]What remains of the flesh and of the bread you shall burn with fire. [33]And you shall not go outside the door of the tabernacle of meeting *for* seven days, until the days of your consecration are ended. For seven days he shall consecrate you. [34]As he has done this day, *so* the LORD has commanded to do, to make atonement for you. [35]Therefore you shall stay *at* the door of the tabernacle of meeting day and night for seven

days, and keep the charge of the LORD, so that you may not die; for so I have been commanded." [36]So Aaron and his sons did all the things that the LORD had commanded by the hand of Moses.

The Priestly Ministry Begins

9 It came to pass on the eighth day that Moses called Aaron and his sons and the elders of Israel. [2]And he said to Aaron, "Take for yourself a young bull as a sin offering and a ram as a burnt offering, without blemish, and offer *them* before the LORD. [3]And to the children of Israel you shall speak, saying, 'Take a kid of the goats as a sin offering, and a calf and a lamb, *both* of the first year, without blemish, as a burnt offering, [4]also a bull and a ram as peace offerings, to sacrifice before the LORD, and a grain offering mixed with oil; for today the LORD will appear to you.'"

[5]So they brought what Moses commanded before the tabernacle of meeting. And all the congregation drew near and stood before the LORD. [6]Then Moses said, "This *is* the thing which the LORD commanded you to do, and the glory of the LORD will appear to you." [7]And Moses said to Aaron, "Go to the altar, offer your sin offering and your burnt offering, and make atonement for yourself and for the people. Offer the offering of the people, and make atonement for them, as the LORD commanded."

[8]Aaron therefore went to the altar and killed the calf of the sin offering, which *was* for himself. [9]Then the sons of Aaron brought the blood to him. And he dipped his finger in the blood, put *it* on the horns of the altar, and poured the blood at the base of the altar. [10]But the fat, the kidneys, and the fatty lobe from the liver of the sin offering he burned on the altar, as the LORD had commanded Moses. [11]The flesh and the hide he burned with fire outside the camp.

[12]And he killed the burnt offering; and Aaron's sons presented to him the blood, which he sprinkled all around on the altar. [13]Then they presented the burnt offering to him, with its pieces and head, and he burned *them* on the altar. [14]And he washed the entrails and the legs, and burned *them* with the burnt offering on the altar.

[15]Then he brought the people's offering, and took the goat, which *was* the sin offering for the people, and killed it and offered it for sin, like the first one. [16]And he brought the burnt offering and offered it according to the prescribed manner. [17]Then he brought the grain offering, took a handful of it, and burned *it* on the altar, besides the burnt sacrifice of the morning.

[18]He also killed the bull and the ram *as* sacrifices of peace offerings, which *were* for the people. And Aaron's sons presented to him the blood, which he sprinkled all around on the altar, [19]and the fat from the bull and the ram—the fatty tail, what covers *the entrails* and the kidneys, and the fatty lobe *attached to* the liver; [20]and they put the fat on the breasts. Then he burned the fat on the altar; [21]but the breasts and the right thigh Aaron waved *as* a wave offering before the LORD, as Moses had commanded.

[22]Then Aaron lifted his hand toward the people, blessed them, and came down from offering the sin offering, the burnt offering, and peace offerings. [23]And Moses and Aaron went into the tabernacle of meeting, and came out and blessed the people. Then the glory of the LORD appeared to all the people, [24]and fire came out from before the LORD and consumed the burnt offering and the fat on the altar. When all the people saw *it,* they shouted and fell on their faces.

The Profane Fire of Nadab and Abihu

10 Then Nadab and Abihu, the sons of Aaron, each took his censer and put fire in it, put incense on it, and offered profane fire before the LORD, which He had not commanded them. [2]So fire went out from the LORD and devoured them, and they died before the LORD. [3]And Moses said to Aaron, "This is what the LORD spoke, saying:

'By those who come near Me
I must be regarded as holy;
And before all the people
I must be glorified.'"

So Aaron held his peace.

[4]Then Moses called Mishael and Elzaphan, the sons of Uzziel the uncle of Aaron, and said to them, "Come near, carry your brethren from before the sanctuary out of the camp." [5]So they went near and carried them by their tunics out of the camp, as Moses had said.

[6]And Moses said to Aaron, and to Eleazar and Ithamar, his sons, "Do not uncover your heads nor tear your clothes, lest you die, and wrath come upon all the people. But let your brethren, the whole house of Israel, bewail the burning which the LORD has kindled. [7]You shall not go out from the door of the tabernacle of meeting, lest you die, for the anointing oil of the LORD *is* upon you." And they did according to the word of Moses.

Nadab and Abihu Break the Law of Solid Ground
(Leviticus 10:1, 2)

God does not take it lightly when the leaders He calls disregard His commandments. When Nadab and Abihu broke God's laws, they never recovered. God executed them on the spot.

Sounds harsh, you say? Consider this. Any movement in its infant stages must set a standard or pattern of operations. If God allowed compromise at the beginning, things would surely grow worse. The same principle came into play in the new church when God took the lives of Ananias and Sapphira (Acts 5:1–11).

Nadab and Abihu broke the Law of Solid Ground. As holy priests and trusted leaders, they were supposed to model obedience for the people. God could not permit them even the slightest renegade move, the smallest maverick act, for that would give permission for others to compromise as well. What was the sin of these leaders?

1. *Independence:* They acted presumptuously, apart from God's leadership.
2. *Impatience:* They failed to wait on the Lord for direction.
3. *Ignorance:* They moved without knowledge of what God wanted.
4. *Illegality:* They acted contrary to God's command.
5. *Impulsivity:* They did what they wanted, driven by ego, not submission.
6. *Insensitivity:* They paid no attention to God's instruction.

Conduct Prescribed for Priests

[8]Then the LORD spoke to Aaron, saying: [9]"Do not drink wine or intoxicating drink, you, nor your sons with you, when you go into the tabernacle of meeting, lest you die. *It shall be* a statute forever throughout your generations, [10]that you may distinguish between holy and unholy, and between unclean and clean, [11]and that you may teach the children of Israel all the statutes which the LORD has spoken to them by the hand of Moses."

[12]And Moses spoke to Aaron, and to Eleazar and Ithamar, his sons who were left: "Take the grain offering that remains of the offerings made by fire to the LORD, and eat it without leaven beside the altar; for it *is* most holy. [13]You shall eat it in a holy place, because it *is* your due and your sons' due, of the sacrifices made by fire to the LORD; for so I have been commanded. [14]The breast of the wave offering and the thigh of the heave offering you shall eat in a clean place, you, your sons, and your daughters with you; for *they are* your due and your sons' due, *which* are given from the sacrifices of peace offerings of the children of Israel. [15]The thigh of the heave offering and the breast of the wave offering they shall bring with the offerings of fat made by fire, to offer *as* a wave offering before the LORD. And it shall be yours and your sons' with you, by a statute forever, as the LORD has commanded."

[16]Then Moses made careful inquiry about the goat of the sin offering, and there it was—burned up. And he was angry with Eleazar and Ithamar, the sons of Aaron *who were* left, saying, [17]"Why have you not eaten the sin offering in a holy place, since it *is* most holy, and *God* has given it to you to bear the guilt of the congregation, to make atonement for them before the LORD? [18]See! Its blood was not brought inside the holy *place;*[a] indeed you should have eaten it in a holy *place,* as I commanded." [19]And Aaron said to Moses, "Look, this day they have offered their sin offering and their burnt offering before the LORD, and such things have befallen me! *If* I had eaten the sin offering today, would it have been accepted in the sight of the LORD?" [20]So when Moses heard *that,* he was content.

Foods Permitted and Forbidden

11 Now the LORD spoke to Moses and Aaron, saying to them, [2]"Speak to the children of Israel, saying, 'These *are* the animals which you may eat among all the animals that *are* on the earth: [3]Among the animals, whatever divides the hoof, having cloven hooves *and* chewing the cud—that you may eat. [4]Nevertheless these you shall not eat among those that

10:18 [a]The Most Holy Place when capitalized

Character: Take It Seriously

(Leviticus 10:1—12:8)

God takes seriously the issue of character. We see His concern repeatedly in Leviticus, from the sin of Aaron's sons to His detailed instructions about clean and unclean food to the purification of a woman after childbirth.

While today we recognize some obvious medical and biological reasons for His precise directions, we can assume God intended through these texts to teach His leaders and His people an important lesson: Put "being" before "doing." Get *yourself* right before you work on anything else.

Far too often we jump to mechanics, methods, and techniques. We put style ahead of substance. We focus on charisma but neglect character. The following axioms beckon us to put our character first:

1. We are given our gifts, but we must develop our character.
2. Our character earns the trust of others.
3. Only good character gives lasting success with people.
4. Sound character communicates credibility and consistency.
5. Our character colors our perspective.
6. Ability may get you to the top, but it takes character to keep you there.
7. We cannot rise above the limitations of our character.

chew the cud or those that have cloven hooves: the camel, because it chews the cud but does not have cloven hooves, is unclean to you; [5]the rock hyrax, because it chews the cud but does not have cloven hooves, *is* unclean to you; [6]the hare, because it chews the cud but does not have cloven hooves, *is* unclean to you; [7]and the swine, though it divides the hoof, having cloven hooves, yet does not chew the cud, *is* unclean to you. [8]Their flesh you shall not eat, and their carcasses you shall not touch. They *are* unclean to you.

[9]These you may eat of all that *are* in the water: whatever in the water has fins and scales, whether in the seas or in the rivers—that you may eat. [10]But all in the seas or in the rivers that do not have fins and scales, all that move in the water or any living thing which *is* in the water, they *are* an abomination to you. [11]They shall be an abomination to you; you shall not eat their flesh, but you shall regard their carcasses as an abomination. [12]Whatever in the water does not have fins or scales—that *shall be* an abomination to you.

[13]And these you shall regard as an abomination among the birds; they shall not be eaten, they *are* an abomination: the eagle, the vulture, the buzzard, [14]the kite, and the falcon after its kind; [15]every raven after its kind, [16]the ostrich, the short-eared owl, the sea gull, and the hawk after its kind; [17]the little owl, the fisher owl, and the screech owl; [18]the white owl, the jackdaw, and the carrion vulture; [19]the stork, the heron after its kind, the hoopoe, and the bat.

[20]"All flying insects that creep on *all* fours *shall be* an abomination to you. [21]Yet these you may eat of every flying insect that creeps on *all* fours: those which have jointed legs above their feet with which to leap on the earth. [22]These you may eat: the locust after its kind, the destroying locust after its kind, the cricket after its kind, and the grasshopper after its kind. [23]But all *other* flying insects which have four feet *shall be* an abomination to you.

Unclean Animals

[24]"By these you shall become unclean; whoever touches the carcass of any of them shall be unclean until evening; [25]whoever carries part of the carcass of any of them shall wash his clothes and be unclean until evening: [26]*The carcass* of any animal which divides the foot, but is not clovenhoofed or does not chew the cud, *is* unclean to you. Everyone who touches it shall be unclean. [27]And whatever goes on its paws, among all kinds of animals that go on *all* fours, those *are* unclean to you. Whoever touches any such carcass shall be unclean until evening. [28]Whoever carries *any such* carcass shall wash his clothes and be unclean until evening. It *is* unclean to you.

[29]"These also *shall be* unclean to you among the creeping things that creep on the earth: the

mole, the mouse, and the large lizard after its kind; [30]the gecko, the monitor lizard, the sand reptile, the sand lizard, and the chameleon. [31]These *are* unclean to you among all that creep. Whoever touches them when they are dead shall be unclean until evening. [32]Anything on which *any* of them falls, when they are dead shall be unclean, whether *it is* any item of wood or clothing or skin or sack, whatever item *it is,* in which *any* work is done, it must be put in water. And it shall be unclean until evening; then it shall be clean. [33]Any earthen vessel into which *any* of them falls you shall break; and whatever *is* in it shall be unclean: [34]in such a vessel, any edible food upon which water falls becomes unclean, and any drink that may be drunk from it becomes unclean. [35]And everything on which *a part* of *any such* carcass falls shall be unclean; *whether it is* an oven or cooking stove, it shall be broken down; *for they are* unclean, and shall be unclean to you. [36]Nevertheless a spring or a cistern, *in which there is* plenty of water, shall be clean, but whatever touches any such carcass becomes unclean. [37]And if a part of *any such* carcass falls on any planting seed which is to be sown, it *remains* clean. [38]But if water is put on the seed, and if *a part* of *any such* carcass falls on it, it *becomes* unclean to you.

[39]And if any animal which you may eat dies, he who touches its carcass shall be unclean until evening. [40]He who eats of its carcass shall wash his clothes and be unclean until evening. He also who carries its carcass shall wash his clothes and be unclean until evening.

[41]And every creeping thing that creeps on the earth *shall be* an abomination. It shall not be eaten. [42]Whatever crawls on its belly, whatever goes on *all* fours, or whatever has many feet among all creeping things that creep on the earth—these you shall not eat, for they *are* an abomination. [43]You shall not make yourselves abominable with any creeping thing that creeps; nor shall you make yourselves unclean with them, lest you be defiled by them. [44]For I *am* the LORD your God. You shall therefore consecrate yourselves, and you shall be holy; for I *am* holy. Neither shall you defile yourselves with any creeping thing that creeps on the earth. [45]For I *am* the LORD who brings you up out of the land of Egypt, to be your God. You shall therefore be holy, for I *am* holy.

[46]This *is* the law of the animals and the birds and every living creature that moves in the waters, and of every creature that creeps on the earth, [47]to distinguish between the unclean and the clean, and between the animal that may be eaten and the animal that may not be eaten.' "

The Ritual After Childbirth

12 Then the LORD spoke to Moses, saying, [2]"Speak to the children of Israel, saying: 'If a woman has conceived, and borne a male child, then she shall be unclean seven days; as in the days of her customary impurity she shall be unclean. [3]And on the eighth day the flesh of his foreskin shall be circumcised. [4]She shall then continue in the blood of *her* purification thirty-three days. She shall not touch any hallowed thing, nor come into the sanctuary until the days of her purification are fulfilled.

[5]But if she bears a female child, then she shall be unclean two weeks, as in her customary impurity, and she shall continue in the blood of *her* purification sixty-six days.

[6]When the days of her purification are fulfilled, whether for a son or a daughter, she shall bring to the priest a lamb of the first year as a burnt offering, and a young pigeon or a turtledove as a sin offering, to the door of the tabernacle of meeting. [7]Then he shall offer it before the LORD, and make atonement for her. And she shall be clean from the flow of her blood. This *is* the law for her who has borne a male or a female.

[8]And if she is not able to bring a lamb, then she may bring two turtledoves or two young pigeons—one as a burnt offering and the other as a sin offering. So the priest shall make atonement for her, and she will be clean.' "

The Law Concerning Leprosy

13 And the LORD spoke to Moses and Aaron, saying: [2]"When a man has on the skin of his body a swelling, a scab, or a bright spot, and it becomes on the skin of his body *like* a leprous[a] sore, then he shall be brought to Aaron the priest or to one of his sons the priests. [3]The priest shall examine the sore on the skin of the body; and if the hair on the sore has turned white, and the sore appears *to be* deeper than the skin of his body, it *is* a leprous sore. Then the priest shall examine him, and pronounce him unclean. [4]But if the bright spot *is* white on the skin of his body, and does not appear *to be* deeper than the skin, and its hair has not turned white, then the priest shall isolate *the one who has* the sore seven days. [5]And the priest shall examine him on the seventh day; and in-

---

13:2 [a]Hebrew *saraath,* disfiguring skin diseases, including leprosy, and so in verses 2–46 and 14:1–32 deed *if* the sore appears to be as it was, *and* the sore has not spread on the skin, then the priest shall isolate him another seven days. [6]Then the priest shall examine him again on the seventh day; and indeed *if* the sore has faded, *and* the sore has not spread on the skin, then the priest shall pronounce him clean; it *is* only a scab, and he shall wash his clothes and be clean. [7]But if the scab should at all spread over the skin, after he has been seen by the priest for his cleansing, he shall be seen by the priest again. [8]And *if* the priest sees that the scab has indeed spread on the skin, then the priest shall pronounce him unclean. It *is* leprosy.

[9]"When the leprous sore is on a person, then he shall be brought to the priest. [10]And the priest shall examine *him;* and indeed *if* the swelling on the skin *is* white, and it has turned the hair white, and *there is* a spot of raw flesh in the swelling, [11]it *is* an old leprosy on the skin of his body. The priest shall pronounce him unclean, and shall not isolate him, for he *is* unclean.

[12]"And if leprosy breaks out all over the skin, and the leprosy covers all the skin of *the one who has* the sore, from his head to his foot, wherever the priest looks, [13]then the priest shall consider; and indeed *if* the leprosy has covered all his body, he shall pronounce *him* clean *who has* the sore. It has all turned white. He *is* clean. [14]But when raw flesh appears on him, he shall be unclean. [15]And the priest shall examine the raw flesh and pronounce him to be unclean; *for* the raw flesh *is* unclean. It *is* leprosy. [16]Or if the raw flesh changes and turns white again, he shall come to the priest. [17]And the priest shall examine him; and indeed *if* the sore has turned white, then the priest shall pronounce *him* clean *who has* the sore. He *is* clean.

[18]"If the body develops a boil in the skin, and it is healed, [19]and in the place of the boil there comes a white swelling or a bright spot, reddish-white, then it shall be shown to the priest; [20]and *if,* when the priest sees it, it indeed *appears* deeper than the skin, and its hair has turned white, the priest shall pronounce him unclean. It *is* a leprous sore which has broken out of the boil. [21]But if the priest examines it, and indeed *there are* no white hairs in it, and it *is* not deeper than the skin, but has faded, then the priest shall isolate him seven days; [22]and if it should at all spread over the skin, then the priest shall pronounce him unclean. It *is* a leprous sore. [23]But if the bright spot stays in one place, *and* has not spread, it *is* the scar of the boil; and the priest shall pronounce him clean.

[24]"Or if the body receives a burn on its skin by fire, and the raw *flesh* of the burn becomes a bright spot, reddish-white or white, [25]then the priest shall examine it; and indeed *if* the hair of the bright spot has turned white, and it appears deeper than the skin, it *is* leprosy broken out in the burn. Therefore the priest shall pronounce him unclean. It *is* a leprous sore. [26]But if the priest examines it, and indeed *there are* no white hairs in the bright spot, and it *is* not deeper than the skin, but has faded, then the priest shall isolate him seven days. [27]And the priest shall examine him on the seventh day. If it has at all spread over the skin, then the priest shall pronounce him unclean. It *is* a leprous sore. [28]But if the bright spot stays in one place, *and* has not spread on the skin, but has faded, it *is* a swelling from the burn. The priest shall pronounce him clean, for it *is* the scar from the burn.

[29]"If a man or woman has a sore on the head or the beard, [30]then the priest shall examine the sore; and indeed if it appears deeper than the skin, *and there is* in it thin yellow hair, then the priest shall pronounce him unclean. It *is* a scaly leprosy of the head or beard. [31]But if the priest examines the scaly sore, and indeed it does not appear deeper than the skin, and *there is* no black hair in it, then the priest shall isolate *the one who has* the scale seven days. [32]And on the seventh day the priest shall examine the sore; and indeed *if* the scale has not spread, and there is no yellow hair in it, and the scale does not appear deeper than the skin, [33]he shall shave himself, but the scale he shall not shave. And the priest shall isolate *the one who has* the scale another seven days. [34]On the seventh day the priest shall examine the scale; and indeed *if* the scale has not spread over the skin, and does not appear deeper than the skin, then the priest shall pronounce him clean. He shall wash his clothes and be clean. [35]But if the scale should at all spread over the skin after his cleansing, [36]then the priest shall examine him; and indeed *if* the scale has spread over the skin, the priest need not seek for yellow hair. He *is* unclean. [37]But if the scale appears to be at a standstill, and there is black hair grown up in it, the scale has healed. He *is* clean, and the priest shall pronounce him clean.

[38]"If a man or a woman has bright spots on the skin of the body, *specifically* white bright spots, [39]then the priest shall look; and indeed *if* the bright spots on the skin of the body *are* dull white, it *is* a white spot *that* grows on the skin. He *is* clean.

[40]"As for the man whose hair has fallen from his head, he *is* bald, *but* he *is* clean. [41]He whose hair has fallen from his forehead, he *is* bald on

the forehead, *but* he *is* clean. [42]And if there is on the bald head or bald forehead a reddish-white sore, it *is* leprosy breaking out on his bald head or his bald forehead. [43]Then the priest shall examine it; and indeed *if* the swelling of the sore *is* reddish-white on his bald head or on his bald forehead, as the appearance of leprosy on the skin of the body, [44]he is a leprous man. He *is* unclean. The priest shall surely pronounce him unclean; his sore *is* on his head.

[45]"Now the leper on whom the sore *is,* his clothes shall be torn and his head bare; and he shall cover his mustache, and cry, 'Unclean! Unclean!' [46]He shall be unclean. All the days he has the sore he shall be unclean. He *is* unclean, and he shall dwell alone; his dwelling *shall be* outside the camp.

The Law Concerning Leprous Garments

[47]"Also, if a garment has a leprous plague[a] in it, *whether it is* a woolen garment or a linen garment, [48]whether *it is* in the warp or woof of linen or wool, whether in leather or in anything made of leather, [49]and if the plague is greenish or reddish in the garment or in the leather, whether in the warp or in the woof, or in anything made of leather, it *is* a leprous plague and shall be shown to the priest. [50]The priest shall examine the plague and isolate *that which has* the plague seven days. [51]And he shall examine the plague on the seventh day. If the plague has spread in the garment, either in the warp or in the woof, in the leather *or* in anything made of leather, the plague *is* an active leprosy. It *is* unclean. [52]He shall therefore burn that garment in which is the plague, whether warp or woof, in wool or in linen, or anything of leather, for it *is* an active leprosy; *the garment* shall be burned in the fire.

[53]"But if the priest examines *it,* and indeed the plague has not spread in the garment, either in the warp or in the woof, or in anything made of leather, [54]then the priest shall command that they wash *the thing* in which *is* the plague; and he shall isolate it another seven days. [55]Then the priest shall examine the plague after it has been washed; and indeed *if* the plague has not changed its color, though the plague has not spread, it *is* unclean, and you shall burn it in the fire; it continues eating away, *whether* the damage *is* outside or inside. [56]If the priest examines *it,* and indeed the plague has faded after washing it, then he shall tear it out of the garment, whether out of the warp or out of the woof, or out of the leather. [57]But if it appears again in the garment, either in the warp or in the woof, or in anything made of leather, it *is* a spreading *plague;* you shall burn with fire that in which is the plague. [58]And

if you wash the garment, either warp or woof, or whatever is made of leather, if the plague has disappeared from it, then it shall be washed a second time, and shall be clean.

[59]"This *is* the law of the leprous plague in a garment of wool or linen, either in the warp or woof, or in anything made of leather, to pronounce it clean or to pronounce it unclean."

The Ritual for Cleansing Healed Lepers

14 Then the LORD spoke to Moses, saying, [2]"This shall be the law of the leper for the day of his cleansing: He shall be brought to the priest. [3]And the priest shall go out of the camp, and the priest shall examine *him;* and indeed, *if* the leprosy is healed in the leper, [4]then the priest shall command to take for him who is to be cleansed two living *and* clean birds, cedar wood, scarlet, and hyssop. [5]And the priest shall command that one of the birds be killed in an earthen vessel over running water. [6]As for the living bird, he shall take it, the cedar wood and the scarlet and the hyssop, and dip them and the living bird in the blood of the bird *that was* killed over the running water. [7]And he shall sprinkle it seven times on him who is to be cleansed from the leprosy, and shall pronounce him clean, and shall let the living bird loose in the open field. [8]He who is to be cleansed shall wash his clothes, shave off all his hair, and wash himself in water, that he may be clean. After that he shall come into the camp, and shall stay outside his tent seven days. [9]But on the seventh day he shall shave all the hair off his head and his beard and his eyebrows—all his hair he shall shave off. He shall wash his clothes and wash his body in water, and he shall be clean.

[10]"And on the eighth day he shall take two male lambs without blemish, one ewe lamb of the first year without blemish, three-tenths *of an ephah* of fine flour mixed with oil as a grain offering, and one log of oil. [11]Then the priest who makes *him* clean shall present the man who is to be made clean, and those things, before the LORD, *at* the door of the tabernacle of meeting. [12]And the priest shall take one male lamb and offer it as a trespass offering, and the log of oil, and wave them *as* a wave offering before the LORD. [13]Then he shall kill the lamb in the place where he kills the sin offering and the burnt offering, in a holy place; for as the sin offering *is* the priest's, so *is* the trespass offering. It *is* most holy. [14]The priest shall take *some* of the blood of the trespass

---

13:47 [a]A mold, fungus, or similar infestation, and so in verses 47–59

offering, and the priest shall put *it* on the tip of the right ear of him who is to be cleansed, on the thumb of his right hand, and on the big toe of his right foot. [15]And the priest shall take *some* of the log of oil, and pour *it* into the palm of his own left hand. [16]Then the priest shall dip his right finger in the oil that *is* in his left hand, and shall sprinkle some of the oil with his finger seven times before the LORD. [17]And of the rest of the oil in his hand, the priest shall put *some* on the tip of the right ear of him who is to be cleansed, on the thumb of his right hand, and on the big toe of his right foot, on the blood of the trespass offering. [18]The rest of the oil that *is* in the priest's hand he shall put on the head of him who is to be cleansed. So the priest shall make atonement for him before the LORD.

[19]"Then the priest shall offer the sin offering, and make atonement for him who is to be cleansed from his uncleanness. Afterward he shall kill the burnt offering. [20]And the priest shall offer the burnt offering and the grain offering on the altar. So the priest shall make atonement for him, and he shall be clean.

[21]"But if he *is* poor and cannot afford it, then he shall take one male lamb *as* a trespass offering to be waved, to make atonement for him, one-tenth *of an ephah* of fine flour mixed with oil as a grain offering, a log of oil, [22]and two turtledoves or two young pigeons, such as he is able to afford: one shall be a sin offering and the other a burnt offering. [23]He shall bring them to the priest on the eighth day for his cleansing, to the door of the tabernacle of meeting, before the LORD. [24]And the priest shall take the lamb of the trespass offering and the log of oil, and the priest shall wave them *as* a wave offering before the LORD. [25]Then he shall kill the lamb of the trespass offering, and the priest shall take *some* of the blood of the trespass offering and put *it* on the tip of the right ear of him who is to be cleansed, on the thumb of his right hand, and on the big toe of his right foot. [26]And the priest shall pour some of the oil into the palm of his own left hand. [27]Then the priest shall sprinkle with his right finger *some* of the oil that *is* in his left hand seven times before the LORD. [28]And the priest shall put *some* of the oil that *is* in his hand on the tip of the right ear of him who is to be cleansed, on the thumb of the right hand, and on the big toe of his right foot, on the place of the blood of the trespass offering. [29]The rest of the oil that *is* in the priest's hand he shall put on the head of him who is to be cleansed, to make atonement for him before the LORD. [30]And he shall offer one of the turtledoves or young pigeons, such as he can afford—

[31]such as he is able to afford, the one *as* a sin offering and the other *as* a burnt offering, with the grain offering. So the priest shall make atonement for him who is to be cleansed before the LORD. [32]This *is* the law *for one* who had a leprous sore, who cannot afford the usual cleansing."

The Law Concerning Leprous Houses

[33]And the LORD spoke to Moses and Aaron, saying: [34]"When you have come into the land of Canaan, which I give you as a possession, and I put the leprous plague[a] in a house in the land of your possession, [35]and he who owns the house comes and tells the priest, saying, 'It seems to me that *there is* some plague in the house,' [36]then the priest shall command that they empty the house, before the priest goes *into it* to examine the plague, that all that *is* in the house may not be made unclean; and afterward the priest shall go in to examine the house. [37]And he shall examine the plague; and indeed *if* the plague *is* on the walls of the house with ingrained streaks, greenish or reddish, which appear to be deep in the wall, [38]then the priest shall go out of the house, to the door of the house, and shut up the house seven days. [39]And the priest shall come again on the seventh day and look; and indeed *if* the plague has spread on the walls of the house, [40]then the priest shall command that they take away the stones in which *is* the plague, and they shall cast them into an unclean place outside the city. [41]And he shall cause the house to be scraped inside, all around, and the dust that they scrape off they shall pour out in an unclean place outside the city. [42]Then they shall take other stones and put *them* in the place of *those* stones, and he shall take other mortar and plaster the house.

[43]"Now if the plague comes back and breaks out in the house, after he has taken away the stones, after he has scraped the house, and after it is plastered, [44]then the priest shall come and look; and indeed *if* the plague has spread in the house, it *is* an active leprosy in the house. It *is* unclean. [45]And he shall break down the house, its stones, its timber, and all the plaster of the house, and he shall carry *them* outside the city to an unclean place. [46]Moreover he who goes into the house at all while it is shut up shall be unclean until evening. [47]And he who lies down in the house shall wash his clothes, and he who eats in the house shall wash his clothes.

[48]"But if the priest comes in and examines *it,* and indeed the plague has not spread in the

---

14:34 [a]Decomposition by mildew, mold, dry rot, etc., and so in verses 34–53

house after the house was plastered, then the priest shall pronounce the house clean, because the plague is healed. ⁴⁹And he shall take, to cleanse the house, two birds, cedar wood, scarlet, and hyssop. ⁵⁰Then he shall kill one of the birds in an earthen vessel over running water; ⁵¹and he shall take the cedar wood, the hyssop, the scarlet, and the living bird, and dip them in the blood of the slain bird and in the running water, and sprinkle the house seven times. ⁵²And he shall cleanse the house with the blood of the bird and the running water and the living bird, with the cedar wood, the hyssop, and the scarlet. ⁵³Then he shall let the living bird loose outside the city in the open field, and make atonement for the house, and it shall be clean.

⁵⁴"This *is* the law for any leprous sore and scale, ⁵⁵for the leprosy of a garment and of a house, ⁵⁶for a swelling and a scab and a bright spot, ⁵⁷to teach when *it is* unclean and when *it is* clean. This *is* the law of leprosy."

The Law Concerning Bodily Discharges

15 And the LORD spoke to Moses and Aaron, saying, ²"Speak to the children of Israel, and say to them: 'When any man has a discharge from his body, his discharge *is* unclean. ³And this shall be his uncleanness in regard to his discharge—whether his body runs with his discharge, or his body is stopped up by his discharge, it *is* his uncleanness. ⁴Every bed is unclean on which he who has the discharge lies, and everything on which he sits shall be unclean. ⁵And whoever touches his bed shall wash his clothes and bathe in water, and be unclean until evening. ⁶He who sits on anything on which he who has the discharge sat shall wash his clothes and bathe in water, and be unclean until evening. ⁷And he who touches the body of him who has the discharge shall wash his clothes and bathe in water, and be unclean until evening. ⁸If he who has the discharge spits on him who is clean, then he shall wash his clothes and bathe in water, and be unclean until evening. ⁹Any saddle on which he who has the discharge rides shall be unclean. ¹⁰Whoever touches anything that was under him shall be unclean until evening. He who carries *any of* those things shall wash his clothes and bathe in water, and be unclean until evening. ¹¹And whomever the one who has the discharge touches, and has not rinsed his hands in water, he shall wash his clothes and bathe in water, and be unclean until evening. ¹²The vessel of earth that he who has the discharge touches shall be broken, and every vessel of wood shall be rinsed in water.

MOSES
GOD'S PROBLEM SOLVER
(Leviticus 15:1–33)

PROFILE IN LEADERSHIP

Have you noticed that rules, regulations, and laws often bring out the human tendency to ask, "But why?"

Sometimes the Lord gives the reasons behind His laws, as He does near the end of Leviticus 15. Here God says He gave the people various ceremonial laws in order to "separate the children of Israel from their uncleanness, lest they die in their uncleanness when they defile My tabernacle that is among them" (Lev. 15:31).

It may seem odd to us that God demonstrated such concern over personal cleanliness, but could it be that God knows something we don't? If Moses harped on one thing, it was this: Be sure to obey your God (whether you understand the *why* or not).

Many of our problems arise from ignoring God's Word when we don't think its instructions make sense. Moses tells us the rules and regulations God gave to His people not only kept them clean—make that *holy*—before Him, but they also protected them from discomfort, sickness, and untimely death.

In some ways, the law can be seen as God solving a problem before it ever occurs. Moses reminds us that God always knows what is best—best for us and best for our relationship with Him.

¹³"And when he who has a discharge is cleansed of his discharge, then he shall count for himself seven days for his cleansing, wash his clothes, and bathe his body in running water; then he shall be clean. ¹⁴On the eighth day he shall take for himself two turtledoves or two young pigeons, and come before the LORD, to the door of the tabernacle of meeting, and give them to the priest. ¹⁵Then the priest shall offer them, the one *as* a sin offering and the other *as* a burnt offering. So the priest shall make atonement for him before the LORD because of his discharge.

¹⁶"If any man has an emission of semen, then he shall wash all his body in water, and be unclean until evening. ¹⁷And any garment and any leather on which there is semen, it shall be washed with water, and be unclean until evening. ¹⁸Also, when a woman lies with a man, and *there is* an emission of semen, they shall bathe in water, and be unclean until evening.

¹⁹"If a woman has a discharge, *and* the discharge from her body is blood, she shall be set apart seven days; and whoever touches her shall be unclean until evening. ²⁰Everything that she lies on during her impurity shall be unclean; also everything that she sits on shall be unclean. ²¹Whoever touches her bed shall wash his clothes and bathe in water, and be unclean until evening. ²²And whoever touches anything that she sat on shall wash his clothes and bathe in water, and be unclean until evening. ²³If *anything* is on *her* bed or on anything on which she sits, when he touches it, he shall be unclean until evening. ²⁴And if any man lies with her at all, so that her impurity is on him, he shall be unclean seven days; and every bed on which he lies shall be unclean.

²⁵"If a woman has a discharge of blood for many days, other than at the time of her *customary* impurity, or if it runs beyond her *usual time of* impurity, all the days of her unclean discharge shall be as the days of her *customary* impurity. She *shall be* unclean. ²⁶Every bed on which she lies all the days of her discharge shall be to her as the bed of her impurity; and whatever she sits on shall be unclean, as the uncleanness of her impurity. ²⁷Whoever touches those things shall be unclean; he shall wash his clothes and bathe in water, and be unclean until evening.

²⁸"But if she is cleansed of her discharge, then she shall count for herself seven days, and after that she shall be clean. ²⁹And on the eighth day she shall take for herself two turtledoves or two young pigeons, and bring them to the priest, to the door of the tabernacle of meeting. ³⁰Then the priest shall offer the one *as* a sin offering and the other *as* a burnt offering, and the priest shall make atonement for her before the LORD for the discharge of her uncleanness.

³¹"Thus you shall separate the children of Israel from their uncleanness, lest they die in their uncleanness when they defile My tabernacle that *is* among them. ³²This *is* the law for one who has a discharge, and *for him* who emits semen and is unclean thereby, ³³and for her who is indisposed because of her *customary* impurity, and for one who has a discharge, either man or woman, and for him who lies with her who is unclean.'"

The Day of Atonement

16 Now the LORD spoke to Moses after the death of the two sons of Aaron, when they offered *profane fire* before the LORD, and died; ²and the LORD said to Moses: "Tell Aaron your brother not to come at *just* any time into the Holy *Place* inside the veil, before the mercy seat which *is* on the ark, lest he die; for I will appear in the cloud above the mercy seat.

³"Thus Aaron shall come into the Holy *Place:* with *the blood of* a young bull as a sin offering, and *of* a ram as a burnt offering. ⁴He shall put the holy linen tunic and the linen trousers on his body; he shall be girded with a linen sash, and with the linen turban he shall be attired. These *are* holy garments. Therefore he shall wash his body in water, and put them on. ⁵And he shall take from the congregation of the children of Israel two kids of the goats as a sin offering, and one ram as a burnt offering.

⁶"Aaron shall offer the bull as a sin offering, which *is* for himself, and make atonement for himself and for his house. ⁷He shall take the two goats and present them before the LORD *at* the door of the tabernacle of meeting. ⁸Then Aaron shall cast lots for the two goats: one lot for the LORD and the other lot for the scapegoat. ⁹And Aaron shall bring the goat on which the LORD's lot fell, and offer it *as* a sin offering. ¹⁰But the goat on which the lot fell to be the scapegoat shall be presented alive before the LORD, to make atonement upon it, *and* to let it go as the scapegoat into the wilderness.

¹¹"And Aaron shall bring the bull of the sin offering, which is for himself, and make atonement for himself and for his house, and shall kill the bull as the sin offering which *is* for himself. ¹²Then he shall take a censer full of burning coals of fire from the altar before the LORD, with his hands full of sweet incense beaten fine, and bring *it* inside the veil. ¹³And he shall put the incense

on the fire before the LORD, that the cloud of incense may cover the mercy seat that *is* on the Testimony, lest he die. [14]He shall take some of the blood of the bull and sprinkle *it* with his finger on the mercy seat on the east *side;* and before the mercy seat he shall sprinkle some of the blood with his finger seven times.

[15]"Then he shall kill the goat of the sin offering, which *is* for the people, bring its blood inside the veil, do with that blood as he did with the blood of the bull, and sprinkle it on the mercy seat and before the mercy seat. [16]So he shall make atonement for the Holy *Place,* because of the uncleanness of the children of Israel, and because of their transgressions, for all their sins; and so he shall do for the tabernacle of meeting which remains among them in the midst of their uncleanness. [17]There shall be no man in the tabernacle of meeting when he goes in to make atonement in the Holy *Place,* until he comes out, that he may make atonement for himself, for his household, and for all the assembly of Israel. [18]And he shall go out to the altar that *is* before the LORD, and make atonement for it, and shall take some of the blood of the bull and some of the blood of the goat, and put it on the horns of the altar all around. [19]Then he shall sprinkle some of the blood on it with his finger seven times, cleanse it, and consecrate it from the uncleanness of the children of Israel.

[20]"And when he has made an end of atoning for the Holy *Place,* the tabernacle of meeting, and the altar, he shall bring the live goat. [21]Aaron shall lay both his hands on the head of the live goat, confess over it all the iniquities of the children of Israel, and all their transgressions, concerning all their sins, putting them on the head of the goat, and shall send *it* away into the wilderness by the hand of a suitable man. [22]The goat shall bear on itself all their iniquities to an uninhabited land; and he shall release the goat in the wilderness.

[23]"Then Aaron shall come into the tabernacle of meeting, shall take off the linen garments which he put on when he went into the Holy *Place,* and shall leave them there. [24]And he shall wash his body with water in a holy place, put on his garments, come out and offer his burnt offering and the burnt offering of the people, and make atonement for himself and for the people. [25]The fat of the sin offering he shall burn on the altar. [26]And he who released the goat as the scapegoat shall wash his clothes and bathe his body in water, and afterward he may come into the camp. [27]The bull *for* the sin offering and the goat *for* the sin offering, whose blood was brought in to make atonement in the Holy *Place,* shall be carried outside the camp. And they shall burn in the fire their skins, their flesh, and their offal. [28]Then he who burns them shall wash his clothes and bathe his body in water, and afterward he may come into the camp.

[29]"*This* shall be a statute forever for you: In the seventh month, on the tenth *day* of the month, you shall afflict your souls, and do no work at all, *whether* a native of your own country or a stranger who dwells among you. [30]For on that day *the priest* shall make atonement for you, to cleanse you, *that* you may be clean from all your sins before the LORD. [31]It *is* a sabbath of solemn rest for you, and you shall afflict your souls. *It is* a statute forever. [32]And the priest, who is anointed and consecrated to minister as priest in his father's place, shall make atonement, and put on the linen clothes, the holy garments; [33]then he shall make atonement for the Holy Sanctuary,[a] and he shall make atonement for the tabernacle of meeting and for the altar, and he shall make atonement for the priests and for all the people of the assembly. [34]This shall be an everlasting statute for you, to make atonement for the children of Israel, for all their sins, once a year." And he did as the LORD commanded Moses.

The Sanctity of Blood

17 And the LORD spoke to Moses, saying, [2]"Speak to Aaron, to his sons, and to all the children of Israel, and say to them, 'This *is* the thing which the LORD has commanded, saying: [3]"Whatever man of the house of Israel who kills an ox or lamb or goat in the camp, or who kills *it* outside the camp, [4]and does not bring it to the door of the tabernacle of meeting to offer an offering to the LORD before the tabernacle of the LORD, the guilt of bloodshed shall be imputed to that man. He has shed blood; and that man shall be cut off from among his people, [5]to the end that the children of Israel may bring their sacrifices which they offer in the open field, that they may bring them to the LORD at the door of the tabernacle of meeting, to the priest, and offer them *as* peace offerings to the LORD. [6]And the priest shall sprinkle the blood on the altar of the LORD *at* the door of the tabernacle of meeting, and burn the fat for a sweet aroma to the LORD. [7]They shall no more offer their sacrifices to demons, after whom they have played the harlot. This shall be a statute forever for them throughout their generations."'

16:33 [a]That is, the Most Holy Place

⁸"Also you shall say to them: 'Whatever man of the house of Israel, or of the strangers who dwell among you, who offers a burnt offering or sacrifice, ⁹and does not bring it to the door of the tabernacle of meeting, to offer it to the LORD, that man shall be cut off from among his people.

¹⁰"And whatever man of the house of Israel, or of the strangers who dwell among you, who eats any blood, I will set My face against that person who eats blood, and will cut him off from among his people. ¹¹For the life of the flesh *is* in the blood, and I have given it to you upon the altar to make atonement for your souls; for it *is* the blood *that* makes atonement for the soul.' ¹²Therefore I said to the children of Israel, 'No one among you shall eat blood, nor shall any stranger who dwells among you eat blood.'

¹³"Whatever man of the children of Israel, or of the strangers who dwell among you, who hunts and catches any animal or bird that may be eaten, he shall pour out its blood and cover it with dust; ¹⁴for *it is* the life of all flesh. Its blood sustains its life. Therefore I said to the children of Israel, 'You shall not eat the blood of any flesh, for the life of all flesh is its blood. Whoever eats it shall be cut off.'

¹⁵"And every person who eats what died *naturally* or what was torn *by beasts, whether he is* a native of your own country or a stranger, he shall both wash his clothes and bathe in water, and be unclean until evening. Then he shall be clean. ¹⁶But if he does not wash *them* or bathe his body, then he shall bear his guilt."

Laws of Sexual Morality

18 Then the LORD spoke to Moses, saying, ²"Speak to the children of Israel, and say to them: 'I am the LORD your God. ³According to the doings of the land of Egypt, where you dwelt, you shall not do; and according to the doings of the land of Canaan, where I am bringing you, you shall not do; nor shall you walk in their ordinances. ⁴You shall observe My judgments and keep My ordinances, to walk in them: I *am* the LORD your God. ⁵You shall therefore keep My statutes and My judgments, which if a man does, he shall live by them: I *am* the LORD.

⁶"None of you shall approach anyone who is

Israel: Raising a Higher Standard
(Leviticus 18:1—21:24)

God calls His people to live at a standard higher than the unbelievers who surround them. In Leviticus 18—20, God reviews His higher standards regarding relationships, religion, and the rights and responsibilities of community members. In the subsequent chapter, He reviews an even higher standard for Israel's leaders, the priests.

Why these higher standards? God intended Israel to be a light and a standard for the rest of the world, and Israel's leaders to be a light and a standard for the Jewish nation. God expects the same of us today. Why must we be faithful in keeping a higher standard than the rest of the world?

1. To be like God.
2. To qualify us for ministry.
3. To guarantee God's blessing on our life.
4. To prepare us for leadership tomorrow.
5. To receive God's reward for faithfulness.

And what characterizes those who choose to pursue life at God's higher standard?

1. They adopt godly values.
2. They care for the interests of others.
3. They live with integrity.
4. They keep their word.
5. They develop their gifts and potential.
6. They manage time and money well.
7. They pass on to others what they have received.

near of kin to him, to uncover his nakedness: I *am* the LORD. [7]The nakedness of your father or the nakedness of your mother you shall not uncover. She *is* your mother; you shall not uncover her nakedness. [8]The nakedness of your father's wife you shall not uncover; it *is* your father's nakedness. [9]The nakedness of your sister, the daughter of your father, or the daughter of your mother, *whether* born at home or elsewhere, their nakedness you shall not uncover. [10]The nakedness of your son's daughter or your daughter's daughter, their nakedness you shall not uncover; for theirs *is* your own nakedness. [11]The nakedness of your father's wife's daughter, begotten by your father—she *is* your sister—you shall not uncover her nakedness. [12]You shall not uncover the nakedness of your father's sister; she *is* near of kin to your father. [13]You shall not uncover the nakedness of your mother's sister, for she *is* near of kin to your mother. [14]You shall not uncover the nakedness of your father's brother. You shall not approach his wife; she *is* your aunt. [15]You shall not uncover the nakedness of your daughter-in-law—she *is* your son's wife—you shall not uncover her nakedness. [16]You shall not uncover the nakedness of your brother's wife; it *is* your brother's nakedness. [17]You shall not uncover the nakedness of a woman and her daughter, nor shall you take her son's daughter or her daughter's daughter, to uncover her nakedness. They *are* near of kin to her. It *is* wickedness. [18]Nor shall you take a woman as a rival to her sister, to uncover her nakedness while the other is alive.

[19]"Also you shall not approach a woman to uncover her nakedness as long as she is in her *customary* impurity. [20]Moreover you shall not lie carnally with your neighbor's wife, to defile yourself with her. [21]And you shall not let any of your descendants pass through *the fire* to Molech, nor shall you profane the name of your God: I *am* the LORD. [22]You shall not lie with a male as with a woman. It *is* an abomination. [23]Nor shall you mate with any animal, to defile yourself with it. Nor shall any woman stand before an animal to mate with it. It *is* perversion.

[24]"Do not defile yourselves with any of these things; for by all these the nations are defiled, which I am casting out before you. [25]For the land is defiled; therefore I visit the punishment of its iniquity upon it, and the land vomits out its inhabitants. [26]You shall therefore keep My statutes and My judgments, and shall not commit *any* of these abominations, *either* any of your own nation or any stranger who dwells among you [27](for all these abominations the men of the land have done, who *were* before you, and thus the land is defiled), [28]lest the land vomit you out also when you defile it, as it vomited out the nations that *were* before you. [29]For whoever commits any of these abominations, the persons who commit *them* shall be cut off from among their people.

[30]"Therefore you shall keep My ordinance, so that *you* do not commit *any* of these abominable customs which were committed before you, and that you do not defile yourselves by them: I *am* the LORD your God.'"

Moral and Ceremonial Laws

19 And the LORD spoke to Moses, saying, [2]"Speak to all the congregation of the children of Israel, and say to them: 'You shall be holy, for I the LORD your God *am* holy.

[3]"Every one of you shall revere his mother and his father, and keep My Sabbaths: I *am* the LORD your God.

[4]"Do not turn to idols, nor make for yourselves molded gods: I *am* the LORD your God.

[5]"And if you offer a sacrifice of a peace offering to the LORD, you shall offer it of your own free will. [6]It shall be eaten the same day you offer *it,* and on the next day. And if any remains until the third day, it shall be burned in the fire. [7]And if it is eaten at all on the third day, it *is* an abomination. It shall not be accepted. [8]Therefore *everyone* who eats it shall bear his iniquity, because he has profaned the hallowed *offering* of the LORD; and that person shall be cut off from his people.

[9]"When you reap the harvest of your land, you shall not wholly reap the corners of your field, nor shall you gather the gleanings of your harvest. [10]And you shall not glean your vineyard, nor shall you gather *every* grape of your vineyard; you shall leave them for the poor and the stranger: I *am* the LORD your God.

[11]"You shall not steal, nor deal falsely, nor lie to one another. [12]And you shall not swear by My name falsely, nor shall you profane the name of your God: I *am* the LORD.

[13]"You shall not cheat your neighbor, nor rob *him.* The wages of him who is hired shall not remain with you all night until morning. [14]You shall not curse the deaf, nor put a stumbling block before the blind, but shall fear your God: I *am* the LORD.

[15]"You shall do no injustice in judgment. You shall not be partial to the poor, nor honor the person of the mighty. In righteousness you shall judge your neighbor. [16]You shall not go about *as* a talebearer among your people; nor shall you take a stand against the life of your neighbor: I *am* the LORD.

¹⁷"You shall not hate your brother in your heart. You shall surely rebuke your neighbor, and not bear sin because of him. ¹⁸You shall not take vengeance, nor bear any grudge against the children of your people, but you shall love your neighbor as yourself: I *am* the LORD.

¹⁹"You shall keep My statutes. You shall not let your livestock breed with another kind. You shall not sow your field with mixed seed. Nor shall a garment of mixed linen and wool come upon you.

²⁰"Whoever lies carnally with a woman who *is* betrothed to a man as a concubine, and who has not at all been redeemed nor given her freedom, for this there shall be scourging; *but* they shall not be put to death, because she was not free. ²¹And he shall bring his trespass offering to the LORD, to the door of the tabernacle of meeting, a ram as a trespass offering. ²²The priest shall make atonement for him with the ram of the trespass offering before the LORD for his sin which he has committed. And the sin which he has committed shall be forgiven him.

²³"When you come into the land, and have planted all kinds of trees for food, then you shall count their fruit as uncircumcised. Three years it shall be as uncircumcised to you. *It* shall not be eaten. ²⁴But in the fourth year all its fruit shall be holy, a praise to the LORD. ²⁵And in the fifth year you may eat its fruit, that it may yield to you its increase: I *am* the LORD your God.

²⁶"You shall not eat *anything* with the blood, nor shall you practice divination or soothsaying. ²⁷You shall not shave around the sides of your head, nor shall you disfigure the edges of your beard. ²⁸You shall not make any cuttings in your flesh for the dead, nor tattoo any marks on you: I *am* the LORD.

²⁹"Do not prostitute your daughter, to cause her to be a harlot, lest the land fall into harlotry, and the land become full of wickedness.

³⁰"You shall keep My Sabbaths and reverence My sanctuary: I *am* the LORD.

³¹"Give no regard to mediums and familiar spirits; do not seek after them, to be defiled by them: I *am* the LORD your God.

³²"You shall rise before the gray headed and honor the presence of an old man, and fear your God: I *am* the LORD.

³³"And if a stranger dwells with you in your land, you shall not mistreat him. ³⁴The stranger who dwells among you shall be to you as one born among you, and you shall love him as yourself; for you were strangers in the land of Egypt: I *am* the LORD your God.

³⁵"You shall do no injustice in judgment, in measurement of length, weight, or volume. ³⁶You shall have honest scales, honest weights, an honest ephah, and an honest hin: I *am* the LORD your God, who brought you out of the land of Egypt.

³⁷"Therefore you shall observe all My statutes and all My judgments, and perform them: I *am* the LORD.'"

Penalties for Breaking the Law

20 Then the LORD spoke to Moses, saying, ²"Again, you shall say to the children of Israel: 'Whoever of the children of Israel, or of the strangers who dwell in Israel, who gives *any* of his descendants to Molech, he shall surely be put to death. The people of the land shall stone him with stones. ³I will set My face against that man, and will cut him off from his people, because he has given *some* of his descendants to Molech, to defile My sanctuary and profane My holy name. ⁴And if the people of the land should in any way hide their eyes from the man, when he gives *some* of his descendants to Molech, and they do not kill him, ⁵then I will set My face against that man and against his family; and I will cut him off from his people, and all who prostitute themselves with him to commit harlotry with Molech.

⁶"And the person who turns to mediums and familiar spirits, to prostitute himself with them, I will set My face against that person and cut him off from his people. ⁷Consecrate yourselves therefore, and be holy, for I *am* the LORD your God. ⁸And you shall keep My statutes, and perform them: I *am* the LORD who sanctifies you.

⁹"For everyone who curses his father or his mother shall surely be put to death. He has cursed his father or his mother. His blood *shall be* upon him.

¹⁰"The man who commits adultery with *another* man's wife, *he* who commits adultery with his neighbor's wife, the adulterer and the adulteress, shall surely be put to death. ¹¹The man who lies with his father's wife has uncovered his father's nakedness; both of them shall surely be put to death. Their blood *shall be* upon them. ¹²If a man lies with his daughter-in-law, both of them shall surely be put to death. They have committed perversion. Their blood *shall be* upon them. ¹³If a man lies with a male as he lies with a woman, both of them have committed an abomination. They shall surely be put to death. Their blood *shall be* upon them. ¹⁴If a man marries a woman and her mother, it *is* wickedness. They shall be burned with fire, both he and they, that there may be no wickedness among you. ¹⁵If a man mates with an animal, he shall surely be put to death,

and you shall kill the animal. [16]If a woman approaches any animal and mates with it, you shall kill the woman and the animal. They shall surely be put to death. Their blood *is* upon them.

[17]'If a man takes his sister, his father's daughter or his mother's daughter, and sees her nakedness and she sees his nakedness, it *is* a wicked thing. And they shall be cut off in the sight of their people. He has uncovered his sister's nakedness. He shall bear his guilt. [18]If a man lies with a woman during her sickness and uncovers her nakedness, he has exposed her flow, and she has uncovered the flow of her blood. Both of them shall be cut off from their people.

[19]'You shall not uncover the nakedness of your mother's sister nor of your father's sister, for that would uncover his near of kin. They shall bear their guilt. [20]If a man lies with his uncle's wife, he has uncovered his uncle's nakedness. They shall bear their sin; they shall die childless. [21]If a man takes his brother's wife, it *is* an unclean thing. He has uncovered his brother's nakedness. They shall be childless.

[22]'You shall therefore keep all My statutes and all My judgments, and perform them, that the land where I am bringing you to dwell may not vomit you out. [23]And you shall not walk in the statutes of the nation which I am casting out before you; for they commit all these things, and therefore I abhor them. [24]But I have said to you, "You shall inherit their land, and I will give it to you to possess, a land flowing with milk and honey." I *am* the LORD your God, who has separated you from the peoples. [25]You shall therefore distinguish between clean animals and unclean, between unclean birds and clean, and you shall not make yourselves abominable by beast or by bird, or by any kind of living thing that creeps on the ground, which I have separated from you as unclean. [26]And you shall be holy to Me, for I the LORD *am* holy, and have separated you from the peoples, that you should be Mine.

[27]'A man or a woman who is a medium, or who has familiar spirits, shall surely be put to death; they shall stone them with stones. Their blood *shall be* upon them.'"

Regulations for Conduct of Priests

21 And the LORD said to Moses, "Speak to the priests, the sons of Aaron, and say to them: 'None shall defile himself for the dead among his people, [2]except for his relatives who are nearest to him: his mother, his father, his son, his daughter, and his brother; [3]also his virgin sister who is near to him, who has had no husband, for her he may defile himself.

[4]*Otherwise* he shall not defile himself, *being* a chief man among his people, to profane himself.

[5]'They shall not make any bald *place* on their heads, nor shall they shave the edges of their beards nor make any cuttings in their flesh. [6]They shall be holy to their God and not profane the name of their God, for they offer the offerings of the LORD made by fire, *and* the bread of their God; therefore they shall be holy. [7]They shall not take a wife *who is* a harlot or a defiled woman, nor shall they take a woman divorced from her husband; for *the priest*[a] is holy to his God. [8]Therefore you shall consecrate him, for he offers the bread of your God. He shall be holy to you, for I the LORD, who sanctify you, *am* holy. [9]The daughter of any priest, if she profanes herself by playing the harlot, she profanes her father. She shall be burned with fire.

[10]'*He who is* the high priest among his brethren, on whose head the anointing oil was poured and who is consecrated to wear the garments, shall not uncover his head nor tear his clothes; [11]nor shall he go near any dead body, nor defile himself for his father or his mother; [12]nor shall he go out of the sanctuary, nor profane the sanctuary of his God; for the consecration of the anointing oil of his God *is* upon him: I *am* the LORD. [13]And he shall take a wife in her virginity. [14]A widow or a divorced woman or a defiled woman *or* a harlot—these he shall not marry; but he shall take a virgin of his own people as wife. [15]Nor shall he profane his posterity among his people, for I the LORD sanctify him.'"

[16]And the LORD spoke to Moses, saying, [17]"Speak to Aaron, saying: 'No man of your descendants in *succeeding* generations, who has *any* defect, may approach to offer the bread of his God. [18]For any man who has a defect shall not approach: a man blind or lame, who has a marred *face* or any *limb* too long, [19]a man who has a broken foot or broken hand, [20]or is a hunchback or a dwarf, or *a man* who has a defect in his eye, or eczema or scab, or is a eunuch. [21]No man of the descendants of Aaron the priest, who has a defect, shall come near to offer the offerings made by fire to the LORD. He has a defect; he shall not come near to offer the bread of his God. [22]He may eat the bread of his God, *both* the most holy and the holy; [23]only he shall not go near the veil or approach the altar, because he has a defect, lest he profane My sanctuaries; for I the LORD sanctify them.'"

[24]And Moses told *it* to Aaron and his sons, and to all the children of Israel.

21:7 [a]Literally *he*

22

Then the LORD spoke to Moses, saying, [2]"Speak to Aaron and his sons, that they separate themselves from the holy things of the children of Israel, and that they do not profane My holy name *by* what they dedicate to Me: I *am* the LORD. [3]Say to them: 'Whoever of all your descendants throughout your generations, who goes near the holy things which the children of Israel dedicate to the LORD, while he has uncleanness upon him, that person shall be cut off from My presence: I *am* the LORD.

[4]"Whatever man of the descendants of Aaron, who *is* a leper or has a discharge, shall not eat the holy offerings until he is clean. And whoever touches anything made unclean *by* a corpse, or a man who has had an emission of semen, [5]or whoever touches any creeping thing by which he would be made unclean, or any person by whom he would become unclean, whatever his uncleanness may be— [6]the person who has touched any such thing shall be unclean until evening, and shall not eat the holy *offerings* unless he washes his body with water. [7]And when the sun goes down he shall be clean; and afterward he may eat the holy *offerings,* because it *is* his food. [8]Whatever dies *naturally* or is torn *by beasts* he shall not eat, to defile himself with it: I *am* the LORD.

[9]"They shall therefore keep My ordinance, lest they bear sin for it and die thereby, if they profane it: I the LORD sanctify them.

[10]"No outsider shall eat the holy *offering;* one who dwells with the priest, or a hired servant, shall not eat the holy thing. [11]But if the priest buys a person with his money, he may eat it; and one who is born in his house may eat his food. [12]If the priest's daughter is married to an outsider, she may not eat of the holy offerings. [13]But if the priest's daughter is a widow or divorced, and has no child, and has returned to her father's house as in her youth, she may eat her father's food; but no outsider shall eat it.

[14]"And if a man eats the holy *offering* unintentionally, then he shall restore a holy *offering* to the priest, and add one-fifth to it. [15]They shall not profane the holy *offerings* of the children of Israel, which they offer to the LORD, [16]or allow them to bear the guilt of trespass when they eat their holy *offerings;* for I the LORD sanctify them.'"

Offerings Accepted and Not Accepted

[17]And the LORD spoke to Moses, saying, [18]"Speak to Aaron and his sons, and to all the children of Israel, and say to them: 'Whatever man of the house of Israel, or of the strangers in Israel, who offers his sacrifice for any of his vows or for any of his freewill offerings, which they offer to the LORD as a burnt offering— [19]*you shall offer* of your own free will a male without blemish from the cattle, from the sheep, or from the goats. [20]Whatever has a defect, you shall not offer, for it shall not be acceptable on your behalf. [21]And whoever offers a sacrifice of a peace offering to the LORD, to fulfill *his* vow, or a freewill offering from the cattle or the sheep, it must be perfect to be accepted; there shall be no defect in it. [22]Those *that are* blind or broken or maimed, or have an ulcer or eczema or scabs, you shall not offer to the LORD, nor make an offering by fire of them on the altar to the LORD. [23]Either a bull or a lamb that has any limb too long or too short you may offer *as* a freewill offering, but for a vow it shall not be accepted.

[24]"You shall not offer to the LORD what is bruised or crushed, or torn or cut; nor shall you make *any offering of them* in your land. [25]Nor from a foreigner's hand shall you offer any of these as the bread of your God, because their corruption *is* in them, *and* defects *are* in them. They shall not be accepted on your behalf.'"

[26]And the LORD spoke to Moses, saying: [27]"When a bull or a sheep or a goat is born, it shall be seven days with its mother; and from the eighth day and thereafter it shall be accepted as an offering made by fire to the LORD. [28]*Whether it is* a cow or ewe, do not kill both her and her young on the same day. [29]And when you offer a sacrifice of thanksgiving to the LORD, offer *it* of your own free will. [30]On the same day it shall be eaten; you shall leave none of it until morning: I *am* the LORD.

[31]"Therefore you shall keep My commandments, and perform them: I *am* the LORD. [32]You shall not profane My holy name, but I will be hallowed among the children of Israel. I *am* the LORD who sanctifies you, [33]who brought you out of the land of Egypt, to be your God: I *am* the LORD."

Feasts of the LORD

23

And the LORD spoke to Moses, saying, [2]"Speak to the children of Israel, and say to them: 'The feasts of the LORD, which you shall proclaim *to be* holy convocations, these *are* My feasts.

The Sabbath

[3]"Six days shall work be done, but the seventh day *is* a Sabbath of solemn rest, a holy convocation. You shall do no work *on it; it is* the Sabbath of the LORD in all your dwellings.

The Passover and Unleavened Bread

4"These *are* the feasts of the LORD, holy convocations which you shall proclaim at their appointed times. 5On the fourteenth *day* of the first month at twilight *is* the LORD's Passover. 6And on the fifteenth day of the same month *is* the Feast of Unleavened Bread to the LORD; seven days you must eat unleavened bread. 7On the first day you shall have a holy convocation; you shall do no customary work on it. 8But you shall offer an offering made by fire to the LORD for seven days. The seventh day *shall be* a holy convocation; you shall do no customary work *on it.*'"

The Feast of Firstfruits

9And the LORD spoke to Moses, saying, 10"Speak to the children of Israel, and say to them: 'When you come into the land which I give to you, and reap its harvest, then you shall bring a sheaf of the firstfruits of your harvest to the priest. 11He shall wave the sheaf before the LORD, to be accepted on your behalf; on the day after the Sabbath the priest shall wave it. 12And you shall offer on that day, when you wave the sheaf, a male lamb of the first year, without blemish, as a burnt offering to the LORD. 13Its grain offering *shall be* two-tenths *of an ephah* of fine flour mixed with oil, an offering made by fire to the LORD, for a sweet aroma; and its drink offering *shall be* of wine, one-fourth of a hin. 14You shall eat neither bread nor parched grain nor fresh grain until the same day that you have brought an offering to your God; *it shall be* a statute forever throughout your generations in all your dwellings.

The Feast of Weeks

15"And you shall count for yourselves from the day after the Sabbath, from the day that you brought the sheaf of the wave offering: seven Sabbaths shall be completed. 16Count fifty days to the day after the seventh Sabbath; then you shall offer a new grain offering to the LORD. 17You shall bring from your dwellings two wave *loaves* of two-tenths *of an ephah.* They shall be of fine flour; they shall be baked with leaven. *They are* the firstfruits to the LORD. 18And you shall offer with the bread seven lambs of the first year, without blemish, one young bull, and two rams. They shall be *as* a burnt offering to the LORD, with their grain offering and their drink offerings, an offering made by fire for a sweet aroma to the LORD. 19Then you shall sacrifice one kid of the goats as a sin offering, and two male lambs of the first year as a sacrifice of a peace offering. 20The priest shall wave them with the bread of the firstfruits *as* a wave offering before the LORD, with the two lambs. They shall be holy to the LORD for the priest. 21And you shall proclaim on the same day *that* it is a holy convocation to you. You shall do no customary work *on it. It shall be* a statute forever in all your dwellings throughout your generations.

22"When you reap the harvest of your land, you shall not wholly reap the corners of your field when you reap, nor shall you gather any gleaning from your harvest. You shall leave them for the poor and for the stranger: I *am* the LORD your God.'"

The Feast of Trumpets

23Then the LORD spoke to Moses, saying, 24"Speak to the children of Israel, saying: 'In the seventh month, on the first *day* of the month, you shall have a sabbath-*rest,* a memorial of blowing of trumpets, a holy convocation. 25You shall do no customary work *on it;* and you shall offer an offering made by fire to the LORD.'"

The Day of Atonement

26And the LORD spoke to Moses, saying: 27"Also the tenth *day* of this seventh month *shall be* the Day of Atonement. It shall be a holy convocation for you; you shall afflict your souls, and offer an offering made by fire to the LORD. 28And you shall do no work on that same day, for it *is* the Day of Atonement, to make atonement for you before the LORD your God. 29For any person who is not afflicted *in soul* on that same day shall be cut off from his people. 30And any person who does any work on that same day, that person I will destroy from among his people. 31You shall do no manner of work; *it shall be* a statute forever throughout your generations in all your dwellings. 32It *shall be* to you a sabbath of *solemn* rest, and you shall afflict your souls; on the ninth *day* of the month at evening, from evening to evening, you shall celebrate your sabbath."

The Feast of Tabernacles

33Then the LORD spoke to Moses, saying, 34"Speak to the children of Israel, saying: 'The fifteenth day of this seventh month *shall be* the Feast of Tabernacles *for* seven days to the LORD. 35On the first day *there shall be* a holy convocation. You shall do no customary work *on it.* 36For seven days you shall offer an offering made by fire to the LORD. On the eighth day you shall have a holy convocation, and you shall offer an offering made by fire to the LORD. It *is* a sacred assembly, *and* you shall do no customary work *on it.*

37"These *are* the feasts of the LORD which you

shall proclaim *to be* holy convocations, to offer an offering made by fire to the LORD, a burnt offering and a grain offering, a sacrifice and drink offerings, everything on its day— ³⁸besides the Sabbaths of the LORD, besides your gifts, besides all your vows, and besides all your freewill offerings which you give to the LORD.

³⁹Also on the fifteenth day of the seventh month, when you have gathered in the fruit of the land, you shall keep the feast of the LORD *for* seven days; on the first day *there shall be* a sabbath-*rest,* and on the eighth day a sabbath-*rest.* ⁴⁰And you shall take for yourselves on the first day the fruit of beautiful trees, branches of palm trees, the boughs of leafy trees, and willows of the brook; and you shall rejoice before the LORD your God for seven days. ⁴¹You shall keep it as a feast to the LORD for seven days in the year. *It shall be* a statute forever in your generations. You shall celebrate it in the seventh month. ⁴²You shall dwell in booths for seven days. All who are native Israelites shall dwell in booths, ⁴³that your generations may know that I made the children of Israel dwell in booths when I brought them out of the land of Egypt: I *am* the LORD your God.'"

⁴⁴So Moses declared to the children of Israel the feasts of the LORD.

Care of the Tabernacle Lamps

24 Then the LORD spoke to Moses, saying: ²"Command the children of Israel that they bring to you pure oil of pressed olives for the light, to make the lamps burn continually. ³Outside the veil of the Testimony, in the tabernacle of meeting, Aaron shall be in charge of it from evening until morning before the LORD continually; *it shall be* a statute forever in your generations. ⁴He shall be in charge of the lamps on the pure *gold* lampstand before the LORD continually.

The Bread of the Tabernacle

⁵"And you shall take fine flour and bake twelve cakes with it. Two-tenths *of an ephah* shall be in each cake. ⁶You shall set them in two rows, six in a row, on the pure *gold* table before the LORD. ⁷And you shall put pure frankincense on *each* row, that it may be on the bread for a memorial, an offering made by fire to the LORD. ⁸Every Sabbath he shall set it in order before the LORD continually, *being taken* from the children of Israel by an everlasting covenant. ⁹And it shall be for Aaron and his sons, and they shall eat it in a holy place; for it *is* most holy to him from the offerings of the LORD made by fire, by a perpetual statute."

The Penalty for Blasphemy

¹⁰Now the son of an Israelite woman, whose father *was* an Egyptian, went out among the children of Israel; and this Israelite *woman's* son and a man of Israel fought each other in the camp. ¹¹And the Israelite woman's son blasphemed the name *of the* LORD and cursed; and so they brought him to Moses. (His mother's name *was* Shelomith the daughter of Dibri, of the tribe of Dan.) ¹²Then they put him in custody, that the mind of the LORD might be shown to them.

¹³And the LORD spoke to Moses, saying, ¹⁴"Take outside the camp him who has cursed; then let all who heard *him* lay their hands on his head, and let all the congregation stone him. ¹⁵"Then you shall speak to the children of Israel, saying: 'Whoever curses his God shall bear his sin. ¹⁶And whoever blasphemes the name of the LORD shall surely be put to death. All the congregation shall certainly stone him, the stranger as well as him who is born in the land. When he blasphemes the name *of the* LORD, he shall be put to death.

¹⁷'Whoever kills any man shall surely be put to death. ¹⁸Whoever kills an animal shall make it good, animal for animal.

¹⁹'If a man causes disfigurement of his neighbor, as he has done, so shall it be done to him— ²⁰fracture for fracture, eye for eye, tooth for tooth; as he has caused disfigurement of a man, so shall it be done to him. ²¹And whoever kills an animal shall restore it; but whoever kills a man shall be put to death. ²²You shall have the same law for the stranger and for one from your own country; for I *am* the LORD your God.'"

²³Then Moses spoke to the children of Israel; and they took outside the camp him who had cursed, and stoned him with stones. So the children of Israel did as the LORD commanded Moses.

The Sabbath of the Seventh Year

25 And the LORD spoke to Moses on Mount Sinai, saying, ²"Speak to the children of Israel, and say to them: 'When you come into the land which I give you, then the land shall keep a sabbath to the LORD. ³Six years you shall sow your field, and six years you shall prune your vineyard, and gather its fruit; ⁴but in the seventh year there shall be a sabbath of solemn rest for the land, a sabbath to the LORD. You shall neither sow your field nor prune your vineyard. ⁵What grows of its own accord of your harvest you shall not reap, nor gather the grapes of your untended vine, *for* it is a year of rest for the land. ⁶And the sabbath

The Year of Jubilee:
A Time to Rest and Sharpen the Ax

(Leviticus 25:1–55)

Ever hear of the Sabbath Year or the Year of Jubilee? Those are the delightful topics of Leviticus 25. The first occurred every seven years, while the second was to take place every fifty years.

These special years called for special behavior. God's people were to stop their usual labor, alter their daily routines, and change their normal existence. Consider a few lessons leaders can learn from these special Sabbaths:

1. *They gave the people a time of rest* (v. 5). God said these special years were seasons for resting the land and their lives.
2. *They gave the people an opportunity for redemption* (vv. 10, 24). Every Israelite could return to ancestral lands and redeem them, just as God did with them.
3. *They gave the people time for reflection* (v. 12). The Jubilee year was to be holy, recognized as a gift from the Lord.
4. *They gave the people time for reward and repair* (vv. 18, 19). As a reward for obedience, God would supply abundant food and time to sharpen the ax.
5. *They gave the people time for relationships* (vv. 35–46). Everyone was to prioritize people over material gain.
6. *They gave the people a time to refocus* (v. 55). God reminds His people that they are His servants and He is their Lord.

produce of the land shall be food for you: for you, your male and female servants, your hired man, and the stranger who dwells with you, ⁷for your livestock and the beasts that *are* in your land—all its produce shall be for food.

The Year of Jubilee

⁸"And you shall count seven sabbaths of years for yourself, seven times seven years; and the time of the seven sabbaths of years shall be to you forty-nine years. ⁹Then you shall cause the trumpet of the Jubilee to sound on the tenth *day* of the seventh month; on the Day of Atonement you shall make the trumpet to sound throughout all your land. ¹⁰And you shall consecrate the fiftieth year, and proclaim liberty throughout *all* the land to all its inhabitants. It shall be a Jubilee for you; and each of you shall return to his possession, and each of you shall return to his family. ¹¹That fiftieth year shall be a Jubilee to you; in it you shall neither sow nor reap what grows of its own accord, nor gather *the grapes* of your untended vine. ¹²For it *is* the Jubilee; it shall be holy to you; you shall eat its produce from the field.

¹³"In this Year of Jubilee, each of you shall return to his possession. ¹⁴And if you sell anything to your neighbor or buy from your neighbor's hand, you shall not oppress one another. ¹⁵According to the number of years after the Jubilee you shall buy from your neighbor, and according to the number of years of crops he shall sell to you. ¹⁶According to the multitude of years you shall increase its price, and according to the fewer number of years you shall diminish its price; for he sells to you *according* to the number *of the years* of the crops. ¹⁷Therefore you shall not oppress one another, but you shall fear your God; for I *am* the LORD your God.

Provisions for the Seventh Year

¹⁸"So you shall observe My statutes and keep My judgments, and perform them; and you will dwell in the land in safety. ¹⁹Then the land will yield its fruit, and you will eat your fill, and dwell there in safety.

²⁰"And if you say, "What shall we eat in the seventh year, since we shall not sow nor gather in our produce?" ²¹Then I will command My blessing on you in the sixth year, and it will bring forth produce enough for three years. ²²And you shall sow in the eighth year, and eat old produce until the ninth year; until its produce comes in, you shall eat *of* the old *harvest*.

Redemption of Property

23'The land shall not be sold permanently, for the land *is* Mine; for you *are* strangers and sojourners with Me. 24And in all the land of your possession you shall grant redemption of the land.

25'If one of your brethren becomes poor, and has sold *some* of his possession, and if his redeeming relative comes to redeem it, then he may redeem what his brother sold. 26Or if the man has no one to redeem it, but he himself becomes able to redeem it, 27then let him count the years since its sale, and restore the remainder to the man to whom he sold it, that he may return to his possession. 28But if he is not able to have *it* restored to himself, then what was sold shall remain in the hand of him who bought it until the Year of Jubilee; and in the Jubilee it shall be released, and he shall return to his possession.

29'If a man sells a house in a walled city, then he may redeem it within a whole year after it is sold; *within* a full year he may redeem it. 30But if it is not redeemed within the space of a full year, then the house in the walled city shall belong permanently to him who bought it, throughout his generations. It shall not be released in the Jubilee. 31However the houses of villages which have no wall around them shall be counted as the fields of the country. They may be redeemed, and they shall be released in the Jubilee. 32Nevertheless the cities of the Levites, *and* the houses in the cities of their possession, the Levites may redeem at any time. 33And if a man purchases a house from the Levites, then the house that was sold in the city of his possession shall be released in the Jubilee; for the houses in the cities of the Levites *are* their possession among the children of Israel. 34But the field of the common-land of their cities may not be sold, for it *is* their perpetual possession.

Lending to the Poor

35'If one of your brethren becomes poor, and falls into poverty among you, then you shall help him, like a stranger or a sojourner, that he may live with you. 36Take no usury or interest from him; but fear your God, that your brother may live with you. 37You shall not lend him your money for usury, nor lend him your food at a profit. 38I *am* the LORD your God, who brought you out of the land of Egypt, to give you the land of Canaan *and* to be your God.

The Law Concerning Slavery

39'And if *one of* your brethren *who dwells* by you becomes poor, and sells himself to you, you shall not compel him to serve as a slave. 40As a hired servant *and* a sojourner he shall be with you, *and* shall serve you until the Year of Jubilee. 41And *then* he shall depart from you—he and his children with him—and shall return to his own family. He shall return to the possession of his fathers. 42For they *are* My servants, whom I brought out of the land of Egypt; they shall not be sold as slaves. 43You shall not rule over him with rigor, but you shall fear your God. 44And as for your male and female slaves whom you may have—from the nations that are around you, from them you may buy male and female slaves. 45Moreover you may buy the children of the strangers who dwell among you, and their families who are with you, which they beget in your land; and they shall become your property. 46And you may take them as an inheritance for your children after you, to inherit *them as* a possession; they shall be your permanent slaves. But regarding your brethren, the children of Israel, you shall not rule over one another with rigor.

47'Now if a sojourner or stranger close to you becomes rich, and *one of* your brethren *who dwells* by him becomes poor, and sells himself to the stranger *or* sojourner close to you, or to a member of the stranger's family, 48after he is sold he may be redeemed again. One of his brothers may redeem him; 49or his uncle or his uncle's son may redeem him; or *anyone* who is near of kin to him in his family may redeem him; or if he is able he may redeem himself. 50Thus he shall reckon with him who bought him: The price of his release shall be according to the number of years, from the year that he was sold to him until the Year of Jubilee; *it shall be* according to the time of a hired servant for him. 51If *there are* still many years *remaining,* according to them he shall repay the price of his redemption from the money with which he was bought. 52And if there remain but a few years until the Year of Jubilee, then he shall reckon with him, *and* according to his years he shall repay him the price of his redemption. 53He shall be with him as a yearly hired servant, and he shall not rule with rigor over him in your sight. 54And if he is not redeemed in these *years,* then he shall be released in the Year of Jubilee—he and his children with him. 55For the children of Israel *are* servants to Me; they *are* My servants whom I brought out of the land of Egypt: I *am* the LORD your God.

Promise of Blessing and Retribution

26 'You shall not make idols for yourselves;
neither a carved image nor a *sacred* pillar shall you rear up for yourselves;

nor shall you set up an engraved stone in your land, to bow down to it;
for I *am* the LORD your God.

2 You shall keep My Sabbaths and reverence My sanctuary:
I *am* the LORD.

3 'If you walk in My statutes and keep My commandments, and perform them,

4 then I will give you rain in its season, the land shall yield its produce, and the trees of the field shall yield their fruit.

5 Your threshing shall last till the time of vintage, and the vintage shall last till the time of sowing;
you shall eat your bread to the full, and dwell in your land safely.

6 I will give peace in the land, and you shall lie down, and none will make *you* afraid;
I will rid the land of evil beasts, and the sword will not go through your land.

7 You will chase your enemies, and they shall fall by the sword before you.

8 Five of you shall chase a hundred, and a hundred of you shall put ten thousand to flight;
your enemies shall fall by the sword before you.

9 'For I will look on you favorably and make you fruitful, multiply you and confirm My covenant with you.

10 You shall eat the old harvest, and clear out the old because of the new.

11 I will set My tabernacle among you, and My soul shall not abhor you.

12 I will walk among you and be your God, and you shall be My people.

13 I *am* the LORD your God, who brought you out of the land of Egypt, that *you* should not be their slaves;
I have broken the bands of your yoke and made you walk upright.

14 'But if you do not obey Me, and do not observe all these commandments,

15 and if you despise My statutes, or if your soul abhors My judgments, so that you do not perform all My commandments, *but* break My covenant,

16 I also will do this to you:
I will even appoint terror over you, wasting disease and fever which shall consume the eyes and cause sorrow of heart.

Sowing and Reaping: Decisions and Consequences

(Leviticus 26:3–39)

Leadership, like life, is the sum total of the decisions we make.

Every decision has consequences. We decide how we will respond to people. We decide how large to make a budget for promotion and marketing. We decide whom to hire. We decide which values are worth going to the mat for.

Toward the end of Leviticus, God lists the blessings He offers to those who obey Him and the punishment they'll receive for disobedience. God, the Ultimate Leader, clearly outlines the consequences for His people's choices.

Leaders who fail to make good decisions . . .

1. Lack commitment.
2. Suffer from a scattered focus.
3. Look for excuses.
4. Forget the big picture.
5. Go public with private thoughts.
6. Adopt the motto, "That's good enough."
7. Don't take God's direction seriously.
8. Behave inconsistently.
9. Create poor relationships.
10. Avoid change.

And you shall sow your seed in vain, for your enemies shall eat it.

17 I will set My face against you, and you shall be defeated by your enemies.
Those who hate you shall reign over you, and you shall flee when no one pursues you.

18 'And after all this, if you do not obey Me, then I will punish you seven times more for your sins.

19 I will break the pride of your power;
I will make your heavens like iron and your earth like bronze.

20 And your strength shall be spent in vain;
for your land shall not yield its produce, nor shall the trees of the land yield their fruit.

21 'Then, if you walk contrary to Me, and are not willing to obey Me, I will bring on

you seven times more plagues, according to your sins.

22 I will also send wild beasts among you, which shall rob you of your children, destroy your livestock, and make you few in number;
and your highways shall be desolate.

23 'And if by these things you are not reformed by Me, but walk contrary to Me,

24 then I also will walk contrary to you, and I will punish you yet seven times for your sins.

25 And I will bring a sword against you that will execute the vengeance of the covenant;
when you are gathered together within your cities I will send pestilence among you;
and you shall be delivered into the hand of the enemy.

26 When I have cut off your supply of bread, ten women shall bake your bread in one oven, and they shall bring back your bread by weight, and you shall eat and not be satisfied.

27 'And after all this, if you do not obey Me, but walk contrary to Me,

28 then I also will walk contrary to you in fury;
and I, even I, will chastise you seven times for your sins.

29 You shall eat the flesh of your sons, and you shall eat the flesh of your daughters.

30 I will destroy your high places, cut down your incense altars, and cast your carcasses on the lifeless forms of your idols;
and My soul shall abhor you.

31 I will lay your cities waste and bring your sanctuaries to desolation, and I will not smell the fragrance of your sweet aromas.

32 I will bring the land to desolation, and your enemies who dwell in it shall be astonished at it.

33 I will scatter you among the nations and draw out a sword after you;
your land shall be desolate and your cities waste.

34 Then the land shall enjoy its sabbaths as long as it lies desolate and you *are* in your enemies' land;
then the land shall rest and enjoy its sabbaths.

35 As long as *it* lies desolate it shall rest—
for the time it did not rest on your sabbaths when you dwelt in it.

36 'And as for those of you who are left, I will send faintness into their hearts in the lands of their enemies;
the sound of a shaken leaf shall cause them to flee;
they shall flee as though fleeing from a sword, and they shall fall when no one pursues.

37 They shall stumble over one another, as it were before a sword, when no one pursues;
and you shall have no *power* to stand before your enemies.

38 You shall perish among the nations, and the land of your enemies shall eat you up.

39 And those of you who are left shall waste away in their iniquity in your enemies' lands;
also in their fathers' iniquities, which are with them, they shall waste away.

40 '*But* if they confess their iniquity and the iniquity of their fathers, with their unfaithfulness in which they were unfaithful to Me, and that they also have walked contrary to Me,

41 and *that* I also have walked contrary to them and have brought them into the land of their enemies;
if their uncircumcised hearts are humbled, and they accept their guilt—

42 then I will remember My covenant with Jacob, and My covenant with Isaac and My covenant with Abraham I will remember;
I will remember the land.

43 The land also shall be left empty by them, and will enjoy its sabbaths while it lies desolate without them;
they will accept their guilt, because they despised My judgments and because their soul abhorred My statutes.

44 Yet for all that, when they are in the land of their enemies, I will not cast them away, nor shall I abhor them, to utterly destroy them and break My covenant with them;
for I *am* the LORD their God.

45 But for their sake I will remember the covenant of their ancestors, whom I brought out of the land of Egypt in the

sight of the nations, that I might be their God:'

I *am* the LORD.'"

⁴⁶These *are* the statutes and judgments and laws which the LORD made between Himself and the children of Israel on Mount Sinai by the hand of Moses.

Redeeming Persons and Property Dedicated to God

27 Now the LORD spoke to Moses, saying, ²"Speak to the children of Israel, and say to them: 'When a man consecrates by a vow certain persons to the LORD, according to your valuation, ³if your valuation is of a male from twenty years old up to sixty years old, then your valuation shall be fifty shekels of silver, according to the shekel of the sanctuary. ⁴If it *is* a female, then your valuation shall be thirty shekels; ⁵and if from five years old up to twenty years old, then your valuation for a male shall be twenty shekels, and for a female ten shekels; ⁶and if from a month old up to five years old, then your valuation for a male shall be five shekels of silver, and for a female your valuation shall be three shekels of silver; ⁷and if from sixty years old and above, if *it is* a male, then your valuation shall be fifteen shekels, and for a female ten shekels.

⁸"But if he is too poor to pay your valuation, then he shall present himself before the priest, and the priest shall set a value for him; according to the ability of him who vowed, the priest shall value him.

⁹"If *it is* an animal that men may bring as an offering to the LORD, all that *anyone* gives to the LORD shall be holy. ¹⁰He shall not substitute it or exchange it, good for bad or bad for good; and if he at all exchanges animal for animal, then both it and the one exchanged for it shall be holy. ¹¹If *it is* an unclean animal which they do not offer as a sacrifice to the LORD, then he shall present the animal before the priest; ¹²and the priest shall set a value for it, whether it is good or bad; as you, the priest, value it, so it shall be. ¹³But if he *wants* at all *to* redeem it, then he must add one-fifth to your valuation.

¹⁴"And when a man dedicates his house *to be* holy to the LORD, then the priest shall set a value for it, whether it is good or bad; as the priest values it, so it shall stand. ¹⁵If he who dedicated it *wants to* redeem his house, then he must add one-fifth of the money of your valuation to it, and it shall be his.

¹⁶"If a man dedicates to the LORD *part* of a field of his possession, then your valuation shall be according to the seed for it. A homer of barley seed *shall be valued* at fifty shekels of silver. ¹⁷If he dedicates his field from the Year of Jubilee, according to your valuation it shall stand. ¹⁸But if he dedicates his field after the Jubilee, then the priest shall reckon to him the money due according to the years that remain till the Year of Jubilee, and it shall be deducted from your valuation. ¹⁹And if he who dedicates the field ever wishes to redeem it, then he must add one-fifth of the money of your valuation to it, and it shall belong to him. ²⁰But if he does not want to redeem the field, or if he has sold the field to another man, it shall not be redeemed anymore; ²¹but the field, when it is released in the Jubilee, shall be holy to the LORD, as a devoted field; it shall be the possession of the priest.

²²"And if a man dedicates to the LORD a field which he has bought, which is not the field of his possession, ²³then the priest shall reckon to him the worth of your valuation, up to the Year of Jubilee, and he shall give your valuation on that day *as* a holy *offering* to the LORD. ²⁴In the Year of Jubilee the field shall return to him from whom it was bought, to the one who *owned* the land as a possession. ²⁵And all your valuations shall be according to the shekel of the sanctuary: twenty gerahs to the shekel.

²⁶"But the firstborn of the animals, which should be the LORD's firstborn, no man shall dedicate; whether *it is* an ox or sheep, it *is* the LORD's. ²⁷And if *it is* an unclean animal, then he shall redeem *it* according to your valuation, and shall add one-fifth to it; or if it is not redeemed, then it shall be sold according to your valuation.

²⁸"Nevertheless no devoted *offering* that a man may devote to the LORD of all that he has, *both* man and beast, or the field of his possession, shall be sold or redeemed; every devoted *offering is* most holy to the LORD. ²⁹No person under the ban, who may become doomed to destruction among men, shall be redeemed, *but* shall surely be put to death. ³⁰And all the tithe of the land, *whether* of the seed of the land *or* of the fruit of the tree, *is* the LORD's. It *is* holy to the LORD. ³¹If a man wants at all to redeem *any* of his tithes, he shall add one-fifth to it. ³²And concerning the tithe of the herd or the flock, of whatever passes under the rod, the tenth one shall be holy to the LORD. ³³He shall not inquire whether it is good or bad, nor shall he exchange it; and if he exchanges it at all, then both it and the one exchanged for it shall be holy; it shall not be redeemed.' "

³⁴These *are* the commandments which the LORD commanded Moses for the children of Israel on Mount Sinai.

NUMBERS
Israel's Leaders Implement the Laws

SUMMARY

While the Book of Leviticus records the ceremonial laws of Israel, the Book of Numbers tells how Israel's leaders implemented those laws.

Numbers describes how the people of Israel learn to function as a camp. It tells how God sets in order their religious, civil, and military economies in preparation for the worshiping, conquering, and journeying that lay ahead.

Like the rest of the Bible, Numbers bluntly records the mistakes as well as the successes of both leaders and followers. Primary among its leadership lessons: Leaders without faith and vision stifle the potential of the group they lead.

The sin of unbelief breaks out repeatedly in the Book of Numbers. Temporal and self-protective perspectives multiply. The prophet Balaam, for example, willingly discards his principles for personal profit. Korah loses sight of God's established chain of care and rebels against Israel's God-given leaders. Ten of the spies sent into Canaan come back fearful, discouraging the nation from moving ahead and accomplishing its goal of possessing the Promised Land.

On the other hand, Numbers also furnishes a picture of healthy, effective leadership. Eleazar, the son of Aaron, assumes the position of high priest after his father's death. He successfully fulfills the role, thanks to godly mentors and role models who support him. And despite their impatience with the Israelites, Moses, Aaron, Joshua, and Caleb all demonstrate godly convictions and principle-centered leadership. Their kind of leadership provides the positive lessons of the book.

God's Role in Numbers

God must exercise both the "rod" and the "staff" as He leads His people through the wilderness. The first generation never made it into the Promised Land, due to their lack of vision, their unbelief, and their disobedience. They suffered the rod of punishment. The second generation did make it in, guided by clear instructions from on high and the divine staff of visionary leaders. The book divides naturally into these two stories.

The book's title comes from two censuses God instructed His leaders to take, thus splitting the book into two logical parts. The first census took place near Sinai at the beginning, just prior to the wilderness journey. The second occurred near the Jordan, almost 40 years later, in preparation for entering the Promised Land.

Near the end, disobedience prevented even Moses from entering the land, and God called on Joshua, Moses' apprentice, to succeed him as leader of Israel.

Leaders in Numbers

Moses, Aaron, Joshua, Balaam, Eleazar, the seventy elders

Other People of Influence in Numbers

Caleb, Korah, Dathan, Abiram, the ten spies, Gad, Reuben, Zelophehad's daughters

Lessons in Leadership

- Trustworthy leaders must have pure motives.

- Commitment separates the doers from the dreamers.

- Vision is essential: You can't seize what you can't see.

- Leaders must be faithful over time and flexible with their schedules.

- Leadership and responsibility must be shared according to giftedness.

- Leaders must understand their resources before they plan their journey.

- Leaders must be secure enough to handle conflict, criticism, and confrontation.

LEADERSHIP

HIGHLIGHTS IN NUMBERS

The First Census of Israel

1 Now the LORD spoke to Moses in the Wilderness of Sinai, in the tabernacle of meeting, on the first *day* of the second month, in the second year after they had come out of the land of Egypt, saying: [2]"Take a census of all the congregation of the children of Israel, by their families, by their fathers' houses, according to the number of names, every male individually, [3]from twenty years old and above—all who *are able to* go to war in Israel. You and Aaron shall number them by their armies. [4]And with you there shall be a man from every tribe, each one the head of his father's house.

[5]"These are the names of the men who shall stand with you: from Reuben, Elizur the son of Shedeur; [6]from Simeon, Shelumiel the son of Zurishaddai; [7]from Judah, Nahshon the son of Amminadab; [8]from Issachar, Nethanel the son of Zuar; [9]from Zebulun, Eliab the son of Helon; [10]from the sons of Joseph: from Ephraim, Elishama the son of Ammihud; from Manasseh, Gamaliel the son of Pedahzur; [11]from Benjamin, Abidan the son of Gideoni; [12]from Dan, Ahiezer the son of Ammishaddai; [13]from Asher, Pagiel the son of Ocran; [14]from Gad, Eliasaph the son of Deuel;[a] [15]from Naphtali, Ahira the son of Enan." [16]These *were* chosen from the congregation, leaders of their fathers' tribes, heads of the divisions in Israel.

[17]Then Moses and Aaron took these men who had been mentioned by name, [18]and they assembled all the congregation together on the first *day* of the second month; and they recited their ancestry by families, by their fathers' houses, according to the number of names, from twenty years old and above, each one individually. [19]As the LORD commanded Moses, so he numbered them in the Wilderness of Sinai.

First Generation Census: Sizing Up the Resources

(Numbers 1:1–54)

Can you imagine the mammoth job of counting the wandering tribes of Israel? That's exactly what Moses and Aaron did. Israel's leaders broke down the huge assignment into many smaller elements, using the tribes, clans, and families already in place in Hebrew culture. Good leaders organize chaos.

---

[20]Now the children of Reuben, Israel's oldest son, their genealogies by their families, by their fathers' house, according to the number of names, every male individually, from twenty years old and above, all who *were able to* go to war: [21]those who were numbered of the tribe of Reuben *were* forty-six thousand five hundred.

[22]From the children of Simeon, their genealogies by their families, by their fathers' house, of those who were numbered, according to the number of names, every male individually, from twenty years old and above, all who *were able to* go to war: [23]those who were numbered of the tribe of Simeon *were* fifty-nine thousand three hundred.

[24]From the children of Gad, their genealogies by their families, by their fathers' house, according to the number of names, from twenty years old and above, all who *were able to* go to war: [25]those who were numbered of the tribe of Gad *were* forty-five thousand six hundred and fifty.

[26]From the children of Judah, their genealogies by their families, by their fathers' house, according to the number of names, from twenty years old and above, all who *were able to* go to war: [27]those who were numbered of the tribe of Judah *were* seventy-four thousand six hundred.

[28]From the children of Issachar, their genealogies by their families, by their fathers' house, according to the number of names, from twenty years old and above, all who *were able to* go to war: [29]those who were numbered of the tribe of Issachar *were* fifty-four thousand four hundred.

[30]From the children of Zebulun, their genealogies by their families, by their fathers' house, according to the number of names, from twenty years old and above, all who *were able to* go to war: [31]those who were numbered of the tribe of Zebulun *were* fifty-seven thousand four hundred.

[32]From the sons of Joseph, the children of Ephraim, their genealogies by their families, by their fathers' house, according to the number of names, from twenty years old and above, all who *were able to* go to war: [33]those who were numbered of the tribe of Ephraim *were* forty thousand five hundred.

[34]From the children of Manasseh, their genealogies by their families, by their fathers' house, according to the number of names, from twenty years old and above, all who *were able to* go to war: [35]those who were numbered of the tribe of Manasseh *were* thirty-two thousand two hundred.

1:14 [a]Spelled *Reuel* in 2:14

³⁶From the children of Benjamin, their genealogies by their families, by their fathers' house, according to the number of names, from twenty years old and above, all who *were able to* go to war: ³⁷those who were numbered of the tribe of Benjamin *were* thirty-five thousand four hundred.

³⁸From the children of Dan, their genealogies by their families, by their fathers' house, according to the number of names, from twenty years old and above, all who *were able to* go to war: ³⁹those who were numbered of the tribe of Dan *were* sixty-two thousand seven hundred.

⁴⁰From the children of Asher, their genealogies by their families, by their fathers' house, according to the number of names, from twenty years old and above, all who *were able to* go to war: ⁴¹those who were numbered of the tribe of Asher *were* forty-one thousand five hundred.

⁴²From the children of Naphtali, their genealogies by their families, by their fathers' house, according to the number of names, from twenty years old and above, all who *were able to* go to war: ⁴³those who were numbered of the tribe of Naphtali *were* fifty-three thousand four hundred.

⁴⁴These are the ones who were numbered, whom Moses and Aaron numbered, with the leaders of Israel, twelve men, each one representing his father's house. ⁴⁵So all who were numbered of the children of Israel, by their fathers' houses, from twenty years old and above, all who *were able to* go to war in Israel— ⁴⁶all who were numbered were six hundred and three thousand five hundred and fifty.

⁴⁷But the Levites were not numbered among them by their fathers' tribe; ⁴⁸for the LORD had spoken to Moses, saying: ⁴⁹"Only the tribe of Levi you shall not number, nor take a census of them among the children of Israel; ⁵⁰but you shall appoint the Levites over the tabernacle of the Testimony, over all its furnishings, and over all things that belong to it; they shall carry the tabernacle and all its furnishings; they shall attend to it and camp around the tabernacle. ⁵¹And when the tabernacle is to go forward, the Levites shall take it down; and when the tabernacle is to be set up, the Levites shall set it up. The outsider who comes near shall be put to death. ⁵²The children of Israel shall pitch their tents, everyone by his own camp, everyone by his own standard, according to their armies; ⁵³but the Levites shall camp around the tabernacle of the Testimony, that there may be no wrath on the congregation of the children of Israel; and the Levites shall keep charge of the tabernacle of the Testimony."

⁵⁴Thus the children of Israel did; according to all that the LORD commanded Moses, so they did.

The Tribes and Leaders by Armies

2 And the LORD spoke to Moses and Aaron, saying: ²"Everyone of the children of Israel shall camp by his own standard, beside the emblems of his father's house; they shall camp some distance from the tabernacle of meeting. ³On the east side, toward the rising of the sun, those of the standard of the forces with Judah shall camp according to their armies; and Nahshon the son of Amminadab *shall be* the leader of the children of Judah." ⁴And his army was numbered at seventy-four thousand six hundred.

⁵"Those who camp next to him *shall be* the tribe of Issachar, and Nethanel the son of Zuar *shall be* the leader of the children of Issachar." ⁶And his army was numbered at fifty-four thousand four hundred.

⁷"Then *comes* the tribe of Zebulun, and Eliab the son of Helon *shall be* the leader of the children of Zebulun." ⁸And his army was numbered at fifty-seven thousand four hundred. ⁹"All who were numbered according to their armies of the forces with Judah, one hundred and eighty-six thousand four hundred—these shall break camp first.

¹⁰"On the south side *shall be* the standard of the forces with Reuben according to their armies, and the leader of the children of Reuben *shall be* Elizur the son of Shedeur." ¹¹And his army was numbered at forty-six thousand five hundred.

¹²"Those who camp next to him *shall be* the tribe of Simeon, and the leader of the children of Simeon *shall be* Shelumiel the son of Zurishaddai." ¹³And his army was numbered at fifty-nine thousand three hundred.

¹⁴"Then *comes* the tribe of Gad, and the leader of the children of Gad *shall be* Eliasaph the son of Reuel."^a ¹⁵And his army was numbered at forty-five thousand six hundred and fifty. ¹⁶"All who were numbered according to their armies of the forces with Reuben, one hundred and fifty-one thousand four hundred and fifty—they shall be the second to break camp.

¹⁷"And the tabernacle of meeting shall move out with the camp of the Levites in the middle of the camps; as they camp, so they shall move out, everyone in his place, by their standards.

¹⁸"On the west side *shall be* the standard of the

2:14 ^aSpelled *Deuel* in 1:14 and 7:42

The Law of Navigation: Planning and Structure

(Numbers 2:1–34)

As a good leader, Moses methodically arranged the tribal camps in the wilderness. He set the tabernacle in the center and arranged the priests around its four sides. Then he symmetrically distributed the Twelve Tribes around the priests and Levites, with three tribes on each of the four sides.

We would do well to plan and organize as Moses did.

1. *Plan to plan.* Give time for planning and organizing.
2. *Determine your primary purpose.* What's the big picture? What are you trying to do?
3. *Assess the situation.* Understand where you sit before trying to develop a strategy.
4. *Prioritize the needs.* Make sure the team agrees on the most important goals.
5. *Ask the right questions.* Ask about market, leadership, revenue, reporting, evaluation.
6. *Set specific goals.* Write goals that are realistic, measurable, convictional.
7. *Clarify and communicate.* Communication links planning and implementation.
8. *Identify possible obstacles.* Mentally walk through all you are trying to pull off.
9. *Have an open system approach to your planning.* Be sympathetic to your environment.
10. *Schedule everything you can.* Get things on the calendar and set deadlines.
11. *Budget everything you can.* Determine both the costs and due dates of projects.
12. *Monitor and correct.* Progress is like a canoe trip; constantly adjust your course.
13. *Study the results.* Evaluation prevents stagnation and exaggeration.

Remember, anyone can steer the ship, but it takes a leader to chart the course.

forces with Ephraim according to their armies, and the leader of the children of Ephraim *shall be* Elishama the son of Ammihud." [19]And his army was numbered at forty thousand five hundred.

[20]"Next to him *comes* the tribe of Manasseh, and the leader of the children of Manasseh *shall be* Gamaliel the son of Pedahzur." [21]And his army was numbered at thirty-two thousand two hundred.

[22]"Then *comes* the tribe of Benjamin, and the leader of the children of Benjamin *shall be* Abidan the son of Gideoni." [23]And his army was numbered at thirty-five thousand four hundred. [24]"All who were numbered according to their armies of the forces with Ephraim, one hundred and eight thousand one hundred—they shall be the third to break camp.

[25]"The standard of the forces with Dan *shall be* on the north side according to their armies, and the leader of the children of Dan *shall be* Ahiezer the son of Ammishaddai." [26]And his army was numbered at sixty-two thousand seven hundred.

[27]"Those who camp next to him *shall be* the tribe of Asher, and the leader of the children of Asher *shall be* Pagiel the son of Ocran." [28]And his army was numbered at forty-one thousand five hundred.

[29]"Then *comes* the tribe of Naphtali, and the leader of the children of Naphtali *shall be* Ahira the son of Enan." [30]And his army was numbered at fifty-three thousand four hundred. [31]"All who were numbered of the forces with Dan, one hundred and fifty-seven thousand six hundred— they shall break camp last, with their standards."

[32]These *are* the ones who were numbered of the children of Israel by their fathers' houses. All who were numbered according to their armies of the forces *were* six hundred and three thousand five hundred and fifty. [33]But the Levites were not numbered among the children of Israel, just as the LORD commanded Moses.

[34]Thus the children of Israel did according to all that the LORD commanded Moses; so they camped by their standards and so they broke camp, each one by his family, according to their fathers' houses.

The Sons of Aaron

3 Now these *are* the records of Aaron and Moses when the LORD spoke with Moses on Mount Sinai. [2]And these *are* the names of the sons of Aaron: Nadab, the firstborn, and Abihu, Eleazar, and Ithamar. [3]These *are* the names of the sons of Aaron, the anointed priests, whom he consecrated to minister as priests.

[4]Nadab and Abihu had died before the LORD when they offered profane fire before the LORD in the Wilderness of Sinai; and they had no children. So Eleazar and Ithamar ministered as priests in the presence of Aaron their father.

The Levites Serve in the Tabernacle

[5]And the LORD spoke to Moses, saying: [6]"Bring the tribe of Levi near, and present them before Aaron the priest, that they may serve him. [7]And they shall attend to his needs and the needs of the whole congregation before the tabernacle of meeting, to do the work of the tabernacle. [8]Also they shall attend to all the furnishings of the tabernacle of meeting, and to the needs of the children of Israel, to do the work of the tabernacle. [9]And you shall give the Levites to Aaron and his sons; they are given entirely to him[a] from among the children of Israel. [10]So you shall appoint Aaron and his sons, and they shall attend to their priesthood; but the outsider who comes near shall be put to death."

[11]Then the LORD spoke to Moses, saying: [12]"Now behold, I Myself have taken the Levites from among the children of Israel instead of every firstborn who opens the womb among the children of Israel. Therefore the Levites shall be Mine, [13]because all the firstborn are Mine. On the day that I struck all the firstborn in the land of Egypt, I sanctified to Myself all the firstborn in Israel, both man and beast. They shall be Mine: I am the LORD."

Census of the Levites Commanded

[14]Then the LORD spoke to Moses in the Wilderness of Sinai, saying: [15]"Number the children of Levi by their fathers' houses, by their families; you shall number every male from a month old and above."

[16]So Moses numbered them according to the word of the LORD, as he was commanded. [17]These were the sons of Levi by their names: Gershon, Kohath, and Merari. [18]And these are the names of the sons of Gershon by their families: Libni and Shimei. [19]And the sons of Kohath by their families: Amram, Izehar, Hebron, and Uzziel. [20]And the sons of Merari by their families: Mahli and Mushi. These are the families of the Levites by their fathers' houses.

[21]From Gershon came the family of the Libnites and the family of the Shimites; these were the families of the Gershonites. [22]Those who were numbered, according to the number of all the males from a month old and above—of those who were numbered there were seven thousand five hundred. [23]The families of the Ger-

shonites were to camp behind the tabernacle westward. [24]And the leader of the father's house of the Gershonites was Eliasaph the son of Lael. [25]The duties of the children of Gershon in the tabernacle of meeting included the tabernacle, the tent with its covering, the screen for the door of the tabernacle of meeting, [26]the screen for the door of the court, the hangings of the court which are around the tabernacle and the altar, and their cords, according to all the work relating to them.

[27]From Kohath came the family of the Amramites, the family of the Izharites, the family of the Hebronites, and the family of the Uzzielites; these were the families of the Kohathites. [28]According to the number of all the males, from a month old and above, there were eight thousand six[a] hundred keeping charge of the sanctuary. [29]The families of the children of Kohath were to camp on the south side of the tabernacle. [30]And the leader of the fathers' house of the families of the Kohathites was Elizaphan the son of Uzziel. [31]Their duty included the ark, the table, the lampstand, the altars, the utensils of the sanctuary with which they ministered, the screen, and all the work relating to them.

[32]And Eleazar the son of Aaron the priest was to be chief over the leaders of the Levites, with oversight of those who kept charge of the sanctuary.

[33]From Merari came the family of the Mahlites and the family of the Mushites; these were the families of Merari. [34]And those who were numbered, according to the number of all the males from a month old and above, were six thousand two hundred. [35]The leader of the fathers' house of the families of Merari was Zuriel the son of Abihail. These were to camp on the north side of the tabernacle. [36]And the appointed duty of the children of Merari included the boards of the tabernacle, its bars, its pillars, its sockets, its utensils, all the work relating to them, [37]and the pillars of the court all around, with their sockets, their pegs, and their cords.

[38]Moreover those who were to camp before the tabernacle on the east, before the tabernacle of meeting, were Moses, Aaron, and his sons, keeping charge of the sanctuary, to meet the needs of the children of Israel; but the outsider who came near was to be put to death. [39]All who were numbered of the Levites, whom Moses and Aaron numbered at the commandment of the

---

3:9 [a]Samaritan Pentateuch and Septuagint read Me.
3:28 [a]Some manuscripts of the Septuagint read three.

LORD, by their families, all the males from a month old and above, *were* twenty-two thousand.

Levites Dedicated Instead of the Firstborn

[40]Then the LORD said to Moses: "Number all the firstborn males of the children of Israel from a month old and above, and take the number of their names. [41]And you shall take the Levites for Me—I *am* the LORD—instead of all the firstborn among the children of Israel, and the livestock of the Levites instead of all the firstborn among the livestock of the children of Israel." [42]So Moses numbered all the firstborn among the children of Israel, as the LORD commanded him. [43]And all the firstborn males, according to the number of names from a month old and above, of those who were numbered of them, were twenty-two thousand two hundred and seventy-three.

[44]Then the LORD spoke to Moses, saying: [45]"Take the Levites instead of all the firstborn among the children of Israel, and the livestock of the Levites instead of their livestock. The Levites shall be Mine: I *am* the LORD. [46]And for the redemption of the two hundred and seventy-three of the firstborn of the children of Israel, who are more than the number of the Levites, [47]you shall take five shekels for each one individually; you shall take *them* in the currency of the shekel of the sanctuary, the shekel of twenty gerahs. [48]And you shall give the money, with which the excess number of them is redeemed, to Aaron and his sons."

[49]So Moses took the redemption money from those who were over and above those who were redeemed by the Levites. [50]From the firstborn of the children of Israel he took the money, one thousand three hundred and sixty-five *shekels,* according to the shekel of the sanctuary. [51]And Moses gave their redemption money to Aaron and his sons, according to the word of the LORD, as the LORD commanded Moses.

Duties of the Sons of Kohath

4 Then the LORD spoke to Moses and Aaron, saying: [2]"Take a census of the sons of Kohath from among the children of Levi, by their families, by their fathers' house, [3]from thirty years old and above, even to fifty years old, all who enter the service to do the work in the tabernacle of meeting.

[4]"This *is* the service of the sons of Kohath in the tabernacle of meeting, *relating to* the most holy things: [5]When the camp prepares to journey, Aaron and his sons shall come, and they shall take down the covering veil and cover the ark of the Testimony with it. [6]Then they shall put on it

a covering of badger skins, and spread over *that* a cloth entirely of blue; and they shall insert its poles.

[7]"On the table of showbread they shall spread a blue cloth, and put on it the dishes, the pans, the bowls, and the pitchers for pouring; and the showbread[a] shall be on it. [8]They shall spread over them a scarlet cloth, and cover the same with a covering of badger skins; and they shall insert its poles. [9]And they shall take a blue cloth and cover the lampstand of the light, with its lamps, its wick-trimmers, its trays, and all its oil vessels, with which they service it. [10]Then they shall put it with all its utensils in a covering of badger skins, and put *it* on a carrying beam.

[11]"Over the golden altar they shall spread a blue cloth, and cover it with a covering of badger skins; and they shall insert its poles. [12]Then they shall take all the utensils of service with which they minister in the sanctuary, put *them* in a blue cloth, cover them with a covering of badger skins, and put *them* on a carrying beam. [13]Also they shall take away the ashes from the altar, and spread a purple cloth over it. [14]They shall put on it all its implements with which they minister there—the firepans, the forks, the shovels, the basins, and all the utensils of the altar—and they shall spread on it a covering of badger skins, and insert its poles. [15]And when Aaron and his sons have finished covering the sanctuary and all the furnishings of the sanctuary, when the camp is set to go, then the sons of Kohath shall come to carry *them;* but they shall not touch any holy thing, lest they die.

"These *are* the things in the tabernacle of meeting which the sons of Kohath are to carry. [16]"The appointed duty of Eleazar the son of Aaron the priest *is* the oil for the light, the sweet incense, the daily grain offering, the anointing oil, the oversight of all the tabernacle, of all that *is* in it, with the sanctuary and its furnishings."

[17]Then the LORD spoke to Moses and Aaron, saying: [18]"Do not cut off the tribe of the families of the Kohathites from among the Levites; [19]but do this in regard to them, that they may live and not die when they approach the most holy things: Aaron and his sons shall go in and appoint each of them to his service and his task. [20]But they shall not go in to watch while the holy things are being covered, lest they die."

Duties of the Sons of Gershon

[21]Then the LORD spoke to Moses, saying: [22]"Also take a census of the sons of Gershon, by

---

4:7 [a]Literally *the continual bread*

their fathers' house, by their families. ²³From thirty years old and above, even to fifty years old, you shall number them, all who enter to perform the service, to do the work in the tabernacle of meeting. ²⁴This *is* the service of the families of the Gershonites, in serving and carrying: ²⁵They shall carry the curtains of the tabernacle and the tabernacle of meeting *with* its covering, the covering of badger skins that *is* on it, the screen for the door of the tabernacle of meeting, ²⁶the screen for the door of the gate of the court, the hangings of the court which *are* around the tabernacle and altar, and their cords, all the furnishings for their service and all that is made for these things: so shall they serve. ²⁷"Aaron and his sons shall assign all the service of the sons of the Gershonites, all their tasks and all their service. And you shall appoint to them all their tasks as their duty. ²⁸This *is* the service of the families of the sons of Gershon in the tabernacle of meeting. And their duties *shall be* under the authority[a] of Ithamar the son of Aaron the priest.

Duties of the Sons of Merari

²⁹"*As for* the sons of Merari, you shall number them by their families and by their fathers' house. ³⁰From thirty years old and above, even to fifty years old, you shall number them, everyone who enters the service to do the work of the tabernacle of meeting. ³¹And this *is* what they must carry as all their service for the tabernacle of meeting: the boards of the tabernacle, its bars, its pillars, its sockets, ³²and the pillars around the court with their sockets, pegs, and cords, with all their furnishings and all their service; and you shall assign *to each man* by name the items he must carry. ³³This *is* the service of the families of the sons of Merari, as all their service for the tabernacle of meeting, under the authority[a] of Ithamar the son of Aaron the priest."

Census of the Levites

³⁴And Moses, Aaron, and the leaders of the congregation numbered the sons of the Kohathites by their families and by their fathers' house, ³⁵from thirty years old and above, even to fifty years old, everyone who entered the service for work in the tabernacle of meeting; ³⁶and those who were numbered by their families were two thousand seven hundred and fifty. ³⁷These *were* the ones who were numbered of the families of the Kohathites, all who might serve in the tabernacle of meeting, whom Moses and Aaron numbered according to the commandment of the LORD by the hand of Moses.

³⁸And those who were numbered of the sons of Gershon, by their families and by their fathers' house, ³⁹from thirty years old and above, even to fifty years old, everyone who entered the service for work in the tabernacle of meeting— ⁴⁰those who were numbered by their families, by their fathers' house, were two thousand six hundred and thirty. ⁴¹These *are* the ones who were numbered of the families of the sons of Gershon, of all who might serve in the tabernacle of meeting, whom Moses and Aaron numbered according to the commandment of the LORD.

⁴²Those of the families of the sons of Merari who were numbered, by their families, by their fathers' house, ⁴³from thirty years old and above, even to fifty years old, everyone who entered the service for work in the tabernacle of meeting— ⁴⁴those who were numbered by their families were three thousand two hundred. ⁴⁵These *are* the ones who were numbered of the families of the sons of Merari, whom Moses and Aaron numbered according to the word of the LORD by the hand of Moses.

⁴⁶All who were numbered of the Levites, whom Moses, Aaron, and the leaders of Israel numbered, by their families and by their fathers' houses, ⁴⁷from thirty years old and above, even to fifty years old, everyone who came to do the work of service and the work of bearing burdens in the tabernacle of meeting— ⁴⁸those who were numbered were eight thousand five hundred and eighty.

⁴⁹According to the commandment of the LORD they were numbered by the hand of Moses, each according to his service and according to his task; thus were they numbered by him, as the LORD commanded Moses.

Ceremonially Unclean Persons Isolated

5 And the LORD spoke to Moses, saying: ²"Command the children of Israel that they put out of the camp every leper, everyone who has a discharge, and whoever becomes defiled by a corpse. ³You shall put out both male and female; you shall put them outside the camp, that they may not defile their camps in the midst of which I dwell." ⁴And the children of Israel did so, and put them outside the camp; as the LORD spoke to Moses, so the children of Israel did.

Confession and Restitution

⁵Then the LORD spoke to Moses, saying, ⁶"Speak to the children of Israel: 'When a man or

---

4:28 [a]Literally *hand* **4:33** [a]Literally *hand*

woman commits any sin that men commit in unfaithfulness against the LORD, and that person is guilty, [7]then he shall confess the sin which he has committed. He shall make restitution for his trespass in full, plus one-fifth of it, and give it to the one he has wronged. [8]But if the man has no relative to whom restitution may be made for the wrong, the restitution for the wrong must go to the LORD for the priest, in addition to the ram of the atonement with which atonement is made for him. [9]Every offering of all the holy things of the children of Israel, which they bring to the priest, shall be his. [10]And every man's holy things shall be his; whatever any man gives the priest shall be his.'"

Concerning Unfaithful Wives

[11]And the LORD spoke to Moses, saying, [12]"Speak to the children of Israel, and say to them: 'If any man's wife goes astray and behaves unfaithfully toward him, [13]and a man lies with her carnally, and it is hidden from the eyes of her husband, and it is concealed that she has defiled herself, and there was no witness against her, nor was she caught— [14]if the spirit of jealousy comes upon him and he becomes jealous of his wife, who has defiled herself; or if the spirit of jealousy comes upon him and he becomes jealous of his wife, although she has not defiled herself— [15]then the man shall bring his wife to the priest. He shall bring the offering required for her, one-tenth of an ephah of barley meal; he shall pour no oil on it and put no frankincense on it, because it is a grain offering of jealousy, an offering for remembering, for bringing iniquity to remembrance.

[16]'And the priest shall bring her near, and set her before the LORD. [17]The priest shall take holy water in an earthen vessel, and take some of the dust that is on the floor of the tabernacle and put it into the water. [18]Then the priest shall stand the woman before the LORD, uncover the woman's head, and put the offering for remembering in her hands, which is the grain offering of jealousy. And the priest shall have in his hand the bitter water that brings a curse. [19]And the priest shall put her under oath, and say to the woman, "If no man has lain with you, and if you have not gone astray to uncleanness while under your husband's authority, be free from this bitter water that brings a curse. [20]But if you have gone astray while under your husband's authority, and if you have defiled yourself and some man other than your husband has lain with you"— [21]then the priest shall put the woman under the oath of the curse, and he shall say to the woman—"the LORD make you a curse and an oath among your people, when the LORD makes your thigh rot and your belly swell; [22]and may this water that causes the curse go into your stomach, and make your belly swell and your thigh rot."

'Then the woman shall say, "Amen, so be it."

[23]'Then the priest shall write these curses in a book, and he shall scrape them off into the bitter water. [24]And he shall make the woman drink the bitter water that brings a curse, and the water that brings the curse shall enter her to become bitter. [25]Then the priest shall take the grain offering of jealousy from the woman's hand, shall wave the offering before the LORD, and bring it to the altar; [26]and the priest shall take a handful of the offering, as its memorial portion, burn it on the altar, and afterward make the woman drink the water. [27]When he has made her drink the water, then it shall be, if she has defiled herself and behaved unfaithfully toward her husband, that the water that brings a curse will enter her and become bitter, and her belly will swell, her thigh will rot, and the woman will become a curse among her people. [28]But if the woman has not defiled herself, and is clean, then she shall be free and may conceive children.

[29]'This is the law of jealousy, when a wife, while under her husband's authority, goes astray and defiles herself, [30]or when the spirit of jealousy comes upon a man, and he becomes jealous of his wife; then he shall stand the woman before the LORD, and the priest shall execute all this law upon her. [31]Then the man shall be free from iniquity, but that woman shall bear her guilt.'"

The Law of the Nazirite

6 Then the LORD spoke to Moses, saying, [2]"Speak to the children of Israel, and say to them: 'When either a man or woman consecrates an offering to take the vow of a Nazirite, to separate himself to the LORD, [3]he shall separate himself from wine and similar drink; he shall drink neither vinegar made from wine nor vinegar made from similar drink; neither shall he drink any grape juice, nor eat fresh grapes or raisins. [4]All the days of his separation he shall eat nothing that is produced by the grapevine, from seed to skin.

[5]'All the days of the vow of his separation no razor shall come upon his head; until the days are fulfilled for which he separated himself to the LORD, he shall be holy. Then he shall let the locks of the hair of his head grow. [6]All the days that he separates himself to the LORD he shall not go near a dead body. [7]He shall not make himself unclean even for his father or his mother, for his

The Law of Sacrifice: Nazirites Give Up to Go Up

(Numbers 6:1–21)

Through the vow of the Nazirite, God provided a way for both men and women to specially consecrate themselves to the Lord for a special time and purpose. Leaders such as Samson (and perhaps Samuel) made this vow, committing to abstain from wine and strong drink, to leave their hair uncut, and to avoid contact with a corpse. They gave up certain rights or options in order to live at a higher standard—in other words, they practiced the Law of Sacrifice. They did so not to stand in judgment of others, but to discipline themselves against the temptations of the day.

How can today's leaders apply the principle behind the Nazirite vow?

Discipline	Application
Abstinence from wine/strong drink	*Indulgence:* discipline to prevent addiction
Uncut hair	*Image:* refuse to allow fashion to lead you
Avoid defilement from corpse	*Integrity:* stay pure; pursue a holy standard

brother or his sister, when they die, because his separation to God *is* on his head. [8]All the days of his separation he shall be holy to the LORD.

[9]"And if anyone dies very suddenly beside him, and he defiles his consecrated head, then he shall shave his head on the day of his cleansing; on the seventh day he shall shave it. [10]Then on the eighth day he shall bring two turtledoves or two young pigeons to the priest, to the door of the tabernacle of meeting; [11]and the priest shall offer one as a sin offering and *the* other as a burnt offering, and make atonement for him, because he sinned in regard to the corpse; and he shall sanctify his head that same day. [12]He shall consecrate to the LORD the days of his separation, and bring a male lamb in its first year as a trespass offering; but the former days shall be lost, because his separation was defiled.

[13]"Now this *is* the law of the Nazirite: When the days of his separation are fulfilled, he shall be brought to the door of the tabernacle of meeting. [14]And he shall present his offering to the LORD: one male lamb in its first year without blemish as a burnt offering, one ewe lamb in its first year without blemish as a sin offering, one ram without blemish as a peace offering, [15]a basket of unleavened bread, cakes of fine flour mixed with oil, unleavened wafers anointed with oil, and their grain offering with their drink offerings.

[16]"Then the priest shall bring *them* before the LORD and offer his sin offering and his burnt offering; [17]and he shall offer the ram as a sacrifice of a peace offering to the LORD, with the basket of unleavened bread; the priest shall also offer its

grain offering and its drink offering. [18]Then the Nazirite shall shave his consecrated head *at* the door of the tabernacle of meeting, and shall take the hair from his consecrated head and put *it* on the fire which is under the sacrifice of the peace offering.

[19]"And the priest shall take the boiled shoulder of the ram, one unleavened cake from the basket, and one unleavened wafer, and put *them* upon the hands of the Nazirite after he has shaved his consecrated *hair,* [20]and the priest shall wave them as a wave offering before the LORD; they *are* holy for the priest, together with the breast of the wave offering and the thigh of the heave offering. After that the Nazirite may drink wine.'

[21]"This is the law of the Nazirite who vows to the LORD the offering for his separation, and besides that, whatever else his hand is able to provide; according to the vow which he takes, so he must do according to the law of his separation."

The Priestly Blessing

[22]And the LORD spoke to Moses, saying: [23]"Speak to Aaron and his sons, saying, 'This is the way you shall bless the children of Israel. Say to them:

[24]   "The LORD bless you and keep you;
[25]   The LORD make His face shine upon you,
         And be gracious to you;
[26]   The LORD lift up His countenance upon you,
         And give you peace."'

²⁷"So they shall put My name on the children of Israel, and I will bless them."

Offerings of the Leaders

7 Now it came to pass, when Moses had finished setting up the tabernacle, that he anointed it and consecrated it and all its furnishings, and the altar and all its utensils; so he anointed them and consecrated them. ²Then the leaders of Israel, the heads of their fathers' houses, who *were* the leaders of the tribes and over those who were numbered, made an offering. ³And they brought their offering before the LORD, six covered carts and twelve oxen, a cart for *every* two of the leaders, and for each one an ox; and they presented them before the tabernacle.

⁴Then the LORD spoke to Moses, saying, ⁵"Accept *these* from them, that they may be used in doing the work of the tabernacle of meeting; and you shall give them to the Levites, *to* every man according to his service." ⁶So Moses took the carts and the oxen, and gave them to the Levites. ⁷Two carts and four oxen he gave to the sons of Gershon, according to their service; ⁸and four carts and eight oxen he gave to the sons of Merari, according to their service, under the authority[a] of Ithamar the son of Aaron the priest. ⁹But to the sons of Kohath he gave none, because theirs *was* the service of the holy things, *which* they carried on their shoulders.

¹⁰Now the leaders offered the dedication *offering* for the altar when it was anointed; so the leaders offered their offering before the altar. ¹¹For the LORD said to Moses, "They shall offer their offering, one leader each day, for the dedication of the altar."

¹²And the one who offered his offering on the first day *was* Nahshon the son of Amminadab, from the tribe of Judah. ¹³His offering *was* one silver platter, the weight of which *was* one hundred and thirty *shekels,* and one silver bowl of seventy shekels, according to the shekel of the sanctuary, both of them full of fine flour mixed with oil as a grain offering; ¹⁴one gold pan of ten *shekels,* full of incense; ¹⁵one young bull, one ram, and one male lamb in its first year, as a burnt offering; ¹⁶one kid of the goats as a sin offering; ¹⁷and for the sacrifice of peace offerings: two oxen, five rams, five male goats, and five male lambs in their first year. This *was* the offering of Nahshon the son of Amminadab.

¹⁸On the second day Nethanel the son of Zuar, leader of Issachar, presented *an offering.* ¹⁹*For* his offering he offered one silver platter, the weight of which *was* one hundred and thirty *shekels,* and one silver bowl of seventy shekels, according to the shekel of the sanctuary, both of them full of fine flour mixed with oil as a grain offering; ²⁰one gold pan of ten *shekels,* full of incense; ²¹one young bull, one ram, and one male lamb in its first year, as a burnt offering; ²²one kid of the goats as a sin offering; ²³and as the sacrifice of peace offerings: two oxen, five rams, five male goats, and five male lambs in their first year. This *was* the offering of Nethanel the son of Zuar.

²⁴On the third day Eliab the son of Helon, leader of the children of Zebulun, *presented an offering.* ²⁵His offering *was* one silver platter, the weight of which *was* one hundred and thirty *shekels,* and one silver bowl of seventy shekels, according to the shekel of the sanctuary, both of them full of fine flour mixed with oil as a grain offering; ²⁶one gold pan of ten *shekels,* full of incense; ²⁷one young bull, one ram, and one male lamb in its first year, as a burnt offering; ²⁸one kid of the goats as a sin offering; ²⁹and for the sacrifice of peace offerings: two oxen, five rams, five male goats, and five male lambs in their first year. This *was* the offering of Eliab the son of Helon.

³⁰On the fourth day Elizur the son of Shedeur, leader of the children of Reuben, *presented an offering.* ³¹His offering *was* one silver platter, the weight of which *was* one hundred and thirty *shekels,* and one silver bowl of seventy shekels, according to the shekel of the sanctuary, both of them full of fine flour mixed with oil as a grain offering; ³²one gold pan of ten *shekels,* full of incense; ³³one young bull, one ram, and one male lamb in its first year, as a burnt offering; ³⁴one kid of the goats as a sin offering; ³⁵and as the sacrifice of peace offerings: two oxen, five rams, five male goats, and five male lambs in their first year. This *was* the offering of Elizur the son of Shedeur.

³⁶On the fifth day Shelumiel the son of Zurishaddai, leader of the children of Simeon, *presented an offering.* ³⁷His offering *was* one silver platter, the weight of which *was* one hundred and thirty *shekels,* and one silver bowl of seventy shekels, according to the shekel of the sanctuary, both of them full of fine flour mixed with oil as a grain offering; ³⁸one gold pan of ten *shekels,* full of incense; ³⁹one young bull, one ram, and one male lamb in its first year, as a burnt offering; ⁴⁰one kid of the goats as a sin offering; ⁴¹and as the sacrifice of peace offerings: two oxen, five rams, five male goats, and five male lambs in their first year. This *was* the offering of Shelumiel the son of Zurishaddai.

7:8 ^aLiterally *hand*

⁴²On the sixth day Eliasaph the son of Deuel,ᵃ leader of the children of Gad, *presented an offering.* ⁴³His offering *was* one silver platter, the weight of which *was* one hundred and thirty *shekels,* and one silver bowl of seventy shekels, according to the shekel of the sanctuary, both of them full of fine flour mixed with oil as a grain offering; ⁴⁴one gold pan of ten *shekels,* full of incense; ⁴⁵one young bull, one ram, and one male lamb in its first year, as a burnt offering; ⁴⁶one kid of the goats as a sin offering; ⁴⁷and as the sacrifice of peace offerings: two oxen, five rams, five male goats, and five male lambs in their first year. This *was* the offering of Eliasaph the son of Deuel.

⁴⁸On the seventh day Elishama the son of Ammihud, leader of the children of Ephraim, *presented an offering.* ⁴⁹His offering *was* one silver platter, the weight of which *was* one hundred and thirty *shekels,* and one silver bowl of seventy shekels, according to the shekel of the sanctuary, both of them full of fine flour mixed with oil as a grain offering; ⁵⁰one gold pan of ten *shekels,* full of incense; ⁵¹one young bull, one ram, and one male lamb in its first year, as a burnt offering; ⁵²one kid of the goats as a sin offering; ⁵³and as the sacrifice of peace offerings: two oxen, five rams, five male goats, and five male lambs in their first year. This *was* the offering of Elishama the son of Ammihud.

⁵⁴On the eighth day Gamaliel the son of Pedahzur, leader of the children of Manasseh, *presented an offering.* ⁵⁵His offering *was* one silver platter, the weight of which *was* one hundred and thirty *shekels,* and one silver bowl of seventy shekels, according to the shekel of the sanctuary, both of them full of fine flour mixed with oil as a grain offering; ⁵⁶one gold pan of ten *shekels,* full of incense; ⁵⁷one young bull, one ram, and one male lamb in its first year, as a burnt offering; ⁵⁸one kid of the goats as a sin offering; ⁵⁹and as the sacrifice of peace offerings: two oxen, five rams, five male goats, and five male lambs in their first year. This *was* the offering of Gamaliel the son of Pedahzur.

⁶⁰On the ninth day Abidan the son of Gideoni, leader of the children of Benjamin, *presented an offering.* ⁶¹His offering *was* one silver platter, the weight of which *was* one hundred and thirty *shekels,* and one silver bowl of seventy shekels, according to the shekel of the sanctuary, both of them full of fine flour mixed with oil as a grain offering; ⁶²one gold pan of ten *shekels,* full of incense; ⁶³one young bull, one ram, and one male lamb in its first year, as a burnt offering; ⁶⁴one kid of the goats as a sin offering; ⁶⁵and as the sacrifice of peace offerings: two oxen, five rams, five male goats, and five male lambs in their first year. This *was* the offering of Abidan the son of Gideoni.

⁶⁶On the tenth day Ahiezer the son of Ammishaddai, leader of the children of Dan, *presented an offering.* ⁶⁷His offering *was* one silver platter, the weight of which *was* one hundred and thirty *shekels,* and one silver bowl of seventy shekels, according to the shekel of the sanctuary, both of them full of fine flour mixed with oil as a grain offering; ⁶⁸one gold pan of ten *shekels,* full of incense; ⁶⁹one young bull, one ram, and one male lamb in its first year, as a burnt offering; ⁷⁰one kid of the goats as a sin offering; ⁷¹and as the sacrifice of peace offerings: two oxen, five rams, five male goats, and five male lambs in their first year. This *was* the offering of Ahiezer the son of Ammishaddai.

⁷²On the eleventh day Pagiel the son of Ocran, leader of the children of Asher, *presented an offering.* ⁷³His offering *was* one silver platter, the weight of which *was* one hundred and thirty *shekels,* and one silver bowl of seventy shekels, according to the shekel of the sanctuary, both of them full of fine flour mixed with oil as a grain offering; ⁷⁴one gold pan of ten *shekels,* full of incense; ⁷⁵one young bull, one ram, and one male lamb in its first year, as a burnt offering; ⁷⁶one kid of the goats as a sin offering; ⁷⁷and as the sacrifice of peace offerings: two oxen, five rams, five male goats, and five male lambs in their first year. This *was* the offering of Pagiel the son of Ocran.

⁷⁸On the twelfth day Ahira the son of Enan, leader of the children of Naphtali, *presented an offering.* ⁷⁹His offering *was* one silver platter, the weight of which *was* one hundred and thirty *shekels,* and one silver bowl of seventy shekels, according to the shekel of the sanctuary, both of them full of fine flour mixed with oil as a grain offering; ⁸⁰one gold pan of ten *shekels,* full of incense; ⁸¹one young bull, one ram, and one male lamb in its first year, as a burnt offering; ⁸²one kid of the goats as a sin offering; ⁸³and as the sacrifice of peace offerings: two oxen, five rams, five male goats, and five male lambs in their first year. This *was* the offering of Ahira the son of Enan.

⁸⁴This *was* the dedication *offering* for the altar from the leaders of Israel, when it was anointed: twelve silver platters, twelve silver bowls, and twelve gold pans. ⁸⁵Each silver platter *weighed* one hundred and thirty *shekels* and each bowl seventy *shekels.* All the silver of the vessels *weighed* two thousand four hundred *shekels,* according to the shekel of the sanctuary. ⁸⁶The twelve gold pans

---

7:42 ᵃSpelled *Reuel* in 2:14

full of incense *weighed* ten *shekels* apiece, according to the shekel of the sanctuary; all the gold of the pans *weighed* one hundred and twenty *shekels.* [87]All the oxen for the burnt offering *were* twelve young bulls, the rams twelve, the male lambs in their first year twelve, with their grain offering, and the kids of the goats as a sin offering twelve. [88]And all the oxen for the sacrifice of peace offerings were twenty-four bulls, the rams sixty, the male goats sixty, and the lambs in their first year sixty. This *was* the dedication *offering* for the altar after it was anointed.

[89]Now when Moses went into the tabernacle of meeting to speak with Him, he heard the voice of One speaking to him from above the mercy seat that *was* on the ark of the Testimony, from between the two cherubim; thus He spoke to him.

Arrangement of the Lamps

8 And the LORD spoke to Moses, saying: [2]"Speak to Aaron, and say to him, 'When you arrange the lamps, the seven lamps shall give light in front of the lampstand.'" [3]And Aaron did so; he arranged the lamps to face toward the front of the lampstand, as the LORD commanded Moses. [4]Now this workmanship of the lampstand *was* hammered gold; from its shaft to its flowers it *was* hammered work. According to the pattern which the LORD had shown Moses, so he made the lampstand.

Cleansing and Dedication of the Levites

[5]Then the LORD spoke to Moses, saying: [6]"Take the Levites from among the children of Israel and cleanse them *ceremonially.* [7]Thus you shall do to them to cleanse them: Sprinkle water of purification on them, and let them shave all their body, and let them wash their clothes, and *so* make themselves clean. [8]Then let them take a young bull with its grain offering of fine flour mixed with oil, and you shall take another young bull as a sin offering. [9]And you shall bring the Levites before the tabernacle of meeting, and you shall gather together the whole congregation of the children of Israel. [10]So you shall bring the Levites before the LORD, and the children of Israel shall lay their hands on the Levites; [11]and Aaron shall offer the Levites before the LORD *like* a wave offering from the children of Israel, that they may perform the work of the LORD. [12]Then the Levites shall lay their hands on the heads of the young bulls, and you shall offer one as a sin offering and the other as a burnt offering to the LORD, to make atonement for the Levites. [13]"And you shall stand the Levites before

Aaron and his sons, and then offer them *like* a wave offering to the LORD. [14]Thus you shall separate the Levites from among the children of Israel, and the Levites shall be Mine. [15]After that the Levites shall go in to service the tabernacle of meeting. So you shall cleanse them and offer them *like* a wave offering. [16]For they *are* wholly given to Me from among the children of Israel; I have taken them for Myself instead of all who open the womb, the firstborn of all the children of Israel. [17]For all the firstborn among the children of Israel *are* Mine, *both* man and beast; on the day that I struck all the firstborn in the land of Egypt I sanctified them to Myself. [18]I have taken the Levites instead of all the firstborn of the children of Israel. [19]And I have given the Levites as a gift to Aaron and his sons from among the children of Israel, to do the work for the children of Israel in the tabernacle of meeting, and to make atonement for the children of Israel, that there be no plague among the children of Israel when the children of Israel come near the sanctuary."

[20]Thus Moses and Aaron and all the congregation of the children of Israel did to the Levites; according to all that the LORD commanded Moses concerning the Levites, so the children of Israel did to them. [21]And the Levites purified themselves and washed their clothes; then Aaron presented them *like* a wave offering before the LORD, and Aaron made atonement for them to cleanse them. [22]After that the Levites went in to do their work in the tabernacle of meeting before Aaron and his sons; as the LORD commanded Moses concerning the Levites, so they did to them.

[23]Then the LORD spoke to Moses, saying, [24]"This *is* what *pertains* to the Levites: From twenty-five years old and above one may enter to perform service in the work of the tabernacle of meeting; [25]and at the age of fifty years they must cease performing this work, and shall work no more. [26]They may minister with their brethren in the tabernacle of meeting, to attend to needs, but they *themselves* shall do no work. Thus you shall do to the Levites regarding their duties."

The Second Passover

9 Now the LORD spoke to Moses in the Wilderness of Sinai, in the first month of the second year after they had come out of the land of Egypt, saying: [2]"Let the children of Israel keep the Passover at its appointed time. [3]On the fourteenth day of this month, at twilight, you shall keep it at its appointed time. According to all its rites and ceremonies you shall

keep it." ⁴So Moses told the children of Israel that they should keep the Passover. ⁵And they kept the Passover on the fourteenth day of the first month, at twilight, in the Wilderness of Sinai; according to all that the LORD commanded Moses, so the children of Israel did.

⁶Now there were *certain* men who were defiled by a human corpse, so that they could not keep the Passover on that day; and they came before Moses and Aaron that day. ⁷And those men said to him, "We *became* defiled by a human corpse. Why are we kept from presenting the offering of the LORD at its appointed time among the children of Israel?"

⁸And Moses said to them, "Stand still, that I may hear what the LORD will command concerning you."

⁹Then the LORD spoke to Moses, saying, ¹⁰"Speak to the children of Israel, saying: 'If anyone of you or your posterity is unclean because of a corpse, or *is* far away on a journey, he may still keep the LORD's Passover. ¹¹On the fourteenth day of the second month, at twilight, they may keep it. They shall eat it with unleavened bread and bitter herbs. ¹²They shall leave none of it until morning, nor break one of its bones. According to all the ordinances of the Passover they shall keep it. ¹³But the man who *is* clean and is not on a journey, and ceases to keep the Passover, that same person shall be cut off from among his people, because he did not bring the offering of the LORD at its appointed time; that man shall bear his sin.

¹⁴'And if a stranger dwells among you, and would keep the LORD's Passover, he must do so according to the rite of the Passover and according to its ceremony; you shall have one ordinance, both for the stranger and the native of the land.'"

The Cloud and the Fire

¹⁵Now on the day that the tabernacle was raised up, the cloud covered the tabernacle, the tent of the Testimony; from evening until morning it was above the tabernacle like the appearance of fire. ¹⁶So it was always: the cloud covered it *by day*, and the appearance of fire by night. ¹⁷Whenever the cloud was taken up from above the tabernacle, after that the children of Israel would journey; and in the place where the cloud settled, there the children of Israel would pitch their tents. ¹⁸At the command of the LORD the children of Israel would journey, and at the command of the LORD they would camp; as long as the cloud stayed above the tabernacle they remained encamped. ¹⁹Even when the cloud

The Law of Timing: God's Dynamic Leadership

(Numbers 9:15–23)

God's people had no way of knowing whether they would camp in a specific location for a few days or a few years. They couldn't slip into a rut and trust in a schedule; they had to remain flexible. They learned to trust God, their Ultimate Leader.

continued long, many days above the tabernacle, the children of Israel kept the charge of the LORD and did not journey. ²⁰So it was, when the cloud was above the tabernacle a few days: according to the command of the LORD they would remain encamped, and according to the command of the LORD they would journey. ²¹So it was, when the cloud remained only from evening until morning: when the cloud was taken up in the morning, then they would journey; whether by day or by night, whenever the cloud was taken up, they would journey. ²²*Whether it was* two days, a month, or a year that the cloud remained above the tabernacle, the children of Israel would remain encamped and not journey; but when it was taken up, they would journey. ²³At the command of the LORD they remained encamped, and at the command of the LORD they journeyed; they kept the charge of the LORD, at the command of the LORD by the hand of Moses.

Two Silver Trumpets

10 And the LORD spoke to Moses, saying: ²"Make two silver trumpets for yourself; you shall make them of hammered work; you shall use them for calling the congregation and for directing the movement of the camps. ³When they blow both of them, all the congregation shall gather before you at the door of the tabernacle of meeting. ⁴But if they blow *only* one, then the leaders, the heads of the divisions of Israel, shall gather to you. ⁵When you sound the advance, the camps that lie on the east side shall then begin their journey. ⁶When you sound the advance the second time, then the camps that lie on the south side shall begin their journey; they shall sound the call for them to begin their journeys. ⁷And when the assembly is to be gathered together, you shall blow, but not sound the advance. [8]The sons of Aaron, the priests, shall blow the trumpets; and these shall be to you as an ordinance forever throughout your generations.

[9]"When you go to war in your land against the enemy who oppresses you, then you shall sound an alarm with the trumpets, and you will be remembered before the LORD your God, and you will be saved from your enemies. [10]Also in the day of your gladness, in your appointed feasts, and at the beginning of your months, you shall blow the trumpets over your burnt offerings and over the sacrifices of your peace offerings; and they shall be a memorial for you before your God: I *am* the LORD your God."

Departure from Sinai

[11]Now it came to pass on the twentieth *day* of the second month, in the second year, that the cloud was taken up from above the tabernacle of the Testimony. [12]And the children of Israel set out from the Wilderness of Sinai on their journeys; then the cloud settled down in the Wilderness of Paran. [13]So they started out for the first time according to the command of the LORD by the hand of Moses.

[14]The standard of the camp of the children of Judah set out first according to their armies; over their army was Nahshon the son of Amminadab. [15]Over the army of the tribe of the children of Issachar *was* Nethanel the son of Zuar. [16]And over the army of the tribe of the children of Zebulun *was* Eliab the son of Helon.

[17]Then the tabernacle was taken down; and the sons of Gershon and the sons of Merari set out, carrying the tabernacle.

[18]And the standard of the camp of Reuben set out according to their armies; over their army *was* Elizur the son of Shedeur. [19]Over the army of the tribe of the children of Simeon *was* Shelumiel the son of Zurishaddai. [20]And over the army of the tribe of the children of Gad *was* Eliasaph the son of Deuel.

[21]Then the Kohathites set out, carrying the holy things. (The tabernacle would be prepared for their arrival.)

[22]And the standard of the camp of the children of Ephraim set out according to their armies; over their army *was* Elishama the son of Ammihud. [23]Over the army of the tribe of the children of Manasseh *was* Gamaliel the son of Pedahzur. [24]And over the army of the tribe of the children of Benjamin *was* Abidan the son of Gideoni.

[25]Then the standard of the camp of the chil-

dren of Dan (the rear guard of all the camps) set out according to their armies; over their army *was* Ahiezer the son of Ammishaddai. [26]Over the army of the tribe of the children of Asher *was* Pagiel the son of Ocran. [27]And over the army of the tribe of the children of Naphtali *was* Ahira the son of Enan.

[28]Thus *was* the order of march of the children of Israel, according to their armies, when they began their journey.

[29]Now Moses said to Hobab the son of Reuel[a] the Midianite, Moses' father-in-law, "We are setting out for the place of which the LORD said, 'I will give it to you.' Come with us, and we will treat you well; for the LORD has promised good things to Israel."

[30]And he said to him, "I will not go, but I will depart to my *own* land and to my relatives."

[31]So *Moses* said, "Please do not leave, inasmuch as you know how we are to camp in the wilderness, and you can be our eyes. [32]And it shall be, if you go with us—indeed it shall be—that whatever good the LORD will do to us, the same we will do to you."

[33]So they departed from the mountain of the LORD on a journey of three days; and the ark of the covenant of the LORD went before them for the three days' journey, to search out a resting place for them. [34]And the cloud of the LORD *was* above them by day when they went out from the camp.

[35]So it was, whenever the ark set out, that Moses said:

"Rise up, O LORD!
Let Your enemies be scattered,
And let those who hate You flee before
You."

[36]And when it rested, he said:

"Return, O LORD,
To the many thousands of Israel."

The People Complain

11 Now *when* the people complained, it displeased the LORD; for the LORD heard *it,* and His anger was aroused. So the fire of the LORD burned among them, and consumed *some* in the outskirts of the camp. [2]Then the people cried out to Moses, and when Moses prayed to the LORD, the fire was quenched. [3]So he called the name of the place

---

10:29 [a]Septuagint reads *Raguel* (compare Exodus 2:18).

Taberah,[a] because the fire of the LORD had burned among them.

⁴Now the mixed multitude who were among them yielded to intense craving; so the children of Israel also wept again and said: "Who will give us meat to eat? ⁵We remember the fish which we ate freely in Egypt, the cucumbers, the melons, the leeks, the onions, and the garlic; ⁶but now our whole being *is* dried up; *there is* nothing at all except this manna *before* our eyes!"

⁷Now the manna *was* like coriander seed, and its color like the color of bdellium. ⁸The people went about and gathered *it,* ground *it* on millstones or beat *it* in the mortar, cooked *it* in pans, and made cakes of it; and its taste was like the taste of pastry prepared with oil. ⁹And when the dew fell on the camp in the night, the manna fell on it.

¹⁰Then Moses heard the people weeping throughout their families, everyone at the door of his tent; and the anger of the LORD was greatly aroused; Moses also was displeased. ¹¹So Moses said to the LORD, "Why have You afflicted Your servant? And why have I not found favor in Your sight, that You have laid the burden of all these people on me? ¹²Did I conceive all these people? Did I beget them, that You should say to me, 'Carry them in your bosom, as a guardian carries a nursing child,' to the land which You swore to their fathers? ¹³Where am I to get meat to give to all these people? For they weep all over me, saying, 'Give us meat, that we may eat.' ¹⁴I am not able to bear all these people alone, because the burden *is* too heavy for me. ¹⁵If You treat me like this, please kill me here and now—if I have found favor in Your sight—and do not let me see my wretchedness!"

The Seventy Elders

¹⁶So the LORD said to Moses: "Gather to Me seventy men of the elders of Israel, whom you know to be the elders of the people and officers over them; bring them to the tabernacle of meeting, that they may stand there with you. ¹⁷Then I will come down and talk with you there. I will take of the Spirit that *is* upon you and will put *the same* upon them; and they shall bear the burden of the people with you, that you may not bear *it* yourself alone. ¹⁸Then you shall say to the people, 'Consecrate yourselves for tomorrow, and you shall eat meat; for you have wept in the hearing of the LORD, saying, "Who

---

11:3 [a]Literally *Burning*

THE SEVENTY ELDERS

SHARING THE BURDEN OF GOD'S ANOINTED

(Numbers 11:11–17)

PROFILE IN LEADERSHIP

We don't know a lot about the seventy elders Moses called to aid him. Scripture does not name them, nor even mention which tribes they represent. What we do know is that they were officers and elders of the people; perhaps all or most were among the rulers of thousands, hundreds, fifties, and tens selected in Exodus 18:25. More than likely they were older men who had gained influence and respect among the people.

The Old Testament mentions the seventy elders only twice, both times to witness God's presence, power, and glory (Ex. 24). But the second time the elders are called, God expands their role. This time they are not only to witness, but to participate—thus revealing something remarkable about how God works with leaders. "I will take of the Spirit that is upon you," God told Moses, "and will put the same upon them; and they shall bear the burden of the people with you, that you may not bear it yourself alone" (Num. 11:17).

When a leader called by God has a burden that becomes too great, God provides help . . . if the leader will ask for it. Not only will the Lord provide helpers to share the load, He will anoint them with His power, just as He did the seventy elders of Israel.

The Law of Empowerment:
What Do Potential Leaders Need?

(Numbers 11:16–30)

Often pastors in traditional churches ask, "Is it really my job to equip people to serve and lead? Am I not merely to be a shepherd and teach the people on Sunday?"

This question demonstrates how our culture has blinded us to the biblical call for leaders to equip other leaders. Numbers 11 demonstrates that equipping laypeople to lead and serve is God's idea, not man's. Leaders are to identify, prepare, and release teams to work.

God left no doubt about how Moses was to train the seventy leaders he had selected. In Numbers 11:16–30 we see the answer to the question: What do potential leaders need? God says:

1. *They need authority* (v. 16, "bring them . . . that they may stand there with you").
2. *They need anointing* (v. 17, "I will take of the Spirit . . . and will put the same upon them").
3. *They need ownership of the vision* (v. 17, "the Spirit that is upon you . . . upon them").
4. *They need responsibility* (v. 17, "they shall bear the burden of the people with you").
5. *They need specific ministry roles* (v. 24, "placed them around the tabernacle").
6. *They need to express their gifts* (v. 25, "when the Spirit rested upon them . . . they prophesied").
7. *They need a secure shepherd who will release them to succeed* (vv. 26–30, Moses).

will give us meat to eat? For *it was* well with us in Egypt." Therefore the LORD will give you meat, and you shall eat. ¹⁹You shall eat, not one day, nor two days, nor five days, nor ten days, nor twenty days, ²⁰but *for* a whole month, until it comes out of your nostrils and becomes loathsome to you, because you have despised the LORD who is among you, and have wept before Him, saying, "Why did we ever come up out of Egypt?' "

²¹And Moses said, "The people whom I *am* among *are* six hundred thousand men on foot; yet You have said, 'I will give them meat, that they may eat *for* a whole month.' ²²Shall flocks and herds be slaughtered for them, to provide enough for them? Or shall all the fish of the sea be gathered together for them, to provide enough for them?"

²³And the LORD said to Moses, "Has the LORD's arm been shortened? Now you shall see whether what I say will happen to you or not."

²⁴So Moses went out and told the people the words of the LORD, and he gathered the seventy men of the elders of the people and placed them around the tabernacle. ²⁵Then the LORD came down in the cloud, and spoke to him, and took of the Spirit that *was* upon him, and placed *the same* upon the seventy elders; and it happened, when the Spirit rested upon them, that they prophesied, although they never did *so* again.ᵃ

²⁶But two men had remained in the camp: the name of one *was* Eldad, and the name of the other Medad. And the Spirit rested upon them. Now they *were* among those listed, but who had not gone out to the tabernacle; yet they prophesied in the camp. ²⁷And a young man ran and told Moses, and said, "Eldad and Medad are prophesying in the camp."

²⁸So Joshua the son of Nun, Moses' assistant, *one* of his choice men, answered and said, "Moses my lord, forbid them!"

²⁹Then Moses said to him, "Are you zealous for my sake? Oh, that all the LORD's people were prophets *and* that the LORD would put His Spirit upon them!" ³⁰And Moses returned to the camp, he and the elders of Israel.

The LORD Sends Quail

³¹Now a wind went out from the LORD, and it brought quail from the sea and left *them* fluttering near the camp, about a day's journey on this side and about a day's journey on the other side, all around the camp, and about two cubits above the surface of the ground. ³²And the people stayed up all that day, all night, and all the next day, and gathered the quail (he who gathered least gathered ten homers); and they spread *them* out for themselves all around the camp.

11:25 ᵃTargum and Vulgate read *did not cease.*

[33]But while the meat *was* still between their teeth, before it was chewed, the wrath of the LORD was aroused against the people, and the LORD struck the people with a very great plague. [34]So he called the name of that place Kibroth Hattaavah,[a] because there they buried the people who had yielded to craving.

[35]From Kibroth Hattaavah the people moved to Hazeroth, and camped at Hazeroth.

Dissension of Aaron and Miriam

12 Then Miriam and Aaron spoke against Moses because of the Ethiopian woman whom he had married; for he had married an Ethiopian woman. [2]So they said, "Has the LORD indeed spoken only through Moses? Has He not spoken through us also?" And the LORD heard *it.* [3](Now the man Moses *was* very humble, more than all men who *were* on the face of the earth.)

[4]Suddenly the LORD said to Moses, Aaron, and Miriam, "Come out, you three, to the tabernacle of meeting!" So the three came out. [5]Then the LORD came down in the pillar of cloud and stood *in* the door of the tabernacle, and called Aaron and Miriam. And they both went forward. [6]Then He said,

"Hear now My words:
  If there is a prophet among you,
  I, the LORD, make Myself known to him
    in a vision;
  I speak to him in a dream.
[7] Not so with My servant Moses;
  He *is* faithful in all My house.
[8] I speak with him face to face,
  Even plainly, and not in dark sayings;
  And he sees the form of the LORD.
  Why then were you not afraid
  To speak against My servant Moses?"

[9]So the anger of the LORD was aroused against them, and He departed. [10]And when the cloud departed from above the tabernacle, suddenly Miriam *became* leprous, as *white as* snow. Then Aaron turned toward Miriam, and there

11:34 [a]Literally *Graves of Craving*

Leadership: Criticism and Confrontation Come with the Territory

(Numbers 12:3–14)

Leaders can bank on two truths. First, they will be criticized. Second, criticism always changes the leader.

Unhappy people tend to attack the point person. Moses' own family criticized him. Notice what God and Moses teach us on how to handle criticism:

1. *Maintain your humility* (v. 3).
2. *Face the criticism squarely* (v. 4).
3. *Be specific about the issue* (vv. 5–8).
4. *Lay out consequences* (vv. 9, 10).
5. *Pray for the criticizers* (vv. 12, 13).
6. *Restore them when appropriate* (v. 14).

Beyond that, consider ten ways leaders should handle criticism:

1. *Understand the difference between constructive and destructive criticism* (who benefits?).
2. *Don't take yourself too seriously* (but take your God very seriously).
3. *Look beyond the criticism to see the critic* (do you respect him? what's her need?).
4. *Guard your own attitude toward the critic* (don't get defensive; stay objective).
5. *Recognize that good people get criticized* (don't beat yourself up).
6. *Keep yourself physically and spiritually in shape* (weariness distorts our perspective).
7. *Don't see only the critic; see the crowd* (is the criticism widespread?).
8. *Wait for time to prove the critic wrong* (be mature enough to be patient).
9. *Associate with people of faith* (spend your optional time with optimists).
10. *Concentrate on your mission; change your mistakes* (focus on the big picture).

she was, a leper. ¹¹So Aaron said to Moses, "Oh, my lord! Please do not lay *this* sin on us, in which we have done foolishly and in which we have sinned. ¹²Please do not let her be as one dead, whose flesh is half consumed when he comes out of his mother's womb!"

¹³So Moses cried out to the LORD, saying, "Please heal her, O God, I pray!"

¹⁴Then the LORD said to Moses, "If her father had but spit in her face, would she not be shamed seven days? Let her be shut out of the camp seven days, and afterward she may be received *again*." ¹⁵So Miriam was shut out of the camp seven days, and the people did not journey till Miriam was brought in *again*. ¹⁶And afterward the people moved from Hazeroth and camped in the Wilderness of Paran.

Spies Sent into Canaan

13 And the LORD spoke to Moses, saying, ²"Send men to spy out the land of Canaan, which I am giving to the children of Israel; from each tribe of their fathers you shall send a man, every one a leader among them."

³So Moses sent them from the Wilderness of Paran according to the command of the LORD, all of them men who *were* heads of the children of Israel. ⁴Now these *were* their names: from the tribe of Reuben, Shammua the son of Zaccur; ⁵from the tribe of Simeon, Shaphat the son of Hori; ⁶from the tribe of Judah, Caleb the son of Jephunneh; ⁷from the tribe of Issachar, Igal the son of Joseph; ⁸from the tribe of Ephraim, Hosheaª the son of Nun; ⁹from the tribe of Benjamin, Palti the son of Raphu; ¹⁰from the tribe of Zebulun, Gaddiel the son of Sodi; ¹¹from the tribe of Joseph, *that is,* from the tribe of Manasseh, Gaddi the son of Susi; ¹²from the tribe of Dan, Ammiel the son of Gemalli; ¹³from the tribe of Asher, Sethur the son of Michael; ¹⁴from the tribe of Naphtali, Nahbi the son of Vophsi; ¹⁵from the tribe of Gad, Geuel the son of Machi.

¹⁶These *are* the names of the men whom Moses sent to spy out the land. And Moses called Hosheaª the son of Nun, Joshua.

¹⁷Then Moses sent them to spy out the land of Canaan, and said to them, "Go up this *way* into the South, and go up to the mountains, ¹⁸and see what the land is like: whether the people who dwell in it *are* strong or weak, few or many; ¹⁹whether the land they dwell in *is* good or bad; whether the cities they inhabit *are* like camps or strongholds; ²⁰whether the land *is* rich or poor; and whether there are forests there or not. Be of good courage. And bring some of the fruit of the land." Now the time *was* the season of the first ripe grapes.

²¹So they went up and spied out the land from the Wilderness of Zin as far as Rehob, near the entrance of Hamath. ²²And they went up through the South and came to Hebron; Ahiman, Sheshai, and Talmai, the descendants of Anak, *were* there. (Now Hebron was built seven years before Zoan in Egypt.) ²³Then they came to the Valley of Eshcol, and there cut down a branch with one cluster of grapes; they carried it between two of them on a pole. *They* also *brought* some of the pomegranates and figs. ²⁴The place was called the Valley of Eshcol,ª because of the cluster which the men of Israel cut down there. ²⁵And they returned from spying out the land after forty days.

²⁶Now they departed and came back to Moses and Aaron and all the congregation of the children of Israel in the Wilderness of Paran, at Kadesh; they brought back word to them and to all the congregation, and showed them the fruit of the land. ²⁷Then they told him, and said: "We went to the land where you sent us. It truly flows with milk and honey, and this *is* its fruit. ²⁸Nevertheless the people who dwell in the land *are* strong; the cities *are* fortified *and* very large; moreover we saw the descendants of Anak there. ²⁹The Amalekites dwell in the land of the South; the Hittites, the Jebusites, and the Amorites dwell in the mountains; and the Canaanites dwell by the sea and along the banks of the Jordan."

³⁰Then Caleb quieted the people before Moses, and said, "Let us go up at once and take possession, for we are well able to overcome it."

³¹But the men who had gone up with him said, "We are not able to go up against the people, for they *are* stronger than we." ³²And they gave the children of Israel a bad report of the land which they had spied out, saying, "The land through which we have gone as spies *is* a land that devours its inhabitants, and all the people whom we saw in it *are* men of *great* stature. ³³There we saw the giantsª (the descendants of Anak came from the giants); and we were like grasshoppers in our own sight, and so we were in their sight."

Israel Refuses to Enter Canaan

14 So all the congregation lifted up their voices and cried, and the people wept that night. ²And all the children of Israel complained against Moses and Aaron, and the whole congregation said to them,

13:8 ªSeptuagint and Vulgate read *Oshea.*
13:16 ªSeptuagint and Vulgate read *Oshea.*
13:24 ªLiterally *Cluster* 13:33 ªHebrew *nephilim*

POSITIVE ATTITUDE

The Ten Spies vs. the Two Spies

(Numbers 13:1—14:10)

As Israel approached the Jordan River, Moses sent out twelve spies to investigate the Promised Land. One spy from each of the twelve tribes of Israel entered Canaan, explored the land, and returned with a report. All twelve had the same external experiences, but the internal conclusions of ten differed markedly from the other two. Joshua and Caleb filed the minority report, but they happened to be right. What could account for these differing opinions?

Similarities

1. All twelve spies were leaders in their tribes (13:2).
2. All twelve spies received the same promise (13:2).
3. All twelve spies received the same opportunities (13:2).

Differences

Majority Report
1. Ten said "no"
2. Misunderstood their mission
3. Saw God in light of their circumstances

Minority Report
1. Two said "go"
2. Understood their mission
3. Saw circumstances in light of their God

After their return, ten of the spies displayed a horrible attitude about the whole endeavor. It's not hard to see why. You can't find God anywhere in their report; they don't mention His name even once. Their sour disposition, pessimistic perspective, and negative report spread like a plague throughout the Israelite camp. "It was, indeed, a land flowing with milk and honey—but there were giants in the land!" they declared. "There is no way we can enter and possess it."

Although Joshua and Caleb took the very same trip and saw the same things witnessed by the other ten spies, they returned with an enthusiastic, positive report. They never doubted the Israelites could take the land. They based their glowing report on God's track record with the nation through the desert. They freely admitted the obstacles, but knew nothing could stand in the way of God. They came back saying, "Yes, there are giants in the land, but they're midgets compared with our God. We can take them *and* the land! And by the way, Canaan really does flow with milk and honey."

The Major Difference: Attitude!

The only difference between those who delivered the majority and minority reports was internal. Their differing reports reflected contrary attitudes toward the land, the divine promises, the people in Canaan, the work involved, the Lord, and themselves. Consider the attitudes of the majority:

1. Disobeyed God
2. Believed the land had no future
3. Displayed cowardice based on fear
4. Utterly ignored God in their report
5. Suffered from a grasshopper complex

The result? These ten naysayers spread anxiety throughout Israel's camp. Their rotten attitudes infected the whole congregation until the spiritual contagion could not be contained. Notice who got blamed for the nation's negative response: "Our brethren have discouraged our hearts, saying, 'The people are greater and taller than we' " (Deut. 1:28). Through a negative majority report, this ancient commission deprived nearly two million people of their inheritance in Canaan. Through their poisonous influence, the Israelites were driven back into the wilderness to die, and God delayed in fulfilling His purpose for His chosen people for 40 frustrating years.

If only they had listened to the minority! Consider their vastly better attitude:

1. Obeyed God
2. Insisted they should enter and possess the land
3. Displayed courage rooted in faith
4. Felt calm assurance
5. Saw themselves in relationship to God

The result? Caleb and Joshua stayed alive for a new era, while the other ten spies perished in the wilderness along with the rest of the adults of that unbelieving generation.

Attitude Axioms

Attitude makes all the difference. The development of a positive attitude is the first conscious step toward becoming an effective leader. Successful leadership cannot be constructed without this crucial building block. Check out the following attitude axioms suggested by the words and actions of Joshua and Caleb:

1. *Our attitude determines our approach to life.*
2. *Our attitude determines our relationships with people.*
3. *Our attitude is often the only difference between success and failure.*
4. *Our attitude at the beginning of a task will affect its outcome more than anything else.*
5. *Our attitude can turn problems into blessings.*
6. *Our attitude can give us an uncommonly positive perspective.*
7. *Our attitude is not automatically good just because we belong to God.*

"If only we had died in the land of Egypt! Or if only we had died in this wilderness! ³Why has the LORD brought us to this land to fall by the sword, that our wives and children should become victims? Would it not be better for us to return to Egypt?" ⁴So they said to one another, "Let us select a leader and return to Egypt."

⁵Then Moses and Aaron fell on their faces before all the assembly of the congregation of the children of Israel.

⁶But Joshua the son of Nun and Caleb the son of Jephunneh, *who were* among those who had spied out the land, tore their clothes; ⁷and they spoke to all the congregation of the children of Israel, saying: "The land we passed through to spy out *is* an exceedingly good land. ⁸If the LORD delights in us, then He will bring us into this land and give it to us, 'a land which flows with milk and honey.'ᵃ ⁹Only do not rebel against the LORD, nor fear the people of the land, for they *are* our bread; their protection has departed from them, and the LORD *is* with us. Do not fear them."

¹⁰And all the congregation said to stone them with stones. Now the glory of the LORD appeared in the tabernacle of meeting before all the children of Israel.

Moses Intercedes for the People

¹¹Then the LORD said to Moses: "How long will these people reject Me? And how long will they not believe Me, with all the signs which I have performed among them? ¹²I will strike them with the pestilence and disinherit them, and I will make of you a nation greater and mightier than they."

¹³And Moses said to the LORD: "Then the Egyptians will hear *it,* for by Your might You brought these people up from among them, ¹⁴and they will tell *it* to the inhabitants of this land. They have heard that You, LORD, *are* among these people; that You, LORD, are seen face to face and Your cloud stands above them, and You go before them in a pillar of cloud by day and in a pillar of fire by night. ¹⁵Now *if* You kill these people as one man, then the nations which have heard of Your fame will speak, saying, ¹⁶'Because the LORD was not able to bring this people to the land which He swore to give them, therefore He killed them in the wilderness.' ¹⁷And now, I pray, let the power of my Lord be great, just as You have spoken, saying, ¹⁸'The LORD is longsuffering and abundant in mercy, forgiving iniquity and transgression; but He by no means clears *the guilty,* visiting the iniquity of the fathers on the children to the third and fourth *generation.*'ᵃ

¹⁹Pardon the iniquity of this people, I pray, according to the greatness of Your mercy, just as You have forgiven this people, from Egypt even until now."

²⁰Then the LORD said: "I have pardoned, according to your word; ²¹but truly, as I live, all the earth shall be filled with the glory of the LORD— ²²because all these men who have seen My glory and the signs which I did in Egypt and in the wilderness, and have put Me to the test now these ten times, and have not heeded My voice, ²³they certainly shall not see the land of which I swore to their fathers, nor shall any of those who rejected Me see it. ²⁴But My servant Caleb, because he has a different spirit in him and has followed Me fully, I will bring into the land where he went, and his descendants shall inherit it. ²⁵Now the Amalekites and the Canaanites dwell in the valley; tomorrow turn and move out into the wilderness by the Way of the Red Sea."

Death Sentence on the Rebels

²⁶And the LORD spoke to Moses and Aaron, saying, ²⁷"How long *shall I bear with* this evil congregation who complain against Me? I have heard the complaints which the children of Israel make against Me. ²⁸Say to them, 'As I live,' says the LORD, 'just as you have spoken in My hearing, so I will do to you: ²⁹The carcasses of you who have complained against Me shall fall in this wilderness, all of you who were numbered, according to your entire number, from twenty years old and above. ³⁰Except for Caleb the son of Jephunneh and Joshua the son of Nun, you shall by no means enter the land which I swore I would make you dwell in. ³¹But your little ones, whom you said would be victims, I will bring in, and they shall know the land which you have despised. ³²But *as for* you, your carcasses shall fall in this wilderness. ³³And your sons shall be shepherds in the wilderness forty years, and bear the brunt of your infidelity, until your carcasses are consumed in the wilderness. ³⁴According to the number of the days in which you spied out the land, forty days, for each day you shall bear your guilt one year, *namely* forty years, and you shall know My rejection. ³⁵I the LORD have spoken this. I will surely do so to all this evil congregation who are gathered together against Me. In this wilderness they shall be consumed, and there they shall die.'"

³⁶Now the men whom Moses sent to spy out the land, who returned and made all the congregation complain against him by bringing a bad report of the land, ³⁷those very men who brought

---

14:8 ᵃExodus 3:8 **14:18** ᵃExodus 34:6, 7

the evil report about the land, died by the plague before the LORD. ³⁸But Joshua the son of Nun and Caleb the son of Jephunneh remained alive, of the men who went to spy out the land.

A Futile Invasion Attempt

³⁹Then Moses told these words to all the children of Israel, and the people mourned greatly. ⁴⁰And they rose early in the morning and went up to the top of the mountain, saying, "Here we are, and we will go up to the place which the LORD has promised, for we have sinned!"

⁴¹And Moses said, "Now why do you transgress the command of the LORD? For this will not succeed. ⁴²Do not go up, lest you be defeated by your enemies, for the LORD *is* not among you. ⁴³For the Amalekites and the Canaanites *are* there before you, and you shall fall by the sword; because you have turned away from the LORD, the LORD will not be with you."

⁴⁴But they presumed to go up to the mountaintop. Nevertheless, neither the ark of the covenant of the LORD nor Moses departed from the camp. ⁴⁵Then the Amalekites and the Canaanites who dwelt in that mountain came down and attacked them, and drove them back as far as Hormah.

Laws of Grain and Drink Offerings

15 And the LORD spoke to Moses, saying, ²"Speak to the children of Israel, and say to them: 'When you have come into the land you are to inhabit, which I am giving to you, ³and you make an offering by fire to the LORD, a burnt offering or a sacrifice, to fulfill a vow or as a freewill offering or in your appointed feasts, to make a sweet aroma to the LORD, from the herd or the flock, ⁴then he who presents his offering to the LORD shall bring a grain offering of one-tenth *of an ephah* of fine flour mixed with one-fourth of a hin of oil; ⁵and one-fourth of a hin of wine as a drink offering you shall prepare with the burnt offering or the sacrifice, for each lamb. ⁶Or for a ram you shall prepare as a grain offering two-tenths *of an ephah* of fine flour mixed with one-third of a hin of oil; ⁷and as a drink offering you shall offer one-third of a hin of wine as a sweet aroma to the LORD. ⁸And when you prepare a young bull as a burnt offering, or as a sacrifice to fulfill a vow, or as a peace offering to the LORD, ⁹then shall be offered with the young bull a grain offering of three-tenths *of an ephah* of fine flour mixed with half a hin of oil; ¹⁰and you shall bring as the drink offering half a hin of wine as an offering made by fire, a sweet aroma to the LORD.

¹¹"Thus it shall be done for each young bull, for each ram, or for each lamb or young goat. ¹²According to the number that you prepare, so you shall do with everyone according to their number. ¹³All who are native-born shall do these things in this manner, in presenting an offering made by fire, a sweet aroma to the LORD. ¹⁴And if a stranger dwells with you, or whoever *is* among you throughout your generations, and would present an offering made by fire, a sweet aroma to the LORD, just as you do, so shall he do. ¹⁵One ordinance *shall be* for you of the assembly and for the stranger who dwells *with you,* an ordinance forever throughout your generations; as you are, so shall the stranger be before the LORD. ¹⁶One law and one custom shall be for you and for the stranger who dwells with you.' "ᵃ

¹⁷Again the LORD spoke to Moses, saying, ¹⁸"Speak to the children of Israel, and say to them: 'When you come into the land to which I bring you, ¹⁹then it will be, when you eat of the bread of the land, that you shall offer up a heave offering to the LORD. ²⁰You shall offer up a cake of the first of your ground meal *as* a heave offering; as a heave offering of the threshing floor, so shall you offer it up. ²¹Of the first of your ground meal you shall give to the LORD a heave offering throughout your generations.

Laws Concerning Unintentional Sin

²²'If you sin unintentionally, and do not observe all these commandments which the LORD has spoken to Moses— ²³all that the LORD has commanded you by the hand of Moses, from the day the LORD gave commandment and onward throughout your generations— ²⁴then it will be, if it is unintentionally committed, without the knowledge of the congregation, that the whole congregation shall offer one young bull as a burnt offering, as a sweet aroma to the LORD, with its grain offering and its drink offering, according to the ordinance, and one kid of the goats as a sin offering. ²⁵So the priest shall make atonement for the whole congregation of the children of Israel, and it shall be forgiven them, for it was unintentional; they shall bring their offering, an offering made by fire to the LORD, and their sin offering before the LORD, for their unintended sin. ²⁶It shall be forgiven the whole congregation of the children of Israel and the stranger who dwells among them, because all the people *did it* unintentionally.

²⁷"And if a person sins unintentionally, then he shall bring a female goat in its first year as a

15:16 ªCompare Exodus 12:49

JOSHUA AND THE LAW OF INFLUENCE

How Did the General Expand His Reach?

(Numbers 14:6–9)

Among the twelve spies who scouted out Canaan, only Joshua and Caleb believed that the Israelites could take the land. Joshua urged the people to move forward, but his influence alone couldn't sway them. At this juncture of his life, Joshua had not matured into a place of great influence. Even though he was right, he couldn't persuade the people to follow. They didn't look to him; they followed the other ten spies.

Joshua's success would eventually grow in proportion to his leadership, but he needed time to deepen his influence. Moses personally mentored him, and eventually Joshua became the obvious leader to take the Israelites into the Promised Land.

The Nature of Leadership

1. *Leadership is influence.*

The true measure of leadership is influence—nothing more, nothing less. Joshua came face-to-face with the true nature of leadership when he failed to influence the people to follow his lead. His position as tribal leader did nothing to help him influence others.

2. *Leaders do not possess influence in every area.*

Those selected to spy out the Promised Land were "every one a leader" (Num. 13:2). That means Joshua was a leader with some influence, but his influence apparently didn't outweigh that of the other 11 leaders.

3. *Our influence is either positive or negative.*

If all twelve spies had given a good report of the Promised Land, the people of Israel likely would have obeyed God and crossed into the land. But influence is a two-edged sword; it cuts both positively and negatively. The ten unfaithful tribal leaders used their influence to lead the people astray—a disaster for those leaders and for all of their followers.

4. *Faithful leaders use their influence to add value.*

Influencers who lead out of a desire to advance their own agendas manipulate the people for their own gain. That's what the other ten spies did. Their fear prompted them to use their influence to frighten Israel. They lied, claiming the land "devours its inhabitants" (Num. 13:32). On the other hand, Joshua and Caleb desired to motivate their countrymen to do what would benefit everyone—always the agenda of great leaders.

5. *With influence comes responsibility.*

Maybe the ten unfaithful tribal leaders didn't want to start a rebellion, yet that's what they did. Following their negative report, the people sought to depose Moses and

Aaron and return to Egypt. As a result, those ten leaders died of plague, and all of their followers died in the desert.

Joshua's Growing Influence

Many individuals who at first seem ineffective as leaders give up. Fortunately for the nation of Israel, Joshua did not fit that mold. He determined to become a better leader. Despite his setback, Joshua continued to be faithful to God and to learn as much as he could from Moses.

1. *Joshua's influence grew because of his relationship with Moses* (Deut. 31:1–8, 23).

Through Moses' mentorship, Joshua not only polished his skills, but the people accepted him as their leader. The Bible says that as Israel prepared to enter the Promised Land, "Then Moses called Joshua and said to him in the sight of all Israel, 'Be strong and of good courage, for you must go with this people to the land which the LORD has sworn to their fathers to give them, and you shall cause them to inherit it'" (Deut. 31:7). In such a way Moses imparted authority to Joshua.

2. *Joshua's influence grew with time and maturity* (Num. 14:1–10; Josh. 18:1–10).

Joshua gave basically the same speech in Numbers 14 that he delivered in Joshua 18. The difference? The second time, a mature Joshua spoke to a new generation. The people had seen his leadership skills in action, and his track record as a leader gave them the confidence to follow his directions.

3. *Joshua's influence grew because of timing* (Josh. 1:16–18).

Sometimes a leader wields little influence until his followers want to go somewhere. Only when the Jews tired of wandering in the desert did they heed the words of Joshua. In Numbers 14, the people responded to Joshua's first exhortation to go in and take the land by loudly suggesting that he be stoned. In Joshua 1, they responded by saying, "All that you command us we will do, and wherever you send us we will go" (v. 16).

4. *Joshua's influence grew because he possessed patience and integrity* (Josh. 1:5–9).

Joshua continued to grow patiently even after the people rejected his words in Numbers 14. While neither he nor Caleb died in the wilderness, as did all those who rebelled against God, nevertheless they both were forced to wander in the desert for 40 years through no fault of their own. Such an "unfair" turn of events could have turned Joshua into an angry, melancholy, disgruntled, and cynical man. Yet he became none of those things. Throughout the long wilderness journey, he continued to display great consistency and credibility—until at last the people were finally ready to follow.

5. *Joshua's influence grew because he was right* (Josh. 23:1–11).

From the beginning, Joshua tried to do the right thing. He attempted to lead the people in the right direction. After the exodus from Egypt, most of Israel considered his words foolhardy and rash—yet Joshua's words stood the test of time. His message never changed, and eventually everyone saw that he was right.

Leadership is all about influence, and Joshua demonstrates that influence comes down to character and conviction.

sin offering. ²⁸So the priest shall make atonement for the person who sins unintentionally, when he sins unintentionally before the LORD, to make atonement for him; and it shall be forgiven him. ²⁹You shall have one law for him who sins unintentionally, *for* him who is native-born among the children of Israel and for the stranger who dwells among them.

Law Concerning Presumptuous Sin

³⁰But the person who does *anything* presumptuously, *whether he is* native-born or a stranger, that one brings reproach on the LORD, and he shall be cut off from among his people. ³¹Because he has despised the word of the LORD, and has broken His commandment, that person shall be completely cut off; his guilt *shall be* upon him.'"

Penalty for Violating the Sabbath

³²Now while the children of Israel were in the wilderness, they found a man gathering sticks on the Sabbath day. ³³And those who found him gathering sticks brought him to Moses and Aaron, and to all the congregation. ³⁴They put him under guard, because it had not been explained what should be done to him.

³⁵Then the LORD said to Moses, "The man must surely be put to death; all the congregation shall stone him with stones outside the camp." ³⁶So, as the LORD commanded Moses, all the congregation brought him outside the camp and stoned him with stones, and he died.

Tassels on Garments

³⁷Again the LORD spoke to Moses, saying, ³⁸"Speak to the children of Israel: Tell them to make tassels on the corners of their garments throughout their generations, and to put a blue thread in the tassels of the corners. ³⁹And you shall have the tassel, that you may look upon it and remember all the commandments of the LORD and do them, and that you *may* not follow the harlotry to which your own heart and your own eyes are inclined, ⁴⁰and that you may remember and do all My commandments, and be holy for your God. ⁴¹I *am* the LORD your God, who brought you out of the land of Egypt, to be your God: I *am* the LORD your God."

Rebellion Against Moses and Aaron

16 Now Korah the son of Izhar, the son of Kohath, the son of Levi, with Dathan and Abiram the sons of Eliab, and On the son of Peleth, sons of Reuben, took *men;* ²and they rose up before Moses with some of the children of Israel, two hundred and

---

KORAH

AN ILLEGITIMATE DESIRE FOR MORE
(Numbers 16:1–11)

PROFILE IN LEADERSHIP

Korah, a talented but insolent Levite, had been set apart to serve in Israel's worship of the living God. His important position gave him both prestige and respect within the nation. Yet he rebelled against both Moses and the Lord, thus illustrating the tragic flaw of many leaders—a desire for power and authority beyond what God has ordained.

Korah's gifted leadership and persuasive speaking abilities earned him the backing of 250 other leaders. Yet his desire for more led to the demise of his followers and their families. Leaders with rebellious hearts always wreak havoc in the lives of those unwise enough to follow them.

Godly leaders must be willing to submit themselves to those in leadership above them. Many who hold leadership positions based on their strength, acumen, and personality find this difficult to accept. Yet willing subordination at one point may very well qualify a person for greater leadership responsibilities down the road.

The Scripture makes it clear that God places people in authority, and it is dangerous to oppose God's anointed. Korah did just that in a classic act of rebellion, and God had to remove him and his followers in order to keep the spiritual plague away from the rest of the nation.

fifty leaders of the congregation, representatives of the congregation, men of renown. ³They gathered together against Moses and Aaron, and said to them, "*You take* too much upon yourselves, for all the congregation *is* holy, every one of them, and the LORD *is* among them. Why then do you exalt yourselves above the assembly of the LORD?"

⁴So when Moses heard *it,* he fell on his face; ⁵and he spoke to Korah and all his company, saying, "Tomorrow morning the LORD will show who *is* His and *who is* holy, and will cause *him* to come near to Him. That one whom He chooses He will cause to come near to Him. ⁶Do this: Take censers, Korah and all your company; ⁷put fire in them and put incense in them before the LORD tomorrow, and it shall be *that* the man whom the LORD chooses *is* the holy one. *You take* too much upon yourselves, you sons of Levi!"

⁸Then Moses said to Korah, "Hear now, you sons of Levi: ⁹*Is it* a small thing to you that the God of Israel has separated you from the congregation of Israel, to bring you near to Himself, to do the work of the tabernacle of the LORD, and to stand before the congregation to serve them; ¹⁰and that He has brought you near to *Himself,* you and all your brethren, the sons of Levi, with you? And are you seeking the priesthood also? ¹¹Therefore you and all your company *are* gathered together against the LORD. And what *is* Aaron that you complain against him?"

¹²And Moses sent to call Dathan and Abiram the sons of Eliab, but they said, "We will not come up! ¹³*Is it* a small thing that you have brought us up out of a land flowing with milk and honey, to kill us in the wilderness, that you should keep acting like a prince over us? ¹⁴Moreover you have not brought us into a land flowing with milk and honey, nor given us inheritance of fields and vineyards. Will you put out the eyes of these men? We will not come up!"

¹⁵Then Moses was very angry, and said to the LORD, "Do not respect their offering. I have not taken one donkey from them, nor have I hurt one of them."

¹⁶And Moses said to Korah, "Tomorrow, you and all your company be present before the LORD—you and they, as well as Aaron. ¹⁷Let each take his censer and put incense in it, and each of you bring his censer before the LORD, two hundred and fifty censers; both you and Aaron, each *with* his censer." ¹⁸So every man took his censer, put fire in it, laid incense on it, and stood at the door of the tabernacle of meeting with Moses and Aaron. ¹⁹And Korah gathered all the congregation against them at the door of the tabernacle of meeting. Then the glory of the LORD appeared to all the congregation.

Self-Appointed Leadership: Moses Defuses Korah's Rebellion

(Numbers 16:1–33)

Two kinds of false leaders emerge within organizations: man-appointed leaders and self-appointed leaders.

Balaam was a false leader of the first kind. Balak persuaded him to do something that God rejected, and the Lord rebuked Balaam for his arrogance. We read his story in Numbers 22—24.

Korah was a false leader of the second kind. Author Frank Damazio writes: "A self-appointed leader takes upon himself the authority and responsibility of a spiritual office to which he has not been divinely called." Korah blatantly and arrogantly rebelled against Moses. In self-will and presumption, Korah followed a process of self-appointment common to many who illegitimately pursue power:

1. He caused others to rise up against existing leadership (16:2).
2. He publicly criticized and questioned existing leadership (16:3).
3. He accused leadership of what he himself was guilty (16:3).
4. He despised as too little the position he had been given—he wanted more (16:10).
5. He continued to murmur, complain, and create a negative atmosphere (16:11).

Unsurprisingly, God always rejects false leadership. He rebuked Balaam, and He put Korah to death. Such leadership lessons might seem harsh, but they last.

²⁰And the LORD spoke to Moses and Aaron, saying, ²¹"Separate yourselves from among this congregation, that I may consume them in a moment."

²²Then they fell on their faces, and said, "O God, the God of the spirits of all flesh, shall one man sin, and You be angry with all the congregation?"

²³So the LORD spoke to Moses, saying, ²⁴"Speak to the congregation, saying, 'Get away from the tents of Korah, Dathan, and Abiram.'"

²⁵Then Moses rose and went to Dathan and Abiram, and the elders of Israel followed him. ²⁶And he spoke to the congregation, saying, "Depart now from the tents of these wicked men! Touch nothing of theirs, lest you be consumed in all their sins." ²⁷So they got away from around the tents of Korah, Dathan, and Abiram; and Dathan and Abiram came out and stood at the door of their tents, with their wives, their sons, and their little children.

²⁸And Moses said: "By this you shall know that the LORD has sent me to do all these works, for I have not done them of my own will. ²⁹If these men die naturally like all men, or if they are visited by the common fate of all men, then the LORD has not sent me. ³⁰But if the LORD creates a new thing, and the earth opens its mouth and swallows them up with all that belongs to them, and they go down alive into the pit, then you will understand that these men have rejected the LORD."

³¹Now it came to pass, as he finished speaking all these words, that the ground split apart under them, ³²and the earth opened its mouth and swallowed them up, with their households and all the men with Korah, with all their goods. ³³So they and all those with them went down alive into the pit; the earth closed over them, and they perished from among the assembly. ³⁴Then all Israel who were around them fled at their cry, for they said, "Lest the earth swallow us up also!"

³⁵And a fire came out from the LORD and consumed the two hundred and fifty men who were offering incense.

³⁶Then the LORD spoke to Moses, saying: ³⁷"Tell Eleazar, the son of Aaron the priest, to pick up the censers out of the blaze, for they are holy, and scatter the fire some distance away. ³⁸The censers of these men who sinned against their own souls, let them be made into hammered plates as a covering for the altar. Because they presented them before the LORD, therefore they are holy; and they shall be a sign to the children of Israel." ³⁹So Eleazar the priest took the bronze censers, which those who were burned up had presented, and they were hammered out as a covering on the altar, ⁴⁰to be a memorial to the children of Israel that no outsider, who is not a descendant of Aaron, should come near to offer incense before the LORD, that he might not become like Korah and his companions, just as the LORD had said to him through Moses.

Complaints of the People

⁴¹On the next day all the congregation of the children of Israel complained against Moses and Aaron, saying, "You have killed the people of the LORD." ⁴²Now it happened, when the congregation had gathered against Moses and Aaron, that they turned toward the tabernacle of meeting; and suddenly the cloud covered it, and the glory of the LORD appeared. ⁴³Then Moses and Aaron came before the tabernacle of meeting.

⁴⁴And the LORD spoke to Moses, saying, ⁴⁵"Get away from among this congregation, that I may consume them in a moment."

And they fell on their faces.

⁴⁶So Moses said to Aaron, "Take a censer and put fire in it from the altar, put incense on it, and take it quickly to the congregation and make atonement for them; for wrath has gone out from the LORD. The plague has begun." ⁴⁷Then Aaron took it as Moses commanded, and ran into the midst of the assembly; and already the plague had begun among the people. So he put in the incense and made atonement for the people. ⁴⁸And he stood between the dead and the living; so the plague was stopped. ⁴⁹Now those who died in the plague were fourteen thousand seven hundred, besides those who died in the Korah incident. ⁵⁰So Aaron returned to Moses at the door of the tabernacle of meeting, for the plague had stopped.

The Budding of Aaron's Rod

17 And the LORD spoke to Moses, saying: ²"Speak to the children of Israel, and get from them a rod from each father's house, all their leaders according to their fathers' houses—twelve rods. Write each man's name on his rod. ³And you shall write Aaron's name on the rod of Levi. For there shall be one rod for the head of each father's house. ⁴Then you shall place them in the tabernacle of meeting before the Testimony, where I meet with you. ⁵And it shall be that the rod of the man whom I choose will blossom; thus I will rid Myself of the complaints of the children of Israel, which they make against you."

⁶So Moses spoke to the children of Israel, and

God Resolves Leadership Issue to Dissolve Grumbling Issue

(Numbers 17:1–10)

To resolve a grumbling issue among the people, God reiterated His calling of the leaders. Everything rises and falls with leadership. Once the leadership issue is addressed, the organization can move forward. Establish the leader, and you establish the organization.

each of their leaders gave him a rod apiece, for each leader according to their fathers' houses, twelve rods; and the rod of Aaron *was* among their rods. 7And Moses placed the rods before the LORD in the tabernacle of witness.

8Now it came to pass on the next day that Moses went into the tabernacle of witness, and behold, the rod of Aaron, of the house of Levi, had sprouted and put forth buds, had produced blossoms and yielded ripe almonds. 9Then Moses brought out all the rods from before the LORD to all the children of Israel; and they looked, and each man took his rod.

10And the LORD said to Moses, "Bring Aaron's rod back before the Testimony, to be kept as a sign against the rebels, that you may put their complaints away from Me, lest they die." 11Thus did Moses; just as the LORD had commanded him, so he did.

12So the children of Israel spoke to Moses, saying, "Surely we die, we perish, we all perish! 13Whoever even comes near the tabernacle of the LORD must die. Shall we all utterly die?"

Duties of Priests and Levites

18 Then the LORD said to Aaron: "You and your sons and your father's house with you shall bear the iniquity *related to* the sanctuary, and you and your sons with you shall bear the iniquity *associated with* your priesthood. 2Also bring with you your brethren of the tribe of Levi, the tribe of your father, that they may be joined with you and serve you while you and your sons *are* with you before the tabernacle of witness. 3They shall attend to your needs and all the needs of the tabernacle; but they shall not come near the articles of the sanctuary and the altar, lest they die—they and you

also. 4They shall be joined with you and attend to the needs of the tabernacle of meeting, for all the work of the tabernacle; but an outsider shall not come near you. 5And you shall attend to the duties of the sanctuary and the duties of the altar, that there *may* be no more wrath on the children of Israel. 6Behold, I Myself have taken your brethren the Levites from among the children of Israel; *they are* a gift to you, given by the LORD, to do the work of the tabernacle of meeting. 7Therefore you and your sons with you shall attend to your priesthood for everything at the altar and behind the veil; and you shall serve. I give your priesthood *to you* as a gift for service, but the outsider who comes near shall be put to death."

Offerings for Support of the Priests

8And the LORD spoke to Aaron: "Here, I Myself have also given you charge of My heave offerings, all the holy gifts of the children of Israel; I have given them as a portion to you and your sons, as an ordinance forever. 9This shall be yours of the most holy things *reserved* from the fire: every offering of theirs, every grain offering and every sin offering and every trespass offering which they render to Me, *shall be* most holy for you and your sons. 10In a most holy *place* you shall eat it; every male shall eat it. It shall be holy to you.

11"This also *is* yours: the heave offering of their gift, with all the wave offerings of the children of Israel; I have given them to you, and your sons and daughters with you, as an ordinance forever. Everyone who is clean in your house may eat it.

12"All the best of the oil, all the best of the new wine and the grain, their firstfruits which they offer to the LORD, I have given them to you. 13Whatever first ripe fruit is in their land, which they bring to the LORD, shall be yours. Everyone who is clean in your house may eat it. 14"Every devoted thing in Israel shall be yours.

15"Everything that first opens the womb of all flesh, which they bring to the LORD, whether man or beast, shall be yours; nevertheless the firstborn of man you shall surely redeem, and the firstborn of unclean animals you shall redeem. 16And those redeemed of the devoted things you shall redeem when one month old, according to your valuation, for five shekels of silver, according to the shekel of the sanctuary, which *is* twenty gerahs. 17But the firstborn of a cow, the firstborn of a sheep, or the firstborn of a goat you shall not redeem; they *are* holy. You shall

Lame Leadership Awards

(Numbers 12—24)

The Book of Numbers offers several "lame leadership" illustrations. Consider just a few acts of indiscretion, foolishness, lack of judgment, poor choices, and just plain old sin:

1. *Korah* (Num. 16)
   Korah recruited two buddies and 250 henchmen to stage an insurrection against Moses. Result? The earth swallowed them up.
2. *The prophet Balaam* (Num. 22—24)
   King Balak paid Balaam to put a curse on Israel. God interceded, even to the point of giving Balaam's donkey a human voice to reason with him. Result? God rebuked Balaam.
3. *Balak* (Num. 22—24)
   King Balak thought he could buy his way into success. He paid Balaam to curse God's people, hoping his plan could override God's sovereignty. Result? It didn't.
4. *Miriam and Aaron* (Num. 12)
   Moses' own sister and brother decided they wanted a bigger piece of the power. Result? Miriam got a case of leprosy, and both got a bigger piece of humble pie.
5. *The ten fearful spies* (Num. 13; 14)
   These men led their clans. They had witnessed God's provision. Yet they turned chicken at the edge of the Promised Land. Result? They destroyed the faith of the people.
6. *Moses* (Num. 20)
   Even Moses had bad days. Once, in a fit of anger, he disobeyed God and struck a rock twice. Result? He forfeited his right to enter Canaan.

sprinkle their blood on the altar, and burn their fat *as* an offering made by fire for a sweet aroma to the LORD. [18]And their flesh shall be yours, just as the wave breast and the right thigh are yours.

[19]"All the heave offerings of the holy things, which the children of Israel offer to the LORD, I have given to you and your sons and daughters with you as an ordinance forever; it *is* a covenant of salt forever before the LORD with you and your descendants with you."

[20]Then the LORD said to Aaron: "You shall have no inheritance in their land, nor shall you have any portion among them; I *am* your portion and your inheritance among the children of Israel.

Tithes for Support of the Levites

[21]"Behold, I have given the children of Levi all the tithes in Israel as an inheritance in return for the work which they perform, the work of the tabernacle of meeting. [22]Hereafter the children of Israel shall not come near the tabernacle of meeting, lest they bear sin and die. [23]But the Levites shall perform the work of the tabernacle of meeting, and they shall bear their iniquity; *it shall be* a statute forever, throughout your generations, that among the children of Israel they

shall have no inheritance. [24]For the tithes of the children of Israel, which they offer up *as* a heave offering to the LORD, I have given to the Levites as an inheritance; therefore I have said to them, 'Among the children of Israel they shall have no inheritance.'"

The Tithe of the Levites

[25]Then the LORD spoke to Moses, saying, [26]"Speak thus to the Levites, and say to them: 'When you take from the children of Israel the tithes which I have given you from them as your inheritance, then you shall offer up a heave offering of it to the LORD, a tenth of the tithe. [27]And your heave offering shall be reckoned to you as though *it were* the grain of the threshing floor and as the fullness of the winepress. [28]Thus you shall also offer a heave offering to the LORD from all your tithes which you receive from the children of Israel, and you shall give the LORD's heave offering from it to Aaron the priest. [29]Of all your gifts you shall offer up every heave offering due to the LORD, from all the best of them, the consecrated part of them.' [30]Therefore you shall say to them: 'When you have lifted up the best of it, then *the rest* shall be accounted to the Levites as the produce of the threshing floor

and as the produce of the winepress. ³¹You may eat it in any place, you and your households, for it *is* your reward for your work in the tabernacle of meeting. ³²And you shall bear no sin because of it, when you have lifted up the best of it. But you shall not profane the holy gifts of the children of Israel, lest you die.'"

Laws of Purification

19 Now the LORD spoke to Moses and Aaron, saying, ²"'This *is* the ordinance of the law which the LORD has commanded, saying: 'Speak to the children of Israel, that they bring you a red heifer without blemish, in which there *is* no defect *and* on which a yoke has never come. ³You shall give it to Eleazar the priest, that he may take it outside the camp, and it shall be slaughtered before him; ⁴and Eleazar the priest shall take some of its blood with his finger, and sprinkle some of its blood seven times directly in front of the tabernacle of meeting. ⁵Then the heifer shall be burned in his sight: its hide, its flesh, its blood, and its offal shall be burned. ⁶And the priest shall take cedar wood and hyssop and scarlet, and cast *them* into the midst of the fire burning the heifer. ⁷Then the priest shall wash his clothes, he shall bathe in water, and afterward he shall come into the camp; the priest shall be unclean until evening. ⁸And the one who burns it shall wash his clothes in water, bathe in water, and shall be unclean until evening. ⁹Then a man *who is* clean shall gather up the ashes of the heifer, and store *them* outside the camp in a clean place; and they shall be kept for the congregation of the children of Israel for the water of purification;ᵃ it *is* for purifying from sin. ¹⁰And the one who gathers the ashes of the heifer shall wash his clothes, and be unclean until evening. It shall be a statute forever to the children of Israel and to the stranger who dwells among them.

¹¹"He who touches the dead body of anyone shall be unclean seven days. ¹²He shall purify himself with the water on the third day and on the seventh day; *then* he will be clean. But if he does not purify himself on the third day and on the seventh day, he will not be clean. ¹³Whoever touches the body of anyone who has died, and does not purify himself, defiles the tabernacle of the LORD. That person shall be cut off from Israel. He shall be unclean, because the water of purification was not sprinkled on him; his uncleanness *is* still on him.

¹⁴"This *is* the law when a man dies in a tent: All who come into the tent and all who *are* in the tent shall be unclean seven days; ¹⁵and every

open vessel, which has no cover fastened on it, *is* unclean. ¹⁶Whoever in the open field touches one who is slain by a sword or who has died, or a bone of a man, or a grave, shall be unclean seven days.

¹⁷"And for an unclean *person* they shall take some of the ashes of the heifer burnt for purification from sin, and running water shall be put on them in a vessel. ¹⁸A clean person shall take hyssop and dip *it* in the water, sprinkle *it* on the tent, on all the vessels, on the persons who were there, or on the one who touched a bone, the slain, the dead, or a grave. ¹⁹The clean *person* shall sprinkle the unclean on the third day and on the seventh day; and on the seventh day he shall purify himself, wash his clothes, and bathe in water; and at evening he shall be clean.

²⁰"But the man who is unclean and does not purify himself, that person shall be cut off from among the assembly, because he has defiled the sanctuary of the LORD. The water of purification has not been sprinkled on him; he *is* unclean. ²¹It shall be a perpetual statute for them. He who sprinkles the water of purification shall wash his clothes; and he who touches the water of purification shall be unclean until evening. ²²Whatever the unclean *person* touches shall be unclean; and the person who touches *it* shall be unclean until evening.'"

Moses' Error at Kadesh

20 Then the children of Israel, the whole congregation, came into the Wilderness of Zin in the first month, and the people stayed in Kadesh; and Miriam died there and was buried there.

²Now there was no water for the congregation; so they gathered together against Moses and Aaron. ³And the people contended with Moses and spoke, saying: "If only we had died when our brethren died before the LORD! ⁴Why have you brought up the assembly of the LORD into this wilderness, that we and our animals should die here? ⁵And why have you made us come up out of Egypt, to bring us to this evil place? It *is* not a place of grain or figs or vines or pomegranates; nor *is* there any water to drink." ⁶So Moses and Aaron went from the presence of the assembly to the door of the tabernacle of meeting, and they fell on their faces. And the glory of the LORD appeared to them.

⁷Then the LORD spoke to Moses, saying, ⁸"Take the rod; you and your brother Aaron gather the congregation together. Speak to the

---

19:9 ᵃLiterally *impurity*

Leadership: Are You Proactive or Reactive?

(Numbers 20:2–13)

We learn something invaluable about leadership at the expense of Moses in Numbers 20. By this point Moses felt unendurably weary of the complaining, the stagnation, and the lack of progress among the people. He was running on empty. And in his weakened condition he made a decision that cost him his future.

Directed by God to speak to a rock in order to get water for the nation, in anger he struck it (as he had earlier). He reacted in fury rather than obeying with poise, and for his disobedience he was barred from entering the Promised Land. This sad incident teaches us at least two lessons.

First, never make a major decision during an emotionally low time. Make decisions in the peak times, not the valley times.

The right time to make a decision

The wrong time to make a decision

Second, choose to be proactive, not reactive, in your leadership. Don't let your mandate come from the grumbling of the crowd. Get your cues from God and the mission He has given you. Ask yourself these questions:

1. Am I a reactor or a creator when I lead?
2. Do I play defense or offense when I lead?
3. Am I a people-pleaser or a God-pleaser when I lead?
4. Do I boss my calendar, or does someone else choose where I give my time?

rock before their eyes, and it will yield its water; thus you shall bring water for them out of the rock, and give drink to the congregation and their animals." ⁹So Moses took the rod from before the LORD as He commanded him.

¹⁰And Moses and Aaron gathered the assembly together before the rock; and he said to them, "Hear now, you rebels! Must we bring water for you out of this rock?" ¹¹Then Moses lifted his hand and struck the rock twice with his rod; and water came out abundantly, and the congregation and their animals drank.

¹²Then the LORD spoke to Moses and Aaron, "Because you did not believe Me, to hallow Me in the eyes of the children of Israel, therefore you shall not bring this assembly into the land which I have given them."

¹³This *was* the water of Meribah,ᵃ because the children of Israel contended with the LORD, and He was hallowed among them.

Passage Through Edom Refused

¹⁴Now Moses sent messengers from Kadesh to the king of Edom. "Thus says your brother Israel: 'You know all the hardship that has befallen

us, ¹⁵how our fathers went down to Egypt, and we dwelt in Egypt a long time, and the Egyptians afflicted us and our fathers. ¹⁶When we cried out to the LORD, He heard our voice and sent the Angel and brought us up out of Egypt; now here we are in Kadesh, a city on the edge of your border. ¹⁷Please let us pass through your country. We will not pass through fields or vineyards, nor will we drink water from wells; we will go along the King's Highway; we will not turn aside to the right hand or to the left until we have passed through your territory.' "

¹⁸Then Edom said to him, "You shall not pass through my *land,* lest I come out against you with the sword."

¹⁹So the children of Israel said to him, "We will go by the Highway, and if I or my livestock drink any of your water, then I will pay for it; let me only pass through on foot, nothing *more.*"

²⁰Then he said, "You shall not pass through." So Edom came out against them with many men and with a strong hand. ²¹Thus Edom refused to

20:13 ᵃLiterally *Contention*

The Four Spiritual Flaws of a Leader

(Numbers 20:10–12)

Moses' disobedience by the rock reminds us of the human flaws that bedevil us all:

- Reacting instead of leading (v. 10)
- Presuming that what worked before will work again (v. 11)
- Compromising our obedience to God so we'll look better (v. 11)
- Failing to trust God to complete what He began (v. 12)

give Israel passage through his territory; so Israel turned away from him.

Death of Aaron

22Now the children of Israel, the whole congregation, journeyed from Kadesh and came to Mount Hor. 23And the LORD spoke to Moses and Aaron in Mount Hor by the border of the land of Edom, saying: 24"Aaron shall be gathered to his people, for he shall not enter the land which I have given to the children of Israel, because you rebelled against My word at the water of Meribah. 25Take Aaron and Eleazar his son, and bring them up to Mount Hor; 26and strip Aaron of his garments and put them on Eleazar his son; for Aaron shall be gathered *to his people* and die there." 27So Moses did just as the LORD commanded, and they went up to Mount Hor in the sight of all the congregation. 28Moses stripped Aaron of his garments and put them on Eleazar his son; and Aaron died there on the top of the mountain. Then Moses and Eleazar came down from the mountain. 29Now when all the congregation saw that Aaron was dead, all the house of Israel mourned for Aaron thirty days.

Canaanites Defeated at Hormah

21 The king of Arad, the Canaanite, who dwelt in the South, heard that Israel was coming on the road to Atharim. Then he fought against Israel and took *some* of them prisoners. 2So Israel made a vow to the LORD, and said, "If You will indeed deliver this people into my hand, then I will utterly destroy their cities." 3And the LORD listened to the voice of Israel and delivered up the Canaanites,

and they utterly destroyed them and their cities. So the name of that place was called Hormah.[a]

The Bronze Serpent

4Then they journeyed from Mount Hor by the Way of the Red Sea, to go around the land of Edom; and the soul of the people became very discouraged on the way. 5And the people spoke against God and against Moses: "Why have you brought us up out of Egypt to die in the wilderness? For *there is* no food and no water, and our soul loathes this worthless bread." 6So the LORD sent fiery serpents among the people, and they bit the people; and many of the people of Israel died.

7Therefore the people came to Moses, and said, "We have sinned, for we have spoken against the LORD and against you; pray to the LORD that He take away the serpents from us." So Moses prayed for the people.

8Then the LORD said to Moses, "Make a fiery *serpent,* and set it on a pole; and it shall be that everyone who is bitten, when he looks at it, shall live." 9So Moses made a bronze serpent, and put it on a pole; and so it was, if a serpent had bitten anyone, when he looked at the bronze serpent, he lived.

From Mount Hor to Moab

10Now the children of Israel moved on and camped in Oboth. 11And they journeyed from Oboth and camped at Ije Abarim, in the wilderness which *is* east of Moab, toward the sunrise. 12From there they moved and camped in the Valley of Zered. 13From there they moved and camped on the other side of the Arnon, which *is* in the wilderness that extends from the border of the Amorites; for the Arnon *is* the border of Moab, between Moab and the Amorites. 14Therefore it is said in the Book of the Wars of the LORD:

> "Waheb in Suphah,[a]
>   The brooks of the Arnon,
> 15   And the slope of the brooks
>   That reaches to the dwelling of Ar,
>   And lies on the border of Moab."

16From there *they went* to Beer, which *is* the well where the LORD said to Moses, "Gather the people together, and I will give them water." 17Then Israel sang this song:

21:3 [a]Literally *Utter Destruction* **21:14** [a]Ancient unknown places; Vulgate reads *What He did in the Red Sea.*

"Spring up, O well!
All of you sing to it—
18 The well the leaders sank,
Dug by the nation's nobles,
By the lawgiver, with their staves."

And from the wilderness *they went* to Mattanah, [19]from Mattanah to Nahaliel, from Nahaliel to Bamoth, [20]and from Bamoth, *in* the valley that *is* in the country of Moab, to the top of Pisgah which looks down on the wasteland.[a]

King Sihon Defeated

[21]Then Israel sent messengers to Sihon king of the Amorites, saying, [22]"Let me pass through your land. We will not turn aside into fields or vineyards; we will not drink water from wells. We will go by the King's Highway until we have passed through your territory." [23]But Sihon would not allow Israel to pass through his territory. So Sihon gathered all his people together and went out against Israel in the wilderness, and he came to Jahaz and fought against Israel. [24]Then Israel defeated him with the edge of the sword, and took possession of his land from the Arnon to the Jabbok, as far as the people of Ammon; for the border of the people of Ammon *was* fortified. [25]So Israel took all these cities, and Israel dwelt in all the cities of the Amorites, in Heshbon and in all its villages. [26]For Heshbon *was* the city of Sihon king of the Amorites, who had fought against the former king of Moab, and had taken all his land from his hand as far as the Arnon. [27]Therefore those who speak in proverbs say:

"Come to Heshbon, let it be built;
Let the city of Sihon be repaired.

28 "For fire went out from Heshbon,
A flame from the city of Sihon;
It consumed Ar of Moab,
The lords of the heights of the Arnon.

29 Woe to you, Moab!
You have perished, O people of Chemosh!
He has given his sons as fugitives,
And his daughters into captivity,
To Sihon king of the Amorites.

30 "But we have shot at them;
Heshbon has perished as far as Dibon.
Then we laid waste as far as Nophah,
Which *reaches* to Medeba."

[31]Thus Israel dwelt in the land of the Amorites. [32]Then Moses sent to spy out Jazer; and they took its villages and drove out the Amorites who *were* there.

King Og Defeated

[33]And they turned and went up by the way to Bashan. So Og king of Bashan went out against them, he and all his people, to battle at Edrei. [34]Then the LORD said to Moses, "Do not fear him, for I have delivered him into your hand, with all his people and his land; and you shall do to him as you did to Sihon king of the Amorites, who dwelt at Heshbon." [35]So they defeated him, his sons, and all his people, until there was no survivor left him; and they took possession of his land.

Balak Sends for Balaam

22 Then the children of Israel moved, and camped in the plains of Moab on the side of the Jordan *across from* Jericho.

[2]Now Balak the son of Zippor saw all that Israel had done to the Amorites. [3]And Moab was exceedingly afraid of the people because they *were* many, and Moab was sick with dread because of the children of Israel. [4]So Moab said to the elders of Midian, "Now this company will lick up everything around us, as an ox licks up the grass of the field." And Balak the son of Zippor *was* king of the Moabites at that time. [5]Then he sent messengers to Balaam the son of Beor at Pethor, which *is* near the River[a] in the land of the sons of his people,[b] to call him, saying: "Look, a people has come from Egypt. See, they cover the face of the earth, and are settling next to me! [6]Therefore please come at once, curse this people for me, for they *are* too mighty for me. Perhaps I shall be able to defeat them and drive them out of the land, for I know that he whom you bless *is* blessed, and he whom you curse is cursed."

[7]So the elders of Moab and the elders of Midian departed with the diviner's fee in their hand, and they came to Balaam and spoke to him the words of Balak. [8]And he said to them, "Lodge here tonight, and I will bring back word to you, as the LORD speaks to me." So the princes of Moab stayed with Balaam.

[9]Then God came to Balaam and said, "Who *are* these men with you?"

[10]So Balaam said to God, "Balak the son of Zippor, king of Moab, has sent to me, *saying,* [11]'Look, a people has come out of Egypt, and

---

21:20 [a]Hebrew *Jeshimon* **22:5** [a]That is, the Euphrates [b]Or *the people of Amau*

they cover the face of the earth. Come now, curse them for me; perhaps I shall be able to overpower them and drive them out.'"

[12]And God said to Balaam, "You shall not go with them; you shall not curse the people, for they *are* blessed."

[13]So Balaam rose in the morning and said to the princes of Balak, "Go back to your land, for the LORD has refused to give me permission to go with you."

[14]And the princes of Moab rose and went to Balak, and said, "Balaam refuses to come with us."

[15]Then Balak again sent princes, more numerous and more honorable than they. [16]And they came to Balaam and said to him, "Thus says Balak the son of Zippor: 'Please let nothing hinder you from coming to me; [17]for I will certainly honor you greatly, and I will do whatever you say to me. Therefore please come, curse this people for me.'"

[18]Then Balaam answered and said to the servants of Balak, "Though Balak were to give me his house full of silver and gold, I could not go beyond the word of the LORD my God, to do less or more. [19]Now therefore, please, you also stay here tonight, that I may know what more the LORD will say to me."

[20]And God came to Balaam at night and said to him, "If the men come to call you, rise *and* go with them; but only the word which I speak to you—that you shall do." [21]So Balaam rose in the morning, saddled his donkey, and went with the princes of Moab.

Balaam, the Donkey, and the Angel

[22]Then God's anger was aroused because he went, and the Angel of the LORD took His stand in the way as an adversary against him. And he was riding on his donkey, and his two servants *were* with him. [23]Now the donkey saw the Angel of the LORD standing in the way with His drawn sword in His hand, and the donkey turned aside out of the way and went into the field. So Balaam struck the donkey to turn her back onto the road. [24]Then the Angel of the LORD stood in a narrow path between the vineyards, *with* a wall on this side and a wall on that side. [25]And when the donkey saw the Angel of the LORD, she pushed herself against the wall and crushed Balaam's foot against the wall; so he struck her again. [26]Then the Angel of the LORD went further, and stood in a narrow place where there *was* no way to turn either to the right hand or to the left. [27]And when the donkey saw the Angel of the LORD, she lay down under Balaam; so Balaam's anger was aroused, and he struck the donkey with his staff.

PROFILE IN LEADERSHIP

BALAAM

GOOD BUT NOT GODLY
(Numbers 22:5—24:25)

One good trait does not a godly leader make—a maxim proven by the life of Balaam.

In one way, this Midianite sorcerer demonstrated good leadership. When Balak, king of Midian, tried to hire Balaam to curse the Israelites, the prophet declared he could speak only what God told him. In the end, Balaam blessed Israel three times (Num. 24:10).

Yet the balance of Scripture denounces Balaam. Joshua 13:22 tells us he practiced soothsaying, an activity condemned by Leviticus 19:26. Both Deuteronomy 23:5 and Joshua 24:9 strongly imply that Balaam asked God for permission to curse Israel. And the New Testament uses Balaam as an example of those who "have forsaken the right way and gone astray" and says, "he was rebuked for his iniquity" (2 Pet. 2:15, 16). Although God would not allow Balaam to curse Israel, apparently the sorcerer suggested a way for Balak to remove God's blessing on the Jewish people. Balaam "taught Balak to put a stumbling block before the children of Israel, to eat things sacrificed to idols, and to commit sexual immorality" (Rev. 2:14; see Num. 25:1–3).

Balaam finally met his demise when, by God's command, the Israelites killed him along with all the other male Midianites (Num. 31:8). And so this "soothsayer" died at the hands of the people he tried to curse.

Balaam Fails to Observe the Law of Buy-In

(Numbers 22:5—24:25)

King Balak was a strong leader with a wrong vision. Balaam was a weaker leader, but had the right vision. The two blended like oil and water. Optimally, the right leader must be in place, with right vision. People buy in to the leader before they buy in to the vision.

²⁸Then the LORD opened the mouth of the donkey, and she said to Balaam, "What have I done to you, that you have struck me these three times?"

²⁹And Balaam said to the donkey, "Because you have abused me. I wish there were a sword in my hand, for now I would kill you!"

³⁰So the donkey said to Balaam, "*Am* I not your donkey on which you have ridden, ever since I *became* yours, to this day? Was I ever disposed to do this to you?"

And he said, "No."

³¹Then the LORD opened Balaam's eyes, and he saw the Angel of the LORD standing in the way with His drawn sword in His hand; and he bowed his head and fell flat on his face. ³²And the Angel of the LORD said to him, "Why have you struck your donkey these three times? Behold, I have come out to stand against you, because *your* way is perverse before Me. ³³The donkey saw Me and turned aside from Me these three times. If she had not turned aside from Me, surely I would also have killed you by now, and let her live."

³⁴And Balaam said to the Angel of the LORD, "I have sinned, for I did not know You stood in the way against me. Now therefore, if it displeases You, I will turn back."

³⁵Then the Angel of the LORD said to Balaam, "Go with the men, but only the word that I speak to you, that you shall speak." So Balaam went with the princes of Balak.

³⁶Now when Balak heard that Balaam was coming, he went out to meet him at the city of Moab, which *is* on the border at the Arnon, the boundary of the territory. ³⁷Then Balak said to Balaam, "Did I not earnestly send to you, calling for you? Why did you not come to me? Am I not able to honor you?"

³⁸And Balaam said to Balak, "Look, I have come to you! Now, have I any power at all to say anything? The word that God puts in my mouth, that I must speak." ³⁹So Balaam went with Balak, and they came to Kirjath Huzoth. ⁴⁰Then Balak offered oxen and sheep, and he sent *some* to Balaam and to the princes who *were* with him.

Balaam's First Prophecy

⁴¹So it was, the next day, that Balak took Balaam and brought him up to the high places of Baal, that from there he might observe the extent of the people.

23 Then Balaam said to Balak, "Build seven altars for me here, and prepare for me here seven bulls and seven rams."

²And Balak did just as Balaam had spoken, and Balak and Balaam offered a bull and a ram on *each* altar. ³Then Balaam said to Balak, "Stand by your burnt offering, and I will go; perhaps the LORD will come to meet me, and whatever He shows me I will tell you." So he went to a desolate height. ⁴And God met Balaam, and he said to Him, "I have prepared the seven altars, and I have offered on *each* altar a bull and a ram."

⁵Then the LORD put a word in Balaam's

Balaam's Hollow, Man-Appointed Leadership

(Numbers 22:14—24:25)

Man-appointed leaders often claim to receive a call from God, but their authority actually derives from human sources and not from the Lord. Eventually, the truth becomes clear to everyone.

In Numbers 22—24 we see an example of a man-appointed leader. Balaam son of Beor tried to curse Israel for profit, but the Lord would not allow it. How can one discern man-appointed leadership?

1. It issues from human ingenuity rather than God's anointing (22:14–16).
2. It often reveals self-serving motives (22:17).
3. It devises plans that oppose what God is doing (22:22).
4. It blinds the leader to God's intentions (22:23–30).
5. Its goals eventually fail because they oppose the work of God (23:1—24:25).

DISCERNMENT

Balaam Just Didn't Get It

(Numbers 22:21–35)

Balaam has borne the brunt of many a joke. Here was a prophet who so lacked discernment that it took a donkey to sense the presence of a threatening angel and to bring the terrible danger to his attention.

Balaam lacked both discernment and intuition about what was happening around him. Note the following observations about Balaam's error:

1. Balaam angered God because he disobeyed what he knew to be right (v. 22).
2. It took the Angel of the Lord standing in the way to stop Balaam (v. 23).
3. The seer could not discern the Angel's blockade (v. 23).
4. Balaam's own agenda so consumed him that he whipped his donkey for responding to the Angel (v. 25).
5. God enabled the donkey to speak when Balaam still didn't perceive his danger (v. 28).
6. The donkey discerned more than Balaam and interpreted reality for him (vv. 28–30).
7. It took a divine miracle for Balaam's eyes to be opened (v. 31).

No leader can long enjoy success without developing a healthy sense of discernment. Lack of discernment nearly got Balaam killed. He did not discern the Lord's presence, and he confessed his lack of discernment (Num. 22:34). God said the prophet would surely have been killed had it not been for his discerning donkey (22:33). When he finally realized his peril, Balaam had to feel both ashamed and embarrassed. It is one thing to lack discernment; it is another for your donkey to possess more it of than you do!

Unfortunately, many leaders today suffer exactly this plight. Many factors conspire to keep us from discerning the needs of the moment. Consider some common factors:

1. An unrelenting schedule leaves no room for listening.
2. An important agenda fosters a stubborn heart rather than a sensitive one.
3. A type-A temperament makes it difficult to slow down and discern.
4. A strong task orientation leaves little time for people or spontaneity.
5. We desire to solve spiritual and emotional problems with external answers.

Do you want to hone your leadership skills? Then make it a priority to pray for greater discernment. Listen for and interpret the root causes of the challenges you face. Consider your gut reaction to others, but also tap your mind. Discernment takes both godly intuition and intellect.

For a positive example of discernment, see p. 383.

mouth, and said, "Return to Balak, and thus you shall speak." [6]So he returned to him, and there he was, standing by his burnt offering, he and all the princes of Moab.

[7]And he took up his oracle and said:

"Balak the king of Moab has brought me
    from Aram,
From the mountains of the east.
'Come, curse Jacob for me,
And come, denounce Israel!'

[8] "How shall I curse whom God has not
    cursed?
And how shall I denounce *whom* the LORD
    has not denounced?
[9] For from the top of the rocks I see him,
And from the hills I behold him;
There! A people dwelling alone,
Not reckoning itself among the nations.

[10] "Who can count the dust[a] of Jacob,
Or number one-fourth of Israel?
Let me die the death of the righteous,
And let my end be like his!"

[11]Then Balak said to Balaam, "What have you done to me? I took you to curse my enemies, and look, you have blessed *them* bountifully!"

[12]So he answered and said, "Must I not take heed to speak what the LORD has put in my mouth?"

Balaam's Second Prophecy

[13]Then Balak said to him, "Please come with me to another place from which you may see them; you shall see only the outer part of them, and shall not see them all; curse them for me from there." [14]So he brought him to the field of Zophim, to the top of Pisgah, and built seven altars, and offered a bull and a ram on *each* altar.

[15]And he said to Balak, "Stand here by your burnt offering while I meet[a] *the* LORD over there."

[16]Then the LORD met Balaam, and put a word in his mouth, and said, "Go back to Balak, and thus you shall speak." [17]So he came to him, and there he was, standing by his burnt offering, and the princes of Moab were with him. And Balak said to him, "What has the LORD spoken?"

[18]Then he took up his oracle and said:

"Rise up, Balak, and hear!
Listen to me, son of Zippor!

[19] "God *is* not a man, that He should lie,
Nor a son of man, that He should repent.

Has He said, and will He not do?
Or has He spoken, and will He not make
    it good?
[20] Behold, I have received *a command* to bless;
He has blessed, and I cannot reverse it.

[21] "He has not observed iniquity in Jacob,
Nor has He seen wickedness in Israel.
The LORD his God *is* with him,
And the shout of a King *is* among them.
[22] God brings them out of Egypt;
He has strength like a wild ox.

[23] "For *there is* no sorcery against Jacob,
Nor any divination against Israel.
It now must be said of Jacob
And of Israel, 'Oh, what God has done!'
[24] Look, a people rises like a lioness,
And lifts itself up like a lion;
It shall not lie down until it devours the
    prey,
And drinks the blood of the slain."

[25]Then Balak said to Balaam, "Neither curse them at all, nor bless them at all!"

[26]So Balaam answered and said to Balak, "Did I not tell you, saying, 'All that the LORD speaks, that I must do'?"

Balaam's Third Prophecy

[27]Then Balak said to Balaam, "Please come, I will take you to another place; perhaps it will please God that you may curse them for me from there." [28]So Balak took Balaam to the top of Peor, that overlooks the wasteland.[a] [29]Then Balaam said to Balak, "Build for me here seven altars, and prepare for me here seven bulls and seven rams." [30]And Balak did as Balaam had said, and offered a bull and a ram on *every* altar.

24 Now when Balaam saw that it pleased the LORD to bless Israel, he did not go as at other times, to seek to use sorcery, but he set his face toward the wilderness. [2]And Balaam raised his eyes, and saw Israel encamped according to their tribes; and the Spirit of God came upon him.

[3]Then he took up his oracle and said:

"The utterance of Balaam the son of Beor,
The utterance of the man whose eyes are
    opened,

23:10 [a]Or *dust cloud* **23:15** [a]Following Masoretic Text, Targum, and Vulgate; Syriac reads *call;* Septuagint reads *go and ask God.* **23:28** [a]Hebrew *Jeshimon*

4 The utterance of him who hears the words
of God,
Who sees the vision of the Almighty,
Who falls down, with eyes wide open:

5 "How lovely are your tents, O Jacob!
Your dwellings, O Israel!
6 Like valleys that stretch out,
Like gardens by the riverside,
Like aloes planted by the LORD,
Like cedars beside the waters.
7 He shall pour water from his buckets,
And his seed *shall be* in many waters.

"His king shall be higher than Agag,
And his kingdom shall be exalted.

8 "God brings him out of Egypt;
He has strength like a wild ox;
He shall consume the nations, his enemies;
He shall break their bones
And pierce *them* with his arrows.
9 'He bows down, he lies down as a lion;
And as a lion, who shall rouse him?'ᵃ

"Blessed *is* he who blesses you,
And cursed *is* he who curses you."

¹⁰Then Balak's anger was aroused against Balaam, and he struck his hands together; and Balak
said to Balaam, "I called you to curse my enemies, and look, you have bountifully blessed *them*
these three times! ¹¹Now therefore, flee to your
place. I said I would greatly honor you, but in
fact, the LORD has kept you back from honor."

¹²So Balaam said to Balak, "Did I not also
speak to your messengers whom you sent to me,
saying, ¹³'If Balak were to give me his house full
of silver and gold, I could not go beyond the
word of the LORD, to do good or bad of my own
will. What the LORD says, that I must speak'?
¹⁴And now, indeed, I am going to my people.
Come, I will advise you what this people will do
to your people in the latter days."

Balaam's Fourth Prophecy

¹⁵So he took up his oracle and said:

"The utterance of Balaam the son of Beor,
And the utterance of the man whose eyes
are opened;
16 The utterance of him who hears the words
of God,
And has the knowledge of the Most High,
Who sees the vision of the Almighty,
Who falls down, with eyes wide open:

17 "I see Him, but not now;
I behold Him, but not near;
A Star shall come out of Jacob;
A Scepter shall rise out of Israel,
And batter the brow of Moab,
And destroy all the sons of tumult.ᵃ

18 "And Edom shall be a possession;
Seir also, his enemies, shall be a possession,
While Israel does valiantly.
19 Out of Jacob One shall have dominion,
And destroy the remains of the city."

²⁰Then he looked on Amalek, and he took up
his oracle and said:

"Amalek *was* first among the nations,
But *shall be* last until he perishes."

²¹Then he looked on the Kenites, and he
took up his oracle and said:

"Firm is your dwelling place,
And your nest is set in the rock;
22 Nevertheless Kain shall be burned.
How long until Asshur carries you away
captive?"

²³Then he took up his oracle and said:

"Alas! Who shall live when God does this?
24 But ships *shall come* from the coasts of
Cyprus,ᵃ
And they shall afflict Asshur and afflict
Eber,
And so shall *Amalek,*ᵇ until he perishes."

²⁵So Balaam rose and departed and returned
to his place; Balak also went his way.

Israel's Harlotry in Moab

25 Now Israel remained in Acacia
Grove,ᵃ and the people began to
commit harlotry with the women of
Moab. ²They invited the people to the sacrifices
of their gods, and the people ate and bowed
down to their gods. ³So Israel was joined to Baal
of Peor, and the anger of the LORD was aroused
against Israel.

⁴Then the LORD said to Moses, "Take all the
leaders of the people and hang the offenders before the LORD, out in the sun, that the fierce
anger of the LORD may turn away from Israel."

24:9 ᵃGenesis 49:9 **24:17** ᵃHebrew *Sheth* (compare
Jeremiah 48:45) **24:24** ᵃHebrew *Kittim* ᵇLiterally
he or *that one* **25:1** ᵃHebrew *Shittim*

[5]So Moses said to the judges of Israel, "Every one of you kill his men who were joined to Baal of Peor."

[6]And indeed, one of the children of Israel came and presented to his brethren a Midianite woman in the sight of Moses and in the sight of all the congregation of the children of Israel, who *were* weeping at the door of the tabernacle of meeting. [7]Now when Phinehas the son of Eleazar, the son of Aaron the priest, saw *it*, he rose from among the congregation and took a javelin in his hand; [8]and he went after the man of Israel into the tent and thrust both of them through, the man of Israel, and the woman through her body. So the plague was stopped among the children of Israel. [9]And those who died in the plague were twenty-four thousand.

[10]Then the LORD spoke to Moses, saying: [11]"Phinehas the son of Eleazar, the son of Aaron the priest, has turned back My wrath from the children of Israel, because he was zealous with My zeal among them, so that I did not consume the children of Israel in My zeal. [12]Therefore say, 'Behold, I give to him My covenant of peace; [13]and it shall be to him and his descendants after him a covenant of an everlasting priesthood, because he was zealous for his God, and made atonement for the children of Israel.' "

[14]Now the name of the Israelite who was killed, who was killed with the Midianite woman, *was* Zimri the son of Salu, a leader of a father's house among the Simeonites. [15]And the name of the Midianite woman who was killed *was* Cozbi the daughter of Zur; he *was* head of the people of a father's house in Midian.

[16]Then the LORD spoke to Moses, saying: [17]"Harass the Midianites, and attack them; [18]for they harassed you with their schemes by which they seduced you in the matter of Peor and in the matter of Cozbi, the daughter of a leader of Midian, their sister, who was killed in the day of the plague because of Peor."

The Second Census of Israel

26 And it came to pass, after the plague, that the LORD spoke to Moses and Eleazar the son of Aaron the priest, saying: [2]"Take a census of all the congregation of the children of Israel from twenty years old and above, by their fathers' houses, all who are able to go to war in Israel." [3]So Moses and Eleazar the priest spoke with them in the plains of Moab by the Jordan, *across from* Jericho, saying: [4]"*Take a census of the people* from twenty years old and above, just as the LORD commanded Moses and the children of Israel who came out of the land of Egypt."

Round Two of the Census: Evaluating What Remains

(Numbers 26:1–63)

As a new generation of Hebrews matured into adulthood, Moses took a second census to size up the Israelite community. At the right time, such an evaluation can be extremely helpful. Leaders must know what resources they have before they develop their plans and design their strategies.

[5]Reuben *was* the firstborn of Israel. The children of Reuben *were: of* Hanoch, the family of the Hanochites; *of* Pallu, the family of the Palluites; [6]*of* Hezron, the family of the Hezronites; *of* Carmi, the family of the Carmites. [7]These *are* the families of the Reubenites: those who were numbered of them were forty-three thousand seven hundred and thirty. [8]And the son of Pallu *was* Eliab. [9]The sons of Eliab *were* Nemuel, Dathan, and Abiram. These *are* the Dathan and Abiram, representatives of the congregation, who contended against Moses and Aaron in the company of Korah, when they contended against the LORD; [10]and the earth opened its mouth and swallowed them up together with Korah when that company died, when the fire devoured two hundred and fifty men; and they became a sign. [11]Nevertheless the children of Korah did not die.

[12]The sons of Simeon according to their families *were: of* Nemuel,[a] the family of the Nemuelites; *of* Jamin, the family of the Jaminites; *of* Jachin,[b] the family of the Jachinites; [13]*of* Zerah,[a] the family of the Zarhites; *of* Shaul, the family of the Shaulites. [14]These *are* the families of the Simeonites: twenty-two thousand two hundred.

[15]The sons of Gad according to their families *were: of* Zephon,[a] the family of the Zephonites; *of* Haggi, the family of the Haggites; *of* Shuni, the family of the Shunites; [16]*of* Ozni,[a] the family of the Oznites; *of* Eri, the family of the Erites; [17]*of* Arod,[a]

26:12 [a]Spelled *Jemuel* in Genesis 46:10 and Exodus 6:15 [b]Called *Jarib* in 1 Chronicles 4:24
26:13 [a]Called *Zohar* in Genesis 46:10
26:15 [a]Called *Ziphion* in Genesis 46:16
26:16 [a]Called *Ezbon* in Genesis 46:16
26:17 [a]Spelled *Arodi* in Samaritan Pentateuch, Syriac, and Genesis 46:16

the family of the Arodites; *of* Areli, the family of the Arelites. ¹⁸These *are* the families of the sons of Gad according to those who were numbered of them: forty thousand five hundred.

¹⁹The sons of Judah *were* Er and Onan; and Er and Onan died in the land of Canaan. ²⁰And the sons of Judah according to their families were: *of* Shelah, the family of the Shelanites; *of* Perez, the family of the Parzites; *of* Zerah, the family of the Zarhites. ²¹And the sons of Perez were: *of* Hezron, the family of the Hezronites; *of* Hamul, the family of the Hamulites. ²²These *are* the families of Judah according to those who were numbered of them: seventy-six thousand five hundred.

²³The sons of Issachar according to their families *were: of* Tola, the family of the Tolaites; *of* Puah,ᵃ the family of the Punites;ᵇ ²⁴of Jashub, the family of the Jashubites; *of* Shimron, the family of the Shimronites. ²⁵These *are* the families of Issachar according to those who were numbered of them: sixty-four thousand three hundred.

²⁶The sons of Zebulun according to their families *were: of* Sered, the family of the Sardites; *of* Elon, the family of the Elonites; *of* Jahleel, the family of the Jahleelites. ²⁷These *are* the families of the Zebulunites according to those who were numbered of them: sixty thousand five hundred.

²⁸The sons of Joseph according to their families, by Manasseh and Ephraim, *were:* ²⁹The sons of Manasseh: of Machir, the family of the Machirites; and Machir begot Gilead; of Gilead, the family of the Gileadites. ³⁰These *are* the sons of Gilead: *of* Jeezer,ᵃ the family of the Jeezerites; of Helek, the family of the Helekites; ³¹*of* Asriel, the family of the Asrielites; *of* Shechem, the family of the Shechemites; ³²*of* Shemida, the family of the Shemidaites; *of* Hepher, the family of the Hepherites. ³³Now Zelophehad the son of Hepher had no sons, but daughters; and the names of the daughters of Zelophehad *were* Mahlah, Noah, Hoglah, Milcah, and Tirzah. ³⁴These *are* the families of Manasseh; and those who were numbered of them *were* fifty-two thousand seven hundred.

³⁵These *are* the sons of Ephraim according to their families: of Shuthelah, the family of the Shuthalhites; of Becher,ᵃ the family of the Bachrites; of Tahan, the family of the Tahanites. ³⁶And these *are* the sons of Shuthelah: of Eran, the family of the Eranites. ³⁷These *are* the families of the sons of Ephraim according to those who were numbered of them: thirty-two thousand five hundred.

These *are* the sons of Joseph according to their families.

³⁸The sons of Benjamin according to their families were: of Bela, the family of the Belaites; of Ashbel, the family of the Ashbelites; of Ahiram, the family of the Ahiramites; ³⁹of Shupham,ᵃ the family of the Shuphamites; of Hupham,ᵇ the family of the Huphamites. ⁴⁰And the sons of Bela were Ardᵃ and Naaman: *of* Ard, the family of the Ardites; of Naaman, the family of the Naamites. ⁴¹These *are* the sons of Benjamin according to their families; and those who were numbered of them *were* forty-five thousand six hundred.

⁴²These *are* the sons of Dan according to their families: of Shuham,ᵃ the family of the Shuhamites. These *are* the families of Dan according to their families. ⁴³All the families of the Shuhamites, according to those who were numbered of them, *were* sixty-four thousand four hundred.

⁴⁴The sons of Asher according to their families *were:* of Jimna, the family of the Jimnites; of Jesui, the family of the Jesuites; of Beriah, the family of the Beriites. ⁴⁵Of the sons of Beriah: of Heber, the family of the Heberites; of Malchiel, the family of the Malchielites. ⁴⁶And the name of the daughter of Asher *was* Serah. ⁴⁷These *are* the families of the sons of Asher according to those who were numbered of them: fifty-three thousand four hundred.

⁴⁸The sons of Naphtali according to their families *were:* of Jahzeel,ᵃ the family of the Jahzeelites; of Guni, the family of the Gunites; ⁴⁹of Jezer, the family of the Jezerites; of Shillem, the family of the Shillemites. ⁵⁰These *are* the families of Naphtali according to their families; and those who were numbered of them *were* forty-five thousand four hundred.

⁵¹These *are* those who were numbered of the children of Israel: six hundred and one thousand seven hundred and thirty.

⁵²Then the LORD spoke to Moses, saying: ⁵³"To these the land shall be divided as an inheritance, according to the number of names. ⁵⁴To a large *tribe* you shall give a larger inheritance, and to a small *tribe* you shall give a smaller inheritance.

26:23 ᵃHebrew *Puvah* (compare Genesis 46:13 and 1 Chronicles 7:1); Samaritan Pentateuch, Septuagint, Syriac, and Vulgate read *Puah.* ᵇSamaritan Pentateuch, Septuagint, Syriac, and Vulgate read *Puaites.* **26:30** ᵃCalled *Abiezer* in Joshua 17:2 **26:35** ᵃCalled *Bered* in 1 Chronicles 7:20 **26:39** ᵃMasoretic Text reads *Shephupham,* spelled *Shephuphan* in 1 Chronicles 8:5. ᵇCalled *Huppim* in Genesis 46:21 **26:40** ᵃCalled *Addar* in 1 Chronicles 8:3 **26:42** ᵃCalled *Hushim* in Genesis 46:23 **26:48** ᵃSpelled *Jahziel* in 1 Chronicles 7:13

Each shall be given its inheritance according to those who were numbered of them. ⁵⁵But the land shall be divided by lot; they shall inherit according to the names of the tribes of their fathers. ⁵⁶According to the lot their inheritance shall be divided between the larger and the smaller."

⁵⁷And these *are* those who were numbered of the Levites according to their families: of Gershon, the family of the Gershonites; of Kohath, the family of the Kohathites; of Merari, the family of the Merarites. ⁵⁸These *are* the families of the Levites: the family of the Libnites, the family of the Hebronites, the family of the Mahlites, the family of the Mushites, and the family of the Korathites. And Kohath begot Amram. ⁵⁹The name of Amram's wife *was* Jochebed the daughter of Levi, who was born to Levi in Egypt; and to Amram she bore Aaron and Moses and their sister Miriam. ⁶⁰To Aaron were born Nadab and Abihu, Eleazar and Ithamar. ⁶¹And Nadab and Abihu died when they offered profane fire before the LORD.

⁶²Now those who were numbered of them were twenty-three thousand, every male from a month old and above; for they were not numbered among the other children of Israel, because there was no inheritance given to them among the children of Israel.

⁶³These *are* those who were numbered by Moses and Eleazar the priest, who numbered the children of Israel in the plains of Moab by the Jordan, *across from* Jericho. ⁶⁴But among these there was not a man of those who were numbered by Moses and Aaron the priest when they numbered the children of Israel in the Wilderness of Sinai. ⁶⁵For the LORD had said of them, "They shall surely die in the wilderness." So there was not left a man of them, except Caleb the son of Jephunneh and Joshua the son of Nun.

Inheritance Laws

27 Then came the daughters of Zelophehad the son of Hepher, the son of Gilead, the son of Machir, the son of Manasseh, from the families of Manasseh the son of Joseph; and these *were* the names of his daughters: Mahlah, Noah, Hoglah, Milcah, and Tirzah. ²And they stood before Moses, before Eleazar the priest, and before the leaders and all the congregation, *by* the doorway of the tabernacle of meeting, saying: ³"Our father died in the wilderness; but he was not in the company of those who gathered together against the LORD, in company with Korah, but he died in his own sin; and he had no sons. ⁴Why should the name of our father be removed from among his family

because he had no son? Give us a possession among our father's brothers."

⁵So Moses brought their case before the LORD.

⁶And the LORD spoke to Moses, saying: ⁷"The daughters of Zelophehad speak *what is* right; you shall surely give them a possession of inheritance among their father's brothers, and cause the inheritance of their father to pass to them. ⁸And you shall speak to the children of Israel, saying: 'If a man dies and has no son, then you shall cause his inheritance to pass to his daughter. ⁹If he has no daughter, then you shall give his inheritance to his brothers. ¹⁰If he has no brothers, then you shall give his inheritance to his father's brothers. ¹¹And if his father has no brothers, then you shall give his inheritance to the relative closest to him in his family, and he shall possess it.'" And it shall be to the children of Israel a statute of judgment, just as the LORD commanded Moses.

Joshua the Next Leader of Israel

¹²Now the LORD said to Moses: "Go up into this Mount Abarim, and see the land which I have given to the children of Israel. ¹³And when you have seen it, you also shall be gathered to your people, as Aaron your brother was gathered. ¹⁴For in the Wilderness of Zin, during the strife of the congregation, you rebelled against My command to hallow Me at the waters before their eyes." (These *are* the waters of Meribah, at Kadesh in the Wilderness of Zin.)

¹⁵Then Moses spoke to the LORD, saying: ¹⁶"Let the LORD, the God of the spirits of all flesh, set a man over the congregation, ¹⁷who may go out before them and go in before them, who may lead them out and bring them in, that the congregation of the LORD may not be like sheep which have no shepherd."

¹⁸And the LORD said to Moses: "Take Joshua the son of Nun with you, a man in whom *is* the Spirit, and lay your hand on him; ¹⁹set him before Eleazar the priest and before all the congregation, and inaugurate him in their sight. ²⁰And you shall give *some* of your authority to him, that all the congregation of the children of Israel may be obedient. ²¹He shall stand before Eleazar the priest, who shall inquire before the LORD for him by the judgment of the Urim. At his word they shall go out, and at his word they shall come in, he and all the children of Israel with him—all the congregation."

²²So Moses did as the LORD commanded him. He took Joshua and set him before Eleazar the priest and before all the congregation. ²³And he

laid his hands on him and inaugurated him, just as the LORD commanded by the hand of Moses.

Daily Offerings

28 Now the LORD spoke to Moses, saying, [2]"Command the children of Israel, and say to them, 'My offering, My food for My offerings made by fire as a sweet aroma to Me, you shall be careful to offer to Me at their appointed time.'

[3]"And you shall say to them, 'This *is* the offering made by fire which you shall offer to the LORD: two male lambs in their first year without blemish, day by day, as a regular burnt offering. [4]The one lamb you shall offer in the morning, the other lamb you shall offer in the evening, [5]and one-tenth of an ephah of fine flour as a grain offering mixed with one-fourth of a hin of pressed oil. [6]*It is* a regular burnt offering which was ordained at Mount Sinai for a sweet aroma, an offering made by fire to the LORD. [7]And its drink offering *shall be* one-fourth of a hin for each lamb; in a holy *place* you shall pour out the drink to the LORD as an offering. [8]The other lamb you shall offer in the evening; as the morning grain offering and its drink offering, you shall offer *it* as an offering made by fire, a sweet aroma to the LORD.

Sabbath Offerings

[9]And on the Sabbath day two lambs in their first year, without blemish, and two-tenths *of an ephah* of fine flour as a grain offering, mixed with oil, with its drink offering— [10]*this is* the burnt offering for every Sabbath, besides the regular burnt offering with its drink offering.

Monthly Offerings

[11]At the beginnings of your months you shall present a burnt offering to the LORD: two young bulls, one ram, and seven lambs in their first year, without blemish; [12]three-tenths *of an ephah* of fine flour as a grain offering, mixed with oil, for each bull; two-tenths *of an ephah* of fine flour as a grain offering, mixed with oil, for the one ram; [13]and one-tenth *of an ephah* of fine flour, mixed with oil, as a grain offering for each lamb, as a burnt offering of sweet aroma, an offering made by fire to the LORD. [14]Their drink offering shall be half a hin of wine for a bull, one-third of a hin for a ram, and one-fourth of a hin for a lamb; this *is* the burnt offering for each month throughout the months of the year. [15]Also one kid of the goats as a sin offering to the LORD shall be offered, besides the regular burnt offering and its drink offering.

Offerings at Passover

[16]"On the fourteenth day of the first month *is* the Passover of the LORD. [17]And on the fifteenth day of this month *is* the feast; unleavened bread shall be eaten for seven days. [18]On the first day *you shall have* a holy convocation. You shall do no customary work. [19]And you shall present an offering made by fire as a burnt offering to the LORD: two young bulls, one ram, and seven lambs in their first year. Be sure they are without blemish. [20]Their grain offering shall be of fine flour mixed with oil: three-tenths *of an ephah* you shall offer for a bull, and two-tenths for a ram; [21]you shall offer one-tenth *of an ephah* for each of the seven lambs; [22]also one goat *as* a sin offering, to make atonement for you. [23]You shall offer these besides the burnt offering of the morning, which *is* for a regular burnt offering. [24]In this manner you shall offer the food of the offering made by fire daily for seven days, as a sweet aroma to the LORD; it shall be offered besides the regular burnt offering and its drink offering. [25]And on the seventh day you shall have a holy convocation. You shall do no customary work.

Offerings at the Feast of Weeks

[26]Also on the day of the firstfruits, when you bring a new grain offering to the LORD at your *Feast of* Weeks, you shall have a holy convocation. You shall do no customary work. [27]You shall present a burnt offering as a sweet aroma to the LORD: two young bulls, one ram, and seven lambs in their first year, [28]with their grain offering of fine flour mixed with oil: three-tenths *of an ephah* for each bull, two-tenths for the one ram, [29]and one-tenth for each of the seven lambs; [30]also one kid of the goats, to make atonement for you. [31]Be sure they are without blemish. You shall present *them* with their drink offerings, besides the regular burnt offering with its grain offering.

Offerings at the Feast of Trumpets

29 'And in the seventh month, on the first *day* of the month, you shall have a holy convocation. You shall do no customary work. For you it is a day of blowing the trumpets. [2]You shall offer a burnt offering as a sweet aroma to the LORD: one young bull, one ram, *and* seven lambs in their first year, without blemish; [3]Their grain offering *shall be* fine flour mixed with oil: three-tenths *of an ephah* for the bull, two-tenths for the ram, [4]and one-tenth for each of the seven lambs; [5]also one kid of the goats *as* a sin offering, to make atonement for you; [6]besides the burnt offering with its grain offering for the New Moon, the regular burnt

MOSES AND JOSHUA AND THE LAW OF REPRODUCTION

It Takes a Leader to Raise Up a Leader
(Numbers 27:18–23)

Of all the wonderful ways Moses expressed his leadership, the most strategic had to be his training of Joshua.

Joshua became the leader who would complete the task of leading the people into the Promised Land. This successful "leadership reproduction" resulted from Moses' example and equipping *and* from Joshua's hunger and giftedness. Moses passed along his authority, abilities, and anointing to Joshua. He gave Joshua his time, his insight, a learning environment, an opportunity to prove himself, and a strong belief in his future. Because Moses spent the time necessary to reproduce himself in Joshua, his dream of Israel entering the Promised Land came to pass, even though he did not personally see it happen.

Moses' Mentoring Process

1. *Moses **empowered** Joshua and gave him **authority*** (Num. 27:20).

When the time came, Moses laid his hands on Joshua and publicly commissioned him. He gave Joshua part of his authority (Num. 27:15–23). Joshua received positive recognition, a leader's approval and acceptance, and Moses' expression of faith in him. After Moses died, no one questioned Joshua's leadership.

2. *Moses gave Joshua **experience** and opportunities for **application*** (Num. 27:21–22).

Joshua's apprenticeship went beyond the merely cerebral or passive. Moses and Joshua did more than talk over coffee; the apprenticeship involved hands-on experience. Moses shared his life and his responsibilities with Joshua by allowing him to prove his leadership as a spy, as a military commander, and as his personal assistant.

3. *Moses gave Joshua **encouragement** and **affirmation*** (Num. 27:23).

Moses repeatedly affirmed his young protégé by taking him along on excursions exclusive of anyone else. They shared a unique intimacy, almost startling considering the difference in their ages. Moses encouraged his apprentice both through his words and his time.

The Needs of Next-Generation Leaders

The interaction of Moses and Joshua demonstrates that reproducing leaders is not a quick, simple process. It closely resembles parenting. It requires time, emotional investment, and sacrifice.

Moses undoubtedly tailored his mentoring to the needs of Joshua. That's important. If you are a parent with more than one child, you understand that each child must be handled differently. Your children have different gifts, interests, talents, and needs.

Still, certain aspects of the parenting process remain fairly constant. When you begin developing the next generation of leaders, recognize that your protégés will need certain things:

1. *From themselves: Conviction, courage, and obedience*

Only emerging leaders themselves can provide some things. You cannot give them the right attitude or the will to learn and obey. When Joshua came to Moses, he had already demonstrated a conviction to follow God, the courage to fight for his beliefs, and the willingness to obey both God and his mentor. That made him a good candidate for further leadership development. As you look for people to mentor, seek those who possess qualities similar to the ones Joshua displayed.

2. *From their mentor: Equipping*

As the mentor, you bear the responsibility for providing emerging leaders with the things they cannot get on their own. Perhaps the following guideline will help you to properly equip them:

P—Purpose: Don't merely spend time with emerging leaders; be strategic. Think of your interaction as an investment based on vision and charged with purpose.

A—Assessment: Give protégés honest feedback. If *you* don't let them know how they are doing, who will?

R—Relationship: Your relationships supply the glue that holds you and your protégés together during the mentoring process. The greater the challenges, the more solid the relationships must be.

E—Encouragement: Protégés will make mistakes and fail; count on that. Your positive words may offer the only things of value they can count on during their most difficult times. Without encouragement, they may lack the will to persevere and keep moving forward.

N—Navigation: The less experienced the emerging leaders, the more help they will need to navigate the obstacle course of life—and the more help they will need in learning how to make good leadership decisions.

T—Tools: Protégés need skills and resources that only a more experienced person can provide.

Above all, as you equip your protégés, approach them as you would dearly loved children: with patience, perspective, and a positive attitude.

3. *From God: Vision*

As you begin to invest in potential leaders, you will invite them to come alongside you and participate in the fulfillment of your vision. That is as it should be.

But there will come a time as you release your protégés when they will need to have a vision of their own. That's not something you can give them. No one can borrow vision; each person must possess his own. Ask God to bless the individuals you mentor with a godly vision that will sustain them as they become leaders in their own right.

4. *From the people: Buy-In*

Without the support and participation of the people, the individuals you mentor cannot make the difficult transition from protégé to leader. So far as it is in your power to do so, publicly invest your authority in your protégés once they appear ready for the responsibility.

offering with its grain offering, and their drink offerings, according to their ordinance, as a sweet aroma, an offering made by fire to the LORD.

Offerings on the Day of Atonement

[7]"On the tenth *day* of this seventh month you shall have a holy convocation. You shall afflict your souls; you shall not do any work. [8]You shall present a burnt offering to the LORD *as* a sweet aroma: one young bull, one ram, *and* seven lambs in their first year. Be sure they are without blemish. [9]Their grain offering *shall be of* fine flour mixed with oil: three-tenths *of an ephah* for the bull, two-tenths for the one ram, [10]and one-tenth for each of the seven lambs; [11]also one kid of the goats *as* a sin offering, besides the sin offering for atonement, the regular burnt offering with its grain offering, and their drink offerings.

Offerings at the Feast of Tabernacles

[12]"On the fifteenth day of the seventh month you shall have a holy convocation. You shall do no customary work, and you shall keep a feast to the LORD seven days. [13]You shall present a burnt offering, an offering made by fire as a sweet aroma to the LORD: thirteen young bulls, two rams, *and* fourteen lambs in their first year. They shall be without blemish. [14]Their grain offering *shall be of* fine flour mixed with oil: three-tenths *of an ephah* for each of the thirteen bulls, two-tenths for each of the two rams, [15]and one-tenth for each of the fourteen lambs; [16]also one kid of the goats *as* a sin offering, besides the regular burnt offering, its grain offering, and its drink offering.

[17]"On the second day *present* twelve young bulls, two rams, fourteen lambs in their first year without blemish, [18]and their grain offering and their drink offerings for the bulls, for the rams, and for the lambs, by their number, according to the ordinance; [19]also one kid of the goats *as* a sin offering, besides the regular burnt offering with its grain offering, and their drink offerings.

[20]"On the third day *present* eleven bulls, two rams, fourteen lambs in their first year without blemish, [21]and their grain offering and their drink offerings for the bulls, for the rams, and for the lambs, by their number, according to the ordinance; [22]also one goat *as* a sin offering, besides the regular burnt offering, its grain offering, and its drink offering.

[23]"On the fourth day *present* ten bulls, two rams, *and* fourteen lambs in their first year, without blemish, [24]and their grain offering and their drink offerings for the bulls, for the rams, and for the lambs, by their number, according to the or-

dinance; [25]also one kid of the goats *as* a sin offering, besides the regular burnt offering, its grain offering, and its drink offering.

[26]"On the fifth day *present* nine bulls, two rams, *and* fourteen lambs in their first year without blemish, [27]and their grain offering and their drink offerings for the bulls, for the rams, and for the lambs, by their number, according to the ordinance; [28]also one goat *as* a sin offering, besides the regular burnt offering, its grain offering, and its drink offering.

[29]"On the sixth day *present* eight bulls, two rams, *and* fourteen lambs in their first year without blemish, [30]and their grain offering and their drink offerings for the bulls, for the rams, and for the lambs, by their number, according to the ordinance; [31]also one goat *as* a sin offering, besides the regular burnt offering, its grain offering, and its drink offering.

[32]"On the seventh day *present* seven bulls, two rams, *and* fourteen lambs in their first year without blemish, [33]and their grain offering and their drink offerings for the bulls, for the rams, and for the lambs, by their number, according to the ordinance; [34]also one goat *as* a sin offering, besides the regular burnt offering, its grain offering, and its drink offering.

[35]"On the eighth day you shall have a sacred assembly. You shall do no customary work. [36]You shall present a burnt offering, an offering made by fire as a sweet aroma to the LORD: one bull, one ram, seven lambs in their first year without blemish, [37]and their grain offering and their drink offerings for the bull, for the ram, and for the lambs, by their number, according to the ordinance; [38]also one goat *as* a sin offering, besides the regular burnt offering, its grain offering, and its drink offering.

[39]"These you shall present to the LORD at your appointed feasts (besides your vowed offerings and your freewill offerings) as your burnt offerings and your grain offerings, as your drink offerings and your peace offerings.'"

[40]So Moses told the children of Israel everything, just as the LORD commanded Moses.

The Law Concerning Vows

30 Then Moses spoke to the heads of the tribes concerning the children of Israel, saying, "This *is* the thing which the LORD has commanded: [2]If a man makes a vow to the LORD, or swears an oath to bind himself by some agreement, he shall not break his word; he shall do according to all that proceeds out of his mouth.

[3]"Or if a woman makes a vow to the LORD,

and binds *herself* by some agreement while in her father's house in her youth, [4]and her father hears her vow and the agreement by which she has bound herself, and her father holds his peace, then all her vows shall stand, and every agreement with which she has bound herself shall stand. [5]But if her father overrules her on the day that he hears, then none of her vows nor her agreements by which she has bound herself shall stand; and the LORD will release her, because her father overruled her.

[6]"If indeed she takes a husband, while bound by her vows or by a rash utterance from her lips by which she bound herself, [7]and her husband hears *it,* and makes no response to her on the day that he hears, then her vows shall stand, and her agreements by which she bound herself shall stand. [8]But if her husband overrules her on the day that he hears *it,* he shall make void her vow which she took and what she uttered with her lips, by which she bound herself, and the LORD will release her.

[9]"Also any vow of a widow or a divorced woman, by which she has bound herself, shall stand against her.

[10]"If she vowed in her husband's house, or bound herself by an agreement with an oath, [11]and her husband heard *it,* and made no response to her *and* did not overrule her, then all her vows shall stand, and every agreement by which she bound herself shall stand. [12]But if her husband truly made them void on the day he heard *them,* then whatever proceeded from her lips concerning her vows or concerning the agreement binding her, it shall not stand; her husband has made them void, and the LORD will release her. [13]Every vow and every binding oath to afflict her soul, her husband may confirm it, or her husband may make it void. [14]Now if her husband makes no response whatever to her from day to day, then he confirms all her vows or all the agreements that bind her; he confirms them, because he made no response to her on the day that he heard *them.* [15]But if he does make them void after he has heard *them,* then he shall bear her guilt."

[16]These *are* the statutes which the LORD commanded Moses, between a man and his wife, and between a father and his daughter in her youth in her father's house.

Vengeance on the Midianites

31 And the LORD spoke to Moses, saying: [2]"Take vengeance on the Midianites for the children of Israel. Afterward you shall be gathered to your people."

[3]So Moses spoke to the people, saying, "Arm some of yourselves for war, and let them go against the Midianites to take vengeance for the LORD on Midian. [4]A thousand from each tribe of all the tribes of Israel you shall send to the war."

[5]So there were recruited from the divisions of Israel one thousand from *each* tribe, twelve thousand armed for war. [6]Then Moses sent them to the war, one thousand from *each* tribe; he sent them to the war with Phinehas the son of Eleazar the priest, with the holy articles and the signal trumpets in his hand. [7]And they warred against the Midianites, just as the LORD commanded Moses, and they killed all the males. [8]They killed the kings of Midian with *the rest of* those who were killed—Evi, Rekem, Zur, Hur, and Reba, the five kings of Midian. Balaam the son of Beor they also killed with the sword.

[9]And the children of Israel took the women of Midian captive, with their little ones, and took as spoil all their cattle, all their flocks, and all their goods. [10]They also burned with fire all the cities where they dwelt, and all their forts. [11]And they took all the spoil and all the booty—of man and beast.

Return from the War

[12]Then they brought the captives, the booty, and the spoil to Moses, to Eleazar the priest, and to the congregation of the children of Israel, to the camp in the plains of Moab by the Jordan, *across from* Jericho. [13]And Moses, Eleazar the priest, and all the leaders of the congregation, went to meet them outside the camp. [14]But Moses was angry with the officers of the army, *with* the captains over thousands and captains over hundreds, who had come from the battle.

[15]And Moses said to them: "Have you kept all the women alive? [16]Look, these *women* caused the children of Israel, through the counsel of Balaam, to trespass against the LORD in the incident of Peor, and there was a plague among the congregation of the LORD. [17]Now therefore, kill every male among the little ones, and kill every woman who has known a man intimately. [18]But keep alive for yourselves all the young girls who have not known a man intimately. [19]And as for you, remain outside the camp seven days; whoever has killed any person, and whoever has touched any slain, purify yourselves and your captives on the third day and on the seventh day. [20]Purify every garment, everything made of leather, everything woven of goats' *hair,* and everything made of wood."

[21]Then Eleazar the priest said to the men of war who had gone to the battle, "This *is* the ordinance of the law which the LORD commanded Moses: [22]Only the gold, the silver, the bronze,

the iron, the tin, and the lead, 23everything that can endure fire, you shall put through the fire, and it shall be clean; and it shall be purified with the water of purification. But all that cannot endure fire you shall put through water. 24And you shall wash your clothes on the seventh day and be clean, and afterward you may come into the camp."

Division of the Plunder

25Now the LORD spoke to Moses, saying: 26"Count up the plunder that was taken—of man and beast—you and Eleazar the priest and the chief fathers of the congregation; 27and divide the plunder into two parts, between those who took part in the war, who went out to battle, and all the congregation. 28And levy a tribute for the LORD on the men of war who went out to battle: one of every five hundred of the persons, the cattle, the donkeys, and the sheep; 29take it from their half, and give it to Eleazar the priest as a heave offering to the LORD. 30And from the children of Israel's half you shall take one of every fifty, drawn from the persons, the cattle, the donkeys, and the sheep, from all the livestock, and give them to the Levites who keep charge of the tabernacle of the LORD." 31So Moses and Eleazar the priest did as the LORD commanded Moses.

32The booty remaining from the plunder, which the men of war had taken, was six hundred and seventy-five thousand sheep, 33seventy-two thousand cattle, 34sixty-one thousand donkeys, 35and thirty-two thousand persons in all, of women who had not known a man intimately. 36And the half, the portion for those who had gone out to war, was in number three hundred and thirty-seven thousand five hundred sheep; 37and the LORD's tribute of the sheep was six hundred and seventy-five. 38The cattle were thirty-six thousand, of which the LORD's tribute was seventy-two. 39The donkeys were thirty thousand five hundred, of which the LORD's tribute was sixty-one. 40The persons were sixteen thousand, of which the LORD's tribute was thirty-two persons. 41So Moses gave the tribute which was the LORD's heave offering to Eleazar the priest, as the LORD commanded Moses.

42And from the children of Israel's half, which Moses separated from the men who fought— 43now the half belonging to the congregation was three hundred and thirty-seven thousand five hundred sheep, 44thirty-six thousand cattle, 45thirty thousand five hundred donkeys, 46and sixteen thousand persons— 47and from the children of Israel's half Moses took one of every fifty, drawn from man and beast, and gave them to the

Levites, who kept charge of the tabernacle of the LORD, as the LORD commanded Moses.

48Then the officers who were over thousands of the army, the captains of thousands and captains of hundreds, came near to Moses; 49and they said to Moses, "Your servants have taken a count of the men of war who are under our command, and not a man of us is missing. 50Therefore we have brought an offering for the LORD, what every man found of ornaments of gold: armlets and bracelets and signet rings and earrings and necklaces, to make atonement for ourselves before the LORD." 51So Moses and Eleazar the priest received the gold from them, all the fashioned ornaments. 52And all the gold of the offering that they offered to the LORD, from the captains of thousands and captains of hundreds, was sixteen thousand seven hundred and fifty shekels. 53(The men of war had taken spoil, every man for himself.) 54And Moses and Eleazar the priest received the gold from the captains of thousands and of hundreds, and brought it into the tabernacle of meeting as a memorial for the children of Israel before the LORD.

The Tribes Settling East of the Jordan

32 Now the children of Reuben and the children of Gad had a very great multitude of livestock; and when they saw the land of Jazer and the land of Gilead, that indeed the region was a place for livestock, 2the children of Gad and the children of Reuben came and spoke to Moses, to Eleazar the priest, and to the leaders of the congregation, saying, 3"Ataroth, Dibon, Jazer, Nimrah, Heshbon, Elealeh, Shebam, Nebo, and Beon, 4the country which the LORD defeated before the congregation of Israel, is a land for livestock, and your servants have livestock." 5Therefore they said, "If we have found favor in your sight, let this land be given to your servants as a possession. Do not take us over the Jordan."

6And Moses said to the children of Gad and to the children of Reuben: "Shall your brethren go to war while you sit here? 7Now why will you discourage the heart of the children of Israel from going over into the land which the LORD has given them? 8Thus your fathers did when I sent them away from Kadesh Barnea to see the land. 9For when they went up to the Valley of Eshcol and saw the land, they discouraged the heart of the children of Israel, so that they did not go into the land which the LORD had given them. 10So the LORD's anger was aroused on that day, and He swore an oath, saying, 11"Surely none of the men who came up from Egypt, from twenty years old and above, shall see the land of which I swore to Abraham, Isaac, and Jacob, because they have not wholly followed Me, [12]except Caleb the son of Jephunneh, the Kenizzite, and Joshua the son of Nun, for they have wholly followed the LORD.' [13]So the LORD's anger was aroused against Israel, and He made them wander in the wilderness forty years, until all the generation that had done evil in the sight of the LORD was gone. [14]And look! You have risen in your fathers' place, a brood of sinful men, to increase still more the fierce anger of the LORD against Israel. [15]For if you turn away from following Him, He will once again leave them in the wilderness, and you will destroy all these people."

[16]Then they came near to him and said: "We will build sheepfolds here for our livestock, and cities for our little ones, [17]but we ourselves will be armed, ready *to go* before the children of Israel until we have brought them to their place; and our little ones will dwell in the fortified cities because of the inhabitants of the land. [18]We will not return to our homes until every one of the children of Israel has received his inheritance. [19]For we will not inherit with them on the other side of the Jordan and beyond, because our inheritance has fallen to us on this eastern side of the Jordan."

[20]Then Moses said to them: "If you do this thing, if you arm yourselves before the LORD for the war, [21]and all your armed men cross over the Jordan before the LORD until He has driven out His enemies from before Him, [22]and the land is subdued before the LORD, then afterward you may return and be blameless before the LORD and before Israel; and this land shall be your possession before the LORD. [23]But if you do not do so, then take note, you have sinned against the LORD; and be sure your sin will find you out. [24]Build cities for your little ones and folds for your sheep, and do what has proceeded out of your mouth."

[25]And the children of Gad and the children of Reuben spoke to Moses, saying: "Your servants will do as my lord commands. [26]Our little ones, our wives, our flocks, and all our livestock will be there in the cities of Gilead; [27]but your servants will cross over, every man armed for war, before the LORD to battle, just as my lord says."

[28]So Moses gave command concerning them to Eleazar the priest, to Joshua the son of Nun, and to the chief fathers of the tribes of the children of Israel. [29]And Moses said to them: "If the children of Gad and the children of Reuben cross over the Jordan with you, every man armed for battle before the LORD, and the land is sub-

dued before you, then you shall give them the land of Gilead as a possession. [30]But if they do not cross over armed with you, they shall have possessions among you in the land of Canaan."

[31]Then the children of Gad and the children of Reuben answered, saying: "As the LORD has said to your servants, so we will do. [32]We will cross over armed before the LORD into the land of Canaan, but the possession of our inheritance *shall remain* with us on this side of the Jordan."

[33]So Moses gave to the children of Gad, to the children of Reuben, and to half the tribe of Manasseh the son of Joseph, the kingdom of Sihon king of the Amorites and the kingdom of Og king of Bashan, the land with its cities within the borders, the cities of the surrounding country. [34]And the children of Gad built Dibon and Ataroth and Aroer, [35]Atroth and Shophan and Jazer and Jogbehah, [36]Beth Nimrah and Beth Haran, fortified cities, and folds for sheep. [37]And the children of Reuben built Heshbon and Elealeh and Kirjathaim, [38]Nebo and Baal Meon (*their* names being changed) and Shibmah; and they gave *other* names to the cities which they built.

[39]And the children of Machir the son of Manasseh went to Gilead and took it, and dispossessed the Amorites who *were* in it. [40]So Moses gave Gilead to Machir the son of Manasseh, and he dwelt in it. [41]Also Jair the son of Manasseh went and took its small towns, and called them Havoth Jair.[a] [42]Then Nobah went and took Kenath and its villages, and he called it Nobah, after his own name.

Israel's Journey from Egypt Reviewed

33 These *are* the journeys of the children of Israel, who went out of the land of Egypt by their armies under the hand of Moses and Aaron. [2]Now Moses wrote down the starting points of their journeys at the command of the LORD. And these *are* their journeys according to their starting points:

[3]They departed from Rameses in the first month, on the fifteenth day of the first month; on the day after the Passover the children of Israel went out with boldness in the sight of all the Egyptians. [4]For the Egyptians were burying all *their* firstborn, whom the LORD had killed among them. Also on their gods the LORD had executed judgments.

[5]Then the children of Israel moved from Rameses and camped at Succoth. [6]They departed from Succoth and camped at Etham, which *is* on

---

32:41 [a]Literally *Towns of Jair*

the edge of the wilderness. [7]They moved from Etham and turned back to Pi Hahiroth, which *is* east of Baal Zephon; and they camped near Migdol. [8]They departed from before Hahiroth[a] and passed through the midst of the sea into the wilderness, went three days' journey in the Wilderness of Etham, and camped at Marah. [9]They moved from Marah and came to Elim. At Elim *were* twelve springs of water and seventy palm trees; so they camped there.

[10]They moved from Elim and camped by the Red Sea. [11]They moved from the Red Sea and camped in the Wilderness of Sin. [12]They journeyed from the Wilderness of Sin and camped at Dophkah. [13]They departed from Dophkah and camped at Alush. [14]They moved from Alush and camped at Rephidim, where there was no water for the people to drink.

[15]They departed from Rephidim and camped in the Wilderness of Sinai. [16]They moved from the Wilderness of Sinai and camped at Kibroth Hattaavah. [17]They departed from Kibroth Hattaavah and camped at Hazeroth. [18]They departed from Hazeroth and camped at Rithmah. [19]They departed from Rithmah and camped at Rimmon Perez. [20]They departed from Rimmon Perez and camped at Libnah. [21]They moved from Libnah and camped at Rissah. [22]They journeyed from Rissah and camped at Kehelathah. [23]They went from Kehelathah and camped at Mount Shepher. [24]They moved from Mount Shepher and camped at Haradah. [25]They moved from Haradah and camped at Makheloth. [26]They moved from Makheloth and camped at Tahath. [27]They departed from Tahath and camped at Terah. [28]They moved from Terah and camped at Mithkah. [29]They went from Mithkah and camped at Hashmonah. [30]They departed from Hashmonah and camped at Moseroth. [31]They departed from Moseroth and camped at Bene Jaakan. [32]They moved from Bene Jaakan and camped at Hor Hagidgad. [33]They went from Hor Hagidgad and camped at Jotbathah. [34]They moved from Jotbathah and camped at Abronah. [35]They departed from Abronah and camped at Ezion Geber. [36]They moved from Ezion Geber and camped in the Wilderness of Zin, which *is* Kadesh. [37]They moved from Kadesh and camped at Mount Hor, on the boundary of the land of Edom.

[38]Then Aaron the priest went up to Mount Hor at the command of the LORD, and died there in the fortieth year after the children of Israel had come out of the land of Egypt, on the first *day* of the fifth month. [39]Aaron *was* one hundred and twenty-three years old when he died on Mount Hor.

[40]Now the king of Arad, the Canaanite, who dwelt in the South in the land of Canaan, heard of the coming of the children of Israel.

[41]So they departed from Mount Hor and camped at Zalmonah. [42]They departed from Zalmonah and camped at Punon. [43]They departed from Punon and camped at Oboth. [44]They departed from Oboth and camped at Ije Abarim, at the border of Moab. [45]They departed from Ijim[a] and camped at Dibon Gad. [46]They moved from Dibon Gad and camped at Almon Diblathaim. [47]They moved from Almon Diblathaim and camped in the mountains of Abarim, before Nebo. [48]They departed from the mountains of Abarim and camped in the plains of Moab by the Jordan, *across from* Jericho. [49]They camped by the Jordan, from Beth Jesimoth as far as the Abel Acacia Grove[a] in the plains of Moab.

Instructions for the Conquest of Canaan

[50]Now the LORD spoke to Moses in the plains of Moab by the Jordan, *across from* Jericho, saying, [51]"Speak to the children of Israel, and say to them: 'When you have crossed the Jordan into the land of Canaan, [52]then you shall drive out all the inhabitants of the land from before you, destroy all their engraved stones, destroy all their molded images, and demolish all their high places; [53]you shall dispossess *the inhabitants of* the land and dwell in it, for I have given you the land to possess. [54]And you shall divide the land by lot as an inheritance among your families; to the larger you shall give a larger inheritance, and to the smaller you shall give a smaller inheritance; there everyone's *inheritance* shall be whatever falls to him by lot. You shall inherit according to the tribes of your fathers. [55]But if you do not drive out the inhabitants of the land from before you, then it shall be that those whom you let remain *shall be* irritants in your eyes and thorns in your sides, and they shall harass you in the land where you dwell. [56]Moreover it shall be *that* I will do to you as I thought to do to them.'"

The Appointed Boundaries of Canaan

34 Then the LORD spoke to Moses, saying, [2]"Command the children of Israel, and say to them: 'When you come into the land of Canaan, this *is* the land that shall fall to you as an inheritance—the land of Canaan to its boundaries. [3]Your southern

33:8 [a]Many Hebrew manuscripts, Samaritan Pentateuch, Syriac, Targum, and Vulgate read *from Pi Hahiroth* (compare verse 7). 33:45 [a]Same as *Ije Abarim*, verse 44 33:49 [a]Hebrew *Abel Shittim*

21 QUALITIES

SELF-DISCIPLINE

Travel on the Inside First

(Numbers 33:1–49)

We must travel on the inside before we can travel on the outside, because the journey of growth and success is first an internal one. The first person you lead is *you*—and you can't lead effectively without self-discipline.

If only the Israelites had remembered this lesson! Numbers 33 provides a review of the entire exodus journey, from Egypt to Jordan. And, boy, was it ever a journey! Tons of manna. Far too much grumbling. And it lasted 40 years.

Why didn't the Israelites get to the Promised Land more quickly? Not because it lay so far away; they could have made the trip in two weeks. The real reason boils down to preparation. The people simply weren't ready for God's blessing until 40 years after they began their trip.

How about you? How is your self-discipline? Plato said, "The first and best victory is to conquer self." If you want to be a leader with self-discipline, follow these action points:

1. *Develop and follow your priorities.*

All leaders are pressed for time, but the successful ones have a plan. If you can determine what's really a priority and release yourself from everything else, it will be much easier to follow through on what's important. That's the essence of self-discipline.

2. *Make a disciplined lifestyle your goal.*

To be successful, self-discipline can't be a one-time event. It has to become a lifestyle. One of the best ways to nurture such a lifestyle is to develop systems and routines, especially in areas crucial to your long-term growth and success. Once you have them, put them to use every day for the rest of your life.

3. *Challenge your excuses.*

Challenge and eliminate any tendency you may have to make excuses. If you can name several reasons why you can't be self-disciplined, realize that they are really just barriers to your success—all of which need to be challenged if you want to go to the next level.

4. *Remove rewards until you finish the job.*

If you lack self-discipline, you may be in the habit of enjoying dessert before eating your vegetables. Mike Delaney offered good counsel: He said that businesses need to differentiate between their shirkers and their workers, because if they reward both the same, they'll soon find they have a lot more of the former than the lattter!

5. *Stay focused on results.*

Anytime you concentrate on the difficulty of the work instead of its results, you're likely to become discouraged. The next time you're facing a must-do task and you're thinking of doing what's convenient instead of paying the price, change your focus. Count the benefits of doing what's right, and then dive in.

For a negative example of self-discipline, see p. 299.

border shall be from the Wilderness of Zin along the border of Edom; then your southern border shall extend eastward to the end of the Salt Sea; ⁴your border shall turn from the southern side of the Ascent of Akrabbim, continue to Zin, and be on the south of Kadesh Barnea; then it shall go on to Hazar Addar, and continue to Azmon; ⁵the border shall turn from Azmon to the Brook of Egypt, and it shall end at the Sea.

⁶"As for the western border, you shall have the Great Sea for a border; this shall be your western border.

⁷"And this shall be your northern border: From the Great Sea you shall mark out your *border* line to Mount Hor; ⁸from Mount Hor you shall mark out *your border* to the entrance of Hamath; then the direction of the border shall be toward Zedad; ⁹the border shall proceed to Ziphron, and it shall end at Hazar Enan. This shall be your northern border.

¹⁰"You shall mark out your eastern border from Hazar Enan to Shepham; ¹¹the border shall go down from Shepham to Riblah on the east side of Ain; the border shall go down and reach to the eastern side of the Sea of Chinnereth; ¹²the border shall go down along the Jordan, and it shall end at the Salt Sea. This shall be your land with its surrounding boundaries.' "

¹³Then Moses commanded the children of Israel, saying: "This *is* the land which you shall inherit by lot, which the LORD has commanded to give to the nine tribes and to the half-tribe. ¹⁴For the tribe of the children of Reuben according to the house of their fathers, and the tribe of the children of Gad according to the house of their fathers, have received *their inheritance;* and the half-tribe of Manasseh has received its inheritance. ¹⁵The two tribes and the half-tribe have received their inheritance on this side of the Jordan, *across from* Jericho eastward, toward the sunrise."

The Leaders Appointed to Divide the Land

¹⁶And the LORD spoke to Moses, saying, ¹⁷"These *are* the names of the men who shall divide the land among you as an inheritance: Eleazar the priest and Joshua the son of Nun. ¹⁸And you shall take one leader of every tribe to divide the land for the inheritance. ¹⁹These *are* the names of the men: from the tribe of Judah, Caleb the son of Jephunneh; ²⁰from the tribe of the children of Simeon, Shemuel the son of Ammihud; ²¹from the tribe of Benjamin, Elidad the son of Chislon; ²²a leader from the tribe of the children of Dan, Bukki the son of Jogli; ²³from

the sons of Joseph: a leader from the tribe of the children of Manasseh, Hanniel the son of Ephod, ²⁴and a leader from the tribe of the children of Ephraim, Kemuel the son of Shiphtan; ²⁵a leader from the tribe of the children of Zebulun, Elizaphan the son of Parnach; ²⁶a leader from the tribe of the children of Issachar, Paltiel the son of Azzan; ²⁷a leader from the tribe of the children of Asher, Ahihud the son of Shelomi; ²⁸and a leader from the tribe of the children of Naphtali, Pedahel the son of Ammihud."

²⁹These *are* the ones the LORD commanded to divide the inheritance among the children of Israel in the land of Canaan.

Cities for the Levites

35 And the LORD spoke to Moses in the plains of Moab by the Jordan *across from* Jericho, saying: ²"Command the children of Israel that they give the Levites cities to dwell in from the inheritance of their possession, and you shall *also* give the Levites common-land around the cities. ³They shall have the cities to dwell in; and their common-land shall be for their cattle, for their herds, and for all their animals. ⁴The common-land of the cities which you will give the Levites *shall extend* from the wall of the city outward a thousand cubits all around. ⁵And you shall measure outside the city on the east side two thousand cubits, on the south side two thousand cubits, on the west side two thousand cubits, and on the north side two thousand cubits. The city *shall be* in the middle. This shall belong to them as common-land for the cities.

⁶"Now among the cities which you will give to the Levites *you shall appoint* six cities of refuge, to which a manslayer may flee. And to these you shall add forty-two cities. ⁷So all the cities you will give to the Levites *shall be* forty-eight; these *you shall give* with their common-land. ⁸And the cities which you will give *shall be* from the possession of the children of Israel; from the larger *tribe* you shall give many, from the smaller you shall give few. Each shall give some of its cities to the Levites, in proportion to the inheritance that each receives."

Cities of Refuge

⁹Then the LORD spoke to Moses, saying, ¹⁰"Speak to the children of Israel, and say to them: 'When you cross the Jordan into the land of Canaan, ¹¹then you shall appoint cities to be cities of refuge for you, that the manslayer who kills any person accidentally may flee there. ¹²They shall be cities of refuge for you from the

avenger, that the manslayer may not die until he stands before the congregation in judgment. [13]And of the cities which you give, you shall have six cities of refuge. [14]You shall appoint three cities on this side of the Jordan, and three cities you shall appoint in the land of Canaan, *which* will be cities of refuge. [15]These six cities shall be for refuge for the children of Israel, for the stranger, and for the sojourner among them, that anyone who kills a person accidentally may flee there.

[16]"But if he strikes him with an iron implement, so that he dies, he *is* a murderer; the murderer shall surely be put to death. [17]And if he strikes him with a stone in the hand, by which one could die, and he does die, he *is* a murderer; the murderer shall surely be put to death. [18]Or *if* he strikes him with a wooden hand weapon, by which one could die, and he does die, he *is* a murderer; the murderer shall surely be put to death. [19]The avenger of blood himself shall put the murderer to death; when he meets him, he shall put him to death. [20]If he pushes him out of hatred or, while lying in wait, hurls something at him so that he dies, [21]or in enmity he strikes him with his hand so that he dies, the one who struck *him* shall surely be put to death. He *is* a murderer. The avenger of blood shall put the murderer to death when he meets him.

[22]"However, if he pushes him suddenly without enmity, or throws anything at him without lying in wait, [23]or uses a stone, by which a man could die, throwing *it* at him without seeing *him,* so that he dies, while he was not his enemy or seeking his harm, [24]then the congregation shall judge between the manslayer and the avenger of blood according to these judgments. [25]So the congregation shall deliver the manslayer from the hand of the avenger of blood, and the congregation shall return him to the city of refuge where he had fled, and he shall remain there until the death of the high priest who was anointed with the holy oil. [26]But if the manslayer at any time goes outside the limits of the city of refuge where he fled, [27]and the avenger of blood finds him outside the limits of his city of refuge, and the avenger of blood kills the manslayer, he shall not be guilty of blood, [28]because he should have remained in his city of refuge until the death of the high priest. But after the death of the high priest the manslayer may return to the land of his possession.

[29]"And these *things* shall be a statute of judgment to you throughout your generations in all your dwellings. [30]Whoever kills a person, the murderer shall be put to death on the testimony of witnesses; but one witness is not *sufficient* testimony against a person for the death *penalty.* [31]Moreover you shall take no ransom for the life of a murderer who *is* guilty of death, but he shall surely be put to death. [32]And you shall take no ransom for him who has fled to his city of refuge, that he may return to dwell in the land before the death of the priest. [33]So you shall not pollute the land where you *are;* for blood defiles the land, and no atonement can be made for the land, for the blood that is shed on it, except by the blood of him who shed it. [34]Therefore do not defile the land which you inhabit, in the midst of which I dwell; for I the LORD dwell among the children of Israel.'"

Marriage of Female Heirs

36 Now the chief fathers of the families of the children of Gilead the son of Machir, the son of Manasseh, of the families of the sons of Joseph, came near and spoke before Moses and before the leaders, the chief fathers of the children of Israel. [2]And they said: "The LORD commanded my lord *Moses* to give the land as an inheritance by lot to the children of Israel, and my lord was commanded by the LORD to give the inheritance of our brother Zelophehad to his daughters. [3]Now if they are married to any of the sons of the *other* tribes of the children of Israel, then their inheritance will be taken from the inheritance of our fathers, and it will be added to the inheritance of the tribe into which they marry; so it will be taken from the lot of our inheritance. [4]And when the Jubilee of the children of Israel comes, then their inheritance will be added to the inheritance of the tribe into which they marry; so their inheritance will be taken away from the inheritance of the tribe of our fathers."

[5]Then Moses commanded the children of Israel according to the word of the LORD, saying: "What the tribe of the sons of Joseph speaks is right. [6]This *is* what the LORD commands concerning the daughters of Zelophehad, saying, 'Let them marry whom they think best, but they may marry only within the family of their father's tribe.' [7]So the inheritance of the children of Israel shall not change hands from tribe to tribe, for every one of the children of Israel shall keep the inheritance of the tribe of his fathers. [8]And every daughter who possesses an inheritance in any tribe of the children of Israel shall be the wife of one of the family of her father's tribe, so that the children of Israel each may possess the inheritance of his fathers. [9]Thus no inheritance shall change hands from *one* tribe to another, but

every tribe of the children of Israel shall keep its own inheritance."

[10] Just as the LORD commanded Moses, so did the daughters of Zelophehad; [11] for Mahlah, Tirzah, Hoglah, Milcah, and Noah, the daughters of Zelophehad, were married to the sons of their father's brothers. [12] They were married into the families of the children of Manasseh the son of Joseph, and their inheritance remained in the tribe of their father's family.

[13] These *are* the commandments and the judgments which the LORD commanded the children of Israel by the hand of Moses in the plains of Moab by the Jordan, *across from* Jericho.

DEUTERONOMY

A Stand-Alone Book on Leadership

SUMMARY

Consider Deuteronomy a stand-alone book on leadership.

It is more, of course, but Deuteronomy is largely the story of a leader, Moses, who challenges a new generation to embrace and implement a God-given vision for the Promised Land. Early on, Moses says, "Go in and possess the land of which the LORD swore to your fathers" (8:1).

The book tells the story of a leader yearning to finish the work he had begun. Moses casts the vision over and over, hoping his people would catch sight of the total picture—namely, that God did not want merely to free them from slavery in Egypt, but to deliver them into the Promised Land. Hear a key verse in Deuteronomy: "He brought us out from there, that He might bring us in, to give us the land of which He swore to our fathers" (6:23).

Deuteronomy begins with Moses recounting all that had happened to the nation. He reminds the people how God had chosen key leaders and placed them over each of the tribes; how He had patiently endured their strife and complaints through 40 years of wandering in the wilderness; how God had led them in conquest over their enemies; and how He had repeated the Ten Commandments to them. Now it was time for this new generation to affirm God's laws, just as their parents had. Although Moses lost his chance to enter the land with them, he patiently interceded for this new generation, trying to lead them into the obedient state that would enable them to inherit the land and finish the conquest.

Deuteronomy consists chiefly of three visionary messages Moses delivered to all Israel, just before he died. His words lead the people to a crossroads at which they must decide their future. Like any good leader, Moses can see the options before the nation and he spells them out in his closing years. It's remarkable how this man, who claimed not to be a good communicator (Ex. 4:10), now casts a clear vision for thousands of Israelites about to end their wandering in the desert! Moses dies at the end of the book, but not before preparing an apprentice, Joshua, to take over and finish the journey into Canaan.

God's Role in Deuteronomy

God promised to Abraham, Isaac, and Jacob that He would make them into a great nation. God uses Moses to fulfill that promise. The events recounted in this book fulfill the original promise to build the descendants of Abraham into a nation of people more numerous than the stars in the sky (Gen. 12:2, 3; Deut. 1:10). God leads Moses, who in turn leads the people to the border of the Promised Land.

Like a brilliant military commander addressing his troops, God displays powerful leadership by steadying His people and readying them for the conquest. He casts vision, providing fresh perspective, provision, purpose, and principles to guide the Israelites. In the very first chapter of the book, God prepares His children to:

1. See the land (*vision*, 1:6–8).
2. Share the load (*delegation*, 1:9–14).
3. Select the leaders (*leadership*, 1:15).
4. Structure the leadership (*organization*, 1:16–18).

Leaders in Deuteronomy

Moses, Joshua

Other People of Influence in Deuteronomy

Canaanites, Hittites, Girgashites, Amorites, Perizzites, Hivites, Jebusites

Lessons in Leadership

- Develop your core values and beliefs before taking new territory.
- Leadership must be proactive, not reactive.
- Activity does not equal accomplishment.
- Leaders must share the benefits of buying into the vision.
- Leaders must constantly remind the people of the vision.
- One person with courage makes a majority.
- The leader must first intercede for the people.
- Leaders must provide for the future, even when they don't get to experience it.

LEADERSHIP HIGHLIGHTS IN DEUTERONOMY

The Previous Command to Enter Canaan

1 These *are* the words which Moses spoke to all Israel on this side of the Jordan in the wilderness, in the plain[a] opposite Suph,[b] between Paran, Tophel, Laban, Hazeroth, and Dizahab. [2]*It is* eleven days' *journey* from Horeb by way of Mount Seir to Kadesh Barnea. [3]Now it came to pass in the fortieth year, in the eleventh month, on the first *day* of the month, *that* Moses spoke to the children of Israel according to all that the LORD had given him as commandments to them, [4]after he had killed Sihon king of the Amorites, who dwelt in Heshbon, and Og king of Bashan, who dwelt at Ashtaroth in[a] Edrei.

[5]On this side of the Jordan in the land of Moab, Moses began to explain this law, saying, [6]"The LORD our God spoke to us in Horeb, saying: 'You have dwelt long enough at this mountain. [7]Turn and take your journey, and go to the mountains of the Amorites, to all the neighboring *places* in the plain,[a] in the mountains and in the lowland, in the South and on the seacoast, to the land of the Canaanites and to Lebanon, as far as the great river, the River Euphrates. [8]See, I have set the land before you; go in and possess the land which the LORD swore to your fathers—to Abraham, Isaac, and Jacob—to give to them and their descendants after them.'

Tribal Leaders Appointed

[9]"And I spoke to you at that time, saying: 'I alone am not able to bear you. [10]The LORD your God has multiplied you, and here you *are* today, as the stars of heaven in multitude. [11]May the LORD God of your fathers make you a thousand times more numerous than you are, and bless you as He has promised you! [12]How can I alone bear your problems and your burdens and your complaints? [13]Choose wise, understanding, and knowledgeable men from among your tribes, and I will make them heads over you.' [14]And you answered me and said, 'The thing which you have told *us* to do *is* good.' [15]So I took the heads of your tribes, wise and knowledgeable men, and made them heads over you, leaders of thousands, leaders of hundreds, leaders of fifties, leaders of tens, and officers for your tribes.

[16]"Then I commanded your judges at that time, saying, 'Hear *the cases* between your

---

1:1 [a]Hebrew *arabah* [b]One manuscript of the Septuagint, also Targum and Vulgate, read *Red Sea*. **1:4** [a]Septuagint, Syriac, and Vulgate read *and* (compare Joshua 12:4). **1:7** [a]Hebrew *arabah*

The Law of the Inner Circle

(Deuteronomy 1:6–18)

The people closest to us determine our level of success. Moses learned this lesson in the wilderness and so implemented a plan to put competent, godly leaders next to him.

When ministers decide to be leaders, they cross a very important line. They no longer judge themselves solely by what they can do themselves; their value depends mainly on what they can get done through others. Moses teaches us that leaders must:

1. See the Land: Vision (vv. 6–8)

Moses saw and reminded everyone of the Lord's faithfulness. God *would* fulfill His promise. Moses could clearly see the outcome, and he motivated others by his vision.

2. Share the Load: Delegation (vv. 9–12)

Moses chose to set his ego aside and share his leadership responsibilities with others. He would give them both the responsibility and authority to do the work; the task now became a team effort.

3. Select the Leaders: Leadership (vv. 13–15)

Moses chose his inner circle from among the spiritually qualified, approved, and appointed according to their abilities.

4. Structure the Leadership: Organization (vv. 16–18)

Moses established a system in which the leaders were to listen fairly, minister boldly, make decisions based on principle, and refer the most difficult cases to him.

brethren, and judge righteously between a man and his brother or the stranger who is with him. [17]You shall not show partiality in judgment; you shall hear the small as well as the great; you shall not be afraid in any man's presence, for the judgment *is* God's. The case that is too hard for you, bring to me, and I will hear it.' [18]And I commanded you at that time all the things which you should do.

Israel's Refusal to Enter the Land

[19]"So we departed from Horeb, and went through all that great and terrible wilderness which you saw on the way to the mountains of the Amorites, as the LORD our God had commanded us. Then we came to Kadesh Barnea. [20]And I said to you, 'You have come to the mountains of the Amorites, which the LORD our God is giving us. [21]Look, the LORD your God has set the land before you; go up *and* possess *it*, as the LORD God of your fathers has spoken to you; do not fear or be discouraged.'

[22]"And every one of you came near to me and said, 'Let us send men before us, and let them search out the land for us, and bring back word to us of the way by which we should go up, and of the cities into which we shall come.'

[23]"The plan pleased me well; so I took twelve of your men, one man from *each* tribe. [24]And they departed and went up into the mountains, and came to the Valley of Eshcol, and spied it out. [25]They also took *some* of the fruit of the land in their hands and brought *it* down to us; and they brought back word to us, saying, '*It is* a good land which the LORD our God is giving us.'

[26]"Nevertheless you would not go up, but rebelled against the command of the LORD your God; [27]and you complained in your tents, and said, 'Because the LORD hates us, He has brought us out of the land of Egypt to deliver us into the hand of the Amorites, to destroy us. [28]Where can we go up? Our brethren have discouraged our hearts, saying, "The people *are* greater and taller than we; the cities *are* great and fortified up to heaven; moreover we have seen the sons of the Anakim there."'

[29]"Then I said to you, 'Do not be terrified, or afraid of them. [30]The LORD your God, who goes before you, He will fight for you, according to all He did for you in Egypt before your eyes, [31]and in the wilderness where you saw how the LORD your God carried you, as a man carries his son, in all the way that you went until you came to this place.' [32]Yet, for all that, you did not believe the LORD your God, [33]who went in the way before you to search out a place for you to pitch your tents, to show you the way you should go, in the fire by night and in the cloud by day.

The Penalty for Israel's Rebellion

[34]"And the LORD heard the sound of your words, and was angry, and took an oath, saying, [35]'Surely not one of these men of this evil generation shall see that good land of which I swore to give to your fathers, [36]except Caleb the son of Jephunneh; he shall see it, and to him and his children I am giving the land on which he walked, because he wholly followed the LORD.' [37]The LORD was also angry with me for your sakes, saying, 'Even you shall not go in there. [38]Joshua the son of Nun, who stands before you, he shall go in there. Encourage him, for he shall cause Israel to inherit it.

[39]"Moreover your little ones and your children, who you say will be victims, who today have no knowledge of good and evil, they shall go in there; to them I will give it, and they shall possess it. [40]But *as for* you, turn and take your journey into the wilderness by the Way of the Red Sea.'

[41]"Then you answered and said to me, 'We have sinned against the LORD; we will go up and fight, just as the LORD our God commanded us.' And when everyone of you had girded on his weapons of war, you were ready to go up into the mountain.

[42]"And the LORD said to me, 'Tell them, "Do not go up nor fight, for I *am* not among you; lest you be defeated before your enemies."' [43]So I spoke to you; yet you would not listen, but rebelled against the command of the LORD, and presumptuously went up into the mountain. [44]And the Amorites who dwelt in that mountain came out against you and chased you as bees do, and drove you back from Seir to Hormah. [45]Then you returned and wept before the LORD, but the LORD would not listen to your voice nor give ear to you.

[46]"So you remained in Kadesh many days, according to the days that you spent *there*.

The Desert Years

2 "Then we turned and journeyed into the wilderness of the Way of the Red Sea, as the LORD spoke to me, and we skirted Mount Seir for many days.

[2]"And the LORD spoke to me, saying: [3]'You have skirted this mountain long enough; turn northward. [4]And command the people, saying, "You *are about to* pass through the territory of your brethren, the descendants of Esau, who live in Seir; and they will be afraid of you. Therefore

watch yourselves carefully. [5]Do not meddle with them, for I will not give you *any* of their land, no, not so much as one footstep, because I have given Mount Seir to Esau *as* a possession. [6]You shall buy food from them with money, that you may eat; and you shall also buy water from them with money, that you may drink.

[7]"For the LORD your God has blessed you in all the work of your hand. He knows your trudging through this great wilderness. These forty years the LORD your God *has been* with you; you have lacked nothing."'

[8]"And when we passed beyond our brethren, the descendants of Esau who dwell in Seir, away from the road of the plain, away from Elath and Ezion Geber, we turned and passed by way of the Wilderness of Moab. [9]Then the LORD said to me, 'Do not harass Moab, nor contend with them in battle, for I will not give you *any* of their land *as* a possession, because I have given Ar to the descendants of Lot *as* a possession.'"

[10](The Emim had dwelt there in times past, a people as great and numerous and tall as the Anakim. [11]They were also regarded as giants,[a] like the Anakim, but the Moabites call them Emim. [12]The Horites formerly dwelt in Seir, but the descendants of Esau dispossessed them and destroyed them from before them, and dwelt in their place, just as Israel did to the land of their possession which the LORD gave them.)

[13]"'Now rise and cross over the Valley of the Zered.' So we crossed over the Valley of the Zered. [14]And the time we took to come from Kadesh Barnea until we crossed over the Valley of the Zered *was* thirty-eight years, until all the generation of the men of war was consumed from the midst of the camp, just as the LORD had sworn to them. [15]For indeed the hand of the LORD was against them, to destroy them from the midst of the camp until they were consumed.

[16]"So it was, when all the men of war had finally perished from among the people, [17]that the LORD spoke to me, saying: [18]'This day you are to cross over at Ar, the boundary of Moab. [19]And *when* you come near the people of Ammon, do not harass them or meddle with them, for I will not give you *any* of the land of the people of Ammon *as* a possession, because I have given it to the descendants of Lot *as* a possession.'"

[20](That was also regarded as a land of giants;[a] giants formerly dwelt there. But the Ammonites call them Zamzummim, [21]a people as great and numerous and tall as the Anakim. But the LORD destroyed them before them, and they dispossessed them and dwelt in their place, [22]just as He had done for the descendants of Esau, who dwelt in Seir, when He destroyed the Horites from before them. They dispossessed them and dwelt in their place, even to this day. [23]And the Avim, who dwelt in villages as far as Gaza—the Caphtorim, who came from Caphtor, destroyed them and dwelt in their place.)

[24]"'Rise, take your journey, and cross over the River Arnon. Look, I have given into your hand Sihon the Amorite, king of Heshbon, and his land. Begin to possess *it,* and engage him in battle. [25]This day I will begin to put the dread and fear of you upon the nations under the whole heaven, who shall hear the report of you, and shall tremble and be in anguish because of you.'

King Sihon Defeated

[26]"And I sent messengers from the Wilderness of Kedemoth to Sihon king of Heshbon, with words of peace, saying, [27]'Let me pass through your land; I will keep strictly to the road, and I will turn neither to the right nor to the left. [28]You shall sell me food for money, that I may eat, and give me water for money, that I may drink; only let me pass through on foot, [29]just as the descendants of Esau who dwell in Seir and the Moabites who dwell in Ar did for me, until I cross the Jordan to the land which the LORD our God is giving us.'

[30]"But Sihon king of Heshbon would not let us pass through, for the LORD your God hardened his spirit and made his heart obstinate, that He might deliver him into your hand, as *it is* this day.

[31]"And the LORD said to me, 'See, I have begun to give Sihon and his land over to you. Begin to possess *it,* that you may inherit his land.' [32]Then Sihon and all his people came out against us to fight at Jahaz. [33]And the LORD our God delivered him over to us; so we defeated him, his sons, and all his people. [34]We took all his cities at that time, and we utterly destroyed the men, women, and little ones of every city; we left none remaining. [35]We took only the livestock as plunder for ourselves, with the spoil of the cities which we took. [36]From Aroer, which *is* on the bank of the River Arnon, and *from* the city that *is* in the ravine, as far as Gilead, there was not one city too strong for us; the LORD our God delivered all to us. [37]Only you did not go near the land of the people of Ammon—anywhere along the River Jabbok, or to the cities of the mountains, or wherever the LORD our God had forbidden us.

2:11 [a]Hebrew *rephaim* **2:20** [a]Hebrew *rephaim*

King Og Defeated

3 "Then we turned and went up the road to Bashan; and Og king of Bashan came out against us, he and all his people, to battle at Edrei. [2]And the LORD said to me, 'Do not fear him, for I have delivered him and all his people and his land into your hand; you shall do to him as you did to Sihon king of the Amorites, who dwelt at Heshbon.'

[3]"So the LORD our God also delivered into our hands Og king of Bashan, with all his people, and we attacked him until he had no survivors remaining. [4]And we took all his cities at that time; there was not a city which we did not take from them: sixty cities, all the region of Argob, the kingdom of Og in Bashan. [5]All these cities *were* fortified with high walls, gates, and bars, besides a great many rural towns. [6]And we utterly destroyed them, as we did to Sihon king of Heshbon, utterly destroying the men, women, and children of every city. [7]But all the livestock and the spoil of the cities we took as booty for ourselves.

The Law of the Big Mo
(Deuteronomy 3:4)

Momentum is a leader's best friend. After defeating the Amorites, the Israelites came to Bashan. God told them to attack. Having tasted military victory already, they didn't hesitate, and once again they triumphed. This led to the defeat of 60 cities in the region. Success breeds success.

[8]"And at that time we took the land from the hand of the two kings of the Amorites who *were* on this side of the Jordan, from the River Arnon to Mount Hermon [9](the Sidonians call Hermon Sirion, and the Amorites call it Senir), [10]all the cities of the plain, all Gilead, and all Bashan, as far as Salcah and Edrei, cities of the kingdom of Og in Bashan.

[11]"For only Og king of Bashan remained of the remnant of the giants.[a] Indeed his bedstead *was* an iron bedstead. (*Is* it not in Rabbah of the people of Ammon?) Nine cubits *is* its length and four cubits its width, according to the standard cubit.

The Land East of the Jordan Divided

[12]"And this land, *which* we possessed at that time, from Aroer, which *is* by the River Arnon,

and half the mountains of Gilead and its cities, I gave to the Reubenites and the Gadites. [13]The rest of Gilead, and all Bashan, the kingdom of Og, I gave to half the tribe of Manasseh. (All the region of Argob, with all Bashan, was called the land of the giants.[a] [14]Jair the son of Manasseh took all the region of Argob, as far as the border of the Geshurites and the Maachathites, and called Bashan after his own name, Havoth Jair,[a] to this day.)

[15]"Also I gave Gilead to Machir. [16]And to the Reubenites and the Gadites I gave from Gilead as far as the River Arnon, the middle of the river as *the* border, as far as the River Jabbok, the border of the people of Ammon; [17]the plain also, with the Jordan as *the* border, from Chinnereth as far as the east side of the Sea of the Arabah (the Salt Sea), below the slopes of Pisgah.

[18]"Then I commanded you at that time, saying: 'The LORD your God has given you this land to possess. All you men of valor shall cross over armed before your brethren, the children of Israel. [19]But your wives, your little ones, and your livestock (I know that you have much livestock) shall stay in your cities which I have given you, [20]until the LORD has given rest to your brethren as to you, and they also possess the land which the LORD your God is giving them beyond the Jordan. Then each of you may return to his possession which I have given you.'

[21]"And I commanded Joshua at that time, saying, 'Your eyes have seen all that the LORD your God has done to these two kings; so will the LORD do to all the kingdoms through which you pass. [22]You must not fear them, for the LORD your God Himself fights for you.'

Moses Forbidden to Enter the Land

[23]"Then I pleaded with the LORD at that time, saying: [24]'O Lord GOD, You have begun to show Your servant Your greatness and Your mighty hand, for what god *is there* in heaven or on earth who can do *anything* like Your works and Your mighty *deeds?* [25]I pray, let me cross over and see the good land beyond the Jordan, those pleasant mountains, and Lebanon.'

[26]"But the LORD was angry with me on your account, and would not listen to me. So the LORD said to me: 'Enough of that! Speak no more to Me of this matter. [27]Go up to the top of Pisgah, and lift your eyes toward the west, the north, the south, and the east; behold *it* with your eyes, for you shall not cross over this Jordan.

3:11 [a]Hebrew *rephaim* **3:13** [a]Hebrew *rephaim*
3:14 [a]Literally *Towns of Jair*

²⁸But command Joshua, and encourage him and strengthen him; for he shall go over before this people, and he shall cause them to inherit the land which you will see.'

²⁹So we stayed in the valley opposite Beth Peor.

Moses Commands Obedience

4 "Now, O Israel, listen to the statutes and the judgments which I teach you to observe, that you may live, and go in and possess the land which the LORD God of your fathers is giving you. ²You shall not add to the word which I command you, nor take from it, that you may keep the commandments of the LORD your God which I command you. ³Your eyes have seen what the LORD did at Baal Peor; for the LORD your God has destroyed from among you all the men who followed Baal of Peor. ⁴But you who held fast to the LORD your God *are* alive today, every one of you.

⁵"Surely I have taught you statutes and judgments, just as the LORD my God commanded me, that you should act according *to them* in the land which you go to possess. ⁶Therefore be careful to observe *them;* for this *is* your wisdom and your understanding in the sight of the peoples who will hear all these statutes, and say, 'Surely this great nation *is* a wise and understanding people.'

⁷"For what great nation *is there* that has God *so* near to it, as the LORD our God *is* to us, for whatever *reason* we may call upon Him? ⁸And what great nation *is there* that has *such* statutes and righteous judgments as are in all this law which I set before you this day? ⁹Only take heed to yourself, and diligently keep yourself, lest you forget the things your eyes have seen, and lest they depart from your heart all the days of your life. And teach them to your children and your grandchildren, ¹⁰*especially concerning* the day you stood before the LORD your God in Horeb, when the LORD said to me, 'Gather the people to Me, and I will let them hear My words, that they may learn to fear Me all the days they live on the earth, and *that* they may teach their children.'

¹¹"Then you came near and stood at the foot of the mountain, and the mountain burned with fire to the midst of heaven, with darkness, cloud, and thick darkness. ¹²And the LORD spoke to you out of the midst of the fire. You heard the sound of the words, but saw no form; *you* only *heard* a voice. ¹³So He declared to you His covenant which He commanded you to perform, the Ten Commandments; and He wrote them on two tablets of stone. ¹⁴And the LORD commanded me

at that time to teach you statutes and judgments, that you might observe them in the land which you cross over to possess.

Beware of Idolatry

¹⁵"Take careful heed to yourselves, for you saw no form when the LORD spoke to you at Horeb out of the midst of the fire, ¹⁶lest you act corruptly and make for yourselves a carved image in the form of any figure: the likeness of male or female, ¹⁷the likeness of any animal that *is* on the earth or the likeness of any winged bird that flies in the air, ¹⁸the likeness of anything that creeps on the ground or the likeness of any fish that *is* in the water beneath the earth. ¹⁹And *take heed,* lest you lift your eyes to heaven, and *when* you see the sun, the moon, and the stars, all the host of heaven, you feel driven to worship them and serve them, which the LORD your God has given to all the peoples under the whole heaven as a heritage. ²⁰But the LORD has taken you and brought you out of the iron furnace, out of Egypt, to be His people, an inheritance, as you are this day. ²¹Furthermore the LORD was angry with me for your sakes, and swore that I would not cross over the Jordan, and that I would not enter the good land which the LORD your God is giving you as an inheritance. ²²But I must die in this land, I must not cross over the Jordan; but you shall cross over and possess that good land. ²³Take heed to yourselves, lest you forget the covenant of the LORD your God which He made with you, and make for yourselves a carved image in the form of anything which the LORD your God has forbidden you. ²⁴For the LORD your God *is* a consuming fire, a jealous God.

²⁵"When you beget children and grandchildren and have grown old in the land, and act corruptly and make a carved image in the form of anything, and do evil in the sight of the LORD your God to provoke Him to anger, ²⁶I call heaven and earth to witness against you this day, that you will soon utterly perish from the land which you cross over the Jordan to possess; you will not prolong *your* days in it, but will be utterly destroyed. ²⁷And the LORD will scatter you among the peoples, and you will be left few in number among the nations where the LORD will drive you. ²⁸And there you will serve gods, the work of men's hands, wood and stone, which neither see nor hear nor eat nor smell. ²⁹But from there you will seek the LORD your God, and you will find *Him* if you seek Him with all your heart and with all your soul. ³⁰When you are in distress, and all these things come upon you in the latter days, when you turn to the LORD your God and

obey His voice. [31](for the LORD your God *is* a merciful God), He will not forsake you nor destroy you, nor forget the covenant of your fathers which He swore to them.

[32]"For ask now concerning the days that are past, which were before you, since the day that God created man on the earth, and *ask* from one end of heaven to the other, whether *any* great *thing* like this has happened, or *anything* like it has been heard. [33]Did *any* people *ever* hear the voice of God speaking out of the midst of the fire, as you have heard, and live? [34]Or did God *ever* try to go *and* take for Himself a nation from the midst of *another* nation, by trials, by signs, by wonders, by war, by a mighty hand and an outstretched arm, and by great terrors, according to all that the LORD your God did for you in Egypt before your eyes? [35]To you it was shown, that you might know that the LORD Himself *is* God; *there is* none other besides Him. [36]Out of heaven He let you hear His voice, that He might instruct you; on earth He showed you His great fire, and you heard His words out of the midst of the fire. [37]And because He loved your fathers, therefore He chose their descendants after them; and He brought you out of Egypt with His Presence, with His mighty power, [38]driving out from before you nations greater and mightier than you, to bring you in, to give you their land *as* an inheritance, as *it is* this day. [39]Therefore know this day, and consider *it* in your heart, that the LORD Himself *is* God in heaven above and on the earth beneath; *there is* no other. [40]You shall therefore keep His statutes and His commandments which I command you today, that it may go well with you and with your children after you, and that you may prolong *your* days in the land which the LORD your God is giving you for all time."

Cities of Refuge East of the Jordan

[41]Then Moses set apart three cities on this side of the Jordan, toward the rising of the sun, [42]that the manslayer might flee there, who kills his neighbor unintentionally, without having hated him in time past, and that by fleeing to one of these cities he might live: [43]Bezer in the wilderness on the plateau for the Reubenites, Ramoth in Gilead for the Gadites, and Golan in Bashan for the Manassites.

Introduction to God's Law

[44]Now this *is* the law which Moses set before the children of Israel. [45]These *are* the testimonies, the statutes, and the judgments which Moses spoke to the children of Israel after they came out of Egypt, [46]on this side of the Jordan, in the

Purpose and Passion

(Deuteronomy 4:32–40)

Moses' speech encourages the people to realize their purpose and calling. This great leader reminds his countrymen of God's faithful provision and imparts to them a sense of destiny.

When leaders project passion for their vision, they create an atmosphere of expectancy among the people. Moses often created at least three such atmospheres for the Jews:

1. **A Sense of Destiny**
   Moses communicated a sense of God's call on Israel's future, a future they were destined to fulfill.
2. **A Sense of Family**
   Moses convinced the people they would enter the land together; cooperatively they could accomplish the vision.
3. **A Militant Spirit**
   Moses called the Israelites to do whatever it took to enter the land; they needed to pay the price to get the job done.

valley opposite Beth Peor, in the land of Sihon king of the Amorites, who dwelt at Heshbon, whom Moses and the children of Israel defeated after they came out of Egypt. [47]And they took possession of his land and the land of Og king of Bashan, two kings of the Amorites, who *were* on this side of the Jordan, toward the rising of the sun, [48]from Aroer, which *is* on the bank of the River Arnon, even to Mount Sion[a] (that is, Hermon), [49]and all the plain on the east side of the Jordan as far as the Sea of the Arabah, below the slopes of Pisgah.

The Ten Commandments Reviewed

5 And Moses called all Israel, and said to them: "Hear, O Israel, the statutes and judgments which I speak in your hearing today, that you may learn them and be careful to observe them. [2]The LORD our God made a covenant with us in Horeb. [3]The LORD did not make this covenant with our fathers, but with us, those who *are* here today, all of us who *are* alive. [4]The LORD talked with you face to face on the mountain from the midst of the fire. [5]I stood be-

---

4:48 [a]Syriac reads *Sirion* (compare 3:9).

Character and Convictions: Foundational for Leaders

(Deuteronomy 5:1–22)

To ensure this new generation entered the Promised Land with solid moral guidelines, Moses repeats the commands he gave earlier in Exodus 20. Former general Norman Schwarzkopf put it this way: "Leadership is a potent combination of character and strategy. But if you must be without one, be without strategy."

tween the LORD and you at that time, to declare to you the word of the LORD; for you were afraid because of the fire, and did not go up the mountain. *He* said:

6 'I *am* the LORD your God who brought you out of the land of Egypt, out of the house of bondage.

7 'You shall have no other gods before Me.

8 'You shall not make for yourself a carved image—any likeness *of anything* that *is* in heaven above, or that *is* in the earth beneath, or that *is* in the water under the earth; 9you shall not bow down to them nor serve them. For I, the LORD your God, *am* a jealous God, visiting the iniquity of the fathers upon the children to the third and fourth *generations* of those who hate Me, 10but showing mercy to thousands, to those who love Me and keep My commandments.

11 'You shall not take the name of the LORD your God in vain, for the LORD will not hold *him* guiltless who takes His name in vain.

12 'Observe the Sabbath day, to keep it holy, as the LORD your God commanded you. 13Six days you shall labor and do all your work, 14but the seventh day *is* the Sabbath of the LORD your God. *In it* you shall do no work: you, nor your son, nor your daughter, nor your male servant, nor your female servant, nor your ox, nor your donkey, nor any of your cattle, nor your stranger who *is* within your gates, that your male servant and your female servant may rest

as well as you. 15And remember that you were a slave in the land of Egypt, and the LORD your God brought you out from there by a mighty hand and by an outstretched arm; therefore the LORD your God commanded you to keep the Sabbath day.

16 'Honor your father and your mother, as the LORD your God has commanded you, that your days may be long, and that it may be well with you in the land which the LORD your God is giving you.

17 'You shall not murder.

18 'You shall not commit adultery.

19 'You shall not steal.

20 'You shall not bear false witness against your neighbor.

21 'You shall not covet your neighbor's wife; and you shall not desire your neighbor's house, his field, his male servant, his female servant, his ox, his donkey, or anything that *is* your neighbor's.'

22"These words the LORD spoke to all your assembly, in the mountain from the midst of the fire, the cloud, and the thick darkness, with a loud voice; and He added no more. And He wrote them on two tablets of stone and gave them to me.

The People Afraid of God's Presence

23"So it was, when you heard the voice from the midst of the darkness, while the mountain was burning with fire, that you came near to me, all the heads of your tribes and your elders. 24And you said: 'Surely the LORD our God has shown us His glory and His greatness, and we have heard His voice from the midst of the fire. We have seen this day that God speaks with man; yet he *still* lives. 25Now therefore, why should we die? For this great fire will consume us; if we hear the voice of the LORD our God anymore, then we shall die. 26For who *is there* of all flesh who has heard the voice of the living God speaking from the midst of the fire, as we *have,* and lived? 27You go near and hear all that the LORD our God may say, and tell us all that the LORD our God says to you, and we will hear and do *it*.'

28"Then the LORD heard the voice of your words when you spoke to me, and the LORD said to me: 'I have heard the voice of the words of this people which they have spoken to you. They are right *in* all that they have spoken. 29Oh, that they had such a heart in them that they would fear Me and always keep all My commandments, that it might be well with them and with their children forever! 30Go and say to them, "Return to your tents." 31But as for you, stand here by Me, and I will speak to you all the commandments, the statutes, and the judgments which you shall teach them, that they may observe *them* in the land which I am giving them to possess.'

[32]"Therefore you shall be careful to do as the LORD your God has commanded you; you shall not turn aside to the right hand or to the left. [33]You shall walk in all the ways which the LORD your God has commanded you, that you may live and *that it may be* well with you, and *that* you may prolong *your* days in the land which you shall possess.

The Greatest Commandment

6 "Now this *is* the commandment, *and these are* the statutes and judgments which the LORD your God has commanded to teach you, that you may observe *them* in the land which you are crossing over to possess, [2]that you may fear the LORD your God, to keep all His statutes and His commandments which I command you, you and your son and your grandson, all the days of your life, and that your days may be prolonged. [3]Therefore hear, O Israel, and be careful to observe *it,* that it may be well with you, and that you may multiply greatly as the LORD God of your fathers has promised you—'a land flowing with milk and honey.'[a]

[4]"Hear, O Israel: The LORD our God, the LORD *is* one![a] [5]You shall love the LORD your God with all your heart, with all your soul, and with all your strength.

[6]"And these words which I command you today shall be in your heart. [7]You shall teach them diligently to your children, and shall talk of them when you sit in your house, when you walk by the way, when you lie down, and when you rise up. [8]You shall bind them as a sign on your hand, and they shall be as frontlets between your eyes. [9]You shall write them on the doorposts of your house and on your gates.

Caution Against Disobedience

[10]"So it shall be, when the LORD your God brings you into the land of which He swore to your fathers, to Abraham, Isaac, and Jacob, to give you large and beautiful cities which you did not build, [11]houses full of all good things, which you did not fill, hewn-out wells which you did not dig, vineyards and olive trees which you did not plant—when you have eaten and are full— [12]then beware, lest you forget the LORD who brought you out of the land of Egypt, from the house of bondage. [13]You shall fear the LORD your God and serve Him, and shall take oaths in His name. [14]You shall not go after other gods, the gods of

The Law of Priorities: Pass Them On!
(Deuteronomy 6:4–9)

An old phrase says, "The leader's job is to keep the main thing, the main thing." Moses attempts to do this in Deuteronomy 6 by reminding the Israelites that their existence revolves around loving God. He also tells family leaders how to transfer truth to their children. Reggie Joiner notes the principles Moses develops:

1. Relationship comes before rules (v. 5).
2. Truth must be in you before it can be in them (v. 6).
3. Each day offers natural opportunities for teaching (v. 7).
   a. When you sit at home: meal time
   b. When you walk along the road: drive time
   c. When you lie down: bedtime
   d. When you get up: get-ready time
4. Repetition is the teacher's best friend (vv. 8, 9).

Make use of all of these opportunities. Decide on issues you can discuss and ask questions of each other. Pray about your priorities together.

the peoples who *are* all around you [15](for the LORD your God *is* a jealous God among you), lest the anger of the LORD your God be aroused against you and destroy you from the face of the earth.

[16]"You shall not tempt the LORD your God as you tempted *Him* in Massah. [17]You shall diligently keep the commandments of the LORD your God, His testimonies, and His statutes which He has commanded you. [18]And you shall do *what is* right and good in the sight of the LORD, that it may be well with you, and that you may go in and possess the good land of which the LORD swore to your fathers, [19]to cast out all your enemies from before you, as the LORD has spoken.

[20]"When your son asks you in time to come, saying, 'What *is the meaning of* the testimonies,

---

6:3 [a]Exodus 3:8 **6:4** [a]Or *The LORD is our God, the LORD alone* (that is, the only one)

the statutes, and the judgments which the LORD our God has commanded you?' [21]then you shall say to your son: 'We were slaves of Pharaoh in Egypt, and the LORD brought us out of Egypt with a mighty hand; [22]and the LORD showed signs and wonders before our eyes, great and severe, against Egypt, Pharaoh, and all his household. [23]Then He brought us out from there, that He might bring us in, to give us the land of which He swore to our fathers. [24]And the LORD commanded us to observe all these statutes, to fear the LORD our God, for our good always, that He might preserve us alive, as *it is* this day. [25]Then it will be righteousness for us, if we are careful to observe all these commandments before the LORD our God, as He has commanded us.'

A Chosen People

7 "When the LORD your God brings you into the land which you go to possess, and has cast out many nations before you, the Hittites and the Girgashites and the Amorites and the Canaanites and the Perizzites and the Hivites and the Jebusites, seven nations greater and mightier than you, [2]and when the LORD your God delivers them over to you, you shall conquer them *and* utterly destroy them. You shall make no covenant with them nor show mercy to them. [3]Nor shall you make marriages with them. You shall not give your daughter to their son, nor take their daughter for your son. [4]For they will turn your sons away from following Me, to serve other gods; so the anger of the LORD will be aroused against you and destroy you suddenly. [5]But thus you shall deal with them: you shall destroy their altars, and break down their *sacred* pillars, and cut down their wooden images,[a] and burn their carved images with fire.

[6]"For you *are* a holy people to the LORD your God; the LORD your God has chosen you to be a people for Himself, a special treasure above all the peoples on the face of the earth. [7]The LORD did not set His love on you nor choose you because you were more in number than any other people, for you were the least of all peoples; [8]but because the LORD loves you, and because He would keep the oath which He swore to your fathers, the LORD has brought you out with a mighty hand, and redeemed you from the house of bondage, from the hand of Pharaoh king of Egypt.

[9]"Therefore know that the LORD your God, He *is* God, the faithful God who keeps covenant and mercy for a thousand generations with those who love Him and keep His commandments; [10]and He repays those who hate Him to their

The Commitment of a Leader
(Deuteronomy 7:7–9)

Good leaders model commitment before they ask anyone else to do so. God promises to keep His commitment to His people "for a thousand generations" (Deut. 7:9). He reminds them that He didn't free them because they deserved it or because they were the largest nation on earth, but because He loved them.

face, to destroy them. He will not be slack with him who hates Him; He will repay him to his face. [11]Therefore you shall keep the commandment, the statutes, and the judgments which I command you today, to observe them.

Blessings of Obedience

[12]"Then it shall come to pass, because you listen to these judgments, and keep and do them, that the LORD your God will keep with you the covenant and the mercy which He swore to your fathers. [13]And He will love you and bless you and multiply you; He will also bless the fruit of your womb and the fruit of your land, your grain and your new wine and your oil, the increase of your cattle and the offspring of your flock, in the land of which He swore to your fathers to give you. [14]You shall be blessed above all peoples; there shall not be a male or female barren among you or among your livestock. [15]And the LORD will take away from you all sickness, and will afflict you with none of the terrible diseases of Egypt which you have known, but will lay *them* on all those who hate you. [16]Also you shall destroy all the peoples whom the LORD your God delivers over to you; your eye shall have no pity on them; nor shall you serve their gods, for that *will be* a snare to you.

[17]"If you should say in your heart, 'These nations are greater than I; how can I dispossess them?'— [18]you shall not be afraid of them, *but* you shall remember well what the LORD your God did to Pharaoh and to all Egypt: [19]the great trials which your eyes saw, the signs and the wonders, the mighty hand and the outstretched arm, by which the LORD your God brought you out. So shall the LORD your God do to all the peoples of

---

7:5 [a]Hebrew *Asherim,* Canaanite deities

The Anointing of a Leader: Its Requirements and Results

(Deuteronomy 7:11–13)

The Old Testament consistently speaks of leaders "anointed by God." Moses was the first such leader in Israel. The anointing represents God's intimate presence and enabling power.

But what determines God's anointing on a person? No doubt, God is sovereign and chooses to place His hand on some and not on others. But while God anoints, Frank Damazio reminds us of some human criteria for anointing. A leader must . . .

1. Obey and teach the people to obey God's Word (Deut. 7:11–13).
2. Desire and pursue the outpouring of the Spirit (Deut. 11:13, 14).
3. Actively build up the "house" of the Lord (Hag. 1:7–11).
4. Recognize God is the source of his blessing and authority (Hos. 2:8, 9).
5. Use his influence for the Lord and not for selfish or evil reasons (Hos. 2:8, 9).
6. Avoid glorifying the anointing more than God Himself (Hos. 2:8, 9).
7. Give himself freely to the work of the Lord (Ex. 35:20–29).
8. Appreciate and guard the anointing (Num. 4:9, 16).

whom you are afraid. ²⁰Moreover the LORD your God will send the hornet among them until those who are left, who hide themselves from you, are destroyed. ²¹You shall not be terrified of them; for the LORD your God, the great and awesome God, *is* among you. ²²And the LORD your God will drive out those nations before you little by little; you will be unable to destroy them at once, lest the beasts of the field become *too* numerous for you. ²³But the LORD your God will deliver them over to you, and will inflict defeat upon them until they are destroyed. ²⁴And He will deliver their kings into your hand, and you will destroy their name from under heaven; no one shall be able to stand against you until you have destroyed

them. ²⁵You shall burn the carved images of their gods with fire; you shall not covet the silver or gold *that is* on them, nor take *it* for yourselves, lest you be snared by it; for it *is* an abomination to the LORD your God. ²⁶Nor shall you bring an abomination into your house, lest you be doomed to destruction like it. You shall utterly detest it and utterly abhor it, for it *is* an accursed thing.

Remember the LORD Your God

8 "Every commandment which I command you today you must be careful to observe, that you may live and multiply, and go in and possess the land of which the LORD swore to your fathers. ²And you shall remember that the LORD your God led you all the way these forty years in the wilderness, to humble you *and* test you, to know what *was* in your heart, whether you would keep His commandments or not. ³So He humbled you, allowed you to hunger, and fed you with manna which you did not know nor did your fathers know, that He might make you know that man shall not live by bread alone; but man lives by every *word* that proceeds from the mouth of the LORD. ⁴Your garments did not wear out on you, nor did your foot swell these forty years. ⁵You should know in your heart that as a man chastens his son, *so* the LORD your God chastens you.

⁶"Therefore you shall keep the commandments of the LORD your God, to walk in His ways and to fear Him. ⁷For the LORD your God is bringing you into a good land, a land of brooks of water, of fountains and springs, that flow out of valleys and hills; ⁸a land of wheat and barley, of vines and fig trees and pomegranates, a land of olive oil and honey; ⁹a land in which you will eat bread without scarcity, in which you will lack nothing; a land whose stones *are* iron and out of whose hills you can dig copper. ¹⁰When you have eaten and are full, then you shall bless the LORD your God for the good land which He has given you.

¹¹"Beware that you do not forget the LORD your God by not keeping His commandments, His judgments, and His statutes which I command you today, ¹²lest—*when* you have eaten and are full, and have built beautiful houses and dwell *in them;* ¹³and *when* your herds and your flocks multiply, and your silver and your gold are multiplied, and all that you have is multiplied; ¹⁴when your heart is lifted up, and you forget the LORD your God who brought you out of the land of Egypt, from the house of bondage; ¹⁵who led you through that great and terrible wilderness, *in which were* fiery serpents and scorpions and thirsty land where there was no water; who brought

Humble Leaders Alone Receive God's Grace

(Deuteronomy 8:1–20)

We all need occasional reminders that it is God who gives His people any power and position they may come to enjoy. God commands His people to remember His blessings in both bad times (Deut. 8:1–10) and good times (8:11–20).

Because that's true, humility is the only appropriate posture—for leaders as well as followers. God constantly reminds leaders of . . .

- The privilege of being a chosen people—God will lead and provide for us.
- The price of being a chosen people—we must rely on His provision, not our own.

It's easy for leaders to succumb to the conceit that they pulled off some victory or objective. Instead, they should acknowledge that the success came to them as an under shepherd from the Master Shepherd. God gives grace to the humble, but opposes the proud (James 4:6). This is the only way to cooperate with the Lord.

water for you out of the flinty rock; [16]who fed you in the wilderness with manna, which your fathers did not know, that He might humble you and that He might test you, to do you good in the end— [17]then you say in your heart, 'My power and the might of my hand have gained me this wealth.'

[18]"And you shall remember the LORD your God, for *it is* He who gives you power to get wealth, that He may establish His covenant which He swore to your fathers, as *it is* this day. [19]Then it shall be, if you by any means forget the LORD your God, and follow other gods, and serve them and worship them, I testify against you this day that you shall surely perish. [20]As the nations which the LORD destroys before you, so you shall perish, because you would not be obedient to the voice of the LORD your God.

Israel's Rebellions Reviewed

9 "Hear, O Israel: You *are* to cross over the Jordan today, and go in to dispossess nations greater and mightier than yourself, cities great and fortified up to heaven, [2]a people great and tall, the descendants of the Anakim, whom you know, and *of whom* you heard *it said,* 'Who can stand before the descendants of Anak?' [3]Therefore understand today that the LORD your God *is* He who goes over before you *as* a consuming fire. He will destroy them and bring them down before you; so you shall drive them out and destroy them quickly, as the LORD has said to you.

[4]"Do not think in your heart, after the LORD your God has cast them out before you, saying, 'Because of my righteousness the LORD has brought me in to possess this land'; but *it is* because of the wickedness of these nations *that* the LORD is driving them out from before you. [5]*It is* not because of your righteousness or the uprightness of your heart *that* you go in to possess their land, but because of the wickedness of these nations *that* the LORD your God drives them out from before you, and that He may fulfill the word which the LORD swore to your fathers, to Abraham, Isaac, and Jacob. [6]Therefore understand that the LORD your God is not giving you this good land to possess because of your righteousness, for you *are* a stiff-necked people.

[7]"Remember! Do not forget how you provoked the LORD your God to wrath in the wilderness. From the day that you departed from the land of Egypt until you came to this place, you have been rebellious against the LORD. [8]Also in Horeb you provoked the LORD to wrath, so that the LORD was angry *enough* with you to have destroyed you. [9]When I went up into the mountain to receive the tablets of stone, the tablets of the covenant which the LORD made with you, then I stayed on the mountain forty days and forty nights. I neither ate bread nor drank water. [10]Then the LORD delivered to me two tablets of stone written with the finger of God, and on them *were* all the words which the LORD had spoken to you on the mountain from the midst of the fire in the day of the assembly. [11]And it came to pass, at the end of forty days and forty nights, *that* the LORD gave me the two tablets of stone, the tablets of the covenant.

[12]"Then the LORD said to me, 'Arise, go down quickly from here, for your people whom you brought out of Egypt have acted corruptly; they have quickly turned aside from the way which I commanded them; they have made themselves a molded image.'

[13]"Furthermore the LORD spoke to me, saying, 'I have seen this people, and indeed they are a stiff-necked people. [14]Let Me alone, that I may destroy them and blot out their name from

under heaven; and I will make of you a nation mightier and greater than they.'

¹⁵"So I turned and came down from the mountain, and the mountain burned with fire; and the two tablets of the covenant *were* in my two hands. ¹⁶And I looked, and behold, you had sinned against the LORD your God—had made for yourselves a molded calf! You had turned aside quickly from the way which the LORD had commanded you. ¹⁷Then I took the two tablets and threw them out of my two hands and broke them before your eyes. ¹⁸And I fell down before the LORD, as at the first, forty days and forty nights; I neither ate bread nor drank water, because of all your sin which you committed in doing wickedly in the sight of the LORD, to provoke Him to anger. ¹⁹For I was afraid of the anger and hot displeasure with which the LORD was angry with you, to destroy you. But the LORD listened to me at that time also. ²⁰And the LORD was very angry with Aaron *and* would have destroyed him; so I prayed for Aaron also at the same time. ²¹Then I took your sin, the calf which you had made, and burned it with fire and crushed it *and* ground *it* very small, until it was as fine as dust; and I threw its dust into the brook that descended from the mountain.

²²"Also at Taberah and Massah and Kibroth Hattaavah you provoked the LORD to wrath. ²³Likewise, when the LORD sent you from Kadesh Barnea, saying, 'Go up and possess the land which I have given you,' then you rebelled against the commandment of the LORD your God, and you did not believe Him nor obey His voice. ²⁴You have been rebellious against the LORD from the day that I knew you.

²⁵"Thus I prostrated myself before the LORD; forty days and forty nights I kept prostrating myself, because the LORD had said He would destroy you. ²⁶Therefore I prayed to the LORD, and said: 'O Lord GOD, do not destroy Your people and Your inheritance whom You have redeemed through Your greatness, whom You have brought out of Egypt with a mighty hand. ²⁷Remember Your servants, Abraham, Isaac, and Jacob; do not look on the stubbornness of this people, or on their wickedness or their sin, ²⁸lest the land from which You brought us should say, "Because the LORD was not able to bring them to the land which He promised them, and because He hated them, He has brought them out to kill them in the wilderness." ²⁹Yet they *are* Your people and Your inheritance, whom You brought out by Your mighty power and by Your outstretched arm.'

The Second Pair of Tablets

10 "At that time the LORD said to me, 'Hew for yourself two tablets of stone like the first, and come up to Me on the mountain and make yourself an ark of wood. ²And I will write on the tablets the words that were on the first tablets, which you broke; and you shall put them in the ark.'

³"So I made an ark of acacia wood, hewed two tablets of stone like the first, and went up the mountain, having the two tablets in my hand. ⁴And He wrote on the tablets according to the first writing, the Ten Commandments, which the LORD had spoken to you in the mountain from the midst of the fire in the day of the assembly; and the LORD gave them to me. ⁵Then I turned and came down from the mountain, and put the tablets in the ark which I had made; and there they are, just as the LORD commanded me."

⁶(Now the children of Israel journeyed from the wells of Bene Jaakan to Moserah, where Aaron died, and where he was buried; and Eleazar his son ministered as priest in his stead. ⁷From there they journeyed to Gudgodah, and from Gudgodah to Jotbathah, a land of rivers of water. ⁸At that time the LORD separated the tribe of Levi to bear the ark of the covenant of the LORD, to stand before the LORD to minister to Him and to bless in His name, to this day. ⁹Therefore Levi has no portion nor inheritance with his brethren; the LORD *is* his inheritance, just as the LORD your God promised him.)

¹⁰"As at the first time, I stayed in the mountain forty days and forty nights; the LORD also heard me at that time, *and* the LORD chose not to destroy you. ¹¹Then the LORD said to me, 'Arise, begin *your* journey before the people, that they may go in and possess the land which I swore to their fathers to give them.'

The Essence of the Law

¹²"And now, Israel, what does the LORD your God require of you, but to fear the LORD your God, to walk in all His ways and to love Him, to serve the LORD your God with all your heart and with all your soul, ¹³and to keep the commandments of the LORD and His statutes which I command you today for your good? ¹⁴Indeed heaven and the highest heavens belong to the LORD your God, *also* the earth with all that *is* in it. ¹⁵The LORD delighted only in your fathers, to love them; and He chose their descendants after them, you above all peoples, as *it is* this day. ¹⁶Therefore circumcise the foreskin of your heart, and be stiff-necked no longer. ¹⁷For the

The Law of Connection: God Touches Their Hearts First

(Deuteronomy 10:1—11:25)

As the Ultimate Leader, God directs His people to obey Him. But He doesn't simply demand obedience without giving sufficient reason. The Lord provides a good rationale for His people to obey Him. He reminds them that He first touched and blessed them—now, the only proper response is loving obedience. God's people were to follow His leadership because of:

1. **Personal Relationship (10:12–22)**
   God communicated His powerful nature, yet personal love for the descendants of Abraham.
2. **Past Record (11:1–7)**
   God reminded the people of the miracles He performed to rescue them from Egypt.
3. **Promised Results (11:8–17)**
   God predicted continued blessings if the Israelites would remain faithful.
4. **Powerful Redemption (11:18–25)**
   God underscored His plan to bless Hebrew families and possessions.

LORD your God *is* God of gods and Lord of lords, the great God, mighty and awesome, who shows no partiality nor takes a bribe. [18]He administers justice for the fatherless and the widow, and loves the stranger, giving him food and clothing. [19]Therefore love the stranger, for you were strangers in the land of Egypt. [20]You shall fear the LORD your God; you shall serve Him, and to Him you shall hold fast, and take oaths in His name. [21]He *is* your praise, and He *is* your God, who has done for you these great and awesome things which your eyes have seen. [22]Your fathers went down to Egypt with seventy persons, and now the LORD your God has made you as the stars of heaven in multitude.

Love and Obedience Rewarded

11 "Therefore you shall love the LORD your God, and keep His charge, His statutes, His judgments, and His commandments always. [2]Know today that *I do* not *speak* with your children, who have not known and who have not seen the chastening of the LORD your God, His greatness and His mighty hand and His outstretched arm— [3]His signs and His acts which He did in the midst of Egypt, to Pharaoh king of Egypt, and to all his land; [4]what He did to the army of Egypt, to their horses and their chariots: how He made the waters of the Red Sea overflow them as they pursued you, and *how* the LORD has destroyed them to this day; [5]what He did for you in the wilderness until you came to this place; [6]and what He did to Dathan and Abiram the sons of Eliab, the son of Reuben: how the earth opened its mouth and swallowed them up, their households, their tents, and all the substance that *was* in their possession, in the midst of all Israel— [7]but your eyes have seen every great act of the LORD which He did.

[8]"Therefore you shall keep every commandment which I command you today, that you may be strong, and go in and possess the land which you cross over to possess, [9]and that you may prolong *your* days in the land which the LORD swore to give your fathers, to them and their descendants, 'a land flowing with milk and honey.'[a] [10]For the land which you go to possess *is* not like the land of Egypt from which you have come, where you sowed your seed and watered *it* by foot, as a vegetable garden; [11]but the land which you cross over to possess *is* a land of hills and valleys, which drinks water from the rain of heaven, [12]a land for which the LORD your God cares; the eyes of the LORD your God *are* always on it, from the beginning of the year to the very end of the year.

[13]"And it shall be that if you earnestly obey My commandments which I command you today, to love the LORD your God and serve Him with all your heart and with all your soul, [14]then I[a] will give *you* the rain for your land in its season, the early rain and the latter rain, that you may gather in your grain, your new wine, and your oil. [15]And I will send grass in your fields for your livestock, that you may eat and be filled.' [16]Take heed to yourselves, lest your heart be deceived, and you turn aside and serve other gods and worship them, [17]lest the LORD's anger be aroused against you, and He shut up the heavens so that there be no rain, and the land yield no produce, and you perish quickly from the good land which the LORD is giving you.

[18]"Therefore you shall lay up these words of mine in your heart and in your soul, and bind them as a sign on your hand, and they shall be as

---

11:9 [a]Exodus 3:8 **11:14** [a]Following Masoretic Text and Targum; Samaritan Pentateuch, Septuagint, and Vulgate read *He.*

frontlets between your eyes. ¹⁹You shall teach them to your children, speaking of them when you sit in your house, when you walk by the way, when you lie down, and when you rise up. ²⁰And you shall write them on the doorposts of your house and on your gates, ²¹that your days and the days of your children may be multiplied in the land of which the LORD swore to your fathers to give them, like the days of the heavens above the earth.

²²"For if you carefully keep all these commandments which I command you to do—to love the LORD your God, to walk in all His ways, and to hold fast to Him— ²³then the LORD will drive out all these nations from before you, and you will dispossess greater and mightier nations than yourselves. ²⁴Every place on which the sole of your foot treads shall be yours: from the wilderness and Lebanon, from the river, the River Euphrates, even to the Western Sea,ᵃ shall be your territory. ²⁵No man shall be able to stand against you; the LORD your God will put the dread of you and the fear of you upon all the land where you tread, just as He has said to you.

²⁶"Behold, I set before you today a blessing and a curse: ²⁷the blessing, if you obey the commandments of the LORD your God which I command you today; ²⁸and the curse, if you do not obey the commandments of the LORD your God, but turn aside from the way which I command you today, to go after other gods which you have not known. ²⁹Now it shall be, when the LORD your God has brought you into the land which you go to possess, that you shall put the blessing on Mount Gerizim and the curse on Mount Ebal. ³⁰Are they not on the other side of the Jordan, toward the setting sun, in the land of the Canaanites who dwell in the plain opposite Gilgal, beside the terebinth trees of Moreh? ³¹For you will cross over the Jordan and go in to possess the land which the LORD your God is giving you, and you will possess it and dwell in it. ³²And you shall be careful to observe all the statutes and judgments which I set before you today.

A Prescribed Place of Worship

12 "These *are* the statutes and judgments which you shall be careful to observe in the land which the LORD God of your fathers is giving you to possess, all the days that you live on the earth. ²You shall utterly destroy all the places where the nations which you shall dispossess served their gods, on the high mountains and on the hills and under every green tree. ³And you shall destroy their al-

tars, break their *sacred* pillars, and burn their wooden images with fire; you shall cut down the carved images of their gods and destroy their names from that place. ⁴You shall not worship the LORD your God *with* such *things*.

⁵"But you shall seek the place where the LORD your God chooses, out of all your tribes, to put His name for His dwelling place; and there you shall go. ⁶There you shall take your burnt offerings, your sacrifices, your tithes, the heave offerings of your hand, your vowed offerings, your freewill offerings, and the firstborn of your herds and flocks. ⁷And there you shall eat before the LORD your God, and you shall rejoice in all to which you have put your hand, you and your households, in which the LORD your God has blessed you.

⁸"You shall not at all do as we are doing here today—every man doing whatever *is* right in his own eyes— ⁹for as yet you have not come to the rest and the inheritance which the LORD your God is giving you. ¹⁰But *when* you cross over the Jordan and dwell in the land which the LORD your God is giving you to inherit, and He gives you rest from all your enemies round about, so that you dwell in safety, ¹¹then there will be the place where the LORD your God chooses to make His name abide. There you shall bring all that I command you: your burnt offerings, your sacrifices, your tithes, the heave offerings of your hand, and all your choice offerings which you vow to the LORD. ¹²And you shall rejoice before the LORD your God, you and your sons and your daughters, your male and female servants, and the Levite who *is* within your gates, since he has no portion nor inheritance with you. ¹³Take heed to yourself that you do not offer your burnt offerings in every place that you see; ¹⁴but in the place which the LORD chooses, in one of your tribes, there you shall offer your burnt offerings, and there you shall do all that I command you.

¹⁵"However, you may slaughter and eat meat within all your gates, whatever your heart desires, according to the blessing of the LORD your God which He has given you; the unclean and the clean may eat of it, of the gazelle and the deer alike. ¹⁶Only you shall not eat the blood; you shall pour it on the earth like water. ¹⁷You may not eat within your gates the tithe of your grain or your new wine or your oil, of the firstborn of your herd or your flock, of any of your offerings which you vow, of your freewill offerings, or of the heave offering of your hand. ¹⁸But you must eat them before the LORD your God in the place

---

11:24 ᵃThat is, the Mediterranean

which the LORD your God chooses, you and your son and your daughter, your male servant and your female servant, and the Levite who *is* within your gates; and you shall rejoice before the LORD your God in all to which you put your hands. [19]Take heed to yourself that you do not forsake the Levite as long as you live in your land.

[20]"When the LORD your God enlarges your border as He has promised you, and you say, 'Let me eat meat,' because you long to eat meat, you may eat as much meat as your heart desires. [21]If the place where the LORD your God chooses to put His name is too far from you, then you may slaughter from your herd and from your flock which the LORD has given you, just as I have commanded you, and you may eat within your gates as much as your heart desires. [22]Just as the gazelle and the deer are eaten, so you may eat them; the unclean and the clean alike may eat them. [23]Only be sure that you do not eat the blood, for the blood *is* the life; you may not eat the life with the meat. [24]You shall not eat it; you shall pour it on the earth like water. [25]You shall not eat it, that it may go well with you and your children after you, when you do *what is* right in the sight of the LORD. [26]Only the holy things which you have, and your vowed offerings, you shall take and go to the place which the LORD chooses. [27]And you shall offer your burnt offerings, the meat and the blood, on the altar of the LORD your God; and the blood of your sacrifices shall be poured out on the altar of the LORD your God, and you shall eat the meat. [28]Observe and obey all these words which I command you, that it may go well with you and your children after you forever, when you do *what is* good and right in the sight of the LORD your God.

Beware of False Gods

[29]"When the LORD your God cuts off from before you the nations which you go to dispossess, and you displace them and dwell in their land, [30]take heed to yourself that you are not ensnared to follow them, after they are destroyed from before you, and that you do not inquire after their gods, saying, 'How did these nations serve their gods? I also will do likewise.' [31]You shall not worship the LORD your God in that way; for every abomination to the LORD which He hates they have done to their gods; for they burn even their sons and daughters in the fire to their gods.

[32]"Whatever I command you, be careful to observe it; you shall not add to it nor take away from it.

Punishment of Apostates

13 "If there arises among you a prophet or a dreamer of dreams, and he gives you a sign or a wonder, [2]and the sign or the wonder comes to pass, of which he spoke to you, saying, 'Let us go after other gods'— which you have not known—'and let us serve them,' [3]you shall not listen to the words of that prophet or that dreamer of dreams, for the LORD your God is testing you to know whether you love the LORD your God with all your heart and with all your soul. [4]You shall walk after the LORD your God and fear Him, and keep His commandments and obey His voice; you shall serve Him and hold fast to Him. [5]But that prophet or that dreamer of dreams shall be put to death, because he has spoken in order to turn *you* away from the LORD your God, who brought you out of the land of Egypt and redeemed you from the house of bondage, to entice you from the way in which the LORD your God commanded you to walk. So you shall put away the evil from your midst.

[6]"If your brother, the son of your mother, your son or your daughter, the wife of your bosom, or your friend who is as your own soul, secretly entices you, saying, 'Let us go and serve other gods,' which you have not known, neither you nor your fathers, [7]of the gods of the people which *are* all around you, near to you or far off from you, from *one* end of the earth to the *other* end of the earth, [8]you shall not consent to him or listen to him, nor shall your eye pity him, nor shall you spare him or conceal him; [9]but you shall surely kill him; your hand shall be first against him to put him to death, and afterward the hand of all the people. [10]And you shall stone him with stones until he dies, because he sought to entice you away from the LORD your God, who brought you out of the land of Egypt, from the house of bondage. [11]So all Israel shall hear and fear, and not again do such wickedness as this among you.

[12]"If you hear someone in one of your cities, which the LORD your God gives you to dwell in, saying, [13]'Corrupt men have gone out from among you and enticed the inhabitants of their city, saying, "Let us go and serve other gods"'— which you have not known— [14]then you shall inquire, search out, and ask diligently. And *if it is* indeed true *and* certain *that* such an abomination was committed among you, [15]you shall surely strike the inhabitants of that city with the edge of the sword, utterly destroying it, all that is in it and its livestock—with the edge of the sword.

[16]And you shall gather all its plunder into the middle of the street, and completely burn with fire the city and all its plunder, for the LORD your God. It shall be a heap forever; it shall not be built again. [17]So none of the accursed things shall remain in your hand, that the LORD may turn from the fierceness of His anger and show you mercy, have compassion on you and multiply you, just as He swore to your fathers, [18]because you have listened to the voice of the LORD your God, to keep all His commandments which I command you today, to do *what is* right in the eyes of the LORD your God.

Improper Mourning

14 "You *are* the children of the LORD your God; you shall not cut yourselves nor shave the front of your head for the dead. [2]For you *are* a holy people to the LORD your God, and the LORD has chosen you to be a people for Himself, a special treasure above all the peoples who *are* on the face of the earth.

Clean and Unclean Meat

[3]"You shall not eat any detestable thing. [4]These *are* the animals which you may eat: the ox, the sheep, the goat, [5]the deer, the gazelle, the roe deer, the wild goat, the mountain goat,[a] the antelope, and the mountain sheep. [6]And you may eat every animal with cloven hooves, having the hoof split into two parts, *and that* chews the cud, among the animals. [7]Nevertheless, of those that chew the cud or have cloven hooves, you shall not eat, *such as* these: the camel, the hare, and the rock hyrax; for they chew the cud but do not have cloven hooves; they *are* unclean for you. [8]Also the swine is unclean for you, because it has cloven hooves, yet *does* not *chew* the cud; you shall not eat their flesh or touch their dead carcasses.

[9]"These you may eat of all that *are* in the waters: you may eat all that have fins and scales. [10]And whatever does not have fins and scales you shall not eat; it *is* unclean for you.

[11]"All clean birds you may eat. [12]But these you shall not eat: the eagle, the vulture, the buzzard, [13]the red kite, the falcon, and the kite after their kinds; [14]every raven after its kind; [15]the ostrich, the short-eared owl, the sea gull, and the hawk after their kinds; [16]the little owl, the screech owl, the white owl, [17]the jackdaw, the carrion vulture, the fisher owl, [18]the stork, the heron after its kind, and the hoopoe and the bat.

[19]"Also every creeping thing that flies is unclean for you; they shall not be eaten. [20]"You may eat all clean birds.

[21]"You shall not eat anything that dies *of itself;* you may give it to the alien who *is* within your gates, that he may eat it, or you may sell it to a foreigner; for you *are* a holy people to the LORD your God.

"You shall not boil a young goat in its mother's milk.

Tithing Principles

[22]"You shall truly tithe all the increase of your grain that the field produces year by year. [23]And you shall eat before the LORD your God, in the place where He chooses to make His name abide, the tithe of your grain and your new wine and your oil, of the firstborn of your herds and your flocks, that you may learn to fear the LORD your God always. [24]But if the journey is too long for you, so that you are not able to carry *the tithe,* or if the place where the LORD your God chooses to put His name is too far from you, when the LORD your God has blessed you, [25]then you shall exchange *it* for money, take the money in your hand, and go to the place which the LORD your God chooses. [26]And you shall spend that money for whatever your heart desires: for oxen or sheep, for wine or similar drink, for whatever your heart desires; you shall eat there before the LORD your God, and you shall rejoice, you and your household. [27]You shall not forsake the Levite who *is* within your gates, for he has no part nor inheritance with you.

[28]"At the end of *every* third year you shall bring out the tithe of your produce of that year and store *it* up within your gates. [29]And the Levite, because he has no portion nor inheritance with you, and the stranger and the fatherless and the widow who *are* within your gates, may come and eat and be satisfied, that the LORD your God may bless you in all the work of your hand which you do.

Debts Canceled Every Seven Years

15 "At the end of *every* seven years you shall grant a release *of debts.* [2]And this *is* the form of the release: Every creditor who has lent *anything* to his neighbor shall release *it;* he shall not require *it* of his neighbor or his brother, because it is called the LORD's release. [3]Of a foreigner you may require *it;* but you shall give up your claim to what is owed by your brother, [4]except when there may be no poor among you; for the LORD will greatly bless you in the land which the LORD your God is giving you to possess *as* an inheritance— [5]only

14:5 [a]Or *addax*

Generosity: A Candle Loses Nothing by Lighting Another

(Deuteronomy 14:27—15:18)

If great leaders err, they do so on the side of generosity. They are givers, not takers. They feel motivated to:

1. **Serve others**—to help them grow and thrive.
2. **Solve problems**—that prevent potential from being reached.
3. **Save causes**—that benefit mankind.

God instructs His leaders and the entire nation of Israel to imitate His generosity and grace. At the end of every seventh year, every Israelite was to cancel all debts owed by fellow citizens. If they would indeed cancel debts, model graciousness and forgiveness, and care for the poor, He would favor their land with abundant crops and freedom from invasion. Imagine! They simply needed to trust that God was in control and let Him worry about rain and sun and fruitful harvest times.

God's instruction here provides us with a reminder of the nature of true leadership. We don't keep score with people; we just keep on giving.

if you carefully obey the voice of the LORD your God, to observe with care all these commandments which I command you today. ⁶For the LORD your God will bless you just as He promised you; you shall lend to many nations, but you shall not borrow; you shall reign over many nations, but they shall not reign over you.

Generosity to the Poor

⁷"If there is among you a poor man of your brethren, within any of the gates in your land which the LORD your God is giving you, you shall not harden your heart nor shut your hand from your poor brother, ⁸but you shall open your hand wide to him and willingly lend him sufficient for his need, whatever he needs. ⁹Beware lest there be a wicked thought in your heart, saying, 'The seventh year, the year of release, is at hand,' and your eye be evil against your poor brother and you give him nothing, and he cry out to the LORD against you, and it become sin

among you. ¹⁰You shall surely give to him, and your heart should not be grieved when you give to him, because for this thing the LORD your God will bless you in all your works and in all to which you put your hand. ¹¹For the poor will never cease from the land; therefore I command you, saying, 'You shall open your hand wide to your brother, to your poor and your needy, in your land.'

The Law Concerning Bondservants

¹²"If your brother, a Hebrew man, or a Hebrew woman, is sold to you and serves you six years, then in the seventh year you shall let him go free from you. ¹³And when you send him away free from you, you shall not let him go away empty-handed; ¹⁴you shall supply him liberally from your flock, from your threshing floor, and from your winepress. *From what* the LORD your God has blessed you with, you shall give to him. ¹⁵You shall remember that you were a slave in the land of Egypt, and the LORD your God redeemed you; therefore I command you this thing today. ¹⁶And if it happens that he says to you, 'I will not go away from you,' because he loves you and your house, since he prospers with you, ¹⁷then you shall take an awl and thrust *it* through his ear to the door, and he shall be your servant forever. Also to your female servant you shall do likewise. ¹⁸It shall not seem hard to you when you send him away free from you; for he has been worth a double hired servant in serving you six years. Then the LORD your God will bless you in all that you do.

The Law Concerning Firstborn Animals

¹⁹"All the firstborn males that come from your herd and your flock you shall sanctify to the LORD your God; you shall do no work with the firstborn of your herd, nor shear the firstborn of your flock. ²⁰You and your household shall eat *it* before the LORD your God year by year in the place which the LORD chooses. ²¹But if there is a defect in it, *if it is* lame or blind *or has* any serious defect, you shall not sacrifice it to the LORD your God. ²²You may eat it within your gates; the unclean and the clean *person* alike *may eat it,* as *if it were* a gazelle or a deer. ²³Only you shall not eat its blood; you shall pour it on the ground like water.

The Passover Reviewed

16 "Observe the month of Abib, and keep the Passover to the LORD your God, for in the month of Abib the LORD your God brought you out of Egypt by night. ²Therefore you shall sacrifice the Passover

---

The Leader as a Servant
(Deuteronomy 15:12–18)

The Old Testament uses several Hebrew terms that we translate as "servant," each one presenting a slightly different picture of the heart of a servant. What can a leader learn from these terms? Plenty. Remember, Jesus forever linked leadership with servanthood (Matt. 20:25–28). Let's take a moment to discover what we might learn about servant leadership from some of these ancient Hebrew words:

1. **Ebed:** a love-slave or servant. This term describes someone who is at the complete disposal of another (Deut. 15:12–18). Likewise, leaders must be at the disposal of the Lord and their people.

2. **Abad:** one who gives up personal rights in order to work in the fields or tabernacle (Num. 18:7, 23). In a similar way, leaders must sacrifice their rights and stay surrendered to the cause.

3. **Sakyir:** a hired servant who works for pay, by day or by year (Lev. 25:39–42). A leader must avoid the perspective of a "paid professional." Remember the lesson of John 10:12, 13?

4. **Sharath:** someone who will perform menial tasks to accomplish an overall goal (Ex. 28:35–43). Leaders must do whatever it takes to serve the mission.

Leaders must never forget that God calls them to serve. If our Lord could wash His disciples' feet as a lowly *sharath*, then how could we frown at becoming an *ebed*?

---

to the LORD your God, from the flock and the herd, in the place where the LORD chooses to put His name. ³You shall eat no leavened bread with it; seven days you shall eat unleavened bread with it, *that is,* the bread of affliction (for you came out of the land of Egypt in haste), that you may remember the day in which you came out of the land of Egypt all the days of your life. ⁴And no leaven shall be seen among you in all your territory for seven days, nor shall *any* of the meat which you sacrifice the first day at twilight remain overnight until morning.

⁵"You may not sacrifice the Passover within any of your gates which the LORD your God gives you; ⁶but at the place where the LORD your God chooses to make His name abide, there you shall sacrifice the Passover at twilight, at the going down of the sun, at the time you came out of Egypt. ⁷And you shall roast and eat *it* in the place which the LORD your God chooses, and in the morning you shall turn and go to your tents. ⁸Six days you shall eat unleavened bread, and on the seventh day there *shall be* a sacred assembly to the LORD your God. You shall do no work *on it.*

The Feast of Weeks Reviewed

⁹"You shall count seven weeks for yourself; begin to count the seven weeks from *the time you* begin *to put* the sickle to the grain. ¹⁰Then you shall keep the Feast of Weeks to the LORD your

God with the tribute of a freewill offering from your hand, which you shall give as the LORD your God blesses you. ¹¹You shall rejoice before the LORD your God, you and your son and your daughter, your male servant and your female servant, the Levite who *is* within your gates, the stranger and the fatherless and the widow who *are* among you, at the place where the LORD your God chooses to make His name abide. ¹²And you shall remember that you were a slave in Egypt, and you shall be careful to observe these statutes.

The Feast of Tabernacles Reviewed

¹³"You shall observe the Feast of Tabernacles seven days, when you have gathered from your threshing floor and from your winepress. ¹⁴And you shall rejoice in your feast, you and your son and your daughter, your male servant and your female servant and the Levite, the stranger and the fatherless and the widow, who *are* within your gates. ¹⁵Seven days you shall keep a sacred feast to the LORD your God in the place which the LORD chooses, because the LORD your God will bless you in all your produce and in all the work of your hands, so that you surely rejoice.

¹⁶"Three times a year all your males shall appear before the LORD your God in the place which He chooses: at the Feast of Unleavened Bread, at the Feast of Weeks, and at the Feast of Tabernacles; and they shall not appear before the

The Law of Navigation:
Moses Provides Future Direction
(Deuteronomy 16:1—25:19)

Much as America's forefathers assembled the U.S. Constitution, Moses furnished clear guidelines for his nation's future. One chief difference: Israel was to live under a theocracy, not a democracy. The nation was to be lovingly ruled by God, not by the whims of the people. Ponder the genius behind the structure and navigation Moses offers in these chapters:

Leadership Action	**Purpose**
1. Established seven annual feasts	1. Reminded people of the big picture
2. Males to worship at central location	2. Provided context for participation
3. Appointed judges for each tribe	3. Furnished leadership at a local level
4. Shared civil duties with the community	4. Created value of justice and social order
5. Communicated criteria for top leaders	5. Cast vision for leadership with integrity
6. Organized offerings for priests/Levites	6. Prioritized holy living and godly priorities
7. Established cities of refuge	7. Esteemed the qualities of mercy and grace
8. Set boundaries for national defense	8. Taught Israel to trust God, not themselves
9. Addressed crimes and moral failure	9. Set consequences prior to criminal acts
10. Tithing to the Lord	10. Taught stewardship as a top priority

LORD empty-handed. [17]Every man *shall give* as he is able, according to the blessing of the LORD your God which He has given you.

Justice Must Be Administered

[18]"You shall appoint judges and officers in all your gates, which the LORD your God gives you, according to your tribes, and they shall judge the people with just judgment. [19]You shall not pervert justice; you shall not show partiality, nor take a bribe, for a bribe blinds the eyes of the wise and twists the words of the righteous. [20]You shall follow what is altogether just, that you may live and inherit the land which the LORD your God is giving you.

[21]"You shall not plant for yourself any tree, as a wooden image, near the altar which you build for yourself to the LORD your God. [22]You shall not set up a *sacred* pillar, which the LORD your God hates.

17 "You shall not sacrifice to the LORD your God a bull or sheep which has any blemish *or* defect, for that *is* an abomination to the LORD your God.

[2]"If there is found among you, within any of your gates which the LORD your God gives you, a man or a woman who has been wicked in the sight of the LORD your God, in transgressing His covenant, [3]who has gone and served other gods and worshiped them, either the sun or moon or any of the host of heaven, which I have not commanded, [4]and it is told you, and you hear *of it,* then you shall inquire diligently. And if *it is* indeed true *and* certain that such an abomination has been committed in Israel, [5]then you shall bring out to your gates that man or woman who has committed that wicked thing, and shall stone to death that man or woman with stones. [6]Whoever is deserving of death shall be put to death on the testimony of two or three witnesses; he shall not be put to death on the testimony of one witness. [7]The hands of the witnesses shall be the first against him to put him to death, and afterward the hands of all the people. So you shall put away the evil from among you.

[8]"If a matter arises which is too hard for you to judge, between degrees of guilt for bloodshed, between one judgment or another, or between one punishment or another, matters of controversy within your gates, then you shall arise and go up to the place which the LORD your God chooses. [9]And you shall come to the priests, the Levites, and to the judge *there* in those days, and inquire *of them;* they shall pronounce upon you the sentence of judgment. [10]You shall do according to the sentence which they pronounce upon you in that place which the LORD chooses. And you shall be careful to do according to all that they order you. [11]According to the sentence of the law in which they

instruct you, according to the judgment which they tell you, you shall do; you shall not turn aside *to* the right hand or *to* the left from the sentence which they pronounce upon you. [12]Now the man who acts presumptuously and will not heed the priest who stands to minister there before the LORD your God, or the judge, that man shall die. So you shall put away the evil from Israel. [13]And all the people shall hear and fear, and no longer act presumptuously.

Principles Governing Kings

[14]"When you come to the land which the LORD your God is giving you, and possess it and dwell in it, and say, 'I will set a king over me like all the nations that *are* around me,' [15]you shall surely set a king over you whom the LORD your God chooses; *one* from among your brethren you shall set as king over you; you may not set a foreigner over you, who *is* not your brother. [16]But he shall not multiply horses for himself, nor cause the people to return to Egypt to multiply horses, for the LORD has said to you, 'You shall not return that way again.' [17]Neither shall he multiply wives for himself, lest his heart turn away; nor shall he greatly multiply silver and gold for himself.

[18]"Also it shall be, when he sits on the throne of his kingdom, that he shall write for himself a copy of this law in a book, from *the one* before the priests, the Levites. [19]And it shall be with him, and he shall read it all the days of his life, that he may learn to fear the LORD his God and be careful to observe all the words of this law and these statutes, [20]that his heart may not be lifted above his brethren, that he may not turn aside from the commandment *to* the right hand or *to* the left, and that he may prolong *his* days in his kingdom, he and his children in the midst of Israel.

The Portion of the Priests and Levites

18 "The priests, the Levites—all the tribe of Levi—shall have no part nor inheritance with Israel; they shall eat the offerings of the LORD made by fire, and His portion. [2]Therefore they shall have no inheritance among their brethren; the LORD is their inheritance, as He said to them.

[3]"And this shall be the priest's due from the people, from those who offer a sacrifice, whether *it is* bull or sheep: they shall give to the priest the shoulder, the cheeks, and the stomach. [4]The first-fruits of your grain and your new wine and your oil, and the first of the fleece of your sheep, you shall give him. [5]For the LORD your God has cho-

sen him out of all your tribes to stand to minister in the name of the LORD, him and his sons forever.

[6]"So if a Levite comes from any of your gates, from where he dwells among all Israel, and comes with all the desire of his mind to the place which the LORD chooses, [7]then he may serve in the name of the LORD his God as all his brethren the Levites *do,* who stand there before the LORD. [8]They shall have equal portions to eat, besides what comes from the sale of his inheritance.

Avoid Wicked Customs

[9]"When you come into the land which the LORD your God is giving you, you shall not learn to follow the abominations of those nations. [10]There shall not be found among you *anyone* who makes his son or his daughter pass through the fire, *or one* who practices witchcraft, *or* a soothsayer, or one who interprets omens, or a sorcerer, [11]or one who conjures spells, or a medium, or a spiritist, or one who calls up the dead. [12]For all who do these things *are* an abomination to the LORD, and because of these abominations the LORD your God drives them out from before you. [13]You shall be blameless before the LORD your God. [14]For these nations which you will dispossess listened to soothsayers and diviners; but as for you, the LORD your God has not appointed such for you.

A New Prophet Like Moses

[15]"The LORD your God will raise up for you a Prophet like me from your midst, from your brethren. Him you shall hear, [16]according to all you desired of the LORD your God in Horeb in the day of the assembly, saying, 'Let me not hear again the voice of the LORD my God, nor let me see this great fire anymore, lest I die.'

[17]"And the LORD said to me: 'What they have spoken is good. [18]I will raise up for them a Prophet like you from among their brethren, and will put My words in His mouth, and He shall speak to them all that I command Him. [19]And it shall be *that* whoever will not hear My words, which He speaks in My name, I will require *it of* him. [20]But the prophet who presumes to speak a word in My name, which I have not commanded him to speak, or who speaks in the name of other gods, that prophet shall die.' [21]And if you say in your heart, 'How shall we know the word which the LORD has not spoken?'— [22]when a prophet speaks in the name of the LORD, if the thing does not happen or come to pass, that *is* the thing which the LORD has not spoken; the

prophet has spoken it presumptuously; you shall not be afraid of him.

Three Cities of Refuge

19 "When the LORD your God has cut off the nations whose land the LORD your God is giving you, and you dispossess them and dwell in their cities and in their houses, ²you shall separate three cities for yourself in the midst of your land which the LORD your God is giving you to possess. ³You shall prepare roads for yourself, and divide into three parts the territory of your land which the LORD your God is giving you to inherit, that any manslayer may flee there.

⁴"And this *is* the case of the manslayer who flees there, that he may live: Whoever kills his neighbor unintentionally, not having hated him in time past— ⁵as when *a man* goes to the woods with his neighbor to cut timber, and his hand swings a stroke with the ax to cut down the tree, and the head slips from the handle and strikes his neighbor so that he dies—he shall flee to one of these cities and live; ⁶lest the avenger of blood, while his anger is hot, pursue the manslayer and overtake him, because the way is long, and kill him, though he *was* not deserving of death, since he had not hated the victim in time past. ⁷Therefore I command you, saying, 'You shall separate three cities for yourself.'

⁸"Now if the LORD your God enlarges your territory, as He swore to your fathers, and gives you the land which He promised to give to your fathers, ⁹and if you keep all these commandments and do them, which I command you today, to love the LORD your God and to walk always in His ways, then you shall add three more cities for yourself besides these three, ¹⁰lest innocent blood be shed in the midst of your land which the LORD your God is giving you *as* an inheritance, and *thus* guilt of bloodshed be upon you.

¹¹"But if anyone hates his neighbor, lies in wait for him, rises against him and strikes him mortally, so that he dies, and he flees to one of these cities, ¹²then the elders of his city shall send and bring him from there, and deliver him over to the hand of the avenger of blood, that he may die. ¹³Your eye shall not pity him, but you shall put away *the guilt of* innocent blood from Israel, that it may go well with you.

Property Boundaries

¹⁴"You shall not remove your neighbor's landmark, which the men of old have set, in your inheritance which you will inherit in the land that the LORD your God is giving you to possess.

The Law Concerning Witnesses

¹⁵"One witness shall not rise against a man concerning any iniquity or any sin that he commits; by the mouth of two or three witnesses the matter shall be established. ¹⁶If a false witness rises against any man to testify against him of wrongdoing, ¹⁷then both men in the controversy shall stand before the LORD, before the priests and the judges who serve in those days. ¹⁸And the judges shall make careful inquiry, and indeed, *if* the witness *is* a false witness, who has testified falsely against his brother, ¹⁹then you shall do to him as he thought to have done to his brother; so you shall put away the evil from among you. ²⁰And those who remain shall hear and fear, and hereafter they shall not again commit such evil among you. ²¹Your eye shall not pity: life *shall be* for life, eye for eye, tooth for tooth, hand for hand, foot for foot.

Principles Governing Warfare

20 "When you go out to battle against your enemies, and see horses and chariots *and* people more numerous than you, do not be afraid of them; for the LORD your God *is* with you, who brought you up from the land of Egypt. ²So it shall be, when you are on the verge of battle, that the priest shall approach and speak to the people. ³And he shall say to them, 'Hear, O Israel: Today you are on the verge of battle with your enemies. Do not let your heart faint, do not be afraid, and do not tremble or be terrified because of them; ⁴for the LORD your God *is* He who goes with you, to fight for you against your enemies, to save you.'

⁵"Then the officers shall speak to the people, saying: 'What man *is there* who has built a new house and has not dedicated it? Let him go and return to his house, lest he die in the battle and another man dedicate it. ⁶Also what man *is there* who has planted a vineyard and has not eaten of it? Let him go and return to his house, lest he die in the battle and another man eat of it. ⁷And what man *is there* who is betrothed to a woman and has not married her? Let him go and return to his house, lest he die in the battle and another man marry her.'

⁸"The officers shall speak further to the people, and say, 'What man *is there who is* fearful and fainthearted? Let him go and return to his house, lest the heart of his brethren faint[a] like his heart.' ⁹And so it shall be, when the officers have

---

20:8 [a]Following Masoretic Text and Targum; Samaritan Pentateuch, Septuagint, Syriac, and Vulgate read *lest he make his brother's heart faint.*

finished speaking to the people, that they shall make captains of the armies to lead the people.

[10]"When you go near a city to fight against it, then proclaim an offer of peace to it. [11]And it shall be that if they accept your offer of peace, and open to you, then all the people *who are* found in it shall be placed under tribute to you, and serve you. [12]Now if *the city* will not make peace with you, but war against you, then you shall besiege it. [13]And when the LORD your God delivers it into your hands, you shall strike every male in it with the edge of the sword. [14]But the women, the little ones, the livestock, and all that is in the city, all its spoil, you shall plunder for yourself; and you shall eat the enemies' plunder which the LORD your God gives you. [15]Thus you shall do to all the cities *which are* very far from you, which *are* not of the cities of these nations.

[16]"But of the cities of these peoples which the LORD your God gives you *as* an inheritance, you shall let nothing that breathes remain alive, [17]but you shall utterly destroy them: the Hittite and the Amorite and the Canaanite and the Perizzite and the Hivite and the Jebusite, just as the LORD your God has commanded you, [18]lest they teach you to do according to all their abomina-

tions which they have done for their gods, and you sin against the LORD your God.

[19]"When you besiege a city for a long time, while making war against it to take it, you shall not destroy its trees by wielding an ax against them; if you can eat of them, do not cut them down to use in the siege, for the tree of the field *is* man's *food*. [20]Only the trees which you know *are* not trees for food you may destroy and cut down, to build siegeworks against the city that makes war with you, until it is subdued.

The Law Concerning Unsolved Murder

21 "If *anyone* is found slain, lying in the field in the land which the LORD your God is giving you to possess, *and* it is not known who killed him, [2]then your elders and your judges shall go out and measure *the distance* from the slain man to the surrounding cities. [3]And it shall be *that* the elders of the city nearest to the slain man will take a heifer which has not been worked *and* which has not pulled with a yoke. [4]The elders of that city shall bring the heifer down to a valley with flowing water, which is neither plowed nor sown, and they shall break the heifer's neck there in the valley. [5]Then the priests, the sons of Levi, shall come near, for

---

MOSES
PROFILE IN LEADERSHIP

THE CONFIDENCE OF GOD'S PRESENCE
(Deuteronomy 20:1–20)

It's always a good idea to have a battle plan if you intend to lead an army into war. Moses possessed a devastating plan for the army of Israel, a set of instructions that came straight from the top—the *very* top.

Imagine the confidence a field commander could instill in his troops knowing that he could not lose. Yet that was just the kind of guarantee God gave Moses and the people of Israel.

How astonishing this must have seemed! For at the time God issued His battle plans, the Hebrews hadn't even settled in their own land, let alone set up a line of defense. Furthermore, the Lord guaranteed His people that they would face military forces far more formidable than their own. Yet God assured them they had nothing to fear—as long as they remembered that He would remain with them always, as He had since the day they left Egypt.

Leaders today can bank on the same promise that gave Moses such courage: "For the LORD your God is He who goes with you, to fight for you against your enemies, to save you" (Deut. 20:4; cf. Heb. 13:5, 6). And so God gives us the same He gave to Moses: "Do not be afraid" (Deut. 20:1).

the LORD your God has chosen them to minister to Him and to bless in the name of the LORD; by their word every controversy and every assault shall be *settled*. [6]And all the elders of that city nearest to the slain *man* shall wash their hands over the heifer whose neck was broken in the valley. [7]Then they shall answer and say, 'Our hands have not shed this blood, nor have our eyes seen *it*. [8]Provide atonement, O LORD, for Your people Israel, whom You have redeemed, and do not lay innocent blood to the charge of Your people Israel.' And atonement shall be provided on their behalf for the blood. [9]So you shall put away the *guilt of* innocent blood from among you when you do *what is* right in the sight of the LORD.

Female Captives

[10]"When you go out to war against your enemies, and the LORD your God delivers them into your hand, and you take them captive, [11]and you see among the captives a beautiful woman, and desire her and would take her for your wife, [12]then you shall bring her home to your house, and she shall shave her head and trim her nails. [13]She shall put off the clothes of her captivity, remain in your house, and mourn her father and her mother a full month; after that you may go in to her and be her husband, and she shall be your wife. [14]And it shall be, if you have no delight in her, then you shall set her free, but you certainly shall not sell her for money; you shall not treat her brutally, because you have humbled her.

Firstborn Inheritance Rights

[15]"If a man has two wives, one loved and the other unloved, and they have borne him children, *both* the loved and the unloved, and *if* the firstborn son is of her who is unloved, [16]then it shall be, on the day he bequeaths his possessions to his sons, *that* he must not bestow firstborn status on the son of the loved wife in preference to the son of the unloved, the *true* firstborn. [17]But he shall acknowledge the son of the unloved wife *as* the firstborn by giving him a double portion of all that he has, for he *is* the beginning of his strength; the right of the firstborn *is* his.

The Rebellious Son

[18]"If a man has a stubborn and rebellious son who will not obey the voice of his father or the voice of his mother, and *who,* when they have chastened him, will not heed them, [19]then his father and his mother shall take hold of him and bring him out to the elders of his city, to the gate of his city. [20]And they shall say to the elders of his city, 'This son of ours is stubborn and rebellious; he will not obey our voice; he is a glutton and a drunkard.' [21]Then all the men of his city shall stone him to death with stones; so you shall put away the evil from among you, and all Israel shall hear and fear.

Miscellaneous Laws

[22]"If a man has committed a sin deserving of death, and he is put to death, and you hang him on a tree, [23]his body shall not remain overnight on the tree, but you shall surely bury him that day, so that you do not defile the land which the LORD your God is giving you *as* an inheritance; for he who is hanged *is* accursed of God.

22 "You shall not see your brother's ox or his sheep going astray, and hide yourself from them; you shall certainly bring them back to your brother. [2]And if your brother *is* not near you, or if you do not know him, then you shall bring it to your own house, and it shall remain with you until your brother seeks it; then you shall restore it to him. [3]You shall do the same with his donkey, and so shall you do with his garment; with any lost thing of your brother's, which he has lost and you have found, you shall do likewise; you must not hide yourself.

[4]"You shall not see your brother's donkey or his ox fall down along the road, and hide yourself from them; you shall surely help him lift *them* up again.

[5]"A woman shall not wear anything that pertains to a man, nor shall a man put on a woman's garment, for all who do so *are* an abomination to the LORD your God.

[6]"If a bird's nest happens to be before you along the way, in any tree or on the ground, with young ones or eggs, with the mother sitting on the young or on the eggs, you shall not take the mother with the young; [7]you shall surely let the mother go, and take the young for yourself, that it may be well with you and *that* you may prolong *your* days.

[8]"When you build a new house, then you shall make a parapet for your roof, that you may not bring guilt of bloodshed on your household if anyone falls from it.

[9]"You shall not sow your vineyard with different kinds of seed, lest the yield of the seed which you have sown and the fruit of your vineyard be defiled.

[10]"You shall not plow with an ox and a donkey together.

[11]"You shall not wear a garment of different sorts, *such as* wool and linen mixed together.

[12]"You shall make tassels on the four corners of the clothing with which you cover *yourself.*

Laws of Sexual Morality

[13]"If any man takes a wife, and goes in to her, and detests her, [14]and charges her with shameful conduct, and brings a bad name on her, and says, 'I took this woman, and when I came to her I found she *was* not a virgin,' [15]then the father and mother of the young woman shall take and bring out *the evidence of* the young woman's virginity to the elders of the city at the gate. [16]And the young woman's father shall say to the elders, 'I gave my daughter to this man as wife, and he detests her. [17]Now he has charged her with shameful conduct, saying, "I found your daughter *was* not a virgin," and yet these *are the evidences of* my daughter's virginity.' And they shall spread the cloth before the elders of the city. [18]Then the elders of that city shall take that man and punish him; [19]and they shall fine him one hundred *shekels* of silver and give *them* to the father of the young woman, because he has brought a bad name on a virgin of Israel. And she shall be his wife; he cannot divorce her all his days.

[20]"But if the thing is true, *and evidences of* virginity are not found for the young woman, [21]then they shall bring out the young woman to the door of her father's house, and the men of her city shall stone her to death with stones, because she has done a disgraceful thing in Israel, to play the harlot in her father's house. So you shall put away the evil from among you.

[22]"If a man is found lying with a woman married to a husband, then both of them shall die—the man that lay with the woman, and the woman; so you shall put away the evil from Israel.

[23]"If a young woman *who is* a virgin is betrothed to a husband, and a man finds her in the city and lies with her, [24]then you shall bring them both out to the gate of that city, and you shall stone them to death with stones, the young woman because she did not cry out in the city, and the man because he humbled his neighbor's wife; so you shall put away the evil from among you.

[25]"But if a man finds a betrothed young woman in the countryside, and the man forces her and lies with her, then only the man who lay with her shall die. [26]But you shall do nothing to the young woman; *there is* in the young woman no sin *deserving* of death, for just as when a man rises against his neighbor and kills him, even so *is* this matter. [27]For he found her in the countryside, *and* the betrothed young woman cried out, but *there was* no one to save her.

[28]"If a man finds a young woman *who is* a virgin, who is not betrothed, and he seizes her and lies with her, and they are found out, [29]then the man who lay with her shall give to the young woman's father fifty *shekels* of silver, and she shall be his wife because he has humbled her; he shall not be permitted to divorce her all his days.

[30]"A man shall not take his father's wife, nor uncover his father's bed.

Those Excluded from the Congregation

23 "He who is emasculated by crushing or mutilation shall not enter the assembly of the LORD.

[2]"One of illegitimate birth shall not enter the assembly of the LORD; even to the tenth generation none of his *descendants* shall enter the assembly of the LORD.

[3]"An Ammonite or Moabite shall not enter the assembly of the LORD; even to the tenth generation none of his *descendants* shall enter the assembly of the LORD forever, [4]because they did not meet you with bread and water on the road when you came out of Egypt, and because they hired against you Balaam the son of Beor from Pethor of Mesopotamia,[a] to curse you. [5]Nevertheless the LORD your God would not listen to Balaam, but the LORD your God turned the curse into a blessing for you, because the LORD your God loves you. [6]You shall not seek their peace nor their prosperity all your days forever.

[7]"You shall not abhor an Edomite, for he *is* your brother. You shall not abhor an Egyptian, because you were an alien in his land. [8]The children of the third generation born to them may enter the assembly of the LORD.

Cleanliness of the Campsite

[9]"When the army goes out against your enemies, then keep yourself from every wicked thing. [10]If there is any man among you who becomes unclean by some occurrence in the night, then he shall go outside the camp; he shall not come inside the camp. [11]But it shall be, when evening comes, that he shall wash with water; and when the sun sets, he may come into the camp.

[12]"Also you shall have a place outside the camp, where you may go out; [13]and you shall have an implement among your equipment, and when you sit down outside, you shall dig with it and turn and cover your refuse. [14]For the LORD your God walks in the midst of your camp, to deliver you and give your enemies over to you; therefore your camp shall be holy, that He may

23:4 [a]Hebrew *Aram Naharaim*

see no unclean thing among you, and turn away from you.

Miscellaneous Laws

[15]"You shall not give back to his master the slave who has escaped from his master to you. [16]He may dwell with you in your midst, in the place which he chooses within one of your gates, where it seems best to him; you shall not oppress him.

[17]"There shall be no *ritual* harlot[a] of the daughters of Israel, or a perverted[b] one of the sons of Israel. [18]You shall not bring the wages of a harlot or the price of a dog to the house of the LORD your God for any vowed offering, for both of these *are* an abomination to the LORD your God.

[19]"You shall not charge interest to your brother—interest on money *or* food *or* anything that is lent out at interest. [20]To a foreigner you may charge interest, but to your brother you shall not charge interest, that the LORD your God may bless you in all to which you set your hand in the land which you are entering to possess.

[21]"When you make a vow to the LORD your God, you shall not delay to pay it; for the LORD your God will surely require it of you, and it would be sin to you. [22]But if you abstain from vowing, it shall not be sin to you. [23]That which has gone from your lips you shall keep and perform, for you voluntarily vowed to the LORD your God what you have promised with your mouth.

[24]"When you come into your neighbor's vineyard, you may eat your fill of grapes at your pleasure, but you shall not put *any* in your container. [25]When you come into your neighbor's standing grain, you may pluck the heads with your hand, but you shall not use a sickle on your neighbor's standing grain.

Law Concerning Divorce

24 "When a man takes a wife and marries her, and it happens that she finds no favor in his eyes because he has found some uncleanness in her, and he writes her a certificate of divorce, puts *it* in her hand, and sends her out of his house, [2]when she has departed from his house, and goes and becomes another man's *wife*, [3]if the latter husband detests her and writes her a certificate of divorce, puts *it* in her hand, and sends her out of his house, or if the latter husband dies who took her as his wife, [4]*then* her former husband who divorced her must not take her back to be his wife after she has been defiled; for that *is* an abomination before the LORD, and you shall not bring sin on the land which the LORD your God is giving you *as* an inheritance.

Miscellaneous Laws

[5]"When a man has taken a new wife, he shall not go out to war or be charged with any business; he shall be free at home one year, and bring happiness to his wife whom he has taken.

[6]"No man shall take the lower or the upper millstone in pledge, for he takes *one's* living in pledge.

[7]"If a man is found kidnapping any of his brethren of the children of Israel, and mistreats him or sells him, then that kidnapper shall die; and you shall put away the evil from among you.

[8]"Take heed in an outbreak of leprosy, that you carefully observe and do according to all that the priests, the Levites, shall teach you; just as I commanded them, *so* you shall be careful to do. [9]Remember what the LORD your God did to Miriam on the way when you came out of Egypt!

[10]"When you lend your brother anything, you shall not go into his house to get his pledge. [11]You shall stand outside, and the man to whom you lend shall bring the pledge out to you. [12]And if the man *is* poor, you shall not keep his pledge overnight. [13]You shall in any case return the pledge to him again when the sun goes down, that he may sleep in his own garment and bless you; and it shall be righteousness to you before the LORD your God.

[14]"You shall not oppress a hired servant *who is* poor and needy, *whether* one of your brethren or one of the aliens who *is* in your land within your gates. [15]Each day you shall give *him* his wages, and not let the sun go down on it, for he *is* poor and has set his heart on it; lest he cry out against you to the LORD, and it be sin to you.

[16]"Fathers shall not be put to death for *their* children, nor shall children be put to death for *their* fathers; a person shall be put to death for his own sin.

[17]"You shall not pervert justice due the stranger or the fatherless, nor take a widow's garment as a pledge. [18]But you shall remember that you were a slave in Egypt, and the LORD your God redeemed you from there; therefore I command you to do this thing.

[19]"When you reap your harvest in your field, and forget a sheaf in the field, you shall not go back to get it; it shall be for the stranger, the

---

23:17 [a]Hebrew *qedeshah,* feminine of *qadesh* (see note *b*) [b]Hebrew *qadesh,* that is, one practicing sodomy and prostitution in religious rituals fatherless, and the widow, that the LORD your God may bless you in all the work of your hands. [20]When you beat your olive trees, you shall not go over the boughs again; it shall be for the stranger, the fatherless, and the widow. [21]When you gather the grapes of your vineyard, you shall not glean it afterward; it shall be for the stranger, the fatherless, and the widow. [22]And you shall remember that you were a slave in the land of Egypt; therefore I command you to do this thing.

25 [1]"If there is a dispute between men, and they come to court, that the judges may judge them, and they justify the righteous and condemn the wicked, [2]then it shall be, if the wicked man deserves to be beaten, that the judge will cause him to lie down and be beaten in his presence, according to his guilt, with a certain number of blows. [3]Forty blows he may give him and no more, lest he should exceed this and beat him with many blows above these, and your brother be humiliated in your sight.

[4]"You shall not muzzle an ox while it treads out the grain.

Marriage Duty of the Surviving Brother

[5]"If brothers dwell together, and one of them dies and has no son, the widow of the dead man shall not be married to a stranger outside the family; her husband's brother shall go in to her, take her as his wife, and perform the duty of a husband's brother to her. [6]And it shall be that the firstborn son which she bears will succeed to the name of his dead brother, that his name may not be blotted out of Israel. [7]But if the man does not want to take his brother's wife, then let his brother's wife go up to the gate to the elders, and say, 'My husband's brother refuses to raise up a name to his brother in Israel; he will not perform the duty of my husband's brother.' [8]Then the elders of his city shall call him and speak to him. But if he stands firm and says, 'I do not want to take her,' [9]then his brother's wife shall come to him in the presence of the elders, remove his sandal from his foot, spit in his face, and answer and say, 'So shall it be done to the man who will not build up his brother's house.' [10]And his name shall be called in Israel, 'The house of him who had his sandal removed.'

Miscellaneous Laws

[11]"If two men fight together, and the wife of one draws near to rescue her husband from the hand of the one attacking him, and puts out her hand and seizes him by the genitals, [12]then you

shall cut off her hand; your eye shall not pity her.

[13]"You shall not have in your bag differing weights, a heavy and a light. [14]You shall not have in your house differing measures, a large and a small. [15]You shall have a perfect and just weight, a perfect and just measure, that your days may be lengthened in the land which the LORD your God is giving you. [16]For all who do such things, all who behave unrighteously, are an abomination to the LORD your God.

Destroy the Amalekites

[17]"Remember what Amalek did to you on the way as you were coming out of Egypt, [18]how he met you on the way and attacked your rear ranks, all the stragglers at your rear, when you were tired and weary; and he did not fear God. [19]Therefore it shall be, when the LORD your God has given you rest from your enemies all around, in the land which the LORD your God is giving you to possess as an inheritance, that you will blot out the remembrance of Amalek from under heaven. You shall not forget.

Offerings of Firstfruits and Tithes

26 [1]"And it shall be, when you come into the land which the LORD your God is giving you as an inheritance, and you possess it and dwell in it, [2]that you shall take some of the first of all the produce of the ground, which you shall bring from your land that the LORD your God is giving you, and put it in a basket and go to the place where the LORD your God chooses to make His name abide. [3]And you shall go to the one who is priest in those days, and say to him, 'I declare today to the LORD your[a] God that I have come to the country which the LORD swore to our fathers to give us.'

[4]"Then the priest shall take the basket out of your hand and set it down before the altar of the LORD your God. [5]And you shall answer and say before the LORD your God: 'My father was a Syrian,[a] about to perish, and he went down to Egypt and dwelt there, few in number; and there he became a nation, great, mighty, and populous. [6]But the Egyptians mistreated us, afflicted us, and laid hard bondage on us. [7]Then we cried out to the LORD God of our fathers, and the LORD heard our voice and looked on our affliction and our labor and our oppression. [8]So the LORD brought us out of Egypt with a mighty hand and with an outstretched arm, with great terror and with signs and wonders. [9]He has brought us to this place and has given us this land, 'a land flowing

26:3 [a]Septuagint reads my. **26:5** [a]Or Aramean

with milk and honey";[a] [10]and now, behold, I have brought the firstfruits of the land which you, O LORD, have given me.'

"Then you shall set it before the LORD your God, and worship before the LORD your God. [11]So you shall rejoice in every good *thing* which the LORD your God has given to you and your house, you and the Levite and the stranger who *is* among you.

[12]"When you have finished laying aside all the tithe of your increase in the third year—the year of tithing—and have given *it* to the Levite, the stranger, the fatherless, and the widow, so that they may eat within your gates and be filled, [13]then you shall say before the LORD your God: 'I have removed the holy *tithe* from *my* house, and also have given them to the Levite, the stranger, the fatherless, and the widow, according to all Your commandments which You have commanded me; I have not transgressed Your commandments, nor have I forgotten *them.* [14]I have not eaten any of it when in mourning, nor have I removed *any* of it for an unclean *use,* nor given *any* of it for the dead. I have obeyed the voice of the LORD my God, and have done according to all that You have commanded me. [15]Look down from Your holy habitation, from heaven, and bless Your people Israel and the land which You have given us, just as You swore to our fathers, "a land flowing with milk and honey." '[a]

A Special People of God

[16]"This day the LORD your God commands you to observe these statutes and judgments; therefore you shall be careful to observe them with all your heart and with all your soul. [17]Today you have proclaimed the LORD to be your God, and that you will walk in His ways and keep His statutes, His commandments, and His judgments, and that you will obey His voice. [18]Also today the LORD has proclaimed you to be His special people, just as He promised you, that *you* should keep all His commandments, [19]and that He will set you high above all nations which He has made, in praise, in name, and in honor, and that you may be a holy people to the LORD your God, just as He has spoken."

The Law Inscribed on Stones

27 Now Moses, with the elders of Israel, commanded the people, saying: "Keep all the commandments which I command you today. [2]And it shall be, on the day when you cross over the Jordan to the land which the LORD your God is giving you, that you shall set up for yourselves large stones, and whitewash them with lime. [3]You shall write on them all the words of this law, when you have crossed over, that you may enter the land which the LORD your God is giving you, 'a land flowing with milk and honey,'[a] just as the LORD God of your fathers promised you. [4]Therefore it shall be, when you have crossed over the Jordan, *that* on Mount Ebal you shall set up these stones, which I command you today, and you shall whitewash them with lime. [5]And there you shall build an altar to the LORD your God, an altar of stones; you shall not use an iron *tool* on them. [6]You shall build with whole stones the altar of the LORD your God, and offer burnt offerings on it to the LORD your God. [7]You shall offer peace offerings, and shall eat there, and rejoice before the LORD your God. [8]And you shall write very plainly on the stones all the words of this law."

[9]Then Moses and the priests, the Levites, spoke to all Israel, saying, "Take heed and listen, O Israel: This day you have become the people of the LORD your God. [10]Therefore you shall obey the voice of the LORD your God, and observe His commandments and His statutes which I command you today."

Curses Pronounced from Mount Ebal

[11]And Moses commanded the people on the same day, saying, [12]"These shall stand on Mount Gerizim to bless the people, when you have crossed over the Jordan: Simeon, Levi, Judah, Issachar, Joseph, and Benjamin; [13]and these shall stand on Mount Ebal to curse: Reuben, Gad, Asher, Zebulun, Dan, and Naphtali.

[14]"And the Levites shall speak with a loud voice and say to all the men of Israel: [15]'Cursed *is* the one who makes a carved or molded image, an abomination to the LORD, the work of the hands of the craftsman, and sets *it* up in secret.'

"And all the people shall answer and say, 'Amen!'

[16]'Cursed *is* the one who treats his father or his mother with contempt.'

"And all the people shall say, 'Amen!'

[17]'Cursed *is* the one who moves his neighbor's landmark.'

"And all the people shall say, 'Amen!'

[18]'Cursed *is* the one who makes the blind to wander off the road.'

"And all the people shall say, 'Amen!'

[19]'Cursed *is* the one who perverts the justice due the stranger, the fatherless, and widow.'

"And all the people shall say, 'Amen!'

26:9 [a]Exodus 3:8 **26:15** [a]Exodus 3:8 **27:3** [a]Exodus 3:8

Double Vision: Moses Enables People to See the Future from Two Angles

(Deuteronomy 27:1—28:68)

Most of the Israelites preparing to enter the Promised Land had grown up in the wilderness and had never seen the miracles in Egypt. Moses recognized that this new generation needed fresh inspiration, and so cast a vision of their future. Moses knew that their prosperity depended far more on a healthy spiritual condition than on military prowess. He therefore exhorted them to grow in their knowledge of the Lord, to trust His holy nature, and to obey His commands.

The vision Moses cast that day looked quite different from anything most leaders have communicated since then: He cast vision for what life would look like if the people obeyed God fully. He told them they would enjoy blessings and fruit beyond what they needed. They would receive favor from neighboring peoples and enjoy great prosperity. They would grow healthy and strong.

But Moses also cast vision for how life would turn out if they failed to obey. Not many leaders do this! From then on, the people could see clearly the blessings of obedience and the curses of disobedience. Moses graphically described both in his speech.

That's the power of vision, from two angles. Such a vision helps people sort out what they will do, because they can think with the end in mind.

---

²⁰"Cursed *is* the one who lies with his father's wife, because he has uncovered his father's bed.'

"And all the people shall say, 'Amen!'

²¹"Cursed *is* the one who lies with any kind of animal.'

"And all the people shall say, 'Amen!'

²²"Cursed *is* the one who lies with his sister, the daughter of his father or the daughter of his mother.'

"And all the people shall say, 'Amen!'

²³"Cursed *is* the one who lies with his mother-in-law.'

"And all the people shall say, 'Amen!'

²⁴"Cursed *is* the one who attacks his neighbor secretly.'

"And all the people shall say, 'Amen!'

²⁵"Cursed *is* the one who takes a bribe to slay an innocent person.'

"And all the people shall say, 'Amen!'

²⁶"Cursed *is* the one who does not confirm *all* the words of this law by observing them.'

"And all the people shall say, 'Amen!'"

Blessings on Obedience

28 "Now it shall come to pass, if you diligently obey the voice of the LORD your God, to observe carefully all His commandments which I command you today, that the LORD your God will set you high above all nations of the earth. ²And all these blessings shall come upon you and overtake you, because you obey the voice of the LORD your God:

³"Blessed *shall* you *be* in the city, and blessed *shall* you *be* in the country.

⁴"Blessed *shall be* the fruit of your body, the produce of your ground and the increase of your herds, the increase of your cattle and the off-spring of your flocks.

⁵"Blessed *shall be* your basket and your kneading bowl.

⁶"Blessed *shall* you *be* when you come in, and blessed *shall* you *be* when you go out.

⁷"The LORD will cause your enemies who rise against you to be defeated before your face; they shall come out against you one way and flee before you seven ways.

⁸"The LORD will command the blessing on you in your storehouses and in all to which you set your hand, and He will bless you in the land which the LORD your God is giving you.

⁹"The LORD will establish you as a holy people to Himself, just as He has sworn to you, if you keep the commandments of the LORD your God and walk in His ways. ¹⁰Then all peoples of the earth shall see that you are called by the name of the LORD, and they shall be afraid of you. ¹¹And the LORD will grant you plenty of goods, in the fruit of your body, in the increase of your livestock, and in the produce of your ground, in the land of which the LORD swore to your fathers to give you. ¹²The LORD will open

to you His good treasure, the heavens, to give the rain to your land in its season, and to bless all the work of your hand. You shall lend to many nations, but you shall not borrow. ¹³And the LORD will make you the head and not the tail; you shall be above only, and not be beneath, if you heed the commandments of the LORD your God, which I command you today, and are careful to observe *them.* ¹⁴So you shall not turn aside from any of the words which I command you this day, *to* the right or the left, to go after other gods to serve them.

Curses on Disobedience

¹⁵"But it shall come to pass, if you do not obey the voice of the LORD your God, to observe carefully all His commandments and His statutes which I command you today, that all these curses will come upon you and overtake you:

¹⁶"Cursed *shall* you *be* in the city, and cursed *shall* you *be* in the country.

¹⁷"Cursed *shall be* your basket and your kneading bowl.

¹⁸"Cursed *shall be* the fruit of your body and the produce of your land, the increase of your cattle and the offspring of your flocks.

¹⁹"Cursed *shall* you *be* when you come in, and cursed *shall* you *be* when you go out.

²⁰"The LORD will send on you cursing, confusion, and rebuke in all that you set your hand to do, until you are destroyed and until you perish quickly, because of the wickedness of your doings in which you have forsaken Me. ²¹The LORD will make the plague cling to you until He has consumed you from the land which you are going to possess. ²²The LORD will strike you with consumption, with fever, with inflammation, with severe burning fever, with the sword, with scorching, and with mildew; they shall pursue you until you perish. ²³And your heavens which *are* over your head shall be bronze, and the earth which is under you *shall be* iron. ²⁴The LORD will change the rain of your land to powder and dust; from the heaven it shall come down on you until you are destroyed.

²⁵"The LORD will cause you to be defeated before your enemies; you shall go out one way against them and flee seven ways before them; and you shall become troublesome to all the kingdoms of the earth. ²⁶Your carcasses shall be food for all the birds of the air and the beasts of the earth, and no one shall frighten *them* away. ²⁷The LORD will strike you with the boils of Egypt, with tumors, with the scab, and with the itch, from which you cannot be healed. ²⁸The LORD will strike you with madness and blindness and confusion of heart. ²⁹And you shall grope at noonday, as a blind man gropes in darkness; you shall not prosper in your ways; you shall be only oppressed and plundered continually, and no one shall save *you.*

³⁰"You shall betroth a wife, but another man shall lie with her; you shall build a house, but you shall not dwell in it; you shall plant a vineyard, but shall not gather its grapes. ³¹Your ox *shall be* slaughtered before your eyes, but you shall not eat of it; your donkey *shall be* violently taken away from before you, and shall not be restored to you; your sheep *shall be* given to your enemies, and you shall have no one to rescue *them.* ³²Your sons and your daughters *shall be* given to another people, and your eyes shall look and fail *with longing* for them all day long; and *there shall be* no strength in your hand. ³³A nation whom you have not known shall eat the fruit of your land and the produce of your labor, and you shall be only oppressed and crushed continually. ³⁴So you shall be driven mad because of the sight which your eyes see. ³⁵The LORD will strike you in the knees and on the legs with severe boils which cannot be healed, and from the sole of your foot to the top of your head.

³⁶"The LORD will bring you and the king whom you set over you to a nation which neither you nor your fathers have known, and there you shall serve other gods—wood and stone. ³⁷And you shall become an astonishment, a proverb, and a byword among all nations where the LORD will drive you.

³⁸"You shall carry much seed out to the field but gather little in, for the locust shall consume it. ³⁹You shall plant vineyards and tend *them,* but you shall neither drink *of* the wine nor gather the *grapes;* for the worms shall eat them. ⁴⁰You shall have olive trees throughout all your territory, but you shall not anoint *yourself* with the oil; for your olives shall drop off. ⁴¹You shall beget sons and daughters, but they shall not be yours; for they shall go into captivity. ⁴²Locusts shall consume all your trees and the produce of your land.

⁴³"The alien who *is* among you shall rise higher and higher above you, and you shall come down lower and lower. ⁴⁴He shall lend to you, but you shall not lend to him; he shall be the head, and you shall be the tail.

⁴⁵"Moreover all these curses shall come upon you and pursue and overtake you, until you are destroyed, because you did not obey the voice of the LORD your God, to keep His commandments and His statutes which He commanded you. ⁴⁶And they shall be upon you for a sign and a wonder, and on your descendants forever.

⁴⁷"Because you did not serve the LORD your God with joy and gladness of heart, for the abundance of everything, ⁴⁸therefore you shall serve your enemies, whom the LORD will send against you, in hunger, in thirst, in nakedness, and in need of everything; and He will put a yoke of iron on your neck until He has destroyed you. ⁴⁹The LORD will bring a nation against you from afar, from the end of the earth, *as swift* as the eagle flies, a nation whose language you will not understand, ⁵⁰a nation of fierce countenance, which does not respect the elderly nor show favor to the young. ⁵¹And they shall eat the increase of your livestock and the produce of your land, until you are destroyed; they shall not leave you grain or new wine or oil, *or* the increase of your cattle or the offspring of your flocks, until they have destroyed you.

⁵²"They shall besiege you at all your gates until your high and fortified walls, in which you trust, come down throughout all your land; and they shall besiege you at all your gates throughout all your land which the LORD your God has given you. ⁵³You shall eat the fruit of your own body, the flesh of your sons and your daughters whom the LORD your God has given you, in the siege and desperate straits in which your enemy shall distress you. ⁵⁴The sensitive and very refined man among you will be hostile toward his brother, toward the wife of his bosom, and toward the rest of his children whom he leaves behind, ⁵⁵so that he will not give any of them the flesh of his children whom he will eat, because he has nothing left in the siege and desperate straits in which your enemy shall distress you at all your gates. ⁵⁶The tender and delicate woman among you, who would not venture to set the sole of her foot on the ground because of her delicateness and sensitivity, will refuse[a] to the husband of her bosom, and to her son and her daughter, ⁵⁷her placenta which comes out from between her feet and her children whom she bears; for she will eat them secretly for lack of everything in the siege and desperate straits in which your enemy shall distress you at all your gates.

⁵⁸"If you do not carefully observe all the words of this law that are written in this book, that you may fear this glorious and awesome name, THE LORD YOUR GOD, ⁵⁹then the LORD will bring upon you and your descendants extraordinary plagues—great and prolonged plagues—and serious and prolonged sicknesses. ⁶⁰Moreover He will bring back on you all the diseases of Egypt, of which you were afraid, and they shall cling to you. ⁶¹Also every sickness and every plague, which *is* not written in this Book of the Law, will the LORD bring upon you until you are destroyed. ⁶²You shall be left few in number, whereas you were as the stars of heaven in multitude, because you would not obey the voice of the LORD your God. ⁶³And it shall be, *that* just as the LORD rejoiced over you to do you good and multiply you, so the LORD will rejoice over you to destroy you and bring you to nothing; and you shall be plucked from off the land which you go to possess.

⁶⁴"Then the LORD will scatter you among all peoples, from one end of the earth to the other, and there you shall serve other gods, which neither you nor your fathers have known—wood and stone. ⁶⁵And among those nations you shall find no rest, nor shall the sole of your foot have a resting place; but there the LORD will give you a trembling heart, failing eyes, and anguish of soul. ⁶⁶Your life shall hang in doubt before you; you shall fear day and night, and have no assurance of life. ⁶⁷In the morning you shall say, 'Oh, that it were evening!' And at evening you shall say, 'Oh, that it were morning!' because of the fear which terrifies your heart, and because of the sight which your eyes see.

⁶⁸"And the LORD will take you back to Egypt in ships, by the way of which I said to you, 'You shall never see it again.' And there you shall be offered for sale to your enemies as male and female slaves, but no one will buy *you*."

The Covenant Renewed in Moab

29 These *are* the words of the covenant which the LORD commanded Moses to make with the children of Israel in the land of Moab, besides the covenant which He made with them in Horeb.

²Now Moses called all Israel and said to them: "You have seen all that the LORD did before your eyes in the land of Egypt, to Pharaoh and to all his servants and to all his land— ³the great trials which your eyes have seen, the signs, and those great wonders. ⁴Yet the LORD has not given you a heart to perceive and eyes to see and ears to hear, to this *very* day. ⁵And I have led you forty years in the wilderness. Your clothes have not worn out on you, and your sandals have not worn out on your feet. ⁶You have not eaten bread, nor have you drunk wine or *similar* drink, that you may know that I *am* the LORD your God. ⁷And when you came to this place, Sihon king of Heshbon and Og king of Bashan came out against us to battle, and we conquered them.

28:56 ᵃLiterally *her eye shall be evil toward*

[8]We took their land and gave it as an inheritance to the Reubenites, to the Gadites, and to half the tribe of Manasseh. [9]Therefore keep the words of this covenant, and do them, that you may prosper in all that you do.

[10]"All of you stand today before the LORD your God: your leaders and your tribes and your elders and your officers, all the men of Israel, [11]your little ones and your wives—also the stranger who *is* in your camp, from the one who cuts your wood to the one who draws your water— [12]that you may enter into covenant with the LORD your God, and into His oath, which the LORD your God makes with you today, [13]that He may establish you today as a people for Himself, and *that* He may be God to you, just as He has spoken to you, and just as He has sworn to your fathers, to Abraham, Isaac, and Jacob.

[14]"I make this covenant and this oath, not with you alone, [15]but with *him* who stands here with us today before the LORD our God, as well as with *him* who *is* not here with us today [16](for you know that we dwelt in the land of Egypt and that we came through the nations which you passed by, [17]and you saw their abominations and their idols which *were* among them—wood and stone and silver and gold); [18]so that there may not be among you man or woman or family or tribe, whose heart turns away today from the LORD our God, to go *and* serve the gods of these nations, and that there may not be among you a root bearing bitterness or wormwood; [19]and so it may not happen, when he hears the words of this curse, that he blesses himself in his heart, saying, 'I shall have peace, even though I follow the dictates[a] of my heart'—as though the drunkard could be included with the sober.

[20]"The LORD would not spare him; for then the anger of the LORD and His jealousy would burn against that man, and every curse that is written in this book would settle on him, and the LORD would blot out his name from under heaven. [21]And the LORD would separate him from all the tribes of Israel for adversity, according to all the curses of the covenant that are written in this Book of the Law, [22]so that the coming generation of your children who rise up after you, and the foreigner who comes from a far land, would say, when they see the plagues of that land and the sicknesses which the LORD has laid on it:

[23]'The whole land *is* brimstone, salt, and burning; it is not sown, nor does it bear, nor does any grass grow there, like the overthrow of Sodom and Gomorrah, Admah, and Zeboiim, which the LORD overthrew in His anger and His wrath.' [24]All nations would say, 'Why has the LORD done so to this land? What does the heat of this great anger mean?' [25]Then *people* would say: 'Because they have forsaken the covenant of the LORD God of their fathers, which He made with them when He brought them out of the land of Egypt; [26]for they went and served other gods and worshiped them, gods that they did not know and that He had not given to them. [27]Then the anger of the LORD was aroused against this land, to bring on it every curse that is written in this book. [28]And the LORD uprooted them from their land in anger, in wrath, and in great indignation, and cast them into another land, as *it is* this day.'

[29]"The secret *things belong* to the LORD our God, but those *things which are* revealed *belong* to us and to our children forever, that *we* may do all the words of this law.

The Blessing of Returning to God

30 "Now it shall come to pass, when all these things come upon you, the blessing and the curse which I have set before you, and you call *them* to mind among all the nations where the LORD your God drives you, [2]and you return to the LORD your God and obey His voice, according to all that I command you today, you and your children, with all your heart and with all your soul, [3]that the LORD your God will bring you back from captivity, and have compassion on you, and gather you again from all the nations where the LORD your God has scattered you. [4]If *any* of you are driven out to the farthest *parts* under heaven, from there the LORD your God will gather you, and from there He will bring you. [5]Then the LORD your God will bring you to the land which your fathers possessed, and you shall possess it. He will prosper you and multiply you more than your fathers. [6]And the LORD your God will circumcise your heart and the heart of your descendants, to love the LORD your God with all your heart and with all your soul, that you may live.

[7]"Also the LORD your God will put all these curses on your enemies and on those who hate you, who persecuted you. [8]And you will again obey the voice of the LORD and do all His commandments which I command you today. [9]The LORD your God will make you abound in all the work of your hand, in the fruit of your body, in the increase of your livestock, and in the produce of your land for good. For the LORD will again rejoice over you for good as He rejoiced over

---

29:19 [a]Or *stubbornness*

your fathers, [10]if you obey the voice of the LORD your God, to keep His commandments and His statutes which are written in this Book of the Law, *and* if you turn to the LORD your God with all your heart and with all your soul.

The Choice of Life or Death

[11]"For this commandment which I command you today *is* not *too* mysterious for you, nor *is* it far off. [12]It *is* not in heaven, that you should say, 'Who will ascend into heaven for us and bring it to us, that we may hear it and do it?' [13]Nor *is* it beyond the sea, that you should say, 'Who will go over the sea for us and bring it to us, that we may hear it and do it?' [14]But the word *is* very near you, in your mouth and in your heart, that you may do it.

[15]"See, I have set before you today life and good, death and evil, [16]in that I command you today to love the LORD your God, to walk in His ways, and to keep His commandments, His statutes, and His judgments, that you may live and multiply; and the LORD your God will bless you in the land which you go to possess. [17]But if your heart turns away so that you do not hear, and are drawn away, and worship other gods and serve them, [18]I announce to you today that you shall surely perish; you shall not prolong *your* days in the land which you cross over the Jordan to go in and possess. [19]I call heaven and earth as witnesses today against you, *that* I have set before you life and death, blessing and cursing; therefore choose life, that both you and your descendants may live; [20]that you may love the LORD your God, that you may obey His voice, and that you may cling to Him, for He *is* your life and the length of your days; and that you may dwell in the land which the LORD swore to your fathers, to Abraham, Isaac, and Jacob, to give them."

Joshua the New Leader of Israel

31 Then Moses went and spoke these words to all Israel. [2]And he said to them: "I *am* one hundred and twenty years old today. I can no longer go out and come in. Also the LORD has said to me, 'You shall not cross over this Jordan.' [3]The LORD your God Himself crosses over before you; He will destroy these nations from before you, and you shall dispossess them. Joshua himself crosses over before you, just as the LORD has said. [4]And the LORD will do to them as He did to Sihon and Og, the kings of the Amorites and their land, when He destroyed them. [5]The LORD will give them over to you, that you may do to them according to every commandment which I have

---

The Law of Legacy: Success Without a Successor Means Failure

(Deuteronomy 31:1–13)

Just before he died, Moses formally presented his successor, Joshua, to the people. Moses had been mentoring him for years in preparation for this day. Knowing that he would not be able to enter the Promised Land himself, he realized he had to equip the next leader to finish what he had started. Note what Moses did for Joshua:

1. He convinced the people that the new must replace the old (vv. 1, 2).
2. He reminded them of God's commitment to fulfill His promise (v. 3).
3. He endorsed the new leader and passed on his authority to Joshua (vv. 3–5).
4. He forecasted victory under Joshua and cited his track record (vv. 3–6).
5. He commissioned Joshua with the task of leading the people into the land (vv. 7, 8).
6. He directed Joshua to read God's Word repeatedly (vv. 9–13).

---

commanded you. [6]Be strong and of good courage, do not fear nor be afraid of them; for the LORD your God, He *is* the One who goes with you. He will not leave you nor forsake you."

[7]Then Moses called Joshua and said to him in the sight of all Israel, "Be strong and of good courage, for you must go with this people to the land which the LORD has sworn to their fathers to give them, and you shall cause them to inherit it. [8]And the LORD, He *is* the One who goes before you. He will be with you, He will not leave you nor forsake you; do not fear nor be dismayed."

The Law to Be Read Every Seven Years

[9]So Moses wrote this law and delivered it to the priests, the sons of Levi, who bore the ark of the covenant of the LORD, and to all the elders of Israel. [10]And Moses commanded them, saying: "At the end of *every* seven years, at the appointed time in the year of release, at the Feast of Tabernacles, [11]when all Israel comes to appear before the LORD your God in the place which He

chooses, you shall read this law before all Israel in their hearing. [12]Gather the people together, men and women and little ones, and the stranger who *is* within your gates, that they may hear and that they may learn to fear the LORD your God and carefully observe all the words of this law, [13]and *that* their children, who have not known it, may hear and learn to fear the LORD your God as long as you live in the land which you cross the Jordan to possess."

Prediction of Israel's Rebellion

[14]Then the LORD said to Moses, "Behold, the days approach when you must die; call Joshua, and present yourselves in the tabernacle of meeting, that I may inaugurate him."

So Moses and Joshua went and presented themselves in the tabernacle of meeting. [15]Now the LORD appeared at the tabernacle in a pillar of cloud, and the pillar of cloud stood above the door of the tabernacle.

[16]And the LORD said to Moses: "Behold, you will rest with your fathers; and this people will rise and play the harlot with the gods of the foreigners of the land, where they go *to be* among them, and they will forsake Me and break My covenant which I have made with them. [17]Then My anger shall be aroused against them in that day, and I will forsake them, and I will hide My face from them, and they shall be devoured. And many evils and troubles shall befall them, so that they will say in that day, 'Have not these evils come upon us because our God *is* not among us?' [18]And I will surely hide My face in that day because of all the evil which they have done, in that they have turned to other gods.

[19]"Now therefore, write down this song for yourselves, and teach it to the children of Israel; put it in their mouths, that this song may be a witness for Me against the children of Israel. [20]When I have brought them to the land flowing with milk and honey, of which I swore to their fathers, and they have eaten and filled themselves and grown fat, then they will turn to other gods and serve them; and they will provoke Me and break My covenant. [21]Then it shall be, when many evils and troubles have come upon them, that this song will testify against them as a witness; for it will not be forgotten in the mouths of their descendants, for I know the inclination of their behavior today, even before I have brought them to the land of which I swore *to give them*."

[22]Therefore Moses wrote this song the same day, and taught it to the children of Israel. [23]Then He inaugurated Joshua the son of Nun, and said, "Be strong and of good courage; for you shall bring the children of Israel into the land of which I swore to them, and I will be with you."

[24]So it was, when Moses had completed writing the words of this law in a book, when they were finished, [25]that Moses commanded the Levites, who bore the ark of the covenant of the LORD, saying: [26]"Take this Book of the Law, and put it beside the ark of the covenant of the LORD your God, that it may be there as a witness against you; [27]for I know your rebellion and your stiff neck. *If* today, while I am yet alive with you, you have been rebellious against the LORD, then how much more after my death? [28]Gather to me all the elders of your tribes, and your officers, that I may speak these words in their hearing and call heaven and earth to witness against them. [29]For I know that after my death you will become utterly corrupt, and turn aside from the way which I have commanded you. And evil will befall you in the latter days, because you will do evil in the sight of the LORD, to provoke Him to anger through the work of your hands."

The Song of Moses

[30]Then Moses spoke in the hearing of all the assembly of Israel the words of this song until they were ended:

32 "Give ear, O heavens, and I will speak;
And hear, O earth, the words of my mouth.

2 Let my teaching drop as the rain,
My speech distill as the dew,
As raindrops on the tender herb,
And as showers on the grass.

3 For I proclaim the name of the LORD:
Ascribe greatness to our God.

4 *He is* the Rock, His work *is* perfect;
For all His ways *are* justice,
A God of truth and without injustice;
Righteous and upright *is* He.

5 "They have corrupted themselves;
They are not His children,
Because of their blemish:
A perverse and crooked generation.

6 Do you thus deal with the LORD,
O foolish and unwise people?
Is He not your Father, *who* bought you?
Has He not made you and established you?

7 "Remember the days of old,
Consider the years of many generations.
Ask your father, and he will show you;
Your elders, and they will tell you:

8 When the Most High divided their
inheritance to the nations,
When He separated the sons of Adam,
He set the boundaries of the peoples
According to the number of the children
of Israel.
9 For the LORD's portion *is* His people;
Jacob *is* the place of His inheritance.

10 "He found him in a desert land
And in the wasteland, a howling
wilderness;
He encircled him, He instructed him,
He kept him as the apple of His eye.
11 As an eagle stirs up its nest,
Hovers over its young,
Spreading out its wings, taking them up,
Carrying them on its wings,
12 *So* the LORD alone led him,
And *there was* no foreign god with him.

13 "He made him ride in the heights of the
earth,
That he might eat the produce of the fields;
He made him draw honey from the rock,
And oil from the flinty rock;
14 Curds from the cattle, and milk of the
flock,
With fat of lambs;
And rams of the breed of Bashan, and
goats,
With the choicest wheat;
And you drank wine, the blood of the
grapes.

15 "But Jeshurun grew fat and kicked;
You grew fat, you grew thick,
You are obese!
Then he forsook God *who* made him,
And scornfully esteemed the Rock of his
salvation.
16 They provoked Him to jealousy with
foreign *gods;*
With abominations they provoked Him to
anger.
17 They sacrificed to demons, not to God,
To gods they did not know,
To new *gods,* new arrivals
That your fathers did not fear.
18 Of the Rock *who* begot you, you are
unmindful,
And have forgotten the God who fathered
you.

19 "And when the LORD saw *it,* He spurned
them,

Because of the provocation of His sons
and His daughters.
20 And He said: 'I will hide My face from
them,
I will see what their end *will be,*
For they *are* a perverse generation,
Children in whom *is* no faith.
21 They have provoked Me to jealousy by
what is not God;
They have moved Me to anger by their
foolish idols.
But I will provoke them to jealousy by
those who are not a nation;
I will move them to anger by a foolish
nation.
22 For a fire is kindled in My anger,
And shall burn to the lowest hell;
It shall consume the earth with her
increase,
And set on fire the foundations of the
mountains.

23 'I will heap disasters on them;
I will spend My arrows on them.
24 *They shall be* wasted with hunger,
Devoured by pestilence and bitter
destruction;
I will also send against them the teeth of
beasts,
With the poison of serpents of the dust.
25 The sword shall destroy outside;
There shall be terror within
For the young man and virgin,
The nursing child with the man of gray
hairs.
26 I would have said, "I will dash them in
pieces,
I will make the memory of them to cease
from among men,"
27 Had I not feared the wrath of the enemy,
Lest their adversaries should
misunderstand,
Lest they should say, "Our hand *is* high;
And it is not the LORD who has done all
this."'

28 "For they *are* a nation void of counsel,
Nor *is there any* understanding in them.
29 Oh, that they were wise, *that* they
understood this,
That they would consider their latter end!
30 How could one chase a thousand,
And two put ten thousand to flight,
Unless their Rock had sold them,
And the LORD had surrendered them?
31 For their rock *is* not like our Rock,

32 Even our enemies themselves *being* judges.
For their vine *is* of the vine of Sodom
And of the fields of Gomorrah;
Their grapes *are* grapes of gall,
Their clusters *are* bitter.

33 Their wine *is* the poison of serpents,
And the cruel venom of cobras.

34 '*Is* this not laid up in store with Me,
Sealed up among My treasures?

35 Vengeance is Mine, and recompense;
Their foot shall slip in *due* time;
For the day of their calamity *is* at hand,
And the things to come hasten upon
them.'

36 "For the LORD will judge His people
And have compassion on His servants,
When He sees that *their* power is gone,
And *there is* no one *remaining,* bond or free.

37 He will say: 'Where *are* their gods,
The rock in which they sought refuge?

38 Who ate the fat of their sacrifices,
And drank the wine of their drink
offering?
Let them rise and help you,
And be your refuge.

39 'Now see that I, *even* I, *am* He,
And *there is* no God besides Me;
I kill and I make alive;
I wound and I heal;
Nor *is there any* who can deliver from My
hand.

40 For I raise My hand to heaven,
And say, "*As* I live forever,

41 If I whet My glittering sword,
And My hand takes hold on judgment,
I will render vengeance to My enemies,
And repay those who hate Me.

42 I will make My arrows drunk with blood,
And My sword shall devour flesh,
With the blood of the slain and the
captives,
From the heads of the leaders of the
enemy."'

43 "Rejoice, O Gentiles, *with* His people;[a]
For He will avenge the blood of His
servants,
And render vengeance to His adversaries;
He will provide atonement for His land
and His people."

44 So Moses came with Joshua[a] the son of
Nun and spoke all the words of this song in the hearing of the people. 45 Moses finished speaking all these words to all Israel, 46 and he said to them: "Set your hearts on all the words which I testify among you today, which you shall command your children to be careful to observe—all the words of this law. 47 For it *is* not a futile thing for you, because it *is* your life, and by this word you shall prolong *your* days in the land which you cross over the Jordan to possess."

Moses to Die on Mount Nebo

48 Then the LORD spoke to Moses that very same day, saying: 49 "Go up this mountain of the Abarim, Mount Nebo, which *is* in the land of Moab, across from Jericho; view the land of Canaan, which I give to the children of Israel as a possession; 50 and die on the mountain which you ascend, and be gathered to your people, just as Aaron your brother died on Mount Hor and was gathered to his people; 51 because you trespassed against Me among the children of Israel at the waters of Meribah Kadesh, in the Wilderness of Zin, because you did not hallow Me in the midst of the children of Israel. 52 Yet you shall see the land before *you,* though you shall not go there, into the land which I am giving to the children of Israel."

Moses' Final Blessing on Israel

33 Now this *is* the blessing with which Moses the man of God blessed the children of Israel before his death. 2 And he said:

"The LORD came from Sinai,
And dawned on them from Seir;
He shone forth from Mount Paran,
And He came with ten thousands of saints;
From His right hand
Came a fiery law for them.

3 Yes, He loves the people;
All His saints *are* in Your hand;
They sit down at Your feet;
everyone receives Your words.

4 Moses commanded a law for us,
A heritage of the congregation of Jacob.

5 And He was King in Jeshurun,
When the leaders of the people were
gathered,
All the tribes of Israel together.

32:43 [a] A Dead Sea Scroll fragment adds *And let all the gods (angels) worship Him* (compare Septuagint and Hebrews 1:6). **32:44** [a] Hebrew *Hoshea* (compare Numbers 13:8, 16)

⁶ "Let Reuben live, and not die,
  Nor let his men be few."

⁷And this he said of Judah:

"Hear, LORD, the voice of Judah,
  And bring him to his people;
  Let his hands be sufficient for him,
  And may You be a help against his
    enemies."

⁸And of Levi he said:

"*Let* Your Thummim and Your Urim *be*
    with Your holy one,
  Whom You tested at Massah,
  And with whom You contended at the
    waters of Meribah,
⁹ Who says of his father and mother,
  'I have not seen them';
  Nor did he acknowledge his brothers,
  Or know his own children;
  For they have observed Your word
  And kept Your covenant.
¹⁰ They shall teach Jacob Your judgments,
  And Israel Your law.
  They shall put incense before You,
  And a whole burnt sacrifice on Your altar.
¹¹ Bless his substance, LORD,
  And accept the work of his hands;
  Strike the loins of those who rise against
    him,
  And of those who hate him, that they rise
    not again."

¹²Of Benjamin he said:

"The beloved of the LORD shall dwell in
    safety by Him,
  Who shelters him all the day long;
  And he shall dwell between His
    shoulders."

¹³And of Joseph he said:

"Blessed of the LORD *is* his land,
  With the precious things of heaven, with
    the dew,
  And the deep lying beneath,
¹⁴ With the precious fruits of the sun,
  With the precious produce of the
    months,
¹⁵ With the best things of the ancient
    mountains,
  With the precious things of the everlasting
    hills,

¹⁶ With the precious things of the earth and
    its fullness,
  And the favor of Him who dwelt in the
    bush.
  Let *the blessing* come 'on the head of
    Joseph,
  And on the crown of the head of him *who
    was* separate from his brothers.'ᵃ
¹⁷ His glory *is like* a firstborn bull,
  And his horns *like* the horns of the wild
    ox;
  Together with them
  He shall push the peoples
  To the ends of the earth;
  They *are* the ten thousands of Ephraim,
  And they *are* the thousands of Manasseh."

¹⁸And of Zebulun he said:

"Rejoice, Zebulun, in your going out,
  And Issachar in your tents!
¹⁹ They shall call the peoples *to the*
    mountain;
  There they shall offer sacrifices of
    righteousness;
  For they shall partake *of* the abundance of
    the seas
  And *of* treasures hidden in the sand."

²⁰And of Gad he said:

"Blessed *is* he who enlarges Gad;
  He dwells as a lion,
  And tears the arm and the crown of his
    head.
²¹ He provided the first *part* for himself,
  Because a lawgiver's portion was reserved
    there.
  He came *with* the heads of the people;
  He administered the justice of the LORD,
  And His judgments with Israel."

²²And of Dan he said:

"Dan *is* a lion's whelp;
  He shall leap from Bashan."

²³And of Naphtali he said:

"O Naphtali, satisfied with favor,
  And full of the blessing of the LORD,
  Possess the west and the south."

²⁴And of Asher he said:

33:16 ᵃGenesis 49:26

"Asher *is* most blessed of sons;
Let him be favored by his brothers,
And let him dip his foot in oil.
25 Your sandals *shall be* iron and bronze;
As your days, *so shall* your strength *be.*

26 " *There is* no one like the God of Jeshurun,
Who rides the heavens to help you,
And in His excellency on the clouds.
27 The eternal God *is* your refuge,
And underneath *are* the everlasting arms;
He will thrust out the enemy from before
you,
And will say, 'Destroy!'
28 Then Israel shall dwell in safety,
The fountain of Jacob alone,
In a land of grain and new wine;
His heavens shall also drop dew.
29 Happy *are* you, O Israel!
Who *is* like you, a people saved by the
LORD,
The shield of your help
And the sword of your majesty!
Your enemies shall submit to you,
And you shall tread down their high
places."

Moses Dies on Mount Nebo

34 Then Moses went up from the plains of Moab to Mount Nebo, to the top of Pisgah, which is across from Jericho. And the LORD showed him all the land of Gilead as far as Dan, [2] all Naphtali and the land of Ephraim and Manasseh, all the land of Judah as far as the Western Sea,[a] [3] the South, and the plain of the Valley of Jericho, the city of palm trees, as far as Zoar. [4] Then the LORD said to him, "This *is* the land of which I swore to give Abraham, Isaac, and Jacob, saying, 'I will give it to your descendants.' I have caused you to see *it* with your eyes, but you shall not cross over there."

[5] So Moses the servant of the LORD died there in the land of Moab, according to the word of the LORD. [6] And He buried him in a valley in the land of Moab, opposite Beth Peor; but no one knows his grave to this day. [7] Moses *was* one hundred and twenty years old when he died. His eyes were not dim nor his natural vigor diminished. [8] And the children of Israel wept for Moses in the plains of Moab thirty days. So the days of weeping *and* mourning for Moses ended.

[9] Now Joshua the son of Nun was full of the spirit of wisdom, for Moses had laid his hands on him; so the children of Israel heeded him, and did as the LORD had commanded Moses.

[10] But since then there has not arisen in Israel a prophet like Moses, whom the LORD knew face to face, [11] in all the signs and wonders which the LORD sent him to do in the land of Egypt, before Pharaoh, before all his servants, and in all his land, [12] and by all that mighty power and all the great terror which Moses performed in the sight of all Israel.

34:2 [a] That is, the Mediterranean

JOSHUA
Encourages Every Second-Generation Leader

Summary

Joshua represents and encourages every second-generation leader. He didn't establish the free nation of Israel—Moses did. But Joshua succeeded Moses respectfully and naturally upon the latter's death. He finished the work Moses could not complete and led the people of Israel to victory in the Promise Land. Joshua challenges us to lay hold of God's promises and walk in His victory despite adversity. We learn a number of valuable lessons from this leader.

First, Joshua remained submissive to the divine chain of care. He never once attempted to displace Moses' leadership, even when Moses had grown old and could no longer do what Joshua could do. Joshua waited until his time came, just as David waited for King Saul to leave the scene. Saul was killed and *then* David became king.

Second, Joshua learned to "let Moses die" and to be strong and courageous in his own style of leadership. At the onset of the book, God commands Joshua to take courage. "Moses my servant is dead," God says to him. "Now therefore, arise, go over this Jordan, you and all this people, to the land which I am giving to them—the children of Israel" (1:2). Joshua was a military leader, different from Moses' diplomatic or reform leadership style. Somewhere, Joshua must have decided not to imitate Moses' style, but to be himself. The timing could not have been more perfect. Joshua entered leadership in a season when Israel needed military leadership, not diplomatic leadership.

Third, as a leader Joshua did "whatever it took." He practiced the Law of Victory as much as anyone in his day—perhaps as much as anyone described in the Bible. His no-nonsense leadership style drove him to pay whatever price seemed necessary to get the job done. He courageously took risks. He often questioned the people, asking things like, "How long will you neglect to go and possess the land which the LORD God of your fathers has given you?" (18:3). He simply couldn't understand why they hesitated. Why didn't they just take the land God had promised them?

This book is all about Israel moving in and settling the Promised Land. Although it took the Israelites many years (and 21 full chapters) to do it, they finally possess all the real estate God had given them. And Joshua led the charge the whole way.

God's Role in Joshua

During Moses' day, God played the role of a patient father, waiting for a new generation to mature so He could lead them into the Promised Land. By the time Joshua takes over, God speaks in a straightforward manner to Israel's commanding officer. He has grown weary of His people's disobedience, hesitance, and complaints. He challenges Joshua not to swerve to the right or to the left, but to do all that He commands. Joshua must compromise nothing, but fulfill everything.

Clearly, we see the Lord lead in a new and appropriate style for the times. His people were entering a season in which they needed to act as a military unit, so both God and Joshua provide direction in a military style.

Leaders in Joshua

Joshua, Caleb, Achan

Other People of Influence in Joshua

Rahab, Eleazar the priest, the Gibeonites

Lessons in Leadership

- Difficult times demand a different style of leadership.
- Good leaders help their people remember past blessings and divine victories.
- Leaders must be willing to take risks and pay the price; courage elicits commitment.
- Compromise on your methods, but never on your convictions or principles.
- Leaders cannot afford to be indecisive; they must give clear and specific directions.
- God will work on behalf of leaders who surrender their hearts completely to Him.
- Good leaders do whatever it takes to get the job done.

LEADERSHIP

HIGHLIGHTS IN JOSHUA

God's Commission to Joshua

1 After the death of Moses the servant of the LORD, it came to pass that the LORD spoke to Joshua the son of Nun, Moses' assistant, saying: 2"Moses My servant is dead. Now therefore, arise, go over this Jordan, you and all this people, to the land which I am giving to them—the children of Israel. 3Every place that the sole of your foot will tread upon I have given you, as I said to Moses. 4From the wilderness and this Lebanon as far as the great river, the River Euphrates, all the land of the Hittites, and to the Great Sea toward the going down of the sun, shall be your territory. 5No man shall *be able to* stand before you all the days of your life; as I was with Moses, *so* I will be with you. I will not leave you nor forsake you. 6Be strong and of good courage, for to this people you shall divide as an inheritance the land which I swore to their fathers to give them. 7Only be strong and very courageous, that you may observe to do according to all the law which Moses My servant commanded you; do not turn from it to the right hand or to the left, that you may prosper wherever you go. 8This Book of the Law shall not depart from your mouth, but you shall meditate in it day and night, that you may observe to do according to all that is written in it. For then you will make your way prosperous, and then you will have good success. 9Have I not commanded you? Be strong and of good courage; do not be afraid, nor be dismayed, for the LORD your God *is* with you wherever you go."

The Order to Cross the Jordan

10Then Joshua commanded the officers of the people, saying, 11"Pass through the camp and command the people, saying, 'Prepare provisions for yourselves, for within three days you will cross over this Jordan, to go in to possess the land which the LORD your God is giving you to possess.'"

12And to the Reubenites, the Gadites, and half the tribe of Manasseh Joshua spoke, saying, 13"Remember the word which Moses the servant of the LORD commanded you, saying, 'The LORD your God is giving you rest and is giving you this land.' 14Your wives, your little ones, and your livestock shall remain in the land which Moses gave you on this side of the Jordan. But you shall pass before your brethren armed, all your mighty men of valor, and help them, 15until the LORD has given your brethren rest, as He *gave* you, and they also have taken possession of the land which the LORD your God is giving them. Then you shall return to the land of your possession and enjoy it, which Moses the LORD's servant gave you on this side of the Jordan toward the sunrise."

16So they answered Joshua, saying, "All that you command us we will do, and wherever you send us we will go. 17Just as we heeded Moses in all things, so we will heed you. Only the LORD

The Law of Timing: Joshua Begins with a Divine Call and Charge

(Joshua 1:1–9)

Consider this: It took 40 years for Joshua's leadership style to match the need of the moment. Moses led diplomatically. He sat and judged the people patiently as they grumbled through long years in the desert. By the time the Israelites reached Canaan, fierce enemies awaited them—and they needed a much more confrontational leader, a military man skilled in war. Enter Joshua. Note the differences between Moses and Joshua and see how timing can dictate appropriate leadership styles:

Moses
1. Led through 40 years of desert travel
2. Was a political, diplomatic leader
3. Patiently listened to complaints
4. Led people as a peacemaking shepherd
5. Provided water from a rock when the people got thirsty

Joshua
1. Led through 30 years of conquering Canaan
2. Was a military, in-your-face leader
3. Confronted laziness and fear of the enemy
4. Led people as a tough commander
5. Told the people to dig their own wells when they got thirsty

your God be with you, as He was with Moses. [18]Whoever rebels against your command and does not heed your words, in all that you command him, shall be put to death. Only be strong and of good courage."

Rahab Hides the Spies

2 Now Joshua the son of Nun sent out two men from Acacia Grove[a] to spy secretly, saying, "Go, view the land, especially Jericho." So they went, and came to the house of a harlot named Rahab, and lodged there. [2]And it was told the king of Jericho, saying, "Behold, men have come here tonight from the children of Israel to search out the country."

[3]So the king of Jericho sent to Rahab, saying, "Bring out the men who have come to you, who have entered your house, for they have come to search out all the country."

The Law of Influence: God Uses Rahab

(Joshua 2:1–21)

The story of Rahab proves that God will use anybody. This woman worked as a prostitute in Jericho as the Israelites approached the city. Although the Hebrew spies needed someone to help them scope out the best approach to conquering the city, there seemed little logical reason why Rahab should have been considered for the role:

1. She occupied no position and held no official title in the city.
2. The Israelites looked upon women as lower class citizens.
3. As a prostitute, she held an even lower social rank than the average woman.

But because leadership depends less on titles than it does on influence, God chose Rahab. She helped the spies by her quick wisdom, gutsy style, and clever plan. By doing so she saved not only her own life, but aided in accomplishing the purposes of God in Jericho. The name "Rahab" even occupies an honored place in the Hall of Faith (Heb. 11:31).

---

[4]Then the woman took the two men and hid them. So she said, "Yes, the men came to me, but I did not know where they *were* from. [5]And it

happened as the gate was being shut, when it was dark, that the men went out. Where the men went I do not know; pursue them quickly, for you may overtake them." [6](But she had brought them up to the roof and hidden them with the stalks of flax, which she had laid in order on the roof.) [7]Then the men pursued them by the road to the Jordan, to the fords. And as soon as those who pursued them had gone out, they shut the gate.

[8]Now before they lay down, she came up to them on the roof, [9]and said to the men: "I know that the LORD has given you the land, that the terror of you has fallen on us, and that all the inhabitants of the land are fainthearted because of you. [10]For we have heard how the LORD dried up the water of the Red Sea for you when you came out of Egypt, and what you did to the two kings of the Amorites who *were* on the other side of the Jordan, Sihon and Og, whom you utterly destroyed. [11]And as soon as we heard *these things,* our hearts melted; neither did there remain any more courage in anyone because of you, for the LORD your God, He *is* God in heaven above and on earth beneath. [12]Now therefore, I beg you, swear to me by the LORD, since I have shown you kindness, that you also will show kindness to my father's house, and give me a true token, [13]and spare my father, my mother, my brothers, my sisters, and all that they have, and deliver our lives from death."

[14]So the men answered her, "Our lives for yours, if none of you tell this business of ours. And it shall be, when the LORD has given us the land, that we will deal kindly and truly with you."

[15]Then she let them down by a rope through the window, for her house *was* on the city wall; she dwelt on the wall. [16]And she said to them, "Get to the mountain, lest the pursuers meet you. Hide there three days, until the pursuers have returned. Afterward you may go your way."

[17]So the men said to her: "We *will be* blameless of this oath of yours which you have made us swear, [18]unless, *when* we come into the land, you bind this line of scarlet cord in the window through which you let us down, and unless you bring your father, your mother, your brothers, and all your father's household to your own home. [19]So it shall be *that* whoever goes outside the doors of your house into the street, his blood *shall be* on his own head, and we *will be* guiltless. And whoever is with you in the house, his blood *shall be* on our head if a hand is laid on him.

2:1 [a]Hebrew *Shittim*

²⁰And if you tell this business of ours, then we will be free from your oath which you made us swear." ²¹Then she said, "According to your words, so *be* it." And she sent them away, and they departed. And she bound the scarlet cord in the window.

²²They departed and went to the mountain, and stayed there three days until the pursuers returned. The pursuers sought *them* all along the way, but did not find *them*. ²³So the two men returned, descended from the mountain, and crossed over; and they came to Joshua the son of Nun, and told him all that had befallen them. ²⁴And they said to Joshua, "Truly the LORD has delivered all the land into our hands, for indeed all the inhabitants of the country are fainthearted because of us."

Israel Crosses the Jordan

3 Then Joshua rose early in the morning; and they set out from Acacia Grove⁴ and came to the Jordan, he and all the children of Israel, and lodged there before they crossed over. ²So it was, after three days, that the officers went through the camp; ³and they commanded the people, saying, "When you see the ark of the covenant of the LORD your God, and the priests,

the Levites, bearing it, then you shall set out from your place and go after it. ⁴Yet there shall be a space between you and it, about two thousand cubits by measure. Do not come near it, that you may know the way by which you must go, for you have not passed *this* way before."

⁵And Joshua said to the people, "Sanctify yourselves, for tomorrow the LORD will do wonders among you." ⁶Then Joshua spoke to the priests, saying, "Take up the ark of the covenant and cross over before the people."

So they took up the ark of the covenant and went before the people.

⁷And the LORD said to Joshua, "This day I will begin to exalt you in the sight of all Israel, that they may know that, as I was with Moses, *so* I will be with you. ⁸You shall command the priests who bear the ark of the covenant, saying, 'When you have come to the edge of the water of the Jordan, you shall stand in the Jordan.'"

⁹So Joshua said to the children of Israel, "Come here, and hear the words of the LORD your God." ¹⁰And Joshua said, "By this you shall know that the living God *is* among you, and *that* He will without fail drive out from before you the Canaanites and the Hittites and the

---

3:1 ³Hebrew *Shittim*

RAHAB   An Unusual Woman of Faith
(Joshua 2:1–21; 6:22–25)

God uses individuals of all temperaments and backgrounds to accomplish His purposes—even prostitutes.

God strategically positioned Rahab, whom the Bible calls a "harlot" (Josh. 2:1), in a home built into the wall of Jericho. When two Hebrew spies came to her for aid, she displayed a clear understanding of spiritual issues. She described how the dread of Israel had overwhelmed her people. She acknowledged that the land belonged to the Israelites and therefore willingly risked her life to hide Joshua's spies (2:4–11). Rahab leveraged her hospitality on behalf of her parents, siblings, and their extended families, begging the spies to spare the lives of all who belonged to her (2:12, 13). They agreed.

Rahab was a woman of her word. Although she could have tipped off her king to the whereabouts of the hiding Israelites, she sent Israel's enemies on a wild goose chase. Why? Because she really believed that God was about to hand her city over to the Hebrews. Even prostitutes can exhibit saving faith (Heb. 11:31).

Wise leaders remember that God sees the human heart; while many would never trust a woman with a personal history like that of Rahab, God selected her. Because Rahab faithfully served God, her family lived and was adopted into Hebrew society—and she became an ancestor of the Lord Jesus Himself (Matt. 1:5).

Hivites and the Perizzites and the Girgashites and the Amorites and the Jebusites: ¹¹Behold, the ark of the covenant of the Lord of all the earth is crossing over before you into the Jordan. ¹²Now therefore, take for yourselves twelve men from the tribes of Israel, one man from every tribe. ¹³And it shall come to pass, as soon as the soles of the feet of the priests who bear the ark of the LORD, the Lord of all the earth, shall rest in the waters of the Jordan, *that* the waters of the Jordan shall be cut off, the waters that come down from upstream, and they shall stand as a heap."

¹⁴So it was, when the people set out from their camp to cross over the Jordan, with the priests bearing the ark of the covenant before the people, ¹⁵and as those who bore the ark came to the Jordan, and the feet of the priests who bore the ark dipped in the edge of the water (for the Jordan overflows all its banks during the whole time of harvest), ¹⁶that the waters which came down from upstream stood *still, and* rose in a heap very far away at Adam, the city that *is* beside Zaretan. So the waters that went down into the Sea of the Arabah, the Salt Sea, failed, *and* were cut off; and the people crossed over opposite Jericho. ¹⁷Then the priests who bore the ark of the covenant of the LORD stood firm on dry ground in the midst of the Jordan; and all Israel crossed over on dry ground, until all the people had crossed completely over the Jordan.

The Memorial Stones

4 And it came to pass, when all the people had completely crossed over the Jordan, that the LORD spoke to Joshua, saying: ²"Take for yourselves twelve men from the people, one man from every tribe, ³and command them, saying, 'Take for yourselves twelve stones from here, out of the midst of the Jordan, from the place where the priests' feet stood firm. You shall carry them over with you and leave them in the lodging place where you lodge tonight.' "

⁴Then Joshua called the twelve men whom he had appointed from the children of Israel, one man from every tribe; ⁵and Joshua said to them: "Cross over before the ark of the LORD your God into the midst of the Jordan, and each one of you take up a stone on his shoulder, according to the number of the tribes of the children of Israel, ⁶that this may be a sign among you when your children ask in time to come, saying, 'What do these stones *mean* to you?' ⁷Then you shall answer them that the waters of the Jordan were cut off before the ark of the covenant of the LORD; when it crossed over the Jordan, the waters of the Jordan were cut off. And these stones shall be for a memorial to the children of Israel forever."

Communication: Joshua Gives Handles to Remember God's Work

(Joshua 4:1–9)

Effective leaders look for ways to use the successes of today to empower their people for the challenges of tomorrow. Joshua did exactly that.

Although God would work a miracle to allow the people to cross the Jordan on dry ground, Joshua knew that only those who saw the incident would remember it—and he wanted to leave a legacy for the next generation, born long after the miracle occurred. Joshua wanted to find a way to communicate God's greatness to the children of Israel yet-to-be-born.

To accomplish his goal, Joshua devised a plan called "Stones of Remembrance." He directed that twelve stones be taken from the middle of the dry riverbed—one for each of the Twelve Tribes who crossed the river—and be piled in a monument on shore. Thereafter, whenever Israel's children or grandchildren asked, "What do those stones mean?" the people would have an opportunity to recast God's vision and recount God's victories. The stones served as "handles" to communicate what God had done.

Good leaders always provide "handles" to enable their people to grab hold of the vision. Effective leaders find a way to communicate future vision and past victories, because their people need to be constantly reminded of both.

⁸And the children of Israel did so, just as Joshua commanded, and took up twelve stones from the midst of the Jordan, as the LORD had spoken to Joshua, according to the number of the tribes of the children of Israel, and carried them over with them to the place where they lodged, and laid them down there. ⁹Then Joshua set up twelve stones in the midst of the Jordan, in the place where the feet of the priests who bore the ark of the covenant stood; and they are there to this day.

¹⁰So the priests who bore the ark stood in the midst of the Jordan until everything was finished that the LORD had commanded Joshua to speak to the people, according to all that Moses had commanded Joshua; and the people hurried and crossed over. ¹¹Then it came to pass, when all the people had completely crossed over, that the ark of the LORD and the priests crossed over in the presence of the people. ¹²And the men of Reuben, the men of Gad, and half the tribe of Manasseh crossed over armed before the children of Israel, as Moses had spoken to them. ¹³About forty thousand prepared for war crossed over before the LORD for battle, to the plains of Jericho. ¹⁴On that day the LORD exalted Joshua in the sight of all Israel; and they feared him, as they had feared Moses, all the days of his life.

¹⁵Then the LORD spoke to Joshua, saying, ¹⁶"Command the priests who bear the ark of the Testimony to come up from the Jordan." ¹⁷Joshua therefore commanded the priests, saying, "Come up from the Jordan." ¹⁸And it came to pass, when the priests who bore the ark of the covenant of the LORD had come from the midst of the Jordan, and the soles of the priests' feet touched the dry land, that the waters of the Jordan returned to their place and overflowed all its banks as before.

¹⁹Now the people came up from the Jordan on the tenth day of the first month, and they camped in Gilgal on the east border of Jericho. ²⁰And those twelve stones which they took out of the Jordan, Joshua set up in Gilgal. ²¹Then he spoke to the children of Israel, saying: "When your children ask their fathers in time to come, saying, 'What are these stones?' ²²then you shall let your children know, saying, 'Israel crossed over this Jordan on dry land'; ²³for the LORD your God dried up the waters of the Jordan before you until you had crossed over, as the LORD your God did to the Red Sea, which He dried up before us until we had crossed over, ²⁴that all the peoples of the earth may know the hand of the LORD, that it is mighty, that you may fear the LORD your God forever."

The Second Generation Circumcised

5 So it was, when all the kings of the Amorites who were on the west side of the Jordan, and all the kings of the Canaanites who were by the sea, heard that the LORD had dried up the waters of the Jordan from before the children of Israel until we[a] had crossed over, that their heart melted; and there was no spirit in them any longer because of the children of Israel.

²At that time the LORD said to Joshua, "Make flint knives for yourself, and circumcise the sons of Israel again the second time." ³So Joshua made flint knives for himself, and circumcised the sons of Israel at the hill of the foreskins.[a] ⁴And this is the reason why Joshua circumcised them: All the people who came out of Egypt who were males, all the men of war, had died in the wilderness on the way, after they had come out of Egypt. ⁵For all the people who came out had been circumcised, but all the people born in the wilderness, on the way as they came out of Egypt, had not been circumcised. ⁶For the children of Israel walked forty years in the wilderness, till all the people who were men of war, who came out of Egypt, were consumed, because they did not obey the voice of the LORD—to whom the LORD swore that He would not show them the land which the LORD had sworn to their fathers that He would give us, "a land flowing with milk and honey."[a] ⁷Then Joshua circumcised their sons whom He raised up in their place; for they were uncircumcised, because they had not been circumcised on the way.

⁸So it was, when they had finished circumcising all the people, that they stayed in their places in the camp till they were healed. ⁹Then the LORD said to Joshua, "This day I have rolled away the reproach of Egypt from you." Therefore the name of the place is called Gilgal[a] to this day.

¹⁰Now the children of Israel camped in Gilgal, and kept the Passover on the fourteenth day of the month at twilight on the plains of Jericho. ¹¹And they ate of the produce of the land on the day after the Passover, unleavened bread and parched grain, on the very same day. ¹²Then the manna ceased on the day after they had eaten the produce of the land; and the children of Israel no longer had manna, but they ate the food of the land of Canaan that year.

5:1 [a]Following Kethib; Qere, some Hebrew manuscripts and editions, Septuagint, Syriac, Targum, and Vulgate read *they.* **5:3** [a]Hebrew *Gibeath Haaraloth* **5:6** [a]Exodus 3:8 **5:9** [a]Literally *Rolling*

The Commander of the Army of the LORD

[13]And it came to pass, when Joshua was by Jericho, that he lifted his eyes and looked, and behold, a Man stood opposite him with His sword drawn in His hand. And Joshua went to Him and said to Him, "*Are* You for us or for our adversaries?"

[14]So He said, "No, but *as* Commander of the army of the LORD I have now come."

And Joshua fell on his face to the earth and worshiped, and said to Him, "What does my Lord say to His servant?"

[15]Then the Commander of the LORD's army said to Joshua, "Take your sandal off your foot, for the place where you stand *is* holy." And Joshua did so.

The Destruction of Jericho

6 Now Jericho was securely shut up because of the children of Israel; none went out, and none came in. [2]And the LORD said to Joshua: "See! I have given Jericho into your hand, its king, *and* the mighty men of valor. [3]You shall march around the city, all *you* men of war; you shall go all around the city once. This you shall do six days. [4]And seven priests shall bear seven trumpets of rams' horns before the ark. But the seventh day you shall march around the city seven times, and the priests shall blow the trumpets. [5]It shall come to pass, when they make a long *blast* with the ram's horn, *and* when you hear the sound of the trumpet, that all the people shall shout with a great shout; then the wall of the city will fall down flat. And the people shall go up every man straight before him."

[6]Then Joshua the son of Nun called the priests and said to them, "Take up the ark of the covenant, and let seven priests bear seven trumpets of rams' horns before the ark of the LORD." [7]And he said to the people, "Proceed, and march around the city, and let him who is armed advance before the ark of the LORD."

[8]So it was, when Joshua had spoken to the people, that the seven priests bearing the seven trumpets of rams' horns before the LORD advanced and blew the trumpets, and the ark of the covenant of the LORD followed them. [9]The armed men went before the priests who blew the trumpets, and the rear guard came after the ark, while *the priests* continued blowing the trumpets. [10]Now Joshua had commanded the people, saying, "You shall not shout or make any noise with your voice, nor shall a word proceed

---

PROFILE IN LEADERSHIP

JOSHUA

A LEADER'S OBEDIENCE SETS THE PACE
(Joshua 5:13–15)

Look at every phase of Joshua's life, and you see a man who gave himself wholeheartedly to completing whatever task was assigned to him.

The first time Joshua appears in Scripture, we see him immediately obeying the instruction of Moses (Ex. 17:9, 10). Thereafter Joshua took on the role of Moses' assistant. Joshua again displayed his obedience when he agreed to spy out the Promised Land. Upon his return from the reconnaissance mission, he and Caleb, alone among the spies, were ready to obey God and enter Canaan. Forty years later when Moses handed the reins of power to his protégé, Joshua again obeyed the call (Josh. 1:5–11).

In the end, the people of Israel followed Joshua's example and did what God asked of them—and as a result inherited the land God had promised. Scripture says that "Israel served the LORD all the days of Joshua" (Josh. 24:31). When the people followed Joshua's lifelong example of obedience, they prospered.

By the time of his death, Joshua was known simply as "the servant of the LORD" (Judg. 2:7, 8). That is high praise! While today we consider Joshua an exceptional leader, nowhere does Scripture describe him as a man of extraordinary might, intellect, or talent. What made him extraordinary was his obedience. And when you're a servant of the Lord, that's all you really need.

out of your mouth, until the day I say to you, 'Shout!' Then you shall shout." ¹¹So he had the ark of the LORD circle the city, going around *it* once. Then they came into the camp and lodged in the camp.

¹²And Joshua rose early in the morning, and the priests took up the ark of the LORD. ¹³Then seven priests bearing seven trumpets of rams' horns before the ark of the LORD went on continually and blew with the trumpets. And the armed men went before them. But the rear guard came after the ark of the LORD, while *the priests* continued blowing the trumpets. ¹⁴And the second day they marched around the city once and returned to the camp. So they did six days.

¹⁵But it came to pass on the seventh day that they rose early, about the dawning of the day, and marched around the city seven times in the same manner. On that day only they marched around the city seven times. ¹⁶And the seventh time it happened, when the priests blew the trumpets, that Joshua said to the people: "Shout, for the LORD has given you the city! ¹⁷Now the city shall be doomed by the LORD to destruction, it and all who *are* in it. Only Rahab the harlot shall live, she and all who *are* with her in the house, because she hid the messengers that we sent. ¹⁸And you, by all means abstain from the accursed

things, lest you become accursed when you take of the accursed things, and make the camp of Israel a curse, and trouble it. ¹⁹But all the silver and gold, and vessels of bronze and iron, *are* consecrated to the LORD; they shall come into the treasury of the LORD."

²⁰So the people shouted when *the priests* blew the trumpets. And it happened when the people heard the sound of the trumpet, and the people shouted with a great shout, that the wall fell down flat. Then the people went up into the city, every man straight before him, and they took the city. ²¹And they utterly destroyed all that *was* in the city, both man and woman, young and old, ox and sheep and donkey, with the edge of the sword.

²²But Joshua had said to the two men who had spied out the country, "Go into the harlot's house, and from there bring out the woman and all that she has, as you swore to her." ²³And the young men who had been spies went in and brought out Rahab, her father, her mother, her brothers, and all that she had. So they brought out all her relatives and left them outside the camp of Israel. ²⁴But they burned the city and all that *was* in it with fire. Only the silver and gold, and the vessels of bronze and iron, they put into the treasury of the house of the LORD. ²⁵And

Joshua Practices the Law of Victory

(Joshua 6:1–20)

Perhaps the most memorable of Joshua's many victories came in the destruction of Jericho. But what a strange story it is!

Try to picture how absurd God's military strategy must have seemed to real men of war. March around Jericho 13 times in one week, blow some trumpets—and that's it? No weapons? No fighting? No plan of attack? No doubt, the residents of Jericho laughed heartily at the weeklong entertainment provided by the dizzy Hebrew army circling their walls.

Yet Joshua was committed to doing whatever it took to gain victory, and if God said shout, then the general would discard his swords and spears and wholeheartedly go with the absurd. Consider ten things to really like about Joshua:

1. He made obedience his first priority.
2. He never waited to see what the crowd wanted to do.
3. He made decisions from an eternal perspective, not a temporary one.
4. He acted decisively.
5. He deeply appreciated the past without worshiping it.
6. He valued results more than image and reputation.
7. He knew that to influence others, he had to stand up and be counted.
8. He never wavered from his understanding of what was right.
9. He trusted his God more than his gift.
10. He made glorifying God his ultimate objective.

Joshua spared Rahab the harlot, her father's household, and all that she had. So she dwells in Israel to this day, because she hid the messengers whom Joshua sent to spy out Jericho.

26Then Joshua charged *them* at that time, saying, "Cursed *be* the man before the LORD who rises up and builds this city Jericho; he shall lay its foundation with his firstborn, and with his youngest he shall set up its gates."

27So the LORD was with Joshua, and his fame spread throughout all the country.

Defeat at Ai

7 But the children of Israel committed a trespass regarding the accursed things, for Achan the son of Carmi, the son of Zabdi,a the son of Zerah, of the tribe of Judah, took of the accursed things; so the anger of the LORD burned against the children of Israel.

2Now Joshua sent men from Jericho to Ai, which *is* beside Beth Aven, on the east side of Bethel, and spoke to them, saying, "Go up and spy out the country." So the men went up and spied out Ai. 3And they returned to Joshua and said to him, "Do not let all the people go up, but let about two or three thousand men go up and attack Ai. Do not weary all the people there, for *the people of Ai are* few." 4So about three thousand

men went up there from the people, but they fled before the men of Ai. 5And the men of Ai struck down about thirty-six men, for they chased them *from* before the gate as far as Shebarim, and struck them down on the descent; therefore the hearts of the people melted and became like water.

6Then Joshua tore his clothes, and fell to the earth on his face before the ark of the LORD until evening, he and the elders of Israel; and they put dust on their heads. 7And Joshua said, "Alas, Lord GOD, why have You brought this people over the Jordan at all—to deliver us into the hand of the Amorites, to destroy us? Oh, that we had been content, and dwelt on the other side of the Jordan! 8O Lord, what shall I say when Israel turns its back before its enemies? 9For the Canaanites and all the inhabitants of the land will hear *it,* and surround us, and cut off our name from the earth. Then what will You do for Your great name?"

The Sin of Achan

10So the LORD said to Joshua: "Get up! Why do you lie thus on your face? 11Israel has sinned, and they have also transgressed My covenant

---

7:1 aCalled *Zimri* in 1 Chronicles 2:6

ACHAN

THE RIPPLE EFFECT OF SIN
(Joshua 7:1–25)

PROFILE IN LEADERSHIP

Things had been going so well. And then, suddenly—*this!*

After an incredible victory over Jericho, an Israelite foot soldier named Achan chose to disobey some clear directives regarding treasures captured in war. Joshua told his men that all the spoils taken from Jericho were to be considered "devoted things," belonging in God's treasury. Achan defied Joshua's orders, taking some valuables and hiding them under his family's tent.

Joshua, unaware of Achan's sin, sent a small contingent of soldiers against Ai—and the confident Israelites suffered a major rout. Joshua immediately recognized that something must be very wrong. He sought God's face for answers and eventually identified Achan as the culprit. In an act of severe judgment, the guilty man, his entire family, their livestock and possessions were all destroyed. By this fearsome act, Joshua determined to follow God and to remove those who would stand in the way of God's work.

The story of Achan illustrates the principle that leaders may become vulnerable following a major success. Although it can be very difficult, leaders must take the appropriate steps to remove those who block God's blessing and work. When a team member like Achan compromises a core value, the ripple effect of his or her action can hurt many others. Godly leaders must stop the ripple before it becomes a flood.

which I commanded them. For they have even taken some of the accursed things, and have both stolen and deceived; and they have also put *it* among their own stuff. ¹²Therefore the children of Israel could not stand before their enemies, *but* turned *their* backs before their enemies, because they have become doomed to destruction. Neither will I be with you anymore, unless you destroy the accursed from among you. ¹³Get up, sanctify the people, and say, 'Sanctify yourselves for tomorrow, because thus says the LORD God of Israel: "*There is* an accursed thing in your midst, O Israel; you cannot stand before your enemies until you take away the accursed thing from among you." ¹⁴In the morning therefore you shall be brought according to your tribes. And it shall be *that* the tribe which the LORD takes shall come according to families; and the family which the LORD takes shall come by households; and the household which the LORD takes shall come man by man. ¹⁵Then it shall be *that* he who is taken with the accursed thing shall be burned with fire, he and all that he has, because he has transgressed the covenant of the LORD, and because he has done a disgraceful thing in Israel.'"

¹⁶So Joshua rose early in the morning and brought Israel by their tribes, and the tribe of Judah was taken. ¹⁷He brought the clan of Judah, and he took the family of the Zarhites; and he brought the family of the Zarhites man by man, and Zabdi was taken. ¹⁸Then he brought his household man by man, and Achan the son of Carmi, the son of Zabdi, the son of Zerah, of the tribe of Judah, was taken.

¹⁹Now Joshua said to Achan, "My son, I beg you, give glory to the LORD God of Israel, and make confession to Him, and tell me now what you have done; do not hide *it* from me."

²⁰And Achan answered Joshua and said, "Indeed I have sinned against the LORD God of Israel, and this is what I have done: ²¹When I saw among the spoils a beautiful Babylonian garment, two hundred shekels of silver, and a wedge of gold weighing fifty shekels, I coveted them and took them. And there they are, hidden in the earth in the midst of my tent, with the silver under it."

²²So Joshua sent messengers, and they ran to the tent; and there it was, hidden in his tent, with the silver under it. ²³And they took them from the midst of the tent, brought them to Joshua and to all the children of Israel, and laid them out before the LORD. ²⁴Then Joshua, and all Israel with him, took Achan the son of Zerah, the silver, the garment, the wedge of gold, his sons,

Convictions: Leaders Don't Allow Compromise to Dilute the Cause

(Joshua 7:1—8:29)

A little city with a short name caused huge problems for the Israelites.

Spies sent out to check out the village of Ai considered it an easy target; its defeat would not even require the whole army, they said. How wrong they were! The contingent dispatched against Ai quickly retreated after suffering frightening losses. What could have happened?

Joshua soon discovered that sin in his camp had caused the debacle. One of his soldiers, Achan, had kept for himself some of the spoils of war, despite God's prohibition against doing so. After a short time of confusion, Joshua dealt decisively with Achan, executing him at the command of God. Joshua would not and could not allow compromise to derail the destiny of his people. Due to his courage and convictions, the next time Israel launched an attack on Ai, the tiny city with the short name presented little problem.

his daughters, his oxen, his donkeys, his sheep, his tent, and all that he had, and they brought them to the Valley of Achor. ²⁵And Joshua said, "Why have you troubled us? The LORD will trouble you this day." So all Israel stoned him with stones; and they burned them with fire after they had stoned them with stones.

²⁶Then they raised over him a great heap of stones, still there to this day. So the LORD turned from the fierceness of His anger. Therefore the name of that place has been called the Valley of Achor[a] to this day.

The Fall of Ai

8 Now the LORD said to Joshua: "Do not be afraid, nor be dismayed; take all the people of war with you, and arise, go up to Ai. See, I have given into your hand the king of Ai, his people, his city, and his land. ²And you shall do to Ai and its king as you did to Jericho and its king. Only its spoil and its cattle you shall take as

7:26 [a]Literally *Trouble*

The Law of Navigation: Joshua Balances Faith and Planning

(Joshua 8:1–29)

When does human planning get in the way of trusting God for results? Or conversely, when does faith become presumption, expecting God to do for us what we must grab hold of ourselves? All Christian leaders must learn the proper balance between divine faith and human preparation.

Joshua demonstrates a beautiful balance as he prepares a second attack on the city of Ai. He begins by asking the Lord whether his army should attack, and if so, when. God ordered the attack and instructed Joshua to set an ambush, but gave no further details. Joshua planned the particulars of the campaign, each step under the inspiration of the Holy Spirit. He divided his troops into two divisions and told one to stage an attack on the city. The other group was to wait in ambush until the men of Ai came out. As the men of Ai chased their attackers, the ambush could close in and allow the Israelites to set the city afire. The plan worked perfectly. When the men of Ai saw the smoke rising above their homes, they lost heart and quickly fell in battle to Israel.

Do you see the synthesis of divine guidance and human strategy? Joshua placed his faith in God for the results, but did not hesitate to lay wise plans and execute them.

booty for yourselves. Lay an ambush for the city behind it."

³So Joshua arose, and all the people of war, to go up against Ai; and Joshua chose thirty thousand mighty men of valor and sent them away by night. ⁴And he commanded them, saying: "Behold, you shall lie in ambush against the city, behind the city. Do not go very far from the city, but all of you be ready. ⁵Then I and all the people who *are* with me will approach the city; and it will come about, when they come out against us as at the first, that we shall flee before them. ⁶For they will come out after us till we have drawn them from the city, for they will say, '*They are* fleeing before us as at the first.' Therefore we

will flee before them. ⁷Then you shall rise from the ambush and seize the city, for the LORD your God will deliver it into your hand. ⁸And it will be, when you have taken the city, *that* you shall set the city on fire. According to the commandment of the LORD you shall do. See, I have commanded you."

⁹Joshua therefore sent them out; and they went to lie in ambush, and stayed between Bethel and Ai, on the west side of Ai; but Joshua lodged that night among the people. ¹⁰Then Joshua rose up early in the morning and mustered the people, and went up, he and the elders of Israel, before the people to Ai. ¹¹And all the people of war who *were* with him went up and drew near; and they came before the city and camped on the north side of Ai. Now a valley *lay* between them and Ai. ¹²So he took about five thousand men and set them in ambush between Bethel and Ai, on the west side of the city. ¹³And when they had set the people, all the army that *was* on the north of the city, and its rear guard on the west of the city, Joshua went that night into the midst of the valley.

¹⁴Now it happened, when the king of Ai saw *it*, that the men of the city hurried and rose early and went out against Israel to battle, he and all his people, at an appointed place before the plain. But he did not know that *there was* an ambush against him behind the city. ¹⁵And Joshua and all Israel made as if they were beaten before them, and fled by the way of the wilderness. ¹⁶So all the people who *were* in Ai were called together to pursue them. And they pursued Joshua and were drawn away from the city. ¹⁷There was not a man left in Ai or Bethel who did not go out after Israel. So they left the city open and pursued Israel.

¹⁸Then the LORD said to Joshua, "Stretch out the spear that *is* in your hand toward Ai, for I will give it into your hand." And Joshua stretched out the spear that *was* in his hand toward the city. ¹⁹So *those in* ambush arose quickly out of their place; they ran as soon as he had stretched out his hand, and they entered the city and took it, and hurried to set the city on fire. ²⁰And when the men of Ai looked behind them, they saw, and behold, the smoke of the city ascended to heaven. So they had no power to flee this way or that way, and the people who had fled to the wilderness turned back on the pursuers.

²¹Now when Joshua and all Israel saw that the ambush had taken the city and that the smoke of the city ascended, they turned back and struck down the men of Ai. ²²Then the others came out of the city against them; so they were *caught in*

the midst of Israel, some on this side and some on that side. And they struck them down, so that they let none of them remain or escape. [23]But the king of Ai they took alive, and brought him to Joshua.

[24]And it came to pass when Israel had made an end of slaying all the inhabitants of Ai in the field, in the wilderness where they pursued them, and when they all had fallen by the edge of the sword until they were consumed, that all the Israelites returned to Ai and struck it with the edge of the sword. [25]So it was that all who fell that day, both men and women, were twelve thousand—all the people of Ai. [26]For Joshua did not draw back his hand, with which he stretched out the spear, until he had utterly destroyed all the inhabitants of Ai. [27]Only the livestock and the spoil of that city Israel took as booty for themselves, according to the word of the LORD which He had commanded Joshua. [28]So Joshua burned Ai and made it a heap forever, a desolation to this day. [29]And the king of Ai he hanged on a tree until evening. And as soon as the sun was down, Joshua commanded that they should take his corpse down from the tree, cast it at the entrance of the gate of the city, and raise over it a great heap of stones that remains to this day.

Joshua Renews the Covenant

[30]Now Joshua built an altar to the LORD God of Israel in Mount Ebal, [31]as Moses the servant of the LORD had commanded the children of Israel, as it is written in the Book of the Law of Moses: "an altar of whole stones over which no man has wielded an iron tool."[a] And they offered on it burnt offerings to the LORD, and sacrificed peace offerings. [32]And there, in the presence of the children of Israel, he wrote on the stones a copy of the law of Moses, which he had written. [33]Then all Israel, with their elders and officers and judges, stood on either side of the ark before the priests, the Levites, who bore the ark of the covenant of the LORD, the stranger as well as he who was born among them. Half of them were in front of Mount Gerizim and half of them in front of Mount Ebal, as Moses the servant of the LORD had commanded before, that they should bless the people of Israel. [34]And afterward he read all the words of the law, the blessings and the cursings, according to all that is written in the Book of the Law. [35]There was not a word of all that Moses had commanded which Joshua did not read before all the assembly of Israel, with the women, the little ones, and the strangers who were living among them.

The Treaty with the Gibeonites

9 And it came to pass when all the kings who were on this side of the Jordan, in the hills and in the lowland and in all the coasts of the Great Sea toward Lebanon—the Hittite, the Amorite, the Canaanite, the Perizzite, the Hivite, and the Jebusite—heard about it, [2]that they gathered together to fight with Joshua and Israel with one accord.

Negotiation and Compromise

(Joshua 9:1–27)

When Israel negotiated with the Gibeonites and ignored God's order to destroy the city, they allowed compromise to jeopardize their mission. While negotiation is not wrong in itself, leaders must never negotiate their convictions, direct orders, or core values. When we start negotiating these, we compromise our mission.

---

[3]But when the inhabitants of Gibeon heard what Joshua had done to Jericho and Ai, [4]they worked craftily, and went and pretended to be ambassadors. And they took old sacks on their donkeys, old wineskins torn and mended, [5]old and patched sandals on their feet, and old garments on themselves; and all the bread of their provision was dry and moldy. [6]And they went to Joshua, to the camp at Gilgal, and said to him and to the men of Israel, "We have come from a far country; now therefore, make a covenant with us."

[7]Then the men of Israel said to the Hivites, "Perhaps you dwell among us; so how can we make a covenant with you?"

[8]But they said to Joshua, "We are your servants."

And Joshua said to them, "Who are you, and where do you come from?"

[9]So they said to him: "From a very far country your servants have come, because of the name of the LORD your God; for we have heard of His fame, and all that He did in Egypt, [10]and all that He did to the two kings of the Amorites who were beyond the Jordan—to Sihon king of Heshbon, and Og king of Bashan, who was at

---

8:31 [a]Deuteronomy 27:5, 6

Ashtaroth. ¹¹Therefore our elders and all the inhabitants of our country spoke to us, saying, 'Take provisions with you for the journey, and go to meet them, and say to them, "We *are* your servants; now therefore, make a covenant with us."' ¹²This bread of ours we took hot *for* our provision from our houses on the day we departed to come to you. But now look, it is dry and moldy. ¹³And these wineskins which we filled *were* new, and see, they are torn; and these our garments and our sandals have become old because of the very long journey."

¹⁴Then the men of Israel took some of their provisions; but they did not ask counsel of the LORD. ¹⁵So Joshua made peace with them, and made a covenant with them to let them live; and the rulers of the congregation swore to them.

¹⁶And it happened at the end of three days, after they had made a covenant with them, that they heard that they *were* their neighbors who dwelt near them. ¹⁷Then the children of Israel journeyed and came to their cities on the third day. Now their cities *were* Gibeon, Chephirah, Beeroth, and Kirjath Jearim. ¹⁸But the children of Israel did not attack them, because the rulers of the congregation had sworn to them by the LORD God of Israel. And all the congregation complained against the rulers.

¹⁹Then all the rulers said to all the congregation, "We have sworn to them by the LORD God of Israel; now therefore, we may not touch them. ²⁰This we will do to them: We will let them live, lest wrath be upon us because of the oath which we swore to them." ²¹And the rulers said to them, "Let them live, but let them be woodcutters and water carriers for all the congregation, as the rulers had promised them."

²²Then Joshua called for them, and he spoke to them, saying, "Why have you deceived us, saying, 'We *are* very far from you,' when you dwell near us? ²³Now therefore, you *are* cursed, and none of you shall be freed from being slaves—woodcutters and water carriers for the house of my God."

²⁴So they answered Joshua and said, "Because your servants were clearly told that the LORD your God commanded His servant Moses to give you all the land, and to destroy all the inhabitants of the land from before you; therefore we were very much afraid for our lives because of you, and have done this thing. ²⁵And now, here we are, in your hands; do with us as it seems good and right to do to us." ²⁶So he did to them, and delivered them out of the hand of the children of Israel, so that they did not kill them. ²⁷And that day Joshua made them woodcutters and water

carriers for the congregation and for the altar of the LORD, in the place which He would choose, even to this day.

The Sun Stands Still

10 Now it came to pass when Adoni-Zedek king of Jerusalem heard how Joshua had taken Ai and had utterly destroyed it—as he had done to Jericho and its king, so he had done to Ai and its king—and how the inhabitants of Gibeon had made peace with Israel and were among them, ²that they feared greatly, because Gibeon *was* a great city, like one of the royal cities, and because it *was* greater than Ai, and all its men *were* mighty. ³Therefore Adoni-Zedek king of Jerusalem sent to Hoham king of Hebron, Piram king of Jarmuth, Japhia king of Lachish, and Debir king of Eglon, saying, ⁴"'Come up to me and help me, that we may attack Gibeon, for it has made peace with Joshua and with the children of Israel.'" ⁵Therefore the five kings of the Amorites, the king of Jerusalem, the king of Hebron, the king of Jarmuth, the king of Lachish, *and* the king of Eglon, gathered together and went up, they and all their armies, and camped before Gibeon and made war against it.

The Integrity of a Leader: Joshua and the Gibeonites

(Joshua 10:1–15)

Joshua compromised his leadership when he made a treaty with the Gibeonites, but once he made a covenant with them, he knew it was his duty to defend them. Integrity means that you keep your oath and "swear to your own hurt" regardless of the cost (see Ps. 15:4).

---

⁶And the men of Gibeon sent to Joshua at the camp at Gilgal, saying, "Do not forsake your servants; come up to us quickly, save us and help us, for all the kings of the Amorites who dwell in the mountains have gathered together against us."

⁷So Joshua ascended from Gilgal, he and all the people of war with him, and all the mighty men of valor. ⁸And the LORD said to Joshua, "Do not fear them, for I have delivered them into your hand; not a man of them shall stand

Joshua and the Law of the Big Mo

(Joshua 10:1–43)

Not only did Joshua lack momentum at the beginning of his campaign, he actually faced several barriers to it. Consider his precarious situation:

1. Israel had just lost its founding leader.
2. Joshua had to follow this hero and revered leader.
3. The Israelites had not realized their dream in 40 years.
4. In front of Israel stood a flooding river and countless walled cities.

So what can a leader without momentum do? The answer: Learn from Joshua.

1. Emphasize that moving forward simply reflects obedience to God.
2. Speak of past conquests under God's direction.
3. Get the people to quickly put some "wins" under their belt.
4. Underscore your own faith in what God has promised.
5. Model courage for everyone.
6. Erect memorials to recall God's pattern of faithfulness.

By chapter ten, Joshua is enjoying the Law of the Big Mo. Israel won victory after victory—and each one made the next one easier to visualize and embrace.

before you." [9] Joshua therefore came upon them suddenly, having marched all night from Gilgal. [10] So the LORD routed them before Israel, killed them with a great slaughter at Gibeon, chased them along the road that goes to Beth Horon, and struck them down as far as Azekah and Makkedah. [11] And it happened, as they fled before Israel *and* were on the descent of Beth Horon, that the LORD cast down large hailstones from heaven on them as far as Azekah, and they died. *There were* more who died from the hailstones than the children of Israel killed with the sword. [12] Then Joshua spoke to the LORD in the day when the LORD delivered up the Amorites before the children of Israel, and he said in the sight of Israel:

"Sun, stand still over Gibeon;
And Moon, in the Valley of Aijalon."
[13] So the sun stood still,
And the moon stopped,
Till the people had revenge
Upon their enemies.

Is this not written in the Book of Jasher? So the sun stood still in the midst of heaven, and did not hasten to go *down* for about a whole day. [14] And there has been no day like that, before it or after it, that the LORD heeded the voice of a man; for the LORD fought for Israel.

[15] Then Joshua returned, and all Israel with him, to the camp at Gilgal.

The Amorite Kings Executed

[16] But these five kings had fled and hidden themselves in a cave at Makkedah. [17] And it was told Joshua, saying, "The five kings have been found hidden in the cave at Makkedah."

[18] So Joshua said, "Roll large stones against the mouth of the cave, and set men by it to guard them. [19] And do not stay *there* yourselves, *but* pursue your enemies, and attack their rear *guard*. Do not allow them to enter their cities, for the LORD your God has delivered them into your hand." [20] Then it happened, while Joshua and the children of Israel made an end of slaying them with a very great slaughter, till they had finished, that those who escaped entered fortified cities. [21] And all the people returned to the camp, to Joshua at Makkedah, in peace.

No one moved his tongue against any of the children of Israel.

[22] Then Joshua said, "Open the mouth of the cave, and bring out those five kings to me from the cave." [23] And they did so, and brought out those five kings to him from the cave: the king of Jerusalem, the king of Hebron, the king of Jarmuth, the king of Lachish, *and* the king of Eglon.

[24] So it was, when they brought out those kings to Joshua, that Joshua called for all the men of Israel, and said to the captains of the men of war who went with him, "Come near, put your feet on the necks of these kings." And they drew near and put their feet on their necks. [25] Then Joshua said to them, "Do not be afraid, nor be dismayed; be strong and of good courage, for thus the LORD will do to all your enemies against whom you fight." [26] And afterward Joshua struck them and killed them, and hanged them on five trees; and they were hanging on the trees until evening. [27] So it was at the time of the going down of the sun *that* Joshua commanded, and they took them down from the trees, cast them

into the cave where they had been hidden, and laid large stones against the cave's mouth, *which remain* until this very day.

Conquest of the Southland

²⁸On that day Joshua took Makkedah, and struck it and its king with the edge of the sword. He utterly destroyed them[a]—all the people who *were* in it. He let none remain. He also did to the king of Makkedah as he had done to the king of Jericho.

²⁹Then Joshua passed from Makkedah, and all Israel with him, to Libnah; and they fought against Libnah. ³⁰And the LORD also delivered it and its king into the hand of Israel; he struck it and all the people who *were* in it with the edge of the sword. He let none remain in it, but did to its king as he had done to the king of Jericho.

³¹Then Joshua passed from Libnah, and all Israel with him, to Lachish; and they encamped against it and fought against it. ³²And the LORD delivered Lachish into the hand of Israel, who took it on the second day, and struck it and all the people who *were* in it with the edge of the sword, according to all that he had done to Libnah. ³³Then Horam king of Gezer came up to help Lachish; and Joshua struck him and his people, until he left him none remaining.

³⁴From Lachish Joshua passed to Eglon, and all Israel with him; and they encamped against it and fought against it. ³⁵They took it on that day and struck it with the edge of the sword; all the people who *were* in it he utterly destroyed that day, according to all that he had done to Lachish.

³⁶So Joshua went up from Eglon, and all Israel with him, to Hebron; and they fought against it. ³⁷And they took it and struck it with the edge of the sword—its king, all its cities, and all the people who *were* in it; he left none remaining, according to all that he had done to Eglon, but utterly destroyed it and all the people who *were* in it.

³⁸Then Joshua returned, and all Israel with him, to Debir; and they fought against it. ³⁹And he took it and its king and all its cities; they struck them with the edge of the sword and utterly destroyed all the people who *were* in it. He left none remaining; as he had done to Hebron, so he did to Debir and its king, as he had done also to Libnah and its king.

⁴⁰So Joshua conquered all the land: the mountain country and the South[a] and the lowland and the wilderness slopes, and all their kings; he left none remaining, but utterly destroyed all that breathed, as the LORD God of Israel had commanded. ⁴¹And Joshua conquered them from Kadesh Barnea as far as Gaza, and all the country of Goshen, even as far as Gibeon. ⁴²All these kings and their land Joshua took at one time, because the LORD God of Israel fought for Israel. ⁴³Then Joshua returned, and all Israel with him, to the camp at Gilgal.

The Northern Conquest

11 And it came to pass, when Jabin king of Hazor heard *these things,* that he sent to Jobab king of Madon, to the king of Shimron, to the king of Achshaph, ²and to the kings who *were* from the north, in the mountains, in the plain south of Chinneroth, in the lowland, and in the heights of Dor on the west, ³to the Canaanites in the east and in the west, the Amorite, the Hittite, the Perizzite, the Jebusite in the mountains, and the Hivite below Hermon in the land of Mizpah. ⁴So they went out, they and all their armies with them, *as* many people *as* the sand that *is* on the seashore in multitude, with very many horses and chariots. ⁵And when all these kings had met together, they came and camped together at the waters of Merom to fight against Israel.

⁶But the LORD said to Joshua, "Do not be afraid because of them, for tomorrow about this time I will deliver all of them slain before Israel. You shall hamstring their horses and burn their chariots with fire." ⁷So Joshua and all the people of war with him came against them suddenly by the waters of Merom, and they attacked them. ⁸And the LORD delivered them into the hand of Israel, who defeated them and chased them to Greater Sidon, to the Brook Misrephoth,[a] and to the Valley of Mizpah eastward; they attacked them until they left none of them remaining. ⁹So Joshua did to them as the LORD had told him: he hamstrung their horses and burned their chariots with fire.

¹⁰Joshua turned back at that time and took Hazor, and struck its king with the sword; for Hazor was formerly the head of all those kingdoms. ¹¹And they struck all the people who *were* in it with the edge of the sword, utterly destroying *them.* There was none left breathing. Then he burned Hazor with fire.

¹²So all the cities of those kings, and all their kings, Joshua took and struck with the edge of

---

10:28 [a]Following Masoretic Text and most authorities; many Hebrew manuscripts, some manuscripts of the Septuagint, and some manuscripts of the Targum read *it.* **10:40** [a]Hebrew *Negev,* and so throughout this book **11:8** [a]Hebrew *Misrephoth Maim*

the sword. He utterly destroyed them, as Moses the servant of the LORD had commanded. [13]But *as for* the cities that stood on their mounds,[a] Israel burned none of them, except Hazor only, *which* Joshua burned. [14]And all the spoil of these cities and the livestock, the children of Israel took as booty for themselves; but they struck every man with the edge of the sword until they had destroyed them, and they left none breathing. [15]As the LORD had commanded Moses his servant, so Moses commanded Joshua, and so Joshua did. He left nothing undone of all that the LORD had commanded Moses.

Summary of Joshua's Conquests

[16]Thus Joshua took all this land: the mountain country, all the South, all the land of Goshen, the lowland, and the Jordan plain[a]—the mountains of Israel and its lowlands, [17]from Mount Halak and the ascent to Seir, even as far as Baal Gad in the Valley of Lebanon below Mount Hermon. He captured all their kings, and struck them down and killed them. [18]Joshua made war a long time with all those kings. [19]There was not a city that made peace with the children of Israel, except the Hivites, the inhabitants of Gibeon. All *the others* they took in battle. [20]For it was of the LORD to harden their hearts, that they should come against Israel in battle, that He might utterly destroy them, *and* that they might receive no mercy, but that He might destroy them, as the LORD had commanded Moses.

[21]And at that time Joshua came and cut off the Anakim from the mountains: from Hebron, from Debir, from Anab, from all the mountains of Judah, and from all the mountains of Israel; Joshua utterly destroyed them with their cities. [22]None of the Anakim were left in the land of the children of Israel; they remained only in Gaza, in Gath, and in Ashdod.

[23]So Joshua took the whole land, according to all that the LORD had said to Moses; and Joshua gave it as an inheritance to Israel according to their divisions by their tribes. Then the land rested from war.

The Kings Conquered by Moses

12 These *are* the kings of the land whom the children of Israel defeated, and whose land they possessed on the other side of the Jordan toward the rising of the sun, from the River Arnon to Mount Hermon, and all the eastern Jordan plain: [2]*One king was* Sihon king of the Amorites, who dwelt in Heshbon *and* ruled half of Gilead, from Aroer, which is on the bank of the River Arnon, from the middle of that river, even as far as the River Jabbok, *which is* the border of the Ammonites, [3]and the eastern Jordan plain from the Sea of Chinneroth as far as the Sea of the Arabah (the Salt Sea), the road to Beth Jeshimoth, and southward below the slopes of Pisgah. [4]*The other king was* Og king of Bashan and his territory, *who was* of the remnant of the giants, who dwelt at Ashtaroth and at Edrei, [5]and reigned over Mount Hermon, over Salcah, over all Bashan, as far as the border of the Geshurites and the Maachathites, and over half of Gilead *to* the border of Sihon king of Heshbon.

[6]These Moses the servant of the LORD and the children of Israel had conquered; and Moses the servant of the LORD had given it *as* a possession to the Reubenites, the Gadites, and half the tribe of Manasseh.

The Kings Conquered by Joshua

[7]And these *are* the kings of the country which Joshua and the children of Israel conquered on this side of the Jordan, on the west, from Baal Gad in the Valley of Lebanon as far as Mount Halak and the ascent to Seir, which Joshua gave to the tribes of Israel *as* a possession according to their divisions, [8]in the mountain country, in the lowlands, in the *Jordan* plain, in the slopes, in the wilderness, and in the South— the Hittites, the Amorites, the Canaanites, the Perizzites, the Hivites, and the Jebusites: [9]the king of Jericho, one; the king of Ai, which *is* beside Bethel, one; [10]the king of Jerusalem, one; the king of Hebron, one; [11]the king of Jarmuth, one; the king of Lachish, one; [12]the king of Eglon, one; the king of Gezer, one; [13]the king of Debir, one; the king of Geder, one; [14]the king of Hormah, one; the king of Arad, one; [15]the king of Libnah, one; the king of Adullam, one; [16]the king of Makkedah, one; the king of Bethel, one; [17]the king of Tappuah, one; the king of Hepher, one; [18]the king of Aphek, one; the king of Lasharon, one; [19]the king of Madon, one; the king of Hazor, one; [20]the king of Shimron Meron, one; the king of Achshaph, one; [21]the king of Taanach, one; the king of Megiddo, one; [22]the king of Kedesh, one; the king of Jokneam in Carmel, one; [23]the king of Dor in the heights of Dor, one; the king of the people of Gilgal, one; [24]the king of Tirzah, one—all the kings, thirty-one.

11:13 [a]Hebrew *tel,* a heap of successive city ruins
11:16 [a]Hebrew *arabah*

21 QUALITIES

COMPETENCE

Joshua Got the Job Done
(Joshua 11:16–23)

Competence rarely happens overnight. Even the great Joshua had to be prepared over many years to handle the enormous task given him. By the time he died, competence could have been his middle name. Consider this:

1. God used Joshua over two generations.
2. God trusted Joshua to lead the military campaigns from the wilderness into Canaan.
3. God called Joshua to spy out the Promised Land.
4. God allowed Joshua to accompany Moses up Mount Sinai.
5. God replaced Moses with Joshua when it came time to lead the people into Canaan.

Ponder the effort God invested in this young leader to make him competent:

1. He was a warrior (Ex. 17:9–11).

Joshua was born to be a warrior. His first opportunity at leadership came as a military leader. God was preparing him for a much larger role, but it all began here.

2. He was a spokesman (Ex. 17:14).

Joshua received a prophetic word from the Lord concerning his lifetime ministry, illustrating how God works in each of us. First, we receive a personal word from the Lord; then we become bearers of His word to others.

3. He was a servant (Ex. 24:13).

Joshua was first known as "the servant of Moses." No one called him a servant of Yahweh until the time of the conquest. He proved his willingness to serve before asking anyone to serve him. Each of us must undergo the same process.

4. He was a faithful coworker (Ex. 32:17).

Moses took Joshua with him to meet with God on Mount Sinai, but when ordered to stop, Joshua halted halfway up. He experienced no glory, no cloud, no voice, and no presence, yet he remained faithful to the big picture.

5. He was an apprentice of Moses and God (Ex. 33:11).

For 40 years, Joshua served as an understudy. His competence grew from Moses' tutoring and his own observations. He would not leave Moses' tent because he wanted to get everything he could from his mentor.

6. He was a zealot (Num. 11:29).

One day when God's presence came down upon the camp and two men began to prophesy, Joshua grew concerned. He forbade them to continue, but Moses said to him, "I wish all God's people were prophets." Joshua's passion later became an asset as it combined with experience.

7. He was a transformed leader (Num. 13:16).

Moses gave the name Joshua to the young man formerly called Hoshea. With that name change came a transformation in identity and character. Joshua became a man ready to delegate, organize, and lead the nation of Israel.

For a negative example of competence, turn to p. 1257.

Remaining Land to Be Conquered

13 Now Joshua was old, advanced in years. And the LORD said to him: "You are old, advanced in years, and there remains very much land yet to be possessed. [2]This is the land that yet remains: all the territory of the Philistines and all *that of* the Geshurites, [3]from Sihor, which *is* east of Egypt, as far as the border of Ekron northward (*which* is counted as Canaanite); the five lords of the Philistines—the Gazites, the Ashdodites, the Ashkelonites, the Gittites, and the Ekronites; also the Avites; [4]from the south, all the land of the Canaanites, and Mearah that belongs to the Sidonians as far as Aphek, to the border of the Amorites; [5]the land of the Gebalites,[a] and all Lebanon, toward the sunrise, from Baal Gad below Mount Hermon as far as the entrance to Hamath; [6]all the inhabitants of the mountains from Lebanon as far as the Brook Misrephoth,[a] *and* all the Sidonians—them I will drive out from before the children of Israel; only divide it by lot to Israel as an inheritance, as I have commanded you. [7]Now therefore, divide this land as an inheritance to the nine tribes and half the tribe of Manasseh."

The Land Divided East of the Jordan

[8]With the other half-tribe the Reubenites and the Gadites received their inheritance, which Moses had given them, beyond the Jordan eastward, as Moses the servant of the LORD had given them: [9]from Aroer which *is* on the bank of the River Arnon, and the town that *is* in the midst of the ravine, and all the plain of Medeba as far as Dibon; [10]all the cities of Sihon king of the Amorites, who reigned in Heshbon, as far as the border of the children of Ammon; [11]Gilead, and the border of the Geshurites and Maachathites, all Mount Hermon, and all Bashan as far as Salcah; [12]all the kingdom of Og in Bashan, who reigned in Ashtaroth and Edrei, who remained of the remnant of the giants; for Moses had defeated and cast out these.

[13]Nevertheless the children of Israel did not drive out the Geshurites or the Maachathites, but the Geshurites and the Maachathites dwell among the Israelites until this day.

[14]Only to the tribe of Levi he had given no inheritance; the sacrifices of the LORD God of

13:5 [a]Or *Giblites* 13:6 [a]Hebrew *Misrephoth Maim*

Confidence and Decisiveness: Joshua Distributes the Land
(Joshua 13:1—19:51)

The time came when Joshua finally felt ready to divide the land God had promised to Abraham hundreds of years earlier. His leadership faced a crucial test when he saw that he needed to exhort the hesitant Jews to occupy their land. "How long will you neglect to go and possess the land which the LORD God of your fathers has given you?" he scolded the faltering tribes (Josh. 18:3).

Joshua's courage left an unmistakable mark on the hearts of his countrymen and reminded them that they were to fulfill the expectations of God. Notice how Joshua led the people in his later years, when decisiveness became especially crucial:

1. Evaluation (13:1—14:5)
Joshua developed a clear picture of the land remaining to be conquered.

2. Imitation (14:6–15)
Joshua blessed Caleb and pointed to him as a model of attitude and determination.

3. Communication (15:1—17:18)
Joshua clearly articulated the boundaries of each tribe's land and what they needed to do.

4. Exhortation (18:1–4)
Joshua challenged the tribes of Israel to take the land God had promised them.

5. Investigation (18:4–10)
Joshua appointed teams to survey the scope of the remaining land and report back to him.

6. Determination (18:11—19:51)
Once he received the commissioned report, Joshua determined who should get what land.

Israel made by fire *are* their inheritance, as He said to them.

The Land of Reuben

[15]And Moses had given to the tribe of the children of Reuben *an inheritance* according to their families. [16]Their territory was from Aroer, which *is* on the bank of the River Arnon, and the city that *is* in the midst of the ravine, and all the plain by Medeba; [17]Heshbon and all its cities that *are* in the plain: Dibon, Bamoth Baal, Beth Baal Meon, [18]Jahaza, Kedemoth, Mephaath, [19]Kirjathaim, Sibmah, Zereth Shahar on the mountain of the valley, [20]Beth Peor, the slopes of Pisgah, and Beth Jeshimoth— [21]all the cities of the plain and all the kingdom of Sihon king of the Amorites, who reigned in Heshbon, whom Moses had struck with the princes of Midian: Evi, Rekem, Zur, Hur, and Reba, who *were* princes of Sihon dwelling in the country. [22]The children of Israel also killed with the sword Balaam the son of Beor, the soothsayer, among those who were killed by them. [23]And the border of the children of Reuben was the bank of the Jordan. This *was* the inheritance of the children of Reuben according to their families, the cities and their villages.

The Land of Gad

[24]Moses also had given *an inheritance* to the tribe of Gad, to the children of Gad according to their families. [25]Their territory was Jazer, and all the cities of Gilead, and half the land of the Ammonites as far as Aroer, which *is* before Rabbah, [26]and from Heshbon to Ramath Mizpah and Betonim, and from Mahanaim to the border of Debir, [27]and in the valley Beth Haram, Beth Nimrah, Succoth, and Zaphon, the rest of the kingdom of Sihon king of Heshbon, with the Jordan as *its* border, as far as the edge of the Sea of Chinnereth, on the other side of the Jordan eastward. [28]This *is* the inheritance of the children of Gad according to their families, the cities and their villages.

Half the Tribe of Manasseh (East)

[29]Moses also had given *an inheritance* to half the tribe of Manasseh; it was for half the tribe of the children of Manasseh according to their families: [30]Their territory was from Mahanaim, all Bashan, all the kingdom of Og king of Bashan, and all the towns of Jair which are in Bashan, sixty cities; [31]half of Gilead, and Ashtaroth and Edrei, cities of the kingdom of Og in Bashan, *were* for the children of Machir the son of Manasseh, for half of the children of Machir according to their families.

[32]These *are the areas* which Moses had distributed as an inheritance in the plains of Moab on the other side of the Jordan, by Jericho eastward. [33]But to the tribe of Levi Moses had given no inheritance; the LORD God of Israel *was* their inheritance, as He had said to them.

The Land Divided West of the Jordan

14 These *are the areas* which the children of Israel inherited in the land of Canaan, which Eleazar the priest, Joshua the son of Nun, and the heads of the fathers of the tribes of the children of Israel distributed as an inheritance to them. [2]Their inheritance *was* by lot, as the LORD had commanded by the hand of Moses, for the nine tribes and the half-tribe. [3]For Moses had given the inheritance of the two tribes and the half-tribe on the other side of the Jordan; but to the Levites he had given no inheritance among them. [4]For the children of Joseph were two tribes: Manasseh and Ephraim. And they gave no part to the Levites in the land, except cities to

Caleb: God Uses Leaders Regardless of Age or Ability

(Joshua 14:6–15)

If you led an army working to conquer hostile territory, and you needed to defeat a community of giants, whom would you send to do the job? Probably not an 85-year-old man—yet that's exactly who topped Joshua's list. Why?

Because that man was Caleb.

Scripture does not indicate that Caleb was a great warrior. But it clearly shows he possessed great faith and passion, qualities that serve leaders today as well as they did in Joshua's day. Author and professor J. Robert Clinton has observed that while effective pastors and church leaders across the nation possess a wide variety of gifts and abilities, almost all of them possess the gift of faith.

Caleb teaches us that leadership has less to do with age than it does with attitude. It's not a matter of position, but of disposition. Growing older does not have to mean growing ineffective. With the power of God and the confidence of Caleb, we can overcome even giants.

dwell *in*, with their common-lands for their livestock and their property. [5]As the LORD had commanded Moses, so the children of Israel did; and they divided the land.

Caleb Inherits Hebron

[6]Then the children of Judah came to Joshua in Gilgal. And Caleb the son of Jephunneh the Kenizzite said to him: "You know the word which the LORD said to Moses the man of God concerning you and me in Kadesh Barnea. [7]I *was* forty years old when Moses the servant of the LORD sent me from Kadesh Barnea to spy out the land, and I brought back word to him as *it was* in my heart. [8]Nevertheless my brethren who went up with me made the heart of the people melt, but I wholly followed the LORD my God. [9]So Moses swore on that day, saying, 'Surely the land where your foot has trodden shall be your inheritance and your children's forever, because you have wholly followed the LORD my God.' [10]And now, behold, the LORD has kept me alive, as He said, these forty-five years, ever since the LORD spoke this word to Moses while Israel wandered in the wilderness; and now, here I am this day, eighty-five years old. [11]As yet I *am as* strong this day as on the day that Moses sent me; just as my strength *was* then, so now *is* my strength for war, both for going out and for coming in. [12]Now therefore, give me this mountain of which the LORD spoke in that day; for you heard in that day how the Anakim *were* there, and *that* the cities *were* great *and* fortified. It may be that the LORD *will be* with me, and I shall be able to drive them out as the LORD said."

[13]And Joshua blessed him, and gave Hebron to Caleb the son of Jephunneh as an inheritance. [14]Hebron therefore became the inheritance of Caleb the son of Jephunneh the Kenizzite to this day, because he wholly followed the LORD God of Israel. [15]And the name of Hebron formerly was Kirjath Arba (*Arba was* the greatest man among the Anakim).

Then the land had rest from war.

The Land of Judah

15 So *this* was the lot of the tribe of the children of Judah according to their families:

The border of Edom at the Wilderness of Zin southward *was* the extreme southern boundary. [2]And their southern border began at the shore of the Salt Sea, from the bay that faces southward. [3]Then it went out to the southern side of the Ascent of Akrabbim, passed along to Zin, ascended on the south side of Kadesh

---

CALEB — OWNER OF A BRAVE HEART
(Joshua 14:10–12)

PROFILE IN LEADERSHIP

The entire Old Testament proclaims God's desire for a pure nation of Israel. Why, then, would the Lord honor Caleb the Kenizzite, a man descended not from Israel, but from his brother Esau?

The answer can be found not in Caleb's blood, but in his heart.

When Caleb and Joshua returned from spying out the Promised Land (Num. 13), the first person to speak up for God wasn't Joshua—the man who one day would lead the nation—but Caleb. After quieting the people, he declared, "Let us go up at once and take possession, for we are well able to overcome it" (Num. 13:30).

Forty-five years later, Caleb still possessed extraordinary amounts of courage and devotion to God. "Here I am this day, eighty-five years old," he declared. "As yet I am as strong this day as on the day that Moses sent me. . . . Now therefore, give me this mountain" (Josh. 14:10–12).

Joshua obviously recognized Caleb's courage and devotion, because he blessed him and declared that Caleb had "wholly followed the LORD God of Israel" (Josh. 14:14). With a word, Joshua made Hebron Caleb's inheritance and fulfilled Moses' promise that God would someday reward him with the land he had walked as a spy all those years before. Caleb courageously fought the intimidating descendants of Anak and captured Hebron, their mountain home.

Barnea, passed along to Hezron, went up to Adar, and went around to Karkaa. [4]*From there* it passed toward Azmon and went out to the Brook of Egypt; and the border ended at the sea. This shall be your southern border.

[5]The east border *was* the Salt Sea as far as the mouth of the Jordan.

And the border on the northern quarter *began* at the bay of the sea at the mouth of the Jordan. [6]The border went up to Beth Hoglah and passed north of Beth Arabah; and the border went up to the stone of Bohan the son of Reuben. [7]Then the border went up toward Debir from the Valley of Achor, and it turned northward toward Gilgal, which *is* before the Ascent of Adummim, which *is* on the south side of the valley. The border continued toward the waters of En Shemesh and ended at En Rogel. [8]And the border went up by the Valley of the Son of Hinnom to the southern slope of the Jebusite *city* (which *is* Jerusalem). The border went up to the top of the mountain that *lies* before the Valley of Hinnom westward, which *is* at the end of the Valley of Rephaim[a] northward. [9]Then the border went around from the top of the hill to the fountain of the water of Nephtoah, and extended to the cities of Mount Ephron. And the border went around to Baalah (which *is* Kirjath Jearim). [10]Then the border turned westward from Baalah to Mount Seir, passed along to the side of Mount Jearim on the north (which *is* Chesalon), went down to Beth Shemesh, and passed on to Timnah. [11]And the border went out to the side of Ekron northward. Then the border went around to Shicron, passed along to Mount Baalah, and extended to Jabneel; and the border ended at the sea.

[12]The west border *was* the coastline of the Great Sea. This *is* the boundary of the children of Judah all around according to their families.

Caleb Occupies Hebron and Debir

[13]Now to Caleb the son of Jephunneh he gave a share among the children of Judah, according to the commandment of the LORD to Joshua, *namely,* Kirjath Arba, which *is* Hebron (*Arba was* the father of Anak). [14]Caleb drove out the three sons of Anak from there: Sheshai, Ahiman, and Talmai, the children of Anak. [15]Then he went up from there to the inhabitants of Debir (formerly the name of Debir *was* Kirjath Sepher).

[16]And Caleb said, "He who attacks Kirjath Sepher and takes it, to him I will give Achsah my daughter as wife." [17]So Othniel the son of Kenaz, the brother of Caleb, took it; and he gave him Achsah his daughter as wife. [18]Now it was so,

when she came *to him,* that she persuaded him to ask her father for a field. So she dismounted from *her* donkey, and Caleb said to her, "What do you wish?" [19]She answered, "Give me a blessing; since you have given me land in the South, give me also springs of water." So he gave her the upper springs and the lower springs.

The Cities of Judah

[20]This *was* the inheritance of the tribe of the children of Judah according to their families:

[21]The cities at the limits of the tribe of the children of Judah, toward the border of Edom in the South, were Kabzeel, Eder, Jagur, [22]Kinah, Dimonah, Adadah, [23]Kedesh, Hazor, Ithnan, [24]Ziph, Telem, Bealoth, [25]Hazor, Hadattah, Kerioth, Hezron (which *is* Hazor), [26]Amam, Shema, Moladah, [27]Hazar Gaddah, Heshmon, Beth Pelet, [28]Hazar Shual, Beersheba, Bizjothjah, [29]Baalah, Ijim, Ezem, [30]Eltolad, Chesil, Hormah, [31]Ziklag, Madmannah, Sansannah, [32]Lebaoth, Shilhim, Ain, and Rimmon: all the cities *are* twenty-nine, with their villages.

[33]In the lowland: Eshtaol, Zorah, Ashnah, [34]Zanoah, En Gannim, Tappuah, Enam, [35]Jarmuth, Adullam, Socoh, Azekah, [36]Sharaim, Adithaim, Gederah, and Gederothaim: fourteen cities with their villages; [37]Zenan, Hadashah, Migdal Gad, [38]Dilean, Mizpah, Joktheel, [39]Lachish, Bozkath, Eglon, [40]Cabbon, Lahmas,[a] Kithlish, [41]Gederoth, Beth Dagon, Naamah, and Makkedah: sixteen cities with their villages; [42]Libnah, Ether, Ashan, [43]Jiphtah, Ashnah, Nezib, [44]Keilah, Achzib, and Mareshah: nine cities with their villages; [45]Ekron, with its towns and villages; [46]from Ekron to the sea, all that *lay* near Ashdod, with their villages; [47]Ashdod with its towns and villages, Gaza with its towns and villages—as far as the Brook of Egypt and the Great Sea with *its* coastline.

[48]And in the mountain country: Shamir, Jattir, Sochoh, [49]Dannah, Kirjath Sannah (which *is* Debir), [50]Anab, Eshtemoh, Anim, [51]Goshen, Holon, and Giloh: eleven cities with their villages; [52]Arab, Dumah, Eshean, [53]Janum, Beth Tappuah, Aphekah, [54]Humtah, Kirjath Arba (which *is* Hebron), and Zior: nine cities with their villages; [55]Maon, Carmel, Ziph, Juttah, [56]Jezreel, Jokdeam, Zanoah, [57]Kain, Gibeah, and Timnah: ten cities with their villages; [58]Halhul, Beth Zur, Gedor, [59]Maarath, Beth Anoth, and Eltekon: six cities with their villages; [60]Kirjath Baal (which *is* Kirjath Jearim) and Rabbah: two cities with their villages.

15:8 [a]Literally *Giants* **15:40** [a]Or *Lahmam*

[61]In the wilderness: Beth Arabah, Middin, Secacah, [62]Nibshan, the City of Salt, and En Gedi: six cities with their villages.

[63]As for the Jebusites, the inhabitants of Jerusalem, the children of Judah could not drive them out; but the Jebusites dwell with the children of Judah at Jerusalem to this day.

Ephraim and West Manasseh

16 The lot fell to the children of Joseph from the Jordan, by Jericho, to the waters of Jericho on the east, to the wilderness that goes up from Jericho through the mountains to Bethel, [2]then went out from Bethel to Luz,[a] passed along to the border of the Archites at Ataroth, [3]and went down westward to the boundary of the Japhletites, as far as the boundary of Lower Beth Horon to Gezer; and it ended at the sea.

[4]So the children of Joseph, Manasseh and Ephraim, took their inheritance.

The Land of Ephraim

[5]The border of the children of Ephraim, according to their families, was *thus:* The border of their inheritance on the east side was Ataroth Addar as far as Upper Beth Horon.

[6]And the border went out toward the sea on the north side of Michmethath; then the border went around eastward to Taanath Shiloh, and passed by it on the east of Janohah. [7]Then it went down from Janohah to Ataroth and Naarah,[a] reached to Jericho, and came out at the Jordan.

[8]The border went out from Tappuah westward to the Brook Kanah, and it ended at the sea. This *was* the inheritance of the tribe of the children of Ephraim according to their families. [9]The separate cities for the children of Ephraim *were* among the inheritance of the children of Manasseh, all the cities with their villages.

[10]And they did not drive out the Canaanites who dwelt in Gezer; but the Canaanites dwell among the Ephraimites to this day and have become forced laborers.

The Other Half-Tribe of Manasseh (West)

17 There was also a lot for the tribe of Manasseh, for he *was* the firstborn of Joseph: *namely* for Machir the firstborn of Manasseh, the father of Gilead, because he was a man of war; therefore he was given Gilead and Bashan. [2]And there was *a lot* for the rest of the children of Manasseh according to their families: for the children of Abiezer,[a] the children of Helek, the children of Asriel, the children of Shechem, the children of Hepher, and the children of Shemida; these *were* the male children of Manasseh the son of Joseph according to their families.

[3]But Zelophehad the son of Hepher, the son of Gilead, the son of Machir, the son of Manasseh, had no sons, but only daughters. And these *are* the names of his daughters: Mahlah, Noah, Hoglah, Milcah, and Tirzah. [4]And they came near before Eleazar the priest, before Joshua the son of Nun, and before the rulers, saying, "The LORD commanded Moses to give us an inheritance among our brothers." Therefore, according to the commandment of the LORD, he gave them an inheritance among their father's brothers. [5]Ten shares fell to Manasseh, besides the land of Gilead and Bashan, which *were* on the other side of the Jordan, [6]because the daughters of Manasseh received an inheritance among his sons; and the rest of Manasseh's sons had the land of Gilead.

[7]And the territory of Manasseh was from Asher to Michmethath, that *lies* east of Shechem; and the border went along south to the inhabitants of En Tappuah. [8]Manasseh had the land of Tappuah, but Tappuah on the border of Manasseh *belonged* to the children of Ephraim. [9]And the border descended to the Brook Kanah, southward to the brook. These cities of Ephraim *are* among the cities of Manasseh. The border of Manasseh *was* on the north side of the brook; and it ended at the sea. [10]Southward *it was* Ephraim's, northward *it was* Manasseh's, and the sea was its border. Manasseh's territory was adjoining Asher on the north and Issachar on the east. [11]And in Issachar and in Asher, Manasseh had Beth Shean and its towns, Ibleam and its towns, the inhabitants of Dor and its towns, the inhabitants of En Dor and its towns, the inhabitants of Taanach and its towns, and the inhabitants of Megiddo and its towns—three hilly regions. [12]Yet the children of Manasseh could not drive out *the inhabitants of* those cities, but the Canaanites were determined to dwell in that land. [13]And it happened, when the children of Israel grew strong, that they put the Canaanites to forced labor, but did not utterly drive them out.

More Land for Ephraim and Manasseh

[14]Then the children of Joseph spoke to Joshua, saying, "Why have you given us *only* one

---

16:2 [a]Septuagint reads *Bethel* (that is, Luz).
16:7 [a]Or *Naaran* (compare 1 Chronicles 7:28)
17:2 [a]Called *Jeezer* in Numbers 26:30

lot and one share to inherit, since we *are* a great people, inasmuch as the LORD has blessed us until now?"

[15]So Joshua answered them, "If you *are* a great people, *then* go up to the forest *country* and clear a place for yourself there in the land of the Perizzites and the giants, since the mountains of Ephraim are too confined for you."

[16]But the children of Joseph said, "The mountain country is not enough for us; and all the Canaanites who dwell in the land of the valley have chariots of iron, *both those* who *are* of Beth Shean and its towns and *those* who *are* of the Valley of Jezreel."

[17]And Joshua spoke to the house of Joseph— to Ephraim and Manasseh—saying, "You *are* a great people and have great power; you shall not have *only* one lot, [18]but the mountain country shall be yours. Although it *is* wooded, you shall cut it down, and its farthest extent shall be yours; for you shall drive out the Canaanites, though they have iron chariots *and* are strong."

The Remainder of the Land Divided

18 Now the whole congregation of the children of Israel assembled together at Shiloh, and set up the tabernacle of meeting there. And the land was subdued before them. [2]But there remained among the children of Israel seven tribes which had not yet received their inheritance.

[3]Then Joshua said to the children of Israel: "How long will you neglect to go and possess the land which the LORD God of your fathers has given you? [4]Pick out from among you three men for *each* tribe, and I will send them; they shall rise and go through the land, survey it according to their inheritance, and come *back* to me. [5]And they shall divide it into seven parts. Judah shall remain in their territory on the south, and the house of Joseph shall remain in their territory on the north. [6]You shall therefore survey the land in seven parts and bring *the survey* here to me, that I may cast lots for you here before the LORD our God. [7]But the Levites have no part among you, for the priesthood of the LORD *is* their inheritance. And Gad, Reuben, and half the tribe of Manasseh have received their inheritance beyond the Jordan on the east, which Moses the servant of the LORD gave them."

[8]Then the men arose to go away; and Joshua charged those who went to survey the land, saying, "Go, walk through the land, survey it, and come back to me, that I may cast lots for you here before the LORD in Shiloh." [9]So the men went, passed through the land, and wrote the survey in a book in seven parts by cities; and they came to Joshua at the camp in Shiloh. [10]Then Joshua cast lots for them in Shiloh before the LORD, and there Joshua divided the land to the children of Israel according to their divisions.

The Land of Benjamin

[11]Now the lot of the tribe of the children of Benjamin came up according to their families, and the territory of their lot came out between the children of Judah and the children of Joseph. [12]Their border on the north side began at the Jordan, and the border went up to the side of Jericho on the north, and went up through the mountains westward; it ended at the Wilderness of Beth Aven. [13]The border went over from there toward Luz, to the side of Luz (which *is* Bethel) southward; and the border descended to Ataroth Addar, near the hill that *lies* on the south side of Lower Beth Horon.

[14]Then the border extended around the west side to the south, from the hill that *lies* before Beth Horon southward; and it ended at Kirjath Baal (which *is* Kirjath Jearim), a city of the children of Judah. This *was* the west side.

[15]The south side *began* at the end of Kirjath Jearim, and the border extended on the west and went out to the spring of the waters of Nephtoah. [16]Then the border came down to the end of the mountain that *lies* before the Valley of the Son of Hinnom, which *is* in the Valley of the Rephaim[a] on the north, descended to the Valley of Hinnom, to the side of the Jebusite *city* on the south, and descended to En Rogel. [17]And it went around from the north, went out to En Shemesh, and extended toward Geliloth, which is before the Ascent of Adummim, and descended to the stone of Bohan the son of Reuben. [18]Then it passed along toward the north side of Arabah,[a] and went down to Arabah. [19]And the border passed along to the north side of Beth Hoglah; then the border ended at the north bay at the Salt Sea, at the south end of the Jordan. This *was* the southern boundary.

[20]The Jordan was its border on the east side. This *was* the inheritance of the children of Benjamin, according to its boundaries all around, according to their families.

[21]Now the cities of the tribe of the children of Benjamin, according to their families, were Jericho, Beth Hoglah, Emek Keziz, [22]Beth Arabah, Zemaraim, Bethel, [23]Avim, Parah, Ophrah, [24]Chephar Haammoni, Ophni, and

---

18:16 [a]Literally *Giants* **18:18** [a]Or *Beth Arabah* (compare 15:6 and 18:22)

Gaba: twelve cities with their villages; [25]Gibeon, Ramah, Beeroth, [26]Mizpah, Chephirah, Mozah, [27]Rekem, Irpeel, Taralah, [28]Zelah, Eleph, Jebus (which *is* Jerusalem), Gibeath, *and* Kirjath: fourteen cities with their villages. This was the inheritance of the children of Benjamin according to their families.

Simeon's Inheritance with Judah

19 The second lot came out for Simeon, for the tribe of the children of Simeon according to their families. And their inheritance was within the inheritance of the children of Judah. [2]They had in their inheritance Beersheba (Sheba), Moladah, [3]Hazar Shual, Balah, Ezem, [4]Eltolad, Bethul, Hormah, [5]Ziklag, Beth Marcaboth, Hazar Susah, [6]Beth Lebaoth, and Sharuhen: thirteen cities and their villages; [7]Ain, Rimmon, Ether, and Ashan: four cities and their villages; [8]and all the villages that *were* all around these cities as far as Baalath Beer, Ramah of the South. This *was* the inheritance of the tribe of the children of Simeon according to their families.

[9]The inheritance of the children of Simeon *was included* in the share of the children of Judah, for the share of the children of Judah was too much for them. Therefore the children of Simeon had *their* inheritance within the inheritance of that people.

The Land of Zebulun

[10]The third lot came out for the children of Zebulun according to their families, and the border of their inheritance was as far as Sarid. [11]Their border went toward the west and to Maralah, went to Dabbasheth, and extended along the brook that is east of Jokneam. [12]Then from Sarid it went eastward toward the sunrise along the border of Chisloth Tabor, and went out toward Daberath, bypassing Japhia. [13]And from there it passed along on the east of Gath Hepher, toward Eth Kazin, and extended to Rimmon, which borders on Neah. [14]Then the border went around it on the north side of Hannathon, and it ended in the Valley of Jiphthah El. [15]Included were Kattath, Nahallal, Shimron, Idalah, and Bethlehem: twelve cities with their villages. [16]This *was* the inheritance of the children of Zebulun according to their families, these cities with their villages.

The Land of Issachar

[17]The fourth lot came out to Issachar, for the children of Issachar according to their families. [18]And their territory went to Jezreel, and *included*

Chesulloth, Shunem, [19]Haphraim, Shion, Anaharath, [20]Rabbith, Kishion, Abez, [21]Remeth, En Gannim, En Haddah, and Beth Pazzez. [22]And the border reached to Tabor, Shahazimah, and Beth Shemesh; their border ended at the Jordan: sixteen cities with their villages. [23]This *was* the inheritance of the tribe of the children of Issachar according to their families, the cities and their villages.

The Land of Asher

[24]The fifth lot came out for the tribe of the children of Asher according to their families. [25]And their territory included Helkath, Hali, Beten, Achshaph, [26]Alammelech, Amad, and Mishal; it reached to Mount Carmel westward, along *the Brook* Shihor Libnath. [27]It turned toward the sunrise to Beth Dagon; and it reached to Zebulun and to the Valley of Jiphthah El, then northward beyond Beth Emek and Neiel, bypassing Cabul *which was* on the left, [28]including Ebron,[a] Rehob, Hammon, and Kanah, as far as Greater Sidon. [29]And the border turned to Ramah and to the fortified city of Tyre; then the border turned to Hosah, and ended at the sea by the region of Achzib. [30]Also Ummah, Aphek, and Rehob *were included:* twenty-two cities with their villages. [31]This *was* the inheritance of the tribe of the children of Asher according to their families, these cities with their villages.

The Land of Naphtali

[32]The sixth lot came out to the children of Naphtali, for the children of Naphtali according to their families. [33]And their border began at Heleph, enclosing the territory from the terebinth tree in Zaanannim, Adami Nekeb, and Jabneel, as far as Lakkum; it ended at the Jordan. [34]From Heleph the border extended westward to Aznoth Tabor, and went out from there toward Hukkok; it adjoined Zebulun on the south side and Asher on the west side, and ended at Judah by the Jordan toward the sunrise. [35]And the fortified cities *are* Ziddim, Zer, Hammath, Rakkath, Chinnereth, [36]Adamah, Ramah, Hazor, [37]Kedesh, Edrei, En Hazor, [38]Iron, Migdal El, Horem, Beth Anath, and Beth Shemesh: nineteen cities with their villages. [39]This *was* the inheritance of the tribe of the children of Naphtali according to their families, the cities and their villages.

19:28 [a]Following Masoretic Text, Targum, and Vulgate; a few Hebrew manuscripts read *Abdon* (compare 21:30 and 1 Chronicles 6:74).

The Land of Dan

⁴⁰The seventh lot came out for the tribe of the children of Dan according to their families. ⁴¹And the territory of their inheritance was Zorah, Eshtaol, Ir Shemesh, ⁴²Shaalabbin, Aijalon, Jethlah, ⁴³Elon, Timnah, Ekron, ⁴⁴Eltekeh, Gibbethon, Baalath, ⁴⁵Jehud, Bene Berak, Gath Rimmon, ⁴⁶Me Jarkon, and Rakkon, with the region near Joppa. ⁴⁷And the border of the children of Dan went beyond these, because the children of Dan went up to fight against Leshem and took it; and they struck it with the edge of the sword, took possession of it, and dwelt in it. They called Leshem, Dan, after the name of Dan their father. ⁴⁸This is the inheritance of the tribe of the children of Dan according to their families, these cities with their villages.

Joshua's Inheritance

⁴⁹When they had made an end of dividing the land as an inheritance according to their borders, the children of Israel gave an inheritance among them to Joshua the son of Nun. ⁵⁰According to the word of the LORD they gave him the city which he asked for, Timnath Serah in the mountains of Ephraim; and he built the city and dwelt in it.

⁵¹These were the inheritances which Eleazar the priest, Joshua the son of Nun, and the heads of the fathers of the tribes of the children of Israel divided as an inheritance by lot in Shiloh before the LORD, at the door of the tabernacle of meeting. So they made an end of dividing the country.

The Cities of Refuge

20 The LORD also spoke to Joshua, saying, ²"Speak to the children of Israel, saying: 'Appoint for yourselves cities of refuge, of which I spoke to you through Moses, ³that the slayer who kills a person accidentally or unintentionally may flee there; and they shall be your refuge from the avenger of blood. ⁴And when he flees to one of those cities, and stands at the entrance of the gate of the city, and declares his case in the hearing of the elders of that city, they shall take him into the city as one of them, and give him a place, that he may dwell among them. ⁵Then if the avenger of blood pursues him, they shall not deliver the slayer into his hand, because he struck his neighbor unintentionally, but did not hate him beforehand. ⁶And he shall dwell in that city until he stands before the congregation for judgment, and until the death of the one who is high priest in those days. Then the slayer may return and come to his own city and his own house, to the city from which he fled.'"

⁷So they appointed Kedesh in Galilee, in the mountains of Naphtali, Shechem in the mountains of Ephraim, and Kirjath Arba (which is Hebron) in the mountains of Judah. ⁸And on the other side of the Jordan, by Jericho eastward, they assigned Bezer in the wilderness on the plain, from the tribe of Reuben, Ramoth in Gilead, from the tribe of Gad, and Golan in Bashan, from the tribe of Manasseh. ⁹These were the cities appointed for all the children of Israel and for the stranger who dwelt among them, that whoever killed a person accidentally might flee there, and not die by the hand of the avenger of blood until he stood before the congregation.

Cities of the Levites

21 Then the heads of the fathers' houses of the Levites came near to Eleazar the priest, to Joshua the son of Nun, and to the heads of the fathers' houses of the tribes of the children of Israel. ²And they spoke to them at Shiloh in the land of Canaan, saying, "The LORD commanded through Moses to give us cities to dwell in, with their common-lands for our livestock." ³So the children of Israel gave to the Levites from their inheritance, at the commandment of the LORD, these cities and their common-lands:

⁴Now the lot came out for the families of the Kohathites. And the children of Aaron the priest, who were of the Levites, had thirteen cities by lot from the tribe of Judah, from the tribe of Simeon, and from the tribe of Benjamin. ⁵The rest of the children of Kohath had ten cities by lot from the families of the tribe of Ephraim, from the tribe of Dan, and from the half-tribe of Manasseh.

⁶And the children of Gershon had thirteen cities by lot from the families of the tribe of Issachar, from the tribe of Asher, from the tribe of Naphtali, and from the half-tribe of Manasseh in Bashan.

⁷The children of Merari according to their families had twelve cities from the tribe of Reuben, from the tribe of Gad, and from the tribe of Zebulun.

⁸And the children of Israel gave these cities with their common-lands by lot to the Levites, as the LORD had commanded by the hand of Moses.

⁹So they gave from the tribe of the children of Judah and from the tribe of the children of Simeon these cities which are designated by name, ¹⁰which were for the children of Aaron,

one of the families of the Kohathites, *who were* of the children of Levi; for the lot was theirs first. [11]And they gave them Kirjath Arba (*Arba was* the father of Anak), which *is* Hebron, in the mountains of Judah, with the common-land surrounding it. [12]But the fields of the city and its villages they gave to Caleb the son of Jephunneh as his possession.

[13]Thus to the children of Aaron the priest they gave Hebron with its common-land (a city of refuge for the slayer), Libnah with its common-land, [14]Jattir with its common-land, Eshtemoa with its common-land, [15]Holon with its common-land, Debir with its common-land, [16]Ain with its common-land, Juttah with its common-land, and Beth Shemesh with its common-land: nine cities from those two tribes; [17]and from the tribe of Benjamin, Gibeon with its common-land, Geba with its common-land, [18]Anathoth with its common-land, and Almon with its common-land: four cities. [19]All the cities of the children of Aaron, the priests, *were* thirteen cities with their common-lands.

[20]And the families of the children of Kohath, the Levites, the rest of the children of Kohath, even they had the cities of their lot from the tribe of Ephraim. [21]For they gave them Shechem with its common-land in the mountains of Ephraim (a city of refuge for the slayer), Gezer with its common-land, [22]Kibzaim with its common-land, and Beth Horon with its common-land: four cities; [23]and from the tribe of Dan, Eltekeh with its common-land, Gibbethon with its common-land, [24]Aijalon with its common-land, *and* Gath Rimmon with its common-land: four cities; [25]and from the half-tribe of Manasseh, Tanach with its common-land and Gath Rimmon with its common-land: two cities. [26]All the ten cities with their common-lands were for the rest of the families of the children of Kohath.

[27]Also to the children of Gershon, of the families of the Levites, from the *other* half-tribe of Manasseh, *they gave* Golan in Bashan with its common-land (a city of refuge for the slayer), and Be Eshterah with its common-land: two cities; [28]and from the tribe of Issachar, Kishion with its common-land, Daberath with its common-land, [29]Jarmuth with its common-land, *and* En Gannim with its common-land: four cities; [30]and from the tribe of Asher, Mishal with its common-land, Abdon with its common-land, [31]Helkath with its common-land, and Rehob with its common-land: four cities; [32]and from the tribe of Naphtali, Kedesh in Galilee with its common-land (a city of refuge for the slayer), Hammoth Dor with its common-land, and Kar-

tan with its common-land: three cities. [33]All the cities of the Gershonites according to their families *were* thirteen cities with their common-lands.

[34]And to the families of the children of Merari, the rest of the Levites, from the tribe of Zebulun, Jokneam with its common-land, Kartah with its common-land, [35]Dimnah with its common-land, *and* Nahalal with its common-land: four cities; [36]and from the tribe of Reuben, Bezer with its common-land, Jahaz with its common-land, [37]Kedemoth with its common-land, and Mephaath with its common-land: four cities;[a] [38]and from the tribe of Gad, Ramoth in Gilead with its common-land (a city of refuge for the slayer), Mahanaim with its common-land, [39]Heshbon with its common-land, *and* Jazer with its common-land: four cities in all. [40]So all the cities for the children of Merari according to their families, the rest of the families of the Levites, were *by* their lot twelve cities.

[41]All the cities of the Levites within the possession of the children of Israel *were* forty-eight cities with their common-lands. [42]Every one of these cities had its common-land surrounding it; thus *were* all these cities.

The Promise Fulfilled

[43]So the LORD gave to Israel all the land of which He had sworn to give to their fathers, and they took possession of it and dwelt in it. [44]The LORD gave them rest all around, according to all that He had sworn to their fathers. And not a man of all their enemies stood against them; the LORD delivered all their enemies into their hand. [45]Not a word failed of any good thing which the LORD had spoken to the house of Israel. All came to pass.

Eastern Tribes Return to Their Lands

22 Then Joshua called the Reubenites, the Gadites, and half the tribe of Manasseh, [2]and said to them: "You have kept all that Moses the servant of the LORD commanded you, and have obeyed my voice in all that I commanded you. [3]You have not left your brethren these many days, up to this day, but have kept the charge of the commandment of the LORD your God. [4]And now the LORD your God has given rest to your brethren, as He promised them; now therefore, return and go to your tents *and* to the land of your possession, which

---

21:37 [a]Following Septuagint and Vulgate (compare 1 Chronicles 6:78, 79); Masoretic Text, Bomberg, and Targum omit verses 36 and 37.

Moses the servant of the LORD gave you on the other side of the Jordan. [5]But take careful heed to do the commandment and the law which Moses the servant of the LORD commanded you, to love the LORD your God, to walk in all His ways, to keep His commandments, to hold fast to Him, and to serve Him with all your heart and with all your soul." [6]So Joshua blessed them and sent them away, and they went to their tents.

[7]Now to half the tribe of Manasseh Moses had given a possession in Bashan, but to the *other* half of it Joshua gave *a possession* among their brethren on this side of the Jordan, westward. And indeed, when Joshua sent them away to their tents, he blessed them, [8]and spoke to them, saying, "Return with much riches to your tents, with very much livestock, with silver, with gold, with bronze, with iron, and with very much clothing. Divide the spoil of your enemies with your brethren."

[9]So the children of Reuben, the children of Gad, and half the tribe of Manasseh returned, and departed from the children of Israel at Shiloh, which *is* in the land of Canaan, to go to the country of Gilead, to the land of their possession, which they had obtained according to the word of the LORD by the hand of Moses.

An Altar by the Jordan

[10]And when they came to the region of the Jordan which *is* in the land of Canaan, the children of Reuben, the children of Gad, and half the tribe of Manasseh built an altar there by the Jordan—a great, impressive altar. [11]Now the children of Israel heard *someone* say, "Behold, the children of Reuben, the children of Gad, and half the tribe of Manasseh have built an altar on the frontier of the land of Canaan, in the region of the Jordan—on the children of Israel's side." [12]And when the children of Israel heard *of it,* the whole congregation of the children of Israel gathered together at Shiloh to go to war against them.

[13]Then the children of Israel sent Phinehas the son of Eleazar the priest to the children of Reuben, to the children of Gad, and to half the tribe of Manasseh, into the land of Gilead, [14]and with him ten rulers, one ruler each from the chief house of every tribe of Israel; and each one *was* the head of the house of his father among the divisions[a] of Israel. [15]Then they came to the children of Reuben, to the children of Gad, and to half the tribe of Manasseh, to the land of Gilead, and they spoke with them, saying, [16]"Thus says the whole congregation of the LORD: 'What treachery *is* this that you have

committed against the God of Israel, to turn away this day from following the LORD, in that you have built for yourselves an altar, that you might rebel this day against the LORD? [17]*Is* the iniquity of Peor not enough for us, from which we are not cleansed till this day, although there was a plague in the congregation of the LORD, [18]but that you must turn away this day from following the LORD? And it shall be, if you rebel today against the LORD, that tomorrow He will be angry with the whole congregation of Israel. [19]Nevertheless, if the land of your possession *is* unclean, *then* cross over to the land of the possession of the LORD, where the LORD's tabernacle stands, and take possession among us; but do not rebel against the LORD, nor rebel against us, by building yourselves an altar besides the altar of the LORD our God. [20]Did not Achan the son of Zerah commit a trespass in the accursed thing, and wrath fell on all the congregation of Israel? And that man did not perish alone in his iniquity.'"

[21]Then the children of Reuben, the children of Gad, and half the tribe of Manasseh answered and said to the heads of the divisions[a] of Israel: [22]"The LORD God of gods, the LORD God of gods, He knows, and let Israel itself know—if *it is* in rebellion, or if in treachery against the LORD, do not save us this day. [23]If we have built ourselves an altar to turn from following the LORD, or if to offer on it burnt offerings or grain offerings, or if to offer peace offerings on it, let the LORD Himself require *an account.* [24]But in fact we have done it for fear, for a reason, saying, 'In time to come your descendants may speak to our descendants, saying, "What have you to do with the LORD God of Israel? [25]For the LORD has made the Jordan a border between you and us, *you* children of Reuben and children of Gad. You have no part in the LORD." So your descendants would make our descendants cease fearing the LORD.' [26]Therefore we said, 'Let us now prepare to build ourselves an altar, not for burnt offering nor for sacrifice, [27]but *that it may be* a witness between you and us and our generations after us, that we may perform the service of the LORD before Him with our burnt offerings, with our sacrifices, and with our peace offerings; that your descendants may not say to our descendants in time to come, "You have no part in the LORD."' [28]Therefore we said that it will be, when they say *this* to us or to our generations in time to come, that we may say, 'Here is the replica of the altar of the LORD which our fathers made,

---

22:14 [a]Literally *thousands* 22:21 [a]Literally *thousands* though not for burnt offerings nor for sacrifices; but it *is* a witness between you and us.' ²⁹Far be it from us that we should rebel against the LORD, and turn from following the LORD this day, to build an altar for burnt offerings, for grain offerings, or for sacrifices, besides the altar of the LORD our God which *is* before His tabernacle."

³⁰Now when Phinehas the priest and the rulers of the congregation, the heads of the divisionsᵃ of Israel who *were* with him, heard the words that the children of Reuben, the children of Gad, and the children of Manasseh spoke, it pleased them. ³¹Then Phinehas the son of Eleazar the priest said to the children of Reuben, the children of Gad, and the children of Manasseh, "This day we perceive that the LORD *is* among us, because you have not committed this treachery against the LORD. Now you have delivered the children of Israel out of the hand of the LORD."

³²And Phinehas the son of Eleazar the priest, and the rulers, returned from the children of Reuben and the children of Gad, from the land of Gilead to the land of Canaan, to the children of Israel, and brought back word to them. ³³So the thing pleased the children of Israel, and the children of Israel blessed God; they spoke no more of going against them in battle, to destroy the land where the children of Reuben and Gad dwelt.

³⁴The children of Reuben and the children of Gadᵃ called the altar, *Witness,* "For *it is* a witness between us that the LORD *is* God."

Joshua's Farewell Address

23 Now it came to pass, a long time after the LORD had given rest to Israel from all their enemies round about, that Joshua was old, advanced in age. ²And Joshua called for all Israel, for their elders, for their heads, for their judges, and for their officers, and said to them:

"I am old, advanced in age. ³You have seen all that the LORD your God has done to all these nations because of you, for the LORD your God *is* He who has fought for you. ⁴See, I have divided to you by lot these nations that remain, to be an inheritance for your tribes, from the Jordan, with all the nations that I have cut off, as far as the Great Sea westward. ⁵And the LORD your God will expel them from before you and drive them out of your sight. So you shall possess their land, as the LORD your God promised you. ⁶Therefore be very courageous to keep and to do all that is written in the Book of the Law of Moses, lest you turn aside from it to the right hand

---

The Law of Magnetism: Joshua Says Good-Bye with Convictions
(Joshua 23:1—24:28)

Joshua's farewell speech urged Israel to stay passionately committed to God. Joshua reminded the people of God's faithfulness, warned them against disobedience and concluded, "But as for me and my house, we will serve the LORD" (Josh. 24:15). Everyone followed Joshua's convictions during his lifetime, for he made them both attractive and magnetic.

---

or to the left, ⁷*and* lest you go among these nations, these who remain among you. You shall not make mention of the name of their gods, nor cause *anyone* to swear *by them;* you shall not serve them nor bow down to them, ⁸but you shall hold fast to the LORD your God, as you have done to this day. ⁹For the LORD has driven out from before you great and strong nations; but *as for* you, no one has been able to stand against you to this day. ¹⁰One man of you shall chase a thousand, for the LORD your God *is* He who fights for you, as He promised you. ¹¹Therefore take careful heed to yourselves, that you love the LORD your God. ¹²Or else, if indeed you do go back, and cling to the remnant of these nations—these that remain among you—and make marriages with them, and go in to them and they to you, ¹³know for certain that the LORD your God will no longer drive out these nations from before you. But they shall be snares and traps to you, and scourges on your sides and thorns in your eyes, until you perish from this good land which the LORD your God has given you.

¹⁴"Behold, this day I *am* going the way of all the earth. And you know in all your hearts and in all your souls that not one thing has failed of all the good things which the LORD your God spoke concerning you. All have come to pass for you; not one word of them has failed. ¹⁵Therefore it shall come to pass, that as all the good things have come upon you which the LORD your God promised you, so the LORD will bring upon you all harmful things, until He has

---

22:30 ᵃLiterally *thousands* **22:34** ᵃSeptuagint adds *and half the tribe of Manasseh.*

destroyed you from this good land which the LORD your God has given you. ¹⁶When you have transgressed the covenant of the LORD your God, which He commanded you, and have gone and served other gods, and bowed down to them, then the anger of the LORD will burn against you, and you shall perish quickly from the good land which He has given you."

The Covenant at Shechem

24 Then Joshua gathered all the tribes of Israel to Shechem and called for the elders of Israel, for their heads, for their judges, and for their officers; and they presented themselves before God. ²And Joshua said to all the people, "Thus says the LORD God of Israel: 'Your fathers, *including* Terah, the father of Abraham and the father of Nahor, dwelt on the other side of the River[a] in old times; and they served other gods. ³Then I took your father Abraham from the other side of the River, led him throughout all the land of Canaan, and multiplied his descendants and gave him Isaac. ⁴To Isaac I gave Jacob and Esau. To Esau I gave the mountains of Seir to possess, but Jacob and his children went down to Egypt. ⁵Also I sent Moses and Aaron, and I plagued Egypt, according to what I did among them. Afterward I brought you out.

⁶"Then I brought your fathers out of Egypt, and you came to the sea; and the Egyptians pursued your fathers with chariots and horsemen to the Red Sea. ⁷So they cried out to the LORD; and He put darkness between you and the Egyptians, brought the sea upon them, and covered them. And your eyes saw what I did in Egypt. Then you dwelt in the wilderness a long time. ⁸And I brought you into the land of the Amorites, who dwelt on the other side of the Jordan, and they fought with you. But I gave them into your hand, that you might possess their land, and I destroyed them from before you. ⁹Then Balak the son of Zippor, king of Moab, arose to make war against Israel, and sent and called Balaam the son of Beor to curse you. ¹⁰But I would not listen to Balaam; therefore he continued to bless you. So I delivered you out of his hand. ¹¹Then you went over the Jordan and came to Jericho. And the men of Jericho fought against you—*also* the Amorites, the Perizzites, the Canaanites, the Hittites, the Girgashites, the Hivites, and the Jebusites. But I delivered them into your hand. ¹²I sent the hornet before you which drove them out from before you, *also* the two kings of the Amorites, *but* not with your sword or with your bow. ¹³I have given you a land for which you did not

labor, and cities which you did not build, and you dwell in them; you eat of the vineyards and olive groves which you did not plant.'

¹⁴"Now therefore, fear the LORD, serve Him in sincerity and in truth, and put away the gods which your fathers served on the other side of the River and in Egypt. Serve the LORD! ¹⁵And if it seems evil to you to serve the LORD, choose for yourselves this day whom you will serve, whether the gods which your fathers served that *were* on the other side of the River, or the gods of the Amorites, in whose land you dwell. But as for me and my house, we will serve the LORD."

¹⁶So the people answered and said: "Far be it from us that we should forsake the LORD to serve other gods; ¹⁷for the LORD our God *is* He who brought us and our fathers up out of the land of Egypt, from the house of bondage, who did those great signs in our sight, and preserved us in all the way that we went and among all the people through whom we passed. ¹⁸And the LORD drove out from before us all the people, including the Amorites who dwelt in the land. We also will serve the LORD, for He *is* our God."

¹⁹But Joshua said to the people, "You cannot serve the LORD, for He *is* a holy God. He *is* a jealous God; He will not forgive your transgressions nor your sins. ²⁰If you forsake the LORD and serve foreign gods, then He will turn and do you harm and consume you, after He has done you good."

²¹And the people said to Joshua, "No, but we will serve the LORD!"

²²So Joshua said to the people, "You *are* witnesses against yourselves that you have chosen the LORD for yourselves, to serve Him."

And they said, "*We are* witnesses!"

²³"Now therefore," *he said,* "put away the foreign gods which *are* among you, and incline your heart to the LORD God of Israel."

²⁴And the people said to Joshua, "The LORD our God we will serve, and His voice we will obey!"

²⁵So Joshua made a covenant with the people that day, and made for them a statute and an ordinance in Shechem. ²⁶Then Joshua wrote these words in the Book of the Law of God. And he took a large stone, and set it up there under the oak that *was* by the sanctuary of the LORD. ²⁷And Joshua said to all the people, "Behold, this stone shall be a witness to us, for it has heard all the words of the LORD which He spoke to us. It shall therefore be a witness to

24:2 [a]Hebrew *Nahar,* the Euphrates, and so in verses 3, 14, and 15

you, lest you deny your God." [28]So Joshua let the people depart, each to his own inheritance.

Death of Joshua and Eleazar

[29]Now it came to pass after these things that Joshua the son of Nun, the servant of the LORD, died, *being* one hundred and ten years old. [30]And they buried him within the border of his inheritance at Timnath Serah, which *is* in the mountains of Ephraim, on the north side of Mount Gaash.

[31]Israel served the LORD all the days of Joshua, and all the days of the elders who outlived Joshua, who had known all the works of the LORD which He had done for Israel.

[32]The bones of Joseph, which the children of Israel had brought up out of Egypt, they buried at Shechem, in the plot of ground which Jacob had bought from the sons of Hamor the father of Shechem for one hundred pieces of silver, and which had become an inheritance of the children of Joseph.

Joshua Fails to Practice the Law of Reproduction

(Joshua 24:29)

Joshua's leadership failed at only one major point: He left no "Joshua" to follow him, as he had followed Moses. Joshua did not reproduce his leadership. Consequently, the Book of Judges records a time of anarchy, when "everyone did what was right in his own eyes" (Judg. 21:25).

[33]And Eleazar the son of Aaron died. They buried him in a hill *belonging to* Phinehas his son, which was given to him in the mountains of Ephraim.

Joshua: Picture of a Faithful Leader

(Joshua 24:29–31)

Joshua provides a superb example of a leader whose faithfulness prompted God to raise him up. Over the three divisions of his life (40 years in Egypt; 40 years in the wilderness; and 30 years in Canaan), God gradually moved this trustworthy man into leadership.

Note the signs of his faithfulness: **Obedience** (Ex. 17:8–16; Num. 32:10–12); **Servanthood** (Ex. 24:13; Josh. 11:15); **Loyalty** (Ex. 33:11; Num. 11:24–30); **Courage** (Num. 13:8, 16, 25–30; 14:5–10); **Promotion** (Num. 27:15–23); **Responsibility** (Deut. 31:7, 8); **Power** (Deut. 34:9); **Credibility** (Deut. 34:9). Joshua's faithfulness challenges us even today to lead as he did:

1. **Live *ahead* of your contemporaries.**
   Joshua spied out the same land at the same time as the other ten spies, but he and Caleb returned with a different report. He lived ahead of his time.
2. **Live *above* your circumstances.**
   Joshua faced several challenges: He followed Moses; he had to conquer mighty Jericho; he had to cross the Jordan with more than one million people. But he did it.
3. **Live *deeper* than your calamities.**
   When Israel began to make progress in taking the Promised Land, some disobeyed God and brought defeat on the nation. Joshua overcame it all.
4. **Live *beyond* your capabilities.**
   Joshua's dream, his determination, and his ability to develop his leadership skills enabled him to soar beyond his own personal gifts.

JUDGES
Responsible for the Nation of Israel

SUMMARY

Judges receives its name from the leaders who assumed responsibility for the nation of Israel from the time of Joshua until the beginning of the monarchy, a period of about 200 years. The term "judge" meant civil magistrate or governor or head of state, clearly a political term for leader.

During the times of the judges, public opinion leaned heavily against a monarchy. Only external pressures applied by prospective invaders eventually prompted the people to demand a king (1 Sam. 8). At the time of the judges, God Himself reigned as Israel's King, while the judges served as under-shepherds.

Under Joshua's leadership, Israel defeated anyone who stood in her way and occupied the land God had promised the nation decades before. After Joshua died, however, the tribes ran into trouble trying to consolidate their inheritance. Turmoil reigned in Palestine. The Philistines pushed in from the Mediterranean Coast, establishing a stranglehold on the region until the time of King David. Other ethnic groups, such as the Midianites, attacked the eastern flank of Israel.

The scattered tribes had grown divided and weak. They lacked a strong leader who could cast a national vision. The last and most famous verse in the book speaks volumes: "In those days there was no king in Israel; everyone did what was right in his own eyes" (Judg. 21:25).

Still, God always raises up a leader for the hour—the theme of this book. Whenever suffering grew terrible and the people cried out in despair, God called forth a judge (or deliverer) to throw off the oppressor's yoke. Sometimes these judges were good and noble men like Gideon or Samuel; at other times erratic and unstable men like Samson rose to the fore.

In any case, the message rings clear: God raises up the weak and unlikely to confound the strong and sensible. Deborah, a woman, led in a time when men were considered the superior gender; Gideon, the runt of the litter in the smallest of the tribes in Israel, rose to greatness in his time; and the strong man Samson ruled for a short while until his inability to control his own appetites led to an impetuous end.

The ultimate lesson here? People need leaders. Jesus echoed this truth when He described the people of Israel as "sheep having no shepherd" (Matt. 9:36). Chaos reigns whenever humankind does whatever is "right in his own eyes." Civilized life becomes impossible when every man has "his own way." We always need healthy, spiritual leaders, and this book illustrates that truth as vividly as any other.

God's Role in Judges

God's role during this period of history cannot be overemphasized. The people relished their conquest of Canaan, but waffled between freedom and chaos. They turned away from God, then turned back to Him for help when oppressed—a pattern often repeated. Yet God always raised up a leader for the hour. Only God ruled as Israel's King, and only He could raise up human leaders to serve under Him.

Leaders in Judges

Othniel, Ehud, Shamgar, Deborah, Gideon, Abimelech, Tola, Jair, Jephthah, Ibzan, Elon, Abdon, Samson

Other People of Influence in Judges

Barak, Jael, the Midianites, the Amalekites, the Philistines, the Ammonites, Micah

Lessons in Leadership

- Leaders who compromise their values eventually compromise their goals.
- It takes strong, spiritual leadership to engineer a turnaround in God's kingdom.
- Leaders should lead from their area of giftedness and strength.
- The one with the plan and insight is the one with the power and influence.
- Leaders must learn to lead themselves before leading others.
- People first buy in to the leader before they buy in to the cause.
- God will often raise up the most unlikely leader to accomplish His purposes.

HIGHLIGHTS IN JUDGES

The Continuing Conquest of Canaan

1 Now after the death of Joshua it came to pass that the children of Israel asked the LORD, saying, "Who shall be first to go up for us against the Canaanites to fight against them?"

[2]And the LORD said, "Judah shall go up. Indeed I have delivered the land into his hand."

[3]So Judah said to Simeon his brother, "Come up with me to my allotted territory, that we may fight against the Canaanites; and I will likewise go with you to your allotted territory." And Simeon went with him. [4]Then Judah went up, and the LORD delivered the Canaanites and the Perizzites into their hand; and they killed ten thousand men at Bezek. [5]And they found Adoni-Bezek in Bezek, and fought against him; and they defeated the Canaanites and the Perizzites. [6]Then Adoni-Bezek fled, and they pursued him and caught him and cut off his thumbs and big toes. [7]And Adoni-Bezek said, "Seventy kings with their thumbs and big toes cut off used to gather *scraps* under my table; as I have done, so God has repaid me." Then they brought him to Jerusalem, and there he died.

[8]Now the children of Judah fought against Jerusalem and took it; they struck it with the edge of the sword and set the city on fire. [9]And afterward the children of Judah went down to fight against the Canaanites who dwelt in the mountains, in the South,[a] and in the lowland. [10]Then Judah went against the Canaanites who dwelt in Hebron. (Now the name of Hebron *was* formerly Kirjath Arba.) And they killed Sheshai, Ahiman, and Talmai.

[11]From there they went against the inhabitants of Debir. (The name of Debir *was* formerly Kirjath Sepher.)

[12]Then Caleb said, "Whoever attacks Kirjath Sepher and takes it, to him I will give my daughter Achsah as wife." [13]And Othniel the son of Kenaz, Caleb's younger brother, took it; so he gave him his daughter Achsah as wife. [14]Now it happened, when she came *to him,* that she urged him[a] to ask her father for a field. And she dismounted from *her* donkey, and Caleb said to her, "What do you wish?" [15]So she said to him, "Give me a blessing; since you have given me land in the South, give me also springs of water."

And Caleb gave her the upper springs and the lower springs.

[16]Now the children of the Kenite, Moses' father-in-law, went up from the City of Palms with the children of Judah into the Wilderness of Judah, which *lies* in the South *near* Arad; and they went and dwelt among the people. [17]And Judah went with his brother Simeon, and they attacked the Canaanites who inhabited Zephath, and utterly destroyed it. So the name of the city was called Hormah. [18]Also Judah took Gaza with its territory, Ashkelon with its territory, and Ekron with its territory. [19]So the LORD was with Judah. And they drove out the mountaineers, but they could not drive out the inhabitants of the lowland, because they had chariots of iron. [20]And they gave Hebron to Caleb, as Moses had said. Then he expelled from there the three sons of Anak. [21]But the children of Benjamin did not drive out the Jebusites who inhabited Jerusalem; so the Jebusites dwell with the children of Benjamin in Jerusalem to this day.

[22]And the house of Joseph also went up against Bethel, and the LORD *was* with them. [23]So the house of Joseph sent men to spy out Bethel. (The name of the city *was* formerly Luz.) [24]And when the spies saw a man coming out of the city, they said to him, "Please show us the entrance to the city, and we will show you mercy." [25]So he showed them the entrance to the city, and they struck the city with the edge of the sword; but they let the man and all his family go. [26]And the man went to the land of the Hittites, built a city, and called its name Luz, which *is* its name to this day.

Incomplete Conquest of the Land

[27]However, Manasseh did not drive out *the inhabitants of* Beth Shean and its villages, or Taanach and its villages, or the inhabitants of Dor and its villages, or the inhabitants of Ibleam and its villages, or the inhabitants of Megiddo and its villages; for the Canaanites were determined to dwell in that land. [28]And it came to pass, when Israel was strong, that they put the Canaanites under tribute, but did not completely drive them out.

[29]Nor did Ephraim drive out the Canaanites who dwelt in Gezer; so the Canaanites dwelt in Gezer among them.

[30]Nor did Zebulun drive out the inhabitants of Kitron or the inhabitants of Nahalol; so the Canaanites dwelt among them, and were put under tribute.

[31]Nor did Asher drive out the inhabitants of Acco or the inhabitants of Sidon, or of Ahlab, Achzib, Helbah, Aphik, or Rehob. [32]So the Asherites dwelt among the Canaanites, the inhabitants of the land; for they did not drive them out.

1:9 [a]Hebrew *Negev,* and so throughout this book
1:14 [a]Septuagint and Vulgate read *he urged her.*

Compromising Values Leads to Compromising Goals

(Judges 1:21–36)

Soon after Joshua died, it became clear how much Israel had failed to fulfill God's calling. The people failed to subdue Canaan, and the Book of Judges reveals a Hebrew nation pressed on the west from the Philistines and on the east from the Midianites. Disregarding God's directions, Israel decided to negotiate some deals and compromise with the inhabitants of Canaan. The people hoped that by doing so they could make friends and avoid confrontation.

How wrong they were!

The Scripture outlines how various tribes failed to drive their enemies out of the land. Compromising their values led to compromising their goals, with tragic results:

Compromises	Consequences
1. Benjamin failed to drive out Jebusites	1. Mixed marriages and diluted faith
2. Manasseh failed to drive out Canaanites	2. Spiritual apathy
3. Ephraim failed to drive out Canaanites	3. Spiritual division
4. Zebulun failed to drive out those in Kitron	4. Tribal strife
5. Dan failed to drive out Amorites	5. Defeat and lack of protection
6. Asher failed to drive out those in Acco	6. Inhabitants became a snare
7. Asher failed to drive out Canaanites	7. Failure to live in the land God had planned
8. Naphtali failed to drive out Bethshemesh	for them

[33]Nor did Naphtali drive out the inhabitants of Beth Shemesh or the inhabitants of Beth Anath; but they dwelt among the Canaanites, the inhabitants of the land. Nevertheless the inhabitants of Beth Shemesh and Beth Anath were put under tribute to them.

[34]And the Amorites forced the children of Dan into the mountains, for they would not allow them to come down to the valley; [35]and the Amorites were determined to dwell in Mount Heres, in Aijalon, and in Shaalbim;[a] yet when the strength of the house of Joseph became greater, they were put under tribute.

[36]Now the boundary of the Amorites *was* from the Ascent of Akrabbim, from Sela, and upward.

Israel's Disobedience

2 Then the Angel of the LORD came up from Gilgal to Bochim, and said: "I led you up from Egypt and brought you to the land of which I swore to your fathers; and I said, 'I will never break My covenant with you. [2]And you shall make no covenant with the inhabitants of this land; you shall tear down their altars.' But you have not obeyed My voice. Why have you done this? [3]Therefore I also said, 'I will not drive them out before you; but they shall be *thorns* in your side,[a] and their gods shall be a snare to you.'" [4]So it was, when the Angel of the LORD spoke these words to all the children of Israel, that the people lifted up their voices and wept.

[5]Then they called the name of that place Bochim;[a] and they sacrificed there to the LORD. [6]And when Joshua had dismissed the people, the children of Israel went each to his own inheritance to possess the land.

Death of Joshua

[7]So the people served the LORD all the days of Joshua, and all the days of the elders who outlived Joshua, who had seen all the great works of the LORD which He had done for Israel. [8]Now Joshua the son of Nun, the servant of the LORD, died *when he was* one hundred and ten years old. [9]And they buried him within the border of his inheritance at Timnath Heres, in the mountains of Ephraim, on the north side of Mount Gaash. [10]When all that generation had been gathered to their fathers, another generation arose after them who did not know the LORD nor the work which He had done for Israel.

1:35 [a]Spelled *Shaalabbin* in Joshua 19:42
2:3 [a]Septuagint, Targum, and Vulgate read *enemies to you.* **2:5** [a]Literally *Weeping*

Organizational Cycle:
Understanding the Pattern of People
(Judges 2:1–6)

Leaders must understand how people think and behave. The Book of Judges provides a vivid biography of leaders, followers, and human nature, and describes a cycle repeated even today. Note the distinct patterns that recur repeatedly in this book:

Rebellion
When things go well, people drop their guard. They relax and pay less attention to details. Peacetime brings a greater chance of rebellion than wartime. In prosperous times, fallen people naturally express their bent toward independence and rebellion.

Repression
Repression follows rebellion. Whether God sends an enemy or the people cause their own misery, they endure hardship, calamity, invasion, or natural disaster. Poor life choices result in retribution.

Repentance
Extreme hardships often trigger community-wide repentance. The repression serves as a wake-up call. Individuals begin to refocus on what is really important and purify their motives and behavior. Organizations cut budgets, downsize, and check egos.

Restoration
Purification leads to restoration. People regain the blessings they once had or acquire what had been intended for them. When they begin to obey God, peace returns to the land once more. And the cycle of fallen human behavior has run its full course.

Israel's Unfaithfulness

[11]Then the children of Israel did evil in the sight of the LORD, and served the Baals; [12]and they forsook the LORD God of their fathers, who had brought them out of the land of Egypt; and they followed other gods from *among* the gods of the people who *were* all around them, and they bowed down to them; and they provoked the LORD to anger. [13]They forsook the LORD and served Baal and the Ashtoreths.[a] [14]And the anger of the LORD was hot against Israel. So He delivered them into the hands of plunderers who despoiled them; and He sold them into the hands of their enemies all around, so that they could no longer stand before their enemies. [15]Wherever they went out, the hand of the LORD was against them for calamity, as the LORD had said, and as the LORD had sworn to them. And they were greatly distressed.

[16]Nevertheless, the LORD raised up judges who delivered them out of the hand of those who plundered them. [17]Yet they would not listen to their judges, but they played the harlot with other gods, and bowed down to them. They turned quickly from the way in which their fathers walked, in obeying the commandments of the LORD; they did not do so. [18]And when the LORD raised up judges for them, the LORD was with the judge and delivered them out of the hand of their enemies all the days of the judge; for the LORD was moved to pity by their groaning because of those who oppressed them and harassed them. [19]And it came to pass, when the judge was dead, that they reverted and behaved more corruptly than their fathers, by following other gods, to serve them and bow down to them. They did not cease from their own doings nor from their stubborn way.

[20]Then the anger of the LORD was hot against Israel; and He said, "Because this nation has transgressed My covenant which I commanded their fathers, and has not heeded My voice, [21]I also will no longer drive out before them any of the nations which Joshua left when he died, [22]so that through them I may test Israel, whether they will keep the ways of the LORD, to walk in them as their fathers kept *them,* or not." [23]Therefore the LORD left those nations, without driving them

---

2:13 [a]Canaanite goddesses

out immediately; nor did He deliver them into the hand of Joshua.

The Nations Remaining in the Land

3 Now these *are* the nations which the LORD left, that He might test Israel by them, *that is,* all who had not known any of the wars in Canaan ²(*this was* only so that the generations of the children of Israel might be taught to know war, at least those who had not formerly known it), ³*namely,* five lords of the Philistines, all the Canaanites, the Sidonians, and the Hivites who dwelt in Mount Lebanon, from Mount Baal Hermon to the entrance of Hamath. ⁴And they were *left, that He might* test Israel by them, to know whether they would obey the commandments of the LORD, which He had commanded their fathers by the hand of Moses.

⁵Thus the children of Israel dwelt among the Canaanites, the Hittites, the Amorites, the Perizzites, the Hivites, and the Jebusites. ⁶And they took their daughters to be their wives, and gave their daughters to their sons; and they served their gods.

Othniel

⁷So the children of Israel did evil in the sight of the LORD. They forgot the LORD their God, and served the Baals and Asherahs.ᵃ ⁸Therefore the anger of the LORD was hot against Israel, and He sold them into the hand of Cushan-Rishathaim king of Mesopotamia; and the children of Israel served Cushan-Rishathaim eight years. ⁹When the children of Israel cried out to the LORD, the LORD raised up a deliverer for the children of Israel, who delivered them: Othniel the son of Kenaz, Caleb's younger brother. ¹⁰The Spirit of the LORD came upon him, and he judged Israel. He went out to war, and the LORD delivered Cushan-Rishathaim king of Mesopotamia into his hand; and his hand prevailed over Cushan-Rishathaim. ¹¹So the land had rest for forty years. Then Othniel the son of Kenaz died.

Ehud

¹²And the children of Israel again did evil in the sight of the LORD. So the LORD strengthened Eglon king of Moab against Israel, because they had done evil in the sight of the LORD. ¹³Then he gathered to himself the people of Ammon and Amalek, went and defeated Israel, and took possession of the City of Palms. ¹⁴So the children of Israel served Eglon king of Moab eighteen years.

¹⁵But when the children of Israel cried out to

The Law of Victory: Three Leaders Find a Way to Deliver Israel

(Judges 3:1–33)

True leaders always find a way to help the team win.

Othniel found his people surrounded by enemies from Mesopotamia. He stepped forward, led the armies of Israel against the pagan king, and prevailed. His victory led to 40 years of peace.

Later, Moab formed an alliance with the Ammonites and Amalekites and attacked Israel. The Hebrews suffered defeat and served these enemies for 18 years. When the people cried out to the Lord, Ehud stepped forward and led them to victory. This peace lasted for 80 years.

A third judge, Shamgar, personally struck down 600 Philistines and rallied his people over Philistia. True leadership starts when a person . . .

- **Perceives a need** (spots a specific problem).
- **Possesses a gift** (has the competence to address the need).
- **Parades a passion** (casts vision for a passion to act).
- **Persuades a people** (attracts others to join the cause).
- **Pursues a purpose** (employs measures to accomplish the desired goal).

---

the LORD, the LORD raised up a deliverer for them: Ehud the son of Gera, the Benjamite, a left-handed man. By him the children of Israel sent tribute to Eglon king of Moab. ¹⁶Now Ehud made himself a dagger (it was double-edged and a cubit in length) and fastened it under his clothes on his right thigh. ¹⁷So he brought the tribute to Eglon king of Moab. (Now Eglon *was* a very fat man.) ¹⁸And when he had finished presenting the tribute, he sent away the people who had carried the tribute. ¹⁹But he himself turned back from the stone images that *were* at Gilgal, and said, "I have a secret message for you, O king."

3:7 ᵃName or symbol for Canaanite goddesses

He said, "Keep silence!" And all who attended him went out from him.

²⁰So Ehud came to him (now he was sitting upstairs in his cool private chamber). Then Ehud said, "I have a message from God for you." So he arose from *his* seat. ²¹Then Ehud reached with his left hand, took the dagger from his right thigh, and thrust it into his belly. ²²Even the hilt went in after the blade, and the fat closed over the blade, for he did not draw the dagger out of his belly; and his entrails came out. ²³Then Ehud went out through the porch and shut the doors of the upper room behind him and locked them.

²⁴When he had gone out, *Eglon's*ᵃ servants came to look, and *to their* surprise, the doors of the upper room were locked. So they said, "He is probably attending to his needs in the cool chamber." ²⁵So they waited till they were embarrassed, and still he had not opened the doors of the upper room. Therefore they took the key and opened *them*. And there was their master, fallen dead on the floor.

²⁶But Ehud had escaped while they delayed, and passed beyond the stone images and escaped to Seirah. ²⁷And it happened, when he arrived, that he blew the trumpet in the mountains of Ephraim, and the children of Israel went down with him from the mountains; and he led them. ²⁸Then he said to them, "Follow *me,* for the LORD has delivered your enemies the Moabites into your hand." So they went down after him, seized the fords of the Jordan leading to Moab, and did not allow anyone to cross over. ²⁹And at that time they killed about ten thousand men of Moab, all stout men of valor; not a man escaped. ³⁰So Moab was subdued that day under the hand of Israel. And the land had rest for eighty years.

Shamgar

³¹After him was Shamgar the son of Anath, who killed six hundred men of the Philistines with an ox goad; and he also delivered Israel.

Deborah

4 When Ehud was dead, the children of Israel again did evil in the sight of the LORD. ²So the LORD sold them into the hand of Jabin king of Canaan, who reigned in Hazor. The commander of his army *was* Sisera, who dwelt in Harosheth Hagoyim. ³And the children of Israel cried out to the LORD; for Jabin had nine hundred chariots of iron, and for twenty years he had harshly oppressed the children of Israel.

⁴Now Deborah, a prophetess, the wife of Lapidoth, was judging Israel at that time. ⁵And she would sit under the palm tree of Deborah between Ramah and Bethel in the mountains of Ephraim. And the children of Israel came up to her for judgment. ⁶Then she sent and called for Barak the son of Abinoam from Kedesh in Naphtali, and said to him, "Has not the LORD God of Israel commanded, 'Go and deploy *troops* at Mount Tabor; take with you ten thousand men of the sons of Naphtali and of the sons of Zebulun; ⁷and against you I will deploy Sisera, the commander of Jabin's army, with his chariots and his multitude at the River Kishon; and I will deliver him into your hand'?"

⁸And Barak said to her, "If you will go with me, then I will go; but if you will not go with me, I will not go!"

⁹So she said, "I will surely go with you; nevertheless there will be no glory for you in the journey you are taking, for the LORD will sell Sisera into the hand of a woman." Then Deborah arose and went with Barak to Kedesh. ¹⁰And Barak called Zebulun and Naphtali to Kedesh; he went up with ten thousand men under his command,ᵃ and Deborah went up with him.

¹¹Now Heber the Kenite, of the children of Hobab the father-in-law of Moses, had separated himself from the Kenites and pitched his tent near the terebinth tree at Zaanaim, which *is* beside Kedesh.

¹²And they reported to Sisera that Barak the son of Abinoam had gone up to Mount Tabor. ¹³So Sisera gathered together all his chariots, nine hundred chariots of iron, and all the people who *were* with him, from Harosheth Hagoyim to the River Kishon.

¹⁴Then Deborah said to Barak, "Up! For this *is* the day in which the LORD has delivered Sisera into your hand. Has not the LORD gone out before you?" So Barak went down from Mount Tabor with ten thousand men following him. ¹⁵And the LORD routed Sisera and all *his* chariots and all *his* army with the edge of the sword before Barak; and Sisera alighted from *his* chariot and fled away on foot. ¹⁶But Barak pursued the chariots and the army as far as Harosheth Hagoyim, and all the army of Sisera fell by the edge of the sword; not a man was left.

¹⁷However, Sisera had fled away on foot to the tent of Jael, the wife of Heber the Kenite; for *there was* peace between Jabin king of Hazor and the house of Heber the Kenite. ¹⁸And Jael went out to meet Sisera, and said to him, "Turn aside, my lord, turn aside to me; do not fear." And when he had turned aside with her into the tent, she covered him with a blanket.

3:24 ᵃLiterally *his* 4:10 ᵃLiterally *at his feet*

21 LAWS

DEBORAH AND THE LAW OF RESPECT

People Naturally Follow Leaders Stronger Than Themselves

(Judges 4:1–16)

People follow those whose leadership they respect. The less skilled follow the more highly skilled. In general, followers seek those who are better leaders than themselves.

The more leadership ability a person has, the more quickly he recognizes leadership—or its lack—in others. When groups of people get together for the first time, take a look at what happens. Leaders in the group immediately take charge. They think about the direction they desire to go and whom they want to take with them. At first, individuals may make tentative moves in several directions, but after they get to know one another, it doesn't take long for them to recognize the strongest leaders and to follow them.

Deborah's leadership gifts commanded the respect of both men and women, even though few women in her day rose to leadership positions. Even Barak, the military commander of the northern tribes of Israel, sought her help.

Take a look at the process any leader (including Deborah) must go through, a process summarized by the word R-E-S-P-E-C-T.

Respect yourself and those with whom you work.

Gaining the respect of others always begins with respecting yourself and your associates. Deborah did this, and people from all over Israel came to her to settle their disputes. If you desire to win the respect of others, first demonstrate a healthy respect for yourself and for your associates.

Exceed the expectations of others.

Few observers might have expected Deborah to change the way the Israelites lived. Yet she raised the standard of living for the common person and returned the nation to peace. Leaders who earn the respect of others go the extra mile, fight to achieve victory, and take others with them.

Stand firm on your convictions.

It must have taken strong convictions for Deborah to summon Barak and command him to fight. Even when Barak doubted the campaign, she did not waver, and proved her convictions by agreeing to accompany Barak to the battle. Followers respect a leader with conviction and a willingness to join the journey.

Possess uncommon security and maturity.

Deborah never tried to take credit for Israel's victory, but recognized those who helped the nation win. Respected leaders don't grab all the credit for themselves. They give as much as they can to others.

Experience personal success.

Leaders cannot help others enjoy success unless they have succeeded themselves. Deborah already had succeeded as a prophetess and a judge before she asked the people to fight.

Contribute to the success of others.

Deborah did everything right in calling the people to battle. She gave them a commander and the resources they needed. She also gave them the word of the Lord that they would win. Under her guidance, "the children of Israel grew stronger and stronger against Jabin king of Canaan, until they destroyed [him]" (Judg. 4:24).

Think ahead of others.

Deborah didn't simply tell Barak to fight; she furnished a plan for his attack. Then she accompanied Barak to the battle. The result: overwhelming victory. How could the people not respect a leader of such strategy and vision?

In general, leaders exercise their authority on one of five levels:

1. Position

Titles or job descriptions provide the lowest level of leadership. People follow these leaders only because they *have* to. That's where Deborah began—as a prophetess. But leadership that stays on this level becomes weaker, not stronger. Leaders who want others to follow simply because they are "the boss" soon lose respect.

2. Permission

As followers grow to like and trust a leader, they begin to follow because they *want* to. People came to Deborah, seeking out her influence. But not even positive relationships, by themselves, can create lasting leadership.

3. Production

At this level, influence grows and respect increases because of what the leader and the people accomplish together. People begin to follow because of what the leader has done for the team or organization. Deborah's success as a judge benefited all the people. If you reach this level, you and your team can achieve many of your goals. But to experience life-changing impact and lasting success, you must make the leap to the next level.

4. People Development

The highest calling of any leader is to help other *leaders* reach their potential. Deborah helped Barak achieve his God-given purpose. Leaders who move to this level change their focus from inspiring and leading followers to developing and leading other leaders.

5. Personhood

Leaders who spend their lives developing individuals and organizations make such an incredible impact for so long that people follow because of who the leader is. Deborah's description as a "mother of Israel" seems to indicate she achieved the personhood level of leadership. Leaders cannot scheme to reach level 5; they arrive at this plateau only through time and God's grace.

¹⁹Then he said to her, "Please give me a little water to drink, for I am thirsty." So she opened a jug of milk, gave him a drink, and covered him. ²⁰And he said to her, "Stand at the door of the tent, and if any man comes and inquires of you, and says, 'Is there any man here?' you shall say, 'No.'"

²¹Then Jael, Heber's wife, took a tent peg and took a hammer in her hand, and went softly to him and drove the peg into his temple, and it went down into the ground; for he was fast asleep and weary. So he died. ²²And then, as Barak pursued Sisera, Jael came out to meet him, and said to him, "Come, I will show you the man whom you seek." And when he went into her *tent,* there lay Sisera, dead with the peg in his temple.

²³So on that day God subdued Jabin king of Canaan in the presence of the children of Israel. ²⁴And the hand of the children of Israel grew stronger and stronger against Jabin king of Canaan, until they had destroyed Jabin king of Canaan.

The Song of Deborah

5 Then Deborah and Barak the son of Abinoam sang on that day, saying:

² "When leaders lead in Israel,
When the people willingly offer
themselves,
Bless the LORD!

³ "Hear, O kings! Give ear, O princes!
I, *even* I, will sing to the LORD;
I will sing praise to the LORD God of
Israel.

⁴ "LORD, when You went out from Seir,
When You marched from the field of
Edom,
The earth trembled and the heavens
poured,
The clouds also poured water;

⁵ The mountains gushed before the LORD,
This Sinai, before the LORD God of Israel.

⁶ "In the days of Shamgar, son of Anath,
In the days of Jael,
The highways were deserted,
And the travelers walked along the
byways.

⁷ Village life ceased, it ceased in Israel,
Until I, Deborah, arose,
Arose a mother in Israel.

⁸ They chose new gods;
Then *there was* war in the gates;

Not a shield or spear was seen among
forty thousand in Israel.

⁹ My heart *is* with the rulers of Israel
Who offered themselves willingly with the
people.
Bless the LORD!

¹⁰ "Speak, you who ride on white donkeys,
Who sit in judges' attire,
And who walk along the road.

¹¹ Far from the noise of the archers, among
the watering places,
There they shall recount the righteous acts
of the LORD,
The righteous acts *for* His villagers in
Israel;
Then the people of the LORD shall go
down to the gates.

¹² "Awake, awake, Deborah!
Awake, awake, sing a song!
Arise, Barak, and lead your captives away,
O son of Abinoam!

¹³ "Then the survivors came down, the people
against the nobles;
The LORD came down for me against the
mighty.

¹⁴ From Ephraim *were* those whose roots
were in Amalek.
After you, Benjamin, with your peoples,
From Machir rulers came down,
And from Zebulun those who bear the
recruiter's staff.

¹⁵ And the princes of Issacharᵃ *were* with
Deborah;
As Issachar, so *was* Barak
Sent into the valley under his command;ᵇ
Among the divisions of Reuben
There were great resolves of heart.

¹⁶ Why did you sit among the sheepfolds,
To hear the pipings for the flocks?
The divisions of Reuben have great
searchings of heart.

¹⁷ Gilead stayed beyond the Jordan,
And why did Dan remain on ships?ᵃ
Asher continued at the seashore,
And stayed by his inlets.

¹⁸ Zebulun *is* a people *who* jeopardized their
lives to the point of death,
Naphtali also, on the heights of the
battlefield.

5:15 ᵃFollowing Septuagint, Syriac, Targum, and Vulgate; Masoretic Text reads *And my princes in Issachar.* ᵇLiterally *at his feet* **5:17** ᵃOr *at ease*

19 "The kings came *and* fought,
Then the kings of Canaan fought
In Taanach, by the waters of Megiddo;
They took no spoils of silver.

20 They fought from the heavens;
The stars from their courses fought against
Sisera.

21 The torrent of Kishon swept them away,
That ancient torrent, the torrent of
Kishon.
O my soul, march on in strength!

22 Then the horses' hooves pounded,
The galloping, galloping of his steeds.

23 'Curse Meroz,' said the angel[a] of the LORD,
'Curse its inhabitants bitterly,
Because they did not come to the help of
the LORD,
To the help of the LORD against the
mighty.'

24 "Most blessed among women is Jael,
The wife of Heber the Kenite;
Blessed is she among women in tents.

25 He asked for water, she gave milk;
She brought out cream in a lordly bowl.

26 She stretched her hand to the tent peg,
Her right hand to the workmen's
hammer;
She pounded Sisera, she pierced his head,
She split and struck through his temple.

27 At her feet he sank, he fell, he lay still;
At her feet he sank, he fell;
Where he sank, there he fell dead.

28 "The mother of Sisera looked through the
window,
And cried out through the lattice,
'Why is his chariot *so* long in coming?
Why tarries the clatter of his chariots?'

29 Her wisest ladies answered her,
Yes, she answered herself,

30 'Are they not finding and dividing the
spoil:
To every man a girl *or* two;
For Sisera, plunder of dyed garments,
Plunder of garments embroidered and
dyed,
Two pieces of dyed embroidery for the
neck of the looter?'

31 "Thus let all Your enemies perish, O
LORD!
But *let* those who love Him *be* like the sun
When it comes out in full strength."

So the land had rest for forty years.

Midianites Oppress Israel

6 Then the children of Israel did evil in the sight of the LORD. So the LORD delivered them into the hand of Midian for seven years, ²and the hand of Midian prevailed against Israel. Because of the Midianites, the children of Israel made for themselves the dens, the caves, and the strongholds which *are* in the mountains. ³So it was, whenever Israel had sown, Midianites would come up; also Amalekites and the people of the East would come up against them. ⁴Then they would encamp against them and destroy the produce of the earth as far as Gaza, and leave no sustenance for Israel, neither sheep nor ox nor donkey. ⁵For they would come up with their livestock and their tents, coming in as numerous as locusts; both they and their camels were without number; and they would enter the land to destroy it. ⁶So Israel was greatly impoverished because of the Midianites, and the children of Israel cried out to the LORD.

⁷And it came to pass, when the children of Israel cried out to the LORD because of the Midianites, ⁸that the LORD sent a prophet to the children of Israel, who said to them, "Thus says the LORD God of Israel: 'I brought you up from Egypt and brought you out of the house of bondage; ⁹and I delivered you out of the hand of the Egyptians and out of the hand of all who oppressed you, and drove them out before you and gave you their land. ¹⁰Also I said to you, "I *am* the LORD your God; do not fear the gods of the Amorites, in whose land you dwell." But you have not obeyed My voice.'"

Gideon

¹¹Now the Angel of the LORD came and sat under the terebinth tree which *was* in Ophrah, which *belonged* to Joash the Abiezrite, while his son Gideon threshed wheat in the winepress, in order to hide *it* from the Midianites. ¹²And the Angel of the LORD appeared to him, and said to him, "The LORD *is* with you, you mighty man of valor!"

¹³Gideon said to Him, "O my lord,[a] if the LORD is with us, why then has all this happened to us? And where *are* all His miracles which our fathers told us about, saying, 'Did not the LORD bring us up from Egypt?' But now the LORD has forsaken us and delivered us into the hands of the Midianites."

¹⁴Then the LORD turned to him and said, "Go in this might of yours, and you shall save

5:23 [a]Or *Angel* 6:13 [a]Hebrew *adoni,* used of man

GIDEON AND THE LAW OF BUY-IN

People Buy In to the Leader, Then the Vision

(*Judges 6:11—8:35*)

At leadership seminars I field a lot of questions about vision. Invariably someone will come up to me during a break, give me a brief description of an evolving vision, and ask, "Do you think my people will buy in to my vision?" I always respond the same way: "First tell me this— do your people buy in to *you*?"

Many believe that if the cause is good enough, people will automatically buy in to it and follow. But that's not how leadership works. People don't at first follow worthy causes; they follow worthy leaders who promote worthwhile causes. People buy in to the leader first, then the leader's vision. Listeners filter every message through the messenger who delivers it. You cannot separate the leader from the cause he promotes. It's not an either/or proposition; the two always go together.

■　　　　■　　　　■　　　　■　　　　■

Who would have picked Gideon as a leader? Certainly not Gideon; he didn't even see himself as a leader. "O my Lord, how can I save Israel?" asked Gideon of the angel who told him that God wanted to use him to defeat the Midianites. "Indeed my clan is the weakest in Manasseh, and I am the least in my father's house" (Judg. 6:15).

Despite Gideon's doubts, God used him. The people rallied around Gideon, and he led Israel to the most lopsided victory in the nation's history.

The Anatomy of Buy-In

Gideon progressed from being an obscure member of a minor clan to a leader of the northern tribes. He grew as a leader through several stages:

1. *Started at home (character)*

A good leader first proves himself to those closest to him. Gideon started with ten household servants. With their help, he destroyed an altar of Baal, built a new altar to God, and offered the sacrifice requested by God.

2. *Won a key influencer (charisma)*

The men of Ophrah grew furious with Gideon when they discovered he had destroyed Baal's altar. "Bring out your son," they ordered his father, Joash, "that he may die" (Judg. 6:30). Yet Gideon won over a powerful ally in his father. Joash stood up for his son and spared Gideon's life.

3. *Broadened his circle (credibility)*

Gideon won over his city by winning the influence of Joash, then quickly won the allegiance of the Abiezrites (the people of his region), along with tribes beyond his borders: Asher, Zebulun, and Naphtali. Even the people of Ephraim joined him. Once a core group of people buy in to your leadership, it's possible to broaden your circle of influence.

4. *Moved at the right time (culmination)*

So many people bought into Gideon's leadership that God had to send a bunch of them home (Judg. 7:2). God reduced the number of Gideon's followers to 300. Yet when they fought under Gideon's leadership, they won a great victory—and God received the glory.

Seven Assets Followers Want in a Leader

People always ask, "Why should I follow you?" Leaders must understand that they themselves go on display before they ever get the chance to display their vision. Once followers gain confidence in the leader, they will feel confident about the vision. Note seven qualities that attract people to a leader:

1. *Calling*

Few things are as compelling as a leader's clear calling. Beforehand, Gideon had lived in fear, doubted himself, and asked for multiple signs to confirm his mission. But once he embraced his calling, passion and boldness filled his heart.

2. *Insight*

People respect a leader with insight, wisdom to see the issues, and vision to see what lies ahead. God gave Gideon insight into the weak hearts of the Midianites. By the time Gideon called his men to battle, he understood that God had assured their victory.

3. *Charisma*

People flock to leaders who make them feel good about themselves. When Gideon invited the people of Ephraim to join in pursuing the Midianites, they reacted angrily. But Gideon helped them see the significance of their role by reminding them that they had captured and killed the princes of Midian (Judg. 8:1–30).

4. *Talent*

Look no further than the entertainment industry for evidence that followers swarm around talent. While we don't know much about Gideon's natural abilities, the angel called him a "mighty man of valor" and instructed him to "go in this might of yours" (Judg. 6:12, 14). More than likely, Gideon possessed both physical strength and courage.

5. *Ability*

People feel a natural attraction to someone who can get things done. Gideon didn't attempt to get the Ephraimites on board until he had proven his ability.

6. *Communication Skills*

A leader who cannot communicate his calling and vision has trouble getting anyone to buy in to his leadership. Whenever Gideon spoke to his people, they understood him and eagerly followed.

7. *Character*

It takes character to win and maintain trust. Gideon started out strong, standing up when others wouldn't. He displayed courage in the face of incredible odds. But in the end, a flaw in his character betrayed both him and the people. After his victories, Gideon created an idol and erected it in Ophrah: "All Israel played the harlot with it there. It became a snare to Gideon and to his house" (Judg. 8:27).

Israel from the hand of the Midianites. Have I not sent you?"

[15]So he said to Him, "O my Lord,[a] how can I save Israel? Indeed my clan *is* the weakest in Manasseh, and I *am* the least in my father's house."

[16]And the LORD said to him, "Surely I will be with you, and you shall defeat the Midianites as one man."

[17]Then he said to Him, "If now I have found favor in Your sight, then show me a sign that it is You who talk with me. [18]Do not depart from here, I pray, until I come to You and bring out my offering and set *it* before You."

And He said, "I will wait until you come back."

[19]So Gideon went in and prepared a young goat, and unleavened bread from an ephah of flour. The meat he put in a basket, and he put the broth in a pot; and he brought *them* out to Him under the terebinth tree and presented *them.* [20]The Angel of God said to him, "Take the meat and the unleavened bread and lay *them* on this rock, and pour out the broth." And he did so. [21]Then the Angel of the LORD put out the end of the staff that *was* in His hand, and touched the meat and the unleavened bread; and fire rose out of the rock and consumed the meat and the unleavened bread. And the Angel of the LORD departed out of his sight.

[22]Now Gideon perceived that He *was* the Angel of the LORD. So Gideon said, "Alas, O Lord GOD! For I have seen the Angel of the LORD face to face."

[23]Then the LORD said to him, "Peace *be* with you; do not fear, you shall not die." [24]So Gideon built an altar there to the LORD, and called it The-LORD-*Is*-Peace.[a] To this day it *is* still in Ophrah of the Abiezrites.

[25]Now it came to pass the same night that the LORD said to him, "Take your father's young bull, the second bull of seven years old, and tear down the altar of Baal that your father has, and cut down the wooden image[a] that *is* beside it; [26]and build an altar to the LORD your God on top of this rock in the proper arrangement, and take the second bull and offer a burnt sacrifice with the wood of the image which you shall cut down." [27]So Gideon took ten men from among his servants and did as the LORD had said to him. But because he feared his father's household and the men of the city too much to do *it* by day, he did *it* by night.

Gideon Destroys the Altar of Baal

[28]And when the men of the city arose early in the morning, there was the altar of Baal, torn down; and the wooden image that *was* beside it was cut down, and the second bull was being offered on the altar *which had been* built. [29]So they said to one another, "Who has done this thing?" And when they had inquired and asked, they said, "Gideon the son of Joash has done this thing." [30]Then the men of the city said to Joash, "Bring out your son, that he may die, because he has torn down the altar of Baal, and because he has cut down the wooden image that *was* beside it."

[31]But Joash said to all who stood against him, "Would you plead for Baal? Would you save him? Let the one who would plead for him be put to death by morning! If he *is* a god, let him plead for himself, because his altar has been torn down!" [32]Therefore on that day he called him Jerubbaal,[a] saying, "Let Baal plead against him, because he has torn down his altar."

[33]Then all the Midianites and Amalekites, the people of the East, gathered together; and they crossed over and encamped in the Valley of Jezreel. [34]But the Spirit of the LORD came upon Gideon; then he blew the trumpet, and the Abiezrites gathered behind him. [35]And he sent messengers throughout all Manasseh, who also gathered behind him. He also sent messengers to Asher, Zebulun, and Naphtali; and they came up to meet them.

The Sign of the Fleece

[36]So Gideon said to God, "If You will save Israel by my hand as You have said— [37]look, I shall put a fleece of wool on the threshing floor; if there is dew on the fleece only, and *it is* dry on all the ground, then I shall know that You will save Israel by my hand, as You have said." [38]And it was so. When he rose early the next morning and squeezed the fleece together, he wrung the dew out of the fleece, a bowlful of water. [39]Then Gideon said to God, "Do not be angry with me, but let me speak just once more: Let me test, I pray, just once more with the fleece; let it now be dry only on the fleece, but on all the ground let there be dew." [40]And God did so that night. It was dry on the fleece only, but there was dew on all the ground.

Gideon's Valiant Three Hundred

7 Then Jerubbaal (that *is,* Gideon) and all the people who *were* with him rose early and encamped beside the well of Harod, so that the camp of the Midianites was on the north side of them by the hill of Moreh in the valley.

6:15 [a]Hebrew *Adonai,* used of God **6:24** [a]Hebrew *YHWH Shalom* **6:25** [a]Hebrew *Asherah,* a Canaanite goddess **6:32** [a]Literally *Let Baal Plead*

Lessons from Gideon About Choosing Leaders

(Judges 7:1–25)

Can you imagine having Gideon's problem? He attracted too many volunteers! To make sure that God would get the glory for the coming victory, God led Gideon in an exercise to eliminate those who would hinder and choose those who would help Israel's cause. Note the lessons we learn from this effective leader:

1. A committed leader always attracts many people.
2. God wants the credit for our victories.
3. Early fallout always occurs before a battle begins (their choice).
4. Later fallout often occurs before the battle begins (God's choice).
5. God doesn't choose the way we choose.
6. God wants *quality* of leaders, not necessarily *quantity*.
7. A few committed leaders with a strategy will bring victory.
8. When a few triumph, the masses rally.

²And the LORD said to Gideon, "The people who *are* with you *are* too many for Me to give the Midianites into their hands, lest Israel claim glory for itself against Me, saying, 'My own hand has saved me.' ³Now therefore, proclaim in the hearing of the people, saying, 'Whoever *is* fearful and afraid, let him turn and depart at once from Mount Gilead.' " And twenty-two thousand of the people returned, and ten thousand remained.

⁴But the LORD said to Gideon, "The people *are* still *too* many; bring them down to the water, and I will test them for you there. Then it will be, *that* of whom I say to you, 'This one shall go with you,' the same shall go with you; and of whomever I say to you, 'This one shall not go with you,' the same shall not go." ⁵So he brought the people down to the water. And the LORD said to Gideon, "Everyone who laps from the water with his tongue, as a dog laps, you shall set apart by himself; likewise everyone who gets down on his knees to drink." ⁶And the number of those who lapped, *putting* their hand to their mouth, was three hundred men; but all the rest of the people got down on their knees to drink water. ⁷Then the LORD said to Gideon, "By the three hundred men who lapped I will save you, and deliver the Midianites into your hand. Let all the *other* people go, every man to his place." ⁸So the people took provisions and their trumpets in their hands. And he sent away all *the rest of* Israel, every man to his tent, and retained those three hundred men. Now the camp of Midian was below him in the valley.

⁹It happened on the same night that the LORD said to him, "Arise, go down against the camp, for I have delivered it into your hand. ¹⁰But if you are afraid to go down, go down to the camp with Purah your servant, ¹¹and you shall hear what they say; and afterward your hands shall be strengthened to go down against the camp." Then he went down with Purah his servant to the outpost of the armed men who *were* in the camp. ¹²Now the Midianites and Amalekites, all the people of the East, were lying in the valley as numerous as locusts; and their camels *were* without number, as the sand by the seashore in multitude.

¹³And when Gideon had come, there was a man telling a dream to his companion. He said, "I have had a dream: *To my* surprise, a loaf of barley bread tumbled into the camp of Midian; it came to a tent and struck it so that it fell and overturned, and the tent collapsed." ¹⁴Then his companion answered and said, "This *is* nothing else but the sword of Gideon the son of Joash, a man of Israel! Into his hand God has delivered Midian and the whole camp."

¹⁵And so it was, when Gideon heard the telling of the dream and its interpretation, that he worshiped. He returned to the camp of Israel, and said, "Arise, for the LORD has delivered the camp of Midian into your hand." ¹⁶Then he divided the three hundred men *into* three companies, and he put a trumpet into every man's hand, with empty pitchers, and torches inside the pitchers. ¹⁷And he said to them, "Look at me and do likewise; watch, and when I come to the edge of the camp you shall do as I do: ¹⁸When I blow the trumpet, I and all who *are* with me, then you also blow the trumpets on every side of the whole camp, and say, '*The sword of* the LORD and of Gideon!' "

¹⁹So Gideon and the hundred men who *were* with him came to the outpost of the camp at the beginning of the middle watch, just as they had posted the watch; and they blew the trumpets and broke the pitchers that *were* in their hands. ²⁰Then the three companies blew the trumpets and broke the pitchers—they held the torches in their left hands and the trumpets in their right hands for blowing—and they cried, "The sword

Why Does God Choose Unlikely Leaders?

(Judges 7:16–25)

Why does God often choose unlikely leaders? Consider the following reasons:

1. To catch the attention of the world
2. To bring honor to Himself
3. To keep the message simple
4. To prompt reliance upon Him, not people
5. To fill us with His power

of the LORD and of Gideon!" 21And every man stood in his place all around the camp; and the whole army ran and cried out and fled. 22When the three hundred blew the trumpets, the LORD set every man's sword against his companion throughout the whole camp; and the army fled to Beth Acacia,ᵃ toward Zererah, as far as the border of Abel Meholah, by Tabbath.

23And the men of Israel gathered together from Naphtali, Asher, and all Manasseh, and pursued the Midianites.

24Then Gideon sent messengers throughout all the mountains of Ephraim, saying, "Come down against the Midianites, and seize from them the watering places as far as Beth Barah and the Jordan." Then all the men of Ephraim gathered together and seized the watering places as far as Beth Barah and the Jordan. 25And they captured two princes of the Midianites, Oreb and Zeeb. They killed Oreb at the rock of Oreb, and Zeeb they killed at the winepress of Zeeb. They pursued Midian and brought the heads of Oreb and Zeeb to Gideon on the other side of the Jordan.

Gideon Subdues the Midianites

8 Now the men of Ephraim said to him, "Why have you done this to us by not calling us when you went to fight with the Midianites?" And they reprimanded him sharply.

2So he said to them, "What have I done now in comparison with you? *Is* not the gleaning *of the grapes* of Ephraim better than the vintage of Abiezer? 3God has delivered into your hands the princes of Midian, Oreb and Zeeb. And what was I able to do in comparison with you?" Then their anger toward him subsided when he said that.

4When Gideon came to the Jordan, he and the three hundred men who *were* with him crossed over, exhausted but still in pursuit. 5Then he said to the men of Succoth, "Please give loaves of bread to the people who follow me, for they are exhausted, and I am pursuing Zebah and Zalmunna, kings of Midian."

6And the leaders of Succoth said, "*Are* the hands of Zebah and Zalmunna now in your hand, that we should give bread to your army?"

7So Gideon said, "For this cause, when the LORD has delivered Zebah and Zalmunna into my hand, then I will tear your flesh with the thorns of the wilderness and with briers!" 8Then he went up from there to Penuel and spoke to them in the same way. And the men of Penuel answered him as the men of Succoth had answered. 9So he also spoke to the men of Penuel, saying, "When I come back in peace, I will tear down this tower!"

10Now Zebah and Zalmunna *were* at Karkor, and their armies with them, about fifteen thousand, all who were left of all the army of the people of the East; for one hundred and twenty thousand men who drew the sword had fallen. 11Then Gideon went up by the road of those who dwell in tents on the east of Nobah and Jogbehah; and he attacked the army while the camp felt secure. 12When Zebah and Zalmunna fled, he pursued them; and he took the two kings of Midian, Zebah and Zalmunna, and routed the whole army.

13Then Gideon the son of Joash returned from battle, from the Ascent of Heres. 14And he caught a young man of the men of Succoth and interrogated him; and he wrote down for him the leaders of Succoth and its elders, seventy-seven men. 15Then he came to the men of Succoth and said, "Here are Zebah and Zalmunna, about whom you ridiculed me, saying, '*Are* the hands of Zebah and Zalmunna now in your hand, that we should give bread to your weary men?'" 16And he took the elders of the city, and thorns of the wilderness and briers, and with them he taught the men of Succoth. 17Then he tore down the tower of Penuel and killed the men of the city.

18And he said to Zebah and Zalmunna, "What kind of men *were they* whom you killed at Tabor?"

So they answered, "As you *are*, so *were* they; each one resembled the son of a king."

19Then he said, "They *were* my brothers, the sons of my mother. *As* the LORD lives, if you had let them live, I would not kill you." 20And he said

---

7:22 ᵃHebrew *Beth Shittah*

to Jether his firstborn, "Rise, kill them!" But the youth would not draw his sword; for he was afraid, because he *was* still a youth.

²¹So Zebah and Zalmunna said, "Rise yourself, and kill us; for as a man *is, so is* his strength." So Gideon arose and killed Zebah and Zalmunna, and took the crescent ornaments that *were* on their camels' necks.

Gideon's Ephod

²²Then the men of Israel said to Gideon, "Rule over us, both you and your son, and your grandson also; for you have delivered us from the hand of Midian."

²³But Gideon said to them, "I will not rule over you, nor shall my son rule over you; the LORD shall rule over you." ²⁴Then Gideon said to them, "I would like to make a request of you, that each of you would give me the earrings from his plunder." For they had golden earrings, because they *were* Ishmaelites.

²⁵So they answered, "We will gladly give *them*." And they spread out a garment, and each man threw into it the earrings from his plunder. ²⁶Now the weight of the gold earrings that he requested was one thousand seven hundred *shekels* of gold, besides the crescent ornaments, pendants, and purple robes which *were* on the kings of Midian, and besides the chains that *were* around their camels' necks. ²⁷Then Gideon made it into an ephod and set it up in his city, Ophrah. And all Israel played the harlot with it there. It became a snare to Gideon and to his house.

²⁸Thus Midian was subdued before the children of Israel, so that they lifted their heads no more. And the country was quiet for forty years in the days of Gideon.

Death of Gideon

²⁹Then Jerubbaal the son of Joash went and dwelt in his own house. ³⁰Gideon had seventy sons who were his own offspring, for he had many wives. ³¹And his concubine who *was* in Shechem also bore him a son, whose name he called Abimelech. ³²Now Gideon the son of Joash died at a good old age, and was buried in the tomb of Joash his father, in Ophrah of the Abiezrites.

³³So it was, as soon as Gideon was dead, that the children of Israel again played the harlot with the Baals, and made Baal-Berith their god. ³⁴Thus the children of Israel did not remember the LORD their God, who had delivered them from the hands of all their enemies on every side; ³⁵nor did they show kindness to the house of Jerubbaal (Gideon) in accordance with the good he had done for Israel.

Abimelech's Conspiracy

9 Then Abimelech the son of Jerubbaal went to Shechem, to his mother's brothers, and spoke with them and with all the family of the house of his mother's father, saying, ²"Please speak in the hearing of all the men of Shechem: 'Which is better for you, that all seventy of the sons of Jerubbaal reign over you, or that one reign over you?' Remember that I *am* your own flesh and bone."

³And his mother's brothers spoke all these words concerning him in the hearing of all the men of Shechem; and their heart was inclined to follow Abimelech, for they said, "He is our brother." ⁴So they gave him seventy *shekels* of silver from the temple of Baal-Berith, with which Abimelech hired worthless and reckless men; and they followed him. ⁵Then he went to his father's house at Ophrah and killed his brothers, the seventy sons of Jerubbaal, on one stone. But Jotham the youngest son of Jerubbaal was left, because he hid himself. ⁶And all the men of Shechem gathered together, all of Beth Millo, and they went and made Abimelech king beside the terebinth tree at the pillar that *was* in Shechem.

The Parable of the Trees

⁷Now when they told Jotham, he went and stood on top of Mount Gerizim, and lifted his voice and cried out. And he said to them:

"Listen to me, you men of Shechem,
    That God may listen to you!

⁸   "The trees once went forth to anoint a king
       over them.
    And they said to the olive tree,
   'Reign over us!'
⁹   But the olive tree said to them,
   'Should I cease giving my oil,
    With which they honor God and men,
    And go to sway over trees?'

¹⁰   "Then the trees said to the fig tree,
   'You come *and* reign over us!'
¹¹   But the fig tree said to them,
   'Should I cease my sweetness and my good
       fruit,
    And go to sway over trees?'

¹²   "Then the trees said to the vine,
   'You come *and* reign over us!'
¹³   But the vine said to them,
   'Should I cease my new wine,
    Which cheers *both* God and men,
    And go to sway over trees?'

14 "Then all the trees said to the bramble,
'You come *and* reign over us!'
15 And the bramble said to the trees,
'If in truth you anoint me as king over
you,
Then come *and* take shelter in my shade;
But if not, let fire come out of the
bramble
And devour the cedars of Lebanon!'

16"Now therefore, if you have acted in truth and sincerity in making Abimelech king, and if you have dealt well with Jerubbaal and his house, and have done to him as he deserves— 17for my father fought for you, risked his life, and delivered you out of the hand of Midian; 18but you have risen up against my father's house this day, and killed his seventy sons on one stone, and made Abimelech, the son of his female servant, king over the men of Shechem, because he is your brother— 19if then you have acted in truth and sincerity with Jerubbaal and with his house this day, *then* rejoice in Abimelech, and let him also rejoice in you. 20But if not, let fire come from Abimelech and devour the men of Shechem and Beth Millo; and let fire come from the men of Shechem and from Beth Millo and devour Abimelech!" 21And Jotham ran away and fled; and he went to Beer and dwelt there, for fear of Abimelech his brother.

Downfall of Abimelech

22After Abimelech had reigned over Israel three years, 23God sent a spirit of ill will between Abimelech and the men of Shechem; and the men of Shechem dealt treacherously with Abimelech, 24that the crime *done* to the seventy sons of Jerubbaal might be settled and their blood be laid on Abimelech their brother, who killed them, and on the men of Shechem, who aided him in the killing of his brothers. 25And the men of Shechem set men in ambush against him on the tops of the mountains, and they robbed all who passed by them along that way; and it was told Abimelech.

26Now Gaal the son of Ebed came with his brothers and went over to Shechem; and the men of Shechem put their confidence in him. 27So they went out into the fields, and gathered *grapes* from their vineyards and trod *them,* and made merry. And they went into the house of their god, and ate and drank, and cursed Abimelech. 28Then Gaal the son of Ebed said, "Who *is* Abimelech, and who *is* Shechem, that we should

ABIMELECH

A PICTURE OF SELF-PROMOTION
(Judges 9:1–57)

PROFILE IN LEADERSHIP

At first glance, Abimelech might seem like an ideal candidate for leadership. A gifted communicator and skilled tactician, he set his heart on becoming the ruler of his people. He had a *passion* to lead.

But passion does not mean fitness.

From the time his father Gideon passed away, ambitious Abimelech kept his eye on the throne of Israel. He effectively used his oratorical abilities to gain power, yet never sought God's view of his career choice. Abimelech hired "worthless and reckless men" (Judg. 9:4) to enforce his will. In his first act as king, he murdered 70 potential rivals—his own brothers, all of whom died on a single stone (9:5). From that point on, God determined to judge both Abimelech and his supporters. The man's arrogance, disobedience, dishonesty, and self-will all should have disqualified him to lead God's people, yet he reigned over the men of Shechem for three years (9:22). In the end, this self-promoting power-seeker and his cronies all died under the terrifying frown of God (9:56, 57).

Self-promotion may "work" in the short run, but over the long haul God makes sure that it fails. Godly leaders must remind themselves of the Lord's instruction: "Humble yourselves under the mighty hand of God, that He may exalt you in due time" (1 Pet. 5:6).

Jotham's Leadership Parable: Power or Service?

(Judges 9:7–15)

Many in our world think the leader must be the biggest, strongest, and most intimidating person in the room. Yet the Bible tells us godly leaders are motivated by service, not power. Jotham used vivid imagery to describe his brother's hollow leadership of Shechem, and warned that Abimelech's power-hungry leadership would bring disaster.

serve him? *Is he* not the son of Jerubbaal, and *is not* Zebul his officer? Serve the men of Hamor the father of Shechem; but why should we serve him? [29]If only this people were under my authority!ᵃ Then I would remove Abimelech." So heᵇ said to Abimelech, "Increase your army and come out!"

[30]When Zebul, the ruler of the city, heard the words of Gaal the son of Ebed, his anger was aroused. [31]And he sent messengers to Abimelech secretly, saying, "Take note! Gaal the son of Ebed and his brothers have come to Shechem; and here they are, fortifying the city against you. [32]Now therefore, get up by night, you and the people who *are* with you, and lie in wait in the field. [33]And it shall be, as soon as the sun is up in the morning, *that* you shall rise early and rush upon the city; and *when* he and the people who are with him come out against you, you may then do to them as you find opportunity."

[34]So Abimelech and all the people who *were* with him rose by night, and lay in wait against Shechem in four companies. [35]When Gaal the son of Ebed went out and stood in the entrance to the city gate, Abimelech and the people who *were* with him rose from lying in wait. [36]And when Gaal saw the people, he said to Zebul, "Look, people are coming down from the tops of the mountains!"

But Zebul said to him, "You see the shadows of the mountains as *if they were* men."

[37]So Gaal spoke again and said, "See, people are coming down from the center of the land, and another company is coming from the Diviners'ᵃ Terebinth Tree."

[38]Then Zebul said to him, "Where indeed *is*

your mouth now, with which you said, 'Who is Abimelech, that we should serve him?' *Are* not these the people whom you despised? Go out, if you will, and fight with them now."

[39]So Gaal went out, leading the men of Shechem, and fought with Abimelech. [40]And Abimelech chased him, and he fled from him; and many fell wounded, to the *very* entrance of the gate. [41]Then Abimelech dwelt at Arumah, and Zebul drove out Gaal and his brothers, so that they would not dwell in Shechem.

[42]And it came about on the next day that the people went out into the field, and they told Abimelech. [43]So he took his people, divided them into three companies, and lay in wait in the field. And he looked, and there were the people, coming out of the city; and he rose against them and attacked them. [44]Then Abimelech and the company that *was* with him rushed forward and stood at the entrance of the gate of the city; and the *other* two companies rushed upon all who *were* in the fields and killed them. [45]So Abimelech fought against the city all that day; he took the city and killed the people who *were* in it; and he demolished the city and sowed it with salt.

[46]Now when all the men of the tower of Shechem had heard *that,* they entered the stronghold of the temple of the god Berith. [47]And it was told Abimelech that all the men of the tower of Shechem were gathered together. [48]Then Abimelech went up to Mount Zalmon, he and all the people who *were* with him. And Abimelech took an ax in his hand and cut down a bough from the trees, and took it and laid *it* on his shoulder; then he said to the people who were with him, "What you have seen me do, make haste *and* do as I *have done.*" [49]So each of the people likewise cut down his own bough and followed Abimelech, put *them* against the stronghold, and set the stronghold on fire above them, so that all the people of the tower of Shechem died, about a thousand men and women.

[50]Then Abimelech went to Thebez, and he encamped against Thebez and took it. [51]But there was a strong tower in the city, and all the men and women—all the people of the city—fled there and shut themselves in; then they went up to the top of the tower. [52]So Abimelech came as far as the tower and fought against it; and he drew near the door of the tower to burn it with fire. [53]But a certain woman dropped an upper

---

9:29 ᵃLiterally *hand* ᵇFollowing Masoretic Text and Targum; Dead Sea Scrolls read *they;* Septuagint reads *I.* **9:37** ᵃHebrew *Meonenim*

millstone on Abimelech's head and crushed his skull. [54]Then he called quickly to the young man, his armorbearer, and said to him, "Draw your sword and kill me, lest men say of me, 'A woman killed him.'" So his young man thrust him through, and he died. [55]And when the men of Israel saw that Abimelech was dead, they departed, every man to his place.

[56]Thus God repaid the wickedness of Abimelech, which he had done to his father by killing his seventy brothers. [57]And all the evil of the men of Shechem God returned on their own heads, and on them came the curse of Jotham the son of Jerubbaal.

Tola

10 After Abimelech there arose to save Israel Tola the son of Puah, the son of Dodo, a man of Issachar; and he dwelt in Shamir in the mountains of Ephraim. [2]He judged Israel twenty-three years; and he died and was buried in Shamir.

Jair

[3]After him arose Jair, a Gileadite; and he judged Israel twenty-two years. [4]Now he had thirty sons who rode on thirty donkeys; they also had thirty towns, which are called "Havoth Jair"[a] to this day, which are in the land of Gilead. [5]And Jair died and was buried in Camon.

Israel Oppressed Again

[6]Then the children of Israel again did evil in the sight of the LORD, and served the Baals and the Ashtoreths, the gods of Syria, the gods of Sidon, the gods of Moab, the gods of the people of Ammon, and the gods of the Philistines; and they forsook the LORD and did not serve Him. [7]So the anger of the LORD was hot against Israel; and He sold them into the hands of the Philistines and into the hands of the people of Ammon. [8]From that year they harassed and oppressed the children of Israel for eighteen years—all the children of Israel who were on the other side of the Jordan in the land of the Amorites, in Gilead. [9]Moreover the people of Ammon crossed over the Jordan to fight against Judah also, against Benjamin, and against the house of Ephraim, so that Israel was severely distressed.

[10]And the children of Israel cried out to the LORD, saying, "We have sinned against You, because we have both forsaken our God and served the Baals!"

[11]So the LORD said to the children of Israel, "Did I not deliver you from the Egyptians and from the Amorites and from the people of Ammon and from the Philistines? [12]Also the Sidonians and Amalekites and Maonites[a] oppressed you; and you cried out to Me, and I delivered you from their hand. [13]Yet you have forsaken Me and served other gods. Therefore I will deliver you no more. [14]Go and cry out to the gods which you have chosen; let them deliver you in your time of distress."

[15]And the children of Israel said to the LORD, "We have sinned! Do to us whatever seems best to You; only deliver us this day, we pray." [16]So they put away the foreign gods from among them and served the LORD. And His soul could no longer endure the misery of Israel.

[17]Then the people of Ammon gathered together and encamped in Gilead. And the children of Israel assembled together and encamped in Mizpah. [18]And the people, the leaders of Gilead, said to one another, "Who is the man who will begin the fight against the people of Ammon? He shall be head over all the inhabitants of Gilead."

The Law of Legacy: Tola and Jair's Influence Dies with Them

(Judges 10:1–6)

Tola and Jair did a fair job of leading the Hebrew people, but Israel immediately did evil upon their deaths, serving the gods of Baal. So what kind of leadership did this pair really exert?

If our leadership leaves no legacy, is it complete? If the people revert to sinful patterns after we depart the scene, have we not failed to practice the Law of Legacy? Remember . . .

- The acid test of our leadership takes place after we are gone.
- Success without a successor is a failure.
- The issue isn't, Can I change them while I'm here? but, Can I do it after I'm gone?
- Reputation is what people think of us now; legacy is what they think of us long after we are gone.

10:4 [a]Literally Towns of Jair (compare Numbers 32:41 and Deuteronomy 3:14) 10:12 [a]Some Septuagint manuscripts read Midianites.

Jephthah

11 Now Jephthah the Gileadite was a mighty man of valor, but he *was* the son of a harlot; and Gilead begot Jephthah. ²Gilead's wife bore sons; and when his wife's sons grew up, they drove Jephthah out, and said to him, "You shall have no inheritance in our father's house, for you *are* the son of another woman." ³Then Jephthah fled from his brothers and dwelt in the land of Tob; and worthless men banded together with Jephthah and went out *raiding* with him.

⁴It came to pass after a time that the people of Ammon made war against Israel. ⁵And so it was, when the people of Ammon made war against Israel, that the elders of Gilead went to get Jephthah from the land of Tob. ⁶Then they said to Jephthah, "Come and be our commander, that we may fight against the people of Ammon."

⁷So Jephthah said to the elders of Gilead, "Did you not hate me, and expel me from my father's house? Why have you come to me now when you are in distress?"

⁸And the elders of Gilead said to Jephthah, "That is why we have turned again to you now, that you may go with us and fight against the people of Ammon, and be our head over all the inhabitants of Gilead."

⁹So Jephthah said to the elders of Gilead, "If you take me back home to fight against the people of Ammon, and the LORD delivers them to me, shall I be your head?"

¹⁰And the elders of Gilead said to Jephthah, "The LORD will be a witness between us, if we do not do according to your words." ¹¹Then Jephthah went with the elders of Gilead, and the people made him head and commander over them; and Jephthah spoke all his words before the LORD in Mizpah.

¹²Now Jephthah sent messengers to the king of the people of Ammon, saying, "What do you have against me, that you have come to fight against me in my land?"

¹³And the king of the people of Ammon answered the messengers of Jephthah, "Because Israel took away my land when they came up out of Egypt, from the Arnon as far as the Jabbok, and to the Jordan. Now therefore, restore those *lands* peaceably."

¹⁴So Jephthah again sent messengers to the king of the people of Ammon, ¹⁵and said to him, "Thus says Jephthah: 'Israel did not take away the land of Moab, nor the land of the people of

---

Ammon; [16]for when Israel came up from Egypt, they walked through the wilderness as far as the Red Sea and came to Kadesh. [17]Then Israel sent messengers to the king of Edom, saying, "Please let me pass through your land." But the king of Edom would not heed. And in like manner they sent to the king of Moab, but he would not *consent*. So Israel remained in Kadesh. [18]And they went along through the wilderness and bypassed the land of Edom and the land of Moab, came to the east side of the land of Moab, and encamped on the other side of the Arnon. But they did not enter the border of Moab, for the Arnon *was* the border of Moab. [19]Then Israel sent messengers to Sihon king of the Amorites, king of Heshbon; and Israel said to him, "Please let us pass through your land into our place." [20]But Sihon did not trust Israel to pass through his territory. So Sihon gathered all his people together, encamped in Jahaz, and fought against Israel. [21]And the LORD God of Israel delivered Sihon and all his people into the hand of Israel, and they defeated them. Thus Israel gained possession of all the land of the Amorites, who inhabited that country. [22]They took possession of all the territory of the Amorites, from the Arnon to the Jabbok and from the wilderness to the Jordan.

[23]"And now the LORD God of Israel has dispossessed the Amorites from before His people Israel; should you then possess it? [24]Will you not possess whatever Chemosh your god gives you to possess? So whatever the LORD our God takes possession of before us, we will possess. [25]And now, *are* you any better than Balak the son of Zippor, king of Moab? Did he ever strive against Israel? Did he ever fight against them? [26]While Israel dwelt in Heshbon and its villages, in Aroer and its villages, and in all the cities along the banks of the Arnon, for three hundred years, why did you not recover *them* within that time? [27]Therefore I have not sinned against you, but you wronged me by fighting against me. May the LORD, the Judge, render judgment this day between the children of Israel and the people of Ammon.'" [28]However, the king of the people of Ammon did not heed the words which Jephthah sent him.

Jephthah's Vow and Victory

[29]Then the Spirit of the LORD came upon Jephthah, and he passed through Gilead and Manasseh, and passed through Mizpah of Gilead; and from Mizpah of Gilead he advanced *toward* the people of Ammon. [30]And Jephthah made a vow to the LORD, and said, "If You will indeed deliver the people of Ammon into my hands, [31]then it will be that whatever comes out of the doors of my house to meet me, when I return in peace from the people of Ammon, shall surely be the LORD's, and I will offer it up as a burnt offering."

[32]So Jephthah advanced toward the people of Ammon to fight against them, and the LORD delivered them into his hands. [33]And he defeated them from Aroer as far as Minnith—twenty cities—and to Abel Keramim,[a] with a very great slaughter. Thus the people of Ammon were subdued before the children of Israel.

Jephthah's Daughter

[34]When Jephthah came to his house at Mizpah, there was his daughter, coming out to meet him with timbrels and dancing; and she *was his* only child. Besides her he had neither son nor daughter. [35]And it came to pass, when he saw her, that he tore his clothes, and said, "Alas, my daughter! You have brought me very low! You are among those who trouble me! For I have given my word to the LORD, and I cannot go back on it."

[36]So she said to him, "My father, *if* you have given your word to the LORD, do to me according to what has gone out of your mouth, because the LORD has avenged you of your enemies, the people of Ammon." [37]Then she said to her father, "Let this thing be done for me: let me alone for two months, that I may go and wander on the mountains and bewail my virginity, my friends and I."

[38]So he said, "Go." And he sent her away *for* two months; and she went with her friends, and bewailed her virginity on the mountains. [39]And it was so at the end of two months that she returned to her father, and he carried out his vow with her which he had vowed. She knew no man.

And it became a custom in Israel [40]*that* the daughters of Israel went four days each year to lament the daughter of Jephthah the Gileadite.

Jephthah's Conflict with Ephraim

12 Then the men of Ephraim gathered together, crossed over toward Zaphon, and said to Jephthah, "Why did you cross over to fight against the people of Ammon, and did not call us to go with you? We will burn your house down on you with fire!"

[2]And Jephthah said to them, "My people and I were in a great struggle with the people of Ammon; and when I called you, you did not de-

---

11:33 [a]Literally *Plain of Vineyards*

liver me out of their hands. ³So when I saw that you would not deliver *me,* I took my life in my hands and crossed over against the people of Ammon; and the LORD delivered them into my hand. Why then have you come up to me this day to fight against me?" ⁴Now Jephthah gathered together all the men of Gilead and fought against Ephraim. And the men of Gilead defeated Ephraim, because they said, "You Gileadites *are* fugitives of Ephraim among the Ephraimites *and* among the Manassites." ⁵The Gileadites seized the fords of the Jordan before the Ephraimites *arrived.* And when *any* Ephraimite who escaped said, "Let me cross over," the men of Gilead would say to him, "*Are* you an Ephraimite?" If he said, "No," ⁶then they would say to him, "Then say, 'Shibboleth'!" And he would say, "Sibboleth," for he could not pronounce *it* right. Then they would take him and kill him at the fords of the Jordan. There fell at that time forty-two thousand Ephraimites.

⁷And Jephthah judged Israel six years. Then Jephthah the Gileadite died and was buried among the cities of Gilead.

Ibzan, Elon, and Abdon

⁸After him, Ibzan of Bethlehem judged Israel. ⁹He had thirty sons. And he gave away thirty daughters in marriage, and brought in thirty daughters from elsewhere for his sons. He judged Israel seven years. ¹⁰Then Ibzan died and was buried at Bethlehem.

¹¹After him, Elon the Zebulunite judged Israel. He judged Israel ten years. ¹²And Elon the Zebulunite died and was buried at Aijalon in the country of Zebulun.

¹³After him, Abdon the son of Hillel the Pirathonite judged Israel. ¹⁴He had forty sons and thirty grandsons, who rode on seventy young donkeys. He judged Israel eight years. ¹⁵Then Abdon the son of Hillel the Pirathonite died and was buried in Pirathon in the land of Ephraim, in the mountains of the Amalekites.

The Birth of Samson

13 Again the children of Israel did evil in the sight of the LORD, and the LORD delivered them into the hand of the Philistines for forty years.

²Now there was a certain man from Zorah, of the family of the Danites, whose name *was* Manoah; and his wife *was* barren and had no children. ³And the Angel of the LORD appeared to the woman and said to her, "Indeed now, you are barren and have borne no children, but you shall conceive and bear a son. ⁴Now therefore, please be careful not to drink wine or *similar* drink, and not to eat anything unclean. ⁵For behold, you shall conceive and bear a son. And no razor shall come upon his head, for the child

---

The Law of Influence:
Judges with Short-Lived Influence

(Judges 12:8–15)

The three leaders who followed Jephthah—Ibzan, Elon, and Abdon—had many sons and daughters and ruled for a total of 25 years. We don't know much about them, except that they cared more for the honor of their own names than that of Yahweh. The subsequent chapter begins by saying that once they were gone, Israel immediately did evil in God's sight (Judg. 13:1). The influence of those judges died when they did. But why? Two reasons become obvious: diminishing vision and growing pride.

When a leader's vision shrinks, so does his or her influence. The smaller the vision, the smaller the influence. These leaders attempted no great things for God because they saw no great things from God. Therefore the record of each of them ends with a mere, he "died and was buried." How sad.

The story grows even sadder when you realize that the shrunken vision of these leaders encompassed only how to further their own names. Even though these leaders trusted God in the beginning, they eventually took their eyes off of Him and believed their own press reports.

It has been well said that the measure of spiritual maturity is the length of time a person can wait between achieving ministry success and being recognized for it. The moment we seek self-promotion, we forget about seeking God.

shall be a Nazirite to God from the womb; and he shall begin to deliver Israel out of the hand of the Philistines."

[6]So the woman came and told her husband, saying, "A Man of God came to me, and His countenance *was* like the countenance of the Angel of God, very awesome; but I did not ask Him where He *was* from, and He did not tell me His name. [7]And He said to me, 'Behold, you shall conceive and bear a son. Now drink no wine or *similar* drink, nor eat anything unclean, for the child shall be a Nazirite to God from the womb to the day of his death.'"

[8]Then Manoah prayed to the LORD, and said, "O my Lord, please let the Man of God whom You sent come to us again and teach us what we shall do for the child who will be born."

[9]And God listened to the voice of Manoah, and the Angel of God came to the woman again as she was sitting in the field; but Manoah her husband *was* not with her. [10]Then the woman ran in haste and told her husband, and said to him, "Look, the Man who came to me the *other* day has just now appeared to me!"

[11]So Manoah arose and followed his wife. When he came to the Man, he said to Him, "Are You the Man who spoke to this woman?"

And He said, "I *am*."

[12]Manoah said, "Now let Your words come *to pass*! What will be the boy's rule of life, and his work?"

[13]So the Angel of the LORD said to Manoah, "Of all that I said to the woman let her be careful. [14]She may not eat anything that comes from the vine, nor may she drink wine or *similar* drink, nor eat anything unclean. All that I commanded her let her observe."

[15]Then Manoah said to the Angel of the LORD, "Please let us detain You, and we will prepare a young goat for You."

[16]And the Angel of the LORD said to Manoah, "Though you detain Me, I will not eat your food. But if you offer a burnt offering, you must offer it to the LORD." (For Manoah did not know He *was* the Angel of the LORD.)

[17]Then Manoah said to the Angel of the LORD, "What *is* Your name, that when Your words come *to pass* we may honor You?"

[18]And the Angel of the LORD said to him, "Why do you ask My name, seeing it *is* wonderful?"

[19]So Manoah took the young goat with the grain offering, and offered it upon the rock to the LORD. And He did a wondrous thing while Manoah and his wife looked on— [20]it happened as the flame went up toward heaven from the altar—the Angel of the LORD ascended in the flame of the altar! When Manoah and his wife saw *this,* they fell on their faces to the ground. [21]When the Angel of the LORD appeared no more to Manoah and his wife, then Manoah knew that He *was* the Angel of the LORD.

[22]And Manoah said to his wife, "We shall surely die, because we have seen God!"

[23]But his wife said to him, "If the LORD had desired to kill us, He would not have accepted a burnt offering and a grain offering from our hands, nor would He have shown us all these *things,* nor would He have told us *such things* as these at this time."

[24]So the woman bore a son and called his name Samson; and the child grew, and the LORD blessed him. [25]And the Spirit of the LORD began to move upon him at Mahaneh Dan[a] between Zorah and Eshtaol.

Samson's Philistine Wife

14 Now Samson went down to Timnah, and saw a woman in Timnah of the daughters of the Philistines. [2]So he went up and told his father and mother, saying, "I have seen a woman in Timnah of the daughters of the Philistines; now therefore, get her for me as a wife."

[3]Then his father and mother said to him, "*Is there* no woman among the daughters of your brethren, or among all my people, that you must go and get a wife from the uncircumcised Philistines?"

And Samson said to his father, "Get her for me, for she pleases me well."

[4]But his father and mother did not know that it was of the LORD—that He was seeking an occasion to move against the Philistines. For at that time the Philistines had dominion over Israel.

[5]So Samson went down to Timnah with his father and mother, and came to the vineyards of Timnah.

Now *to his* surprise, a young lion *came* roaring against him. [6]And the Spirit of the LORD came mightily upon him, and he tore the lion apart as one would have torn apart a young goat, though *he had* nothing in his hand. But he did not tell his father or his mother what he had done.

[7]Then he went down and talked with the woman; and she pleased Samson well. [8]After some time, when he returned to get her, he turned aside to see the carcass of the lion. And behold, a swarm of bees and honey *were* in the carcass of the lion. [9]He took some of it in his

---

13:25 [a]Literally *Camp of Dan* (compare 18:12)

hands and went along, eating. When he came to his father and mother, he gave *some* to them, and they also ate. But he did not tell them that he had taken the honey out of the carcass of the lion.

[10]So his father went down to the woman. And Samson gave a feast there, for young men used to do so. [11]And it happened, when they saw him, that they brought thirty companions to be with him.

[12]Then Samson said to them, "Let me pose a riddle to you. If you can correctly solve and explain it to me within the seven days of the feast, then I will give you thirty linen garments and thirty changes of clothing. [13]But if you cannot explain *it* to me, then you shall give me thirty linen garments and thirty changes of clothing."

And they said to him, "Pose your riddle, that we may hear it."

[14]So he said to them:

"Out of the eater came something to eat,
    And out of the strong came something
       sweet."

Now for three days they could not explain the riddle.

[15]But it came to pass on the seventh[a] day that they said to Samson's wife, "Entice your husband, that he may explain the riddle to us, or else we will burn you and your father's house with fire. Have you invited us in order to take what is ours? *Is that* not *so?*"

[16]Then Samson's wife wept on him, and said, "You only hate me! You do not love me! You have posed a riddle to the sons of my people, but you have not explained *it* to me."

And he said to her, "Look, I have not explained *it* to my father or my mother; so should I explain *it* to you?" [17]Now she had wept on him the seven days while their feast lasted. And it happened on the seventh day that he told her, because she pressed him so much. Then she explained the riddle to the sons of her people. [18]So the men of the city said to him on the seventh day before the sun went down:

"What *is* sweeter than honey?
    And what *is* stronger than a lion?"

And he said to them:

"If you had not plowed with my heifer,
    You would not have solved my riddle!"

[19]Then the Spirit of the LORD came upon him mightily, and he went down to Ashkelon

and killed thirty of their men, took their apparel, and gave the changes *of clothing* to those who had explained the riddle. So his anger was aroused, and he went back up to his father's house. [20]And Samson's wife was *given* to his companion, who had been his best man.

Samson Defeats the Philistines

15 After a while, in the time of wheat harvest, it happened that Samson visited his wife with a young goat. And he said, "Let me go in to my wife, into *her* room." But her father would not permit him to go in.

[2]Her father said, "I really thought that you thoroughly hated her; therefore I gave her to your companion. *Is* not her younger sister better than she? Please, take her instead."

[3]And Samson said to them, "This time I shall be blameless regarding the Philistines if I harm them!" [4]Then Samson went and caught three hundred foxes; and he took torches, turned *the foxes* tail to tail, and put a torch between each pair of tails. [5]When he had set the torches on fire, he let *the foxes* go into the standing grain of the Philistines, and burned up both the shocks and the standing grain, as well as the vineyards *and* olive groves.

[6]Then the Philistines said, "Who has done this?"

And they answered, "Samson, the son-in-law of the Timnite, because he has taken his wife and given her to his companion." So the Philistines came up and burned her and her father with fire.

[7]Samson said to them, "Since you would do a thing like this, I will surely take revenge on you, and after that I will cease." [8]So he attacked them hip and thigh with a great slaughter; then he went down and dwelt in the cleft of the rock of Etam.

[9]Now the Philistines went up, encamped in Judah, and deployed themselves against Lehi. [10]And the men of Judah said, "Why have you come up against us?"

So they answered, "We have come up to arrest Samson, to do to him as he has done to us."

[11]Then three thousand men of Judah went down to the cleft of the rock of Etam, and said to Samson, "Do you not know that the Philistines rule over us? What *is* this you have done to us?"

And he said to them, "As they did to me, so I have done to them."

14:15 [a]Following Masoretic Text, Targum, and Vulgate; Septuagint and Syriac read *fourth*.

SAMSON AND THE LAW OF SOLID GROUND

Trust Is the Foundation of Leadership

(Judges 13:24—16:31)

Aleader's history of successes and failures makes or breaks his credibility. It's a little like earning and spending pocket change. Each time you make a good leadership decision, it puts change into your pocket. Each time you make a poor one, you have to pay out some of your change. Every leader has a certain amount of change in his pocket when he starts in a new leadership position. From then on, he either builds up his change or pays it out.

To build trust, a leader must exemplify three qualities: competence, connection, and character. People will forgive occasional mistakes based on ability, especially if they can see that you're still growing as a leader. But they won't trust someone who slips in character. In that area, even occasional lapses are lethal. No leader can break trust with his people and expect to keep influencing them. Trust makes leadership possible.

By all accounts, Samson could have become one of Israel's greatest leaders, yet he turned out to be one of the worst. How could someone with such a strong start finish so poorly?

Samson learned the hard way that trust provides the foundation for all genuine leadership. This impetuous, volatile, lustful, moody, emotional, and unpredictable man provides a very good example of a very bad leader. Since no one could trust him, none followed his leadership.

Signs of Leaders in Trouble

Leaders who erode the solid ground of trustworthy leadership usually exhibit one or more of the following signs. Leaders in trouble . . .

1. *Fail to address glaring character weaknesses.*

Samson struggled with sexual impurity. He asked for a pagan wife, slept with prostitutes, and ultimately Delilah destroyed him. Any time a leader neglects to repair his character flaws, they worsen.

2. *Count on deception to safeguard themselves.*

People who flirt with disobedience often deceive others to protect themselves. Samson liked using riddles to outwit others. He didn't tell the whole truth, which later led to distrust and betrayal.

3. *Act impulsively.*

Time after time, Samson displayed his impetuosity. He chose his wife rashly. He made wagers without thinking. And more than once his impulsive spirit led him into a bloody battle. A leader who cannot control his temper endangers both himself and others.

4. *Are overcome by an area of weakness.*

Sin eventually consumes anyone who gives it free rein. Samson met his match in Delilah. The deceiver was deceived; the seducer, seduced. He lost a dangerous game and it cost him everything.

5. *Misuse their God-given gifts.*

Samson possessed immense strength and godly anointing, but he took both for granted. Many times Samson exploited his God-given gift, intended for the deliverance of his people, for personal revenge. When a leader misuses God's gifts, serious consequences inevitably follow.

When Leaders Lose Their Teachability

Samson's self-centered, undisciplined, and arrogant nature made him unteachable. What happens when leaders lose their teachability?

1. *They lean on their own strength and understanding.*

Unteachable leaders lose touch with God and His people. They lean on their own strength and do not seek guidance from God or others. Samson repeatedly used brute force and violence to cope with difficulties. When embarrassed at his wedding feast, he killed 30 men. When the men of Judah turned him over to Philistia, he bludgeoned to death a thousand men. When caught with a prostitute, he ripped apart the city gates of Gaza. Samson didn't take the advice of his parents, never took advice from his people, and didn't look to God for guidance. Worse still, Samson never acknowledged God as the source of his strength. He went from a man of anointing to a man of arrogance.

2. *They fail to learn from their mistakes.*

A person's life runs uphill or downhill, depending on whether he fails forward or backward. It's a mistake only if you don't learn from it. Samson's life reveals no record of improvement, only a downward spiral. For leaders to learn from their mistakes, they must be . . .

- Big enough to admit mistakes. Samson blamed everyone else for his problems. He never once admitted his sin or humbled himself before God.
- Smart enough to profit from them. It's one thing to know you're wrong; it's another to figure out *why* you erred.
- Strong enough to correct them. If you can't implement necessary changes, you can't improve yourself or your situation.

3. *They react rather than lead.*

While good leaders are proactive, unteachable people almost exclusively react. When Samson saw the daughter of Timnah, he immediately asked for her in marriage. When his wife married his best man, he burned down the Philistines' fields. Samson reacted right up to his death—and left his people groaning under Philistine oppression.

4. *They are easily defeated.*

Unteachable people always lose. Even great talent (like Samson's) can take a person only so far. Samson's character flaw, left unrepaired because of an unteachable spirit, led to moral erosion and unchecked sin—and that led to his destruction.

Who knows what might have happened had Samson ever humbly connected with God or sought the guidance and accountability of his people?

[12]But they said to him, "We have come down to arrest you, that we may deliver you into the hand of the Philistines."

Then Samson said to them, "Swear to me that you will not kill me yourselves."

[13]So they spoke to him, saying, "No, but we will tie you securely and deliver you into their hand; but we will surely not kill you." And they bound him with two new ropes and brought him up from the rock.

[14]When he came to Lehi, the Philistines came shouting against him. Then the Spirit of the LORD came mightily upon him; and the ropes that *were* on his arms became like flax that is burned with fire, and his bonds broke loose from his hands. [15]He found a fresh jawbone of a donkey, reached out his hand and took it, and killed a thousand men with it. [16]Then Samson said:

"With the jawbone of a donkey,
    Heaps upon heaps,
With the jawbone of a donkey
    I have slain a thousand men!"

[17]And so it was, when he had finished speaking, that he threw the jawbone from his hand, and called that place Ramath Lehi.[a]

[18]Then he became very thirsty; so he cried out to the LORD and said, "You have given this great deliverance by the hand of Your servant; and now shall I die of thirst and fall into the hand of the uncircumcised?" [19]So God split the hollow place that *is* in Lehi,[a] and water came out, and he drank; and his spirit returned, and he revived. Therefore he called its name En Hakkore,[b] which is in Lehi to this day. [20]And he judged Israel twenty years in the days of the Philistines.

Samson and Delilah

16 Now Samson went to Gaza and saw a harlot there, and went in to her. [2]*When* the Gazites *were told,* "Samson has come here!" they surrounded *the place* and lay in wait for him all night at the gate of the city. They were quiet all night, saying, "In the morning, when it is daylight, we will kill him." [3]And Samson lay *low* till midnight; then he arose at midnight, took hold of the doors of the gate of the city and the two gateposts, pulled them up, bar and all, put *them* on his shoulders, and carried them to the top of the hill that faces Hebron.

[4]Afterward it happened that he loved a woman in the Valley of Sorek, whose name *was* Delilah. [5]And the lords of the Philistines came up to her and said to her, "Entice him, and find out where his great strength *lies,* and by what *means*

we may overpower him, that we may bind him to afflict him; and every one of us will give you eleven hundred *pieces* of silver."

[6]So Delilah said to Samson, "Please tell me where your great strength *lies,* and with what you may be bound to afflict you."

[7]And Samson said to her, "If they bind me with seven fresh bowstrings, not yet dried, then I shall become weak, and be like any *other* man."

[8]So the lords of the Philistines brought up to her seven fresh bowstrings, not yet dried, and she bound him with them. [9]Now *men were* lying in wait, staying with her in the room. And she said to him, "The Philistines *are* upon you, Samson!" But he broke the bowstrings as a strand of yarn breaks when it touches fire. So the secret of his strength was not known.

[10]Then Delilah said to Samson, "Look, you have mocked me and told me lies. Now, please tell me what you may be bound with."

[11]So he said to her, "If they bind me securely with new ropes that have never been used, then I shall become weak, and be like any *other* man."

[12]Therefore Delilah took new ropes and bound him with them, and said to him, "The Philistines *are* upon you, Samson!" And *men were* lying in wait, staying in the room. But he broke them off his arms like a thread.

[13]Delilah said to Samson, "Until now you have mocked me and told me lies. Tell me what you may be bound with."

And he said to her, "If you weave the seven locks of my head into the web of the loom"—

[14]So she wove *it* tightly with the batten of the loom, and said to him, "The Philistines *are* upon you, Samson!" But he awoke from his sleep, and pulled out the batten and the web from the loom.

[15]Then she said to him, "How can you say, 'I love you,' when your heart *is* not with me? You have mocked me these three times, and have not told me where your great strength *lies.*" [16]And it came to pass, when she pestered him daily with her words and pressed him, *so* that his soul was vexed to death, [17]that he told her all his heart, and said to her, "No razor has ever come upon my head, for I *have been* a Nazirite to God from my mother's womb. If I am shaven, then my strength will leave me, and I shall become weak, and be like any *other* man."

[18]When Delilah saw that he had told her all his heart, she sent and called for the lords of the Philistines, saying, "Come up once more, for he

---

15:17 [a]Literally *Jawbone Height* **15:19** [a]Literally *Jawbone* (compare verse 14) [b]Literally *Spring of the Caller*

SELF-DISCIPLINE

Samson Had It, Then Lost It
(Judges 16:1–20)

We must determine to lead our own lives well, before expecting anyone else to follow. Samson seemed to begin his leadership journey as a very disciplined man. He could delay some gratification (although he always struggled with a weakness for women) and kept his Nazirite vow. As he grew older, it was as though he left the foundation of self-discipline and lustfully consumed whatever he wanted: food, women, drink, Philistines.

Discipline does not automatically make someone a leader, but no one can long remain a leader without it. More government leaders have failed from poor discipline than poor policies. More pastors have failed due to bad discipline than bad theology. More business leaders have sabotaged their careers from lack of discipline than by lack of cash flow.

Consider the following list of disciplines that followers want in a leader:

1. They want to see *character* in their leader.
2. They want to observe *competence* in their leader.
3. They want to witness *compassion* in their leader.
4. They want to sense *commitment* in their leader.
5. They want to feel *connection* to their leader.
6. They want to make a *contribution* with their leader.
7. They want to see *contrition* in their leader.
8. They want to join a *cause* with their leader.
9. They want to observe *consistency* in their leader.
10. They want to feel *confidence* in their leader.
11. They want to sense *courage* from their leader.
12. They want to spot *convictions* in their leader.

How to Build Convictions in Your Life

How does a leader become disciplined? Scores of books try to answer that question, but let's underscore here the spiritual dimension of discipline. Spiritual discipline begins when a leader develops personal convictions, those principles we live and die for—the values that guide our life. This is our starting point. Convictions come when . . .

1. We have studied and learned what God's Word says on a given issue.
2. We choose to apply and obey the Word of God in everyday life.
3. We have exposed ourselves to a need.
4. We meditate on specific truths over a period of six months to a year.
5. We have decided what is worth living and dying for.
6. We associate with people who possess convictions in the same areas.
7. We settle an issue before we are forced to do so.

Why not make a list now of those principles you most believe in? Then ask yourself: *Am I disciplined in those areas?* If not, begin to build convictions there first!

For a positive example of self-discipline, see p. 197.

has told me all his heart." So the lords of the Philistines came up to her and brought the money in their hand. ¹⁹Then she lulled him to sleep on her knees, and called for a man and had him shave off the seven locks of his head. Then she began to torment him,ᵃ and his strength left him. ²⁰And she said, "The Philistines *are* upon you, Samson!" So he awoke from his sleep, and said, "I will go out as before, at other times, and shake myself free!" But he did not know that the LORD had departed from him.

²¹Then the Philistines took him and put out his eyes, and brought him down to Gaza. They bound him with bronze fetters, and he became a grinder in the prison. ²²However, the hair of his head began to grow again after it had been shaven.

Samson Dies with the Philistines

²³Now the lords of the Philistines gathered together to offer a great sacrifice to Dagon their god, and to rejoice. And they said:

"Our god has delivered into our hands Samson our enemy!"

²⁴When the people saw him, they praised their god; for they said:

"Our god has delivered into our hands our enemy,
The destroyer of our land,
And the one who multiplied our dead."

²⁵So it happened, when their hearts were merry, that they said, "Call for Samson, that he may perform for us." So they called for Samson from the prison, and he performed for them. And they stationed him between the pillars. ²⁶Then Samson said to the lad who held him by the hand, "Let me feel the pillars which support the temple, so that I can lean on them." ²⁷Now the tem-

16:19 ᵃFollowing Masoretic Text, Targum, and Vulgate; Septuagint reads *he began to be weak.*

The Cry for Leadership:
Judges Who Failed to Finish Well
(*Judges 6:11—8:32; 14:1—16:27*)

Why do so few leaders in the Bible finish well? More than two thirds of biblical leaders finish poorly. Consider, for example, the two most famous judges in the Book of Judges: Gideon and Samson.

Gideon

Early Career (Judg. 6:11—7:25)
1. Chosen by God
2. Hated idols
3. Had an angelic vision
4. Destroyed idols
5. Great deliverer

Later Career (Judg. 8:1–32)
1. Rejected by God
2. Made an idol
3. Caused Israel to sin
4. Became a stumbling stone
5. His good ruined by his evil

Samson

Early Career (Judg. 14:1—16:19)
1. Dedicated to God
2. Great warrior
3. Exceedingly strong
4. Killed thousands of soldiers
5. Man of faith
6. Killed a lion
7. Broke strong bands
8. Carried off the gates of Gaza

Later Career (Judg. 16:20–27)
1. Lost dedication to God
2. Deceived by a woman
3. Had eyes burned out
4. Imprisoned; hair shaved
5. Left by the Lord
6. Mocked and ridiculed
7. Never fulfilled potential
8. Lost his anointing

Many leaders fail toward the end of their life because 1. they somehow dilute the original vision that drove them; 2. their success distorts them; and 3. their weaknesses go unaddressed.
Don't let this happen to you. While a good start helps, a good finish is up to you.

ple was full of men and women. All the lords of the Philistines *were* there—about three thousand men and women on the roof watching while Samson performed.

[28]Then Samson called to the LORD, saying, "O Lord GOD, remember me, I pray! Strengthen me, I pray, just this once, O God, that I may with one *blow* take vengeance on the Philistines for my two eyes!" [29]And Samson took hold of the two middle pillars which supported the temple, and he braced himself against them, one on his right and the other on his left. [30]Then Samson said, "Let me die with the Philistines!" And he pushed with *all his* might, and the temple fell on the lords and all the people who *were* in it. So the dead that he killed at his death were more than he had killed in his life.

[31]And his brothers and all his father's household came down and took him, and brought *him* up and buried him between Zorah and Eshtaol in the tomb of his father Manoah. He had judged Israel twenty years.

Micah's Idolatry

17Now there was a man from the mountains of Ephraim, whose name *was* Micah. [2]And he said to his mother, "The eleven hundred *shekels* of silver that were taken from you, and on which you put a curse, even saying it in my ears—here *is* the silver with me; I took it."

And his mother said, "*May you be* blessed by the LORD, my son!" [3]So when he had returned the eleven hundred *shekels* of silver to his mother, his mother said, "I had wholly dedicated the silver from my hand to the LORD for my son, to make a carved image and a molded image; now therefore, I will return it to you." [4]Thus he returned the silver to his mother. Then his mother took two hundred *shekels* of silver and gave them to the silversmith, and he made it into a carved image and a molded image; and they were in the house of Micah.

[5]The man Micah had a shrine, and made an ephod and household idols;[a] and he consecrated one of his sons, who became his priest. [6]In those days *there was* no king in Israel; everyone did *what was* right in his own eyes.

[7]Now there was a young man from Bethlehem in Judah, of the family of Judah; he *was* a Levite, and was staying there. [8]The man departed from the city of Bethlehem in Judah to stay wherever he could find *a place*. Then he came to the mountains of Ephraim, to the house of Micah, as he journeyed. [9]And Micah said to him, "Where do you come from?"

So he said to him, "I *am* a Levite from Bethlehem in Judah, and I am on my way to find *a place* to stay."

[10]Micah said to him, "Dwell with me, and be a father and a priest to me, and I will give you ten *shekels* of silver per year, a suit of clothes, and your sustenance." So the Levite went in. [11]Then the Levite was content to dwell with the man; and the young man became like one of his sons to him. [12]So Micah consecrated the Levite, and the young man became his priest, and lived in the house of Micah. [13]Then Micah said, "Now I know that the LORD will be good to me, since I have a Levite as priest!"

The Danites Adopt Micah's Idolatry

18In those days *there was* no king in Israel. And in those days the tribe of the Danites was seeking an inheritance for itself to dwell in; for until that day *their* inheritance among the tribes of Israel had not fallen to them. [2]So the children of Dan sent five men of their family from their territory, men of valor from Zorah and Eshtaol, to spy out the land and search it. They said to them, "Go, search the land." So they went to the mountains of Ephraim, to the house of Micah, and lodged there. [3]While they *were* at the house of Micah, they recognized the voice of the young Levite. They turned aside and said to him, "Who brought you here? What are you doing in this *place?* What do you have here?"

[4]He said to them, "Thus and so Micah did for me. He has hired me, and I have become his priest."

[5]So they said to him, "Please inquire of God, that we may know whether the journey on which we go will be prosperous."

[6]And the priest said to them, "Go in peace. The presence of the LORD *be* with you on your way."

[7]So the five men departed and went to Laish. They saw the people who *were* there, how they dwelt safely, in the manner of the Sidonians, quiet and secure. *There were* no rulers in the land who might put *them* to shame for anything. They *were* far from the Sidonians, and they had no ties with anyone.[a]

[8]Then *the spies* came back to their brethren at Zorah and Eshtaol, and their brethren said to them, "What *is* your *report?*"

[9]So they said, "Arise, let us go up against

17:5 [a]Hebrew *teraphim* **18:7** [a]Following Masoretic Text, Targum, and Vulgate; Septuagint reads *with Syria.*

them. For we have seen the land, and indeed it *is* very good. *Would* you *do* nothing? Do not hesitate to go, *and* enter to possess the land. [10]When you go, you will come to a secure people and a large land. For God has given it into your hands, a place where *there is* no lack of anything that *is* on the earth."

[11]And six hundred men of the family of the Danites went from there, from Zorah and Eshtaol, armed with weapons of war. [12]Then they went up and encamped in Kirjath Jearim in Judah. (Therefore they call that place Mahaneh Dan[a] to this day. There *it is,* west of Kirjath Jearim.) [13]And they passed from there to the mountains of Ephraim, and came to the house of Micah.

[14]Then the five men who had gone to spy out the country of Laish answered and said to their brethren, "Do you know that there are in these houses an ephod, household idols, a carved image, and a molded image? Now therefore, consider what you should do." [15]So they turned aside there, and came to the house of the young Levite man—to the house of Micah—and greeted him. [16]The six hundred men armed with their weapons of war, who *were* of the children of Dan, stood by the entrance of the gate. [17]Then the five men who had gone to spy out the land went up. Entering there, they took the carved image, the ephod, the household idols, and the molded image. The priest stood at the entrance of the gate with the six hundred men *who were* armed with weapons of war.

[18]When these went into Micah's house and took the carved image, the ephod, the household idols, and the molded image, the priest said to them, "What are you doing?"

[19]And they said to him, "Be quiet, put your hand over your mouth, and come with us; be a father and a priest to us. *Is it* better for you to be a priest to the household of one man, or that you be a priest to a tribe and a family in Israel?" [20]So the priest's heart was glad; and he took the ephod, the household idols, and the carved image, and took his place among the people.

[21]Then they turned and departed, and put the little ones, the livestock, and the goods in front of them. [22]When they were a good way from the house of Micah, the men who *were* in the houses near Micah's house gathered together and overtook the children of Dan. [23]And they called out to the children of Dan. So they turned around and said to Micah, "What ails you, that you have gathered such a company?"

[24]So he said, "You have taken away my gods which I made, and the priest, and you have gone away. Now what more do I have? How can you say to me, 'What ails you?'"

[25]And the children of Dan said to him, "Do not let your voice be heard among us, lest angry men fall upon you, and you lose your life, with the lives of your household!" [26]Then the children of Dan went their way. And when Micah saw that they *were* too strong for him, he turned and went back to his house.

Danites Settle in Laish

[27]So they took *the things* Micah had made, and the priest who had belonged to him, and went to Laish, to a people quiet and secure; and they struck them with the edge of the sword and burned the city with fire. [28]*There was* no deliverer, because it *was* far from Sidon, and they had no ties with anyone. It was in the valley that belongs to Beth Rehob. So they rebuilt the city and dwelt there. [29]And they called the name of the city Dan, after the name of Dan their father, who was born to Israel. However, the name of the city formerly *was* Laish.

[30]Then the children of Dan set up for themselves the carved image; and Jonathan the son of Gershom, the son of Manasseh,[a] and his sons were priests to the tribe of Dan until the day of the captivity of the land. [31]So they set up for themselves Micah's carved image which he made, all the time that the house of God was in Shiloh.

The Levite's Concubine

19 And it came to pass in those days, when *there was* no king in Israel, that there was a certain Levite staying in the remote mountains of Ephraim. He took for himself a concubine from Bethlehem in Judah. [2]But his concubine played the harlot against him, and went away from him to her father's house at Bethlehem in Judah, and was there four whole months. [3]Then her husband arose and went after her, to speak kindly to her *and* bring her back, having his servant and a couple of donkeys with him. So she brought him into her father's house; and when the father of the young woman saw him, he was glad to meet him. [4]Now his father-in-law, the young woman's father, detained him; and he stayed with him three days. So they ate and drank and lodged there.

[5]Then it came to pass on the fourth day that they arose early in the morning, and he stood to depart; but the young woman's father said to his

---

18:12 [a]Literally *Camp of Dan* **18:30** [a]Septuagint and Vulgate read *Moses.*

son-in-law, "Refresh your heart with a morsel of bread, and afterward go your way."

⁶So they sat down, and the two of them ate and drank together. Then the young woman's father said to the man, "Please be content to stay all night, and let your heart be merry." ⁷And when the man stood to depart, his father-in-law urged him; so he lodged there again. ⁸Then he arose early in the morning on the fifth day to depart, but the young woman's father said, "Please refresh your heart." So they delayed until afternoon; and both of them ate.

⁹And when the man stood to depart—he and his concubine and his servant—his father-in-law, the young woman's father, said to him, "Look, the day is now drawing toward evening; please spend the night. See, the day is coming to an end; lodge here, that your heart may be merry. Tomorrow go your way early, so that you may get home."

¹⁰However, the man was not willing to spend that night; so he rose and departed, and came opposite Jebus (that is, Jerusalem). With him were the two saddled donkeys; his concubine was also with him. ¹¹They were near Jebus, and the day was far spent; and the servant said to his master, "Come, please, and let us turn aside into this city of the Jebusites and lodge in it."

¹²But his master said to him, "We will not turn aside here into a city of foreigners, who are not of the children of Israel; we will go on to Gibeah." ¹³So he said to his servant, "Come, let us draw near to one of these places, and spend the night in Gibeah or in Ramah." ¹⁴And they passed by and went their way; and the sun went down on them near Gibeah, which belongs to Benjamin. ¹⁵They turned aside there to go in to lodge in Gibeah. And when he went in, he sat down in the open square of the city, for no one would take them into his house to spend the night.

¹⁶Just then an old man came in from his work in the field at evening, who also was from the mountains of Ephraim; he was staying in Gibeah, whereas the men of the place were Benjamites. ¹⁷And when he raised his eyes, he saw the traveler in the open square of the city; and the old man said, "Where are you going, and where do you come from?"

¹⁸So he said to him, "We are passing from Bethlehem in Judah toward the remote mountains of Ephraim; I am from there. I went to Bethlehem in Judah; now I am going to the house of the LORD. But there is no one who will take me into his house, ¹⁹although we have both straw and fodder for our donkeys, and bread and wine for myself, for your female servant, and for the young man who is with your servant; there is no lack of anything."

²⁰And the old man said, "Peace be with you! However, let all your needs be my responsibility; only do not spend the night in the open square." ²¹So he brought him into his house, and gave fodder to the donkeys. And they washed their feet, and ate and drank.

Gibeah's Crime

²²As they were enjoying themselves, suddenly certain men of the city, perverted men,ᵃ surrounded the house and beat on the door. They spoke to the master of the house, the old man, saying, "Bring out the man who came to your house, that we may know him carnally!"

²³But the man, the master of the house, went out to them and said to them, "No, my brethren! I beg you, do not act so wickedly! Seeing this man has come into my house, do not commit this outrage. ²⁴Look, here is my virgin daughter and the man'sᵃ concubine; let me bring them out now. Humble them, and do with them as you please; but to this man do not do such a vile thing!" ²⁵But the men would not heed him. So the man took his concubine and brought her out to them. And they knew her and abused her all night until morning; and when the day began to break, they let her go.

²⁶Then the woman came as the day was dawning, and fell down at the door of the man's house where her master was, till it was light.

²⁷When her master arose in the morning, and opened the doors of the house and went out to go his way, there was his concubine, fallen at the door of the house with her hands on the threshold. ²⁸And he said to her, "Get up and let us be going." But there was no answer. So the man lifted her onto the donkey; and the man got up and went to his place.

²⁹When he entered his house he took a knife, laid hold of his concubine, and divided her into twelve pieces, limb by limb,ᵃ and sent her throughout all the territory of Israel. ³⁰And so it was that all who saw it said, "No such deed has been done or seen from the day that the children of Israel came up from the land of Egypt until this day. Consider it, confer, and speak up!"

Israel's War with the Benjamites

20 So all the children of Israel came out, from Dan to Beersheba, as well as from the land of Gilead, and the congregation gathered together as one man before the LORD at Mizpah. ²And the leaders of all

---

19:22 ᵃLiterally *sons of Belial*   **19:24** ᵃLiterally *his*
19:29 ᵃLiterally *with her bones*

the people, all the tribes of Israel, presented themselves in the assembly of the people of God, four hundred thousand foot soldiers who drew the sword. ³(Now the children of Benjamin heard that the children of Israel had gone up to Mizpah.)

Then the children of Israel said, "Tell *us,* how did this wicked deed happen?"

⁴So the Levite, the husband of the woman who was murdered, answered and said, "My concubine and I went into Gibeah, which belongs to Benjamin, to spend the night. ⁵And the men of Gibeah rose against me, and surrounded the house at night because of me. They intended to kill me, but instead they ravished my concubine so that she died. ⁶So I took hold of my concubine, cut her in pieces, and sent her throughout all the territory of the inheritance of Israel, because they committed lewdness and outrage in Israel. ⁷Look! All of you *are* children of Israel; give your advice and counsel here and now!"

⁸So all the people arose as one man, saying, "None *of us* will go to his tent, nor will any turn back to his house; ⁹but now this *is* the thing which we will do to Gibeah: *We will go up* against it by lot. ¹⁰We will take ten men out of *every* hundred throughout all the tribes of Israel, a hundred out of *every* thousand, and a thousand out of *every* ten thousand, to make provisions for the people, that when they come to Gibeah in Benjamin, they may repay all the vileness that they have done in Israel." ¹¹So all the men of Israel were gathered against the city, united together as one man.

¹²Then the tribes of Israel sent men through all the tribe of Benjamin, saying, "What *is* this wickedness that has occurred among you? ¹³Now therefore, deliver up the men, the perverted menᵃ who *are* in Gibeah, that we may put them to death and remove the evil from Israel!" But the children of Benjamin would not listen to the voice of their brethren, the children of Israel. ¹⁴Instead, the children of Benjamin gathered together from their cities to Gibeah, to go to battle against the children of Israel. ¹⁵And from their cities at that time the children of Benjamin numbered twenty-six thousand men who drew the sword, besides the inhabitants of Gibeah, who numbered seven hundred select men. ¹⁶Among all this people *were* seven hundred select men *who were* left-handed; every one could sling a stone at a hair's *breadth* and not miss. ¹⁷Now besides Benjamin, the men of Israel numbered four hundred thousand men who drew the sword; all of these *were* men of war.

¹⁸Then the children of Israel arose and went up to the house of Godᵃ to inquire of God. They said, "Which of us shall go up first to battle against the children of Benjamin?"

The LORD said, "Judah first!"

¹⁹So the children of Israel rose in the morning and encamped against Gibeah. ²⁰And the men of Israel went out to battle against Benjamin, and the men of Israel put themselves in battle array to fight against them at Gibeah. ²¹Then the children of Benjamin came out of Gibeah, and on that day cut down to the ground twenty-two thousand men of the Israelites. ²²And the people, that is, the men of Israel, encouraged themselves and again formed the battle line at the place where they had put themselves in array on the first day. ²³Then the children of Israel went up and wept before the LORD until evening, and asked counsel of the LORD, saying, "Shall I again draw near for battle against the children of my brother Benjamin?"

And the LORD said, "Go up against him."

²⁴So the children of Israel approached the children of Benjamin on the second day. ²⁵And Benjamin went out against them from Gibeah on the second day, and cut down to the ground eighteen thousand more of the children of Israel; all these drew the sword.

²⁶Then all the children of Israel, that is, all the people, went up and came to the house of Godᵃ and wept. They sat there before the LORD and fasted that day until evening; and they offered burnt offerings and peace offerings before the LORD. ²⁷So the children of Israel inquired of the LORD (the ark of the covenant of God *was* there in those days, ²⁸and Phinehas the son of Eleazar, the son of Aaron, stood before it in those days), saying, "Shall I yet again go out to battle against the children of my brother Benjamin, or shall I cease?"

And the LORD said, "Go up, for tomorrow I will deliver them into your hand."

²⁹Then Israel set men in ambush all around Gibeah. ³⁰And the children of Israel went up against the children of Benjamin on the third day, and put themselves in battle array against Gibeah as at the other times. ³¹So the children of Benjamin went out against the people, *and* were drawn away from the city. They began to strike down *and* kill some of the people, as at the other times, in the highways (one of which goes up to Bethel and the other to Gibeah) and in the field, about thirty men of Israel. ³²And the children of Benjamin said, "They *are* defeated before us, as at first."

20:13 ᵃLiterally *sons of Belial* 20:18 ᵃOr *Bethel*
20:26 ᵃOr *Bethel*

But the children of Israel said, "Let us flee and draw them away from the city to the highways." ³³So all the men of Israel rose from their place and put themselves in battle array at Baal Tamar. Then Israel's men in ambush burst forth from their position in the plain of Geba. ³⁴And ten thousand select men from all Israel came against Gibeah, and the battle was fierce. But *the Benjamites*ᵃ did not know that disaster *was* upon them. ³⁵The LORD defeated Benjamin before Israel. And the children of Israel destroyed that day twenty-five thousand one hundred Benjamites; all these drew the sword.

³⁶So the children of Benjamin saw that they were defeated. The men of Israel had given ground to the Benjamites, because they relied on the men in ambush whom they had set against Gibeah. ³⁷And the men in ambush quickly rushed upon Gibeah; the men in ambush spread out and struck the whole city with the edge of the sword. ³⁸Now the appointed signal between the men of Israel and the men in ambush was that they would make a great cloud of smoke rise up from the city, ³⁹whereupon the men of Israel would turn in battle. Now Benjamin had begun to strike *and* kill about thirty of the men of Israel. For they said, "Surely they are defeated before us, as *in* the first battle." ⁴⁰But when the cloud began to rise from the city in a column of smoke, the Benjamites looked behind them, and there was the whole city going up *in smoke* to heaven. ⁴¹And when the men of Israel turned back, the men of Benjamin panicked, for they saw that disaster had come upon them. ⁴²Therefore they turned *their backs* before the men of Israel in the direction of the wilderness; but the battle overtook them, and whoever *came* out of the cities they destroyed in their midst. ⁴³They surrounded the Benjamites, chased them, *and* easily trampled them down as far as the front of Gibeah toward the east. ⁴⁴And eighteen thousand men of Benjamin fell; all these *were* men of valor. ⁴⁵Then theyᵃ turned and fled toward the wilderness to the rock of Rimmon; and they cut down five thousand of them on the highways. Then they pursued them relentlessly up to Gidom, and killed two thousand of them. ⁴⁶So all who fell of Benjamin that day were twenty-five thousand men who drew the sword; all these *were* men of valor.

⁴⁷But six hundred men turned and fled toward the wilderness to the rock of Rimmon, and they stayed at the rock of Rimmon for four months. ⁴⁸And the men of Israel turned back against the children of Benjamin, and struck them down with the edge of the sword—from *every* city, men and beasts, all who were found. They also set fire to all the cities they came to.

Wives Provided for the Benjamites

21 Now the men of Israel had sworn an oath at Mizpah, saying, "None of us shall give his daughter to Benjamin as a wife." ²Then the people came to the house of God,ᵃ and remained there before God till evening. They lifted up their voices and wept bitterly, ³and said, "O LORD God of Israel, why has this come to pass in Israel, that today there should be one tribe *missing* in Israel?"

⁴So it was, on the next morning, that the people rose early and built an altar there, and offered burnt offerings and peace offerings. ⁵The children of Israel said, "Who *is there* among all the tribes of Israel who did not come up with the assembly to the LORD?" For they had made a great oath concerning anyone who had not come up to the LORD at Mizpah, saying, "He shall surely be put to death." ⁶And the children of Israel grieved for Benjamin their brother, and said, "One tribe is cut off from Israel today. ⁷What shall we do for wives for those who remain, seeing we have sworn by the LORD that we will not give them our daughters as wives?"

⁸And they said, "What one *is there* from the tribes of Israel who did not come up to Mizpah to the LORD?" And, in fact, no one had come to the camp from Jabesh Gilead to the assembly. ⁹For when the people were counted, indeed, not one of the inhabitants of Jabesh Gilead *was* there. ¹⁰So the congregation sent out there twelve thousand of their most valiant men, and commanded them, saying, "Go and strike the inhabitants of Jabesh Gilead with the edge of the sword, including the women and children. ¹¹And this *is* the thing that you shall do: You shall utterly destroy every male, and every woman who has known a man intimately." ¹²So they found among the inhabitants of Jabesh Gilead four hundred young virgins who had not known a man intimately; and they brought them to the camp at Shiloh, which is in the land of Canaan.

¹³Then the whole congregation sent *word* to the children of Benjamin who *were* at the rock of Rimmon, and announced peace to them. ¹⁴So Benjamin came back at that time, and they gave them the women whom they had saved alive of the women of Jabesh Gilead; and yet they had not found enough for them.

¹⁵And the people grieved for Benjamin,

20:34 ᵃLiterally *they*   **20:45** ᵃSeptuagint reads *the rest.*   **21:2** ᵃOr *Bethel* because the LORD had made a void in the tribes of Israel.

[16]Then the elders of the congregation said, "What shall we do for wives for those who remain, since the women of Benjamin have been destroyed?" [17]And they said, "*There must be* an inheritance for the survivors of Benjamin, that a tribe may not be destroyed from Israel. [18]However, we cannot give them wives from our daughters, for the children of Israel have sworn an oath, saying, 'Cursed *be* the one who gives a wife to Benjamin.'" [19]Then they said, "In fact, *there is* a yearly feast of the LORD in Shiloh, which *is* north of Bethel, on the east side of the highway that goes up from Bethel to Shechem, and south of Lebonah."

[20]Therefore they instructed the children of Benjamin, saying, "Go, lie in wait in the vineyards, [21]and watch; and just when the daughters of Shiloh come out to perform their dances, then come out from the vineyards, and every man catch a wife for himself from the daughters of Shiloh; then go to the land of Benjamin. [22]Then it shall be, when their fathers or their brothers come to us to complain, that we will say to them, 'Be kind to them for our sakes, because we did not take a wife for any of them in the war; for *it is* not *as though* you have given the *women* to them at this time, making yourselves guilty of your oath.'"

[23]And the children of Benjamin did so; they took enough wives for their number from those who danced, whom they caught. Then they went and returned to their inheritance, and they rebuilt the cities and dwelt in them. [24]So the children of Israel departed from there at that time, every man to his tribe and family; they went out from there, every man to his inheritance.

[25]In those days *there was* no king in Israel; everyone did *what was* right in his own eyes.

RUTH
God Honors Loyalty and Integrity

SUMMARY

The Book of Ruth reminds us that God honors and emphasizes the leadership qualities of loyalty and integrity.

Ruth, a Moabite woman widowed at an early age, found herself faced with the option of abandoning her widowed mother-in-law or risking life in a foreign land. She chose to stay committed to her friend and mentor, Naomi, and her uncommon decision ultimately paid off.

Ruth's commitment to stay with her mother-in-law, despite the death of her husband, revealed her remarkable character and showcased her sense of loyalty and responsibility. When she remained faithful to Naomi, demonstrated an impeccable work ethic, and maintained fidelity as she gleaned every day in a rich man's field, she set herself apart as unique.

Where did this non-Hebrew learn such character and trust in God to meet her needs? From her deceased husband? From Naomi? We do not know, but we do know that Ruth remained committed to doing the right thing, and God surprised her by meeting every need she had, and more. God provided for Ruth through Boaz, a man with similar character—and perhaps this is the most profound lesson of the book.

Ruth illustrates that when leaders focus on doing what is right, God will bless the fruit of their labors. To qualify for such a blessing means placing responsibilities before results. Character must precede conduct. Faithfulness must precede fruitfulness.

"Seek first the kingdom of God and His righteousness," Jesus reminds us, "and all these things shall be added to you" (Matt. 6:33). This is how God's kingdom works. Jesus taught that if you get the tree right, the fruit will be right (Matt. 12:33–35). As in the Book of Ruth, Jesus prioritizes *being* before *doing*.

Our leadership must flow out of our very being, a natural outgrowth of what we have incarnated. And yet most leaders struggle at exactly this point. By definition, most leaders are result-oriented. They jump immediately to the visible and the measurable, to the exterior results that people affirm. Who affirms their private, personal disciplines? Who asks about their character on Monday morning when they walk into the office? Most leaders tend to talk about the "bottom line."

Although we all agree character is paramount, it just seems too hard to track. So most people, even leaders, jump to results. For some, "the end justifies the means." God says, however, that when we work on the *depth* of our ministry, He'll work on its *breadth*.

Leaders need to read the beautiful story of Ruth, for it will remind them of two fundamental truths:

1. God does indeed reward character.
2. God will accomplish His purposes in the end—even if He has to use a Moabite woman to do it.

God's Role in Ruth

Why did God in His providence preserve the Book of Ruth? Perhaps He did so because Ruth would take an honored place in the messianic family line. God moves throughout this book as the divine director of events—orchestrating a plan to graft young Ruth into the family tree of David and leading ultimately to Jesus.

God accomplishes His work and leadership through all the joys and tragedies of life. Famine, loneliness, death, voluntary exile, and unshakable fidelity become the tools He uses to fulfill His sovereign plan. As a phenomenal leader, God brokered the resources and circumstances of this time in Israel's history to pull off what He intended.

Leaders in Ruth

Naomi, Boaz

Other People of Influence in Ruth

Ruth

Lessons in Leadership

- God rewards the integrity and loyalty of leaders.
- God will sovereignly accomplish His purposes through unlikely people.
- Leaders must place character and spiritual formation before conduct and skill formation.

LEADERSHIP

HIGHLIGHTS IN RUTH

Elimelech's Family Goes to Moab

1 Now it came to pass, in the days when the judges ruled, that there was a famine in the land. And a certain man of Bethlehem, Judah, went to dwell in the country of Moab, he and his wife and his two sons. ²The name of the man *was* Elimelech, the name of his wife *was* Naomi, and the names of his two sons *were* Mahlon and Chilion—Ephrathites of Bethlehem, Judah. And they went to the country of Moab and remained there. ³Then Elimelech, Naomi's husband, died; and she was left, and her two sons. ⁴Now they took wives of the women of Moab: the name of the one *was* Orpah, and the name of the other Ruth. And they dwelt there about ten years. ⁵Then both Mahlon and Chilion also died; so the woman survived her two sons and her husband.

Commitment Precedes Resources

(Ruth 1:1–22)

While every leader needs financial and human resources to reach his or her goals, commitment should always precede those resources. When a leader demonstrates a commitment to the mission and goals of the organization, the resources always follow.

In the very first chapter of the book that bears her name, Ruth chooses to stay with Naomi, her mother-in-law, even after she loses her husband. She didn't know it, but her commitment would lead to all kinds of open doors. Ruth finds work during a difficult time, makes friends in a foreign land, and eventually gains a new husband, Boaz. Most impressively, God includes her—a Moabite adopted into the family of Israel—in the line of Christ. The child she bore became part of the lineage of the Messiah!

The key? Commitment. Until a leader commits, a hesitancy lingers. But the moment that leader definitely commits, then God moves and a whole stream of events begins to flow. All manner of unforeseen incidents, meetings, persons, and material assistance—which no one could ever dream up—begin to occur. And it all starts to happen the moment a leader makes a firm commitment.

Naomi Returns with Ruth

⁶Then she arose with her daughters-in-law that she might return from the country of Moab, for she had heard in the country of Moab that the LORD had visited His people by giving them bread. ⁷Therefore she went out from the place where she was, and her two daughters-in-law with her; and they went on the way to return to the land of Judah. ⁸And Naomi said to her two daughters-in-law, "Go, return each to her mother's house. The LORD deal kindly with you, as you have dealt with the dead and with me. ⁹The LORD grant that you may find rest, each in the house of her husband."

So she kissed them, and they lifted up their voices and wept. ¹⁰And they said to her, "Surely we will return with you to your people."

¹¹But Naomi said, "Turn back, my daughters; why will you go with me? *Are* there still sons in my womb, that they may be your husbands? ¹²Turn back, my daughters, go—for I am too old to have a husband. If I should say I have hope, *if* I should have a husband tonight and should also bear sons, ¹³would you wait for them till they were grown? Would you restrain yourselves from having husbands? No, my daughters; for it grieves me very much for your sakes that the hand of the LORD has gone out against me!"

¹⁴Then they lifted up their voices and wept again; and Orpah kissed her mother-in-law, but Ruth clung to her.

¹⁵And she said, "Look, your sister-in-law has gone back to her people and to her gods; return after your sister-in-law."

¹⁶But Ruth said:

"Entreat me not to leave you,
    Or to turn back from following after you;
    For wherever you go, I will go;
    And wherever you lodge, I will lodge;
    Your people *shall be* my people,
    And your God, my God.
¹⁷   Where you die, I will die,
    And there will I be buried.
    The LORD do so to me, and more also,
    If *anything but* death parts you and me."

¹⁸When she saw that she was determined to go with her, she stopped speaking to her.

¹⁹Now the two of them went until they came to Bethlehem. And it happened, when they had come to Bethlehem, that all the city was excited because of them; and the women said, "*Is* this Naomi?"

²⁰But she said to them, "Do not call me

Naomi;[a] call me Mara,[b] for the Almighty has dealt very bitterly with me. [21]I went out full, and the LORD has brought me home again empty. Why do you call me Naomi, since the LORD has testified against me, and the Almighty has afflicted me?"

[22]So Naomi returned, and Ruth the Moabitess her daughter-in-law with her, who returned from the country of Moab. Now they came to Bethlehem at the beginning of barley harvest.

Ruth Meets Boaz

2 There was a relative of Naomi's husband, a man of great wealth, of the family of Elimelech. His name *was* Boaz. [2]So Ruth the Moabitess said to Naomi, "Please let me go to the field, and glean heads of grain after *him* in whose sight I may find favor."

And she said to her, "Go, my daughter."

[3]Then she left, and went and gleaned in the field after the reapers. And she happened to come to the part of the field *belonging* to Boaz, who *was* of the family of Elimelech.

[4]Now behold, Boaz came from Bethlehem, and said to the reapers, "The LORD *be* with you!"

And they answered him, "The LORD bless you!"

[5]Then Boaz said to his servant who was in charge of the reapers, "Whose young woman *is* this?"

[6]So the servant who was in charge of the reapers answered and said, "It *is* the young Moabite woman who came back with Naomi from the country of Moab. [7]And she said, 'Please let me glean and gather after the reapers among the sheaves.' So she came and has continued from morning until now, though she rested a little in the house."

[8]Then Boaz said to Ruth, "You will listen, my daughter, will you not? Do not go to glean in another field, nor go from here, but stay close by my young women. [9]*Let* your eyes *be* on the field which they reap, and go after them. Have I not commanded the young men not to touch you? And when you are thirsty, go to the vessels and drink from what the young men have drawn."

[10]So she fell on her face, bowed down to the ground, and said to him, "Why have I found favor in your eyes, that you should take notice of me, since I *am* a foreigner?"

[11]And Boaz answered and said to her, "It has been fully reported to me, all that you have done for your mother-in-law since the death of your

1:20 [a]Literally *Pleasant* [b]Literally *Bitter*

RUTH

WILLINGLY FOLLOWS NAOMI
(Ruth 1:8–18)

PROFILE IN LEADERSHIP

The Book of Ruth tells a tale of love and respect between two women from vastly different worlds.

Gentle and loving Ruth, a Moabite, cared deeply for her mother-in-law, Naomi. Ruth willingly left her comfort zone and the only world she had ever known to travel with Naomi to foreign Bethlehem. She exemplifies the strength and determination leaders must have to venture out and follow God, even if it means leaving family and friends behind.

Ruth submitted herself to the directions Naomi gave her in this new and strange culture. Her kinsman-redeemer, Boaz, eventually married her and blessed her with security and protection. But when Ruth first made the choice to follow Naomi's directions, the young Moabite had no way of knowing how it would all turn out. She simply stepped out in faith.

Naomi prayed that Ruth would become famous throughout Israel for her good deeds, and God is still answering that prayer today as millions turn to the Book of Ruth for memorable lessons on love and faithfulness. As the great-grandmother of King David, the foreigner Ruth found a lasting place in the lineage of our Savior, Jesus Christ.

husband, and *how* you have left your father and your mother and the land of your birth, and have come to a people whom you did not know before. [12]The LORD repay your work, and a full reward be given you by the LORD God of Israel, under whose wings you have come for refuge."

[13]Then she said, "Let me find favor in your sight, my lord; for you have comforted me, and have spoken kindly to your maidservant, though I am not like one of your maidservants."

[14]Now Boaz said to her at mealtime, "Come here, and eat of the bread, and dip your piece of bread in the vinegar." So she sat beside the reapers, and he passed parched *grain* to her; and she ate and was satisfied, and kept some back. [15]And when she rose up to glean, Boaz commanded his young men, saying, "Let her glean even among the sheaves, and do not reproach her. [16]Also let *grain* from the bundles fall purposely for her; leave *it* that she may glean, and do not rebuke her."

[17]So she gleaned in the field until evening, and beat out what she had gleaned, and it was about an ephah of barley. [18]Then she took *it* up and went into the city, and her mother-in-law saw what she had gleaned. So she brought out and gave to her what she had kept back after she had been satisfied.

[19]And her mother-in-law said to her, "Where have you gleaned today? And where did you work? Blessed be the one who took notice of you."

So she told her mother-in-law with whom she had worked, and said, "The man's name with whom I worked today *is* Boaz."

[20]Then Naomi said to her daughter-in-law, "Blessed *be* he of the LORD, who has not forsaken His kindness to the living and the dead!" And Naomi said to her, "This man *is* a relation of ours, one of our close relatives."

[21]Ruth the Moabitess said, "He also said to me, 'You shall stay close by my young men until they have finished all my harvest.'"

[22]And Naomi said to Ruth her daughter-in-law, "*It is* good, my daughter, that you go out with his young women, and that people do not meet you in any other field." [23]So she stayed close by the young women of Boaz, to glean until the end of barley harvest and wheat harvest; and she dwelt with her mother-in-law.

BOAZ
MODEL OF KINDNESS AND SPIRITUAL LEADERSHIP
(Ruth 2:4–17)

PROFILE IN LEADERSHIP

The first words we hear from an individual often make the most lasting impression on us.

The first recorded words of Boaz, a wealthy and influential landowner and farmer from Bethlehem, tell us that he loved God and wanted God's blessings on those around him—including those who worked his fields.

On the day Ruth asked to gather grain left behind by his servants, Boaz arrived at his field and greeted the harvesters with a hearty, "The LORD be with you!" (Ruth 2:4).

"The LORD bless you!" the servants replied (2:4).

Why did these workers so enthusiastically respond in kind to Boaz's blessing? Apparently, they knew something about this extraordinary man, his relationship with God, and how he treated people.

We see Boaz's special nature in how he treated Ruth. When he heard the story of this poor Moabite widow, he showed her great kindness and consideration—even to the point of affording her special protection from men in the field and special permission to gather grain *with* his servants. He also gave her all the water she needed and later invited her to join him and his workers for lunch.

Boaz models the sort of kindness required in all godly leaders. He knew when to reach out and welcome those God brought into his circle of influence, even while remaining compassionate and caring toward his own.

GENEROSITY

Boaz Doesn't Keep Score, He Just Keeps Giving
(Ruth 2:8—4:10)

Leaders must be generous, predisposed to give their resources to others. They believe a candle loses nothing when it lights another.

No one models this better than Boaz, the spiritual leader who became Ruth's husband. He owned a large field, and like other landowners, employed reapers to gather his harvest. When the reapers finished, the less fortunate were allowed to "glean" in the field, taking whatever remained of the harvested crops. Ruth was one such person.

Boaz's generous spirit surfaced immediately when he saw Ruth. He asked the reapers about her identity, then expressed his generosity to her. Boaz displayed his generous leadership in several ways:

1. **He was generous with his compassion (2:8, 9).**
   He told Ruth not to glean anywhere else; she would get all she needed from him.
2. **He was generous with his compliments (2:11, 12).**
   He noticed her sacrifice and complimented her efforts.
3. **He was generous with his courtesy (2:14).**
   He invited her to join his staff for a meal, kindly serving her all she wanted.
4. **He was generous with his crops (2:15, 16).**
   He told his reapers to put out extra bundles of grain for her to find.
5. **He was generous with his credibility (3:11–13).**
   He showed respect by doing what was right by her request.
6. **He was generous with his commitment (4:9, 10).**
   He committed himself to ensuring that Ruth's former husband had offspring to carry on his name.

You can give without loving, but you cannot love without giving. Leaders who fail to display generosity should ask themselves, *Do I really love the people I lead?* When great leaders err, they always err on the side of generosity. If they err in paying salaries, they err in paying too much. If they err in firing a staff member, they err on the side of excessive emotional support, severance package, and affirmation. No leader gets ahead by mimicking Ebenezer Scrooge.

Jesus talked about this generous spirit when he said, "If anyone wants to sue you and take away your tunic, let him have your cloak also. And whoever compels you to go one mile, go with him two" (Matt. 5:40, 41).

A generous spirit drove Boaz to go the second mile with Ruth, even before he suspected she might become his wife. (He assumed she would be attracted to a younger man, Ruth 3:10.) Even so, Boaz gave her extra time, attention, grain, respect, favor, and honor.

How about you? Who would describe your leadership as generous?

For a negative example of generosity, see p. 1323.

Ruth's Redemption Assured

3 Then Naomi her mother-in-law said to her, "My daughter, shall I not seek security for you, that it may be well with you? [2]Now Boaz, whose young women you were with, *is he* not our relative? In fact, he is winnowing barley tonight at the threshing floor. [3]Therefore wash yourself and anoint yourself, put on your *best* garment and go down to the threshing floor; *but* do not make yourself known to the man until he has finished eating and drinking. [4]Then it shall be, when he lies down, that you shall notice the place where he lies; and you shall go in, uncover his feet, and lie down; and he will tell you what you should do."

[5]And she said to her, "All that you say to me I will do."

[6]So she went down to the threshing floor and did according to all that her mother-in-law instructed her. [7]And after Boaz had eaten and drunk, and his heart was cheerful, he went to lie down at the end of the heap of grain; and she came softly, uncovered his feet, and lay down.

[8]Now it happened at midnight that the man was startled, and turned himself; and there, a woman was lying at his feet. [9]And he said, "Who *are* you?"

So she answered, "I *am* Ruth, your maidservant. Take your maidservant under your wing,[a] for you are a close relative."

[10]Then he said, "Blessed *are* you of the LORD, my daughter! For you have shown more kindness at the end than at the beginning, in that you did not go after young men, whether poor or rich. [11]And now, my daughter, do not fear. I will

---

The Law of Solid Ground: Both Ruth and Boaz Benefit

(Ruth 3:1–15)

Naomi knew how a woman could properly communicate her interest in a man. She told Ruth to enter the room where Boaz slept, uncover his feet, and sleep there. When Boaz awoke and discovered Ruth, he immediately understood the overture. Yet his sense of integrity would not allow him to sleep with her; he was committed to practicing what he preached. That's what the word "integrity" means: oneness. A person's words, thoughts, and actions are one.

The ancient Greek word for "sincerity" carries a similar meaning. Statues were baked in ovens, usually emerging from the kiln with small cracks. Artists tried to hide these flaws by filling in the cracks with hot wax. Once in a while, a statue without blemishes would appear. On the bottom of these works, the artist would write *sinceros*—"without wax."

Is your leadership "without wax"? Are your words, intentions, and actions one? Are you a Boaz-type of leader?

---

do for you all that you request, for all the people of my town know that you *are* a virtuous woman. [12]Now it is true that I *am* a close relative; however, there is a relative closer than I. [13]Stay this night, and in the morning it shall be *that* if he will perform the duty of a close relative for you—good; let him do it. But if he does not want to perform the duty for you, then I will perform the duty for you, *as* the LORD lives! Lie down until morning."

[14]So she lay at his feet until morning, and she arose before one could recognize another. Then he said, "Do not let it be known that the woman came to the threshing floor." [15]Also he said, "Bring the shawl that *is* on you and hold it." And when she held it, he measured six *ephahs* of barley, and laid *it* on her. Then she[a] went into the city.

Courage: Ruth Steps Out and Takes a Risk

(Ruth 3:1–6)

Ruth took a risk in following her mother-in-law's instruction. What allows a leader to risk?

Responsibility: Sense the need to step out.
Initiative: Act even when no one else goes before.
Sacrifice: Make sacrifices to make things work.
Knowledge: Possess enough information to trust the decision.

3:9 [a]Or *Spread the corner of your garment over your maidservant* **3:15** [a]Many Hebrew manuscripts, Syriac, and Vulgate read *she;* Masoretic Text, Septuagint, and Targum read *he.*

[16]When she came to her mother-in-law, she said, "*Is* that you, my daughter?"

Then she told her all that the man had done for her. [17]And she said, "These six *ephahs* of barley he gave me; for he said to me, 'Do not go empty-handed to your mother-in-law.'"

[18]Then she said, "Sit still, my daughter, until you know how the matter will turn out; for the man will not rest until he has concluded the matter this day."

Boaz Redeems Ruth

4 Now Boaz went up to the gate and sat down there; and behold, the close relative of whom Boaz had spoken came by. So Boaz said, "Come aside, friend,[a] sit down here." So he came aside and sat down. [2]And he took ten men of the elders of the city, and said, "Sit down here." So they sat down. [3]Then he said to the close relative, "Naomi, who has come back from the country of Moab, sold the piece of land which *belonged* to our brother Elimelech. [4]And I thought to inform you, saying, 'Buy *it* back in the presence of the inhabitants and the elders of my people. If you will redeem *it,* redeem *it;* but if you[a] will not redeem *it, then* tell me, that I may know; for *there is* no one but you to redeem *it,* and I *am* next after you.'"

And he said, "I will redeem *it.*"

[5]Then Boaz said, "On the day you buy the field from the hand of Naomi, you must also buy *it* from Ruth the Moabitess, the wife of the dead, to perpetuate[a] the name of the dead through his inheritance."

[6]And the close relative said, "I cannot redeem *it* for myself, lest I ruin my own inheritance. You redeem my right of redemption for yourself, for I cannot redeem *it.*"

[7]Now this *was the custom* in former times in Israel concerning redeeming and exchanging, to confirm anything: one man took off his sandal and gave *it* to the other, and this *was* a confirmation in Israel.

[8]Therefore the close relative said to Boaz,

4:1 [a]Hebrew *peloni almoni;* literally *so and so*
4:4 [a]Following many Hebrew manuscripts, Septuagint, Syriac, Targum, and Vulgate; Masoretic Text reads *he.* **4:5** [a]Literally *raise up*

Women Who Made a Difference

(Ruth 4:13–17)

Ruth and Naomi provide just two examples of women in Scripture who made a difference. Such heroines show up everywhere in both the Old and New Testaments. Study these ladies and be encouraged:

Abigail (1 Sam. 25:1–42)
Anna (Luke 2:36–38)
Deborah (Judg. 4; 5)
Dorcas (Acts 9:36–42)
Elizabeth (Luke 1:5–80)
Esther (Book of Esther)
Eunice (Acts 16:1–3; 2 Tim. 1:5)
Eve (Gen. 2; 3; 2 Cor. 11:3)
Hannah (1 Sam. 1:1—2:21)
Jochebed (Ex. 2:1–11; 6:20)
Lois (2 Tim. 1:5)
Lydia (Acts 16:12–15, 40)
Martha (Luke 10:38–41; John 11)
Mary (Luke 10:38–42; John 12)
Mary, Jesus' mother (Matt. 1; 2; Luke 1; 2)
Mary Magdalene (Matt. 20:1–18; 27:56, 61)
Miriam (Ex. 15:20, 21)
Phoebe (Rom. 16:1, 2)
Priscilla (Acts 18:2, 18, 26)
Rachel (Gen. 29—31)
Rahab (Josh. 2; 6:17–25)
Rebekah (Gen. 24; 25:20–28)
Sarah (Gen. 11; 12; 16; 18)
Susanna (Luke 8:3)
Widow in temple (Mark 12:41–44)
Wife of Pilate (Matt. 27:19–24)
Woman of Samaria (John 4)
Woman who washes Jesus' feet (Luke 7:36–50)

Boaz and Ruth Exhibit Character . . . and It Pays Off

(Ruth 4:1–6)

Both Ruth and Boaz wanted their relationship to go further, yet when the truth came to light, Boaz informed Ruth he must take the decision before the city leaders. Ruth submitted, never pushing her desire to be remarried. Character enables a leader to do what is right, even when it's difficult.

"Buy *it* for yourself." So he took off his sandal. [9] And Boaz said to the elders and all the people, "You *are* witnesses this day that I have bought all that was Elimelech's, and all that *was* Chilion's and Mahlon's, from the hand of Naomi. [10] Moreover, Ruth the Moabitess, the widow of Mahlon, I have acquired as my wife, to perpetuate the name of the dead through his inheritance, that the name of the dead may not be cut off from among his brethren and from his position at the gate.[a] You *are* witnesses this day."

[11] And all the people who *were* at the gate, and the elders, said, "*We are* witnesses. The LORD make the woman who is coming to your house like Rachel and Leah, the two who built the house of Israel; and may you prosper in Ephrathah and be famous in Bethlehem. [12] May your house be like the house of Perez, whom Tamar bore to Judah, because of the offspring which the LORD will give you from this young woman."

Descendants of Boaz and Ruth

[13] So Boaz took Ruth and she became his wife; and when he went in to her, the LORD gave her conception, and she bore a son. [14] Then the women said to Naomi, "Blessed *be* the LORD, who has not left you this day without a close relative; and may his name be famous in Israel! [15] And may he be to you a restorer of life and a nourisher of your old age; for your daughter-in-law, who loves you, who is better to you than seven sons, has borne him." [16] Then Naomi took the child and laid him on her bosom, and became a nurse to him. [17] Also the neighbor women gave him a name, saying, "There is a son born to Naomi." And they called his name Obed. He *is* the father of Jesse, the father of David.

[18] Now this *is* the genealogy of Perez: Perez begot Hezron; [19] Hezron begot Ram, and Ram begot Amminadab; [20] Amminadab begot Nahshon, and Nahshon begot Salmon;[a] [21] Salmon begot Boaz, and Boaz begot Obed; [22] Obed begot Jesse, and Jesse begot David.

4:10 [a] Probably his civic office 4:20 [a] Hebrew *Salmah*

1 SAMUEL
Leaders with a Treasure Trove of Insight

SUMMARY

Samuel was a leader of leaders—a chief advisor to the kings and military captains of Israel. When he spoke, everyone listened.

As the prophet of God, Samuel anointed kings; as the interpreter of the divine Word, he counseled and challenged kings. Serving as judge in the years just prior to Saul's monarchy, Samuel embodied the three great functions of prophet, priest, and king, as Jesus Christ would later.

Samuel and Saul illustrate vividly how a ministry leader and a marketplace leader might relate to one another.

The book begins with Samuel's birth and describes how Eli the priest mentored him as a young boy. The first several chapters depict his role as a judge and show how he led Israel back to God from Baal worship. As Samuel grew older, he appointed his sons to judge Israel, but these men did not "walk in his ways" (8:3) and the people demanded a king. Samuel anoints Saul in chapter nine, and the king's flawed reign takes up the next 20 chapters of the book.

Saul's insecurity leads to a volatile monarchy. He projects his fears onto others, presumes upon the priestly role of Samuel, and jealously pursues David after the young man defeats Goliath. Samuel dies in chapter 25, leaving the leadership of Israel in chaos. By the end of the book, Saul lies dead in battle.

God's Role in 1 Samuel

It has been said that organizations move through at least four stages of growth.

The first is the entrepreneurial stage, where the group seeks viability (this happened for Israel under Moses). The second is the emerging stage, where the group seeks credibility (occurred under Joshua). The third is the established stage, where the group seeks stability (occurred under the judges, ending with Samuel). By this third stage, Israel had a problem. They forgot who they were!

First Samuel describes how God desperately tries calling His people back to Him through the godly leadership of Samuel. But they refuse, demand a king, and crown Saul.

That leads the nation to the fourth and final stage of organizations: erosion, a stage marked by vulnerability. Unless the people can return to their roots and mission, they will crumble from within.

Leaders in 1 Samuel

Eli, Samuel, Saul, David, Jonathan

Other People of Influence in 1 Samuel

Hannah, the Philistines, the prophets, David's mighty men, Abigail, the spirit medium

Lessons in Leadership

- If your leadership doesn't work at home, don't export it.
- Trouble comes when leaders spend more time trying to keep their job than to do their job.
- Leaders must hear from God before they speak for God.
- God selects leaders based on their heart, not just their head and hands.
- Human promotion does not equal divine empowerment.

LEADERSHIP

HIGHLIGHTS IN 1 SAMUEL

The Family of Elkanah

1 Now there was a certain man of Ramathaim Zophim, of the mountains of Ephraim, and his name *was* Elkanah the son of Jeroham, the son of Elihu,[a] the son of Tohu,[b] the son of Zuph, an Ephraimite. [2]And he had two wives: the name of one *was* Hannah, and the name of the other Peninnah. Peninnah had children, but Hannah had no children. [3]This man went up from his city yearly to worship and sacrifice to the LORD of hosts in Shiloh. Also the two sons of Eli, Hophni and Phinehas, the priests of the LORD, *were* there. [4]And whenever the time came for Elkanah to make an offering, he would give portions to Peninnah his wife and to all her sons and daughters. [5]But to Hannah he would give a double portion, for he loved Hannah, although the LORD had closed her womb. [6]And her rival also provoked her severely, to make her miserable, because the LORD had closed her womb. [7]So it was, year by year, when she went up to the house of the LORD, that she provoked her; therefore she wept and did not eat.

Hannah's Vow

[8]Then Elkanah her husband said to her, "Hannah, why do you weep? Why do you not eat? And why is your heart grieved? *Am* I not better to you than ten sons?"

[9]So Hannah arose after they had finished eating and drinking in Shiloh. Now Eli the priest was sitting on the seat by the doorpost of the tabernacle[a] of the LORD. [10]And she *was* in bitterness of soul, and prayed to the LORD and wept in anguish. [11]Then she made a vow and said, "O LORD of hosts, if You will indeed look on the affliction of Your maidservant and remember me, and not forget Your maidservant, but will give Your maidservant a male child, then I will give him to the LORD all the days of his life, and no razor shall come upon his head."

[12]And it happened, as she continued praying before the LORD, that Eli watched her mouth. [13]Now Hannah spoke in her heart; only her lips moved, but her voice was not heard. Therefore Eli thought she was drunk. [14]So Eli said to her, "How long will you be drunk? Put your wine away from you!"

[15]But Hannah answered and said, "No, my lord, I *am* a woman of sorrowful spirit. I have drunk neither wine nor intoxicating drink, but have poured out my soul before the LORD. [16]Do not consider your maidservant a wicked woman,[a]

1:1 [a]Spelled *Eliel* in 1 Chronicles 6:34 [b]Spelled *Toah* in 1 Chronicles 6:34 **1:9** [a]Hebrew *heykal,* palace or temple **1:16** [a]Literally *daughter of Belial*

HANNAH

THE POWER OF PERSISTENCE
(1 Samuel 1:1–28)

PROFILE IN LEADERSHIP

When you think of Hannah, think of persistence and faith.

At a time in history when infertility earned a woman both scorn and ridicule, Hannah faced an added heartache: She became the object of cruel mocking by her husband's other wife. Had you been Hannah, how would you have responded?

Hannah refused to lash out at her rival, but instead took her sorrow and loss to God. She prayed earnestly to her Lord, begging Him for a son. She refused to believe that her difficult situation had to remain permanent.

Hannah prayed sincerely, specifically, and sacrificially. She did not back away from her request, even when rebuked by an uncomprehending priest—and God rewarded her faith with a son, Samuel. When the time came for her to keep her word and give Samuel to the service of the Lord, she did so with a thankful heart.

Prayer changed the course of Hannah's life and impacted an entire nation. God used her son in a key role as prophet during the lifetime of King David, and his influence outlived him as he gave great impetus to the prophetic movement. God also blessed Hannah with many other children, proving once again His delight in the faith and persistence of His people.

for out of the abundance of my complaint and grief I have spoken until now."

[17]Then Eli answered and said, "Go in peace, and the God of Israel grant your petition which you have asked of Him."

[18]And she said, "Let your maidservant find favor in your sight." So the woman went her way and ate, and her face was no longer *sad*.

Samuel Is Born and Dedicated

[19]Then they rose early in the morning and worshiped before the LORD, and returned and came to their house at Ramah. And Elkanah knew Hannah his wife, and the LORD remembered her. [20]So it came to pass in the process of time that Hannah conceived and bore a son, and called his name Samuel,[a] *saying,* "Because I have asked for him from the LORD."

[21]Now the man Elkanah and all his house went up to offer to the LORD the yearly sacrifice and his vow. [22]But Hannah did not go up, for she said to her husband, "*Not* until the child is weaned; then I will take him, that he may appear before the LORD and remain there forever."

[23]So Elkanah her husband said to her, "Do what seems best to you; wait until you have weaned him. Only let the LORD establish His[a] word." Then the woman stayed and nursed her son until she had weaned him.

[24]Now when she had weaned him, she took him up with her, with three bulls,[a] one ephah of flour, and a skin of wine, and brought him to the house of the LORD in Shiloh. And the child *was* young. [25]Then they slaughtered a bull, and brought the child to Eli. [26]And she said, "O my lord! As your soul lives, my lord, I *am* the woman who stood by you here, praying to the LORD. [27]For this child I prayed, and the LORD has granted me my petition which I asked of Him. [28]Therefore I also have lent him to the LORD; as long as he lives he shall be lent to the LORD." So they worshiped the LORD there.

Hannah's Prayer

2 And Hannah prayed and said:

"My heart rejoices in the LORD;
　My horn[a] is exalted in the LORD.
I smile at my enemies,
　Because I rejoice in Your salvation.

[2] "No one is holy like the LORD,
　For *there is* none besides You,
　Nor *is there* any rock like our God.

[3] "Talk no more so very proudly;
　Let no arrogance come from your mouth,
For the LORD *is* the God of knowledge;
　And by Him actions are weighed.

[4] "The bows of the mighty men *are* broken,
　And those who stumbled are girded with
　　strength.
[5] *Those who were* full have hired themselves
　　out for bread,
　And the hungry have ceased *to hunger.*
Even the barren has borne seven,
　And she who has many children has
　　become feeble.

[6] "The LORD kills and makes alive;
　He brings down to the grave and brings
　　up.
[7] The LORD makes poor and makes rich;
　He brings low and lifts up.
[8] He raises the poor from the dust
　And lifts the beggar from the ash heap,
To set *them* among princes
　And make them inherit the throne of
　　glory.

"For the pillars of the earth *are* the LORD's,
　And He has set the world upon them.
[9] He will guard the feet of His saints,
　But the wicked shall be silent in darkness.

"For by strength no man shall prevail.
[10] The adversaries of the LORD shall be
　　broken in pieces;
From heaven He will thunder against
　　them.
The LORD will judge the ends of the
　　earth.

"He will give strength to His king,
　And exalt the horn of His anointed."

[11]Then Elkanah went to his house at Ramah. But the child ministered to the LORD before Eli the priest.

The Wicked Sons of Eli

[12]Now the sons of Eli *were* corrupt;[a] they did not know the LORD. [13]And the priests' custom

---

1:20 [a]Literally *Heard by God* **1:23** [a]Following Masoretic Text, Targum, and Vulgate; Dead Sea Scrolls, Septuagint, and Syriac read *your.*
1:24 [a]Dead Sea Scrolls, Septuagint, and Syriac read *a three-year-old bull.* **2:1** [a]That is, strength
2:12 [a]Literally *sons of Belial*

with the people *was that* when any man offered a sacrifice, the priest's servant would come with a three-pronged fleshhook in his hand while the meat was boiling. [14]Then he would thrust *it* into the pan, or kettle, or caldron, or pot; and the priest would take for himself all that the fleshhook brought up. So they did in Shiloh to all the Israelites who came there. [15]Also, before they burned the fat, the priest's servant would come and say to the man who sacrificed, "Give meat for roasting to the priest, for he will not take boiled meat from you, but raw."

[16]And *if* the man said to him, "They should really burn the fat first; *then* you may·take *as much* as your heart desires," he would then answer him, "*No,* but you must give *it* now; and if not, I will take *it* by force."

[17]Therefore the sin of the young men was very great before the LORD, for men abhorred the offering of the LORD.

Eli's Leadership: Success as a Priest, Not as a Parent

(1 Samuel 2:12–17, 22–36)

Eli's failure to lead his family eventually led to his downfall as a religious leader. This revered judge in Israel failed to discipline his two sons and ended up rearing spiritual rebels. Eli lost his credibility, his job, and eventually his life.

The Scripture teaches that if we do not faithfully lead our own household, we lack the qualifications to lead beyond the home (1 Tim. 3:4, 5)—in other words, if it doesn't work at home, don't export it.

How could a priest like Eli miss the mark? By making some crucial errors.

1. **Emphasis:** Eli emphasized teaching his colleagues and clients, not his family.
2. **Expectation:** Eli thought his sons would "get it" just because they lived in the house of the Lord.
3. **Example:** Eli failed to live out in his home what he taught in his work.
4. **Entanglements:** Eli got so caught up with his profession, he blinded himself to his failure.

Samuel's Childhood Ministry

[18]But Samuel ministered before the LORD, *even as* a child, wearing a linen ephod. [19]Moreover his mother used to make him a little robe, and bring *it* to him year by year when she came up with her husband to offer the yearly sacrifice. [20]And Eli would bless Elkanah and his wife, and say, "The LORD give you descendants from this woman for the loan that was given to the LORD." Then they would go to their own home.

[21]And the LORD visited Hannah, so that she conceived and bore three sons and two daughters. Meanwhile the child Samuel grew before the LORD.

Prophecy Against Eli's Household

[22]Now Eli was very old; and he heard everything his sons did to all Israel,[a] and how they lay with the women who assembled at the door of the tabernacle of meeting. [23]So he said to them, "Why do you do such things? For I hear of your evil dealings from all the people. [24]No, my sons! For *it is* not a good report that I hear. You make the LORD's people transgress. [25]If one man sins against another, God will judge him. But if a man sins against the LORD, who will intercede for him?" Nevertheless they did not heed the voice of their father, because the LORD desired to kill them.

[26]And the child Samuel grew in stature, and in favor both with the LORD and men.

[27]Then a man of God came to Eli and said to him, "Thus says the LORD: 'Did I not clearly reveal Myself to the house of your father when they were in Egypt in Pharaoh's house? [28]Did I not choose him out of all the tribes of Israel *to be* My priest, to offer upon My altar, to burn incense, and to wear an ephod before Me? And did I not give to the house of your father all the offerings of the children of Israel made by fire? [29]Why do you kick at My sacrifice and My offering which I have commanded *in My* dwelling place, and honor your sons more than Me, to make yourselves fat with the best of all the offerings of Israel My people?' [30]Therefore the LORD God of Israel says: 'I said indeed *that* your house and the house of your father would walk before Me forever.' But now the LORD says: 'Far be it from Me; for those who honor Me I will honor, and those who despise Me shall be lightly esteemed. [31]Behold, the days are coming that I will cut off your arm and the arm of your father's house, so that there will not be an old man in

---

2:22 [a]Following Masoretic Text, Targum, and Vulgate; Dead Sea Scrolls and Septuagint omit the rest of this verse.

your house. [32]And you will see an enemy *in My* dwelling place, *despite* all the good which God does for Israel. And there shall not be an old man in your house forever. [33]But any of your men *whom* I do not cut off from My altar shall consume your eyes and grieve your heart. And all the descendants of your house shall die in the flower of their age. [34]Now this *shall be* a sign to you that will come upon your two sons, on Hophni and Phinehas: in one day they shall die, both of them. [35]Then I will raise up for Myself a faithful priest *who* shall do according to what *is* in My heart and in My mind. I will build him a sure house, and he shall walk before My anointed forever. [36]And it shall come to pass that everyone who is left in your house will come *and* bow down to him for a piece of silver and a morsel of bread, and say, "Please, put me in one of the priestly positions, that I may eat a piece of bread." ' "

Samuel's First Prophecy

3 Now the boy Samuel ministered to the LORD before Eli. And the word of the LORD was rare in those days; *there was* no widespread revelation. [2]And it came to pass at that time, while Eli *was* lying down in his place, and when his eyes had begun to grow so dim

---

Samuel Learns to Listen to and Speak for God
(1 Samuel 3:1–3)

Samuel teaches us that we hear from God through:

- **Proper Practice:** Samuel was already obeying all he knew (v. 1).
- **Proper Position:** Samuel lay quiet and still and removed all distractions (v. 3).
- **Proper Proximity:** Samuel lived in the presence of God (v. 3).

---

that he could not see, [3]and before the lamp of God went out in the tabernacle[a] of the LORD where the ark of God *was,* and while Samuel was lying down, [4]that the LORD called Samuel. And he answered, "Here I am!" [5]So he ran to Eli and said, "Here I am, for you called me."

And he said, "I did not call; lie down again." And he went and lay down.

3:3 [a]Hebrew *heykal,* palace or temple

SAMUEL

A LEADER WHO LEARNED TO LISTEN
(1 Samuel 3:1–21)

All leaders need to learn to recognize the voice of God, even as young Samuel did.

While he lay on the floor one night near the ark of God, the Lord called out to him, "Samuel! Samuel!" At first, Samuel heard but didn't recognize the Father's voice. He kept listening, however, and eventually he received word regarding a coming judgment against the priest Eli and his family.

Samuel spent a long and sleepless night, paralyzed with fear at the thought of repeating what God had told him. But Eli convinced Samuel it was far more dangerous to withhold the truth than to reveal what God had shown him (1 Sam. 3:17). So Samuel laid out the whole truth—and because of his obedience, God raised the young man up as a leader and prophet among his people (3:20).

Samuel is a great biblical example of godly leadership. He demonstrates that the man or woman who is fit to lead God's people is the one who has learned to hear His voice, heed His words, and speak His truth, no matter the earthly consequences.

God has never chosen His leaders based on their charisma or eloquence of speech. Rather, He looks for those with the courage to hear and speak exactly what He tells them.

[6]Then the LORD called yet again, "Samuel!"

So Samuel arose and went to Eli, and said, "Here I am, for you called me." He answered, "I did not call, my son; lie down again." [7](Now Samuel did not yet know the LORD, nor was the word of the LORD yet revealed to him.)

[8]And the LORD called Samuel again the third time. So he arose and went to Eli, and said, "Here I am, for you did call me."

Then Eli perceived that the LORD had called the boy. [9]Therefore Eli said to Samuel, "Go, lie down; and it shall be, if He calls you, that you must say, 'Speak, LORD, for Your servant hears.'" So Samuel went and lay down in his place.

[10]Now the LORD came and stood and called as at other times, "Samuel! Samuel!"

And Samuel answered, "Speak, for Your servant hears."

[11]Then the LORD said to Samuel: "Behold, I will do something in Israel at which both ears of everyone who hears it will tingle. [12]In that day I will perform against Eli all that I have spoken concerning his house, from beginning to end. [13]For I have told him that I will judge his house forever for the iniquity which he knows, because his sons made themselves vile, and he did not restrain them. [14]And therefore I have sworn to the house of Eli that the iniquity of Eli's house shall not be atoned for by sacrifice or offering forever."

[15]So Samuel lay down until morning,[a] and opened the doors of the house of the LORD. And Samuel was afraid to tell Eli the vision. [16]Then Eli called Samuel and said, "Samuel, my son!"

He answered, "Here I am."

[17]And he said, "What is the word that the LORD spoke to you? Please do not hide it from me. God do so to you, and more also, if you hide anything from me of all the things that He said to you." [18]Then Samuel told him everything, and hid nothing from him. And he said, "It is the LORD. Let Him do what seems good to Him."

[19]So Samuel grew, and the LORD was with him and let none of his words fall to the ground. [20]And all Israel from Dan to Beersheba knew that Samuel had been established as a prophet of the LORD. [21]Then the LORD appeared again in Shiloh. For the LORD revealed Himself to Samuel in Shiloh by the word of the LORD.

4 And the word of Samuel came to all Israel.[a]

The Ark of God Captured

Now Israel went out to battle against the Philistines, and encamped beside Ebenezer; and the Philistines encamped in Aphek. [2]Then the Philistines put themselves in battle array against Israel. And when they joined battle, Israel was defeated by the Philistines, who killed about four thousand men of the army in the field. [3]And when the people had come into the camp, the elders of Israel said, "Why has the LORD defeated us today before the Philistines? Let us bring the ark of the covenant of the LORD from Shiloh to us, that when it comes among us it may save us from the hand of our enemies." [4]So the people sent to Shiloh, that they might bring from there the ark of the covenant of the LORD of hosts, who dwells between the cherubim. And the two sons of Eli, Hophni and Phinehas, were there with the ark of the covenant of God.

[5]And when the ark of the covenant of the LORD came into the camp, all Israel shouted so loudly that the earth shook. [6]Now when the Philistines heard the noise of the shout, they said, "What does the sound of this great shout in the camp of the Hebrews mean?" Then they understood that the ark of the LORD had come into the camp. [7]So the Philistines were afraid, for they said, "God has come into the camp!" And they said, "Woe to us! For such a thing has never happened before. [8]Woe to us! Who will deliver us from the hand of these mighty gods? These are the gods who struck the Egyptians with all the plagues in the wilderness. [9]Be strong and conduct yourselves like men, you Philistines, that you do not become servants of the Hebrews, as they have been to you. Conduct yourselves like men, and fight!"

[10]So the Philistines fought, and Israel was defeated, and every man fled to his tent. There was a very great slaughter, and there fell of Israel thirty thousand foot soldiers. [11]Also the ark of God was captured; and the two sons of Eli, Hophni and Phinehas, died.

Death of Eli

[12]Then a man of Benjamin ran from the battle line the same day, and came to Shiloh with his clothes torn and dirt on his head. [13]Now when he came, there was Eli, sitting on a seat by the wayside watching,[a] for his heart trembled for the ark of God. And when the man came into the

---

3:15 [a]Following Masoretic Text, Targum, and Vulgate; Septuagint adds *and he arose in the morning.*
4:1 [a]Following Masoretic Text and Targum; Septuagint and Vulgate add *And it came to pass in those days that the Philistines gathered themselves together to fight;* Septuagint adds further *against Israel.*
4:13 [a]Following Masoretic Text and Vulgate; Septuagint reads *beside the gate watching the road.*

city and told *it,* all the city cried out. [14]When Eli heard the noise of the outcry, he said, "What *does* the sound of this tumult *mean?*" And the man came quickly and told Eli. [15]Eli was ninety-eight years old, and his eyes were so dim that he could not see.

[16]Then the man said to Eli, "I *am* he who came from the battle. And I fled today from the battle line."

And he said, "What happened, my son?"

[17]So the messenger answered and said, "Israel has fled before the Philistines, and there has been a great slaughter among the people. Also your two sons, Hophni and Phinehas, are dead; and the ark of God has been captured."

[18]Then it happened, when he made mention of the ark of God, that Eli fell off the seat backward by the side of the gate; and his neck was broken and he died, for the man was old and heavy. And he had judged Israel forty years.

Ichabod

[19]Now his daughter-in-law, Phinehas' wife, was with child, *due* to be delivered; and when she heard the news that the ark of God was captured, and that her father-in-law and her husband were dead, she bowed herself and gave birth, for her labor pains came upon her. [20]And about the time of her death the women who stood by her said to her, "Do not fear, for you have borne a son." But she did not answer, nor did she regard *it.* [21]Then she named the child Ichabod,[a] saying, "The glory has departed from Israel!" because the ark of God had been captured and because of her father-in-law and her husband. [22]And she said, "The glory has departed from Israel, for the ark of God has been captured."

The Philistines and the Ark

5 Then the Philistines took the ark of God and brought it from Ebenezer to Ashdod. [2]When the Philistines took the ark of God, they brought it into the house of Dagon[a] and set it by Dagon. [3]And when the people of Ashdod arose early in the morning, there was Dagon, fallen on its face to the earth before the ark of the LORD. So they took Dagon and set it in its place again. [4]And when they arose early the next morning, there was Dagon, fallen on its face to the ground before the ark of the LORD. The head of Dagon and both the palms of its hands *were* broken off on the threshold; only Dagon's torso[a] was left of it. [5]Therefore neither the priests of Dagon nor any who come into Dagon's house tread on the threshold of Dagon in Ashdod to this day.

[6]But the hand of the LORD was heavy on the people of Ashdod, and He ravaged them and struck them with tumors,[a] *both* Ashdod and its territory. [7]And when the men of Ashdod saw how *it was,* they said, "The ark of the God of Israel must not remain with us, for His hand is harsh toward us and Dagon our god." [8]Therefore they sent and gathered to themselves all the lords of the Philistines, and said, "What shall we do with the ark of the God of Israel?"

And they answered, "Let the ark of the God of Israel be carried away to Gath." So they carried the ark of the God of Israel away. [9]So it was, after they had carried it away, that the hand of the LORD was against the city with a very great destruction; and He struck the men of the city, both small and great, and tumors broke out on them.

[10]Therefore they sent the ark of God to Ekron. So it was, as the ark of God came to Ekron, that the Ekronites cried out, saying, "They have brought the ark of the God of Israel to us, to kill us and our people!" [11]So they sent and gathered together all the lords of the Philistines, and said, "Send away the ark of the God of Israel, and let it go back to its own place, so that it does not kill us and our people." For there was a deadly destruction throughout all the city; the hand of God was very heavy there. [12]And the men who did not die were stricken with the tumors, and the cry of the city went up to heaven.

The Ark Returned to Israel

6 Now the ark of the LORD was in the country of the Philistines seven months. [2]And the Philistines called for the priests and the diviners, saying, "What shall we do with the ark of the LORD? Tell us how we should send it to its place."

[3]So they said, "If you send away the ark of the God of Israel, do not send it empty; but by all means return *it* to Him *with* a trespass offering. Then you will be healed, and it will be known to you why His hand is not removed from you."

[4]Then they said, "What *is* the trespass offering which we shall return to Him?"

They answered, "Five golden tumors and five golden rats, *according to* the number of the lords of the Philistines. For the same plague *was* on all

---

4:21 [a]Literally *Inglorious* **5:2** [a]A Philistine idol
5:4 [a]Following Septuagint, Syriac, Targum, and Vulgate; Masoretic Text reads *Dagon.* **5:6** [a]Probably bubonic plague. Septuagint and Vulgate add here *And in the midst of their land rats sprang up, and there was a great death panic in the city.*

21 LAWS

SAMUEL AND THE LAW OF E. F. HUTTON

A Shepherd Gains an Audience Through Service
(1 Samuel 4:1)

Have you ever wondered what gave Samuel such credibility with others? When he spoke, people listened.

Few descriptions offer a greater compliment than the one given to Samuel's leadership in 1 Samuel 3:19, 20: "So Samuel grew, and the LORD was with him and let none of his words fall to the ground. And all of Israel from Dan to Beersheba knew that Samuel had been established as a prophet of the LORD."

Samuel's success began when he was just a boy, under his mentor Eli. God spoke to Samuel during the night, then the lad spoke for God to Eli (1 Sam. 3:11–18). Despite the hardness of God's message to Eli, Samuel spoke the truth in love. This encounter began a long pattern for Samuel.

Soon, the Israelites sought out Samuel to speak words of direction for their future. They needed help to retrieve the Ark of the Covenant. They needed strategy against their enemy, the Philistines. They eventually sought his permission to crown a king, like the other nations around them.

The influence of the prophet just kept growing. It grew so vast, that when King Saul failed in his leadership, Samuel removed him. Imagine, having the sole authority to kick out even the reigning king! Samuel lived long enough to give the Israelites two kings. Samuel exhorted, he affirmed, he corrected, he prophesied, he reminded, and he taught the people. When he died, all of Israel gathered to mourn his loss (25:1). Indeed, this was a man of impact!

Images of Leadership from Samuel's Life

1. *Shepherd*

   The key descriptive word here is *relationships*. The Bible loves to describe God's leaders as shepherds. Even the Lord is described as a Shepherd (Ps. 23; John 10:11). A shepherd knows, loves, protects, and leads his sheep. Samuel drew from this imagery. He spoke out of relationship. He identified with the people and could be both tough and tender because of this relationship. People listened because of relationship.

2. *Steward*

   The key word here is *responsibility*. A steward acts on behalf of an owner, overseeing others and managing possessions. Stewards are accountable to the owner. Jesus taught this principle in Luke 12:42–48. Samuel lived this truth as he confronted kings and peasants, as he wept over the disobedience of Israel, and as he sought guidance for his nation. He remained faithful to his calling, accountable to God, and responsible to people. That is why they listened.

3. *Seer*

The key word here is *revelation*. Leaders must possess a vision and communicate fresh direction to the people. Samuel, like other Old Testament prophets, brought the word of God to bear on contemporary issues. He spoke with divine conviction about past lessons, present situations, and future direction. He moved from being merely a judge to becoming a prophet, speaking with skill as a visionary leader. People listened because of his revelation.

4. *Servant*

The key word here is *rights*. A biblically informed leader gives up his rights instead of gaining them when he reaches the top. Leaders sacrifice for the good of the people they lead. Samuel modeled this as he interceded for Israel, as he made sacrifices on the altar on their behalf, and as he wept for their welfare. Power did not motivate him, but service. People listened because of his servant's heart.

From Serving to Leading

God calls every leader to be a servant, but not every servant is to be a leader. So, how do we take the step to leadership?

In Hebrew, the word we translate as "leader" (*nagiyd*) comes from a root that conveys the idea of servanthood and being an example to others. The word is variously translated in Scripture as captain, ruler, prince, governor, and noble.

Leader vs. King

The Hebrew term for "leader" stands in sharp contrast to the word for "king." The fairly neutral Hebrew term for "king" (*melech*) allowed for the possibility of independence, for being a maverick. Samuel warned against this very thing when the Israelites asked for a king. *Melechs* might be renegades, but *nagiyds* were those under authority, subject to a higher power and fulfilling the wishes of that higher power. Saul was a *melech*, while Samuel was a *nagiyd*.

To be a captain, ruler, prince, governor, or noble of the people of God, a person must first come squarely under the authority of God. We can go no further without first understanding this element. Yet a second element is just as important. The Hebrew term *nagiyd* also means to stand boldly, to announce, to manifest—the natural outgrowth of receiving commands from God. The leader is to boldly stand and communicate God's commands with conviction.

God's leader is first to be a servant of the Lord, then an example, then a proclaimer and communicator to the people. And no one did this better than Samuel.

of you and on your lords. [5]Therefore you shall make images of your tumors and images of your rats that ravage the land, and you shall give glory to the God of Israel; perhaps He will lighten His hand from you, from your gods, and from your land. [6]Why then do you harden your hearts as the Egyptians and Pharaoh hardened their hearts? When He did mighty things among them, did they not let the people go, that they might depart? [7]Now therefore, make a new cart, take two milk cows which have never been yoked, and hitch the cows to the cart; and take their calves home, away from them. [8]Then take the ark of the LORD and set it on the cart; and put the articles of gold which you are returning to Him *as* a trespass offering in a chest by its side. Then send it away, and let it go. [9]And watch: if it goes up the road to its own territory, to Beth Shemesh, *then* He has done us this great evil. But if not, then we shall know that *it is* not His hand *that* struck us—it happened to us by chance."

[10]Then the men did so; they took two milk cows and hitched them to the cart, and shut up their calves at home. [11]And they set the ark of the LORD on the cart, and the chest with the gold rats and the images of their tumors. [12]Then the cows headed straight for the road to Beth Shemesh, *and* went along the highway, lowing as they went, and did not turn aside to the right hand or the left. And the lords of the Philistines went after them to the border of Beth Shemesh.

[13]Now *the people of* Beth Shemesh *were* reaping their wheat harvest in the valley; and they lifted their eyes and saw the ark, and rejoiced to see *it.* [14]Then the cart came into the field of Joshua of Beth Shemesh, and stood there; a large stone *was* there. So they split the wood of the cart and offered the cows as a burnt offering to the LORD. [15]The Levites took down the ark of the LORD and the chest that *was* with it, in which *were* the articles of gold, and put *them* on the large stone. Then the men of Beth Shemesh offered burnt offerings and made sacrifices the same day to the LORD. [16]So when the five lords of the Philistines had seen *it,* they returned to Ekron the same day.

[17]These *are* the golden tumors which the Philistines returned *as* a trespass offering to the LORD: one for Ashdod, one for Gaza, one for Ashkelon, one for Gath, one for Ekron; [18]and the golden rats, *according to* the number of all the cities of the Philistines *belonging to* the five lords, *both* fortified cities and country villages, even as far as the large *stone of* Abel on which they set the ark of the LORD, *which stone remains* to this day in the field of Joshua of Beth Shemesh.

[19]Then He struck the men of Beth Shemesh, because they had looked into the ark of the LORD. He struck fifty thousand and seventy men[a] of the people, and the people lamented because the LORD had struck the people with a great slaughter.

The Ark at Kirjath Jearim

[20]And the men of Beth Shemesh said, "Who is able to stand before this holy LORD God? And to whom shall it go up from us?" [21]So they sent messengers to the inhabitants of Kirjath Jearim, saying, "The Philistines have brought back the ark of the LORD; come down *and* take it up with you."

7 Then the men of Kirjath Jearim came and took the ark of the LORD, and brought it into the house of Abinadab on the hill, and consecrated Eleazar his son to keep the ark of the LORD.

Samuel Judges Israel

[2]So it was that the ark remained in Kirjath Jearim a long time; it was there twenty years. And all the house of Israel lamented after the LORD.

[3]Then Samuel spoke to all the house of Israel, saying, "If you return to the LORD with all your hearts, *then* put away the foreign gods and the Ashtoreths[a] from among you, and prepare your hearts for the LORD, and serve Him only; and He will deliver you from the hand of the Philistines." [4]So the children of Israel put away the Baals and the Ashtoreths,[a] and served the LORD only.

[5]And Samuel said, "Gather all Israel to Mizpah, and I will pray to the LORD for you." [6]So they gathered together at Mizpah, drew water, and poured *it* out before the LORD. And they fasted that day, and said there, "We have sinned against the LORD." And Samuel judged the children of Israel at Mizpah.

[7]Now when the Philistines heard that the children of Israel had gathered together at Mizpah, the lords of the Philistines went up against Israel. And when the children of Israel heard *of it,* they were afraid of the Philistines. [8]So the children of Israel said to Samuel, "Do not cease to cry out to the LORD our God for us, that He may save us from the hand of the Philistines."

[9]And Samuel took a suckling lamb and offered *it as* a whole burnt offering to the LORD.

6:19 [a]Or *He struck seventy men of the people and fifty oxen of a man* **7:3** [a]Canaanite goddesses **7:4** [a]Canaanite goddesses

Samuel's Influence:
One Person with Courage Makes a Majority
(1 Samuel 7:1–17)

It didn't take long for the Israelites to get a taste of the leadership of their new judge and prophet, Samuel. The prophet's influence grew daily. When the people trusted him, they were delivered from the Philistines, saw the ark returned to their land, and enjoyed peace in the land. He became by far the most influential leader of his day.

But how did he gain such influence? What made everyone listen to him? At least three indispensable qualities gained him the influence he won:

1. Competence
God blessed Samuel with many gifts. He heard from the Lord, he could see the future unfold, and he wisely knew what to do in crisis. His abilities provided one reason that everyone listened to him.

2. Character
Unlike Eli, Samuel exuded integrity and honestly faced each area of his life. People trusted him and knew that he had Israel's best interests in mind. They considered Samuel utterly trustworthy and depended upon him to intercede for them with God.

3. Connection
Samuel knew how to connect with people; he spoke their language. He expressed compassion for their predicaments and brought courage to their pursuits.

Fortunately for us, the formula for Samuel's success still works today:

Competence + Character + Connection = Influence

Then Samuel cried out to the LORD for Israel, and the LORD answered him. [10]Now as Samuel was offering up the burnt offering, the Philistines drew near to battle against Israel. But the LORD thundered with a loud thunder upon the Philistines that day, and so confused them that they were overcome before Israel. [11]And the men of Israel went out of Mizpah and pursued the Philistines, and drove them back as far as below Beth Car. [12]Then Samuel took a stone and set *it* up between Mizpah and Shen, and called its name Ebenezer,[a] saying, "Thus far the LORD has helped us."

[13]So the Philistines were subdued, and they did not come anymore into the territory of Israel. And the hand of the LORD was against the Philistines all the days of Samuel. [14]Then the cities which the Philistines had taken from Israel were restored to Israel, from Ekron to Gath; and Israel recovered its territory from the hands of the Philistines. Also there was peace between Israel and the Amorites.

[15]And Samuel judged Israel all the days of his life. [16]He went from year to year on a circuit to Bethel, Gilgal, and Mizpah, and judged Israel in all those places. [17]But he always returned to Ramah, for his home *was* there. There he judged Israel, and there he built an altar to the LORD.

Israel Demands a King

8 Now it came to pass when Samuel was old that he made his sons judges over Israel. [2]The name of his firstborn was Joel, and the name of his second, Abijah; *they were* judges in Beersheba. [3]But his sons did not walk in his ways; they turned aside after dishonest gain, took bribes, and perverted justice.

[4]Then all the elders of Israel gathered together and came to Samuel at Ramah, [5]and said to him, "Look, you are old, and your sons do not walk in your ways. Now make us a king to judge us like all the nations."

[6]But the thing displeased Samuel when they said, "Give us a king to judge us." So Samuel prayed to the LORD. [7]And the LORD said to Samuel, "Heed the voice of the people in all that they say to you; for they have not rejected you, but they have rejected Me, that I should not

7:12 [a]Literally *Stone of Help*

Human Promotion Does Not Equal a Divine Call

(1 Samuel 8:4, 5)

Samuel's sons had neither the character nor the calling of their dad; the people wanted nothing to do with them. Their lack of credibility moved the nation to request a king! Yet a human verdict does not equal a divine calling—especially when it comes to leadership.

reign over them. [8]According to all the works which they have done since the day that I brought them up out of Egypt, even to this day—with which they have forsaken Me and served other gods—so they are doing to you also. [9]Now therefore, heed their voice. However, you shall solemnly forewarn them, and show them the behavior of the king who will reign over them."

[10]So Samuel told all the words of the LORD to the people who asked him for a king. [11]And he said, "This will be the behavior of the king who will reign over you: He will take your sons and appoint *them* for his own chariots and *to be* his horsemen, and *some* will run before his chariots. [12]He will appoint captains over his thousands and captains over his fifties, *will set some* to plow his ground and reap his harvest, and *some* to make his weapons of war and equipment for his chariots. [13]He will take your daughters *to be* perfumers, cooks, and bakers. [14]And he will take the best of your fields, your vineyards, and your olive groves, and give *them* to his servants. [15]He will take a tenth of your grain and your vintage, and give it to his officers and servants. [16]And he will take your male servants, your female servants, your finest young men,[a] and your donkeys, and put *them* to his work. [17]He will take a tenth of your sheep. And you will be his servants. [18]And you will cry out in that day because of your king whom you have chosen for yourselves, and the LORD will not hear you in that day."

[19]Nevertheless the people refused to obey the voice of Samuel; and they said, "No, but we will have a king over us, [20]that we also may be like all the nations, and that our king may judge us and go out before us and fight our battles."

[21]And Samuel heard all the words of the people, and he repeated them in the hearing of the LORD. [22]So the LORD said to Samuel, "Heed their voice, and make them a king."

And Samuel said to the men of Israel, "Every man go to his city."

Saul Chosen to Be King

9 There was a man of Benjamin whose name *was* Kish the son of Abiel, the son of Zeror, the son of Bechorath, the son of Aphiah, a Benjamite, a mighty man of power. [2]And he had a choice and handsome son whose name *was* Saul. *There was* not a more handsome person than he among the children of Israel. From his shoulders upward *he was* taller than any of the people.

[3]Now the donkeys of Kish, Saul's father, were lost. And Kish said to his son Saul, "Please take one of the servants with you, and arise, go and look for the donkeys." [4]So he passed through the mountains of Ephraim and through the land of Shalisha, but they did not find *them*. Then they passed through the land of Shaalim, and *they were* not *there*. Then he passed through the land of the Benjamites, but they did not find *them*.

[5]When they had come to the land of Zuph, Saul said to his servant who *was* with him, "Come, let us return, lest my father cease *caring* about the donkeys and become worried about us."

[6]And he said to him, "Look now, *there is* in this city a man of God, and *he is* an honorable man; all that he says surely comes to pass. So let us go there; perhaps he can show us the way that we should go."

[7]Then Saul said to his servant, "But look, *if* we go, what shall we bring the man? For the bread in our vessels is all gone, and *there is* no present to bring to the man of God. What do we have?"

[8]And the servant answered Saul again and said, "Look, I have here at hand one-fourth of a shekel of silver. I will give *that* to the man of God, to tell us our way." [9](Formerly in Israel, when a man went to inquire of God, he spoke thus: "Come, let us go to the seer"; for *he who is* now *called* a prophet was formerly called a seer.)

[10]Then Saul said to his servant, "Well said; come, let us go." So they went to the city where the man of God *was*.

[11]As they went up the hill to the city, they met some young women going out to draw water, and said to them, "Is the seer here?"

[12]And they answered them and said, "Yes, there he is, just ahead of you. Hurry now; for today he came to this city, because there is a sacrifice of the people today on the high place. [13]As

8:16 [a]Septuagint reads *cattle*.

soon as you come into the city, you will surely find him before he goes up to the high place to eat. For the people will not eat until he comes, because he must bless the sacrifice; afterward those who are invited will eat. Now therefore, go up, for about this time you will find him." [14]So they went up to the city. As they were coming into the city, there was Samuel, coming out toward them on his way up to the high place.

[15]Now the LORD had told Samuel in his ear the day before Saul came, saying, [16]"Tomorrow about this time I will send you a man from the land of Benjamin, and you shall anoint him commander over My people Israel, that he may save My people from the hand of the Philistines; for I have looked upon My people, because their cry has come to Me."

[17]So when Samuel saw Saul, the LORD said to him, "There he is, the man of whom I spoke to you. This one shall reign over My people." [18]Then Saul drew near to Samuel in the gate, and said, "Please tell me, where *is* the seer's house?"

[19]Samuel answered Saul and said, "I *am* the seer. Go up before me to the high place, for you shall eat with me today; and tomorrow I will let you go and will tell you all that *is* in your heart. [20]But as for your donkeys that were lost three days ago, do not be anxious about them, for they have been found. And on whom *is* all the desire of Israel? *Is it* not on you and on all your father's house?"

[21]And Saul answered and said, "*Am* I not a Benjamite, of the smallest of the tribes of Israel, and my family the least of all the families of the tribe[a] of Benjamin? Why then do you speak like this to me?"

[22]Now Samuel took Saul and his servant and brought them into the hall, and had them sit in the place of honor among those who were invited; there *were* about thirty persons. [23]And Samuel said to the cook, "Bring the portion which I gave you, of which I said to you, 'Set it apart.'" [24]So the cook took up the thigh with its upper part and set *it* before Saul. And *Samuel* said, "Here it is, what was kept back. *It* was set apart for you. Eat; for until this time it has been kept for you, since I said I invited the people." So Saul ate with Samuel that day.

[25]When they had come down from the high place into the city, *Samuel* spoke with Saul on the top of the house.[a] [26]They arose early; and it was about the dawning of the day that Samuel called to Saul on the top of the house, saying, "Get up, that I may send you on your way." And Saul arose, and both of them went outside, he and Samuel.

Saul Anointed King

[27]As they were going down to the outskirts of the city, Samuel said to Saul, "Tell the servant to go on ahead of us." And he went on. "But you stand here awhile, that I may announce to you the word of God."

10 Then Samuel took a flask of oil and poured *it* on his head, and kissed him and said: "*Is it* not because the LORD has anointed you commander over His inheritance?[a] [2]When you have departed from me today, you will find two men by Rachel's tomb in the territory of Benjamin at Zelzah; and they will say to you, 'The donkeys which you went to look for have been found. And now your father has ceased caring about the donkeys and is worrying about you, saying, "What shall I do about my son?"' [3]Then you shall go on forward from there and come to the terebinth tree of Tabor. There three men going up to God at Bethel will meet you, one carrying three young goats, another carrying three loaves of bread, and another carrying a skin of wine. [4]And they will greet you and give you two *loaves* of bread, which you shall receive from their hands. [5]After that you shall come to the hill of God where the Philistine garrison *is.* And it will happen, when you have come there to the city, that you will meet a group of prophets coming down from the high place with a stringed instrument, a tambourine, a flute, and a harp before them; and they will be prophesying. [6]Then the Spirit of the LORD will come upon you, and you will prophesy with them and be turned into another man. [7]And let it be, when these signs come to you, *that* you do as the occasion demands; for God *is* with you. [8]You shall go down before me to Gilgal; and surely I will come down to you to offer burnt offerings *and* make sacrifices of peace offerings. Seven days you shall wait, till I come to you and show you what you should do."

[9]So it was, when he had turned his back to go from Samuel, that God gave him another heart; and all those signs came to pass that day. [10]When

---

9:21 [a]Literally *tribes* **9:25** [a]Following Masoretic Text and Targum; Septuagint omits *He spoke with Saul on the top of the house;* Septuagint and Vulgate add *And he prepared a bed for Saul on the top of the house, and he slept.* **10:1** [a]Following Masoretic Text, Targum, and Vulgate; Septuagint reads *His people Israel; and you shall rule the people of the Lord;* Septuagint and Vulgate add *And you shall deliver His people from the hands of their enemies all around them. And this shall be a sign to you, that God has anointed you to be a prince.*

Strategic Partnerships:
Ministry and Marketplace Leaders
How Saul and Samuel Partnered Together to Lead God's People

(1 Samuel 9:1—15:31)

The Scripture provides a marvelous picture of how pastors and business leaders can partner together to fulfill a God-given vision. First Samuel shows how God sovereignly uses both Samuel the priest (ministry leader) and Saul the king (marketplace leader).

Because he feels secure, Samuel is able to fulfill his role as spiritual leader to big and strong Saul. He finds his security in his divine call and in the One who called him, not in people. While Saul could be an intimidating, daunting leader (1 Sam. 9:2), Samuel does not envy Saul's role, nor can he be diverted from his work in Saul's life. Note the following observations regarding the partnership of these two in fulfilling God's plan.

1. *Samuel could speak into Saul's life because he felt secure in his calling* (9:17–19).

   While God told Samuel to anoint Saul as king, the prophet never considered the son of Kish to be a celebrity. Saul became king over Samuel—but Samuel never placed his security or emotional health in a mere man. With poise and confidence he said to Saul, "I am the prophet." He then instructed Saul concerning the spiritual matters he would face as king.

2. *Samuel affirmed Saul's complementary role and honored him for it* (9:21–23).

   Although Samuel had been the visible leader in Israel, he intentionally gave away his status by publicly honoring Saul. He reserved special food for him and a special place at the table, so no one would question whom they were to follow.

3. *Samuel took initiative and anointed Saul for the role he was to fulfill* (10:1).

   Samuel didn't feel competition or envy over this new king; he knew that both would serve as leaders among God's people as complementary partners. As Coach Bill McCartney once said to some Promise Keeper speakers, "We are not here to compete with each other, but to complete each other."

4. *Samuel helped Saul to receive a new heart for serving people* (10:6–9).

   At this point Samuel had every reason to feel awkward or displaced; now Saul was doing the very thing Samuel had been gifted to do. But Samuel didn't resist helping Saul to develop into the spiritual leader God called him to be.

5. *Samuel encouraged Saul to use his spiritual gifts* (10:10–13).

   Samuel faithfully brought God's word to Saul. He prepared Saul to receive his spiritual gifts by explaining what would happen and when to look for it.

6. *Samuel did not feel intimidated by or envious of Saul's conquests* (13:8–13).

   Samuel allowed neither Saul's position as king nor his success as conqueror to move him. While Samuel affirmed the king, he also understood his role in Israel and in the king's life. Samuel confronted Saul's disobedience and clarified each of their roles.

7. *Samuel spoke words of direction to Saul* (15:1–3).

   Even after confronting Saul's disobedience, Samuel was able to provide direction for the king and affirm his work on the battlefield. He didn't shrink from playing his role in Saul's life and again clarified Saul's place in the scheme of things. He furnished Saul with great confidence and support as he led the armies of Israel.

Continued on next page

Continued

8. *Samuel prayed and hurt for Saul when the king failed* (15:10, 11).

Samuel grieved when God rejected the disobedient Saul. He knew that God intended great things for Saul—and the king's failure broke Samuel's heart. As Saul's spiritual leader, Samuel hurt for the king.

9. *Samuel could confront Saul when he sinned and provide him perspective* (15:12–23).

Samuel felt called to continually provide the big-picture perspective to Saul and remind him of his roots, of God's call and mission. He offered an eternal perspective to the king and refused to let him try to do God's will in his own way.

10. *Samuel possessed the spiritual credibility to call for repentance and worship from Saul* (15:24–31).

Samuel ministered to Saul with a beautiful combination of grace and truth. He spoke the truth in love, never out of spite or superiority. And when he returned with Saul, he did it not out of intimidation, but to leave Saul with as much dignity as possible.

What Every Pastor Should Know About These Partnerships

The Scripture illustrates the partnership role that ministry leaders and marketplace leaders can enjoy, if only they will work cooperatively.

1. *Samuel* illustrates the role of the *pastor* (the ministry leader). *Saul* illustrates the role of the *entrepreneur* (the marketplace leader).
2. The issue ministry leaders (pastors) must settle: *personal security*. The issue marketplace leaders (laymen) must settle: *personal submission*.
3. The pastor often envies the entrepreneur's *success* (the money). The entrepreneur often envies the pastor's *significance* (the mission).
4. Pastors must develop a *vision* big enough to attract entrepreneurs. Entrepreneurs must develop a *generous spirit* to enable pastors to fulfill it.
5. Pastors must include business leaders in *decisions* so they can own the ministry. Entrepreneurs must include pastors in both their *checkbook* and *calendar*.
6. Pastors must give the *church's ministry* to entrepreneurs/marketplace leaders. Entrepreneurs must give their *spiritual gifts* to the church's ministry.
7. Pastors fail in this partnership because they feel *intimidated*. Entrepreneurs fail in this partnership because they feel *independent*.
8. Pastors can offer one thing that entrepreneurs want most: *fulfillment*. Entrepreneurs can offer one thing that pastors need most: *resources*.

they came there to the hill, there was a group of prophets to meet him; then the Spirit of God came upon him, and he prophesied among them. [11]And it happened, when all who knew him formerly saw that he indeed prophesied among the prophets, that the people said to one another, "What *is* this *that* has come upon the son of Kish? *Is* Saul also among the prophets?" [12]Then a man from there answered and said, "But who *is* their father?" Therefore it became a proverb: "*Is* Saul also among the prophets?" [13]And when he had finished prophesying, he went to the high place.

[14]Then Saul's uncle said to him and his servant, "Where did you go?"

So he said, "To look for the donkeys. When we saw that *they were* nowhere *to be found,* we went to Samuel."

[15]And Saul's uncle said, "Tell me, please, what Samuel said to you."

[16]So Saul said to his uncle, "He told us plainly that the donkeys had been found." But about the matter of the kingdom, he did not tell him what Samuel had said.

Saul Proclaimed King

[17]Then Samuel called the people together to the LORD at Mizpah, [18]and said to the children of Israel, "Thus says the LORD God of Israel: 'I brought up Israel out of Egypt, and delivered you from the hand of the Egyptians *and* from the hand of all kingdoms and from those who

oppressed you.' [19]But you have today rejected your God, who Himself saved you from all your adversities and your tribulations; and you have said to Him, 'No, set a king over us!' Now therefore, present yourselves before the LORD by your tribes and by your clans."[a]

[20]And when Samuel had caused all the tribes of Israel to come near, the tribe of Benjamin was chosen. [21]When he had caused the tribe of Benjamin to come near by their families, the family of Matri was chosen. And Saul the son of Kish was chosen. But when they sought him, he could not be found. [22]Therefore they inquired of the LORD further, "Has the man come here yet?"

And the LORD answered, "There he is, hidden among the equipment."

[23]So they ran and brought him from there; and when he stood among the people, he was taller than any of the people from his shoulders upward. [24]And Samuel said to all the people, "Do you see him whom the LORD has chosen, that there is no one like him among all the people?"

So all the people shouted and said, "Long live the king!"

[25]Then Samuel explained to the people the behavior of royalty, and wrote it in a book and laid it up before the LORD. And Samuel sent all the people away, every man to his house. [26]And Saul also went home to Gibeah; and valiant men went with him, whose hearts God had touched. [27]But some rebels said, "How can this man save us?" So they despised him, and brought him no presents. But he held his peace.

Saul Saves Jabesh Gilead

11 Then Nahash the Ammonite came up and encamped against Jabesh Gilead; and all the men of Jabesh said to Nahash, "Make a covenant with us, and we will serve you."

[2]And Nahash the Ammonite answered them, "On this condition I will make a covenant with you, that I may put out all your right eyes, and bring reproach on all Israel."

[3]Then the elders of Jabesh said to him, "Hold off for seven days, that we may send messengers to all the territory of Israel. And then, if there is no one to save us, we will come out to you."

[4]So the messengers came to Gibeah of Saul and told the news in the hearing of the people. And all the people lifted up their voices and wept. [5]Now there was Saul, coming behind the herd from the field; and Saul said, "What troubles the people, that they weep?" And they told him the words of the men of Jabesh. [6]Then the Spirit of God came upon Saul when he heard this

news, and his anger was greatly aroused. [7]So he took a yoke of oxen and cut them in pieces, and sent them throughout all the territory of Israel by the hands of messengers, saying, "Whoever does not go out with Saul and Samuel to battle, so it shall be done to his oxen."

And the fear of the LORD fell on the people, and they came out with one consent. [8]When he numbered them in Bezek, the children of Israel were three hundred thousand, and the men of Judah thirty thousand. [9]And they said to the messengers who came, "Thus you shall say to the men of Jabesh Gilead: 'Tomorrow, by the time the sun is hot, you shall have help.'" Then the messengers came and reported it to the men of Jabesh, and they were glad. [10]Therefore the men of Jabesh said, "Tomorrow we will come out to you, and you may do with us whatever seems good to you."

[11]So it was, on the next day, that Saul put the people in three companies; and they came into the midst of the camp in the morning watch, and killed Ammonites until the heat of the day. And it happened that those who survived were scattered, so that no two of them were left together.

[12]Then the people said to Samuel, "Who is he who said, 'Shall Saul reign over us?' Bring the men, that we may put them to death."

[13]But Saul said, "Not a man shall be put to death this day, for today the LORD has accomplished salvation in Israel."

[14]Then Samuel said to the people, "Come, let us go to Gilgal and renew the kingdom there."

[15]So all the people went to Gilgal, and there they made Saul king before the LORD in Gilgal. There they made sacrifices of peace offerings before the LORD, and there Saul and all the men of Israel rejoiced greatly.

Samuel's Address at Saul's Coronation

12 Now Samuel said to all Israel: "Indeed I have heeded your voice in all that you said to me, and have made a king over you. [2]And now here is the king, walking before you; and I am old and grayheaded, and look, my sons are with you. I have walked before you from my childhood to this day. [3]Here I am. Witness against me before the LORD and before His anointed: Whose ox have I taken, or whose donkey have I taken, or whom have I cheated? Whom have I oppressed, or from whose hand have I received any bribe with which to blind my eyes? I will restore it to you."

[4]And they said, "You have not cheated us or

10:19 [a]Literally thousands

21 QUALITIES

COMMUNICATION

Samuel and the Importance of Clear Communication
(1 Samuel 10:3—12:25)

Dr. J. Robert Clinton did a formal study of Christian leaders and discovered that, without exception, all of them possessed word gifts: teaching, prophecy, evangelism, preaching, words of knowledge or wisdom, exhortation, etc. More than anything else, they used their gifts of communication to lead their people.

Peter Drucker, the father of American management, believes that 60 percent of all management problems result from faulty communication. Having a message doesn't matter if leaders don't communicate clearly and motivate others.

It is amazing how God wired us. We can listen to a leader flap his gums for 30 minutes, flinging thoughts and ideas about the room. He just talks, opens his mouth to make a few sounds—and yet we want to get up and pursue those ideas.

This is the power of communication. Proverbs 18:21 tells us, "Death and life are in the power of the tongue."

During his day, Samuel was Mr. Communication. Everyone listened to him. What kind of communicator was he? Look at the following examples:

1. *He spoke words of revelation* (7:3).
   His communication contained divine revelation, insights the people lacked.
2. *He spoke words of inspiration* (10:3–6).
   His communication inspired Saul to overcome his fears and step out.
3. *He spoke words of exhortation* (10:24).
   His communication encouraged the people to act and follow Saul as their new king.
4. *He spoke words of affirmation* (10:24).
   His communication affirmed, supported, and endorsed Saul publicly.
5. *He spoke words of information* (10:25).
   His communication overflowed with good content, edifying and teaching others.
6. *He spoke words of declaration* (12:20–25).
   His communication gave clear direction to the people and hope for their future.

How Did He Do It?

Each time Samuel spoke, he followed the rules below:

1. *Simplify the message.*
   He spoke forthrightly, clearly, and simply. No one wondered what he meant.
2. *See the person.*
   He always empathized with others. He knew his audience.
3. *Show the truth.*
   He demonstrated credibility with his passion and his life. He lived what he said.
4. *Seek the response.*
   He always spoke with a purpose. When finished, he urged the people to obey God.

For a negative example of communication, see p. 5.

oppressed us, nor have you taken anything from any man's hand."

[5]Then he said to them, "The LORD *is* witness against you, and His anointed *is* witness this day, that you have not found anything in my hand."

And they answered, "*He is* witness."

[6]Then Samuel said to the people, "*It is* the LORD who raised up Moses and Aaron, and who brought your fathers up from the land of Egypt. [7]Now therefore, stand still, that I may reason with you before the LORD concerning all the righteous acts of the LORD which He did to you and your fathers: [8]When Jacob had gone into Egypt,[a] and your fathers cried out to the LORD, then the LORD sent Moses and Aaron, who brought your fathers out of Egypt and made them dwell in this place. [9]And when they forgot the LORD their God, He sold them into the hand of Sisera, commander of the army of Hazor, into the hand of the Philistines, and into the hand of the king of Moab; and they fought against them. [10]Then they cried out to the LORD, and said, 'We have sinned, because we have forsaken the LORD and served the Baals and Ashtoreths;[a] but now deliver us from the hand of our enemies, and we will serve You.' [11]And the LORD sent Jerubbaal,[a] Bedan,[b] Jephthah, and Samuel,[c] and delivered you out of the hand of your enemies on every side; and you dwelt in safety. [12]And when you saw that Nahash king of the Ammonites came against you, you said to me, 'No, but a king shall reign over us,' when the LORD your God *was* your king.

[13]"Now therefore, here is the king whom you have chosen *and* whom you have desired. And take note, the LORD has set a king over you. [14]If you fear the LORD and serve Him and obey His voice, and do not rebel against the commandment of the LORD, then both you and the king who reigns over you will continue following the LORD your God. [15]However, if you do not obey the voice of the LORD, but rebel against the commandment of the LORD, then the hand of the LORD will be against you, as *it was* against your fathers.

[16]"Now therefore, stand and see this great thing which the LORD will do before your eyes: [17]*Is* today not the wheat harvest? I will call to the LORD, and He will send thunder and rain, that you may perceive and see that your wickedness *is* great, which you have done in the sight of the LORD, in asking a king for yourselves."

[18]So Samuel called to the LORD, and the LORD sent thunder and rain that day; and all the people greatly feared the LORD and Samuel.

[19]And all the people said to Samuel, "Pray for your servants to the LORD your God, that we may not die; for we have added to all our sins the evil of asking a king for ourselves."

[20]Then Samuel said to the people, "Do not fear. You have done all this wickedness; yet do not turn aside from following the LORD, but serve the LORD with all your heart. [21]And do not turn aside; for *then you would go* after empty things which cannot profit or deliver, for they *are* nothing. [22]For the LORD will not forsake His people, for His great name's sake, because it has pleased the LORD to make you His people. [23]Moreover, as for me, far be it from me that I should sin against the LORD in ceasing to pray for you; but I will teach you the good and the right way. [24]Only fear the LORD, and serve Him in truth with all your heart; for consider what great things He has done for you. [25]But if you still do wickedly, you shall be swept away, both you and your king."

Saul's Unlawful Sacrifice

13 Saul reigned one year; and when he had reigned two years over Israel,[a] [2]Saul chose for himself three thousand *men* of Israel. Two thousand were with Saul in Michmash and in the mountains of Bethel, and a thousand were with Jonathan in Gibeah of Benjamin. The rest of the people he sent away, every man to his tent.

[3]And Jonathan attacked the garrison of the Philistines that *was* in Geba, and the Philistines heard *of it*. Then Saul blew the trumpet throughout all the land, saying, "Let the Hebrews hear!" [4]Now all Israel heard it said *that* Saul had attacked a garrison of the Philistines, and *that* Israel had also become an abomination to the Philistines. And the people were called together to Saul at Gilgal.

[5]Then the Philistines gathered together to fight with Israel, thirty[a] thousand chariots and six thousand horsemen, and people as the sand which *is* on the seashore in multitude. And they came up and encamped in Michmash, to the east

---

12:8 [a]Following Masoretic Text, Targum, and Vulgate; Septuagint adds *and the Egyptians afflicted them.* **12:10** [a]Canaanite goddesses **12:11** [a]Syriac reads *Deborah;* Targum reads *Gideon.* [b]Septuagint and Syriac read *Barak;* Targum reads *Simson.* [c]Syriac reads *Simson.* **13:1** [a]The Hebrew is difficult (compare 2 Samuel 5:4; 2 Kings 14:2; see also 2 Samuel 2:10; Acts 13:21). **13:5** [a]Following Masoretic Text, Septuagint, Targum, and Vulgate; Syriac and some manuscripts of the Septuagint read *three.*

21 QUALITIES

COURAGE

The One Item Saul Forgot to Pack

(1 Samuel 10:17—13:14)

Although Saul became king chiefly through his striking appearance, he never won the inward battles. On the outside, he was tall, good-looking and well-built (1 Sam. 9:2). On the inside, however, he amounted to little more than a shrimp. Observe the leadership of Saul:

1. When the time arrives to anoint Saul as king, he hides among the baggage.
2. When Samuel asks Saul to lead, he excuses himself as unable.
3. When Saul's soldiers begin to scatter, he panics and disobeys his divine orders.
4. When confronted over his sin, Saul makes excuses for himself.
5. When Saul attacks the Amalekites, he is afraid to trust God and destroy the enemy.
6. When Saul fears losing the allegiance of the people, he builds a statue of himself.
7. When the Philistines face Israel, Saul's fear prevents him from negotiating.
8. When David gains popularity, Saul's insecurity drives him to attempted murder.

Lessons from Saul

- *Courage and cowardice are both contagious.*
  When Goliath challenged Saul's men, they fled to their tents; when David's men faced vastly superior forces, they stood their ground, fought . . . and won (2 Sam. 23:8–12).
- *Without courage, it doesn't matter how good your intentions are.*
  Saul had good intentions when he presented burnt offerings to the Lord. But he let his fear that the people would desert him control his actions (1 Sam. 13:13, 14).
- *Only courage allows you to do what you are afraid of doing.*
  Saul showed his lack of courage from the beginning, when he hid among the baggage to avoid becoming king (1 Sam. 10:22).
- *Without courage, we're slaves of our own insecurity and possessiveness.*
  King Saul momentarily repented on several occasions when confronted about his repeated attempts to kill David. But later, captive to his fears and insecurities, he always resumed his evil pursuit.
- *If the leader lacks courage, the people will lack commitment.*
  Contrary to God's command, Saul and the people spared the best of the livestock they captured from the Amalekites. Saul let it happen because, as he admitted, "I feared the people and obeyed their voice" (1 Sam. 15:24).
- *A leader without courage will never let go of the familiar.*
  Saul employed a medium to ask counsel of Samuel's departed spirit—in direct violation of God's law (1 Sam. 28:5–20). He lacked the courage to trust God to help him step into an unknown future.
- *Lack of courage will eventually sabotage a leader.*
  Saul's lack of courage eventually cost him not only the throne of Israel, but also his own life and the life of his faithful son, Jonathan (1 Sam. 31:1–6).

For a positive example of courage, see p. 434.

of Beth Aven. [6]When the men of Israel saw that they were in danger (for the people were distressed), then the people hid in caves, in thickets, in rocks, in holes, and in pits. [7]And *some of* the Hebrews crossed over the Jordan to the land of Gad and Gilead.

As for Saul, he *was* still in Gilgal, and all the people followed him trembling. [8]Then he waited seven days, according to the time set by Samuel. But Samuel did not come to Gilgal; and the people were scattered from him. [9]So Saul said, "Bring a burnt offering and peace offerings here to me." And he offered the burnt offering. [10]Now it happened, as soon as he had finished presenting the burnt offering, that Samuel came; and Saul went out to meet him, that he might greet him.

[11]And Samuel said, "What have you done?"

Saul said, "When I saw that the people were scattered from me, and *that* you did not come within the days appointed, and *that* the Philistines gathered together at Michmash, [12]then I said, 'The Philistines will now come down on me at Gilgal, and I have not made supplication to the LORD.' Therefore I felt compelled, and offered a burnt offering."

[13]And Samuel said to Saul, "You have done foolishly. You have not kept the commandment of the LORD your God, which He commanded you. For now the LORD would have established your kingdom over Israel forever. [14]But now your kingdom shall not continue. The LORD has sought for Himself a man after His own heart, and the LORD has commanded him *to be* commander over His people, because you have not kept what the LORD commanded you."

[15]Then Samuel arose and went up from Gilgal to Gibeah of Benjamin.[a] And Saul numbered the people present with him, about six hundred men.

No Weapons for the Army

[16]Saul, Jonathan his son, and the people present with them remained in Gibeah of Benjamin. But the Philistines encamped in Michmash. [17]Then raiders came out of the camp of the Philistines in three companies. One company turned onto the road to Ophrah, to the land of Shual, [18]another company turned to the road *to* Beth Horon, and another company turned *to* the road of the border that overlooks the Valley of Zeboim toward the wilderness.

[19]Now there was no blacksmith to be found throughout all the land of Israel, for the Philistines said, "Lest the Hebrews make swords or spears." [20]But all the Israelites would go down to the Philistines to sharpen each man's plowshare, his mattock, his ax, and his sickle; [21]and the

charge for a sharpening was a pim[a] for the plowshares, the mattocks, the forks, and the axes, and to set the points of the goads. [22]So it came about, on the day of battle, that there was neither sword nor spear found in the hand of any of the people who *were* with Saul and Jonathan. But they were found with Saul and Jonathan his son.

[23]And the garrison of the Philistines went out to the pass of Michmash.

Jonathan Defeats the Philistines

14 Now it happened one day that Jonathan the son of Saul said to the young man who bore his armor, "Come, let us go over to the Philistines' garrison that *is* on the other side." But he did not tell his father. [2]And Saul was sitting in the outskirts of Gibeah under a pomegranate tree which *is* in Migron. The people who *were* with him *were* about six hundred men. [3]Ahijah the son of Ahitub, Ichabod's brother, the son of Phinehas, the son of Eli, the LORD's priest in Shiloh, was wearing an ephod. But the people did not know that Jonathan had gone.

[4]Between the passes, by which Jonathan sought to go over to the Philistines' garrison, *there was* a sharp rock on one side and a sharp rock on the other side. And the name of one *was* Bozez, and the name of the other Seneh. [5]The front of one faced northward opposite Michmash, and the other southward opposite Gibeah.

[6]Then Jonathan said to the young man who bore his armor, "Come, let us go over to the garrison of these uncircumcised; it may be that the LORD will work for us. For nothing restrains the LORD from saving by many or by few."

[7]So his armorbearer said to him, "Do all that is in your heart. Go then; here I am with you, according to your heart."

[8]Then Jonathan said, "Very well, let us cross over to *these* men, and we will show ourselves to them. [9]If they say thus to us, 'Wait until we come to you,' then we will stand still in our place and not go up to them. [10]But if they say thus, 'Come up to us,' then we will go up. For the LORD has delivered them into our hand, and this *will be* a sign to us."

[11]So both of them showed themselves to the garrison of the Philistines. And the Philistines said, "Look, the Hebrews are coming out of the

---

13:15 [a]Following Masoretic Text and Targum; Septuagint and Vulgate add *And the rest of the people went up after Saul to meet the people who fought against them, going from Gilgal to Gibeah in the hill of Benjamin.* **13:21** [a]About two-thirds shekel weight holes where they have hidden." [12]Then the men of the garrison called to Jonathan and his armorbearer, and said, "Come up to us, and we will show you something."

Jonathan said to his armorbearer, "Come up after me, for the LORD has delivered them into the hand of Israel." [13]And Jonathan climbed up on his hands and knees with his armorbearer after him; and they fell before Jonathan. And as he came after him, his armorbearer killed them. [14]That first slaughter which Jonathan and his armorbearer made was about twenty men within about half an acre of land.[a]

[15]And there was trembling in the camp, in the field, and among all the people. The garrison and the raiders also trembled; and the earth quaked, so that it was a very great trembling. [16]Now the watchmen of Saul in Gibeah of Benjamin looked, and *there* was the multitude, melting away; and they went here and there. [17]Then Saul said to the people who *were* with him, "Now call the roll and see who has gone from us." And when they had called the roll, surprisingly, Jonathan and his armorbearer *were* not *there.* [18]And Saul said to Ahijah, "Bring the ark[a] of God here" (for at that time the ark[b] of God was with the children of Israel). [19]Now it happened, while Saul talked to the priest, that the noise which *was* in the camp of the Philistines continued to increase; so Saul said to the priest, "Withdraw your hand." [20]Then Saul and all the people who *were* with him assembled, and they went to the battle; and indeed every man's sword was against his neighbor, *and there was* very great confusion. [21]Moreover the Hebrews *who* were with the Philistines before that time, who went up with them into the camp *from the* surrounding *country,* they also joined the Israelites who *were* with Saul and Jonathan. [22]Likewise all the men of Israel who had hidden in the mountains of Ephraim, *when* they heard that the Philistines fled, they also followed hard after them in the battle. [23]So the LORD saved Israel that day, and the battle shifted to Beth Aven.

Saul's Rash Oath

[24]And the men of Israel were distressed that day, for Saul had placed the people under oath, saying, "Cursed *is* the man who eats *any* food until evening, before I have taken vengeance on my enemies." So none of the people tasted food. [25]Now all *the people* of the land came to a forest; and there was honey on the ground. [26]And when the people had come into the woods, there was the honey, dripping; but no one put his hand to his mouth, for the people feared the oath. [27]But Jonathan had not heard his father charge the people with the oath; therefore he stretched out the end of the rod that *was* in his hand and dipped it in a honeycomb, and put his hand to his mouth; and his countenance brightened. [28]Then one of the people said, "Your father strictly charged the people with an oath, saying, 'Cursed *is* the man who eats food this day.'" And the people were faint.

[29]But Jonathan said, "My father has troubled the land. Look now, how my countenance has brightened because I tasted a little of this honey. [30]How much better if the people had eaten freely today of the spoil of their enemies which they found! For now would there not have been a much greater slaughter among the Philistines?"

[31]Now they had driven back the Philistines that day from Michmash to Aijalon. So the people were very faint. [32]And the people rushed on the spoil, and took sheep, oxen, and calves, and slaughtered *them* on the ground; and the people ate *them* with the blood. [33]Then they told Saul, saying, "Look, the people are sinning against the LORD by eating with the blood!"

So he said, "You have dealt treacherously; roll a large stone to me this day." [34]Then Saul said, "Disperse yourselves among the people, and say to them, 'Bring me here every man's ox and every man's sheep, slaughter *them* here, and eat; and do not sin against the LORD by eating with the blood.'" So every one of the people brought his ox with him that night, and slaughtered *it* there. [35]Then Saul built an altar to the LORD. This was the first altar that he built to the LORD.

[36]Now Saul said, "Let us go down after the Philistines by night, and plunder them until the morning light; and let us not leave a man of them."

And they said, "Do whatever seems good to you."

Then the priest said, "Let us draw near to God here."

[37]So Saul asked counsel of God, "Shall I go down after the Philistines? Will You deliver them into the hand of Israel?" But He did not answer him that day. [38]And Saul said, "Come over here, all you chiefs of the people, and know and see what this sin was today. [39]For *as* the LORD lives, who saves Israel, though it be in Jonathan my son, he shall surely die." But not a man among all the people answered him. [40]Then he said to all

---

14:14 [a]Literally *half the area plowed by a yoke* (of oxen in a day) 14:18 [a]Following Masoretic Text, Targum, and Vulgate; Septuagint reads *ephod.* [b]Following Masoretic Text, Targum, and Vulgate; Septuagint reads *ephod.*

Israel, "You be on one side, and my son Jonathan and I will be on the other side."

And the people said to Saul, "Do what seems good to you."

[41]Therefore Saul said to the LORD God of Israel, "Give a perfect *lot.*"[a] So Saul and Jonathan were taken, but the people escaped. [42]And Saul said, "Cast *lots* between my son Jonathan and me." So Jonathan was taken. [43]Then Saul said to Jonathan, "Tell me what you have done."

And Jonathan told him, and said, "I only tasted a little honey with the end of the rod that *was* in my hand. So now I must die!"

[44]Saul answered, "God do so and more also; for you shall surely die, Jonathan."

[45]But the people said to Saul, "Shall Jonathan die, who has accomplished this great deliverance in Israel? Certainly not! *As* the LORD lives, not one hair of his head shall fall to the ground, for he has worked with God this day." So the people rescued Jonathan, and he did not die.

[46]Then Saul returned from pursuing the Philistines, and the Philistines went to their own place.

Saul's Continuing Wars

[47]So Saul established his sovereignty over Israel, and fought against all his enemies on every side, against Moab, against the people of Ammon, against Edom, against the kings of Zobah, and against the Philistines. Wherever he turned, he harassed *them.*[a] [48]And he gathered an army and attacked the Amalekites, and delivered Israel from the hands of those who plundered them.

[49]The sons of Saul were Jonathan, Jishui,[a] and Malchishua. And the names of his two daughters *were these:* the name of the firstborn Merab, and the name of the younger Michal. [50]The name of Saul's wife *was* Ahinoam the daughter of Ahimaaz. And the name of the commander of his army *was* Abner the son of Ner, Saul's uncle. [51]Kish *was* the father of Saul, and Ner the father of Abner *was* the son of Abiel.

[52]Now there was fierce war with the Philistines all the days of Saul. And when Saul saw any strong man or any valiant man, he took him for himself.

Saul Spares King Agag

15 Samuel also said to Saul, "The LORD sent me to anoint you king over His people, over Israel. Now therefore, heed the voice of the words of the LORD. [2]Thus says the LORD of hosts: 'I will punish Amalek *for* what he did to Israel, how he ambushed him on the way when he came up from Egypt. [3]Now go

and attack Amalek, and utterly destroy all that they have, and do not spare them. But kill both man and woman, infant and nursing child, ox and sheep, camel and donkey.' "

[4]So Saul gathered the people together and numbered them in Telaim, two hundred thousand foot soldiers and ten thousand men of Judah. [5]And Saul came to a city of Amalek, and lay in wait in the valley.

[6]Then Saul said to the Kenites, "Go, depart, get down from among the Amalekites, lest I destroy you with them. For you showed kindness to all the children of Israel when they came up out of Egypt." So the Kenites departed from among the Amalekites. [7]And Saul attacked the Amalekites, from Havilah all the way to Shur, which is east of Egypt. [8]He also took Agag king of the Amalekites alive, and utterly destroyed all the people with the edge of the sword. [9]But Saul and the people spared Agag and the best of the sheep, the oxen, the fatlings, the lambs, and all *that was* good, and were unwilling to utterly destroy them. But everything despised and worthless, that they utterly destroyed.

Saul Rejected as King

[10]Now the word of the LORD came to Samuel, saying, [11]"I greatly regret that I have set up Saul *as* king, for he has turned back from following Me, and has not performed My commandments." And it grieved Samuel, and he cried out to the LORD all night. [12]So when Samuel rose early in the morning to meet Saul, it was told Samuel, saying, "Saul went to Carmel, and indeed, he set up a monument for himself; and he has gone on around, passed by, and gone down to Gilgal." [13]Then Samuel went to Saul, and Saul said to him, "Blessed *are* you of the LORD! I have performed the commandment of the LORD."

[14]But Samuel said, "What then *is* this bleating of the sheep in my ears, and the lowing of the oxen which I hear?"

[15]And Saul said, "They have brought them from the Amalekites; for the people spared the best of the sheep and the oxen, to sacrifice to the LORD your God; and the rest we have utterly destroyed."

14:41 [a]Following Masoretic Text and Targum; Septuagint and Vulgate read *Why do You not answer Your servant today? If the injustice is with me or Jonathan my son, O LORD God of Israel, give proof; and if You say it is with Your people Israel, give holiness.*
14:47 [a]Septuagint and Vulgate read *prospered.*
14:49 [a]Called *Abinadab* in 1 Chronicles 8:33 and 9:39

[16]Then Samuel said to Saul, "Be quiet! And I will tell you what the LORD said to me last night." And he said to him, "Speak on."

[17]So Samuel said, "When you *were* little in your own eyes, *were* you not head of the tribes of Israel? And did not the LORD anoint you king over Israel? [18]Now the LORD sent you on a mission, and said, 'Go, and utterly destroy the sinners, the Amalekites, and fight against them until they are consumed.' [19]Why then did you not obey the voice of the LORD? Why did you swoop down on the spoil, and do evil in the sight of the LORD?"

[20]And Saul said to Samuel, "But I have obeyed the voice of the LORD, and gone on the mission on which the LORD sent me, and brought back Agag king of Amalek; I have utterly destroyed the Amalekites. [21]But the people took of the plunder, sheep and oxen, the best of the things which should have been utterly destroyed, to sacrifice to the LORD your God in Gilgal."

[22]So Samuel said:

"Has the LORD *as great* delight in burnt offerings and sacrifices,
As in obeying the voice of the LORD?
Behold, to obey is better than sacrifice,
And to heed than the fat of rams.

[23] For rebellion *is as* the sin of witchcraft,
And stubbornness *is as* iniquity and idolatry.
Because you have rejected the word of the LORD,
He also has rejected you from *being* king."

[24]Then Saul said to Samuel, "I have sinned, for I have transgressed the commandment of the LORD and your words, because I feared the people and obeyed their voice. [25]Now therefore, please pardon my sin, and return with me, that I may worship the LORD."

[26]But Samuel said to Saul, "I will not return with you, for you have rejected the word of the LORD, and the LORD has rejected you from being king over Israel."

[27]And as Samuel turned around to go away, *Saul* seized the edge of his robe, and it tore. [28]So Samuel said to him, "The LORD has torn the kingdom of Israel from you today, and has given it to a neighbor of yours, *who is* better than you. [29]And also the Strength of Israel will not lie nor relent. For He *is* not a man, that He should relent." [30]Then he said, "I have sinned; *yet* honor me now, please, before the elders of my people and before Israel, and return with me, that I may

SAUL — STOPPED LEADING TO SERVE HIS OWN INTERESTS
(1 Samuel 15:1–26)

PROFILE IN LEADERSHIP

The Lord could not have been more specific. Speaking through the prophet Samuel, God commanded King Saul to destroy the Amalekites and everything they owned; no one and no thing was to be spared.

This was to be the supreme test of Saul's fitness to lead God's people—a test he failed miserably. Although he and his army routed the people of Amalek, he disobeyed God by sparing Agag, king of the Amalekites, and took for himself the best of their livestock.

When Samuel confronted Saul about his disobedience, he offered the lame excuse that he intended to sacrifice the livestock to the Lord. His rationalization didn't wash—not in Samuel's eyes and certainly not in God's. From that moment on, his days as king were numbered. And so ended what had looked to be a promising reign.

It is only a matter of time before a leader's heart reveals its true nature: soft and obedient toward the Lord? or hard and self-serving?

Truly godly leaders commit themselves to obeying the commands of God, whether they fully understand those commands or not. What they do know is the truth of Samuel's words: "Behold, to obey is better than sacrifice, and to heed than the fat of rams" (1 Sam. 15:22).

worship the LORD your God." [31]So Samuel turned back after Saul, and Saul worshiped the LORD.

[32]Then Samuel said, "Bring Agag king of the Amalekites here to me." So Agag came to him cautiously.

And Agag said, "Surely the bitterness of death is past."

[33]But Samuel said, "As your sword has made women childless, so shall your mother be childless among women." And Samuel hacked Agag in pieces before the LORD in Gilgal.

[34]Then Samuel went to Ramah, and Saul went up to his house at Gibeah of Saul. [35]And Samuel went no more to see Saul until the day of his death. Nevertheless Samuel mourned for Saul, and the LORD regretted that He had made Saul king over Israel.

David Anointed King

16 Now the LORD said to Samuel, "How long will you mourn for Saul, seeing I have rejected him from reigning over Israel? Fill your horn with oil, and go; I am sending you to Jesse the Bethlehemite. For I have provided Myself a king among his sons."

[2]And Samuel said, "How can I go? If Saul hears it, he will kill me."

But the LORD said, "Take a heifer with you, and say, 'I have come to sacrifice to the LORD.' [3]Then invite Jesse to the sacrifice, and I will show you what you shall do; you shall anoint for Me the one I name to you."

[4]So Samuel did what the LORD said, and went to Bethlehem. And the elders of the town trembled at his coming, and said, "Do you come peaceably?"

[5]And he said, "Peaceably; I have come to sacrifice to the LORD. Sanctify yourselves, and come with me to the sacrifice." Then he consecrated Jesse and his sons, and invited them to the sacrifice.

[6]So it was, when they came, that he looked at Eliab and said, "Surely the LORD's anointed is before Him!"

[7]But the LORD said to Samuel, "Do not look at his appearance or at his physical stature, because I have refused him. For the LORD does not see as man sees;[a] for man looks at the outward appearance, but the LORD looks at the heart."

16:7 [a]Septuagint reads *For God does not see as man sees;* Targum reads *It is not by the appearance of a man;* Vulgate reads *Nor do I judge according to the looks of a man.*

DAVID

A LEADER AFTER GOD'S OWN HEART
(1 Samuel 16:1–13)

PROFILE IN LEADERSHIP

The selection of David to be Israel's king illustrates how God often disregards human customs and traditions to accomplish His purposes.

By human standards, David, as the youngest son of Jesse, appeared least likely to be considered for a leadership position. But God saw the heart of this young man and knew that His people needed a leader with a tenderness of spirit. David might have become a warrior, but gentleness was his defining trait.

David developed into a leader of courage with wisdom and strength beyond his years. He demonstrated his godly spirit through his willingness to take on Goliath while the great warriors of Israel hid in their tents (1 Sam. 17:40–50). David enjoyed a clear sense of dependence on God and made sure God would get the glory for any success in his life.

David began his leadership journey as low man on the totem pole. He did what was asked of him with a great attitude, having fun along the way. While his own brothers looked down on him, God lifted him up.

David's life illustrates that faithfulness in small things often results in much larger assignments and greater responsibility down the road. David loved the Lord and lived his life as a man after God's own heart (13:14).

[8]So Jesse called Abinadab, and made him pass before Samuel. And he said, "Neither has the LORD chosen this one." [9]Then Jesse made Shammah pass by. And he said, "Neither has the LORD chosen this one." [10]Thus Jesse made seven of his sons pass before Samuel. And Samuel said to Jesse, "The LORD has not chosen these."

How Do You Recognize a Leader?

(1 Samuel 16:6–10)

When did David first become a leader? The Bible makes it clear that the young man had become a leader long before he ever received a title.

This young leader first began to surface in 1 Samuel 16—but only God and Samuel recognized his leadership at first. Only after his great and unexpected victory over Goliath did everyone else recognize his special abilities (1 Sam. 17:55–58).

David's example shows that true leaders always declare themselves without making any announcements. It becomes obvious. Too often, we feel forced to pick someone to lead, whether or not they are a leader—and that's when wrong motives and false criteria emerge. What can we learn from 1 Samuel 16?

Mistakes We Make When Picking a Leader

1. Looking at looks (vv. 6, 7)
2. Picking from the past (vv. 6, 7)
3. Picking from the pecking order (vv. 8–10)
4. Opting for age and tenure over ability (vv. 8–10)

---

[11]And Samuel said to Jesse, "Are all the young men here?" Then he said, "There remains yet the youngest, and there he is, keeping the sheep."

And Samuel said to Jesse, "Send and bring him. For we will not sit down[a] till he comes here." [12]So he sent and brought him in. Now he *was* ruddy, with bright eyes, and good-looking. And the LORD said, "Arise, anoint him; for this *is* the one!" [13]Then Samuel took the horn of oil and anointed him in the midst of his brothers; and the Spirit of the LORD came upon David from that day forward. So Samuel arose and went to Ramah.

A Distressing Spirit Troubles Saul

[14]But the Spirit of the LORD departed from Saul, and a distressing spirit from the LORD troubled him. [15]And Saul's servants said to him, "Surely, a distressing spirit from God is troubling you. [16]Let our master now command your servants, *who are* before you, to seek out a man *who is* a skillful player on the harp. And it shall be that he will play it with his hand when the distressing spirit from God is upon you, and you shall be well."

[17]So Saul said to his servants, "Provide me now a man who can play well, and bring *him* to me."

[18]Then one of the servants answered and said, "Look, I have seen a son of Jesse the Bethlehemite, *who is* skillful in playing, a mighty man of valor, a man of war, prudent in speech, and a handsome person; and the LORD *is* with him."

[19]Therefore Saul sent messengers to Jesse, and said, "Send me your son David, who *is* with the sheep." [20]And Jesse took a donkey *loaded with* bread, a skin of wine, and a young goat, and sent *them* by his son David to Saul. [21]So David came to Saul and stood before him. And he loved him greatly, and he became his armorbearer. [22]Then Saul sent to Jesse, saying, "Please let David stand before me, for he has found favor in my sight." [23]And so it was, whenever the spirit from God was upon Saul, that David would take a harp and play *it* with his hand. Then Saul would become refreshed and well, and the distressing spirit would depart from him.

David and Goliath

17 Now the Philistines gathered their armies together to battle, and were gathered at Sochoh, which *belongs to* Judah; they encamped between Sochoh and Azekah, in Ephes Dammim. [2]And Saul and the men of Israel were gathered together, and they encamped in the Valley of Elah, and drew up in battle array against the Philistines. [3]The Philistines stood on a mountain on one side, and Israel stood on a mountain on the other side, with a valley between them.

[4]And a champion went out from the camp of the Philistines, named Goliath, from Gath, whose height *was* six cubits and a span. [5]*He had* a bronze helmet on his head, and he *was* armed with a coat of mail, and the weight of the coat *was* five thousand shekels of bronze. [6]And *he had* bronze

---

16:11 [a]Following Septuagint and Vulgate; Masoretic Text reads *turn around;* Targum and Syriac read *turn away.*

armor on his legs and a bronze javelin between his shoulders. [7]Now the staff of his spear *was* like a weaver's beam, and his iron spearhead *weighed* six hundred shekels; and a shield-bearer went before him. [8]Then he stood and cried out to the armies of Israel, and said to them, "Why have you come out to line up for battle? *Am* I not a Philistine, and you the servants of Saul? Choose a man for yourselves, and let him come down to me. [9]If he is able to fight with me and kill me, then we will be your servants. But if I prevail against him and kill him, then you shall be our servants and serve us." [10]And the Philistine said, "I defy the armies of Israel this day; give me a man, that we may fight together." [11]When Saul and all Israel heard these words of the Philistine, they were dismayed and greatly afraid.

[12]Now David *was* the son of that Ephrathite of Bethlehem Judah, whose name *was* Jesse, and who had eight sons. And the man was old, advanced *in years,* in the days of Saul. [13]The three oldest sons of Jesse had gone to follow Saul to the battle. The names of his three sons who went to the battle *were* Eliab the firstborn, next to him

Abinadab, and the third Shammah. [14]David *was* the youngest. And the three oldest followed Saul. [15]But David occasionally went and returned from Saul to feed his father's sheep at Bethlehem.

[16]And the Philistine drew near and presented himself forty days, morning and evening.

[17]Then Jesse said to his son David, "Take now for your brothers an ephah of this dried *grain* and these ten loaves, and run to your brothers at the camp. [18]And carry these ten cheeses to the captain of *their* thousand, and see how your brothers fare, and bring back news of them." [19]Now Saul and they and all the men of Israel *were* in the Valley of Elah, fighting with the Philistines.

[20]So David rose early in the morning, left the sheep with a keeper, and took *the things* and went as Jesse had commanded him. And he came to the camp as the army was going out to the fight and shouting for the battle. [21]For Israel and the Philistines had drawn up in battle array, army against army. [22]And David left his supplies in the hand of the supply keeper, ran to the army, and came and greeted his brothers. [23]Then as he talked with them, there was the champion, the

The Law of Victory:
David Defeats Goliath and Everyone Wins
(1 Samuel 17:19–58)

Victory is always fun. No one likes to lose. But when a leader practices the Law of Victory, it impacts more than the leader. It affects everyone around the leader.

Consider David in his battle with Goliath. By practicing this law, he transformed the once-paralyzed Israelite soldiers into a force capable of defeating the "invincible" Philistine army. Here's how he did it:

1. *His perspective differed from others.*
   He didn't see what everyone else saw, an invincible giant. He saw an opportunity.
2. *His methods differed from others.*
   He decided to use proven weapons that he knew would work, not the conventional ones.
3. *His conviction differed from others.*
   He recognized Goliath had no covenant with God, while he felt passionately committed to God's covenant.
4. *His motives differed from others.*
   He heard Goliath's threats against the God of Israel and knew God could beat him.
5. *His vision differed from others.*
   He wanted to make Yahweh known to the world as the most powerful God on earth.
6. *His experience differed from others.*
   He brought to the battlefield past victories over a lion and bear, not months of paralyzing fear.
7. *His attitude differed from others.*
   He saw Goliath not as a threat too big to hit, but as a target too big to miss!

Philistine of Gath, Goliath by name, coming up from the armies of the Philistines; and he spoke according to the same words. So David heard *them*. ²⁴And all the men of Israel, when they saw the man, fled from him and were dreadfully afraid. ²⁵So the men of Israel said, "Have you seen this man who has come up? Surely he has come up to defy Israel; and it shall be *that* the man who kills him the king will enrich with great riches, will give him his daughter, and give his father's house exemption *from taxes* in Israel."

²⁶Then David spoke to the men who stood by him, saying, "What shall be done for the man who kills this Philistine and takes away the reproach from Israel? For who *is* this uncircumcised Philistine, that he should defy the armies of the living God?"

²⁷And the people answered him in this manner, saying, "So shall it be done for the man who kills him."

²⁸Now Eliab his oldest brother heard when he spoke to the men; and Eliab's anger was aroused against David, and he said, "Why did you come down here? And with whom have you left those few sheep in the wilderness? I know your pride and the insolence of your heart, for you have come down to see the battle."

²⁹And David said, "What have I done now? *Is there* not a cause?" ³⁰Then he turned from him toward another and said the same thing; and these people answered him as the first ones *did*.

³¹Now when the words which David spoke were heard, they reported *them* to Saul; and he sent for him. ³²Then David said to Saul, "Let no man's heart fail because of him; your servant will go and fight with this Philistine."

³³And Saul said to David, "You are not able to go against this Philistine to fight with him; for you *are* a youth, and he a man of war from his youth."

³⁴But David said to Saul, "Your servant used to keep his father's sheep, and when a lion or a bear came and took a lamb out of the flock, ³⁵I went out after it and struck it, and delivered *the lamb* from its mouth; and when it arose against me, I caught *it* by its beard, and struck and killed it. ³⁶Your servant has killed both lion and bear; and this uncircumcised Philistine will be like one of them, seeing he has defied the armies of the living God." ³⁷Moreover David said, "The LORD, who delivered me from the paw of the lion and from the paw of the bear, He will deliver me from the hand of this Philistine."

And Saul said to David, "Go, and the LORD be with you!"

³⁸So Saul clothed David with his armor, and

The Law of the Lid: Leadership Determined Saul and David's Success

(1 Samuel 17:24–40)

When Goliath taunted the armies of Israel, the frightened Hebrew soldiers forgot how to fight. They lacked a leader who could provide a strategy for success.

Saul was a very experienced soldier, but he cowered in fear with his men. David, on the other hand, sized up the situation, determined his weapon (a sling and five smooth stones) and ran toward Goliath.

Saul suffered under a lid of fear, paralyzed from leading. David labored under no such lid. Once he conquered the giant, the Israelite armies joined him to finish off the Philistines.

he put a bronze helmet on his head; he also clothed him with a coat of mail. ³⁹David fastened his sword to his armor and tried to walk, for he had not tested *them*. And David said to Saul, "I cannot walk with these, for I have not tested *them*." So David took them off.

⁴⁰Then he took his staff in his hand; and he chose for himself five smooth stones from the brook, and put them in a shepherd's bag, in a pouch which he had, and his sling was in his hand. And he drew near to the Philistine. ⁴¹So the Philistine came, and began drawing near to David, and the man who bore the shield *went* before him. ⁴²And when the Philistine looked about and saw David, he disdained him; for he was *only* a youth, ruddy and good-looking. ⁴³So the Philistine said to David, "*Am* I a dog, that you come to me with sticks?" And the Philistine cursed David by his gods. ⁴⁴And the Philistine said to David, "Come to me, and I will give your flesh to the birds of the air and the beasts of the field!"

⁴⁵Then David said to the Philistine, "You come to me with a sword, with a spear, and with a javelin. But I come to you in the name of the LORD of hosts, the God of the armies of Israel, whom you have defied. ⁴⁶This day the LORD will deliver you into my hand, and I will strike you and take your head from you. And this day I will give the carcasses of the camp of the Philistines to the birds of the air and the wild beasts of the

earth, that all the earth may know that there is a God in Israel. [47]Then all this assembly shall know that the LORD does not save with sword and spear; for the battle *is* the LORD's, and He will give you into our hands."

[48]So it was, when the Philistine arose and came and drew near to meet David, that David hurried and ran toward the army to meet the Philistine. [49]Then David put his hand in his bag and took out a stone; and he slung *it* and struck the Philistine in his forehead, so that the stone sank into his forehead, and he fell on his face to the earth. [50]So David prevailed over the Philistine with a sling and a stone, and struck the Philistine and killed him. But *there was* no sword in the hand of David. [51]Therefore David ran and stood over the Philistine, took his sword and drew it out of its sheath and killed him, and cut off his head with it.

And when the Philistines saw that their champion was dead, they fled. [52]Now the men of Israel and Judah arose and shouted, and pursued the Philistines as far as the entrance of the valley[a] and to the gates of Ekron. And the wounded of the Philistines fell along the road to Shaaraim, even as far as Gath and Ekron. [53]Then the children of Israel returned from chasing the Philistines, and they plundered their tents. [54]And David took the head of the Philistine and brought it to Jerusalem, but he put his armor in his tent.

[55]When Saul saw David going out against the Philistine, he said to Abner, the commander of the army, "Abner, whose son *is* this youth?"

And Abner said, "As your soul lives, O king, I do not know."

[56]So the king said, "Inquire whose son this young man *is*."

[57]Then, as David returned from the slaughter of the Philistine, Abner took him and brought him before Saul with the head of the Philistine in his hand. [58]And Saul said to him, "Whose son *are* you, young man?"

So David answered, "*I am* the son of your servant Jesse the Bethlehemite."

Saul Resents David

18 Now when he had finished speaking to Saul, the soul of Jonathan was knit to the soul of David, and Jonathan loved him as his own soul. [2]Saul took him that day, and would not let him go home to his father's house anymore. [3]Then Jonathan and David made a covenant, because he loved him as his own soul. [4]And Jonathan took off the robe that *was* on him and gave it to David, with his armor, even to his sword and his bow and his belt.

[5]So David went out wherever Saul sent him, *and* behaved wisely. And Saul set him over the men of war, and he was accepted in the sight of all the people and also in the sight of Saul's servants. [6]Now it had happened as they were coming *home,* when David was returning from the slaughter of the Philistine, that the women had come out of all the cities of Israel, singing and dancing, to meet King Saul, with tambourines, with joy, and with musical instruments. [7]So the women sang as they danced, and said:

"Saul has slain his thousands,
    And David his ten thousands."

[8]Then Saul was very angry, and the saying displeased him; and he said, "They have ascribed to David ten thousands, and to me they have ascribed *only* thousands. Now *what* more can he have but the kingdom?" [9]So Saul eyed David from that day forward.

[10]And it happened on the next day that the distressing spirit from God came upon Saul, and he prophesied inside the house. So David played *music* with his hand, as at other times; but *there was* a spear in Saul's hand. [11]And Saul cast the spear, for he said, "I will pin David to the wall!" But David escaped his presence twice.

[12]Now Saul was afraid of David, because the LORD was with him, but had departed from Saul. [13]Therefore Saul removed him from his presence, and made him his captain over a thousand; and he went out and came in before the people. [14]And David behaved wisely in all his ways, and the LORD *was* with him. [15]Therefore, when Saul saw that he behaved very wisely, he was afraid of him. [16]But all Israel and Judah loved David, because he went out and came in before them.

David Marries Michal

[17]Then Saul said to David, "Here is my older daughter Merab; I will give her to you as a wife. Only be valiant for me, and fight the LORD's battles." For Saul thought, "Let my hand not be against him, but let the hand of the Philistines be against him."

[18]So David said to Saul, "Who *am* I, and what *is* my life *or* my father's family in Israel, that I should be son-in-law to the king?" [19]But it happened at the time when Merab, Saul's daughter, should have been given to David, that she was given to Adriel the Meholathite as a wife.

[20]Now Michal, Saul's daughter, loved David.

17:52 [a]Following Masoretic Text, Syriac, Targum, and Vulgate; Septuagint reads *Gath.*

The Law of Empowerment:
Saul Couldn't Give Away His Power

(1 Samuel 18:7–29)

King Saul clearly recognized David as a mighty warrior, a valuable team member, an obedient servant, a favored man, and an effective leader. He also clearly saw him as a potential successor and threat.

Things didn't get better when he heard the Israelite ladies compare the two—and Saul came out second best (1 Sam. 18:7). Saul's insecurity and fear drove him to turn against David. Insecurity often drives a leader to do stupid and self-sabotaging things.

1. Saul looked at David's every activity with suspicion (v. 9).
2. Saul hurled his spear at David to try to kill him (v. 11).
3. Saul feared David because God's Spirit was with him (v. 12).
4. Saul changed David's position to prevent them from seeing each other (v. 13).
5. Saul dreaded being compared to David in any way (vv. 15, 16).
6. Saul put David in charge of 1,000 troops in hopes that the Philistines would kill him (vv. 13, 17).
7. Saul gave his daughter Michal to David, hoping she would be a snare to him (vv. 20, 21).
8. Saul sponsored secrets to deceive David (v. 22).
9. Saul perceived himself as David's enemy (v. 29).

And they told Saul, and the thing pleased him. ²¹So Saul said, "I will give her to him, that she may be a snare to him, and that the hand of the Philistines may be against him." Therefore Saul said to David a second time, "You shall be my son-in-law today."

²²And Saul commanded his servants, "Communicate with David secretly, and say, 'Look, the king has delight in you, and all his servants love you. Now therefore, become the king's son-in-law.'"

²³So Saul's servants spoke those words in the hearing of David. And David said, "Does it seem to you a light thing to be a king's son-in-law, seeing I am a poor and lightly esteemed man?" ²⁴And the servants of Saul told him, saying, "In this manner David spoke."

²⁵Then Saul said, "Thus you shall say to David: 'The king does not desire any dowry but one hundred foreskins of the Philistines, to take vengeance on the king's enemies.'" But Saul thought to make David fall by the hand of the Philistines. ²⁶So when his servants told David these words, it pleased David well to become the king's son-in-law. Now the days had not expired; ²⁷therefore David arose and went, he and his men, and killed two hundred men of the Philistines. And David brought their foreskins, and they gave them in full count to the king, that he might become the king's son-in-law. Then Saul gave him Michal his daughter as a wife.

²⁸Thus Saul saw and knew that the LORD was with David, and that Michal, Saul's daughter, loved him; ²⁹and Saul was still more afraid of David. So Saul became David's enemy continually. ³⁰Then the princes of the Philistines went out to war. And so it was, whenever they went out, that David behaved more wisely than all the servants of Saul, so that his name became highly esteemed.

Saul Persecutes David

19 Now Saul spoke to Jonathan his son and to all his servants, that they should kill David; but Jonathan, Saul's son, delighted greatly in David. ²So Jonathan told David, saying, "My father Saul seeks to kill you. Therefore please be on your guard until morning, and stay in a secret place and hide. ³And I will go out and stand beside my father in the field where you are, and I will speak with my father about you. Then what I observe, I will tell you."

⁴Thus Jonathan spoke well of David to Saul his father, and said to him, "Let not the king sin against his servant, against David, because he has not sinned against you, and because his works have been very good toward you. ⁵For he took his

life in his hands and killed the Philistine, and the LORD brought about a great deliverance for all Israel. You saw *it* and rejoiced. Why then will you sin against innocent blood, to kill David without a cause?"

⁶So Saul heeded the voice of Jonathan, and Saul swore, "*As* the LORD lives, he shall not be killed." ⁷Then Jonathan called David, and Jonathan told him all these things. So Jonathan brought David to Saul, and he was in his presence as in times past.

⁸And there was war again; and David went out and fought with the Philistines, and struck them with a mighty blow, and they fled from him.

⁹Now the distressing spirit from the LORD came upon Saul as he sat in his house with his spear in his hand. And David was playing *music* with *his* hand. ¹⁰Then Saul sought to pin David to the wall with the spear, but he slipped away from Saul's presence; and he drove the spear into the wall. So David fled and escaped that night.

¹¹Saul also sent messengers to David's house to watch him and to kill him in the morning. And Michal, David's wife, told him, saying, "If you do not save your life tonight, tomorrow you will be killed." ¹²So Michal let David down through a window. And he went and fled and escaped. ¹³And Michal took an image and laid *it* in the bed, put a cover of goats' *hair* for his head, and covered *it* with clothes. ¹⁴So when Saul sent messengers to take David, she said, "He *is* sick."

¹⁵Then Saul sent the messengers *back* to see David, saying, "Bring him up to me in the bed, that I may kill him." ¹⁶And when the messengers had come in, there was the image in the bed, with a cover of goats' *hair* for his head. ¹⁷Then Saul said to Michal, "Why have you deceived me like this, and sent my enemy away, so that he has escaped?"

And Michal answered Saul, "He said to me, 'Let me go! Why should I kill you?'"

¹⁸So David fled and escaped, and went to Samuel at Ramah, and told him all that Saul had done to him. And he and Samuel went and stayed in Naioth. ¹⁹Now it was told Saul, saying, "Take note, David *is* at Naioth in Ramah!" ²⁰Then Saul sent messengers to take David. And when they saw the group of prophets prophesying, and Samuel standing *as* leader over them, the Spirit of God came upon the messengers of Saul, and they also prophesied. ²¹And when Saul was told, he sent other messengers, and they prophesied likewise. Then Saul sent messengers again

DAVID
PARTNERSHIP WITH JONATHAN ENABLES HIM TO ENDURE
(1 Samuel 19:1—23:18)

PROFILE IN LEADERSHIP

No leader succeeds on his own—not even a great leader whom God called "a man after My own heart" (Acts 13:22), and "the apple of [My] eye" (Ps. 17:8). Even David needed his Jonathan.

In the dark days when he scrambled from cave to cave to escape the murderous threats of King Saul, David turned to his friend, Jonathan, for strength and encouragement. At great risk to himself, Jonathan warned David and told him to hide out for a time (1 Sam. 19:2). Jonathan, hoping to pacify his father and reconcile the king to his friend, spoke well of David. And for a short while Saul relented, promising that David would not die by his hand.

Soon the old animosities reasserted themselves, however, and Jonathan once again risked his life to help his dear friend (20:30–33). Even though he knew that God had chosen David—and not him—to rule Israel, Jonathan remained faithful to his comrade until the very end of his life. One verse in particular describes Jonathan's invaluable ministry to David: "Then Jonathan, Saul's son, arose and went to David in the woods and strengthened his hand in God" (23:16).

Do you have someone who "strengthens your hand in God"? All leaders need loyal friends who can help them to persevere through the tough times.

the third time, and they prophesied also. ²²Then he also went to Ramah, and came to the great well that *is* at Sechu. So he asked, and said, "Where *are* Samuel and David?"

And *someone* said, "Indeed *they are* at Naioth in Ramah." ²³So he went there to Naioth in Ramah. Then the Spirit of God was upon him also, and he went on and prophesied until he came to Naioth in Ramah. ²⁴And he also stripped off his clothes and prophesied before Samuel in like manner, and lay down naked all that day and all that night. Therefore they say, "*Is* Saul also among the prophets?"[a]

Jonathan's Loyalty to David

20 Then David fled from Naioth in Ramah, and went and said to Jonathan, "What have I done? What *is* my iniquity, and what *is* my sin before your father, that he seeks my life?"

²So Jonathan said to him, "By no means! You shall not die! Indeed, my father will do nothing either great or small without first telling me. And why should my father hide this thing from me? It *is* not *so!*"

³Then David took an oath again, and said, "Your father certainly knows that I have found favor in your eyes, and he has said, 'Do not let Jonathan know this, lest he be grieved.' But truly, *as* the LORD lives and *as* your soul lives, *there is* but a step between me and death."

⁴So Jonathan said to David, "Whatever you yourself desire, I will do *it* for you."

⁵And David said to Jonathan, "Indeed tomorrow *is* the New Moon, and I should not fail to sit with the king to eat. But let me go, that I may hide in the field until the third *day* at evening. ⁶If your father misses me at all, then say, 'David earnestly asked *permission* of me that he might run over to Bethlehem, his city, for *there is* a yearly sacrifice there for all the family.' ⁷If he says thus: '*It is* well,' your servant will be safe. But if he is very angry, be sure that evil is determined by him. ⁸Therefore you shall deal kindly with your servant, for you have brought your servant into a covenant of the LORD with you. Nevertheless, if there is iniquity in me, kill me yourself, for why should you bring me to your father?"

⁹But Jonathan said, "Far be it from you! For if I knew certainly that evil was determined by my father to come upon you, then would I not tell you?"

¹⁰Then David said to Jonathan, "Who will tell me, or what *if* your father answers you roughly?"

¹¹And Jonathan said to David, "Come, let us go out into the field." So both of them went out

The Law of Connection: Covenant Love Draws Commitment

(1 Samuel 20:1–41)

Although Jonathan was the royal prince, he exalted and encouraged David, knowing he risked his future throne. First Samuel 20 describes the four characteristics of their friendship. Jonathan was: available (vv. 1–4); dependable (vv. 5–17); vulnerable (vv. 18–33); and responsible (vv. 34–42). And so Jonathan won David's loyalty (v. 41).

into the field. ¹²Then Jonathan said to David: "The LORD God of Israel *is witness!* When I have sounded out my father sometime tomorrow, *or* the third *day,* and indeed *there is* good toward David, and I do not send to you and tell you, ¹³may the LORD do so and much more to Jonathan. But if it pleases my father *to do* you evil, then I will report it to you and send you away, that you may go in safety. And the LORD be with you as He has been with my father. ¹⁴And you shall not only show me the kindness of the LORD while I still live, that I may not die; ¹⁵but you shall not cut off your kindness from my house forever, no, not when the LORD has cut off every one of the enemies of David from the face of the earth." ¹⁶So Jonathan made *a covenant* with the house of David, *saying,* "Let the LORD require *it* at the hand of David's enemies."

¹⁷Now Jonathan again caused David to vow, because he loved him; for he loved him as he loved his own soul. ¹⁸Then Jonathan said to David, "Tomorrow *is* the New Moon; and you will be missed, because your seat will be empty. ¹⁹And *when* you have stayed three days, go down quickly and come to the place where you hid on the day of the deed; and remain by the stone Ezel. ²⁰Then I will shoot three arrows to the side, as though I shot at a target; ²¹and there I will send a lad, *saying,* 'Go, find the arrows.' If I expressly say to the lad, 'Look, the arrows *are* on this side of you; get them and come'—then, as the LORD lives, *there is* safety for you and no harm. ²²But if I say thus to the young man, 'Look, the arrows *are* beyond you'—go your way, for the LORD has sent you away. ²³And as for the matter which you

19:24 [a]Compare 1 Samuel 10:12

and I have spoken of, indeed the LORD *be* between you and me forever."

²⁴Then David hid in the field. And when the New Moon had come, the king sat down to eat the feast. ²⁵Now the king sat on his seat, as at other times, on a seat by the wall. And Jonathan arose,ª and Abner sat by Saul's side, but David's place was empty. ²⁶Nevertheless Saul did not say anything that day, for he thought, "Something has happened to him; he *is* unclean, surely he *is* unclean." ²⁷And it happened the next day, the second *day* of the month, that David's place was empty. And Saul said to Jonathan his son, "Why has the son of Jesse not come to eat, either yesterday or today?"

²⁸So Jonathan answered Saul, "David earnestly asked *permission* of me *to go* to Bethlehem. ²⁹And he said, 'Please let me go, for our family has a sacrifice in the city, and my brother has commanded me *to be there*. And now, if I have found favor in your eyes, please let me get away and see my brothers.' Therefore he has not come to the king's table."

³⁰Then Saul's anger was aroused against Jonathan, and he said to him, "You son of a perverse, rebellious *woman!* Do I not know that you have chosen the son of Jesse to your own shame and to the shame of your mother's nakedness? ³¹For as long as the son of Jesse lives on the earth, you shall not be established, nor your kingdom. Now therefore, send and bring him to me, for he shall surely die."

³²And Jonathan answered Saul his father, and said to him, "Why should he be killed? What has he done?" ³³Then Saul cast a spear at him to kill him, by which Jonathan knew that it was determined by his father to kill David.

³⁴So Jonathan arose from the table in fierce anger, and ate no food the second day of the month, for he was grieved for David, because his father had treated him shamefully.

³⁵And so it was, in the morning, that Jonathan went out into the field at the time appointed with David, and a little lad *was* with him. ³⁶Then he said to his lad, "Now run, find the arrows which I shoot." As the lad ran, he shot an arrow beyond him. ³⁷When the lad had come to the place where the arrow was which Jonathan had shot, Jonathan cried out after the lad and said, "*Is* not the arrow beyond you?" ³⁸And Jonathan cried out after the lad, "Make haste, hurry, do not delay!" So Jonathan's lad gathered up the arrows and came back to his master. ³⁹But the lad did not know anything. Only Jonathan and David knew of the matter. ⁴⁰Then Jonathan gave his weapons to his lad, and said to him, "Go, carry *them* to the city."

⁴¹As soon as the lad had gone, David arose from *a place* toward the south, fell on his face to the ground, and bowed down three times. And they kissed one another; and they wept together, but David more so. ⁴²Then Jonathan said to David, "Go in peace, since we have both sworn in the name of the LORD, saying, 'May the LORD be between you and me, and between your descendants and my descendants, forever.'" So he arose and departed, and Jonathan went into the city.

David and the Holy Bread

21 Now David came to Nob, to Ahimelech the priest. And Ahimelech was afraid when he met David, and said to him, "Why *are* you alone, and no one is with you?"

²So David said to Ahimelech the priest, "The king has ordered me on some business, and said to me, 'Do not let anyone know anything about the business on which I send you, or what I have commanded you.' And I have directed *my* young men to such and such a place. ³Now therefore, what have you on hand? Give *me* five *loaves of* bread in my hand, or whatever can be found."

⁴And the priest answered David and said, "*There is* no common bread on hand; but there is holy bread, if the young men have at least kept themselves from women."

⁵Then David answered the priest, and said to him, "Truly, women *have been* kept from us about three days since I came out. And the vessels of the young men are holy, and *the bread is* in effect common, even though it was consecrated in the vessel this day."

⁶So the priest gave him holy *bread;* for there was no bread there but the showbread which had been taken from before the LORD, in order to put hot bread *in its place* on the day when it was taken away.

⁷Now a certain man of the servants of Saul *was* there that day, detained before the LORD. And his name *was* Doeg, an Edomite, the chief of the herdsmen who *belonged* to Saul.

⁸And David said to Ahimelech, "Is there not here on hand a spear or a sword? For I have brought neither my sword nor my weapons with me, because the king's business required haste."

⁹So the priest said, "The sword of Goliath the Philistine, whom you killed in the Valley of Elah, there it is, wrapped in a cloth behind the ephod.

20:25 ªFollowing Masoretic Text, Syriac, Targum, and Vulgate; Septuagint reads *he sat across from Jonathan.*

If you will take that, take *it*. For *there is* no other except that one here."

And David said, "*There is* none like it; give it to me."

David Flees to Gath

[10]Then David arose and fled that day from before Saul, and went to Achish the king of Gath. [11]And the servants of Achish said to him, "*Is* this not David the king of the land? Did they not sing of him to one another in dances, saying:

'Saul has slain his thousands,
And David his ten thousands'?"[a]

[12]Now David took these words to heart, and was very much afraid of Achish the king of Gath. [13]So he changed his behavior before them, pretended madness in their hands, scratched on the doors of the gate, and let his saliva fall down on his beard. [14]Then Achish said to his servants, "Look, you see the man is insane. Why have you brought him to me? [15]Have I need of madmen, that you have brought this *fellow* to play the madman in my presence? Shall this *fellow* come into my house?"

David's Four Hundred Men

22 David therefore departed from there and escaped to the cave of Adullam. So when his brothers and all his father's house heard *it,* they went down there to him. [2]And everyone *who was* in distress, everyone who *was* in debt, and everyone *who was* discontented gathered to him. So he became captain over them. And there were about four hundred men with him.

[3]Then David went from there to Mizpah of Moab; and he said to the king of Moab, "Please let my father and mother come here with you, till I know what God will do for me." [4]So he brought them before the king of Moab, and they dwelt with him all the time that David was in the stronghold.

[5]Now the prophet Gad said to David, "Do not stay in the stronghold; depart, and go to the land of Judah." So David departed and went into the forest of Hereth.

Saul Murders the Priests

[6]When Saul heard that David and the men who *were* with him had been discovered—now Saul was staying in Gibeah under a tamarisk tree in Ramah, with his spear in his hand, and all his servants standing about him— [7]then Saul said to his servants who stood about him, "Hear now,

you Benjamites! Will the son of Jesse give every one of you fields and vineyards, *and* make you all captains of thousands and captains of hundreds? [8]All of you have conspired against me, and *there is* no one who reveals to me that my son has made a covenant with the son of Jesse; and *there is* not one of you who is sorry for me or reveals to me that my son has stirred up my servant against me, to lie in wait, as *it is* this day."

[9]Then answered Doeg the Edomite, who was set over the servants of Saul, and said, "I saw the son of Jesse going to Nob, to Ahimelech the son of Ahitub. [10]And he inquired of the LORD for him, gave him provisions, and gave him the sword of Goliath the Philistine."

[11]So the king sent to call Ahimelech the priest, the son of Ahitub, and all his father's house, the priests who *were* in Nob. And they all came to the king. [12]And Saul said, "Hear now, son of Ahitub!"

He answered, "Here I am, my lord."

[13]Then Saul said to him, "Why have you conspired against me, you and the son of Jesse, in that you have given him bread and a sword, and have inquired of God for him, that he should rise against me, to lie in wait, as it is this day?"

[14]So Ahimelech answered the king and said, "And who among all your servants *is as* faithful as David, who is the king's son-in-law, who goes at your bidding, and is honorable in your house? [15]Did I then begin to inquire of God for him? Far be it from me! Let not the king impute anything to his servant, *or* to any in the house of my father. For your servant knew nothing of all this, little or much."

[16]And the king said, "You shall surely die, Ahimelech, you and all your father's house!" [17]Then the king said to the guards who stood about him, "Turn and kill the priests of the LORD, because their hand also *is* with David, and because they knew when he fled and did not tell it to me." But the servants of the king would not lift their hands to strike the priests of the LORD. [18]And the king said to Doeg, "You turn and kill the priests!" So Doeg the Edomite turned and struck the priests, and killed on that day eighty-five men who wore a linen ephod. [19]Also Nob, the city of the priests, he struck with the edge of the sword, both men and women, children and nursing infants, oxen and donkeys and sheep—with the edge of the sword.

[20]Now one of the sons of Ahimelech the son of Ahitub, named Abiathar, escaped and fled after David. [21]And Abiathar told David that Saul had

---

21:11 [a]Compare 1 Samuel 18:7

The Law of Buy-In: David Draws Loyal Renegades

(1 Samuel 22:1—23:29)

After David fled from Saul to the cave of Adullam, four hundred men sought him out to follow his leadership. The Bible describes these men as in distress, in debt, and discontented. Obviously, David had to train these "losers" if he was to create an effective army. And he did.

These men eventually became like David. Some even killed giants, as he did—a classic example of the Law of Buy-In. They first bought into David, then into his vision and leadership. Observe what David teaches us about his leadership:

1. David attracted these men even without pursuing them.
2. David drew deep loyalty out of them without ever trying to get it.
3. David transformed these men without disenchanting them over their initial state.
4. David fought alongside these "losers" and turned them into winners.

Consider the astounding exploits of some of these men. Second Samuel 23 tells us that Adino slew 800 men with a spear in one battle (v. 8); Eleazar struck down the enemy until his hand clung to his sword (vv. 9, 10); Shammah defended a plot of ground against an enemy army (vv. 11, 12). Three of these men snuck behind enemy lines just to get David a drink of water from a well in Bethlehem (vv. 15–17). David attracted men like him—souls in distress. He also reproduced men like him—warriors and conquerors.

killed the LORD's priests. ²²So David said to Abiathar, "I knew that day, when Doeg the Edomite *was* there, that he would surely tell Saul. I have caused *the death* of all the persons of your father's house. ²³Stay with me; do not fear. For he who seeks my life seeks your life, but with me you *shall be safe.*"

David Saves the City of Keilah

23 Then they told David, saying, "Look, the Philistines are fighting against Keilah, and they are robbing the threshing floors."

²Therefore David inquired of the LORD, saying, "Shall I go and attack these Philistines?"

And the LORD said to David, "Go and attack the Philistines, and save Keilah."

³But David's men said to him, "Look, we are afraid here in Judah. How much more then if we go to Keilah against the armies of the Philistines?"

⁴Then David inquired of the LORD once again.

And the LORD answered him and said, "Arise, go down to Keilah. For I will deliver the Philistines into your hand." ⁵And David and his men went to Keilah and fought with the Philistines, struck them with a mighty blow, and took away their livestock. So David saved the inhabitants of Keilah.

⁶Now it happened, when Abiathar the son of Ahimelech fled to David at Keilah, *that* he went down *with* an ephod in his hand.

⁷And Saul was told that David had gone to Keilah. So Saul said, "God has delivered him into my hand, for he has shut himself in by entering a town that has gates and bars." ⁸Then Saul called all the people together for war, to go down to Keilah to besiege David and his men.

⁹When David knew that Saul plotted evil against him, he said to Abiathar the priest, "Bring the ephod here." ¹⁰Then David said, "O LORD God of Israel, Your servant has certainly heard that Saul seeks to come to Keilah to destroy the city for my sake. ¹¹Will the men of Keilah deliver me into his hand? Will Saul come down, as Your servant has heard? O LORD God of Israel, I pray, tell Your servant."

And the LORD said, "He will come down."

¹²Then David said, "Will the men of Keilah deliver me and my men into the hand of Saul?"

And the LORD said, "They will deliver *you.*"

¹³So David and his men, about six hundred, arose and departed from Keilah and went wherever they could go. Then it was told Saul that David had escaped from Keilah; so he halted the expedition.

David in Wilderness Strongholds

¹⁴And David stayed in strongholds in the wilderness, and remained in the mountains in the Wilderness of Ziph. Saul sought him every day, but God did not deliver him into his hand. ¹⁵So David saw that Saul had come out to seek

his life. And David *was* in the Wilderness of Ziph in a forest.[a] [16]Then Jonathan, Saul's son, arose and went to David in the woods and strengthened his hand in God. [17]And he said to him, "Do not fear, for the hand of Saul my father shall not find you. You shall be king over Israel, and I shall be next to you. Even my father Saul knows that." [18]So the two of them made a covenant before the LORD. And David stayed in the woods, and Jonathan went to his own house.

[19]Then the Ziphites came up to Saul at Gibeah, saying, "Is David not hiding with us in strongholds in the woods, in the hill of Hachilah, which *is* on the south of Jeshimon? [20]Now therefore, O king, come down according to all the desire of your soul to come down; and our part *shall be* to deliver him into the king's hand."

[21]And Saul said, "Blessed *are* you of the LORD, for you have compassion on me. [22]Please go and find out for sure, and see the place where his hideout is, *and* who has seen him there. For I am told he is very crafty. [23]See therefore, and take knowledge of all the lurking places where he hides; and come back to me with certainty, and I will go with you. And it shall be, if he is in the land, that I will search for him throughout all the clans[a] of Judah."

[24]So they arose and went to Ziph before Saul. But David and his men *were* in the Wilderness of Maon, in the plain on the south of Jeshimon. [25]When Saul and his men went to seek *him,* they told David. Therefore he went down to the rock, and stayed in the Wilderness of Maon. And when Saul heard *that,* he pursued David in the Wilderness of Maon. [26]Then Saul went on one side of the mountain, and David and his men on the other side of the mountain. So David made haste to get away from Saul, for Saul and his men were encircling David and his men to take them.

[27]But a messenger came to Saul, saying, "Hurry and come, for the Philistines have invaded the land!" [28]Therefore Saul returned from pursuing David, and went against the Philistines; so they called that place the Rock of Escape.[a] [29]Then David went up from there and dwelt in strongholds at En Gedi.

David Spares Saul

24 Now it happened, when Saul had returned from following the Philistines, that it was told him, saying, "Take note! David *is* in the Wilderness of En Gedi." [2]Then Saul took three thousand chosen men from all Israel, and went to seek David and his men on the Rocks of the Wild Goats. [3]So he came to the sheepfolds by the road, where there

was a cave; and Saul went in to attend to his needs. (David and his men were staying in the recesses of the cave.) [4]Then the men of David said to him, "This is the day of which the LORD said to you, 'Behold, I will deliver your enemy into your hand, that you may do to him as it seems good to you.'" And David arose and secretly cut off a corner of Saul's robe. [5]Now it happened afterward that David's heart troubled him because he had cut Saul's *robe.* [6]And he said to his men, "The LORD forbid that I should do this thing to my master, the LORD's anointed, to stretch out my hand against him, seeing he *is* the anointed of the LORD." [7]So David restrained his servants with *these* words, and did not allow them to rise against Saul. And Saul got up from the cave and went on *his* way.

[8]David also arose afterward, went out of the cave, and called out to Saul, saying, "My lord the king!" And when Saul looked behind him, David stooped with his face to the earth, and bowed down. [9]And David said to Saul: "Why do you listen to the words of men who say, 'Indeed David seeks your harm'? [10]Look, this day your eyes have seen that the LORD delivered you today into my hand in the cave, and *someone* urged *me* to kill you. But *my eye* spared you, and I said, 'I will not stretch out my hand against my lord, for he *is* the LORD's anointed.' [11]Moreover, my father, see! Yes, see the corner of your robe in my hand! For in that I cut off the corner of your robe, and did not kill you, know and see that *there is* neither evil nor rebellion in my hand, and I have not sinned against you. Yet you hunt my life to take it. [12]Let the LORD judge between you and me, and let the LORD avenge me on you. But my hand shall not be against you. [13]As the proverb of the ancients says, 'Wickedness proceeds from the wicked.' But my hand shall not be against you. [14]After whom has the king of Israel come out? Whom do you pursue? A dead dog? A flea? [15]Therefore let the LORD be judge, and judge between you and me, and see and plead my case, and deliver me out of your hand."

[16]So it was, when David had finished speaking these words to Saul, that Saul said, "*Is* this your voice, my son David?" And Saul lifted up his voice and wept. [17]Then he said to David: "You *are* more righteous than I; for you have rewarded me with good, whereas I have rewarded you with evil. [18]And you have shown this day how you have dealt well with me; for when the LORD delivered me into your hand, you did not

---

23:15 [a]Or *in Horesh* **23:23** [a]Literally *thousands*
23:28 [a]Hebrew *Sela Hammahlekoth*

The Law of Solid Ground: David's Respect for Saul Earns Him Trust

(1 Samuel 24:1–22)

Leadership operates on the basis of trust. Before David became king, he showed respect for the king who preceded him. Saul failed to practice this law, and lost his kingdom. The Bible provides a vivid contrast between Saul and David's leadership.

Saul	David
1. Self-conscious from the beginning	1. Displayed God-confidence from the beginning
2. Presumed on the priestly office	2. Didn't assume any right or privilege
3. Disobeyed God in the little things	3. Obeyed God in the little things
4. Lost integrity by covering his sin	4. Maintained integrity by respecting Saul
5. Failed to submit to God-given authority	5. Consistently submitted to authority
6. Preoccupied with his own fame	6. Desired to increase God's reputation

kill me. ¹⁹For if a man finds his enemy, will he let him get away safely? Therefore may the LORD reward you with good for what you have done to me this day. ²⁰And now I know indeed that you shall surely be king, and that the kingdom of Israel shall be established in your hand. ²¹Therefore swear now to me by the LORD that you will not cut off my descendants after me, and that you will not destroy my name from my father's house."

²²So David swore to Saul. And Saul went home, but David and his men went up to the stronghold.

Death of Samuel

25 Then Samuel died; and the Israelites gathered together and lamented for him, and buried him at his home in Ramah. And David arose and went down to the Wilderness of Paran.ᵃ

David and the Wife of Nabal

²Now *there was* a man in Maon whose business *was* in Carmel, and the man *was* very rich. He had three thousand sheep and a thousand goats. And he was shearing his sheep in Carmel. ³The name of the man *was* Nabal, and the name of his wife Abigail. And *she was* a woman of good understanding and beautiful appearance; but the man *was* harsh and evil in *his* doings. He *was* of the house of Caleb.

⁴When David heard in the wilderness that Nabal was shearing his sheep, ⁵David sent ten young men; and David said to the young men, "Go up to Carmel, go to Nabal, and greet him

in my name. ⁶And thus you shall say to him who lives *in prosperity:* 'Peace *be* to you, peace to your house, and peace to all that you have! ⁷Now I have heard that you have shearers. Your shepherds were with us, and we did not hurt them, nor was there anything missing from them all the while they were in Carmel. ⁸Ask your young men, and they will tell you. Therefore let *my* young men find favor in your eyes, for we come on a feast day. Please give whatever comes to your hand to your servants and to your son David.'"

⁹So when David's young men came, they spoke to Nabal according to all these words in the name of David, and waited.

¹⁰Then Nabal answered David's servants, and said, "Who *is* David, and who *is* the son of Jesse? There are many servants nowadays who break away each one from his master. ¹¹Shall I then take my bread and my water and my meat that I have killed for my shearers, and give *it* to men when I do not know where they *are* from?"

¹²So David's young men turned on their heels and went back; and they came and told him all these words. ¹³Then David said to his men, "Every man gird on his sword." So every man girded on his sword, and David also girded on his sword. And about four hundred men went with David, and two hundred stayed with the supplies.

¹⁴Now one of the young men told Abigail, Nabal's wife, saying, "Look, David sent messengers from the wilderness to greet our master; and

---

25:1 ᵃFollowing Masoretic Text, Syriac, Targum, and Vulgate; Septuagint reads *Maon.*

he reviled them. [15]But the men *were* very good to us, and we were not hurt, nor did we miss anything as long as we accompanied them, when we were in the fields. [16]They were a wall to us both by night and day, all the time we were with them keeping the sheep. [17]Now therefore, know and consider what you will do, for harm is determined against our master and against all his household. For he *is such* a scoundrel[a] that *one* cannot speak to him."

[18]Then Abigail made haste and took two hundred *loaves* of bread, two skins of wine, five sheep already dressed, five seahs of roasted *grain,* one hundred clusters of raisins, and two hundred cakes of figs, and loaded *them* on donkeys. [19]And she said to her servants, "Go on before me; see, I am coming after you." But she did not tell her husband Nabal.

[20]So it was, *as* she rode on the donkey, that she went down under cover of the hill; and there were David and his men, coming down toward her, and she met them. [21]Now David had said, "Surely in vain I have protected all that this *fellow* has in the wilderness, so that nothing was missed of all that *belongs* to him. And he has repaid me evil for good. [22]May God do so, and more also, to the enemies of David, if I leave one male of all who *belong* to him by morning light."

[23]Now when Abigail saw David, she dismounted quickly from the donkey, fell on her face before David, and bowed down to the ground. [24]So she fell at his feet and said: "On me, my lord, *on me let* this iniquity *be!* And please let your maidservant speak in your ears, and hear the words of your maidservant. [25]Please, let not my lord regard this scoundrel Nabal. For as his name *is,* so *is* he: Nabal[a] *is* his name, and folly *is* with him! But I, your maidservant, did not see the young men of my lord whom you sent. [26]Now therefore, my lord, *as* the LORD lives and *as* your soul lives, since the LORD has held you back from coming to bloodshed and from avenging yourself with your own hand, now then, let your enemies and those who seek harm for my lord be as Nabal. [27]And now this present which your maidservant has brought to my lord, let it be given to the young men who follow my lord. [28]Please forgive the trespass of your maidservant. For the LORD will certainly make for my lord an enduring house, because my lord fights the battles of the LORD, and evil is not found in you throughout your days. [29]Yet a man has risen to pursue you and seek your life, but the life of my lord shall be bound in the bundle of the living

25:17 [a]Literally *son of Belial* **25:25** [a]Literally *Fool*

ABIGAIL — THE LAW OF CONNECTION
(1 Samuel 25:1–42)

PROFILE IN LEADERSHIP

Following Samuel's death, David moved to the Wilderness of Paran. There he encountered shepherds tending the flocks of the wealthy Nabal—an insolent, rude, and contentious man. Nabal happened to be married to a beautiful, intelligent, and intuitive woman named Abigail, and his wise wife saved his miserable life.

When Nabal offended David, Abigail very quickly took steps to defuse a volatile situation. She gathered a great feast and went out to meet David. Abigail's decisive actions met the immediate need of feeding David's men. They also calmed David and diverted him from avenging himself. Abigail lived the Law of Connection.

Upon her return home, Abigail kept her head and chose not to deal with Nabal until he was sober. Regardless of her husband's rudeness and inappropriate behavior, Abigail responded forthrightly and respectfully. God Himself later avenged David and chose to remove Nabal from the equation.

David never forgot this encounter. He knew a woman of God when he saw one, and after Nabal's death he chose Abigail to be his wife. Her patience and submission during difficult times, as well as her wisdom and problem-solving skills, prepared her to be an excellent wife for David. David valued Abigail's strength and felt greatly attracted to this highly capable female leader.

RELATIONSHIPS

Healthy Abigail vs. Despicable Nabal
(1 Samuel 25:1–42)

Ask people to name their favorite person in the Bible, and likely you'll hear the name Abigail. Due to her rare courage, common sense, and some fabulous relational skills, she single-handedly saved her family from certain destruction.

Her husband Nabal, on the other hand, almost provoked the slaughter of his whole household. Nabal's name means "fool," and he lived up to his name. A man without discernment, he selfishly refused to provide for David and his men. An enraged David gathered his troops to kill every male in Nabal's home, and he would have done it—except for Abigail. Note the following relationship lessons she teaches us:

Relationship Lessons from Abigail

1. *Risky initiative:* Abigail took the first step with David to resolve a sticky situation.
2. *Emotional security:* Abigail demonstrated inward security in her identity.
3. *Genuine humility:* Abigail submitted to David by falling at his feet and seeking his favor.
4. *Personal responsibility:* Abigail took responsibility for Nabal and explained his wicked behavior.
5. *Selfless attitude:* Abigail focused completely on David's welfare and future success.
6. *Generous spirit:* Abigail gave David and his men a choice gift for their journey.
7. *Forthright approach:* Abigail directly asked David to forgive Nabal.
8. *Quick wit:* Abigail suggested David didn't want a slaughter on his conscience.
9. *Eternal perspective:* Abigail saw David and their relationship from a divine viewpoint.
10. *Kind affirmation:* Abigail sought David's benefit and gave him encouraging words.

The Stuff Good Relationships Are Made Of

Effective leaders grow their relational skills in the following manner:

- *Have a Leader's Head: Understand People*
  Abigail knew how to appeal to David in order to accomplish her goal.
- *Have a Leader's Heart: Love People*
  Abigail assumed the role of a servant, submitting to both David and her husband. She felt secure enough to serve.
- *Have a Leader's Hand: Help People*
  Abigail gave David and his men what they needed. She added value to him and thereby saved the life of her family.

Nabal: The Other Shoe Drops

Nabal's wife may have excelled in relationships, but Nabal floundered. Their marriage illustrates that opposites really do attract.

As David and his men were getting ready to pass through Nabal's property, David sent a few men ahead to ask Nabal if he could spare anything: food, wool, drinks, anything—they weren't choosy. But Nabal refused to give them even the time of day. He grumbled loudly and sent them away with insults. How foolish!

Nabal should have known that David had saved his nation from Goliath and the Philistines. He should have known the prophet Samuel had anointed David to be the next king. He should have known that David had long protected Nabal's men and possessions. But if Nabal knew any of these things, they didn't matter to him. Nabal still refused to return David's favor.

So was Nabal a criminal? Did he do anything illegal or immoral? Not really. He simply sabotaged his leadership by his lack of people skills.

Nabal serves as a prototype of many pastors and leaders today. Like Nabal, we become so consumed with our own work and personal life that we neglect the only eternal resource on this earth: people. How exactly did Nabal fail to develop healthy relationship skills?

Why Did Nabal Fail?

1. Nabal grew wealthy and satisfied and didn't think he needed to build relationships (v. 2).
2. Nabal became selfish and distrustful of others; he couldn't overcome his evil temperament (v. 3).
3. Nabal neither gave nor received encouragement; he had grown numb to positive attitudes (v. 6).
4. Nabal forgot how others had blessed him in the past; he counted only his losses (vv. 7, 8).
5. Nabal belittled people and forgot their names; his insecurity prevented generosity (v. 10).
6. Nabal saw no reason to help others; he suffered from self-centered motives (v. 11).
7. Nabal wanted to build only his own "kingdom," not God's (v. 11).

Do you or someone you know suffer from similar symptoms? Relational skills are paramount in the kingdom of God. Jesus summarized the kingdom in two phrases: 1. Love God with all your heart; and 2. Love your neighbor as yourself. Our faith doesn't revolve around some sterile creed or doctrine, although creeds remain important. Faith revolves around relationships, vertical with God and horizontal with people. It's all about relationships.

Four Word Pictures

What could Nabal have done to improve his relational skills? He could have started by embracing the following word pictures:

1. *The Host*
   Just as a host takes initiative and makes a guest feel comfortable in his or her home, so we are to host the relationships of our lives.
2. *The Doctor*
   Just as a doctor does not give a prescription before first making a diagnosis, we are to poke and prod others with questions, so that our responses match the relevant need.
3. *The Counselor*
   A good counselor actively listens. Since the number one emotional need of people today is the need to be understood, we must deepen our listening skills.
4. *The Tour Guide*
   You hire a tour guide to help you reach your planned destination. God wants us to serve as spiritual "tour guides" for others, helping them to reach their potential.

with the LORD your God; and the lives of your enemies He shall sling out, *as from* the pocket of a sling. [30]And it shall come to pass, when the LORD has done for my lord according to all the good that He has spoken concerning you, and has appointed you ruler over Israel, [31]that this will be no grief to you, nor offense of heart to my lord, either that you have shed blood without cause, or that my lord has avenged himself. But when the LORD has dealt well with my lord, then remember your maidservant."

[32]Then David said to Abigail: "Blessed *is* the LORD God of Israel, who sent you this day to meet me! [33]And blessed *is* your advice and blessed *are* you, because you have kept me this day from coming to bloodshed and from avenging myself with my own hand. [34]For indeed, *as* the LORD God of Israel lives, who has kept me back from hurting you, unless you had hurried and come to meet me, surely by morning light no males would have been left to Nabal!" [35]So David received from her hand what she had brought him, and said to her, "Go up in peace to your house. See, I have heeded your voice and respected your person."

[36]Now Abigail went to Nabal, and there he was, holding a feast in his house, like the feast of a king. And Nabal's heart *was* merry within him, for he *was* very drunk; therefore she told him nothing, little or much, until morning light. [37]So it was, in the morning, when the wine had gone from Nabal, and his wife had told him these things, that his heart died within him, and he became *like* a stone. [38]Then it happened, *after* about ten days, that the LORD struck Nabal, and he died.

[39]So when David heard that Nabal was dead, he said, "Blessed *be* the LORD, who has pleaded the cause of my reproach from the hand of Nabal, and has kept His servant from evil! For the LORD has returned the wickedness of Nabal on his own head."

And David sent and proposed to Abigail, to take her as his wife. [40]When the servants of David had come to Abigail at Carmel, they spoke to her saying, "David sent us to you, to ask you to become his wife."

[41]Then she arose, bowed her face to the earth, and said, "Here is your maidservant, a servant to wash the feet of the servants of my lord." [42]So Abigail rose in haste and rode on a donkey, attended by five of her maidens; and she followed the messengers of David, and became his wife. [43]David also took Ahinoam of Jezreel, and so both of them were his wives.

[44]But Saul had given Michal his daughter, David's wife, to Palti[a] the son of Laish, who *was* from Gallim.

David Spares Saul a Second Time

26 Now the Ziphites came to Saul at Gibeah, saying, "Is David not hiding in the hill of Hachilah, opposite Jeshimon?" [2]Then Saul arose and went down to the Wilderness of Ziph, having three thousand chosen men of Israel with him, to seek David in the Wilderness of Ziph. [3]And Saul encamped in the hill of Hachilah, which *is* opposite Jeshimon, by the road. But David stayed in the wilderness, and he saw that Saul came after him into the wilderness. [4]David therefore sent out spies, and understood that Saul had indeed come.

[5]So David arose and came to the place where Saul had encamped. And David saw the place where Saul lay, and Abner the son of Ner, the commander of his army. Now Saul lay within the camp, with the people encamped all around him. [6]Then David answered, and said to Ahimelech the Hittite and to Abishai the son of Zeruiah, brother of Joab, saying, "Who will go down with me to Saul in the camp?"

And Abishai said, "I will go down with you."

[7]So David and Abishai came to the people by night; and there Saul lay sleeping within the camp, with his spear stuck in the ground by his head. And Abner and the people lay all around him. [8]Then Abishai said to David, "God has delivered your enemy into your hand this day. Now therefore, please, let me strike him at once with the spear, right to the earth; and I will not *have* to strike him a second time!"

[9]But David said to Abishai, "Do not destroy him; for who can stretch out his hand against the LORD's anointed, and be guiltless?" [10]David said furthermore, "*As* the LORD lives, the LORD shall strike him, or his day shall come to die, or he shall go out to battle and perish. [11]The LORD forbid that I should stretch out my hand against the LORD's anointed. But please, take now the spear and the jug of water that *are* by his head, and let us go." [12]So David took the spear and the jug of water *by* Saul's head, and they got away; and no man saw or knew *it* or awoke. For they *were* all asleep, because a deep sleep from the LORD had fallen on them.

[13]Now David went over to the other side, and stood on the top of a hill afar off, a great distance *being* between them. [14]And David called out to the people and to Abner the son of Ner, saying, "Do you not answer, Abner?"

25:44 [a]Spelled *Paltiel* in 2 Samuel 3:15

21 QUALITIES

LISTENING

David's Conflict Resolution Strategy Wins Saul Over
(1 Samuel 26:1–25)

Through listening, leaders earn the right to speak into the lives of their people. Because they listen, they speak with relevance. And as they listen, they display love, compassion, and understanding.

David led well because he listened well. First Samuel 26 describes how he gained the opportunity to take Saul's life for the second time. David snuck up on the king while he slept. But instead of killing him, David took the king's spear and water jug and later, from a distance, confronted him with questions. David shows that a leader who listens possesses genuine love.

1. *Genuine love is not always popular—be different.*

Remember David's men? Malcontents. Disgruntled. More than once they encouraged him to look out for himself and take Saul's life—but David refused. We must be careful how we interpret circumstances and whose advice we accept.

2. *Genuine love needs a clear perspective—be humble.*

After David took Saul's spear and jug, he called to the king from a distance. He submitted himself and humbly asked for perspective. "What have I done?" he asked. We will never be able to love people correctly until we see them clearly, with God's eyes.

3. *Genuine love is not defensive—be patient.*

David knew God put him in this situation for a purpose and trusted Him to deliver him. David offers to make a sacrifice if he has harmed Saul or done anything wrong, and he waits to hear Saul's rationale. Impatience indicates we lack trust and want our rights.

4. *Genuine love is powerful—be forgiving.*

Saul later apologizes to David and admits his wrong. He promises to go home. At this point, David sits in the driver's seat; he still has Saul's spear and jug. But he returns them and forgives Saul of everything. Like David, we must trust God to make things right.

What Steps Did David Take?

Note the following steps David walked through with Saul (1 Sam. 26):

1. He initiated the contact with Saul and set the stage for communication (v. 14).
2. He appealed to Saul's sense of right and wrong (vv. 15, 16).
3. He asked questions and listened for the king's heart's response (v. 18).
4. He asked them to listen so he could share his perspective (v. 19).
5. He determined to own up to anything he had done wrong (v. 19).
6. He submitted himself to Saul (v. 20).
7. He offered forgiveness and reconciliation as an act of trust in God (vv. 22–24).

How about you? Do you display love for others by listening? Are you a good listener?

For a negative example of listening, see p. 528.

Then Abner answered and said, "Who *are* you, calling out to the king?"

[15]So David said to Abner, "*Are* you not a man? And who *is* like you in Israel? Why then have you not guarded your lord the king? For one of the people came in to destroy your lord the king. [16]This thing that you have done *is* not good. *As* the LORD lives, you deserve to die, because you have not guarded your master, the LORD's anointed. And now see where the king's spear *is,* and the jug of water that *was* by his head."

[17]Then Saul knew David's voice, and said, "*Is* that your voice, my son David?"

David said, "*It is* my voice, my lord, O king." [18]And he said, "Why does my lord thus pursue his servant? For what have I done, or what evil *is* in my hand? [19]Now therefore, please, let my lord the king hear the words of his servant: If the LORD has stirred you up against me, let Him accept an offering. But if *it is* the children of men, *may* they *be* cursed before the LORD, for they have driven me out this day from sharing in the inheritance of the LORD, saying, 'Go, serve other gods.' [20]So now, do not let my blood fall to the earth before the face of the LORD. For the king of Israel has come out to seek a flea, as when one hunts a partridge in the mountains."

[21]Then Saul said, "I have sinned. Return, my son David. For I will harm you no more, because my life was precious in your eyes this day. Indeed I have played the fool and erred exceedingly."

[22]And David answered and said, "Here is the king's spear. Let one of the young men come over and get it. [23]May the LORD repay every man *for* his righteousness and his faithfulness; for the LORD delivered you into *my* hand today, but I would not stretch out my hand against the LORD's anointed. [24]And indeed, as your life was valued much this day in my eyes, so let my life be valued much in the eyes of the LORD, and let Him deliver me out of all tribulation."

[25]Then Saul said to David, "*May* you *be* blessed, my son David! You shall both do great things and also still prevail."

So David went on his way, and Saul returned to his place.

David Allied with the Philistines

27 And David said in his heart, "Now I shall perish someday by the hand of Saul. *There is* nothing better for me than that I should speedily escape to the land of the Philistines; and Saul will despair of me, to seek me anymore in any part of Israel. So I shall escape out of his hand." [2]Then David arose and went over with the six hundred men who *were* with him to Achish the son of Maoch, king of Gath. [3]So David dwelt with Achish at Gath, he and his men, each man with his household, *and* David with his two wives, Ahinoam the Jezreelitess, and Abigail the Carmelitess, Nabal's widow. [4]And it was told Saul that David had fled to Gath; so he sought him no more.

[5]Then David said to Achish, "If I have now found favor in your eyes, let them give me a place in some town in the country, that I may dwell there. For why should your servant dwell in the royal city with you?" [6]So Achish gave him Ziklag that day. Therefore Ziklag has belonged to the kings of Judah to this day. [7]Now the time that David dwelt in the country of the Philistines was one full year and four months.

[8]And David and his men went up and raided the Geshurites, the Girzites,[a] and the Amalekites. For those nations were the inhabitants of the land from of old, as you go to Shur, even as far as the land of Egypt. [9]Whenever David attacked the land, he left neither man nor woman alive, but took away the sheep, the oxen, the donkeys, the camels, and the apparel, and returned and came to Achish. [10]Then Achish would say, "Where have you made a raid today?" And David would say, "Against the southern *area* of Judah, or against the southern *area* of the Jerahmeelites, or against the southern *area* of the Kenites." [11]David would save neither man nor woman alive, to bring *news* to Gath, saying, "Lest they should inform on us, saying, 'Thus David did.'" And thus *was* his behavior all the time he dwelt in the country of the Philistines. [12]So Achish believed David, saying, "He has made his people Israel utterly abhor him; therefore he will be my servant forever."

28 Now it happened in those days that the Philistines gathered their armies together for war, to fight with Israel. And Achish said to David, "You assuredly know that you will go out with me to battle, you and your men."

[2]So David said to Achish, "Surely you know what your servant can do."

And Achish said to David, "Therefore I will make you one of my chief guardians forever."

Saul Consults a Medium

[3]Now Samuel had died, and all Israel had lamented for him and buried him in Ramah, in his own city. And Saul had put the mediums and the spiritists out of the land.

27:8 [a]Or *Gezrites*

[4]Then the Philistines gathered together, and came and encamped at Shunem. So Saul gathered all Israel together, and they encamped at Gilboa. [5]When Saul saw the army of the Philistines, he was afraid, and his heart trembled greatly. [6]And when Saul inquired of the LORD, the LORD did not answer him, either by dreams or by Urim or by the prophets.

[7]Then Saul said to his servants, "Find me a woman who is a medium, that I may go to her and inquire of her."

And his servants said to him, "In fact, *there is* a woman who is a medium at En Dor."

[8]So Saul disguised himself and put on other clothes, and he went, and two men with him; and they came to the woman by night. And he said, "Please conduct a séance for me, and bring up for me the one I shall name to you."

[9]Then the woman said to him, "Look, you know what Saul has done, how he has cut off the mediums and the spiritists from the land. Why then do you lay a snare for my life, to cause me to die?"

[10]And Saul swore to her by the LORD, saying, "*As* the LORD lives, no punishment shall come upon you for this thing."

[11]Then the woman said, "Whom shall I bring up for you?"

And he said, "Bring up Samuel for me."

[12]When the woman saw Samuel, she cried out with a loud voice. And the woman spoke to Saul, saying, "Why have you deceived me? For you *are* Saul!"

[13]And the king said to her, "Do not be afraid. What did you see?"

And the woman said to Saul, "I saw a spirit[a] ascending out of the earth."

[14]So he said to her, "What *is* his form?"

And she said, "An old man is coming up, and he *is* covered with a mantle." And Saul perceived that it *was* Samuel, and he stooped with *his* face to the ground and bowed down.

[15]Now Samuel said to Saul, "Why have you disturbed me by bringing me up?"

And Saul answered, "I am deeply distressed; for the Philistines make war against me, and God has departed from me and does not answer me anymore, neither by prophets nor by dreams. Therefore I have called you, that you may reveal to me what I should do."

[16]Then Samuel said: "So why do you ask me, seeing the LORD has departed from you and has become your enemy? [17]And the LORD has done for Himself[a] as He spoke by me. For the LORD has torn the kingdom out of your hand and given it to your neighbor, David. [18]Because you

did not obey the voice of the LORD nor execute His fierce wrath upon Amalek, therefore the LORD has done this thing to you this day. [19]Moreover the LORD will also deliver Israel with you into the hand of the Philistines. And tomorrow you and your sons *will be* with me. The LORD will also deliver the army of Israel into the hand of the Philistines."

[20]Immediately Saul fell full length on the ground, and was dreadfully afraid because of the words of Samuel. And there was no strength in him, for he had eaten no food all day or all night.

[21]And the woman came to Saul and saw that he was severely troubled, and said to him, "Look, your maidservant has obeyed your voice, and I have put my life in my hands and heeded the words which you spoke to me. [22]Now therefore, please, heed also the voice of your maidservant, and let me set a piece of bread before you; and eat, that you may have strength when you go on *your* way."

[23]But he refused and said, "I will not eat."

So his servants, together with the woman, urged him; and he heeded their voice. Then he arose from the ground and sat on the bed. [24]Now the woman had a fatted calf in the house, and she hastened to kill it. And she took flour and kneaded *it*, and baked unleavened bread from it. [25]So she brought *it* before Saul and his servants, and they ate. Then they rose and went away that night.

The Philistines Reject David

29 Then the Philistines gathered together all their armies at Aphek, and the Israelites encamped by a fountain which *is* in Jezreel. [2]And the lords of the Philistines passed in review by hundreds and by thousands, but David and his men passed in review at the rear with Achish. [3]Then the princes of the Philistines said, "What *are* these Hebrews *doing here?*"

And Achish said to the princes of the Philistines, "*Is* this not David, the servant of Saul king of Israel, who has been with me these days, or these years? And to this day I have found no fault in him since he defected *to* me."

[4]But the princes of the Philistines were angry with him; so the princes of the Philistines said to him, "Make this fellow return, that he may go back to the place which you have appointed for him, and do not let him go down with us to battle, lest in the battle he become our adversary. For with what could he reconcile himself to his master, if not with the heads of these men? [5]*Is*

28:13 [a]Hebrew *elohim* **28:17** [a]Or *him,* that is, David

David Fails to Trust God and Visits the Carnal Corral

(1 Samuel 29:1–11)

Over time David grew weary of Saul's pursuit and chose to escape to the land of the Philistines. He became vague about his purpose, defensive about his leadership, and lost the trust of Israel. Even great leaders become vulnerable when they grow tired, lonely, angry, or hungry.

this not David, of whom they sang to one another in dances, saying:

'Saul has slain his thousands,
And David his ten thousands'?"[a]

[6]Then Achish called David and said to him, "Surely, *as* the LORD lives, you have been upright, and your going out and your coming in with me in the army *is* good in my sight. For to this day I have not found evil in you since the day of your coming to me. Nevertheless the lords do not favor you. [7]Therefore return now, and go in peace, that you may not displease the lords of the Philistines."

[8]So David said to Achish, "But what have I done? And to this day what have you found in your servant as long as I have been with you, that I may not go and fight against the enemies of my lord the king?"

[9]Then Achish answered and said to David, "I know that you *are* as good in my sight as an angel of God; nevertheless the princes of the Philistines have said, 'He shall not go up with us to the battle.' [10]Now therefore, rise early in the morning with your master's servants who have come with you.[a] And as soon as you are up early in the morning and have light, depart."

[11]So David and his men rose early to depart in the morning, to return to the land of the Philistines. And the Philistines went up to Jezreel.

David's Conflict with the Amalekites

30 Now it happened, when David and his men came to Ziklag, on the third day, that the Amalekites had invaded the South and Ziklag, attacked Ziklag and burned it with fire, [2]and had taken captive the women and those who *were* there, from small to great; they did not kill anyone, but carried *them* away and went their way. [3]So David and his men came to the city, and there it was, burned with fire; and their wives, their sons, and their daughters had been taken captive. [4]Then David and the people who *were* with him lifted up their voices and wept, until they had no more power to weep. [5]And David's two wives, Ahinoam the Jezreelitess, and Abigail the widow of Nabal the Carmelite, had been taken captive. [6]Now David was greatly distressed, for the people spoke of stoning him, because the soul of all the people was grieved, every man for his sons and his daughters. But David strengthened himself in the LORD his God.

[7]Then David said to Abiathar the priest, Ahimelech's son, "Please bring the ephod here to me." And Abiathar brought the ephod to David. [8]So David inquired of the LORD, saying, "Shall I pursue this troop? Shall I overtake them?"

And He answered him, "Pursue, for you shall surely overtake *them* and without fail recover *all*."

[9]So David went, he and the six hundred men who *were* with him, and came to the Brook Besor, where those stayed who were left behind. [10]But David pursued, he and four hundred men; for two hundred stayed *behind,* who were so weary that they could not cross the Brook Besor.

[11]Then they found an Egyptian in the field, and brought him to David; and they gave him bread and he ate, and they let him drink water. [12]And they gave him a piece of a cake of figs and two clusters of raisins. So when he had eaten, his strength came back to him; for he had eaten no bread nor drunk water for three days and three nights. [13]Then David said to him, "To whom do you *belong,* and where *are* you from?"

And he said, "I *am* a young man from Egypt, servant of an Amalekite; and my master left me behind, because three days ago I fell sick. [14]We made an invasion of the southern *area* of the Cherethites, in the *territory* which *belongs* to Judah, and of the southern *area* of Caleb; and we burned Ziklag with fire."

[15]And David said to him, "Can you take me down to this troop?"

So he said, "Swear to me by God that you will neither kill me nor deliver me into the hands of my master, and I will take you down to this troop."

29:5 [a]Compare 1 Samuel 18:7 **29:10** [a]Following Masoretic Text, Targum, and Vulgate; Septuagint adds *and go to the place which I have selected for you there; and set no bothersome word in your heart, for you are good before me. And rise on your way.*

¹⁶And when he had brought him down, there they were, spread out over all the land, eating and drinking and dancing, because of all the great spoil which they had taken from the land of the Philistines and from the land of Judah. ¹⁷Then David attacked them from twilight until the evening of the next day. Not a man of them escaped, except four hundred young men who rode on camels and fled. ¹⁸So David recovered all that the Amalekites had carried away, and David rescued his two wives. ¹⁹And nothing of theirs was lacking, either small or great, sons or daughters, spoil or anything which they had taken from them; David recovered all. ²⁰Then David took all the flocks and herds they had driven before those *other* livestock, and said, "This *is* David's spoil."

²¹Now David came to the two hundred men who had been so weary that they could not follow David, whom they also had made to stay at the Brook Besor. So they went out to meet David and to meet the people who *were* with him.

David's Partnership: To Get Ahead, Put Others First

(1 Samuel 30:17–20)

When David pursued the Amalekites who had raided his city, some of his older troops stayed back to help with supplies. When the victorious troops returned home, some "wicked and worthless men" (1 Sam. 30:22) suggested that those who stayed behind should receive none of the spoil. David resolved the conflict by declaring that since God had given them victory, even those who had protected the supplies had played a role and therefore should share equally in the plunder.

Clearly, David valued partnership. What did his act of partnership do for his leadership?

1. It helped others see the contribution of every man's gift.
2. It reminded everyone that God was the true source of every good gift.
3. It promoted goodwill in potential allies.
4. It enabled David to prepare for the future and make friends all over Israel.
5. It developed a nationwide value of mutual benefit and good faith.

And when David came near the people, he greeted them. ²²Then all the wicked and worthless men^a of those who went with David answered and said, "Because they did not go with us, we will not give them *any* of the spoil that we have recovered, except for every man's wife and children, that they may lead *them* away and depart."

²³But David said, "My brethren, you shall not do so with what the LORD has given us, who has preserved us and delivered into our hand the troop that came against us. ²⁴For who will heed you in this matter? But as his part *is* who goes down to the battle, so *shall* his part *be* who stays by the supplies; they shall share alike." ²⁵So it was, from that day forward; he made it a statute and an ordinance for Israel to this day.

²⁶Now when David came to Ziklag, he sent *some* of the spoil to the elders of Judah, to his friends, saying, "Here is a present for you from the spoil of the enemies of the LORD"— ²⁷to *those* who *were* in Bethel, *those* who *were* in Ramoth of the South, *those* who *were* in Jattir, ²⁸*those* who *were* in Aroer, *those* who *were* in Siphmoth, *those* who *were* in Eshtemoa, ²⁹*those* who *were* in Rachal, *those* who *were* in the cities of the Jerahmeelites, *those* who *were* in the cities of the Kenites, ³⁰*those* who *were* in Hormah, *those* who *were* in Chorashan,^a *those* who *were* in Athach, ³¹*those* who *were* in Hebron, and to all the places where David himself and his men were accustomed to rove.

The Tragic End of Saul and His Sons

31 Now the Philistines fought against Israel; and the men of Israel fled from before the Philistines, and fell slain on Mount Gilboa. ²Then the Philistines followed hard after Saul and his sons. And the Philistines killed Jonathan, Abinadab, and Malchishua, Saul's sons. ³The battle became fierce against Saul. The archers hit him, and he was severely wounded by the archers.

⁴Then Saul said to his armorbearer, "Draw your sword, and thrust me through with it, lest these uncircumcised men come and thrust me through and abuse me."

But his armorbearer would not, for he was greatly afraid. Therefore Saul took a sword and fell on it. ⁵And when his armorbearer saw that Saul was dead, he also fell on his sword, and died with him. ⁶So Saul, his three sons, his armorbearer, and all his men died together that same day.

30:22 ^aLiterally *men of Belial* **30:30** ^aOr *Borashan*

⁷And when the men of Israel who *were* on the other side of the valley, and *those* who *were* on the other side of the Jordan, saw that the men of Israel had fled and that Saul and his sons were dead, they forsook the cities and fled; and the Philistines came and dwelt in them. ⁸So it happened the next day, when the Philistines came to strip the slain, that they found Saul and his three sons fallen on Mount Gilboa. ⁹And they cut off his head and stripped off his armor, and sent *word* throughout the land of the Philistines, to proclaim *it in* the temple of their idols and among the people. ¹⁰Then they put his armor in the temple of the Ashtoreths, and they fastened his body to the wall of Beth Shan.ᵃ

¹¹Now when the inhabitants of Jabesh Gilead heard what the Philistines had done to Saul, ¹²all the valiant men arose and traveled all night, and took the body of Saul and the bodies of his sons from the wall of Beth Shan; and they came to Jabesh and burned them there. ¹³Then they took their bones and buried *them* under the tamarisk tree at Jabesh, and fasted seven days.

31:10 ᵃSpelled *Beth Shean* in Joshua 17:11 and elsewhere

2 SAMUEL
Continuous Account of the First Kings of Israel

SUMMARY

I n the original Hebrew manuscripts of the Old Testament, the books of 1 and 2 Samuel form a single volume. Together they give one continuous account of the first kings of Israel.

Second Samuel begins with the death of King Saul and Prince Jonathan. Although the prophet Samuel had anointed David king long before, only after this incident does he begin his monarchy. David refused to assume any royal authority until Saul, God's anointed king, had died.

A turbulent transition period brought civil war between David's military forces, led by Joab, and Saul's army, led by Abner. David's army grew steadily stronger, while Abner's weakened by the day. When Joab murdered Abner, all of Israel lost heart, and Judah and Israel finally joined as one under David's leadership.

The rest of the book tells the intriguing story of a leader every bit as human as he was noble. David quickly became a much stronger leader than Saul, due in large measure to the Law of the Lid. In addition, David practiced every one of the 21 Laws of Leadership. He developed a standing army; he established a capital where the ark of God could be housed; he laid plans to build a temple; and he conquered every army he faced. He wrote more than one hundred psalms expressing his own intimacy with God. Two verses tell his story early on: "David went on and became great, and the LORD God of hosts was with him" (5:10), and "The LORD preserved David wherever he went" (8:14).

Sadly, none of this kept David from indulging the baser side of his nature. Before the book is half finished, David has committed adultery with Bathsheba. When she becomes pregnant, he tries to cover up his sin and orders her soldier husband to the front lines to ensure his death. David never fully recovered from this sin. He neglected his family, leaving both sons and daughters to wonder how Dad could be such a great king, but such a distant father.

Despite all of this, David remains the only person in Scripture whom God calls a "man after His own heart" (1 Sam. 13:14). In 2 Samuel we see both the qualities of an effective leader and the quirks of an ineffective leader who loses sight of the big picture. David's life proves that every leader needs an inner circle to keep him or her in check.

God's Role in 2 Samuel

God intended for Israel to become a light to the nations, goading the surrounding kingdoms to jealousy over the special relationship between Israel and God. The Lord blessed the Hebrews in order that they might bless the nations of the world (Gen. 12:1–3). Under David's reign, Israel comes close to God's goal. David takes a country the size of the state of New Jersey and develops it into a world-class nation. Everyone recognized the strength of Israel's leadership, economy, military force, and natural resources.

God desired to develop and maintain a close relationship with David, knowing that as the leader goes, so goes the nation. Even when David sinned, he managed to stay in touch with God.

Leaders in 2 Samuel

David, Joab, Abner, Ishbosheth, Absalom

Other People of Influence in 2 Samuel

Michal, Bathsheba, Nathan, Hushai

Lessons in Leadership

- Leaders mature when they allow God to break them.
- Leaders must be both tough and tender.
- When leaders stop sacrificing, they stop succeeding.
- People do what people see.
- Leadership is about relationships—if you get along, they'll go along.
- If you won't carry the ball, you can't lead the team.
- The first person you must lead is you.
- The leader's source is God—not people, material resources, or money.

HIGHLIGHTS IN 2 SAMUEL

The Report of Saul's Death

1 Now it came to pass after the death of Saul, when David had returned from the slaughter of the Amalekites, and David had stayed two days in Ziklag, ²on the third day, behold, it happened that a man came from Saul's camp with his clothes torn and dust on his head. So it was, when he came to David, that he fell to the ground and prostrated himself.

³And David said to him, "Where have you come from?"

So he said to him, "I have escaped from the camp of Israel."

⁴Then David said to him, "How did the matter go? Please tell me."

And he answered, "The people have fled from the battle, many of the people are fallen and dead, and Saul and Jonathan his son are dead also."

⁵So David said to the young man who told him, "How do you know that Saul and Jonathan his son are dead?"

⁶Then the young man who told him said, "As I happened by chance to be on Mount Gilboa, there was Saul, leaning on his spear; and indeed the chariots and horsemen followed hard after him. ⁷Now when he looked behind him, he saw me and called to me. And I answered, 'Here I am.' ⁸And he said to me, 'Who are you?' So I answered him, 'I am an Amalekite.' ⁹He said to me again, 'Please stand over me and kill me, for anguish has come upon me, but my life still remains in me.' ¹⁰So I stood over him and killed him, because I was sure that he could not live after he had fallen. And I took the crown that was on his head and the bracelet that was on his arm, and have brought them here to my lord."

¹¹Therefore David took hold of his own clothes and tore them, and so did all the men who were with him. ¹²And they mourned and wept and fasted until evening for Saul and for Jonathan his son, for the people of the LORD and for the house of Israel, because they had fallen by the sword.

¹³Then David said to the young man who told him, "Where are you from?"

And he answered, "I am the son of an alien, an Amalekite."

¹⁴So David said to him, "How was it you were not afraid to put forth your hand to destroy the LORD's anointed?" ¹⁵Then David called one of the young men and said, "Go near, and execute him!" And he struck him so that he died. ¹⁶So David said to him, "Your blood is on your own head, for your own mouth has testified against you, saying, 'I have killed the LORD's anointed.'"

The Song of the Bow

¹⁷Then David lamented with this lamentation over Saul and over Jonathan his son, ¹⁸and he told them to teach the children of Judah the Song of the Bow; indeed it is written in the Book of Jasher:

¹⁹ "The beauty of Israel is slain on your high places!
    How the mighty have fallen!
²⁰ Tell it not in Gath,
    Proclaim it not in the streets of Ashkelon—
    Lest the daughters of the Philistines rejoice,
    Lest the daughters of the uncircumcised triumph.

²¹ "O mountains of Gilboa,
    Let there be no dew nor rain upon you,
    Nor fields of offerings.
    For the shield of the mighty is cast away there!
    The shield of Saul, not anointed with oil.

The Authority Test: David Submits Until the End

(2 Samuel 1:17–27)

When David hears that Saul and Jonathan have died in battle, he mourns deeply for his friend Jonathan. But he also weeps for Saul, the man who: 1. tried to murder him in the palace; 2. tried to get the Philistines to kill him in battle; and 3. chased him through hills and caves in order to execute him. Why honor such a man?

In David's mind, submission to authority has little to do with the person in charge. In fact, when a young Amalekite tells David that he put Saul out of his misery at the king's request, David orders his execution, saying, "Your blood is on your own head, for your own mouth has testified against you, saying, 'I have killed the LORD's anointed'" (2 Sam. 1:16).

While leaders earn their influence, God gives them their authority. We owe our submission to whatever authorities God installs, regardless of who they may be (Rom. 13:1).

22 From the blood of the slain,
From the fat of the mighty,
The bow of Jonathan did not turn back,
And the sword of Saul did not return
empty.

23 "Saul and Jonathan *were* beloved and
pleasant in their lives,
And in their death they were not divided;
They were swifter than eagles,
They were stronger than lions.

24 "O daughters of Israel, weep over Saul,
Who clothed you in scarlet, with luxury;
Who put ornaments of gold on your
apparel.

25 "How the mighty have fallen in the midst
of the battle!
Jonathan *was* slain in your high places.
26 I am distressed for you, my brother
Jonathan;
You have been very pleasant to me;
Your love to me was wonderful,
Surpassing the love of women.

27 "How the mighty have fallen,
And the weapons of war perished!"

David Anointed King of Judah

2 It happened after this that David inquired
of the LORD, saying, "Shall I go up to any
of the cities of Judah?"
And the LORD said to him, "Go up."
David said, "Where shall I go up?"
And He said, "To Hebron."

2So David went up there, and his two wives
also, Ahinoam the Jezreelitess, and Abigail the
widow of Nabal the Carmelite. 3And David
brought up the men who *were* with him, every
man with his household. So they dwelt in the
cities of Hebron.

4Then the men of Judah came, and there they
anointed David king over the house of Judah.
And they told David, saying, "The men of Jabesh
Gilead *were the ones* who buried Saul." 5So David
sent messengers to the men of Jabesh Gilead, and
said to them, "You *are* blessed of the LORD, for
you have shown this kindness to your lord, to
Saul, and have buried him. 6And now may the
LORD show kindness and truth to you. I also will
repay you this kindness, because you have done
this thing. 7Now therefore, let your hands be
strengthened, and be valiant; for your master Saul
is dead, and also the house of Judah has anointed
me king over them."

Conflict at the Top

(2 Samuel 2:4–11)

Saul's death led to all kinds of turmoil over
who would become the next king. Despite
David's anointing by Samuel, others saw a
tempting opportunity to seize power.

Transitions often bring difficult times. Leaders who fail to plan for their departure invite
trouble. Saul could have been a hero had he
cooperated with God in preparing David to
succeed him. He didn't have a more submissive staff person in his entire palace than
David.

Saul suffered from an "I" problem, an over-
size ego that blinded him. Saul could've helped
himself had he recognized these truths:

1. Since change makes people insecure,
   leaders must see ahead and prepare for
   them.
2. People can live without certainty, but not
   without clarity regarding future direction.
3. Wise choices today put "change in the
   pocket" of a leader regarding future
   choices.
4. Problem-solving skills and effective communication earn the leader trust and
   credibility.

Ishbosheth Made King of Israel

8But Abner the son of Ner, commander of
Saul's army, took Ishbosheth[a] the son of Saul and
brought him over to Mahanaim; 9and he made
him king over Gilead, over the Ashurites, over
Jezreel, over Ephraim, over Benjamin, and over
all Israel. 10Ishbosheth, Saul's son, *was* forty years
old when he began to reign over Israel, and he
reigned two years. Only the house of Judah followed David. 11And the time that David was king
in Hebron over the house of Judah was seven
years and six months.

Israel and Judah at War

12Now Abner the son of Ner, and the servants
of Ishbosheth the son of Saul, went out from
Mahanaim to Gibeon. 13And Joab the son of
Zeruiah, and the servants of David, went out and
met them by the pool of Gibeon. So they sat

2:8 aCalled *Esh-Baal* in 1 Chronicles 8:33 and 9:39

down, one on one side of the pool and the other on the other side of the pool. [14]Then Abner said to Joab, "Let the young men now arise and compete before us."

And Joab said, "Let them arise."

[15]So they arose and went over by number, twelve from Benjamin, *followers* of Ishbosheth the son of Saul, and twelve from the servants of David. [16]And each one grasped his opponent by the head and *thrust* his sword in his opponent's side; so they fell down together. Therefore that place was called the Field of Sharp Swords,[a] which *is* in Gibeon. [17]So there was a very fierce battle that day, and Abner and the men of Israel were beaten before the servants of David.

[18]Now the three sons of Zeruiah were there: Joab and Abishai and Asahel. And Asahel *was as* fleet of foot as a wild gazelle. [19]So Asahel pursued Abner, and in going he did not turn to the right hand or to the left from following Abner.

[20]Then Abner looked behind him and said, "*Are* you Asahel?"

He answered, "I *am.*"

[21]And Abner said to him, "Turn aside to your right hand or to your left, and lay hold on one of the young men and take his armor for yourself." But Asahel would not turn aside from following him. [22]So Abner said again to Asahel, "Turn aside from following me. Why should I strike you to the ground? How then could I face your brother Joab?" [23]However, he refused to turn aside. Therefore Abner struck him in the stomach with the blunt end of the spear, so that the spear came out of his back; and he fell down there and died on the spot. So it was *that* as many as came to the place where Asahel fell down and died, stood still.

[24]Joab and Abishai also pursued Abner. And the sun was going down when they came to the hill of Ammah, which *is* before Giah by the road to the Wilderness of Gibeon. [25]Now the children of Benjamin gathered together behind Abner and became a unit, and took their stand on top of a hill. [26]Then Abner called to Joab and said, "Shall the sword devour forever? Do you not know that it will be bitter in the latter end? How long will it be then until you tell the people to return from pursuing their brethren?"

[27]And Joab said, "*As* God lives, unless you had spoken, surely then by morning all the people would have given up pursuing their brethren." [28]So Joab blew a trumpet; and all the people stood still and did not pursue Israel anymore, nor did they fight anymore. [29]Then Abner and his men went on all that night through the plain, crossed over the Jordan, and went through all Bithron; and they came to Mahanaim.

[30]So Joab returned from pursuing Abner. And when he had gathered all the people together, there were missing of David's servants nineteen men and Asahel. [31]But the servants of David had struck down, of Benjamin and Abner's men, three hundred and sixty men who died. [32]Then they took up Asahel and buried him in his father's tomb, which *was in* Bethlehem. And Joab and his men went all night, and they came to Hebron at daybreak.

3 Now there was a long war between the house of Saul and the house of David. But David grew stronger and stronger, and the house of Saul grew weaker and weaker.

Sons of David

[2]Sons were born to David in Hebron: His firstborn was Amnon by Ahinoam the Jezreelitess; [3]his second, Chileab, by Abigail the widow of Nabal the Carmelite; the third, Absalom the son of Maacah, the daughter of Talmai, king of Geshur; [4]the fourth, Adonijah the son of Haggith; the fifth, Shephatiah the son of Abital; [5]and the sixth, Ithream, by David's wife Eglah. These were born to David in Hebron.

Abner Joins Forces with David

[6]Now it was so, while there was war between the house of Saul and the house of David, that Abner was strengthening *his hold* on the house of Saul. [7]And Saul had a concubine, whose name *was* Rizpah, the daughter of Aiah. So *Ishbosheth* said to Abner, "Why have you gone in to my father's concubine?"

[8]Then Abner became very angry at the words of Ishbosheth, and said, "*Am* I a dog's head that belongs to Judah? Today I show loyalty to the house of Saul your father, to his brothers, and to his friends, and have not delivered you into the hand of David; and you charge me today with a fault concerning this woman? [9]May God do so to Abner, and more also, if I do not do for David as the LORD has sworn to him— [10]to transfer the kingdom from the house of Saul, and set up the throne of David over Israel and over Judah, from Dan to Beersheba." [11]And he could not answer Abner another word, because he feared him.

[12]Then Abner sent messengers on his behalf to David, saying, "Whose *is* the land?" saying *also,* "Make your covenant with me, and indeed my hand *shall be* with you to bring all Israel to you."

[13]And *David* said, "Good, I will make a covenant with you. But one thing I require of you:

2:16 [a]Hebrew *Helkath Hazzurim*

you shall not see my face unless you first bring Michal, Saul's daughter, when you come to see my face." [14]So David sent messengers to Ishbosheth, Saul's son, saying, "Give *me* my wife Michal, whom I betrothed to myself for a hundred foreskins of the Philistines." [15]And Ishbosheth sent and took her from *her* husband, from Paltiel[a] the son of Laish. [16]Then her husband went along with her to Bahurim, weeping behind her. So Abner said to him, "Go, return!" And he returned.

[17]Now Abner had communicated with the elders of Israel, saying, "In time past you were seeking for David *to be* king over you. [18]Now then, do *it!* For the LORD has spoken of David, saying, 'By the hand of My servant David, I[a] will save My people Israel from the hand of the Philistines and the hand of all their enemies.'" [19]And Abner also spoke in the hearing of Benjamin. Then Abner also went to speak in the hearing of David in Hebron all that seemed good to Israel and the whole house of Benjamin.

[20]So Abner and twenty men with him came to David at Hebron. And David made a feast for Abner and the men who *were* with him. [21]Then Abner said to David, "I will arise and go, and gather all Israel to my lord the king, that they may make a covenant with you, and that you

may reign over all that your heart desires." So David sent Abner away, and he went in peace.

Joab Murders Abner

[22]At that moment the servants of David and Joab came from a raid and brought much spoil with them. But Abner *was* not with David in Hebron, for he had sent him away, and he had gone in peace. [23]When Joab and all the troops that *were* with him had come, they told Joab, saying, "Abner the son of Ner came to the king, and he sent him away, and he has gone in peace." [24]Then Joab came to the king and said, "What have you done? Look, Abner came to you; why *is* it *that* you sent him away, and he has already gone? [25]Surely you realize that Abner the son of Ner came to deceive you, to know your going out and your coming in, and to know all that you are doing."

[26]And when Joab had gone from David's presence, he sent messengers after Abner, who brought him back from the well of Sirah. But David did not know *it*. [27]Now when Abner had

---

3:15 [a]Spelled *Palti* in 1 Samuel 25:44
3:18 [a]Following many Hebrew manuscripts, Septuagint, Syriac, and Targum; Masoretic Text reads *he*.

JOAB	THE GENERAL WHO FORGOT THE REAL BOSS
	(2 Samuel 3:6–39)

PROFILE IN LEADERSHIP

When you forget whom you serve, you quickly fall prey to the basest human instincts. And leaders are not exempt.

Joab, a nephew of King David and a successful army commander, showed great arrogance toward the king by chiding him for entering into a treaty with Abner, a former enemy. Joab basically called David a fool for allowing Abner to escape unharmed. Then he moved secretly to deal with Abner as he saw fit.

Joab plotted to kill Abner, not because he posed a threat to David's kingdom, but out of personal vengeance (2 Sam. 3:30). Without telling the king his plans, he sent messengers to retrieve Abner so that he could murder him in cold blood. When David heard what Joab had done, he praised the dead man, but pronounced a curse upon Joab and his family (3:28, 29).

Many things can disqualify someone from godly leadership, and unrestrained vengeance is one of the most effective. God tells us that vengeance belongs to Him (Deut. 32:35). Those who cannot humble themselves to serve God and those He has raised up will eventually act out of selfish motives and hurt the kingdom.

When Joab lost sight of his true calling, he launched out to serve his own selfish interests. In the end, his actions cost him everything (1 Kin. 2:28–35).

returned to Hebron, Joab took him aside in the gate to speak with him privately, and there stabbed him in the stomach, so that he died for the blood of Asahel his brother.

[28]Afterward, when David heard *it,* he said, "My kingdom and I *are* guiltless before the LORD forever of the blood of Abner the son of Ner. [29]Let it rest on the head of Joab and on all his father's house; and let there never fail to be in the house of Joab one who has a discharge or is a leper, who leans on a staff or falls by the sword, or who lacks bread." [30]So Joab and Abishai his brother killed Abner, because he had killed their brother Asahel at Gibeon in the battle.

David's Mourning for Abner

[31]Then David said to Joab and to all the people who were with him, "Tear your clothes, gird yourselves with sackcloth, and mourn for Abner." And King David followed the coffin. [32]So they buried Abner in Hebron; and the king lifted up his voice and wept at the grave of Abner, and all the people wept. [33]And the king sang *a lament* over Abner and said:

"Should Abner die as a fool dies?
[34]   Your hands were not bound
  Nor your feet put into fetters;

As a man falls before wicked men, *so* you fell."

Then all the people wept over him again.

[35]And when all the people came to persuade David to eat food while it was still day, David took an oath, saying, "God do so to me, and more also, if I taste bread or anything else till the sun goes down!" [36]Now all the people took note *of it,* and it pleased them, since whatever the king did pleased all the people. [37]For all the people and all Israel understood that day that it had not been the king's *intent* to kill Abner the son of Ner. [38]Then the king said to his servants, "Do you not know that a prince and a great man has fallen this day in Israel? [39]And I *am* weak today, though anointed king; and these men, the sons of Zeruiah, *are* too harsh for me. The LORD shall repay the evildoer according to his wickedness."

Ishbosheth Is Murdered

4 When Saul's son[a] heard that Abner had died in Hebron, he lost heart, and all Israel was troubled. [2]Now Saul's son *had* two men *who were* captains of troops. The name of one *was* Baanah and the name of the other Rechab, the

4:1 [a]That is, Ishbosheth

DAVID   THE HEART OF A GREAT KING
(2 Samuel 4:5–12)

PROFILE IN LEADERSHIP

As a young teen anointed by the prophet Samuel to one day become king, David patiently awaited his ascent to the throne. Both his influence and his skills continued to grow as he faced many challenges, reflecting the process all leaders must undergo in the leadership journey.

David's honorable actions reveal his integrity and commitment to the legitimate holder of the throne, King Saul, "the LORD's anointed." David refused to usurp power and grew angry when overzealous partisans murdered Ishbosheth in a wicked effort to speed up God's timetable.

By conducting himself in such an honorable way, David modeled the Law of Solid Ground. He recognized that by manipulating his way to power he would only break trust. David clearly understood the Law of Timing; as the chosen leader, he refused to sacrifice his mission and calling on the altar of inappropriate timing.

David's greatness and influence vastly increased as those around him recognized he had committed himself to higher principles. He would not tolerate subordinates who felt free to take matters into their own hands. David sacrificed personal gain for those who sought to destroy him—a classic servant leader. His kept his heart close to God, and consequently his behavior reflected strong inner character and the utmost respect for God's timing.

SAUL AND DAVID AND THE LAW OF THE LID

Leadership Ability Determines a Person's Level of Effectiveness

(2 Samuel 5:1–4)

Success lies within the reach of nearly everyone. But personal success without leadership ability brings only limited effectiveness, achieving only a fraction of what might have occurred with good leadership. The higher you want to climb, the more you need leadership. The greater the impact you want to make, the greater your influence needs to be.

Leadership ability is the lid that determines a person's level of effectiveness. The lower an individual's ability to lead, the lower the lid on his potential. The higher the leadership, the greater the effectiveness. Your leadership ability—for better or for worse—always determines your effectiveness and the potential impact of your organization. To reach the highest level of effectiveness, you have to raise the lid on your leadership ability.

■   ■   ■   ■   ■

Why did Saul fail as Israel's king, while David succeeded? The answer can be found in the Law of the Lid: Leadership ability determines a person's level of effectiveness. While David lifted many lids, Saul's attitude kept the lid clamped down firmly on his leadership. Take a look at the similar paths the men traveled:

1. *Both received counsel from godly men.*

Samuel, the last judge of Israel, anointed both men. And both received the benefit of godly counsel—Saul from Samuel, and David from Samuel and later Nathan the prophet.

2. *Both faced great challenges.*

Every leader faces obstacles, tests, and trials. Saul and David sometimes faced the same ones. Take Goliath, for example: When the huge Philistine offered to fight Israel's champion, both Saul and David heard the challenge. Saul, Israel's greatest warrior, hid in fear. But David, a mere boy, eagerly faced the challenge and won honor for God.

3. *Both had the choice to change and grow.*

Saul and David reacted very differently when confronted with their shortcomings. When Samuel rebuked Saul for making an unauthorized burnt offering to God, the king spoke not a whisper of sorrow or repentance. Evidently Saul kept on the same course.

David possessed an entirely different kind of heart. When Nathan confronted the king after the sordid incident with Bathsheba, David broke down and sorrowfully repented.

The Lids That Limited Saul

God removed all the external lids from Saul's life when the son of Kish ascended Israel's throne. But even without any external lids to his leadership, he still labored under several *internal* lids:

Fear: Saul began his reign by hiding among the equipment.

Impatience: Saul refused to wait for Samuel and offered an illegal sacrifice.

Denial: Saul continued as though all was well even after Samuel declared that God had rejected him as king.

Impulsiveness: Saul rashly made an oath that almost cost him the life of his son.

Deceit: Saul offered his daughter Michal to David, hoping the young man would die in battle to win her hand in marriage.

Jealousy: Saul became enraged when the people compared him to David, and from then on kept a jealous eye on the young man.

Anger: Saul repeatedly tried to kill David.

Because Saul never removed the lids from his leadership, God had to remove him from the throne of Israel.

The Lids That Did *Not* Limit David

David also had many lids on his life, both internal and external, but they did not stop him:

1. *His family*

David's limitations started at home. When Samuel asked Jesse to gather all his sons so God could reveal the next king of Israel, no one thought to invite David. His brothers thought no better of him than did his father. When David visited the battlefront, they scorned him. When David spoke out against Goliath's blasphemy, his brothers insulted him and told him to go home.

2. *His leader*

Saul continually tried to sabotage David's leadership and effectiveness. When David offered to fight Goliath, Saul told him, "You are not able to go against this Philistine to fight with him" (1 Sam. 17:33). Then Saul tried to put his heavy armor on the boy—*he* certainly wasn't going to use it! For many years, Saul tried repeatedly to kill David.

3. *His background*

David came from a family of poor shepherds. His father, Jesse the Bethlehemite, lacked both lofty lineage and powerful position. David wasn't even the eldest son in his family; seven older brothers all came before him.

4. *His youthfulness and inexperience*

At the time Samuel anointed David, the boy had no experience leading anything but sheep. When he stepped forward to fight Goliath, others considered him "only a youth," and he had never fought a wartime battle. Time and again, people underestimated and disrespected him.

The One Who Lifted the Lid

Ultimately David became a great leader—yet not because he lacked limitations in life. He achieved much because he became a lid lifter.

Every leader has lids on his life; nobody is born without them. And they don't disappear when a person receives a title, achieves a position, or gets invested with power. The issue is not whether you have lids, but what you are going to do about them.

sons of Rimmon the Beerothite, of the children of Benjamin. (For Beeroth also was *part* of Benjamin, [3]because the Beerothites fled to Gittaim and have been sojourners there until this day.)

[4]Jonathan, Saul's son, had a son *who was* lame in *his* feet. He was five years old when the news about Saul and Jonathan came from Jezreel; and his nurse took him up and fled. And it happened, as she made haste to flee, that he fell and became lame. His name *was* Mephibosheth.[a]

[5]Then the sons of Rimmon the Beerothite, Rechab and Baanah, set out and came at about the heat of the day to the house of Ishbosheth, who was lying on his bed at noon. [6]And they came there, all the way into the house, *as though* to get wheat, and they stabbed him in the stomach. Then Rechab and Baanah his brother escaped. [7]For when they came into the house, he was lying on his bed in his bedroom; then they struck him and killed him, beheaded him and took his head, and were all night escaping through the plain. [8]And they brought the head of Ishbosheth to David at Hebron, and said to the king, "Here is the head of Ishbosheth, the son of Saul your enemy, who sought your life; and the LORD has avenged my lord the king this day of Saul and his descendants."

[9]But David answered Rechab and Baanah his brother, the sons of Rimmon the Beerothite, and said to them, "*As* the LORD lives, who has redeemed my life from all adversity, [10]when someone told me, saying, 'Look, Saul is dead,' thinking to have brought good news, I arrested him and had him executed in Ziklag—the one who *thought* I would give him a reward for *his* news. [11]How much more, when wicked men have killed a righteous person in his own house on his bed? Therefore, shall I not now require his blood at your hand and remove you from the earth?" [12]So David commanded his young men, and they executed them, cut off their hands and feet, and hanged *them* by the pool in Hebron. But they took the head of Ishbosheth and buried *it* in the tomb of Abner in Hebron.

David Reigns over All Israel

5 Then all the tribes of Israel came to David at Hebron and spoke, saying, "Indeed we *are* your bone and your flesh. [2]Also, in time past, when Saul was king over us, you were the one who led Israel out and brought them in; and the LORD said to you, 'You shall shepherd My people Israel, and be ruler over Israel.'" [3]Therefore all the elders of Israel came to the king at Hebron, and King David made a covenant with them at Hebron before the LORD. And they

---

The Value of Vision
(2 Samuel 5:1–12)

David's vision energized the Hebrew nation far beyond anything Saul had ever imagined. Notice what the vision of David did for the Israelite nation:

1. **Vision unites (vv. 1–3).**
   For the first time in years, "all the tribes" and "all the elders" came together.

2. **Vision provides a center for leadership (vv. 4, 5).**
   David began his reign from Hebron, but desired to unite a divided land and lead from Jerusalem.

3. **Vision dominates inner conversation (vv. 6–8).**
   All of us indulge in "inner conversation." David's vision focused his men as they neared Jerusalem.

4. **Vision inspires greatness (vv. 9, 10).**
   David's dream for Jerusalem helped him and his people realize a great goal together.

5. **Vision attracts others to the leader (vv. 11, 12).**
   Once David had taken Jerusalem, others began to join the cause.

---

anointed David king over Israel. [4]David *was* thirty years old when he began to reign, *and* he reigned forty years. [5]In Hebron he reigned over Judah seven years and six months, and in Jerusalem he reigned thirty-three years over all Israel and Judah.

The Conquest of Jerusalem

[6]And the king and his men went to Jerusalem against the Jebusites, the inhabitants of the land, who spoke to David, saying, "You shall not come in here; but the blind and the lame will repel you," thinking, "David cannot come in here." [7]Nevertheless David took the stronghold of Zion (that *is,* the City of David).

[8]Now David said on that day, "Whoever climbs up by way of the water shaft and defeats the Jebusites (the lame and the blind, *who are*

4:4 [a]Called *Merib-Baal* in 1 Chronicles 8:34 and 9:40

hated by David's soul), *he shall be chief and captain.*"[a] Therefore they say, "The blind and the lame shall not come into the house."

[9]Then David dwelt in the stronghold, and called it the City of David. And David built all around from the Millo[a] and inward. [10]So David went on and became great, and the LORD God of hosts *was* with him.

[11]Then Hiram king of Tyre sent messengers to David, and cedar trees, and carpenters and masons. And they built David a house. [12]So David knew that the LORD had established him as king over Israel, and that He had exalted His kingdom for the sake of His people Israel.

[13]And David took more concubines and wives from Jerusalem, after he had come from Hebron. Also more sons and daughters were born to David. [14]Now these *are* the names of those who were born to him in Jerusalem: Shammua,[a] Shobab, Nathan, Solomon, [15]Ibhar, Elishua,[a] Nepheg, Japhia, [16]Elishama, Eliada, and Eliphelet.

The Philistines Defeated

[17]Now when the Philistines heard that they had anointed David king over Israel, all the Philistines went up to search for David. And David heard *of it* and went down to the stronghold. [18]The Philistines also went and deployed themselves in the Valley of Rephaim. [19]So David inquired of the LORD, saying, "Shall I go up against the Philistines? Will You deliver them into my hand?"

And the LORD said to David, "Go up, for I will doubtless deliver the Philistines into your hand."

[20]So David went to Baal Perazim, and David defeated them there; and he said, "The LORD has broken through my enemies before me, like a breakthrough of water." Therefore he called the name of that place Baal Perazim.[a] [21]And they left their images there, and David and his men carried them away.

[22]Then the Philistines went up once again and deployed themselves in the Valley of Rephaim. [23]Therefore David inquired of the LORD, and He said, "You shall not go up; circle around behind them, and come upon them in front of the mulberry trees. [24]And it shall be, when you hear the sound of marching in the tops of the mulberry trees, then you shall advance quickly. For then the LORD will go out before you to strike the camp of the Philistines." [25]And David did so, as the LORD commanded him; and he drove back the Philistines from Geba[a] as far as Gezer.

Communication: Don't Go Until You Know
(2 Samuel 5:19, 23; 7:3–16)

One of the most crucial leadership questions of all has nothing to do with finding resources, attracting competent team members, or setting a target date. This critical question employs four small but potent words: "What does God say?"

David discovered the importance of this question in two quite different ways. In 2 Samuel 5, he twice hears the Philistines have gathered to attack him. Both times, he inquires of the Lord before he acts. Both times he gets divine instructions, follows them, and succeeds.

Two chapters later, Nathan the prophet speaks for God before receiving divine instructions. God corrects him that night, and he is forced to return to David and amend what he has spoken.

The lesson: Don't act or speak for God until you are sure you represent Him correctly. For the spiritual leader, listening always comes before speaking.

The Ark Brought to Jerusalem

[6] Again David gathered all *the* choice *men* of Israel, thirty thousand. [2]And David arose and went with all the people who *were* with him from Baale Judah to bring up from there the ark of God, whose name is called by the Name,[a] the LORD of Hosts, who dwells *between* the cherubim. [3]So they set the ark of God on a new cart, and brought it out of the house of Abinadab, which *was* on the hill; and Uzzah and Ahio, the sons of Abinadab, drove the new cart.[a] [4]And they brought it out of the house of Abinadab, which *was* on the hill, accompanying the

---

5:8 [a]Compare 1 Chronicles 11:6　**5:9** [a]Literally *The Landfill*　**5:14** [a]Spelled *Shimea* in 1 Chronicles 3:5　**5:15** [a]Spelled *Elishama* in 1 Chronicles 3:6　**5:20** [a]Literally *Master of Breakthroughs*　**5:25** [a]Following Masoretic Text, Targum, and Vulgate; Septuagint reads *Gibeon.*　**6:2** [a]Septuagint, Targum, and Vulgate omit *by the Name;* many Hebrew manuscripts and Syriac read *there.*　**6:3** [a]Septuagint adds *with the ark.*

ark of God; and Ahio went before the ark. [5]Then David and all the house of Israel played *music* before the LORD on all kinds of *instruments of* fir wood, on harps, on stringed instruments, on tambourines, on sistrums, and on cymbals.

[6]And when they came to Nachon's threshing floor, Uzzah put out *his hand* to the ark of God and took hold of it, for the oxen stumbled. [7]Then the anger of the LORD was aroused against Uzzah, and God struck him there for *his* error; and he died there by the ark of God. [8]And David became angry because of the LORD's outbreak against Uzzah; and he called the name of the place Perez Uzzah[a] to this day.

[9]David was afraid of the LORD that day; and he said, "How can the ark of the LORD come to me?" [10]So David would not move the ark of the LORD with him into the City of David; but David took it aside into the house of Obed-Edom the Gittite. [11]The ark of the LORD remained in the house of Obed-Edom the Gittite three months. And the LORD blessed Obed-Edom and all his household.

[12]Now it was told King David, saying, "The LORD has blessed the house of Obed-Edom and all that *belongs* to him, because of the ark of God." So David went and brought up the ark of God from the house of Obed-Edom to the City of David with gladness. [13]And so it was, when those bearing the ark of the LORD had gone six paces, that he sacrificed oxen and fatted sheep. [14]Then David danced before the LORD with all *his* might; and David *was* wearing a linen ephod. [15]So David and all the house of Israel brought up the ark of the LORD with shouting and with the sound of the trumpet.

[16]Now as the ark of the LORD came into the City of David, Michal, Saul's daughter, looked through a window and saw King David leaping and whirling before the LORD; and she despised him in her heart. [17]So they brought the ark of the LORD, and set it in its place in the midst of the tabernacle that David had erected for it. Then David offered burnt offerings and peace offerings before the LORD. [18]And when David had finished offering burnt offerings and peace offerings, he blessed the people in the name of the LORD of hosts. [19]Then he distributed among all the people, among the whole multitude of Israel, both the women and the men, to everyone a loaf of bread, a piece *of meat,* and a cake of raisins. So all the people departed, everyone to his house.

[20]Then David returned to bless his household. And Michal the daughter of Saul came out

---

6:8 [a]Literally *Outburst Against Uzzah*

David's Intimacy with God: People-Pleasing vs. God-Pleasing

(2 Samuel 6:1–23)

What excitement must have filled the air the day David led the parade to bring the Ark of the Covenant to Jerusalem! The marching quickly turned into a celebration, for the "ark of the LORD"—the physical representation of God's presence and blessing—was returning to its rightful place.

David felt so exhilarated by the grand event that he stripped down to a "linen ephod" and "danced before the LORD with all his might," twirling and leaping with joy (2 Sam. 6:14). This radical display disgusted David's image-conscious wife, Michal. She turned on her husband and rebuked him for acting so unsophisticated. Mockingly she said, "How glorious was the king of Israel today, uncovering himself today in the eyes of the maids of his servants, as one of the base fellows shamelessly uncovers himself!" (6:20).

David responded by contrasting two pursuits: people-pleasing vs. God-pleasing. He told her, "It was before the LORD [that I danced]. . . . Therefore I will play music before the LORD. And I will be even more undignified than this, and will be humble in my own sight" (6:21, 22).

God-pleasing leaders can learn three important things from David:

1. **Sacrifice:** David made many sacrifices en route to Jerusalem.
2. **Surrender:** David danced and shouted with reckless abandon before the Lord.
3. **Service:** David gave food generously to all in Israel.

Michal: Obsessed with Image and Reputation

(2 Samuel 6:20)

David's wife, Michal, worried far more about image than authenticity. When David danced before the Lord, she felt ashamed of him. She wanted to guard her family's reputation, remain oh-so sophisticated. But when we focus on appearance rather than substance, we wind up with shallow spirits.

to meet David, and said, "How glorious was the king of Israel today, uncovering himself today in the eyes of the maids of his servants, as one of the base fellows shamelessly uncovers himself!"

²¹So David said to Michal, "*It was* before the LORD, who chose me instead of your father and all his house, to appoint me ruler over the people of the LORD, over Israel. Therefore I will play *music* before the LORD. ²²And I will be even more undignified than this, and will be humble in my own sight. But as for the maidservants of whom you have spoken, by them I will be held in honor."

²³Therefore Michal the daughter of Saul had no children to the day of her death.

God's Covenant with David

7 Now it came to pass when the king was dwelling in his house, and the LORD had given him rest from all his enemies all around, ²that the king said to Nathan the prophet, "See now, I dwell in a house of cedar, but the ark of God dwells inside tent curtains."

³Then Nathan said to the king, "Go, do all that *is* in your heart, for the LORD *is* with you."

⁴But it happened that night that the word of the LORD came to Nathan, saying, ⁵"Go and tell My servant David, 'Thus says the LORD: "Would you build a house for Me to dwell in? ⁶For I have not dwelt in a house since the time that I brought the children of Israel up from Egypt, even to this day, but have moved about in a tent and in a tabernacle. ⁷Wherever I have moved about with all the children of Israel, have I ever spoken a word to anyone from the tribes of Israel, whom I commanded to shepherd My people Israel, saying, 'Why have you not built Me a house of cedar?'"'⁸Now therefore, thus shall you say to My servant David, 'Thus says the LORD of

hosts: "I took you from the sheepfold, from following the sheep, to be ruler over My people, over Israel. ⁹And I have been with you wherever you have gone, and have cut off all your enemies from before you, and have made you a great name, like the name of the great men who *are* on the earth. ¹⁰Moreover I will appoint a place for My people Israel, and will plant them, that they may dwell in a place of their own and move no more; nor shall the sons of wickedness oppress them anymore, as previously, ¹¹since the time that I commanded judges *to be* over My people Israel, and have caused you to rest from all your enemies. Also the LORD tells you that He will make you a house.ᵃ

¹²"When your days are fulfilled and you rest with your fathers, I will set up your seed after you, who will come from your body, and I will establish his kingdom. ¹³He shall build a house for My name, and I will establish the throne of his kingdom forever. ¹⁴I will be his Father, and he

7:11 ᵃThat is, a royal dynasty

The Law of Intuition and Decision Making

(2 Samuel 6:1—7:17)

Within a few years of his ascent to the throne, David's leadership is in full swing. He begins to exercise broad decision-making skills as the king of Israel. Consider several principles we learn from David, the decision maker:

1. Good leaders influence the decisions of others (6:1, 2).
2. Good decision makers want God in the center of the process (6:3–5).
3. Good decision making respects the power of God (6:6–11).
4. Good decisions foster joy and celebration (6:12–15).
5. Good leaders place God's agenda ahead of their own (7:1–3).
6. Good decision makers listen to others (7:4–11).
7. Good leaders positively affect future generations (7:12, 13).
8. Present decisions determine future conditions (7:14–17).

shall be My son. If he commits iniquity, I will chasten him with the rod of men and with the blows of the sons of men. [15]But My mercy shall not depart from him, as I took *it* from Saul, whom I removed from before you. [16]And your house and your kingdom shall be established forever before you.[a] Your throne shall be established forever.'"'

[17]According to all these words and according to all this vision, so Nathan spoke to David.

David's Thanksgiving to God

[18]Then King David went in and sat before the LORD; and he said: "Who *am* I, O Lord GOD? And what is my house, that You have brought me this far? [19]And yet this was a small thing in Your sight, O Lord GOD; and You have also spoken of Your servant's house for a great while to come. *Is* this the manner of man, O Lord GOD? [20]Now what more can David say to You? For You, Lord GOD, know Your servant. [21]For Your word's sake, and according to Your own heart, You have done all these great things, to make Your servant know *them*. [22]Therefore You are great, O Lord GOD.[a] For *there is* none like You, nor *is there any* God besides You, according to all that we have heard with our ears. [23]And who *is* like Your people, like Israel, the one nation on the earth whom God went to redeem for Himself as a people, to make for Himself a name—and to do for Yourself great and awesome deeds for Your land—before Your people whom You redeemed for Yourself from Egypt, the nations, and their gods? [24]For You have made Your people Israel Your very own people forever; and You, LORD, have become their God.

[25]"Now, O LORD God, the word which You have spoken concerning Your servant and concerning his house, establish *it* forever and do as You have said. [26]So let Your name be magnified forever, saying, 'The LORD of hosts *is* the God over Israel.' And let the house of Your servant David be established before You. [27]For You, O LORD of hosts, God of Israel, have revealed *this* to Your servant, saying, 'I will build you a house.' Therefore Your servant has found it in his heart to pray this prayer to You.

[28]"And now, O Lord GOD, You are God, and Your words are true, and You have promised this goodness to Your servant. [29]Now therefore, let it please You to bless the house of Your servant, that it may continue before You forever; for You, O Lord GOD, have spoken *it,* and with Your blessing let the house of Your servant be blessed forever."

David's Further Conquests

8 After this it came to pass that David attacked the Philistines and subdued them. And David took Metheg Ammah from the hand of the Philistines.

[2]Then he defeated Moab. Forcing them down to the ground, he measured them off with a line. With two lines he measured off those to be put to death, and with one full line those to be kept alive. So the Moabites became David's servants, *and* brought tribute.

[3]David also defeated Hadadezer the son of Rehob, king of Zobah, as he went to recover his territory at the River Euphrates. [4]David took from him one thousand *chariots,* seven hundred[a] horsemen, and twenty thousand foot soldiers. Also David hamstrung all the chariot horses, except that he spared *enough* of them for one hundred chariots.

[5]When the Syrians of Damascus came to help Hadadezer king of Zobah, David killed twenty-two thousand of the Syrians. [6]Then David put garrisons in Syria of Damascus; and the Syrians became David's servants, *and* brought tribute. So the LORD preserved David wherever he went. [7]And David took the shields of gold that had belonged to the servants of Hadadezer, and brought them to Jerusalem. [8]Also from Betah[a] and from Berothai, cities of Hadadezer, King David took a large amount of bronze.

[9]When Toi[a] king of Hamath heard that David had defeated all the army of Hadadezer, [10]then Toi sent Joram[a] his son to King David, to greet him and bless him, because he had fought against Hadadezer and defeated him (for Hadadezer had been at war with Toi); and *Joram* brought with him articles of silver, articles of gold, and articles of bronze. [11]King David also dedicated these to the LORD, along with the silver and gold that he had dedicated from all the nations which he had subdued— [12]from Syria,[a] from Moab, from the people of Ammon, from the Philistines, from Amalek, and from the spoil of Hadadezer the son of Rehob, king of Zobah.

[13]And David made *himself* a name when he returned from killing eighteen thousand Syrians[a]

7:16 [a]Septuagint reads *Me.* **7:22** [a]Targum and Syriac read *O LORD God.* **8:4** [a]Or *seven thousand* (compare 1 Chronicles 18:4) **8:8** [a]Spelled *Tibhath* in 1 Chronicles 18:8 **8:9** [a]Spelled *Tou* in 1 Chronicles 18:9 **8:10** [a]Spelled *Hadoram* in 1 Chronicles 18:10 **8:12** [a]Septuagint, Syriac, and some Hebrew manuscripts read *Edom.* **8:13** [a]Septuagint, Syriac, and some Hebrew manuscripts read *Edomites* (compare 1 Chronicles 18:12).

The Law of Victory and Team Building

(2 Samuel 8:1—10:12)

Repeatedly in 2 Samuel King David gives us good illustrations of both the Law of Victory and effective teamwork. David finds a way to help Israel conquer again and again, and he keeps the people working together to achieve new goals. What can we learn about winning teams from David?

A Winning Team . . .

1. Starts with a plan (8:1–3).
2. Develops a structure (8:6, 14).
3. Has an anointed leader (8:6, 14).
4. Puts the interests of others first (8:15).
5. Shares responsibilities with others (8:16–18).
6. Helps each other out (10:9–12).
7. Develops winning team members (23:8–12).
8. Breeds loyalty (23:13–17).

in the Valley of Salt. [14]He also put garrisons in Edom; throughout all Edom he put garrisons, and all the Edomites became David's servants. And the LORD preserved David wherever he went.

David's Administration

[15]So David reigned over all Israel; and David administered judgment and justice to all his people. [16]Joab the son of Zeruiah *was* over the army; Jehoshaphat the son of Ahilud *was* recorder; [17]Zadok the son of Ahitub and Ahimelech the son of Abiathar *were* the priests; Seraiah[a] *was* the scribe; [18]Benaiah the son of Jehoiada *was over* both the Cherethites and the Pelethites; and David's sons were chief ministers.

David's Kindness to Mephibosheth

9 Now David said, "Is there still anyone who is left of the house of Saul, that I may show him kindness for Jonathan's sake?"

[2]And *there was* a servant of the house of Saul whose name *was* Ziba. So when they had called him to David, the king said to him, "*Are* you Ziba?"

He said, "At your service!"

[3]Then the king said, "*Is* there not still some-

one of the house of Saul, to whom I may show the kindness of God?"

And Ziba said to the king, "There is still a son of Jonathan *who is* lame in *his* feet."

[4]So the king said to him, "Where *is* he?"

And Ziba said to the king, "Indeed he *is* in the house of Machir the son of Ammiel, in Lo Debar."

[5]Then King David sent and brought him out of the house of Machir the son of Ammiel, from Lo Debar.

[6]Now when Mephibosheth the son of Jonathan, the son of Saul, had come to David, he fell on his face and prostrated himself. Then David said, "Mephibosheth?"

And he answered, "Here is your servant!"

[7]So David said to him, "Do not fear, for I will surely show you kindness for Jonathan your father's sake, and will restore to you all the land of Saul your grandfather; and you shall eat bread at my table continually."

[8]Then he bowed himself, and said, "What *is* your servant, that you should look upon such a dead dog as I?"

[9]And the king called to Ziba, Saul's servant, and said to him, "I have given to your master's son all that belonged to Saul and to all his house. [10]You therefore, and your sons and your servants, shall work the land for him, and you shall bring in *the harvest,* that your master's son may have food to eat. But Mephibosheth your master's son shall eat bread at my table always." Now Ziba had fifteen sons and twenty servants.

[11]Then Ziba said to the king, "According to all that my lord the king has commanded his servant, so will your servant do."

"As for Mephibosheth," *said the king,* "he

8:17 [a]Spelled *Shavsha* in 1 Chronicles 18:16

Gratitude: David Returns a Favor

(2 Samuel 9:1–13)

Long after Jonathan's death, David returned a favor to his old friend through a kindness shown to Mephibosheth, Jonathan's disabled son. He restored to him all of Saul's belongings; he ordered servants to cultivate his land; and he provided food, income, and a role at court. Gratitude cultivates generosity.

shall eat at my table[a] like one of the king's sons." [12]Mephibosheth had a young son whose name *was* Micha. And all who dwelt in the house of Ziba *were* servants of Mephibosheth. [13]So Mephibosheth dwelt in Jerusalem, for he ate continually at the king's table. And he was lame in both his feet.

The Ammonites and Syrians Defeated

10 It happened after this that the king of the people of Ammon died, and Hanun his son reigned in his place. [2]Then David said, "I will show kindness to Hanun the son of Nahash, as his father showed kindness to me."

So David sent by the hand of his servants to comfort him concerning his father. And David's servants came into the land of the people of Ammon. [3]And the princes of the people of Ammon said to Hanun their lord, "Do you think that David really honors your father because he has sent comforters to you? Has David not *rather* sent his servants to you to search the city, to spy it out, and to overthrow it?"

[4]Therefore Hanun took David's servants, shaved off half of their beards, cut off their garments in the middle, at their buttocks, and sent them away. [5]When they told David, he sent to meet them, because the men were greatly ashamed. And the king said, "Wait at Jericho until your beards have grown, and *then* return."

[6]When the people of Ammon saw that they had made themselves repulsive to David, the people of Ammon sent and hired the Syrians of Beth Rehob and the Syrians of Zoba, twenty thousand foot soldiers; and from the king of Maacah one thousand men, and from Ish-Tob twelve thousand men. [7]Now when David heard *of it,* he sent Joab and all the army of the mighty men. [8]Then the people of Ammon came out and put themselves in battle array at the entrance of the gate. And the Syrians of Zoba, Beth Rehob, Ish-Tob, and Maacah *were* by themselves in the field.

[9]When Joab saw that the battle line was against him before and behind, he chose some of Israel's best and put *them* in battle array against the Syrians. [10]And the rest of the people he put under the command of Abishai his brother, that he might set *them* in battle array against the people of Ammon. [11]Then he said, "If the Syrians are too strong for me, then you shall help me; but if the people of Ammon are too strong for you, then I will come and help you. [12]Be of good courage, and let us be strong for our people and for the cities of our God. And may the LORD do *what is* good in His sight."

[13]So Joab and the people who *were* with him drew near for the battle against the Syrians, and they fled before him. [14]When the people of Ammon saw that the Syrians were fleeing, they also fled before Abishai, and entered the city. So Joab returned from the people of Ammon and went to Jerusalem.

[15]When the Syrians saw that they had been defeated by Israel, they gathered together. [16]Then Hadadezer[a] sent and brought out the Syrians who *were* beyond the River,[b] and they came to Helam. And Shobach the commander of Hadadezer's army *went* before them. [17]When it was told David, he gathered all Israel, crossed over the Jordan, and came to Helam. And the Syrians set themselves in battle array against David and fought with him. [18]Then the Syrians fled before Israel; and David killed seven hundred charioteers and forty thousand horsemen of the Syrians, and struck Shobach the commander of their army, who died there. [19]And when all the kings *who were* servants to Hadadezer[a] saw that they were defeated by Israel, they made peace with Israel and served them. So the Syrians were afraid to help the people of Ammon anymore.

David, Bathsheba, and Uriah

11 It happened in the spring of the year, at the time when kings go out *to battle,* that David sent Joab and his servants with him, and all Israel; and they destroyed the people of Ammon and besieged Rabbah. But David remained at Jerusalem.

[2]Then it happened one evening that David arose from his bed and walked on the roof of the king's house. And from the roof he saw a woman bathing, and the woman *was* very beautiful to behold. [3]So David sent and inquired about the woman. And *someone* said, "*Is* this not Bathsheba, the daughter of Eliam, the wife of Uriah the Hittite?" [4]Then David sent messengers, and took her; and she came to him, and he lay with her, for she was cleansed from her impurity; and she returned to her house. [5]And the woman conceived; so she sent and told David, and said, "I *am* with child."

[6]Then David sent to Joab, *saying,* "Send me Uriah the Hittite." And Joab sent Uriah to David. [7]When Uriah had come to him, David asked how Joab was doing, and how the people were doing, and how the war prospered. [8]And David said to Uriah, "Go down to your house and wash

---

9:11 [a]Septuagint reads *David's table.* 10:16 [a]Hebrew *Hadarezer* [b]That is, the Euphrates 10:19 [a]Hebrew *Hadarezer*

The Law of Solid Ground:
Five Expressions of Power Abuse
(2 Samuel 11:1–27)

Pittacus wrote, "The measure of a man is what he does with power." When David used Bathsheba for his own selfish purposes, he began a long spiral downward into deceit, adultery, and murder.

Second Samuel 11 tells the story of a king who forgot that leaders wield power for one reason only: to serve. Consider the "Path to Abusive Power" in leaders:

Stage One: Surprise—"I get this?"
Stage Two: Self-Esteem—"I need this."
Stage Three: Satisfaction—"I deserve this."
Stage Four: Selfishness—"I demand this."

By watching King David weave a tangled web following his sin with Bathsheba, we notice five common abuses of power that still trip up leaders today. Calvin Miller describes them this way:

1. Drifting away from those disciplines we still demand of our people (v. 1).
2. Believing that others owe us whatever use we can make of them (vv. 2, 3).
3. Attempting to fix things up rather than make things right (v. 6).
4. Refusing to accept that we could be blindly out of God's will (v. 11).
5. Believing that people in our way are expendable (v. 14).

your feet." So Uriah departed from the king's house, and a gift *of food* from the king followed him. [9]But Uriah slept at the door of the king's house with all the servants of his lord, and did not go down to his house. [10]So when they told David, saying, "Uriah did not go down to his house," David said to Uriah, "Did you not come from a journey? Why did you not go down to your house?"

[11]And Uriah said to David, "The ark and Israel and Judah are dwelling in tents, and my lord Joab and the servants of my lord are encamped in the open fields. Shall I then go to my house to eat and drink, and to lie with my wife? *As* you live, and *as* your soul lives, I will not do this thing."

[12]Then David said to Uriah, "Wait here today also, and tomorrow I will let you depart." So Uriah remained in Jerusalem that day and the next. [13]Now when David called him, he ate and drank before him; and he made him drunk. And at evening he went out to lie on his bed with the servants of his lord, but he did not go down to his house.

[14]In the morning it happened that David wrote a letter to Joab and sent *it* by the hand of Uriah. [15]And he wrote in the letter, saying, "Set Uriah in the forefront of the hottest battle, and retreat from him, that he may be struck down and die." [16]So it was, while Joab besieged the city,

that he assigned Uriah to a place where he knew there *were* valiant men. [17]Then the men of the city came out and fought with Joab. And *some* of the people of the servants of David fell; and Uriah the Hittite died also.

[18]Then Joab sent and told David all the things concerning the war, [19]and charged the messenger, saying, "When you have finished telling the matters of the war to the king, [20]if it happens that the king's wrath rises, and he says to you: 'Why did you approach so near to the city when you fought? Did you not know that they would shoot from the wall? [21]Who struck Abimelech the son of Jerubbesheth?[a] Was it not a woman who cast a piece of a millstone on him from the wall, so that he died in Thebez? Why did you go near the wall?'—then you shall say, 'Your servant Uriah the Hittite is dead also.'"

[22]So the messenger went, and came and told David all that Joab had sent by him. [23]And the messenger said to David, "Surely the men prevailed against us and came out to us in the field; then we drove them back as far as the entrance of the gate. [24]The archers shot from the wall at your servants; and *some* of the king's servants are dead, and your servant Uriah the Hittite is dead also."

11:21 [a]Same as *Jerubbaal* (Gideon), Judges 6:32ff

The Law of Sacrifice: Leaders Who Stop Sacrificing Stop Succeeding

(2 Samuel 11:1—12:31)

David is a different man in 2 Samuel 11; 12 than in 1 Samuel 11; 12. Somewhere along the way, he decided he didn't need to sacrifice in order to lead well. He no longer prepared for new challenges. When we stop growing, we stop leading. When we stop sacrificing, we stop succeeding.

²⁵Then David said to the messenger, "Thus you shall say to Joab: 'Do not let this thing displease you, for the sword devours one as well as another. Strengthen your attack against the city, and overthrow it.' So encourage him."

²⁶When the wife of Uriah heard that Uriah her husband was dead, she mourned for her husband. ²⁷And when her mourning was over, David sent and brought her to his house, and she became his wife and bore him a son. But the thing that David had done displeased the LORD.

Nathan's Parable and David's Confession

12 Then the LORD sent Nathan to David. And he came to him, and said to him: "There were two men in one city, one rich and the other poor. ²The rich *man* had exceedingly many flocks and herds. ³But the poor *man* had nothing, except one little ewe lamb which he had bought and nourished; and it grew up together with him and with his children. It ate of his own food and drank from his own cup and lay in his bosom; and it was like a daughter to him. ⁴And a traveler came to the rich man, who refused to take from his own flock and from his own herd to prepare one for the wayfaring man who had come to him; but he took the poor man's lamb and prepared it for the man who had come to him."

⁵So David's anger was greatly aroused against the man, and he said to Nathan, "*As* the LORD lives, the man who has done this shall surely die! ⁶And he shall restore fourfold for the lamb, because he did this thing and because he had no pity."

⁷Then Nathan said to David, "You *are* the man! Thus says the LORD God of Israel: 'I anointed you king over Israel, and I delivered you from the hand of Saul. ⁸I gave you your master's house and your master's wives into your keeping, and gave you the house of Israel and Judah. And if *that had been* too little, I also would have given you much more! ⁹Why have you despised the commandment of the LORD, to do evil in His sight? You have killed Uriah the Hittite with the sword; you have taken his wife *to be* your wife, and have killed him with the sword of the people of Ammon. ¹⁰Now therefore, the sword shall never depart from your house, because you have despised Me, and have taken the wife of Uriah the Hittite to be your wife.' ¹¹Thus says the LORD: 'Behold, I will raise up adversity against you from your own house; and I will take your wives before your eyes and give *them* to your neighbor, and he shall lie with your wives in the sight of this sun. ¹²For you did *it* secretly, but I will do this thing before all Israel, before the sun.'"

¹³So David said to Nathan, "I have sinned against the LORD."

And Nathan said to David, "The LORD also has put away your sin; you shall not die. ¹⁴However, because by this deed you have given great occasion to the enemies of the LORD to blaspheme, the child also *who is* born to you shall surely die." ¹⁵Then Nathan departed to his house.

The Death of David's Son

And the LORD struck the child that Uriah's wife bore to David, and it became ill. ¹⁶David therefore pleaded with God for the child, and David fasted and went in and lay all night on the ground. ¹⁷So the elders of his house arose *and went* to him, to raise him up from the ground. But he would not, nor did he eat food with them. ¹⁸Then on the seventh day it came to pass that the child died. And the servants of David were afraid to tell him that the child was dead. For they said, "Indeed, while the child was alive, we spoke to him, and he would not heed our voice. How can we tell him that the child is dead? He may do some harm!"

¹⁹When David saw that his servants were whispering, David perceived that the child was dead. Therefore David said to his servants, "Is the child dead?"

And they said, "He is dead."

²⁰So David arose from the ground, washed and anointed himself, and changed his clothes; and he went into the house of the LORD and worshiped. Then he went to his own house; and

21 QUALITIES

SECURITY

Nathan Feared No One

(2 Samuel 12:1–14)

Security provides the foundation for strong leadership. When we feel insecure, we drift from our mission whenever trouble arises. We must feel secure, or when people stop liking us; when funding drops; when morale dips; or when others reject or criticize us—we will crumble. If we do not feel secure, fear will eventually cause us to sabotage our leadership.

Imagine what might have happened had Nathan lacked security. Consider the odds stacked against him. He knew he had to confront David in his sin, yet David had covered up everything so well; no one else knew what had happened. That meant Nathan could expect no moral support. Further, the popular David had led Israel to prominence among the nations, and most Israelites would side with David if he put up a fight. Finally, from a technical viewpoint, David hadn't done anything illegal to Uriah. He had set up the man to be killed in battle by the Ammonites, but it wasn't his spear or sword that took Uriah's life. Nathan had to feel utterly secure in his plan of attack, or it would backfire.

What enabled Nathan to demonstrate secure leadership?

1. *Nathan had God's truth behind him.* He didn't have to stand alone against David.
2. *Nathan had a relationship with David.* Their friendship created the bridge that allowed Nathan to do what God called him to do.
3. *Nathan's identity depended upon his divine call, not his popularity.* Nathan determined to speak God's truth regardless of the popular reaction.
4. *Nathan understood his personal mission.* He operated out of deep conviction.
5. *Nathan was humble and broken.* He had nothing to lose, for he had died to personal ambition.

Common Symptoms of Insecurity

The following symptoms usually indicate feelings of insecurity:

1. *Comparison*—We compare ourselves with others and keep score.
2. *Compensation*—We feel like a victim and must compensate for our losses.
3. *Competition*—We become self-consumed and try to outdo others for attention.
4. *Compulsion*—We feel driven to perform in order to gain other's approval.
5. *Condemnation*—We judge others or ourselves, resulting in self-pity or conceit.
6. *Control*—We feel we must take charge, protect our interests, and manipulate.

Four Keys to Security

To reduce personal insecurities, build the following four ingredients into your life:

1. *Identity:* Establish your identity in Christ, not in performance.
2. *Brokenness:* Allow God to break you of self-sufficiency and self-promotion.
3. *Purpose:* Discover and practice your God-given purpose in life, not someone else's.
4. *Give and receive the blessing:* Learn to affirm others and receive affirmation.

For a negative example of security, see p. 1150.

The Law of the Inner Circle: Nathan Confronts David

(2 Samuel 12:1–15)

"Be sure your sins will find you out," we say almost flippantly, but David's life illustrates the reality of the phrase.

Nathan confronted David as part of the king's "inner circle." He had permission to speak hard truth in love, so he used a clever narrative to bring his point home. David had failed miserably. But his failure wasn't final. Look at what's needed in order to survive a major failure:

1. An open and transparent heart
It's easier to tolerate mistakes admitted than mistakes denied.

2. A spirit of forgiveness toward followers
A follower you treat with charity is more prone to forgive you when you are caught failing.

3. A responsible attitude
A leader who owns up to his or her behavior will last longer and fare better.

4. The ability to change
Leaders must demonstrate they are humble and teachable and willing to grow or change.

5. A hunger to grow and stretch
Followers will stay with a leader in process if he or she is moving in the right direction.

David must have blanched when Nathan pointed a finger at him and shouted, "You are the man!" (2 Sam. 12:7). Yet thank God for Nathan! All leaders need a Nathan in their inner circle, and if they don't have one, they need to find one. Soon.

---

when he requested, they set food before him, and he ate. [21]Then his servants said to him, "What *is* this that you have done? You fasted and wept for the child *while he was* alive, but when the child died, you arose and ate food."

[22]And he said, "While the child was alive, I fasted and wept; for I said, 'Who can tell *whether* the LORD[a] will be gracious to me, that the child may live?' [23]But now he is dead; why should I fast? Can I bring him back again? I shall go to him, but he shall not return to me."

Solomon Is Born

[24]Then David comforted Bathsheba his wife, and went in to her and lay with her. So she bore a son, and he[a] called his name Solomon. Now the LORD loved him, [25]and He sent *word* by the hand of Nathan the prophet: So he[a] called his name Jedidiah,[b] because of the LORD.

Rabbah Is Captured

[26]Now Joab fought against Rabbah of the people of Ammon, and took the royal city. [27]And Joab sent messengers to David, and said, "I have fought against Rabbah, and I have taken the city's water *supply*. [28]Now therefore, gather the rest of the people together and encamp against the city and take it, lest I take the city and it be called after my name." [29]So David gath-

ered all the people together and went to Rabbah, fought against it, and took it. [30]Then he took their king's crown from his head. Its weight *was* a talent of gold, with precious stones. And it was *set* on David's head. Also he brought out the spoil of the city in great abundance. [31]And he brought out the people who *were* in it, and put *them to work* with saws and iron picks and iron axes, and made them cross over to the brick works. So he did to all the cities of the people of Ammon. Then David and all the people returned to Jerusalem.

Amnon and Tamar

13 After this Absalom the son of David had a lovely sister, whose name *was* Tamar; and Amnon the son of David loved her. [2]Amnon was so distressed over his sister Tamar that he became sick; for she *was* a virgin. And it was improper for Amnon to do anything to her. [3]But Amnon had a friend whose name *was* Jonadab the son of Shimeah, David's

---

12:22 [a]A few Hebrew manuscripts and Syriac read *God.* **12:24** [a]Following Kethib, Septuagint, and Vulgate; Qere, a few Hebrew manuscripts, Syriac, and Targum read *she.* **12:25** [a]Qere, some Hebrew manuscripts, Syriac, and Targum read *she.* [b]Literally *Beloved of the LORD*

DISCERNMENT

Nathan Saw Below the Surface
(2 Samuel 12:1–15)

Like Samuel before him, the prophet Nathan served as a leader to the leaders. God used Nathan to correct his erring leader.

Nathan knew David had slept with another man's wife and subsequently caused the man's death. Although the king had multiple wives, he still insisted on having one more. Nathan saw a greedy and selfish heart in Israel's king. Few individuals in David's reign wielded the influence or had the guts to confront him in his sin. Once Nathan discerned what David had done, he gained an audience with the king, told him a compelling story, and with great poise dealt with the problem in a caring but firm manner.

Nathan could act as he did because of his keen, God-given discernment. He knew what had happened and what lay beneath the surface of David's wicked behavior. Discernment goes deeper than knowledge, resembling intuition. At times, discernment is a gift; at other times, it results from much experience. Discernment brings a profound perception of what is occurring, either on the outside or the inside of a person. What gave Nathan such keen discernment?

1. *He had been listening to God* (v. 1).
   The text says God "sent" him to David. Obviously, God had been speaking to His prophet.
2. *He knew David's circumstances* (vv. 1–6).
   Nathan had watched David for many years and so recognized the egregious changes when they came.
3. *He was objective in his perspective* (vv. 7, 8).
   Nathan could speak for God and provide God's viewpoint on the king's situation.
4. *He understood the root issues* (vv. 9–12).
   Nathan saw more than symptoms; he saw root problems and consequences.
5. *He saw the ultimate cause and effect* (v. 14).
   Nathan passionately championed the name and reputation of God. He hated how the pagan nations surrounding Israel might mock the Lord should they hear of David's sin.

How Do We Grow in Our Discernment?

To improve your discernment as a leader, do the following:

1. *Learn to hear God's voice.* Get quiet and read Scripture. Reflect on the mind of God.
2. *Build problem-solving skills.* If you can see root issues of problems, you can solve those difficulties.
3. *Analyze your successes.* What worked? Can you identify the heart of the matter?
4. *Evaluate your options.* Discernment involves both your gut and your head.
5. *Expand your opportunities.* Get more experience to help you deepen your wisdom.
6. *Explore what others think.* Choose some leaders you admire and study how they think.
7. *Listen to your gut.* Most people are afraid to listen to their God-given intuition.

For a negative example of discernment, see p. 183.

Responsibility: If You Won't Carry the Ball, You Can't Lead the Team

(2 Samuel 13:1–39)

David suffers the first of several horrible consequences of his sin with Bathsheba shortly after some military conquests. David's son, Amnon, rapes his half sister, Tamar. When David hears about it, he does nothing—surprising and upsetting David's son, Absalom. After two years, Absalom murders Amnon. The whole mess plays out almost like a soap opera.

By this point, David's leadership has shrunk to a mere shadow of its former self. Note the changes in David's leadership:

1. He no longer works proactively, but passively interacts with those closest to him (vv. 30, 31).
2. He no longer expresses joy, but is full of grief and mourning (v. 31).
3. He no longer acts on his convictions, but buys into rationalizations about his loss (vv. 32, 33, 39).
4. He no longer solves problems, but licks his wounds (vv. 34–36).
5. He no longer pursues his desires, but remains paralyzed regarding Absalom (v. 39).

brother. Now Jonadab *was* a very crafty man. ⁴And he said to him, "Why *are* you, the king's son, becoming thinner day after day? Will you not tell me?"

Amnon said to him, "I love Tamar, my brother Absalom's sister."

⁵So Jonadab said to him, "Lie down on your bed and pretend to be ill. And when your father comes to see you, say to him, 'Please let my sister Tamar come and give me food, and prepare the food in my sight, that I may see *it* and eat it from her hand.' " ⁶Then Amnon lay down and pretended to be ill; and when the king came to see him, Amnon said to the king, "Please let Tamar my sister come and make a couple of cakes for me in my sight, that I may eat from her hand."

⁷And David sent home to Tamar, saying, "Now go to your brother Amnon's house, and prepare food for him." ⁸So Tamar went to her brother Amnon's house; and he was lying down. Then she took flour and kneaded *it,* made cakes in his sight, and baked the cakes. ⁹And she took the pan and placed *them* out before him, but he refused to eat. Then Amnon said, "Have everyone go out from me." And they all went out from him. ¹⁰Then Amnon said to Tamar, "Bring the food into the bedroom, that I may eat from your hand." And Tamar took the cakes which she had made, and brought *them* to Amnon her brother in the bedroom. ¹¹Now when she had brought *them* to him to eat, he took hold of her and said to her, "Come, lie with me, my sister."

¹²But she answered him, "No, my brother, do not force me, for no such thing should be done in Israel. Do not do this disgraceful thing! ¹³And I, where could I take my shame? And as for you, you would be like one of the fools in Israel. Now therefore, please speak to the king; for he will not withhold me from you." ¹⁴However, he would not heed her voice; and being stronger than she, he forced her and lay with her.

¹⁵Then Amnon hated her exceedingly, so that the hatred with which he hated her *was* greater than the love with which he had loved her. And Amnon said to her, "Arise, be gone!"

¹⁶So she said to him, "No, indeed! This evil of sending me away *is* worse than the other that you did to me."

But he would not listen to her. ¹⁷Then he called his servant who attended him, and said, "Here! Put this *woman* out, away from me, and bolt the door behind her." ¹⁸Now she had on a robe of many colors, for the king's virgin daughters wore such apparel. And his servant put her out and bolted the door behind her.

¹⁹Then Tamar put ashes on her head, and tore her robe of many colors that *was* on her, and laid her hand on her head and went away crying bitterly. ²⁰And Absalom her brother said to her, "Has Amnon your brother been with you? But now hold your peace, my sister. He *is* your brother; do not take this thing to heart." So Tamar remained desolate in her brother Absalom's house.

²¹But when King David heard of all these things, he was very angry. ²²And Absalom spoke to his brother Amnon neither good nor bad. For Absalom hated Amnon, because he had forced his sister Tamar.

Absalom Murders Amnon

²³And it came to pass, after two full years, that Absalom had sheepshearers in Baal Hazor, which *is* near Ephraim; so Absalom invited all the king's

21 QUALITIES

PASSION

Absalom Ruins His Own Cause
(2 Samuel 13:22—18:9)

After David sinned with Bathsheba, the prophet Nathan warned the king that the sword would never depart from his house (2 Sam. 12:10). True to the prediction, David endured domestic problems from that day on—deception, adultery, incest, even murder. David never figured out how to deal with the rebellion effectively; it was as though his anointing and authority had left him.

No one saw this more clearly than his son, Absalom. When Amnon raped his sister Tamar and David did nothing about it, Absalom became irate (13:22). His fury grew the longer the king delayed justice. Further, Absalom tried and failed to get an audience with his father. It was as though David had abandoned his role as spiritual leader over his family.

Finally, Absalom could take it no longer. He got everyone's attention by committing two crimes. First, he avenged his sister Tamar by murdering Amnon; for this crime his father David banished him (13:37, 38). After he was permitted to return, Absalom got angry with general Joab and set his field on fire (14:30).

Despite his actions, Absalom couldn't get the fatherly attention he wanted so desperately. Past the boiling point, he used his passion to sabotage his father's leadership. He played politics and convinced people to bring their lawsuits to him. He lobbied for support of his leadership. Finally he raised an army to rebel against the king.

In the end, Absalom died as a maverick leader whose passion went awry. As you study his story in 2 Samuel 13—18, look for those lessons about passion gone bad:

1. Passion without perspective brings death (13:22–29).
2. Passion *will* find expression, in either healthy or unhealthy ways (14:28–30).
3. People follow passion over orthodoxy, even when it's unwise (15:1–12).
4. Leaders who follow passion defeat leaders who follow protocol (15:13, 14).
5. Self-centered passion always skews the judgment of a leader (16:22).
6. Unchanneled and unbridled passion damages everyone near it (17; 18).
7. When passion outweighs wisdom, leaders sabotage themselves (18:9).

The Good News

Absalom represents a leader who can't bridle his passion. When a leader embraces passion before he learns submission, trouble always follows.

Does this mean we should condemn passion? Absolutely not! Passion is one of the 21 Indispensable Qualities of a Leader. Consider the benefits of passion:

1. Passion is the first step to achievement.
2. Passion increases your willpower.
3. Passion changes you.
4. Passion makes the impossible possible.

Passion helps develop your leadership. Passion must, however, pour from the heart of a leader who is wise, accountable, submissive, and unselfish.

For a positive example of passion, see p. 1232.

sons. [24]Then Absalom came to the king and said, "Kindly note, your servant has sheepshearers; please, let the king and his servants go with your servant."

[25]But the king said to Absalom, "No, my son, let us not all go now, lest we be a burden to you." Then he urged him, but he would not go; and he blessed him.

[26]Then Absalom said, "If not, please let my brother Amnon go with us."

And the king said to him, "Why should he go with you?" [27]But Absalom urged him; so he let Amnon and all the king's sons go with him.

[28]Now Absalom had commanded his servants, saying, "Watch now, when Amnon's heart is merry with wine, and when I say to you, 'Strike Amnon!' then kill him. Do not be afraid. Have I not commanded you? Be courageous and valiant." [29]So the servants of Absalom did to Amnon as Absalom had commanded. Then all the king's sons arose, and each one got on his mule and fled.

[30]And it came to pass, while they were on the way, that news came to David, saying, "Absalom has killed all the king's sons, and not one of them is left!" [31]So the king arose and tore his garments and lay on the ground, and all his servants stood by with their clothes torn. [32]Then Jonadab the son of Shimeah, David's brother, answered and said, "Let not my lord suppose they have killed all the young men, the king's sons, for only Amnon is dead. For by the command of Absalom this has been determined from the day that he forced his sister Tamar. [33]Now therefore, let not my lord the king take the thing to his heart, to think that all the king's sons are dead. For only Amnon is dead."

Absalom Flees to Geshur

[34]Then Absalom fled. And the young man who was keeping watch lifted his eyes and looked, and there, many people were coming from the road on the hillside behind him.[a] [35]And Jonadab said to the king, "Look, the king's sons are coming; as your servant said, so it is." [36]So it was, as soon as he had finished speaking, that the king's sons indeed came, and they lifted up their voice and wept. Also the king and all his servants wept very bitterly.

[37]But Absalom fled and went to Talmai the son of Ammihud, king of Geshur. And *David* mourned for his son every day. [38]So Absalom fled and went to Geshur, and was there three years. [39]And King David[a] longed to go to[b] Absalom. For he had been comforted concerning Amnon, because he was dead.

Absalom Returns to Jerusalem

14 So Joab the son of Zeruiah perceived that the king's heart *was* concerned about Absalom. [2]And Joab sent to Tekoa and brought from there a wise woman, and said to her, "Please pretend to be a mourner, and put on mourning apparel; do not anoint yourself with oil, but act like a woman who has been mourning a long time for the dead. [3]Go to the king and speak to him in this manner." So Joab put the words in her mouth.

[4]And when the woman of Tekoa spoke[a] to the king, she fell on her face to the ground and prostrated herself, and said, "Help, O king!"

[5]Then the king said to her, "What troubles you?"

And she answered, "Indeed I *am* a widow, my husband is dead. [6]Now your maidservant had two sons; and the two fought with each other in the field, and *there was* no one to part them, but the one struck the other and killed him. [7]And now the whole family has risen up against your maidservant, and they said, 'Deliver him who struck his brother, that we may execute him for the life of his brother whom he killed; and we will destroy the heir also.' So they would extinguish my ember that is left, and leave to my husband *neither* name nor remnant on the earth."

[8]Then the king said to the woman, "Go to your house, and I will give orders concerning you."

[9]And the woman of Tekoa said to the king, "My lord, O king, *let* the iniquity *be* on me and on my father's house, and the king and his throne *be* guiltless."

[10]So the king said, "Whoever says *anything* to you, bring him to me, and he shall not touch you anymore."

[11]Then she said, "Please let the king remember the LORD your God, and do not permit the avenger of blood to destroy anymore, lest they destroy my son."

And he said, "*As* the LORD lives, not one hair of your son shall fall to the ground."

[12]Therefore the woman said, "Please, let your maidservant speak *another* word to my lord the king."

13:34 [a]Septuagint adds *And the watchman went and told the king, and said, "I see men from the way of Horonaim, from the regions of the mountains."*
13:39 [a]Following Masoretic Text, Syriac, and Vulgate; Septuagint reads *the spirit of the king;* Targum reads *the soul of King David.* [b]Following Masoretic Text and Targum; Septuagint and Vulgate read *ceased to pursue after.* **14:4** [a]Many Hebrew manuscripts, Septuagint, Syriac, and Vulgate read *came.*

And he said, "Say on."

[13]So the woman said: "Why then have you schemed such a thing against the people of God? For the king speaks this thing as one who is guilty, *in that* the king does not bring his banished one home again. [14]For we will surely die and *become* like water spilled on the ground, which cannot be gathered up again. Yet God does not take away a life; but He devises means, so that His banished ones are not expelled from Him. [15]Now therefore, I have come to speak of this thing to my lord the king because the people have made me afraid. And your maidservant said, 'I will now speak to the king; it may be that the king will perform the request of his maidservant. [16]For the king will hear and deliver his maidservant from the hand of the man *who would* destroy me and my son together from the inheritance of God.' [17]Your maidservant said, 'The word of my lord the king will now be comforting; for as the angel of God, so *is* my lord the king in discerning good and evil. And may the Lord your God be with you.' "

[18]Then the king answered and said to the woman, "Please do not hide from me anything that I ask you."

And the woman said, "Please, let my lord the king speak."

[19]So the king said, "*Is* the hand of Joab with you in all this?" And the woman answered and said, "*As* you live, my lord the king, no one can turn to the right hand or to the left from anything that my lord the king has spoken. For your servant Joab commanded me, and he put all these words in the mouth of your maidservant. [20]To bring about this change of affairs your servant Joab has done this thing; but my lord *is* wise, according to the wisdom of the angel of God, to know everything that *is* in the earth."

[21]And the king said to Joab, "All right, I have granted this thing. Go therefore, bring back the young man Absalom."

[22]Then Joab fell to the ground on his face and bowed himself, and thanked the king. And Joab said, "Today your servant knows that I have found favor in your sight, my lord, O king, in that the king has fulfilled the request of his servant." [23]So Joab arose and went to Geshur, and brought Absalom to Jerusalem. [24]And the king said, "Let him return to his own house, but do not let him see my face." So Absalom returned to his own house, but did not see the king's face.

David Forgives Absalom

[25]Now in all Israel there was no one who was praised as much as Absalom for his good looks. From the sole of his foot to the crown of his head there was no blemish in him. [26]And when he cut the hair of his head—at the end of every year he cut *it* because it was heavy on him— when he cut it, he weighed the hair of his head at two hundred shekels according to the king's standard. [27]To Absalom were born three sons, and one daughter whose name *was* Tamar. She was a woman of beautiful appearance.

[28]And Absalom dwelt two full years in Jerusalem, but did not see the king's face. [29]Therefore Absalom sent for Joab, to send him to the king, but he would not come to him. And when he sent again the second time, he would not come. [30]So he said to his servants, "See, Joab's field is near mine, and he has barley there; go and set it on fire." And Absalom's servants set the field on fire.

[31]Then Joab arose and came to Absalom's house, and said to him, "Why have your servants set my field on fire?"

[32]And Absalom answered Joab, "Look, I sent to you, saying, 'Come here, so that I may send you to the king, to say, "Why have I come from Geshur? *It would be* better for me *to be* there still." ' Now therefore, let me see the king's face; but if there is iniquity in me, let him execute me."

[33]So Joab went to the king and told him. And when he had called for Absalom, he came to the king and bowed himself on his face to the ground before the king. Then the king kissed Absalom.

Absalom's Treason

15 After this it happened that Absalom provided himself with chariots and horses, and fifty men to run before him. [2]Now Absalom would rise early and stand beside the way to the gate. *So it was, whenever anyone who had a lawsuit came to the king for a decision, that Absalom would call to him and say, "What city *are* you from?" And he would say, "Your servant *is* from such and such a tribe of Israel." [3]Then Absalom would say to him, "Look, your case *is* good and right; but *there is* no deputy of the king to hear you." [4]Moreover Absalom would say, "Oh, that I were made judge in the land, and everyone who has any suit or cause would come to me; then I would give him justice." [5]And *so* it was, whenever anyone came near to bow down to him, that he would put out his hand and take him and kiss him. [6]In this manner Absalom acted toward all Israel who came to the king for judgment. So Absalom stole the hearts of the men of Israel.

The Law of Respect:
Absalom Assumes Power, David Flees
(2 Samuel 15:1–37)

Some time after he returns to Jerusalem following the murder of his brother Amnon, Absalom rises to power and assumes a position of leadership in Israel. In the intervening years he becomes a stronger, more forceful leader than his father, David.

Despite David's natural leadership abilities, somehow he lost his conviction and resolve. Before the chapter ends, we see David running from his own son—thus reminding us of the Law of Respect. People usually follow leaders who are stronger than themselves. It's not hard to see why Absalom could rally so many Israelites to his side:

Absalom
1. Provides himself with resources and weapons
2. Speaks about justice and meeting other's needs
3. Steals the people's hearts with his charisma
4. Rallies the people behind his vision
5. Rises up in courage to lead Israel

David
1. No longer goes out to battle
2. Doesn't provide enough deputies
3. Becomes distant and out of touch with people
4. Maintains politically correct view
5. Flees in fear of Absalom

---

[7]Now it came to pass after forty[a] years that Absalom said to the king, "Please, let me go to Hebron and pay the vow which I made to the LORD. [8]For your servant took a vow while I dwelt at Geshur in Syria, saying, 'If the LORD indeed brings me back to Jerusalem, then I will serve the LORD.'"

[9]And the king said to him, "Go in peace." So he arose and went to Hebron.

[10]Then Absalom sent spies throughout all the tribes of Israel, saying, "As soon as you hear the sound of the trumpet, then you shall say, 'Absalom reigns in Hebron!'" [11]And with Absalom went two hundred men invited from Jerusalem, and they went along innocently and did not know anything. [12]Then Absalom sent for Ahithophel the Gilonite, David's counselor, from his city—from Giloh—while he offered sacrifices. And the conspiracy grew strong, for the people with Absalom continually increased in number.

David Escapes from Jerusalem

[13]Now a messenger came to David, saying, "The hearts of the men of Israel are with Absalom."

[14]So David said to all his servants who *were* with him at Jerusalem, "Arise, and let us flee, or we shall not escape from Absalom. Make haste to depart, lest he overtake us suddenly and bring disaster upon us, and strike the city with the edge of the sword."

[15]And the king's servants said to the king, "We *are* your servants, *ready to do* whatever my lord the king commands." [16]Then the king went out with all his household after him. But the king left ten women, concubines, to keep the house. [17]And the king went out with all the people after him, and stopped at the outskirts. [18]Then all his servants passed before him; and all the Cherethites, all the Pelethites, and all the Gittites, six hundred men who had followed him from Gath, passed before the king.

[19]Then the king said to Ittai the Gittite, "Why are you also going with us? Return and remain with the king. For you *are* a foreigner and also an exile from your own place. [20]In fact, you came *only* yesterday. Should I make you wander up and down with us today, since I go I know not where? Return, and take your brethren back. Mercy and truth *be* with you."

[21]But Ittai answered the king and said, "*As* the LORD lives, and *as* my lord the king lives, surely in whatever place my lord the king shall be, whether in death or life, even there also your servant will be."

15:7 [a]Septuagint manuscripts, Syriac, and Josephus read *four*.

²²So David said to Ittai, "Go, and cross over." Then Ittai the Gittite and all his men and all the little ones who *were* with him crossed over. ²³And all the country wept with a loud voice, and all the people crossed over. The king himself also crossed over the Brook Kidron, and all the people crossed over toward the way of the wilderness.

²⁴There was Zadok also, and all the Levites with him, bearing the ark of the covenant of God. And they set down the ark of God, and Abiathar went up until all the people had finished crossing over from the city. ²⁵Then the king said to Zadok, "Carry the ark of God back into the city. If I find favor in the eyes of the LORD, He will bring me back and show me *both* it and His dwelling place. ²⁶But if He says thus: 'I have no delight in you,' here I am, let Him do to me as seems good to Him." ²⁷The king also said to Zadok the priest, "*Are* you *not* a seer? Return to the city in peace, and your two sons with you, Ahimaaz your son, and Jonathan the son of Abiathar. ²⁸See, I will wait in the plains of the wilderness until word comes from you to inform me." ²⁹Therefore Zadok and Abiathar carried the ark of God back to Jerusalem. And they remained there.

³⁰So David went up by the Ascent of the *Mount of* Olives, and wept as he went up; and he had his head covered and went barefoot. And all the people who *were* with him covered their heads and went up, weeping as they went up. ³¹Then *someone* told David, saying, "Ahithophel *is* among the conspirators with Absalom." And David said, "O LORD, I pray, turn the counsel of Ahithophel into foolishness!"

³²Now it happened when David had come to the top *of the mountain,* where he worshiped God—there was Hushai the Archite coming to meet him with his robe torn and dust on his head. ³³David said to him, "If you go on with me, then you will become a burden to me. ³⁴But if you return to the city, and say to Absalom, 'I will be your servant, O king; as I *was* your father's servant previously, so I *will* now also *be* your servant,' then you may defeat the counsel of Ahithophel for me. ³⁵And *do* you not *have* Zadok and Abiathar the priests with you there? Therefore it will be *that* whatever you hear from the king's house, you shall tell to Zadok and Abiathar the priests. ³⁶Indeed *they have* there with them their two sons, Ahimaaz, Zadok's *son,* and Jonathan, Abiathar's *son;* and by them you shall send me everything you hear."

³⁷So Hushai, David's friend, went into the city. And Absalom came into Jerusalem.

Mephibosheth's Servant

16 When David was a little past the top *of the mountain,* there was Ziba the servant of Mephibosheth, who met him with a couple of saddled donkeys, and on them two hundred *loaves* of bread, one hundred clusters of raisins, one hundred summer fruits, and a skin of wine. ²And the king said to Ziba, "What do you mean to do with these?"

So Ziba said, "The donkeys *are* for the king's household to ride on, the bread and summer fruit for the young men to eat, and the wine for those who are faint in the wilderness to drink."

³Then the king said, "And where *is* your master's son?"

And Ziba said to the king, "Indeed he is staying in Jerusalem, for he said, 'Today the house of Israel will restore the kingdom of my father to me.'"

⁴So the king said to Ziba, "Here, all that *belongs* to Mephibosheth *is* yours."

And Ziba said, "I humbly bow before you, *that* I may find favor in your sight, my lord, O king!"

Shimei Curses David

⁵Now when King David came to Bahurim, there was a man from the family of the house of Saul, whose name *was* Shimei the son of Gera, coming from there. He came out, cursing continuously as he came. ⁶And he threw stones at David and at all the servants of King David. And all the people and all the mighty men *were* on his right hand and on his left. ⁷Also Shimei said thus when he cursed: "Come out! Come out! You bloodthirsty man, you rogue! ⁸The LORD has brought upon you all the blood of the house of Saul, in whose place you have reigned; and the LORD has delivered the kingdom into the hand of Absalom your son. So now you *are caught* in your own evil, because you are a bloodthirsty man!"

⁹Then Abishai the son of Zeruiah said to the king, "Why should this dead dog curse my lord the king? Please, let me go over and take off his head!"

¹⁰But the king said, "What have I to do with you, you sons of Zeruiah? So let him curse, because the LORD has said to him, 'Curse David.' Who then shall say, 'Why have you done so?'"

¹¹And David said to Abishai and all his servants, "See how my son who came from my own body seeks my life. How much more now *may this* Benjamite? Let him alone, and let him curse; for so the LORD has ordered him. ¹²It may

be that the LORD will look on my affliction,[a] and that the LORD will repay me with good for his cursing this day." [13]And as David and his men went along the road, Shimei went along the hillside opposite him and cursed as he went, threw stones at him and kicked up dust. [14]Now the king and all the people who *were* with him became weary; so they refreshed themselves there.

The Advice of Ahithophel

[15]Meanwhile Absalom and all the people, the men of Israel, came to Jerusalem; and Ahithophel *was* with him. [16]And so it was, when Hushai the Archite, David's friend, came to Absalom, that Hushai said to Absalom, "*Long* live the king! *Long* live the king!"

[17]So Absalom said to Hushai, "*Is* this your loyalty to your friend? Why did you not go with your friend?"

[18]And Hushai said to Absalom, "No, but whom the LORD and this people and all the men of Israel choose, his I will be, and with him I will remain. [19]Furthermore, whom should I serve? *Should I* not *serve* in the presence of his son? As I have served in your father's presence, so will I be in your presence."

[20]Then Absalom said to Ahithophel, "Give advice as to what we should do."

[21]And Ahithophel said to Absalom, "Go in to your father's concubines, whom he has left to keep the house; and all Israel will hear that you are abhorred by your father. Then the hands of all who are with you will be strong." [22]So they pitched a tent for Absalom on the top of the house, and Absalom went in to his father's concubines in the sight of all Israel.

[23]Now the advice of Ahithophel, which he gave in those days, *was* as if one had inquired at the oracle of God. So *was* all the advice of Ahithophel both with David and with Absalom.

17 Moreover Ahithophel said to Absalom, "Now let me choose twelve thousand men, and I will arise and pursue David tonight. [2]I will come upon him while he *is* weary and weak, and make him afraid. And all the people who *are* with him will flee, and I will strike only the king. [3]Then I will

16:12 [a]Following Kethib, Septuagint, Syriac, and Vulgate; Qere reads *my eyes;* Targum reads *tears of my eyes.*

ABSALOM

A TRAGIC CASE OF LEADERSHIP GONE BAD
(2 Samuel 16:1—18:18)

PROFILE IN LEADERSHIP

Study the Bible from cover to cover, and it would be hard to find a more tragic case study on leadership gone bad than the story of Absalom.

Absalom grew up as a child of privilege in the royal palace. He was charismatic, attractive, and very powerful. Eventually he used his personal magnetism and abilities to displace David, God's anointed. For all of David's strengths as a leader, he failed as a father and never helped Absalom acquire a heart for God.

Absalom's inner circle of advisors greatly influenced his treachery by giving him wicked counsel. Absalom chose to listen to their evil voices precisely because he had already allowed them to greatly influence his thinking. His misplaced passion to acquire the throne constituted an act of treason. And it should surprise no one that those who gathered around Absalom were themselves persons of evil intent who recognized opportunities—however despicable—for personal gain.

Absalom's abuse of positional power, won through great natural talents, inflicted enormous pain on many Israelites. His lack of respect for authority, combined with a lack of respect for God, led to chaos in the kingdom. One cannot help but wonder what might have happened had David shed his tears for Absalom as the boy grew up under his roof, rather than at his funeral (2 Sam. 18:33).

bring back all the people to you. When all return except the man whom you seek, all the people will be at peace." [4]And the saying pleased Absalom and all the elders of Israel.

The Advice of Hushai

[5]Then Absalom said, "Now call Hushai the Archite also, and let us hear what he says too." [6]And when Hushai came to Absalom, Absalom spoke to him, saying, "Ahithophel has spoken in this manner. Shall we do as he says? If not, speak up."

[7]So Hushai said to Absalom: "The advice that Ahithophel has given *is* not good at this time. [8]For," said Hushai, "you know your father and his men, that they *are* mighty men, and they *are* enraged in their minds, like a bear robbed of her cubs in the field; and your father *is* a man of war, and will not camp with the people. [9]Surely by now he is hidden in some pit, or in some *other* place. And it will be, when some of them are overthrown at the first, that whoever hears *it* will say, 'There is a slaughter among the people who follow Absalom.' [10]And even he *who is* valiant, whose heart *is* like the heart of a lion, will melt completely. For all Israel knows that your father *is* a mighty man, and *those* who *are* with him *are* valiant men. [11]Therefore I advise that all Israel be fully gathered to you, from Dan to Beersheba, like the sand that *is* by the sea for multitude, and that you go to battle in person. [12]So we will come upon him in some place where he may be found, and we will fall on him as the dew falls on the ground. And of him and all the men who *are* with him there shall not be left so much as one. [13]Moreover, if he has withdrawn into a city, then all Israel shall bring ropes to that city; and we will pull it into the river, until there is not one small stone found there."

[14]So Absalom and all the men of Israel said, "The advice of Hushai the Archite *is* better than the advice of Ahithophel." For the LORD had purposed to defeat the good advice of Ahithophel, to the intent that the LORD might bring disaster on Absalom.

Hushai Warns David to Escape

[15]Then Hushai said to Zadok and Abiathar the priests, "Thus and so Ahithophel advised Absalom and the elders of Israel, and thus and so I have advised. [16]Now therefore, send quickly and tell David, saying, 'Do not spend this night in the plains of the wilderness, but speedily cross over, lest the king and all the people who *are* with him be swallowed up.'" [17]Now Jonathan and Ahimaaz stayed at En Rogel, for they dared not be seen coming into the city; so a female servant would come and tell them, and they would go and tell King David. [18]Nevertheless a lad saw them, and told Absalom. But both of them went away quickly and came to a man's house in Bahurim, who had a well in his court; and they went down into it. [19]Then the woman took and spread a covering over the well's mouth, and spread ground grain on it; and the thing was not known. [20]And when Absalom's servants came to the woman at the house, they said, "Where *are* Ahimaaz and Jonathan?"

So the woman said to them, "They have gone over the water brook."

And when they had searched and could not find *them,* they returned to Jerusalem. [21]Now it came to pass, after they had departed, that they came up out of the well and went and told King David, and said to David, "Arise and cross over the water quickly. For thus has Ahithophel advised against you." [22]So David and all the people who *were* with him arose and crossed over the Jordan. By morning light not one of them was left who had not gone over the Jordan.

[23]Now when Ahithophel saw that his advice was not followed, he saddled a donkey, and arose and went home to his house, to his city. Then he put his household in order, and hanged himself, and died; and he was buried in his father's tomb.

[24]Then David went to Mahanaim. And Absalom crossed over the Jordan, he and all the men of Israel with him. [25]And Absalom made Amasa captain of the army instead of Joab. This Amasa *was* the son of a man whose name *was* Jithra,[a] an Israelite,[b] who had gone in to Abigail the daughter of Nahash, sister of Zeruiah, Joab's mother. [26]So Israel and Absalom encamped in the land of Gilead.

[27]Now it happened, when David had come to Mahanaim, that Shobi the son of Nahash from Rabbah of the people of Ammon, Machir the son of Ammiel from Lo Debar, and Barzillai the Gileadite from Rogelim, [28]brought beds and basins, earthen vessels and wheat, barley and flour, parched *grain* and beans, lentils and parched *seeds,* [29]honey and curds, sheep and cheese of the herd, for David and the people who *were* with him to eat. For they said, "The people are hungry and weary and thirsty in the wilderness."

17:25 [a]Spelled *Jether* in 1 Chronicles 2:17 and elsewhere   [b]Following Masoretic Text, some manuscripts of the Septuagint, and Targum; some manuscripts of the Septuagint read *Ishmaelite* (compare 1 Chronicles 2:17); Vulgate reads *of Jezrael.*

Absalom's Defeat and Death

18 And David numbered the people who *were* with him, and set captains of thousands and captains of hundreds over them. [2]Then David sent out one third of the people under the hand of Joab, one third under the hand of Abishai the son of Zeruiah, Joab's brother, and one third under the hand of Ittai the Gittite. And the king said to the people, "I also will surely go out with you myself."

[3]But the people answered, "You shall not go out! For if we flee away, they will not care about us; nor if half of us die, will they care about us. But *you are* worth ten thousand of us now. For you are now more help to us in the city."

[4]Then the king said to them, "Whatever seems best to you I will do." So the king stood beside the gate, and all the people went out by hundreds and by thousands. [5]Now the king had commanded Joab, Abishai, and Ittai, saying, "*Deal gently for my sake with the young man Absalom.*" And all the people heard when the king gave all the captains orders concerning Absalom.

[6]So the people went out into the field of battle against Israel. And the battle was in the woods of Ephraim. [7]The people of Israel were overthrown there before the servants of David, and a great slaughter of twenty thousand took place there that day. [8]For the battle there was scattered over the face of the whole countryside, and the woods devoured more people that day than the sword devoured.

[9]Then Absalom met the servants of David. Absalom rode on a mule. The mule went under the thick boughs of a great terebinth tree, and his head caught in the terebinth; so he was left hanging between heaven and earth. And the mule which *was* under him went on. [10]Now a certain man saw *it* and told Joab, and said, "I just saw Absalom hanging in a terebinth tree!"

[11]So Joab said to the man who told him, "You just saw *him!* And why did you not strike him there to the ground? I would have given you ten *shekels* of silver and a belt."

[12]But the man said to Joab, "Though I were to receive a thousand *shekels* of silver in my hand, I would not raise my hand against the king's son. For in our hearing the king commanded you and Abishai and Ittai, saying, 'Beware lest anyone *touch* the young man Absalom!'[a] [13]Otherwise I would have dealt falsely against my own life. For there is nothing hidden from the king, and you yourself would have set yourself against *me.*"

[14]Then Joab said, "I cannot linger with you." And he took three spears in his hand and thrust

them through Absalom's heart, while he was *still* alive in the midst of the terebinth tree. [15]And ten young men who bore Joab's armor surrounded Absalom, and struck and killed him.

[16]So Joab blew the trumpet, and the people returned from pursuing Israel. For Joab held back the people. [17]And they took Absalom and cast him into a large pit in the woods, and laid a very large heap of stones over him. Then all Israel fled, everyone to his tent.

[18]Now Absalom in his lifetime had taken and set up a pillar for himself, which *is* in the King's Valley. For he said, "I have no son to keep my name in remembrance." He called the pillar after his own name. And to this day it is called Absalom's Monument.

David Hears of Absalom's Death

[19]Then Ahimaaz the son of Zadok said, "Let me run now and take the news to the king, how the LORD has avenged him of his enemies."

18:12 [a]The ancient versions read *'Protect the young man Absalom for me!'*

Brokenness: Maturity Comes When God Breaks a Leader

(2 Samuel 18:19–33)

The armies of Absalom and King David came to blows over who would lead Israel, and the old king reasserted his rule.

David's troops not only routed his son's armies; they also killed Absalom himself. Yet David couldn't rejoice, even though his rebellious son's death ended the war. His family had fallen far. Absalom was dead. Amnon was dead. Tamar had been raped. Many who remained had grown twisted and sick.

And David cried out in brokenness.

In this broken state, God began to restore David to the man he once was, the man after His own heart. David regained his resolve to lead his country and leave a worthwhile legacy. He crushed other revolts, killed other giants, restored Israel. In many ways, David matured to a new level as a leader through this awful season of brokenness. Broken boldness now characterized his leadership.

^{20}And Joab said to him, "You shall not take the news this day, for you shall take the news another day. But today you shall take no news, because the king's son is dead." ^{21}Then Joab said to the Cushite, "Go, tell the king what you have seen." So the Cushite bowed himself to Joab and ran.

^{22}And Ahimaaz the son of Zadok said again to Joab, "But whatever happens, please let me also run after the Cushite."

So Joab said, "Why will you run, my son, since you have no news ready?"

^{23}"But whatever happens," he said, "let me run."

So he said to him, "Run." Then Ahimaaz ran by way of the plain, and outran the Cushite.

^{24}Now David was sitting between the two gates. And the watchman went up to the roof over the gate, to the wall, lifted his eyes and looked, and there was a man, running alone. ^{25}Then the watchman cried out and told the king. And the king said, "If he is alone, there is news in his mouth." And he came rapidly and drew near.

^{26}Then the watchman saw another man running, and the watchman called to the gatekeeper and said, "There is another man, running alone!"

And the king said, "He also brings news."

^{27}So the watchman said, "I think the running of the first is like the running of Ahimaaz the son of Zadok."

And the king said, "He is a good man, and comes with good news."

^{28}So Ahimaaz called out and said to the king, "All is well!" Then he bowed down with his face to the earth before the king, and said, "Blessed be the LORD your God, who has delivered up the men who raised their hand against my lord the king!"

^{29}The king said, "Is the young man Absalom safe?"

Ahimaaz answered, "When Joab sent the king's servant and me your servant, I saw a great tumult, but I did not know what it was about."

^{30}And the king said, "Turn aside and stand here." So he turned aside and stood still.

^{31}Just then the Cushite came, and the Cushite said, "There is good news, my lord the king! For the LORD has avenged you this day of all those who rose against you."

^{32}And the king said to the Cushite, "Is the young man Absalom safe?"

So the Cushite answered, "May the enemies of my lord the king, and all who rise against you to do harm, be like that young man!"

David's Mourning for Absalom

^{33}Then the king was deeply moved, and went up to the chamber over the gate, and wept. And as he went, he said thus: "O my son Absalom—my son, my son Absalom—if only I had died in your place! O Absalom my son, my son!"

19 And Joab was told, "Behold, the king is weeping and mourning for Absalom." ^{2}So the victory that day was turned into mourning for all the people. For the people heard it said that day, "The king is grieved for his son." ^{3}And the people stole back into the city that day, as people who are ashamed steal away when they flee in battle. ^{4}But the king covered his face, and the king cried out with a loud voice, "O my son Absalom! O Absalom, my son, my son!"

^{5}Then Joab came into the house to the king, and said, "Today you have disgraced all your servants who today have saved your life, the lives of your sons and daughters, the lives of your wives and the lives of your concubines, ^{6}in that you love your enemies and hate your friends. For you have declared today that you regard neither princes nor servants; for today I perceive that if Absalom had lived and all of us had died today, then it would have pleased you well. ^{7}Now therefore, arise, go out and speak comfort to your servants. For I swear by the LORD, if you do not go out, not one will stay with you this night. And that will be worse for you than all the evil that has befallen you from your youth until now." ^{8}Then the king arose and sat in the gate. And they told all the people, saying, "There is the king, sitting in the gate." So all the people came before the king.

For everyone of Israel had fled to his tent.

David Returns to Jerusalem

^{9}Now all the people were in a dispute throughout all the tribes of Israel, saying, "The king saved us from the hand of our enemies, he delivered us from the hand of the Philistines, and now he has fled from the land because of Absalom. ^{10}But Absalom, whom we anointed over us, has died in battle. Now therefore, why do you say nothing about bringing back the king?"

^{11}So King David sent to Zadok and Abiathar the priests, saying, "Speak to the elders of Judah, saying, 'Why are you the last to bring the king back to his house, since the words of all Israel have come to the king, to his very house? ^{12}You are my brethren, you are my bone and my flesh. Why then are you the last to bring back the king?' ^{13}And say to Amasa, 'Are you not my bone and my flesh? God do so to me, and more also, if you are not commander of the army before me continually in place of Joab.'" [14]So he swayed the hearts of all the men of Judah, just as *the heart of* one man, so that they sent *this word* to the king: "Return, you and all your servants!"

[15]Then the king returned and came to the Jordan. And Judah came to Gilgal, to go to meet the king, to escort the king across the Jordan. [16]And Shimei the son of Gera, a Benjamite, who *was* from Bahurim, hurried and came down with the men of Judah to meet King David. [17]*There were* a thousand men of Benjamin with him, and Ziba the servant of the house of Saul, and his fifteen sons and his twenty servants with him; and they went over the Jordan before the king. [18]Then a ferryboat went across to carry over the king's household, and to do what he thought good.

David's Mercy to Shimei

Now Shimei the son of Gera fell down before the king when he had crossed the Jordan. [19]Then he said to the king, "Do not let my lord impute iniquity to me, or remember what wrong your servant did on the day that my lord the king left Jerusalem, that the king should take *it* to heart. [20]For I, your servant, know that I have sinned. Therefore here I am, the first to come today of all the house of Joseph to go down to meet my lord the king."

[21]But Abishai the son of Zeruiah answered and said, "Shall not Shimei be put to death for this, because he cursed the LORD's anointed?"

[22]And David said, "What have I to do with you, you sons of Zeruiah, that you should be adversaries to me today? Shall any man be put to death today in Israel? For do I not know that today I *am* king over Israel?" [23]Therefore the king said to Shimei, "You shall not die." And the king swore to him.

David and Mephibosheth Meet

[24]Now Mephibosheth the son of Saul came down to meet the king. And he had not cared for his feet, nor trimmed his mustache, nor washed his clothes, from the day the king departed until the day he returned in peace. [25]So it was, when he had come to Jerusalem to meet the king, that the king said to him, "Why did you not go with me, Mephibosheth?"

[26]And he answered, "My lord, O king, my servant deceived me. For your servant said, 'I will saddle a donkey for myself, that I may ride on it and go to the king,' because your servant *is* lame. [27]And he has slandered your servant to my lord the king, but my lord the king *is* like the angel of God. Therefore do *what is* good in your eyes. [28]For all my father's house were but dead men before my lord the king. Yet you set your servant among those who eat at your own table. Therefore what right have I still to cry out anymore to the king?"

[29]So the king said to him, "Why do you speak anymore of your matters? I have said, 'You and Ziba divide the land.'"

[30]Then Mephibosheth said to the king, "Rather, let him take it all, inasmuch as my lord the king has come back in peace to his own house."

David's Kindness to Barzillai

[31]And Barzillai the Gileadite came down from Rogelim and went across the Jordan with the king, to escort him across the Jordan. [32]Now Barzillai was a very aged man, eighty years old. And he had provided the king with supplies while he stayed at Mahanaim, for he *was* a very rich man. [33]And the king said to Barzillai, "Come across with me, and I will provide for you while you are with me in Jerusalem."

[34]But Barzillai said to the king, "How long have I to live, that I should go up with the king to Jerusalem? [35]I *am* today eighty years old. Can I discern between the good and bad? Can your servant taste what I eat or what I drink? Can I hear any longer the voice of singing men and singing women? Why then should your servant be a further burden to my lord the king? [36]Your servant will go a little way across the Jordan with the king. And why should the king repay me *with* such a reward? [37]Please let your servant turn back again, that I may die in my own city, near the grave of my father and mother. But here is your servant Chimham; let him cross over with my lord the king, and do for him what seems good to you."

[38]And the king answered, "Chimham shall cross over with me, and I will do for him what seems good to you. Now whatever you request of me, I will do for you." [39]Then all the people went over the Jordan. And when the king had crossed over, the king kissed Barzillai and blessed him, and he returned to his own place.

The Quarrel About the King

[40]Now the king went on to Gilgal, and Chimham[a] went on with him. And all the people of Judah escorted the king, and also half the people of Israel. [41]Just then all the men of Israel came to the king, and said to the king, "Why

---

19:40 [a]Masoretic Text reads *Chimhan*.

have our brethren, the men of Judah, stolen you away and brought the king, his household, and all David's men with him across the Jordan?"

⁴²So all the men of Judah answered the men of Israel, "Because the king *is* a close relative of ours. Why then are you angry over this matter? Have we ever eaten at the king's *expense?* Or has he given us any gift?"

⁴³And the men of Israel answered the men of Judah, and said, "We have ten shares in the king; therefore we also have more *right* to David than you. Why then do you despise us—were we not the first to advise bringing back our king?"

Yet the words of the men of Judah were fiercer than the words of the men of Israel.

The Rebellion of Sheba

20 And there happened to be there a rebel,ᵃ whose name *was* Sheba the son of Bichri, a Benjamite. And he blew a trumpet, and said:

"We have no share in David,
    Nor do we have inheritance in the son of Jesse;
    Every man to his tents, O Israel!"

²So every man of Israel deserted David, *and* followed Sheba the son of Bichri. But the men of Judah, from the Jordan as far as Jerusalem, remained loyal to their king.

³Now David came to his house at Jerusalem. And the king took the ten women, his concubines whom he had left to keep the house, and put them in seclusion and supported them, but did not go in to them. So they were shut up to the day of their death, living in widowhood.

⁴And the king said to Amasa, "Assemble the men of Judah for me within three days, and be present here yourself." ⁵So Amasa went to assemble *the men of* Judah. But he delayed longer than the set time which David had appointed him. ⁶And David said to Abishai, "Now Sheba the son of Bichri will do us more harm than Absalom. Take your lord's servants and pursue him, lest he find for himself fortified cities, and escape us." ⁷So Joab's men, with the Cherethites, the Pelethites, and all the mighty men, went out after him. And they went out of Jerusalem to pursue Sheba the son of Bichri. ⁸When they *were* at the large stone which *is* in Gibeon, Amasa came before them. Now Joab was dressed in battle armor; on it was a belt *with* a sword fastened in its sheath at his hips; and as he was going forward, it fell out. ⁹Then Joab said to Amasa, "*Are* you in health, my brother?" And Joab took Amasa by

the beard with his right hand to kiss him. ¹⁰But Amasa did not notice the sword that *was* in Joab's hand. And he struck him with it in the stomach, and his entrails poured out on the ground; and he did not *strike* him again. Thus he died.

Then Joab and Abishai his brother pursued Sheba the son of Bichri. ¹¹Meanwhile one of Joab's men stood near Amasa, and said, "Whoever favors Joab and whoever *is* for David—follow Joab!" ¹²But Amasa wallowed in *his* blood in the middle of the highway. And when the man saw that all the people stood still, he moved Amasa from the highway to the field and threw a garment over him, when he saw that everyone who came upon him halted. ¹³When he was removed from the highway, all the people went on after Joab to pursue Sheba the son of Bichri.

¹⁴And he went through all the tribes of Israel to Abel and Beth Maachah and all the Berites. So they were gathered together and also went after *Sheba.*ᵃ ¹⁵Then they came and besieged him in Abel of Beth Maachah; and they cast up a siege mound against the city, and it stood by the rampart. And all the people who *were* with Joab battered the wall to throw it down.

¹⁶Then a wise woman cried out from the city, "Hear, hear! Please say to Joab, 'Come nearby, that I may speak with you.'" ¹⁷When he had come near to her, the woman said, "*Are* you Joab?"

He answered, "I *am.*"

Then she said to him, "Hear the words of your maidservant."

And he answered, "I am listening."

¹⁸So she spoke, saying, "They used to talk in former times, saying, 'They shall surely seek *guidance* at Abel,' and so they would end *disputes.* ¹⁹I *am among the* peaceable *and* faithful in Israel. You seek to destroy a city and a mother in Israel. Why would you swallow up the inheritance of the LORD?"

²⁰And Joab answered and said, "Far be it, far be it from me, that I should swallow up or destroy! ²¹That *is* not so. But a man from the mountains of Ephraim, Sheba the son of Bichri by name, has raised his hand against the king, against David. Deliver him only, and I will depart from the city."

So the woman said to Joab, "Watch, his head will be thrown to you over the wall." ²²Then the woman in her wisdom went to all the people. And they cut off the head of Sheba the son of Bichri, and threw *it* out to Joab. Then he blew a trumpet, and they withdrew from the city, every man to his tent. So Joab returned to the king at Jerusalem.

20:1 ᵃLiterally *man of Belial* **20:14** ᵃLiterally *him*

David's Government Officers

[23]And Joab *was* over all the army of Israel; Benaiah the son of Jehoiada *was* over the Cherethites and the Pelethites; [24]Adoram *was* in charge of revenue; Jehoshaphat the son of Ahilud *was* recorder; [25]Sheva *was* scribe; Zadok and Abiathar *were* the priests; [26]and Ira the Jairite was a chief minister under David.

David Avenges the Gibeonites

21 Now there was a famine in the days of David for three years, year after year; and David inquired of the LORD. And the LORD answered, "*It is* because of Saul and *his* bloodthirsty house, because he killed the Gibeonites." [2]So the king called the Gibeonites and spoke to them. Now the Gibeonites *were* not of the children of Israel, but of the remnant of the Amorites; the children of Israel had sworn protection to them, but Saul had sought to kill them in his zeal for the children of Israel and Judah.

[3]Therefore David said to the Gibeonites, "What shall I do for you? And with what shall I make atonement, that you may bless the inheritance of the LORD?"

[4]And the Gibeonites said to him, "We will have no silver or gold from Saul or from his house, nor shall you kill any man in Israel for us."

So he said, "Whatever you say, I will do for you."

[5]Then they answered the king, "As for the man who consumed us and plotted against us, *that* we should be destroyed from remaining in any of the territories of Israel, [6]let seven men of his descendants be delivered to us, and we will hang them before the LORD in Gibeah of Saul, *whom* the LORD chose."

And the king said, "I will give *them.*"

[7]But the king spared Mephibosheth the son of Jonathan, the son of Saul, because of the LORD's oath that *was* between them, between David and Jonathan the son of Saul. [8]So the king took Armoni and Mephibosheth, the two sons of Rizpah the daughter of Aiah, whom she bore to Saul, and the five sons of Michal[a] the daughter of Saul, whom she brought up for Adriel the son of Barzillai the Meholathite; [9]and he delivered them into the hands of the Gibeonites, and they hanged them on the hill before the LORD. So they fell, *all* seven together, and were put to death in the days of harvest, in the first *days,* in the beginning of barley harvest.

[10]Now Rizpah the daughter of Aiah took sackcloth and spread it for herself on the rock, from the beginning of harvest until the late rains poured on them from heaven. And she did not allow the birds of the air to rest on them by day nor the beasts of the field by night.

[11]And David was told what Rizpah the

21:8 [a]Or *Merab* (compare 1 Samuel 18:19 and 25:44; 2 Samuel 3:14 and 6:23)

Relationships: Coping with Difficult People

(2 Samuel 21:1–14)

Every leader faces difficult people and draining circumstances. The following difficult personality types commonly accost leaders today:

Type	Strategy
1. *The Sherman Tank:* rides over people	1. Consider the issue; stand up if important.
2. *The Space Cadet:* lives in another world	2. Find and develop their unique gifts.
3. *The Volcano:* explosive, unpredictable	3. Remove from crowd, listen, be direct.
4. *The Thumb Sucker:* self-pity, pouts	4. Don't reward; expose them to real trouble.
5. *The Wet Blanket:* always down	5. Be honest, don't cater; don't let them lead.
6. *The Garbage Collector:* attracts the worst	6. Challenge their statements; force honesty.
7. *The User:* demands lots of time, energy	7. Set boundaries; require accountability.

The Gibeonites became one of David's difficult people. Answer the following questions about how David chose to deal with them:

1. Why did God send the famine and the Gibeonites to David (vv. 1, 2)?
2. How far should the leader go to satisfy the complaints of a critic (vv. 3, 4)?
3. Did David go too far in trying to appease the Gibeonites or Rizpah (vv. 5–14)?

daughter of Aiah, the concubine of Saul, had done. [12]Then David went and took the bones of Saul, and the bones of Jonathan his son, from the men of Jabesh Gilead who had stolen them from the street of Beth Shan,[a] where the Philistines had hung them up, after the Philistines had struck down Saul in Gilboa. [13]So he brought up the bones of Saul and the bones of Jonathan his son from there; and they gathered the bones of those who had been hanged. [14]They buried the bones of Saul and Jonathan his son in the country of Benjamin in Zelah, in the tomb of Kish his father. So they performed all that the king commanded. And after that God heeded the prayer for the land.

Philistine Giants Destroyed

[15]When the Philistines were at war again with Israel, David and his servants with him went down and fought against the Philistines; and David grew faint. [16]Then Ishbi-Benob, who *was* one of the sons of the giant, the weight of whose bronze spear *was* three hundred *shekels,* who was bearing a new *sword,* thought he could kill David. [17]But Abishai the son of Zeruiah came to his aid, and struck the Philistine and killed him. Then the men of David swore to him, saying, "You shall go out no more with us to battle, lest you quench the lamp of Israel."

[18]Now it happened afterward that there was again a battle with the Philistines at Gob. Then Sibbechai the Hushathite killed Saph,[a] who *was* one of the sons of the giant. [19]Again there was war at Gob with the Philistines, where Elhanan the son of Jaare-Oregim[a] the Bethlehemite killed *the brother of* Goliath the Gittite, the shaft of whose spear *was* like a weaver's beam.

[20]Yet again there was war at Gath, where there was a man of *great* stature, who had six fingers on each hand and six toes on each foot, twenty-four in number; and he also was born to the giant. [21]So when he defied Israel, Jonathan the son of Shimea,[a] David's brother, killed him.

[22]These four were born to the giant in Gath, and fell by the hand of David and by the hand of his servants.

Praise for God's Deliverance

22 Then David spoke to the LORD the words of this song, on the day when the LORD had delivered him from the hand of all his enemies, and from the hand of Saul. [2]And he said:[a]

"The LORD *is* my rock and my fortress and my deliverer;

[3] The God of my strength, in whom I will trust;
My shield and the horn of my salvation,
My stronghold and my refuge;
My Savior, You save me from violence.
[4] I will call upon the LORD, *who is worthy* to be praised;
So shall I be saved from my enemies.

[5] "When the waves of death surrounded me,
The floods of ungodliness made me afraid.
[6] The sorrows of Sheol surrounded me;
The snares of death confronted me.
[7] In my distress I called upon the LORD,
And cried out to my God;
He heard my voice from His temple,
And my cry *entered* His ears.

[8] "Then the earth shook and trembled;
The foundations of heaven[a] quaked and were shaken,
Because He was angry.
[9] Smoke went up from His nostrils,
And devouring fire from His mouth;
Coals were kindled by it.
[10] He bowed the heavens also, and came down
With darkness under His feet.
[11] He rode upon a cherub, and flew;
And He was seen[a] upon the wings of the wind.
[12] He made darkness canopies around Him,
Dark waters *and* thick clouds of the skies.
[13] From the brightness before Him
Coals of fire were kindled.

[14] "The LORD thundered from heaven,
And the Most High uttered His voice.
[15] He sent out arrows and scattered them;
Lightning bolts, and He vanquished them.
[16] Then the channels of the sea were seen,
The foundations of the world were uncovered,
At the rebuke of the LORD,
At the blast of the breath of His nostrils.

21:12 [a]Spelled *Beth Shean* in Joshua 17:11 and elsewhere **21:18** [a]Spelled *Sippai* in 1 Chronicles 20:4 **21:19** [a]Spelled *Jair* in 1 Chronicles 20:5 **21:21** [a]Spelled *Shammah* in 1 Samuel 16:9 and elsewhere **22:2** [a]Compare Psalm 18 **22:8** [a]Following Masoretic Text, Septuagint, and Targum; Syriac and Vulgate read *hills* (compare Psalm 18:7). **22:11** [a]Following Masoretic Text and Septuagint; many Hebrew manuscripts, Syriac, and Vulgate read *He flew* (compare Psalm 18:10); Targum reads *He spoke with power.*

God Is the Source, Not People or Material Resources

(2 Samuel 22:1–51; 24:1–15)

Despite David's serious lapses in both judgment and godliness, he continued to seek the Lord out of the depths of his soul, from the beginning of his life to its very end.

In the twilight of his years, David sang a beautiful song declaring God as the source of his victory (2 Sam. 22). He declared that neither horses nor chariots could deliver him, but only the hand of the living God.

When toward the end of his reign David took a census against God's will, the Lord gave him his choice of punishment: seven years of famine; three months of fleeing from his enemies; or three days' pestilence. David chose the epidemic, saying, "I am in great distress. Please let us fall into the hand of the LORD, for His mercies are great; but do not let me fall into the hand of man" (2 Sam. 24:14).

Whether in punishment or provision, David knew that God is always the right choice. He still is.

17 "He sent from above, He took me,
   He drew me out of many waters.
18 He delivered me from my strong enemy,
   From those who hated me;
   For they were too strong for me.
19 They confronted me in the day of my
      calamity,
   But the LORD was my support.
20 He also brought me out into a broad
      place;
   He delivered me because He delighted in
      me.

21 "The LORD rewarded me according to my
      righteousness;
   According to the cleanness of my hands
   He has recompensed me.
22 For I have kept the ways of the LORD,
   And have not wickedly departed from my
      God.
23 For all His judgments *were* before me;
   And *as for* His statutes, I did not depart
      from them.

24 I was also blameless before Him,
   And I kept myself from my iniquity.
25 Therefore the LORD has recompensed me
      according to my righteousness,
   According to my cleanness in His eyes.[a]

26 "With the merciful You will show Yourself
      merciful;
   With a blameless man You will show
      Yourself blameless;
27 With the pure You will show Yourself pure;
   And with the devious You will show
      Yourself shrewd.
28 You will save the humble people;
   But Your eyes *are* on the haughty, *that* You
      may bring *them* down.

29 "For You *are* my lamp, O LORD;
   The LORD shall enlighten my darkness.
30 For by You I can run against a troop;
   By my God I can leap over a wall.
31 *As for* God, His way *is* perfect;
   The word of the LORD *is* proven;
   He *is* a shield to all who trust in Him.

32 "For who *is* God, except the LORD?
   And who *is* a rock, except our God?
33 God *is* my strength *and* power,[a]
   And He makes my[b] way perfect.
34 He makes my[a] feet like the *feet* of deer,
   And sets me on my high places.
35 He teaches my hands to make war,
   So that my arms can bend a bow of bronze.

36 "You have also given me the shield of Your
      salvation;
   Your gentleness has made me great.
37 You enlarged my path under me;
   So my feet did not slip.

38 "I have pursued my enemies and destroyed
      them;
   Neither did I turn back again till they
      were destroyed.

22:25 [a]Septuagint, Syriac, and Vulgate read *the cleanness of my hands in His sight* (compare Psalm 18:24); Targum reads *my cleanness before His word.* **22:33** [a]Dead Sea Scrolls, Septuagint, Syriac, and Vulgate read *It is God who arms me with strength* (compare Psalm 18:32); Targum reads *It is God who sustains me with strength.* [b]Following Qere, Septuagint, Syriac, Targum, and Vulgate (compare Psalm 18:32); Kethib reads *His.* **22:34** [a]Following Qere, Septuagint, Syriac, Targum, and Vulgate (compare Psalm 18:33); Kethib reads *His.*

39 And I have destroyed them and wounded
them,
So that they could not rise;
They have fallen under my feet.
40 For You have armed me with strength for
the battle;
You have subdued under me those who
rose against me.
41 You have also given me the necks of my
enemies,
So that I destroyed those who hated me.
42 They looked, but *there was* none to save;
Even to the LORD, but He did not answer
them.
43 Then I beat them as fine as the dust of the
earth;
I trod them like dirt in the streets,
And I spread them out.

44 "You have also delivered me from the
strivings of my people;
You have kept me as the head of the
nations.
A people I have not known shall serve me.
45 The foreigners submit to me;
As soon as they hear, they obey me.
46 The foreigners fade away,
And come frightened[a] from their
hideouts.

47 "The LORD lives!
Blessed *be* my Rock!
Let God be exalted,
The Rock of my salvation!
48 *It is* God who avenges me,
And subdues the peoples under me;
49 He delivers me from my enemies.
You also lift me up above those who rise
against me;
You have delivered me from the violent
man.
50 Therefore I will give thanks to You, O
LORD, among the Gentiles,
And sing praises to Your name.

51 "*He* is the tower of salvation to His king,
And shows mercy to His anointed,
To David and his descendants
forevermore."

David's Last Words

23 Now these *are* the last words of David.

Thus says David the son of Jesse;
Thus says the man raised up on high,

The anointed of the God of Jacob,
And the sweet psalmist of Israel:

2 "The Spirit of the LORD spoke by me,
And His word *was* on my tongue.
3 The God of Israel said,
The Rock of Israel spoke to me:
'He who rules over men *must* be just
Ruling in the fear of God.
4 And *he shall be* like the light of the
morning *when* the sun rises,
A morning without clouds,
Like the tender grass *springing* out of the
earth,
By clear shining after rain.'

5 "Although my house *is* not so with God,
Yet He has made with me an everlasting
covenant,
Ordered in all *things* and secure.
For *this is* all my salvation and all *my*
desire;
Will He not make *it* increase?
6 But *the sons* of rebellion *shall* all *be* as
thorns thrust away,
Because they cannot be taken with hands.
7 But the man *who* touches them
Must be armed with iron and the shaft of
a spear,
And they shall be utterly burned with fire
in *their* place."

David's Mighty Men

8 These *are* the names of the mighty men
whom David had: Josheb-Basshebeth[a] the Tach-
monite, chief among the captains.[b] He was called
Adino the Eznite, because he had killed eight
hundred men at one time. 9 And after him *was*
Eleazar the son of Dodo,[a] the Ahohite, *one* of the
three mighty men with David when they defied
the Philistines *who* were gathered there for battle,
and the men of Israel had retreated. 10 He arose
and attacked the Philistines until his hand was
weary, and his hand stuck to the sword. The
LORD brought about a great victory that day; and
the people returned after him only to plunder.
11 And after him *was* Shammah the son of Agee
the Hararite. The Philistines had gathered

22:46 [a]Following Septuagint, Targum, and Vulgate
(compare Psalm 18:45); Masoretic Text reads *gird
themselves.* **23:8** [a]Literally *One Who Sits in the Seat*
(compare 1 Chronicles 11:11) [b]Following
Masoretic Text and Targum; Septuagint and Vulgate
read *the three.* **23:9** [a]Spelled *Dodai* in 1 Chronicles
27:4

together into a troop where there was a piece of ground full of lentils. So the people fled from the Philistines. [12]But he stationed himself in the middle of the field, defended it, and killed the Philistines. So the LORD brought about a great victory.

[13]Then three of the thirty chief men went down at harvest time and came to David at the cave of Adullam. And the troop of Philistines encamped in the Valley of Rephaim. [14]David *was* then in the stronghold, and the garrison of the Philistines *was* then *in* Bethlehem. [15]And David said with longing, "Oh, that someone would give me a drink of the water from the well of Bethlehem, which *is* by the gate!" [16]So the three mighty men broke through the camp of the Philistines, drew water from the well of Bethlehem that *was* by the gate, and took it and brought *it* to David. Nevertheless he would not drink it, but poured it out to the LORD. [17]And he said, "Far be it from me, O LORD, that I should do this! Is *this not* the blood of the men who went in *jeopardy of* their lives?" Therefore he would not drink it.

These things were done by the three mighty men.

[18]Now Abishai the brother of Joab, the son of Zeruiah, was chief of *another* three.[a] He lifted his spear against three hundred *men,* killed *them,* and won a name among *these* three. [19]Was he not the most honored of three? Therefore he became their captain. However, he did not attain to the *first* three.

[20]Benaiah *was* the son of Jehoiada, the son of a valiant man from Kabzeel, who had done many deeds. He had killed two lion-like heroes of Moab. He also had gone down and killed a lion in the midst of a pit on a snowy day. [21]And he killed an Egyptian, a spectacular man. The Egyptian *had* a spear in his hand; so he went down to him with a staff, wrested the spear out of the Egyptian's hand, and killed him with his own spear. [22]These *things* Benaiah the son of Jehoiada did, and won a name among three mighty men. [23]He was more honored than the thirty, but he did not attain to the *first* three. And David appointed him over his guard.

[24]Asahel the brother of Joab *was* one of the thirty; Elhanan the son of Dodo of Bethlehem, [25]Shammah the Harodite, Elika the Harodite, [26]Helez the Paltite, Ira the son of Ikkesh the Tekoite, [27]Abiezer the Anathothite, Mebunnai the Hushathite, [28]Zalmon the Ahohite, Maharai the Netophathite, [29]Heleb the son of Baanah (the Netophathite), Ittai the son of Ribai from Gibeah of the children of Benjamin, [30]Benaiah a Pirathonite, Hiddai from the brooks of Gaash,

[31]Abi-Albon the Arbathite, Azmaveth the Barhumite, [32]Eliahba the Shaalbonite (of the sons of Jashen), Jonathan, [33]Shammah the Hararite, Ahiam the son of Sharar the Hararite, [34]Eliphelet the son of Ahasbai, the son of the Maachathite, Eliam the son of Ahithophel the Gilonite, [35]Hezrai[a] the Carmelite, Paarai the Arbite, [36]Igal the son of Nathan of Zobah, Bani the Gadite, [37]Zelek the Ammonite, Naharai the Beerothite (armorbearer of Joab the son of Zeruiah), [38]Ira the Ithrite, Gareb the Ithrite, [39]*and* Uriah the Hittite: thirty-seven in all.

23:18 [a]Following Masoretic Text, Septuagint, and Vulgate; some Hebrew manuscripts and Syriac read *thirty;* Targum reads *the mighty men.* 23:35 [a]Spelled *Hezro* in 1 Chronicles 11:37

The Law of the Inner Circle
(2 Samuel 23:14–17)

It was just a casual remark. Not a command. Not an order. Not even a request.

And yet the moment David's men heard their leader mutter how he'd love to sip a cool drink from a certain Bethlehem well, they immediately broke through enemy lines and braved Philistine swords and spears to retrieve a cup of the precious liquid. David had invested so much in his inner circle that fierce loyalty was the natural result.

Such astonishing loyalty doesn't come from a mere job description. It doesn't develop because the leader is scheduled for a promotion. It doesn't appear on demand. Loyalty like this comes only through modeling. David got this kind of "second-mile" effort because he had long modeled such loyalty for his men.

And it is that loyalty that drove him to do what he did next. When his comrades returned with the cup of water dripping in their hands, David honored their sacrifice by presenting it to the Lord rather than drinking it. "Far be it from me, O LORD, that I should do this!" he cried. "Is this not the blood of the men who went in jeopardy of their lives?" (2 Sam. 23:17). So David poured out the water as an offering to God.

Who wouldn't go the extra mile for a leader like that?

David's Census of Israel and Judah

24 Again the anger of the LORD was aroused against Israel, and He moved David against them to say, "Go, number Israel and Judah."

[2]So the king said to Joab the commander of the army who *was* with him, "Now go throughout all the tribes of Israel, from Dan to Beersheba, and count the people, that I may know the number of the people."

[3]And Joab said to the king, "Now may the LORD your God add to the people a hundred times more than there are, and may the eyes of my lord the king see *it.* But why does my lord the king desire this thing?" [4]Nevertheless the king's word prevailed against Joab and against the captains of the army. Therefore Joab and the captains of the army went out from the presence of the king to count the people of Israel.

[5]And they crossed over the Jordan and camped in Aroer, on the right side of the town which *is* in the midst of the ravine of Gad, and toward Jazer. [6]Then they came to Gilead and to the land of Tahtim Hodshi; they came to Dan Jaan and around to Sidon; [7]and they came to the stronghold of Tyre and to all the cities of the Hivites and the Canaanites. Then they went out to South Judah *as far as* Beersheba. [8]So when they had gone through all the land, they came to Jerusalem at the end of nine months and twenty days. [9]Then Joab gave the sum of the number of the people to the king. And there were in Israel eight hundred thousand valiant men who drew the sword, and the men of Judah were five hundred thousand men.

The Judgment on David's Sin

[10]And David's heart condemned him after he had numbered the people. So David said to the LORD, "I have sinned greatly in what I have done; but now, I pray, O LORD, take away the iniquity of Your servant, for I have done very foolishly."

[11]Now when David arose in the morning, the word of the LORD came to the prophet Gad, David's seer, saying, [12]"Go and tell David, 'Thus says the LORD: "I offer you three *things;* choose one of them for yourself, that I may do *it* to you."'" [13]So Gad came to David and told him; and he said to him, "Shall seven[a] years of famine come to you in your land? Or shall you flee three months before your enemies, while they pursue you? Or shall there be three days' plague in your land? Now consider and see what answer I should take back to Him who sent me."

[14]And David said to Gad, "I am in great distress. Please let us fall into the hand of the LORD, for His mercies *are* great; but do not let me fall into the hand of man."

[15]So the LORD sent a plague upon Israel from the morning till the appointed time. From Dan to Beersheba seventy thousand men of the people died. [16]And when the angel[a] stretched out His hand over Jerusalem to destroy it, the LORD relented from the destruction, and said to the angel who was destroying the people, "It is enough; now restrain your hand." And the angel of the LORD was by the threshing floor of Araunah[b] the Jebusite.

[17]Then David spoke to the LORD when he saw the angel who was striking the people, and said, "Surely I have sinned, and I have done wickedly; but these sheep, what have they done? Let Your hand, I pray, be against me and against my father's house."

The Altar on the Threshing Floor

[18]And Gad came that day to David and said to him, "Go up, erect an altar to the LORD on the threshing floor of Araunah the Jebusite." [19]So David, according to the word of Gad, went up as the LORD commanded. [20]Now Araunah looked, and saw the king and his servants coming toward him. So Araunah went out and bowed before the king with his face to the ground.

[21]Then Araunah said, "Why has my lord the king come to his servant?"

And David said, "To buy the threshing floor from you, to build an altar to the LORD, that the plague may be withdrawn from the people."

[22]Now Araunah said to David, "Let my lord the king take and offer up whatever *seems* good to him. Look, *here are* oxen for burnt sacrifice, and threshing implements and the yokes of the oxen for wood. [23]All these, O king, Araunah has given to the king."

And Araunah said to the king, "May the LORD your God accept you."

[24]Then the king said to Araunah, "No, but I will surely buy *it* from you for a price; nor will I offer burnt offerings to the LORD my God with that which costs me nothing." So David bought the threshing floor and the oxen for fifty shekels of silver. [25]And David built there an altar to the LORD, and offered burnt offerings and peace offerings. So the LORD heeded the prayers for the land, and the plague was withdrawn from Israel.

24:13 [a]Following Masoretic Text, Syriac, Targum, and Vulgate; Septuagint reads *three* (compare 1 Chronicles 21:12). **24:16** [a]Or *Angel* [b]Spelled *Ornan* in 1 Chronicles 21:15

1 KINGS

The Necessity of Purpose-Driven Leadership

SUMMARY

First and Second Kings give an account of the leaders who followed David: kings such as Solomon, Jeroboam, and Rehoboam; prophets such as Elijah, Elisha, and Micaiah. These men picture the necessity of purpose-driven leadership—leadership motivated by core values and strong convictions.

Some call purpose-driven leadership *visionary leadership.* Visionary leadership is motivated by something that not only *could* be done, but *should* be done. The leader carries a sense of moral obligation about the vision.

First Kings describes the reign of King Solomon. Despite his wisdom, he lacked focused leadership. He begins well, but by chapter 11 he becomes distracted from any moral obligation.

The book begins with a skirmish over who will succeed David as king of Israel. David selects Solomon, who takes over as the final king to reign over a united Israel. Solomon recognizes the overwhelming responsibility of his position and goes to the proper Source for wisdom. This pleases God immensely, to the point that God gives him all the necessary wisdom—and everything else he *didn't* ask for!

Yet Solomon illustrates a fundamental principle every leader must understand. While this man became the wisest human leader who ever lived and authored a number of books, the king's poor choices and failure to apply what God told him weakened his leadership.

Before Solomon left the way of God, the Lord greatly used him. Kings and queens from distant lands visited him and became acquainted with the God of Israel—precisely what God had in mind for the Jews. Israel was to become a light to the nations, and for a while its beacon of hope shone brightly.

But when Solomon began trusting his own wisdom and failed to stay focused on God, the Lord divided his kingdom and ripped it away. The nation remained split until outsiders like Assyria and Babylon conquered one kingdom, then the next. In the difficult years in between, God had to raise up prophets as His leaders and spokesmen, since the kings frequently would not listen to His voice.

God's Role in 1 Kings

By the end of 1 Kings, the Hebrew nation lies divided, torn both by civil wars and invaders. God seeks out godly leaders like David—men who would listen to His voice and obey it.

As in so many Old Testament books, God's interaction in 1 Kings appears almost entirely limited to leaders—for if He can raise up leaders to model the life He intended for Israel, the people would almost certainly follow suit.

Leaders in 1 Kings

David, Adonijah, Solomon, Rehoboam, Jeroboam, Abijam, Asa, Jehoshaphat, Ahab, Jezebel

Other People of Influence in 1 Kings

Nathan, Ahijah, Elijah, a widow, Obadiah, Micaiah

Lessons in Leadership

- Success without a successor is a failure.
- Decision making and problem solving is the fastest way to gain influence.
- Check your motives before you lead anything.
- The issue is not prioritizing our schedule, but scheduling our priorities.
- Influencing followers is addition; influencing leaders is multiplication.
- Keep first things first; distraction is the enemy of direction.
- Leaders must touch a heart before they ask for a hand.
- A divided leader eventually produces a divided nation.
- Passion and conviction mark the difference between a great leader and a mediocre one.
- Principles, not emotions, should guide your leadership.

LEADERSHIP HIGHLIGHTS IN 1 KINGS

Adonijah Presumes to Be King

1 Now King David was old, advanced in years; and they put covers on him, but he could not get warm. [2]Therefore his servants said to him, "Let a young woman, a virgin, be sought for our lord the king, and let her stand before the king, and let her care for him; and let her lie in your bosom, that our lord the king may be warm." [3]So they sought for a lovely young woman throughout all the territory of Israel, and found Abishag the Shunammite, and brought her to the king. [4]The young woman *was* very lovely; and she cared for the king, and served him; but the king did not know her.

[5]Then Adonijah the son of Haggith exalted himself, saying, "I will be king"; and he prepared for himself chariots and horsemen, and fifty men to run before him. [6](And his father had not rebuked him at any time by saying, "Why have you done so?" He *was* also very good-looking. *His mother* had borne him after Absalom.) [7]Then he conferred with Joab the son of Zeruiah and with Abiathar the priest, and they followed and helped Adonijah. [8]But Zadok the priest, Benaiah the son of Jehoiada, Nathan the prophet, Shimei, Rei, and the mighty men who *belonged* to David were not with Adonijah.

[9]And Adonijah sacrificed sheep and oxen and fattened cattle by the stone of Zoheleth, which *is* by En Rogel; he also invited all his brothers, the king's sons, and all the men of Judah, the king's servants. [10]But he did not invite Nathan the prophet, Benaiah, the mighty men, or Solomon his brother.

[11]So Nathan spoke to Bathsheba the mother of Solomon, saying, "Have you not heard that Adonijah the son of Haggith has become king, and David our lord does not know *it?* [12]Come, please, let me now give you advice, that you may save your own life and the life of your son Solomon. [13]Go immediately to King David and say to him, 'Did you not, my lord, O king, swear to your maidservant, saying, "Assuredly your son Solomon shall reign after me, and he shall sit on my throne"? Why then has Adonijah become king?' [14]Then, while you are still talking there with the king, I also will come in after you and confirm your words."

[15]So Bathsheba went into the chamber to the king. (Now the king was very old, and Abishag the Shunammite was serving the king.) [16]And Bathsheba bowed and did homage to the king. Then the king said, "What is your wish?"

[17]Then she said to him, "My lord, you swore by the LORD your God to your maidservant, saying, 'Assuredly Solomon your son shall reign after me, and he shall sit on my throne.' [18]So now, look! Adonijah has become king; and now, my lord the king, you do not know about *it.* [19]He has sacrificed oxen and fattened cattle and sheep in abundance, and has invited all the sons of the king, Abiathar the priest, and Joab the commander of the army; but Solomon your servant he has not invited. [20]And as for you, my lord, O king, the eyes of all Israel *are* on you, that you should tell them who will sit on the throne of my lord the king after him. [21]Otherwise it will happen, when my lord the king rests with his fathers, that I and my son Solomon will be counted as offenders."

[22]And just then, while she was still talking with the king, Nathan the prophet also came in. [23]So they told the king, saying, "Here is Nathan the prophet." And when he came in before the king, he bowed down before the king with his face to the ground. [24]And Nathan said, "My lord, O king, have you said, 'Adonijah shall reign after me, and he shall sit on my throne'? [25]For he has gone down today, and has sacrificed oxen and fattened cattle and sheep in abundance, and has invited all the king's sons, and the commanders of the army, and Abiathar the priest; and look! They are eating and drinking before him; and they say, 'Long live King Adonijah!' [26]But he has not invited me—me your servant—nor Zadok the priest, nor Benaiah the son of Jehoiada, nor your servant Solomon. [27]Has this thing been done by my lord the king, and you have not told your servant who should sit on the throne of my lord the king after him?"

David Proclaims Solomon King

[28]Then King David answered and said, "Call Bathsheba to me." So she came into the king's presence and stood before the king. [29]And the king took an oath and said, "*As* the LORD lives, who has redeemed my life from every distress, [30]just as I swore to you by the LORD God of Israel, saying, 'Assuredly Solomon your son shall be king after me, and he shall sit on my throne in my place,' so I certainly will do this day."

[31]Then Bathsheba bowed with *her* face to the earth, and paid homage to the king, and said, "Let my lord King David live forever!"

[32]And King David said, "Call to me Zadok the priest, Nathan the prophet, and Benaiah the son of Jehoiada." So they came before the king. [33]The king also said to them, "Take with you the servants of your lord, and have Solomon my son ride on my own mule, and take him down to Gihon. [34]There let Zadok the priest and Nathan

The Law of Legacy: David and Solomon

(1 Kings 1:28–40)

Two things greatly helped Solomon in his succession to the throne of Israel; both gave him the authority he required to rule. First, God chose him to be the next king. Second, David chose him as his successor.

Transitions in leadership often cause significant problems for groups and organizations. Notice what David did to smooth the transition process in his kingdom:

1. He made a public commitment (vv. 28–30).
2. He brought key influencers into the process (v. 32).
3. He gave Solomon some of his own resources, easily recognizable to the people (v. 33).
4. He set up a public commissioning for Solomon (vv. 34, 35).
5. He publicly endorsed Solomon's leadership (v. 35).
6. He initiated a celebration to transition the leadership to his successor (vv. 39, 40).

the prophet anoint him king over Israel; and blow the horn, and say, 'Long live King Solomon!' ³⁵Then you shall come up after him, and he shall come and sit on my throne, and he shall be king in my place. For I have appointed him to be ruler over Israel and Judah."

³⁶Benaiah the son of Jehoiada answered the king and said, "Amen! May the LORD God of my lord the king say so *too.* ³⁷As the LORD has been with my lord the king, even so may He be with Solomon, and make his throne greater than the throne of my lord King David."

³⁸So Zadok the priest, Nathan the prophet, Benaiah the son of Jehoiada, the Cherethites, and the Pelethites went down and had Solomon ride on King David's mule, and took him to Gihon. ³⁹Then Zadok the priest took a horn of oil from the tabernacle and anointed Solomon. And they blew the horn, and all the people said, *"Long* live King Solomon!" ⁴⁰And all the people went up after him; and the people played the flutes and rejoiced with great joy, so that the earth *seemed to* split with their sound.

⁴¹Now Adonijah and all the guests who *were* with him heard *it* as they finished eating. And when Joab heard the sound of the horn, he said, "Why *is* the city in such a noisy uproar?" ⁴²While he was still speaking, there came Jonathan, the son of Abiathar the priest. And Adonijah said to him, "Come in, for you *are* a prominent man, and bring good news."

⁴³Then Jonathan answered and said to Adonijah, "No! Our lord King David has made Solomon king. ⁴⁴The king has sent with him Zadok the priest, Nathan the prophet, Benaiah the son of Jehoiada, the Cherethites, and the Pelethites; and they have made him ride on the king's mule. ⁴⁵So Zadok the priest and Nathan the prophet have anointed him king at Gihon; and they have gone up from there rejoicing, so that the city is in an uproar. This *is* the noise that you have heard. ⁴⁶Also Solomon sits on the throne of the kingdom. ⁴⁷And moreover the king's servants have gone to bless our lord King David, saying, 'May God make the name of Solomon better than your name, and may He make his throne greater than your throne.' Then the king bowed himself on the bed. ⁴⁸Also the king said thus, 'Blessed *be* the LORD God of Israel, who has given *one* to sit on my throne this day, while my eyes see *it!*'"

⁴⁹So all the guests who were with Adonijah were afraid, and arose, and each one went his way.

⁵⁰Now Adonijah was afraid of Solomon; so he arose, and went and took hold of the horns of the altar. ⁵¹And it was told Solomon, saying, "Indeed Adonijah is afraid of King Solomon; for look, he has taken hold of the horns of the altar, saying, 'Let King Solomon swear to me today that he will not put his servant to death with the sword.'"

⁵²Then Solomon said, "If he proves himself a worthy man, not one hair of him shall fall to the earth; but if wickedness is found in him, he shall die." ⁵³So King Solomon sent them to bring him down from the altar. And he came and fell down before King Solomon; and Solomon said to him, "Go to your house."

David's Instructions to Solomon

2 Now the days of David drew near that he should die, and he charged Solomon his son, saying: ²"I go the way of all the earth; be strong, therefore, and prove yourself a man. ³And keep the charge of the LORD your God: to walk in His ways, to keep His statutes, His commandments, His judgments, and His testimonies, as it is written in the Law of Moses, that you may prosper in all that you do and wherever you turn;

The Law of the Inner Circle: Solomon Ensures Loyalty

(1 Kings 2:1–46)

Solomon had to make some tough but crucial leadership decisions at the beginning of his reign. First, he had to deal with men scheming for power; even his own brother, Adonijah, tried to set up his own kingdom. One by one, King Solomon discerned the loyalties of his associates, then removed all who refused to cooperate with him.

Solomon knew he could never work with renegades, no matter how influential or strategic they might seem. The young king ensured that his inner circle would include only loyal men who wanted to work with him.

David had seen these troubles brewing on the horizon. He knew he was placing his son in a precarious leadership situation, but twice he confidently declared that Solomon would know what to do (1 Kin. 2:6, 9). David understood that those closest to Solomon would greatly hinder or improve his level of success. Solomon understood the same thing—and wisely acted on it.

⁴that the LORD may fulfill His word which He spoke concerning me, saying, 'If your sons take heed to their way, to walk before Me in truth with all their heart and with all their soul,' He said, 'you shall not lack a man on the throne of Israel.'

⁵"Moreover you know also what Joab the son of Zeruiah did to me, *and* what he did to the two commanders of the armies of Israel, to Abner the son of Ner and Amasa the son of Jether, whom he killed. And he shed the blood of war in peacetime, and put the blood of war on his belt that *was* around his waist, and on his sandals that *were* on his feet. ⁶Therefore do according to your wisdom, and do not let his gray hair go down to the grave in peace.

⁷"But show kindness to the sons of Barzillai the Gileadite, and let them be among those who eat at your table, for so they came to me when I fled from Absalom your brother.

⁸"And see, *you have* with you Shimei the son of Gera, a Benjamite from Bahurim, who cursed me with a malicious curse in the day when I went to Mahanaim. But he came down to meet me at the Jordan, and I swore to him by the LORD, saying, 'I will not put you to death with the sword.' ⁹Now therefore, do not hold him guiltless, for you *are* a wise man and know what you ought to do to him; but bring his gray hair down to the grave with blood."

Death of David

¹⁰So David rested with his fathers, and was buried in the City of David. ¹¹The period that David reigned over Israel *was* forty years; seven years he reigned in Hebron, and in Jerusalem he reigned thirty-three years. ¹²Then Solomon sat on the throne of his father David; and his kingdom was firmly established.

Solomon Executes Adonijah

¹³Now Adonijah the son of Haggith came to Bathsheba the mother of Solomon. So she said, "Do you come peaceably?"

And he said, "Peaceably." ¹⁴Moreover he said, "I have something *to say* to you."

And she said, "Say it."

¹⁵Then he said, "You know that the kingdom was mine, and all Israel had set their expectations on me, that I should reign. However, the kingdom has been turned over, and has become my brother's; for it was his from the LORD. ¹⁶Now I ask one petition of you; do not deny me."

And she said to him, "Say it."

¹⁷Then he said, "Please speak to King Solomon, for he will not refuse you, that he may give me Abishag the Shunammite as wife."

¹⁸So Bathsheba said, "Very well, I will speak for you to the king."

¹⁹Bathsheba therefore went to King Solomon, to speak to him for Adonijah. And the king rose up to meet her and bowed down to her, and sat down on his throne and had a throne set for the king's mother; so she sat at his right hand. ²⁰Then she said, "I desire one small petition of you; do not refuse me."

And the king said to her, "Ask it, my mother, for I will not refuse you."

²¹So she said, "Let Abishag the Shunammite be given to Adonijah your brother as wife."

²²And King Solomon answered and said to his mother, "Now why do you ask Abishag the Shunammite for Adonijah? Ask for him the kingdom also—for he *is* my older brother—for him, and for Abiathar the priest, and for Joab the son of Zeruiah." ²³Then King Solomon swore by the LORD, saying, "May God do so to me, and more also, if Adonijah has not spoken this word against

his own life! [24]Now therefore, *as* the LORD lives, who has confirmed me and set me on the throne of David my father, and who has established a house[a] for me, as He promised, Adonijah shall be put to death today!"

[25]So King Solomon sent by the hand of Benaiah the son of Jehoiada; and he struck him down, and he died.

Abiathar Exiled, Joab Executed

[26]And to Abiathar the priest the king said, "Go to Anathoth, to your own fields, for you *are* deserving of death; but I will not put you to death at this time, because you carried the ark of the Lord GOD before my father David, and because you were afflicted every time my father was afflicted." [27]So Solomon removed Abiathar from being priest to the LORD, that he might fulfill the word of the LORD which He spoke concerning the house of Eli at Shiloh.

[28]Then news came to Joab, for Joab had defected to Adonijah, though he had not defected to Absalom. So Joab fled to the tabernacle of the LORD, and took hold of the horns of the altar. [29]And King Solomon was told, "Joab has fled to the tabernacle of the LORD; there *he is,* by the altar." Then Solomon sent Benaiah the son of Jehoiada, saying, "Go, strike him down." [30]So Benaiah went to the tabernacle of the LORD, and said to him, "Thus says the king, 'Come out!'"

And he said, "No, but I will die here." And Benaiah brought back word to the king, saying, "Thus said Joab, and thus he answered me." [31]Then the king said to him, "Do as he has said, and strike him down and bury him, that you may take away from me and from the house of my father the innocent blood which Joab shed. [32]So the LORD will return his blood on his head, because he struck down two men more righteous and better than he, and killed them with the sword—Abner the son of Ner, the commander of the army of Israel, and Amasa the son of Jether, the commander of the army of Judah—though my father David did not know *it.* [33]Their blood shall therefore return upon the head of Joab and upon the head of his descendants forever. But upon David and his descendants, upon his house and his throne, there shall be peace forever from the LORD."

[34]So Benaiah the son of Jehoiada went up and struck and killed him; and he was buried in his own house in the wilderness. [35]The king put Benaiah the son of Jehoiada in his place over the army, and the king put Zadok the priest in the place of Abiathar.

Shimei Executed

[36]Then the king sent and called for Shimei, and said to him, "Build yourself a house in Jerusalem and dwell there, and do not go out from there anywhere. [37]For it shall be, on the day you go out and cross the Brook Kidron, know for certain you shall surely die; your blood shall be on your own head."

[38]And Shimei said to the king, "The saying *is* good. As my lord the king has said, so your servant will do." So Shimei dwelt in Jerusalem many days.

[39]Now it happened at the end of three years, that two slaves of Shimei ran away to Achish the son of Maachah, king of Gath. And they told Shimei, saying, "Look, your slaves *are* in Gath!" [40]So Shimei arose, saddled his donkey, and went to Achish at Gath to seek his slaves. And Shimei went and brought his slaves from Gath. [41]And Solomon was told that Shimei had gone from Jerusalem to Gath and had come back. [42]Then the king sent and called for Shimei, and said to him, "Did I not make you swear by the LORD, and warn you, saying, 'Know for certain that on the day you go out and travel anywhere, you shall surely die'? And you said to me, 'The word I have heard *is* good.' [43]Why then have you not kept the oath of the LORD and the commandment that I gave you?" [44]The king said moreover to Shimei, "You know, as your heart acknowledges, all the wickedness that you did to my father David; therefore the LORD will return your wickedness on your own head. [45]But King Solomon *shall be* blessed, and the throne of David shall be established before the LORD forever."

[46]So the king commanded Benaiah the son of Jehoiada; and he went out and struck him down, and he died. Thus the kingdom was established in the hand of Solomon.

Solomon Requests Wisdom

3 Now Solomon made a treaty with Pharaoh king of Egypt, and married Pharaoh's daughter; then he brought her to the City of David until he had finished building his own house, and the house of the LORD, and the wall all around Jerusalem. [2]Meanwhile the people sacrificed at the high places, because there was no house built for the name of the LORD until those days. [3]And Solomon loved the LORD, walking in the statutes of his father David, except that he sacrificed and burned incense at the high places.

[4]Now the king went to Gibeon to sacrifice there, for that *was* the great high place: Solomon

---

2:24 [a]That is, a royal dynasty

SOLOMON AND THE LAW OF THE BIG MO

Momentum Is a Leader's Best Friend

(1 Kings 2:1—4:24)

It takes a leader to create momentum. Followers catch it. And managers are able to continue it once it has begun. But *creating* it requires someone who can motivate others, not one who needs to be motivated. Harry Truman once said, "If you can't stand the heat, get out of the kitchen." For leaders, that statement should be changed to read, "If you can't *make* some heat, get out of the kitchen."

All leaders face the challenge of creating change in an organization. Just as every sailor knows you can't steer a ship that isn't moving forward, strong leaders understand that to change direction, you first have to create forward progress. Without momentum, even the simplest tasks can seem insurmountable. But with momentum on your side, the future looks bright, obstacles appear small, and trouble seems temporary. With enough momentum, nearly any kind of change is possible.

The time of transition from one leader to another presents the most critical challenge to continuing momentum. How did Solomon so successfully take the reins from his father? Consider the following actions the young king took to ensure a smooth transition:

1. *He started with what David provided.*

Solomon's father gave him everything he needed to start his reign: a stable kingdom, plentiful resources, wise counsel, and his public endorsement. David made it clear to everyone in Israel that he had chosen Solomon as king.

2. *He humbly asked for leadership wisdom above all else.*

Solomon probably became king at about 18 years of age, yet despite his youth, he recognized the difficulties of leadership. He knew he needed wisdom above all else, so he asked for an understanding heart to judge God's people. That request kept his motives pure and made it possible for him to avoid momentum breakers.

3. *He made wise decisions that won him credibility.*

Solomon made several deft decisions concerning enemies to his throne. He exiled one opponent, executed two others, and put a fourth under house arrest. But even more important, he cemented his credibility with the people. The wisdom he displayed in a domestic dispute profoundly impacted the people: "All Israel heard of the judgment which the king had rendered; and they feared the king" (1 Kin. 3:28).

4. *He maintained the peace.*

Solomon's bold moves against enemies within Israel maintained peace at home, thus preventing a bloody civil war. But Solomon wisely took additional measures to keep other nations from threatening his country's progress—and therefore "he had peace on every side all around him" (1 Kin. 4:24).

5. *He surrounded himself with wise associates.*

Only Solomon among the kings of Israel can challenge David as the architect of a great inner circle. Solomon kept on a few of David's trusted servants in his own administration, but not many. Most of them he nurtured himself.

What It Takes to Sustain Momentum

How does a winning team keep winning? What makes it possible for an organization to keep the momentum going? The answer is not *what*, but *who*. It takes a leader to sustain momentum, a leader who possesses . . .

1. *A willingness to accept responsibility for the organization's momentum.*

Most leaders happily accept responsibility so long as an organization succeeds, but hedge when the organization starts to slip. Yet momentum—positive, negative, or nonexistent—is always the leader's responsibility. Olan Hendrix, C.E.O. of the Leadership Resource Group, maintains that after you've led an organization for three years, *every* problem is *your* problem.

2. *A willingness to direct momentum instead of letting it direct him.*

Momentum always has a direction. Most people in an organization have little impact on its momentum; it simply carries them. But leaders cannot afford to *surf* momentum; they must *steer* it. Before Solomon became king, an outstanding military leader, David, created the nation's momentum. Yet Solomon never led an army; his goals weren't military in nature. He gave most of his attention to trade and construction—and that meant he had to change the direction of the nation's momentum.

3. *A willingness to be enthusiastic at all times.*

Remain positive! Some personality types find it easy to remain enthusiastic; others don't. Reflect on the following secrets to keeping leadership positive all the time:

- *The work I'm doing is most important.* Make sure your vision, your mission, and your actions all line up. It's easy to stay excited when what you're doing really matters.
- *The people I work with are the best.* Place a high value on everyone you work with. Expect the best of them, and they'll give their best.
- *The results will be positive.* For the most part, you get what you expect. Only occasionally will you be surprised—but even then, you'll just as often be surprised by *better* results as by worse ones.

Have you ever met a leader with a chronically negative attitude who was able to continually sustain positive momentum? Probably not.

No leader can ignore the impact of momentum. If you've got it, you and your people will be able to accomplish things you never thought possible. If you don't, the smallest tasks will seem difficult. As the leader, you must make the choice to have it.

The Law of Intuition: Solomon's Problem Solving Gave Him Influence

(1 Kings 3:3–28)

What would you choose if God offered to give you anything you named? King Solomon came face-to-face with that delightful dilemma when Yahweh presented the young king with His equivalent of the genie in the bottle. "Ask! What shall I give you?" the Lord said to Solomon one night (1 Kin. 3:5).

Solomon displayed a good amount of wisdom by asking for more of it to lead the people of Israel. God not only answered his request, but also gave him what he did not ask for: riches, honor, long life, and conquest. Leadership wisdom allowed Solomon to:

1. Make wise decisions for his nation.
2. Choose the right staff for his palace.
3. Judge wisely between disputing parties.
4. Recognize priorities and gain perspective.

Before chapter three ends, Solomon has the chance to demonstrate his wisdom. Two women bring a child to him, both claiming to be the mother. Solomon tells them to cut the baby in half and let each woman have part of the child. He wisely used his knowledge of the overpowering maternal instinct to reveal the identity of the true mother.

offered a thousand burnt offerings on that altar. ⁵At Gibeon the LORD appeared to Solomon in a dream by night; and God said, "Ask! What shall I give you?"

⁶And Solomon said: "You have shown great mercy to Your servant David my father, because he walked before You in truth, in righteousness, and in uprightness of heart with You; You have continued this great kindness for him, and You have given him a son to sit on his throne, as *it is* this day. ⁷Now, O LORD my God, You have made Your servant king instead of my father David, but I *am* a little child; I do not know *how* to go out or come in. ⁸And Your servant *is* in the midst of Your people whom You have chosen, a great people, too numerous to be num-

bered or counted. ⁹Therefore give to Your servant an understanding heart to judge Your people, that I may discern between good and evil. For who is able to judge this great people of Yours?"

¹⁰The speech pleased the LORD, that Solomon had asked this thing. ¹¹Then God said to him: "Because you have asked this thing, and have not asked long life for yourself, nor have asked riches for yourself, nor have asked the life of your enemies, but have asked for yourself understanding to discern justice, ¹²behold, I have done according to your words; see, I have given you a wise and understanding heart, so that there has not been anyone like you before you, nor shall any like you arise after you. ¹³And I have also given you what you have not asked: both riches and honor, so that there shall not be anyone like you among the kings all your days. ¹⁴So if you walk in My ways, to keep My statutes and My commandments, as your father David walked, then I will lengthen your days."

¹⁵Then Solomon awoke; and indeed it had been a dream. And he came to Jerusalem and stood before the ark of the covenant of the LORD, offered up burnt offerings, offered peace offerings, and made a feast for all his servants.

Solomon's Wise Judgment

¹⁶Now two women *who were* harlots came to the king, and stood before him. ¹⁷And one woman said, "O my lord, this woman and I dwell in the same house; and I gave birth while she *was* in the house. ¹⁸Then it happened, the third day after I had given birth, that this woman also gave birth. And we *were* together; no one *was* with us in the house, except the two of us in the house. ¹⁹And this woman's son died in the night, because she lay on him. ²⁰So she arose in the middle of the night and took my son from my side, while your maidservant slept, and laid him in her bosom, and laid her dead child in my bosom. ²¹And when I rose in the morning to nurse my son, there he was, dead. But when I had examined him in the morning, indeed, he was not my son whom I had borne."

²²Then the other woman said, "No! But the living one *is* my son, and the dead one *is* your son."

And the first woman said, "No! But the dead one *is* your son, and the living one *is* my son."

Thus they spoke before the king.

²³And the king said, "The one says, 'This *is* my son, who lives, and your son *is* the dead one'; and the other says, 'No! But your son *is* the dead

one, and my son *is* the living one.'" 24Then the king said, "Bring me a sword." So they brought a sword before the king. 25And the king said, "Divide the living child in two, and give half to one, and half to the other."

26Then the woman whose son *was* living spoke to the king, for she yearned with compassion for her son; and she said, "O my lord, give her the living child, and by no means kill him!"

But the other said, "Let him be neither mine nor yours, *but* divide *him*."

27So the king answered and said, "Give the first woman the living child, and by no means kill him; she *is* his mother."

28And all Israel heard of the judgment which the king had rendered; and they feared the king, for they saw that the wisdom of God *was* in him to administer justice.

Solomon's Administration

4 So King Solomon was king over all Israel. 2And these *were* his officials: Azariah the son of Zadok, the priest; 3Elihoreph and Ahijah, the sons of Shisha, scribes; Jehoshaphat the son of Ahilud, the recorder; 4Benaiah the son of Jehoiada, over the army; Zadok and Abiathar, the priests; 5Azariah the son of Nathan, over the officers; Zabud the son of Nathan, a priest *and* the king's friend; 6Ahishar, over the household; and Adoniram the son of Abda, over the labor force.

7And Solomon had twelve governors over all Israel, who provided food for the king and his household; each one made provision for one month of the year. 8These *are* their names: Ben-Hur,a in the mountains of Ephraim; 9Ben-Deker,a in Makaz, Shaalbim, Beth Shemesh, and Elon Beth Hanan; 10Ben-Hesed,a in Arubboth; to him *belonged* Sochoh and all the land of Hepher; 11Ben-Abinadab,a *in* all the regions of Dor; he had Taphath the daughter of Solomon as wife; 12Baana the son of Ahilud, *in* Taanach, Megiddo, and all Beth Shean, which *is* beside Zaretan below Jezreel, from Beth Shean to Abel Meholah, as far as the other side of Jokneam; 13Ben-Geber,a in Ramoth Gilead; to him *belonged* the towns of Jair the son of Manasseh, in Gilead; to him *also belonged* the region of Argob in Bashan—sixty large cities with walls and bronze gate-bars; 14Ahinadab the son of Iddo, *in* Mahanaim; 15Ahimaaz, in Naphtali; he also took Basemath the daughter of Solomon as wife; 16Baanah the son of Hushai, in Asher and Aloth; 17Jehoshaphat the son of Paruah, in Issachar; 18Shimei the son of Elah, in Benjamin; 19Geber the son of Uri, in the land of Gilead, *in* the country of Sihon king of the Amorites, and of Og king of Bashan. *He was* the only governor who *was* in the land.

Prosperity and Wisdom of Solomon's Reign

20Judah and Israel *were* as numerous as the sand by the sea in multitude, eating and drinking and rejoicing. 21So Solomon reigned over all kingdoms from the Rivera *to* the land of the Philistines, as far as the border of Egypt. *They* brought tribute and served Solomon all the days of his life.

22Now Solomon's provision for one day was thirty kors of fine flour, sixty kors of meal, 23ten fatted oxen, twenty oxen from the pastures, and one hundred sheep, besides deer, gazelles, roebucks, and fatted fowl.

24For he had dominion over all *the region* on this side of the Rivera from Tiphsah even to Gaza, namely over all the kings on this side of the River; and he had peace on every side all around him. 25And Judah and Israel dwelt safely, each man under his vine and his fig tree, from Dan as far as Beersheba, all the days of Solomon.

26Solomon had fortya thousand stalls of horses for his chariots, and twelve thousand horsemen. 27And these governors, each man in his month, provided food for King Solomon and for all who came to King Solomon's table. There was no lack in their supply. 28They also brought barley and straw to the proper place, for the horses and steeds, each man according to his charge.

29And God gave Solomon wisdom and exceedingly great understanding, and largeness of heart like the sand on the seashore. 30Thus Solomon's wisdom excelled the wisdom of all the men of the East and all the wisdom of Egypt. 31For he was wiser than all men—than Ethan the Ezrahite, and Heman, Chalcol, and Darda, the sons of Mahol; and his fame was in all the surrounding nations. 32He spoke three thousand proverbs, and his songs were one thousand and five. 33Also he spoke of trees, from the cedar tree of Lebanon even to the hyssop that springs out of the wall; he spoke also of animals, of birds, of

---

4:8 aLiterally *Son of Hur* **4:9** aLiterally *Son of Deker* **4:10** aLiterally *Son of Hesed* **4:11** aLiterally *Son of Abinadab* **4:13** aLiterally *Son of Geber* **4:21** aThat is, the Euphrates **4:24** aThat is, the Euphrates **4:26** aFollowing Masoretic Text and most other authorities; some manuscripts of the Septuagint read *four* (compare 2 Chronicles 9:25).

creeping things, and of fish. [34]And men of all nations, from all the kings of the earth who had heard of his wisdom, came to hear the wisdom of Solomon.

Solomon Prepares to Build the Temple

5 Now Hiram king of Tyre sent his servants to Solomon, because he heard that they had anointed him king in place of his father, for Hiram had always loved David. [2]Then Solomon sent to Hiram, saying:

[3] You know how my father David could not build a house for the name of the LORD his God because of the wars which were fought against him on every side, until the LORD put *his foes*[a] under the soles of his feet.

[4] But now the LORD my God has given me rest on every side; *there is* neither adversary nor evil occurrence.

[5] And behold, I propose to build a house for the name of the LORD my God, as the LORD spoke to my father David, saying, "Your son, whom I will set on your throne in your place, he shall build the house for My name."

[6] Now therefore, command that they cut

Partnerships Allow Leaders to Achieve Far More

(1 Kings 5:1–10)

When Solomon began his rule, Hiram, the king of Tyre, congratulated him on his new position. Solomon capitalized on the relationship and invited Hiram to help him build the temple. Together, the two leaders achieved far more than they could have alone. That's partnership.

down cedars for me from Lebanon; and my servants will be with your servants, and I will pay you wages for your servants according to whatever you say. For you know *there is* none among us who has skill to cut timber like the Sidonians.

5:3 [a]Literally *them*

SOLOMON — A WISE KING WHO FORGOT THE FIRST PRINCIPLE OF WISDOM

(1 Kings 4:29–34)

PROFILE IN LEADERSHIP

For a smart guy, he sure ended up doing some dumb things.

Near the beginning of Solomon's reign, God approached the young king with a proposal: Ask Me for anything you want. Much to God's delight, Solomon didn't ask for great riches, respect among world leaders, or an invincible nation. Solomon asked for wisdom, and God answered abundantly.

The Bible tells us that the Lord gave the king "wisdom and exceedingly great understanding, and largeness of heart like the sand on the seashore," and that his wisdom exceeded that of any other man (1 Kin. 4:29–31). Solomon's expansive mind explored the disciplines of botany, zoology, and musicology, and pondered topics ranging from economics to communication to love.

The wisdom of King Solomon helped Israel to prosper greatly. His kingdom annually took in untold amounts of gold and silver and other precious commodities. Solomon himself amassed wealth greater than all the kings of his time (1 Kin. 10:23).

But by the end of his reign, this brilliant king somehow forgot the first principle of wisdom: "The fear of the LORD is the beginning of wisdom" (Ps. 111:10). When Solomon was old, "his wives turned his heart after other gods; and his heart was not loyal to the LORD his God" (1 Kin. 11:4). Only wisdom energized by a vibrant walk with God makes godly leaders.

[7]So it was, when Hiram heard the words of Solomon, that he rejoiced greatly and said,

Blessed *be* the LORD this day, for He has given David a wise son over this great people!

[8]Then Hiram sent to Solomon, saying:

I have considered *the message* which you sent me, *and* I will do all you desire concerning the cedar and cypress logs. [9] My servants shall bring *them* down from Lebanon to the sea; I will float them in rafts by sea to the place you indicate to me, and will have them broken apart there; then you can take *them* away. And you shall fulfill my desire by giving food for my household.

[10]Then Hiram gave Solomon cedar and cypress logs *according to* all his desire. [11]And Solomon gave Hiram twenty thousand kors of wheat *as* food for his household, and twenty[a] kors of pressed oil. Thus Solomon gave to Hiram year by year.

[12]So the LORD gave Solomon wisdom, as He had promised him; and there was peace between Hiram and Solomon, and the two of them made a treaty together.

[13]Then King Solomon raised up a labor force out of all Israel; and the labor force was thirty thousand men. [14]And he sent them to Lebanon, ten thousand a month in shifts: they were one month in Lebanon *and* two months at home; Adoniram *was* in charge of the labor force. [15]Solomon had seventy thousand who carried burdens, and eighty thousand who quarried *stone* in the mountains, [16]besides three thousand three hundred[a] from the chiefs of Solomon's deputies, who supervised the people who labored in the work. [17]And the king commanded them to quarry large stones, costly stones, *and* hewn stones, to lay the foundation of the temple.[a] [18]So Solomon's builders, Hiram's builders, and the Gebalites quarried *them;* and they prepared timber and stones to build the temple.

Solomon Builds the Temple

6 And it came to pass in the four hundred and eightieth[a] year after the children of Israel had come out of the land of Egypt, in the fourth year of Solomon's reign over Israel, in the month of Ziv, which *is* the second month, that he began to build the house of the LORD. [2]Now the house which King Solomon built for the LORD, its length *was* sixty cubits, its width twenty, and its height thirty cubits. [3]The vestibule in front of the sanctuary[a] of the house *was* twenty cubits long across the width of the house, *and* the width of *the vestibule*[b] extended ten cubits from the front of the house. [4]And he made for the house windows with beveled frames.

[5]Against the wall of the temple he built chambers all around, *against* the walls of the temple, all around the sanctuary and the inner sanctuary.[a] Thus he made side chambers all around it. [6]The lowest chamber *was* five cubits wide, the middle *was* six cubits wide, and the third *was* seven cubits wide; for he made narrow ledges around the outside of the temple, so that *the support beams* would not be fastened into the walls of the temple. [7]And the temple, when it was being built, was built with stone finished at the quarry, so that no hammer or chisel *or* any iron tool was heard in the temple while it was being built. [8]The doorway for the middle story[a] *was* on the right side of the temple. They went up by stairs to the middle *story,* and from the middle to the third.

[9]So he built the temple and finished it, and he paneled the temple with beams and boards of cedar. [10]And he built side chambers against the entire temple, each five cubits high; they were attached to the temple with cedar beams.

[11]Then the word of the LORD came to Solomon, saying: [12]"*Concerning* this temple which you are building, if you walk in My statutes, execute My judgments, keep all My commandments, and walk in them, then I will perform My word with you, which I spoke to your father David. [13]And I will dwell among the children of Israel, and will not forsake My people Israel."

[14]So Solomon built the temple and finished it. [15]And he built the inside walls of the temple with cedar boards; from the floor of the temple to the ceiling he paneled the inside with wood;

5:11 [a]Following Masoretic Text, Targum, and Vulgate; Septuagint and Syriac read *twenty thousand.* **5:16** [a]Following Masoretic Text, Targum, and Vulgate; Septuagint reads *three thousand six hundred.* **5:17** [a]Literally *house,* and so frequently throughout this book **6:1** [a]Following Masoretic Text, Targum, and Vulgate; Septuagint reads *fortieth.* **6:3** [a]Hebrew *heykal;* here the main room of the temple, elsewhere called the holy place (compare Exodus 26:33 and Ezekiel 41:1) [b]Literally *it* **6:5** [a]Hebrew *debir;* here the inner room of the temple, elsewhere called the Most Holy Place (compare verse 16) **6:8** [a]Following Masoretic Text and Vulgate; Septuagint reads *upper story;* Targum reads *ground story.*

The Difficulty of Handling Power

(1 Kings 6:1–38)

Solomon built the temple with excellence, sparing no expense and caring for each detail. He finished even the "invisible parts" with high quality and precision. Through his building program, Solomon became known everywhere and his power vastly increased.

And that may be the very thing that led to his later problems.

Every leader has power, gained in a variety of ways. Ponder the following "power platforms" and ask yourself: *Which ones do I use with others?*

1. **Coercive Power:** based on fear; failure to comply brings punishment
   Weakness: Volunteers cannot be forced to act.
2. **Connection Power:** based on who you know, not who you are
   Weakness: It becomes political.
3. **Charisma Power:** based on personality
   Weakness: Smiles and warm feelings cannot replace truth.
4. **Competence Power:** based on ability to get results
   Weakness: Raw ability is good, but not if it alienates or fails to empower people.
5. **Christmas Power:** based on gifts bestowed
   Weakness: People want what they don't need, and need what they don't want.

and he covered the floor of the temple with planks of cypress. [16]Then he built the twenty-cubit room at the rear of the temple, from floor to ceiling, with cedar boards; he built *it* inside as the inner sanctuary, as the Most Holy *Place.* [17]And in front of it the temple sanctuary was forty cubits *long.* [18]The inside of the temple was cedar, carved with ornamental buds and open flowers. All *was* cedar; there was no stone *to be* seen.

[19]And he prepared the inner sanctuary inside the temple, to set the ark of the covenant of the LORD there. [20]The inner sanctuary *was* twenty cubits long, twenty cubits wide, and twenty cubits high. He overlaid it with pure gold, and overlaid the altar of cedar. [21]So Solomon overlaid the inside of the temple with pure gold. He stretched gold chains across the front of the inner sanctuary, and overlaid it with gold. [22]The whole temple he overlaid with gold, until he had finished all the temple; also he overlaid with gold the entire altar that *was* by the inner sanctuary.

[23]Inside the inner sanctuary he made two cherubim *of* olive wood, *each* ten cubits high. [24]One wing of the cherub *was* five cubits, and the other wing of the cherub five cubits: ten cubits from the tip of one wing to the tip of the other. [25]And the other cherub *was* ten cubits; both cherubim *were* of the same size and shape. [26]The height of one cherub *was* ten cubits, and so *was* the other cherub. [27]Then he set the cherubim inside the inner room;[a] and they stretched out the wings of the cherubim so that the wing of the one touched *one* wall, and the wing of the other cherub touched the other wall. And their wings touched each other in the middle of the room. [28]Also he overlaid the cherubim with gold.

[29]Then he carved all the walls of the temple all around, both the inner and outer *sanctuaries,* with carved figures of cherubim, palm trees, and open flowers. [30]And the floor of the temple he overlaid with gold, both the inner and outer *sanctuaries.*

[31]For the entrance of the inner sanctuary he made doors *of* olive wood; the lintel *and* doorposts *were* one-fifth *of the wall.* [32]The two doors *were of* olive wood; and he carved on them figures of cherubim, palm trees, and open flowers, and overlaid *them* with gold; and he spread gold on the cherubim and on the palm trees. [33]So for the door of the sanctuary he also made doorposts *of* olive wood, one-fourth *of the wall.* [34]And the two doors *were of* cypress wood; two panels *comprised* one folding door, and two panels *comprised* the other folding door. [35]Then he carved cherubim, palm trees, and open flowers *on them,* and overlaid *them* with gold applied evenly on the carved work.

[36]And he built the inner court with three rows of hewn stone and a row of cedar beams.

[37]In the fourth year the foundation of the

6:27 [a]Literally *house*

house of the LORD was laid, in the month of Ziv. [38]And in the eleventh year, in the month of Bul, which is the eighth month, the house was finished in all its details and according to all its plans. So he was seven years in building it.

Solomon's Other Buildings

7 But Solomon took thirteen years to build his own house; so he finished all his house. [2]He also built the House of the Forest of Lebanon; its length *was* one hundred cubits, its width fifty cubits, and its height thirty cubits, with four rows of cedar pillars, and cedar beams on the pillars. [3]And *it was* paneled with cedar above the beams that *were* on forty-five pillars, fifteen *to* a row. [4]*There were* windows *with beveled frames in* three rows, and window *was* opposite window *in* three tiers. [5]And all the doorways and doorposts *had* rectangular frames; and window *was* opposite window *in* three tiers.

[6]He also made the Hall of Pillars: its length *was* fifty cubits, and its width thirty cubits; and in front of them *was* a portico with pillars, and a canopy *was* in front of them.

[7]Then he made a hall for the throne, the Hall of Judgment, where he might judge; and *it was* paneled with cedar from floor to ceiling.[a]

[8]And the house where he dwelt *had* another court inside the hall, of like workmanship. Solomon also made a house like this hall for Pharaoh's daughter, whom he had taken *as wife.*

[9]All these *were of* costly stones cut to size, trimmed with saws, inside and out, from the foundation to the eaves, and also on the outside to the great court. [10]The foundation *was of* costly stones, large stones, some ten cubits and some eight cubits. [11]And above *were* costly stones, hewn to size, and cedar wood. [12]The great court *was* enclosed with three rows of hewn stones and a row of cedar beams. So were the inner court of the house of the LORD and the vestibule of the temple.

Hiram the Craftsman

[13]Now King Solomon sent and brought Huram[a] from Tyre. [14]He *was* the son of a widow from the tribe of Naphtali, and his father *was* a man of Tyre, a bronze worker; he was filled with wisdom and understanding and skill in working with all kinds of bronze work. So he came to King Solomon and did all his work.

The Bronze Pillars for the Temple

[15]And he cast two pillars of bronze, each one eighteen cubits high, and a line of twelve cubits measured the circumference of each. [16]Then he made two capitals *of* cast bronze, to set on the tops of the pillars. The height of one capital *was* five cubits, and the height of the other capital *was* five cubits. [17]*He made* a lattice network, with wreaths of chainwork, for the capitals which *were* on top of the pillars: seven chains for one capital and seven for the other capital. [18]So he made the pillars, and two rows of pomegranates above the network all around to cover the capitals that *were* on top; and thus he did for the other capital.

[19]The capitals which *were* on top of the pillars in the hall *were* in the shape of lilies, four cubits. [20]The capitals on the two pillars also *had pomegranates* above, by the convex surface which *was* next to the network; and there *were* two hundred such pomegranates in rows on each of the capitals all around.

[21]Then he set up the pillars by the vestibule of the temple; he set up the pillar on the right and called its name Jachin, and he set up the pillar on the left and called its name Boaz. [22]The tops of the pillars were in the shape of lilies. So the work of the pillars was finished.

The Sea and the Oxen

[23]And he made the Sea of cast bronze, ten cubits from one brim to the other; *it was* completely round. Its height *was* five cubits, and a line of thirty cubits measured its circumference. [24]Below its brim *were* ornamental buds encircling it all around, ten to a cubit, all the way around the Sea. The ornamental buds *were* cast in two rows when it was cast. [25]It stood on twelve oxen: three looking toward the north, three looking toward the west, three looking toward the south, and three looking toward the east; the Sea *was set* upon them, and all their back parts *pointed* inward. [26]It *was* a handbreadth thick; and its brim was shaped like the brim of a cup, *like* a lily blossom. It contained two thousand[a] baths.

The Carts and the Lavers

[27]He also made ten carts of bronze; four cubits *was* the length of each cart, four cubits its width, and three cubits its height. [28]And this *was* the design of the carts: They had panels, and the panels *were* between frames; [29]on the panels that *were* between the frames *were* lions, oxen, and cherubim. And on the frames *was* a pedestal on top. Below the lions and oxen *were* wreaths of plaited work. [30]Every cart had four bronze wheels

---

7:7 [a]Literally *floor,* that is, of the upper level
7:13 [a]Hebrew *Hiram* (compare 2 Chronicles 2:13, 14) **7:26** [a]Or *three thousand* (compare 2 Chronicles 4:5)

and axles of bronze, and its four feet had supports. Under the laver *were* supports of cast *bronze* beside each wreath. ³¹Its opening inside the crown at the top *was* one cubit in diameter; and the opening *was* round, shaped *like* a pedestal, one and a half cubits in outside diameter; and also on the opening *were* engravings, but the panels were square, not round. ³²Under the panels *were* the four wheels, and the axles of the wheels *were joined* to the cart. The height of a wheel *was* one and a half cubits. ³³The workmanship of the wheels *was* like the workmanship of a chariot wheel; their axle pins, their rims, their spokes, and their hubs *were* all of cast *bronze*. ³⁴And *there were* four supports at the four corners of each cart; its supports *were* part of the cart itself. ³⁵On the top of the cart, at the height of half a cubit, *it was* perfectly round. And on the top of the cart, its flanges and its panels *were* of the same casting. ³⁶On the plates of its flanges and on its panels he engraved cherubim, lions, and palm trees, wherever there was a clear space on each, with wreaths all around. ³⁷Thus he made the ten carts. All of them were of the same mold, one measure, *and* one shape.

³⁸Then he made ten lavers of bronze; each laver contained forty baths, *and* each laver *was* four cubits. On each of the ten carts *was* a laver. ³⁹And he put five carts on the right side of the house, and five on the left side of the house. He set the Sea on the right side of the house, toward the southeast.

Furnishings of the Temple

⁴⁰Huram[a] made the lavers and the shovels and the bowls. So Huram finished doing all the work that he was to do for King Solomon *for* the house of the LORD: ⁴¹the two pillars, the *two* bowl-shaped capitals that *were* on top of the two pillars; the two networks covering the two bowl-shaped capitals which *were* on top of the pillars; ⁴²four hundred pomegranates for the two networks (two rows of pomegranates for each network, to cover the two bowl-shaped capitals that *were* on top of the pillars); ⁴³the ten carts, and ten lavers on the carts; ⁴⁴one Sea, and twelve oxen under the Sea; ⁴⁵the pots, the shovels, and the bowls.

All these articles which Huram[a] made for King Solomon *for* the house of the LORD *were of* burnished bronze. ⁴⁶In the plain of Jordan the king had them cast in clay molds, between Succoth and Zaretan. ⁴⁷And Solomon did not weigh all the articles, because *there were* so many; the weight of the bronze was not determined.

⁴⁸Thus Solomon had all the furnishings made for the house of the LORD: the altar of gold, and the table of gold on which *was* the showbread; ⁴⁹the lampstands of pure gold, five on the right *side* and five on the left in front of the inner sanctuary, with the flowers and the lamps and the wick-trimmers of gold; ⁵⁰the basins, the trimmers, the bowls, the ladles, and the censers of pure gold; and the hinges of gold, *both* for the doors of the inner room (the Most Holy *Place*) *and* for the doors of the main hall of the temple.

⁵¹So all the work that King Solomon had done for the house of the LORD was finished; and Solomon brought in the things which his father David had dedicated: the silver and the gold and the furnishings. He put them in the treasuries of the house of the LORD.

The Ark Brought into the Temple

8 Now Solomon assembled the elders of Israel and all the heads of the tribes, the chief fathers of the children of Israel, to King Solomon in Jerusalem, that they might bring up the ark of the covenant of the LORD from the City of David, which *is* Zion. ²Therefore all the men of Israel assembled with King Solomon at the feast in the month of Ethanim, which *is* the seventh month. ³So all the elders of Israel came, and the priests took up the ark. ⁴Then they brought up the ark of the LORD, the tabernacle of meeting, and all the holy furnishings that *were* in the tabernacle. The priests and the Levites brought them up. ⁵Also King Solomon, and all the congregation of Israel who were assembled with him, *were* with him before the ark, sacrificing sheep and oxen that could not be counted or numbered for multitude. ⁶Then the priests brought in the ark of the covenant of the LORD to its place, into the inner sanctuary of the temple, to the Most Holy *Place,* under the wings of the cherubim. ⁷For the cherubim spread *their* two wings over the place of the ark, and the cherubim overshadowed the ark and its poles. ⁸The poles extended so that the ends of the poles could be seen from the holy *place,* in front of the inner sanctuary; but they could not be seen from outside. And they are there to this day. ⁹Nothing *was* in the ark except the two tablets of stone which Moses put there at Horeb, when the LORD made *a covenant* with the children of Israel, when they came out of the land of Egypt.

¹⁰And it came to pass, when the priests came out of the holy *place,* that the cloud filled the

---

7:40 [a]Hebrew *Hiram* (compare 2 Chronicles 2:13, 14) **7:45** [a]Hebrew *Hiram* (compare 2 Chronicles 2:13, 14)

house of the LORD, [11]so that the priests could not continue ministering because of the cloud; for the glory of the LORD filled the house of the LORD.

[12]Then Solomon spoke:

"The LORD said He would dwell in the
 dark cloud.
[13] I have surely built You an exalted house,
 And a place for You to dwell in forever."

Solomon's Speech at Completion of the Work

[14]Then the king turned around and blessed the whole assembly of Israel, while all the assembly of Israel was standing. [15]And he said: "Blessed be the LORD God of Israel, who spoke with His mouth to my father David, and with His hand has fulfilled it, saying, [16]'Since the day that I brought My people Israel out of Egypt, I have chosen no city from any tribe of Israel in which to build a house, that My name might be there; but I chose David to be over My people Israel.' [17]Now it was in the heart of my father David to build a temple[a] for the name of the LORD God of Israel. [18]But the LORD said to my father David, 'Whereas it was in your heart to build a temple for My name, you did well that it was in your heart. [19]Nevertheless you shall not build the temple, but your son who will come from your body, he shall build the temple for My name.' [20]So the LORD has fulfilled His word which He spoke; and I have filled the position of my father David, and sit on the throne of Israel, as the LORD promised; and I have built a temple for the name of the LORD God of Israel. [21]And there I have made a place for the ark, in which is the

---

Leaders Know Their Source and Give God Credit

(1 Kings 8:12–61)

After Solomon built a magnificent temple to house the ark of the covenant, he prayed a dedication prayer committing the temple to God. Despite his hard work, Solomon knew all the glory belonged to God. All leaders must recognize that lasting fruit appears only by the blessing of God.

---

covenant of the LORD which He made with our fathers, when He brought them out of the land of Egypt."

Solomon's Prayer of Dedication

[22]Then Solomon stood before the altar of the LORD in the presence of all the assembly of Israel, and spread out his hands toward heaven; [23]and he said: "LORD God of Israel, there is no God in heaven above or on earth below like You, who keep Your covenant and mercy with Your servants who walk before You with all their hearts. [24]You have kept what You promised Your servant David my father; You have both spoken with Your mouth and fulfilled it with Your hand, as it is this day. [25]Therefore, LORD God of Israel, now keep what You promised Your servant David my father, saying, 'You shall not fail to have a man sit before Me on the throne of Israel, only if your sons take heed to their way, that they walk before Me as you have walked before Me.' [26]And now I pray, O God of Israel, let Your word come true, which You have spoken to Your servant David my father.

[27]"But will God indeed dwell on the earth? Behold, heaven and the heaven of heavens cannot contain You. How much less this temple which I have built! [28]Yet regard the prayer of Your servant and his supplication, O LORD my God, and listen to the cry and the prayer which Your servant is praying before You today: [29]that Your eyes may be open toward this temple night and day, toward the place of which You said, 'My name shall be there,' that You may hear the prayer which Your servant makes toward this place. [30]And may You hear the supplication of Your servant and of Your people Israel, when they pray toward this place. Hear in heaven Your dwelling place; and when You hear, forgive.

[31]"When anyone sins against his neighbor, and is forced to take an oath, and comes and takes an oath before Your altar in this temple, [32]then hear in heaven, and act, and judge Your servants, condemning the wicked, bringing his way on his head, and justifying the righteous by giving him according to his righteousness.

[33]"When Your people Israel are defeated before an enemy because they have sinned against You, and when they turn back to You and confess Your name, and pray and make supplication to You in this temple, [34]then hear in heaven, and forgive the sin of Your people Israel, and bring them back to the land which You gave to their fathers.

8:17 [a]Literally house, and so in verses 18–20

³⁵"When the heavens are shut up and there is no rain because they have sinned against You, when they pray toward this place and confess Your name, and turn from their sin because You afflict them, ³⁶then hear in heaven, and forgive the sin of Your servants, Your people Israel, that You may teach them the good way in which they should walk; and send rain on Your land which You have given to Your people as an inheritance.

³⁷"When there is famine in the land, pestilence *or* blight *or* mildew, locusts *or* grasshoppers; when their enemy besieges them in the land of their cities; whatever plague or whatever sickness *there is;* ³⁸whatever prayer, whatever supplication is made by anyone, *or* by all Your people Israel, when each one knows the plague of his own heart, and spreads out his hands toward this temple: ³⁹then hear in heaven Your dwelling place, and forgive, and act, and give to everyone according to all his ways, whose heart You know (for You alone know the hearts of all the sons of men), ⁴⁰that they may fear You all the days that they live in the land which You gave to our fathers.

⁴¹"Moreover, concerning a foreigner, who *is* not of Your people Israel, but has come from a far country for Your name's sake ⁴²(for they will hear of Your great name and Your strong hand and Your outstretched arm), when he comes and prays toward this temple, ⁴³hear in heaven Your dwelling place, and do according to all for which the foreigner calls to You, that all peoples of the earth may know Your name and fear You, as *do* Your people Israel, and that they may know that this temple which I have built is called by Your name.

⁴⁴"When Your people go out to battle against their enemy, wherever You send them, and when they pray to the LORD toward the city which You have chosen and the temple which I have built for Your name, ⁴⁵then hear in heaven their prayer and their supplication, and maintain their cause.

⁴⁶"When they sin against You (for *there is* no one who does not sin), and You become angry with them and deliver them to the enemy, and they take them captive to the land of the enemy, far or near; ⁴⁷yet when they come to themselves in the land where they were carried captive, and repent, and make supplication to You in the land of those who took them captive, saying, 'We have sinned and done wrong, we have committed wickedness'; ⁴⁸and *when* they return to You with all their heart and with all their soul in the land of their enemies who led them away captive, and pray to You toward their land which You gave to their fathers, the city which You have chosen and the temple which I have built

for Your name: ⁴⁹then hear in heaven Your dwelling place their prayer and their supplication, and maintain their cause, ⁵⁰and forgive Your people who have sinned against You, and all their transgressions which they have transgressed against You; and grant them compassion before those who took them captive, that they may have compassion on them ⁵¹(for they *are* Your people and Your inheritance, whom You brought out of Egypt, out of the iron furnace), ⁵²that Your eyes may be open to the supplication of Your servant and the supplication of Your people Israel, to listen to them whenever they call to You. ⁵³For You separated them from among all the peoples of the earth *to be* Your inheritance, as You spoke by Your servant Moses, when You brought our fathers out of Egypt, O Lord GOD."

Solomon Blesses the Assembly

⁵⁴And so it was, when Solomon had finished praying all this prayer and supplication to the LORD, that he arose from before the altar of the LORD, from kneeling on his knees with his hands spread up to heaven. ⁵⁵Then he stood and blessed all the assembly of Israel with a loud voice, saying: ⁵⁶"Blessed *be* the LORD, who has given rest to His people Israel, according to all that He promised. There has not failed one word of all His good promise, which He promised through His servant Moses. ⁵⁷May the LORD our God be with us, as He was with our fathers. May He not leave us nor forsake us, ⁵⁸that He may incline our hearts to Himself, to walk in all His ways, and to keep His commandments and His statutes and His judgments, which He commanded our fathers. ⁵⁹And may these words of mine, with which I have made supplication before the LORD, be near the LORD our God day and night, that He may maintain the cause of His servant and the cause of His people Israel, as each day may require, ⁶⁰that all the peoples of the earth may know that the LORD *is* God; *there is* no other. ⁶¹Let your heart therefore be loyal to the LORD our God, to walk in His statutes and keep His commandments, as at this day."

Solomon Dedicates the Temple

⁶²Then the king and all Israel with him offered sacrifices before the LORD. ⁶³And Solomon offered a sacrifice of peace offerings, which he offered to the LORD, twenty-two thousand bulls and one hundred and twenty thousand sheep. So the king and all the children of Israel dedicated the house of the LORD. ⁶⁴On the same day the king consecrated the middle of the court that *was* in front of the house of the LORD; for there

he offered burnt offerings, grain offerings, and the fat of the peace offerings, because the bronze altar that *was* before the LORD *was* too small to receive the burnt offerings, the grain offerings, and the fat of the peace offerings.

[65]At that time Solomon held a feast, and all Israel with him, a great assembly from the entrance of Hamath to the Brook of Egypt, before the LORD our God, seven days and seven *more* days—fourteen days. [66]On the eighth day he sent the people away; and they blessed the king, and went to their tents joyful and glad of heart for all the good that the LORD had done for His servant David, and for Israel His people.

God's Second Appearance to Solomon

And it came to pass, when Solomon had finished building the house of the LORD and the king's house, and all Solomon's desire which he wanted to do, [2]that the LORD appeared to Solomon the second time, as He had appeared to him at Gibeon. [3]And the LORD said to him: "I have heard your prayer and your supplication that you have made before Me; I have consecrated this house which you have built to put My name there forever, and My eyes and My heart will be there perpetually. [4]Now if you walk before Me as your father David walked, in integrity of heart and in uprightness, to do according to all that I have commanded you, *and if* you keep My statutes and My judgments, [5]then I will establish the throne of your kingdom over Israel forever, as I promised David your father, saying, 'You shall not fail to have a man on the throne of Israel.' [6]*But* if you or your sons at all turn from following Me, and do not keep My commandments *and* My statutes which I have set before you, but go and serve other gods and worship them, [7]then I will cut off Israel from the land which I have given them; and this house which I have consecrated for My name I will cast out of My sight. Israel will be a proverb and a byword among all peoples. [8]And *as for* this house, *which* is exalted, everyone who passes by it will be astonished and will hiss, and say, 'Why has the LORD done thus to this land and to this house?' [9]Then they will answer, 'Because they forsook the LORD their God, who brought their fathers out of the land of Egypt, and have embraced other gods, and worshiped them and served them; therefore the LORD has brought all this calamity on them.'"

Solomon and Hiram Exchange Gifts

[10]Now it happened at the end of twenty years, when Solomon had built the two houses, the house of the LORD and the king's house [11](Hiram the king of Tyre had supplied Solomon with cedar and cypress and gold, as much as he desired), *that* King Solomon then gave Hiram twenty cities in the land of Galilee. [12]Then Hiram went from Tyre to see the cities which Solomon had given him, but they did not please him. [13]So he said, "What *kind of* cities *are* these which you have given me, my brother?" And he called them the land of Cabul,[a] as they are to this day. [14]Then Hiram sent the king one hundred and twenty talents of gold.

Solomon's Additional Achievements

[15]And this *is* the reason for the labor force which King Solomon raised: to build the house of the LORD, his own house, the Millo,[a] the wall of Jerusalem, Hazor, Megiddo, and Gezer. [16](Pharaoh king of Egypt had gone up and taken Gezer and burned it with fire, had killed the Canaanites who dwelt in the city, and had given it *as* a dowry to his daughter, Solomon's wife.) [17]And Solomon built Gezer, Lower Beth Horon, [18]Baalath, and Tadmor in the wilderness, in the land *of Judah,* [19]all the storage cities that Solomon had, cities for his chariots and cities for his cavalry, and whatever Solomon desired to build in Jerusalem, in Lebanon, and in all the land of his dominion.

[20]All the people *who were* left of the Amorites, Hittites, Perizzites, Hivites, and Jebusites, who *were* not of the children of Israel— [21]that is, their descendants who were left in the land after them, whom the children of Israel had not been able to destroy completely—from these Solomon raised forced labor, as it is to this day. [22]But of the children of Israel Solomon made no forced laborers, because they *were* men of war and his servants: his officers, his captains, commanders of his chariots, and his cavalry.

[23]Others *were* chiefs of the officials who *were* over Solomon's work: five hundred and fifty, who ruled over the people who did the work.

[24]But Pharaoh's daughter came up from the City of David to her house which *Solomon*[a] had built for her. Then he built the Millo.

[25]Now three times a year Solomon offered burnt offerings and peace offerings on the altar which he had built for the LORD, and he burned incense with them *on the altar* that *was* before the LORD. So he finished the temple.

[26]King Solomon also built a fleet of ships at

9:13 [a]Literally *Good for Nothing* 9:15 [a]Literally *The Landfill* 9:24 [a]Literally *he* (compare 2 Chronicles 8:11)

Ezion Geber, which *is* near Elath[a] on the shore of the Red Sea, in the land of Edom. [27]Then Hiram sent his servants with the fleet, seamen who knew the sea, to work with the servants of Solomon. [28]And they went to Ophir, and acquired four hundred and twenty talents of gold from there, and brought *it* to King Solomon.

The Queen of Sheba's Praise of Solomon

10 Now when the queen of Sheba heard of the fame of Solomon concerning the name of the LORD, she came to test him with hard questions. [2]She came to Jerusalem with a very great retinue, with camels that bore spices, very much gold, and precious stones; and when she came to Solomon, she spoke with him about all that was in her heart. [3]So Solomon answered all her questions; there was nothing so difficult for the king that he could not explain *it* to her. [4]And when the queen of Sheba had seen all the wisdom of Solomon, the house that he had built, [5]the food on his table, the seating of his servants, the service of his waiters and their apparel, his cupbearers, and his entryway by which he went up to the house of the LORD, there was no more spirit in her. [6]Then she said to the king: "It was a true report which I heard in my own land about your words and your wisdom. [7]However I did not believe the words until I came and saw with my own eyes; and indeed the half was not told me. Your wisdom and prosperity exceed the fame of which I heard. [8]*Happy are* your men and happy *are* these your servants, who stand continually before you *and* hear your wisdom! [9]Blessed be the LORD your God, who delighted in you, setting you on the throne of Israel! Because the LORD has loved Israel forever, therefore He made you king, to do justice and righteousness."

[10]Then she gave the king one hundred and twenty talents of gold, spices in great quantity, and precious stones. There never again came such abundance of spices as the queen of Sheba gave to King Solomon. [11]Also, the ships of Hiram, which brought gold from Ophir, brought great *quantities* of almug[a] wood and precious stones from Ophir. [12]And the king made steps of the almug wood for the house of the LORD and for the king's house, also harps and stringed instruments for singers. There never again came such almug wood, nor has the like been seen to this day.

[13]Now King Solomon gave the queen of Sheba all she desired, whatever she asked, besides what Solomon had given her according to the royal generosity. So she turned and went to her own country, she and her servants.

Play to Your Strength: The 70-25-5 Principle

(1 Kings 10:1–9)

Great leaders play to their strength. They don't spend vast amounts of time attempting to be a jack-of-all-trades. Instead, they deepen their ability to do what they do best, until they do it as well as anyone.

Solomon certainly lived by this principle. God made him the wisest and richest king of his day (1 Kin. 3:12, 13). Other monarchs heard of his wisdom and wealth and eagerly sought an audience with him. From all over the known world, powerful rulers from distant lands made the long trek to Israel to catch a glimpse of this young phenom. Solomon provided rich counsel and gifts to others, and quickly became known for his breadth of mind and depth of insight.

How did Solomon gain such fame? He focused on what he did best. Leaders would be wise to follow a similar pattern, called the 70-25-5 principle:

- Give 70 percent of your time to your areas of strength.
- Give 25 percent of your time to the areas you want to improve.
- Give 5 percent of your time to the areas of your weakness.

Solomon's Great Wealth

[14]The weight of gold that came to Solomon yearly was six hundred and sixty-six talents of gold, [15]besides *that* from the traveling merchants, from the income of traders, from all the kings of Arabia, and from the governors of the country.

[16]And King Solomon made two hundred large shields *of* hammered gold; six hundred *shekels* of gold went into each shield. [17]He also *made* three hundred shields *of* hammered gold; three minas of gold went into each shield. The king put them in the House of the Forest of Lebanon.

[18]Moreover the king made a great throne of ivory, and overlaid it with pure gold. [19]The throne had six steps, and the top of the throne

9:26 [a]Hebrew *Eloth* (compare 2 Kings 14:22)
10:11 [a]Or *algum* (compare 2 Chronicles 9:10, 11)

The Law of Explosive Growth

(1 Kings 10:24, 25)

Solomon impacted other leaders and multiplied his vision in them. To follow his example:

1. Bring something to the table.
2. What do you contribute best to your world?
3. What do you want to accomplish?
4. How can you serve other leaders?

was round at the back; *there were* armrests on either side of the place of the seat, and two lions stood beside the armrests. [20]Twelve lions stood there, one on each side of the six steps; nothing like *this* had been made for any *other* kingdom.

[21]All King Solomon's drinking vessels *were* gold, and all the vessels of the House of the Forest of Lebanon *were* pure gold. Not *one was* silver, for this was accounted as nothing in the days of Solomon. [22]For the king had merchant ships[a] at sea with the fleet of Hiram. Once every three years the merchant ships came bringing gold, silver, ivory, apes, and monkeys.[b] [23]So King Solomon surpassed all the kings of the earth in riches and wisdom.

[24]Now all the earth sought the presence of Solomon to hear his wisdom, which God had put in his heart. [25]Each man brought his present: articles of silver and gold, garments, armor, spices, horses, and mules, at a set rate year by year.

[26]And Solomon gathered chariots and horsemen; he had one thousand four hundred chariots and twelve thousand horsemen, whom he stationed[a] in the chariot cities and with the king at Jerusalem. [27]The king made silver *as common* in Jerusalem as stones, and he made cedar trees as abundant as the sycamores which *are* in the lowland.

[28]Also Solomon had horses imported from Egypt and Keveh; the king's merchants bought them in Keveh at the *current* price. [29]Now a chariot that was imported from Egypt cost six hundred *shekels* of silver, and a horse one hundred and fifty; and thus, through their agents,[a] they exported *them* to all the kings of the Hittites and the kings of Syria.

Solomon's Heart Turns from the LORD

11 But King Solomon loved many foreign women, as well as the daughter of Pharaoh: women of the Moabites, Ammonites, Edomites, Sidonians, *and* Hittites— [2]from the nations of whom the LORD had said to the children of Israel, "You shall not intermarry with them, nor they with you. Surely they will turn away your hearts after their gods." Solomon clung to these in love. [3]And he had seven hundred wives, princesses, and three hundred concubines; and his wives turned away his heart. [4]For it was so, when Solomon was old, that his wives turned his heart after other gods; and his heart was not loyal to the LORD his God, as *was* the heart of his father David. [5]For Solomon went

10:22 [a]Literally *ships of Tarshish,* deep-sea vessels [b]Or *peacocks* **10:26** [a]Following Septuagint, Syriac, Targum, and Vulgate (compare 2 Chronicles 9:25); Masoretic Text reads *led.* **10:29** [a]Literally *by their hands*

Distraction, the Enemy of Direction

(1 Kings 11:1–43)

How could the wisest man in history turn away from God? How could the leader whose gifts and focus once made him the talk of the world get distracted from his calling?

The temptations that enticed Solomon continue to attack every leader. Once we "arrive," it becomes easy to stop feeling hungry for growth and excellence. How quickly we become satisfied—and how soon we begin to spiral downward. Note how this process of decay looked for Solomon:

1. **Distractions:** He deviated from his call to lead and be a light to the nations.
2. **Adversaries:** God raised up adversaries to steer him back to his priorities and call.
3. **Self-absorption:** He became consumed with himself rather than his call.
4. **Loss of God's presence:** God withdrew His anointing.
5. **Pursuit of pleasure:** He became even more obsessed with his own pleasure.
6. **Emptiness:** He finally grew weary of his pursuits and recognized his emptiness.

after Ashtoreth the goddess of the Sidonians, and after Milcom the abomination of the Ammonites. [6]Solomon did evil in the sight of the LORD, and did not fully follow the LORD, as *did* his father David. [7]Then Solomon built a high place for Chemosh the abomination of Moab, on the hill that *is* east of Jerusalem, and for Molech the abomination of the people of Ammon. [8]And he did likewise for all his foreign wives, who burned incense and sacrificed to their gods.

[9]So the LORD became angry with Solomon, because his heart had turned from the LORD God of Israel, who had appeared to him twice, [10]and had commanded him concerning this thing, that he should not go after other gods; but he did not keep what the LORD had commanded. [11]Therefore the LORD said to Solomon, "Because you have done this, and have not kept My covenant and My statutes, which I have commanded you, I will surely tear the kingdom away from you and give it to your servant. [12]Nevertheless I will not do it in your days, for the sake of your father David; I will tear it out of the hand of your son. [13]However I will not tear away the whole kingdom; I will give one tribe to your son for the sake of My servant David, and for the sake of Jerusalem which I have chosen."

Adversaries of Solomon

[14]Now the LORD raised up an adversary against Solomon, Hadad the Edomite; he *was* a descendant of the king in Edom. [15]For it happened, when David was in Edom, and Joab the commander of the army had gone up to bury the slain, after he had killed every male in Edom [16](because for six months Joab remained there with all Israel, until he had cut down every male in Edom), [17]that Hadad fled to go to Egypt, he and certain Edomites of his father's servants with him. Hadad *was* still a little child. [18]Then they arose from Midian and came to Paran; and they took men with them from Paran and came to Egypt, to Pharaoh king of Egypt, who gave him a house, apportioned food for him, and gave him land. [19]And Hadad found great favor in the sight of Pharaoh, so that he gave him as wife the sister of his own wife, that is, the sister of Queen Tahpenes. [20]Then the sister of Tahpenes bore him Genubath his son, whom Tahpenes weaned in Pharaoh's house. And Genubath was in Pharaoh's household among the sons of Pharaoh.

[21]So when Hadad heard in Egypt that David rested with his fathers, and that Joab the commander of the army was dead, Hadad said to Pharaoh, "Let me depart, that I may go to my own country."

[22]Then Pharaoh said to him, "But what have you lacked with me, that suddenly you seek to go to your own country?"

So he answered, "Nothing, but do let me go anyway."

[23]And God raised up *another* adversary against him, Rezon the son of Eliadah, who had fled from his lord, Hadadezer king of Zobah. [24]So he gathered men to him and became captain over a band *of raiders,* when David killed those *of Zobah.* And they went to Damascus and dwelt there, and reigned in Damascus. [25]He was an adversary of Israel all the days of Solomon (besides the trouble that Hadad *caused*); and he abhorred Israel, and reigned over Syria.

Jeroboam's Rebellion

[26]Then Solomon's servant, Jeroboam the son of Nebat, an Ephraimite from Zereda, whose mother's name *was* Zeruah, a widow, also rebelled against the king.

[27]And this *is* what caused him to rebel against the king: Solomon had built the Millo *and* repaired the damages to the City of David his father. [28]The man Jeroboam *was* a mighty man of valor; and Solomon, seeing that the young man was industrious, made him the officer over all the labor force of the house of Joseph.

[29]Now it happened at that time, when Jeroboam went out of Jerusalem, that the prophet Ahijah the Shilonite met him on the way; and he had clothed himself with a new garment, and the two *were* alone in the field. [30]Then Ahijah took hold of the new garment that *was* on him, and tore it *into* twelve pieces. [31]And he said to Jeroboam, "Take for yourself ten pieces, for thus says the LORD, the God of Israel: 'Behold, I will tear the kingdom out of the hand of Solomon and will give ten tribes to you [32](but he shall have one tribe for the sake of My servant David, and for the sake of Jerusalem, the city which I have chosen out of all the tribes of Israel), [33]because they have[a] forsaken Me, and worshiped Ashtoreth the goddess of the Sidonians, Chemosh the god of the Moabites, and Milcom the god of the people of Ammon, and have not walked in My ways to do *what is* right in My eyes and *keep* My statutes and My judgments, as *did* his father David. [34]However I will not take the whole kingdom out of his hand, because I have made him ruler all the days of his life for the sake of My servant David, whom I chose because he kept My commandments and My statutes. [35]But I will

---

11:33 [a]Following Masoretic Text and Targum; Septuagint, Syriac, and Vulgate read *he has.*

take the kingdom out of his son's hand and give it to you—ten tribes. [36]And to his son I will give one tribe, that My servant David may always have a lamp before Me in Jerusalem, the city which I have chosen for Myself, to put My name there. [37]So I will take you, and you shall reign over all your heart desires, and you shall be king over Israel. [38]Then it shall be, if you heed all that I command you, walk in My ways, and do *what is* right in My sight, to keep My statutes and My commandments, as My servant David did, then I will be with you and build for you an enduring house, as I built for David, and will give Israel to you. [39]And I will afflict the descendants of David because of this, but not forever.'"

[40]Solomon therefore sought to kill Jeroboam. But Jeroboam arose and fled to Egypt, to Shishak king of Egypt, and was in Egypt until the death of Solomon.

Death of Solomon

[41]Now the rest of the acts of Solomon, all that he did, and his wisdom, *are* they not written in the book of the acts of Solomon? [42]And the period that Solomon reigned in Jerusalem over all Israel *was* forty years. [43]Then Solomon rested with his fathers, and was buried in the City of David his father. And Rehoboam his son reigned in his place.

The Revolt Against Rehoboam

12 And Rehoboam went to Shechem, for all Israel had gone to Shechem to make him king. [2]So it happened, when Jeroboam the son of Nebat heard *it* (he was still in Egypt, for he had fled from the presence of King Solomon and had been dwelling in Egypt), [3]that they sent and called him. Then Jeroboam and the whole assembly of Israel came and spoke to Rehoboam, saying, [4]"Your father made our yoke heavy; now therefore, lighten the burdensome service of your father, and his heavy yoke which he put on us, and we will serve you."

[5]So he said to them, "Depart *for* three days, then come back to me." And the people departed.

[6]Then King Rehoboam consulted the elders who stood before his father Solomon while he still lived, and he said, "How do you advise *me* to answer these people?"

[7]And they spoke to him, saying, "If you will be a servant to these people today, and serve them, and answer them, and speak good words to them, then they will be your servants forever."

[8]But he rejected the advice which the elders had given him, and consulted the young men who had grown up with him, who stood before him. [9]And he said to them, "What advice do you give? How should we answer this people who have spoken to me, saying, 'Lighten the yoke which your father put on us'?"

[10]Then the young men who had grown up with him spoke to him, saying, "Thus you should speak to this people who have spoken to you, saying, 'Your father made our yoke heavy, but you make *it* lighter on us'—thus you shall say to them: 'My little *finger* shall be thicker than my father's waist! [11]And now, whereas my father put a heavy yoke on you, I will add to your yoke; my father chastised you with whips, but I will chastise you with scourges!'"[a]

[12]So Jeroboam and all the people came to Rehoboam the third day, as the king had directed, saying, "Come back to me the third day." [13]Then the king answered the people roughly, and rejected the advice which the elders had given him; [14]and he spoke to them according to the advice of the young men, saying, "My father made your yoke heavy, but I will add to your yoke; my father chastised you with whips, but I will chastise you with scourges!"[a] [15]So the king did not listen to the people; for the turn *of events* was from the LORD, that He might fulfill His word, which the LORD had spoken by Ahijah the Shilonite to Jeroboam the son of Nebat.

[16]Now when all Israel saw that the king did not listen to them, the people answered the king, saying:

"What share have we in David?
We have no inheritance in the son of Jesse.
To your tents, O Israel!
Now, see to your own house, O David!"

So Israel departed to their tents. [17]But Rehoboam reigned over the children of Israel who dwelt in the cities of Judah.

[18]Then King Rehoboam sent Adoram, who *was* in charge of the revenue; but all Israel stoned him with stones, and he died. Therefore King Rehoboam mounted his chariot in haste to flee to Jerusalem. [19]So Israel has been in rebellion against the house of David to this day.

[20]Now it came to pass when all Israel heard that Jeroboam had come back, they sent for him and called him to the congregation, and made him king over all Israel. There was none who followed the house of David, but the tribe of Judah only.

[21]And when Rehoboam came to Jerusalem,

12:11 [a]Literally *scorpions* **12:14** [a]Literally *scorpions*

21 LAWS

REHOBOAM AND THE LAW OF CONNECTION

Leaders Touch a Heart Before They Ask for a Hand

(1 Kings 12:1–24)

A leader can't connect with people only when he is communicating to groups; he must connect with individuals. The stronger the relationship and connection between individuals, the more likely the follower will want to help the leader. Some leaders have problems because they believe that followers must take the responsibility to connect. But successful leaders always initiate. They take the first step and then make the effort to continue building relationships.

When a leader has done the work to connect with his people, you can see it in the way the organization functions. Employees show incredible loyalty and a strong work ethic. The people aspire to the vision of the leader. The impact is incredible.

■ ■ ■ ● ● ■ ■ ■

Connecting requires giving. The power-hungry Rehoboam wanted to flex his political muscles more than he desired to connect with his people. Rehoboam never learned the Law of Connection. If you desire to connect with others, check your motives:

1. *Get beyond yourself.*

Dr. Albert Schweitzer asserted, "Whatever you have received more than others—in health, in talents, in ability, in success . . . all this you must not take to yourself as a matter of course. In gratitude for good fortune, you must render some sacrifice of your own life for another life."

Selfishness and insecurity usually lie at the heart of those who fail to get beyond themselves. Clearly, Rehoboam never got beyond himself. His bullying earned him not more respect, but contempt. To connect with people, remain others-minded and remember that leadership is a privilege.

2. *Grow beyond yourself.*

Mahatma Gandhi once remarked, "The difference between what we do and what we are capable of doing would suffice to solve most of the world's problems."

Had Rehoboam gleaned from the experience of the elders, he would have discovered how little he knew about leading. But this cocky and unteachable young man missed a great opportunity for growth—and so destroyed the nation. If you want to grow beyond yourself, remain humble and teachable.

3. *Give beyond yourself.*

Individuals with low self-esteem almost always focus chiefly on themselves. Conversely, a study from the University of Michigan revealed that people who regularly volunteer their time heighten their zest for living and increase their life expectancy.

Rehoboam had no interest in what he could give; he aimed to get the maximum. Effective leaders must persistently ask themselves, "What am I doing for others?" Be a river, not a reservoir.

4. *Go beyond yourself.*

"When you were born, you cried, and the world rejoiced," goes a Middle Eastern saying. "May you live your life so that when you die, the world will cry, and you will rejoice."

Every great leader has the ability to connect. If you want to be a better leader, you must learn to connect with people. Do it, and you will dramatically raise your level of leadership. Do it well, and people will follow you anywhere.

When You Connect with People

Connecting with people isn't complicated, but it takes effort. Observe how Rehoboam neglected this priority:

1. *Your people are more willing to take action when you first move them with emotion.*

Even when King Solomon's elders advised Rehoboam that he could win the people's hearts forever by lightening their workload, he turned a deaf ear. When he showed no concern for their welfare, they sought another leader who would listen.

When you remain open to your people's needs, they will remain open to your vision. When you take action to meet their needs, they will take action to fulfill your vision. Wise leaders discern and meet the needs of their people.

2. *When you give first, your people will give in return.*

Rehoboam squandered multiple opportunities to give to his people. It may seem paradoxical, but a leader gets more by giving more. When you give of your time, talent, and possessions, you receive much more in return.

3. *When you connect with individuals, you gain the attention of crowds.*

Too arrogant to walk among his people, Rehoboam tried to lead Israel impersonally from behind the palace walls. While the nature of leadership often requires speaking before groups, effective leaders understand that true connection happens one-on-one.

4. *When you reach out to your people, they will reach back toward you.*

The initial confrontation between Rehoboam and his people took place when they came to him; he was so out of touch he couldn't see they were on the verge of revolting. Rehoboam was a *reactive* leader rather than a *proactive* one. When it became clear he had caused his people's displeasure, he pointed a finger at them. As a result, his kingdom ripped apart.

Whether you have just taken over a leadership position or are well established, you must connect with your people if you are to succeed. Remember, the telltale sign of a great leader is not what he has accomplished on his own, but what he has been able to accomplish through others. That happens only through connection.

he assembled all the house of Judah with the tribe of Benjamin, one hundred and eighty thousand chosen *men* who were warriors, to fight against the house of Israel, that he might restore the kingdom to Rehoboam the son of Solomon. [22]But the word of God came to Shemaiah the man of God, saying, [23]"Speak to Rehoboam the son of Solomon, king of Judah, to all the house of Judah and Benjamin, and to the rest of the people, saying, [24]'Thus says the LORD: "You shall not go up nor fight against your brethren the children of Israel. Let every man return to his house, for this thing is from Me."'" Therefore they obeyed the word of the LORD, and turned back, according to the word of the LORD.

Jeroboam's Gold Calves

[25]Then Jeroboam built Shechem in the mountains of Ephraim, and dwelt there. Also he went out from there and built Penuel. [26]And Jeroboam said in his heart, "Now the kingdom may return to the house of David: [27]If these people go up to offer sacrifices in the house of the LORD at Jerusalem, then the heart of this people will turn back to their lord, Rehoboam king of Judah, and they will kill me and go back to Rehoboam king of Judah."

[28]Therefore the king asked advice, made two calves of gold, and said to the people, "It is too much for you to go up to Jerusalem. Here are your gods, O Israel, which brought you up from the land of Egypt!" [29]And he set up one in Bethel, and the other he put in Dan. [30]Now this thing became a sin, for the people went *to worship* before the one as far as Dan. [31]He made shrines[a] on the high places, and made priests from every class of people, who were not of the sons of Levi.

[32]Jeroboam ordained a feast on the fifteenth day of the eighth month, like the feast that *was* in Judah, and offered sacrifices on the altar. So he did at Bethel, sacrificing to the calves that he had made. And at Bethel he installed the priests of the high places which he had made. [33]So he made offerings on the altar which he had made at Bethel on the fifteenth day of the eighth month, in the month which he had devised in his own heart. And he ordained a feast for the children of Israel, and offered sacrifices on the altar and burned incense.

The Message of the Man of God

13 And behold, a man of God went from Judah to Bethel by the word of the LORD, and Jeroboam stood by the altar to burn incense. [2]Then he cried out against the altar by the word of the LORD, and said, "O altar, altar! Thus says the LORD: 'Behold, a child, Josiah by name, shall be born to the house of David; and on you he shall sacrifice the priests of the high places who burn incense on you, and men's bones shall be burned on you.'" [3]And he gave a sign the same day, saying, "This *is* the sign which the LORD has spoken: Surely the altar shall split apart, and the ashes on it shall be poured out."

[4]So it came to pass when King Jeroboam heard the saying of the man of God, who cried out against the altar in Bethel, that he stretched out his hand from the altar, saying, "Arrest him!" Then his hand, which he stretched out toward him, withered, so that he could not pull it back to himself. [5]The altar also was split apart, and the ashes poured out from the altar, according to the sign which the man of God had given by the word of the LORD. [6]Then the king answered and said to the man of God, "Please entreat the favor of the LORD your God, and pray for me, that my hand may be restored to me."

So the man of God entreated the LORD, and the king's hand was restored to him, and became as before. [7]Then the king said to the man of God, "Come home with me and refresh yourself, and I will give you a reward."

[8]But the man of God said to the king, "If you were to give me half your house, I would not go in with you; nor would I eat bread nor drink water in this place. [9]For so it was commanded me by the word of the LORD, saying, 'You shall not eat bread, nor drink water, nor return by the same way you came.'" [10]So he went another way and did not return by the way he came to Bethel.

Death of the Man of God

[11]Now an old prophet dwelt in Bethel, and his sons came and told him all the works that the man of God had done that day in Bethel; they also told their father the words which he had spoken to the king. [12]And their father said to them, "Which way did he go?" For his sons had seen[a] which way the man of God went who came from Judah. [13]Then he said to his sons, "Saddle the donkey for me." So they saddled the donkey for him; and he rode on it, [14]and went after the man of God, and found him sitting under an oak. Then he said to him, "*Are* you the man of God who came from Judah?"

And he said, "I *am.*"

[15]Then he said to him, "Come home with me and eat bread."

12:31 [a]Literally *a house* **13:12** [a]Septuagint, Syriac, Targum, and Vulgate read *showed him.*

The Consequences of Compromise

(1 Kings 13:11–24)

An unnamed, elderly prophet illustrates both the power of a leader living by his convictions, and how compromise can steal away conviction. He triumphed when he stood, but perished when he turned back. Just so, we gain when we stand strong, but can lose it all when we slip.

[16]And he said, "I cannot return with you nor go in with you; neither can I eat bread nor drink water with you in this place. [17]For I have been told by the word of the LORD, 'You shall not eat bread nor drink water there, nor return by going the way you came.'"

[18]He said to him, "I too *am* a prophet as you *are,* and an angel spoke to me by the word of the LORD, saying, 'Bring him back with you to your house, that he may eat bread and drink water.'" (He was lying to him.)

[19]So he went back with him, and ate bread in his house, and drank water.

[20]Now it happened, as they sat at the table, that the word of the LORD came to the prophet who had brought him back; [21]and he cried out to the man of God who came from Judah, saying, "Thus says the LORD: 'Because you have disobeyed the word of the LORD, and have not kept the commandment which the LORD your God commanded you, [22]but you came back, ate bread, and drank water in the place of which *the LORD* said to you, "Eat no bread and drink no water," your corpse shall not come to the tomb of your fathers.'"

[23]So it was, after he had eaten bread and after he had drunk, that he saddled the donkey for him, the prophet whom he had brought back. [24]When he was gone, a lion met him on the road and killed him. And his corpse was thrown on the road, and the donkey stood by it. The lion also stood by the corpse. [25]And there, men passed by and saw the corpse thrown on the road, and the lion standing by the corpse. Then they went and told *it* in the city where the old prophet dwelt.

[26]Now when the prophet who had brought him back from the way heard *it,* he said, "It *is* the man of God who was disobedient to the word of the LORD. Therefore the LORD has delivered him to the lion, which has torn him and killed him, according to the word of the LORD which He spoke to him." [27]And he spoke to his sons, saying, "Saddle the donkey for me." So they saddled *it.* [28]Then he went and found his corpse thrown on the road, and the donkey and the lion standing by the corpse. The lion had not eaten the corpse nor torn the donkey. [29]And the prophet took up the corpse of the man of God, laid it on the donkey, and brought it back. So the old prophet came to the city to mourn, and to bury him. [30]Then he laid the corpse in his own tomb; and they mourned over him, *saying,* "Alas, my brother!" [31]So it was, after he had buried him, that he spoke to his sons, saying, "When I am dead, then bury me in the tomb where the man of God *is* buried; lay my bones beside his bones. [32]For the saying which he cried out by the word of the LORD against the altar in Bethel, and against all the shrines[a] on the high places which *are* in the cities of Samaria, will surely come to pass."

[33]After this event Jeroboam did not turn from his evil way, but again he made priests from every class of people for the high places; whoever wished, he consecrated him, and he became *one* of the priests of the high places. [34]And this thing was the sin of the house of Jeroboam, so as to exterminate and destroy *it* from the face of the earth.

Judgment on the House of Jeroboam

14 At that time Abijah the son of Jeroboam became sick. [2]And Jeroboam said to his wife, "Please arise, and disguise yourself, that they may not recognize you as the wife of Jeroboam, and go to Shiloh. Indeed, Ahijah the prophet *is* there, who told me that *I would be* king over this people. [3]Also take with you ten loaves, *some* cakes, and a jar of honey, and go to him; he will tell you what will become of the child." [4]And Jeroboam's wife did so; she arose and went to Shiloh, and came to the house of Ahijah. But Ahijah could not see, for his eyes were glazed by reason of his age.

[5]Now the LORD had said to Ahijah, "Here is the wife of Jeroboam, coming to ask you something about her son, for he *is* sick. Thus and thus you shall say to her; for it will be, when she comes in, that she will pretend *to be* another *woman.*"

[6]And so it was, when Ahijah heard the sound of her footsteps as she came through the door, he

---

13:32 [a]Literally *houses*

The Law of the Lid:
As the Leader Goes, So Goes the Nation
(1 Kings 14:1—15:34)

Leadership ability is the lid on the success of a nation or organization. When Israel or Judah lived under good kings, things went well. Under bad kings, things went sour.

The heart and skill of a leader will always tremendously affect the life of the people under his direction. This is a law, both timeless and universal. See how this law played out under the Hebrew kings of the Old Testament:

Good Kings
1. Drew loyalty from their people
2. Enjoyed victory over sin
3. Enjoyed peace within the kingdom
4. Were affirmed by God's prophets
5. Enjoyed prosperity
6. Opposed evil kings

Bad Kings
1. Drew rebellion from their people
2. Saw bondage to sin
3. Suffered turmoil within the kingdom
4. Were rebuked by God's prophets
5. Often endured natural disasters and war
6. Opposed good kings

said, "Come in, wife of Jeroboam. Why do you pretend *to be* another *person?* For I *have been* sent to you *with* bad *news.* [7]Go, tell Jeroboam, 'Thus says the LORD God of Israel: "Because I exalted you from among the people, and made you ruler over My people Israel, [8]and tore the kingdom away from the house of David, and gave it to you; and *yet* you have not been as My servant David, who kept My commandments and who followed Me with all his heart, to do only *what was* right in My eyes; [9]but you have done more evil than all who were before you, for you have gone and made for yourself other gods and molded images to provoke Me to anger, and have cast Me behind your back— [10]therefore behold! I will bring disaster on the house of Jeroboam, and will cut off from Jeroboam every male in Israel, bond and free; I will take away the remnant of the house of Jeroboam, as one takes away refuse until it is all gone. [11]The dogs shall eat whoever belongs to Jeroboam and dies in the city, and the birds of the air shall eat whoever dies in the field; for the LORD has spoken!"' [12]Arise therefore, go to your own house. When your feet enter the city, the child shall die. [13]And all Israel shall mourn for him and bury him, for he is the only one of Jeroboam who shall come to the grave, because in him there is found something good toward the LORD God of Israel in the house of Jeroboam.

[14]"Moreover the LORD will raise up for Himself a king over Israel who shall cut off the house of Jeroboam; this is the day. What? Even now!

[15]For the LORD will strike Israel, as a reed is shaken in the water. He will uproot Israel from this good land which He gave to their fathers, and will scatter them beyond the River,[a] because they have made their wooden images,[b] provoking the LORD to anger. [16]And He will give Israel up because of the sins of Jeroboam, who sinned and who made Israel sin."

[17]Then Jeroboam's wife arose and departed, and came to Tirzah. When she came to the threshold of the house, the child died. [18]And they buried him; and all Israel mourned for him, according to the word of the LORD which He spoke through His servant Ahijah the prophet.

Death of Jeroboam

[19]Now the rest of the acts of Jeroboam, how he made war and how he reigned, indeed they *are* written in the book of the chronicles of the kings of Israel. [20]The period that Jeroboam reigned *was* twenty-two years. So he rested with his fathers. Then Nadab his son reigned in his place.

Rehoboam Reigns in Judah

[21]And Rehoboam the son of Solomon reigned in Judah. Rehoboam *was* forty-one years old when he became king. He reigned seventeen years in Jerusalem, the city which the LORD had chosen out of all the tribes of Israel, to put His

---

14:15 [a]That is, the Euphrates [b]Hebrew *Asherim,* Canaanite deities name there. His mother's name *was* Naamah, an Ammonitess. [22]Now Judah did evil in the sight of the LORD, and they provoked Him to jealousy with their sins which they committed, more than all that their fathers had done. [23]For they also built for themselves high places, *sacred* pillars, and wooden images on every high hill and under every green tree. [24]And there were also perverted persons[a] in the land. They did according to all the abominations of the nations which the LORD had cast out before the children of Israel.

[25]It happened in the fifth year of King Rehoboam *that* Shishak king of Egypt came up against Jerusalem. [26]And he took away the treasures of the house of the LORD and the treasures of the king's house; he took away everything. He also took away all the gold shields which Solomon had made. [27]Then King Rehoboam made bronze shields in their place, and committed *them* to the hands of the captains of the guard, who guarded the doorway of the king's house. [28]And whenever the king entered the house of the LORD, the guards carried them, then brought them back into the guardroom.

[29]Now the rest of the acts of Rehoboam, and all that he did, *are* they not written in the book of the chronicles of the kings of Judah? [30]And there was war between Rehoboam and Jeroboam all *their* days. [31]So Rehoboam rested with his fathers, and was buried with his fathers in the City of David. His mother's name *was* Naamah, an Ammonitess. Then Abijam[a] his son reigned in his place.

Abijam Reigns in Judah

15 In the eighteenth year of King Jeroboam the son of Nebat, Abijam became king over Judah. [2]He reigned three years in Jerusalem. His mother's name *was* Maachah the granddaughter of Abishalom. [3]And he walked in all the sins of his father, which he had done before him; his heart was not loyal to the LORD his God, as was the heart of his father David. [4]Nevertheless for David's sake the LORD his God gave him a lamp in Jerusalem, by setting up his son after him and by establishing Jerusalem; [5]because David did *what was* right in the eyes of the LORD, and had not turned aside from anything that He commanded him all the days of his life, except in the matter of Uriah the Hittite. [6]And there was war between Rehoboam[a] and Jeroboam all the days of his life. [7]Now the rest of the acts of Abijam, and all that he did, *are* they not written in the book of the chronicles of the kings of Judah? And there was war between Abijam and Jeroboam.

[8]So Abijam rested with his fathers, and they buried him in the City of David. Then Asa his son reigned in his place.

Asa Reigns in Judah

[9]In the twentieth year of Jeroboam king of Israel, Asa became king over Judah. [10]And he reigned forty-one years in Jerusalem. His grandmother's name *was* Maachah the granddaughter of Abishalom. [11]Asa did *what was* right in the eyes of the LORD, as *did* his father David. [12]And he banished the perverted persons[a] from the land, and removed all the idols that his fathers had made. [13]Also he removed Maachah his grandmother from *being* queen mother, because she had made an obscene image of Asherah.[a] And Asa cut down her obscene image and burned *it* by the Brook Kidron. [14]But the high places were not removed. Nevertheless Asa's heart was loyal to the LORD all his days. [15]He also brought into the house of the LORD the things which his father had dedicated, and the things which he himself had dedicated: silver and gold and utensils.

[16]Now there was war between Asa and Baasha king of Israel all their days. [17]And Baasha king of Israel came up against Judah, and built Ramah, that he might let none go out or come in to Asa king of Judah. [18]Then Asa took all the silver and gold *that was* left in the treasuries of the house of the LORD and the treasuries of the king's house, and delivered them into the hand of his servants. And King Asa sent them to Ben-Hadad the son of Tabrimmon, the son of Hezion, king of Syria, who dwelt in Damascus, saying, [19]"*Let there be* a treaty between you and me, as there was between my father and your father. See, I have sent you a present of silver and gold. Come and break your treaty with Baasha king of Israel, so that he will withdraw from me."

[20]So Ben-Hadad heeded King Asa, and sent the captains of his armies against the cities of Israel. He attacked Ijon, Dan, Abel Beth Maachah, and all Chinneroth, with all the land of Naphtali. [21]Now it happened, when Baasha heard *it,* that he stopped building Ramah, and remained in Tirzah.

[22]Then King Asa made a proclamation

14:24 [a]Hebrew *qadesh,* that is, one practicing sodomy and prostitution in religious rituals
14:31 [a]Spelled *Abijah* in 2 Chronicles 12:16ff
15:6 [a]Following Masoretic Text, Septuagint, Targum, and Vulgate; some Hebrew manuscripts and Syriac read *Abijam.* **15:12** [a]Hebrew *qedeshim,* that is, those practicing sodomy and prostitution in religious rituals **15:13** [a]A Canaanite goddess

throughout all Judah; none *was* exempted. And they took away the stones and timber of Ramah, which Baasha had used for building; and with them King Asa built Geba of Benjamin, and Mizpah.

²³The rest of all the acts of Asa, all his might, all that he did, and the cities which he built, *are* they not written in the book of the chronicles of the kings of Judah? But in the time of his old age he was diseased in his feet. ²⁴So Asa rested with his fathers, and was buried with his fathers in the City of David his father. Then Jehoshaphat his son reigned in his place.

Nadab Reigns in Israel

²⁵Now Nadab the son of Jeroboam became king over Israel in the second year of Asa king of Judah, and he reigned over Israel two years. ²⁶And he did evil in the sight of the LORD, and walked in the way of his father, and in his sin by which he had made Israel sin.

²⁷Then Baasha the son of Ahijah, of the house of Issachar, conspired against him. And Baasha killed him at Gibbethon, which *belonged* to the Philistines, while Nadab and all Israel laid siege to Gibbethon. ²⁸Baasha killed him in the third year of Asa king of Judah, and reigned in his place. ²⁹And it was so, when he became king, *that* he killed all the house of Jeroboam. He did not leave to Jeroboam anyone that breathed, until he had destroyed him, according to the word of the LORD which He had spoken by His servant Ahijah the Shilonite, ³⁰because of the sins of Jeroboam, which he had sinned and by which he had made Israel sin, because of his provocation with which he had provoked the LORD God of Israel to anger.

³¹Now the rest of the acts of Nadab, and all that he did, *are* they not written in the book of the chronicles of the kings of Israel? ³²And there was war between Asa and Baasha king of Israel all their days.

Baasha Reigns in Israel

³³In the third year of Asa king of Judah, Baasha the son of Ahijah became king over all Israel in Tirzah, and *reigned* twenty-four years. ³⁴He did evil in the sight of the LORD, and walked in the way of Jeroboam, and in his sin by which he had made Israel sin.

16 Then the word of the LORD came to Jehu the son of Hanani, against Baasha, saying: ²"Inasmuch as I lifted you out of the dust and made you ruler over My people Israel, and you have walked in the way of Jeroboam, and have made My people Israel sin, to provoke Me to anger with their sins, ³surely I will take away the posterity of Baasha and the posterity of his house, and I will make your house like the house of Jeroboam the son of Nebat. ⁴The dogs shall eat whoever belongs to Baasha and dies in the city, and the birds of the air shall eat whoever dies in the fields."

⁵Now the rest of the acts of Baasha, what he did, and his might, *are* they not written in the book of the chronicles of the kings of Israel? ⁶So Baasha rested with his fathers and was buried in Tirzah. Then Elah his son reigned in his place.

⁷And also the word of the LORD came by the prophet Jehu the son of Hanani against Baasha and his house, because of all the evil that he did in the sight of the LORD in provoking Him to anger with the work of his hands, in being like the house of Jeroboam, and because he killed them.

Elah Reigns in Israel

⁸In the twenty-sixth year of Asa king of Judah, Elah the son of Baasha became king over Israel, *and reigned* two years in Tirzah. ⁹Now his servant Zimri, commander of half *his* chariots, conspired against him as he was in Tirzah drinking himself drunk in the house of Arza, steward of *his* house in Tirzah. ¹⁰And Zimri went in and struck him and killed him in the twenty-seventh year of Asa king of Judah, and reigned in his place.

¹¹Then it came to pass, when he began to reign, as soon as he was seated on his throne, *that* he killed all the household of Baasha; he did not leave him one male, neither of his relatives nor of his friends. ¹²Thus Zimri destroyed all the household of Baasha, according to the word of the LORD, which He spoke against Baasha by Jehu the prophet, ¹³for all the sins of Baasha and the sins of Elah his son, by which they had sinned and by which they had made Israel sin, in provoking the LORD God of Israel to anger with their idols.

¹⁴Now the rest of the acts of Elah, and all that he did, *are* they not written in the book of the chronicles of the kings of Israel?

Zimri Reigns in Israel

¹⁵In the twenty-seventh year of Asa king of Judah, Zimri had reigned in Tirzah seven days. And the people *were* encamped against Gibbethon, which *belonged* to the Philistines. ¹⁶Now the people *who were* encamped heard it said, "Zimri has conspired and also has killed the king." So all Israel made Omri, the commander of the army, king over Israel that day in the

camp. [17]Then Omri and all Israel with him went up from Gibbethon, and they besieged Tirzah. [18]And it happened, when Zimri saw that the city was taken, that he went into the citadel of the king's house and burned the king's house down upon himself with fire, and died, [19]because of the sins which he had committed in doing evil in the sight of the LORD, in walking in the way of Jeroboam, and in his sin which he had committed to make Israel sin.

[20]Now the rest of the acts of Zimri, and the treason he committed, *are* they not written in the book of the chronicles of the kings of Israel?

Omri Reigns in Israel

[21]Then the people of Israel were divided into two parts: half of the people followed Tibni the son of Ginath, to make him king, and half followed Omri. [22]But the people who followed Omri prevailed over the people who followed Tibni the son of Ginath. So Tibni died and Omri reigned. [23]In the thirty-first year of Asa king of Judah, Omri became king over Israel, *and reigned* twelve years. Six years he reigned in Tirzah. [24]And he bought the hill of Samaria from Shemer for two talents of silver; then he built on the hill, and called the name of the city which he built, Samaria, after the name of Shemer, owner of the hill. [25]Omri did evil in the eyes of the LORD, and did worse than all who *were* before him. [26]For he walked in all the ways of Jeroboam the son of Nebat, and in his sin by which he had made Israel sin, provoking the LORD God of Israel to anger with their idols.

[27]Now the rest of the acts of Omri which he did, and the might that he showed, *are* they not written in the book of the chronicles of the kings of Israel?

[28]So Omri rested with his fathers and was buried in Samaria. Then Ahab his son reigned in his place.

Ahab Reigns in Israel

[29]In the thirty-eighth year of Asa king of Judah, Ahab the son of Omri became king over Israel; and Ahab the son of Omri reigned over Israel in Samaria twenty-two years. [30]Now Ahab the son of Omri did evil in the sight of the LORD, more than all who *were* before him. [31]And it came to pass, as though it had been a trivial thing for him to walk in the sins of Jeroboam the son of Nebat, that he took as wife Jezebel the daughter of Ethbaal, king of the Sidonians; and he went and served Baal and worshiped him. [32]Then he set up an altar for Baal in the temple of Baal, which he had built in Samaria. [33]And Ahab made a wooden image.[a] Ahab did more to provoke the LORD God of Israel to anger than all the kings of Israel who were before him. [34]In his days Hiel of Bethel built Jericho. He laid its foundation with Abiram his firstborn, and with his youngest *son* Segub he set up its gates, according to the word of the LORD, which He had spoken through Joshua the son of Nun.[a]

Elijah Proclaims a Drought

17 And Elijah the Tishbite, of the inhabitants of Gilead, said to Ahab, "*As* the LORD God of Israel lives, before whom I stand, there shall not be dew nor rain these years, except at my word."

Convictions: When God Is Behind You, One Is a Majority

(1 Kings 17:1)

Some consider Elijah the greatest prophet of the Old Testament. When he predicts a drought, he's not out to make a popular speech or gain friends in high places. Elijah spoke to the people when God spoke to him. God plus one equals a majority.

---

[2]Then the word of the LORD came to him, saying, [3]"Get away from here and turn eastward, and hide by the Brook Cherith, which flows into the Jordan. [4]And it will be *that* you shall drink from the brook, and I have commanded the ravens to feed you there."

[5]So he went and did according to the word of the LORD, for he went and stayed by the Brook Cherith, which flows into the Jordan. [6]The ravens brought him bread and meat in the morning, and bread and meat in the evening; and he drank from the brook. [7]And it happened after a while that the brook dried up, because there had been no rain in the land.

Elijah and the Widow

[8]Then the word of the LORD came to him, saying, [9]"Arise, go to Zarephath, which *belongs* to Sidon, and dwell there. See, I have commanded a

---

16:33 [a]Hebrew *Asherah,* a Canaanite goddess
16:34 [a]Compare Joshua 6:26

widow there to provide for you." [10]So he arose and went to Zarephath. And when he came to the gate of the city, indeed a widow *was* there gathering sticks. And he called to her and said, "Please bring me a little water in a cup, that I may drink." [11]And as she was going to get *it,* he called to her and said, "Please bring me a morsel of bread in your hand."

[12]So she said, "As the LORD your God lives, I do not have bread, only a handful of flour in a bin, and a little oil in a jar; and see, I *am* gathering a couple of sticks that I may go in and prepare it for myself and my son, that we may eat it, and die."

[13]And Elijah said to her, "Do not fear; go *and* do as you have said, but make me a small cake from it first, and bring *it* to me; and afterward make *some* for yourself and your son. [14]For thus says the LORD God of Israel: 'The bin of flour shall not be used up, nor shall the jar of oil run dry, until the day the LORD sends rain on the earth.' "

[15]So she went away and did according to the word of Elijah; and she and he and her household ate for *many* days. [16]The bin of flour was not used up, nor did the jar of oil run dry, according to the word of the LORD which He spoke by Elijah.

Elijah Revives the Widow's Son

[17]Now it happened after these things *that* the son of the woman who owned the house became sick. And his sickness was so serious that there was no breath left in him. [18]So she said to Elijah, "What have I to do with you, O man of God? Have you come to me to bring my sin to remembrance, and to kill my son?"

[19]And he said to her, "Give me your son." So he took him out of her arms and carried him to the upper room where he was staying, and laid him on his own bed. [20]Then he cried out to the LORD and said, "O LORD my God, have You also brought tragedy on the widow with whom I lodge, by killing her son?" [21]And he stretched himself out on the child three times, and cried out to the LORD and said, "O LORD my God, I pray, let this child's soul come back to him." [22]Then the LORD heard the voice of Elijah; and the soul of the child came back to him, and he revived.

[23]And Elijah took the child and brought him down from the upper room into the house, and gave him to his mother. And Elijah said, "See, your son lives!"

[24]Then the woman said to Elijah, "Now by this I know that you *are* a man of God, *and* that the word of the LORD in your mouth *is* the truth."

ELIJAH
STANDING ALONE, SPEAKING TRUTH
(1 Kings 17:1—18:40)

PROFILE IN LEADERSHIP

The prophet Elijah knew about the idolatry of Israel and the wickedness of King Ahab. He knew the time for judgment had arrived. And he also knew that drought and famine were about to devastate Israel.

He knew because he himself had announced God's judgment.

This all took place during a very sad time in the history of Israel, when the people had all but turned their backs on God and their king had sinned against the Lord openly and boldly. Elijah, consumed with holy indignation, prayed that it might not rain in Israel—and for more than three years, not a drop of rain fell. Streams dried up, crops failed, and people starved.

Later, all alone, the prophet stood on Mt. Carmel among 450 prophets of Baal, giving the people visual proof of the impotence of their puny god. In a spectacular demonstration of the awesomeness of the true and living God, Elijah called fire down from heaven—and then directed the execution of Baal's priests.

Imagine the courage it took for one solitary man to pray for judgment on his own people, confront a wicked king, then stand before hundreds of false prophets and challenge their piety! Although the Lord took Elijah to heaven long ago (2 Kin. 2:11), this courageous prophet still proclaims today that true leadership may mean standing alone and speaking difficult truth.

Elijah's Message to Ahab

18 And it came to pass *after* many days that the word of the LORD came to Elijah, in the third year, saying, "Go, present yourself to Ahab, and I will send rain on the earth."

[2]So Elijah went to present himself to Ahab; and *there was* a severe famine in Samaria. [3]And Ahab had called Obadiah, who *was* in charge of *his* house. (Now Obadiah feared the LORD greatly. [4]For so it was, while Jezebel massacred the prophets of the LORD, that Obadiah had taken one hundred prophets and hidden them, fifty to a cave, and had fed them with bread and water.) [5]And Ahab had said to Obadiah, "Go into the land to all the springs of water and to all the brooks; perhaps we may find grass to keep the horses and mules alive, so that we will not have to kill any livestock." [6]So they divided the land between them to explore it; Ahab went one way by himself, and Obadiah went another way by himself.

[7]Now as Obadiah was on his way, suddenly Elijah met him; and he recognized him, and fell on his face, and said, "*Is* that you, my lord Elijah?"

[8]And he answered him, "*It is* I. Go, tell your master, 'Elijah *is* here.'"

[9]So he said, "How have I sinned, that you are delivering your servant into the hand of Ahab, to kill me? [10]*As* the LORD your God lives, there is no nation or kingdom where my master has not sent someone to hunt for you; and when they said, '*He is* not *here,*' he took an oath from the kingdom or nation that they could not find you. [11]And now you say, 'Go, tell your master, "Elijah *is* here"'! [12]And it shall come to pass, *as soon as* I am gone from you, that the Spirit of the LORD will carry you to a place I do not know; so when I go and tell Ahab, and he cannot find you, he will kill me. But I your servant have feared the LORD from my youth. [13]Was it not reported to my lord what I did when Jezebel killed the prophets of the LORD, how I hid one hundred men of the LORD's prophets, fifty to a cave, and fed them with bread and water? [14]And now you say, 'Go, tell your master, "Elijah *is* here."' He will kill me!"

[15]Then Elijah said, "*As* the LORD of hosts lives, before whom I stand, I will surely present myself to him today."

[16]So Obadiah went to meet Ahab, and told him; and Ahab went to meet Elijah. [17]Then it happened, when Ahab saw Elijah, that Ahab said to him, "*Is that* you, O troubler of Israel?"

[18]And he answered, "I have not troubled Israel, but you and your father's house *have,* in that you have forsaken the commandments of the LORD and have followed the Baals. [19]Now therefore, send *and* gather all Israel to me on Mount Carmel, the four hundred and fifty prophets of Baal, and the four hundred prophets of Asherah,[a] who eat at Jezebel's table."

Elijah's Mount Carmel Victory

[20]So Ahab sent for all the children of Israel, and gathered the prophets together on Mount Carmel. [21]And Elijah came to all the people, and said, "How long will you falter between two opinions? If the LORD *is* God, follow Him; but if Baal, follow him." But the people answered him not a word. [22]Then Elijah said to the people, "I alone am left a prophet of the LORD; but Baal's prophets *are* four hundred and fifty men. [23]Therefore let them give us two bulls; and let them choose one bull for themselves, cut it in pieces, and lay *it* on the wood, but put no fire *under it;* and I will prepare the other bull, and lay *it* on the wood, but put no fire *under it.* [24]Then you call on the name of your gods, and I will call on the name of the LORD; and the God who answers by fire, He is God."

So all the people answered and said, "It is well spoken."

[25]Now Elijah said to the prophets of Baal, "Choose one bull for yourselves and prepare *it* first, for you *are* many; and call on the name of your god, but put no fire *under it.*"

[26]So they took the bull which was given them, and they prepared *it,* and called on the name of Baal from morning even till noon, saying, "O Baal, hear us!" But *there was* no voice; no one answered. Then they leaped about the altar which they had made.

[27]And so it was, at noon, that Elijah mocked them and said, "Cry aloud, for he *is* a god; either he is meditating, or he is busy, or he is on a journey, *or* perhaps he is sleeping and must be awakened." [28]So they cried aloud, and cut themselves, as was their custom, with knives and lances, until the blood gushed out on them. [29]And when midday was past, they prophesied until the *time* of the offering of the *evening* sacrifice. But *there was* no voice; no one answered, no one paid attention.

[30]Then Elijah said to all the people, "Come near to me." So all the people came near to him. And he repaired the altar of the LORD *that was* broken down. [31]And Elijah took twelve stones,

---

18:19 [a]A Canaanite goddess

21 QUALITIES

COURAGE

Elijah's Fire and Passion Attract Others
(1 Kings 18:1–40)

Not only did the crowds see the fire of God in Elijah, they soon saw it in his ministry—literally.

Elijah grew tired of his people's spiritual rebellion and angry with the false prophets of Baal. He confronted both forces atop Mt. Carmel and there defeated the devil's henchmen, although they outnumbered him 850 to 1 (1 Kin. 18:19). No one had seen anything like his courage since the day David fought Goliath unremembered years before. And like the underdog David, Elijah met the enemy with passion. His eyes drank in the greatness of God, not the numbers of his enemies. This heavenly vision provided the fire that fueled his courage.

Leaders always need courage. No one who wants to bring about change can manage without courage. Courage flamed in Elijah's heart because:

1. *His resolution outweighed his reservations.*
   Although greatly outnumbered, Elijah resolved that Baal had to be confronted at any cost.
2. *His desires outweighed his desperation.*
   Although it meant risk, Elijah wanted to honor Yahweh more than anything else.
3. *His compassion outweighed his complaints.*
   Although Elijah hated the people's attitude, he wanted them to find and follow Yahweh.

Let the Fire Fall

As Elijah worshiped and prayed all alone atop the mountain, he mustered the courage to call down fire from heaven. The fire inside of him drew down the fire of God, decisively defeating Baal.

This poses a good question for leaders today. When will the "fire" come down in our leadership? According to Elijah, the fire comes . . .

1. When we know our message is from God (v. 1).
2. When we stand for what is right, regardless of the cost (vv. 2–20).
3. When our need is the greatest (vv. 2, 5, 21, 22).
4. When we take our message to the people (vv. 20, 21).
5. When we bring others to a point of decision (v. 21).
6. When we repair and use the altar of God (vv. 23–32).
7. When we face circumstances that only God's fire will light (vv. 33–35).
8. When we publicly trust God to do what only He can do (vv. 33–37).
9. When we hunger for God to receive glory (vv. 36–39).
10. When we desire to see others return to the Lord (v. 37).

For a negative example of courage, see p. 335.

according to the number of the tribes of the sons of Jacob, to whom the word of the LORD had come, saying, "Israel shall be your name."[a] [32]Then with the stones he built an altar in the name of the LORD; and he made a trench around the altar large enough to hold two seahs of seed. [33]And he put the wood in order, cut the bull in pieces, and laid it on the wood, and said, "Fill four waterpots with water, and pour it on the burnt sacrifice and on the wood." [34]Then he said, "Do it a second time," and they did it a second time; and he said, "Do it a third time," and they did it a third time. [35]So the water ran all around the altar; and he also filled the trench with water.

[36]And it came to pass, at the time of the offering of the evening sacrifice, that Elijah the prophet came near and said, "LORD God of Abraham, Isaac, and Israel, let it be known this day that You are God in Israel and I am Your servant, and that I have done all these things at Your word. [37]Hear me, O LORD, hear me, that this people may know that You are the LORD God, and that You have turned their hearts back to You again."

[38]Then the fire of the LORD fell and consumed the burnt sacrifice, and the wood and the stones and the dust, and it licked up the water that was in the trench. [39]Now when all the people saw it, they fell on their faces; and they said,

"The LORD, He is God! The LORD, He is God!"

[40]And Elijah said to them, "Seize the prophets of Baal! Do not let one of them escape!" So they seized them; and Elijah brought them down to the Brook Kishon and executed them there.

The Drought Ends

[41]Then Elijah said to Ahab, "Go up, eat and drink; for there is the sound of abundance of rain." [42]So Ahab went up to eat and drink. And Elijah went up to the top of Carmel; then he bowed down on the ground, and put his face between his knees, [43]and said to his servant, "Go up now, look toward the sea."

So he went up and looked, and said, "There is nothing." And seven times he said, "Go again."

[44]Then it came to pass the seventh time, that he said, "There is a cloud, as small as a man's hand, rising out of the sea!" So he said, "Go up, say to Ahab, 'Prepare your chariot, and go down before the rain stops you.'"

[45]Now it happened in the meantime that the sky became black with clouds and wind, and there was a heavy rain. So Ahab rode away and went to Jezreel. [46]Then the hand of the LORD came upon Elijah; and he girded up his loins and ran ahead of Ahab to the entrance of Jezreel.

18:31 [a]Genesis 32:28

Elijah and the Law of E. F. Hutton

(1 Kings 18:27–38)

When the man spoke, people jumped.

"Cry aloud," he told the false prophets; and they did (v. 27).

"Come near to me," he commanded the Israelites; and they did (v. 30).

"Fill four waterpots with water, and pour it on the burnt sacrifice and on the wood," he told some servants; and they did (v. 33).

"Do it a second time," he ordered; and they did (v. 34).

"Do it a third time," he said; and they did (v. 34).

But most amazing of all, by the end of the day after all the theatrics, Elijah turned his face toward heaven and cried, "Hear me, O LORD, hear me, that this people may know that You are the LORD God, and that You have turned their hearts back to You again"; and God did (1 Kin. 18:37, 38)!

When Elijah spoke, everyone listened. How did the prophet gain the ear of everyone who heard his voice? We can discern a number of reasons:

1. *His courage:* He was willing to stand alone for God.
2. *His conviction:* He had a passion for what he believed.
3. *His character:* He was honest and forthright with everyone.
4. *His connection:* He magnetically drew the people to himself and to God.
5. *His credibility:* He eventually gained the people's ear because he got the results he was after.

Elijah Escapes from Jezebel

19 And Ahab told Jezebel all that Elijah had done, also how he had executed all the prophets with the sword. [2]Then Jezebel sent a messenger to Elijah, saying, "So let the gods do *to me,* and more also, if I do not make your life as the life of one of them by tomorrow about this time." [3]And when he saw *that,* he arose and ran for his life, and went to Beersheba, which *belongs* to Judah, and left his servant there.

[4]But he himself went a day's journey into the wilderness, and came and sat down under a broom tree. And he prayed that he might die, and said, "It is enough! Now, LORD, take my life, for I *am* no better than my fathers!"

[5]Then as he lay and slept under a broom tree, suddenly an angel[a] touched him, and said to him, "Arise *and* eat." [6]Then he looked, and there by his head *was* a cake baked on coals, and a jar of water. So he ate and drank, and lay down again. [7]And the angel[a] of the LORD came back the second time, and touched him, and said, "Arise *and* eat, because the journey *is* too great for you." [8]So he arose, and ate and drank; and he went in the strength of that food forty days and forty nights as far as Horeb, the mountain of God.

[9]And there he went into a cave, and spent the night in that place; and behold, the word of the LORD *came* to him, and He said to him, "What are you doing here, Elijah?"

[10]So he said, "I have been very zealous for the LORD God of hosts; for the children of Israel have forsaken Your covenant, torn down Your altars, and killed Your prophets with the sword. I alone am left; and they seek to take my life."

God's Revelation to Elijah

[11]Then He said, "Go out, and stand on the mountain before the LORD." And behold, the LORD passed by, and a great and strong wind tore into the mountains and broke the rocks in pieces before the LORD, *but* the LORD *was* not in the wind; and after the wind an earthquake, *but* the LORD *was* not in the earthquake; [12]and after the earthquake a fire, *but* the LORD *was* not in the fire; and after the fire a still small voice.

[13]So it was, when Elijah heard *it,* that he wrapped his face in his mantle and went out and stood in the entrance of the cave. Suddenly a voice *came* to him, and said, "What are you doing here, Elijah?"

19:5 [a]Or *Angel* **19:7** [a]Or *Angel*

Burnout: Principles, Not Emotions, Must Guide Leaders

(1 Kings 19:1–3)

Emotions are wonderful servants, but poor leaders.

How ironic that Elijah would flee from Jezebel! The courageous leader who successfully confronted 450 prophets of Baal and 400 prophets of Asherah turned on his heels and ran from a wicked woman who threatened his life.

How could it happen? The phenomenon of emotional burnout helps us make sense of the incident. Leaders burn out when they pay out huge emotional expenses without replenishing the inner person. Review what happened . . .

Elijah's Emotional Expense

- Predicted a drought to King Ahab
- Supernaturally receives food from a widow and the birds
- Announces the end of the drought
- Challenges the 450 prophets of Baal
- Mobilizes people to eliminate idols
- Prays down torrential rain in Judah
- Outruns the storm and Ahab's chariot
- Confronted by Jezebel; leaves his servant

Elijah's Eventual Consequence

- Isolation: he cut himself off from friends
- Paranoia: he felt totally alone in serving God; imagined everyone was trying to kill him
- Exhaustion: he felt famished and lay down
- Hiding: he got lost in a cave
- Self-pity: he complained of no reward
- Depression: he prayed that he might die
- Messiah complex: he alone remained as God's prophet
- Empty: he had no fresh word from the Lord

CHARISMA

Ahab and Jezebel Manipulate People Because They Cannot Move Them

(1 Kings 19:1—22:40)

Few couples in Scripture look less attractive than King Ahab and Queen Jezebel. We get acquainted with their ugly style at the end of 1 Kings. Because they suffered an almost total lack of leadership charisma, they had to use manipulation, selfishness, and cunning to get what they wanted.

Charisma has been defined as a magnetic personal attraction that draws others to the leader, making them feel better about themselves. Effective leaders do well to develop some level of charisma.

In Greek, the word *charisma* means "gift." God gives a degree of charisma to everyone. Leaders are to give it away to others; charismatic people are others-centered. So why did Ahab and Jezebel fail to demonstrate any charisma?

1. They set out to selfishly build their own kingdoms (22:8).
2. They used people in order to get ahead; anyone was expendable (19:2).
3. They worried about image and lived under false pretenses (21:8–13).
4. They sulked and got angry when they didn't get their way (21:4).
5. They pretended to be someone they were not (21:25–27).
6. They abused the authority they had been given (21:18, 19).

Ahab and Jezebel felt no incentive to develop charisma because their position allowed them to use people. Why would they need to inspire others to cooperate with them? Wasn't their word law? Godly leaders must avoid this wicked attitude at all costs.

Roadblocks to Charisma

To build charisma, be others-minded. Leaders who think about others and their concerns before thinking of themselves quickly develop charisma.

How would you rate your own charisma? Are other people naturally attracted to you? Are you well liked? Consider the following roadblocks to charisma. Do you possess any of these?

- **Pride:** Nobody wants to follow a leader who thinks he is better than everyone else. Arrogant leaders lose the respect of others.
- **Insecurity:** If you are uncomfortable with yourself, others will be, too. Only secure leaders can provide a secure atmosphere.
- **Moodiness:** If people never know what to expect from you, they stop expecting anything. Eventually, they won't even approach you.
- **Selfishness:** People can tell if you are using them merely to reach your own goal. No healthy person stays for long in such an unhealthy environment.
- **Perfectionism:** People respect the desire for excellence, but loathe unrealistic expectations. No one wants to feel the program is more important than they are.
- **Cynicism:** People don't want to be rained on by someone who sees a cloud around every silver lining. Negative leaders repulse healthy followers.

For a positive look at charisma, see p. 1317.

The Law of the Inner Circle: Development Beats Discouragement

(1 Kings 19:4–10)

Discouragement buries many landmines in our path: It hurts our self-image; it causes us to evade our responsibilities; it prompts us to blame others for our problems; it tempts us to blur the facts. We tend to lead according to the way we feel about ourselves.

Elijah became one discouraged leader after his confrontation with Jezebel. Emotionally drained, physically spent, full of self-pity and ready to die, he looked haggard and nearly done in. So what did God do to help the prophet through his deep discouragement? He told him to select and develop another leader, Elisha. Their relationship suggests several observations about leadership:

1. God desires to continually raise up leaders (1 Kin. 19:16).
2. The leader finds and challenges the potential leader (1 Kin. 19:19, 20).
3. The potential leader counts the cost, pays the price and follows (1 Kin. 19:20, 21).
4. The potential leader stays close to and shadows the leader (2 Kin. 2:2–8).
5. The potential leader covets the power of God that he sees in the leader (2 Kin. 2:9, 10).
6. The leader passes his authority to the potential leader (2 Kin. 2:11–13).
7. Others recognize the transfer of spiritual authority (2 Kin. 2:14, 15).

[14]And he said, "I have been very zealous for the LORD God of hosts; because the children of Israel have forsaken Your covenant, torn down Your altars, and killed Your prophets with the sword. I alone am left; and they seek to take my life."

[15]Then the LORD said to him: "Go, return on your way to the Wilderness of Damascus; and when you arrive, anoint Hazael *as* king over Syria. [16]Also you shall anoint Jehu the son of Nimshi *as* king over Israel. And Elisha the son of Shaphat of Abel Meholah you shall anoint *as* prophet in your place. [17]It shall be *that* whoever escapes the sword of Hazael, Jehu will kill; and whoever escapes the sword of Jehu, Elisha will kill. [18]Yet I have reserved seven thousand in Israel, all whose knees have not bowed to Baal, and every mouth that has not kissed him."

Elisha Follows Elijah

[19]So he departed from there, and found Elisha the son of Shaphat, who *was* plowing *with* twelve yoke *of* oxen before him, and he was with the twelfth. Then Elijah passed by him and threw his mantle on him. [20]And he left the oxen and ran after Elijah, and said, "Please let me kiss my father and my mother, and *then* I will follow you."

And he said to him, "Go back again, for what have I done to you?"

[21]So *Elisha* turned back from him, and took a yoke of oxen and slaughtered them and boiled their flesh, using the oxen's equipment, and gave it to the people, and they ate. Then he arose and followed Elijah, and became his servant.

Ahab Defeats the Syrians

20 Now Ben-Hadad the king of Syria gathered all his forces together; thirty-two kings *were* with him, with horses and chariots. And he went up and besieged Samaria, and made war against it. [2]Then he sent messengers into the city to Ahab king of Israel, and said to him, "Thus says Ben-Hadad: [3]'Your silver and your gold *are* mine; your loveliest wives and children are mine.'"

[4]And the king of Israel answered and said, "My lord, O king, just as you say, I and all that I have *are* yours."

[5]Then the messengers came back and said, "Thus speaks Ben-Hadad, saying, 'Indeed I have sent to you, saying, "You shall deliver to me your silver and your gold, your wives and your children"; [6]but I will send my servants to you tomorrow about this time, and they shall search your house and the houses of your servants. And it shall be, *that* whatever is pleasant in your eyes, they will put *it* in their hands and take *it*.'"

[7]So the king of Israel called all the elders of the land, and said, "Notice, please, and see how

this *man* seeks trouble, for he sent to me for my wives, my children, my silver, and my gold; and I did not deny him."

[8]And all the elders and all the people said to him, "Do not listen or consent."

[9]Therefore he said to the messengers of Ben-Hadad, "Tell my lord the king, 'All that you sent for to your servant the first time I will do, but this thing I cannot do.'"

And the messengers departed and brought back word to him.

[10]Then Ben-Hadad sent to him and said, "The gods do so to me, and more also, if enough dust is left of Samaria for a handful for each of the people who follow me."

[11]So the king of Israel answered and said, "Tell *him*, 'Let not the one who puts on *his armor* boast like the one who takes *it off.*'"

[12]And it happened when *Ben-Hadad* heard this message, as he and the kings *were* drinking at the command post, that he said to his servants, "Get ready." And they got ready to attack the city.

[13]Suddenly a prophet approached Ahab king of Israel, saying, "Thus says the LORD: 'Have you seen all this great multitude? Behold, I will deliver it into your hand today, and you shall know that I *am* the LORD.'"

[14]So Ahab said, "By whom?"

And he said, "Thus says the LORD: 'By the young leaders of the provinces.'"

Then he said, "Who will set the battle in order?"

And he answered, "You."

[15]Then he mustered the young leaders of the provinces, and there were two hundred and thirty-two; and after them he mustered all the people, all the children of Israel—seven thousand.

[16]So they went out at noon. Meanwhile Ben-Hadad and the thirty-two kings helping him were getting drunk at the command post. [17]The young leaders of the provinces went out first. And Ben-Hadad sent out *a patrol,* and they told him, saying, "Men are coming out of Samaria!" [18]So he said, "If they have come out for peace, take them alive; and if they have come out for war, take them alive."

[19]Then these young leaders of the provinces went out of the city with the army which followed them. [20]And each one killed his man; so the Syrians fled, and Israel pursued them; and Ben-Hadad the king of Syria escaped on a horse with the cavalry. [21]Then the king of Israel went out and attacked the horses and chariots, and killed the Syrians with a great slaughter.

[22]And the prophet came to the king of Israel and said to him, "Go, strengthen yourself; take note, and see what you should do, for in the spring of the year the king of Syria will come up against you."

The Syrians Again Defeated

[23]Then the servants of the king of Syria said to him, "Their gods *are* gods of the hills. Therefore they were stronger than we; but if we fight against them in the plain, surely we will be stronger than they. [24]So do this thing: Dismiss the kings, each from his position, and put captains in their places; [25]and you shall muster an army like the army that you have lost, horse for horse and chariot for chariot. Then we will fight against them in the plain; surely we will be stronger than they."

And he listened to their voice and did so.

[26]So it was, in the spring of the year, that Ben-Hadad mustered the Syrians and went up to Aphek to fight against Israel. [27]And the children of Israel were mustered and given provisions, and they went against them. Now the children of Israel encamped before them like two little flocks of goats, while the Syrians filled the countryside.

[28]Then a man of God came and spoke to the king of Israel, and said, "Thus says the LORD: 'Because the Syrians have said, "The LORD *is* God of the hills, but He *is* not God of the valleys," therefore I will deliver all this great multitude into your hand, and you shall know that I *am* the LORD.' " [29]And they encamped opposite each other for seven days. So it was that on the seventh day the battle was joined; and the children of Israel killed one hundred thousand foot soldiers *of* the Syrians in one day. [30]But the rest fled to Aphek, into the city; then a wall fell on twenty-seven thousand of the men *who were* left.

And Ben-Hadad fled and went into the city, into an inner chamber.

Ahab's Treaty with Ben-Hadad

[31]Then his servants said to him, "Look now, we have heard that the kings of the house of Israel *are* merciful kings. Please, let us put sackcloth around our waists and ropes around our heads, and go out to the king of Israel; perhaps he will spare your life." [32]So they wore sackcloth around their waists and *put* ropes around their heads, and came to the king of Israel and said, "Your servant Ben-Hadad says, 'Please let me live.'"

And he said, "*Is* he still alive? He *is* my brother."

[33]Now the men were watching closely to see whether *any sign of mercy would come* from him;

and they quickly grasped *at this word* and said, "Your brother Ben–Hadad."

So he said, "Go, bring him." Then Ben-Hadad came out to him; and he had him come up into the chariot.

³⁴So *Ben-Hadad* said to him, "The cities which my father took from your father I will restore; and you may set up marketplaces for yourself in Damascus, as my father did in Samaria."

Then *Ahab said,* "I will send you away with this treaty." So he made a treaty with him and sent him away.

Ahab Condemned

³⁵Now a certain man of the sons of the prophets said to his neighbor by the word of the LORD, "Strike me, please." And the man refused to strike him. ³⁶Then he said to him, "Because you have not obeyed the voice of the LORD, surely, as soon as you depart from me, a lion shall kill you." And as soon as he left him, a lion found him and killed him.

³⁷And he found another man, and said, "Strike me, please." So the man struck him, inflicting a wound. ³⁸Then the prophet departed and waited for the king by the road, and disguised himself with a bandage over his eyes. ³⁹Now as the king passed by, he cried out to the king and said, "Your servant went out into the midst of the battle; and there, a man came over and brought a man to me, and said, 'Guard this man; if by any means he is missing, your life shall be for his life, or else you shall pay a talent of silver.' ⁴⁰While your servant was busy here and there, he was gone."

Then the king of Israel said to him, "So *shall* your judgment *be;* you yourself have decided *it.*"

⁴¹And he hastened to take the bandage away from his eyes; and the king of Israel recognized him as one of the prophets. ⁴²Then he said to him, "Thus says the LORD: 'Because you have let slip out of *your* hand a man whom I appointed to utter destruction, therefore your life shall go for his life, and your people for his people.'"

⁴³So the king of Israel went to his house sullen and displeased, and came to Samaria.

Naboth Is Murdered for His Vineyard

21 And it came to pass after these things *that* Naboth the Jezreelite had a vineyard which *was* in Jezreel, next to the palace of Ahab king of Samaria. ²So Ahab spoke to Naboth, saying, "Give me your vineyard, that I may have it for a vegetable garden, because it *is* near, next to my house; and for it I will give you a vineyard better than it. *Or,* if it seems good to you, I will give you its worth in money."

³But Naboth said to Ahab, "The LORD forbid that I should give the inheritance of my fathers to you!"

⁴So Ahab went into his house sullen and displeased because of the word which Naboth the Jezreelite had spoken to him; for he had said, "I will not give you the inheritance of my fathers." And he lay down on his bed, and turned away his face, and would eat no food. ⁵But Jezebel his wife came to him, and said to him, "Why is your spirit so sullen that you eat no food?"

⁶He said to her, "Because I spoke to Naboth the Jezreelite, and said to him, 'Give me your vineyard for money; or else, if it pleases you, I will give you *another* vineyard for it.' And he answered, 'I will not give you my vineyard.'"

⁷Then Jezebel his wife said to him, "You now exercise authority over Israel! Arise, eat food, and let your heart be cheerful; I will give you the vineyard of Naboth the Jezreelite."

⁸And she wrote letters in Ahab's name, sealed *them* with his seal, and sent the letters to the elders and the nobles who *were* dwelling in the city with Naboth. ⁹She wrote in the letters, saying,

Proclaim a fast, and seat Naboth with high honor among the people; ¹⁰and seat two men, scoundrels, before him to bear witness against him, saying, "You have blasphemed God and the king." *Then* take him out, and stone him, that he may die.

¹¹So the men of his city, the elders and nobles who were inhabitants of his city, did as Jezebel had sent to them, as it *was* written in the letters which she had sent to them. ¹²They proclaimed a fast, and seated Naboth with high honor among the people. ¹³And two men, scoundrels, came in and sat before him; and the scoundrels witnessed against him, against Naboth, in the presence of the people, saying, "Naboth has blasphemed God and the king!" Then they took him outside the city and stoned him with stones, so that he died. ¹⁴Then they sent to Jezebel, saying, "Naboth has been stoned and is dead."

¹⁵And it came to pass, when Jezebel heard that Naboth had been stoned and was dead, that Jezebel said to Ahab, "Arise, take possession of the vineyard of Naboth the Jezreelite, which he refused to give you for money; for Naboth is not alive, but dead." ¹⁶So it was, when Ahab heard that Naboth was dead, that Ahab got up and

went down to take possession of the vineyard of Naboth the Jezreelite.

The LORD Condemns Ahab

[17]Then the word of the LORD came to Elijah the Tishbite, saying, [18]"Arise, go down to meet Ahab king of Israel, who *lives* in Samaria. There *he is,* in the vineyard of Naboth, where he has gone down to take possession of it. [19]You shall speak to him, saying, 'Thus says the LORD: "Have you murdered and also taken possession?" ' And you shall speak to him, saying, 'Thus says the LORD: "In the place where dogs licked the blood of Naboth, dogs shall lick your blood, even yours." ' "

[20]So Ahab said to Elijah, "Have you found me, O my enemy?"

And he answered, "I have found *you,* because you have sold yourself to do evil in the sight of the LORD: [21]Behold, I will bring calamity on you. I will take away your posterity, and will cut off from Ahab every male in Israel, both bond and free. [22]I will make your house like the house of Jeroboam the son of Nebat, and like the house of Baasha the son of Ahijah, because of the provocation with which you have provoked *Me* to anger, and made Israel sin.' [23]And concerning Jezebel the LORD also spoke, saying, 'The dogs shall eat Jezebel by the wall[a] of Jezreel.' [24]The dogs shall eat whoever belongs to Ahab and dies in the city, and the birds of the air shall eat whoever dies in the field."

[25]But there was no one like Ahab who sold himself to do wickedness in the sight of the LORD, because Jezebel his wife stirred him up. [26]And he behaved very abominably in following idols, according to all *that* the Amorites had done, whom the LORD had cast out before the children of Israel.

[27]So it was, when Ahab heard those words, that he tore his clothes and put sackcloth on his body, and fasted and lay in sackcloth, and went about mourning.

[28]And the word of the LORD came to Elijah the Tishbite, saying, [29]"See how Ahab has humbled himself before Me? Because he has humbled himself before Me, I will not bring the calamity in his days. In the days of his son I will bring the calamity on his house."

Micaiah Warns Ahab

22 Now three years passed without war between Syria and Israel. [2]Then it came to pass, in the third year, that Jehoshaphat the king of Judah went down to *visit* the king of Israel.

[3]And the king of Israel said to his servants, "Do you know that Ramoth in Gilead *is* ours, but we hesitate to take it out of the hand of the king of Syria?" [4]So he said to Jehoshaphat, "Will you go with me to fight at Ramoth Gilead?"

Jehoshaphat said to the king of Israel, "I *am* as you *are,* my people as your people, my horses as your horses." [5]Also Jehoshaphat said to the king of Israel, "Please inquire for the word of the LORD today."

[6]Then the king of Israel gathered the prophets together, about four hundred men, and said to them, "Shall I go against Ramoth Gilead to fight, or shall I refrain?"

So they said, "Go up, for the Lord will deliver *it* into the hand of the king."

[7]And Jehoshaphat said, "*Is there* not still a prophet of the LORD here, that we may inquire of Him?"[a]

[8]So the king of Israel said to Jehoshaphat, "*There is* still one man, Micaiah the son of Imlah, by whom we may inquire of the LORD; but I hate him, because he does not prophesy good concerning me, but evil."

And Jehoshaphat said, "Let not the king say such things!"

[9]Then the king of Israel called an officer and said, "Bring Micaiah the son of Imlah quickly!"

[10]The king of Israel and Jehoshaphat the king of Judah, having put on *their* robes, sat each on his throne, at a threshing floor at the entrance of the gate of Samaria; and all the prophets prophesied before them. [11]Now Zedekiah the son of Chenaanah had made horns of iron for himself; and he said, "Thus says the LORD: 'With these you shall gore the Syrians until they are destroyed.' " [12]And all the prophets prophesied so, saying, "Go up to Ramoth Gilead and prosper, for the LORD will deliver *it* into the king's hand."

[13]Then the messenger who had gone to call Micaiah spoke to him, saying, "Now listen, the words of the prophets with one accord encourage the king. Please, let your word be like the word of one of them, and speak encouragement."

[14]And Micaiah said, "*As* the LORD lives, whatever the LORD says to me, that I will speak."

[15]Then he came to the king; and the king said to him, "Micaiah, shall we go to war against Ramoth Gilead, or shall we refrain?"

21:23 [a]Following Masoretic Text and Septuagint; some Hebrew manuscripts, Syriac, Targum, and Vulgate read *plot of ground* (compare 2 Kings 9:36).
22:7 [a]Or *him*

And he answered him, "Go and prosper, for the LORD will deliver *it* into the hand of the king!"

[16]So the king said to him, "How many times shall I make you swear that you tell me nothing but the truth in the name of the LORD?"

[17]Then he said, "I saw all Israel scattered on the mountains, as sheep that have no shepherd. And the LORD said, 'These have no master. Let each return to his house in peace.'"

[18]And the king of Israel said to Jehoshaphat, "Did I not tell you he would not prophesy good concerning me, but evil?"

[19]Then *Micaiah* said, "Therefore hear the word of the LORD: I saw the LORD sitting on His throne, and all the host of heaven standing by, on His right hand and on His left. [20]And the LORD said, 'Who will persuade Ahab to go up, that he may fall at Ramoth Gilead?' So one spoke in this manner, and another spoke in that manner. [21]Then a spirit came forward and stood before the LORD, and said, 'I will persuade him.' [22]The LORD said to him, 'In what way?' So he said, 'I will go out and be a lying spirit in the mouth of all his prophets.' And the LORD said, 'You shall persuade *him,* and also prevail. Go out and do so.' [23]Therefore look! The LORD has put a lying spirit in the mouth of all these prophets of yours, and the LORD has declared disaster against you."

[24]Now Zedekiah the son of Chenaanah went near and struck Micaiah on the cheek, and said, "Which way did the spirit from the LORD go from me to speak to you?"

[25]And Micaiah said, "Indeed, you shall see on that day when you go into an inner chamber to hide!"

[26]So the king of Israel said, "Take Micaiah, and return him to Amon the governor of the city and to Joash the king's son; [27]and say, 'Thus says the king: "Put this *fellow* in prison, and feed him with bread of affliction and water of affliction, until I come in peace."'"

[28]But Micaiah said, "If you ever return in peace, the LORD has not spoken by me." And he said, "Take heed, all you people!"

Ahab Dies in Battle

[29]So the king of Israel and Jehoshaphat the king of Judah went up to Ramoth Gilead. [30]And the king of Israel said to Jehoshaphat, "I will disguise myself and go into battle; but you put on your robes." So the king of Israel disguised himself and went into battle.

[31]Now the king of Syria had commanded the thirty-two captains of his chariots, saying, "Fight with no one small or great, but only with the king of Israel." [32]So it was, when the captains of the chariots saw Jehoshaphat, that they said, "Surely it *is* the king of Israel!" Therefore they turned aside to fight against him, and Jehoshaphat cried out. [33]And it happened, when the captains of the chariots saw that it *was* not the king of Israel, that they turned back from pursuing him. [34]Now a *certain* man drew a bow at random, and struck the king of Israel between the joints of his armor. So he said to the driver of his chariot, "Turn around and take me out of the battle, for I am wounded."

[35]The battle increased that day; and the king was propped up in his chariot, facing the Syrians, and died at evening. The blood ran out from the wound onto the floor of the chariot. [36]Then, as the sun was going down, a shout went throughout the army, saying, "Every man to his city, and every man to his own country!"

[37]So the king died, and was brought to Samaria. And they buried the king in Samaria. [38]Then *someone* washed the chariot at a pool in Samaria, and the dogs licked up his blood while the harlots bathed,[a] according to the word of the LORD which He had spoken.

[39]Now the rest of the acts of Ahab, and all that he did, the ivory house which he built and all the cities that he built, *are* they not written in the book of the chronicles of the kings of Israel? [40]So Ahab rested with his fathers. Then Ahaziah his son reigned in his place.

Jehoshaphat Reigns in Judah

[41]Jehoshaphat the son of Asa had become king over Judah in the fourth year of Ahab king of Israel. [42]Jehoshaphat *was* thirty-five years old when he became king, and he reigned twenty-five years in Jerusalem. His mother's name *was* Azubah the daughter of Shilhi. [43]And he walked in all the ways of his father Asa. He did not turn aside from them, doing *what was* right in the eyes of the LORD. Nevertheless the high places were not taken away, *for* the people offered sacrifices and burned incense on the high places. [44]Also Jehoshaphat made peace with the king of Israel.

[45]Now the rest of the acts of Jehoshaphat, the might that he showed, and how he made war, *are* they not written in the book of the chronicles of the kings of Judah? [46]And the rest of the perverted persons,[a] who remained in the days of his

---

22:38 [a]Syriac and Targum read *they washed his armor.*
22:46 [a]Hebrew *qadesh,* that is, one practicing sodomy and prostitution in religious rituals

father Asa, he banished from the land. [47]*There was* then no king in Edom, only a deputy of the king.

[48]Jehoshaphat made merchant ships[a] to go to Ophir for gold; but they never sailed, for the ships were wrecked at Ezion Geber. [49]Then Ahaziah the son of Ahab said to Jehoshaphat, "Let my servants go with your servants in the ships." But Jehoshaphat would not.

[50]And Jehoshaphat rested with his fathers, and was buried with his fathers in the City of David his father. Then Jehoram his son reigned in his place.

Ahaziah Reigns in Israel

[51]Ahaziah the son of Ahab became king over Israel in Samaria in the seventeenth year of Jehoshaphat king of Judah, and reigned two years over Israel. [52]He did evil in the sight of the LORD, and walked in the way of his father and in the way of his mother and in the way of Jeroboam the son of Nebat, who had made Israel sin; [53]for he served Baal and worshiped him, and provoked the LORD God of Israel to anger, according to all that his father had done.

22:48 [a]Or *ships of Tarshish*

2 KINGS

Final Days of the Divided Kingdom

SUMMARY

The second book of the kings of Israel and Judah describes the final days of the divided kingdom before both halves fall into captivity. As much as anything, it is a story of failed leadership.

God had a difficult time finding leaders with character, competence, and compassion for the people. The people consistently reflect the deficiencies of their leaders, just as the Law of Magnetism would predict.

Many have said that leaders cannot lead others beyond where they have gone themselves. It's true. The division of Israel and Judah simply reflects the divided heart of each leader. To whom would each king show allegiance? To be sure, some good kings arise and bring about positive reform. Once they die, however, the new leaders neglect to follow through on the reforms, and the people return to their rebellion and apathy. Second Kings offers a sad commentary on the human condition. We discover far more negative than positive leadership examples in this book.

A few highlights may be noted, however. The prophets Elijah and Elisha never back off of their uncompromising message. Elijah ministers to the ruling elite of Israel, while Elisha focuses on the common people of many nations. King Hezekiah enjoys a personal renewal during his reign, then asks for his days to be lengthened so he can finish needed reforms. God lengthens his life and Hezekiah makes a difference. God also uses another good leader, the prophet Isaiah, to speak into Hezekiah's life and to carry the answer to his prayers. King Josiah goes down as one of the few good kings in Judah. He ascends to the throne at eight years of age, and before he dies, he leads Judah in massive repentance and reform, beginning with the renovation of the house of the Lord.

Unfortunately, these strong, healthy spiritual leaders make up the minority in 2 Kings. Most of the book chronicles the decline and fall of both Israel and Judah, beginning with their leaders. The book illustrates repeatedly that leaders never find what they are looking for when they abandon the higher cause of God for their own interests.

God's Role in 2 Kings

As He did in 1 Kings, God spends most of His time beckoning leaders to follow Him. When they do so, He displays His goodness, answers their prayers, and provides for their needs.

Unfortunately, most Hebrew leaders pay little attention to Him. Even when the prophets confront them, they listen only when the news tickles their fancy. Most either abandon the true God for Baal worship, or consider Yahweh a mere superstition to be held for good luck (the continuing practice of many current political leaders). Still, God chose to speak to these leaders through His prophets.

Leaders in 2 Kings

Elijah, Elisha, Jehoram, Ben-Hadad, Hazael, Ahaziah, Jehu, Jezebel, Ahab, Joash, Ahaz, Isaiah, Hezekiah, Josiah, Nebuchadnezzar

Other People of Influence in 2 Kings

Jehoiada, Naaman, Gehazi, the Babylonians, the Assyrians

Lessons in Leadership

- The measure of a man is what he does with power.
- Choose your mentors well and ask for what you want.
- Don't sweat the small stuff—think strategically as you make your battle plans.
- Stay focused with your mission, stay flexible with your methods.
- Maintain an eternal perspective.
- If you compromise the ultimate, you'll become slave to the immediate.
- Never underestimate the power of God.
- Outward, public reform begins with inward, personal renewal.

HIGHLIGHTS IN 2 KINGS

God Judges Ahaziah

1 Moab rebelled against Israel after the death of Ahab.

[2]Now Ahaziah fell through the lattice of his upper room in Samaria, and was injured; so he sent messengers and said to them, "Go, inquire of Baal-Zebub, the god of Ekron, whether I shall recover from this injury." [3]But the angel[a] of the LORD said to Elijah the Tishbite, "Arise, go up to meet the messengers of the king of Samaria, and say to them, '*Is it* because *there is* no God in Israel *that* you are going to inquire of Baal-Zebub, the god of Ekron?' [4]Now therefore, thus says the LORD: 'You shall not come down from the bed to which you have gone up, but you shall surely die.'" So Elijah departed.

[5]And when the messengers returned to him, he said to them, "Why have you come back?"

[6]So they said to him, "A man came up to meet us, and said to us, 'Go, return to the king who sent you, and say to him, "Thus says the LORD: '*Is it* because *there is* no God in Israel *that* you are sending to inquire of Baal-Zebub, the god of Ekron? Therefore you shall not come down from the bed to which you have gone up, but you shall surely die.'"'"

[7]Then he said to them, "What kind of man *was it* who came up to meet you and told you these words?"

[8]So they answered him, "A hairy man wearing a leather belt around his waist."

And he said, "It *is* Elijah the Tishbite."

[9]Then the king sent to him a captain of fifty with his fifty men. So he went up to him; and there he was, sitting on the top of a hill. And he spoke to him: "Man of God, the king has said, 'Come down!'"

[10]So Elijah answered and said to the captain of fifty, "If I *am* a man of God, then let fire come down from heaven and consume you and your fifty men." And fire came down from heaven and consumed him and his fifty. [11]Then he sent to him another captain of fifty with his fifty men.

And he answered and said to him: "Man of God, thus has the king said, 'Come down quickly!'"

[12]So Elijah answered and said to them, "If I *am* a man of God, let fire come down from heaven and consume you and your fifty men." And the fire of God came down from heaven and consumed him and his fifty.

[13]Again, he sent a third captain of fifty with his fifty men. And the third captain of fifty went up, and came and fell on his knees before Elijah, and pleaded with him, and said to him: "Man of God, please let my life and the life of these fifty servants of yours be precious in your sight. [14]Look, fire has come down from heaven and burned up the first two captains of fifties with their fifties. But let my life now be precious in your sight."

[15]And the angel[a] of the LORD said to Elijah, "Go down with him; do not be afraid of him." So he arose and went down with him to the king. [16]Then he said to him, "Thus says the LORD: 'Be-

---

1:3 [a]Or *Angel* **1:15** [a]Or *Angel*

The Measure of a Man Is How He Handles Power

(2 Kings 1:1–17)

When Ahaziah, the king of Israel, injured himself in a fall, he wanted to know whether he would recover—but he inquired of the false god Baal, not of Yahweh, the God of Israel. This angered the Lord, who sent a prophecy through Elijah to the king, informing him that he would die.

The king in turn sent a captain and 50 soldiers to capture Elijah, but the prophet called down fire from heaven and killed them. After this happened a second time, a third delegation approached Elijah and begged for mercy. An angel told the prophet to go with the men and visit the king.

We can make some observations about this episode. Notice the humanity of this great prophet:

1. Elijah possessed both spiritual authority and anxiety at the same time (vv. 13–15).
2. Elijah spoke harshly and with power (vv. 10, 12).
3. Elijah showed no respect for the authority of the king (vv. 9–14).
4. Elijah required an angel to appear to confirm that he should spare the soldiers and go with them to meet the king (v. 15).

cause you have sent messengers to inquire of Baal-Zebub, the god of Ekron, *is it* because *there is* no God in Israel to inquire of His word? Therefore you shall not come down from the bed to which you have gone up, but you shall surely die.'"

[17]So *Ahaziah* died according to the word of the LORD which Elijah had spoken. Because he had no son, Jehoram[a] became king in his place, in the second year of Jehoram the son of Jehoshaphat, king of Judah.

[18]Now the rest of the acts of Ahaziah which he did, *are* they not written in the book of the chronicles of the kings of Israel?

Elijah Ascends to Heaven

2 And it came to pass, when the LORD was about to take up Elijah into heaven by a whirlwind, that Elijah went with Elisha from Gilgal. [2]Then Elijah said to Elisha, "Stay here, please, for the LORD has sent me on to Bethel."

But Elisha said, "*As* the LORD lives, and *as* your soul lives, I will not leave you!" So they went down to Bethel.

[3]Now the sons of the prophets who *were* at Bethel came out to Elisha, and said to him, "Do you know that the LORD will take away your master from over you today?"

And he said, "Yes, I know; keep silent!"

[4]Then Elijah said to him, "Elisha, stay here, please, for the LORD has sent me on to Jericho."

But he said, "*As* the LORD lives, and *as* your soul lives, I will not leave you!" So they came to Jericho.

[5]Now the sons of the prophets who *were* at Jericho came to Elisha and said to him, "Do you know that the LORD will take away your master from over you today?"

So he answered, "Yes, I know; keep silent!"

[6]Then Elijah said to him, "Stay here, please, for the LORD has sent me on to the Jordan."

But he said, "*As* the LORD lives, and *as* your soul lives, I will not leave you!" So the two of them went on. [7]And fifty men of the sons of the prophets went and stood facing *them* at a distance, while the two of them stood by the Jordan. [8]Now Elijah took his mantle, rolled *it* up, and struck the water; and it was divided this way and that, so that the two of them crossed over on dry ground.

[9]And so it was, when they had crossed over, that Elijah said to Elisha, "Ask! What may I do for you, before I am taken away from you?"

Elisha said, "Please let a double portion of your spirit be upon me."

1:17 [a]The son of Ahab king of Israel (compare 3:1)

Choose Your Mentors Well: Elisha Risks the "Big Ask"

(2 Kings 2:9, 10)

Every leader needs mentors, especially emerging leaders. After watching the great Elijah for many years, Elisha reached down and found the guts to ask Elijah for a double portion of his spirit.

God took Elisha through the preparation necessary under Elijah. The younger man waited for the right time, then made his request. The result? Scripture records that Elisha performed twice as many miracles as did his mentor. Note several principles outlined in 1 Kings 19 and 2 Kings 2 underlying his preparation:

Elisha's Preparation	Leadership Principle
1. He was anointed to replace Elijah.	1. Leaders must understand their call and role.
2. Elijah found him plowing a field.	2. Leaders must have a servant's heart.
3. Elisha touched Elijah's mantle long before he entered his ministry.	3. Leaders must wait patiently on God's perfect timing for their authority.
4. He asked to kiss his parents good-bye.	4. Leaders must respect parental authority.
5. He burned his farming tools.	5. Leaders must surrender former ambitions.
6. He stuck with Elijah wherever he went.	6. Leaders must pursue good mentors.
7. He absorbed all he could from Elijah.	7. Leaders must hunger to grow and develop.

THE LAW OF MAGNETISM

Elijah and Elisha Cut from the Same Cloth

(2 Kings 2:1–15)

Effective leaders are always on the lookout for good people. Each of us carries around a mental list of what kind of people we would like in our organization. Believe it or not, whom you get is not determined by what you *want*, but by who you *are*. In most situations, you draw people who possess the same qualities you do.

It is possible for a leader to go out and recruit people unlike himself, but it's crucial to recognize that people who are different will not naturally be attracted to him. Their quality does not depend on a hiring process, a human resources department, or even what you consider to be the quality of your area's applicant pool. It depends on you. If you think the people you attract could be better, then it's time for you to improve yourself.

What enabled Elijah to draw like-minded people to his side? The answer is found in the Law of Magnetism. Who you are is who you attract.

1. *Every leader has a measure of magnetism.*

All leaders attract others. Highly charismatic leaders often attract large numbers of followers, but even modest leaders gain a following. If they didn't, they wouldn't be leaders, would they?

2. *A leader's magnetism may impact others intellectually, emotionally, or volitionally.*

Not all leaders affect people in the same way, nor do they use the same means of influence. The greatest leaders connect on multiple levels: with followers' minds, hearts, and wills.

Elijah's magnetism affected others on every level. When he defeated the false prophets of Baal, he connected with the people first by calling down fire from heaven so even confirmed skeptics saw the reality of God. But that alone was not enough. To give his message more emotional impact, Elijah drenched his sacrifice in gallons of water. When God's fire licked up the sacrifice, water and all, the people declared, "The LORD, He is God!" (1 Kin. 18:39). And the prophet connected on a volitional level when he cried, "Seize the prophets of Baal!" (18:40) and the people obeyed.

3. *Magnetism is neither good nor bad in itself—it depends on what a leader does with it.*

Charismatic leaders come in all shapes and sizes. There are Adolf Hitlers and Mother Teresas, Ahabs and Elijahs. Magnetism is like money; it's a useful tool, neither good nor bad in itself. Elijah used his ability to attract like-minded people in order to fulfill his mission and extend his influence.

4. *Secure leaders draw both similar and complementary followers.*

All leaders tend to attract people similar to themselves in values, age, attitude, etc. Elijah's leadership attracted people who loved God and who were gifted in prophecy.

But secure leaders—ones who acknowledge and accept their weaknesses as well as their strengths—also attract people with complementary abilities.

5. *A leader's magnetism never remains static.*

A leader can cultivate, shape, and mature his magnetism. Before Elijah drew crowds, he labored in obscurity, helping a widow and her son. God provided him with time to cultivate a vision for his life, to make his purpose clear, and to give him confidence. All those things increased his level of magnetism.

It's More Than Mere Chemistry

Mutual attraction is more than chemistry. At least four elements combine to make it happen:

1. *Mutual Vision*

Followers do not naturally line up with a leader whose vision they don't respect. Both Elijah and Elisha possessed a vision to serve God for the sake of Israel. When Elisha had the opportunity to share Elijah's work, he turned away from his old life of farming and adopted Elijah's vision of leadership.

2. *Mutual Expectations*

Mutual expectations develop naturally from mutual vision. Both Elijah and Elisha expected to do great things for God. Elisha expected and received a double portion of the anointing on Elijah.

3. *Mutual Contribution*

Individuals follow leaders because they believe those leaders can take them where they want to go. Leaders enlist followers because they understand that followers help them to realize their vision. Each contributes something to fulfill the other's expectations. Elijah led and mentored Elisha, giving him the opportunity to learn how to be a godly leader. Elisha needed to humble himself, follow the older prophet, and learn. The arrangement made both of them better leaders.

4. *Mutual Commitment*

Without a strong mutual commitment, leaders and followers cannot achieve their mutual goals. As Elijah neared the end of his leadership, Elisha renewed his commitment to his mentor. Three times when Elijah offered to release his protégé, Elisha responded, "As the LORD lives, and as your soul lives, I will not leave you!" (2 Kin. 2:2, 4, 6). Elijah's commitment to Elisha had grown equally strong, culminating in his offer to do whatever he could for his servant—including the blessing of a double portion of his spirit.

Do You Like What You See?

What do you have to offer followers? Is the attraction mutual?

You will discover a lot about yourself by looking at the people your leadership has been attracting. What you observe may please you, but if you aren't getting the kind or the number of followers you'd like, there's good news. You need not be stuck where you are. You can grow and change in this area of your leadership.

¹⁰So he said, "You have asked a hard thing. *Nevertheless,* if you see me *when I am* taken from you, it shall be so for you; but if not, it shall not be *so.*" ¹¹Then it happened, as they continued on and talked, that suddenly a chariot of fire *appeared* with horses of fire, and separated the two of them; and Elijah went up by a whirlwind into heaven.

¹²And Elisha saw *it,* and he cried out, "My father, my father, the chariot of Israel and its horsemen!" So he saw him no more. And he took hold of his own clothes and tore them into two pieces. ¹³He also took up the mantle of Elijah that had fallen from him, and went back and stood by the bank of the Jordan. ¹⁴Then he took the mantle of Elijah that had fallen from him, and struck the water, and said, "Where *is* the LORD God of Elijah?" And when he also had struck the water, it was divided this way and that; and Elisha crossed over.

¹⁵Now when the sons of the prophets who *were* from Jericho saw him, they said, "The spirit of Elijah rests on Elisha." And they came to meet him, and bowed to the ground before him. ¹⁶Then they said to him, "Look now, there are fifty strong men with your servants. Please let them go and search for your master, lest perhaps the Spirit of the LORD has taken him up and cast him upon some mountain or into some valley."

And he said, "You shall not send anyone."

¹⁷But when they urged him till he was ashamed, he said, "Send *them!*" Therefore they sent fifty men, and they searched for three days but did not find him. ¹⁸And when they came back to him, for he had stayed in Jericho, he said to them, "Did I not say to you, 'Do not go'?"

Elisha Performs Miracles

¹⁹Then the men of the city said to Elisha, "Please notice, the situation of this city *is* pleasant, as my lord sees; but the water *is* bad, and the ground barren."

²⁰And he said, "Bring me a new bowl, and put salt in it." So they brought *it* to him. ²¹Then he went out to the source of the water, and cast in the salt there, and said, "Thus says the LORD: 'I have healed this water; from it there shall be no more death or barrenness.'" ²²So the water remains healed to this day, according to the word of Elisha which he spoke.

²³Then he went up from there to Bethel; and as he was going up the road, some youths came from the city and mocked him, and said to him, "Go up, you baldhead! Go up, you baldhead!"

²⁴So he turned around and looked at them, and pronounced a curse on them in the name of the LORD. And two female bears came out of the woods and mauled forty-two of the youths.

²⁵Then he went from there to Mount Carmel, and from there he returned to Samaria.

Moab Rebels Against Israel

3 Now Jehoram the son of Ahab became king over Israel at Samaria in the eighteenth year of Jehoshaphat king of Judah, and reigned twelve years. ²And he did evil in the sight of the LORD, but not like his father and mother; for he put away the *sacred* pillar of Baal that his father had made. ³Nevertheless he persisted in the sins of Jeroboam the son of Nebat, who had made Israel sin; he did not depart from them.

⁴Now Mesha king of Moab was a sheepbreeder, and he regularly paid the king of Israel one hundred thousand lambs and the wool of one hundred thousand rams. ⁵But it happened, when Ahab died, that the king of Moab rebelled against the king of Israel.

⁶So King Jehoram went out of Samaria at that time and mustered all Israel. ⁷Then he went and sent to Jehoshaphat king of Judah, saying, "The king of Moab has rebelled against me. Will you go with me to fight against Moab?"

And he said, "I will go up; I *am* as you *are,* my people as your people, my horses as your horses." ⁸Then he said, "Which way shall we go up?"

And he answered, "By way of the Wilderness of Edom."

⁹So the king of Israel went with the king of Judah and the king of Edom, and they marched on that roundabout route seven days; and there was no water for the army, nor for the animals that followed them. ¹⁰And the king of Israel said, "Alas! For the LORD has called these three kings together to deliver them into the hand of Moab."

¹¹But Jehoshaphat said, "*Is there* no prophet of the LORD here, that we may inquire of the LORD by him?"

So one of the servants of the king of Israel answered and said, "Elisha the son of Shaphat *is* here, who poured water on the hands of Elijah."

¹²And Jehoshaphat said, "The word of the LORD is with him." So the king of Israel and Jehoshaphat and the king of Edom went down to him.

¹³Then Elisha said to the king of Israel, "What have I to do with you? Go to the prophets of your father and the prophets of your mother."

But the king of Israel said to him, "No, for the LORD has called these three kings *together* to deliver them into the hand of Moab."

¹⁴And Elisha said, "*As* the LORD of hosts lives, before whom I stand, surely were it not that I regard the presence of Jehoshaphat king of Judah, I would not look at you, nor see you. ¹⁵But now bring me a musician."

Then it happened, when the musician played, that the hand of the LORD came upon him. ¹⁶And he said, "Thus says the LORD: 'Make this valley full of ditches.' ¹⁷For thus says the LORD: 'You shall not see wind, nor shall you see rain; yet that valley shall be filled with water, so that you, your cattle, and your animals may drink.' ¹⁸And this is a simple matter in the sight of the LORD; He will also deliver the Moabites into your hand. ¹⁹Also you shall attack every fortified city and every choice city, and shall cut down every good tree, and stop up every spring of water, and ruin every good piece of land with stones."

²⁰Now it happened in the morning, when the grain offering was offered, that suddenly water came by way of Edom, and the land was filled with water.

²¹And when all the Moabites heard that the kings had come up to fight against them, all who were able to bear arms and older were gathered; and they stood at the border. ²²Then they rose up early in the morning, and the sun was shining on the water; and the Moabites saw the water on the other side *as* red as blood. ²³And they said, "This is blood; the kings have surely struck swords and have killed one another; now therefore, Moab, to the spoil!"

²⁴So when they came to the camp of Israel, Israel rose up and attacked the Moabites, so that they fled before them; and they entered *their* land, killing the Moabites. ²⁵Then they destroyed the cities, and each man threw a stone on every good piece of land and filled it; and they stopped up all the springs of water and cut down all the good trees. But they left the stones of Kir Haraseth *intact*. However the slingers surrounded and attacked it.

²⁶And when the king of Moab saw that the battle was too fierce for him, he took with him seven hundred men who drew swords, to break through to the king of Edom, but they could not. ²⁷Then he took his eldest son who would have reigned in his place, and offered him *as* a burnt offering upon the wall; and there was great indignation against Israel. So they departed from him and returned to *their own* land.

Elisha and the Widow's Oil

4 A certain woman of the wives of the sons of the prophets cried out to Elisha, saying, "Your servant my husband is dead, and you know that your servant feared the LORD. And the creditor is coming to take my two sons to be his slaves."

The Law of Intuition: Good Leaders Think Strategically

(2 Kings 3:9–27)

The kings of Judah, Israel, and Edom ally themselves to fight Moab. But in the middle of the desert they make a horrifying discovery: They have run out of water! Panic strikes until they remember Elisha and his connection to the God of miracles.

Elisha responds differently to their request than they had imagined. He declares God will give them plenty of water—that was easy. But he also predicts God will give them Moab itself (2 Kin. 3:17, 18)!

The principle is this: These kings were diverted from their big-picture mission with a logistical matter. No doubt, water was important. But God reminded them that they had asked only for the small thing, not the ultimate thing.

Years ago, *Discipleship Journal* published an article on this very lesson. Our prayers as leaders must become strategic.

- **Logistical prayer:** We pray logistically when we ask God for the small things: "Lord, help the microphones to work today as I teach."
- **Tactical prayer:** We pray tactically when we pray for more meaningful things, but still not for the ultimate: "Lord, help me to say something meaningful today to my people."
- **Strategic prayer:** We pray strategically when we pray for the ultimate purposes of God: "Lord, may You be glorified today and may You raise up disciples from this meeting."

²So Elisha said to her, "What shall I do for you? Tell me, what do you have in the house?" And she said, "Your maidservant has nothing in the house but a jar of oil."

³Then he said, "Go, borrow vessels from everywhere, from all your neighbors—empty vessels; do not gather just a few. ⁴And when you have come in, you shall shut the door behind you and your sons; then pour it into all those vessels, and set aside the full ones."

⁵So she went from him and shut the door behind her and her sons, who brought *the vessels* to her; and she poured *it* out. ⁶Now it came to pass, when the vessels were full, that she said to her son, "Bring me another vessel."

And he said to her, "*There is* not another vessel." So the oil ceased. ⁷Then she came and told the man of God. And he said, "Go, sell the oil and pay your debt; and you *and* your sons live on the rest."

Elisha Raises the Shunammite's Son

⁸Now it happened one day that Elisha went to Shunem, where there *was* a notable woman, and she persuaded him to eat some food. So it was, as often as he passed by, he would turn in there to eat some food. ⁹And she said to her husband, "Look now, I know that this *is* a holy man of God, who passes by us regularly. ¹⁰Please, let us make a small upper room on the wall; and let us put a bed for him there, and a table and a chair and a lampstand; so it will be, whenever he comes to us, he can turn in there."

¹¹And it happened one day that he came there, and he turned in to the upper room and lay down there. ¹²Then he said to Gehazi his servant, "Call this Shunammite woman." When he had called her, she stood before him. ¹³And he said to him, "Say now to her, 'Look, you have been concerned for us with all this care. What *can I* do for you? Do you want me to speak on your behalf to the king or to the commander of the army?'"

She answered, "I dwell among my own people."

¹⁴So he said, "What then *is* to be done for her?"

And Gehazi answered, "Actually, she has no son, and her husband is old."

¹⁵So he said, "Call her." When he had called her, she stood in the doorway. ¹⁶Then he said, "About this time next year you shall embrace a son."

And she said, "No, my lord. Man of God, do not lie to your maidservant!"

¹⁷But the woman conceived, and bore a son when the appointed time had come, of which Elisha had told her.

¹⁸And the child grew. Now it happened one day that he went out to his father, to the reapers. ¹⁹And he said to his father, "My head, my head!"

So he said to a servant, "Carry him to his

Running on Empty

(2 Kings 4:1–7)

Did you know that emptiness can be a wonderful gift? That's the lesson a destitute woman learned from the prophet Elisha.

One day Elisha meets a woman with nothing—no husband, no income, no food, no prospects. The prophet tells her to gather what she has, and she returns with a jar of oil and several empty jars from neighbors. Elijah begins to pour her oil into the empty jars, and he just keeps on pouring until all the jars are full. Only then does the oil in the first jar run out. Interestingly, the woman gets as much oil as she has empty jars.

There is something about "nothing" that moves God's hand. He loves leading us to empty places where we can lean on nothing except His provision. If we are not experiencing God's presence and provision, could it be that we aren't empty enough? Could we still be distracted and dependent on ourselves? This story teaches us that . . .

1. Emptiness is a gift from the Lord.
2. Emptiness tells us we have a need.
3. It is possible that we may not be empty enough.
4. We must admit our emptiness.
5. Only God can truly fill us.

mother." ²⁰When he had taken him and brought him to his mother, he sat on her knees till noon, and *then* died. ²¹And she went up and laid him on the bed of the man of God, shut *the door* upon him, and went out. ²²Then she called to her husband, and said, "Please send me one of the young men and one of the donkeys, that I may run to the man of God and come back."

²³So he said, "Why are you going to him today? *It is* neither the New Moon nor the Sabbath."

And she said, "*It is* well." ²⁴Then she saddled a donkey, and said to her servant, "Drive, and go forward; do not slacken the pace for me unless I tell you." ²⁵And so she departed, and went to the man of God at Mount Carmel.

So it was, when the man of God saw her afar off, that he said to his servant Gehazi, "Look, the Shunammite woman! ²⁶Please run now to meet her, and say to her, '*Is it* well with you? *Is it* well with your husband? *Is it* well with the child?'"

And she answered, "*It is* well." ²⁷Now when she came to the man of God at the hill, she caught him by the feet, but Gehazi came near to push her away. But the man of God said, "Let her alone; for her soul *is* in deep distress, and the LORD has hidden *it* from me, and has not told me."

²⁸So she said, "Did I ask a son of my lord? Did I not say, 'Do not deceive me'?"

²⁹Then he said to Gehazi, "Get yourself ready, and take my staff in your hand, and be on your way. If you meet anyone, do not greet him; and if anyone greets you, do not answer him; but lay my staff on the face of the child."

³⁰And the mother of the child said, "*As the* LORD lives, and *as* your soul lives, I will not leave you." So he arose and followed her. ³¹Now Gehazi went on ahead of them, and laid the staff on the face of the child; but *there was* neither voice nor hearing. Therefore he went back to meet him, and told him, saying, "The child has not awakened."

³²When Elisha came into the house, there was the child, lying dead on his bed. ³³He went in therefore, shut the door behind the two of them, and prayed to the LORD. ³⁴And he went up and lay on the child, and put his mouth on his mouth, his eyes on his eyes, and his hands on his hands; and he stretched himself out on the child, and the flesh of the child became warm. ³⁵He returned and walked back and forth in the house, and again went up and stretched himself out on him; then the child sneezed seven times, and the child opened his eyes. ³⁶And he called Gehazi and said, "Call this Shunammite woman." So he called her. And when she came in to him, he

ELISHA

A PROPHET WITH HEART
(2 Kings 4:1–44)

PROFILE *IN LEADERSHIP*

His name sounds a lot like that of his mentor, Elijah. Both prophets struggled against the idolatrous Baal cult; both wielded great influence over the leaders of their day. But they differed markedly in how they carried out their spiritual duties.

The prophet Elisha relied more on miracles than did his fiery mentor, Elijah, and a greater number of his signs and wonders demonstrated God's mercy and gentleness. The Bible says Elisha performed twice as many miracles as Elijah and more wonders than any Old Testament character other than Moses.

But while these two men differed in their methods, they pursued the same objective: to turn their people from idolatry and bring them back to the true and living God.

In a way, the differences between Elijah and Elisha reflect the complex nature of the God they served. Elijah most often proclaimed God's judgment and wrath, while Elisha tended to declare His love and grace. Together they provide a human illustration of Romans 11:22, which urges us to "consider the goodness and severity of God."

The life of Elisha demonstrates that God uses leaders of all kinds, both those who emphasize His judgment and wrath and those who draw men and women to Himself through tender demonstrations of divine love and grace.

said, "Pick up your son." [37]So she went in, fell at his feet, and bowed to the ground; then she picked up her son and went out.

Elisha Purifies the Pot of Stew

[38]And Elisha returned to Gilgal, and *there was* a famine in the land. Now the sons of the prophets *were* sitting before him; and he said to his servant, "Put on the large pot, and boil stew for the sons of the prophets." [39]So one went out into the field to gather herbs, and found a wild vine, and gathered from it a lapful of wild gourds, and came and sliced *them* into the pot of stew, though they did not know *what they were.* [40]Then they served it to the men to eat. Now it happened, as they were eating the stew, that they cried out and said, "Man of God, *there is* death in the pot!" And they could not eat *it.*

[41]So he said, "Then bring some flour." And he put *it* into the pot, and said, "Serve *it* to the people, that they may eat." And there was nothing harmful in the pot.

Elisha Feeds One Hundred Men

[42]Then a man came from Baal Shalisha, and brought the man of God bread of the firstfruits, twenty loaves of barley bread, and newly ripened grain in his knapsack. And he said, "Give *it* to the people, that they may eat."

[43]But his servant said, "What? Shall I set this before one hundred men?"

He said again, "Give it to the people, that they may eat; for thus says the LORD: 'They shall eat and have *some* left over.'" [44]So he set *it* before them; and they ate and had *some* left over, according to the word of the LORD.

Naaman's Leprosy Healed

5 Now Naaman, commander of the army of the king of Syria, was a great and honorable man in the eyes of his master, because by him the LORD had given victory to Syria. He was also a mighty man of valor, *but* a leper. [2]And the Syrians had gone out on raids, and had brought back captive a young girl from the land

---

NAAMAN

A NEW LESSON LEARNED
(2 Kings 5:1–14)

PROFILE IN **LEADERSHIP**

Naaman, one of the great military leaders of his time, had earned the love and respect of his king. Yet for all his strength and might, Naaman suffered from the dreaded disease of leprosy. When his king learned of a Hebrew prophet named Elisha who might be able to help, he sent Naaman off with great expectations, perhaps anticipating a grand healing in the courts of a great man.

But rather than an impressive meeting with the prophet, Naaman received instructions (by messenger) to wash seven times in the Jordan River. This enraged Naaman and he angrily refused to follow the prescription. He wasn't teachable. He struggled with pride, faulty expectations, and inflexibility. Much like many leaders today . . .

1. He wanted a quick fix.
2. He expected special treatment.
3. He held certain assumptions about a solution.
4. He grew angry about perceived unfair treatment.
5. He rejected the new solution.

Yet as a strong leader, Naaman had surrounded himself with individuals who could speak up and disagree with him, and his inner circle provided good counsel. Naaman changed his mind, followed the prophet's directives, and was healed.

Leaders who remain teachable receive ongoing and sometimes unexpected blessings. But unteachable leaders will be left behind as our world changes and as God does new things in our culture.

of Israel. She waited on Naaman's wife. ³Then she said to her mistress, "If only my master *were* with the prophet who *is* in Samaria! For he would heal him of his leprosy." ⁴And *Naaman* went in and told his master, saying, "Thus and thus said the girl who *is* from the land of Israel."

⁵Then the king of Syria said, "Go now, and I will send a letter to the king of Israel."

So he departed and took with him ten talents of silver, six thousand *shekels* of gold, and ten changes of clothing. ⁶Then he brought the letter to the king of Israel, which said,

Now be advised, when this letter comes to you, that I have sent Naaman my servant to you, that you may heal him of his leprosy.

⁷And it happened, when the king of Israel read the letter, that he tore his clothes and said, "*Am I God*, to kill and make alive, that this man sends a man to me to heal him of his leprosy? Therefore please consider, and see how he seeks a quarrel with me."

⁸So it was, when Elisha the man of God heard that the king of Israel had torn his clothes, that he sent to the king, saying, "Why have you torn your clothes? Please let him come to me, and he shall know that there is a prophet in Israel."

⁹Then Naaman went with his horses and chariot, and he stood at the door of Elisha's house. ¹⁰And Elisha sent a messenger to him, saying, "Go and wash in the Jordan seven times, and your flesh shall be restored to you, and *you shall be clean.*" ¹¹But Naaman became furious, and went away and said, "Indeed, I said to myself, 'He will surely come out *to me*, and stand and call on the name of the LORD his God, and wave his hand over the place, and heal the leprosy.' ¹²*Are* not the Abanah[a] and the Pharpar, the rivers of Damascus, better than all the waters of Israel? Could I not wash in them and be clean?" So he turned and went away in a rage. ¹³And his servants came near and spoke to him, and said, "My father, *if* the prophet had told you *to do* something great, would you not have done *it?* How much more then, when he says to you, 'Wash, and be clean'?" ¹⁴So he went down and dipped seven times in the Jordan, according to the saying of the man of God; and his flesh was restored like the flesh of a little child, and he was clean.

¹⁵And he returned to the man of God, he and all his aides, and came and stood before him; and he said, "Indeed, now I know that *there is* no God in all the earth, except in Israel; now therefore, please take a gift from your servant."

Accountability: Gehazi Got Some from Elisha
(2 Kings 5:15–27)

Elisha turned down the money and gifts Naaman offered him, but Elisha's servant, Gehazi, went after them by rationalizing his greed. Like Gehazi, we possess a boundless ability to deceive ourselves. That is why leaders need others to ask them difficult questions. We must welcome accountability partners.

¹⁶But he said, "*As* the LORD lives, before whom I stand, I will receive nothing." And he urged him to take *it,* but he refused.

¹⁷So Naaman said, "Then, if not, please let your servant be given two mule-loads of earth; for your servant will no longer offer either burnt offering or sacrifice to other gods, but to the LORD. ¹⁸Yet in this thing may the LORD pardon your servant: when my master goes into the temple of Rimmon to worship there, and he leans on my hand, and I bow down in the temple of Rimmon—when I bow down in the temple of Rimmon, may the LORD please pardon your servant in this thing."

¹⁹Then he said to him, "Go in peace." So he departed from him a short distance.

Gehazi's Greed

²⁰But Gehazi, the servant of Elisha the man of God, said, "Look, my master has spared Naaman this Syrian, while not receiving from his hands what he brought; but *as* the LORD lives, I will run after him and take something from him." ²¹So Gehazi pursued Naaman. When Naaman saw *him* running after him, he got down from the chariot to meet him, and said, "*Is* all well?"

²²And he said, "All *is* well. My master has sent me, saying, 'Indeed, just now two young men of the sons of the prophets have come to me from the mountains of Ephraim. Please give them a talent of silver and two changes of garments.'"

²³So Naaman said, "Please, take two talents." And he urged him, and bound two talents of silver in two bags, with two changes of garments, and handed *them* to two of his servants; and they

---

5:12 [a]Following Kethib, Septuagint, and Vulgate; Qere, Syriac, and Targum read *Amanah.*

carried *them* on ahead of him. ²⁴When he came to the citadel, he took *them* from their hand, and stored *them* away in the house; then he let the men go, and they departed. ²⁵Now he went in and stood before his master. Elisha said to him, "Where *did you go*, Gehazi?"

And he said, "Your servant did not go anywhere."

²⁶Then he said to him, "Did not my heart go *with you* when the man turned back from his chariot to meet you? *Is it* time to receive money and to receive clothing, olive groves and vineyards, sheep and oxen, male and female servants? ²⁷Therefore the leprosy of Naaman shall cling to you and your descendants forever." And he went out from his presence leprous, *as white* as snow.

The Floating Ax Head

6 And the sons of the prophets said to Elisha, "See now, the place where we dwell with you is too small for us. ²Please, let us go to the Jordan, and let every man take a beam from there, and let us make there a place where we may dwell."

So he answered, "Go."

³Then one said, "Please consent to go with your servants."

And he answered, "I will go." ⁴So he went with them. And when they came to the Jordan, they cut down trees. ⁵But as one was cutting down a tree, the iron *ax head* fell into the water; and he cried out and said, "Alas, master! For it was borrowed."

⁶So the man of God said, "Where did it fall?" And he showed him the place. So he cut off a stick, and threw *it* in there; and he made the iron float. ⁷Therefore he said, "Pick *it* up for yourself." So he reached out his hand and took it.

The Blinded Syrians Captured

⁸Now the king of Syria was making war against Israel; and he consulted with his servants, saying, "My camp *will be* in such and such a place." ⁹And the man of God sent to the king of Israel, saying, "Beware that you do not pass this place, for the Syrians are coming down there." ¹⁰Then the king of Israel sent *someone* to the place of which the man of God had told him. Thus he warned him, and he was watchful there, not just once or twice.

¹¹Therefore the heart of the king of Syria was greatly troubled by this thing; and he called his servants and said to them, "Will you not show me which of us *is* for the king of Israel?"

¹²And one of his servants said, "None, my lord, O king; but Elisha, the prophet who *is* in Is-

---

Vision: Elisha Helps Others to See His Divine Perspective

(2 Kings 6:8–17)

How can a leader help an associate catch his vision? The story of Elisha and his servant gives us some clues.

The king of Aram had pursued Elisha into Dothan, surrounding him with an army large enough to frighten the servant. Elisha simply prayed that God would show the servant the true situation. Elisha's example reminds us of some important truths about perspective:

1. Elisha felt unmoved by the physical realm and its opposition.
2. Elisha showed poise and calmly assured his servant he had nothing to fear.
3. Elisha communicated a vision invisible to others.
4. Elisha prayed that his servant would be able to see what he saw.

Perspective separates leaders and followers more than any other characteristic. Leaders see *before* followers do; they see *beyond* what followers do; and they see *bigger* than followers do.

---

rael, tells the king of Israel the words that you speak in your bedroom."

¹³So he said, "Go and see where he *is*, that I may send and get him."

And it was told him, saying, "Surely *he is* in Dothan."

¹⁴Therefore he sent horses and chariots and a great army there, and they came by night and surrounded the city. ¹⁵And when the servant of the man of God arose early and went out, there was an army, surrounding the city with horses and chariots. And his servant said to him, "Alas, my master! What shall we do?"

¹⁶So he answered, "Do not fear, for those who *are* with us *are* more than those who *are* with them." ¹⁷And Elisha prayed, and said, "LORD, I pray, open his eyes that he may see." Then the LORD opened the eyes of the young man, and he saw. And behold, the mountain *was* full of horses and chariots of fire all around Elisha. ¹⁸So when *the Syrians* came down to him, Elisha prayed to the LORD, and said, "Strike this people, I pray,

with blindness." And He struck them with blindness according to the word of Elisha.

[19]Now Elisha said to them, "This *is* not the way, nor *is* this the city. Follow me, and I will bring you to the man whom you seek." But he led them to Samaria.

[20]So it was, when they had come to Samaria, that Elisha said, "LORD, open the eyes of these *men,* that they may see." And the LORD opened their eyes, and they saw; and there *they were,* inside Samaria!

[21]Now when the king of Israel saw them, he said to Elisha, "My father, shall I kill *them?* Shall I kill *them?*"

[22]But he answered, "You shall not kill *them.* Would you kill those whom you have taken captive with your sword and your bow? Set food and water before them, that they may eat and drink and go to their master." [23]Then he prepared a great feast for them; and after they ate and drank, he sent them away and they went to their master. So the bands of Syrian *raiders* came no more into the land of Israel.

Syria Besieges Samaria in Famine

[24]And it happened after this that Ben-Hadad king of Syria gathered all his army, and went up and besieged Samaria. [25]And there was a great famine in Samaria; and indeed they besieged it until a donkey's head was *sold* for eighty *shekels* of silver, and one-fourth of a kab of dove droppings for five *shekels* of silver.

[26]Then, as the king of Israel was passing by on the wall, a woman cried out to him, saying, "Help, my lord, O king!"

[27]And he said, "If the LORD does not help you, where can I find help for you? From the threshing floor or from the winepress?" [28]Then the king said to her, "What is troubling you?"

And she answered, "This woman said to me, 'Give your son, that we may eat him today, and we will eat my son tomorrow.' [29]So we boiled my son, and ate him. And I said to her on the next day, 'Give your son, that we may eat him'; but she has hidden her son."

[30]Now it happened, when the king heard the words of the woman, that he tore his clothes; and as he passed by on the wall, the people looked, and there underneath *he had* sackcloth on his body. [31]Then he said, "God do so to me and more also, if the head of Elisha the son of Shaphat remains on him today!"

[32]But Elisha was sitting in his house, and the elders were sitting with him. And *the king* sent a man ahead of him, but before the messenger came to him, he said to the elders, "Do you see how this son of a murderer has sent someone to take away my head? Look, when the messenger comes, shut the door, and hold him fast at the door. *Is* not the sound of his master's feet behind him?" [33]And while he was still talking with them, there was the messenger, coming down to him; and then *the king* said, "Surely this calamity *is* from the LORD; why should I wait for the LORD any longer?"

7 Then Elisha said, "Hear the word of the LORD. Thus says the LORD: 'Tomorrow about this time a seah of fine flour *shall be sold* for a shekel, and two seahs of barley for a shekel, at the gate of Samaria.'"

[2]So an officer on whose hand the king leaned answered the man of God and said, "Look, *if* the LORD would make windows in heaven, could this thing be?"

And he said, "In fact, you shall see *it* with your eyes, but you shall not eat of it."

The Syrians Flee

[3]Now there were four leprous men at the entrance of the gate; and they said to one another, "Why are we sitting here until we die? [4]If we say, 'We will enter the city,' the famine *is* in the city, and we shall die there. And if we sit here, we die also. Now therefore, come, let us surrender to the army of the Syrians. If they keep us alive, we shall live; and if they kill us, we shall only die." [5]And they rose at twilight to go to the camp of the Syrians; and when they had come to the outskirts of the Syrian camp, to their surprise no one *was* there. [6]For the LORD had caused the army of the Syrians to hear the noise of chariots and the noise of horses—the noise of a great army; so they said to one another, "Look, the king of Israel has hired against us the kings of the Hittites and the kings of the Egyptians to attack us!" [7]Therefore they arose and fled at twilight, and left the camp intact—their tents, their horses, and their donkeys—and they fled for their lives. [8]And when these lepers came to the outskirts of the camp, they went into one tent and ate and drank, and carried from it silver and gold and clothing, and went and hid *them;* then they came back and entered another tent, and carried *some* from there *also,* and went and hid *it.*

[9]Then they said to one another, "We are not doing right. This day *is* a day of good news, and we remain silent. If we wait until morning light, some punishment will come upon us. Now therefore, come, let us go and tell the king's household." [10]So they went and called to the gatekeepers of the city, and told them, saying, "We went to the Syrian camp, and surprisingly

no one *was* there, not a human sound—only horses and donkeys tied, and the tents intact." ¹¹And the gatekeepers called out, and they told *it* to the king's household inside.

¹²So the king arose in the night and said to his servants, "Let me now tell you what the Syrians have done to us. They know that we *are* hungry; therefore they have gone out of the camp to hide themselves in the field, saying, 'When they come out of the city, we shall catch them alive, and get into the city.'"

¹³And one of his servants answered and said, "Please, let several *men* take five of the remaining horses which are left in the city. Look, they *may either become* like all the multitude of Israel that are left in it; or indeed, *I say,* they *may become* like all the multitude of Israel left from those who are consumed; so let us send them and see." ¹⁴Therefore they took two chariots with horses; and the king sent them in the direction of the Syrian army, saying, "Go and see." ¹⁵And they went after them to the Jordan; and indeed all the road *was* full of garments and weapons which the Syrians had thrown away in their haste. So the messengers returned and told the king. ¹⁶Then the people went out and plundered the tents of the Syrians. So a seah of fine flour was *sold* for a shekel, and two seahs of barley for a shekel, according to the word of the LORD.

¹⁷Now the king had appointed the officer on whose hand he leaned to have charge of the gate. But the people trampled him in the gate, and he died, just as the man of God had said, who spoke when the king came down to him. ¹⁸So it happened just as the man of God had spoken to the king, saying, "Two seahs of barley for a shekel, and a seah of fine flour for a shekel, shall be *sold* tomorrow about this time in the gate of Samaria."

¹⁹Then that officer had answered the man of God, and said, "Now look, *if* the LORD would make windows in heaven, could such a thing be?"

And he had said, "In fact, you shall see *it* with your eyes, but you shall not eat of it." ²⁰And so it happened to him, for the people trampled him in the gate, and he died.

The King Restores the Shunammite's Land

8 Then Elisha spoke to the woman whose son he had restored to life, saying, "Arise and go, you and your household, and stay wherever you can; for the LORD has called for a famine, and furthermore, it will come upon the land for seven years." ²So the woman arose and did according to the saying of the man of God, and she went with her household and dwelt in the land of the Philistines seven years.

³It came to pass, at the end of seven years, that the woman returned from the land of the Philistines; and she went to make an appeal to the king for her house and for her land. ⁴Then the king talked with Gehazi, the servant of the man of God, saying, "Tell me, please, all the great things Elisha has done." ⁵Now it happened, as he was telling the king how he had restored the dead to life, that there was the woman whose son he had restored to life, appealing to the king for her house and for her land. And Gehazi said, "My lord, O king, this *is* the woman, and this *is* her son whom Elisha restored to life." ⁶And when the king asked the woman, she told him.

So the king appointed a certain officer for her, saying, "Restore all that *was* hers, and all the proceeds of the field from the day that she left the land until now."

Death of Ben-Hadad

⁷Then Elisha went to Damascus, and Ben-Hadad king of Syria was sick; and it was told him, saying, "The man of God has come here." ⁸And the king said to Hazael, "Take a present in your hand, and go to meet the man of God, and inquire of the LORD by him, saying, 'Shall I recover from this disease?' " ⁹So Hazael went to meet him and took a present with him, of every good thing of Damascus, forty camel-loads; and he came and stood before him, and said, "Your son Ben-Hadad king of Syria has sent me to you, saying, 'Shall I recover from this disease?' "

¹⁰And Elisha said to him, "Go, say to him,

The Law of Solid Ground: Hazael Breaks It and Pays

(2 Kings 8:7–15)

Hazael began his leadership by breaking trust with his leader, yet he never thought about the consequences of his example. How could he expect anything different from his people? Leaders who break the Law of Solid Ground may expect a haunting ripple effect.

'You shall certainly recover.' However the LORD has shown me that he will really die." [11]Then he set his countenance in a stare until he was ashamed; and the man of God wept. [12]And Hazael said, "Why is my lord weeping?"

He answered, "Because I know the evil that you will do to the children of Israel: Their strongholds you will set on fire, and their young men you will kill with the sword; and you will dash their children, and rip open their women with child."

[13]So Hazael said, "But what is your servant—a dog, that he should do this gross thing?"

And Elisha answered, "The LORD has shown me that you will become king over Syria."

[14]Then he departed from Elisha, and came to his master, who said to him, "What did Elisha say to you?" And he answered, "He told me you would surely recover." [15]But it happened on the next day that he took a thick cloth and dipped it in water, and spread it over his face so that he died; and Hazael reigned in his place.

Jehoram Reigns in Judah

[16]Now in the fifth year of Joram the son of Ahab, king of Israel, Jehoshaphat having been king of Judah, Jehoram the son of Jehoshaphat began to reign as king of Judah. [17]He was thirty-two years old when he became king, and he reigned eight years in Jerusalem. [18]And he walked in the way of the kings of Israel, just as the house of Ahab had done, for the daughter of Ahab was his wife; and he did evil in the sight of the LORD. [19]Yet the LORD would not destroy Judah, for the sake of His servant David, as He promised him to give a lamp to him and his sons forever.

[20]In his days Edom revolted against Judah's authority, and made a king over themselves. [21]So Joram[a] went to Zair, and all his chariots with him. Then he rose by night and attacked the Edomites who had surrounded him and the captains of the chariots; and the troops fled to their tents. [22]Thus Edom has been in revolt against Judah's authority to this day. And Libnah revolted at that time.

[23]Now the rest of the acts of Joram, and all that he did, are they not written in the book of the chronicles of the kings of Judah? [24]So Joram rested with his fathers, and was buried with his fathers in the City of David. Then Ahaziah his son reigned in his place.

Ahaziah Reigns in Judah

[25]In the twelfth year of Joram the son of Ahab, king of Israel, Ahaziah the son of Jehoram, king of Judah, began to reign. [26]Ahaziah was twenty-two years old when he became king, and he reigned one year in Jerusalem. His mother's name was Athaliah the granddaughter of Omri, king of Israel. [27]And he walked in the way of the house of Ahab, and did evil in the sight of the LORD, like the house of Ahab, for he was the son-in-law of the house of Ahab.

[28]Now he went with Joram the son of Ahab to war against Hazael king of Syria at Ramoth Gilead; and the Syrians wounded Joram. [29]Then King Joram went back to Jezreel to recover from the wounds which the Syrians had inflicted on him at Ramah, when he fought against Hazael king of Syria. And Ahaziah the son of Jehoram, king of Judah, went down to see Joram the son of Ahab in Jezreel, because he was sick.

Jehu Anointed King of Israel

9 And Elisha the prophet called one of the sons of the prophets, and said to him, "Get yourself ready, take this flask of oil in your hand, and go to Ramoth Gilead. [2]Now when you arrive at that place, look there for Jehu the son of Jehoshaphat, the son of Nimshi, and go in and make him rise up from among his associates, and take him to an inner room. [3]Then take the flask of oil, and pour it on his head, and say, 'Thus says the LORD: "I have anointed you king over Israel."' Then open the door and flee, and do not delay."

[4]So the young man, the servant of the prophet, went to Ramoth Gilead. [5]And when he arrived, there were the captains of the army sitting; and he said, "I have a message for you, Commander."

Jehu said, "For which one of us?"

And he said, "For you, Commander." [6]Then he arose and went into the house. And he poured the oil on his head, and said to him, "Thus says the LORD God of Israel: 'I have anointed you king over the people of the LORD, over Israel. [7]You shall strike down the house of Ahab your master, that I may avenge the blood of My servants the prophets, and the blood of all the servants of the LORD, at the hand of Jezebel. [8]For the whole house of Ahab shall perish; and I will cut off from Ahab all the males in Israel, both bond and free. [9]So I will make the house of Ahab like the house of Jeroboam the son of Nebat, and like the house of Baasha the son of Ahijah. [10]The dogs shall eat Jezebel on the plot of ground at Jezreel, and there shall be none to bury her.'" And he opened the door and fled.

[11]Then Jehu came out to the servants of his

8:21 [a]Spelled Jehoram in verse 16

master, and *one* said to him, "*Is* all well? Why did this madman come to you?"

And he said to them, "You know the man and his babble."

¹²And they said, "A lie! Tell us now."

So he said, "Thus and thus he spoke to me, saying, 'Thus says the LORD: "I have anointed you king over Israel."'"

¹³Then each man hastened to take his garment and put *it* under him on the top of the steps; and they blew trumpets, saying, "Jehu is king!"

Joram of Israel Killed

¹⁴So Jehu the son of Jehoshaphat, the son of Nimshi, conspired against Joram. (Now Joram had been defending Ramoth Gilead, he and all Israel, against Hazael king of Syria. ¹⁵But King Joram had returned to Jezreel to recover from the wounds which the Syrians had inflicted on him when he fought with Hazael king of Syria.) And Jehu said, "If you are so minded, let no one leave *or* escape from the city to go and tell *it* in Jezreel." ¹⁶So Jehu rode in a chariot and went to Jezreel, for Joram was laid up there; and Ahaziah king of Judah had come down to see Joram.

¹⁷Now a watchman stood on the tower in Jezreel, and he saw the company of Jehu as he came, and said, "I see a company of men."

And Joram said, "Get a horseman and send him to meet them, and let him say, '*Is it* peace?'"

¹⁸So the horseman went to meet him, and said, "Thus says the king: '*Is it* peace?'"

And Jehu said, "What have you to do with peace? Turn around and follow me."

So the watchman reported, saying, "The messenger went to them, but is not coming back."

¹⁹Then he sent out a second horseman who came to them, and said, "Thus says the king: '*Is it* peace?'"

And Jehu answered, "What have you to do with peace? Turn around and follow me."

²⁰So the watchman reported, saying, "He went up to them and is not coming back; and the driving *is* like the driving of Jehu the son of Nimshi, for he drives furiously!"

²¹Then Joram said, "Make ready." And his chariot was made ready. Then Joram king of Israel and Ahaziah king of Judah went out, each in his chariot; and they went out to meet Jehu, and met him on the property of Naboth the Jezreelite. ²²Now it happened, when Joram saw Jehu, that he said, "*Is it* peace, Jehu?"

So he answered, "What peace, as long as the harlotries of your mother Jezebel and her witch-craft *are so* many?"

²³Then Joram turned around and fled, and said to Ahaziah, "Treachery, Ahaziah!" ²⁴Now Jehu drew his bow with full strength and shot Jehoram between his arms; and the arrow came out at his heart, and he sank down in his chariot. ²⁵Then *Jehu* said to Bidkar his captain, "Pick *him* up, *and* throw him into the tract of the field of Naboth the Jezreelite; for remember, when you and I were riding together behind Ahab his father, that the LORD laid this burden upon him: ²⁶Surely I saw yesterday the blood of Naboth and the blood of his sons,' says the LORD, 'and I will repay you in this plot,' says the LORD. Now therefore, take *and* throw him on the plot *of ground,* according to the word of the LORD."

Ahaziah of Judah Killed

²⁷But when Ahaziah king of Judah saw *this,* he fled by the road to Beth Haggan.ᵃ So Jehu pursued him, and said, "Shoot him also in the chariot." *And they shot him* at the Ascent of Gur, which is by Ibleam. Then he fled to Megiddo, and died there. ²⁸And his servants carried him in the chariot to Jerusalem, and buried him in his tomb with his fathers in the City of David. ²⁹In the eleventh year of Joram the son of Ahab, Ahaziah had become king over Judah.

Jezebel's Violent Death

³⁰Now when Jehu had come to Jezreel, Jezebel heard *of it;* and she put paint on her eyes and adorned her head, and looked through a window. ³¹Then, as Jehu entered at the gate, she said, "*Is it* peace, Zimri, murderer of your master?"

³²And he looked up at the window, and said, "Who *is* on my side? Who?" So two *or* three eunuchs looked out at him. ³³Then he said, "Throw her down." So they threw her down, and *some* of her blood spattered on the wall and on the horses; and he trampled her underfoot. ³⁴And when he had gone in, he ate and drank. Then he said, "Go now, see to this accursed *woman,* and bury her, for she was a king's daughter." ³⁵So they went to bury her, but they found no more of her than the skull and the feet and the palms of *her* hands. ³⁶Therefore they came back and told him. And he said, "This *is* the word of the LORD, which He spoke by His servant Elijah the Tishbite, saying, 'On the plot *of ground* at Jezreel dogs shall eat the flesh of Jezebel;ᵃ ³⁷and the corpse of Jezebel shall be as refuse on the surface of the field, in the plot at Jezreel, so that they shall not say, "Here *lies* Jezebel."'"

9:27 ᵃLiterally *The Garden House* **9:36** ᵃ1 Kings 21:23

Ahab's Seventy Sons Killed

10 Now Ahab had seventy sons in Samaria. And Jehu wrote and sent letters to Samaria, to the rulers of Jezreel,[a] to the elders, and to those who reared Ahab's *sons,* saying:

2 Now as soon as this letter comes to you, since your master's sons *are* with you, and you have chariots and horses, a fortified city also, and weapons, 3choose the best qualified of your master's sons, set *him* on his father's throne, and fight for your master's house.

4But they were exceedingly afraid, and said, "Look, two kings could not stand up to him; how then can we stand?" 5And he who *was* in charge of the house, and he who *was* in charge of the city, the elders also, and those who reared *the sons,* sent to Jehu, saying, "We *are* your servants, we will do all you tell us; but we will not make anyone king. Do *what is* good in your sight." 6Then he wrote a second letter to them, saying:

If you *are* for me and will obey my voice, take the heads of the men, your master's sons, and come to me at Jezreel by this time tomorrow.

Now the king's sons, seventy persons, *were* with the great men of the city, *who* were rearing them. 7So it was, when the letter came to them, that they took the king's sons and slaughtered seventy persons, put their heads in baskets and sent *them* to him at Jezreel.

8Then a messenger came and told him, saying, "They have brought the heads of the king's sons."

And he said, "Lay them in two heaps at the entrance of the gate until morning."

9So it was, in the morning, that he went out and stood, and said to all the people, "You *are* righteous. Indeed I conspired against my master and killed him; but who killed all these? 10Know now that nothing shall fall to the earth of the word of the LORD which the LORD spoke concerning the house of Ahab; for the LORD has done what He spoke by His servant Elijah." 11So Jehu killed all who remained of the house of Ahab in Jezreel, and all his great men and his close acquaintances and his priests, until he left him none remaining.

10:1 [a]Following Masoretic Text, Syriac, and Targum; Septuagint reads *Samaria;* Vulgate reads *city.*

JEHU   COMPROMISE LEADS TO IDOLATRY
(2 Kings 10:1–36)

PROFILE IN LEADERSHIP

Call him a man with a mission. Jehu not only accepted a charge from God to lead Israel as king, he also embraced divine instructions to destroy the house of Ahab and the worship of Baal. God told him not to spare anyone from Ahab's family and to eliminate all traces of Baal worship in Israel.

Jehu led brilliantly in fulfilling God's commands. He rid the nation of the family of Ahab and of the worshipers of Baal. He even laid waste to Baal's temple and everything in it. The Bible tells us that God commended Jehu for carrying out his mission, even promising him great blessing because of his obedience (2 Kin. 10:30).

But a problem eventually arose. While Jehu obeyed God to the last detail concerning the destruction of Ahab and the worship of Baal, he compromised his devotion to God by leaving intact some idols from Israel's past. Even after such great success, "Jehu took no heed to walk in the law of the LORD God of Israel with all his heart" (10:31). In time, idols of a different kind corrupted his heart.

Jehu accomplished great things for the Lord and the kingdom of Israel, but his compromise led to another vile form of idolatry. In the end, his disobedience overshadowed his accomplishments as a leader.

Ahaziah's Forty-two Brothers Killed

[12]And he arose and departed and went to Samaria. On the way, at Beth Eked[a] of the Shepherds, [13]Jehu met with the brothers of Ahaziah king of Judah, and said, "Who *are* you?"

So they answered, "We *are* the brothers of Ahaziah; we have come down to greet the sons of the king and the sons of the queen mother."

[14]And he said, "Take them alive!" So they took them alive, and killed them at the well of Beth Eked, forty-two men; and he left none of them.

The Rest of Ahab's Family Killed

[15]Now when he departed from there, he met Jehonadab the son of Rechab, *coming* to meet him; and he greeted him and said to him, "Is your heart right, as my heart *is* toward your heart?"

And Jehonadab answered, "It is."

Jehu said, "If it is, give *me* your hand." So he gave *him* his hand, and he took him up to him into the chariot. [16]Then he said, "Come with me, and see my zeal for the LORD." So they had him ride in his chariot. [17]And when he came to Samaria, he killed all who remained to Ahab in Samaria, till he had destroyed them, according to the word of the LORD which He spoke to Elijah.

Worshipers of Baal Killed

[18]Then Jehu gathered all the people together, and said to them, "Ahab served Baal a little, Jehu will serve him much. [19]Now therefore, call to me all the prophets of Baal, all his servants, and all his priests. Let no one be missing, for I have a great sacrifice for Baal. Whoever is missing shall not live." But Jehu acted deceptively, with the intent of destroying the worshipers of Baal. [20]And Jehu said, "Proclaim a solemn assembly for Baal." So they proclaimed *it*. [21]Then Jehu sent throughout all Israel; and all the worshipers of Baal came, so that there was not a man left who did not come. So they came into the temple[a] of Baal, and the temple of Baal was full from one end to the other. [22]And he said to the one in charge of the wardrobe, "Bring out vestments for all the worshipers of Baal." So he brought out vestments for them. [23]Then Jehu and Jehonadab the son of Rechab went into the temple of Baal, and said to the worshipers of Baal, "Search and see that no servants of the LORD are here with you, but only the worshipers of Baal." [24]So they went in to offer sacrifices and burnt offerings. Now Jehu had appointed for himself eighty men on the outside, and had said, "*If* any of the men whom I have brought into your hands escapes, *whoever lets him escape, it shall be* his life for the life of the other."

[25]Now it happened, as soon as he had made an end of offering the burnt offering, that Jehu said to the guard and to the captains, "Go in *and* kill them; let no one come out!" And they killed them with the edge of the sword; then the guards and the officers threw *them* out, and went into the inner room of the temple of Baal. [26]And they brought the *sacred* pillars out of the temple of Baal and burned them. [27]Then they broke down the *sacred* pillar of Baal, and tore down the temple of Baal and made it a refuse dump to this day. [28]Thus Jehu destroyed Baal from Israel.

[29]However Jehu did not turn away from the sins of Jeroboam the son of Nebat, who had made Israel sin, *that is,* from the golden calves that *were* at Bethel and Dan. [30]And the LORD said to Jehu, "Because you have done well in doing *what is* right in My sight, *and* have done to the house of Ahab all that *was* in My heart, your sons shall sit on the throne of Israel to the fourth *generation.*" [31]But Jehu took no heed to walk in the law of the LORD God of Israel with all his heart; for he did not depart from the sins of Jeroboam, who had made Israel sin.

Death of Jehu

[32]In those days the LORD began to cut off *parts* of Israel; and Hazael conquered them in all the territory of Israel [33]from the Jordan eastward: all the land of Gilead—Gad, Reuben, and Manasseh—from Aroer, which *is* by the River Arnon, including Gilead and Bashan.

[34]Now the rest of the acts of Jehu, all that he did, and all his might, *are* they not written in the book of the chronicles of the kings of Israel? [35]So Jehu rested with his fathers, and they buried him in Samaria. Then Jehoahaz his son reigned in his place. [36]And the period that Jehu reigned over Israel in Samaria *was* twenty-eight years.

Athaliah Reigns in Judah

11 When Athaliah the mother of Ahaziah saw that her son was dead, she arose and destroyed all the royal heirs. [2]But Jehosheba, the daughter of King Joram, sister of Ahaziah, took Joash the son of Ahaziah, and stole him away from among the king's sons *who were* being murdered; and they hid him and his nurse in the bedroom, from Athaliah, so that he was not killed. [3]So he was

---

10:12 [a]Or *The Shearing House* **10:21** [a]Literally *house,* and so elsewhere in this chapter hidden with her in the house of the LORD for six years, while Athaliah reigned over the land.

Joash Crowned King of Judah

[4] In the seventh year Jehoiada sent and brought the captains of hundreds—of the bodyguards and the escorts—and brought them into the house of the LORD to him. And he made a covenant with them and took an oath from them in the house of the LORD, and showed them the king's son. [5] Then he commanded them, saying, "This *is* what you shall do: One-third of you who come on duty on the Sabbath shall be keeping watch over the king's house, [6] one-third *shall be* at the gate of Sur, and one-third at the gate behind the escorts. You shall keep the watch of the house, lest it be broken down. [7] The two contingents of you who go off duty on the Sabbath shall keep the watch of the house of the LORD for the king. [8] But you shall surround the king on all sides, every man with his weapons in his hand; and whoever comes within range, let him be put to death. You are to be with the king as he goes out and as he comes in."

[9] So the captains of the hundreds did according to all that Jehoiada the priest commanded. Each of them took his men who were to be on duty on the Sabbath, with those who were going off duty on the Sabbath, and came to Jehoiada the priest. [10] And the priest gave the captains of hundreds the spears and shields which *had belonged* to King David, that were in the temple of the LORD. [11] Then the escorts stood, every man with his weapons in his hand, all around the king, from the right side of the temple to the left side of the temple, by the altar and the house. [12] And he brought out the king's son, put the crown on him, and *gave him* the Testimony;[a] they made him king and anointed him, and they clapped their hands and said, "Long live the king!"

Death of Athaliah

[13] Now when Athaliah heard the noise of the escorts *and* the people, she came to the people *in* the temple of the LORD. [14] When she looked, there was the king standing by a pillar according to custom; and the leaders and the trumpeters were by the king. All the people of the land were rejoicing and blowing trumpets. So Athaliah tore her clothes and cried out, "Treason! Treason!"

[15] And Jehoiada the priest commanded the captains of the hundreds, the officers of the army, and said to them, "Take her outside under guard, and slay with the sword whoever follows her." For the priest had said, "Do not let her be killed in the house of the LORD." [16] So they seized her; and she went by way of the horses' entrance *into* the king's house, and there she was killed.

[17] Then Jehoiada made a covenant between the LORD, the king, and the people, that they should be the LORD's people, and *also* between the king and the people. [18] And all the people of the land went to the temple of Baal, and tore it down. They thoroughly broke in pieces its altars and images, and killed Mattan the priest of Baal before the altars. And the priest appointed officers over the house of the LORD. [19] Then he took the captains of hundreds, the bodyguards, the escorts, and all the people of the land; and they brought the king down from the house of the LORD, and went by way of the gate of the escorts to the king's house. Then he sat on the throne of the kings. [20] So all the people of the land rejoiced; and the city was quiet, for they had slain Athaliah with the sword *in* the king's house. [21] Jehoash *was* seven years old when he became king.

Jehoash Repairs the Temple

12 In the seventh year of Jehu, Jehoash[a] became king, and he reigned forty years in Jerusalem. His mother's name *was* Zibiah of Beersheba. [2] Jehoash did *what was* right in the sight of the LORD all the days in which Jehoiada the priest instructed him. [3] But the high places were not taken away; the people still sacrificed and burned incense on the high places.

[4] And Jehoash said to the priests, "All the money of the dedicated gifts that are brought into the house of the LORD—each man's census money, each man's assessment money[a]—*and* all the money that a man purposes in his heart to bring into the house of the LORD, [5] let the priests take *it* themselves, each from his constituency; and let them repair the damages of the temple, wherever any dilapidation is found."

[6] Now it was so, by the twenty-third year of King Jehoash, *that* the priests had not repaired the damages of the temple. [7] So King Jehoash called Jehoiada the priest and the *other* priests, and said to them, "Why have you not repaired the damages of the temple? Now therefore, do not take *more* money from your constituency, but deliver it for repairing the damages of the temple." [8] And the priests agreed that they would neither receive *more* money from the people, nor repair the damages of the temple.

11:12 [a]That is, the Law (compare Exodus 25:16, 21 and Deuteronomy 31:9) **12:1** [a]Spelled *Joash* in 11:2ff **12:4** [a]Compare Leviticus 27:2ff

The Law of Navigation: Jehoash Charts the Course to Repair the Temple

(2 Kings 12:4–16)

Jehoash well navigated the temple repairs, even though he had to fire the priests who oversaw the initial fund-raising efforts. Jehoash efficiently collected the money, cast the vision, and held the people accountable until the job was finished. Good leaders understand how to get the job done.

[9]Then Jehoiada the priest took a chest, bored a hole in its lid, and set it beside the altar, on the right side as one comes into the house of the LORD; and the priests who kept the door put there all the money brought into the house of the LORD. [10]So it was, whenever they saw that *there was* much money in the chest, that the king's scribe and the high priest came up and put it in bags, and counted the money that was found in the house of the LORD. [11]Then they gave the money, which had been apportioned, into the hands of those who did the work, who had the oversight of the house of the LORD; and they paid it out to the carpenters and builders who worked on the house of the LORD, [12]and to masons and stonecutters, and for buying timber and hewn stone, to repair the damage of the house of the LORD, and for all that was paid out to repair the temple. [13]However there were not made for the house of the LORD basins of silver, trimmers, sprinkling-bowls, trumpets, any articles of gold or articles of silver, from the money brought into the house of the LORD. [14]But they gave that to the workmen, and they repaired the house of the LORD with it. [15]Moreover they did not require an account from the men into whose hand they delivered the money to be paid to workmen, for they dealt faithfully. [16]The money from the trespass offerings and the money from the sin offerings was not brought into the house of the LORD. It belonged to the priests.

Hazael Threatens Jerusalem

[17]Hazael king of Syria went up and fought against Gath, and took it; then Hazael set his face to go up to Jerusalem. [18]And Jehoash king of Judah took all the sacred things that his fathers, Jehoshaphat and Jehoram and Ahaziah, kings of Judah, had dedicated, and his own sacred things, and all the gold found in the treasuries of the house of the LORD and in the king's house, and sent *them* to Hazael king of Syria. Then he went away from Jerusalem.

Death of Joash

[19]Now the rest of the acts of Joash,[a] and all that he did, *are* they not written in the book of the chronicles of the kings of Judah? [20]And his servants arose and formed a conspiracy, and killed Joash in the house of the Millo,[a] which goes down to Silla. [21]For Jozachar[a] the son of Shimeath and Jehozabad the son of Shomer,[b] his servants, struck him. So he died, and they buried him with his fathers in the City of David. Then Amaziah his son reigned in his place.

Jehoahaz Reigns in Israel

13 In the twenty-third year of Joash[a] the son of Ahaziah, king of Judah, Jehoahaz the son of Jehu became king over Israel in Samaria, *and reigned* seventeen years. [2]And he did evil in the sight of the LORD, and followed the sins of Jeroboam the son of Nebat, who had made Israel sin. He did not depart from them. [3]Then the anger of the LORD was aroused against Israel, and He delivered them into the hand of Hazael king of Syria, and into the hand of Ben-Hadad the son of Hazael, all *their* days. [4]So Jehoahaz pleaded with the LORD, and the LORD listened to him; for He saw the oppression of Israel, because the king of Syria oppressed them. [5]Then the LORD gave Israel a deliverer, so that they escaped from under the hand of the Syrians; and the children of Israel dwelt in their tents as before. [6]Nevertheless they did not depart from the sins of the house of Jeroboam, who had made Israel sin, *but* walked in them; and the wooden image[a] also remained in Samaria. [7]For He left of the army of Jehoahaz only fifty horsemen, ten chariots, and ten thousand foot soldiers; for the king of Syria had destroyed them and made them like the dust at threshing.

[8]Now the rest of the acts of Jehoahaz, all that he did, and his might, *are* they not written in the book of the chronicles of the kings of Israel? [9]So Jehoahaz rested with his fathers, and they buried

12:19 [a]Spelled *Jehoash* in 12:1ff **12:20** [a]Literally *The Landfill* **12:21** [a]Called *Zabad* in 2 Chronicles 24:26 [b]Called *Shimrith* in 2 Chronicles 24:26 **13:1** [a]Spelled *Jehoash* in 12:1ff **13:6** [a]Hebrew *Asherah,* a Canaanite goddess him in Samaria. Then Joash his son reigned in his place.

Jehoash Reigns in Israel

[10]In the thirty-seventh year of Joash king of Judah, Jehoash[a] the son of Jehoahaz became king over Israel in Samaria, *and reigned* sixteen years. [11]And he did evil in the sight of the LORD. He did not depart from all the sins of Jeroboam the son of Nebat, who made Israel sin, *but* walked in them.

[12]Now the rest of the acts of Joash, all that he did, and his might with which he fought against Amaziah king of Judah, *are* they not written in the book of the chronicles of the kings of Israel? [13]So Joash rested with his fathers. Then Jeroboam sat on his throne. And Joash was buried in Samaria with the kings of Israel.

Death of Elisha

[14]Elisha had become sick with the illness of which he would die. Then Joash the king of Israel came down to him, and wept over his face, and said, "O my father, my father, the chariots of Israel and their horsemen!"

[15]And Elisha said to him, "Take a bow and some arrows." So he took himself a bow and some arrows. [16]Then he said to the king of Israel, "Put your hand on the bow." So he put his hand *on it,* and Elisha put his hands on the king's hands. [17]And he said, "Open the east window"; and he opened *it.* Then Elisha said, "Shoot"; and he shot. And he said, "The arrow of the LORD's deliverance and the arrow of deliverance from Syria; for you must strike the Syrians at Aphek till you have destroyed *them."* [18]Then he said, "Take the arrows"; so he took *them.* And he said to the king of Israel, "Strike the ground"; so he struck three times, and stopped. [19]And the man of God was angry with him, and said, "You should have struck five or six times; then you would have struck Syria till you had destroyed *it!* But now you will strike Syria *only* three times."

13:10 [a]Spelled *Joash* in verse 9

The Rule of Management: People Do What People See

(2 Kings 3:1—23:37)

The Bible provides ample confirmation of a key management principle: People don't do what they hear; they do what they see. The example of the leader determines the experience of the people.

For the most part, God's people endured hard times during the days of the Book of 2 Kings. Below is a list of kings in Judah and Israel. Only two kings on this list, Hezekiah and Josiah, wholeheartedly worshiped God. Remember: A nation's leadership determines the direction of the whole country. People do what people see.

Judah	Israel
Jehoram (2 Kin. 8)	Joram (2 Kin. 3)
Ahaziah (2 Kin. 8)	Jehu (2 Kin. 10)
Athaliah (2 Kin. 11)	Jehoahaz (2 Kin. 13)
Joash (2 Kin. 11)	Jehoash (2 Kin. 13)
Amaziah (2 Kin. 14)	Jeroboam II (2 Kin. 14)
Azariah (2 Kin. 15)	Zechariah (2 Kin. 15)
Jotham (2 Kin. 15)	Shallum (2 Kin. 15)
Ahaz (2 Kin. 16)	Menahem (2 Kin. 15)
Hezekiah (2 Kin. 18)	Pekahiah (2 Kin. 15)
Manasseh (2 Kin. 21)	Pekah (2 Kin. 15)
Amon (2 Kin. 21)	Hoshea (2 Kin. 17)
Josiah (2 Kin. 22)	
Jehoahaz (2 Kin. 23)	
Jehoiakim (2 Kin. 23)	
Jehoiakin (2 Kin. 24)	
Zedekiah (2 Kin. 24)	

²⁰Then Elisha died, and they buried him. And the *raiding* bands from Moab invaded the land in the spring of the year. ²¹So it was, as they were burying a man, that suddenly they spied a band *of raiders;* and they put the man in the tomb of Elisha; and when the man was let down and touched the bones of Elisha, he revived and stood on his feet.

Israel Recaptures Cities from Syria

²²And Hazael king of Syria oppressed Israel all the days of Jehoahaz. ²³But the LORD was gracious to them, had compassion on them, and regarded them, because of His covenant with Abraham, Isaac, and Jacob, and would not yet destroy them or cast them from His presence.

²⁴Now Hazael king of Syria died. Then Ben-Hadad his son reigned in his place. ²⁵And Jehoash[a] the son of Jehoahaz recaptured from the hand of Ben-Hadad, the son of Hazael, the cities which he had taken out of the hand of Jehoahaz his father by war. Three times Joash defeated him and recaptured the cities of Israel.

Amaziah Reigns in Judah

14 In the second year of Joash the son of Jehoahaz, king of Israel, Amaziah the son of Joash, king of Judah, became king. ²He was twenty-five years old when he became king, and he reigned twenty-nine years in Jerusalem. His mother's name was Jehoaddan of Jerusalem. ³And he did *what was* right in the sight of the LORD, yet not like his father David; he did everything as his father Joash had done. ⁴However the high places were not taken away, and the people still sacrificed and burned incense on the high places.

⁵Now it happened, as soon as the kingdom was established in his hand, that he executed his servants who had murdered his father the king. ⁶But the children of the murderers he did not execute, according to what is written in the Book of the Law of Moses, in which the LORD commanded, saying, "Fathers shall not be put to death for their children, nor shall children be put to death for their fathers; but a person shall be put to death for his own sin."[a]

⁷He killed ten thousand Edomites in the Valley of Salt, and took Sela by war, and called its name Joktheel to this day.

⁸Then Amaziah sent messengers to Jehoash[a] the son of Jehoahaz, the son of Jehu, king of Israel, saying, "Come, let us face one another *in battle.*" ⁹And Jehoash king of Israel sent to Amaziah king of Judah, saying, "The thistle that *was* in Lebanon sent to the cedar that *was* in Leb-

anon, saying, 'Give your daughter to my son as wife'; and a wild beast that *was* in Lebanon passed by and trampled the thistle. ¹⁰You have indeed defeated Edom, and your heart has lifted you up. Glory *in that,* and stay at home; for why should you meddle with trouble so that you fall—you and Judah with you?"

¹¹But Amaziah would not heed. Therefore Jehoash king of Israel went out; so he and Amaziah king of Judah faced one another at Beth Shemesh, which *belongs* to Judah. ¹²And Judah was defeated by Israel, and every man fled to his tent. ¹³Then Jehoash king of Israel captured Amaziah king of Judah, the son of Jehoash, the son of Ahaziah, at Beth Shemesh; and he went to Jerusalem, and broke down the wall of Jerusalem from the Gate of Ephraim to the Corner Gate—four hundred cubits. ¹⁴And he took all the gold and silver, all the articles that were found in the house of the LORD and in the treasuries of the king's house, and hostages, and returned to Samaria.

¹⁵Now the rest of the acts of Jehoash which he did—his might, and how he fought with Amaziah king of Judah—*are* they not written in the book of the chronicles of the kings of Israel? ¹⁶So Jehoash rested with his fathers, and was buried in Samaria with the kings of Israel. Then Jeroboam his son reigned in his place.

¹⁷Amaziah the son of Joash, king of Judah, lived fifteen years after the death of Jehoash the son of Jehoahaz, king of Israel. ¹⁸Now the rest of the acts of Amaziah, *are* they not written in the book of the chronicles of the kings of Judah? ¹⁹And they formed a conspiracy against him in Jerusalem, and he fled to Lachish; but they sent after him to Lachish and killed him there. ²⁰Then they brought him on horses, and he was buried at Jerusalem with his fathers in the City of David.

²¹And all the people of Judah took Azariah,[a] who *was* sixteen years old, and made him king instead of his father Amaziah. ²²He built Elath and restored it to Judah, after the king rested with his fathers.

Jeroboam II Reigns in Israel

²³In the fifteenth year of Amaziah the son of Joash, king of Judah, Jeroboam the son of Joash, king of Israel, became king in Samaria, *and reigned* forty-one years. ²⁴And he did evil in the sight of the LORD; he did not depart from all the

---

13:25 [a]Spelled *Joash* in verses 12–14, 25
14:6 [a]Deuteronomy 24:16 **14:8** [a]Spelled *Joash* in 13:12ff and 2 Chronicles 25:17ff **14:21** [a]Called *Uzziah* in 2 Chronicles 26:1ff, Isaiah 6:1, and elsewhere

sins of Jeroboam the son of Nebat, who had made Israel sin. [25]He restored the territory of Israel from the entrance of Hamath to the Sea of the Arabah, according to the word of the LORD God of Israel, which He had spoken through His servant Jonah the son of Amittai, the prophet who *was* from Gath Hepher. [26]For the LORD saw *that* the affliction of Israel *was* very bitter; and whether bond or free, there was no helper for Israel. [27]And the LORD did not say that He would blot out the name of Israel from under heaven; but He saved them by the hand of Jeroboam the son of Joash.

[28]Now the rest of the acts of Jeroboam, and all that he did—his might, how he made war, and how he recaptured for Israel, from Damascus and Hamath, *what had belonged* to Judah—*are* they not written in the book of the chronicles of the kings of Israel? [29]So Jeroboam rested with his fathers, the kings of Israel. Then Zechariah his son reigned in his place.

Azariah Reigns in Judah

15 In the twenty-seventh year of Jeroboam king of Israel, Azariah the son of Amaziah, king of Judah, became king. [2]He was sixteen years old when he became king, and he reigned fifty-two years in Jerusalem. His mother's name *was* Jecholiah of Jerusalem. [3]And he did *what was* right in the sight of the LORD, according to all that his father Amaziah had done, [4]except that the high places were not removed; the people still sacrificed and burned incense on the high places. [5]Then the LORD struck the king, so that he was a leper until the day of his death; so he dwelt in an isolated house. And Jotham the king's son *was* over the *royal* house, judging the people of the land.

[6]Now the rest of the acts of Azariah, and all that he did, *are* they not written in the book of the chronicles of the kings of Judah? [7]So Azariah rested with his fathers, and they buried him with his fathers in the City of David. Then Jotham his son reigned in his place.

Zechariah Reigns in Israel

[8]In the thirty-eighth year of Azariah king of Judah, Zechariah the son of Jeroboam reigned over Israel in Samaria six months. [9]And he did evil in the sight of the LORD, as his fathers had done; he did not depart from the sins of Jeroboam the son of Nebat, who had made Israel sin. [10]Then Shallum the son of Jabesh conspired against him, and struck and killed him in front of the people; and he reigned in his place. [11]Now the rest of the acts of Zechariah, indeed they *are* written in the book of the chronicles of the kings of Israel.

[12]This *was* the word of the LORD which He spoke to Jehu, saying, "Your sons shall sit on the throne of Israel to the fourth *generation*."[a] And so it was.

Shallum Reigns in Israel

[13]Shallum the son of Jabesh became king in the thirty-ninth year of Uzziah[a] king of Judah; and he reigned a full month in Samaria. [14]For Menahem the son of Gadi went up from Tirzah, came to Samaria, and struck Shallum the son of Jabesh in Samaria and killed him; and he reigned in his place.

[15]Now the rest of the acts of Shallum, and the conspiracy which he led, indeed they *are* written in the book of the chronicles of the kings of Israel. [16]Then from Tirzah, Menahem attacked Tiphsah, all who *were* there, and its territory. Because they did not surrender, therefore he attacked *it*. All the women there who were with child he ripped open.

Menahem Reigns in Israel

[17]In the thirty-ninth year of Azariah king of Judah, Menahem the son of Gadi became king over Israel, *and reigned* ten years in Samaria. [18]And he did evil in the sight of the LORD; he did not depart all his days from the sins of Jeroboam the son of Nebat, who had made Israel sin. [19]Pul[a] king of Assyria came against the land; and Menahem gave Pul a thousand talents of silver, that his hand might be with him to strengthen the kingdom under his control. [20]And Menahem exacted the money from Israel, from all the very wealthy, from each man fifty shekels of silver, to give to the king of Assyria. So the king of Assyria turned back, and did not stay there in the land.

[21]Now the rest of the acts of Menahem, and all that he did, *are* they not written in the book of the chronicles of the kings of Israel? [22]So Menahem rested with his fathers. Then Pekahiah his son reigned in his place.

Pekahiah Reigns in Israel

[23]In the fiftieth year of Azariah king of Judah, Pekahiah the son of Menahem became king over Israel in Samaria, *and reigned* two years. [24]And he did evil in the sight of the LORD; he did not depart from the sins of Jeroboam the son of Nebat, who had made Israel sin. [25]Then Pekah the son of Remaliah, an officer of his, conspired against

---

15:12 [a]2 Kings 10:30 **15:13** [a]Called *Azariah* in 14:21ff and 15:1ff **15:19** [a]That is, Tiglath-Pileser III (compare verse 29)

him and killed him in Samaria, in the citadel of the king's house, along with Argob and Arieh; and with him were fifty men of Gilead. He killed him and reigned in his place.

²⁶Now the rest of the acts of Pekahiah, and all that he did, indeed they *are* written in the book of the chronicles of the kings of Israel.

Pekah Reigns in Israel

²⁷In the fifty-second year of Azariah king of Judah, Pekah the son of Remaliah became king over Israel in Samaria, *and reigned* twenty years. ²⁸And he did evil in the sight of the LORD; he did not depart from the sins of Jeroboam the son of Nebat, who had made Israel sin. ²⁹In the days of Pekah king of Israel, Tiglath-Pileser king of Assyria came and took Ijon, Abel Beth Maachah, Janoah, Kedesh, Hazor, Gilead, and Galilee, all the land of Naphtali; and he carried them captive to Assyria. ³⁰Then Hoshea the son of Elah led a conspiracy against Pekah the son of Remaliah, and struck and killed him; so he reigned in his place in the twentieth year of Jotham the son of Uzziah.

³¹Now the rest of the acts of Pekah, and all that he did, indeed they *are* written in the book of the chronicles of the kings of Israel.

Jotham Reigns in Judah

³²In the second year of Pekah the son of Remaliah, king of Israel, Jotham the son of Uzziah, king of Judah, began to reign. ³³He was twenty-five years old when he became king, and he reigned sixteen years in Jerusalem. His mother's name *was* Jerusha[a] the daughter of Zadok. ³⁴And he did *what was* right in the sight of the LORD; he did according to all that his father Uzziah had done. ³⁵However the high places were not removed; the people still sacrificed and burned incense on the high places. He built the Upper Gate of the house of the LORD.

³⁶Now the rest of the acts of Jotham, and all that he did, *are* they not written in the book of the chronicles of the kings of Judah? ³⁷In those days the LORD began to send Rezin king of Syria and Pekah the son of Remaliah against Judah. ³⁸So Jotham rested with his fathers, and was buried with his fathers in the City of David his father. Then Ahaz his son reigned in his place.

Ahaz Reigns in Judah

16 In the seventeenth year of Pekah the son of Remaliah, Ahaz the son of Jotham, king of Judah, began to reign. ²Ahaz *was* twenty years old when he became king, and he reigned sixteen years in Jeru-

salem; and he did not do *what was* right in the sight of the LORD his God, as his father David *had done.* ³But he walked in the way of the kings of Israel; indeed he made his son pass through the fire, according to the abominations of the nations whom the LORD had cast out from before the children of Israel. ⁴And he sacrificed and burned incense on the high places, on the hills, and under every green tree.

⁵Then Rezin king of Syria and Pekah the son of Remaliah, king of Israel, came up to Jerusalem to *make* war; and they besieged Ahaz but could not overcome *him.* ⁶At that time Rezin king of Syria captured Elath for Syria, and drove the men of Judah from Elath. Then the Edomites[a] went to Elath, and dwell there to this day.

⁷So Ahaz sent messengers to Tiglath-Pileser king of Assyria, saying, "I *am* your servant and your son. Come up and save me from the hand of the king of Syria and from the hand of the king of Israel, who rise up against me." ⁸And Ahaz took the silver and gold that was found in the house of the LORD, and in the treasuries of the king's house, and sent *it as* a present to the king of Assyria. ⁹So the king of Assyria heeded him; for the king of Assyria went up against Damascus and took it, carried *its people* captive to Kir, and killed Rezin.

¹⁰Now King Ahaz went to Damascus to meet Tiglath-Pileser king of Assyria, and saw an altar that *was* at Damascus; and King Ahaz sent to Urijah the priest the design of the altar and its pattern, according to all its workmanship. ¹¹Then Urijah the priest built an altar according to all that King Ahaz had sent from Damascus. So Urijah the priest made *it* before King Ahaz came back from Damascus. ¹²And when the king came back from Damascus, the king saw the altar; and the king approached the altar and made offerings on it. ¹³So he burned his burnt offering and his grain offering; and he poured his drink offering and sprinkled the blood of his peace offerings on the altar. ¹⁴He also brought the bronze altar which *was* before the LORD, from the front of the temple—from between the *new* altar and the house of the LORD—and put it on the north side of the *new* altar. ¹⁵Then King Ahaz commanded Urijah the priest, saying, "On the great *new* altar burn the morning burnt offering, the evening grain offering, the king's burnt sacrifice, and his grain offering, with the burnt offering of all the people of the land, their grain offering, and their

---

15:33 [a]Spelled *Jerushah* in 2 Chronicles 27:1
16:6 [a]Some ancient authorities read *Syrians.*

drink offerings; and sprinkle on it all the blood of the burnt offering and all the blood of the sacrifice. And the bronze altar shall be for me to inquire *by*." [16]Thus did Urijah the priest, according to all that King Ahaz commanded.

[17]And King Ahaz cut off the panels of the carts, and removed the lavers from them; and he took down the Sea from the bronze oxen that *were* under it, and put it on a pavement of stones. [18]Also he removed the Sabbath pavilion which they had built in the temple, and he removed the king's outer entrance from the house of the LORD, on account of the king of Assyria.

[19]Now the rest of the acts of Ahaz which he did, *are* they not written in the book of the chronicles of the kings of Judah? [20]So Ahaz rested with his fathers, and was buried with his fathers in the City of David. Then Hezekiah his son reigned in his place.

Hoshea Reigns in Israel

17 In the twelfth year of Ahaz king of Judah, Hoshea the son of Elah became king of Israel in Samaria, *and he reigned* nine years. [2]And he did evil in the sight of the LORD, but not as the kings of Israel who were before him. [3]Shalmaneser king of Assyria came up against him; and Hoshea became his vassal, and paid him tribute money. [4]And the king of Assyria uncovered a conspiracy by Hoshea; for he had sent messengers to So, king of Egypt, and brought no tribute to the king of Assyria, as *he had done* year by year. Therefore the king of Assyria shut him up, and bound him in prison.

Israel Carried Captive to Assyria

[5]Now the king of Assyria went throughout all the land, and went up to Samaria and besieged it for three years. [6]In the ninth year of Hoshea, the king of Assyria took Samaria and carried Israel away to Assyria, and placed them in Halah and by the Habor, the River of Gozan, and in the cities of the Medes.

[7]For so it was that the children of Israel had sinned against the LORD their God, who had brought them up out of the land of Egypt, from under the hand of Pharaoh king of Egypt; and they had feared other gods, [8]and had walked in the statutes of the nations whom the LORD had cast out from before the children of Israel, and of the kings of Israel, which they had made. [9]Also the children of Israel secretly did against the LORD their God things that *were* not right, and they built for themselves high places in all their cities, from watchtower to fortified city. [10]They set up for themselves *sacred* pillars and wooden images[a] on every high hill and under every green tree. [11]There they burned incense on all the high places, like the nations whom the LORD had carried away before them; and they did wicked things to provoke the LORD to anger, [12]for they served idols, of which the LORD had said to them, "You shall not do this thing."

[13]Yet the LORD testified against Israel and against Judah, by all of His prophets, every seer, saying, "Turn from your evil ways, and keep My commandments *and* My statutes, according to all the law which I commanded your fathers, and which I sent to you by My servants the prophets." [14]Nevertheless they would not hear, but stiffened their necks, like the necks of their fathers, who did not believe in the LORD their God. [15]And they rejected His statutes and His covenant that He had made with their fathers, and His testimonies which He had testified against them; they followed idols, became idolaters, and *went* after the nations who *were* all around them, *concerning* whom the LORD had charged them that they should not do like them. [16]So they left all the commandments of the LORD their God, made for themselves a molded image *and* two calves, made a wooden image and worshiped all the host of heaven, and served Baal. [17]And they caused their sons and daughters to pass through the fire, practiced witchcraft and soothsaying, and sold themselves to do evil in the sight of the LORD, to provoke Him to anger. [18]Therefore the LORD was very angry with Israel, and removed them from His sight; there was none left but the tribe of Judah alone.

[19]Also Judah did not keep the commandments of the LORD their God, but walked in the statutes of Israel which they made. [20]And the LORD rejected all the descendants of Israel, afflicted them, and delivered them into the hand of plunderers, until He had cast them from His sight. [21]For He tore Israel from the house of David, and they made Jeroboam the son of Nebat king. Then Jeroboam drove Israel from following the LORD, and made them commit a great sin. [22]For the children of Israel walked in all the sins of Jeroboam which he did; they did not depart from them, [23]until the LORD removed Israel out of His sight, as He had said by all His servants the prophets. So Israel was carried away from their own land to Assyria, *as it is* to this day.

17:10 [a]Hebrew *Asherim,* Canaanite deities

Assyria Resettles Samaria

²⁴Then the king of Assyria brought *people* from Babylon, Cuthah, Ava, Hamath, and from Sepharvaim, and placed *them* in the cities of Samaria instead of the children of Israel; and they took possession of Samaria and dwelt in its cities. ²⁵And it was so, at the beginning of their dwelling there, *that* they did not fear the LORD; therefore the LORD sent lions among them, which killed *some* of them. ²⁶So they spoke to the king of Assyria, saying, "The nations whom you have removed and placed in the cities of Samaria do not know the rituals of the God of the land; therefore He has sent lions among them, and indeed, they are killing them because they do not know the rituals of the God of the land." ²⁷Then the king of Assyria commanded, saying, "Send there one of the priests whom you brought from there; let him go and dwell there, and let him teach them the rituals of the God of the land." ²⁸Then one of the priests whom they had carried away from Samaria came and dwelt in Bethel, and taught them how they should fear the LORD.

²⁹However every nation continued to make gods of its own, and put *them* in the shrines on the high places which the Samaritans had made, *every* nation in the cities where they dwelt. ³⁰The men of Babylon made Succoth Benoth, the men of Cuth made Nergal, the men of Hamath made Ashima, ³¹and the Avites made Nibhaz and Tartak; and the Sepharvites burned their children in fire to Adrammelech and Anammelech, the gods of Sepharvaim. ³²So they feared the LORD, and from every class they appointed for themselves priests of the high places, who sacrificed for them in the shrines of the high places. ³³They feared the LORD, yet served their own gods—according to the rituals of the nations from among whom they were carried away.

³⁴To this day they continue practicing the former rituals; they do not fear the LORD, nor do they follow their statutes or their ordinances, or the law and commandment which the LORD had commanded the children of Jacob, whom He named Israel, ³⁵with whom the LORD had made a covenant and charged them, saying: "You shall not fear other gods, nor bow down to them nor serve them nor sacrifice to them; ³⁶but the LORD, who brought you up from the land of Egypt with great power and an outstretched arm, Him you shall fear, Him you shall worship, and to Him you shall offer sacrifice. ³⁷And the statutes, the ordinances, the law, and the commandment which He wrote for you, you shall be careful to observe forever; you shall not fear other gods. ³⁸And the covenant that I have made with you, you shall not forget, nor shall you fear other gods. ³⁹But the LORD your God you shall fear; and He will deliver you from the hand of all your enemies." ⁴⁰However they did not obey, but they followed their former rituals. ⁴¹So these nations feared the LORD, yet served their carved images; also their children and their children's children have continued doing as their fathers did, even to this day.

Hezekiah Reigns in Judah

18 Now it came to pass in the third year of Hoshea the son of Elah, king of Israel, *that* Hezekiah the son of Ahaz, king of Judah, began to reign. ²He was twenty-five years old when he became king, and he reigned twenty-nine years in Jerusalem. His mother's name *was* Abi[a] the daughter of Zechariah. ³And he did *what was* right in the sight of the LORD, according to all that his father David had done.

⁴He removed the high places and broke the *sacred* pillars, cut down the wooden image[a] and broke in pieces the bronze serpent that Moses had made; for until those days the children of Israel burned incense to it, and called it Nehushtan.[b] ⁵He trusted in the LORD God of Israel, so that after him was none like him among all the kings of Judah, nor who were before him. ⁶For he held fast to the LORD; he did not depart from following Him, but kept His commandments, which the LORD had commanded Moses. ⁷The LORD was with him; he prospered wherever he went. And he rebelled against the king of Assyria and did not serve him. ⁸He subdued the Philistines, as far as Gaza and its territory, from watchtower to fortified city.

⁹Now it came to pass in the fourth year of King Hezekiah, which *was* the seventh year of Hoshea the son of Elah, king of Israel, *that* Shalmaneser king of Assyria came up against Samaria and besieged it. ¹⁰And at the end of three years they took it. In the sixth year of Hezekiah, that *is,* the ninth year of Hoshea king of Israel, Samaria was taken. ¹¹Then the king of Assyria carried Israel away captive to Assyria, and put them in Halah and by the Habor, the River of Gozan, and in the cities of the Medes, ¹²because they did not obey the voice of the LORD their God, but transgressed His covenant *and* all that Moses the servant of the LORD had commanded; and they would neither hear nor do *them.*

18:2 [a]Called *Abijah* in 2 Chronicles 29:1ff
18:4 [a]Hebrew *Asherah,* a Canaanite goddess
[b]Literally *Bronze Thing*

[13]And in the fourteenth year of King Hezekiah, Sennacherib king of Assyria came up against all the fortified cities of Judah and took them. [14]Then Hezekiah king of Judah sent to the king of Assyria at Lachish, saying, "I have done wrong; turn away from me; whatever you impose on me I will pay." And the king of Assyria assessed Hezekiah king of Judah three hundred talents of silver and thirty talents of gold. [15]So Hezekiah gave *him* all the silver that was found in the house of the LORD and in the treasuries of the king's house. [16]At that time Hezekiah stripped *the gold from* the doors of the temple of the LORD, and *from* the pillars which Hezekiah king of Judah had overlaid, and gave it to the king of Assyria.

Sennacherib Boasts Against the LORD

[17]Then the king of Assyria sent *the* Tartan,[a] *the* Rabsaris,[b] *and the* Rabshakeh[c] from Lachish, with a great army against Jerusalem, to King Hezekiah. And they went up and came to Jerusalem. When they had come up, they went and stood by the aqueduct from the upper pool, which *was* on the highway to the Fuller's Field. [18]And when they had called to the king, Eliakim the son of Hilkiah, who *was* over the household, Shebna the scribe, and Joah the son of Asaph, the recorder, came out to them. [19]Then *the* Rabshakeh said to them, "Say now to Hezekiah, 'Thus says the great king, the king of Assyria: "What confidence *is* this in which you trust? [20]You speak of *having* plans and power for war; but *they are* mere words. And in whom do you trust, that you rebel against me? [21]Now look! You are trusting in the staff of this broken reed, Egypt, on which if a man leans, it will go into his hand and pierce it. So *is* Pharaoh king of Egypt to all who trust in him. [22]But if you say to me, 'We trust in the LORD our God,' *is* it not He whose high places and whose altars Hezekiah has taken away, and said to Judah and Jerusalem, 'You shall worship before this altar in Jerusalem'?"' [23]Now therefore, I urge you, give a pledge to my master the king of Assyria, and I will give you two thousand horses—if you are able on your part to put riders on them! [24]How then will you repel one captain of the least of my master's servants, and put your trust in Egypt for chariots and horsemen? [25]Have I now come up without the LORD against this place to destroy it? The LORD said to me, 'Go up against this land, and destroy it.'"

[26]Then Eliakim the son of Hilkiah, Shebna, and Joah said to *the* Rabshakeh, "Please speak to your servants in Aramaic, for we understand *it;* and do not speak to us in Hebrew[a] in the hearing of the people who *are* on the wall."

[27]But *the* Rabshakeh said to them, "Has my master sent me to your master and to you to speak these words, and not to the men who sit on the wall, who will eat and drink their own waste with you?"

[28]Then *the* Rabshakeh stood and called out with a loud voice in Hebrew, and spoke, saying, "Hear the word of the great king, the king of Assyria! [29]Thus says the king: 'Do not let Hezekiah deceive you, for he shall not be able to deliver you from his hand; [30]nor let Hezekiah make you trust in the LORD, saying, "The LORD will surely deliver us; this city shall not be given into the hand of the king of Assyria."' [31]Do not listen to Hezekiah; for thus says the king of Assyria: 'Make *peace* with me by a present and come out to me; and every one of you eat from his own vine and every one from his own fig tree, and every one of you drink the waters of his own cistern; [32]until I come and take you away to a land like your own land, a land of grain and new wine, a land of bread and vineyards, a land of olive groves and honey, that you may live and not die. But do not listen to Hezekiah, lest he persuade you, saying, "The LORD will deliver us." [33]Has any of the gods of the nations at all delivered its land from the hand of the king of Assyria? [34]Where *are* the gods of Hamath and Arpad? Where *are* the gods of Sepharvaim and Hena and Ivah? Indeed, have they delivered Samaria from my hand? [35]Who among all the gods of the lands have delivered their countries from my hand, that the LORD should deliver Jerusalem from my hand?'"

[36]But the people held their peace and answered him not a word; for the king's commandment was, "Do not answer him." [37]Then Eliakim the son of Hilkiah, who *was* over the household, Shebna the scribe, and Joah the son of Asaph, the recorder, came to Hezekiah with *their* clothes torn, and told him the words of *the* Rabshakeh.

Isaiah Assures Deliverance

19 And so it was, when King Hezekiah heard *it,* that he tore his clothes, covered himself with sackcloth, and went into the house of the LORD. [2]Then he sent Eliakim, who *was* over the household, Shebna the scribe, and the elders of the priests, covered with sackcloth, to Isaiah the prophet, the son of Amoz. [3]And they said to him, "Thus says Hezekiah: 'This

---

18:17 [a]A title, probably *Commander in Chief*   [b]A title, probably *Chief Officer*   [c]A title, probably *Chief of Staff* or *Governor*   **18:26** [a]Literally *Judean*

day *is* a day of trouble, and rebuke, and blasphemy; for the children have come to birth, but *there is* no strength to bring them forth. 4It may be that the LORD your God will hear all the words of *the* Rabshakeh, whom his master the king of Assyria has sent to reproach the living God, and will rebuke the words which the LORD your God has heard. Therefore lift up *your* prayer for the remnant that is left.'"

5So the servants of King Hezekiah came to Isaiah. 6And Isaiah said to them, "Thus you shall say to your master, 'Thus says the LORD: "Do not be afraid of the words which you have heard, with which the servants of the king of Assyria have blasphemed Me. 7Surely I will send a spirit upon him, and he shall hear a rumor and return to his own land; and I will cause him to fall by the sword in his own land."'"

Sennacherib's Threat and Hezekiah's Prayer

8Then *the* Rabshakeh returned and found the king of Assyria warring against Libnah, for he heard that he had departed from Lachish. 9And the king heard concerning Tirhakah king of Ethiopia, "Look, he has come out to make war with you." So he again sent messengers to Hezekiah, saying, 10"Thus you shall speak to Hezekiah king of Judah, saying: 'Do not let your God in whom you trust deceive you, saying, "Jerusalem shall not be given into the hand of the king of Assyria." 11Look! You have heard what the kings of Assyria have done to all lands by utterly destroying them; and shall you be delivered? 12Have the gods of the nations delivered those whom my fathers have destroyed, Gozan and Haran and Rezeph, and the people of Eden who *were* in Telassar? 13Where *is* the king of Hamath, the king of Arpad, and the king of the city of Sepharvaim, Hena, and Ivah?'"

14And Hezekiah received the letter from the hand of the messengers, and read it; and Hezekiah went up to the house of the LORD, and spread it before the LORD. 15Then Hezekiah prayed before the LORD, and said: "O LORD God of Israel, *the* One who dwells *between* the cherubim, You are God, You alone, of all the kingdoms of the earth. You have made heaven and earth. 16Incline Your ear, O LORD, and hear; open Your eyes, O LORD, and see; and hear the words of Sennacherib, which he has sent to reproach the living God. 17Truly, LORD, the kings of Assyria have laid waste the nations and their lands, 18and have cast their gods into the fire; for they *were* not gods, but the work of men's hands—wood and stone. Therefore they destroyed them. 19Now

therefore, O LORD our God, I pray, save us from his hand, that all the kingdoms of the earth may know that You *are* the LORD God, You alone."

The Word of the LORD Concerning Sennacherib

20Then Isaiah the son of Amoz sent to Hezekiah, saying, "Thus says the LORD God of Israel: 'Because you have prayed to Me against Sennacherib king of Assyria, I have heard.' 21This *is* the word which the LORD has spoken concerning him:

'The virgin, the daughter of Zion,
　Has despised you, laughed you to scorn;
The daughter of Jerusalem
　Has shaken *her* head behind your back!

22 'Whom have you reproached and
　　blasphemed?
Against whom have you raised *your* voice,
And lifted up your eyes on high?
Against the Holy *One* of Israel.
23 By your messengers you have reproached
　　the Lord,
And said: "By the multitude of my
　　chariots
I have come up to the height of the
　　mountains,
To the limits of Lebanon;
I will cut down its tall cedars
And its choice cypress trees;
I will enter the extremity of its borders,
To its fruitful forest.
24 I have dug and drunk strange water,
And with the soles of my feet I have dried
　　up
All the brooks of defense."

25 'Did you not hear long ago
How I made it,
From ancient times that I formed it?
Now I have brought it to pass,
That you should be
For crushing fortified cities *into* heaps of
　　ruins.
26 Therefore their inhabitants had little
　　power;
They were dismayed and confounded;
They were *as* the grass of the field
And the green herb,
As the grass on the housetops
And *grain* blighted before it is grown.

27 'But I know your dwelling place,
Your going out and your coming in,

And your rage against Me.
28 Because your rage against Me and your
tumult
Have come up to My ears,
Therefore I will put My hook in your
nose
And My bridle in your lips,
And I will turn you back
By the way which you came.

29"This *shall be* a sign to you:

You shall eat this year such as grows of
itself,
And in the second year what springs from
the same;
Also in the third year sow and reap,
Plant vineyards and eat the fruit of them.
30 And the remnant who have escaped of the
house of Judah
Shall again take root downward,
And bear fruit upward.
31 For out of Jerusalem shall go a remnant,
And those who escape from Mount Zion.
The zeal of the LORD of hosts[a] will do
this.'

32"Therefore thus says the LORD concerning
the king of Assyria:

'He shall not come into this city,
Nor shoot an arrow there,
Nor come before it with shield,
Nor build a siege mound against it.
33 By the way that he came,
By the same shall he return;
And he shall not come into this city,'
Says the LORD.
34 'For I will defend this city, to save it
For My own sake and for My servant
David's sake.'"

Sennacherib's Defeat and Death

35And it came to pass on a certain night that
the angel[a] of the LORD went out, and killed in
the camp of the Assyrians one hundred and
eighty-five thousand; and when *people* arose early
in the morning, there were the corpses—all
dead. 36So Sennacherib king of Assyria departed
and went away, returned *home,* and remained at
Nineveh. 37Now it came to pass, as he was worshiping in the temple of Nisroch his god, that his
sons Adrammelech and Sharezer struck him
down with the sword; and they escaped into the
land of Ararat. Then Esarhaddon his son reigned
in his place.

Hezekiah's Life Extended

20 In those days Hezekiah was sick
and near death. And Isaiah the
prophet, the son of Amoz, went to
him and said to him, "Thus says the LORD: 'Set
your house in order, for you shall die, and not
live.'"

2Then he turned his face toward the wall, and
prayed to the LORD, saying, 3"Remember now,
O LORD, I pray, how I have walked before You
in truth and with a loyal heart, and have done
what was good in Your sight." And Hezekiah
wept bitterly.

4And it happened, before Isaiah had gone out
into the middle court, that the word of the
LORD came to him, saying, 5"Return and tell
Hezekiah the leader of My people, 'Thus says the
LORD, the God of David your father: "I have
heard your prayer, I have seen your tears; surely I
will heal you. On the third day you shall go up
to the house of the LORD. 6And I will add to
your days fifteen years. I will deliver you and this
city from the hand of the king of Assyria; and I
will defend this city for My own sake, and for the
sake of My servant David."'"

7Then Isaiah said, "Take a lump of figs." So
they took and laid *it* on the boil, and he recovered.

8And Hezekiah said to Isaiah, "What *is* the
sign that the LORD will heal me, and that I shall
go up to the house of the LORD the third day?"

9Then Isaiah said, "This is the sign to you
from the LORD, that the LORD will do the thing
which He has spoken: *shall* the shadow go forward ten degrees or go backward ten degrees?"

10And Hezekiah answered, "It is an easy thing
for the shadow to go down ten degrees; no, but
let the shadow go backward ten degrees."

11So Isaiah the prophet cried out to the
LORD, and He brought the shadow ten degrees
backward, by which it had gone down on the
sundial of Ahaz.

The Babylonian Envoys

12At that time Berodach-Baladan[a] the son of
Baladan, king of Babylon, sent letters and a present to Hezekiah, for he heard that Hezekiah had
been sick. 13And Hezekiah was attentive to them,
and showed them all the house of his treasures—
the silver and gold, the spices and precious

19:31 [a]Following many Hebrew manuscripts and
ancient versions (compare Isaiah 37:32); Masoretic
Text omits *of hosts.* **19:35** [a]Or *Angel*
20:12 [a]Spelled *Merodach-Baladan* in Isaiah 39:1

Never Underestimate the Power of God

(2 Kings 20:1–7)

Hezekiah was one of only two kings in Judah who completely followed the Lord. In the days of Esarhaddon king of Assyria, Hezekiah lay on his deathbed. Isaiah the prophet had predicted the king's imminent death and told him to get his house in order.

But Hezekiah poured out his heart to the Lord and reminded God of His covenant, and how the king had faithfully led Judah. As Isaiah left the royal court, God heard Hezekiah's prayer and determined to heal him. God kept the king alive for another 15 years.

God did for the king what Hezekiah could not do for himself. Both God and Hezekiah knew their roles:

Hezekiah's Role	God's Role
1. Maintain a humble heart.	1. Demonstrate grace and power.
2. Submit to God's values.	2. Control the destiny of the land.
3. Ask God to meet needs.	3. Respond to needs of people.
4. Stay faithful to the covenant.	4. Stay faithful to the covenant.

ointment, and all[a] his armory—all that was found among his treasures. There was nothing in his house or in all his dominion that Hezekiah did not show them.

[14]Then Isaiah the prophet went to King Hezekiah, and said to him, "What did these men say, and from where did they come to you?"

So Hezekiah said, "They came from a far country, from Babylon."

[15]And he said, "What have they seen in your house?"

So Hezekiah answered, "They have seen all that is in my house; there is nothing among my treasures that I have not shown them."

[16]Then Isaiah said to Hezekiah, "Hear the word of the LORD: [17]'Behold, the days are coming when all that is in your house, and what your fathers have accumulated until this day, shall be carried to Babylon; nothing shall be left,' says the LORD. [18]'And they shall take away some of your sons who will descend from you, whom you will beget; and they shall be eunuchs in the palace of the king of Babylon.'"

[19]So Hezekiah said to Isaiah, "The word of the LORD which you have spoken is good!" For he said, "Will there not be peace and truth at least in my days?"

Death of Hezekiah

[20]Now the rest of the acts of Hezekiah—all his might, and how he made a pool and a tunnel and brought water into the city—are they not written in the book of the chronicles of the kings of Judah? [21]So Hezekiah rested with his fa-thers. Then Manasseh his son reigned in his place.

Manasseh Reigns in Judah

21 Manasseh was twelve years old when he became king, and he reigned fifty-five years in Jerusalem. His mother's name was Hephzibah. [2]And he did evil in the sight of the LORD, according to the abominations of the nations whom the LORD had cast out before the children of Israel. [3]For he rebuilt the high places which Hezekiah his father had destroyed; he raised up altars for Baal, and made a wooden image,[a] as Ahab king of Israel had done; and he worshiped all the host of heaven[b] and served them. [4]He also built altars in the house of the LORD, of which the LORD had said, "In Jerusalem I will put My name." [5]And he built altars for all the host of heaven in the two courts of the house of the LORD. [6]Also he made his son pass through the fire, practiced soothsaying, used witchcraft, and consulted spiritists and mediums. He did much evil in the sight of the LORD, to provoke Him to anger. [7]He even set a carved image of Asherah[a] that he had made, in the house of which the LORD had said to David and to Solomon his son, "In this house and in Jerusalem, which I have chosen out of all the tribes of Israel, I will put My name forever; [8]and I will not

---

20:13 [a]Following many Hebrew manuscripts, Syriac, and Targum; Masoretic Text omits all.
21:3 [a]Hebrew Asherah, a Canaanite goddess [b]The gods of the Assryians **21:7** [a]A Canaanite goddess

make the feet of Israel wander anymore from the land which I gave their fathers—only if they are careful to do according to all that I have commanded them, and according to all the law that My servant Moses commanded them." [9]But they paid no attention, and Manasseh seduced them to do more evil than the nations whom the LORD had destroyed before the children of Israel.

[10]And the LORD spoke by His servants the prophets, saying, [11]"Because Manasseh king of Judah has done these abominations (he has acted more wickedly than all the Amorites who *were* before him, and has also made Judah sin with his idols), [12]therefore thus says the LORD God of Israel: 'Behold, *I* am bringing *such* calamity upon Jerusalem and Judah, that whoever hears of it, both his ears will tingle. [13]And I will stretch over Jerusalem the measuring line of Samaria and the plummet of the house of Ahab; I will wipe Jerusalem as *one* wipes a dish, wiping *it* and turning *it* upside down. [14]So I will forsake the remnant of My inheritance and deliver them into the hand of their enemies; and they shall become victims of plunder to all their enemies, [15]because they have done evil in My sight, and have provoked Me to anger since the day their fathers came out of Egypt, even to this day.'"

[16]Moreover Manasseh shed very much innocent blood, till he had filled Jerusalem from one end to another, besides his sin by which he made Judah sin, in doing evil in the sight of the LORD.

[17]Now the rest of the acts of Manasseh—all that he did, and the sin that he committed—*are* they not written in the book of the chronicles of the kings of Judah? [18]So Manasseh rested with his fathers, and was buried in the garden of his own house, in the garden of Uzza. Then his son Amon reigned in his place.

Amon's Reign and Death

[19]Amon *was* twenty-two years old when he became king, and he reigned two years in Jerusalem. His mother's name *was* Meshullemeth the daughter of Haruz of Jotbah. [20]And he did evil in the sight of the LORD, as his father Manasseh had done. [21]So he walked in all the ways that his father had walked; and he served the idols that his father had served, and worshiped them. [22]He forsook the LORD God of his fathers, and did not walk in the way of the LORD.

[23]Then the servants of Amon conspired against him, and killed the king in his own house. [24]But the people of the land executed all those who had conspired against King Amon. Then the people of the land made his son Josiah king in his place.

[25]Now the rest of the acts of Amon which he did, *are* they not written in the book of the chronicles of the kings of Judah? [26]And he was buried in his tomb in the garden of Uzza. Then Josiah his son reigned in his place.

Josiah Reigns in Judah

22 Josiah *was* eight years old when he became king, and he reigned thirty-one years in Jerusalem. His mother's name *was* Jedidah the daughter of Adaiah of Bozkath. [2]And he did *what was* right in the sight of the LORD, and walked in all the ways of his father David; he did not turn aside to the right hand or to the left.

Hilkiah Finds the Book of the Law

[3]Now it came to pass, in the eighteenth year of King Josiah, *that* the king sent Shaphan the scribe, the son of Azaliah, the son of Meshullam, to the house of the LORD, saying: [4]"Go up to Hilkiah the high priest, that he may count the money which has been brought into the house of the LORD, which the doorkeepers have gathered from the people. [5]And let them deliver it into the hand of those doing the work, who are the overseers in the house of the LORD; let them give it to those who *are* in the house of the LORD doing the work, to repair the damages of the house— [6]to carpenters and builders and masons—and to buy timber and hewn stone to repair the house. [7]However there need be no accounting made with them of the money delivered into their hand, because they deal faithfully."

[8]Then Hilkiah the high priest said to Shaphan the scribe, "I have found the Book of the Law in the house of the LORD." And Hilkiah gave the book to Shaphan, and he read it. [9]So Shaphan the scribe went to the king, bringing the king word, saying, "Your servants have gathered the money that was found in the house, and have delivered it into the hand of those who do the work, who oversee the house of the LORD." [10]Then Shaphan the scribe showed the king, saying, "Hilkiah the priest has given me a book." And Shaphan read it before the king.

[11]Now it happened, when the king heard the words of the Book of the Law, that he tore his clothes. [12]Then the king commanded Hilkiah the priest, Ahikam the son of Shaphan, Achbor[a] the son of Michaiah, Shaphan the scribe, and Asaiah a servant of the king, saying, [13]"Go, inquire of the LORD for me, for the people and for all Judah,

---

22:12 [a]*Abdon the son of Micah* in 2 Chronicles 34:20

concerning the words of this book that has been found; for great *is* the wrath of the LORD that is aroused against us, because our fathers have not obeyed the words of this book, to do according to all that is written concerning us."

[14] So Hilkiah the priest, Ahikam, Achbor, Shaphan, and Asaiah went to Huldah the prophetess, the wife of Shallum the son of Tikvah, the son of Harhas, keeper of the wardrobe. (She dwelt in Jerusalem in the Second Quarter.) And they spoke with her. [15] Then she said to them, "Thus says the LORD God of Israel, 'Tell the man who sent you to Me, [16] "Thus says the LORD: 'Behold, I will bring calamity on this place and on its inhabitants—all the words of the book which the king of Judah has read— [17] because they have forsaken Me and burned incense to other gods, that they might provoke Me to anger with all the works of their hands. Therefore My wrath shall be aroused against this place and shall not be quenched.' " ' [18] But as for the king of Judah, who sent you to inquire of the LORD, in this manner you shall speak to him, 'Thus says the LORD God of Israel: "*Concerning* the words which you have heard— [19] because your heart was tender, and you humbled yourself before the LORD when you heard what I spoke

against this place and against its inhabitants, that they would become a desolation and a curse, and you tore your clothes and wept before Me, I also have heard *you*," says the LORD. [20] "Surely, therefore, I will gather you to your fathers, and you shall be gathered to your grave in peace; and your eyes shall not see all the calamity which I will bring on this place." ' " So they brought back word to the king.

Josiah Restores True Worship

23 Now the king sent them to gather all the elders of Judah and Jerusalem to him. [2] The king went up to the house of the LORD with all the men of Judah, and with him all the inhabitants of Jerusalem—the priests and the prophets and all the people, both small and great. And he read in their hearing all the words of the Book of the Covenant which had been found in the house of the LORD.

[3] Then the king stood by a pillar and made a covenant before the LORD, to follow the LORD and to keep His commandments and His testimonies and His statutes, with all *his* heart and all *his* soul, to perform the words of this covenant that were written in this book. And all the people took a stand for the covenant. [4] And the king

PROFILE IN LEADERSHIP

JOSIAH

A KING WHO COULD DO NO WRONG

(2 Kings 22:1—23:30)

Josiah became king of Judah at age eight, following the murder of his wicked father (2 Kin. 21:23–26). Yet unlike his father, the Bible says Josiah "did what was right in the sight of the LORD, and walked in all the ways of his father David; he did not turn aside to the right hand or to the left" (22:2). Josiah's inner circle must have included righteous men and women—no doubt including his mother, Jedidah—who nurtured Josiah in the ways of God.

Josiah respected the role of spiritual leaders. He maintained a teachable spirit, desiring to hear the words of God. He listened to scriptural rebuke and responded with brokenness, realizing how far from God's Law his people had strayed. Josiah's reign brought about the restoration of the temple, and his godly influence helped reduce the effects of decades of evil leadership. Josiah, God's servant, passionately pursued the things of God rather than personal prestige.

God rewarded Josiah by allowing him to live in peace. He died in battle, but never saw the devastation poised to sweep over his nation. Scripture devotes two entire chapters to his life and influence, compared with barely a sentence for the many wicked leaders. Unlike Josiah, their lives were like chaff blown away by the wind.

Josiah: Outward Reform Begins with Inward Renewal

(2 Kings 22:10—23:25)

Throughout his 31 years of godly leadership, King Josiah wholeheartedly followed the Lord and devoted himself to leading the people well. His own spiritual passion soon began to influence Judah and eventually brought about public reform.

Even today Josiah remains a vivid example of a key biblical principle: Outward reform begins with inward renewal. The leader must experience personal change before he or she can implement public change. Leaders make an impact the same way an atomic bomb does: They implode before they explode.

How did the young king "implode" before he "exploded"? After ten years on the throne, while he was still a teenager, Josiah sent several men to the high priest to reenergize the process of repairing the temple. While cleaning up the rubble, the high priest found "the Book of the Law" (2 Kin. 22:8). Shaphan the scribe read it, then reported its contents to the young king. And how did Josiah respond? He imploded: "When the king heard the words of the Book of the Law . . . he tore his clothes" (22:11). His tender heart and humility prompted him to embark on a national program of spiritual reform. The cycle worked this way for King Josiah:

Personal Renewal

Public Reform Occurs　　　　　　　　　　**Personal Change Occurs**

Public Change Implemented

---

commanded Hilkiah the high priest, the priests of the second order, and the doorkeepers, to bring out of the temple of the LORD all the articles that were made for Baal, for Asherah,[a] and for all the host of heaven;[b] and he burned them outside Jerusalem in the fields of Kidron, and carried their ashes to Bethel. [5]Then he removed the idolatrous priests whom the kings of Judah had ordained to burn incense on the high places in the cities of Judah and in the places all around Jerusalem, and those who burned incense to Baal, to the sun, to the moon, to the constellations, and to all the host of heaven. [6]And he brought out the wooden image[a] from the house of the LORD, to the Brook Kidron outside Jerusalem, burned it at the Brook Kidron and ground it to ashes, and threw its ashes on the graves of the common people. [7]Then he tore down the ritual booths of the perverted persons[a] that were in the house of the LORD, where the women wove hangings for the wooden image. [8]And he brought all the priests from the cities of Judah, and defiled the high places where the priests had burned incense, from Geba to Beersheba; also he broke down the high places at the gates which were at the entrance of the Gate of Joshua the governor of the city, which were to the left of the city gate. [9]Nevertheless the priests of the high places did not come up to the altar of the LORD in Jerusalem, but they ate unleavened bread among their brethren.

[10]And he defiled Topheth, which is in the Valley of the Son[a] of Hinnom, that no man might make his son or his daughter pass through the fire to Molech. [11]Then he removed the horses that the kings of Judah had dedicated to the sun, at the entrance to the house of the LORD, by the chamber of Nathan-Melech, the officer who was in the court; and he burned the chariots of the sun with fire. [12]The altars that were on the roof, the upper chamber of Ahaz, which the kings of Judah had made, and the altars which Manasseh had made in the two courts of the house of the LORD, the king broke down and pulverized there, and threw their dust into the Brook Kidron. [13]Then the king defiled the high places that were east of Jerusalem, which were on the south of the Mount of Corruption, which

---

23:4 [a]A Canaanite goddess [b]The gods of the Assyrians **23:6** [a]Hebrew *Asherah*, a Canaanite goddess **23:7** [a]Hebrew *qedeshim*, that is, those practicing sodomy and prostitution in religious rituals **23:10** [a]Kethib reads *Sons*.

Solomon king of Israel had built for Ashtoreth the abomination of the Sidonians, for Chemosh the abomination of the Moabites, and for Milcom the abomination of the people of Ammon. [14]And he broke in pieces the *sacred* pillars and cut down the wooden images, and filled their places with the bones of men.

[15]Moreover the altar that *was* at Bethel, *and* the high place which Jeroboam the son of Nebat, who made Israel sin, had made, both that altar and the high place he broke down; and he burned the high place *and* crushed *it* to powder, and burned the wooden image. [16]As Josiah turned, he saw the tombs that *were* there on the mountain. And he sent and took the bones out of the tombs and burned *them* on the altar, and defiled it according to the word of the LORD which the man of God proclaimed, who proclaimed these words. [17]Then he said, "What gravestone *is* this that I see?"

So the men of the city told him, "*It is* the tomb of the man of God who came from Judah and proclaimed these things which you have done against the altar of Bethel."

[18]And he said, "Let him alone; let no one move his bones." So they let his bones alone, with the bones of the prophet who came from Samaria.

[19]Now Josiah also took away all the shrines of the high places that *were* in the cities of Samaria, which the kings of Israel had made to provoke the LORD[a] to anger; and he did to them according to all the deeds he had done in Bethel. [20]He executed all the priests of the high places who *were* there, on the altars, and burned men's bones on them; and he returned to Jerusalem.

[21]Then the king commanded all the people, saying, "Keep the Passover to the LORD your God, as *it is* written in this Book of the Covenant." [22]Such a Passover surely had never been held since the days of the judges who judged Israel, nor in all the days of the kings of Israel and the kings of Judah. [23]But in the eighteenth year of King Josiah this Passover was held before the LORD in Jerusalem. [24]Moreover Josiah put away those who consulted mediums and spiritists, the household gods and idols, all the abominations that were seen in the land of Judah and in Jerusalem, that he might perform the words of the law which were written in the book that Hilkiah the priest found in the house of the LORD. [25]Now before him there was no king like him, who turned to the LORD with all his heart, with all his soul, and with all his might, according to all the Law of Moses; nor after him did *any* arise like him.

Impending Judgment on Judah

[26]Nevertheless the LORD did not turn from the fierceness of His great wrath, with which His anger was aroused against Judah, because of all the provocations with which Manasseh had provoked Him. [27]And the LORD said, "I will also remove Judah from My sight, as I have removed Israel, and will cast off this city Jerusalem which I have chosen, and the house of which I said, 'My name shall be there.'"[a]

Josiah Dies in Battle

[28]Now the rest of the acts of Josiah, and all that he did, *are* they not written in the book of the chronicles of the kings of Judah? [29]In his days Pharaoh Necho king of Egypt went to the aid of the king of Assyria, to the River Euphrates; and King Josiah went against him. And *Pharaoh Necho* killed him at Megiddo when he confronted him. [30]Then his servants moved his body in a chariot from Megiddo, brought him to Jerusalem, and buried him in his own tomb. And the people of the land took Jehoahaz the son of Josiah, anointed him, and made him king in his father's place.

The Reign and Captivity of Jehoahaz

[31]Jehoahaz *was* twenty-three years old when he became king, and he reigned three months in Jerusalem. His mother's name *was* Hamutal the daughter of Jeremiah of Libnah. [32]And he did evil in the sight of the LORD, according to all that his fathers had done. [33]Now Pharaoh Necho put him in prison at Riblah in the land of Hamath, that he might not reign in Jerusalem; and he imposed on the land a tribute of one hundred talents of silver and a talent of gold. [34]Then Pharaoh Necho made Eliakim the son of Josiah king in place of his father Josiah, and changed his name to Jehoiakim. And *Pharaoh* took Jehoahaz and went to Egypt, and he[a] died there.

Jehoiakim Reigns in Judah

[35]So Jehoiakim gave the silver and gold to Pharaoh; but he taxed the land to give money according to the command of Pharaoh; he exacted the silver and gold from the people of the land, from every one according to his assessment, to give *it* to Pharaoh Necho. [36]Jehoiakim *was* twenty-five years old when he became king, and he reigned eleven years in Jerusalem. His

---

23:19 [a]Following Septuagint, Syriac, and Vulgate; Masoretic Text and Targum omit *the LORD*. **23:27** [a]1 Kings 8:29 **23:34** [a]That is, Jehoahaz mother's name *was* Zebudah the daughter of Pedaiah of Rumah. [37]And he did evil in the sight of the LORD, according to all that his fathers had done.

Judah Overrun by Enemies

24 In his days Nebuchadnezzar king of Babylon came up, and Jehoiakim became his vassal *for* three years. Then he turned and rebelled against him. [2]And the LORD sent against him *raiding* bands of Chaldeans, bands of Syrians, bands of Moabites, and bands of the people of Ammon; He sent them against Judah to destroy it, according to the word of the LORD which He had spoken by His servants the prophets. [3]Surely at the commandment of the LORD *this* came upon Judah, to remove *them* from His sight because of the sins of Manasseh, according to all that he had done, [4]and also because of the innocent blood that he had shed; for he had filled Jerusalem with innocent blood, which the LORD would not pardon.

[5]Now the rest of the acts of Jehoiakim, and all that he did, *are* they not written in the book of the chronicles of the kings of Judah? [6]So Jehoiakim rested with his fathers. Then Jehoiachin his son reigned in his place.

[7]And the king of Egypt did not come out of his land anymore, for the king of Babylon had taken all that belonged to the king of Egypt from the Brook of Egypt to the River Euphrates.

The Reign and Captivity of Jehoiachin

[8]Jehoiachin *was* eighteen years old when he became king, and he reigned in Jerusalem three months. His mother's name *was* Nehushta the daughter of Elnathan of Jerusalem. [9]And he did evil in the sight of the LORD, according to all that his father had done.

[10]At that time the servants of Nebuchadnezzar king of Babylon came up against Jerusalem, and the city was besieged. [11]And Nebuchadnezzar king of Babylon came against the city, as his servants were besieging it. [12]Then Jehoiachin king of Judah, his mother, his servants, his princes, and his officers went out to the king of Babylon; and the king of Babylon, in the eighth year of his reign, took him prisoner.

The Captivity of Jerusalem

[13]And he carried out from there all the treasures of the house of the LORD and the treasures of the king's house, and he cut in pieces all the articles of gold which Solomon king of Israel had made in the temple of the LORD, as the LORD had said. [14]Also he carried into captivity all Jerusalem: all the captains and all the mighty men of valor, ten thousand captives, and all the craftsmen and smiths. None remained except the poorest people of the land. [15]And he carried Jehoiachin captive to Babylon. The king's mother, the king's wives, his officers, and the mighty of the land he carried into captivity from Jerusalem to Babylon. [16]All the valiant men, seven thousand, and craftsmen and smiths, one thousand, all *who were* strong *and* fit for war, these the king of Babylon brought captive to Babylon.

Zedekiah Reigns in Judah

[17]Then the king of Babylon made Mattaniah, *Jehoiachin's*[a] uncle, king in his place, and changed his name to Zedekiah.

[18]Zedekiah *was* twenty-one years old when he became king, and he reigned eleven years in Jerusalem. His mother's name *was* Hamutal the daughter of Jeremiah of Libnah. [19]He also did evil in the sight of the LORD, according to all that Jehoiakim had done. [20]For because of the anger of the LORD *this* happened in Jerusalem and Judah, that He finally cast them out from His presence. Then Zedekiah rebelled against the king of Babylon.

The Fall and Captivity of Judah

25 Now it came to pass in the ninth year of his reign, in the tenth month, on the tenth *day* of the month, *that* Nebuchadnezzar king of Babylon and all his army came against Jerusalem and encamped against it; and they built a siege wall against it all around. [2]So the city was besieged until the eleventh year of King Zedekiah. [3]By the ninth *day* of the *fourth* month the famine had become so severe in the city that there was no food for the people of the land.

[4]Then the city wall was broken through, and all the men of war *fled* at night by way of the gate between two walls, which was by the king's garden, even though the Chaldeans *were* still encamped all around against the city. And *the king*[a] went by way of the plain.[b] [5]But the army of the Chaldeans pursued the king, and they overtook him in the plains of Jericho. All his army was scattered from him. [6]So they took the king and brought him up to the king of Babylon at Riblah, and they pronounced judgment on him. [7]Then they killed the sons of Zedekiah before his eyes, put out the eyes of Zedekiah, bound him with bronze fetters, and took him to Babylon.

24:17 [a]Literally *his* **25:4** [a]Literally *he* [b]Or *Arabah,* that is, the Jordan Valley

[8]And in the fifth month, on the seventh *day* of the month (which *was* the nineteenth year of King Nebuchadnezzar king of Babylon), Nebuzaradan the captain of the guard, a servant of the king of Babylon, came to Jerusalem. [9]He burned the house of the LORD and the king's house; all the houses of Jerusalem, that is, all the houses of the great, he burned with fire. [10]And all the army of the Chaldeans who *were with* the captain of the guard broke down the walls of Jerusalem all around.

[11]Then Nebuzaradan the captain of the guard carried away captive the rest of the people *who* remained in the city and the defectors who had deserted to the king of Babylon, with the rest of the multitude. [12]But the captain of the guard left *some* of the poor of the land as vinedressers and farmers. [13]The bronze pillars that *were* in the house of the LORD, and the carts and the bronze Sea that *were* in the house of the LORD, the Chaldeans broke in pieces, and carried their bronze to Babylon. [14]They also took away the pots, the shovels, the trimmers, the spoons, and all the bronze utensils with which the priests ministered. [15]The firepans and the basins, the things of solid gold and solid silver, the captain of the guard took away. [16]The two pillars, one Sea, and the carts, which Solomon had made for the house of the LORD, the bronze of all these articles was beyond measure. [17]The height of one pillar *was* eighteen cubits, and the capital on it *was* of bronze. The height of the capital was three cubits, and the network and pomegranates all around the capital were all of bronze. The second pillar was the same, with a network.

[18]And the captain of the guard took Seraiah the chief priest, Zephaniah the second priest, and the three doorkeepers. [19]He also took out of the city an officer who had charge of the men of war, five men of the king's close associates who were found in the city, the chief recruiting officer of the army, who mustered the people of the land, and sixty men of the people of the land *who* were found in the city. [20]So Nebuzaradan, captain of the guard, took these and brought them to the king of Babylon at Riblah. [21]Then the king of Babylon struck them and put them to death at Riblah in the land of Hamath. Thus Judah was carried away captive from its own land.

Gedaliah Made Governor of Judah

[22]Then he made Gedaliah the son of Ahikam, the son of Shaphan, governor over the people who remained in the land of Judah, whom Nebuchadnezzar king of Babylon had left. [23]Now when all the captains of the armies, they and *their* men, heard that the king of Babylon had made Gedaliah governor, they came to Gedaliah at Mizpah—Ishmael the son of Nethaniah, Johanan the son of Careah, Seraiah the son of Tanhumeth the Netophathite, and Jaazaniah[a] the son of a Maachathite, they and their men. [24]And Gedaliah took an oath before them and their men, and said to them, "Do not be afraid of the servants of the Chaldeans. Dwell in the land and serve the king of Babylon, and it shall be well with you."

[25]But it happened in the seventh month that Ishmael the son of Nethaniah, the son of Elishama, of the royal family, came with ten men and struck and killed Gedaliah, the Jews, as well as the Chaldeans who were with him at Mizpah. [26]And all the people, small and great, and the captains of the armies, arose and went to Egypt; for they were afraid of the Chaldeans.

Jehoiachin Released from Prison

[27]Now it came to pass in the thirty-seventh year of the captivity of Jehoiachin king of Judah, in the twelfth month, on the twenty-seventh *day* of the month, *that* Evil-Merodach[a] king of Babylon, in the year that he began to reign, released Jehoiachin king of Judah from prison. [28]He spoke kindly to him, and gave him a more prominent seat than those of the kings who *were* with him in Babylon. [29]So Jehoiachin changed from his prison garments, and he ate bread regularly before the king all the days of his life. [30]And as for his provisions, *there was* a regular ration given him by the king, a portion for each day, all the days of his life.

25:23 [a]Spelled *Jezaniah* in Jeremiah 40:8
25:27 [a]Literally *Man of Marduk*

1 CHRONICLES

The Public Office of Leaders

SUMMARY

If the books of Samuel and Kings teach us about the personal weaknesses of Israel's leaders, then 1 and 2 Chronicles outline the public office of those leaders and detail their leadership successes from a civil and religious point of view.

Rather than merely retelling the story of David's struggle with Saul, his sin with Bathsheba, and his rebellious household under Absalom, for example, 1 Chronicles focuses on the recovery of the ark of the covenant, the temple construction and dedication, and Israel's worship. It emphasizes God's mercy (especially in relation to David's shortcomings) and stresses the king's service to God.

The book begins with nine chapters of genealogies, thereby demonstrating the enormous value of heritage to the Jewish people. Ancestors often foreshadowed the lives of later descendants. Leaders could cite exactly their family trees; centuries later the apostle Paul spoke of being from the tribe of Benjamin, a Pharisee of the Pharisees. Following the genealogies, the text examines the leaders of Israel, beginning with King Saul. First Chronicles tells us precisely why Saul was killed and why David replaced him as king.

Immediately in David's leadership we observe the Law of the Lid, the Law of Respect, the Law of the Inner Circle, the Law of Timing, the Law of Solid Ground, the Law of Connection, the Law of Reproduction, the Law of Explosive Growth, and the Law of Influence. His 40 years as king bring a series of remarkable accomplishments. He builds a standing army; defeats the inhabitants of Jerusalem and relocates his capital there; establishes national policy and order; and gathers the resources to build the temple (even though God will not allow him to build it himself). The book ends with David turning the kingdom over to Solomon, his son—and gaining the pledges of all his staff to faithfully serve the new king.

God's Role in 1 Chronicles

In 1 Chronicles we see God as the grand Supervisor of Israel's exploits. Because the book does not delve much into the personal lives of the kings, but rather examines their public leadership, God plays the part of a divine Coach. He encourages, inspires, rewards, and disciplines His key players, so that the nation's spiritual climate can flourish.

God shows His pleasure when His leaders share His priorities, and displays great displeasure when they don't. The Lord affirmed King David and the citizens of Israel during his coronation, for example, but chastised the king when he usurped authority and called for a nationwide census. Again, we notice that God limits His dealings with the nation primarily to direct interaction with its leaders. God desired to lead the leaders and thus influence the whole country.

Leaders in 1 Chronicles

Saul, David, Nathan, Gad, Solomon

Other People of Influence in 1 Chronicles

Joab, Jashobeam, Eleazar, and the thirty leaders of David's mighty men

Lessons in Leadership

- Leadership is influence, nothing more and nothing less.
- Leaders who develop people win their fierce loyalty.
- Leaders increase their power when they share it with others.
- Effective leaders keep first things first.
- Leaders who last are marked by humility.
- Spiritual leaders trust God's mercy over man's justice.
- Healthy leaders assume responsibility for everything that happens under their watch.
- Great leaders expect to pay a price.
- Great leaders lead by example.
- Great leaders set up their successor for success.

LEADERSHIP

HIGHLIGHTS IN 1 CHRONICLES

AMNON: The High Cost of No Self-Discipline (3:1)	*page 486*
THE LAW OF MAGNETISM: David Attracted Loyal Risk Takers (11:10–23)	*page 494*
DAVID AND THE LAW OF THE INNER CIRCLE: A Leader's Potential Is Determined by Those Closest to Him (11:10—12:40)	*pages 496, 497*
THE LAW OF REPRODUCTION: David Raised Up Leaders (12:1–38)	*page 498*
DAVID: Willingness to Assume the Blame (21:1–17)	*page 506*
PERSPECTIVE AND VISION: David Sees a Bigger Picture (22:1–19)	*page 507*
THE LAW OF LEGACY: David Sets Up Solomon to Succeed (29:1–5)	*page 514*

The Family of Adam—Seth to Abraham

1 Adam, Seth, Enosh, ²Cainan,ᵃ Mahalalel, Jared, ³Enoch, Methuselah, Lamech, ⁴Noah,ᵃ Shem, Ham, and Japheth.

⁵The sons of Japheth *were* Gomer, Magog, Madai, Javan, Tubal, Meshech, and Tiras. ⁶The sons of Gomer *were* Ashkenaz, Diphath,ᵃ and Togarmah. ⁷The sons of Javan *were* Elishah, Tarshishah,ᵃ Kittim, and Rodanim.ᵇ

⁸The sons of Ham *were* Cush, Mizraim, Put, and Canaan. ⁹The sons of Cush *were* Seba, Havilah, Sabta,ᵃ Raama,ᵇ and Sabtecha. The sons of Raama *was* Sheba and Dedan. ¹⁰Cush begot Nimrod; he began to be a mighty one on the earth. ¹¹Mizraim begot Ludim, Anamim, Lehabim, Naphtuhim, ¹²Pathrusim, Casluhim (from whom came the Philistines and the Caphtorim). ¹³Canaan begot Sidon, his firstborn, and Heth; ¹⁴the Jebusite, the Amorite, and the Girgashite; ¹⁵the Hivite, the Arkite, and the Sinite; ¹⁶the Arvadite, the Zemarite, and the Hamathite.

¹⁷The sons of Shem *were* Elam, Asshur, Arphaxad, Lud, Aram, Uz, Hul, Gether, and Meshech.ᵃ ¹⁸Arphaxad begot Shelah, and Shelah begot Eber. ¹⁹To Eber were born two sons: the name of one *was* Peleg,ᵃ for in his days the earth was divided; and his brother's name *was* Joktan. ²⁰Joktan begot Almodad, Sheleph, Hazarmaveth, Jerah, ²¹Hadoram, Uzal, Diklah, ²²Ebal,ᵃ Abimael, Sheba, ²³Ophir, Havilah, and Jobab. All these *were* the sons of Joktan.

²⁴Shem, Arphaxad, Shelah, ²⁵Eber, Peleg, Reu, ²⁶Serug, Nahor, Terah, ²⁷and Abram, who *is* Abraham. ²⁸The sons of Abraham *were* Isaac and Ishmael.

The Family of Ishmael

²⁹These *are* their genealogies: The firstborn of Ishmael *was* Nebajoth; then Kedar, Adbeel, Mibsam, ³⁰Mishma, Dumah, Massa, Hadad,ᵃ Tema, ³¹Jetur, Naphish, and Kedemah. These *were* the sons of Ishmael.

The Family of Keturah

³²Now the sons born to Keturah, Abraham's concubine, *were* Zimran, Jokshan, Medan, Midian, Ishbak, and Shuah. The sons of Jokshan *were* Sheba and Dedan. ³³The sons of Midian *were* Ephah, Epher, Hanoch, Abida, and Eldaah. All these were the children of Keturah.

The Family of Isaac

³⁴And Abraham begot Isaac. The sons of Isaac *were* Esau and Israel. ³⁵The sons of Esau *were* Eliphaz, Reuel, Jeush, Jaalam, and Korah. ³⁶And the sons of Eliphaz *were* Teman, Omar, Zephi,ᵃ

Genealogies: The Impact of a Leader's Heritage

(1 Chronicles 1:1—9:44)

The first nine chapters of 1 Chronicles furnish a genealogy of Israel's leaders—almost a third of the book! The enormous space given to these ancestral lists illustrates the vast importance of heritage to a Hebrew leader.

Such an emphasis can teach us several important lessons. Our generation and culture seem to place a much lower value on family stock and past tradition than did others in history. What do we learn from the lineages of these Jewish leaders?

1. They remained connected to their heritage.
2. They saw their place in history and gained perspective from it.
3. They were able to honor and pay respect to their forefathers.
4. They saw their lineage as a family blessing and passed on this blessing.
5. They used their heritage to provide a sense of stability for their children.
6. They sensed tendencies of ancestral giftedness and calling.
7. They could retain their identity even when exiled to a foreign land.

Gatam, *and* Kenaz; and *by* Timna,ᵇ Amalek. ³⁷The sons of Reuel *were* Nahath, Zerah, Shammah, and Mizzah.

The Family of Seir

³⁸The sons of Seir *were* Lotan, Shobal, Zibeon, Anah, Dishon, Ezer, and Dishan. ³⁹And the sons of Lotan *were* Hori and Homam; Lotan's sister *was* Timna. ⁴⁰The sons of Shobal *were*

1:2 ᵃHebrew *Qenan* **1:4** ᵃFollowing Masoretic Text and Vulgate; Septuagint adds *the sons of Noah.* **1:6** ᵃSpelled *Riphath* in Genesis 10:3 **1:7** ᵃSpelled *Tarshish* in Genesis 10:4 ᵇSpelled *Dodanim* in Genesis 10:4 **1:9** ᵃSpelled *Sabtah* in Genesis 10:7 ᵇSpelled *Raamah* in Genesis 10:7 **1:17** ᵃSpelled *Mash* in Genesis 10:23 **1:19** ᵃLiterally *Division* **1:22** ᵃSpelled *Obal* in Genesis 10:28 **1:30** ᵃSpelled *Hadar* in Genesis 25:15 **1:36** ᵃSpelled *Zepho* in Genesis 36:11 ᵇCompare Genesis 36:12

Alian,[a] Manahath, Ebal, Shephi,[b] and Onam. The sons of Zibeon were Ajah and Anah. [41]The son of Anah was Dishon. The sons of Dishon were Hamran,[a] Eshban, Ithran, and Cheran. [42]The sons of Ezer were Bilhan, Zaavan, and Jaakan.[a] The sons of Dishan were Uz and Aran.

The Kings of Edom

[43]Now these were the kings who reigned in the land of Edom before a king reigned over the children of Israel: Bela the son of Beor, and the name of his city was Dinhabah. [44]And when Bela died, Jobab the son of Zerah of Bozrah reigned in his place. [45]When Jobab died, Husham of the land of the Temanites reigned in his place. [46]And when Husham died, Hadad the son of Bedad, who attacked Midian in the field of Moab, reigned in his place. The name of his city was Avith. [47]When Hadad died, Samlah of Masrekah reigned in his place. [48]And when Samlah died, Saul of Rehoboth-by-the-River reigned in his place. [49]When Saul died, Baal-Hanan the son of Achbor reigned in his place. [50]And when Baal-Hanan died, Hadad[a] reigned in his place; and the name of his city was Pai.[b] His wife's name was Mehetabel the daughter of Matred, the daughter of Mezahab. [51]Hadad died also. And the chiefs of Edom were Chief Timnah, Chief Aliah,[a] Chief Jetheth, [52]Chief Aholibamah, Chief Elah, Chief Pinon, [53]Chief Kenaz, Chief Teman, Chief Mibzar, [54]Chief Magdiel, and Chief Iram. These were the chiefs of Edom.

The Family of Israel

2 These were the sons of Israel: Reuben, Simeon, Levi, Judah, Issachar, Zebulun, [2]Dan, Joseph, Benjamin, Naphtali, Gad, and Asher.

From Judah to David

[3]The sons of Judah were Er, Onan, and Shelah. These three were born to him by the daughter of Shua, the Canaanitess. Er, the firstborn of Judah, was wicked in the sight of the LORD; so He killed him. [4]And Tamar, his daughter-in-law, bore him Perez and Zerah. All the sons of Judah were five.

[5]The sons of Perez were Hezron and Hamul. [6]The sons of Zerah were Zimri, Ethan, Heman, Calcol, and Dara—five of them in all.

[7]The son of Carmi was Achar,[a] the troubler of Israel, who transgressed in the accursed thing. [8]The son of Ethan was Azariah.

[9]Also the sons of Hezron who were born to him were Jerahmeel, Ram, and Chelubai.[a] [10]Ram begot Amminadab, and Amminadab begot Nahshon, leader of the children of Judah; [11]Nahshon begot Salma,[a] and Salma begot Boaz; [12]Boaz begot Obed, and Obed begot Jesse; [13]Jesse begot Eliab his firstborn, Abinadab the second, Shimea[a] the third, [14]Nethanel the fourth, Raddai the fifth, [15]Ozem the sixth, and David the seventh.

[16]Now their sisters were Zeruiah and Abigail. And the sons of Zeruiah were Abishai, Joab, and Asahel—three. [17]Abigail bore Amasa; and the father of Amasa was Jether the Ishmaelite.[a]

The Family of Hezron

[18]Caleb the son of Hezron had children by Azubah, his wife, and by Jerioth. Now these were her sons: Jesher, Shobab, and Ardon. [19]When Azubah died, Caleb took Ephrath[a] as his wife, who bore him Hur. [20]And Hur begot Uri, and Uri begot Bezalel.

[21]Now afterward Hezron went in to the daughter of Machir the father of Gilead, whom he married when he was sixty years old; and she bore him Segub. [22]Segub begot Jair, who had twenty-three cities in the land of Gilead. [23](Geshur and Syria took from them the towns of Jair, with Kenath and its towns—sixty towns.) All these belonged to the sons of Machir the father of Gilead. [24]After Hezron died in Caleb Ephrathah, Hezron's wife Abijah bore him Ashhur the father of Tekoa.

The Family of Jerahmeel

[25]The sons of Jerahmeel, the firstborn of Hezron, were Ram, the firstborn, and Bunah, Oren, Ozem, and Ahijah. [26]Jerahmeel had another wife, whose name was Atarah; she was the mother of Onam. [27]The sons of Ram, the firstborn of Jerahmeel, were Maaz, Jamin, and Eker. [28]The sons of Onam were Shammai and Jada. The sons of Shammai were Nadab and Abishur.

[29]And the name of the wife of Abishur was Abihail, and she bore him Ahban and Molid. [30]The sons of Nadab were Seled and Appaim; Seled died without children. [31]The son of Ap-

---

1:40 [a]Spelled *Alvan* in Genesis 36:23 [b]Spelled *Shepho* in Genesis 36:23 **1:41** [a]Spelled *Hemdan* in Genesis 36:26 **1:42** [a]Spelled *Akan* in Genesis 36:27 **1:50** [a]Spelled *Hadar* in Genesis 36:39 [b]Spelled *Pau* in Genesis 36:39 **1:51** [a]Spelled *Alvah* in Genesis 36:40 **2:7** [a]Spelled *Achan* in Joshua 7:1 and elsewhere **2:9** [a]Spelled *Caleb* in 2:18, 42 **2:11** [a]Spelled *Salmon* in Ruth 4:21 and Luke 3:32 **2:13** [a]Spelled *Shammah* in 1 Samuel 16:9 and elsewhere **2:17** [a]Compare 2 Samuel 17:25 **2:19** [a]Spelled *Ephrathah* elsewhere paim *was* Ishi, the son of Ishi *was* Sheshan, and Sheshan's son *was* Ahlai. ³²The sons of Jada, the brother of Shammai, *were* Jether and Jonathan; Jether died without children. ³³The sons of Jonathan *were* Peleth and Zaza. These were the sons of Jerahmeel.

³⁴Now Sheshan had no sons, only daughters. And Sheshan had an Egyptian servant whose name *was* Jarha. ³⁵Sheshan gave his daughter to Jarha his servant as wife, and she bore him Attai. ³⁶Attai begot Nathan, and Nathan begot Zabad; ³⁷Zabad begot Ephlal, and Ephlal begot Obed; ³⁸Obed begot Jehu, and Jehu begot Azariah; ³⁹Azariah begot Helez, and Helez begot Eleasah; ⁴⁰Eleasah begot Sismai, and Sismai begot Shallum; ⁴¹Shallum begot Jekamiah, and Jekamiah begot Elishama.

The Family of Caleb

⁴²The descendants of Caleb the brother of Jerahmeel *were* Mesha, his firstborn, who was the father of Ziph, and the sons of Mareshah the father of Hebron. ⁴³The sons of Hebron *were* Korah, Tappuah, Rekem, and Shema. ⁴⁴Shema begot Raham the father of Jorkoam, and Rekem begot Shammai. ⁴⁵And the son of Shammai *was* Maon, and Maon *was* the father of Beth Zur.

⁴⁶Ephah, Caleb's concubine, bore Haran, Moza, and Gazez; and Haran begot Gazez. ⁴⁷And the sons of Jahdai *were* Regem, Jotham, Geshan, Pelet, Ephah, and Shaaph.

⁴⁸Maachah, Caleb's concubine, bore Sheber and Tirhanah. ⁴⁹She also bore Shaaph the father of Madmannah, Sheva the father of Machbenah and the father of Gibea. And the daughter of Caleb *was* Achsah.

⁵⁰These were the descendants of Caleb: The sons of Hur, the firstborn of Ephrathah, *were* Shobal the father of Kirjath Jearim, ⁵¹Salma the father of Bethlehem, *and* Hareph the father of Beth Gader.

⁵²And Shobal the father of Kirjath Jearim had descendants: Haroeh, *and* half of the *families of* Manuhoth.ᵃ ⁵³The families of Kirjath Jearim *were* the Ithrites, the Puthites, the Shumathites, and the Mishraites. From these came the Zorathites and the Eshtaolites.

⁵⁴The sons of Salma *were* Bethlehem, the Netophathites, Atroth Beth Joab, half of the Manahethites, and the Zorites.

⁵⁵And the families of the scribes who dwelt at Jabez *were* the Tirathites, the Shimeathites, *and* the Suchathites. These *were* the Kenites who came from Hammath, the father of the house of Rechab.

The Family of David

3 Now these were the sons of David who were born to him in Hebron: The firstborn *was* Amnon, by Ahinoam the Jezreelitess; the second, Daniel,ᵃ by Abigail the Carmelitess; ²the third, Absalom the son of Maacah, the daughter of Talmai, king of Geshur; the fourth, Adonijah the son of Haggith; ³the fifth, Shephatiah, by Abital; the sixth, Ithream, by his wife Eglah.

⁴*These* six were born to him in Hebron. There he reigned seven years and six months, and in Jerusalem he reigned thirty-three years. ⁵And these were born to him in Jerusalem: Shimea,ᵃ Shobab, Nathan, and Solomon—four by Bathshuaᵇ the daughter of Ammiel.ᶜ ⁶Also *there* were Ibhar, Elishama,ᵃ Eliphelet,ᵇ ⁷Nogah, Nepheg, Japhia, ⁸Elishama, Eliada,ᵃ and Eliphelet—nine *in all.* ⁹*These were* all the sons of David, besides the sons of the concubines, and Tamar their sister.

The Family of Solomon

¹⁰Solomon's son *was* Rehoboam; Abijahᵃ *was* his son, Asa his son, Jehoshaphat his son, ¹¹Joramᵃ his son, Ahaziah his son, Joashᵇ his son, ¹²Amaziah his son, Azariahᵃ his son, Jotham his son, ¹³Ahaz his son, Hezekiah his son, Manasseh his son, ¹⁴Amon his son, *and* Josiah his son. ¹⁵The sons of Josiah *were* Johanan the firstborn, the second Jehoiakim, the third Zedekiah, and the fourth Shallum.ᵃ ¹⁶The sons of Jehoiakim *were* Jeconiah his son *and* Zedekiahᵃ his son.

The Family of Jeconiah

¹⁷And the sons of Jeconiahᵃ *were* Assir,ᵇ Shealtiel his son, ¹⁸*and* Malchiram, Pedaiah, Shenazzar, Jecamiah, Hoshama, and Nedabiah. ¹⁹The sons of Pedaiah *were* Zerubbabel and Shimei. The sons of Zerubbabel *were* Meshullam, Hananiah, Shelomith their sister, ²⁰and Hashubah, Ohel, Berechiah, Hasadiah, and Jushab-Hesed—five *in all.*

2:52 ᵃSame as *the Manahethites,* verse 54 **3:1** ᵃCalled *Chileab* in 2 Samuel 3:3 **3:5** ᵃSpelled *Shammua* in 14:4 and 2 Samuel 5:14 ᵇSpelled *Bathsheba* in 2 Samuel 11:3 ᶜCalled *Eliam* in 2 Samuel 11:3 **3:6** ᵃSpelled *Elishua* in 14:5 and 2 Samuel 5:15 ᵇSpelled *Elpelet* in 14:5 **3:8** ᵃSpelled *Beeliada* in 14:7 **3:10** ᵃSpelled *Abijam* in 1 Kings 15:1 **3:11** ᵃSpelled *Jehoram* in 2 Kings 1:17 and 8:16 ᵇSpelled *Jehoash* in 2 Kings 12:1 **3:12** ᵃCalled *Uzziah* in Isaiah 6:1 **3:15** ᵃCalled *Jehoahaz* in 2 Kings 23:31 **3:16** ᵃCompare 2 Kings 24:17 **3:17** ᵃAlso called *Coniah* in Jeremiah 22:24 and *Jehoiachin* in 2 Kings 24:8 ᵇOr *Jeconiah the captive were*

²¹The sons of Hananiah *were* Pelatiah and Jeshaiah, the sons of Rephaiah, the sons of Arnan, the sons of Obadiah, and the sons of Shechaniah. ²²The son of Shechaniah was Shemaiah. The sons of Shemaiah *were* Hattush, Igal, Bariah, Neariah, and Shaphat—six *in all.* ²³The sons of Neariah *were* Elioenai, Hezekiah, and Azrikam—three *in all.* ²⁴The sons of Elioenai *were* Hodaviah, Eliashib, Pelaiah, Akkub, Johanan, Delaiah, and Anani—seven *in all.*

The Family of Judah

4 The sons of Judah *were* Perez, Hezron, Carmi, Hur, and Shobal. ²And Reaiah the son of Shobal begot Jahath, and Jahath begot Ahumai and Lahad. These *were* the families of the Zorathites. ³These *were* the sons *of the father* of Etam: Jezreel, Ishma, and Idbash; and the name of their sister *was* Hazelelponi; ⁴and Penuel *was* the father of Gedor, and Ezer *was the* father of Hushah.

These *were* the sons of Hur, the firstborn of Ephrathah the father of Bethlehem.

⁵And Ashhur the father of Tekoa had two wives, Helah and Naarah. ⁶Naarah bore him Ahuzzam, Hepher, Temeni, and Haahashtari. These *were* the sons of Naarah. ⁷The sons of Helah *were* Zereth, Zohar, and Ethnan; ⁸and Koz begot Anub, Zobebah, and the families of Aharhel the son of Harum.

⁹Now Jabez was more honorable than his brothers, and his mother called his name Jabez,ᵃ saying, "Because I bore *him* in pain." ¹⁰And Jabez called on the God of Israel saying, "Oh, that You would bless me indeed, and enlarge my territory, that Your hand would be with me, and that You would keep *me* from evil, that I may not cause pain!" So God granted him what he requested.

¹¹Chelub the brother of Shuhah begot Mehir, who *was* the father of Eshton. ¹²And Eshton begot Beth-Rapha, Paseah, and Tehinnah the father of Ir-Nahash. These *were* the men of Rechah.

¹³The sons of Kenaz *were* Othniel and Seraiah. The sons of Othniel *were* Hathath,ᵃ ¹⁴and Meonothai *who* begot Ophrah. Seraiah begot Joab the father of Ge Harashim,ᵃ for they were craftsmen. ¹⁵The sons of Caleb the son of Jephunneh *were* Iru, Elah, and Naam. The son of Elah *was* Kenaz. ¹⁶The sons of Jehallelel *were* Ziph, Ziphah, Tiria, and Asarel. ¹⁷The sons of

4:9 ᵃLiterally *He Will Cause Pain* **4:13** ᵃSeptuagint and Vulgate add *and Meonothai.* **4:14** ᵃLiterally *Valley of Craftsmen*

AMNON — THE HIGH COST OF NO SELF-DISCIPLINE
(1 Chronicles 3:1)

PROFILE IN LEADERSHIP

One might suppose the firstborn son of the greatest king of Israel to be almost foreordained to do great things for God and His people. Yet David's firstborn, Amnon, wound up as little more than a quick and sad footnote to the early chapters of 1 Chronicles.

Amnon forfeited any claim to leadership of his people because he could not control himself—specifically his fleshly lusts (2 Sam. 13:1–19). This lack of self-control led to the disgrace of his family, and eventually to his death at the hands of a vengeful brother (13:22–29).

Amnon's demise began the day he fixed his eyes upon his lovely half sister, Tamar, and lusted after her beauty. The Law expressly forbade this kind of union and laid out severe penalties for those who violated its provisions (Lev. 18:9; 20:17). But this didn't deter Amnon, who hatched a plot to lie with his sister. Despite Tamar's horrified protests, Amnon forced himself on her and then sent her away in disgrace. When Absalom, Tamar's brother, heard what his half brother had done, he plotted revenge. At an opportune time, Absalom's men murdered Amnon and fled the scene.

A miserable, sordid story—and all because of a lack of discipline. No leader can afford to do without self-discipline. Amnon tried, and wished he hadn't.

Jabez's Honorable Mention

(1 Chronicles 4:9, 10)

God singled out one man from more than 600 others for special recognition in the genealogical lists of 1 Chronicles. Why did the Lord say Jabez lived above average? Because he modeled three qualities that make leaders rise to the top: 1. great ambition; 2. great faith; and 3. great prayer.

Ezrah *were* Jether, Mered, Epher, and Jalon. And *Mered's wife*[a] bore Miriam, Shammai, and Ishbah the father of Eshtemoa. [18](His wife Jehudijah[a] bore Jered the father of Gedor, Heber the father of Sochoh, and Jekuthiel the father of Zanoah.) And these were the sons of Bithiah the daughter of Pharaoh, whom Mered took.

[19]The sons of Hodiah's wife, the sister of Naham, *were* the fathers of Keilah the Garmite and of Eshtemoa the Maachathite. [20]And the sons of Shimon *were* Amnon, Rinnah, Ben-Hanan, and Tilon. And the sons of Ishi *were* Zoheth and Ben-Zoheth.

[21]The sons of Shelah the son of Judah *were* Er the father of Lecah, Laadah the father of Mareshah, and the families of the house of the linen workers of the house of Ashbea; [22]also Jokim, the men of Chozeba, and Joash; Saraph, who ruled in Moab, and Jashubi-Lehem. Now the records are ancient. [23]These *were* the potters and those who dwell at Netaim[a] and Gederah;[b] there they dwelt with the king for his work.

The Family of Simeon

[24]The sons of Simeon *were* Nemuel, Jamin, Jarib,[a] Zerah,[b] *and* Shaul, [25]Shallum his son, Mibsam his son, and Mishma his son. [26]And the sons of Mishma *were* Hamuel his son, Zacchur his son, and Shimei his son. [27]Shimei had sixteen sons and six daughters; but his brothers did not have many children, nor did any of their families multiply as much as the children of Judah.

[28]They dwelt at Beersheba, Moladah, Hazar Shual, [29]Bilhah, Ezem, Tolad, [30]Bethuel, Hormah, Ziklag, [31]Beth Marcaboth, Hazar Susim, Beth Biri, and at Shaaraim. These *were* their cities until the reign of David. [32]And their villages *were* Etam, Ain, Rimmon, Tochen, and Ashan—five cities— [33]and all the villages that *were* around these cities as far as Baal.[a] These *were* their

dwelling places, and they maintained their genealogy: [34]Meshobab, Jamlech, and Joshah the son of Amaziah; [35]Joel, and Jehu the son of Joshibiah, the son of Seraiah, the son of Asiel; [36]Elioenai, Jaakobah, Jeshohaiah, Asaiah, Adiel, Jesimiel, and Benaiah; [37]Ziza the son of Shiphi, the son of Allon, the son of Jedaiah, the son of Shimri, the son of Shemaiah— [38]these mentioned by name *were* leaders in their families, and their father's house increased greatly.

[39]So they went to the entrance of Gedor, as far as the east side of the valley, to seek pasture for their flocks. [40]And they found rich, good pasture, and the land *was* broad, quiet, and peaceful; for some Hamites formerly lived there.

[41]These recorded by name came in the days of Hezekiah king of Judah; and they attacked their tents and the Meunites who were found there, and utterly destroyed them, as it is to this day. So they dwelt in their place, because *there was* pasture for their flocks there. [42]Now *some* of them, five hundred men of the sons of Simeon, went to Mount Seir, having as their captains Pelatiah, Neariah, Rephaiah, and Uzziel, the sons of Ishi. [43]And they defeated the rest of the Amalekites who had escaped. They have dwelt there to this day.

The Family of Reuben

5 Now the sons of Reuben the firstborn of Israel—he *was* indeed the firstborn, but because he defiled his father's bed, his birthright was given to the sons of Joseph, the son of Israel, so that the genealogy is not listed according to the birthright; [2]yet Judah prevailed over his brothers, and from him *came* a ruler, although the birthright was Joseph's— [3]the sons of Reuben the firstborn of Israel were Hanoch, Pallu, Hezron, and Carmi.

[4]The sons of Joel *were* Shemaiah his son, Gog his son, Shimei his son, [5]Micah his son, Reaiah his son, Baal his son, [6]and Beerah his son, whom Tiglath-Pileser[a] king of Assyria carried into captivity. He *was* leader of the Reubenites. [7]And his brethren by their families, when the genealogy of their generations was registered: the chief, Jeiel, and Zechariah, [8]and Bela the son of Azaz, the son of Shema, the son of Joel, who dwelt in Aroer, as far as Nebo and Baal Meon. [9]Eastward they settled as far as the entrance of the wilderness this

---

4:17 [a]Literally *she* **4:18** [a]Or *His Judean wife*
4:23 [a]Literally *Plants* [b]Literally *Hedges* **4:24** [a]Called *Jachin* in Genesis 46:10 [b]Called *Zohar* in Genesis 46:10 **4:33** [a]Or *Baalath Beer* (compare Joshua 19:8)
5:6 [a]Hebrew *Tilgath-Pilneser*

side of the River Euphrates, because their cattle had multiplied in the land of Gilead.

[10]Now in the days of Saul they made war with the Hagrites, who fell by their hand; and they dwelt in their tents throughout the entire *area* east of Gilead.

The Family of Gad

[11]And the children of Gad dwelt next to them in the land of Bashan as far as Salcah: [12]Joel *was* the chief, Shapham the next, then Jaanai and Shaphat in Bashan, [13]and their brethren of their father's house: Michael, Meshullam, Sheba, Jorai, Jachan, Zia, and Eber—seven *in all.* [14]These *were* the children of Abihail the son of Huri, the son of Jaroah, the son of Gilead, the son of Michael, the son of Jeshishai, the son of Jahdo, the son of Buz; [15]Ahi the son of Abdiel, the son of Guni, *was* chief of their father's house. [16]And *the Gadites* dwelt in Gilead, in Bashan and in its villages, and in all the common-lands of Sharon within their borders. [17]All these were registered by genealogies in the days of Jotham king of Judah, and in the days of Jeroboam king of Israel.

[18]The sons of Reuben, the Gadites, and half the tribe of Manasseh *had* forty-four thousand seven hundred and sixty valiant men, men able to bear shield and sword, to shoot with the bow, and skillful in war, who went to war. [19]They made war with the Hagrites, Jetur, Naphish, and Nodab. [20]And they were helped against them, and the Hagrites were delivered into their hand, and all who *were* with them, for they cried out to God in the battle. He heeded their prayer, because they put their trust in Him. [21]Then they took away their livestock—fifty thousand of their camels, two hundred and fifty thousand of their sheep, and two thousand of their donkeys—also one hundred thousand of their men; [22]for many fell dead, because the war *was* God's. And they dwelt in their place until the captivity.

The Family of Manasseh (East)

[23]So the children of the half-tribe of Manasseh dwelt in the land. Their *numbers* increased from Bashan to Baal Hermon, that is, to Senir, or Mount Hermon. [24]These *were* the heads of their fathers' houses: Epher, Ishi, Eliel, Azriel, Jeremiah, Hodaviah, and Jahdiel. They were mighty men of valor, famous men, *and* heads of their fathers' houses.

[25]And they were unfaithful to the God of their fathers, and played the harlot after the gods of the peoples of the land, whom God had destroyed before them. [26]So the God of Israel stirred up the spirit of Pul king of Assyria, that

is, Tiglath-Pileser[a] king of Assyria. He carried the Reubenites, the Gadites, and the half-tribe of Manasseh into captivity. He took them to Halah, Habor, Hara, and the river of Gozan to this day.

The Family of Levi

6 The sons of Levi *were* Gershon, Kohath, and Merari. [2]The sons of Kohath *were* Amram, Izhar, Hebron, and Uzziel. [3]The children of Amram *were* Aaron, Moses, and Miriam. And the sons of Aaron *were* Nadab, Abihu, Eleazar, and Ithamar. [4]Eleazar begot Phinehas, *and* Phinehas begot Abishua; [5]Abishua begot Bukki, and Bukki begot Uzzi; [6]Uzzi begot Zerahiah, and Zerahiah begot Meraioth; [7]Meraioth begot Amariah, and Amariah begot Ahitub; [8]Ahitub begot Zadok, and Zadok begot Ahimaaz; [9]Ahimaaz begot Azariah, and Azariah begot Johanan; [10]Johanan begot Azariah (it was he who ministered as priest in the temple that Solomon built in Jerusalem); [11]Azariah begot Amariah, and Amariah begot Ahitub; [12]Ahitub begot Zadok, and Zadok begot Shallum; [13]Shallum begot Hilkiah, and Hilkiah begot Azariah; [14]Azariah begot Seraiah, and Seraiah begot Jehozadak. [15]Jehozadak went *into captivity* when the LORD carried Judah and Jerusalem into captivity by the hand of Nebuchadnezzar.

[16]The sons of Levi *were* Gershon,[a] Kohath, and Merari. [17]These are the names of the sons of Gershon: Libni and Shimei. [18]The sons of Kohath *were* Amram, Izhar, Hebron, and Uzziel. [19]The sons of Merari *were* Mahli and Mushi. Now these *are* the families of the Levites according to their fathers: [20]Of Gershon *were* Libni his son, Jahath his son, Zimmah his son, [21]Joah his son, Iddo his son, Zerah his son, *and* Jeatherai his son. [22]The sons of Kohath *were* Amminadab his son, Korah his son, Assir his son, [23]Elkanah his son, Ebiasaph his son, Assir his son, [24]Tahath his son, Uriel his son, Uzziah his son, and Shaul his son. [25]The sons of Elkanah *were* Amasai and Ahimoth. [26]*As for* Elkanah,[a] the sons of Elkanah *were* Zophai[b] his son, Nahath[c] his son, [27]Eliab[a] his son, Jeroham his son, *and* Elkanah his son. [28]The sons of Samuel *were* Joel[a] the firstborn, and Abijah the second.[b] [29]The sons of Merari *were* Mahli, Libni his son,

---

5:26 [a]Hebrew *Tilgath-Pilneser* **6:16** [a]Hebrew *Gershom* (alternate spelling of *Gershon,* as in verses 1, 17, 20, 43, 62, and 71) **6:26** [a]Compare verse 35 [b]Spelled *Zuph* in verse 35 and 1 Samuel 1:1 [c]Compare verse 34 **6:27** [a]Compare verse 34 **6:28** [a]Following Septuagint, Syriac, and Arabic (compare verse 33 and 1 Samuel 8:2) [b]Hebrew *Vasheni*

Shimei his son, Uzzah his son, [30]Shimea his son, Haggiah his son, *and* Asaiah his son.

Musicians in the House of the LORD

[31]Now these are the men whom David appointed over the service of song in the house of the LORD, after the ark came to rest. [32]They were ministering with music before the dwelling place of the tabernacle of meeting, until Solomon had built the house of the LORD in Jerusalem, and they served in their office according to their order.

[33]And these *are* the ones who ministered with their sons: Of the sons of the Kohathites *were* Heman the singer, the son of Joel, the son of Samuel, [34]the son of Elkanah, the son of Jeroham, the son of Eliel,[a] the son of Toah,[b] [35]the son of Zuph, the son of Elkanah, the son of Mahath, the son of Amasai, [36]the son of Elkanah, the son of Joel, the son of Azariah, the son of Zephaniah, [37]the son of Tahath, the son of Assir, the son of Ebiasaph, the son of Korah, [38]the son of Izhar, the son of Kohath, the son of Levi, the son of Israel. [39]And his brother Asaph, who stood at his right hand, *was* Asaph the son of Berachiah, the son of Shimea, [40]the son of Michael, the son of Baaseiah, the son of Malchijah, [41]the son of Ethni, the son of Zerah, the son of Adaiah, [42]the son of Ethan, the son of Zimmah, the son of Shimei, [43]the son of Jahath, the son of Gershon, the son of Levi.

[44]Their brethren, the sons of Merari, on the left hand, *were* Ethan the son of Kishi, the son of Abdi, the son of Malluch, [45]the son of Hashabiah, the son of Amaziah, the son of Hilkiah, [46]the son of Amzi, the son of Bani, the son of Shamer, [47]the son of Mahli, the son of Mushi, the son of Merari, the son of Levi.

[48]And their brethren, the Levites, *were* appointed to every kind of service of the tabernacle of the house of God.

The Family of Aaron

[49]But Aaron and his sons offered sacrifices on the altar of burnt offering and on the altar of incense, for all the work of the Most Holy *Place,* and to make atonement for Israel, according to all that Moses the servant of God had commanded. [50]Now these *are* the sons of Aaron: Eleazar his son, Phinehas his son, Abishua his son, [51]Bukki his son, Uzzi his son, Zerahiah his son, [52]Meraioth his son, Amariah his son, Ahitub his son, [53]Zadok his son, *and* Ahimaaz his son.

Dwelling Places of the Levites

[54]Now these *are* their dwelling places throughout their settlements in their territory, for they were *given* by lot to the sons of Aaron, of the family of the Kohathites: [55]They gave them Hebron in the land of Judah, with its surrounding common-lands. [56]But the fields of the city and its villages they gave to Caleb the son of Jephunneh. [57]And to the sons of Aaron they gave *one of* the cities of refuge, Hebron; also Libnah with its common-lands, Jattir, Eshtemoa with its common-lands, [58]Hilen[a] with its common-lands, Debir with its common-lands, [59]Ashan[a] with its common-lands, and Beth Shemesh with its common-lands. [60]And from the tribe of Benjamin: Geba with its common-lands, Alemeth[a] with its common-lands, and Anathoth with its common-lands. All their cities among their families *were* thirteen.

[61]To the rest of the family of the tribe of the Kohathites *they gave* by lot ten cities from half the tribe of Manasseh. [62]And to the sons of Gershon, throughout their families, *they gave* thirteen cities from the tribe of Issachar, from the tribe of Asher, from the tribe of Naphtali, and from the tribe of Manasseh in Bashan. [63]To the sons of Merari, throughout their families, *they gave* twelve cities from the tribe of Reuben, from the tribe of Gad, and from the tribe of Zebulun. [64]So the children of Israel gave *these* cities with their common-lands to the Levites. [65]And they gave by lot from the tribe of the children of Judah, from the tribe of the children of Simeon, and from the tribe of the children of Benjamin these cities which are called by *their* names.

[66]Now some of the families of the sons of Kohath *were given* cities as their territory from the tribe of Ephraim. [67]And they gave them *one of* the cities of refuge, Shechem with its common-lands, in the mountains of Ephraim, also Gezer with its common-lands, [68]Jokmeam with its common-lands, Beth Horon with its common-lands, [69]Aijalon with its common-lands, and Gath Rimmon with its common-lands. [70]And from the half-tribe of Manasseh: Aner with its common-lands and Bileam with its common-lands, for the rest of the family of the sons of Kohath.

[71]From the family of the half-tribe of Manasseh the sons of Gershon *were given* Golan in Bashan with its common-lands and Ashtaroth with its common-lands. [72]And from the tribe of Issachar: Kedesh with its common-lands, Daberath with its common-lands, [73]Ramoth with

---

6:34 [a]Spelled *Elihu* in 1 Samuel 1:1   [b]Spelled *Tohu* in 1 Samuel 1:1   **6:58** [a]Spelled *Holon* in Joshua 21:15   **6:59** [a]Spelled *Ain* in Joshua 21:16   **6:60** [a]Spelled *Almon* in Joshua 21:18

its common-lands, and Anem with its common-lands. [74]And from the tribe of Asher: Mashal with its common-lands, Abdon with its common-lands, [75]Hukok with its common-lands, and Rehob with its common-lands. [76]And from the tribe of Naphtali: Kedesh in Galilee with its common-lands, Hammon with its common-lands, and Kirjathaim with its common-lands.

[77]From the tribe of Zebulun the rest of the children of Merari *were given* Rimmon[a] with its common-lands and Tabor with its common-lands. [78]And on the other side of the Jordan, across from Jericho, on the east side of the Jordan, *they were given* from the tribe of Reuben: Bezer in the wilderness with its common-lands, Jahzah with its common-lands, [79]Kedemoth with its common-lands, and Mephaath with its common-lands. [80]And from the tribe of Gad: Ramoth in Gilead with its common-lands, Mahanaim with its common-lands, [81]Heshbon with its common-lands, and Jazer with its common-lands.

The Family of Issachar

7 The sons of Issachar *were* Tola, Puah,[a] Jashub, and Shimron—four *in all.* [2]The sons of Tola *were* Uzzi, Rephaiah, Jeriel, Jahmai, Jibsam, and Shemuel, heads of their father's house. *The sons* of Tola *were* mighty men of valor in their generations; their number in the days of David *was* twenty-two thousand six hundred. [3]The son of Uzzi *was* Izrahiah, and the sons of Izrahiah *were* Michael, Obadiah, Joel, and Ishiah. All five of them *were* chief men. [4]And with them, by their generations, according to their fathers' houses, *were* thirty-six thousand troops ready for war; for they had many wives and sons.

[5]Now their brethren among all the families of Issachar *were* mighty men of valor, listed by their genealogies, eighty-seven thousand in all.

The Family of Benjamin

[6]*The sons* of Benjamin *were* Bela, Becher, and Jediael—three *in all.* [7]The sons of Bela were Ezbon, Uzzi, Uzziel, Jerimoth, and Iri—five *in all.* They *were* heads of *their* fathers' houses, and they were listed by their genealogies, twenty-two thousand and thirty-four mighty men of valor.

[8]The sons of Becher *were* Zemirah, Joash, Eliezer, Elioenai, Omri, Jerimoth, Abijah, Anathoth, and Alemeth. All these *are* the sons of Becher. [9]And they were recorded by genealogy according to their generations, heads of their fathers' houses, twenty thousand two hundred mighty men of valor. [10]The son of Jediael *was*

Bilhan, and the sons of Bilhan *were* Jeush, Benjamin, Ehud, Chenaanah, Zethan, Tharshish, and Ahishahar.

[11]All these sons of Jediael *were* heads of their fathers' houses; *there were* seventeen thousand two hundred mighty men of valor fit to go out for war *and* battle. [12]Shuppim and Huppim[a] *were* the sons of Ir, *and* Hushim *was* the son of Aher.

The Family of Naphtali

[13]The sons of Naphtali *were* Jahziel,[a] Guni, Jezer, and Shallum,[b] the sons of Bilhah.

The Family of Manasseh (West)

[14]The descendants of Manasseh: his Syrian concubine bore him Machir the father of Gilead, the father of Asriel.[a] [15]Machir took as his wife *the sister* of Huppim and Shuppim,[a] whose name *was* Maachah. The name of *Gilead's* grandson[b] *was* Zelophehad,[c] but Zelophehad begot only daughters. [16](Maachah the wife of Machir bore a son, and she called his name Peresh. The name of his brother *was* Sheresh, and his sons *were* Ulam and Rakem. [17]The son of Ulam *was* Bedan.) These *were* the descendants of Gilead the son of Machir, the son of Manasseh.

[18]His sister Hammoleketh bore Ishhod, Abiezer, and Mahlah.

[19]And the sons of Shemida were Ahian, Shechem, Likhi, and Aniam.

The Family of Ephraim

[20]The sons of Ephraim *were* Shuthelah, Bered his son, Tahath his son, Eladah his son, Tahath his son, [21]Zabad his son, Shuthelah his son, and Ezer and Elead. The men of Gath who were born in *that* land killed *them* because they came down to take away their cattle. [22]Then Ephraim their father mourned many days, and his brethren came to comfort him.

[23]And when he went in to his wife, she conceived and bore a son; and he called his name Beriah,[a] because tragedy had come upon his house. [24]Now his daughter *was* Sheerah, who built Lower and Upper Beth Horon and Uzzen Sheerah; [25]and Rephah *was* his son, *as well as* Resheph, and Telah his son, Tahan his son,

---

6:77 [a]Hebrew *Rimmono,* alternate spelling of *Rimmon;* see 4:32 **7:1** [a]Spelled *Puvah* in Genesis 46:13 **7:12** [a]Called *Hupham* in Numbers 26:39 **7:13** [a]Spelled *Jahzeel* in Genesis 46:24 [b]Spelled *Shillem* in Genesis 46:24 **7:14** [a]The son of Gilead (compare Numbers 26:30, 31) **7:15** [a]Compare verse 12 [b]Literally *the second* [c]Compare Numbers 26:30–33 **7:23** [a]Literally *In Tragedy*

[26]Laadan his son, Ammihud his son, Elishama his son, [27]Nun[a] his son, and Joshua his son.

[28]Now their possessions and dwelling places were Bethel and its towns: to the east Naaran, to the west Gezer and its towns, and Shechem and its towns, as far as Ayyah[a] and its towns; [29]and by the borders of the children of Manasseh were Beth Shean and its towns, Taanach and its towns, Megiddo and its towns, Dor and its towns. In these dwelt the children of Joseph, the son of Israel.

The Family of Asher

[30]The sons of Asher were Imnah, Ishvah, Ishvi, Beriah, and their sister Serah. [31]The sons of Beriah were Heber and Malchiel, who was the father of Birzaith.[a] [32]And Heber begot Japhlet, Shomer,[a] Hotham,[b] and their sister Shua. [33]The sons of Japhlet were Pasach, Bimhal, and Ashvath. These were the children of Japhlet. [34]The sons of Shemer were Ahi, Rohgah, Jehubbah, and Aram. [35]And the sons of his brother Helem were Zophah, Imna, Shelesh, and Amal. [36]The sons of Zophah were Suah, Harnepher, Shual, Beri, Imrah, [37]Bezer, Hod, Shamma, Shilshah, Jithran,[a] and Beera. [38]The sons of Jether were Jephunneh, Pispah, and Ara. [39]The sons of Ulla were Arah, Haniel, and Rizia.

[40]All these were the children of Asher, heads of their fathers' houses, choice men, mighty men of valor, chief leaders. And they were recorded by genealogies among the army fit for battle; their number was twenty-six thousand.

The Family Tree of King Saul of Benjamin

8 Now Benjamin begot Bela his firstborn, Ashbel the second, Aharah[a] the third, [2]Nohah the fourth, and Rapha the fifth. [3]The sons of Bela were Addar,[a] Gera, Abihud, [4]Abishua, Naaman, Ahoah, [5]Gera, Shephuphan, and Huram.

[6]These are the sons of Ehud, who were the heads of the fathers' houses of the inhabitants of Geba, and who forced them to move to Manahath: [7]Naaman, Ahijah, and Gera who forced them to move. He begot Uzza and Ahihud.

[8]Also Shaharaim had children in the country of Moab, after he had sent away Hushim and Baara his wives. [9]By Hodesh his wife he begot Jobab, Zibia, Mesha, Malcam, [10]Jeuz, Sachiah, and Mirmah. These were his sons, heads of their fathers' houses.

[11]And by Hushim he begot Abitub and Elpaal. [12]The sons of Elpaal were Eber, Misham, and Shemed, who built Ono and Lod with its towns; [13]and Beriah and Shema, who were heads of their fathers' houses of the inhabitants of Aijalon, who drove out the inhabitants of Gath. [14]Ahio, Shashak, Jeremoth, [15]Zebadiah, Arad, Eder, [16]Michael, Ispah, and Joha were the sons of Beriah. [17]Zebadiah, Meshullam, Hizki, Heber, [18]Ishmerai, Jizliah, and Jobab were the sons of Elpaal. [19]Jakim, Zichri, Zabdi, [20]Elienai, Zillethai, Eliel, [21]Adaiah, Beraiah, and Shimrath were the sons of Shimei. [22]Ishpan, Eber, Eliel, [23]Abdon, Zichri, Hanan, [24]Hananiah, Elam, Antothijah, [25]Iphdeiah, and Penuel were the sons of Shashak. [26]Shamsherai, Shehariah, Athaliah, [27]Jaareshiah, Elijah, and Zichri were the sons of Jeroham.

[28]These were heads of the fathers' houses by their generations, chief men. These dwelt in Jerusalem.

[29]Now the father of Gibeon, whose wife's name was Maacah, dwelt at Gibeon. [30]And his firstborn son was Abdon, then Zur, Kish, Baal, Nadab, [31]Gedor, Ahio, Zecher, [32]and Mikloth, who begot Shimeah.[a] They also dwelt alongside their relatives in Jerusalem, with their brethren. [33]Ner[a] begot Kish, Kish begot Saul, and Saul begot Jonathan, Malchishua, Abinadab,[b] and Esh-Baal.[c] [34]The son of Jonathan was Merib-Baal,[a] and Merib-Baal begot Micah. [35]The sons of Micah were Pithon, Melech, Tarea, and Ahaz. [36]And Ahaz begot Jehoaddah;[a] Jehoaddah begot Alemeth, Azmaveth, and Zimri; and Zimri begot Moza. [37]Moza begot Binea, Raphah[a] his son, Eleasah his son, and Azel his son.

[38]Azel had six sons whose names were these: Azrikam, Bocheru, Ishmael, Sheariah, Obadiah, and Hanan. All these were the sons of Azel. [39]And the sons of Eshek his brother were Ulam his firstborn, Jeush the second, and Eliphelet the third.

[40]The sons of Ulam were mighty men of valor—archers. They had many sons and grandsons, one hundred and fifty in all. These were all sons of Benjamin.

7:27 [a]Hebrew Non 7:28 [a]Many Hebrew manuscripts, Bomberg, Septuagint, Targum, and Vulgate read Gazza. 7:31 [a]Or Birzavith or Birzoth 7:32 [a]Spelled Shemer in verse 34 [b]Spelled Helem in verse 35 7:37 [a]Spelled Jether in verse 38 8:1 [a]Spelled Ahiram in Numbers 26:38 8:3 [a]Called Ard in Numbers 26:40 8:32 [a]Spelled Shimeam in 9:38 8:33 [a]Also the son of Gibeon (compare 9:36, 39) [b]Called Jishui in 1 Samuel 14:49 [c]Called Ishbosheth in 2 Samuel 2:8 and elsewhere 8:34 [a]Called Mephibosheth in 2 Samuel 4:4 8:36 [a]Spelled Jarah in 9:42 8:37 [a]Spelled Rephaiah in 9:43

9 So all Israel was recorded by genealogies, and indeed, they *were* inscribed in the book of the kings of Israel. But Judah was carried away captive to Babylon because of their unfaithfulness. ²And the first inhabitants who *dwelt* in their possessions in their cities *were* Israelites, priests, Levites, and the Nethinim.

Dwellers in Jerusalem

³Now in Jerusalem the children of Judah dwelt, and some of the children of Benjamin, and of the children of Ephraim and Manasseh: ⁴Uthai the son of Ammihud, the son of Omri, the son of Imri, the son of Bani, of the descendants of Perez, the son of Judah. ⁵Of the Shilonites: Asaiah the firstborn and his sons. ⁶Of the sons of Zerah: Jeuel, and their brethren—six hundred and ninety. ⁷Of the sons of Benjamin: Sallu the son of Meshullam, the son of Hodaviah, the son of Hassenuah; ⁸Ibneiah the son of Jeroham; Elah the son of Uzzi, the son of Michri; Meshullam the son of Shephatiah, the son of Reuel, the son of Ibnijah; ⁹and their brethren, according to their generations—nine hundred and fifty-six. All these men *were* heads of a father's *house* in their fathers' houses.

The Priests at Jerusalem

¹⁰Of the priests: Jedaiah, Jehoiarib, and Jachin; ¹¹Azariah the son of Hilkiah, the son of Meshullam, the son of Zadok, the son of Meraioth, the son of Ahitub, the officer over the house of God; ¹²Adaiah the son of Jeroham, the son of Pashur, the son of Malchijah; Maasai the son of Adiel, the son of Jahzerah, the son of Meshullam, the son of Meshillemith, the son of Immer; ¹³and their brethren, heads of their fathers' *houses*—one thousand seven hundred and sixty. *They were* very able men for the work of the service of the house of God.

The Levites at Jerusalem

¹⁴Of the Levites: Shemaiah the son of Hasshub, the son of Azrikam, the son of Hashabiah, of the sons of Merari; ¹⁵Bakbakkar, Heresh, Galal, and Mattaniah the son of Micah, the son of Zichri, the son of Asaph; ¹⁶Obadiah the son of Shemaiah, the son of Galal, the son of Jeduthun; and Berechiah the son of Asa, the son of Elkanah, who lived in the villages of the Netophathites.

The Levite Gatekeepers

¹⁷And the gatekeepers *were* Shallum, Akkub, Talmon, Ahiman, and their brethren. Shallum *was* the chief. ¹⁸Until then *they had been* gatekeepers for the camps of the children of Levi at the King's Gate on the east.

¹⁹Shallum the son of Kore, the son of Ebiasaph, the son of Korah, and his brethren, from his father's house, the Korahites, *were* in charge of the work of the service, gatekeepers of the tabernacle. Their fathers had been keepers of the entrance to the camp of the LORD. ²⁰And Phinehas the son of Eleazar had been the officer over them in time past; the LORD *was* with him. ²¹Zechariah the son of Meshelemiah *was* keeper of the door of the tabernacle of meeting.

²²All those chosen as gatekeepers *were* two hundred and twelve. They were recorded by their genealogy, in their villages. David and Samuel the seer had appointed them to their trusted office. ²³So they and their children *were* in charge of the gates of the house of the LORD, the house of the tabernacle, by assignment. ²⁴The gatekeepers were assigned to the four directions: the east, west, north, and south. ²⁵And their brethren in their villages *had* to come with them from time to time for seven days. ²⁶For in this trusted office *were* four chief gatekeepers; they were Levites. And they had charge over the chambers and treasuries of the house of God. ²⁷And they lodged *all* around the house of God because they *had* the responsibility, and they *were* in charge of opening *it* every morning.

Other Levite Responsibilities

²⁸Now *some* of them were in charge of the serving vessels, for they brought them in and took them out by count. ²⁹*Some* of them *were* appointed over the furnishings and over all the implements of the sanctuary, and over the fine flour and the wine and the oil and the incense and the spices. ³⁰And *some* of the sons of the priests made the ointment of the spices.

³¹Mattithiah of the Levites, the firstborn of Shallum the Korahite, had the trusted office over the things that were baked in the pans. ³²And some of their brethren of the sons of the Kohathites *were* in charge of preparing the showbread for every Sabbath.

³³These are the singers, heads of the fathers' *houses* of the Levites, *who lodged* in the chambers, *and were* free *from other duties;* for they were employed in *that* work day and night. ³⁴These heads of the fathers' *houses* of the Levites *were* heads throughout their generations. They dwelt at Jerusalem.

The Family of King Saul

³⁵Jeiel the father of Gibeon, whose wife's name *was* Maacah, dwelt at Gibeon. ³⁶His first-

born son *was* Abdon, then Zur, Kish, Baal, Ner, Nadab, [37]Gedor, Ahio, Zechariah,[a] and Mikloth. [38]And Mikloth begot Shimeam.[a] They also dwelt alongside their relatives in Jerusalem, with their brethren. [39]Ner begot Kish, Kish begot Saul, and Saul begot Jonathan, Malchishua, Abinadab, and Esh-Baal. [40]The son of Jonathan *was* Merib-Baal, and Merib-Baal begot Micah. [41]The sons of Micah *were* Pithon, Melech, Tahrea,[a] and *Ahaz*.[b] [42]And Ahaz begot Jarah;[a] Jarah begot Alemeth, Azmaveth, and Zimri; and Zimri begot Moza; [43]Moza begot Binea, Rephaiah[a] his son, Eleasah his son, and Azel his son.

[44]And Azel had six sons whose names *were* these: Azrikam, Bocheru, Ishmael, Sheariah, Obadiah, and Hanan; these *were* the sons of Azel.

Tragic End of Saul and His Sons

10 Now the Philistines fought against Israel; and the men of Israel fled from before the Philistines, and fell slain on Mount Gilboa. [2]Then the Philistines followed hard after Saul and his sons. And the Philistines killed Jonathan, Abinadab, and Malchishua, Saul's sons. [3]The battle became fierce against Saul. The archers hit him, and he was wounded by the archers. [4]Then Saul said to his armorbearer, "Draw your sword, and thrust me through with it, lest these uncircumcised men come and abuse me." But his armorbearer would not, for he was greatly afraid. Therefore Saul took a sword and fell on it. [5]And when his armorbearer saw that Saul was dead, he also fell on his sword and died. [6]So Saul and his three sons died, and all his house died together. [7]And when all the men of Israel who *were* in the valley saw that they had fled and that Saul and his sons were dead, they forsook their cities and fled; then the Philistines came and dwelt in them.

[8]So it happened the next day, when the Philistines came to strip the slain, that they found Saul and his sons fallen on Mount Gilboa. [9]And they stripped him and took his head and his armor, and sent word *throughout* the land of the Philistines to proclaim the news *in the temple* of their idols and among the people. [10]Then they put his armor in the temple of their gods, and fastened his head in the temple of Dagon.

[11]And when all Jabesh Gilead heard all that the Philistines had done to Saul, [12]all the valiant men arose and took the body of Saul and the bodies of his sons; and they brought them to Jabesh, and buried their bones under the tamarisk tree at Jabesh, and fasted seven days.

[13]So Saul died for his unfaithfulness which he had committed against the LORD, because he did not keep the word of the LORD, and also because he consulted a medium for guidance. [14]But *he* did not inquire of the LORD; therefore He killed him, and turned the kingdom over to David the son of Jesse.

David Made King over All Israel

11 Then all Israel came together to David at Hebron, saying, "Indeed we *are* your bone and your flesh. [2]Also, in time past, even when Saul was king, you *were* the one who led Israel out and brought them in; and the LORD your God said to you, 'You shall shepherd My people Israel, and be ruler over My people Israel.'" [3]Therefore all the elders of Israel came to the king at Hebron, and David made a covenant with them at Hebron before the LORD. And they anointed David king over Israel, according to the word of the LORD by Samuel.

9:37 [a]Called *Zecher* in 8:31 **9:38** [a]Spelled *Shimeah* in 8:32 **9:41** [a]Spelled *Tarea* in 8:35 [b]Following Arabic, Syriac, Targum, and Vulgate (compare 8:35); Masoretic Text and Septuagint omit *and Ahaz*. **9:42** [a]Spelled *Jehoaddah* in 8:36 **9:43** [a]Spelled *Raphah* in 8:37

The Law of Influence: David Led Before Saul Left Office

(1 Chronicles 11:1–3)

As the most influential man in the country, David was leading long before Saul lost his throne.

Like it or not, position doesn't make a person a leader. Title may give someone authority, but not influence. Influence comes from the person; it must be earned. David had earned it and Saul had not. Why was this so?

1. *Unity:* David rallied the people and created unity (v. 1).
2. *Identification:* David identified with his followers as family (v. 1).
3. *Credibility:* David effectively led various military campaigns (v. 2).
4. *Anointing:* David enjoyed God's hand and power on his life (v. 2).
5. *Partnership:* David worked cooperatively *with* key leaders, not *over* them (v. 3).

The City of David

⁴And David and all Israel went to Jerusalem, which is Jebus, where the Jebusites *were,* the inhabitants of the land. ⁵But the inhabitants of Jebus said to David, "You shall not come in here!" Nevertheless David took the stronghold of Zion (that is, the City of David). ⁶Now David said, "Whoever attacks the Jebusites first shall be chief and captain." And Joab the son of Zeruiah went up first, and became chief. ⁷Then David dwelt in the stronghold; therefore they called it the City of David. ⁸And he built the city around it, from the Milloᵃ to the surrounding area. Joab repaired the rest of the city. ⁹So David went on and became great, and the LORD of hosts *was* with him.

The Mighty Men of David

¹⁰Now these *were* the heads of the mighty men whom David had, who strengthened themselves with him in his kingdom, with all Israel, to make him king, according to the word of the LORD concerning Israel.

¹¹And this *is* the number of the mighty men whom David had: Jashobeam the son of a Hachmonite, chief of the captains;ᵃ he had lifted up his spear against three hundred, killed *by him* at one time.

¹²After him *was* Eleazar the son of Dodo, the Ahohite, who *was* one of the three mighty men. ¹³He was with David at Pasdammim. Now there the Philistines were gathered for battle, and there was a piece of ground full of barley. So the peo-

ple fled from the Philistines. ¹⁴But they stationed themselves in the middle of *that* field, defended it, and killed the Philistines. So the LORD brought about a great victory.

¹⁵Now three of the thirty chief men went down to the rock to David, into the cave of Adullam; and the army of the Philistines encamped in the Valley of Rephaim. ¹⁶David *was* then in the stronghold, and the garrison of the Philistines *was* then in Bethlehem. ¹⁷And David said with longing, "Oh, that someone would give me a drink of water from the well of Bethlehem, which is by the gate!" ¹⁸So the three broke through the camp of the Philistines, drew water from the well of Bethlehem that *was* by the gate, and took *it* and brought *it* to David. Nevertheless David would not drink it, but poured it out to the LORD. ¹⁹And he said, "Far be it from me, O my God, that I should do this! Shall I drink the blood of these men *who have put* their lives *in jeopardy?* For at the risk of their lives they brought it." Therefore he would not drink it. These things were done by the three mighty men.

²⁰Abishai the brother of Joab was chief of *another* three.ᵃ He had lifted up his spear against three hundred *men,* killed *them,* and won a name

11:8 ᵃLiterally *The Landfill* **11:11** ᵃFollowing Qere; Kethib, Septuagint, and Vulgate read *the thirty* (compare 2 Samuel 23:8). **11:20** ᵃFollowing Masoretic Text, Septuagint, and Vulgate; Syriac reads *thirty.*

The Law of Magnetism:
David Attracted Loyal Risk Takers

(1 Chronicles 11:10–23)

The Scripture offers an impressive list of military leaders connected to David, calling them his "mighty men" and describing several of their incredible exploits.

Have you ever wondered how David was able to attract such a qualified and extraordinary group of leaders? The answer lies in the Law of Magnetism. Leaders attract people like themselves.

David's Qualities	Parallels from David's Men
1. Submissive and loyal to Saul	1. Submissive and loyal to David (v. 10)
2. Slew many enemy soldiers in battle	2. Slew many enemy soldiers in battle (v. 11)
3. Took a stand against the Philistines	3. Took a stand against the Philistines (v. 14)
4. Risked his life and went the extra mile	4. Risked life and went the extra mile (v. 18)
5. Killed a lion single-handedly	5. Killed a lion single-handedly (v. 22)
6. Slew a giant	6. Slew a giant (v. 23)

among *these* three. ²¹Of the three he was more honored than the other two men. Therefore he became their captain. However he did not attain to the *first* three.

²²Benaiah was the son of Jehoiada, the son of a valiant man from Kabzeel, who had done many deeds. He had killed two lion-like heroes of Moab. He also had gone down and killed a lion in the midst of a pit on a snowy day. ²³And he killed an Egyptian, a man of *great* height, five cubits tall. In the Egyptian's hand *there was* a spear like a weaver's beam; and he went down to him with a staff, wrested the spear out of the Egyptian's hand, and killed him with his own spear. ²⁴These *things* Benaiah the son of Jehoiada did, and won a name among three mighty men. ²⁵Indeed he was more honored than the thirty, but he did not attain to the *first* three. And David appointed him over his guard.

²⁶Also the mighty warriors *were* Asahel the brother of Joab, Elhanan the son of Dodo of Bethlehem, ²⁷Shammoth the Harorite,ᵃ Helez the Pelonite,ᵇ ²⁸Ira the son of Ikkesh the Tekoite, Abiezer the Anathothite, ²⁹Sibbechai the Hushathite, Ilai the Ahohite, ³⁰Maharai the Netophathite, Heledᵃ the son of Baanah the Netophathite, ³¹Ithaiᵃ the son of Ribai of Gibeah, of the sons of Benjamin, Benaiah the Pirathonite, ³²Huraiᵃ of the brooks of Gaash, Abielᵇ the Arbathite, ³³Azmaveth the Baharumite,ᵃ Eliahba the Shaalbonite, ³⁴the sons of Hashem the Gizonite, Jonathan the son of Shageh the Hararite, ³⁵Ahiam the son of Sacar the Hararite, Eliphal the son of Ur, ³⁶Hepher the Mecherathite, Ahijah the Pelonite, ³⁷Hezro the Carmelite, Naarai the son of Ezbai, ³⁸Joel the brother of Nathan, Mibhar the son of Hagri, ³⁹Zelek the Ammonite, Naharai the Berothiteᵃ (the armorbearer of Joab the son of Zeruiah), ⁴⁰Ira the Ithrite, Gareb the Ithrite, ⁴¹Uriah the Hittite, Zabad the son of Ahlai, ⁴²Adina the son of Shiza the Reubenite (a chief of the Reubenites) and thirty with him, ⁴³Hanan the son of Maachah, Joshaphat the Mithnite, ⁴⁴Uzzia the Ashterathite, Shama and Jeiel the sons of Hotham the Aroerite, ⁴⁵Jediael the son of Shimri, and Joha his brother, the Tizite, ⁴⁶Eliel the Mahavite, Jeribai and Joshaviah the sons of Elnaam, Ithmah the Moabite, ⁴⁷Eliel, Obed, and Jaasiel the Mezobaite.

The Growth of David's Army

12 Now these *were* the men who came to David at Ziklag while he was still a fugitive from Saul the son of Kish; and they *were* among the mighty men, helpers in the war, ²armed with bows, using both the right hand and the left in *hurling* stones and *shooting* arrows with the bow. *They were* of Benjamin, Saul's brethren.

³The chief *was* Ahiezer, then Joash, the sons of Shemaah the Gibeathite; Jeziel and Pelet the sons of Azmaveth; Berachah, and Jehu the Anathothite; ⁴Ishmaiah the Gibeonite, a mighty man among the thirty, and over the thirty; Jeremiah, Jahaziel, Johanan, and Jozabad the Gederathite; ⁵Eluzai, Jerimoth, Bealiah, Shemariah, and Shephatiah the Haruphite; ⁶Elkanah, Jisshiah, Azarel, Joezer, and Jashobeam, the Korahites; ⁷and Joelah and Zebadiah the sons of Jeroham of Gedor.

⁸*Some* Gadites joined David at the stronghold in the wilderness, mighty men of valor, men trained for battle, who could handle shield and spear, whose faces *were like* the faces of lions, and *were* as swift as gazelles on the mountains: ⁹Ezer the first, Obadiah the second, Eliab the third, ¹⁰Mishmannah the fourth, Jeremiah the fifth, ¹¹Attai the sixth, Eliel the seventh, ¹²Johanan the eighth, Elzabad the ninth, ¹³Jeremiah the tenth, and Machbanai the eleventh. ¹⁴These *were* from the sons of Gad, captains of the army; the least was over a hundred, and the greatest was over a thousand. ¹⁵These *are* the ones who crossed the Jordan in the first month, when it had overflowed all its banks; and they put to flight all *those* in the valleys, to the east and to the west.

¹⁶Then some of the sons of Benjamin and Judah came to David at the stronghold. ¹⁷And David went out to meet them, and answered and said to them, "If you have come peaceably to me to help me, my heart will be united with you; but if to betray me to my enemies, since *there is* no wrong in my hands, may the God of our fathers look and bring judgment." ¹⁸Then the Spirit came upon Amasai, chief of the captains, *and he said:*

" *We are* yours, O David;
  We *are* on your side, O son of Jesse!
  Peace, peace to you,
  And peace to your helpers!
  For your God helps you."

11:27 ᵃSpelled *Harodite* in 2 Samuel 23:25 ᵇCalled *Paltite* in 2 Samuel 23:26 **11:30** ᵃSpelled *Heleb* in 2 Samuel 23:29 and *Heldai* in 1 Chronicles 27:15 **11:31** ᵃSpelled *Ittai* in 2 Samuel 23:29 **11:32** ᵃSpelled *Hiddai* in 2 Samuel 23:30 ᵇSpelled *Abi-Albon* in 2 Samuel 23:31 **11:33** ᵃSpelled *Barhumite* in 2 Samuel 23:31 **11:39** ᵃSpelled *Beerothite* in 2 Samuel 23:37

21 LAWS

DAVID AND THE LAW OF THE INNER CIRCLE

A Leader's Potential Is Determined by Those Closest to Him

(1 Chronicles 11:10—12:40)

There are no Lone Ranger leaders. If you're alone, you're not *leading* anybody.

Think of any highly effective leader, and you will find someone surrounded by a strong inner circle.

Hire the best staff you can find, develop them as much as you can, and hand off everything you possibly can to them. When you have the right staff, potential skyrockets.

You see, every leader's potential is determined by the people closest to him. If those people are strong, then the leader can make a huge impact. If they are weak, he can't.

Examine the way David pulled together the core people who made him great:

1. *He started building a strong inner circle before he needed it.*

David began building his team long before he was crowned king. First Chronicles emphasizes how many of the warriors who flocked to David were leaders (1 Chr. 12:14). David didn't attract just anyone; he attracted strong leaders.

2. *He attracted people with varied gifts.*

David attracted men of diverse abilities. We read of experienced warriors with a variety of skills—ambidextrous bowmen, slingers, and spearmen—many mighty men of valor, and hundreds of captains. With the help of these men, David felt ready for anything.

3. *He engendered loyalty.*

David's followers displayed incredible loyalty to him throughout his life. In the early days, three of his men risked their lives to get him some water from a favorite well in Bethlehem. Decades later his closest men stayed with him even when it looked as though Absalom might crush his father (2 Sam. 15:21). Those closest to David always seemed willing to put their lives on the line for him.

4. *He delegated responsibility based on ability.*

David continually gave authority to others. He designated Joab as commander of the army, and he felt equally secure in giving others civil authority (1 Chr. 18:14–17). Of course, delegating authority always entails risk—witness Joab's unilateral decision to kill Abner (2 Sam. 3:22–30). But great leaders risk delegation in order to reach the highest level of leadership.

Inner-Circle Qualities

The following qualities spell out the words *inner circle*. Look for these traits in the people you depend on most:

Influential—Everything begins with influence. If you want to extend your reach, you must attract and lead other leaders. More than twelve hundred leaders are mentioned in the list of warriors who came to David (1 Chr. 12:23–37).

Networking—*Who* people know is just as important as *what* they know. When David hid from Saul, he was able to escape with the help of those who cared about him.

Nurturing—People who care about each other take care of each other. Your inner circle should prop you up. Certainly Jonathan is the best example of a nurturer in David's life. He loved David unconditionally, encouraged him, and guarded his life.

Empowering—The members of your inner circle should enable you to achieve more than you could alone. David's mighty men empowered him to accomplish incredible things.

Resourceful—Inner-circle members should always add value. When David desired to conquer Jerusalem, he offered to make the man who led the charge chief over his army (2 Sam. 5:6–10)—and Joab won control of the armed forces.

Character-driven—The character of an inner-circle member matters more than any other quality. People of weak character in David's inner circle cost him dearly. But people of strong character often helped to steer him out of trouble.

Intuitive—While every person is naturally intuitive in his area of gifting, that doesn't mean everyone uses his or her intuition. As you seek members for your inner circle, rely on those who have learned to trust their instincts.

Responsible—Those closest to you should never leave you hanging. If you ask them to carry the ball, they must follow through. David's companions made his cause their own.

Competent—You can't get anything done if your people can't do their jobs. You don't need world-class performers exclusively, but all of your inner-circle people must perform with excellence. The skill of David's people helped make him great.

Loyal—Loyalty alone does not make people candidates for your inner circle, but lack of loyalty definitely disqualifies them. David's people stuck with him even to death. Don't keep anyone close to you whom you cannot trust.

Energetic—Energy covers a multitude of mistakes, for it helps a person to keep coming back, failure after failure. Without tenacity, David and his men never would have survived in the wilderness, nor would they have made the nation secure from its enemies.

Look Around!

When God wants a leader to do something of value for Him, He provides that leader with the individuals to get the job done. That was true for David, and it will be true for you. All you need to do is look around.

The Law of Reproduction: David Raised Up Leaders

(1 Chronicles 12:1–38)

We can conclude from the list of warriors who joined David in Ziklag that his ragtag team was diverse, loyal, and hungry for victory. So what did David do to reproduce his leadership in them?

1. *He was relational.*
   Unlike Saul, who lived in fear, David's personable and approachable manner enticed hundreds of misfit volunteers to serve him. David accepted anyone.
2. *He was resourceful.*
   David made use of every situation and got the best out of it—even in the wilderness. He resourced his team to become all they could be and enabled it to succeed.
3. *He was rewarding.*
   David quickly shared both rewards and recognition for victory. He affirmed his men and motivated them with words of encouragement and spoils from battle.
4. *He was respectable.*
   David modeled a leadership style that others wanted to imitate. Friends and foes alike respected him; people saw in David an example of good leadership.

The chronicler says simply, "All these men of war, who could keep ranks, came to Hebron with a loyal heart, to make David king over all Israel; and all the rest of Israel were of one mind to make David king" (1 Chr. 12:38). And he concludes, "There was joy in Israel" (1 Chr. 12:40).

So David received them, and made them captains of the troop.

19And *some* from Manasseh defected to David when he was going with the Philistines to battle against Saul; but they did not help them, for the lords of the Philistines sent him away by agreement, saying, "He may defect to his master Saul *and endanger* our heads." 20When he went to Ziklag, those of Manasseh who defected to him were Adnah, Jozabad, Jediael, Michael, Jozabad, Elihu, and Zillethai, captains of the thousands who *were* from Manasseh. 21And they helped David against the bands *of raiders,* for they *were* all mighty men of valor, and they were captains in the army. 22For at *that* time they came to David day by day to help him, until *it was* a great army, like the army of God.

David's Army at Hebron

23Now these *were* the numbers of the divisions *that were* equipped for war, *and* came to David at Hebron to turn *over* the kingdom of Saul to him, according to the word of the LORD: 24of the sons of Judah bearing shield and spear, six thousand eight hundred armed for war; 25of the sons of Simeon, mighty men of valor fit for war, seven thousand one hundred; 26of the sons of Levi four thousand six hundred; 27Jehoiada, the leader of the Aaronites, and with him three thousand seven hundred; 28Zadok, a young man, a valiant warrior, and from his father's house twenty-two captains; 29of the sons of Benjamin, relatives of Saul, three thousand (until then the greatest part of them had remained loyal to the house of Saul); 30of the sons of Ephraim twenty thousand eight hundred, mighty men of valor, famous men throughout their father's house; 31of the half-tribe of Manasseh eighteen thousand, who were designated by name to come and make David king; 32of the sons of Issachar who had understanding of the times, to know what Israel ought to do, their chiefs were two hundred; and all their brethren were at their command; 33of Zebulun there were fifty thousand who went out to battle, expert in war with all weapons of war, stouthearted men who could keep ranks; 34of Naphtali one thousand captains, and with them thirty-seven thousand with shield and spear; 35of the Danites who could keep battle formation, twenty-eight thousand six hundred; 36of Asher, those who could go out to war, able to keep battle formation, forty thousand; 37of the Reubenites and the Gadites and the half-tribe of Manasseh, from the other side of the Jordan, one hundred and twenty thousand armed for battle with every *kind* of weapon of war.

38All these men of war, who could keep ranks,

The Law of Intuition: Discernment Comes Before Decision

(1 Chronicles 12:32)

One of the more popular passages in 1 Chronicles is found in chapter 12. The sons of Issachar are there described as men who "had understanding of the times, to know what Israel ought to do" (v. 32). What a description of the Law of Intuition! Before Israel made a decision, they got discernment. The sons of Issachar understood three key factors:

1. *The culture:* They understood the population and the place where they lived.
2. *The timing:* They understood the times and discerned when to move.
3. *The strategy:* They knew what Israel ought to do, the steps that should be taken.

How about you? Are you a "son of Issachar"? Do you understand your culture—its trends, its myths, its strengths, its dangers? Do you understand the age in which you're living—its tenor and general movement? And do you have a strategy to grapple with both the culture and the times?

came to Hebron with a loyal heart, to make David king over all Israel; and all the rest of Israel *were* of one mind to make David king. ³⁹And they were there with David three days, eating and drinking, for their brethren had prepared for them. ⁴⁰Moreover those who were near to them, from as far away as Issachar and Zebulun and Naphtali, were bringing food on donkeys and camels, on mules and oxen—provisions of flour and cakes of figs and cakes of raisins, wine and oil and oxen and sheep abundantly, for *there was* joy in Israel.

The Ark Brought from Kirjath Jearim

13 Then David consulted with the captains of thousands and hundreds, *and* with every leader. ²And David said to all the assembly of Israel, "If *it seems* good to you, and if it is of the LORD our God, let us send out to our brethren everywhere *who are* left in all the land of Israel, and with them to the priests and Levites *who are* in their cities *and* their commonlands, that they may gather together to us; ³and

let us bring the ark of our God back to us, for we have not inquired at it since the days of Saul." ⁴Then all the assembly said that they would do so, for the thing was right in the eyes of all the people.

⁵So David gathered all Israel together, from Shihor in Egypt to as far as the entrance of Hamath, to bring the ark of God from Kirjath Jearim. ⁶And David and all Israel went up to Baalah,ᵃ to Kirjath Jearim, which belonged to Judah, to bring up from there the ark of God the LORD, who dwells *between* the cherubim, where *His* name is proclaimed. ⁷So they carried the ark of God on a new cart from the house of Abinadab, and Uzza and Ahio drove the cart. ⁸Then David and all Israel played *music* before God with all *their* might, with singing, on harps, on stringed instruments, on tambourines, on cymbals, and with trumpets.

⁹And when they came to Chidon'sᵃ threshing floor, Uzza put out his hand to hold the ark, for the oxen stumbled. ¹⁰Then the anger of the LORD was aroused against Uzza, and He struck him because he put his hand to the ark; and he died there before God. ¹¹And David became angry because of the LORD's outbreak against Uzza; therefore that place is called Perez Uzzaᵃ to this day. ¹²David was afraid of God that day, saying, "How can I bring the ark of God to me?"

Leaders Must Be Teachable

(1 Chronicles 13:5–12)

David grew both angry and frightened when God struck down Uzzah during an accident involving the transport of the ark of God. Leaders must remain teachable. We must not presume we know exactly how things will play out or what tomorrow will bring. Leaders must be learners.

¹³So David would not move the ark with him into the City of David, but took it aside into the house of Obed-Edom the Gittite. ¹⁴The ark of God remained with the family of Obed-Edom in his house three months. And the LORD blessed the house of Obed-Edom and all that he had.

13:6 ᵃCalled *Baale Judah* in 2 Samuel 6:2
13:9 ᵃCalled *Nachon* in 2 Samuel 6:6
13:11 ᵃLiterally *Outburst Against Uzza*

David Established at Jerusalem

14 Now Hiram king of Tyre sent messengers to David, and cedar trees, with masons and carpenters, to build him a house. ²So David knew that the LORD had established him as king over Israel, for his kingdom was highly exalted for the sake of His people Israel.

³Then David took more wives in Jerusalem, and David begot more sons and daughters. ⁴And these are the names of his children whom he had in Jerusalem: Shammua,ᵃ Shobab, Nathan, Solomon, ⁵Ibhar, Elishua,ᵃ Elpelet,ᵇ ⁶Nogah, Nepheg, Japhia, ⁷Elishama, Beeliada,ᵃ and Eliphelet.

The Philistines Defeated

⁸Now when the Philistines heard that David had been anointed king over all Israel, all the Philistines went up to search for David. And David heard *of it* and went out against them. ⁹Then the Philistines went and made a raid on the Valley of Rephaim. ¹⁰And David inquired of God, saying, "Shall I go up against the Philistines? Will You deliver them into my hand?"

The LORD said to him, "Go up, for I will deliver them into your hand."

¹¹So they went up to Baal Perazim, and David defeated them there. Then David said, "God has broken through my enemies by my hand like a breakthrough of water." Therefore they called the name of that place Baal Perazim.ᵃ ¹²And when they left their gods there, David gave a commandment, and they were burned with fire.

¹³Then the Philistines once again made a raid on the valley. ¹⁴Therefore David inquired again of God, and God said to him, "You shall not go up after them; circle around them, and come upon them in front of the mulberry trees. ¹⁵And it shall be, when you hear a sound of marching in the tops of the mulberry trees, then you shall go out to battle, for God has gone out before you to strike the camp of the Philistines." ¹⁶So David did as God commanded him, and they drove back the army of the Philistines from Gibeon as far as Gezer. ¹⁷Then the fame of David went out into all lands, and the LORD brought the fear of him upon all nations.

The Ark Brought to Jerusalem

15 *David* built houses for himself in the City of David; and he prepared a place for the ark of God, and pitched a tent for it. ²Then David said, "No one may carry the ark of God but the Levites, for the LORD has chosen them to carry the ark of God and to minister before Him forever." ³And David gathered all Israel together at Jerusalem, to bring up the ark of the LORD to its place, which he had prepared for it. ⁴Then David assembled the children of Aaron and the Levites: ⁵of the sons of Kohath, Uriel the chief, and one hundred and twenty of his brethren; ⁶of the sons of Merari, Asaiah the chief, and two hundred and twenty of his brethren; ⁷of the sons of Gershom, Joel the chief, and one hundred and thirty of his brethren; ⁸of the sons of Elizaphan, Shemaiah the chief, and two hundred of his brethren; ⁹of the sons of Hebron, Eliel the chief, and eighty of his brethren; ¹⁰of the sons of Uzziel, Amminadab the chief, and one hundred and twelve of his brethren.

¹¹And David called for Zadok and Abiathar the priests, and for the Levites: for Uriel, Asaiah, Joel, Shemaiah, Eliel, and Amminadab. ¹²He said to them, "You *are* the heads of the fathers' *houses* of the Levites; sanctify yourselves, you and your brethren, that you may bring up the ark of the LORD God of Israel to *the place* I have prepared for it. ¹³For because you *did* not *do it* the first *time*, the LORD our God broke out against us, because we did not consult Him about the proper order."

¹⁴So the priests and the Levites sanctified themselves to bring up the ark of the LORD God of Israel. ¹⁵And the children of the Levites bore the ark of God on their shoulders, by its poles, as Moses had commanded according to the word of the LORD.

¹⁶Then David spoke to the leaders of the Levites to appoint their brethren *to be* the singers accompanied by instruments of music, stringed instruments, harps, and cymbals, by raising the voice with resounding joy. ¹⁷So the Levites appointed Heman the son of Joel; and of his brethren, Asaph the son of Berechiah; and of their brethren, the sons of Merari, Ethan the son of Kushaiah; ¹⁸and with them their brethren of the second *rank*: Zechariah, Ben,ᵃ Jaaziel, Shemiramoth, Jehiel, Unni, Eliab, Benaiah, Maaseiah, Mattithiah, Elipheleh, Mikneiah, Obed-Edom, and Jeiel, the gatekeepers; ¹⁹the singers, Heman, Asaph, and Ethan, *were* to sound the cymbals of bronze; ²⁰Zechariah, Aziel, Shemiramoth, Jehiel, Unni, Eliab, Maaseiah, and Benaiah, with strings according to Alamoth; ²¹Mattithiah, Elipheleh, Mikneiah, Obed-Edom, Jeiel, and Azaziah, to direct with harps on the Sheminith; ²²Chenaniah, leader of the Levites, was instructor *in charge of* the music, because he *was* skillful; ²³Berechiah

---

14:4 ᵃSpelled *Shimea* in 3:5 **14:5** ᵃSpelled *Elishama* in 3:6 ᵇSpelled *Eliphelet* in 3:6 **14:7** ᵃSpelled *Eliada* in 3:8 **14:11** ᵃLiterally *Master of Breakthroughs* **15:18** ᵃFollowing Masoretic Text and Vulgate; Septuagint omits *Ben*.

and Elkanah *were* doorkeepers for the ark; [24]Sheb-aniah, Joshaphat, Nethanel, Amasai, Zechariah, Benaiah, and Eliezer, the priests, were to blow the trumpets before the ark of God; and Obed-Edom and Jehiah, doorkeepers for the ark.

[25]So David, the elders of Israel, and the captains over thousands went to bring up the ark of the covenant of the LORD from the house of Obed-Edom with joy. [26]And so it was, when God helped the Levites who bore the ark of the covenant of the LORD, that they offered seven bulls and seven rams. [27]David was clothed with a robe of fine linen, as were all the Levites who bore the ark, the singers, and Chenaniah the music master *with* the singers. David also wore a linen ephod. [28]Thus all Israel brought up the ark of the covenant of the LORD with shouting and with the sound of the horn, with trumpets and with cymbals, making music with stringed instruments and harps.

[29]And it happened, *as* the ark of the covenant of the LORD came to the City of David, that Michal, Saul's daughter, looked through a window and saw King David whirling and playing music; and she despised him in her heart.

The Ark Placed in the Tabernacle

16 So they brought the ark of God, and set it in the midst of the tabernacle that David had erected for it. Then they offered burnt offerings and peace offerings before God. [2]And when David had finished offering the burnt offerings and the peace offerings, he blessed the people in the name of the LORD. [3]Then he distributed to everyone of Israel, both man and woman, to everyone a loaf of bread, a piece *of meat,* and a cake of raisins.

[4]And he appointed some of the Levites to minister before the ark of the LORD, to commemorate, to thank, and to praise the LORD God of Israel: [5]Asaph the chief, and next to him Zechariah, *then* Jeiel, Shemiramoth, Jehiel, Mattithiah, Eliab, Benaiah, and Obed-Edom: Jeiel with stringed instruments and harps, but Asaph made music with cymbals; [6]Benaiah and Jahaziel the priests regularly *blew* the trumpets before the ark of the covenant of God.

David's Song of Thanksgiving

[7]On that day David first delivered *this psalm* into the hand of Asaph and his brethren, to thank the LORD:

[8]   Oh, give thanks to the LORD!
    Call upon His name;
    Make known His deeds among the peoples!
[9]   Sing to Him, sing psalms to Him;
    Talk of all His wondrous works!
[10]   Glory in His holy name;
    Let the hearts of those rejoice who seek
      the LORD!
[11]   Seek the LORD and His strength;
    Seek His face evermore!
[12]   Remember His marvelous works which
      He has done,
    His wonders, and the judgments of His
      mouth,
[13]   O seed of Israel His servant,
    You children of Jacob, His chosen ones!

[14]   He *is* the LORD our God;
    His judgments *are* in all the earth.
[15]   Remember His covenant forever,
    The word which He commanded, for a
      thousand generations,
[16]   *The covenant which* He made with
      Abraham,
    And His oath to Isaac,
[17]   And confirmed it to Jacob for a statute,
    To Israel *for* an everlasting covenant,
[18]   Saying, "To you I will give the land of
      Canaan
    As the allotment of your inheritance,"
[19]   When you were few in number,
    Indeed very few, and strangers in it.

[20]   When they went from one nation to
      another,
    And from *one* kingdom to another people,
[21]   He permitted no man to do them wrong;
    Yes, He rebuked kings for their sakes,
[22]   *Saying,* "Do not touch My anointed ones,
    And do My prophets no harm."[a]

[23]   Sing to the LORD, all the earth;
    Proclaim the good news of His salvation
      from day to day.
[24]   Declare His glory among the nations,
    His wonders among all peoples.
[25]   For the LORD *is* great and greatly to be
      praised;
    He *is* also to be feared above all gods.
[26]   For all the gods of the peoples *are* idols,
    But the LORD made the heavens.
[27]   Honor and majesty *are* before Him;
    Strength and gladness are in His place.
[28]   Give to the LORD, O families of the
      peoples,
    Give to the LORD glory and strength.

16:22 [a]Compare verses 8–22 with Psalm 105:1–15

29 Give to the LORD the glory *due* His name;
 Bring an offering, and come before Him.
 Oh, worship the LORD in the beauty of
  holiness!
30 Tremble before Him, all the earth.
 The world also is firmly established,
 It shall not be moved.

31 Let the heavens rejoice, and let the earth
  be glad;
 And let them say among the nations, "The
  LORD reigns."
32 Let the sea roar, and all its fullness;
 Let the field rejoice, and all that *is* in it.
33 Then the trees of the woods shall rejoice
  before the LORD,
 For He is coming to judge the earth.[a]

34 Oh, give thanks to the LORD, for *He is*
  good!
 For His mercy *endures* forever.[a]
35 And say, "Save us, O God of our salvation;
 Gather us together, and deliver us from the
  Gentiles,
 To give thanks to Your holy name,
 To triumph in Your praise."

36 Blessed *be* the LORD God of Israel
 From everlasting to everlasting![a]

And all the people said, "Amen!" and praised the
LORD.

Regular Worship Maintained

37So he left Asaph and his brothers there before the ark of the covenant of the LORD to minister before the ark regularly, as every day's work required; 38and Obed-Edom with his sixty-eight brethren, including Obed-Edom the son of Jeduthun, and Hosah, *to be* gatekeepers; 39and Zadok the priest and his brethren the priests, before the tabernacle of the LORD at the high place that *was* at Gibeon, 40to offer burnt offerings to the LORD on the altar of burnt offering regularly morning and evening, and *to do* according to all that is written in the Law of the LORD which He commanded Israel; 41and with them Heman and Jeduthun and the rest who were chosen, who were designated by name, to give thanks to the LORD, because His mercy *endures* forever; 42and with them Heman and Jeduthun, to sound aloud with trumpets and cymbals and the musical instruments of God. Now the sons of Jeduthun *were* gatekeepers.

43Then all the people departed, every man to his house; and David returned to bless his house.

God's Covenant with David

17 Now it came to pass, when David was dwelling in his house, that David said to Nathan the prophet, "See now, I dwell in a house of cedar, but the ark of the covenant of the LORD *is* under tent curtains."

2Then Nathan said to David, "Do all that *is* in your heart, for God *is* with you."

3But it happened that night that the word of God came to Nathan, saying, "'Go and tell My servant David, 'Thus says the LORD: "You shall not build Me a house to dwell in. 5For I have not dwelt in a house since the time that I brought up Israel, even to this day, but have gone from tent to tent, and from *one* tabernacle *to another.* 6Wherever I have moved about with all Israel, have I ever spoken a word to any of the judges of Israel, whom I commanded to shepherd My people, saying, 'Why have you not built Me a house of cedar?' '' 7Now therefore, thus shall you say to My servant David, 'Thus says the LORD of hosts: "I took you from the sheepfold, from following the sheep, to be ruler over My people Israel. 8And I have been with you wherever you have gone, and have cut off all your enemies from before you, and have made you a name like the name of the great men who *are* on the earth. 9Moreover I will appoint a place for My people Israel, and will plant them, that they may dwell in a place of their own and move no more; nor shall the sons of wickedness oppress them anymore, as previously, 10since the time that I commanded judges *to be* over My people Israel. Also I will subdue all your enemies. Furthermore I tell you that the LORD will build you a house.[a] 11And it shall be, when your days are fulfilled, when you must go *to be* with your fathers, that I will set up your seed after you, who will be of your sons; and I will establish his kingdom. 12He shall build Me a house, and I will establish his throne forever. 13I will be his Father, and he shall be My son; and I will not take My mercy away from him, as I took *it* from *him* who was before you. 14And I will establish him in My house and in My kingdom forever; and his throne shall be established forever."'"

15According to all these words and according to all this vision, so Nathan spoke to David.

16Then King David went in and sat before the LORD; and he said: "Who *am* I, O LORD God? And what is my house, that You have brought

---

16:33 [a]Compare verses 23–33 with Psalm 96:1–13
16:34 [a]Compare verse 34 with Psalm 106:1
16:36 [a]Compare verses 35, 36 with Psalm 106:47, 48
17:10 [a]That is, a royal dynasty

me this far? [17]And *yet* this was a small thing in Your sight, O God; and You have *also* spoken of Your servant's house for a great while to come, and have regarded me according to the rank of a man of high degree, O LORD God. [18]What more can David *say* to You for the honor of Your servant? For You know Your servant. [19]O LORD, for Your servant's sake, and according to Your own heart, You have done all this greatness, in making known all these great things. [20]O LORD, *there is* none like You, nor *is there any* God besides You, according to all that we have heard with our ears. [21]And who *is* like Your people Israel, the one nation on the earth whom God went to redeem for Himself *as* a people—to make for Yourself a name by great and awesome deeds, by driving out nations from before Your people whom You redeemed from Egypt? [22]For You have made Your people Israel Your very own people forever; and You, LORD, have become their God.

[23]"And now, O LORD, the word which You have spoken concerning Your servant and concerning his house, *let it* be established forever, and do as You have said. [24]So let it be established, that Your name may be magnified forever, saying, 'The LORD of hosts, the God of Israel, *is* Israel's God.' And let the house of Your servant David be established before You. [25]For You, O my God, have revealed to Your servant that You will build him a house. Therefore Your servant has found it *in his heart* to pray before You. [26]And now, LORD, You are God, and have promised this goodness to Your servant. [27]Now You have been pleased to bless the house of Your servant, that it may continue before You forever; for You have blessed it, O LORD, and *it shall be* blessed forever."

Humility: The Mark of a Leader Who Finishes Well

(1 Chronicles 17:1–27)

Both Nathan and David showed genuine humility. Nathan had to modify his instructions to David after he too quickly spoke for God, and David responded with grace when he learned he would not build the temple. Humility keeps leaders on track and enables them to see beyond themselves.

David's Further Conquests

18 After this it came to pass that David attacked the Philistines, subdued them, and took Gath and its towns from the hand of the Philistines. [2]Then he defeated Moab, and the Moabites became David's servants, *and* brought tribute.

[3]And David defeated Hadadezer[a] king of Zobah *as far as* Hamath, as he went to establish his power by the River Euphrates. [4]David took from him one thousand chariots, seven thousand[a] horsemen, and twenty thousand foot soldiers. Also David hamstrung all the chariot *horses,* except that he spared enough of them for one hundred chariots.

[5]When the Syrians of Damascus came to help Hadadezer king of Zobah, David killed twenty-two thousand of the Syrians. [6]Then David put *garrisons* in Syria of Damascus; and the Syrians became David's servants, *and* brought tribute. So the LORD preserved David wherever he went. [7]And David took the shields of gold that were on the servants of Hadadezer, and brought them to Jerusalem. [8]Also from Tibhath[a] and from Chun, cities of Hadadezer, David brought a large amount of bronze, with which Solomon made the bronze Sea, the pillars, and the articles of bronze.

[9]Now when Tou[a] king of Hamath heard that David had defeated all the army of Hadadezer king of Zobah, [10]he sent Hadoram[a] his son to King David, to greet him and bless him, because he had fought against Hadadezer and defeated him (for Hadadezer had been at war with Tou); and *Hadoram brought with him* all kinds of articles of gold, silver, and bronze. [11]King David also dedicated these to the LORD, along with the silver and gold that he had brought from all *these* nations—from Edom, from Moab, from the people of Ammon, from the Philistines, and from Amalek.

[12]Moreover Abishai the son of Zeruiah killed eighteen thousand Edomites[a] in the Valley of Salt. [13]He also put garrisons in Edom, and all the Edomites became David's servants. And the LORD preserved David wherever he went.

David's Administration

[14]So David reigned over all Israel, and administered judgment and justice to all his people.

18:3 [a]Hebrew *Hadarezer,* and so throughout chapters 18 and 19 **18:4** [a]Or *seven hundred* (compare 2 Samuel 8:4) **18:8** [a]Spelled *Betah* in 2 Samuel 8:8 **18:9** [a]Spelled *Toi* in 2 Samuel 8:9, 10 **18:10** [a]Spelled *Joram* in 2 Samuel 8:10 **18:12** [a]Or *Syrians* (compare 2 Samuel 8:13)

¹⁵Joab the son of Zeruiah *was* over the army; Jehoshaphat the son of Ahilud *was* recorder; ¹⁶Zadok the son of Ahitub and Abimelech the son of Abiathar *were* the priests; Shavshaᵃ *was* the scribe; ¹⁷Benaiah the son of Jehoiada *was* over the Cherethites and the Pelethites; and David's sons *were* chief ministers at the king's side.

Leaders Broker Human Resources

(1 Chronicles 18:14–17)

David understood that he was to broker human gifts and talents. As Scripture says, he "administered judgment and justice to all his people" (1 Chr. 18:14). The next verses report how the king placed individuals in appropriate tasks according to their gifts: Joab led the army; Jehoshaphat was the recorder; Shavsha served as the scribe; and so on.

Effective leaders know their primary job isn't to amass personal accomplishments, but to accomplish as much as possible through the gifts of others. How do leaders inspire their associates to such great heights?

1. *Know the keys to their heart:* What do they sing about, cry about, dream about?
2. *Know the gifts in their possession:* What do they do well that gets results?
3. *Know the opportunities in their path:* What next step fits their maturity?

The Ammonites and Syrians Defeated

19 It happened after this that Nahash the king of the people of Ammon died, and his son reigned in his place. ²Then David said, "I will show kindness to Hanun the son of Nahash, because his father showed kindness to me." So David sent messengers to comfort him concerning his father. And David's servants came to Hanun in the land of the people of Ammon to comfort him.

³And the princes of the people of Ammon said to Hanun, "Do you think that David really honors your father because he has sent comforters to you? Did his servants not come to you to search and to overthrow and to spy out the land?"

⁴Therefore Hanun took David's servants, shaved them, and cut off their garments in the middle, at their buttocks, and sent them away. ⁵Then *some* went and told David about the men; and he sent to meet them, because the men were greatly ashamed. And the king said, "Wait at Jericho until your beards have grown, and *then* return."

⁶When the people of Ammon saw that they had made themselves repulsive to David, Hanun and the people of Ammon sent a thousand talents of silver to hire for themselves chariots and horsemen from Mesopotamia,ᵃ from Syrian Maacah, and from Zobah.ᵇ ⁷So they hired for themselves thirty-two thousand chariots, with the king of Maacah and his people, who came and encamped before Medeba. Also the people of Ammon gathered together from their cities, and came to battle.

⁸Now when David heard *of it,* he sent Joab and all the army of the mighty men. ⁹Then the people of Ammon came out and put themselves in battle array before the gate of the city, and the kings who had come *were* by themselves in the field.

¹⁰When Joab saw that the battle line was against him before and behind, he chose some of Israel's best, and put *them* in battle array against the Syrians. ¹¹And the rest of the people he put under the command of Abishai his brother, and they set *themselves* in battle array against the people of Ammon. ¹²Then he said, "If the Syrians are too strong for me, then you shall help me; but if the people of Ammon are too strong for you, then I will help you. ¹³Be of good courage, and let us be strong for our people and for the cities of our God. And may the LORD do *what is* good in His sight."

¹⁴So Joab and the people who *were* with him drew near for the battle against the Syrians, and they fled before him. ¹⁵When the people of Ammon saw that the Syrians were fleeing, they also fled before Abishai his brother, and entered the city. So Joab went to Jerusalem.

¹⁶Now when the Syrians saw that they had been defeated by Israel, they sent messengers and brought the Syrians who were beyond the River,ᵃ and Shophachᵇ the commander of Hadadezer's army *went* before them. ¹⁷When it was told David, he gathered all Israel, crossed over the Jordan and came upon them, and set up in battle array against them. So when David had set up in *battle* array against the Syrians, they fought with him.

18:16 ᵃSpelled *Seraiah* in 2 Samuel 8:17
19:6 ᵃHebrew *Aram Naharaim* ᵇSpelled *Zoba* in 2 Samuel 10:6 **19:16** ᵃThat is, the Euphrates ᵇSpelled *Shobach* in 2 Samuel 10:16

[18]Then the Syrians fled before Israel; and David killed seven thousand[a] charioteers and forty thousand foot soldiers[b] of the Syrians, and killed Shophach the commander of the army. [19]And when the servants of Hadadezer saw that they were defeated by Israel, they made peace with David and became his servants. So the Syrians were not willing to help the people of Ammon anymore.

Rabbah Is Conquered

20 It happened in the spring of the year, at the time kings go out *to battle,* that Joab led out the armed forces and ravaged the country of the people of Ammon, and came and besieged Rabbah. But David stayed at Jerusalem. And Joab defeated Rabbah and overthrew it. [2]Then David took their king's crown from his head, and found it to weigh a talent of gold, and *there were* precious stones in it. And it was set on David's head. Also he brought out the spoil of the city in great abundance. [3]And he brought out the people who *were* in it, and put *them* to work[a] with saws, with iron picks, and with axes. So David did to all the cities of the people of Ammon. Then David and all the people returned *to* Jerusalem.

Philistine Giants Destroyed

[4]Now it happened afterward that war broke out at Gezer with the Philistines, at which time Sibbechai the Hushathite killed Sippai,[a] *who was one* of the sons of the giant. And they were subdued.

[5]Again there was war with the Philistines, and Elhanan the son of Jair[a] killed Lahmi the brother of Goliath the Gittite, the shaft of whose spear *was* like a weaver's beam.

[6]Yet again there was war at Gath, where there was a man of *great* stature, with twenty-four fingers and toes, six *on each hand* and six *on each foot;* and he also was born to the giant. [7]So when he defied Israel, Jonathan the son of Shimea,[a] David's brother, killed him.

[8]These were born to the giant in Gath, and they fell by the hand of David and by the hand of his servants.

The Census of Israel and Judah

21 Now Satan stood up against Israel, and moved David to number Israel. [2]So David said to Joab and to the leaders of the people, "Go, number Israel from Beersheba to Dan, and bring the number of them to me that I may know *it.*"

[3]And Joab answered, "May the LORD make His

The Law of Reproduction: Giant Killers Grow Under David's Leadership

(1 Chronicles 20:4–8)

You might call it, "Déjà vu all over again." First Chronicles 20 describes David's army battling and beating Philistine giants. You can't help but recall 1 Samuel 17, when young David killed Goliath. His men had simply learned the second verse of the same song.

By this point in Israel's history, David had selected and trained giant killers just like himself—the story of the Law of Reproduction. Giant killers come only from other giant killers. Leaders can reproduce only what they have become themselves. We teach what we know, but we reproduce what we are. Consider the following truths:

1. *It takes one to know one.* We tend to see what we possess ourselves.
2. *It takes one to show one.* We cannot model for someone what we haven't done.
3. *It takes one to grow one.* We cannot train someone until we've done it ourselves.

---

people a hundred times more than they are. But, my lord the king, *are* they not all my lord's servants? Why then does my lord require this thing? Why should he be a cause of guilt in Israel?"

[4]Nevertheless the king's word prevailed against Joab. Therefore Joab departed and went throughout all Israel and came to Jerusalem. [5]Then Joab gave the sum of the number of the people to David. All Israel *had* one million one hundred thousand men who drew the sword, and Judah *had* four hundred and seventy thousand men who drew the sword. [6]But he did not count Levi and Benjamin among them, for the king's word was abominable to Joab.

19:18 [a]Or *seven hundred* (compare 2 Samuel 10:18) [b]Or *horsemen* (compare 2 Samuel 10:18) **20:3** [a]Septuagint reads *cut them.* **20:4** [a]Spelled *Saph* in 2 Samuel 21:18 **20:5** [a]Spelled *Jaare-Oregim* in 2 Samuel 21:19 **20:7** [a]Spelled *Shimeah* in 2 Samuel 21:21 and *Shammah* in 1 Samuel 16:9

Pay the Price, Depend on God

(1 Chronicles 21:1–13)

David's choice to count his soldiers revealed he was beginning to place more confidence in his troops than in the power of God. Fortunately, he placed himself in the hands of the Lord when he chose his punishment—once again demonstrating the "divine dependency" that got him to the top.

[7]And God was displeased with this thing; therefore He struck Israel. [8]So David said to God, "I have sinned greatly, because I have done this thing; but now, I pray, take away the iniquity of Your servant, for I have done very foolishly."

[9]Then the LORD spoke to Gad, David's seer, saying, [10]"Go and tell David, saying, 'Thus says the LORD: "I offer you three *things;* choose one of them for yourself, that I may do *it* to you."'"

[11]So Gad came to David and said to him, "Thus says the LORD: 'Choose for yourself, [12]either three[a] years of famine, or three months to be defeated by your foes with the sword of your enemies overtaking *you,* or else for three days the sword of the LORD—the plague in the land, with the angel[b] of the LORD destroying throughout all the territory of Israel.' Now consider what answer I should take back to Him who sent me."

[13]And David said to Gad, "I am in great distress. Please let me fall into the hand of the LORD, for His mercies *are* very great; but do not let me fall into the hand of man."

[14]So the LORD sent a plague upon Israel, and seventy thousand men of Israel fell. [15]And God sent an angel to Jerusalem to destroy it. As he[a] was destroying, the LORD looked and relented of the disaster, and said to the angel who was destroying, "It is enough; now restrain your[b] hand." And the angel of the LORD stood by the threshing floor of Ornan[c] the Jebusite.

[16]Then David lifted his eyes and saw the angel of the LORD standing between earth and heaven, having in his hand a drawn sword stretched out over Jerusalem. So David and the elders, clothed in sackcloth, fell on their faces. [17]And David said

21:12 [a]Or *seven* (compare 2 Samuel 24:13) [b]Or *Angel,* and so elsewhere in this chapter **21:15** [a]Or *He* [b]Or *Your* [c]Spelled *Araunah* in 2 Samuel 24:16

DAVID — WILLINGNESS TO ASSUME THE BLAME

(1 Chronicles 21:1–17)

PROFILE IN LEADERSHIP

Times of failure not only reveal a leader's true character, but also present opportunities for significant leadership lessons.

Following a major victory over the Philistines, King David made a major mistake. The king chose to listen to Satan, stopped trusting God for the defense of his nation, and undertook a census. His pride in the growth of his kingdom blinded his judgment. Had his spiritual advisors temporarily left the area? Or had David ignored their counsel? Either way, David failed miserably—as do most leaders at some point in the journey.

David's willingness to take responsibility for his foolish action demonstrated his depth of character. The king refused to project blame, even though the Scripture states that Satan provoked him. David repented and accepted punishment from the hand of God, acknowledging the mercy of God and trusting in the grace of God. Even so, David's error snuffed out the lives of seventy thousand Israelites. When leaders mess up, many people suffer.

Many leaders attempt to hide failures, blame others, or run from God. Not David. He admitted his failure and repented. Although he faced many difficulties, David worked to restore his relationship with God and did whatever he could to minimize the consequences of his failure in the lives of others (1 Chr. 21:16, 17).

to God, "Was it not I who commanded the people to be numbered? I am the one who has sinned and done evil indeed; but these sheep, what have they done? Let Your hand, I pray, O LORD my God, be against me and my father's house, but not against Your people that they should be plagued."

[18]Therefore, the angel of the LORD commanded Gad to say to David that David should go and erect an altar to the LORD on the threshing floor of Ornan the Jebusite. [19]So David went up at the word of Gad, which he had spoken in the name of the LORD. [20]Now Ornan turned and saw the angel; and his four sons who were with him hid themselves, but Ornan continued threshing wheat. [21]So David came to Ornan, and Ornan looked and saw David. And he went out from the threshing floor, and bowed before David with his face to the ground. [22]Then David said to Ornan, "Grant me the place of this threshing floor, that I may build an altar on it to the LORD. You shall grant it to me at the full price, that the plague may be withdrawn from the people."

[23]But Ornan said to David, "Take it to yourself, and let my lord the king do what is good in his eyes. Look, I also give you the oxen for burnt offerings, the threshing implements for wood, and the wheat for the grain offering; I give it all."

[24]Then King David said to Ornan, "No, but I will surely buy it for the full price, for I will not take what is yours for the LORD, nor offer burnt offerings with that which costs me nothing." [25]So David gave Ornan six hundred shekels of gold by weight for the place. [26]And David built there an altar to the LORD, and offered burnt offerings and peace offerings, and called on the LORD; and He answered him from heaven by fire on the altar of burnt offering.

[27]So the LORD commanded the angel, and he returned his sword to its sheath.

[28]At that time, when David saw that the LORD had answered him on the threshing floor of Ornan the Jebusite, he sacrificed there. [29]For the tabernacle of the LORD and the altar of the burnt offering, which Moses had made in the wilderness, were at that time at the high place in Gibeon. [30]But David could not go before it to inquire of God, for he was afraid of the sword of the angel of the LORD.

David Prepares to Build the Temple

22 Then David said, "This is the house of the LORD God, and this is the altar of burnt offering for Israel." [2]So David commanded to gather the aliens who were in the land of Israel; and he appointed masons to cut hewn stones to build the house of God. [3]And David prepared iron in abundance for the nails of the doors of the gates and for the joints, and bronze in abundance beyond measure, [4]and cedar

---

Perspective and Vision: David Sees a Bigger Picture
(1 Chronicles 22:1–19)

David's personal vision and passion extended far beyond his own lifetime. Although he knew Solomon would build the temple, he did some long-range planning and preparation for its construction. "Solomon my son is young and inexperienced," he explained, "and the house to be built for the LORD must be exceedingly magnificent, famous and glorious throughout all countries. I will now make preparation for it" (1 Chr. 22:5).

David appointed stone cutters, gathered cedar logs, acquired mounds of iron for the nails, and even gave Solomon a solemn charge to finish the job (22:11–19). This is the kind of thing that separates leaders from followers. Leaders see . . .

- **Beyond Others:** They look past their own future to the generations that follow.
- **Before Others:** They see what must happen long before others are ready.
- **Bigger Than Others:** They have a larger than usual vision of what can happen.

David not only prepared the materials for the construction of the temple and challenged his son to faithfully build the Lord's house, but he also commanded all the leaders of Israel to help Solomon complete the task. "Now set your heart and your soul to seek the LORD your God," he told them. "Therefore arise and build the sanctuary of the LORD God" (22:19). Worthy visions outlast those who cast them.

trees in abundance; for the Sidonians and those from Tyre brought much cedar wood to David.

⁵Now David said, "Solomon my son *is* young and inexperienced, and the house to be built for the LORD *must be* exceedingly magnificent, famous and glorious throughout all countries. I will now make preparation for it." So David made abundant preparations before his death.

⁶Then he called for his son Solomon, and charged him to build a house for the LORD God of Israel. ⁷And David said to Solomon: "My son, as for me, it was in my mind to build a house to the name of the LORD my God; ⁸but the word of the LORD came to me, saying, 'You have shed much blood and have made great wars; you shall not build a house for My name, because you have shed much blood on the earth in My sight. ⁹Behold, a son shall be born to you, who shall be a man of rest; and I will give him rest from all his enemies all around. His name shall be Solomon,ᵃ for I will give peace and quietness to Israel in his days. ¹⁰He shall build a house for My name, and he shall be My son, and I *will be* his Father; and I will establish the throne of his kingdom over Israel forever.' ¹¹Now, my son, may the LORD be with you; and may you prosper, and build the house of the LORD your God, as He has said to you. ¹²Only may the LORD give you wisdom and understanding, and give you charge concerning Israel, that you may keep the law of the LORD your God. ¹³Then you will prosper, if you take care to fulfill the statutes and judgments with which the LORD charged Moses concerning Israel. Be strong and of good courage; do not fear nor be dismayed. ¹⁴Indeed I have taken much trouble to prepare for the house of the LORD one hundred thousand talents of gold and one million talents of silver, and bronze and iron beyond measure, for it is so abundant. I have prepared timber and stone also, and you may add to them. ¹⁵Moreover *there are* workmen with you in abundance: woodsmen and stonecutters, and all types of skillful men for every kind of work. ¹⁶Of gold and silver and bronze and iron *there is* no limit. Arise and begin working, and the LORD be with you."

¹⁷David also commanded all the leaders of Israel to help Solomon his son, *saying,* ¹⁸"*Is* not the LORD your God with you? And has He *not* given you rest on every side? For He has given the inhabitants of the land into my hand, and the land is subdued before the LORD and before His people. ¹⁹Now set your heart and your soul to seek the LORD your God. Therefore arise and build the sanctuary of the LORD God, to bring the ark of the covenant of the LORD and the holy arti-

cles of God into the house that is to be built for the name of the LORD."

The Divisions of the Levites

23 So when David was old and full of days, he made his son Solomon king over Israel.

²And he gathered together all the leaders of Israel, with the priests and the Levites. ³Now the Levites were numbered from the age of thirty years and above; and the number of individual males was thirty-eight thousand. ⁴Of these, twenty-four thousand *were* to look after the work of the house of the LORD, six thousand *were* officers and judges, ⁵four thousand *were* gatekeepers, and four thousand praised the LORD with *musical* instruments, "which I made," *said David,* "for giving praise."

⁶Also David separated them into divisions among the sons of Levi: Gershon, Kohath, and Merari.

⁷Of the Gershonites: Laadanᵃ and Shimei. ⁸The sons of Laadan: the first Jehiel, then Zetham and Joel—three *in all.* ⁹The sons of Shimei: Shelomith, Haziel, and Haran—three *in all.* These were the heads of the fathers' *houses* of Laadan. ¹⁰And the sons of Shimei: Jahath, Zina,ᵃ Jeush, and Beriah. These *were* the four sons of Shimei. ¹¹Jahath was the first and Zizah the second. But Jeush and Beriah did not have many sons; therefore they were assigned as one father's house.

¹²The sons of Kohath: Amram, Izhar, Hebron, and Uzziel—four *in all.* ¹³The sons of Amram: Aaron and Moses; and Aaron was set apart, he and his sons forever, that he should sanctify the most holy things, to burn incense before the LORD, to minister to Him, and to give the blessing in His name forever. ¹⁴Now the sons of Moses the man of God were reckoned to the tribe of Levi. ¹⁵The sons of Moses *were* Gershonᵃ and Eliezer. ¹⁶Of the sons of Gershon, Shebuelᵃ *was* the first. ¹⁷Of the descendants of Eliezer, Rehabiah was the first. And Eliezer had no other sons, but the sons of Rehabiah were very many. ¹⁸Of the sons of Izhar, Shelomith *was* the first. ¹⁹Of the sons of Hebron, Jeriah *was* the first, Amariah the second, Jahaziel the third, and Jekameam the fourth. ²⁰Of the sons of Uzziel, Michah *was* the first and Jesshiah the second.

²¹The sons of Merari *were* Mahli and Mushi. The sons of Mahli *were* Eleazar and Kish. ²²And

22:9 ᵃLiterally *Peaceful* **23:7** ᵃSpelled *Libni* in Exodus 6:17 **23:10** ᵃSeptuagint and Vulgate read *Zizah* (compare verse 11). **23:15** ᵃHebrew *Gershom* (compare 6:16) **23:16** ᵃSpelled *Shubael* in 24:20

Eleazar died, and had no sons, but only daughters; and their brethren, the sons of Kish, took them *as wives.* [23]The sons of Mushi *were* Mahli, Eder, and Jeremoth—three *in all.*

[24]These *were* the sons of Levi by their fathers' houses—the heads of the fathers' *houses* as they were counted individually by the number of their names, who did the work for the service of the house of the LORD, from the age of twenty years and above.

[25]For David said, "The LORD God of Israel has given rest to His people, that they may dwell in Jerusalem forever"; [26]and also to the Levites, "They shall no longer carry the tabernacle, or any of the articles for its service." [27]For by the last words of David the Levites *were* numbered from twenty years old and above; [28]because their duty *was* to help the sons of Aaron in the service of the house of the LORD, in the courts and in the chambers, in the purifying of all holy things and the work of the service of the house of God, [29]both with the showbread and the fine flour for the grain offering, with the unleavened cakes and *what is baked in* the pan, with what is mixed and with all kinds of measures and sizes; [30]to stand every morning to thank and praise the LORD, and likewise at evening; [31]and at every presentation of a burnt offering to the LORD on the Sabbaths and on the New Moons and on the set feasts, by number according to the ordinance governing them, regularly before the LORD; [32]and that they should attend to the needs of the tabernacle of meeting, the needs of the holy *place,* and the needs of the sons of Aaron their brethren in the work of the house of the LORD.

The Divisions of the Priests

24 Now *these are* the divisions of the sons of Aaron. The sons of Aaron *were* Nadab, Abihu, Eleazar, and Ithamar. [2]And Nadab and Abihu died before their father, and had no children; therefore Eleazar and Ithamar ministered as priests. [3]Then David with Zadok of the sons of Eleazar, and Ahimelech of the sons of Ithamar, divided them according to the schedule of their service.

[4]There were more leaders found of the sons of Eleazar than of the sons of Ithamar, and *thus* they were divided. Among the sons of Eleazar *were* sixteen heads of *their* fathers' houses, and eight heads of their fathers' houses among the sons of Ithamar. [5]Thus they were divided by lot, one group as another, for there were officials of the sanctuary and officials *of the house* of God, from the sons of Eleazar and from the sons of Ithamar. [6]And the scribe, Shemaiah the son of

Nethanel, *one of* the Levites, wrote them down before the king, the leaders, Zadok the priest, Ahimelech the son of Abiathar, and the heads of the fathers' *houses* of the priests and Levites, one father's house taken for Eleazar and *one* for Ithamar.

[7]Now the first lot fell to Jehoiarib, the second to Jedaiah, [8]the third to Harim, the fourth to Seorim, [9]the fifth to Malchijah, the sixth to Mijamin, [10]the seventh to Hakkoz, the eighth to Abijah, [11]the ninth to Jeshua, the tenth to Shecaniah, [12]the eleventh to Eliashib, the twelfth to Jakim, [13]the thirteenth to Huppah, the fourteenth to Jeshebeab, [14]the fifteenth to Bilgah, the sixteenth to Immer, [15]the seventeenth to Hezir, the eighteenth to Happizzez,[a] [16]the nineteenth to Pethahiah, the twentieth to Jehezekel,[a] [17]the twenty-first to Jachin, the twenty-second to Gamul, [18]the twenty-third to Delaiah, the twenty-fourth to Maaziah.

[19]This *was* the schedule of their service for coming into the house of the LORD according to their ordinance by the hand of Aaron their father, as the LORD God of Israel had commanded him.

Other Levites

[20]And the rest of the sons of Levi: of the sons of Amram, Shubael;[a] of the sons of Shubael, Jehdeiah. [21]Concerning Rehabiah, of the sons of Rehabiah, the first *was* Isshiah. [22]Of the Izharites, Shelomoth;[a] of the sons of Shelomoth, Jahath. [23]Of the sons *of Hebron,*[a] Jeriah *was the first,*[b] Amariah the second, Jahaziel the third, *and* Jekameam the fourth. [24]*Of* the sons of Uzziel, Michah; of the sons of Michah, Shamir. [25]The brother of Michah, Isshiah; of the sons of Isshiah, Zechariah. [26]The sons of Merari *were* Mahli and Mushi; the son of Jaaziah, Beno. [27]The sons of Merari by Jaaziah *were* Beno, Shoham, Zaccur, and Ibri. [28]Of Mahli: Eleazar, who had no sons. [29]Of Kish: the son of Kish, Jerahmeel. [30]Also the sons of Mushi *were* Mahli, Eder, and Jerimoth. These *were* the sons of the Levites according to their fathers' houses.

[31]These also cast lots just as their brothers the sons of Aaron did, in the presence of King

---

24:15 [a]Septuagint and Vulgate read *Aphses.*
24:16 [a]Masoretic Text reads *Jehezkel.*
24:20 [a]Spelled *Shebuel* in 23:16 **24:22** [a]Spelled *Shelomith* in 23:18 **24:23** [a]Supplied from 23:19 (following some Hebrew manuscripts and Septuagint manuscripts) [b]Supplied from 23:19 (following some Hebrew manuscripts and Septuagint manuscripts)

David, Zadok, Ahimelech, and the heads of the fathers' *houses* of the priests and Levites. The chief fathers *did* just as their younger brethren.

The Musicians

25 Moreover David and the captains of the army separated for the service *some* of the sons of Asaph, of Heman, and of Jeduthun, who *should* prophesy with harps, stringed instruments, and cymbals. And the number of the skilled men performing their service was: [2]Of the sons of Asaph: Zaccur, Joseph, Nethaniah, and Asharelah;[a] the sons of Asaph *were* under the direction of Asaph, who prophesied according to the order of the king. [3]Of Jeduthun, the sons of Jeduthun: Gedaliah, Zeri,[a] Jeshaiah, Shimei, Hashabiah, and Mattithiah, six,[b] under the direction of their father Jeduthun, who prophesied with a harp to give thanks and to praise the LORD. [4]Of Heman, the sons of Heman: Bukkiah, Mattaniah, Uzziel,[a] Shebuel,[b] Jerimoth,[c] Hananiah, Hanani, Eliathah, Giddalti, Romamti-Ezer, Joshbekashah, Mallothi, Hothir, *and* Mahazioth. [5]All these *were* the sons of Heman the king's seer in the words of God, to exalt his horn.[a] For God gave Heman fourteen sons and three daughters.

[6]All these *were* under the direction of their father for the music *in* the house of the LORD, with cymbals, stringed instruments, and harps, for the service of the house of God. Asaph, Jeduthun, and Heman *were* under the authority of the king. [7]So the number of them, with their brethren who were instructed in the songs of the LORD, all who were skillful, *was* two hundred and eighty-eight.

[8]And they cast lots for their duty, the small as well as the great, the teacher with the student.

[9]Now the first lot for Asaph came out for Joseph; the second for Gedaliah, him with his brethren and sons, twelve; [10]the third for Zaccur, his sons and his brethren, twelve; [11]the fourth for Jizri,[a] his sons and his brethren, twelve; [12]the fifth for Nethaniah, his sons and his brethren, twelve; [13]the sixth for Bukkiah, his sons and his brethren, twelve; [14]the seventh for Jesharelah,[a] his sons and his brethren, twelve; [15]the eighth for Jeshaiah, his sons and his brethren, twelve; [16]the ninth for Mattaniah, his sons and his brethren, twelve; [17]the tenth for Shimei, his sons and his brethren, twelve; [18]the eleventh for Azarel,[a] his sons and his brethren, twelve; [19]the twelfth for Hashabiah, his sons and his brethren, twelve; [20]the thirteenth for Shubael,[a] his sons and his brethren, twelve; [21]the fourteenth for Mattithiah, his sons and his brethren, twelve; [22]the fifteenth for Jeremoth,[a] his sons and his brethren, twelve; [23]the sixteenth for Hananiah, his sons and his brethren, twelve; [24]the seventeenth for Joshbekashah, his sons and his brethren, twelve; [25]the eighteenth for Hanani, his sons and his brethren, twelve; [26]the nineteenth for Mallothi, his sons and his brethren, twelve; [27]the twentieth for Eliathah, his sons and his brethren, twelve; [28]the twenty-first for Hothir, his sons and his brethren, twelve; [29]the twenty-second for Giddalti, his sons and his brethren, twelve; [30]the twenty-third for Mahazioth, his sons and his brethren, twelve; [31]the twenty-fourth for Romamti-Ezer, his sons and his brethren, twelve.

The Gatekeepers

26 Concerning the divisions of the gatekeepers: of the Korahites, Meshelemiah the son of Kore, of the sons of Asaph. [2]And the sons of Meshelemiah *were* Zechariah the firstborn, Jediael the second, Zebadiah the third, Jathniel the fourth, [3]Elam the fifth, Jehohanan the sixth, Eliehoenai the seventh.

[4]Moreover the sons of Obed-Edom *were* Shemaiah the firstborn, Jehozabad the second, Joah the third, Sacar the fourth, Nethanel the fifth, [5]Ammiel the sixth, Issachar the seventh, Peulthai the eighth; for God blessed him.

[6]Also to Shemaiah his son were sons born who governed their fathers' houses, because they *were* men of great ability. [7]The sons of Shemaiah *were* Othni, Rephael, Obed, and Elzabad, whose brothers Elihu and Semachiah *were* able men.

[8]All these *were* of the sons of Obed-Edom, they and their sons and their brethren, able men with strength for the work: sixty-two of Obed-Edom.

[9]And Meshelemiah had sons and brethren, eighteen able men.

[10]Also Hosah, of the children of Merari, had sons: Shimri the first (for *though* he was not the firstborn, his father made him the first), [11]Hilkiah the second, Tebaliah the third, Zechariah the fourth; all the sons and brethren of Hosah *were* thirteen.

25:2 [a]Spelled *Jesharelah* in verse 14 **25:3** [a]Spelled *Jizri* in verse 11 [b]*Shimei,* appearing in one Hebrew and several Septuagint manuscripts, completes the total of six sons (compare verse 17). **25:4** [a]Spelled *Azarel* in verse 18 [b]Spelled *Shubael* in verse 20 [c]Spelled *Jeremoth* in verse 22 **25:5** [a]That is, to increase his power or influence **25:11** [a]Spelled *Zeri* in verse 3 **25:14** [a]Spelled *Asharelah* in verse 2 **25:18** [a]Spelled *Uzziel* in verse 4 **25:20** [a]Spelled *Shebuel* in verse 4 **25:22** [a]Spelled *Jerimoth* in verse 4

Competence: David's Royal Administration

(1 Chronicles 26:1—27:34)

Toward the end of 1 Chronicles we see David's flow chart of army divisions, tribal officers, treasurers, and royal overseers. God selected a leader with a compass in his head and a magnet in his heart. David had mastered the three Ps of organization: planning, preparation, and personnel.

[12] Among these *were* the divisions of the gatekeepers, among the chief men, *having* duties just like their brethren, to serve in the house of the LORD. [13] And they cast lots for each gate, the small as well as the great, according to their father's house. [14] The lot for the East *Gate* fell to Shelemiah. Then they cast lots *for* his son Zechariah, a wise counselor, and his lot came out for the North Gate; [15] to Obed-Edom the South Gate, and to his sons the storehouse.[a] [16] To Shuppim and Hosah *the lot came out* for the West Gate, with the Shallecheth Gate on the ascending highway—watchman opposite watchman. [17] On the east were *six* Levites, on the north four each day, on the south four each day, and for the storehouse[a] two by two. [18] As for the Parbar[a] on the west, *there were* four on the highway *and* two at the Parbar. [19] These were the divisions of the gatekeepers among the sons of Korah and among the sons of Merari.

The Treasuries and Other Duties

[20] Of the Levites, Ahijah *was* over the treasuries of the house of God and over the treasuries of the dedicated things. [21] The sons of Laadan, the descendants of the Gershonites of Laadan, heads of their fathers' *houses,* of Laadan the Gershonite: Jehieli. [22] The sons of Jehieli, Zetham and Joel his brother, *were* over the treasuries of the house of the LORD. [23] Of the Amramites, the Izharites, the Hebronites, and the Uzzielites: [24] Shebuel the son of Gershom, the son of Moses, *was* overseer of the treasuries. [25] And his brethren by Eliezer *were* Rehabiah his son, Jeshaiah his son, Joram his son, Zichri his son, and Shelomith his son.

[26] This Shelomith and his brethren *were* over all the treasuries of the dedicated things which King David and the heads of fathers' *houses,* the captains over thousands and hundreds, and the captains of the army, had dedicated. [27] Some of the spoils won in battles they dedicated to maintain the house of the LORD. [28] And all that Samuel the seer, Saul the son of Kish, Abner the son of Ner, and Joab the son of Zeruiah had dedicated, every dedicated *thing,* was under the hand of Shelomith and his brethren.

[29] Of the Izharites, Chenaniah and his sons *performed* duties as officials and judges over Israel outside Jerusalem.

[30] Of the Hebronites, Hashabiah and his brethren, one thousand seven hundred able men, had the oversight of Israel on the west side of the Jordan for all the business of the LORD, and in the service of the king. [31] Among the Hebronites, Jerijah *was* head of the Hebronites according to his genealogy of the fathers. In the fortieth year of the reign of David they were sought, and there were found among them capable men at Jazer of Gilead. [32] And his brethren *were* two thousand seven hundred able men, heads of fathers' *houses,* whom King David made officials over the Reubenites, the Gadites, and the half-tribe of Manasseh, for every matter pertaining to God and the affairs of the king.

The Military Divisions

27 And the children of Israel, according to their number, the heads of fathers' *houses,* the captains of thousands and hundreds and their officers, served the king in every matter of the *military* divisions. *These divisions* came in and went out month by month throughout all the months of the year, each division *having* twenty-four thousand.

[2] Over the first division for the first month *was* Jashobeam the son of Zabdiel, and in his division *were* twenty-four thousand; [3] he *was* of the children of Perez, and the chief of all the captains of the army for the first month. [4] Over the division of the second month *was* Dodai[a] an Ahohite, and of his division Mikloth also *was* the leader; in his division *were* twenty-four thousand. [5] The third captain of the army for the third month *was* Benaiah, the son of Jehoiada the priest, who was chief; in his division *were* twenty-four thousand. [6] This was the Benaiah *who was* mighty *among* the thirty, and was over the thirty; in his division *was* Ammizabad his son. [7] The fourth *captain* for the fourth month *was* Asahel the brother of Joab, and Zebadiah his son after

---

26:15 [a]Hebrew *asuppim* **26:17** [a]Hebrew *asuppim* **26:18** [a]Probably a court or colonnade extending west of the temple **27:4** [a]Hebrew *Dodai,* usually spelled *Dodo* (compare 2 Samuel 23:9)

him; in his division *were* twenty-four thousand. [8]The fifth *captain* for the fifth month *was* Shamhuth[a] the Izrahite; in his division were twenty-four thousand. [9]The sixth *captain* for the sixth month *was* Ira the son of Ikkesh the Tekoite; in his division *were* twenty-four thousand. [10]The seventh *captain* for the seventh month *was* Helez the Pelonite, of the children of Ephraim; in his division *were* twenty-four thousand. [11]The eighth *captain* for the eighth month *was* Sibbechai the Hushathite, of the Zarhites; in his division *were* twenty-four thousand. [12]The ninth *captain* for the ninth month *was* Abiezer the Anathothite, of the Benjamites; in his division *were* twenty-four thousand. [13]The tenth *captain* for the tenth month *was* Maharai the Netophathite, of the Zarhites; in his division *were* twenty-four thousand. [14]The eleventh *captain* for the eleventh month *was* Benaiah the Pirathonite, of the children of Ephraim; in his division *were* twenty-four thousand. [15]The twelfth *captain* for the twelfth month *was* Heldai[a] the Netophathite, of Othniel; in his division *were* twenty-four thousand.

Leaders of Tribes

[16]Furthermore, over the tribes of Israel: the officer over the Reubenites *was* Eliezer the son of Zichri; over the Simeonites, Shephatiah the son of Maachah; [17]over the Levites, Hashabiah the son of Kemuel; over the Aaronites, Zadok; [18]over Judah, Elihu, *one* of David's brothers; *over* Issachar, Omri the son of Michael; [19]over Zebulun, Ishmaiah the son of Obadiah; *over* Naphtali, Jerimoth the son of Azriel; [20]over the children of Ephraim, Hoshea the son of Azaziah; *over* the half-tribe of Manasseh, Joel the son of Pedaiah; [21]over the half-*tribe* of Manasseh in Gilead, Iddo the son of Zechariah; *over* Benjamin, Jaasiel the son of Abner; [22]over Dan, Azarel the son of Jeroham. These *were* the leaders of the tribes of Israel.

[23]But David did not take the number of those twenty years old and under, because the LORD had said He would multiply Israel like the stars of the heavens. [24]Joab the son of Zeruiah began a census, but he did not finish, for wrath came upon Israel because of this census; nor was the number recorded in the account of the chronicles of King David.

Other State Officials

[25]And Azmaveth the son of Adiel *was* over the king's treasuries; and Jehonathan the son of Uzziah was over the storehouses in the field, in the cities, in the villages, and in the fortresses. [26]Ezri the son of Chelub was over those who did the work of the field for tilling the ground. [27]And Shimei the Ramathite *was* over the vineyards, and Zabdi the Shiphmite was over the produce of the vineyards for the supply of wine. [28]Baal-Hanan the Gederite was over the olive trees and the sycamore trees that *were* in the lowlands, and Joash *was* over the store of oil. [29]And Shitrai the Sharonite *was* over the herds that fed in Sharon, and Shaphat the son of Adlai was over the herds *that were* in the valleys. [30]Obil the Ishmaelite *was* over the camels, Jehdeiah the Meronothite *was* over the donkeys, [31]and Jaziz the Hagrite *was* over the flocks. All these *were* the officials over King David's property.

[32]Also Jehonathan, David's uncle, *was* a counselor, a wise man, and a scribe; and Jehiel the son of Hachmoni *was* with the king's sons. [33]Ahithophel *was* the king's counselor, and Hushai the Archite *was* the king's companion. [34]After Ahithophel *was* Jehoiada the son of Benaiah, then Abiathar. And the general of the king's army *was* Joab.

Solomon Instructed to Build the Temple

28 Now David assembled at Jerusalem all the leaders of Israel: the officers of the tribes and the captains of the divisions who served the king, the captains over thousands and captains over hundreds, and the stewards over all the substance and possessions of the king and of his sons, with the officials, the valiant men, and all the mighty men of valor.

[2]Then King David rose to his feet and said, "Hear me, my brethren and my people: I *had* it in my heart to build a house of rest for the ark of the covenant of the LORD, and for the footstool of our God, and had made preparations to build it. [3]But God said to me, 'You shall not build a house for My name, because you *have been* a man of war and have shed blood.' [4]However the LORD God of Israel chose me above all the house of my father to be king over Israel forever, for He has chosen Judah *to be* the ruler. And of the house of Judah, the house of my father, and among the sons of my father, He was pleased with me to make *me* king over all Israel. [5]And of all my sons (for the LORD has given me many sons) He has chosen my son Solomon to sit on the throne of the kingdom of the LORD over Israel. [6]Now He said to me, 'It is your son Solomon *who* shall build My house and My courts; for I have chosen him *to be* My son, and I will be

---

27:8 [a]Spelled *Shammoth* in 11:27 and *Shammah* in 2 Samuel 23:11 **27:15** [a]Spelled *Heled* in 11:30 and *Heleb* in 2 Samuel 23:29

his Father. [7]Moreover I will establish his kingdom forever, if he is steadfast to observe My commandments and My judgments, as it is this day.' [8]Now therefore, in the sight of all Israel, the assembly of the LORD, and in the hearing of our God, be careful to seek out all the commandments of the LORD your God, that you may possess this good land, and leave it as an inheritance for your children after you forever.

[9]"As for you, my son Solomon, know the God of your father, and serve Him with a loyal heart and with a willing mind; for the LORD searches all hearts and understands all the intent of the thoughts. If you seek Him, He will be found by you; but if you forsake Him, He will cast you off forever. [10]Consider now, for the LORD has chosen you to build a house for the sanctuary; be strong, and do it."

[11]Then David gave his son Solomon the plans for the vestibule, its houses, its treasuries, its upper chambers, its inner chambers, and the place of the mercy seat; [12]and the plans for all that he had by the Spirit, of the courts of the house of the LORD, of all the chambers all around, of the treasuries of the house of God, and of the treasuries for the dedicated things; [13]also for the division of the priests and the Levites, for all the work of the service of the house of the LORD, and for all the articles of service in the house of the LORD. [14]He gave gold by weight for things of gold, for all articles used in every kind of service; also silver for all articles of silver by weight, for all articles used in every kind of service; [15]the weight for the lampstands of gold, and their lamps of gold, by weight for each lampstand and its lamps; for the lampstands of silver by weight, for the lampstand and its lamps, according to the use of each lampstand. [16]And by weight he gave gold for the tables of the showbread, for each table, and silver for the tables of silver; [17]also pure gold for the forks, the basins, the pitchers of pure gold, and the golden bowls—he gave gold by weight for every bowl; and for the silver bowls, silver by weight for every bowl; [18]and refined gold by weight for the altar of incense, and for the construction of the chariot, that is, the gold cherubim that spread their wings and overshadowed the ark of the covenant of the LORD. [19]"All this," said David, "the LORD made me understand in writing, by His hand upon me, all the works of these plans."

[20]And David said to his son Solomon, "Be strong and of good courage, and do it; do not fear nor be dismayed, for the LORD God—my God—will be with you. He will not leave you nor forsake you, until you have finished all the work for the service of the house of the LORD. [21]Here are the divisions of the priests and the Levites for all the service of the house of God; and every willing craftsman will be with you for all manner of workmanship, for every kind of service; also the leaders and all the people will be completely at your command."

Offerings for Building the Temple

29Furthermore King David said to all the assembly: "My son Solomon, whom alone God has chosen, is young and inexperienced; and the work is great, because the temple[a] is not for man but for the LORD God. [2]Now for the house of my God I have prepared with all my might: gold for things to be made of gold, silver for things of silver, bronze for things of bronze, iron for things of iron, wood for things of wood, onyx stones, stones to be set, glistening stones of various colors, all kinds of precious stones, and marble slabs in abundance. [3]Moreover, because I have set my affection on the house of my God, I have given to the house of my God, over and above all that I have prepared for the holy house, my own special treasure of gold and silver: [4]three thousand talents of gold, of the gold of Ophir, and seven thousand talents of refined silver, to overlay the walls of the houses; [5]the gold for things of gold and the silver for things of silver, and for all kinds of work to be done by the hands of craftsmen. Who then is willing to consecrate himself this day to the LORD?"

[6]Then the leaders of the fathers' houses, leaders of the tribes of Israel, the captains of thousands and of hundreds, with the officers over the king's work, offered willingly. [7]They gave for the work of the house of God five thousand talents and ten thousand darics of gold, ten thousand talents of silver, eighteen thousand talents of bronze, and one hundred thousand talents of iron. [8]And whoever had precious stones gave them to the treasury of the house of the LORD, into the hand of Jehiel[a] the Gershonite. [9]Then the people rejoiced, for they had offered willingly, because with a loyal heart they had offered willingly to the LORD; and King David also rejoiced greatly.

David's Praise to God

[10]Therefore David blessed the LORD before all the assembly; and David said:

"Blessed are You, LORD God of Israel, our Father, forever and ever.

29:1 [a]Literally palace **29:8** [a]Possibly the same as Jehieli (compare 26:21, 22)

The Law of Legacy: David Sets Up Solomon to Succeed

(1 Chronicles 29:1–5)

As his life begins ebbing away, we see David preparing his son Solomon to give oversight to the construction of the temple. The old king is determined to ensure his legacy by setting up the next leader and committing him to the care of God Almighty. Look closely at what he did:

1. He rallied all the people together (v. 1).
2. He affirmed God's choice of his successor (v. 1).
3. He identified the great need for help (v. 1).
4. He reminded the people of his own commitment (v. 2).
5. He declared that the people were well on their way to the goal (vv. 3–5).
6. He asked for commitment (v. 5).

The people loved this old king, and they knew he was not asking them to do anything he had not already demonstrated an eagerness to complete himself. Because people do what people see, David was able to motivate the Israelites to do three things:

- Sacrificially give toward the temple project
- Support Solomon and his leadership
- Rejoice in what God was doing among them

And so the Book of 1 Chronicles comes to a close, saying of David, "So he died in a good old age, full of days and riches and honor; and Solomon his son reigned in his place" (29:28).

11 Yours, O LORD, *is* the greatness,
The power and the glory,
The victory and the majesty;
For all *that is* in heaven and in earth *is*
Yours;
Yours *is* the kingdom, O LORD,
And You are exalted as head over all.

12 Both riches and honor *come* from You,
And You reign over all.
In Your hand *is* power and might;
In Your hand *it is* to make great
And to give strength to all.

13 "Now therefore, our God,
We thank You
And praise Your glorious name.

14 But who *am* I, and who *are* my people,
That we should be able to offer so
willingly as this?
For all things *come* from You,
And of Your own we have given You.

15 For we *are* aliens and pilgrims before You,
As *were* all our fathers;
Our days on earth *are* as a shadow,
And without hope.

16 "O LORD our God, all this abundance that we have prepared to build You a house for Your holy name is from Your hand, and *is* all Your own. 17 I know also, my God, that You test the heart and have pleasure in uprightness. As for me, in the uprightness of my heart I have willingly offered all these *things;* and now with joy I have seen Your people, who are present here to offer willingly to You. 18 O LORD God of Abraham, Isaac, and Israel, our fathers, keep this forever in the intent of the thoughts of the heart of Your people, and fix their heart toward You. 19 And give my son Solomon a loyal heart to keep Your commandments and Your testimonies and Your statutes, to do all *these things,* and to build the temple[a] for which I have made provision."

20 Then David said to all the assembly, "Now bless the LORD your God." So all the assembly blessed the LORD God of their fathers, and bowed their heads and prostrated themselves before the LORD and the king.

Solomon Anointed King

21 And they made sacrifices to the LORD and offered burnt offerings to the LORD on the next day: a thousand bulls, a thousand rams, a thousand lambs, with their drink offerings, and sacri-

---

29:19 [a]Literally *palace*

fices in abundance for all Israel. ²²So they ate and drank before the LORD with great gladness on that day. And they made Solomon the son of David king the second time, and anointed *him* before the LORD *to be* the leader, and Zadok *to be* priest. ²³Then Solomon sat on the throne of the LORD as king instead of David his father, and prospered; and all Israel obeyed him. ²⁴All the leaders and the mighty men, and also all the sons of King David, submitted themselves to King Solomon. ²⁵So the LORD exalted Solomon exceedingly in the sight of all Israel, and bestowed on him *such* royal majesty as had not been on any king before him in Israel.

The Close of David's Reign

²⁶Thus David the son of Jesse reigned over all Israel. ²⁷And the period that he reigned over Israel *was* forty years; seven years he reigned in Hebron, and thirty-three *years* he reigned in Jerusalem. ²⁸So he died in a good old age, full of days and riches and honor; and Solomon his son reigned in his place. ²⁹Now the acts of King David, first and last, indeed they *are* written in the book of Samuel the seer, in the book of Nathan the prophet, and in the book of Gad the seer, ³⁰with all his reign and his might, and the events that happened to him, to Israel, and to all the kingdoms of the lands.

SUMMARY

If 2 Chronicles develops one major theme or offers one major lesson, it is this: Leaders need to finish well.

Four kings—Solomon, Asa, Uzziah, and Jehoshaphat—all began their monarchies well, but failed to finish strongly. Each enjoyed both success and fame as a leader, but they let the good times get to them. Their perspective got fuzzy; they began to overestimate their own importance; they grew blind to their weaknesses and refused accountability; and they started to trust in human ingenuity rather than in God—all "alarm bells" appropriate for leaders yet today!

What accounts for these poor finishes? Second Chronicles considers the Jerusalem worship center as symbolic of God's covenant with His people (ch. 7). The temple represented His presence, His promises, His provision, and His protection. Indeed, it symbolized His very Person. As each leader drifted away from his calling, his worship grew cold and sterile, becoming nothing more than an item to be checked off of a "to-do" list. While God was still there, they grew emotionally absent—and eventually God's presence and blessings began to fade.

Second Chronicles delivers a sobering warning to leaders who are drifting from their passion. When our leadership activities become mere routine, we have wandered from our original call. When we become distracted by peripheral issues and deviate from the purpose that first drove us to lead, we have wandered from our original call. When we overestimate our importance and allow ourselves to become exceptions to the rules—we have wandered away from our leadership call.

Second Chronicles demonstrates that leaders cannot separate their spiritual condition from their success as a leader. While intimacy with God does not automatically make anyone a great leader—plenty of deeply spiritual people do not lead well—yet one cannot be a godly leader apart from intimacy with God. Our leadership must begin with our relationship with God. Had the kings of Israel and Judah remained intimate with Yahweh, they would have avoided many of their mistakes, pride, blindness, presumption, and failures. Nearly every king desired to lead his people in reform, yet most of them failed. The lesson for us? Leaders cannot execute public reform until they experience personal repentance.

God's Role in 2 Chronicles

God intended to call the Hebrew leaders into close, personal encounters with Him. Josiah most clearly illustrates God's goal.

Josiah became king at eight years of age (34:1). As he grew older, God increasingly led this young man's life (34:3–7). Josiah led strongly to the very end: "Thus Josiah removed all the abominations from all the country that belonged to the children of Israel, and made all who were present in Israel diligently serve the LORD their God" (34:33).

Leaders in 2 Chronicles

Solomon, Rehoboam, Jeroboam, Abijah, Asa, Jehoshaphat, Ahab, Jehoram, Ahaziah, Joash, Amaziah, Uzziah, Jotham, Ahaz, Hezekiah, Manasseh, Josiah, Jehoahaz

Other People of Influence in 2 Chronicles

Rehoboam's young counselors, Shemaiah, Micaiah, Jehoiada, Oded

Lessons in Leadership

- Priorities must be in place: all's well that begins well.
- Leaders committed to excellence will excel themselves.
- Healthy leaders seek wise counsel, even if it's not what they want to hear.
- When things go wrong, check the humility of the leader.
- God blesses His people so that they will bless the nations.
- Leaders who maintain God's rule over their life maintain their rule.
- Leaders cannot pursue power and love at the same time.
- Leaders can undo their accomplishments by failing to finish well.
- Example is the main ingredient in influencing others.
- Leaders find a way to reach the goal and enable the team to win.

HIGHLIGHTS IN 2 CHRONICLES

Solomon Requests Wisdom

1 Now Solomon the son of David was strengthened in his kingdom, and the LORD his God *was* with him and exalted him exceedingly.

²And Solomon spoke to all Israel, to the captains of thousands and of hundreds, to the judges, and to every leader in all Israel, the heads of the fathers' *houses*. ³Then Solomon, and all the assembly with him, went to the high place that *was* at Gibeon; for the tabernacle of meeting with God was there, which Moses the servant of the LORD had made in the wilderness. ⁴But David had brought up the ark of God from Kirjath Jearim to *the place* David had prepared for it, for he had pitched a tent for it at Jerusalem. ⁵Now the bronze altar that Bezalel the son of Uri, the son of Hur, had made, he put[a] before the tabernacle of the LORD; Solomon and the assembly sought Him *there*. ⁶And Solomon went up there to the bronze altar before the LORD, which *was* at the tabernacle of meeting, and offered a thousand burnt offerings on it.

⁷On that night God appeared to Solomon, and said to him, "Ask! What shall I give you?"

⁸And Solomon said to God: "You have shown great mercy to David my father, and have made me king in his place. ⁹Now, O LORD God, let Your promise to David my father be established, for You have made me king over a people like the dust of the earth in multitude. ¹⁰Now give me wisdom and knowledge, that I may go out and come in before this people; for who can judge this great people of Yours?"

¹¹Then God said to Solomon: "Because this was in your heart, and you have not asked riches or wealth or honor or the life of your enemies, nor have you asked long life—but have asked wisdom and knowledge for yourself, that you may judge My people over whom I have made you king— ¹²wisdom and knowledge *are* granted to you; and I will give you riches and wealth and honor, such as none of the kings have had who *were* before you, nor shall any after you have the like."

Solomon's Military and Economic Power

¹³So Solomon came to Jerusalem from the high place that *was* at Gibeon, from before the tabernacle of meeting, and reigned over Israel. ¹⁴And Solomon gathered chariots and horsemen; he had one thousand four hundred chariots and twelve thousand horsemen, whom he stationed in the chariot cities and with the king in Jerusalem. ¹⁵Also the king made silver and gold as common in Jerusalem as stones, and he made cedars as abundant as the sycamores which *are* in the

---

The Law of Priorities: Solomon Gets It All
(2 Chronicles 1:3–12)

Every leader must establish a list of priorities, then learn to put first things first. Second Chronicles begins with a lesson in priorities.

When Solomon became king of Israel, he was given the opportunity to ask God for anything. Instead of requesting riches or fame, he asked for wisdom to lead his people well. Good answer! God responded by rewarding him not only with the thing he asked for, but also with all the benefits he didn't request.

This incident illustrates how effective prioritizing often works. When you put first things first, you frequently gain the time for nonessentials. Solomon narrowed his wedge, and got it all. No doubt, King Solomon faced the same options we have today:

1. *Easy Things First:* He could've chosen to focus on the easy tasks ahead of him.
2. *Fun Things First:* He could've chosen to focus on riches or fame.
3. *Urgent Things First:* He could've asked for help in building the temple.
4. *Hard Things First:* He could've sought favor with those who didn't like him.
5. *First Things First:* Instead, he chose to seek wisdom so he could glorify God.

---

lowland. ¹⁶And Solomon had horses imported from Egypt and Keveh; the king's merchants bought them in Keveh at the *current* price. ¹⁷They also acquired and imported from Egypt a chariot for six hundred *shekels* of silver, and a horse for one hundred and fifty; thus, through their agents,[a] they exported them to all the kings of the Hittites and the kings of Syria.

Solomon Prepares to Build the Temple

2 Then Solomon determined to build a temple for the name of the LORD, and a royal house for himself. ²Solomon selected seventy thousand men to bear burdens, eighty thousand to quarry *stone* in the mountains, and three thousand six hundred to oversee them.

1:5 [a]Some authorities read *it was there.*
1:17 [a]Literally *by their hands*

[3]Then Solomon sent to Hiram[a] king of Tyre, saying:

As you have dealt with David my father, and sent him cedars to build himself a house to dwell in, *so deal with me.* [4]Behold, I am building a temple for the name of the LORD my God, to dedicate *it* to Him, to burn before Him sweet incense, for the continual showbread, for the burnt offerings morning and evening, on the Sabbaths, on the New Moons, and on the set feasts of the LORD our God. This *is an ordinance* forever to Israel.

[5] And the temple which I build *will be* great, for our God is greater than all gods. [6]But who is able to build Him a temple, since heaven and the heaven of heavens cannot contain Him? Who *am* I then, that I should build Him a temple, except to burn sacrifice before Him?

[7] Therefore send me at once a man skillful to work in gold and silver, in bronze and iron, in purple and crimson and blue, who has skill to engrave with the skillful men who are with me in Judah and Jerusalem, whom David my father provided. [8]Also send me cedar and cypress and algum logs from Lebanon, for I know that your servants have skill to cut timber in Lebanon; and indeed my servants *will be* with your servants, [9]to prepare timber for me in abundance, for the temple which I am about to build *shall be* great and wonderful.

[10] And indeed I will give to your servants, the woodsmen who cut timber, twenty thousand kors of ground wheat, twenty thousand kors of barley, twenty thousand baths of wine, and twenty thousand baths of oil.

[11]Then Hiram king of Tyre answered in writing, which he sent to Solomon:

Because the LORD loves His people, He has made you king over them.

[12]Hiram[a] also said:

Blessed *be* the LORD God of Israel, who made heaven and earth, for He has given King David a wise son, endowed with prudence and understanding, who will build a temple for the LORD and a royal house for himself!

[13] And now I have sent a skillful man, endowed with understanding, Huram[a] my master[b] *craftsman* [14](the son of a woman of the daughters of Dan, and his father was a

2:3 [a]Hebrew *Huram* (compare 1 Kings 5:1)
2:12 [a]Hebrew *Huram* (compare 1 Kings 5:1)
2:13 [a]Spelled *Hiram* in 1 Kings 7:13   [b]Literally *father* (compare 1 Kings 7:13, 14)

The Law of Navigation:
Solomon Commits Himself to Excellence
(2 Chronicles 2:1—6:42)

Solomon saw to it that excellence controlled both the design and construction of the temple. He committed himself to excellence every step of the way, including hidden areas. If you were to ask him, "Why bother with the details of an area that no one would ever see? Who would know whether it was done right or not?" he would respond, "*I* would know and *God* would know."

Leaders who model a commitment to excellence reap great rewards, and their people tend to emulate that same concern. Look at how Solomon's commitment to excellence shows up:

Chapter	Subject	Commitment to Excellence
2	Preparation of temple	He offers sacrifices daily consecrating the work.
3	Design and dimensions	He specifies exact sizes and decorations in rooms.
4	Furnishings	He furnishes it with extravagant accessories.
5	The ark	He takes great care transporting the ark.
6	The dedication	He models godly motives for building a temple.

man of Tyre), skilled to work in gold and silver, bronze and iron, stone and wood, purple and blue, fine linen and crimson, and to make any engraving and to accomplish any plan which may be given to him, with your skillful men and with the skillful men of my lord David your father.

15 Now therefore, the wheat, the barley, the oil, and the wine which my lord has spoken of, let him send to his servants. 16And we will cut wood from Lebanon, as much as you need; we will bring it to you in rafts by sea to Joppa, and you will carry it up to Jerusalem.

17Then Solomon numbered all the aliens who were in the land of Israel, after the census in which David his father had numbered them; and there were found to be one hundred and fifty-three thousand six hundred. 18And he made seventy thousand of them bearers of burdens, eighty thousand stonecutters in the mountain, and three thousand six hundred overseers to make the people work.

Solomon Builds the Temple

3 Now Solomon began to build the house of the LORD at Jerusalem on Mount Moriah, where the LORDª had appeared to his father David, at the place that David had prepared on the threshing floor of Ornanᵇ the Jebusite. 2And he began to build on the second day of the second month in the fourth year of his reign.

3This is the foundation which Solomon laid for building the house of God: The length was sixty cubits (by cubits according to the former measure) and the width twenty cubits. 4And the vestibule that was in front of the sanctuaryª was twenty cubits long across the width of the house, and the height was one hundred andᵇ twenty. He overlaid the inside with pure gold. 5The larger roomª he paneled with cypress which he overlaid with fine gold, and he carved palm trees and chainwork on it. 6And he decorated the house with precious stones for beauty, and the gold was gold from Parvaim. 7He also overlaid the house—the beams and doorposts, its walls and doors—with gold; and he carved cherubim on the walls.

8And he made the Most Holy Place. Its length was according to the width of the house, twenty cubits, and its width twenty cubits. He overlaid it with six hundred talents of fine gold. 9The weight of the nails was fifty shekels of gold; and he overlaid the upper area with gold. 10In the

Most Holy Place he made two cherubim, fashioned by carving, and overlaid them with gold. 11The wings of the cherubim were twenty cubits in overall length: one wing of the one cherub was five cubits, touching the wall of the room, and the other wing was five cubits, touching the wing of the other cherub; 12one wing of the other cherub was five cubits, touching the wall of the room, and the other wing also was five cubits, touching the wing of the other cherub. 13The wings of these cherubim spanned twenty cubits overall. They stood on their feet, and they faced inward. 14And he made the veil of blue, purple, crimson, and fine linen, and wove cherubim into it.

15Also he made in front of the templeª two pillars thirty-fiveᵇ cubits high, and the capital that was on the top of each of them was five cubits. 16He made wreaths of chainwork, as in the inner sanctuary, and put them on top of the pillars; and he made one hundred pomegranates, and put them on the wreaths of chainwork. 17Then he set up the pillars before the temple, one on the right hand and the other on the left; he called the name of the one on the right hand Jachin, and the name of the one on the left Boaz.

Furnishings of the Temple

4 Moreover he made a bronze altar: twenty cubits was its length, twenty cubits its width, and ten cubits its height.

2Then he made the Sea of cast bronze, ten cubits from one brim to the other; it was completely round. Its height was five cubits, and a line of thirty cubits measured its circumference. 3And under it was the likeness of oxen encircling it all around, ten to a cubit, all the way around the Sea. The oxen were cast in two rows, when it was cast. 4It stood on twelve oxen: three looking toward the north, three looking toward the west, three looking toward the south, and three looking toward the east; the Sea was set upon them, and all their back parts pointed inward. 5It was a handbreadth thick; and its brim was shaped like

3:1 ªLiterally He, following Masoretic Text and Vulgate; Septuagint reads the LORD; Targum reads the Angel of the LORD. ᵇSpelled Araunah in 2 Samuel 24:16ff 3:4 ªThe main room of the temple; elsewhere called the holy place (compare 1 Kings 6:3) ᵇFollowing Masoretic Text, Septuagint, and Vulgate; Arabic, some manuscripts of the Septuagint, and Syriac omit one hundred and. 3:5 ªLiterally house 3:15 ªLiterally house ᵇOr eighteen (compare 1 Kings 7:15; 2 Kings 25:17; and Jeremiah 52:21) the brim of a cup, *like* a lily blossom. It contained three thousand[a] baths.

[6]He also made ten lavers, and put five on the right side and five on the left, to wash in them; such things as they offered for the burnt offering they would wash in them, but the Sea *was* for the priests to wash in. [7]And he made ten lampstands of gold according to their design, and set *them* in the temple, five on the right side and five on the left. [8]He also made ten tables, and placed *them* in the temple, five on the right side and five on the left. And he made one hundred bowls of gold.

[9]Furthermore he made the court of the priests, and the great court and doors for the court; and he overlaid these doors with bronze. [10]He set the Sea on the right side, toward the southeast.

[11]Then Huram made the pots and the shovels and the bowls. So Huram finished doing the work that he was to do for King Solomon for the house of God: [12]the two pillars and the bowl-shaped capitals *that were* on top of the two pillars; the two networks covering the two bowl-shaped capitals which *were* on top of the pillars; [13]four hundred pomegranates for the two networks (two rows of pomegranates for each network, to cover the two bowl-shaped capitals that *were* on the pillars); [14]he also made carts and the lavers on the carts; [15]one Sea and twelve oxen under it; [16]also the pots, the shovels, the forks—and all their articles Huram his master[a] *craftsman* made of burnished bronze for King Solomon for the house of the LORD.

[17]In the plain of Jordan the king had them cast in clay molds, between Succoth and Zeredah.[a] [18]And Solomon had all these articles made in such great abundance that the weight of the bronze was not determined.

[19]Thus Solomon had all the furnishings made for the house of God: the altar of gold and the tables on which *was* the showbread; [20]the lampstands with their lamps of pure gold, to burn in the prescribed manner in front of the inner sanctuary, [21]with the flowers and the lamps and the wick-trimmers of gold, of purest gold; [22]the trimmers, the bowls, the ladles, and the censers of pure gold. As for the entry of the sanctuary, its inner doors to the Most Holy *Place,* and the doors of the main hall of the temple, *were* gold.

5 So all the work that Solomon had done for the house of the LORD was finished; and Solomon brought in the things which his father David had dedicated: the silver and the gold and all the furnishings. And he put *them* in the treasuries of the house of God.

The Ark Brought into the Temple

[2]Now Solomon assembled the elders of Israel and all the heads of the tribes, the chief fathers of the children of Israel, in Jerusalem, that they might bring the ark of the covenant of the LORD up from the City of David, which *is* Zion. [3]Therefore all the men of Israel assembled with the king at the feast, which *was* in the seventh month. [4]So all the elders of Israel came, and the Levites took up the ark. [5]Then they brought up the ark, the tabernacle of meeting, and all the holy furnishings that *were* in the tabernacle. The priests and the Levites brought them up. [6]Also King Solomon, and all the congregation of Israel who were assembled with him before the ark, were sacrificing sheep and oxen that could not be counted or numbered for multitude. [7]Then the priests brought in the ark of the covenant of the LORD to its place, into the inner sanctuary of the temple,[a] to the Most Holy *Place,* under the wings of the cherubim. [8]For the cherubim spread *their* wings over the place of the ark, and the cherubim overshadowed the ark and its poles. [9]The poles extended so that the ends of the poles of the ark could be seen from *the holy place,* in front of the inner sanctuary; but they could not be seen from outside. And they are there to this day. [10]Nothing was in the ark except the two tablets which Moses put *there* at Horeb, when the LORD made *a covenant* with the children of Israel, when they had come out of Egypt.

[11]And it came to pass when the priests came out of the *Most* Holy *Place* (for all the priests who *were* present had sanctified themselves, without keeping to their divisions), [12]and the Levites *who were* the singers, all those of Asaph and Heman and Jeduthun, with their sons and their brethren, stood at the east end of the altar, clothed in white linen, having cymbals, stringed instruments and harps, and with them one hundred and twenty priests sounding with trumpets— [13]indeed it came to pass, when the trumpeters and singers *were* as one, to make one sound to be heard in praising and thanking the LORD, and when they lifted up their voice with the trumpets and cymbals and instruments of music, and praised the LORD, *saying:*

" *For He is* good,
For His mercy *endures* forever,"[a]

4:5 [a]Or *two thousand* (compare 1 Kings 7:26)
4:16 [a]Literally *father* **4:17** [a]Spelled *Zaretan* in 1 Kings 7:46 **5:7** [a]Literally *house* **5:13** [a]Compare Psalm 106:1

that the house, the house of the LORD, was filled with a cloud, [14]so that the priests could not continue ministering because of the cloud; for the glory of the LORD filled the house of God.

6 Then Solomon spoke:

"The LORD said He would dwell in the dark cloud.
[2] I have surely built You an exalted house,
And a place for You to dwell in forever."

Solomon's Speech upon Completion of the Work

[3]Then the king turned around and blessed the whole assembly of Israel, while all the assembly of Israel was standing. [4]And he said: "Blessed be the LORD God of Israel, who has fulfilled with His hands what He spoke with His mouth to my father David, saying, [5]'Since the day that I brought My people out of the land of Egypt, I have chosen no city from any tribe of Israel in which to build a house, that My name might be there, nor did I choose any man to be a ruler over My people Israel. [6]Yet I have chosen Jerusalem, that My name may be there, and I have chosen David to be over My people Israel.' [7]Now it was in the heart of my father David to build a temple[a] for the name of the LORD God of Israel. [8]But the LORD said to my father David, 'Whereas it was in your heart to build a temple for My name, you did well in that it was in your heart. [9]Nevertheless you shall not build the temple, but your son who will come from your body, he shall build the temple for My name.' [10]So the LORD has fulfilled His word which He spoke, and I have filled the position of my father David, and sit on the throne of Israel, as the LORD promised; and I have built the temple for the name of the LORD God of Israel. [11]And there I have put the ark, in which is the covenant of the LORD which He made with the children of Israel."

Solomon's Prayer of Dedication

[12]Then Solomon[a] stood before the altar of the LORD in the presence of all the assembly of Israel, and spread out his hands [13](for Solomon had made a bronze platform five cubits long, five cubits wide, and three cubits high, and had set it in the midst of the court; and he stood on it, knelt down on his knees before all the assembly of Israel, and spread out his hands toward heaven); [14]and he said: "LORD God of Israel, there is no God in heaven or on earth like You, who keep Your covenant and mercy with Your servants who walk before You with all their hearts. [15]You

have kept what You promised Your servant David my father; You have both spoken with Your mouth and fulfilled it with Your hand, as it is this day. [16]Therefore, LORD God of Israel, now keep what You promised Your servant David my father, saying, 'You shall not fail to have a man sit before Me on the throne of Israel, only if your sons take heed to their way, that they walk in My law as you have walked before Me.' [17]And now, O LORD God of Israel, let Your word come true, which You have spoken to Your servant David.

[18]"But will God indeed dwell with men on the earth? Behold, heaven and the heaven of heavens cannot contain You. How much less this temple[a] which I have built! [19]Yet regard the prayer of Your servant and his supplication, O LORD my God, and listen to the cry and the prayer which Your servant is praying before You: [20]that Your eyes may be open toward this temple day and night, toward the place where You said You would put Your name, that You may hear the prayer which Your servant makes toward this place. [21]And may You hear the supplications of Your servant and of Your people Israel, when they pray toward this place. Hear from heaven Your dwelling place, and when You hear, forgive.

[22]"If anyone sins against his neighbor, and is forced to take an oath, and comes and takes an oath before Your altar in this temple, [23]then hear from heaven, and act, and judge Your servants, bringing retribution on the wicked by bringing his way on his own head, and justifying the righteous by giving him according to his righteousness.

[24]"Or if Your people Israel are defeated before an enemy because they have sinned against You, and return and confess Your name, and pray and make supplication before You in this temple, [25]then hear from heaven and forgive the sin of Your people Israel, and bring them back to the land which You gave to them and their fathers.

[26]"When the heavens are shut up and there is no rain because they have sinned against You, when they pray toward this place and confess Your name, and turn from their sin because You afflict them, [27]then hear in heaven, and forgive the sin of Your servants, Your people Israel, that You may teach them the good way in which they should walk; and send rain on Your land which You have given to Your people as an inheritance.

[28]"When there is famine in the land, pesti-

6:7 [a]Literally house, and so in verses 8–10
6:12 [a]Literally he (compare 1 Kings 8:22)
6:18 [a]Literally house

lence or blight or mildew, locusts or grasshoppers; when their enemies besiege them in the land of their cities; whatever plague or whatever sickness *there is;* [29]whatever prayer, whatever supplication is *made* by anyone, or by all Your people Israel, when each one knows his own burden and his own grief, and spreads out his hands to this temple: [30]then hear from heaven Your dwelling place, and forgive, and give to everyone according to all his ways, whose heart You know (for You alone know the hearts of the sons of men), [31]that they may fear You, to walk in Your ways as long as they live in the land which You gave to our fathers.

[32]"Moreover, concerning a foreigner, who is not of Your people Israel, but has come from a far country for the sake of Your great name and Your mighty hand and Your outstretched arm, when they come and pray in this temple; [33]then hear from heaven Your dwelling place, and do according to all for which the foreigner calls to You, that all peoples of the earth may know Your name and fear You, as *do* Your people Israel, and that they may know that this temple which I have built is called by Your name.

[34]"When Your people go out to battle against their enemies, wherever You send them, and when they pray to You toward this city which You have chosen and the temple which I have built for Your name, [35]then hear from heaven their prayer and their supplication, and maintain their cause.

[36]"When they sin against You (for *there is* no one who does not sin), and You become angry with them and deliver them to the enemy, and they take them captive to a land far or near; [37]yet when they come to themselves in the land where they were carried captive, and repent, and make supplication to You in the land of their captivity, saying, 'We have sinned, we have done wrong, and have committed wickedness'; [38]and *when* they return to You with all their heart and with all their soul in the land of their captivity, where they have been carried captive, and pray toward their land which You gave to their fathers, the city which You have chosen, and toward the temple which I have built for Your name: [39]then hear from heaven Your dwelling place their prayer and their supplications, and maintain their cause, and forgive Your people who have sinned against You. [40]Now, my God, I pray, let Your eyes be open and *let* Your ears *be* attentive to the prayer *made* in this place.

[41] "Now therefore,
Arise, O LORD God, to Your resting place,

You and the ark of Your strength.
Let Your priests, O LORD God, be clothed with salvation,
And let Your saints rejoice in goodness.

[42] "O LORD God, do not turn away the face of Your Anointed;
Remember the mercies of Your servant David."[a]

Solomon Dedicates the Temple

7 When Solomon had finished praying, fire came down from heaven and consumed the burnt offering and the sacrifices; and the glory of the LORD filled the temple.[a] [2]And the priests could not enter the house of the LORD, because the glory of the LORD had filled the LORD's house. [3]When all the children of Israel saw how the fire came down, and the glory of the LORD on the temple, they bowed their faces to the ground on the pavement, and worshiped and praised the LORD, *saying:*

"For *He is* good,
For His mercy *endures* forever."[a]

[4]Then the king and all the people offered sacrifices before the LORD. [5]King Solomon offered a sacrifice of twenty-two thousand bulls and one hundred and twenty thousand sheep. So the king and all the people dedicated the house of God. [6]And the priests attended to their services; the Levites also with instruments of the music of the LORD, which King David had made to praise the LORD, saying, "For His mercy *endures* forever,"[a] whenever David offered praise by their ministry. The priests sounded trumpets opposite them, while all Israel stood.

[7]Furthermore Solomon consecrated the middle of the court that *was* in front of the house of the LORD; for there he offered burnt offerings and the fat of the peace offerings, because the bronze altar which Solomon had made was not able to receive the burnt offerings, the grain offerings, and the fat.

[8]At that time Solomon kept the feast seven days, and all Israel with him, a very great assembly from the entrance of Hamath to the Brook of Egypt.[a] [9]And on the eighth day they held a sacred assembly, for they observed the dedication of the altar seven days, and the feast seven days.

6:42 [a]Compare Psalm 132:8–10 **7:1** [a]Literally *house*
7:3 [a]Compare Psalm 106:1 **7:6** [a]Compare Psalm
106:1 **7:8** [a]That is, the Shihor (compare
1 Chronicles 13:5)

[10]On the twenty-third day of the seventh month he sent the people away to their tents, joyful and glad of heart for the good that the LORD had done for David, for Solomon, and for His people Israel. [11]Thus Solomon finished the house of the LORD and the king's house; and Solomon successfully accomplished all that came into his heart to make in the house of the LORD and in his own house.

God's Second Appearance to Solomon

[12]Then the LORD appeared to Solomon by night, and said to him: "I have heard your prayer, and have chosen this place for Myself as a house of sacrifice. [13]When I shut up heaven and there is no rain, or command the locusts to devour the land, or send pestilence among My people, [14]if My people who are called by My name will humble themselves, and pray and seek My face, and turn from their wicked ways, then I will hear from heaven, and will forgive their sin and heal their land. [15]Now My eyes will be open and My ears attentive to prayer made in this place. [16]For now I have chosen and sanctified this house, that My name may be there forever; and My eyes and My heart will be there perpetually. [17]As for you, if you walk before Me as your father David walked, and do according to all that I have commanded you, and if you keep My statutes and My judgments, [18]then I will establish the throne of your kingdom, as I covenanted with David your father, saying, 'You shall not fail to have a man as ruler in Israel.'

[19]"But if you turn away and forsake My statutes and My commandments which I have set before you, and go and serve other gods, and worship them, [20]then I will uproot them from My land which I have given them; and this house which I have sanctified for My name I will cast out of My sight, and will make it a proverb and a byword among all peoples.

[21]"And as for this house, which is exalted, everyone who passes by it will be astonished and say, 'Why has the LORD done thus to this land and this house?' [22]Then they will answer, 'Because they forsook the LORD God of their fathers, who brought them out of the land of Egypt, and embraced other gods, and worshiped them and served them; therefore He has brought all this calamity on them.'"

Solomon's Additional Achievements

8 It came to pass at the end of twenty years, when Solomon had built the house of the LORD and his own house, [2]that the cities which Hiram[a] had given to Solomon, Solomon built them; and he settled the children of Israel there. [3]And Solomon went to Hamath Zobah and seized it. [4]He also built Tadmor in the wilderness, and all the storage cities which he built in Hamath. [5]He built Upper Beth Horon and Lower Beth Horon, fortified cities with walls, gates, and bars, [6]also Baalath and all the storage cities that Solomon had, and all the chariot cities and the cities of the cavalry, and all that Solomon desired to build in Jerusalem, in Lebanon, and in all the land of his dominion.

[7]All the people who were left of the Hittites, Amorites, Perizzites, Hivites, and Jebusites, who were not of Israel— [8]that is, their descendants who were left in the land after them, whom the children of Israel did not destroy—from these Solomon raised forced labor, as it is to this day. [9]But Solomon did not make the children of Israel servants for his work. Some were men of war, captains of his officers, captains of his chariots, and his cavalry. [10]And others were chiefs of the officials of King Solomon: two hundred and fifty, who ruled over the people.

[11]Now Solomon brought the daughter of Pharaoh up from the City of David to the house he had built for her, for he said, "My wife shall not dwell in the house of David king of Israel, because the places to which the ark of the LORD has come are holy."

[12]Then Solomon offered burnt offerings to the LORD on the altar of the LORD which he had built before the vestibule, [13]according to the daily rate, offering according to the commandment of Moses, for the Sabbaths, the New Moons, and the three appointed yearly feasts—the Feast of Unleavened Bread, the Feast of Weeks, and the Feast of Tabernacles. [14]And, according to the order of David his father, he appointed the divisions of the priests for their service, the Levites for their duties (to praise and serve before the priests) as the duty of each day required, and the gatekeepers by their divisions at each gate; for so David the man of God had commanded. [15]They did not depart from the command of the king to the priests and Levites concerning any matter or concerning the treasuries.

[16]Now all the work of Solomon was well-ordered from[a] the day of the foundation of the house of the LORD until it was finished. So the house of the LORD was completed.

[17]Then Solomon went to Ezion Geber and Elath[a] on the seacoast, in the land of Edom.

8:2 [a]Hebrew Huram (compare 2 Chronicles 2:3)
8:16 [a]Following Septuagint, Syriac, and Vulgate; Masoretic Text reads as far as. 8:17 [a]Hebrew Eloth (compare 2 Kings 14:22)

[18]And Hiram sent him ships by the hand of his servants, and servants who knew the sea. They went with the servants of Solomon to Ophir, and acquired four hundred and fifty talents of gold from there, and brought it to King Solomon.

The Queen of Sheba's Praise of Solomon

9 Now when the queen of Sheba heard of the fame of Solomon, she came to Jerusalem to test Solomon with hard questions, *having* a very great retinue, camels that bore spices, gold in abundance, and precious stones; and when she came to Solomon, she spoke with him about all that was in her heart. [2]So Solomon answered all her questions; there was nothing so difficult for Solomon that he could not explain it to her. [3]And when the queen of Sheba had seen the wisdom of Solomon, the house that he had built, [4]the food on his table, the seating of his servants, the service of his waiters and their apparel, his cupbearers and their apparel, and his entryway by which he went up to the house of the LORD, there was no more spirit in her.

[5]Then she said to the king: "*It was* a true report which I heard in my own land about your words and your wisdom. [6]However I did not believe their words until I came and saw with my own eyes; and indeed the half of the greatness of your wisdom was not told me. You exceed the fame of which I heard. [7]Happy *are* your men and happy *are* these your servants, who stand continually before you and hear your wisdom! [8]Blessed be the LORD your God, who delighted in you, setting you on His throne *to be* king for the LORD your God! Because your God has loved Israel, to establish them forever, therefore He made you king over them, to do justice and righteousness."

[9]And she gave the king one hundred and twenty talents of gold, spices in great abundance, and precious stones; there never were any spices such as those the queen of Sheba gave to King Solomon.

[10]Also, the servants of Hiram and the servants of Solomon, who brought gold from Ophir, brought algum[a] wood and precious stones. [11]And the king made walkways *of* the algum[a] wood for the house of the LORD and for the king's house, also harps and stringed instruments for singers; and there were none such *as these* seen before in the land of Judah.

[12]Now King Solomon gave to the queen of

9:10 [a]Or *almug* (compare 1 Kings 10:11, 12)
9:11 [a]Or *almug* (compare 1 Kings 10:11, 12)

B efore he careened off course in his later years, Solomon began to fulfill God's dream of blessing the nations through the nation of Israel. When leaders from the surrounding countries heard of his great wisdom, they hopped aboard their camels and made the long trek to Jerusalem to see whether the reports could be trusted. The Queen of Sheba spoke for these wide-eyed visitors when she said, "Blessed be the LORD your God, who delighted in you, setting you on His throne to be king for the LORD your God!" (2 Chr. 9:8).

After the queen saw Solomon's splendor, he sent her away with much more than she brought (9:12). So she returned to her own land, blessed by God. Many other interested leaders visited Solomon after she left (9:23).

Centuries later, the Lord Jesus Christ would tell His followers that what they had received freely, they should freely give (Matt. 10:8). Solomon had asked for godly wisdom that he might rule in a way pleasing to God. The Lord freely gave him that wisdom, so he freely shared it with others—in his words, in his music, and in his writings.

Effective, godly leadership means giving what you have so that God may be glorified in all you do. What you have freely received, freely give—and so bless others.

Sheba all she desired, whatever she asked, *much more* than she had brought to the king. So she turned and went to her own country, she and her servants.

Solomon's Great Wealth

¹³The weight of gold that came to Solomon yearly was six hundred and sixty-six talents of gold, ¹⁴besides *what* the traveling merchants and traders brought. And all the kings of Arabia and governors of the country brought gold and silver to Solomon. ¹⁵And King Solomon made two hundred large shields of hammered gold; six hundred *shekels* of hammered gold went into each shield. ¹⁶*He* also *made* three hundred shields of hammered gold; three hundred *shekels*ᵃ of gold went into each shield. The king put them in the House of the Forest of Lebanon.

¹⁷Moreover the king made a great throne of ivory, and overlaid it with pure gold. ¹⁸The throne *had* six steps, with a footstool of gold, *which were* fastened to the throne; there were armrests on either side of the place of the seat, and two lions stood beside the armrests. ¹⁹Twelve lions stood there, one on each side of the six steps; nothing like *this* had been made for any *other* kingdom.

²⁰All King Solomon's drinking vessels *were* gold, and all the vessels of the House of the Forest of Lebanon *were* pure gold. Not *one was* silver, for this was accounted as nothing in the days of Solomon. ²¹For the king's ships went to Tarshish with the servants of Hiram.ᵃ Once every three years the merchant shipsᵇ came, bringing gold, silver, ivory, apes, and monkeys.ᶜ

²²So King Solomon surpassed all the kings of the earth in riches and wisdom. ²³And all the kings of the earth sought the presence of Solomon to hear his wisdom, which God had put in his heart. ²⁴Each man brought his present: articles of silver and gold, garments, armor, spices, horses, and mules, at a set rate year by year.

²⁵Solomon had four thousand stalls for horses and chariots, and twelve thousand horsemen whom he stationed in the chariot cities and with the king at Jerusalem.

²⁶So he reigned over all the kings from the Riverᵃ to the land of the Philistines, as far as the border of Egypt. ²⁷The king made silver *as common* in Jerusalem as stones, and he made cedar trees as abundant as the sycamores which *are* in the lowland. ²⁸And they brought horses to Solomon from Egypt and from all lands.

Death of Solomon

²⁹Now the rest of the acts of Solomon, first and last, *are* they not written in the book of Na-than the prophet, in the prophecy of Ahijah the Shilonite, and in the visions of Iddo the seer concerning Jeroboam the son of Nebat? ³⁰Solomon reigned in Jerusalem over all Israel forty years. ³¹Then Solomon rested with his fathers, and was buried in the City of David his father. And Rehoboam his son reigned in his place.

The Revolt Against Rehoboam

10 And Rehoboam went to Shechem, for all Israel had gone to Shechem to make him king. ²So it happened, when Jeroboam the son of Nebat heard *it* (he was in Egypt, where he had fled from the presence of King Solomon), that Jeroboam returned from Egypt. ³Then they sent for him and called him. And Jeroboam and all Israel came and spoke to Rehoboam, saying, ⁴"Your father made our yoke heavy; now therefore, lighten the burdensome service of your father and his heavy yoke which he put on us, and we will serve you."

Rehoboam Violates the Law of Intuition and Pays

(2 Chronicles 10:1–17)

Rehoboam, the successor to Solomon, knew little about good leadership. Instead of sizing up his situation and culture, he went on a power trip. He failed to discern, listen, or follow wise counsel from those who could help him most—and lost more than half of the kingdom.

---

⁵So he said to them, "Come back to me after three days." And the people departed.

⁶Then King Rehoboam consulted the elders who stood before his father Solomon while he still lived, saying, "How do you advise *me* to answer these people?"

⁷And they spoke to him, saying, "If you are kind to these people, and please them, and speak good words to them, they will be your servants forever."

⁸But he rejected the advice which the elders had given him, and consulted the young men

---

9:16 ᵃOr *three minas* (compare 1 Kings 10:17)
9:21 ᵃHebrew *Huram* (compare 1 Kings 10:22)
ᵇLiterally *ships of Tarshish,* deep-sea vessels ᶜOr *peacocks* **9:26** ᵃThat is, the Euphrates

Rehoboam and the Law of the Inner Circle

(2 Chronicles 10:6–8)

Be careful what kind of inner circle you choose! King Rehoboam had the benefit of his father's inner circle, men who gave him wise counsel. But the foolish young king rejected their advice and instead looked for advice that agreed with his own opinion. Horrible move! He should have gone with a core team who possessed the qualities of a solid inner circle:

1. *Experience:* People who have been down the road of life and understand it.
2. *Heart for God:* People who place God first and uphold His values.
3. *Objectivity:* People who see the pros and cons of the issues.
4. *Love for people:* People who love others and value them more than things.
5. *Complementary gifts:* People who bring diverse gifts to the relationship.
6. *Loyalty to the leader:* People who truly love and are concerned for the leader.

who had grown up with him, who stood before him. [9]And he said to them, "What advice do you give? How should we answer this people who have spoken to me, saying, 'Lighten the yoke which your father put on us'?"

[10]Then the young men who had grown up with him spoke to him, saying, "Thus you should speak to the people who have spoken to you, saying, 'Your father made our yoke heavy, but you make *it* lighter on us'—thus you shall say to them: 'My little *finger* shall be thicker than my father's waist! [11]And now, whereas my father put a heavy yoke on you, I will add to your yoke; my father chastised you with whips, but I *will chastise you* with scourges!'"[a]

[12]So Jeroboam and all the people came to Rehoboam on the third day, as the king had directed, saying, "Come back to me the third day." [13]Then the king answered them roughly. King Rehoboam rejected the advice of the elders, [14]and he spoke to them according to the advice of the young men, saying, "My father[a] made your yoke heavy, but I will add to it; my father chastised you with whips, but I *will chastise you* with scourges!"[b] [15]So the king did not listen to

the people; for the turn *of events* was from God, that the LORD might fulfill His word, which He had spoken by the hand of Ahijah the Shilonite to Jeroboam the son of Nebat.

[16]Now when all Israel *saw* that the king did not listen to them, the people answered the king, saying:

"What share have we in David?
　We have no inheritance in the son of Jesse.
Every man to your tents, O Israel!
Now see to your own house, O David!"

So all Israel departed to their tents. [17]But Rehoboam reigned over the children of Israel who dwelt in the cities of Judah.

[18]Then King Rehoboam sent Hadoram, who *was* in charge of revenue; but the children of Israel stoned him with stones, and he died. Therefore King Rehoboam mounted *his* chariot in haste to flee to Jerusalem. [19]So Israel has been in rebellion against the house of David to this day.

11 Now when Rehoboam came to Jerusalem, he assembled from the house of Judah and Benjamin one hundred and eighty thousand chosen *men* who were warriors, to fight against Israel, that he might restore the kingdom to Rehoboam.

[2]But the word of the LORD came to Shemaiah the man of God, saying, [3]"Speak to Rehoboam the son of Solomon, king of Judah, and to all Israel in Judah and Benjamin, saying, [4]'Thus says the LORD: "You shall not go up or fight against your brethren! Let every man return to his house, for this thing is from Me."'" Therefore they obeyed the words of the LORD, and turned back from attacking Jeroboam.

Rehoboam Fortifies the Cities

[5]So Rehoboam dwelt in Jerusalem, and built cities for defense in Judah. [6]And he built Bethlehem, Etam, Tekoa, [7]Beth Zur, Sochoh, Adullam, [8]Gath, Mareshah, Ziph, [9]Adoraim, Lachish, Azekah, [10]Zorah, Aijalon, and Hebron, which are in Judah and Benjamin, fortified cities. [11]And he fortified the strongholds, and put captains in them, and stores of food, oil, and wine. [12]Also in every city he *put* shields and spears, and made them very strong, having Judah and Benjamin on his side.

10:11 [a]Literally *scorpions* **10:14** [a]Following many Hebrew manuscripts, Septuagint, Syriac, and Vulgate (compare verse 10 and 1 Kings 12:14); Masoretic Text reads *I.* [b]Literally *scorpions*

LISTENING

Rehoboam Fails to Listen to the Right People
(2 Chronicles 10:15)

King Rehoboam's dysfunctional leadership split the nation of Israel in two. His hunger for power, unreasonable demands, poor decision making, and lack of compassion for those who worked under him all conspired to doom his leadership. But probably the root of his problem can be found in 2 Chronicles 10:15: "So the king did not listen to the people. . . ."

Listening is one of the 21 Indispensable Qualities of a Leader. Leaders must listen for two reasons: 1. to connect with others; and 2. to learn from others. President Woodrow Wilson said, "The ear of the leader must ring with the voices of the people." What's more, a good leader encourages followers to tell him what he needs to know, not what he wants to hear. Sometimes 50 percent of your leadership involves simple listening. So why did Rehoboam fail at this simple task?

1. *Narrow Vision*
   The people promised to serve him if he lightened their load; he didn't see it.
2. *Poor Decision-making Skills*
   He wavered on what to do about their request and told them to come back later.
3. *Self-centered Focus*
   He rejected wise counsel after deciding it didn't match his desires.
4. *Demanding and Impatient Style*
   He promised to make life tougher, not easier, for his people.

We learn from King Rehoboam the difference between "hearing" and "listening." Hearing is a function of the ears; the king heard all the spoken words. Listening, however, is a function of the will; leaders listen to connect and to learn. Rehoboam failed to do both, as he refused to listen to history, his followers, the wise counsel of his staff, and to God.

Certainly we cannot listen to everyone—far too many opposing voices and views cry out for that. So to whom should leaders be listening? Listen especially well to the following:

1. *Your Followers*
   Good leaders take the time to get a feel for each team member as a person.
2. *Your Customers*
   Good leaders make it a priority to keep in contact with those they serve.
3. *Your Competitors*
   Good leaders don't imitate the competition, but they listen in order to learn from the encounter.
4. *Your Mentors*
   No leader can afford to be without a mentor's insight.
5. *Your Inner Circle*
   Leaders must listen to those closest to them to confirm the pulse of the organization.

For a positive example of listening, turn to p. 357.

Priests and Levites Move to Judah

[13]And from all their territories the priests and the Levites who *were* in all Israel took their stand with him. [14]For the Levites left their common-lands and their possessions and came to Judah and Jerusalem, for Jeroboam and his sons had rejected them from serving as priests to the LORD. [15]Then he appointed for himself priests for the high places, for the demons, and the calf idols which he had made. [16]And after *the Levites left,*[a] those from all the tribes of Israel, such as set their heart to seek the LORD God of Israel, came to Jerusalem to sacrifice to the LORD God of their fathers. [17]So they strengthened the kingdom of Judah, and made Rehoboam the son of Solomon strong for three years, because they walked in the way of David and Solomon for three years.

The Family of Rehoboam

[18]Then Rehoboam took for himself as wife Mahalath the daughter of Jerimoth the son of David, *and of* Abihail the daughter of Eliab the son of Jesse. [19]And she bore him children: Jeush, Shamariah, and Zaham. [20]After her he took Maachah the granddaughter[a] of Absalom; and she bore him Abijah, Attai, Ziza, and Shelomith. [21]Now Rehoboam loved Maachah the granddaughter of Absalom more than all his wives and his concubines; for he took eighteen wives and sixty concubines, and begot twenty-eight sons and sixty daughters. [22]And Rehoboam appointed Abijah the son of Maachah as chief, *to be* leader among his brothers; for he *intended* to make him king. [23]He dealt wisely, and dispersed some of his sons throughout all the territories of Judah and Benjamin, to every fortified city; and he gave them provisions in abundance. He also sought many wives *for them.*

Egypt Attacks Judah

12 Now it came to pass, when Rehoboam had established the kingdom and had strengthened himself, that he forsook the law of the LORD, and all Israel along with him. [2]And it happened in the fifth year of King Rehoboam *that* Shishak king of Egypt came up against Jerusalem, because they had transgressed against the LORD, [3]with twelve hundred chariots, sixty thousand horsemen, and people without number who came with him out of Egypt—the Lubim and the Sukkiim and the Ethiopians. [4]And he took the fortified cities of Judah and came to Jerusalem.

[5]Then Shemaiah the prophet came to Rehoboam and the leaders of Judah, who were gathered together in Jerusalem because of Shishak, and said to them, "Thus says the LORD: 'You have forsaken Me, and therefore I also have left you in the hand of Shishak.'"

[6]So the leaders of Israel and the king humbled themselves; and they said, "The LORD *is* righteous."

[7]Now when the LORD saw that they humbled themselves, the word of the LORD came to Shemaiah, saying, "They have humbled themselves; *therefore* I will not destroy them, but I will grant them some deliverance. My wrath shall not be poured out on Jerusalem by the hand of Shishak. [8]Nevertheless they will be his servants, that they may distinguish My service from the service of the kingdoms of the nations."

[9]So Shishak king of Egypt came up against Jerusalem, and took away the treasures of the house of the LORD and the treasures of the king's house; he took everything. He also carried away the gold shields which Solomon had made. [10]Then King Rehoboam made bronze shields in their place, and committed *them* to the hands of the captains of the guard, who guarded the doorway of the king's house. [11]And whenever the king entered the house of the LORD, the guard would go and bring them out; then they would take them back into the guardroom. [12]When he humbled himself, the wrath of the LORD turned from him, so as not to destroy *him* completely; and things also went well in Judah.

The End of Rehoboam's Reign

[13]Thus King Rehoboam strengthened himself in Jerusalem and reigned. Now Rehoboam *was* forty-one years old when he became king; and he reigned seventeen years in Jerusalem, the city which the LORD had chosen out of all the tribes of Israel, to put His name there. His mother's name *was* Naamah, an Ammonitess. [14]And he did evil, because he did not prepare his heart to seek the LORD.

[15]The acts of Rehoboam, first and last, *are* they not written in the book of Shemaiah the prophet, and of Iddo the seer concerning genealogies? And *there were* wars between Rehoboam and Jeroboam all their days. [16]So Rehoboam rested with his fathers, and was buried in the City of David. Then Abijah[a] his son reigned in his place.

11:16 [a]Literally *after them* **11:20** [a]Literally *daughter,* but in the broader sense of granddaughter (compare 2 Chronicles 13:2) **12:16** [a]Spelled *Abijam* in 1 Kings 14:31

Abijah Reigns in Judah

13 In the eighteenth year of King Jeroboam, Abijah became king over Judah. [2]He reigned three years in Jerusalem. His mother's name *was* Michaiah[a] the daughter of Uriel of Gibeah.

And there was war between Abijah and Jeroboam. [3]Abijah set the battle in order with an army of valiant warriors, four hundred thousand choice men. Jeroboam also drew up in battle formation against him with eight hundred thousand choice men, mighty men of valor.

[4]Then Abijah stood on Mount Zemaraim, which *is* in the mountains of Ephraim, and said, "Hear me, Jeroboam and all Israel: [5]Should you not know that the LORD God of Israel gave the dominion over Israel to David forever, to him and his sons, by a covenant of salt? [6]Yet Jeroboam the son of Nebat, the servant of Solomon the son of David, rose up and rebelled against his lord. [7]Then worthless rogues gathered to him, and strengthened themselves against Rehoboam the son of Solomon, when Rehoboam was young and inexperienced and could not withstand them. [8]And now you think to withstand the kingdom of the LORD, which is in the hand of the sons of David; and you *are* a great multitude, and with you are the gold calves which Jeroboam made for you as gods. [9]Have you not cast out the priests of the LORD, the sons of Aaron, and the Levites, and made for yourselves priests, like the peoples of *other* lands, so that whoever comes to consecrate himself with a young bull and seven rams may be a priest of *things that are* not gods? [10]But as for us, the LORD *is* our God, and we have not forsaken Him; and the priests who minister to the LORD *are* the sons of Aaron, and the Levites *attend* to *their* duties. [11]And they burn to the LORD every morning and every evening burnt sacrifices and sweet incense; *they* also *set* the showbread *in order on* the pure *gold* table, and the lampstand of gold with its lamps to burn every evening; for we keep the command of the LORD our God, but you have forsaken Him. [12]Now look, God Himself is with us as *our* head, and His priests with sounding trumpets to sound the alarm against you. O children of Israel, do not fight against the LORD God of your fathers, for you shall not prosper!"

[13]But Jeroboam caused an ambush to go around behind them; so they were in front of Judah, and the ambush *was* behind them. [14]And when Judah looked around, to their surprise the battle line *was* at both front and rear; and they cried out to the LORD, and the priests sounded the trumpets. [15]Then the men of Judah gave a shout; and as the men of Judah shouted, it happened that God struck Jeroboam and all Israel before Abijah and Judah. [16]And the children of Is-

---

13:2 [a]Spelled *Maachah* in 11:20, 21 and 1 Kings 15:2

Vision: Abijah Learns the Right Vision, Gets the Right Results

(2 Chronicles 13:1–18)

An unusual king named Abijah reminds us that the right vision at the right time brings the right results.

Abijah followed Rehoboam as king of Judah. He tried to warn the leaders of Israel (the northern kingdom) against their folly in rebelling against the Lord. He cast the vision, reminded them of their heritage, and encouraged them to follow it. "Now look," he said, "God Himself is with us as our head, and His priests with sounding trumpets to sound the alarm against you. O children of Israel, do not fight against the LORD God of your fathers, for you shall not prosper!" (2 Chr. 13:12).

When king Jeroboam refused to listen, God honored Abijah and delivered him from Jeroboam's ambush. That day five hundred thousand enemy soldiers fell on the battlefield. Abijah's vision led to his victory. Consider this:

- The wrong vision at the wrong time = Disaster
- The wrong vision at the right time = Mistake
- The right vision at the wrong time = Blunder
- The right vision at the right time = Success

rael fled before Judah, and God delivered them into their hand. [17]Then Abijah and his people struck them with a great slaughter; so five hundred thousand choice men of Israel fell slain. [18]Thus the children of Israel were subdued at that time; and the children of Judah prevailed, because they relied on the LORD God of their fathers. [19]And Abijah pursued Jeroboam and took cities from him: Bethel with its villages, Jeshanah with its villages, and Ephrain[a] with its villages. [20]So Jeroboam did not recover strength again in the days of Abijah; and the LORD struck him, and he died.

[21]But Abijah grew mighty, married fourteen wives, and begot twenty-two sons and sixteen daughters. [22]Now the rest of the acts of Abijah, his ways, and his sayings *are* written in the annals of the prophet Iddo.

14 So Abijah rested with his fathers, and they buried him in the City of David. Then Asa his son reigned in his place. In his days the land was quiet for ten years.

Asa Reigns in Judah

[2]Asa did *what was* good and right in the eyes of the LORD his God, [3]for he removed the altars of the foreign *gods* and the high places, and broke down the *sacred* pillars and cut down the wooden images. [4]He commanded Judah to seek the LORD God of their fathers, and to observe the law and the commandment. [5]He also removed the high places and the incense altars from all the cities of Judah, and the kingdom was quiet under him. [6]And he built fortified cities in Judah, for the land had rest; he had no war in those years, because the LORD had given him rest. [7]Therefore he said to Judah, "Let us build these cities and make walls around *them,* and towers, gates, and bars, *while* the land *is* yet before us, because we have sought the LORD our God; we have sought *Him,* and He has given us rest on every side." So they built and prospered. [8]And Asa had an army of three hundred thousand from Judah who carried shields and spears, and from Benjamin two hundred and eighty thousand men who carried shields and drew bows; all these *were* mighty men of valor.

[9]Then Zerah the Ethiopian came out against them with an army of a million men and three hundred chariots, and he came to Mareshah. [10]So Asa went out against him, and they set the troops in battle array in the Valley of Zephathah at Mareshah. [11]And Asa cried out to the LORD his God, and said, "LORD, *it is* nothing for You to help, whether with many or with those who have no power; help us, O LORD our God, for

we rest on You, and in Your name we go against this multitude. O LORD, You *are* our God; do not let man prevail against You!"

[12]So the LORD struck the Ethiopians before Asa and Judah, and the Ethiopians fled. [13]And Asa and the people who *were* with him pursued them to Gerar. So the Ethiopians were overthrown, and they could not recover, for they were broken before the LORD and His army. And they carried away very much spoil. [14]Then they defeated all the cities around Gerar, for the fear of the LORD came upon them; and they plundered all the cities, for there was exceedingly much spoil in them. [15]They also attacked the livestock enclosures, and carried off sheep and camels in abundance, and returned to Jerusalem.

The Reforms of Asa

15 Now the Spirit of God came upon Azariah the son of Oded. [2]And he went out to meet Asa, and said to him: "Hear me, Asa, and all Judah and Benjamin. The LORD *is* with you while you are with Him. If you seek Him, He will be found by you; but if you forsake Him, He will forsake you. [3]For a long time Israel *has been* without the true God, without a teaching priest, and without law; [4]but when in their trouble they turned to the LORD God of Israel, and sought Him, He was found by them. [5]And in those times *there was* no peace to the one who went out, nor to the one who came in, but great turmoil *was* on all the inhabitants of the lands. [6]So nation was destroyed by nation, and city by city, for God troubled them with every adversity. [7]But you, be strong and do not let your hands be weak, for your work shall be rewarded!"

[8]And when Asa heard these words and the prophecy of Oded[a] the prophet, he took courage, and removed the abominable idols from all the land of Judah and Benjamin and from the cities which he had taken in the mountains of Ephraim; and he restored the altar of the LORD that *was* before the vestibule of the LORD. [9]Then he gathered all Judah and Benjamin, and those who dwelt with them from Ephraim, Manasseh, and Simeon, for they came over to him in great numbers from Israel when they saw that the LORD his God was with him.

[10]So they gathered together at Jerusalem in the third month, in the fifteenth year of the reign of Asa. [11]And they offered to the LORD at that

---

13:19 [a]Or *Ephron* **15:8** [a]Following Masoretic Text and Septuagint; Syriac and Vulgate read *Azariah the son of Oded* (compare verse 1).

time seven hundred bulls and seven thousand sheep from the spoil they had brought. [12]Then they entered into a covenant to seek the LORD God of their fathers with all their heart and with all their soul; [13]and whoever would not seek the LORD God of Israel was to be put to death, whether small or great, whether man or woman. [14]Then they took an oath before the LORD with a loud voice, with shouting and trumpets and rams' horns. [15]And all Judah rejoiced at the oath, for they had sworn with all their heart and sought Him with all their soul; and He was found by them, and the LORD gave them rest all around.

[16]Also he removed Maachah, the mother of Asa the king, from *being* queen mother, because she had made an obscene image of Asherah;[a] and Asa cut down her obscene image, then crushed and burned *it* by the Brook Kidron. [17]But the high places were not removed from Israel. Nevertheless the heart of Asa was loyal all his days.

[18]He also brought into the house of God the things that his father had dedicated and that he himself had dedicated: silver and gold and utensils. [19]And there was no war until the thirty-fifth year of the reign of Asa.

Asa's Treaty with Syria

16 In the thirty-sixth year of the reign of Asa, Baasha king of Israel came up against Judah and built Ramah, that he might let none go out or come in to Asa king of Judah. [2]Then Asa brought silver and gold from the treasuries of the house of the LORD and of the king's house, and sent to Ben-Hadad king of Syria, who dwelt in Damascus, saying, [3]"*Let there be* a treaty between you and me, as there was between my father and your father. See, I have sent you silver and gold; come, break your treaty with

---

15:16 [a]A Canaanite deity

ASA — THE DIFFICULTY OF FINISHING WELL

(2 Chronicles 15:1—16:13)

King Asa is one of many Old Testament kings who failed to finish well. At the beginning of his time of leadership he discovered this timeless principle: The Lord is with you when you are with Him (2 Chr. 15:2). Immediately after the king learned this truth from the prophet Azariah, he initiated sweeping national reforms. After several years, however, he returned to his old leadership patterns and relied on men instead of God (16:7–12). When God's prophet warned him against this pattern, he grew angry and imprisoned him. He also "oppressed some of the people at that time" (16:10). Asa eventually died, a hollow leader who failed to finish well.

Asa stands with the majority who fail to finish well. Often, the pattern of failure stems from secret sin in the leader's life. Look at how this worked with David and Solomon:

David
1. Anointed king
2. Mighty warrior
3. Musician of the Lord
4. Faithful, loyal man
5. Great leader who made preparations for the temple

Tragic Ending
1. Disloyal to his men
2. Committed adultery
3. Committed murder
4. Tried to cover his sins
5. Brought judgment on family

Solomon
1. Anointed king
2. Humble person of prayer
3. Temple builder
4. Greatest wealth and wisdom
5. Authored proverbs and songs

Tragic Ending
1. Turned his heart from God
2. Became idol worshiper
3. Bought into vain philosophy
4. Selfishly sinned against the Lord
5. Sought to kill Jeroboam

Baasha king of Israel, so that he will withdraw from me."

4So Ben-Hadad heeded King Asa, and sent the captains of his armies against the cities of Israel. They attacked Ijon, Dan, Abel Maim, and all the storage cities of Naphtali. 5Now it happened, when Baasha heard *it,* that he stopped building Ramah and ceased his work. 6Then King Asa took all Judah, and they carried away the stones and timber of Ramah, which Baasha had used for building; and with them he built Geba and Mizpah.

Hanani's Message to Asa

7And at that time Hanani the seer came to Asa king of Judah, and said to him: "Because you have relied on the king of Syria, and have not relied on the LORD your God, therefore the army of the king of Syria has escaped from your hand. 8Were the Ethiopians and the Lubim not a huge army with very many chariots and horsemen? Yet, because you relied on the LORD, He delivered them into your hand. 9For the eyes of the LORD run to and fro throughout the whole earth, to show Himself strong on behalf of *those* whose heart *is* loyal to Him. In this you have done foolishly; therefore from now on you shall have wars." 10Then Asa was angry with the seer, and put him in prison, for *he was* enraged at him because of this. And Asa oppressed *some* of the people at that time.

Illness and Death of Asa

11Note that the acts of Asa, first and last, are indeed written in the book of the kings of Judah and Israel. 12And in the thirty-ninth year of his reign, Asa became diseased in his feet, and his malady was severe; yet in his disease he did not seek the LORD, but the physicians.

13So Asa rested with his fathers; he died in the forty-first year of his reign. 14They buried him in his own tomb, which he had made for himself in the City of David; and they laid him in the bed which was filled with spices and various ingredients prepared in a mixture of ointments. They made a very great burning for him.

Jehoshaphat Reigns in Judah

17 Then Jehoshaphat his son reigned in his place, and strengthened himself against Israel. 2And he placed troops in all the fortified cities of Judah, and set garrisons in the land of Judah and in the cities of Ephraim which Asa his father had taken. 3Now the LORD was with Jehoshaphat, because he walked in the former ways of his father David;

he did not seek the Baals, 4but sought the God[a] of his father, and walked in His commandments and not according to the acts of Israel. 5Therefore the LORD established the kingdom in his hand; and all Judah gave presents to Jehoshaphat, and he had riches and honor in abundance. 6And his heart took delight in the ways of the LORD; moreover he removed the high places and wooden images from Judah.

7Also in the third year of his reign he sent his leaders, Ben-Hail, Obadiah, Zechariah, Nethanel, and Michaiah, to teach in the cities of Judah. 8And with them *he sent* Levites: Shemaiah, Nethaniah, Zebadiah, Asahel, Shemiramoth, Jehonathan, Adonijah, Tobijah, and Tobadonijah—the Levites; and with them Elishama and Jehoram, the priests. 9So they taught in Judah, and *had* the Book of the Law of the LORD with them; they went throughout all the cities of Judah and taught the people.

10And the fear of the LORD fell on all the kingdoms of the lands that *were* around Judah, so that they did not make war against Jehoshaphat. 11Also *some* of the Philistines brought Jehoshaphat presents and silver as tribute; and the Arabians brought him flocks, seven thousand seven hundred rams and seven thousand seven hundred male goats.

12So Jehoshaphat became increasingly powerful, and he built fortresses and storage cities in Judah. 13He had much property in the cities of Judah; and the men of war, mighty men of valor, *were* in Jerusalem.

14These *are* their numbers, according to their fathers' houses. Of Judah, the captains of thousands: Adnah the captain, and with him three hundred thousand mighty men of valor; 15and next to him *was* Jehohanan the captain, and with him two hundred and eighty thousand; 16and next to him *was* Amasiah the son of Zichri, who willingly offered himself to the LORD, and with him two hundred thousand mighty men of valor. 17Of Benjamin: Eliada a mighty man of valor, and with him two hundred thousand men armed with bow and shield; 18and next to him *was* Jehozabad, and with him one hundred and eighty thousand prepared for war. 19These served the king, besides those the king put in the fortified cities throughout all Judah.

Micaiah Warns Ahab

18 Jehoshaphat had riches and honor in abundance; and by marriage he allied himself with Ahab. 2After some years he went down to *visit* Ahab in Samaria; and Ahab killed sheep and oxen in abundance for him and

---

17:4 [a]Septuagint reads LORD God.

Compromise: Sometimes There's No Room for Tolerance

(2 Chronicles 18:1–31)

There are times when tolerance cannot be tolerated. King Jehoshaphat formed an alliance with King Ahab of Israel to fight a common enemy, failing to understand that when you partner with an immoral or deceitful leader, you are asking for trouble. Moral failure impacts every part of leadership.

the people who were with him, and persuaded him to go up *with him* to Ramoth Gilead. ³So Ahab king of Israel said to Jehoshaphat king of Judah, "Will you go with me *against* Ramoth Gilead?"

And he answered him, "I *am* as you *are,* and my people as your people; *we will be* with you in the war."

⁴Also Jehoshaphat said to the king of Israel, "Please inquire for the word of the LORD today."

⁵Then the king of Israel gathered the prophets together, four hundred men, and said to them, "Shall we go to war against Ramoth Gilead, or shall I refrain?"

So they said, "Go up, for God will deliver it into the king's hand."

⁶But Jehoshaphat said, "*Is there* not still a prophet of the LORD here, that we may inquire of Him?"ᵃ

⁷So the king of Israel said to Jehoshaphat, "*There is* still one man by whom we may inquire of the LORD; but I hate him, because he never prophesies good concerning me, but always evil. He *is* Micaiah the son of Imla."

And Jehoshaphat said, "Let not the king say such things!"

⁸Then the king of Israel called one *of his* officers and said, "Bring Micaiah the son of Imla quickly!"

⁹The king of Israel and Jehoshaphat king of Judah, clothed in *their* robes, sat each on his throne; and they sat at a threshing floor at the entrance of the gate of Samaria; and all the prophets prophesied before them. ¹⁰Now Zedekiah the son of Chenaanah had made horns of iron for himself; and he said, "Thus says the LORD: 'With these you shall gore the Syrians until they are destroyed.'"

¹¹And all the prophets prophesied so, saying, "Go up to Ramoth Gilead and prosper, for the LORD will deliver *it* into the king's hand."

¹²Then the messenger who had gone to call Micaiah spoke to him, saying, "Now listen, the words of the prophets with one accord encourage the king. Therefore please let your word be like *the word of* one of them, and speak encouragement."

¹³And Micaiah said, "*As* the LORD lives, whatever my God says, that I will speak."

¹⁴Then he came to the king; and the king said to him, "Micaiah, shall we go to war against Ramoth Gilead, or shall I refrain?"

And he said, "Go and prosper, and they shall be delivered into your hand!"

¹⁵So the king said to him, "How many times shall I make you swear that you tell me nothing but the truth in the name of the LORD?"

¹⁶Then he said, "I saw all Israel scattered on the mountains, as sheep that have no shepherd. And the LORD said, 'These have no master. Let each return to his house in peace.'"

¹⁷And the king of Israel said to Jehoshaphat, "Did I not tell you he would not prophesy good concerning me, but evil?"

¹⁸Then *Micaiah* said, "Therefore hear the word of the LORD: I saw the LORD sitting on His throne, and all the host of heaven standing on His right hand and His left. ¹⁹And the LORD said, 'Who will persuade Ahab king of Israel to go up, that he may fall at Ramoth Gilead?' So one spoke in this manner, and another spoke in that manner. ²⁰Then a spirit came forward and stood before the LORD, and said, 'I will persuade him.' The LORD said to him, 'In what way?' ²¹So he said, 'I will go out and be a lying spirit in the mouth of all his prophets.' And *the* LORD said, 'You shall persuade *him* and also prevail; go out and do so.' ²²Therefore look! The LORD has put a lying spirit in the mouth of these prophets of yours, and the LORD has declared disaster against you."

²³Then Zedekiah the son of Chenaanah went near and struck Micaiah on the cheek, and said, "Which way did the spirit from the LORD go from me to speak to you?"

²⁴And Micaiah said, "Indeed you shall see on that day when you go into an inner chamber to hide!"

²⁵Then the king of Israel said, "Take Micaiah, and return him to Amon the governor of the city and to Joash the king's son; ²⁶and say, 'Thus says the king: "Put this *fellow* in prison, and feed

18:6 ᵃOr *him*

him with bread of affliction and water of affliction, until I return in peace."'"

²⁷But Micaiah said, "If you ever return in peace, the LORD has not spoken by me." And he said, "Take heed, all you people!"

Ahab Dies in Battle

²⁸So the king of Israel and Jehoshaphat the king of Judah went up to Ramoth Gilead. ²⁹And the king of Israel said to Jehoshaphat, "I will disguise myself and go into battle; but you put on your robes." So the king of Israel disguised himself, and they went into battle.

³⁰Now the king of Syria had commanded the captains of the chariots who *were* with him, saying, "Fight with no one small or great, but only with the king of Israel."

³¹So it was, when the captains of the chariots saw Jehoshaphat, that they said, "It *is* the king of Israel!" Therefore they surrounded him to attack; but Jehoshaphat cried out, and the LORD helped him, and God diverted them from him. ³²For so it was, when the captains of the chariots saw that it was not the king of Israel, that they turned back from pursuing him. ³³Now a certain man drew a bow at random, and struck the king of Israel between the joints of his armor. So he said to the driver of his chariot, "Turn around and take me out of the battle, for I am wounded." ³⁴The battle increased that day, and the king of Israel propped *himself* up in *his* chariot facing the Syrians until evening; and about the time of sunset he died.

19 Then Jehoshaphat the king of Judah returned safely to his house in Jerusalem. ²And Jehu the son of Hanani the seer went out to meet him, and said to King Jehoshaphat, "Should you help the wicked and love those who hate the LORD? Therefore the wrath of the LORD *is* upon you. ³Nevertheless good things are found in you, in that you have removed the wooden images from the land, and have prepared your heart to seek God."

The Reforms of Jehoshaphat

⁴So Jehoshaphat dwelt at Jerusalem; and he went out again among the people from Beersheba to the mountains of Ephraim, and brought them back to the LORD God of their fathers. ⁵Then he set judges in the land throughout all the fortified cities of Judah, city by city, ⁶and said to the judges, "Take heed to what you are doing, for you do not judge for man but for the LORD, who *is* with you in the judgment. ⁷Now therefore, let the fear of the LORD be upon you; take care and do *it,* for *there is* no iniquity with the

LORD our God, no partiality, nor taking of bribes."

⁸Moreover in Jerusalem, for the judgment of the LORD and for controversies, Jehoshaphat appointed some of the Levites and priests, and some of the chief fathers of Israel, when they returned to Jerusalem.ᵃ ⁹And he commanded them, saying, "Thus you shall act in the fear of the LORD, faithfully and with a loyal heart: ¹⁰Whatever case comes to you from your brethren who dwell in their cities, whether of bloodshed or offenses against law or commandment, against statutes or ordinances, you shall warn them, lest they trespass against the LORD and wrath come upon you and your brethren. Do this, and you will not be guilty. ¹¹And take notice: Amariah the chief priest *is* over you in all matters of the LORD; and Zebadiah the son of Ishmael, the ruler of the house of Judah, for all the king's matters; also the Levites *will be* officials before you. Behave courageously, and the LORD will be with the good."

Ammon, Moab, and Mount Seir Defeated

20 It happened after this *that* the people of Moab with the people of Ammon, and *others* with them besides the Ammonites,ᵃ came to battle against Jehoshaphat. ²Then some came and told Jehoshaphat, saying, "A great multitude is coming against you from beyond the sea, from Syria;ᵃ and they are in Hazazon Tamar" (which *is* En Gedi). ³And Jehoshaphat feared, and set himself to seek the LORD, and proclaimed a fast throughout all Judah. ⁴So Judah gathered together to ask *help* from the LORD; and from all the cities of Judah they came to seek the LORD.

⁵Then Jehoshaphat stood in the assembly of Judah and Jerusalem, in the house of the LORD, before the new court, ⁶and said: "O LORD God of our fathers, *are* You not God in heaven, and do You *not* rule over all the kingdoms of the nations, and in Your hand *is there not* power and might, so that no one is able to withstand You? ⁷*Are* You not our God, *who* drove out the inhabitants of this land before Your people Israel, and gave it to the descendants of Abraham Your friend forever? ⁸And they dwell in it, and have

---

19:8 ᵃSeptuagint and Vulgate read *for the inhabitants of Jerusalem.* **20:1** ᵃFollowing Masoretic Text and Vulgate; Septuagint reads *Meunites* (compare 26:7). **20:2** ᵃFollowing Masoretic Text, Septuagint, and Vulgate; some Hebrew manuscripts and Old Latin read *Edom.*

21 QUALITIES

RESPONSIBILITY

Leaders Cannot Give It Away

(2 Chronicles 20:1–25)

A leader can delegate anything except responsibility. Leaders simply cannot give it away. They can model it; they can teach it; they can share it. But in the words of President Harry Truman, the buck stops with the leader.

Responsibility—"the ability to meet obligations; the act of being accountable; a duty of trust"—is one of the 21 Indispensable Qualities of a Leader. It's the ability to make and keep commitments.

When Jehoshaphat became king of Judah, he assumed a trust. Like all kings, he was to lead the people, protect the people, and manage the resources of the nation. Second Chronicles 20 records his greatest challenge to that point in his leadership. An army from three countries laid plans to attack Judah. Reports of their activity frightened the king (2 Chr. 20:3). No doubt, he faced the same options we all face in a crisis: give up, back up, or stand up. At such times we find out the quality of our leadership:

1. *The dropouts:* leaders who give up and fail to take responsibility.
2. *The cop-outs:* leaders who make excuses for why they aren't responsible.
3. *The hold-outs:* leaders who waiver too long to take responsibility.
4. *The all-outs:* leaders who own the responsibility and take action.

What Steps Did Jehoshaphat Take?

Second Chronicles 20 provides us with a beautiful story of a human leader who did what was right. Consider the appropriate steps he took:

1. *He fought his fear* (vv. 2, 3).
   Jehoshaphat was terrified, but he didn't let it paralyze him. He stayed calm enough to think.
2. *He sought the Lord* (vv. 3, 6–13).
   Before he did anything else, he sought perspective by praying and seeking wisdom from God.
3. *He brought the synergy* (vv. 3, 4).
   He didn't act alone, but gathered the people to inform them of the issue.
4. *He caught the vision* (vv. 14–17).
   He listened to the voice of the Lord until he knew what to do.
5. *He bought the idea* (vv. 18, 19).
   He bowed his head and began to embrace the steps he and his nation had to take.
6. *He taught the plan* (vv. 20–23).
   He assembled the key players and gave them instructions on what each had to do.
7. *He got the victory* (vv. 24, 25).
   He followed through with precision and succeeded, just as God predicted.

For a negative example of responsibility, see p. 1190.

built You a sanctuary in it for Your name, saying, [9]'If disaster comes upon us—sword, judgment, pestilence, or famine—we will stand before this temple and in Your presence (for Your name *is* in this temple), and cry out to You in our affliction, and You will hear and save.' [10]And now, here are the people of Ammon, Moab, and Mount Seir— whom You would not let Israel invade when they came out of the land of Egypt, but they turned from them and did not destroy them— [11]here they are, rewarding us by coming to throw us out of Your possession which You have given us to inherit. [12]O our God, will You not judge them? For we have no power against this great multitude that is coming against us; nor do we know what to do, but our eyes *are* upon You."

[13]Now all Judah, with their little ones, their wives, and their children, stood before the LORD.

[14]Then the Spirit of the LORD came upon Jahaziel the son of Zechariah, the son of Benaiah, the son of Jeiel, the son of Mattaniah, a Levite of the sons of Asaph, in the midst of the assembly. [15]And he said, "Listen, all you of Judah and you inhabitants of Jerusalem, and you, King Jehoshaphat! Thus says the LORD to you: 'Do not be afraid nor dismayed because of this great multitude, for the battle *is* not yours, but God's. [16]To-morrow go down against them. They will surely come up by the Ascent of Ziz, and you will find them at the end of the brook before the Wilderness of Jeruel. [17]You will not *need* to fight in this *battle*. Position yourselves, stand still and see the salvation of the LORD, who is with you, O Judah and Jerusalem!' Do not fear or be dismayed; to-morrow go out against them, for the LORD *is* with you."

[18]And Jehoshaphat bowed his head with *his* face to the ground, and all Judah and the inhabitants of Jerusalem bowed before the LORD, worshiping the LORD. [19]Then the Levites of the children of the Kohathites and of the children of the Korahites stood up to praise the LORD God of Israel with voices loud and high.

[20]So they rose early in the morning and went out into the Wilderness of Tekoa; and as they went out, Jehoshaphat stood and said, "Hear me, O Judah and you inhabitants of Jerusalem: Believe in the LORD your God, and you shall be established; believe His prophets, and you shall prosper." [21]And when he had consulted with the people, he appointed those who should sing to the LORD, and who should praise the beauty of holiness, as they went out before the army and were saying:

PROFILE IN LEADERSHIP

JEHOSHAPHAT

FINISHED POORLY BY FORMING DESTRUCTIVE ALLIANCES
(2 Chronicles 20:1–37)

King Jehoshaphat of Judah handled a major national crisis the way any great leader should: by leading his people to God in prayer.

Judah faced almost certain defeat. A great army of Moabites, Ammonites, and others stood poised to attack. The badly outnumbered forces of Judah stared destruction in the face and trembled over their fate. In his most desperate hour, the king called his people from all over Judah to pray in Jerusalem for national deliverance. "We have no power against this great multitude that is coming against us," he admitted to God, "nor do we know what to do, but our eyes are upon You" (2 Chr. 20:12).

The Lord answered Jehoshaphat's prayers and miraculously delivered His people from death—and He did so without one soldier of Judah marching off to battle.

Sadly, the king did not spend all his years on the throne expressing such great faith. Late in his reign, Jehoshaphat allowed pagan influences to corrupt his people. He also made an unwise alliance with King Ahaziah of Israel, a wicked man who worshiped Baal (20:33, 35).

Jehoshaphat somehow forgot that God calls leaders not only to begin a race, but to finish it. That is the only way to stand in the winner's circle at heaven's reward ceremonies.

"Praise the LORD,
  For His mercy *endures* forever."[a]

[22]Now when they began to sing and to praise, the LORD set ambushes against the people of Ammon, Moab, and Mount Seir, who had come against Judah; and they were defeated. [23]For the people of Ammon and Moab stood up against the inhabitants of Mount Seir to utterly kill and destroy *them*. And when they had made an end of the inhabitants of Seir, they helped to destroy one another.

[24]So when Judah came to a place overlooking the wilderness, they looked toward the multitude; and there *were* their dead bodies, fallen on the earth. No one had escaped. [25]When Jehoshaphat and his people came to take away their spoil, they found among them an abundance of valuables on the dead bodies,[a] and precious jewelry, which they stripped off for themselves, more than they could carry away; and they were three days gathering the spoil because there was so much. [26]And on the fourth day they assembled in the Valley of Berachah, for there they blessed the LORD; therefore the name of that place was called The Valley of Berachah[a] until this day. [27]Then they returned, every man of Judah and Jerusalem, with Jehoshaphat in front of them, to go back to Jerusalem with joy, for the LORD had made them rejoice over their enemies. [28]So they came to Jerusalem, with stringed instruments and harps and trumpets, to the house of the LORD. [29]And the fear of God was on all the kingdoms of *those* countries when they heard that the LORD had fought against the enemies of Israel. [30]Then the realm of Jehoshaphat was quiet, for his God gave him rest all around.

The End of Jehoshaphat's Reign

[31]So Jehoshaphat was king over Judah. *He was* thirty-five years old when he became king, and he reigned twenty-five years in Jerusalem. His mother's name *was* Azubah the daughter of Shilhi. [32]And he walked in the way of his father Asa, and did not turn aside from it, doing *what was* right in the sight of the LORD. [33]Nevertheless the high places were not taken away, for as yet the people had not directed their hearts to the God of their fathers.

[34]Now the rest of the acts of Jehoshaphat, first and last, indeed they *are* written in the book of Jehu the son of Hanani, which *is* mentioned in the book of the kings of Israel.

[35]After this Jehoshaphat king of Judah allied himself with Ahaziah king of Israel, who acted very wickedly. [36]And he allied himself with him to make ships to go to Tarshish, and they made the ships in Ezion Geber. [37]But Eliezer the son of Dodavah of Mareshah prophesied against Jehoshaphat, saying, "Because you have allied yourself with Ahaziah, the LORD has destroyed your works." Then the ships were wrecked, so that they were not able to go to Tarshish.

Jehoram Reigns in Judah

21 And Jehoshaphat rested with his fathers, and was buried with his fathers in the City of David. Then Jehoram his son reigned in his place. [2]He had brothers, the sons of Jehoshaphat: Azariah, Jehiel, Zechariah, Azaryahu, Michael, and Shephatiah; all these *were* the sons of Jehoshaphat king of Israel. [3]Their father gave them great gifts of silver and gold and precious things, with fortified cities in Judah; but he gave the kingdom to Jehoram, because he *was* the firstborn.

[4]Now when Jehoram was established over the kingdom of his father, he strengthened himself and killed all his brothers with the sword, and also *others* of the princes of Israel.

[5]Jehoram *was* thirty-two years old when he became king, and he reigned eight years in Jerusalem. [6]And he walked in the way of the kings of Israel, just as the house of Ahab had done, for he had the daughter of Ahab as a wife; and he did evil in the sight of the LORD. [7]Yet the LORD would not destroy the house of David, because of the covenant that He had made with David, and since He had promised to give a lamp to him and to his sons forever.

[8]In his days Edom revolted against Judah's authority, and made a king over themselves. [9]So Jehoram went out with his officers, and all his chariots with him. And he rose by night and attacked the Edomites who had surrounded him and the captains of the chariots. [10]Thus Edom has been in revolt against Judah's authority to this day. At that time Libnah revolted against his rule, because he had forsaken the LORD God of his fathers. [11]Moreover he made high places in the mountains of Judah, and caused the inhabitants of Jerusalem to commit harlotry, and led Judah astray.

[12]And a letter came to him from Elijah the prophet, saying,

---

20:21 [a]Compare Psalm 106:1 **20:25** [a]A few Hebrew manuscripts, Old Latin, and Vulgate read *garments;* Septuagint reads *armor.* **20:26** [a]Literally *Blessing*

Thus says the LORD God of your father David:

Because you have not walked in the ways of Jehoshaphat your father, or in the ways of Asa king of Judah, [13]but have walked in the way of the kings of Israel, and have made Judah and the inhabitants of Jerusalem to play the harlot like the harlotry of the house of Ahab, and also have killed your brothers, those of your father's household, *who were* better than yourself, [14]behold, the LORD will strike your people with a serious affliction— your children, your wives, and all your possessions; [15]and you *will become* very sick with a disease of your intestines, until your intestines come out by reason of the sickness, day by day.

[16]Moreover the LORD stirred up against Jehoram the spirit of the Philistines and the Arabians who *were* near the Ethiopians. [17]And they came up into Judah and invaded it, and carried away all the possessions that were found in the king's house, and also his sons and his wives, so that there was not a son left to him except Jehoahaz,[a] the youngest of his sons.

[18]After all this the LORD struck him in his intestines with an incurable disease. [19]Then it happened in the course of time, after the end of two years, that his intestines came out because of his sickness; so he died in severe pain. And his people made no burning for him, like the burning for his fathers.

[20]He was thirty-two years old when he became king. He reigned in Jerusalem eight years and, to no one's sorrow, departed. However they buried him in the City of David, but not in the tombs of the kings.

Ahaziah Reigns in Judah

22 Then the inhabitants of Jerusalem made Ahaziah his youngest son king in his place, for the raiders who came with the Arabians into the camp had killed all the older *sons.* So Ahaziah the son of Jehoram, king of Judah, reigned. [2]Ahaziah *was* forty-two[a] years old when he became king, and he reigned one year in Jerusalem. His mother's name *was* Athaliah the granddaughter of Omri. [3]He also walked in the ways of the house of Ahab, for his mother advised him to do wickedly. [4]Therefore he did evil in the sight of the LORD, like the house of Ahab; for they were his counselors after

---

21:17 [a]Elsewhere called *Ahaziah* (compare 2 Chronicles 22:1) **22:2** [a]Or *twenty-two* (compare 2 Kings 8:26)

Servanthood: Leaders Serve Their People and Their Purpose

(2 Chronicles 22:1–9)

What impact can godless character have on leaders and nations? We find out in the life of King Ahaziah.

The young king and several other political and military leaders lost their lives and their positions through a self-centered pursuit of power. They forgot that a leader must serve his people and his purpose. Leaders are not given authority to better themselves, to enlarge their income or social status, or to improve their standard of living. They are first and always servants of others.

This biblical idea appears throughout the Scripture, but finds special emphasis in the Gospels through the teaching of Jesus Christ. Consider what our Lord teaches us about servant leadership:

Human Economy	God's Economy
1. Pursuit of power and prestige	1. Pursuit of love and service to others
2. Improve wealth and status of the leader	2. Improve the welfare of the people
3. See others as enemies and competitors	3. See others as brothers who complement
4. Motive is to remove or kill opposition	4. Motive is to meet needs and grow the cause
5. The result: the leader is glorified	5. The result: God is glorified

the death of his father, to his destruction. ⁵He also followed their advice, and went with Jehoramᵃ the son of Ahab king of Israel to war against Hazael king of Syria at Ramoth Gilead; and the Syrians wounded Joram. ⁶Then he returned to Jezreel to recover from the wounds which he had received at Ramah, when he fought against Hazael king of Syria. And Azariahᵃ the son of Jehoram, king of Judah, went down to see Jehoram the son of Ahab in Jezreel, because he was sick.

⁷His going to Joram was God's occasion for Ahaziah's downfall; for when he arrived, he went out with Jehoram against Jehu the son of Nimshi, whom the LORD had anointed to cut off the house of Ahab. ⁸And it happened, when Jehu was executing judgment on the house of Ahab, and found the princes of Judah and the sons of Ahaziah's brothers who served Ahaziah, that he killed them. ⁹Then he searched for Ahaziah; and they caught him (he was hiding in Samaria), and brought him to Jehu. When they had killed him, they buried him, "because," they said, "he is the son of Jehoshaphat, who sought the LORD with all his heart."

So the house of Ahaziah had no one to assume power over the kingdom.

Athaliah Reigns in Judah

¹⁰Now when Athaliah the mother of Ahaziah saw that her son was dead, she arose and destroyed all the royal heirs of the house of Judah. ¹¹But Jehoshabeath,ᵃ the daughter of the king, took Joash the son of Ahaziah, and stole him away from among the king's sons who were being murdered, and put him and his nurse in a bedroom. So Jehoshabeath, the daughter of King Jehoram, the wife of Jehoiada the priest (for she was the sister of Ahaziah), hid him from Athaliah so that she did not kill him. ¹²And he was hidden with them in the house of God for six years, while Athaliah reigned over the land.

Joash Crowned King of Judah

23 In the seventh year Jehoiada strengthened himself, *and made a* covenant with the captains of hundreds: Azariah the son of Jeroham, Ishmael the son of Jehohanan, Azariah the son of Obed, Maaseiah

---

22:5 ᵃAlso spelled *Joram* (compare verses 5 and 7; 2 Kings 8:28; and elsewhere) **22:6** ᵃSome Hebrew manuscripts, Septuagint, Syriac, Vulgate, and 2 Kings 8:29 read *Ahaziah*. **22:11** ᵃSpelled *Jehosheba* in 2 Kings 11:2

PROFILE IN LEADERSHIP

ATHALIA

PURSUING POWER RATHER THAN LOVE
(2 Chronicles 22:10—23:15)

Some leaders step into positions of power out of love and a sense of mission. Others seek leadership merely to gain power over others and to revel in a smug feeling of superiority. Normally it doesn't take long to determine which sort of leader you've got.

It took no time at all to decide in the case of Athalia.

As soon as she heard that her son, King Ahaziah, had been killed by Jehu, "she arose and destroyed all the royal heirs of the house of Judah" (2 Chr. 22:10)—including all her grandsons. She missed only one, Joash, who escaped her murderous rampage only when a godly young woman named Jehoshabeath hid him in the house of God for six years. Athaliah did not care in the slightest that God had promised His people that the Messiah would come through the royal line of David.

This is a picture of a leader so thirsty for power that she would do anything to attain and hold her illegitimate title—including murdering her own kin. Athaliah ruled over Judah for seven years. In the end, the people violently removed her from power (23:12–15).

Queen Athaliah is an extreme example of a leader motivated not by love, but by power, prestige, and position. It never takes long to spot the difference.

the son of Adaiah, and Elishaphat the son of Zichri. [2]And they went throughout Judah and gathered the Levites from all the cities of Judah, and the chief fathers of Israel, and they came to Jerusalem.

[3]Then all the assembly made a covenant with the king in the house of God. And he said to them, "Behold, the king's son shall reign, as the LORD has said of the sons of David. [4]This *is* what you shall do: One-third of you entering on the Sabbath, of the priests and the Levites, *shall be* keeping watch over the doors; [5]one-third *shall be* at the king's house; and one-third at the Gate of the Foundation. All the people *shall be* in the courts of the house of the LORD. [6]But let no one come into the house of the LORD except the priests and those of the Levites who serve. They may go in, for they *are* holy; but all the people shall keep the watch of the LORD. [7]And the Levites shall surround the king on all sides, every man with his weapons in his hand; and whoever comes into the house, let him be put to death. You are to be with the king when he comes in and when he goes out."

[8]So the Levites and all Judah did according to all that Jehoiada the priest commanded. And each man took his men who were to be on duty on the Sabbath, with those who were going *off duty* on the Sabbath; for Jehoiada the priest had not dismissed the divisions. [9]And Jehoiada the priest gave to the captains of hundreds the spears and the large and small shields which *had belonged* to King David, that *were* in the temple of God. [10]Then he set all the people, every man with his weapon in his hand, from the right side of the temple to the left side of the temple, along by the altar and by the temple, all around the king. [11]And they brought out the king's son, put the crown on him, *gave him* the Testimony,[a] and made him king. Then Jehoiada and his sons anointed him, and said, "*Long* live the king!"

Death of Athaliah

[12]Now when Athaliah heard the noise of the people running and praising the king, she came to the people *in* the temple of the LORD. [13]*When* she looked, there was the king standing by his pillar at the entrance; and the leaders and the trumpeters *were* by the king. All the people of the land were rejoicing and blowing trumpets, also the singers with musical instruments, and those who led in praise. So Athaliah tore her clothes and said, "Treason! Treason!"

[14]And Jehoiada the priest brought out the captains of hundreds who were set over the army, and said to them, "Take her outside under

guard, and slay with the sword whoever follows her." For the priest had said, "Do not kill her in the house of the LORD."

[15]So they seized her; and she went by way of the entrance of the Horse Gate *into* the king's house, and they killed her there.

[16]Then Jehoiada made a covenant between himself, the people, and the king, that they should be the LORD's people. [17]And all the people went to the temple[a] of Baal, and tore it down. They broke in pieces its altars and images, and killed Mattan the priest of Baal before the altars. [18]Also Jehoiada appointed the oversight of the house of the LORD to the hand of the priests, the Levites, whom David had assigned in the house of the LORD, to offer the burnt offerings of the LORD, as *it is* written in the Law of Moses, with rejoicing and with singing, *as it was established* by David. [19]And he set the gatekeepers at the gates of the house of the LORD, so that no one *who was* in any way unclean should enter.

[20]Then he took the captains of hundreds, the nobles, the governors of the people, and all the people of the land, and brought the king down from the house of the LORD; and they went through the Upper Gate to the king's house, and set the king on the throne of the kingdom. [21]So all the people of the land rejoiced; and the city was quiet, for they had slain Athaliah with the sword.

Joash Repairs the Temple

24 Joash *was* seven years old when he became king, and he reigned forty years in Jerusalem. His mother's name *was* Zibiah of Beersheba. [2]Joash did *what was* right in the sight of the LORD all the days of Jehoiada the priest. [3]And Jehoiada took two wives for him, and he had sons and daughters.

[4]Now it happened after this *that* Joash set his heart on repairing the house of the LORD. [5]Then he gathered the priests and the Levites, and said to them, "Go out to the cities of Judah, and gather from all Israel money to repair the house of your God from year to year, and see that you do it quickly."

However the Levites did not do it quickly. [6]So the king called Jehoiada the chief *priest,* and said to him, "Why have you not required the Levites to bring in from Judah and from Jerusalem the collection, *according to the commandment* of Moses the servant of the LORD and of the assembly of Israel, for the tabernacle of witness?" [7]For the sons of Athaliah, that wicked woman,

23:11 [a]That is, the Law (compare Exodus 25:16, 21; 31:18) **23:17** [a]Literally *house*

Motives: *Why* You Do Determines *What* You Do

(2 Chronicles 24:4–18)

As a young man, Joash committed himself to restoring the temple. He remained true as long as the high priest Jehoiada was alive. When Jehoiada died, however, the king abandoned the temple and worshiped idols. *Why* we do something ultimately determines *what* we do.

had broken into the house of God, and had also presented all the dedicated things of the house of the LORD to the Baals.

8Then at the king's command they made a chest, and set it outside at the gate of the house of the LORD. 9And they made a proclamation throughout Judah and Jerusalem to bring to the LORD the collection *that* Moses the servant of God *had imposed* on Israel in the wilderness. 10Then all the leaders and all the people rejoiced, brought their contributions, and put *them* into the chest until all had given. 11So it was, at that time, when the chest was brought to the king's official by the hand of the Levites, and when they saw that *there was* much money, that the king's scribe and the high priest's officer came and emptied the chest, and took it and returned it to its place. Thus they did day by day, and gathered money in abundance.

12The king and Jehoiada gave it to those who did the work of the service of the house of the LORD; and they hired masons and carpenters to repair the house of the LORD, and also those who worked in iron and bronze to restore the house of the LORD. 13So the workmen labored, and the work was completed by them; they restored the house of God to its original condition and reinforced it. 14When they had finished, they brought the rest of the money before the king and Jehoiada; they made from it articles for the house of the LORD, articles for serving and offering, spoons and vessels of gold and silver. And they offered burnt offerings in the house of the LORD continually all the days of Jehoiada.

Apostasy of Joash

15But Jehoiada grew old and was full of days, and he died; *he was* one hundred and thirty years

old when he died. 16And they buried him in the City of David among the kings, because he had done good in Israel, both toward God and His house.

17Now after the death of Jehoiada the leaders of Judah came and bowed down to the king. And the king listened to them. 18Therefore they left the house of the LORD God of their fathers, and served wooden images and idols; and wrath came upon Judah and Jerusalem because of their trespass. 19Yet He sent prophets to them, to bring them back to the LORD; and they testified against them, but they would not listen.

20Then the Spirit of God came upon Zechariah the son of Jehoiada the priest, who stood above the people, and said to them, "Thus says God: 'Why do you transgress the commandments of the LORD, so that you cannot prosper? Because you have forsaken the LORD, He also has forsaken you.'" 21So they conspired against him, and at the command of the king they stoned him with stones in the court of the house of the LORD. 22Thus Joash the king did not remember the kindness which Jehoiada his father had done to him, but killed his son; and as he died, he said, "The LORD look on *it,* and repay!"

Death of Joash

23So it happened in the spring of the year *that* the army of Syria came up against him; and they came to Judah and Jerusalem, and destroyed all the leaders of the people from among the people, and sent all their spoil to the king of Damascus. 24For the army of the Syrians came with a small company of men; but the LORD delivered a very great army into their hand, because they had forsaken the LORD God of their fathers. So they executed judgment against Joash. 25And when they had withdrawn from him (for they left him severely wounded), his own servants conspired against him because of the blood of the sonsa of Jehoiada the priest, and killed him on his bed. So he died. And they buried him in the City of David, but they did not bury him in the tombs of the kings.

26These are the ones who conspired against him: Zabada the son of Shimeath the Ammonitess, and Jehozabad the son of Shimrithb the Moabitess. 27Now *concerning* his sons, and the many oracles about him, and the repairing of the house of God, indeed they *are* written in the annals of the book of the kings. Then Amaziah his son reigned in his place.

24:25 aSeptuagint and Vulgate read *son* (compare verses 20–22). **24:26** aOr *Jozachar* (compare 2 Kings 12:21) bOr *Shomer* (compare 2 Kings 12:21)

Amaziah Reigns in Judah

25 Amaziah *was* twenty-five years old *when* he became king, and he reigned twenty-nine years in Jerusalem. His mother's name *was* Jehoaddan of Jerusalem. ²And he did *what was* right in the sight of the LORD, but not with a loyal heart.

³Now it happened, as soon as the kingdom was established for him, that he executed his servants who had murdered his father the king. ⁴However he did not execute their children, but *did* as *it is* written in the Law in the Book of Moses, where the LORD commanded, saying, "The fathers shall not be put to death for their children, nor shall the children be put to death for their fathers; but a person shall die for his own sin."ᵃ

The War Against Edom

⁵Moreover Amaziah gathered Judah together and set over them captains of thousands and captains of hundreds, according to *their* fathers' houses, throughout all Judah and Benjamin; and he numbered them from twenty years old and above, and found them to be three hundred thousand choice *men, able* to go to war, who could handle spear and shield. ⁶He also hired one hundred thousand mighty men of valor from Israel for one hundred talents of silver. ⁷But a man of God came to him, saying, "O king, do not let the army of Israel go with you, for the LORD *is* not with Israel—*not with* any of the children of Ephraim. ⁸But if you go, be gone! Be strong in battle! *Even so,* God shall make you fall before the enemy; for God has power to help and to overthrow."

⁹Then Amaziah said to the man of God, "But what *shall we* do about the hundred talents which I have given to the troops of Israel?"

And the man of God answered, "The LORD is able to give you much more than this." ¹⁰So Amaziah discharged the troops that had come to him from Ephraim, to go back home. Therefore their anger was greatly aroused against Judah, and they returned home in great anger.

¹¹Then Amaziah strengthened himself, and leading his people, he went to the Valley of Salt and killed ten thousand of the people of Seir. ¹²Also the children of Judah took captive ten thousand alive, brought them to the top of the rock, and cast them down from the top of the rock, so that they all were dashed in pieces.

¹³But as for the soldiers of the army which Amaziah had discharged, so that they would not go with him to battle, they raided the cities of Judah from Samaria to Beth Horon, killed three thousand in them, and took much spoil.

¹⁴Now it was so, after Amaziah came from the slaughter of the Edomites, that he brought the gods of the people of Seir, set them up *to be* his gods, and bowed down before them and burned incense to them. ¹⁵Therefore the anger of the LORD was aroused against Amaziah, and He sent him a prophet who said to him, "Why have you sought the gods of the people, which could not rescue their own people from your hand?"

¹⁶So it was, as he talked with him, that *the king* said to him, "Have we made you the king's counselor? Cease! Why should you be killed?"

Then the prophet ceased, and said, "I know that God has determined to destroy you, because you have done this and have not heeded my advice."

Israel Defeats Judah

¹⁷Now Amaziah king of Judah asked advice and sent to Joashᵃ the son of Jehoahaz, the son of Jehu, king of Israel, saying, "Come, let us face one another *in battle.*"

¹⁸And Joash king of Israel sent to Amaziah king of Judah, saying, "The thistle that *was* in Lebanon sent to the cedar that was in Lebanon, saying, 'Give your daughter to my son as wife'; and a wild beast that *was* in Lebanon passed by and trampled the thistle. ¹⁹Indeed you say that you have defeated the Edomites, and your heart is lifted up to boast. Stay at home now; why should you meddle with trouble, that you should fall—you and Judah with you?"

²⁰But Amaziah would not heed, for it *came* from God, that He might give them into the hand *of their enemies,* because they sought the gods of Edom. ²¹So Joash king of Israel went out; and he and Amaziah king of Judah faced one another at Beth Shemesh, which *belongs* to Judah. ²²And Judah was defeated by Israel, and every man fled to his tent. ²³Then Joash the king of Israel captured Amaziah king of Judah, the son of Joash, the son of Jehoahaz, at Beth Shemesh; and he brought him to Jerusalem, and broke down the wall of Jerusalem from the Gate of Ephraim to the Corner Gate—four hundred cubits. ²⁴And *he took* all the gold and silver, all the articles that were found in the house of God with Obed-Edom, the treasures of the king's house, and hostages, and returned to Samaria.

Death of Amaziah

²⁵Amaziah the son of Joash, king of Judah, lived fifteen years after the death of Joash the son

---

25:4 ᵃDeuteronomy 24:16 **25:17** ᵃSpelled *Jehoash* in 2 Kings 14:8ff of Jehoahaz, king of Israel. [26]Now the rest of the acts of Amaziah, from first to last, indeed *are* they not written in the book of the kings of Judah and Israel? [27]After the time that Amaziah turned away from following the LORD, they made a conspiracy against him in Jerusalem, and he fled to Lachish; but they sent after him to Lachish and killed him there. [28]Then they brought him on horses and buried him with his fathers in the City of Judah.

Uzziah Reigns in Judah

26 Now all the people of Judah took Uzziah,[a] who *was* sixteen years old, and made him king instead of his father Amaziah. [2]He built Elath[a] and restored it to Judah, after the king rested with his fathers.

[3]Uzziah *was* sixteen years old when he became king, and he reigned fifty-two years in Jerusalem. His mother's name was Jecholiah of Jerusalem. [4]And he did *what was* right in the sight of the LORD, according to all that his father Amaziah had done. [5]He sought God in the days of Zechariah, who had understanding in the visions[a] of God; and as long as he sought the LORD, God made him prosper.

[6]Now he went out and made war against the Philistines, and broke down the wall of Gath, the wall of Jabneh, and the wall of Ashdod; and he built cities *around* Ashdod and among the Philistines. [7]God helped him against the Philistines, against the Arabians who lived in Gur Baal, and against the Meunites. [8]Also the Ammonites brought tribute to Uzziah. His fame spread as far as the entrance of Egypt, for he became exceedingly strong.

[9]And Uzziah built towers in Jerusalem at the Corner Gate, at the Valley Gate, and at the corner buttress of the wall; then he fortified them. [10]Also he built towers in the desert. He dug many wells, for he had much livestock, both in the lowlands and in the plains; *he also had* farmers and vinedressers in the mountains and in Carmel, for he loved the soil.

[11]Moreover Uzziah had an army of fighting men who went out to war by companies, according to the number on their roll as prepared by Jeiel the scribe and Maaseiah the officer, under the hand of Hananiah, *one* of the king's

---

26:1 [a]Called *Azariah* in 2 Kings 14:21ff
26:2 [a]Hebrew *Eloth* **26:5** [a]Several Hebrew manuscripts, Septuagint, Syriac, Targum, and Arabic read *fear*.

UZZIAH

BUILT HIS MILITARY, LATER HIS OWN POWER
(2 Chronicles 26:1–23)

PROFILE IN LEADERSHIP

The ancient kings of Israel and Judah died centuries ago, yet like all leaders, the choices they made nearly always reflected their true character. Uzziah's reign mirrored that of Asa, Josiah, and Amaziah—it began very strong and ended in disgrace.

In the early years, Uzziah displayed strong, godly leadership skills. The Lord blessed him with military success. During this time, his inner circle included a godly spiritual counselor, Zechariah, who exerted significant influence for good. Uzziah sought after God, and the Lord prospered him.

As Uzziah's kingdom and wealth increased, however, he lost focus. His priorities shifted to personal success and fame rather than the things that delighted God's heart. His eyes drifted from God, and sin blinded his actions.

Like many highly successful leaders, Uzziah developed an attitude of superiority. He exhibited an astonishing lack of discernment when he usurped the priestly role by offering incense in the temple. A raw desire for power consumed his soul, and the king intentionally stepped out of his God-ordained role. As a result, Uzziah left a legacy of disgrace. The Word of God says of him: "He dwelt in an isolated house, because he was a leper; for he was cut off from the house of the LORD" (2 Chr. 26:21). A sad ending to a promising start.

captains. [12]The total number of chief officers[a] of the mighty men of valor *was* two thousand six hundred. [13]And under their authority *was* an army of three hundred and seven thousand five hundred, that made war with mighty power, to help the king against the enemy. [14]Then Uzziah prepared for them, for the entire army, shields, spears, helmets, body armor, bows, and slings *to cast* stones. [15]And he made devices in Jerusalem, invented by skillful men, to be on the towers and the corners, to shoot arrows and large stones. So his fame spread far and wide, for he was marvelously helped till he became strong.

The Penalty for Uzziah's Pride

[16]But when he was strong his heart was lifted up, to *his* destruction, for he transgressed against the LORD his God by entering the temple of the LORD to burn incense on the altar of incense. [17]So Azariah the priest went in after him, and with him were eighty priests of the LORD—valiant men. [18]And they withstood King Uzziah, and said to him, "*It is* not for you, Uzziah, to burn incense to the LORD, but for the priests, the sons of Aaron, who are consecrated to burn incense. Get out of the sanctuary, for you have trespassed! You *shall have* no honor from the LORD God."

[19]Then Uzziah became furious; and he *had* a censer in his hand to burn incense. And while he was angry with the priests, leprosy broke out on his forehead, before the priests in the house of the LORD, beside the incense altar. [20]And Azariah the chief priest and all the priests looked at him, and there, on his forehead, he *was* leprous; so they thrust him out of that place. Indeed he also hurried to get out, because the LORD had struck him.

[21]King Uzziah was a leper until the day of his death. He dwelt in an isolated house, because he was a leper; for he was cut off from the house of the LORD. Then Jotham his son *was* over the king's house, judging the people of the land.

[22]Now the rest of the acts of Uzziah, from first to last, the prophet Isaiah the son of Amoz wrote. [23]So Uzziah rested with his fathers, and they buried him with his fathers in the field of burial which *belonged* to the kings, for they said, "He is a leper." Then Jotham his son reigned in his place.

Jotham Reigns in Judah

27 Jotham *was* twenty-five years old when he became king, and he reigned sixteen years in Jerusalem. His mother's name *was* Jerushah[a] the daughter of Zadok. [2]And he did *what was* right in the sight

of the LORD, according to all that his father Uzziah had done (although he did not enter the temple of the LORD). But still the people acted corruptly.

[3]He built the Upper Gate of the house of the LORD, and he built extensively on the wall of Ophel. [4]Moreover he built cities in the mountains of Judah, and in the forests he built fortresses and towers. [5]He also fought with the king of the Ammonites and defeated them. And the people of Ammon gave him in that year one hundred talents of silver, ten thousand kors of wheat, and ten thousand of barley. The people of Ammon paid this to him in the second and third years also. [6]So Jotham became mighty, because he prepared his ways before the LORD his God.

[7]Now the rest of the acts of Jotham, and all his wars and his ways, indeed they *are* written in the book of the kings of Israel and Judah. [8]He was twenty-five years old when he became king, and he reigned sixteen years in Jerusalem. [9]So Jotham rested with his fathers, and they buried him in the City of David. Then Ahaz his son reigned in his place.

Ahaz Reigns in Judah

28 Ahaz *was* twenty years old when he became king, and he reigned sixteen years in Jerusalem; and he did not do *what was* right in the sight of the LORD, as his father David *had* done. [2]For he walked in the ways of the kings of Israel, and made molded images for the Baals. [3]He burned incense in the Valley of the Son of Hinnom, and burned his children in the fire, according to the abominations of the nations whom the LORD had cast out before the children of Israel. [4]And he sacrificed and burned incense on the high places, on the hills, and under every green tree.

Syria and Israel Defeat Judah

[5]Therefore the LORD his God delivered him into the hand of the king of Syria. They defeated him, and carried away a great multitude of them as captives, and brought *them* to Damascus. Then he was also delivered into the hand of the king of Israel, who defeated him with a great slaughter. [6]For Pekah the son of Remaliah killed one hundred and twenty thousand in Judah in one day, all valiant men, because they had forsaken the LORD God of their fathers. [7]Zichri, a mighty man of Ephraim, killed Maaseiah the king's son, Azrikam the officer over the house, and Elkanah

26:12 [a]Literally *chief fathers*   **27:1** [a]Spelled *Jerusha* in 2 Kings 15:33

Hezekiah: Leaders Must Be Examples, Not Exceptions
(2 Chronicles 29:1–36)

Far too often, leaders drift. Once they get some experience under their belt and a track record of accomplishments, they often abandon the lifestyle that helped them reach the top. They chafe under the very rules that they established or endorsed. They continue to call the people to follow them, but they see themselves as exceptions to the rules, not examples of keeping the rules.

Sadly, leaders like these forget the number one management principle in the world: People do what people see. If they want to succeed, leaders must incarnate the life they desire in their followers.

Hezekiah teaches us this principle. He inherited an unholy mess, left by his father, King Ahaz. He repaired the temple, restored legitimate worship, removed the idols, repented for the people, and required a change in the land. Once the population saw his example of worship, they followed suit.

Second Chronicles 29 ends with these wonderful words: "Then Hezekiah and all the people rejoiced that God had prepared the people, since the events took place so suddenly" (v. 36). These events took place so quickly not only because of a sovereign God who replaced Ahaz with the king's godly son, but because Hezekiah modeled the life he expected of others.

who was second to the king. ⁸And the children of Israel carried away captive of their brethren two hundred thousand women, sons, and daughters; and they also took away much spoil from them, and brought the spoil to Samaria.

Israel Returns the Captives

⁹But a prophet of the LORD was there, whose name *was* Oded; and he went out before the army that came to Samaria, and said to them: "Look, because the LORD God of your fathers was angry with Judah, He has delivered them into your hand; but you have killed them in a rage *that* reaches up to heaven. ¹⁰And now you propose to force the children of Judah and Jerusalem to be your male and female slaves; *but are* you not also guilty before the LORD your God? ¹¹Now hear me, therefore, and return the captives, whom you have taken captive from your brethren, for the fierce wrath of the LORD *is* upon you."

¹²Then some of the heads of the children of Ephraim, Azariah the son of Johanan, Berechiah the son of Meshillemoth, Jehizkiah the son of Shallum, and Amasa the son of Hadlai, stood up against those who came from the war, ¹³and said to them, "You shall not bring the captives here, for we *already* have offended the LORD. You intend to add to our sins and to our guilt; for our guilt is great, and *there is* fierce wrath against Israel." ¹⁴So the armed men left the captives and the spoil before the leaders and all the assembly. ¹⁵Then the men who were designated by name rose up and took the captives, and from the spoil they clothed all who were naked among them, dressed them and gave them sandals, gave them food and drink, and anointed them; and they let all the feeble ones ride on donkeys. So they brought them to their brethren at Jericho, the city of palm trees. Then they returned to Samaria.

Assyria Refuses to Help Judah

¹⁶At the same time King Ahaz sent to the kingsᵃ of Assyria to help him. ¹⁷For again the Edomites had come, attacked Judah, and carried away captives. ¹⁸The Philistines also had invaded the cities of the lowland and of the South of Judah, and had taken Beth Shemesh, Aijalon, Gederoth, Sochoh with its villages, Timnah with its villages, and Gimzo with its villages; and they dwelt there. ¹⁹For the LORD brought Judah low because of Ahaz king of Israel, for he had encouraged moral decline in Judah and had been continually unfaithful to the LORD. ²⁰Also Tiglath-Pileserᵃ king of Assyria came to him and distressed him, and did not assist him. ²¹For Ahaz took part *of the treasures* from the house of the LORD, from the house of the king, and from the

28:16 ᵃSeptuagint, Syriac, and Vulgate read *king* (compare verse 20). **28:20** ᵃHebrew *Tilgath-Pilneser*

leaders, and he gave *it* to the king of Assyria; but he did not help him.

Apostasy and Death of Ahaz

[22]Now in the time of his distress King Ahaz became increasingly unfaithful to the LORD. This *is that* King Ahaz. [23]For he sacrificed to the gods of Damascus which had defeated him, saying, "Because the gods of the kings of Syria help them, I will sacrifice to them that they may help me." But they were the ruin of him and of all Israel. [24]So Ahaz gathered the articles of the house of God, cut in pieces the articles of the house of God, shut up the doors of the house of the LORD, and made for himself altars in every corner of Jerusalem. [25]And in every single city of Judah he made high places to burn incense to other gods, and provoked to anger the LORD God of his fathers.

[26]Now the rest of his acts and all his ways, from first to last, indeed they *are* written in the book of the kings of Judah and Israel. [27]So Ahaz rested with his fathers, and they buried him in the city, in Jerusalem; but they did not bring him into the tombs of the kings of Israel. Then Hezekiah his son reigned in his place.

Hezekiah Reigns in Judah

29 Hezekiah became king *when he was* twenty-five years old, and he reigned twenty-nine years in Jerusalem. His mother's name *was* Abijah[a] the daughter of Zechariah. [2]And he did *what was* right in the sight of the LORD, according to all that his father David had done.

Hezekiah Cleanses the Temple

[3]In the first year of his reign, in the first month, he opened the doors of the house of the LORD and repaired them. [4]Then he brought in the priests and the Levites, and gathered them in the East Square, [5]and said to them: "Hear me, Levites! Now sanctify yourselves, sanctify the house of the LORD God of your fathers, and carry out the rubbish from the holy *place*. [6]For our fathers have trespassed and done evil in the eyes of the LORD our God; they have forsaken Him, have turned their faces away from the dwelling place of the LORD, and turned *their* backs *on Him*. [7]They have also shut up the doors of the vestibule, put out the lamps, and have not burned incense or offered burnt offerings in the holy *place* to the God of Israel. [8]Therefore the wrath of the LORD fell upon Judah and Jerusalem, and He has given them up to trouble, to desolation, and to jeering, as you see with your

eyes. [9]For indeed, because of this our fathers have fallen by the sword; and our sons, our daughters, and our wives *are* in captivity.

[10]"Now *it is* in my heart to make a covenant with the LORD God of Israel, that His fierce wrath may turn away from us. [11]My sons, do not be negligent now, for the LORD has chosen you to stand before Him, to serve Him, and that you should minister to Him and burn incense."

[12]Then these Levites arose: Mahath the son of Amasai and Joel the son of Azariah, of the sons of the Kohathites; of the sons of Merari, Kish the son of Abdi and Azariah the son of Jehallelel; of the Gershonites, Joah the son of Zimmah and Eden the son of Joah; [13]of the sons of Elizaphan, Shimri and Jeiel; of the sons of Asaph, Zechariah and Mattaniah; [14]of the sons of Heman, Jehiel and Shimei; and of the sons of Jeduthun, Shemaiah and Uzziel.

[15]And they gathered their brethren, sanctified themselves, and went according to the commandment of the king, at the words of the LORD, to cleanse the house of the LORD. [16]Then the priests went into the inner part of the house of the LORD to cleanse *it,* and brought out all the debris that they found in the temple of the LORD to the court of the house of the LORD. And the Levites took *it* out and carried *it* to the Brook Kidron.

[17]Now they began to sanctify on the first *day* of the first month, and on the eighth day of the month they came to the vestibule of the LORD. So they sanctified the house of the LORD in eight days, and on the sixteenth day of the first month they finished.

[18]Then they went in to King Hezekiah and said, "We have cleansed all the house of the LORD, the altar of burnt offerings with all its articles, and the table of the showbread with all its articles. [19]Moreover all the articles which King Ahaz in his reign had cast aside in his transgression we have prepared and sanctified; and there they *are,* before the altar of the LORD."

Hezekiah Restores Temple Worship

[20]Then King Hezekiah rose early, gathered the rulers of the city, and went up to the house of the LORD. [21]And they brought seven bulls, seven rams, seven lambs, and seven male goats for a sin offering for the kingdom, for the sanctuary, and for Judah. Then he commanded the priests, the sons of Aaron, to offer *them* on the altar of the LORD. [22]So they killed the bulls, and the priests received the blood and sprinkled *it* on

---

29:1 [a]Spelled *Abi* in 2 Kings 18:2

the altar. Likewise they killed the rams and sprinkled the blood on the altar. They also killed the lambs and sprinkled the blood on the altar. [23]Then they brought out the male goats *for the* sin offering before the king and the assembly, and they laid their hands on them. [24]And the priests killed them; and they presented their blood on the altar as a sin offering to make an atonement for all Israel, for the king commanded *that* the burnt offering and the sin offering *be made* for all Israel.

[25]And he stationed the Levites in the house of the LORD with cymbals, with stringed instruments, and with harps, according to the commandment of David, of Gad the king's seer, and of Nathan the prophet; for thus *was* the commandment of the LORD by His prophets. [26]The Levites stood with the instruments of David, and the priests with the trumpets. [27]Then Hezekiah commanded *them* to offer the burnt offering on the altar. And when the burnt offering began, the song of the LORD *also* began, with the trumpets and with the instruments of David king of Israel. [28]So all the assembly worshiped, the singers sang, and the trumpeters sounded; all *this continued* until the burnt offering was finished. [29]And when they had finished offering, the king and all who were present with him bowed and worshiped. [30]Moreover King Hezekiah and the leaders commanded the Levites to sing praise to the LORD with the words of David and of Asaph the seer. So they sang praises with gladness, and they bowed their heads and worshiped.

[31]Then Hezekiah answered and said, "Now *that* you have consecrated yourselves to the LORD, come near, and bring sacrifices and thank offerings into the house of the LORD." So the assembly brought in sacrifices and thank offerings, and as many as were of a willing heart *brought* burnt offerings. [32]And the number of the burnt offerings which the assembly brought was seventy bulls, one hundred rams, *and* two hundred lambs; all these *were* for a burnt offering to the LORD. [33]The consecrated things *were* six hundred bulls and three thousand sheep. [34]But the priests were too few, so that they could not skin all the burnt offerings; therefore their brethren the Levites helped them until the work was ended and until the *other* priests had sanctified themselves, for the Levites were more diligent in sanctifying themselves than the priests. [35]Also the burnt offerings *were* in abundance, with the fat of the peace offerings and *with* the drink offerings for *every* burnt offering.

So the service of the house of the LORD was set in order. [36]Then Hezekiah and all the people rejoiced that God had prepared the people, since the events took place so suddenly.

Hezekiah Keeps the Passover

30 And Hezekiah sent to all Israel and Judah, and also wrote letters to Ephraim and Manasseh, that they should come to the house of the LORD at Jerusalem, to keep the Passover to the LORD God of Israel. [2]For the king and his leaders and all the assembly in Jerusalem had agreed to keep the Passover in the second month. [3]For they could not keep it at the regular time,[a] because a sufficient number of priests had not consecrated themselves, nor had the people gathered together at Jerusalem. [4]And the matter pleased the king and all the assembly. [5]So they resolved to make a proclamation throughout all Israel, from Beersheba to Dan, that they should come to keep the Passover to the LORD God of Israel at Jerusalem, since they had not done *it* for a long *time* in the *prescribed* manner.

[6]Then the runners went throughout all Israel and Judah with the letters from the king and his leaders, and spoke according to the command of the king: "Children of Israel, return to the LORD God of Abraham, Isaac, and Israel; then He will return to the remnant of you who have escaped from the hand of the kings of Assyria. [7]And do not be like your fathers and your brethren, who trespassed against the LORD God of their fathers, so that He gave them up to desolation, as you see. [8]Now do not be stiff-necked, as your fathers *were, but* yield yourselves to the LORD; and enter His sanctuary, which He has sanctified forever, and serve the LORD your God, that the fierceness of His wrath may turn away from you. [9]For if you return to the LORD, your brethren and your children *will be treated* with compassion by those who lead them captive, so that they may come back to this land; for the LORD your God *is* gracious and merciful, and will not turn *His* face from you if you return to Him."

[10]So the runners passed from city to city through the country of Ephraim and Manasseh, as far as Zebulun; but they laughed at them and mocked them. [11]Nevertheless some from Asher, Manasseh, and Zebulun humbled themselves and came to Jerusalem. [12]Also the hand of God was on Judah to give them singleness of heart to obey the command of the king and the leaders, at the word of the LORD.

30:3 [a]That is, the first month (compare Leviticus 23:5); literally *at that time*

¹³Now many people, a very great assembly, gathered at Jerusalem to keep the Feast of Unleavened Bread in the second month. ¹⁴They arose and took away the altars that *were* in Jerusalem, and they took away all the incense altars and cast *them* into the Brook Kidron. ¹⁵Then they slaughtered the Passover *lambs* on the fourteenth *day* of the second month. The priests and the Levites were ashamed, and sanctified themselves, and brought the burnt offerings to the house of the LORD. ¹⁶They stood in their place according to their custom, according to the Law of Moses the man of God; the priests sprinkled the blood *received* from the hand of the Levites. ¹⁷For *there were* many in the assembly who had not sanctified themselves; therefore the Levites had charge of the slaughter of the Passover *lambs* for everyone *who was* not clean, to sanctify *them* to the LORD. ¹⁸For a multitude of the people, many from Ephraim, Manasseh, Issachar, and Zebulun, had not cleansed themselves, yet they ate the Passover contrary to what was written. But Hezekiah prayed for them, saying, "May the good LORD provide atonement for everyone ¹⁹*who* prepares his heart to seek God, the LORD God of his fathers, though *he is* not *cleansed* according to the purification of the sanctuary." ²⁰And the LORD listened to Hezekiah and healed the people.

²¹So the children of Israel who were present at Jerusalem kept the Feast of Unleavened Bread seven days with great gladness; and the Levites and the priests praised the LORD day by day, *singing* to the LORD, accompanied by loud instruments. ²²And Hezekiah gave encouragement to all the Levites who taught the good knowledge of the LORD; and they ate throughout the feast seven days, offering peace offerings and making confession to the LORD God of their fathers.

²³Then the whole assembly agreed to keep *the feast* another seven days, and they kept it *another* seven days with gladness. ²⁴For Hezekiah king of Judah gave to the assembly a thousand bulls and seven thousand sheep, and the leaders gave to the assembly a thousand bulls and ten thousand sheep; and a great number of priests sanctified themselves. ²⁵The whole assembly of Judah rejoiced, also the priests and Levites, all the assembly that came from Israel, the sojourners who came from the land of Israel, and those who dwelt in Judah. ²⁶So there was great joy in Jerusalem, for since the time of Solomon the son of David, king of Israel, *there had* been nothing like this in Jerusalem. ²⁷Then the priests, the Levites, arose and blessed the people, and their voice was heard; and their prayer came *up* to His holy dwelling place, to heaven.

The Reforms of Hezekiah

31 Now when all this was finished, all Israel who were present went out to the cities of Judah and broke the *sacred* pillars in pieces, cut down the wooden images, and threw down the high places and the altars—from all Judah, Benjamin, Ephraim, and Manasseh—until they had utterly destroyed them all. Then all the children of Israel returned to their own cities, every man to his possession.

²And Hezekiah appointed the divisions of the priests and the Levites according to their divisions, each man according to his service, the priests and Levites for burnt offerings and peace offerings, to serve, to give thanks, and to praise in the gates of the camp[a] of the LORD. ³The king also *appointed* a portion of his possessions for the burnt offerings: for the morning and evening burnt offerings, the burnt offerings for the Sabbaths and the New Moons and the set feasts, as *it is* written in the Law of the LORD.

⁴Moreover he commanded the people who dwelt in Jerusalem to contribute support for the priests and the Levites, that they might devote themselves to the Law of the LORD.

⁵As soon as the commandment was circulated, the children of Israel brought in abundance the firstfruits of grain and wine, oil and honey, and of all the produce of the field; and they brought in abundantly the tithe of everything. ⁶And the children of Israel and Judah, who dwelt in the cities of Judah, brought the tithe of oxen and sheep; also the tithe of holy things which were consecrated to the LORD their God they laid in heaps.

⁷In the third month they began laying them in heaps, and they finished in the seventh month. ⁸And when Hezekiah and the leaders came and saw the heaps, they blessed the LORD and His people Israel. ⁹Then Hezekiah questioned the priests and the Levites concerning the heaps. ¹⁰And Azariah the chief priest, from the house of Zadok, answered him and said, "Since *the people* began to bring the offerings into the house of the LORD, we have had enough to eat and have plenty left, for the LORD has blessed His people; and what is left *is* this great abundance."

¹¹Now Hezekiah commanded *them* to prepare rooms in the house of the LORD, and they prepared them. ¹²Then they faithfully brought in the offerings, the tithes, and the dedicated things; Cononiah the Levite had charge of them, and Shimei his brother *was* the next. ¹³Jehiel, Azaziah,

---

31:2 ᵃThat is, the temple

Nahath, Asahel, Jerimoth, Jozabad, Eliel, Is-machiah, Mahath, and Benaiah *were* overseers under the hand of Cononiah and Shimei his brother, at the commandment of Hezekiah the king and Azariah the ruler of the house of God. [14]Kore the son of Imnah the Levite, the keeper of the East Gate, *was* over the freewill offerings to God, to distribute the offerings of the LORD and the most holy things. [15]And under him *were* Eden, Miniamin, Jeshua, Shemaiah, Amariah, and Shecaniah, *his* faithful assistants in the cities of the priests, to distribute allotments to their brethren by divisions, to the great as well as the small.

[16]Besides those males from three years old and up who were written in the genealogy, they distributed to everyone who entered the house of the LORD his daily portion for the work of his service, by his division, [17]and to the priests who were written in the genealogy according to their father's house, and to the Levites from twenty years old and up according to their work, by their divisions, [18]and to all who were written in the genealogy—their little ones and their wives, their sons and daughters, the whole company of them—for in their faithfulness they sanctified themselves in holiness.

[19]Also for the sons of Aaron the priests, *who were* in the fields of the common-lands of their cities, in every single city, *there were* men who were designated by name to distribute portions to all the males among the priests and to all who were listed by genealogies among the Levites.

[20]Thus Hezekiah did throughout all Judah, and he did what *was* good and right and true before the LORD his God. [21]And in every work that he began in the service of the house of God, in the law and in the commandment, to seek his God, he did *it* with all his heart. So he prospered.

Sennacherib Boasts Against the LORD

32 After these deeds of faithfulness, Sennacherib king of Assyria came and entered Judah; he encamped against the fortified cities, thinking to win them over to himself. [2]And when Hezekiah saw that Sennacherib had come, and that his purpose was to make war against Jerusalem, [3]he consulted with his leaders and commanders[a] to stop the water from the springs which *were* outside the city; and they helped him. [4]Thus many people gathered together who stopped all the springs and the brook that ran through the land, saying, "Why should the kings[a] of Assyria come and find much water?" [5]And he strengthened himself, built up all the wall that was broken, raised *it* up

---

Commitment: Hezekiah Has What It Takes

(2 Chronicles 31:20, 21)

The Bible describes King Hezekiah as a leader who "did what was good and right and true before the LORD his God. And in every work that he began . . . he did it with all his heart. So he prospered" (2 Chr. 31:20, 21).

Hezekiah paid the price to get the job done. But what is the price of commitment?

1. *Change of lifestyle:* Hezekiah couldn't live the way his father lived.
2. *Loneliness:* Hezekiah stepped out in obedience, alone at first.
3. *Faith in God:* Hezekiah believed that God would bless his efforts.
4. *Criticism:* Hezekiah weathered the harsh questions of an older generation.
5. *Hard work and money:* The king gave up time, energy, and budget to reach his goal.
6. *Daily discipline:* Hezekiah had to instill a daily regimen to bring about reform.
7. *Constant pressure:* The king endured the pressure of potential failure and misunderstanding.

---

to the towers, and *built* another wall outside; also he repaired the Millo[a] *in* the City of David, and made weapons and shields in abundance. [6]Then he set military captains over the people, gathered them together to him in the open square of the city gate, and gave them encouragement, saying, [7]"Be strong and courageous; do not be afraid nor dismayed before the king of Assyria, nor before all the multitude that *is* with him; for *there are* more with us than with him. [8]With him *is* an arm of flesh; but with us *is* the LORD our God, to help us and to fight our battles." And the people were strengthened by the words of Hezekiah king of Judah.

[9]After this Sennacherib king of Assyria sent his servants to Jerusalem (but he and all the forces with him *laid siege* against Lachish), to Hezekiah king of Judah, and to all Judah who *were* in Jerusalem, saying, [10]"Thus says Sen-

---

32:3 [a]Literally *mighty men* **32:4** [a]Following Masoretic Text and Vulgate; Arabic, Septuagint, and Syriac read *king.* **32:5** [a]Literally *The Landfill* nacherib king of Assyria: 'In what do you trust, that you remain under siege in Jerusalem? ¹¹Does not Hezekiah persuade you to give yourselves over to die by famine and by thirst, saying, "The LORD our God will deliver us from the hand of the king of Assyria"? ¹²Has not the same Hezekiah taken away His high places and His altars, and commanded Judah and Jerusalem, saying, "You shall worship before one altar and burn incense on it"? ¹³Do you not know what I and my fathers have done to all the peoples of *other* lands? Were the gods of the nations of those lands in any way able to deliver their lands out of my hand? ¹⁴Who *was there* among all the gods of those nations that my fathers utterly destroyed that could deliver his people from my hand, that your God should be able to deliver you from my hand? ¹⁵Now therefore, do not let Hezekiah deceive you or persuade you like this, and do not believe him; for no god of any nation or kingdom was able to deliver his people from my hand or the hand of my fathers. How much less will your God deliver you from my hand?'"

¹⁶Furthermore, his servants spoke against the LORD God and against His servant Hezekiah.

¹⁷He also wrote letters to revile the LORD God of Israel, and to speak against Him, saying, "As the gods of the nations of *other* lands have not delivered their people from my hand, so the God of Hezekiah will not deliver His people from my hand." ¹⁸Then they called out with a loud voice in Hebrew[a] to the people of Jerusalem who *were* on the wall, to frighten them and trouble them, that they might take the city. ¹⁹And they spoke against the God of Jerusalem, as against the gods of the people of the earth—the work of men's hands.

Sennacherib's Defeat and Death

²⁰Now because of this King Hezekiah and the prophet Isaiah, the son of Amoz, prayed and cried out to heaven. ²¹Then the LORD sent an angel who cut down every mighty man of valor, leader, and captain in the camp of the king of Assyria. So he returned shamefaced to his own land. And when he had gone into the temple of his god, some of his own offspring struck him down with the sword there.

²²Thus the LORD saved Hezekiah and the inhabitants of Jerusalem from the hand of Sennacherib the king of Assyria, and from the hand of all *others,* and guided them[a] on every side. ²³And many brought gifts to the LORD at Jerusalem, and presents to Hezekiah king of Judah, so that he was exalted in the sight of all nations thereafter.

Hezekiah Humbles Himself

²⁴In those days Hezekiah was sick and near death, and he prayed to the LORD; and He spoke to him and gave him a sign. ²⁵But Hezekiah did not repay according to the favor *shown* him, for his heart was lifted up; therefore wrath was looming over him and over Judah and Jerusalem. ²⁶Then Hezekiah humbled himself for the pride of his heart, he and the inhabitants of Jerusalem, so that the wrath of the LORD did not come upon them in the days of Hezekiah.

Hezekiah's Wealth and Honor

²⁷Hezekiah had very great riches and honor. And he made himself treasuries for silver, for gold, for precious stones, for spices, for shields, and for all kinds of desirable items; ²⁸storehouses for the harvest of grain, wine, and oil; and stalls for all kinds of livestock, and folds for flocks.[a] ²⁹Moreover he provided cities for himself, and possessions of flocks and herds in abundance; for God had given him very much property. ³⁰This same Hezekiah also stopped the water outlet of Upper Gihon, and brought the water by tunnel[a] to the west side of the City of David. Hezekiah prospered in all his works.

³¹However, *regarding* the ambassadors of the princes of Babylon, whom they sent to him to inquire about the wonder that was *done* in the land, God withdrew from him, in order to test him, that He might know all *that was* in his heart.

Death of Hezekiah

³²Now the rest of the acts of Hezekiah, and his goodness, indeed they *are* written in the vision of Isaiah the prophet, the son of Amoz, *and* in the book of the kings of Judah and Israel. ³³So Hezekiah rested with his fathers, and they buried him in the upper tombs of the sons of David; and all Judah and the inhabitants of Jerusalem honored him at his death. Then Manasseh his son reigned in his place.

Manasseh Reigns in Judah

33 Manasseh *was* twelve years old when he became king, and he reigned fifty-five years in Jerusalem. ²But he did evil in the sight of the LORD, according to the abominations of the nations whom the

---

32:18 [a]Literally *Judean* **32:22** [a]Septuagint reads *gave them rest;* Vulgate reads *gave them treasures.* **32:28** [a]Following Septuagint and Vulgate; Arabic and Syriac omit *folds for flocks;* Masoretic Text reads *flocks for sheepfolds.* **32:30** [a]Literally *brought it straight* (compare 2 Kings 20:20)

LORD had cast out before the children of Israel. [3]For he rebuilt the high places which Hezekiah his father had broken down; he raised up altars for the Baals, and made wooden images; and he worshiped all the host of heaven[a] and served them. [4]He also built altars in the house of the LORD, of which the LORD had said, "In Jerusalem shall My name be forever." [5]And he built altars for all the host of heaven in the two courts of the house of the LORD. [6]Also he caused his sons to pass through the fire in the Valley of the Son of Hinnom; he practiced soothsaying, used witchcraft and sorcery, and consulted mediums and spiritists. He did much evil in the sight of the LORD, to provoke Him to anger. [7]He even set a carved image, the idol which he had made, in the house of God, of which God had said to David and to Solomon his son, "In this house and in Jerusalem, which I have chosen out of all the tribes of Israel, I will put My name forever; [8]and I will not again remove the foot of Israel from the land which I have appointed for your fathers—only if they are careful to do all that I have commanded them, according to the whole law and the statutes and the ordinances by the hand of Moses." [9]So Manasseh seduced Judah and the inhabitants of Jerusalem to do more evil than the nations whom the LORD had destroyed before the children of Israel.

Manasseh Restored After Repentance

[10]And the LORD spoke to Manasseh and his people, but they would not listen. [11]Therefore the LORD brought upon them the captains of the army of the king of Assyria, who took Manasseh with hooks,[a] bound him with bronze *fetters*, and carried him off to Babylon. [12]Now when he was in affliction, he implored the LORD his God, and humbled himself greatly before the God of his fathers, [13]and prayed to Him; and He received his entreaty, heard his supplication, and brought him back to Jerusalem into his kingdom. Then Manasseh knew that the LORD *was* God.

[14]After this he built a wall outside the City of David on the west side of Gihon, in the valley, as far as the entrance of the Fish Gate; and *it* enclosed Ophel, and he raised it to a very great height. Then he put military captains in all the fortified cities of Judah. [15]He took away the foreign gods and the idol from the house of the LORD, and all the altars that he had built in the mount of the house of the LORD and in Jerusalem; and he cast *them* out of the city. [16]He also repaired the altar of the LORD, sacrificed peace offerings and thank offerings on it, and commanded Judah to serve the LORD God of Israel.

[17]Nevertheless the people still sacrificed on the high places, *but* only to the LORD their God.

Death of Manasseh

[18]Now the rest of the acts of Manasseh, his prayer to his God, and the words of the seers who spoke to him in the name of the LORD God of Israel, indeed they *are written* in the book[a] of the kings of Israel. [19]Also his prayer and *how God* received his entreaty, and all his sin and trespass, and the sites where he built high places and set up wooden images and carved images, before he was humbled, indeed they *are* written among the sayings of Hozai.[a] [20]So Manasseh rested with his fathers, and they buried him in his own house. Then his son Amon reigned in his place.

Amon's Reign and Death

[21]Amon *was* twenty-two years old when he became king, and he reigned two years in Jerusalem. [22]But he did evil in the sight of the LORD, as his father Manasseh had done; for Amon sacrificed to all the carved images which his father Manasseh had made, and served them. [23]And he did not humble himself before the LORD, as his father Manasseh had humbled himself; but Amon trespassed more and more.

[24]Then his servants conspired against him, and killed him in his own house. [25]But the people of the land executed all those who had conspired against King Amon. Then the people of the land made his son Josiah king in his place.

Josiah Reigns in Judah

34 Josiah *was* eight years old when he became king, and he reigned thirty-one years in Jerusalem. [2]And he did *what was* right in the sight of the LORD, and walked in the ways of his father David; *he did not* turn aside to the right hand or to the left.

[3]For in the eighth year of his reign, while he was still young, he began to seek the God of his father David; and in the twelfth year he began to purge Judah and Jerusalem of the high places, the wooden images, the carved images, and the molded images. [4]They broke down the altars of the Baals in his presence, and the incense altars which *were* above them he cut down; and the wooden images, the carved images, and the molded images he broke in pieces, and made dust of them and scattered *it* on the graves of

33:3 [a]The gods of the Assyrians 33:11 [a]That is, nose hooks (compare 2 Kings 19:28)
33:18 [a]Literally *words* 33:19 [a]Septuagint reads *the seers.*

those who had sacrificed to them. [5]He also burned the bones of the priests on their altars, and cleansed Judah and Jerusalem. [6]And *so he did* in the cities of Manasseh, Ephraim, and Simeon, as far as Naphtali and all around, with axes.[a] [7]When he had broken down the altars and the wooden images, had beaten the carved images into powder, and cut down all the incense altars throughout all the land of Israel, he returned to Jerusalem.

Hilkiah Finds the Book of the Law

[8]In the eighteenth year of his reign, when he had purged the land and the temple,[a] he sent Shaphan the son of Azaliah, Maaseiah the governor of the city, and Joah the son of Joahaz the recorder, to repair the house of the LORD his God. [9]When they came to Hilkiah the high priest, they delivered the money that was brought into the house of God, which the Levites who kept the doors had gathered from the hand of Manasseh and Ephraim, from all the remnant of Israel, from all Judah and Benjamin, and *which* they had brought back to Jerusalem. [10]Then they put *it* in the hand of the foremen who had the oversight of the house of the LORD; and they gave it to the workmen who

worked in the house of the LORD, to repair and restore the house. [11]They gave *it* to the craftsmen and builders to buy hewn stone and timber for beams, and to floor the houses which the kings of Judah had destroyed. [12]And the men did the work faithfully. Their overseers *were* Jahath and Obadiah the Levites, of the sons of Merari, and Zechariah and Meshullam, of the sons of the Kohathites, to supervise. *Others of* the Levites, all of whom were skillful with instruments of music, [13]*were* over the burden bearers and *were* overseers of all who did work in any kind of service. And *some* of the Levites *were* scribes, officers, and gatekeepers.

[14]Now when they brought out the money that was brought into the house of the LORD, Hilkiah the priest found the Book of the Law of the LORD *given* by Moses. [15]Then Hilkiah answered and said to Shaphan the scribe, "I have found the Book of the Law in the house of the LORD." And Hilkiah gave the book to Shaphan. [16]So Shaphan carried the book to the king, bringing the king word, saying, "All that was committed to your servants they are doing. [17]And they have gathered the money that was found in

34:6 [a]Literally *swords* **34:8** [a]Literally *house*

JOSIAH — PERSONAL REPENTANCE PRECEDES PUBLIC REFORM
(2 Chronicles 34:3–33)

PROFILE IN LEADERSHIP

As the leader goes, so go the people. Over and over in the history of Israel, we see that pattern repeated—for both evil and good.

When young King Josiah heard the words of God's long-forgotten law, sorrow gripped his heart (2 Chr. 34:8, 15, 19–21). He tore his clothes in repentance and directed several godly men to petition the Lord to see what he needed to do.

For years already Josiah had busied himself doing everything he could to purify the kingdom from idolatry. He had ordered images of Baal, altars to false gods, and other religious shrines destroyed. He even burned the bones of deceased pagan priests over their altars. And then he turned his attention toward purifying and renovating the temple.

God saw the repentant heart of Judah's king and told Josiah that He would withhold His wrath against the people until after Josiah had died. The genuine repentance of this godly leader led to changes in behavior among the people of Judah. They, too, renewed their covenant with the God of their ancestors. And for the rest of Josiah's life, the people stayed devoted to the Lord and His law.

Such is the power of a leader modeling godliness. As the leader goes, so go the people—for good or for evil.

21 LAWS

JOSIAH AND THE LAW OF VICTORY

Leaders Find a Way for the Team to Win

(2 Chronicles 34:3—35:19)

Have you ever thought about what separates the leaders who achieve victory from those who suffer defeat? What does it take to be a winner? Victorious leaders share an inability to accept defeat. The alternative to winning seems totally unacceptable to them, so they figure out what must be done to achieve victory, and then they go after it with everything at their disposal.

Leaders who practice the Law of Victory believe that anything less than success is unacceptable. And they have no Plan B. That keeps them fighting.

■   ■   ■   ■   ■

Winning is an inside job. The team that achieves victory is the one that first wins its internal battles. And the first one to face and win these internal battles is the leader.

Achieving a Personal Victory

How does a leader seek victory over self? Consider how Josiah conquered himself:

1. *He remained open and teachable.*

Leaders who remain willing to learn and open to change put themselves in a position to win. Josiah demonstrated that kind of openness and teachability. As a 16-year-old, instead of trying to convince everyone that he knew it all, he humbled himself. He departed from the ways of his arrogant father and sought God.

2. *He removed obstacles carried forward from the past.*

All leaders have to deal with baggage. One way or another, a leader has to win battles involving past problems. For Josiah, a major battle involved idol worship, a problem since the time of King Solomon. He courageously swept the country clean of idols. As you seek victory in your organization, you must face and overcome problems from the past. They may be ineffective traditions, incompetent players who need to be released, errors in judgment, or unrepented-of sins. Whatever they are, you must find the courage to face and resolve them.

3. *He realized what he needed to give and gave it.*

Victory always carries a personal cost. For Josiah, that meant repairing the temple and reinstating the Passover. Out of his own holdings, he gave thirty thousand lambs and young goats and three thousand cattle to be sacrificed (2 Chr. 35:7, 18).

4. *He recognized the key to victory.*

Every leader must find the key to victory. For Josiah, that key was repentance. After the Book of the Law was discovered and read, he genuinely repented of his own sins and of those of his people, then prompted his countrymen to follow his lead. Every leadership situation contains a key to victory. If you are the leader, you must find that key and turn it.

5. *He retained a personal commitment to succeed.*

People never become more committed than their leader. Josiah's personal commitment inspired the people to be faithful despite their evil desires and history (2 Chr. 34:31). If members of an organization discover they have greater commitment than their leaders, they will find another organization with another leader.

Helping Others Break Through for Victory

If you're fighting the necessary inside battles, you are putting yourself in the best place to lead your team to victory. But that may not be enough. For your organization to reach the next level, your people need their own breakthroughs. Here's a good way to help them achieve their own triumphs:

1. *Understand breakthrough timing.*

There are three prime times for leading people to a breakthrough. People are ripe for a change when . . .

• they hurt enough that they need a breakthrough.
• they learn enough that they want a breakthrough.
• they receive enough that they are able to break through.

Provide your people with learning opportunities, give them resources and encouragement, and pay attention to where they are mentally, spiritually, and emotionally. Then, when they're ready, give a little nudge to help them over the hump.

2. *Pray for a breakthrough.*

The best thing you can do for your people is to pray for them. The eminent evangelist John Wesley observed, "God does nothing but in answer to prayer." Ask God for a breakthrough. Then ask God to help you do your part, to reveal to the people their part, and to fulfill His part.

3. *Become a breakthrough person.*

If you show what it means to be a breakthrough person, your people will value breakthroughs. Most breakthrough people exhibit these qualities:

• *Vulnerability:* They realize they aren't perfect, they can't do it all, and they need God to make up the difference.
• *Humility:* They're not out to prove anything and they don't care who gets the credit. They're glad to share the spotlight with others.
• *Transparency:* They live their lives as open books. They admit where they're coming short as well as where God is working in their lives.

4. *Find breakthrough leaders.*

Gathering strong leaders adept at breakthroughs can make a difference in your organization. It's like having a team of breakthrough catalysts working alongside you.

If you want a winning team, you must have winning players. The best way to do that is to create breakthroughs. If you can become a breakthrough person who leads a team of breakthrough leaders who oversee an organization filled with breakthrough people, then victory becomes almost inevitable.

the house of the LORD, and have delivered it into the hand of the overseers and the workmen." [18]Then Shaphan the scribe told the king, saying, "Hilkiah the priest has given me a book." And Shaphan read it before the king.

[19]Thus it happened, when the king heard the words of the Law, that he tore his clothes. [20]Then the king commanded Hilkiah, Ahikam the son of Shaphan, Abdon[a] the son of Micah, Shaphan the scribe, and Asaiah a servant of the king, saying, [21]"Go, inquire of the LORD for me, and for those who are left in Israel and Judah, concerning the words of the book that is found; for great is the wrath of the LORD that is poured out on us, because our fathers have not kept the word of the LORD, to do according to all that is written in this book."

[22]So Hilkiah and those the king had appointed went to Huldah the prophetess, the wife of Shallum the son of Tokhath,[a] the son of Hasrah,[b] keeper of the wardrobe. (She dwelt in Jerusalem in the Second Quarter.) And they spoke to her to that effect.

[23]Then she answered them, "Thus says the LORD God of Israel, 'Tell the man who sent you to Me, [24]"Thus says the LORD: 'Behold, I will bring calamity on this place and on its inhabitants, all the curses that are written in the book which they have read before the king of Judah, [25]because they have forsaken Me and burned incense to other gods, that they might provoke Me to anger with all the works of their hands. Therefore My wrath will be poured out on this place, and not be quenched.'"' [26]But as for the king of Judah, who sent you to inquire of the LORD, in this manner you shall speak to him, 'Thus says the LORD God of Israel: "Concerning the words which you have heard— [27]because your heart was tender, and you humbled yourself before God when you heard His words against this place and against its inhabitants, and you humbled yourself before Me, and you tore your clothes and wept before Me, I also have heard you," says the LORD. [28]"Surely I will gather you to your fathers, and you shall be gathered to your grave in peace; and your eyes shall not see all the calamity which I will bring on this place and its inhabitants."'" So they brought back word to the king.

Josiah Restores True Worship

[29]Then the king sent and gathered all the elders of Judah and Jerusalem. [30]The king went up to the house of the LORD, with all the men of Judah and the inhabitants of Jerusalem—the priests and the Levites, and all the people, great

and small. And he read in their hearing all the words of the Book of the Covenant which had been found in the house of the LORD. [31]Then the king stood in his place and made a covenant before the LORD, to follow the LORD, and to keep His commandments and His testimonies and His statutes with all his heart and all his soul, to perform the words of the covenant that were written in this book. [32]And he made all who were present in Jerusalem and Benjamin take a stand. So the inhabitants of Jerusalem did according to the covenant of God, the God of their fathers. [33]Thus Josiah removed all the abominations from all the country that belonged to the children of Israel, and made all who were present in Israel diligently serve the LORD their God. All his days they did not depart from following the LORD God of their fathers.

Josiah Keeps the Passover

35 Now Josiah kept a Passover to the LORD in Jerusalem, and they slaughtered the Passover lambs on the fourteenth day of the first month. [2]And he set the priests in their duties and encouraged them for the service of the house of the LORD. [3]Then he said to the Levites who taught all Israel, who were holy to the LORD: "Put the holy ark in the house which Solomon the son of David, king of Israel, built. It shall no longer be a burden on your shoulders. Now serve the LORD your God and His people Israel. [4]Prepare yourselves according to your fathers' houses, according to your divisions, following the written instruction of David king of Israel and the written instruction of Solomon his son. [5]And stand in the holy place according to the divisions of the fathers' houses of your brethren the lay people, and according to the division of the father's house of the Levites. [6]So slaughter the Passover offerings, consecrate yourselves, and prepare them for your brethren, that they may do according to the word of the LORD by the hand of Moses."

[7]Then Josiah gave the lay people lambs and young goats from the flock, all for Passover offerings for all who were present, to the number of thirty thousand, as well as three thousand cattle; these were from the king's possessions. [8]And his leaders gave willingly to the people, to the priests, and to the Levites. Hilkiah, Zechariah, and Jehiel, rulers of the house of God, gave to the priests for the Passover offerings two thousand

---

34:20 [a]Achbor the son of Michaiah in 2 Kings 22:12
34:22 [a]Spelled Tikvah in 2 Kings 22:14 [b]Spelled Harhas in 2 Kings 22:14

six hundred *from the flock,* and three hundred cattle. [9]Also Conaniah, his brothers Shemaiah and Nethanel, and Hashabiah and Jeiel and Jozabad, chief of the Levites, gave to the Levites for Passover *offerings* five thousand *from the flock* and five hundred cattle.

[10]So the service was prepared, and the priests stood in their places, and the Levites in their divisions, according to the king's command. [11]And they slaughtered the Passover *offerings;* and the priests sprinkled *the blood* with their hands, while the Levites skinned *the animals.* [12]Then they removed the burnt offerings that *they* might give them to the divisions of the fathers' houses of the *lay* people, to offer to the LORD, as *it is* written in the Book of Moses. And so *they did* with the cattle. [13]Also they roasted the Passover *offerings* with fire according to the ordinance; but the *other* holy *offerings* they boiled in pots, in caldrons, and in pans, and divided *them* quickly among all the *lay* people. [14]Then afterward they prepared portions for themselves and for the priests, because the priests, the sons of Aaron, *were busy* in offering burnt offerings and fat until night; therefore the Levites prepared portions for themselves and for the priests, the sons of Aaron. [15]And the singers, the sons of Asaph, *were* in their places, according to the command of David, Asaph, Heman, and Jeduthun the king's seer. Also the gatekeepers were at each gate; they did not have to leave their position, because their brethren the Levites prepared portions for them.

[16]So all the service of the LORD was prepared the same day, to keep the Passover and to offer burnt offerings on the altar of the LORD, according to the command of King Josiah. [17]And the children of Israel who were present kept the Passover at that time, and the Feast of Unleavened Bread for seven days. [18]There had been no Passover kept in Israel like that since the days of Samuel the prophet; and none of the kings of Israel had kept such a Passover as Josiah kept, with the priests and the Levites, all Judah and Israel who were present, and the inhabitants of Jerusalem. [19]In the eighteenth year of the reign of Josiah this Passover was kept.

Josiah Dies in Battle

[20]After all this, when Josiah had prepared the temple, Necho king of Egypt came up to fight against Carchemish by the Euphrates; and Josiah went out against him. [21]But he sent messengers to him, saying, "What have I to do with you, king of Judah? *I have* not *come* against you this day, but against the house with which I have war; for God commanded me to make haste. Refrain *from* meddling with* God, who *is* with me, lest He destroy you." [22]Nevertheless Josiah would not turn his face from him, but disguised himself so that he might fight with him, and did not heed the words of Necho from the mouth of God. So he came to fight in the Valley of Megiddo.

[23]And the archers shot King Josiah; and the king said to his servants, "Take me away, for I am severely wounded." [24]His servants therefore took him out of that chariot and put him in the second chariot that he had, and they brought him to Jerusalem. So he died, and was buried in *one of* the tombs of his fathers. And all Judah and Jerusalem mourned for Josiah.

[25]Jeremiah also lamented for Josiah. And to this day all the singing men and the singing women speak of Josiah in their lamentations. They made it a custom in Israel; and indeed they *are* written in the Laments.

[26]Now the rest of the acts of Josiah and his goodness, according to *what was* written in the Law of the LORD, [27]and his deeds from first to last, indeed they *are* written in the book of the kings of Israel and Judah.

The Reign and Captivity of Jehoahaz

36 Then the people of the land took Jehoahaz the son of Josiah, and made him king in his father's place in Jerusalem. [2]Jehoahaz[a] *was* twenty-three years old when he became king, and he reigned three months in Jerusalem. [3]Now the king of Egypt deposed him at Jerusalem; and he imposed on the land a tribute of one hundred talents of silver and a talent of gold. [4]Then the king of Egypt made *Jehoahaz's*[a] brother Eliakim king over Judah and Jerusalem, and changed his name to Jehoiakim. And Necho took Jehoahaz[b] his brother and carried him off to Egypt.

The Reign and Captivity of Jehoiakim

[5]Jehoiakim *was* twenty-five years old when he became king, and he reigned eleven years in Jerusalem. And he did evil in the sight of the LORD his God. [6]Nebuchadnezzar king of Babylon came up against him, and bound him in bronze *fetters* to carry him off to Babylon. [7]Nebuchadnezzar also carried off *some* of the articles from the house of the LORD to Babylon, and put them in his temple at Babylon. [8]Now the rest of the acts of Jehoiakim, the abominations which he did, and what was found against him, indeed they *are* written in the book of the kings of

---

36:2 [a]Masoretic Text reads *Joahaz.* 36:4 [a]Literally *his* [b]Masoretic Text reads *Joahaz.*

Israel and Judah. Then Jehoiachin his son reigned in his place.

The Reign and Captivity of Jehoiachin

[9]Jehoiachin *was* eight[a] years old when he became king, and he reigned in Jerusalem three months and ten days. And he did evil in the sight of the LORD. [10]At the turn of the year King Nebuchadnezzar summoned *him* and took him to Babylon, with the costly articles from the house of the LORD, and made Zedekiah, *Jehoiakim's*[a] brother, king over Judah and Jerusalem.

Zedekiah Reigns in Judah

[11]Zedekiah *was* twenty-one years old when he became king, and he reigned eleven years in Jerusalem. [12]He did evil in the sight of the LORD his God, *and* did not humble himself before Jeremiah the prophet, *who spoke* from the mouth of the LORD. [13]And he also rebelled against King Nebuchadnezzar, who had made him swear *an oath* by God; but he stiffened his neck and hardened his heart against turning to the LORD God of Israel. [14]Moreover all the leaders of the priests and the people transgressed more and more, *according* to all the abominations of the nations, and defiled the house of the LORD which He had consecrated in Jerusalem.

The Fall of Jerusalem

[15]And the LORD God of their fathers sent *warnings* to them by His messengers, rising up early and sending *them,* because He had compassion on His people and on His dwelling place. [16]But they mocked the messengers of God, despised His words, and scoffed at His prophets, until the wrath of the LORD arose against His people, till *there was* no remedy.

[17]Therefore He brought against them the king of the Chaldeans, who killed their young men with the sword in the house of their sanctuary, and had no compassion on young man or virgin, on the aged or the weak; He gave *them* all into his hand. [18]And all the articles from the house of God, great and small, the treasures of the house of the LORD, and the treasures of the king and of his leaders, all *these* he took to Babylon. [19]Then they burned the house of God, broke down the wall of Jerusalem, burned all its palaces with fire, and destroyed all its precious possessions. [20]And those who escaped from the sword he carried away to Babylon, where they became servants to him and his sons until the rule of the kingdom of Persia, [21]to fulfill the word of the LORD by the mouth of Jeremiah, until the land had enjoyed her Sabbaths. As long as she lay desolate she kept Sabbath, to fulfill seventy years.

The Proclamation of Cyrus

[22]Now in the first year of Cyrus king of Persia, that the word of the LORD by the mouth of Jeremiah might be fulfilled, the LORD stirred up the spirit of Cyrus king of Persia, so that he made a proclamation throughout all his kingdom, and also *put it* in writing, saying,

[23] Thus says Cyrus king of Persia:
   All the kingdoms of the earth the LORD
   God of heaven has given me. And He has
   commanded me to build Him a house at
   Jerusalem which is in Judah. Who *is* among
   you of all His people? May the LORD his
   God *be* with him, and let him go up!

36:9 [a]Some Hebrew manuscripts, Septuagint, Syriac, and 2 Kings 24:8 read *eighteen.*
36:10 [a]Literally *his* (compare 2 Kings 24:17)

EZRA

The Jews Return from Babylonian Captivity to Israel

SUMMARY

The scribe Ezra and the cupbearer-turned-building-contractor Nehemiah both led the Jews in their return from Babylonian captivity to Israel. Their leadership roles complemented one another.

Nehemiah restored the people's hope as he enabled them to rebuild the Jerusalem wall in record time. Ezra restored their faith as he enabled them to become "people of the Book" once more. Ezra helped supervise the reconstruction of the Jerusalem temple in anticipation of the restoration of Israel's true worship.

While Zerubbabel led the first group of Jews back to Jerusalem to rebuild the temple, Ezra led a second group. God had commissioned him to rebuild the temple worship. Both men had to endure tremendous discouragement, yet overcame long odds to reach their goals. Both displayed tenacious leadership.

Like some other Old Testament leaders, Ezra might be considered a "teaching leader" who led mostly with his word gifts. He organized and directed and provided vision for the people. He shepherded those who were prone to wander. But more than anything, he used his teaching gift to lead the people back to where they belonged spiritually.

Ezra not only spoke, he wrote. Many believe that he wrote four biblical books: 1 and 2 Chronicles, Ezra, and Nehemiah. He also delivered sermons that communicated God's dream of gathering His people to Himself again in the Holy City.

His leadership skills appear throughout this book. Perhaps we could best describe him in four words:

1. *Pioneer:* Ezra blazed the trail and helped the Jews restart their temple worship.
2. *Model:* Ezra committed himself first to study God's Word, then to practice it, then to communicate it to the rest of Israel.
3. *Catalyst:* Ezra's courage and decisiveness in the face of opposition prompted the Jews to finish the work they had started.
4. *Teacher:* Ezra put into understandable words the very thoughts of God.

God's Role in Ezra

The Book of Ezra records the fulfillment of God's promise through Jeremiah to bring the Israelites back to their land after 70 years of captivity.

God provided direction to a variety of leaders. First, He led the leaders of Persia. God softened the hearts of Cyrus, Darius, and Artaxerxes to let the Jews return to Jerusalem and rebuild their lives, both physically and spiritually. Second, He directed Ezra, Zerubbabel, and Nehemiah as they led the Jews in their return to faith in God. More than any other man, Ezra shaped the returning Jews into the spiritual leaders God intended for them to be. Through the protection of the three Persian kings and the leadership of such great and godly Jews as Zerubbabel, Joshua, Haggai, Zechariah, and Ezra, the people completed the second temple, and true worship at last returned to Jerusalem.

Leaders in Ezra

Darius, Cyrus, Artaxerxes, Ezra, Zerubbabel

Other People of Influence in Ezra

Zechariah, Haggai

Lessons in Leadership

- God's leadership may seem subtle or absent, but He steadily finishes the work He starts.
- Both courage and fear are contagious.
- In times of conflict, leaders must act decisively.
- If workers are to give their perspiration, leaders must give them inspiration.
- Most people need a catalyst before they'll do anything risky.
- Incarnational leadership studies the truth, practices the truth, then teaches the truth.

LEADERSHIP

HIGHLIGHTS IN EZRA

End of the Babylonian Captivity

1 Now in the first year of Cyrus king of Persia, that the word of the LORD by the mouth of Jeremiah might be fulfilled, the LORD stirred up the spirit of Cyrus king of Persia, so that he made a proclamation throughout all his kingdom, and also *put it* in writing, saying,

2 Thus says Cyrus king of Persia:

All the kingdoms of the earth the LORD God of heaven has given me. And He has commanded me to build Him a house at Jerusalem which *is* in Judah. ³Who *is* among you of all His people? May his God be with him, and let him go up to Jerusalem which *is* in Judah, and build the house of the LORD God of Israel (He *is* God), which *is* in Jerusalem. ⁴And whoever is left in any place where he dwells, let the men of his place help him with silver and gold, with goods and livestock, besides the freewill offerings for the house of God which *is* in Jerusalem.

⁵Then the heads of the fathers' *houses* of Judah and Benjamin, and the priests and the Levites, with all whose spirits God had moved, arose to go up and build the house of the LORD which *is* in Jerusalem. ⁶And all those who *were* around them encouraged them with articles of silver and gold, with goods and livestock, and with precious things, besides all *that* was willingly offered.

⁷King Cyrus also brought out the articles of the house of the LORD, which Nebuchadnezzar had taken from Jerusalem and put in the temple of his gods; ⁸and Cyrus king of Persia brought them out by the hand of Mithredath the treasurer, and counted them out to Sheshbazzar the prince of Judah. ⁹This *is* the number of them: thirty gold platters, one thousand silver platters, twenty-nine knives, ¹⁰thirty gold basins, four hundred and ten silver basins of a similar *kind, and* one thousand other articles. ¹¹All the articles of gold and silver *were* five thousand four hundred. All *these* Sheshbazzar took with the captives who were brought from Babylon to Jerusalem.

The Captives Who Returned to Jerusalem

2 Now[a] these *are* the people of the province who came back from the captivity, of those who had been carried away, whom Nebuchadnezzar the king of Babylon had carried away to Babylon, and who returned to Jerusalem and Judah, everyone to his *own* city.

2:1 [a]Compare this chapter with Nehemiah 7:6–73.

The Law of Connection:
Cyrus Rules People by Relating to Them
(Ezra 1:1–7)

Unlike King Rehoboam, the Persian king Cyrus was able to connect with God's people. He first displayed mercy and then identified with the values and heart of his people. This allowed him to strengthen his reign.

What enabled King Cyrus to connect with the people? Ezra tells us he practiced . . .

1. *Humility:* He realized his power came from God and should honor God (v. 2).
2. *Responsibility:* He felt strongly he should build a place of worship for the Jews (v. 2).
3. *Empowerment:* He allowed those who had a heart to build to fulfill their call (v. 3).
4. *Resources:* He issued a decree to support the builders (v. 4).
5. *Stewardship:* He managed people's gifts, enabling them to play to their strengths (v. 5).
6. *Priorities:* He valued what was most important to the people (v. 7).

It was no accident that Cyrus arose to help Israel. Many years before these events transpired, God predicted through the prophet Isaiah that Cyrus would "subdue nations before him and loose the armor of kings." He declared, "For Jacob My servant's sake, and Israel My elect, I have even called you by your name; I have named you, though you have not known Me. I am the LORD, and there is no other; there is no God besides Me" (Is. 45:1, 4, 5).

[2]*Those* who came with Zerubbabel *were* Jeshua, Nehemiah, Seraiah, Reelaiah, Mordecai, Bilshan, Mispar,[a] Bigvai, Rehum,[b] *and* Baanah. The number of the men of the people of Israel: [3]the people of Parosh, two thousand one hundred and seventy-two; [4]the people of Shephatiah, three hundred and seventy-two; [5]the people of Arah, seven hundred and seventy-five; [6]the people of Pahath-Moab, of the people of Jeshua *and* Joab, two thousand eight hundred and twelve; [7]the people of Elam, one thousand two hundred and fifty-four; [8]the people of Zattu, nine hundred and forty-five; [9]the people of Zaccai, seven hundred and sixty; [10]the people of Bani,[a] six hundred and forty-two; [11]the people of Bebai, six hundred and twenty-three; [12]the people of Azgad, one thousand two hundred and twenty-two; [13]the people of Adonikam, six hundred and sixty-six; [14]the people of Bigvai, two thousand and fifty-six; [15]the people of Adin, four hundred and fifty-four; [16]the people of Ater of Hezekiah, ninety-eight; [17]the people of Bezai, three hundred and twenty-three; [18]the people of Jorah,[a] one hundred and twelve; [19]the people of Hashum, two hundred and twenty-three; [20]the people of Gibbar,[a] ninety-five; [21]the people of Bethlehem, one hundred and twenty-three; [22]the men of Netophah, fifty-six; [23]the men of Anathoth, one hundred and twenty-eight; [24]the people of Azmaveth,[a] forty-two; [25]the people of Kirjath Arim,[a] Chephirah, and Beeroth, seven hundred and forty-three; [26]the people of Ramah and Geba, six hundred and twenty-one; [27]the men of Michmas, one hundred and twenty-two; [28]the men of Bethel and Ai, two hundred and twenty-three; [29]the people of Nebo, fifty-two; [30]the people of Magbish, one hundred and fifty-six; [31]the people of the other Elam, one thousand two hundred and fifty-four; [32]the people of Harim, three hundred and twenty; [33]the people of Lod, Hadid, and Ono, seven hundred and twenty-five; [34]the people of Jericho, three hundred and forty-five; [35]the people of Senaah, three thousand six hundred and thirty.

[36]The priests: the sons of Jedaiah, of the house of Jeshua, nine hundred and seventy-three; [37]the sons of Immer, one thousand and fifty-two; [38]the sons of Pashhur, one thousand two hundred and forty-seven; [39]the sons of Harim, one thousand and seventeen.

[40]The Levites: the sons of Jeshua and Kadmiel, of the sons of Hodaviah,[a] seventy-four.

[41]The singers: the sons of Asaph, one hundred and twenty-eight.

[42]The sons of the gatekeepers: the sons of Shallum, the sons of Ater, the sons of Talmon, the sons of Akkub, the sons of Hatita, and the sons of Shobai, one hundred and thirty-nine *in* all.

[43]The Nethinim: the sons of Ziha, the sons of Hasupha, the sons of Tabbaoth, [44]the sons of Keros, the sons of Siaha,[a] the sons of Padon, [45]the sons of Lebanah, the sons of Hagabah, the sons of Akkub, [46]the sons of Hagab, the sons of Shalmai, the sons of Hanan, [47]the sons of Giddel, the sons of Gahar, the sons of Reaiah, [48]the sons of Rezin, the sons of Nekoda, the sons of Gazzam, [49]the sons of Uzza, the sons of Paseah, the sons of Besai, [50]the sons of Asnah, the sons of Meunim, the sons of Nephusim,[a] [51]the sons of Bakbuk, the sons of Hakupha, the sons of Harhur, [52]the sons of Bazluth,[a] the sons of Mehida, the sons of Harsha, [53]the sons of Barkos, the sons of Sisera, the sons of Tamah, [54]the sons of Neziah, and the sons of Hatipha.

[55]The sons of Solomon's servants: the sons of Sotai, the sons of Sophereth, the sons of Peruda,[a] [56]the sons of Jaala, the sons of Darkon, the sons of Giddel, [57]the sons of Shephatiah, the sons of Hattil, the sons of Pochereth of Zebaim, and the sons of Ami.[a] [58]All the Nethinim and the children of Solomon's servants were three hundred and ninety-two.

[59]And these *were* the ones who came up from Tel Melah, Tel Harsha, Cherub, Addan,[a] and Immer; but they could not identify their father's house or their genealogy,[b] whether they *were* of Israel: [60]the sons of Delaiah, the sons of Tobiah, and the sons of Nekoda, six hundred and fifty-two; [61]and of the sons of the priests: the sons of Habaiah, the sons of Koz,[a] and the sons of Barzillai, who took a wife of the daughters of Barzillai the Gileadite, and was called by their name. [62]These sought their listing *among* those who were registered by genealogy, but they were not found; therefore they *were excluded* from the priesthood as defiled. [63]And the governor[a] said to

---

2:2 [a]Spelled *Mispereth* in Nehemiah 7:7 [b]Spelled *Nehum* in Nehemiah 7:7 **2:10** [a]Spelled *Binnui* in Nehemiah 7:15 **2:18** [a]Called *Hariph* in Nehemiah 7:24 **2:20** [a]Called *Gibeon* in Nehemiah 7:25 **2:24** [a]Called *Beth Azmaveth* in Nehemiah 7:28 **2:25** [a]Called *Kirjath Jearim* in Nehemiah 7:29 **2:40** [a]Spelled *Hodevah* in Nehemiah 7:43 **2:44** [a]Spelled *Sia* in Nehemiah 7:47 **2:50** [a]Spelled *Nephishesim* in Nehemiah 7:52 **2:52** [a]Spelled *Bazlith* in Nehemiah 7:54 **2:55** [a]Spelled *Perida* in Nehemiah 7:57 **2:57** [a]Spelled *Amon* in Nehemiah 7:59 **2:59** [a]Spelled *Addon* in Nehemiah 7:61 [b]Literally *seed* **2:61** [a]Or *Hakkoz* **2:63** [a]Hebrew *Tirshatha* them that they should not eat of the most holy things till a priest could consult with the Urim and Thummim.

[64]The whole assembly together *was* forty-two thousand three hundred *and* sixty, [65]besides their male and female servants, of whom *there were* seven thousand three hundred and thirty-seven; and they had two hundred men and women singers. [66]Their horses *were* seven hundred and thirty-six, their mules two hundred and forty-five, [67]their camels four hundred and thirty-five, and *their* donkeys six thousand seven hundred and twenty.

[68]*Some* of the heads of the fathers' *houses,* when they came to the house of the LORD which *is* in Jerusalem, offered freely for the house of God, to erect it in its place: [69]According to their ability, they gave to the treasury for the work sixty-one thousand gold drachmas, five thousand minas of silver, and one hundred priestly garments.

[70]So the priests and the Levites, *some* of the people, the singers, the gatekeepers, and the Nethinim, dwelt in their cities, and all Israel in their cities.

Worship Restored at Jerusalem

3 And when the seventh month had come, and the children of Israel *were* in the cities, the people gathered together as one man to Jerusalem. [2]Then Jeshua the son of Jozadak[a] and his brethren the priests, and Zerubbabel the son of Shealtiel and his brethren, arose and built the altar of the God of Israel, to offer burnt offerings on it, as *it is* written in the Law of Moses the man of God. [3]Though fear *had come* upon them because of the people of those countries, they set the altar on its bases; and they offered burnt offerings on it to the LORD, *both* the morning and evening burnt offerings. [4]They also kept the Feast of Tabernacles, as *it is* written, and *offered* the daily burnt offerings in the number required by ordinance for each day. [5]Afterwards *they offered* the regular burnt offering, and *those* for New Moons and for all the appointed feasts of the LORD that were consecrated, and *those* of everyone who willingly offered a freewill offering to the LORD. [6]From the first day of the seventh month they began to offer burnt offerings to the LORD, although the foundation of the temple of the LORD had not been laid. [7]They also gave money to the masons and the carpenters, and food, drink, and oil to the people of Sidon and Tyre to bring cedar logs from Lebanon to the sea, to Joppa, according to the permission which they had from Cyrus king of Persia.

Courage: People Need Permission to Take Risks

(Ezra 3:7)

Most people need permission to take a risk. By issuing his proclamation, King Cyrus modeled another leadership principle.

Cyrus issued a decree to all the Jews that they could return to their homeland and begin life again there. You might think that every Jew would jump at this opportunity to leave a land of captivity and go home, but out of a population of hundreds of thousands of Jews (in 538 B.C.), only 49,897 responded to the offer. The ones who did return gave up a life of comfort and familiarity to pursue a life of rebuilding.

A risk like this is tough for most people. Usually, a leader must step forward and give men and women permission to take a risk, step out, and make sacrifices. Most people generally take the path of least resistance and migrate toward comfort zones. This is why leaders must both model courage and call forth courage from others.

Restoration of the Temple Begins

[8]Now in the second month of the second year of their coming to the house of God at Jerusalem, Zerubbabel the son of Shealtiel, Jeshua the son of Jozadak,[a] and the rest of their brethren the priests and the Levites, and all those who had come out of the captivity to Jerusalem, began *work* and appointed the Levites from twenty years old and above to oversee the work of the house of the LORD. [9]Then Jeshua *with* his sons and brothers, Kadmiel *with* his sons, and the sons of Judah,[a] arose as one to oversee those working on the house of God: the sons of Henadad *with* their sons and their brethren the Levites.

[10]When the builders laid the foundation of the temple of the LORD, the priests stood[a] in their apparel with trumpets, and the Levites, the

3:2 [a]Spelled *Jehozadak* in 1 Chronicles 6:14
3:8 [a]Spelled *Jehozadak* in 1 Chronicles 6:14
3:9 [a]Or *Hodaviah* (compare 2:40)   3:10 [a]Following Septuagint, Syriac, and Vulgate; Masoretic Text reads *they stationed the priests.*

sons of Asaph, with cymbals, to praise the LORD, according to the ordinance of David king of Israel. [11]And they sang responsively, praising and giving thanks to the LORD:

> "For *He is* good,
> For His mercy *endures* forever toward Israel."[a]

Then all the people shouted with a great shout, when they praised the LORD, because the foundation of the house of the LORD was laid.

[12]But many of the priests and Levites and heads of the fathers' *houses,* old men who had seen the first temple, wept with a loud voice when the foundation of this temple was laid before their eyes. Yet many shouted aloud for joy, [13]so that the people could not discern the noise of the shout of joy from the noise of the weeping of the people, for the people shouted with a loud shout, and the sound was heard afar off.

Resistance to Rebuilding the Temple

Now when the adversaries of Judah and Benjamin heard that the descendants of the captivity were building the temple of the LORD God of Israel, [2]they came to Zerubbabel and the heads of the fathers' *houses,* and said to them, "Let us build with you, for we seek your God as you *do;* and we have sacrificed to Him since the days of Esarhaddon king of Assyria, who brought us here." [3]But Zerubbabel and Jeshua and the rest of the heads of the fathers' *houses* of Israel said to them, "You may do nothing with us to build a house for our God; but we alone will build to the LORD God of Israel, as King Cyrus the king of Persia has commanded us." [4]Then the people of the land tried to discourage the people of Judah. They troubled them in building, [5]and hired counselors against them to frustrate their purpose all the days of Cyrus king of Persia, even until the reign of Darius king of Persia.

Rebuilding of Jerusalem Opposed

[6]In the reign of Ahasuerus, in the beginning of his reign, they wrote an accusation against the inhabitants of Judah and Jerusalem.

[7]In the days of Artaxerxes also, Bishlam, Mithredath, Tabel, and the rest of their companions wrote to Artaxerxes king of Persia; and the letter *was* written in Aramaic script, and translated into the Aramaic language. [8]Rehum[a] the commander and Shimshai the scribe wrote a letter against Jerusalem to King Artaxerxes in this fashion:

Discernment: Zerubbabel Reads the People, Then Acts

(Ezra 4:1–3)

Leaders must practice discernment. Relationships can get messy; people often harbor personal agendas and attempt to mask their true motives or to make them sound more noble than they really are.

Such was the case when a group of outsiders approached Zerubbabel and offered to help. "Let us build with you, for we seek your God as you do; and we have sacrificed to Him since the days of Esarhaddon king of Assyria, who brought us here," they said (Ezra 4:2). Zerubbabel sized them up and read the situation perfectly. He quickly recognized these folks had really arrived only to discourage and poison the minds of the builders. His relational discernment kept these negative influences from infiltrating the flock.

Leaders must *read* the people, then *lead* the people. They must understand the timing, the people, the situation, and the priorities, then act accordingly. Their action depends upon how they read these factors. Discernment always precedes decision. Analysis always precedes action.

---

[9] From[a] Rehum the commander, Shimshai the scribe, and the rest of their companions—*representatives* of the Dinaites, the Apharsathchites, the Tarpelites, the people of Persia and Erech and Babylon and Shushan,[b] the Dehavites, the Elamites, [10]and the rest of the nations whom the great and noble Osnapper took captive and settled in the cities of Samaria and the remainder beyond the River[a]—and so forth.[b]

[11](This *is* a copy of the letter that they sent him)

3:11 [a]Compare Psalm 136:1   **4:8** [a]The original language of Ezra 4:8 through 6:18 is Aramaic. **4:9** [a]Literally *Then* [b]Or *Susa*   **4:10** [a]That is, the Euphrates [b]Literally *and now*

To King Artaxerxes from your servants, the men *of the region* beyond the River, and so forth:[a]

12 Let it be known to the king that the Jews who came up from you have come to us at Jerusalem, and are building the rebellious and evil city, and are finishing *its* walls and repairing the foundations. [13]Let it now be known to the king that, if this city is built and the walls completed, they will not pay tax, tribute, or custom, and the king's treasury will be diminished. [14]Now because we receive support from the palace, it was not proper for us to see the king's dishonor; therefore we have sent and informed the king, [15]that search may be made in the book of the records of your fathers. And you will find in the book of the records and know that this city *is* a rebellious city, harmful to kings and provinces, and that they have incited sedition within the city in former times, for which cause this city was destroyed.

16 We inform the king that if this city is rebuilt and its walls are completed, the result will be that you will have no dominion beyond the River.

[17]The king sent an answer:

To Rehum the commander, *to* Shimshai the scribe, *to* the rest of their companions who dwell in Samaria, and *to* the remainder beyond the River:

Peace, and so forth.[a]

18 The letter which you sent to us has been clearly read before me. [19]And I gave the command, and a search has been made, and it was found that this city in former times has revolted against kings, and rebellion and sedition have been fostered in it. [20]There have also been mighty kings over Jerusalem, who have ruled over all *the region* beyond the River; and tax, tribute, and custom were paid to them. [21]Now give the command to make these men cease, that this city may not be built until the command is given by me.

22 Take heed now that you do not fail to do this. Why should damage increase to the hurt of the kings?

[23]Now when the copy of King Artaxerxes' letter *was* read before Rehum, Shimshai the scribe, and their companions, they went up in haste to Jerusalem against the Jews, and by force of arms made them cease. [24]Thus the work of the house of God which *is* at Jerusalem ceased, and it was discontinued until the second year of the reign of Darius king of Persia.

Restoration of the Temple Resumed

5 Then the prophet Haggai and Zechariah the son of Iddo, prophets, prophesied to the Jews who *were* in Judah and Jerusalem, in the name of the God of Israel, *who was* over them. [2]So Zerubbabel the son of Shealtiel and Jeshua the son of Jozadak[a] rose up and began to build the house of God which *is* in Jerusalem; and the prophets of God *were* with them, helping them.

[3]At the same time Tattenai the governor of *the region* beyond the River[a] and Shethar-Boznai and their companions came to them and spoke thus to them: "Who has commanded you to build this temple and finish this wall?" [4]Then, accordingly, we told them the names of the men who were constructing this building. [5]But the eye of their God was upon the elders of the Jews, so that they could not make them cease till a report could go to Darius. Then a written answer was returned concerning this *matter.* [6]This is a copy of the letter that Tattenai sent:

The governor of *the region* beyond the River, and Shethar-Boznai, and his companions, the Persians who *were in the region* beyond the River, to Darius the king.

[7](They sent a letter to him, in which was written thus)

To Darius the king:

All peace.

8 Let it be known to the king that we went into the province of Judea, to the temple of the great God, which is being built with heavy stones, and timber is being laid in the walls; and this work goes on diligently and prospers in their hands.

9 Then we asked those elders, *and* spoke thus to them: "Who commanded you to build

---

4:11 [a]Literally *and now*   4:17 [a]Literally *and now*
5:2 [a]Spelled *Jehozadak* in 1 Chronicles 6:14
5:3 [a]That is, the Euphrates

this temple and to finish these walls?" [10]We also asked them their names to inform you, that we might write the names of the men who *were* chief among them.

[11] And thus they returned us an answer, saying: "We are the servants of the God of heaven and earth, and we are rebuilding the temple that was built many years ago, which a great king of Israel built and completed. [12]But because our fathers provoked the God of heaven to wrath, He gave them into the hand of Nebuchadnezzar king of Babylon, the Chaldean, *who* destroyed this temple and carried the people away to Babylon. [13]However, in the first year of Cyrus king of Babylon, King Cyrus issued a decree to build this house of God. [14]Also, the gold and silver articles of the house of God, which Nebuchadnezzar had taken from the temple that *was* in Jerusalem and carried into the temple of Babylon—those King Cyrus took from the temple of Babylon, and they were given to one named Sheshbazzar, whom he had made governor. [15]And he said to him, 'Take these articles; go, carry them to the temple *site* that *is* in Jerusalem, and let the house of God be rebuilt on its former site.' [16]Then the same Sheshbazzar came *and* laid the foundation of the house of God which *is* in Jerusalem; but from that time even until now it has been under construction, and it is not finished."

[17] Now therefore, if *it seems* good to the king, let a search be made in the king's treasure house, which *is* there in Babylon, whether it is *so* that a decree was issued by King Cyrus to build this house of God at Jerusalem, and let the king send us his pleasure concerning this *matter*.

The Decree of Darius

6 Then King Darius issued a decree, and a search was made in the archives,[a] where the treasures were stored in Babylon. [2]And at Achmetha,[a] in the palace that *is* in the province of Media, a scroll was found, and in it a record *was* written thus:

[3] In the first year of King Cyrus, King Cyrus issued a decree *concerning* the house of God at Jerusalem: "Let the house be rebuilt, the place where they offered sacrifices; and let the foundations of it be firmly laid, its height sixty cubits *and* its width sixty cubits,

[4]*with* three rows of heavy stones and one row of new timber. Let the expenses be paid from the king's treasury. [5]Also let the gold and silver articles of the house of God, which Nebuchadnezzar took from the temple which *is* in Jerusalem and brought to Babylon, be restored and taken back to the temple which *is* in Jerusalem, *each* to its place; and deposit *them* in the house of God"—

[6] Now *therefore,* Tattenai, governor of *the region* beyond the River, and Shethar-Boznai, and your companions the Persians who *are* beyond the River, keep yourselves far from there. [7]Let the work of this house of God alone; let the governor of the Jews and the elders of the Jews build this house of God on its site.

[8] Moreover I issue a decree *as to* what you shall do for the elders of these Jews, for the building of this house of God: Let the cost be paid at the king's expense from taxes *on the region* beyond the River; this is to be given immediately to these men, so that they are not hindered. [9]And whatever they need—young bulls, rams, and lambs for the burnt offerings of the God of heaven, wheat, salt, wine, and oil, according to the request of the priests who *are* in Jerusalem—let it be given them day by day without fail, [10]that they may offer sacrifices of sweet aroma to the God of heaven, and pray for the life of the king and his sons.

[11] Also I issue a decree that whoever alters this edict, let a timber be pulled from his house and erected, and let him be hanged on it; and let his house be made a refuse heap because of this. [12]And may the God who causes His name to dwell there destroy any king or people who put their hand to alter it, or to destroy this house of God which is in Jerusalem. I Darius issue a decree; let it be done diligently.

The Temple Completed and Dedicated

[13]Then Tattenai, governor of *the region* beyond the River, Shethar-Boznai, and their companions diligently did according to what King Darius had sent. [14]So the elders of the Jews built, and they prospered through the prophesying of

---

6:1 [a]Literally *house of the scrolls*   **6:2** [a]Probably *Ecbatana,* the ancient capital of Media

Zechariah Learns Motivation Comes Before Mobilization

(Ezra 6:14)

Opposition and conflict delayed temple construction for 14 years. Only the leadership of Haggai and Zechariah motivated the people to finish what they had begun. Leaders make sure the team follows through on what it begins. Through the influence of these two prophets, construction was completed in 516 B.C.

Haggai the prophet and Zechariah the son of Iddo. And they built and finished *it,* according to the commandment of the God of Israel, and according to the command of Cyrus, Darius, and Artaxerxes king of Persia. ¹⁵Now the temple was finished on the third day of the month of Adar, which was in the sixth year of the reign of King Darius. ¹⁶Then the children of Israel, the priests and the Levites and the rest of the descendants of the captivity, celebrated the dedication of this house of God with joy. ¹⁷And they offered sacrifices at the dedication of this house of God, one hundred bulls, two hundred rams, four hundred lambs, and as a sin offering for all Israel twelve male goats, according to the number of the tribes of Israel. ¹⁸They assigned the priests to their divisions and the Levites to their divisions, over the service of God in Jerusalem, as it is written in the Book of Moses.

The Passover Celebrated

¹⁹And the descendants of the captivity kept the Passover on the fourteenth *day* of the first month. ²⁰For the priests and the Levites had purified themselves; all of them *were ritually* clean. And they slaughtered the Passover *lambs* for all the descendants of the captivity, for their brethren the priests, and for themselves. ²¹Then the children of Israel who had returned from the captivity ate together with all who had separated themselves from the filth of the nations of the land in order to seek the LORD God of Israel. ²²And they kept the Feast of Unleavened Bread seven days with joy; for the LORD made them joyful, and turned the heart of the king of Assyria toward them, to strengthen their hands in the work of the house of God, the God of Israel.

The Arrival of Ezra

7 Now after these things, in the reign of Artaxerxes king of Persia, Ezra the son of Seraiah, the son of Azariah, the son of Hilkiah, ²the son of Shallum, the son of Zadok, the son of Ahitub, ³the son of Amariah, the son of Azariah, the son of Meraioth, ⁴the son of Zerahiah, the son of Uzzi, the son of Bukki, ⁵the son of Abishua, the son of Phinehas, the son of Eleazar, the son of Aaron the chief priest— ⁶this Ezra came up from Babylon; and he *was* a skilled scribe in the Law of Moses, which the LORD God of Israel had given. The king granted him all his request, according to the hand of the LORD his God upon him. ⁷Some of the children of Israel, the priests, the Levites, the singers, the gatekeepers, and the Nethinim came up to Jerusalem in the seventh year of King Artaxerxes. ⁸And Ezra came to Jerusalem in the fifth month, which *was* in the seventh year of the king. ⁹On the first *day* of the first month he began *his* journey from Babylon, and on the first *day* of the fifth month he came to Jerusalem, according to the good hand of his God upon him. ¹⁰For Ezra had prepared his heart to seek the Law of the LORD, and to do *it,* and to teach statutes and ordinances in Israel.

The Letter of Artaxerxes to Ezra

¹¹This *is* a copy of the letter that King Artaxerxes gave Ezra the priest, the scribe, expert in the words of the commandments of the LORD, and of His statutes to Israel:

¹² Artaxerxes,ᵃ king of kings,

To Ezra the priest, a scribe of the Law of the God of heaven:

Perfect *peace,* and so forth.ᵇ

¹³ I issue a decree that all those of the people of Israel and the priests and Levites in my realm, who volunteer to go up to Jerusalem, may go with you. ¹⁴And whereas you are being sent by the king and his seven counselors to inquire concerning Judah and Jerusalem, with regard to the Law of your God which *is* in your hand; ¹⁵and *whereas you are* to carry the silver and gold which the king and his counselors have freely offered to the God of Israel, whose dwelling

---

7:12 ᵃThe original language of Ezra 7:12–26 is Aramaic. ᵇLiterally *and now*

is in Jerusalem; [16]and *whereas* all the silver and gold that you may find in all the province of Babylon, along with the freewill offering of the people and the priests, *are to be* freely offered for the house of their God in Jerusalem— [17]now therefore, be careful to buy with this money bulls, rams, and lambs, with their grain offerings and their drink offerings, and offer them on the altar of the house of your God in Jerusalem.

[18] And whatever seems good to you and your brethren to do with the rest of the silver and the gold, do it according to the will of your God. [19]Also the articles that are given to you for the service of the house of your God, deliver in full before the God of Jerusalem. [20]And whatever more may be needed for the house of your God, which you may have occasion to provide, pay *for it* from the king's treasury.

[21] And I, *even* I, Artaxerxes the king, issue a decree to all the treasurers who *are in the region* beyond the River, that whatever Ezra the priest, the scribe of the Law of the God of heaven, may require of you, let it be done diligently, [22]up to one hundred talents of silver, one hundred kors of wheat, one hundred baths of wine, one hundred baths of oil, and salt without prescribed limit. [23]Whatever is commanded by the God of heaven, let it diligently be done for the house of the God of heaven. For why should there be wrath against the realm of the king and his sons?

[24] Also we inform you that it shall not be lawful to impose tax, tribute, or custom *on* any of the priests, Levites, singers, gatekeepers, Nethinim, or servants of this house of God. [25]And you, Ezra, according to your God-given wisdom, set magistrates and judges who may judge all the people who *are in the region* beyond the River, all such as know the laws of your God; and teach those who do not know *them*. [26]Whoever will not observe the law of your God and the law of the king, let judgment be executed speedily on him, whether *it be* death, or banishment, or confiscation of goods, or imprisonment.

[27]Blessed *be* the LORD God of our fathers, who has put *such a thing* as this in the king's

---

PROFILE IN LEADERSHIP

EZRA

MANY YEARS OF DOING THE RIGHT THING
(Ezra 7:6–10)

Even at a young age, Ezra diligently studied and learned to become a scholar. He won the respect of many, including the political leader of the land of his exile, King Artaxerxes. Although Ezra's passion and vision centered on Jerusalem, he clearly kept himself busy doing God's work while in exile. He established his connections and influence over time—a necessary step if the dream of restoring Jerusalem were to be fulfilled.

As a result of many years of consistently doing the right thing, the king finally trusted Ezra with great power and resources, acknowledging his character qualities in writing. He provided all that Ezra needed to get the job done.

Ezra led many Israelites back to Jerusalem during this time of restoration. As a spiritual leader, Ezra had prepared, studied, and connected with many ordinary Jews, and his pronounced influence prompted many to follow him to Jerusalem. Ezra did not utilize his power, intellect, and influence for personal gain, but rather to restore Jerusalem.

When Ezra arrived in Jerusalem and found that a remnant of Jews had disobeyed God and polluted the bloodlines of His people, he did not shrink from making the tough call (Ezra 9; 10). Throughout his life, Ezra exercised the very best leadership qualities with both passion and zeal, which God utilized to fulfill His call.

Ezra: *Being Before Doing*

(Ezra 7:10)

On the basis of King Artaxerxes' decree, Ezra traveled from Babylon to Jerusalem (Ezra 7:1–10). As a priest, he felt committed to establishing spiritual priorities among the people, especially as it pertained to their new temple. One verse reflects the heart of a leader fully committed to his God: "For Ezra had prepared his heart to seek the Law of the LORD, and to do it, and to teach statutes and ordinances in Israel" (7:10). Do you see the order of priorities in his leadership?

1. *Learn it:* Ezra studied and discovered the truth himself.
2. *Live it:* Ezra practiced and applied what he had learned.
3. *Loan it:* Ezra passed on to others what he had already embraced.

Successful leaders must learn to follow Ezra's model. Dwight L. Moody suggested the greatest tragedy of his day was that Christian leaders attempted to traffic in unlived truth. It is our tragedy as well. We cannot give away what we don't incarnate. We must import truth before we export truth. God wants to construct our "being" before our "doing."

heart, to beautify the house of the LORD which *is* in Jerusalem, [28]and has extended mercy to me before the king and his counselors, and before all the king's mighty princes.

So I was encouraged, as the hand of the LORD my God *was* upon me; and I gathered leading men of Israel to go up with me.

Heads of Families Who Returned with Ezra

8 These *are* the heads of their fathers' *houses,* and *this is* the genealogy of those who went up with me from Babylon, in the reign of King Artaxerxes: [2]of the sons of Phinehas, Gershom; of the sons of Ithamar, Daniel; of the sons of David, Hattush; [3]of the sons of Shecaniah, of the sons of Parosh, Zechariah; and registered with him *were* one hundred and fifty males; [4]of the sons of Pahath-Moab, Eliehoenai the son of Zerahiah, and with him two hundred males; [5]of the sons of Shechaniah,[a] Ben-Jahaziel,

and with him three hundred males; [6]of the sons of Adin, Ebed the son of Jonathan, and with him fifty males; [7]of the sons of Elam, Jeshaiah the son of Athaliah, and with him seventy males; [8]of the sons of Shephatiah, Zebadiah the son of Michael, and with him eighty males; [9]of the sons of Joab, Obadiah the son of Jehiel, and with him two hundred and eighteen males; [10]of the sons of Shelomith,[a] Ben-Josiphiah, and with him one hundred and sixty males; [11]of the sons of Bebai, Zechariah the son of Bebai, and with him twenty-eight males; [12]of the sons of Azgad, Johanan the son of Hakkatan, and with him one hundred and ten males; [13]of the last sons of Adonikam, whose names *are* these—Eliphelet, Jeiel, and Shemaiah—and with them sixty males; [14]also of the sons of Bigvai, Uthai and Zabbud, and with them seventy males.

Servants for the Temple

[15]Now I gathered them by the river that flows to Ahava, and we camped there three days. And I looked among the people and the priests, and found none of the sons of Levi there. [16]Then I sent for Eliezer, Ariel, Shemaiah, Elnathan, Jarib, Elnathan, Nathan, Zechariah, and Meshullam, leaders; also for Joiarib and Elnathan, men of understanding. [17]And I gave them a command for Iddo the chief man at the place Casiphia, and I told them what they should say to Iddo *and his* brethren[a] the Nethinim at the place Casiphia— that they should bring us servants for the house of our God. [18]Then, by the good hand of our God upon us, they brought us a man of understanding, of the sons of Mahli the son of Levi, the son of Israel, namely Sherebiah, with his sons and brothers, eighteen men; [19]and Hashabiah, and with him Jeshaiah of the sons of Merari, his brothers and their sons, twenty men; [20]also of the Nethinim, whom David and the leaders had appointed for the service of the Levites, two hundred and twenty Nethinim. All of them were designated by name.

Fasting and Prayer for Protection

[21]Then I proclaimed a fast there at the river of Ahava, that we might humble ourselves before our God, to seek from Him the right way for us and our little ones and all our possessions. [22]For I

8:5 [a]Following Masoretic Text and Vulgate; Septuagint reads *the sons of Zatho, Shechaniah.*
8:10 [a]Following Masoretic Text and Vulgate; Septuagint reads *the sons of Banni, Shelomith.*
8:17 [a]Following Vulgate; Masoretic Text reads *to Iddo his brother;* Septuagint reads *to their brethren.*

was ashamed to request of the king an escort of soldiers and horsemen to help us against the enemy on the road, because we had spoken to the king, saying, "The hand of our God *is* upon all those for good who seek Him, but His power and His wrath *are* against all those who forsake Him." [23]So we fasted and entreated our God for this, and He answered our prayer.

Gifts for the Temple

[24]And I separated twelve of the leaders of the priests—Sherebiah, Hashabiah, and ten of their brethren with them— [25]and weighed out to them the silver, the gold, and the articles, the offering for the house of our God which the king and his counselors and his princes, and all Israel *who were* present, had offered. [26]I weighed into their hand six hundred and fifty talents of silver, silver articles *weighing* one hundred talents, one hundred talents of gold, [27]twenty gold basins *worth* a thousand drachmas, and two vessels of fine polished bronze, precious as gold. [28]And I said to them, "You *are* holy to the LORD; the articles *are* holy also; and the silver and the gold *are* a freewill offering to the LORD God of your fathers. [29]Watch and keep *them* until you weigh *them* before the leaders of the priests and the Levites and heads of the fathers' *houses* of Israel in Jerusalem, *in* the chambers of the house of the LORD." [30]So the priests and the Levites received the silver and the gold and the articles by weight, to bring *them* to Jerusalem to the house of our God.

The Return to Jerusalem

[31]Then we departed from the river of Ahava on the twelfth *day* of the first month, to go to Jerusalem. And the hand of our God was upon us, and He delivered us from the hand of the enemy and from ambush along the road. [32]So we came to Jerusalem, and stayed there three days. [33]Now on the fourth day the silver and the gold and the articles were weighed in the house of our God by the hand of Meremoth the son of Uriah the priest, and with him *was* Eleazar the son of Phinehas; with them *were* the Levites, Jozabad the son of Jeshua and Noadiah the son of Binnui, [34]with the number *and* weight of everything. All the weight was written down at that time.

[35]The children of those who had been carried away captive, who had come from the captivity, offered burnt offerings to the God of Israel: twelve bulls for all Israel, ninety-six rams, seventy-seven lambs, and twelve male goats *as* a sin offering. All *this was* a burnt offering to the LORD.

[36]And they delivered the king's orders to the king's satraps and the governors *in the region* beyond the River. So they gave support to the people and the house of God.

Intermarriage with Pagans

9 When these things were done, the leaders came to me, saying, "The people of Israel and the priests and the Levites have not separated themselves from the peoples of the lands, with respect to the abominations of the Canaanites, the Hittites, the Perizzites, the Jebusites, the Ammonites, the Moabites, the Egyptians, and the Amorites. [2]For they have taken some of their daughters *as wives* for themselves and their sons, so that the holy seed is mixed with the peoples of *those* lands. Indeed, the hand of the leaders and rulers has been foremost in this trespass." [3]So when I heard this thing, I tore my garment and my robe, and plucked out some

---

Ezra and the Number One Management Principle in the World
(Ezra 9:1—10:44)

Like all great leaders, we see Ezra demonstrate the number one management principle in the world: People do what people see. When Ezra heard of the sin and compromise of the Israelites, he mourned and fasted. He then took logical steps to bring about change. The steps he took are transferable, and led to the repentance of a nation. Ponder the sequence of events in this example of pure leadership:

1. He felt genuine remorse over national sin (10:6).
2. He issued a proclamation for the Jews to gather in Jerusalem (10:7).
3. He spoke clearly and directly concerning the issue (10:10).
4. He challenged the people to repent and change (10:11).
5. He accepted a plan for leaders to meet with the transgressors (10:13–17).
6. He started with the leaders who failed, then moved to the people (10:18–24).
7. He brought about public repentance and reformation (10:25–44).

of the hair of my head and beard, and sat down astonished. [4]Then everyone who trembled at the words of the God of Israel assembled to me, because of the transgression of those who had been carried away captive, and I sat astonished until the evening sacrifice.

[5]At the evening sacrifice I arose from my fasting; and having torn my garment and my robe, I fell on my knees and spread out my hands to the LORD my God. [6]And I said: "O my God, I am too ashamed and humiliated to lift up my face to You, my God; for our iniquities have risen higher than *our* heads, and our guilt has grown up to the heavens. [7]Since the days of our fathers to this day we *have been* very guilty, and for our iniquities we, our kings, *and* our priests have been delivered into the hand of the kings of the lands, to the sword, to captivity, to plunder, and to humiliation, as *it is* this day. [8]And now for a little while grace has been *shown* from the LORD our God, to leave us a remnant to escape, and to give us a peg in His holy place, that our God may enlighten our eyes and give us a measure of revival in our bondage. [9]For we *were* slaves. Yet our God did not forsake us in our bondage; but He extended mercy to us in the sight of the kings of Persia, to revive us, to repair the house of our God, to rebuild its ruins, and to give us a wall in Judah and Jerusalem. [10]And now, O our God, what shall we say after this? For we have forsaken Your commandments, [11]which You commanded by Your servants the prophets, saying, 'The land which you are entering to possess is an unclean land, with the uncleanness of the peoples of the lands, with their abominations which have filled it from one end to another with their impurity. [12]Now therefore, do not give your daughters as wives for their sons, nor take their daughters to your sons; and never seek their peace or prosperity, that you may be strong and eat the good of the land, and leave *it* as an inheritance to your children forever.' [13]And after all that has come upon us for our evil deeds and for our great guilt, since You our God have punished us less than our iniquities *deserve*, and have given us *such* deliverance as this, [14]should we again break Your commandments, and join in marriage with the people *committing* these abominations? Would You not be angry with us until You had consumed *us,* so that *there would be* no remnant or survivor? [15]O LORD God of Israel, You *are* righteous, for we are left as a remnant, as *it is* this day. Here we *are* before You, in our guilt, though no one can stand before You because of this!"

Confession of Improper Marriages

10 Now while Ezra was praying, and while he was confessing, weeping, and bowing down before the house of God, a very large assembly of men, women, and children gathered to him from Israel; for the people wept very bitterly. [2]And Shechaniah the son of Jehiel, *one* of the sons of Elam, spoke up and said to Ezra, "We have trespassed against our God, and have taken pagan wives from the peoples of the land; yet now there is hope in Israel in spite of this. [3]Now therefore, let us make a covenant with our God to put away all these wives and those who have been born to them, according to the advice of my master and of those who tremble at the commandment of our God; and let it be done according to the law. [4]Arise, for *this* matter *is* your *responsibility.* We also *are* with you. Be of good courage, and do *it.*"

[5]Then Ezra arose, and made the leaders of the priests, the Levites, and all Israel swear an oath that they would do according to this word. So they swore an oath. [6]Then Ezra rose up from before the house of God, and went into the chamber of Jehohanan the son of Eliashib; and *when* he came there, he ate no bread and drank no water, for he mourned because of the guilt of those from the captivity.

[7]And they issued a proclamation throughout Judah and Jerusalem to all the descendants of the captivity, that they must gather at Jerusalem, [8]and that whoever would not come within three days, according to the instructions of the leaders and elders, all his property would be confiscated, and he himself would be separated from the assembly of those from the captivity.

[9]So all the men of Judah and Benjamin gathered at Jerusalem within three days. It *was* the ninth month, on the twentieth of the month; and all the people sat in the open square of the house of God, trembling because of *this* matter and because of heavy rain. [10]Then Ezra the priest stood up and said to them, "You have transgressed and have taken pagan wives, adding to the guilt of Israel. [11]Now therefore, make confession to the LORD God of your fathers, and do His will; separate yourselves from the peoples of the land, and from the pagan wives."

[12]Then all the assembly answered and said with a loud voice, "Yes! As you have said, so we must do. [13]But *there are* many people; *it is* the season for heavy rain, and we are not able to stand outside. Nor *is this* the work of one or two days, for *there are* many of us who have transgressed in this matter. [14]Please, let the leaders of our entire

assembly stand; and let all those in our cities who have taken pagan wives come at appointed times, together with the elders and judges of their cities, until the fierce wrath of our God is turned away from us in this matter." [15]Only Jonathan the son of Asahel and Jahaziah the son of Tikvah opposed this, and Meshullam and Shabbethai the Levite gave them support.

[16]Then the descendants of the captivity did so. And Ezra the priest, *with* certain heads of the fathers' *households,* were set apart by the fathers' *households,* each of them by name; and they sat down on the first day of the tenth month to examine the matter. [17]By the first day of the first month they finished *questioning* all the men who had taken pagan wives.

Pagan Wives Put Away

[18]And among the sons of the priests who had taken pagan wives *the following* were found of the sons of Jeshua the son of Jozadak,[a] and his brothers: Maaseiah, Eliezer, Jarib, and Gedaliah. [19]And they gave their promise that they would put away their wives; and *being* guilty, *they* presented a ram of the flock as their trespass offering.

[20]Also of the sons of Immer: Hanani and Zebadiah; [21]of the sons of Harim: Maaseiah, Elijah, Shemaiah, Jehiel, and Uzziah; [22]of the sons of Pashhur: Elioenai, Maaseiah, Ishmael, Nethanel, Jozabad, and Elasah.

[23]Also of the Levites: Jozabad, Shimei, Kelaiah (the same *is* Kelita), Pethahiah, Judah, and Eliezer.

[24]Also of the singers: Eliashib; and of the gatekeepers: Shallum, Telem, and Uri.

[25]And others of Israel: of the sons of Parosh: Ramiah, Jeziah, Malchiah, Mijamin, Eleazar, Malchijah, and Benaiah; [26]of the sons of Elam: Mattaniah, Zechariah, Jehiel, Abdi, Jeremoth, and Eliah; [27]of the sons of Zattu: Elioenai, Eliashib, Mattaniah, Jeremoth, Zabad, and Aziza; [28]of the sons of Bebai: Jehohanan, Hananiah, Zabbai, *and* Athlai; [29]of the sons of Bani: Meshullam, Malluch, Adaiah, Jashub, Sheal, *and* Ramoth;[a] [30]of the sons of Pahath-Moab: Adna, Chelal, Benaiah, Maaseiah, Mattaniah, Bezalel, Binnui, and Manasseh; [31]of the sons of Harim: Eliezer, Ishijah, Malchijah, Shemaiah, Shimeon, [32]Benjamin, Malluch, *and* Shemariah; [33]of the sons of Hashum: Mattenai, Mattattah, Zabad, Eliphelet, Jeremai, Manasseh, *and* Shimei; [34]of the sons of Bani: Maadai, Amram, Uel, [35]Benaiah, Bedeiah, Cheluh,[a] [36]Vaniah, Meremoth, Eliashib, [37]Mattaniah, Mattenai, Jaasai,[a] [38]Bani, Binnui, Shimei, [39]Shelemiah, Nathan, Adaiah, [40]Machnadebai, Shashai, Sharai, [41]Azarel, Shelemiah, Shemariah, [42]Shallum, Amariah, *and* Joseph; [43]of the sons of Nebo: Jeiel, Mattithiah, Zabad, Zebina, Jaddai,[a] Joel, *and* Benaiah.

[44]All these had taken pagan wives, and *some of* them had wives *by whom* they had children.

10:18 [a]Spelled *Jehozadak* in 1 Chronicles 6:14
10:29 [a]Or *Jeremoth*　**10:35** [a]Or *Cheluhi,* or *Cheluhu*
10:37 [a]Or *Jaasu*　**10:43** [a]Or *Jaddu*

NEHEMIAH

In a Nutshell—a Classic Case Study in Leadership

SUMMARY

The man saw a need, rose up, captured a vision, laid a plan, and mobilized others to join him in his cause. In a nutshell, that's the story of Nehemiah, a classic case study in leadership.

In fact, one distinctive of Nehemiah is that no overt miracles occur in the book. Nobody is healed or raised from the dead. God simply answers prayer by providing a leader with favor, strength, and wisdom. Then the work of God is fleshed out in the day-to-day grind of committed workers under one man's gifted leadership—ordinary people enjoying God's blessing as they follow a gifted leader. If you want a study in the fundamentals of leadership, this book is a good place to begin.

A contemporary of Ezra, Nehemiah served as cupbearer for King Artaxerxes. He instinctively understood the laws of navigation, connection, timing, buy-in, priorities, the "big mo," and victory; you see them all in action in these few chapters.

One day Nehemiah heard that the walls surrounding Jerusalem lay in ruins, a disgrace to the Hebrews. Other nations mocked them. This terrible news burdened Nehemiah, and he knew something had to be done. Once he decided to take on the rebuilding project, the walls that for years had been nothing but rubble were completed in just 52 days.

Nehemiah stationed workers in logical positions, and they all labored successfully until they finished the work. Yet it took a coach for them to work as a team. Israel had never lacked for workers; what the nation needed was a leader to chart the course and set the people in motion. Zerubbabel had led the way to restore Jerusalem's temple; Ezra led the way to restore Jerusalem's worship. Now, a new leader was needed to restore Jerusalem's walls.

Under Nehemiah's leadership, the Jews received a permit for the rebuilding job, gathered the resources, identified workers' gifts, assigned positions, overcame criticism, and labored until the walls stood firm and tall once more. And it all happened in record time.

God's Role in Nehemiah

God works behind the scenes to set up Nehemiah's success. He influences the influencers.

When Nehemiah began to weep and pray over the disgrace of Jerusalem's ruins, God furnished him with the vision to rebuild the wall. Then God provided favor as Nehemiah sought permission from the king to leave his post and return to Jerusalem to inspect the city. Through the wealth of the Persian Empire, God even supplied the resources Nehemiah would need for rebuilding the wall.

While this book provides extremely pragmatic lessons in sound leadership principles, God remains clearly visible from the beginning. Before he did anything else, Nehemiah took time to pray. Each step of the way, Nehemiah sought the Lord for direction. As the walls rose, so did the hopes of the Jews living in Jerusalem. They saw the rebuilt walls as a symbol that God had not abandoned them and was ready to restore their lives.

Leaders in Nehemiah

Nehemiah, King Artaxerxes, the leaders of each family

Other People of Influence in Nehemiah

Sanballat, Tobiah, Geshem

Lessons in Leadership

- You cannot separate good leadership from clear vision.
- Lasting leaders feel the burden of a need before they receive the vision to meet it.
- Leaders act from a deep sense of responsibility.
- The greater the preparation, the easier the motivation.
- Leaders are more fulfilled by empowering others than by doing the work themselves.

LEADERSHIP

HIGHLIGHTS IN NEHEMIAH

Nehemiah Prays for His People

1 The words of Nehemiah the son of Hachaliah.

It came to pass in the month of Chislev, *in* the twentieth year, as I was in Shushan[a] the citadel, [2]that Hanani one of my brethren came with men from Judah; and I asked them concerning the Jews who had escaped, who had survived the captivity, and concerning Jerusalem. [3]And they said to me, "The survivors who are left from the captivity in the province *are* there in great distress and reproach. The wall of Jerusalem *is* also broken down, and its gates *are* burned with fire."

[4]So it was, when I heard these words, that I sat down and wept, and mourned *for many* days; I was fasting and praying before the God of heaven.

Nehemiah Prays First!

(Nehemiah 1:4)

When Nehemiah heard that the walls of Jerusalem lay in ruins, that its charred gates sat rotting, and that the Jewish survivors lived in distress and reproach, he did what every great leader must do: He fasted and prayed.

Something powerful happens when a leader prays and stands in the gap for his people. Intercession must always be a primary role for a leader. The apostle Peter once declared his top two leadership priorities: prayer and the ministry of God's Word (Acts 6:4). A leader's prayer accomplishes four things:

1. Prayer internalizes the burden, deepening our ownership of a need.
2. Prayer insists that we quiet our hearts and wait, slowing us down to receive from God.
3. Prayer infuses the vision, enabling us to see what God wants to do.
4. Prayer initiates the vision's fulfillment, acting as a catalyst for us to act.

---

[5]And I said: "I pray, LORD God of heaven, O great and awesome God, *You* who keep *Your* covenant and mercy with those who love You[a] and observe Your[b] commandments, [6]please let Your ear be attentive and Your eyes open, that You may hear the prayer of Your servant which I pray before You now, day and night, for the children of Israel Your servants, and confess the sins of the children of Israel which we have sinned against You. Both my father's house and I have sinned. [7]We have acted very corruptly against You, and have not kept the commandments, the statutes, nor the ordinances which You commanded Your servant Moses. [8]Remember, I pray, the word that You commanded Your servant Moses, saying, '*If* you are unfaithful, I will scatter you among the nations;[a] but *if* you return to Me, and keep My commandments and do them, though some of you were cast out to the farthest part of the heavens, *yet* I will gather them from there, and bring them to the place which I have chosen as a dwelling for My name.'[a] [10]Now these *are* Your servants and Your people, whom You have redeemed by Your great power, and by Your strong hand. [11]O Lord, I pray, please let Your ear be attentive to the prayer of Your servant, and to the prayer of Your servants who desire to fear Your name; and let Your servant prosper this day, I pray, and grant him mercy in the sight of this man."

For I was the king's cupbearer.

Nehemiah Sent to Judah

2 And it came to pass in the month of Nisan, in the twentieth year of King Artaxerxes, *when* wine *was* before him, that I took the wine and gave it to the king. Now I had never been sad in his presence before. [2]Therefore the king said to me, "Why *is* your face sad, since you *are* not sick? This *is* nothing but sorrow of heart."

So I became dreadfully afraid, [3]and said to the king, "May the king live forever! Why should my face not be sad, when the city, the place of my fathers' tombs, *lies* waste, and its gates are burned with fire?"

[4]Then the king said to me, "What do you request?"

So I prayed to the God of heaven. [5]And I said to the king, "If it pleases the king, and if your servant has found favor in your sight, I ask that you send me to Judah, to the city of my fathers' tombs, that I may rebuild it."

[6]Then the king said to me (the queen also sitting beside him), "How long will your journey be? And when will you return?" So it pleased the king to send me; and I set him a time.

[7]Furthermore I said to the king, "If it pleases the king, let letters be given to me for the

---

1:1 [a]Or *Susa* **1:5** [a]Literally *Him* [b]Literally *His*
1:8 [a]Leviticus 26:33 **1:9** [a]Deuteronomy 30:2–5

NEHEMIAH AND THE LAW OF NAVIGATION

Anyone Can Steer the Ship, but It Takes a Leader to Chart the Course
(Nehemiah 1:1—3:32)

Leaders who navigate do even more than control the direction in which they and their people travel. They see the whole trip in their minds before they leave the dock. They have a vision for their destination, they understand what it will take to get there, they know who they'll need on the team to be successful, and they recognize the obstacles long before they appear on the horizon.

Sometimes it's difficult balancing optimism and realism, intuition and planning, faith and fact. But that's what it takes to be effective as a navigating leader.

Above everything else, the secret to the Law of Navigation is preparation. When you prepare well, you convey confidence and trust to the people. It's not the size of the project that determines its acceptance, support, and success. It's the size of the leader. Leaders who are good navigators are capable of taking their people just about anywhere.

It seems remarkable, but Nehemiah could see both the problem and the solution even though he had never visited Jerusalem. That's an incredible characteristic of all great leaders: They have uncommon vision. And that's why they can navigate groups of people.

A leader sees . . .

- *Farther than others see.* Nehemiah was able to see the problem even though he lived hundreds of miles away from Jerusalem. And he could picture the solution in his head.
- *More than others see.* Nehemiah knew that the wall could and should be rebuilt, and he knew what it would take to do it. Before he left Shushan, he asked the king to provide him with letters allowing him to gather materials and granting him safe passage to Judah.
- *Before others see.* None of Jerusalem's neighbors wanted to see the Jews rebuild their wall, and several enemy leaders conspired against Nehemiah and the people. But Nehemiah saw the danger and planned accordingly; he refused to give in to enemy plots. And when the people sensed danger, he formulated strategies to defend the city and keep the people working at the same time.

The Jews needed only 52 days to rebuild a city wall that had lain in ruins for more than 120 years. And they were able to do it because they had a great leader to navigate for them.

Nehemiah knew his purpose, made his plans, and led the people through the process. His is truly one of the most remarkable stories of leadership ever recorded.

Nehemiah's Navigation

Before the building process could begin, Nehemiah spent time getting himself and his people ready.

1. *He identified with the problem* (1:2–4).

Nehemiah first inquired about the status of the Jews and the wall around Jerusalem. When he heard that the wall remained a rubble and that God's name was being mocked, he wept. The people's problem became his problem and his burden to bear.

2. *He spent time in prayer* (1:4–11).

Almost immediately Nehemiah went to his knees to pray. He confessed his wrongdoing and that of the people and he interceded for them. Then he asked for God's favor. No doubt he got the vision and plan to rebuild the wall during his time of connection with God.

3. *He approached the key influencers* (2:1–9).

In any leadership endeavor, key people of influence can make or break the whole undertaking. In this case, it was the Persian king Artaxerxes. From him, Nehemiah received not only permission to rebuild the wall, but also resources and support. Nehemiah undoubtedly also selected and approached other key people to take with him.

4. *He assessed the situation* (2:11–15).

When he finally arrived in Jerusalem, Nehemiah surveyed firsthand the challenge facing him. He did it quietly, at night, personally assessing the damage and planning the project without interference or unwanted advice.

5. *He met with the people and cast the vision* (2:16, 17).

We don't know exactly how Nehemiah approached the people or with whom he met first, but we do know he spoke with the Jews, the priests, the nobles, the officials, and the people who did the work. He described his vision for rebuilding the wall and the spiritual ramifications of the project.

6. *He encouraged them with past successes* (2:18).

With a task as daunting as the rebuilding of the wall, Nehemiah knew he needed to encourage the people. So he "told them of the hand of [his] God which had been good upon [him], and also of the king's words that he had spoken to [him]" (2:18).

7. *He received buy-in from the people* (2:18).

Two short sentences record the turning point for the whole rebuilding process: "So they said, 'Let us rise up and build.' Then they set their hands to this good work" (2:18). The people had bought in. They dedicated themselves to Nehemiah's leadership and vision.

8. *He organized the people and got them working* (3:1–32).

The people didn't work haphazardly. Nehemiah organized them by family and set them to work according to planned priorities, beginning with the city's gates.

Nehemiah put a lot of work into realizing his vision. Without his great leadership and careful planning, the wall may never have been built.

The Law of Timing: Nehemiah Chose the Moment to See the King

(Nehemiah 2:1–5)

Good leaders understand that timing is everything. Nehemiah spoke to the king about Jerusalem, but not until four months *after* he first heard about its broken wall. He began praying about the ruined wall in December, but not until April did he approach the king about rebuilding them. What was he waiting on?

No one knows for sure, but Nehemiah might well have been waiting on . . .

1. His ownership of the burden and vision.
2. A foundation of prayer to be laid.
3. His own readiness with a plan.
4. The king's mental and emotional mood.
5. The season when he could move quickly.
6. A trust to deepen between him and the king.

governors *of the region* beyond the River,[a] that they must permit me to pass through till I come to Judah, [8]and a letter to Asaph the keeper of the king's forest, that he must give me timber to make beams for the gates of the citadel which *pertains* to the temple,[a] for the city wall, and for the house that I will occupy." And the king granted *them* to me according to the good hand of my God upon me.

[9]Then I went to the governors *in the region* beyond the River, and gave them the king's letters. Now the king had sent captains of the army and horsemen with me. [10]When Sanballat the Horonite and Tobiah the Ammonite official[a] heard *of it,* they were deeply disturbed that a man had come to seek the well-being of the children of Israel.

Nehemiah Views the Wall of Jerusalem

[11]So I came to Jerusalem and was there three days. [12]Then I arose in the night, I and a few men with me; I told no one what my God had put in my heart to do at Jerusalem; nor was there any animal with me, except the one on which I rode. [13]And I went out by night through the Valley Gate to the Serpent Well and the Refuse Gate, and viewed the walls of Jerusalem which were broken down and its gates which were burned with fire. [14]Then I went on to the Fountain Gate and to the King's Pool, but *there was* no room for the animal under me to pass. [15]So I went up in the night by the valley, and viewed the wall; then I turned back and entered by the Valley Gate, and so returned. [16]And the officials did not know where I had gone or what I had done; I had not yet told the Jews, the priests, the nobles, the officials, or the others who did the work.

[17]Then I said to them, "You see the distress that we *are* in, how Jerusalem *lies* waste, and its gates are burned with fire. Come and let us build the wall of Jerusalem, that we may no longer be a reproach." [18]And I told them of the hand of my God which had been good upon me, and also of the king's words that he had spoken to me.

2:7 [a]That is, the Euphrates, and so elsewhere in this book **2:8** [a]Literally *house* **2:10** [a]Literally *servant,* and so elsewhere in this book

The Law of Buy-In: Nehemiah Shares the *Why* Before the *What*

(Nehemiah 2:5–17)

Nehemiah takes three days to size things up in Jerusalem before he speaks to the Jews, the officials, the priests, and the nobles. When he does speak, he practices the Law of Buy-In. He knows his countrymen would have to buy in to *him* before they would buy in to his *plan.*

Notice how this man declares the *why* before he explains the *what.* He provides the following reasons to get his colleagues to buy in to his vision for rebuilding the wall:

1. He had committed himself to oversee the project (2:5).
2. Asaph had approved timber for the beams and gates (2:8).
3. The situation was a reproach to Israel (2:17).
4. The ruined walls could not protect any of them (2:17).
5. God's hand was on him and had given him favor (2:18).
6. King Artaxerxes had given him permission to come and rebuild (2:18).

INITIATIVE

Nehemiah Takes the Lead
(Nehemiah 1:4—2:8)

Nehemiah might have served as the poster boy for the philosophy, "You never have to recover from a good start." He powerfully illustrates the role of initiative in a leader's life.

This godly leader took initiative in praying for Jerusalem's problem, in planning the rebuilding project, in persuading the people to act, and in pursuing the product they all wanted. And he did it in that order. His initiative showed great insight.

Nehemiah couldn't imagine sitting still when he heard the walls of Jerusalem lay in shambles. He *had* to act. Of all the things a leader should fear, complacency ought to head the list.

But what enables good leaders to initiate? Nehemiah demonstrates that leaders know something in their heart or in their gut that prompts them to move. They don't know everything, but they know enough to act. Nehemiah had insight into the following areas:

1. *He knew how long the project would take* (2:6).
   Nehemiah gave King Artaxerxes a definite time period for his absence.
2. *He knew how to get there* (2:7).
   Nehemiah asked for letters of permission to pass through the provinces beyond the river to Judah.
3. *He knew what he would need to get the job done* (2:8).
   Nehemiah requested timbers from Asaph to make beams and gates for the wall.
4. *He knew that God's hand was upon him* (2:8).
   Nehemiah got all that he requested because the hand of God rested on him.

Qualities of Initiators
Nehemiah displayed the qualities that make for initiative in leaders:

1. *They know what they want.*
   Desire is the starting point of all achievement. Nehemiah knew that he wanted that wall up.
2. *They push themselves to act.*
   At first, Nehemiah acted alone. He pushed to get the facts that would move others.
3. *They take more risks.*
   Nehemiah took some major risks as he got permission to go, to get wood, and to survey the job.
4. *They make more mistakes.*
   Nehemiah wasn't afraid to mobilize men who weren't professional contracters or soldiers to build and fight.
5. *They go with their gut.*
   What Nehemiah lacked in experience, he made up for with the passion of his heart.

For a negative example of initiative, see p. 1085.

The Law of Connection: Nehemiah's Construction Follows Connection

(Nehemiah 2:17, 18)

Nehemiah connected with the hearts of his volunteers before asking them to sacrifice their time and energy. He appealed to their sense of dignity, identity, and responsibility. The wall went up in record time because he won the hearts of the builders prior to winning the hands of the builders.

So they said, "Let us rise up and build." Then they set their hands to *this* good *work*.

[19]But when Sanballat the Horonite, Tobiah the Ammonite official, and Geshem the Arab heard *of it,* they laughed at us and despised us, and said, "What *is* this thing that you are doing? Will you rebel against the king?"

[20]So I answered them, and said to them, "The God of heaven Himself will prosper us; therefore we His servants will arise and build, but you have no heritage or right or memorial in Jerusalem."

Rebuilding the Wall

3 Then Eliashib the high priest rose up with his brethren the priests and built the Sheep Gate; they consecrated it and hung its doors. They built as far as the Tower of the Hundred,[a] *and* consecrated it, then as far as the Tower of Hananel. [2]Next to *Eliashib*[a] the men of Jericho built. And next to them Zaccur the son of Imri built.

[3]Also the sons of Hassenaah built the Fish Gate; they laid its beams and hung its doors with its bolts and bars. [4]And next to them Meremoth the son of Urijah, the son of Koz,[a] made repairs. Next to them Meshullam the son of Berechiah, the son of Meshezabel, made repairs. Next to them Zadok the son of Baana made repairs. [5]Next to them the Tekoites made repairs; but their nobles did not put their shoulders[a] to the work of their Lord.

[6]Moreover Jehoiada the son of Paseah and Meshullam the son of Besodeiah repaired the Old Gate; they laid its beams and hung its doors, with its bolts and bars. [7]And next to them Melatiah the Gibeonite, Jadon the Meronothite, the men of Gibeon and Mizpah, repaired the residence[a] of the governor *of the region* beyond the River. [8]Next to him Uzziel the son of Harhaiah, one of the goldsmiths, made repairs. Also next to him Hananiah, one[a] of the perfumers, made repairs; and they fortified Jerusalem as far as the Broad Wall. [9]And next to them Rephaiah the son of Hur, leader of half the district of Jerusalem, made repairs. [10]Next to them Jedaiah the son of Harumaph made repairs in front of his house. And next to him Hattush the son of Hashabniah made repairs.

[11]Malchijah the son of Harim and Hashub the son of Pahath-Moab repaired another section, as well as the Tower of the Ovens. [12]And next to him was Shallum the son of Hallohesh,

---

3:1 [a]Hebrew *Hammeah,* also at 12:39 **3:2** [a]Literally *On his hand* **3:4** [a]Or *Hakkoz* **3:5** [a]Literally *necks* **3:7** [a]Literally *throne* **3:8** [a]Literally *the son*

The Law of Reproduction: Nehemiah Develops Others to Carry On

(Nehemiah 2:5—6:14)

The Book of Nehemiah is one grand narrative on effective leadership. Consider the following list, "Ten Things I Know About Leadership." As you may have guessed, Nehemiah models every one of these truths:

1. Leadership is influence (2:5–8, 16–18).
2. Great leaders are effective communicators of vision (2:17, 18).
3. Leaders possess tremendous faith in people (3:1–32).
4. Great leadership is always assisted by others (3:1–32; 13:13).
5. Problem solving is the quickest way to gain leadership (4:7–23).
6. Everything rises and falls on leadership (4:9–15).
7. Leadership can be taught (4:21–23).
8. Leadership must be in the hands of few, ministry in the hands of many (5:1–7).
9. The most important ingredient to leadership is credibility/integrity (5:14–19).
10. Leadership takes responsibility for every area of the task (6:1–14).

The Law of Priorities: Nehemiah Wisely Uses His Resources

(Nehemiah 3:1–32)

Thomas Jefferson once said, "No duty the executive has to perform is so trying as to put the right man in the right place." Shortly after his arrival in Jerusalem, we see Nehemiah busily at work putting the right men in the right places.

The text lists specific men as the builders of specific gates. Why? Nehemiah has placed them in stations according to their natural gifts and interests and has them build the portion of the wall right in front of their homes. Talk about self-motivation!

Nehemiah recognized the principles that make organizations progress:

1. Motivation without organization equals frustration.
2. The strongest organizations are the simplest.
3. Leaders love everybody, but move with the movers.
4. Good organizations establish clear lines of authority.
5. People do what you inspect, not what you expect.
6. Leaders provide a supportive climate of trust and teamwork.
7. Successful organizations recognize and reward effort.

leader of half the district of Jerusalem; he and his daughters made repairs.

[13] Hanun and the inhabitants of Zanoah repaired the Valley Gate. They built it, hung its doors with its bolts and bars, and *repaired* a thousand cubits of the wall as far as the Refuse Gate. [14] Malchijah the son of Rechab, leader of the district of Beth Haccerem, repaired the Refuse Gate; he built it and hung its doors with its bolts and bars. [15] Shallun the son of Col-Hozeh, leader of the district of Mizpah, repaired the Fountain Gate; he built it, covered it, hung its doors with its bolts and bars, and repaired the wall of the Pool of Shelah by the King's Garden, as far as the stairs that go down from the City of David. [16] After

him Nehemiah the son of Azbuk, leader of half the district of Beth Zur, made repairs as far as *the place* in front of the tombs[a] of David, to the man-made pool, and as far as the House of the Mighty.

[17] After him the Levites, *under* Rehum the son of Bani, made repairs. Next to him Hashabiah, leader of half the district of Keilah, made repairs for his district. [18] After him their brethren, *under* Bavai[a] the son of Henadad, leader of the *other* half of the district of Keilah, made repairs. [19] And next to him Ezer the son of Jeshua, the leader of Mizpah, repaired another section in front of the Ascent to the Armory at the buttress. [20] After him Baruch the son of Zabbai[a] carefully repaired the other section, from the buttress to the door of the house of Eliashib the high priest. [21] After him Meremoth the son of Urijah, the son of Koz,[a] repaired another section, from the door of the house of Eliashib to the end of the house of Eliashib.

[22] And after him the priests, the men of the plain, made repairs. [23] After him Benjamin and Hasshub made repairs opposite their house. After them Azariah the son of Maaseiah, the son of Ananiah, made repairs by his house. [24] After him Binnui the son of Henadad repaired another section, from the house of Azariah to the buttress, even as far as the corner. [25] Palal the son of Uzai *made repairs* opposite the buttress, and on the tower which projects from the king's upper house that *was* by the court of the prison. After him Pedaiah the son of Parosh *made repairs.*

[26] Moreover the Nethinim who dwelt in Ophel *made repairs* as far as *the place* in front of the Water Gate toward the east, and on the projecting tower. [27] After them the Tekoites repaired another section, next to the great projecting tower, and as far as the wall of Ophel.

[28] Beyond the Horse Gate the priests made repairs, each in front of his *own* house. [29] After them Zadok the son of Immer made repairs in front of his *own* house. After him Shemaiah the son of Shechaniah, the keeper of the East Gate, made repairs. [30] After him Hananiah the son of Shelemiah, and Hanun, the sixth son of Zalaph, repaired another section. After him Meshullam the son of Berechiah made repairs in front of his dwelling. [31] After him Malchijah, one of the

---

3:16 [a]Septuagint, Syriac, and Vulgate read *tomb.*
3:18 [a]Following Masoretic Text and Vulgate; some Hebrew manuscripts, Septuagint, and Syriac read *Binnui* (compare verse 24). **3:20** [a]A few Hebrew manuscripts, Syriac, and Vulgate read *Zaccai.*
3:21 [a]Or *Hakkoz*

goldsmiths, made repairs as far as the house of the Nethinim and of the merchants, in front of the Miphkad[a] Gate, and as far as the upper room at the corner. [32]And between the upper room at the corner, as far as the Sheep Gate, the goldsmiths and the merchants made repairs.

The Wall Defended Against Enemies

4 But it so happened, when Sanballat heard that we were rebuilding the wall, that he was furious and very indignant, and mocked the Jews. [2]And he spoke before his brethren and the army of Samaria, and said, "What are these feeble Jews doing? Will they fortify themselves? Will they offer sacrifices? Will they complete it in a day? Will they revive the stones from the heaps of rubbish—*stones* that are burned?"

[3]Now Tobiah the Ammonite *was* beside him, and he said, "Whatever they build, if even a fox goes up *on it,* he will break down their stone wall."

[4]Hear, O our God, for we are despised; turn their reproach on their own heads, and give them as plunder to a land of captivity! [5]Do not cover their iniquity, and do not let their sin be blotted out from before You; for they have provoked *You* to anger before the builders.

[6]So we built the wall, and the entire wall was joined together up to half its *height,* for the people had a mind to work.

[7]Now it happened, when Sanballat, Tobiah, the Arabs, the Ammonites, and the Ashdodites heard that the walls of Jerusalem were being restored and the gaps were beginning to be closed, that they became very angry, [8]and all of them conspired together to come *and* attack Jerusalem and create confusion. [9]Nevertheless we made our prayer to our God, and because of them we set a watch against them day and night.

[10]Then Judah said, "The strength of the laborers is failing, and *there is* so much rubbish that we are not able to build the wall."

[11]And our adversaries said, "They will neither know nor see anything, till we come into their midst and kill them and cause the work to cease."

[12]So it was, when the Jews who dwelt near them came, that they told us ten times, "From whatever place you turn, *they will be* upon us."

3:31 [a]Literally *Inspection* or *Recruiting*

Commitment: How to Beat Your Problems

(Nehemiah 4:1—5:13)

One of the great tests of leadership is how you handle opposition. Nehemiah faced the usual tactics of the opposition: ridicule (Neh. 4:1–3); resistance (4:7, 8); and rumor (4:11, 12). Nehemiah modeled the right response to all three of these challenges. He . . .

1. Relied on God (4:4, 5).
2. Respected the opposition (4:9).
3. Reinforced his weak points (4:13).
4. Reassured the people (4:14).
5. Refused to quit (4:15).
6. Renewed the people's strength continually (4:16–23).

While Nehemiah 4 concerns problems from without, chapter 5 deals with problems from within—disputes about food, property, and taxes.

Persistence is the ultimate gauge of our leadership; the secret is to outlast our critics. Nehemiah taught us this lesson by staying committed to his ultimate calling.

[13]Therefore I positioned *men* behind the lower parts of the wall, at the openings; and I set the people according to their families, with their swords, their spears, and their bows. [14]And I looked, and arose and said to the nobles, to the leaders, and to the rest of the people, "Do not be afraid of them. Remember the Lord, great and awesome, and fight for your brethren, your sons, your daughters, your wives, and your houses."

[15]And it happened, when our enemies heard that it was known to us, and *that* God had brought their plot to nothing, that all of us returned to the wall, everyone to his work. [16]So it was, from that time on, *that* half of my servants worked at construction, while the other half held the spears, the shields, the bows, and *wore* armor; and the leaders *were* behind all the house of Judah. [17]Those who built on the wall, and those who carried burdens, loaded themselves so that with one hand they worked at construction, and with the other held a weapon. [18]Every one of the builders had his sword girded at his side as he built. And the one who sounded the trumpet *was* beside me.

[19]Then I said to the nobles, the rulers, and the rest of the people, "The work *is* great and extensive, and we are separated far from one another on the wall. [20]Wherever you hear the sound of the trumpet, rally to us there. Our God will fight for us."

[21]So we labored in the work, and half of *the men*[a] held the spears from daybreak until the stars appeared. [22]At the same time I also said to the people, "Let each man and his servant stay at night in Jerusalem, that they may be our guard by night and a working party by day." [23]So neither I, my brethren, my servants, nor the men of the guard who followed me took off our clothes, *except* that everyone took them off for washing.

4:21 [a]Literally *them*

The Law of the Big Mo: Nehemiah's Best Friend

(Nehemiah 4:9–20)

Momentum is a leader's best friend. When leaders lack momentum, they appear worse than they really are. When they have momentum, they appear better than they really are.

Nehemiah saw his momentum grind to a halt when opponents ridiculed and mocked the wall rebuilding project. Workers became discouraged. After prayer and a word of encouragement from their leader, the work continued, and momentum kicked in once more. Nehemiah regained momentum by these actions:

1. He prayed for the work and the workers (4:9, 10).
2. He created a plan to address the problems (4:12, 13).
3. He called for the best out of his workers (4:14).
4. He reminded them of God's help in their divine mission (4:14).
5. He provided a new strategy for victory (4:16).
6. He furnished new tools (weapons) for the workers (4:16, 17).
7. He rallied the people to support each other (4:19, 20).

Nehemiah Deals with Oppression

5 And there was a great outcry of the people and their wives against their Jewish brethren. [2]For there were those who said, "We, our sons, and our daughters *are* many; therefore let us get grain, that we may eat and live."

[3]There were also *some* who said, "We have mortgaged our lands and vineyards and houses, that we might buy grain because of the famine."

[4]There were also those who said, "We have borrowed money for the king's tax *on* our lands and vineyards. [5]Yet now our flesh *is* as the flesh of our brethren, our children as their children; and indeed we are forcing our sons and our daughters to be slaves, and *some* of our daughters have been brought into slavery. *It is* not in our power *to redeem them,* for other men have our lands and vineyards."

[6]And I became very angry when I heard their outcry and these words. [7]After serious thought, I rebuked the nobles and rulers, and said to them, "Each of you is exacting usury from his brother." So I called a great assembly against them. [8]And I said to them, "According to our ability we have redeemed our Jewish brethren who were sold to the nations. Now indeed, will you even sell your brethren? Or should they be sold to us?"

Then they were silenced and found nothing *to say.* [9]Then I said, "What you are doing *is* not good. Should you not walk in the fear of our God because of the reproach of the nations, our enemies? [10]I also, *with* my brethren and my servants, am lending them money and grain. Please, let us stop this usury! [11]Restore now to them, even this day, their lands, their vineyards, their olive groves, and their houses, also a hundredth oᶠ the money and the grain, the new wine and the oil, that you have charged them."

[12]So they said, "We will restore *it,* and will require nothing from them; we will do as you say." Then I called the priests, and required an oath from them that they would do according to this promise. [13]Then I shook out the fold of my garment[a] and said, "So may God shake out each man from his house, and from his property, who does not perform this promise. Even thus may he be shaken out and emptied."

And all the assembly said, "Amen!" and praised the LORD. Then the people did according to this promise.

The Generosity of Nehemiah

[14]Moreover, from the time that I was appointed to be their governor in the land of Ju-

---

The Law of Victory: Nehemiah Finishes the Wall in Record Time
(Nehemiah 5:14—6:9)

Nehemiah did nearly everything right as a leader. He never distanced himself from his people by eating from the governor's allowance; he didn't levy heavy taxes; he stayed committed to hands-on construction; and he refused to buy real estate, unlike previous governors (Neh. 5:14–19).

As the wall neared completion, Sanballat and Tobiah invited Nehemiah to come down from his work for a chat. He responded, "I am doing a great work, so that I cannot come down. Why should the work cease while I leave it and go down to you?" (Neh. 6:3). Before long the wall was completed, finished in record time. We can learn at least four significant leadership lessons from studying Nehemiah's leadership:

1. The quickest way to stop a great work is to stop a great leader.
2. Problems and projects seem to go together.
3. The tide turns once the project is successful.
4. A successful project will bring glory to God.

---

dah, from the twentieth year until the thirty-second year of King Artaxerxes, twelve years, neither I nor my brothers ate the governor's provisions. [15]But the former governors who *were* before me laid burdens on the people, and took from them bread and wine, besides forty shekels of silver. Yes, even their servants bore rule over the people, but I did not do so, because of the fear of God. [16]Indeed, I also continued the work on this wall, and we[a] did not buy any land. All my servants *were* gathered there for the work.

[17]And at my table *were* one hundred and fifty Jews and rulers, besides those who came to us from the nations around us. [18]Now *that* which was prepared daily *was* one ox *and* six choice sheep. Also fowl were prepared for me, and once every ten days an abundance of all kinds of wine.

5:13 [a]Literally *my lap* **5:16** [a]Following Masoretic Text; Septuagint, Syriac, and Vulgate read *I.*

Yet in spite of this I did not demand the governor's provisions, because the bondage was heavy on this people.

[19]Remember me, my God, for good, *according to* all that I have done for this people.

Conspiracy Against Nehemiah

6 Now it happened when Sanballat, Tobiah, Geshem the Arab, and the rest of our enemies heard that I had rebuilt the wall, and *that* there were no breaks left in it (though at that time I had not hung the doors in the gates), [2]that Sanballat and Geshem sent to me, saying, "Come, let us meet together among the villages in the plain of Ono." But they thought to do me harm.

[3]So I sent messengers to them, saying, "I *am* doing a great work, so that I cannot come down. Why should the work cease while I leave it and go down to you?"

[4]But they sent me this message four times, and I answered them in the same manner.

[5]Then Sanballat sent his servant to me as before, the fifth time, with an open letter in his hand. [6]In it *was* written:

It is reported among the nations, and Geshem[a] says, *that* you and the Jews plan to rebel; therefore, according to these rumors, you are rebuilding the wall, that you may be their king. [7]And you have also appointed prophets to proclaim concerning you at Jerusalem, saying, "*There is* a king in Judah!" Now these matters will be reported to the king. So come, therefore, and let us consult together.

[8]Then I sent to him, saying, "No such things as you say are being done, but you invent them in your own heart."

[9]For they all *were trying to* make us afraid, saying, "Their hands will be weakened in the work, and it will not be done." Now therefore, *O God,* strengthen my hands.

[10]Afterward I came to the house of Shemaiah the son of Delaiah, the son of Mehetabel, who *was* a secret informer; and he said, "Let us meet together in the house of God, within the temple, and let us close the doors of the temple, for they are coming to kill you; indeed, at night they will come to kill you."

[11]And I said, "Should such a man as I flee? And who *is there* such as I who would go into the temple to save his life? I will not go in!"

[12]Then I perceived that God had not sent him at all, but that he pronounced *this* prophecy against

me because Tobiah and Sanballat had hired him. [13]For this reason he *was* hired, that I should be afraid and act that way and sin, so *that* they might have *cause* for an evil report, that they might reproach me.

[14]My God, remember Tobiah and Sanballat, according to these their works, and the prophetess Noadiah and the rest of the prophets who would have made me afraid.

The Wall Completed

[15]So the wall was finished on the twenty-fifth *day* of Elul, in fifty-two days. [16]And it happened, when all our enemies heard *of it,* and all the nations around us saw *these things,* that they were very disheartened in their own eyes; for they perceived that this work was done by our God.

Commitment: Four Characteristics of Those Who Complete a Task

(Nehemiah 6:15, 16)

Commitment comes before anything else in a leader's life. Because Nehemiah had it and drew it out of others, the people finished the wall in 52 days, despite many adversities. Their great accomplishment so thrilled Nehemiah that he wrote, "When all our enemies heard of it, and all the nations around us saw these things . . . they were very disheartened in their own eyes; for they perceived that this work was done by our God" (Neh. 6:16).

Leaders who complete a task possess at least four characteristics:

1. *A compelling purpose:* They make a great commitment to a great cause.
2. *A clear perspective:* They don't let fear cloud their view of the future.
3. *A continual prayer:* They pray about everything and gain God's favor.
4. *A courageous persistence:* They move ahead despite the odds.

---

[17]Also in those days the nobles of Judah sent many letters to Tobiah, and *the letters of* Tobiah came to them. [18]For many in Judah were pledged to him, because he was the son-in-law of

6:6 [a]Hebrew *Gashmu*

Shechaniah the son of Arah, and his son Jehohanan had married the daughter of Meshullam the son of Berechiah. [19]Also they reported his good deeds before me, and reported my words to him. Tobiah sent letters to frighten me.

7 Then it was, when the wall was built and I had hung the doors, when the gatekeepers, the singers, and the Levites had been appointed, [2]that I gave the charge of Jerusalem to my brother Hanani, and Hananiah the leader of the citadel, for he *was* a faithful man and feared God more than many.

[3]And I said to them, "Do not let the gates of Jerusalem be opened until the sun is hot; and while they stand *guard,* let them shut and bar the doors; and appoint guards from among the inhabitants of Jerusalem, one at his watch station and another in front of his own house."

The Captives Who Returned to Jerusalem

[4]Now the city *was* large and spacious, but the people in it *were* few, and the houses *were* not rebuilt. [5]Then my God put it into my heart to gather the nobles, the rulers, and the people, that they might be registered by genealogy. And I found a register of the genealogy of those who had come up in the first *return,* and found written in it:

[6] These[a] *are* the people of the province who came back from the captivity, of those who had been carried away, whom Nebuchadnezzar the king of Babylon had carried away, and who returned to Jerusalem and Judah, everyone to his city.

[7] Those who came with Zerubbabel *were* Jeshua, Nehemiah, Azariah, Raamiah, Nahamani, Mordecai, Bilshan, Mispereth,[a] Bigvai, Nehum, and Baanah.

The number of the men of the people of Israel: [8]the sons of Parosh, two thousand one hundred and seventy-two;
[9]the sons of Shephatiah, three hundred and seventy-two;
[10]the sons of Arah, six hundred and fifty-two;
[11]the sons of Pahath-Moab, of the sons of Jeshua and Joab, two thousand eight hundred and eighteen;
[12]the sons of Elam, one thousand two hundred and fifty-four;
[13]the sons of Zattu, eight hundred and forty-five;
[14]the sons of Zaccai, seven hundred and sixty;
[15]the sons of Binnui,[a] six hundred and forty-eight;
[16]the sons of Bebai, six hundred and twenty-eight;
[17]the sons of Azgad, two thousand three hundred and twenty-two;

7:6 [a]Compare verses 6–72 with Ezra 2:1–70
7:7 [a]Spelled *Mispar* in Ezra 2:2 **7:15** [a]Spelled *Bani* in Ezra 2:10

Changing with the Times

(Nehemiah 7:1, 2)

Two emotions usually follow a great achievement: first, a sigh of relief and celebration; and second, a sense of . . . *now what?*

How we handle achievement tells us a lot about our character. The period following a success can become a dangerous time. Sometimes we feel tempted toward complacency, especially if we lack another goal. We can become satisfied and let down our guard. Momentum leaks.

The moment of victory is a crucial time for any organization. The leader must be able to change—or face a transitional problem. The transitional problem occurs when the leader does not know how to grow with the organization. Nehemiah's life illustrates the problem:

Two Types of Leadership Seasons

1. *Catalyst:* Gets it going
2. *Designer:* Thinks it up
3. *Motivator:* Encourages
4. *Entrepreneur:* Relies on self

1. *Consolidator:* Keeps it going
2. *Developer:* Follows it up
3. *Manager:* Organizes
4. *Executive:* Relies on others

[18]the sons of Adonikam, six hundred and sixty-seven;

[19]the sons of Bigvai, two thousand and sixty-seven;

[20]the sons of Adin, six hundred and fifty-five;

[21]the sons of Ater of Hezekiah, ninety-eight;

[22]the sons of Hashum, three hundred and twenty-eight;

[23]the sons of Bezai, three hundred and twenty-four;

[24]the sons of Hariph,[a] one hundred and twelve;

[25]the sons of Gibeon,[a] ninety-five;

[26]the men of Bethlehem and Netophah, one hundred and eighty-eight;

[27]the men of Anathoth, one hundred and twenty-eight;

[28]the men of Beth Azmaveth,[a] forty-two;

[29]the men of Kirjath Jearim, Chephirah, and Beeroth, seven hundred and forty-three;

[30]the men of Ramah and Geba, six hundred and twenty-one;

[31]the men of Michmas, one hundred and twenty-two;

[32]the men of Bethel and Ai, one hundred and twenty-three;

[33]the men of the other Nebo, fifty-two;

[34]the sons of the other Elam, one thousand two hundred and fifty-four;

[35]the sons of Harim, three hundred and twenty;

[36]the sons of Jericho, three hundred and forty-five;

[37]the sons of Lod, Hadid, and Ono, seven hundred and twenty-one;

[38]the sons of Senaah, three thousand nine hundred and thirty.

[39] The priests: the sons of Jedaiah, of the house of Jeshua, nine hundred and seventy-three;

[40]the sons of Immer, one thousand and fifty-two;

[41]the sons of Pashhur, one thousand two hundred and forty-seven;

[42]the sons of Harim, one thousand and seventeen.

[43] The Levites: the sons of Jeshua, of Kadmiel, *and* of the sons of Hodevah,[a] seventy-four.

[44] The singers: the sons of Asaph, one hundred and forty-eight.

[45] The gatekeepers: the sons of Shallum, the sons of Ater,

the sons of Talmon,
the sons of Akkub,
the sons of Hatita,
the sons of Shobai, one hundred and thirty-eight.

[46] The Nethinim: the sons of Ziha,
the sons of Hasupha,
the sons of Tabbaoth,
[47]the sons of Keros,
the sons of Sia,[a]
the sons of Padon,
[48]the sons of Lebana,[a]
the sons of Hagaba,[b]
the sons of Salmai,[c]
[49]the sons of Hanan,
the sons of Giddel,
the sons of Gahar,
[50]the sons of Reaiah,
the sons of Rezin,
the sons of Nekoda,
[51]the sons of Gazzam,
the sons of Uzza,
the sons of Paseah,
[52]the sons of Besai,
the sons of Meunim,
the sons of Nephishesim,[a]
[53]the sons of Bakbuk,
the sons of Hakupha,
the sons of Harhur,
[54]the sons of Bazlith,[a]
the sons of Mehida,
the sons of Harsha,
[55]the sons of Barkos,
the sons of Sisera,
the sons of Tamah,
[56]the sons of Neziah,
and the sons of Hatipha.

[57] The sons of Solomon's servants: the sons of Sotai,
the sons of Sophereth,
the sons of Perida,[a]
[58]the sons of Jaala,
the sons of Darkon,
the sons of Giddel,
[59]the sons of Shephatiah,

7:24 [a]Called *Jorah* in Ezra 2:18 **7:25** [a]Called *Gibbar* in Ezra 2:20 **7:28** [a]Called *Azmaveth* in Ezra 2:24 **7:43** [a]Spelled *Hodaviah* in Ezra 2:40 **7:47** [a]Spelled *Siaha* in Ezra 2:44 **7:48** [a]Masoretic Text reads *Lebanah.* [b]Masoretic Text reads *Hogabah.* [c]Or *Shalmai,* or *Shamlai* **7:52** [a]Spelled *Nephusim* in Ezra 2:50 **7:54** [a]Spelled *Bazluth* in Ezra 2:52 **7:57** [a]Spelled *Peruda* in Ezra 2:55

the sons of Hattil,
the sons of Pochereth of Zebaim,
and the sons of Amon.[a]
[60]All the Nethinim, and the sons of
Solomon's servants, were three hundred
and ninety-two.

[61] And these were the ones who came up from
Tel Melah, Tel Harsha, Cherub, Addon,[a] and
Immer, but they could not identify their
father's house nor their lineage, whether
they were of Israel: [62]the sons of Delaiah,
the sons of Tobiah,
the sons of Nekoda, six hundred and forty-
two;
[63]and of the priests: the sons of Habaiah,
the sons of Koz,[a]
the sons of Barzillai, who took a wife of the
daughters of Barzillai the Gileadite, and was
called by their name.
[64]These sought their listing among those who
were registered by genealogy, but it was not
found; therefore they were excluded from
the priesthood as defiled. [65]And the
governor[a] said to them that they should not
eat of the most holy things till a priest could
consult with the Urim and Thummim.

[66] Altogether the whole assembly was forty-
two thousand three hundred and sixty,
[67]besides their male and female servants, of
whom there were seven thousand three
hundred and thirty-seven; and they had two
hundred and forty-five men and women
singers. [68]Their horses were seven hundred
and thirty-six, their mules two hundred and
forty-five, [69]their camels four hundred and
thirty-five, and donkeys six thousand seven
hundred and twenty.

[70] And some of the heads of the fathers'
houses gave to the work. The governor[a]
gave to the treasury one thousand gold
drachmas, fifty basins, and five hundred and
thirty priestly garments. [71]Some of the heads
of the fathers' houses gave to the treasury of
the work twenty thousand gold drachmas,
and two thousand two hundred silver minas.
[72]And that which the rest of the people gave
was twenty thousand gold drachmas, two
thousand silver minas, and sixty-seven
priestly garments.

[73]So the priests, the Levites, the gatekeepers,
the singers, some of the people, the Nethinim,
and all Israel dwelt in their cities.

Ezra Reads the Law

When the seventh month came, the children
of Israel were in their cities.

8 Now all the people gathered together as
one man in the open square that was in
front of the Water Gate; and they told Ezra
the scribe to bring the Book of the Law of Moses, which the LORD had commanded Israel. [2]So
Ezra the priest brought the Law before the assembly of men and women and all who could
hear with understanding on the first day of the
seventh month. [3]Then he read from it in the
open square that was in front of the Water Gate
from morning until midday, before the men and
women and those who could understand; and
the ears of all the people were attentive to the
Book of the Law.

[4]So Ezra the scribe stood on a platform of
wood which they had made for the purpose; and
beside him, at his right hand, stood Mattithiah,
Shema, Anaiah, Urijah, Hilkiah, and Maaseiah;
and at his left hand Pedaiah, Mishael, Malchijah,
Hashum, Hashbadana, Zechariah, and Meshullam. [5]And Ezra opened the book in the sight of all
the people, for he was standing above all the people; and when he opened it, all the people stood
up. [6]And Ezra blessed the LORD, the great God.

Then all the people answered, "Amen,
Amen!" while lifting up their hands. And they
bowed their heads and worshiped the LORD
with their faces to the ground.

[7]Also Jeshua, Bani, Sherebiah, Jamin, Akkub,
Shabbethai, Hodijah, Maaseiah, Kelita, Azariah,
Jozabad, Hanan, Pelaiah, and the Levites, helped
the people to understand the Law; and the people stood in their place. [8]So they read distinctly

---

7:59 [a]Spelled *Ami* in Ezra 2:57 **7:61** [a]Spelled
Addan in Ezra 2:59 **7:63** [a]Or *Hakkoz*
7:65 [a]Hebrew *Tirshatha* **7:70** [a]Hebrew *Tirshatha*

The Practical Leader

(Nehemiah 8:8)

Nehemiah and Ezra both wanted the rebuilt wall to symbolize rebuilt spiritual
lives. "So they read distinctly from the book, in
the Law of God; and they gave the sense, and
helped them to understand the reading" (Neh.
8:8). These leaders wanted their people to understand and apply what they heard.

from the book, in the Law of God; and they gave the sense, and helped *them* to understand the reading.

[9]And Nehemiah, who *was* the governor,[a] Ezra the priest *and* scribe, and the Levites who taught the people said to all the people, "This day *is* holy to the LORD your God; do not mourn nor weep." For all the people wept, when they heard the words of the Law.

[10]Then he said to them, "Go your way, eat the fat, drink the sweet, and send portions to those for whom nothing is prepared; for *this* day *is* holy to our Lord. Do not sorrow, for the joy of the LORD is your strength."

[11]So the Levites quieted all the people, saying, "Be still, for the day *is* holy; do not be grieved." [12]And all the people went their way to eat and drink, to send portions and rejoice greatly, because they understood the words that were declared to them.

The Feast of Tabernacles

[13]Now on the second day the heads of the fathers' *houses* of all the people, with the priests and Levites, were gathered to Ezra the scribe, in order to understand the words of the Law. [14]And they found written in the Law, which the LORD had commanded by Moses, that the children of Israel should dwell in booths during the feast of the seventh month, [15]and that they should announce and proclaim in all their cities and in Jerusalem, saying, "Go out to the mountain, and bring olive branches, branches of oil trees, myrtle branches, palm branches, and branches of leafy trees, to make booths, as *it is* written."

[16]Then the people went out and brought *them* and made themselves booths, each one on the roof of his house, or in their courtyards or the courts of the house of God, and in the open square of the Water Gate and in the open square of the Gate of Ephraim. [17]So the whole assembly of those who had returned from the captivity made booths and sat under the booths; for since the days of Joshua the son of Nun until that day the children of Israel had not done so. And there was very great gladness. [18]Also day by day, from the first day until the last day, he read from the Book of the Law of God. And they kept the feast seven days; and on the eighth day *there was* a sacred assembly, according to the *prescribed* manner.

The People Confess Their Sins

9 Now on the twenty-fourth day of this month the children of Israel were assembled with fasting, in sackcloth, and with dust on their heads.[a] [2]Then those of Israelite lineage separated themselves from all foreigners; and they stood and confessed their sins and the iniquities of their fathers. [3]And they stood up in their place and read from the Book of the Law of the LORD their God *for one*-fourth of the day; and *for another* fourth they confessed and worshiped the LORD their God.

[4]Then Jeshua, Bani, Kadmiel, Shebaniah, Bunni, Sherebiah, Bani, *and* Chenani stood on the stairs of the Levites and cried out with a loud voice to the LORD their God. [5]And the Levites, Jeshua, Kadmiel, Bani, Hashabniah, Sherebiah, Hodijah, Shebaniah, *and* Pethahiah, said:

> "Stand up *and* bless the LORD your God
> Forever and ever!

> "Blessed be Your glorious name,
> Which is exalted above all blessing and
> praise!

[6] You alone *are* the LORD;
> You have made heaven,
> The heaven of heavens, with all their host,
> The earth and everything on it,
> The seas and all that is in them,
> And You preserve them all.
> The host of heaven worships You.

[7] "You *are* the LORD God,
> Who chose Abram,
> And brought him out of Ur of the
> Chaldeans,
> And gave him the name Abraham;
[8] You found his heart faithful before You,
> And made a covenant with him
> To give the land of the Canaanites,
> The Hittites, the Amorites,
> The Perizzites, the Jebusites,
> And the Girgashites—
> To give *it* to his descendants.
> You have performed Your words,
> For You *are* righteous.

[9] "You saw the affliction of our fathers in
> Egypt,
> And heard their cry by the Red Sea.
[10] You showed signs and wonders against
> Pharaoh,
> Against all his servants,
> And against all the people of his land.
> For You knew that they acted proudly
> against them.
> So You made a name for Yourself, as *it is*
> this day.

8:9 [a]Hebrew *Tirshatha* **9:1** [a]Literally *earth on them*

11 And You divided the sea before them,
So that they went through the midst of
the sea on the dry land;
And their persecutors You threw into the
deep,
As a stone into the mighty waters.
12 Moreover You led them by day with a
cloudy pillar,
And by night with a pillar of fire,
To give them light on the road
Which they should travel.

13 "You came down also on Mount Sinai,
And spoke with them from heaven,
And gave them just ordinances and true
laws,
Good statutes and commandments.
14 You made known to them Your holy
Sabbath,
And commanded them precepts, statutes
and laws,
By the hand of Moses Your servant.
15 You gave them bread from heaven for their
hunger,
And brought them water out of the rock
for their thirst,
And told them to go in to possess the land
Which You had sworn to give them.

16 "But they and our fathers acted proudly,
Hardened their necks,
And did not heed Your commandments.
17 They refused to obey,
And they were not mindful of Your
wonders
That You did among them.
But they hardened their necks,
And in their rebellion[a]
They appointed a leader
To return to their bondage.
But You *are* God,
Ready to pardon,
Gracious and merciful,
Slow to anger,
Abundant in kindness,
And did not forsake them.

18 "Even when they made a molded calf for
themselves,
And said, 'This *is* your god
That brought you up out of Egypt,'
And worked great provocations,
19 Yet in Your manifold mercies
You did not forsake them in the wilderness.
The pillar of the cloud did not depart
from them by day,

To lead them on the road;
Nor the pillar of fire by night,
To show them light,
And the way they should go.
20 You also gave Your good Spirit to instruct
them,
And did not withhold Your manna from
their mouth,
And gave them water for their thirst.
21 Forty years You sustained them in the
wilderness;
They lacked nothing;
Their clothes did not wear out[a]
And their feet did not swell.

22 "Moreover You gave them kingdoms and
nations,
And divided them into districts.[a]
So they took possession of the land of
Sihon,
The land of[b] the king of Heshbon,
And the land of Og king of Bashan.
23 You also multiplied their children as the
stars of heaven,
And brought them into the land
Which You had told their fathers
To go in and possess.
24 So the people went in
And possessed the land;
You subdued before them the inhabitants
of the land,
The Canaanites,
And gave them into their hands,
With their kings
And the people of the land,
That they might do with them as they
wished.
25 And they took strong cities and a rich
land,
And possessed houses full of all goods,
Cisterns *already* dug, vineyards, olive
groves,
And fruit trees in abundance.
So they ate and were filled and grew fat,
And delighted themselves in Your great
goodness.

26 "Nevertheless they were disobedient
And rebelled against You,
Cast Your law behind their backs

9:17 [a]Following Masoretic Text and Vulgate;
Septuagint reads *in Egypt.* **9:21** [a]Compare
Deuteronomy 29:5 **9:22** [a]Literally *corners*
[b]Following Masoretic Text and Vulgate; Septuagint
omits *The land of.*

And killed Your prophets, who testified
    against them
To turn them to Yourself;
And they worked great provocations.
27 Therefore You delivered them into the
    hand of their enemies,
Who oppressed them;
And in the time of their trouble,
When they cried to You,
You heard from heaven;
And according to Your abundant mercies
You gave them deliverers who saved them
From the hand of their enemies.

28 "But after they had rest,
They again did evil before You.
Therefore You left them in the hand of
    their enemies,
So that they had dominion over them;
Yet when they returned and cried out to
    You,
You heard from heaven;
And many times You delivered them
    according to Your mercies,
29 And testified against them,
That You might bring them back to Your
    law.
Yet they acted proudly,
And did not heed Your commandments,
But sinned against Your judgments,
'Which if a man does, he shall live by
    them.'[a]
And they shrugged their shoulders,
Stiffened their necks,
And would not hear.
30 Yet for many years You had patience with
    them,
And testified against them by Your Spirit
    in Your prophets.
Yet they would not listen;
Therefore You gave them into the hand of
    the peoples of the lands.
31 Nevertheless in Your great mercy
You did not utterly consume them nor
    forsake them;
For You are God, gracious and merciful.

32 "Now therefore, our God,
The great, the mighty, and awesome God,
Who keeps covenant and mercy:
Do not let all the trouble seem small
    before You
That has come upon us,
Our kings and our princes,
Our priests and our prophets,
Our fathers and on all Your people,

From the days of the kings of Assyria until
    this day.
33 However You are just in all that has
    befallen us;
For You have dealt faithfully,
But we have done wickedly.
34 Neither our kings nor our princes,
Our priests nor our fathers,
Have kept Your law,
Nor heeded Your commandments and
    Your testimonies,
With which You testified against them.
35 For they have not served You in their
    kingdom,
Or in the many good things that You gave
    them,
Or in the large and rich land which You
    set before them;
Nor did they turn from their wicked
    works.

36 "Here we are, servants today!
And the land that You gave to our fathers,
To eat its fruit and its bounty,
Here we are, servants in it!
37 And it yields much increase to the kings
You have set over us,
Because of our sins;
Also they have dominion over our bodies
    and our cattle
At their pleasure;
And we are in great distress.

38 "And because of all this,
We make a sure covenant and write it;
Our leaders, our Levites, and our priests
    seal it."

The People Who Sealed the Covenant

10 Now those who placed their seal on
the document were:
Nehemiah the governor, the son of
Hacaliah, and Zedekiah, 2Seraiah, Azariah, Jeremiah, 3Pashhur, Amariah, Malchijah, 4Hattush,
Shebaniah, Malluch, 5Harim, Meremoth, Obadiah, 6Daniel, Ginnethon, Baruch, 7Meshullam,
Abijah, Mijamin, 8Maaziah, Bilgai, and Shemaiah.
These were the priests.

9The Levites: Jeshua the son of Azaniah, Binnui of the sons of Henadad, and Kadmiel.

10Their brethren: Shebaniah, Hodijah, Kelita,
Pelaiah, Hanan, 11Micha, Rehob, Hashabiah,
12Zaccur, Sherebiah, Shebaniah, 13Hodijah, Bani,
and Beninu.

9:29 [a]Leviticus 18:5

¹⁴The leaders of the people: Parosh, Pahath-Moab, Elam, Zattu, Bani, ¹⁵Bunni, Azgad, Bebai, ¹⁶Adonijah, Bigvai, Adin, ¹⁷Ater, Hezekiah, Azzur, ¹⁸Hodijah, Hashum, Bezai, ¹⁹Hariph, Anathoth, Nebai, ²⁰Magpiash, Meshullam, Hezir, ²¹Meshezabel, Zadok, Jaddua, ²²Pelatiah, Hanan, Anaiah, ²³Hoshea, Hananiah, Hasshub, ²⁴Hallohesh, Pilha, Shobek, ²⁵Rehum, Hashabnah, Maaseiah, ²⁶Ahijah, Hanan, Anan, ²⁷Malluch, Harim, *and* Baanah.

The Covenant That Was Sealed

²⁸Now the rest of the people—the priests, the Levites, the gatekeepers, the singers, the Nethinim, and all those who had separated themselves from the peoples of the lands to the Law of God, their wives, their sons, and their daughters, everyone who had knowledge and understanding— ²⁹these joined with their brethren, their nobles, and entered into a curse and an oath to walk in God's Law, which was given by Moses the servant of God, and to observe and do all the commandments of the LORD our Lord, and His ordinances and His statutes: ³⁰We would not give our daughters as wives to the peoples of the land, nor take their daughters for our sons; ³¹*if* the peoples of the land brought wares or any grain to sell on the Sabbath day, we would not buy it from them on the Sabbath, or on a holy day; and we would forego the seventh year's *produce* and the exacting of every debt.

³²Also we made ordinances for ourselves, to exact from ourselves yearly one-third of a shekel for the service of the house of our God: ³³for the showbread, for the regular grain offering, for the regular burnt offering of the Sabbaths, the New Moons, and the set feasts; for the holy things, for the sin offerings to make atonement for Israel, and all the work of the house of our God. ³⁴We cast lots among the priests, the Levites, and the people, for *bringing* the wood offering into the house of our God, according to our fathers' houses, at the appointed times year by year, to burn on the altar of the LORD our God as *it is* written in the Law.

³⁵And *we made ordinances* to bring the firstfruits of our ground and the firstfruits of all fruit of all trees, year by year, to the house of the LORD; ³⁶to bring the firstborn of our sons and our cattle, as *it is* written in the Law, and the firstborn of our herds and our flocks, to the house of our God, to the priests who minister in the house of our God; ³⁷to bring the firstfruits of

NEHEMIAH

COMMITTED TO THE WAY OF GOD
(Nehemiah 10:1–29)

PROFILE IN LEADERSHIP

Nehemiah and the rest of Israel's leaders well understood the gravity of entering into covenants, making promises, and signing contracts. So can there be any doubt that a reverent hush fell over them when they determined together to sign a covenant with the true and living God?

After Nehehiah had led his countrymen through a time of confession and repentance, the governor decided it was time to commit themselves to obey the laws and commands that God had given Israel so long before. It was time to commit their hearts to the Lord Himself.

Nehemiah made sure the people did not sign this agreement lightly. Following the example of Moses centuries earlier, he urged the people to swear an oath to God, accepting both blessings for obedience and curses for rebellion. They promised to faithfully adhere to every word of God's Law and not deviate from it in any way (Neh. 10:29).

As governor and top leader of his people, Nehemiah signed the document first. In doing so, he showed his commitment to sticking with the agreement and set an example for the rest of the leadership and the nation. As always, he acted as a "leader's leader."

When leaders step forward the way Nehemiah did, they make possible a climate for renewal and revival. Even today we rightly look to him as an example of true leadership.

our dough, our offerings, the fruit from all kinds of trees, *the* new wine and oil, to the priests, to the storerooms of the house of our God; and to bring the tithes of our land to the Levites, for the Levites should receive the tithes in all our farming communities. [38]And the priest, the descendant of Aaron, shall be with the Levites when the Levites receive tithes; and the Levites shall bring up a tenth of the tithes to the house of our God, to the rooms of the storehouse.

[39]For the children of Israel and the children of Levi shall bring the offering of the grain, of the new wine and the oil, to the storerooms where the articles of the sanctuary *are, where* the priests who minister and the gatekeepers and the singers *are;* and we will not neglect the house of our God.

The People Dwelling in Jerusalem

11 Now the leaders of the people dwelt at Jerusalem; the rest of the people cast lots to bring one out of ten to dwell in Jerusalem, the holy city, and nine-tenths *were to dwell* in *other* cities. [2]And the people blessed all the men who willingly offered themselves to dwell at Jerusalem.

[3]These *are* the heads of the province who dwelt in Jerusalem. (But in the cities of Judah everyone dwelt in his own possession in their cities—Israelites, priests, Levites, Nethinim, and descendants of Solomon's servants.) [4]Also in Jerusalem dwelt *some* of the children of Judah and of the children of Benjamin.

The children of Judah: Athaiah the son of Uzziah, the son of Zechariah, the son of Amariah, the son of Shephatiah, the son of Mahalalel, of the children of Perez; [5]and Maaseiah the son of Baruch, the son of Col-Hozeh, the son of Hazaiah, the son of Adaiah, the son of Joiarib, the son of Zechariah, the son of Shiloni. [6]All the sons of Perez who dwelt at Jerusalem *were* four hundred and sixty-eight valiant men.

[7]And these are the sons of Benjamin: Sallu the son of Meshullam, the son of Joed, the son of Pedaiah, the son of Kolaiah, the son of Maaseiah, the son of Ithiel, the son of Jeshaiah; [8]and after him Gabbai *and* Sallai, nine hundred and twenty-eight. [9]Joel the son of Zichri *was* their overseer, and Judah the son of Senuah[a] *was* second over the city.

[10]Of the priests: Jedaiah the son of Joiarib, and Jachin; [11]Seraiah the son of Hilkiah, the son of Meshullam, the son of Zadok, the son of Meraioth, the son of Ahitub, *was* the leader of the house of God. [12]Their brethren who did the work of the house *were* eight hundred and twenty-two; and Adaiah the son of Jeroham, the son of Pelaliah, the son of Amzi, the son of Zechariah, the son of Pashhur, the son of Malchijah, [13]and his brethren, heads of the fathers' *houses, were* two hundred and forty-two; and Amashai the son of Azarel, the son of Ahzai, the son of Meshillemoth, the son of Immer, [14]and their brethren, mighty men of valor, *were* one hundred and twenty-eight. Their overseer *was* Zabdiel the son of *one of* the great men.[a]

[15]Also of the Levites: Shemaiah the son of Hasshub, the son of Azrikam, the son of Hashabiah, the son of Bunni; [16]Shabbethai and Jozabad, of the heads of the Levites, *had* the oversight of the business outside of the house of God; [17]Mattaniah the son of Micha,[a] the son of Zabdi, the son of Asaph, the leader *who* began the thanksgiving with prayer; Bakbukiah, the second among his brethren; and Abda the son of Shammua, the son of Galal, the son of Jeduthun. [18]All the Levites in the holy city *were* two hundred and eighty-four.

[19]Moreover the gatekeepers, Akkub, Talmon, and their brethren who kept the gates, *were* one hundred and seventy-two.

[20]And the rest of Israel, of the priests *and* Levites, *were* in all the cities of Judah, everyone in his inheritance. [21]But the Nethinim dwelt in Ophel. And Ziha and Gishpa *were* over the Nethinim.

[22]Also the overseer of the Levites at Jerusalem *was* Uzzi the son of Bani, the son of Hashabiah, the son of Mattaniah, the son of Micha, of the sons of Asaph, the singers in charge of the service of the house of God. [23]For *it was* the king's command concerning them that a certain portion should be for the singers, a quota day by day. [24]Pethahiah the son of Meshezabel, of the children of Zerah the son of Judah, *was* the king's deputy[a] in all matters concerning the people.

The People Dwelling Outside Jerusalem

[25]And as for the villages with their fields, *some* of the children of Judah dwelt in Kirjath Arba and its villages, Dibon and its villages, Jekabzeel and its villages; [26]in Jeshua, Moladah, Beth Pelet, [27]Hazar Shual, and Beersheba and its villages; [28]in Ziklag and Meconah and its villages; [29]in En Rimmon, Zorah, Jarmuth, [30]Zanoah, Adullam, and their villages; in Lachish and its fields; in Azekah and its villages. They dwelt from Beersheba to the Valley of Hinnom.

11:9 [a]Or *Hassenuah* **11:14** [a]Or *the son of Haggedolim* **11:17** [a]Or *Michah* **11:24** [a]Literally *at the king's hand*

[31]Also the children of Benjamin from Geba *dwelt* in Michmash, Aija, and Bethel, and their villages; [32]in Anathoth, Nob, Ananiah; [33]in Hazor, Ramah, Gittaim; [34]in Hadid, Zeboim, Neballat; [35]in Lod, Ono, *and* the Valley of Craftsmen. [36]Some of the Judean divisions of Levites *were* in Benjamin.

The Priests and Levites

12 Now these *are* the priests and the Levites who came up with Zerubbabel the son of Shealtiel, and Jeshua: Seraiah, Jeremiah, Ezra, [2]Amariah, Malluch, Hattush, [3]Shechaniah, Rehum, Meremoth, [4]Iddo, Ginnethoi,[a] Abijah, [5]Mijamin, Maadiah, Bilgah, [6]Shemaiah, Joiarib, Jedaiah, [7]Sallu, Amok, Hilkiah, *and* Jedaiah.

These *were* the heads of the priests and their brethren in the days of Jeshua.

[8]Moreover the Levites *were* Jeshua, Binnui, Kadmiel, Sherebiah, Judah, *and* Mattaniah *who led* the thanksgiving *psalms,* he and his brethren. [9]Also Bakbukiah and Unni, their brethren, *stood* across from them in *their* duties.

[10]Jeshua begot Joiakim, Joiakim begot Eliashib, Eliashib begot Joiada, [11]Joiada begot Jonathan, and Jonathan begot Jaddua.

[12]Now in the days of Joiakim, the priests, the heads of the fathers' *houses were:* of Seraiah, Meraiah; of Jeremiah, Hananiah; [13]of Ezra, Meshullam; of Amariah, Jehohanan; [14]of Melichu,[a] Jonathan; of Shebaniah,[b] Joseph; [15]of Harim,[a] Adna; of Meraioth,[b] Helkai; [16]of Iddo, Zechariah; of Ginnethon, Meshullam; [17]of Abijah, Zichri; *the son* of Minjamin;[a] of Moadiah,[b] Piltai; [18]of Bilgah, Shammua; of Shemaiah, Jehonathan; [19]of Joiarib, Mattenai; of Jedaiah, Uzzi; [20]of Sallai,[a] Kallai; of Amok, Eber; [21]of Hilkiah, Hashabiah; *and* of Jedaiah, Nethanel.

[22]During the reign of Darius the Persian, a record *was also kept* of the Levites and priests *who had been* heads of their fathers' *houses* in the days of Eliashib, Joiada, Johanan, and Jaddua. [23]The sons of Levi, the heads of the fathers' *houses* until the days of Johanan the son of Eliashib, *were* written in the book of the chronicles.

[24]And the heads of the Levites *were* Hashabiah, Sherebiah, and Jeshua the son of Kadmiel, with their brothers across from them, to praise *and* give thanks, group alternating with group, according to the command of David the man of God. [25]Mattaniah, Bakbukiah, Obadiah, Meshullam, Talmon, and Akkub *were* gatekeepers keeping the watch at the storerooms of the gates. [26]These *lived* in the days of Joiakim the son of Jeshua, the son of Jozadak,[a] and in the days of Nehemiah the governor, and of Ezra the priest, the scribe.

Nehemiah Dedicates the Wall

[27]Now at the dedication of the wall of Jerusalem they sought out the Levites in all their places, to bring them to Jerusalem to celebrate the dedication with gladness, both with thanksgivings and singing, *with* cymbals and stringed instruments and harps. [28]And the sons of the singers gathered together from the countryside around Jerusalem, from the villages of the Netophathites, [29]from the house of Gilgal, and from the fields of Geba and Azmaveth; for the singers had built themselves villages all around Jerusalem. [30]Then the priests and Levites purified themselves, and purified the people, the gates, and the wall.

[31]So I brought the leaders of Judah up on the wall, and appointed two large thanksgiving choirs. *One* went to the right hand on the wall toward the Refuse Gate. [32]After them went Hoshaiah and half of the leaders of Judah, [33]and Azariah, Ezra, Meshullam, [34]Judah, Benjamin, Shemaiah, Jeremiah, [35]and some of the priests' sons with trumpets—Zechariah the son of Jonathan, the son of Shemaiah, the son of Mattaniah, the son of Michaiah, the son of Zaccur, the son of Asaph, [36]and his brethren, Shemaiah, Azarel, Milalai, Gilalai, Maai, Nethanel, Judah, *and* Hanani, with the musical instruments of David the man of God. And Ezra the scribe *went* before them. [37]By the Fountain Gate, in front of them, they went up the stairs of the City of David, on the stairway of the wall, beyond the house of David, as far as the Water Gate eastward.

[38]The other thanksgiving choir went the opposite *way,* and I *was* behind them with half of the people on the wall, going past the Tower of the Ovens as far as the Broad Wall, [39]and above the Gate of Ephraim, above the Old Gate, above the Fish Gate, the Tower of Hananel, the Tower of the Hundred, as far as the Sheep Gate; and they stopped by the Gate of the Prison.

[40]So the two thanksgiving choirs stood in the house of God, likewise I and the half of the rulers with me; [41]and the priests, Eliakim, Maaseiah, Minjamin,[a] Michaiah, Elioenai, Zechariah,

---

12:4 [a]Or *Ginnethon* (compare verse 16) **12:14** [a]Or *Malluch* (compare verse 2) [b]Or *Shechaniah* (compare verse 3) **12:15** [a]Or *Rehum* (compare verse 3) [b]Or *Meremoth* (compare verse 3) **12:17** [a]Or *Mijamin* (compare verse 5) [b]Or *Maadiah* (compare verse 5) **12:20** [a]Or *Sallu* (compare verse 7) **12:26** [a]Spelled *Jehozadak* in 1 Chronicles 6:14 **12:41** [a]Or *Mijamin* (compare verse 5) *and* Hananiah, with trumpets; [42]also Maaseiah, Shemaiah, Eleazar, Uzzi, Jehohanan, Malchijah, Elam, and Ezer. The singers sang loudly with Jezrahiah the director.

[43]Also that day they offered great sacrifices, and rejoiced, for God had made them rejoice with great joy; the women and the children also rejoiced, so that the joy of Jerusalem was heard afar off.

Temple Responsibilities

[44]And at the same time some were appointed over the rooms of the storehouse for the offerings, the firstfruits, and the tithes, to gather into them from the fields of the cities the portions specified by the Law for the priests and Levites; for Judah rejoiced over the priests and Levites who ministered. [45]Both the singers and the gatekeepers kept the charge of their God and the charge of the purification, according to the command of David *and* Solomon his son. [46]For in the days of David and Asaph of old *there were* chiefs of the singers, and songs of praise and thanksgiving to God. [47]In the days of Zerubbabel and in the days of Nehemiah all Israel gave the portions for the singers and the gatekeepers, a portion for each day. They also consecrated *holy things* for the Levites, and the Levites consecrated *them* for the children of Aaron.

Principles of Separation

13 On that day they read from the Book of Moses in the hearing of the people, and in it was found written that no Ammonite or Moabite should ever come into the assembly of God, [2]because they had not met the children of Israel with bread and water, but hired Balaam against them to curse them. However, our God turned the curse into a blessing. [3]So it was, when they had heard the Law, that they separated all the mixed multitude from Israel.

The Reforms of Nehemiah

[4]Now before this, Eliashib the priest, having authority over the storerooms of the house of our God, *was* allied with Tobiah. [5]And he had prepared for him a large room, where previously they had stored the grain offerings, the frankincense, the articles, the tithes of grain, the new wine and oil, which were commanded *to be given* to the Levites and singers and gatekeepers, and the offerings for the priests. [6]But during all this I was not in Jerusalem, for in the thirty-second year of Artaxerxes king of Babylon I had returned to the king. Then after certain days I ob-

---

The Law of Legacy: There Is No Success Without a Successor

(Nehemiah 13:1–31)

Even after Nehemiah returned to King Artaxerxes, he felt the necessity to follow up on the work in Jerusalem. When he returned to visit the walled city, he learned the people already had compromised God's statutes—and he knew he had to do something to ensure the success of the last several months of labor.

Nehemiah learned that when the leader is away, the people tend to stray. Consider the following problems he encountered:

1. *Compromising companionship* (vv. 1–9)
2. *Financial fiasco* (vv. 10–14)
3. *Secularized Sabbath* (vv. 15–22)
4. *Domestic disobedience* (vv. 23–31)

When Nehemiah failed to develop a strong inner circle and reproduce his vision in a team of leaders, everyone drifted. He witnessed firsthand the second law of thermodynamics: Things don't wind up; they wind down, unless energy is applied. A sound legacy develops only when a team has been trained and positioned to carry on.

---

tained leave from the king, [7]and I came to Jerusalem and discovered the evil that Eliashib had done for Tobiah, in preparing a room for him in the courts of the house of God. [8]And it grieved me bitterly; therefore I threw all the household goods of Tobiah out of the room. [9]Then I commanded them to cleanse the rooms; and I brought back into them the articles of the house of God, with the grain offering and the frankincense.

[10]I also realized that the portions for the Levites had not been given *them;* for each of the Levites and the singers who did the work had gone back to his field. [11]So I contended with the rulers, and said, "Why is the house of God forsaken?" And I gathered them together and set them in their place. [12]Then all Judah brought the tithe of the grain and the new wine and the oil to the storehouse. [13]And I appointed as treasurers over the storehouse Shelemiah the priest and Zadok the scribe, and of the Levites, Pedaiah; and next to them *was* Hanan the son of Zaccur,

the son of Mattaniah; for they were considered faithful, and their task *was* to distribute to their brethren.

¹⁴Remember me, O my God, concerning this, and do not wipe out my good deeds that I have done for the house of my God, and for its services!

¹⁵In those days I saw *people* in Judah treading wine presses on the Sabbath, and bringing in sheaves, and loading donkeys with wine, grapes, figs, and all *kinds of* burdens, which they brought into Jerusalem on the Sabbath day. And I warned *them* about the day on which they were selling provisions. ¹⁶Men of Tyre dwelt there also, who brought in fish and all kinds of goods, and sold *them* on the Sabbath to the children of Judah, and in Jerusalem.

¹⁷Then I contended with the nobles of Judah, and said to them, "What evil thing *is* this that you do, by which you profane the Sabbath day? ¹⁸Did not your fathers do thus, and did not our God bring all this disaster on us and on this city? Yet you bring added wrath on Israel by profaning the Sabbath."

¹⁹So it was, at the gates of Jerusalem, as it began to be dark before the Sabbath, that I commanded the gates to be shut, and charged that they must not be opened till after the Sabbath. Then I posted *some* of my servants at the gates, *so that* no burdens would be brought in on the Sabbath day. ²⁰Now the merchants and sellers of all kinds of wares lodged outside Jerusalem once or twice. ²¹Then I warned them, and said to them, "Why do you spend the night around the wall? If you do *so* again, I will lay hands on you!" From that time on they came no *more* on the Sabbath. ²²And I commanded the Levites that

they should cleanse themselves, and that they should go and guard the gates, to sanctify the Sabbath day.

Remember me, O my God, *concerning* this also, and spare me according to the greatness of Your mercy!

²³In those days I also saw Jews *who* had married women of Ashdod, Ammon, *and* Moab. ²⁴And half of their children spoke the language of Ashdod, and could not speak the language of Judah, but spoke according to the language of one or the other people.

²⁵So I contended with them and cursed them, struck some of them and pulled out their hair, and made them swear by God, *saying,* "You shall not give your daughters as wives to their sons, nor take their daughters for your sons or yourselves. ²⁶Did not Solomon king of Israel sin by these things? Yet among many nations there was no king like him, who was beloved of his God; and God made him king over all Israel. Nevertheless pagan women caused even him to sin. ²⁷Should we then hear of your doing all this great evil, transgressing against our God by marrying pagan women?"

²⁸And *one* of the sons of Joiada, the son of Eliashib the high priest, *was* a son-in-law of Sanballat the Horonite; therefore I drove him from me.

²⁹Remember them, O my God, because they have defiled the priesthood and the covenant of the priesthood and the Levites.

³⁰Thus I cleansed them of everything pagan. I also assigned duties to the priests and the Levites, each to his service, ³¹and to bringing the wood offering and the firstfruits at appointed times.

Remember me, O my God, for good!

ESTHER

The Story of a Woman—Beautiful Inside and Out

SUMMARY

While leadership principles can be found throughout the Scriptures, they are not taught systematically—just as no single doctrine is taught systematically through the 66 books of the Bible. Instead, God chooses to teach these principles experientially, through the lives of ordinary persons in history. That is precisely how leadership shows up in the Book of Esther.

If you look closely, you can spot a divine pattern. God always takes the initiative in executing His plan. Then He looks for a person who will submit to Him, makes that individual aware of a need, and the need quickly becomes the personal burden of the person God has chosen. Ultimately, the individual embraces God's plan and feels morally compelled to act on it. The vision becomes his or her possession. Finally, the person calls others to join the cause, often at great personal risk.

The Book of Esther tells the story of a woman who is beautiful both inside and out. Mordecai, an older cousin, takes her under his wing in her early years; in a sense, he becomes her mentor. As a gorgeous young Jewish woman, Esther is chosen to replace Queen Vashti as the consort of King Ahasuerus. She marries into the royal family and over the years deepens her influence.

Somewhere in the midst of her reign, a man named Haman feels snubbed by Mordecai and responds by making plans to exterminate the Jewish people. When Mordecai learns of the plot, he returns to his protégé, Queen Esther, and tries to convince her that she must stop this genocidal plan. After a moment of indecision, she agrees to take the enormous risk. Her courageous initiative, quick wit, charm, and poise in this desperate moment testify to the Jews that God will always raise up sufficient leadership for each crisis that emerges.

Esther joined the company of such illustrious deliverers as Joseph, who kept his people alive during the famine in Egypt; Moses, who led Israel out of slavery; Samson and David, who delivered the Hebrews from the Philistines; and Gideon, who delivered the people from the hand of the Midianites.

Esther tells the story of an ordinary person who fulfills an extraordinary leadership challenge in an unlikely context. She is a Jew in a foreign land and a woman in a male-dominated world—a minority within a minority. But God raised her up at exactly the right time.

God's Role in Esther

Esther is one of only two books in Scripture where the name of God does not appear even once (the Song of Solomon is the other). Why this amazing omission? Some have conjectured that the writer simply could not risk open worship of God. Whatever the reason, it doesn't really matter. While we may not see God's face anywhere in the book, we see His hand everywhere.

God's work can be clearly seen through His inner prompting of three leaders: Mordecai, King Xerxes, and Esther. In this great book, God's providence and Esther's preparation meet. We see this in Mordecai's phrase: "Yet who knows whether you have come to the kingdom for such a time as this?" (4:14).

The word "providence" comes from two root words: *pro*, meaning "before," and *video*, meaning "to see." God sees beforehand and orchestrates events to accomplish His purposes. First, God took Queen Vashti off the throne. Then, He gave the throne to Esther. Finally, He put the right people in the right places.

Leaders in Esther

King Xerxes, Mordecai, Haman, Esther

Other People of Influence in Esther

Hathach

Lessons in Leadership

- The first step a leader takes may be alone and at great risk.
- God is at work behind the scenes whenever you act on His Word.
- Every leader needs mentors.
- Great leaders act on behalf of their people and serve them.
- Timing is everything.

LEADERSHIP

HIGHLIGHTS IN ESTHER

ESTHER: Protector of the Messianic Line (2:1–17)	*page 600*
THE LAW OF RESPECT: Esther Stays Accountable to Mordecai (2:20–22)	*page 601*
MORDECAI: Refusing the Smallest Compromise (3:1–6)	*page 602*
ESTHER AND THE LAW OF TIMING: When to Lead Is As Important As What to Do and Where to Go (4:6–17)	*pages 604, 605*
THE LAW OF SOLID GROUND: God, Esther, and Haman (7:1–10)	*page 607*

The King Dethrones Queen Vashti

1 Now it came to pass in the days of Ahasuerus[a] (this *was* the Ahasuerus who reigned over one hundred and twenty-seven provinces, from India to Ethiopia), [2]in those days when King Ahasuerus sat on the throne of his kingdom, which *was* in Shushan[a] the citadel, [3]*that* in the third year of his reign he made a feast for all his officials and servants—the powers of Persia and Media, the nobles, and the princes of the provinces *being* before him— [4]when he showed the riches of his glorious kingdom and the splendor of his excellent majesty for many days, one hundred and eighty days *in all*.

[5]And when these days were completed, the king made a feast lasting seven days for all the people who were present in Shushan the citadel, from great to small, in the court of the garden of the king's palace. [6]*There were* white and blue linen *curtains* fastened with cords of fine linen and purple on silver rods and marble pillars; *and the* couches *were* of gold and silver on a *mosaic* pavement of alabaster, turquoise, and white and black marble. [7]And they served drinks in golden vessels, each vessel being different from the other, with royal wine in abundance, according to the generosity of the king. [8]In accordance with the law, the drinking was not compulsory; for so the king had ordered all the officers of his household, that they should do according to each man's pleasure.

[9]Queen Vashti also made a feast for the women *in* the royal palace which *belonged* to King Ahasuerus.

[10]On the seventh day, when the heart of the king was merry with wine, he commanded Mehuman, Biztha, Harbona, Bigtha, Abagtha, Zethar, and Carcas, seven eunuchs who served in the presence of King Ahasuerus, [11]to bring Queen Vashti before the king, *wearing* her royal crown, in order to show her beauty to the people and the officials, for she *was* beautiful to behold. [12]But Queen Vashti refused to come at the king's command *brought* by *his* eunuchs; therefore the king was furious, and his anger burned within him.

[13]Then the king said to the wise men who understood the times (for this *was* the king's manner toward all who knew law and justice, [14]those closest to him *being* Carshena, Shethar, Admatha, Tarshish, Meres, Marsena, and Memucan, the seven princes of Persia and Media, who had access to the king's presence, *and* who ranked highest in the kingdom): [15]"What *shall we* do to Queen Vashti, according to law, because she did not obey the command of King Ahasuerus *brought to her* by the eunuchs?"

The Law of Influence
(Esther 1:12)

When Queen Vashti refused to be put on display, King Ahasuerus grew angry. At the counsel of his advisors, he removed her from office, opening the door for Esther to take her spot. Esther serves as a marvelous illustration of how God uses one person's influence to accomplish His plans!

---

[16]And Memucan answered before the king and the princes: "Queen Vashti has not only wronged the king, but also all the princes, and all the people who *are* in all the provinces of King Ahasuerus. [17]For the queen's behavior will become known to all women, so that they will despise their husbands in their eyes, when they report, 'King Ahasuerus commanded Queen Vashti to be brought in before him, but she did not come.' [18]This very day the *noble* ladies of Persia and Media will say to all the king's officials that they have heard of the behavior of the queen. Thus *there will be* excessive contempt and wrath. [19]If it pleases the king, let a royal decree go out from him, and let it be recorded in the laws of the Persians and the Medes, so that it will not be altered, that Vashti shall come no more before King Ahasuerus; and let the king give her royal position to another who is better than she. [20]When the king's decree which he will make is proclaimed throughout all his empire (for it is great), all wives will honor their husbands, both great and small."

[21]And the reply pleased the king and the princes, and the king did according to the word of Memucan. [22]Then he sent letters to all the king's provinces, to each province in its own script, and to every people in their own language, that each man should be master in his own house, and speak in the language of his own people.

Esther Becomes Queen

2 After these things, when the wrath of King Ahasuerus subsided, he remembered Vashti, what she had done, and what had been decreed against her. [2]Then the king's servants who attended him said: "Let beautiful young virgins be sought for the king; [3]and let the

---

1:1 [a]Generally identified with Xerxes I (485–464 B.C.) **1:2** [a]Or *Susa,* and so throughout this book king appoint officers in all the provinces of his kingdom, that they may gather all the beautiful young virgins to Shushan the citadel, into the women's quarters, under the custody of Hegai[a] the king's eunuch, custodian of the women. And let beauty preparations be given *them*. [4]Then let the young woman who pleases the king be queen instead of Vashti."

This thing pleased the king, and he did so.

[5]In Shushan the citadel there was a certain Jew whose name *was* Mordecai the son of Jair, the son of Shimei, the son of Kish, a Benjamite. [6]*Kish*[a] had been carried away from Jerusalem with the captives who had been captured with Jeconiah[b] king of Judah, whom Nebuchadnezzar the king of Babylon had carried away. [7]And *Mordecai* had brought up Hadassah, that *is,* Esther, his uncle's daughter, for she had neither father nor mother. The young woman *was* lovely and beautiful. When her father and mother died, Mordecai took her as his own daughter.

[8]So it was, when the king's command and decree were heard, and when many young women were gathered at Shushan the citadel, *under* the custody of Hegai, that Esther also was taken to the king's palace, into the care of Hegai the custodian of the women. [9]Now the young woman pleased him, and she obtained his favor; so he readily gave beauty preparations to her, besides her allowance. Then seven choice maidservants were provided for her from the king's palace, and he moved her and her maidservants to the best *place* in the house of the women.

[10]Esther had not revealed her people or family, for Mordecai had charged her not to reveal *it*. [11]And every day Mordecai paced in front of the court of the women's quarters, to learn of Esther's welfare and what was happening to her.

[12]Each young woman's turn came to go in to King Ahasuerus after she had completed twelve months' preparation, according to the regulations for the women, for thus were the days of their preparation apportioned: six months with oil of myrrh, and six months with perfumes and preparations for beautifying women. [13]Thus *prepared,* each young woman went to the king, and she was given whatever she desired to take with her from the women's quarters to the king's palace. [14]In the evening she went, and in the morning she returned to the second house of the women, to the custody of Shaashgaz, the king's eunuch who kept the concubines. She would not go in to the

2:3 [a]Hebrew *Hege* **2:6** [a]Literally *Who* [b]Same as *Jehoiachin*, 2 Kings 24:6 and elsewhere

ESTHER PROTECTOR OF THE MESSIANIC LINE
(Esther 2:1–17)

PROFILE IN LEADERSHIP

By risking her life after rising to prominence, Esther, the captive Jewish orphan, protected the lineage of the coming Messiah. Her gift of intuition and exquisite sense of timing energized her leadership. Through the whole ordeal she remained humbly committed to her people and used her influence to save them all.

Through her kindness and gracious spirit, Esther found favor with the eunuch in charge of the candidates for queen. He rewarded her with a position of prominence and high visibility. During this time, Esther remained close to her foster father, Mordecai. She maintained a teachable spirit and did not lose sight of her origins. Thanks to these godly qualities, Mordecai was able to guide Esther through many potential land mines.

One sees the true nature of Esther's heart following her selection as queen. Here was a former peasant girl who easily could have gotten caught up in the pageantry and fame of royalty. Instead, Esther constantly reminded herself that she had received a God-given status for a reason. Her servant heart enabled her to risk her life for others. She had earned the trust of the king, used her intuition well, and really did come to the kingdom "for such a time as this" (Esth. 4:14).

king again unless the king delighted in her and called for her by name.

[15]Now when the turn came for Esther the daughter of Abihail the uncle of Mordecai, who had taken her as his daughter, to go in to the king, she requested nothing but what Hegai the king's eunuch, the custodian of the women, advised. And Esther obtained favor in the sight of all who saw her. [16]So Esther was taken to King Ahasuerus, into his royal palace, in the tenth month, which *is* the month of Tebeth, in the seventh year of his reign. [17]The king loved Esther more than all the *other* women, and she obtained grace and favor in his sight more than all the virgins; so he set the royal crown upon her head and made her queen instead of Vashti. [18]Then the king made a great feast, the Feast of Esther, for all his officials and servants; and he proclaimed a holiday in the provinces and gave gifts according to the generosity of a king.

Mordecai Discovers a Plot

[19]When virgins were gathered together a second time, Mordecai sat within the king's gate. [20]*Now* Esther had not revealed her family and her people, just as Mordecai had charged her, for Esther obeyed the command of Mordecai as when she was brought up by him.

[21]In those days, while Mordecai sat within the king's gate, two of the king's eunuchs, Bigthan and Teresh, doorkeepers, became furious and sought to lay hands on King Ahasuerus. [22]So the matter became known to Mordecai, who told Queen Esther, and Esther informed the king in Mordecai's name. [23]And when an inquiry was made into the matter, it was confirmed, and both were hanged on a gallows; and it was written in the book of the chronicles in the presence of the king.

Haman's Conspiracy Against the Jews

3 After these things King Ahasuerus promoted Haman, the son of Hammedatha the Agagite, and advanced him and set his seat above all the princes who *were* with him. [2]And all the king's servants who *were* within the king's gate bowed and paid homage to Haman, for so the king had commanded concerning him. But Mordecai would not bow or pay homage. [3]Then the king's servants who *were* within the king's gate said to Mordecai, "Why do you transgress the king's command?" [4]Now it happened, when they spoke to him daily and he would not listen to them, that they told *it* to Haman, to see whether Mordecai's words would stand; for *Mordecai* had told them that he *was* a Jew. [5]When Haman saw that Mordecai did not bow or pay him homage, Haman was filled with wrath. [6]But he disdained to lay hands on Mordecai alone, for they had told him of the people of Mordecai. Instead, Haman sought to destroy all the Jews who *were* throughout the

The Law of Respect:
Esther Stays Accountable to Mordecai
(Esther 2:20–22)

Esther was a beautiful young Jew being reared by her older cousin, Mordecai, in the days of the Persian captivity. When Esther found favor with the king and was chosen to become his next queen, the choice surprised both her and Mordecai. She would now hold a significant place of influence in the empire, even as a Jewish captive!

Because she had learned well the Law of Respect, she remained accountable to Mordecai's leadership and mentoring even after she moved into the palace. She listened and followed his counsel about concealing her identity as a Jew. His advice paid off, and the king selected her to be the queen of Persia.

What allowed Mordecai to continue to be a persuasive mentor in Esther's life, even though she became rich, famous, and influential? We see four reasons in chapter two:

1. *Relationship:* He had raised her and known her for years.
2. *Wisdom:* He intuitively knew what she should do when campaigning to be queen.
3. *Concern:* Every day he paced in front of Esther's court out of love and concern.
4. *Courage:* He informed Esther when he discovered a plot against the king.

whole kingdom of Ahasuerus—the people of Mordecai.

[7]In the first month, which is the month of Nisan, in the twelfth year of King Ahasuerus, they cast Pur (that *is,* the lot), before Haman to determine the day and the month,[a] until *it fell on the* twelfth *month,*[b] which *is* the month of Adar.

[8]Then Haman said to King Ahasuerus, "There is a certain people scattered and dispersed among the people in all the provinces of your kingdom; their laws *are* different from all *other* people's, and they do not keep the king's laws. Therefore it *is* not fitting for the king to let them remain. [9]If it pleases the king, let *a decree* be written that they be destroyed, and I will pay ten thousand talents of silver into the hands of those who do the work, to bring *it* into the king's treasuries."

[10]So the king took his signet ring from his hand and gave it to Haman, the son of Hammedatha the Agagite, the enemy of the Jews. [11]And the king said to Haman, "The money and the people *are* given to you, to do with them as seems good to you."

[12]Then the king's scribes were called on the thirteenth day of the first month, and *a decree* was written according to all that Haman com-

manded—to the king's satraps, to the governors who *were* over each province, to the officials of all people, to every province according to its script, and to every people in their language. In the name of King Ahasuerus it was written, and sealed with the king's signet ring. [13]And the letters were sent by couriers into all the king's provinces, to destroy, to kill, and to annihilate all the Jews, both young and old, little children and women, in one day, on the thirteenth *day* of the twelfth *month,* which *is* the month of Adar, and to plunder their possessions.[a] [14]A copy of the document was to be issued as law in every province, being published for all people, that they should be ready for that day. [15]The couriers went out, hastened by the king's command; and the decree was proclaimed in Shushan the citadel. So the king and Haman sat down to drink, but the city of Shushan was perplexed.

3:7 [a]Septuagint adds *to destroy the people of Mordecai in one day;* Vulgate adds *the nation of the Jews should be destroyed.* [b]Following Masoretic Text and Vulgate; Septuagint reads *and the lot fell on the fourteenth of the month.* **3:13** [a]Septuagint adds the text of the letter here.

MORDECAI

REFUSING THE SMALLEST COMPROMISE
(Esther 3:1–6)

PROFILE IN LEADERSHIP

Being God's kind of leader means refusing even the smallest compromise in what you believe. Mordecai was that kind of leader.

Mordecai wasn't going to bend—not one bit—when Haman, the newly appointed prime minister of Persia, demanded a show of reverence bordering on worship (Esth. 3:2). When the palace officials asked Mordecai why he refused to reverence the prime minister, he told them he was a Jew. And what difference did that make? The Lord Himself had said, "You shall have no other gods before Me. . . . You shall not bow down to them nor serve them" (Ex. 20:3, 5). Day after day these men tried to "talk some sense" into Mordecai; didn't Haman have the authority to execute him for his insolence?

Haman, in his arrogance and pride, decided not to challenge Mordecai directly, but to wipe out his whole race. In a plot eerily similar to the one carried out many centuries later in Nazi Germany, Haman decreed that Mordecai's people, the Jews, should be exterminated.

Mordecai, of course, paled at the news. Still, he held steadfastly to his refusal to dishonor his God by bowing before a mere man. In the end, through a twist utterly characteristic of the Lord, God honored Mordecai and exalted him before the very people who had begged him to compromise his principles.

Esther Agrees to Help the Jews

4 When Mordecai learned all that had happened, he tore his clothes and put on sackcloth and ashes, and went out into the midst of the city. He cried out with a loud and bitter cry. ²He went as far as the front of the king's gate, for no one *might* enter the king's gate clothed with sackcloth. ³And in every province where the king's command and decree arrived, *there was* great mourning among the Jews, with fasting, weeping, and wailing; and many lay in sackcloth and ashes.

⁴So Esther's maids and eunuchs came and told her, and the queen was deeply distressed. Then she sent garments to clothe Mordecai and take his sackcloth away from him, but he would not accept *them.* ⁵Then Esther called Hathach, *one* of the king's eunuchs whom he had appointed to attend her, and she gave him a command concerning Mordecai, to learn what and why this *was.* ⁶So Hathach went out to Mordecai in the city square that *was* in front of the king's gate. ⁷And Mordecai told him all that had happened to him, and the sum of money that Haman had promised to pay into the king's treasuries to destroy the Jews. ⁸He also gave him a copy of the written decree for their destruction, which was given at Shushan, that he might show it to Esther and explain it to her, and that he might command her to go in to the king to make supplication to him and plead before him for her people. ⁹So Hathach returned and told Esther the words of Mordecai.

¹⁰Then Esther spoke to Hathach, and gave him a command for Mordecai: ¹¹"All the king's servants and the people of the king's provinces know that any man or woman who goes into the inner court to the king, who has not been called, *he has* but one law: put *all* to death, except the one to whom the king holds out the golden scepter, that he may live. Yet I myself have not been called to go in to the king these thirty days." ¹²So they told Mordecai Esther's words.

¹³And Mordecai told *them* to answer Esther: "Do not think in your heart that you will escape in the king's palace any more than all the other Jews. ¹⁴For if you remain completely silent at this time, relief and deliverance will arise for the Jews from another place, but you and your father's house will perish. Yet who knows whether you have come to the kingdom for *such* a time as this?"

¹⁵Then Esther told *them* to reply to Mordecai: ¹⁶"Go, gather all the Jews who are present in Shushan, and fast for me; neither eat nor drink for three days, night or day. My maids and I will

The Law of Sacrifice: Esther Is Willing to Give Her Life for the People
(Esther 4:11–16)

After Mordecai confronts Esther about risking her life for her people, she makes a commitment to approach the king uninvited—even though such an appearance invited death (Esth. 4:11). Esther says simply, "I will go to the king, which is against the law; and if I perish, I perish!" (4:16). She took the step; she informed the king; she changed his mind; she saved the day.

Such is the life of a leader who practices the Law of Sacrifice. A leader must be willing to give up to go up.

Of course, leaders do this only when their cause becomes more important than their life. Jesus called His staff to deny themselves, take up their cross, and follow Him (Matt. 16:24). He told them that those who saved their lives would lose them. Esther put the cause of her people above her instinct for self-preservation—and not only lived, but enabled many others to live as well.

fast likewise. And so I will go to the king, which *is* against the law; and if I perish, I perish!"

¹⁷So Mordecai went his way and did according to all that Esther commanded him.ᵃ

Esther's Banquet

5 Now it happened on the third day that Esther put on *her* royal *robes* and stood in the inner court of the king's palace, across from the king's house, while the king sat on his royal throne in the royal house, facing the entrance of the house.ᵃ ²So it was, when the king saw Queen Esther standing in the court, *that* she found favor in his sight, and the king held out to Esther the golden scepter that *was* in his hand. Then Esther went near and touched the top of the scepter.

³And the king said to her, "What do you wish, Queen Esther? What *is* your request? It shall be given to you—up to half the kingdom!"

4:17 ᵃSeptuagint adds a prayer of Mordecai here.
5:1 ᵃSeptuagint adds many extra details in verses 1 and 2.

ESTHER AND THE LAW OF TIMING

When to Lead Is As Important As What to Do and Where to Go

(Esther 4:6–17)

When the right leader and the right moment come together, incredible things happen. Winston Churchill described it like this: "There comes a special moment in everyone's life, a moment for which that person was born. That special opportunity, when he seizes it, will fulfill his mission—a mission for which he is uniquely qualified. In that moment he finds greatness. It is his finest hour."

Reading a situation and knowing what to do are not enough to make you succeed in leadership. Only the right action at the right time will bring success. Anything else exacts a high price.

To be an effective leader, you must overcome whatever keeps you from moving forward. Like Esther, you must learn that if you don't seize the moment . . .

1. *Your fate will be like that of the rest of the crowd.*

Sometimes it's easy to buy in to the notion that we are special and won't have to take the risks of earlier generations. But that is a myth. If we don't take risks, we can never expect to rise to the occasion. Mordecai reminded Esther that even though she was queen, she would fare no better than the rest of the Jews if she didn't talk to the king.

2. *God will replace you with someone else.*

Mordecai motivated Esther by reminding her that God would accomplish His purposes even if she sat on the sidelines. It's not necessarily the giftedness of the leader that prompts God's blessing; it's more often the leader's willingness to move when and where He indicates.

3. *You could lose more than an opportunity.*

Mordecai reminded Esther that if she sat back and did nothing, she could lose more than a chance to do the right thing—she could lose her life. Although doing the right thing at the right time can seem risky, in the long run, leaders incur a greater risk by *not* taking action.

4. *You could miss out on your mission in life.*

Mordecai speculated that if Esther failed to act on behalf of her people, she might miss out on God's purpose for her life. You will never accomplish your mission by remaining idle. What paralyzes you? Fear? Image? Regardless of what keeps you from pursuing an opportunity, you will succeed only by making one timely decision after another.

There is no such thing as zero risk in leadership. But when you determine to seize a ripe opportunity despite the risk, you build momentum.

The Test of Timing

Make sure that each decision you make stands the test of timing. To help determine if it's the right time to seize an opportunity, consider the following:

1. *The Needs Around You*

When you keep a finger on the pulse of your people's basic needs, you will always find opportune times to lead.

Esther understood the needs of her people. She understood not only what they needed, but also what they needed *from her*. Get in touch with your people's needs. Then make a point to continually ask: What is their mood? What do they desire to accomplish? What do they need from me, their leader?

2. *The Opportunities Before You*

You find ripe opportunities only by looking for them. Early in Esther's leadership, Mordecai did much of the "spotting." He let her know each time he discerned a small window of opportunity. Esther learned from Mordecai's insight, and later discerned the opportune time to inform the king of Mordecai's actions. When you take the time to spot golden opportunities, they start to stick out.

3. *The Influencers Behind You*

Esther came to value Mordecai's opinion so much that she made sure he remained by her side throughout her reign. Before you make an important decision, ask your key influencers what they are feeling. Do they see the same opportunity you do? Are they discerning the same timing? When trying to discern the right time to take action, you must get feedback from your key people.

4. *The Successes Under You*

Experience provides practical advice, so take a minute to recall your successes. Have you done anything like this before? Is it reasonable to expect the same outcome from this decision?

Mordecai had to convince Esther about the right time to approach the king. Success in that incident gave her confidence for the future. Before long, Esther had gained so much influence with the king that he was asking her for advice.

5. *The Courage Within You*

Leadership requires courage—the courage to risk, to reach, and to put yourself on the line to seize an opportunity. The word *courage* comes from a French word that means "heart." Taking advantage of an opportunity at the right time requires heart.

Esther demonstrated tremendous courage, time after time. It took great heart to stand before the king. Fear tried to get her to back down—and fear will also try to get the better of you. But good leaders understand that ripe opportunities never come without fear. So they move forward despite a moment of hesitation.

[4]So Esther answered, "If it pleases the king, let the king and Haman come today to the banquet that I have prepared for him."

[5]Then the king said, "Bring Haman quickly, that he may do as Esther has said." So the king and Haman went to the banquet that Esther had prepared.

[6]At the banquet of wine the king said to Esther, "What *is* your petition? It shall be granted you. What *is* your request, up to half the kingdom? It shall be done!"

[7]Then Esther answered and said, "My petition and request *is this:* [8]If I have found favor in the sight of the king, and if it pleases the king to grant my petition and fulfill my request, then let the king and Haman come to the banquet which I will prepare for them, and tomorrow I will do as the king has said."

Haman's Plot Against Mordecai

[9]So Haman went out that day joyful and with a glad heart; but when Haman saw Mordecai in the king's gate, and that he did not stand or tremble before him, he was filled with indignation against Mordecai. [10]Nevertheless Haman restrained himself and went home, and he sent and called for his friends and his wife Zeresh. [11]Then Haman told them of his great riches, the multitude of his children, everything in which the king had promoted him, and how he had advanced him above the officials and servants of the king.

[12]Moreover Haman said, "Besides, Queen Esther invited no one but me to come in with the king to the banquet that she prepared; and tomorrow I am again invited by her, along with the king. [13]Yet all this avails me nothing, so long as I see Mordecai the Jew sitting at the king's gate."

[14]Then his wife Zeresh and all his friends said to him, "Let a gallows be made, fifty cubits high, and in the morning suggest to the king that Mordecai be hanged on it; then go merrily with the king to the banquet."

And the thing pleased Haman; so he had the gallows made.

The King Honors Mordecai

6 That night the king could not sleep. So one was commanded to bring the book of the records of the chronicles; and they were read before the king. [2]And it was found written that Mordecai had told of Bigthana and Teresh, two of the king's eunuchs, the doorkeepers who had sought to lay hands on King Ahasuerus. [3]Then the king said, "What honor or dignity has been bestowed on Mordecai for this?"

And the king's servants who attended him said, "Nothing has been done for him."

[4]So the king said, "Who *is* in the court?" Now Haman had *just* entered the outer court of the king's palace to suggest that the king hang Mordecai on the gallows that he had prepared for him.

[5]The king's servants said to him, "Haman is there, standing in the court."

And the king said, "Let him come in."

[6]So Haman came in, and the king asked him, "What shall be done for the man whom the king delights to honor?"

Now Haman thought in his heart, "Whom would the king delight to honor more than me?" [7]And Haman answered the king, "*For* the man whom the king delights to honor, [8]let a royal robe be brought which the king has worn, and a horse on which the king has ridden, which has a royal crest placed on its head. [9]Then let this robe and horse be delivered to the hand of one of the king's most noble princes, that he may array the man whom the king delights to honor. Then parade him on horseback through the city square, and proclaim before him: 'Thus shall it be done to the man whom the king delights to honor!'"

[10]Then the king said to Haman, "Hurry, take the robe and the horse, as you have suggested, and do so for Mordecai the Jew who sits within the king's gate! Leave nothing undone of all that you have spoken."

[11]So Haman took the robe and the horse, arrayed Mordecai and led him on horseback through the city square, and proclaimed before him, "Thus shall it be done to the man whom the king delights to honor!"

[12]Afterward Mordecai went back to the king's gate. But Haman hurried to his house, mourning and with his head covered. [13]When Haman told his wife Zeresh and all his friends everything that had happened to him, his wise men and his wife Zeresh said to him, "If Mordecai, before whom you have begun to fall, is of Jewish descent, you will not prevail against him but will surely fall before him."

[14]While they *were* still talking with him, the king's eunuchs came, and hastened to bring Haman to the banquet which Esther had prepared.

Haman Hanged Instead of Mordecai

7 So the king and Haman went to dine with Queen Esther. [2]And on the second day, at the banquet of wine, the king again said to Esther, "What *is* your petition, Queen Esther? It shall be granted you. And what *is* your request, up to half the kingdom? It shall be done!"

The Law of Solid Ground: God, Esther, and Haman

(Esther 7:1–10)

God, Esther, and Haman each play a leading role in the Book of Esther. God is the Leader in control; Esther is the leader under control; and Haman is the leader out of control. Consider each one.

God: The Leader in Control
1. He took Queen Vashti off the throne.
2. He gave Esther the throne.
3. He used Mordecai to supply information.
4. He put everyone in place before the crisis.

Esther: The Leader Under Control
1. Her position didn't steal her compassion.
2. She felt limited in what she could do.
3. She knew her place in the organization.
4. She felt the need to fast and pray.
5. She depended on the prayers of others.
6. She was willing to take a risk and obey.
7. She didn't take advantage of generosity.
8. She recognized the importance of timing.

Haman: The Leader out of Control
1. He misunderstood the times.
2. He lost joy over little problems.
3. He needed friends to build his self-image.
4. His greed and ambition made him unhappy.
5. He listened to the wrong people.
6. He thought too highly of himself.
7. He set himself up for a fall.
8. He reaped what he sowed.

³Then Queen Esther answered and said, "If I have found favor in your sight, O king, and if it pleases the king, let my life be given me at my petition, and my people at my request. ⁴For we have been sold, my people and I, to be destroyed, to be killed, and to be annihilated. Had we been sold as male and female slaves, I would have held my tongue, although the enemy could never compensate for the king's loss."

⁵So King Ahasuerus answered and said to Queen Esther, "Who is he, and where is he, who would dare presume in his heart to do such a thing?"

⁶And Esther said, "The adversary and enemy *is* this wicked Haman!"

So Haman was terrified before the king and queen.

⁷Then the king arose in his wrath from the banquet of wine *and went* into the palace garden; but Haman stood before Queen Esther, pleading for his life, for he saw that evil was determined against him by the king. ⁸When the king returned from the palace garden to the place of the banquet of wine, Haman had fallen across the couch where Esther *was.* Then the king said, "Will he also assault the queen while I *am* in the house?"

As the word left the king's mouth, they covered Haman's face. ⁹Now Harbonah, one of the eunuchs, said to the king, "Look! The gallows, fifty cubits high, which Haman made for Mordecai, who spoke good on the king's behalf, is standing at the house of Haman."

Then the king said, "Hang him on it!"

¹⁰So they hanged Haman on the gallows that he had prepared for Mordecai. Then the king's wrath subsided.

Esther Saves the Jews

8 On that day King Ahasuerus gave Queen Esther the house of Haman, the enemy of the Jews. And Mordecai came before the king, for Esther had told how he *was related* to her. ²So the king took off his signet ring, which he had taken from Haman, and gave it to Mordecai; and Esther appointed Mordecai over the house of Haman.

³Now Esther spoke again to the king, fell down at his feet, and implored him with tears to counteract the evil of Haman the Agagite, and

The Law of Solid Ground: Mordecai Gets a Reward

(Esther 8:1, 2)

Twice Mordecai protected the king from destructive leaders, and twice he was rewarded. He reaped the benefits of a track record that showed him to be a leader who could be trusted. He demonstrates that a leader cannot be successful unless other people want him to be.

the scheme which he had devised against the Jews. [4]And the king held out the golden scepter toward Esther. So Esther arose and stood before the king, [5]and said, "If it pleases the king, and if I have found favor in his sight and the thing *seems* right to the king and I am pleasing in his eyes, let it be written to revoke the letters devised by Haman, the son of Hammedatha the Agagite, which he wrote to annihilate the Jews who *are* in all the king's provinces. [6]For how can I endure to see the evil that will come to my people? Or how can I endure to see the destruction of my countrymen?"

[7]Then King Ahasuerus said to Queen Esther and Mordecai the Jew, "Indeed, I have given Esther the house of Haman, and they have hanged him on the gallows because he *tried to* lay his hand on the Jews. [8]You yourselves write *a decree* concerning the Jews, as you please, in the king's name, and seal *it* with the king's signet ring; for whatever is written in the king's name and sealed with the king's signet ring no one can revoke."

[9]So the king's scribes were called at that time, in the third month, which *is* the month of Sivan, on the twenty-third *day;* and it was written, according to all that Mordecai commanded, to the Jews, the satraps, the governors, and the princes of the provinces from India to Ethiopia, one hundred and twenty-seven provinces *in all,* to every province in its own script, to every people in their own language, and to the Jews in their own script and language. [10]And he wrote in the name of King Ahasuerus, sealed *it* with the king's signet ring, and sent letters by couriers on horseback, riding on royal horses bred from swift steeds.[a]

[11]By these letters the king permitted the Jews who *were* in every city to gather together and protect their lives—to destroy, kill, and annihilate all the forces of any people or province that would assault them, *both* little children and women, and to plunder their possessions, [12]on one day in all the provinces of King Ahasuerus, on the thirteenth *day* of the twelfth month, which *is* the month of Adar.[a] [13]A copy of the document was to be issued as a decree in every province and published for all people, so that the Jews would be ready on that day to avenge themselves on their enemies. [14]The couriers who rode on royal horses went out, hastened and pressed on by the king's command. And the decree was issued in Shushan the citadel.

[15]So Mordecai went out from the presence of the king in royal apparel of blue and white, with a great crown of gold and a garment of fine linen and purple; and the city of Shushan rejoiced and was glad. [16]The Jews had light and gladness, joy and honor. [17]And in every province and city, wherever the king's command and decree came, the Jews had joy and gladness, a feast and a holiday. Then many of the people of the land became Jews, because fear of the Jews fell upon them.

The Jews Destroy Their Tormentors

9 Now in the twelfth month, that *is,* the month of Adar, on the thirteenth day, *the time* came for the king's command and his decree to be executed. On the day that the enemies of the Jews had hoped to overpower them, the opposite occurred, in that the Jews themselves overpowered those who hated them. [2]The Jews gathered together in their cities throughout all the provinces of King Ahasuerus to lay hands on those who sought their harm. And no one could withstand them, because fear of them fell upon all people. [3]And all the officials of the provinces, the satraps, the governors, and all those doing the king's work, helped the Jews, because the fear of Mordecai fell upon them. [4]For Mordecai *was* great in the king's palace, and his fame spread throughout all the provinces; for this man Mordecai became increasingly prominent. [5]Thus the Jews defeated all their enemies with the stroke of the sword, with slaughter and destruction, and did what they pleased with those who hated them.

[6]And in Shushan the citadel the Jews killed and destroyed five hundred men. [7]Also Parshandatha, Dalphon, Aspatha, [8]Poratha, Adalia, Aridatha, [9]Parmashta, Arisai, Aridai, and Vajezatha— [10]the ten sons of Haman the son of Hammedatha, the enemy of the Jews—they killed; but they did not lay a hand on the plunder.

[11]On that day the number of those who were killed in Shushan the citadel was brought to the king. [12]And the king said to Queen Esther, "The Jews have killed and destroyed five hundred men in Shushan the citadel, and the ten sons of Haman. What have they done in the rest of the king's provinces? Now what *is* your petition? It shall be granted to you. Or what *is* your further request? It shall be done."

[13]Then Esther said, "If it pleases the king, let it be granted to the Jews who *are* in Shushan to do again tomorrow according to today's decree, and let Haman's ten sons be hanged on the gallows."

8:10 [a]Literally *sons of the swift horses*
8:12 [a]Septuagint adds the text of the letter here.

[14]So the king commanded this to be done; the decree was issued in Shushan, and they hanged Haman's ten sons.

[15]And the Jews who *were* in Shushan gathered together again on the fourteenth day of the month of Adar and killed three hundred men at Shushan; but they did not lay a hand on the plunder.

[16]The remainder of the Jews in the king's provinces gathered together and protected their lives, had rest from their enemies, and killed seventy-five thousand of their enemies; but they did not lay a hand on the plunder. [17]This *was* on the thirteenth day of the month of Adar. And on the fourteenth of *the month*[a] they rested and made it a day of feasting and gladness.

The Feast of Purim

[18]But the Jews who *were* at Shushan assembled together on the thirteenth *day,* as well as on the fourteenth; and on the fifteenth of *the month*[a] they rested, and made it a day of feasting and gladness. [19]Therefore the Jews of the villages who dwelt in the unwalled towns celebrated the fourteenth day of the month of Adar *with* gladness and feasting, as a holiday, and for sending presents to one another.

[20]And Mordecai wrote these things and sent letters to all the Jews, near and far, who *were* in all the provinces of King Ahasuerus, [21]to establish among them that they should celebrate yearly the fourteenth and fifteenth days of the month of Adar, [22]as the days on which the Jews had rest from their enemies, as the month which was turned from sorrow to joy for them, and from mourning to a holiday; that they should make them days of feasting and joy, of sending presents to one another and gifts to the poor. [23]So the Jews accepted the custom which they had begun, as Mordecai had written to them, [24]because Haman, the son of Hammedatha the Agagite, the enemy of all the Jews, had plotted against the Jews to annihilate them, and had cast Pur (that *is,* the lot), to consume them and destroy them; [25]but when *Esther*[a] came before the king, he commanded by letter that this[b] wicked plot which *Haman* had devised against the Jews should return on his own head, and that he and his sons should be hanged on the gallows.

[26]So they called these days Purim, after the name Pur. Therefore, because of all the words of this letter, what they had seen concerning this matter, and what had happened to them, [27]the Jews established and imposed it upon themselves and their descendants and all who would join them, that without fail they should celebrate these two days every year, according to the written *instructions* and according to the *prescribed* time, [28]that these days *should be* remembered and kept throughout every generation, every family, every province, and every city, that these days of Purim should not fail *to be observed* among the Jews, and *that* the memory of them should not perish among their descendants.

[29]Then Queen Esther, the daughter of Abihail, with Mordecai the Jew, wrote with full authority to confirm this second letter about Purim. [30]And *Mordecai* sent letters to all the Jews, to the one hundred and twenty-seven provinces of the kingdom of Ahasuerus, *with* words of peace and truth, [31]to confirm these days of Purim at their *appointed* time, as Mordecai the Jew and Queen Esther had prescribed for them, and as they had decreed for themselves and their descendants concerning matters of their fasting and lamenting. [32]So the decree of Esther confirmed these matters of Purim, and it was written in the book.

Mordecai's Advancement

10 And King Ahasuerus imposed tribute on the land and *on* the islands of the sea. [2]Now all the acts of his power and his might, and the account of the greatness of Mordecai, to which the king advanced him, *are* they not written in the book of the chronicles of the kings of Media and Persia? [3]For Mordecai the Jew *was* second to King Ahasuerus, and was great among the Jews and well received by the multitude of his brethren, seeking the good of his people and speaking peace to all his countrymen.[a]

9:17 [a]Literally *it* **9:18** [a]Literally *it* **9:25** [a]Literally *she* or *it* [b]Literally *his* **10:3** [a]Literally *seed.* Septuagint and Vulgate add a dream of Mordecai here; Vulgate adds six more chapters.

JOB
Reputation for Integrity Makes a Strong Leader

SUMMARY

Job's 42 chapters describe one man's hellish loss of nearly everything he holds dear, including his ten children. The book begins by describing Job as blameless and upright, a man who shuns evil. His reputation for integrity makes him a strong leader within his family and community. He has amassed a considerable fortune and demonstrates great wisdom in his business and community affairs. It would be difficult to imagine a better leadership model than Job—discerning, industrious, devoted to God and family, successful, and well-thought-of by his colleagues.

And that is exactly what makes his story so troubling. In no time at all, he loses it all. Through no fault of his own, he must deal with tragedy in its deepest forms. Yet how he deals with it provides a beautiful case study in character, integrity, credibility, patience, and poise.

First, Job maintains perspective. Immediately after hearing the first round of tragic news, he falls to the ground and worships (1:20). He knows that unless he consciously remains subject to God's authority, he will react with bitterness and rancor. He maintains a big-picture perspective.

Next, Job does some soul searching. He looks within and asks whether anything needs correction—something only a secure person can do.

Third, Job begins to ask questions of God and others. Yet even in his complaints, he never abandons his commitment to God or his core values.

Finally, Job determines to continue trusting the process. At one point he declares, "Though He slay me, yet will I trust Him" (13:15). Job decides to await God's response; he will continue to rely on divine insight.

Yet that is not the end of his sad story. To compound his dilemma, four "friends" approach Job to offer their counsel. They offer several explanations for why all of this is happening, centering around the theme, "You must have sinned."

The majority of the book features three cycles of debate between Eliphaz, Bildad, Zophar (and Elihu) on one side, and Job on the other. After Job's "friends" present their futile arguments, God steps in with a series of probing questions. Job realizes his presumption and sincerely repents. He acknowledges that God is God and that he has no right to second-guess the Omniscient One. Then, as a leader who always takes the "high road," Job prays for his four friends that God would show them mercy for their foolish words.

God's Role in Job

God plays the part of the C.E.O. who finds Himself needing to cast the vision to those who have lost sight of it. In the same way that a supervisor must repeatedly communicate the "big picture" to employees who see things only from their departmental perspective, God shows up at the end of the book to correct all five speakers. He asks, "Where were you when I laid the foundations of the earth?" (38:4). God plays the leader's role, providing perspective for the characters in the story.

Leaders in Job

Job

Other People of Influence in Job

Eliphaz, Bildad, Zophar, Elihu

Lessons in Leadership

- Mature leaders maintain perspective, especially when things don't go according to plan.
- Good leaders remain teachable and choose their counselors wisely.
- Integrity and character are the foundations for leadership.
- Never pretend or presume to have all the answers.
- We can live without having all the answers.
- Effective leaders can adjust when things go wrong.

LEADERSHIP

HIGHLIGHTS IN JOB

Job and His Family in Uz

1 There was a man in the land of Uz, whose name *was* Job; and that man was blameless and upright, and one who feared God and shunned evil. ²And seven sons and three daughters were born to him. ³Also, his possessions were seven thousand sheep, three thousand camels, five hundred yoke of oxen, five hundred female donkeys, and a very large household, so that this man was the greatest of all the people of the East.

⁴And his sons would go and feast *in their* houses, each on his *appointed* day, and would send and invite their three sisters to eat and drink with them. ⁵So it was, when the days of feasting had run their course, that Job would send and sanctify them, and he would rise early in the morning and offer burnt offerings *according to* the number of them all. For Job said, "It may be that my sons have sinned and cursed[a] God in their hearts." Thus Job did regularly.

Satan Attacks Job's Character

⁶Now there was a day when the sons of God came to present themselves before the LORD, and Satan[a] also came among them. ⁷And the LORD said to Satan, "From where do you come?"

So Satan answered the LORD and said, "From going to and fro on the earth, and from walking back and forth on it."

⁸Then the LORD said to Satan, "Have you considered My servant Job, that *there is* none like him on the earth, a blameless and upright man, one who fears God and shuns evil?"

⁹So Satan answered the LORD and said, "Does Job fear God for nothing? ¹⁰Have You not made a hedge around him, around his household, and around all that he has on every side? You have blessed the work of his hands, and his possessions have increased in the land. ¹¹But now, stretch out Your hand and touch all that he has, and he will surely curse You to Your face!"

¹²And the LORD said to Satan, "Behold, all that he has *is* in your power; only do not lay a hand on his *person*."

So Satan went out from the presence of the LORD.

Job Loses His Property and Children

¹³Now there was a day when his sons and daughters *were* eating and drinking wine in their oldest brother's house; ¹⁴and a messenger came to Job and said, "The oxen were plowing and the donkeys feeding beside them, ¹⁵when the Sabeans[a] raided *them* and took them away—indeed they have killed the servants with the edge of the sword; and I alone have escaped to tell you!"

¹⁶While he *was* still speaking, another also came and said, "The fire of God fell from heaven and burned up the sheep and the servants, and consumed them; and I alone have escaped to tell you!"

1:5 [a]Literally *blessed,* but used here in the evil sense, and so in verse 11 and 2:5, 9　**1:6** [a]Literally *the Adversary,* and so throughout this book
1:15 [a]Literally *Sheba* (compare 6:19)

Self-Discipline: Job Maintains Perspective

(Job 1:1–22)

All hell broke loose. The man lost almost everything: his livestock, his land, his home, and even his children.

Job was a disciplined person, however. He lived his life from his character, not his emotions. Consequently, Job maintained perspective when terrible tragedy struck him: "Then Job arose, tore his robe, and shaved his head; and he fell to the ground and worshiped" (Job 1:20). The Scripture later tells us that in all the crises he faced, Job never sinned against God with his words (2:10). He maintained his sense of integrity all the way through his ordeal.

Wow! What discipline! Job modeled a valuable leadership posture for us. Note the sequence of remarkable events in his life:

1. *Worship:* Job worshiped and articulated God's sovereignty in his life.
2. *Perspective:* Worship enabled Job to capture God's perspective and power.
3. *Humility:* Perspective allowed Job to see his limited knowledge.
4. *Teachability:* Humility caused Job to hunger and seek God's insight.
5. *Victory:* Teachability ultimately led Job to gain victory over his losses.

¹⁷While he *was* still speaking, another also came and said, "The Chaldeans formed three bands, raided the camels and took them away, yes, and killed the servants with the edge of the sword; and I alone have escaped to tell you!"

¹⁸While he *was* still speaking, another also came and said, "Your sons and daughters *were* eating and drinking wine in their oldest brother's house, ¹⁹and suddenly a great wind came from across[a] the wilderness and struck the four corners of the house, and it fell on the young people, and they are dead; and I alone have escaped to tell you!"

²⁰Then Job arose, tore his robe, and shaved his head; and he fell to the ground and worshiped. ²¹And he said:

"Naked I came from my mother's womb,
  And naked shall I return there.
  The LORD gave, and the LORD has taken away;
  Blessed be the name of the LORD."

²²In all this Job did not sin nor charge God with wrong.

Satan Attacks Job's Health

2 Again there was a day when the sons of God came to present themselves before the LORD, and Satan came also among them to present himself before the LORD. ²And the LORD said to Satan, "From where do you come?"

Satan answered the LORD and said, "From going to and fro on the earth, and from walking back and forth on it."

³Then the LORD said to Satan, "Have you considered My servant Job, that *there is* none like him on the earth, a blameless and upright man, one who fears God and shuns evil? And still he holds fast to his integrity, although you incited Me against him, to destroy him without cause."

⁴So Satan answered the LORD and said, "Skin for skin! Yes, all that a man has he will give for his life. ⁵But stretch out Your hand now, and touch his bone and his flesh, and he will surely curse You to Your face!"

⁶And the LORD said to Satan, "Behold, he *is* in your hand, but spare his life."

⁷So Satan went out from the presence of the LORD, and struck Job with painful boils from the sole of his foot to the crown of his head. ⁸And he took for himself a potsherd with which to scrape himself while he sat in the midst of the ashes.

⁹Then his wife said to him, "Do you still hold fast to your integrity? Curse God and die!"

¹⁰But he said to her, "You speak as one of the foolish women speaks. Shall we indeed accept good from God, and shall we not accept adversity?" In all this Job did not sin with his lips.

Job's Three Friends

¹¹Now when Job's three friends heard of all this adversity that had come upon him, each one came from his own place—Eliphaz the Temanite, Bildad the Shuhite, and Zophar the Naamathite. For they had made an appointment together to come and mourn with him, and to comfort him. ¹²And when they raised their eyes from afar, and did not recognize him, they lifted their voices and wept; and each one tore his robe and sprinkled dust on his head toward heaven. ¹³So they sat down with him on the ground seven days and seven nights, and no one spoke a word to him, for they saw that *his* grief was very great.

1:19 [a]Septuagint omits *across*.

Listening: To Connect with Job, His Friends Listen for a Week

(Job 2:11–13)

When Job's friends hear about his catastrophe, they want to help. By this time, boils have broken out all over Job's body, and his friends don't even recognize him. They feel his pain and are horrified to see a friend in such need. Mercifully, they keep their mouths shut for one whole week (if only they had continued their silence!). They sit with their friend and listen.

Somehow these friends realized an important truth: People don't lose intimacy when they stop talking, but when they stop listening. Leaders seldom realize how much their listening empowers the other person. Because they are leaders, the sheer act of listening speaks volumes that even a great speech can't communicate. Listening . . .

- Communicates the value of the other person and his or her thoughts.
- Communicates love and understanding and care for their needs.
- Communicates a desire to grow, learn, and remain teachable.

Job Deplores His Birth

3 After this Job opened his mouth and cursed the day of his *birth*. ²And Job spoke, and said:

³ "May the day perish on which I was
        born,
    And the night *in which* it was said,
  'A male child is conceived.'
⁴ May that day be darkness;
    May God above not seek it,
    Nor the light shine upon it.
⁵ May darkness and the shadow of death
        claim it;
    May a cloud settle on it;
    May the blackness of the day terrify it.
⁶ *As for* that night, may darkness seize it;
    May it not rejoiceᵃ among the days of the
        year,
    May it not come into the number of the
        months.
⁷ Oh, may that night be barren!
    May no joyful shout come into it!
⁸ May those curse it who curse the day,
    Those who are ready to arouse Leviathan.
⁹ May the stars of its morning be dark;
    May it look for light, but *have* none,
    And not see the dawning of the day;
¹⁰ Because it did not shut up the doors of my
        mother's womb,
    Nor hide sorrow from my eyes.

¹¹ "Why did I not die at birth?
    Why did I *not* perish when I came from
        the womb?
¹² Why did the knees receive me?
    Or why the breasts, that I should nurse?
¹³ For now I would have lain still and been
        quiet,
    I would have been asleep;
    Then I would have been at rest
¹⁴ With kings and counselors of the earth,
    Who built ruins for themselves,
¹⁵ Or with princes who had gold,
    Who filled their houses *with* silver;
¹⁶ Or *why* was I not hidden like a stillborn
        child,
    Like infants who never saw light?
¹⁷ There the wicked cease *from* troubling,
    And there the weary are at rest.
¹⁸ *There* the prisoners rest together;
    They do not hear the voice of the
        oppressor.
¹⁹ The small and great are there,
    And the servant *is* free from his master.

²⁰ "Why is light given to him who is in
        misery,
    And life to the bitter of soul,
²¹ Who long for death, but it does not *come,*
    And search for it more than hidden
        treasures;
²² Who rejoice exceedingly,
    And are glad when they can find the
        grave?
²³ *Why is light given* to a man whose way is
        hidden,
    And whom God has hedged in?
²⁴ For my sighing comes before I eat,ᵃ
    And my groanings pour out like water.
²⁵ For the thing I greatly feared has come
        upon me,
    And what I dreaded has happened to me.
²⁶ I am not at ease, nor am I quiet;
    I have no rest, for trouble comes."

Eliphaz: Job Has Sinned

4 Then Eliphaz the Temanite answered and said:

² "*If* one attempts a word with you, will you
        become weary?
    But who can withhold himself from
        speaking?
³ Surely you have instructed many,
    And you have strengthened weak hands.
⁴ Your words have upheld him who was
        stumbling,
    And you have strengthened the feeble
        knees;
⁵ But now it comes upon you, and you are
        weary;
    It touches you, and you are troubled.
⁶ *Is* not your reverence your confidence?
    And the integrity of your ways your hope?

⁷ "Remember now, who *ever* perished being
        innocent?
    Or where were the upright *ever* cut off?
⁸ Even as I have seen,
    Those who plow iniquity
    And sow trouble reap the same.
⁹ By the blast of God they perish,
    And by the breath of His anger they are
        consumed.
¹⁰ The roaring of the lion,
    The voice of the fierce lion,
    And the teeth of the young lions are
        broken.

3:6 ᵃSeptuagint, Syriac, Targum, and Vulgate read *be joined.* **3:24** ᵃLiterally *my bread*

11 The old lion perishes for lack of prey,
And the cubs of the lioness are scattered.

12 "Now a word was secretly brought to me,
And my ear received a whisper of it.

13 In disquieting thoughts from the visions of
the night,
When deep sleep falls on men,

14 Fear came upon me, and trembling,
Which made all my bones shake.

15 Then a spirit passed before my face;
The hair on my body stood up.

16 It stood still,
But I could not discern its appearance.
A form *was* before my eyes;
There was silence;
Then I heard a voice *saying:*

17 'Can a mortal be more righteous than God?
Can a man be more pure than his Maker?

18 If He puts no trust in His servants,
If He charges His angels with error,

19 How much more those who dwell in
houses of clay,
Whose foundation is in the dust,
Who are crushed before a moth?

20 They are broken in pieces from morning
till evening;
They perish forever, with no one
regarding.

21 Does not their own excellence go away?
They die, even without wisdom.'

Eliphaz: Job Is Chastened by God

5 "Call out now;
Is there anyone who will answer you?
And to which of the holy ones will you
turn?

2 For wrath kills a foolish man,
And envy slays a simple one.

3 I have seen the foolish taking root,
But suddenly I cursed his dwelling place.

4 His sons are far from safety,
They are crushed in the gate,
And *there is* no deliverer.

5 Because the hungry eat up his harvest,
Taking it even from the thorns,[a]
And a snare snatches their substance.[b]

6 For affliction does not come from the
dust,
Nor does trouble spring from the ground;

7 Yet man is born to trouble,
As the sparks fly upward.

8 "But as for me, I would seek God,
And to God I would commit my cause—

9 Who does great things, and unsearchable,

Marvelous things without number.

10 He gives rain on the earth,
And sends waters on the fields.

11 He sets on high those who are lowly,
And those who mourn are lifted to safety.

12 He frustrates the devices of the crafty,
So that their hands cannot carry out their
plans.

13 He catches the wise in their own
craftiness,
And the counsel of the cunning comes
quickly upon them.

14 They meet with darkness in the daytime,
And grope at noontime as in the night.

15 But He saves the needy from the sword,
From the mouth of the mighty,
And from their hand.

16 So the poor have hope,
And injustice shuts her mouth.

17 "Behold, happy *is* the man whom God
corrects;
Therefore do not despise the chastening of
the Almighty.

18 For He bruises, but He binds up;
He wounds, but His hands make whole.

19 He shall deliver you in six troubles,
Yes, in seven no evil shall touch you.

20 In famine He shall redeem you from
death,
And in war from the power of the sword.

21 You shall be hidden from the scourge of
the tongue,
And you shall not be afraid of destruction
when it comes.

22 You shall laugh at destruction and famine,
And you shall not be afraid of the beasts of
the earth.

23 For you shall have a covenant with the
stones of the field,
And the beasts of the field shall be at
peace with you.

24 You shall know that your tent *is* in peace;
You shall visit your dwelling and find
nothing amiss.

25 You shall also know that your descendants
shall be many,
And your offspring like the grass of the
earth.

26 You shall come to the grave at a full age,

5:5 [a]Septuagint reads *They shall not be taken from evil
men;* Vulgate reads *And the armed man shall take him
by violence.* [b]Septuagint reads *The might shall draw
them off;* Vulgate reads *And the thirsty shall drink up
their riches.*

As a sheaf of grain ripens in its season.

27 Behold, this we have searched out;
It *is* true.
Hear it, and know for yourself."

Job: My Complaint Is Just

6 Then Job answered and said:

2 "Oh, that my grief were fully
weighed,
And my calamity laid with it on the
scales!

3 For then it would be heavier than the sand
of the sea—
Therefore my words have been rash.

4 For the arrows of the Almighty *are* within
me;
My spirit drinks in their poison;
The terrors of God are arrayed against me.

5 Does the wild donkey bray when it has
grass,
Or does the ox low over its fodder?

6 Can flavorless food be eaten without salt?
Or is there *any* taste in the white of an
egg?

7 My soul refuses to touch *them*;
They *are* as loathsome food to me.

8 "Oh, that I might have my request,
That God would grant *me* the thing that I
long for!

9 That it would please God to crush me,
That He would loose His hand and cut
me off!

10 Then I would still have comfort;
Though in anguish I would exult,
He will not spare;
For I have not concealed the words of the
Holy One.

11 "What strength do I have, that I should
hope?
And what *is* my end, that I should prolong
my life?

12 *Is* my strength the strength of stones?
Or is my flesh bronze?

13 *Is* my help not within me?
And is success driven from me?

14 "To him who is afflicted, kindness *should be
shown* by his friend,
Even though he forsakes the fear of the
Almighty.

15 My brothers have dealt deceitfully like a
brook,
Like the streams of the brooks that pass
away,

16 Which are dark because of the ice,
And into which the snow vanishes.

17 When it is warm, they cease to flow;
When it is hot, they vanish from their place.

18 The paths of their way turn aside,

Integrity: Job Challenges His Friends to Identify His Flaws

(Job 6:1—7:21)

All of Job's friends posed a theory about his troubles, but Job simply asked them to survey his life and point out any place where he lacked integrity. He felt so certain of the blamelessness of his heart that he invited the scrutiny of his peers. Only a leader with strong character and a strong sense of security can do that!

C. S. Lewis calls this quality, "Leaders with chests." Lewis likened the properly ordered soul to the human body: the head (reason) must rule the belly (the sensual appetites) through the chest (character and spirit). The chest is the indispensable liaison between reason and the appetites. Without a strong "chest," men would succumb to excuses, relativism, and compromise. Lewis called those with no character or integrity, "men without chests."

What enabled Job to possess such integrity as a leader?

1. *Strong Security:* He felt emotionally secure enough to take criticism.
2. *Clear Conscience:* He kept a clear and sensitive conscience regarding sin.
3. *Pure Motives:* He refused to entertain self-indulgent motives.
4. *Solid Character:* He was committed to doing the right thing at any cost.

19 They go nowhere and perish.
The caravans of Tema look,
The travelers of Sheba hope for them.
20 They are disappointed because they were
confident;
They come there and are confused.
21 For now you are nothing,
You see terror and are afraid.
22 Did I ever say, 'Bring *something* to me'?
Or, 'Offer a bribe for me from your wealth'?
23 Or, 'Deliver me from the enemy's hand'?
Or, 'Redeem me from the hand of
oppressors'?

24 "Teach me, and I will hold my tongue;
Cause me to understand wherein I have
erred.
25 How forceful are right words!
But what does your arguing prove?
26 Do you intend to rebuke *my* words,
And the speeches of a desperate one, *which
are* as wind?
27 Yes, you overwhelm the fatherless,
And you undermine your friend.
28 Now therefore, be pleased to look at me;
For I would never lie to your face.
29 Yield now, let there be no injustice!
Yes, concede, my righteousness still stands!
30 Is there injustice on my tongue?
Cannot my taste discern the unsavory?

Job: My Suffering Is Comfortless

7 "*Is there* not a time of hard service for man
on earth?
Are not his days also like the days of a hired
man?
2 Like a servant who earnestly desires the
shade,
And like a hired man who eagerly looks
for his wages,
3 So I have been allotted months of futility,
And wearisome nights have been
appointed to me.
4 When I lie down, I say, 'When shall I arise,
And the night be ended?'
For I have had my fill of tossing till dawn.
5 My flesh is caked with worms and dust,
My skin is cracked and breaks out afresh.

6 "My days are swifter than a weaver's
shuttle,
And are spent without hope.
7 Oh, remember that my life *is* a breath!
My eye will never again see good.
8 The eye of him who sees me will see me
no *more*;

While your *eyes* are upon me, I shall no
longer *be*.
9 *As* the cloud disappears and vanishes away,
So he who goes down to the grave does
not come up.
10 He shall never return to his house,
Nor shall his place know him anymore.

11 "Therefore I will not restrain my mouth;
I will speak in the anguish of my spirit;
I will complain in the bitterness of my soul.
12 *Am* I a sea, or a sea serpent,
That You set a guard over me?
13 When I say, 'My bed will comfort me,
My couch will ease my complaint,'
14 Then You scare me with dreams
And terrify me with visions,
15 So that my soul chooses strangling
And death rather than my body.[a]
16 I loathe *my life;*
I would not live forever.
Let me alone,
For my days *are but* a breath.

17 "What *is* man, that You should exalt him,
That You should set Your heart on him,
18 That You should visit him every morning,
And test him every moment?
19 How long?
Will You not look away from me,
And let me alone till I swallow my saliva?
20 Have I sinned?
What have I done to You, O watcher of
men?
Why have You set me as Your target,
So that I am a burden to myself?[a]
21 Why then do You not pardon my
transgression,
And take away my iniquity?
For now I will lie down in the dust,
And You will seek me diligently,
But I *will* no longer *be*."

Bildad: Job Should Repent

8 Then Bildad the Shuhite answered and
said:

2 "How long will you speak these *things,*
And the words of your mouth *be* like a
strong wind?
3 Does God subvert judgment?
Or does the Almighty pervert justice?

7:15 [a]Literally *my bones*   **7:20** [a]Following
Masoretic Text, Targum, and Vulgate; Septuagint
and Jewish tradition read *to You.*

4 If your sons have sinned against Him,
He has cast them away for their
transgression.
5 If you would earnestly seek God
And make your supplication to the
Almighty,
6 If you *were* pure and upright,
Surely now He would awake for you,
And prosper your rightful dwelling place.
7 Though your beginning was small,
Yet your latter end would increase
abundantly.

8 "For inquire, please, of the former age,
And consider the things discovered by
their fathers;
9 For we *were born* yesterday, and know
nothing,
Because our days on earth *are* a shadow.
10 Will they not teach you and tell you,
And utter words from their heart?

11 "Can the papyrus grow up without a
marsh?
Can the reeds flourish without water?
12 While it *is* yet green *and* not cut down,
It withers before any *other* plant.
13 So *are* the paths of all who forget God;
And the hope of the hypocrite shall
perish,
14 Whose confidence shall be cut off,
And whose trust *is* a spider's web.
15 He leans on his house, but it does not
stand.
He holds it fast, but it does not endure.
16 He grows green in the sun,
And his branches spread out in his
garden.
17 His roots wrap around the rock heap,
And look for a place in the stones.
18 If he is destroyed from his place,
Then *it* will deny him, *saying,* 'I have not
seen you.'

19 "Behold, this is the joy of His way,
And out of the earth others will grow.
20 Behold, God will not cast away the
blameless,
Nor will He uphold the evildoers.
21 He will yet fill your mouth with
laughing,
And your lips with rejoicing.
22 Those who hate you will be clothed with
shame,
And the dwelling place of the wicked will
come to nothing.'"[a]

Job: There Is No Mediator

9 Then Job answered and said:

2 "Truly I know *it is* so,
But how can a man be righteous before
God?
3 If one wished to contend with Him,
He could not answer Him one time out of
a thousand.
4 God is wise in heart and mighty in
strength.
Who has hardened *himself* against Him and
prospered?
5 He removes the mountains, and they do
not know
When He overturns them in His anger;
6 He shakes the earth out of its place,
And its pillars tremble;
7 He commands the sun, and it does not
rise;
He seals off the stars;
8 He alone spreads out the heavens,
And treads on the waves of the sea;
9 He made the Bear, Orion, and the
Pleiades,
And the chambers of the south;
10 He does great things past finding out,
Yes, wonders without number.
11 If He goes by me, I do not see *Him;*
If He moves past, I do not perceive
Him;
12 If He takes away, who can hinder Him?
Who can say to Him, 'What are You
doing?'
13 God will not withdraw His anger,
The allies of the proud[a] lie prostrate
beneath Him.

14 "How then can I answer Him,
And choose my words *to reason* with Him?
15 For though I were righteous, I could not
answer Him;
I would beg mercy of my Judge.
16 If I called and He answered me,
I would not believe that He was listening
to my voice.
17 For He crushes me with a tempest,
And multiplies my wounds without cause.
18 He will not allow me to catch my breath,
But fills me with bitterness.
19 If *it is a matter* of strength, indeed *He is*
strong;
And if of justice, who will appoint my day
in court?

8:22 [a]Literally *will not be*   **9:13** [a]Hebrew *rahab*

20 Though I were righteous, my own mouth
would condemn me;
Though I *were* blameless, it would prove
me perverse.

21 "I am blameless, yet I do not know myself;
I despise my life.

22 It *is* all one *thing;*
Therefore I say, 'He destroys the blameless
and the wicked.'

23 If the scourge slays suddenly,
He laughs at the plight of the innocent.

24 The earth is given into the hand of the
wicked.
He covers the faces of its judges.
If it is not *He,* who else could it be?

25 "Now my days are swifter than a runner;
They flee away, they see no good.

26 They pass by like swift ships,
Like an eagle swooping on its prey.

27 If I say, 'I will forget my complaint,
I will put off my sad face and wear a
smile,'

28 I am afraid of all my sufferings;
I know that You will not hold me
innocent.

29 *If* I am condemned,
Why then do I labor in vain?

30 If I wash myself with snow water,
And cleanse my hands with soap,

31 Yet You will plunge me into the pit,
And my own clothes will abhor me.

32 "For *He is* not a man, as I *am,*
That I may answer Him,
And *that* we should go to court together.

33 Nor is there any mediator between us,
Who may lay his hand on us both.

34 Let Him take His rod away from me,
And do not let dread of Him terrify me.

35 *Then* I would speak and not fear Him,
But it is not so with me.

Job: I Would Plead with God

10 "My soul loathes my life;
I will give free course to my
complaint,
I will speak in the bitterness of my soul.

2 I will say to God, 'Do not condemn me;
Show me why You contend with me.

3 *Does it* seem good to You that You should
oppress,
That You should despise the work of Your
hands,
And smile on the counsel of the wicked?

4 Do You have eyes of flesh?
Or do You see as man sees?

5 *Are* Your days like the days of a mortal
man?
Are Your years like the days of a mighty
man,

6 That You should seek for my iniquity
And search out my sin,

7 Although You know that I am not wicked,
And *there is* no one who can deliver from
Your hand?

8 'Your hands have made me and fashioned
me,
An intricate unity;
Yet You would destroy me.

9 Remember, I pray, that You have made me
like clay.
And will You turn me into dust again?

10 Did You not pour me out like milk,
And curdle me like cheese,

11 Clothe me with skin and flesh,
And knit me together with bones and
sinews?

12 You have granted me life and favor,
And Your care has preserved my spirit.

13 'And these *things* You have hidden in Your
heart;
I know that this *was* with You:

14 If I sin, then You mark me,
And will not acquit me of my iniquity.

15 If I am wicked, woe to me;
Even *if* I am righteous, I cannot lift up my
head.
I am full of disgrace;
See my misery!

16 If *my head* is exalted,
You hunt me like a fierce lion,
And again You show Yourself awesome
against me.

17 You renew Your witnesses against me,
And increase Your indignation toward me;
Changes and war are *ever* with me.

18 'Why then have You brought me out of
the womb?
Oh, that I had perished and no eye had
seen me!

19 I would have been as though I had not
been.
I would have been carried from the womb
to the grave.

20 Are not my days few?
Cease! Leave me alone, that I may take a
little comfort,

21 Before I go *to the place from which* I shall
   not return,
   To the land of darkness and the shadow of
   death,
22 A land as dark as darkness *itself,*
   As the shadow of death, without any order,
   Where even the light *is* like darkness.'"

Zophar Urges Job to Repent

11 Then Zophar the Naamathite answered and said:

2 "Should not the multitude of words be
   answered?
   And should a man full of talk be
   vindicated?
3 Should your empty talk make men hold
   their peace?
   And when you mock, should no one
   rebuke you?
4 For you have said,
   'My doctrine *is* pure,
   And I am clean in your eyes.'
5 But oh, that God would speak,
   And open His lips against you,
6 That He would show you the secrets of
   wisdom!
   For *they would* double *your* prudence.
   Know therefore that God exacts from you
   Less than your iniquity *deserves.*

7 "Can you search out the deep things of
   God?
   Can you find out the limits of the
   Almighty?
8 *They are* higher than heaven— what can
   you do?
   Deeper than Sheol— what can you know?
9 Their measure *is* longer than the earth
   And broader than the sea.

10 "If He passes by, imprisons, and gathers *to
   judgment,*
   Then who can hinder Him?
11 For He knows deceitful men;
   He sees wickedness also.
   Will He not then consider *it?*
12 For an empty-headed man will be wise,
   When a wild donkey's colt is born a man.

13 "If you would prepare your heart,
   And stretch out your hands toward Him;
14 If iniquity *were* in your hand, *and you* put it
   far away,
   And would not let wickedness dwell in
   your tents;

15 Then surely you could lift up your face
   without spot;
   Yes, you could be steadfast, and not fear;
16 Because you would forget *your* misery,
   And remember *it* as waters *that have* passed
   away,
17 And *your* life would be brighter than
   noonday.
   Though you were dark, you would be like
   the morning.
18 And you would be secure, because there is
   hope;
   Yes, you would dig *around you, and* take
   your rest in safety.
19 You would also lie down, and no one
   would make *you* afraid;
   Yes, many would court your favor.
20 But the eyes of the wicked will fail,
   And they shall not escape,
   And their hope—loss of life!"

Job Answers His Critics

12 Then Job answered and said:

2 "No doubt you *are* the people,
   And wisdom will die with you!
3 But I have understanding as well as you;
   I *am* not inferior to you.
   Indeed, who does not *know* such things as
   these?

4 "I am one mocked by his friends,
   Who called on God, and He answered
   him,
   The just and blameless *who is* ridiculed.
5 A lamp[a] is despised in the thought of one
   who is at ease;
   It is made ready for those whose feet slip.
6 The tents of robbers prosper,
   And those who provoke God are secure—
   In what God provides by His hand.

7 "But now ask the beasts, and they will teach
   you;
   And the birds of the air, and they will tell
   you;
8 Or speak to the earth, and it will teach
   you;
   And the fish of the sea will explain to you.
9 Who among all these does not know
   That the hand of the LORD has done
   this,
10 In whose hand *is* the life of every living
   thing,

12:5 [a]Or *disaster*

And the breath of all mankind?
11 Does not the ear test words
And the mouth taste its food?
12 Wisdom *is* with aged men,
And with length of days, understanding.

13 "With Him *are* wisdom and strength,
He has counsel and understanding.
14 If He breaks *a thing* down, it cannot be rebuilt;
If He imprisons a man, there can be no release.
15 If He withholds the waters, they dry up;
If He sends them out, they overwhelm the earth.
16 With Him *are* strength and prudence.
The deceived and the deceiver *are* His.
17 He leads counselors away plundered,
And makes fools of the judges.
18 He loosens the bonds of kings,
And binds their waist with a belt.
19 He leads princes[a] away plundered,
And overthrows the mighty.
20 He deprives the trusted ones of speech,
And takes away the discernment of the elders.
21 He pours contempt on princes,
And disarms the mighty.
22 He uncovers deep things out of darkness,
And brings the shadow of death to light.
23 He makes nations great, and destroys them;
He enlarges nations, and guides them.
24 He takes away the understanding[a] of the chiefs of the people of the earth,
And makes them wander in a pathless wilderness.
25 They grope in the dark without light,
And He makes them stagger like a drunken *man*.

13 "Behold, my eye has seen all *this*,
My ear has heard and understood it.
2 What you know, I also know;
I *am* not inferior to you.
3 But I would speak to the Almighty,
And I desire to reason with God.
4 But you forgers of lies,
You *are* all worthless physicians.
5 Oh, that you would be silent,
And it would be your wisdom!
6 Now hear my reasoning,
And heed the pleadings of my lips.
7 Will you speak wickedly for God,
And talk deceitfully for Him?
8 Will you show partiality for Him?

9 Will you contend for God?
Will it be well when He searches you out?
Or can you mock Him as one mocks a man?
10 He will surely rebuke you
If you secretly show partiality.
11 Will not His excellence make you afraid,
And the dread of Him fall upon you?
12 Your platitudes *are* proverbs of ashes,
Your defenses are defenses of clay.

13 "Hold your peace with me, and let me speak,
Then let come on me what *may!*
14 Why do I take my flesh in my teeth,
And put my life in my hands?
15 Though He slay me, yet will I trust Him.
Even so, I will defend my own ways before Him.
16 He also *shall* be my salvation,
For a hypocrite could not come before Him.

12:19 [a]Literally *priests,* but not in a technical sense
12:24 [a]Literally *heart*

Commitment: Job Stays Steady at All Costs

(Job 13:15)

The statement confounds nominal Christians, yet it is exactly the kind of affirmation that God uses to build His kingdom in the darkest places on earth. "Though He slay me," Job says, "yet will I trust Him" (Job 13:15).

Statements like this shake the very gates of hell. What can stop a leader who has made this kind of commitment? Not pain. Not death. Not hardship.

Why has terrorism, for instance, become such an international problem? Because terrorists already have given up their lives for their cause. They will drive a truck full of explosives into enemy headquarters because they no longer hold their lives dear.

This is where Job finally ended up—willing to give up his life for God. Only in that position do we find complete liberation—free from any temptation, threat, bribe, sin, or enticement. When we can say, with the apostle Paul, that we have already died (Gal. 2:20), then we will have reached the place where God can really use us.

17 Listen carefully to my speech,
And to my declaration with your ears.
18 See now, I have prepared *my* case,
I know that I shall be vindicated.
19 Who *is* he *who* will contend with me?
If now I hold my tongue, I perish.

Job's Despondent Prayer

20 "Only two *things* do not do to me,
Then I will not hide myself from You:
21 Withdraw Your hand far from me,
And let not the dread of You make me
afraid.
22 Then call, and I will answer;
Or let me speak, then You respond to me.
23 How many *are* my iniquities and sins?
Make me know my transgression and my
sin.
24 Why do You hide Your face,
And regard me as Your enemy?
25 Will You frighten a leaf driven to and fro?
And will You pursue dry stubble?
26 For You write bitter things against me,
And make me inherit the iniquities of my
youth.
27 You put my feet in the stocks,
And watch closely all my paths.
You set a limit[a] for the soles of my feet.

28 "*Man*[a] decays like a rotten thing,
Like a garment that is moth-eaten.

14 "Man *who is* born of woman
Is of few days and full of
trouble.
2 He comes forth like a flower and fades
away;
He flees like a shadow and does not
continue.
3 And do You open Your eyes on such a one,
And bring me[a] to judgment with Yourself?
4 Who can bring a clean *thing* out of an
unclean?
No one!
5 Since his days *are* determined,
The number of his months *is* with You;
You have appointed his limits, so that he
cannot pass.
6 Look away from him that he may rest,
Till like a hired man he finishes his day.

7 "For there is hope for a tree,
If it is cut down, that it will sprout again,
And that its tender shoots will not cease.

13:27 [a]Literally *inscribe a print* **13:28** [a]Literally *He*
14:3 [a]Septuagint, Syriac, and Vulgate read *him*.

JOB   PUZZLED, NOT UNBELIEVING
(Job 13:20—14:22)

PROFILE IN LEADERSHIP

God doesn't mind questions; it's doubt that He hates.

For many wearying hours, the three friends of Job— Eliphaz, Bildad, and Zophar—accused Job of all kinds of evil. They spoke the kind of foolish words that the healthy and ill-informed often speak to those in pain.

O, how Job wanted to take his case to the Lord Himself! "Why did I not die at birth?" he asked the Lord. "How long? Will You not look away from me, and let me alone till I swallow my saliva?" (Job 3:11; 7:19).

Job's words reflect the kind of torment we would expect from a godly man in deep pain. But God says nothing. Only at the end of the book does God at last break His silence. And while He answers not one of Job's questions, neither does He chastise him for asking them. God rebukes Job for only one thing: doubting His righteous character (40:8).

Leaders must never be afraid to ask hard questions of God, but neither must they demand that He answer. And no matter how dark our circumstances may grow, we must resist the temptation to doubt God's holy nature. When we, like Job, through trembling lips confess the awesome majesty of God, we may at last be ready for the awesome blessing of God.

8   Though its root may grow old in the earth,
     And its stump may die in the ground,
9   *Yet* at the scent of water it will bud
     And bring forth branches like a plant.
10   But man dies and is laid away;
     Indeed he breathes his last
     And where *is* he?
11   *As* water disappears from the sea,
     And a river becomes parched and dries up,
12   So man lies down and does not rise.
     Till the heavens *are* no more,
     They will not awake
     Nor be roused from their sleep.

13   "Oh, that You would hide me in the grave,
     That You would conceal me until Your
         wrath is past,
     That You would appoint me a set time,
         and remember me!
14   If a man dies, shall he live *again?*
     All the days of my hard service I will wait,
     Till my change comes.
15   You shall call, and I will answer You;
     You shall desire the work of Your hands.
16   For now You number my steps,
     But do not watch over my sin.
17   My transgression *is* sealed up in a bag,
     And You cover[a] my iniquity.

18   "But *as* a mountain falls *and* crumbles away,
     And *as* a rock is moved from its place;
19   *As* water wears away stones,
     And as torrents wash away the soil of the
         earth;
     So You destroy the hope of man.
20   You prevail forever against him, and he
         passes on;
     You change his countenance and send him
         away.
21   His sons come to honor, and he does not
         know *it;*
     They are brought low, and he does not
         perceive *it.*
22   But his flesh will be in pain over it,
     And his soul will mourn over it."

Eliphaz Accuses Job of Folly

15   Then Eliphaz the Temanite answered
     and said:

2   "Should a wise man answer with empty
         knowledge,
     And fill himself with the east wind?
3   Should he reason with unprofitable talk,
     Or by speeches with which he can do no
         good?

4   Yes, you cast off fear,
     And restrain prayer before God.
5   For your iniquity teaches your mouth,
     And you choose the tongue of the crafty.
6   Your own mouth condemns you, and not I;
     Yes, your own lips testify against you.

7   "*Are* you the first man *who* was born?
     Or were you made before the hills?
8   Have you heard the counsel of God?
     Do you limit wisdom to yourself?
9   What do you know that we do not know?
     What do you understand that *is* not in us?
10   Both the gray-haired and the aged *are*
         among us,
     Much older than your father.
11   *Are* the consolations of God too small for
         you,
     And the word *spoken* gently[a] with you?
12   Why does your heart carry you away,
     And what do your eyes wink at,
13   That you turn your spirit against God,
     And let *such* words go out of your mouth?

14   "What *is* man, that he could be pure?
     And *he who is* born of a woman, that he
         could be righteous?
15   If *God* puts no trust in His saints,
     And the heavens are not pure in His sight,
16   How much less man, *who is* abominable
         and filthy,
     Who drinks iniquity like water!

17   "I will tell you, hear me;
     What I have seen I will declare,
18   What wise men have told,
     Not hiding *anything received* from their
         fathers,
19   To whom alone the land was given,
     And no alien passed among them:
20   The wicked man writhes with pain all *his*
         days,
     And the number of years is hidden from
         the oppressor.
21   Dreadful sounds *are* in his ears;
     In prosperity the destroyer comes upon him.
22   He does not believe that he will return
         from darkness,
     For a sword is waiting for him.
23   He wanders about for bread, *saying,*
     'Where *is* it?'
     He knows that a day of darkness is ready
         at his hand.

14:17 [a]Literally *plaster over*   **15:11** [a]Septuagint
reads *a secret thing.*

24 Trouble and anguish make him afraid;
They overpower him, like a king ready for
battle.
25 For he stretches out his hand against God,
And acts defiantly against the Almighty,
26 Running stubbornly against Him
With his strong, embossed shield.

27 "Though he has covered his face with his
fatness,
And made *his* waist heavy with fat,
28 He dwells in desolate cities,
In houses which no one inhabits,
Which are destined to become ruins.
29 He will not be rich,
Nor will his wealth continue,
Nor will his possessions overspread the
earth.
30 He will not depart from darkness;
The flame will dry out his branches,
And by the breath of His mouth he will
go away.
31 Let him not trust in futile *things,* deceiving
himself,
For futility will be his reward.
32 It will be accomplished before his time,
And his branch will not be green.
33 He will shake off his unripe grape like a
vine,
And cast off his blossom like an olive tree.
34 For the company of hypocrites *will be*
barren,
And fire will consume the tents of bribery.

35 They conceive trouble and bring forth
futility;
Their womb prepares deceit."

Job Reproaches His Pitiless Friends

16 Then Job answered and said:

2 "I have heard many such things;
Miserable comforters *are* you all!
3 Shall words of wind have an end?
Or what provokes you that you answer?
4 I also could speak as you *do,*
If your soul were in my soul's place.
I could heap up words against you,
And shake my head at you;
5 *But* I would strengthen you with my
mouth,
And the comfort of my lips would relieve
your grief.

6 "Though I speak, my grief is not
relieved;
And *if* I remain silent, how am I eased?
7 But now He has worn me out;
You have made desolate all my company.
8 You have shriveled me up,
And it is a witness *against me;*
My leanness rises up against me
And bears witness to my face.
9 He tears *me* in His wrath, and hates me;
He gnashes at me with His teeth;
My adversary sharpens His gaze on me.
10 They gape at me with their mouth,

Job's Friends Fail at the Law of Connection
(Job 16:2)

Eliphaz, Bildad, and Zophar accused Job of acting foolishly, of speaking wrongly, of leading wickedly. But they never got their message across for two reasons: First, they didn't have all the facts; and second, they didn't practice the Law of Connection.

Many leaders are tempted to make the same mistakes. We voice our opinions even though we remain ignorant of important information and lack any heart connection to our audience. Job called his friends, "miserable comforters." Every good communicator seeks first to understand before being understood. Note how they differ from public speakers:

Public Speaker	Communicator
1. Seeks to be understood and liked	1. Seeks to understand and connect
2. Asks: What do I have?	2. Asks: What do they need?
3. Focuses on techniques	3. Focuses on atmosphere
4. Is self-conscious	4. Is audience-oriented
5. Wants to complete the speech	5. Wants to complete the people
6. Content-oriented	6. Change-oriented

They strike me reproachfully on the cheek,
They gather together against me.

11 God has delivered me to the ungodly,
And turned me over to the hands of the
   wicked.

12 I was at ease, but He has shattered me;
He also has taken *me* by my neck, and
   shaken me to pieces;
He has set me up for His target,

13 His archers surround me.
He pierces my heart[a] and does not pity;
He pours out my gall on the ground.

14 He breaks me with wound upon wound;
He runs at me like a warrior.[a]

15 "I have sewn sackcloth over my skin,
And laid my head[a] in the dust.

16 My face is flushed from weeping,
And on my eyelids *is* the shadow of death;

17 Although no violence *is* in my hands,
And my prayer *is* pure.

18 "O earth, do not cover my blood,
And let my cry have no *resting* place!

19 Surely even now my witness *is* in heaven,
And my evidence *is* on high.

20 My friends scorn me;
My eyes pour out *tears* to God.

21 Oh, that one might plead for a man with
   God,
As a man *pleads* for his neighbor!

22 For when a few years are finished,
I shall go the way of no return.

Job Prays for Relief

17 "My spirit is broken,
   My days are extinguished,
   The grave *is ready* for me.

2 *Are* not mockers with me?
And does not my eye dwell on their
   provocation?

3 "Now put down a pledge for me with
   Yourself.
Who *is* he *who* will shake hands with me?

4 For You have hidden their heart from
   understanding;
Therefore You will not exalt *them*.

5 He who speaks flattery to *his* friends,
Even the eyes of his children will fail.

6 "But He has made me a byword of the
   people,
And I have become one in whose face
   men spit.

7 My eye has also grown dim because of
   sorrow,

And all my members *are* like shadows.

8 Upright *men* are astonished at this,
And the innocent stirs himself up against
   the hypocrite.

9 Yet the righteous will hold to his way,
And he who has clean hands will be
   stronger and stronger.

10 "But please, come back again, all of you,[a]
For I shall not find *one* wise *man* among
   you.

11 My days are past,
My purposes are broken off,
Even the thoughts of my heart.

12 They change the night into day;
'The light *is* near,' *they say,* in the face of
   darkness.

13 If I wait *for* the grave *as* my house,
If I make my bed in the darkness,

14 If I say to corruption, 'You *are* my father,'
And to the worm, 'You *are* my mother and
   my sister,'

15 Where then *is* my hope?
As for my hope, who can see it?

16 *Will* they go down to the gates of Sheol?
Shall *we have* rest together in the dust?"

Bildad: The Wicked Are Punished

18 Then Bildad the Shuhite answered
   and said:

2 "How long *till* you put an end to words?
Gain understanding, and afterward we will
   speak.

3 Why are we counted as beasts,
And regarded as stupid in your sight?

4 You who tear yourself in anger,
Shall the earth be forsaken for you?
Or shall the rock be removed from its
   place?

5 "The light of the wicked indeed goes out,
And the flame of his fire does not shine.

6 The light is dark in his tent,
And his lamp beside him is put out.

7 The steps of his strength are shortened,
And his own counsel casts him down.

8 For he is cast into a net by his own feet,
And he walks into a snare.

9 The net takes *him* by the heel,
And a snare lays hold of him.

16:13 [a]Literally *kidneys*   **16:14** [a]Vulgate reads *giant*.
16:15 [a]Literally *horn*   **17:10** [a]Following some
Hebrew manuscripts, Septuagint, Syriac, and
Vulgate; Masoretic Text and Targum read *all of them.*

10 A noose *is* hidden for him on the ground,
And a trap for him in the road.
11 Terrors frighten him on every side,
And drive him to his feet.
12 His strength is starved,
And destruction *is* ready at his side.
13 It devours patches of his skin;
The firstborn of death devours his limbs.
14 He is uprooted from the shelter of his tent,
And they parade him before the king of terrors.
15 They dwell in his tent *who are* none of his;
Brimstone is scattered on his dwelling.
16 His roots are dried out below,
And his branch withers above.
17 The memory of him perishes from the earth,
And he has no name among the renowned.[a]
18 He is driven from light into darkness,
And chased out of the world.
19 He has neither son nor posterity among his people,
Nor any remaining in his dwellings.
20 Those in the west are astonished at his day,
As those in the east are frightened.
21 Surely such *are* the dwellings of the wicked,
And this *is* the place *of him who* does not know God."

Job Trusts in His Redeemer

19 Then Job answered and said:

2 "How long will you torment my soul,
And break me in pieces with words?
3 These ten times you have reproached me;
You are not ashamed *that* you have wronged me.[a]
4 And if indeed I have erred,
My error remains with me.
5 If indeed you exalt *yourselves* against me,
And plead my disgrace against me,
6 Know then that God has wronged me,
And has surrounded me with His net.

7 "If I cry out concerning wrong, I am not heard.
If I cry aloud, *there is* no justice.
8 He has fenced up my way, so that I cannot pass;
And He has set darkness in my paths.
9 He has stripped me of my glory,
And taken the crown *from* my head.

10 He breaks me down on every side,
And I am gone;
My hope He has uprooted like a tree.
11 He has also kindled His wrath against me,
And He counts me as *one* of His enemies.
12 His troops come together
And build up their road against me;
They encamp all around my tent.

13 "He has removed my brothers far from me,
And my acquaintances are completely estranged from me.
14 My relatives have failed,
And my close friends have forgotten me.
15 Those who dwell in my house, and my maidservants,
Count me as a stranger;
I am an alien in their sight.
16 I call my servant, but he gives no answer;
I beg him with my mouth.
17 My breath is offensive to my wife,
And I am repulsive to the children of my own body.
18 Even young children despise me;
I arise, and they speak against me.
19 All my close friends abhor me,
And those whom I love have turned against me.
20 My bone clings to my skin and to my flesh,
And I have escaped by the skin of my teeth.

21 "Have pity on me, have pity on me, O you my friends,
For the hand of God has struck me!
22 Why do you persecute me as God *does,*
And are not satisfied with my flesh?

23 "Oh, that my words were written!
Oh, that they were inscribed in a book!
24 That they were engraved on a rock
With an iron pen and lead, forever!
25 For I know *that* my Redeemer lives,
And He shall stand at last on the earth;
26 And after my skin is destroyed, this *I know,*
That in my flesh I shall see God,
27 Whom I shall see for myself,
And my eyes shall behold, and not another.
How my heart yearns within me!
28 If you should say, 'How shall we persecute him?'—

18:17 [a]Literally *before the outside,* meaning distinguished, famous   **19:3** [a]A Jewish tradition reads *make yourselves strange to me.*

Vision: Job's Perspective Separates Him from the Others

(Job 19:25–27)

The first difference separating leaders from followers is perspective. Both can have character and integrity; both can love others; both can obey God. But leaders think differently than followers.

Job and his friends held profoundly different perspectives. Throughout the book, Job maintains an eternal perspective. "For I know that my Redeemer lives, and He shall stand at last on the earth," he says (Job 19:25). In the following two verses he continues to cast vision for the reality of life beyond the grave. Unlike his wife, who told him to curse God and die; unlike his friends, who told him none of this would have happened had he just lived better—Job saw beyond the superficial to the eternal. What enabled Job to see what God saw?

1. *He renewed his perspective:* He clung to the justice and character of God.
2. *He released his past:* He was willing to let go of what he had lost.
3. *He remembered his purpose:* He realized that he existed only to glorify God.

Since the root of the matter is found in me,

29 Be afraid of the sword for yourselves;
For wrath *brings* the punishment of the sword,
That you may know *there is* a judgment."

Zophar's Sermon on the Wicked Man

20 Then Zophar the Naamathite answered and said:

2 "Therefore my anxious thoughts make me answer,
Because of the turmoil within me.

3 I have heard the rebuke that reproaches me,
And the spirit of my understanding causes me to answer.

4 "Do you *not* know this of old,
Since man was placed on earth,

5 That the triumphing of the wicked is short,
And the joy of the hypocrite is *but* for a moment?

6 Though his haughtiness mounts up to the heavens,
And his head reaches to the clouds,

7 *Yet* he will perish forever like his own refuse;
Those who have seen him will say, 'Where is he?'

8 He will fly away like a dream, and not be found;

Yes, he will be chased away like a vision of the night.

9 The eye *that* saw him will *see him* no more,
Nor will his place behold him anymore.

10 His children will seek the favor of the poor,
And his hands will restore his wealth.

11 His bones are full of his youthful vigor,
But it will lie down with him in the dust.

12 "Though evil is sweet in his mouth,
And he hides it under his tongue,

13 *Though* he spares it and does not forsake it,
But still keeps it in his mouth,

14 *Yet* his food in his stomach turns sour;
It becomes cobra venom within him.

15 He swallows down riches
And vomits them up again;
God casts them out of his belly.

16 He will suck the poison of cobras;
The viper's tongue will slay him.

17 He will not see the streams,
The rivers flowing with honey and cream.

18 He will restore that for which he labored,
And will not swallow *it* down;
From the proceeds of business
He will get no enjoyment.

19 For he has oppressed *and* forsaken the poor,
He has violently seized a house which he did not build.

20 "Because he knows no quietness in his heart,[a]
He will not save anything he desires.

20:20 [a]Literally *belly*

21 Nothing is left for him to eat;
Therefore his well-being will not last.
22 In his self-sufficiency he will be in distress;
Every hand of misery will come against
him.
23 *When* he is about to fill his stomach,
God will cast on him the fury of His
wrath,
And will rain *it* on him while he is eating.
24 He will flee from the iron weapon;
A bronze bow will pierce him through.
25 It is drawn, and comes out of the body;
Yes, the glittering *point comes* out of his
gall.
Terrors *come* upon him;
26 Total darkness *is* reserved for his treasures.
An unfanned fire will consume him;
It shall go ill with him who is left in his
tent.
27 The heavens will reveal his iniquity,
And the earth will rise up against him.
28 The increase of his house will depart,
And his goods will flow away in the day of
His wrath.
29 This *is* the portion from God for a wicked
man,
The heritage appointed to him by God."

Job's Discourse on the Wicked

21 Then Job answered and said:
2 "Listen carefully to my speech,
And let this be your consolation.
3 Bear with me that I may speak,
And after I have spoken, keep mocking.

4 "As for me, *is* my complaint against man?
And if *it were,* why should I not be
impatient?
5 Look at me and be astonished;
Put *your* hand over *your* mouth.
6 Even when I remember I am terrified,
And trembling takes hold of my flesh.
7 Why do the wicked live *and* become old,
Yes, become mighty in power?
8 Their descendants are established with
them in their sight,
And their offspring before their eyes.
9 Their houses *are* safe from fear,
Neither *is* the rod of God upon them.
10 Their bull breeds without failure;
Their cow calves without miscarriage.
11 They send forth their little ones like a
flock,
And their children dance.
12 They sing to the tambourine and harp,

And rejoice to the sound of the flute.
13 They spend their days in wealth,
And in a moment go down to the grave.[a]
14 Yet they say to God, 'Depart from us,
For we do not desire the knowledge of
Your ways.
15 Who *is* the Almighty, that we should serve
Him?
And what profit do we have if we pray to
Him?'
16 Indeed their prosperity *is* not in their hand;
The counsel of the wicked is far from me.

17 "How often is the lamp of the wicked put
out?
How often does their destruction come
upon them,
The sorrows *God* distributes in His anger?
18 They are like straw before the wind,
And like chaff that a storm carries away.
19 *They say,* 'God lays up one's[a] iniquity for
his children';
Let Him recompense him, that he may
know *it.*
20 Let his eyes see his destruction,
And let him drink of the wrath of the
Almighty.
21 For what does he care about his household
after him,
When the number of his months is cut in
half?

22 "Can *anyone* teach God knowledge,
Since He judges those on high?
23 One dies in his full strength,
Being wholly at ease and secure;
24 His pails[a] are full of milk,
And the marrow of his bones is moist.
25 Another man dies in the bitterness of his
soul,
Never having eaten with pleasure.
26 They lie down alike in the dust,
And worms cover them.

27 "Look, I know your thoughts,
And the schemes *with which* you would
wrong me.
28 For you say,
'Where *is* the house of the prince?
And where *is* the tent,[a]
The dwelling place of the wicked?'

21:13 [a]Or *Sheol* **21:19** [a]Literally *his*
21:24 [a]Septuagint and Vulgate read *bowels;* Syriac
reads *sides;* Targum reads *breasts.* **21:28** [a]Vulgate
omits *the tent.*

29 Have you not asked those who travel the road?
And do you not know their signs?
30 For the wicked are reserved for the day of doom;
They shall be brought out on the day of wrath.
31 Who condemns his way to his face?
And who repays him *for what* he has done?
32 Yet he shall be brought to the grave,
And a vigil kept over the tomb.
33 The clods of the valley shall be sweet to him;
Everyone shall follow him,
As countless *have gone* before him.
34 How then can you comfort me with empty words,
Since falsehood remains in your answers?"

Eliphaz Accuses Job of Wickedness

22 Then Eliphaz the Temanite answered and said:

2 "Can a man be profitable to God,
Though he who is wise may be profitable to himself?
3 *Is it* any pleasure to the Almighty that you are righteous?
Or *is it* gain *to Him* that you make your ways blameless?

4 "Is it because of your fear of Him that He corrects you,
And enters into judgment with you?
5 *Is* not your wickedness great,
And your iniquity without end?
6 For you have taken pledges from your brother for no reason,
And stripped the naked of their clothing.
7 You have not given the weary water to drink,
And you have withheld bread from the hungry.
8 But the mighty man possessed the land,
And the honorable man dwelt in it.
9 You have sent widows away empty,
And the strength of the fatherless was crushed.
10 Therefore snares *are* all around you,
And sudden fear troubles you,
11 Or darkness *so that* you cannot see;
And an abundance of water covers you.

12 "Is not God in the height of heaven?
And see the highest stars, how lofty they are!

13 And you say, 'What does God know?
Can He judge through the deep darkness?
14 Thick clouds cover Him, so that He cannot see,
And He walks above the circle of heaven.'
15 Will you keep to the old way
Which wicked men have trod,
16 Who were cut down before their time,
Whose foundations were swept away by a flood?
17 They said to God, 'Depart from us!
What can the Almighty do to them?'[a]
18 Yet He filled their houses with good *things;*
But the counsel of the wicked is far from me.

19 "The righteous see *it* and are glad,
And the innocent laugh at them:
20 'Surely our adversaries[a] are cut down,
And the fire consumes their remnant.'

21 "Now acquaint yourself with Him, and be at peace;
Thereby good will come to you.
22 Receive, please, instruction from His mouth,
And lay up His words in your heart.
23 If you return to the Almighty, you will be built up;
You will remove iniquity far from your tents.
24 Then you will lay your gold in the dust,
And the *gold* of Ophir among the stones of the brooks.
25 Yes, the Almighty will be your gold[a]
And your precious silver;
26 For then you will have your delight in the Almighty,
And lift up your face to God.
27 You will make your prayer to Him,
He will hear you,
And you will pay your vows.
28 You will also declare a thing,
And it will be established for you;
So light will shine on your ways.
29 When they cast *you* down, and you say,
'Exaltation *will come!'*
Then He will save the humble *person.*
30 He will *even* deliver one who is not innocent;

22:17 [a]Septuagint and Syriac read *us.*
22:20 [a]Septuagint reads *substance.* 22:25 [a]The ancient versions suggest *defense;* Hebrew reads *gold* as in verse 24.

Yes, he will be delivered by the purity of your hands."

Job Proclaims God's Righteous Judgments

23 Then Job answered and said:

2 "Even today my complaint is bitter;
My[a] hand is listless because of my groaning.

3 Oh, that I knew where I might find Him,
That I might come to His seat!

4 I would present *my* case before Him,
And fill my mouth with arguments.

5 I would know the words *which* He would answer me,
And understand what He would say to me.

6 Would He contend with me in His great power?
No! But He would take *note* of me.

7 There the upright could reason with Him,
And I would be delivered forever from my Judge.

8 "Look, I go forward, but He is not *there,*
And backward, but I cannot perceive Him;

9 When He works on the left hand, I cannot behold *Him;*
When He turns to the right hand, I cannot see *Him.*

10 But He knows the way that I take;
When He has tested me, I shall come forth as gold.

11 My foot has held fast to His steps;
I have kept His way and not turned aside.

12 I have not departed from the commandment of His lips;
I have treasured the words of His mouth
More than my necessary *food.*

13 "But He *is* unique, and who can make Him change?
And *whatever* His soul desires, *that* He does.

14 For He performs *what is* appointed for me,
And many such *things are* with Him.

15 Therefore I am terrified at His presence;
When I consider *this,* I am afraid of Him.

16 For God made my heart weak,
And the Almighty terrifies me;

17 Because I was not cut off from the presence of darkness,
And He did *not* hide deep darkness from my face.

Job Complains of Violence on the Earth

24 "*Since* times are not hidden from the Almighty,
Why do those who know Him see not His days?

2 "*Some* remove landmarks;
They seize flocks violently and feed *on* them;

3 They drive away the donkey of the fatherless;
They take the widow's ox as a pledge.

4 They push the needy off the road;
All the poor of the land are forced to hide.

5 Indeed, *like* wild donkeys in the desert,
They go out to their work, searching for food.
The wilderness *yields* food for them *and* for *their* children.

6 They gather their fodder in the field
And glean in the vineyard of the wicked.

7 They spend the night naked, without clothing,
And have no covering in the cold.

8 They are wet with the showers of the mountains,
And huddle around the rock for want of shelter.

9 "*Some* snatch the fatherless from the breast,
And take a pledge from the poor.

10 They cause *the poor* to go naked, without clothing;
And they take away the sheaves from the hungry.

11 They press out oil within their walls,
And tread winepresses, yet suffer thirst.

12 The dying groan in the city,
And the souls of the wounded cry out;
Yet God does not charge *them* with wrong.

13 "There are those who rebel against the light;
They do not know its ways
Nor abide in its paths.

14 The murderer rises with the light;
He kills the poor and needy;
And in the night he is like a thief.

15 The eye of the adulterer waits for the twilight,
Saying, 'No eye will see me';
And he disguises *his* face.

16 In the dark they break into houses

23:2 [a]Following Masoretic Text, Targum, and Vulgate; Septuagint and Syriac read *His.*

Which they marked for themselves in the daytime;
They do not know the light.
17 For the morning is the same to them as the shadow of death;
If *someone* recognizes *them*,
They are in the terrors of the shadow of death.

18 "They *should be* swift on the face of the waters,
Their portion *should be* cursed in the earth,
So that no *one would* turn into the way of their vineyards.
19 As drought and heat consume the snow waters,
So the grave[a] *consumes those who* have sinned.
20 The womb *should* forget him,
The worm *should* feed sweetly on him;
He *should* be remembered no more,
And wickedness *should* be broken like a tree.
21 For he preys on the barren *who* do not bear,
And does no good for the widow.

22 "But *God* draws the mighty away with His power;
He rises up, but no *man* is sure of life.
23 He gives them security, and they rely *on it;*
Yet His eyes *are* on their ways.
24 They are exalted for a little while,
Then they are gone.
They are brought low;
They are taken out of the way like all *others;*
They dry out like the heads of grain.

25 "Now if *it is* not *so,* who will prove me a liar,
And make my speech worth nothing?"

Bildad: How Can Man Be Righteous?

25 Then Bildad the Shuhite answered and said:

2 "Dominion and fear *belong* to Him;
He makes peace in His high places.
3 Is there any number to His armies?
Upon whom does His light not rise?

24:19 [a]Or *Sheol*

JOB'S FRIENDS

MISGUIDED COMPANIONS WHO MEANT WELL
(Job 24:25)

PROFILE IN LEADERSHIP

At a time when Job most needed the love and encouragement of his friends, he received only their condemnation, torment, and wrath. Eliphaz argued from experience, Bildad from tradition, and Zophar from legalism, and as is often the case, many of their arguments contained elements of truth. These three friends could have become major obstacles—lids—in Job's life. And yet he did not allow that to happen.

Job's friends believed he must have behaved treacherously to meet with such awful tragedy. Would God treat a good friend like this? They accused him of many specific sins, adding their names to a long list of amateur theologians who assume that people in pain have done something to deserve their suffering. While that may indeed be the case (see John 5:14), it is not universally so.

False accusation can debilitate the falsely accused. At the most vulnerable time of his life, Job's friends continued to slander him—yet he continued to depend on God. He fought hard against depression and discouragement. In the midst of great pain and loss, Job demonstrated solid character and great strength; nothing was able to destroy his faith in God. In the end, truth prevailed and God blessed Job greatly. Job's story reminds us that all leaders must filter the counsel of their inner circle through the truth of God's Word.

4 How then can man be righteous before
God?
Or how can he be pure *who is* born of a
woman?
5 If even the moon does not shine,
And the stars are not pure in His sight,
6 How much less man, *who is* a maggot,
And a son of man, *who is* a worm?"

Job: Man's Frailty and God's Majesty

26 But Job answered and said:

2 "How have you helped *him who is*
without power?
How have you saved the arm *that has* no
strength?
3 How have you counseled *one who has* no
wisdom?
And *how* have you declared sound advice
to many?
4 To whom have you uttered words?
And whose spirit came from you?

5 "The dead tremble,
Those under the waters and those
inhabiting them.
6 Sheol *is* naked before Him,
And Destruction has no covering.
7 He stretches out the north over empty
space;
He hangs the earth on nothing.
8 He binds up the water in His thick clouds,
Yet the clouds are not broken under it.
9 He covers the face of *His* throne,
And spreads His cloud over it.
10 He drew a circular horizon on the face of
the waters,
At the boundary of light and darkness.
11 The pillars of heaven tremble,
And are astonished at His rebuke.
12 He stirs up the sea with His power,
And by His understanding He breaks up
the storm.
13 By His Spirit He adorned the heavens;
His hand pierced the fleeing serpent.
14 Indeed these *are* the mere edges of His ways,
And how small a whisper we hear of
Him!
But the thunder of His power who can
understand?"

Job Maintains His Integrity

27 Moreover Job continued his discourse, and said:

2 "*As* God lives, *who* has taken away my
justice,

And the Almighty, *who* has made my soul
bitter,
3 As long as my breath *is* in me,
And the breath of God in my nostrils,
4 My lips will not speak wickedness,
Nor my tongue utter deceit.
5 Far be it from me
That I should say you are right;
Till I die I will not put away my integrity
from me.
6 My righteousness I hold fast, and will not
let it go;
My heart shall not reproach *me* as long as I
live.

7 "May my enemy be like the wicked,
And he who rises up against me like the
unrighteous.
8 For what is the hope of the hypocrite,
Though he may gain *much*,
If God takes away his life?
9 Will God hear his cry
When trouble comes upon him?
10 Will he delight himself in the Almighty?
Will he always call on God?

11 "I will teach you about the hand of God;
What *is* with the Almighty I will not
conceal.
12 Surely all of you have seen *it*;
Why then do you behave with complete
nonsense?

13 "This is the portion of a wicked man with
God,
And the heritage of oppressors, received
from the Almighty:
14 If his children are multiplied, *it is* for the
sword;
And his offspring shall not be satisfied with
bread.
15 Those who survive him shall be buried in
death,
And their[a] widows shall not weep,
16 Though he heaps up silver like dust,
And piles up clothing like clay—
17 He may pile *it* up, but the just will
wear *it*,
And the innocent will divide the silver.
18 He builds his house like a moth,[a]
Like a booth *which* a watchman makes.
19 The rich man will lie down,

27:15 [a]Literally *his*   **27:18** [a]Following Masoretic
Text and Vulgate; Septuagint and Syriac read *spider*
(compare 8:14); Targum reads *decay*.

But not be gathered *up;*[a]
He opens his eyes,
And he *is* no more.

20 Terrors overtake him like a flood;
A tempest steals him away in the night.

21 The east wind carries him away, and he is
gone;
It sweeps him out of his place.

22 It hurls against him and does not spare;
He flees desperately from its power.

23 *Men* shall clap their hands at him,
And shall hiss him out of his place.

Job's Discourse on Wisdom

28 "Surely there is a mine for silver,
And a place *where* gold is
refined.

2 Iron is taken from the earth,
And copper *is* smelted *from* ore.

3 *Man* puts an end to darkness,
And searches every recess
For ore in the darkness and the shadow of
death.

4 He breaks open a shaft away from people;
In places forgotten by feet
They hang far away from men;
They swing to and fro.

5 *As for* the earth, from it comes bread,
But underneath it is turned up as by fire;

6 Its stones *are* the source of sapphires,
And it contains gold dust.

7 *That* path no bird knows,
Nor has the falcon's eye seen it.

8 The proud lions[a] have not trodden it,
Nor has the fierce lion passed over it.

9 He puts his hand on the flint;
He overturns the mountains at the roots.

10 He cuts out channels in the rocks,
And his eye sees every precious thing.

11 He dams up the streams from trickling;
What is hidden he brings forth to light.

12 "But where can wisdom be found?
And where *is* the place of understanding?

13 Man does not know its value,
Nor is it found in the land of the
living.

14 The deep says, '*It is* not in me';
And the sea says, '*It is* not with me.'

15 It cannot be purchased for gold,
Nor can silver be weighed *for* its price.

16 It cannot be valued in the gold of Ophir,
In precious onyx or sapphire.

17 Neither gold nor crystal can equal it,
Nor can it be exchanged for jewelry of
fine gold.

18 No mention shall be made of coral or
quartz,
For the price of wisdom *is* above rubies.

19 The topaz of Ethiopia cannot equal it,
Nor can it be valued in pure gold.

20 "From where then does wisdom come?
And where *is* the place of understanding?

21 It is hidden from the eyes of all living,
And concealed from the birds of the air.

22 Destruction and Death say,
'We have heard a report about it with our
ears.'

23 God understands its way,
And He knows its place.

24 For He looks to the ends of the earth,
And sees under the whole heavens,

25 To establish a weight for the wind,
And apportion the waters by measure.

26 When He made a law for the rain,
And a path for the thunderbolt,

27 Then He saw *wisdom*[a] and declared it;
He prepared it, indeed, He searched it out.

28 And to man He said,
'Behold, the fear of the Lord, that *is*
wisdom,
And to depart from evil *is* understanding.'"

Job's Summary Defense

29 Job further continued his discourse,
and said:

2 "Oh, that I were as *in* months past,
As *in* the days *when* God watched over me;

3 When His lamp shone upon my head,
And when by His light I walked *through*
darkness;

4 Just as I was in the days of my prime,
When the friendly counsel of God *was*
over my tent;

5 When the Almighty *was* yet with me,
When my children *were* around me;

6 When my steps were bathed with cream,[a]
And the rock poured out rivers of oil for
me!

7 "When I went out to the gate by the city,
When I took my seat in the open square,

27:19 [a]Following Masoretic Text and Targum;
Septuagint and Syriac read *But shall not add* (that is,
do it again); Vulgate reads *But take away nothing.*
28:8 [a]Literally *sons of pride,* figurative of the great
lions **28:27** [a]Literally *it* **29:6** [a]Masoretic Text
reads *wrath;* ancient versions and some Hebrew
manuscripts read *cream* (compare 20:17).

Wisdom: Job Recognizes His Source of Wisdom and Seeks It

(Job 28:23–28)

Despite his confusion and pain, Job makes it clear that he looks to God alone for wisdom. He understands that He cannot lead himself, much less his family, without God as his never-ending source of perspective and understanding. Job has heard from his friends and knows their theories ring hollow. The best they can muster is the wisdom of men; Job will not be satisfied until he has the wisdom of God.

The third chapter of James distinguishes between these two radically different sources of wisdom:

Wisdom from Below	Wisdom from Above
1. Works temporarily in a few situations	1. Is universal and timeless, yet eternally relevant
2. Seems logical for the moment	2. Often seems illogical or even backwards
3. Limited in scope	3. Always big picture and unlimited in scope
4. Competitive: it is win/lose	4. Complementary: it is win/win

8 The young men saw me and hid,
And the aged arose *and* stood;
9 The princes refrained from talking,
And put *their* hand on their mouth;
10 The voice of nobles was hushed,
And their tongue stuck to the roof of their mouth.
11 When the ear heard, then it blessed me,
And when the eye saw, then it approved me;
12 Because I delivered the poor who cried out,
The fatherless and *the one who* had no helper.
13 The blessing of a perishing *man* came upon me,
And I caused the widow's heart to sing for joy.
14 I put on righteousness, and it clothed me;
My justice *was* like a robe and a turban.
15 I *was* eyes to the blind,
And I *was* feet to the lame.
16 I *was* a father to the poor,
And I searched out the case *that* I did not know.
17 I broke the fangs of the wicked,
And plucked the victim from his teeth.

18 "Then I said, 'I shall die in my nest,
And multiply *my* days as the sand.
19 My root *is* spread out to the waters,
And the dew lies all night on my branch.

20 My glory *is* fresh within me,
And my bow is renewed in my hand.'

21 "*Men* listened to me and waited,
And kept silence for my counsel.
22 After my words they did not speak again,
And my speech settled on them *as dew.*
23 They waited for me *as* for the rain,
And they opened their mouth wide *as* for the spring rain.
24 *If* I mocked at them, they did not believe *it,*
And the light of my countenance they did not cast down.
25 I chose the way for them, and sat as chief;
So I dwelt as a king in the army,
As one *who* comforts mourners.

30 "But now they mock at me, *men* younger than I,
Whose fathers I disdained to put with the dogs of my flock.
2 Indeed, what *profit is* the strength of their hands to me?
Their vigor has perished.
3 *They are* gaunt from want and famine,
Fleeing late to the wilderness, desolate and waste,
4 Who pluck mallow by the bushes,
And broom tree roots *for* their food.
5 They were driven out from among *men,*
They shouted at them as *at* a thief.
6 *They had* to live in the clefts of the valleys,

In caves of the earth and the rocks.
7   Among the bushes they brayed,
Under the nettles they nestled.
8   *They were* sons of fools,
Yes, sons of vile men;
They were scourged from the land.

9   "And now I am their taunting song;
Yes, I am their byword.
10   They abhor me, they keep far from me;
They do not hesitate to spit in my face.
11   Because He has loosed my[a] bowstring and
afflicted me,
They have cast off restraint before me.
12   At *my* right *hand* the rabble arises;
They push away my feet,
And they raise against me their ways of
destruction.
13   They break up my path,
They promote my calamity;
They have no helper.
14   They come as broad breakers;
Under the ruinous storm they roll along.
15   Terrors are turned upon me;
They pursue my honor as the wind,
And my prosperity has passed like a cloud.

16   "And now my soul is poured out because of
my *plight*;
The days of affliction take hold of me.
17   My bones are pierced in me at night,
And my gnawing pains take no rest.
18   By great force my garment is disfigured;
It binds me about as the collar of my coat.
19   He has cast me into the mire,
And I have become like dust and ashes.

20   "I cry out to You, but You do not answer
me;
I stand up, and You regard me.
21   *But* You have become cruel to me;
With the strength of Your hand You
oppose me.
22   You lift me up to the wind and cause me
to ride *on it*;
You spoil my success.
23   For I know *that* You will bring me *to*
death,
And *to* the house appointed for all living.

24   "Surely He would not stretch out *His* hand
against a heap of ruins,
If they cry out when He destroys *it*.
25   Have I not wept for him who was in
trouble?
Has *not* my soul grieved for the poor?

26   But when I looked for good, evil came *to*
me;
And when I waited for light, then came
darkness.
27   My heart is in turmoil and cannot rest;
Days of affliction confront me.
28   I go about mourning, but not in the sun;
I stand up in the assembly *and* cry out for
help.
29   I am a brother of jackals,
And a companion of ostriches.
30   My skin grows black and falls from me;
My bones burn with fever.
31   My harp is *turned* to mourning,
And my flute to the voice of those who
weep.

31

"I have made a covenant with my
eyes;
Why then should I look upon a
young woman?
2   For what *is* the allotment of God from above,
And the inheritance of the Almighty from
on high?
3   *Is* it not destruction for the wicked,
And disaster for the workers of iniquity?
4   Does He not see my ways,
And count all my steps?

5   "If I have walked with falsehood,
Or if my foot has hastened to deceit,
6   Let me be weighed on honest scales,
That God may know my integrity.
7   If my step has turned from the way,
Or my heart walked after my eyes,
Or if any spot adheres to my hands,
8   *Then* let me sow, and another eat;
Yes, let my harvest be rooted out.

9   "If my heart has been enticed by a woman,
Or *if* I have lurked at my neighbor's door,
10   *Then* let my wife grind for another,
And let others bow down over her.
11   For that *would be* wickedness;
Yes, it *would be* iniquity *deserving of*
judgment.
12   For that *would be* a fire *that* consumes to
destruction,
And would root out all my increase.

13   "If I have despised the cause of my male or
female servant
When they complained against me,

30:11 [a]Following Masoretic Text, Syriac, and
Targum; Septuagint and Vulgate read *His.*

Character and Consistency: Job Affirms His Promise

(Job 31:1–40)

One of the beautiful facets of the Book of Job is that it displays how a man can be very human, and yet very heavenly at the same time.

Job feels all the emotions of a man who has endured great loss. He becomes angry, depressed, and anxious, and declares his feelings openly. At the same time, he never drifts from his strong character; he remains consistent through everything. The moment it appears he will curse God and give up on Him, he affirms his promise to be faithful even when he doesn't understand what is happening. Job pledges to maintain his integrity despite his circumstances.

Such a commitment is a crucial key to leadership. Here's why:

1. Leaders must be visionary, but they cannot see everything in the future.
2. Instead of pretending to be in control, leaders must model being under control.
3. Leaders must model humanity and identify with the limitations of followers.
4. Leaders must model an anchored life, living from character, not emotions.
5. While leaders don't know what tomorrow holds, they do know who holds tomorrow.

---

14 What then shall I do when God rises up?
When He punishes, how shall I answer Him?

15 Did not He who made me in the womb make them?
Did not the same One fashion us in the womb?

16 "If I have kept the poor from *their* desire,
Or caused the eyes of the widow to fail,

17 Or eaten my morsel by myself,
So that the fatherless could not eat of it

18 (But from my youth I reared him as a father,
And from my mother's womb I guided *the widow*[a]);

19 If I have seen anyone perish for lack of clothing,
Or any poor *man* without covering;

20 If his heart[a] has not blessed me,
And *if* he was *not* warmed with the fleece of my sheep;

21 If I have raised my hand against the fatherless,
When I saw I had help in the gate;

22 *Then* let my arm fall from my shoulder,
Let my arm be torn from the socket.

23 For destruction *from* God *is* a terror to me,
And because of His magnificence I cannot endure.

24 "If I have made gold my hope,
Or said to fine gold, 'You *are* my confidence';

25 If I have rejoiced because my wealth *was* great,
And because my hand had gained much;

26 If I have observed the sun[a] when it shines,
Or the moon moving *in* brightness,

27 So that my heart has been secretly enticed,
And my mouth has kissed my hand;

28 This also *would be* an iniquity *deserving of* judgment,
For I would have denied God who is above.

29 "If I have rejoiced at the destruction of him who hated me,
Or lifted myself up when evil found him

30 (Indeed I have not allowed my mouth to sin
By asking for a curse on his soul);

31 If the men of my tent have not said,
'Who is there that has not been satisfied with his meat?'

32 (*But* no sojourner had to lodge in the street,
For I have opened my doors to the traveler[a]);

33 If I have covered my transgressions as Adam,

31:18 [a]Literally *her* (compare verse 16)
31:20 [a]Literally *loins*   **31:26** [a]Literally *light*
31:32 [a]Following Septuagint, Syriac, Targum, and Vulgate; Masoretic Text reads *road.*

By hiding my iniquity in my bosom,
34 Because I feared the great multitude,
And dreaded the contempt of families,
So that I kept silence
And did not go out of the door—
35 Oh, that I had one to hear me!
Here is my mark.
Oh, that the Almighty would answer me,
That my Prosecutor had written a book!
36 Surely I would carry it on my shoulder,
And bind it on me *like* a crown;
37 I would declare to Him the number of my
steps;
Like a prince I would approach Him.

38 "If my land cries out against me,
And its furrows weep together;
39 If I have eaten its fruit[a] without money,
Or caused its owners to lose their lives;
40 *Then* let thistles grow instead of wheat,
And weeds instead of barley."

The words of Job are ended.

Elihu Contradicts Job's Friends

32 So these three men ceased answering
Job, because he *was* righteous in his
own eyes. ²Then the wrath of Elihu,
the son of Barachel the Buzite, of the family of
Ram, was aroused against Job; his wrath was
aroused because he justified himself rather than
God. ³Also against his three friends his wrath was
aroused, because they had found no answer, and
yet had condemned Job.

⁴Now because they *were* years older than he,
Elihu had waited to speak to Job.[a] ⁵When Elihu
saw that *there was* no answer in the mouth of
these three men, his wrath was aroused.

⁶So Elihu, the son of Barachel the Buzite, answered and said:

"I *am* young in years, and you *are* very old;
Therefore I was afraid,
And dared not declare my opinion to you.
7 I said, 'Age[a] should speak,
And multitude of years should teach
wisdom.'
8 But *there is* a spirit in man,
And the breath of the Almighty gives him
understanding.
9 Great men[a] are not *always* wise,
Nor do the aged *always* understand justice.

10 "Therefore I say, 'Listen to me,
I also will declare my opinion.'
11 Indeed I waited for your words,

I listened to your reasonings, while you
searched out what to say.
12 I paid close attention to you;
And surely not one of you convinced Job,
Or answered his words—
13 Lest you say,
'We have found wisdom';
God will vanquish him, not man.
14 Now he has not directed *his* words against
me;
So I will not answer him with your words.

15 "They are dismayed and answer no more;
Words escape them.
16 And I have waited, because they did not
speak,
Because they stood still *and* answered no
more.
17 I also will answer my part,
I too will declare my opinion.
18 For I am full of words;
The spirit within me compels me.
19 Indeed my belly *is* like wine *that* has no
vent;
It is ready to burst like new wineskins.
20 I will speak, that I may find relief;
I must open my lips and answer.
21 Let me not, I pray, show partiality to
anyone;
Nor let me flatter any man.
22 For I do not know how to flatter,
Else my Maker would soon take me away.

Elihu Contradicts Job

33 "But please, Job, hear my speech,
And listen to all my words.
2 Now, I open my mouth;
My tongue speaks in my mouth.
3 My words *come* from my upright heart;
My lips utter pure knowledge.
4 The Spirit of God has made me,
And the breath of the Almighty gives me
life.
5 If you can answer me,
Set *your* words in order before me;
Take your stand.
6 Truly I *am* as your spokesman[a] before God;
I also have been formed out of clay.
7 Surely no fear of me will terrify you,
Nor will my hand be heavy on you.

31:39 [a]Literally *its strength* **32:4** [a]Vulgate reads *till
Job had spoken.* **32:7** [a]Literally *Days,* that is, years
32:9 [a]Or *Men of many years* **33:6** [a]Literally *as your
mouth*

8 "Surely you have spoken in my hearing,
  And I have heard the sound of *your* words,
    saying,
9 'I *am* pure, without transgression;
  I *am* innocent, and *there is* no iniquity in me.
10 Yet He finds occasions against me,
  He counts me as His enemy;
11 He puts my feet in the stocks,
  He watches all my paths.'

12 "Look, *in* this you are not righteous.
  I will answer you,
  For God is greater than man.
13 Why do you contend with Him?
  For He does not give an accounting of any
    of His words.
14 For God may speak in one way, or in
    another,
  Yet man does not perceive it.
15 In a dream, in a vision of the night,
  When deep sleep falls upon men,
  While slumbering on their beds,
16 Then He opens the ears of men,
  And seals their instruction.
17 In order to turn man *from his* deed,
  And conceal pride from man,
18 He keeps back his soul from the Pit,
  And his life from perishing by the sword.

19 "*Man* is also chastened with pain on his bed,
  And with strong *pain* in many of his
    bones,
20 So that his life abhors bread,
  And his soul succulent food.
21 His flesh wastes away from sight,
  And his bones stick out *which once* were
    not seen.
22 Yes, his soul draws near the Pit,
  And his life to the executioners.

23 "If there is a messenger for him,
  A mediator, one among a thousand,
  To show man His uprightness,
24 Then He is gracious to him, and says,
  'Deliver him from going down to the Pit;
  I have found a ransom';
25 His flesh shall be young like a child's,
  He shall return to the days of his youth.
26 He shall pray to God, and He will delight
    in him,
  He shall see His face with joy,
  For He restores to man His righteousness.
27 Then he looks at men and says,
  'I have sinned, and perverted *what was*
    right,
  And it did not profit me.'

28 He will redeem his[a] soul from going down
    to the Pit,
  And his[b] life shall see the light.

29 "Behold, God works all these *things,*
  Twice, *in fact,* three *times* with a man,
30 To bring back his soul from the Pit,
  That he may be enlightened with the light
    of life.

31 "Give ear, Job, listen to me;
  Hold your peace, and I will speak.
32 If you have anything to say, answer me;
  Speak, for I desire to justify you.
33 If not, listen to me;
  Hold your peace, and I will teach you
    wisdom."

Elihu Proclaims God's Justice

34 Elihu further answered and said:

2 "Hear my words, you wise *men;*
  Give ear to me, you who have knowledge.
3 For the ear tests words
  As the palate tastes food.
4 Let us choose justice for ourselves;
  Let us know among ourselves what *is*
    good.

5 "For Job has said, 'I am righteous,
  But God has taken away my justice;
6 Should I lie concerning my right?
  My wound *is* incurable, *though I am*
    without transgression.'
7 What man *is* like Job,
  Who drinks scorn like water,
8 Who goes in company with the workers
    of iniquity,
  And walks with wicked men?
9 For he has said, 'It profits a man nothing
  That he should delight in God.'

10 "Therefore listen to me, you men of
    understanding:
  Far be it from God *to do* wickedness,
  And *from* the Almighty to *commit* iniquity.
11 For He repays man *according to* his work,
  And makes man to find a reward according
    to *his* way.
12 Surely God will never do wickedly,
  Nor will the Almighty pervert justice.
13 Who gave Him charge over the earth?
  Or who appointed *Him over* the whole
    world?

33:28 [a]Or *my* (Kethib) [b]Or *my* (Kethib)

14 If He should set His heart on it,
    If He should gather to Himself His Spirit
        and His breath,
15 All flesh would perish together,
    And man would return to dust.

16 "If *you have* understanding, hear this;
    Listen to the sound of my words:
17 Should one who hates justice govern?
    Will you condemn *Him who is* most just?
18 *Is it fitting* to say to a king, 'You are
        worthless,'
    And to nobles, 'You are wicked'?
19 Yet He is not partial to princes,
    Nor does He regard the rich more than
        the poor;
    For they *are* all the work of His hands.
20 In a moment they die, in the middle of
        the night;
    The people are shaken and pass away;
    The mighty are taken away without a
        hand.

21 "For His eyes *are* on the ways of man,
    And He sees all his steps.
22 There is no darkness nor shadow of death
    Where the workers of iniquity may hide
        themselves.
23 For He need not further consider a man,
    That he should go before God in
        judgment.
24 He breaks in pieces mighty men without
        inquiry,
    And sets others in their place.
25 Therefore He knows their works;
    He overthrows *them* in the night,
    And they are crushed.
26 He strikes them as wicked *men*
    In the open sight of others,
27 Because they turned back from Him,
    And would not consider any of His ways,
28 So that they caused the cry of the poor to
        come to Him;
    For He hears the cry of the afflicted.
29 When He gives quietness, who then can
        make trouble?
    And when He hides *His* face, who then
        can see Him,
    Whether *it is* against a nation or a man
        alone?—
30 That the hypocrite should not reign,
    Lest the people be ensnared.

31 "For has *anyone* said to God,
    'I have borne *chastening;*
    I will offend no more;

32 Teach me *what* I do not see;
    If I have done iniquity, I will do no more'?
33 Should He repay *it* according to your *terms,*
    Just because you disavow it?
    You must choose, and not I;
    Therefore speak what you know.

34 "Men of understanding say to me,
    Wise men who listen to me:
35 'Job speaks without knowledge,
    His words *are* without wisdom.'
36 Oh, that Job were tried to the utmost,
    Because *his* answers *are like* those of
        wicked men!
37 For he adds rebellion to his sin;
    He claps *his hands* among us,
    And multiplies his words against God."

Elihu Condemns Self-Righteousness

35 Moreover Elihu answered and said:

2 "Do you think this is right?
    Do you say,
    'My righteousness is more than God's'?
3 For you say,
    'What advantage will it be to You?
    What profit shall I have, more than *if* I had
        sinned?'

4 "I will answer you,
    And your companions with you.
5 Look to the heavens and see;
    And behold the clouds—
    They are higher than you.
6 If you sin, what do you accomplish against
        Him?
    Or, *if* your transgressions are multiplied,
        what do you do to Him?
7 If you are righteous, what do you give
        Him?
    Or what does He receive from your
        hand?
8 Your wickedness affects a man such as you,
    And your righteousness a son of man.

9 "Because of the multitude of oppressions
        they cry out;
    They cry out for help because of the arm
        of the mighty.
10 But no one says, 'Where *is* God my
        Maker,
    Who gives songs in the night,
11 Who teaches us more than the beasts of
        the earth,
    And makes us wiser than the birds of
        heaven?'

12 There they cry out, but He does not answer,
Because of the pride of evil men.
13 Surely God will not listen to empty *talk,*
Nor will the Almighty regard it.
14 Although you say you do not see Him,
Yet justice *is* before Him, and you must wait for Him.
15 And now, because He has not punished in His anger,
Nor taken much notice of folly,
16 Therefore Job opens his mouth in vain;
He multiplies words without knowledge."

Elihu Proclaims God's Goodness

36 Elihu also proceeded and said:
2 "Bear with me a little, and I will show you
That *there are* yet words to speak on God's behalf.
3 I will fetch my knowledge from afar;
I will ascribe righteousness to my Maker.
4 For truly my words *are* not false;
One who is perfect in knowledge *is* with you.

5 "Behold, God *is* mighty, but despises *no one;*
He is mighty in strength of understanding.
6 He does not preserve the life of the wicked,
But gives justice to the oppressed.
7 He does not withdraw His eyes from the righteous;
But *they are* on the throne with kings,
For He has seated them forever,
And they are exalted.
8 And if *they are* bound in fetters,
Held in the cords of affliction,
9 Then He tells them their work and their transgressions—
That they have acted defiantly.
10 He also opens their ear to instruction,
And commands that they turn from iniquity.
11 If they obey and serve *Him,*
They shall spend their days in prosperity,
And their years in pleasures.
12 But if they do not obey,
They shall perish by the sword,
And they shall die without knowledge.[a]

13 "But the hypocrites in heart store up wrath;
They do not cry for help when He binds them.
14 They die in youth,
And their life *ends* among the perverted persons.[a]
15 He delivers the poor in their affliction,
And opens their ears in oppression.

16 "Indeed He would have brought you out of dire distress,
Into a broad place where *there is* no restraint;
And what is set on your table *would be* full of richness.
17 But you are filled with the judgment due the wicked;
Judgment and justice take hold *of you.*
18 Because *there is* wrath, *beware* lest He take you away with *one* blow;
For a large ransom would not help you avoid *it.*
19 Will your riches,
Or all the mighty forces,
Keep you from distress?
20 Do not desire the night,
When people are cut off in their place.
21 Take heed, do not turn to iniquity,
For you have chosen this rather than affliction.

22 "Behold, God is exalted by His power;
Who teaches like Him?
23 Who has assigned Him His way,
Or who has said, 'You have done wrong'?

Elihu Proclaims God's Majesty

24 "Remember to magnify His work,
Of which men have sung.
25 Everyone has seen it;
Man looks on *it* from afar.

26 "Behold, God *is* great, and we do not know *Him;*
Nor can the number of His years *be* discovered.
27 For He draws up drops of water,
Which distill as rain from the mist,
28 Which the clouds drop down
And pour abundantly on man.
29 Indeed, can *anyone* understand the spreading of clouds,
The thunder from His canopy?
30 Look, He scatters His light upon it,
And covers the depths of the sea.
31 For by these He judges the peoples;

36:12 [a]Masoretic Text reads *as one without knowledge.*
36:14 [a]Hebrew *qedeshim,* that is, those practicing sodomy and prostitution in religious rituals

He gives food in abundance.
³² He covers *His* hands with lightning,
And commands it to strike.
³³ His thunder declares it,
The cattle also, concerning the rising *storm*.

37

¹ "At this also my heart trembles,
And leaps from its place.
² Hear attentively the thunder of
His voice,
And the rumbling *that* comes from His
mouth.
³ He sends it forth under the whole heaven,
His lightning to the ends of the earth.
⁴ After it a voice roars;
He thunders with His majestic voice,
And He does not restrain them when His
voice is heard.
⁵ God thunders marvelously with His voice;
He does great things which we cannot
comprehend.
⁶ For He says to the snow, 'Fall *on* the earth';
Likewise to the gentle rain and the heavy
rain of His strength.
⁷ He seals the hand of every man,
That all men may know His work.
⁸ The beasts go into dens,
And remain in their lairs.
⁹ From the chamber *of the south* comes the
whirlwind,
And cold from the scattering winds *of the
north*.
¹⁰ By the breath of God ice is given,
And the broad waters are frozen.
¹¹ Also with moisture He saturates the thick
clouds;
He scatters His bright clouds.
¹² And they swirl about, being turned by His
guidance,
That they may do whatever He commands
them
On the face of the whole earth.^a
¹³ He causes it to come,
Whether for correction,
Or for His land,
Or for mercy.

¹⁴ "Listen to this, O Job;
Stand still and consider the wondrous
works of God.
¹⁵ Do you know when God dispatches them,
And causes the light of His cloud to shine?
¹⁶ Do you know how the clouds are
balanced,
Those wondrous works of Him who is
perfect in knowledge?

¹⁷ Why *are* your garments hot,
When He quiets the earth by the south
wind?
¹⁸ With Him, have you spread out the skies,
Strong as a cast metal mirror?

¹⁹ "Teach us what we should say to Him,
For we can prepare nothing because of the
darkness.
²⁰ Should He be told that I *wish to* speak?
If a man were to speak, surely he would be
swallowed up.
²¹ Even now *men* cannot look at the light
when it is bright in the skies,
When the wind has passed and cleared
them.
²² He comes from the north *as* golden
splendor;
With God *is* awesome majesty.
²³ *As for* the Almighty, we cannot find Him;
He is excellent in power,
In judgment and abundant justice;
He does not oppress.
²⁴ Therefore men fear Him;
He shows no partiality to any *who are* wise
of heart."

The LORD Reveals His Omnipotence to Job

38

Then the LORD answered Job out of
the whirlwind, and said:

² "Who *is* this who darkens counsel
By words without knowledge?
³ Now prepare yourself like a man;
I will question you, and you shall answer
Me.

⁴ "Where were you when I laid the
foundations of the earth?
Tell *Me,* if you have understanding.
⁵ Who determined its measurements?
Surely you know!
Or who stretched the line upon it?
⁶ To what were its foundations fastened?
Or who laid its cornerstone,
⁷ When the morning stars sang together,
And all the sons of God shouted for joy?

⁸ "Or *who* shut in the sea with doors,
When it burst forth *and* issued from the
womb;
⁹ When I made the clouds its garment,
And thick darkness its swaddling band;

37:12 ^aLiterally *the world of the earth*

God Rebukes Men for Questioning His Justice

(Job 38:1–7)

When God finally enters the scene in Job 38, He brings justice and perspective with Him. He rebukes Eliphaz, Bildad, and Zophar for projecting their opinions as though they represented the mind of God (a danger every spiritual leader faces!). Before God is finished, He poses His own question: Where were you when I created the world?

Many leaders feel a great temptation to pretend they know everything that's coming down the pike. They feel an unreasonable need to project self-confidence, not realizing that people soon recognize their pretension. Leaders often fail to understand that people do not need a leader to have every answer.

Consider this: Individuals can live without certainty from a leader, but not without clarity. Leaders must be genuine with their people. Unless a word has come to us directly from the mouth of the Lord, we cannot know what is coming in the future. Don't speak with certainty on an issue of which you are unsure! Yet when you do speak, speak with clarity, even if your words paint only a small part of the whole picture. Your people do not need certainty on every issue, but they do need clarity on every issue. It is clarity that helps organizations to progress.

10 When I fixed My limit for it,
And set bars and doors;
11 When I said,
'This far you may come, but no farther,
And here your proud waves must stop!'

12 "Have you commanded the morning since
your days *began,*
And caused the dawn to know its place,
13 That it might take hold of the ends of the
earth,
And the wicked be shaken out of it?
14 It takes on form like clay *under* a seal,
And stands out like a garment.
15 From the wicked their light is withheld,
And the upraised arm is broken.

16 "Have you entered the springs of the sea?
Or have you walked in search of the
depths?
17 Have the gates of death been revealed to
you?
Or have you seen the doors of the shadow
of death?
18 Have you comprehended the breadth of
the earth?
Tell *Me,* if you know all this.

19 "Where *is* the way *to* the dwelling of light?
And darkness, where *is* its place,
20 That you may take it to its territory,
That you may know the paths *to* its home?

21 Do you know *it,* because you were born
then,
Or *because* the number of your days *is*
great?

22 "Have you entered the treasury of snow,
Or have you seen the treasury of hail,
23 Which I have reserved for the time of
trouble,
For the day of battle and war?
24 By what way is light diffused,
Or the east wind scattered over the earth?

25 "Who has divided a channel for the
overflowing *water,*
Or a path for the thunderbolt,
26 To cause it to rain on a land *where there is*
no one,
A wilderness in which *there is* no man;
27 To satisfy the desolate waste,
And cause to spring forth the growth of
tender grass?
28 Has the rain a father?
Or who has begotten the drops of dew?
29 From whose womb comes the ice?
And the frost of heaven, who gives it
birth?
30 The waters harden like stone,
And the surface of the deep is frozen.

31 "Can you bind the cluster of the Pleiades,
Or loose the belt of Orion?

32 Can you bring out Mazzaroth[a] in its
   season?
   Or can you guide the Great Bear with its
   cubs?
33 Do you know the ordinances of the
   heavens?
   Can you set their dominion over the earth?

34 "Can you lift up your voice to the clouds,
   That an abundance of water may cover
   you?
35 Can you send out lightnings, that they may
   go,
   And say to you, 'Here we are!'?
36 Who has put wisdom in the mind?[a]
   Or who has given understanding to the
   heart?
37 Who can number the clouds by wisdom?
   Or who can pour out the bottles of heaven,
38 When the dust hardens in clumps,
   And the clods cling together?

39 "Can you hunt the prey for the lion,
   Or satisfy the appetite of the young lions,
40 When they crouch in *their* dens,
   Or lurk in their lairs to lie in wait?
41 Who provides food for the raven,
   When its young ones cry to God,
   And wander about for lack of food?

39

1 "Do you know the time when the
   wild mountain goats bear young?
   Or can you mark when the deer
   gives birth?
2 Can you number the months *that* they
   fulfill?
   Or do you know the time when they bear
   young?
3 They bow down,
   They bring forth their young,
   They deliver their offspring.[a]
4 Their young ones are healthy,
   They grow strong with grain;
   They depart and do not return to them.

5 "Who set the wild donkey free?
   Who loosed the bonds of the onager,
6 Whose home I have made the wilderness,
   And the barren land his dwelling?
7 He scorns the tumult of the city;
   He does not heed the shouts of the driver.
8 The range of the mountains *is* his pasture,
   And he searches after every green thing.

9 "Will the wild ox be willing to serve you?
   Will he bed by your manger?

10 Can you bind the wild ox in the furrow
   with ropes?
   Or will he plow the valleys behind you?
11 Will you trust him because his strength *is*
   great?
   Or will you leave your labor to him?
12 Will you trust him to bring home your
   grain,
   And gather it to your threshing floor?

13 "The wings of the ostrich wave proudly,
   But are her wings and pinions *like the*
   kindly stork's?
14 For she leaves her eggs on the ground,
   And warms them in the dust;
15 She forgets that a foot may crush them,
   Or that a wild beast may break them.
16 She treats her young harshly, as though
   they were not hers;
   Her labor is in vain, without concern,
17 Because God deprived her of wisdom,
   And did not endow her with
   understanding.
18 When she lifts herself on high,
   She scorns the horse and its rider.

19 "Have you given the horse strength?
   Have you clothed his neck with thunder?[a]
20 Can you frighten him like a locust?
   His majestic snorting strikes terror.
21 He paws in the valley, and rejoices in *his*
   strength;
   He gallops into the clash of arms.
22 He mocks at fear, and is not frightened;
   Nor does he turn back from the sword.
23 The quiver rattles against him,
   The glittering spear and javelin.
24 He devours the distance with fierceness
   and rage;
   Nor does he come to a halt because the
   trumpet *has* sounded.
25 At *the blast of* the trumpet he says, 'Aha!'
   He smells the battle from afar,
   The thunder of captains and shouting.

26 "Does the hawk fly by your wisdom,
   And spread its wings toward the south?
27 Does the eagle mount up at your
   command,
   And make its nest on high?
28 On the rock it dwells and resides,
   On the crag of the rock and the stronghold.

38:32 [a]Literally *Constellations*   **38:36** [a]Literally
inward parts   **39:3** [a]Literally *pangs,* figurative of
offspring   **39:19** [a]Or *a mane*

29 From there it spies out the prey;
Its eyes observe from afar.
30 Its young ones suck up blood;
And where the slain *are*, there it *is*."

40 Moreover the LORD answered Job, and said:

2 "Shall the one who contends with the
Almighty correct *Him*?
He who rebukes God, let him answer it."

Job's Response to God

³Then Job answered the LORD and said:

4 "Behold, I am vile;
What shall I answer You?
I lay my hand over my mouth.
5 Once I have spoken, but I will not answer;
Yes, twice, but I will proceed no further."

Humility: Like All Good Leaders, Job Acknowledges His Weakness

(Job 40:3–5; 42:1–6)

When God confronts Job with His power and majesty, Job responds with absolute humility (Job 40:3–5). The chastened man doesn't try to defend himself or rationalize his feelings. He confesses his humanity, then shuts his mouth.

And still God is not finished with His awesome lesson.

Even after Job acknowledges his insignificance and presumption, God delivers a second speech, graphically describing His power to control everything. He glories in the might of Behemoth and the ferocity of Leviathan, and asks Job if he dare go near either one. This time Job responds with deep repentance (42:1–6), clearly marking the difference between his friends and him.

Good leaders feel secure enough to repent when wrong. They don't have to project their self-worth, defend their every move, or make excuses for their failures. In the end, God rebuked Job's friends and rewarded Job—but not until the end.

God's Challenge to Job

⁶Then the LORD answered Job out of the whirlwind, and said:

7 "Now prepare yourself like a man;
I will question you, and you shall answer
Me:

8 "Would you indeed annul My judgment?
Would you condemn Me that you may be
justified?
9 Have you an arm like God?
Or can you thunder with a voice like
His?
10 Then adorn yourself *with* majesty and
splendor,
And array yourself with glory and beauty.
11 Disperse the rage of your wrath;
Look on everyone *who is* proud, and
humble him.
12 Look on everyone *who is* proud, *and* bring
him low;
Tread down the wicked in their place.
13 Hide them in the dust together,
Bind their faces in hidden *darkness*.
14 Then I will also confess to you
That your own right hand can save you.

15 "Look now at the behemoth,ᵃ which I
made *along* with you;
He eats grass like an ox.
16 See now, his strength *is* in his hips,
And his power *is* in his stomach muscles.
17 He moves his tail like a cedar;
The sinews of his thighs are tightly knit.
18 His bones *are like* beams of bronze,
His ribs like bars of iron.
19 He *is* the first of the ways of God;
Only He who made him can bring near
His sword.
20 Surely the mountains yield food for him,
And all the beasts of the field play there.
21 He lies under the lotus trees,
In a covert of reeds and marsh.
22 The lotus trees cover him *with* their
shade;
The willows by the brook surround him.
23 Indeed the river may rage,
Yet he is not disturbed;
He is confident, though the Jordan gushes
into his mouth,
24 *Though* he takes it in his eyes,
Or one pierces *his* nose with a snare.

40:15 ᵃA large animal, exact identity unknown

41 "Can you draw out Leviathan[a] with a hook,
  Or *snare* his tongue with a line
    which you lower?
2 Can you put a reed through his nose,
  Or pierce his jaw with a hook?
3 Will he make many supplications to you?
  Will he speak softly to you?
4 Will he make a covenant with you?
  Will you take him as a servant forever?
5 Will you play with him as *with* a bird,
  Or will you leash him for your maidens?
6 Will *your* companions make a banquet[a] of him?
  Will they apportion him among the merchants?
7 Can you fill his skin with harpoons,
  Or his head with fishing spears?
8 Lay your hand on him;
  Remember the battle—
  Never do it again!
9 Indeed, *any* hope of *overcoming* him is false;
  Shall *one not* be overwhelmed at the sight of him?
10 No one *is so* fierce that he would dare stir him up.
  Who then is able to stand against Me?
11 Who has preceded Me, that I should pay *him?*
  Everything under heaven is Mine.

12 "I will not conceal[a] his limbs,
  His mighty power, or his graceful proportions.
13 Who can remove his outer coat?
  Who can approach *him* with a double bridle?
14 Who can open the doors of his face,
  With his terrible teeth all around?
15 *His* rows of scales are *his* pride,
  Shut up tightly *as with* a seal;
16 One is so near another
  That no air can come between them;
17 They are joined one to another,
  They stick together and cannot be parted.
18 His sneezings flash forth light,
  And his eyes *are* like the eyelids of the morning.
19 Out of his mouth go burning lights;
  Sparks of fire shoot out.
20 Smoke goes out of his nostrils,
  As *from* a boiling pot and burning rushes.
21 His breath kindles coals,
  And a flame goes out of his mouth.
22 Strength dwells in his neck,
  And sorrow dances before him.

23 The folds of his flesh are joined together;
  They are firm on him and cannot be moved.
24 His heart is as hard as stone,
  Even as hard as the lower *millstone.*
25 When he raises himself up, the mighty are afraid;
  Because of his crashings they are beside[a] themselves.
26 *Though* the sword reaches him, it cannot avail;
  Nor does spear, dart, or javelin.
27 He regards iron as straw,
  And bronze as rotten wood.
28 The arrow cannot make him flee;
  Slingstones become like stubble to him.
29 Darts are regarded as straw;
  He laughs at the threat of javelins.
30 His undersides *are* like sharp potsherds;
  He spreads pointed *marks* in the mire.
31 He makes the deep boil like a pot;
  He makes the sea like a pot of ointment.
32 He leaves a shining wake behind him;
  One would think the deep had white hair.
33 On earth there is nothing like him,
  Which is made without fear.
34 He beholds every high *thing;*
  He *is* king over all the children of pride."

Job's Repentance and Restoration

42 Then Job answered the LORD and said:

2 "I know that You can do everything,
  And that no purpose *of Yours* can be withheld from You.
3 *You asked,* 'Who *is* this who hides counsel without knowledge?'
  Therefore I have uttered what I did not understand,
  Things too wonderful for me, which I did not know.
4 Listen, please, and let me speak;
  You said, 'I will question you, and you shall answer Me.'

5 "I have heard of You by the hearing of the ear,
  But now my eye sees You.
6 Therefore I abhor *myself,*
  And repent in dust and ashes."

41:1 [a]A large sea creature, exact identity unknown
41:6 [a]Or *bargain over him*   **41:12** [a]Literally *keep silent about*   **41:25** [a]Or *purify themselves*

[7]And so it was, after the LORD had spoken these words to Job, that the LORD said to Eliphaz the Temanite, "My wrath is aroused against you and your two friends, for you have not spoken of Me *what is* right, as My servant Job *has.* [8]Now therefore, take for yourselves seven bulls and seven rams, go to My servant Job, and offer up for yourselves a burnt offering; and My servant Job shall pray for you. For I will accept him, lest I deal with you *according to your* folly; because you have not spoken of Me *what is* right, as My servant Job *has.*"

[9]So Eliphaz the Temanite and Bildad the Shuhite *and* Zophar the Naamathite went and did as the LORD commanded them; for the LORD had accepted Job. [10]And the LORD restored Job's losses[a] when he prayed for his friends. Indeed the LORD gave Job twice as much as he had before. [11]Then all his brothers, all his sisters, and all those who had been his acquaintances before, came to him and ate food with him in his house; and they consoled him and comforted him for all the adversity that the LORD had brought upon him. Each one gave him a piece of silver and each a ring of gold.

[12]Now the LORD blessed the latter *days* of Job more than his beginning; for he had fourteen thousand sheep, six thousand camels, one thousand yoke of oxen, and one thousand female donkeys. [13]He also had seven sons and three daughters. [14]And he called the name of the first Jemimah, the name of the second Keziah, and the name of the third Keren-Happuch. [15]In all the land were found no women *so* beautiful as the daughters of Job; and their father gave them an inheritance among their brothers.

[16]After this Job lived one hundred and forty years, and saw his children and grandchildren *for* four generations. [17]So Job died, old and full of days.

42:10 [a]Literally *Job's captivity,* that is, what was captured from Job

Relationships: Job Takes the High Road

(Job 42:10)

After enduring nearly 40 chapters of criticism and condemnation from Eliphaz, Bildad, and Zophar, Job has the opportunity to get even. God announces His displeasure with them, apparently giving Job a wonderful chance to say, "I told you so." Instead, Job prays for his foolish friends.

Like all great leaders, Job refused to take vengeance or hold grudges. Instead, he took the high road. He forgave his friends, interceded for them, and sent them on their way. Remind yourself of the differences between the low road and the high road:

Low Road
1. Revenge and retaliation when wronged
2. Plays the same game as others
3. Guided by emotions; is up and down
4. Reactive: lives no better than anyone else

High Road
1. Unconditional love and forgiveness
2. Refuses to play games; lives by principles
3. Guided by character and values
4. Proactive: lives above merely human standards

PSALMS
Poetic Words Reflect Human Emotions

SUMMARY

Bible readers through the ages have flocked to the Book of Psalms. Its poetic words reflect the entire range of human emotions. The various writers of the psalms aim to express their deepest feelings and longings—as well as the truth of God's wisdom.

These ancient Hebrew songs contribute to our understanding of leadership in both definitive and dynamic ways. They are *definitive* because they contain God's thoughts and values; they help leaders to understand how God thinks, what He values, and how He might respond to a leader's circumstances. They are *dynamic* because they explore the ups and downs of a leader's humanity. David, who wrote the majority of the psalms, expressed every emotion he felt as a leader, from the joy of God's victories, to deep contrition for his sin and shortcomings, anger over national injustice and lack of vision, and sadness over his weakness and lack of understanding.

Several writers contributed over many years to the collection we know as the Psalms. David, Asaph, the sons of Korah, Solomon, Moses, Heman, Ethan, and a handful of anonymous authors all made unique contributions to this amazing "hymnal of Israel." We learn at least two great leadership lessons from them:

1. *Leaders remain human.*
2. *Leadership is relationships.*

Leadership always concerns more than cold, sterile strategy or achievement of goals. It demands that leaders shepherd others, exhort them, and build internal motivation in the hearts of their followers. David, especially, speaks continually about his relationships—both his vertical relationship with God and his horizontal relationships with people. The people loved him because of his competency and compassion.

God's Role in Psalms

Can anyone doubt that Psalm 23 would win a contest for "Most Popular Psalm"? It portrays the Lord not as the omnipotent Creator, not as the brilliant Strategist or the mighty Captain, but as a loving Shepherd who leads and guides His people with a rod and a staff.

David worked as a shepherd in his youth and later, as king, tapped the lessons he had learned in the fields. The psalms picture the intimate nature of God's relationship to His people.

Leaders in Psalms

David, Asaph, Solomon, the sons of Korah, Moses, Heman, Ethan

Other People of Influence in Psalms

The enemies of Israel, the wicked, the people of Israel

Lessons in Leadership

- Leaders never lose their humanity; they hurt when their people hurt.

- Leaders must be guided by principles and values worth dying for.

- Leaders gain credibility through their own vulnerability and transparency.

- Leaders take refuge in the Lord and allow Him to fight battles through them.

- Leaders must be honest about their emotions.

- Leaders recognize that the good in their lives comes from above.

- A leader's highest aim should be to honor and glorify God.

- The primary difference between a follower and a leader is perspective.

LEADERSHIP

HIGHLIGHTS IN PSALMS

Book One: Psalms 1—41

PSALM 1

The Way of the Righteous and the End of the Ungodly

1 Blessed *is* the man
Who walks not in the counsel of the ungodly,
Nor stands in the path of sinners,
Nor sits in the seat of the scornful;
2 But his delight *is* in the law of the LORD,
And in His law he meditates day and night.
3 He shall be like a tree
Planted by the rivers of water,
That brings forth its fruit in its season,
Whose leaf also shall not wither;
And whatever he does shall prosper.

4 The ungodly *are* not so,
But *are* like the chaff which the wind drives away.
5 Therefore the ungodly shall not stand in the judgment,
Nor sinners in the congregation of the righteous.
6 For the LORD knows the way of the righteous,
But the way of the ungodly shall perish.

PSALM 2

The Messiah's Triumph and Kingdom

1 Why do the nations rage,
And the people plot a vain thing?
2 The kings of the earth set themselves,
And the rulers take counsel together,
Against the LORD and against His Anointed, *saying,*
3 "Let us break Their bonds in pieces
And cast away Their cords from us."

4 He who sits in the heavens shall laugh;
The LORD shall hold them in derision.
5 Then He shall speak to them in His wrath,
And distress them in His deep displeasure:
6 "Yet I have set My King
On My holy hill of Zion."

7 "I will declare the decree:
The LORD has said to Me,
'You *are* My Son,
Today I have begotten You.

The Law of the Inner Circle: Be Careful Where You Get Your Counsel

(Psalm 1:1–3)

The brilliant first psalm contrasts the righteous and the wicked. Leaders, take note, for the difference between the two seems to be where they get their counsel! Observe how a foolish leader can be led astray by a corrupt inner circle:

1. The leader begins to browse for the wrong counsel (v. 1).
2. The leader begins to listen to the wrong voices (v. 1).
3. The leader joins the wrong inner circle (v. 1).

Psalm 1:2 tells us that a wise leader meditates on God's Word day and night. To meditate means to examine, to experience, and to evaluate. Note the results of receiving counsel from the right inner circle:

1. Stability (v. 3)
2. Inward nourishment and refreshment (v. 3)
3. Fruitfulness and productivity (v. 3)
4. Strength and durability (v. 3)
5. Success (v. 3)

8 Ask of Me, and I will give *You*
The nations *for* Your inheritance,
And the ends of the earth *for* Your possession.
9 You shall break[a] them with a rod of iron;
You shall dash them to pieces like a potter's vessel.' "

10 Now therefore, be wise, O kings;
Be instructed, you judges of the earth.
11 Serve the LORD with fear,
And rejoice with trembling.
12 Kiss the Son,[a] lest He[b] be angry,

2:9 [a]Following Masoretic Text and Targum; Septuagint, Syriac, and Vulgate read *rule* (compare Revelation 2:27). **2:12** [a]Septuagint and Vulgate read *Embrace discipline;* Targum reads *Receive instruction.* [b]Septuagint reads *the* LORD.

And you perish *in* the way,
When His wrath is kindled but a little.
Blessed *are* all those who put their trust in
Him.

PSALM 3

The LORD Helps His Troubled People

A Psalm of David when he fled
from Absalom his son.

1 LORD, how they have increased who
trouble me!
Many *are* they who rise up against me.
2 Many *are* they who say of me,
"*There is* no help for him in God." Selah

3 But You, O LORD, *are* a shield for me,
My glory and the One who lifts up my
head.
4 I cried to the LORD with my voice,
And He heard me from His holy hill.
Selah

5 I lay down and slept;
I awoke, for the LORD sustained me.
6 I will not be afraid of ten thousands of
people
Who have set *themselves* against me all
around.

7 Arise, O LORD;
Save me, O my God!
For You have struck all my enemies on the
cheekbone;
You have broken the teeth of the ungodly.
8 Salvation *belongs* to the LORD.
Your blessing *is* upon Your people. Selah

PSALM 4

The Safety of the Faithful

To the Chief Musician. With stringed instruments.
A Psalm of David.

1 Hear me when I call, O God of my
righteousness!
You have relieved me in *my* distress;
Have mercy on me, and hear my prayer.

2 How long, O you sons of men,
Will you turn my glory to shame?
How long will you love worthlessness
And seek falsehood? Selah
3 But know that the LORD has set apart[a] for
Himself him who is godly;
The LORD will hear when I call to Him.

4 Be angry, and do not sin.
Meditate within your heart on your bed,
and be still. Selah
5 Offer the sacrifices of righteousness,
And put your trust in the LORD.

6 *There are* many who say,
"Who will show us *any* good?"
LORD, lift up the light of Your
countenance upon us.
7 You have put gladness in my heart,
More than in the season that their grain
and wine increased.
8 I will both lie down in peace, and sleep;
For You alone, O LORD, make me dwell in
safety.

PSALM 5

A Prayer for Guidance

To the Chief Musician. With flutes.[a]
A Psalm of David.

1 Give ear to my words, O LORD,
Consider my meditation.
2 Give heed to the voice of my cry,
My King and my God,
For to You I will pray.
3 My voice You shall hear in the morning,
O LORD;
In the morning I will direct *it* to You,
And I will look up.

4 For You *are* not a God who takes pleasure
in wickedness,
Nor shall evil dwell with You.
5 The boastful shall not stand in Your sight;
You hate all workers of iniquity.
6 You shall destroy those who speak
falsehood;
The LORD abhors the bloodthirsty and
deceitful man.

7 But as for me, I will come into Your house
in the multitude of Your mercy;
In fear of You I will worship toward Your
holy temple.
8 Lead me, O LORD, in Your righteousness
because of my enemies;
Make Your way straight before my face.

9 For *there is* no faithfulness in their mouth;
Their inward part *is* destruction;

4:3 [a]Many Hebrew manuscripts, Septuagint,
Targum, and Vulgate read *made wonderful.*
5:title [a]Hebrew *nehiloth*

Their throat *is* an open tomb;
They flatter with their tongue.
10 Pronounce them guilty, O God!
Let them fall by their own counsels;
Cast them out in the multitude of their
    transgressions,
For they have rebelled against You.

11 But let all those rejoice who put their trust
    in You;
Let them ever shout for joy, because You
    defend them;
Let those also who love Your name
Be joyful in You.
12 For You, O LORD, will bless the righteous;
With favor You will surround him as *with*
    a shield.

PSALM 6

A Prayer of Faith in Time of Distress

To the Chief Musician. With stringed instruments.
   On an eight-stringed harp.[a] A Psalm of David.

1 O LORD, do not rebuke me in Your
    anger,
Nor chasten me in Your hot displeasure.
2 Have mercy on me, O LORD, for I *am*
    weak;
O LORD, heal me, for my bones are
    troubled.
3 My soul also is greatly troubled;
But You, O LORD—how long?

4 Return, O LORD, deliver me!
Oh, save me for Your mercies' sake!
5 For in death *there is* no remembrance of
    You;
In the grave who will give You thanks?

6 I am weary with my groaning;
All night I make my bed swim;
I drench my couch with my tears.
7 My eye wastes away because of grief;
It grows old because of all my enemies.

8 Depart from me, all you workers of
    iniquity;
For the LORD has heard the voice of my
    weeping.
9 The LORD has heard my supplication;
The LORD will receive my prayer.
10 Let all my enemies be ashamed and greatly
    troubled;
Let them turn back *and* be ashamed
    suddenly.

The Leader's Humanity: Don't Hide It

(Psalm 6:1–10)

David was a "man after [God's] own heart" (Acts 13:22), but he never hesitated to reveal his emotions or his weakness. Even as king of Israel, he declared his fears, his anxieties, and his ambitions. Good leaders know how to balance transparency with being an example. Good leaders feel secure enough to be vulnerable.

PSALM 7

Prayer and Praise for Deliverance from Enemies

A Meditation[a] of David, which he sang to the
    LORD concerning the words of Cush, a
                    Benjamite.

1 O LORD my God, in You I put my trust;
Save me from all those who persecute me;
And deliver me,
2 Lest they tear me like a lion,
Rending *me* in pieces, while *there is* none
    to deliver.

3 O LORD my God, if I have done this:
If there is iniquity in my hands,
4 If I have repaid evil to him who was at
    peace with me,
Or have plundered my enemy without
    cause,
5 Let the enemy pursue me and overtake *me*;
Yes, let him trample my life to the earth,
And lay my honor in the dust.   Selah

6 Arise, O LORD, in Your anger;
Lift Yourself up because of the rage of my
    enemies;
Rise up for me[a] *to* the judgment You have
    commanded!
7 So the congregation of the peoples shall
    surround You;
For their sakes, therefore, return on high.
8 The LORD shall judge the peoples;

6:title [a]Hebrew *sheminith* 7:title [a]Hebrew *Shiggaion*
7:6 [a]Following Masoretic Text, Targum, and
Vulgate; Septuagint reads O LORD *my God.*

Judge me, O LORD, according to my
righteousness,
And according to my integrity within me.

9 Oh, let the wickedness of the wicked
come to an end,
But establish the just;
For the righteous God tests the hearts and
minds.
10 My defense *is* of God,
Who saves the upright in heart.

11 God *is* a just judge,
And God is angry *with the wicked* every
day.
12 If he does not turn back,
He will sharpen His sword;
He bends His bow and makes it ready.
13 He also prepares for Himself instruments
of death;
He makes His arrows into fiery shafts.

14 Behold, *the wicked* brings forth iniquity;
Yes, he conceives trouble and brings forth
falsehood.
15 He made a pit and dug it out,
And has fallen into the ditch *which* he
made.
16 His trouble shall return upon his own
head,

And his violent dealing shall come down
on his own crown.

17 I will praise the LORD according to His
righteousness,
And will sing praise to the name of the
LORD Most High.

PSALM 8

The Glory of the LORD in Creation

To the Chief Musician. On the instrument of
Gath.[a] A Psalm of David.

1 O LORD, our Lord,
How excellent *is* Your name in all the earth,
Who have set Your glory above the
heavens!

2 Out of the mouth of babes and nursing
infants
You have ordained strength,
Because of Your enemies,
That You may silence the enemy and the
avenger.

3 When I consider Your heavens, the work
of Your fingers,

8:title [a]Hebrew *Al Gittith*

Identity: A Balanced Perspective of God's Role and the Leader's Role

(Psalm 8:3–9)

Have you ever asked, "When does a leader's confidence become arrogance? How self-assured should I be as a leader? What does humility look like in a leader's life?"
Psalm 8 answers those questions. This passage shows leaders how to balance their identity with their self-esteem. Consider how David perceives his identity and maintains both confidence and humility:

1. David sees clearly his own weakness and humanity (vv. 3, 4).
David begins by asking a question: "Why does God even give any thought to me?" He realizes that in the sweep of the galaxy, man accounts for only a very small part. Remembering this helps us to remain humble.

2. David sees his God-given position and privileges (vv. 5–8).
David knows that God has made humankind a little lower than Himself. The Lord put men and women in charge of the whole earth and gave them authority over creation.

3. David sees a balance by giving all the glory to God (v. 9).
David closes the psalm the way he began. He magnifies the Lord and gives Him the credit for the good that has come from his life and leadership.

The moon and the stars, which You have
ordained,
4 What is man that You are mindful of him,
And the son of man that You visit him?
5 For You have made him a little lower than
the angels,[a]
And You have crowned him with glory
and honor.

6 You have made him to have dominion
over the works of Your hands;
You have put all *things* under his feet,
7 All sheep and oxen—
Even the beasts of the field,
8 The birds of the air,
And the fish of the sea
That pass through the paths of the seas.

9 O LORD, our Lord,
How excellent *is* Your name in all the
earth!

PSALM 9

Prayer and Thanksgiving for the LORD's Righteous Judgments

To the Chief Musician. To *the tune of*
"Death of the Son."[a] A Psalm of David.

1 I will praise *You,* O LORD, with my whole
heart;
I will tell of all Your marvelous works.
2 I will be glad and rejoice in You;
I will sing praise to Your name, O Most
High.

3 When my enemies turn back,
They shall fall and perish at Your
presence.
4 For You have maintained my right and my
cause;
You sat on the throne judging in
righteousness.
5 You have rebuked the nations,
You have destroyed the wicked;
You have blotted out their name forever
and ever.

6 O enemy, destructions are finished forever!
And you have destroyed cities;
Even their memory has perished.
7 But the LORD shall endure forever;
He has prepared His throne for judgment.
8 He shall judge the world in righteousness,
And He shall administer judgment for the
peoples in uprightness.

9 The LORD also will be a refuge for the
oppressed,
A refuge in times of trouble.
10 And those who know Your name will put
their trust in You;
For You, LORD, have not forsaken those
who seek You.

11 Sing praises to the LORD, who dwells in
Zion!
Declare His deeds among the people.
12 When He avenges blood, He remembers
them;
He does not forget the cry of the
humble.

13 Have mercy on me, O LORD!
Consider my trouble from those who hate
me,
You who lift me up from the gates of
death,
14 That I may tell of all Your praise
In the gates of the daughter of Zion.
I will rejoice in Your salvation.

15 The nations have sunk down in the pit
which they made;
In the net which they hid, their own foot
is caught.
16 The LORD is known *by* the judgment He
executes;
The wicked is snared in the work of his
own hands.
Meditation.[a]   Selah

17 The wicked shall be turned into hell,
And all the nations that forget God.
18 For the needy shall not always be
forgotten;
The expectation of the poor shall *not*
perish forever.

19 Arise, O LORD,
Do not let man prevail;
Let the nations be judged in Your sight.
20 Put them in fear, O LORD,
That the nations may know themselves to
be but men.   Selah

8:5 [a]Hebrew *Elohim, God;* Septuagint, Syriac,
Targum, and Jewish tradition translate as *angels.*
9:title [a]Hebrew *Muth Labben* **9:16** [a]Hebrew
Higgaion

PSALM 10

A Song of Confidence in God's Triumph over Evil

1 Why do You stand afar off, O LORD?
Why do You hide in times of trouble?
2 The wicked in *his* pride persecutes the poor;
Let them be caught in the plots which they have devised.

3 For the wicked boasts of his heart's desire;
He blesses the greedy *and* renounces the LORD.
4 The wicked in his proud countenance does not seek *God;*
God *is* in none of his thoughts.

5 His ways are always prospering;
Your judgments *are* far above, out of his sight;
As for all his enemies, he sneers at them.
6 He has said in his heart, "I shall not be moved;
I shall never be in adversity."
7 His mouth is full of cursing and deceit and oppression;
Under his tongue *is* trouble and iniquity.

8 He sits in the lurking places of the villages;
In the secret places he murders the innocent;
His eyes are secretly fixed on the helpless.
9 He lies in wait secretly, as a lion in his den;
He lies in wait to catch the poor;
He catches the poor when he draws him into his net.
10 So he crouches, he lies low,
That the helpless may fall by his strength.
11 He has said in his heart,
"God has forgotten;
He hides His face;
He will never see."

12 Arise, O LORD!
O God, lift up Your hand!
Do not forget the humble.
13 Why do the wicked renounce God?
He has said in his heart,
"You will not require *an account.*"

14 But You have seen, for You observe trouble and grief,
To repay *it* by Your hand.
The helpless commits himself to You;
You are the helper of the fatherless.

15 Break the arm of the wicked and the evil *man;*
Seek out his wickedness *until* You find none.
16 The LORD *is* King forever and ever;
The nations have perished out of His land.
17 LORD, You have heard the desire of the humble;
You will prepare their heart;
You will cause Your ear to hear,
18 To do justice to the fatherless and the oppressed,
That the man of the earth may oppress no more.

PSALM 11

Faith in the LORD's Righteousness

To the Chief Musician. A Psalm of David.

1 In the LORD I put my trust;
How can you say to my soul,
"Flee *as* a bird to your mountain"?
2 For look! The wicked bend *their* bow,
They make ready their arrow on the string,
That they may shoot secretly at the upright in heart.
3 If the foundations are destroyed,
What can the righteous do?

4 The LORD *is* in His holy temple,
The LORD's throne *is* in heaven;
His eyes behold,
His eyelids test the sons of men.
5 The LORD tests the righteous,
But the wicked and the one who loves violence His soul hates.
6 Upon the wicked He will rain coals;
Fire and brimstone and a burning wind
Shall be the portion of their cup.

7 For the LORD *is* righteous,
He loves righteousness;
His countenance beholds the upright.[a]

PSALM 12

Man's Treachery and God's Constancy

To the Chief Musician. On an eight-stringed harp.[a] A Psalm of David.

1 Help, LORD, for the godly man ceases!
For the faithful disappear from among the sons of men.

11:7 [a]Or *The upright beholds His countenance*
12:title [a]Hebrew *sheminith*

2 They speak idly everyone with his
neighbor;
With flattering lips *and* a double heart they
speak.

3 May the LORD cut off all flattering lips,
And the tongue that speaks proud things,
4 Who have said,
"With our tongue we will prevail;
Our lips *are* our own;
Who *is* lord over us?"

5 "For the oppression of the poor, for the
sighing of the needy,
Now I will arise," says the LORD;
"I will set *him* in the safety for which he
yearns."

6 The words of the LORD *are* pure words,
Like silver tried in a furnace of earth,
Purified seven times.
7 You shall keep them, O LORD,
You shall preserve them from this
generation forever.

8 The wicked prowl on every side,
When vileness is exalted among the sons
of men.

PSALM 13

Trust in the Salvation of the LORD

To the Chief Musician. A Psalm of David.

1 How long, O LORD? Will You forget me
forever?
How long will You hide Your face from
me?
2 How long shall I take counsel in my
soul,
Having sorrow in my heart daily?
How long will my enemy be exalted over
me?

3 Consider *and* hear me, O LORD my God;
Enlighten my eyes,
Lest I sleep the *sleep of* death;
4 Lest my enemy say,
"I have prevailed against him";
Lest those who trouble me rejoice when I
am moved.

5 But I have trusted in Your mercy;
My heart shall rejoice in Your salvation.
6 I will sing to the LORD,
Because He has dealt bountifully with me.

PSALM 14

Folly of the Godless, and God's Final Triumph

To the Chief Musician. A Psalm of David.

1 The fool has said in his heart,
" *There is* no God."
They are corrupt,
They have done abominable works,
There is none who does good.

2 The LORD looks down from heaven upon
the children of men,
To see if there are any who understand,
who seek God.
3 They have all turned aside,
They have together become corrupt;
There is none who does good,
No, not one.

4 Have all the workers of iniquity no
knowledge,
Who eat up my people *as* they eat bread,
And do not call on the LORD?
5 There they are in great fear,
For God *is* with the generation of the
righteous.
6 You shame the counsel of the poor,
But the LORD *is* his refuge.

7 Oh, that the salvation of Israel *would come*
out of Zion!
When the LORD brings back the captivity
of His people,
Let Jacob rejoice *and* Israel be glad.

PSALM 15

The Character of Those Who May Dwell with the LORD

A Psalm of David.

1 LORD, who may abide in Your tabernacle?
Who may dwell in Your holy hill?

2 He who walks uprightly,
And works righteousness,
And speaks the truth in his heart;
3 He *who* does not backbite with his tongue,
Nor does evil to his neighbor,
Nor does he take up a reproach against
his friend;
4 In whose eyes a vile person is despised,
But he honors those who fear the
LORD;

Value-Driven Leadership

(Psalm 15:1–5)

What qualities should every leader possess? Psalm 15 furnishes us with a list of many of the necessary traits.

David describes a righteous man who walks in integrity and gains not only the respect of others, but also an audience with God (Ps. 15:1, 2). He demonstrates why predetermined values and ethics, not expediency, must drive our leadership. How does David picture a godly leader? The leader . . .

- possesses integrity (v. 2)
- does what is right (v. 2)
- is honest and trustworthy (v. 2)
- does not gossip (v. 3)
- does not listen to gossip (v. 3)
- does no harm to others (v. 3)
- speaks out against wrong (v. 4)
- honors others who walk in truth (v. 4)
- keeps their word even when it costs them (v. 4)
- isn't greedy to gain at the expense of others (v. 5)
- takes no bribes against anyone (v. 5)
- is strong and stable (v. 5)

He *who* swears to his own hurt and does not change;

5 He *who* does not put out his money at usury,
Nor does he take a bribe against the innocent.

He who does these *things* shall never be moved.

PSALM 16

The Hope of the Faithful, and the Messiah's Victory

A Michtam of David.

1 Preserve me, O God, for in You I put my trust.

2 *O my soul,* you have said to the LORD,
"You *are* my Lord,
My goodness is nothing apart from You."

3 As for the saints who *are* on the earth,

"They are the excellent ones, in whom is all my delight."

4 Their sorrows shall be multiplied who hasten *after* another *god;*
Their drink offerings of blood I will not offer,
Nor take up their names on my lips.

5 O LORD, *You are* the portion of my inheritance and my cup;
You maintain my lot.

6 The lines have fallen to me in pleasant *places;*
Yes, I have a good inheritance.

7 I will bless the LORD who has given me counsel;
My heart also instructs me in the night seasons.

8 I have set the LORD always before me;
Because *He is* at my right hand I shall not be moved.

9 Therefore my heart is glad, and my glory rejoices;
My flesh also will rest in hope.

10 For You will not leave my soul in Sheol,
Nor will You allow Your Holy One to see corruption.

11 You will show me the path of life;
In Your presence *is* fullness of joy;
At Your right hand *are* pleasures forevermore.

PSALM 17

Prayer with Confidence in Final Salvation

A Prayer of David.

1 Hear a just cause, O LORD,
Attend to my cry;
Give ear to my prayer *which is* not from deceitful lips.

2 Let my vindication come from Your presence;
Let Your eyes look on the things that are upright.

3 You have tested my heart;
You have visited *me* in the night;
You have tried me and have found nothing;
I have purposed that my mouth shall not transgress.

4 Concerning the works of men,
By the word of Your lips,

I have kept away from the paths of the
destroyer.

5 Uphold my steps in Your paths,
That my footsteps may not slip.

6 I have called upon You, for You will hear
me, O God;
Incline Your ear to me, *and* hear my speech.

7 Show Your marvelous lovingkindness by
Your right hand,
O You who save those who trust *in You*
From those who rise up *against them*.

8 Keep me as the apple of Your eye;
Hide me under the shadow of Your wings,

9 From the wicked who oppress me,
From my deadly enemies who surround me.

10 They have closed up their fat *hearts;*
With their mouths they speak proudly.

11 They have now surrounded us in our steps;
They have set their eyes, crouching down
to the earth,

12 As a lion is eager to tear his prey,
And like a young lion lurking in secret
places.

13 Arise, O LORD,
Confront him, cast him down;

Deliver my life from the wicked with Your
sword,

14 With Your hand from men, O LORD,
From men of the world *who have* their
portion in *this* life,
And whose belly You fill with Your
hidden treasure.
They are satisfied with children,
And leave the rest of their *possession* for
their babes.

15 As for me, I will see Your face in
righteousness;
I shall be satisfied when I awake in Your
likeness.

PSALM 18

God the Sovereign Savior

To the Chief Musician. A Psalm of David the
servant of the LORD, who spoke to the LORD the
words of this song on the day that the LORD
delivered him from the hand of all his enemies
and from the hand of Saul. And he said:

1 I will love You, O LORD, my strength.

2 The LORD is my rock and my fortress and
my deliverer;

God: An Absolute Leader in a Relative World

(Psalm 18:1–34)

God is an absolute in a relative world. So how can leaders learn to rely on Him? Psalm 18 gives
some answers.

David not only models what it means to be a leader, but also how to lean completely on the God
who transcends the universe and judges it. Human leaders can find refuge in God's absolute
leadership for two reasons:

1. The Lord is a mighty Protector.
2. The Lord is an effective Equipper.

Psalm 18:1–29 describes the tangible benefits of living according to this truth. When leaders
adopt it, they can perform beyond their abilities. Why? Because God enables them to do so. The
psalmist declares that God "teaches" or "trains" their hands for battle (18:34). Leaders are to
emulate both roles, in addition to several others pictured throughout the psalms:

1. The leader as a king (20:9)
2. The leader as a shepherd (23:1)
3. The leader as a guide/counselor (48:14)
4. The leader as a disciplinarian (50:16–21)
5. The leader as a provider (72:6)
6. The leader as a creator/innovator (95:5)
7. The leader as a worker/producer (107:37)

My God, my strength, in whom I will
    trust;
My shield and the horn of my salvation,
    my stronghold.

3 I will call upon the LORD, *who is worthy* to
    be praised;
So shall I be saved from my enemies.

4 The pangs of death surrounded me,
And the floods of ungodliness made me
    afraid.
5 The sorrows of Sheol surrounded me;
The snares of death confronted me.
6 In my distress I called upon the LORD,
And cried out to my God;
He heard my voice from His temple,
And my cry came before Him, *even* to His
    ears.

7 Then the earth shook and trembled;
The foundations of the hills also quaked
    and were shaken,
Because He was angry.
8 Smoke went up from His nostrils,
And devouring fire from His mouth;
Coals were kindled by it.
9 He bowed the heavens also, and came
    down
With darkness under His feet.
10 And He rode upon a cherub, and flew;
He flew upon the wings of the wind.
11 He made darkness His secret place;
His canopy around Him *was* dark waters
And thick clouds of the skies.
12 From the brightness before Him,
His thick clouds passed with hailstones and
    coals of fire.

13 The LORD thundered from heaven,
And the Most High uttered His voice,
Hailstones and coals of fire.[a]
14 He sent out His arrows and scattered the
    foe,
Lightnings in abundance, and He
    vanquished them.
15 Then the channels of the sea were seen,
The foundations of the world were
    uncovered
At Your rebuke, O LORD,
At the blast of the breath of Your nostrils.

16 He sent from above, He took me;
He drew me out of many waters.
17 He delivered me from my strong enemy,
From those who hated me,
For they were too strong for me.

18 They confronted me in the day of my
    calamity,
But the LORD was my support.
19 He also brought me out into a broad place;
He delivered me because He delighted in
    me.

20 The LORD rewarded me according to my
    righteousness;
According to the cleanness of my hands
He has recompensed me.
21 For I have kept the ways of the LORD,
And have not wickedly departed from my
    God.
22 For all His judgments *were* before me,
And I did not put away His statutes from
    me.
23 I was also blameless before Him,
And I kept myself from my iniquity.
24 Therefore the LORD has recompensed me
    according to my righteousness,
According to the cleanness of my hands in
    His sight.

25 With the merciful You will show Yourself
    merciful;
With a blameless man You will show
    Yourself blameless;
26 With the pure You will show Yourself
    pure;
And with the devious You will show
    Yourself shrewd.
27 For You will save the humble people,
But will bring down haughty looks.

28 For You will light my lamp;
The LORD my God will enlighten my
    darkness.
29 For by You I can run against a troop,
By my God I can leap over a wall.
30 *As for* God, His way *is* perfect;
The word of the LORD is proven;
He *is* a shield to all who trust in Him.

31 For who *is* God, except the LORD?
And who *is* a rock, except our God?
32 *It is* God who arms me with strength,
And makes my way perfect.
33 He makes my feet like the *feet of* deer,
And sets me on my high places.
34 He teaches my hands to make war,
So that my arms can bend a bow of bronze.

18:13 [a]Following Masoretic Text, Targum, and
Vulgate; a few Hebrew manuscripts and Septuagint
omit *Hailstones and coals of fire.*

35 You have also given me the shield of Your
    salvation;
Your right hand has held me up,
Your gentleness has made me great.

36 You enlarged my path under me,
So my feet did not slip.

37 I have pursued my enemies and overtaken
    them;
Neither did I turn back again till they
    were destroyed.

38 I have wounded them,
So that they could not rise;
They have fallen under my feet.

39 For You have armed me with strength for
    the battle;
You have subdued under me those who
    rose up against me.

40 You have also given me the necks of my
    enemies,
So that I destroyed those who hated me.

41 They cried out, but *there was* none to save;
Even to the LORD, but He did not answer
    them.

42 Then I beat them as fine as the dust before
    the wind;
I cast them out like dirt in the streets.

43 You have delivered me from the strivings
    of the people;
You have made me the head of the
    nations;
A people I have not known shall serve me.

44 As soon as they hear of me they obey me;
The foreigners submit to me.

45 The foreigners fade away,
And come frightened from their hideouts.

46 The LORD lives!
Blessed *be* my Rock!
Let the God of my salvation be exalted.

47 *It is* God who avenges me,
And subdues the peoples under me;

48 He delivers me from my enemies.
You also lift me up above those who rise
    against me;
You have delivered me from the violent
    man.

49 Therefore I will give thanks to You, O
    LORD, among the Gentiles,
And sing praises to Your name.

50 Great deliverance He gives to His king,
And shows mercy to His anointed,
To David and his descendants
    forevermore.

PSALM 19

The Perfect Revelation of the LORD

To the Chief Musician. A Psalm of David.

1 The heavens declare the glory of God;
And the firmament shows His handiwork.

2 Day unto day utters speech,
And night unto night reveals knowledge.

3 *There is* no speech nor language
Where their voice is not heard.

4 Their line[a] has gone out through all the
    earth,
And their words to the end of the world.

In them He has set a tabernacle for the
    sun,

5 Which *is* like a bridegroom coming out of
    his chamber,
And rejoices like a strong man to run its
    race.

6 Its rising *is* from one end of heaven,
And its circuit to the other end;
And there is nothing hidden from its heat.

7 The law of the LORD *is* perfect, converting
    the soul;
The testimony of the LORD *is* sure,
    making wise the simple;

8 The statutes of the LORD *are* right,
    rejoicing the heart;
The commandment of the LORD *is* pure,
    enlightening the eyes;

9 The fear of the LORD *is* clean, enduring
    forever;
The judgments of the LORD *are* true *and*
    righteous altogether.

10 More to be desired *are they* than gold,
Yea, than much fine gold;
Sweeter also than honey and the
    honeycomb.

11 Moreover by them Your servant is warned,
And in keeping them *there is* great reward.

12 Who can understand *his* errors?
Cleanse me from secret *faults.*

13 Keep back Your servant also from
    presumptuous *sins;*
Let them not have dominion over me.
Then I shall be blameless,
And I shall be innocent of great
    transgression.

19:4 [a]Septuagint, Syriac, and Vulgate read *sound;*
Targum reads *business.*

Leaders Communicate

(Psalm 19:1–14)

God is not only the Ultimate Leader, but the Ultimate Communicator. The creation declares God's power and glory (Ps. 19:1–6). The Law declares God's wisdom and will (19:7–14). God precisely reveals His message to His followers through both. Three simple verses (19:7–9) declare the results of this ultimate communication:

God's Revelation	Description	The Results
1. His Law	1. Perfect	1. Restores the soul
2. Testimony	2. Sure	2. Makes us wise
3. Statutes	3. Right	3. Gives joy to the heart
4. Commandments	4. Pure	4. Enlightens our perception
5. Fear and reverence	5. Clean	5. Endures forever
6. Judgments	6. True	6. Completely right

14 Let the words of my mouth and the
    meditation of my heart
Be acceptable in Your sight,
O LORD, my strength and my Redeemer.

PSALM 20

The Assurance of God's Saving Work

To the Chief Musician. A Psalm of David.

1 May the LORD answer you in the day of
    trouble;
May the name of the God of Jacob defend
    you;
2 May He send you help from the sanctuary,
And strengthen you out of Zion;
3 May He remember all your offerings,
And accept your burnt sacrifice. Selah

4 May He grant you according to your
    heart's *desire,*
And fulfill all your purpose.
5 We will rejoice in your salvation,
And in the name of our God we will set
    up *our* banners!
May the LORD fulfill all your petitions.

6 Now I know that the LORD saves His
    anointed;
He will answer him from His holy heaven
With the saving strength of His right hand.

7 Some *trust* in chariots, and some in horses;
But we will remember the name of the
    LORD our God.

8 They have bowed down and fallen;
But we have risen and stand upright.

9 Save, LORD!
May the King answer us when we call.

PSALM 21

Joy in the Salvation of the LORD

To the Chief Musician.
A Psalm of David.

1 The king shall have joy in Your strength,
    O LORD;
And in Your salvation how greatly shall he
    rejoice!
2 You have given him his heart's desire,
And have not withheld the request of his
    lips. Selah

3 For You meet him with the blessings of
    goodness;
You set a crown of pure gold upon his
    head.
4 He asked life from You, *and* You gave *it* to
    him—
Length of days forever and ever.
5 His glory *is* great in Your salvation;
Honor and majesty You have placed upon
    him.
6 For You have made him most blessed
    forever;
You have made him exceedingly glad with
    Your presence.
7 For the king trusts in the LORD,

And through the mercy of the Most High
he shall not be moved.

8 Your hand will find all Your enemies;
Your right hand will find those who hate
You.

9 You shall make them as a fiery oven in the
time of Your anger;
The LORD shall swallow them up in His
wrath,
And the fire shall devour them.

10 Their offspring You shall destroy from the
earth,
And their descendants from among the
sons of men.

11 For they intended evil against You;
They devised a plot *which* they are not able
to perform.

12 Therefore You will make them turn their
back;
You will make ready *Your arrows* on Your
string toward their faces.

13 Be exalted, O LORD, in Your own
strength!
We will sing and praise Your power.

PSALM 22

The Suffering, Praise, and Posterity of
the Messiah

To the Chief Musician. Set to "The Deer of the
Dawn."[a] A Psalm of David.

1 My God, My God, why have You forsaken
Me?
Why are You so far from helping Me,
And from the words of My groaning?

2 O My God, I cry in the daytime, but You
do not hear;
And in the night season, and am not silent.

3 But You *are* holy,
Enthroned in the praises of Israel.

4 Our fathers trusted in You;
They trusted, and You delivered them.

5 They cried to You, and were delivered;
They trusted in You, and were not
ashamed.

6 But I *am* a worm, and no man;
A reproach of men, and despised by the
people.

7 All those who see Me ridicule Me;
They shoot out the lip, they shake the
head, *saying,*

8 "He trusted[a] in the LORD, let Him rescue
Him;
Let Him deliver Him, since He delights in
Him!"

9 But You *are* He who took Me out of the
womb;
You made Me trust *while* on My mother's
breasts.

10 I was cast upon You from birth.
From My mother's womb
You *have been* My God.

11 Be not far from Me,
For trouble *is* near;
For *there is* none to help.

12 Many bulls have surrounded Me;
Strong *bulls* of Bashan have encircled Me.

13 They gape at Me *with* their mouths,
Like a raging and roaring lion.

14 I am poured out like water,
And all My bones are out of joint;
My heart is like wax;
It has melted within Me.

15 My strength is dried up like a potsherd,
And My tongue clings to My jaws;
You have brought Me to the dust of death.

16 For dogs have surrounded Me;
The congregation of the wicked has
enclosed Me.
They pierced[a] My hands and My feet;

17 I can count all My bones.
They look *and* stare at Me.

18 They divide My garments among them,
And for My clothing they cast lots.

19 But You, O LORD, do not be far from Me;
O My Strength, hasten to help Me!

20 Deliver Me from the sword,
My precious *life* from the power of the dog.

21 Save Me from the lion's mouth
And from the horns of the wild oxen!

You have answered Me.

22 I will declare Your name to My brethren;
In the midst of the assembly I will praise
You.

22:title [a]Hebrew *Aijeleth Hashahar*
22:8 [a]Septuagint, Syriac, and Vulgate read *hoped;*
Targum reads *praised.* **22:16** [a]Following some
Hebrew manuscripts, Septuagint, Syriac, Vulgate;
Masoretic Text reads *Like a lion.*

23 You who fear the LORD, praise Him!
All you descendants of Jacob, glorify Him,
And fear Him, all you offspring of Israel!
24 For He has not despised nor abhorred the
affliction of the afflicted;
Nor has He hidden His face from Him;
But when He cried to Him, He heard.

25 My praise *shall be* of You in the great
assembly;
I will pay My vows before those who fear
Him.
26 The poor shall eat and be satisfied;
Those who seek Him will praise the
LORD.
Let your heart live forever!

27 All the ends of the world
Shall remember and turn to the LORD,
And all the families of the nations
Shall worship before You.ª
28 For the kingdom *is* the LORD's,
And He rules over the nations.

29 All the prosperous of the earth
Shall eat and worship;
All those who go down to the dust
Shall bow before Him,
Even he who cannot keep himself alive.

30 A posterity shall serve Him.
It will be recounted of the Lord to the
next generation,
31 They will come and declare His
righteousness to a people who will be
born,
That He has done *this.*

PSALM 23

The LORD the Shepherd of His People

A Psalm of David.

1 The LORD *is* my shepherd;
I shall not want.
2 He makes me to lie down in green pastures;
He leads me beside the still waters.
3 He restores my soul;
He leads me in the paths of righteousness
For His name's sake.

4 Yea, though I walk through the valley of
the shadow of death,
I will fear no evil;
For You *are* with me;
Your rod and Your staff, they comfort me.

22:27 ªFollowing Masoretic Text, Septuagint, and
Targum; Arabic, Syriac, and Vulgate read *Him.*

The Leader as a Shepherd

(Psalm 23:1–6)

No psalm has gained more admirers than Psalm 23. In it, we learn not only about God's nature, but also about His leadership. David describes the Lord as a Shepherd, no doubt seeing Him this way because of his own leadership bias. David also had been a model shepherd.

Both Old and New Testaments use the term "shepherd" to illustrate leadership. The word communicates the love, nurture, intimacy, and spiritual care a godly leader provides. It involves both the rod (correction) and the staff (direction). Psalm 23 describes the Ultimate Shepherd performing several functions. The Shepherd . . .

- provides (v. 1)
- gives rest (v. 2)
- confidently leads (v. 3)
- renews and restores (v. 3)
- guides and directs (v. 3)
- protects (v. 4)
- corrects and comforts (v. 4)
- feeds and anoints (v. 5)
- loves (v. 6)
- furnishes permanent shelter (v. 6)

5 You prepare a table before me in the
presence of my enemies;
You anoint my head with oil;
My cup runs over.
6 Surely goodness and mercy shall follow me
All the days of my life;
And I will dwell[a] in the house of the
LORD
Forever.

The Leader and Stress
(Psalm 23:1–6)

Have you discovered the difference between problems and facts? Problems are things we can do something about; we can solve problems. Facts are things we can do nothing about; therefore we do well not to worry about them. We apply energy only to those things we can change. We can feel peace and act with poise, because we no longer beat our heads against an unbreakable wall.

Psalm 23 reminds us of what God alone can control and what we can control. It distinguishes between problems and facts. It defines God as . . .

- our possession (v. 1)
- our provision (v. 1)
- our peace (v. 2)
- our pardon (v. 3)
- our partner (v. 4)
- our preparation (v. 5)
- our praise (v. 5)
- our paradise (v. 6)

PSALM 24

The King of Glory and His Kingdom

A Psalm of David.

1 The earth *is* the LORD's, and all its fullness,
The world and those who dwell therein.
2 For He has founded it upon the seas,
And established it upon the waters.

3 Who may ascend into the hill of the
LORD?
Or who may stand in His holy place?
4 He who has clean hands and a pure
heart,
Who has not lifted up his soul to an idol,

Nor sworn deceitfully.
5 He shall receive blessing from the LORD,
And righteousness from the God of his
salvation.
6 This *is* Jacob, the generation of those who
seek Him,
Who seek Your face.   Selah

7 Lift up your heads, O you gates!
And be lifted up, you everlasting doors!
And the King of glory shall come in.
8 Who *is* this King of glory?
The LORD strong and mighty,
The LORD mighty in battle.
9 Lift up your heads, O you gates!
Lift up, you everlasting doors!
And the King of glory shall come in.
10 Who is this King of glory?
The LORD of hosts,
He *is* the King of glory.   Selah

PSALM 25

A Plea for Deliverance and Forgiveness

A Psalm of David.

1 To You, O LORD, I lift up my soul.
2 O my God, I trust in You;
Let me not be ashamed;
Let not my enemies triumph over me.
3 Indeed, let no one who waits on You be
ashamed;
Let those be ashamed who deal
treacherously without cause.

4 Show me Your ways, O LORD;
Teach me Your paths.
5 Lead me in Your truth and teach me,
For You *are* the God of my salvation;
On You I wait all the day.

6 Remember, O LORD, Your tender mercies
and Your lovingkindnesses,
For they *are* from of old.
7 Do not remember the sins of my youth,
nor my transgressions;
According to Your mercy remember me,
For Your goodness' sake, O LORD.

8 Good and upright *is* the LORD;
Therefore He teaches sinners in the way.
9 The humble He guides in justice,
And the humble He teaches His way.

23:6 [a]Following Septuagint, Syriac, Targum, and Vulgate; Masoretic Text reads *return*.

10 All the paths of the LORD *are* mercy and
truth,
To such as keep His covenant and His
testimonies.

11 For Your name's sake, O LORD,
Pardon my iniquity, for it *is* great.

12 Who *is* the man that fears the LORD?
Him shall He[a] teach in the way He[b]
chooses.

13 He himself shall dwell in prosperity,
And his descendants shall inherit the earth.

14 The secret of the LORD *is* with those who
fear Him,
And He will show them His covenant.

15 My eyes *are* ever toward the LORD,
For He shall pluck my feet out of the net.

16 Turn Yourself to me, and have mercy on me,
For I *am* desolate and afflicted.

17 The troubles of my heart have enlarged;
Bring me out of my distresses!

18 Look on my affliction and my pain,
And forgive all my sins.

19 Consider my enemies, for they are many;
And they hate me with cruel hatred.

20 Keep my soul, and deliver me;
Let me not be ashamed, for I put my trust
in You.

21 Let integrity and uprightness preserve me,
For I wait for You.

22 Redeem Israel, O God,
Out of all their troubles!

PSALM 26

A Prayer for Divine Scrutiny and Redemption

A Psalm of David.

1 Vindicate me, O LORD,
For I have walked in my integrity.
I have also trusted in the LORD;
I shall not slip.

2 Examine me, O LORD, and prove me;
Try my mind and my heart.

3 For Your lovingkindness *is* before my eyes,
And I have walked in Your truth.

4 I have not sat with idolatrous mortals,
Nor will I go in with hypocrites.

5 I have hated the assembly of evildoers,
And will not sit with the wicked.

6 I will wash my hands in innocence;
So I will go about Your altar, O LORD,

7 That I may proclaim with the voice of
thanksgiving,
And tell of all Your wondrous works.

8 LORD, I have loved the habitation of Your
house,
And the place where Your glory dwells.

9 Do not gather my soul with sinners,
Nor my life with bloodthirsty men,

10 In whose hands *is* a sinister scheme,
And whose right hand is full of bribes.

11 But as for me, I will walk in my integrity;
Redeem me and be merciful to me.

12 My foot stands in an even place;
In the congregations I will bless the LORD.

PSALM 27

An Exuberant Declaration of Faith

A Psalm of David.

1 The LORD *is* my light and my salvation;
Whom shall I fear?
The LORD *is* the strength of my life;
Of whom shall I be afraid?

2 When the wicked came against me
To eat up my flesh,
My enemies and foes,
They stumbled and fell.

3 Though an army may encamp against me,
My heart shall not fear;
Though war may rise against me,
In this I *will be* confident.

4 One *thing* I have desired of the LORD,
That will I seek:
That I may dwell in the house of the
LORD
All the days of my life,
To behold the beauty of the LORD,
And to inquire in His temple.

5 For in the time of trouble
He shall hide me in His pavilion;
In the secret place of His tabernacle
He shall hide me;
He shall set me high upon a rock.

6 And now my head shall be lifted up above
my enemies all around me;
Therefore I will offer sacrifices of joy in
His tabernacle;
I will sing, yes, I will sing praises to the
LORD.

25:12 [a]Or *he* [b]Or *he*

7 Hear, O LORD, *when* I cry with my voice!
Have mercy also upon me, and answer me.
8 *When You said,* "Seek My face,"
My heart said to You, "Your face, LORD, I
will seek."
9 Do not hide Your face from me;
Do not turn Your servant away in anger;
You have been my help;
Do not leave me nor forsake me,
O God of my salvation.
10 When my father and my mother forsake
me,
Then the LORD will take care of me.

11 Teach me Your way, O LORD,
And lead me in a smooth path, because of
my enemies.
12 Do not deliver me to the will of my
adversaries;
For false witnesses have risen against me,
And such as breathe out violence.
13 *I would have lost heart,* unless I had believed
That I would see the goodness of the
LORD
In the land of the living.

14 Wait on the LORD;
Be of good courage,
And He shall strengthen your heart;
Wait, I say, on the LORD!

PSALM 28

Rejoicing in Answered Prayer

A Psalm of David.

1 To You I will cry, O LORD my Rock:
Do not be silent to me,
Lest, if You *are* silent to me,
I become like those who go down to the
pit.
2 Hear the voice of my supplications
When I cry to You,
When I lift up my hands toward Your holy
sanctuary.

3 Do not take me away with the wicked
And with the workers of iniquity,
Who speak peace to their neighbors,
But evil *is* in their hearts.
4 Give them according to their deeds,
And according to the wickedness of their
endeavors;
Give them according to the work of their
hands;
Render to them what they deserve.

5 Because they do not regard the works of
the LORD,
Nor the operation of His hands,
He shall destroy them
And not build them up.

6 Blessed *be* the LORD,
Because He has heard the voice of my
supplications!
7 The LORD *is* my strength and my shield;
My heart trusted in Him, and I am helped;
Therefore my heart greatly rejoices,
And with my song I will praise Him.

8 The LORD *is* their strength,[a]
And He *is* the saving refuge of His
anointed.
9 Save Your people,
And bless Your inheritance;
Shepherd them also,
And bear them up forever.

PSALM 29

Praise to God in His Holiness and Majesty

A Psalm of David.

1 Give unto the LORD, O you mighty ones,
Give unto the LORD glory and strength.
2 Give unto the LORD the glory due to His
name;
Worship the LORD in the beauty of
holiness.

3 The voice of the LORD *is* over the waters;
The God of glory thunders;
The LORD *is* over many waters.
4 The voice of the LORD *is* powerful;
The voice of the LORD *is* full of majesty.

5 The voice of the LORD breaks the cedars,
Yes, the LORD splinters the cedars of
Lebanon.
6 He makes them also skip like a calf,
Lebanon and Sirion like a young wild ox.
7 The voice of the LORD divides the flames
of fire.

8 The voice of the LORD shakes the
wilderness;
The LORD shakes the Wilderness of
Kadesh.

28:8 [a]Following Masoretic Text and Targum;
Septuagint, Syriac, and Vulgate read *the strength of
His people.*

9 The voice of the LORD makes the deer
 give birth,
And strips the forests bare;
And in His temple everyone says, "Glory!"

10 The LORD sat *enthroned* at the Flood,
And the LORD sits as King forever.
11 The LORD will give strength to His people;
The LORD will bless His people with
 peace.

PSALM 30

The Blessedness of Answered Prayer

*A Psalm. A Song at the dedication
of the house of David.*

1 I will extol You, O LORD, for You have
 lifted me up,
And have not let my foes rejoice over me.
2 O LORD my God, I cried out to You,
And You healed me.
3 O LORD, You brought my soul up from
 the grave;
You have kept me alive, that I should not
 go down to the pit.[a]

4 Sing praise to the LORD, you saints of His,
And give thanks at the remembrance of
 His holy name.[a]
5 For His anger *is but for* a moment,
His favor *is for* life;
Weeping may endure for a night,
But joy *comes* in the morning.

6 Now in my prosperity I said,
"I shall never be moved."
7 LORD, by Your favor You have made my
 mountain stand strong;
You hid Your face, *and* I was troubled.

8 I cried out to You, O LORD;
And to the LORD I made supplication:
9 "What profit *is there* in my blood,
When I go down to the pit?
Will the dust praise You?
Will it declare Your truth?
10 Hear, O LORD, and have mercy on me;
LORD, be my helper!"

11 You have turned for me my mourning
 into dancing;
You have put off my sackcloth and clothed
 me with gladness,
12 To the end that *my* glory may sing praise
 to You and not be silent.

O LORD my God, I will give thanks to
 You forever.

PSALM 31

The LORD a Fortress in Adversity

To the Chief Musician. A Psalm of David.

1 In You, O LORD, I put my trust;
Let me never be ashamed;
Deliver me in Your righteousness.
2 Bow down Your ear to me,
Deliver me speedily;
Be my rock of refuge,
A fortress of defense to save me.

3 For You *are* my rock and my fortress;
Therefore, for Your name's sake,
Lead me and guide me.
4 Pull me out of the net which they have
 secretly laid for me,
For You *are* my strength.
5 Into Your hand I commit my spirit;
You have redeemed me, O LORD God of
 truth.

6 I have hated those who regard useless
 idols;
But I trust in the LORD.
7 I will be glad and rejoice in Your mercy,
For You have considered my trouble;
You have known my soul in adversities;
8 And have not shut me up into the hand of
 the enemy;
You have set my feet in a wide place.

9 Have mercy on me, O LORD, for I am in
 trouble;
My eye wastes away with grief,
Yes, my soul and my body!
10 For my life is spent with grief,
And my years with sighing;
My strength fails because of my iniquity,
And my bones waste away.
11 I am a reproach among all my enemies,
But especially among my neighbors,
And *am* repulsive to my acquaintances;
Those who see me outside flee from me.
12 I am forgotten like a dead man, out of
 mind;
I am like a broken vessel.
13 For I hear the slander of many;

30:3 [a]Following Qere and Targum; Kethib,
Septuagint, Syriac, and Vulgate read *from those who
descend to the pit.* **30:4** [a]Or *His holiness*

Fear *is* on every side;
While they take counsel together against
me,
They scheme to take away my life.

14 But as for me, I trust in You, O LORD;
I say, "You *are* my God."
15 My times *are* in Your hand;
Deliver me from the hand of my enemies,
And from those who persecute me.
16 Make Your face shine upon Your servant;
Save me for Your mercies' sake.
17 Do not let me be ashamed, O LORD, for I
have called upon You;
Let the wicked be ashamed;
Let them be silent in the grave.
18 Let the lying lips be put to silence,
Which speak insolent things proudly and
contemptuously against the righteous.

19 Oh, how great *is* Your goodness,
Which You have laid up for those who
fear You,
Which You have prepared for those who
trust in You
In the presence of the sons of men!
20 You shall hide them in the secret place of
Your presence
From the plots of man;
You shall keep them secretly in a pavilion
From the strife of tongues.

21 Blessed *be* the LORD,
For He has shown me His marvelous
kindness in a strong city!
22 For I said in my haste,
"I am cut off from before Your eyes";
Nevertheless You heard the voice of my
supplications
When I cried out to You.

23 Oh, love the LORD, all you His saints!
For the LORD preserves the faithful,
And fully repays the proud person.
24 Be of good courage,
And He shall strengthen your heart,
All you who hope in the LORD.

PSALM 32

The Joy of Forgiveness

A Psalm of David. A Contemplation.[a]

1 Blessed *is he whose* transgression *is*
forgiven,
Whose sin *is* covered.

2 Blessed *is* the man to whom the LORD
does not impute iniquity,
And in whose spirit *there is* no deceit.

3 When I kept silent, my bones grew old
Through my groaning all the day long.
4 For day and night Your hand was heavy
upon me;
My vitality was turned into the drought of
summer. Selah
5 I acknowledged my sin to You,
And my iniquity I have not hidden.
I said, "I will confess my transgressions to
the LORD,"
And You forgave the iniquity of my sin.
Selah

6 For this cause everyone who is godly shall
pray to You
In a time when You may be found;
Surely in a flood of great waters
They shall not come near him.
7 You *are* my hiding place;
You shall preserve me from trouble;
You shall surround me with songs of
deliverance. Selah

8 I will instruct you and teach you in the
way you should go;
I will guide you with My eye.
9 Do not be like the horse *or* like the mule,
Which have no understanding,
Which must be harnessed with bit and
bridle,
Else they will not come near you.

10 Many sorrows *shall be* to the wicked;
But he who trusts in the LORD, mercy
shall surround him.
11 Be glad in the LORD and rejoice, you
righteous;
And shout for joy, all *you* upright in heart!

PSALM 33

The Sovereignty of the LORD in Creation and History

1 Rejoice in the LORD, O you righteous!
For praise from the upright is beautiful.
2 Praise the LORD with the harp;
Make melody to Him with an instrument
of ten strings.

32:title [a]Hebrew *Maschil*

Guidance: Leaders Are Not Perfect, but Whole

(Psalm 32:8)

God does not expect leaders to be perfect, but to be whole. Have you appreciated the enormous difference? To have integrity means to be whole, as in a whole number (an "integer"). Despite his or her human frailties, a leader can effectively guide those who follow.

Psalm 32:8 reminds us that leaders must closely observe the flock for its needs and problems. God expects spiritual leaders to serve as guides. A guide gets a person or group safely to a planned destination. The Hebrew word for "guide" gives us several clues as to what God expects from those He uses as leaders:

1. A guide is a spiritual head who unites and directs people in their walk with God.
2. A guide takes people on the straight path that leads to fellowship with God.
3. A guide gives accurate and godly counsel to those who need it.
4. A guide leads with gentleness and trustworthiness, making others feel safe.
5. A guide bases his or her direction on the Spirit and the Word of God.

3 Sing to Him a new song;
Play skillfully with a shout of joy.

4 For the word of the LORD *is* right,
And all His work *is* done in truth.

5 He loves righteousness and justice;
The earth is full of the goodness of the LORD.

6 By the word of the LORD the heavens were made,
And all the host of them by the breath of His mouth.

7 He gathers the waters of the sea together as a heap;[a]
He lays up the deep in storehouses.

8 Let all the earth fear the LORD;
Let all the inhabitants of the world stand in awe of Him.

9 For He spoke, and it was *done;*
He commanded, and it stood fast.

10 The LORD brings the counsel of the nations to nothing;
He makes the plans of the peoples of no effect.

11 The counsel of the LORD stands forever,
The plans of His heart to all generations.

12 Blessed *is* the nation whose God *is* the LORD,
The people He has chosen as His own inheritance.

13 The LORD looks from heaven;
He sees all the sons of men.

14 From the place of His dwelling He looks
On all the inhabitants of the earth;

15 He fashions their hearts individually;
He considers all their works.

16 No king *is* saved by the multitude of an army;
A mighty man is not delivered by great strength.

17 A horse *is* a vain hope for safety;
Neither shall it deliver *any* by its great strength.

18 Behold, the eye of the LORD *is* on those who fear Him,
On those who hope in His mercy,

19 To deliver their soul from death,
And to keep them alive in famine.

20 Our soul waits for the LORD;
He *is* our help and our shield.

21 For our heart shall rejoice in Him,
Because we have trusted in His holy name.

22 Let Your mercy, O LORD, be upon us,
Just as we hope in You.

PSALM 34

The Happiness of Those Who Trust in God

A Psalm of David when he pretended madness before Abimelech, who drove him away, and he departed.

1 I will bless the LORD at all times;
His praise *shall* continually *be* in my mouth.

2 My soul shall make its boast in the LORD;

33:7 [a]Septuagint, Targum, and Vulgate read *in a vessel.*

The humble shall hear *of it* and be glad.

3 Oh, magnify the LORD with me,
And let us exalt His name together.

4 I sought the LORD, and He heard me,
And delivered me from all my fears.

5 They looked to Him and were radiant,
And their faces were not ashamed.

6 This poor man cried out, and the LORD
heard *him*,
And saved him out of all his troubles.

7 The angel[a] of the LORD encamps all
around those who fear Him,
And delivers them.

8 Oh, taste and see that the LORD *is* good;
Blessed *is* the man *who* trusts in Him!

9 Oh, fear the LORD, you His saints!
There is no want to those who fear Him.

10 The young lions lack and suffer hunger;
But those who seek the LORD shall not
lack any good *thing*.

11 Come, you children, listen to me;
I will teach you the fear of the LORD.

12 Who *is* the man *who* desires life,
And loves *many* days, that he may see
good?

13 Keep your tongue from evil,
And your lips from speaking deceit.

14 Depart from evil and do good;
Seek peace and pursue it.

15 The eyes of the LORD *are* on the
righteous,
And His ears *are open* to their cry.

16 The face of the LORD *is* against those who
do evil,
To cut off the remembrance of them from
the earth.

17 *The righteous* cry out, and the LORD hears,
And delivers them out of all their troubles.

18 The LORD *is* near to those who have a
broken heart,
And saves such as have a contrite spirit.

19 Many *are* the afflictions of the righteous,
But the LORD delivers him out of them all.

20 He guards all his bones;
Not one of them is broken.

21 Evil shall slay the wicked,
And those who hate the righteous shall be
condemned.

22 The LORD redeems the soul of His
servants,

And none of those who trust in Him shall
be condemned.

PSALM 35

The LORD the Avenger of His People

A Psalm of David.

1 Plead *my cause,* O LORD, with those who
strive with me;
Fight against those who fight against me.

2 Take hold of shield and buckler,
And stand up for my help.

3 Also draw out the spear,
And stop those who pursue me.
Say to my soul,
"I *am* your salvation."

4 Let those be put to shame and brought to
dishonor
Who seek after my life;
Let those be turned back and brought to
confusion
Who plot my hurt.

5 Let them be like chaff before the wind,
And let the angel[a] of the LORD chase
them.

6 Let their way be dark and slippery,
And let the angel of the LORD pursue
them.

7 For without cause they have hidden their
net for me *in* a pit,
Which they have dug without cause for my
life.

8 Let destruction come upon him
unexpectedly,
And let his net that he has hidden catch
himself;
Into that very destruction let him fall.

9 And my soul shall be joyful in the LORD;
It shall rejoice in His salvation.

10 All my bones shall say,
"LORD, who *is* like You,
Delivering the poor from him who is too
strong for him,
Yes, the poor and the needy from him
who plunders him?"

11 Fierce witnesses rise up;
They ask me *things* that I do not know.

12 They reward me evil for good,
To the sorrow of my soul.

13 But as for me, when they were sick,

34:7 [a]Or *Angel* **35:5** [a]Or *Angel*

My clothing *was* sackcloth;
I humbled myself with fasting;
And my prayer would return to my own
heart.
14 I paced about as though *he were* my friend
or brother;
I bowed down heavily, as one who mourns
for his mother.

15 But in my adversity they rejoiced
And gathered together;
Attackers gathered against me,
And I did not know *it;*
They tore *at me* and did not cease;
16 With ungodly mockers at feasts
They gnashed at me with their teeth.

17 Lord, how long will You look on?
Rescue me from their destructions,
My precious *life* from the lions.
18 I will give You thanks in the great
assembly;
I will praise You among many people.

19 Let them not rejoice over me who are
wrongfully my enemies;
Nor let them wink with the eye who hate
me without a cause.
20 For they do not speak peace,
But they devise deceitful matters
Against *the* quiet ones in the land.
21 They also opened their mouth wide
against me,
And said, "Aha, aha!
Our eyes have seen *it.*"

22 *This* You have seen, O LORD;
Do not keep silence.
O Lord, do not be far from me.
23 Stir up Yourself, and awake to my
vindication,
To my cause, my God and my Lord.
24 Vindicate me, O LORD my God, according
to Your righteousness;
And let them not rejoice over me.
25 Let them not say in their hearts, "Ah, so
we would have it!"
Let them not say, "We have swallowed him
up."

26 Let them be ashamed and brought to
mutual confusion
Who rejoice at my hurt;
Let them be clothed with shame and
dishonor
Who exalt themselves against me.

27 Let them shout for joy and be glad,
Who favor my righteous cause;
And let them say continually,
"Let the LORD be magnified,
Who has pleasure in the prosperity of His
servant."
28 And my tongue shall speak of Your
righteousness
And of Your praise all the day long.

PSALM 36

Man's Wickedness and God's Perfections

To the Chief Musician. A Psalm of David the
servant of the LORD.

1 An oracle within my heart concerning the
transgression of the wicked:
There is no fear of God before his eyes.
2 For he flatters himself in his own eyes,
When he finds out his iniquity *and* when
he hates.
3 The words of his mouth *are* wickedness
and deceit;
He has ceased to be wise *and* to do good.
4 He devises wickedness on his bed;
He sets himself in a way *that is* not good;
He does not abhor evil.

5 Your mercy, O LORD, *is* in the heavens;
Your faithfulness *reaches* to the clouds.
6 Your righteousness *is* like the great
mountains;
Your judgments *are* a great deep;
O LORD, You preserve man and beast.

7 How precious *is* Your lovingkindness, O
God!
Therefore the children of men put their
trust under the shadow of Your wings.
8 They are abundantly satisfied with the
fullness of Your house,
And You give them drink from the river
of Your pleasures.
9 For with You *is* the fountain of life;
In Your light we see light.

10 Oh, continue Your lovingkindness to those
who know You,
And Your righteousness to the upright in
heart.
11 Let not the foot of pride come against me,
And let not the hand of the wicked drive
me away.
12 There the workers of iniquity have fallen;

They have been cast down and are not able to rise.

PSALM 37

The Heritage of the Righteous and the Calamity of the Wicked

A Psalm of David.

1 Do not fret because of evildoers,
Nor be envious of the workers of iniquity.

2 For they shall soon be cut down like the grass,
And wither as the green herb.

3 Trust in the LORD, and do good;
Dwell in the land, and feed on His faithfulness.

4 Delight yourself also in the LORD,
And He shall give you the desires of your heart.

5 Commit your way to the LORD,
Trust also in Him,
And He shall bring *it* to pass.

6 He shall bring forth your righteousness as the light,
And your justice as the noonday.

7 Rest in the LORD, and wait patiently for Him;
Do not fret because of him who prospers in his way,
Because of the man who brings wicked schemes to pass.

8 Cease from anger, and forsake wrath;
Do not fret—*it* only *causes* harm.

9 For evildoers shall be cut off;
But those who wait on the LORD,
They shall inherit the earth.

10 For yet a little while and the wicked *shall be* no *more;*
Indeed, you will look carefully for his place,
But it *shall be* no *more.*

11 But the meek shall inherit the earth,
And shall delight themselves in the abundance of peace.

12 The wicked plots against the just,
And gnashes at him with his teeth.

13 The Lord laughs at him,
For He sees that his day is coming.

14 The wicked have drawn the sword
And have bent their bow,
To cast down the poor and needy,
To slay those who are of upright conduct.

15 Their sword shall enter their own heart,
And their bows shall be broken.

16 A little that a righteous man has
Is better than the riches of many wicked.

17 For the arms of the wicked shall be broken,
But the LORD upholds the righteous.

18 The LORD knows the days of the upright,
And their inheritance shall be forever.

The Law of Intuition: David Makes Decisions Wisely

(Psalm 37:3–9)

Do you ever feel as though you need a therapist? If so, then Psalm 37 is for you.

David writes as a counselor, providing wise steps to take as you face crises and decisions. Whenever you feel the pressure of competition in the market, the compulsion to perform, or to compare your lot with other leaders, pause and remember these words. David brings eternal perspective and long-term vision that prevents mistakes in short-term decisions:

1. Trust in the Lord and do good; do what is right despite what others do (v. 3).
2. Cultivate faithfulness and don't move too quickly; don't rush anything (v. 3).
3. Prioritize God and His values; He will reward and satisfy you in the end (v. 4).
4. Commit your plans to Him and trust Him; the results are in His hand (v. 5).
5. Be quiet and patient; perspective comes when we grow still and think (v. 7).
6. Don't fret or compare; such anxiety always gives bad motivation (v. 7).
7. Refuse to get angry at competition; anger does not bring the results you desire (v. 8).
8. Put your hope in the Lord; ultimately, He will guide and use your decision (v. 9).

19 They shall not be ashamed in the evil time,
And in the days of famine they shall be
satisfied.
20 But the wicked shall perish;
And the enemies of the LORD,
Like the splendor of the meadows, shall
vanish.
Into smoke they shall vanish away.

21 The wicked borrows and does not repay,
But the righteous shows mercy and gives.
22 For *those* blessed by Him shall inherit the
earth,
But *those* cursed by Him shall be cut off.

23 The steps of a *good* man are ordered by the
LORD,
And He delights in his way.
24 Though he fall, he shall not be utterly cast
down;
For the LORD upholds *him with* His hand.

25 I have been young, and *now* am old;
Yet I have not seen the righteous forsaken,
Nor his descendants begging bread.
26 *He is* ever merciful, and lends;
And his descendants *are* blessed.

27 Depart from evil, and do good;
And dwell forevermore.
28 For the LORD loves justice,
And does not forsake His saints;
They are preserved forever,
But the descendants of the wicked shall be
cut off.

29 The righteous shall inherit the land,
And dwell in it forever.

30 The mouth of the righteous speaks wisdom,
And his tongue talks of justice.
31 The law of his God *is* in his heart;
None of his steps shall slide.

32 The wicked watches the righteous,
And seeks to slay him.
33 The LORD will not leave him in his hand,
Nor condemn him when he is judged.

34 Wait on the LORD,
And keep His way,
And He shall exalt you to inherit the land;
When the wicked are cut off, you shall
see *it.*
35 I have seen the wicked in great power,
And spreading himself like a native green
tree.

36 Yet he passed away,[a] and behold, he *was* no
more;
Indeed I sought him, but he could not be
found.

37 Mark the blameless *man,* and observe the
upright;
For the future of *that* man *is* peace.
38 But the transgressors shall be destroyed
together;
The future of the wicked shall be cut off.

39 But the salvation of the righteous *is* from
the LORD;
He is their strength in the time of trouble.
40 And the LORD shall help them and deliver
them;
He shall deliver them from the wicked,
And save them,
Because they trust in Him.

PSALM 38

Prayer in Time of Chastening

A Psalm of David. To bring to remembrance.

1 O LORD, do not rebuke me in Your wrath,
Nor chasten me in Your hot displeasure!
2 For Your arrows pierce me deeply,
And Your hand presses me down.

3 *There is* no soundness in my flesh
Because of Your anger,
Nor *any* health in my bones
Because of my sin.
4 For my iniquities have gone over my head;
Like a heavy burden they are too heavy for
me.
5 My wounds are foul *and* festering
Because of my foolishness.

6 I am troubled, I am bowed down greatly;
I go mourning all the day long.
7 For my loins are full of inflammation,
And *there is* no soundness in my flesh.
8 I am feeble and severely broken;
I groan because of the turmoil of my heart.

9 Lord, all my desire *is* before You;
And my sighing is not hidden from You.
10 My heart pants, my strength fails me;
As for the light of my eyes, it also has gone
from me.

37:36 [a]Following Masoretic Text, Septuagint, and
Targum; Syriac and Vulgate read *I passed by.*

11 My loved ones and my friends stand aloof
     from my plague,
   And my relatives stand afar off.
12 Those also who seek my life lay snares
     for me;
   Those who seek my hurt speak of
     destruction,
   And plan deception all the day long.

13 But I, like a deaf *man,* do not hear;
   And *I am* like a mute *who* does not open
     his mouth.
14 Thus I am like a man who does not hear,
   And in whose mouth *is* no response.

15 For in You, O LORD, I hope;
   You will hear, O Lord my God.
16 For I said, *"Hear me,* lest they rejoice over me,
   Lest, when my foot slips, they exalt
     themselves against me."

17 For I *am* ready to fall,
   And my sorrow *is* continually before me.
18 For I will declare my iniquity;
   I will be in anguish over my sin.
19 But my enemies *are* vigorous, *and* they are
     strong;
   And those who hate me wrongfully have
     multiplied.
20 Those also who render evil for good,
   They are my adversaries, because I follow
     what is good.

21 Do not forsake me, O LORD;
   O my God, be not far from me!
22 Make haste to help me,
   O Lord, my salvation!

PSALM 39

Prayer for Wisdom and Forgiveness

**To the Chief Musician. To Jeduthun.
A Psalm of David.**

1 I said, "I will guard my ways,
   Lest I sin with my tongue;
   I will restrain my mouth with a muzzle,
   While the wicked are before me."
2 I was mute with silence,
   I held my peace *even* from good;
   And my sorrow was stirred up.
3 My heart was hot within me;
   While I was musing, the fire burned.
   Then I spoke with my tongue:

4 "LORD, make me to know my end,
   And what *is* the measure of my days,

That I may know how frail I *am.*
5 Indeed, You have made my days *as*
   handbreadths,
   And my age *is* as nothing before You;
   Certainly every man at his best state *is* but
     vapor.   Selah
6 Surely every man walks about like a
     shadow;
   Surely they busy themselves in vain;
   He heaps up *riches,*
   And does not know who will gather them.

7 "And now, Lord, what do I wait for?
   My hope *is* in You.
8 Deliver me from all my transgressions;
   Do not make me the reproach of the foolish.

The Law of Timing: Leaders Value Time, They Don't Kill It

(Psalm 39:4, 5)

Like Moses in Psalm 90, David shows his mindfulness of his brief time on earth. He asks God to help him number his days (Ps. 39:4, 5), which ought to be the prayer of every leader. Wise leaders work to redeem the time they have (Eph. 5:16, 17).

Management expert Peter Drucker identified this leadership principle: He said that good leaders need to regard first of all not their *task,* but their *time.*

A leader needs to wonder if the task is worth the time investment. What would happen if the leader wasn't the one doing it? Would there be someone else who could do it just as well, and for whom the task would be time better spent?

A good leader knows that time is like gold, and good "spending habits" are essential. It's just that in this case the units are minutes, not dollars.

If you don't know where your time goes—that's a danger signal. If you can save small bits of time and consolidate them into a chunk of time that can be spent on something worthwhile—that's like "found money."

If leaders can number their minutes and hours, "numbering their days" will be easier.

9 I was mute, I did not open my mouth,
Because it was You who did *it*.
10 Remove Your plague from me;
I am consumed by the blow of Your hand.
11 When with rebukes You correct man for
iniquity,
You make his beauty melt away like a moth;
Surely every man *is* vapor.   Selah

12 "Hear my prayer, O LORD,
And give ear to my cry;
Do not be silent at my tears;
For I *am* a stranger with You,
A sojourner, as all my fathers *were*.
13 Remove Your gaze from me, that I may
regain strength,
Before I go away and am no more."

PSALM 40

Faith Persevering in Trial

To the Chief Musician. A Psalm of David.

1 I waited patiently for the LORD;
And He inclined to me,
And heard my cry.
2 He also brought me up out of a horrible
pit,

Out of the miry clay,
And set my feet upon a rock,
And established my steps.
3 He has put a new song in my mouth—
Praise to our God;
Many will see *it* and fear,
And will trust in the LORD.

4 Blessed *is* that man who makes the LORD
his trust,
And does not respect the proud, nor such
as turn aside to lies.
5 Many, O LORD my God, *are* Your
wonderful works
Which You have done;
And Your thoughts toward us
Cannot be recounted to You in order;
If I would declare and speak *of them,*
They are more than can be numbered.

6 Sacrifice and offering You did not desire;
My ears You have opened.
Burnt offering and sin offering You did
not require.
7 Then I said, "Behold, I come;
In the scroll of the book *it is* written of me.
8 I delight to do Your will, O my God,
And Your law *is* within my heart."

DAVID   TRUSTING IN GOD ALONE
(Psalm 40:1–17)

PROFILE IN LEADERSHIP

King David knew something about suffering, particularly suffering caused by his own actions. But he also knew to whom he could turn during those times of trouble. This "man after [God's] own heart" (Acts 13:22) made it a point to seek the Lord in difficult days and to make the news of God's goodness known to everyone who would listen.

David knew that God would always remain faithful to Himself and to His holy nature—even when David acted unfaithfully. David knew that at just the right time, God would deliver him from despair. He knew the freedom and security that come from trusting in God alone as his deliverer.

What great comfort and joy come to us when we understand that God is rich in grace and mercy, that He not only forgives, but restores and redeems! The Lord lifts us up from our personal pits of despair and puts us in right standing with Him.

David was far from a perfect man, but he understood something all godly leaders must grasp: When times of trouble arrive—even trouble we bring on ourselves—we must turn to God and wait patiently for His help. He'll never fail us. Remember these truths about the God you serve, then proclaim them to everyone who will hear.

9 I have proclaimed the good news of
righteousness
In the great assembly;
Indeed, I do not restrain my lips,
O LORD, You Yourself know.
10 I have not hidden Your righteousness
within my heart;
I have declared Your faithfulness and Your
salvation;
I have not concealed Your lovingkindness
and Your truth
From the great assembly.

11 Do not withhold Your tender mercies
from me, O LORD;
Let Your lovingkindness and Your truth
continually preserve me.
12 For innumerable evils have surrounded
me;
My iniquities have overtaken me, so that I
am not able to look up;
They are more than the hairs of my head;
Therefore my heart fails me.

13 Be pleased, O LORD, to deliver me;
O LORD, make haste to help me!
14 Let them be ashamed and brought to
mutual confusion
Who seek to destroy my life;
Let them be driven backward and brought
to dishonor
Who wish me evil.
15 Let them be confounded because of their
shame,
Who say to me, "Aha, aha!"

16 Let all those who seek You rejoice and be
glad in You;
Let such as love Your salvation say
continually,
"The LORD be magnified!"
17 But I *am* poor and needy;
Yet the LORD thinks upon me.
You *are* my help and my deliverer;
Do not delay, O my God.

PSALM 41

The Blessing and Suffering of the Godly

To the Chief Musician. A Psalm of David.

1 Blessed *is* he who considers the poor;
The LORD will deliver him in time of
trouble.
2 The LORD will preserve him and keep him
alive,

And he will be blessed on the earth;
You will not deliver him to the will of his
enemies.
3 The LORD will strengthen him on his bed
of illness;
You will sustain him on his sickbed.

4 I said, "LORD, be merciful to me;
Heal my soul, for I have sinned against
You."
5 My enemies speak evil of me:
"When will he die, and his name perish?"
6 And if he comes to see *me,* he speaks lies;
His heart gathers iniquity to itself;
When he goes out, he tells *it.*

7 All who hate me whisper together against
me;
Against me they devise my hurt.
8 "An evil disease," *they say,* "clings to him.
And *now* that he lies down, he will rise up
no more."
9 Even my own familiar friend in whom I
trusted,
Who ate my bread,
Has lifted up *his* heel against me.

10 But You, O LORD, be merciful to me, and
raise me up,
That I may repay them.
11 By this I know that You are well pleased
with me,
Because my enemy does not triumph over
me.
12 As for me, You uphold me in my integrity,
And set me before Your face forever.

13 Blessed *be* the LORD God of Israel
From everlasting to everlasting!
Amen and Amen.

Book Two: Psalms 42—72

PSALM 42

Yearning for God in the Midst of Distresses

To the Chief Musician. A Contemplation[a]
of the sons of Korah.

1 As the deer pants for the water brooks,
So pants my soul for You, O God.
2 My soul thirsts for God, for the living
God.

42:title [a]Hebrew *Maschil*

When shall I come and appear before God?[a]

3 My tears have been my food day and night,
   While they continually say to me,
   "Where *is* your God?"

4 When I remember these *things,*
   I pour out my soul within me.
   For I used to go with the multitude;
   I went with them to the house of God,
   With the voice of joy and praise,
   With a multitude that kept a pilgrim feast.

5 Why are you cast down, O my soul?
   And *why* are you disquieted within me?
   Hope in God, for I shall yet praise Him
   For the help of His countenance.[a]

6 O my God,[a] my soul is cast down within
      me;
   Therefore I will remember You from the
      land of the Jordan,
   And from the heights of Hermon,
   From the Hill Mizar.

7 Deep calls unto deep at the noise of Your
      waterfalls;
   All Your waves and billows have gone over
      me.

8 The LORD will command His
      lovingkindness in the daytime,
   And in the night His song *shall be* with
      me—
   A prayer to the God of my life.

9 I will say to God my Rock,
   "Why have You forgotten me?
   Why do I go mourning because of the
      oppression of the enemy?"

10 *As* with a breaking of my bones,
   My enemies reproach me,
   While they say to me all day long,
   "Where *is* your God?"

11 Why are you cast down, O my soul?
   And why are you disquieted within me?
   Hope in God;
   For I shall yet praise Him,
   The help of my countenance and my God.

PSALM 43

Prayer to God in Time of Trouble

1 Vindicate me, O God,
   And plead my cause against an ungodly
      nation;
   Oh, deliver me from the deceitful and
      unjust man!

2 For You *are* the God of my strength;
   Why do You cast me off?
   Why do I go mourning because of the
      oppression of the enemy?

3 Oh, send out Your light and Your truth!
   Let them lead me;
   Let them bring me to Your holy hill
   And to Your tabernacle.

4 Then I will go to the altar of God,
   To God my exceeding joy;
   And on the harp I will praise You,
   O God, my God.

5 Why are you cast down, O my soul?
   And why are you disquieted within me?
   Hope in God;
   For I shall yet praise Him,
   The help of my countenance and my God.

PSALM 44

Redemption Remembered in Present Dishonor

To the Chief Musician. A Contemplation[a]
   of the sons of Korah.

1 We have heard with our ears, O God,
   Our fathers have told us,
   The deeds You did in their days,
   In days of old:

2 You drove out the nations with Your hand,
   But them You planted;
   You afflicted the peoples, and cast them out.

3 For they did not gain possession of the
      land by their own sword,
   Nor did their own arm save them;
   But it was Your right hand, Your arm, and
      the light of Your countenance,
   Because You favored them.

4 You are my King, O God;[a]
   Command[b] victories for Jacob.

42:2 [a]Following Masoretic Text and Vulgate; some
Hebrew manuscripts, Septuagint, Syriac, and
Targum read *I see the face of God.* **42:5** [a]Following
Masoretic Text and Targum; a few Hebrew
manuscripts, Septuagint, Syriac, and Vulgate read
The help of my countenance, my God. **42:6** [a]Following
Masoretic Text and Targum; a few Hebrew
manuscripts, Septuagint, Syriac, and Vulgate put *my
God* at the end of verse 5. **44:title** [a]Hebrew *Maschil*
44:4 [a]Following Masoretic Text and Targum;
Septuagint and Vulgate read *and my God.*
[b]Following Masoretic Text and Targum; Septuagint,
Syriac, and Vulgate read *Who commands.*

5   Through You we will push down our
     enemies;
     Through Your name we will trample those
       who rise up against us.
6   For I will not trust in my bow,
     Nor shall my sword save me.
7   But You have saved us from our enemies,
     And have put to shame those who hated
       us.
8   In God we boast all day long,
     And praise Your name forever.   Selah

9   But You have cast us off and put us to
     shame,
     And You do not go out with our armies.
10   You make us turn back from the enemy,
     And those who hate us have taken spoil
       for themselves.
11   You have given us up like sheep intended
     for food,
     And have scattered us among the nations.
12   You sell Your people for next to nothing,
     And are not enriched by selling them.

13   You make us a reproach to our neighbors,
     A scorn and a derision to those all around
       us.
14   You make us a byword among the nations,
     A shaking of the head among the peoples.
15   My dishonor is continually before me,
     And the shame of my face has covered
       me,
16   Because of the voice of him who
     reproaches and reviles,
     Because of the enemy and the avenger.

17   All this has come upon us;
     But we have not forgotten You,
     Nor have we dealt falsely with Your
       covenant.
18   Our heart has not turned back,
     Nor have our steps departed from Your
       way;
19   But You have severely broken us in the
     place of jackals,
     And covered us with the shadow of death.

20   If we had forgotten the name of our God,
     Or stretched out our hands to a foreign
       god,
21   Would not God search this out?
     For He knows the secrets of the heart.
22   Yet for Your sake we are killed all day
     long;
     We are accounted as sheep for the
       slaughter.

23   Awake! Why do You sleep, O Lord?
     Arise! Do not cast us off forever.
24   Why do You hide Your face,
     And forget our affliction and our
       oppression?
25   For our soul is bowed down to the dust;
     Our body clings to the ground.
26   Arise for our help,
     And redeem us for Your mercies' sake.

PSALM 45

The Glories of the Messiah and His Bride

To the Chief Musician.
Set to "The Lilies."[a] A Contemplation[b]
of the sons of Korah. A Song of Love.

1   My heart is overflowing with a good
     theme;
     I recite my composition concerning the
       King;
     My tongue is the pen of a ready writer.

2   You are fairer than the sons of men;
     Grace is poured upon Your lips;
     Therefore God has blessed You forever.
3   Gird Your sword upon Your thigh, O
     Mighty One,
     With Your glory and Your majesty.
4   And in Your majesty ride prosperously
     because of truth, humility, and
     righteousness;
     And Your right hand shall teach You
       awesome things.
5   Your arrows are sharp in the heart of the
     King's enemies;
     The peoples fall under You.

6   Your throne, O God, is forever and ever;
     A scepter of righteousness is the scepter of
       Your kingdom.
7   You love righteousness and hate
     wickedness;
     Therefore God, Your God, has anointed
       You
     With the oil of gladness more than Your
       companions.
8   All Your garments are scented with myrrh
     and aloes and cassia,
     Out of the ivory palaces, by which they
       have made You glad.
9   Kings' daughters are among Your
     honorable women;

45:title [a]Hebrew Shoshannim   [b]Hebrew Maschil

At Your right hand stands the queen in gold from Ophir.

10 Listen, O daughter,
Consider and incline your ear;
Forget your own people also, and your father's house;
11 So the King will greatly desire your beauty;
Because He *is* your Lord, worship Him.
12 And the daughter of Tyre *will come* with a gift;
The rich among the people will seek your favor.

13 The royal daughter *is* all glorious within *the palace;*
Her clothing *is* woven with gold.
14 She shall be brought to the King in robes of many colors;
The virgins, her companions who follow her, shall be brought to You.
15 With gladness and rejoicing they shall be brought;
They shall enter the King's palace.

16 Instead of Your fathers shall be Your sons,
Whom You shall make princes in all the earth.
17 I will make Your name to be remembered in all generations;
Therefore the people shall praise You forever and ever.

PSALM 46

God the Refuge of His People and Conqueror of the Nations

To the Chief Musician. A Psalm of the sons of Korah. A Song for Alamoth.

1 God *is* our refuge and strength,
A very present help in trouble.
2 Therefore we will not fear,
Even though the earth be removed,
And though the mountains be carried into the midst of the sea;
3 *Though* its waters roar *and* be troubled,
Though the mountains shake with its swelling. Selah

4 *There is* a river whose streams shall make glad the city of God,
The holy *place* of the tabernacle of the Most High.

5 God *is* in the midst of her, she shall not be moved;
God shall help her, just at the break of dawn.
6 The nations raged, the kingdoms were moved;
He uttered His voice, the earth melted.

7 The LORD of hosts *is* with us;
The God of Jacob *is* our refuge. Selah

8 Come, behold the works of the LORD,
Who has made desolations in the earth.
9 He makes wars cease to the end of the earth;
He breaks the bow and cuts the spear in two;
He burns the chariot in the fire.
10 Be still, and know that I *am* God;
I will be exalted among the nations,
I will be exalted in the earth!

11 The LORD of hosts *is* with us;
The God of Jacob *is* our refuge. Selah

PSALM 47

Praise to God, the Ruler of the Earth

To the Chief Musician.
A Psalm of the sons of Korah.

1 Oh, clap your hands, all you peoples!
Shout to God with the voice of triumph!
2 For the LORD Most High *is* awesome;
He is a great King over all the earth.
3 He will subdue the peoples under us,
And the nations under our feet.
4 He will choose our inheritance for us,
The excellence of Jacob whom He loves. Selah

5 God has gone up with a shout,
The LORD with the sound of a trumpet.
6 Sing praises to God, sing praises!
Sing praises to our King, sing praises!
7 For God *is* the King of all the earth;
Sing praises with understanding.

8 God reigns over the nations;
God sits on His holy throne.
9 The princes of the people have gathered together,
The people of the God of Abraham.

For the shields of the earth *belong* to
   God;
He is greatly exalted.

PSALM 48

The Glory of God in Zion

   A Song. A Psalm of the sons of Korah.

1 Great *is* the LORD, and greatly to be
    praised
  In the city of our God,
  In His holy mountain.
2 Beautiful in elevation,
  The joy of the whole earth,
  Is Mount Zion *on* the sides of the north,
  The city of the great King.
3 God *is* in her palaces;
  He is known as her refuge.

4 For behold, the kings assembled,
  They passed by together.
5 They saw *it, and* so they marveled;
  They were troubled, they hastened away.
6 Fear took hold of them there,
  And pain, as of a woman in birth pangs,
7 *As when* You break the ships of Tarshish
  With an east wind.

8 As we have heard,
  So we have seen
  In the city of the LORD of hosts,
  In the city of our God:
  God will establish it forever.   **Selah**

9 We have thought, O God, on Your
    lovingkindness,
  In the midst of Your temple.
10 According to Your name, O God,
  So *is* Your praise to the ends of the earth;
  Your right hand is full of righteousness.
11 Let Mount Zion rejoice,
  Let the daughters of Judah be glad,
  Because of Your judgments.

12 Walk about Zion,
  And go all around her.
  Count her towers;
13 Mark well her bulwarks;
  Consider her palaces;
  That you may tell *it* to the generation
    following.
14 For this *is* God,
  Our God forever and ever;
  He will be our guide
  Even to death.[a]

PSALM 49

The Confidence of the Foolish

   To the Chief Musician.
   A Psalm of the sons of Korah.

1 Hear this, all peoples;
  Give ear, all inhabitants of the world,
2 Both low and high,
  Rich and poor together.
3 My mouth shall speak wisdom,
  And the meditation of my heart *shall give*
    understanding.
4 I will incline my ear to a proverb;
  I will disclose my dark saying on the harp.

5 Why should I fear in the days of evil,
  When the iniquity at my heels surrounds
    me?
6 Those who trust in their wealth
  And boast in the multitude of their riches,
7 None *of them* can by any means redeem *his*
    brother,
  Nor give to God a ransom for him—
8 For the redemption of their souls *is* costly,
  And it shall cease forever—
9 That he should continue to live eternally,
  And not see the Pit.

10 For he sees wise men die;
  Likewise the fool and the senseless person
    perish,
  And leave their wealth to others.
11 Their inner thought *is that* their houses
    will last forever,[a]
  Their dwelling places to all generations;
  They call *their* lands after their own names.
12 Nevertheless man, *though* in honor, does
    not remain;[a]
  He is like the beasts *that* perish.

13 This is the way of those who *are* foolish,
  And of their posterity who approve their
    sayings.   **Selah**
14 Like sheep they are laid in the grave;
  Death shall feed on them;
  The upright shall have dominion over
    them in the morning;

48:14 [a]Following Masoretic Text and Syriac;
Septuagint and Vulgate read *Forever.*
49:11 [a]Septuagint, Syriac, Targum, and Vulgate read
Their graves shall be their houses forever.
49:12 [a]Following Masoretic Text and Targum;
Septuagint, Syriac, and Vulgate read *understand*
(compare verse 20).

The Law of Priorities:
When Activity Becomes Achievement

(Psalm 49:12–17)

God encourages us to fix our eyes on the things that endure. In light of eternity, leaders cannot become consumed with the temporary. Leaders cannot allow the pursuit of wealth or power to move them (Ps. 49:12, 13). Only a vision that outlives them, a vision connected to eternity, will fulfill a godly leader.

In other words, we must build a legacy. What are we going to leave behind when we die? Psalm 49:17 reminds us we will take nothing with us, no matter how rich we become. So what will we leave behind that counts?

A huge difference exists between a legacy and an inheritance. Anyone can leave an inheritance. An inheritance is something you leave *to* your family or loved ones, and it also fades. A legacy is something you leave *in* your family and loved ones. Consider the differences between the two:

Inheritance	Legacy
1. Something tangible you give *to* others	1. Something tangible you place *in* others
2. Temporarily brings them happiness	2. Permanently transforms them
3. Eventually fades as it is spent	3. Lives on long after you die
4. Your activity may or may not pay off	4. Your activity becomes achievement

And their beauty shall be consumed in the
grave, far from their dwelling.
15 But God will redeem my soul from the
power of the grave,
For He shall receive me.   Selah

16 Do not be afraid when one becomes rich,
When the glory of his house is increased;
17 For when he dies he shall carry nothing
away;
His glory shall not descend after him.
18 Though while he lives he blesses himself
(For *men* will praise you when you do well
for yourself),
19 He shall go to the generation of his fathers;
They shall never see light.
20 A man *who is* in honor, yet does not
understand,
Is like the beasts *that* perish.

PSALM 50

God the Righteous Judge

A Psalm of Asaph.

1 The Mighty One, God the LORD,
Has spoken and called the earth
From the rising of the sun to its going
down.

2 Out of Zion, the perfection of beauty,
God will shine forth.
3 Our God shall come, and shall not keep
silent;
A fire shall devour before Him,
And it shall be very tempestuous all
around Him.

4 He shall call to the heavens from above,
And to the earth, that He may judge His
people:
5 "Gather My saints together to Me,
Those who have made a covenant with
Me by sacrifice."
6 Let the heavens declare His righteousness,
For God Himself *is* Judge.   Selah

7 "Hear, O My people, and I will speak,
O Israel, and I will testify against you;
I *am* God, your God!
8 I will not rebuke you for your sacrifices
Or your burnt offerings,
Which are continually before Me.
9 I will not take a bull from your house,
Nor goats out of your folds.
10 For every beast of the forest *is* Mine,
And the cattle on a thousand hills.
11 I know all the birds of the mountains,
And the wild beasts of the field *are* Mine.

12 "If I were hungry, I would not tell you;
For the world *is* Mine, and all its fullness.
13 Will I eat the flesh of bulls,
Or drink the blood of goats?
14 Offer to God thanksgiving,
And pay your vows to the Most High.
15 Call upon Me in the day of trouble;
I will deliver you, and you shall glorify
Me."

16 But to the wicked God says:
"What *right* have you to declare My
statutes,
Or take My covenant in your mouth,
17 Seeing you hate instruction
And cast My words behind you?
18 When you saw a thief, you consented[a]
with him,
And have been a partaker with adulterers.
19 You give your mouth to evil,
And your tongue frames deceit.
20 You sit *and* speak against your brother;
You slander your own mother's son.
21 These *things* you have done, and I kept
silent;
You thought that I was altogether like
you;
But I will rebuke you,
And set *them* in order before your eyes.

22 "Now consider this, you who forget God,
Lest I tear *you* in pieces,
And *there be* none to deliver:

23 Whoever offers praise glorifies Me;
And to him who orders *his* conduct *aright*
I will show the salvation of God."

PSALM 51

A Prayer of Repentance

To the Chief Musician. A Psalm of David when
Nathan the prophet went to him, after he had
gone in to Bathsheba.

1 Have mercy upon me, O God,
According to Your lovingkindness;
According to the multitude of Your tender
mercies,
Blot out my transgressions.
2 Wash me thoroughly from my iniquity,
And cleanse me from my sin.

3 For I acknowledge my transgressions,
And my sin *is* always before me.
4 Against You, You only, have I sinned,
And done *this* evil in Your sight—
That You may be found just when You
speak,[a]
And blameless when You judge.

5 Behold, I was brought forth in iniquity,
And in sin my mother conceived me.

50:18 [a]Septuagint, Syriac, Targum, and Vulgate read
ran. **51:4** [a]Septuagint, Targum, and Vulgate read *in
Your words.*

The Law of Solid Ground:
David Faces His Sin, Remains King
(Psalm 51:3, 4)

David wrote Psalm 51 shortly after he committed adultery with Bathsheba (2 Sam. 11:1—12:15).
When Nathan confronted him about his sin, the king fell to the floor and wept in bitter repentance. He publicly sought restoration as a king and as a spiritual man, as this great psalm
demonstrates. Because of his repentant heart, God allowed him to remain in office until he died.
Why, then, are some leaders removed from office when they fail morally? Why could David remain king? The answer may lie in the Law of Solid Ground. David practiced this law and maintained his trust in God. Those who do not repent after some failure—or who do so only for public
show—often lose their positions. Some sins no doubt disqualify leaders from continuing in leadership, but more fail in leadership from their deceptions than from their mistakes. History
teaches that the public usually forgives a leader who owns up to his mistakes, but refuses to forgive those who remain unrepentant.
Mistakes don't have to prove fatal; we all make them. But when a leader deceives the people
and loses their trust, they will no longer follow him or her.

6 Behold, You desire truth in the inward
parts,
And in the hidden *part* You will make me
to know wisdom.

7 Purge me with hyssop, and I shall be clean;
Wash me, and I shall be whiter than snow.
8 Make me hear joy and gladness,
That the bones You have broken may
rejoice.
9 Hide Your face from my sins,
And blot out all my iniquities.

10 Create in me a clean heart, O God,
And renew a steadfast spirit within me.
11 Do not cast me away from Your presence,
And do not take Your Holy Spirit from me.

12 Restore to me the joy of Your salvation,
And uphold me *by Your* generous Spirit.
13 *Then* I will teach transgressors Your ways,
And sinners shall be converted to You.

14 Deliver me from the guilt of bloodshed, O
God,
The God of my salvation,
And my tongue shall sing aloud of Your
righteousness.
15 O Lord, open my lips,
And my mouth shall show forth Your
praise.
16 For You do not desire sacrifice, or else I
would give *it;*
You do not delight in burnt offering.
17 The sacrifices of God *are* a broken spirit,
A broken and a contrite heart—
These, O God, You will not despise.

18 Do good in Your good pleasure to Zion;
Build the walls of Jerusalem.
19 Then You shall be pleased with the
sacrifices of righteousness,
With burnt offering and whole burnt
offering;
Then they shall offer bulls on Your altar.

PSALM 52

The End of the Wicked and the Peace of the Godly

To the Chief Musician. A Contemplation[a] of
David when Doeg the Edomite went and told
Saul, and said to him, "David has gone to the
house of Ahimelech."

1 Why do you boast in evil, O mighty man?
The goodness of God *endures* continually.

2 Your tongue devises destruction,
Like a sharp razor, working deceitfully.
3 You love evil more than good,
Lying rather than speaking righteousness.
Selah
4 You love all devouring words,
You deceitful tongue.

5 God shall likewise destroy you forever;
He shall take you away, and pluck you out
of *your* dwelling place,
And uproot you from the land of the
living. Selah
6 The righteous also shall see and fear,
And shall laugh at him, *saying,*
7 "Here is the man *who* did not make God
his strength,
But trusted in the abundance of his riches,
And strengthened himself in his
wickedness."

8 But I *am* like a green olive tree in the
house of God;
I trust in the mercy of God forever and
ever.
9 I will praise You forever,
Because You have done *it;*
And in the presence of Your saints
I will wait on Your name, for *it is* good.

PSALM 53

Folly of the Godless, and the Restoration of Israel

To the Chief Musician. Set to "Mahalath."
A Contemplation[a] of David.

1 The fool has said in his heart,
"*There is* no God."
They are corrupt, and have done
abominable iniquity;
There is none who does good.

2 God looks down from heaven upon the
children of men,
To see if there are *any* who understand,
who seek God.
3 Every one of them has turned aside;
They have together become corrupt;
There is none who does good,
No, not one.

4 Have the workers of iniquity no
knowledge,

52:title [a]Hebrew *Maschil* **53:title** [a]Hebrew *Maschil*

Who eat up my people *as* they eat bread,
And do not call upon God?
5 There they are in great fear
Where no fear was,
For God has scattered the bones of him
who encamps against you;
You have put *them* to shame,
Because God has despised them.

6 Oh, that the salvation of Israel would
come out of Zion!
When God brings back the captivity of
His people,
Let Jacob rejoice *and* Israel be glad.

PSALM 54

Answered Prayer for Deliverance from Adversaries

To the Chief Musician. With stringed
instruments.[a] A Contemplation[b] of David
when the Ziphites went and said to Saul,
"Is David not hiding with us?"

1 Save me, O God, by Your name,
And vindicate me by Your strength.
2 Hear my prayer, O God;
Give ear to the words of my mouth.
3 For strangers have risen up against me,
And oppressors have sought after my life;
They have not set God before them. Selah

4 Behold, God *is* my helper;
The Lord *is* with those who uphold my
life.
5 He will repay my enemies for their evil.
Cut them off in Your truth.

6 I will freely sacrifice to You;
I will praise Your name, O LORD, for *it is*
good.
7 For He has delivered me out of all trouble;
And my eye has seen *its desire* upon my
enemies.

PSALM 55

Trust in God Concerning the Treachery of Friends

To the Chief Musician. With stringed
instruments.[a] A Contemplation[b] of David.

1 Give ear to my prayer, O God,
And do not hide Yourself from my
supplication.
2 Attend to me, and hear me;

I am restless in my complaint, and moan
noisily,
3 Because of the voice of the enemy,
Because of the oppression of the wicked;
For they bring down trouble upon me,
And in wrath they hate me.

4 My heart is severely pained within me,
And the terrors of death have fallen upon
me.
5 Fearfulness and trembling have come upon
me,
And horror has overwhelmed me.
6 So I said, "Oh, that I had wings like a
dove!
I would fly away and be at rest.
7 Indeed, I would wander far off,
And remain in the wilderness. Selah
8 I would hasten my escape
From the windy storm *and* tempest."

9 Destroy, O Lord, *and* divide their tongues,
For I have seen violence and strife in the
city.
10 Day and night they go around it on its
walls;
Iniquity and trouble *are* also in the midst
of it.
11 Destruction *is* in its midst;
Oppression and deceit do not depart from
its streets.

12 For *it is* not an enemy *who* reproaches me;
Then I could bear *it.*
Nor *is it* one *who* hates me who has
exalted *himself* against me;
Then I could hide from him.
13 But *it was* you, a man my equal,
My companion and my acquaintance.
14 We took sweet counsel together,
And walked to the house of God in the
throng.

15 Let death seize them;
Let them go down alive into hell,
For wickedness *is* in their dwellings *and*
among them.

16 As for me, I will call upon God,
And the LORD shall save me.
17 Evening and morning and at noon
I will pray, and cry aloud,
And He shall hear my voice.

54:title [a]Hebrew *neginoth* [b]Hebrew *Maschil*
55:title [a]Hebrew *neginoth* [b]Hebrew *Maschil*

¹⁸ He has redeemed my soul in peace from
    the battle *that was* against me,
For there were many against me.
¹⁹ God will hear, and afflict them,
    Even He who abides from of old. Selah
Because they do not change,
Therefore they do not fear God.

²⁰ He has put forth his hands against those
    who were at peace with him;
He has broken his covenant.
²¹ *The words* of his mouth were smoother
    than butter,
But war *was* in his heart;
His words were softer than oil,
Yet they *were* drawn swords.

²² Cast your burden on the LORD,
    And He shall sustain you;
He shall never permit the righteous to be
    moved.

²³ But You, O God, shall bring them down
    to the pit of destruction;
Bloodthirsty and deceitful men shall not
    live out half their days;
But I will trust in You.

PSALM 56

Prayer for Relief from Tormentors

To the Chief Musician. Set to "The Silent Dove
in Distant Lands."[a] A Michtam of David when the
Philistines captured him in Gath.

¹ Be merciful to me, O God, for man would
    swallow me up;
Fighting all day he oppresses me.
² My enemies would hound *me* all day,
For *there are* many who fight against me, O
    Most High.

³ Whenever I am afraid,
    I will trust in You.
⁴ In God (I will praise His word),
    In God I have put my trust;
I will not fear.
What can flesh do to me?

⁵ All day they twist my words;
    All their thoughts *are* against me for
    evil.
⁶ They gather together,
    They hide, they mark my steps,
When they lie in wait for my life.
⁷ Shall they escape by iniquity?

In anger cast down the peoples, O
    God!
⁸ You number my wanderings;
    Put my tears into Your bottle;
Are they not in Your book?
⁹ When I cry out *to You,*
    Then my enemies will turn back;
This I know, because God *is* for me.
¹⁰ In God (I will praise *His* word),
    In the LORD (I will praise *His* word),
¹¹ In God I have put my trust;
    I will not be afraid.
What can man do to me?

¹² Vows *made* to You *are binding* upon me, O
    God;
I will render praises to You,
¹³ For You have delivered my soul from
    death.
Have You not *kept* my feet from falling,
That I may walk before God
In the light of the living?

PSALM 57

Prayer for Safety from Enemies

To the Chief Musician. Set to
"Do Not Destroy."[a] A Michtam of David
when he fled from Saul into the cave.

¹ Be merciful to me, O God, be merciful to
    me!
For my soul trusts in You;
And in the shadow of Your wings I will
    make my refuge,
Until *these* calamities have passed by.

² I will cry out to God Most High,
    To God who performs *all things* for me.
³ He shall send from heaven and save me;
    He reproaches the one who would
    swallow me up. Selah
God shall send forth His mercy and His
    truth.

⁴ My soul *is* among lions;
    I lie *among* the sons of men
Who are set on fire,
Whose teeth *are* spears and arrows,
And their tongue a sharp sword.
⁵ Be exalted, O God, above the heavens;
    Let Your glory *be* above all the earth.

56:title [a]Hebrew *Jonath Elem Rechokim*
57:title [a]Hebrew *Al Tashcheth*

6   They have prepared a net for my
       steps;
    My soul is bowed down;
    They have dug a pit before me;
    Into the midst of it they *themselves* have
       fallen.   Selah

7   My heart is steadfast, O God, my heart is
       steadfast;
    I will sing and give praise.
8   Awake, my glory!
    Awake, lute and harp!
    I will awaken the dawn.

9   I will praise You, O Lord, among the
       peoples;
    I will sing to You among the nations.
10 For Your mercy reaches unto the
       heavens,
    And Your truth unto the clouds.

11 Be exalted, O God, above the heavens;
    Let Your glory *be* above all the earth.

Leaders Practice Telling Themselves the Truth

(Psalm 57:1–11)

Psalm 57 gives us a beautiful picture of a leader in touch with his humanity. David composed it as he fled from Saul in the mountains and caves of Israel. The psalm expresses anxiety and fear, yet it ends with triumph: "Be exalted, O God, above the heavens; let Your glory be above all the earth" (Ps. 57:11).

Author Philip Yancey suggests that David wrote and sang the psalms as therapy for himself. Somehow, telling himself the truth enabled him to rise above his fear and see a transcendent God who remained in control.

Fortunately, few of us live with such danger. Like David, however, we all have times when nerves fail and fear creeps in. We feel surrounded by adversaries. Telling ourselves the truth, as David did, will heal and comfort us, as it did him. The truth of Psalm 57 can serve as our counselor. Successful leaders tell themselves the truth and gain perspective in the midst of volatile emotions.

PSALM 58

The Just Judgment of the Wicked

To the Chief Musician. Set to "Do Not Destroy."[a]
A Michtam of David.

1   Do you indeed speak righteousness, you
       silent ones?
    Do you judge uprightly, you sons of men?
2   No, in heart you work wickedness;
    You weigh out the violence of your hands
       in the earth.

3   The wicked are estranged from the womb;
    They go astray as soon as they are born,
       speaking lies.
4   Their poison *is* like the poison of a serpent;
    They are like the deaf cobra *that* stops its ear,
5   Which will not heed the voice of charmers,
    Charming ever so skillfully.

6   Break their teeth in their mouth, O God!
    Break out the fangs of the young lions, O
       LORD!
7   Let them flow away as waters *which* run
       continually;
    When he bends *his bow,*
    Let his arrows be as if cut in pieces.
8   *Let them be* like a snail which melts away as
       it goes,
    Like a stillborn child of a woman, that they
       may not see the sun.

9   Before your pots can feel *the burning* thorns,
    He shall take them away as with a
       whirlwind,
    As in His living and burning wrath.
10 The righteous shall rejoice when he sees
       the vengeance;
    He shall wash his feet in the blood of the
       wicked,
11 So that men will say,
    "Surely *there is* a reward for the righteous;
    Surely He is God who judges in the earth."

PSALM 59

The Assured Judgment of the Wicked

To the Chief Musician. Set to "Do Not Destroy."[a]
A Michtam of David when Saul sent men, and
they watched the house in order to kill him.

1   Deliver me from my enemies, O my God;
    Defend me from those who rise up against
       me.

58:title [a]Hebrew *Al Tashcheth*   **59:title** [a]Hebrew *Al Tashcheth*

2 Deliver me from the workers of iniquity,
And save me from bloodthirsty men.

3 For look, they lie in wait for my life;
The mighty gather against me,
Not *for* my transgression nor *for* my sin, O
LORD.

4 They run and prepare themselves through
no fault *of mine.*

Awake to help me, and behold!
5 You therefore, O LORD God of hosts, the
God of Israel,
Awake to punish all the nations;
Do not be merciful to any wicked
transgressors. Selah

6 At evening they return,
They growl like a dog,
And go all around the city.
7 Indeed, they belch with their mouth;
Swords *are* in their lips;
For *they say,* "Who hears?"

8 But You, O LORD, shall laugh at them;
You shall have all the nations in derision.
9 I will wait for You, O You his Strength;[a]
For God *is* my defense.
10 My God of mercy[a] shall come to meet me;
God shall let me see *my desire* on my
enemies.

11 Do not slay them, lest my people forget;
Scatter them by Your power,
And bring them down,
O Lord our shield.
12 *For* the sin of their mouth *and* the words
of their lips,
Let them even be taken in their pride,
And for the cursing and lying *which* they
speak.
13 Consume *them* in wrath, consume *them,*
That they *may* not *be;*
And let them know that God rules in
Jacob
To the ends of the earth. Selah

14 And at evening they return,
They growl like a dog,
And go all around the city.
15 They wander up and down for food,
And howl[a] if they are not satisfied.

16 But I will sing of Your power;
Yes, I will sing aloud of Your mercy in the
morning;

For You have been my defense
And refuge in the day of my trouble.
17 To You, O my Strength, I will sing praises;
For God *is* my defense,
My God of mercy.

PSALM 60

Urgent Prayer for the Restored Favor of God

To the Chief Musician. Set to "Lily of the
Testimony."[a] A Michtam of David. For teaching.
When he fought against Mesopotamia and Syria
of Zobah, and Joab returned and killed twelve
thousand Edomites in the Valley of Salt.

1 O God, You have cast us off;
You have broken us down;
You have been displeased;
Oh, restore us again!
2 You have made the earth tremble;
You have broken it;
Heal its breaches, for it is shaking.
3 You have shown Your people hard things;
You have made us drink the wine of
confusion.

4 You have given a banner to those who fear
You,
That it may be displayed because of the
truth. Selah
5 That Your beloved may be delivered,
Save *with* Your right hand, and hear me.

6 God has spoken in His holiness:
"I will rejoice;
I will divide Shechem
And measure out the Valley of Succoth.
7 Gilead *is* Mine, and Manasseh *is* Mine;
Ephraim also *is* the helmet for My head;
Judah *is* My lawgiver.
8 Moab *is* My washpot;
Over Edom I will cast My shoe;
Philistia, shout in triumph because of Me."

59:9 [a]Following Masoretic Text and Syriac; some
Hebrew manuscripts, Septuagint, Targum, and
Vulgate read *my Strength.* **59:10** [a]Following Qere;
some Hebrew manuscripts, Septuagint, and Vulgate
read *My God, His mercy;* Kethib, some Hebrew
manuscripts and Targum read *O God, my mercy;*
Syriac reads *O God, Your mercy.* **59:15** [a]Following
Septuagint and Vulgate; Masoretic Text, Syriac, and
Targum read *spend the night.* **60:title** [a]Hebrew
Shushan Eduth

9   Who will bring me *to* the strong city?
Who will lead me to Edom?

10   *Is it* not You, O God, *who* cast us off?
And You, O God, *who* did not go out with
our armies?

11   Give us help from trouble,
For the help of man *is* useless.

12   Through God we will do valiantly,
For *it is* He *who* shall tread down our
enemies.[a]

PSALM 61

Assurance of God's Eternal Protection

To the Chief Musician. On a stringed instrument.[a]
A Psalm of David.

1   Hear my cry, O God;
Attend to my prayer.

2   From the end of the earth I will cry to You,
When my heart is overwhelmed;
Lead me to the rock that is higher than I.

3   For You have been a shelter for me,
A strong tower from the enemy.

4   I will abide in Your tabernacle forever;
I will trust in the shelter of Your wings.
Selah

5   For You, O God, have heard my vows;
You have given *me* the heritage of those
who fear Your name.

6   You will prolong the king's life,
His years as many generations.

7   He shall abide before God forever.
Oh, prepare mercy and truth, *which* may
preserve him!

8   So I will sing praise to Your name forever,
That I may daily perform my vows.

PSALM 62

A Calm Resolve to Wait for the Salvation of God

To the Chief Musician. To Jeduthun.
A Psalm of David.

1   Truly my soul silently *waits* for God;
From Him *comes* my salvation.

2   He only *is* my rock and my salvation;
He is my defense;
I shall not be greatly moved.

3   How long will you attack a man?
You shall be slain, all of you,

Like a leaning wall and a tottering fence.

4   They only consult to cast *him* down from
his high position;
They delight in lies;
They bless with their mouth,
But they curse inwardly.   *Selah*

5   My soul, wait silently for God alone,
For my expectation *is* from Him.

6   He only *is* my rock and my salvation;
He is my defense;
I shall not be moved.

7   In God *is* my salvation and my glory;
The rock of my strength,
And my refuge, *is* in God.

8   Trust in Him at all times, you people;
Pour out your heart before Him;
God *is* a refuge for us.   *Selah*

9   Surely men of low degree *are* a vapor,
Men of high degree *are* a lie;
If they are weighed on the scales,
They *are* altogether *lighter* than vapor.

10   Do not trust in oppression,
Nor vainly hope in robbery;
If riches increase,
Do not set *your* heart *on them*.

11   God has spoken once,
Twice I have heard this:
That power *belongs* to God.

12   Also to You, O Lord, *belongs* mercy;
For You render to each one according to
his work.

PSALM 63

Joy in the Fellowship of God

A Psalm of David when he was
in the wilderness of Judah.

1   O God, You *are* my God;
Early will I seek You;
My soul thirsts for You;
My flesh longs for You
In a dry and thirsty land
Where there is no water.

2   So I have looked for You in the sanctuary,
To see Your power and Your glory.

3   Because Your lovingkindness *is* better than
life,

60:12 [a]Compare verses 5–12 with 108:6–13
61:title [a]Hebrew *neginah*

My lips shall praise You.
4 Thus I will bless You while I live;
I will lift up my hands in Your name.
5 My soul shall be satisfied as with marrow
and fatness,
And my mouth shall praise *You* with joyful
lips.

6 When I remember You on my bed,
I meditate on You in the *night* watches.
7 Because You have been my help,
Therefore in the shadow of Your wings I
will rejoice.
8 My soul follows close behind You;
Your right hand upholds me.

9 But those *who* seek my life, to destroy *it,*
Shall go into the lower parts of the earth.
10 They shall fall by the sword;
They shall be a portion for jackals.

11 But the king shall rejoice in God;
Everyone who swears by Him shall glory;
But the mouth of those who speak lies
shall be stopped.

PSALM 64

Oppressed by the Wicked but Rejoicing in the LORD

To the Chief Musician. A Psalm of David.

1 Hear my voice, O God, in my meditation;
Preserve my life from fear of the enemy.
2 Hide me from the secret plots of the
wicked,
From the rebellion of the workers of
iniquity,
3 Who sharpen their tongue like a sword,
And bend *their bows to shoot* their arrows—
bitter words,
4 That they may shoot in secret at the
blameless;
Suddenly they shoot at him and do not fear.

5 They encourage themselves *in* an evil
matter;
They talk of laying snares secretly;
They say, "Who will see them?"
6 They devise iniquities:
"We have perfected a shrewd scheme."
Both the inward thought and the heart of
man are deep.

7 But God shall shoot at them *with* an
arrow;

Suddenly they shall be wounded.
8 So He will make them stumble over their
own tongue;
All who see them shall flee away.
9 All men shall fear,
And shall declare the work of God;
For they shall wisely consider His doing.

10 The righteous shall be glad in the LORD,
and trust in Him.
And all the upright in heart shall glory.

PSALM 65

Praise to God for His Salvation and Providence

To the Chief Musician.
A Psalm of David. A Song.

1 Praise is awaiting You, O God, in Zion;
And to You the vow shall be performed.
2 O You who hear prayer,
To You all flesh will come.
3 Iniquities prevail against me;
As for our transgressions,
You will provide atonement for them.

4 Blessed *is the man* You choose,
And cause to approach *You,*
That he may dwell in Your courts.
We shall be satisfied with the goodness of
Your house,
Of Your holy temple.

5 *By* awesome deeds in righteousness You
will answer us,
O God of our salvation,
You who are the confidence of all the ends
of the earth,
And of the far-off seas;
6 Who established the mountains by His
strength,
Being clothed with power;
7 You who still the noise of the seas,
The noise of their waves,
And the tumult of the peoples.
8 They also who dwell in the farthest parts
are afraid of Your signs;
You make the outgoings of the morning
and evening rejoice.

9 You visit the earth and water it,
You greatly enrich it;
The river of God is full of water;
You provide their grain,
For so You have prepared it.

10 You water its ridges abundantly,
You settle its furrows;
You make it soft with showers,
You bless its growth.

11 You crown the year with Your goodness,
And Your paths drip *with* abundance.

12 They drop *on* the pastures of the
wilderness,
And the little hills rejoice on every side.

13 The pastures are clothed with flocks;
The valleys also are covered with grain;
They shout for joy, they also sing.

PSALM 66

Praise to God for His Awesome Works

To the Chief Musician. A Song. A Psalm.

1 Make a joyful shout to God, all the
earth!

2 Sing out the honor of His name;
Make His praise glorious.

3 Say to God,
"How awesome are Your works!
Through the greatness of Your power
Your enemies shall submit themselves to
You.

4 All the earth shall worship You
And sing praises to You;
They shall sing praises *to* Your name."
Selah

5 Come and see the works of God;
He is awesome *in His* doing toward the
sons of men.

6 He turned the sea into dry *land;*
They went through the river on foot.
There we will rejoice in Him.

7 He rules by His power forever;
His eyes observe the nations;
Do not let the rebellious exalt themselves.
Selah

8 Oh, bless our God, you peoples!
And make the voice of His praise to be
heard,

9 Who keeps our soul among the living,
And does not allow our feet to be
moved.

10 For You, O God, have tested us;
You have refined us as silver is refined.

11 You brought us into the net;
You laid affliction on our backs.

12 You have caused men to ride over our
heads;

We went through fire and through water;
But You brought us out to rich *fulfillment.*

13 I will go into Your house with burnt
offerings;
I will pay You my vows,

14 Which my lips have uttered
And my mouth has spoken when I was in
trouble.

15 I will offer You burnt sacrifices of fat
animals,
With the sweet aroma of rams;
I will offer bulls with goats.   Selah

16 Come *and* hear, all you who fear God,
And I will declare what He has done for
my soul.

17 I cried to Him with my mouth,
And He was extolled with my tongue.

18 If I regard iniquity in my heart,
The Lord will not hear.

19 *But* certainly God has heard *me;*
He has attended to the voice of my prayer.

20 Blessed *be* God,
Who has not turned away my prayer,
Nor His mercy from me!

PSALM 67

An Invocation and a Doxology

To the Chief Musician. On stringed instruments.[a]
A Psalm. A Song.

1 God be merciful to us and bless us,
And cause His face to shine upon us, Selah

2 That Your way may be known on earth,
Your salvation among all nations.

3 Let the peoples praise You, O God;
Let all the peoples praise You.

4 Oh, let the nations be glad and sing for
joy!
For You shall judge the people righteously,
And govern the nations on earth.   Selah

5 Let the peoples praise You, O God;
Let all the peoples praise You.

6 *Then* the earth shall yield her increase;
God, our own God, shall bless us.

7 God shall bless us,
And all the ends of the earth shall fear
Him.

67:title [a]Hebrew *neginoth*

The Law of Intuition:
Vision for the World Drives God's Leaders
(Psalm 67:1–7)

God's blessings follow leaders who adopt His vision for the nations of the world.

Psalm 67 contains both the "top line" and the "bottom line" of the covenant God invites us to enter. The top line represents God's blessings for His people; the bottom line represents the natural response to that blessing. When God blesses us, we are to turn around and bless all the unblessed nations of the earth.

Psalm 67:1 asks God to be gracious, to bless, and to make His face to shine upon His people (the *top line* of the covenant). Verse 2 says, "That Your way may be known on earth, Your salvation among all nations" (the *bottom line* of the covenant). The last two verses of the psalm reiterate the top and bottom lines.

God blesses His people so that they can bless those who have yet to be blessed. Godly leaders feel driven by this vision. Maintenance is not the goal. Getting blessed is not the goal. The top line represents only half of the deal; the goal is to participate in the bottom line. World conquest motivates God's heart, and He accomplishes this mission through leaders who cast vision for participating in bottom-line living.

PSALM 68

The Glory of God in His Goodness to Israel

To the Chief Musician.
A Psalm of David. A Song.

1 Let God arise,
Let His enemies be scattered;
Let those also who hate Him flee before
Him.
2 As smoke is driven away,
So drive *them* away;
As wax melts before the fire,
So let the wicked perish at the presence of
God.
3 But let the righteous be glad;
Let them rejoice before God;
Yes, let them rejoice exceedingly.

4 Sing to God, sing praises to His name;
Extol Him who rides on the clouds,[a]
By His name YAH,
And rejoice before Him.

5 A father of the fatherless, a defender of
widows,
Is God in His holy habitation.
6 God sets the solitary in families;
He brings out those who are bound into
prosperity;
But the rebellious dwell in a dry *land.*

7 O God, when You went out before Your
people,
When You marched through the
wilderness,　　　Selah
8 The earth shook;
The heavens also dropped *rain* at the
presence of God;
Sinai itself *was* moved at the presence of
God, the God of Israel.
9 You, O God, sent a plentiful rain,
Whereby You confirmed Your inheritance,
When it was weary.
10 Your congregation dwelt in it;
You, O God, provided from Your goodness
for the poor.

11 The Lord gave the word;
Great *was* the company of those who
proclaimed *it:*
12 "Kings of armies flee, they flee,
And she who remains at home divides the
spoil.
13 Though you lie down among the
sheepfolds,
You will be like the wings of a dove
covered with silver,
And her feathers with yellow gold."
14 When the Almighty scattered kings in it,
It was *white* as snow in Zalmon.

68:4 [a]Masoretic Text reads *deserts;* Targum reads
heavens (compare verse 34 and Isaiah 19:1).

15 A mountain of God *is* the mountain of
Bashan;
A mountain *of many* peaks *is* the mountain
of Bashan.
16 Why do you fume with envy, you
mountains of *many* peaks?
This is the mountain *which* God desires to
dwell in;
Yes, the LORD will dwell *in it* forever.
17 The chariots of God *are* twenty thousand,
Even thousands of thousands;
The Lord is among them *as in* Sinai, in the
Holy *Place.*
18 You have ascended on high,
You have led captivity captive;
You have received gifts among men,
Even *from* the rebellious,
That the LORD God might dwell *there.*

19 Blessed *be* the Lord,
Who daily loads us *with benefits,*
The God of our salvation!   Selah
20 Our God *is* the God of salvation;
And to GOD the Lord *belong* escapes from
death.

21 But God will wound the head of His
enemies,
The hairy scalp of the one who still goes
on in his trespasses.
22 The Lord said, "I will bring back from
Bashan,
I will bring *them* back from the depths of
the sea,
23 That your foot may crush *them*[a] in blood,
And the tongues of your dogs *may have*
their portion from *your* enemies."

24 They have seen Your procession, O God,
The procession of my God, my King, into
the sanctuary.
25 The singers went before, the players on
instruments *followed* after;
Among *them were* the maidens playing
timbrels.
26 Bless God in the congregations,
The Lord, from the fountain of Israel.
27 There *is* little Benjamin, their leader,
The princes of Judah *and* their company,
The princes of Zebulun *and* the princes of
Naphtali.

28 Your God has commanded[a] your strength;
Strengthen, O God, what You have done
for us.

29 Because of Your temple at Jerusalem,
Kings will bring presents to You.
30 Rebuke the beasts of the reeds,
The herd of bulls with the calves of the
peoples,
Till everyone submits himself with pieces of
silver.
Scatter the peoples *who* delight in war.
31 Envoys will come out of Egypt;
Ethiopia will quickly stretch out her hands
to God.

32 Sing to God, you kingdoms of the earth;
Oh, sing praises to the Lord,   Selah
33 To Him who rides on the heaven of
heavens, *which were* of old!
Indeed, He sends out His voice, a mighty
voice.
34 Ascribe strength to God;
His excellence *is* over Israel,
And His strength *is* in the clouds.
35 O God, *You are* more awesome than Your
holy places.
The God of Israel *is* He who gives
strength and power to *His* people.

Blessed *be* God!

PSALM 69

An Urgent Plea for Help in Trouble

To the Chief Musician. Set to "The Lilies."[a]
A Psalm of David.

1 Save me, O God!
For the waters have come up to *my* neck.
2 I sink in deep mire,
Where *there is* no standing;
I have come into deep waters,
Where the floods overflow me.
3 I am weary with my crying;
My throat is dry;
My eyes fail while I wait for my God.

4 Those who hate me without a cause
Are more than the hairs of my head;
They are mighty who would destroy me,
Being my enemies wrongfully;
Though I have stolen nothing,
I *still* must restore *it.*

68:23 [a]Septuagint, Syriac, Targum, and Vulgate read
you may dip your foot. **68:28** [a]Septuagint, Syriac,
Targum, and Vulgate read *Command, O God.*
69:title [a]Hebrew *Shoshannim*

5 O God, You know my foolishness;
And my sins are not hidden from You.
6 Let not those who wait for You, O Lord
GOD of hosts, be ashamed because of me;
Let not those who seek You be confounded
because of me, O God of Israel.
7 Because for Your sake I have borne
reproach;
Shame has covered my face.
8 I have become a stranger to my brothers,
And an alien to my mother's children;
9 Because zeal for Your house has eaten me
up,
And the reproaches of those who reproach
You have fallen on me.
10 When I wept *and chastened* my soul with
fasting,
That became my reproach.
11 I also made sackcloth my garment;
I became a byword to them.
12 Those who sit in the gate speak against me,
And I *am* the song of the drunkards.

13 But as for me, my prayer *is* to You,
O LORD, *in* the acceptable time;
O God, in the multitude of Your mercy,
Hear me in the truth of Your salvation.
14 Deliver me out of the mire,
And let me not sink;
Let me be delivered from those who hate
me,
And out of the deep waters.
15 Let not the floodwater overflow me,
Nor let the deep swallow me up;
And let not the pit shut its mouth on me.

16 Hear me, O LORD, for Your
lovingkindness *is* good;
Turn to me according to the multitude of
Your tender mercies.
17 And do not hide Your face from Your
servant,
For I am in trouble;
Hear me speedily.
18 Draw near to my soul, *and* redeem it;
Deliver me because of my enemies.

19 You know my reproach, my shame, and
my dishonor;
My adversaries *are* all before You.
20 Reproach has broken my heart,
And I am full of heaviness;
I looked *for someone* to take pity, but *there
was* none;
And for comforters, but I found none.
21 They also gave me gall for my food,

And for my thirst they gave me vinegar to
drink.
22 Let their table become a snare before them,
And their well-being a trap.
23 Let their eyes be darkened, so that they do
not see;
And make their loins shake continually.
24 Pour out Your indignation upon them,
And let Your wrathful anger take hold of
them.
25 Let their dwelling place be desolate;
Let no one live in their tents.
26 For they persecute the *ones* You have struck,
And talk of the grief of those You have
wounded.
27 Add iniquity to their iniquity,
And let them not come into Your
righteousness.
28 Let them be blotted out of the book of
the living,
And not be written with the righteous.

29 But I *am* poor and sorrowful;
Let Your salvation, O God, set me up on
high.
30 I will praise the name of God with a song,
And will magnify Him with thanksgiving.
31 *This* also shall please the LORD better than
an ox *or* bull,
Which has horns and hooves.
32 The humble shall see *this and* be glad;
And you who seek God, your hearts shall
live.
33 For the LORD hears the poor,
And does not despise His prisoners.

34 Let heaven and earth praise Him,
The seas and everything that moves in
them.
35 For God will save Zion
And build the cities of Judah,
That they may dwell there and possess it.
36 Also, the descendants of His servants shall
inherit it,
And those who love His name shall dwell
in it.

PSALM 70

Prayer for Relief from Adversaries

To the Chief Musician. *A Psalm* of David.
To bring to remembrance.

1 *Make haste,* O God, to deliver me!
Make haste to help me, O LORD!

2 Let them be ashamed and confounded
Who seek my life;
Let them be turned back[a] and confused
Who desire my hurt.
3 Let them be turned back because of their
shame,
Who say, "Aha, aha!"

4 Let all those who seek You rejoice and be
glad in You;
And let those who love Your salvation say
continually,
"Let God be magnified!"

5 But I *am* poor and needy;
Make haste to me, O God!
You *are* my help and my deliverer;
O LORD, do not delay.

PSALM 71

God the Rock of Salvation

1 In You, O LORD, I put my trust;
Let me never be put to shame.
2 Deliver me in Your righteousness, and
cause me to escape;
Incline Your ear to me, and save me.
3 Be my strong refuge,
To which I may resort continually;
You have given the commandment to save
me,
For You *are* my rock and my fortress.

4 Deliver me, O my God, out of the hand of
the wicked,
Out of the hand of the unrighteous and
cruel man.
5 For You are my hope, O Lord GOD;
You are my trust from my youth.
6 By You I have been upheld from birth;
You are He who took me out of my
mother's womb.
My praise *shall be* continually of You.

7 I have become as a wonder to many,
But You *are* my strong refuge.
8 Let my mouth be filled *with* Your praise
And with Your glory all the day.

9 Do not cast me off in the time of old age;
Do not forsake me when my strength fails.
10 For my enemies speak against me;
And those who lie in wait for my life take
counsel together,
11 Saying, "God has forsaken him;

Pursue and take him, for *there is* none to
deliver *him.*"

12 O God, do not be far from me;
O my God, make haste to help me!
13 Let them be confounded *and* consumed
Who are adversaries of my life;
Let them be covered *with* reproach and
dishonor
Who seek my hurt.
14 But I will hope continually,
And will praise You yet more and more.
15 My mouth shall tell of Your righteousness
And Your salvation all the day,
For I do not know *their* limits.
16 I will go in the strength of the Lord GOD;
I will make mention of Your
righteousness, of Yours only.

17 O God, You have taught me from my
youth;
And to this *day* I declare Your wondrous
works.
18 Now also when *I am* old and grayheaded,
O God, do not forsake me,
Until I declare Your strength to *this*
generation,
Your power to everyone *who* is to come.

19 Also Your righteousness, O God, *is* very
high,
You who have done great things;
O God, who *is* like You?
20 *You,* who have shown me great and severe
troubles,
Shall revive me again,
And bring me up again from the depths of
the earth.
21 You shall increase my greatness,
And comfort me on every side.

22 Also with the lute I will praise You—
And Your faithfulness, O my God!
To You I will sing with the harp,
O Holy One of Israel.
23 My lips shall greatly rejoice when I sing to
You,
And my soul, which You have redeemed.
24 My tongue also shall talk of Your
righteousness all the day long;
For they are confounded,

70:2 [a]Following Masoretic Text, Septuagint,
Targum, and Vulgate; some Hebrew manuscripts
and Syriac read *be appalled* (compare 40:15).

For they are brought to shame
Who seek my hurt.

PSALM 72

Glory and Universality of the Messiah's Reign

A Psalm of Solomon.

1 Give the king Your judgments, O God,
And Your righteousness to the king's Son.
2 He will judge Your people with
righteousness,
And Your poor with justice.
3 The mountains will bring peace to the
people,
And the little hills, by righteousness.
4 He will bring justice to the poor of the
people;
He will save the children of the needy,
And will break in pieces the oppressor.

5 They shall fear You[a]
As long as the sun and moon endure,
Throughout all generations.
6 He shall come down like rain upon the
grass before mowing,
Like showers *that* water the earth.
7 In His days the righteous shall flourish,
And abundance of peace,
Until the moon is no more.

8 He shall have dominion also from sea to
sea,
And from the River to the ends of the
earth.
9 Those who dwell in the wilderness will
bow before Him,
And His enemies will lick the dust.
10 The kings of Tarshish and of the isles
Will bring presents;
The kings of Sheba and Seba
Will offer gifts.
11 Yes, all kings shall fall down before Him;
All nations shall serve Him.

12 For He will deliver the needy when he
cries,
The poor also, and *him* who has no
helper.
13 He will spare the poor and needy,
And will save the souls of the needy.
14 He will redeem their life from oppression
and violence;
And precious shall be their blood in His
sight.

15 And He shall live;
And the gold of Sheba will be given to
Him;
Prayer also will be made for Him
continually,
And daily He shall be praised.

16 There will be an abundance of grain in
the earth,
On the top of the mountains;
Its fruit shall wave like Lebanon;
And *those* of the city shall flourish like
grass of the earth.

17 His name shall endure forever;
His name shall continue as long as the sun.
And *men* shall be blessed in Him;
All nations shall call Him blessed.

18 Blessed *be* the LORD God, the God of
Israel,
Who only does wondrous things!
19 And blessed *be* His glorious name forever!
And let the whole earth be filled *with* His
glory.
Amen and Amen.

20 The prayers of David the son of Jesse are
ended.

Book Three: Psalms 73—89

PSALM 73

The Tragedy of the Wicked, and the Blessedness of Trust in God

A Psalm of Asaph.

1 Truly God *is* good to Israel,
To such as are pure in heart.
2 But as for me, my feet had almost
stumbled;
My steps had nearly slipped.
3 For I *was* envious of the boastful,
When I saw the prosperity of the wicked.

4 For *there are* no pangs in their death,
But their strength *is* firm.
5 They *are* not in trouble *as other* men,
Nor are they plagued like *other* men.
6 Therefore pride serves as their necklace;
Violence covers them *like* a garment.

72:5 [a]Following Masoretic Text and Targum;
Septuagint and Vulgate read *They shall continue.*

Vision: The Difference Between Followers and Leaders

(Psalm 73:1–17)

Vision is the friend of every leader, helping them to keep perspective and stay the course. When Asaph sees the final destiny of the wicked, he is able to endure his season of oppression. Without hope in the future, we lack power in the present.

7 Their eyes bulge[a] with abundance;
They have more than heart could wish.
8 They scoff and speak wickedly *concerning* oppression;
They speak loftily.
9 They set their mouth against the heavens,
And their tongue walks through the earth.
10 Therefore his people return here,
And waters of a full *cup* are drained by them.
11 And they say, "How does God know?
And is there knowledge in the Most High?"
12 Behold, these *are* the ungodly,
Who are always at ease;
They increase *in* riches.
13 Surely I have cleansed my heart *in* vain,
And washed my hands in innocence.
14 For all day long I have been plagued,
And chastened every morning.

15 If I had said, "I will speak thus,"
Behold, I would have been untrue to the generation of Your children.
16 When I thought *how* to understand this,
It *was* too painful for me—
17 Until I went into the sanctuary of God;
Then I understood their end.

18 Surely You set them in slippery places;
You cast them down to destruction.
19 Oh, how they are *brought* to desolation, as in a moment!
They are utterly consumed with terrors.
20 As a dream when *one* awakes,
So, Lord, when You awake,
You shall despise their image.

21 Thus my heart was grieved,
And I was vexed in my mind.
22 I *was* so foolish and ignorant;
I was *like* a beast before You.
23 Nevertheless I *am* continually with You;
You hold *me* by my right hand.
24 You will guide me with Your counsel,
And afterward receive me *to* glory.

25 Whom have I in heaven *but* You?
And *there is* none upon earth *that* I desire besides You.
26 My flesh and my heart fail;
But God *is* the strength of my heart and my portion forever.

27 For indeed, those who are far from You shall perish;
You have destroyed all those who desert You for harlotry.
28 But *it is* good for me to draw near to God;
I have put my trust in the Lord GOD,
That I may declare all Your works.

PSALM 74

A Plea for Relief from Oppressors

A Contemplation[a] of Asaph.

1 O God, why have You cast *us* off forever?
Why does Your anger smoke against the sheep of Your pasture?
2 Remember Your congregation, *which* You have purchased of old,
The tribe of Your inheritance, *which* You have redeemed—
This Mount Zion where You have dwelt.
3 Lift up Your feet to the perpetual desolations.
The enemy has damaged everything in the sanctuary.
4 Your enemies roar in the midst of Your meeting place;
They set up their banners *for* signs.
5 They seem like men who lift up
Axes among the thick trees.
6 And now they break down its carved work, all at once,
With axes and hammers.
7 They have set fire to Your sanctuary;
They have defiled the dwelling place of Your name to the ground.

73:7 [a]Targum reads *face bulges;* Septuagint, Syriac, and Vulgate read *iniquity bulges.* **74:title** [a]Hebrew *Maschil*

8   They said in their hearts,
    "Let us destroy them altogether."
    They have burned up all the meeting
        places of God in the land.

9   We do not see our signs;
    There is no longer any prophet;
    Nor *is there* any among us who knows
        how long.

10 O God, how long will the adversary
        reproach?
    Will the enemy blaspheme Your name
        forever?

11 Why do You withdraw Your hand, even
        Your right hand?
    Take it out of Your bosom and destroy
        them.

12 For God *is* my King from of old,
    Working salvation in the midst of the
        earth.

13 You divided the sea by Your strength;
    You broke the heads of the sea serpents in
        the waters.

14 You broke the heads of Leviathan in
        pieces,
    And gave him *as* food to the people
        inhabiting the wilderness.

15 You broke open the fountain and the
        flood;
    You dried up mighty rivers.

16 The day *is* Yours, the night also *is* Yours;
    You have prepared the light and the sun.

17 You have set all the borders of the earth;
    You have made summer and winter.

18 Remember this, *that* the enemy has
        reproached, O LORD,
    And *that* a foolish people has blasphemed
        Your name.

19 Oh, do not deliver the life of Your
        turtledove to the wild beast!
    Do not forget the life of Your poor
        forever.

20 Have respect to the covenant;
    For the dark places of the earth are full of
        the haunts of cruelty.

21 Oh, do not let the oppressed return
        ashamed!
    Let the poor and needy praise Your name.

22 Arise, O God, plead Your own cause;
    Remember how the foolish man
        reproaches You daily.

23 Do not forget the voice of Your enemies;
    The tumult of those who rise up against
        You increases continually.

PSALM 75

Thanksgiving for God's Righteous Judgment

To the Chief Musician. Set to "Do Not Destroy."[a]
A Psalm of Asaph. A Song.

1   We give thanks to You, O God, we give
        thanks!
    For Your wondrous works declare *that*
        Your name is near.

2   "When I choose the proper time,
    I will judge uprightly.

3   The earth and all its inhabitants are
        dissolved;
    I set up its pillars firmly.   Selah

4   "I said to the boastful, 'Do not deal
        boastfully,'
    And to the wicked, 'Do not lift up the
        horn.

5   Do not lift up your horn on high;
    Do *not* speak with a stiff neck.'"

6   For exaltation *comes* neither from the east
    Nor from the west nor from the south.

7   But God *is* the Judge:
    He puts down one,
    And exalts another.

8   For in the hand of the LORD *there is* a cup,
    And the wine is red;
    It is fully mixed, and He pours it out;
    Surely its dregs shall all the wicked of the
        earth
    Drain *and* drink down.

9   But I will declare forever,
    I will sing praises to the God of Jacob.

10 "All the horns of the wicked I will also cut
        off,
    But the horns of the righteous shall be
        exalted."

PSALM 76

The Majesty of God in Judgment

To the Chief Musician. On stringed instruments.[a]
A Psalm of Asaph. A Song.

1   In Judah God *is* known;
    His name *is* great in Israel.

75:title [a]Hebrew *Al Tashcheth* **76:title** [a]Hebrew
neginoth

2 In Salem[a] also is His tabernacle,
And His dwelling place in Zion.
3 There He broke the arrows of the bow,
The shield and sword of battle.   Selah

4 You *are* more glorious and excellent
Than the mountains of prey.
5 The stouthearted were plundered;
They have sunk into their sleep;
And none of the mighty men have found
the use of their hands.
6 At Your rebuke, O God of Jacob,
Both the chariot and horse were cast into
a dead sleep.

7 You, Yourself, *are* to be feared;
And who may stand in Your presence
When once You are angry?
8 You caused judgment to be heard from
heaven;
The earth feared and was still,
9 When God arose to judgment,
To deliver all the oppressed of the earth.
Selah

10 Surely the wrath of man shall praise You;
With the remainder of wrath You shall
gird Yourself.

11 Make vows to the LORD your God, and
pay *them;*
Let all who are around Him bring presents
to Him who ought to be feared.
12 He shall cut off the spirit of princes;
He is awesome to the kings of the earth.

PSALM 77

The Consoling Memory of God's Redemptive Works

To the Chief Musician. To Jeduthun.
A Psalm of Asaph.

1 I cried out to God with my voice—
To God with my voice;
And He gave ear to me.
2 In the day of my trouble I sought the Lord;
My hand was stretched out in the night
without ceasing;
My soul refused to be comforted.
3 I remembered God, and was troubled;
I complained, and my spirit was
overwhelmed.   Selah

4 You hold my eyelids *open;*
I am so troubled that I cannot speak.

5 I have considered the days of old,
The years of ancient times.
6 I call to remembrance my song in the night;
I meditate within my heart,
And my spirit makes diligent search.

7 Will the Lord cast off forever?
And will He be favorable no more?
8 Has His mercy ceased forever?
Has *His* promise failed forevermore?
9 Has God forgotten to be gracious?
Has He in anger shut up His tender
mercies?   Selah

10 And I said, "This *is* my anguish;
But I will remember the years of the right
hand of the Most High."
11 I will remember the works of the LORD;
Surely I will remember Your wonders of
old.
12 I will also meditate on all Your work,
And talk of Your deeds.
13 Your way, O God, *is* in the sanctuary;
Who *is* so great a God as *our* God?
14 You *are* the God who does wonders;
You have declared Your strength among
the peoples.
15 You have with *Your* arm redeemed Your
people,
The sons of Jacob and Joseph.   Selah

16 The waters saw You, O God;
The waters saw You, they were afraid;
The depths also trembled.
17 The clouds poured out water;
The skies sent out a sound;
Your arrows also flashed about.
18 The voice of Your thunder *was* in the
whirlwind;
The lightnings lit up the world;
The earth trembled and shook.
19 Your way *was* in the sea,
Your path in the great waters,
And Your footsteps were not known.
20 You led Your people like a flock
By the hand of Moses and Aaron.

PSALM 78

God's Kindness to Rebellious Israel

A Contemplation[a] of Asaph.

1 Give ear, O my people, *to* my law;
Incline your ears to the words of my
mouth.

76:2 [a]That is, Jerusalem **78:title** [a]Hebrew *Maschil*

2 I will open my mouth in a parable;
I will utter dark sayings of old,
3 Which we have heard and known,
And our fathers have told us.
4 We will not hide *them* from their children,
Telling to the generation to come the
praises of the LORD,
And His strength and His wonderful works
that He has done.

5 For He established a testimony in Jacob,
And appointed a law in Israel,
Which He commanded our fathers,
That they should make them known to
their children;
6 That the generation to come might know
them,
The children *who* would be born,
That they may arise and declare *them* to
their children,
7 That they may set their hope in God,
And not forget the works of God,
But keep His commandments;
8 And may not be like their fathers,
A stubborn and rebellious generation,
A generation *that* did not set its heart
aright,
And whose spirit was not faithful to God.

9 The children of Ephraim, *being* armed *and*
carrying bows,
Turned back in the day of battle.
10 They did not keep the covenant of God;
They refused to walk in His law,
11 And forgot His works
And His wonders that He had shown them.

12 Marvelous things He did in the sight of
their fathers,
In the land of Egypt, *in* the field of Zoan.
13 He divided the sea and caused them to
pass through;
And He made the waters stand up like a
heap.
14 In the daytime also He led them with the
cloud,
And all the night with a light of fire.
15 He split the rocks in the wilderness,
And gave *them* drink in abundance like the
depths.
16 He also brought streams out of the rock,
And caused waters to run down like rivers.

17 But they sinned even more against Him
By rebelling against the Most High in the
wilderness.

18 And they tested God in their heart
By asking for the food of their fancy.
19 Yes, they spoke against God:
They said, "Can God prepare a table in the
wilderness?
20 Behold, He struck the rock,
So that the waters gushed out,
And the streams overflowed.
Can He give bread also?
Can He provide meat for His people?"

21 Therefore the LORD heard *this* and was
furious;
So a fire was kindled against Jacob,
And anger also came up against Israel,
22 Because they did not believe in God,
And did not trust in His salvation.
23 Yet He had commanded the clouds above,
And opened the doors of heaven,
24 Had rained down manna on them to eat,
And given them of the bread of heaven.
25 Men ate angels' food;
He sent them food to the full.

26 He caused an east wind to blow in the
heavens;
And by His power He brought in the
south wind.
27 He also rained meat on them like the dust,
Feathered fowl like the sand of the seas;
28 And He let *them* fall in the midst of their
camp,
All around their dwellings.
29 So they ate and were well filled,
For He gave them their own desire.
30 They were not deprived of their craving;
But while their food *was* still in their
mouths,
31 The wrath of God came against them,
And slew the stoutest of them,
And struck down the choice *men* of Israel.

32 In spite of this they still sinned,
And did not believe in His wondrous
works.
33 Therefore their days He consumed in
futility,
And their years in fear.

34 When He slew them, then they sought
Him;
And they returned and sought earnestly
for God.
35 Then they remembered that God *was* their
rock,
And the Most High God their Redeemer.

36 Nevertheless they flattered Him with their
mouth,
And they lied to Him with their tongue;
37 For their heart was not steadfast with Him,
Nor were they faithful in His covenant.
38 But He, *being* full of compassion, forgave
their iniquity,
And did not destroy *them*.
Yes, many a time He turned His anger
away,
And did not stir up all His wrath;
39 For He remembered that they *were but*
flesh,
A breath that passes away and does not
come again.

40 How often they provoked Him in the
wilderness,
And grieved Him in the desert!
41 Yes, again and again they tempted God,
And limited the Holy One of Israel.
42 They did not remember His power:
The day when He redeemed them from
the enemy,
43 When He worked His signs in Egypt,
And His wonders in the field of Zoan;
44 Turned their rivers into blood,
And their streams, that they could not
drink.
45 He sent swarms of flies among them,
which devoured them,
And frogs, which destroyed them.
46 He also gave their crops to the caterpillar,
And their labor to the locust.
47 He destroyed their vines with hail,
And their sycamore trees with frost.
48 He also gave up their cattle to the hail,
And their flocks to fiery lightning.
49 He cast on them the fierceness of His
anger,
Wrath, indignation, and trouble,
By sending angels of destruction *among
them*.
50 He made a path for His anger;
He did not spare their soul from death,
But gave their life over to the plague,
51 And destroyed all the firstborn in Egypt,
The first of *their* strength in the tents of
Ham.
52 But He made His own people go forth
like sheep,
And guided them in the wilderness like a
flock;
53 And He led them on safely, so that they
did not fear;
But the sea overwhelmed their enemies.

54 And He brought them to His holy border,
This mountain *which* His right hand had
acquired.
55 He also drove out the nations before them,
Allotted them an inheritance by survey,
And made the tribes of Israel dwell in
their tents.

56 Yet they tested and provoked the Most
High God,
And did not keep His testimonies,
57 But turned back and acted unfaithfully like
their fathers;
They were turned aside like a deceitful
bow.
58 For they provoked Him to anger with
their high places,
And moved Him to jealousy with their
carved images.
59 When God heard *this*, He was furious,
And greatly abhorred Israel,
60 So that He forsook the tabernacle of
Shiloh,
The tent He had placed among men,
61 And delivered His strength into captivity,
And His glory into the enemy's hand.
62 He also gave His people over to the sword,
And was furious with His inheritance.
63 The fire consumed their young men,
And their maidens were not given in
marriage.
64 Their priests fell by the sword,
And their widows made no lamentation.

65 Then the Lord awoke as *from* sleep,
Like a mighty man who shouts because of
wine.
66 And He beat back His enemies;
He put them to a perpetual reproach.

67 Moreover He rejected the tent of Joseph,
And did not choose the tribe of Ephraim,
68 But chose the tribe of Judah,
Mount Zion which He loved.
69 And He built His sanctuary like the
heights,
Like the earth which He has established
forever.
70 He also chose David His servant,
And took him from the sheepfolds;
71 From following the ewes that had young
He brought him,
To shepherd Jacob His people,
And Israel His inheritance.
72 So he shepherded them according to the
integrity of his heart,

Skill and Competence: Eleven Keys to Excellence

(Psalm 78:72)

David's leadership succeeded through a two-sided coin: his hands and his heart, or outward skill and inward integrity. Every great spiritual leader must have this combination. David's excellent leadership combined both heart and art. To have one without the other leads to failure.

Consider the following list of 11 keys to excellence, aimed at helping us to develop our leadership skills today. Leaders must . . .

- first value excellence
- not settle for average
- pay attention to detail
- remain committed to what really matters
- display integrity and sound ethics
- show genuine respect for others
- go the second mile
- demonstrate consistency
- never stop improving
- always give 100%
- make excellence a lifestyle

And guided them by the skillfulness of his
hands.

PSALM 79

A Dirge and a Prayer for Israel, Destroyed by Enemies

A Psalm of Asaph.

1 O God, the nations have come into Your
inheritance;
Your holy temple they have defiled;
They have laid Jerusalem in heaps.
2 The dead bodies of Your servants
They have given *as* food for the birds of
the heavens,
The flesh of Your saints to the beasts of
the earth.
3 Their blood they have shed like water all
around Jerusalem,
And *there was* no one to bury *them*.
4 We have become a reproach to our
neighbors,

A scorn and derision to those who are
around us.
5 How long, LORD?
Will You be angry forever?
Will Your jealousy burn like fire?
6 Pour out Your wrath on the nations that
do not know You,
And on the kingdoms that do not call on
Your name.
7 For they have devoured Jacob,
And laid waste his dwelling place.

8 Oh, do not remember former iniquities
against us!
Let Your tender mercies come speedily to
meet us,
For we have been brought very low.
9 Help us, O God of our salvation,
For the glory of Your name;
And deliver us, and provide atonement for
our sins,
For Your name's sake!
10 Why should the nations say,
"Where *is* their God?"
Let there be known among the nations in
our sight
The avenging of the blood of Your
servants *which has been* shed.
11 Let the groaning of the prisoner come
before You;
According to the greatness of Your power
Preserve those who are appointed to die;
12 And return to our neighbors sevenfold
into their bosom
Their reproach with which they have
reproached You, O Lord.
13 So we, Your people and sheep of Your
pasture,
Will give You thanks forever;
We will show forth Your praise to all
generations.

PSALM 80

Prayer for Israel's Restoration

To the Chief Musician. Set to "The Lilies."[a]
A Testimony[b] of Asaph. A Psalm.

1 Give ear, O Shepherd of Israel,
You who lead Joseph like a flock;
You who dwell *between* the cherubim,
shine forth!

80:title [a]Hebrew *Shoshannim* [b]Hebrew *Eduth*

2 Before Ephraim, Benjamin, and Manasseh,
Stir up Your strength,
And come *and* save us!

3 Restore us, O God;
Cause Your face to shine,
And we shall be saved!

4 O LORD God of hosts,
How long will You be angry
Against the prayer of Your people?
5 You have fed them with the bread of tears,
And given them tears to drink in great
measure.
6 You have made us a strife to our
neighbors,
And our enemies laugh among themselves.

7 Restore us, O God of hosts;
Cause Your face to shine,
And we shall be saved!

8 You have brought a vine out of Egypt;
You have cast out the nations, and
planted it.
9 You prepared *room* for it,
And caused it to take deep root,
And it filled the land.
10 The hills were covered with its shadow,
And the mighty cedars with its boughs.
11 She sent out her boughs to the Sea,[a]
And her branches to the River.[b]

12 Why have You broken down her hedges,
So that all who pass by the way pluck her
fruit?
13 The boar out of the woods uproots it,
And the wild beast of the field devours it.

14 Return, we beseech You, O God of hosts;
Look down from heaven and see,
And visit this vine
15 And the vineyard which Your right hand
has planted,
And the branch *that* You made strong for
Yourself.
16 *It is* burned with fire, *it is* cut down;
They perish at the rebuke of Your
countenance.
17 Let Your hand be upon the man of Your
right hand,
Upon the son of man *whom* You made
strong for Yourself.
18 Then we will not turn back from You;
Revive us, and we will call upon Your
name.

19 Restore us, O LORD God of hosts;
Cause Your face to shine,
And we shall be saved!

PSALM 81

An Appeal for Israel's Repentance

*To the Chief Musician. On an instrument of
Gath.[a] A Psalm of Asaph.*

1 Sing aloud to God our strength;
Make a joyful shout to the God of Jacob.
2 Raise a song and strike the timbrel,
The pleasant harp with the lute.

3 Blow the trumpet at the time of the New
Moon,
At the full moon, on our solemn feast day.
4 For this *is* a statute for Israel,
A law of the God of Jacob.
5 This He established in Joseph *as* a
testimony,
When He went throughout the land of
Egypt,
Where I heard a language I did not
understand.

6 "I removed his shoulder from the burden;
His hands were freed from the baskets.
7 You called in trouble, and I delivered you;
I answered you in the secret place of
thunder;
I tested you at the waters of Meribah.
Selah

8 "Hear, O My people, and I will admonish
you!
O Israel, if you will listen to Me!
9 There shall be no foreign god among you;
Nor shall you worship any foreign god.
10 I *am* the LORD your God,
Who brought you out of the land of Egypt;
Open your mouth wide, and I will fill it.

11 "But My people would not heed My
voice,
And Israel would *have* none of Me.
12 So I gave them over to their own stubborn
heart,
To walk in their own counsels.

13 "Oh, that My people would listen to Me,
That Israel would walk in My ways!

80:11 [a]That is, the Mediterranean [b]That is, the
Euphrates **81:title** [a]Hebrew *Al Gittith*

14 I would soon subdue their enemies,
And turn My hand against their
adversaries.
15 The haters of the LORD would pretend
submission to Him,
But their fate would endure forever.
16 He would have fed them also with the
finest of wheat;
And with honey from the rock I would
have satisfied you."

PSALM 82

A Plea for Justice

A Psalm of Asaph.

1 God stands in the congregation of the
mighty;
He judges among the gods.[a]
2 How long will you judge unjustly,
And show partiality to the wicked?   Selah
3 Defend the poor and fatherless;
Do justice to the afflicted and needy.
4 Deliver the poor and needy;
Free *them* from the hand of the wicked.

5 They do not know, nor do they understand;
They walk about in darkness;
All the foundations of the earth are
unstable.

6 I said, "You *are* gods,[a]
And all of you *are* children of the Most
High.

7 But you shall die like men,
And fall like one of the princes."

8 Arise, O God, judge the earth;
For You shall inherit all nations.

PSALM 83

Prayer to Frustrate Conspiracy Against Israel

A Song. A Psalm of Asaph.

1 Do not keep silent, O God!
Do not hold Your peace,
And do not be still, O God!
2 For behold, Your enemies make a tumult;
And those who hate You have lifted up
their head.
3 They have taken crafty counsel against
Your people,
And consulted together against Your
sheltered ones.
4 They have said, "Come, and let us cut
them off from *being* a nation,
That the name of Israel may be
remembered no more."

5 For they have consulted together with one
consent;
They form a confederacy against You:
6 The tents of Edom and the Ishmaelites;

82:1 [a]Hebrew *elohim, mighty ones;* that is, the judges
82:6 [a]Hebrew *elohim, mighty ones;* that is, the judges

The Law of Influence: Measuring Your Leadership

(Psalm 82:1–8)

Many passages in Scripture declare God to be the Ultimate Judge (Pss. 7:8; 9:8; 10:18; 26:1; Prov. 31:9; Is. 1:17; etc.). A judge brings justice to bear, punishing the criminal and rewarding the righteous.

But before the final Day of Judgment, God uses His leaders to vindicate His people and urge the wicked to repent. God has entrusted His leaders with the gospel of Jesus Christ, through which men can be delivered from final judgment. Listen to the Lord's promise to His people: "I will restore your judges as at the first" (Is. 1:26). Spiritual leaders are to take this task seriously and to use their influence to promote justice. This differentiates true judges from false judges:

True Judges	False Judges
1. Chosen and appointed by God (Deut. 16:18)	1. Rule by their own power (Jer. 5:30, 31)
2. Responsible for certain areas (2 Chr. 19:5)	2. Lead others astray (Mic. 3:5)
3. Righteous and trustworthy (Deut. 16:18)	3. Irresponsible, selfish (Mic. 3:1, 2)

Moab and the Hagrites;
7 Gebal, Ammon, and Amalek;
Philistia with the inhabitants of Tyre;
8 Assyria also has joined with them;
They have helped the children of Lot.
Selah

9 Deal with them as *with* Midian,
As *with* Sisera,
As *with* Jabin at the Brook Kishon,
10 Who perished at En Dor,
Who became *as* refuse on the earth.
11 Make their nobles like Oreb and like
Zeeb,
Yes, all their princes like Zebah and
Zalmunna,
12 Who said, "Let us take for ourselves
The pastures of God for a possession."

13 O my God, make them like the whirling
dust,
Like the chaff before the wind!
14 As the fire burns the woods,
And as the flame sets the mountains on fire,
15 So pursue them with Your tempest,
And frighten them with Your storm.
16 Fill their faces with shame,
That they may seek Your name, O LORD.
17 Let them be confounded and dismayed
forever;
Yes, let them be put to shame and perish,
18 That they may know that You, whose
name alone *is* the LORD,
Are the Most High over all the earth.

PSALM 84

The Blessedness of Dwelling in the House of God

To the Chief Musician. On an instrument of
Gath.[a] A Psalm of the sons of Korah.

1 How lovely *is* Your tabernacle,
O LORD of hosts!
2 My soul longs, yes, even faints
For the courts of the LORD;
My heart and my flesh cry out for the
living God.

3 Even the sparrow has found a home,
And the swallow a nest for herself,
Where she may lay her young—
Even Your altars, O LORD of hosts,
My King and my God.
4 Blessed *are* those who dwell in Your house;
They will still be praising You.   Selah

5 Blessed *is* the man whose strength *is* in
You,
Whose heart *is* set on pilgrimage.
6 *As they* pass through the Valley of Baca,
They make it a spring;
The rain also covers it with pools.
7 They go from strength to strength;
Each one appears before God in Zion.[a]

8 O LORD God of hosts, hear my prayer;
Give ear, O God of Jacob!   Selah
9 O God, behold our shield,
And look upon the face of Your anointed.

10 For a day in Your courts *is* better than a
thousand.
I would rather be a doorkeeper in the
house of my God
Than dwell in the tents of wickedness.
11 For the LORD God *is* a sun and shield;
The LORD will give grace and glory;
No good *thing* will He withhold
From those who walk uprightly.

12 O LORD of hosts,
Blessed *is* the man who trusts in You!

PSALM 85

Prayer that the LORD Will Restore Favor to the Land

To the Chief Musician.
A Psalm of the sons of Korah.

1 LORD, You have been favorable to Your
land;
You have brought back the captivity of
Jacob.
2 You have forgiven the iniquity of Your
people;
You have covered all their sin.   Selah
3 You have taken away all Your wrath;
You have turned from the fierceness of
Your anger.

4 Restore us, O God of our salvation,
And cause Your anger toward us to cease.
5 Will You be angry with us forever?
Will You prolong Your anger to all
generations?
6 Will You not revive us again,
That Your people may rejoice in You?

84:title [a]Hebrew *Al Gittith* **84:7** [a]Septuagint,
Syriac, and Vulgate read *The God of gods shall be
seen.*

7 Show us Your mercy, LORD,
And grant us Your salvation.

8 I will hear what God the LORD will
speak,
For He will speak peace
To His people and to His saints;
But let them not turn back to folly.
9 Surely His salvation *is* near to those who
fear Him,
That glory may dwell in our land.

10 Mercy and truth have met together;
Righteousness and peace have kissed.
11 Truth shall spring out of the earth,
And righteousness shall look down from
heaven.
12 Yes, the LORD will give *what is* good;
And our land will yield its increase.
13 Righteousness will go before Him,
And shall make His footsteps *our* pathway.

PSALM 86

Prayer for Mercy, with Meditation on the Excellencies of the LORD

A Prayer of David.

1 Bow down Your ear, O LORD, hear me;
For I *am* poor and needy.
2 Preserve my life, for I *am* holy;
You are my God;
Save Your servant who trusts in You!
3 Be merciful to me, O Lord,
For I cry to You all day long.
4 Rejoice the soul of Your servant,
For to You, O Lord, I lift up my soul.
5 For You, Lord, *are* good, and ready to
forgive,
And abundant in mercy to all those who
call upon You.
6 Give ear, O LORD, to my prayer;
And attend to the voice of my
supplications.
7 In the day of my trouble I will call upon
You,
For You will answer me.

8 Among the gods *there is* none like You, O
Lord;
Nor *are there any works* like Your works.
9 All nations whom You have made
Shall come and worship before You, O
Lord,
And shall glorify Your name.

10 For You *are* great, and do wondrous things;
You alone *are* God.

11 Teach me Your way, O LORD;
I will walk in Your truth;
Unite my heart to fear Your name.
12 I will praise You, O Lord my God, with all
my heart,
And I will glorify Your name forevermore.
13 For great *is* Your mercy toward me,
And You have delivered my soul from the
depths of Sheol.

14 O God, the proud have risen against me,
And a mob of violent *men* have sought my
life,
And have not set You before them.
15 But You, O Lord, *are* a God full of
compassion, and gracious,
Longsuffering and abundant in mercy and
truth.

16 Oh, turn to me, and have mercy on me!
Give Your strength to Your servant,
And save the son of Your maidservant.
17 Show me a sign for good,
That those who hate me may see *it* and be
ashamed,
Because You, LORD, have helped me and
comforted me.

PSALM 87

The Glories of the City of God

A Psalm of the sons of Korah. A Song.

1 His foundation *is* in the holy mountains.
2 The LORD loves the gates of Zion
More than all the dwellings of Jacob.
3 Glorious things are spoken of you,
O city of God! Selah

4 "I will make mention of Rahab and
Babylon to those who know Me;
Behold, O Philistia and Tyre, with
Ethiopia:
'This *one* was born there.'"

5 And of Zion it will be said,
"This *one* and that *one* were born in her;
And the Most High Himself shall establish
her."
6 The LORD will record,
When He registers the peoples:
"This *one* was born there." Selah

⁷ Both the singers and the players on
instruments *say,*
"All my springs *are* in you."

PSALM 88

A Prayer for Help in Despondency

A Song. A Psalm of the sons of Korah. To the
Chief Musician. Set to "Mahalath Leannoth." A
Contemplation[a] of Heman the Ezrahite.

¹ O Lᴏʀᴅ, God of my salvation,
I have cried out day and night before You.
² Let my prayer come before You;
Incline Your ear to my cry.

³ For my soul is full of troubles,
And my life draws near to the grave.
⁴ I am counted with those who go down to
the pit;
I am like a man *who has* no strength,
⁵ Adrift among the dead,
Like the slain who lie in the grave,
Whom You remember no more,
And who are cut off from Your hand.

⁶ You have laid me in the lowest pit,
In darkness, in the depths.
⁷ Your wrath lies heavy upon me,
And You have afflicted *me* with all Your
waves.   Selah
⁸ You have put away my acquaintances far
from me;
You have made me an abomination to them;
I am shut up, and I cannot get out;
⁹ My eye wastes away because of affliction.

Lᴏʀᴅ, I have called daily upon You;
I have stretched out my hands to You.
¹⁰ Will You work wonders for the dead?
Shall the dead arise *and* praise You? Selah
¹¹ Shall Your lovingkindness be declared in
the grave?
Or Your faithfulness in the place of
destruction?
¹² Shall Your wonders be known in the dark?
And Your righteousness in the land of
forgetfulness?

¹³ But to You I have cried out, O Lᴏʀᴅ,
And in the morning my prayer comes
before You.
¹⁴ Lᴏʀᴅ, why do You cast off my soul?
Why do You hide Your face from me?
¹⁵ I *have been* afflicted and ready to die from
my youth;

I suffer Your terrors;
I am distraught.
¹⁶ Your fierce wrath has gone over me;
Your terrors have cut me off.
¹⁷ They came around me all day long like
water;
They engulfed me altogether.
¹⁸ Loved one and friend You have put far
from me,
And my acquaintances into darkness.

PSALM 89

Remembering the Covenant with David, and Sorrow for Lost Blessings

A Contemplation[a] of Ethan the Ezrahite.

¹ I will sing of the mercies of the Lᴏʀᴅ
forever;
With my mouth will I make known Your
faithfulness to all generations.
² For I have said, "Mercy shall be built up
forever;
Your faithfulness You shall establish in the
very heavens."

³ "I have made a covenant with My chosen,
I have sworn to My servant David:
⁴ 'Your seed I will establish forever,
And build up your throne to all
generations.'"   Selah

⁵ And the heavens will praise Your wonders,
O Lᴏʀᴅ;
Your faithfulness also in the assembly of
the saints.
⁶ For who in the heavens can be compared
to the Lᴏʀᴅ?
Who among the sons of the mighty can be
likened to the Lᴏʀᴅ?
⁷ God is greatly to be feared in the assembly
of the saints,
And to be held in reverence by all *those*
around Him.
⁸ O Lᴏʀᴅ God of hosts,
Who *is* mighty like You, O Lᴏʀᴅ?
Your faithfulness also surrounds You.
⁹ You rule the raging of the sea;
When its waves rise, You still them.
¹⁰ You have broken Rahab in pieces, as one
who is slain;
You have scattered Your enemies with
Your mighty arm.

88:title [a]Hebrew *Maschil*   **89:title** [a]Hebrew
Maschil

11 The heavens *are* Yours, the earth also *is*
Yours;
The world and all its fullness, You have
founded them.

12 The north and the south, You have created
them;
Tabor and Hermon rejoice in Your name.

13 You have a mighty arm;
Strong is Your hand, *and* high is Your right
hand.

14 Righteousness and justice *are* the
foundation of Your throne;
Mercy and truth go before Your face.

15 Blessed *are* the people who know the
joyful sound!
They walk, O LORD, in the light of Your
countenance.

16 In Your name they rejoice all day long,
And in Your righteousness they are
exalted.

17 For You *are* the glory of their strength,
And in Your favor our horn is exalted.

18 For our shield *belongs* to the LORD,
And our king to the Holy One of Israel.

19 Then You spoke in a vision to Your holy
one,[a]
And said: "I have given help to *one who is*
mighty;
I have exalted one chosen from the people.

20 I have found My servant David;
With My holy oil I have anointed him,

21 With whom My hand shall be established;
Also My arm shall strengthen him.

22 The enemy shall not outwit him,
Nor the son of wickedness afflict him.

23 I will beat down his foes before his face,
And plague those who hate him.

24 "But My faithfulness and My mercy *shall be*
with him,
And in My name his horn shall be exalted.

25 Also I will set his hand over the sea,
And his right hand over the rivers.

26 He shall cry to Me, 'You *are* my Father,
My God, and the rock of my salvation.'

27 Also I will make him *My* firstborn,
The highest of the kings of the earth.

28 My mercy I will keep for him forever,
And My covenant shall stand firm with him.

29 His seed also I will make *to endure* forever,
And his throne as the days of heaven.

30 "If his sons forsake My law
And do not walk in My judgments,

31 If they break My statutes

The Fruit That Comes from God's Anointing

(Psalm 89:19–29)

All leaders should seek the anointing of
God. They need to be empowered by the
hand of God, and show evidence of this by
leading in a way far superior to what they
could have achieved on their own.

What does God promise leaders anointed by
His Spirit?

1. God's help (v. 19)
2. Being called God's servant (v. 20)
3. God's strength (v. 21)
4. God's hand with them (v. 21)
5. Freedom from affliction (v. 22)
6. Freedom from deception (v. 22)
7. Victory over the enemy (v. 23)
8. God's faithfulness and kindness (v. 24)
9. Influence in the world (v. 25)
10. God's saving power (v. 26)
11. A Father-son relationship (v. 26)
12. Exaltation and authority (vv. 27–29)
13. Partaking of the covenant (v. 28)
14. Promise of descendants (v. 29)

And do not keep My commandments,

32 Then I will punish their transgression with
the rod,
And their iniquity with stripes.

33 Nevertheless My lovingkindness I will not
utterly take from him,
Nor allow My faithfulness to fail.

34 My covenant I will not break,
Nor alter the word that has gone out of
My lips.

35 Once I have sworn by My holiness;
I will not lie to David:

36 His seed shall endure forever,
And his throne as the sun before Me;

37 It shall be established forever like the moon,
Even *like* the faithful witness in the sky."
Selah

38 But You have cast off and abhorred,
You have been furious with Your
anointed.

89:19 [a]Following many Hebrew manuscripts;
Masoretic Text, Septuagint, Targum, and Vulgate
read *holy ones.*

39 You have renounced the covenant of Your
servant;
You have profaned his crown *by casting it*
to the ground.
40 You have broken down all his hedges;
You have brought his strongholds to ruin.
41 All who pass by the way plunder him;
He is a reproach to his neighbors.
42 You have exalted the right hand of his
adversaries;
You have made all his enemies rejoice.
43 You have also turned back the edge of his
sword,
And have not sustained him in the battle.
44 You have made his glory cease,
And cast his throne down to the ground.
45 The days of his youth You have shortened;
You have covered him with shame.   Selah

46 How long, LORD?
Will You hide Yourself forever?
Will Your wrath burn like fire?
47 Remember how short my time is;
For what futility have You created all the
children of men?
48 What man can live and not see death?
Can he deliver his life from the power of
the grave?   Selah

49 Lord, where *are* Your former
lovingkindnesses,
Which You swore to David in Your truth?
50 Remember, Lord, the reproach of Your
servants—
How I bear in my bosom *the reproach of* all
the many peoples,
51 With which Your enemies have
reproached, O LORD,
With which they have reproached the
footsteps of Your anointed.

52 Blessed *be* the LORD forevermore!
Amen and Amen.

Book Four: Psalms 90—106

PSALM 90

The Eternity of God, and Man's Frailty

A Prayer of Moses the man of God.

1 Lord, You have been our dwelling place[a] in
all generations.
2 Before the mountains were brought forth,
Or ever You had formed the earth and the
world,

Even from everlasting to everlasting, You
are God.

3 You turn man to destruction,
And say, "Return, O children of men."
4 For a thousand years in Your sight
Are like yesterday when it is past,
And *like* a watch in the night.
5 You carry them away *like* a flood;
They are like a sleep.
In the morning they are like grass *which*
grows up:
6 In the morning it flourishes and grows up;
In the evening it is cut down and withers.

7 For we have been consumed by Your
anger,
And by Your wrath we are terrified.
8 You have set our iniquities before You,
Our secret *sins* in the light of Your
countenance.
9 For all our days have passed away in Your
wrath;
We finish our years like a sigh.
10 The days of our lives *are* seventy years;
And if by reason of strength *they are* eighty
years,
Yet their boast *is* only labor and sorrow;
For it is soon cut off, and we fly away.
11 Who knows the power of Your anger?
For as the fear of You, *so is* Your wrath.
12 So teach *us* to number our days,
That we may gain a heart of wisdom.

13 Return, O LORD!
How long?

90:1 [a]Septuagint, Targum, and Vulgate read *refuge.*

Leaders Manage Their Time and Do More with Less

(Psalm 90:12, 17)

Moses had seen a generation squander 40
years in the wilderness. He believed that
if leaders could only gain a keen sense of the
swift passage of time, and if they would work
for something significant, they could die with a
great sense of satisfaction. Leaders don't kill
time, they execute it.

And have compassion on Your servants.

14 Oh, satisfy us early with Your mercy,
That we may rejoice and be glad all our
days!

15 Make us glad according to the days *in
which* You have afflicted us,
The years *in which* we have seen evil.

16 Let Your work appear to Your servants,
And Your glory to their children.

17 And let the beauty of the LORD our God
be upon us,
And establish the work of our hands for
us;
Yes, establish the work of our hands.

PSALM 91

Safety of Abiding in the Presence of God

1 He who dwells in the secret place of the
Most High
Shall abide under the shadow of the
Almighty.

2 I will say of the LORD, "*He is* my refuge
and my fortress;
My God, in Him I will trust."

3 Surely He shall deliver you from the snare
of the fowler[a]
And from the perilous pestilence.

4 He shall cover you with His feathers,
And under His wings you shall take
refuge;

His truth *shall be your* shield and buckler.

5 You shall not be afraid of the terror by
night,
Nor of the arrow *that* flies by day,

6 Nor of the pestilence *that* walks in
darkness,
Nor of the destruction *that* lays waste at
noonday.

7 A thousand may fall at your side,
And ten thousand at your right hand;
But it shall not come near you.

8 Only with your eyes shall you look,
And see the reward of the wicked.

9 Because you have made the LORD, *who is*
my refuge,
Even the Most High, your dwelling place,

10 No evil shall befall you,
Nor shall any plague come near your
dwelling;

11 For He shall give His angels charge over
you,
To keep you in all your ways.

12 In *their* hands they shall bear you up,
Lest you dash your foot against a stone.

13 You shall tread upon the lion and the
cobra,
The young lion and the serpent you shall
trample underfoot.

91:3 [a]That is, one who catches birds in a trap or
snare

The Leader's Refuge

(Psalm 91:1–16)

We discover one of the most comforting chapters in the Bible in Psalm 91. It describes the
security believers can enjoy through faith in God. Leaders can especially benefit from this
set of promises. Study them and enjoy them:

Promise	Leader's Benefit
1. God's presence (vv. 1, 2)	1. It doesn't have to be lonely at the top.
2. God's protection (vv. 3, 4)	2. As you take initiative and risks, God keeps you safe.
3. God's peace (vv. 5, 6)	3. You don't have to feel insecure in unknown territory.
4. God's perspective (vv. 7–10)	4. God gives an eternal view of life that keeps you steady.
5. God's provision (vv. 11–13)	5. Regardless of your needs, God meets them.
6. God's power (vv. 14–16)	6. In adversity, God delivers and helps you reach your goal.

¹⁴ "Because he has set his love upon Me,
  therefore I will deliver him;
  I will set him on high, because he has
  known My name.
¹⁵ He shall call upon Me, and I will answer
  him;
  I *will be* with him in trouble;
  I will deliver him and honor him.
¹⁶ With long life I will satisfy him,
  And show him My salvation."

PSALM 92

Praise to the LORD for His Love and Faithfulness

A Psalm. A Song for the Sabbath day.

¹ *It is* good to give thanks to the LORD,
  And to sing praises to Your name, O Most
  High;
² To declare Your lovingkindness in the
  morning,
  And Your faithfulness every night,
³ On an instrument of ten strings,
  On the lute,
  And on the harp,
  With harmonious sound.
⁴ For You, LORD, have made me glad
  through Your work;
  I will triumph in the works of Your hands.

⁵ O LORD, how great are Your works!
  Your thoughts are very deep.
⁶ A senseless man does not know,
  Nor does a fool understand this.
⁷ When the wicked spring up like grass,
  And when all the workers of iniquity
  flourish,
  It is that they may be destroyed forever.

⁸ But You, LORD, *are* on high forevermore.
⁹ For behold, Your enemies, O LORD,
  For behold, Your enemies shall perish;
  All the workers of iniquity shall be
  scattered.

¹⁰ But my horn You have exalted like a wild
  ox;
  I have been anointed with fresh oil.
¹¹ My eye also has seen *my desire* on my
  enemies;
  My ears hear *my desire* on the wicked
  Who rise up against me.

¹² The righteous shall flourish like a palm tree,
  He shall grow like a cedar in Lebanon.

¹³ Those who are planted in the house of the
  LORD
  Shall flourish in the courts of our God.
¹⁴ They shall still bear fruit in old age;
  They shall be fresh and flourishing,
¹⁵ To declare that the LORD is upright;
  He is my rock, and *there is* no
  unrighteousness in Him.

PSALM 93

The Eternal Reign of the LORD

¹ The LORD reigns, He is clothed with
  majesty;
  The LORD is clothed,
  He has girded Himself with strength.
  Surely the world is established, so that it
  cannot be moved.
² Your throne *is* established from of old;
  You *are* from everlasting.

³ The floods have lifted up, O LORD,
  The floods have lifted up their voice;
  The floods lift up their waves.
⁴ The LORD on high *is* mightier
  Than the noise of many waters,
  Than the mighty waves of the sea.

⁵ Your testimonies are very sure;
  Holiness adorns Your house,
  O LORD, forever.

PSALM 94

God the Refuge of the Righteous

¹ O LORD God, to whom vengeance
  belongs—
  O God, to whom vengeance belongs,
  shine forth!
² Rise up, O Judge of the earth;
  Render punishment to the proud.
³ LORD, how long will the wicked,
  How long will the wicked triumph?

⁴ They utter speech, *and* speak insolent
  things;
  All the workers of iniquity boast in
  themselves.
⁵ They break in pieces Your people, O LORD,
  And afflict Your heritage.
⁶ They slay the widow and the stranger,
  And murder the fatherless.
⁷ Yet they say, "The LORD does not see,
  Nor does the God of Jacob understand."

8 Understand, you senseless among the
    people;
  And *you* fools, when will you be wise?
9 He who planted the ear, shall He not hear?
  He who formed the eye, shall He not see?
10 He who instructs the nations, shall He not
    correct,
  He who teaches man knowledge?
11 The LORD knows the thoughts of man,
  That they *are* futile.

12 Blessed *is* the man whom You instruct, O
    LORD,
  And teach out of Your law,
13 That You may give him rest from the days
    of adversity,
  Until the pit is dug for the wicked.
14 For the LORD will not cast off His people,
  Nor will He forsake His inheritance.
15 But judgment will return to righteousness,
  And all the upright in heart will follow it.

16 Who will rise up for me against the
    evildoers?
  Who will stand up for me against the
    workers of iniquity?
17 Unless the LORD *had been* my help,
  My soul would soon have settled in silence.
18 If I say, "My foot slips,"
  Your mercy, O LORD, will hold me up.
19 In the multitude of my anxieties within me,
  Your comforts delight my soul.

20 Shall the throne of iniquity, which devises
    evil by law,
  Have fellowship with You?
21 They gather together against the life of the
    righteous,
  And condemn innocent blood.
22 But the LORD has been my defense,
  And my God the rock of my refuge.
23 He has brought on them their own
    iniquity,
  And shall cut them off in their own
    wickedness;
  The LORD our God shall cut them off.

PSALM 95

A Call to Worship and Obedience

1 Oh come, let us sing to the LORD!
  Let us shout joyfully to the Rock of our
    salvation.
2 Let us come before His presence with
    thanksgiving;

Let us shout joyfully to Him with psalms.
3 For the LORD *is* the great God,
  And the great King above all gods.
4 In His hand *are* the deep places of the
    earth;
  The heights of the hills *are* His also.
5 The sea *is* His, for He made it;
  And His hands formed the dry *land.*

6 Oh come, let us worship and bow down;
  Let us kneel before the LORD our Maker.
7 For He *is* our God,
  And we *are* the people of His pasture,
  And the sheep of His hand.

  Today, if you will hear His voice:
8 "Do not harden your hearts, as in the
    rebellion,[a]
  As *in* the day of trial[b] in the wilderness,
9 When your fathers tested Me;
  They tried Me, though they saw My work.
10 For forty years I was grieved with *that*
    generation,
  And said, 'It *is* a people who go astray in
    their hearts,
  And they do not know My ways.'
11 So I swore in My wrath,
  'They shall not enter My rest.'"

PSALM 96

A Song of Praise to God Coming in Judgment

1 Oh, sing to the LORD a new song!
  Sing to the LORD, all the earth.
2 Sing to the LORD, bless His name;
  Proclaim the good news of His salvation
    from day to day.
3 Declare His glory among the nations,
  His wonders among all peoples.

4 For the LORD *is* great and greatly to be
    praised;
  He *is* to be feared above all gods.
5 For all the gods of the peoples *are* idols,
  But the LORD made the heavens.
6 Honor and majesty *are* before Him;
  Strength and beauty *are* in His sanctuary.

7 Give to the LORD, O families of the
    peoples,
  Give to the LORD glory and strength.
8 Give to the LORD the glory *due* His name;
  Bring an offering, and come into His courts.

95:8 [a]Or *Meribah* [b]Or *Massah*

9 Oh, worship the LORD in the beauty of
holiness!
Tremble before Him, all the earth.

10 Say among the nations, "The LORD reigns;
The world also is firmly established,
It shall not be moved;
He shall judge the peoples righteously."

11 Let the heavens rejoice, and let the earth
be glad;
Let the sea roar, and all its fullness;

12 Let the field be joyful, and all that *is* in it.
Then all the trees of the woods will
rejoice before the LORD.

13 For He is coming, for He is coming to
judge the earth.
He shall judge the world with righteousness,
And the peoples with His truth.

PSALM 97

A Song of Praise to the Sovereign LORD

1 The LORD reigns;
Let the earth rejoice;
Let the multitude of isles be glad!

2 Clouds and darkness surround Him;
Righteousness and justice *are* the
foundation of His throne.

3 A fire goes before Him,
And burns up His enemies round about.

4 His lightnings light the world;
The earth sees and trembles.

5 The mountains melt like wax at the
presence of the LORD,
At the presence of the Lord of the whole
earth.

6 The heavens declare His righteousness,
And all the peoples see His glory.

7 Let all be put to shame who serve carved
images,
Who boast of idols.
Worship Him, all *you* gods.

8 Zion hears and is glad,
And the daughters of Judah rejoice
Because of Your judgments, O LORD.

9 For You, LORD, *are* most high above all the
earth;
You are exalted far above all gods.

10 You who love the LORD, hate evil!
He preserves the souls of His saints;
He delivers them out of the hand of the
wicked.

11 Light is sown for the righteous,
And gladness for the upright in heart.

12 Rejoice in the LORD, you righteous,
And give thanks at the remembrance of
His holy name.[a]

PSALM 98

A Song of Praise to the LORD for His Salvation and Judgment

A Psalm.

1 Oh, sing to the LORD a new song!
For He has done marvelous things;
His right hand and His holy arm have
gained Him the victory.

2 The LORD has made known His salvation;
His righteousness He has revealed in the
sight of the nations.

3 He has remembered His mercy and His
faithfulness to the house of Israel;
All the ends of the earth have seen the
salvation of our God.

4 Shout joyfully to the LORD, all the earth;
Break forth in song, rejoice, and sing
praises.

5 Sing to the LORD with the harp,
With the harp and the sound of a psalm,

6 With trumpets and the sound of a horn;
Shout joyfully before the LORD, the King.

7 Let the sea roar, and all its fullness,
The world and those who dwell in it;

8 Let the rivers clap *their* hands;
Let the hills be joyful together before the
LORD,

9 For He is coming to judge the earth.
With righteousness He shall judge the
world,
And the peoples with equity.

PSALM 99

Praise to the LORD for His Holiness

1 The LORD reigns;
Let the peoples tremble!
He dwells *between* the cherubim;
Let the earth be moved!

2 The LORD *is* great in Zion,
And He *is* high above all the peoples.

3 Let them praise Your great and awesome
name—
He *is* holy.

97:12 [a]Or *His holiness*

4 The King's strength also loves justice;
You have established equity;
You have executed justice and
righteousness in Jacob.
5 Exalt the LORD our God,
And worship at His footstool—
He *is* holy.

6 Moses and Aaron were among His priests,
And Samuel was among those who called
upon His name;
They called upon the LORD, and He
answered them.
7 He spoke to them in the cloudy pillar;
They kept His testimonies and the
ordinance He gave them.

8 You answered them, O LORD our God;
You were to them God-Who-Forgives,
Though You took vengeance on their deeds.
9 Exalt the LORD our God,
And worship at His holy hill;
For the LORD our God *is* holy.

PSALM 100

A Song of Praise for the LORD's Faithfulness to His People

A Psalm of Thanksgiving.

1 Make a joyful shout to the LORD, all you
lands!
2 Serve the LORD with gladness;
Come before His presence with singing.
3 Know that the LORD, He *is* God;
It is He *who* has made us, and not we
ourselves;[a]
We are His people and the sheep of His
pasture.

4 Enter into His gates with thanksgiving,
And into His courts with praise.
Be thankful to Him, *and* bless His name.
5 For the LORD *is* good;
His mercy *is* everlasting,
And His truth *endures* to all generations.

PSALM 101

Promised Faithfulness to the LORD

A Psalm of David.

1 I will sing of mercy and justice;
To You, O LORD, I will sing praises.

2 I will behave wisely in a perfect way.
Oh, when will You come to me?

I will walk within my house with a perfect
heart.

3 I will set nothing wicked before my eyes;
I hate the work of those who fall away;
It shall not cling to me.
4 A perverse heart shall depart from me;
I will not know wickedness.

5 Whoever secretly slanders his neighbor,
Him I will destroy;
The one who has a haughty look and a
proud heart,
Him I will not endure.

6 My eyes *shall be* on the faithful of the land,
That they may dwell with me;
He who walks in a perfect way,
He shall serve me.
7 He who works deceit shall not dwell
within my house;
He who tells lies shall not continue in my
presence.
8 Early I will destroy all the wicked of the
land,
That I may cut off all the evildoers from
the city of the LORD.

PSALM 102

The LORD's Eternal Love

*A Prayer of the afflicted, when he is overwhelmed
and pours out his complaint before the LORD.*

1 Hear my prayer, O LORD,
And let my cry come to You.
2 Do not hide Your face from me in the day
of my trouble;
Incline Your ear to me;
In the day that I call, answer me speedily.

3 For my days are consumed like smoke,
And my bones are burned like a hearth.
4 My heart is stricken and withered like grass,
So that I forget to eat my bread.
5 Because of the sound of my groaning
My bones cling to my skin.
6 I am like a pelican of the wilderness;
I am like an owl of the desert.
7 I lie awake,
And am like a sparrow alone on the
housetop.

100:3 [a]Following Kethib, Septuagint, and Vulgate;
Qere, many Hebrew manuscripts, and Targum read
we are His.

8 My enemies reproach me all day long;
Those who deride me swear an oath
against me.
9 For I have eaten ashes like bread,
And mingled my drink with weeping,
10 Because of Your indignation and Your
wrath;
For You have lifted me up and cast me
away.
11 My days *are* like a shadow that lengthens,
And I wither away like grass.

12 But You, O LORD, shall endure forever,
And the remembrance of Your name to all
generations.
13 You will arise *and* have mercy on Zion;
For the time to favor her,
Yes, the set time, has come.
14 For Your servants take pleasure in her
stones,
And show favor to her dust.
15 So the nations shall fear the name of the
LORD,
And all the kings of the earth Your glory.
16 For the LORD shall build up Zion;
He shall appear in His glory.
17 He shall regard the prayer of the destitute,
And shall not despise their prayer.

18 This will be written for the generation to
come,
That a people yet to be created may praise
the LORD.
19 For He looked down from the height of
His sanctuary;
From heaven the LORD viewed the earth,
20 To hear the groaning of the prisoner,
To release those appointed to death,
21 To declare the name of the LORD in Zion,
And His praise in Jerusalem,
22 When the peoples are gathered together,
And the kingdoms, to serve the LORD.

23 He weakened my strength in the way;
He shortened my days.
24 I said, "O my God,
Do not take me away in the midst of my
days;
Your years *are* throughout all generations.
25 Of old You laid the foundation of the earth,
And the heavens *are* the work of Your
hands.
26 They will perish, but You will endure;
Yes, they will all grow old like a garment;
Like a cloak You will change them,
And they will be changed.

27 But You *are* the same,
And Your years will have no end.
28 The children of Your servants will
continue,
And their descendants will be established
before You."

PSALM 103

Praise for the LORD's Mercies

A Psalm of David.

1 Bless the LORD, O my soul;
And all that is within me, *bless* His holy
name!
2 Bless the LORD, O my soul,
And forget not all His benefits:
3 Who forgives all your iniquities,
Who heals all your diseases,
4 Who redeems your life from destruction,
Who crowns you with lovingkindness and
tender mercies,
5 Who satisfies your mouth with good *things,*
So that your youth is renewed like the
eagle's.

6 The LORD executes righteousness
And justice for all who are oppressed.
7 He made known His ways to Moses,
His acts to the children of Israel.

How God Raises a Leader

(Psalm 103:1–5)

The benefits of trusting the Lord listed in this text correspond to the stages God uses in building someone into a healthy, spiritual leader. The psalmist lists the benefits in this order:

1. **God pardons (v. 3)**—Leaders must put their past shame or blame behind them.
2. **God heals (v. 3)**—They must become healthy and be liberated from old wounds.
3. **God redeems (v. 4)**—They see their abilities and personality redeemed.
4. **God crowns (v. 4)**—They are crowned with gifts and a place to serve.
5. **God satisfies (v. 5)**—They feel satisfied and fulfilled as they live out their role.

8 The LORD *is* merciful and gracious,
Slow to anger, and abounding in mercy.
9 He will not always strive *with us,*
Nor will He keep *His anger* forever.
10 He has not dealt with us according to our sins,
Nor punished us according to our iniquities.

11 For as the heavens are high above the earth,
So great is His mercy toward those who fear Him;
12 As far as the east is from the west,
So far has He removed our transgressions from us.
13 As a father pities *his* children,
So the LORD pities those who fear Him.
14 For He knows our frame;
He remembers that we *are* dust.

15 *As for* man, his days *are* like grass;
As a flower of the field, so he flourishes.
16 For the wind passes over it, and it is gone,
And its place remembers it no more.[a]

17 But the mercy of the LORD *is* from everlasting to everlasting
On those who fear Him,
And His righteousness to children's children,
18 To such as keep His covenant,
And to those who remember His commandments to do them.

19 The LORD has established His throne in heaven,
And His kingdom rules over all.

20 Bless the LORD, you His angels,
Who excel in strength, who do His word,
Heeding the voice of His word.
21 Bless the LORD, all *you* His hosts,
You ministers of His, who do His pleasure.
22 Bless the LORD, all His works,
In all places of His dominion.

Bless the LORD, O my soul!

103:16 [a]Compare Job 7:10

Natural Leadership vs. Spiritual Leadership

(Psalm 103:13–18)

Good leaders remember where they came from and who their source is—a memory that separates spiritual leaders from natural leaders.

God leads His people more like a parent than a boss. He maintains a vision of the big picture and sticks with the right priorities. While natural leaders display obvious leadership abilities, they often drift from this style of leadership. They tend to lean more on their gifts than on God. Consider the differences between the two types of leaders:

Natural Leader	Spiritual Leader
1. Self-confident	1. Confident in God (Pss. 56:9; 118:6)
2. Knows men	2. Knows God (John 10:14)
3. Makes own decisions	3. Seeks to find God's will (Rom. 12:2; Eph. 5:17)
4. Ambitious	4. Self-sacrificing (Matt. 20:25–28; Luke 9:23)
5. Originates own methods	5. Finds and follows God's methods (Pss. 40:8; 143:10)
6. Enjoys commanding others	6. Servant of all (Mark 10:42–45)
7. Motivated by self-interest	7. Motivated by love for God and man (1 John 4:7–21)
8. Independent	8. God-dependent (Is. 42:1; John 15:5)
9. Gets power through personality	9. Empowered by the Holy Spirit (Acts 1:8)
10. Cowboy driving the herd	10. Shepherd leading the flock (1 Pet. 5:2, 3)

PSALM 104

Praise to the Sovereign LORD for His Creation and Providence

1   Bless the LORD, O my soul!

  O LORD my God, You are very great:
  You are clothed with honor and majesty,
2   Who cover *Yourself* with light as *with* a
    garment,
  Who stretch out the heavens like a curtain.

3   He lays the beams of His upper chambers
    in the waters,
  Who makes the clouds His chariot,
  Who walks on the wings of the wind,
4   Who makes His angels spirits,
  His ministers a flame of fire.

Leaders Are Stewards, Not Owners

(Psalm 104:1–5)

The earth belongs to the Lord, not to humankind. Therefore, leaders should never act as if they own the place. While we can feel confident of our mission, we must remember we are stewards, not owners. We simply manage what He has established, based on His values and vision.

---

5   *You who* laid the foundations of the earth,
  So *that* it should not be moved forever,
6   You covered it with the deep as *with* a
    garment;
  The waters stood above the mountains.
7   At Your rebuke they fled;
  At the voice of Your thunder they
    hastened away.
8   They went up over the mountains;
  They went down into the valleys,
  To the place which You founded for them.
9   You have set a boundary that they may not
    pass over,
  That they may not return to cover the
    earth.

10   He sends the springs into the valleys;
  They flow among the hills.
11   They give drink to every beast of the field;

  The wild donkeys quench their thirst.
12   By them the birds of the heavens have
    their home;
  They sing among the branches.
13   He waters the hills from His upper
    chambers;
  The earth is satisfied with the fruit of Your
    works.

14   He causes the grass to grow for the cattle,
  And vegetation for the service of man,
  That he may bring forth food from the
    earth,
15   And wine *that* makes glad the heart of man,
  Oil to make *his* face shine,
  And bread *which* strengthens man's heart.
16   The trees of the LORD are full *of sap,*
  The cedars of Lebanon which He planted,
17   Where the birds make their nests;
  The stork has her home in the fir trees.
18   The high hills *are* for the wild goats;
  The cliffs are a refuge for the rock badgers.[a]

19   He appointed the moon for seasons;
  The sun knows its going down.
20   You make darkness, and it is night,
  In which all the beasts of the forest creep
    about.
21   The young lions roar after their prey,
  And seek their food from God.
22   *When* the sun rises, they gather together
  And lie down in their dens.
23   Man goes out to his work
  And to his labor until the evening.

24   O LORD, how manifold are Your works!
  In wisdom You have made them all.
  The earth is full of Your possessions—
25   This great and wide sea,
  In which *are* innumerable teeming things,
  Living things both small and great.
26   There the ships sail about;
  There is that Leviathan
  Which You have made to play there.

27   These all wait for You,
  That You may give *them* their food in due
    season.
28   *What* You give them they gather in;
  You open Your hand, they are filled with
    good.
29   You hide Your face, they are troubled;
  You take away their breath, they die and
    return to their dust.

104:18 [a]Or *rock hyrax* (compare Leviticus 11:5)

30 You send forth Your Spirit, they are
   created;
   And You renew the face of the earth.

31 May the glory of the LORD endure
   forever;
   May the LORD rejoice in His works.
32 He looks on the earth, and it trembles;
   He touches the hills, and they smoke.

33 I will sing to the LORD as long as I live;
   I will sing praise to my God while I have
   my being.
34 May my meditation be sweet to Him;
   I will be glad in the LORD.
35 May sinners be consumed from the earth,
   And the wicked be no more.

   Bless the LORD, O my soul!
   Praise the LORD!

PSALM 105

The Eternal Faithfulness of the LORD

1 Oh, give thanks to the LORD!
   Call upon His name;
   Make known His deeds among the
   peoples!
2 Sing to Him, sing psalms to Him;
   Talk of all His wondrous works!
3 Glory in His holy name;
   Let the hearts of those rejoice who seek
   the LORD!
4 Seek the LORD and His strength;
   Seek His face evermore!
5 Remember His marvelous works which
   He has done,
   His wonders, and the judgments of His
   mouth,
6 O seed of Abraham His servant,
   You children of Jacob, His chosen ones!

7 He is the LORD our God;
   His judgments are in all the earth.
8 He remembers His covenant forever,
   The word which He commanded, for a
   thousand generations,
9 The covenant which He made with
   Abraham,
   And His oath to Isaac,
10 And confirmed it to Jacob for a statute,
   To Israel as an everlasting covenant,
11 Saying, "To you I will give the land of
   Canaan
   As the allotment of your inheritance,"

12 When they were few in number,
   Indeed very few, and strangers in it.
13 When they went from one nation to
   another,
   From one kingdom to another people,
14 He permitted no one to do them wrong;
   Yes, He rebuked kings for their sakes,
15 Saying, "Do not touch My anointed ones,
   And do My prophets no harm."

16 Moreover He called for a famine in the
   land;
   He destroyed all the provision of bread.
17 He sent a man before them—
   Joseph—who was sold as a slave.
18 They hurt his feet with fetters,
   He was laid in irons.
19 Until the time that his word came to pass,
   The word of the LORD tested him.
20 The king sent and released him,
   The ruler of the people let him go free.
21 He made him lord of his house,
   And ruler of all his possessions,
22 To bind his princes at his pleasure,
   And teach his elders wisdom.

23 Israel also came into Egypt,
   And Jacob dwelt in the land of Ham.
24 He increased His people greatly,
   And made them stronger than their
   enemies.
25 He turned their heart to hate His people,
   To deal craftily with His servants.

26 He sent Moses His servant,
   And Aaron whom He had chosen.
27 They performed His signs among them,
   And wonders in the land of Ham.
28 He sent darkness, and made it dark;
   And they did not rebel against His word.
29 He turned their waters into blood,
   And killed their fish.
30 Their land abounded with frogs,
   Even in the chambers of their kings.
31 He spoke, and there came swarms of flies,
   And lice in all their territory.
32 He gave them hail for rain,
   And flaming fire in their land.
33 He struck their vines also, and their fig
   trees,
   And splintered the trees of their territory.
34 He spoke, and locusts came,
   Young locusts without number,
35 And ate up all the vegetation in their land,
   And devoured the fruit of their ground.

36 He also destroyed all the firstborn in their
land,
The first of all their strength.

37 He also brought them out with silver and
gold,
And *there was* none feeble among His tribes.

38 Egypt was glad when they departed,
For the fear of them had fallen upon
them.

39 He spread a cloud for a covering,
And fire to give light in the night.

40 *The people* asked, and He brought quail,
And satisfied them with the bread of
heaven.

41 He opened the rock, and water gushed
out;
It ran in the dry places *like* a river.

42 For He remembered His holy promise,
And Abraham His servant.

43 He brought out His people with joy,
His chosen ones with gladness.

44 He gave them the lands of the Gentiles,
And they inherited the labor of the
nations,

45 That they might observe His statutes
And keep His laws.

Praise the LORD!

PSALM 106

Joy in Forgiveness of Israel's Sins

1 Praise the LORD!

Oh, give thanks to the LORD, for *He is*
good!
For His mercy *endures* forever.

2 Who can utter the mighty acts of the
LORD?
Who can declare all His praise?

3 Blessed *are* those who keep justice,
And he who does[a] righteousness at all
times!

4 Remember me, O LORD, with the favor
You have toward Your people.
Oh, visit me with Your salvation,

5 That I may see the benefit of Your chosen
ones,
That I may rejoice in the gladness of Your
nation,
That I may glory with Your inheritance.

6 We have sinned with our fathers,
We have committed iniquity,
We have done wickedly.

7 Our fathers in Egypt did not understand
Your wonders;
They did not remember the multitude of
Your mercies,
But rebelled by the sea—the Red Sea.

8 Nevertheless He saved them for His
name's sake,
That He might make His mighty power
known.

9 He rebuked the Red Sea also, and it dried
up;
So He led them through the depths,
As through the wilderness.

10 He saved them from the hand of him who
hated *them,*
And redeemed them from the hand of the
enemy.

11 The waters covered their enemies;
There was not one of them left.

12 Then they believed His words;
They sang His praise.

13 They soon forgot His works;
They did not wait for His counsel,

14 But lusted exceedingly in the wilderness,
And tested God in the desert.

15 And He gave them their request,
But sent leanness into their soul.

16 When they envied Moses in the camp,
And Aaron the saint of the LORD,

17 The earth opened up and swallowed
Dathan,
And covered the faction of Abiram.

18 A fire was kindled in their company;
The flame burned up the wicked.

19 They made a calf in Horeb,
And worshiped the molded image.

20 Thus they changed their glory
Into the image of an ox that eats grass.

21 They forgot God their Savior,
Who had done great things in Egypt,

22 Wondrous works in the land of Ham,
Awesome things by the Red Sea.

23 Therefore He said that He would destroy
them,
Had not Moses His chosen one stood
before Him in the breach,

106:3 [a]Septuagint, Syriac, Targum, and Vulgate read
those who do.

To turn away His wrath, lest He destroy
them.

24 Then they despised the pleasant land;
They did not believe His word,
25 But complained in their tents,
And did not heed the voice of the LORD.
26 Therefore He raised His hand *in an oath*
against them,
To overthrow them in the wilderness,
27 To overthrow their descendants among the
nations,
And to scatter them in the lands.

28 They joined themselves also to Baal of
Peor,
And ate sacrifices made to the dead.
29 Thus they provoked *Him* to anger with
their deeds,
And the plague broke out among them.
30 Then Phinehas stood up and intervened,
And the plague was stopped.
31 And that was accounted to him for
righteousness
To all generations forevermore.

32 They angered *Him* also at the waters of
strife,[a]
So that it went ill with Moses on account
of them;
33 Because they rebelled against His Spirit,
So that he spoke rashly with his lips.

34 They did not destroy the peoples,
Concerning whom the LORD had
commanded them,
35 But they mingled with the Gentiles
And learned their works;
36 They served their idols,
Which became a snare to them.
37 They even sacrificed their sons
And their daughters to demons,
38 And shed innocent blood,
The blood of their sons and daughters,
Whom they sacrificed to the idols of
Canaan;
And the land was polluted with blood.
39 Thus they were defiled by their own
works,
And played the harlot by their own deeds.

40 Therefore the wrath of the LORD was
kindled against His people,
So that He abhorred His own inheritance.
41 And He gave them into the hand of the
Gentiles,

And those who hated them ruled over
them.
42 Their enemies also oppressed them,
And they were brought into subjection
under their hand.
43 Many times He delivered them;
But they rebelled in their counsel,
And were brought low for their iniquity.

44 Nevertheless He regarded their affliction,
When He heard their cry;
45 And for their sake He remembered His
covenant,
And relented according to the multitude
of His mercies.
46 He also made them to be pitied
By all those who carried them away
captive.

47 Save us, O LORD our God,
And gather us from among the Gentiles,
To give thanks to Your holy name,
To triumph in Your praise.

48 Blessed *be* the LORD God of Israel
From everlasting to everlasting!
And let all the people say, "Amen!"

Praise the LORD!

Book Five: Psalms 107—150

PSALM 107

Thanksgiving to the LORD for His Great Works of Deliverance

1 Oh, give thanks to the LORD, for *He is*
good!
For His mercy *endures* forever.
2 Let the redeemed of the LORD say *so*,
Whom He has redeemed from the hand of
the enemy,
3 And gathered out of the lands,
From the east and from the west,
From the north and from the south.

4 They wandered in the wilderness in a
desolate way;
They found no city to dwell in.
5 Hungry and thirsty,
Their soul fainted in them.
6 Then they cried out to the LORD in their
trouble,

106:32 [a]Or *Meribah*

And He delivered them out of their
distresses.
7 And He led them forth by the right way,
That they might go to a city for a dwelling
place.
8 Oh, that *men* would give thanks to the
LORD *for* His goodness,
And *for* His wonderful works to the
children of men!
9 For He satisfies the longing soul,
And fills the hungry soul with goodness.

10 Those who sat in darkness and in the
shadow of death,
Bound in affliction and irons—
11 Because they rebelled against the words of
God,
And despised the counsel of the Most High,
12 Therefore He brought down their heart
with labor;
They fell down, and *there was* none to help.
13 Then they cried out to the LORD in their
trouble,
And He saved them out of their distresses.
14 He brought them out of darkness and the
shadow of death,
And broke their chains in pieces.
15 Oh, that *men* would give thanks to the
LORD *for* His goodness,
And *for* His wonderful works to the
children of men!
16 For He has broken the gates of bronze,
And cut the bars of iron in two.

17 Fools, because of their transgression,
And because of their iniquities, were
afflicted.
18 Their soul abhorred all manner of food,
And they drew near to the gates of death.
19 Then they cried out to the LORD in their
trouble,
And He saved them out of their distresses.
20 He sent His word and healed them,
And delivered *them* from their destructions.
21 Oh, that *men* would give thanks to the
LORD *for* His goodness,
And *for* His wonderful works to the
children of men!
22 Let them sacrifice the sacrifices of
thanksgiving,
And declare His works with rejoicing.

23 Those who go down to the sea in ships,
Who do business on great waters,
24 They see the works of the LORD,
And His wonders in the deep.

25 For He commands and raises the stormy
wind,
Which lifts up the waves of the sea.
26 They mount up to the heavens,
They go down again to the depths;
Their soul melts because of trouble.
27 They reel to and fro, and stagger like a
drunken man,
And are at their wits' end.
28 Then they cry out to the LORD in their
trouble,
And He brings them out of their distresses.
29 He calms the storm,
So that its waves are still.
30 Then they are glad because they are quiet;
So He guides them to their desired haven.
31 Oh, that *men* would give thanks to the
LORD *for* His goodness,
And *for* His wonderful works to the
children of men!
32 Let them exalt Him also in the assembly of
the people,
And praise Him in the company of the
elders.

33 He turns rivers into a wilderness,
And the watersprings into dry ground;
34 A fruitful land into barrenness,
For the wickedness of those who dwell
in it.
35 He turns a wilderness into pools of water,
And dry land into watersprings.
36 There He makes the hungry dwell,
That they may establish a city for a
dwelling place,
37 And sow fields and plant vineyards,
That they may yield a fruitful harvest.
38 He also blesses them, and they multiply
greatly;
And He does not let their cattle decrease.

39 When they are diminished and brought
low
Through oppression, affliction, and sorrow,
40 He pours contempt on princes,
And causes them to wander in the
wilderness *where there is* no way;
41 Yet He sets the poor on high, far from
affliction,
And makes *their* families like a flock.
42 The righteous see *it* and rejoice,
And all iniquity stops its mouth.

43 Whoever *is* wise will observe these *things,*
And they will understand the
lovingkindness of the LORD.

PSALM 108

Assurance of God's Victory over Enemies

A Song. A Psalm of David.

1 O God, my heart is steadfast;
   I will sing and give praise, even with my glory.
2 Awake, lute and harp!
   I will awaken the dawn.
3 I will praise You, O LORD, among the peoples,
   And I will sing praises to You among the nations.
4 For Your mercy *is* great above the heavens,
   And Your truth *reaches* to the clouds.

5 Be exalted, O God, above the heavens,
   And Your glory above all the earth;
6 That Your beloved may be delivered,
   Save *with* Your right hand, and hear me.

7 God has spoken in His holiness:
   "I will rejoice;
   I will divide Shechem
   And measure out the Valley of Succoth.
8 Gilead *is* Mine; Manasseh *is* Mine;
   Ephraim also *is* the helmet for My head;
   Judah *is* My lawgiver.
9 Moab *is* My washpot;
   Over Edom I will cast My shoe;
   Over Philistia I will triumph."

10 Who will bring me *into* the strong city?
   Who will lead me to Edom?
11 *Is it* not You, O God, *who* cast us off?
   And *You,* O God, *who* did not go out with our armies?
12 Give us help from trouble,
   For the help of man is useless.
13 Through God we will do valiantly,
   For *it is* He *who* shall tread down our enemies.[a]

PSALM 109

Plea for Judgment of False Accusers

To the Chief Musician. A Psalm of David.

1 Do not keep silent,
   O God of my praise!
2 For the mouth of the wicked and the mouth of the deceitful
   Have opened against me;

They have spoken against me with a lying tongue.
3 They have also surrounded me with words of hatred,
   And fought against me without a cause.
4 In return for my love they are my accusers,
   But I *give myself to* prayer.
5 Thus they have rewarded me evil for good,
   And hatred for my love.

6 Set a wicked man over him,
   And let an accuser[a] stand at his right hand.
7 When he is judged, let him be found guilty,
   And let his prayer become sin.
8 Let his days be few,
   And let another take his office.
9 Let his children be fatherless,
   And his wife a widow.
10 Let his children continually be vagabonds, and beg;
   Let them seek *their bread*[a] also from their desolate places.
11 Let the creditor seize all that he has,
   And let strangers plunder his labor.
12 Let there be none to extend mercy to him,
   Nor let there be any to favor his fatherless children.
13 Let his posterity be cut off,
   And in the generation following let their name be blotted out.
14 Let the iniquity of his fathers be remembered before the LORD,
   And let not the sin of his mother be blotted out.
15 Let them be continually before the LORD,
   That He may cut off the memory of them from the earth;
16 Because he did not remember to show mercy,
   But persecuted the poor and needy man,
   That he might even slay the broken in heart.
17 As he loved cursing, so let it come to him;
   As he did not delight in blessing, so let it be far from him.
18 As he clothed himself with cursing as with his garment,
   So let it enter his body like water,

108:13 [a]Compare verses 6–13 with 60:5–12
109:6 [a]Hebrew *satan*   **109:10** [a]Following Masoretic Text and Targum; Septuagint and Vulgate read *be cast out.*

And like oil into his bones.
19 Let it be to him like the garment which
covers him,
And for a belt with which he girds himself
continually.
20 Let this be the LORD's reward to my
accusers,
And to those who speak evil against my
person.

21 But You, O GOD the Lord,
Deal with me for Your name's sake;
Because Your mercy is good, deliver me.
22 For I am poor and needy,
And my heart is wounded within me.
23 I am gone like a shadow when it
lengthens;
I am shaken off like a locust.
24 My knees are weak through fasting,
And my flesh is feeble from lack of fatness.
25 I also have become a reproach to them;
When they look at me, they shake their
heads.

26 Help me, O LORD my God!
Oh, save me according to Your mercy,
27 That they may know that this is Your
hand—
That You, LORD, have done it!
28 Let them curse, but You bless;
When they arise, let them be ashamed,
But let Your servant rejoice.
29 Let my accusers be clothed with shame,
And let them cover themselves with their
own disgrace as with a mantle.

30 I will greatly praise the LORD with my
mouth;
Yes, I will praise Him among the
multitude.
31 For He shall stand at the right hand of the
poor,
To save him from those who condemn
him.

PSALM 110

Announcement of the Messiah's Reign

A Psalm of David.

1 The LORD said to my Lord,
"Sit at My right hand,
Till I make Your enemies Your footstool."
2 The LORD shall send the rod of Your
strength out of Zion.
Rule in the midst of Your enemies!

3 Your people shall be volunteers
In the day of Your power;
In the beauties of holiness, from the womb
of the morning,
You have the dew of Your youth.
4 The LORD has sworn
And will not relent,
"You are a priest forever
According to the order of Melchizedek."

5 The Lord is at Your right hand;
He shall execute kings in the day of His
wrath.
6 He shall judge among the nations,
He shall fill the places with dead bodies,
He shall execute the heads of many
countries.
7 He shall drink of the brook by the
wayside;
Therefore He shall lift up the head.

PSALM 111

Praise to God for His Faithfulness and Justice

1 Praise the LORD!

I will praise the LORD with my whole
heart,
In the assembly of the upright and in the
congregation.

2 The works of the LORD are great,
Studied by all who have pleasure in
them.
3 His work is honorable and glorious,
And His righteousness endures forever.
4 He has made His wonderful works to be
remembered;
The LORD is gracious and full of
compassion.
5 He has given food to those who fear Him;
He will ever be mindful of His covenant.
6 He has declared to His people the power
of His works,
In giving them the heritage of the nations.

7 The works of His hands are verity and
justice;
All His precepts are sure.
8 They stand fast forever and ever,
And are done in truth and uprightness.
9 He has sent redemption to His people;
He has commanded His covenant forever:
Holy and awesome is His name.

10 The fear of the LORD *is* the beginning of
wisdom;
A good understanding have all those who
do *His commandments.*
His praise endures forever.

PSALM 112

The Blessed State of the Righteous

1 Praise the LORD!

Blessed *is* the man *who* fears the LORD,
Who delights greatly in His
commandments.
2 His descendants will be mighty on earth;
The generation of the upright will be
blessed.
3 Wealth and riches *will be* in his house,
And his righteousness endures forever.
4 Unto the upright there arises light in the
darkness;
He is gracious, and full of compassion, and
righteous.
5 A good man deals graciously and lends;
He will guide his affairs with discretion.
6 Surely he will never be shaken;
The righteous will be in everlasting
remembrance.
7 He will not be afraid of evil tidings;
His heart is steadfast, trusting in the LORD.
8 His heart *is* established;
He will not be afraid,
Until he sees *his desire* upon his enemies.

9 He has dispersed abroad,
He has given to the poor;
His righteousness endures forever;
His horn will be exalted with honor.
10 The wicked will see *it* and be grieved;
He will gnash his teeth and melt away;
The desire of the wicked shall perish.

PSALM 113

The Majesty and Condescension of God

1 Praise the LORD!

Praise, O servants of the LORD,
Praise the name of the LORD!
2 Blessed be the name of the LORD
From this time forth and forevermore!
3 From the rising of the sun to its going
down
The LORD's name *is* to be praised.

4 The LORD *is* high above all nations,
His glory above the heavens.
5 Who *is* like the LORD our God,
Who dwells on high,
6 Who humbles Himself to behold
The things that are in the heavens and in the
earth?

7 He raises the poor out of the dust,
And lifts the needy out of the ash heap,
8 That He may seat *him* with princes—
With the princes of His people.
9 He grants the barren woman a home,
Like a joyful mother of children.

Praise the LORD!

PSALM 114

The Power of God in His Deliverance of Israel

1 When Israel went out of Egypt,
The house of Jacob from a people of
strange language,
2 Judah became His sanctuary,
And Israel His dominion.

3 The sea saw *it* and fled;
Jordan turned back.
4 The mountains skipped like rams,
The little hills like lambs.
5 What ails you, O sea, that you fled?
O Jordan, *that* you turned back?
6 O mountains, *that* you skipped like rams?
O little hills, like lambs?

7 Tremble, O earth, at the presence of the
Lord,
At the presence of the God of Jacob,
8 Who turned the rock *into* a pool of water,
The flint into a fountain of waters.

PSALM 115

The Futility of Idols and the Trustworthiness of God

1 Not unto us, O LORD, not unto us,
But to Your name give glory,
Because of Your mercy,
Because of Your truth.
2 Why should the Gentiles say,
"So where *is* their God?"

3 But our God *is* in heaven;
He does whatever He pleases.

4 Their idols *are* silver and gold,
The work of men's hands.
5 They have mouths, but they do not speak;
Eyes they have, but they do not see;
6 They have ears, but they do not hear;
Noses they have, but they do not smell;
7 They have hands, but they do not handle;
Feet they have, but they do not walk;
Nor do they mutter through their throat.
8 Those who make them are like them;
So is everyone who trusts in them.

9 O Israel, trust in the LORD;
He *is* their help and their shield.
10 O house of Aaron, trust in the LORD;
He *is* their help and their shield.
11 You who fear the LORD, trust in the LORD;
He *is* their help and their shield.

12 The LORD has been mindful of *us;*
He will bless us;
He will bless the house of Israel;
He will bless the house of Aaron.
13 He will bless those who fear the LORD,
Both small and great.

14 May the LORD give you increase more and
more,
You and your children.
15 *May* you *be* blessed by the LORD,
Who made heaven and earth.

16 The heaven, *even* the heavens, *are* the LORD's;
But the earth He has given to the children
of men.
17 The dead do not praise the LORD,
Nor any who go down into silence.
18 But we will bless the LORD
From this time forth and forevermore.

Praise the LORD!

PSALM 116

Thanksgiving for Deliverance from Death

1 I love the LORD, because He has heard
My voice *and* my supplications.
2 Because He has inclined His ear to me,
Therefore I will call *upon Him* as long as I
live.

3 The pains of death surrounded me,
And the pangs of Sheol laid hold of me;
I found trouble and sorrow.

4 Then I called upon the name of the LORD:
"O LORD, I implore You, deliver my soul!"

5 Gracious *is* the LORD, and righteous;
Yes, our God *is* merciful.
6 The LORD preserves the simple;
I was brought low, and He saved me.
7 Return to your rest, O my soul,
For the LORD has dealt bountifully with
you.

8 For You have delivered my soul from death,
My eyes from tears,
And my feet from falling.
9 I will walk before the LORD
In the land of the living.
10 I believed, therefore I spoke,
"I am greatly afflicted."
11 I said in my haste,
"All men *are* liars."

12 What shall I render to the LORD
For all His benefits toward me?
13 I will take up the cup of salvation,
And call upon the name of the LORD.
14 I will pay my vows to the LORD
Now in the presence of all His people.

15 Precious in the sight of the LORD
Is the death of His saints.

16 O LORD, truly I *am* Your servant;
I *am* Your servant, the son of Your
maidservant;
You have loosed my bonds.
17 I will offer to You the sacrifice of
thanksgiving,
And will call upon the name of the LORD.
18 I will pay my vows to the LORD
Now in the presence of all His people,
19 In the courts of the LORD's house,
In the midst of you, O Jerusalem.

Praise the LORD!

PSALM 117

Let All Peoples Praise the LORD

1 Praise the LORD, all you Gentiles!
Laud Him, all you peoples!
2 For His merciful kindness is great toward us,
And the truth of the LORD *endures* forever.

Praise the LORD!

PSALM 118

Praise to God for His Everlasting Mercy

1 Oh, give thanks to the LORD, for *He is* good!
For His mercy *endures* forever.

2 Let Israel now say,
"His mercy *endures* forever."

3 Let the house of Aaron now say,
"His mercy *endures* forever."

4 Let those who fear the LORD now say,
"His mercy *endures* forever."

5 I called on the LORD in distress;
The LORD answered me *and set me* in a broad place.

6 The LORD *is* on my side;
I will not fear.
What can man do to me?

7 The LORD is for me among those who help me;
Therefore I shall see *my desire* on those who hate me.

8 *It is* better to trust in the LORD
Than to put confidence in man.

9 *It is* better to trust in the LORD
Than to put confidence in princes.

10 All nations surrounded me,
But in the name of the LORD I will destroy them.

11 They surrounded me,
Yes, they surrounded me;
But in the name of the LORD I will destroy them.

12 They surrounded me like bees;
They were quenched like a fire of thorns;
For in the name of the LORD I will destroy them.

13 You pushed me violently, that I might fall,
But the LORD helped me.

14 The LORD *is* my strength and song,
And He has become my salvation.[a]

15 The voice of rejoicing and salvation
Is in the tents of the righteous;
The right hand of the LORD does valiantly.

16 The right hand of the LORD is exalted;
The right hand of the LORD does valiantly.

17 I shall not die, but live,
And declare the works of the LORD.

18 The LORD has chastened me severely,
But He has not given me over to death.

19 Open to me the gates of righteousness;
I will go through them,
And I will praise the LORD.

20 This is the gate of the LORD,
Through which the righteous shall enter.

21 I will praise You,
For You have answered me,
And have become my salvation.

22 The stone *which* the builders rejected
Has become the chief cornerstone.

23 This was the LORD's doing;
It *is* marvelous in our eyes.

24 This *is* the day the LORD has made;
We will rejoice and be glad in it.

25 Save now, I pray, O LORD;
O LORD, I pray, send now prosperity.

26 Blessed *is* he who comes in the name of the LORD!
We have blessed you from the house of the LORD.

27 God *is* the LORD,
And He has given us light;
Bind the sacrifice with cords to the horns of the altar.

28 You *are* my God, and I will praise You;
You are my God, I will exalt You.

29 Oh, give thanks to the LORD, for *He is* good!
For His mercy *endures* forever.

PSALM 119

Meditations on the Excellencies of the Word of God

א ALEPH

1 Blessed *are* the undefiled in the way,
Who walk in the law of the LORD!

2 Blessed *are* those who keep His testimonies,
Who seek Him with the whole heart!

3 They also do no iniquity;
They walk in His ways.

4 You have commanded *us*
To keep Your precepts diligently.

5 Oh, that my ways were directed
To keep Your statutes!

6 Then I would not be ashamed,
When I look into all Your commandments.

7 I will praise You with uprightness of heart,
When I learn Your righteous judgments.

118:14 [a]Compare Exodus 15:2

Leaders Cannot Show the Way
Until They Know the Way
(Psalm 119:1–176)

The longest psalm in the Bible is a song about the priority of the Word of God. For 176 verses, Psalm 119 holds high the words and wisdom of God and convinces us to treasure it more than anything else in life.

Why is this challenge so crucial for us? Leaders in our world face two realities:

1. Change happens faster than ever, so leaders must remain adaptable.
2. We need timeless values more than ever, so leaders must remain principle-driven.

Psalm 119 provides a roadmap for getting the wisdom, values, and principles we need to lead effectively. Consider what Psalm 119 teaches about adopting God's Word as our source for leadership principles. Our leadership will . . .

- be blessed (vv. 1, 2)
- remain pure and ethical (vv. 9–11)
- be strengthened and revitalized (vv. 28, 149, 154–159)
- insightfully answer criticism (v. 42)
- enjoy liberty (v. 45)
- gain wise counsel when needed (v. 66)
- remain steady even when afflicted (vv. 67–72, 92)
- display more insight than our teachers (vv. 99, 100)
- be enlightened and intuitive (vv. 105, 130)
- have a reliable guide even for new issues (vv. 129, 160)
- enjoy inward peace and poise (v. 165)
- get divine help (vv. 173–175)

---

8 I will keep Your statutes;
   Oh, do not forsake me utterly!

ב BETH
9 How can a young man cleanse his way?
   By taking heed according to Your word.
10 With my whole heart I have sought You;
   Oh, let me not wander from Your commandments!
11 Your word I have hidden in my heart,
   That I might not sin against You.
12 Blessed *are* You, O LORD!
   Teach me Your statutes.
13 With my lips I have declared
   All the judgments of Your mouth.
14 I have rejoiced in the way of Your testimonies,
   As *much as* in all riches.
15 I will meditate on Your precepts,
   And contemplate Your ways.
16 I will delight myself in Your statutes;
   I will not forget Your word.

ג GIMEL
17 Deal bountifully with Your servant,
   That I may live and keep Your word.
18 Open my eyes, that I may see
   Wondrous things from Your law.
19 I *am* a stranger in the earth;
   Do not hide Your commandments from me.
20 My soul breaks with longing
   For Your judgments at all times.
21 You rebuke the proud—the cursed,
   Who stray from Your commandments.
22 Remove from me reproach and contempt,
   For I have kept Your testimonies.
23 Princes also sit *and* speak against me,
   But Your servant meditates on Your statutes.
24 Your testimonies also *are* my delight
   And my counselors.

ד DALETH
25 My soul clings to the dust;
   Revive me according to Your word.

26 I have declared my ways, and You
    answered me;
    Teach me Your statutes.
27 Make me understand the way of Your
    precepts;
    So shall I meditate on Your wonderful
    works.
28 My soul melts from heaviness;
    Strengthen me according to Your word.
29 Remove from me the way of lying,
    And grant me Your law graciously.
30 I have chosen the way of truth;
    Your judgments I have laid *before me*.
31 I cling to Your testimonies;
    O LORD, do not put me to shame!
32 I will run the course of Your
    commandments,
    For You shall enlarge my heart.

ה HE
33 Teach me, O LORD, the way of Your
    statutes,
    And I shall keep it *to the end*.
34 Give me understanding, and I shall keep
    Your law;
    Indeed, I shall observe it with *my* whole
    heart.
35 Make me walk in the path of Your
    commandments,
    For I delight in it.
36 Incline my heart to Your testimonies,
    And not to covetousness.
37 Turn away my eyes from looking at
    worthless things,
    And revive me in Your way.[a]
38 Establish Your word to Your servant,
    Who *is devoted* to fearing You.
39 Turn away my reproach which I dread,
    For Your judgments *are* good.
40 Behold, I long for Your precepts;
    Revive me in Your righteousness.

ו WAW
41 Let Your mercies come also to me, O
    LORD—
    Your salvation according to Your word.
42 So shall I have an answer for him who
    reproaches me,
    For I trust in Your word.
43 And take not the word of truth utterly out
    of my mouth,
    For I have hoped in Your ordinances.
44 So shall I keep Your law continually,
    Forever and ever.
45 And I will walk at liberty,
    For I seek Your precepts.

46 I will speak of Your testimonies also before
    kings,
    And will not be ashamed.
47 And I will delight myself in Your
    commandments,
    Which I love.
48 My hands also I will lift up to Your
    commandments,
    Which I love,
    And I will meditate on Your statutes.

ז ZAYIN
49 Remember the word to Your servant,
    Upon which You have caused me to hope.
50 This *is* my comfort in my affliction,
    For Your word has given me life.
51 The proud have me in great derision,
    Yet I do not turn aside from Your law.
52 I remembered Your judgments of old, O
    LORD,
    And have comforted myself.
53 Indignation has taken hold of me
    Because of the wicked, who forsake Your
    law.
54 Your statutes have been my songs
    In the house of my pilgrimage.
55 I remember Your name in the night, O
    LORD,
    And I keep Your law.
56 This has become mine,
    Because I kept Your precepts.

ח HETH
57 *You are* my portion, O LORD;
    I have said that I would keep Your words.
58 I entreated Your favor with *my* whole
    heart;
    Be merciful to me according to Your
    word.
59 I thought about my ways,
    And turned my feet to Your testimonies.
60 I made haste, and did not delay
    To keep Your commandments.
61 The cords of the wicked have bound me,
    But I have not forgotten Your law.
62 At midnight I will rise to give thanks to
    You,
    Because of Your righteous judgments.
63 I *am* a companion of all who fear You,
    And of those who keep Your precepts.
64 The earth, O LORD, is full of Your mercy;
    Teach me Your statutes.

119:37 [a]Following Masoretic Text, Septuagint, and
Vulgate; Targum reads *Your words*.

ט TETH

65 You have dealt well with Your servant,
O LORD, according to Your word.

66 Teach me good judgment and knowledge,
For I believe Your commandments.

67 Before I was afflicted I went astray,
But now I keep Your word.

68 You *are* good, and do good;
Teach me Your statutes.

69 The proud have forged a lie against me,
But I will keep Your precepts with *my*
whole heart.

70 Their heart is as fat as grease,
But I delight in Your law.

71 *It is* good for me that I have been afflicted,
That I may learn Your statutes.

72 The law of Your mouth *is* better to me
Than thousands of *coins of* gold and silver.

י YOD

73 Your hands have made me and fashioned
me;
Give me understanding, that I may learn
Your commandments.

74 Those who fear You will be glad when
they see me,
Because I have hoped in Your word.

75 I know, O LORD, that Your judgments *are*
right,
And *that* in faithfulness You have afflicted
me.

76 Let, I pray, Your merciful kindness be for
my comfort,
According to Your word to Your servant.

77 Let Your tender mercies come to me, that
I may live;
For Your law *is* my delight.

78 Let the proud be ashamed,
For they treated me wrongfully with
falsehood;
But I will meditate on Your precepts.

79 Let those who fear You turn to me,
Those who know Your testimonies.

80 Let my heart be blameless regarding Your
statutes,
That I may not be ashamed.

כ KAPH

81 My soul faints for Your salvation,
But I hope in Your word.

82 My eyes fail *from searching* Your word,
Saying, "When will You comfort me?"

83 For I have become like a wineskin in
smoke,
Yet I do not forget Your statutes.

84 How many *are* the days of Your servant?

When will You execute judgment on
those who persecute me?

85 The proud have dug pits for me,
Which *is* not according to Your law.

86 All Your commandments *are* faithful;
They persecute me wrongfully;
Help me!

87 They almost made an end of me on earth,
But I did not forsake Your precepts.

88 Revive me according to Your
lovingkindness,
So that I may keep the testimony of Your
mouth.

ל LAMED

89 Forever, O LORD,
Your word is settled in heaven.

90 Your faithfulness *endures* to all generations;
You established the earth, and it abides.

91 They continue this day according to Your
ordinances,
For all *are* Your servants.

92 Unless Your law *had been* my delight,
I would then have perished in my affliction.

93 I will never forget Your precepts,
For by them You have given me life.

94 I *am* Yours, save me;
For I have sought Your precepts.

95 The wicked wait for me to destroy me,
But I will consider Your testimonies.

96 I have seen the consummation of all
perfection,
But Your commandment *is* exceedingly
broad.

מ MEM

97 Oh, how I love Your law!
It *is* my meditation all the day.

98 You, through Your commandments, make
me wiser than my enemies;
For they *are* ever with me.

99 I have more understanding than all my
teachers,
For Your testimonies *are* my meditation.

100 I understand more than the ancients,
Because I keep Your precepts.

101 I have restrained my feet from every evil
way,
That I may keep Your word.

102 I have not departed from Your judgments,
For You Yourself have taught me.

103 How sweet are Your words to my taste,
Sweeter than honey to my mouth!

104 Through Your precepts I get
understanding;
Therefore I hate every false way.

ב NUN

105 Your word *is* a lamp to my feet
And a light to my path.
106 I have sworn and confirmed
That I will keep Your righteous judgments.
107 I am afflicted very much;
Revive me, O LORD, according to Your word.
108 Accept, I pray, the freewill offerings of my mouth, O LORD,
And teach me Your judgments.
109 My life *is* continually in my hand,
Yet I do not forget Your law.
110 The wicked have laid a snare for me,
Yet I have not strayed from Your precepts.
111 Your testimonies I have taken as a heritage forever,
For they *are* the rejoicing of my heart.
112 I have inclined my heart to perform Your statutes
Forever, to the very end.

ס SAMEK

113 I hate the double-minded,
But I love Your law.
114 You *are* my hiding place and my shield;
I hope in Your word.
115 Depart from me, you evildoers,
For I will keep the commandments of my God!
116 Uphold me according to Your word, that I may live;
And do not let me be ashamed of my hope.
117 Hold me up, and I shall be safe,
And I shall observe Your statutes continually.
118 You reject all those who stray from Your statutes,
For their deceit *is* falsehood.
119 You put away all the wicked of the earth *like* dross;
Therefore I love Your testimonies.
120 My flesh trembles for fear of You,
And I am afraid of Your judgments.

ע AYIN

121 I have done justice and righteousness;
Do not leave me to my oppressors.
122 Be surety for Your servant for good;
Do not let the proud oppress me.
123 My eyes fail *from seeking* Your salvation
And Your righteous word.
124 Deal with Your servant according to Your mercy,
And teach me Your statutes.
125 I *am* Your servant;

Give me understanding,
That I may know Your testimonies.
126 *It is* time for *You* to act, O LORD,
For they have regarded Your law as void.
127 Therefore I love Your commandments
More than gold, yes, than fine gold!
128 Therefore all *Your* precepts *concerning* all things
I consider *to be* right;
I hate every false way.

פ PE

129 Your testimonies are wonderful;
Therefore my soul keeps them.
130 The entrance of Your words gives light;
It gives understanding to the simple.
131 I opened my mouth and panted,
For I longed for Your commandments.
132 Look upon me and be merciful to me,
As Your custom *is* toward those who love Your name.
133 Direct my steps by Your word,
And let no iniquity have dominion over me.
134 Redeem me from the oppression of man,
That I may keep Your precepts.
135 Make Your face shine upon Your servant,
And teach me Your statutes.
136 Rivers of water run down from my eyes,
Because *men* do not keep Your law.

צ TSADDE

137 Righteous *are* You, O LORD,
And upright *are* Your judgments.
138 Your testimonies, *which* You have commanded,
Are righteous and very faithful.
139 My zeal has consumed me,
Because my enemies have forgotten Your words.
140 Your word *is* very pure;
Therefore Your servant loves it.
141 I *am* small and despised,
Yet I do not forget Your precepts.
142 Your righteousness *is* an everlasting righteousness,
And Your law *is* truth.
143 Trouble and anguish have overtaken me,
Yet Your commandments *are* my delights.
144 The righteousness of Your testimonies *is* everlasting;
Give me understanding, and I shall live.

ק QOPH

145 I cry out with *my* whole heart;
Hear me, O LORD!
I will keep Your statutes.

146 I cry out to You;
    Save me, and I will keep Your testimonies.
147 I rise before the dawning of the morning,
    And cry for help;
    I hope in Your word.
148 My eyes are awake through the *night*
        watches,
    That I may meditate on Your word.
149 Hear my voice according to Your
        lovingkindness;
    O LORD, revive me according to Your
        justice.
150 They draw near who follow after
        wickedness;
    They are far from Your law.
151 You *are* near, O LORD,
    And all Your commandments *are* truth.
152 Concerning Your testimonies,
    I have known of old that You have
        founded them forever.

ר RESH
153 Consider my affliction and deliver me,
    For I do not forget Your law.
154 Plead my cause and redeem me;
    Revive me according to Your word.
155 Salvation *is* far from the wicked,
    For they do not seek Your statutes.
156 Great *are* Your tender mercies, O LORD;
    Revive me according to Your judgments.
157 Many *are* my persecutors and my enemies,
    Yet I do not turn from Your testimonies.
158 I see the treacherous, and am disgusted,
    Because they do not keep Your word.
159 Consider how I love Your precepts;
    Revive me, O LORD, according to Your
        lovingkindness.
160 The entirety of Your word *is* truth,
    And every one of Your righteous
        judgments *endures* forever.

ש SHIN
161 Princes persecute me without a cause,
    But my heart stands in awe of Your word.
162 I rejoice at Your word
    As one who finds great treasure.
163 I hate and abhor lying,
    But I love Your law.
164 Seven times a day I praise You,
    Because of Your righteous judgments.
165 Great peace have those who love Your law,
    And nothing causes them to stumble.
166 LORD, I hope for Your salvation,
    And I do Your commandments.
167 My soul keeps Your testimonies,
    And I love them exceedingly.

168 I keep Your precepts and Your testimonies,
    For all my ways *are* before You.

ת TAU
169 Let my cry come before You, O LORD;
    Give me understanding according to Your
       word.
170 Let my supplication come before You;
    Deliver me according to Your word.
171 My lips shall utter praise,
    For You teach me Your statutes.
172 My tongue shall speak of Your word,
    For all Your commandments *are*
       righteousness.
173 Let Your hand become my help,
    For I have chosen Your precepts.
174 I long for Your salvation, O LORD,
    And Your law *is* my delight.
175 Let my soul live, and it shall praise You;
    And let Your judgments help me.
176 I have gone astray like a lost sheep;
    Seek Your servant,
    For I do not forget Your commandments.

PSALM 120

Plea for Relief from Bitter Foes

A Song of Ascents.

1 In my distress I cried to the LORD,
    And He heard me.
2 Deliver my soul, O LORD, from lying lips
    And from a deceitful tongue.

3 What shall be given to you,
    Or what shall be done to you,
    You false tongue?
4 Sharp arrows of the warrior,
    With coals of the broom tree!

5 Woe is me, that I dwell in Meshech,
    That I dwell among the tents of Kedar!
6 My soul has dwelt too long
    With one who hates peace.
7 I *am for* peace;
    But when I speak, they *are* for war.

PSALM 121

God the Help of Those Who Seek Him

A Song of Ascents.

1 I will lift up my eyes to the hills—
    From whence comes my help?
2 My help *comes* from the LORD,
    Who made heaven and earth.

3 He will not allow your foot to be moved;
He who keeps you will not slumber.
4 Behold, He who keeps Israel
Shall neither slumber nor sleep.

5 The LORD is your keeper;
The LORD is your shade at your right
hand.
6 The sun shall not strike you by day,
Nor the moon by night.

7 The LORD shall preserve you from all evil;
He shall preserve your soul.
8 The LORD shall preserve your going out
and your coming in
From this time forth, and even
forevermore.

PSALM 122

The Joy of Going to the House of the LORD

A Song of Ascents. Of David.

1 I was glad when they said to me,
"Let us go into the house of the LORD."
2 Our feet have been standing
Within your gates, O Jerusalem!

3 Jerusalem is built
As a city that is compact together,
4 Where the tribes go up,
The tribes of the LORD,
To the Testimony of Israel,
To give thanks to the name of the LORD.
5 For thrones are set there for judgment,
The thrones of the house of David.

6 Pray for the peace of Jerusalem:
"May they prosper who love you.
7 Peace be within your walls,
Prosperity within your palaces."
8 For the sake of my brethren and
companions,
I will now say, "Peace be within you."
9 Because of the house of the LORD our
God
I will seek your good.

PSALM 123

Prayer for Relief from Contempt

A Song of Ascents.

1 Unto You I lift up my eyes,
O You who dwell in the heavens.

2 Behold, as the eyes of servants *look* to the
hand of their masters,
As the eyes of a maid to the hand of her
mistress,
So our eyes *look* to the LORD our God,
Until He has mercy on us.

3 Have mercy on us, O LORD, have mercy
on us!
For we are exceedingly filled with
contempt.
4 Our soul is exceedingly filled
With the scorn of those who are at ease,
With the contempt of the proud.

PSALM 124

The LORD the Defense of His People

A Song of Ascents. Of David.

1 "If it had not been the LORD who was on
our side,"
Let Israel now say—
2 "If it had not been the LORD who was on
our side,
When men rose up against us,
3 Then they would have swallowed us alive,
When their wrath was kindled against us;
4 Then the waters would have overwhelmed
us,
The stream would have gone over our
soul;
5 Then the swollen waters
Would have gone over our soul."

6 Blessed be the LORD,
Who has not given us as prey to their
teeth.
7 Our soul has escaped as a bird from the
snare of the fowlers;[a]
The snare is broken, and we have escaped.
8 Our help is in the name of the LORD,
Who made heaven and earth.

PSALM 125

The LORD the Strength of His People

A Song of Ascents.

1 Those who trust in the LORD
Are like Mount Zion,
Which cannot be moved, *but* abides forever.
2 As the mountains surround Jerusalem,

124:7 [a]That is, persons who catch birds in a trap or
snare

So the LORD surrounds His people
From this time forth and forever.

3 For the scepter of wickedness shall not rest
On the land allotted to the righteous,
Lest the righteous reach out their hands to
iniquity.

4 Do good, O LORD, to *those who are* good,
And to *those who are* upright in their hearts.

5 As for such as turn aside to their crooked
ways,
The LORD shall lead them away
With the workers of iniquity.

Peace *be* upon Israel!

PSALM 126

A Joyful Return to Zion

A Song of Ascents.

1 When the LORD brought back the
captivity of Zion,
We were like those who dream.
2 Then our mouth was filled with laughter,
And our tongue with singing.
Then they said among the nations,
"The LORD has done great things for them."
3 The LORD has done great things for us,
And we are glad.

4 Bring back our captivity, O LORD,
As the streams in the South.

5 Those who sow in tears
Shall reap in joy.
6 He who continually goes forth weeping,
Bearing seed for sowing,
Shall doubtless come again with rejoicing,
Bringing his sheaves *with him.*

PSALM 127

Laboring and Prospering with the LORD

A Song of Ascents. Of Solomon.

1 Unless the LORD builds the house,
They labor in vain who build it;
Unless the LORD guards the city,
The watchman stays awake in vain.
2 *It is* vain for you to rise up early,
To sit up late,
To eat the bread of sorrows;
For so He gives His beloved sleep.

Security Is Found in the Lord, Not in Followers

(Psalm 127:1)

Psalm 127:1 says it all. Unless God remains at the center of your efforts, you labor in vain.

Whether we lead in the military, in construction, or sit behind a desk, we cannot fight, build, or plan well enough to gain anything permanent. Smart leaders not only include God in their strategy, they place Him at its center. He alone can provide leaders with security; we cannot get it from followers. Consider the following list of rules regarding security and people:

1. People cannot provide permanent security for a leader.
2. Leaders should never put their emotional health in the hands of someone else.
3. Spiritual and emotional health requires the truth.
4. Leaders must remember that hurting people naturally hurt people.
5. Trouble arises when leaders depend on people to do what only God can do.

---

3 Behold, children *are* a heritage from the
LORD,
The fruit of the womb *is* a reward.
4 Like arrows in the hand of a warrior,
So *are* the children of one's youth.
5 Happy *is* the man who has his quiver full
of them;
They shall not be ashamed,
But shall speak with their enemies in the
gate.

PSALM 128

Blessings of Those Who Fear the LORD

A Song of Ascents.

1 Blessed *is* every one who fears the LORD,
Who walks in His ways.

2 When you eat the labor of your hands,
You *shall be* happy, and *it shall be* well with
you.
3 Your wife *shall be* like a fruitful vine
In the very heart of your house,

Your children like olive plants
All around your table.
4 Behold, thus shall the man be blessed
Who fears the LORD.

5 The LORD bless you out of Zion,
And may you see the good of Jerusalem
All the days of your life.
6 Yes, may you see your children's children.

Peace be upon Israel!

PSALM 129

Song of Victory over Zion's Enemies

A Song of Ascents.

1 "Many a time they have afflicted me from
my youth,"
Let Israel now say—
2 "Many a time they have afflicted me from
my youth;
Yet they have not prevailed against me.
3 The plowers plowed on my back;
They made their furrows long."
4 The LORD is righteous;
He has cut in pieces the cords of the wicked.

5 Let all those who hate Zion
Be put to shame and turned back.
6 Let them be as the grass on the housetops,
Which withers before it grows up,
7 With which the reaper does not fill his
hand,
Nor he who binds sheaves, his arms.
8 Neither let those who pass by them say,
"The blessing of the LORD be upon you;
We bless you in the name of the LORD!"

PSALM 130

Waiting for the Redemption of the LORD

A Song of Ascents.

1 Out of the depths I have cried to You, O
LORD;
2 Lord, hear my voice!
Let Your ears be attentive
To the voice of my supplications.

3 If You, LORD, should mark iniquities,
O Lord, who could stand?
4 But there is forgiveness with You,
That You may be feared.

5 I wait for the LORD, my soul waits,
And in His word I do hope.

6 My soul waits for the Lord
More than those who watch for the
morning—
Yes, more than those who watch for the
morning.

7 O Israel, hope in the LORD;
For with the LORD there is mercy,
And with Him is abundant redemption.
8 And He shall redeem Israel
From all his iniquities.

PSALM 131

Simple Trust in the LORD

A Song of Ascents. Of David.

1 LORD, my heart is not haughty,
Nor my eyes lofty.
Neither do I concern myself with great
matters,
Nor with things too profound for me.

2 Surely I have calmed and quieted my soul,
Like a weaned child with his mother;
Like a weaned child is my soul within me.

3 O Israel, hope in the LORD
From this time forth and forever.

Balancing Childlike and Childish Styles

(Psalm 131:1–3)

The Christian leader is mature enough to
not act childish, yet remains trusting
enough to stay childlike. David describes himself as a "weaned child" (Ps. 131:2)—not a
helpless baby, but neither a self-sufficient
maverick. He must trust his mother for help
and strength. This illustrates the balance of
spiritual maturity.

PSALM 132

The Eternal Dwelling of God in Zion

A Song of Ascents.

1 LORD, remember David
And all his afflictions;
2 How he swore to the LORD,
And vowed to the Mighty One of Jacob:

3 "Surely I will not go into the chamber of
    my house,
  Or go up to the comfort of my bed;
4 I will not give sleep to my eyes
  Or slumber to my eyelids,
5 Until I find a place for the LORD,
  A dwelling place for the Mighty One of
    Jacob."

6 Behold, we heard of it in Ephrathah;
  We found it in the fields of the woods.[a]
7 Let us go into His tabernacle;
  Let us worship at His footstool.
8 Arise, O LORD, to Your resting place,
  You and the ark of Your strength.
9 Let Your priests be clothed with
    righteousness,
  And let Your saints shout for joy.

10 For Your servant David's sake,
   Do not turn away the face of Your
     Anointed.

11 The LORD has sworn *in* truth to David;
   He will not turn from it:
   "I will set upon your throne the fruit of
     your body.
12 If your sons will keep My covenant
   And My testimony which I shall teach
     them,
   Their sons also shall sit upon your throne
     forevermore."

13 For the LORD has chosen Zion;
   He has desired *it* for His dwelling place:
14 "This *is* My resting place forever;
   Here I will dwell, for I have desired it.
15 I will abundantly bless her provision;
   I will satisfy her poor with bread.
16 I will also clothe her priests with
     salvation,
   And her saints shall shout aloud for joy.
17 There I will make the horn of David
     grow;
   I will prepare a lamp for My Anointed.
18 His enemies I will clothe with shame,
   But upon Himself His crown shall
     flourish."

PSALM 133

Blessed Unity of the People of God

A Song of Ascents. Of David.

1 Behold, how good and how pleasant *it is*
  For brethren to dwell together in unity!

2 *It is* like the precious oil upon the head,
  Running down on the beard,
  The beard of Aaron,
  Running down on the edge of his
    garments.
3 *It is* like the dew of Hermon,
  Descending upon the mountains of Zion;
  For there the LORD commanded the
    blessing—
  Life forevermore.

PSALM 134

Praising the LORD in His House at Night

A Song of Ascents.

1 Behold, bless the LORD,
  All *you* servants of the LORD,
  Who by night stand in the house of the
    LORD!
2 Lift up your hands *in* the sanctuary,
  And bless the LORD.

3 The LORD who made heaven and earth
  Bless you from Zion!

PSALM 135

Praise to God in Creation and Redemption

1 Praise the LORD!

  Praise the name of the LORD;
  Praise *Him,* O you servants of the LORD!
2 You who stand in the house of the LORD,
  In the courts of the house of our God,
3 Praise the LORD, for the LORD *is* good;
  Sing praises to His name, for *it is* pleasant.
4 For the LORD has chosen Jacob for
    Himself,
  Israel for His special treasure.

5 For I know that the LORD *is* great,
  And our Lord *is* above all gods.
6 Whatever the LORD pleases He does,
  In heaven and in earth,
  In the seas and in all deep places.
7 He causes the vapors to ascend from the
    ends of the earth;
  He makes lightning for the rain;
  He brings the wind out of His treasuries.

8 He destroyed the firstborn of Egypt,
  Both of man and beast.

132:6 [a]Hebrew *Jaar*

9 He sent signs and wonders into the midst
of you, O Egypt,
Upon Pharaoh and all his servants.
10 He defeated many nations
And slew mighty kings—
11 Sihon king of the Amorites,
Og king of Bashan,
And all the kingdoms of Canaan—
12 And gave their land *as* a heritage,
A heritage to Israel His people.

13 Your name, O LORD, *endures* forever,
Your fame, O LORD, throughout all
generations.
14 For the LORD will judge His people,
And He will have compassion on His
servants.

15 The idols of the nations *are* silver and gold,
The work of men's hands.
16 They have mouths, but they do not speak;
Eyes they have, but they do not see;
17 They have ears, but they do not hear;
Nor is there *any* breath in their mouths.
18 Those who make them are like them;
So is everyone who trusts in them.

19 Bless the LORD, O house of Israel!
Bless the LORD, O house of Aaron!
20 Bless the LORD, O house of Levi!
You who fear the LORD, bless the LORD!
21 Blessed be the LORD out of Zion,
Who dwells in Jerusalem!

Praise the LORD!

PSALM 136

Thanksgiving to God for His Enduring Mercy

1 Oh, give thanks to the LORD, for *He is*
good!
For His mercy *endures* forever.
2 Oh, give thanks to the God of gods!
For His mercy *endures* forever.
3 Oh, give thanks to the Lord of lords!
For His mercy *endures* forever:

4 To Him who alone does great wonders,
For His mercy *endures* forever;
5 To Him who by wisdom made the heavens,
For His mercy *endures* forever;
6 To Him who laid out the earth above the
waters,
For His mercy *endures* forever;

7 To Him who made great lights,
For His mercy *endures* forever—
8 The sun to rule by day,
For His mercy *endures* forever;
9 The moon and stars to rule by night,
For His mercy *endures* forever.

10 To Him who struck Egypt in their
firstborn,
For His mercy *endures* forever;
11 And brought out Israel from among them,
For His mercy *endures* forever;
12 With a strong hand, and with an
outstretched arm,
For His mercy *endures* forever;
13 To Him who divided the Red Sea in two,
For His mercy *endures* forever;
14 And made Israel pass through the midst
of it,
For His mercy *endures* forever;
15 But overthrew Pharaoh and his army in
the Red Sea,
For His mercy *endures* forever;
16 To Him who led His people through the
wilderness,
For His mercy *endures* forever;
17 To Him who struck down great kings,
For His mercy *endures* forever;
18 And slew famous kings,
For His mercy *endures* forever—
19 Sihon king of the Amorites,
For His mercy *endures* forever;
20 And Og king of Bashan,
For His mercy *endures* forever—
21 And gave their land as a heritage,
For His mercy *endures* forever;
22 A heritage to Israel His servant,
For His mercy *endures* forever.

23 Who remembered us in our lowly state,
For His mercy *endures* forever;
24 And rescued us from our enemies,
For His mercy *endures* forever;
25 Who gives food to all flesh,
For His mercy *endures* forever.

26 Oh, give thanks to the God of heaven!
For His mercy *endures* forever.

PSALM 137

Longing for Zion in a Foreign Land

1 By the rivers of Babylon,
There we sat down, yea, we wept
When we remembered Zion.

2 We hung our harps
Upon the willows in the midst of it.
3 For there those who carried us away
captive asked of us a song,
And those who plundered us *requested*
mirth,
Saying, "Sing us *one* of the songs of
Zion!"

4 How shall we sing the LORD's song
In a foreign land?
5 If I forget you, O Jerusalem,
Let my right hand forget *its skill!*
6 If I do not remember you,
Let my tongue cling to the roof of my
mouth—
If I do not exalt Jerusalem
Above my chief joy.

7 Remember, O LORD, against the sons of
Edom
The day of Jerusalem,
Who said, "Raze *it,* raze *it,*
To its very foundation!"

8 O daughter of Babylon, who are to be
destroyed,
Happy the one who repays you as you
have served us!
9 Happy the one who takes and dashes
Your little ones against the rock!

PSALM 138

The LORD's Goodness to the Faithful

A Psalm of David.

1 I will praise You with my whole heart;
Before the gods I will sing praises to You.
2 I will worship toward Your holy temple,
And praise Your name
For Your lovingkindness and Your truth;
For You have magnified Your word above
all Your name.
3 In the day when I cried out, You answered
me,
And made me bold *with* strength in my
soul.

4 All the kings of the earth shall praise You,
O LORD,
When they hear the words of Your mouth.
5 Yes, they shall sing of the ways of the
LORD,
For great *is* the glory of the LORD.
6 Though the LORD *is* on high,
Yet He regards the lowly;
But the proud He knows from afar.

7 Though I walk in the midst of trouble,
You will revive me;
You will stretch out Your hand
Against the wrath of my enemies,

Three Questions for Christian Leaders

(Psalm 137:1–6)

Three great issues erupt from the lyrics of this psalm: the writer dreams, the writer cries, and the writer sings.

No wonder the people wept—the Jews had been taken from Israel against their will and exiled to Babylon. No wonder they sang—they could not forget Zion, the land of their birth. No wonder they dreamed—they hoped and prayed for the day of their return home.

These issues pose great questions for every leader:

1. What do you dream about?

The psalmist remembered Zion; he longed to live again in his homeland. What are the dreams of your heart? What would you do if you had no fear of failure?

2. What do you cry about?

The psalmist cried about living in Babylon; he wept over the captivity of his people. What makes you cry? What burdens drive you to become passionate?

3. What do you sing about?

The psalmist sang about the blessings of God; he sang his remembrances of God's justice. What do you sing about? What causes you to rejoice or express joy?

And Your right hand will save me.

8 The LORD will perfect *that which* concerns me;
Your mercy, O LORD, *endures* forever;
Do not forsake the works of Your hands.

PSALM 139

God's Perfect Knowledge of Man

For the Chief Musician. A Psalm of David.

1 O LORD, You have searched me and known *me.*
2 You know my sitting down and my rising up;
You understand my thought afar off.
3 You comprehend my path and my lying down,
And are acquainted with all my ways.
4 For *there is* not a word on my tongue,
But behold, O LORD, You know it altogether.
5 You have hedged me behind and before,
And laid Your hand upon me.
6 *Such* knowledge *is* too wonderful for me;
It is high, I cannot *attain* it.

7 Where can I go from Your Spirit?
Or where can I flee from Your presence?
8 If I ascend into heaven, You *are* there;
If I make my bed in hell, behold, You *are* there.

9 *If* I take the wings of the morning,
And dwell in the uttermost parts of the sea,
10 Even there Your hand shall lead me,
And Your right hand shall hold me.
11 If I say, "Surely the darkness shall fall[a] on me,"
Even the night shall be light about me;
12 Indeed, the darkness shall not hide from You,
But the night shines as the day;
The darkness and the light *are* both alike *to You.*

13 For You formed my inward parts;
You covered me in my mother's womb.
14 I will praise You, for I am fearfully *and* wonderfully made;[a]
Marvelous are Your works,
And *that* my soul knows very well.
15 My frame was not hidden from You,
When I was made in secret,
And skillfully wrought in the lowest parts of the earth.
16 Your eyes saw my substance, being yet unformed.
And in Your book they all were written,
The days fashioned for me,
When *as yet there were* none of them.

139:11 [a]Vulgate and Symmachus read *cover.*
139:14 [a]Following Masoretic Text and Targum; Septuagint, Syriac, and Vulgate read *You are fearfully wonderful.*

A Leader's Relationship with God Shapes His or Her Perspective

(Psalm 139:1–24)

Talk about seeing the big picture! In this psalm David explores the depths of God's omniscience, omnipotence, and omnipresence.

David's dynamic and intimate relationship with God shapes his perspective on life. The king of Israel knew he wasn't alone. He rejoiced that he could draw upon God's infinite wisdom, that he could never run from God or His justice, and that he could count on God's power whenever he needed it. The leader of Israel had a Leader himself, named Yahweh. Ponder the benefits of an intimate relationship with God as Leader:

1. God knows our every thought, every word, and every move (vv. 1–6).
2. God directs us, no matter where we go (vv. 7–10).
3. God knows no hopeless or helpless situations (vv. 11, 12).
4. God formed every complex detail of our bodies, minds, and spirits (vv. 13–16).
5. God constantly thinks of us and is concerned with the details of our lives (vv. 17, 18).
6. God searches our hearts and will purify our motives (vv. 23, 24).

17 How precious also are Your thoughts to
    me, O God!
How great is the sum of them!
18 If I should count them, they would be
    more in number than the sand;
When I awake, I am still with You.

19 Oh, that You would slay the wicked, O God!
Depart from me, therefore, you
    bloodthirsty men.
20 For they speak against You wickedly;
Your enemies take *Your name* in vain.[a]
21 Do I not hate them, O LORD, who hate You?
And do I not loathe those who rise up
    against You?
22 I hate them with perfect hatred;
I count them my enemies.

23 Search me, O God, and know my heart;
Try me, and know my anxieties;
24 And see if *there is any* wicked way in me,
And lead me in the way everlasting.

PSALM 140

Prayer for Deliverance from Evil Men

To the Chief Musician. A Psalm of David.

1 Deliver me, O LORD, from evil men;
Preserve me from violent men,
2 Who plan evil things in *their* hearts;
They continually gather together *for* war.
3 They sharpen their tongues like a serpent;
The poison of asps *is* under their lips.   Selah

4 Keep me, O LORD, from the hands of the
    wicked;
Preserve me from violent men,
Who have purposed to make my steps
    stumble.
5 The proud have hidden a snare for me, and
    cords;
They have spread a net by the wayside;
They have set traps for me.   Selah

6 I said to the LORD: "You *are* my God;
Hear the voice of my supplications, O
    LORD.
7 O GOD the Lord, the strength of my
    salvation,
You have covered my head in the day of
    battle.
8 Do not grant, O LORD, the desires of the
    wicked;
Do not further his *wicked* scheme,
Lest they be exalted.   Selah

9 "*As for* the head of those who surround me,
Let the evil of their lips cover them;
10 Let burning coals fall upon them;
Let them be cast into the fire,
Into deep pits, that they rise not up again.
11 Let not a slanderer be established in the
    earth;
Let evil hunt the violent man to
    overthrow *him*."

12 I know that the LORD will maintain
The cause of the afflicted,
And justice for the poor.
13 Surely the righteous shall give thanks to
    Your name;
The upright shall dwell in Your presence.

PSALM 141

Prayer for Safekeeping from Wickedness

A Psalm of David.

1 LORD, I cry out to You;
Make haste to me!
Give ear to my voice when I cry out to
    You.
2 Let my prayer be set before You *as* incense,
The lifting up of my hands *as* the evening
    sacrifice.

3 Set a guard, O LORD, over my mouth;
Keep watch over the door of my lips.
4 Do not incline my heart to any evil thing,
To practice wicked works
With men who work iniquity;
And do not let me eat of their delicacies.

5 Let the righteous strike me;
It shall be a kindness.
And let him rebuke me;
It shall be as excellent oil;
Let my head not refuse it.

For still my prayer *is* against the deeds of
    the wicked.
6 Their judges are overthrown by the sides
    of the cliff,
And they hear my words, for they are sweet.
7 Our bones are scattered at the mouth of
    the grave,
As when one plows and breaks up the earth.

139:20 [a]Septuagint and Vulgate read *They take your
cities in vain.*

8 But my eyes *are* upon You, O GOD the Lord;
In You I take refuge;
Do not leave my soul destitute.
9 Keep me from the snares they have laid for
me,
And from the traps of the workers of
iniquity.
10 Let the wicked fall into their own nets,
While I escape safely.

PSALM 142

A Plea for Relief from Persecutors

*A Contemplation[a] of David. A Prayer when he
was in the cave.*

1 I cry out to the LORD with my voice;
With my voice to the LORD I make my
supplication.
2 I pour out my complaint before Him;
I declare before Him my trouble.

3 When my spirit was overwhelmed within
me,
Then You knew my path.
In the way in which I walk
They have secretly set a snare for me.
4 Look on *my* right hand and see,
For *there is* no one who acknowledges me;
Refuge has failed me;
No one cares for my soul.

5 I cried out to You, O LORD:
I said, "You *are* my refuge,
My portion in the land of the living.
6 Attend to my cry,
For I am brought very low;
Deliver me from my persecutors,
For they are stronger than I.
7 Bring my soul out of prison,
That I may praise Your name;
The righteous shall surround me,
For You shall deal bountifully with me."

PSALM 143

An Earnest Appeal for Guidance and Deliverance

A Psalm of David.

1 Hear my prayer, O LORD,
Give ear to my supplications!
In Your faithfulness answer me,
And in Your righteousness.
2 Do not enter into judgment with Your
servant,

For in Your sight no one living is
righteous.

3 For the enemy has persecuted my soul;
He has crushed my life to the ground;
He has made me dwell in darkness,
Like those who have long been dead.
4 Therefore my spirit is overwhelmed within
me;
My heart within me is distressed.

5 I remember the days of old;
I meditate on all Your works;
I muse on the work of Your hands.
6 I spread out my hands to You;
My soul *longs* for You like a thirsty land.
Selah

7 Answer me speedily, O LORD;
My spirit fails!
Do not hide Your face from me,
Lest I be like those who go down into the
pit.
8 Cause me to hear Your lovingkindness in
the morning,
For in You do I trust;
Cause me to know the way in which I
should walk,
For I lift up my soul to You.

9 Deliver me, O LORD, from my enemies;
In You I take shelter.[a]
10 Teach me to do Your will,
For You *are* my God;
Your Spirit *is* good.
Lead me in the land of uprightness.

11 Revive me, O LORD, for Your name's
sake!
For Your righteousness' sake bring my soul
out of trouble.
12 In Your mercy cut off my enemies,
And destroy all those who afflict my soul;
For I *am* Your servant.

PSALM 144

A Song to the LORD Who Preserves and Prospers His People

A Psalm of David.

1 Blessed *be* the LORD my Rock,
Who trains my hands for war,
And my fingers for battle—

142:title [a]Hebrew *Maschil*   **143:9** [a]Septuagint and
Vulgate read *To You I flee.*

2 My lovingkindness and my fortress,
My high tower and my deliverer,
My shield and *the One* in whom I take
refuge,
Who subdues my people[a] under me.

3 LORD, what *is* man, that You take
knowledge of him?
Or the son of man, that You are mindful
of him?
4 Man is like a breath;
His days *are* like a passing shadow.

5 Bow down Your heavens, O LORD, and
come down;
Touch the mountains, and they shall
smoke.
6 Flash forth lightning and scatter them;
Shoot out Your arrows and destroy
them.
7 Stretch out Your hand from above;
Rescue me and deliver me out of great
waters,
From the hand of foreigners,
8 Whose mouth speaks lying words,
And whose right hand *is* a right hand of
falsehood.

9 I will sing a new song to You, O God;
On a harp of ten strings I will sing praises
to You,
10 *The One* who gives salvation to kings,
Who delivers David His servant
From the deadly sword.

11 Rescue me and deliver me from the hand
of foreigners,
Whose mouth speaks lying words,
And whose right hand *is* a right hand of
falsehood—
12 That our sons *may be* as plants grown up in
their youth;
That our daughters *may be* as pillars,
Sculptured in palace style;
13 *That* our barns *may be* full,
Supplying all kinds of produce;
That our sheep may bring forth
thousands
And ten thousands in our fields;
14 *That* our oxen *may be* well laden;
That there be no breaking in or going out;
That there be no outcry in our streets.
15 Happy *are* the people who are in such a
state;
Happy *are* the people whose God *is* the
LORD!

PSALM 145

A Song of God's Majesty and Love

A Praise of David.

1 I will extol You, my God, O King;
And I will bless Your name forever and
ever.
2 Every day I will bless You,
And I will praise Your name forever and
ever.
3 Great *is* the LORD, and greatly to be
praised;
And His greatness *is* unsearchable.

4 One generation shall praise Your works to
another,
And shall declare Your mighty acts.
5 I[a] will meditate on the glorious splendor
of Your majesty,
And on Your wondrous works.[b]
6 *Men* shall speak of the might of Your
awesome acts,
And I will declare Your greatness.
7 They shall utter the memory of Your great
goodness,
And shall sing of Your righteousness.

8 The LORD *is* gracious and full of
compassion,
Slow to anger and great in mercy.
9 The LORD *is* good to all,
And His tender mercies *are* over all His
works.

10 All Your works shall praise You, O LORD,
And Your saints shall bless You.
11 They shall speak of the glory of Your
kingdom,
And talk of Your power,
12 To make known to the sons of men His
mighty acts,
And the glorious majesty of His kingdom.
13 Your kingdom *is* an everlasting kingdom,
And Your dominion *endures* throughout all
generations.[a]

144:2 [a]Following Masoretic Text, Septuagint, and
Vulgate; Syriac and Targum read *the peoples*
(compare 18:47).   **145:5** [a]Following Masoretic
Text and Targum; Dead Sea Scrolls, Septuagint,
Syriac, and Vulgate read *They.*   [b]Literally *on the words
of Your wondrous works*   **145:13** [a]Following
Masoretic Text and Targum; Dead Sea Scrolls,
Septuagint, Syriac, and Vulgate add *The LORD is
faithful in all His words, And holy in all His works.*

Commitment Comes Before Provision

(Psalm 145:8–20)

If Psalm 145 communicates just one message, it is that God deserves our unconditional commitment. David praises God for His goodness and His provisions. But he also makes it clear that leaders must walk in reckless abandon to the ways of God.

Once leaders make a commitment, they find that God provides the people, resources, and strategy necessary to fulfill their dream. In one sense, God enters a partnership with His leaders and promises to fulfill His role as we fulfill ours:

God's Role: Provision (vv. 8–17)
1. He is gracious and merciful.
2. His acts are mighty.
3. His kingdom is everlasting.
4. His dominion endures through all generations.
5. He satisfies our desires.
6. He is righteous and kind in all His ways.

Our Role: Commitment (vv. 18–20)
1. To those who call upon Him.
2. To those who fear Him.
3. To those who love Him.

14 The LORD upholds all who fall,
And raises up all *who are* bowed down.
15 The eyes of all look expectantly to You,
And You give them their food in due season.
16 You open Your hand
And satisfy the desire of every living thing.
17 The LORD *is* righteous in all His ways,
Gracious in all His works.
18 The LORD *is* near to all who call upon Him,
To all who call upon Him in truth.
19 He will fulfill the desire of those who fear Him;
He also will hear their cry and save them.
20 The LORD preserves all who love Him,
But all the wicked He will destroy.
21 My mouth shall speak the praise of the LORD,
And all flesh shall bless His holy name
Forever and ever.

PSALM 146

The Happiness of Those Whose Help Is the LORD

1 Praise the LORD!

Praise the LORD, O my soul!
2 While I live I will praise the LORD;
I will sing praises to my God while I have my being.

3 Do not put your trust in princes,
Nor in a son of man, in whom *there is* no help.
4 His spirit departs, he returns to his earth;
In that very day his plans perish.

5 Happy *is* he who *has* the God of Jacob for his help,
Whose hope *is* in the LORD his God,
6 Who made heaven and earth,
The sea, and all that *is* in them;
Who keeps truth forever,
7 Who executes justice for the oppressed,
Who gives food to the hungry.
The LORD gives freedom to the prisoners.

8 The LORD opens *the eyes of* the blind;
The LORD raises those who are bowed down;
The LORD loves the righteous.
9 The LORD watches over the strangers;
He relieves the fatherless and widow;
But the way of the wicked He turns upside down.

10 The LORD shall reign forever—
Your God, O Zion, to all generations.

Praise the LORD!

PSALM 147

Praise to God for His Word and Providence

1 Praise the LORD!
For *it is* good to sing praises to our God;
For *it is* pleasant, *and* praise is beautiful.

2 The LORD builds up Jerusalem;
He gathers together the outcasts of Israel.
3 He heals the brokenhearted
And binds up their wounds.
4 He counts the number of the stars;

He calls them all by name.
5 Great *is* our Lord, and mighty in power;
His understanding *is* infinite.
6 The LORD lifts up the humble;
He casts the wicked down to the ground.

7 Sing to the LORD with thanksgiving;
Sing praises on the harp to our God,
8 Who covers the heavens with clouds,
Who prepares rain for the earth,
Who makes grass to grow on the
mountains.
9 He gives to the beast its food,
And to the young ravens that cry.

10 He does not delight in the strength of the
horse;
He takes no pleasure in the legs of a man.
11 The LORD takes pleasure in those who fear
Him,
In those who hope in His mercy.

12 Praise the LORD, O Jerusalem!
Praise your God, O Zion!
13 For He has strengthened the bars of your
gates;
He has blessed your children within you.
14 He makes peace *in* your borders,
And fills you with the finest wheat.

15 He sends out His command *to the* earth;
His word runs very swiftly.
16 He gives snow like wool;
He scatters the frost like ashes;
17 He casts out His hail like morsels;
Who can stand before His cold?
18 He sends out His word and melts them;
He causes His wind to blow, *and the*
waters flow.

19 He declares His word to Jacob,
His statutes and His judgments to Israel.
20 He has not dealt thus with any nation;
And *as for His* judgments, they have not
known them.

Praise the LORD!

PSALM 148

Praise to the LORD from Creation

1 Praise the LORD!

Praise the LORD from the heavens;
Praise Him in the heights!

2 Praise Him, all His angels;
Praise Him, all His hosts!
3 Praise Him, sun and moon;
Praise Him, all you stars of light!
4 Praise Him, you heavens of heavens,
And you waters above the heavens!

5 Let them praise the name of the
LORD,
For He commanded and they were
created.
6 He also established them forever and
ever;
He made a decree which shall not pass
away.

7 Praise the LORD from the earth,
You great sea creatures and all the
depths;
8 Fire and hail, snow and clouds;
Stormy wind, fulfilling His word;
9 Mountains and all hills;
Fruitful trees and all cedars;
10 Beasts and all cattle;
Creeping things and flying fowl;
11 Kings of the earth and all peoples;
Princes and all judges of the earth;
12 Both young men and maidens;
Old men and children.

13 Let them praise the name of the
LORD,
For His name alone is exalted;
His glory *is* above the earth and
heaven.
14 And He has exalted the horn of His
people,
The praise of all His saints—
Of the children of Israel,
A people near to Him.

Praise the LORD!

PSALM 149

Praise to God for His Salvation and Judgment

1 Praise the LORD!

Sing to the LORD a new song,
And His praise in the assembly of saints.

2 Let Israel rejoice in their Maker;
Let the children of Zion be joyful in their
King.

3 Let them praise His name with the dance;
Let them sing praises to Him with the timbrel and harp.
4 For the LORD takes pleasure in His people;
He will beautify the humble with salvation.

5 Let the saints be joyful in glory;
Let them sing aloud on their beds.
6 *Let* the high praises of God *be* in their mouth,
And a two-edged sword in their hand,
7 To execute vengeance on the nations,
And punishments on the peoples;
8 To bind their kings with chains,
And their nobles with fetters of iron;
9 To execute on them the written judgment—
This honor have all His saints.

Praise the LORD!

PSALM 150

Let All Things Praise the LORD

1 Praise the LORD!

Praise God in His sanctuary;
Praise Him in His mighty firmament!

2 Praise Him for His mighty acts;
Praise Him according to His excellent greatness!

3 Praise Him with the sound of the trumpet;
Praise Him with the lute and harp!
4 Praise Him with the timbrel and dance;
Praise Him with stringed instruments and flutes!
5 Praise Him with loud cymbals;
Praise Him with clashing cymbals!

6 Let everything that has breath praise the LORD.

Praise the LORD!

PROVERBS
Principles for Guiding One's Life

SUMMARY

A vast amount of leadership wisdom lies within the 31 chapters of Proverbs. Its excellent principles for guiding one's life come to us in the form of poetry, like the Psalms. But where Psalms portrays the relationships and emotions of a leader, Proverbs displays the principles, values, and intellect of a leader. The Law of Navigation, the Law of Solid Ground, and the Law of Intuition surface repeatedly in this book.

Proverbs is all about the mind of a leader, how a leader thinks. Who would dispute that leaders think differently from followers? Good leaders see things *before* followers do; they see *beyond* what followers do; and they see *bigger* than followers do. While followers may barely feel able to see and plan beyond next week, leaders must think, envision, and plan well into the future.

Fuller Seminary professor Bobby Clinton has said, "The primary difference between a follower and a leader is perspective. The primary difference between a leader and an effective leader is better perspective." Both leaders and followers can have strong character. Both can possess warm relational skills. Both can even have a strong personality and a strong will. What separates them is how they think and perceive reality.

Because the Scripture teaches that we were all made to rule (Gen. 1:26–28), everyone possesses the capacity to raise their level of leadership ability. Each of us can improve the way we influence others. We must, however, begin with our perspective—and that is what makes the Book of Proverbs so profound. It is a book about improving the way we think and therefore act. It is a book about raising the "lid" on our leadership ability—first by the way we lead our own lives, then by the way we lead others.

In this book you will encounter wisdom principles that appear so simple, yet are tremendously deep and profound. Soak in every verse through the eyes of a leader. The wisdom lies in front of every one of us, "crying out loudly in the streets," longing to be noticed (1:20–23). Embrace the disciplines and the character that Solomon suggests, and you will be on your way to transforming your leadership.

God's Role in Proverbs

God is the ultimate source of wisdom and of life itself. He mentors leaders who seek wisdom for their decision making. Proverbs paints a picture of wisdom as a person calling out for listeners, but finding few. God is also the divine Parent disciplining His children. He furnishes words of correction and guidance, again beseeching us to listen. Finally, this book presents God as the divine Preacher or Teacher. He contrasts the diligent and the sluggard, the good and the wicked, the wise and the foolish. The axioms flow off His tongue, teaching the student how the Master thinks and acts.

Leaders in Proverbs

Solomon, wise men, Agur, Lemuel

Other People of Influence in Proverbs

The wise person, the harlot, the sluggard, the wicked person, the fool

Lessons in Leadership

- Good leadership begins with good wisdom and insight.
- Competency cannot substitute for lack of character.
- Leadership development begins with "being" before "doing."
- Leaders who solve problems will never lack followers.
- Wisdom is available to leaders who pursue it diligently, but it is not automatic.
- Laziness can steal everything a leader has worked to achieve.
- God rewards leaders who do right.

LEADERSHIP

HIGHLIGHTS IN PROVERBS

The Beginning of Knowledge

1 The proverbs of Solomon the son of David, king of Israel:

2 To know wisdom and instruction,
To perceive the words of understanding,

3 To receive the instruction of wisdom,
Justice, judgment, and equity;

4 To give prudence to the simple,
To the young man knowledge and
discretion—

5 A wise *man* will hear and increase
learning,
And a man of understanding will attain
wise counsel,

6 To understand a proverb and an enigma,
The words of the wise and their riddles.

7 The fear of the LORD *is* the beginning of
knowledge,
But fools despise wisdom and instruction.

Shun Evil Counsel

8 My son, hear the instruction of your
father,
And do not forsake the law of your
mother;

9 For they *will be* a graceful ornament on
your head,
And chains about your neck.

10 My son, if sinners entice you,
Do not consent.

11 If they say, "Come with us,
Let us lie in wait to *shed* blood;
Let us lurk secretly for the innocent
without cause;

12 Let us swallow them alive like Sheol,ᵃ
And whole, like those who go down to
the Pit;

13 We shall find all *kinds* of precious
possessions,
We shall fill our houses with spoil;

14 Cast in your lot among us,
Let us all have one purse"—

15 My son, do not walk in the way with them,
Keep your foot from their path;

16 For their feet run to evil,
And they make haste to shed blood.

17 Surely, in vain the net is spread
In the sight of any bird;

18 But they lie in wait for their *own* blood,
They lurk secretly for their *own* lives.

19 So *are* the ways of everyone who is greedy
for gain;
It takes away the life of its owners.

Decision Making: The Fast Way to Gain Leadership

(Proverbs 1:7–33)

Wisdom can be a leader's best friend, especially in times of decision. Suppose you find yourself in a large committee meeting in which a crucial decision must be made. The committee reaches an impasse and everything stops. Who will become the most influential person in that room? Answer: the one with the wisdom to draw a conclusion that not only works, but which receives the blessing of that committee.

Proverbs 1 describes wisdom as a woman crying out in the streets (v. 20). What a beautiful picture! Wisdom does not hide herself, but shouts publicly! We must go out and find her and build a friendship with her. What can we learn about decision making from Proverbs 1?

1. The foundation for every decision is to honor and revere God (v. 7).
2. We must build off our heritage and conscience: what values are we to embrace? (vv. 8, 9).
3. We must avoid the counsel of the ungodly (vv. 10–19).
4. We must pursue wisdom. What are the facts? What are the options? (vv. 20–23).
5. We must move toward inward peace (vv. 32, 33).

The Call of Wisdom

20 Wisdom calls aloud outside;
She raises her voice in the open squares.

21 She cries out in the chief concourses,ᵃ
At the openings of the gates in the city
She speaks her words:

22 "How long, you simple ones, will you love
simplicity?
For scorners delight in their scorning,
And fools hate knowledge.

23 Turn at my rebuke;
Surely I will pour out my spirit on you;

1:12 ᵃOr *the grave*   **1:21** ᵃSeptuagint, Syriac, and Targum read *top of the walls;* Vulgate reads *the head of multitudes.*

I will make my words known to you.

24 Because I have called and you refused,
I have stretched out my hand and no one
regarded,

25 Because you disdained all my counsel,
And would have none of my rebuke,

26 I also will laugh at your calamity;
I will mock when your terror comes,

27 When your terror comes like a storm,
And your destruction comes like a
whirlwind,
When distress and anguish come upon
you.

28 "Then they will call on me, but I will not
answer;
They will seek me diligently, but they will
not find me.

29 Because they hated knowledge
And did not choose the fear of the LORD,

30 They would have none of my counsel
And despised my every rebuke.

31 Therefore they shall eat the fruit of their
own way,
And be filled to the full with their own
fancies.

32 For the turning away of the simple will
slay them,

And the complacency of fools will destroy
them;

33 But whoever listens to me will dwell safely,
And will be secure, without fear of evil."

The Value of Wisdom

2 My son, if you receive my words,
And treasure my commands within you,
2 So that you incline your ear to
wisdom,
And apply your heart to understanding;

3 Yes, if you cry out for discernment,
And lift up your voice for understanding,

4 If you seek her as silver,
And search for her as *for* hidden treasures;

5 Then you will understand the fear of the
LORD,
And find the knowledge of God.

6 For the LORD gives wisdom;
From His mouth *come* knowledge and
understanding;

7 He stores up sound wisdom for the upright;
He is a shield to those who walk uprightly;

8 He guards the paths of justice,
And preserves the way of His saints.

9 Then you will understand righteousness
and justice,
Equity *and* every good path.

Desire: What Separates Leaders from Followers

(Proverbs 2:1–4)

Good leaders seem to know what steps to take into a bright future. But what enables them to know what to do? How do they differ from followers? Proverbs 2 tells us the key difference may be desire. We all must answer three great questions in life:

1. What do we want?
2. Why do we want it?
3. How badly do we want it?

Consider the phrases Proverbs 2 uses to talk about the passionate search for wisdom:

- *receive* my words (v. 1)
- *treasure* my commands (v. 1)
- *incline* your ear to wisdom (v. 2)
- *apply* your heart to understanding (v. 2)
- *cry out* for discernment (v. 3)
- *lift up* your voice for understanding (v. 3)
- *seek* her as silver (v. 4)
- *search for* her as for hidden treasure (v. 4)

Good leaders hunt for wisdom as though it were diamonds and rubies. So—for what are *you* searching?

10 When wisdom enters your heart,
And knowledge is pleasant to your soul,
11 Discretion will preserve you;
Understanding will keep you,
12 To deliver you from the way of evil,
From the man who speaks perverse things,
13 From those who leave the paths of
uprightness
To walk in the ways of darkness;
14 Who rejoice in doing evil,
And delight in the perversity of the wicked;
15 Whose ways *are* crooked,
And *who are* devious in their paths;
16 To deliver you from the immoral woman,
From the seductress *who* flatters with her
words,
17 Who forsakes the companion of her
youth,
And forgets the covenant of her God.
18 For her house leads down to death,
And her paths to the dead;
19 None who go to her return,
Nor do they regain the paths of life—
20 So you may walk in the way of goodness,
And keep *to* the paths of righteousness.
21 For the upright will dwell in the land,
And the blameless will remain in it;
22 But the wicked will be cut off from the
earth,
And the unfaithful will be uprooted
from it.

Guidance for the Young

3 My son, do not forget my law,
But let your heart keep my commands;
2 For length of days and long life
And peace they will add to you.

3 Let not mercy and truth forsake you;
Bind them around your neck,
Write them on the tablet of your heart,
4 *And* so find favor and high esteem
In the sight of God and man.

5 Trust in the LORD with all your heart,
And lean not on your own understanding;
6 In all your ways acknowledge Him,
And He shall direct[a] your paths.

7 Do not be wise in your own eyes;
Fear the LORD and depart from evil.
8 It will be health to your flesh,[a]
And strength[b] to your bones.

9 Honor the LORD with your possessions,
And with the firstfruits of all your
increase;
10 So your barns will be filled with plenty,
And your vats will overflow with new
wine.

3:6 [a]Or *make smooth* or *straight* **3:8** [a]Literally *navel,*
figurative of the body [b]Literally *drink* or *refreshment*

The Irony of Spiritual Leadership:
Get Understanding but Don't Lean On It
(Proverbs 3:5, 6)

Proverbs 2 and 3 poses an apparent paradox in spiritual leadership. We are to get wisdom and understanding (2:1–5), yet we are not to lean on it apart from the Lord (3:5, 6). Even good wisdom divorced from God can become a snare. So how are godly leaders to think?

1. Godly leaders think *big:* They realize God's vision is usually bigger than theirs.
2. Godly leaders think *other people:* They always include others in the mix.
3. Godly leaders think *continually:* They're not satisfied with today's answers.
4. Godly leaders think *bottom line:* They want to see results and fruit.
5. Godly leaders think *continual growth:* They want to keep improving.
6. Godly leaders think *without lines:* They let God outside of the box.
7. Godly leaders think *victory:* They want to see God's rule come to earth.
8. Godly leaders think *intuitively:* They have a sense of what will work.
9. Godly leaders think *servanthood:* They want to serve and add value to people.
10. Godly leaders think *quickly:* They evaluate quickly and see possible answers.

11 My son, do not despise the chastening of
the LORD,
Nor detest His correction;
12 For whom the LORD loves He corrects,
Just as a father the son *in whom* he
delights.

13 Happy *is* the man *who* finds wisdom,
And the man *who* gains understanding;
14 For her proceeds *are* better than the profits
of silver,
And her gain than fine gold.
15 She *is* more precious than rubies,
And all the things you may desire cannot
compare with her.
16 Length of days *is* in her right hand,
In her left hand riches and honor.
17 Her ways *are* ways of pleasantness,
And all her paths *are* peace.
18 She *is* a tree of life to those who take hold
of her,
And happy *are* all who retain her.

19 The LORD by wisdom founded the earth;
By understanding He established the
heavens;
20 By His knowledge the depths were broken
up,
And clouds drop down the dew.

21 My son, let them not depart from your
eyes—
Keep sound wisdom and discretion;
22 So they will be life to your soul
And grace to your neck.
23 Then you will walk safely in your way,
And your foot will not stumble.
24 When you lie down, you will not be
afraid;
Yes, you will lie down and your sleep will
be sweet.
25 Do not be afraid of sudden terror,
Nor of trouble from the wicked when it
comes;
26 For the LORD will be your confidence,
And will keep your foot from being
caught.

27 Do not withhold good from those to
whom it is due,
When it is in the power of your hand to
do *so.*
28 Do not say to your neighbor,
"Go, and come back,
And tomorrow I will give *it,*"
When *you have* it with you.

29 Do not devise evil against your neighbor,
For he dwells by you for safety's sake.
30 Do not strive with a man without cause,
If he has done you no harm.

31 Do not envy the oppressor,
And choose none of his ways;
32 For the perverse *person is* an abomination
to the LORD,
But His secret counsel *is* with the
upright.
33 The curse of the LORD *is* on the house of
the wicked,
But He blesses the home of the just.
34 Surely He scorns the scornful,
But gives grace to the humble.
35 The wise shall inherit glory,
But shame shall be the legacy of fools.

Security in Wisdom

4 Hear, *my* children, the instruction of a
father,
And give attention to know
understanding;
2 For I give you good doctrine:
Do not forsake my law.
3 When I was my father's son,
Tender and the only one in the sight of
my mother,
4 He also taught me, and said to me:
"Let your heart retain my words;
Keep my commands, and live.
5 Get wisdom! Get understanding!
Do not forget, nor turn away from the
words of my mouth.
6 Do not forsake her, and she will preserve
you;
Love her, and she will keep you.
7 Wisdom *is* the principal thing;
Therefore get wisdom.
And in all your getting, get understanding.
8 Exalt her, and she will promote you;
She will bring you honor, when you
embrace her.
9 She will place on your head an ornament
of grace;
A crown of glory she will deliver to
you."

10 Hear, my son, and receive my sayings,
And the years of your life will be many.
11 I have taught you in the way of wisdom;
I have led you in right paths.
12 When you walk, your steps will not be
hindered,
And when you run, you will not stumble.

13 Take firm hold of instruction, do not let
go;
Keep her, for she *is* your life.

14 Do not enter the path of the wicked,
And do not walk in the way of evil.

15 Avoid it, do not travel on it;
Turn away from it and pass on.

16 For they do not sleep unless they have
done evil;
And their sleep is taken away unless they
make *someone* fall.

17 For they eat the bread of wickedness,
And drink the wine of violence.

18 But the path of the just *is* like the shining
sun,ᵃ
That shines ever brighter unto the perfect
day.

19 The way of the wicked *is* like darkness;
They do not know what makes them
stumble.

20 My son, give attention to my words;
Incline your ear to my sayings.

21 Do not let them depart from your eyes;
Keep them in the midst of your heart;

22 For they *are* life to those who find them,
And health to all their flesh.

23 Keep your heart with all diligence,
For out of it *spring* the issues of life.

24 Put away from you a deceitful mouth,
And put perverse lips far from you.

25 Let your eyes look straight ahead,
And your eyelids look right before you.

26 Ponder the path of your feet,
And let all your ways be established.

27 Do not turn to the right or the left;
Remove your foot from evil.

The Peril of Adultery

5 My son, pay attention to my wisdom;
Lend your ear to my understanding,
2 That you may preserve discretion,
And your lips may keep knowledge.

3 For the lips of an immoral woman drip
honey,
And her mouth *is* smoother than oil;

4 But in the end she is bitter as wormwood,
Sharp as a two-edged sword.

5 Her feet go down to death,
Her steps lay hold of hell.ᵃ

6 Lest you ponder *her* path of life—
Her ways are unstable;
You do not know *them*.

Principle-Centered Leadership

(Proverbs 4:20–27)

Leaders who last do not merely react to
their culture; they base their leadership
on timeless and universal principles. They remain relevant because they marry cultural
context to timeless truth. Proverbs 4 encourages leaders to become principle centered.
Verses 20–27 teach us that God's principles
give us three crucial tools:

1. They are a *guide;* they help us stay on the
right path.
2. They are a *guard;* they keep our hearts
and bodies protected.
3. They are a *gauge;* they enable us to evaluate where we are.

These principles build our character, direct
our decisions, and correct our lifestyles. Every
leader ought to consume God's Word, then put
the truths he or she discovers in the form of
principles that can guide, guard, and gauge his
or her life.

---

7 Therefore hear me now, *my* children,
And do not depart from the words of my
mouth.

8 Remove your way far from her,
And do not go near the door of her house,

9 Lest you give your honor to others,
And your years to the cruel *one;*

10 Lest aliens be filled with your wealth,
And your labors *go* to the house of a
foreigner;

11 And you mourn at last,
When your flesh and your body are
consumed,

12 And say:
"How I have hated instruction,
And my heart despised correction!

13 I have not obeyed the voice of my
teachers,
Nor inclined my ear to those who
instructed me!

14 I was on the verge of total ruin,
In the midst of the assembly and
congregation."

4:18 ᵃLiterally *light* 5:5 ᵃOr *Sheol*

15 Drink water from your own cistern,
And running water from your own well.
16 Should your fountains be dispersed abroad,
Streams of water in the streets?
17 Let them be only your own,
And not for strangers with you.
18 Let your fountain be blessed,
And rejoice with the wife of your youth.
19 As a loving deer and a graceful doe,
Let her breasts satisfy you at all times;
And always be enraptured with her love.
20 For why should you, my son, be
enraptured by an immoral woman,
And be embraced in the arms of a
seductress?

21 For the ways of man are before the eyes of
the LORD,
And He ponders all his paths.
22 His own iniquities entrap the wicked man,
And he is caught in the cords of his sin.
23 He shall die for lack of instruction,
And in the greatness of his folly he shall
go astray.

Dangerous Promises

6 My son, if you become surety for your
friend,
If you have shaken hands in pledge for a
stranger,
2 You are snared by the words of your
mouth;
You are taken by the words of your
mouth.
3 So do this, my son, and deliver yourself;
For you have come into the hand of your
friend:
Go and humble yourself;
Plead with your friend.
4 Give no sleep to your eyes,
Nor slumber to your eyelids.
5 Deliver yourself like a gazelle from the
hand of the hunter,
And like a bird from the hand of the
fowler.[a]

6:5 [a]That is, one who catches birds in a trap or
snare

SOLOMON

IT IS MORE BLESSED TO FOLLOW GOOD ADVICE THAN TO GIVE IT

(Proverbs 5:3–21)

PROFILE IN LEADERSHIP

It doesn't take a leader very long to realize that it's easier to give good advice than to follow it. Solomon proves the point.

This wisest of kings didn't hold back when it came to warning his people against adultery. He tells us repeatedly and with great conviction that only fools fall into adultery. Perhaps he spoke so forcefully after pondering the fate of his own father, David, who brought on himself no end of trouble through his illicit affair with Bathsheba (2 Sam. 12:10). Solomon therefore counseled other men to stay at home and find contentment "with the wife of your youth" (Prov. 5:18). The king knew very well the spiritual issues at stake in marriage, for he declares, "The ways of man are before the eyes of the LORD, and He ponders all his paths" (5:21).

And yet, somehow, this same leader failed to heed God's explicit warning against kings taking many wives (Deut. 17:17). Solomon blatantly disobeyed this command and married *seven hundred* women. The result? "His wives turned his heart after other gods; and his heart was not loyal to the LORD his God" (1 Kin. 11:4).

Wise leaders not only give good advice; they heed it. How different the fortunes of Israel might have turned out had Solomon acted on the wisdom he so forcefully expressed to others!

Moral Failure: Disciplines Prevent Nightmares

(Proverbs 5:3–23)

How many leaders have ruined their lives and damaged the lives of others through immorality? Character has become a crucial issue today precisely because of the myriad leaders in the political, business, and religious worlds who have fallen morally. No doubt spiritual warfare has played a big role in the tens of thousands of leaders who have failed. They fall partly because the enemy has targeted leaders for attack.

Leaders need to remember that they influence many others beyond themselves; they never fall in a vacuum. They also need to realize that replacing fallen leaders is a slow and difficult process.

So how can we guard against falling? First, we must take care not to emphasize the gifts of a leader over his or her character. We have an unhealthy tendency to see and reward the gift more than the character, but both are to be developed. We must strike the following balance if we are to finish well:

GIFT DEPOSITED   CHARACTER BUILT

WHAT I AM	WHAT I DO	THE RESULT
Humble	Rely on God	God's Power
Visionary	Set Goals	High Morale
Convictional	Do Right	Credibility

The Folly of Indolence

6   Go to the ant, you sluggard!
    Consider her ways and be wise,
7   Which, having no captain,
    Overseer or ruler,
8   Provides her supplies in the summer,
    And gathers her food in the harvest.
9   How long will you slumber, O sluggard?
    When will you rise from your sleep?
10   A little sleep, a little slumber,
    A little folding of the hands to sleep—
11   So shall your poverty come on you like a
      prowler,
    And your need like an armed man.

The Wicked Man

12   A worthless person, a wicked man,
    Walks with a perverse mouth;
13   He winks with his eyes,
    He shuffles his feet,
    He points with his fingers;
14   Perversity *is* in his heart,
    He devises evil continually,
    He sows discord.
15   Therefore his calamity shall come suddenly;

Suddenly he shall be broken without
    remedy.
16   These six *things* the LORD hates,
    Yes, seven *are* an abomination to Him:
17   A proud look,
    A lying tongue,
    Hands that shed innocent blood,
18   A heart that devises wicked plans,
    Feet that are swift in running to evil,
19   A false witness *who* speaks lies,
    And one who sows discord among brethren.

Beware of Adultery

20   My son, keep your father's command,
    And do not forsake the law of your
      mother.
21   Bind them continually upon your heart;
    Tie them around your neck.
22   When you roam, they[a] will lead you;
    When you sleep, they will keep you;
    And *when* you awake, they will speak with
      you.

6:22 [a]Literally *it*

Leadership Lessons from the Ant

(Proverbs 6:6–8)

Do you want to make a difference? Then pay attention to the metaphor of the ant. It's amazing that one of the smallest of God's creatures can become one of His greatest teachers. The lessons the ant teaches us can be summarized this way:

A—Attitude of Initiative
Ants don't need a commander to tell them to get started.

N—Nature of Integrity
Ants work faithfully and need no outside accountability to keep them doing right.

T—Thirst for Industry
Ants work hard and will replace their anthill when it gets ruined.

S—Source of Insight
Ants store provisions in summer.

If we consider and learn from the ways of the ant, we can grow wise.

---

23 For the commandment *is* a lamp,
   And the law a light;
   Reproofs of instruction *are* the way of life,
24 To keep you from the evil woman,
   From the flattering tongue of a seductress.
25 Do not lust after her beauty in your heart,
   Nor let her allure you with her eyelids.
26 For by means of a harlot
   A man is reduced to a crust of bread;
   And an adulteress[a] will prey upon his precious life.
27 Can a man take fire to his bosom,
   And his clothes not be burned?
28 Can one walk on hot coals,
   And his feet not be seared?
29 So *is* he who goes in to his neighbor's wife;
   Whoever touches her shall not be innocent.
30 *People* do not despise a thief
   If he steals to satisfy himself when he is starving.
31 Yet *when* he is found, he must restore sevenfold;
   He may have to give up all the substance of his house.

32 Whoever commits adultery with a woman lacks understanding;
   He *who* does so destroys his own soul.
33 Wounds and dishonor he will get,
   And his reproach will not be wiped away.
34 For jealousy *is* a husband's fury;
   Therefore he will not spare in the day of vengeance.
35 He will accept no recompense,
   Nor will he be appeased though you give many gifts.

7 My son, keep my words,
   And treasure my commands within you.
2   Keep my commands and live,
   And my law as the apple of your eye.
3 Bind them on your fingers;
   Write them on the tablet of your heart.
4 Say to wisdom, "You *are* my sister,"
   And call understanding *your* nearest kin,
5 That they may keep you from the immoral woman,
   From the seductress *who* flatters with her words.

The Crafty Harlot

6 For at the window of my house
   I looked through my lattice,
7 And saw among the simple,
   I perceived among the youths,
   A young man devoid of understanding,
8 Passing along the street near her corner;
   And he took the path to her house
9 In the twilight, in the evening,
   In the black and dark night.

10 And there a woman met him,
   With the attire of a harlot, and a crafty heart.
11 She *was* loud and rebellious,
   Her feet would not stay at home.
12 At times *she was* outside, at times in the open square,
   Lurking at every corner.
13 So she caught him and kissed him;
   With an impudent face she said to him:
14 " *I have* peace offerings with me;
   Today I have paid my vows.
15 So I came out to meet you,
   Diligently to seek your face,
   And I have found you.
16 I have spread my bed with tapestry,
   Colored coverings of Egyptian linen.
17 I have perfumed my bed

6:26 [a]Literally *a man's wife,* that is, of another

With myrrh, aloes, and cinnamon.

18 Come, let us take our fill of love until
    morning;
    Let us delight ourselves with love.

19 For my husband *is* not at home;
    He has gone on a long journey;

20 He has taken a bag of money with him,
    And will come home on the appointed day."

21 With her enticing speech she caused him
    to yield,
    With her flattering lips she seduced him.

22 Immediately he went after her, as an ox
    goes to the slaughter,
    Or as a fool to the correction of the
    stocks,[a]

23 Till an arrow struck his liver.
    As a bird hastens to the snare,
    He did not know it *would cost* his life.

24 Now therefore, listen to me, *my* children;
    Pay attention to the words of my mouth:

25 Do not let your heart turn aside to her
    ways,
    Do not stray into her paths;

26 For she has cast down many wounded,

And all who were slain by her were strong
men.

27 Her house *is* the way to hell,[a]
    Descending to the chambers of death.

The Excellence of Wisdom

8 Does not wisdom cry out,
    And understanding lift up her voice?

2 She takes her stand on the top of the
    high hill,
    Beside the way, where the paths meet.

3 She cries out by the gates, at the entry of
    the city,
    At the entrance of the doors:

4 "To you, O men, I call,
    And my voice *is* to the sons of men.

5 O you simple ones, understand prudence,
    And you fools, be of an understanding
    heart.

6 Listen, for I will speak of excellent things,
    And from the opening of my lips *will come*
    right things;

7:22 [a]Septuagint, Syriac, and Targum read *as a dog
to bonds;* Vulgate reads *as a lamb . . . to bonds.*
7:27 [a]Or *Sheol*

THE SLUGGARD

WORTHLESS TO THE KINGDOM
(Proverbs 6:6, 9–11)

PROFILE IN LEADERSHIP

King Solomon had plenty to say about the "sluggard," or the habitually lazy person. He contrasts the sluggard with the ant, who works diligently during the summer to gather enough food for the winter. In Proverbs 20:4, Solomon describes the sluggard as one who refuses to work hard during the growing season and so has nothing at harvest time. The sluggard makes only one commitment: to his leisure. He'll try any excuse to shy away from honest labor, even excusing himself through irrational claims of danger (Prov. 22:13).

The sluggard in the physical sense does nothing for the world around him; he leaves it unchanged, except for pillaging some of its resources. The sluggard in the spiritual sense is little different; he leaves the world no better than he found it, and perhaps a little poorer. When leaders become lazy and lose their diligence in doing good for God, they become spiritual sluggards and worthless to the kingdom (Matt. 5:13).

Wise leaders know their time is limited. They know they have no way to retrieve misused or wasted time. Jesus stressed this when He said, "I must work the works of Him who sent Me while it is day; the night is coming when no one can work" (John 9:4). Leaders in the body of Christ must remain diligent in doing good and in encouraging others to do likewise.

7 For my mouth will speak truth;
Wickedness *is* an abomination to my lips.
8 All the words of my mouth *are* with
righteousness;
Nothing crooked or perverse *is* in them.
9 They *are* all plain to him who understands,
And right to those who find knowledge.
10 Receive my instruction, and not silver,
And knowledge rather than choice gold;
11 For wisdom *is* better than rubies,
And all the things one may desire cannot
be compared with her.

12 "I, wisdom, dwell with prudence,
And find out knowledge *and* discretion.
13 The fear of the LORD *is* to hate evil;
Pride and arrogance and the evil way
And the perverse mouth I hate.
14 Counsel *is* mine, and sound wisdom;
I *am* understanding, I have strength.
15 By me kings reign,
And rulers decree justice.
16 By me princes rule, and nobles,
All the judges of the earth.[a]
17 I love those who love me,
And those who seek me diligently will
find me.
18 Riches and honor *are* with me,
Enduring riches and righteousness.
19 My fruit *is* better than gold, yes, than fine
gold,
And my revenue than choice silver.
20 I traverse the way of righteousness,
In the midst of the paths of justice,
21 That I may cause those who love me to
inherit wealth,
That I may fill their treasuries.

The Law of Intuition: Wisdom Makes the Difference

(Proverbs 8:15, 16)

Leadership begins with our thoughts even before our actions. When our mind and our attitudes are right, we position ourselves to lead well. Wisdom desires to be the best friend of any leader. Wise leaders also have discernment in relationships, a hatred for what is wrong, and influence.

22 "The LORD possessed me at the beginning
of His way,
Before His works of old.
23 I have been established from everlasting,
From the beginning, before there was ever
an earth.
24 When *there were* no depths I was brought
forth,
When *there were* no fountains abounding
with water.
25 Before the mountains were settled,
Before the hills, I was brought forth;
26 While as yet He had not made the earth
or the fields,
Or the primal dust of the world.
27 When He prepared the heavens, I *was*
there,
When He drew a circle on the face of the
deep,
28 When He established the clouds above,
When He strengthened the fountains of
the deep,
29 When He assigned to the sea its
limit,
So that the waters would not transgress
His command,
When He marked out the foundations of
the earth,
30 Then I was beside Him *as* a master
craftsman;[a]
And I was daily *His* delight,
Rejoicing always before Him,
31 Rejoicing in His inhabited world,
And my delight *was* with the sons of
men.

32 "Now therefore, listen to me, *my*
children,
For blessed *are* those who keep my ways.
33 Hear instruction and be wise,
And do not disdain *it.*
34 Blessed is the man who listens to me,
Watching daily at my gates,
Waiting at the posts of my doors.
35 For whoever finds me finds life,
And obtains favor from the LORD;
36 But he who sins against me wrongs his
own soul;
All those who hate me love death."

8:16 [a]Masoretic Text, Syriac, Targum, and Vulgate read *righteousness;* Septuagint, Bomberg, and some manuscripts and editions read *earth.* **8:30** [a]A Jewish tradition reads *one brought up.*

The Way of Wisdom

9 Wisdom has built her house,
She has hewn out her seven pillars;
2   She has slaughtered her meat,
She has mixed her wine,
She has also furnished her table.
3   She has sent out her maidens,
She cries out from the highest places of
the city,
4   "Whoever *is* simple, let him turn in
here!"
As for him who lacks understanding, she
says to him,
5   "Come, eat of my bread
And drink of the wine I have mixed.
6   Forsake foolishness and live,
And go in the way of understanding.

7   "He who corrects a scoffer gets shame for
himself,
And he who rebukes a wicked *man only*
harms himself.
8   Do not correct a scoffer, lest he hate you;
Rebuke a wise *man,* and he will love
you.
9   Give *instruction* to a wise *man,* and he will
be still wiser;
Teach a just *man,* and he will increase in
learning.

10   "The fear of the LORD *is* the beginning of
wisdom,
And the knowledge of the Holy One *is*
understanding.
11   For by me your days will be multiplied,
And years of life will be added to you.
12   If you are wise, you are wise for yourself,
And *if* you scoff, you will bear *it* alone."

The Way of Folly
13   A foolish woman is clamorous;
She is simple, and knows nothing.
14   For she sits at the door of her house,
On a seat *by* the highest places of the
city,
15   To call to those who pass by,
Who go straight on their way:
16   "Whoever *is* simple, let him turn in here";
And *as for* him who lacks understanding,
she says to him,
17   "Stolen water is sweet,
And bread *eaten* in secret is pleasant."
18   But he does not know that the dead *are*
there,
That her guests *are* in the depths of hell.[a]

Wise Sayings of Solomon

10 The proverbs of Solomon:

A wise son makes a glad father,
But a foolish son *is* the grief of his mother.

2   Treasures of wickedness profit nothing,
But righteousness delivers from death.
3   The LORD will not allow the righteous
soul to famish,
But He casts away the desire of the
wicked.

4   He who has a slack hand becomes poor,
But the hand of the diligent makes rich.
5   He who gathers in summer *is* a wise son;
He who sleeps in harvest *is* a son who
causes shame.

6   Blessings *are* on the head of the righteous,
But violence covers the mouth of the
wicked.

9:18 [a]Or *Sheol*

The Law of E. F. Hutton: Leaders Must Have Skillful Tongues

(Proverbs 10:6–32)

A number of verses in Proverbs speak of
the tongue and how to use it as a positive
influence. Leaders who use words skillfully
increase their influence. Leaders who understand the power of their words accomplish
the following:

1. They proclaim justice and are blessed
   (v. 6).
2. They speak hope for the future, becoming
   a fountain of life to others (v. 11).
3. They speak forth wisdom and save others
   from ruin (vv. 13, 14).
4. They know when silence is more powerful
   than words (v. 19).
5. Their words feed and nourish many others (v. 21).
6. They express what is right and nurture
   the right in the hearts of those who follow (vv. 31, 32).

7 The memory of the righteous *is* blessed,
But the name of the wicked will rot.

8 The wise in heart will receive commands,
But a prating fool will fall.

9 He who walks with integrity walks
securely,
But he who perverts his ways will become
known.

10 He who winks with the eye causes trouble,
But a prating fool will fall.

11 The mouth of the righteous *is* a well of
life,
But violence covers the mouth of the
wicked.

12 Hatred stirs up strife,
But love covers all sins.

13 Wisdom is found on the lips of him who
has understanding,
But a rod *is* for the back of him who is
devoid of understanding.

14 Wise *people* store up knowledge,
But the mouth of the foolish *is* near
destruction.

15 The rich man's wealth *is* his strong city;
The destruction of the poor *is* their
poverty.

16 The labor of the righteous *leads* to life,
The wages of the wicked to sin.

17 He who keeps instruction *is in* the way of
life,
But he who refuses correction goes astray.

18 Whoever hides hatred *has* lying lips,
And whoever spreads slander *is* a fool.

19 In the multitude of words sin is not
lacking,
But he who restrains his lips *is* wise.

20 The tongue of the righteous *is* choice
silver;
The heart of the wicked *is worth* little.

21 The lips of the righteous feed many,
But fools die for lack of wisdom.[a]

22 The blessing of the LORD makes *one* rich,
And He adds no sorrow with it.

23 To do evil *is* like sport to a fool,
But a man of understanding has wisdom.

24 The fear of the wicked will come upon him,
And the desire of the righteous will be
granted.

25 When the whirlwind passes by, the wicked
is no more,
But the righteous *has* an everlasting
foundation.

26 As vinegar to the teeth and smoke to the
eyes,
So *is* the lazy *man* to those who send him.

27 The fear of the LORD prolongs days,
But the years of the wicked will be
shortened.

28 The hope of the righteous *will be* gladness,
But the expectation of the wicked will
perish.

29 The way of the LORD *is* strength for the
upright,
But destruction *will come* to the workers of
iniquity.

30 The righteous will never be removed,
But the wicked will not inhabit the earth.

31 The mouth of the righteous brings forth
wisdom,
But the perverse tongue will be cut out.

32 The lips of the righteous know what is
acceptable,
But the mouth of the wicked *what is*
perverse.

11 Dishonest scales *are* an abomination
to the LORD,
But a just weight *is* His delight.

2 When pride comes, then comes shame;
But with the humble *is* wisdom.

3 The integrity of the upright will guide
them,
But the perversity of the unfaithful will
destroy them.

4 Riches do not profit in the day of wrath,
But righteousness delivers from death.

5 The righteousness of the blameless will
direct[a] his way aright,
But the wicked will fall by his own
wickedness.

10:21 [a]Literally *heart* **11:5** [a]Or *make smooth* or
straight

6 The righteousness of the upright will
      deliver them,
   But the unfaithful will be caught by *their*
      lust.

7 When a wicked man dies, *his* expectation
      will perish,
   And the hope of the unjust perishes.

8 The righteous is delivered from trouble,
   And it comes to the wicked instead.

9 The hypocrite with *his* mouth destroys his
      neighbor,
   But through knowledge the righteous will
      be delivered.

10 When it goes well with the righteous, the
      city rejoices;
   And when the wicked perish, *there is*
      jubilation.

11 By the blessing of the upright the city is
      exalted,
   But it is overthrown by the mouth of the
      wicked.

12 He who is devoid of wisdom despises his
      neighbor,
   But a man of understanding holds his
      peace.

13 A talebearer reveals secrets,
   But he who is of a faithful spirit conceals a
      matter.

14 Where *there is* no counsel, the people fall;
   But in the multitude of counselors *there is*
      safety.

15 He who is surety for a stranger will suffer,
   But one who hates being surety is secure.

16 A gracious woman retains honor,
   But ruthless *men* retain riches.

17 The merciful man does good for his own
      soul,
   But *he who is* cruel troubles his own flesh.

18 The wicked *man* does deceptive work,
   But he who sows righteousness *will have* a
      sure reward.

19 As righteousness *leads* to life,
   So he who pursues evil *pursues it* to his
      own death.

20 Those who are of a perverse heart *are* an
      abomination to the LORD,
   But *the* blameless in their ways *are* His
      delight.

21 *Though they* join forces,[a] the wicked will
      not go unpunished;

The Law of the Inner Circle: Your Advisors Will Make or Break You

(Proverbs 11:14)

Every leader ought to build an inner circle that adds value to him or her and to the leadership of the organization. But choose well, for the members of this inner circle will become your closest confidantes; your inner circle will make you or break you.

Proverbs 11:14 says, "Where there is no counsel, the people fall; but in the multitude of counselors there is safety." So who belongs in the "council," in this inner circle? Strive for the following:

1. Creative people
2. Loyal people
3. People who share your vision
4. Wise and intelligent people
5. People with complementary gifts
6. People with influence
7. People of faith
8. People of integrity

   But the posterity of the righteous will be
      delivered.

22 *As* a ring of gold in a swine's snout,
   So is a lovely woman who lacks discretion.

23 The desire of the righteous *is* only good,
   But the expectation of the wicked *is*
      wrath.

24 There is *one* who scatters, yet increases
      more;
   And there is *one* who withholds more than
      is right,
   But it *leads* to poverty.

25 The generous soul will be made rich,
   And he who waters will also be watered
      himself.

26 The people will curse him who withholds
      grain,
   But blessing *will be* on the head of him
      who sells *it*.

11:21 [a]Literally *hand to hand*

27 He who earnestly seeks good finds favor,
But trouble will come to him who seeks *evil*.

28 He who trusts in his riches will fall,
But the righteous will flourish like foliage.

29 He who troubles his own house will inherit the wind,
And the fool *will be* servant to the wise of heart.

30 The fruit of the righteous *is a* tree of life,
And he who wins souls *is* wise.

31 If the righteous will be recompensed on the earth,
How much more the ungodly and the sinner.

12 Whoever loves instruction loves knowledge,
But he who hates correction *is* stupid.

2 A good *man* obtains favor from the LORD,
But a man of wicked intentions He will condemn.

3 A man is not established by wickedness,
But the root of the righteous cannot be moved.

4 An excellent[a] wife *is* the crown of her husband,
But she who causes shame *is* like rottenness in his bones.

5 The thoughts of the righteous *are* right,
But the counsels of the wicked *are* deceitful.

6 The words of the wicked *are,* "Lie in wait for blood,"
But the mouth of the upright will deliver them.

7 The wicked are overthrown and *are* no more,
But the house of the righteous will stand.

8 A man will be commended according to his wisdom,
But he who is of a perverse heart will be despised.

9 Better *is the one* who is slighted but has a servant,
Than he who honors himself but lacks bread.

10 A righteous *man* regards the life of his animal,
But the tender mercies of the wicked *are* cruel.

11 He who tills his land will be satisfied with bread,
But he who follows frivolity *is* devoid of understanding.[a]

12 The wicked covet the catch of evil *men,*
But the root of the righteous yields *fruit.*

13 The wicked is ensnared by the transgression of *his* lips,
But the righteous will come through trouble.

14 A man will be satisfied with good by the fruit of *his* mouth,
And the recompense of a man's hands will be rendered to him.

15 The way of a fool *is* right in his own eyes,
But he who heeds counsel *is* wise.

16 A fool's wrath is known at once,
But a prudent *man* covers shame.

17 He *who* speaks truth declares righteousness,
But a false witness, deceit.

18 There is one who speaks like the piercings of a sword,
But the tongue of the wise *promotes* health.

19 The truthful lip shall be established forever,
But a lying tongue *is* but for a moment.

20 Deceit is in the heart of those who devise evil,
But counselors of peace have joy.

21 No grave trouble will overtake the righteous,
But the wicked shall be filled with evil.

22 Lying lips *are* an abomination to the LORD,
But those who deal truthfully *are* His delight.

23 A prudent man conceals knowledge,
But the heart of fools proclaims foolishness.

24 The hand of the diligent will rule,
But the lazy *man* will be put to forced labor.

12:4 [a]Literally *A wife of valor* **12:11** [a]Literally *heart*

25 Anxiety in the heart of man causes
    depression,
    But a good word makes it glad.

26 The righteous should choose his friends
    carefully,
    For the way of the wicked leads them astray.

27 The lazy *man* does not roast what he took
    in hunting,
    But diligence *is* man's precious possession.

28 In the way of righteousness *is* life,
    And in *its* pathway *there is* no death.

13

A wise son *heeds* his father's
instruction,
But a scoffer does not listen to
rebuke.

2 A man shall eat well by the fruit of *his*
    mouth,
    But the soul of the unfaithful feeds on
    violence.

3 He who guards his mouth preserves his
    life,
    But he who opens wide his lips shall have
    destruction.

4 The soul of a lazy *man* desires, and *has*
    nothing;
    But the soul of the diligent shall be made
    rich.

5 A righteous *man* hates lying,
    But a wicked *man* is loathsome and comes
    to shame.

6 Righteousness guards *him whose* way is
    blameless,
    But wickedness overthrows the sinner.

7 There is one who makes himself rich, yet
    has nothing;
    And one who makes himself poor, yet *has*
    great riches.

8 The ransom of a man's life *is* his riches,
    But the poor does not hear rebuke.

9 The light of the righteous rejoices,
    But the lamp of the wicked will be put
    out.

10 By pride comes nothing but strife,
    But with the well-advised *is* wisdom.

11 Wealth *gained by* dishonesty will be
    diminished,
    But he who gathers by labor will increase.

12 Hope deferred makes the heart sick,
    But *when* the desire comes, *it is* a tree of
    life.

13 He who despises the word will be destroyed,
    But he who fears the commandment will
    be rewarded.

14 The law of the wise *is* a fountain of life,
    To turn *one* away from the snares of death.

15 Good understanding gains favor,
    But the way of the unfaithful *is* hard.

16 Every prudent *man* acts with knowledge,
    But a fool lays open *his* folly.

17 A wicked messenger falls into trouble,
    But a faithful ambassador *brings* health.

18 Poverty and shame *will come* to him who
    disdains correction,
    But he who regards a rebuke will be
    honored.

19 A desire accomplished is sweet to the soul,
    But *it is* an abomination to fools to depart
    from evil.

20 He who walks with wise *men* will be wise,
    But the companion of fools will be
    destroyed.

Effective Leadership Invites Partnerships

(Proverbs 13:20)

Y ou become like those with whom you partner. Choose your partners for many of the
same reasons a leader chooses his or her
inner circle. Choose those who add value to
you and can benefit from you. Both leaders
and organizations should see improvement for
having entered into partnership.

21 Evil pursues sinners,
    But to the righteous, good shall be repaid.

22 A good *man* leaves an inheritance to his
    children's children,

But the wealth of the sinner is stored up
for the righteous.

23 Much food *is* in the fallow *ground* of the
poor,
And for lack of justice there is waste.[a]

24 He who spares his rod hates his son,
But he who loves him disciplines him
promptly.

25 The righteous eats to the satisfying of his
soul,
But the stomach of the wicked shall be in
want.

14

The wise woman builds her house,
But the foolish pulls it down with
her hands.

2 He who walks in his uprightness fears the
LORD,
But *he who is* perverse in his ways despises
Him.

3 In the mouth of a fool *is* a rod of pride,
But the lips of the wise will preserve them.

4 Where no oxen *are,* the trough *is* clean;
But much increase *comes* by the strength of
an ox.

5 A faithful witness does not lie,
But a false witness will utter lies.

6 A scoffer seeks wisdom and does not *find
it,*
But knowledge *is* easy to him who
understands.

7 Go from the presence of a foolish man,
When you do not perceive *in him* the lips
of knowledge.

8 The wisdom of the prudent *is* to
understand his way,
But the folly of fools *is* deceit.

9 Fools mock at sin,
But among the upright *there is* favor.

10 The heart knows its own bitterness,
And a stranger does not share its joy.

11 The house of the wicked will be
overthrown,
But the tent of the upright will flourish.

12 There is a way *that seems* right to a man,
But its end *is* the way of death.

13 Even in laughter the heart may sorrow,
And the end of mirth *may be* grief.

14 The backslider in heart will be filled with
his own ways,
But a good man *will be satisfied* from above.[a]

15 The simple believes every word,
But the prudent considers well his steps.

16 A wise *man* fears and departs from evil,
But a fool rages and is self-confident.

17 A quick-tempered *man* acts foolishly,
And a man of wicked intentions is hated.

18 The simple inherit folly,
But the prudent are crowned with
knowledge.

19 The evil will bow before the good,
And the wicked at the gates of the
righteous.

20 The poor *man* is hated even by his own
neighbor,
But the rich *has* many friends.

21 He who despises his neighbor sins;
But he who has mercy on the poor, happy
is he.

22 Do they not go astray who devise evil?
But mercy and truth *belong* to those who
devise good.

23 In all labor there is profit,
But idle chatter[a] *leads* only to poverty.

24 The crown of the wise is their riches,
But the foolishness of fools *is* folly.

25 A true witness delivers souls,
But a deceitful *witness* speaks lies.

26 In the fear of the LORD *there is* strong
confidence,
And His children will have a place of
refuge.

27 The fear of the LORD *is* a fountain of life,
To turn *one* away from the snares of death.

28 In a multitude of people *is* a king's honor,
But in the lack of people *is* the downfall
of a prince.

13:23 [a]Literally *what is swept away* **14:14** [a]Literally
from above himself **14:23** [a]Literally *talk of the lips*

29 *He who is* slow to wrath has great
understanding,
But *he who is* impulsive[a] exalts folly.

30 A sound heart *is* life to the body,
But envy *is* rottenness to the bones.

31 He who oppresses the poor reproaches his
Maker,
But he who honors Him has mercy on the
needy.

32 The wicked is banished in his wickedness,
But the righteous has a refuge in his death.

33 Wisdom rests in the heart of him who has
understanding,
But *what is* in the heart of fools is made
known.

34 Righteousness exalts a nation,
But sin *is* a reproach to *any* people.

35 The king's favor *is* toward a wise servant,
But his wrath *is against* him who causes
shame.

15 A soft answer turns away wrath,
But a harsh word stirs up anger.
2 The tongue of the wise uses
knowledge rightly,
But the mouth of fools pours forth
foolishness.

3 The eyes of the LORD *are* in every place,
Keeping watch on the evil and the good.

4 A wholesome tongue *is* a tree of life,
But perverseness in it breaks the spirit.

5 A fool despises his father's instruction,
But he who receives correction is prudent.

6 *In* the house of the righteous *there is* much
treasure,
But in the revenue of the wicked is trouble.

7 The lips of the wise disperse knowledge,
But the heart of the fool *does* not *do* so.

8 The sacrifice of the wicked *is* an
abomination to the LORD,
But the prayer of the upright *is* His delight.

9 The way of the wicked *is* an abomination
to the LORD,
But He loves him who follows
righteousness.

10 Harsh discipline *is* for him who forsakes
the way,
And he who hates correction will die.

11 Hell[a] and Destruction[b] *are* before the
LORD;

14:29 [a]Literally *short of spirit* **15:11** [a]Or *Sheol*
[b]Hebrew *Abaddon*

Master Communication and You Manage Conflict

(Proverbs 15:1–7)

God rightly expects leaders to manage conflict within their organizations. But how can you best accomplish this?

A good place to start is Proverbs 15:1—yet while we often quote this verse, we seldom practice it. Sometimes only the leaders are given liberty to express anger, and sooner or later this kind of unhealthy environment comes back to haunt them. Leaders must create safe places for communication. Master communication and you manage conflict. Look at the first seven verses of Proverbs 15 and note its counsel about managing conflict:

1. Remain calm and gentle when confronting conflict, and your example will become contagious (v. 1).
2. Speak wisely, making sure your information is truthful and accurate (v. 2).
3. Remember, God is the ultimate Judge and will execute justice (v. 3).
4. Use your words to foster healing; fix the problem, not the blame (v. 4).
5. Stay teachable; be open to correction and quick to apologize when wrong (v. 5).
6. Add value to everyone who contacts you, even when you disagree (v. 6).
7. Speak words that spread knowledge and understanding (v. 7).

So how much more the hearts of the sons
of men.

12 A scoffer does not love one who corrects
him,
Nor will he go to the wise.

13 A merry heart makes a cheerful
countenance,
But by sorrow of the heart the spirit is
broken.

14 The heart of him who has understanding
seeks knowledge,
But the mouth of fools feeds on
foolishness.

15 All the days of the afflicted *are* evil,
But he who is of a merry heart *has* a
continual feast.

16 Better *is* a little with the fear of the LORD,
Than great treasure with trouble.

17 Better *is* a dinner of herbs[a] where love is,
Than a fatted calf with hatred.

18 A wrathful man stirs up strife,
But *he who is* slow to anger allays
contention.

19 The way of the lazy *man is* like a hedge of
thorns,
But the way of the upright *is* a highway.

20 A wise son makes a father glad,
But a foolish man despises his mother.

21 Folly *is* joy *to him who is* destitute of
discernment,
But a man of understanding walks
uprightly.

22 Without counsel, plans go awry,
But in the multitude of counselors they
are established.

23 A man has joy by the answer of his
mouth,
And a word *spoken* in due season, how
good *it is!*

24 The way of life *winds* upward for the wise,
That he may turn away from hell[a] below.

25 The LORD will destroy the house of the
proud,

But He will establish the boundary of the
widow.

26 The thoughts of the wicked *are* an
abomination to the LORD,
But *the words* of the pure *are* pleasant.

27 He who is greedy for gain troubles his
own house,
But he who hates bribes will live.

28 The heart of the righteous studies how to
answer,
But the mouth of the wicked pours forth
evil.

29 The LORD *is* far from the wicked,
But He hears the prayer of the righteous.

30 The light of the eyes rejoices the heart,
And a good report makes the bones
healthy.[a]

31 The ear that hears the rebukes of life
Will abide among the wise.

32 He who disdains instruction despises his
own soul,
But he who heeds rebuke gets
understanding.

33 The fear of the LORD *is* the instruction of
wisdom,
And before honor *is* humility.

16 The preparations of the heart *belong*
to man,
But the answer of the tongue *is* from
the LORD.

2 All the ways of a man *are* pure in his own
eyes,
But the LORD weighs the spirits.

3 Commit your works to the LORD,
And your thoughts will be established.

4 The LORD has made all for Himself,
Yes, even the wicked for the day of doom.

5 Everyone proud in heart *is* an abomination
to the LORD;
Though they join forces,[a] none will go
unpunished.

15:17 [a]Or *vegetables* **15:24** [a]Or *Sheol*
15:30 [a]Literally *fat* **16:5** [a]Literally *hand to hand*

6 In mercy and truth
Atonement is provided for iniquity;
And by the fear of the LORD *one* departs
from evil.

7 When a man's ways please the LORD,
He makes even his enemies to be at peace
with him.

8 Better *is* a little with righteousness,
Than vast revenues without justice.

9 A man's heart plans his way,
But the LORD directs his steps.

10 Divination *is* on the lips of the king;
His mouth must not transgress in judgment.

11 Honest weights and scales *are* the LORD's;
All the weights in the bag *are* His work.

12 *It is* an abomination for kings to commit
wickedness,
For a throne is established by
righteousness.

13 Righteous lips *are* the delight of kings,
And they love him who speaks *what is*
right.

14 As messengers of death *is* the king's wrath,
But a wise man will appease it.

15 In the light of the king's face *is* life,
And his favor *is* like a cloud of the latter
rain.

16 How much better to get wisdom than
gold!
And to get understanding is to be chosen
rather than silver.

17 The highway of the upright *is* to depart
from evil;
He who keeps his way preserves his soul.

18 Pride *goes* before destruction,
And a haughty spirit before a fall.

19 Better *to be* of a humble spirit with the
lowly,
Than to divide the spoil with the proud.

20 He who heeds the word wisely will find
good,
And whoever trusts in the LORD, happy
is he.

21 The wise in heart will be called prudent,
And sweetness of the lips increases
learning.

22 Understanding *is* a wellspring of life to
him who has it.
But the correction of fools *is* folly.

23 The heart of the wise teaches his
mouth,
And adds learning to his lips.

The Law of Navigation

(Proverbs 16:1–3)

Effective leaders practice the Law of Navigation. Proverbs 16 opens with these words: "The preparations of the heart belong to man, but the answer of the tongue is from the LORD. All the ways of a man are pure in his own eyes, but the LORD weighs the spirits. Commit your works to the LORD, and your thoughts will be established" (vv. 1–3).

These verses teach us to:

- check the source of our wisdom
- check our motives
- check the outcome we are pursuing

Consider five key words to understanding how God helps leaders to navigate their way through life:

1. *Process:* God's plan usually unfolds over time. What is He revealing progressively?
2. *Purpose:* God wants to accomplish His purposes. Why were you created?
3. *Potential:* God will use your gifts and passion. Does this goal fit who you are?
4. *Prioritize:* God will ask you to adjust your time and energy. What steps must you take?
5. *Proceed:* God will eventually require you to act. When should you start?

24 Pleasant words *are like* a honeycomb,
   Sweetness to the soul and health to the
      bones.

25 There is a way *that seems* right to a man,
   But its end *is* the way of death.

26 The person who labors, labors for himself,
   For his *hungry* mouth drives him *on.*

27 An ungodly man digs up evil,
   And *it is* on his lips like a burning fire.
28 A perverse man sows strife,
   And a whisperer separates the best of
      friends.
29 A violent man entices his neighbor,
   And leads him in a way *that is* not good.
30 He winks his eye to devise perverse things;
   He purses his lips *and* brings about evil.

31 The silver-haired head *is* a crown of glory,
   If it is found in the way of righteousness.

32 *He who is* slow to anger *is* better than the
      mighty,
   And he who rules his spirit than he who
      takes a city.

33 The lot is cast into the lap,
   But its every decision *is* from the LORD.

17 Better *is* a dry morsel with quietness,
   Than a house full of feasting[a] *with*
      strife.

2 A wise servant will rule over a son who
      causes shame,
   And will share an inheritance among the
      brothers.

3 The refining pot *is* for silver and the
      furnace for gold,
   But the LORD tests the hearts.

4 An evildoer gives heed to false lips;
   A liar listens eagerly to a spiteful tongue.

5 He who mocks the poor reproaches his
      Maker;
   He who is glad at calamity will not go
      unpunished.

6 Children's children *are* the crown of old
      men,
   And the glory of children *is* their father.

7 Excellent speech is not becoming to a fool,
   Much less lying lips to a prince.

It's Not About Position, but Empowerment

(Proverbs 17:2)

Our influence has less to do with our position or title than it does with the life we live. It's not about position, but production. It is not the education we get, but the empowerment we give, that makes a difference to others.

The key word is *credibility.* We gain credibility when our life matches our talk and when both add value to others. In the words of Proverbs 17:2, it's better to be a wise slave than a foolish son. Answer the following vital questions:

1. *Consistency:* Are you the same person no matter who's with you?
2. *Choices:* Do you make decisions based on how they benefit *you* or *others?*
3. *Credit:* Are you quick to recognize others for their efforts when you succeed?
4. *Character:* Do you work harder at your image or your integrity?
5. *Credibility:* Have you recognized that credibility is a victory, not a gift?

---

8 A present *is* a precious stone in the eyes of
      its possessor;
   Wherever he turns, he prospers.

9 He who covers a transgression seeks love,
   But he who repeats a matter separates
      friends.

10 Rebuke is more effective for a wise *man*
   Than a hundred blows on a fool.

11 An evil *man* seeks only rebellion;
   Therefore a cruel messenger will be sent
      against him.

12 Let a man meet a bear robbed of her cubs,
   Rather than a fool in his folly.

13 Whoever rewards evil for good,
   Evil will not depart from his house.

17:1 [a]*Or sacrificial meals*

14 The beginning of strife *is like* releasing
water;
Therefore stop contention before a quarrel
starts.

15 He who justifies the wicked, and he who
condemns the just,
Both of them alike *are* an abomination to
the LORD.

16 Why *is there* in the hand of a fool the
purchase price of wisdom,
Since *he has* no heart *for it?*

17 A friend loves at all times,
And a brother is born for adversity.

18 A man devoid of understanding shakes
hands in a pledge,
And becomes surety for his friend.

19 He who loves transgression loves strife,
And he who exalts his gate seeks
destruction.

20 He who has a deceitful heart finds no good,
And he who has a perverse tongue falls
into evil.

21 He who begets a scoffer *does so* to his
sorrow,
And the father of a fool has no joy.

22 A merry heart does good, *like* medicine,[a]
But a broken spirit dries the bones.

23 A wicked *man* accepts a bribe behind the
back[a]
To pervert the ways of justice.

24 Wisdom *is* in the sight of him who has
understanding,
But the eyes of a fool *are* on the ends of
the earth.

25 A foolish son *is* a grief to his father,
And bitterness to her who bore him.

26 Also, to punish the righteous *is* not good,
Nor to strike princes for *their* uprightness.

27 He who has knowledge spares his words,
And a man of understanding is of a calm
spirit.

28 Even a fool is counted wise when he holds
his peace;

When he shuts his lips, *he is* considered
perceptive.

18 A man who isolates himself seeks his
own desire;
He rages against all wise judgment.

2 A fool has no delight in understanding,
But in expressing his own heart.

3 When the wicked comes, contempt comes
also;
And with dishonor *comes* reproach.

4 The words of a man's mouth *are* deep
waters;
The wellspring of wisdom *is* a flowing
brook.

5 *It is* not good to show partiality to the
wicked,
Or to overthrow the righteous in
judgment.

6 A fool's lips enter into contention,
And his mouth calls for blows.

7 A fool's mouth *is* his destruction,
And his lips *are* the snare of his soul.

8 The words of a talebearer *are* like tasty
trifles,[a]
And they go down into the inmost body.

9 He who is slothful in his work
Is a brother to him who is a great destroyer.

10 The name of the LORD *is* a strong tower;
The righteous run to it and are safe.

11 The rich man's wealth *is* his strong city,
And like a high wall in his own esteem.

12 Before destruction the heart of a man is
haughty,
And before honor *is* humility.

13 He who answers a matter before he
hears *it,*
It *is* folly and shame to him.

14 The spirit of a man will sustain him in
sickness,
But who can bear a broken spirit?

17:22 [a]Or *makes medicine even better* **17:23** [a]*Literally
from the bosom* **18:8** [a]A Jewish tradition reads
wounds.

The Law of E. F. Hutton: The Evolution of Leadership

(Proverbs 18:21)

Few muscles in a body wield more power than the little one inside the mouth. The Bible says, "Death and life are in the power of the tongue, and those who love it will eat its fruit" (Prov. 18:21). Leaders who understand this greatly increase their influence.

Our understanding of leadership has evolved over the last five or six decades. The way people expect leaders to lead has changed. Many have said our culture has witnessed four styles of leadership since 1950:

1. *The Military Commander:* Leaders came out of the army and expected unquestioning obedience from subordinates. Many of our presidents had military backgrounds.
2. *The Chief Executive Officer:* Most leaders migrated to a different style driven by vision and shared by everyone. Yet it was still top down and possibly very narrow in scope.
3. *The Coach:* Leaders moved toward a coach model where they saw employees as players on a team. This produced even better results, but still limited the possibilities to the vision of the coach.
4. *The Poet and Gardener:* Today, leaders see the need to express the heart of the team, as a poet gives words to the heart of readers. They develop players using encouragement and direction. They recognize the power of words and use them wisely.

---

15 The heart of the prudent acquires
   knowledge,
   And the ear of the wise seeks knowledge.

16 A man's gift makes room for him,
   And brings him before great men.

17 The first *one* to plead his cause *seems* right,
   Until his neighbor comes and examines
   him.

18 Casting lots causes contentions to cease,
   And keeps the mighty apart.

19 A brother offended *is harder to win* than a
   strong city,
   And contentions *are* like the bars of a
   castle.

20 A man's stomach shall be satisfied from the
   fruit of his mouth;
   From the produce of his lips he shall be
   filled.

21 Death and life *are* in the power of the
   tongue,
   And those who love it will eat its fruit.

22 *He who* finds a wife finds a good *thing,*
   And obtains favor from the LORD.

23 The poor *man* uses entreaties,
   But the rich answers roughly.

24 A man *who has* friends must himself be
   friendly,[a]
   But there is a friend *who* sticks closer than
   a brother.

19 Better *is* the poor who walks in his
   integrity
   Than *one who is* perverse in his lips,
   and is a fool.

2 Also it is not good *for* a soul *to be* without
   knowledge,
   And he sins who hastens with *his* feet.

3 The foolishness of a man twists his way,
   And his heart frets against the LORD.

4 Wealth makes many friends,
   But the poor is separated from his friend.

5 A false witness will not go unpunished,
   And *he who* speaks lies will not escape.

18:24 [a]Following Greek manuscripts, Syriac, Targum, and Vulgate; Masoretic Text reads *may come to ruin.*

6 Many entreat the favor of the nobility,
And every man *is* a friend to one who
gives gifts.

7 All the brothers of the poor hate him;
How much more do his friends go far
from him!
He may pursue *them with* words, *yet* they
abandon *him.*

8 He who gets wisdom loves his own soul;
He who keeps understanding will find
good.

9 A false witness will not go unpunished,
And *he who* speaks lies shall perish.

10 Luxury is not fitting for a fool,
Much less for a servant to rule over
princes.

11 The discretion of a man makes him slow
to anger,
And his glory *is* to overlook a
transgression.

12 The king's wrath *is* like the roaring of a
lion,
But his favor *is* like dew on the grass.

13 A foolish son *is* the ruin of his father,
And the contentions of a wife *are* a
continual dripping.

14 Houses and riches *are* an inheritance from
fathers,
But a prudent wife *is* from the LORD.

15 Laziness casts *one* into a deep sleep,
And an idle person will suffer hunger.

16 He who keeps the commandment keeps
his soul;
But he who is careless[a] of his ways will die.

17 He who has pity on the poor lends to the
LORD,
And He will pay back what he has given.

18 Chasten your son while there is hope,
And do not set your heart on his
destruction.[a]

19 *A man of* great wrath will suffer
punishment;
For if you rescue *him,* you will have to do
it again.

20 Listen to counsel and receive instruction,
That you may be wise in your latter days.

21 There are many plans in a man's heart,
Nevertheless the LORD's counsel—that will
stand.

22 What is desired in a man is kindness,
And a poor man is better than a liar.

23 The fear of the LORD *leads* to life,
And *he who has it* will abide in satisfaction;
He will not be visited with evil.

24 A lazy *man* buries his hand in the bowl,[a]
And will not so much as bring it to his
mouth again.

25 Strike a scoffer, and the simple will
become wary;
Rebuke one who has understanding, *and*
he will discern knowledge.

26 He who mistreats *his* father *and* chases
away *his* mother
Is a son who causes shame and brings
reproach.

27 Cease listening to instruction, my son,
And you will stray from the words of
knowledge.

28 A disreputable witness scorns justice,
And the mouth of the wicked devours
iniquity.

29 Judgments are prepared for scoffers,
And beatings for the backs of fools.

20 Wine *is* a mocker,
Strong drink *is* a brawler,
And whoever is led astray by it is not
wise.

2 The wrath[a] of a king *is* like the roaring of
a lion;
Whoever provokes him to anger sins *against*
his own life.

19:16 [a]Literally *despises,* figurative of recklessness
or carelessness **19:18** [a]Literally *to put him to
death;* a Jewish tradition reads *on his crying.*
19:24 [a]Septuagint and Syriac read *bosom;* Targum
and Vulgate read *armpit.* **20:2** [a]Literally *fear* or *terror*
which is produced by the king's wrath

3 *It is* honorable for a man to stop
striving,
Since any fool can start a quarrel.

4 The lazy *man* will not plow because of
winter;
He will beg during harvest and *have*
nothing.

5 Counsel in the heart of man *is like* deep
water,
But a man of understanding will draw it
out.

6 Most men will proclaim each his own
goodness,
But who can find a faithful man?

7 The righteous *man* walks in his integrity;
His children *are* blessed after him.

8 A king who sits on the throne of
judgment
Scatters all evil with his eyes.

9 Who can say, "I have made my heart
clean,
I am pure from my sin"?

10 Diverse weights *and* diverse measures,
They *are* both alike, an abomination to the
LORD.

11 Even a child is known by his deeds,
Whether what he does *is* pure and right.

12 The hearing ear and the seeing eye,
The LORD has made them both.

13 Do not love sleep, lest you come to
poverty;
Open your eyes, *and* you will be satisfied
with bread.

14 " *It is* good for nothing,"[a] cries the buyer;
But when he has gone his way, then he
boasts.

15 There is gold and a multitude of rubies,
But the lips of knowledge *are* a precious
jewel.

16 Take the garment of one who is surety *for*
a stranger,
And hold it as a pledge *when it* is for a
seductress.

17 Bread gained by deceit *is* sweet to a man,
But afterward his mouth will be filled with
gravel.

18 Plans are established by counsel;
By wise counsel wage war.

19 He who goes about *as* a talebearer reveals
secrets;
Therefore do not associate with one who
flatters with his lips.

20 Whoever curses his father or his mother,
His lamp will be put out in deep darkness.

21 An inheritance gained hastily at the
beginning
Will not be blessed at the end.

22 Do not say, "I will recompense evil";
Wait for the LORD, and He will save you.

23 Diverse weights *are* an abomination to the
LORD,
And dishonest scales *are* not good.

24 A man's steps *are* of the LORD;
How then can a man understand his own
way?

25 *It is* a snare for a man to devote rashly
something as holy,
And afterward to reconsider *his* vows.

26 A wise king sifts out the wicked,
And brings the threshing wheel over
them.

27 The spirit of a man *is* the lamp of the
LORD,
Searching all the inner depths of his heart.[a]

28 Mercy and truth preserve the king,
And by lovingkindness he upholds his
throne.

29 The glory of young men *is* their strength,
And the splendor of old men *is* their gray
head.

30 Blows that hurt cleanse away evil,
As *do* stripes the inner depths of the heart.[a]

20:14 [a]Literally *evil, evil* **20:27** [a]Literally *the rooms of
the belly* **20:30** [a]Literally *the rooms of the belly*

21

The king's heart *is* in the hand of the LORD,
Like the rivers of water; He turns it wherever He wishes.

Leaders Know the Difference

(Proverbs 21:1)

Leaders can and should make their plans, but they must never forget that it is God who controls the future. "The king's heart is in the hand of the LORD," says the Bible. "Like the rivers of water; He turns it wherever He wishes" (Prov. 21:1). Successful leaders remember this and therefore know the difference between being in charge and being in control.

We kid ourselves if we think we are in control. We may have charge of a group, but the best we can do is remain *under* control. God is the Ultimate Leader, and He is forever *in* control. It has been rightly said: "We don't know what the future holds, but we do know the One who holds the future."

2 Every way of a man *is* right in his own eyes,
But the LORD weighs the hearts.

3 To do righteousness and justice
Is more acceptable to the LORD than sacrifice.

4 A haughty look, a proud heart,
And the plowing[a] of the wicked *are* sin.

5 The plans of the diligent *lead* surely to plenty,
But *those of* everyone who *is* hasty, surely to poverty.

6 Getting treasures by a lying tongue
Is the fleeting fantasy of those who seek death.[a]

7 The violence of the wicked will destroy them,[a]
Because they refuse to do justice.

8 The way of a guilty man *is* perverse;[a]
But *as for* the pure, his work *is* right.

9 Better to dwell in a corner of a housetop,
Than in a house shared with a contentious woman.

10 The soul of the wicked desires evil;
His neighbor finds no favor in his eyes.

11 When the scoffer is punished, the simple is made wise;
But when the wise is instructed, he receives knowledge.

12 The righteous *God* wisely considers the house of the wicked,
Overthrowing the wicked for *their* wickedness.

13 Whoever shuts his ears to the cry of the poor
Will also cry himself and not be heard.

14 A gift in secret pacifies anger,
And a bribe behind the back,[a] strong wrath.

15 *It is* a joy for the just to do justice,
But destruction *will come* to the workers of iniquity.

16 A man who wanders from the way of understanding
Will rest in the assembly of the dead.

17 He who loves pleasure *will be* a poor man;
He who loves wine and oil will not be rich.

18 The wicked *shall be* a ransom for the righteous,
And the unfaithful for the upright.

19 Better to dwell in the wilderness,
Than with a contentious and angry woman.

20 *There is* desirable treasure,
And oil in the dwelling of the wise,
But a foolish man squanders it.

21:4 [a]Or *lamp* **21:6** [a]Septuagint reads *Pursue vanity on the snares of death;* Vulgate reads *Is vain and foolish, and shall stumble on the snares of death;* Targum reads *They shall be destroyed, and they shall fall who seek death.* **21:7** [a]Literally *drag them away* **21:8** [a]Or *The way of a man is perverse and strange* **21:14** [a]Literally *in the bosom*

²¹ He who follows righteousness and mercy
Finds life, righteousness, and honor.

²² A wise *man* scales the city of the mighty,
And brings down the trusted stronghold.

²³ Whoever guards his mouth and tongue
Keeps his soul from troubles.

²⁴ A proud *and* haughty *man*—"Scoffer" *is* his
name;
He acts with arrogant pride.

²⁵ The desire of the lazy *man* kills him,
For his hands refuse to labor.
²⁶ He covets greedily all day long,
But the righteous gives and does not spare.

²⁷ The sacrifice of the wicked *is* an
abomination;
How much more *when* he brings it with
wicked intent!

²⁸ A false witness shall perish,
But the man who hears *him* will speak
endlessly.

²⁹ A wicked man hardens his face,
But *as for* the upright, he establishes[a] his way.

³⁰ *There is* no wisdom or understanding
Or counsel against the LORD.

³¹ The horse *is* prepared for the day of battle,
But deliverance *is* of the LORD.

22 A *good* name is to be chosen rather
than great riches,
Loving favor rather than silver and
gold.

² The rich and the poor have this in
common,
The LORD *is* the maker of them all.

³ A prudent *man* foresees evil and hides
himself,
But the simple pass on and are punished.

⁴ By humility *and* the fear of the LORD
Are riches and honor and life.

⁵ Thorns *and* snares *are* in the way of the
perverse;
He who guards his soul will be far from
them.

⁶ Train up a child in the way he should go,
And when he is old he will not depart
from it.

⁷ The rich rules over the poor,
And the borrower *is* servant to the
lender.

⁸ He who sows iniquity will reap sorrow,
And the rod of his anger will fail.

⁹ He who has a generous eye will be
blessed,
For he gives of his bread to the poor.

¹⁰ Cast out the scoffer, and contention will
leave;
Yes, strife and reproach will cease.

¹¹ He who loves purity of heart
And has grace on his lips,
The king *will be* his friend.

¹² The eyes of the LORD preserve
knowledge,
But He overthrows the words of the
faithless.

¹³ The lazy *man* says, "*There is* a lion outside!
I shall be slain in the streets!"

¹⁴ The mouth of an immoral woman *is* a
deep pit;
He who is abhorred by the LORD will fall
there.

¹⁵ Foolishness *is* bound up in the heart of a
child;
The rod of correction will drive it far
from him.

¹⁶ He who oppresses the poor to increase his
riches,
And he who gives to the rich, *will* surely
come to poverty.

Sayings of the Wise
¹⁷ Incline your ear and hear the words of the
wise,
And apply your heart to my knowledge;
¹⁸ For *it is* a pleasant thing if you keep them
within you;
Let them all be fixed upon your lips,
¹⁹ So that your trust may be in the LORD;

21:29 [a]Qere and Septuagint read *understands.*

Leading Our Children

(Proverbs 22:6)

God calls parents to lead their children. He tells them that if they train up a child in the way he should go, when he is old he will not depart from it (Prov. 22:6). And just how does a parent become a good leader for a child? Partly by focusing on three key words:

1. **Modeling:** Abraham Lincoln said, "There is but one way to train up a child in the way he should go, and that is to travel it yourself." A good example is worth a thousand sermons. What you do has more impact on your child than all the lectures you could ever give.

2. **Management:** Good management is the ability to discern the uniqueness of a child and teach him or her accordingly. We are to train up a child in the way *he* should go. This may mean we will have to adapt our style, depending on the child's temperament and wiring.

3. **Memories:** Parents should create memories. Why? Because memories are more important than things. Note that the verse says, "When he is old, he will not depart. . . ." This implies that the child retains some memories of his early experiences and embraces them later in life.

I have instructed you today, even you.
20 Have I not written to you excellent
things
Of counsels and knowledge,
21 That I may make you know the certainty
of the words of truth,
That you may answer words of truth
To those who send to you?

22 Do not rob the poor because he *is* poor,
Nor oppress the afflicted at the gate;
23 For the LORD will plead their cause,
And plunder the soul of those who
plunder them.

24 Make no friendship with an angry man,
And with a furious man do not go,
25 Lest you learn his ways
And set a snare for your soul.

26 Do not be one of those who shakes hands
in a pledge,
One of those who is surety for debts;
27 If you have nothing *with which* to pay,
Why should he take away your bed from
under you?

28 Do not remove the ancient landmark
Which your fathers have set.

29 Do you see a man *who* excels in his work?
He will stand before kings;
He will not stand before unknown *men.*

23 When you sit down to eat with a
ruler,
Consider carefully what *is* before
you;
2 And put a knife to your throat
If you *are* a man given to appetite.
3 Do not desire his delicacies,
For they *are* deceptive food.

4 Do not overwork to be rich;
Because of your own understanding, cease!
5 Will you set your eyes on that which is
not?
For *riches* certainly make themselves wings;
They fly away like an eagle *toward* heaven.

6 Do not eat the bread of a miser,[a]
Nor desire his delicacies;
7 For as he thinks in his heart, so *is* he.
"Eat and drink!" he says to you,
But his heart is not with you.
8 The morsel you have eaten, you will vomit
up,
And waste your pleasant words.

9 Do not speak in the hearing of a fool,
For he will despise the wisdom of your
words.

10 Do not remove the ancient landmark,
Nor enter the fields of the fatherless;

23:6 [a]Literally *one who has an evil eye*

Vision: Hope for a Preferred Future

(Proverbs 23:7–19)

Leaders understand the importance of their minds to the future of their organizations. Consider some of the timeless principles offered in Proverbs 23 about our minds and a godly vision for tomorrow:

1. Your thoughts determine your character (v. 7).
2. Be careful of your thoughts; they may break into words at any time (v. 7).
3. Don't waste your thoughts on those who don't hunger for them (v. 9).
4. The first person you lead is you, and the first organ you master is your mind (v. 12).
5. Don't let your mind drift away from God's truth and into vain envy (v. 17).
6. Stay confident that your vision will come to pass (v. 18).
7. Discipline your thoughts to remain steadfast in what you know is right (v. 19).

11 For their Redeemer *is* mighty;
He will plead their cause against you.

12 Apply your heart to instruction,
And your ears to words of knowledge.

13 Do not withhold correction from a child,
For *if* you beat him with a rod, he will not die.

14 You shall beat him with a rod,
And deliver his soul from hell.[a]

15 My son, if your heart is wise,
My heart will rejoice—indeed, I myself;

16 Yes, my inmost being will rejoice
When your lips speak right things.

17 Do not let your heart envy sinners,
But *be zealous* for the fear of the LORD all the day;

18 For surely there is a hereafter,
And your hope will not be cut off.

19 Hear, my son, and be wise;
And guide your heart in the way.

20 Do not mix with winebibbers,
Or with gluttonous eaters of meat;

21 For the drunkard and the glutton will come to poverty,
And drowsiness will clothe *a man* with rags.

22 Listen to your father who begot you,
And do not despise your mother when she is old.

23 Buy the truth, and do not sell *it,*
Also wisdom and instruction and understanding.

24 The father of the righteous will greatly rejoice,
And he who begets a wise *child* will delight in him.

25 Let your father and your mother be glad,
And let her who bore you rejoice.

26 My son, give me your heart,
And let your eyes observe my ways.

27 For a harlot *is* a deep pit,
And a seductress *is* a narrow well.

28 She also lies in wait as *for* a victim,
And increases the unfaithful among men.

29 Who has woe?
Who has sorrow?
Who has contentions?
Who has complaints?
Who has wounds without cause?
Who has redness of eyes?

30 Those who linger long at the wine,
Those who go in search of mixed wine.

31 Do not look on the wine when it is red,
When it sparkles in the cup,
When it swirls around smoothly;

32 At the last it bites like a serpent,
And stings like a viper.

33 Your eyes will see strange things,
And your heart will utter perverse things.

34 Yes, you will be like one who lies down in the midst of the sea,
Or like one who lies at the top of the mast, *saying:*

35 "They have struck me, *but* I was not hurt;
They have beaten me, but I did not feel *it.*
When shall I awake, that I may seek another *drink?*"

23:14 ᵃOr *Sheol*

24

Do not be envious of evil men,
Nor desire to be with them;
2   For their heart devises violence,
And their lips talk of troublemaking.

3   Through wisdom a house is built,
And by understanding it is established;
4   By knowledge the rooms are filled
With all precious and pleasant riches.

5   A wise man *is* strong,
Yes, a man of knowledge increases
strength;
6   For by wise counsel you will wage your
own war,
And in a multitude of counselors *there is*
safety.

7   Wisdom *is* too lofty for a fool;
He does not open his mouth in the gate.

8   He who plots to do evil
Will be called a schemer.
9   The devising of foolishness *is* sin,
And the scoffer *is* an abomination to
men.

10   *If* you faint in the day of adversity,
Your strength *is* small.

11   Deliver *those who* are drawn toward death,
And hold back *those* stumbling to the
slaughter.
12   If you say, "Surely we did not know this,"
Does not He who weighs the hearts
consider *it?*
He who keeps your soul, does He *not*
know *it?*
And will He *not* render to *each* man
according to his deeds?

13   My son, eat honey because *it is* good,
And the honeycomb *which is* sweet to your
taste;
14   So *shall* the knowledge of wisdom *be* to
your soul;
If you have found *it,* there is a prospect,
And your hope will not be cut off.

15   Do not lie in wait, O wicked *man,* against
the dwelling of the righteous;
Do not plunder his resting place;
16   For a righteous *man* may fall seven times
And rise again,
But the wicked shall fall by calamity.

17   Do not rejoice when your enemy falls,
And do not let your heart be glad when
he stumbles;
18   Lest the LORD see *it,* and it displease Him,
And He turn away His wrath from him.

19   Do not fret because of evildoers,
Nor be envious of the wicked;
20   For there will be no prospect for the evil
man;
The lamp of the wicked will be put out.

21   My son, fear the LORD and the king;
Do not associate with those given to
change;
22   For their calamity will rise suddenly,
And who knows the ruin those two can
bring?

Further Sayings of the Wise

23These *things* also *belong* to the wise:

It *is* not good to show partiality in
judgment.
24   He who says to the wicked, "You *are*
righteous,"
Him the people will curse;
Nations will abhor him.
25   But those who rebuke *the wicked* will have
delight,
And a good blessing will come upon them.

26   He who gives a right answer kisses the
lips.

27   Prepare your outside work,
Make it fit for yourself in the field;
And afterward build your house.

28   Do not be a witness against your neighbor
without cause,
For would you deceive[a] with your lips?
29   Do not say, "I will do to him just as he has
done to me;
I will render to the man according to his
work."

30   I went by the field of the lazy *man,*
And by the vineyard of the man devoid of
understanding;
31   And there it was, all overgrown with
thorns;
Its surface was covered with nettles;
Its stone wall was broken down.

24:28 [a]Septuagint and Vulgate read *Do not deceive.*

32 When I saw *it,* I considered *it* well;
I looked on *it and* received instruction:
33 A little sleep, a little slumber,
A little folding of the hands to rest;
34 So shall your poverty come *like* a prowler,
And your need like an armed man.

Further Wise Sayings of Solomon

25 These also *are* proverbs of Solomon which the men of Hezekiah king of Judah copied:

2 *It is* the glory of God to conceal a matter,
But the glory of kings *is* to search out a matter.

3 *As* the heavens for height and the earth for depth,
So the heart of kings *is* unsearchable.

4 Take away the dross from silver,
And it will go to the silversmith *for* jewelry.
5 Take away the wicked from before the king,
And his throne will be established in righteousness.

6 Do not exalt yourself in the presence of the king,
And do not stand in the place of the great;
7 For *it is* better that he say to you,
"Come up here,"
Than that you should be put lower in the presence of the prince,
Whom your eyes have seen.

8 Do not go hastily to court;
For what will you do in the end,
When your neighbor has put you to shame?
9 Debate your case with your neighbor,
And do not disclose the secret to another;
10 Lest he who hears *it* expose your shame,
And your reputation be ruined.

11 A word fitly spoken *is like* apples of gold
In settings of silver.
12 *Like* an earring of gold and an ornament of fine gold
Is a wise rebuker to an obedient ear.

13 Like the cold of snow in time of harvest
Is a faithful messenger to those who send him,
For he refreshes the soul of his masters.

14 Whoever falsely boasts of giving
Is like clouds and wind without rain.

15 By long forbearance a ruler is persuaded,
And a gentle tongue breaks a bone.

16 Have you found honey?
Eat only as much as you need,
Lest you be filled with it and vomit.

17 Seldom set foot in your neighbor's house,
Lest he become weary of you and hate you.

18 A man who bears false witness against his neighbor
Is like a club, a sword, and a sharp arrow.

19 Confidence in an unfaithful *man* in time of trouble
Is like a bad tooth and a foot out of joint.

20 *Like* one who takes away a garment in cold weather,
And like vinegar on soda,
Is one who sings songs to a heavy heart.

21 If your enemy is hungry, give him bread to eat;
And if he is thirsty, give him water to drink;
22 For *so* you will heap coals of fire on his head,
And the LORD will reward you.

23 The north wind brings forth rain,
And a backbiting tongue an angry countenance.

24 *It is* better to dwell in a corner of a housetop,
Than in a house shared with a contentious woman.

25 *As* cold water to a weary soul,
So *is* good news from a far country.

26 A righteous *man* who falters before the wicked
Is like a murky spring and a polluted well.

27 *It is* not good to eat much honey;
So to seek one's own glory *is not* glory.

28 Whoever *has* no rule over his own spirit
Is like a city broken down, without walls.

Situational Leaders: Read the Need, Then Lead

(Proverbs 25:21, 22)

Leaders need to respond to individuals based on their needs rather than their faults. Proverbs 25:21, 22 encourages us to see what others need—even our enemies—and respond accordingly.

Good leaders do this well. They don't lead out of a predetermined package of behaviors, but size up every situation and discern what must happen to reach the desired goal. Like a quarterback who reads the defense, then calls an audible from the line of scrimmage, good leaders remain flexible and may change their response, based not on what a person deserves, but on what they need to succeed. Good leaders follow this path in difficult situations:

1. **They need:** They aren't afraid to admit they need to listen and get understanding.
2. **They read:** They evaluate what has happened and what steps are best to take.
3. **They feed:** They communicate what they've observed to key players.
4. **They heed:** They act on the basis of their discovery, even if it means change.
5. **They lead:** They provide direction to those involved.

26

As snow in summer and rain in
  harvest,
So honor is not fitting for a fool.

2 Like a flitting sparrow, like a flying
  swallow,
So a curse without cause shall not alight.

3 A whip for the horse,
A bridle for the donkey,
And a rod for the fool's back.

4 Do not answer a fool according to his
  folly,
Lest you also be like him.

5 Answer a fool according to his folly,
Lest he be wise in his own eyes.

6 He who sends a message by the hand of a
  fool
Cuts off *his own* feet *and* drinks violence.

7 *Like* the legs of the lame that hang limp
Is a proverb in the mouth of fools.

8 Like one who binds a stone in a sling
Is he who gives honor to a fool.

9 *Like* a thorn *that* goes into the hand of a
  drunkard
Is a proverb in the mouth of fools.

10 The great *God* who formed everything
Gives the fool *his* hire and the transgressor
  his wages.[a]

11 As a dog returns to his own vomit,
So a fool repeats his folly.

12 Do you see a man wise in his own eyes?
There is more hope for a fool than for him.

13 The lazy *man* says, "*There is* a lion in the
  road!
A fierce lion *is* in the streets!"

14 *As* a door turns on its hinges,
So *does* the lazy *man* on his bed.

15 The lazy *man* buries his hand in the bowl;[a]
It wearies him to bring it back to his
  mouth.

16 The lazy *man is* wiser in his own eyes
Than seven men who can answer sensibly.

17 He who passes by *and* meddles in a quarrel
  not his own
Is like one who takes a dog by the ears.

18 Like a madman who throws firebrands,
  arrows, and death,

19 *Is* the man *who* deceives his neighbor,
And says, "I was only joking!"

20 Where *there is* no wood, the fire goes out;
And where *there is* no talebearer, strife
  ceases.

21 *As* charcoal *is* to burning coals, and wood
  to fire,
So *is* a contentious man to kindle strife.

22 The words of a talebearer *are* like tasty
  trifles,
And they go down into the inmost body.

26:10 [a]The Hebrew is difficult; ancient and modern translators differ greatly. **26:15** [a]Compare 19:24

23 Fervent lips with a wicked heart
Are like earthenware covered with silver
dross.

24 He who hates, disguises *it* with his lips,
And lays up deceit within himself;

25 When he speaks kindly, do not believe him,
For *there are* seven abominations in his
heart;

26 *Though his* hatred is covered by deceit,
His wickedness will be revealed before the
assembly.

27 Whoever digs a pit will fall into it,
And he who rolls a stone will have it roll
back on him.

28 A lying tongue hates *those who are* crushed
by it,
And a flattering mouth works ruin.

27 Do not boast about tomorrow,
For you do not know what a day
may bring forth.

2 Let another man praise you, and not your
own mouth;
A stranger, and not your own lips.

3 A stone *is* heavy and sand *is* weighty,
But a fool's wrath *is* heavier than both of
them.

4 Wrath *is* cruel and anger a torrent,
But who *is* able to stand before jealousy?

5 Open rebuke *is* better
Than love carefully concealed.

6 Faithful *are* the wounds of a friend,
But the kisses of an enemy *are* deceitful.

7 A satisfied soul loathes the honeycomb,
But to a hungry soul every bitter thing *is*
sweet.

8 Like a bird that wanders from its nest
Is a man who wanders from his place.

9 Ointment and perfume delight the heart,
And the sweetness of a man's friend *gives
delight* by hearty counsel.

10 Do not forsake your own friend or your
father's friend,
Nor go to your brother's house in the day
of your calamity;
Better *is* a neighbor nearby than a brother
far away.

11 My son, be wise, and make my heart glad,
That I may answer him who reproaches me.

12 A prudent *man* foresees evil *and* hides
himself;
The simple pass on *and* are punished.

Relationships: When People Are Esteemed, Relationships Are Redeemed

(Proverbs 27:1–21)

Leaders understand that people represent an organization's most appreciable asset. No resource is more valuable than people. Therefore, people skills represent a leader's most important attribute.

This text presents some fundamentals on relationships. It teaches that if people are esteemed, relationships are redeemed. Leaders can learn at least the following principles from this chapter:

1. *Don't brag* (vv. 1, 2)—Leaders understand how little they get from self-promotion.
2. *Don't envy* (v. 4)—Leaders sabotage themselves if their motive is to keep up with others.
3. *Be forthright* (vv. 5, 6)—Leaders don't fear confrontation, but speak the truth in love.
4. *Don't forsake your roots* (v. 8)—Leaders understand the power of relational heritage.
5. *Stay close* (vv. 9, 10)—Leaders work at maintaining relationships and meeting needs.
6. *Add value* (v. 17)—Leaders sharpen those with whom they come in contact.
7. *Don't be moved by flattery* (v. 21)—Stay humble or you will stumble.

13 Take the garment of him who is surety for
a stranger,
And hold it in pledge *when* he is surety for
a seductress.

14 He who blesses his friend with a loud
voice, rising early in the morning,
It will be counted a curse to him.

15 A continual dripping on a very rainy day
And a contentious woman are alike;
16 Whoever restrains her restrains the wind,
And grasps oil with his right hand.

17 *As* iron sharpens iron,
So a man sharpens the countenance of his
friend.

18 Whoever keeps the fig tree will eat its
fruit;
So he who waits on his master will be
honored.

19 As in water face *reflects* face,
So a man's heart *reveals* the man.

20 Hell[a] and Destruction[b] are never full;
So the eyes of man are never satisfied.

21 The refining pot *is* for silver and the
furnace for gold,
And a man *is valued* by what others say of
him.

22 Though you grind a fool in a mortar with
a pestle along with crushed grain,
Yet his foolishness will not depart from
him.

23 Be diligent to know the state of your
flocks,
And attend to your herds;
24 For riches *are* not forever,
Nor does a crown *endure* to all
generations.
25 *When* the hay is removed, and the tender
grass shows itself,
And the herbs of the mountains are
gathered in,
26 The lambs *will provide* your clothing,
And the goats the price of a field;
27 *You shall have* enough goats' milk for your
food,
For the food of your household,
And the nourishment of your
maidservants.

28 The wicked flee when no one
pursues,
But the righteous are bold as a lion.

2 Because of the transgression of a land,
many *are* its princes;
But by a man of understanding *and*
knowledge
Right will be prolonged.

3 A poor man who oppresses the poor
Is like a driving rain which leaves no food.

4 Those who forsake the law praise the
wicked,
But such as keep the law contend with
them.

5 Evil men do not understand justice,
But those who seek the LORD understand
all.

6 Better *is* the poor who walks in his
integrity
Than one perverse *in his* ways, though he
be rich.

7 Whoever keeps the law *is* a discerning
son,
But a companion of gluttons shames his
father.

8 One who increases his possessions by
usury and extortion
Gathers it for him who will pity the poor.

9 One who turns away his ear from hearing
the law,
Even his prayer *is* an abomination.

10 Whoever causes the upright to go astray in
an evil way,
He himself will fall into his own pit;
But the blameless will inherit good.

11 The rich man *is* wise in his own eyes,
But the poor who has understanding
searches him out.

12 When the righteous rejoice, *there is* great
glory;
But when the wicked arise, men hide
themselves.

27:20 [a]Or *Sheol* [b]Hebrew *Abaddon*

13 He who covers his sins will not prosper,
But whoever confesses and forsakes *them*
will have mercy.

14 Happy *is* the man who is always reverent,
But he who hardens his heart will fall into
calamity.

15 *Like* a roaring lion and a charging bear
Is a wicked ruler over poor people.

16 A ruler who lacks understanding *is* a great
oppressor,
But he who hates covetousness will
prolong *his* days.

17 A man burdened with bloodshed will flee
into a pit;
Let no one help him.

18 Whoever walks blamelessly will be saved,
But *he who is* perverse *in his* ways will
suddenly fall.

19 He who tills his land will have plenty of
bread,
But he who follows frivolity will have
poverty enough!

20 A faithful man will abound with blessings,
But he who hastens to be rich will not go
unpunished.

21 To show partiality *is* not good,
Because for a piece of bread a man will
transgress.

22 A man with an evil eye hastens after
riches,
And does not consider that poverty will
come upon him.

23 He who rebukes a man will find more
favor afterward
Than he who flatters with the tongue.

24 Whoever robs his father or his mother,
And says, "*It is* no transgression,"
The same *is* companion to a destroyer.

25 He who is of a proud heart stirs up strife,
But he who trusts in the LORD will be
prospered.

26 He who trusts in his own heart is a fool,
But whoever walks wisely will be delivered.

27 He who gives to the poor will not lack,
But he who hides his eyes will have many
curses.

28 When the wicked arise, men hide
themselves;
But when they perish, the righteous
increase.

29 He who is often rebuked, *and*
hardens *his* neck,
Will suddenly be destroyed, and that
without remedy.

2 When the righteous are in authority, the
people rejoice;
But when a wicked *man* rules, the people
groan.

3 Whoever loves wisdom makes his father
rejoice,
But a companion of harlots wastes *his*
wealth.

4 The king establishes the land by justice,
But he who receives bribes overthrows it.

5 A man who flatters his neighbor
Spreads a net for his feet.

6 By transgression an evil man is snared,
But the righteous sings and rejoices.

7 The righteous considers the cause of the
poor,
But the wicked does not understand *such*
knowledge.

8 Scoffers set a city aflame,
But wise *men* turn away wrath.

9 *If* a wise man contends with a foolish man,
Whether *the fool* rages or laughs, *there is* no
peace.

10 The bloodthirsty hate the blameless,
But the upright seek his well-being.[a]

11 A fool vents all his feelings,[a]
But a wise *man* holds them back.

12 If a ruler pays attention to lies,
All his servants *become* wicked.

29:10 [a]Literally *soul* **29:11** [a]Literally *spirit*

The Law of Influence:
The Leader Causes People to Thrive or Groan
(Proverbs 29:2–18)

People reflect their leader. We cannot expect followers to grow beyond their leader. We cannot expect followers to turn out fundamentally different from their leader. People feel attracted to leaders like them; they also reflect those who lead them. Consider what Proverbs 29 tells us about the influence of good and bad leaders:

1. **Attitudes (v. 2)**
   When good leaders rule, people rejoice; when the wicked reign, people groan.
2. **Stability (v. 4)**
   When moral leaders rule, they establish justice; compromising leaders tear things down.
3. **Compassion (v. 7)**
   Good leaders express concern for the poor; bad leaders reflect no compassion for anyone.
4. **Honesty (v. 12)**
   When leaders pay attention to lies, their staff begins to esteem the same deceptions.
5. **Vision (v. 18)**
   Solid vision keeps everyone on track; chaos reigns wherever the vision lapses.

13 The poor *man* and the oppressor have this
in common:
The LORD gives light to the eyes of both.

14 The king who judges the poor with truth,
His throne will be established forever.

15 The rod and rebuke give wisdom,
But a child left *to himself* brings shame to
his mother.

16 When the wicked are multiplied,
transgression increases;
But the righteous will see their fall.

17 Correct your son, and he will give you
rest;
Yes, he will give delight to your soul.

18 Where *there is* no revelation,[a] the people
cast off restraint;
But happy *is* he who keeps the law.

19 A servant will not be corrected by mere
words;
For though he understands, he will not
respond.

20 Do you see a man hasty in his words?
There is more hope for a fool than for him.

21 He who pampers his servant from
childhood
Will have him as a son in the end.

22 An angry man stirs up strife,
And a furious man abounds in
transgression.

23 A man's pride will bring him low,
But the humble in spirit will retain honor.

24 Whoever is a partner with a thief hates his
own life;
He swears to tell the truth,[a] but reveals
nothing.

25 The fear of man brings a snare,
But whoever trusts in the LORD shall be
safe.

26 Many seek the ruler's favor,
But justice for man *comes* from the LORD.

27 An unjust man *is* an abomination to the
righteous,
And *he who is* upright in the way *is* an
abomination to the wicked.

29:18 [a]Or *prophetic vision*   **29:24** [a]Literally *hears the adjuration*

The Wisdom of Agur

30 The words of Agur the son of Jakeh, *his* utterance. This man declared to Ithiel—to Ithiel and Ucal:

2 Surely I *am* more stupid than *any* man,
And do not have the understanding of a man.
3 I neither learned wisdom
Nor have knowledge of the Holy One.

4 Who has ascended into heaven, or descended?
Who has gathered the wind in His fists?
Who has bound the waters in a garment?
Who has established all the ends of the earth?
What *is* His name, and what *is* His Son's name,
If you know?

5 Every word of God *is* pure;
He *is* a shield to those who put their trust in Him.
6 Do not add to His words,
Lest He rebuke you, and you be found a liar.

7 Two *things* I request of You
(Deprive me not before I die):
8 Remove falsehood and lies far from me;
Give me neither poverty nor riches—
Feed me with the food allotted to me;
9 Lest I be full and deny *You,*
And say, "Who *is* the LORD?"
Or lest I be poor and steal,
And profane the name of my God.

10 Do not malign a servant to his master,
Lest he curse you, and you be found guilty.

11 *There is* a generation *that* curses its father,
And does not bless its mother.
12 *There is* a generation *that is* pure in its own eyes,
Yet is not washed from its filthiness.
13 *There is* a generation—oh, how lofty are their eyes!
And their eyelids are lifted up.
14 *There is* a generation whose teeth *are like* swords,
And whose fangs *are like* knives,
To devour the poor from off the earth,
And the needy from *among* men.

15 The leech has two daughters—
Give *and* Give!

There are three *things that* are never satisfied,
Four never say, "Enough!":
16 The grave,[a]
The barren womb,
The earth *that* is not satisfied with water—
And the fire never says, "Enough!"

17 The eye *that* mocks *his* father,
And scorns obedience to *his* mother,
The ravens of the valley will pick it out,
And the young eagles will eat it.

18 There are three *things which* are too wonderful for me,
Yes, four *which* I do not understand:
19 The way of an eagle in the air,
The way of a serpent on a rock,
The way of a ship in the midst of the sea,
And the way of a man with a virgin.

20 This *is* the way of an adulterous woman:
She eats and wipes her mouth,
And says, "I have done no wickedness."

21 For three *things* the earth is perturbed,
Yes, for four it cannot bear up:
22 For a servant when he reigns,
A fool when he is filled with food,
23 A hateful *woman* when she is married,
And a maidservant who succeeds her mistress.

24 There are four *things which* are little on the earth,
But they *are* exceedingly wise:
25 The ants *are* a people not strong,
Yet they prepare their food in the summer;
26 The rock badgers[a] *are* a feeble folk,
Yet they make their homes in the crags;
27 The locusts have no king,
Yet they all advance in ranks;
28 The spider[a] skillfully grasps with its hands,
And it is in kings' palaces.

29 There are three *things which* are majestic in pace,
Yes, four *which* are stately in walk:
30 A lion, *which is* mighty among beasts
And does not turn away from any;

30:16 [a]Or *Sheol* **30:26** [a]Or *hyraxes* **30:28** [a]Or *lizard*

31 A greyhound,[a]
A male goat also,
And a king *whose* troops *are* with him.[b]

32 If you have been foolish in exalting
yourself,
Or if you have devised evil, *put your* hand
on *your* mouth.

33 For *as* the churning of milk produces
butter,
And wringing the nose produces blood,
So the forcing of wrath produces strife.

The Words of King Lemuel's Mother

31 The words of King Lemuel, the utterance which his mother taught
him:

2 What, my son?
And what, son of my womb?
And what, son of my vows?

3 Do not give your strength to women,
Nor your ways to that which destroys
kings.

4 *It is* not for kings, O Lemuel,
It is not for kings to drink wine,
Nor for princes intoxicating drink;

5 Lest they drink and forget the law,
And pervert the justice of all the afflicted.

6 Give strong drink to him who is perishing,
And wine to those who are bitter of heart.

7 Let him drink and forget his poverty,
And remember his misery no more.

8 Open your mouth for the speechless,
In the cause of all *who are* appointed to
die.[a]

9 Open your mouth, judge righteously,
And plead the cause of the poor and
needy.

The Virtuous Wife

10 Who[a] can find a virtuous[b] wife?
For her worth *is* far above rubies.

11 The heart of her husband safely trusts her;
So he will have no lack of gain.

12 She does him good and not evil
All the days of her life.

13 She seeks wool and flax,
And willingly works with her hands.

14 She is like the merchant ships,
She brings her food from afar.

15 She also rises while it is yet night,
And provides food for her household,
And a portion for her maidservants.

A Woman of Influence

(Proverbs 31:10–31)

Proverbs 31 no doubt gets more airtime on Mother's Day than any other passage of Scripture. The majority of the proverb describes a virtuous woman who leads her home with integrity, discipline, and giftedness. This wife and mother is a leader not because she tries to be one, but because of who she is.

Her Assets
1. She is trustworthy (v. 11).
2. She is a positive influence (v. 12).
3. She is a hard worker (vv. 13, 14, 19, 24–27).
4. She is a planner (vv. 21, 22).
5. She is protective (v. 27).

Her Achievements
1. She meets the needs of her home (v. 15).
2. She invests for her household (v. 16).
3. She keeps herself in shape (v. 17).
4. She helps her husband become successful (v. 23).

Her Attitudes
1. Delightful (v. 13)
2. Healthy (v. 18)
3. Compassionate (v. 20)
4. Unselfish (v. 20)
5. Public (v. 25)

Her Applause
1. From her family (v. 28)
2. From her husband (vv. 28, 29)
3. From God's Word (v. 30)
4. From her works (v. 31)

---

16 She considers a field and buys it;
From her profits she plants a vineyard.

17 She girds herself with strength,
And strengthens her arms.

18 She perceives that her merchandise *is*
good,
And her lamp does not go out by night.

19 She stretches out her hands to the distaff,
And her hand holds the spindle.

30:31 [a]Exact identity unknown [b]A Jewish tradition reads *a king against whom there is no uprising.*
31:8 [a]Literally *sons of passing away* **31:10** [a]Verses 10 through 31 are an alphabetic acrostic in Hebrew (compare Psalm 119). [b]Literally *a wife of valor,* in the sense of all forms of excellence

20 She extends her hand to the poor,
Yes, she reaches out her hands to the needy.
21 She is not afraid of snow for her
household,
For all her household *is* clothed with
scarlet.
22 She makes tapestry for herself;
Her clothing *is* fine linen and purple.
23 Her husband is known in the gates,
When he sits among the elders of the
land.
24 She makes linen garments and sells *them,*
And supplies sashes for the merchants.
25 Strength and honor *are* her clothing;
She shall rejoice in time to come.

26 She opens her mouth with wisdom,
And on her tongue *is* the law of kindness.
27 She watches over the ways of her
household,
And does not eat the bread of idleness.
28 Her children rise up and call her blessed;
Her husband *also,* and he praises her:
29 "Many daughters have done well,
But you excel them all."
30 Charm *is* deceitful and beauty *is* passing,
But a woman *who* fears the LORD, she shall
be praised.
31 Give her of the fruit of her hands,
And let her own works praise her in the
gates.

SUMMARY

Ecclesiastes, like the Book of Job, presents one of the greatest challenges to understanding in the Bible. Ancient Hebrews used to debate its meaning and whether it should even be included in the canon of Scripture. Fortunately for us, by divine providence, Ecclesiastes did make it into the Bible with its unique message for leaders.

The central themes of the book focus on the meaning of life, motives for behavior, and where God fits into our personal mission—paramount issues for every leader.

Our leadership must be about something much bigger than us. If our leadership advances merely our own "kingdom," only increases the profits of our company, or only benefits ourselves—we have failed the higher call of leadership. All leadership must bring honor to God, serve and benefit others, and utilize the gifts of each team member to their fullest potential.

The tone of this book displays an overriding pessimism, as expressed through the words "under the sun" or "under heaven." The writer explores life almost devoid of a divine perspective, lived from a selfish, humanistic worldview. He generally leaves God out of his deliberations, leaving himself with human reason alone and resulting in superficial and shallow leadership.

A second theme of the book deals with our motives. *Why* we do something ultimately determines *what* we do. The author shows from personal experience that all earthly goals and blessings, when pursued as an end in themselves, lead to dissatisfaction and emptiness.

Finally, the book answers the question, Where does God fit into our personal mission? All good leaders operate from a personal and corporate mission statement. Vision drives them. In chapter two alone, this book questions the materialistic mission of building buildings, making money, controlling workers, and pursuing pleasure. Of course, there's nothing wrong with buildings, money, or workers—as long as they serve only as a means to an eternal end, not an end in themselves.

Instead, leaders ought to wrestle with how they might change eternity through their leadership. After reading this book, leaders should ask themselves: "Who am I? Why am I attempting to lead others? Where am I trying to go? What values guide my life?" The final chapter reminds us that a day of reckoning awaits when God will bring all these issues to light.

God's Role in Ecclesiastes

Leaders cannot find genuine fulfillment outside of linking their lives to God's purposes for the world. As "the Preacher" explores various avenues for satisfaction—power, possessions, prestige, pleasure—he finds them hollow. God moves him along the path of discovery until he finds no real meaning to life "under heaven," but only in relationship to God and His eternal purposes. God provides all meaning and fulfillment in this life. The author could not find anything of value apart from a life lived in obedience to God's calling.

Leaders in Ecclesiastes

"The Preacher," God

Other People of Influence in Ecclesiastes

Wise men, fools

Lessons in Leadership

- No real meaning exists apart from linking our lives to God's purpose.
- Humanism and materialism provide incomplete counsel for decision making.
- Possessions, people, pleasure, prestige, and power make great servants but poor masters.
- Timing is key: *When* to lead is as important as *what* to do and *where* to go.
- People are motivated by a variety of incentives.
- Divine wisdom provides direction, protection, correction, and resolution.
- Leaders must invest themselves generously, knowing the payoff comes later.

LEADERSHIP

HIGHLIGHTS IN ECCLESIASTES

The Vanity of Life

1 The words of the Preacher, the son of David, king in Jerusalem.

2 "Vanity[a] of vanities," says the Preacher;
"Vanity of vanities, all *is* vanity."

3 What profit has a man from all his labor
In which he toils under the sun?
4 *One* generation passes away, and *another*
generation comes;
But the earth abides forever.
5 The sun also rises, and the sun goes down,
And hastens to the place where it arose.
6 The wind goes toward the south,
And turns around to the north;
The wind whirls about continually,
And comes again on its circuit.
7 All the rivers run into the sea,
Yet the sea *is* not full;
To the place from which the rivers come,
There they return again.
8 All things *are* full of labor;

Man cannot express *it.*
The eye is not satisfied with seeing,
Nor the ear filled with hearing.

9 That which has been *is* what will be,
That which *is* done is what will be done,
And *there is* nothing new under the sun.
10 Is there anything of which it may be said,
"See, this *is* new"?
It has already been in ancient times before
us.
11 *There is* no remembrance of former *things,*
Nor will there be any remembrance of
things that are to come
By *those* who will come after.

The Grief of Wisdom

12 I, the Preacher, was king over Israel in Jerusalem. 13 And I set my heart to seek and search out by wisdom concerning all that is done under

---

1:2 [a]Or *Absurdity, Frustration, Futility, Nonsense;* and so throughout this book

---

Vision: If Life Has No Meaning, Leadership Has No Mission

(Ecclesiastes 1:3–11)

"Life is vanity," writes Solomon. Imagine the wisest, richest, most powerful man in his time, proclaiming everything worthless! Solomon's name means "peace," but he enjoyed none of it while writing most of this book. He grew deflated, depressed, and disillusioned about life "under the sun." Here we see a leader who lost the air in his sails because he abandoned his true mission. He teaches us . . .

1. There is no profit (vv. 3, 4).
Life without God is an exercise in futility. Generations come and go; all we do is move things around.

2. There is no purpose (vv. 5–7).
The sun rises only to set again, endlessly repeating a meaningless cycle. Wind blows, river flows, all in monotony.

3. There is no progress (vv. 8–11).
There is no satisfaction; there's nothing new under the sun, nor pleasant remembrance of earlier life.

Leadership without an eternal perspective falls into the trap of meaninglessness. Leadership must work toward significant, meaningful goals. We are forced to conclude that:

1. If nothing worthwhile exists under the sun, our only hope must lie above it.
2. If the man with everything investigated every visible delight and still wound up unsatisfied, then what satisfies must be invisible.
3. If the wisest man on earth finds no answers under heaven, then we must look to heaven itself for those answers.

heaven; this burdensome task God has given to the sons of man, by which they may be exercised. ¹⁴I have seen all the works that are done under the sun; and indeed, all *is* vanity and grasping for the wind.

¹⁵   *What is* crooked cannot be made straight,
    And what is lacking cannot be numbered.

¹⁶I communed with my heart, saying, "Look, I have attained greatness, and have gained more wisdom than all who were before me in Jerusalem. My heart has understood great wisdom and knowledge." ¹⁷And I set my heart to know wisdom and to know madness and folly. I perceived that this also is grasping for the wind.

¹⁸   For in much wisdom *is* much grief,
    And he who increases knowledge increases
    sorrow.

The Vanity of Pleasure

2 I said in my heart, "Come now, I will test you with mirth; therefore enjoy pleasure"; but surely, this also *was* vanity. ²I said of laughter—"Madness!"; and of mirth, "What does it accomplish?" ³I searched in my heart *how* to gratify my flesh with wine, while guiding my heart with wisdom, and how to lay hold on folly, till I might see what *was* good for the sons of men to do under heaven all the days of their lives.

⁴I made my works great, I built myself houses, and planted myself vineyards. ⁵I made myself gardens and orchards, and I planted all *kinds* of fruit trees in them. ⁶I made myself water pools from which to water the growing trees of the grove. ⁷I acquired male and female servants, and had servants born in my house. Yes, I had greater possessions of herds and flocks than all who were in Jerusalem before me. ⁸I also gathered for myself silver and gold and the special treasures of kings and of the provinces. I acquired male and female singers, the delights of the sons of men, *and* musical instruments[a] of all kinds.

⁹So I became great and excelled more than all who were before me in Jerusalem. Also my wisdom remained with me.

¹⁰   Whatever my eyes desired I did not keep
    from them.
    I did not withhold my heart from any
    pleasure,
    For my heart rejoiced in all my labor;
    And this was my reward from all my labor.
¹¹   Then I looked on all the works that my
    hands had done

And on the labor in which I had toiled;
    And indeed all *was* vanity and grasping for
    the wind.
    There was no profit under the sun.

The End of the Wise and the Fool

¹²   Then I turned myself to consider wisdom
    and madness and folly;
    For what *can* the man *do* who succeeds the
    king?—
    Only what he has already done.
¹³   Then I saw that wisdom excels folly
    As light excels darkness.
¹⁴   The wise man's eyes *are* in his head,
    But the fool walks in darkness.
    Yet I myself perceived
    That the same event happens to them all.

¹⁵   So I said in my heart,
    "As it happens to the fool,
    It also happens to me,
    And why was I then more wise?"
    Then I said in my heart,
    "This also *is* vanity."
¹⁶   For *there is* no more remembrance of the
    wise than of the fool forever,
    Since all that now *is* will be forgotten in
    the days to come.
    And how does a wise *man* die?
    As the fool!

¹⁷Therefore I hated life because the work that was done under the sun *was* distressing to me, for all *is* vanity and grasping for the wind. ¹⁸Then I hated all my labor in which I had toiled under the sun, because I must leave it to the man who will come after me. ¹⁹And who knows whether he will be wise or a fool? Yet he will rule over all my labor in which I toiled and in which I have shown myself wise under the sun. This also *is* vanity. ²⁰Therefore I turned my heart and despaired of all the labor in which I had toiled under the sun. ²¹For there is a man whose labor *is* with wisdom, knowledge, and skill; yet he must leave his heritage to a man who has not labored for it. This also *is* vanity and a great evil. ²²For what has man for all his labor, and for the striving of his heart with which he has toiled under the sun? ²³For all his days *are* sorrowful, and his work burdensome; even in the night his heart takes no rest. This also is vanity.

²⁴Nothing *is* better for a man *than* that he should eat and drink, and *that* his soul should enjoy good in his labor. This also, I saw, was from

---

2:8 ᵃExact meaning unknown

21 QUALITIES

We can learn from Solomon's costly mistakes. The King of Israel desperately pursued several unrelated goals in a vain attempt to satisfy himself. Ecclesiastes 2:1–11 provides a good example of a leader who didn't know how to get what he wanted.

By the time Solomon wrote these words, he had reached a high level of success—but still felt empty. He couldn't put his finger on why fulfillment continued to escape him. Because he lacked focus, he searched high and low, experimenting with all kinds of goals, yet never achieved satisfaction. Sadly, he attempted to solve an inward problem with an outward solution.

The old axiom remains true: If you chase two rabbits, both will escape. This was certainly true of Solomon's futile attempts to reach his varied goals. (He pursued eight goals in Ecclesiastes 2 alone!) So, what can we learn from this leader about focus?

1. He pursued too many things in too short a time.
2. He pursued the wrong goals to reach his desired outcome.
3. His self-serving goals were all wrong.
4. He despaired because he never identified what he really wanted.

A Checklist for Making Decisions

Solomon eventually did narrow his focus, but it took him a lifetime and an entire book to do so (see Eccl. 12). He finally determined what really mattered and what he really wanted.

How about you? Have you figured out your focus? How do you make major decisions? Do you have a way of determining your focus, based on what really matters or what really counts? Consider the following checklist as you make decisions about where to invest your time and energy. When faced with a decision, ask yourself:

1. Is this consistent with my priorities?
2. Is this within my area of competence?
3. Can someone else do it better?
4. What do my trusted friends say?
5. Do I have the time?

When you say "yes" to an opportunity, get ready to focus. Make to-do lists. Set your priorities. Avoid clutter. Pursue excellence, but avoid perfectionism. Question everything. Work to prevent procrastination. Control interruptions and distractions. Use the calendar. Narrow your wedge—don't try to do everything. That means you'll have to say no to some good things. And how can you say no gracefully?

1. Say no to the proposition, not to the person.
2. Respond in terms that convey the best interests of the person who's requesting your involvement.
3. Defer creatively; suggest an alternative.

For a positive example of focus, see page 1450.

The Law of Priorities and the Law of Sacrifice: Things Don't Make a Leader

(Ecclesiastes 2:1–26)

Solomon attempted to find satisfaction in accumulating things: houses, gardens, vineyards, flocks, slaves, etc. He found all of it empty.

Many leaders succumb to the same temptation. They begin well, but once they reach their first level of goals—if they don't continue to stretch—they shrink. Their shrinking often takes the form of accumulating. Their success gains them a nice discretionary income. So they spend and gain. Spend and gain. Spend and gain. But none of this fills the void inside.

All leaders have two major voids:

1. The God-sized vacuum inside their heart; only the Lord can fill it.
2. The life-sized vacuum inside their heart; only their life mission can fulfill it.

To reach these goals, leaders must give up the pursuit of lesser things. C. S. Lewis wrote, "Indeed, if we consider the unblushing promises of reward . . . promised in the Gospels, it would seem that our Lord finds our desires, not too strong, but too weak. We are halfhearted creatures, fooling about with drink and sex and ambition when infinite joy is offered us, like an ignorant child who wants to go on making mud pies in a slum because he cannot imagine what is meant by an offer of a holiday at the sea. We are far too easily pleased."

the hand of God. ²⁵For who can eat, or who can have enjoyment, more than I?[a] ²⁶For *God* gives wisdom and knowledge and joy to a man who *is* good in His sight; but to the sinner He gives the work of gathering and collecting, that he may give to *him who is* good before God. This also *is* vanity and grasping for the wind.

Everything Has Its Time

3 To everything *there is* a season,
A time for every purpose under heaven:

² A time to be born,
And a time to die;
A time to plant,
And a time to pluck *what is* planted;
³ A time to kill,
And a time to heal;
A time to break down,
And a time to build up;
⁴ A time to weep,
And a time to laugh;
A time to mourn,
And a time to dance;
⁵ A time to cast away stones,
And a time to gather stones;
A time to embrace,
And a time to refrain from embracing;
⁶ A time to gain,
And a time to lose;

A time to keep,
And a time to throw away;
⁷ A time to tear,
And a time to sew;
A time to keep silence,
And a time to speak;
⁸ A time to love,
And a time to hate;
A time of war,
And a time of peace.

The God-Given Task

⁹What profit has the worker from that in which he labors? ¹⁰I have seen the God-given task with which the sons of men are to be occupied. ¹¹He has made everything beautiful in its time. Also He has put eternity in their hearts, except that no one can find out the work that God does from beginning to end.

¹²I know that nothing *is* better for them than to rejoice, and to do good in their lives, ¹³and also that every man should eat and drink and enjoy the good of all his labor—it *is* the gift of God.

¹⁴ I know that whatever God does,
It shall be forever.

2:25 [a]Following Masoretic Text, Targum, and Vulgate; some Hebrew manuscripts, Septuagint, and Syriac read *without Him.*

The Law of Timing: There's a Season for Everything

(Ecclesiastes 3:1–8)

Solomon knew quite a bit about the Law of Timing. He tells us there exists an appointed time for everything under heaven. Then he lists several examples: birth, death, planting, reaping, weeping, laughing, etc.

We don't *control* the timing of most events; the best we can do is to *recognize* the timing. Ecclesiastes 3 teaches leaders several important lessons:

1. It is our responsibility to recognize God's timing, not to change it.
2. It is our responsibility to accept and cooperate with God's timing.
3. Our alignment with God's timing makes a great difference.
4. God has made everything appropriate in its time.
5. God has put eternity in our hearts, so we must trust God to communicate His timing.
6. We can do nothing better during our lifetime than to rejoice and do good.

Nothing can be added to it,
And nothing taken from it.
God does *it,* that men should fear before
 Him.
15 That which is has already been,
And what is to be has already been;
And God requires an account of what is past.

Injustice Seems to Prevail

16Moreover I saw under the sun:

In the place of judgment,
Wickedness *was* there;
And *in* the place of righteousness,
Iniquity *was* there.

17I said in my heart,

"God shall judge the righteous and the
 wicked,
For *there is* a time there for every purpose
 and for every work."

18I said in my heart, "Concerning the condition of the sons of men, God tests them, that they may see that they themselves are *like* animals." 19For what happens to the sons of men also happens to animals; one thing befalls them: as one dies, so dies the other. Surely, they all have one breath; man has no advantage over animals, for all *is* vanity. 20All go to one place: all are from the dust, and all return to dust. 21Who knows the spirit of the sons of men, which goes upward, and the spirit of the animal, which goes down to the earth?a 22So I perceived that nothing *is* better than that a man should rejoice in his own works, for that *is* his heritage. For who can bring him to see what will happen after him?

4 Then I returned and considered all the oppression that is done under the sun:

And look! The tears of the oppressed,
But they have no comforter—
On the side of their oppressors *there is*
 power,
But they have no comforter.
2 Therefore I praised the dead who were
 already dead,
More than the living who are still alive.
3 Yet, better than both *is he* who has never
 existed,
Who has not seen the evil work that is
 done under the sun.

The Vanity of Selfish Toil

4Again, I saw that for all toil and every skillful work a man is envied by his neighbor. This also *is* vanity and grasping for the wind.

5 The fool folds his hands
And consumes his own flesh.
6 Better a handful *with* quietness
Than both hands full, *together with* toil and
 grasping for the wind.

7Then I returned, and I saw vanity under the sun:

8 There is one alone, without companion:
He has neither son nor brother.
Yet *there is* no end to all his labors,
Nor is his eye satisfied with riches.
But he never asks,
"For whom do I toil and deprive myself of
 good?"
This also *is* vanity and a grave misfortune.

3:21 aSeptuagint, Syriac, Targum, and Vulgate read *Who knows whether the spirit . . . goes upward, and whether . . . goes downward to the earth?*

The Rewards of Partnership

(Ecclesiastes 4:9–12)

Most leaders recognize they need partnerships to reach big goals. Note the rewards of a healthy partnership:

1. Partners accomplish more (v. 9).
2. Partners complement each other (v. 10).
3. Partners supply support and warmth for each other (v. 11).
4. Partners give strength to each other (v. 12).

The Value of a Friend

9 Two *are* better than one,
Because they have a good reward for their labor.
10 For if they fall, one will lift up his companion.
But woe to him *who is* alone when he falls,
For *he has* no one to help him up.
11 Again, if two lie down together, they will keep warm;
But how can one be warm *alone?*
12 Though one may be overpowered by another, two can withstand him.
And a threefold cord is not quickly broken.

Popularity Passes Away

13 Better a poor and wise youth
Than an old and foolish king who will be admonished no more.
14 For he comes out of prison to be king,
Although he was born poor in his kingdom.
15 I saw all the living who walk under the sun;
They were with the second youth who stands in his place.
16 *There was* no end of all the people over whom he was made king;
Yet those who come afterward will not rejoice in him.
Surely this also *is* vanity and grasping for the wind.

Fear God, Keep Your Vows

5 Walk prudently when you go to the house of God; and draw near to hear rather than to give the sacrifice of fools, for they do not know that they do evil.

Motivational Needs: What Every Leader Needs to Know

(Ecclesiastes 4:1–8)

While Ecclesiastes 4 seems to continue the theme of futility, it actually attempts to address the issue of motivation. Solomon says that he observes people in a variety of contexts, and nothing seems to satisfy them.

Where do people search for satisfaction? What do they seek in life? Note Solomon's observations about what motivates most men and women:

1. Comfort and fulfillment (vv. 1–3)
2. Competition and triumph (vv. 4–6)
3. Consumption and greed (vv. 7, 8)

As leaders, we must understand people's motivational needs. A scholar named David McClellan identified three main motivations, or "drivers," that people exhibit in their work. According to McClellan, each person generally has a primary driver, and perhaps another driver as their backup.

One driver is achievement. Achievers like to perform, to finish a task. Getting across the goal line is what satisfies them.

Another driver is affiliation. Affiliators put emphasis on belonging to a group and relating well to others. They're "people people," and they want everybody to be happy.

The third driver is influence. Influencers seek to have power over whatever situation they're in. They like things their way. Status is important to them. For them, the name of the game is control.

To work well with others, it helps to know what motivations "make them tick."

2   Do not be rash with your mouth,
   And let not your heart utter anything
      hastily before God.
   For God *is* in heaven, and you on earth;
   Therefore let your words be few.

3   For a dream comes through much activity,
   And a fool's voice *is known* by *his* many
      words.

4   When you make a vow to God, do not
      delay to pay it;
   For *He has* no pleasure in fools.
   Pay what you have vowed—

5   Better not to vow than to vow and not
      pay.

6 Do not let your mouth cause your flesh to sin, nor say before the messenger *of God* that it *was* an error. Why should God be angry at your excuse[a] and destroy the work of your hands? 7 For in the multitude of dreams and many words *there is* also vanity. But fear God.

Leadership Pitfalls

(Ecclesiastes 5:2–7)

Do you ever make promises to God? Scripture advises caution before we commit something to God—good advice for *any* decision a leader must make. Solomon describes three major pitfalls lying in wait for careless leaders:

1. **Hasty Speech (vv. 2, 3)**
   Leaders must listen as much as they speak. It takes more than words to fulfill dreams.
2. **Empty Promises (vv. 4, 5)**
   Leaders tend to say what others want to hear. Don't promise what you can't deliver.
3. **Lame Excuses (vv. 6, 7)**
   Leaders diminish their influence when they try to reverse a mistake with a lame excuse.

The Vanity of Gain and Honor

8 If you see the oppression of the poor, and the violent perversion of justice and righteousness in a province, do not marvel at the matter; for high official watches over high official, and higher officials are over them.

9 Moreover the profit of the land is for all; *even* the king is served from the field.

10   He who loves silver will not be satisfied
      with silver;
   Nor he who loves abundance, with
      increase.
   This also *is* vanity.

11   When goods increase,
   They increase who eat them;
   So what profit have the owners
   Except to see *them* with their eyes?

12   The sleep of a laboring man *is* sweet,
   Whether he eats little or much;
   But the abundance of the rich will not
      permit him to sleep.

13   There is a severe evil *which* I have seen
      under the sun:
   Riches kept for their owner to his hurt.

14   But those riches perish through
      misfortune;
   When he begets a son, *there is* nothing in
      his hand.

15   As he came from his mother's womb,
      naked shall he return,
   To go as he came;
   And he shall take nothing from his labor
   Which he may carry away in his hand.

16   And this also *is* a severe evil—
   Just exactly as he came, so shall he go.
   And what profit has he who has labored
      for the wind?

17   All his days he also eats in darkness,
   And *he has* much sorrow and sickness and
      anger.

18 Here is what I have seen: *It is* good and fitting *for one* to eat and drink, and to enjoy the good of all his labor in which he toils under the sun all the days of his life which God gives him; for it *is* his heritage. 19 As for every man to whom God has given riches and wealth, and given him power to eat of it, to receive his heritage and rejoice in his labor—this *is* the gift of God. 20 For he will not dwell unduly on the days of his life, because God keeps *him* busy with the joy of his heart.

5:6 [a]Literally *voice*

6 There is an evil which I have seen under the sun, and it *is* common among men: [2]A man to whom God has given riches and wealth and honor, so that he lacks nothing for himself of all he desires; yet God does not give him power to eat of it, but a foreigner consumes it. This *is* vanity, and it *is* an evil affliction.

[3]If a man begets a hundred *children* and lives many years, so that the days of his years are many, but his soul is not satisfied with goodness, or indeed he has no burial, I say *that* a stillborn child *is* better than he— [4]for it comes in vanity and departs in darkness, and its name is covered with darkness. [5]Though it has not seen the sun or known *anything,* this has more rest than that man, [6]even if he lives a thousand years twice— but has not seen goodness. Do not all go to one place?

[7]
All the labor of man *is* for his mouth,
And yet the soul is not satisfied.
[8]
For what more has the wise *man* than the fool?
What does the poor man have,
Who knows *how* to walk before the living?
[9]
Better *is* the sight of the eyes than the wandering of desire.
This also *is* vanity and grasping for the wind.

[10]
Whatever one is, he has been named already,
For it is known that he *is* man;
And he cannot contend with Him who is mightier than he.
[11]
Since there are many things that increase vanity,
How *is* man the better?

[12]For who knows what *is* good for man in life, all the days of his vain life which he passes like a shadow? Who can tell a man what will happen after him under the sun?

The Value of Practical Wisdom

7 A good name *is* better than precious ointment,
And the day of death than the day of one's birth;
[2]
Better to go to the house of mourning
Than to go to the house of feasting,
For that *is* the end of all men;
And the living will take *it* to heart.
[3]
Sorrow *is* better than laughter,
For by a sad countenance the heart is made better.

[4]
The heart of the wise *is* in the house of mourning,
But the heart of fools *is* in the house of mirth.

[5]
It is better to hear the rebuke of the wise
Than for a man to hear the song of fools.
[6]
For like the crackling of thorns under a pot,
So *is* the laughter of the fool.
This also is vanity.
[7]
Surely oppression destroys a wise *man's* reason,
And a bribe debases the heart.

[8]
The end of a thing *is* better than its beginning;
The patient in spirit *is* better than the proud in spirit.
[9]
Do not hasten in your spirit to be angry,
For anger rests in the bosom of fools.
[10]
Do not say,
"Why were the former days better than these?"
For you do not inquire wisely concerning this.

[11]
Wisdom *is* good with an inheritance,
And profitable to those who see the sun.
[12]
For wisdom *is* a defense *as* money *is* a defense,
But the excellence of knowledge *is that* wisdom gives life to those who have it.

[13]
Consider the work of God;
For who can make straight what He has made crooked?
[14]
In the day of prosperity be joyful,
But in the day of adversity consider:
Surely God has appointed the one as well as the other,
So that man can find out nothing *that will come* after him.

[15]I have seen everything in my days of vanity:

There is a just *man* who perishes in his righteousness,
And there is a wicked *man* who prolongs *life* in his wickedness.

[16]
Do not be overly righteous,
Nor be overly wise:
Why should you destroy yourself?
[17]
Do not be overly wicked,
Nor be foolish:

Why should you die before your time?

18 *It is* good that you grasp this,
And also not remove your hand from the other;
For he who fears God will escape them all.

19 Wisdom strengthens the wise
More than ten rulers of the city.

20 For *there is* not a just man on earth who does good
And does not sin.

21 Also do not take to heart everything people say,
Lest you hear your servant cursing you.

22 For many times, also, your own heart has known
That even you have cursed others.

23 All this I have proved by wisdom.
I said, "I will be wise";
But it *was* far from me.

24 As for that which is far off and exceedingly deep,
Who can find it out?

25 I applied my heart to know,
To search and seek out wisdom and the reason *of things,*
To know the wickedness of folly,
Even of foolishness *and* madness.

26 And I find more bitter than death
The woman whose heart *is* snares and nets,
Whose hands *are* fetters.
He who pleases God shall escape from her,
But the sinner shall be trapped by her.

27 "Here is what I have found," says the Preacher,
"*Adding* one thing to the other to find out the reason,

28 Which my soul still seeks but I cannot find:
One man among a thousand I have found,
But a woman among all these I have not found.

29 Truly, this only I have found:
That God made man upright,
But they have sought out many schemes."

8 Who *is* like a wise *man?*
And who knows the interpretation of a thing?
A man's wisdom makes his face shine,
And the sternness of his face is changed.

Obey Authorities for God's Sake

2 I *say,* "Keep the king's commandment for the sake of your oath to God. 3 Do not be hasty to go from his presence. Do not take your stand for an evil thing, for he does whatever pleases him."

4 Where the word of a king *is, there is* power;
And who may say to him, "What are you doing?"

5 He who keeps his command will experience nothing harmful;
And a wise man's heart discerns both time and judgment,

6 Because for every matter there is a time and judgment,
Though the misery of man increases greatly.

Servanthood: The Quality of a Leader Who Lasts

(Ecclesiastes 8:1–9)

Solomon reminds us about our relationship to leaders above us. We are to submit to them, not because the person deserves it, but because the office deserves it and God decrees it.

And what about leaders in authority? Solomon also issues a warning. When leaders try to exercise authority without a servant's heart, they eventually hurt themselves. Consider what he says:

Role of the Follower
1. Submit to God-given authority.
2. Trust God to accomplish His purpose.
3. Don't quit or become divisive.

Role of the Leader
1. Exercise authority with wisdom and caution.
2. Recognize no human controls all of life.
3. Lead others by serving not bossing them.

7 For he does not know what will happen;
So who can tell him when it will occur?

8 No one has power over the spirit to retain
the spirit,
And no one has power in the day of
death.
There is no release from that war,
And wickedness will not deliver those who
are given to it.

⁹All this I have seen, and applied my heart to every work that is done under the sun: *There is* a time in which one man rules over another to his own hurt.

Death Comes to All

¹⁰Then I saw the wicked buried, who had come and gone from the place of holiness, and they were forgotten[a] in the city where they had so done. This also *is* vanity. ¹¹Because the sentence against an evil work is not executed speedily, therefore the heart of the sons of men is fully set in them to do evil. ¹²Though a sinner does evil a hundred *times,* and his *days* are prolonged, yet I surely know that it will be well with those who fear God, who fear before Him. ¹³But it will not be well with the wicked; nor will he prolong *his* days, *which are* as a shadow, because he does not fear before God.

¹⁴There is a vanity which occurs on earth, that there are just *men* to whom it happens according to the work of the wicked; again, there are wicked *men* to whom it happens according to the work of the righteous. I said that this also *is* vanity.

¹⁵So I commended enjoyment, because a man has nothing better under the sun than to eat, drink, and be merry; for this will remain with him in his labor *all* the days of his life which God gives him under the sun.

¹⁶When I applied my heart to know wisdom and to see the business that is done on earth, even though one sees no sleep day or night, ¹⁷then I saw all the work of God, that a man cannot find out the work that is done under the sun. For though a man labors to discover *it,* yet he will not find *it;* moreover, though a wise *man* attempts to know *it,* he will not be able to find *it.*

9 For I considered all this in my heart, so that I could declare it all: that the righteous and the wise and their works *are* in the hand of God. People know neither love nor hatred *by* anything *they* see before them. ²All things *come* alike to all:

One event *happens* to the righteous and
the wicked;
To the good,[a] the clean, and the unclean;
To him who sacrifices and him who does
not sacrifice.
As is the good, so *is* the sinner;
He who takes an oath as *he* who fears an
oath.

³This *is* an evil in all that is done under the sun: that one thing *happens* to all. Truly the hearts of the sons of men are full of evil; madness *is* in their hearts while they live, and after that *they go* to the dead. ⁴But for him who is joined to all the living there is hope, for a living dog is better than a dead lion.

5 For the living know that they will die;
But the dead know nothing,
And they have no more reward,
For the memory of them is forgotten.

6 Also their love, their hatred, and their envy
have now perished;
Nevermore will they have a share
In anything done under the sun.

7 Go, eat your bread with joy,
And drink your wine with a merry heart;
For God has already accepted your works.

8 Let your garments always be white,
And let your head lack no oil.

⁹Live joyfully with the wife whom you love all the days of your vain life which He has given you under the sun, all your days of vanity; for

---

8:10 [a]Some Hebrew manuscripts, Septuagint, and Vulgate read *praised.* **9:2** [a]Septuagint, Syriac, and Vulgate read *good and bad.*

You Have a Work to Do

(Ecclesiastes 9:7–18)

Since everyone on earth has a work to do— a task uniquely suited to our lives—then . . .

- Work joyfully, since our approval comes from God (vv. 7–9).
- Work energetically, even if the results seem uncertain (vv. 10–12).
- Work wisely, with the benefit of God's perspective (vv. 13–18).

that *is* your portion in life, and in the labor which you perform under the sun.

[10]Whatever your hand finds to do, do *it* with your might; for *there is* no work or device or knowledge or wisdom in the grave where you are going.

[11]I returned and saw under the sun that—

The race *is* not to the swift,
Nor the battle to the strong,
Nor bread to the wise,
Nor riches to men of understanding,
Nor favor to men of skill;
But time and chance happen to them all.

[12] For man also does not know his time:
Like fish taken in a cruel net,
Like birds caught in a snare,
So the sons of men *are* snared in an evil time,
When it falls suddenly upon them.

Wisdom Superior to Folly

[13]This wisdom I have also seen under the sun, and it *seemed* great to me: [14]*There was* a little city with few men in it; and a great king came against it, besieged it, and built great snares[a] around it. [15]Now there was found in it a poor wise man, and he by his wisdom delivered the city. Yet no one remembered that same poor man.

[16]Then I said:

"Wisdom *is* better than strength.
Nevertheless the poor man's wisdom *is* despised,
And his words are not heard.

[17] Words of the wise, *spoken* quietly, *should be* heard
Rather than the shout of a ruler of fools.

[18] Wisdom *is* better than weapons of war;
But one sinner destroys much good."

10 Dead flies putrefy[a] the perfumer's ointment,
And cause it to give off a foul odor;
So does a little folly to one respected for wisdom *and* honor.

[2] A wise man's heart *is* at his right hand,
But a fool's heart at his left.

[3] Even when a fool walks along the way,
He lacks wisdom,
And he shows everyone *that* he *is* a fool.

[4] If the spirit of the ruler rises against you,
Do not leave your post;
For conciliation pacifies great offenses.

[5] There is an evil I have seen under the sun,
As an error proceeding from the ruler:

[6] Folly is set in great dignity,
While the rich sit in a lowly place.

[7] I have seen servants on horses,
While princes walk on the ground like servants.

[8] He who digs a pit will fall into it,
And whoever breaks through a wall will be bitten by a serpent.

[9] He who quarries stones may be hurt by them,
And he who splits wood may be endangered by it.

[10] If the ax is dull,
And one does not sharpen the edge,
Then he must use more strength;
But wisdom brings success.

[11] A serpent may bite when *it is* not charmed;
The babbler is no different.

[12] The words of a wise man's mouth *are* gracious,
But the lips of a fool shall swallow him up;

[13] The words of his mouth begin with foolishness,
And the end of his talk *is* raving madness.

[14] A fool also multiplies words.
No man knows what is to be;
Who can tell him what will be after him?

[15] The labor of fools wearies them,
For they do not even know how to go to the city!

[16] Woe to you, O land, when your king *is* a child,
And your princes feast in the morning!

[17] Blessed *are* you, O land, when your king *is* the son of nobles,
And your princes feast at the proper time—
For strength and not for drunkenness!

[18] Because of laziness the building decays,
And through idleness of hands the house leaks.

[19] A feast is made for laughter,
And wine makes merry;
But money answers everything.

[20] Do not curse the king, even in your thought;
Do not curse the rich, even in your bedroom;

9:14 [a]Septuagint, Syriac, and Vulgate read *bulwarks*.
10:1 [a]Targum and Vulgate omit *putrefy*.

For a bird of the air may carry your voice,
And a bird in flight may tell the matter.

The Value of Diligence

11 Cast your bread upon the waters,
For you will find it after many
days.

2 Give a serving to seven, and also to eight,
For you do not know what evil will be on
the earth.

Generosity: Leaders Give Before They Receive

(Ecclesiastes 11:1–9)

Solomon knew a thing or two about wise investing. He counsels leaders to be generous, giving before they receive. And why should leaders initiate giving? Because they know they will eventually receive a hefty return. Wise leaders embrace the following truths about generosity:

1. Givers go first (v. 1).
2. Givers receive a return (v. 1).
3. The return may not be immediate (v. 1).
4. Giving does not keep us from misfortune (vv. 2, 3).
5. If you do not give, you cannot expect a return (v. 4).
6. The return will be in proportion to your giving (v. 6).
7. The motive for giving is love for God (v. 9).

---

3 If the clouds are full of rain,
They empty *themselves* upon the earth;
And if a tree falls to the south or the
north,
In the place where the tree falls, there it
shall lie.

4 He who observes the wind will not sow,
And he who regards the clouds will not
reap.

5 As you do not know what *is* the way of
the wind,[a]
Or how the bones *grow* in the womb of
her who is with child,
So you do not know the works of God
who makes everything.

6 In the morning sow your seed,

And in the evening do not withhold your
hand;
For you do not know which will prosper,
Either this or that,
Or whether both alike *will be* good.

7 Truly the light is sweet,
And *it is* pleasant for the eyes to behold
the sun;

8 But if a man lives many years
And rejoices in them all,
Yet let him remember the days of darkness,
For they will be many.
All that is coming *is* vanity.

Seek God in Early Life

9 Rejoice, O young man, in your youth,
And let your heart cheer you in the days
of your youth;
Walk in the ways of your heart,
And in the sight of your eyes;
But know that for all these
God will bring you into judgment.

10 Therefore remove sorrow from your heart,
And put away evil from your flesh,
For childhood and youth *are* vanity.

12 Remember now your Creator in the
days of your youth,
Before the difficult days come,
And the years draw near when you say,
"I have no pleasure in them":

2 While the sun and the light,
The moon and the stars,
Are not darkened,
And the clouds do not return after the
rain;

3 In the day when the keepers of the house
tremble,
And the strong men bow down;
When the grinders cease because they are
few,
And those that look through the windows
grow dim;

4 When the doors are shut in the streets,
And the sound of grinding is low;
When one rises up at the sound of a bird,
And all the daughters of music are brought
low.

5 Also they are afraid of height,
And of terrors in the way;
When the almond tree blossoms,
The grasshopper is a burden,
And desire fails.

11:5 [a]*Or spirit*

Wise Words for Leaders on How to Finish Well

(Ecclesiastes 12:1–14)

Amazing how God can bring sunshine out of the cloudiest day, isn't it? So it is with the Book of Ecclesiastes. An otherwise pessimistic and discouraging book ends, by God's grace, on a significant "up" note.

Chapter 12 concludes Solomon's meditation with some wise words that should direct every leader. They sound like the lecture of an experienced mentor attempting to counsel an emerging leader, trying to keep him or her from making some of the same mistakes he made. Consider Solomon's wisdom in this grand finale:

1. Don't lose sight of the big picture, especially when you are young (vv. 1–4).
2. Do what is right before it is too late to correct yourself (vv. 5–8).
3. Use your words like tools to shepherd and add value to others (v. 11).
4. Don't try to master everything in life, just what is important (v. 12).
5. Trust and obey God, because He is the ultimate Judge (vv. 13, 14).

For man goes to his eternal home,
And the mourners go about the streets.

6 *Remember your Creator* before the silver
cord is loosed,[a]
Or the golden bowl is broken,
Or the pitcher shattered at the fountain,
Or the wheel broken at the well.

7 Then the dust will return to the earth as it
was,
And the spirit will return to God who
gave it.

8 "Vanity of vanities," says the Preacher,
"All *is* vanity."

The Whole Duty of Man

9 And moreover, because the Preacher was wise, he still taught the people knowledge; yes, he pondered and sought out *and* set in order many proverbs. [10]The Preacher sought to find ac-

ceptable words; and *what was* written *was* upright—words of truth. [11]The words of the wise are like goads, and the words of scholars[a] are like well-driven nails, given by one Shepherd. [12]And further, my son, be admonished by these. Of making many books *there is* no end, and much study *is* wearisome to the flesh.

[13]Let us hear the conclusion of the whole matter:

Fear God and keep His commandments,
For this is man's all.
14 For God will bring every work into
judgment,
Including every secret thing,
Whether good or evil.

12:6 [a]Following Qere and Targum; Kethib reads
removed; Septuagint and Vulgate read *broken*.
12:11 [a]Literally *masters of the assemblies*

SONG OF SOLOMON

God's Love for His People

SUMMARY

The Song of Solomon stands alone among 1,005 songs that Solomon wrote (1 Kin. 4:32). It is often called "The Song of Songs" because many consider it the best of his songs, the most excellent composition he ever wrote. Pious Jews read it every year on the eighth day of the Passover.

The Song proclaims a husband's love for his wife and illustrates God's love for His people, the love that Christ has for the Church, His bride. It describes how a lover cherishes his beloved and how he enjoys the way she completes him.

The song implies that leaders must learn to love the people God has placed within their sphere of influence. We cannot separate leadership from relationship. This book vividly portrays the mutual love both parties have for each other, a love that drives them to appreciate each other and serve each other extravagantly. This kind of love prompts the spiritual leader and the follower to "go the extra mile" and do more than the expected. The book frequently exhibits the "and then some" principle—the lover relishes his beloved, cares for her, provides for her . . . *and then some*. Healthy, intimate relationships create this kind of generous attitude.

Far too often, leaders believe their position forces them to remain distant from their people. They imagine they must remain aloof, even a bit mysterious, living at a level unattainable by others. This is *not* a biblical idea. This song reveals a transparent and vulnerable spiritual leader who speaks intimately of both his strengths and his needs. He feels secure enough to quit hiding behind smokescreens, as leaders today often do. What kind of smokescreens trouble us? Consider two: "I just cannot open up with my people." "I don't have time to build relationships—I'm too busy trying to reach my goals." The lover in this song is honest enough to quit believing the kind of lies we often believe today. He wouldn't think of saying, "If my people are going to submit to me as a leader, I cannot let them get too close to me," or, "If I become vulnerable, my people won't respect me."

The Song of Solomon may give you a whole new perspective on the love a spiritual leader can have for his people. You can also apply these principles to the expressive, vulnerable relationships you find in your church, office, or neighborhood.

God's Role in the Song of Solomon

Scholars have interpreted this book in four primary ways:

1. *Allegory.* This view sees the book expressing the love of God for His chosen people. Each part of the song contains some symbolic meaning.
2. *Dramatic narrative.* The song expresses Solomon's own love affair with a Shulamite woman, whom he takes as wife to his palace in Jerusalem.
3. *Extended parable.* This view sees the song not as an allegory seeking meaning in every verse, but as a parable of Christ and His church.
4. *Literal.* This view sees Solomon celebrating the virtues of human love.

However you view the book, think of God's role as the Ultimate Leader whose love for His people motivates Him to lead and to act on their behalf.

Leaders in the Song of Solomon

The husband (or God)

Other People of Influence in the Song of Solomon

The wife or the beloved (the body of Christ), the friends

Lessons in Leadership

- The best leaders feel motivated by love and compassion for their people.
- You cannot separate leadership from relationships.
- When leaders practice transparency, respect goes up, not down.
- Both the leader and the people need each other.
- Even the toughest of problems can be solved when relationships are managed well.

LEADERSHIP

HIGHLIGHTS IN THE SONG OF SOLOMON

THE PASSIONATE, Consuming Love of God (1:1)	*page 800*
AFFIRMATION: Leaders Identify and Affirm Qualities in Others (1:10–15)	*page 801*
LEADERS HONOR THEIR TEAMS: Put 10s on Their Foreheads (4:1–16)	*page 803*

1
The song of songs, which *is* Solomon's.

The Banquet

THE SHULAMITE[a]

2 Let him kiss me with the kisses of his
       mouth—
   For your[b] love *is* better than wine.
3 Because of the fragrance of your good
       ointments,
   Your name *is* ointment poured forth;
   Therefore the virgins love you.
4 Draw me away!

THE DAUGHTERS OF JERUSALEM

   We will run after you.[a]

THE SHULAMITE

   The king has brought me into his
       chambers.

THE DAUGHTERS OF JERUSALEM

   We will be glad and rejoice in you.[b]

   We will remember your[c] love more than
       wine.

THE SHULAMITE

   Rightly do they love you.[d]

5 I *am* dark, but lovely,
   O daughters of Jerusalem,
   Like the tents of Kedar,
   Like the curtains of Solomon.
6 Do not look upon me, because I *am* dark,
   Because the sun has tanned me.
   My mother's sons were angry with me;
   They made me the keeper of the
       vineyards,
   But my own vineyard I have not kept.

(TO HER BELOVED)

7 Tell me, O you whom I love,
   Where you feed *your flock,*
   Where you make *it* rest at noon.
   For why should I be as one who veils
       herself[a]
   By the flocks of your companions?

THE BELOVED

8 If you do not know, O fairest among
       women,
   Follow in the footsteps of the flock,
   And feed your little goats
   Beside the shepherds' tents.

1:2 [a]A Palestinian young woman (compare 6:13).
The speaker and audience are identified according
to the number, gender, and person of the Hebrew
words. Occasionally the identity is not certain.
[b]Masculine singular, that is, the Beloved
1:4 [a]Masculine singular, that is, the Beloved
[b]Feminine singular, that is, the Shulamite
[c]Masculine singular, that is, the Beloved [d]Masculine
singular, that is, the Beloved **1:7** [a]Septuagint,
Syriac, and Vulgate read *wanders.*

The Passionate, Consuming Love of God

(Song of Solomon 1:1)

Most of the time when we use words like "passion" and "love," we speak of the affection between a man and a woman. But have you ever thought of God's love in terms of *passion?*

In the Song of Solomon, we see a beautiful picture of the tender devotion that God means to be shared between a husband and wife. But we also see a picture of the love God wants His people to share with Jesus Christ.

King Solomon understood that this love was unearned and unmerited, that in many ways God poured it out on His people despite themselves. This kind of love represents an actual communion between Christ and His church. On His part, it's a love that gives all to those with nothing to give in exchange. On our part, it is the kind of love that inspires us to hunger for more of Him, to thirst for Him to shine out through us.

Godly leaders understand that the relationship between Christ and His people amounts to far more than some kind of religious arrangement or contractual agreement. Rather, it is a relationship of love, tenderness, and passion, a relationship in which we, the bride, remain aware of our unworthiness of the Bridegroom's love—yet bask in its limitless depths.

9 I have compared you, my love,
   To my filly among Pharaoh's chariots.
10 Your cheeks are lovely with ornaments,
   Your neck with chains *of gold.*

Affirmation: Leaders Identify and Affirm Qualities in Others

(Song of Solomon 1:10–15)

Leaders whom others love and loyally follow are usually those who express appreciation to their followers. They live the principle of affirmation.

The Song of Solomon reveals a spiritual leader who identifies specific qualities he appreciates about his beloved, then expresses his appreciation. This marvelous love letter shows a spiritual leader communicating love and affirmation. The follower almost always reciprocates the sentiment. Notice what Solomon and all great leaders do to encourage those in their care:

1. **Identify**—Declare what it is you appreciate. Name it.
2. **Specify**—Be as specific as you can. No generalizations about their style!
3. **Quantify**—Express how they have made a measurable difference in your life.
4. **Magnify**—Encourage your followers liberally in public, before their peers.

THE DAUGHTERS OF JERUSALEM
11 We will make you[a] ornaments of gold
   With studs of silver.

THE SHULAMITE
12 While the king *is* at his table,
   My spikenard sends forth its fragrance.
13 A bundle of myrrh *is* my beloved to me,
   That lies all night between my breasts.
14 My beloved *is* to me a cluster of henna
   blooms
   In the vineyards of En Gedi.

THE BELOVED
15 Behold, you *are* fair, my love!
   Behold, you *are* fair!
   You *have* dove's eyes.

THE SHULAMITE
16 Behold, you *are* handsome, my beloved!
   Yes, pleasant!
   Also our bed *is* green.
17 The beams of our houses *are* cedar,
   And our rafters of fir.

2 I *am* the rose of Sharon,
   And the lily of the valleys.

THE BELOVED
2 Like a lily among thorns,
   So is my love among the daughters.

THE SHULAMITE
3 Like an apple tree among the trees of the
     woods,
   So *is* my beloved among the sons.
   I sat down in his shade with great delight,
   And his fruit *was* sweet to my taste.

THE SHULAMITE TO THE DAUGHTERS OF JERUSALEM
4 He brought me to the banqueting house,
   And his banner over me *was* love.
5 Sustain me with cakes of raisins,
   Refresh me with apples,
   For I *am* lovesick.

6 His left hand *is* under my head,
   And his right hand embraces me.
7 I charge you, O daughters of Jerusalem,
   By the gazelles or by the does of the field,
   Do not stir up nor awaken love
   Until it pleases.

The Beloved's Request

THE SHULAMITE
8 The voice of my beloved!
   Behold, he comes
   Leaping upon the mountains,
   Skipping upon the hills.
9 My beloved is like a gazelle or a young
     stag.
   Behold, he stands behind our wall;
   He is looking through the windows,
   Gazing through the lattice.

10 My beloved spoke, and said to me:
   "Rise up, my love, my fair one,
   And come away.
11 For lo, the winter is past,
   The rain is over *and* gone.

1:11 [a]Feminine singular, that is, the Shulamite

12 The flowers appear on the earth;
The time of singing has come,
And the voice of the turtledove
Is heard in our land.
13 The fig tree puts forth her green figs,
And the vines *with* the tender grapes
Give a good smell.
Rise up, my love, my fair one,
And come away!

14 "O my dove, in the clefts of the rock,
In the secret *places* of the cliff,
Let me see your face,
Let me hear your voice;
For your voice *is* sweet,
And your face *is* lovely."

HER BROTHERS

15 Catch us the foxes,
The little foxes that spoil the vines,
For our vines *have* tender grapes.

Catching the Little Foxes

(*Song of Solomon 2:15*)

It's the "little foxes" that often ruin an organization—bad attitudes, lack of encouragement, no time off, impatient supervisors, or gossip. Leaders must listen for the sounds of little fox feet. Remember, it's better to build a fence at the top of the cliff than a hospital at the bottom.

THE SHULAMITE

16 My beloved *is* mine, and I *am* his.
He feeds *his flock* among the lilies.

(TO HER BELOVED)

17 Until the day breaks
And the shadows flee away,
Turn, my beloved,
And be like a gazelle
Or a young stag
Upon the mountains of Bether.[a]

A Troubled Night

THE SHULAMITE

3 By night on my bed I sought the one I love;
I sought him, but I did not find him.
2 "I will rise now," *I said,*

"And go about the city;
In the streets and in the squares
I will seek the one I love."
I sought him, but I did not find him.
3 The watchmen who go about the city found me;
I said,
"Have you seen the one I love?"

4 Scarcely had I passed by them,
When I found the one I love.
I held him and would not let him go,
Until I had brought him to the house of my mother,
And into the chamber of her who conceived me.

5 I charge you, O daughters of Jerusalem,
By the gazelles or by the does of the field,
Do not stir up nor awaken love
Until it pleases.

The Coming of Solomon

THE SHULAMITE

6 Who *is* this coming out of the wilderness
Like pillars of smoke,
Perfumed with myrrh and frankincense,
With all the merchant's fragrant powders?
7 Behold, it *is* Solomon's couch,
With sixty valiant men around it,
Of the valiant of Israel.
8 They all hold swords,
Being expert in war.
Every man *has* his sword on his thigh
Because of fear in the night.

9 Of the wood of Lebanon
Solomon the King
Made himself a palanquin:[a]
10 He made its pillars *of* silver,
Its support *of* gold,
Its seat *of* purple,
Its interior paved *with* love
By the daughters of Jerusalem.
11 Go forth, O daughters of Zion,
And see King Solomon with the crown
With which his mother crowned him
On the day of his wedding,
The day of the gladness of his heart.

2:17 [a]Literally *Separation* **3:9** [a]A portable enclosed chair

The Bridegroom Praises the Bride

THE BELOVED

4 Behold, you *are* fair, my love!
Behold, you *are* fair!
You *have* dove's eyes behind your veil.
Your hair *is* like a flock of goats,
Going down from Mount Gilead.

2 Your teeth *are* like a flock of shorn *sheep*
Which have come up from the washing,
Every one of which bears twins,
And none *is* barren among them.

3 Your lips *are* like a strand of scarlet,
And your mouth is lovely.
Your temples behind your veil
Are like a piece of pomegranate.

4 Your neck *is* like the tower of David,
Built for an armory,
On which hang a thousand bucklers,
All shields of mighty men.

5 Your two breasts *are* like two fawns,
Twins of a gazelle,
Which feed among the lilies.

6 Until the day breaks
And the shadows flee away,
I will go my way to the mountain of
myrrh
And to the hill of frankincense.

7 You *are* all fair, my love,
And *there is* no spot in you.

8 Come with me from Lebanon, *my*
spouse,
With me from Lebanon.
Look from the top of Amana,
From the top of Senir and Hermon,
From the lions' dens,
From the mountains of the leopards.

9 You have ravished my heart,
My sister, *my* spouse;
You have ravished my heart
With one *look* of your eyes,
With one link of your necklace.

10 How fair is your love,
My sister, *my* spouse!
How much better than wine is your love,
And the scent of your perfumes
Than all spices!

11 Your lips, O *my* spouse,
Drip as the honeycomb;
Honey and milk *are* under your tongue;
And the fragrance of your garments
Is like the fragrance of Lebanon.

12 A garden enclosed
Is my sister, *my* spouse,
A spring shut up,
A fountain sealed.

13 Your plants *are* an orchard of
pomegranates
With pleasant fruits,
Fragrant henna with spikenard,

Leaders Honor Their Teams: Put 10s on Their Foreheads

(Song of Solomon 4:1–16)

Solomon spoke delightful words that honored and lifted up his bride. Many scholars believe this song is actually a metaphor for Christ's love for His people. The song also gives leaders a beautiful picture about how to communicate honor from the heart. How can we best communicate compliments to those we lead?

1. **Make them sincere.** Be genuine and authentic about what you say.
2. **Make them specific.** Get very pointed and detailed about what you say.
3. **Make them public.** Declare these honoring words in front of others.
4. **Make them personal.** Be personal about what you say.

Whenever I see my staff, I put an imaginary "10" on the forehead of each individual. This helps me treat each person like a "10," a high performer who makes a difference to me and the organization. Inevitably, they respond as if they *are* a 10!

If you don't already do this, why not start today? Put "10s" on the people you lead. Treat them based on their potential, not their performance. You'll be amazed how both will rise.

14 Spikenard and saffron,
　　Calamus and cinnamon,
　　With all trees of frankincense,
　　Myrrh and aloes,
　　With all the chief spices—
15 A fountain of gardens,
　　A well of living waters,
　　And streams from Lebanon.

THE SHULAMITE

16 Awake, O north *wind,*
　　And come, O south!
　　Blow upon my garden,
　　That its spices may flow out.
　　Let my beloved come to his garden
　　And eat its pleasant fruits.

Leaders Bless People

(Song of Solomon 4:1–16)

Good leaders give the "blessing" to those they lead. In the Hebrew culture, fathers or patriarchs usually gave the blessing to their sons; rabbis and other spiritual leaders also pronounced blessings. Gary Smalley and John Trent remind us that the blessing contains five key elements:

1. *Affirming words:* words that give hope and encouragement to the listener.
2. *Meaningful touch:* an embrace or a hand on a shoulder communicating care.
3. *Expression of high value:* a statement on the value that person adds to everyone.
4. *Vision of a special future:* provides word pictures that communicate potential.
5. *Application of genuine commitment:* do everything in your power to see that blessing comes to pass.

THE BELOVED

5 I have come to my garden, my sister, *my*
　　spouse;
　　I have gathered my myrrh with my spice;
　　I have eaten my honeycomb with my
　　honey;
　　I have drunk my wine with my milk.

(TO HIS FRIENDS)

　　Eat, O friends!
　　Drink, yes, drink deeply,
　　O beloved ones!

The Shulamite's Troubled Evening

THE SHULAMITE

2 I sleep, but my heart is awake;
　　It is the voice of my beloved!
　　He knocks, *saying,*
　　"Open for me, my sister, my love,
　　My dove, my perfect one;
　　For my head is covered with dew,
　　My locks with the drops of the night."

3 I have taken off my robe;
　　How can I put it on *again?*
　　I have washed my feet;
　　How can I defile them?
4 My beloved put his hand
　　By the latch *of the door,*
　　And my heart yearned for him.
5 I arose to open for my beloved,
　　And my hands dripped *with* myrrh,
　　My fingers with liquid myrrh,
　　On the handles of the lock.

6 I opened for my beloved,
　　But my beloved had turned away *and* was
　　　gone.
　　My heart leaped up when he spoke.
　　I sought him, but I could not find him;
　　I called him, but he gave me no answer.
7 The watchmen who went about the city
　　　found me.
　　They struck me, they wounded me;
　　The keepers of the walls
　　Took my veil away from me.
8 I charge you, O daughters of Jerusalem,
　　If you find my beloved,
　　That you tell him I *am* lovesick!

THE DAUGHTERS OF JERUSALEM

9 What *is* your beloved
　　More than *another* beloved,
　　O fairest among women?
　　What *is* your beloved
　　More than *another* beloved,
　　That you so charge us?

THE SHULAMITE

10 My beloved *is* white and ruddy,
　　Chief among ten thousand.
11 His head *is like* the finest gold;
　　His locks *are* wavy,
　　And black as a raven.
12 His eyes *are* like doves
　　By the rivers of waters,
　　Washed with milk,
　　And fitly set.

13 His cheeks *are* like a bed of spices,
Banks of scented herbs.
His lips *are* lilies,
Dripping liquid myrrh.

14 His hands *are* rods of gold
Set with beryl.
His body *is* carved ivory
Inlaid *with* sapphires.

15 His legs *are* pillars of marble
Set on bases of fine gold.
His countenance *is* like Lebanon,
Excellent as the cedars.

16 His mouth *is* most sweet,
Yes, he *is* altogether lovely.
This *is* my beloved,
And this *is* my friend,
O daughters of Jerusalem!

THE DAUGHTERS OF JERUSALEM

6 Where has your beloved gone,
O fairest among women?
Where has your beloved turned aside,
That we may seek him with you?

THE SHULAMITE

2 My beloved has gone to his garden,
To the beds of spices,
To feed *his flock* in the gardens,
And to gather lilies.

3 I *am* my beloved's,
And my beloved *is* mine.
He feeds *his flock* among the lilies.

Praise of the Shulamite's Beauty

THE BELOVED

4 O my love, you *are as* beautiful as Tirzah,
Lovely as Jerusalem,
Awesome as *an army* with banners!

5 Turn your eyes away from me,
For they have overcome me.
Your hair *is* like a flock of goats
Going down from Gilead.

6 Your teeth *are* like a flock of sheep
Which have come up from the washing;
Every one bears twins,
And none *is* barren among them.

7 Like a piece of pomegranate
Are your temples behind your veil.

8 There are sixty queens
And eighty concubines,
And virgins without number.

9 My dove, my perfect one,
Is the only one,

The only one of her mother,
The favorite of the one who bore her.
The daughters saw her
And called her blessed,
The queens and the concubines,
And they praised her.

10 Who is she who looks forth as the
morning,
Fair as the moon,
Clear as the sun,
Awesome as *an army* with banners?

THE SHULAMITE

11 I went down to the garden of nuts
To see the verdure of the valley,
To see whether the vine had budded
And the pomegranates had bloomed.

12 Before I was even aware,
My soul had made me
As the chariots of my noble people.[a]

THE BELOVED AND HIS FRIENDS

13 Return, return, O Shulamite;
Return, return, that we may look upon you!

6:12 [a]Hebrew *Ammi Nadib*

Leaders Practice Good People Skills

(Song of Solomon 5:1—6:13)

The Song of Solomon overflows with heart, describing a passionate relationship between two people who deeply love each other.

What can leaders learn from this book? Leaders must relate to their people from the soul, not merely by protocol. The best way to overcome problems is to involve your heart, not just your head.

Unfortunately, we're tempted toward another direction. When we fail at something, we tend to see why it happened and cut ourselves some slack; we may even make excuses for our mistakes. In other words, we deal with ourselves using our heart. Yet we often neglect the heart when dealing with others. We can be direct and even demanding. It really works best to switch the whole thing around. When dealing with yourself, use your head. When dealing with others, use your heart.

THE SHULAMITE

What would you see in the Shulamite—
As it were, the dance of the two camps?[a]

Expressions of Praise

THE BELOVED

7 How beautiful are your feet in sandals,
O prince's daughter!
The curves of your thighs *are* like jewels,
The work of the hands of a skillful
workman.

2 Your navel *is* a rounded goblet;
It lacks no blended beverage.
Your waist *is* a heap of wheat
Set about with lilies.

3 Your two breasts *are* like two fawns,
Twins of a gazelle.

4 Your neck *is* like an ivory tower,
Your eyes *like* the pools in Heshbon
By the gate of Bath Rabbim.
Your nose *is* like the tower of Lebanon
Which looks toward Damascus.

5 Your head *crowns* you like *Mount* Carmel,
And the hair of your head *is* like purple;
A king *is* held captive by *your* tresses.

6 How fair and how pleasant you are,
O love, with your delights!

7 This stature of yours is like a palm tree,
And your breasts *like* its clusters.

8 I said, "I will go up to the palm tree,
I will take hold of its branches."
Let now your breasts be like clusters of the
vine,
The fragrance of your breath like apples,

9 And the roof of your mouth like the best
wine.

THE SHULAMITE

The wine goes *down* smoothly for my
beloved,
Moving gently the lips of sleepers.[a]

10 I *am* my beloved's,
And his desire *is* toward me.

11 Come, my beloved,
Let us go forth to the field;
Let us lodge in the villages.

12 Let us get up early to the vineyards;
Let us see if the vine has budded,
Whether the grape blossoms are open,
And the pomegranates are in bloom.
There I will give you my love.

13 The mandrakes give off a fragrance,
And at our gates *are* pleasant *fruits,*

All manner, new and old,
Which I have laid up for you, my beloved.

8 Oh, that you were like my brother,
Who nursed at my mother's breasts!
If I should find you outside,
I would kiss you;
I would not be despised.

2 I would lead you *and* bring you
Into the house of my mother,
She *who* used to instruct me.
I would cause you to drink of spiced wine,
Of the juice of my pomegranate.

(TO THE DAUGHTERS OF JERUSALEM)

3 His left hand *is* under my head,
And his right hand embraces me.

4 I charge you, O daughters of Jerusalem,
Do not stir up nor awaken love
Until it pleases.

Love Renewed in Lebanon

A RELATIVE

5 Who *is* this coming up from the
wilderness,
Leaning upon her beloved?

I awakened you under the apple tree.
There your mother brought you forth;
There she *who* bore you brought *you* forth.

THE SHULAMITE TO HER BELOVED

6 Set me as a seal upon your heart,
As a seal upon your arm;
For love *is as* strong as death,
Jealousy *as* cruel as the grave;[a]
Its flames *are* flames of fire,
A most vehement flame.[b]

7 Many waters cannot quench love,
Nor can the floods drown it.
If a man would give for love
All the wealth of his house,
It would be utterly despised.

THE SHULAMITE'S BROTHERS

8 We have a little sister,
And she has no breasts.
What shall we do for our sister
In the day when she is spoken for?

6:13 [a]Hebrew *Mahanaim* 7:9 [a]Septuagint, Syriac,
and Vulgate read *lips and teeth.* 8:6 [a]Or *Sheol*
[b]Literally *A flame of YAH* (a poetic form of *YHWH,*
the LORD)

9 If she *is* a wall,
We will build upon her
A battlement of silver;
And if she *is* a door,
We will enclose her
With boards of cedar.

THE SHULAMITE

10 I *am* a wall,
And my breasts like towers;
Then I became in his eyes
As one who found peace.

11 Solomon had a vineyard at Baal Hamon;
He leased the vineyard to keepers;
Everyone was to bring for its fruit
A thousand silver coins.

(TO SOLOMON)

12 My own vineyard *is* before me.
You, O Solomon, *may have* a thousand,
And those who tend its fruit two
hundred.

THE BELOVED

13 You who dwell in the gardens,
The companions listen for your voice—
Let me hear it!

THE SHULAMITE

14 Make haste, my beloved,
And be like a gazelle
Or a young stag
On the mountains of spices.

ISAIAH

Consistent Lifestyle . . . Uncompromising Convictions . . . Clear Vision

SUMMARY

We remember Isaiah as one of the greatest prophets in Jewish history and as one of the most powerful models in the Bible. The book that bears his name describes his consistent lifestyle, his uncompromising convictions, and his clear vision that drove him to continue speaking out despite the unfaithfulness of his people.

Isaiah's lifestyle reminds us that we cannot separate a leader's words and walk. A leader must first be an example to the people. People do what people see. Isaiah led with integrity. Integrity means "oneness," the quality of purity and consistency. When we speak of the integrity of Scripture, we mean that it proclaims one consistent message. This word describes Isaiah, a man of God full of consistency.

Isaiah's convictions teach us about avoiding ungodly compromise. He and his contemporary, the prophet Micah, both raised the bar for the people by holding to God's standards with unswerving determination. While leaders must remain flexible with their methods, they cannot compromise their convictions.

Finally, Isaiah furnishes a beautiful case study of a leader who led from vision. He describes a God-given vision that drives him to fulfill his calling as a leader. He clings to it despite rejection (6:9). Throughout the book he communicates his vision to the people and warns them to repent. Before he finishes, he has influenced King Hezekiah to bring about national reforms. Through his tenacious intercession with God, Sennacherib's entire army is destroyed (2 Kin. 19:36, 37; 2 Chr. 32:20–23; Is. 37:36–38).

God's Role in Isaiah

As the One who inspired both Isaiah's ministry and his writings, God again reveals Himself as the Leader of leaders. We see the Lord telling Isaiah what to say to the people and warning them of the impending judgment if they fail to repent. God also gives Isaiah visions about the future. While the first 39 chapters lay out some bleak moments, the remaining 27 provide strong hope. Isaiah predicts the coming Messiah as the Ultimate Leader for the people of Israel. The Messiah embodies all the positive qualities of an effective leader.

Leaders in Isaiah

Isaiah, King Hezekiah, the Messiah

Other People of Influence in Isaiah

Kings of Judah and Israel, leaders of Assyria, Babylon, Edom, Egypt, Tyre, Cush, Philistia, Moab, Damascus (Syria), Dedan, and Kedar

Lessons in Leadership

- Vision is born out of values and ethics—they must align.
- The measure of a person is what he or she does with power.
- Leaders create atmospheres and environments for growth and success.
- Ability, opportunity, and desire make up the components of a call to lead.
- God reduces prideful leaders but resources humble leaders.
- Strategic planning that ignores God and the changing culture is doomed to fail.
- Insecure leaders inevitably destroy people; secure leaders develop people.
- The higher leaders climb, the fewer there are who can hold them accountable.
- God Himself provides the ultimate model of servant leadership.

LEADERSHIP

HIGHLIGHTS IN ISAIAH

1 The vision of Isaiah the son of Amoz, which he saw concerning Judah and Jerusalem in the days of Uzziah, Jotham, Ahaz, *and* Hezekiah, kings of Judah.

The Wickedness of Judah

2 Hear, O heavens, and give ear, O earth!
    For the LORD has spoken:
    "I have nourished and brought up children,
    And they have rebelled against Me;
3 The ox knows its owner
    And the donkey its master's crib;
    But Israel does not know,
    My people do not consider."

4 Alas, sinful nation,
    A people laden with iniquity,
    A brood of evildoers,
    Children who are corrupters!
    They have forsaken the LORD,
    They have provoked to anger
    The Holy One of Israel,
    They have turned away backward.

5 Why should you be stricken again?
    You will revolt more and more.
    The whole head is sick,
    And the whole heart faints.
6 From the sole of the foot even to the
        head,
    There is no soundness in it,
    But wounds and bruises and putrefying
        sores;
    They have not been closed or bound up,
    Or soothed with ointment.

7 Your country *is* desolate,
    Your cities *are* burned with fire;
    Strangers devour your land in your
        presence;
    And *it is* desolate, as overthrown by
        strangers.
8 So the daughter of Zion is left as a booth
        in a vineyard,
    As a hut in a garden of cucumbers,
    As a besieged city.
9 Unless the LORD of hosts
    Had left to us a very small remnant,
    We would have become like Sodom,
    We would have been made like
        Gomorrah.

10 Hear the word of the LORD,
    You rulers of Sodom;
    Give ear to the law of our God,
    You people of Gomorrah:

Growth Occurs When Vision and Values Match

(Isaiah 1:10–17)

God scolds the leaders of Judah and Jerusalem—even calling them rulers of Sodom and people of Gomorrah, the wicked cities He wiped out in Genesis 19—because they continued to perform religious rituals long after their hearts had grown cold and distant toward God. In other words, they continued to pursue a godly vision far from the values that birthed it. They had become empty, hollow leaders.

God resents perfunctory behavior. He doesn't want leaders who merely go through the motions. Leaders can look good while pursuing a worthwhile vision that they no longer consider valuable. Leaders find power only when . . .

1. Their vision and values match.
2. Their lifestyle and lip service match.
3. Their conduct and character match.
4. Their image and integrity match.
5. Their promises and production match.
6. Their strategy and support match.

11 "To what purpose *is* the multitude of your
        sacrifices to Me?"
    Says the LORD.
    "I have had enough of burnt offerings of
        rams
    And the fat of fed cattle.
    I do not delight in the blood of bulls,
    Or of lambs or goats.

12 "When you come to appear before Me,
    Who has required this from your hand,
    To trample My courts?
13 Bring no more futile sacrifices;
    Incense is an abomination to Me.
    The New Moons, the Sabbaths, and the
        calling of assemblies—
    I cannot endure iniquity and the sacred
        meeting.
14 Your New Moons and your appointed
        feasts
    My soul hates;
    They are a trouble to Me,
    I am weary of bearing *them*.

15 When you spread out your hands,
   I will hide My eyes from you;
   Even though you make many prayers,
   I will not hear.
   Your hands are full of blood.

16 "Wash yourselves, make yourselves clean;
   Put away the evil of your doings from
      before My eyes.
   Cease to do evil,
17 Learn to do good;
   Seek justice,
   Rebuke the oppressor;[a]
   Defend the fatherless,
   Plead for the widow.

18 "Come now, and let us reason together,"
      Says the LORD,
   "Though your sins are like scarlet,
   They shall be as white as snow;
   Though they are red like crimson,
   They shall be as wool.
19 If you are willing and obedient,
   You shall eat the good of the land;
20 But if you refuse and rebel,
   You shall be devoured by the sword";
   For the mouth of the LORD has spoken.

The Degenerate City

21 How the faithful city has become a
      harlot!
   It was full of justice;
   Righteousness lodged in it,
   But now murderers.
22 Your silver has become dross,
   Your wine mixed with water.
23 Your princes are rebellious,
   And companions of thieves;
   Everyone loves bribes,
   And follows after rewards.
   They do not defend the fatherless,
   Nor does the cause of the widow come
      before them.

24 Therefore the Lord says,
   The LORD of hosts, the Mighty One of
      Israel,
   "Ah, I will rid Myself of My adversaries,
   And take vengeance on My enemies.
25 I will turn My hand against you,
   And thoroughly purge away your dross,
   And take away all your alloy.
26 I will restore your judges as at the first,
   And your counselors as at the beginning.
   Afterward you shall be called the city of
      righteousness, the faithful city."

27 Zion shall be redeemed with justice,
   And her penitents with righteousness.
28 The destruction of transgressors and of
      sinners shall be together,
   And those who forsake the LORD shall be
      consumed.
29 For they[a] shall be ashamed of the terebinth
      trees
   Which you have desired;
   And you shall be embarrassed because of
      the gardens
   Which you have chosen.
30 For you shall be as a terebinth whose leaf
      fades,
   And as a garden that has no water.
31 The strong shall be as tinder,
   And the work of it as a spark;
   Both will burn together,
   And no one shall quench them.

The Future House of God

2 The word that Isaiah the son of Amoz saw
   concerning Judah and Jerusalem.

2 Now it shall come to pass in the latter days
   That the mountain of the LORD's house
   Shall be established on the top of the
      mountains,
   And shall be exalted above the hills;
   And all nations shall flow to it.
3 Many people shall come and say,
   "Come, and let us go up to the mountain
      of the LORD,
   To the house of the God of Jacob;
   He will teach us His ways,
   And we shall walk in His paths."
   For out of Zion shall go forth the law,
   And the word of the LORD from
      Jerusalem.
4 He shall judge between the nations,
   And rebuke many people;
   They shall beat their swords into
      plowshares,
   And their spears into pruning hooks;
   Nation shall not lift up sword against
      nation,
   Neither shall they learn war anymore.

The Day of the LORD

5 O house of Jacob, come and let us walk
   In the light of the LORD.

1:17 [a]Some ancient versions read the oppressed.
1:29 [a]Following Masoretic Text, Septuagint, and
Vulgate; some Hebrew manuscripts and Targum
read you.

6 For You have forsaken Your people, the
house of Jacob,
Because they are filled with eastern ways;
They *are* soothsayers like the Philistines,
And they are pleased with the children of
foreigners.

7 Their land is also full of silver and gold,
And there is no end to their treasures;
Their land is also full of horses,
And there is no end to their chariots.

8 Their land is also full of idols;
They worship the work of their own hands,
That which their own fingers have made.

9 People bow down,
And each man humbles himself;
Therefore do not forgive them.

10 Enter into the rock, and hide in the dust,
From the terror of the LORD
And the glory of His majesty.

11 The lofty looks of man shall be humbled,
The haughtiness of men shall be bowed
down,
And the LORD alone shall be exalted in
that day.

12 For the day of the LORD of hosts
Shall come upon everything proud and
lofty,
Upon everything lifted up—
And it shall be brought low—

13 Upon all the cedars of Lebanon *that are*
high and lifted up,
And upon all the oaks of Bashan;

14 Upon all the high mountains,
And upon all the hills *that are* lifted up;

15 Upon every high tower,
And upon every fortified wall;

16 Upon all the ships of Tarshish,
And upon all the beautiful sloops.

17 The loftiness of man shall be bowed down,
And the haughtiness of men shall be
brought low;
The LORD alone will be exalted in that
day,

18 But the idols He shall utterly abolish.

19 They shall go into the holes of the rocks,
And into the caves of the earth,
From the terror of the LORD
And the glory of His majesty,
When He arises to shake the earth
mightily.

20 In that day a man will cast away his idols
of silver

And his idols of gold,
Which they made, *each* for himself to
worship,
To the moles and bats,

21 To go into the clefts of the rocks,
And into the crags of the rugged rocks,
From the terror of the LORD
And the glory of His majesty,
When He arises to shake the earth
mightily.

22 Sever yourselves from such a man,
Whose breath *is* in his nostrils;
For of what account is he?

Judgment on Judah and Jerusalem

3 For behold, the Lord, the LORD of hosts,
Takes away from Jerusalem and from
Judah
The stock and the store,
The whole supply of bread and the whole
supply of water;

2 The mighty man and the man of war,
The judge and the prophet,
And the diviner and the elder;

3 The captain of fifty and the honorable
man,
The counselor and the skillful artisan,
And the expert enchanter.

Judah's Lousy Leaders: Everything Rises and Falls on Leadership

(Isaiah 3:1–4)

God had a strategy for judging Judah, and
part of His judgment involved removing
good leaders from the nation. No organization
or nation can prosper without good leadership. People suffer with poor leaders at the
helm. God knew the way to impact the nation
was to change its leadership.

---

4 "I will give children *to be* their princes,
And babes shall rule over them.

5 The people will be oppressed,
Every one by another and every one by
his neighbor;
The child will be insolent toward the
elder,
And the base toward the honorable."

6 When a man takes hold of his brother
In the house of his father, *saying,*
"You have clothing;
You be our ruler,
And *let* these ruins *be* under your power,"[a]
7 In that day he will protest, saying,
"I cannot cure *your* ills,
For in my house *is* neither food nor
clothing;
Do not make me a ruler of the people."

8 For Jerusalem stumbled,
And Judah is fallen,
Because their tongue and their doings
Are against the LORD,
To provoke the eyes of His glory.
9 The look on their countenance witnesses
against them,
And they declare their sin as Sodom;
They do not hide *it.*
Woe to their soul!
For they have brought evil upon
themselves.

10 "Say to the righteous that *it shall be* well
with them,
For they shall eat the fruit of their doings.
11 Woe to the wicked! *It shall be* ill *with him,*
For the reward of his hands shall be given
him.
12 *As for* My people, children *are* their
oppressors,

And women rule over them.
O My people! Those who lead you cause
you to err,
And destroy the way of your paths."

Oppression and Luxury Condemned

13 The LORD stands up to plead,
And stands to judge the people.
14 The LORD will enter into judgment
With the elders of His people
And His princes:
"For you have eaten up the vineyard;
The plunder of the poor *is* in your houses.
15 What do you mean by crushing My
people
And grinding the faces of the poor?"
Says the Lord GOD of hosts.

16 Moreover the LORD says:

"Because the daughters of Zion are haughty,
And walk with outstretched necks
And wanton eyes,
Walking and mincing *as* they go,
Making a jingling with their feet,
17 Therefore the Lord will strike with a scab
The crown of the head of the daughters of
Zion,
And the LORD will uncover their secret
parts."

3:6 [a] Literally *hand*

The Law of Navigation: How Leaders Lead

(Isaiah 3:14, 15)

The more power leaders gain, the more they reveal of themselves. Power causes the heart to disclose its contents.

The leaders described in Isaiah 3 displayed their corrupt hearts the moment they won a position of authority. Good or bad, leaders determine where and when the organization goes; this is the ripple effect of the Law of Navigation. The Lord responded to these corrupt leaders by sounding judgment against them.

Leaders must consider the impact of their every move. Leaders always lead. There are no time-outs! There never comes a time when it doesn't matter what you do. Think of your leadership like a diet. Suppose you eat right in the restaurant with friends, but then go home and consume a whole strawberry cheesecake. You won't lose weight that way! What you eat eventually shows. In the same way, those you lead eventually reflect your leadership. Your navigation as a leader depends on the following:

1. When you know where you are going, you gain *conviction.*
2. When you have been there before, you gain *credibility.*
3. When you can take someone with you, you gain *connection.*

18 In that day the Lord will take away the finery:
The jingling anklets, the scarves, and the crescents;
19 The pendants, the bracelets, and the veils;
20 The headdresses, the leg ornaments, and the headbands;
21 The perfume boxes, the charms, and the rings;
22 The nose jewels,
the festal apparel, and the mantles;
The outer garments, the purses,
23 and the mirrors;
The fine linen, the turbans, and the robes.

24 And so it shall be:

Instead of a sweet smell there will be a stench;
Instead of a sash, a rope;
Instead of well-set hair, baldness;
Instead of a rich robe, a girding of sackcloth;
And branding instead of beauty.
25 Your men shall fall by the sword,
And your mighty in the war.

26 Her gates shall lament and mourn,
And she being desolate shall sit on the ground.

4 And in that day seven women shall take hold of one man, saying,
"We will eat our own food and wear our own apparel;
Only let us be called by your name,
To take away our reproach."

The Renewal of Zion

2 In that day the Branch of the LORD shall be beautiful and glorious;
And the fruit of the earth shall be excellent and appealing
For those of Israel who have escaped.

3 And it shall come to pass that he who is left in Zion and remains in Jerusalem will be called holy—everyone who is recorded among the living in Jerusalem. 4 When the Lord has washed away the filth of the daughters of Zion, and purged the blood of Jerusalem from her midst, by the spirit of judgment and by the spirit of burning, 5 then the LORD will create above every dwelling place of Mount Zion, and above her assemblies, a cloud and smoke by day and the shining of a flaming fire by night. For over all the glory there will be a covering. 6 And there will be a tabernacle for shade in the daytime from the heat, for a place of refuge, and for a shelter from storm and rain.

The Value of Vision

(Isaiah 4:2–6)

Isaiah 4 illustrates how good leaders create a climate for growth based on a picture of a preferred future. A strong God-given vision drove all the worthwhile accomplishments recorded in the Bible. Consider the following examples:

Leader	Vision
1. Abraham (Gen. 12)	To create a great nation of people of faith
2. Moses (Ex. 3; 4)	To lead the people of Israel out of Egypt
3. Joshua (Num. 27)	To lead the people of Israel into the Promised Land
4. David (1 Chr. 22)	To build the temple in Jerusalem
5. Solomon (2 Chr. 28)	To complete the building of the temple
6. Nehemiah (Neh. 2)	To rebuild the Jerusalem wall
7. Esther (Esth. 4)	To save the Jewish people from Haman
8. Zerubbabel (Hag. 1)	To rebuild the temple
9. Jesus (Matt. 28; Luke 15)	To seek and save the lost, and to disciple men to do the same
10. Paul (Acts 9)	To take the gospel to the Jews and Gentiles

God's Disappointing Vineyard

5 Now let me sing to my Well-beloved
A song of my Beloved regarding His
vineyard:

My Well-beloved has a vineyard
On a very fruitful hill.
2 He dug it up and cleared out its stones,
And planted it with the choicest vine.
He built a tower in its midst,
And also made a winepress in it;
So He expected *it* to bring forth *good*
grapes,
But it brought forth wild grapes.

3 "And now, O inhabitants of Jerusalem and
men of Judah,
Judge, please, between Me and My
vineyard.
4 What more could have been done to My
vineyard
That I have not done in it?
Why then, when I expected *it* to bring
forth *good* grapes,
Did it bring forth wild grapes?
5 And now, please let Me tell you what I
will do to My vineyard:
I will take away its hedge, and it shall be
burned;
And break down its wall, and it shall be
trampled down.
6 I will lay it waste;
It shall not be pruned or dug,
But there shall come up briers and thorns.
I will also command the clouds
That they rain no rain on it."

7 For the vineyard of the LORD of hosts *is*
the house of Israel,
And the men of Judah are His pleasant
plant.
He looked for justice, but behold,
oppression;
For righteousness, but behold, a cry *for*
help.

Impending Judgment on Excesses

8 Woe to those who join house to house;
They add field to field,
Till *there is* no place
Where they may dwell alone in the midst
of the land!
9 In my hearing the LORD of hosts *said*,
"Truly, many houses shall be desolate,
Great and beautiful ones, without
inhabitant.

10 For ten acres of vineyard shall yield one
bath,
And a homer of seed shall yield one
ephah."

11 Woe to those who rise early in the
morning,
That they may follow intoxicating drink;
Who continue until night, *till* wine
inflames them!
12 The harp and the strings,
The tambourine and flute,
And wine are in their feasts;
But they do not regard the work of the
LORD,
Nor consider the operation of His hands.

13 Therefore my people have gone into
captivity,
Because *they have* no knowledge;
Their honorable men *are* famished,
And their multitude dried up with thirst.
14 Therefore Sheol has enlarged itself
And opened its mouth beyond measure;
Their glory and their multitude and their
pomp,
And he who is jubilant, shall descend
into it.
15 People shall be brought down,
Each man shall be humbled,
And the eyes of the lofty shall be
humbled.
16 But the LORD of hosts shall be exalted in
judgment,
And God who is holy shall be hallowed in
righteousness.
17 Then the lambs shall feed in their pasture,
And in the waste places of the fat ones
strangers shall eat.

18 Woe to those who draw iniquity with
cords of vanity,
And sin as if with a cart rope;
19 That say, "Let Him make speed *and* hasten
His work,
That we may see *it;*
And let the counsel of the Holy One of
Israel draw near and come,
That we may know *it.*"

20 Woe to those who call evil good, and
good evil;
Who put darkness for light, and light for
darkness;
Who put bitter for sweet, and sweet for
bitter!

21 Woe to *those who are* wise in their own
eyes,
And prudent in their own sight!

22 Woe to men mighty at drinking wine,
Woe to men valiant for mixing
intoxicating drink,
23 Who justify the wicked for a bribe,
And take away justice from the righteous
man!

24 Therefore, as the fire devours the stubble,
And the flame consumes the chaff,
So their root will be as rottenness,
And their blossom will ascend like dust;
Because they have rejected the law of the
LORD of hosts,
And despised the word of the Holy One
of Israel.
25 Therefore the anger of the LORD is
aroused against His people;
He has stretched out His hand against
them
And stricken them,
And the hills trembled.
Their carcasses *were* as refuse in the midst
of the streets.

For all this His anger is not turned away,
But His hand *is* stretched out still.

26 He will lift up a banner to the nations
from afar,
And will whistle to them from the end of
the earth;
Surely they shall come with speed, swiftly.
27 No one will be weary or stumble among
them,
No one will slumber or sleep;
Nor will the belt on their loins be loosed,
Nor the strap of their sandals be broken;
28 Whose arrows *are* sharp,
And all their bows bent;
Their horses' hooves will seem like flint,
And their wheels like a whirlwind.
29 Their roaring *will be* like a lion,
They will roar like young lions;
Yes, they will roar
And lay hold of the prey;
They will carry *it* away safely,
And no one will deliver.
30 In that day they will roar against them
Like the roaring of the sea.
And if *one* looks to the land,
Behold, darkness *and* sorrow;
And the light is darkened by the clouds.

Isaiah Called to Be a Prophet

6 In the year that King Uzziah died, I saw
the Lord sitting on a throne, high and lifted
up, and the train of His *robe* filled the temple. [2]Above it stood seraphim; each one had six
wings: with two he covered his face, with two he
covered his feet, and with two he flew. [3]And one
cried to another and said:

"Holy, holy, holy *is* the LORD of hosts;
The whole earth *is* full of His glory!"

[4]And the posts of the door were shaken by the
voice of him who cried out, and the house was
filled with smoke.
[5]So I said:

"Woe *is* me, for I am undone!
Because I *am* a man of unclean lips,
And I dwell in the midst of a people of
unclean lips;
For my eyes have seen the King,
The LORD of hosts."

[6]Then one of the seraphim flew to me, having in his hand a live coal *which* he had taken
with the tongs from the altar. [7]And he touched
my mouth *with it,* and said:

The Call of a Leader
(Isaiah 6:1–8)

The first eight verses of Isaiah 6 illustrate
how God calls many leaders. After Isaiah
captures a vision for God, the Lord lays out a
need for someone to speak for Him. God has a
message and is looking for a messenger. God
issued a general call, for anyone, and Isaiah
took it personally. He did so because of three
factors that make up a divine call to lead:

1. **Opportunity:** We see a specific place
where we can make a difference. This has
to do with timing (v. 1).
2. **Ability:** We recognize that we have the
God-given gifts to do something about
the need. This has to do with competence
(vv. 6, 7).
3. **Desire:** We want to step out and address
the need; our hunger pushes us. This has
to do with our passion (v. 8).

Responding to a Divine Call
(Isaiah 6:1–8)

Have you ever noticed that the experience of Isaiah parallels our own process of responding to a divine call to lead?

Isaiah gets a vision of God (Is. 6:1–4), a vision of himself (6:5–7) and a vision of ministry (6:8). At least five stages in this process apply to us:

Stage One: *The Revelation of God* (vv. 1, 2)
Isaiah saw the Lord in a face-to-face encounter that changed him forever.

Stage Two: *The Realization of God's Holiness* (vv. 3, 4)
Isaiah experiences God as holy. Through this encounter, the Lord becomes more than an abstract idea. Isaiah learns of God's awesome personality.

Stage Three: *The Recognition of His Own Sinfulness* (v. 5)
Isaiah sees the vast distance between God and himself. He sees the infinite contrast and is broken of self.

Stage Four: *The Renewal of His Perspective* (vv. 6, 7)
An angel touches the prophet, cleansing him and giving him a new outlook. He is ready to serve.

Stage Five: *The Response of His Lifestyle* (v. 8)
When God calls, Isaiah eagerly steps forward. A call is marked by a fruitful life.

"Behold, this has touched your lips;
Your iniquity is taken away,
And your sin purged."

[8]Also I heard the voice of the Lord, saying:

"Whom shall I send,
And who will go for Us?"

Then I said, "Here *am* I! Send me."
[9]And He said, "Go, and tell this people:

'Keep on hearing, but do not understand;
Keep on seeing, but do not perceive.'

[10] "Make the heart of this people dull,
And their ears heavy,
And shut their eyes;
Lest they see with their eyes,
And hear with their ears,
And understand with their heart,
And return and be healed."

[11]Then I said, "Lord, how long?"
And He answered:

"Until the cities are laid waste and without inhabitant,
The houses are without a man,

The land is utterly desolate,
[12] The LORD has removed men far away,
And the forsaken places *are* many in the midst of the land.
[13] But yet a tenth *will be* in it,
And will return and be for consuming,
As a terebinth tree or as an oak,
Whose stump *remains* when it is cut down.
So the holy seed *shall be* its stump."

Isaiah Sent to King Ahaz

7 Now it came to pass in the days of Ahaz the son of Jotham, the son of Uzziah, king of Judah, *that* Rezin king of Syria and Pekah the son of Remaliah, king of Israel, went up to Jerusalem to *make* war against it, but could not prevail against it. [2]And it was told to the house of David, saying, "Syria's forces are deployed in Ephraim." So his heart and the heart of his people were moved as the trees of the woods are moved with the wind.

[3]Then the LORD said to Isaiah, "Go out now to meet Ahaz, you and Shear-Jashub[a] your son, at the end of the aqueduct from the upper pool, on the highway to the Fuller's Field, [4]and say to him: 'Take heed, and be quiet; do not fear or be

7:3 [a]Literally *A Remnant Shall Return*

fainthearted for these two stubs of smoking firebrands, for the fierce anger of Rezin and Syria, and the son of Remaliah. [5]Because Syria, Ephraim, and the son of Remaliah have plotted evil against you, saying, [6]"Let us go up against Judah and trouble it, and let us make a gap in its wall for ourselves, and set a king over them, the son of Tabel"— [7]thus says the Lord GOD:

"It shall not stand,
Nor shall it come to pass.
[8] For the head of Syria is Damascus,
And the head of Damascus is Rezin.
Within sixty-five years Ephraim will be broken,
So that it will not be a people.
[9] The head of Ephraim is Samaria,
And the head of Samaria is Remaliah's son.
If you will not believe,
Surely you shall not be established."'"

The Immanuel Prophecy

[10]Moreover the LORD spoke again to Ahaz, saying, [11]"Ask a sign for yourself from the LORD your God; ask it either in the depth or in the height above."
[12]But Ahaz said, "I will not ask, nor will I test the LORD!"

[13]Then he said, "Hear now, O house of David! Is it a small thing for you to weary men, but will you weary my God also? [14]Therefore the Lord Himself will give you a sign: Behold, the virgin shall conceive and bear a Son, and shall call His name Immanuel.[a] [15]Curds and honey He shall eat, that He may know to refuse the evil and choose the good. [16]For before the Child shall know to refuse the evil and choose the good, the land that you dread will be forsaken by both her kings. [17]The LORD will bring the king of Assyria upon you and your people and your father's house—days that have not come since the day that Ephraim departed from Judah."

[18] And it shall come to pass in that day
That the LORD will whistle for the fly
That is in the farthest part of the rivers of Egypt,
And for the bee that is in the land of Assyria.
[19] They will come, and all of them will rest
In the desolate valleys and in the clefts of the rocks,
And on all thorns and in all pastures.

7:14 [a]Literally God-With-Us

The Law of Connection:
The Call Pushes Leaders to Communicate
(Isaiah 7:1–17)

Isaiah wants to communicate a message that begins to burn inside of him (as it did with Jeremiah). The divine message gives him an urgency to connect with others and spread God's word. God's call gives him a divine compulsion to speak and act.

A leader's sense of call provides divine energy. Ponder a few other examples of this phenomenon:

1. Abraham was called by God through a divine visitation (Gen. 12).
2. Joseph was called by God through a dream (Gen. 37).
3. Moses was called by God through a voice in a burning bush (Ex. 3; 4).
4. Aaron was called by God through his brother Moses (Ex. 4).
5. Joshua was called by God through Moses (Ex. 17).
6. Gideon was called by God through an angel (Judg. 6).
7. Samuel was called by God through God's audible voice (1 Sam. 3).
8. David was called by God through the prophet Samuel (1 Sam. 16).
9. Paul was called by God through a vision while he traveled (Acts 9).
10. Timothy was called by God by Paul's preaching and through his upbringing (1 Tim. 1; 2 Tim. 1; 2).

20 In the same day the Lord will shave with a
    hired razor,
    With those from beyond the River,[a] with
    the king of Assyria,
    The head and the hair of the legs,
    And will also remove the beard.

21 It shall be in that day
    That a man will keep alive a young cow
    and two sheep;
22 So it shall be, from the abundance of milk
    they give,
    That he will eat curds;
    For curds and honey everyone will eat
    who is left in the land.

23 It shall happen in that day,
    That wherever there could be a thousand
    vines
    Worth a thousand *shekels* of silver,
    It will be for briers and thorns.
24 With arrows and bows men will come
    there,
    Because all the land will become briers
    and thorns.

25 And to any hill which could be dug with
    the hoe,
    You will not go there for fear of briers and
    thorns;
    But it will become a range for oxen
    And a place for sheep to roam.

Assyria Will Invade the Land

8 Moreover the LORD said to me, "Take a
large scroll, and write on it with a man's
pen concerning Maher-Shalal-Hash-Baz.[a]
²And I will take for Myself faithful witnesses to
record, Uriah the priest and Zechariah the son of
Jeberechiah."

³Then I went to the prophetess, and she conceived and bore a son. Then the LORD said to
me, "Call his name Maher-Shalal-Hash-Baz; ⁴for
before the child shall have knowledge to cry 'My
father' and 'My mother,' the riches of Damascus
and the spoil of Samaria will be taken away before the king of Assyria."

⁵The LORD also spoke to me again, saying:

6 "Inasmuch as these people refused
    The waters of Shiloah that flow softly,
    And rejoice in Rezin and in Remaliah's
    son;
7 Now therefore, behold, the Lord brings up
    over them
    The waters of the River,[a] strong and
    mighty—

The king of Assyria and all his glory;
    He will go up over all his channels
    And go over all his banks.
8 He will pass through Judah,
    He will overflow and pass over,
    He will reach up to the neck;
    And the stretching out of his wings
    Will fill the breadth of Your land,
    O Immanuel.[a]

9 "Be shattered, O you peoples, and be
    broken in pieces!
    Give ear, all you from far countries.
    Gird yourselves, but be broken in pieces;
    Gird yourselves, but be broken in pieces.
10 Take counsel together, but it will come to
    nothing;
    Speak the word, but it will not stand,
    For God *is* with us."[a]

Fear God, Heed His Word

¹¹For the LORD spoke thus to me with a
strong hand, and instructed me that I should not
walk in the way of this people, saying:

12 "Do not say, 'A conspiracy,'
    Concerning all that this people call a
    conspiracy,
    Nor be afraid of their threats, nor be
    troubled.
13 The LORD of hosts, Him you shall hallow;
    Let Him *be* your fear,
    And *let* Him *be* your dread.
14 He will be as a sanctuary,
    But a stone of stumbling and a rock of
    offense
    To both the houses of Israel,
    As a trap and a snare to the inhabitants of
    Jerusalem.
15 And many among them shall stumble;
    They shall fall and be broken,
    Be snared and taken."

16 Bind up the testimony,
    Seal the law among my disciples.
17 And I will wait on the LORD,
    Who hides His face from the house of
    Jacob;
    And I will hope in Him.
18 Here am I and the children whom the
    LORD has given me!
    We are for signs and wonders in Israel

7:20 [a]That is, the Euphrates 8:1 [a]Literally *Speed the
Spoil, Hasten the Booty* 8:7 [a]That is, the Euphrates
8:8 [a]Literally *God-With-Us* 8:10 [a]Hebrew *Immanuel*

From the LORD of hosts,
Who dwells in Mount Zion.

[19]And when they say to you, "Seek those who are mediums and wizards, who whisper and mutter," should not a people seek their God? *Should they seek* the dead on behalf of the living? [20]To the law and to the testimony! If they do not speak according to this word, *it is* because *there is* no light in them.
[21]They will pass through it hard-pressed and hungry; and it shall happen, when they are hungry, that they will be enraged and curse their king and their God, and look upward. [22]Then they will look to the earth, and see trouble and darkness, gloom of anguish; and *they will be* driven into darkness.

The Government of the Promised Son

9 Nevertheless the gloom *will* not *be* upon her who *is* distressed,
As when at first He lightly esteemed
The land of Zebulun and the land of Naphtali,
And afterward more heavily oppressed *her,*
By the way of the sea, beyond the Jordan,
In Galilee of the Gentiles.
[2] The people who walked in darkness
Have seen a great light;
Those who dwelt in the land of the shadow of death,
Upon them a light has shined.

[3] You have multiplied the nation
And increased its joy;[a]
They rejoice before You
According to the joy of harvest,
As *men* rejoice when they divide the spoil.
[4] For You have broken the yoke of his burden
And the staff of his shoulder,
The rod of his oppressor,
As in the day of Midian.
[5] For every warrior's sandal from the noisy battle,
And garments rolled in blood,
Will be used for burning *and* fuel of fire.

[6] For unto us a Child is born,
Unto us a Son is given;
And the government will be upon His shoulder.
And His name will be called
Wonderful, Counselor, Mighty God,
Everlasting Father, Prince of Peace.

[7] Of the increase of *His* government and peace
There will be no end,
Upon the throne of David and over His kingdom,
To order it and establish it with judgment and justice
From that time forward, even forever.
The zeal of the LORD of hosts will perform this.

The Punishment of Samaria

[8] The LORD sent a word against Jacob,
And it has fallen on Israel.
[9] All the people will know—
Ephraim and the inhabitant of Samaria—
Who say in pride and arrogance of heart:
[10] "The bricks have fallen down,
But we will rebuild with hewn stones;
The sycamores are cut down,
But we will replace *them* with cedars."
[11] Therefore the LORD shall set up
The adversaries of Rezin against him,
And spur his enemies on,
[12] The Syrians before and the Philistines behind;
And they shall devour Israel with an open mouth.

For all this His anger is not turned away,
But His hand *is* stretched out still.

[13] For the people do not turn to Him who strikes them,
Nor do they seek the LORD of hosts.
[14] Therefore the LORD will cut off head and tail from Israel,
Palm branch and bulrush in one day.
[15] The elder and honorable, he *is* the head;
The prophet who teaches lies, he *is* the tail.
[16] For the leaders of this people cause *them* to err,
And *those who are* led by them are destroyed.
[17] Therefore the Lord will have no joy in their young men,
Nor have mercy on their fatherless and widows;
For everyone *is* a hypocrite and an evildoer,
And every mouth speaks folly.

9:3 [a]Following Qere and Targum; Kethib and Vulgate read *not increased joy;* Septuagint reads *Most of the people You brought down in Your joy.*

For all this His anger is not turned away,
But His hand *is* stretched out still.

18 For wickedness burns as the fire;
It shall devour the briers and thorns,
And kindle in the thickets of the forest;
They shall mount up *like* rising smoke.
19 Through the wrath of the LORD of hosts
The land is burned up,
And the people shall be as fuel for the fire;
No man shall spare his brother.
20 And he shall snatch on the right hand
And be hungry;
He shall devour on the left hand
And not be satisfied;
Every man shall eat the flesh of his own
arm.
21 Manasseh *shall devour* Ephraim, and
Ephraim Manasseh;
Together they *shall be* against Judah.

For all this His anger is not turned away,
But His hand *is* stretched out still.

10 "Woe to those who decree
unrighteous decrees,
Who write misfortune,
Which they have prescribed
2 To rob the needy of justice,
And to take what is right from the poor of
My people,
That widows may be their prey,
And *that* they may rob the fatherless.
3 What will you do in the day of punishment,
And in the desolation *which* will come
from afar?
To whom will you flee for help?
And where will you leave your glory?
4 Without Me they shall bow down among
the prisoners,
And they shall fall among the slain."

For all this His anger is not turned away,
But His hand *is* stretched out still.

Arrogant Assyria Also Judged

5 "Woe to Assyria, the rod of My anger
And the staff in whose hand is My
indignation.
6 I will send him against an ungodly nation,
And against the people of My wrath
I will give him charge,
To seize the spoil, to take the prey,
And to tread them down like the mire of
the streets.

The Benefits of Humility, the Liabilities of Pride

(Isaiah 10:1–6)

Beware of treating followers unjustly! God reserves a stern condemnation for oppressive leaders.

In Isaiah 10, God speaks to both Assyria and Israel to declare the benefits of humility and the liabilities of pride. Later, God even models the leadership style He wants every leader to embrace by sending the Suffering Servant. The Messiah will come to serve, not to be served (Is. 52; 53; Mark 10:45). God perfectly illustrates servant leadership. Followers come when leaders serve. Look how often God calls His leaders "servants":

1. *Abraham:* called God's servant (Gen. 26:24)
2. *Moses:* called God's servant (Ex. 14:31)
3. *Joshua:* called Moses' servant (Ex. 33:11)
4. *Caleb:* called God's servant (Num. 14:24)
5. *Samuel:* called God's servant (1 Sam. 3:9)
6. *David:* called Saul's servant (1 Sam. 29:3)
7. *Elijah:* called God's servant (2 Kin. 9:36)
8. *Isaiah:* called God's servant (Is. 20:3)

7 Yet he does not mean so,
Nor does his heart think so;
But *it is* in his heart to destroy,
And cut off not a few nations.
8 For he says,
'*Are* not my princes altogether kings?
9 *Is* not Calno like Carchemish?
Is not Hamath like Arpad?
Is not Samaria like Damascus?
10 As my hand has found the kingdoms of
the idols,
Whose carved images excelled those of
Jerusalem and Samaria,
11 As I have done to Samaria and her idols,
Shall I not do also to Jerusalem and her
idols?'"

12 Therefore it shall come to pass, when the Lord has performed all His work on Mount Zion and on Jerusalem, *that He will say,* "I will punish the fruit of the arrogant heart of the king of Assyria, and the glory of his haughty looks."

13 For he says:

"By the strength of my hand I have done *it,*
And by my wisdom, for I am prudent;
Also I have removed the boundaries of the
    people,
And have robbed their treasuries;
So I have put down the inhabitants like a
    valiant *man.*
14 My hand has found like a nest the riches
    of the people,
And as one gathers eggs *that are* left,
I have gathered all the earth;
And there was no one who moved *his*
    wing,
Nor opened *his* mouth with even a
    peep."

15 Shall the ax boast itself against him who
    chops with it?
Or shall the saw exalt itself against him
    who saws with it?
As if a rod could wield *itself* against those
    who lift it up,
Or as if a staff could lift up, *as if it were* not
    wood!
16 Therefore the Lord, the Lord[a] of hosts,
Will send leanness among his fat ones;
And under his glory
He will kindle a burning
Like the burning of a fire.
17 So the Light of Israel will be for a fire,
And his Holy One for a flame;
It will burn and devour
His thorns and his briers in one day.
18 And it will consume the glory of his forest
    and of his fruitful field,
Both soul and body;
And they will be as when a sick man
    wastes away.
19 Then the rest of the trees of his forest
Will be so few in number
That a child may write them.

The Returning Remnant of Israel
20 And it shall come to pass in that day
That the remnant of Israel,
And such as have escaped of the house of
    Jacob,
Will never again depend on him who
    defeated them,
But will depend on the LORD, the Holy
    One of Israel, in truth.
21 The remnant will return, the remnant of
    Jacob,
To the Mighty God.
22 For though your people, O Israel, be as the
    sand of the sea,

A remnant of them will return;
The destruction decreed shall overflow
    with righteousness.
23 For the Lord GOD of hosts
Will make a determined end
In the midst of all the land.

24Therefore thus says the Lord GOD of hosts:
"O My people, who dwell in Zion, do not be
afraid of the Assyrian. He shall strike you with
a rod and lift up his staff against you, in the
manner of Egypt. 25For yet a very little while
and the indignation will cease, as will My anger
in their destruction." 26And the LORD of hosts
will stir up a scourge for him like the slaughter
of Midian at the rock of Oreb; *as* His rod was
on the sea, so will He lift it up in the manner
of Egypt.

27 It shall come to pass in that day
That his burden will be taken away from
    your shoulder,
And his yoke from your neck,
And the yoke will be destroyed because of
    the anointing oil.

28 He has come to Aiath,
He has passed Migron;
At Michmash he has attended to his
    equipment.
29 They have gone along the ridge,
They have taken up lodging at Geba.
Ramah is afraid,
Gibeah of Saul has fled.
30 Lift up your voice,
O daughter of Gallim!
Cause it to be heard as far as Laish—
O poor Anathoth![a]
31 Madmenah has fled,
The inhabitants of Gebim seek refuge.
32 As yet he will remain at Nob that day;
He will shake his fist at the mount of the
    daughter of Zion,
The hill of Jerusalem.

33 Behold, the Lord,
The LORD of hosts,
Will lop off the bough with terror;
Those of high stature *will be* hewn down,
And the haughty will be humbled.

10:16 [a]Following Bomberg; Masoretic Text and
Dead Sea Scrolls read *YHWH (the* LORD).
10:30 [a]Following Masoretic Text, Targum, and
Vulgate; Septuagint and Syriac read *Listen to her,
O Anathoth.*

34   He will cut down the thickets of the forest
      with iron,
    And Lebanon will fall by the Mighty One.

The Reign of Jesse's Offspring

11   There shall come forth a Rod from
       the stem of Jesse,
       And a Branch shall grow out of his
       roots.

2   The Spirit of the LORD shall rest upon
      Him,
    The Spirit of wisdom and understanding,
    The Spirit of counsel and might,
    The Spirit of knowledge and of the fear of
      the LORD.

3   His delight *is* in the fear of the LORD,
    And He shall not judge by the sight of His
      eyes,
    Nor decide by the hearing of His ears;

4   But with righteousness He shall judge the
      poor,
    And decide with equity for the meek of
      the earth;
    He shall strike the earth with the rod of
      His mouth,
    And with the breath of His lips He shall
      slay the wicked.

5   Righteousness shall be the belt of His
      loins,
    And faithfulness the belt of His waist.

6   "The wolf also shall dwell with the lamb,
    The leopard shall lie down with the young
      goat,
    The calf and the young lion and the
      fatling together;
    And a little child shall lead them.

7   The cow and the bear shall graze;
    Their young ones shall lie down together;
    And the lion shall eat straw like the ox.

8   The nursing child shall play by the cobra's
      hole,
    And the weaned child shall put his hand in
      the viper's den.

9   They shall not hurt nor destroy in all My
      holy mountain,
    For the earth shall be full of the
      knowledge of the LORD
    As the waters cover the sea.

10   "And in that day there shall be a Root of
      Jesse,
    Who shall stand as a banner to the people;
    For the Gentiles shall seek Him,
    And His resting place shall be glorious."

11   It shall come to pass in that day
    That the Lord shall set His hand again the
      second time
    To recover the remnant of His people who
      are left,
    From Assyria and Egypt,
    From Pathros and Cush,
    From Elam and Shinar,
    From Hamath and the islands of the sea.

12   He will set up a banner for the nations,
    And will assemble the outcasts of Israel,
    And gather together the dispersed of Judah
    From the four corners of the earth.

13   Also the envy of Ephraim shall depart,
    And the adversaries of Judah shall be cut
      off;
    Ephraim shall not envy Judah,
    And Judah shall not harass Ephraim.

14   But they shall fly down upon the shoulder
      of the Philistines toward the west;
    Together they shall plunder the people of
      the East;
    They shall lay their hand on Edom and
      Moab;
    And the people of Ammon shall obey
      them.

15   The LORD will utterly destroy[a] the tongue
      of the Sea of Egypt;
    With His mighty wind He will shake His
      fist over the River,[b]
    And strike it in the seven streams,
    And make *men* cross over dryshod.

16   There will be a highway for the remnant
      of His people
    Who will be left from Assyria,
    As it was for Israel
    In the day that he came up from the land
      of Egypt.

A Hymn of Praise

12   And in that day you will say:

    "O LORD, I will praise You;
    Though You were angry with me,
    Your anger is turned away, and You
      comfort me.

2   Behold, God *is* my salvation,
    I will trust and not be afraid;
    'For YAH, the LORD, *is* my strength and
      song;
    He also has become my salvation.'"[a]

11:15 [a]Following Masoretic Text and Vulgate;
Septuagint, Syriac, and Targum read *dry up.* [b]That
is, the Euphrates **12:2** [a]Exodus 15:2

3   Therefore with joy you will draw water
From the wells of salvation.

4 And in that day you will say:

"Praise the LORD, call upon His name;
Declare His deeds among the peoples,
Make mention that His name is exalted.
5   Sing to the LORD,
For He has done excellent things;
This is known in all the earth.
6   Cry out and shout, O inhabitant of Zion,
For great is the Holy One of Israel in your
midst!"

Proclamation Against Babylon

13 The burden against Babylon which
Isaiah the son of Amoz saw.

2   "Lift up a banner on the high mountain,
Raise your voice to them;
Wave your hand, that they may enter the
gates of the nobles.
3   I have commanded My sanctified ones;
I have also called My mighty ones for My
anger—
Those who rejoice in My exaltation."

4   The noise of a multitude in the
mountains,
Like that of many people!
A tumultuous noise of the kingdoms of
nations gathered together!
The LORD of hosts musters
The army for battle.
5   They come from a far country,
From the end of heaven—
The LORD and His weapons of
indignation,
To destroy the whole land.

6   Wail, for the day of the LORD is at hand!
It will come as destruction from the
Almighty.
7   Therefore all hands will be limp,
Every man's heart will melt,
8   And they will be afraid.
Pangs and sorrows will take hold of them;
They will be in pain as a woman in
childbirth;
They will be amazed at one another;
Their faces will be like flames.

9   Behold, the day of the LORD comes,
Cruel, with both wrath and fierce anger,
To lay the land desolate;

And He will destroy its sinners from it.
10   For the stars of heaven and their
constellations
Will not give their light;
The sun will be darkened in its going
forth,
And the moon will not cause its light to
shine.

11   "I will punish the world for its evil,
And the wicked for their iniquity;
I will halt the arrogance of the proud,
And will lay low the haughtiness of the
terrible.
12   I will make a mortal more rare than fine
gold,
A man more than the golden wedge of
Ophir.
13   Therefore I will shake the heavens,
And the earth will move out of her place,
In the wrath of the LORD of hosts
And in the day of His fierce anger.
14   It shall be as the hunted gazelle,
And as a sheep that no man takes up;
Every man will turn to his own people,
And everyone will flee to his own land.
15   Everyone who is found will be thrust
through,
And everyone who is captured will fall by
the sword.
16   Their children also will be dashed to
pieces before their eyes;
Their houses will be plundered
And their wives ravished.

17   "Behold, I will stir up the Medes against
them,
Who will not regard silver;
And as for gold, they will not delight in it.
18   Also their bows will dash the young men
to pieces,
And they will have no pity on the fruit of
the womb;
Their eye will not spare children.
19   And Babylon, the glory of kingdoms,
The beauty of the Chaldeans' pride,
Will be as when God overthrew Sodom
and Gomorrah.
20   It will never be inhabited,
Nor will it be settled from generation to
generation;
Nor will the Arabian pitch tents there,
Nor will the shepherds make their
sheepfolds there.
21   But wild beasts of the desert will lie
there,

And their houses will be full of owls;
Ostriches will dwell there,
And wild goats will caper there.
22 The hyenas will howl in their citadels,
And jackals in their pleasant palaces.
Her time *is* near to come,
And her days will not be prolonged."

Mercy on Jacob

For the LORD will have mercy on Jacob, and will still choose Israel, and settle them in their own land. The strangers will be joined with them, and they will cling to the house of Jacob. ²Then people will take them and bring them to their place, and the house of Israel will possess them for servants and maids in the land of the LORD; they will take them captive whose captives they were, and rule over their oppressors.

Fall of the King of Babylon

³It shall come to pass in the day the LORD gives you rest from your sorrow, and from your fear and the hard bondage in which you were made to serve, ⁴that you will take up this proverb against the king of Babylon, and say:

"How the oppressor has ceased,
The golden[a] city ceased!
5 The LORD has broken the staff of the
   wicked,
The scepter of the rulers;
6 He who struck the people in wrath with a
   continual stroke,
He who ruled the nations in anger,
Is persecuted *and* no one hinders.
7 The whole earth is at rest *and* quiet;
They break forth into singing.
8 Indeed the cypress trees rejoice over
   you,
And the cedars of Lebanon,
Saying, 'Since you were cut down,
No woodsman has come up against us.'

9 "Hell from beneath is excited about you,
To meet *you* at your coming;
It stirs up the dead for you,
All the chief ones of the earth;
It has raised up from their thrones
All the kings of the nations.
10 They all shall speak and say to you:
'Have you also become as weak as we?
Have you become like us?
11 Your pomp is brought down to Sheol,
And the sound of your stringed
   instruments;

The maggot is spread under you,
And worms cover you.'

The Fall of Lucifer

12 "How you are fallen from heaven,
O Lucifer,[a] son of the morning!
How you are cut down to the ground,
You who weakened the nations!
13 For you have said in your heart:
'I will ascend into heaven,
I will exalt my throne above the stars of
   God;
I will also sit on the mount of the
   congregation
On the farthest sides of the north;
14 I will ascend above the heights of the
   clouds,
I will be like the Most High.'
15 Yet you shall be brought down to Sheol,
To the lowest depths of the Pit.

16 "Those who see you will gaze at you,
And consider you, *saying:*
'*Is* this the man who made the earth
   tremble,
Who shook kingdoms,
17 Who made the world as a wilderness
And destroyed its cities,
Who did not open the house of his
   prisoners?'

18 "All the kings of the nations,
All of them, sleep in glory,
Everyone in his own house;
19 But you are cast out of your grave
Like an abominable branch,
Like the garment of those who are slain,
Thrust through with a sword,
Who go down to the stones of the pit,
Like a corpse trodden underfoot.
20 You will not be joined with them in
   burial,
Because you have destroyed your land
And slain your people.
The brood of evildoers shall never be
   named.
21 Prepare slaughter for his children
Because of the iniquity of their fathers,
Lest they rise up and possess the land,
And fill the face of the world with cities."

Babylon Destroyed

22 "For I will rise up against them," says the
   LORD of hosts,

14:4 [a]Or *insolent* **14:12** [a]Literally *Day Star*

A Riches to Rags Story

(Isaiah 14:3–23)

Proverbs 16:18 reminds us that pride comes before a fall and that a haughty spirit causes one to stumble. We see that truth in action in Isaiah 14.

While we see the immediate fulfillment of this passage in the king of Babylon, many scholars believe the text also speaks of Satan. Note the arrogant words in verses 12–17. What a sobering picture of a leader who goes astray! Both the oppressive king and Satan had one common characteristic: a lust for pride and power. Consider the devil's fall from his original place in heaven, as described in Isaiah 14, Ezekiel 28, and Revelation 12; 20:

1. The one cast down (to the bottomless pit) (Is. 14:15; Rev. 12:10; 20:3)
2. Full of wisdom (Ezek. 28:12)
3. Perfect in beauty (Ezek. 28:12)
4. Song leader and musician of heaven (Ezek. 28:13)
5. The anointed cherub (Ezek. 28:14)
6. One who covered the throne (Ezek. 28:14, 16)
7. Great dragon (Rev. 12:9)
8. The serpent (Rev. 12:9; 20:2)
9. The devil; the spirit of deception (Rev. 12:9; 20:10)
10. Accuser of the brethren (Rev. 20:10)

"And cut off from Babylon the name and remnant,
And offspring and posterity," says the LORD.

23 "I will also make it a possession for the porcupine,
And marshes of muddy water;
I will sweep it with the broom of destruction," says the LORD of hosts.

Assyria Destroyed

24 The LORD of hosts has sworn, saying,
"Surely, as I have thought, so it shall come to pass,
And as I have purposed, *so* it shall stand:

25 That I will break the Assyrian in My land,
And on My mountains tread him underfoot.
Then his yoke shall be removed from them,
And his burden removed from their shoulders.

26 This *is* the purpose that is purposed against the whole earth,
And this *is* the hand that is stretched out over all the nations.

27 For the LORD of hosts has purposed,
And who will annul *it?*

His hand *is* stretched out,
And who will turn it back?"

Philistia Destroyed

28 This is the burden which came in the year that King Ahaz died.

29 "Do not rejoice, all you of Philistia,
Because the rod that struck you is broken;
For out of the serpent's roots will come forth a viper,
And its offspring *will be* a fiery flying serpent.

30 The firstborn of the poor will feed,
And the needy will lie down in safety;
I will kill your roots with famine,
And it will slay your remnant.

31 Wail, O gate! Cry, O city!
All you of Philistia *are* dissolved;
For smoke will come from the north,
And no one *will be* alone in his appointed times."

32 What will they answer the messengers of the nation?
That the LORD has founded Zion,
And the poor of His people shall take refuge in it.

Proclamation Against Moab

15 The burden against Moab.

Because in the night Ar of Moab is laid waste
And destroyed,
Because in the night Kir of Moab is laid waste
And destroyed,

2 He has gone up to the temple[a] and Dibon,
To the high places to weep.
Moab will wail over Nebo and over Medeba;
On all their heads *will be* baldness,
And every beard cut off.

3 In their streets they will clothe themselves with sackcloth;
On the tops of their houses
And in their streets
Everyone will wail, weeping bitterly.

4 Heshbon and Elealeh will cry out,
Their voice shall be heard as far as Jahaz;
Therefore the armed soldiers[a] of Moab will cry out;
His life will be burdensome to him.

5 "My heart will cry out for Moab;
His fugitives *shall flee* to Zoar,
Like a three-year-old heifer.[a]
For by the Ascent of Luhith
They will go up with weeping;
For in the way of Horonaim
They will raise up a cry of destruction,

6 For the waters of Nimrim will be desolate,
For the green grass has withered away;
The grass fails, there is nothing green.

7 Therefore the abundance they have gained,
And what they have laid up,
They will carry away to the Brook of the Willows.

8 For the cry has gone all around the borders of Moab,
Its wailing to Eglaim
And its wailing to Beer Elim.

15:2 [a]Hebrew *bayith,* literally *house*
15:4 [a]Following Masoretic Text, Targum, and Vulgate; Septuagint and Syriac read *loins.* **15:5** [a]Or *The Third Eglath,* an unknown city (compare Jeremiah 48:34)

ISAIAH — A LEADER'S HEART OF LOVE FOR THE UNLOVELY
(Isaiah 15:5; 16:9, 11)

PROFILE IN LEADERSHIP

Someone must have forgotten to tell the prophet Isaiah that he lived in Old Testament times.

You know the picture most have of ancient Hebrew leaders—eye-for-an-eye types, angry, hair akimbo, and eager for God's righteous judgment to fall upon the pagans and the wicked. And yet, here stands Isaiah, crying out for heathen Moab and weeping for wayward Heshbon.

Isaiah demonstrates for us the attitude of a godly leader who sees approaching judgment on unbelievers. He actually *grieves* over what is coming on lost souls. While he acknowledges and even celebrates God's righteousness and sovereignty in judging those who reject Him, he also proclaims that the calamity about to descend is nothing other than a terrible tragedy.

Isaiah's lament over the fate of these ancient nations reveals the attitude of a truly godly leader. While he knew those erring nations surely deserved God's judgment, he also knew that without God's grace and mercy, none of us could expect anything else.

We ought to stand in awed silence when we see the judgment of God falling on those who have forsaken His way. But we should never see His judgment as an occasion to celebrate our own righteousness. Rather, we ought to grieve for the lost and reflect deeply on the grace and mercy God has extended to us.

9 For the waters of Dimon[a] will be full of
blood;
Because I will bring more upon Dimon,[b]
Lions upon him who escapes from Moab,
And on the remnant of the land."

Moab Destroyed

16 Send the lamb to the ruler of the
land,
From Sela to the wilderness,
To the mount of the daughter of Zion.
2 For it shall be as a wandering bird thrown
out of the nest;
So shall be the daughters of Moab at the
fords of the Arnon.

3 "Take counsel, execute judgment;
Make your shadow like the night in the
middle of the day;
Hide the outcasts,
Do not betray him who escapes.
4 Let My outcasts dwell with you, O Moab;
Be a shelter to them from the face of the
spoiler.
For the extortioner is at an end,
Devastation ceases,
The oppressors are consumed out of the
land.
5 In mercy the throne will be established;
And One will sit on it in truth, in the
tabernacle of David,
Judging and seeking justice and hastening
righteousness."

6 We have heard of the pride of Moab—
He is very proud—
Of his haughtiness and his pride and his
wrath;
But his lies *shall* not *be* so.
7 Therefore Moab shall wail for Moab;
Everyone shall wail.
For the foundations of Kir Hareseth you
shall mourn;
Surely *they are* stricken.

8 For the fields of Heshbon languish,
And the vine of Sibmah;
The lords of the nations have broken
down its choice plants,
Which have reached to Jazer
And wandered through the wilderness.
Her branches are stretched out,
They are gone over the sea.
9 Therefore I will bewail the vine of
Sibmah,
With the weeping of Jazer;

I will drench you with my tears,
O Heshbon and Elealeh;
For battle cries have fallen
Over your summer fruits and your harvest.

10 Gladness is taken away,
And joy from the plentiful field;
In the vineyards there will be no singing,
Nor will there be shouting;
No treaders will tread out wine in the
presses;
I have made their shouting cease.
11 Therefore my heart shall resound like a
harp for Moab,
And my inner being for Kir Heres.

12 And it shall come to pass,
When it is seen that Moab is weary on the
high place,
That he will come to his sanctuary to
pray;
But he will not prevail.

13This *is* the word which the LORD has spoken concerning Moab since that time. 14But
now the LORD has spoken, saying, "Within
three years, as the years of a hired man, the glory
of Moab will be despised with all that great
multitude, and the remnant *will be* very small *and*
feeble."

Proclamation Against Syria and Israel

17 The burden against Damascus.

"Behold, Damascus will cease from
being a city,
And it will be a ruinous heap.
2 The cities of Aroer *are* forsaken;[a]
They will be for flocks
Which lie down, and no one will make
them afraid.
3 The fortress also will cease from Ephraim,
The kingdom from Damascus,
And the remnant of Syria;
They will be as the glory of the children
of Israel,"
Says the LORD of hosts.

15:9 [a]Following Masoretic Text and Targum; Dead
Sea Scrolls and Vulgate read *Dibon*; Septuagint reads
Rimon. [b]Following Masoretic Text and Targum;
Dead Sea Scrolls and Vulgate read *Dibon*; Septuagint
reads *Rimon*. **17:2** [a]Following Masoretic Text and
Vulgate; Septuagint reads *It shall be forsaken forever;*
Targum reads *Its cities shall be forsaken and desolate.*

4 "In that day it shall come to pass
That the glory of Jacob will wane,
And the fatness of his flesh grow lean.
5 It shall be as when the harvester gathers
the grain,
And reaps the heads with his arm;
It shall be as he who gathers heads of grain
In the Valley of Rephaim.
6 Yet gleaning grapes will be left in it,
Like the shaking of an olive tree,
Two *or* three olives at the top of the
uppermost bough,
Four *or* five in its most fruitful branches,"
Says the LORD God of Israel.

7 In that day a man will look to his Maker,
And his eyes will have respect for the Holy
One of Israel.
8 He will not look to the altars,
The work of his hands;
He will not respect what his fingers have
made,
Nor the wooden images[a] nor the incense
altars.

9 In that day his strong cities will be as a
forsaken bough[a]
And an uppermost branch,[b]
Which they left because of the children of
Israel;
And there will be desolation.

10 Because you have forgotten the God of
your salvation,
And have not been mindful of the Rock
of your stronghold,
Therefore you will plant pleasant plants
And set out foreign seedlings;
11 In the day you will make your plant to
grow,
And in the morning you will make your
seed to flourish;
But the harvest *will be* a heap of ruins
In the day of grief and desperate sorrow.

12 Woe to the multitude of many people
Who make a noise like the roar of the seas,
And to the rushing of nations
That make a rushing like the rushing of
mighty waters!
13 The nations will rush like the rushing of
many waters;
But *God* will rebuke them and they will
flee far away,
And be chased like the chaff of the
mountains before the wind,
Like a rolling thing before the whirlwind.

14 Then behold, at eventide, trouble!
And before the morning, he *is* no more.
This *is* the portion of those who plunder us,
And the lot of those who rob us.

Proclamation Against Ethiopia

18 Woe to the land shadowed with
buzzing wings,
Which *is* beyond the rivers of
Ethiopia,
2 Which sends ambassadors by sea,
Even in vessels of reed on the waters,
saying,
"Go, swift messengers, to a nation tall and
smooth *of skin,*
To a people terrible from their beginning
onward,
A nation powerful and treading down,
Whose land the rivers divide."

3 All inhabitants of the world and dwellers
on the earth:
When he lifts up a banner on the
mountains, you see *it;*
And when he blows a trumpet, you hear *it.*
4 For so the LORD said to me,
"I will take My rest,
And I will look from My dwelling place
Like clear heat in sunshine,
Like a cloud of dew in the heat of
harvest."
5 For before the harvest, when the bud is
perfect
And the sour grape is ripening in the
flower,
He will both cut off the sprigs with
pruning hooks
And take away *and* cut down the branches.
6 They will be left together for the
mountain birds of prey
And for the beasts of the earth;
The birds of prey will summer on them,
And all the beasts of the earth will winter
on them.

7 In that time a present will be brought to
the LORD of hosts
From[a] a people tall and smooth *of skin,*

17:8 [a]Hebrew *Asherim,* Canaanite deities
17:9 [a]Septuagint reads *Hivites;* Targum reads *laid
waste;* Vulgate reads *as the plows.* [b]Septuagint reads
Amorites; Targum reads *in ruins;* Vulgate reads *corn.*
18:7 [a]Following Dead Sea Scrolls, Septuagint,
and Vulgate; Masoretic Text omits *From;* Targum
reads *To.*

And from a people terrible from their
   beginning onward,
A nation powerful and treading down,
Whose land the rivers divide—
To the place of the name of the LORD of
   hosts,
To Mount Zion.

Proclamation Against Egypt

19 The burden against Egypt.

Behold, the LORD rides on a swift
   cloud,
And will come into Egypt;
The idols of Egypt will totter at His
   presence,
And the heart of Egypt will melt in its
   midst.

2 "I will set Egyptians against Egyptians;
Everyone will fight against his brother,
And everyone against his neighbor,
City against city, kingdom against
   kingdom.
3 The spirit of Egypt will fail in its midst;
I will destroy their counsel,
And they will consult the idols and the
   charmers,
The mediums and the sorcerers.
4 And the Egyptians I will give
Into the hand of a cruel master,
And a fierce king will rule over them,"
Says the Lord, the LORD of hosts.

5 The waters will fail from the sea,
And the river will be wasted and dried up.
6 The rivers will turn foul;
The brooks of defense will be emptied and
   dried up;
The reeds and rushes will wither.
7 The papyrus reeds by the River,[a] by the
   mouth of the River,
And everything sown by the River,
Will wither, be driven away, and be no
   more.
8 The fishermen also will mourn;
All those will lament who cast hooks into
   the River,
And they will languish who spread nets on
   the waters.
9 Moreover those who work in fine flax
And those who weave fine fabric will be
   ashamed;
10 And its foundations will be broken.
All who make wages *will be* troubled of
   soul.

11 Surely the princes of Zoan *are* fools;
Pharaoh's wise counselors give foolish
   counsel.
How do you say to Pharaoh, "I *am* the son
   of the wise,
The son of ancient kings?"
12 Where *are* they?
Where are your wise men?

19:7 [a]That is, the Nile

Personal Qualifications of Leadership

(Isaiah 19:11–15)

What qualifies a person to be a leader? Most natural leaders don't aspire to be great *leaders;* they aspire to be great *persons.* Personal qualifications lead to leadership qualifications. When leaders lead their own lives well, others naturally want to follow.

Consider Mother Teresa of Calcutta, India. It's doubtful she ever said, "I am going to set out to be a great leader!" Yet that is what she became by determining to be the person God created her to be. She developed personal qualities that became leadership qualities.

Isaiah illustrates this from a negative viewpoint. The senseless, naïve leaders of Zoan and Noph lacked the foresight to lead others. Their incompetence prompted God to compare them with a drunken man who can't even walk straight. If we want our leadership to last, we must pay attention to four crucial elements:

1. **Character**—enables us to do what is right even when it seems difficult.
2. **Perspective**—enables us to understand what must happen to reach a goal.
3. **Courage**—enables us to initiate and take the risks to step out toward a worthy goal.
4. **Favor**—enables us to attract and empower others to join us in the cause.

Let them tell you now,
And let them know what the LORD of
hosts has purposed against Egypt.
13 The princes of Zoan have become fools;
The princes of Noph[a] are deceived;
They have also deluded Egypt,
Those who are the mainstay of its tribes.
14 The LORD has mingled a perverse spirit in
her midst;
And they have caused Egypt to err in all
her work,
As a drunken man staggers in his vomit.
15 Neither will there be *any* work for
Egypt,
Which the head or tail,
Palm branch or bulrush, may do.[a]

[16]In that day Egypt will be like women, and
will be afraid and fear because of the waving of
the hand of the LORD of hosts, which He waves
over it. [17]And the land of Judah will be a terror
to Egypt; everyone who makes mention of it will
be afraid in himself, because of the counsel of
the LORD of hosts which He has determined
against it.

Egypt, Assyria, and Israel Blessed

[18]In that day five cities in the land of Egypt
will speak the language of Canaan and swear by
the LORD of hosts; one will be called the City of
Destruction.[a]

[19]In that day there will be an altar to the
LORD in the midst of the land of Egypt, and a
pillar to the LORD at its border. [20]And it will be
for a sign and for a witness to the LORD of hosts
in the land of Egypt; for they will cry to the
LORD because of the oppressors, and He will
send them a Savior and a Mighty One, and He
will deliver them. [21]Then the LORD will be
known to Egypt, and the Egyptians will know
the LORD in that day, and will make sacrifice and
offering; yes, they will make a vow to the LORD
and perform *it*. [22]And the LORD will strike
Egypt, He will strike and heal *it;* they will return
to the LORD, and He will be entreated by them
and heal them.

[23]In that day there will be a highway from
Egypt to Assyria, and the Assyrian will come into
Egypt and the Egyptian into Assyria, and the
Egyptians will serve with the Assyrians.

[24]In that day Israel will be one of three with
Egypt and Assyria—a blessing in the midst of
the land, [25]whom the LORD of hosts shall bless,
saying, "Blessed *is* Egypt My people, and Assyria
the work of My hands, and Israel My inheritance."

The Sign Against Egypt and Ethiopia

20 In the year that Tartan[a] came to Ashdod, when Sargon the king of Assyria sent him, and he fought against
Ashdod and took it, [2]at the same time the LORD
spoke by Isaiah the son of Amoz, saying, "Go,
and remove the sackcloth from your body, and
take your sandals off your feet." And he did so,
walking naked and barefoot.

[3]Then the LORD said, "Just as My servant Isaiah has walked naked and barefoot three years *for*
a sign and a wonder against Egypt and Ethiopia,
[4]so shall the king of Assyria lead away the Egyptians as prisoners and the Ethiopians as captives,
young and old, naked and barefoot, with their
buttocks uncovered, to the shame of Egypt.
[5]Then they shall be afraid and ashamed of Ethiopia their expectation and Egypt their glory.
[6]And the inhabitant of this territory will say in
that day, 'Surely such *is* our expectation, wherever we flee for help to be delivered from the
king of Assyria; and how shall we escape?'"

The Fall of Babylon Proclaimed

21 The burden against the Wilderness
of the Sea.

As whirlwinds in the South pass through,
So it comes from the desert, from a
terrible land.
2 A distressing vision is declared to me;
The treacherous dealer deals treacherously,
And the plunderer plunders.
Go up, O Elam!
Besiege, O Media!
All its sighing I have made to cease.

3 Therefore my loins are filled with pain;
Pangs have taken hold of me, like the
pangs of a woman in labor.
I was distressed when *I* heard *it;*
I was dismayed when *I* saw *it.*
4 My heart wavered, fearfulness frightened
me;
The night for which I longed He turned
into fear for me.
5 Prepare the table,
Set a watchman in the tower,
Eat and drink.

19:13 [a]That is, ancient Memphis **19:15** [a]Compare
Isaiah 9:14–16 **19:18** [a]Some Hebrew manuscripts,
Arabic, Dead Sea Scrolls, Targum, and Vulgate read
Sun; Septuagint reads *Asedek* (literally *Righteousness*).
20:1 [a]Or *the Commander in Chief*

Arise, you princes,
Anoint the shield!

6 For thus has the Lord said to me:
"Go, set a watchman,
Let him declare what he sees."
7 And he saw a chariot *with* a pair of
horsemen,
A chariot of donkeys, *and* a chariot of
camels,
And he listened earnestly with great care.
8 Then he cried, "A lion,[a] my Lord!
I stand continually on the watchtower in
the daytime;
I have sat at my post every night.
9 And look, here comes a chariot of men
with a pair of horsemen!"
Then he answered and said,
"Babylon is fallen, is fallen!
And all the carved images of her gods
He has broken to the ground."

10 Oh, my threshing and the grain of my
floor!
That which I have heard from the LORD
of hosts,
The God of Israel,
I have declared to you.

Proclamation Against Edom

11The burden against Dumah.

He calls to me out of Seir,
"Watchman, what of the night?
Watchman, what of the night?"
12 The watchman said,
"The morning comes, and also the night.
If you will inquire, inquire;
Return! Come back!"

Proclamation Against Arabia

13The burden against Arabia.

In the forest in Arabia you will lodge,
O you traveling companies of Dedanites.
14 O inhabitants of the land of Tema,
Bring water to him who is thirsty;
With their bread they met him who fled.
15 For they fled from the swords, from the
drawn sword,
From the bent bow, and from the distress
of war.

16For thus the LORD has said to me: "Within
a year, according to the year of a hired man, all
the glory of Kedar will fail; 17and the remainder

of the number of archers, the mighty men of the
people of Kedar, will be diminished; for the
LORD God of Israel has spoken *it*."

Proclamation Against Jerusalem

22 The burden against the Valley of
Vision.

What ails you now, that you have all gone
up to the housetops,
2 You who are full of noise,
A tumultuous city, a joyous city?
Your slain *men are* not slain with the
sword,
Nor dead in battle.
3 All your rulers have fled together;
They are captured by the archers.
All who are found in you are bound
together;
They have fled from afar.
4 Therefore I said, "Look away from me,
I will weep bitterly;
Do not labor to comfort me
Because of the plundering of the daughter
of my people."

5 For *it is* a day of trouble and treading
down and perplexity
By the Lord GOD of hosts
In the Valley of Vision—
Breaking down the walls
And of crying to the mountain.
6 Elam bore the quiver
With chariots of men *and* horsemen,
And Kir uncovered the shield.
7 It shall come to pass *that* your choicest
valleys
Shall be full of chariots,
And the horsemen shall set themselves in
array at the gate.
8 He removed the protection of Judah.
You looked in that day to the armor of the
House of the Forest;
9 You also saw the damage to the city of
David,
That it was great;
And you gathered together the waters of
the lower pool.
10 You numbered the houses of Jerusalem,
And the houses you broke down
To fortify the wall.
11 You also made a reservoir between the two
walls

21:8 [a]Dead Sea Scrolls read *Then the observer cried.*

For the water of the old pool.
But you did not look to its Maker,
Nor did you have respect for Him who
   fashioned it long ago.

12 And in that day the Lord GOD of hosts
Called for weeping and for mourning,
For baldness and for girding with
   sackcloth.
13 But instead, joy and gladness,
Slaying oxen and killing sheep,
Eating meat and drinking wine:
"Let us eat and drink, for tomorrow we die!"

14 Then it was revealed in my hearing by the
   LORD of hosts,
"Surely for this iniquity there will be no
   atonement for you,
Even to your death," says the Lord GOD of
   hosts.

The Judgment on Shebna

15 Thus says the Lord GOD of hosts:

" Go, proceed to this steward,
To Shebna, who *is* over the house, *and say:*
16 'What have you here, and whom have you
   here,
That you have hewn a sepulcher here,
As he who hews himself a sepulcher on
   high,
Who carves a tomb for himself in a rock?
17 Indeed, the LORD will throw you away
   violently,
O mighty man,
And will surely seize you.
18 He will surely turn violently and toss you
   like a ball
Into a large country;
There you shall die, and there your
   glorious chariots
Shall be the shame of your master's house.
19 So I will drive you out of your office,
And from your position he will pull you
   down.ᵃ

20 'Then it shall be in that day,
That I will call My servant Eliakim the son
   of Hilkiah;
21 I will clothe him with your robe
And strengthen him with your belt;
I will commit your responsibility into his
   hand.
He shall be a father to the inhabitants of
   Jerusalem
And to the house of Judah.

22 The key of the house of David
I will lay on his shoulder;
So he shall open, and no one shall shut;
And he shall shut, and no one shall open.
23 I will fasten him *as* a peg in a secure place,
And he will become a glorious throne to
   his father's house.

24 "They will hang on him all the glory of his father's house, the offspring and the posterity, all vessels of small quantity, from the cups to all the pitchers. 25 In that day,' says the LORD of hosts, 'the peg that is fastened in the secure place will be removed and be cut down and fall, and the burden that *was* on it will be cut off; for the LORD has spoken.'"

Proclamation Against Tyre

23

The burden against Tyre.

Wail, you ships of Tarshish!
For it is laid waste,
So that there is no house, no harbor;
From the land of Cyprusᵃ it is revealed to
   them.

God's Providence: He Raises Up Leaders and Brings Them Down

(Isaiah 23:1–18)

The city of Tyre wielded great international influence during Isaiah's day. Its wealthy merchants created a high standard of living. But when God chose to bring them down, no one could stop Him. We can position people, but only God exalts them. We can develop others, but only God raises them up.

---

2 Be still, you inhabitants of the coastland,
You merchants of Sidon,
Whom those who cross the sea have
   filled.ᵃ

22:19 ᵃSeptuagint omits *he will pull you down;* Syriac, Targum, and Vulgate read *I will pull you down.* **23:1** ᵃHebrew *Kittim,* western lands, especially Cyprus **23:2** ᵃFollowing Masoretic Text and Vulgate; Septuagint and Targum read *Passing over the water;* Dead Sea Scrolls read *Your messengers passing over the sea.*

3 And on great waters the grain of Shihor,
The harvest of the River,[a] *is* her revenue;
And she is a marketplace for the nations.

4 Be ashamed, O Sidon;
For the sea has spoken,
The strength of the sea, saying,
"I do not labor, nor bring forth children;
Neither do I rear young men,
Nor bring up virgins."
5 When the report *reaches* Egypt,
They also will be in agony at the report of
Tyre.

6 Cross over to Tarshish;
Wail, you inhabitants of the coastland!
7 *Is* this your joyous *city,*
Whose antiquity *is* from ancient days,
Whose feet carried her far off to dwell?
8 Who has taken this counsel against Tyre,
the crowning *city,*
Whose merchants *are* princes,
Whose traders *are* the honorable of the
earth?
9 The LORD of hosts has purposed it,
To bring to dishonor the pride of all glory,
To bring into contempt all the honorable
of the earth.

10 Overflow through your land like the
River,[a]
O daughter of Tarshish;
There is no more strength.
11 He stretched out His hand over the sea,
He shook the kingdoms;
The LORD has given a commandment
against Canaan
To destroy its strongholds.
12 And He said, "You will rejoice no more,
O you oppressed virgin daughter of Sidon.
Arise, cross over to Cyprus;
There also you will have no rest."

13 Behold, the land of the Chaldeans,
This people *which* was not;
Assyria founded it for wild beasts of the
desert.
They set up its towers,
They raised up its palaces,
And brought it to ruin.

14 Wail, you ships of Tarshish!
For your strength is laid waste.

15 Now it shall come to pass in that day that
Tyre will be forgotten seventy years, according to

the days of one king. At the end of seventy years
it will happen to Tyre as *in* the song of the harlot:

16 "Take a harp, go about the city,
You forgotten harlot;
Make sweet melody, sing many songs,
That you may be remembered."

17 And it shall be, at the end of seventy years,
that the LORD will deal with Tyre. She will return to her hire, and commit fornication with all
the kingdoms of the world on the face of the
earth. 18 Her gain and her pay will be set apart for
the LORD; it will not be treasured nor laid up, for
her gain will be for those who dwell before the
LORD, to eat sufficiently, and for fine clothing.

Impending Judgment on the Earth

24 Behold, the LORD makes the earth
empty and makes it waste,
Distorts its surface
And scatters abroad its inhabitants.
2 And it shall be:
As with the people, so with the priest;
As with the servant, so with his master;
As with the maid, so with her mistress;
As with the buyer, so with the seller;
As with the lender, so with the borrower;
As with the creditor, so with the debtor.
3 The land shall be entirely emptied and
utterly plundered,
For the LORD has spoken this word.

4 The earth mourns *and* fades away,
The world languishes *and* fades away;
The haughty people of the earth languish.
5 The earth is also defiled under its
inhabitants,
Because they have transgressed the laws,
Changed the ordinance,
Broken the everlasting covenant.
6 Therefore the curse has devoured the
earth,
And those who dwell in it are desolate.
Therefore the inhabitants of the earth are
burned,
And few men *are* left.

7 The new wine fails, the vine languishes,
All the merry-hearted sigh.
8 The mirth of the tambourine ceases,
The noise of the jubilant ends,
The joy of the harp ceases.

23:3 [a]That is, the Nile 23:10 [a]That is, the Nile

9 They shall not drink wine with a song;
Strong drink is bitter to those who
drink it.
10 The city of confusion is broken down;
Every house is shut up, so that none may
go in.
11 *There is* a cry for wine in the streets,
All joy is darkened,
The mirth of the land is gone.
12 In the city desolation is left,
And the gate is stricken with destruction.
13 When it shall be thus in the midst of the
land among the people,
It shall be like the shaking of an olive tree,
Like the gleaning of grapes when the
vintage is done.

14 They shall lift up their voice, they shall
sing;
For the majesty of the LORD
They shall cry aloud from the sea.
15 Therefore glorify the LORD in the
dawning light,
The name of the LORD God of Israel in
the coastlands of the sea.
16 From the ends of the earth we have heard
songs:
"Glory to the righteous!"
But I said, "I am ruined, ruined!
Woe to me!
The treacherous dealers have dealt
treacherously,
Indeed, the treacherous dealers have dealt
very treacherously."

17 Fear and the pit and the snare
Are upon you, O inhabitant of the earth.
18 And it shall be
That he who flees from the noise of the
fear
Shall fall into the pit,
And he who comes up from the midst of
the pit
Shall be caught in the snare;
For the windows from on high are open,
And the foundations of the earth are
shaken.

19 The earth is violently broken,
The earth is split open,
The earth is shaken exceedingly.
20 The earth shall reel to and fro like a
drunkard,
And shall totter like a hut;
Its transgression shall be heavy upon it,
And it will fall, and not rise again.

21 It shall come to pass in that day
That the LORD will punish on high the
host of exalted ones,
And on the earth the kings of the earth.
22 They will be gathered together,
As prisoners are gathered in the pit,
And will be shut up in the prison;
After many days they will be punished.
23 Then the moon will be disgraced
And the sun ashamed;
For the LORD of hosts will reign
On Mount Zion and in Jerusalem
And before His elders, gloriously.

Praise to God

25 O LORD, You *are* my God.
I will exalt You,
I will praise Your name,
For You have done wonderful *things;*
Your counsels of old *are* faithfulness *and*
truth.
2 For You have made a city a ruin,
A fortified city a ruin,
A palace of foreigners to be a city no more;
It will never be rebuilt.
3 Therefore the strong people will glorify
You;
The city of the terrible nations will fear
You.
4 For You have been a strength to the poor,
A strength to the needy in his distress,
A refuge from the storm,
A shade from the heat;
For the blast of the terrible ones *is* as a
storm *against* the wall.
5 You will reduce the noise of aliens,
As heat in a dry place;
As heat in the shadow of a cloud,
The song of the terrible ones will be
diminished.

6 And in this mountain
The LORD of hosts will make for all
people
A feast of choice pieces,
A feast of wines on the lees,
Of fat things full of marrow,
Of well-refined wines on the lees.
7 And He will destroy on this mountain
The surface of the covering cast over all
people,
And the veil that is spread over all nations.
8 He will swallow up death forever,
And the Lord GOD will wipe away tears
from all faces;
The rebuke of His people

Vision: Great Leaders Never Lose Sight of the Big Picture

(Isaiah 25:1–12)

Good leaders never shrink from dealing with the realities of the here and now, no matter how depressing they might be. Yet they never lose sight of the big picture and what the ultimate future looks like.

While Isaiah 25 boasts a wonderful vision for the future, it comes on the heels of chapter 24, which predicts doom and gloom for the immediate future. One chapter deals with a temporary situation; the next pictures the ultimate situation. Leadership must stay in touch with both. Vision separates leaders from followers:

Followers	Leaders
1. See the here and now	1. See the ultimate goals and potential
2. Driven by the atmosphere of today	2. Driven by their vision for tomorrow
3. Limited perspective on their abilities	3. Larger perspective on everyone's abilities
4. Can be diverted by today's losses	4. Stays on track by focusing on the goal
5. Key word: immediate	5. Key word: ultimate

He will take away from all the earth;
For the LORD has spoken.

9 And it will be said in that day:
"Behold, this *is* our God;
We have waited for Him, and He will save
us.
This *is* the LORD;
We have waited for Him;
We will be glad and rejoice in His salvation."

10 For on this mountain the hand of the
LORD will rest,
And Moab shall be trampled down under
Him,
As straw is trampled down for the refuse
heap.

11 And He will spread out His hands in their
midst
As a swimmer reaches out to swim,
And He will bring down their pride
Together with the trickery of their hands.

12 The fortress of the high fort of your walls
He will bring down, lay low,
And bring to the ground, down to the dust.

A Song of Salvation

26 In that day this song will be sung in
the land of Judah:

"We have a strong city;
God will appoint salvation *for* walls and
bulwarks.

2 Open the gates,
That the righteous nation which keeps the
truth may enter in.

3 You will keep *him* in perfect peace,
Whose mind *is* stayed *on* You,
Because he trusts in You.

4 Trust in the LORD forever,
For in YAH, the LORD, *is* everlasting
strength.[a]

5 For He brings down those who dwell on
high,
The lofty city;
He lays it low,
He lays it low to the ground,

26:4 [a]Or *Rock of Ages*

Leaders Manage Stress by Managing Perspective

(Isaiah 26:3, 4)

Those who fix their eyes on the past risk a severe collision with the future. Those who see only the future hit much too hard the speed bumps of today. Only those who fix their eyes on God can effectively negotiate the right pace of life.

He brings it down to the dust.
6 The foot shall tread it down—
The feet of the poor
And the steps of the needy."

7 The way of the just *is* uprightness;
O Most Upright,
You weigh the path of the just.
8 Yes, in the way of Your judgments,
O LORD, we have waited for You;
The desire of *our* soul *is* for Your name
And for the remembrance of You.
9 With my soul I have desired You in the
night,
Yes, by my spirit within me I will seek
You early;
For when Your judgments *are* in the earth,
The inhabitants of the world will learn
righteousness.

10 Let grace be shown to the wicked,
Yet he will not learn righteousness;
In the land of uprightness he will deal
unjustly,
And will not behold the majesty of the
LORD.
11 LORD, *when* Your hand is lifted up, they
will not see.
But they will see and be ashamed
For *their* envy of people;
Yes, the fire of Your enemies shall devour
them.

12 LORD, You will establish peace for us,
For You have also done all our works
in us.
13 O LORD our God, masters besides You
Have had dominion over us;
But by You only we make mention of
Your name.
14 *They are* dead, they will not live;
They are deceased, they will not rise.
Therefore You have punished and
destroyed them,
And made all their memory to perish.
15 You have increased the nation, O LORD,
You have increased the nation;
You are glorified;
You have expanded all the borders of the
land.

16 LORD, in trouble they have visited You,
They poured out a prayer *when* Your
chastening *was* upon them.
17 As a woman with child
Is in pain and cries out in her pangs,

When she draws near the time of her
delivery,
So have we been in Your sight, O LORD.
18 We have been with child, we have been in
pain;
We have, as it were, brought forth wind;
We have not accomplished any deliverance
in the earth,
Nor have the inhabitants of the world
fallen.

19 Your dead shall live;
Together with my dead body[a] they shall arise.
Awake and sing, you who dwell in dust;
For your dew *is like* the dew of herbs,
And the earth shall cast out the dead.

Take Refuge from the Coming Judgment

20 Come, my people, enter your chambers,
And shut your doors behind you;
Hide yourself, as it were, for a little
moment,
Until the indignation is past.
21 For behold, the LORD comes out of His
place
To punish the inhabitants of the earth for
their iniquity;
The earth will also disclose her blood,
And will no more cover her slain.

27 In that day the LORD with His
severe sword, great and strong,
Will punish Leviathan the fleeing
serpent,
Leviathan that twisted serpent;
And He will slay the reptile that *is* in the
sea.

The Restoration of Israel

2 In that day sing to her,
"A vineyard of red wine!"[a]
3 I, the LORD, keep it,
I water it every moment;
Lest any hurt it,
I keep it night and day.
4 Fury *is* not in Me.
Who would set briers *and* thorns
Against Me in battle?

26:19 [a]Following Masoretic Text and Vulgate;
Syriac and Targum read *their dead bodies;* Septuagint
reads *those in the tombs.* **27:2** [a]Following Masoretic
Text (Kittel's *Biblia Hebraica*), Bomberg, and Vulgate;
Masoretic Text (*Biblia Hebraica Stuttgartensia*), some
Hebrew manuscripts, and Septuagint read *delight;*
Targum reads *choice vineyard.*

I would go through them,
I would burn them together.
5 Or let him take hold of My strength,
That he may make peace with Me;
And he shall make peace with Me."

6 Those who come He shall cause to take
root in Jacob;
Israel shall blossom and bud,
And fill the face of the world with fruit.

7 Has He struck Israel as He struck those
who struck him?
Or has He been slain according to the
slaughter of those who were slain by
Him?
8 In measure, by sending it away,
You contended with it.
He removes *it* by His rough wind
In the day of the east wind.
9 Therefore by this the iniquity of Jacob will
be covered;
And this *is* all the fruit of taking away his
sin:
When he makes all the stones of the altar
Like chalkstones that are beaten to dust,
Wooden images[a] and incense altars shall
not stand.

10 Yet the fortified city *will be* desolate,
The habitation forsaken and left like a
wilderness;
There the calf will feed, and there it will
lie down
And consume its branches.
11 When its boughs are withered, they will
be broken off;
The women come *and* set them on fire.
For it *is* a people of no understanding;
Therefore He who made them will not
have mercy on them,
And He who formed them will show
them no favor.

12 And it shall come to pass in that day
That the LORD will thresh,
From the channel of the River[a] to the
Brook of Egypt;
And you will be gathered one by one,
O you children of Israel.

13 So it shall be in that day:
The great trumpet will be blown;
They will come, who are about to perish
in the land of Assyria,

And they who are outcasts in the land of
Egypt,
And shall worship the LORD in the holy
mount at Jerusalem.

Woe to Ephraim and Jerusalem

28 Woe to the crown of pride, to the
drunkards of Ephraim,
Whose glorious beauty *is* a fading
flower
Which *is* at the head of the verdant valleys,
To those who are overcome with wine!
2 Behold, the Lord has a mighty and strong
one,
Like a tempest of hail and a destroying
storm,
Like a flood of mighty waters overflowing,
Who will bring *them* down to the earth
with *His* hand.
3 The crown of pride, the drunkards of
Ephraim,
Will be trampled underfoot;
4 And the glorious beauty is a fading flower
Which *is* at the head of the verdant valley,
Like the first fruit before the summer,
Which an observer sees;
He eats it up while it is still in his hand.

5 In that day the LORD of hosts will be
For a crown of glory and a diadem of
beauty
To the remnant of His people,
6 For a spirit of justice to him who sits in
judgment,
And for strength to those who turn back
the battle at the gate.

7 But they also have erred through wine,
And through intoxicating drink are out of
the way;
The priest and the prophet have erred
through intoxicating drink,
They are swallowed up by wine,
They are out of the way through
intoxicating drink;
They err in vision, they stumble *in*
judgment.
8 For all tables are full of vomit *and* filth;
No place *is* clean.

9 "Whom will he teach knowledge?
And whom will he make to understand
the message?

27:9 [a]Hebrew *Asherim*, Canaanite deities
27:12 [a]That is, the Euphrates

Those *just* weaned from milk?
Those *just* drawn from the breasts?
10 For precept *must be* upon precept, precept
upon precept,
Line upon line, line upon line,
Here a little, there a little."

11 For with stammering lips and another
tongue
He will speak to this people,
12 To whom He said, "This *is* the rest *with
which*
You may cause the weary to rest,"
And, "This *is* the refreshing";
Yet they would not hear.
13 But the word of the LORD was to them,
"Precept upon precept, precept upon
precept,
Line upon line, line upon line,
Here a little, there a little,"
That they might go and fall backward, and
be broken
And snared and caught.

14 Therefore hear the word of the LORD, you
scornful men,
Who rule this people who *are* in
Jerusalem,
15 Because you have said, "We have made a
covenant with death,
And with Sheol we are in agreement.
When the overflowing scourge passes
through,
It will not come to us,
For we have made lies our refuge,
And under falsehood we have hidden
ourselves."

A Cornerstone in Zion

16 Therefore thus says the Lord GOD:

"Behold, I lay in Zion a stone for a
foundation,
A tried stone, a precious cornerstone, a
sure foundation;
Whoever believes will not act hastily.
17 Also I will make justice the measuring
line,
And righteousness the plummet;
The hail will sweep away the refuge of lies,
And the waters will overflow the hiding
place.
18 Your covenant with death will be
annulled,
And your agreement with Sheol will not
stand;

When the overflowing scourge passes
through,
Then you will be trampled down by it.
19 As often as it goes out it will take you;
For morning by morning it will pass over,
And by day and by night;
It will be a terror just to understand the
report."

20 For the bed is too short to stretch out *on,*
And the covering so narrow that one
cannot wrap himself *in it.*
21 For the LORD will rise up as *at* Mount
Perazim,
He will be angry as in the Valley of
Gibeon—
That He may do His work, His awesome
work,
And bring to pass His act, His unusual act.
22 Now therefore, do not be mockers,
Lest your bonds be made strong;
For I have heard from the Lord GOD of
hosts,
A destruction determined even upon the
whole earth.

Listen to the Teaching of God

23 Give ear and hear my voice,
Listen and hear my speech.
24 Does the plowman keep plowing all day to
sow?
Does he keep turning his soil and breaking
the clods?
25 When he has leveled its surface,
Does he not sow the black cummin
And scatter the cummin,
Plant the wheat in rows,
The barley in the appointed place,
And the spelt in its place?
26 For He instructs him in right judgment,
His God teaches him.

27 For the black cummin is not threshed with
a threshing sledge,
Nor is a cartwheel rolled over the
cummin;
But the black cummin is beaten out with a
stick,
And the cummin with a rod.
28 Bread *flour* must be ground;
Therefore he does not thresh it forever,
Break *it with* his cartwheel,
Or crush *it with* his horsemen.
29 This also comes from the LORD of hosts,
Who is wonderful in counsel *and* excellent
in guidance.

Woe to Jerusalem

29 ¹"Woe to Ariel,ᵃ to Ariel, the city
where David dwelt!
Add year to year;
Let feasts come around.
² Yet I will distress Ariel;
There shall be heaviness and sorrow,
And it shall be to Me as Ariel.
³ I will encamp against you all around,
I will lay siege against you with a mound,
And I will raise siegeworks against you.
⁴ You shall be brought down,
You shall speak out of the ground;
Your speech shall be low, out of the dust;
Your voice shall be like a medium's, out of
the ground;
And your speech shall whisper out of the
dust.

⁵ "Moreover the multitude of your foes
Shall be like fine dust,
And the multitude of the terrible ones
Like chaff that passes away;
Yes, it shall be in an instant, suddenly.
⁶ You will be punished by the LORD of
hosts
With thunder and earthquake and great
noise,
With storm and tempest
And the flame of devouring fire.
⁷ The multitude of all the nations who fight
against Ariel,
Even all who fight against her and her
fortress,
And distress her,
Shall be as a dream of a night vision.
⁸ It shall even be as when a hungry man
dreams,
And look—he eats;
But he awakes, and his soul is still empty;
Or as when a thirsty man dreams,
And look—he drinks;
But he awakes, and indeed *he is* faint,
And his soul still craves:
So the multitude of all the nations shall
be,
Who fight against Mount Zion."

The Blindness of Disobedience

⁹ Pause and wonder!
Blind yourselves and be blind!
They are drunk, but not with wine;
They stagger, but not with intoxicating
drink.
¹⁰ For the LORD has poured out on you
The spirit of deep sleep,

And has closed your eyes, namely, the
prophets;
And He has covered your heads, *namely,*
the seers.

¹¹The whole vision has become to you like the
words of a book that is sealed, which *men* deliver
to one who is literate, saying, "Read this, please."
And he says, "I cannot, for it *is* sealed."
¹²Then the book is delivered to one who is il-
literate, saying, "Read this, please."
And he says, "I am not literate."
¹³Therefore the Lord said:

"Inasmuch as these people draw near with
their mouths
And honor Me with their lips,
But have removed their hearts far from
Me,
And their fear toward Me is taught by the
commandment of men,
¹⁴ Therefore, behold, I will again do a
marvelous work
Among this people,
A marvelous work and a wonder;
For the wisdom of their wise *men* shall
perish,
And the understanding of their prudent
men shall be hidden."

¹⁵ Woe to those who seek deep to hide their
counsel far from the LORD,
And their works are in the dark;
They say, "Who sees us?" and, "Who
knows us?"
¹⁶ Surely you have things turned around!
Shall the potter be esteemed as the clay;
For shall the thing made say of him who
made it,
"He did not make me"?
Or shall the thing formed say of him who
formed it,
"He has no understanding"?

Future Recovery of Wisdom

¹⁷ *Is* it not yet a very little while
Till Lebanon shall be turned into a fruitful
field,
And the fruitful field be esteemed as a
forest?
¹⁸ In that day the deaf shall hear the words of
the book,
And the eyes of the blind shall see out of
obscurity and out of darkness.

29:1 ᵃThat is, Jerusalem

19 The humble also shall increase *their* joy in
the LORD,
And the poor among men shall rejoice
In the Holy One of Israel.
20 For the terrible one is brought to nothing,
The scornful one is consumed,
And all who watch for iniquity are cut
off—
21 Who make a man an offender by a word,
And lay a snare for him who reproves in
the gate,
And turn aside the just by empty words.

22Therefore thus says the LORD, who redeemed Abraham, concerning the house of Jacob:

"Jacob shall not now be ashamed,
Nor shall his face now grow pale;
23 But when he sees his children,
The work of My hands, in his midst,
They will hallow My name,
And hallow the Holy One of Jacob,
And fear the God of Israel.
24 These also who erred in spirit will come
to understanding,
And those who complained will learn
doctrine."

Futile Confidence in Egypt

30 "Woe to the rebellious children,"
says the LORD,
"Who take counsel, but not of Me,
And who devise plans, but not of My
Spirit,
That they may add sin to sin;
2 Who walk to go down to Egypt,
And have not asked My advice,
To strengthen themselves in the strength of
Pharaoh,
And to trust in the shadow of Egypt!
3 Therefore the strength of Pharaoh
Shall be your shame,
And trust in the shadow of Egypt
Shall be *your* humiliation.
4 For his princes were at Zoan,
And his ambassadors came to Hanes.
5 They were all ashamed of a people *who*
could not benefit them,
Or be help or benefit,
But a shame and also a reproach."

6The burden against the beasts of the South.

Through a land of trouble and anguish,
From which *came* the lioness and lion,

The viper and fiery flying serpent,
They will carry their riches on the backs
of young donkeys,
And their treasures on the humps of
camels,
To a people *who* shall not profit;
7 For the Egyptians shall help in vain and to
no purpose.
Therefore I have called her
Rahab-Hem-Shebeth.[a]

Strategic Planning: Where God Fits In
(Isaiah 30:1–5)

Leaders and organizations constantly make
plans. This is one reason why leaders are
in demand; they plan for and negotiate the future. Yet Isaiah issues a warning to every
leader who develops plans without asking if
they fit the mind of God.

Leaders must remember just how tentative
strategic plans need to be. No one knows the
future except God. Keep in mind the following
equation as you plan:

Our Preparation + God's Providence = Success

Leaders must constantly ask if their plans
fit God's revealed will for them and their organization. Then they must ask if their plans
remain relevant to the needs of their mission,
their values, their vision, and their long-range
objectives. Finally, they need to ask if their
plans fit the needs of their culture and time.
This makes for wise leadership and strategic
planning.

A Rebellious People

8 Now go, write it before them on a tablet,
And note it on a scroll,
That it may be for time to come,
Forever and ever:
9 That this *is* a rebellious people,
Lying children,
Children *who* will not hear the law of the
LORD;
10 Who say to the seers, "Do not see,"
And to the prophets, "Do not prophesy to
us right things;

30:7 [a]Literally *Rahab Sits Idle*

Speak to us smooth things, prophesy
deceits.
11 Get out of the way,
Turn aside from the path,
Cause the Holy One of Israel
To cease from before us."

12Therefore thus says the Holy One of Israel:

"Because you despise this word,
And trust in oppression and perversity,
And rely on them,
13 Therefore this iniquity shall be to you
Like a breach ready to fall,
A bulge in a high wall,
Whose breaking comes suddenly, in an
instant.
14 And He shall break it like the breaking of
the potter's vessel,
Which is broken in pieces;
He shall not spare.
So there shall not be found among its
fragments
A shard to take fire from the hearth,
Or to take water from the cistern."

15For thus says the Lord GOD, the Holy One
of Israel:

"In returning and rest you shall be saved;
In quietness and confidence shall be your
strength."
But you would not,
16 And you said, "No, for we will flee on
horses"—
Therefore you shall flee!
And, "We will ride on swift *horses*"—
Therefore those who pursue you shall be
swift!

17 One thousand *shall flee* at the threat of one,
At the threat of five you shall flee,
Till you are left as a pole on top of a
mountain
And as a banner on a hill.

God Will Be Gracious
18 Therefore the LORD will wait, that He
may be gracious to you;
And therefore He will be exalted, that He
may have mercy on you.
For the LORD *is* a God of justice;
Blessed *are* all those who wait for Him.

19 For the people shall dwell in Zion at
Jerusalem;

You shall weep no more.
He will be very gracious to you at the
sound of your cry;
When He hears it, He will answer you.
20 And *though* the Lord gives you
The bread of adversity and the water of
affliction,
Yet your teachers will not be moved into a
corner anymore,
But your eyes shall see your teachers.
21 Your ears shall hear a word behind you,
saying,
"This *is* the way, walk in it,"
Whenever you turn to the right hand
Or whenever you turn to the left.
22 You will also defile the covering of your
images of silver,
And the ornament of your molded images
of gold.
You will throw them away as an unclean
thing;
You will say to them, "Get away!"

23 Then He will give the rain for your seed
With which you sow the ground,
And bread of the increase of the earth;
It will be fat and plentiful.
In that day your cattle will feed
In large pastures.
24 Likewise the oxen and the young donkeys
that work the ground
Will eat cured fodder,
Which has been winnowed with the
shovel and fan.
25 There will be on every high mountain
And on every high hill
Rivers *and* streams of waters,
In the day of the great slaughter,
When the towers fall.
26 Moreover the light of the moon will be as
the light of the sun,
And the light of the sun will be sevenfold,
As the light of seven days,
In the day that the LORD binds up the
bruise of His people
And heals the stroke of their wound.

Judgment on Assyria
27 Behold, the name of the LORD comes
from afar,
Burning *with* His anger,
And *His* burden *is* heavy;
His lips are full of indignation,
And His tongue like a devouring fire.
28 His breath is like an overflowing stream,
Which reaches up to the neck,

To sift the nations with the sieve of
   futility;
And *there shall be* a bridle in the jaws of
   the people,
Causing *them* to err.

29 You shall have a song
As in the night *when* a holy festival is kept,
And gladness of heart as when one goes
   with a flute,
To come into the mountain of the LORD,
To the Mighty One of Israel.
30 The LORD will cause His glorious voice to
   be heard,
And show the descent of His arm,
With the indignation of *His* anger
And the flame of a devouring fire,
With scattering, tempest, and hailstones.
31 For through the voice of the LORD
Assyria will be beaten down,
As He strikes with the rod.
32 And *in* every place where the staff of
   punishment passes,
Which the LORD lays on him,
It will be with tambourines and harps;
And in battles of brandishing He will fight
   with it.
33 For Tophet *was* established of old,
Yes, for the king it is prepared.
He has made *it* deep and large;
Its pyre *is* fire with much wood;
The breath of the LORD, like a stream of
   brimstone,
Kindles it.

The Folly of Not Trusting God

31 Woe to those who go down to
   Egypt for help,
   And rely on horses,
Who trust in chariots because *they are*
   many,
And in horsemen because they are very
   strong,
But who do not look to the Holy One of
   Israel,
Nor seek the LORD!
2 Yet He also *is* wise and will bring disaster,
And will not call back His words,
But will arise against the house of
   evildoers,
And against the help of those who work
   iniquity.
3 Now the Egyptians *are* men, and not God;
And their horses are flesh, and not spirit.
When the LORD stretches out His hand,
Both he who helps will fall,

And he who is helped will fall down;
They all will perish together.

God Will Deliver Jerusalem

4 For thus the LORD has spoken to me:

" As a lion roars,
And a young lion over his prey
(When a multitude of shepherds is
   summoned against him,
He will not be afraid of their voice
Nor be disturbed by their noise),
So the LORD of hosts will come down
To fight for Mount Zion and for its hill.
5 Like birds flying about,
So will the LORD of hosts defend
   Jerusalem.
Defending, He will also deliver *it;*
Passing over, He will preserve *it.*"

6 Return *to Him* against whom the children of
Israel have deeply revolted. 7 For in that day every
man shall throw away his idols of silver and his
idols of gold—sin, which your own hands have
made for yourselves.

8 " Then Assyria shall fall by a sword not of
   man,
And a sword not of mankind shall devour
   him.
But he shall flee from the sword,
And his young men shall become forced
   labor.
9 He shall cross over to his stronghold for
   fear,
And his princes shall be afraid of the
   banner,"
Says the LORD,
Whose fire *is* in Zion
And whose furnace *is* in Jerusalem.

A Reign of Righteousness

32 Behold, a king will reign in
   righteousness,
   And princes will rule with justice.
2 A man will be as a hiding place from the
   wind,
And a cover from the tempest,
As rivers of water in a dry place,
As the shadow of a great rock in a weary
   land.
3 The eyes of those who see will not be
   dim,
And the ears of those who hear will listen.
4 Also the heart of the rash will understand
   knowledge,

And the tongue of the stammerers will be
ready to speak plainly.

5 The foolish person will no longer be
called generous,
Nor the miser said *to be* bountiful;
6 For the foolish person will speak
foolishness,
And his heart will work iniquity:
To practice ungodliness,
To utter error against the LORD,
To keep the hungry unsatisfied,
And he will cause the drink of the thirsty
to fail.
7 Also the schemes of the schemer *are* evil;
He devises wicked plans
To destroy the poor with lying words,
Even when the needy speaks justice.
8 But a generous man devises generous
things,
And by generosity he shall stand.

Consequences of Complacency

9 Rise up, you women who are at ease,
Hear my voice;
You complacent daughters,
Give ear to my speech.
10 In a year and *some* days
You will be troubled, you complacent
women;
For the vintage will fail,
The gathering will not come.
11 Tremble, you *women* who are at ease;
Be troubled, you complacent ones;
Strip yourselves, make yourselves bare,
And gird *sackcloth* on *your* waists.

12 People shall mourn upon their breasts
For the pleasant fields, for the fruitful
vine.
13 On the land of my people will come up
thorns *and* briers,
Yes, on all the happy homes *in* the joyous
city;
14 Because the palaces will be forsaken,
The bustling city will be deserted.
The forts and towers will become lairs
forever,
A joy of wild donkeys, a pasture of
flocks—
15 Until the Spirit is poured upon us from on
high,
And the wilderness becomes a fruitful
field,
And the fruitful field is counted as a
forest.

The Peace of God's Reign

16 Then justice will dwell in the wilderness,
And righteousness remain in the fruitful
field.
17 The work of righteousness will be peace,
And the effect of righteousness, quietness
and assurance forever.
18 My people will dwell in a peaceful
habitation,
In secure dwellings, and in quiet resting
places,
19 Though hail comes down on the forest,
And the city is brought low in
humiliation.

20 Blessed *are* you who sow beside all waters,
Who send out freely the feet of the ox and
the donkey.

A Prayer in Deep Distress

33 Woe to you who plunder, though
you *have* not *been* plundered;
And you who deal treacherously,
though they have not dealt
treacherously with you!
When you cease plundering,
You will be plundered;
When you make an end of dealing
treacherously,
They will deal treacherously with you.

2 O LORD, be gracious to us;
We have waited for You.
Be their[a] arm every morning,
Our salvation also in the time of trouble.
3 At the noise of the tumult the people shall
flee;
When You lift Yourself up, the nations
shall be scattered;
4 And Your plunder shall be gathered
Like the gathering of the caterpillar;
As the running to and fro of locusts,
He shall run upon them.

5 The LORD is exalted, for He dwells on
high;
He has filled Zion with justice and
righteousness.
6 Wisdom and knowledge will be the
stability of your times,
And the strength of salvation;
The fear of the LORD *is* His treasure.

33:2 [a]Septuagint omits *their;* Syriac, Targum, and
Vulgate read *our.*

7 Surely their valiant ones shall cry outside,
The ambassadors of peace shall weep
bitterly.
8 The highways lie waste,
The traveling man ceases.
He has broken the covenant,
He has despised the cities,[a]
He regards no man.
9 The earth mourns *and* languishes,
Lebanon is shamed *and* shriveled;
Sharon is like a wilderness,
And Bashan and Carmel shake off *their
fruits.*

Impending Judgment on Zion

10 "Now I will rise," says the LORD;
"Now I will be exalted,
Now I will lift Myself up.
11 You shall conceive chaff,
You shall bring forth stubble;
Your breath, *as* fire, shall devour you.
12 And the people shall be *like* the burnings
of lime;
Like thorns cut up they shall be burned in
the fire.
13 Hear, you *who are* afar off, what I have done;
And you *who are* near, acknowledge My
might."

14 The sinners in Zion are afraid;
Fearfulness has seized the hypocrites:
"Who among us shall dwell with the
devouring fire?
Who among us shall dwell with everlasting
burnings?"
15 He who walks righteously and speaks
uprightly,
He who despises the gain of oppressions,
Who gestures with his hands, refusing
bribes,
Who stops his ears from hearing of
bloodshed,
And shuts his eyes from seeing evil:
16 He will dwell on high;
His place of defense *will be* the fortress of
rocks;
Bread will be given him,
His water *will be* sure.

The Land of the Majestic King

17 Your eyes will see the King in His beauty;
They will see the land that is very far off.
18 Your heart will meditate on terror:
"Where *is* the scribe?
Where *is* he who weighs?
Where *is* he who counts the towers?"

The Law of Solid Ground: Leaders Must Earn Trust

(Isaiah 33:14–16)

Who can stand up under the purification process of God? Who can remain unchanged through the fire of God?

That's the question Isaiah asks and then answers. He lays out a list of traits for the kind of people who can stand in a crisis. Ponder his description:

1. *Integrity:* The leader's life and words match (v. 15).
2. *Justice:* The leader rejects dishonest gain (v. 15).
3. *Convictions:* The leader's values won't allow him to accept bribes (v. 15).
4. *Positive focus:* The leader refuses to dwell on destructive issues (v. 15).
5. *Pure:* The leader disciplines his or her mind to remain clean and pure (v. 15).
6. *Secure:* The leader is firm, stable in his identity and source of strength (v. 16).

Characteristics like these earn the trust of others. When leaders possess them, they feel secure enough to develop others, rather than destroy them. Remember, only secure leaders empower others.

---

19 You will not see a fierce people,
A people of obscure speech, beyond
perception,
Of a stammering tongue *that you* cannot
understand.
20 Look upon Zion, the city of our
appointed feasts;
Your eyes will see Jerusalem, a quiet home,
A tabernacle *that* will not be taken down;
Not one of its stakes will ever be removed,
Nor will any of its cords be broken.
21 But there the majestic LORD *will be* for us
A place of broad rivers *and* streams,
In which no galley with oars will sail,
Nor majestic ships pass by

33:8 [a]Following Masoretic Text and Vulgate; Dead
Sea Scrolls read *witnesses;* Septuagint omits *cities;*
Targum reads *They have been removed from their cities.*

22 (For the LORD *is* our Judge,
The LORD *is* our Lawgiver,
The LORD *is* our King;
He will save us);
23 Your tackle is loosed,
They could not strengthen their mast,
They could not spread the sail.

Then the prey of great plunder is divided;
The lame take the prey.
24 And the inhabitant will not say, "I am sick";
The people who dwell in it *will be*
forgiven *their* iniquity.

Judgment on the Nations

34 Come near, you nations, to hear;
And heed, you people!
Let the earth hear, and all that is
in it,
The world and all things that come forth
from it.
2 For the indignation of the LORD *is* against
all nations,
And *His* fury against all their armies;
He has utterly destroyed them,
He has given them over to the slaughter.
3 Also their slain shall be thrown out;
Their stench shall rise from their corpses,
And the mountains shall be melted with
their blood.
4 All the host of heaven shall be dissolved,
And the heavens shall be rolled up like a
scroll;
All their host shall fall down
As the leaf falls from the vine,
And as *fruit* falling from a fig tree.

5 "For My sword shall be bathed in heaven;
Indeed it shall come down on Edom,
And on the people of My curse, for
judgment.
6 The sword of the LORD is filled with
blood,
It is made overflowing with fatness,
With the blood of lambs and goats,
With the fat of the kidneys of rams.
For the LORD has a sacrifice in Bozrah,
And a great slaughter in the land of Edom.
7 The wild oxen shall come down with them,
And the young bulls with the mighty bulls;
Their land shall be soaked with blood,
And their dust saturated with fatness."

8 For *it is* the day of the LORD's vengeance,
The year of recompense for the cause of
Zion.

9 Its streams shall be turned into pitch,
And its dust into brimstone;
Its land shall become burning pitch.
10 It shall not be quenched night or day;
Its smoke shall ascend forever.
From generation to generation it shall lie
waste;
No one shall pass through it forever and
ever.
11 But the pelican and the porcupine shall
possess it,
Also the owl and the raven shall dwell
in it.
And He shall stretch out over it
The line of confusion and the stones of
emptiness.
12 They shall call its nobles to the kingdom,
But none *shall be* there, and all its princes
shall be nothing.

13 And thorns shall come up in its palaces,
Nettles and brambles in its fortresses;
It shall be a habitation of jackals,
A courtyard for ostriches.
14 The wild beasts of the desert shall also
meet with the jackals,
And the wild goat shall bleat to its
companion;
Also the night creature shall rest there,
And find for herself a place of rest.
15 There the arrow snake shall make her nest
and lay *eggs*
And hatch, and gather *them* under her
shadow;
There also shall the hawks be gathered,
Every one with her mate.

16 "Search from the book of the LORD, and
read:
Not one of these shall fail;
Not one shall lack her mate.
For My mouth has commanded it, and His
Spirit has gathered them.
17 He has cast the lot for them,
And His hand has divided it among them
with a measuring line.
They shall possess it forever;
From generation to generation they shall
dwell in it."

The Future Glory of Zion

35 The wilderness and the wasteland
shall be glad for them,
And the desert shall rejoice and
blossom as the rose;
2 It shall blossom abundantly and rejoice,

Even with joy and singing.
The glory of Lebanon shall be given to it,
The excellence of Carmel and Sharon.
They shall see the glory of the LORD,
The excellency of our God.

3 Strengthen the weak hands,
And make firm the feeble knees.
4 Say to those *who are* fearful-hearted,
"Be strong, do not fear!
Behold, your God will come *with*
vengeance,
With the recompense of God;
He will come and save you."

5 Then the eyes of the blind shall be
opened,
And the ears of the deaf shall be
unstopped.
6 Then the lame shall leap like a deer,
And the tongue of the dumb sing.
For waters shall burst forth in the
wilderness,
And streams in the desert.
7 The parched ground shall become a pool,
And the thirsty land springs of water;
In the habitation of jackals, where each lay,
There shall be grass with reeds and rushes.

8 A highway shall be there, and a road,
And it shall be called the Highway of
Holiness.
The unclean shall not pass over it,
But it *shall be* for others.
Whoever walks the road, although a fool,
Shall not go astray.
9 No lion shall be there,
Nor shall *any* ravenous beast go up on it;
It shall not be found there.
But the redeemed shall walk *there,*
10 And the ransomed of the LORD shall
return,
And come to Zion with singing,
With everlasting joy on their heads.
They shall obtain joy and gladness,
And sorrow and sighing shall flee away.

Sennacherib Boasts Against the LORD

36 Now it came to pass in the four-teenth year of King Hezekiah *that* Sennacherib king of Assyria came up against all the fortified cities of Judah and took them. ²Then the king of Assyria sent *the* Rab-shakeh[a] with a great army from Lachish to King Hezekiah at Jerusalem. And he stood by the aqueduct from the upper pool, on the highway to the Fuller's Field. ³And Eliakim the son of Hilkiah, who was over the household, Shebna the scribe, and Joah the son of Asaph, the recorder, came out to him.

⁴Then *the* Rabshakeh said to them, "Say now to Hezekiah, 'Thus says the great king, the king of Assyria: "What confidence is this in which you trust? ⁵I say you speak of having plans and power for war; but *they are* mere words. Now in whom do you trust, that you rebel against me? ⁶Look! You are trusting in the staff of this broken reed, Egypt, on which if a man leans, it will go into his hand and pierce it. So *is* Pharaoh king of Egypt to all who trust in him.

⁷"But if you say to me, 'We trust in the LORD our God,' *is it* not He whose high places and whose altars Hezekiah has taken away, and said to Judah and Jerusalem, 'You shall worship before this altar'?"' ⁸Now therefore, I urge you, give a pledge to my master the king of Assyria, and I will give you two thousand horses—if you are able on your part to put riders on them! ⁹How then will you repel one captain of the least of my master's servants, and put your trust in Egypt for chariots and horsemen? ¹⁰Have I now come up without the LORD against this land to destroy it? The LORD said to me, 'Go up against this land, and destroy it.'"

¹¹Then Eliakim, Shebna, and Joah said to *the* Rabshakeh, "Please speak to your servants in Aramaic, for we understand *it;* and do not speak to us in Hebrew[a] in the hearing of the people who *are* on the wall."

¹²But *the* Rabshakeh said, "Has my master sent me to your master and to you to speak these words, and not to the men who sit on the wall, who will eat and drink their own waste with you?"

¹³Then *the* Rabshakeh stood and called out with a loud voice in Hebrew, and said, "Hear the words of the great king, the king of Assyria! ¹⁴Thus says the king: 'Do not let Hezekiah deceive you, for he will not be able to deliver you; ¹⁵nor let Hezekiah make you trust in the LORD, saying, "The LORD will surely deliver us; this city will not be given into the hand of the king of Assyria."' ¹⁶Do not listen to Hezekiah; for thus says the king of Assyria: 'Make *peace* with me *by a* present and come out to me; and every one of you eat from his own vine and every one from his own fig tree, and every one of you drink the waters of his own cistern; ¹⁷until I come and take you away to a land like your own land, a land of

---

36:2 ᵃA title, probably *Chief of Staff* or *Governor*
36:11 ᵃLiterally *Judean*

grain and new wine, a land of bread and vineyards. ¹⁸*Beware* lest Hezekiah persuade you, saying, "The Lord will deliver us." Has any one of the gods of the nations delivered its land from the hand of the king of Assyria? ¹⁹Where *are* the gods of Hamath and Arpad? Where *are* the gods of Sepharvaim? Indeed, have they delivered Samaria from my hand? ²⁰Who among all the gods of these lands have delivered their countries from my hand, that the Lord should deliver Jerusalem from my hand?'"

²¹But they held their peace and answered him not a word; for the king's commandment was, "Do not answer him." ²²Then Eliakim the son of Hilkiah, who *was* over the household, Shebna the scribe, and Joah the son of Asaph, the recorder, came to Hezekiah with *their* clothes torn, and told him the words of *the* Rabshakeh.

Isaiah Assures Deliverance

37 And so it was, when King Hezekiah heard *it*, that he tore his clothes, covered himself with sackcloth, and went into the house of the Lord. ²Then he sent Eliakim, who *was* over the household, Shebna the scribe, and the elders of the priests, covered with sackcloth, to Isaiah the prophet, the son of Amoz. ³And they said to him, "Thus says Hezekiah: 'This day *is* a day of trouble and rebuke and blasphemy; for the children have come to birth, but *there is* no strength to bring them forth. ⁴It may be that the Lord your God will hear the words of *the* Rabshakeh, whom his master the king of Assyria has sent to reproach the living God, and will rebuke the words which the Lord your God has heard. Therefore lift up *your* prayer for the remnant that is left.'"

⁵So the servants of King Hezekiah came to Isaiah. ⁶And Isaiah said to them, "Thus you shall say to your master, 'Thus says the Lord: "Do not be afraid of the words which you have heard, with which the servants of the king of Assyria have blasphemed Me. ⁷Surely I will send a spirit upon him, and he shall hear a rumor and return to his own land; and I will cause him to fall by the sword in his own land."'"

Sennacherib's Threat and Hezekiah's Prayer

⁸Then *the* Rabshakeh returned, and found the king of Assyria warring against Libnah, for he heard that he had departed from Lachish. ⁹And the king heard concerning Tirhakah king of Ethiopia, "He has come out to make war with you." So when he heard *it,* he sent messengers to Hezekiah, saying, ¹⁰"Thus you shall speak to

Hezekiah king of Judah, saying: 'Do not let your God in whom you trust deceive you, saying, "Jerusalem shall not be given into the hand of the king of Assyria." ¹¹Look! You have heard what the kings of Assyria have done to all lands by utterly destroying them; and shall you be delivered? ¹²Have the gods of the nations delivered those whom my fathers have destroyed, Gozan and Haran and Rezeph, and the people of Eden who *were* in Telassar? ¹³Where *is* the king of Hamath, the king of Arpad, and the king of the city of Sepharvaim, Hena, and Ivah?'"

¹⁴And Hezekiah received the letter from the hand of the messengers, and read it; and Hezekiah went up to the house of the Lord, and spread it before the Lord. ¹⁵Then Hezekiah prayed to the Lord, saying: ¹⁶"O Lord of hosts, God of Israel, *the* One who dwells *between* the cherubim, You *are* God, You alone, of all the kingdoms of the earth. You have made heaven and earth. ¹⁷Incline Your ear, O Lord, and hear; open Your eyes, O Lord, and see; and hear all the words of Sennacherib, which he has sent to reproach the living God. ¹⁸Truly, Lord, the kings of Assyria have laid waste all the nations and their lands, ¹⁹and have cast their gods into the fire; for they *were* not gods, but the work of men's hands—wood and stone. Therefore they destroyed them. ²⁰Now therefore, O Lord our God, save us from his hand, that all the kingdoms of the earth may know that You *are* the Lord, You alone."

The Word of the Lord Concerning Sennacherib

²¹Then Isaiah the son of Amoz sent to Hezekiah, saying, "Thus says the Lord God of Israel, 'Because you have prayed to Me against Sennacherib king of Assyria, ²²this *is* the word which the Lord has spoken concerning him:

"The virgin, the daughter of Zion,
    Has despised you, laughed you to scorn;
The daughter of Jerusalem
    Has shaken *her* head behind your back!

²³ "Whom have you reproached and
    blasphemed?
Against whom have you raised *your* voice,
And lifted up your eyes on high?
Against the Holy One of Israel.
²⁴ By your servants you have reproached the
    Lord,
And said, 'By the multitude of my chariots
    I have come up to the height of the
    mountains,

To the limits of Lebanon;
I will cut down its tall cedars
And its choice cypress trees;
I will enter its farthest height,
To its fruitful forest.
25 I have dug and drunk water,
And with the soles of my feet I have dried
up
All the brooks of defense.'

26 "Did you not hear long ago
How I made it,
From ancient times that I formed it?
Now I have brought it to pass,
That you should be
For crushing fortified cities *into* heaps of
ruins.
27 Therefore their inhabitants *had* little power;
They were dismayed and confounded;
They were *as* the grass of the field
And the green herb,
As the grass on the housetops
And grain blighted before it is grown.

28 "But I know your dwelling place,
Your going out and your coming in,
And your rage against Me.
29 Because your rage against Me and your
tumult
Have come up to My ears,
Therefore I will put My hook in your nose
And My bridle in your lips,
And I will turn you back
By the way which you came."'

30 "This *shall be* a sign to you:

You shall eat this year such as grows of
itself,
And the second year what springs from the
same;
Also in the third year sow and reap,
Plant vineyards and eat the fruit of them.
31 And the remnant who have escaped of the
house of Judah
Shall again take root downward,
And bear fruit upward.
32 For out of Jerusalem shall go a remnant,
And those who escape from Mount Zion.
The zeal of the LORD of hosts will do this.

33 "Therefore thus says the LORD concerning
the king of Assyria:

'He shall not come into this city,
Nor shoot an arrow there,

Nor come before it with shield,
Nor build a siege mound against it.
34 By the way that he came,
By the same shall he return;
And he shall not come into this city,'
Says the LORD.
35 'For I will defend this city, to save it
For My own sake and for My servant
David's sake.'"

The Law of Navigation: The Role of Planning and Praying

(Isaiah 37:1–37)

King Hezekiah provides an example of a leader who does what is humanly possible, then leans on God for the outcome. God had to do what the king could not do. A place exists for both preparation and prayer. To employ only one is naïve and incomplete.

Sennacherib's Defeat and Death

36 Then the angel[a] of the LORD went out, and killed in the camp of the Assyrians one hundred and eighty-five thousand; and when *people* arose early in the morning, there were the corpses—all dead. 37 So Sennacherib king of Assyria departed and went away, returned *home,* and remained at Nineveh. 38 Now it came to pass, as he was worshiping in the house of Nisroch his god, that his sons Adrammelech and Sharezer struck him down with the sword; and they escaped into the land of Ararat. Then Esarhaddon his son reigned in his place.

Hezekiah's Life Extended

38 In those days Hezekiah was sick and near death. And Isaiah the prophet, the son of Amoz, went to him and said to him, "Thus says the LORD: 'Set your house in order, for you shall die and not live.'" 2 Then Hezekiah turned his face toward the wall, and prayed to the LORD, 3 and said, "Remember now, O LORD, I pray, how I have walked before You in truth and with a loyal heart, and have done *what is* good in Your sight." And Hezekiah wept bitterly.
4 And the word of the LORD came to Isaiah,

37:36 [a]Or *Angel*

saying, [5]"Go and tell Hezekiah, 'Thus says the LORD, the God of David your father: "I have heard your prayer, I have seen your tears; surely I will add to your days fifteen years. [6]I will deliver you and this city from the hand of the king of Assyria, and I will defend this city."' [7]And this *is* the sign to you from the LORD, that the LORD will do this thing which He has spoken: [8]Behold, I will bring the shadow on the sundial, which has gone down with the sun on the sundial of Ahaz, ten degrees backward." So the sun returned ten degrees on the dial by which it had gone down.

[9]This is the writing of Hezekiah king of Judah, when he had been sick and had recovered from his sickness:

[10] I said,
"In the prime of my life
I shall go to the gates of Sheol;
I am deprived of the remainder of my
    years."
[11] I said,
"I shall not see YAH,
The LORD[a] in the land of the living;
I shall observe man no more among the
    inhabitants of the world.[b]
[12] My life span is gone,
Taken from me like a shepherd's tent;

I have cut off my life like a weaver.
He cuts me off from the loom;
From day until night You make an end of
    me.
[13] I have considered until morning—
Like a lion,
So He breaks all my bones;
From day until night You make an end of
    me.
[14] Like a crane *or* a swallow, so I chattered;
I mourned like a dove;
My eyes fail *from looking* upward.
O LORD,[a] I am oppressed;
Undertake for me!

[15] "What shall I say?
He has both spoken to me,[a]
And He Himself has done *it*.
I shall walk carefully all my years

38:11 [a]Hebrew *YAH, YAH* [b]Following some Hebrew manuscripts; Masoretic Text and Vulgate read *rest;* Septuagint omits *among the inhabitants of the world;* Targum reads *land.* **38:14** [a]Following Bomberg; Masoretic Text and Dead Sea Scrolls read *Lord.* **38:15** [a]Following Masoretic Text and Vulgate; Dead Sea Scrolls and Targum read *And shall I say to Him;* Septuagint omits first half of this verse.

HEZEKIAH — THE ART OF THANKSGIVING
(Isaiah 38:9–20)

PROFILE IN LEADERSHIP

Nothing brings out gratefulness like a reprieve from imminent death. When King Hezekiah of Judah, a good and godly king, heard from the prophet Isaiah that he was about to die, he immediately turned to the God he had faithfully served. He begged God for an extension of life—and the Lord granted him an additional 15 years. When Hezekiah learned that the Lord would lengthen his life, he did what any godly leader would do: He thanked and praised his God. Upon his recovery, he wrote to the Lord a poem of thanksgiving and praise for the good He had done.

As the godly king meditated on God's goodness, he realized that the Lord had used even his sickness for his good. In verse 17 he wrote, "Indeed it was for my own peace that I had great bitterness"—the same sentiment expressed many years before by his revered ancestor, David: "It is good for me that I have been afflicted, that I may learn Your statutes" (Ps. 119:71).

Hezekiah's hymn of gratitude not only thanked the Lord for sparing his life, it also expressed his commitment to "sing my songs with stringed instruments all the days of [my] life" (Is. 38:20). He realized that expressing gratitude to God ought to be more than a one-time event; it must be a lifestyle.

In the bitterness of my soul.

16 O Lord, by these *things men* live;
And in all these *things is* the life of my
spirit;
So You will restore me and make me live.

17 Indeed *it was* for *my own* peace
That I had great bitterness;
But You have lovingly *delivered* my soul
from the pit of corruption,
For You have cast all my sins behind Your
back.

18 For Sheol cannot thank You,
Death cannot praise You;
Those who go down to the pit cannot
hope for Your truth.

19 The living, the living man, he shall praise
You,
As I *do* this day;
The father shall make known Your truth
to the children.

20 "The LORD *was ready* to save me;
Therefore we will sing my songs with
stringed instruments
All the days of our life, in the house of the
LORD."

21Now Isaiah had said, "Let them take a lump
of figs, and apply *it* as a poultice on the boil, and
he shall recover."

22And Hezekiah had said, "What *is* the sign
that I shall go up to the house of the LORD?"

The Babylonian Envoys

39 At that time Merodach-Baladan[a] the
son of Baladan, king of Babylon, sent
letters and a present to Hezekiah, for
he heard that he had been sick and had recovered. 2And Hezekiah was pleased with them, and
showed them the house of his treasures—the silver and gold, the spices and precious ointment,
and all his armory—all that was found among his
treasures. There was nothing in his house or in all
his dominion that Hezekiah did not show them.

3Then Isaiah the prophet went to King
Hezekiah, and said to him, "What did these men
say, and from where did they come to you?"

So Hezekiah said, "They came to me from a
far country, from Babylon."

4And he said, "What have they seen in your
house?"

So Hezekiah answered, "They have seen all
that *is* in my house; there is nothing among my
treasures that I have not shown them."

5Then Isaiah said to Hezekiah, "Hear the
word of the LORD of hosts: 6'Behold, the days are

coming when all that *is* in your house, and what
your fathers have accumulated until this day, shall
be carried to Babylon; nothing shall be left,' says
the LORD. 7'And they shall take away *some* of
your sons who will descend from you, whom
you will beget; and they shall be eunuchs in the
palace of the king of Babylon.'"

8So Hezekiah said to Isaiah, "The word of the
LORD which you have spoken *is* good!" For he
said, "At least there will be peace and truth in my
days."

God's People Are Comforted

40 "Comfort, yes, comfort My
people!"
Says your God.

2 "Speak comfort to Jerusalem, and cry out to
her,
That her warfare is ended,
That her iniquity is pardoned;
For she has received from the LORD's hand
Double for all her sins."

3 The voice of one crying in the wilderness:
"Prepare the way of the LORD;
Make straight in the desert[a]
A highway for our God.

4 Every valley shall be exalted
And every mountain and hill brought low;
The crooked places shall be made straight
And the rough places smooth;

5 The glory of the LORD shall be revealed,
And all flesh shall see *it* together;
For the mouth of the LORD has spoken."

6 The voice said, "Cry out!"
And he[a] said, "What shall I cry?"

"All flesh *is* grass,
And all its loveliness *is* like the flower of
the field.

7 The grass withers, the flower fades,
Because the breath of the LORD blows
upon it;
Surely the people *are* grass.

8 The grass withers, the flower fades,
But the word of our God stands forever."

9 O Zion,
You who bring good tidings,

39:1 [a]Spelled *Berodach-Baladan* in 2 Kings 20:12
40:3 [a]Following Masoretic Text, Targum, and
Vulgate; Septuagint omits *in the desert*.
40:6 [a]Following Masoretic Text and Targum; Dead
Sea Scrolls, Septuagint, and Vulgate read *I*.

Get up into the high mountain;
O Jerusalem,
You who bring good tidings,
Lift up your voice with strength,
Lift *it* up, be not afraid;
Say to the cities of Judah, "Behold your God!"

10 Behold, the Lord GOD shall come with a strong *hand,*
And His arm shall rule for Him;
Behold, His reward *is* with Him,
And His work before Him.

11 He will feed His flock like a shepherd;
He will gather the lambs with His arm,
And carry *them* in His bosom,
And gently lead those who are with young.

12 Who has measured the waters[a] in the hollow of His hand,
Measured heaven with a span
And calculated the dust of the earth in a measure?
Weighed the mountains in scales
And the hills in a balance?

13 Who has directed the Spirit of the LORD,
Or *as* His counselor has taught Him?

14 With whom did He take counsel, and *who* instructed Him,
And taught Him in the path of justice?
Who taught Him knowledge,

And showed Him the way of understanding?

15 Behold, the nations *are* as a drop in a bucket,
And are counted as the small dust on the scales;
Look, He lifts up the isles as a very little thing.

16 And Lebanon *is* not sufficient to burn,
Nor its beasts sufficient for a burnt offering.

17 All nations before Him *are* as nothing,
And they are counted by Him less than nothing and worthless.

18 To whom then will you liken God?
Or what likeness will you compare to Him?

19 The workman molds an image,
The goldsmith overspreads it with gold,
And the silversmith casts silver chains.

20 Whoever *is* too impoverished for *such* a contribution
Chooses a tree *that* will not rot;
He seeks for himself a skillful workman
To prepare a carved image *that* will not totter.

40:12 [a]Following Masoretic Text, Septuagint, and Vulgate; Dead Sea Scrolls read *waters of the sea;* Targum reads *waters of the world.*

The Model for Leadership

(Isaiah 40:1–31)

We must never forget that the greatest model for leadership always comes from the life of God Himself. Isaiah 40 makes it clear that God as the Ultimate Leader models:

1. Comfort and Security
God supplies comfort and cleansing to His people (vv. 1, 2).

2. Empowerment and Delegation
God makes the path straight for others, then has them speak His words (vv. 3–8).

3. Shepherding and Direction
God proclaims good news and guides His people like a Shepherd (vv. 9–11).

4. Power and Authority
No one can challenge God's strength. He is a Leader with unequaled power (vv. 12–17).

5. Creator and Developer
God is the transcendent Leader who builds and develops others (vv. 21–26).

6. Wise Counselor and Provider
God is the source for every need we may have (vv. 27–31).

21 Have you not known?
Have you not heard?
Has it not been told you from the
beginning?
Have you not understood from the
foundations of the earth?

22 *It is* He who sits above the circle of the
earth,
And its inhabitants *are* like grasshoppers,
Who stretches out the heavens like a
curtain,
And spreads them out like a tent to dwell
in.

23 He brings the princes to nothing;
He makes the judges of the earth useless.

24 Scarcely shall they be planted,
Scarcely shall they be sown,
Scarcely shall their stock take root in the
earth,
When He will also blow on them,
And they will wither,
And the whirlwind will take them away
like stubble.

25 "To whom then will you liken Me,
Or *to whom* shall I be equal?" says the Holy
One.

26 Lift up your eyes on high,
And see who has created these *things,*
Who brings out their host by number;
He calls them all by name,
By the greatness of His might
And the strength of *His* power;
Not one is missing.

27 Why do you say, O Jacob,
And speak, O Israel:
"My way is hidden from the LORD,
And my just claim is passed over by my
God"?

28 Have you not known?
Have you not heard?
The everlasting God, the LORD,
The Creator of the ends of the earth,
Neither faints nor is weary.
His understanding is unsearchable.

29 He gives power to the weak,
And to *those who have* no might He
increases strength.

30 Even the youths shall faint and be weary,
And the young men shall utterly fall,

31 But those who wait on the LORD
Shall renew *their* strength;
They shall mount up with wings like
eagles,

They shall run and not be weary,
They shall walk and not faint.

Israel Assured of God's Help

41 "Keep silence before Me, O
coastlands,
And let the people renew *their*
strength!
Let them come near, then let them speak;
Let us come near together for judgment.

2 "Who raised up one from the east?
Who in righteousness called him to His
feet?
Who gave the nations before him,
And made *him* rule over kings?
Who gave *them* as the dust *to* his sword,
As driven stubble to his bow?

3 Who pursued them, *and* passed safely
By the way *that* he had not gone with his
feet?

4 Who has performed and done *it,*
Calling the generations from the
beginning?
'I, the LORD, am the first;
And with the last I *am* He.'"

5 The coastlands saw *it* and feared,
The ends of the earth were afraid;
They drew near and came.

6 Everyone helped his neighbor,
And said to his brother,
"Be of good courage!"

7 So the craftsman encouraged the goldsmith;
He who smooths *with* the hammer *inspired*
him who strikes the anvil,
Saying, "It *is* ready for the soldering";
Then he fastened it with pegs,
That it might not totter.

8 "But you, Israel, *are* My servant,
Jacob whom I have chosen,
The descendants of Abraham My friend.

9 *You* whom I have taken from the ends of
the earth,
And called from its farthest regions,
And said to you,
'You *are* My servant,
I have chosen you and have not cast you
away:

10 Fear not, for I *am* with you;
Be not dismayed, for I *am* your God.
I will strengthen you,
Yes, I will help you,
I will uphold you with My righteous right
hand.'

11 "Behold, all those who were incensed
        against you
    Shall be ashamed and disgraced;
    They shall be as nothing,
    And those who strive with you shall perish.
12 You shall seek them and not find them—
    Those who contended with you.
    Those who war against you
    Shall be as nothing,
    As a nonexistent thing.
13 For I, the LORD your God, will hold your
        right hand,
    Saying to you, 'Fear not, I will help you.'

14 "Fear not, you worm Jacob,
    You men of Israel!
    I will help you," says the LORD
    And your Redeemer, the Holy One of
        Israel.
15 "Behold, I will make you into a new
        threshing sledge with sharp teeth;
    You shall thresh the mountains and beat
        them small,
    And make the hills like chaff.
16 You shall winnow them, the wind shall
        carry them away,
    And the whirlwind shall scatter them;
    You shall rejoice in the LORD,
    And glory in the Holy One of Israel.

17 "The poor and needy seek water, but there
        is none,
    Their tongues fail for thirst.
    I, the LORD, will hear them;
    I, the God of Israel, will not forsake them.
18 I will open rivers in desolate heights,
    And fountains in the midst of the valleys;
    I will make the wilderness a pool of water,
    And the dry land springs of water.
19 I will plant in the wilderness the cedar and
        the acacia tree,
    The myrtle and the oil tree;
    I will set in the desert the cypress tree and
        the pine
    And the box tree together,
20 That they may see and know,
    And consider and understand together,
    That the hand of the LORD has done this,
    And the Holy One of Israel has created it.

The Futility of Idols

21 "Present your case," says the LORD.
    "Bring forth your strong reasons," says the
        King of Jacob.
22 "Let them bring forth and show us what
        will happen;

    Let them show the former things, what
        they were,
    That we may consider them,
    And know the latter end of them;
    Or declare to us things to come.
23 Show the things that are to come
        hereafter,
    That we may know that you are gods;
    Yes, do good or do evil,
    That we may be dismayed and see it
        together.
24 Indeed you are nothing,
    And your work is nothing;
    He who chooses you is an abomination.

25 "I have raised up one from the north,
    And he shall come;
    From the rising of the sun he shall call on
        My name;
    And he shall come against princes as
        though mortar,
    As the potter treads clay.
26 Who has declared from the beginning, that
        we may know?
    And former times, that we may say, 'He is
        righteous'?
    Surely there is no one who shows,
    Surely there is no one who declares,
    Surely there is no one who hears your
        words.
27 The first time I said to Zion,
    'Look, there they are!'
    And I will give to Jerusalem one who
        brings good tidings.
28 For I looked, and there was no man;
    I looked among them, but there was no
        counselor,
    Who, when I asked of them, could answer
        a word.
29 Indeed they are all worthless;[a]
    Their works are nothing;
    Their molded images are wind and
        confusion.

The Servant of the LORD

42 "Behold! My Servant whom I
        uphold,
        My Elect One in whom My soul
            delights!
    I have put My Spirit upon Him;
    He will bring forth justice to the Gentiles.
2   He will not cry out, nor raise His voice,

41:29 [a]Following Masoretic Text and Vulgate; Dead
Sea Scrolls, Syriac, and Targum read nothing;
Septuagint omits the first line.

Nor cause His voice to be heard in the
    street.
3 A bruised reed He will not break,
    And smoking flax He will not quench;
    He will bring forth justice for truth.
4 He will not fail nor be discouraged,
    Till He has established justice in the
      earth;
    And the coastlands shall wait for His law."

5 Thus says God the LORD,
    Who created the heavens and stretched
      them out,
    Who spread forth the earth and that which
      comes from it,
    Who gives breath to the people on it,
    And spirit to those who walk on it:
6 "I, the LORD, have called You in
      righteousness,
    And will hold Your hand;
    I will keep You and give You as a covenant
      to the people,
    As a light to the Gentiles,
7 To open blind eyes,
    To bring out prisoners from the prison,
    Those who sit in darkness from the prison
      house.
8 I am the LORD, that is My name;
    And My glory I will not give to another,
    Nor My praise to carved images.
9 Behold, the former things have come to
      pass,
    And new things I declare;
    Before they spring forth I tell you of
      them."

Praise to the LORD

10 Sing to the LORD a new song,
    And His praise from the ends of the earth,
    You who go down to the sea, and all that
      is in it,
    You coastlands and you inhabitants of
      them!
11 Let the wilderness and its cities lift up their
      voice,
    The villages that Kedar inhabits.
    Let the inhabitants of Sela sing,
    Let them shout from the top of the
      mountains.
12 Let them give glory to the LORD,
    And declare His praise in the coastlands.
13 The LORD shall go forth like a mighty
      man;
    He shall stir up His zeal like a man of war.
    He shall cry out, yes, shout aloud;
    He shall prevail against His enemies.

Promise of the LORD's Help

14 "I have held My peace a long time,
    I have been still and restrained Myself.
    Now I will cry like a woman in labor,
    I will pant and gasp at once.
15 I will lay waste the mountains and hills,
    And dry up all their vegetation;
    I will make the rivers coastlands,
    And I will dry up the pools.
16 I will bring the blind by a way they did
      not know;
    I will lead them in paths they have not
      known.
    I will make darkness light before them,
    And crooked places straight.
    These things I will do for them,
    And not forsake them.
17 They shall be turned back,
    They shall be greatly ashamed,
    Who trust in carved images,
    Who say to the molded images,
    'You are our gods.'

18 "Hear, you deaf;
    And look, you blind, that you may see.
19 Who is blind but My servant,
    Or deaf as My messenger whom I send?
    Who is blind as he who is perfect,
    And blind as the LORD's servant?
20 Seeing many things, but you do not
      observe;
    Opening the ears, but he does not hear."

Israel's Obstinate Disobedience

21 The LORD is well pleased for His
      righteousness' sake;
    He will exalt the law and make it
      honorable.
22 But this is a people robbed and plundered;
    All of them are snared in holes,
    And they are hidden in prison houses;
    They are for prey, and no one delivers;
    For plunder, and no one says, "Restore!"

23 Who among you will give ear to this?
    Who will listen and hear for the time to
      come?
24 Who gave Jacob for plunder, and Israel to
      the robbers?
    Was it not the LORD,
    He against whom we have sinned?
    For they would not walk in His ways,
    Nor were they obedient to His law.
25 Therefore He has poured on him the fury
      of His anger
    And the strength of battle;

It has set him on fire all around,
Yet he did not know;
And it burned him,
Yet he did not take *it* to heart.

The Redeemer of Israel

43 But now, thus says the LORD, who
created you, O Jacob,
And He who formed you, O Israel:
"Fear not, for I have redeemed you;
I have called *you* by your name;
You *are* Mine.
2 When you pass through the waters, I *will*
be with you;
And through the rivers, they shall not
overflow you.
When you walk through the fire, you shall
not be burned,
Nor shall the flame scorch you.
3 For I *am* the LORD your God,
The Holy One of Israel, your Savior;
I gave Egypt for your ransom,
Ethiopia and Seba in your place.
4 Since you were precious in My sight,
You have been honored,
And I have loved you;
Therefore I will give men for you,
And people for your life.
5 Fear not, for I *am* with you;
I will bring your descendants from the
east,
And gather you from the west;
6 I will say to the north, 'Give them up!'
And to the south, 'Do not keep them
back!'
Bring My sons from afar,
And My daughters from the ends of the
earth—
7 Everyone who is called by My name,
Whom I have created for My glory;
I have formed him, yes, I have made him."

The Law of Sacrifice

(Isaiah 43:1–7)

God, as the Ultimate Leader, consistently
practices the Law of Sacrifice. Leaders
will do the illogical and surrender valuable
possessions in order to fulfill and capture
their dream. Fortunately for us, *we* are God's
dream. Only through the prophet Isaiah does
God say directly to His people, "I love you."

---

8 Bring out the blind people who have eyes,
And the deaf who have ears.
9 Let all the nations be gathered together,
And let the people be assembled.
Who among them can declare this,
And show us former things?
Let them bring out their witnesses, that
they may be justified;
Or let them hear and say, "It is truth."
10 "You *are* My witnesses," says the LORD,
"And My servant whom I have chosen,
That you may know and believe Me,
And understand that I *am* He.
Before Me there was no God formed,
Nor shall there be after Me.
11 I, *even* I, *am* the LORD,
And besides Me *there is* no savior.
12 I have declared and saved,
I have proclaimed,
And *there was* no foreign *god* among you;
Therefore you *are* My witnesses,"
Says the LORD, "that I *am* God.
13 Indeed before the day *was,* I *am* He;
And *there is* no one who can deliver out of
My hand;
I work, and who will reverse it?"

14 Thus says the LORD, your Redeemer,
The Holy One of Israel:
"For your sake I will send to Babylon,
And bring them all down as fugitives—
The Chaldeans, who rejoice in their ships.
15 I *am* the LORD, your Holy One,
The Creator of Israel, your King."

16 Thus says the LORD, who makes a way in
the sea
And a path through the mighty waters,
17 Who brings forth the chariot and horse,
The army and the power
(They shall lie down together, they shall
not rise;
They are extinguished, they are quenched
like a wick):
18 "Do not remember the former things,
Nor consider the things of old.
19 Behold, I will do a new thing,
Now it shall spring forth;
Shall you not know it?
I will even make a road in the wilderness
And rivers in the desert.
20 The beast of the field will honor Me,
The jackals and the ostriches,
Because I give waters in the wilderness
And rivers in the desert,
To give drink to My people, My chosen.

21 This people I have formed for Myself;
They shall declare My praise.

Pleading with Unfaithful Israel

22 "But you have not called upon Me, O Jacob;
And you have been weary of Me, O Israel.

23 You have not brought Me the sheep for your burnt offerings,
Nor have you honored Me with your sacrifices.
I have not caused you to serve with grain offerings,
Nor wearied you with incense.

24 You have bought Me no sweet cane with money,
Nor have you satisfied Me with the fat of your sacrifices;
But you have burdened Me with your sins,
You have wearied Me with your iniquities.

25 "I, *even* I, *am* He who blots out your transgressions for My own sake;
And I will not remember your sins.

26 Put Me in remembrance;
Let us contend together;
State your *case,* that you may be acquitted.

27 Your first father sinned,
And your mediators have transgressed against Me.

28 Therefore I will profane the princes of the sanctuary;
I will give Jacob to the curse,
And Israel to reproaches.

God's Blessing on Israel

44 "Yet hear me now, O Jacob My servant,
And Israel whom I have chosen.

2 Thus says the LORD who made you
And formed you from the womb, *who* will help you:
'Fear not, O Jacob My servant;
And you, Jeshurun, whom I have chosen.

3 For I will pour water on him who is thirsty,
And floods on the dry ground;
I will pour My Spirit on your descendants,
And My blessing on your offspring;

4 They will spring up among the grass
Like willows by the watercourses.'

5 One will say, 'I *am* the LORD's';
Another will call *himself* by the name of Jacob;
Another will write *with* his hand, 'The LORD's,'
And name *himself* by the name of Israel.

Revival Fire: Man-Made or God-Given?

(Isaiah 44:1–8)

What godly leader has no desire in their heart to see the fire of God? We all long for fire to descend from heaven to empower us to accomplish a great task. Sometimes, however, when it seems hard to wait for the "heavenly" fire, we resort to "homemade" fire. Consider four kinds of homemade fire:

1. **The fire of association:** We feel this fire when we're enjoying a revival atmosphere. It serves as a hot poker.
2. **The fire of yesterday:** This fire comes from hearing testimonies of saints who talk about the good old days.
3. **The fire of selfish desires:** This fire comes as a spark when we see how it will benefit me to serve God today.
4. **The fire of tradition:** This fire comes when we feel warm and comfortable with the way we've always done it.

So what distinguishes divine fire from man-made fire?

Man-Made Fires	God-Given Fires
1. Have a tendency to go out	1. Remain as long as our focus stays on Him
2. Are not sufficient for today	2. Are more than enough to meet our needs
3. Are not contagious	3. Are contagious for those who see them

There Is No Other God

6 "Thus says the LORD, the King of Israel,
  And his Redeemer, the LORD of hosts:
  'I *am* the First and I *am* the Last;
  Besides Me *there is* no God.
7 And who can proclaim as I do?
  Then let him declare it and set it in order
    for Me,
  Since I appointed the ancient people.
  And the things that are coming and shall
    come,
  Let them show these to them.
8 Do not fear, nor be afraid;
  Have I not told you from that time, and
    declared *it*?
  You *are* My witnesses.
  Is there a God besides Me?
  Indeed *there is* no other Rock;
  I know not *one.*'"

Idolatry Is Foolishness

9 Those who make an image, all of them *are*
    useless,
  And their precious things shall not profit;
  They *are* their own witnesses;
  They neither see nor know, that they may
    be ashamed.
10 Who would form a god or mold an image
    That profits him nothing?
11 Surely all his companions would be
    ashamed;
  And the workmen, they *are* mere men.
  Let them all be gathered together,
  Let them stand up;
  Yet they shall fear,
  They shall be ashamed together.

12 The blacksmith with the tongs works one
    in the coals,
  Fashions it with hammers,
  And works it with the strength of his arms.
  Even so, he is hungry, and his strength fails;
  He drinks no water and is faint.

13 The craftsman stretches out *his* rule,
  He marks one out with chalk;
  He fashions it with a plane,
  He marks it out with the compass,
  And makes it like the figure of a man,
  According to the beauty of a man, that it
    may remain in the house.
14 He cuts down cedars for himself,
  And takes the cypress and the oak;
  He secures *it* for himself among the trees
    of the forest.
  He plants a pine, and the rain nourishes *it.*

15 Then it shall be for a man to burn,
  For he will take some of it and warm
    himself;
  Yes, he kindles *it* and bakes bread;
  Indeed he makes a god and worships *it;*
  He makes it a carved image, and falls down
    to it.
16 He burns half of it in the fire;
  With this half he eats meat;
  He roasts a roast, and is satisfied.
  He even warms *himself* and says,
  "Ah! I am warm,
  I have seen the fire."
17 And the rest of it he makes into a god,
  His carved image.
  He falls down before it and worships *it,*
  Prays to it and says,
  "Deliver me, for you *are* my god!"

18 They do not know nor understand;
  For He has shut their eyes, so that they
    cannot see,
  And their hearts, so that they cannot
    understand.
19 And no one considers in his heart,
  Nor *is there* knowledge nor understanding
    to say,
  "I have burned half of it in the fire,
  Yes, I have also baked bread on its coals;
  I have roasted meat and eaten *it;*
  And shall I make the rest of it an
    abomination?
  Shall I fall down before a block of
    wood?"
20 He feeds on ashes;
  A deceived heart has turned him aside;
  And he cannot deliver his soul,
  Nor say, "*Is there* not a lie in my right
    hand?"

Israel Is Not Forgotten

21 "Remember these, O Jacob,
  And Israel, for you *are* My servant;
  I have formed you, you *are* My servant;
  O Israel, you will not be forgotten by Me!
22 I have blotted out, like a thick cloud, your
    transgressions,
  And like a cloud, your sins.
  Return to Me, for I have redeemed you."

23 Sing, O heavens, for the LORD has done *it!*
  Shout, you lower parts of the earth;
  Break forth into singing, you mountains,
  O forest, and every tree in it!
  For the LORD has redeemed Jacob,
  And glorified Himself in Israel.

Judah Will Be Restored

24 Thus says the LORD, your Redeemer,
And He who formed you from the
womb:
"I *am* the LORD, who makes all *things,*
Who stretches out the heavens all alone,
Who spreads abroad the earth by Myself;

25 Who frustrates the signs of the babblers,
And drives diviners mad;
Who turns wise men backward,
And makes their knowledge foolishness;

26 Who confirms the word of His servant,
And performs the counsel of His
messengers;
Who says to Jerusalem, 'You shall be
inhabited,'
To the cities of Judah, 'You shall be built,'
And I will raise up her waste places;

27 Who says to the deep, 'Be dry!
And I will dry up your rivers';

28 Who says of Cyrus, '*He is* My shepherd,
And he shall perform all My pleasure,
Saying to Jerusalem, "You shall be built,"
And to the temple, "Your foundation shall
be laid."'

Cyrus, God's Instrument

45 "Thus says the LORD to His
anointed,
To Cyrus, whose right hand I have
held—
To subdue nations before him
And loose the armor of kings,
To open before him the double doors,
So that the gates will not be shut:

2 'I will go before you
And make the crooked places[a] straight;
I will break in pieces the gates of bronze
And cut the bars of iron.

3 I will give you the treasures of darkness
And hidden riches of secret places,
That you may know that I, the LORD,
Who call *you* by your name,
Am the God of Israel.

4 For Jacob My servant's sake,
And Israel My elect,
I have even called you by your name;
I have named you, though you have not
known Me.

5 I *am* the LORD, and *there is* no other;
There is no God besides Me.
I will gird you, though you have not
known Me,

6 That they may know from the rising of
the sun to its setting
That *there is* none besides Me.

I *am* the LORD, and *there is* no other;

7 I form the light and create darkness,
I make peace and create calamity;
I, the LORD, do all these *things.*'

8 "Rain down, you heavens, from above,
And let the skies pour down righteousness;
Let the earth open, let them bring forth
salvation,
And let righteousness spring up together.
I, the LORD, have created it.

9 "Woe to him who strives with his Maker!
Let the potsherd *strive* with the potsherds
of the earth!
Shall the clay say to him who forms it,
'What are you making?'
Or shall your handiwork *say,* 'He has no
hands'?

10 Woe to him who says to *his* father, 'What
are you begetting?'
Or to the woman, 'What have you
brought forth?'"

11 Thus says the LORD,
The Holy One of Israel, and his Maker:
"Ask Me of things to come concerning My
sons;
And concerning the work of My hands,
you command Me.

12 I have made the earth,
And created man on it.
I—My hands—stretched out the heavens,
And all their host I have commanded.

13 I have raised him up in righteousness,
And I will direct all his ways;
He shall build My city
And let My exiles go free,
Not for price nor reward,"
Says the LORD of hosts.

The LORD, the Only Savior

14 Thus says the LORD:

"The labor of Egypt and merchandise of
Cush
And of the Sabeans, men of stature,
Shall come over to you, and they shall be
yours;
They shall walk behind you,
They shall come over in chains;
And they shall bow down to you.

45:2 [a]Dead Sea Scrolls and Septuagint read
mountains; Targum reads *I will trample down the walls;*
Vulgate reads *I will humble the great ones of the earth.*

They will make supplication to you, *saying,*
  'Surely God *is* in you,
And *there is* no other;
There *is* no other God.' "

15 Truly You *are* God, who hide Yourself,
  O God of Israel, the Savior!
16 They shall be ashamed
  And also disgraced, all of them;
  They shall go in confusion together,
  Who are makers of idols.
17 *But* Israel shall be saved by the LORD
  With an everlasting salvation;
  You shall not be ashamed or disgraced
  Forever and ever.

18 For thus says the LORD,
  Who created the heavens,
  Who is God,
  Who formed the earth and made it,
  Who has established it,
  Who did not create it in vain,
  Who formed it to be inhabited:
  "I *am* the LORD, and *there is* no other.
19 I have not spoken in secret,
  In a dark place of the earth;
  I did not say to the seed of Jacob,
  'Seek Me in vain';
  I, the LORD, speak righteousness,
  I declare things that are right.

20 "Assemble yourselves and come;
  Draw near together,
  You *who have* escaped from the nations.
  They have no knowledge,
  Who carry the wood of their carved
    image,
  And pray to a god *that* cannot save.
21 Tell and bring forth *your* case;
  Yes, let them take counsel together.
  Who has declared this from ancient time?
  Who has told it from that time?
  Have not I, the LORD?
  And *there is* no other God besides Me,
  A just God and a Savior;
  There is none besides Me.

22 "Look to Me, and be saved,
  All you ends of the earth!
  For I *am* God, and *there is* no other.
23 I have sworn by Myself;
  The word has gone out of My mouth *in*
    righteousness,
  And shall not return,
  That to Me every knee shall bow,
  Every tongue shall take an oath.

24 He shall say,
  'Surely in the LORD I have righteousness
    and strength.
  To Him *men* shall come,
  And all shall be ashamed
  Who are incensed against Him.
25 In the LORD all the descendants of Israel
  Shall be justified, and shall glory.' "

Dead Idols and the Living God

46 Bel bows down, Nebo stoops;
  Their idols were on the beasts and
    on the cattle.
  Your carriages *were* heavily loaded,
  A burden to the weary *beast.*
2 They stoop, they bow down together;
  They could not deliver the burden,
  But have themselves gone into captivity.

3 "Listen to Me, O house of Jacob,
  And all the remnant of the house of Israel,
  Who have been upheld *by Me* from birth,
  Who have been carried from the womb:
4 Even to *your* old age, I *am* He,
  And *even* to gray hairs I will carry *you!*
  I have made, and I will bear;
  Even I will carry, and will deliver *you.*

5 "To whom will you liken Me, and make *Me*
    equal
  And compare Me, that we should be
    alike?
6 They lavish gold out of the bag,
  And weigh silver on the scales;
  They hire a goldsmith, and he makes it a
    god;
  They prostrate themselves, yes, they
    worship.
7 They bear it on the shoulder, they carry it
  And set it in its place, and it stands;
  From its place it shall not move.
  Though *one* cries out to it, yet it cannot
    answer
  Nor save him out of his trouble.

8 "Remember this, and show yourselves men;
  Recall to mind, O you transgressors.
9 Remember the former things of old,
  For I *am* God, and *there is* no other;
  I am God, and *there is* none like Me,
10 Declaring the end from the beginning,
  And from ancient times *things* that are not
    yet done,
  Saying, 'My counsel shall stand,
  And I will do all My pleasure,'
11 Calling a bird of prey from the east,

The man who executes My counsel, from
a far country.
Indeed I have spoken *it;*
I will also bring it to pass.
I have purposed *it;*
I will also do it.

12 "Listen to Me, you stubborn-hearted,
Who *are* far from righteousness:
13 I bring My righteousness near, it shall not
be far off;
My salvation shall not linger.
And I will place salvation in Zion,
For Israel My glory.

The Humiliation of Babylon

47 "Come down and sit in the dust,
O virgin daughter of Babylon;
Sit on the ground without a throne,
O daughter of the Chaldeans!
For you shall no more be called
Tender and delicate.
2 Take the millstones and grind meal.
Remove your veil,
Take off the skirt,
Uncover the thigh,
Pass through the rivers.
3 Your nakedness shall be uncovered,
Yes, your shame will be seen;
I will take vengeance,
And I will not arbitrate with a man."

4 As *for* our Redeemer, the LORD of hosts *is*
His name,
The Holy One of Israel.

5 "Sit in silence, and go into darkness,
O daughter of the Chaldeans;
For you shall no longer be called
The Lady of Kingdoms.
6 I was angry with My people;
I have profaned My inheritance,
And given them into your hand.
You showed them no mercy;
On the elderly you laid your yoke very
heavily.
7 And you said, 'I shall be a lady forever,'
So that you did not take these *things* to
heart,
Nor remember the latter end of them.

8 "Therefore hear this now, *you who are* given
to pleasures,
Who dwell securely,
Who say in your heart, 'I *am,* and *there is*
no one else besides me;

I shall not sit *as* a widow,
Nor shall I know the loss of children';
9 But these two *things* shall come to you
In a moment, in one day:
The loss of children, and widowhood.
They shall come upon you in their fullness
Because of the multitude of your sorceries,
For the great abundance of your
enchantments.

10 "For you have trusted in your wickedness;
You have said, 'No one sees me';
Your wisdom and your knowledge have
warped you;
And you have said in your heart,
'I *am,* and *there is* no one else besides me.'
11 Therefore evil shall come upon you;
You shall not know from where it arises.
And trouble shall fall upon you;
You will not be able to put it off.
And desolation shall come upon you
suddenly,
Which you shall not know.

12 "Stand now with your enchantments
And the multitude of your sorceries,
In which you have labored from your
youth—
Perhaps you will be able to profit,
Perhaps you will prevail.
13 You are wearied in the multitude of your
counsels;
Let now the astrologers, the stargazers,
And the monthly prognosticators
Stand up and save you
From what shall come upon you.
14 Behold, they shall be as stubble,
The fire shall burn them;
They shall not deliver themselves
From the power of the flame;
It shall not *be* a coal to be warmed by,
Nor a fire to sit before!
15 Thus shall they be to you
With whom you have labored,
Your merchants from your youth;
They shall wander each one to his quarter.
No one shall save you.

Israel Refined for God's Glory

48 "Hear this, O house of Jacob,
Who are called by the name of
Israel,
And have come forth from the wellsprings
of Judah;
Who swear by the name of the LORD,
And make mention of the God of Israel,

But not in truth or in righteousness;

2 For they call themselves after the holy city,
And lean on the God of Israel;
The LORD of hosts *is* His name:

3 "I have declared the former things from the
beginning;
They went forth from My mouth, and I
caused them to hear it.
Suddenly I did *them,* and they came to
pass.

4 Because I knew that you *were* obstinate,
And your neck *was* an iron sinew,
And your brow bronze,

5 Even from the beginning I have declared *it*
to you;
Before it came to pass I proclaimed *it* to
you,
Lest you should say, 'My idol has done
them,
And my carved image and my molded
image
Have commanded them.'

6 "You have heard;
See all this.
And will you not declare *it?*
I have made you hear new things from this
time,
Even hidden things, and you did not know
them.

7 They are created now and not from the
beginning;
And before this day you have not heard
them,
Lest you should say, 'Of course I knew
them.'

8 Surely you did not hear,
Surely you did not know;
Surely from long ago your ear was not
opened.
For I knew that you would deal very
treacherously,
And were called a transgressor from the
womb.

9 "For My name's sake I will defer My anger,
And *for* My praise I will restrain it from
you,
So that I do not cut you off.

10 Behold, I have refined you, but not as
silver;
I have tested you in the furnace of
affliction.

11 For My own sake, for My own sake, I will
do *it;*

For how should *My name* be profaned?
And I will not give My glory to another.

God's Ancient Plan to Redeem Israel

12 "Listen to Me, O Jacob,
And Israel, My called:
I *am* He, I *am* the First,
I *am* also the Last.

13 Indeed My hand has laid the foundation of
the earth,
And My right hand has stretched out the
heavens;
When I call to them,
They stand up together.

14 "All of you, assemble yourselves, and hear!
Who among them has declared these
things?
The LORD loves him;
He shall do His pleasure on Babylon,
And His arm *shall be against* the Chaldeans.

15 I, *even* I, have spoken;
Yes, I have called him,
I have brought him, and his way will
prosper.

16 "Come near to Me, hear this:
I have not spoken in secret from the
beginning;
From the time that it was, I *was* there.
And now the Lord GOD and His Spirit
Have[a] sent Me."

17 Thus says the LORD, your Redeemer,
The Holy One of Israel:
"I *am* the LORD your God,
Who teaches you to profit,
Who leads you by the way you should go.

18 Oh, that you had heeded My
commandments!
Then your peace would have been like a
river,
And your righteousness like the waves of
the sea.

19 Your descendants also would have been
like the sand,
And the offspring of your body like the
grains of sand;
His name would not have been cut off
Nor destroyed from before Me."

20 Go forth from Babylon!
Flee from the Chaldeans!
With a voice of singing,

48:16 [a]The Hebrew verb is singular.

Declare, proclaim this,
Utter it to the end of the earth;
Say, "The LORD has redeemed
His servant Jacob!"

21 And they did not thirst
When He led them through the deserts;
He caused the waters to flow from the
rock for them;
He also split the rock, and the waters
gushed out.

22 "*There is* no peace," says the LORD, "for the
wicked."

The Servant, the Light to the Gentiles

49 "Listen, O coastlands, to Me,
And take heed, you peoples from
afar!
The LORD has called Me from the womb;
From the matrix of My mother He has
made mention of My name.

2 And He has made My mouth like a sharp
sword;

The Mission and Vision of a Leader

(Isaiah 49:1–3)

Leaders must give their lives to causes that count. They must sense that what they do matters to God. Only then will they feel deep satisfaction for their work. Isaiah speaks some incredible words about the Messiah's mission as a Leader:

1. He was called from His mother's womb (v. 1).
2. He was gifted with specific resources (v. 2).
3. He was protected supernaturally by God (v. 2).
4. He was given a particular divine mission (v. 2).
5. He was ordained to reflect God's glory (v. 3).

While any leader might well covet these descriptions, only in the life of the Messiah, God's servant sent from heaven to redeem earth, were they perfectly fulfilled. Yet they serve as a model for us as we pursue our God-given mission and vision.

In the shadow of His hand He has hidden
Me,
And made Me a polished shaft;
In His quiver He has hidden Me."

3 "And He said to me,
'You *are* My servant, O Israel,
In whom I will be glorified.'
4 Then I said, 'I have labored in vain,
I have spent my strength for nothing and
in vain;
Yet surely my just reward *is* with the LORD,
And my work with my God.'"

5 "And now the LORD says,
Who formed Me from the womb *to be* His
Servant,
To bring Jacob back to Him,
So that Israel is gathered to Him[a]
(For I shall be glorious in the eyes of the
LORD,
And My God shall be My strength),
6 Indeed He says,
'It is too small a thing that You should be
My Servant
To raise up the tribes of Jacob,
And to restore the preserved ones of Israel;
I will also give You as a light to the
Gentiles,
That You should be My salvation to the
ends of the earth.'"

7 Thus says the LORD,
The Redeemer of Israel, their Holy One,
To Him whom man despises,
To Him whom the nation abhors,
To the Servant of rulers:
"Kings shall see and arise,
Princes also shall worship,
Because of the LORD who is faithful,
The Holy One of Israel;
And He has chosen You."

8 Thus says the LORD:

"In an acceptable time I have heard You,
And in the day of salvation I have helped
You;
I will preserve You and give You
As a covenant to the people,
To restore the earth,
To cause them to inherit the desolate
heritages;

49:5 [a]Qere, Dead Sea Scrolls, and Septuagint read *is gathered to Him;* Kethib reads *is not gathered.*

9 That You may say to the prisoners, 'Go
forth,'
To those who *are* in darkness, 'Show
yourselves.'

"They shall feed along the roads,
And their pastures *shall be* on all desolate
heights.
10 They shall neither hunger nor thirst,
Neither heat nor sun shall strike them;
For He who has mercy on them will lead
them,
Even by the springs of water He will
guide them.
11 I will make each of My mountains a road,
And My highways shall be elevated.
12 Surely these shall come from afar;
Look! Those from the north and the west,
And these from the land of Sinim."

13 Sing, O heavens!
Be joyful, O earth!
And break out in singing, O mountains!
For the LORD has comforted His people,
And will have mercy on His afflicted.

God Will Remember Zion

14 But Zion said, "The LORD has forsaken
me,
And my Lord has forgotten me."

15 "Can a woman forget her nursing child,
And not have compassion on the son of
her womb?
Surely they may forget,
Yet I will not forget you.
16 See, I have inscribed you on the palms *of*
My hands;
Your walls *are* continually before Me.
17 Your sons[a] shall make haste;
Your destroyers and those who laid you
waste
Shall go away from you.
18 Lift up your eyes, look around and see;
All these gather together *and* come to you.
As I live," says the LORD,
"You shall surely clothe yourselves with
them all as an ornament,
And bind them *on you* as a bride *does.*

19 "For your waste and desolate places,
And the land of your destruction,
Will even now be too small for the
inhabitants;
And those who swallowed you up will be
far away.

20 The children you will have,
After you have lost the others,
Will say again in your ears,
'The place *is* too small for me;
Give me a place where I may dwell.'
21 Then you will say in your heart,
'Who has begotten these for me,
Since I have lost my children and am
desolate,
A captive, and wandering to and fro?
And who has brought these up?
There I was, left alone;
But these, where *were* they?'"

22 Thus says the Lord GOD:

"Behold, I will lift My hand in an oath to
the nations,
And set up My standard for the peoples;
They shall bring your sons in *their* arms,
And your daughters shall be carried on
their shoulders;
23 Kings shall be your foster fathers,
And their queens your nursing mothers;
They shall bow down to you with *their*
faces to the earth,
And lick up the dust of your feet.
Then you will know that I *am* the LORD,
For they shall not be ashamed who wait
for Me."

24 Shall the prey be taken from the mighty,
Or the captives of the righteous[a] be
delivered?

25 But thus says the LORD:

"Even the captives of the mighty shall be
taken away,
And the prey of the terrible be delivered;
For I will contend with him who contends
with you,
And I will save your children.
26 I will feed those who oppress you with
their own flesh,
And they shall be drunk with their own
blood as with sweet wine.
All flesh shall know
That I, the LORD, *am* your Savior,
And your Redeemer, the Mighty One of
Jacob."

49:17 [a]Dead Sea Scrolls, Septuagint, Targum, and
Vulgate read *builders.* **49:24** [a]Following Masoretic
Text and Targum; Dead Sea Scrolls, Syriac, and
Vulgate read *the mighty;* Septuagint reads *unjustly.*

The Servant, Israel's Hope

50

Thus says the LORD:

"Where *is* the certificate of your
  mother's divorce,
Whom I have put away?
Or which of My creditors *is it* to whom I
  have sold you?
For your iniquities you have sold
  yourselves,
And for your transgressions your mother
  has been put away.

2 Why, when I came, *was there* no man?
Why, when I called, *was there* none to
  answer?
Is My hand shortened at all that it cannot
  redeem?
Or have I no power to deliver?
Indeed with My rebuke I dry up the sea,
I make the rivers a wilderness;
Their fish stink because *there is* no water,
And die of thirst.

3 I clothe the heavens with blackness,
And I make sackcloth their covering."

4 "The Lord GOD has given Me
The tongue of the learned,
That I should know how to speak
A word in season to *him who is* weary.
He awakens Me morning by morning,
He awakens My ear
To hear as the learned.

5 The Lord GOD has opened My ear;
And I was not rebellious,
Nor did I turn away.

6 I gave My back to those who struck *Me,*
And My cheeks to those who plucked out
  the beard;
I did not hide My face from shame and
  spitting.

7 "For the Lord GOD will help Me;
Therefore I will not be disgraced;
Therefore I have set My face like a
  flint,
And I know that I will not be ashamed.

8 *He is* near who justifies Me;
Who will contend with Me?
Let us stand together.
Who *is* My adversary?
Let him come near Me.

9 Surely the Lord GOD will help Me;
Who *is* he *who* will condemn Me?
Indeed they will all grow old like a
  garment;
The moth will eat them up.

10 "Who among you fears the LORD?
Who obeys the voice of His Servant?
Who walks in darkness
And has no light?
Let him trust in the name of the LORD
And rely upon his God.

11 Look, all you who kindle a fire,
Who encircle *yourselves* with sparks:
Walk in the light of your fire and in the
  sparks you have kindled—
This you shall have from My hand:
You shall lie down in torment.

The LORD Comforts Zion

51

"Listen to Me, you who follow after
  righteousness,
You who seek the LORD:
Look to the rock *from which* you were
  hewn,
And to the hole of the pit *from which* you
  were dug.

2 Look to Abraham your father,
And to Sarah *who* bore you;
For I called him alone,
And blessed him and increased him."

3 For the LORD will comfort Zion,
He will comfort all her waste places;
He will make her wilderness like Eden,
And her desert like the garden of the
  LORD;
Joy and gladness will be found in it,
Thanksgiving and the voice of melody.

4 "Listen to Me, My people;
And give ear to Me, O My nation:
For law will proceed from Me,
And I will make My justice rest
As a light of the peoples.

5 My righteousness *is* near,
My salvation has gone forth,
And My arms will judge the peoples;
The coastlands will wait upon Me,
And on My arm they will trust.

6 Lift up your eyes to the heavens,
And look on the earth beneath.
For the heavens will vanish away like
  smoke,
The earth will grow old like a garment,
And those who dwell in it will die in like
  manner;
But My salvation will be forever,
And My righteousness will not be
  abolished.

7 "Listen to Me, you who know righteousness,
You people in whose heart *is* My law:

Do not fear the reproach of men,
Nor be afraid of their insults.
8 For the moth will eat them up like a
garment,
And the worm will eat them like wool;
But My righteousness will be forever,
And My salvation from generation to
generation."

9 Awake, awake, put on strength,
O arm of the LORD!
Awake as in the ancient days,
In the generations of old.
Are You not *the arm* that cut Rahab apart,
And wounded the serpent?

10 *Are* You not *the One* who dried up the sea,
The waters of the great deep;
That made the depths of the sea a road
For the redeemed to cross over?
11 So the ransomed of the LORD shall return,
And come to Zion with singing,
With everlasting joy on their heads.
They shall obtain joy and gladness;
Sorrow and sighing shall flee away.

12 "I, *even* I, *am* He who comforts you.
Who *are* you that you should be afraid
Of a man *who* will die,
And of the son of a man *who* will be made
like grass?
13 And you forget the LORD your Maker,
Who stretched out the heavens
And laid the foundations of the earth;
You have feared continually every day
Because of the fury of the oppressor,
When *he has* prepared to destroy.
And where *is* the fury of the oppressor?
14 The captive exile hastens, that he may be
loosed,
That he should not die in the pit,
And that his bread should not fail.
15 But I *am* the LORD your God,
Who divided the sea whose waves
roared—
The LORD of hosts *is* His name.
16 And I have put My words in your mouth;
I have covered you with the shadow of
My hand,
That I may plant the heavens,
Lay the foundations of the earth,
And say to Zion, 'You *are* My people.'"

God's Fury Removed

17 Awake, awake!
Stand up, O Jerusalem,

You who have drunk at the hand of the
LORD
The cup of His fury;
You have drunk the dregs of the cup of
trembling,
And drained *it* out.
18 *There is* no one to guide her
Among all the sons she has brought forth;
Nor *is there any* who takes her by the hand
Among all the sons she has brought up.
19 These two *things* have come to you;
Who will be sorry for you?—
Desolation and destruction, famine and
sword—
By whom will I comfort you?
20 Your sons have fainted,
They lie at the head of all the streets,
Like an antelope in a net;
They are full of the fury of the LORD,
The rebuke of your God.

21 Therefore please hear this, you afflicted,
And drunk but not with wine.
22 Thus says your Lord,
The LORD and your God,
Who pleads the cause of His people:
"See, I have taken out of your hand
The cup of trembling,
The dregs of the cup of My fury;
You shall no longer drink it.
23 But I will put it into the hand of those
who afflict you,
Who have said to you,[a]
'Lie down, that we may walk over you.'
And you have laid your body like the
ground,
And as the street, for those who walk
over."

God Redeems Jerusalem

52 Awake, awake!
Put on your strength, O Zion;
Put on your beautiful garments,
O Jerusalem, the holy city!
For the uncircumcised and the unclean
Shall no longer come to you.
2 Shake yourself from the dust, arise;
Sit down, O Jerusalem!
Loose yourself from the bonds of your
neck,
O captive daughter of Zion!

3 For thus says the LORD:

51:23 [a]Literally *your soul*

"You have sold yourselves for nothing,
And you shall be redeemed without
money."

⁴For thus says the Lord GOD:

"My people went down at first
Into Egypt to dwell there;
Then the Assyrian oppressed them without
cause.

⁵ Now therefore, what have I here," says the
LORD,
"That My people are taken away for
nothing?
Those who rule over them
Make them wail,"ᵃ says the LORD,
"And My name is blasphemed continually
every day.

⁶ Therefore My people shall know My
name;
Therefore they shall know in that day
That I am He who speaks:
'Behold, it is I.'"

⁷ How beautiful upon the mountains
Are the feet of him who brings good
news,
Who proclaims peace,
Who brings glad tidings of good things,
Who proclaims salvation,
Who says to Zion,
"Your God reigns!"

⁸ Your watchmen shall lift up their voices,
With their voices they shall sing
together;
For they shall see eye to eye
When the LORD brings back Zion.

⁹ Break forth into joy, sing together,
You waste places of Jerusalem!
For the LORD has comforted His people,
He has redeemed Jerusalem.

¹⁰ The LORD has made bare His holy arm
In the eyes of all the nations;
And all the ends of the earth shall see
The salvation of our God.

¹¹ Depart! Depart! Go out from there,
Touch no unclean thing;
Go out from the midst of her,
Be clean,
You who bear the vessels of the LORD.

¹² For you shall not go out with haste,
Nor go by flight;
For the LORD will go before you,
And the God of Israel will be your rear
guard.

The Sin-Bearing Servant

¹³ Behold, My Servant shall deal prudently;
He shall be exalted and extolled and be
very high.

¹⁴ Just as many were astonished at you,
So His visage was marred more than any
man,
And His form more than the sons of men;

¹⁵ So shall He sprinkleᵃ many nations.
Kings shall shut their mouths at Him;
For what had not been told them they
shall see,
And what they had not heard they shall
consider.

53 Who has believed our report?
And to whom has the arm of the
LORD been revealed?

² For He shall grow up before Him as a
tender plant,
And as a root out of dry ground.
He has no form or comeliness;
And when we see Him,
There is no beauty that we should desire
Him.

³ He is despised and rejected by men,
A Man of sorrows and acquainted with
grief.
And we hid, as it were, our faces from Him;
He was despised, and we did not esteem
Him.

⁴ Surely He has borne our griefs
And carried our sorrows;
Yet we esteemed Him stricken,
Smitten by God, and afflicted.

⁵ But He was wounded for our
transgressions,
He was bruised for our iniquities;
The chastisement for our peace was upon
Him,
And by His stripes we are healed.

⁶ All we like sheep have gone astray;
We have turned, every one, to his own
way;
And the LORD has laid on Him the
iniquity of us all.

⁷ He was oppressed and He was afflicted,
Yet He opened not His mouth;
He was led as a lamb to the slaughter,

52:5 ᵃDead Sea Scrolls read Mock; Septuagint reads
Marvel and wail; Targum reads Boast themselves;
Vulgate reads Treat them unjustly. **52:15** ᵃOr startle

Servant Leadership Modeled by the Messiah

(Isaiah 52:13—53:12)

Beyond all question, Jesus Christ modeled the Law of Sacrifice. He gave up for a time the riches of heaven in order to fulfill his divinely ordained role on earth.

Isaiah 53 describes what is often called "the exchanged life." Jesus took our sin, pain, and failures so we could have His righteousness, healing, and victory. While He offers this package to everyone, leaders have the opportunity to benefit from this sacrifice in a particularly tangible fashion.

Ponder for a moment what Christ gave up and what we obtain. Imagine what might happen if you were to implement the entire gift of redemption that Christ paid for on your behalf! He sacrificed greatly so that we might enjoy the following gifts:

His Sacrifice
1. Grief, infirmities, insecurities
2. Sins and transgressions
3. Sicknesses and diseases
4. Mental turmoil and pain
5. Weaknesses

Our Gain
1. Security and solid emotions
2. Forgiveness from guilt
3. Health and wholeness
4. Peace of mind
5. His strength

And as a sheep before its shearers is silent,
So He opened not His mouth.
8 He was taken from prison and from
judgment,
And who will declare His generation?
For He was cut off from the land of the
living;
For the transgressions of My people He
was stricken.
9 And they[a] made His grave with the
wicked—
But with the rich at His death,
Because He had done no violence,
Nor *was any* deceit in His mouth.

10 Yet it pleased the LORD to bruise Him;
He has put *Him* to grief.
When You make His soul an offering for
sin,
He shall see *His* seed, He shall prolong *His*
days,
And the pleasure of the LORD shall
prosper in His hand.
11 He shall see the labor of His soul,[a] *and* be
satisfied.
By His knowledge My righteous Servant
shall justify many,
For He shall bear their iniquities.
12 Therefore I will divide Him a portion
with the great,
And He shall divide the spoil with the
strong,

Because He poured out His soul unto death,
And He was numbered with the
transgressors,
And He bore the sin of many,
And made intercession for the
transgressors.

A Perpetual Covenant of Peace

54 "Sing, O barren,
You *who* have not borne!
Break forth into singing, and cry
aloud,
You *who* have not labored with child!
For more *are* the children of the desolate
Than the children of the married woman,"
says the LORD.
2 "Enlarge the place of your tent,
And let them stretch out the curtains of
your dwellings;
Do not spare;
Lengthen your cords,
And strengthen your stakes.
3 For you shall expand to the right and to
the left,
And your descendants will inherit the
nations,
And make the desolate cities inhabited.

53:9 [a]Literally *he* or *He* **53:11** [a]Following
Masoretic Text, Targum, and Vulgate; Dead Sea
Scrolls and Septuagint read *From the labor of His soul
He shall see light.*

4 "Do not fear, for you will not be
ashamed;
Neither be disgraced, for you will not be
put to shame;
For you will forget the shame of your
youth,
And will not remember the reproach of
your widowhood anymore.
5 For your Maker *is* your husband,
The LORD of hosts *is* His name;
And your Redeemer *is* the Holy One of
Israel;
He is called the God of the whole earth.
6 For the LORD has called you
Like a woman forsaken and grieved in
spirit,
Like a youthful wife when you were
refused,"
Says your God.
7 "For a mere moment I have forsaken you,
But with great mercies I will gather you.
8 With a little wrath I hid My face from you
for a moment;
But with everlasting kindness I will have
mercy on you,"
Says the LORD, your Redeemer.

9 "For this *is* like the waters of Noah to
Me;
For as I have sworn
That the waters of Noah would no longer
cover the earth,
So have I sworn
That I would not be angry with you, nor
rebuke you.
10 For the mountains shall depart
And the hills be removed,
But My kindness shall not depart from
you,
Nor shall My covenant of peace be
removed,"
Says the LORD, who has mercy on you.

11 "O you afflicted one,
Tossed with tempest, *and* not comforted,
Behold, I will lay your stones with colorful
gems,
And lay your foundations with sapphires.
12 I will make your pinnacles of rubies,
Your gates of crystal,
And all your walls of precious stones.
13 All your children *shall be* taught by the
LORD,
And great *shall be* the peace of your
children.
14 In righteousness you shall be established;

You shall be far from oppression, for you
shall not fear;
And from terror, for it shall not come near
you.
15 Indeed they shall surely assemble, *but* not
because of Me.
Whoever assembles against you shall fall
for your sake.

16 "Behold, I have created the blacksmith
Who blows the coals in the fire,
Who brings forth an instrument for his
work;
And I have created the spoiler to destroy.
17 No weapon formed against you shall
prosper,
And every tongue *which* rises against you
in judgment
You shall condemn.
This *is* the heritage of the servants of the
LORD,
And their righteousness *is* from Me,"
Says the LORD.

An Invitation to Abundant Life

55 "Ho! Everyone who thirsts,
Come to the waters;
And you who have no money,
Come, buy and eat.
Yes, come, buy wine and milk
Without money and without price.
2 Why do you spend money for *what is* not
bread,
And your wages for *what* does not satisfy?
Listen carefully to Me, and eat *what is*
good,
And let your soul delight itself in
abundance.
3 Incline your ear, and come to Me.
Hear, and your soul shall live;
And I will make an everlasting covenant
with you—
The sure mercies of David.
4 Indeed I have given him *as* a witness to
the people,
A leader and commander for the people.
5 Surely you shall call a nation you do not
know,
And nations *who* do not know you shall
run to you,
Because of the LORD your God,
And the Holy One of Israel;
For He has glorified you."

6 Seek the LORD while He may be found,
Call upon Him while He is near.

The Law of Victory:
Leaders Communicate Until They See Results

(Isaiah 55:1–11)

Isaiah 55 offers the words of a great communicator. In this passage God invites everyone to participate in His offer to quench their thirst. He tries to convince His hearers that He alone can fulfill their desires and permanently meet their needs. Then He beckons them to seek Him while He may be found.

Verses 10–12 contain a marvelous promise. God says that just as the rain and snow fall from the sky and do not return without watering the earth, so His Word will also accomplish the goals He sets for it. God's Word *will* bear fruit. From these three simple verses, note how God evaluates good communication:

1. His Word will get results (v. 10).
2. His Word will furnish tools and resources (v. 10).
3. His Word will meet needs (v. 10).
4. His Word will perform His will (v. 11).
5. His Word will satisfy the soul of the hearers (v. 12).

How about you? Can you, as a leader, make those claims? How do you evaluate your communication? What fruit does your communication produce?

7 Let the wicked forsake his way,
And the unrighteous man his thoughts;
Let him return to the LORD,
And He will have mercy on him;
And to our God,
For He will abundantly pardon.

8 "For My thoughts *are* not your thoughts,
Nor *are* your ways My ways," says the
LORD.
9 "For *as* the heavens are higher than the
earth,
So are My ways higher than your
ways,
And My thoughts than your thoughts.

10 "For as the rain comes down, and the snow
from heaven,
And do not return there,
But water the earth,
And make it bring forth and bud,
That it may give seed to the sower
And bread to the eater,
11 So shall My word be that goes forth from
My mouth;
It shall not return to Me void,
But it shall accomplish what I please,
And it shall prosper *in the thing* for which I
sent it.

12 "For you shall go out with joy,
And be led out with peace;
The mountains and the hills
Shall break forth into singing before you,
And all the trees of the field shall clap *their*
hands.
13 Instead of the thorn shall come up the
cypress tree,
And instead of the brier shall come up the
myrtle tree;
And it shall be to the LORD for a name,
For an everlasting sign *that* shall not be cut
off."

Salvation for the Gentiles

56 Thus says the LORD:

"Keep justice, and do righteousness,
For My salvation *is* about to come,
And My righteousness to be revealed.
2 Blessed *is* the man *who* does this,
And the son of man *who* lays hold on it;
Who keeps from defiling the Sabbath,
And keeps his hand from doing any
evil."

3 Do not let the son of the foreigner
Who has joined himself to the LORD
Speak, saying,

"The LORD has utterly separated me from
His people";
Nor let the eunuch say,
"Here I am, a dry tree."
4 For thus says the LORD:
"To the eunuchs who keep My Sabbaths,
And choose what pleases Me,
And hold fast My covenant,
5 Even to them I will give in My house
And within My walls a place and a name
Better than that of sons and daughters;
I will give them[a] an everlasting name
That shall not be cut off.

6 "Also the sons of the foreigner
Who join themselves to the LORD, to
serve Him,
And to love the name of the LORD, to be
His servants—
Everyone who keeps from defiling the
Sabbath,
And holds fast My covenant—
7 Even them I will bring to My holy
mountain,
And make them joyful in My house of
prayer.
Their burnt offerings and their sacrifices
Will be accepted on My altar;
For My house shall be called a house of
prayer for all nations."
8 The Lord GOD, who gathers the outcasts
of Israel, says,
"Yet I will gather to him
Others besides those who are gathered to
him."

Israel's Irresponsible Leaders

9 All you beasts of the field, come to devour,
All you beasts in the forest.
10 His watchmen are blind,
They are all ignorant;
They are all dumb dogs,
They cannot bark;
Sleeping, lying down, loving to slumber.
11 Yes, they are greedy dogs
Which never have enough.
And they are shepherds
Who cannot understand;
They all look to their own way,
Every one for his own gain,
From his own territory.
12 "Come," one says, "I will bring wine,
And we will fill ourselves with intoxicating
drink;
Tomorrow will be as today,
And much more abundant."

Israel's Futile Idolatry

57 The righteous perishes,
And no man takes it to heart;
Merciful men are taken away,
While no one considers
That the righteous is taken away from evil.
2 He shall enter into peace;
They shall rest in their beds,
Each one walking in his uprightness.

3 "But come here,
You sons of the sorceress,
You offspring of the adulterer and the
harlot!
4 Whom do you ridicule?
Against whom do you make a wide mouth
And stick out the tongue?
Are you not children of transgression,
Offspring of falsehood,
5 Inflaming yourselves with gods under
every green tree,
Slaying the children in the valleys,
Under the clefts of the rocks?
6 Among the smooth stones of the stream
Is your portion;
They, they, are your lot!
Even to them you have poured a drink
offering,
You have offered a grain offering.
Should I receive comfort in these?

7 "On a lofty and high mountain
You have set your bed;
Even there you went up
To offer sacrifice.
8 Also behind the doors and their posts
You have set up your remembrance;
For you have uncovered yourself to those
other than Me,
And have gone up to them;
You have enlarged your bed
And made a covenant with them;
You have loved their bed,
Where you saw their nudity.[a]
9 You went to the king with ointment,
And increased your perfumes;
You sent your messengers far off,
And even descended to Sheol.
10 You are wearied in the length of your
way;
Yet you did not say, 'There is no hope.'
You have found the life of your hand;
Therefore you were not grieved.

56:5 [a]Literally him **57:8** [a]Literally hand, a
euphemism

11 "And of whom have you been afraid, or
        feared,
    That you have lied
    And not remembered Me,
    Nor taken *it* to your heart?
    Is it not because I have held My peace
        from of old
    That you do not fear Me?
12 I will declare your righteousness
    And your works,
    For they will not profit you.
13 When you cry out,
    Let your collection *of idols* deliver you.
    But the wind will carry them all away,
    A breath will take *them.*
    But he who puts his trust in Me shall
        possess the land,
    And shall inherit My holy mountain."

Healing for the Backslider

14 And one shall say,
    "Heap it up! Heap it up!
    Prepare the way,
    Take the stumbling block out of the way
        of My people."

15 For thus says the High and Lofty One
    Who inhabits eternity, whose name *is*
        Holy:
    "I dwell in the high and holy *place,*
    With him *who* has a contrite and humble
        spirit,
    To revive the spirit of the humble,
    And to revive the heart of the contrite
        ones.
16 For I will not contend forever,
    Nor will I always be angry;
    For the spirit would fail before Me,
    And the souls *which* I have made.
17 For the iniquity of his covetousness
    I was angry and struck him;
    I hid and was angry,
    And he went on backsliding in the way of
        his heart.
18 I have seen his ways, and will heal him;
    I will also lead him,
    And restore comforts to him
    And to his mourners.
19 "I create the fruit of the lips:
    Peace, peace to *him who is* far off and to
        him who is near,"
    Says the LORD,
    "And I will heal him."
20 But the wicked *are* like the troubled sea,
    When it cannot rest,
    Whose waters cast up mire and dirt.
21 "*There is* no peace,"
    Says my God, "for the wicked."

Fasting that Pleases God

58 "Cry aloud, spare not;
    Lift up your voice like a trumpet;
    Tell My people their transgression,
    And the house of Jacob their sins.
2 Yet they seek Me daily,
    And delight to know My ways,
    As a nation that did righteousness,
    And did not forsake the ordinance of their
        God.
    They ask of Me the ordinances of justice;
    They take delight in approaching God.
3 'Why have we fasted,' *they say,* 'and You
        have not seen?
    Why have we afflicted our souls, and You
        take no notice?'

    "In fact, in the day of your fast you find
        pleasure,
    And exploit all your laborers.
4 Indeed you fast for strife and debate,
    And to strike with the fist of wickedness.
    You will not fast as *you do* this day,
    To make your voice heard on high.
5 Is it a fast that I have chosen,
    A day for a man to afflict his soul?
    Is it to bow down his head like a bulrush,
    And to spread out sackcloth and ashes?
    Would you call this a fast,
    And an acceptable day to the LORD?

6 "*Is* this not the fast that I have chosen:
    To loose the bonds of wickedness,
    To undo the heavy burdens,
    To let the oppressed go free,
    And that you break every yoke?
7 *Is it* not to share your bread with the
        hungry,
    And that you bring to your house the
        poor who are cast out;
    When you see the naked, that you cover
        him,
    And not hide yourself from your own
        flesh?
8 Then your light shall break forth like the
        morning,
    Your healing shall spring forth speedily,
    And your righteousness shall go before
        you;
    The glory of the LORD shall be your rear
        guard.

Leadership Must Reflect God's Values and Ethics

(Isaiah 58:1–14)

The practice of fasting goes much deeper than the act of going without food. God declares that He delights not merely in His people going without some daily staples, but in loosing the "bonds of wickedness" and undoing "heavy burdens" of those they have oppressed (Is. 58:6).

Leaders would do well to learn from these words. God is calling us to live from His set of values and ethics. Fasting is fine and good—and these days we don't do it enough—but to fast while continuing to harbor destructive thoughts and oppressive attitudes does not reflect godly leadership. Ethics supply the foundation for our values. Values supply the power that drives our leadership. Consider what God expects from the "fasted life":

1. Liberate those who are oppressed (v. 6).
2. Share resources with the needy (v. 7).
3. Provide shelter to the homeless (v. 7).
4. Supply clothing to the naked (v. 7).
5. Stop accusing and judging others (v. 9).

9 Then you shall call, and the LORD will
   answer;
   You shall cry, and He will say, 'Here I *am*.'

   "If you take away the yoke from your
   midst,
   The pointing of the finger, and speaking
   wickedness,
10 *If* you extend your soul to the hungry
   And satisfy the afflicted soul,
   Then your light shall dawn in the
   darkness,
   And your darkness shall *be* as the noonday.
11 The LORD will guide you continually,
   And satisfy your soul in drought,
   And strengthen your bones;
   You shall be like a watered garden,
   And like a spring of water, whose waters
   do not fail.
12 Those from among you
   Shall build the old waste places;
   You shall raise up the foundations of many
   generations;

And you shall be called the Repairer of
   the Breach,
   The Restorer of Streets to Dwell In.

13 "If you turn away your foot from the
   Sabbath,
   From doing your pleasure on My holy day,
   And call the Sabbath a delight,
   The holy *day* of the LORD honorable,
   And shall honor Him, not doing your own
   ways,
   Nor finding your own pleasure,
   Nor speaking *your own* words,
14 Then you shall delight yourself in the
   LORD;
   And I will cause you to ride on the high
   hills of the earth,
   And feed you with the heritage of Jacob
   your father.
   The mouth of the LORD has spoken."

Separated from God

59 Behold, the LORD's hand is not
   shortened,
   That it cannot save;
   Nor His ear heavy,
   That it cannot hear.
2 But your iniquities have separated you
   from your God;
   And your sins have hidden *His* face from
   you,
   So that He will not hear.
3 For your hands are defiled with blood,
   And your fingers with iniquity;
   Your lips have spoken lies,
   Your tongue has muttered perversity.

4 No one calls for justice,
   Nor does *any* plead for truth.
   They trust in empty words and speak lies;
   They conceive evil and bring forth
   iniquity.
5 They hatch vipers' eggs and weave the
   spider's web;
   He who eats of their eggs dies,
   And *from* that which is crushed a viper
   breaks out.

6 Their webs will not become garments,
   Nor will they cover themselves with their
   works;
   Their works *are* works of iniquity,
   And the act of violence *is* in their hands.
7 Their feet run to evil,
   And they make haste to shed innocent
   blood;

Their thoughts *are* thoughts of iniquity;
Wasting and destruction *are* in their paths.
8 The way of peace they have not known,
And *there is* no justice in their ways;
They have made themselves crooked paths;
Whoever takes that way shall not know
peace.

Sin Confessed

9 Therefore justice is far from us,
Nor does righteousness overtake us;
We look for light, but there is darkness!
For brightness, *but* we walk in blackness!
10 We grope for the wall like the blind,
And we grope as if *we had* no eyes;
We stumble at noonday as at twilight;
We are as dead *men* in desolate places.
11 We all growl like bears,
And moan sadly like doves;
We look for justice, but *there is* none;
For salvation, *but* it is far from us.
12 For our transgressions are multiplied before
You,
And our sins testify against us;
For our transgressions *are* with us,
And *as for* our iniquities, we know them:
13 In transgressing and lying against the
LORD,
And departing from our God,
Speaking oppression and revolt,
Conceiving and uttering from the heart
words of falsehood.
14 Justice is turned back,
And righteousness stands afar off;
For truth is fallen in the street,
And equity cannot enter.
15 So truth fails,
And he *who* departs from evil makes
himself a prey.

The Redeemer of Zion

Then the LORD saw *it,* and it displeased
Him
That *there was* no justice.
16 He saw that *there was* no man,
And wondered that *there was* no
intercessor;
Therefore His own arm brought salvation
for Him;
And His own righteousness, it sustained
Him.
17 For He put on righteousness as a
breastplate,
And a helmet of salvation on His head;
He put on the garments of vengeance for
clothing,

And was clad with zeal as a cloak.
18 According to *their* deeds, accordingly He
will repay,
Fury to His adversaries,
Recompense to His enemies;
The coastlands He will fully repay.
19 So shall they fear
The name of the LORD from the west,
And His glory from the rising of the sun;
When the enemy comes in like a flood,
The Spirit of the LORD will lift up a
standard against him.

20 "The Redeemer will come to Zion,
And to those who turn from transgression
in Jacob,"
Says the LORD.

21"As for Me," says the LORD, "this *is* My covenant with them: My Spirit who *is* upon you,
and My words which I have put in your mouth,
shall not depart from your mouth, nor from the
mouth of your descendants, nor from the mouth
of your descendants' descendants," says the
LORD, "from this time and forevermore."

The Gentiles Bless Zion

60 Arise, shine;
For your light has come!
And the glory of the LORD is risen
upon you.
2 For behold, the darkness shall cover the
earth,
And deep darkness the people;
But the LORD will arise over you,
And His glory will be seen upon you.
3 The Gentiles shall come to your light,
And kings to the brightness of your rising.

4 "Lift up your eyes all around, and see:
They all gather together, they come to
you;
Your sons shall come from afar,
And your daughters shall be nursed at *your*
side.
5 Then you shall see and become radiant,
And your heart shall swell with joy;
Because the abundance of the sea shall be
turned to you,
The wealth of the Gentiles shall come to
you.
6 The multitude of camels shall cover your
land,
The dromedaries of Midian and Ephah;
All those from Sheba shall come;
They shall bring gold and incense,

And they shall proclaim the praises of the
LORD.

7 All the flocks of Kedar shall be gathered
together to you,
The rams of Nebaioth shall minister to
you;
They shall ascend with acceptance on My
altar,
And I will glorify the house of My glory.

8 "Who *are* these *who* fly like a cloud,
And like doves to their roosts?
9 Surely the coastlands shall wait for Me;
And the ships of Tarshish *will come* first,
To bring your sons from afar,
Their silver and their gold with them,
To the name of the LORD your God,
And to the Holy One of Israel,
Because He has glorified you.

10 "The sons of foreigners shall build up your
walls,
And their kings shall minister to you;
For in My wrath I struck you,
But in My favor I have had mercy on you.
11 Therefore your gates shall be open
continually;
They shall not be shut day or night,
That *men* may bring to you the wealth of
the Gentiles,
And their kings in procession.
12 For the nation and kingdom which will
not serve you shall perish,
And *those* nations shall be utterly ruined.

13 "The glory of Lebanon shall come to you,
The cypress, the pine, and the box tree
together,
To beautify the place of My sanctuary;
And I will make the place of My feet
glorious.
14 Also the sons of those who afflicted you
Shall come bowing to you,
And all those who despised you shall fall
prostrate at the soles of your feet;
And they shall call you The City of the
LORD,
Zion of the Holy One of Israel.

15 "Whereas you have been forsaken and
hated,
So that no one went through *you,*
I will make you an eternal excellence,
A joy of many generations.
16 You shall drink the milk of the Gentiles,
And milk the breast of kings;

You shall know that I, the LORD, *am* your
Savior
And your Redeemer, the Mighty One of
Jacob.

17 "Instead of bronze I will bring gold,
Instead of iron I will bring silver,
Instead of wood, bronze,
And instead of stones, iron.
I will also make your officers peace,
And your magistrates righteousness.
18 Violence shall no longer be heard in your
land,
Neither wasting nor destruction within
your borders;
But you shall call your walls Salvation,
And your gates Praise.

God the Glory of His People

19 "The sun shall no longer be your light by
day,
Nor for brightness shall the moon give
light to you;
But the LORD will be to you an everlasting
light,
And your God your glory.
20 Your sun shall no longer go down,
Nor shall your moon withdraw itself;
For the LORD will be your everlasting
light,
And the days of your mourning shall be
ended.
21 Also your people *shall* all *be* righteous;
They shall inherit the land forever,
The branch of My planting,
The work of My hands,
That I may be glorified.
22 A little one shall become a thousand,
And a small one a strong nation.
I, the LORD, will hasten it in its time."

The Good News of Salvation

61 "The Spirit of the Lord GOD *is*
upon Me,
Because the LORD has anointed Me
To preach good tidings to the poor;
He has sent Me to heal the brokenhearted,
To proclaim liberty to the captives,
And the opening of the prison to *those who
are* bound;
2 To proclaim the acceptable year of the
LORD,
And the day of vengeance of our God;
To comfort all who mourn,
3 To console those who mourn in Zion,
To give them beauty for ashes,

The Purpose of God's Anointing

(Isaiah 61:1–3)

What does God call His anointed Leader to do? Isaiah describes how God's Servant comes to preach good tidings to the poor, to heal the brokenhearted, to proclaim liberty to the captives, and to proclaim the acceptable year of the Lord. God is the One who anoints, who prepares His leaders for service. But what is the purpose of the anointing?

God anoints leaders to enable them to speak the supernatural words and perform the supernatural tasks He has called them to do. Consider the purposes of God's anointing, according to Isaiah:

1. To supernaturally enable men and women to perform their ministries
2. To bring hope and good news to the afflicted
3. To heal the brokenhearted
4. To proclaim liberty to the captives
5. To set prisoners free
6. To proclaim the acceptable year of the Lord
7. To announce the day of God's vengeance and justice
8. To comfort all who mourn
9. To furnish beauty for those who have lost it
10. To provide happiness and a glad heart
11. To supply an opportunity to praise God's name
12. To glorify the Lord and not man

The oil of joy for mourning,
The garment of praise for the spirit of
heaviness;
That they may be called trees of
righteousness,
The planting of the LORD, that He may be
glorified."

4 And they shall rebuild the old ruins,
They shall raise up the former desolations,
And they shall repair the ruined cities,
The desolations of many generations.
5 Strangers shall stand and feed your flocks,
And the sons of the foreigner
Shall be your plowmen and your
vinedressers.
6 But you shall be named the priests of the
LORD,
They shall call you the servants of our God.
You shall eat the riches of the Gentiles,
And in their glory you shall boast.
7 Instead of your shame *you shall have* double
honor,
And *instead of* confusion they shall rejoice
in their portion.
Therefore in their land they shall possess
double;
Everlasting joy shall be theirs.

8 "For I, the LORD, love justice;
I hate robbery for burnt offering;
I will direct their work in truth,
And will make with them an everlasting
covenant.
9 Their descendants shall be known among
the Gentiles,
And their offspring among the people.
All who see them shall acknowledge them,
That they *are* the posterity *whom* the LORD
has blessed."

10 I will greatly rejoice in the LORD,
My soul shall be joyful in my God;
For He has clothed me with the garments
of salvation,
He has covered me with the robe of
righteousness,
As a bridegroom decks *himself* with
ornaments,
And as a bride adorns *herself* with her
jewels.
11 For as the earth brings forth its bud,
As the garden causes the things that are
sown in it to spring forth,
So the Lord GOD will cause righteousness
and praise to spring forth before all the
nations.

Assurance of Zion's Salvation

62 For Zion's sake I will not hold My peace,
And for Jerusalem's sake I will not rest,
Until her righteousness goes forth as brightness,
And her salvation as a lamp *that* burns.
2 The Gentiles shall see your righteousness,
And all kings your glory.
You shall be called by a new name,
Which the mouth of the LORD will name.
3 You shall also be a crown of glory
In the hand of the LORD,
And a royal diadem
In the hand of your God.
4 You shall no longer be termed Forsaken,
Nor shall your land any more be termed Desolate;
But you shall be called Hephzibah,[a] and your land Beulah;[b]
For the LORD delights in you,
And your land shall be married.
5 For *as* a young man marries a virgin,
So shall your sons marry you;
And *as* the bridegroom rejoices over the bride,
So shall your God rejoice over you.

6 I have set watchmen on your walls, O Jerusalem;
They shall never hold their peace day or night.
You who make mention of the LORD, do not keep silent,
7 And give Him no rest till He establishes
And till He makes Jerusalem a praise in the earth.

8 The LORD has sworn by His right hand
And by the arm of His strength:
"Surely I will no longer give your grain
As food for your enemies;
And the sons of the foreigner shall not drink your new wine,
For which you have labored.
9 But those who have gathered it shall eat it,
And praise the LORD;
Those who have brought it together shall drink it in My holy courts."

10 Go through,
Go through the gates!
Prepare the way for the people;
Build up,
Build up the highway!
Take out the stones,
Lift up a banner for the peoples!

11 Indeed the LORD has proclaimed
To the end of the world:
"Say to the daughter of Zion,
'Surely your salvation is coming;
Behold, His reward *is* with Him,
And His work before Him.'"
12 And they shall call them The Holy People,
The Redeemed of the LORD;
And you shall be called Sought Out,
A City Not Forsaken.

The LORD in Judgment and Salvation

63 Who *is* this who comes from Edom,
With dyed garments from Bozrah,
This *One who is* glorious in His apparel,
Traveling in the greatness of His strength?—

"I who speak in righteousness, mighty to save."

2 Why *is* Your apparel red,
And Your garments like one who treads in the winepress?

3 "I have trodden the winepress alone,
And from the peoples no one *was* with Me.
For I have trodden them in My anger,
And trampled them in My fury;
Their blood is sprinkled upon My garments,
And I have stained all My robes.
4 For the day of vengeance *is* in My heart,
And the year of My redeemed has come.
5 I looked, but *there was* no one to help,
And I wondered
That *there was* no one to uphold;
Therefore My own arm brought salvation for Me;
And My own fury, it sustained Me.
6 I have trodden down the peoples in My anger,
Made them drunk in My fury,
And brought down their strength to the earth."

God's Mercy Remembered

7 I will mention the lovingkindnesses of the LORD

62:4 [a]Literally *My Delight Is in Her* [b]Literally *Married*

And the praises of the LORD,
According to all that the LORD has
bestowed on us,
And the great goodness toward the house
of Israel,
Which He has bestowed on them
according to His mercies,
According to the multitude of His
lovingkindnesses.
8 For He said, "Surely they *are* My people,
Children *who* will not lie."
So He became their Savior.
9 In all their affliction He was afflicted,
And the Angel of His Presence saved
them;
In His love and in His pity He redeemed
them;
And He bore them and carried them
All the days of old.
10 But they rebelled and grieved His Holy
Spirit;
So He turned Himself against them as an
enemy,
And He fought against them.

11 Then he remembered the days of old,
Moses *and* his people, *saying:*
"Where *is* He who brought them up out of
the sea
With the shepherd of His flock?
Where *is* He who put His Holy Spirit
within them,
12 Who led *them* by the right hand of Moses,
With His glorious arm,
Dividing the water before them
To make for Himself an everlasting name,
13 Who led them through the deep,
As a horse in the wilderness,
That they might not stumble?"

Daring Courage Comes from Deep Conviction

(Isaiah 63:11–14)

Isaiah recalls that Moses received his courage from his God-given convictions. Moses' relationship with God came first; next came a foundation of convictions; and finally the courage to lead others without compromise. Popularity with God controlled Moses' life, not popularity with people.

14 As a beast goes down into the valley,
And the Spirit of the LORD causes him to
rest,
So You lead Your people,
To make Yourself a glorious name.

A Prayer of Penitence

15 Look down from heaven,
And see from Your habitation, holy and
glorious.
Where *are* Your zeal and Your strength,
The yearning of Your heart and Your
mercies toward me?
Are they restrained?
16 Doubtless You *are* our Father,
Though Abraham was ignorant of us,
And Israel does not acknowledge us.
You, O LORD, *are* our Father;
Our Redeemer from Everlasting *is* Your
name.
17 O LORD, why have You made us stray
from Your ways,
And hardened our heart from Your fear?
Return for Your servants' sake,
The tribes of Your inheritance.
18 Your holy people have possessed *it* but a
little while;
Our adversaries have trodden down Your
sanctuary.
19 We have become *like* those of old, over
whom You never ruled,
Those who were never called by Your
name.

64 Oh, that You would rend the
heavens!
That You would come down!
That the mountains might shake at Your
presence—
2 As fire burns brushwood,
As fire causes water to boil—
To make Your name known to Your
adversaries,
That the nations may tremble at Your
presence!
3 When You did awesome things *for which*
we did not look,
You came down,
The mountains shook at Your presence.
4 For since the beginning of the world
Men have not heard nor perceived by the
ear,
Nor has the eye seen any God besides You,
Who acts for the one who waits for Him.
5 You meet him who rejoices and does
righteousness,

Who remembers You in Your ways.
You are indeed angry, for we have
   sinned—
In these ways we continue;
And we need to be saved.

6 But we are all like an unclean *thing,*
And all our righteousnesses *are* like filthy
   rags;
We all fade as a leaf,
And our iniquities, like the wind,
Have taken us away.

7 And *there is* no one who calls on Your
   name,
Who stirs himself up to take hold of You;
For You have hidden Your face from us,
And have consumed us because of our
   iniquities.

8 But now, O LORD,
You *are* our Father;
We *are* the clay, and You our potter;
And all we *are* the work of Your hand.

9 Do not be furious, O LORD,
Nor remember iniquity forever;
Indeed, please look—we all *are* Your
   people!

10 Your holy cities are a wilderness,
Zion is a wilderness,
Jerusalem a desolation.

11 Our holy and beautiful temple,
Where our fathers praised You,
Is burned up with fire;
And all our pleasant things are laid waste.

12 Will You restrain Yourself because of these
   things, O LORD?
Will You hold Your peace, and afflict us
   very severely?

The Righteousness of God's Judgment

65 "I was sought by *those who* did not
      ask *for* Me;
I was found by *those who* did not
      seek Me.
I said, 'Here I am, here I am,'
To a nation *that* was not called by My
   name.

2 I have stretched out My hands all day long
   to a rebellious people,
Who walk in a way *that is* not good,
According to their own thoughts;

3 A people who provoke Me to anger
   continually to My face;
Who sacrifice in gardens,
And burn incense on altars of brick;

4 Who sit among the graves,

And spend the night in the tombs;
Who eat swine's flesh,
And the broth of abominable things is *in*
   their vessels;

5 Who say, 'Keep to yourself,
Do not come near me,
For I am holier than you!'
These *are* smoke in My nostrils,
A fire that burns all the day.

6 "Behold, *it is* written before Me:
I will not keep silence, but will repay—
Even repay into their bosom—

7 Your iniquities and the iniquities of your
   fathers together,"
Says the LORD,
"Who have burned incense on the
   mountains
And blasphemed Me on the hills;
Therefore I will measure their former
   work into their bosom."

8 Thus says the LORD:

"As the new wine is found in the cluster,
And *one* says, 'Do not destroy it,
For a blessing *is* in it,'
So will I do for My servants' sake,
That I may not destroy them all.

9 I will bring forth descendants from Jacob,
And from Judah an heir of My mountains;
My elect shall inherit it,
And My servants shall dwell there.

10 Sharon shall be a fold of flocks,
And the Valley of Achor a place for herds
   to lie down,
For My people who have sought Me.

11 "But you *are* those who forsake the LORD,
Who forget My holy mountain,
Who prepare a table for Gad,[a]
And who furnish a drink offering for
   Meni.[b]

12 Therefore I will number you for the sword,
And you shall all bow down to the
   slaughter;
Because, when I called, you did not
   answer;
When I spoke, you did not hear,
But did evil before My eyes,
And chose *that* in which I do not delight."

13 Therefore thus says the Lord GOD:

65:11 [a]Literally *Troop* or *Fortune,* a pagan deity
[b]Literally *Number* or *Destiny,* a pagan deity

"Behold, My servants shall eat,
But you shall be hungry;
Behold, My servants shall drink,
But you shall be thirsty;
Behold, My servants shall rejoice,
But you shall be ashamed;
14 Behold, My servants shall sing for joy of
heart,
But you shall cry for sorrow of heart,
And wail for grief of spirit.
15 You shall leave your name as a curse to
My chosen;
For the Lord GOD will slay you,
And call His servants by another name;
16 So that he who blesses himself in the earth
Shall bless himself in the God of truth;
And he who swears in the earth
Shall swear by the God of truth;
Because the former troubles are forgotten,
And because they are hidden from My
eyes.

The Glorious New Creation

17 "For behold, I create new heavens and a
new earth;
And the former shall not be remembered
or come to mind.
18 But be glad and rejoice forever in what I
create;
For behold, I create Jerusalem as a
rejoicing,
And her people a joy.
19 I will rejoice in Jerusalem,
And joy in My people;
The voice of weeping shall no longer be
heard in her,
Nor the voice of crying.

20 "No more shall an infant from there live but
a few days,
Nor an old man who has not fulfilled his
days;
For the child shall die one hundred years
old,
But the sinner being one hundred years old
shall be accursed.
21 They shall build houses and inhabit them;
They shall plant vineyards and eat their
fruit.
22 They shall not build and another inhabit;
They shall not plant and another eat;
For as the days of a tree, so shall be the days
of My people,
And My elect shall long enjoy the work of
their hands.
23 They shall not labor in vain,

Nor bring forth children for trouble;
For they shall be the descendants of the
blessed of the LORD,
And their offspring with them.

24 "It shall come to pass
That before they call, I will answer;
And while they are still speaking, I will
hear.
25 The wolf and the lamb shall feed together,
The lion shall eat straw like the ox,
And dust shall be the serpent's food.
They shall not hurt nor destroy in all My
holy mountain,"
Says the LORD.

True Worship and False

66 Thus says the LORD:

"Heaven is My throne,
And earth is My footstool.
Where is the house that you will build
Me?
And where is the place of My rest?
2 For all those things My hand has made,
And all those things exist,"
Says the LORD.
"But on this one will I look:
On him who is poor and of a contrite
spirit,
And who trembles at My word.

3 "He who kills a bull is as if he slays a man;
He who sacrifices a lamb, as if he breaks a
dog's neck;
He who offers a grain offering, as if he
offers swine's blood;
He who burns incense, as if he blesses an
idol.
Just as they have chosen their own ways,
And their soul delights in their
abominations,
4 So will I choose their delusions,
And bring their fears on them;
Because, when I called, no one answered,
When I spoke they did not hear;
But they did evil before My eyes,
And chose that in which I do not delight."

The LORD Vindicates Zion

5 Hear the word of the LORD,
You who tremble at His word:
"Your brethren who hated you,
Who cast you out for My name's sake,
said,
'Let the LORD be glorified,

That we may see your joy.'
But they shall be ashamed."

6 The sound of noise from the city!
A voice from the temple!
The voice of the LORD,
Who fully repays His enemies!

7 "Before she was in labor, she gave birth;
Before her pain came,
She delivered a male child.
8 Who has heard such a thing?
Who has seen such things?
Shall the earth be made to give birth in
one day?
Or shall a nation be born at once?
For as soon as Zion was in labor,
She gave birth to her children.
9 Shall I bring to the time of birth, and not
cause delivery?" says the LORD.
"Shall I who cause delivery shut up *the
womb?*" says your God.
10 "Rejoice with Jerusalem,
And be glad with her, all you who love
her;
Rejoice for joy with her, all you who
mourn for her;
11 That you may feed and be satisfied
With the consolation of her bosom,
That you may drink deeply and be
delighted
With the abundance of her glory."

12 For thus says the LORD:

"Behold, I will extend peace to her like a
river,
And the glory of the Gentiles like a
flowing stream.
Then you shall feed;
On *her* sides shall you be carried,
And be dandled on *her* knees.
13 As one whom his mother comforts,
So I will comfort you;
And you shall be comforted in Jerusalem."

The Reign and Indignation of God

14 When you see *this,* your heart shall rejoice,
And your bones shall flourish like grass;
The hand of the LORD shall be known to
His servants,
And *His* indignation to His enemies.
15 For behold, the LORD will come with fire
And with His chariots, like a whirlwind,

To render His anger with fury,
And His rebuke with flames of fire.
16 For by fire and by His sword
The LORD will judge all flesh;
And the slain of the LORD shall be many.

17 "Those who sanctify themselves and purify
themselves,
To go to the gardens
After an *idol* in the midst,
Eating swine's flesh and the abomination
and the mouse,
Shall be consumed together," says the
LORD.

18 "For I *know* their works and their thoughts. It shall be that I will gather all nations and tongues; and they shall come and see My glory. 19 I will set a sign among them; and those among them who escape I will send to the nations: *to* Tarshish and Pul[a] and Lud, who draw the bow, and Tubal and Javan, *to* the coastlands afar off who have not heard My fame nor seen My glory. And they shall declare My glory among the Gentiles. 20 Then they shall bring all your brethren for an offering to the LORD out of all nations, on horses and in chariots and in litters, on mules and on camels, to My holy mountain Jerusalem," says the LORD, "as the children of Israel bring an offering in a clean vessel into the house of the LORD. 21 And I will also take some of them for priests *and* Levites," says the LORD.

22 "For as the new heavens and the new
earth
Which I will make shall remain before
Me," says the LORD,
"So shall your descendants and your name
remain.
23 And it shall come to pass
That from one New Moon to another,
And from one Sabbath to another,
All flesh shall come to worship before
Me," says the LORD.

24 "And they shall go forth and look
Upon the corpses of the men
Who have transgressed against Me.
For their worm does not die,
And their fire is not quenched.
They shall be an abhorrence to all flesh."

66:19 [a]Following Masoretic Text and Targum;
Septuagint reads *Put* (compare Jeremiah 46:9).

JEREMIAH
A Call to Change and Repentance

SUMMARY

Without question the prophet Jeremiah received one of the toughest assignments of any leader in the Old Testament. God called him to lead a stubborn people, then informed him that the people would not follow his lead (7:27, 28).

Jeremiah was born toward the end of the reign of King Josiah, the last good king of Judah. The prophet's leadership came at a time of moral, political, and religious decline, ending in the Babylonian exile. God called Jeremiah as a youth and immediately began to prepare him to serve as a prophet to the nations. He was a priest called to prophetic service at a most unhappy time.

God directed Jeremiah to deliver a hard message, a message of critical evaluation rather than of salvation. He was to call the people to change and repentance, to raise the standard they had dropped, and to call them to recapture their values and heritage. Think of him as a new C.E.O., called in to turn around a failing organization—only Jeremiah had a country to overhaul, not a mere corporation. He couldn't fire anyone; and in fact, those he attempted to influence rejected him. Jeremiah led the Hebrews during tough times, yet he never lost his vision.

We understand Jeremiah's personality more thoroughly than any other prophet. He clung tenaciously to his assigned task through long years of rejection and persecution, and still stands as a tribute to God's grace and the mettle of a strong leader. What's more, we call Jeremiah "the weeping prophet" because he shed so many tears over the hardness of his people and the severity of their judgment.

This embattled leader embraced core convictions, yet never lost his compassion. His heart didn't grow cold and crusty, despite the calloused hearts of his listeners. He continued to invest himself in his cause even though the people considered him a meddler and a traitor. Jewish men, nobles, and kings all tried to assassinate him at one time or another. While God warned Jeremiah from the start that the masses would reject his leadership, he continued to set the pace for what was right.

God's Role in Jeremiah

Jeremiah learned early to rely on God for sustaining grace. In chapter one, God tells him that even before his body took shape in his mother's womb, the Lord had ordained him as a prophet to the nations—to pluck up, tear down, and build again.

Several times during his career, Jeremiah determined to quit, but God reminded him of the vision and strengthened him. This divine call became the very reason Jeremiah remained true to his task.

At one point, the prophet likened God's word to an inner fire that would consume him if he didn't continue to speak. Jeremiah provides an example of a leader who continued in tough times through the supernatural work of God. Divine conviction drove him, along with a divine compassion and a divine call.

Leaders in Jeremiah

Jeremiah, King Jehoiakim, Hananiah

Other People of Influence in Jeremiah

Pashhur, false prophets

Lessons in Leadership

- God's calling of a leader matches His empowerment.

- Leaders must expect criticism and sometimes must confront.

- Leaders must not only endure change, but create it.

- Effective leaders identify with the sins and failures of their people.

- Leaders can be compared to both watchmen and shepherds.

- Great leaders never lose their ability to empathize.

- Successful leaders find memorable and creative ways to communicate truth.

- Leaders must cling to their God-given vision even when the people stray.

LEADERSHIP

HIGHLIGHTS IN JEREMIAH

1 The words of Jeremiah the son of Hilkiah, of the priests who *were* in Anathoth in the land of Benjamin, ²to whom the word of the LORD came in the days of Josiah the son of Amon, king of Judah, in the thirteenth year of his reign. ³It came also in the days of Jehoiakim the son of Josiah, king of Judah, until the end of the eleventh year of Zedekiah the son of Josiah, king of Judah, until the carrying away of Jerusalem captive in the fifth month.

The Prophet Is Called

⁴Then the word of the LORD came to me, saying:

5 "Before I formed you in the womb I knew you;
  Before you were born I sanctified you;
  I ordained you a prophet to the nations."

⁶Then said I:

"Ah, Lord GOD!
  Behold, I cannot speak, for I *am* a youth."

⁷But the LORD said to me:

"Do not say, 'I *am* a youth,'
  For you shall go to all to whom I send you,

And whatever I command you, you shall speak.
8 Do not be afraid of their faces,
  For I *am* with you to deliver you," says the LORD.

⁹Then the LORD put forth His hand and touched my mouth, and the LORD said to me:

"Behold, I have put My words in your mouth.
10 See, I have this day set you over the nations and over the kingdoms,
  To root out and to pull down,
  To destroy and to throw down,
  To build and to plant."

¹¹Moreover the word of the LORD came to me, saying, "Jeremiah, what do you see?"
And I said, "I see a branch of an almond tree."
¹²Then the LORD said to me, "You have seen well, for I am ready to perform My word."
¹³And the word of the LORD came to me the second time, saying, "What do you see?"
And I said, "I see a boiling pot, and it is facing away from the north."
¹⁴Then the LORD said to me:

"Out of the north calamity shall break forth
  On all the inhabitants of the land.

God's Call and Empowerment Match

(Jeremiah 1:4–10)

Jeremiah's call to become a prophet to the nations came early in his life—and it scared him terribly. Why? He failed to see that God's call and His empowerment always match. When God calls you to do something, He always provides the empowerment to fulfill that calling.

If God calls you, heed the call. He will also give you the resources to accomplish the work. But if He hasn't called you, don't conjure up some self-appointment. If He doesn't send you, you will not ultimately succeed (Jer. 23:21, 32). Jeremiah received his call through a "word of the LORD," one of several Jewish leaders called this way (Jer. 1:4; Ezek. 1:3; Hos. 1:1; Joel 1:1; Jon. 1:1). Note the circumstances of God's call on Jeremiah's life given in Jeremiah 1:4–10:

- God created Jeremiah for a purpose (v. 5).
- Jeremiah felt inadequate (v. 6).
- God wanted total control (v. 7).
- God gave the promise of a blessing (v. 8).
- God gave Jeremiah spiritual anointing (v. 9).
- God gave Jeremiah a difficult ministry (v. 10).

God's call, whether from birth or otherwise (see Acts 9 for other types of calls), eventually gets confirmed when God endorses a person's vocation. They feel they can do nothing else. How about you? What are your earliest memories of the call of God on your life?

15 For behold, I am calling
All the families of the kingdoms of the
    north," says the LORD;
"They shall come and each one set his
    throne
At the entrance of the gates of Jerusalem,
Against all its walls all around,
And against all the cities of Judah.
16 I will utter My judgments
Against them concerning all their
    wickedness,
Because they have forsaken Me,
Burned incense to other gods,
And worshiped the works of their own
    hands.

17 "Therefore prepare yourself and arise,
And speak to them all that I command you.
Do not be dismayed before their faces,
Lest I dismay you before them.
18 For behold, I have made you this day
A fortified city and an iron pillar,
And bronze walls against the whole land—
Against the kings of Judah,
Against its princes,
Against its priests,

And against the people of the land.
19 They will fight against you,
But they shall not prevail against you.
For I *am* with you," says the LORD, "to
    deliver you."

God's Case Against Israel

2 Moreover the word of the LORD came to
me, saying, 2"Go and cry in the hearing of
Jerusalem, saying, 'Thus says the LORD:

"I remember you,
The kindness of your youth,
The love of your betrothal,
When you went after Me in the
    wilderness,
In a land not sown.
3 Israel *was* holiness to the LORD,
The firstfruits of His increase.
All that devour him will offend;
Disaster will come upon them," says the
    LORD.' "

4Hear the word of the LORD, O house of Jacob and all the families of the house of Israel.
5Thus says the LORD:

The Law of Sacrifice: Jeremiah Gave Up Loads to Lead

(Jeremiah 1:18, 19)

Leaders must practice the Law of Sacrifice. We must give up to go up. Our call to lead is no cakewalk, but calls for responsibility and sacrifice.

The opportunity to practice this law provides a motive check for us. Leaders always gain a chance to evaluate their motives when leadership becomes difficult and requires more sacrifice. Jeremiah endured several occasions to practice this law:

1. **He was called to a ministry of opposition (1:18, 19).**
   Jeremiah never gained popularity. People didn't flock to hear him denounce their wickedness.
2. **He was not permitted to marry (16:1, 2).**
   Jeremiah lived a life of solitude without the joys of family and loved ones.
3. **He was beaten and put into stocks (20:1–3).**
   The people responded to the prophet's message with physical punishment.
4. **He was publicly disgraced to depict the judgment of Israel (27:1–3).**
   God told Jeremiah to put bonds and stocks around his neck to illustrate the coming yoke of Babylon.
5. **He was imprisoned in a dungeon (38:1–6).**
   Jeremiah was treated worse than thieves or murderers; he almost suffocated in this dry well.

Do you suddenly feel a little better about your plight as a leader? Jeremiah faced horrible odds, yet never walked away from his message or his call from God.

Communication: Effective Leaders Use Memorable Imagery

(Jeremiah 2:1–16)

We increase our ability to cast vision when we improve our communication. Effective leaders find memorable ways to communicate with their people.

Jeremiah uses vivid analogies and metaphors to describe how Israel has drifted from the Lord. He uses word pictures like a bride running to and then from her husband, a man digging a cistern, and a slave who has lost his freedom.

God challenged Jeremiah to communicate with those who refused to listen to him. This likely stretched him to become an even better communicator than if he had been given an easy task. As you scan the pages of his book, notice that Jeremiah, along with other Old Testament prophets, used five tools in an attempt to drive home his message:

1. **Strong Beginning**
   Jeremiah didn't waste words as he grabbed the people's attention.
2. **Simple Language**
   Jeremiah didn't try to impress anyone with huge, theological terms.
3. **One Theme**
   Jeremiah stuck with one profound issue per message, not seventeen.
4. **Pictures**
   Jeremiah used word pictures, illustrations, and object lessons to drive home his message.
5. **Emotional Ending**
   Jeremiah closed his communication with an appeal to strike both heart and head.

"What injustice have your fathers found in Me,
That they have gone far from Me,
Have followed idols,
And have become idolaters?
6 Neither did they say, 'Where *is* the LORD,
Who brought us up out of the land of Egypt,
Who led us through the wilderness,
Through a land of deserts and pits,
Through a land of drought and the shadow of death,
Through a land that no one crossed
And where no one dwelt?'
7 I brought you into a bountiful country,
To eat its fruit and its goodness.
But when you entered, you defiled My land
And made My heritage an abomination.
8 The priests did not say, 'Where *is* the LORD?'
And those who handle the law did not know Me;
The rulers also transgressed against Me;
The prophets prophesied by Baal,
And walked after *things that* do not profit.

9 "Therefore I will yet bring charges against you," says the LORD,
"And against your children's children I will bring charges.
10 For pass beyond the coasts of Cyprus[a] and see,
Send to Kedar[b] and consider diligently,
And see if there has been such *a thing.*
11 Has a nation changed *its* gods,
Which *are* not gods?
But My people have changed their Glory
For *what* does not profit.
12 Be astonished, O heavens, at this,
And be horribly afraid;
Be very desolate," says the LORD.
13 "For My people have committed two evils:
They have forsaken Me, the fountain of living waters,
And hewn themselves cisterns—broken cisterns that can hold no water.

2:10 [a]Hebrew *Kittim,* western lands, especially Cyprus [b]In the northern Arabian desert, representative of the eastern cultures

14 "*Is* Israel a servant?
    Is he a homeborn *slave?*
    Why is he plundered?
15 The young lions roared at him, *and*
        growled;
    They made his land waste;
    His cities are burned, without inhabitant.
16 Also the people of Noph[a] and Tahpanhes
    Have broken the crown of your head.
17 Have you not brought this on yourself,
    In that you have forsaken the LORD your
        God
    When He led you in the way?
18 And now why take the road to Egypt,
    To drink the waters of Sihor?
    Or why take the road to Assyria,
    To drink the waters of the River?[a]
19 Your own wickedness will correct you,
    And your backslidings will rebuke you.
    Know therefore and see that *it is* an evil
        and bitter *thing*
    That you have forsaken the LORD your
        God,
    And the fear of Me *is* not in you,"
    Says the Lord GOD of hosts.

20 "For of old I have broken your yoke *and*
        burst your bonds;
    And you said, 'I will not transgress,'
    When on every high hill and under every
        green tree
    You lay down, playing the harlot.
21 Yet I had planted you a noble vine, a seed
        of highest quality.
    How then have you turned before Me
    Into the degenerate plant of an alien vine?
22 For though you wash yourself with lye,
        and use much soap,
    Yet your iniquity is marked before Me,"
    says the Lord GOD.

23 "How can you say, 'I am not polluted,
    I have not gone after the Baals'?
    See your way in the valley;
    Know what you have done:
    You are a swift dromedary breaking loose
        in her ways,
24 A wild donkey used to the wilderness,
    That sniffs at the wind in her desire;
    In her time of mating, who can turn her
        away?
    All those who seek her will not weary
        themselves;
    In her month they will find her.
25 Withhold your foot from being unshod,
        and your throat from thirst.

But you said, 'There is no hope.
    No! For I have loved aliens, and after them
        I will go.'

26 "As the thief is ashamed when he is found
        out,
    So is the house of Israel ashamed;
    They and their kings and their princes, and
        their priests and their prophets,
27 Saying to a tree, 'You *are* my father,'
    And to a stone, 'You gave birth to me.'
    For they have turned *their* back to Me, and
        not *their* face.
    But in the time of their trouble
    They will say, 'Arise and save us.'
28 But where *are* your gods that you have
        made for yourselves?
    Let them arise,
    If they can save you in the time of your
        trouble;
    For *according to* the number of your cities
    Are your gods, O Judah.

29 "Why will you plead with Me?
    You all have transgressed against Me," says
        the LORD.
30 "In vain I have chastened your children;
    They received no correction.
    Your sword has devoured your prophets
    Like a destroying lion.

31 "O generation, see the word of the LORD!
    Have I been a wilderness to Israel,
    Or a land of darkness?
    Why do My people say, 'We are lords;
    We will come no more to You'?
32 Can a virgin forget her ornaments,
    Or a bride her attire?
    Yet My people have forgotten Me days
        without number.

33 "Why do you beautify your way to seek
        love?
    Therefore you have also taught
    The wicked women your ways.
34 Also on your skirts is found
    The blood of the lives of the poor
        innocents.
    I have not found it by secret search,
    But plainly on all these things.
35 Yet you say, 'Because I am innocent,
    Surely His anger shall turn from me.'
    Behold, I will plead My case against you,

2:16 [a]That is, Memphis in ancient Egypt
2:18 [a]That is, the Euphrates

Because you say, 'I have not sinned.'

36 Why do you gad about so much to change
your way?
Also you shall be ashamed of Egypt as you
were ashamed of Assyria.

37 Indeed you will go forth from him
With your hands on your head;
For the LORD has rejected your trusted
allies,
And you will not prosper by them.

Israel Is Shameless

3 "They say, 'If a man divorces his wife,
And she goes from him
And becomes another man's,
May he return to her again?'
Would not that land be greatly polluted?
But you have played the harlot with many
lovers;
Yet return to Me," says the LORD.

2 "Lift up your eyes to the desolate heights
and see:
Where have you not lain *with men?*
By the road you have sat for them
Like an Arabian in the wilderness;
And you have polluted the land
With your harlotries and your wickedness.

3 Therefore the showers have been
withheld,
And there has been no latter rain.
You have had a harlot's forehead;
You refuse to be ashamed.

4 Will you not from this time cry to Me,
'My Father, You *are* the guide of my youth?

5 Will He remain angry forever?
Will He keep it to the end?'
Behold, you have spoken and done evil
things,
As you were able."

A Call to Repentance

6 The LORD said also to me in the days of
Josiah the king: "Have you seen what backsliding
Israel has done? She has gone up on every high
mountain and under every green tree, and there
played the harlot. 7 And I said, after she had done
all these *things,* 'Return to Me.' But she did not
return. And her treacherous sister Judah saw it.
8 Then I saw that for all the causes for which
backsliding Israel had committed adultery, I had
put her away and given her a certificate of divorce; yet her treacherous sister Judah did not
fear, but went and played the harlot also. 9 So it
came to pass, through her casual harlotry, that she
defiled the land and committed adultery with

stones and trees. 10 And yet for all this her treacherous sister Judah has not turned to Me with her
whole heart, but in pretense," says the LORD.

11 Then the LORD said to me, "Backsliding Israel has shown herself more righteous than
treacherous Judah. 12 Go and proclaim these
words toward the north, and say:

'Return, backsliding Israel,' says the LORD;
'I will not cause My anger to fall on you.
For I *am* merciful,' says the LORD;
'I will not remain angry forever.

13 Only acknowledge your iniquity,
That you have transgressed against the
LORD your God,
And have scattered your charms
To alien deities under every green tree,
And you have not obeyed My voice,' says
the LORD.

14 "Return, O backsliding children," says the
LORD; "for I am married to you. I will take you,
one from a city and two from a family, and I will
bring you to Zion. 15 And I will give you shepherds according to My heart, who will feed you
with knowledge and understanding.

16 "Then it shall come to pass, when you are
multiplied and increased in the land in those
days," says the LORD, "that they will say no more,
'The ark of the covenant of the LORD.' It shall not
come to mind, nor shall they remember it, nor
shall they visit *it,* nor shall it be made anymore.

17 "At that time Jerusalem shall be called The
Throne of the LORD, and all the nations shall be
gathered to it, to the name of the LORD, to Jerusalem. No more shall they follow the dictates of
their evil hearts.

18 "In those days the house of Judah shall walk
with the house of Israel, and they shall come together out of the land of the north to the land
that I have given as an inheritance to your fathers.

19 "But I said:

'How can I put you among the children
And give you a pleasant land,
A beautiful heritage of the hosts of
nations?'

"And I said:

'You shall call Me, "My Father,"
And not turn away from Me.'

20 Surely, *as* a wife treacherously departs from
her husband,
So have you dealt treacherously with Me,
O house of Israel," says the LORD.

God's Criteria for Leaders: Shepherds After His Heart

(Jeremiah 3:15)

God tells us His criteria for leadership when He promises through Jeremiah that He will give the people shepherds after His own heart—the same description given to David in the Book of 1 Samuel. What does this mean? God says these shepherds are to lead His people with "knowledge and understanding."

This kind of leader doesn't develop automatically. Most seminaries still struggle with providing practical, usable tools for the men and women they are preparing for ministry. A "shepherd after God's own heart" must possess at least four skills:

1. Attitude Skills
A servant's heart, both positive and persistent.

2. People Skills
The ability to relate to others: communicate, delegate, motivate, confront, etc.

3. Equipping Skills
The ability to train and develop others for service.

4. Leadership Skills
The ability to cast vision, plan strategy, direct teams, and empower others.

21 A voice was heard on the desolate heights,
Weeping *and* supplications of the children
of Israel.
For they have perverted their way;
They have forgotten the LORD their God.

22 "Return, you backsliding children,
And I will heal your backslidings."

"Indeed we do come to You,
For You are the LORD our God.

23 Truly, in vain *is salvation hoped for* from the
hills,
And from the multitude of mountains;
Truly, in the LORD our God
Is the salvation of Israel.

24 For shame has devoured

The labor of our fathers from our youth—
Their flocks and their herds,
Their sons and their daughters.

25 We lie down in our shame,
And our reproach covers us.
For we have sinned against the LORD our
God,
We and our fathers,
From our youth even to this day,
And have not obeyed the voice of the
LORD our God."

4 "If you will return, O Israel," says the
LORD,
"Return to Me;
And if you will put away your
abominations out of My sight,
Then you shall not be moved.

2 And you shall swear, 'The LORD lives,'
In truth, in judgment, and in righteousness;
The nations shall bless themselves in Him,
And in Him they shall glory."

3 For thus says the LORD to the men of Judah
and Jerusalem:

"Break up your fallow ground,
And do not sow among thorns.

4 Circumcise yourselves to the LORD,
And take away the foreskins of your hearts,
You men of Judah and inhabitants of
Jerusalem,
Lest My fury come forth like fire,
And burn so that no one can quench *it*,
Because of the evil of your doings."

An Imminent Invasion

5 Declare in Judah and proclaim in Jerusalem,
and say:

"Blow the trumpet in the land;
Cry, 'Gather together,'
And say, 'Assemble yourselves,
And let us go into the fortified cities.'

6 Set up the standard toward Zion.
Take refuge! Do not delay!
For I will bring disaster from the north,
And great destruction."

7 The lion has come up from his thicket,
And the destroyer of nations is on his way.
He has gone forth from his place
To make your land desolate.
Your cities will be laid waste,
Without inhabitant.

8 For this, clothe yourself with sackcloth,
  Lament and wail.
  For the fierce anger of the LORD
  Has not turned back from us.

9 "And it shall come to pass in that day," says
    the LORD,
  "*That* the heart of the king shall perish,
  And the heart of the princes;
  The priests shall be astonished,
  And the prophets shall wonder."

10 Then I said, "Ah, Lord GOD!
  Surely You have greatly deceived this
    people and Jerusalem,
  Saying, 'You shall have peace,'
  Whereas the sword reaches to the heart."

11 At that time it will be said
  To this people and to Jerusalem,
  "A dry wind of the desolate heights *blows* in
    the wilderness
  Toward the daughter of My people—
  Not to fan or to cleanse—

12 A wind too strong for these will come for
    Me;
  Now I will also speak judgment against
    them."

13 "Behold, he shall come up like clouds,
  And his chariots like a whirlwind.
  His horses are swifter than eagles.
  Woe to us, for we are plundered!"

14 O Jerusalem, wash your heart from
    wickedness,
  That you may be saved.
  How long shall your evil thoughts lodge
    within you?

15 For a voice declares from Dan
  And proclaims affliction from Mount
    Ephraim:

16 "Make mention to the nations,
  Yes, proclaim against Jerusalem,
  That watchers come from a far country
  And raise their voice against the cities of
    Judah.

17 Like keepers of a field they are against her
    all around,
  Because she has been rebellious against
    Me," says the LORD.

18 "Your ways and your doings
  Have procured these *things* for you.
  This *is* your wickedness,
  Because it is bitter,
  Because it reaches to your heart."

Sorrow for the Doomed Nation

19 O my soul, my soul!
  I am pained in my very heart!
  My heart makes a noise in me;
  I cannot hold my peace,
  Because you have heard, O my soul,
  The sound of the trumpet,
  The alarm of war.

20 Destruction upon destruction is cried,
  For the whole land is plundered.
  Suddenly my tents are plundered,
  And my curtains in a moment.

21 How long will I see the standard,
  And hear the sound of the trumpet?

Compassion: Leaders Must Empathize with Human Flaws

(Jeremiah 4:19–26)

Compassion drove Jeremiah. He empathized with the flaws of his people, and even though he warned them of coming judgment, his proclamation sounded far from cold and sterile. He identified with the Israelites and anguished over their plight. This enabled him to lead over the long haul.

22 "For My people *are* foolish,
  They have not known Me.
  They *are* silly children,
  And they have no understanding.
  They *are* wise to do evil,
  But to do good they have no
    knowledge."

23 I beheld the earth, and indeed *it was*
    without form, and void;
  And the heavens, they *had* no light.

24 I beheld the mountains, and indeed they
    trembled,
  And all the hills moved back and forth.

25 I beheld, and indeed *there was* no man,
  And all the birds of the heavens had
    fled.

26 I beheld, and indeed the fruitful land *was* a
    wilderness,
  And all its cities were broken down
  At the presence of the LORD,
  By His fierce anger.

²⁷For thus says the LORD:

"The whole land shall be desolate;
  Yet I will not make a full end.
²⁸ For this shall the earth mourn,
  And the heavens above be black,
  Because I have spoken.
  I have purposed and will not relent,
  Nor will I turn back from it.
²⁹ The whole city shall flee from the noise of
    the horsemen and bowmen.
  They shall go into thickets and climb up
    on the rocks.
  Every city *shall be* forsaken,
  And not a man shall dwell in it.

³⁰ "And *when* you *are* plundered,
  What will you do?
  Though you clothe yourself with
    crimson,
  Though you adorn *yourself* with ornaments
    of gold,
  Though you enlarge your eyes with
    paint,
  In vain you will make yourself fair;
  Your lovers will despise you;
  They will seek your life.

³¹ "For I have heard a voice as of a woman in
    labor,
  The anguish as of her who brings forth
    her first child,
  The voice of the daughter of Zion
    bewailing herself;
  She spreads her hands, *saying,*
  'Woe *is* me now, for my soul is weary
  Because of murderers!'

The Justice of God's Judgment

5 "Run to and fro through the streets of
    Jerusalem;
  See now and know;
  And seek in her open places
  If you can find a man,
  If there is *anyone* who executes judgment,
  Who seeks the truth,
  And I will pardon her.
² Though they say, '*As* the LORD lives,'
  Surely they swear falsely."

³ O LORD, *are* not Your eyes on the truth?
  You have stricken them,
  But they have not grieved;
  You have consumed them,
  But they have refused to receive
    correction.

They have made their faces harder than
    rock;
They have refused to return.

⁴ Therefore I said, "Surely these *are* poor.
  They are foolish;
  For they do not know the way of the
    LORD,
  The judgment of their God.
⁵ I will go to the great men and speak to
    them,
  For they have known the way of the LORD,
  The judgment of their God."

But these have altogether broken the yoke
And burst the bonds.
⁶ Therefore a lion from the forest shall slay
    them,
  A wolf of the deserts shall destroy them;
  A leopard will watch over their cities.
  Everyone who goes out from there shall
    be torn in pieces,
  Because their transgressions are many;
  Their backslidings have increased.

⁷ "How shall I pardon you for this?
  Your children have forsaken Me
  And sworn by *those that are* not gods.
  When I had fed them to the full,
  Then they committed adultery
  And assembled themselves by troops in the
    harlots' houses.
⁸ They were *like* well-fed lusty stallions;
  Every one neighed after his neighbor's
    wife.
⁹ Shall I not punish *them* for these *things?*"
    says the LORD.
"And shall I not avenge Myself on such a
    nation as this?

¹⁰ "Go up on her walls and destroy,
  But do not make a complete end.
  Take away her branches,
  For they *are* not the LORD's.
¹¹ For the house of Israel and the house of
    Judah
  Have dealt very treacherously with Me,"
    says the LORD.

¹² They have lied about the LORD,
  And said, "*It is* not He.
  Neither will evil come upon us,
  Nor shall we see sword or famine.
¹³ And the prophets become wind,
  For the word *is* not in them.
  Thus shall it be done to them."

¹⁴Therefore thus says the LORD God of hosts:

"Because you speak this word,
Behold, I will make My words in your
mouth fire,
And this people wood,
And it shall devour them.

15 Behold, I will bring a nation against you
from afar,
O house of Israel," says the LORD.
"It is a mighty nation,
It is an ancient nation,
A nation whose language you do not
know,
Nor can you understand what they say.

16 Their quiver is like an open tomb;
They are all mighty men.

17 And they shall eat up your harvest and
your bread,
Which your sons and daughters should eat.
They shall eat up your flocks and your
herds;
They shall eat up your vines and your fig
trees;
They shall destroy your fortified cities,
In which you trust, with the sword.

¹⁸"Nevertheless in those days," says the LORD,
"I will not make a complete end of you. ¹⁹And it
will be when you say, 'Why does the LORD our
God do all these things to us?' then you shall answer them, 'Just as you have forsaken Me and
served foreign gods in your land, so you shall
serve aliens in a land that is not yours.'

20 "Declare this in the house of Jacob
And proclaim it in Judah, saying,

21 'Hear this now, O foolish people,
Without understanding,
Who have eyes and see not,
And who have ears and hear not:

22 Do you not fear Me?' says the LORD.
'Will you not tremble at My presence,
Who have placed the sand as the bound of
the sea,
By a perpetual decree, that it cannot pass
beyond it?
And though its waves toss to and fro,
Yet they cannot prevail;
Though they roar, yet they cannot pass
over it.

23 But this people has a defiant and rebellious
heart;
They have revolted and departed.

24 They do not say in their heart,
"Let us now fear the LORD our God,

Who gives rain, both the former and the
latter, in its season.
He reserves for us the appointed weeks of
the harvest."

25 Your iniquities have turned these things away,
And your sins have withheld good from you.

26 'For among My people are found wicked
men;
They lie in wait as one who sets snares;
They set a trap;
They catch men.

27 As a cage is full of birds,
So their houses are full of deceit.
Therefore they have become great and
grown rich.

28 They have grown fat, they are sleek;
Yes, they surpass the deeds of the wicked;
They do not plead the cause,
The cause of the fatherless;
Yet they prosper,
And the right of the needy they do not
defend.

29 Shall I not punish them for these things?'
says the LORD.
'Shall I not avenge Myself on such a nation
as this?'

30 "An astonishing and horrible thing
Has been committed in the land:

31 The prophets prophesy falsely,
And the priests rule by their own power;
And My people love to have it so.
But what will you do in the end?

Impending Destruction from the North

6 "O you children of Benjamin,
Gather yourselves to flee from the midst
of Jerusalem!
Blow the trumpet in Tekoa,
And set up a signal-fire in Beth Haccerem;
For disaster appears out of the north,
And great destruction.

2 I have likened the daughter of Zion
To a lovely and delicate woman.

3 The shepherds with their flocks shall come
to her.
They shall pitch their tents against her all
around.
Each one shall pasture in his own place."

4 "Prepare war against her;
Arise, and let us go up at noon.
Woe to us, for the day goes away,
For the shadows of the evening are
lengthening.

5 Arise, and let us go by night,
And let us destroy her palaces."

6 For thus has the LORD of hosts said:

"Cut down trees,
And build a mound against Jerusalem.
This *is* the city to be punished.
She *is* full of oppression in her midst.
7 As a fountain wells up with water,
So she wells up with her wickedness.
Violence and plundering are heard in her.
Before Me continually *are* grief and
wounds.
8 Be instructed, O Jerusalem,
Lest My soul depart from you;
Lest I make you desolate,
A land not inhabited."

9 Thus says the LORD of hosts:

"They shall thoroughly glean as a vine the
remnant of Israel;
As a grape-gatherer, put your hand back
into the branches."

10 To whom shall I speak and give warning,
That they may hear?
Indeed their ear *is* uncircumcised,
And they cannot give heed.
Behold, the word of the LORD is a
reproach to them;
They have no delight in it.
11 Therefore I am full of the fury of the LORD.
I am weary of holding *it* in.
"I will pour it out on the children outside,
And on the assembly of young men
together;
For even the husband shall be taken with
the wife,
The aged with *him who is* full of days.
12 And their houses shall be turned over to
others,
Fields and wives together;
For I will stretch out My hand
Against the inhabitants of the land," says
the LORD.
13 "Because from the least of them even to the
greatest of them,
Everyone *is* given to covetousness;
And from the prophet even to the priest,
Everyone deals falsely.
14 They have also healed the hurt of My
people slightly,
Saying, 'Peace, peace!'
When *there is* no peace.

15 Were they ashamed when they had
committed abomination?
No! They were not at all ashamed;
Nor did they know how to blush.
Therefore they shall fall among those who
fall;
At the time I punish them,
They shall be cast down," says the LORD.

16 Thus says the LORD:

"Stand in the ways and see,
And ask for the old paths, where the good
way *is,*
And walk in it;
Then you will find rest for your souls.
But they said, 'We will not walk *in it.*'
17 Also, I set watchmen over you, *saying,*
'Listen to the sound of the trumpet!'
But they said, 'We will not listen.'
18 Therefore hear, you nations,

The Leader Is a Watchman Who Guards and Guides the Flock

(Jeremiah 6:16–19)

Jeremiah illustrates the leader's job as a watchman. God appointed watchmen over His people to sound the trumpet in times of danger and to serve as His voice.

A watchman provides an outstanding metaphor for a leader. Watchmen guard and guide those they supervise. They guard against anything that would endanger the vision. They guide those they oversee, encouraging them to continue on the path toward that vision. They watch out for danger and maintain quality control. They cry out warnings to those who drift from the vision. They commit themselves to finishing the task they began. Watchmen must possess strong moral fiber and must remain committed to a strong sense of right and wrong.

Jeremiah served well as a watchman, but he never convinced the masses to get on board with what was right. In your own leadership, where do you draw the line between doing what is right and doing what will retain followers?

And know, O congregation, what *is* among them.
19 Hear, O earth!
Behold, I will certainly bring calamity on this people—
The fruit of their thoughts,
Because they have not heeded My words
Nor My law, but rejected it.
20 For what purpose to Me
Comes frankincense from Sheba,
And sweet cane from a far country?
Your burnt offerings *are* not acceptable,
Nor your sacrifices sweet to Me."

²¹Therefore thus says the LORD:

"Behold, I will lay stumbling blocks before this people,
And the fathers and the sons together shall fall on them.
The neighbor and his friend shall perish."

²²Thus says the LORD:

"Behold, a people comes from the north country,
And a great nation will be raised from the farthest parts of the earth.
23 They will lay hold on bow and spear;
They *are* cruel and have no mercy;
Their voice roars like the sea;
And they ride on horses,
As men of war set in array against you, O daughter of Zion."

24 We have heard the report of it;
Our hands grow feeble.
Anguish has taken hold of us,
Pain as of a woman in labor.
25 Do not go out into the field,
Nor walk by the way.
Because of the sword of the enemy,
Fear *is* on every side.
26 O daughter of my people,
Dress in sackcloth
And roll about in ashes!
Make mourning *as for* an only son, most bitter lamentation;
For the plunderer will suddenly come upon us.

27 "I have set you *as* an assayer *and* a fortress among My people,
That you may know and test their way.
28 They *are* all stubborn rebels, walking as slanderers.

They are bronze and iron,
They *are* all corrupters;
29 The bellows blow fiercely,
The lead is consumed by the fire;
The smelter refines in vain,
For the wicked are not drawn off.
30 *People* will call them rejected silver,
Because the LORD has rejected them."

Trusting in Lying Words

7 The word that came to Jeremiah from the LORD, saying, ²"Stand in the gate of the LORD's house, and proclaim there this word, and say, 'Hear the word of the LORD, all *you of* Judah who enter in at these gates to worship the LORD!'" ³Thus says the LORD of hosts, the God of Israel: "Amend your ways and your doings, and I will cause you to dwell in this place. ⁴Do not trust in these lying words, saying, 'The temple of the LORD, the temple of the LORD, the temple of the LORD *are* these.'

⁵"For if you thoroughly amend your ways and your doings, if you thoroughly execute judgment between a man and his neighbor, ⁶*if* you do not oppress the stranger, the fatherless, and the widow, and do not shed innocent blood in this place, or walk after other gods to your hurt, ⁷then I will cause you to dwell in this place, in the land that I gave to your fathers forever and ever.

⁸"Behold, you trust in lying words that cannot profit. ⁹Will you steal, murder, commit adultery, swear falsely, burn incense to Baal, and walk after other gods whom you do not know, ¹⁰and *then* come and stand before Me in this house which is called by My name, and say, 'We are delivered to do all these abominations'? ¹¹Has this house, which is called by My name, become a den of thieves in your eyes? Behold, I, even I, have seen *it,*" says the LORD.

¹²"But go now to My place which *was* in Shiloh, where I set My name at the first, and see what I did to it because of the wickedness of My people Israel. ¹³And now, because you have done all these works," says the LORD, "and I spoke to you, rising up early and speaking, but you did not hear, and I called you, but you did not answer, ¹⁴therefore I will do to the house which is called by My name, in which you trust, and to this place which I gave to you and your fathers, as I have done to Shiloh. ¹⁵And I will cast you out of My sight, as I have cast out all your brethren—the whole posterity of Ephraim.

¹⁶"Therefore do not pray for this people, nor lift up a cry or prayer for them, nor make intercession to Me; for I will not hear you. ¹⁷Do you not see what they do in the cities of Judah and

in the streets of Jerusalem? [18]The children gather wood, the fathers kindle the fire, and the women knead dough, to make cakes for the queen of heaven; and *they* pour out drink offerings to other gods, that they may provoke Me to anger. [19]Do they provoke Me to anger?" says the LORD. "*Do they* not *provoke* themselves, to the shame of their own faces?"

[20]Therefore thus says the Lord GOD: "Behold, My anger and My fury will be poured out on this place—on man and on beast, on the trees of the field and on the fruit of the ground. And it will burn and not be quenched."

[21]Thus says the LORD of hosts, the God of Israel: "Add your burnt offerings to your sacrifices and eat meat. [22]For I did not speak to your fathers, or command them in the day that I brought them out of the land of Egypt, concerning burnt offerings or sacrifices. [23]But this is what I commanded them, saying, 'Obey My voice, and I will be your God, and you shall be My people. And walk in all the ways that I have commanded you, that it may be well with you.' [24]Yet they did not obey or incline their ear, but followed the counsels *and* the dictates of their evil hearts, and went backward and not forward. [25]Since the day that your fathers came out of the land of Egypt until this day, I have even sent to you all My servants the prophets, daily rising up early and sending *them*. [26]Yet they did not obey Me or incline their ear, but stiffened their neck. They did worse than their fathers.

[27]"Therefore you shall speak all these words to them, but they will not obey you. You shall also call to them, but they will not answer you.

Judgment on Obscene Religion

[28]"So you shall say to them, 'This *is* a nation that does not obey the voice of the LORD their God nor receive correction. Truth has perished and has been cut off from their mouth. [29]Cut off your hair and cast *it* away, and take up a lamentation on the desolate heights; for the LORD has rejected and forsaken the generation of His wrath.' [30]For the children of Judah have done evil in My sight," says the LORD. "They have set their abominations in the house which is called by My name, to pollute it. [31]And they have built the high places of Tophet, which *is* in the Valley of the Son of Hinnom, to burn their sons and their daughters in the fire, which I did not command, nor did it come into My heart. [32]Therefore behold, the days are coming," says the LORD, "when it will no more be called Tophet, or the Valley of the Son of Hinnom, but the Valley of Slaughter; for they will bury in

Tophet until there is no room. [33]The corpses of this people will be food for the birds of the heaven and for the beasts of the earth. And no one will frighten *them away*. [34]Then I will cause to cease from the cities of Judah and from the streets of Jerusalem the voice of mirth and the voice of gladness, the voice of the bridegroom and the voice of the bride. For the land shall be desolate.

8 "At that time," says the LORD, "they shall bring out the bones of the kings of Judah, and the bones of its princes, and the bones of the priests, and the bones of the prophets, and the bones of the inhabitants of Jerusalem, out of their graves. [2]They shall spread them before the sun and the moon and all the host of heaven, which they have loved and which they have served and after which they have walked, which they have sought and which they have worshiped. They shall not be gathered nor buried; they shall be like refuse on the face of the earth. [3]Then death shall be chosen rather than life by all the residue of those who remain of this evil family, who remain in all the places where I have driven them," says the LORD of hosts.

The Peril of False Teaching

[4]"Moreover you shall say to them, 'Thus says the LORD:

> "Will they fall and not rise?
>   Will one turn away and not return?
> [5] Why has this people slidden back,
>   Jerusalem, in a perpetual backsliding?
>   They hold fast to deceit,
>   They refuse to return.
> [6] I listened and heard,
>   *But* they do not speak aright.
>   No man repented of his wickedness,
>   Saying, 'What have I done?'
>   Everyone turned to his own course,
>   As the horse rushes into the battle.
>
> [7] "Even the stork in the heavens
>   Knows her appointed times;
>   And the turtledove, the swift, and the
>   swallow
>   Observe the time of their coming.
>   But My people do not know the
>   judgment of the LORD.
>
> [8] "How can you say, 'We *are* wise,
>   And the law of the LORD *is* with us'?
>   Look, the false pen of the scribe certainly
>   works falsehood.
> [9] The wise men are ashamed,
>   They are dismayed and taken.

Behold, they have rejected the word of the
LORD;
So what wisdom do they have?

10 Therefore I will give their wives to others,
And their fields to those who will inherit
them;
Because from the least even to the greatest
Everyone is given to covetousness;
From the prophet even to the priest
Everyone deals falsely.

11 For they have healed the hurt of the
daughter of My people slightly,
Saying, 'Peace, peace!'
When *there is* no peace.

12 Were they ashamed when they had
committed abomination?
No! They were not at all ashamed,
Nor did they know how to blush.
Therefore they shall fall among those who
fall;
In the time of their punishment
They shall be cast down," says the LORD.

13 "I will surely consume them," says the
LORD.
"No grapes *shall be* on the vine,

Nor figs on the fig tree,
And the leaf shall fade;
And *the things* I have given them shall pass
away from them."'"

14 "Why do we sit still?
Assemble yourselves,
And let us enter the fortified cities,
And let us be silent there.
For the LORD our God has put us to silence
And given us water of gall to drink,
Because we have sinned against the LORD.

15 "*We* looked for peace, but no good *came;*
And for a time of health, and there was
trouble!

16 The snorting of His horses was heard from
Dan.
The whole land trembled at the sound of
the neighing of His strong ones;
For they have come and devoured the land
and all that is in it,
The city and those who dwell in it."

17 "For behold, I will send serpents among
you,

JEREMIAH

SPEAKING HARD TRUTH WITHOUT COMPROMISE
(Jeremiah 8:1–13)

PROFILE IN LEADERSHIP

Jeremiah did not receive a pleasant message from God to deliver to his
people. The Lord ordered him to declare judgment and destruction on
Judah. God told the prophet that He was about to destroy a sinful generation,
a group of stubborn men and women who had turned to the basest kind of
idolatry.

The Lord had patiently borne with these people. For many years He had
issued stern warnings about their sin—yet they refused to surrender to Him.
They had grown so depraved and shameless that God told Jeremiah they could
no longer even blush over their vile conduct (Jer. 8:12).

The truly godly leader takes no pleasure in announcing divine judgment. It is
a grievous thing to have to announce that the time for retribution has come.
God Himself grieves when His people's sin sinks to the point of no return. On
the other hand, a truly godly leader never shrinks from confronting sin or
from declaring the message of God. Effective leaders faithfully confront sin and
call the sinner to repentance.

It could not have been easy for Jeremiah to communicate God's words of
judgment. Neither is it easy to communicate today with people who need to be
confronted over their sin. But leadership means speaking all the truth—
sometimes unpleasant and painful truth—that God has entrusted to us.

Vipers which cannot be charmed,
And they shall bite you," says the LORD.

The Prophet Mourns for the People

18 I would comfort myself in sorrow;
My heart *is* faint in me.
19 Listen! The voice,
The cry of the daughter of my people
From a far country:
"*Is* not the LORD in Zion?
Is not her King in her?"

"Why have they provoked Me to anger
With their carved images—
With foreign idols?"

20 "The harvest is past,
The summer is ended,
And we are not saved!"

21 For the hurt of the daughter of my people
I am hurt.
I am mourning;
Astonishment has taken hold of me.
22 *Is there* no balm in Gilead,
Is there no physician there?
Why then is there no recovery
For the health of the daughter of my
people?

9 Oh, that my head were waters,
And my eyes a fountain of tears,
That I might weep day and night
For the slain of the daughter of my people!
2 Oh, that I had in the wilderness
A lodging place for travelers;
That I might leave my people,
And go from them!
For they *are* all adulterers,
An assembly of treacherous men.

3 "And *like* their bow they have bent their
tongues *for* lies.
They are not valiant for the truth on the
earth.
For they proceed from evil to evil,
And they do not know Me," says the
LORD.
4 "Everyone take heed to his neighbor,
And do not trust any brother;
For every brother will utterly supplant,
And every neighbor will walk with
slanderers.
5 Everyone will deceive his neighbor,
And will not speak the truth;

They have taught their tongue to speak
lies;
They weary themselves to commit
iniquity.
6 Your dwelling place *is* in the midst of
deceit;
Through deceit they refuse to know Me,"
says the LORD.

7 Therefore thus says the LORD of hosts:

"Behold, I will refine them and try them;
For how shall I deal with the daughter of
My people?
8 Their tongue *is* an arrow shot out;
It speaks deceit;
One speaks peaceably to his neighbor with
his mouth,
But in his heart he lies in wait.
9 Shall I not punish them for these *things?*"
says the LORD.
"Shall I not avenge Myself on such a nation
as this?"

10 I will take up a weeping and wailing for
the mountains,
And for the dwelling places of the
wilderness a lamentation,
Because they are burned up,
So that no one can pass through;
Nor can *men* hear the voice of the cattle.
Both the birds of the heavens and the
beasts have fled;
They are gone.

11 "I will make Jerusalem a heap of ruins, a
den of jackals.
I will make the cities of Judah desolate,
without an inhabitant."

12 Who *is* the wise man who may understand this? And *who is he* to whom the mouth of the LORD has spoken, that he may declare it? Why does the land perish *and* burn up like a wilderness, so that no one can pass through? 13 And the LORD said, "Because they have forsaken My law which I set before them, and have not obeyed My voice, nor walked according to it, 14 but they have walked according to the dictates of their own hearts and after the Baals, which their fathers taught them," 15 therefore thus says the LORD of hosts, the God of Israel: "Behold, I will feed them, this people, with wormwood, and give them water of gall to drink. 16 I will scatter them also among the Gentiles, whom neither they nor their fathers have known. And I

will send a sword after them until I have consumed them."

The People Mourn in Judgment

¹⁷Thus says the LORD of hosts:

"Consider and call for the mourning
women,
That they may come;
And send for skillful wailing women,
That they may come.
¹⁸ Let them make haste
And take up a wailing for us,
That our eyes may run with tears,
And our eyelids gush with water.
¹⁹ For a voice of wailing is heard from Zion:
'How we are plundered!
We are greatly ashamed,
Because we have forsaken the land,
Because we have been cast out of our
dwellings.'"

²⁰ Yet hear the word of the LORD, O
women,
And let your ear receive the word of His
mouth;
Teach your daughters wailing,
And everyone her neighbor a lamentation.
²¹ For death has come through our windows,
Has entered our palaces,
To kill off the children—*no longer to be*
outside!
And the young men—*no longer* on the
streets!

²² Speak, "Thus says the LORD:

'Even the carcasses of men shall fall as
refuse on the open field,
Like cuttings after the harvester,
And no one shall gather *them.*'"

²³Thus says the LORD:

"Let not the wise *man* glory in his wisdom,
Let not the mighty *man* glory in his might,
Nor let the rich *man* glory in his riches;
²⁴ But let him who glories glory in this,
That he understands and knows Me,
That I *am* the LORD, exercising
lovingkindness, judgment, and
righteousness in the earth.
For in these I delight," says the LORD.

²⁵"Behold, the days are coming," says the
LORD, "that I will punish all *who are* circumcised
with the uncircumcised— ²⁶Egypt, Judah, Edom,
the people of Ammon, Moab, and all *who are* in
the farthest corners, who dwell in the wilderness.
For all *these* nations *are* uncircumcised, and all the
house of Israel *are* uncircumcised in the heart."

Idols and the True God

10 Hear the word which the LORD
speaks to you, O house of Israel.
²Thus says the LORD:

"Do not learn the way of the Gentiles;
Do not be dismayed at the signs of heaven,

Priorities: Leaders Must Know What's Really Valuable

(*Jeremiah 9:23, 24*)

What is our ultimate priority? What should we pursue more than anything else? What is
worth boasting about? Some business leaders would answer, "Wealth and investments."
Some educational or political leaders would reply, "Intelligence and strategy." Some athletic or
sports leaders might respond, "Strength and speed."

But Jeremiah warns us against boasting about any of these. These are valuable resources, but
not ultimate priorities. The only thing worth boasting about is a vital relationship with God. The
others are merely a means to an end.

Leaders must recognize the difference between these two:

The Ultimate	The Immediate
1. God is the source.	1. The others are a resource.
2. He provides a life.	2. These provide a living.
3. Spiritual things are the end.	3. Material things are a means to an end.

For the Gentiles are dismayed at them.

3 For the customs of the peoples *are* futile;
For *one* cuts a tree from the forest,
The work of the hands of the workman,
    with the ax.

4 They decorate it with silver and gold;
They fasten it with nails and hammers
So that it will not topple.

5 They *are* upright, like a palm tree,
And they cannot speak;
They must be carried,
Because they cannot go *by themselves.*
Do not be afraid of them,
For they cannot do evil,
Nor can they do any good."

6 Inasmuch as *there is* none like You, O LORD
(You *are* great, and Your name *is* great in
    might),

7 Who would not fear You, O King of the
    nations?
For this is Your rightful due.
For among all the wise *men* of the
    nations,
And in all their kingdoms,
There is none like You.

8 But they are altogether dull-hearted and
    foolish;
A wooden idol *is* a worthless doctrine.

9 Silver is beaten into plates;
It is brought from Tarshish,
And gold from Uphaz,
The work of the craftsman
And of the hands of the metalsmith;
Blue and purple *are* their clothing;
They *are* all the work of skillful *men.*

10 But the LORD *is* the true God;
He *is* the living God and the everlasting
    King.
At His wrath the earth will tremble,
And the nations will not be able to endure
    His indignation.

11 Thus you shall say to them: "The gods that
have not made the heavens and the earth shall
perish from the earth and from under these
heavens."

12 He has made the earth by His power,
He has established the world by His
    wisdom,
And has stretched out the heavens at His
    discretion.

13 When He utters His voice,
There is a multitude of waters in the
    heavens:

"And He causes the vapors to ascend from
    the ends of the earth.
He makes lightning for the rain,
He brings the wind out of His treasuries."[a]

14 Everyone is dull-hearted, without
    knowledge;
Every metalsmith is put to shame by an
    image;
For his molded image *is* falsehood,
And *there is* no breath in them.

15 They *are* futile, a work of errors;
In the time of their punishment they shall
    perish.

16 The Portion of Jacob *is* not like them,
For He *is* the Maker of all *things,*
And Israel *is* the tribe of His inheritance;
The LORD of hosts *is* His name.

The Coming Captivity of Judah

17 Gather up your wares from the land,
O inhabitant of the fortress!

18 For thus says the LORD:

"Behold, I will throw out at this time
The inhabitants of the land,
And will distress them,
That they may find *it* so."

19 Woe is me for my hurt!
My wound is severe.
But I say, "Truly this *is* an infirmity,
And I must bear it."

20 My tent is plundered,
And all my cords are broken;
My children have gone from me,
And they *are* no more.
There is no one to pitch my tent anymore,
Or set up my curtains.

21 For the shepherds have become dull-
    hearted,
And have not sought the LORD;
Therefore they shall not prosper,
And all their flocks shall be scattered.

22 Behold, the noise of the report has come,
And a great commotion out of the north
    country,
To make the cities of Judah desolate, a den
    of jackals.

23 O LORD, I know the way of man *is* not in
    himself;

10:13 [a]Psalm 135:7

It is not in man who walks to direct his
own steps.

24 O LORD, correct me, but with justice;
Not in Your anger, lest You bring me to
nothing.

25 Pour out Your fury on the Gentiles, who
do not know You,
And on the families who do not call on
Your name;
For they have eaten up Jacob,
Devoured him and consumed him,
And made his dwelling place desolate.

The Broken Covenant

11 The word that came to Jeremiah
from the LORD, saying, [2]"Hear the
words of this covenant, and speak to
the men of Judah and to the inhabitants of Jerusalem; [3]and say to them, 'Thus says the LORD
God of Israel: "Cursed *is* the man who does not
obey the words of this covenant [4]which I commanded your fathers in the day I brought them
out of the land of Egypt, from the iron furnace,
saying, 'Obey My voice, and do according to all
that I command you; so shall you be My people,
and I will be your God,' [5]that I may establish the
oath which I have sworn to your fathers, to give
them 'a land flowing with milk and honey,'[a] as *it
is* this day." '"

And I answered and said, "So be it, LORD."

[6]Then the LORD said to me, "Proclaim all
these words in the cities of Judah and in the
streets of Jerusalem, saying: 'Hear the words of
this covenant and do them. [7]For I earnestly exhorted your fathers in the day I brought them up
out of the land of Egypt, until this day, rising
early and exhorting, saying, "Obey My voice."
[8]Yet they did not obey or incline their ear, but
everyone followed the dictates of his evil heart;
therefore I will bring upon them all the words of
this covenant, which I commanded *them* to do,
but *which* they have not done.' "

[9]And the LORD said to me, "A conspiracy has
been found among the men of Judah and among
the inhabitants of Jerusalem. [10]They have turned
back to the iniquities of their forefathers who refused to hear My words, and they have gone after
other gods to serve them; the house of Israel and
the house of Judah have broken My covenant
which I made with their fathers."

[11]Therefore thus says the LORD: "Behold, I
will surely bring calamity on them which they
will not be able to escape; and though they cry
out to Me, I will not listen to them. [12]Then the
cities of Judah and the inhabitants of Jerusalem
will go and cry out to the gods to whom they

offer incense, but they will not save them at all in
the time of their trouble. [13]For *according to* the
number of your cities were your gods, O Judah;
and *according to* the number of the streets of Jerusalem you have set up altars to *that* shameful
thing, altars to burn incense to Baal.

[14]"So do not pray for this people, or lift up a
cry or prayer for them; for I will not hear *them* in
the time that they cry out to Me because of their
trouble.

15 "What has My beloved to do in My house,
Having done lewd deeds with many?
And the holy flesh has passed from you.
When you do evil, then you rejoice.

16 The LORD called your name,
Green Olive Tree, Lovely *and* of Good
Fruit.
With the noise of a great tumult
He has kindled fire on it,
And its branches are broken.

[17]"For the LORD of hosts, who planted you,
has pronounced doom against you for the evil of
the house of Israel and of the house of Judah,
which they have done against themselves to provoke Me to anger in offering incense to Baal."

Jeremiah's Life Threatened

[18]Now the LORD gave me knowledge *of it,*
and I know *it;* for You showed me their doings.
[19]But I *was* like a docile lamb brought to the
slaughter; and I did not know that they had devised schemes against me, *saying,* "Let us destroy
the tree with its fruit, and let us cut him off from
the land of the living, that his name may be remembered no more."

20 But, O LORD of hosts,
You who judge righteously,
Testing the mind and the heart,
Let me see Your vengeance on them,
For to You I have revealed my cause.

[21]"Therefore thus says the LORD concerning
the men of Anathoth who seek your life, saying,
'Do not prophesy in the name of the LORD, lest
you die by our hand'— [22]therefore thus says the
LORD of hosts: 'Behold, I will punish them. The
young men shall die by the sword, their sons and
their daughters shall die by famine; [23]and there
shall be no remnant of them, for I will bring catastrophe on the men of Anathoth, *even* the year
of their punishment.' "

11:5 [a]Exodus 3:8

Jeremiah's Question

12 Righteous *are* You, O LORD, when
I plead with You;
Yet let me talk with You about *Your*
judgments.
Why does the way of the wicked prosper?
Why are those happy who deal so
treacherously?

2   You have planted them, yes, they have
taken root;
They grow, yes, they bear fruit.
You *are* near in their mouth
But far from their mind.

3   But You, O LORD, know me;
You have seen me,
And You have tested my heart toward
You.
Pull them out like sheep for the slaughter,
And prepare them for the day of slaughter.

4   How long will the land mourn,
And the herbs of every field wither?
The beasts and birds are consumed,
For the wickedness of those who dwell
there,
Because they said, "He will not see our
final end."

Attitude: Leaders Don't Get Lost in the Problems

(Jeremiah 12:1–4)

If Jeremiah complained about relatively easy
days, then how could God use him in hard
times? Like us, Jeremiah suffered from hard-
ening of the attitudes. We lose perspective on
what real problems look like and what God is
able to do. Let's focus on His promise, not our
problems.

The LORD Answers Jeremiah

5   "If you have run with the footmen, and
they have wearied you,
Then how can you contend with horses?
And *if* in the land of peace,
In which you trusted, *they wearied you,*
Then how will you do in the floodplain[a]
of the Jordan?

6   For even your brothers, the house of your
father,

Even they have dealt treacherously with
you;
Yes, they have called a multitude after you.
Do not believe them,
Even though they speak smooth words to
you.

7   "I have forsaken My house, I have left My
heritage;
I have given the dearly beloved of My soul
into the hand of her enemies.

8   My heritage is to Me like a lion in the
forest;
It cries out against Me;
Therefore I have hated it.

9   My heritage *is* to Me *like* a speckled
vulture;
The vultures all around *are* against her.
Come, assemble all the beasts of the field,
Bring them to devour!

10 "Many rulers[a] have destroyed My vineyard,
They have trodden My portion underfoot;
They have made My pleasant portion a
desolate wilderness.

11 They have made it desolate;
Desolate, it mourns to Me;
The whole land is made desolate,
Because no one takes *it* to heart.

12 The plunderers have come
On all the desolate heights in the
wilderness,
For the sword of the LORD shall devour
From *one* end of the land to the *other* end
of the land;
No flesh shall have peace.

13 They have sown wheat but reaped thorns;
They have put themselves to pain *but* do
not profit.
But be ashamed of your harvest
Because of the fierce anger of the LORD."

14 Thus says the LORD: "Against all My evil
neighbors who touch the inheritance which I
have caused My people Israel to inherit—behold, I will pluck them out of their land and
pluck out the house of Judah from among them.
15 Then it shall be, after I have plucked them out,
that I will return and have compassion on them
and bring them back, everyone to his heritage
and everyone to his land. 16 And it shall be, if they
will learn carefully the ways of My people, to
swear by My name, 'As the LORD lives,' as they
taught My people to swear by Baal, then they

12:5 [a]Or *thicket* **12:10** [a]Literally *shepherds* or *pastors* shall be established in the midst of My people. [17]But if they do not obey, I will utterly pluck up and destroy that nation," says the LORD.

Symbol of the Linen Sash

13 Thus the LORD said to me: "Go and get yourself a linen sash, and put it around your waist, but do not put it in water." [2]So I got a sash according to the word of the LORD, and put *it* around my waist.

[3]And the word of the LORD came to me the second time, saying, [4]"'Take the sash that you acquired, which *is* around your waist, and arise, go to the Euphrates,[a] and hide it there in a hole in the rock." [5]So I went and hid it by the Euphrates, as the LORD commanded me.

[6]Now it came to pass after many days that the LORD said to me, "Arise, go to the Euphrates, and take from there the sash which I commanded you to hide there." [7]Then I went to the Euphrates and dug, and I took the sash from the place where I had hidden it; and there was the sash, ruined. It was profitable for nothing.

[8]Then the word of the LORD came to me, saying, [9]"'Thus says the LORD: 'In this manner I will ruin the pride of Judah and the great pride of Jerusalem. [10]This evil people, who refuse to hear My words, who follow the dictates of their hearts, and walk after other gods to serve them and worship them, shall be just like this sash which is profitable for nothing. [11]For as the sash clings to the waist of a man, so I have caused the whole house of Israel and the whole house of Judah to cling to Me,' says the LORD, 'that they may become My people, for renown, for praise, and for glory; but they would not hear.'

Symbol of the Wine Bottles

[12]"Therefore you shall speak to them this word: 'Thus says the LORD God of Israel: "Every bottle shall be filled with wine."'

"And they will say to you, 'Do we not certainly know that every bottle will be filled with wine?'

[13]"Then you shall say to them, 'Thus says the LORD: "Behold, I will fill all the inhabitants of this land—even the kings who sit on David's throne, the priests, the prophets, and all the inhabitants of Jerusalem—with drunkenness! [14]And I will dash them one against another, even the fathers and the sons together," says the LORD. "I will not pity nor spare nor have mercy, but will destroy them."'"

Pride Precedes Captivity

[15]   Hear and give ear:
    Do not be proud,
    For the LORD has spoken.
[16]   Give glory to the LORD your God
    Before He causes darkness,
    And before your feet stumble
    On the dark mountains,
    And while you are looking for light,
    He turns it into the shadow of death

13:4 [a]Hebrew *Perath*

The Linen Sash:
An Analogy for Leaders Who Want to Be Useful
(Jeremiah 13:1–11)

God instructed Jeremiah to wear a linen sash for a while, then bury it. What happened? The once useful sash became useless.

Through this sash, God provides a teaching analogy for His people. The ruined piece of clothing represented the people of Israel who once served and worshiped God, but then became useless through their disobedience. Leaders have special reasons to pay close attention to this object lesson. Consider the parallels between leaders and the linen sash:

Remain useful when:	Become useless when:
1. *They are stretched.*	1. *They are soiled.*
We must be stretched and challenged.	We cannot live with sin and apathy.
2. *They are secure.*	2. *They are separated.*
We must draw our identity from God.	We cannot live as mavericks.
3. *They are solid.*	3. *They are shrunk.*
We must possess stable values.	We aren't useful when we think small.

And makes it dense darkness.

17 But if you will not hear it,
My soul will weep in secret for your pride;
My eyes will weep bitterly
And run down with tears,
Because the LORD's flock has been taken
captive.

18 Say to the king and to the queen mother,
"Humble yourselves;
Sit down,
For your rule shall collapse, the crown of
your glory."

19 The cities of the South shall be shut up,
And no one shall open them;
Judah shall be carried away captive, all of
it;
It shall be wholly carried away captive.

20 Lift up your eyes and see
Those who come from the north.
Where is the flock that was given to you,
Your beautiful sheep?

21 What will you say when He punishes you?
For you have taught them
To be chieftains, to be head over you.
Will not pangs seize you,
Like a woman in labor?

22 And if you say in your heart,
"Why have these things come upon me?"
For the greatness of your iniquity
Your skirts have been uncovered,
Your heels made bare.

23 Can the Ethiopian change his skin or the
leopard its spots?
Then may you also do good who are
accustomed to do evil.

24 "Therefore I will scatter them like stubble
That passes away by the wind of the
wilderness.

25 This is your lot,
The portion of your measures from Me,"
says the LORD,
"Because you have forgotten Me
And trusted in falsehood.

26 Therefore I will uncover your skirts over
your face,
That your shame may appear.

27 I have seen your adulteries
And your lustful neighings,
The lewdness of your harlotry,
Your abominations on the hills in the
fields.
Woe to you, O Jerusalem!
Will you still not be made clean?"

Sword, Famine, and Pestilence

14 The word of the LORD that came to
Jeremiah concerning the droughts.

2 "Judah mourns,
And her gates languish;
They mourn for the land,
And the cry of Jerusalem has gone up.

3 Their nobles have sent their lads for water;
They went to the cisterns and found no
water.
They returned with their vessels empty;
They were ashamed and confounded
And covered their heads.

4 Because the ground is parched,
For there was no rain in the land,
The plowmen were ashamed;
They covered their heads.

5 Yes, the deer also gave birth in the field,
But left because there was no grass.

6 And the wild donkeys stood in the
desolate heights;
They sniffed at the wind like jackals;
Their eyes failed because there was no
grass."

7 O LORD, though our iniquities testify
against us,
Do it for Your name's sake;
For our backslidings are many,
We have sinned against You.

8 O the Hope of Israel, his Savior in time of
trouble,
Why should You be like a stranger in the
land,
And like a traveler who turns aside to tarry
for a night?

9 Why should You be like a man astonished,
Like a mighty one who cannot save?
Yet You, O LORD, are in our midst,
And we are called by Your name;
Do not leave us!

10 Thus says the LORD to this people:

"Thus they have loved to wander;
They have not restrained their feet.
Therefore the LORD does not accept
them;
He will remember their iniquity now,
And punish their sins."

11 Then the LORD said to me, "Do not pray
for this people, for their good. 12 When they fast, I
will not hear their cry; and when they offer
burnt offering and grain offering, I will not

accept them. But I will consume them by the sword, by the famine, and by the pestilence."

¹³Then I said, "Ah, Lord GOD! Behold, the prophets say to them, 'You shall not see the sword, nor shall you have famine, but I will give you assured peace in this place.'"

¹⁴And the LORD said to me, "The prophets prophesy lies in My name. I have not sent them, commanded them, nor spoken to them; they prophesy to you a false vision, divination, a worthless thing, and the deceit of their heart. ¹⁵Therefore thus says the LORD concerning the prophets who prophesy in My name, whom I did not send, and who say, 'Sword and famine shall not be in this land'—'By sword and famine those prophets shall be consumed! ¹⁶And the people to whom they prophesy shall be cast out in the streets of Jerusalem because of the famine and the sword; they will have no one to bury them—them nor their wives, their sons nor their daughters—for I will pour their wickedness on them.'

¹⁷"Therefore you shall say this word to them:

'Let my eyes flow with tears night and day,
And let them not cease;
For the virgin daughter of my people
Has been broken with a mighty stroke,
with a very severe blow.
18　If I go out to the field,
Then behold, those slain with the sword!
And if I enter the city,

Then behold, those sick from famine!
Yes, both prophet and priest go about in a
land they do not know.'"

The People Plead for Mercy

19　Have You utterly rejected Judah?
Has Your soul loathed Zion?
Why have You stricken us so that *there is*
no healing for us?
We looked for peace, but *there was* no good;
And for the time of healing, and there was
trouble.
20　We acknowledge, O LORD, our wickedness
And the iniquity of our fathers,
For we have sinned against You.
21　Do not abhor *us,* for Your name's sake;
Do not disgrace the throne of Your glory.
Remember, do not break Your covenant
with us.
22　Are there any among the idols of the
nations that can cause rain?
Or can the heavens give showers?
Are You not He, O LORD our God?
Therefore we will wait for You,
Since You have made all these.

The LORD Will Not Relent

15 Then the LORD said to me, "*Even* if Moses and Samuel stood before Me, My mind *would* not *be* favorable toward this people. Cast *them* out of My sight, and let them go forth. ²And it shall be, if they say to

---

What Happens to Leaders Who Mislead and Damage Others?

(Jeremiah 14:14–16)

A group of false prophets spoke about the future, as Jeremiah did, yet they proclaimed a much more positive message than his. People liked them because they spoke what they wanted to hear. Nevertheless, God told Jeremiah to continue speaking truthfully. The very drought, famine, and sword the false prophets denied would soon kill them.

God reserves special judgment for leaders who speak out of turn and who give the people merely what they want to hear. Note the sharp contrast between these prophets and Jeremiah:

Jeremiah	False Leaders
1. Spoke the truth even when it hurt	1. Spoke only what made people feel good
2. Constantly checked and purified his motives	2. Were motivated by selfish gain and popularity
3. Gave direction tied to an eternal hope	3. Gave direction tied to temporary pleasure
4. Was eventually proven right	4. Lost their lives because of what they said

you, 'Where should we go?' then you shall tell them, 'Thus says the LORD:

"Such as *are* for death, to death;
    And such as *are* for the sword, to the
       sword;
    And such as *are* for the famine, to the
       famine;
    And such as *are* for the captivity, to the
       captivity."'

3 "And I will appoint over them four forms *of destruction*," says the LORD: "the sword to slay, the dogs to drag, the birds of the heavens and the beasts of the earth to devour and destroy. 4 I will hand them over to trouble, to all kingdoms of the earth, because of Manasseh the son of Hezekiah, king of Judah, for what he did in Jerusalem.

5   "For who will have pity on you, O
       Jerusalem?
    Or who will bemoan you?
    Or who will turn aside to ask how you are
       doing?
6   You have forsaken Me," says the LORD,
    "You have gone backward.
    Therefore I will stretch out My hand
       against you and destroy you;
    I am weary of relenting!
7   And I will winnow them with a
       winnowing fan in the gates of the land;
    I will bereave *them* of children;
    I will destroy My people,
    Since they do not return from their ways.
8   Their widows will be increased to Me
       more than the sand of the seas;
    I will bring against them,
    Against the mother of the young men,
    A plunderer at noonday;
    I will cause anguish and terror to fall on
       them suddenly.
9   "She languishes who has borne seven;
    She has breathed her last;
    Her sun has gone down
    While *it was* yet day;
    She has been ashamed and confounded.
    And the remnant of them I will deliver to
       the sword
    Before their enemies," says the LORD.

Jeremiah's Dejection

10   Woe is me, my mother,
    That you have borne me,
    A man of strife and a man of contention
       to the whole earth!

    I have neither lent for interest,
    Nor have men lent to me for interest.
    Every one of them curses me.

11 The LORD said:

   "Surely it will be well with your remnant;
    Surely I will cause the enemy to intercede
       with you
    In the time of adversity and in the time of
       affliction.
12   Can anyone break iron,
    The northern iron and the bronze?
13   Your wealth and your treasures
    I will give as plunder without price,
    Because of all your sins,
    Throughout your territories.
14   And I will make *you* cross over with[a] your
       enemies
    Into a land *which* you do not know;
    For a fire is kindled in My anger,
    Which shall burn upon you."

15   O LORD, You know;
    Remember me and visit me,
    And take vengeance for me on my
       persecutors.
    In Your enduring patience, do not take me
       away.
    Know that for Your sake I have suffered
       rebuke.
16   Your words were found, and I ate them,
    And Your word was to me the joy and
       rejoicing of my heart;
    For I am called by Your name,
    O LORD God of hosts.
17   I did not sit in the assembly of the
       mockers,
    Nor did I rejoice;
    I sat alone because of Your hand,
    For You have filled me with indignation.
18   Why is my pain perpetual
    And my wound incurable,
    Which refuses to be healed?
    Will You surely be to me like an unreliable
       stream,
    As waters *that* fail?

The LORD Reassures Jeremiah

19 Therefore thus says the LORD:

   "If you return,
    Then I will bring you back;

15:14 [a]Following Masoretic Text and Vulgate; Septuagint, Syriac, and Targum read *cause you to serve* (compare 17:4).

You shall stand before Me;
If you take out the precious from the vile,
You shall be as My mouth.
Let them return to you,
But you must not return to them.
20 And I will make you to this people a
    fortified bronze wall;
And they will fight against you,
But they shall not prevail against you;
For I *am* with you to save you
And deliver you," says the LORD.
21 "I will deliver you from the hand of the
    wicked,
And I will redeem you from the grip of
    the terrible."

Courage: One Person Standing with God Is Invincible

(Jeremiah 15:15–21)

Jeremiah asked God to remember the stand he took. This leader acted with courage when no one else seemed to be able to do so. In three short verses, we read what Jeremiah endured in his struggle to stand courageously:

1. He was neglected (v. 15).
2. He was mistreated (v. 15).
3. He was lonely (v. 17).
4. He endured continual discouragement (v. 18).
5. He felt let down by God (v. 18).

In verses 19–21, God gave His prophet courage by giving him a . . .

1. *Picture of Himself*—God allowed him to stand and see a vision of Yahweh.
2. *Picture of the people*—God confirms Jeremiah's view: The people *are* stubborn.
3. *Picture of victory*—God reminds him that the Lord is greater than any circumstance.

Jeremiah's Lifestyle and Message

16 The word of the LORD also came to me, saying, 2"You shall not take a wife, nor shall you have sons or daughters in this place." 3For thus says the LORD concerning the sons and daughters who are born in this place, and concerning their mothers who bore them and their fathers who begot them in this land: 4"They shall die gruesome deaths; they shall not be lamented nor shall they be buried, *but* they shall be like refuse on the face of the earth. They shall be consumed by the sword and by famine, and their corpses shall be meat for the birds of heaven and for the beasts of the earth."

5For thus says the LORD: "Do not enter the house of mourning, nor go to lament or bemoan them; for I have taken away My peace from this people," says the LORD, "lovingkindness and mercies. 6Both the great and the small shall die in this land. They shall not be buried; neither shall men lament for them, cut themselves, nor make themselves bald for them. 7Nor shall *men* break *bread* in mourning for them, to comfort them for the dead; nor shall *men* give them the cup of consolation to drink for their father or their mother. 8Also you shall not go into the house of feasting to sit with them, to eat and drink."

9For thus says the LORD of hosts, the God of Israel: "Behold, I will cause to cease from this place, before your eyes and in your days, the voice of mirth and the voice of gladness, the voice of the bridegroom and the voice of the bride.

10"And it shall be, when you show this people all these words, and they say to you, 'Why has the LORD pronounced all this great disaster against us? Or what *is* our iniquity? Or what *is* our sin that we have committed against the LORD our God?' 11then you shall say to them, 'Because your fathers have forsaken Me,' says the LORD; 'they have walked after other gods and have served them and worshiped them, and have forsaken Me and not kept My law. 12And you have done worse than your fathers, for behold, each one follows the dictates of his own evil heart, so that no one listens to Me. 13Therefore I will cast you out of this land into a land that you do not know, neither you nor your fathers; and there you shall serve other gods day and night, where I will not show you favor.'

God Will Restore Israel

14"Therefore behold, the days are coming," says the LORD, "that it shall no more be said, 'The LORD lives who brought up the children of Israel from the land of Egypt,' 15but, 'The LORD lives who brought up the children of Israel from the land of the north and from all the lands where He had driven them.' For I will bring them back into their land which I gave to their fathers.

16"Behold, I will send for many fishermen," says the LORD, "and they shall fish them; and afterward I will send for many hunters, and they shall hunt them from every mountain and every hill, and out of the holes of the rocks. [17]For My eyes *are* on all their ways; they are not hidden from My face, nor is their iniquity hidden from My eyes. [18]And first I will repay double for their iniquity and their sin, because they have defiled My land; they have filled My inheritance with the carcasses of their detestable and abominable idols."

[19] O LORD, my strength and my fortress,
My refuge in the day of affliction,
The Gentiles shall come to You
From the ends of the earth and say,
"Surely our fathers have inherited lies,
Worthlessness and unprofitable *things*."
[20] Will a man make gods for himself,
Which *are* not gods?

[21] "Therefore behold, I will this once cause
    them to know,
I will cause them to know
My hand and My might;
And they shall know that My name *is* the
    LORD.

Judah's Sin and Punishment

17 "The sin of Judah *is* written with a pen of iron;
        With the point of a diamond *it is* engraved
On the tablet of their heart,
And on the horns of your altars,
[2]   While their children remember
Their altars and their wooden images[a]
By the green trees on the high hills.
[3]   O My mountain in the field,
I will give as plunder your wealth, all your treasures,
And your high places of sin within all your borders.
[4]   And you, even yourself,
Shall let go of your heritage which I gave you;
And I will cause you to serve your enemies
In the land which you do not know;
For you have kindled a fire in My anger *which* shall burn forever."

[5]Thus says the LORD:

"Cursed *is* the man who trusts in man
And makes flesh his strength,
Whose heart departs from the LORD.

[6] For he shall be like a shrub in the desert,
And shall not see when good comes,
But shall inhabit the parched places in the wilderness,
In a salt land *which is* not inhabited.

[7] "Blessed *is* the man who trusts in the LORD,
And whose hope is the LORD.
[8] For he shall be like a tree planted by the waters,
Which spreads out its roots by the river,
And will not fear[a] when heat comes;
But its leaf will be green,
And will not be anxious in the year of drought,
Nor will cease from yielding fruit.

[9] "The heart *is* deceitful above all *things*,
And desperately wicked;
Who can know it?
[10] I, the LORD, search the heart,
I test the mind,
Even to give every man according to his ways,
According to the fruit of his doings.

[11] "*As* a partridge that broods but does not hatch,
So is he who gets riches, but not by right;
It will leave him in the midst of his days,
And at his end he will be a fool."

[12] A glorious high throne from the beginning
Is the place of our sanctuary.
[13] O LORD, the hope of Israel,
All who forsake You shall be ashamed.

"Those who depart from Me
Shall be written in the earth,
Because they have forsaken the LORD,
The fountain of living waters."

Jeremiah Prays for Deliverance

[14]   Heal me, O LORD, and I shall be healed;
Save me, and I shall be saved,
For You *are* my praise.
[15]   Indeed they say to me,
"Where *is* the word of the LORD?
Let it come now!"
[16]   As for me, I have not hurried away from
being a shepherd *who* follows You,
Nor have I desired the woeful day;

17:2 [a]Hebrew *Asherim,* Canaanite deities
17:8 [a]Qere and Targum read *see*.

You know what came out of my lips;
It was right there before You.

17 Do not be a terror to me;
You *are* my hope in the day of doom.

18 Let them be ashamed who persecute me,
But do not let me be put to shame;
Let them be dismayed,
But do not let me be dismayed,
Bring on them the day of doom,
And destroy them with double destruction!

Hallow the Sabbath Day

19 Thus the LORD said to me: "Go and stand in the gate of the children of the people, by which the kings of Judah come in and by which they go out, and in all the gates of Jerusalem; 20 and say to them, 'Hear the word of the LORD, you kings of Judah, and all Judah, and all the inhabitants of Jerusalem, who enter by these gates. 21 Thus says the LORD: "Take heed to yourselves, and bear no burden on the Sabbath day, nor bring *it* in by the gates of Jerusalem; 22 nor carry a burden out of your houses on the Sabbath day, nor do any work, but hallow the Sabbath day, as I commanded your fathers. 23 But they did not obey nor incline their ear, but made their neck stiff, that they might not hear nor receive instruction.

24 "And it shall be, if you heed Me carefully," says the LORD, "to bring no burden through the gates of this city on the Sabbath day, but hallow the Sabbath day, to do no work in it, 25 then shall enter the gates of this city kings and princes sitting on the throne of David, riding in chariots and on horses, they and their princes, accompanied by the men of Judah and the inhabitants of Jerusalem; and this city shall remain forever. 26 And they shall come from the cities of Judah and from the places around Jerusalem, from the land of Benjamin and from the lowland, from the mountains and from the South, bringing burnt offerings and sacrifices, grain offerings and incense, bringing sacrifices of praise to the house of the LORD.

27 "But if you will not heed Me to hallow the Sabbath day, such as not carrying a burden when entering the gates of Jerusalem on the Sabbath day, then I will kindle a fire in its gates, and it shall devour the palaces of Jerusalem, and it shall not be quenched."'"

The Potter and the Clay

18 The word which came to Jeremiah from the LORD, saying: 2 "Arise and go down to the potter's house, and there I will cause you to hear My words." 3 Then I went down to the potter's house, and there he was, making something at the wheel. 4 And the vessel that he made of clay was marred in the hand of the potter; so he made it again into another vessel, as it seemed good to the potter to make.

5 Then the word of the LORD came to me, saying: 6 "O house of Israel, can I not do with you as this potter?" says the LORD. "Look, as the clay *is* in the potter's hand, so *are* you in My hand, O house of Israel! 7 The instant I speak concerning a nation and concerning a kingdom, to pluck up, to pull down, and to destroy *it,* 8 if that nation against whom I have spoken turns from its evil, I will relent of the disaster that I thought to bring upon it. 9 And the instant I speak concerning a nation and concerning a kingdom, to build and to plant *it,* 10 if it does evil in My sight so that it does not obey My voice, then I will relent concerning the good with which I said I would benefit it.

11 "Now therefore, speak to the men of Judah and to the inhabitants of Jerusalem, saying, 'Thus says the LORD: "Behold, I am fashioning a disaster and devising a plan against you. Return now every one from his evil way, and make your ways and your doings good."'"

God's Warning Rejected

12 And they said, "That is hopeless! So we will walk according to our own plans, and we will every one obey the dictates of his evil heart."

13 Therefore thus says the LORD:

"Ask now among the Gentiles,
Who has heard such things?
The virgin of Israel has done a very horrible thing.

14 Will *a* man leave the snow water of Lebanon,
Which comes from the rock of the field?
Will the cold flowing waters be forsaken for strange waters?

15 "Because My people have forgotten Me,
They have burned incense to worthless idols.
And they have caused themselves to stumble in their ways,
From the ancient paths,
To walk in pathways and not on a highway,

16 To make their land desolate *and* a perpetual hissing;
Everyone who passes by it will be astonished
And shake his head.

17 I will scatter them as with an east wind
  before the enemy;
I will show them[a] the back and not the
  face
In the day of their calamity."

Jeremiah Persecuted

18 Then they said, "Come and let us devise
plans against Jeremiah; for the law shall not perish from the priest, nor counsel from the wise,
nor the word from the prophet. Come and let us
attack him with the tongue, and let us not give
heed to any of his words."

Teachability: To Keep Leading, Keep Learning

(Jeremiah 18:18)

If you want to keep leading, you must keep learning. Yesterday's growth cannot suffice for today. We must remain teachable and flexible. God is the Potter; we are the clay. He will do what He wishes. We must allow Him to mold us in the way He desires.

---

19 Give heed to me, O LORD,
  And listen to the voice of those who
    contend with me!
20 Shall evil be repaid for good?
  For they have dug a pit for my life.
  Remember that I stood before You
  To speak good for them,
  To turn away Your wrath from them.
21 Therefore deliver up their children to the
    famine,
  And pour out their *blood*
  By the force of the sword;
  Let their wives *become* widows
  And bereaved of their children.
  Let their men be put to death,
  Their young men *be* slain
  By the sword in battle.
22 Let a cry be heard from their houses,
  When You bring a troop suddenly upon
    them;
  For they have dug a pit to take me,
  And hidden snares for my feet.
23 Yet, LORD, You know all their counsel
  Which is against me, to slay *me*.
  Provide no atonement for their iniquity,
  Nor blot out their sin from Your sight;

But let them be overthrown before You.
  Deal *thus* with them
  In the time of Your anger.

The Sign of the Broken Flask

19 Thus says the LORD: "Go and get a potter's earthen flask, and *take* some of the elders of the people and some of the elders of the priests. 2 And go out to the Valley of the Son of Hinnom, which *is* by the entry of the Potsherd Gate; and proclaim there the words that I will tell you, 3 and say, 'Hear the word of the LORD, O kings of Judah and inhabitants of Jerusalem. Thus says the LORD of hosts, the God of Israel: "Behold, I will bring such a catastrophe on this place, that whoever hears of it, his ears will tingle.

4 "Because they have forsaken Me and made this an alien place, because they have burned incense in it to other gods whom neither they, their fathers, nor the kings of Judah have known, and have filled this place with the blood of the innocents 5 (they have also built the high places of Baal, to burn their sons with fire *for* burnt offerings to Baal, which I did not command or speak, nor did it come into My mind), 6 therefore behold, the days are coming," says the LORD, "that this place shall no more be called Tophet or the Valley of the Son of Hinnom, but the Valley of Slaughter. 7 And I will make void the counsel of Judah and Jerusalem in this place, and I will cause them to fall by the sword before their enemies and by the hands of those who seek their lives; their corpses I will give as meat for the birds of the heaven and for the beasts of the earth. 8 I will make this city desolate and a hissing; everyone who passes by it will be astonished and hiss because of all its plagues. 9 And I will cause them to eat the flesh of their sons and the flesh of their daughters, and everyone shall eat the flesh of his friend in the siege and in the desperation with which their enemies and those who seek their lives shall drive them to despair."'

10 "Then you shall break the flask in the sight of the men who go with you, 11 and say to them, 'Thus says the LORD of hosts: "Even so I will break this people and this city, as *one* breaks a potter's vessel, which cannot be made whole again; and they shall bury *them* in Tophet till *there* is no place to bury. 12 Thus I will do to this place," says the LORD, "and to its inhabitants, and make this city like Tophet. 13 And the houses of Jerusalem and the houses of the kings of Judah shall be

---

18:17 [a] Following Septuagint, Syriac, Targum, and Vulgate; Masoretic Text reads *look them in.*

defiled like the place of Tophet, because of all the houses on whose roofs they have burned incense to all the host of heaven, and poured out drink offerings to other gods.'"'"

14Then Jeremiah came from Tophet, where the LORD had sent him to prophesy; and he stood in the court of the Lord's house and said to all the people, 15"Thus says the LORD of hosts, the God of Israel: 'Behold, I will bring on this city and on all her towns all the doom that I have pronounced against it, because they have stiffened their necks that they might not hear My words.'"

The Word of God to Pashhur

20 Now Pashhur the son of Immer, the priest who *was* also chief governor in the house of the LORD, heard that Jeremiah prophesied these things. 2Then Pashhur struck Jeremiah the prophet, and put him in the stocks that *were* in the high gate of Benjamin, which *was* by the house of the LORD.

3And it happened on the next day that Pashhur brought Jeremiah out of the stocks. Then Jeremiah said to him, "The LORD has not called your name Pashhur, but Magor-Missabib.a 4For

thus says the LORD: 'Behold, I will make you a terror to yourself and to all your friends; and they shall fall by the sword of their enemies, and your eyes shall see *it*. I will give all Judah into the hand of the king of Babylon, and he shall carry them captive to Babylon and slay them with the sword. 5Moreover I will deliver all the wealth of this city, all its produce, and all its precious things; all the treasures of the kings of Judah I will give into the hand of their enemies, who will plunder them, seize them, and carry them to Babylon. 6And you, Pashhur, and all who dwell in your house, shall go into captivity. You shall go to Babylon, and there you shall die, and be buried there, you and all your friends, to whom you have prophesied lies.'"

Jeremiah's Unpopular Ministry

7 O LORD, You induced me, and I was
   persuaded;
   You are stronger than I, and have
   prevailed.
   I am in derision daily;
   Everyone mocks me.

20:3 aLiterally *Fear on Every Side*

Convictions: Turning Defeat into Dividends

(Jeremiah 20:1–18)

Every leader experiences both good and bad days. Even God's greatest leaders become discouraged.

Jeremiah 20 allows us to see into the heart of a great leader. Jeremiah complains to God in the first ten verses. He praises God for his victories in the next four verses. And in the next five verses he curses the day he was born.

The key question on *your* bad day is: Are you going to give up or get up? And how *can* you get up?

1. **Rise above self-pity.** Failure is an attitude, not just an outcome.
2. **Think positively.** Success comes by going from failure to failure without losing enthusiasm.
3. **Learn from your experiences.** Failure isn't failure unless you learn nothing from it.
4. **Seek alternatives.** All successful leaders vary their approaches.
5. **Develop a sense of humor.** Laughter is the shortest distance between two people and the fastest way to get perspective.
6. **Be realistic.** The first job of the leader is to define reality.
7. **Establish new goals.** Failure is an opportunity to begin again, but more intelligently.
8. **Develop a passion.** Your own resolution to succeed counts for more than anything else.
9. **Broaden your base of support.** No single venture should support your entire emotional life.
10. **Separate your self-worth from your performance.** A positive self-image prepares you for success.

8 For when I spoke, I cried out;
   I shouted, "Violence and plunder!"
   Because the word of the LORD was made
      to me
   A reproach and a derision daily.
9 Then I said, "I will not make mention of
      Him,
   Nor speak anymore in His name."
   But *His word* was in my heart like a
      burning fire
   Shut up in my bones;
   I was weary of holding *it* back,
   And I could not.
10 For I heard many mocking:
   "Fear on every side!"
   "Report," *they say,* "and we will report it!"
   All my acquaintances watched for my
      stumbling, *saying,*
   "Perhaps he can be induced;
   Then we will prevail against him,
   And we will take our revenge on him."

11 But the LORD *is* with me as a mighty,
      awesome One.
   Therefore my persecutors will stumble,
      and will not prevail.
   They will be greatly ashamed, for they will
      not prosper.
   Their everlasting confusion will never be
      forgotten.
12 But, O LORD of hosts,
   You who test the righteous,
   And see the mind and heart,
   Let me see Your vengeance on them;
   For I have pleaded my cause before You.

13 Sing to the LORD! Praise the LORD!
   For He has delivered the life of the poor
   From the hand of evildoers.

14 Cursed *be* the day in which I was born!
   Let the day not be blessed in which my
      mother bore me!
15 Let the man *be* cursed
   Who brought news to my father, saying,
   "A male child has been born to you!"
   Making him very glad.
16 And let that man be like the cities
   Which the LORD overthrew, and did not
      relent;
   Let him hear the cry in the morning
   And the shouting at noon,
17 Because he did not kill me from the
      womb,
   That my mother might have been my
      grave,

   And her womb always enlarged *with me.*
18 Why did I come forth from the womb to
      see labor and sorrow,
   That my days should be consumed with
      shame?

Jerusalem's Doom Is Sealed

21 The word which came to Jeremiah from the LORD when King Zedekiah sent to him Pashhur the son of Melchiah, and Zephaniah the son of Maaseiah, the priest, saying, [2]"Please inquire of the LORD for us, for Nebuchadnezzar[a] king of Babylon makes war against us. Perhaps the LORD will deal with us according to all His wonderful works, that *the king* may go away from us."

[3]Then Jeremiah said to them, "Thus you shall say to Zedekiah, "Thus says the LORD God of Israel: "Behold, I will turn back the weapons of war that *are* in your hands, with which you fight against the king of Babylon and the Chaldeans[a] who besiege you outside the walls; and I will assemble them in the midst of this city. [5]I Myself will fight against you with an outstretched hand and with a strong arm, even in anger and fury and great wrath. [6]I will strike the inhabitants of this city, both man and beast; they shall die of a great pestilence. [7]And afterward," says the LORD, "I will deliver Zedekiah king of Judah, his servants and the people, and such as are left in this city from the pestilence and the sword and the famine, into the hand of Nebuchadnezzar king of Babylon, into the hand of their enemies, and into the hand of those who seek their life; and he shall strike them with the edge of the sword. He shall not spare them, or have pity or mercy."'

[8]"Now you shall say to this people, 'Thus says the LORD: "Behold, I set before you the way of life and the way of death. [9]He who remains in this city shall die by the sword, by famine, and by pestilence; but he who goes out and defects to the Chaldeans who besiege you, he shall live, and his life shall be as a prize to him. [10]For I have set My face against this city for adversity and not for good," says the LORD. "It shall be given into the hand of the king of Babylon, and he shall burn it with fire."'

Message to the House of David

[11]"And concerning the house of the king of Judah, *say,* 'Hear the word of the LORD, [12]O house of David! Thus says the LORD:

21:2 [a]Hebrew *Nebuchadrezzar,* and so elsewhere
21:4 [a]Or *Babylonians*

"Execute judgment in the morning;
And deliver *him who is* plundered
Out of the hand of the oppressor,
Lest My fury go forth like fire
And burn so that no one can quench *it,*
Because of the evil of your doings.

13 "Behold, I *am* against you, O inhabitant of
the valley,
And rock of the plain," says the LORD,
"Who say, 'Who shall come down against us?
Or who shall enter our dwellings?'
14 But I will punish you according to the
fruit of your doings," says the LORD;
"I will kindle a fire in its forest,
And it shall devour all things around it."'"

22 Thus says the LORD: "Go down to
the house of the king of Judah, and
there speak this word, ²and say, 'Hear
the word of the LORD, O king of Judah, you who
sit on the throne of David, you and your servants
and your people who enter these gates! ³Thus says
the LORD: "Execute judgment and righteousness,
and deliver the plundered out of the hand of the
oppressor. Do no wrong and do no violence to
the stranger, the fatherless, or the widow, nor shed
innocent blood in this place. ⁴For if you indeed
do this thing, then shall enter the gates of this
house, riding on horses and in chariots, accompanied by servants and people, kings who sit on the
throne of David. ⁵But if you will not hear these
words, I swear by Myself," says the LORD, "that
this house shall become a desolation."'"
⁶For thus says the LORD to the house of the
king of Judah:

The Measure of
a Man Is What He
Does with Power

(Jeremiah 22:6–30)

Leaders who use their power or influence
for personal gain offend God. Jeremiah
cautions leaders who build their own "kingdoms" but fail to exhibit wisdom. He warns
them against preoccupation with their own
welfare rather than the people God has given
them. God considers such misuse of power
grounds for removal.

"You *are* Gilead to Me,
The head of Lebanon;
Yet I surely will make you a wilderness,
Cities *which* are not inhabited.
7 I will prepare destroyers against you,
Everyone with his weapons;
They shall cut down your choice cedars
And cast *them* into the fire.

⁸And many nations will pass by this city; and
everyone will say to his neighbor, 'Why has the
LORD done so to this great city?' ⁹Then they will
answer, 'Because they have forsaken the covenant
of the LORD their God, and worshiped other
gods and served them.'"

10 Weep not for the dead, nor bemoan him;
Weep bitterly for him who goes away,
For he shall return no more,
Nor see his native country.

Message to the Sons of Josiah

11For thus says the LORD concerning Shallum[a] the son of Josiah, king of Judah, who
reigned instead of Josiah his father, who went
from this place: "He shall not return here anymore, 12but he shall die in the place where they
have led him captive, and shall see this land no
more.

13 "Woe to him who builds his house by
unrighteousness
And his chambers by injustice,
Who uses his neighbor's service without
wages
And gives him nothing for his work,
14 Who says, 'I will build myself a wide
house with spacious chambers,
And cut out windows for it,
Paneling *it* with cedar
And painting *it* with vermilion.'
15 "Shall you reign because you enclose
yourself in cedar?
Did not your father eat and drink,
And do justice and righteousness?
Then *it was* well with him.
16 He judged the cause of the poor and
needy;
Then *it was* well.
Was not this knowing Me?" says the
LORD.
17 "Yet your eyes and your heart *are* for
nothing but your covetousness,

22:11 [a]Also called *Jehoahaz*

For shedding innocent blood,
And practicing oppression and violence."

[18]Therefore thus says the LORD concerning Jehoiakim the son of Josiah, king of Judah:

"They shall not lament for him,
Saying, 'Alas, my brother!' or 'Alas, my sister!'
They shall not lament for him,
Saying, 'Alas, master!' or 'Alas, his glory!'
[19] He shall be buried with the burial of a donkey,
Dragged and cast out beyond the gates of Jerusalem.

[20] "Go up to Lebanon, and cry out,
And lift up your voice in Bashan;
Cry from Abarim,
For all your lovers are destroyed.
[21] I spoke to you in your prosperity,
But you said, 'I will not hear.'
This *has been* your manner from your youth,
That you did not obey My voice.
[22] The wind shall eat up all your rulers,
And your lovers shall go into captivity;
Surely then you will be ashamed and humiliated
For all your wickedness.
[23] O inhabitant of Lebanon,
Making your nest in the cedars,
How gracious will you be when pangs come upon you,
Like the pain of a woman in labor?

Message to Coniah

[24]"*As* I live," says the LORD, "though Coniah[a] the son of Jehoiakim, king of Judah, were the signet on My right hand, yet I would pluck you off; [25]and I will give you into the hand of those who seek your life, and into the hand *of those* whose face you fear—the hand of Nebuchadnezzar king of Babylon and the hand of the Chaldeans. [26]So I will cast you out, and your mother who bore you, into another country where you were not born; and there you shall die. [27]But to the land to which they desire to return, there they shall not return.

[28] "Is this man Coniah a despised, broken idol—
A vessel in which *is* no pleasure?
Why are they cast out, he and his descendants,
And cast into a land which they do not know?

[29] O earth, earth, earth,
Hear the word of the LORD!
[30] Thus says the LORD:
'Write this man down as childless,
A man *who* shall not prosper in his days;
For none of his descendants shall prosper,
Sitting on the throne of David,
And ruling anymore in Judah.'"

The Branch of Righteousness

23 "Woe to the shepherds who destroy and scatter the sheep of My pasture!" says the LORD. [2]Therefore thus says the LORD God of Israel against the shepherds who feed My people: "You have scattered My flock, driven them away, and not attended to them. Behold, I will attend to you for the evil of your doings," says the LORD. [3]"But I will gather the remnant of My flock out of all countries where I have driven them, and bring them back to their folds; and they shall be fruitful and increase. [4]I will set up shepherds over them who will feed them; and they shall fear no more, nor be dismayed, nor shall they be lacking," says the LORD.

[5] "Behold, *the* days are coming," says the LORD,
"That I will raise to David a Branch of righteousness;
A King shall reign and prosper,
And execute judgment and righteousness in the earth.
[6] In His days Judah will be saved,
And Israel will dwell safely;
Now this *is* His name by which He will be called:

THE LORD OUR RIGHTEOUSNESS.[a]

[7]"Therefore, behold, *the* days are coming," says the LORD, "that they shall no longer say, 'As the LORD lives who brought up the children of Israel from the land of Egypt,' [8]but, 'As the LORD lives who brought up and led the descendants of the house of Israel from the north country and from all the countries where I had driven them.' And they shall dwell in their own land."

False Prophets and Empty Oracles

[9] My heart within me is broken
Because of the prophets;
All my bones shake.
I am like a drunken man,

22:24 [a]Also called *Jeconiah* and *Jehoiachin*
23:6 [a]Hebrew *YHWH Tsidkenu*

The Changing of the Guard:
When Leaders Need to Be Replaced

(Jeremiah 23:1–16)

God does not hesitate to remove poor or wicked leaders—and beyond their removal, God pronounces His judgment on them.

Jeremiah 23 supplies us with a good evaluation tool to recognize what God values in a leader and what constitutes grounds for dismissal and replacement. Study the characteristics of the kind of leaders God promised to replace:

1. Leaders who destroy their people instead of developing them (v. 1)
2. Leaders who scatter their people instead of uniting them in a cause (v. 1)
3. Leaders who abandon their people in fear instead of remaining responsible (v. 4)
4. Leaders who act in self-serving and unjust ways instead of standing for the truth (v. 10)
5. Leaders who lie, as though there were no God (v. 11)
6. Leaders who lead their people astray instead of guiding them into security (v. 13)
7. Leaders who foster evil and deceit instead of integrity and honesty (v. 14)
8. Leaders who fill people with false hope rather than speaking God's Word (v. 16)

God didn't merely threaten to remove bad leaders; He also promised to raise up a Righteous Branch from the line of David to replace these artificial leaders. Today we know that Righteous Branch has a beautiful name: Jesus Christ!

And like a man whom wine has
   overcome,
Because of the LORD,
And because of His holy words.
10 For the land is full of adulterers;
For because of a curse the land mourns.
The pleasant places of the wilderness are
   dried up.
Their course of life is evil,
And their might *is* not right.

11 "For both prophet and priest are profane;
Yes, in My house I have found their
   wickedness," says the LORD.
12 "Therefore their way shall be to them
Like slippery *ways;*
In the darkness they shall be driven on
And fall in them;
For I will bring disaster on them,
The year of their punishment," says the
   LORD.
13 "And I have seen folly in the prophets of
   Samaria:
They prophesied by Baal
And caused My people Israel to err.
14 Also I have seen a horrible thing in the
   prophets of Jerusalem:
They commit adultery and walk in lies;

They also strengthen the hands of evildoers,
So that no one turns back from his
   wickedness.
All of them are like Sodom to Me,
And her inhabitants like Gomorrah.

15 "Therefore thus says the LORD of hosts
concerning the prophets:

'Behold, I will feed them with wormwood,
And make them drink the water of gall;
For from the prophets of Jerusalem
Profaneness has gone out into all the land.'"

16 Thus says the LORD of hosts:

"Do not listen to the words of the prophets
   who prophesy to you.
They make you worthless;
They speak a vision of their own heart,
Not from the mouth of the LORD.
17 They continually say to those who despise
   Me,
'The LORD has said, "You shall have
   peace"';
And *to* everyone who walks according to
   the dictates of his own heart, they say,
'No evil shall come upon you.'"

Vision: God-Given or Man-Made?

(Jeremiah 23:13–40)

How do we recognize a vision as God-given or as man-made? First, does it align with the Word of God, the nature of God, and the ways of God? Second, does it advance God's kingdom, and not necessarily the leader's? Third, does it bless other people? Finally, does the vision stand the test of time?

18 For who has stood in the counsel of the LORD,
And has perceived and heard His word?
Who has marked His word and heard *it*?
19 Behold, a whirlwind of the LORD has gone forth in fury—
A violent whirlwind!
It will fall violently on the head of the wicked.
20 The anger of the LORD will not turn back
Until He has executed and performed the thoughts of His heart.
In the latter days you will understand it perfectly.

21 "I have not sent these prophets, yet they ran.
I have not spoken to them, yet they prophesied.
22 But if they had stood in My counsel,
And had caused My people to hear My words,
Then they would have turned them from their evil way
And from the evil of their doings.

23 "*Am* I a God near at hand," says the LORD,
"And not a God afar off?
24 Can anyone hide himself in secret places,
So I shall not see him?" says the LORD;
"Do I not fill heaven and earth?" says the LORD.

25 "I have heard what the prophets have said who prophesy lies in My name, saying, 'I have dreamed, I have dreamed!' 26 How long will *this* be in the heart of the prophets who prophesy lies? Indeed *they are* prophets of the deceit of their own heart, 27 who try to make My people forget My name by their dreams which everyone tells his neighbor, as their fathers forgot My name for Baal.

28 "The prophet who has a dream, let him tell a dream;
And he who has My word, let him speak My word faithfully.
What *is* the chaff to the wheat?" says the LORD.
29 "*Is* not My word like a fire?" says the LORD,
"And like a hammer *that* breaks the rock in pieces?

30 "Therefore behold, I *am* against the prophets," says the LORD, "who steal My words every one from his neighbor. 31 Behold, I *am* against the prophets," says the LORD, "who use their tongues and say, 'He says.' 32 Behold, I *am* against those who prophesy false dreams," says the LORD, "and tell them, and cause My people to err by their lies and by their recklessness. Yet I did not send them or command them; therefore they shall not profit this people at all," says the LORD.

33 "So when these people or the prophet or the priest ask you, saying, 'What is the oracle of the LORD?' you shall then say to them, 'What oracle?'[a] I will even forsake you," says the LORD. 34 "And *as for* the prophet and the priest and the people who say, 'The oracle of the LORD!' I will even punish that man and his house. 35 Thus every one of you shall say to his neighbor, and every one to his brother, 'What has the LORD answered?' and, 'What has the LORD spoken?' 36 And the oracle of the LORD you shall mention no more. For every man's word will be his oracle, for you have perverted the words of the living God, the LORD of hosts, our God. 37 Thus you shall say to the prophet, 'What has the LORD answered you?' and, 'What has the LORD spoken?' 38 But since you say, 'The oracle of the LORD!' therefore thus says the LORD: 'Because you say this word, "The oracle of the LORD!" and I have sent to you, saying, "Do not say, 'The oracle of the LORD!'" 39 therefore behold, I, even I, will utterly forget you and forsake you, and the city that I gave you and your fathers, and *will cast you* out of My presence. 40 And I will bring an everlasting reproach upon you, and a perpetual shame, which shall not be forgotten.'"

23:33 [a]Septuagint, Targum, and Vulgate read '*You are the burden*.'

The Sign of Two Baskets of Figs

24 The LORD showed me, and there were two baskets of figs set before the temple of the LORD, after Nebuchadnezzar king of Babylon had carried away captive Jeconiah the son of Jehoiakim, king of Judah, and the princes of Judah with the craftsmen and smiths, from Jerusalem, and had brought them to Babylon. ²One basket *had* very good figs, like the figs *that are* first ripe; and the other basket *had* very bad figs which could not be eaten, they were so bad. ³Then the LORD said to me, "What do you see, Jeremiah?"

And I said, "Figs, the good figs, very good; and the bad, very bad, which cannot be eaten, they are so bad."

⁴Again the word of the LORD came to me, saying, ⁵"Thus says the LORD, the God of Israel: 'Like these good figs, so will I acknowledge those who are carried away captive from Judah, whom I have sent out of this place for *their own* good, into the land of the Chaldeans. ⁶For I will set My eyes on them for good, and I will bring them back to this land; I will build them and not pull *them* down, and I will plant them and not pluck *them* up. ⁷Then I will give them a heart to know Me, that I *am* the LORD; and they shall be My people, and I will be their God, for they shall return to Me with their whole heart.

⁸'And as the bad figs which cannot be eaten, they are so bad'—surely thus says the LORD—'so will I give up Zedekiah the king of Judah, his princes, the residue of Jerusalem who remain in this land, and those who dwell in the land of Egypt. ⁹I will deliver them to trouble into all the kingdoms of the earth, for *their* harm, *to be* a reproach and a byword, a taunt and a curse, in all places where I shall drive them. ¹⁰And I will send the sword, the famine, and the pestilence among them, till they are consumed from the land that I gave to them and their fathers.'"

Seventy Years of Desolation

25 The word that came to Jeremiah concerning all the people of Judah, in the fourth year of Jehoiakim the son of Josiah, king of Judah (which *was* the first year of Nebuchadnezzar king of Babylon), ²which Jeremiah the prophet spoke to all the people of Judah and to all the inhabitants of Jerusalem, saying: ³"From the thirteenth year of Josiah the son of Amon, king of Judah, even to this day, this *is* the twenty-third year in which the word of the LORD has come to me; and I have spoken to you, rising early and speaking, but you

have not listened. ⁴And the LORD has sent to you all His servants the prophets, rising early and sending *them,* but you have not listened nor inclined your ear to hear. ⁵They said, 'Repent now everyone of his evil way and his evil doings, and dwell in the land that the LORD has given to you and your fathers forever and ever. ⁶Do not go after other gods to serve them and worship them, and do not provoke Me to anger with the works of your hands; and I will not harm you.' ⁷Yet you have not listened to Me," says the LORD, "that you might provoke Me to anger with the works of your hands to your own hurt.

⁸"Therefore thus says the LORD of hosts: 'Because you have not heard My words, ⁹behold, I will send and take all the families of the north,' says the LORD, 'and Nebuchadnezzar the king of Babylon, My servant, and will bring them against this land, against its inhabitants, and against these nations all around, and will utterly destroy them, and make them an astonishment, a hissing, and perpetual desolations. ¹⁰Moreover I will take from them the voice of mirth and the voice of gladness, the voice of the bridegroom and the voice of the bride, the sound of the millstones and the light of the lamp. ¹¹And this whole land shall be a desolation *and* an astonishment, and these nations shall serve the king of Babylon seventy years.

¹²'Then it will come to pass, when seventy years are completed, *that* I will punish the king of Babylon and that nation, the land of the Chaldeans, for their iniquity,' says the LORD; 'and I will make it a perpetual desolation. ¹³So I will bring on that land all My words which I have pronounced against it, all that is written in this book, which Jeremiah has prophesied concerning all the nations. ¹⁴(For many nations and great kings shall be served by them also; and I will repay them according to their deeds and according to the works of their own hands.)'"

Judgment on the Nations

¹⁵For thus says the LORD God of Israel to me: "Take this wine cup of fury from My hand, and cause all the nations, to whom I send you, to drink it. ¹⁶And they will drink and stagger and go mad because of the sword that I will send among them."

¹⁷Then I took the cup from the LORD's hand, and made all the nations drink, to whom the LORD had sent me: ¹⁸Jerusalem and the cities of Judah, its kings and its princes, to make them a desolation, an astonishment, a hissing, and a curse, as *it is* this day; ¹⁹Pharaoh king of Egypt, his servants, his princes, and all his people; ²⁰all the

mixed multitude, all the kings of the land of Uz, all the kings of the land of the Philistines (namely, Ashkelon, Gaza, Ekron, and the remnant of Ashdod); 21Edom, Moab, and the people of Ammon; 22all the kings of Tyre, all the kings of Sidon, and the kings of the coastlands which *are* across the sea; 23Dedan, Tema, Buz, and all *who are* in the farthest corners; 24all the kings of Arabia and all the kings of the mixed multitude who dwell in the desert; 25all the kings of Zimri, all the kings of Elam, and all the kings of the Medes; 26all the kings of the north, far and near, one with another; and all the kingdoms of the world which *are* on the face of the earth. Also the king of Sheshach[a] shall drink after them.

27"Therefore you shall say to them, 'Thus says the LORD of hosts, the God of Israel: "Drink, be drunk, and vomit! Fall and rise no more, because of the sword which I will send among you." ' 28And it shall be, if they refuse to take the cup from your hand to drink, then you shall say to them, 'Thus says the LORD of hosts: "You shall certainly drink! 29For behold, I begin to bring calamity on the city which is called by My name, and should you be utterly unpunished? You shall not be unpunished, for I will call for a sword on all the inhabitants of the earth," says the LORD of hosts.'

30"Therefore prophesy against them all these words, and say to them:

'The LORD will roar from on high,
And utter His voice from His holy
   habitation;
He will roar mightily against His fold.
He will give a shout, as those who tread
   the grapes,
Against all the inhabitants of the earth.
31 A noise will come to the ends of the
   earth—
For the LORD has a controversy with the
   nations;
He will plead His case with all flesh.
He will give those *who are* wicked to the
   sword,' says the LORD."

32Thus says the LORD of hosts:

"Behold, disaster shall go forth
   From nation to nation,
And a great whirlwind shall be raised up
   From the farthest parts of the earth.

33"And at that day the slain of the LORD shall be from *one* end of the earth even to the *other* end of the earth. They shall not be lamented, or gath-ered, or buried; they shall become refuse on the ground.

34 "Wail, shepherds, and cry!
Roll about *in the ashes,*
You leaders of the flock!
For the days of your slaughter and your
   dispersions are fulfilled;
You shall fall like a precious vessel.
35 And the shepherds will have no way to
   flee,
Nor the leaders of the flock to escape.
36 A voice of the cry of the shepherds,
And a wailing of the leaders to the flock
   will be heard.
For the LORD has plundered their pasture,
37 And the peaceful dwellings are cut down
Because of the fierce anger of the LORD.
38 He has left His lair like the lion;
For their land is desolate
Because of the fierceness of the Oppressor,
And because of His fierce anger."

Jeremiah Saved from Death

26 In the beginning of the reign of Jehoiakim the son of Josiah, king of Judah, this word came from the LORD, saying, 2"Thus says the LORD: 'Stand in the court of the LORD's house, and speak to all the cities of Judah, which come to worship *in* the LORD's house, all the words that I command you to speak to them. Do not diminish a word. 3Perhaps everyone will listen and turn from his evil way, that I may relent concerning the calamity which I purpose to bring on them because of the evil of their doings.' 4And you shall say to them, 'Thus says the LORD: "If you will not listen to Me, to walk in My law which I have set before you, 5to heed the words of My servants the prophets whom I sent to you, both rising up early and sending *them* (but you have not heeded), 6then I will make this house like Shiloh, and will make this city a curse to all the nations of the earth." ' "

7So the priests and the prophets and all the people heard Jeremiah speaking these words in the house of the LORD. 8Now it happened, when Jeremiah had made an end of speaking all that the LORD had commanded *him* to speak to all the people, that the priests and the prophets and all the people seized him, saying, "You will surely die! 9Why have you prophesied in the name of the LORD, saying, 'This house shall be like Shiloh, and this city shall be desolate, without an

---

25:26 [a]A code word for Babylon (compare 51:41)

inhabitant'?" And all the people were gathered against Jeremiah in the house of the LORD.

[10]When the princes of Judah heard these things, they came up from the king's house to the house of the LORD and sat down in the entry of the New Gate of the LORD's *house.* [11]And the priests and the prophets spoke to the princes and all the people, saying, "This man deserves to die! For he has prophesied against this city, as you have heard with your ears."

[12]Then Jeremiah spoke to all the princes and all the people, saying: "The LORD sent me to prophesy against this house and against this city with all the words that you have heard. [13]Now therefore, amend your ways and your doings, and obey the voice of the LORD your God; then the LORD will relent concerning the doom that He has pronounced against you. [14]As for me, here I am, in your hand; do with me as seems good and proper to you. [15]But know for certain that if you put me to death, you will surely bring innocent blood on yourselves, on this city, and on its inhabitants; for truly the LORD has sent me to you to speak all these words in your hearing."

[16]So the princes and all the people said to the priests and the prophets, "This man does not deserve to die. For he has spoken to us in the name of the LORD our God."

[17]Then certain of the elders of the land rose up and spoke to all the assembly of the people, saying: [18]"Micah of Moresheth prophesied in the days of Hezekiah king of Judah, and spoke to all the people of Judah, saying, 'Thus says the LORD of hosts:

> "Zion shall be plowed *like* a field,
> Jerusalem shall become heaps of ruins,
> And the mountain of the temple[a]
> Like the bare hills of the forest." '[b]

[19]Did Hezekiah king of Judah and all Judah ever put him to death? Did he not fear the LORD and seek the LORD's favor? And the LORD relented concerning the doom which He had pronounced against them. But we are doing great evil against ourselves."

[20]Now there was also a man who prophesied in the name of the LORD, Urijah the son of Shemaiah of Kirjath Jearim, who prophesied against this city and against this land according to all the words of Jeremiah. [21]And when Jehoiakim the king, with all his mighty men and all the princes, heard his words, the king sought to put him to death; but when Urijah heard *it,* he was afraid and fled, and went to Egypt. [22]Then Jehoiakim the king sent men to Egypt: Elnathan the son of Achbor, and *other* men *who went* with him to Egypt. [23]And they brought Urijah from Egypt and brought him to Jehoiakim the king, who killed him with the sword and cast his dead body into the graves of the common people.

[24]Nevertheless the hand of Ahikam the son of Shaphan was with Jeremiah, so that they should not give him into the hand of the people to put him to death.

Symbol of the Bonds and Yokes

27 In the beginning of the reign of Jehoiakim[a] the son of Josiah, king of Judah, this word came to Jeremiah from the LORD, saying,[b] [2]"Thus says the LORD to me: 'Make for yourselves bonds and yokes, and put them on your neck, [3]and send them to the king of Edom, the king of Moab, the king of the Ammonites, the king of Tyre, and the king of Sidon, by the hand of the messengers who come to Jerusalem to Zedekiah king of Judah. [4]And command them to say to their masters, "Thus says the LORD of hosts, the God of Israel—thus you shall say to your masters: [5]'I have made the earth, the man and the beast that *are* on the ground, by My great power and by My outstretched arm, and have given it to whom it seemed proper to Me. [6]And now I have given all these lands into the hand of Nebuchadnezzar the king of Babylon, My servant; and the beasts of the field I have also given him to serve him. [7]So all nations shall serve him and his son and his son's son, until the time of his land comes; and then many nations and great kings shall make him serve them. [8]And it shall be, *that* the nation and kingdom which will not serve Nebuchadnezzar the king of Babylon, and which will not put its neck under the yoke of the king of Babylon, that nation I will punish,' says the LORD, 'with the sword, the famine, and the pestilence, until I have consumed them by his hand. [9]Therefore do not listen to your prophets, your diviners, your dreamers, your soothsayers, or your sorcerers, who speak to you, saying, "You shall not serve the king of Babylon." [10]For they prophesy a lie to you, to remove you far from your land; and I will drive you out, and you will perish. [11]But the nations that bring their necks under the yoke of the king of Babylon and serve him, I will let them remain in their own land,' says the LORD, 'and they shall till it and dwell in it.' " ' "

26:18 [a]Literally *house* [b]Compare Micah 3:12
27:1 [a]Following Masoretic Text, Targum, and Vulgate; some Hebrew manuscripts, Arabic, and Syriac read *Zedekiah* (compare 27:3, 12; 28:1). [b]Septuagint omits verse 1.

God Uses the Unrighteous Leader to Prune the Righteous

(Jeremiah 27:1–8)

While God never ordains false leaders, He may use wicked leaders—even self-appointed ones—to perform His purposes. What an irony! God warns against false leaders and simultaneously uses an evil king (the Babylonian Nebuchadnezzar) to prune the people He calls His own. Jeremiah 27 helps us to see an important truth regarding how God carries out His will in history:

1. **His Moral Will**

   God instructs us to lead with a heart of integrity. We must not lead without His approval. But it is our choice. We learn this lesson from the false prophets of Jeremiah's day.

2. **His Sovereign Will**

   God may choose to use any leader to accomplish His purposes. It is God's choice. We learn this lesson from King Nebuchadnezzar of Babylon.

¹²I also spoke to Zedekiah king of Judah according to all these words, saying, "Bring your necks under the yoke of the king of Babylon, and serve him and his people, and live! ¹³Why will you die, you and your people, by the sword, by the famine, and by the pestilence, as the LORD has spoken against the nation that will not serve the king of Babylon? ¹⁴Therefore do not listen to the words of the prophets who speak to you, saying, 'You shall not serve the king of Babylon,' for they prophesy a lie to you; ¹⁵for I have not sent them," says the LORD, "yet they prophesy a lie in My name, that I may drive you out, and that you may perish, you and the prophets who prophesy to you."

¹⁶Also I spoke to the priests and to all this people, saying, "Thus says the LORD: 'Do not listen to the words of your prophets who prophesy to you, saying, "Behold, the vessels of the LORD's house will now shortly be brought back from Babylon"; for they prophesy a lie to you. ¹⁷Do not listen to them; serve the king of Babylon, and live! Why should this city be laid waste? ¹⁸But if they *are* prophets, and if the word of the

LORD is with them, let them now make intercession to the LORD of hosts, that the vessels which are left in the house of the LORD, *in* the house of the king of Judah, and at Jerusalem, do not go to Babylon.'

¹⁹"For thus says the LORD of hosts concerning the pillars, concerning the Sea, concerning the carts, and concerning the remainder of the vessels that remain in this city, ²⁰which Nebuchadnezzar king of Babylon did not take, when he carried away captive Jeconiah the son of Jehoiakim, king of Judah, from Jerusalem to Babylon, and all the nobles of Judah and Jerusalem— ²¹yes, thus says the LORD of hosts, the God of Israel, concerning the vessels that remain in the house of the LORD, and in the house of the king of Judah and of Jerusalem: ²²'They shall be carried to Babylon, and there they shall be until the day that I visit them,' says the LORD. 'Then I will bring them up and restore them to this place.'"

Hananiah's Falsehood and Doom

28 And it happened in the same year, at the beginning of the reign of Zedekiah king of Judah, in the fourth year *and* in the fifth month, *that* Hananiah the son of Azur the prophet, who *was* from Gibeon, spoke to me in the house of the LORD in the presence of the priests and of all the people, saying, ²"Thus speaks the LORD of hosts, the God of Israel, saying: 'I have broken the yoke of the king of Babylon. ³Within two full years I will bring back to this place all the vessels of the LORD's house, that Nebuchadnezzar king of Babylon took away from this place and carried to Babylon. ⁴And I will bring back to this place Jeconiah the son of Jehoiakim, king of Judah, with all the captives of Judah who went to Babylon,' says the LORD, 'for I will break the yoke of the king of Babylon.'"

⁵Then the prophet Jeremiah spoke to the prophet Hananiah in the presence of the priests and in the presence of all the people who stood in the house of the LORD, ⁶and the prophet Jeremiah said, "Amen! The LORD do so; the LORD perform your words which you have prophesied, to bring back the vessels of the LORD's house and all who were carried away captive, from Babylon to this place. ⁷Nevertheless hear now this word that I speak in your hearing and in the hearing of all the people: ⁸The prophets who have been before me and before you of old prophesied against many countries and great kingdoms—of war and disaster and pestilence. ⁹As for the prophet who prophesies of peace, when the word of the prophet comes to pass, the

prophet will be known *as* one whom the LORD has truly sent."

¹⁰Then Hananiah the prophet took the yoke off the prophet Jeremiah's neck and broke it. ¹¹And Hananiah spoke in the presence of all the people, saying, "Thus says the LORD: 'Even so I will break the yoke of Nebuchadnezzar king of Babylon from the neck of all nations within the space of two full years.'" And the prophet Jeremiah went his way.

¹²Now the word of the LORD came to Jeremiah, after Hananiah the prophet had broken the yoke from the neck of the prophet Jeremiah, saying, ¹³"Go and tell Hananiah, saying, 'Thus says the LORD: "You have broken the yokes of wood, but you have made in their place yokes of iron." ¹⁴For thus says the LORD of hosts, the God of Israel: "I have put a yoke of iron on the neck of all these nations, that they may serve Nebuchadnezzar king of Babylon; and they shall serve him. I have given him the beasts of the field also."'"

¹⁵Then the prophet Jeremiah said to Hananiah the prophet, "Hear now, Hananiah, the LORD has not sent you, but you make this people trust in a lie. ¹⁶Therefore thus says the LORD: 'Behold, I will cast you from the face of the earth. This year you shall die, because you have taught rebellion against the LORD.'"

¹⁷So Hananiah the prophet died the same year in the seventh month.

Jeremiah's Letter to the Captives

29 Now these *are* the words of the letter that Jeremiah the prophet sent from Jerusalem to the remainder of the elders who were carried away captive—to the priests, the prophets, and all the people whom Nebuchadnezzar had carried away captive from Jerusalem to Babylon. ²(This happened after Jeconiah the king, the queen mother, the eunuchs, the princes of Judah and Jerusalem, the craftsmen, and the smiths had departed from Jerusalem.) ³*The letter was sent* by the hand of Elasah the son of Shaphan, and Gemariah the son of Hilkiah, whom Zedekiah king of Judah sent to Babylon, to Nebuchadnezzar king of Babylon, saying,

4   Thus says the LORD of hosts, the God of Israel, to all who were carried away captive, whom I have caused to be carried away from Jerusalem to Babylon:

5   Build houses and dwell *in them;* plant gardens and eat their fruit. ⁶Take wives and beget sons and daughters; and take wives for your sons and give your daughters to husbands, so that they may bear sons and daughters—that you may be increased there, and not diminished. ⁷And seek the peace of the city where I have caused you to be carried away captive, and pray to the LORD for it; for in its peace you will have peace. ⁸For thus says the LORD of hosts, the God of Israel: Do not let your prophets and your diviners who are in your midst deceive you, nor listen to your dreams which you cause to be dreamed. ⁹For they prophesy falsely to you in My name; I have not sent them, says the LORD.

10   For thus says the LORD: After seventy years are completed at Babylon, I will visit you and perform My good word toward you, and cause you to return to this place. ¹¹For I know the thoughts that I think toward you, says the LORD, thoughts of peace and not of evil, to give you a future and a hope. ¹²Then you will call upon Me and go and pray to Me, and I will listen to you. ¹³And you will seek Me and find *Me,* when you search for Me with all your heart. ¹⁴I will be found by you, says the LORD, and I will bring you back from your captivity; I will gather you from all the nations and from all the places where I have driven you, says the LORD, and I will bring you to the place from which I cause you to be carried away captive.

Rewards: Leaders with Integrity Can Remain Optimistic

(Jeremiah 29:11–14)

Even in Israel's darkest hour, God assured the people of His plans to prosper them and give them a hopeful future. Just so, even when we don't see immediate results, we can remain assured of God's ultimate blessing and benefit. The fruit may not come immediately, but it will come ultimately.

15   Because you have said, "The LORD has raised up prophets for us in Babylon"— ¹⁶therefore thus says the LORD concerning the king who sits on the throne of David,

concerning all the people who dwell in this city, and concerning your brethren who have not gone out with you into captivity—17thus says the LORD of hosts: Behold, I will send on them the sword, the famine, and the pestilence, and will make them like rotten figs that cannot be eaten, they are so bad. 18And I will pursue them with the sword, with famine, and with pestilence; and I will deliver them to trouble among all the kingdoms of the earth—to be a curse, an astonishment, a hissing, and a reproach among all the nations where I have driven them, 19because they have not heeded My words, says the LORD, which I sent to them by My servants the prophets, rising up early and sending them; neither would you heed, says the LORD. 20Therefore hear the word of the LORD, all you of the captivity, whom I have sent from Jerusalem to Babylon.

21 Thus says the LORD of hosts, the God of Israel, concerning Ahab the son of Kolaiah, and Zedekiah the son of Maaseiah, who prophesy a lie to you in My name: Behold, I will deliver them into the hand of Nebuchadnezzar king of Babylon, and he shall slay them before your eyes. 22And because of them a curse shall be taken up by all the captivity of Judah who are in Babylon, saying, "The LORD make you like Zedekiah and Ahab, whom the king of Babylon roasted in the fire"; 23because they have done disgraceful things in Israel, have committed adultery with their neighbors' wives, and have spoken lying words in My name, which I have not commanded them. Indeed I know, and am a witness, says the LORD.

24 You shall also speak to Shemaiah the Nehelamite, saying, 25Thus speaks the LORD of hosts, the God of Israel, saying: You have sent letters in your name to all the people who are at Jerusalem, to Zephaniah the son of Maaseiah the priest, and to all the priests, saying, 26"The LORD has made you priest instead of Jehoiada the priest, so that there should be officers in the house of the LORD over every man who is demented and considers himself a prophet, that you should put him in prison and in the stocks. 27Now therefore, why have you not rebuked Jeremiah of Anathoth who makes himself a prophet to you? 28For he has sent to us in Babylon, saying, 'This captivity is long; build

houses and dwell in them, and plant gardens and eat their fruit.'"

29 Now Zephaniah the priest read this letter in the hearing of Jeremiah the prophet. 30Then the word of the LORD came to Jeremiah, saying: 31Send to all those in captivity, saying, Thus says the LORD concerning Shemaiah the Nehelamite: Because Shemaiah has prophesied to you, and I have not sent him, and he has caused you to trust in a lie—32therefore thus says the LORD: Behold, I will punish Shemaiah the Nehelamite and his family: he shall not have anyone to dwell among this people, nor shall he see the good that I will do for My people, says the LORD, because he has taught rebellion against the LORD.

Restoration of Israel and Judah

30 The word that came to Jeremiah from the LORD, saying, 2"Thus speaks the LORD God of Israel, saying: 'Write in a book for yourself all the words that I have spoken to you. 3For behold, the days are coming,' says the LORD, 'that I will bring back from captivity My people Israel and Judah,' says the LORD. 'And I will cause them to return to the land that I gave to their fathers, and they shall possess it.'"

4Now these are the words that the LORD spoke concerning Israel and Judah.

5"For thus says the LORD:

'We have heard a voice of trembling,
　Of fear, and not of peace.
6 Ask now, and see,
　Whether a man is ever in labor with child?
　So why do I see every man with his hands on his loins
　Like a woman in labor,
　And all faces turned pale?
7 Alas! For that day is great,
　So that none is like it;
　And it is the time of Jacob's trouble,
　But he shall be saved out of it.

8 'For it shall come to pass in that day,'
　Says the LORD of hosts,
'That I will break his yoke from your neck,
　And will burst your bonds;
　Foreigners shall no more enslave them.
9 But they shall serve the LORD their God,
　And David their king,
　Whom I will raise up for them.

10 'Therefore do not fear, O My servant
  Jacob,' says the LORD,
'Nor be dismayed, O Israel;
For behold, I will save you from afar,
And your seed from the land of their
  captivity.
Jacob shall return, have rest and be quiet,
And no one shall make *him* afraid.
11 For I *am* with you,' says the LORD, 'to save
  you;
Though I make a full end of all nations
  where I have scattered you,
Yet I will not make a complete end of
  you.
But I will correct you in justice,
And will not let you go altogether
  unpunished.'

God Punishes with Bad Leaders, Rewards with Good Ones

(Jeremiah 30:10–22)

Jeremiah declares that God's way of punishing His people is to give them bad leaders (Jer. 30:10, 11), while the Lord's way of
rewarding them is to give them good leaders
(30:21, 22). Everything rises and falls on leadership. As the leader goes, so go the people.
Why is this true?

1. **Because leaders represent the people
   they oversee.**
2. **Because people reflect the leader they
   follow.**
3. **Because leaders are usually the most influential individuals among the people.**
4. **Because when God starts a movement,
   He uses one person to spearhead it.**
5. **Because people are like sheep and look to
   leaders for models.**

---

12 "For thus says the LORD:

'Your affliction *is* incurable,
Your wound *is* severe.
13 *There is* no one to plead your cause,
That you may be bound up;
You have no healing medicines.
14 All your lovers have forgotten you;
They do not seek you;

For I have wounded you with the wound
  of an enemy,
With the chastisement of a cruel one,
For the multitude of your iniquities,
Because your sins have increased.
15 Why do you cry about your affliction?
Your sorrow *is* incurable.
Because of the multitude of your
  iniquities,
Because your sins have increased,
I have done these things to you.

16 'Therefore all those who devour you shall
  be devoured;
And all your adversaries, every one of
  them, shall go into captivity;
Those who plunder you shall become
  plunder,
And all who prey upon you I will make a
  prey.
17 For I will restore health to you
And heal you of your wounds,' says the
  LORD,
'Because they called you an outcast *saying*:
"This *is* Zion;
No one seeks her."'

18 "Thus says the LORD:

'Behold, I will bring back the captivity of
  Jacob's tents,
And have mercy on his dwelling places;
The city shall be built upon its own
  mound,
And the palace shall remain according to
  its own plan.
19 Then out of them shall proceed
  thanksgiving
And the voice of those who make merry;
I will multiply them, and they shall not
  diminish;
I will also glorify them, and they shall not
  be small.
20 Their children also shall be as before,
And their congregation shall be established
  before Me;
And I will punish all who oppress them.
21 Their nobles shall be from among them,
And their governor shall come from their
  midst;
Then I will cause him to draw near,
And he shall approach Me;
For who *is* this who pledged his heart to
  approach Me?' says the LORD.
22 'You shall be My people,
And I will be your God.'"

23 Behold, the whirlwind of the LORD
Goes forth with fury,
A continuing whirlwind;
It will fall violently on the head of the
wicked.
24 The fierce anger of the LORD will not
return until He has done it,
And until He has performed the intents of
His heart.

In the latter days you will consider it.

The Remnant of Israel Saved

31 "At the same time," says the LORD, "I
will be the God of all the families of
Israel, and they shall be My people."
2 Thus says the LORD:

"The people who survived the sword
Found grace in the wilderness—
Israel, when I went to give him rest."

3 The LORD has appeared of old to me,
saying:
"Yes, I have loved you with an everlasting
love;
Therefore with lovingkindness I have
drawn you.
4 Again I will build you, and you shall be
rebuilt,
O virgin of Israel!
You shall again be adorned with your
tambourines,
And shall go forth in the dances of those
who rejoice.
5 You shall yet plant vines on the mountains
of Samaria;
The planters shall plant and eat *them* as
ordinary food.
6 For there shall be a day
When the watchmen will cry on Mount
Ephraim,
'Arise, and let us go up *to* Zion,
To the LORD our God.'"

7 For thus says the LORD:

"Sing with gladness for Jacob,
And shout among the chief of the nations;
Proclaim, give praise, and say,
'O LORD, save Your people,
The remnant of Israel!'
8 Behold, I will bring them from the north
country,
And gather them from the ends of the
earth,

Among them the blind and the lame,
The woman with child
And the one who labors with child,
together;
A great throng shall return there.
9 They shall come with weeping,
And with supplications I will lead them.
I will cause them to walk by the rivers of
waters,
In a straight way in which they shall not
stumble;
For I am a Father to Israel,
And Ephraim *is* My firstborn.

10 "Hear the word of the LORD, O nations,
And declare *it* in the isles afar off, and say,
'He who scattered Israel will gather him,
And keep him as a shepherd *does* his flock.'
11 For the LORD has redeemed Jacob,
And ransomed him from the hand of one
stronger than he.
12 Therefore they shall come and sing in the
height of Zion,
Streaming to the goodness of the LORD—
For wheat and new wine and oil,
For the young of the flock and the herd;
Their souls shall be like a well-watered
garden,
And they shall sorrow no more at all.

13 "Then shall the virgin rejoice in the dance,
And the young men and the old, together;
For I will turn their mourning to joy,
Will comfort them,
And make them rejoice rather than sorrow.
14 I will satiate the soul of the priests with
abundance,
And My people shall be satisfied with My
goodness, says the LORD."

Mercy on Ephraim

15 Thus says the LORD:

"A voice was heard in Ramah,
Lamentation *and* bitter weeping,
Rachel weeping for her children,
Refusing to be comforted for her
children,
Because they *are* no more."

16 Thus says the LORD:

"Refrain your voice from weeping,
And your eyes from tears;
For your work shall be rewarded, says the
LORD,

And they shall come back from the land of the enemy.

17 There is hope in your future, says the LORD,
That *your* children shall come back to their own border.

18 "I have surely heard Ephraim bemoaning himself:
'You have chastised me, and I was chastised, Like an untrained bull;
Restore me, and I will return,
For You *are* the LORD my God.

19 Surely, after my turning, I repented;
And after I was instructed, I struck myself on the thigh;
I was ashamed, yes, even humiliated,
Because I bore the reproach of my youth.'

20 *Is* Ephraim My dear son?
Is he a pleasant child?
For though I spoke against him,
I earnestly remember him still;
Therefore My heart yearns for him;
I will surely have mercy on him, says the LORD.

21 "Set up signposts,
Make landmarks;
Set your heart toward the highway,
The way in *which* you went.
Turn back, O virgin of Israel,
Turn back to these your cities.

22 How long will you gad about,
O you backsliding daughter?
For the LORD has created a new thing in the earth—
A woman shall encompass a man."

Future Prosperity of Judah

23 Thus says the LORD of hosts, the God of Israel: "They shall again use this speech in the land of Judah and in its cities, when I bring back their captivity: 'The LORD bless you, O home of justice, *and* mountain of holiness!' 24 And there shall dwell in Judah itself, and in all its cities together, farmers and those going out with flocks. 25 For I have satiated the weary soul, and I have replenished every sorrowful soul."

26 After this I awoke and looked around, and my sleep was sweet to me.

27 "Behold, the days are coming, says the LORD, that I will sow the house of Israel and the house of Judah with the seed of man and the seed of beast. 28 And it shall come to pass, *that* as I have watched over them to pluck up, to break down, to throw down, to destroy, and to afflict,

so I will watch over them to build and to plant, says the LORD. 29 In those days they shall say no more:

'The fathers have eaten sour grapes,
And the children's teeth are set on edge.'

30 But every one shall die for his own iniquity; every man who eats the sour grapes, his teeth shall be set on edge.

A New Covenant

31 "Behold, the days are coming, says the LORD, when I will make a new covenant with the house of Israel and with the house of Judah— 32 not according to the covenant that I made with their fathers in the day *that* I took them by the hand to lead them out of the land of Egypt, My covenant which they broke, though I was a husband to them,[a] says the LORD. 33 But this *is* the covenant that I will make with the house of Israel after those days, says the LORD: I will put My law in their minds, and write it on their hearts; and I will be their God, and they shall be My people. 34 No more shall every man teach his neighbor, and every man his brother, saying, 'Know the LORD,' for they all shall know Me, from the least of them to the greatest of them, says the LORD. For I will forgive their iniquity, and their sin I will remember no more."

35 Thus says the LORD,
Who gives the sun for a light by day,
The ordinances of the moon and the stars for a light by night,
Who disturbs the sea,
And its waves roar
(The LORD of hosts *is* His name):

36 "If those ordinances depart
From before Me, says the LORD,
Then the seed of Israel shall also cease
From being a nation before Me forever."

37 Thus says the LORD:

"If heaven above can be measured,
And the foundations of the earth searched out beneath,
I will also cast off all the seed of Israel
For all that they have done, says the LORD.

31:32 [a]Following Masoretic Text, Targum, and Vulgate; Septuagint and Syriac read *and I turned away from them.*

³⁸"Behold, the days are coming, says the LORD, that the city shall be built for the LORD from the Tower of Hananel to the Corner Gate. ³⁹The surveyor's line shall again extend straight forward over the hill Gareb; then it shall turn toward Goath. ⁴⁰And the whole valley of the dead bodies and of the ashes, and all the fields as far as the Brook Kidron, to the corner of the Horse Gate toward the east, *shall be* holy to the LORD. It shall not be plucked up or thrown down anymore forever."

Jeremiah Buys a Field

32 The word that came to Jeremiah from the LORD in the tenth year of Zedekiah king of Judah, which was the eighteenth year of Nebuchadnezzar. ²For then the king of Babylon's army besieged Jerusalem, and Jeremiah the prophet was shut up in the court of the prison, which *was in* the king of Judah's house. ³For Zedekiah king of Judah had shut him up, saying, "Why do you prophesy and say, 'Thus says the LORD: "Behold, I will give this city into the hand of the king of Babylon, and he shall take it; ⁴and Zedekiah king of Judah shall not escape from the hand of the Chaldeans, but shall surely be delivered into the hand of the king of Babylon, and shall speak with him face to face,ᵃ and see him eye to eye; ⁵then he shall lead Zedekiah to Babylon, and there he shall be until I visit him," says the LORD; "though you fight with the Chaldeans, you shall not succeed"?'"

⁶And Jeremiah said, "The word of the LORD came to me, saying, ⁷'Behold, Hanamel the son of Shallum your uncle will come to you, saying, "Buy my field which *is* in Anathoth, for the right of redemption *is* yours to buy *it*."' ⁸Then Hanamel my uncle's son came to me in the court of the prison according to the word of the LORD, and said to me, 'Please buy my field that *is* in Anathoth, which *is* in the country of Benjamin; for the right of inheritance *is* yours, and the redemption yours; buy *it* for yourself.' Then I knew that this was the word of the LORD. ⁹So I bought the field from Hanamel, the son of my uncle who *was* in Anathoth, and weighed *out to* him the money—seventeen shekels of silver. ¹⁰And I signed the deed and sealed *it,* took witnesses, and weighed the money on the scales. ¹¹So I took the purchase deed, *both* that which was sealed *according* to the law and custom, and that which was open; ¹²and I gave the purchase deed to Baruch the son of Neriah, son of Mahseiah, in the presence of Hanamel my uncle's *son,* and in the presence of the witnesses who signed the purchase deed, before all the Jews who sat in the court of the prison.

¹³"Then I charged Baruch before them, saying, ¹⁴"Thus says the LORD of hosts, the God of Israel: "Take these deeds, both this purchase deed which is sealed and this deed which is open, and put them in an earthen vessel, that they may last many days." ¹⁵For thus says the LORD of hosts, the God of Israel: "Houses and fields and vineyards shall be possessed again in this land."'

Jeremiah Prays for Understanding

¹⁶"Now when I had delivered the purchase deed to Baruch the son of Neriah, I prayed to the LORD, saying: ¹⁷'Ah, Lord GOD! Behold, You have made the heavens and the earth by Your great power and outstretched arm. There is nothing too hard for You. ¹⁸*You* show lovingkindness to thousands, and repay the iniquity of the fathers into the bosom of their children after them—the Great, the Mighty God, whose name *is* the LORD of hosts. ¹⁹*You are* great in counsel and mighty in work, for Your eyes *are* open to all the ways of the sons of men, to give everyone according to his ways and according to the fruit of his doings. ²⁰You have set signs and wonders in the land of Egypt, to this day, and in Israel and among *other* men; and You have made Yourself a name, as it is this day. ²¹You have brought Your people Israel out of the land of Egypt with signs and wonders, with a strong hand and an outstretched arm, and with great terror; ²²You have given them this land, of which You swore to their fathers to give them—"a land flowing with milk and honey."ᵃ ²³And they came in and took possession of it, but they have not obeyed Your voice or walked in Your law. They have done nothing of all that You commanded them to do; therefore You have caused all this calamity to come upon them.

²⁴"Look, the siege mounds! They have come to the city to take it; and the city has been given into the hand of the Chaldeans who fight against it, because of the sword and famine and pestilence. What You have spoken has happened; there You see *it!* ²⁵And You have said to me, O Lord GOD, "Buy the field for money, and take witnesses"!—yet the city has been given into the hand of the Chaldeans.'"

God's Assurance of the People's Return

²⁶Then the word of the LORD came to Jeremiah, saying, ²⁷"Behold, I *am* the LORD, the God of all flesh. Is there anything too hard for

---

32:4 ᵃLiterally *mouth to mouth* **32:22** ᵃExodus 3:8

Me? [28]Therefore thus says the LORD: 'Behold, I will give this city into the hand of the Chaldeans, into the hand of Nebuchadnezzar king of Babylon, and he shall take it. [29]And the Chaldeans who fight against this city shall come and set fire to this city and burn it, with the houses on whose roofs they have offered incense to Baal and poured out drink offerings to other gods, to provoke Me to anger; [30]because the children of Israel and the children of Judah have done only evil before Me from their youth. For the children of Israel have provoked Me only to anger with the work of their hands,' says the LORD. [31]'For this city has been to Me *a provocation of* My anger and My fury from the day that they built it, even to this day; so I will remove it from before My face [32]because of all the evil of the children of Israel and the children of Judah, which they have done to provoke Me to anger—they, their kings, their princes, their priests, their prophets, the men of Judah, and the inhabitants of Jerusalem. [33]And they have turned to Me the back, and not the face; though I taught them, rising up early and teaching *them,* yet they have not listened to receive instruction. [34]But they set their abominations in the house which is called by My name, to defile it. [35]And they built the high places of Baal which *are* in the Valley of the Son of Hinnom, to cause their sons and their daughters to pass through *the fire* to Molech, which I did not command them, nor did it come into My mind that they should do this abomination, to cause Judah to sin.'

[36]'Now therefore, thus says the LORD, the God of Israel, concerning this city of which you say, 'It shall be delivered into the hand of the king of Babylon by the sword, by the famine, and by the pestilence: [37]Behold, I will gather them out of all countries where I have driven them in My anger, in My fury, and in great wrath; I will bring them back to this place, and I will cause them to dwell safely. [38]They shall be My people, and I will be their God; [39]then I will give them one heart and one way, that they may fear Me forever, for the good of them and their children after them. [40]And I will make an everlasting covenant with them, that I will not turn away from doing them good; but I will put My fear in their hearts so that they will not depart from Me. [41]Yes, I will rejoice over them to do them good, and I will assuredly plant them in this land, with all My heart and with all My soul.'

[42]'For thus says the LORD: 'Just as I have brought all this great calamity on this people, so I will bring on them all the good that I have promised them. [43]And fields will be bought in this land of which you say, "*It is* desolate, without man or beast; it has been given into the hand of the Chaldeans." [44]Men will buy fields for money, sign deeds and seal *them,* and take witnesses, in the land of Benjamin, in the places around Jerusalem, in the cities of Judah, in the cities of the mountains, in the cities of the lowland, and in the cities of the South; for I will cause their captives to return,' says the LORD."

Excellence of the Restored Nation

33 Moreover the word of the LORD came to Jeremiah a second time, while he was still shut up in the court of the prison, saying, [2]"Thus says the LORD who made it, the LORD who formed it to establish it (the LORD *is* His name): [3]'Call to Me, and I will answer you, and show you great and mighty things, which you do not know.'

[4]"For thus says the LORD, the God of Israel, concerning the houses of this city and the houses of the kings of Judah, which have been pulled down *to fortify*[a] against the siege mounds and the sword: [5]'They come to fight with the Chaldeans, but *only* to fill their places[a] with the dead bodies of men whom I will slay in My anger and My fury, all for whose wickedness I have hidden My face from this city. [6]Behold, I will bring it health and healing; I will heal them and reveal to them the abundance of peace and truth. [7]And I will cause the captives of Judah and the captives of Israel to return, and will rebuild those places as at the first. [8]I will cleanse them from all their iniquity by which they have sinned against Me, and I will pardon all their iniquities by which they have sinned and by which they have transgressed against Me. [9]Then it shall be to Me a name of joy, a praise, and an honor before all nations of the earth, who shall hear all the good that I do to them; they shall fear and tremble for all the goodness and all the prosperity that I provide for it.'

[10]"Thus says the LORD: 'Again there shall be heard in this place—of which you say, "It *is* desolate, without man and without beast"—in the cities of Judah, in the streets of Jerusalem that are desolate, without man and without inhabitant and without beast, [11]the voice of joy and the voice of gladness, the voice of the bridegroom and the voice of the bride, the voice of those who will say:

33:4 [a]Compare Isaiah 22:10 **33:5** [a]Compare 2 Kings 23:14

"Praise the LORD of hosts,
For the LORD *is* good,
For His mercy *endures* forever"—

and of those *who will* bring the sacrifice of praise into the house of the LORD. For I will cause the captives of the land to return as at the first,' says the LORD.

12"Thus says the LORD of hosts: 'In this place which is desolate, without man and without beast, and in all its cities, there shall again be a dwelling place of shepherds causing *their* flocks to lie down. 13In the cities of the mountains, in the cities of the lowland, in the cities of the South, in the land of Benjamin, in the places around Jerusalem, and in the cities of Judah, the flocks shall again pass under the hands of him who counts *them*,' says the LORD.

14"Behold, the days are coming,' says the LORD, 'that I will perform that good thing which I have promised to the house of Israel and to the house of Judah:

15   ' In those days and at that time
       I will cause to grow up to David
       A Branch of righteousness;
       He shall execute judgment and
          righteousness in the earth.
16   In those days Judah will be saved,
       And Jerusalem will dwell safely.
       And this *is the name* by which she will be
          called:

THE LORD OUR RIGHTEOUSNESS.'a

17"For thus says the LORD: 'David shall never lack a man to sit on the throne of the house of Israel; 18nor shall the priests, the Levites, lack a man to offer burnt offerings before Me, to kindle grain offerings, and to sacrifice continually.'"

The Permanence of God's Covenant

19And the word of the LORD came to Jeremiah, saying, 20"Thus says the LORD: 'If you can break My covenant with the day and My covenant with the night, so that there will not be day and night in their season, 21then My covenant may also be broken with David My servant, so that he shall not have a son to reign on his throne, and with the Levites, the priests, My ministers. 22As the host of heaven cannot be numbered, nor the sand of the sea measured, so will I multiply the descendants of David My servant and the Levites who minister to Me.'"

23Moreover the word of the LORD came to Jeremiah, saying, 24"Have you not considered what these people have spoken, saying, 'The two

families which the LORD has chosen, He has also cast them off'? Thus they have despised My people, as if they should no more be a nation before them. 25"Thus says the LORD: 'If My covenant *is* not with day and night, *and if* I have not appointed the ordinances of heaven and earth, 26then I will cast away the descendants of Jacob and David My servant, *so* that I will not take *any* of his descendants *to be* rulers over the descendants of Abraham, Isaac, and Jacob. For I will cause their captives to return, and will have mercy on them.'"

Zedekiah Warned by God

34 The word which came to Jeremiah from the LORD, when Nebuchadnezzar king of Babylon and all his army, all the kingdoms of the earth under his dominion, and all the people, fought against Jerusalem and all its cities, saying, 2"Thus says the LORD, the God of Israel: 'Go and speak to Zedekiah king of Judah and tell him, "Thus says the LORD: 'Behold, I will give this city into the hand of the king of Babylon, and he shall burn it with fire. 3And you shall not escape from his hand, but shall surely be taken and delivered into his hand; your eyes shall see the eyes of the king of Babylon, he shall speak with you face to face,a and you shall go to Babylon.'"' 4Yet hear the word of the LORD, O Zedekiah king of Judah! Thus says the LORD concerning you: 'You shall not die by the sword. 5You shall die in peace; as in the ceremonies of your fathers, the former kings who were before you, so they shall burn incense for you and lament for you, *saying,* "Alas, lord!" For I have pronounced the word, says the LORD.'"

6Then Jeremiah the prophet spoke all these words to Zedekiah king of Judah in Jerusalem, 7when the king of Babylon's army fought against Jerusalem and all the cities of Judah that were left, against Lachish and Azekah; for *only* these fortified cities remained of the cities of Judah.

Treacherous Treatment of Slaves

8*This is* the word that came to Jeremiah from the LORD, after King Zedekiah had made a covenant with all the people who *were* at Jerusalem to proclaim liberty to them: 9that every man should set free his male and female slave—a Hebrew man or woman—that no one should keep a Jewish brother in bondage. 10Now when all the

---

33:16 aCompare 23:5, 6   34:3 aLiterally *mouth to mouth*

princes and all the people, who had entered into the covenant, heard that everyone should set free his male and female slaves, that no one should keep them in bondage anymore, they obeyed and let *them* go. ¹¹But afterward they changed their minds and made the male and female slaves return, whom they had set free, and brought them into subjection as male and female slaves.

¹²Therefore the word of the LORD came to Jeremiah from the LORD, saying, ¹³"Thus says the LORD, the God of Israel: 'I made a covenant with your fathers in the day that I brought them out of the land of Egypt, out of the house of bondage, saying, ¹⁴"At the end of seven years let every man set free his Hebrew brother, who has been sold to him; and when he has served you six years, you shall let him go free from you." But your fathers did not obey Me nor incline their ear. ¹⁵Then you recently turned and did what was right in My sight—every man proclaiming liberty to his neighbor; and you made a covenant before Me in the house which is called by My name. ¹⁶Then you turned around and profaned My name, and every one of you brought back his male and female slaves, whom you had set at liberty, at their pleasure, and brought them back into subjection, to be your male and female slaves.'

¹⁷"Therefore thus says the LORD: 'You have not obeyed Me in proclaiming liberty, every one to his brother and every one to his neighbor. Behold, I proclaim liberty to you,' says the LORD—'to the sword, to pestilence, and to famine! And I will deliver you to trouble among all the kingdoms of the earth. ¹⁸And I will give the men who have transgressed My covenant, who have not performed the words of the covenant which they made before Me, when they cut the calf in two and passed between the parts of it— ¹⁹the princes of Judah, the princes of Jerusalem, the eunuchs, the priests, and all the people of the land who passed between the parts of the calf— ²⁰I will give them into the hand of their enemies and into the hand of those who seek their life. Their dead bodies shall be for meat for the birds of the heaven and the beasts of the earth. ²¹And I will give Zedekiah king of Judah and his princes into the hand of their enemies, into the hand of those who seek their life, and into the hand of the king of Babylon's army which has gone back from you. ²²Behold, I will command,' says the LORD, 'and cause them to return to this city. They will fight against it and take it and burn it with fire; and I will make the cities of Judah a desolation without inhabitant.'"

The Obedient Rechabites

35 The word which came to Jeremiah from the LORD in the days of Jehoiakim the son of Josiah, king of Judah, saying, ²"Go to the house of the Rechabites, speak to them, and bring them into the house of the LORD, into one of the chambers, and give them wine to drink."

³Then I took Jaazaniah the son of Jeremiah, the son of Habazziniah, his brothers and all his sons, and the whole house of the Rechabites, ⁴and I brought them into the house of the LORD, into the chamber of the sons of Hanan the son of Igdaliah, a man of God, which *was* by the chamber of the princes, above the chamber of Maaseiah the son of Shallum, the keeper of the door. ⁵Then I set before the sons of the house of the Rechabites bowls full of wine, and cups; and I said to them, "Drink wine."

⁶But they said, "We will drink no wine, for Jonadab the son of Rechab, our father, commanded us, saying, 'You shall drink no wine, you nor your sons, forever. ⁷You shall not build a house, sow seed, plant a vineyard, nor have *any of these;* but all your days you shall dwell in tents, that you may live many days in the land where you are sojourners.' ⁸Thus we have obeyed the voice of Jonadab the son of Rechab, our father, in all that he charged us, to drink no wine all our days, we, our wives, our sons, or our daughters, ⁹nor to build ourselves houses to dwell in; nor do we have vineyard, field, or seed. ¹⁰But we have dwelt in tents, and have obeyed and done according to all that Jonadab our father commanded us. ¹¹But it came to pass, when Nebuchadnezzar king of Babylon came up into the land, that we said, 'Come, let us go to Jerusalem for fear of the army of the Chaldeans and for fear of the army of the Syrians.' So we dwell at Jerusalem."

¹²Then came the word of the LORD to Jeremiah, saying, ¹³"Thus says the LORD of hosts, the God of Israel: 'Go and tell the men of Judah and the inhabitants of Jerusalem, "Will you not receive instruction to obey My words?" says the LORD. ¹⁴"The words of Jonadab the son of Rechab, which he commanded his sons, not to drink wine, are performed; for to this day they drink none, and obey their father's commandment. But although I have spoken to you, rising early and speaking, you did not obey Me. ¹⁵I have also sent to you all My servants the prophets, rising up early and sending *them,* saying, 'Turn now everyone from his evil way, amend your doings, and do not go after other gods to serve them; then you will dwell in the land which I have given you

and your fathers.' But you have not inclined your ear, nor obeyed Me. [16]Surely the sons of Jonadab the son of Rechab have performed the commandment of their father, which he commanded them, but this people has not obeyed Me."'

[17]"Therefore thus says the LORD God of hosts, the God of Israel: 'Behold, I will bring on Judah and on all the inhabitants of Jerusalem all the doom that I have pronounced against them; because I have spoken to them but they have not heard, and I have called to them but they have not answered.'"

[18]And Jeremiah said to the house of the Rechabites, "Thus says the LORD of hosts, the God of Israel: 'Because you have obeyed the commandment of Jonadab your father, and kept all his precepts and done according to all that he commanded you, [19]therefore thus says the LORD of hosts, the God of Israel: "Jonadab the son of Rechab shall not lack a man to stand before Me forever."'"

The Scroll Read in the Temple

36 Now it came to pass in the fourth year of Jehoiakim the son of Josiah, king of Judah, *that* this word came to Jeremiah from the LORD, saying: [2]"Take a scroll of a book and write on it all the words that I

have spoken to you against Israel, against Judah, and against all the nations, from the day I spoke to you, from the days of Josiah even to this day. [3]It may be that the house of Judah will hear all the adversities which I purpose to bring upon them, that everyone may turn from his evil way, that I may forgive their iniquity and their sin."

[4]Then Jeremiah called Baruch the son of Neriah; and Baruch wrote on a scroll of a book, at the instruction of Jeremiah,[a] all the words of the LORD which He had spoken to him. [5]And Jeremiah commanded Baruch, saying, "I *am* confined, I cannot go into the house of the LORD. [6]You go, therefore, and read from the scroll which you have written at my instruction,[a] the words of the LORD, in the hearing of the people in the LORD's house on the day of fasting. And you shall also read them in the hearing of all Judah who come from their cities. [7]It may be that they will present their supplication before the LORD, and everyone will turn from his evil way. For great *is* the anger and the fury that the LORD has pronounced against this people." [8]And Baruch the son of Neriah did according to all that Jeremiah

---

36:4 [a]Literally *from Jeremiah's mouth* **36:6** [a]Literally *from my mouth*

PROFILE IN LEADERSHIP

BAD LEADERS

REFUSE TO HEED WARNINGS
(Jeremiah 36:1—40:16)

History offers countless examples of leaders who failed because they refused to heed warnings. Just before the outbreak of World War II, British Prime Minister Neville Chamberlain failed to heed warnings from several parties concerning the threat posed by Adolf Hitler. Instead, Chamberlain pursued a policy of "appeasement" and confidently announced "peace in our time." He died a year after the Nazi invasion of Poland.

Two leaders described in the Book of Jeremiah—King Jehoiakim of Judah and Gedaliah, governor of Judah—also failed to heed dire warnings, and it cost them dearly.

Jehoiakim received a scroll containing Jeremiah's prophecies of destruction. But instead of heeding them, the king burned the scroll and called for the arrest of Jeremiah and his scribe (Jer. 36:1–24). The result: divine judgment on him and his family.

Gedaliah, appointed governor of Judah by the Babylonian king, failed to heed a warning of his impending assassination. He learned of the plot, who was involved, and what could be done to prevent it. But instead of taking the advice offered him, he chose to ignore the threat—and an assassin soon took his life.

A good leader knows when to heed warnings and advice. God has given us His Word, His Spirit, and one another to keep us on the right track. Wise leaders carefully consider the words of all three.

the prophet commanded him, reading from the book the words of the LORD in the LORD's house.

[9]Now it came to pass in the fifth year of Jehoiakim the son of Josiah, king of Judah, in the ninth month, *that* they proclaimed a fast before the LORD to all the people in Jerusalem, and to all the people who came from the cities of Judah to Jerusalem. [10]Then Baruch read from the book the words of Jeremiah in the house of the LORD, in the chamber of Gemariah the son of Shaphan the scribe, in the upper court at the entry of the New Gate of the LORD's house, in the hearing of all the people.

The Scroll Read in the Palace

[11]When Michaiah the son of Gemariah, the son of Shaphan, heard all the words of the LORD from the book, [12]he then went down to the king's house, into the scribe's chamber; and there all the princes were sitting—Elishama the scribe, Delaiah the son of Shemaiah, Elnathan the son of Achbor, Gemariah the son of Shaphan, Zedekiah the son of Hananiah, and all the princes. [13]Then Michaiah declared to them all the words that he had heard when Baruch read the book in the hearing of the people. [14]Therefore all the princes sent Jehudi the son of Nethaniah, the son of Shelemiah, the son of Cushi, to Baruch, saying, "Take in your hand the scroll from which you have read in the hearing of the people, and come." So Baruch the son of Neriah took the scroll in his hand and came to them. [15]And they said to him, "Sit down now, and read it in our hearing." So Baruch read *it* in their hearing.

[16]Now it happened, when they had heard all the words, that they looked in fear from one to another, and said to Baruch, "We will surely tell the king of all these words." [17]And they asked Baruch, saying, "Tell us now, how did you write all these words—at his instruction?"[a]

[18]So Baruch answered them, "He proclaimed with his mouth all these words to me, and I wrote *them* with ink in the book."

[19]Then the princes said to Baruch, "Go and hide, you and Jeremiah; and let no one know where you are."

The King Destroys Jeremiah's Scroll

[20]And they went to the king, into the court; but they stored the scroll in the chamber of Elishama the scribe, and told all the words in the hearing of the king. [21]So the king sent Jehudi to bring the scroll, and he took it from Elishama the scribe's chamber. And Jehudi read it in the hearing of the king and in the hearing of all the princes who stood beside the king. [22]Now the

king was sitting in the winter house in the ninth month, with *a fire* burning on the hearth before him. [23]And it happened, when Jehudi had read three or four columns, *that the king* cut it with the scribe's knife and cast *it* into the fire that *was* on the hearth, until all the scroll was consumed in the fire that *was* on the hearth. [24]Yet they were not afraid, nor did they tear their garments, the king nor any of his servants who heard all these words. [25]Nevertheless Elnathan, Delaiah, and Gemariah implored the king not to burn the scroll; but he would not listen to them. [26]And the king commanded Jerahmeel the king's[a] son, Seraiah the son of Azriel, and Shelemiah the son of Abdeel, to seize Baruch the scribe and Jeremiah the prophet, but the LORD hid them.

Jeremiah Rewrites the Scroll

[27]Now after the king had burned the scroll with the words which Baruch had written at the instruction of Jeremiah,[a] the word of the LORD came to Jeremiah, saying: [28]"Take yet another scroll, and write on it all the former words that were in the first scroll which Jehoiakim the king of Judah has burned. [29]And you shall say to Jehoiakim king of Judah, 'Thus says the LORD: "You have burned this scroll, saying, 'Why have you written in it that the king of Babylon will certainly come and destroy this land, and cause man and beast to cease from here?'" [30]Therefore thus says the LORD concerning Jehoiakim king of Judah: "He shall have no one to sit on the throne of David, and his dead body shall be cast out to the heat of the day and the frost of the night. [31]I will punish him, his family, and his servants for their iniquity; and I will bring on them, on the inhabitants of Jerusalem, and on the men of Judah all the doom that I have pronounced against them; but they did not heed."'"

[32]Then Jeremiah took another scroll and gave it to Baruch the scribe, the son of Neriah, who wrote on it at the instruction of Jeremiah[a] all the words of the book which Jehoiakim king of Judah had burned in the fire. And besides, there were added to them many similar words.

Zedekiah's Vain Hope

37 Now King Zedekiah the son of Josiah reigned instead of Coniah the son of Jehoiakim, whom Nebuchadnezzar king of Babylon made king in the land of Judah. [2]But neither he nor his servants nor the

---

36:17 [a]Literally *with his mouth* 36:26 [a]Hebrew *Hammelech* 36:27 [a]Literally *from Jeremiah's mouth* 36:32 [a]Literally *from Jeremiah's mouth* people of the land gave heed to the words of the LORD which He spoke by the prophet Jeremiah.

³And Zedekiah the king sent Jehucal the son of Shelemiah, and Zephaniah the son of Maaseiah, the priest, to the prophet Jeremiah, saying, "Pray now to the LORD our God for us." ⁴Now Jeremiah was coming and going among the people, for they had not *yet* put him in prison. ⁵Then Pharaoh's army came up from Egypt; and when the Chaldeans who were besieging Jerusalem heard news of them, they departed from Jerusalem.

⁶Then the word of the LORD came to the prophet Jeremiah, saying, ⁷"Thus says the LORD, the God of Israel, 'Thus you shall say to the king of Judah, who sent you to Me to inquire of Me: "Behold, Pharaoh's army which has come up to help you will return to Egypt, to their own land. ⁸And the Chaldeans shall come back and fight against this city, and take it and burn it with fire."' ⁹Thus says the LORD: 'Do not deceive yourselves, saying, "The Chaldeans will surely depart from us," for they will not depart. ¹⁰For though you had defeated the whole army of the Chaldeans who fight against you, and there remained *only* wounded men among them, they would rise up, every man in his tent, and burn the city with fire.'"

Jeremiah Imprisoned

¹¹And it happened, when the army of the Chaldeans left *the siege* of Jerusalem for fear of Pharaoh's army, ¹²that Jeremiah went out of Jerusalem to go into the land of Benjamin to claim his property there among the people. ¹³And when he was in the Gate of Benjamin, a captain of the guard *was* there whose name *was* Irijah the son of Shelemiah, the son of Hananiah; and he seized Jeremiah the prophet, saying, "You are defecting to the Chaldeans!"

¹⁴Then Jeremiah said, "False! I am not defecting to the Chaldeans." But he did not listen to him.

So Irijah seized Jeremiah and brought him to the princes. ¹⁵Therefore the princes were angry with Jeremiah, and they struck him and put him in prison in the house of Jonathan the scribe. For they had made that the prison.

¹⁶When Jeremiah entered the dungeon and the cells, and Jeremiah had remained there many days, ¹⁷then Zedekiah the king sent and took him *out*. The king asked him secretly in his house, and said, "Is there *any* word from the LORD?"

And Jeremiah said, "There is." Then he said, "You shall be delivered into the hand of the king of Babylon!"

¹⁸Moreover Jeremiah said to King Zedekiah, "What offense have I committed against you, against your servants, or against this people, that you have put me in prison? ¹⁹Where now *are* your prophets who prophesied to you, saying, 'The king of Babylon will not come against you or against this land'? ²⁰Therefore please hear now, O my lord the king. Please, let my petition be accepted before you, and do not make me return to the house of Jonathan the scribe, lest I die there."

²¹Then Zedekiah the king commanded that they should commit Jeremiah to the court of the prison, and that they should give him daily a piece of bread from the bakers' street, until all the bread in the city was gone. Thus Jeremiah remained in the court of the prison.

Jeremiah in the Dungeon

38 Now Shephatiah the son of Mattan, Gedaliah the son of Pashhur, Jucal[a] the son of Shelemiah, and Pashhur the son of Malchiah heard the words that Jeremiah had spoken to all the people, saying, ²"Thus says the LORD: 'He who remains in this city shall die by the sword, by famine, and by pestilence; but he who goes over to the Chaldeans shall live; his life shall be as a prize to him, and he shall live.'[a] ³Thus says the LORD: 'This city shall surely be given into the hand of the king of Babylon's army, which shall take it.'"

⁴Therefore the princes said to the king, "Please, let this man be put to death, for thus he weakens the hands of the men of war who remain in this city, and the hands of all the people, by speaking such words to them. For this man does not seek the welfare of this people, but their harm."

⁵Then Zedekiah the king said, "Look, he *is* in your hand. For the king can *do* nothing against you." ⁶So they took Jeremiah and cast him into the dungeon of Malchiah the king's[a] son, which *was* in the court of the prison, and they let Jeremiah down with ropes. And in the dungeon *there was* no water, but mire. So Jeremiah sank in the mire.

⁷Now Ebed-Melech the Ethiopian, one of the eunuchs, who was in the king's house, heard that they had put Jeremiah in the dungeon. When the king was sitting at the Gate of Benjamin, ⁸Ebed-Melech went out of the king's house and spoke to the king, saying: ⁹"'My lord the king, these men have done evil in all that they have done to Jeremiah the prophet, whom they have cast into the dungeon, and he is likely to die

38:1 [a]Same as *Jehucal* (compare 37:3)
38:2 [a]Compare 21:9 **38:6** [a]Hebrew *Hammelech*

from hunger in the place where he is. For *there is* no more bread in the city." [10]Then the king commanded Ebed-Melech the Ethiopian, saying, "Take from here thirty men with you, and lift Jeremiah the prophet out of the dungeon before he dies." [11]So Ebed-Melech took the men with him and went into the house of the king under the treasury, and took from there old clothes and old rags, and let them down by ropes into the dungeon to Jeremiah. [12]Then Ebed-Melech the Ethiopian said to Jeremiah, "Please put these old clothes and rags under your armpits, under the ropes." And Jeremiah did so. [13]So they pulled Jeremiah up with ropes and lifted him out of the dungeon. And Jeremiah remained in the court of the prison.

Responsibility: Like It or Not, the Buck Stops with the Leader

(Jeremiah 38:1–6)

Power abuse occurs not only when evil leaders act out of selfishness, but when good leaders neglect to do what they should. In this case, King Zedekiah delegated an undesirable task to someone else, declaring himself powerless to act. The king lacked the courage to use his power to protect God's prophet.

Jeremiah, on the other hand, remained responsible to a call he didn't like. He proclaimed destruction against his own people, naming Babylon as the executioner. Imagine that you were an evangelist standing in church today, declaring that God was raising up the communists to punish America. You declare that God cares nothing for the Declaration of Independence or the Constitution; in fact, the things we emphasize offend God. If you try to stop speaking this message, you feel disobedient. The word burns inside you and you *must* speak. So you pursue responsibility, not popularity.

Such was the man and the message of Jeremiah.

Zedekiah's Fears and Jeremiah's Advice

[14]Then Zedekiah the king sent and had Jeremiah the prophet brought to him at the third entrance of the house of the LORD. And the king said to Jeremiah, "I will ask you something. Hide nothing from me."

[15]Jeremiah said to Zedekiah, "If I declare *it* to you, will you not surely put me to death? And if I give you advice, you will not listen to me."

[16]So Zedekiah the king swore secretly to Jeremiah, saying, "*As* the LORD lives, who made our very souls, I will not put you to death, nor will I give you into the hand of these men who seek your life."

[17]Then Jeremiah said to Zedekiah, "Thus says the LORD, the God of hosts, the God of Israel: 'If you surely surrender to the king of Babylon's princes, then your soul shall live; this city shall not be burned with fire, and you and your house shall live. [18]But if you do not surrender to the king of Babylon's princes, then this city shall be given into the hand of the Chaldeans; they shall burn it with fire, and you shall not escape from their hand.'"

[19]And Zedekiah the king said to Jeremiah, "I am afraid of the Jews who have defected to the Chaldeans, lest they deliver me into their hand, and they abuse me."

[20]But Jeremiah said, "They shall not deliver *you*. Please, obey the voice of the LORD which I speak to you. So it shall be well with you, and your soul shall live. [21]But if you refuse to surrender, this *is* the word that the LORD has shown me: [22]'Now behold, all the women who are left in the king of Judah's house *shall be* surrendered to the king of Babylon's princes, and those *women* shall say:

"Your close friends have set upon you
    And prevailed against you;
Your feet have sunk in the mire,
    And they have turned away again."

[23]"So they shall surrender all your wives and children to the Chaldeans. You shall not escape from their hand, but shall be taken by the hand of the king of Babylon. And you shall cause this city to be burned with fire.'"

[24]Then Zedekiah said to Jeremiah, "Let no one know of these words, and you shall not die. [25]But if the princes hear that I have talked with you, and they come to you and say to you, 'Declare to us now what you have said to the king, and also what the king said to you; do not hide *it* from us, and we will not put you to death,' [26]then you shall say to them, 'I presented my request before the king, that he would not make me return to Jonathan's house to die there.'"

[27]Then all the princes came to Jeremiah and asked him. And he told them according to all

these words that the king had commanded. So they stopped speaking with him, for the conversation had not been heard. [28]Now Jeremiah remained in the court of the prison until the day that Jerusalem was taken. And he was *there* when Jerusalem was taken.

The Fall of Jerusalem

39 In the ninth year of Zedekiah king of Judah, in the tenth month, Nebuchadnezzar king of Babylon and all his army came against Jerusalem, and besieged it. [2]In the eleventh year of Zedekiah, in the fourth month, on the ninth *day* of the month, the city was penetrated.

[3]Then all the princes of the king of Babylon came in and sat in the Middle Gate: Nergal-Sharezer, Samgar-Nebo, Sarsechim, Rabsaris,[a] Nergal-Sarezer, Rabmag,[b] with the rest of the princes of the king of Babylon.

[4]So it was, when Zedekiah the king of Judah and all the men of war saw them, that they fled and went out of the city by night, by way of the king's garden, by the gate between the two walls. And he went out by way of the plain.[a] [5]But the Chaldean army pursued them and overtook Zedekiah in the plains of Jericho. And when they had captured him, they brought him up to Nebuchadnezzar king of Babylon, to Riblah in the land of Hamath, where he pronounced judgment on him. [6]Then the king of Babylon killed the sons of Zedekiah before his eyes in Riblah; the king of Babylon also killed all the nobles of Judah. [7]Moreover he put out Zedekiah's eyes, and bound him with bronze fetters to carry him off to Babylon. [8]And the Chaldeans burned the king's house and the houses of the people with fire, and broke down the walls of Jerusalem. [9]Then Nebuzaradan the captain of the guard carried away captive to Babylon the remnant of the people who remained in the city and those who defected to him, with the rest of the people who remained. [10]But Nebuzaradan the captain of the guard left in the land of Judah the poor people, who had nothing, and gave them vineyards and fields at the same time.

Jeremiah Goes Free

[11]Now Nebuchadnezzar king of Babylon gave charge concerning Jeremiah to Nebuzaradan the captain of the guard, saying, [12]"Take him and look after him, and do him no harm; but do to him just as he says to you." [13]So Nebuzaradan the captain of the guard sent Nebushasban, Rabsaris, Nergal-Sharezer, Rabmag, and all the king of Babylon's chief officers; [14]then they sent *someone* to take Jeremiah from the court of the prison, and committed him to Gedaliah the son of Ahikam, the son of Shaphan, that he should take him home. So he dwelt among the people.

[15]Meanwhile the word of the LORD had come to Jeremiah while he was shut up in the court of the prison, saying, [16]"Go and speak to Ebed-Melech the Ethiopian, saying, 'Thus says the LORD of hosts, the God of Israel: "Behold, I will bring My words upon this city for adversity and not for good, and they shall be *performed* in that day before you. [17]But I will deliver you in that day," says the LORD, "and you shall not be given into the hand of the men of whom you *are* afraid. [18]For I will surely deliver you, and you shall not fall by the sword; but your life shall be as a prize to you, because you have put your trust in Me," says the LORD.'"

Jeremiah with Gedaliah the Governor

40 The word that came to Jeremiah from the LORD after Nebuzaradan the captain of the guard had let him go from Ramah, when he had taken him bound in chains among all who were carried away captive from Jerusalem and Judah, who were carried away captive to Babylon.

[2]And the captain of the guard took Jeremiah and said to him: "The LORD your God has pronounced this doom on this place. [3]Now the LORD has brought *it,* and has done just as He said. Because you *people* have sinned against the LORD, and not obeyed His voice, therefore this thing has come upon you. [4]And now look, I free you this day from the chains that *were* on your hand. If it seems good to you to come with me to Babylon, come, and I will look after you. But if it seems wrong for you to come with me to Babylon, remain here. See, all the land *is* before you; wherever it seems good and convenient for you to go, go there." [5]Now while Jeremiah had not yet gone back, *Nebuzaradan said,* "Go back to Gedaliah the son of Ahikam, the son of Shaphan, whom the king of Babylon has made governor over the cities of Judah, and dwell with him among the people. Or go wherever it seems convenient for you to go." So the captain of the guard gave him rations and a gift and let him go. [6]Then Jeremiah went to Gedaliah the son of Ahikam, to Mizpah, and dwelt with him among the people who were left in the land.

39:3 [a]A title, probably *Chief Officer;* also verse 13
[b]A title, probably *Troop Commander;* also verse 13
39:4 [a]Or *the Arabah,* that is, the Jordan Valley

Gedaliah's Poor Decision-Making Skills Lead to Disaster

(Jeremiah 40:5—41:2)

The Babylonians appointed Gedaliah the governor of Judah and put him in charge of the poor who had not been taken into exile. But the man failed to develop good decision-making skills. In fact, he made one disastrous decision because he neglected to process available information. A man named Ishmael eventually assassinated him, preventing him from ever reaching his potential as a leader.

What could Gedaliah have done to better approach the decisions before him?

1. Maintain a vision of the big picture.
2. Gather all the information possible.
3. Listen to those closest to the situation.
4. Narrow the best options.
5. Imagine the outcome of each option.
6. Note the moral and spiritual ramifications to the decision.
7. Make choices based on the following criteria:
   a) Which best reflects the mind of God?
   b) Which benefits the whole of the people?
   c) Which aligns itself with the mission you are to accomplish?

⁷And when all the captains of the armies who *were* in the fields, they and their men, heard that the king of Babylon had made Gedaliah the son of Ahikam governor in the land, and had committed to him men, women, children, and the poorest of the land who had not been carried away captive to Babylon, ⁸then they came to Gedaliah at Mizpah—Ishmael the son of Nethaniah, Johanan and Jonathan the sons of Kareah, Seraiah the son of Tanhumeth, the sons of Ephai the Netophathite, and Jezaniahª the son of a Maachathite, they and their men. ⁹And Gedaliah the son of Ahikam, the son of Shaphan, took an oath before them and their men, saying, "Do not be afraid to serve the Chaldeans. Dwell in the land and serve the king of Babylon, and it shall be well with you. ¹⁰As for me, I will indeed dwell at Mizpah and serve

the Chaldeans who come to us. But you, gather wine and summer fruit and oil, put *them* in your vessels, and dwell in your cities that you have taken." ¹¹Likewise, when all the Jews who *were* in Moab, among the Ammonites, in Edom, and who *were* in all the countries, heard that the king of Babylon had left a remnant of Judah, and that he had set over them Gedaliah the son of Ahikam, the son of Shaphan, ¹²then all the Jews returned out of all places where they had been driven, and came to the land of Judah, to Gedaliah at Mizpah, and gathered wine and summer fruit in abundance.

¹³Moreover Johanan the son of Kareah and all the captains of the forces that *were* in the fields came to Gedaliah at Mizpah, ¹⁴and said to him, "Do you certainly know that Baalis the king of the Ammonites has sent Ishmael the son of Nethaniah to murder you?" But Gedaliah the son of Ahikam did not believe them.

¹⁵Then Johanan the son of Kareah spoke secretly to Gedaliah in Mizpah, saying, "Let me go, please, and I will kill Ishmael the son of Nethaniah, and no one will know *it*. Why should he murder you, so that all the Jews who are gathered to you would be scattered, and the remnant in Judah perish?"

¹⁶But Gedaliah the son of Ahikam said to Johanan the son of Kareah, "You shall not do this thing, for you speak falsely concerning Ishmael."

Insurrection Against Gedaliah

41 Now it came to pass in the seventh month *that* Ishmael the son of Nethaniah, the son of Elishama, of the royal family and of the officers of the king, came with ten men to Gedaliah the son of Ahikam, at Mizpah. And there they ate bread together in Mizpah. ²Then Ishmael the son of Nethaniah, and the ten men who were with him, arose and struck Gedaliah the son of Ahikam, the son of Shaphan, with the sword, and killed him whom the king of Babylon had made governor over the land. ³Ishmael also struck down all the Jews who were with him, *that is,* with Gedaliah at Mizpah, and the Chaldeans who were found there, the men of war.

⁴And it happened, on the second day after he had killed Gedaliah, when as yet no one knew *it,* ⁵that certain men came from Shechem, from Shiloh, and from Samaria, eighty men with their beards shaved and their clothes torn, having cut themselves, with offerings and incense in their hand, to bring *them* to the house

40:8 ªSpelled *Jaazaniah* in 2 Kings 25:23

of the LORD. ⁶Now Ishmael the son of Nethaniah went out from Mizpah to meet them, weeping as he went along; and it happened as he met them that he said to them, "Come to Gedaliah the son of Ahikam!" ⁷So it was, when they came into the midst of the city, that Ishmael the son of Nethaniah killed them *and cast them* into the midst of a pit, he and the men who were with him. ⁸But ten men were found among them who said to Ishmael, "Do not kill us, for we have treasures of wheat, barley, oil, and honey in the field." So he desisted and did not kill them among their brethren. ⁹Now the pit into which Ishmael had cast all the dead bodies of the men whom he had slain, because of Gedaliah, *was* the same one Asa the king had made for fear of Baasha king of Israel. Ishmael the son of Nethaniah filled it with *the* slain. ¹⁰Then Ishmael carried away captive all the rest of the people who *were* in Mizpah, the king's daughters and all the people who remained in Mizpah, whom Nebuzaradan the captain of the guard had committed to Gedaliah the son of Ahikam. And Ishmael the son of Nethaniah carried them away captive and departed to go over to the Ammonites.

¹¹But when Johanan the son of Kareah and all the captains of the forces that *were* with him heard of all the evil that Ishmael the son of Nethaniah had done, ¹²they took all the men and went to fight with Ishmael the son of Nethaniah; and they found him by the great pool that *is* in Gibeon. ¹³So it was, when all the people who *were* with Ishmael saw Johanan the son of Kareah, and all the captains of the forces who *were* with him, that they were glad. ¹⁴Then all the people whom Ishmael had carried away captive from Mizpah turned around and came back, and went to Johanan the son of Kareah. ¹⁵But Ishmael the son of Nethaniah escaped from Johanan with eight men and went to the Ammonites.

¹⁶Then Johanan the son of Kareah, and all the captains of the forces that were with him, took from Mizpah all the rest of the people whom he had recovered from Ishmael the son of Nethaniah after he had murdered Gedaliah the son of Ahikam—the mighty men of war and the women and the children and the eunuchs, whom he had brought back from Gibeon. ¹⁷And they departed and dwelt in the habitation of Chimham, which is near Bethlehem, as they went on their way to Egypt, ¹⁸because of the Chaldeans; for they were afraid of them, because Ishmael the son of Nethaniah had murdered Gedaliah the son of Ahikam,

whom the king of Babylon had made governor in the land.

The Flight to Egypt Forbidden

42 Now all the captains of the forces, Johanan the son of Kareah, Jezaniah the son of Hoshaiah, and all the people, from the least to the greatest, came near ²and said to Jeremiah the prophet, "Please, let our petition be acceptable to you, and pray for us to the LORD your God, for all this remnant (since we are left *but* a few of many, as you can see), ³that the LORD your God may show us the way in which we should walk and the thing we should do."

Jeremiah Makes a Tough Call

(*Jeremiah 42:1—43:13*)

Most leaders don't look forward to making tough calls. Jeremiah had to make a tough call when his people rejected God's solution to a dilemma. Jeremiah had to remind them of their disobedience and explain the consequences of their choice (Jer. 42:19–22).

Many leaders fail because of an inability to make tough decisions. Consider some guidelines for making a tough call:

1. Accept tough calls as a requirement of leadership.
2. Do your homework. Research can make or break a decision.
3. Set a deadline.
4. Make sure the timing is right.
5. Seek counsel from the right people.
6. Make your decisions on the principles and values you believe in.
7. Develop systems that enable you to make the tough call.
8. Understand the emotional expense of making the tough call.
9. Recognize your part and God's part.
10. Pray for discernment and courage.

---

⁴Then Jeremiah the prophet said to them, "I have heard. Indeed, I will pray to the LORD your God according to your words, and it shall be, *that* whatever the LORD answers you, I will declare *it* to you. I will keep nothing back from you."

[5]So they said to Jeremiah, "Let the LORD be a true and faithful witness between us, if we do not do according to everything which the LORD your God sends us by you. [6]Whether *it is* pleasing or displeasing, we will obey the voice of the LORD our God to whom we send you, that it may be well with us when we obey the voice of the LORD our God."

[7]And it happened after ten days that the word of the LORD came to Jeremiah. [8]Then he called Johanan the son of Kareah, all the captains of the forces which *were* with him, and all the people from the least even to the greatest, [9]and said to them, "Thus says the LORD, the God of Israel, to whom you sent me to present your petition before Him: [10]'If you will still remain in this land, then I will build you and not pull *you* down, and I will plant you and not pluck *you* up. For I relent concerning the disaster that I have brought upon you. [11]Do not be afraid of the king of Babylon, of whom you are afraid; do not be afraid of him,' says the LORD, 'for I *am* with you, to save you and deliver you from his hand. [12]And I will show you mercy, that he may have mercy on you and cause you to return to your own land.'

[13]"But if you say, 'We will not dwell in this land,' disobeying the voice of the LORD your God, [14]saying, 'No, but we will go to the land of Egypt where we shall see no war, nor hear the sound of the trumpet, nor be hungry for bread, and there we will dwell'— [15]Then hear now the word of the LORD, O remnant of Judah! Thus says the LORD of hosts, the God of Israel: 'If you wholly set your faces to enter Egypt, and go to dwell there, [16]then it shall be *that* the sword which you feared shall overtake you there in the land of Egypt; the famine of which you were afraid shall follow close after you there *in* Egypt; and there you shall die. [17]So shall it be with all the men who set their faces to go to Egypt to dwell there. They shall die by the sword, by famine, and by pestilence. And none of them shall remain or escape from the disaster that I will bring upon them.'

[18]"For thus says the LORD of hosts, the God of Israel: 'As My anger and My fury have been poured out on the inhabitants of Jerusalem, so will My fury be poured out on you when you enter Egypt. And you shall be an oath, an astonishment, a curse, and a reproach; and you shall see this place no more.'

[19]"The LORD has said concerning you, O remnant of Judah, 'Do not go to Egypt!' Know certainly that I have admonished you this day. [20]For you were hypocrites in your hearts when you sent me to the LORD your God, saying, 'Pray for us to the LORD our God, and according to all that the LORD your God says, so declare to us and we will do *it*.' [21]And I have this day declared *it* to you, but you have not obeyed the voice of the LORD your God, or anything which He has sent you by me. [22]Now therefore, know certainly that you shall die by the sword, by famine, and by pestilence in the place where you desire to go to dwell."

Jeremiah Taken to Egypt

43 Now it happened, when Jeremiah had stopped speaking to all the people all the words of the LORD their God, for which the LORD their God had sent him to them, all these words, [2]that Azariah the son of Hoshaiah, Johanan the son of Kareah, and all the proud men spoke, saying to Jeremiah, "You speak falsely! The LORD our God has not sent you to say, 'Do not go to Egypt to dwell there.' [3]But Baruch the son of Neriah has set you against us, to deliver us into the hand of the Chaldeans, that they may put us to death or carry us away captive to Babylon." [4]So Johanan the son of Kareah, all the captains of the forces, and all the people would not obey the voice of the LORD, to remain in the land of Judah. [5]But Johanan the son of Kareah and all the captains of the forces took all the remnant of Judah who had returned to dwell in the land of Judah, from all nations where they had been driven— [6]men, women, children, the king's daughters, and every person whom Nebuzaradan the captain of the guard had left with Gedaliah the son of Ahikam, the son of Shaphan, and Jeremiah the prophet and Baruch the son of Neriah. [7]So they went to the land of Egypt, for they did not obey the voice of the LORD. And they went as far as Tahpanhes.

[8]Then the word of the LORD came to Jeremiah in Tahpanhes, saying, [9]"Take large stones in your hand, and hide them in the sight of the men of Judah, in the clay in the brick courtyard which *is* at the entrance to Pharaoh's house in Tahpanhes; [10]and say to them, 'Thus says the LORD of hosts, the God of Israel: "Behold, I will send and bring Nebuchadnezzar the king of Babylon, My servant, and will set his throne above these stones that I have hidden. And he will spread his royal pavilion over them. [11]When he comes, he shall strike the land of Egypt *and deliver* to death *those appointed* for death, and to captivity *those appointed* for captivity, and to the sword *those appointed* for the sword. [12]I[a] will kin-

---

43:12 [a]Following Masoretic Text and Targum; Septuagint, Syriac, and Vulgate read *He.*

dle a fire in the houses of the gods of Egypt, and he shall burn them and carry them away captive. And he shall array himself with the land of Egypt, as a shepherd puts on his garment, and he shall go out from there in peace. [13]He shall also break the *sacred* pillars of Beth Shemesh[a] that *are* in the land of Egypt; and the houses of the gods of the Egyptians he shall burn with fire."'"

Communication: Jeremiah Uses Word Pictures

(Jeremiah 43:8–13)

Jeremiah led the people primarily through his word gifts. He expressed his leadership using gifts of prophecy, teaching, and exhortation. Through wise use of these gifts, he became a master communicator.

His book features at least 12 metaphors, or word pictures, that he used to communicate God's message to God's people. Effective leaders find similar analogies and object lessons to make their point. Study and learn from Jeremiah, a master communicator.

Jeremiah's twelve object lessons:
1. The almond branch (1:11, 12)
2. The boiling pot (1:13–19)
3. The ruined linen sash (13:1–11)
4. The wine bottles (13:12–14)
5. The drought (14:1–9)
6. The partridge (17:9–11)
7. The potter and the clay (18:1–17)
8. The broken flask (19:1–13)
9. Two baskets of figs (24:1–10)
10. The bonds and yokes (27:1–11)
11. The command to buy a field (32:6–25)
12. The parable of the stones (43:8–13)

Israelites Will Be Punished in Egypt

44 The word that came to Jeremiah concerning all the Jews who dwell in the land of Egypt, who dwell at Migdol, at Tahpanhes, at Noph,[a] and in the country of Pathros, saying, [2]"Thus says the LORD of hosts, the God of Israel: 'You have seen all the calamity that I have brought on Jerusalem and on all the cities of Judah; and behold, this day they *are* a desolation, and no one dwells in them, [3]because of their wickedness which they have committed

to provoke Me to anger, in that they went to burn incense *and* to serve other gods whom they did not know, they nor you nor your fathers. [4]However I have sent to you all My servants the prophets, rising early and sending *them,* saying, "Oh, do not do this abominable thing that I hate!" [5]But they did not listen or incline their ear to turn from their wickedness, to burn no incense to other gods. [6]So My fury and My anger were poured out and kindled in the cities of Judah and in the streets of Jerusalem; and they are wasted *and* desolate, as it is this day.'

[7]"Now therefore, thus says the LORD, the God of hosts, the God of Israel: 'Why do you commit *this* great evil against yourselves, to cut off from you man and woman, child and infant, out of Judah, leaving none to remain, [8]in that you provoke Me to wrath with the works of your hands, burning incense to other gods in the land of Egypt where you have gone to dwell, that you may cut yourselves off and be a curse and a reproach among all the nations of the earth? [9]Have you forgotten the wickedness of your fathers, the wickedness of the kings of Judah, the wickedness of their wives, your own wickedness, and the wickedness of your wives, which they committed in the land of Judah and in the streets of Jerusalem? [10]They have not been humbled, to this day, nor have they feared; they have not walked in My law or in My statutes that I set before you and your fathers.'

[11]"Therefore thus says the LORD of hosts, the God of Israel: 'Behold, I will set My face against you for catastrophe and for cutting off all Judah. [12]And I will take the remnant of Judah who have set their faces to go into the land of Egypt to dwell there, and they shall all be consumed *and* fall in the land of Egypt. They shall be consumed by the sword *and* by famine. They shall die, from the least to the greatest, by the sword and by famine; and they shall be an oath, an astonishment, a curse and a reproach! [13]For I will punish those who dwell in the land of Egypt, as I have punished Jerusalem, by the sword, by famine, and by pestilence, [14]so that none of the remnant of Judah who have gone into the land of Egypt to dwell there shall escape or survive, lest they return to the land of Judah, to which they desire to return and dwell. For none shall return except those who escape.'"

[15]Then all the men who knew that their wives had burned incense to other gods, with all the women who stood by, a great multitude, and

---

43:13 [a]Literally *House of the Sun,* ancient On; later called Heliopolis **44:1** [a]That is, ancient Memphis all the people who dwelt in the land of Egypt, in Pathros, answered Jeremiah, saying: [16]"*As for the* word that you have spoken to us in the name of the LORD, we will not listen to you! [17]But we will certainly do whatever has gone out of our own mouth, to burn incense to the queen of heaven and pour out drink offerings to her, as we have done, we and our fathers, our kings and our princes, in the cities of Judah and in the streets of Jerusalem. For *then* we had plenty of food, were well-off, and saw no trouble. [18]But since we stopped burning incense to the queen of heaven and pouring out drink offerings to her, we have lacked everything and have been consumed by the sword and by famine."

[19]*The women also said,* "And when we burned incense to the queen of heaven and poured out drink offerings to her, did we make cakes for her, to worship her, and pour out drink offerings to her without our husbands' *permission?*"

[20]Then Jeremiah spoke to all the people—the men, the women, and all the people who had given him *that* answer—saying: [21]"The incense that you burned in the cities of Judah and in the streets of Jerusalem, you and your fathers, your kings and your princes, and the people of the land, did not the LORD remember them, and did it *not* come into His mind? [22]So the LORD could no longer bear *it,* because of the evil of your do-ings *and* because of the abominations which you committed. Therefore your land is a desolation, an astonishment, a curse, and without an inhab-itant, as *it is* this day. [23]Because you have burned incense and because you have sinned against the LORD, and have not obeyed the voice of the LORD or walked in His law, in His statutes or in His testimonies, therefore this calamity has hap-pened to you, as *at* this day."

[24]Moreover Jeremiah said to all the people and to all the women, "Hear the word of the LORD, all Judah who *are* in the land of Egypt! [25]Thus says the LORD of hosts, the God of Israel, saying: 'You and your wives have spoken with your mouths and fulfilled with your hands, say-ing, "We will surely keep our vows that we have made, to burn incense to the queen of heaven and pour out drink offerings to her." You will surely keep your vows and perform your vows!' [26]Therefore hear the word of the LORD, all Judah who dwell in the land of Egypt: 'Behold, I have sworn by My great name,' says the LORD, 'that My name shall no more be named in the mouth of any man of Judah in all the land of Egypt, say-ing, "The Lord GOD lives." [27]Behold, I will watch over them for adversity and not for good. And all the men of Judah who *are* in the land of Egypt shall be consumed by the sword and by famine, until there is an end to them. [28]Yet a small num-ber who escape the sword shall return from the land of Egypt to the land of Judah; and all the remnant of Judah, who have gone to the land of Egypt to dwell there, shall know whose words will stand, Mine or theirs. [29]And this *shall be* a sign to you,' says the LORD, 'that I will punish you in this place, that you may know that My words will surely stand against you for adversity.'

[30]"Thus says the LORD: 'Behold, I will give Pharaoh Hophra king of Egypt into the hand of his enemies and into the hand of those who seek his life, as I gave Zedekiah king of Judah into the hand of Nebuchadnezzar king of Babylon, his enemy who sought his life.'"

Assurance to Baruch

45 The word that Jeremiah the prophet spoke to Baruch the son of Neriah, when he had written these words in a book at the instruction of Jeremiah,[a] in the fourth year of Jehoiakim the son of Josiah, king of Judah, saying, [2]"Thus says the LORD, the God of Israel, to you, O Baruch: [3]"You said, "Woe is me now! For the LORD has added grief to my sorrow. I fainted in my sighing, and I find no rest."'

[4]"Thus you shall say to him, 'Thus says the LORD: "Behold, what I have built I will break down, and what I have planted I will pluck up, that is, this whole land. [5]And do you seek great things for yourself? Do not seek *them;* for be-hold, I will bring adversity on all flesh," says the LORD. "But I will give your life to you as a prize in all places, wherever you go."'"

Judgment on Egypt

46 The word of the LORD which came to Jeremiah the prophet against the nations. [2]Against Egypt.

Concerning the army of Pharaoh Necho, king of Egypt, which was by the River Eu-phrates in Carchemish, and which Nebuchad-nezzar king of Babylon defeated in the fourth year of Jehoiakim the son of Josiah, king of Ju-dah:

[3] "Order the buckler and shield,
And draw near to battle!
[4] Harness the horses,
And mount up, you horsemen!
Stand forth with *your* helmets,
Polish the spears,

45:1 [a]Literally *from Jeremiah's mouth*

Put on the armor!
5 Why have I seen them dismayed *and*
  turned back?
  Their mighty ones are beaten down;
  They have speedily fled,
  And did not look back,
  For fear *was* all around," says the LORD.
6 "Do not let the swift flee away,
  Nor the mighty man escape;
  They will stumble and fall
  Toward the north, by the River Euphrates.

7 "Who *is* this coming up like a flood,
  Whose waters move like the rivers?
8 Egypt rises up like a flood,
  And *its* waters move like the rivers;
  And he says, 'I will go up *and* cover the
  earth,
  I will destroy the city and its inhabitants.'
9 Come up, O horses, and rage, O chariots!
  And let the mighty men come forth:
  The Ethiopians and the Libyans who
  handle the shield,
  And the Lydians who handle *and* bend the
  bow.
10 For this *is* the day of the Lord GOD of
  hosts,
  A day of vengeance,
  That He may avenge Himself on His
  adversaries.
  The sword shall devour;
  It shall be satiated and made drunk with
  their blood;
  For the Lord GOD of hosts has a sacrifice
  In the north country by the River
  Euphrates.

11 "Go up to Gilead and take balm,
  O virgin, the daughter of Egypt;
  In vain you will use many medicines;
  You shall not be cured.
12 The nations have heard of your shame,
  And your cry has filled the land;
  For the mighty man has stumbled against
  the mighty;
  They both have fallen together."

Babylonia Will Strike Egypt

13 The word that the LORD spoke to Jeremiah
the prophet, how Nebuchadnezzar king of Babylon would come *and* strike the land of Egypt.

14 "Declare in Egypt, and proclaim in Migdol;
  Proclaim in Noph[a] and in Tahpanhes;
  Say, 'Stand fast and prepare yourselves,
  For the sword devours all around you.'

15 Why are your valiant *men* swept away?
  They did not stand
  Because the LORD drove them away.
16 He made many fall;
  Yes, one fell upon another.
  And they said, 'Arise!
  Let us go back to our own people
  And to the land of our nativity
  From the oppressing sword.'
17 They cried there,
  'Pharaoh, king of Egypt, *is but* a noise.
  He has passed by the appointed time!'

18 "*As* I live," says the King,
  Whose name *is* the LORD of hosts,
  "Surely as Tabor *is* among the mountains
  And as Carmel by the sea, *so* he shall
  come.
19 O you daughter dwelling in Egypt,
  Prepare yourself to go into captivity!
  For Noph[a] shall be waste and desolate,
  without inhabitant.

20 "Egypt *is* a very pretty heifer,
  But destruction comes, it comes from the
  north.
21 Also her mercenaries are in her midst like
  fat bulls,
  For they also are turned back,
  They have fled away together.
  They did not stand,
  For the day of their calamity had come
  upon them,
  The time of their punishment.
22 Her noise shall go like a serpent,
  For they shall march with an army
  And come against her with axes,
  Like those who chop wood.

23 "They shall cut down her forest," says the
  LORD,
  "Though it cannot be searched,
  Because they *are* innumerable,
  And more numerous than grasshoppers.
24 The daughter of Egypt shall be ashamed;
  She shall be delivered into the hand
  Of the people of the north."

25 The LORD of hosts, the God of Israel, says:
"Behold, I will bring punishment on Amon[a] of
No,[b] and Pharaoh and Egypt, with their gods
and their kings—Pharaoh and those who trust in

46:14 [a]That is, ancient Memphis 46:19 [a]That is,
ancient Memphis 46:25 [a]A sun god [b]That is,
ancient Thebes

him. [26]And I will deliver them into the hand of those who seek their lives, into the hand of Nebuchadnezzar king of Babylon and the hand of his servants. Afterward it shall be inhabited as in the days of old," says the LORD.

God Will Preserve Israel

[27] "But do not fear, O My servant Jacob,
And do not be dismayed, O Israel!
For behold, I will save you from afar,
And your offspring from the land of their captivity;
Jacob shall return, have rest and be at ease;
No one shall make him afraid.
[28] Do not fear, O Jacob My servant," says the LORD,
"For I am with you;
For I will make a complete end of all the nations
To which I have driven you,
But I will not make a complete end of you.
I will rightly correct you,
For I will not leave you wholly unpunished."

Judgment on Philistia

47 The word of the LORD that came to Jeremiah the prophet against the Philistines, before Pharaoh attacked Gaza.

[2]Thus says the LORD:

"Behold, waters rise out of the north,
And shall be an overflowing flood;
They shall overflow the land and all that is in it,
The city and those who dwell within;
Then the men shall cry,
And all the inhabitants of the land shall wail.
[3] At the noise of the stamping hooves of his strong horses,
At the rushing of his chariots,
At the rumbling of his wheels,
The fathers will not look back for their children,
Lacking courage,
[4] Because of the day that comes to plunder all the Philistines,
To cut off from Tyre and Sidon every helper who remains;
For the LORD shall plunder the Philistines,
The remnant of the country of Caphtor.
[5] Baldness has come upon Gaza,
Ashkelon is cut off

With the remnant of their valley.
How long will you cut yourself?
[6] "O you sword of the LORD,
How long until you are quiet?
Put yourself up into your scabbard,
Rest and be still!
[7] How can it be quiet,
Seeing the LORD has given it a charge
Against Ashkelon and against the seashore?
There He has appointed it."

Judgment on Moab

48 Against Moab.
Thus says the LORD of hosts, the God of Israel:

"Woe to Nebo!
For it is plundered,
Kirjathaim is shamed and taken;
The high stronghold[a] is shamed and dismayed—
[2] No more praise of Moab.
In Heshbon they have devised evil against her:
'Come, and let us cut her off as a nation.'
You also shall be cut down, O Madmen![a]
The sword shall pursue you;
[3] A voice of crying shall be from Horonaim:
'Plundering and great destruction!'

[4] "Moab is destroyed;
Her little ones have caused a cry to be heard;[a]
[5] For in the Ascent of Luhith they ascend with continual weeping;
For in the descent of Horonaim the enemies have heard a cry of destruction.

[6] "Flee, save your lives!
And be like the juniper[a] in the wilderness.
[7] For because you have trusted in your works and your treasures,
You also shall be taken.
And Chemosh shall go forth into captivity,
His priests and his princes together.
[8] And the plunderer shall come against every city;
No one shall escape.
The valley also shall perish,
And the plain shall be destroyed,
As the LORD has spoken.

48:1 [a]Hebrew Misgab 48:2 [a]A city of Moab
48:4 [a]Following Masoretic Text, Targum, and Vulgate; Septuagint reads Proclaim it in Zoar.
48:6 [a]Or Aroer, a city of Moab

9 "Give wings to Moab,
That she may flee and get away;
For her cities shall be desolate,
Without any to dwell in them.

10 Cursed *is* he who does the work of the
LORD deceitfully,
And cursed *is* he who keeps back his
sword from blood.

11 "Moab has been at ease from his[a] youth;
He has settled on his dregs,
And has not been emptied from vessel to
vessel,
Nor has he gone into captivity.
Therefore his taste remained in him,
And his scent has not changed.

12 "Therefore behold, the days are coming,"
says the LORD,
"That I shall send him wine-workers
Who will tip him over
And empty his vessels
And break the bottles.

13 Moab shall be ashamed of Chemosh,
As the house of Israel was ashamed of
Bethel, their confidence.

14 "How can you say, 'We *are* mighty
And strong men for the war'?
15 Moab is plundered and gone up *from* her
cities;
Her chosen young men have gone down
to the slaughter," says the King,
Whose name *is* the LORD of hosts.

16 "The calamity of Moab *is* near at hand,
And his affliction comes quickly.
17 Bemoan him, all you who are around him;
And all you who know his name,
Say, 'How the strong staff is broken,
The beautiful rod!'

18 "O daughter inhabiting Dibon,
Come down from *your* glory,
And sit in thirst;
For the plunderer of Moab has come
against you,
He has destroyed your strongholds.
19 O inhabitant of Aroer,
Stand by the way and watch;
Ask him who flees
And her who escapes;
Say, 'What has happened?'

20 Moab is shamed, for he is broken down.
Wail and cry!
Tell it in Arnon, that Moab is plundered.

21 "And judgment has come on the plain
country:
On Holon and Jahzah and Mephaath,
22 On Dibon and Nebo and Beth
Diblathaim,
23 On Kirjathaim and Beth Gamul and Beth
Meon,
24 On Kerioth and Bozrah,
On all the cities of the land of Moab,
Far or near.
25 The horn of Moab is cut off,
And his arm is broken," says the LORD.

26 "Make him drunk,
Because he exalted *himself* against the
LORD.
Moab shall wallow in his vomit,
And he shall also be in derision.
27 For was not Israel a derision to you?
Was he found among thieves?
For whenever you speak of him,
You shake *your head in scorn.*
28 You who dwell in Moab,
Leave the cities and dwell in the rock,
And be like the dove *which* makes her nest
In the sides of the cave's mouth.

29 "We have heard the pride of Moab
(He *is* exceedingly proud),
Of his loftiness and arrogance and pride,
And of the haughtiness of his heart."
30 "I know his wrath," says the LORD,
"But it *is* not right;
His lies have made nothing right.
31 Therefore I will wail for Moab,
And I will cry out for all Moab;
I[a] will mourn for the men of Kir Heres.
32 O vine of Sibmah! I will weep for you
with the weeping of Jazer.
Your plants have gone over the sea,
They reach to the sea of Jazer.
The plunderer has fallen on your summer
fruit and your vintage.
33 Joy and gladness are taken
From the plentiful field
And from the land of Moab;
I have caused wine to fail from the
winepresses;
No one will tread with joyous shouting—
Not joyous shouting!

48:11 [a]The Hebrew uses masculine and feminine
pronouns interchangeably in this chapter.
48:31 [a]Following Dead Sea Scrolls, Septuagint, and
Vulgate; Masoretic Text reads *He.*

Leadership Brings Temptations

(Jeremiah 48:26–30)

The nation of Moab dominated several others in her most powerful years, but God pronounced a severe judgment against her. Why? Moab's leaders, caught up in their own power, defied the Lord. Pride, conceit, and arrogance began to drive her leaders.

The same danger often ruins leaders today. Several related temptations commonly lead to the destruction of contemporary leaders:

1. **Pride:** We enjoy thinking that we did it on our own.
2. **Possessions:** We pursue the perks that come with our visibility.
3. **Popularity:** We begin to believe our own press.
4. **Power:** We recognize our clout and use it to advance ourselves.
5. **Prestige:** We love the feeling of being important and irreplaceable.
6. **Pleasure:** We think we deserve special treatment not given to others.
7. **People:** We cross a line from serving others to pleasing people.

After enjoying leadership success, a sequence of events often follows:

1. **Satisfaction:** We enjoy the victory we have achieved.
2. **Indulgence:** We unconsciously feel we deserve a pleasurable reward.
3. **Compromise:** We rationalize our behavior.
4. **Denial:** We continue leading, not realizing our impure motives.
5. **Adultery:** We give ourselves to another, sexually, emotionally, or financially.
6. **Obsession:** We get trapped in a pattern that consumes us.

---

34 "From the cry of Heshbon to Elealeh and
　　to Jahaz
　They have uttered their voice,
　From Zoar to Horonaim,
　Like a three-year-old heifer;[a]
　For the waters of Nimrim also shall be
　　desolate.

35 "Moreover," says the LORD,
　"I will cause to cease in Moab
　The one who offers *sacrifices* in the high
　　places
　And burns incense to his gods.

36 Therefore My heart shall wail like flutes
　　for Moab,
　And like flutes My heart shall wail
　For the men of Kir Heres.
　Therefore the riches they have acquired
　　have perished.

37 "For every head *shall be* bald, and every
　　beard clipped;
　On all the hands *shall be* cuts, and on the
　　loins sackcloth—

38 A general lamentation
　On all the housetops of Moab,
　And in its streets;

For I have broken Moab like a vessel in
　　which *is* no pleasure," says the LORD.

39 "They shall wail:
　'How she is broken down!
　How Moab has turned her back with
　　shame!'
　So Moab shall be a derision
　And a dismay to all those about her."

40 For thus says the LORD:

"Behold, one shall fly like an eagle,
　And spread his wings over Moab.

41 Kerioth is taken,
　And the strongholds are surprised;
　The mighty men's hearts in Moab on that
　　day shall be
　Like the heart of a woman in birth pangs.

42 And Moab shall be destroyed as a people,
　Because he exalted *himself* against the
　　LORD.

43 Fear and the pit and the snare *shall be* upon
　　you,
　O inhabitant of Moab," says the LORD.

48:34 [a]Or *The Third Eglath,* an unknown city
(compare Isaiah 15:5)

44 "He who flees from the fear shall fall into
         the pit,
     And he who gets out of the pit shall be
         caught in the snare.
     For upon Moab, upon it I will bring
     The year of their punishment," says the
         LORD.

45 "Those who fled stood under the shadow
         of Heshbon
     Because of exhaustion.
     But a fire shall come out of Heshbon,
     A flame from the midst of Sihon,
     And shall devour the brow of Moab,
     The crown of the head of the sons of
         tumult.
46 Woe to you, O Moab!
     The people of Chemosh perish;
     For your sons have been taken captive,
     And your daughters captive.

47 "Yet I will bring back the captives of Moab
     In the latter days," says the LORD.

Thus far *is* the judgment of Moab.

Judgment on Ammon

49

Against the Ammonites.
Thus says the LORD:

"Has Israel no sons?
     Has he no heir?
     Why *then* does Milcom[a] inherit Gad,
     And his people dwell in its cities?
2 Therefore behold, the days are coming,"
         says the LORD,
     "That I will cause to be heard an alarm of
         war
     In Rabbah of the Ammonites;
     It shall be a desolate mound,
     And her villages shall be burned with fire.
     Then Israel shall take possession of his
         inheritance," says the LORD.

3 "Wail, O Heshbon, for Ai is plundered!
     Cry, you daughters of Rabbah,
     Gird yourselves with sackcloth!
     Lament and run to and fro by the walls;
     For Milcom shall go into captivity
     With his priests and his princes together.
4 Why do you boast in the valleys,
     Your flowing valley, O backsliding daughter?
     Who trusted in her treasures, *saying,*
     'Who will come against me?'
5 Behold, I will bring fear upon you,"
     Says the Lord GOD of hosts,

"From all those who are around you;
     You shall be driven out, everyone
         headlong,
     And no one will gather those who wander
         off.
6 But afterward I will bring back
     The captives of the people of Ammon,"
     says the LORD.

Judgment on Edom

7 Against Edom.
Thus says the LORD of hosts:

"*Is* wisdom no more in Teman?
     Has counsel perished from the prudent?
     Has their wisdom vanished?
8 Flee, turn back, dwell in the depths, O
         inhabitants of Dedan!
     For I will bring the calamity of Esau upon
         him,
     The time *that* I will punish him.
9 If grape-gatherers came to you,
     Would they not leave *some* gleaning
         grapes?
     If thieves by night,
     Would they not destroy until they have
         enough?
10 But I have made Esau bare;
     I have uncovered his secret places,[a]
     And he shall not be able to hide himself.
     His descendants are plundered,
     His brethren and his neighbors,
     And he *is* no more.
11 Leave your fatherless children,
     I will preserve *them* alive;
     And let your widows trust in Me."

12 For thus says the LORD: "Behold, those
whose judgment *was* not to drink of the cup
have assuredly drunk. And *are* you the one who
will altogether go unpunished? You shall not go
unpunished, but you shall surely drink *of it.* 13 For
I have sworn by Myself," says the LORD, "that
Bozrah shall become a desolation, a reproach, a
waste, and a curse. And all its cities shall be perpetual wastes."

14   I have heard a message from the LORD,
     And an ambassador has been sent to the
         nations:
     "Gather together, come against her,
     And rise up to battle!

49:1 [a]Hebrew *Malcam,* literally *their king,* a god of
the Ammonites; also called *Molech* (compare verse 3)
49:10 [a]Compare Obadiah 5, 6

15 "For indeed, I will make you small among
    nations,
    Despised among men.
16 Your fierceness has deceived you,
    The pride of your heart,
    O you who dwell in the clefts of the rock,
    Who hold the height of the hill!
    Though you make your nest as high as the
    eagle,
    I will bring you down from there," says the
    LORD.[a]

17 "Edom also shall be an astonishment;
    Everyone who goes by it will be
    astonished
    And will hiss at all its plagues.
18 As in the overthrow of Sodom and
    Gomorrah
    And their neighbors," says the LORD,
    "No one shall remain there,
    Nor shall a son of man dwell in it.

19 "Behold, he shall come up like a lion from
    the floodplain[a] of the Jordan
    Against the dwelling place of the strong;
    But I will suddenly make him run away
    from her.
    And who is a chosen man that I may
    appoint over her?
    For who is like Me?
    Who will arraign Me?
    And who is that shepherd
    Who will withstand Me?"

20 Therefore hear the counsel of the LORD
    that He has taken against Edom,
    And His purposes that He has proposed
    against the inhabitants of Teman:
    Surely the least of the flock shall draw
    them out;
    Surely He shall make their dwelling places
    desolate with them.
21 The earth shakes at the noise of their fall;
    At the cry its noise is heard at the Red
    Sea.
22 Behold, He shall come up and fly like the
    eagle,
    And spread His wings over Bozrah;
    The heart of the mighty men of Edom in
    that day shall be
    Like the heart of a woman in birth pangs.

Judgment on Damascus

23 Against Damascus.

    "Hamath and Arpad are shamed,
    For they have heard bad news.

    They are fainthearted;
    There is trouble on the sea;
    It cannot be quiet.
24 Damascus has grown feeble;
    She turns to flee,
    And fear has seized her.
    Anguish and sorrows have taken her like a
    woman in labor.
25 Why is the city of praise not deserted, the
    city of My joy?
26 Therefore her young men shall fall in her
    streets,
    And all the men of war shall be cut off in
    that day," says the LORD of hosts.
27 "I will kindle a fire in the wall of
    Damascus,
    And it shall consume the palaces of Ben-
    Hadad."[a]

Judgment on Kedar and Hazor

28 Against Kedar and against the kingdoms of
Hazor, which Nebuchadnezzar king of Babylon
shall strike.

    Thus says the LORD:

    "Arise, go up to Kedar,
    And devastate the men of the East!
29 Their tents and their flocks they shall take
    away.
    They shall take for themselves their
    curtains,
    All their vessels and their camels;
    And they shall cry out to them,
    'Fear is on every side!'

30 "Flee, get far away! Dwell in the depths,
    O inhabitants of Hazor!" says the LORD.
    "For Nebuchadnezzar king of Babylon has
    taken counsel against you,
    And has conceived a plan against you.

31 "Arise, go up to the wealthy nation that
    dwells securely," says the LORD,
    "Which has neither gates nor bars,
    Dwelling alone.
32 Their camels shall be for booty,
    And the multitude of their cattle for
    plunder.
    I will scatter to all winds those in the
    farthest corners,
    And I will bring their calamity from all its
    sides," says the LORD.
33 "Hazor shall be a dwelling for jackals, a
    desolation forever;

49:16 [a]Compare Obadiah 3, 4 49:19 [a]Or thicket
49:27 [a]Compare Amos 1:4

No one shall reside there,
Nor son of man dwell in it."

Judgment on Elam

[34]The word of the LORD that came to Jeremiah the prophet against Elam, in the beginning of the reign of Zedekiah king of Judah, saying, [35]"Thus says the LORD of hosts:

'Behold, I will break the bow of Elam,
The foremost of their might.
[36] Against Elam I will bring the four winds
From the four quarters of heaven,
And scatter them toward all those winds;
There shall be no nations where the
outcasts of Elam will not go.
[37] For I will cause Elam to be dismayed
before their enemies
And before those who seek their life.
I will bring disaster upon them,
My fierce anger,' says the LORD;
'And I will send the sword after them
Until I have consumed them.
[38] I will set My throne in Elam,
And will destroy from there the king and
the princes,' says the LORD.

[39] 'But it shall come to pass in the latter days:
I will bring back the captives of Elam,' says
the LORD."

Judgment on Babylon and Babylonia

50 The word that the LORD spoke against Babylon and against the land of the Chaldeans by Jeremiah the prophet.

[2] "Declare among the nations,
Proclaim, and set up a standard;
Proclaim—do not conceal it—
Say, 'Babylon is taken, Bel is shamed.
Merodach[a] is broken in pieces;
Her idols are humiliated,
Her images are broken in pieces.'
[3] For out of the north a nation comes up
against her,
Which shall make her land desolate,
And no one shall dwell therein.
They shall move, they shall depart,
Both man and beast.

[4] "In those days and in that time," says the
LORD,
"The children of Israel shall come,
They and the children of Judah together;
With continual weeping they shall come,

And seek the LORD their God.
[5] They shall ask the way to Zion,
With their faces toward it, saying,
'Come and let us join ourselves to the
LORD
In a perpetual covenant
That will not be forgotten.'

[6] "My people have been lost sheep.
Their shepherds have led them astray;
They have turned them away on the
mountains.
They have gone from mountain to hill;
They have forgotten their resting place.
[7] All who found them have devoured them;
And their adversaries said, 'We have not
offended,
Because they have sinned against the
LORD, the habitation of justice,
The LORD, the hope of their fathers.'

[8] "Move from the midst of Babylon,
Go out of the land of the Chaldeans;
And be like the rams before the flocks.
[9] For behold, I will raise and cause to come
up against Babylon
An assembly of great nations from the
north country,
And they shall array themselves against
her;
From there she shall be captured.
Their arrows shall be like those of an expert
warrior;[a]
None shall return in vain.
[10] And Chaldea shall become plunder;
All who plunder her shall be satisfied," says
the LORD.

[11] "Because you were glad, because you
rejoiced,
You destroyers of My heritage,
Because you have grown fat like a heifer
threshing grain,
And you bellow like bulls,
[12] Your mother shall be deeply ashamed;
She who bore you shall be ashamed.
Behold, the least of the nations shall be a
wilderness,
A dry land and a desert.
[13] Because of the wrath of the LORD
She shall not be inhabited,

50:2 [a]A Babylonian god; sometimes spelled *Marduk*
50:9 [a]Following some Hebrew manuscripts, Septuagint, and Syriac; Masoretic Text, Targum, and Vulgate read *a warrior who makes childless.*

But she shall be wholly desolate.
Everyone who goes by Babylon shall be horrified
And hiss at all her plagues.

14 "Put yourselves in array against Babylon all around,
All you who bend the bow;
Shoot at her, spare no arrows,
For she has sinned against the LORD.
15 Shout against her all around;
She has given her hand,
Her foundations have fallen,
Her walls are thrown down;
For it *is* the vengeance of the LORD.
Take vengeance on her.
As she has done, so do to her.
16 Cut off the sower from Babylon,
And him who handles the sickle at harvest time.
For fear of the oppressing sword
Everyone shall turn to his own people,
And everyone shall flee to his own land.

17 "Israel *is* like scattered sheep;
The lions have driven *him* away.
First the king of Assyria devoured him;
Now at last this Nebuchadnezzar king of Babylon has broken his bones."

18 Therefore thus says the LORD of hosts, the God of Israel:

"Behold, I will punish the king of Babylon and his land,
As I have punished the king of Assyria.
19 But I will bring back Israel to his home,
And he shall feed on Carmel and Bashan;
His soul shall be satisfied on Mount Ephraim and Gilead.
20 In those days and in that time," says the LORD,
"The iniquity of Israel shall be sought, but *there shall be* none;
And the sins of Judah, but they shall not be found;
For I will pardon those whom I preserve.

21 "Go up against the land of Merathaim, against it,
And against the inhabitants of Pekod.
Waste and utterly destroy them," says the LORD,
"And do according to all that I have commanded you.
22 A sound of battle *is* in the land,
And of great destruction.
23 How the hammer of the whole earth has been cut apart and broken!
How Babylon has become a desolation among the nations!
I have laid a snare for you;
24 You have indeed been trapped, O Babylon,
And you were not aware;
You have been found and also caught,
Because you have contended against the LORD.
25 The LORD has opened His armory,
And has brought out the weapons of His indignation;
For this *is* the work of the Lord GOD of hosts
In the land of the Chaldeans.
26 Come against her from the farthest border;
Open her storehouses;
Cast her up as heaps of ruins,
And destroy her utterly;
Let nothing of her be left.
27 Slay all her bulls,
Let them go down to the slaughter.
Woe to them!
For their day has come, the time of their punishment.
28 The voice of those who flee and escape from the land of Babylon
Declares in Zion the vengeance of the LORD our God,
The vengeance of His temple.

29 "Call together the archers against Babylon.
All you who bend the bow, encamp against it all around;
Let none of them escape.[a]
Repay her according to her work;
According to all she has done, do to her;
For she has been proud against the LORD,
Against the Holy One of Israel.
30 Therefore her young men shall fall in the streets,
And all her men of war shall be cut off in that day," says the LORD.
31 "Behold, I *am* against you,
O most haughty one!" says the Lord GOD of hosts;
"For your day has come,
The time *that* I will punish you.[a]

50:29 [a]Qere, some Hebrew manuscripts, Septuagint, and Targum add *to her*.
50:31 [a]Following Masoretic Text and Targum; Septuagint and Vulgate read *The time of your punishment*.

32 The most proud shall stumble and fall,
   And no one will raise him up;
   I will kindle a fire in his cities,
   And it will devour all around him."

33 Thus says the LORD of hosts:

"The children of Israel *were* oppressed,
   Along with the children of Judah;
   All who took them captive have held them
      fast;
   They have refused to let them go.
34 Their Redeemer *is* strong;
   The LORD of hosts *is* His name.
   He will thoroughly plead their case,
   That He may give rest to the land,
   And disquiet the inhabitants of Babylon.

35 "A sword *is* against the Chaldeans," says the
      LORD,
   "Against the inhabitants of Babylon,
   And against her princes and her wise men.
36 A sword *is* against the soothsayers, and they
      will be fools.
   A sword *is* against her mighty men, and
      they will be dismayed.
37 A sword *is* against their horses,
   Against their chariots,
   And against all the mixed peoples who *are*
      in her midst;
   And they will become like women.
   A sword *is* against her treasures, and they
      will be robbed.
38 A drought[a] *is* against her waters, and they
      will be dried up.
   For it *is* the land of carved images,
   And they are insane with *their* idols.

39 "Therefore the wild desert beasts shall dwell
      there with the jackals,
   And the ostriches shall dwell in it.
   It shall be inhabited no more forever,
   Nor shall it be dwelt in from generation to
      generation.
40 As God overthrew Sodom and Gomorrah
   And their neighbors," says the LORD,
   "So no one shall reside there,
   Nor son of man dwell in it.

41 "Behold, a people shall come from the
      north,
   And a great nation and many kings
   Shall be raised up from the ends of the
      earth.
42 They shall hold the bow and the lance;
   They *are* cruel and shall not show mercy.

   Their voice shall roar like the sea;
   They shall ride on horses,
   Set in array, like a man for the battle,
   Against you, O daughter of Babylon.

43 "The king of Babylon has heard the report
      about them,
   And his hands grow feeble;
   Anguish has taken hold of him,
   Pangs as of a woman in childbirth.

44 "Behold, he shall come up like a lion from
      the floodplain[a] of the Jordan
   Against the dwelling place of the strong;
   But I will make them suddenly run away
      from her.
   And who *is* a chosen *man that* I may
      appoint over her?
   For who *is* like Me?
   Who will arraign Me?
   And who *is* that shepherd
   Who will withstand Me?"

45 Therefore hear the counsel of the LORD
      that He has taken against Babylon,
   And His purposes that He has proposed
      against the land of the Chaldeans:
   Surely the least of the flock shall draw
      them out;
   Surely He will make their dwelling place
      desolate with them.
46 At the noise of the taking of Babylon
   The earth trembles,
   And the cry is heard among the nations.

The Utter Destruction of Babylon

51 Thus says the LORD:

"Behold, I will raise up against
      Babylon,
   Against those who dwell in Leb Kamai,[a]
   A destroying wind.
2 And I will send winnowers to Babylon,
   Who shall winnow her and empty her
      land.
   For in the day of doom
   They shall be against her all around.
3 Against *her* let the archer bend his bow,
   And lift himself up against *her* in his
      armor.

50:38 [a]Following Masoretic Text, Targum, and
Vulgate; Syriac reads *sword;* Septuagint omits *A
drought is.* **50:44** [a]Or *thicket* **51:1** [a]A code word for
Chaldea (Babylonia); may be translated *The Midst of
Those Who Rise Up Against Me*

Do not spare her young men;
Utterly destroy all her army.

4 Thus the slain shall fall in the land of the
     Chaldeans,
   And *those* thrust through in her streets.

5 For Israel is not forsaken, nor Judah,
   By his God, the LORD of hosts,
   Though their land was filled with sin
     against the Holy One of Israel."

6 Flee from the midst of Babylon,
   And every one save his life!
   Do not be cut off in her iniquity,
   For this *is* the time of the LORD's
     vengeance;
   He shall recompense her.

7 Babylon *was* a golden cup in the LORD's
     hand,
   That made all the earth drunk.
   The nations drank her wine;
   Therefore the nations are deranged.

8 Babylon has suddenly fallen and been
     destroyed.
   Wail for her!
   Take balm for her pain;
   Perhaps she may be healed.

9 We would have healed Babylon,
   But she is not healed.
   Forsake her, and let us go everyone to his
     own country;
   For her judgment reaches to heaven and is
     lifted up to the skies.

10 The LORD has revealed our righteousness.
   Come and let us declare in Zion the work
     of the LORD our God.

11 Make the arrows bright!
   Gather the shields!
   The LORD has raised up the spirit of the
     kings of the Medes.
   For His plan *is* against Babylon to destroy
     it,
   Because it *is* the vengeance of the LORD,
   The vengeance for His temple.

12 Set up the standard on the walls of
     Babylon;
   Make the guard strong,
   Set up the watchmen,
   Prepare the ambushes.
   For the LORD has both devised and done
   What He spoke against the inhabitants of
     Babylon.

13 O you who dwell by many waters,
   Abundant in treasures,
   Your end has come,
   The measure of your covetousness.

14 The LORD of hosts has sworn by Himself:
   "Surely I will fill you with men, as with
     locusts,
   And they shall lift up a shout against you."

15 He has made the earth by His power;
   He has established the world by His
     wisdom,
   And stretched out the heaven by His
     understanding.

16 When He utters *His* voice—
   There is a multitude of waters in the
     heavens:
   "He causes the vapors to ascend from the
     ends of the earth;
   He makes lightnings for the rain;
   He brings the wind out of His treasuries."[a]

17 Everyone is dull-hearted, without
     knowledge;
   Every metalsmith is put to shame by the
     carved image;
   For his molded image *is* falsehood,
   And *there is* no breath in them.

18 They *are* futile, a work of errors;
   In the time of their punishment they shall
     perish.

19 The Portion of Jacob *is* not like them,
   For He *is* the Maker of all things;
   And *Israel is* the tribe of His inheritance.
   The LORD of hosts *is* His name.

20 "You *are* My battle-ax *and* weapons of war:
   For with you I will break the nation in
     pieces;
   With you I will destroy kingdoms;

21 With you I will break in pieces the horse
     and its rider;
   With you I will break in pieces the chariot
     and its rider;

22 With you also I will break in pieces man
     and woman;
   With you I will break in pieces old and
     young;
   With you I will break in pieces the young
     man and the maiden;

23 With you also I will break in pieces the
     shepherd and his flock;
   With you I will break in pieces the farmer
     and his yoke of oxen;
   And with you I will break in pieces
     governors and rulers.

51:16 [a]Psalm 135:7

24 "And I will repay Babylon
And all the inhabitants of Chaldea
For all the evil they have done
In Zion in your sight," says the LORD.

25 "Behold, I *am* against you, O destroying
mountain,
Who destroys all the earth," says the LORD.
"And I will stretch out My hand against you,
Roll you down from the rocks,
And make you a burnt mountain.

26 They shall not take from you a stone for a
corner
Nor a stone for a foundation,
But you shall be desolate forever," says the
LORD.

27 Set up a banner in the land,
Blow the trumpet among the nations!
Prepare the nations against her,
Call the kingdoms together against her:
Ararat, Minni, and Ashkenaz.
Appoint a general against her;
Cause the horses to come up like the
bristling locusts.

28 Prepare against her the nations,
With the kings of the Medes,
Its governors and all its rulers,
All the land of his dominion.

29 And the land will tremble and sorrow;
For every purpose of the LORD shall be
performed against Babylon,
To make the land of Babylon a desolation
without inhabitant.

30 The mighty men of Babylon have ceased
fighting,
They have remained in their strongholds;
Their might has failed,
They became *like* women;
They have burned her dwelling places,
The bars of her *gate* are broken.

31 One runner will run to meet another,
And one messenger to meet another,
To show the king of Babylon that his city
is taken on *all* sides;

32 The passages are blocked,
The reeds they have burned with fire,
And the men of war are terrified.

33 For thus says the LORD of hosts, the God of
Israel:

"The daughter of Babylon *is* like a
threshing floor
When it is time to thresh her;
Yet a little while
And the time of her harvest will come."

34 "Nebuchadnezzar the king of Babylon
Has devoured me, he has crushed me;
He has made me an empty vessel,
He has swallowed me up like a monster;
He has filled his stomach with my delicacies,
He has spit me out.

35 Let the violence *done* to me and my flesh
be upon Babylon,"
The inhabitant of Zion will say;
"And my blood be upon the inhabitants of
Chaldea!"
Jerusalem will say.

36 Therefore thus says the LORD:

"Behold, I will plead your case and take
vengeance for you.
I will dry up her sea and make her springs
dry.

37 Babylon shall become a heap,
A dwelling place for jackals,
An astonishment and a hissing,
Without an inhabitant.

38 They shall roar together like lions,
They shall growl like lions' whelps.

39 In their excitement I will prepare their
feasts;
I will make them drunk,
That they may rejoice,
And sleep a perpetual sleep
And not awake," says the LORD.

40 "I will bring them down
Like lambs to the slaughter,
Like rams with male goats.

41 "Oh, how Sheshach[a] is taken!
Oh, how the praise of the whole earth is
seized!
How Babylon has become desolate among
the nations!

42 The sea has come up over Babylon;
She is covered with the multitude of its
waves.

43 Her cities are a desolation,
A dry land and a wilderness,
A land where no one dwells,
Through which no son of man passes.

44 I will punish Bel in Babylon,
And I will bring out of his mouth what he
has swallowed;
And the nations shall not stream to him
anymore.
Yes, the wall of Babylon shall fall.

51:41 [a]A code word for Babylon (compare
Jeremiah 25:26)

⁴⁵ "My people, go out of the midst of her!
And let everyone deliver himself from the
fierce anger of the LORD.
⁴⁶ And lest your heart faint,
And you fear for the rumor that *will be*
heard in the land
(A rumor will come *one* year,
And after that, in *another* year
A rumor *will come,*
And violence in the land,
Ruler against ruler),
⁴⁷ Therefore behold, the days are coming
That I will bring judgment on the carved
images of Babylon;
Her whole land shall be ashamed,
And all her slain shall fall in her midst.
⁴⁸ Then the heavens and the earth and all
that *is* in them
Shall sing joyously over Babylon;
For the plunderers shall come to her from
the north," says the LORD.

⁴⁹ As Babylon *has caused* the slain of Israel to
fall,
So at Babylon the slain of all the earth
shall fall.
⁵⁰ You who have escaped the sword,
Get away! Do not stand still!
Remember the LORD afar off,
And let Jerusalem come to your mind.

⁵¹ We are ashamed because we have heard
reproach.
Shame has covered our faces,
For strangers have come into the
sanctuaries of the LORD's house.

⁵² "Therefore behold, the days are coming,"
says the LORD,
"That I will bring judgment on her carved
images,
And throughout all her land the wounded
shall groan.
⁵³ Though Babylon were to mount up to
heaven,
And though she were to fortify the height
of her strength,
Yet from Me plunderers would come to
her," says the LORD.

⁵⁴ The sound of a cry *comes* from Babylon,
And great destruction from the land of the
Chaldeans,
⁵⁵ Because the LORD is plundering Babylon
And silencing her loud voice,
Though her waves roar like great waters,

And the noise of their voice is uttered,
⁵⁶ Because the plunderer comes against her,
against Babylon,
And her mighty men are taken.
Every one of their bows is broken;
For the LORD *is* the God of recompense,
He will surely repay.

⁵⁷ "And I will make drunk
Her princes and wise men,
Her governors, her deputies, and her
mighty men.
And they shall sleep a perpetual sleep
And not awake," says the King,
Whose name *is* the LORD of hosts.

⁵⁸Thus says the LORD of hosts:

"The broad walls of Babylon shall be utterly
broken,
And her high gates shall be burned with
fire;
The people will labor in vain,
And the nations, because of the fire;
And they shall be weary."

Jeremiah's Command to Seraiah

⁵⁹The word which Jeremiah the prophet
commanded Seraiah the son of Neriah, the son
of Mahseiah, when he went with Zedekiah the
king of Judah to Babylon in the fourth year of
his reign. And Seraiah *was* the quartermaster. ⁶⁰So
Jeremiah wrote in a book all the evil that would
come upon Babylon, all these words that are
written against Babylon. ⁶¹And Jeremiah said to
Seraiah, "When you arrive in Babylon and see it,
and read all these words, ⁶²then you shall say, 'O
LORD, You have spoken against this place to cut
it off, so that none shall remain in it, neither man
nor beast, but it shall be desolate forever.' ⁶³Now
it shall be, when you have finished reading this
book, *that* you shall tie a stone to it and throw it
out into the Euphrates. ⁶⁴Then you shall say,
'Thus Babylon shall sink and not rise from the
catastrophe that I will bring upon her. And they
shall be weary.'"

Thus far *are* the words of Jeremiah.

The Fall of Jerusalem Reviewed

52 Zedekiah *was* twenty-one years old
when he became king, and he
reigned eleven years in Jerusalem.
His mother's name *was* Hamutal the daughter of
Jeremiah of Libnah. ²He also did evil in the sight
of the LORD, according to all that Jehoiakim had
done. ³For because of the anger of the LORD *this*

happened in Jerusalem and Judah, till He finally cast them out from His presence. Then Zedekiah rebelled against the king of Babylon.

⁴Now it came to pass in the ninth year of his reign, in the tenth month, on the tenth *day* of the month, *that* Nebuchadnezzar king of Babylon and all his army came against Jerusalem and encamped against it; and *they* built a siege wall against it all around. ⁵So the city was besieged until the eleventh year of King Zedekiah. ⁶By the fourth month, on the ninth day of the month, the famine had become so severe in the city that there was no food for the people of the land. ⁷Then the city wall was broken through, and all the men of war fled and went out of the city at night by way of the gate between the two walls, which *was* by the king's garden, even though the Chaldeans *were* near the city all around. And they went by way of the plain.ª

⁸But the army of the Chaldeans pursued the king, and they overtook Zedekiah in the plains of Jericho. All his army was scattered from him. ⁹So they took the king and brought him up to the king of Babylon at Riblah in the land of Hamath, and he pronounced judgment on him. ¹⁰Then the king of Babylon killed the sons of Zedekiah before his eyes. And he killed all the princes of Judah in Riblah. ¹¹He also put out the eyes of Zedekiah; and the king of Babylon bound him in bronze fetters, took him to Babylon, and put him in prison till the day of his death.

The Law of Connection: Leaders Must Achieve Reception, Not Rebellion
(Jeremiah 52:1–11)

God judged Zedekiah because he rebelled against the king of Babylon. Zedekiah forgot that even the leader works for someone. His rebellion led to the downfall of Jerusalem. Leaders must remember they are stewards of the people God has given them. A leader's rebellion leads to rebellion among the people.

The Temple and City Plundered and Burned
¹²Now in the fifth month, on the tenth *day* of the month (which *was* the nineteenth year of King Nebuchadnezzar king of Babylon), Neb-

uzaradan, the captain of the guard, *who* served the king of Babylon, came to Jerusalem. ¹³He burned the house of the LORD and the king's house; all the houses of Jerusalem, that is, all the houses of the great, he burned with fire. ¹⁴And all the army of the Chaldeans who *were* with the captain of the guard broke down all the walls of Jerusalem all around. ¹⁵Then Nebuzaradan the captain of the guard carried away captive *some* of the poor people, the rest of the people who remained in the city, the defectors who had deserted to the king of Babylon, and the rest of the craftsmen. ¹⁶But Nebuzaradan the captain of the guard left *some* of the poor of the land as vinedressers and farmers.

¹⁷The bronze pillars that *were* in the house of the LORD, and the carts and the bronze Sea that *were* in the house of the LORD, the Chaldeans broke in pieces, and carried all their bronze to Babylon. ¹⁸They also took away the pots, the shovels, the trimmers, the bowls, the spoons, and all the bronze utensils with which the priests ministered. ¹⁹The basins, the firepans, the bowls, the pots, the lampstands, the spoons, and the cups, whatever *was* solid gold and whatever *was* solid silver, the captain of the guard took away. ²⁰The two pillars, one Sea, the twelve bronze bulls which *were* under *it, and* the carts, which King Solomon had made for the house of the LORD—the bronze of all these articles was beyond measure. ²¹Now *concerning* the pillars: the height of one pillar *was* eighteen cubits, a measuring line of twelve cubits could measure its circumference, and its thickness *was* four fingers; *it was* hollow. ²²A capital of bronze *was* on it; and the height of one capital *was* five cubits, with a network and pomegranates all around the capital, all of bronze. The second pillar, with pomegranates was the same. ²³There were ninety-six pomegranates on the sides; all the pomegranates, all around on the network, *were* one hundred.

The People Taken Captive to Babylonia
²⁴The captain of the guard took Seraiah the chief priest, Zephaniah the second priest, and the three doorkeepers. ²⁵He also took out of the city an officer who had charge of the men of war, seven men of the king's close associates who were found in the city, the principal scribe of the army who mustered the people of the land, and sixty men of the people of the land who were found in the midst of the city. ²⁶And Nebuzaradan the captain of the guard took these and brought them to the king of Babylon at Riblah. ²⁷Then

---

52:7 ªOr *the Arabah,* that is, the Jordan Valley

the king of Babylon struck them and put them to death at Riblah in the land of Hamath. Thus Judah was carried away captive from its own land.

[28]These *are* the people whom Nebuchadnezzar carried away captive: in the seventh year, three thousand and twenty-three Jews; [29]in the eighteenth year of Nebuchadnezzar he carried away captive from Jerusalem eight hundred and thirty-two persons; [30]in the twenty-third year of Nebuchadnezzar, Nebuzaradan the captain of the guard carried away captive of the Jews seven hundred and forty-five persons. All the persons *were* four thousand six hundred.

Jehoiachin Released from Prison

[31]Now it came to pass in the thirty-seventh year of the captivity of Jehoiachin king of Judah, in the twelfth month, on the twenty-fifth *day* of the month, *that* Evil-Merodach[a] king of Babylon, in the first *year* of his reign, lifted up the head of Jehoiachin king of Judah and brought him out of prison. [32]And he spoke kindly to him and gave him a more prominent seat than those of the kings who *were* with him in Babylon. [33]So Jehoiachin changed from his prison garments, and he ate bread regularly before the king all the days of his life. [34]And as for his provisions, there was a regular ration given him by the king of Babylon, a portion for each day until the day of his death, all the days of his life.

52:31 [a]Or *Awil-Marduk*

LAMENTATIONS
Reflecting the Heart of a Leader

SUMMARY

The prophet Jeremiah wrote the passionate little Book of Lamentations after the Babylonians captured and destroyed Jerusalem. It is a deeply personal work, displaying the raw emotions of the prophet in response to the brutalization of Judah. Although he had predicted his people's exile and rebuked them for their unrepentant hearts, he deeply felt their pain and hurt when foreigners killed many of them and forced most of the others into exile in a pagan land.

This book feels like the Book of Psalms, full of emotion and reflecting the heart of a leader who desires the best for the people he once influenced. At the same time, it captures the mind of a leader who never waivers from his convictions, even when he must stand by them all alone. Midway through the book, Jeremiah reminds the people that repentance is all God requires and that He renews His mercies every morning (3:22, 23).

Jeremiah is rightly called the "weeping prophet," and Lamentations summarizes his cry for the people. We learn again that a leader cannot divorce himself or herself from the people he or she leads. Good leaders model both the heart and the behavior they want others to embrace. Someone once said, "Don't get too far out in front of your people or they will mistake you for the enemy." While standards must be upheld, the leader cannot hold those standards in some cold, distant fashion, unfeeling of the people's heart.

Good leaders are more than entrepreneurs. Entrepreneurs can act alone, but leaders cannot. By definition, they have followers whom they always want to take with them. Jeremiah knew what was best for the people, but he did not force them to cooperate. He pled with them to obey, but they refused. As a result, he lamented their apathy and their wasted potential.

As you read this book, allow the emotions of this "weeping prophet" to penetrate your own heart. Do you care for the people you lead to this degree? Are you as concerned for the "one lost sheep" who fails to take the journey, as you are for the 99 who go? Do you really love the people you lead? Perhaps Jeremiah can mentor us.

God's Role in Lamentations

God must play the disciplinarian in this book. He informed Jeremiah that unless the Jews repented, they would fall into captivity. God continued to remind Jeremiah of His divine standards and imperatives: repentance and obedience.

At the same time, God communicates His mercy and is seen as the Lord who weeps over the state of His people. How difficult it must be for God! He foreknows the decline of His people and how simple it would be for them to avoid disaster, yet He chooses to wait for their decision and repentance, like a parent who awaits a prodigal's return. This book is not merely about Jeremiah's lament, but God's as well.

Leaders in Lamentations

Jeremiah, Zedekiah

Other People of Influence in Lamentations

Babylonians

Lessons in Leadership

- God must break leaders over a need before they can implement a vision for that need.

- In tough spots, the person who leads best maintains compassion for the followers.

- Even the most noble endeavors fail with immoral leadership.

- Good leaders provide justice, but never without mercy on those who repent.

LEADERSHIP

HIGHLIGHTS IN LAMENTATIONS

WE SUSTAIN God's Conquest When We Maintain Our Character (1:7, 8)	*page 955*
COMPASSION for a Need Brings Commitment to a Vision (2:20)	*page 958*
JEREMIAH: Hope in the Midst of Calamity (3:1–66)	*page 959*
THE PRINCIPLE of Rewards (4:6–8)	*page 962*

Jerusalem in Affliction

1
How lonely sits the city
That was full of people!
How like a widow is she,
Who *was* great among the nations!
The princess among the provinces
Has become a slave!

2 She weeps bitterly in the night,
Her tears *are* on her cheeks;
Among all her lovers
She has none to comfort *her.*
All her friends have dealt treacherously
  with her;
They have become her enemies.

3 Judah has gone into captivity,
Under affliction and hard servitude;
She dwells among the nations,
She finds no rest;
All her persecutors overtake her in dire
  straits.

4 The roads to Zion mourn
Because no one comes to the set feasts.
All her gates are desolate;
Her priests sigh,
Her virgins are afflicted,
And she *is* in bitterness.

5 Her adversaries have become the master,
Her enemies prosper;
For the LORD has afflicted her
Because of the multitude of her
  transgressions.
Her children have gone into captivity
  before the enemy.

6 And from the daughter of Zion
All her splendor has departed.
Her princes have become like deer
That find no pasture,
That flee without strength
Before the pursuer.

7 In the days of her affliction and roaming,
Jerusalem remembers all her pleasant things
That she had in the days of old.
When her people fell into the hand of the
  enemy,
With no one to help her,
The adversaries saw her
And mocked at her downfall.[a]

8 Jerusalem has sinned gravely,
Therefore she has become vile.[a]

1:7 [a]Vulgate reads *her Sabbaths.* **1:8** [a]Septuagint and
Vulgate read *moved* or *removed.*

We Sustain God's Conquest When We Maintain Our Character

(Lamentations 1:7, 8)

God had given His people so many possessions. For centuries they had enjoyed conquest of the Promised Land. Now they lost everything—and all because they had sinned greatly.

Great conquests must be supported by great character. Whatever gains leaders make, they can lose in a heartbeat, unless they simultaneously develop the character to support those gains. Over the last 20 years we have watched many leaders fall morally. Generally speaking, their charisma (gifts) exceeded their character (moral infrastructure). The gift grew bigger than the person.

It has been said, "Nothing is so hard to gain, and so easy to lose, as a good reputation." Leaders must recognize how fleeting is their fame or popularity. Instead, they must give themselves to constructing their character. Only then will they keep the gains God gives them through their leadership.

We usually recognize . . .	We should equally recognize . . .
1. Talents and gifts.	1. Solid character and integrity.
2. The superb product.	2. The process that develops on the way.
3. Excellence in performance.	3. Excellence in discipline.
4. External appearances.	4. Internal stability and obedience.

All who honored her despise her
Because they have seen her nakedness;
Yes, she sighs and turns away.

9 Her uncleanness *is* in her skirts;
She did not consider her destiny;
Therefore her collapse was awesome;
She had no comforter.
"O LORD, behold my affliction,
For *the* enemy is exalted!"

10 The adversary has spread his hand
Over all her pleasant things;
For she has seen the nations enter her
    sanctuary,
Those whom You commanded
Not to enter Your assembly.

11 All her people sigh,
They seek bread;
They have given their valuables for food to
    restore life.
"See, O LORD, and consider,
For I am scorned."

12 "*Is it* nothing to you, all you who pass by?
Behold and see
If there is any sorrow like my sorrow,
Which has been brought on me,
Which the LORD has inflicted
In the day of His fierce anger.

13 "From above He has sent fire into my
    bones,
And it overpowered them;
He has spread a net for my feet
And turned me back;
He has made me desolate
And faint all the day.

14 "The yoke of my transgressions was bound;[a]
They were woven together by His hands,
And thrust upon my neck.
He made my strength fail;
The Lord delivered me into the hands of
those whom I am not able to withstand.

15 "The Lord has trampled underfoot all my
    mighty *men* in my midst;
He has called an assembly against me
To crush my young men;
The Lord trampled *as* in a winepress
The virgin daughter of Judah.

16 "For these *things* I weep;
My eye, my eye overflows with water;

Because the comforter, who should restore
    my life,
Is far from me.
My children are desolate
Because the enemy prevailed."

17 Zion spreads out her hands,
But no one comforts her;
The LORD has commanded concerning
    Jacob
That those around him *become* his adversaries;
Jerusalem has become an unclean thing
    among them.

18 "The LORD is righteous,
For I rebelled against His commandment.
Hear now, all peoples,
And behold my sorrow;
My virgins and my young men
Have gone into captivity.

19 "I called for my lovers,
But they deceived me;
My priests and my elders
Breathed their last in the city,
While they sought food
To restore their life.

20 "See, O LORD, that I *am* in distress;
My soul is troubled;
My heart is overturned within me,
For I have been very rebellious.
Outside the sword bereaves,
At home *it is* like death.

21 "They have heard that I sigh,
But no one comforts me.
All my enemies have heard of my trouble;
They are glad that You have done *it*.
Bring on the day You have announced,
That they may become like me.

22 "Let all their wickedness come before You,
And do to them as You have done to me
For all my transgressions;
For my sighs *are* many,
And my heart *is* faint."

God's Anger with Jerusalem

2 How the Lord has covered the daughter
    of Zion
With a cloud in His anger!
He cast down from heaven to the earth
The beauty of Israel,

1:14 [a]Following Masoretic Text and Targum;
Septuagint, Syriac, and Vulgate read *watched over.*

And did not remember His footstool
In the day of His anger.

2 The Lord has swallowed up and has not
pitied
All the dwelling places of Jacob.
He has thrown down in His wrath
The strongholds of the daughter of Judah;
He has brought *them* down to the
ground;
He has profaned the kingdom and its
princes.

3 He has cut off in fierce anger
Every horn of Israel;
He has drawn back His right hand
From before the enemy.
He has blazed against Jacob like a flaming
fire
Devouring all around.

4 Standing like an enemy, He has bent His
bow;
With His right hand, like an adversary,
He has slain all *who were* pleasing to His
eye;
On the tent of the daughter of Zion,
He has poured out His fury like fire.

5 The Lord was like an enemy.
He has swallowed up Israel,
He has swallowed up all her palaces;
He has destroyed her strongholds,
And has increased mourning and
lamentation
In the daughter of Judah.

6 He has done violence to His tabernacle,
As if it were a garden;
He has destroyed His place of assembly;
The LORD has caused
The appointed feasts and Sabbaths to be
forgotten in Zion.
In His burning indignation He has
spurned the king and the priest.

7 The Lord has spurned His altar,
He has abandoned His sanctuary;
He has given up the walls of her palaces
Into the hand of the enemy.
They have made a noise in the house of
the LORD
As on the day of a set feast.

8 The LORD has purposed to destroy
The wall of the daughter of Zion.
He has stretched out a line;
He has not withdrawn His hand from
destroying;
Therefore He has caused the rampart and
wall to lament;
They languished together.

9 Her gates have sunk into the ground;
He has destroyed and broken her bars.
Her king and her princes *are* among the
nations;
The Law *is* no *more,*
And her prophets find no vision from the
LORD.

10 The elders of the daughter of Zion
Sit on the ground *and* keep silence;
They throw dust on their heads
And gird themselves with sackcloth.
The virgins of Jerusalem
Bow their heads to the ground.

11 My eyes fail with tears,
My heart is troubled;
My bile is poured on the ground
Because of the destruction of the daughter
of my people,
Because the children and the infants
Faint in the streets of the city.

12 They say to their mothers,
"Where *is* grain and wine?"
As they swoon like the wounded
In the streets of the city,
As their life is poured out
In their mothers' bosom.

13 How shall I console you?
To what shall I liken you,
O daughter of Jerusalem?
What shall I compare with you, that I may
comfort you,
O virgin daughter of Zion?
For your ruin *is* spread wide as the sea;
Who can heal you?

14 Your prophets have seen for you
False and deceptive visions;
They have not uncovered your iniquity,
To bring back your captives,
But have envisioned for you false
prophecies and delusions.

15 All who pass by clap *their* hands at you;
They hiss and shake their heads
At the daughter of Jerusalem:

"*Is* this the city that is called
'The perfection of beauty,
The joy of the whole earth'?"

16 All your enemies have opened their mouth
against you;
They hiss and gnash *their* teeth.
They say, "We have swallowed *her* up!
Surely this *is* the day we have waited for;
We have found *it,* we have seen *it!*"

17 The LORD has done what He purposed;
He has fulfilled His word
Which He commanded in days of old.
He has thrown down and has not pitied,
And He has caused an enemy to rejoice
over you;
He has exalted the horn of your
adversaries.

18 Their heart cried out to the Lord,
"O wall of the daughter of Zion,
Let tears run down like a river day and
night;
Give yourself no relief;
Give your eyes no rest.

19 "Arise, cry out in the night,
At the beginning of the watches;
Pour out your heart like water before the
face of the Lord.

Lift your hands toward Him
For the life of your young children,
Who faint from hunger at the head of
every street."

20 "See, O LORD, and consider!
To whom have You done this?
Should the women eat their offspring,
The children they have cuddled?[a]
Should the priest and prophet be slain
In the sanctuary of the Lord?

21 "Young and old lie
On the ground in the streets;
My virgins and my young men
Have fallen by the sword;
You have slain *them* in the day of Your
anger,
You have slaughtered *and* not pitied.

22 "You have invited as to a feast day
The terrors that surround me.
In the day of the LORD's anger
There was no refugee or survivor.
Those whom I have borne and brought
up
My enemies have destroyed."

2:20 [a]Vulgate reads *a span long.*

Compassion for a Need Brings Commitment to a Vision

(Lamentations 2:20)

Although for many years Jeremiah had predicted the captivity of his rebellious people, he weeps when his prophecy comes true. In Lamentations 2:20 he begs the Lord to stop the punishment. He asks for pity.

This dialogue between Jeremiah and God about the Hebrews offers a rare glimpse into the heart-shaping work God did in Jeremiah, the leader. While the prophet has a passion for righteousness and justice, at the same time he has compassion for the very people who so anger him. Like Moses, Jeremiah often displayed one face to the people—usually judgment and threats—but another to God in prayer. He begged Yahweh not to abandon His people. Compassion enabled Jeremiah to remain committed to the vision that one day God would restore His people.

This is what makes a godly leader great: clear and firm leadership, yet a compassionate heart as an intercessor. Reggie McNeal writes, "One mark of genuine spiritual greatness is compassion for one's tormentors."

Leaders must first feel burdened for the people's needs; only then will they commit themselves to a vision of their deliverance. Jeremiah's compassion kept him in the game when it would have been easier to walk away. He teaches us that while people may reject your messages and oppose your arguments, they remain helpless against your prayers.

The Prophet's Anguish and Hope

3 I *am* the man *who* has seen affliction by
the rod of His wrath.
2 He has led me and made *me* walk
In darkness and not *in* light.
3 Surely He has turned His hand against me
Time and time again throughout the day.

4 He has aged my flesh and my skin,
And broken my bones.
5 He has besieged me
And surrounded *me* with bitterness and woe.
6 He has set me in dark places
Like the dead of long ago.

7 He has hedged me in so that I cannot get
out;
He has made my chain heavy.
8 Even when I cry and shout,
He shuts out my prayer.
9 He has blocked my ways with hewn stone;
He has made my paths crooked.

10 He *has been* to me a bear lying in wait,
Like a lion in ambush.

11 He has turned aside my ways and torn me
in pieces;
He has made me desolate.
12 He has bent His bow
And set me up as a target for the arrow.
13 He has caused the arrows of His quiver
To pierce my loins.[a]
14 I have become the ridicule of all my
people—
Their taunting song all the day.
15 He has filled me with bitterness,
He has made me drink wormwood.

16 He has also broken my teeth with gravel,
And covered me with ashes.
17 You have moved my soul far from peace;
I have forgotten prosperity.
18 And I said, "My strength and my hope
Have perished from the LORD."

19 Remember my affliction and roaming,
The wormwood and the gall.

3:13 [a]Literally *kidneys*

JEREMIAH

HOPE IN THE MIDST OF CALAMITY
(Lamentations 3:1–66)

PROFILE IN LEADERSHIP

As Jeremiah trudged through his ruined city, he smelled destruction everywhere. He knew the invading Babylonians had devastated Jerusalem because the people of Judah had forsaken their God. The Lord's people had brought this misery on themselves—yet his heart still broke.

For two whole chapters Jeremiah laments the calamity. He recognizes the chastening hand of God, for he says, "Is it not from the mouth of the Most High that woe and well-being proceed?" (Lam. 3:38). Right in the middle of his dirge he pauses to express one of the most hopeful pronouncements in the Old Testament: "Through the LORD's mercies we are not consumed, because His compassions fail not. They are new every morning; great is Your faithfulness" (3:22, 23).

In the midst of the carnage, in the midst of his own wailing, the prophet finds hope in knowing that God still reigns. He knows that restoration and repentance can occur. God's anger will not burn against His people forever. And so Jeremiah can continue. Oh, there will still be tears—the last two chapters of Lamentations again play the mournful sounds of a funeral march. Yet because God lives, hope lives!

Effective leaders bank on hope, even in the face of God's judgment. They know that, for those who call on the name of the Lord Jesus Christ, restoration and redemption can indeed follow destruction.

20 My soul still remembers
And sinks within me.
21 This I recall to my mind,
Therefore I have hope.

God Is Ultimately in Control and Will Mercifully Act for His People

(Lamentations 3:21–36)

Jeremiah the leader wisely remains fixed on a vision of God's sovereignty: God is more powerful than the Babylonians. He focuses on God's nature: God is full of mercy and compassion. He dwells on his vision of God's plans: God will deliver His people and give them a hopeful future.

---

22 *Through* the LORD's mercies we are not
consumed,
Because His compassions fail not.
23 *They are* new every morning;
Great *is* Your faithfulness.
24 "The LORD *is* my portion," says my soul,
"Therefore I hope in Him!"

25 The LORD *is* good to those who wait for
Him,
To the soul *who* seeks Him.
26 *It is* good that *one* should hope and wait
quietly
For the salvation of the LORD.
27 *It is* good for a man to bear
The yoke in his youth.

28 Let him sit alone and keep silent,
Because *God* has laid *it* on him;
29 Let him put his mouth in the dust—
There may yet be hope.
30 Let him give *his* cheek to the one who
strikes him,
And be full of reproach.

31 For the Lord will not cast off forever.
32 Though He causes grief,
Yet He will show compassion
According to the multitude of His mercies.
33 For He does not afflict willingly,
Nor grieve the children of men.

34 To crush under one's feet
All the prisoners of the earth,
35 To turn aside the justice *due* a man
Before the face of the Most High,
36 Or subvert a man in his cause—
The Lord does not approve.

37 Who *is* he *who* speaks and it comes to pass,
When the Lord has not commanded *it?*
38 *Is it* not from the mouth of the Most High
That woe and well-being proceed?
39 Why should a living man complain,
A man for the punishment of his sins?

40 Let us search out and examine our ways,
And turn back to the LORD;
41 Let us lift our hearts and hands
To God in heaven.
42 We have transgressed and rebelled;
You have not pardoned.

43 You have covered *Yourself* with anger
And pursued us;
You have slain *and* not pitied.
44 You have covered Yourself with a cloud,
That prayer should not pass through.
45 You have made us an offscouring and
refuse
In the midst of the peoples.

46 All our enemies
Have opened their mouths against us.
47 Fear and a snare have come upon us,
Desolation and destruction.
48 My eyes overflow with rivers of water
For the destruction of the daughter of my
people.

49 My eyes flow and do not cease,
Without interruption,
50 Till the LORD from heaven
Looks down and sees.
51 My eyes bring suffering to my soul
Because of all the daughters of my city.

52 My enemies without cause
Hunted me down like a bird.
53 They silenced[a] my life in the pit
And threw stones at me.
54 The waters flowed over my head;
I said, "I am cut off!"

55 I called on Your name, O LORD,
From the lowest pit.

3:53 [a]Septuagint reads *put to death.*

56 You have heard my voice:
"Do not hide Your ear
From my sighing, from my cry for help."

57 You drew near on the day I called on You,
And said, "Do not fear!"

58 O Lord, You have pleaded the case for my
soul;
You have redeemed my life.

59 O LORD, You have seen *how* I am
wronged;
Judge my case.

60 You have seen all their vengeance,
All their schemes against me.

61 You have heard their reproach, O LORD,
All their schemes against me,

62 The lips of my enemies
And their whispering against me all the day.

63 Look at their sitting down and their rising
up;
I *am* their taunting song.

64 Repay them, O LORD,
According to the work of their hands.

65 Give them a veiled[a] heart;
Your curse *be* upon them!

66 In Your anger,
Pursue and destroy them
From under the heavens of the LORD.

The Degradation of Zion

4 How the gold has become dim!
How changed the fine gold!
The stones of the sanctuary are scattered
At the head of every street.

2 The precious sons of Zion,
Valuable as fine gold,
How they are regarded as clay pots,
The work of the hands of the potter!

3 Even the jackals present their breasts
To nurse their young;
But the daughter of my people *is* cruel,
Like ostriches in the wilderness.

4 The tongue of the infant clings
To the roof of its mouth for thirst;
The young children ask for bread,
But no one breaks *it* for them.

5 Those who ate delicacies
Are desolate in the streets;
Those who were brought up in scarlet
Embrace ash heaps.

6 The punishment of the iniquity of the
daughter of my people
Is greater than the punishment of the sin
of Sodom,
Which was overthrown in a moment,
With no hand to help her!

7 Her Nazirites[a] were brighter than snow
And whiter than milk;
They were more ruddy in body than
rubies,
Like sapphire in their appearance.

8 *Now* their appearance is blacker than soot;
They go unrecognized in the streets;
Their skin clings to their bones,
It has become as dry as wood.

9 *Those* slain by the sword are better off
Than *those* who die of hunger;
For these pine away,
Stricken *for lack* of the fruits of the field.

10 The hands of the compassionate women
Have cooked their own children;
They became food for them
In the destruction of the daughter of my
people.

11 The LORD has fulfilled His fury,
He has poured out His fierce anger.
He kindled a fire in Zion,
And it has devoured its foundations.

12 The kings of the earth,
And all inhabitants of the world,
Would not have believed
That the adversary and the enemy
Could enter the gates of Jerusalem—

13 Because of the sins of her prophets
And the iniquities of her priests,
Who shed in her midst
The blood of the just.

14 They wandered blind in the streets;
They have defiled themselves with blood,
So that no one would touch their
garments.

15 They cried out to them,
"Go away, unclean!
Go away, go away,

3:65 [a]A Jewish tradition reads *sorrow of.* **4:7** [a]Or
nobles

The Principle of Rewards

(Lamentations 4:6–8)

You might call it the principle of rewards: What gets rewarded gets done. Good leaders recognize how to attach both rewards and consequences to team members' performance. Any system of rewards should prioritize the most important conduct, then reward it publicly. In addition, the system ought to prioritize the non-negotiable negatives, because they damage the team. A price should be attached to these, as well.

Jeremiah gives us a snapshot of how God did this with His people. He says the consequences for their sin exceeded that of Sodom, for while that ancient city vanished in a moment, Judah's punishment dragged on and on.

How do we communicate rewards to our people? To what do we pay attention? Do our people know what is important? When team members don't produce the results the leader desires, usually just a few reasons explain why:

1. They are not sure what to do.
2. They don't know what to do first.
3. They don't know how to do it.
4. The reward system does not align with the group goals.
5. The leader presents unnecessary obstacles.

Do not touch us!"
When they fled and wandered,
Those among the nations said,
"They shall no longer dwell *here*."

16 The face[a] of the LORD scattered them;
He no longer regards them.
The people do not respect the priests
Nor show favor to the elders.

17 Still our eyes failed us,
Watching vainly for our help;
In our watching we watched
For a nation *that* could not save *us*.

18 They tracked our steps
So that we could not walk in our streets.
Our end was near;
Our days were over,
For our end had come.

19 Our pursuers were swifter
Than the eagles of the heavens.
They pursued us on the mountains
And lay in wait for us in the wilderness.

20 The breath of our nostrils, the anointed of
the LORD,
Was caught in their pits,
Of whom we said, "Under his shadow
We shall live among the nations."

21 Rejoice and be glad, O daughter of Edom,
You who dwell in the land of Uz!
The cup shall also pass over to you
And you shall become drunk and make
yourself naked.

22 *The punishment of* your iniquity is
accomplished,
O daughter of Zion;
He will no longer send you into captivity.
He will punish your iniquity,
O daughter of Edom;
He will uncover your sins!

A Prayer for Restoration

5 Remember, O LORD, what has come
upon us;
Look, and behold our reproach!
2 Our inheritance has been turned over to
aliens,
And our houses to foreigners.
3 We have become orphans and waifs,
Our mothers *are* like widows.

4 We pay for the water we drink,
And our wood comes at a price.
5 *They* pursue at our heels;[a]
We labor *and* have no rest.
6 We have given our hand *to* the Egyptians

4:16 [a]Targum reads *anger.* **5:5** [a]Literally *necks*

And the Assyrians, to be satisfied with
bread.

7   Our fathers sinned *and are* no more,
But we bear their iniquities.
8   Servants rule over us;
There is none to deliver *us* from their
hand.
9   We get our bread *at the risk* of our lives,
Because of the sword in the wilderness.

10   Our skin is hot as an oven,
Because of the fever of famine.
11   They ravished the women in Zion,
The maidens in the cities of Judah.
12   Princes were hung up by their hands,
And elders were not respected.
13   Young men ground at the millstones;
Boys staggered under *loads of* wood.
14   The elders have ceased *gathering at the*
gate,
And the young men from their music.

15   The joy of our heart has ceased;
Our dance has turned into mourning.
16   The crown has fallen *from* our head.
Woe to us, for we have sinned!
17   Because of this our heart is faint;
Because of these *things* our eyes grow dim;

18   Because of Mount Zion which is desolate,
With foxes walking about on it.

19   You, O LORD, remain forever;
Your throne from generation to generation.
20   Why do You forget us forever,
And forsake us for so long a time?
21   Turn us back to You, O LORD, and we
will be restored;
Renew our days as of old,
22   Unless You have utterly rejected us,
And are very angry with us!

Successful Leaders Depend on God

(Lamentations 5:14–19)

Successful leaders depend not on their own
wit and wisdom, but on God. Jeremiah
confesses both the sin of the people and that
God reigns forever and will ultimately restore
what has been lost. Leaders act according to
their gifts and calling, but trust God to bring
about the desired results.

EZEKIEL
A Leader with Backbone and Conviction

SUMMARY

God raised up Ezekiel to serve as a prophet during a most difficult time in Israel's history. He provides a tremendous illustration of a leader with backbone and conviction.

From the beginning, God warned Ezekiel that he would speak to a stubborn group. He faced opposition at almost every turn—a level of opposition that might cause many leaders to reevaluate their position and move on. Ezekiel chose to remain and stay true to his convictions. Appropriately enough, the name of this strong prophet means "God strengthens."

Ezekiel demonstrates for us three leadership skills. First, a leader can lead off of vision, even in tough times. Second, a leader can stay true to core values, even in tough times. Third, a leader can compel people to grapple even with hard truth.

Ezekiel clearly led out of vision. God consistently provided him with unusual visions that drove him to speak in unusual ways. From hands and scrolls descending from heaven, to four abominations committed in the temple, to vines, eagles, lions, dry bones, and fires, Ezekiel trafficked in strange but memorable pictures. These pictures often arrived with a divine interpretation and instructions on how he was to communicate God's Word to the people. Ezekiel closely followed the leadership axiom on vision: See it clearly, show it creatively, and say it constantly.

Ezekiel managed to stay true to his convictions and core values despite the people's response. God said from the beginning: "As for them, whether they hear or whether they refuse—for they are a rebellious house—yet they will know that a prophet has been among them. And you, son of man, do not be afraid of them nor be afraid of their words . . . or dismayed by their looks, though they are a rebellious house. You shall speak My words to them, whether they hear or whether they refuse, for they are rebellious. But you, son of man, hear what I say to you. Do not be rebellious like that rebellious house; open your mouth and eat what I give you" (2:5–8).

Ezekiel compelled the people to hear him and wrestle with the pressing issues. He was an extremely creative communicator, often using visual aids or dramatically acting out his message. He quickly obeyed the Lord's instructions, even when many of the symbolic actions God called him to enact looked difficult or embarrassing. His dynamic ministry won the respect, attention, and admiration of Judah's elders. But while they listened to him, they refused to act on what he said. This disappointed Ezekiel, for no one took greater pains to cast a vision to his own generation than he did.

God's Role in Ezekiel

God described Ezekiel as a watchman. He called the prophet to warn the Jews of impending danger if they did not repent. Like a watchman who sees an invading army en route, he admonishes the people to get ready or be destroyed. God describes Himself to Ezekiel as the One who supplies the right words. God is the Director of this great drama that Ezekiel acts out. He is the Writer of the script Ezekiel is to read to the people. And He is the Author who closes the curtain when the play ends—a finale in the form of the invading Babylonian army—when it's too late for the people to discover the play is no mere act.

Leaders in Ezekiel

Ezekiel

Other People of Influence in Ezekiel

Pelatiah, Jaazaniah, Nebuchadnezzar, Pharaoh

Lessons in Leadership

- One leader with courage is a majority.
- Effective leaders communicate creatively and unforgettably.
- Leaders are stewards of the people and of the resources they oversee.
- We must lead ourselves before we lead anyone else.
- A leader stands between God's goals and the people's problems.
- Often, a leader takes his or her first step alone.

LEADERSHIP

HIGHLIGHTS IN EZEKIEL

Ezekiel's Vision of God

1 Now it came to pass in the thirtieth year, in the fourth *month,* on the fifth *day* of the month, as I *was* among the captives by the River Chebar, *that* the heavens were opened and I saw visions[a] of God. [2]On the fifth *day* of the month, which *was* in the fifth year of King Jehoiachin's captivity, [3]the word of the LORD came expressly to Ezekiel the priest, the son of Buzi, in the land of the Chaldeans[a] by the River Chebar; and the hand of the LORD was upon him there.

[4]Then I looked, and behold, a whirlwind was coming out of the north, a great cloud with raging fire engulfing itself; and brightness *was* all around it and radiating out of its midst like the color of amber, out of the midst of the fire. [5]Also from within it *came* the likeness of four living creatures. And this *was* their appearance: they had the likeness of a man. [6]Each one had four faces, and each one had four wings. [7]Their legs *were* straight, and the soles of their feet *were* like the soles of calves' feet. They sparkled like the color of burnished bronze. [8]The hands of a man *were* under their wings on their four sides; and each of the four had faces and wings. [9]Their wings touched one another. *The creatures* did not turn when they went, but each one went straight forward.

[10]As for the likeness of their faces, *each* had the face of a man; each of the four had the face of a lion on the right side, each of the four had the face of an ox on the left side, and each of the four had the face of an eagle. [11]Thus *were* their faces. Their wings stretched upward; two *wings* of each one touched one another, and two covered their bodies. [12]And each one went straight forward; they went wherever the spirit wanted to go, and they did not turn when they went.

[13]As for the likeness of the living creatures, their appearance *was* like burning coals of fire, like the appearance of torches going back and forth among the living creatures. The fire was bright, and out of the fire went lightning. [14]And the living creatures ran back and forth, in appearance like a flash of lightning.

[15]Now as I looked at the living creatures, behold, a wheel *was* on the earth beside each living creature with its four faces. [16]The appearance of the wheels and their workings *was* like the color

---

1:1 [a]Following Masoretic Text, Septuagint, and Vulgate; Syriac and Targum read *a vision.* **1:3** [a]Or *Babylonians,* and so elsewhere in this book

---

Communicating Vision

(Ezekiel 1:1–3)

Like Jeremiah, Ezekiel knew how to communicate a message so that every listener understood and knew what to do. This is the mark of a successful communicator. Note how he communicated:

1. His vision was memorable; his words inventive.

God instructed the prophet how to cast his vision. He is told to use object lessons, using materials like a brick, an iron plate, his own body, ropes, ingredients for bread, human dung, and cow manure. God's instructions seemed so radical that even Ezekiel felt repulsed by them. Yet no one would ever forget the lessons.

2. His vision was measurable; his words insightful.

Ezekiel spoke specifically about future events. He gave no fuzzy, ambiguous word about how God wanted the people to follow, should they decide to cooperate. He delivered a compelling and detailed word about how long Israel had drifted from God, the siege of Jerusalem, how long the exile would last, and what conditions would be like when God brought about His long-threatened punishment.

3. His vision was motivational; his words gave incentive.

Ezekiel didn't talk merely to pronounce judgment. He wanted to compel the Israelites to repent and return to God. He discussed how defiling life would be under a foreign leader and the horror of submitting to a power that didn't understand them. He gave them a reason to act.

Vision: You Can Seize Only What You Can See

(Ezekiel 1:4–28)

This great book begins with a vision. Ezekiel receives a revelation from God of four angelic figures. In this vision, God calls the prophet to be His spokesman and watchman to the Hebrew exiles. This vision is the first of four in the book:

1. The vision of the four angels (Ezek. 1—3)
2. The vision of glory and godlessness (Ezek. 8—11)
3. The vision of the burning vine (Ezek. 15)
4. The vision of the dry bones (Ezek. 37)

Ezekiel describes this first vision in vivid detail. Like all effective leaders, he spoke as clearly as possible. A pastor once said, "If it's fuzzy in the pulpit, it's foggy in the pew."

Ezekiel provided vision by way of analogies, then applied those visions. He communicated a picture (Ezek. 1), then communicated his point (Ezek. 2). Divine visions always help a leader and the people move in the right direction. A divine vision also seems to include these components:

1. *A clear mental image:* It serves as a sort of blueprint inside of us.
2. *A positive change:* It serves to improve present conditions.
3. *A future focus:* It furnishes insight and direction for the unseen future.
4. *A gift from God:* It is divinely inspired, not humanly manipulated.
5. *A chosen people and time:* It is for a select leader and group at a given time.

of beryl, and all four had the same likeness. The appearance of their workings *was*, as it were, a wheel in the middle of a wheel. [17]When they moved, they went toward any one of four directions; they did not turn aside when they went. [18]As for their rims, they were so high they were awesome; and their rims *were* full of eyes, all around the four of them. [19]When the living creatures went, the wheels went beside them; and when the living creatures were lifted up from the earth, the wheels were lifted up. [20]Wherever the spirit wanted to go, they went, *because* there the spirit went; and the wheels were lifted together with them, for the spirit of the living creatures[a] *was* in the wheels. [21]When those went, *these* went; when those stood, *these* stood; and when those were lifted up from the earth, the wheels were lifted up together with them, for the spirit of the living creatures[a] *was* in the wheels.

[22]The likeness of the firmament above the heads of the living creatures[a] *was* like the color of an awesome crystal, stretched out over their heads. [23]And under the firmament their wings *spread out* straight, one toward another. Each one had two which covered one side, and each one had two which covered the other side of the body. [24]When they went, I heard the noise of their wings, like the noise of many waters, like the voice of the Almighty, a tumult like the noise

of an army; and when they stood still, they let down their wings. [25]A voice came from above the firmament that *was* over their heads; whenever they stood, they let down their wings.

[26]And above the firmament over their heads *was* the likeness of a throne, in appearance like a sapphire stone; on the likeness of the throne *was* a likeness with the appearance of a man high above it. [27]Also from the appearance of His waist and upward I saw, as it were, the color of amber with the appearance of fire all around within it; and from the appearance of His waist and downward I saw, as it were, the appearance of fire with brightness all around. [28]Like the appearance of a rainbow in a cloud on a rainy day, so *was* the appearance of the brightness all around it. This *was* the appearance of the likeness of the glory of the LORD.

Ezekiel Sent to Rebellious Israel

So when I saw *it*, I fell on my face, and I heard a voice of One speaking.

1:20 [a]Literally *living creature*; Septuagint and Vulgate read *spirit of life*; Targum reads *creatures*.
1:21 [a]Literally *living creature*; Septuagint and Vulgate read *spirit of life*; Targum reads *creatures*.
1:22 [a]Following Septuagint, Targum, and Vulgate; Masoretic Text reads *living creature*.

And He said to me, "Son of man, stand on your feet, and I will speak to you." [2]Then the Spirit entered me when He spoke to me, and set me on my feet; and I heard Him who spoke to me. [3]And He said to me: "Son of man, I am sending you to the children of Israel, to a rebellious nation that has rebelled against Me; they and their fathers have transgressed against Me to this very day. [4]For *they are* impudent and stubborn children. I am sending you to them, and you shall say to them, 'Thus says the Lord GOD.' [5]As for them, whether they hear or whether they refuse—for they *are* a rebellious house—yet they will know that a prophet has been among them.

[6]"And you, son of man, do not be afraid of them nor be afraid of their words, though briers and thorns *are* with you and you dwell among scorpions; do not be afraid of their words or dismayed by their looks, though they *are* a rebellious house. [7]You shall speak My words to them, whether they hear or whether they refuse, for they *are* rebellious. [8]But you, son of man, hear what I say to you. Do not be rebellious like that rebellious house; open your mouth and eat what I give you."

[9]Now when I looked, there was a hand stretched out to me; and behold, a scroll of a book *was* in it. [10]Then He spread it before me; and *there was* writing on the inside and on the outside, and written on it *were* lamentations and mourning and woe.

Moreover He said to me, "Son of man, eat what you find; eat this scroll, and go, speak to the house of Israel." [2]So I opened my mouth, and He caused me to eat that scroll.

[3]And He said to me, "Son of man, feed your belly, and fill your stomach with this scroll that I give you." So I ate, and it was in my mouth like honey in sweetness.

[4]Then He said to me: "Son of man, go to the house of Israel and speak with My words to them. [5]For you *are* not sent to a people of unfamiliar speech and of hard language, *but* to the house of Israel, [6]not to many people of unfamiliar speech and of hard language, whose words you cannot understand. Surely, had I sent you to them, they would have listened to you. [7]But the house of Israel will not listen to you, because they will not listen to Me; for all the house of Israel *are* impudent and hard-hearted. [8]Behold, I have made your face strong against their faces, and your forehead strong against their foreheads. [9]Like adamant stone, harder than flint, I have made your forehead; do not be afraid of them, nor be dismayed at their looks, though they *are* a rebellious house."

[10]Moreover He said to me: "Son of man, receive into your heart all My words that I speak to you, and hear with your ears. [11]And go, get to the

The Necessity of a Call in Tough Times

(Ezekiel 2:1–10)

God described not only what He wanted Ezekiel to do, but also the conditions in which he would serve. God told him He was sending him to a rebellious people who acted like stubborn children. Yet he was to continue speaking whether they listened or not (Ezek. 2:7). God's call didn't depend on the people's response. Ezekiel had to stand strong even when the people ignored him.

God has Ezekiel eat a scroll (representing the divine words he is to speak), inscribed both on the front and the back, leaving him no room to change or add to the message he is to speak (2:10). Ezekiel had to stay honest and true to those words.

This presents a challenge to leaders. What role does God play and what role do we play? Are leaders never permitted to speak from their own mind and emotions? Consider the roles of both God and people:

God's Role
1. He calls us into service.
2. He gives us gifts and graces.
3. He provides words of direction.
4. He supplies a compelling fire inside us.
5. He controls the outcome.

The Human Role
1. People confirm our call.
2. People cooperate with their gifts.
3. We use our mind and emotions.
4. Others recognize and respect the fire.
5. We are to be faithful to the end.

Adaptability: Effective Leaders Adapt to Changing Needs
(Ezekiel 3:8, 9)

Because Israel acted like a stubborn mule and would not listen to the prophet's words, Ezekiel had to adapt to the needs of his audience. God spoke these words to him: "I have made your face strong against their faces, and your forehead strong against their foreheads. Like adamant stone, harder than flint, I have made your forehead; do not be afraid of them, nor be dismayed at their looks, though they are a rebellious house" (Ezek. 3:8, 9).

Effective leaders allow God to shape them into the kind of people they need to be for each situation they encounter. They don't get stuck on one method or mode of operation. When approaching a new and different context, leaders should read . . .

1. **Situations:** Do my circumstances tell me it is time to move forward?
2. **People:** Are the people ready and willing to make a move?
3. **Timing:** Is this the right time to make a move?
4. **Staff:** Does my team have the gifts and the influence to lead the way?
5. **Opportunity:** Do we have the opportunity to be successful if we move?
6. **Resources:** Do we possess the resources to move now?
7. **Themselves:** Am I the right person to lead the way?

captives, to the children of your people, and speak to them and tell them, 'Thus says the Lord GOD,' whether they hear, or whether they refuse."

¹²Then the Spirit lifted me up, and I heard behind me a great thunderous voice: "Blessed *is* the glory of the LORD from His place!" ¹³*I* also *heard* the noise of the wings of the living creatures that touched one another, and the noise of the wheels beside them, and a great thunderous noise. ¹⁴So the Spirit lifted me up and took me away, and I went in bitterness, in the heat of my spirit; but the hand of the LORD was strong upon me. ¹⁵Then I came to the captives at Tel Abib, who dwelt by the River Chebar; and I sat where they sat, and remained there astonished among them seven days.

Ezekiel Is a Watchman

¹⁶Now it came to pass at the end of seven days that the word of the LORD came to me, saying, ¹⁷"Son of man, I have made you a watchman for the house of Israel; therefore hear a word from My mouth, and give them warning from Me: ¹⁸When I say to the wicked, 'You shall surely die,' and you give him no warning, nor speak to warn the wicked from his wicked way, to save his life, that same wicked *man* shall die in his iniquity; but his blood I will require at your hand. ¹⁹Yet, if you warn the wicked, and he does not turn from his wickedness, nor from his wicked way, he shall die in his iniquity; but you have delivered your soul.

²⁰"Again, when a righteous *man* turns from his righteousness and commits iniquity, and I lay a stumbling block before him, he shall die; because you did not give him warning, he shall die in his sin, and his righteousness which he has done shall not be remembered; but his blood I will require at your hand. ²¹Nevertheless if you warn the righteous *man* that the righteous should not sin, and he does not sin, he shall surely live because he took warning; also you will have delivered your soul."

²²Then the hand of the LORD was upon me there, and He said to me, "Arise, go out into the plain, and there I shall talk with you."

²³So I arose and went out into the plain, and behold, the glory of the LORD stood there, like the glory which I saw by the River Chebar; and I fell on my face. ²⁴Then the Spirit entered me and set me on my feet, and spoke with me and said to me: "Go, shut yourself inside your house. ²⁵And you, O son of man, surely they will put ropes on you and bind you with them, so that you cannot go out among them. ²⁶I will make your tongue cling to the roof of your mouth, so that you shall be mute and not be one to rebuke them, for they *are* a rebellious house. ²⁷But when I speak with you, I will open your mouth, and you shall say to them, 'Thus says the Lord GOD.' He who hears, let him hear; and he who refuses, let him refuse; for they *are* a rebellious house.

The Siege of Jerusalem Portrayed

4 "You also, son of man, take a clay tablet and lay it before you, and portray on it a city, Jerusalem. ²Lay siege against it, build a siege wall against it, and heap up a mound against it; set camps against it also, and place battering rams against it all around. ³Moreover take for yourself an iron plate, and set it *as* an iron wall between you and the city. Set your face against it, and it shall be besieged, and you shall lay siege against it. This *will be* a sign to the house of Israel.

⁴"Lie also on your left side, and lay the iniquity of the house of Israel upon it. *According* to the number of the days that you lie on it, you shall bear their iniquity. ⁵For I have laid on you the years of their iniquity, according to the number of the days, three hundred and ninety days; so you shall bear the iniquity of the house of Israel. ⁶And when you have completed them, lie again on your right side; then you shall bear the iniquity of the house of Judah forty days. I have laid on you a day for each year.

⁷"Therefore you shall set your face toward the siege of Jerusalem; your arm *shall be* uncovered, and you shall prophesy against it. ⁸And surely I will restrain you so that you cannot turn from one side to another till you have ended the days of your siege.

⁹"Also take for yourself wheat, barley, beans, lentils, millet, and spelt; put them into one vessel, and make bread of them for yourself. *During* the number of days that you lie on your side, three hundred and ninety days, you shall eat it. ¹⁰And your food which you eat *shall be* by weight, twenty shekels a day; from time to time you shall eat it. ¹¹You shall also drink water by measure, one-sixth of a hin; from time to time you shall drink. ¹²And you shall eat it *as* barley cakes; and bake it using fuel of human waste in their sight."

¹³Then the LORD said, "So shall the children of Israel eat their defiled bread among the Gentiles, where I will drive them."

¹⁴So I said, "Ah, Lord GOD! Indeed I have never defiled myself from my youth till now; I have never eaten what died of itself or was torn by beasts, nor has abominable flesh ever come into my mouth."

¹⁵Then He said to me, "See, I am giving you cow dung instead of human waste, and you shall prepare your bread over it."

¹⁶Moreover He said to me, "Son of man, surely I will cut off the supply of bread in Jerusalem; they shall eat bread by weight and with anxiety, and shall drink water by measure and with dread, ¹⁷that they may lack bread and water,

and be dismayed with one another, and waste away because of their iniquity.

A Sword Against Jerusalem

5 "And you, son of man, take a sharp sword, take it as a barber's razor, and pass *it* over your head and your beard; then take scales to weigh and divide the hair. ²You shall burn with fire one-third in the midst of the city, when the days of the siege are finished; then you shall take one-third and strike around *it* with the sword, and one-third you shall scatter in the wind: I will draw out a sword after them. ³You shall also take a small number of them and bind them in the edge of your *garment*. ⁴Then take some of them again and throw them into the midst of the fire, and burn them in the fire. From there a fire will go out into all the house of Israel.

⁵"Thus says the Lord GOD: 'This *is* Jerusalem; I have set her in the midst of the nations and the countries all around her. ⁶She has rebelled against My judgments by doing wickedness more than the nations, and against My statutes more than the countries that *are* all around her; for they have refused My judgments, and they have not walked in My statutes.' ⁷Therefore thus says the Lord GOD: 'Because you have multiplied *disobedience* more than the nations that *are* all around you, have not walked in My statutes nor kept My judgments, nor even done[a] according to the judgments of the nations that *are* all around you'— ⁸therefore thus says the Lord GOD: 'Indeed I, even I, *am* against you and will execute judgments in your midst in the sight of the nations. ⁹And I will do among you what I have never done, and the like of which I will never do again, because of all your abominations. ¹⁰Therefore fathers shall eat *their* sons in your midst, and sons shall eat their fathers; and I will execute judgments among you, and all of you who remain I will scatter to all the winds.

¹¹"Therefore, *as* I live,' says the Lord GOD, 'surely, because you have defiled My sanctuary with all your detestable things and with all your abominations, therefore I will also diminish *you;* My eye will not spare, nor will I have any pity. ¹² One-third of you shall die of the pestilence, and be consumed with famine in your midst; and one-third shall fall by the sword all around you; and I will scatter another third to all the winds, and I will draw out a sword after them.

¹³"Thus shall My anger be spent, and I will

5:7 [a]Following Masoretic Text, Septuagint, Targum, and Vulgate; many Hebrew manuscripts and Syriac read *but have done* (compare 11:12).

cause My fury to rest upon them, and I will be avenged; and they shall know that I, the LORD, have spoken *it* in My zeal, when I have spent My fury upon them. [14]Moreover I will make you a waste and a reproach among the nations that *are* all around you, in the sight of all who pass by.

[15]"So it[a] shall be a reproach, a taunt, a lesson, and an astonishment to the nations that *are* all around you, when I execute judgments among you in anger and in fury and in furious rebukes. I, the LORD, have spoken. [16]When I send against them the terrible arrows of famine which shall be for destruction, which I will send to destroy you, I will increase the famine upon you and cut off your supply of bread. [17]So I will send against you famine and wild beasts, and they will bereave you. Pestilence and blood shall pass through you, and I will bring the sword against you. I, the LORD, have spoken.'"

Judgment on Idolatrous Israel

6 Now the word of the LORD came to me, saying: [2]"Son of man, set your face toward the mountains of Israel, and prophesy against them, [3]and say, 'O mountains of Israel, hear the word of the Lord GOD! Thus says the Lord GOD to the mountains, to the hills, to the ravines, and to the valleys: "Indeed I, *even* I, will bring a sword against you, and I will destroy your high places. [4]Then your altars shall be desolate, your incense altars shall be broken, and I will cast down your slain *men* before your idols. [5]And I will lay the corpses of the children of Israel before their idols, and I will scatter your bones all around your altars. [6]In all your dwelling places the cities shall be laid waste, and the high places shall be desolate, so that your altars may be laid waste and made desolate, your idols may be broken and made to cease, your incense altars may be cut down, and your works may be abolished. [7]The slain shall fall in your midst, and you shall know that I *am* the LORD.

[8]"Yet I will leave a remnant, so that you may have *some* who escape the sword among the nations, when you are scattered through the countries. [9]Then those of you who escape will remember Me among the nations where they are carried captive, because I was crushed by their adulterous heart which has departed from Me, and by their eyes which play the harlot after their idols; they will loathe themselves for the evils

---

5:15 [a]Septuagint, Syriac, Targum, and Vulgate read *you.*

---

which they committed in all their abominations. [10]And they shall know that I *am* the LORD; I have not said in vain that I would bring this calamity upon them."

[11]Thus says the Lord GOD: "Pound your fists and stamp your feet, and say, 'Alas, for all the evil abominations of the house of Israel! For they shall fall by the sword, by famine, and by pestilence. [12]He who is far off shall die by the pestilence, he who is near shall fall by the sword, and he who remains and is besieged shall die by the famine. Thus will I spend My fury upon them. [13]Then you shall know that I *am* the LORD, when their slain are among their idols all around their altars, on every high hill, on all the mountaintops, under every green tree, and under every thick oak, wherever they offered sweet incense to all their idols. [14]So I will stretch out My hand against them and make the land desolate, yes, more desolate than the wilderness toward Diblah, in all their dwelling places. Then they shall know that I *am* the LORD.' " ' "

Judgment on Israel Is Near

7 Moreover the word of the LORD came to me, saying, [2]"And you, son of man, thus says the Lord GOD to the land of Israel:

'An end! The end has come upon the four
   corners of the land.
[3]Now the end *has come* upon you,
And I will send My anger against you;
I will judge you according to your ways,
And I will repay you for all your
   abominations.
[4]My eye will not spare you,
Nor will I have pity;
But I will repay your ways,
And your abominations will be in your
   midst;
Then you shall know that I *am* the
   LORD!'

[5]"Thus says the Lord GOD:

'A disaster, a singular disaster;
Behold, it has come!
[6]An end has come,
The end has come;
It has dawned for you;
Behold, it has come!
[7]Doom has come to you, you who dwell in
   the land;
The time has come,
A day of trouble *is* near,
And not of rejoicing in the mountains.

[8]Now upon you I will soon pour out My
   fury,
And spend My anger upon you;
I will judge you according to your ways,
And I will repay you for all your
   abominations.

[9]'My eye will not spare,
Nor will I have pity;
I will repay you according to your ways,
And your abominations will be in your
   midst.
Then you shall know that I *am* the LORD
   who strikes.

[10]'Behold, the day!
Behold, it has come!
Doom has gone out;
The rod has blossomed,
Pride has budded.
[11]Violence has risen up into a rod of
   wickedness;
None of them *shall remain,*
None of their multitude,
None of them;
Nor *shall there be* wailing for them.
[12]The time has come,
The day draws near.

'Let not the buyer rejoice,
Nor the seller mourn,
For wrath *is* on their whole multitude.
[13]For the seller shall not return to what has
   been sold,
Though he may still be alive;
For the vision concerns the whole
   multitude,
And it shall not turn back;
No one will strengthen himself
Who lives in iniquity.

[14]'They have blown the trumpet and made
   everyone ready,
But no one goes to battle;
For My wrath *is* on all their multitude.
[15]The sword *is* outside,
And the pestilence and famine within.
Whoever *is* in the field
Will die by the sword;
And whoever *is* in the city,
Famine and pestilence will devour him.

[16]'Those who survive will escape and be on
   the mountains
Like doves of the valleys,
All of them mourning,

Each for his iniquity.

¹⁷ Every hand will be feeble,
And every knee will be *as* weak *as* water.
¹⁸ They will also be girded with sackcloth;
Horror will cover them;
Shame *will be* on every face,
Baldness on all their heads.

¹⁹ 'They will throw their silver into the
streets,
And their gold will be like refuse;
Their silver and their gold will not be able
to deliver them
In the day of the wrath of the LORD;
They will not satisfy their souls,
Nor fill their stomachs,
Because it became their stumbling block of
iniquity.

²⁰ 'As for the beauty of his ornaments,
He set it in majesty;
But they made from it
The images of their abominations—
Their detestable things;
Therefore I have made it
Like refuse to them.
²¹ I will give it as plunder
Into the hands of strangers,
And to the wicked of the earth as spoil;
And they shall defile it.
²² I will turn My face from them,
And they will defile My secret place;
For robbers shall enter it and defile it.

²³ 'Make a chain,
For the land is filled with crimes of blood,
And the city is full of violence.
²⁴ Therefore I will bring the worst of the
Gentiles,
And they will possess their houses;
I will cause the pomp of the strong to
cease,
And their holy places shall be defiled.
²⁵ Destruction comes;
They will seek peace, but *there shall be*
none.
²⁶ Disaster will come upon disaster,
And rumor will be upon rumor.
Then they will seek a vision from a
prophet;
But the law will perish from the priest,
And counsel from the elders.
²⁷ 'The king will mourn,
The prince will be clothed with
desolation,

And the hands of the common people will
tremble.
I will do to them according to their way,
And according to what they deserve I will
judge them;
Then they shall know that I *am* the
LORD!'"

Abominations in the Temple

8 And it came to pass in the sixth year, in the sixth *month,* on the fifth *day* of the month, as I sat in my house with the elders of Judah sitting before me, that the hand of the Lord GOD fell upon me there. ²Then I looked, and there was a likeness, like the appearance of fire—from the appearance of His waist and downward, fire; and from His waist and upward, like the appearance of brightness, like the color of amber. ³He stretched out the form of a hand, and took me by a lock of my hair; and the Spirit lifted me up between earth and heaven, and brought me in visions of God to Jerusalem, to the door of the north gate of the inner *court,* where the seat of the image of jealousy *was,* which provokes to jealousy. ⁴And behold, the glory of the God of Israel *was* there, like the vision that I saw in the plain.

⁵Then He said to me, "Son of man, lift your eyes now toward the north." So I lifted my eyes toward the north, and there, north of the altar gate, was this image of jealousy in the entrance.

⁶Furthermore He said to me, "Son of man, do you see what they are doing, the great abominations that the house of Israel commits here, to make Me go far away from My sanctuary? Now turn again, you will see greater abominations." ⁷So He brought me to the door of the court; and when I looked, there was a hole in the wall. ⁸Then He said to me, "Son of man, dig into the wall"; and when I dug into the wall, there was a door.

⁹And He said to me, "Go in, and see the wicked abominations which they are doing there." ¹⁰So I went in and saw, and there—every sort of creeping thing, abominable beasts, and all the idols of the house of Israel, portrayed all around on the walls. ¹¹And there stood before them seventy men of the elders of the house of Israel, and in their midst stood Jaazaniah the son of Shaphan. Each man had a censer in his hand, and a thick cloud of incense went up. ¹²Then He said to me, "Son of man, have you seen what the elders of the house of Israel do in the dark, every man in the room of his idols? For they say, 'The LORD does not see us, the LORD has forsaken the land.'"

The Law of Solid Ground: Leaders Pay for Conduct No One Sees

(Ezekiel 8:12, 13)

When leaders believe they can do whatever they want in private even if it contradicts what they do in public, they violate their calling. Leaders who last commit themselves to personal integrity, even when no one is watching, because they know it will pay off in public, when many may be watching.

[13]And He said to me, "Turn again, *and* you will see greater abominations that they are doing." [14]So He brought me to the door of the north gate of the LORD's house; and to my dismay, women were sitting there weeping for Tammuz.

[15]Then He said to me, "Have you seen *this,* O son of man? Turn again, you will see greater abominations than these." [16]So He brought me into the inner court of the LORD's house; and there, at the door of the temple of the LORD, between the porch and the altar, *were* about twenty-five men with their backs toward the temple of the LORD and their faces toward the east, and they were worshiping the sun toward the east.

[17]And He said to me, "Have you seen *this,* O son of man? Is it a trivial thing to the house of Judah to commit the abominations which they commit here? For they have filled the land with violence; then they have returned to provoke Me to anger. Indeed they put the branch to their nose. [18]Therefore I also will act in fury. My eye will not spare nor will I have pity; and though they cry in My ears with a loud voice, I will not hear them."

The Wicked Are Slain

9 Then He called out in my hearing with a loud voice, saying, "Let those who have charge over the city draw near, each *with* a deadly weapon in his hand." [2]And suddenly six men came from the direction of the upper gate, which faces north, each with his battle-ax in his hand. One man among them *was* clothed with linen and had a writer's inkhorn at his side. They went in and stood beside the bronze altar.

[3]Now the glory of the God of Israel had gone up from the cherub, where it had been, to the threshold of the temple.[a] And He called to the man clothed with linen, who *had* the writer's inkhorn at his side; [4]and the LORD said to him, "Go through the midst of the city, through the midst of Jerusalem, and put a mark on the foreheads of the men who sigh and cry over all the abominations that are done within it."

[5]To the others He said in my hearing, "Go after him through the city and kill; do not let your eye spare, nor have any pity. [6]Utterly slay old *and* young men, maidens and little children and women; but do not come near anyone on whom *is* the mark; and begin at My sanctuary." So they began with the elders who *were* before the temple. [7]Then He said to them, "Defile the temple, and fill the courts with the slain. Go out!" And they went out and killed in the city.

[8]So it was, that while they were killing them, I was left *alone;* and I fell on my face and cried out, and said, "Ah, Lord GOD! Will You destroy all the remnant of Israel in pouring out Your fury on Jerusalem?"

[9]Then He said to me, "The iniquity of the house of Israel and Judah *is* exceedingly great, and the land is full of bloodshed, and the city full of perversity; for they say, 'The LORD has forsaken the land, and the LORD does not see!' [10]And as for Me also, My eye will neither spare, nor will I have pity, *but* I will recompense their deeds on their own head."

[11]Just then, the man clothed with linen, who *had* the inkhorn at his side, reported back and said, "I have done as You commanded me."

The Glory Departs from the Temple

10 And I looked, and there in the firmament that was above the head of the cherubim, there appeared something like a sapphire stone, having the appearance of the likeness of a throne. [2]Then He spoke to the man clothed with linen, and said, "Go in among the wheels, under the cherub, fill your hands with coals of fire from among the cherubim, and scatter *them* over the city." And he went in as I watched.

[3]Now the cherubim were standing on the south side of the temple[a] when the man went in, and the cloud filled the inner court. [4]Then the glory of the LORD went up from the cherub, *and paused* over the threshold of the temple; and the house was filled with the cloud, and the court

9:3 [a]Literally *house* **10:3** [a]Literally *house,* also in verses 4 and 18

was full of the brightness of the LORD's glory. [5]And the sound of the wings of the cherubim was heard *even* in the outer court, like the voice of Almighty God when He speaks.

[6]Then it happened, when He commanded the man clothed in linen, saying, "Take fire from among the wheels, from among the cherubim," that he went in and stood beside the wheels. [7]And the cherub stretched out his hand from among the cherubim to the fire that *was* among the cherubim, and took *some of it* and put *it* into the hands of the *man* clothed with linen, who took *it* and went out. [8]The cherubim appeared to have the form of a man's hand under their wings.

[9]And when I looked, there were four wheels by the cherubim, one wheel by one cherub and another wheel by each other cherub; the wheels appeared *to have* the color of a beryl stone. [10]*As for* their appearance, all four looked alike—as it were, a wheel in the middle of a wheel. [11]When they went, they went toward *any of* their four directions; they did not turn aside when they went, but followed in the direction the head was facing. They did not turn aside when they went. [12]And their whole body, with their back, their hands, their wings, and the wheels that the four had, *were* full of eyes all around. [13]As for the wheels, they were called in my hearing, "Wheel."

[14]Each one had four faces: the first face *was* the face of a cherub, the second face the face of a man, the third the face of a lion, and the fourth the face of an eagle. [15]And the cherubim were lifted up. This *was* the living creature I saw by the River Chebar. [16]When the cherubim went, the wheels went beside them; and when the cherubim lifted their wings to mount up from the earth, the same wheels also did not turn from beside them. [17]When *the cherubim*[a] stood still, *the wheels* stood still, and when *one*[b] was lifted up, *the other*[c] lifted itself up, for the spirit of the living creature *was* in them.

[18]Then the glory of the LORD departed from the threshold of the temple and stood over the cherubim. [19]And the cherubim lifted their wings and mounted up from the earth in my sight. When they went out, the wheels *were* beside them; and they stood at the door of the east gate of the LORD's house, and the glory of the God of Israel *was* above them.

[20]This *is* the living creature I saw under the God of Israel by the River Chebar; and I knew they *were* cherubim. [21]Each one had four faces and each one four wings, and the likeness of the hands of a man *was* under their wings. [22]And the likeness of their faces *was* the same *as* the faces

which I had seen by the River Chebar, their appearance and their persons. They each went straight forward.

Judgment on Wicked Counselors

11 Then the Spirit lifted me up and brought me to the East Gate of the LORD's house, which faces eastward; and there at the door of the gate were twenty-five men, among whom I saw Jaazaniah the son of Azzur, and Pelatiah the son of Benaiah, princes of the people. [2]And He said to me: "Son of man, these *are* the men who devise iniquity and give wicked counsel in this city, [3]who say, '*The time is* not near to build houses; this *city is* the caldron, and we *are* the meat.' [4]Therefore prophesy against them, prophesy, O son of man!"

[5]Then the Spirit of the LORD fell upon me, and said to me, "Speak! 'Thus says the LORD: "Thus you have said, O house of Israel; for I

10:17 [a]Literally *they* [b]Literally *they* [c]Literally *they*

God Looks at the Leader's Heart

(Ezekiel 11:1–13)

When God measures the greatness of a leader, He puts His tape measure around the heart, not the head. Ezekiel 11 echoes the message we learn from King David in 1 Samuel 16. When God punishes evil leaders, their followers also get punished. We may conclude from this that no nation rises above its leadership.

What can we learn from these failed leaders? The chief lesson lies in their hearts. God desires that leaders first develop the following heart characteristics:

1. Healthy personal security
2. Strong biblical identity
3. Growing intimacy with Him
4. Consistent personal disciplines
5. Pure motives and ambitions
6. Biblical values and priorities
7. Humble servant's heart
8. Healthy community relationships
9. Principle-centered decisions
10. Compassionate love for people

know the things that come into your mind. ⁶You have multiplied your slain in this city, and you have filled its streets with the slain." ⁷Therefore thus says the Lord GOD: "Your slain whom you have laid in its midst, they *are* the meat, and this *city is* the caldron; but I shall bring you out of the midst of it. ⁸You have feared the sword; and I will bring a sword upon you," says the Lord GOD. ⁹"And I will bring you out of its midst, and deliver you into the hands of strangers, and execute judgments on you. ¹⁰You shall fall by the sword. I will judge you at the border of Israel. Then you shall know that I *am* the LORD. ¹¹This *city* shall not be your caldron, nor shall you be the meat in its midst. I will judge you at the border of Israel. ¹²And you shall know that I *am* the LORD; for you have not walked in My statutes nor executed My judgments, but have done according to the customs of the Gentiles which *are* all around you.' "

¹³Now it happened, while I was prophesying, that Pelatiah the son of Benaiah died. Then I fell on my face and cried with a loud voice, and said, "Ah, Lord GOD! Will You make a complete end of the remnant of Israel?"

God Will Restore Israel

¹⁴Again the word of the LORD came to me, saying, ¹⁵"Son of man, your brethren, your relatives, your countrymen, and all the house of Israel in its entirety, *are* those about whom the inhabitants of Jerusalem have said, 'Get far away from the LORD; this land has been given to us as a possession.' ¹⁶Therefore say, 'Thus says the Lord GOD: "Although I have cast them far off among the Gentiles, and although I have scattered them among the countries, yet I shall be a little sanctuary for them in the countries where they have gone." ' ¹⁷Therefore say, 'Thus says the Lord GOD: "I will gather you from the peoples, assemble you from the countries where you have been scattered, and I will give you the land of Israel." ' ¹⁸And they will go there, and they will take away all its detestable things and all its abominations from there. ¹⁹Then I will give them one heart, and I will put a new spirit within them,ᵃ and take the stony heart out of their flesh, and give them a heart of flesh, ²⁰that they may walk in My statutes and keep My judgments and do them; and they shall be My people, and I will be their God. ²¹But *as for those* whose hearts follow the desire for their detestable things and their abominations, I will recompense their deeds on their own heads," says the Lord GOD.

²²So the cherubim lifted up their wings, with the wheels beside them, and the glory of the God of Israel *was* high above them. ²³And the glory of the LORD went up from the midst of the city and stood on the mountain, which *is* on the east side of the city.

²⁴Then the Spirit took me up and brought me in a vision by the Spirit of God into Chaldea,ᵃ to those in captivity. And the vision that I had seen went up from me. ²⁵So I spoke to those in captivity of all the things the LORD had shown me.

Judah's Captivity Portrayed

12 Now the word of the LORD came to me, saying: ²"Son of man, you dwell in the midst of a rebellious house, which has eyes to see but does not see, and ears to hear but does not hear; for they *are* a rebellious house.

³"Therefore, son of man, prepare your belongings for captivity, and go into captivity by day in their sight. You shall go from your place into captivity to another place in their sight. It may be that they will consider, though they *are* a rebellious house. ⁴By day you shall bring out your belongings in their sight, as though going into captivity; and at evening you shall go in their sight, like those who go into captivity. ⁵Dig through the wall in their sight, and carry your belongings out through it. ⁶In their sight you shall bear *them* on *your* shoulders *and* carry *them* out at twilight; you shall cover your face, so that you cannot see the ground, for I have made you a sign to the house of Israel."

⁷So I did as I was commanded. I brought out my belongings by day, as though going into captivity, and at evening I dug through the wall with my hand. I brought *them* out at twilight, *and* I bore *them* on *my* shoulder in their sight.

⁸And in the morning the word of the LORD came to me, saying, ⁹"Son of man, has not the house of Israel, the rebellious house, said to you, 'What are you doing?' ¹⁰Say to them, 'Thus says the Lord GOD: "This burden *concerns* the prince in Jerusalem and all the house of Israel who are among them." ' ¹¹Say, 'I *am* a sign to you. As I have done, so shall it be done to them; they shall be carried away into captivity.' ¹²And the prince who *is* among them shall bear *his belongings* on *his* shoulder at twilight and go out. They shall dig through the wall to carry *them* out through it. He shall cover his face, so that he cannot see the ground with *his* eyes. ¹³I will also spread My net over him, and he shall be caught in My snare. I

11:19 ᵃLiterally *you* **11:24** ᵃOr *Babylon,* and so elsewhere in this book

---

Vision: A Revelation Without Action Fades

(Ezekiel 12:1–28)

God told Ezekiel to pack up his belongings and symbolically act out the exile awaiting the Jews, once again using creative means to communicate vision.

In Ezekiel 12:21–28 God speaks of the powerlessness of visions unless someone puts feet to them. Visions lose their strength without action to support them. Good leaders always share both the vision and the steps to its implementation.

Yet the first step always must be to catch the God-given vision. Consider one process to go through as you attempt to catch God's vision for the people:

1. *Look within you:* What do you feel?
2. *Look behind you:* What have you learned?
3. *Look around you:* What is happening to others?
4. *Look ahead of you:* What is the big picture?
5. *Look above you:* What does God expect of you?
6. *Look beside you:* What resources are available to you?

---

will bring him to Babylon, *to* the land of the Chaldeans; yet he shall not see it, though he shall die there. [14]I will scatter to every wind all who *are* around him to help him, and all his troops; and I will draw out the sword after them.

[15]"Then they shall know that I *am* the LORD, when I scatter them among the nations and disperse them throughout the countries. [16]But I will spare a few of their men from the sword, from famine, and from pestilence, that they may declare all their abominations among the Gentiles wherever they go. Then they shall know that I *am* the LORD."

Judgment Not Postponed

[17]Moreover the word of the LORD came to me, saying, [18]"Son of man, eat your bread with quaking, and drink your water with trembling and anxiety. [19]And say to the people of the land, 'Thus says the Lord GOD to the inhabitants of Jerusalem *and* to the land of Israel: "They shall eat their bread with anxiety, and drink their water with dread, so

that her land may be emptied of all who are in it, because of the violence of all those who dwell in it. [20]Then the cities that are inhabited shall be laid waste, and the land shall become desolate; and you shall know that I *am* the LORD." ' "

[21]And the word of the LORD came to me, saying, [22]"Son of man, what *is* this proverb *that* you *people* have about the land of Israel, which says, 'The days are prolonged, and every vision fails'? [23]Tell them therefore, 'Thus says the Lord GOD: "I will lay this proverb to rest, and they shall no more use it as a proverb in Israel." But say to them, "The days are at hand, and the fulfillment of every vision. [24]For no more shall there be any false vision or flattering divination within the house of Israel. [25]For I *am* the LORD. I speak, and the word which I speak will come to pass; it will no more be postponed; for in your days, O rebellious house, I will say the word and perform it," says the Lord GOD.' "

[26]Again the word of the LORD came to me, saying, [27]"Son of man, look, the house of Israel is saying, 'The vision that he sees *is* for many days *from now,* and he prophesies of times far off.' [28]Therefore say to them, 'Thus says the Lord GOD: "None of My words will be postponed any more, but the word which I speak will be done," says the Lord GOD.' "

Woe to Foolish Prophets

13 And the word of the LORD came to me, saying, [2]"Son of man, prophesy against the prophets of Israel who prophesy, and say to those who prophesy out of their own heart, 'Hear the word of the LORD!' "

[3]Thus says the Lord GOD: "Woe to the foolish prophets, who follow their own spirit and have seen nothing! [4]O Israel, your prophets are like foxes in the deserts. [5]You have not gone up into the gaps to build a wall for the house of Israel to stand in battle on the day of the LORD. [6]They have envisioned futility and false divination, saying, 'Thus says the LORD!' But the LORD has not sent them; yet they hope that the word may be confirmed. [7]Have you not seen a futile vision, and have you not spoken false divination? You say, 'The LORD says,' but I have not spoken."

[8]Therefore thus says the Lord GOD: "Because you have spoken nonsense and envisioned lies, therefore I *am* indeed against you," says the Lord GOD. [9]"My hand will be against the prophets who envision futility and who divine lies; they shall not be in the assembly of My people, nor be written in the record of the house of Israel, nor shall they enter into the land of Israel. Then you shall know that I *am* the Lord GOD.

¹⁰"Because, indeed, because they have seduced My people, saying, 'Peace!' when *there is* no peace—and one builds a wall, and they plaster it with untempered *mortar*— ¹¹say to those who plaster *it* with untempered *mortar,* that it will fall. There will be flooding rain, and you, O great hailstones, shall fall; and a stormy wind shall tear *it* down. ¹²Surely, when the wall has fallen, will it not be said to you, 'Where *is* the mortar with which you plastered *it?*'"

¹³Therefore thus says the Lord GOD: "I will cause a stormy wind to break forth in My fury; and there shall be a flooding rain in My anger, and great hailstones in fury to consume *it*. ¹⁴So I will break down the wall you have plastered with untempered *mortar,* and bring it down to the ground, so that its foundation will be uncovered; it will fall, and you shall be consumed in the midst of it. Then you shall know that I *am* the LORD.

¹⁵"Thus will I accomplish My wrath on the wall and on those who have plastered it with untempered *mortar;* and I will say to you, 'The wall *is* no *more,* nor those who plastered it, ¹⁶that is, the prophets of Israel who prophesy concerning Jerusalem, and who see visions of peace for her when *there is* no peace,'" says the Lord GOD.

¹⁷"Likewise, son of man, set your face against the daughters of your people, who prophesy out of their own heart; prophesy against them, ¹⁸and say, 'Thus says the Lord GOD: "Woe to the *women* who sew *magic* charms on their sleeves[a] and make veils for the heads of people of every height to hunt souls! Will you hunt the souls of My people, and keep yourselves alive? ¹⁹And will you profane Me among My people for handfuls of barley and for pieces of bread, killing people who should not die, and keeping people alive who should not live, by your lying to My people who listen to lies?"

²⁰"Therefore thus says the Lord GOD: "Behold, I *am* against your *magic* charms by which you hunt souls there like birds. I will tear them from your arms, and let the souls go, the souls you hunt like birds. ²¹I will also tear off your veils and deliver My people out of your hand, and they shall no longer be as prey in your hand. Then you shall know that I *am* the LORD. ²²Because with lies you have made the heart of the righteous sad, whom I have not made sad; and you have strengthened the hands of the wicked, so that he does not turn from his wicked way to save his life. ²³Therefore you shall no longer envision futility nor practice divination; for I will deliver My people out of your hand, and you shall know that I *am* the LORD."'"

Idolatry Will Be Punished

14 Now some of the elders of Israel came to me and sat before me. ²And the word of the LORD came to me, saying, ³"Son of man, these men have set up their idols in their hearts, and put before them that which causes them to stumble into iniquity. Should I let Myself be inquired of at all by them?

⁴"Therefore speak to them, and say to them, 'Thus says the Lord GOD: "Everyone of the house of Israel who sets up his idols in his heart, and puts before him what causes him to stumble into iniquity, and then comes to the prophet, I the LORD will answer him who comes, according to the multitude of his idols, ⁵that I may seize the house of Israel by their heart, because they are all estranged from Me by their idols."'

⁶"Therefore say to the house of Israel, 'Thus says the Lord GOD: "Repent, turn away from your idols, and turn your faces away from all your abominations. ⁷For anyone of the house of Israel, or of the strangers who dwell in Israel, who separates himself from Me and sets up his idols in his heart and puts before him what causes him to stumble into iniquity, then comes to a prophet to inquire of him concerning Me, I the LORD will answer him by Myself. ⁸I will set My face against that man and make him a sign and a proverb, and I will cut him off from the midst of My people. Then you shall know that I *am* the LORD.

⁹"And if the prophet is induced to speak anything, I the LORD have induced that prophet, and I will stretch out My hand against him and destroy him from among My people Israel. ¹⁰And they shall bear their iniquity; the punishment of the prophet shall be the same as the punishment of the one who inquired, ¹¹that the house of Israel may no longer stray from Me, nor be profaned anymore with all their transgressions, but that they may be My people and I may be their God," says the Lord GOD.'"

Judgment on Persistent Unfaithfulness

¹²The word of the LORD came again to me, saying: ¹³"Son of man, when a land sins against Me by persistent unfaithfulness, I will stretch out My hand against it; I will cut off its supply of bread, send famine on it, and cut off man and beast from it. ¹⁴Even *if* these three men, Noah, Daniel, and

---

13:18 [a]Literally *over all the joints of My hands;* Vulgate reads *under every elbow;* Septuagint and Targum read *on all elbows of the hands.*

The Law of Influence: Even the Best Leaders Can't Force Action

(Ezekiel 14:12–14)

Even the best leaders cannot force followers to act. God says even three of His choice servants—Noah, Daniel, and Job—could not save rebellious Judah. All three were full of integrity, character, and discipline, totally competent and responsible to do the right thing. Yet God says even they could save only themselves.

Job, were in it, they would deliver *only* themselves by their righteousness," says the Lord GOD.

15"If I cause wild beasts to pass through the land, and they empty it, and make it so desolate that no man may pass through because of the beasts, 16*even though* these three men *were* in it, *as* I live," says the Lord GOD, "they would deliver neither sons nor daughters; only they would be delivered, and the land would be desolate.

17"Or *if* I bring a sword on that land, and say, 'Sword, go through the land,' and I cut off man and beast from it, 18*even though* these three men *were* in it, *as* I live," says the Lord GOD, "they would deliver neither sons nor daughters, but only they themselves would be delivered.

19"Or *if* I send a pestilence into that land and pour out My fury on it in blood, and cut off from it man and beast, 20*even though* Noah, Daniel, and Job *were* in it, *as* I live," says the Lord GOD, "they would deliver neither son nor daughter; they would deliver *only* themselves by their righteousness."

21For thus says the Lord GOD: "How much more it shall be when I send My four severe judgments on Jerusalem—the sword and famine and wild beasts and pestilence—to cut off man and beast from it? 22Yet behold, there shall be left in it a remnant who will be brought out, *both* sons and daughters; surely they will come out to you, and you will see their ways and their doings. Then you will be comforted concerning the disaster that I have brought upon Jerusalem, all that I have brought upon it. 23And they will comfort you, when you see their ways and their doings; and you shall know that I have done nothing without cause that I have done in it," says the Lord GOD.

The Outcast Vine

15 Then the word of the LORD came to me, saying: 2"Son of man, how is the wood of the vine *better* than any other wood, the vine branch which is among the trees of the forest? 3Is wood taken from it to make any object? Or can *men* make a peg from it to hang any vessel on? 4Instead, it is thrown into the fire for fuel; the fire devours both ends of it, and its middle is burned. Is it useful for *any* work? 5Indeed, when it was whole, no object could be made from it. How much less will it be useful for *any* work when the fire has devoured it, and it is burned?

6"Therefore thus says the Lord GOD: 'Like the wood of the vine among the trees of the forest, which I have given to the fire for fuel, so I will give up the inhabitants of Jerusalem; 7and I will set My face against them. They will go out from *one* fire, but *another* fire shall devour them. Then you shall know that I *am* the LORD, when I set My face against them. 8Thus I will make the land desolate, because they have persisted in unfaithfulness,' says the Lord GOD."

God's Love for Jerusalem

16 Again the word of the LORD came to me, saying, 2"Son of man, cause Jerusalem to know her abominations, 3and say, 'Thus says the Lord GOD to Jerusalem: "Your birth and your nativity *are* from the land of Canaan; your father *was* an Amorite and your mother a Hittite. 4*As for* your nativity, on the day you were born your navel cord was not cut, nor were you washed in water to cleanse *you;* you were not rubbed with salt nor wrapped in swaddling cloths. 5No eye pitied you, to do any of these things for you, to have compassion on you; but you were thrown out into the open field, when you yourself were loathed on the day you were born.

6"And when I passed by you and saw you struggling in your own blood, I said to you in your blood, 'Live!' Yes, I said to you in your blood, 'Live!' 7I made you thrive like a plant in the field; and you grew, matured, and became very beautiful. *Your* breasts were formed, your hair grew, but you *were* naked and bare.

8"When I passed by you again and looked upon you, indeed your time *was* the time of love; so I spread My wing over you and covered your nakedness. Yes, I swore an oath to you and entered into a covenant with you, and you became Mine," says the Lord GOD.

9"Then I washed you in water; yes, I

thoroughly washed off your blood, and I anointed you with oil. [10]I clothed you in embroidered cloth and gave you sandals of badger skin; I clothed you with fine linen and covered you with silk. [11]I adorned you with ornaments, put bracelets on your wrists, and a chain on your neck. [12]And I put a jewel in your nose, earrings in your ears, and a beautiful crown on your head. [13]Thus you were adorned with gold and silver, and your clothing *was of* fine linen, silk, and embroidered cloth. You ate *pastry of* fine flour, honey, and oil. You were exceedingly beautiful, and succeeded to royalty. [14]Your fame went out among the nations because of your beauty, for it *was* perfect through My splendor which I had bestowed on you," says the Lord GOD.

Jerusalem's Harlotry

[15]"But you trusted in your own beauty, played the harlot because of your fame, and poured out your harlotry on everyone passing by who *would have* it. [16]You took some of your garments and adorned multicolored high places for yourself, and played the harlot on them. *Such* things should not happen, nor be. [17]You have also taken your beautiful jewelry from My gold and My silver, which I had given you, and made for yourself male images and played the harlot with them. [18]You took your embroidered garments and covered them, and you set My oil and My incense before them. [19]Also My food which I gave you—the pastry of fine flour, oil, and honey *which* I fed you—you set it before them as sweet incense; and *so* it was," says the Lord GOD.

[20]"Moreover you took your sons and your daughters, whom you bore to Me, and these you sacrificed to them to be devoured. *Were* your *acts* of harlotry a small matter, [21]that you have slain My children and offered them up to them by causing them to pass through *the fire?* [22]And in all your abominations and acts of harlotry you did not remember the days of your youth, when you were naked and bare, struggling in your blood.

[23]"Then it was so, after all your wickedness— 'Woe, woe to you!' says the Lord GOD— [24]*that* you also built for yourself a shrine, and made a high place for yourself in every street. [25]You built your high places at the head of every road, and made your beauty to be abhorred. You offered yourself to everyone who passed by, and multiplied your acts of harlotry. [26]You also committed harlotry with the Egyptians, your very fleshly neighbors, and increased your acts of harlotry to provoke Me to anger.

[27]"Behold, therefore, I stretched out My hand against you, diminished your allotment, and gave

---

The Law of Magnetism: God's People Become Like Pagan Leaders

(Ezekiel 16:23–29)

We attract who we are, not who we want. Consider the following:

1. **Attraction:** We tend to attract those similar to us.
2. **Reflection:** We tend to reflect those who lead or follow us.
3. **Repercussion:** We tend to face similar consequences as those who are like us.

---

you up to the will of those who hate you, the daughters of the Philistines, who were ashamed of your lewd behavior. [28]You also played the harlot with the Assyrians, because you were insatiable; indeed you played the harlot with them and still were not satisfied. [29]Moreover you multiplied your acts of harlotry as far as the land of the trader, Chaldea; and even then you were not satisfied.

[30]"How degenerate is your heart!" says the Lord GOD, "seeing you do all these *things,* the deeds of a brazen harlot.

Jerusalem's Adultery

[31]"You erected your shrine at the head of every road, and built your high place in every street. Yet you were not like a harlot, because you scorned payment. [32]*You are* an adulterous wife, *who* takes strangers instead of her husband. [33]Men make payment to all harlots, but you made your payments to all your lovers, and hired them to come to you from all around for your harlotry. [34]You are the opposite of *other* women in your harlotry, because no one solicited you to be a harlot. In that you gave payment but no payment was given you, therefore you are the opposite."

Jerusalem's Lovers Will Abuse Her

[35]"Now then, O harlot, hear the word of the LORD! [36]Thus says the Lord GOD: "Because your filthiness was poured out and your nakedness uncovered in your harlotry with your lovers, and with all your abominable idols, and because of the blood of your children which you gave to them, [37]surely, therefore, I will gather all your lovers with whom you took pleasure, all those you loved, *and* all those you hated; I will gather

them from all around against you and will uncover your nakedness to them, that they may see all your nakedness. [38]And I will judge you as women who break wedlock or shed blood are judged; I will bring blood upon you in fury and jealousy. [39]I will also give you into their hand, and they shall throw down your shrines and break down your high places. They shall also strip you of your clothes, take your beautiful jewelry, and leave you naked and bare.

[40]"They shall also bring up an assembly against you, and they shall stone you with stones and thrust you through with their swords. [41]They shall burn your houses with fire, and execute judgments on you in the sight of many women; and I will make you cease playing the harlot, and you shall no longer hire lovers. [42]So I will lay to rest My fury toward you, and My jealousy shall depart from you. I will be quiet, and be angry no more. [43]Because you did not remember the days of your youth, but agitated Me[a] with all these *things,* surely I will also recompense your deeds on *your own* head," says the Lord GOD. "And you shall not commit lewdness in addition to all your abominations.

More Wicked than Samaria and Sodom

[44]"Indeed everyone who quotes proverbs will use *this* proverb against you: 'Like mother, like daughter!' [45]You *are* your mother's daughter, loathing husband and children; and you *are* the sister of your sisters, who loathed their husbands and children; your mother *was* a Hittite and your father an Amorite.

[46]"Your elder sister *is* Samaria, who dwells with her daughters to the north of you; and your younger sister, who dwells to the south of you, *is* Sodom and her daughters. [47]You did not walk in their ways nor act according to their abominations; but, as *if that were* too little, you became more corrupt than they in all your ways.

[48]"*As* I live," says the Lord GOD, "neither your sister Sodom nor her daughters have done as you and your daughters have done. [49]Look, this was the iniquity of your sister Sodom: She and her daughter had pride, fullness of food, and abundance of idleness; neither did she strengthen the hand of the poor and needy. [50]And they were haughty and committed abomination before Me; therefore I took them away as I saw *fit.*[a]

[51]"Samaria did not commit half of your sins; but you have multiplied your abominations more than they, and have justified your sisters by all the abominations which you have done. [52]You who judged your sisters, bear your own shame also, because the sins which you committed were more

abominable than theirs; they are more righteous than you. Yes, be disgraced also, and bear your own shame, because you justified your sisters.

[53]"When I bring back their captives, the captives of Sodom and her daughters, and the captives of Samaria and her daughters, then *I will also bring back* the captives of your captivity among them, [54]that you may bear your own shame and be disgraced by all that you did when you comforted them. [55]When your sisters, Sodom and her daughters, return to their former state, and Samaria and her daughters return to their former state, then you and your daughters will return to your former state. [56]For your sister Sodom was not a byword in your mouth in the days of your pride, [57]before your wickedness was uncovered. It was like the time of the reproach of the daughters of Syria[a] and all *those* around her, and of the daughters of the Philistines, who despise you everywhere. [58]You have paid for your lewdness and your abominations," says the LORD. [59]For thus says the Lord GOD: "I will deal with you as you have done, who despised the oath by breaking the covenant.

An Everlasting Covenant

[60]"Nevertheless I will remember My covenant with you in the days of your youth, and I will establish an everlasting covenant with you. [61]Then you will remember your ways and be ashamed, when you receive your older and your younger sisters; for I will give them to you for daughters, but not because of My covenant with you. [62]And I will establish My covenant with you. Then you shall know that I *am* the LORD, [63]that you may remember and be ashamed, and never open your mouth anymore because of your shame, when I provide you an atonement for all you have done," says the Lord GOD.'"

The Eagles and the Vine

17 And the word of the LORD came to me, saying, [2]"Son of man, pose a riddle, and speak a parable to the house of Israel, [3]and say, 'Thus says the Lord GOD:

" A great eagle with large wings and long pinions,

16:43 [a]Following Septuagint, Syriac, Targum, and Vulgate; Masoretic Text reads *were agitated with Me.* **16:50** [a]Vulgate reads *you saw;* Septuagint reads *he saw;* Targum reads *as was revealed to Me.*
16:57 [a]Following Masoretic Text, Septuagint, Targum, and Vulgate; many Hebrew manuscripts and Syriac read *Edom.*

Full of feathers of various colors,
Came to Lebanon
And took from the cedar the highest
    branch.
4 He cropped off its topmost young twig
And carried it to a land of trade;
He set it in a city of merchants.
5 Then he took some of the seed of the
    land
And planted it in a fertile field;
He placed *it* by abundant waters
And set it like a willow tree.
6 And it grew and became a spreading vine
    of low stature;
Its branches turned toward him,
But its roots were under it.
So it became a vine,
Brought forth branches,
And put forth shoots.

7 "But there was another[a] great eagle with
    large wings and many feathers;
And behold, this vine bent its roots toward
    him,
And stretched its branches toward him,
From the garden terrace where it had been
    planted,
That he might water it.
8 It was planted in good soil by many
    waters,
To bring forth branches, bear fruit,
And become a majestic vine."'

9 "Say, 'Thus says the Lord GOD:

"Will it thrive?
Will he not pull up its roots,
Cut off its fruit,
And leave it to wither?
All of its spring leaves will wither,
And no great power or many people
Will be needed to pluck it up by its
    roots.
10 Behold, *it is* planted,
Will it thrive?
Will it not utterly wither when the east
    wind touches it?
It will wither in the garden terrace where
    it grew."'"

11 Moreover the word of the LORD came to me, saying, 12 "Say now to the rebellious house: 'Do you not know what these *things* mean?' Tell *them,* 'Indeed the king of Babylon went to Jerusalem and took its king and princes, and led them with him to Babylon. 13 And he took the king's offspring, made a covenant with him, and put him under oath. He also took away the mighty of the land, 14 that the kingdom might be brought low and not lift itself up, *but* that by keeping his covenant it might stand. 15 But he rebelled against him by sending his ambassadors to Egypt, that they might give him horses and many people. Will he prosper? Will he who does such *things* escape? Can he break a covenant and still be delivered?

16 'As I live,' says the Lord GOD, 'surely in the place *where* the king *dwells* who made him king, whose oath he despised and whose covenant he broke—with him in the midst of Babylon he shall die. 17 Nor will Pharaoh with *his* mighty army and great company do anything in the war, when they heap up a siege mound and build a wall to cut off many persons. 18 Since he despised the oath by breaking the covenant, and in fact gave his hand and still did all these *things,* he shall not escape.'"

19 Therefore thus says the Lord GOD: "As I live, surely My oath which he despised, and My covenant which he broke, I will recompense on his own head. 20 I will spread My net over him, and he shall be taken in My snare. I will bring him to Babylon and try him there for the treason which he committed against Me. 21 All his fugitives[a] with all his troops shall fall by the sword, and those who remain shall be scattered to every wind; and you shall know that I, the LORD, have spoken."

Israel Exalted at Last

22 Thus says the Lord GOD: "I will take also *one* of the highest branches of the high cedar and set *it* out. I will crop off from the topmost of its young twigs a tender one, and will plant *it* on a high and prominent mountain. 23 On the mountain height of Israel I will plant it; and it will bring forth boughs, and bear fruit, and be a majestic cedar. Under it will dwell birds of every sort; in the shadow of its branches they will dwell. 24 And all the trees of the field shall know that I, the LORD, have brought down the high tree and exalted the low tree, dried up the green tree and made the dry tree flourish; I, the LORD, have spoken and have done *it.*"

17:7 [a]Following Septuagint, Syriac, and Vulgate; Masoretic Text and Targum read *one.*
17:21 [a]Following Masoretic Text and Vulgate; many Hebrew manuscripts and Syriac read *choice men;* Targum reads *mighty men;* Septuagint omits *All his fugitives.*

A False Proverb Refuted

18 The word of the LORD came to me again, saying, [2]"What do you mean when you use this proverb concerning the land of Israel, saying:

'The fathers have eaten sour grapes,
And the children's teeth are set on edge'?

[3]"As I live," says the Lord GOD, "you shall no longer use this proverb in Israel.

[4] "Behold, all souls are Mine;
The soul of the father
As well as the soul of the son is Mine;
The soul who sins shall die.

[5] But if a man is just
And does what is lawful and right;

[6] If he has not eaten on the mountains,
Nor lifted up his eyes to the idols of the
  house of Israel,
Nor defiled his neighbor's wife,
Nor approached a woman during her
  impurity;

[7] If he has not oppressed anyone,
But has restored to the debtor his pledge;
Has robbed no one by violence,
But has given his bread to the hungry
And covered the naked with clothing;

[8] If he has not exacted usury
Nor taken any increase,

But has withdrawn his hand from iniquity
And executed true judgment between man
  and man;

[9] If he has walked in My statutes
And kept My judgments faithfully—
He *is* just;
He shall surely live!"
Says the Lord GOD.

[10] "If he begets a son *who is* a robber
Or a shedder of blood,
Who does any of these *things*

[11] And does none of those *duties,*
But has eaten on the mountains
Or defiled his neighbor's wife;

[12] If he has oppressed the poor and needy,
Robbed by violence,
Not restored the pledge,
Lifted his eyes to the idols,
Or committed abomination;

[13] If he has exacted usury
Or taken increase—
Shall he then live?
He shall not live!
If he has done any of these abominations,
He shall surely die;
His blood shall be upon him.

[14] "*If,* however, he begets a son
Who sees all the sins which his father has
  done,

Discernment: Leaders Assess Situations, Then Respond

(Ezekiel 18:1–32)

God handles each circumstance based on His assessment of the individual situation. In Ezekiel 18 God reminds us to use discernment in each situation we face. Don't package everyone together, but size everyone up, one at a time. Respond correctly to each situation.

Consider a few rules of thumb to increase your leadership discernment:

1. Analyze past successes.
   Try to identify the root issues of problems you have already solved. What patterns do you see? What enabled you to succeed?

2. Assess each person based on their particular situation.
   Don't fall into such a rut that you begin to stereotype everyone. Let each team member be an individual and discern what is right for him or her, without the baggage of others.

3. Listen to your gut.
   Try to recall times when your intuition "spoke" to you correctly. Get data, but go beyond mere information to your heart's sense of the right thing.

4. Learn from wise leaders.
   What great leaders do you admire? Study and read the lives of other leaders with gifting similar to yours and discover how they think and make decisions.

And considers but does not do likewise;

15 *Who* has not eaten on the mountains,
Nor lifted his eyes to the idols of the
house of Israel,
Nor defiled his neighbor's wife;

16 Has not oppressed anyone,
Nor withheld a pledge,
Nor robbed by violence,
But has given his bread to the hungry
And covered the naked with clothing;

17 *Who* has withdrawn his hand from the
poor[a]
And not received usury or increase,
But has executed My judgments
And walked in My statutes—
He shall not die for the iniquity of his
father;
He shall surely live!

18 "*As for* his father,
Because he cruelly oppressed,
Robbed his brother by violence,
And did what *is* not good among his
people,
Behold, he shall die for his iniquity.

Turn and Live

19 "Yet you say, 'Why should the son not bear the guilt of the father?' Because the son has done what is lawful and right, and has kept all My statutes and observed them, he shall surely live. 20 The soul who sins shall die. The son shall not bear the guilt of the father, nor the father bear the guilt of the son. The righteousness of the righteous shall be upon himself, and the wickedness of the wicked shall be upon himself.

21 "But if a wicked man turns from all his sins which he has committed, keeps all My statutes, and does what is lawful and right, he shall surely live; he shall not die. 22 None of the transgressions which he has committed shall be remembered against him; because of the righteousness which he has done, he shall live. 23 Do I have any pleasure at all that the wicked should die?" says the Lord GOD, "*and* not that he should turn from his ways and live?

24 "But when a righteous man turns away from his righteousness and commits iniquity, and does according to all the abominations that the wicked *man* does, shall he live? All the righteousness which he has done shall not be remembered; because of the unfaithfulness of which he is guilty and the sin which he has committed, because of them he shall die.

25 "Yet you say, 'The way of the Lord is not fair.' Hear now, O house of Israel, is it not My way which is fair, and your ways which are not fair? 26 When a righteous *man* turns away from his righteousness, commits iniquity, and dies in it, it is because of the iniquity which he has done that he dies. 27 Again, when a wicked *man* turns away from the wickedness which he committed, and does what is lawful and right, he preserves himself alive. 28 Because he considers and turns away from all the transgressions which he committed, he shall surely live; he shall not die. 29 Yet the house of Israel says, 'The way of the Lord is not fair.' O house of Israel, is it not My ways which are fair, and your ways which are not fair?

30 "Therefore I will judge you, O house of Israel, every one according to his ways," says the Lord GOD. "Repent, and turn from all your transgressions, so that iniquity will not be your ruin. 31 Cast away from you all the transgressions which you have committed, and get yourselves a new heart and a new spirit. For why should you die, O house of Israel? 32 For I have no pleasure in the death of one who dies," says the Lord GOD. "Therefore turn and live!"

Israel Degraded

19 "Moreover take up a lamentation for the princes of Israel, 2 and say:

'What *is* your mother? A lioness:
She lay down among the lions;
Among the young lions she nourished her
cubs.

3 She brought up one of her cubs,
And he became a young lion;
He learned to catch prey,
And he devoured men.

4 The nations also heard of him;
He was trapped in their pit,
And they brought him with chains to the
land of Egypt.

5 'When she saw that she waited, *that* her
hope was lost,
She took another of her cubs *and* made
him a young lion.

6 He roved among the lions,
And became a young lion;
He learned to catch prey;
He devoured men.

7 He knew their desolate places,[a]

18:17 [a]Following Masoretic Text, Targum, and Vulgate; Septuagint reads *iniquity* (compare verse 8). **19:7** [a]Septuagint reads *He stood in insolence;* Targum reads *He destroyed its palaces;* Vulgate reads *He learned to make widows.*

And laid waste their cities;
The land with its fullness was desolated
By the noise of his roaring.
⁸ Then the nations set against him from the
provinces on every side,
And spread their net over him;
He was trapped in their pit.
⁹ They put him in a cage with chains,
And brought him to the king of Babylon;
They brought him in nets,
That his voice should no longer be heard
on the mountains of Israel.

¹⁰ 'Your mother *was* like a vine in your
bloodline,ᵃ
Planted by the waters,
Fruitful and full of branches
Because of many waters.
¹¹ She had strong branches for scepters of
rulers.
She towered in stature above the thick
branches,
And was seen in her height amid the dense
foliage.
¹² But she was plucked up in fury,
She was cast down to the ground,
And the east wind dried her fruit,
Her strong branches were broken and
withered;
The fire consumed them.
¹³ And now she *is* planted in the wilderness,
In a dry and thirsty land.
¹⁴ Fire has come out from a rod of her
branches
And devoured her fruit,
So that she has no strong branch— a
scepter for ruling.' "

Discipline: If Leaders Can't Rule Themselves, They Can't Rule Others

(Ezekiel 19:1–14)

There is no leadership without self-discipline. Since the "princes" of Ezekiel 19 lacked the discipline to lead their own lives well, they also failed to lead anyone else well. Leaders must first lead themselves and earn the right to attract followers. The best leader serves as a model for others.

This *is* a lamentation, and has become a lamentation.

The Rebellions of Israel

20 It came to pass in the seventh year, in the fifth *month,* on the tenth *day* of the month, *that* certain of the elders of Israel came to inquire of the LORD, and sat before me. ²Then the word of the LORD came to me, saying, ³"Son of man, speak to the elders of Israel, and say to them, 'Thus says the Lord GOD: "Have you come to inquire of Me? *As* I live," says the Lord GOD, "I will not be inquired of by you." '⁴Will you judge them, son of man, will you judge *them?* Then make known to them the abominations of their fathers.

⁵"Say to them, 'Thus says the Lord GOD: "On the day when I chose Israel and raised My hand in an oath to the descendants of the house of Jacob, and made Myself known to them in the land of Egypt, I raised My hand in an oath to them, saying, 'I *am* the LORD your God.' ⁶On that day I raised My hand in an oath to them, to bring them out of the land of Egypt into a land that I had searched out for them, 'flowing with milk and honey,'ᵃ the glory of all lands. ⁷Then I said to them, 'Each of you, throw away the abominations which are before his eyes, and do not defile yourselves with the idols of Egypt. I *am* the LORD your God.' ⁸But they rebelled against Me and would not obey Me. They did not all cast away the abominations which were before their eyes, nor did they forsake the idols of Egypt. Then I said, 'I will pour out My fury on them and fulfill My anger against them in the midst of the land of Egypt.' ⁹But I acted for My name's sake, that it should not be profaned before the Gentiles among whom they *were,* in whose sight I had made Myself known to them, to bring them out of the land of Egypt.

¹⁰"Therefore I made them go out of the land of Egypt and brought them into the wilderness. ¹¹And I gave them My statutes and showed them My judgments, 'which, *if* a man does, he shall live by them.'ᵃ ¹²Moreover I also gave them My Sabbaths, to be a sign between them and Me, that they might know that I *am* the LORD who sanctifies them. ¹³Yet the house of Israel rebelled against Me in the wilderness; they did not walk in My statutes; they despised My judgments,

19:10 ᵃLiterally *blood,* following Masoretic Text, Syriac, and Vulgate; Septuagint reads *like a flower on a pomegranate tree;* Targum reads *in your likeness.*
20:6 ᵃExodus 3:8 **20:11** ᵃLeviticus 18:5

'which, *if* a man does, he shall live by them';[a] and they greatly defiled My Sabbaths. Then I said I would pour out My fury on them in the wilderness, to consume them. [14]But I acted for My name's sake, that it should not be profaned before the Gentiles, in whose sight I had brought them out. [15]So I also raised My hand in an oath to them in the wilderness, that I would not bring them into the land which I had given *them,* 'flowing with milk and honey,'[a] the glory of all lands, [16]because they despised My judgments and did not walk in My statutes, but profaned My Sabbaths; for their heart went after their idols. [17]Nevertheless My eye spared them from destruction. I did not make an end of them in the wilderness.

[18]"But I said to their children in the wilderness, 'Do not walk in the statutes of your fathers, nor observe their judgments, nor defile yourselves with their idols. [19]I *am* the LORD your God: Walk in My statutes, keep My judgments, and do them; [20]hallow My Sabbaths, and they will be a sign between Me and you, that you may know that I *am* the LORD your God.'

[21]"Notwithstanding, the children rebelled against Me; they did not walk in My statutes, and were not careful to observe My judgments, 'which, *if* a man does, he shall live by them';[a] but they profaned My Sabbaths. Then I said I would pour out My fury on them and fulfill My anger against them in the wilderness. [22]Nevertheless I withdrew My hand and acted for My name's sake, that it should not be profaned in the sight of the Gentiles, in whose sight I had brought them out. [23]Also I raised My hand in an oath to those in the wilderness, that I would scatter them among the Gentiles and disperse them throughout the countries, [24]because they had not executed My judgments, but had despised My statutes, profaned My Sabbaths, and their eyes were fixed on their fathers' idols.

[25]"Therefore I also gave them up to statutes *that were* not good, and judgments by which they could not live; [26]and I pronounced them unclean because of their ritual gifts, in that they caused all their firstborn to pass through *the fire,* that I might make them desolate and that they might know that I am the LORD.' "

[27]"Therefore, son of man, speak to the house of Israel, and say to them, 'Thus says the Lord GOD: "In this too your fathers have blasphemed Me, by being unfaithful to Me. [28]When I brought them into the land *concerning* which I had raised My hand in an oath to give them, and they saw all the high hills and all the thick trees, there they offered their sacrifices and provoked Me with their offerings. There they also sent up their sweet aroma and poured out their drink offerings. [29]Then I said to them, 'What *is* this high place to which you go?' So its name is called Bamah[a] to this day." ' [30]Therefore say to the house of Israel, 'Thus says the Lord GOD: "Are you defiling yourselves in the manner of your fathers, and committing harlotry according to their abominations? [31]For when you offer your gifts and make your sons pass through the fire, you defile yourselves with all your idols, even to this day. So shall I be inquired of by you, O house of Israel? *As* I live," says the Lord GOD, "I will not be inquired of by you. [32]What you have in your mind shall never be, when you say, 'We will be like the Gentiles, like the families in other countries, serving wood and stone.'

God Will Restore Israel

[33]"*As* I live," says the Lord GOD, "surely with a mighty hand, with an outstretched arm, and with fury poured out, I will rule over you. [34]I will bring you out from the peoples and gather you out of the countries where you are scattered, with a mighty hand, with an outstretched arm, and with fury poured out. [35]And I will bring you into the wilderness of the peoples, and there I will plead My case with you face to face. [36]Just as I pleaded My case with your fathers in the wilderness of the land of Egypt, so I will plead My case with you," says the Lord GOD.

[37]"I will make you pass under the rod, and I will bring you into the bond of the covenant; [38]I will purge the rebels from among you, and those who transgress against Me; I will bring them out of the country where they dwell, but they shall not enter the land of Israel. Then you will know that I *am* the LORD.

[39]"As for you, O house of Israel," thus says the Lord GOD: "Go, serve every one of you his idols—and hereafter—if you will not obey Me; but profane My holy name no more with your gifts and your idols. [40]For on My holy mountain, on the mountain height of Israel," says the Lord GOD, "there all the house of Israel, all of them in the land, shall serve Me; there I will accept them, and there I will require your offerings and the firstfruits of your sacrifices, together with all your holy things. [41]I will accept you as a sweet aroma when I bring you out from the peoples and gather you out of the countries where you have been scattered; and I will be hallowed in

---

20:13 [a]Leviticus 18:5 20:15 [a]Exodus 3:8
20:21 [a]Leviticus 18:5 20:29 [a]Literally *High Place*

you before the Gentiles. [42]Then you shall know that I *am* the LORD, when I bring you into the land of Israel, into the country *for* which I raised My hand in an oath to give to your fathers. [43]And there you shall remember your ways and all your doings with which you were defiled; and you shall loathe yourselves in your own sight because of all the evils that you have committed. [44]Then you shall know that I *am* the LORD, when I have dealt with you for My name's sake, not according to your wicked ways nor according to your corrupt doings, O house of Israel," says the Lord GOD.'"

Fire in the Forest

[45]Furthermore the word of the LORD came to me, saying, [46]"Son of man, set your face toward the south; preach against the south and prophesy against the forest land, the South,[a] [47]and say to the forest of the South, 'Hear the word of the LORD! Thus says the Lord GOD: "Behold, I will kindle a fire in you, and it shall devour every green tree and every dry tree in you; the blazing flame shall not be quenched, and all faces from the south to the north shall be scorched by it. [48]All flesh shall see that I, the LORD, have kindled it; it shall not be quenched."'"

[49]Then I said, "Ah, Lord GOD! They say of me, 'Does he not speak parables?'"

Babylon, the Sword of God

21 And the word of the LORD came to me, saying, [2]"Son of man, set your face toward Jerusalem, preach against the holy places, and prophesy against the land of Israel; [3]and say to the land of Israel, 'Thus says the LORD: "Behold, I *am* against you, and I will draw My sword out of its sheath and cut off both righteous and wicked from you. [4]Because I will cut off both righteous and wicked from you, therefore My sword shall go out of its sheath against all flesh from south *to* north, [5]that all flesh may know that I, the LORD, have drawn My sword out of its sheath; it shall not return anymore." [6]Sigh therefore, son of man, with a breaking heart, and sigh with bitterness before their eyes. [7]And it shall be when they say to you, 'Why are you sighing?' that you shall answer, 'Because of the news; when it comes, every heart will melt, all hands will be feeble, every spirit will faint, and all knees will be weak *as* water. Behold, it is coming and shall be brought to pass,' says the Lord GOD."

[8]Again the word of the LORD came to me, saying, [9]"Son of man, prophesy and say, 'Thus says the LORD!' Say:

'A sword, a sword is sharpened
And also polished!
[10] Sharpened to make a dreadful slaughter,
Polished to flash like lightning!
Should we then make mirth?
It despises the scepter of My son,
As it does all wood.
[11] And He has given it to be polished,
That it may be handled;
This sword is sharpened, and it is polished
To be given into the hand of the slayer.'

[12] "Cry and wail, son of man;
For it will be against My people,
Against all the princes of Israel.
Terrors including the sword will be against My people;
Therefore strike *your* thigh.

[13] "Because *it is* a testing,
And what if *the sword* despises even the scepter?
The scepter shall be no *more*,"

says the Lord GOD.

[14] "You therefore, son of man, prophesy,
And strike *your* hands together.
The third time let the sword do double *damage*.
It *is* the sword *that* slays,
The sword that slays the great *men,*
That enters their private chambers.
[15] I have set the point of the sword against all their gates,
That the heart may melt and many may stumble.
Ah! *It is* made bright;
It is grasped for slaughter:

[16] . "Swords at the ready!
Thrust right!
Set your blade!
Thrust left—
Wherever your edge is ordered!

[17] "I also will beat My fists together,
And I will cause My fury to rest;
I, the LORD, have spoken."

[18]The word of the LORD came to me again, saying: [19]"And son of man, appoint for yourself two ways for the sword of the king of Babylon to go; both of them shall go from the same land.

20:46 [a]Hebrew *Negev*

Make a sign; put *it* at the head of the road to the city. [20]Appoint a road for the sword to go to Rabbah of the Ammonites, and to Judah, into fortified Jerusalem. [21]For the king of Babylon stands at the parting of the road, at the fork of the two roads, to use divination: he shakes the arrows, he consults the images, he looks at the liver. [22]In his right hand is the divination for Jerusalem: to set up battering rams, to call for a slaughter, to lift the voice with shouting, to set battering rams against the gates, to heap up a *siege* mound, and to build a wall. [23]And it will be to them like a false divination in the eyes of those who have sworn oaths with them; but he will bring their iniquity to remembrance, that they may be taken.

[24]"Therefore thus says the Lord GOD: 'Because you have made your iniquity to be remembered, in that your transgressions are uncovered, so that in all your doings your sins appear—because you have come to remembrance, you shall be taken in hand.

[25]"Now to you, O profane, wicked prince of Israel, whose day has come, whose iniquity *shall* end, [26]thus says the Lord GOD:

"Remove the turban, and take off the
        crown;
    Nothing *shall remain* the same.
    Exalt the humble, and humble the exalted.
[27] Overthrown, overthrown,
    I will make it overthrown!
    It shall be no *longer*,
    Until He comes whose right it is,
    And I will give it *to Him*."'

A Sword Against the Ammonites

[28]"And you, son of man, prophesy and say, 'Thus says the Lord GOD concerning the Ammonites and concerning their reproach,' and say:

'A sword, a sword *is* drawn,
    Polished for slaughter,
    For consuming, for flashing—
[29] While they see false visions for you,
    While they divine a lie to you,
    To bring you on the necks of the wicked,
        the slain
    Whose day has come,
    Whose iniquity *shall* end.

[30] 'Return *it* to its sheath.
    I will judge you
    In the place where you were created,
    In the land of your nativity.
[31] I will pour out My indignation on you;

I will blow against you with the fire of My
    wrath,
    And deliver you into the hands of brutal
        men *who are* skillful to destroy.
[32] You shall be fuel for the fire;
    Your blood shall be in the midst of the
        land.
    You shall not be remembered,
    For I the LORD have spoken.'"

Sins of Jerusalem

22 Moreover the word of the LORD came to me, saying, [2]"Now, son of man, will you judge, will you judge the bloody city? Yes, show her all her abominations! [3]Then say, 'Thus says the Lord GOD: "The city sheds blood in her own midst, that her time may come; and she makes idols within herself to defile herself. [4]You have become guilty by the blood which you have shed, and have defiled yourself with the idols which you have made. You have caused your days to draw near, and have come to *the end* of your years; therefore I have made you a reproach to the nations, and a mockery to all countries. [5]*Those* near and *those* far from you will mock you as infamous *and* full of tumult.

[6]"Look, the princes of Israel: each one has used his power to shed blood in you. [7]In you they have made light of father and mother; in your midst they have oppressed the stranger; in you they have mistreated the fatherless and the widow. [8]You have despised My holy things and profaned My Sabbaths. [9]In you are men who slander to cause bloodshed; in you are those who eat on the mountains; in your midst they commit lewdness. [10]In you men uncover their fathers' nakedness; in you they violate women who are set apart during their impurity. [11]One commits abomination with his neighbor's wife; another lewdly defiles his daughter-in-law; and another in you violates his sister, his father's daughter. [12]In you they take bribes to shed blood; you take usury and increase; you have made profit from your neighbors by extortion, and have forgotten Me," says the Lord GOD.

[13]"Behold, therefore, I beat My fists at the dishonest profit which you have made, and at the bloodshed which has been in your midst. [14]Can your heart endure, or can your hands remain strong, in the days when I shall deal with you? I, the LORD, have spoken, and will do *it*. [15]I will scatter you among the nations, disperse you throughout the countries, and remove your filthiness completely from you. [16]You shall defile yourself in the sight of the nations; then you shall know that I *am* the LORD."'"

The Position of a Leader: Standing in the Gap

(Ezekiel 22:24–31)

God contrasts the poor leader with the godly leader in Ezekiel 22. The poor leader oppresses and destroys his or her followers, while the godly leader "stands in the gap" on behalf of the land and the people (v. 30). These leaders represent God to the people, and represent the people to God. They serve as "middlemen," serving God and serving the needs of the people. This text describes ten traits of the leader God affirms:

1. **Consecration:** They set themselves apart and remain committed to their call.
2. **Discipline:** They do what is right even when it is difficult.
3. **Servanthood:** They model a selfless life, lived for the benefit of others.
4. **Vision:** They see what God sees and live off the power of potential.
5. **Compassion:** Love for their cause and their people moves them to action.
6. **Trustworthiness:** They keep their word regardless of what others do.
7. **Decisiveness:** They make good decisions in a timely manner.
8. **Wisdom:** They think like God thinks and avoid impetuous moves.
9. **Courage:** They take risks for what is right.
10. **Passion:** They demonstrate enthusiasm for their divine calling.

Israel in the Furnace

[17]The word of the LORD came to me, saying, [18]"Son of man, the house of Israel has become dross to Me; they *are* all bronze, tin, iron, and lead, in the midst of a furnace; they have become dross from silver. [19]Therefore thus says the Lord GOD: 'Because you have all become dross, therefore behold, I will gather you into the midst of Jerusalem. [20]*As men* gather silver, bronze, iron, lead, and tin into the midst of a furnace, to blow fire on it, to melt *it;* so I will gather *you* in My anger and in My fury, and I will leave *you there* and melt you. [21]Yes, I will gather you and blow on you with the fire of My wrath, and you shall be melted in its midst. [22]As silver is melted in the midst of a furnace, so shall you be melted in its midst; then you shall know that I, the LORD, have poured out My fury on you.' "

Israel's Wicked Leaders

[23]And the word of the LORD came to me, saying, [24]"Son of man, say to her: 'You *are* a land that is not cleansed[a] or rained on in the day of indignation.' [25]The conspiracy of her prophets[a] in her midst is like a roaring lion tearing the prey; they have devoured people; they have taken treasure and precious things; they have made many widows in her midst. [26]Her priests have violated My law and profaned My holy things; they have not distinguished between the holy and unholy, nor have they made known *the dif-* ference between the unclean and the clean; and they have hidden their eyes from My Sabbaths, so

22:24 [a]Following Masoretic Text, Syriac, and Vulgate; Septuagint reads *showered upon.*
22:25 [a]Following Masoretic Text and Vulgate; Septuagint reads *princes;* Targum reads *scribes.*

What Does God Look for in a Leader?

(Ezekiel 22:30)

This single verse contains a good description of the kind of leader God looks for. Take a look at what God was seeking in Ezekiel's day:

1. **A man:** God wasn't looking for a large committee, but a single person.
2. **Among them:** This person would relate best to people within his own culture.
3. **A builder of walls:** He must be constructive and hard working.
4. **Stand in the gap:** He must bridge the gap between people and God.
5. **On behalf of the land:** He carries a burden and vision for where he lives.

that I am profaned among them. ²⁷Her princes in her midst *are* like wolves tearing the prey, to shed blood, to destroy people, and to get dishonest gain. ²⁸Her prophets plastered them with untempered *mortar,* seeing false visions, and divining lies for them, saying, 'Thus says the Lord GOD,' when the LORD had not spoken. ²⁹The people of the land have used oppressions, committed robbery, and mistreated the poor and needy; and they wrongfully oppress the stranger. ³⁰So I sought for a man among them who would make a wall, and stand in the gap before Me on behalf of the land, that I should not destroy it; but I found no one. ³¹Therefore I have poured out My indignation on them; I have consumed them with the fire of My wrath; and I have recompensed their deeds on their own heads," says the Lord GOD.

Two Harlot Sisters

23 The word of the LORD came again to me, saying:

²   "Son of man, there were two women,
     The daughters of one mother.
³   They committed harlotry in Egypt,
     They committed harlotry in their youth;
     Their breasts were there embraced,
     Their virgin bosom was there pressed.
⁴   Their names: Oholah[a] the elder and
        Oholibah[b] her sister;
     They were Mine,
     And they bore sons and daughters.
     As for their names,
     Samaria *is* Oholah, and Jerusalem *is*
        Oholibah.

The Older Sister, Samaria

⁵   "Oholah played the harlot even though she
        was Mine;
     And she lusted for her lovers, the
        neighboring Assyrians,
⁶   *Who were* clothed in purple,
     Captains and rulers,
     All of them desirable young men,
     Horsemen riding on horses.
⁷   Thus she committed her harlotry with
        them,
     All of them choice men of Assyria;
     And with all for whom she lusted,
     With all their idols, she defiled herself.
⁸   She has never given up her harlotry *brought*
        from Egypt,
     For in her youth they had lain with her,
     Pressed her virgin bosom,
     And poured out their immorality upon
        her.

⁹   "Therefore I have delivered her
     Into the hand of her lovers,
     Into the hand of the Assyrians,
     For whom she lusted.
¹⁰   They uncovered her nakedness,
     Took away her sons and daughters,
     And slew her with the sword;
     She became a byword among women,
     For they had executed judgment on her.

The Younger Sister, Jerusalem

¹¹"Now although her sister Oholibah saw *this,* she became more corrupt in her lust than she, and in her harlotry more corrupt than her sister's harlotry.

¹²   "She lusted for the neighboring Assyrians,
     Captains and rulers,
     Clothed most gorgeously,
     Horsemen riding on horses,
     All of them desirable young men.
¹³   Then I saw that she was defiled;
     Both *took* the same way.
¹⁴   But she increased her harlotry;
     She looked at men portrayed on the wall,
     Images of Chaldeans portrayed in
        vermilion,
¹⁵   Girded with belts around their waists,
     Flowing turbans on their heads,
     All of them looking like captains,
     In the manner of the Babylonians of
        Chaldea,
     The land of their nativity.
¹⁶   As soon as her eyes saw them,
     She lusted for them
     And sent messengers to them in Chaldea.

¹⁷   "Then the Babylonians came to her, into
        the bed of love,
     And they defiled her with their
        immorality;
     So she was defiled by them, and alienated
        herself from them.
¹⁸   She revealed her harlotry and uncovered
        her nakedness.
     Then I alienated Myself from her,
     As I had alienated Myself from her sister.

¹⁹   "Yet she multiplied her harlotry
     In calling to remembrance the days of her
        youth,
     When she had played the harlot in the
        land of Egypt.

23:4 [a]Literally *Her Own Tabernacle* [b]Literally *My Tabernacle Is in Her*

20 For she lusted for her paramours,
   Whose flesh *is like* the flesh of donkeys,
   And whose issue *is like* the issue of horses.
21 Thus you called to remembrance the
      lewdness of your youth,
   When the Egyptians pressed your bosom
   Because of your youthful breasts.

Judgment on Jerusalem

22 "Therefore, Oholibah, thus says the Lord
GOD:

   'Behold, I will stir up your lovers against
      you,
   From whom you have alienated yourself,
   And I will bring them against you from
      every side:
23   The Babylonians,
   All the Chaldeans,
   Pekod, Shoa, Koa,
   All the Assyrians with them,
   All of them desirable young men,
   Governors and rulers,
   Captains and men of renown,
   All of them riding on horses.
24   And they shall come against you
   With chariots, wagons, and war-horses,
   With a horde of people.
   They shall array against you
   Buckler, shield, and helmet all around.

   'I will delegate judgment to them,
   And they shall judge you according to
      their judgments.
25   I will set My jealousy against you,
   And they shall deal furiously with you;
   They shall remove your nose and your
      ears,
   And your remnant shall fall by the sword;
   They shall take your sons and your
      daughters,
   And your remnant shall be devoured by
      fire.
26   They shall also strip you of your clothes
   And take away your beautiful jewelry.

27   'Thus I will make you cease your lewdness
      and your harlotry
   Brought from the land of Egypt,
   So that you will not lift your eyes to them,
   Nor remember Egypt anymore.'

28 "For thus says the Lord GOD: 'Surely I will
deliver you into the hand of those you hate, into
the hand *of those* from whom you alienated yourself. 29 They will deal hatefully with you, take

away all you have worked for, and leave you
naked and bare. The nakedness of your harlotry
shall be uncovered, both your lewdness and your
harlotry. 30 I will do these *things* to you because
you have gone as a harlot after the Gentiles, because you have become defiled by their idols.
31 You have walked in the way of your sister;
therefore I will put her cup in your hand.'

32 "Thus says the Lord GOD:

   'You shall drink of your sister's cup,
   The deep and wide one;
   You shall be laughed to scorn
   And held in derision;
   It contains much.
33   You will be filled with drunkenness and
      sorrow,
   The cup of horror and desolation,
   The cup of your sister Samaria.
34   You shall drink and drain it,
   You shall break its shards,
   And tear at your own breasts;
   For I have spoken,'
   Says the Lord GOD.

35 "Therefore thus says the Lord GOD:

   'Because you have forgotten Me and cast
      Me behind your back,
   Therefore you shall bear the *penalty*
   Of your lewdness and your harlotry.'"

Both Sisters Judged

36 The LORD also said to me: "Son of man,
will you judge Oholah and Oholibah? Then declare to them their abominations. 37 For they have
committed adultery, and blood *is* on their hands.
They have committed adultery with their idols,
and even sacrificed their sons whom they bore to
Me, passing them through *the fire,* to devour
them. 38 Moreover they have done this to Me:
They have defiled My sanctuary on the same day
and profaned My Sabbaths. 39 For after they had
slain their children for their idols, on the same
day they came into My sanctuary to profane it;
and indeed thus they have done in the midst of
My house.
40 "Furthermore you sent for men to come
from afar, to whom a messenger *was* sent; and
there they came. And you washed yourself for
them, painted your eyes, and adorned yourself
with ornaments. 41 You sat on a stately couch,
with a table prepared before it, on which you
had set My incense and My oil. 42 The sound of a
carefree multitude *was* with her, and Sabeans *were*
brought from the wilderness with men of the

common sort, who put bracelets on their wrists and beautiful crowns on their heads. ⁴³Then I said concerning *her who had grown* old in adulteries, 'Will they commit harlotry with her now, and she *with them?*' ⁴⁴Yet they went in to her, as men go in to a woman who plays the harlot; thus they went in to Oholah and Oholibah, the lewd women. ⁴⁵But righteous men will judge them after the manner of adulteresses, and after the manner of women who shed blood, because they *are* adulteresses, and blood *is* on their hands.

Confrontation: It Comes with the Territory

(Ezekiel 23:36–39)

God told Ezekiel to confront His people using colorful and striking imagery. "Oholah" and "Oholibah" are symbolic names for sinful Israel and Judah. God describes the sins they have committed and demands that Ezekiel confront the people with their rebellion.

At times a leader must confront sinful or destructive behavior in the ranks. No healthy leader enjoys confrontation, but no healthy leader avoids it, either. What can we learn from God and Ezekiel about confrontation?

1. *Be compassionate.* Ezekiel hurt as he recalled the sins of Israel.
2. *Be forthright.* Ezekiel spoke honestly and directly to the issues.
3. *Be specific.* Ezekiel didn't drop hints, but gave specifics about the problem.
4. *Be clear.* Ezekiel spoke simply about the consequences of such behavior.
5. *Be redemptive.* Ezekiel communicated for the purpose of restoring the people.
6. *Be hopeful.* Ezekiel ended with words of hope for the future.

⁴⁶"For thus says the Lord GOD: 'Bring up an assembly against them, give them up to trouble and plunder. ⁴⁷The assembly shall stone them with stones and execute them with their swords; they shall slay their sons and their daughters, and burn their houses with fire. ⁴⁸Thus I will cause lewdness to cease from the land, that all women may be taught not to practice your lewdness. ⁴⁹They shall repay you for your lewdness, and

you shall pay for your idolatrous sins. Then you shall know that I *am* the Lord GOD.'"

Symbol of the Cooking Pot

24 Again, in the ninth year, in the tenth month, on the tenth *day* of the month, the word of the LORD came to me, saying, ²"Son of man, write down the name of the day, this very day—the king of Babylon started his siege against Jerusalem this very day. ³And utter a parable to the rebellious house, and say to them, 'Thus says the Lord GOD:

"Put on a pot, set *it* on,
        And also pour water into it.
⁴   Gather pieces *of* meat in it,
        Every good piece,
        The thigh and the shoulder.
        Fill *it* with choice cuts;
⁵   Take the choice of the flock.
        Also pile *fuel* bones under it,
        Make it boil well,
        And let the cuts simmer in it."

⁶"Therefore thus says the Lord GOD:

"Woe to the bloody city,
        To the pot whose scum *is* in it,
        And whose scum is not gone from it!
        Bring it out piece by piece,
        On which no lot has fallen.
⁷   For her blood is in her midst;
        She set it on top of a rock;
        She did not pour it on the ground,
        To cover it with dust.
⁸   That it may raise up fury and take vengeance,
        I have set her blood on top of a rock,
        That it may not be covered."

⁹"Therefore thus says the Lord GOD:

"Woe to the bloody city!
        I too will make the pyre great.
¹⁰   Heap on the wood,
        Kindle the fire;
        Cook the meat well,
        Mix in the spices,
        And let the cuts be burned up.

¹¹   "Then set the pot empty on the coals,
        That it may become hot and its bronze may burn,
        That its filthiness may be melted in it,
        That its scum may be consumed.
¹²   She has grown weary with lies,

And her great scum has not gone from
her.

Let her scum *be* in the fire!

13 In your filthiness *is* lewdness.

Because I have cleansed you, and you were
not cleansed,

You will not be cleansed of your filthiness
anymore,

Till I have caused My fury to rest upon
you.

14 I, the LORD, have spoken *it;*

It shall come to pass, and I will do *it;*

I will not hold back,

Nor will I spare,

Nor will I relent;

According to your ways

And according to your deeds

They[a] will judge you,"

Says the Lord GOD.' "

The Prophet's Wife Dies

15 Also the word of the LORD came to me,
saying, 16 "Son of man, behold, I take away from
you the desire of your eyes with one stroke; yet
you shall neither mourn nor weep, nor shall your
tears run down. 17 Sigh in silence, make no
mourning for the dead; bind your turban on
your head, and put your sandals on your feet; do
not cover *your* lips, and do not eat man's bread *of
sorrow.*"

18 So I spoke to the people in the morning,
and at evening my wife died; and the next morning I did as I was commanded.

19 And the people said to me, "Will you not
tell us what these *things signify* to us, that you behave so?"

20 Then I answered them, "The word of the
LORD came to me, saying, 21 Speak to the house
of Israel, "Thus says the Lord GOD: 'Behold, I
will profane My sanctuary, your arrogant boast,
the desire of your eyes, the delight of your soul;
and your sons and daughters whom you left behind shall fall by the sword. 22 And you shall do as
I have done; you shall not cover *your* lips nor eat
man's bread *of sorrow.* 23 Your turbans shall be on
your heads and your sandals on your feet; you
shall neither mourn nor weep, but you shall pine
away in your iniquities and mourn with one another. 24 Thus Ezekiel is a sign to you; according
to all that he has done you shall do; and when
this comes, you shall know that I *am* the Lord
GOD.' "

25 'And you, son of man—*will it* not *be* in the
day when I take from them their stronghold,
their joy and their glory, the desire of their eyes,
and that on which they set their minds, their sons

and their daughters: 26 *that* on that day one who
escapes will come to you to let *you* hear *it* with
your ears? 27 On that day your mouth will be
opened to him who has escaped; you shall speak
and no longer be mute. Thus you will be a sign
to them, and they shall know that I *am* the
LORD.' "

Proclamation Against Ammon

25 The word of the LORD came to me,
saying, 2 "Son of man, set your face
against the Ammonites, and prophesy
against them. 3 Say to the Ammonites, 'Hear the
word of the Lord GOD! Thus says the Lord GOD:
"Because you said, 'Aha!' against My sanctuary
when it was profaned, and against the land of Israel when it was desolate, and against the house
of Judah when they went into captivity, 4 indeed,
therefore, I will deliver you as a possession to the
men of the East, and they shall set their encamp-
ments among you and make their dwellings
among you; they shall eat your fruit, and they
shall drink your milk. 5 And I will make Rabbah
a stable for camels and Ammon a resting place
for flocks. Then you shall know that I *am* the
LORD."

6 "For thus says the Lord GOD: "Because you
clapped *your* hands, stamped your feet, and rejoiced in heart with all your disdain for the land
of Israel, 7 indeed, therefore, I will stretch out My
hand against you, and give you as plunder to the
nations; I will cut you off from the peoples, and
I will cause you to perish from the countries; I
will destroy you, and you shall know that I *am*
the LORD."

Proclamation Against Moab

8 "Thus says the Lord GOD: "Because Moab
and Seir say, 'Look! The house of Judah *is* like all
the nations,' 9 therefore, behold, I will clear the
territory of Moab of cities, of the cities on its
frontier, the glory of the country, Beth Jeshimoth, Baal Meon, and Kirjathaim. 10 To the men
of the East I will give it as a possession, together
with the Ammonites, that the Ammonites may
not be remembered among the nations. 11 And I
will execute judgments upon Moab, and they
shall know that I *am* the LORD."

Proclamation Against Edom

12 "Thus says the Lord GOD: "Because of what
Edom did against the house of Judah by taking
vengeance, and has greatly offended by avenging

24:14 [a]Septuagint, Syriac, Targum, and Vulgate
read *I.*

itself on them," ¹³therefore thus says the Lord GOD: "I will also stretch out My hand against Edom, cut off man and beast from it, and make it desolate from Teman; Dedan shall fall by the sword. ¹⁴I will lay My vengeance on Edom by the hand of My people Israel, that they may do in Edom according to My anger and according to My fury; and they shall know My vengeance," says the Lord GOD.

Proclamation Against Philistia

¹⁵Thus says the Lord GOD: "Because the Philistines dealt vengefully and took vengeance with a spiteful heart, to destroy because of the old hatred," ¹⁶therefore thus says the Lord GOD: "I will stretch out My hand against the Philistines, and I will cut off the Cherethites and destroy the remnant of the seacoast. ¹⁷I will execute great vengeance on them with furious rebukes; and they shall know that I *am* the LORD, when I lay My vengeance upon them."'"

Proclamation Against Tyre

26 And it came to pass in the eleventh year, on the first *day* of the month, *that* the word of the LORD came to me, saying, ²"Son of man, because Tyre has said against Jerusalem, 'Aha! She is broken who *was* the gateway of the peoples; now she is turned over to me; I shall be filled; she is laid waste.'

³"Therefore thus says the Lord GOD: 'Behold, I *am* against you, O Tyre, and will cause many nations to come up against you, as the sea causes its waves to come up. ⁴And they shall destroy the walls of Tyre and break down her towers; I will also scrape her dust from her, and make her like the top of a rock. ⁵It shall be *a place for* spreading nets in the midst of the sea, for I have spoken,' says the Lord GOD; 'it shall become plunder for the nations. ⁶Also her daughter *villages* which *are* in the fields shall be slain by the sword. Then they shall know that I am the LORD.'

⁷"For thus says the Lord GOD: 'Behold, I will bring against Tyre from the north Nebuchadnezzar[a] king of Babylon, king of kings, with horses, with chariots, and with horsemen, and an army with many people. ⁸He will slay with the sword your daughter *villages* in the fields; he will heap up a siege mound against you, build a wall against you, and raise a defense against you. ⁹He will direct his battering rams against your walls, and with his axes he will break down your towers. ¹⁰Because of the abundance of his horses, their dust will cover you; your walls will shake at the noise of the horsemen, the wagons, and the

chariots, when he enters your gates, as men enter a city that has been breached. ¹¹With the hooves of his horses he will trample all your streets; he will slay your people by the sword, and your strong pillars will fall to the ground. ¹²They will plunder your riches and pillage your merchandise; they will break down your walls and destroy your pleasant houses; they will lay your stones, your timber, and your soil in the midst of the water. ¹³I will put an end to the sound of your songs, and the sound of your harps shall be heard no more. ¹⁴I will make you like the top of a rock; you shall be *a place for* spreading nets, and you shall never be rebuilt, for I the LORD have spoken,' says the Lord GOD.

¹⁵"Thus says the Lord GOD to Tyre: 'Will the coastlands not shake at the sound of your fall, when the wounded cry, when slaughter is made in the midst of you? ¹⁶Then all the princes of the sea will come down from their thrones, lay aside their robes, and take off their embroidered garments; they will clothe themselves with trembling; they will sit on the ground, tremble *every* moment, and be astonished at you. ¹⁷And they will take up a lamentation for you, and say to you:

"How you have perished,
    O one inhabited by seafaring men,
    O renowned city,
    Who was strong at sea,
    She and her inhabitants,
    Who caused their terror *to be* on all her
        inhabitants!
¹⁸   Now the coastlands tremble on the day of
        your fall;
    Yes, the coastlands by the sea are troubled
        at your departure."'

¹⁹"For thus says the Lord GOD: 'When I make you a desolate city, like cities that are not inhabited, when I bring the deep upon you, and great waters cover you, ²⁰then I will bring you down with those who descend into the Pit, to the people of old, and I will make you dwell in the lowest part of the earth, in places desolate from antiquity, with those who go down to the Pit, so that you may never be inhabited; and I shall establish glory in the land of the living. ²¹I will make you a terror, and you *shall be* no *more;* though you are sought for, you will never be found again,' says the Lord GOD."

26:7 [a]Hebrew *Nebuchadrezzar,* and so elsewhere in this book

Lamentation for Tyre

27 The word of the LORD came again to me, saying, [2]"Now, son of man, take up a lamentation for Tyre, [3]and say to Tyre, 'You who are situated at the entrance of the sea, merchant of the peoples on many coastlands, thus says the Lord GOD:

" O Tyre, you have said,
' I *am* perfect in beauty.'
[4] Your borders *are* in the midst of the seas.
   Your builders have perfected your beauty.
[5] They made all *your* planks of fir trees from Senir;
   They took a cedar from Lebanon to make you a mast.
[6] *Of* oaks from Bashan they made your oars;
   The company of Ashurites have inlaid your planks
   With ivory from the coasts of Cyprus.[a]
[7] Fine embroidered linen from Egypt was what you spread for your sail;
   Blue and purple from the coasts of Elishah was what covered you.

[8] "Inhabitants of Sidon and Arvad were your oarsmen;
   Your wise men, O Tyre, were in you;
   They became your pilots.
[9] Elders of Gebal and its wise men
   Were in you to caulk your seams;
   All the ships of the sea
   And their oarsmen were in you
   To market your merchandise.

[10] "Those from Persia, Lydia,[a] and Libya[b]
   Were in your army as men of war;
   They hung shield and helmet in you;
   They gave splendor to you.
[11] Men of Arvad with your army *were* on your walls *all* around,
   And the men of Gammad were in your towers;
   They hung their shields on your walls *all* around;
   They made your beauty perfect.

[12]"Tarshish *was* your merchant because of your many luxury goods. They gave you silver, iron, tin, and lead for your goods. [13]Javan, Tubal, and Meshech *were* your traders. They bartered human lives and vessels of bronze for your merchandise. [14]Those from the house of Togarmah traded for your wares with horses, steeds, and mules. [15]The men of Dedan *were* your traders; many isles *were* the market of your hand. They brought you ivory tusks and ebony as payment. [16]Syria *was* your merchant because of the abundance of goods you made. They gave you for your wares emeralds, purple, embroidery, fine linen, corals, and rubies. [17]Judah and the land of Israel *were* your traders. They traded for your merchandise wheat of Minnith, millet, honey, oil, and balm. [18]Damascus *was* your merchant because of the abundance of goods you made, because of your many luxury items, with the wine of Helbon and with white wool. [19]Dan and Javan paid for your wares, traversing back and forth. Wrought iron, cassia, and cane were among your merchandise. [20]Dedan *was* your merchant in saddlecloths for riding. [21]Arabia and all the princes of Kedar *were* your regular merchants. They traded with you in lambs, rams, and goats. [22]The merchants of Sheba and Raamah *were* your merchants. They traded for your wares the choicest spices, all kinds of precious stones, and gold. [23]Haran, Canneh, Eden, the merchants of Sheba, Assyria, *and* Chilmad *were* your merchants. [24]These *were* your merchants in choice items—in purple clothes, in embroidered garments, in chests of multicolored apparel, in sturdy woven cords, which were in your marketplace.

[25] "The ships of Tarshish were carriers of your merchandise.
   You were filled and very glorious in the midst of the seas.
[26] Your oarsmen brought you into many waters,
   But the east wind broke you in the midst of the seas.

[27] "Your riches, wares, and merchandise,
   Your mariners and pilots,
   Your caulkers and merchandisers,
   All your men of war who *are* in you,
   And the entire company which *is* in your midst,
   Will fall into the midst of the seas on the day of your ruin.
[28] The common-land will shake at the sound of the cry of your pilots.

[29] " All who handle the oar,
   The mariners,
   All the pilots of the sea
   Will come down from their ships *and* stand on the shore.

27:6 [a]Hebrew *Kittim,* western lands, especially Cyprus **27:10** [a]Hebrew *Lud* [b]Hebrew *Put*

30 They will make their voice heard because of you;
They will cry bitterly and cast dust on their heads;
They will roll about in ashes;
31 They will shave themselves completely bald because of you,
Gird themselves with sackcloth,
And weep for you
With bitterness of heart *and* bitter wailing.
32 In their wailing for you
They will take up a lamentation,
And lament for you:
'What *city is* like Tyre,
Destroyed in the midst of the sea?
33 'When your wares went out by sea,
You satisfied many people;
You enriched the kings of the earth
With your many luxury goods and your merchandise.
34 But you are broken by the seas in the depths of the waters;
Your merchandise and the entire company will fall in your midst.
35 All the inhabitants of the isles will be astonished at you;
Their kings will be greatly afraid,
And *their* countenance will be troubled.
36 The merchants among the peoples will hiss at you;
You will become a horror, and *be* no more forever.' ""

Proclamation Against the King of Tyre

28 The word of the LORD came to me again, saying, 2"Son of man, say to the prince of Tyre, 'Thus says the Lord GOD:

"Because your heart *is* lifted up,
And you say, 'I *am* a god,
I sit *in* the seat of gods,
In the midst of the seas,'
Yet you *are* a man, and not a god,
Though you set your heart as the heart of a god
3 (Behold, you *are* wiser than Daniel!
There is no secret that can be hidden from you!
4 With your wisdom and your understanding
You have gained riches for yourself,
And gathered gold and silver into your treasuries;

Ezekiel Speaks with Courage

(Ezekiel 28:1–19)

Ezekiel could speak hard truth to the king of Tyre because God had deposited in him a . . .

1. **Dream:** He saw what God saw—a preferred future with just leaders.
2. **Desire:** He had a desire to see change and to be part of the solution.
3. **Decisiveness:** He recognized what needed to be done and he chose to step in.
4. **Daring:** His courage to act outweighed his fear of the king.
5. **Dedication:** He remained committed to fulfilling his call, whatever the cost.
6. **Direction:** He had a clear plan for change.
7. **Dependence on God:** He relied on God to do what only He could do.

---

5 By your great wisdom in trade you have increased your riches,
And your heart is lifted up because of your riches),"

6"Therefore thus says the Lord GOD:

"Because you have set your heart as the heart of a god,
7 Behold, therefore, I will bring strangers against you,
The most terrible of the nations;
And they shall draw their swords against the beauty of your wisdom,
And defile your splendor.
8 They shall throw you down into the Pit,
And you shall die the death of the slain
In the midst of the seas.

9 "Will you still say before him who slays you,
'I *am* a god'?
But you *shall be* a man, and not a god,
In the hand of him who slays you.
10 You shall die the death of the uncircumcised
By the hand of aliens;
For I have spoken," says the Lord GOD.'"

Lamentation for the King of Tyre

[11]Moreover the word of the LORD came to me, saying, [12]"Son of man, take up a lamentation for the king of Tyre, and say to him, 'Thus says the Lord GOD:

"You *were* the seal of perfection,
   Full of wisdom and perfect in beauty.
[13]   You were in Eden, the garden of God;
   Every precious stone *was* your covering:
   The sardius, topaz, and diamond,
   Beryl, onyx, and jasper,
   Sapphire, turquoise, and emerald with gold.
   The workmanship of your timbrels and pipes
   Was prepared for you on the day you were created.

[14]   "You *were* the anointed cherub who covers;
   I established you;
   You were on the holy mountain of God;
   You walked back and forth in the midst of fiery stones.
[15]   You *were* perfect in your ways from the day you were created,
   Till iniquity was found in you.

[16]   "By the abundance of your trading
   You became filled with violence within,
   And you sinned;
   Therefore I cast you as a profane thing
   Out of the mountain of God;
   And I destroyed you, O covering cherub,
   From the midst of the fiery stones.

[17]   "Your heart was lifted up because of your beauty;
   You corrupted your wisdom for the sake of your splendor;
   I cast you to the ground,
   I laid you before kings,
   That they might gaze at you.

[18]   "You defiled your sanctuaries
   By the multitude of your iniquities,
   By the iniquity of your trading;
   Therefore I brought fire from your midst;
   It devoured you,
   And I turned you to ashes upon the earth
   In the sight of all who saw you.
[19]   All who knew you among the peoples are astonished at you;
   You have become a horror,
   And *shall be* no more forever.'"'"

Proclamation Against Sidon

[20]Then the word of the LORD came to me, saying, [21]"Son of man, set your face toward Sidon, and prophesy against her, [22]and say, 'Thus says the Lord GOD:

"Behold, I *am* against you, O Sidon;
   I will be glorified in your midst;
   And they shall know that I *am* the LORD,
   When I execute judgments in her and am hallowed in her.
[23]   For I will send pestilence upon her,
   And blood in her streets;
   The wounded shall be judged in her midst
   By the sword against her on every side;
   Then they shall know that I *am* the LORD.

[24]"And there shall no longer be a pricking brier or a painful thorn for the house of Israel from among all *who are* around them, who despise them. Then they shall know that I *am* the Lord GOD."

Israel's Future Blessing

[25]'Thus says the Lord GOD: "When I have gathered the house of Israel from the peoples among whom they are scattered, and am hallowed in them in the sight of the Gentiles, then they will dwell in their own land which I gave to My servant Jacob. [26]And they will dwell safely there, build houses, and plant vineyards; yes, they will dwell securely, when I execute judgments on all those around them who despise them. Then they shall know that I *am* the LORD their God."'"

Proclamation Against Egypt

29 In the tenth year, in the tenth *month*, on the twelfth *day* of the month, the word of the LORD came to me, saying, [2]"Son of man, set your face against Pharaoh king of Egypt, and prophesy against him, and against all Egypt. [3]Speak, and say, 'Thus says the Lord GOD:

"Behold, I *am* against you,
   O Pharaoh king of Egypt,
   O great monster who lies in the midst of his rivers,
   Who has said, 'My River[a] *is* my own;
   I have made *it* for myself.'
[4]   But I will put hooks in your jaws,
   And cause the fish of your rivers to stick to your scales;

29:3 [a]That is, the Nile

I will bring you up out of the midst of
    your rivers,
And all the fish in your rivers will stick to
    your scales.
5 I will leave you in the wilderness,
    You and all the fish of your rivers;
    You shall fall on the open field;
    You shall not be picked up or gathered.[a]
    I have given you as food
    To the beasts of the field
    And to the birds of the heavens.

6   "Then all the inhabitants of Egypt
    Shall know that I *am* the LORD,
    Because they have been a staff of reed to
      the house of Israel.
7   When they took hold of you with the
      hand,
    You broke and tore all their
      shoulders;[a]
    When they leaned on you,
    You broke and made all their backs
      quiver."

[8]"Therefore thus says the Lord GOD: "Surely
I will bring a sword upon you and cut off from
you man and beast. [9]And the land of Egypt shall
become desolate and waste; then they will know
that I *am* the LORD, because he said, 'The River
is mine, and I have made *it*.' [10]Indeed, therefore,
I *am* against you and against your rivers, and I
will make the land of Egypt utterly waste and
desolate, from Migdol[a] *to* Syene, as far as the
border of Ethiopia. [11]Neither foot of man shall
pass through it nor foot of beast pass through it,
and it shall be uninhabited forty years. [12]I will
make the land of Egypt desolate in the midst of
the countries *that are* desolate; and among the
cities *that are* laid waste, her cities shall be desolate forty years; and I will scatter the Egyptians
among the nations and disperse them throughout the countries."

[13]Yet, thus says the Lord GOD: "At the end of
forty years I will gather the Egyptians from the
peoples among whom they were scattered. [14]I
will bring back the captives of Egypt and cause
them to return to the land of Pathros, to the land
of their origin, and there they shall be a lowly
kingdom. [15]It shall be the lowliest of kingdoms;
it shall never again exalt itself above the nations,
for I will diminish them so that they will not rule
over the nations anymore. [16]No longer shall it be
the confidence of the house of Israel, but will remind them of *their* iniquity when they turned to
follow them. Then they shall know that I *am* the
Lord GOD." "

Babylonia Will Plunder Egypt

[17]And it came to pass in the twenty-seventh
year, in the first *month,* on the first *day* of the
month, *that* the word of the LORD came to me,
saying, [18]"Son of man, Nebuchadnezzar king of
Babylon caused his army to labor strenuously
against Tyre; every head *was* made bald, and
every shoulder rubbed raw; yet neither he nor
his army received wages from Tyre, for the labor
which they expended on it. [19]Therefore thus says
the Lord GOD: 'Surely I will give the land of
Egypt to Nebuchadnezzar king of Babylon; he
shall take away her wealth, carry off her spoil,
and remove her pillage; and that will be the
wages for his army. [20]I have given him the land of
Egypt *for* his labor, because they worked for Me,'
says the Lord GOD.

[21]"In that day I will cause the horn of the
house of Israel to spring forth, and I will open
your mouth to speak in their midst. Then they
shall know that I *am* the LORD.'"

Egypt and Her Allies Will Fall

30 The word of the LORD came to me
again, saying, [2]"Son of man, prophesy
and say, 'Thus says the Lord GOD:

  "Wail, 'Woe to the day!'
3   For the day *is* near,
    Even the day of the LORD *is* near;
    It will be a day of clouds, the time of the
      Gentiles.
4   The sword shall come upon Egypt,
    And great anguish shall be in Ethiopia,
    When the slain fall in Egypt,
    And they take away her wealth,
    And her foundations are broken down.

[5]"Ethiopia, Libya,[a] Lydia,[b] all the mingled
people, Chub, and the men of the lands who are
allied, shall fall with them by the sword."

[6]Thus says the LORD:

  "Those who uphold Egypt shall fall,
    And the pride of her power shall come
      down.
    From Migdol *to* Syene
    Those within her shall fall by the sword,"
    Says the Lord GOD.

29:5 [a]Following Masoretic Text, Septuagint, and
Vulgate; some Hebrew manuscripts and Targum
read *buried.* **29:7** [a]Following Masoretic Text and
Vulgate; Septuagint and Syriac read *hand.*
29:10 [a]Or *tower* **30:5** [a]Hebrew *Put* [b]Hebrew *Lud*

7 "They shall be desolate in the midst of the
  desolate countries,
  And her cities shall be in the midst of the
  cities *that are* laid waste.
8 Then they will know that I *am* the LORD,
  When I have set a fire in Egypt
  And all her helpers are destroyed.
9 On that day messengers shall go forth from
  Me in ships
  To make the careless Ethiopians afraid,
  And great anguish shall come upon them,
  As on the day of Egypt;
  For indeed it is coming!"

10 "Thus says the Lord GOD:

  "I will also make a multitude of Egypt to
  cease
  By the hand of Nebuchadnezzar king of
  Babylon.
11 He and his people with him, the most
  terrible of the nations,
  Shall be brought to destroy the land;
  They shall draw their swords against Egypt,
  And fill the land with the slain.
12 I will make the rivers dry,
  And sell the land into the hand of the
  wicked;
  I will make the land waste, and all that is
  in it,
  By the hand of aliens.
  I, the LORD, have spoken."

13 "Thus says the Lord GOD:

  "I will also destroy the idols,
  And cause the images to cease from Noph;[a]
  There shall no longer be princes from the
  land of Egypt;
  I will put fear in the land of Egypt.
14 I will make Pathros desolate,
  Set fire to Zoan,
  And execute judgments in No.[a]
15 I will pour My fury on Sin,[a] the strength
  of Egypt;
  I will cut off the multitude of No,
16 And set a fire in Egypt;
  Sin shall have great pain,
  No shall be split open,
  And Noph *shall be in* distress daily.
17 The young men of Aven[a] and Pi Beseth
  shall fall by the sword,
  And these *cities* shall go into captivity.
18 At Tehaphnehes[a] the day shall also be
  darkened,[b]
  When I break the yokes of Egypt there.

  And her arrogant strength shall cease in her;
  As for her, a cloud shall cover her,
  And her daughters shall go into captivity.
19 Thus I will execute judgments on Egypt,
  Then they shall know that I *am* the
  LORD."' "

Proclamation Against Pharaoh

20 And it came to pass in the eleventh year, in
the first *month,* on the seventh *day* of the month,
that the word of the LORD came to me, saying,
21 "Son of man, I have broken the arm of Pharaoh
king of Egypt; and see, it has not been bandaged
for healing, nor a splint put on to bind it, to
make it strong enough to hold a sword. 22 Therefore thus says the Lord GOD: 'Surely I *am* against
Pharaoh king of Egypt, and will break his arms,
both the strong one and the one that was broken;
and I will make the sword fall out of his hand. 23 I
will scatter the Egyptians among the nations, and
disperse them throughout the countries. 24 I will
strengthen the arms of the king of Babylon and
put My sword in his hand; but I will break
Pharaoh's arms, and he will groan before him
with the groanings of a mortally wounded *man.*
25 Thus I will strengthen the arms of the king of
Babylon, but the arms of Pharaoh shall fall
down; they shall know that I *am* the LORD, when
I put My sword into the hand of the king of
Babylon and he stretches it out against the land

30:13 [a]That is, ancient Memphis **30:14** [a]That is,
ancient Thebes **30:15** [a]That is, ancient Pelusium
30:17 [a]That is, ancient On (Heliopolis)
30:18 [a]Spelled *Tahpanhes* in Jeremiah 43:7 and
elsewhere [b]Following many Hebrew manuscripts,
Bomberg, Septuagint, Syriac, Targum, and Vulgate;
Masoretic Text reads *refrained.*

God Is the One Who Raises Up and Removes Leaders

(Ezekiel 30:20–26)

It is God who raises up leaders and who removes them from office; our job is to submit
to His bidding. Leaders commonly misunderstand this truth. God says that whether leaders are good or evil, He ultimately is the One
who puts them there—and He will remove
them.

of Egypt. ²⁶I will scatter the Egyptians among the nations and disperse them throughout the countries. Then they shall know that I *am* the LORD.'"

Egypt Cut Down Like a Great Tree

31 Now it came to pass in the eleventh year, in the third *month,* on the first *day* of the month, *that* the word of the LORD came to me, saying, ²"Son of man, say to Pharaoh king of Egypt and to his multitude:

'Whom are you like in your greatness?
³　Indeed Assyria *was* a cedar in Lebanon,
　With fine branches that shaded the forest,
　And of high stature;
　And its top was among the thick boughs.
⁴　The waters made it grow;
　Underground waters gave it height,
　With their rivers running around the place
　　where it was planted,
　And sent out rivulets to all the trees of the
　　field.

⁵　'Therefore its height was exalted above all
　　the trees of the field;
　Its boughs were multiplied,
　And its branches became long because of
　　the abundance of water,
　As it sent them out.
⁶　All the birds of the heavens made their
　　nests in its boughs;
　Under its branches all the beasts of the
　　field brought forth their young;
　And in its shadow all great nations made
　　their home.

⁷　'Thus it was beautiful in greatness and in
　　the length of its branches,
　Because its roots reached to abundant
　　waters.
⁸　The cedars in the garden of God could
　　not hide it;
　The fir trees were not like its boughs,
　And the chestnut^a trees were not like its
　　branches;
　No tree in the garden of God was like it
　　in beauty.
⁹　I made it beautiful with a multitude of
　　branches,
　So that all the trees of Eden envied it,
　That *were* in the garden of God.'

¹⁰"Therefore thus says the Lord GOD: 'Because you have increased in height, and it set its top among the thick boughs, and its heart was lifted up in its height, ¹¹therefore I will deliver it

into the hand of the mighty one of the nations, and he shall surely deal with it; I have driven it out for its wickedness. ¹²And aliens, the most terrible of the nations, have cut it down and left it; its branches have fallen on the mountains and in all the valleys; its boughs lie broken by all the rivers of the land; and all the peoples of the earth have gone from under its shadow and left it.

¹³　'On its ruin will remain all the birds of the
　　heavens,
　And all the beasts of the field will come to
　　its branches—

¹⁴"So that no trees by the waters may ever again exalt themselves for their height, nor set their tops among the thick boughs, that no tree which drinks water may ever be high enough to reach up to them.

　'For they have all been delivered to death,
　To the depths of the earth,
　Among the children of men who go down
　　to the Pit.'

¹⁵"Thus says the Lord GOD: 'In the day when it went down to hell, I caused mourning. I covered the deep because of it. I restrained its rivers, and the great waters were held back. I caused Lebanon to mourn for it, and all the trees of the field wilted because of it. ¹⁶I made the nations shake at the sound of its fall, when I cast it down to hell together with those who descend into the Pit; and all the trees of Eden, the choice and best of Lebanon, all that drink water, were comforted in the depths of the earth. ¹⁷They also went down to hell with it, with those *slain* by the sword; and *those who were* its *strong* arm dwelt in its shadows among the nations.

¹⁸"To which of the trees in Eden will you then be likened in glory and greatness? Yet you shall be brought down with the trees of Eden to the depths of the earth; you shall lie in the midst of the uncircumcised, with *those* slain by the sword. This *is* Pharaoh and all his multitude,' says the Lord GOD."

Lamentation for Pharaoh and Egypt

32 And it came to pass in the twelfth year, in the twelfth *month,* on the first *day* of the month, *that* the word of the LORD came to me, saying, ²"Son of man, take up a lamentation for Pharaoh king of Egypt, and say to him:

31:8 ^aHebrew *armon*

'You are like a young lion among the
    nations,
And you *are* like a monster in the seas,
Bursting forth in your rivers,
Troubling the waters with your feet,
And fouling their rivers.'

3"Thus says the Lord GOD:

'I will therefore spread My net over you
    with a company of many people,
And they will draw you up in My net.
4   Then I will leave you on the land;
I will cast you out on the open fields,
And cause to settle on you all the birds of
    the heavens.
And with you I will fill the beasts of the
    whole earth.
5   I will lay your flesh on the mountains,
And fill the valleys with your carcass.

6   'I will also water the land with the flow of
    your blood,
Even to the mountains;
And the riverbeds will be full of you.
7   When *I* put out your light,
I will cover the heavens, and make its stars
    dark;
I will cover the sun with a cloud,
And the moon shall not give her light.
8   All the bright lights of the heavens I will
    make dark over you,
And bring darkness upon your land,'
Says the Lord GOD.

9"I will also trouble the hearts of many peoples, when I bring your destruction among the
nations, into the countries which you have not
known. 10Yes, I will make many peoples astonished at you, and their kings shall be horribly
afraid of you when I brandish My sword before
them; and they shall tremble *every* moment, every
man for his own life, in the day of your fall.'

11"For thus says the Lord GOD: 'The sword of
the king of Babylon shall come upon you. 12By
the swords of the mighty warriors, all of them
the most terrible of the nations, I will cause your
multitude to fall.

'They shall plunder the pomp of Egypt,
And all its multitude shall be destroyed.
13   Also I will destroy all its animals
From beside its great waters;
The foot of man shall muddy them no more,
Nor shall the hooves of animals muddy
    them.

14   Then I will make their waters clear,
And make their rivers run like oil,'
Says the Lord GOD.

15   'When I make the land of Egypt desolate,
And the country is destitute of all that
    once filled it,
When I strike all who dwell in it,
Then they shall know that I *am* the LORD.

16   'This *is* the lamentation
With which they shall lament her;
The daughters of the nations shall lament
    her;
They shall lament for her, for Egypt,
And for all her multitude,'
Says the Lord GOD."

Egypt and Others Consigned to the Pit

17It came to pass also in the twelfth year, on
the fifteenth *day* of the month, *that* the word of
the LORD came to me, saying:

18   "Son of man, wail over the multitude of
    Egypt,
And cast them down to the depths of the
    earth,
Her and the daughters of the famous
    nations,
With those who go down to the Pit:
19   'Whom do you surpass in beauty?
Go down, be placed with the
    uncircumcised.'

20   "They shall fall in the midst of *those* slain by
    the sword;
She is delivered to the sword,
Drawing her and all her multitudes.
21   The strong among the mighty
Shall speak to him out of the midst of hell
With those who help him:
'They have gone down,
They lie with the uncircumcised, slain by
    the sword.'

22   "Assyria *is* there, and all her company,
With their graves all around her,
All of them slain, fallen by the sword.
23   Her graves are set in the recesses of the Pit,
And her company is all around her grave,
All of them slain, fallen by the sword,
Who caused terror in the land of the
    living.

24   "There *is* Elam and all her multitude,
All around her grave,

All of them slain, fallen by the sword,
Who have gone down uncircumcised to
  the lower parts of the earth,
Who caused their terror in the land of the
  living;
Now they bear their shame with those
  who go down to the Pit.
25 They have set her bed in the midst of the
  slain,
With all her multitude,
With her graves all around it,
All of them uncircumcised, slain by the
  sword;
Though their terror was caused
In the land of the living,
Yet they bear their shame
With those who go down to the Pit;
It was put in the midst of the slain.

26 "There *are* Meshech and Tubal and all their
  multitudes,
With all their graves around it,
All of them uncircumcised, slain by the
  sword,
Though they caused their terror in the
  land of the living.
27 They do not lie with the mighty
Who are fallen of the uncircumcised,
Who have gone down to hell with their
  weapons of war;
They have laid their swords under their
  heads,
But their iniquities will be on their
  bones,
Because of the terror of the mighty in the
  land of the living.
28 Yes, you shall be broken in the midst of
  the uncircumcised,
And lie with *those* slain by the sword.

29 "There *is* Edom,
Her kings and all her princes,
Who despite their might
Are laid beside *those* slain by the sword;
They shall lie with the uncircumcised,
And with those who go down to the
  Pit.
30 There *are* the princes of the north,
All of them, and all the Sidonians,
Who have gone down with the slain
In shame at the terror which they caused
  by their might;
They lie uncircumcised with *those* slain by
  the sword,
And bear their shame with those who go
  down to the Pit.

31 "Pharaoh will see them
And be comforted over all his multitude,
Pharaoh and all his army,
Slain by the sword,"
Says the Lord GOD.

32 "For I have caused My terror in the land of
  the living;
And he shall be placed in the midst of the
  uncircumcised
With *those* slain by the sword,
Pharaoh and all his multitude,"
Says the Lord GOD.

The Watchman and His Message

33 Again the word of the LORD came to me, saying, 2"Son of man, speak to the children of your people, and say to them: 'When I bring the sword upon a land, and the people of the land take a man from their territory and make him their watchman, 3when he sees the sword coming upon the land, if he blows the trumpet and warns the people, 4then whoever hears the sound of the trumpet and does not take warning, if the sword comes and takes him away, his blood shall be on his *own* head. 5He heard the sound of the trumpet, but did not take warning; his blood shall be upon himself. But he who takes warning will save his life. 6But if the watchman sees the sword coming and does not blow the trumpet, and the people are not warned, and the sword comes and takes *any* person from among them, he is taken away in his iniquity; but his blood I will require at the watchman's hand.'

7"So you, son of man: I have made you a watchman for the house of Israel; therefore you

Watchmen: All Leaders Are Stewards of Their God-Given Resources

(Ezekiel 33:1–6)

If a leader sees calamity approaching and sounds the trumpet to warn the people, he has done his work. If the watchman fails to warn the people of approaching disaster, God will hold the watchman accountable for the lives lost—a sobering truth about the awesome responsibility of leadership.

shall hear a word from My mouth and warn them for Me. [8]When I say to the wicked, 'O wicked *man,* you shall surely die!' and you do not speak to warn the wicked from his way, that wicked *man* shall die in his iniquity; but his blood I will require at your hand. [9]Nevertheless if you warn the wicked to turn from his way, and he does not turn from his way, he shall die in his iniquity; but you have delivered your soul.

[10]"Therefore you, O son of man, say to the house of Israel: 'Thus you say, "If our transgressions and our sins *lie* upon us, and we pine away in them, how can we then live?"' [11]Say to them: '*As* I live,' says the Lord GOD, 'I have no pleasure in the death of the wicked, but that the wicked turn from his way and live. Turn, turn from your evil ways! For why should you die, O house of Israel?'

The Fairness of God's Judgment

[12]"Therefore you, O son of man, say to the children of your people: 'The righteousness of the righteous man shall not deliver him in the day of his transgression; as for the wickedness of the wicked, he shall not fall because of it in the day that he turns from his wickedness; nor shall the righteous be able to live because of *his righteousness* in the day that he sins.' [13]When I say to the righteous *that* he shall surely live, but he trusts in his own righteousness and commits iniquity, none of his righteous works shall be remembered; but because of the iniquity that he has committed, he shall die. [14]Again, when I say to the wicked, 'You shall surely die,' if he turns from his sin and does what is lawful and right, [15]if the wicked restores the pledge, gives back what he has stolen, and walks in the statutes of life without committing iniquity, he shall surely live; he shall not die. [16]None of his sins which he has committed shall be remembered against him; he has done what is lawful and right; he shall surely live.

[17]"Yet the children of your people say, 'The way of the LORD is not fair.' But it is their way which is not fair! [18]When the righteous turns from his righteousness and commits iniquity, he shall die because of it. [19]But when the wicked turns from his wickedness and does what is lawful and right, he shall live because of it. [20]Yet you say, 'The way of the LORD is not fair.' O house of Israel, I will judge every one of you according to his own ways."

The Fall of Jerusalem

[21]And it came to pass in the twelfth year of our captivity, in the tenth *month,* on the fifth *day* of the month, *that* one who had escaped from Jerusalem came to me and said, "The city has been captured!"

[22]Now the hand of the LORD had been upon me the evening before the man came who had escaped. And He had opened my mouth; so when he came to me in the morning, my mouth was opened, and I was no longer mute.

The Cause of Judah's Ruin

[23]Then the word of the LORD came to me, saying: [24]"Son of man, they who inhabit those ruins in the land of Israel are saying, 'Abraham was only one, and he inherited the land. But we *are* many; the land has been given to us as a possession.'

[25]"Therefore say to them, 'Thus says the Lord GOD: "You eat *meat* with blood, you lift up your eyes toward your idols, and shed blood. Should you then possess the land? [26]You rely on your sword, you commit abominations, and you defile one another's wives. Should you then possess the land?"'

[27]"Say thus to them, 'Thus says the Lord GOD: "*As* I live, surely those who *are* in the ruins shall fall by the sword, and the one who *is* in the open field I will give to the beasts to be devoured, and those who *are* in the strongholds and caves shall die of the pestilence. [28]For I will make the land most desolate, her arrogant strength shall cease, and the mountains of Israel shall be so desolate that no one will pass through. [29]Then they shall know that I *am* the LORD, when I have made the land most desolate because of all their abominations which they have committed."'

Hearing and Not Doing

[30]"As for you, son of man, the children of your people are talking about you beside the walls and in the doors of the houses; and they speak to one another, everyone saying to his brother, 'Please come and hear what the word is that comes from the LORD.' [31]So they come to you as people do, they sit before you *as* My people, and they hear your words, but they do not do them; for with their mouth they show much love, *but* their hearts pursue their *own* gain. [32]Indeed you *are* to them as a very lovely song of one who has a pleasant voice and can play well on an instrument; for they hear your words, but they do not do them. [33]And when this comes to pass—surely it will come—then they will know that a prophet has been among them."

Irresponsible Shepherds

34 And the word of the LORD came to me, saying, [2]"Son of man, prophesy against the shepherds of Israel, prophesy and say to them, 'Thus says the Lord GOD to the shepherds: "Woe to the shepherds of Israel who feed themselves! Should not the shepherds feed the flocks? [3]You eat the fat and clothe yourselves with the wool; you slaughter the fatlings, *but* you do not feed the flock. [4]The weak you have not strengthened, nor have you healed those who were sick, nor bound up the broken, nor brought back what was driven away, nor sought what was lost; but with force and cruelty you have ruled them. [5]So they were scattered because *there was* no shepherd; and they became food for all the beasts of the field when they were scattered. [6]My sheep wandered through all the mountains, and on every high hill; yes, My flock was scattered over the whole face of the earth, and no one was seeking or searching *for them*."

[7]"Therefore, you shepherds, hear the word of the LORD: [8]"*As* I live," says the Lord GOD, "surely because My flock became a prey, and My flock became food for every beast of the field, because *there was* no shepherd, nor did My shepherds search for My flock, but the shepherds fed themselves and did not feed My flock"— [9]therefore, O shepherds, hear the word of the LORD!

[10]Thus says the Lord GOD: "Behold, I *am* against the shepherds, and I will require My flock at their hand; I will cause them to cease feeding the sheep, and the shepherds shall feed themselves no more; for I will deliver My flock from their mouths, that they may no longer be food for them."

God, the True Shepherd

[11]"For thus says the Lord GOD: "Indeed I Myself will search for My sheep and seek them out. [12]As a shepherd seeks out his flock on the day he is among his scattered sheep, so will I seek out My sheep and deliver them from all the places where they were scattered on a cloudy and dark day. [13]And I will bring them out from the peoples and gather them from the countries, and will bring them to their own land; I will feed them on the mountains of Israel, in the valleys and in all the inhabited places of the country. [14]I will feed them in good pasture, and their fold shall be on the high mountains of Israel. There they shall lie down in a good fold and feed in rich pasture on the mountains of Israel. [15]I will feed My flock, and I will make them lie down," says the Lord GOD. [16]"I will seek what was lost and bring back what was driven away, bind up the broken and strengthen what was sick; but I will destroy the fat and the strong, and feed them in judgment."

Leaders Are to Relate as Shepherds to People

(Ezekiel 34:11–24)

The Lord of ancient Israel was the Great Shepherd to His flock, Israel. He calls all spiritual leaders to view their role in the same way. The word picture of the shepherd enables us to see what kind of relational skills and attitudes we are to build into our leadership. Ezekiel 34 describes how the shepherd cares for his flock. The shepherd . . .

1. Searches out the lost sheep (vv. 11–16).
2. Delivers the captive sheep (v. 12).
3. Gathers the dispersed sheep (v. 13).
4. Feeds the hungry sheep (v. 13).
5. Rests the weary sheep (v. 15).
6. Binds up the hurt sheep (v. 16).
7. Strengthens the weak sheep (v. 16).
8. Protects the vulnerable sheep (vv. 17–22).
9. Equips the needy sheep (v. 23).
10. Directs all the sheep (v. 24).

You may want to compare this text to Psalm 23, another picture of the leader as a shepherd. In that psalm God is the Shepherd, providing guidance, restoration, preparation, resources, comfort, and anointing for His sheep.

¹⁷"And *as for* you, O My flock, thus says the Lord GOD: "Behold, I shall judge between sheep and sheep, between rams and goats. ¹⁸*Is it* too little for you to have eaten up the good pasture, that you must tread down with your feet the residue of your pasture—and to have drunk of the clear waters, that you must foul the residue with your feet? ¹⁹And *as for* My flock, they eat what you have trampled with your feet, and they drink what you have fouled with your feet."

²⁰"Therefore thus says the Lord GOD to them: "Behold, I Myself will judge between the fat and the lean sheep. ²¹Because you have pushed with side and shoulder, butted all the weak ones with your horns, and scattered them abroad, ²²therefore I will save My flock, and they shall no longer be a prey; and I will judge between sheep and sheep. ²³I will establish one shepherd over them, and he shall feed them—My servant David. He shall feed them and be their shepherd. ²⁴And I, the LORD, will be their God, and My servant David a prince among them; I, the LORD, have spoken.

²⁵"I will make a covenant of peace with them, and cause wild beasts to cease from the land; and they will dwell safely in the wilderness and sleep in the woods. ²⁶I will make them and the places all around My hill a blessing; and I will cause showers to come down in their season; there shall be showers of blessing. ²⁷Then the trees of the field shall yield their fruit, and the earth shall yield her increase. They shall be safe in their land; and they shall know that I *am* the LORD, when I have broken the bands of their yoke and delivered them from the hand of those who enslaved them. ²⁸And they shall no longer be a prey for the nations, nor shall beasts of the land devour them; but they shall dwell safely, and no one shall make *them* afraid. ²⁹I will raise up for them a garden of renown, and they shall no longer be consumed with hunger in the land, nor bear the shame of the Gentiles anymore. ³⁰Thus they shall know that I, the LORD their God, *am* with them, and they, the house of Israel, *are* My people," says the Lord GOD.'"

³¹"You are My flock, the flock of My pasture; you *are* men, *and* I *am* your God," says the Lord GOD.

Judgment on Mount Seir

35 Moreover the word of the LORD came to me, saying, ²"Son of man, set your face against Mount Seir and prophesy against it, ³and say to it, 'Thus says the Lord GOD:

"Behold, O Mount Seir, I *am* against you; I will stretch out My hand against you, And make you most desolate; ⁴ I shall lay your cities waste, And you shall be desolate. Then you shall know that I *am* the LORD.

⁵"Because you have had an ancient hatred, and have shed *the blood of* the children of Israel by the power of the sword at the time of their calamity, *when* their iniquity *came to an* end, ⁶therefore, *as* I live," says the Lord GOD, "I will prepare you for blood, and blood shall pursue you; since you have not hated blood, therefore blood shall pursue you. ⁷Thus I will make Mount Seir most desolate, and cut off from it the one who leaves and the one who returns. ⁸And I will fill its mountains with the slain; on your hills and in your valleys and in all your ravines those who are slain by the sword shall fall. ⁹I will make you perpetually desolate, and your cities shall be uninhabited; then you shall know that I *am* the LORD.

¹⁰"Because you have said, 'These two nations and these two countries shall be mine, and we will possess them,' although the LORD was there, ¹¹therefore, *as* I live," says the Lord GOD, "I will do according to your anger and according to the envy which you showed in your hatred against them; and I will make Myself known among them when I judge you. ¹²Then you shall know that I *am* the LORD. I have heard all your blasphemies which you have spoken against the mountains of Israel, saying, 'They are desolate; they are given to us to consume.' ¹³Thus with your mouth you have boasted against Me and multiplied your words against Me; I have heard *them.*"

¹⁴"Thus says the Lord GOD: "The whole earth will rejoice when I make you desolate. ¹⁵As you rejoiced because the inheritance of the house of Israel was desolate, so I will do to you; you shall be desolate, O Mount Seir, as well as all of Edom—all of it! Then they shall know that I *am* the LORD."'

Blessing on Israel

36 "And you, son of man, prophesy to the mountains of Israel, and say, 'O mountains of Israel, hear the word of the LORD! ²Thus says the Lord GOD: "Because the enemy has said of you, 'Aha! The ancient heights have become our possession,'"' ³therefore prophesy, and say, 'Thus says the Lord GOD: "Because they made *you* desolate and swallowed you up on every side, so that you became the possession of the rest of the nations, and you are taken up by the lips of talkers and slandered by the people"— [4]therefore, O mountains of Israel, hear the word of the Lord GOD! Thus says the Lord GOD to the mountains, the hills, the rivers, the valleys, the desolate wastes, and the cities that have been forsaken, which became plunder and mockery to the rest of the nations all around— [5]therefore thus says the Lord GOD: "Surely I have spoken in My burning jealousy against the rest of the nations and against all Edom, who gave My land to themselves as a possession, with whole-hearted joy *and* spiteful minds, in order to plunder its open country."'

[6]"Therefore prophesy concerning the land of Israel, and say to the mountains, the hills, the rivers, and the valleys, 'Thus says the Lord GOD: "Behold, I have spoken in My jealousy and My fury, because you have borne the shame of the nations." [7]Therefore thus says the Lord GOD: "I have raised My hand in an oath that surely the nations that *are* around you shall bear their own shame. [8]But you, O mountains of Israel, you shall shoot forth your branches and yield your fruit to My people Israel, for they are about to come. [9]For indeed I *am* for you, and I will turn to you, and you shall be tilled and sown. [10]I will multiply men upon you, all the house of Israel, all of it; and the cities shall be inhabited and the ruins rebuilt. [11]I will multiply upon you man and beast; and they shall increase and bear young; I will make you inhabited as in former times, and do better *for you* than at your beginnings. Then you shall know that I *am* the LORD. [12]Yes, I will cause men to walk on you, My people Israel; they shall take possession of you, and you shall be their inheritance; no more shall you bereave them *of children*."

[13]"Thus says the Lord GOD: "Because they say to you, 'You devour men and bereave your nation *of children*,' [14]therefore you shall devour men no more, nor bereave your nation anymore," says the Lord GOD. [15]"Nor will I let you hear the taunts of the nations anymore, nor bear the reproach of the peoples anymore, nor shall you cause your nation to stumble anymore," says the Lord GOD.'"

The Renewal of Israel

[16]Moreover the word of the LORD came to me, saying: [17]"Son of man, when the house of Israel dwelt in their own land, they defiled it by their own ways and deeds; to Me their way was like the uncleanness of a woman in her customary impurity. [18]Therefore I poured out My fury on them for the blood they had shed on the land, and for their idols *with which* they had defiled it. [19]So I scattered them among the nations, and they were dispersed throughout the countries; I judged them according to their ways and their deeds. [20]When they came to the nations, wherever they went, they profaned My holy name— when they said of them, 'These *are* the people of the LORD, *and* yet they have gone out of His land.' [21]But I had concern for My holy name, which the house of Israel had profaned among the nations wherever they went.

[22]"Therefore say to the house of Israel, 'Thus says the Lord GOD: "I do not do *this* for your sake, O house of Israel, but for My holy name's sake, which you have profaned among the nations wherever you went. [23]And I will sanctify My great name, which has been profaned among the nations, which you have profaned in their midst; and the nations shall know that I *am* the LORD," says the Lord GOD, "when I am hallowed in you before their eyes. [24]For I will take you from among the nations, gather you out of all countries, and bring you into your own land. [25]Then I will sprinkle clean water on you, and you shall be clean; I will cleanse you from all your filthiness and from all your idols. [26]I will give you a new heart and put a new spirit within you; I will take the heart of stone out of your flesh and give you a heart of flesh. [27]I will put My Spirit within you and cause you to walk in My statutes, and you will keep My judgments and do *them*. [28]Then you shall dwell in the land that I gave to your fathers; you shall be My people, and I will be your God. [29]I will deliver you from all your uncleannesses. I will call for the grain and multiply it, and bring no famine upon you. [30]And I will multiply the fruit of your trees and the increase of your fields, so that you need never again bear the reproach of famine among the nations. [31]Then you will remember your evil ways and your deeds that *were* not good; and you will loathe yourselves in your own sight, for your iniquities and your abominations. [32]Not for your sake do I do *this*," says the Lord GOD, "let it be known to you. Be ashamed and confounded for your own ways, O house of Israel!"

[33]"Thus says the Lord GOD: "On the day that I cleanse you from all your iniquities, I will also enable *you* to dwell in the cities, and the ruins shall be rebuilt. [34]The desolate land shall be tilled instead of lying desolate in the sight of all who pass by. [35]So they will say, 'This land that was desolate has become like the garden of Eden; and the wasted, desolate, and ruined cities *are now* fortified *and* inhabited.' [36]Then the nations which are left all around you shall know that I, the

LORD, have rebuilt the ruined places *and* planted what was desolate. I, the LORD, have spoken *it,* and I will do *it.*"

37"Thus says the Lord GOD: "I will also let the house of Israel inquire of Me to do this for them: I will increase their men like a flock. 38Like a flock *offered as* holy *sacrifices,* like the flock at Jerusalem on its feast days, so shall the ruined cities be filled with flocks of men. Then they shall know that I *am* the LORD."'"

The Dry Bones Live

37 The hand of the LORD came upon me and brought me out in the Spirit of the LORD, and set me down in the midst of the valley; and it *was* full of bones. 2Then He caused me to pass by them all around, and behold, *there were* very many in the open valley; and indeed *they were* very dry. 3And He said to me, "Son of man, can these bones live?"

So I answered, "O Lord GOD, You know."

4Again He said to me, "Prophesy to these bones, and say to them, 'O dry bones, hear the word of the LORD! 5Thus says the Lord GOD to these bones: "Surely I will cause breath to enter into you, and you shall live. 6I will put sinews on you and bring flesh upon you, cover you with skin and put breath in you; and you shall live. Then you shall know that I *am* the LORD."'"

7So I prophesied as I was commanded; and as I prophesied, there was a noise, and suddenly a rattling; and the bones came together, bone to bone. 8Indeed, as I looked, the sinews and the flesh came upon them, and the skin covered them over; but *there was* no breath in them.

9Also He said to me, "Prophesy to the breath, prophesy, son of man, and say to the breath, 'Thus says the Lord GOD: "Come from the four winds, O breath, and breathe on these slain, that they may live."'" 10So I prophesied as He commanded me, and breath came into them, and they lived, and stood upon their feet, an exceedingly great army.

11Then He said to me, "Son of man, these bones are the whole house of Israel. They indeed say, 'Our bones are dry, our hope is lost, and we ourselves are cut off!' 12Therefore prophesy and say to them, 'Thus says the Lord GOD: "Behold, O My people, I will open your graves and cause you to come up from your graves, and bring you into the land of Israel. 13Then you shall know that I *am* the LORD, when I have opened your graves, O My people, and brought you up from your graves. 14I will put My Spirit in you, and you shall live, and I will place you in your own land. Then you shall know that I, the LORD, have spoken *it* and performed *it,*" says the LORD.'"

One Kingdom, One King

15Again the word of the LORD came to me, saying, 16"As for you, son of man, take a stick for yourself and write on it: 'For Judah and for the children of Israel, his companions.' Then take another stick and write on it, 'For Joseph, the stick of Ephraim, and *for* all the house of Israel, his companions.' 17Then join them one to another for yourself into one stick, and they will become one in your hand.

18"And when the children of your people speak to you, saying, 'Will you not show us what you *mean* by these?'— 19say to them, 'Thus says the Lord GOD: "Surely I will take the stick of Joseph, which *is* in the hand of Ephraim, and the tribes of Israel, his companions; and I will join them with it, with the stick of Judah, and make them one stick, and they will be one in My hand."' 20And the sticks on which you write will be in your hand before their eyes.

21"Then say to them, 'Thus says the Lord GOD: "Surely I will take the children of Israel from among the nations, wherever they have gone, and will gather them from every side and bring them into their own land; 22and I will make them one nation in the land, on the mountains of Israel; and one king shall be king over them all; they shall no longer be two nations, nor shall they ever be divided into two kingdoms again. 23They shall not defile themselves anymore with their idols, nor with their detestable things, nor with any of their transgressions; but I will deliver them from all their dwelling places in which they have sinned, and will cleanse them. Then they shall be My people, and I will be their God.

24"David My servant *shall be* king over them, and they shall all have one shepherd; they shall also walk in My judgments and observe My statutes, and do them. 25Then they shall dwell in the land that I have given to Jacob My servant, where your fathers dwelt; and they shall dwell there, they, their children, and their children's children, forever; and My servant David *shall be* their prince forever. 26Moreover I will make a covenant of peace with them, and it shall be an everlasting covenant with them; I will establish them and multiply them, and I will set My sanctuary in their midst forevermore. 27My tabernacle also shall be with them; indeed I will be their God, and they shall be My people. 28The nations also will know that I, the LORD, sanctify Israel, when My sanctuary is in their midst forevermore."'"

Gog and Allies Attack Israel

38 Now the word of the LORD came to me, saying, [2]"Son of man, set your face against Gog, of the land of Magog, the prince of Rosh,[a] Meshech, and Tubal, and prophesy against him, [3]and say, 'Thus says the Lord GOD: "Behold, I *am* against you, O Gog, the prince of Rosh, Meshech, and Tubal. [4]I will turn you around, put hooks into your jaws, and lead you out, with all your army, horses, and horsemen, all splendidly clothed, a great company *with* bucklers and shields, all of them handling swords. [5]Persia, Ethiopia,[a] and Libya[b] are with them, all of them *with* shield and helmet; [6]Gomer and all its troops; the house of Togarmah *from* the far north and all its troops—many people *are* with you.

[7]"Prepare yourself and be ready, you and all your companies that are gathered about you; and be a guard for them. [8]After many days you will be visited. In the latter years you will come into the land of those brought back from the sword *and* gathered from many people on the mountains of Israel, which had long been desolate; they were brought out of the nations, and now all of them dwell safely. [9]You will ascend, coming like a storm, covering the land like a cloud, you and all your troops and many peoples with you."

[10]"Thus says the Lord GOD: "On that day it shall come to pass *that* thoughts will arise in your mind, and you will make an evil plan: [11]You will say, 'I will go up against a land of unwalled villages; I will go to a peaceful people, who dwell safely, all of them dwelling without walls, and having neither bars nor gates'— [12]to take plunder and to take booty, to stretch out your hand against the waste places *that are again* inhabited, and against a people gathered from the nations, who have acquired livestock and goods, who dwell in the midst of the land. [13]Sheba, Dedan, the merchants of Tarshish, and all their young lions will say to you, 'Have you come to take plunder? Have you gathered your army to take booty, to carry away silver and gold, to take away livestock and goods, to take great plunder?'"'

[14]"Therefore, son of man, prophesy and say to Gog, 'Thus says the Lord GOD: "On that day when My people Israel dwell safely, will you not know *it*? [15]Then you will come from your place out of the far north, you and many peoples with you, all of them riding on horses, a great company and a mighty army. [16]You will come up against My people Israel like a cloud, to cover the land. It will be in the latter days that I will bring you against My land, so that the nations may know Me, when I am hallowed in you, O Gog, before their eyes." [17]Thus says the Lord GOD: "Are *you* he of whom I have spoken in former days by My servants the prophets of Israel, who prophesied for years in those days that I would bring you against them?

Judgment on Gog

[18]"And it will come to pass at the same time, when Gog comes against the land of Israel," says the Lord GOD, "*that* My fury will show in My face. [19]For in My jealousy *and* in the fire of My wrath I have spoken: 'Surely in that day there shall be a great earthquake in the land of Israel, [20]so that the fish of the sea, the birds of the heavens, the beasts of the field, all creeping things that creep on the earth, and all men who *are* on the face of the earth shall shake at My presence. The mountains shall be thrown down, the steep places shall fall, and every wall shall fall to the ground.' [21]I will call for a sword against Gog throughout all My mountains," says the Lord GOD. "Every man's sword will be against his brother. [22]And I will bring him to judgment with pestilence and bloodshed; I will rain down on him, on his troops, and on the many peoples who *are* with him, flooding rain, great hailstones, fire, and brimstone. [23]Thus I will magnify Myself and sanctify Myself, and I will be known in the eyes of many nations. Then they shall know that I *am* the LORD."'

Gog's Armies Destroyed

39 "And you, son of man, prophesy against Gog, and say, 'Thus says the Lord GOD: "Behold, I *am* against you, O Gog, the prince of Rosh,[a] Meshech, and Tubal; [2]and I will turn you around and lead you on, bringing you up from the far north, and bring you against the mountains of Israel. [3]Then I will knock the bow out of your left hand, and cause the arrows to fall out of your right hand. [4]You shall fall upon the mountains of Israel, you and all your troops and the peoples who *are* with you; I will give you to birds of prey of every sort and to the beasts of the field to be devoured. [5]You shall fall on the open field; for I have spoken," says the Lord GOD. [6]"And I will send fire on Magog and on those who live in security in the coastlands. Then they shall know that I *am* the LORD. [7]So I will make My holy name known in

---

38:2 [a]Targum, Vulgate, and Aquila read *chief prince of* (also verse 3). **38:5** [a]Hebrew *Cush* [b]Hebrew *Put* **39:1** [a]Targum, Vulgate and Aquila read *chief prince of.*

the midst of My people Israel, and I will not *let them* profane My holy name anymore. Then the nations shall know that *I am* the LORD, the Holy One in Israel. [8]Surely it is coming, and it shall be done," says the Lord GOD. "This *is* the day of which I have spoken.

[9]"Then those who dwell in the cities of Israel will go out and set on fire and burn the weapons, both the shields and bucklers, the bows and arrows, the javelins and spears; and they will make fires with them for seven years. [10]They will not take wood from the field nor cut down *any* from the forests, because they will make fires with the weapons; and they will plunder those who plundered them, and pillage those who pillaged them," says the Lord GOD.

The Burial of Gog

[11]"It will come to pass in that day *that* I will give Gog a burial place there in Israel, the valley of those who pass by east of the sea; and it will obstruct travelers, because there they will bury Gog and all his multitude. Therefore they will call *it* the Valley of Hamon Gog.[a] [12]For seven months the house of Israel will be burying them, in order to cleanse the land. [13]Indeed all the people of the land will be burying, and they will gain renown for it on the day that I am glorified," says the Lord GOD. [14]"They will set apart men regularly employed, with the help of a search party,[a] to pass through the land and bury those bodies remaining on the ground, in order to cleanse it. At the end of seven months they will make a search. [15]The search party will pass through the land; and *when anyone* sees a man's bone, he shall set up a marker by it, till the buriers have buried it in the Valley of Hamon Gog. [16]*The* name of *the* city *will* also *be* Hamonah. Thus they shall cleanse the land."'

A Triumphant Festival

[17]"And as for you, son of man, thus says the Lord GOD, 'Speak to every sort of bird and to every beast of the field:

" Assemble yourselves and come;
    Gather together from all sides to My
       sacrificial meal
    Which I am sacrificing for you,
    A great sacrificial meal on the mountains
       of Israel,
    That you may eat flesh and drink blood.
[18] You shall eat the flesh of the mighty,
    Drink the blood of the princes of the
       earth,
    Of rams and lambs,

    Of goats and bulls,
    All of them fatlings of Bashan.
[19] You shall eat fat till you are full,
    And drink blood till you are drunk,
    At My sacrificial meal
    Which I am sacrificing for you.
[20] You shall be filled at My table
    With horses and riders,
    With mighty men
    And with all the men of war," says the
       Lord GOD.

Israel Restored to the Land

[21]"I will set My glory among the nations; all the nations shall see My judgment which I have executed, and My hand which I have laid on them. [22]So the house of Israel shall know that I *am* the LORD their God from that day forward. [23]The Gentiles shall know that the house of Israel went into captivity for their iniquity; because they were unfaithful to Me, therefore I hid My face from them. I gave them into the hand of their enemies, and they all fell by the sword. [24]According to their uncleanness and according to their transgressions I have dealt with them, and hidden My face from them."'

[25]"Therefore thus says the Lord GOD: 'Now I will bring back the captives of Jacob, and have mercy on the whole house of Israel; and I will be jealous for My holy name— [26]after they have borne their shame, and all their unfaithfulness in which they were unfaithful to Me, when they dwelt safely in their *own* land and no one made *them* afraid. [27]When I have brought them back from the peoples and gathered them out of their enemies' lands, and I am hallowed in them in the sight of many nations, [28]then they shall know that I *am* the LORD their God, who sent them into captivity among the nations, but also brought them back to their land, and left none of them captive any longer. [29]And I will not hide My face from them anymore; for I shall have poured out My Spirit on the house of Israel,' says the Lord GOD."

A New City, a New Temple

40 In the twenty-fifth year of our captivity, at the beginning of the year, on the tenth *day* of the month, in the fourteenth year after the city was captured, on the very same day the hand of the LORD was upon me; and He took me there. [2]In the visions of God He took me into the land of Israel and

---

39:11 [a]Literally *The Multitude of Gog*
39:14 [a]Literally *those who pass through*

set me on a very high mountain; on it toward the south *was* something like the structure of a city. ³He took me there, and behold, *there was* a man whose appearance *was* like the appearance of bronze. He had a line of flax and a measuring rod in his hand, and he stood in the gateway.

⁴And the man said to me, "Son of man, look with your eyes and hear with your ears, and fix your mind on everything I show you; for you *were* brought here so that I might show *them* to you. Declare to the house of Israel everything you see." ⁵Now there was a wall all around the outside of the temple.ᵃ In the man's hand was a measuring rod six cubits *long, each being a* cubit and a handbreadth; and he measured the width of the wall structure, one rod; and the height, one rod.

Great Leaders See the Big Picture and the Little Process

(Ezekiel 40:1—44:31)

God, the Ultimate Leader, never loses sight of the whole, but never ignores details, either. What does God communicate in these chapters?

1. I care about the details.
2. No one is unimportant.
3. We have a bigger purpose for what we do.
4. The labor of each individual has meaning.

The Eastern Gateway of the Temple

⁶Then he went to the gateway which faced east; and he went up its stairs and measured the threshold of the gateway, *which was* one rod wide, and the other threshold *was* one rod wide. ⁷Each gate chamber *was* one rod long and one rod wide; between the gate chambers *was a space of* five cubits; and the threshold of the gateway by the vestibule of the inside gate *was* one rod. ⁸He also measured the vestibule of the inside gate, one rod. ⁹Then he measured the vestibule of the gateway, eight cubits; and the gateposts, two cubits. The vestibule of the gate *was* on the inside. ¹⁰In the eastern gateway *were* three gate chambers on one side and three on the other; the three *were* all the same size; also the gateposts were of the same size on this side and that side.

¹¹He measured the width of the entrance to the gateway, ten cubits; *and* the length of the gate, thirteen cubits. ¹²There was a space in front of the gate chambers, one cubit *on this side* and one cubit on that side; the gate chambers *were* six cubits on this side and six cubits on that side. ¹³Then he measured the gateway from the roof of *one* gate chamber to the roof of the other; the width *was* twenty-five cubits, as door faces door. ¹⁴He measured the gateposts, sixty cubits high, and the court all around the gateway *extended* to the gatepost. ¹⁵*From* the front of the entrance gate to the front of the vestibule of the inner gate *was* fifty cubits. ¹⁶*There were* beveled window *frames* in the gate chambers and in their intervening archways on the inside of the gateway all around, and likewise in the vestibules. *There were* windows all around on the inside. And on each gatepost *were* palm trees.

The Outer Court

¹⁷Then he brought me into the outer court; and *there were* chambers and a pavement made all around the court; thirty chambers faced the pavement. ¹⁸The pavement was by the side of the gateways, corresponding to the length of the gateways; *this was* the lower pavement. ¹⁹Then he measured the width from the front of the lower gateway to the front of the inner court exterior, one hundred cubits toward the east and the north.

The Northern Gateway

²⁰On the outer court was also a gateway facing north, and he measured its length and its width. ²¹Its gate chambers, three on this side and three on that side, its gateposts and its archways, had the same measurements as the first gate; its length *was* fifty cubits and its width twenty-five cubits. ²²Its windows and those of its archways, and also its palm trees, *had* the same measurements as the gateway facing east; it was ascended by seven steps, and its archway *was* in front of it. ²³A gate of the inner court was opposite the northern gateway, just as the eastern *gateway;* and he measured from gateway to gateway, one hundred cubits.

The Southern Gateway

²⁴After that he brought me toward the south, and there a gateway was facing south; and he measured its gateposts and archways according to these same measurements. ²⁵*There were* windows in it and in its archways all around like those windows; its length *was* fifty cubits and its width

---

40:5 ᵃLiterally *house,* and so elsewhere in this book

twenty-five cubits. ²⁶Seven steps led up to it, and its archway *was* in front of them; and it had palm trees on its gateposts, one on this side and one on that side. ²⁷*There was* also a gateway on the inner court, facing south; and he measured from gateway to gateway toward the south, one hundred cubits.

Gateways of the Inner Court

²⁸Then he brought me to the inner court through the southern gateway; he measured the southern gateway according to these same measurements. ²⁹Also its gate chambers, its gateposts, and its archways *were* according to these same measurements; *there were* windows in it and in its archways all around; *it was* fifty cubits long and twenty-five cubits wide. ³⁰*There were* archways all around, twenty-five cubits long and five cubits wide. ³¹Its archways faced the outer court, palm trees *were* on its gateposts, and going up to it *were* eight steps.

³²And he brought me into the inner court facing east; he measured the gateway according to these same measurements. ³³Also its gate chambers, its gateposts, and its archways *were* according to these same measurements; and *there were* windows in it and in its archways all around; *it was* fifty cubits long and twenty-five cubits wide. ³⁴Its archways faced the outer court, and palm trees *were* on its gateposts on this side and on that side; and going up to it *were* eight steps.

³⁵Then he brought me to the north gateway and measured *it* according to these same measurements—³⁶also its gate chambers, its gateposts, and its archways. It had windows all around; its length *was* fifty cubits and its width twenty-five cubits. ³⁷Its gateposts faced the outer court, palm trees *were* on its gateposts on this side and on that side, and going up to it *were* eight steps.

Where Sacrifices Were Prepared

³⁸*There was* a chamber and its entrance by the gateposts of the gateway, where they washed the burnt offering. ³⁹In the vestibule of the gateway *were* two tables on this side and two tables on that side, on which to slay the burnt offering, the sin offering, and the trespass offering. ⁴⁰At the outer side of the vestibule, as one goes up to the entrance of the northern gateway, *were* two tables; and on the other side of the vestibule of the gateway *were* two tables. ⁴¹Four tables *were* on this side and four tables on that side, by the side of the gateway, eight tables on which they slaughtered *the sacrifices.* ⁴²*There were* also four tables of hewn stone for the burnt offering, one cubit and a half long, one cubit and a half wide, and one

cubit high; on these they laid the instruments with which they slaughtered the burnt offering and the sacrifice. ⁴³Inside *were* hooks, a handbreadth wide, fastened all around; and the flesh of the sacrifices *was* on the tables.

Chambers for Singers and Priests

⁴⁴Outside the inner gate *were* the chambers for the singers in the inner court, one facing south at the side of the northern gateway, and the other facing north at the side of the southern gateway. ⁴⁵Then he said to me, "This chamber which faces south *is* for the priests who have charge of the temple. ⁴⁶The chamber which faces north *is* for the priests who have charge of the altar; these *are* the sons of Zadok, from the sons of Levi, who come near the LORD to minister to Him."

Dimensions of the Inner Court and Vestibule

⁴⁷And he measured the court, one hundred cubits long and one hundred cubits wide, foursquare. The altar *was* in front of the temple. ⁴⁸Then he brought me to the vestibule of the temple and measured the doorposts of the vestibule, five cubits on this side and five cubits on that side; and the width of the gateway *was* three cubits on this side and three cubits on that side. ⁴⁹The length of the vestibule *was* twenty cubits, and the width eleven cubits; and by the steps which led up to it *there were* pillars by the doorposts, one on this side and another on that side.

Dimensions of the Sanctuary

41 Then he brought me into the sanctuaryᵃ and measured the doorposts, six cubits wide on one side and six cubits wide on the other side—the width of the tabernacle. ²The width of the entryway *was* ten cubits, and the side walls of the entrance *were* five cubits on this side and five cubits on the other side; and he measured its length, forty cubits, and its width, twenty cubits.

³Also he went inside and measured the doorposts, two cubits; and the entrance, six cubits *high;* and the width of the entrance, seven cubits. ⁴He measured the length, twenty cubits; and the width, twenty cubits, beyond the sanctuary; and he said to me, "This *is* the Most Holy *Place.*"

41:1 ᵃHebrew *heykal,* here the main room of the temple, sometimes called the *holy place* (compare Exodus 26:33)

The Side Chambers on the Wall

[5]Next, he measured the wall of the temple, six cubits. The width of each side chamber all around the temple *was* four cubits on every side. [6]The side chambers *were* in three stories, one above the other, thirty chambers in each story; they rested on ledges which *were* for the side chambers all around, that they might be supported, but not fastened to the wall of the temple. [7]As one went up from story to story, the side chambers became wider all around, because their supporting ledges in the wall of the temple ascended like steps; therefore the width of the structure increased as one went up *from* the lowest *story* to the highest by way of the middle one. [8]I also saw an elevation all around the temple; it was the foundation of the side chambers, a full rod, *that is,* six cubits high. [9]The thickness of the outer wall of the side chambers *was* five cubits, and so also the remaining terrace by the place of the side chambers of the temple. [10]And between *it and* the *wall* chambers was a width of twenty cubits all around the temple on every side. [11]The doors of the side chambers opened on the terrace, one door toward the north and another toward the south; and the width of the terrace *was* five cubits all around.

The Building at the Western End

[12]The building that faced the separating courtyard at its western end *was* seventy cubits wide; the wall of the building *was* five cubits thick all around, and its length ninety cubits.

Dimensions and Design of the Temple Area

[13]So he measured the temple, one hundred cubits long; and the separating courtyard with the building and its walls *was* one hundred cubits long; [14]also the width of the eastern face of the temple, including the separating courtyard, *was* one hundred cubits. [15]He measured the length of the building behind it, facing the separating courtyard, with its galleries on the one side and on the other side, one hundred cubits, as well as the inner temple and the porches of the court, [16]their doorposts and the beveled window frames. And the galleries all around their three stories opposite the threshold were paneled with wood from the ground to the windows—the windows were covered— [17]from the space above the door, even to the inner room,[a] as well as outside, and on every wall all around, inside and outside, by measure.

[18]And *it was* made with cherubim and palm trees, a palm tree between cherub and cherub. *Each* cherub had two faces, [19]so that the face of a man *was* toward a palm tree on one side, and the face of a young lion toward a palm tree on the other side; thus *it was* made throughout the temple all around. [20]From the floor to the space above the door, and on the wall of the sanctuary, cherubim and palm trees *were* carved.

[21]The doorposts of the temple *were* square, *as* was the front of the sanctuary; their appearance was similar. [22]The altar *was* of wood, three cubits high, and its length two cubits. Its corners, its length, and its sides *were* of wood; and he said to me, "This *is* the table that *is* before the LORD."

[23]The temple and the sanctuary had two doors. [24]The doors had two panels apiece, two folding panels: two *panels* for one door and two panels for the other *door.* [25]Cherubim and palm trees *were* carved on the doors of the temple just as they *were* carved on the walls. A wooden canopy *was* on the front of the vestibule outside. [26]*There were* beveled window *frames* and palm trees on one side and on the other, on the sides of the vestibule—also on the side chambers of the temple and on the canopies.

The Chambers for the Priests

42 Then he brought me out into the outer court, by the way toward the north; and he brought me into the chamber which *was* opposite the separating courtyard, and which *was* opposite the building toward the north. [2]Facing the length, *which was* one hundred cubits (the width was fifty cubits), was the north door. [3]Opposite the inner court of twenty *cubits,* and opposite the pavement of the outer court, *was* gallery against gallery in three *stories.* [4]In front of the chambers, toward the inside, *was* a walk ten cubits wide, at a distance of one cubit; and their doors faced north. [5]Now the upper chambers *were* shorter, because the galleries took away *space* from them more than from the lower and middle stories of the building. [6]For they *were* in three *stories* and did not have pillars like the pillars of the courts; therefore *the upper level* was shortened more than the lower and middle levels from the ground up. [7]And a wall which *was* outside ran parallel to the chambers, at the front of the chambers, toward the outer court; its length *was* fifty cubits. [8]The length of the chambers toward the outer court *was* fifty cubits, whereas that facing the temple *was* one hundred cubits. [9]At the lower chambers *was* the entrance on the east side, as one goes into them from the outer court.

41:17 [a]Literally *house,* here the Most Holy Place

¹⁰Also *there were* chambers in the thickness of the wall of the court toward the east, opposite the separating courtyard and opposite the building. ¹¹*There was* a walk in front of them also, and their appearance *was* like the chambers which *were* toward the north; they *were* as long and as wide as the others, and all their exits and entrances *were* according to plan. ¹²And corresponding to the doors of the chambers that *were* facing south, as one enters them, *there was* a door in front of the walk, the way directly in front of the wall toward the east.

¹³Then he said to me, "The north chambers *and* the south chambers, which *are* opposite the separating courtyard, *are* the holy chambers where the priests who approach the LORD shall eat the most holy offerings. There they shall lay the most holy offerings—the grain offering, the sin offering, and the trespass offering—for the place *is* holy. ¹⁴When the priests enter them, they shall not go out of the holy *chamber* into the outer court; but there they shall leave their garments in which they minister, for they *are* holy. They shall put on other garments; then they may approach *that* which *is* for the people."

Outer Dimensions of the Temple

¹⁵Now when he had finished measuring the inner temple, he brought me out through the gateway that faces toward the east, and measured it all around. ¹⁶He measured the east side with the measuring rod,ᵃ five hundred rods by the measuring rod all around. ¹⁷He measured the north side, five hundred rods by the measuring rod all around. ¹⁸He measured the south side, five hundred rods by the measuring rod. ¹⁹He came around to the west side *and* measured five hundred rods by the measuring rod. ²⁰He measured it on the four sides; it had a wall all around, five hundred *cubits* long and five hundred wide, to separate the holy areas from the common.

The Temple, the LORD's Dwelling Place

43 Afterward he brought me to the gate, the gate that faces toward the east. ²And behold, the glory of the God of Israel came from the way of the east. His voice *was* like the sound of many waters; and the earth shone with His glory. ³*It was* like the appearance of the vision which I saw—like the vision which I saw when Iᵃ came to destroy the city. The visions *were* like the vision which I saw by the River Chebar; and I fell on my face. ⁴And the glory of the LORD came into the temple by way of the gate which faces toward the east. ⁵The Spirit lifted me up and brought me into the inner court; and behold, the glory of the LORD filled the temple.

⁶Then I heard *Him* speaking to me from the temple, while a man stood beside me. ⁷And He said to me, "Son of man, *this is* the place of My throne and the place of the soles of My feet, where I will dwell in the midst of the children of Israel forever. No more shall the house of Israel defile My holy name, they nor their kings, by their harlotry or with the carcasses of their kings on their high places. ⁸When they set their threshold by My threshold, and their doorpost by My doorpost, with a wall between them and Me, they defiled My holy name by the abominations which they committed; therefore I have consumed them in My anger. ⁹Now let them put their harlotry and the carcasses of their kings far away from Me, and I will dwell in their midst forever.

¹⁰"Son of man, describe the temple to the house of Israel, that they may be ashamed of their iniquities; and let them measure the pattern. ¹¹And if they are ashamed of all that they have done, make known to them the design of the temple and its arrangement, its exits and its entrances, its entire design and all its ordinances, all its forms and all its laws. Write *it* down in their sight, so that they may keep its whole design and all its ordinances, and perform them. ¹²This *is* the law of the temple: The whole area surrounding the mountaintop *is* most holy. Behold, this *is* the law of the temple.

Dimensions of the Altar

¹³"These are the measurements of the altar in cubits (the *cubit is* one cubit and a handbreadth): the base one cubit high and one cubit wide, with a rim all around its edge of one span. This *is* the height of the altar: ¹⁴from the base on the ground to the lower ledge, two cubits; the width of the ledge, one cubit; from the smaller ledge to the larger ledge, four cubits; and the width of the ledge, *one* cubit. ¹⁵The altar hearth *is* four cubits high, with four horns extending upward from the hearth. ¹⁶The altar hearth *is* twelve cubits long, twelve wide, square at its four corners; ¹⁷the ledge, fourteen *cubits* long and fourteen wide on its four sides, with a rim of half a cubit around it; its base, one cubit all around; and its steps face toward the east."

Consecrating the Altar

¹⁸And He said to me, "Son of man, thus says the Lord GOD: 'These *are* the ordinances for the

42:16 ᵃCompare 40:5　**43:3** ᵃSome Hebrew manuscripts and Vulgate read *He*.

altar on the day when it is made, for sacrificing burnt offerings on it, and for sprinkling blood on it. [19]You shall give a young bull for a sin offering to the priests, the Levites, who are of the seed of Zadok, who approach Me to minister to Me,' says the Lord GOD. [20]'You shall take some of its blood and put *it* on the four horns of the altar, on the four corners of the ledge, and on the rim around it; thus you shall cleanse it and make atonement for it. [21]Then you shall also take the bull of the sin offering, and burn it in the appointed place of the temple, outside the sanctuary. [22]On the second day you shall offer a kid of the goats without blemish for a sin offering; and they shall cleanse the altar, as they cleansed *it* with the bull. [23]When you have finished cleansing *it,* you shall offer a young bull without blemish, and a ram from the flock without blemish. [24]When you offer them before the LORD, the priests shall throw salt on them, and they will offer them up *as* a burnt offering to the LORD. [25]Every day for seven days you shall prepare a goat *for* a sin offering; they shall also prepare a young bull and a ram from the flock, both without blemish. [26]Seven days they shall make atonement for the altar and purify it, and so consecrate *it.* [27]When these days are over it shall be, on the eighth day and thereafter, that the priests shall offer your burnt offerings and your peace offerings on the altar; and I will accept you,' says the Lord GOD."

The East Gate and the Prince

44 Then He brought me back to the outer gate of the sanctuary which faces toward the east, but it *was* shut. [2]And the LORD said to me, "This gate shall be shut; it shall not be opened, and no man shall enter by it, because the LORD God of Israel has entered by it; therefore it shall be shut. [3]*As for* the prince, *because* he *is* the prince, he may sit in it to eat bread before the LORD; he shall enter by way of the vestibule of the gateway, and go out the same way."

Those Admitted to the Temple

[4]Also He brought me by way of the north gate to the front of the temple; so I looked, and behold, the glory of the LORD filled the house of the LORD; and I fell on my face. [5]And the LORD said to me, "Son of man, mark well, see with your eyes and hear with your ears, all that I say to you concerning all the ordinances of the house of the LORD and all its laws. Mark well who may enter the house and all who go out from the sanctuary.

[6]"Now say to the rebellious, to the house of Israel, Thus says the Lord GOD: "O house of Israel, let Us have no more of all your abominations. [7]When you brought in foreigners, uncircumcised in heart and uncircumcised in flesh, to be in My sanctuary to defile it—My house—and when you offered My food, the fat and the blood, then they broke My covenant because of all your abominations. [8]And you have not kept charge of My holy things, but you have set *others* to keep charge of My sanctuary for you." [9]Thus says the Lord GOD: "No foreigner, uncircumcised in heart or uncircumcised in flesh, shall enter My sanctuary, including any foreigner who *is* among the children of Israel.

Laws Governing Priests

[10]"And the Levites who went far from Me, when Israel went astray, who strayed away from Me after their idols, they shall bear their iniquity. [11]Yet they shall be ministers in My sanctuary, *as* gatekeepers of the house and ministers of the house; they shall slay the burnt offering and the sacrifice for the people, and they shall stand before them to minister to them. [12]Because they ministered to them before their idols and caused the house of Israel to fall into iniquity, therefore I have raised My hand in an oath against them," says the Lord GOD, "that they shall bear their iniquity. [13]And they shall not come near Me to minister to Me as priest, nor come near any of My holy things, nor into the Most Holy *Place;* but they shall bear their shame and their abominations which they have committed. [14]Nevertheless I will make them keep charge of the temple, for all its work, and for all that has to be done in it.

[15]"But the priests, the Levites, the sons of Zadok, who kept charge of My sanctuary when the children of Israel went astray from Me, they shall come near Me to minister to Me; and they shall stand before Me to offer to Me the fat and the blood," says the Lord GOD. [16]"They shall enter My sanctuary, and they shall come near My table to minister to Me, and they shall keep My charge. [17]And it shall be, whenever they enter the gates of the inner court, that they shall put on linen garments; no wool shall come upon them while they minister within the gates of the inner court or within the house. [18]They shall have linen turbans on their heads and linen trousers on their bodies; they shall not clothe themselves with *anything that causes* sweat. [19]When they go out to the outer court, to the *outer* court to the people, they shall take off their garments in which they have ministered, leave them in the holy chambers, and

put on other garments; and in their holy garments they shall not sanctify the people.

20"They shall neither shave their heads, nor let their hair grow long, but they shall keep their hair well trimmed. 21No priest shall drink wine when he enters the inner court. 22They shall not take as wife a widow or a divorced woman, but take virgins of the descendants of the house of Israel, or widows of priests.

23"And they shall teach My people *the differ-ence* between the holy and the unholy, and cause them to discern between the unclean and the clean. 24In controversy they shall stand as judges, *and* judge it according to My judgments. They shall keep My laws and My statutes in all My appointed meetings, and they shall hallow My Sabbaths.

25"They shall not defile *themselves* by coming near a dead person. Only for father or mother, for son or daughter, for brother or unmarried sister may they defile themselves. 26After he is cleansed, they shall count seven days for him. 27And on the day that he goes to the sanctuary to minister in the sanctuary, he must offer his sin offering in the inner court," says the Lord GOD.

28"It shall be, in regard to their inheritance, *that* I *am* their inheritance. You shall give them no possession in Israel, for I *am* their possession. 29They shall eat the grain offering, the sin offering, and the trespass offering; every dedicated thing in Israel shall be theirs. 30The best of all firstfruits of any kind, and every sacrifice of any kind from all your sacrifices, shall be the priest's; also you shall give to the priest the first of your ground meal, to cause a blessing to rest on your house. 31The priests shall not eat anything, bird or beast, that died naturally or was torn *by wild beasts.*

The Holy District

45 "Moreover, when you divide the land by lot into inheritance, you shall set apart a district for the LORD, a holy section of the land; its length *shall be* twenty-five thousand *cubits,* and the width ten thousand. It *shall be* holy throughout its territory all around. 2Of this there shall be a square plot for the sanctuary, five hundred by five hundred *rods,* with fifty cubits around it for an open space. 3So this is the district you shall measure: twenty-five thousand *cubits* long and ten thousand wide; in it shall be the sanctuary, the Most Holy *Place.* 4It shall be a holy *section* of the land, belonging to the priests, the ministers of the sanctuary, who come near to minister to the LORD; it shall be a place for their houses and a holy place for the sanctuary. 5*An area* twenty-five thousand *cubits* long and ten thousand wide shall belong to the Levites, the ministers of the temple; they shall have twenty chambers as a possession.[a]

Properties of the City and the Prince

6"You shall appoint as the property of the city *an area* five thousand *cubits* wide and twenty-five thousand long, adjacent to the district of the holy *section;* it shall belong to the whole house of Israel.

7"The prince shall have *a section* on one side and the other of the holy district and the city's property; and bordering on the holy district and the city's property, extending westward on the west side and eastward on the east side, the length *shall be* side by side with one of the *tribal* portions, from the west border to the east border. 8The land shall be his possession in Israel; and My princes shall no more oppress My people, but they shall give *the rest of* the land to the house of Israel, according to their tribes."

Laws Governing the Prince

9Thus says the Lord GOD: "Enough, O princes of Israel! Remove violence and plundering, execute justice and righteousness, and stop dispossessing My people," says the Lord GOD. 10"You shall have honest scales, an honest ephah, and an honest bath. 11The ephah and the bath shall be of the same measure, so that the bath contains one-tenth of a homer, and the ephah one-tenth of a homer; their measure shall be according to the homer. 12The shekel *shall be* twenty gerahs; twenty shekels, twenty-five shekels, *and* fifteen shekels shall be your mina.

13"This *is* the offering which you shall offer: you shall give one-sixth of an ephah from a homer of wheat, and one-sixth of an ephah from a homer of barley. 14The ordinance concerning oil, the bath of oil, *is* one-tenth of a bath from a kor. A kor *is* a homer or ten baths, for ten baths *are* a homer. 15And one lamb shall be given from a flock of two hundred, from the rich pastures of Israel. These shall be for grain offerings, burnt offerings, and peace offerings, to make atonement for them," says the Lord GOD. 16"All the people of the land shall give this offering for the prince in Israel. 17Then it shall be the prince's part *to give* burnt offerings, grain offerings, and drink offerings, at the feasts, the New Moons, the Sabbaths, and at all the appointed seasons of

---

45:5 [a]Following Masoretic Text, Targum, and Vulgate; Septuagint reads *a possession, cities of dwelling.*

the house of Israel. He shall prepare the sin offering, the grain offering, the burnt offering, and the peace offerings to make atonement for the house of Israel."

Keeping the Feasts

[18]"Thus says the Lord GOD: "In the first *month,* on the first *day* of the month, you shall take a young bull without blemish and cleanse the sanctuary. [19]The priest shall take some of the blood of the sin offering and put *it* on the doorposts of the temple, on the four corners of the ledge of the altar, and on the gateposts of the gate of the inner court. [20]And so you shall do on the seventh *day* of the month for everyone who has sinned unintentionally or in ignorance. Thus you shall make atonement for the temple.

[21]"In the first *month,* on the fourteenth day of the month, you shall observe the Passover, a feast of seven days; unleavened bread shall be eaten. [22]And on that day the prince shall prepare for himself and for all the people of the land a bull *for* a sin offering. [23]On the seven days of the feast he shall prepare a burnt offering to the LORD, seven bulls and seven rams without blemish, daily for seven days, and a kid of the goats daily *for* a sin offering. [24]And he shall prepare a grain offering of one ephah for each bull and one ephah for each ram, together with a hin of oil for each ephah.

[25]"In the seventh *month,* on the fifteenth day of the month, at the feast, he shall do likewise for seven days, according to the sin offering, the burnt offering, the grain offering, and the oil."

The Manner of Worship

46 'Thus says the Lord GOD: "The gateway of the inner court that faces toward the east shall be shut the six working days; but on the Sabbath it shall be opened, and on the day of the New Moon it shall be opened. [2]The prince shall enter by way of the vestibule of the gateway from the outside, and stand by the gatepost. The priests shall prepare his burnt offering and his peace offerings. He shall worship at the threshold of the gate. Then he shall go out, but the gate shall not be shut until evening. [3]Likewise the people of the land shall worship at the entrance to this gateway before the LORD on the Sabbaths and the New Moons. [4]The burnt offering that the prince offers to the LORD on the Sabbath day *shall be* six lambs without blemish, and a ram without blemish; [5]and the grain offering *shall be one* ephah for a ram, and the grain offering for the lambs, as much as he wants to give, as well as a hin of oil

with every ephah. [6]On the day of the New Moon *it shall be* a young bull without blemish, six lambs, and a ram; they shall be without blemish. [7]He shall prepare a grain offering of an ephah for a bull, an ephah for a ram, as much as he wants to give for the lambs, and a hin of oil with every ephah. [8]When the prince enters, he shall go in by way of the vestibule of the gateway, and go out the same way.

[9]"But when the people of the land come before the LORD on the appointed feast days, whoever enters by way of the north gate to worship shall go out by way of the south gate; and whoever enters by way of the south gate shall go out by way of the north gate. He shall not return by way of the gate through which he came, but shall go out through the opposite gate. [10]The prince shall then be in their midst. When they go in, he shall go in; and when they go out, he shall go out. [11]At the festivals and the appointed feast days the grain offering shall be an ephah for a bull, an ephah for a ram, as much as he wants to give for the lambs, and a hin of oil with every ephah.

[12]"Now when the prince makes a voluntary burnt offering or voluntary peace offering to the LORD, the gate that faces toward the east shall then be opened for him; and he shall prepare his burnt offering and his peace offerings as he did on the Sabbath day. Then he shall go out, and after he goes out the gate shall be shut.

[13]"You shall daily make a burnt offering to the LORD *of* a lamb of the first year without blemish; you shall prepare it every morning. [14]And you shall prepare a grain offering with it every morning, a sixth of an ephah, and a third of a hin of oil to moisten the fine flour. This grain offering is a perpetual ordinance, to be made regularly to the LORD. [15]Thus they shall prepare the lamb, the grain offering, and the oil, *as* a regular burnt offering every morning."

The Prince and Inheritance Laws

[16]'Thus says the Lord GOD: "If the prince gives a gift *of some* of his inheritance to any of his sons, it shall belong to his sons; it is their possession by inheritance. [17]But if he gives a gift of some of his inheritance to one of his servants, it shall be his until the year of liberty, after which it shall return to the prince. But his inheritance shall belong to his sons; it shall become theirs. [18]Moreover the prince shall not take any of the people's inheritance by evicting them from their property; he shall provide an inheritance for his sons from his own property, so that none of My people may be scattered from his property." '"

How the Offerings Were Prepared

[19]Now he brought me through the entrance, which *was* at the side of the gate, into the holy chambers of the priests which face toward the north; and there a place *was* situated at their extreme western end. [20]And he said to me, "This *is* the place where the priests shall boil the trespass offering and the sin offering, *and* where they shall bake the grain offering, so that they do not bring *them* out into the outer court to sanctify the people."

[21]Then he brought me out into the outer court and caused me to pass by the four corners of the court; and in fact, in every corner of the court *there was another* court. [22]In the four corners of the court *were* enclosed courts, forty *cubits* long and thirty wide; all four corners *were* the same size. [23]*There was* a row *of building stones* all around in them, all around the four of them; and cooking hearths were made under the rows of stones all around. [24]And he said to me, "These *are* the kitchens where the ministers of the temple shall boil the sacrifices of the people."

The Healing Waters and Trees

47 Then he brought me back to the door of the temple; and there was water, flowing from under the threshold of the temple toward the east, for the front of the temple faced east; the water was flowing from under the right side of the temple, south of the altar. [2]He brought me out by way of the north gate, and led me around on the outside to the outer gateway that faces east; and there was water, running out on the right side.

[3]And when the man went out to the east with the line in his hand, he measured one thousand cubits, and he brought me through the waters; the water *came up to my* ankles. [4]Again he measured one thousand and brought me through the waters; the water *came up to my* knees. Again he measured one thousand and brought me through; the water *came up to my* waist. [5]Again he measured one thousand, *and it was* a river that I could not cross; for the water was too deep, water in which one must swim, a river that could not be crossed. [6]He said to me, "Son of man, have you seen *this*?" Then he brought me and returned me to the bank of the river.

[7]When I returned, there, along the bank of the river, *were* very many trees on one side and the other. [8]Then he said to me: "This water flows toward the eastern region, goes down into the valley, and enters the sea. *When it* reaches the sea, *its* waters are healed. [9]And it shall be *that* every living thing that moves, wherever the rivers go, will live. There will be a very great multitude of fish, because these waters go there; for they will be healed, and everything will live wherever the river goes. [10]It shall be *that* fishermen will stand by it from En Gedi to En Eglaim; they will be *places* for spreading their nets. Their fish will be of the same kinds as the fish of the Great Sea, exceedingly many. [11]But its swamps and marshes will not be healed; they will be given over to salt. [12]Along the bank of the river, on this side and that, will grow all *kinds of* trees used for food; their leaves will not wither, and their fruit will not fail. They will bear fruit every month, because their water flows from the sanctuary. Their fruit will be for food, and their leaves for medicine."

Borders of the Land

[13]Thus says the Lord GOD: "These *are* the borders by which you shall divide the land as an inheritance among the twelve tribes of Israel. Joseph *shall have two* portions. [14]You shall inherit it equally with one another; for I raised My hand in an oath to give it to your fathers, and this land shall fall to you as your inheritance.

[15]"This *shall be* the border of the land on the north: from the Great Sea, *by* the road to Hethlon, as one goes to Zedad, [16]Hamath, Berothah, Sibraim (which *is* between the border of Damascus and the border of Hamath), to Hazar Hatticon (which *is* on the border of Hauran). [17]Thus the boundary shall be from the Sea to Hazar Enan, the border of Damascus; and as for the north, northward, it is the border of Hamath. *This is* the north side.

[18]"On the east side you shall mark out the border from between Hauran and Damascus, and between Gilead and the land of Israel, along the Jordan, and along the eastern side of the sea. *This is* the east side.

[19]"The south side, toward the South,[a] *shall be* from Tamar to the waters of Meribah by Kadesh, along the brook to the Great Sea. *This is* the south side, toward the South.

[20]"The west side *shall be* the Great Sea, from the *southern* boundary until one comes to a point opposite Hamath. This *is* the west side.

[21]"Thus you shall divide this land among yourselves according to the tribes of Israel. [22]It shall be that you will divide it by lot as an inheritance for yourselves, and for the strangers who dwell among you and who bear children among you. They shall be to you as native-born among the children of Israel; they shall have an inheritance with you among the tribes of Israel. [23]And

---

47:19 [a]Hebrew *Negev*

it shall be *that* in whatever tribe the stranger dwells, there you shall give *him* his inheritance," says the Lord GOD.

Division of the Land

48 "Now these *are* the names of the tribes: From the northern border along the road to Hethlon at the entrance of Hamath, to Hazar Enan, the border of Damascus northward, in the direction of Hamath, *there shall be* one *section for* Dan from its east to its west side; ²by the border of Dan, from the east side to the west, one *section for* Asher; ³by the border of Asher, from the east side to the west, one *section for* Naphtali; ⁴by the border of Naphtali, from the east side to the west, one *section for* Manasseh; ⁵by the border of Manasseh, from the east side to the west, one *section for* Ephraim; ⁶by the border of Ephraim, from the east side to the west, one *section for* Reuben; ⁷by the border of Reuben, from the east side to the west, one *section for* Judah; ⁸by the border of Judah, from the east side to the west, shall be the district which you shall set apart, twenty-five thousand *cubits* in width, and *in* length the same as one of the *other* portions, from the east side to the west, with the sanctuary in the center.

⁹"The district that you shall set apart for the LORD *shall be* twenty-five thousand *cubits* in length and ten thousand in width. ¹⁰To these—to the priests—the holy district shall belong: on the north twenty-five thousand *cubits in length,* on the west ten thousand in width, on the east ten thousand in width, and on the south twenty-five thousand in length. The sanctuary of the LORD shall be in the center. ¹¹*It shall be* for the priests of the sons of Zadok, who are sanctified, who have kept My charge, who did not go astray when the children of Israel went astray, as the Levites went astray. ¹²And *this* district of land that is set apart shall be to them a thing most holy by the border of the Levites.

¹³"Opposite the border of the priests, the Levites *shall have an area* twenty-five thousand *cubits* in length and ten thousand in width; its entire length *shall be* twenty-five thousand and its width ten thousand. ¹⁴And they shall not sell or exchange any of it; they may not alienate this best *part* of the land, for *it is* holy to the LORD.

¹⁵"The five thousand *cubits* in width that remain, along the edge of the twenty-five thousand, shall be for general use by the city, for dwellings and common-land; and the city shall be in the center. ¹⁶These *shall be* its measurements: the north side four thousand five hun-

dred *cubits,* the south side four thousand five hundred, the east side four thousand five hundred, and the west side four thousand five hundred. ¹⁷The common-land of the city shall be: to the north two hundred and fifty *cubits,* to the south two hundred and fifty, to the east two hundred and fifty, and to the west two hundred and fifty. ¹⁸The rest of the length, alongside the district of the holy *section, shall be* ten thousand *cubits* to the east and ten thousand to the west. It shall be adjacent to the district of the holy *section,* and its produce shall be food for the workers of the city. ¹⁹The workers of the city, from all the tribes of Israel, shall cultivate it. ²⁰The entire district *shall be* twenty-five thousand *cubits* by twenty-five thousand *cubits,* foursquare. You shall set apart the holy district with the property of the city.

²¹"The rest *shall belong* to the prince, on one side and on the other of the holy district and of the city's property, next to the twenty-five thousand *cubits* of the *holy* district as far as the eastern border, and westward next to the twenty-five thousand as far as the western border, adjacent to the *tribal* portions; *it shall belong* to the prince. It shall be the holy district, and the sanctuary of the temple *shall be* in the center. ²²Moreover, apart from the possession of the Levites and the possession of the city *which are* in the midst of what *belongs* to the prince, *the area* between the border of Judah and the border of Benjamin shall belong to the prince.

²³"As for the rest of the tribes, from the east side to the west, Benjamin *shall have* one *section;* ²⁴by the border of Benjamin, from the east side to the west, Simeon *shall have* one *section;* ²⁵by the border of Simeon, from the east side to the west, Issachar *shall have* one *section;* ²⁶by the border of Issachar, from the east side to the west, Zebulun *shall have* one *section;* ²⁷by the border of Zebulun, from the east side to the west, Gad *shall have* one *section;* ²⁸by the border of Gad, on the south side, toward the South,[a] the border shall be from Tamar *to* the waters of Meribah *by* Kadesh, along the brook to the Great Sea. ²⁹This *is* the land which you shall divide by lot as an inheritance among the tribes of Israel, and these *are* their portions," says the Lord GOD.

The Gates of the City and Its Name

³⁰"These *are* the exits of the city. On the north side, measuring four thousand five hundred *cubits* ³¹(the gates of the city *shall be* named after the tribes of Israel), the three gates north-

---

48:28 ᵃHebrew *Negev*

ward: one gate for Reuben, one gate for Judah, and one gate for Levi; [32]on the east side, four thousand five hundred *cubits,* three gates: one gate for Joseph, one gate for Benjamin, and one gate for Dan; [33]on the south side, measuring four thousand five hundred *cubits,* three gates: one gate for Simeon, one gate for Issachar, and one gate for Zebulun; [34]on the west side, four thou-sand five hundred *cubits* with their three gates: one gate for Gad, one gate for Asher, and one gate for Naphtali. [35]All the way around *shall be* eighteen thousand *cubits;* and the name of the city from *that* day *shall be:* THE LORD *IS* THERE."[a]

48:35 [a]Hebrew *YHWH Shammah*

DANIEL
Faith and Leadership in Action

SUMMARY

The exemplary personal character of Daniel makes him a favorite Bible personality for many. He is one of only a handful of men in the Bible about whom God says nothing negative. Although he shared the human nature of all other biblical leaders, he seems to rise above the others because of a combination of qualities:

- **Character**—He displays character by refusing to do wrong before foreign kings.
- **Competence**—Kings offer to pay him for his ability to interpret dreams.
- **Convictions**—He refuses to eat the king's meat or drink his wine.
- **Courage**—He faces the lions' den without flinching.
- **Charisma**—He is so winsome that royalty wants him to play key roles in government.
- **Commitment**—He remains committed to his God despite pressure to compromise.
- **Compassion**—He never loses his love for others, even in an enemy culture.

In the early chapters of the book, we see Daniel and his Hebrew friends in action as they live out their faith and leadership in a foreign land. Daniel stands up to king Nebuchadnezzar and requests that he and his friends be allowed to eat something other than what fills the plates of the other young men in the palace. He negotiates terms and ends up stronger and healthier for his decision. This catches the attention of the Babylonian officials and Daniel becomes a man of influence, even as a youth. Soon, he is interpreting dreams for the king, offering wise counsel to officials, and demonstrating a commitment to his faith rare for anyone, young or old.

Before he is through, Daniel has left a legacy stretching over the reigns of three kings, both Babylonian and Persian. He was a leader who lived the life God meant him to live. As he aged, he moved from interpreter of dreams to a dreamer himself—providing prophetic insight into the end times. He delivered his deep and complex words from a pure heart, showing himself to be a man who loved God, lived his faith, and wanted to influence many others to embrace Yahweh. As you read the book, watch for Daniel, Shadrach, Meshach, and Abednego to demonstrate leadership powerful enough to influence entire people groups to follow.

God's Role in Daniel

Old Testament leaders succeeded as long as they stayed intimately connected to God. Daniel proves this pattern. God continually blessed Daniel with wisdom, skills, and favor, as long as Daniel maintained his character and courage.

God led Daniel faithfully from the time he was a young boy. By the time of the Babylonian captivity, Daniel and his friends had followed Yahweh for years. They continued this lifestyle as adults, and God not only blessed them but bailed them out of dangerous and even deadly situations.

The Book of Daniel serves as a powerful illustration of what can happen when God and a healthy, spiritual leader cooperate to reach their world.

Leaders in Daniel

Daniel, Nebuchadnezzar, Darius, Belshazzar

Other People of Influence in Daniel

Shardrach, Meshach, Abednego, the king's officials

Lessons in Leadership

- Leaders must first possess godly qualities before they develop skills.
- Commitment precedes everything—resources will follow a leader's resolve.
- Leaders must often stand alone as they begin their journey.
- To identify the leader in a group, look for the one to whom everyone listens.
- A gift may take a leader to the top, but humility enables him to endure.
- Spiritual leaders talk to God about people before talking to people about God.
- Godly leaders do not pursue their own fame, but are out to make God famous.

LEADERSHIP

HIGHLIGHTS IN DANIEL

CHARACTER: Daniel Had What It Took! (2:48)	*page 1025*
NEBUCHADNEZZAR: Face-to-Face with the Majesty of God (3:1–30)	*page 1027*
SHADRACH, MESHACH, AND ABED-NEGO: Courage Fueled by Faith (3:16–18)	*page 1028*
TEACHABILITY: The King Is Slow to Learn (4:1–37)	*page 1031*
THE LAW OF E. F. HUTTON: When Daniel Speaks, People Listen (5:13, 14)	*page 1033*
DANIEL: A Man Who Sought Understanding (8:15, 17, 27)	*page 1037*

Daniel and His Friends Obey God

1 In the third year of the reign of Jehoiakim king of Judah, Nebuchadnezzar king of Babylon came to Jerusalem and besieged it. [2]And the Lord gave Jehoiakim king of Judah into his hand, with some of the articles of the house of God, which he carried into the land of Shinar to the house of his god; and he brought the articles into the treasure house of his god.

[3]Then the king instructed Ashpenaz, the master of his eunuchs, to bring some of the children of Israel and some of the king's descendants and some of the nobles, [4]young men in whom *there was* no blemish, but good-looking, gifted in all wisdom, possessing knowledge and quick to understand, who *had* ability to serve in the king's palace, and whom they might teach the language and literature of the Chaldeans. [5]And the king appointed for them a daily provision of the king's delicacies and of the wine which he drank, and three years of training for them, so that at the end of *that time* they might serve before the king. [6]Now from among those of the sons of Judah were Daniel, Hananiah, Mishael, and Azariah. [7]To them the chief of the eunuchs gave names: he gave Daniel *the name* Belteshazzar; to Hananiah, Shadrach; to Mishael, Meshach; and to Azariah, Abed-Nego.

[8]But Daniel purposed in his heart that he would not defile himself with the portion of the king's delicacies, nor with the wine which he drank; therefore he requested of the chief of the eunuchs that he might not defile himself. [9]Now God had brought Daniel into the favor and goodwill of the chief of the eunuchs. [10]And the chief of the eunuchs said to Daniel, "I fear my lord the king, who has appointed your food and drink. For why should he see your faces looking worse than the young men who *are* your age? Then you would endanger my head before the king."

[11]So Daniel said to the steward[a] whom the chief of the eunuchs had set over Daniel, Hananiah, Mishael, and Azariah, [12]"Please test your servants for ten days, and let them give us vegetables to eat and water to drink. [13]Then let our appearance be examined before you, and the appearance of the young men who eat the portion of the king's delicacies; and as you see fit, *so deal* with your servants." [14]So he consented with them in this matter, and tested them ten days.

[15]And at the end of ten days their features appeared better and fatter in flesh than all the young men who ate the portion of the king's

---

1:11 [a]Hebrew *Melzar*, also in verse 16

Leadership Qualifications:
Prerequisite for Responsibility
(Daniel 1:4–19)

The victorious Babylonians took Daniel and other sharp, young Hebrews to their king, who wanted to groom them as leaders. What qualities did the king seek? Take a look and see if you would like to have such emerging leaders working alongside of you!

1. **Young (v. 4).** They were youths, still young enough to be trained.
2. **Sharp looking (v. 4).** They were well-groomed and well-dressed.
3. **Intelligent (v. 4).** They had good minds and could process information quickly.
4. **Diverse skills (v. 4).** They displayed a variety of skills.
5. **Competent (v. 4).** They showed wisdom in using their skills to achieve results.
6. **Servant's heart (v. 4).** They served others however they might be needed.
7. **Teachable (vv. 4, 5).** They were able and hungry to learn new concepts.
8. **Convictional (v. 8).** They possessed inward strength and values.
9. **Favor with people (v. 9).** They enjoyed influence with others.
10. **Submissive (v. 12).** They willingly became team players.
11. **Relational (v. 12).** They had good people skills and charisma.
12. **Well-informed (v. 17).** They possessed knowledge in a variety of areas.
13. **Gifted (v. 17).** They had valuable abilities obvious to others.
14. **Excellence (v. 19).** They were men of excellence and high standards.

delicacies. [16]Thus the steward took away their portion of delicacies and the wine that they were to drink, and gave them vegetables.

[17]As for these four young men, God gave them knowledge and skill in all literature and wisdom; and Daniel had understanding in all visions and dreams.

[18]Now at the end of the days, when the king had said that they should be brought in, the chief of the eunuchs brought them in before Nebuchadnezzar. [19]Then the king interviewed[a] them, and among them all none was found like Daniel, Hananiah, Mishael, and Azariah; therefore they served before the king. [20]And in all matters of wisdom *and* understanding about which the king examined them, he found them ten times better than all the magicians *and* astrologers who *were* in all his realm. [21]Thus Daniel continued until the first year of King Cyrus.

Nebuchadnezzar's Dream

2 Now in the second year of Nebuchadnezzar's reign, Nebuchadnezzar had dreams; and his spirit was *so* troubled that his sleep left him. [2]Then the king gave the command to call the magicians, the astrologers, the sorcerers, and the Chaldeans to tell the king his dreams. So they came and stood before the king. [3]And the king said to them, "I have had a dream, and my spirit is anxious to know the dream."

[4]Then the Chaldeans spoke to the king in Aramaic,[a] "O king, live forever! Tell your servants the dream, and we will give the interpretation."

[5]The king answered and said to the Chaldeans, "My decision is firm: if you do not make known the dream to me, and its interpretation, you shall be cut in pieces, and your houses shall be made an ash heap. [6]However, if you tell the dream and its interpretation, you shall receive from me gifts, rewards, and great honor. Therefore tell me the dream and its interpretation."

[7]They answered again and said, "Let the king tell his servants the dream, and we will give its interpretation."

[8]The king answered and said, "I know for certain that you would gain time, because you see that my decision is firm: [9]if you do not make known the dream to me, *there is only* one decree for you! For you have agreed to speak lying and corrupt words before me till the time has changed. Therefore tell me the dream, and I shall know that you can give me its interpretation."

[10]The Chaldeans answered the king, and said, "There is not a man on earth who can tell the king's matter; therefore no king, lord, or ruler has

ever asked such things of any magician, astrologer, or Chaldean. [11]*It is* a difficult thing that the king requests, and there is no other who can tell it to the king except the gods, whose dwelling is not with flesh."

[12]For this reason the king was angry and very furious, and gave the command to destroy all the wise *men* of Babylon. [13]So the decree went out, and they began killing the wise *men;* and they sought Daniel and his companions, to kill *them.*

Nebuchadnezzar and Daniel: A Contrast in Pride and Humility

(Daniel 2:1–28)

When the magicians of Babylon fail to interpret a troubling dream, Nebuchadnezzar threatens to kill them all. He embodies pride and arrogance. Contrast him with Daniel, who steps forward to interpret the dream, yet refuses to accept personal glory. Instead, he honors the God of heaven.

God Reveals Nebuchadnezzar's Dream

[14]Then with counsel and wisdom Daniel answered Arioch, the captain of the king's guard, who had gone out to kill the wise *men* of Babylon; [15]he answered and said to Arioch the king's captain, "Why is the decree from the king so urgent?" Then Arioch made the decision known to Daniel.

[16]So Daniel went in and asked the king to give him time, that he might tell the king the interpretation. [17]Then Daniel went to his house, and made the decision known to Hananiah, Mishael, and Azariah, his companions, [18]that they might seek mercies from the God of heaven concerning this secret, so that Daniel and his companions might not perish with the rest of the wise *men* of Babylon. [19]Then the secret was revealed to Daniel in a night vision. So Daniel blessed the God of heaven.

[20]Daniel answered and said:

"Blessed be the name of God forever and ever,
For wisdom and might are His.

1:19 [a]Literally *talked with them* **2:4** [a]The original language of Daniel 2:4b through 7:28 is Aramaic.

21 And He changes the times and the seasons;
   He removes kings and raises up kings;
   He gives wisdom to the wise
   And knowledge to those who have
      understanding.
22 He reveals deep and secret things;
   He knows what *is* in the darkness,
   And light dwells with Him.

23 "I thank You and praise You,
   O God of my fathers;
   You have given me wisdom and might,
   And have now made known to me what
      we asked of You,
   For You have made known to us the king's
      demand."

Daniel Explains the Dream

24Therefore Daniel went to Arioch, whom the king had appointed to destroy the wise *men* of Babylon. He went and said thus to him: "Do not destroy the wise *men* of Babylon; take me before the king, and I will tell the king the interpretation."

25Then Arioch quickly brought Daniel before the king, and said thus to him, "I have found a man of the captives[a] of Judah, who will make known to the king the interpretation."

26The king answered and said to Daniel, whose name *was* Belteshazzar, "Are you able to make known to me the dream which I have seen, and its interpretation?"

27Daniel answered in the presence of the king, and said, "The secret which the king has demanded, the wise *men,* the astrologers, the magicians, and the soothsayers cannot declare to the king. 28But there is a God in heaven who reveals secrets, and He has made known to King Nebuchadnezzar what will be in the latter days. Your dream, and the visions of your head upon your bed, were these: 29As for you, O king, thoughts came *to* your *mind while* on your bed, *about* what would come to pass after this; and He who reveals secrets has made known to you what will be. 30But as for me, this secret has not been revealed to me because I have more wisdom than anyone living, but for *our* sakes who make known the interpretation to the king, and that you may know the thoughts of your heart.

31"You, O king, were watching; and behold, a great image! This great image, whose splendor *was* excellent, stood before you; and its form *was* awesome. 32This image's head *was* of fine gold, its chest and arms of silver, its belly and thighs[a] of bronze, 33its legs of iron, its feet partly of iron and partly of clay.[a] 34You watched while a stone was

cut out without hands, which struck the image on its feet of iron and clay, and broke them in pieces. 35Then the iron, the clay, the bronze, the silver, and the gold were crushed together, and became like chaff from the summer threshing floors; the wind carried them away so that no trace of them was found. And the stone that struck the image became a great mountain and filled the whole earth.

36"This *is* the dream. Now we will tell the interpretation of it before the king. 37You, O king, *are* a king of kings. For the God of heaven has given you a kingdom, power, strength, and glory; 38and wherever the children of men dwell, or the beasts of the field and the birds of the heaven, He has given *them* into your hand, and has made you ruler over them all—you *are* this head of gold. 39But after you shall arise another kingdom inferior to yours; then another, a third kingdom of bronze, which shall rule over all the earth. 40And the fourth kingdom shall be as strong as iron, inasmuch as iron breaks in pieces and shatters everything; and like iron that crushes, *that kingdom* will break in pieces and crush all the others. 41Whereas you saw the feet and toes, partly of potter's clay and partly of iron, the kingdom shall be divided; yet the strength of the iron shall be in it, just as you saw the iron mixed with ceramic clay. 42And *as* the toes of the feet *were* partly of iron and partly of clay, *so* the kingdom shall be partly strong and partly fragile. 43As you saw iron mixed with ceramic clay, they will mingle with the seed of men; but they will not adhere to one another, just as iron does not mix with clay. 44And in the days of these kings the God of heaven will set up a kingdom which shall never be destroyed; and the kingdom shall not be left to other people; it shall break in pieces and consume all these kingdoms, and it shall stand forever. 45Inasmuch as you saw that the stone was cut out of the mountain without hands, and that it broke in pieces the iron, the bronze, the clay, the silver, and the gold—the great God has made known to the king what will come to pass after this. The dream is certain, and its interpretation is sure."

Daniel and His Friends Promoted

46Then King Nebuchadnezzar fell on his face, prostrate before Daniel, and commanded that they should present an offering and incense to him. 47The king answered Daniel, and said, "Truly your God *is* the God of gods, the Lord of

---

2:25 [a]Literally *of the sons of the captivity* **2:32** [a]Or *sides* **2:33** [a]Or *baked clay,* and so in verses 34, 35, and 42

21 QUALITIES

CHARACTER

Daniel Had What It Took!

(Daniel 2:48)

Does the private life of a leader truly impact his or her public life? No question about it. Daniel illustrates why character plays such a vital role.

Daniel could have tried merely to survive his experience as a captive in a foreign land. Instead, he never left his disciplined life of character and personal commitment. Ponder the character he displayed during his times of testing under the kings of Babylon:

1. **His Diet:** He wouldn't compromise on ritually unclean foods, but ate only vegetables.
2. **His Motives:** He didn't take credit for interpreting dreams, but glorified God instead.
3. **His Honesty:** He spoke the truth to authorities, regardless of its unpopularity.
4. **His Disciplines:** He continued praying daily, even though it might cost him his life.
5. **His Integrity:** He had no interest in bribes or payoffs.
6. **His Convictions:** He stayed committed to his friends and beliefs even as he rose through the ranks.

How a leader deals with the circumstances of life tells you many things about his character. Crisis doesn't necessarily *make* character, but it certainly does *reveal* it. Adversity makes a person choose one of two paths: character or compromise. Every time a leader chooses character, he grows stronger.

Character is the foundation on which a leader builds his or her life. It all begins with character, because leadership operates on the basis of trust. People will follow a leader only so far as they trust him or her. Character communicates credibility, harnesses respect, creates consistency, and earns trust.

Every leader must know the following about character:

1. **Character is more than talk.** Anyone can *say* that he has integrity, but action is the real indicator of character. Your character determines who you are and what you do. That's why you can never separate a leader's character from his actions. If a leader's actions and intentions continually work against each other, look to his character to find out why.
2. **Talent is a gift, but character is a choice.** We have no control over a lot of things in life. We don't get to choose our parents or the circumstances of our birth and upbringing. But we do choose our character. We create it each time we make choices.
3. **Character brings lasting success with people.** True leadership always involves others. Followers do not trust leaders whose character they know to be flawed, and they will not continue to follow them.
4. **Leaders cannot rise above the limitations of their character.** Character will either limit or support a leader, depending on its strength. It will always determine whether a leader finishes well.

For a negative example of character, see p. 1340.

kings, and a revealer of secrets, since you could reveal this secret." [48]Then the king promoted Daniel and gave him many great gifts; and he made him ruler over the whole province of Babylon, and chief administrator over all the wise *men* of Babylon. [49]Also Daniel petitioned the king, and he set Shadrach, Meshach, and Abed-Nego over the affairs of the province of Babylon; but Daniel *sat* in the gate[a] of the king.

The Image of Gold

3 Nebuchadnezzar the king made an image of gold, whose height *was* sixty cubits *and* its width six cubits. He set it up in the plain of Dura, in the province of Babylon. [2]And King Nebuchadnezzar sent *word* to gather together the satraps, the administrators, the governors, the counselors, the treasurers, the judges, the magistrates, and all the officials of the provinces, to come to the dedication of the image which King Nebuchadnezzar had set up. [3]So the satraps, the administrators, the governors, the counselors, the treasurers, the judges, the magistrates, and all the officials of the provinces gathered together for the dedication of the image that King Nebuchadnezzar had set up; and they stood before the image that Nebuchadnezzar had set up. [4]Then a herald cried aloud: "To you it is commanded, O peoples, nations, and languages, [5]*that* at the time you hear the sound of the horn, flute, harp, lyre, *and* psaltery, in symphony with all kinds of music, you shall fall down and worship the gold image that King Nebuchadnezzar has set up; [6]and whoever does not fall down and worship shall be cast immediately into the midst of a burning fiery furnace."

[7]So at that time, when all the people heard the sound of the horn, flute, harp, *and* lyre, in symphony with all kinds of music, all the people, nations, and languages fell down *and* worshiped the gold image which King Nebuchadnezzar had set up.

Daniel's Friends Disobey the King

[8]Therefore at that time certain Chaldeans came forward and accused the Jews. [9]They spoke and said to King Nebuchadnezzar, "O king, live forever! [10]You, O king, have made a decree that everyone who hears the sound of the horn, flute, harp, lyre, *and* psaltery, in symphony with all kinds of music, shall fall down and worship the gold image; [11]and whoever does not fall down and worship shall be cast into the midst of a burning fiery furnace. [12]There are certain Jews whom you have set over the affairs of the province of Babylon: Shadrach, Meshach, and Abed-Nego; these

men, O king, have not paid due regard to you. They do not serve your gods or worship the gold image which you have set up."

Commitment: When a Leader Has Resolve, Resources Follow

(Daniel 3:1–18)

When the three friends of Daniel refused to worship a statue Nebuchadnezzar had made, they told the king that they expected their God to deliver them. Immediately afterwards they made a bold statement of commitment: "But if not, let it be known to you, O king, that we do not serve your gods, nor will we worship the gold image which you have set up" (Dan. 3:18). The second statement did not dilute the first, but simply declared the men's resolve.

Once we make a commitment, the resources follow—but they seldom follow until we declare our commitment. From this text we learn the following about developing commitment:

1. It usually begins with a struggle.
2. It seldom surrounds abilities or gifts.
3. It is the result of choice, not condition.
4. It is fostered when we settle the issue before it arises.
5. It is enhanced by deep trust in God.
6. It lasts when we remain single-minded.

[13]Then Nebuchadnezzar, in rage and fury, gave the command to bring Shadrach, Meshach, and Abed-Nego. So they brought these men before the king. [14]Nebuchadnezzar spoke, saying to them, "*Is it* true, Shadrach, Meshach, and Abed-Nego, *that* you do not serve my gods or worship the gold image which I have set up? [15]Now if you are ready at the time you hear the sound of the horn, flute, harp, lyre, *and* psaltery, in symphony with all kinds of music, and you fall down and worship the image which I have made, *good!* But if you do not worship, you shall be cast immediately into the midst of a burning fiery furnace. And who *is* the god who will deliver you from my hands?"

[16]Shadrach, Meshach, and Abed-Nego answered and said to the king, "O Nebuchadnez-

2:49 [a]That is, the king's court

zar, we have no need to answer you in this matter. [17]If that *is the case,* our God whom we serve is able to deliver us from the burning fiery furnace, and He will deliver *us* from your hand, O king. [18]But if not, let it be known to you, O king, that we do not serve your gods, nor will we worship the gold image which you have set up."

Saved in Fiery Trial

[19]Then Nebuchadnezzar was full of fury, and the expression on his face changed toward Shadrach, Meshach, and Abed-Nego. He spoke and commanded that they heat the furnace seven times more than it was usually heated. [20]And he commanded certain mighty men of valor who *were* in his army to bind Shadrach, Meshach, and Abed-Nego, *and* cast *them* into the burning fiery furnace. [21]Then these men were bound in their coats, their trousers, their turbans, and their *other* garments, and were cast into the midst of the burning fiery furnace. [22]Therefore, because the king's command was urgent, and the furnace exceedingly hot, the flame of the fire killed those men who took up Shadrach, Meshach, and Abed-Nego. [23]And these three men, Shadrach, Meshach, and Abed-Nego, fell down bound into the midst of the burning fiery furnace.

[24]Then King Nebuchadnezzar was astonished; and he rose in haste *and* spoke, saying to his counselors, "Did we not cast three men bound into the midst of the fire?"

They answered and said to the king, "True, O king."

[25]"Look!" he answered, "I see four men loose, walking in the midst of the fire; and they are not hurt, and the form of the fourth is like the Son of God."[a]

Nebuchadnezzar Praises God

[26]Then Nebuchadnezzar went near the mouth of the burning fiery furnace *and* spoke, saying, "Shadrach, Meshach, and Abed-Nego, servants of the Most High God, come out, and come *here.*" Then Shadrach, Meshach, and Abed-Nego came from the midst of the fire. [27]And the satraps, administrators, governors, and the king's counselors gathered together, and they saw these men on whose bodies the fire had no power; the hair of their head was not singed nor were their garments affected, and the smell of fire was not on them.

[28]Nebuchadnezzar spoke, saying, "Blessed be

3:25 [a]Or *a son of the gods*

NEBUCHADNEZZAR

FACE-TO-FACE WITH THE MAJESTY OF GOD
(Daniel 3:1–30)

PROFILE IN LEADERSHIP

While King Nebuchadnezzar provides a great example of a leader with seriously misplaced passion, he provides an even better example of what happens when a man comes face-to-face with the majesty of the living God.

Nebuchadnezzar, full of pride, created a 90-foot-high golden "god" whom all of his subjects were ordered to worship. It must have been a magnificent sight, gleaming brightly and all alone in the glare of the hot Mesopotamian sun.

But it was *just* a statue.

Nebuchadnezzar, a leader of great passion, threatened to kill anyone who disobeyed his orders. When three of God's servants refused to bow down, the king flew into a rage and ordered them burned alive. On that day, the king saw up close the infinite difference between the God of Israel and the idol he had set up. Before the king's bedazzled eyes, God performed a great miracle that left Nebuchadnezzar and the other witnesses gaping in awe.

The king would never be the same. He turned from his idol to the God whose people he had once persecuted. He praised the Lord and demanded that his subjects worship Him alone.

Godly leaders should ask the Lord to show them regular glimpses of His power and glory. When He does that, it becomes much easier to direct our passion toward serving the one, true God.

the God of Shadrach, Meshach, and Abed-Nego, who sent His Angel[a] and delivered His servants who trusted in Him, and they have frustrated the king's word, and yielded their bodies, that they should not serve nor worship any god except their own God! [29]Therefore I make a decree that any people, nation, or language which speaks anything amiss against the God of Shadrach, Meshach, and Abed-Nego shall be cut in pieces, and their houses shall be made an ash heap; because there is no other God who can deliver like this."

[30]Then the king promoted Shadrach, Meshach, and Abed-Nego in the province of Babylon.

Nebuchadnezzar's Second Dream

4 Nebuchadnezzar the king,

To all peoples, nations, and languages that dwell in all the earth:

Peace be multiplied to you.

[2] I thought it good to declare the signs and wonders that the Most High God has worked for me.

[3] How great *are* His signs,
And how mighty His wonders!
His kingdom *is* an everlasting kingdom,
And His dominion *is* from generation to generation.

[4] I, Nebuchadnezzar, was at rest in my house, and flourishing in my palace. [5]I saw a dream which made me afraid, and the thoughts on my bed and the visions of my head troubled me. [6]Therefore I issued a decree to bring in all the wise *men* of Babylon before me, that they might make known to me the interpretation of the dream. [7]Then the magicians, the astrologers, the Chaldeans, and the soothsayers came in, and I told them the dream; but they did not make known to me its interpretation. [8]But at last Daniel came before me (his name *is* Belteshazzar, according to the name of my god; in him *is* the Spirit of the Holy God), and I told the dream before him, *saying:* [9]"Belteshazzar, chief of the magicians, because I know that the Spirit of the Holy

3:28 [a]Or *angel*

SHADRACH, MESHACH, AND ABED-NEGO

COURAGE FUELED BY FAITH
(Daniel 3:16–18)

Every leader will at some point reach a crossroads of faith, when he or she has to take a stand—even at the risk of great personal loss.

Shadrach, Meshach, and Abed-Nego faced such a moment. They were given one simple choice: bow or die. There would be no bargaining, no compromise, no "meeting halfway." Nebuchadnezzar ordered them to bow to his idol, or be reduced to ashes. They chose the furnace.

How could they resist such peer pressure and deadly threats? Their speech gives us several clues:

1. *"Our God . . . is able to deliver us"* (v. 17). They believed in the *omnipotence* of God, that nothing was too hard for Him.
2. *"He will deliver us"* (v. 17). They believed in the *love* of God that acts on behalf of the beloved.
3. *"But if not . . ."* (v. 18). They believed in the *sovereignty* of God, that He acts on the basis of His own pleasure and will.
4. *"Our God whom we serve . . ."* (v. 17). They not only believed certain things, they acted on them, and had done so all of their lives.

All leaders will face times of testing when they will be ordered to "bow." During those times they need the courage and conviction to say, "I will *never* bow!"

Competence: People Come to See a Gift in Action

(Daniel 4:8)

Although Nebuchadnezzar pays lip service to the Most High God after seeing Him in action, he still thinks too highly of himself. So God gives him a vision about how he will be humbled. Once again, Daniel is called upon to interpret a dream, since all recognize him as the only one with the ability to explain such visions.

When a leader operates in the area of his or her gift, people *will* watch and listen. Competence is a key attribute for every leader. Without even knowing it, followers ask four questions of every leader:

1. **Knowledge:** Does the leader know where he is going?
2. **Desire:** Do I want to go where the leader is going?
3. **Ability:** Can the leader get me there?
4. **Trust:** Do I trust this leader?

Because Daniel could answer "yes" to each of these questions, he entered each challenge primed to succeed. He enjoyed peace, not panic; faith, not fear; and commitment, not compromise.

Every leader must ask, "What is my gift? What do I offer that people need? What unique contribution do I make that makes people want to follow me?"

God *is* in you, and no secret troubles you, explain to me the visions of my dream that I have seen, and its interpretation.

10 "These *were* the visions of my head *while* on my bed:

I was looking, and behold,
A tree in the midst of the earth,
And its height was great.
11 The tree grew and became strong;
Its height reached to the heavens,
And it could be seen to the ends of all the earth.
12 Its leaves *were* lovely,
Its fruit abundant,
And in it *was* food for all.
The beasts of the field found shade under it,
The birds of the heavens dwelt in its branches,
And all flesh was fed from it.

13 "I saw in the visions of my head *while* on my bed, and there was a watcher, a holy one, coming down from heaven. 14 He cried aloud and said thus:

'Chop down the tree and cut off its branches,
Strip off its leaves and scatter its fruit.

Let the beasts get out from under it,
And the birds from its branches.
15 Nevertheless leave the stump and roots in the earth,
Bound with a band of iron and bronze,
In the tender grass of the field.
Let it be wet with the dew of heaven,
And *let* him graze with the beasts
On the grass of the earth.
16 Let his heart be changed from *that of* a man,
Let him be given the heart of a beast,
And let seven times[a] pass over him.

17 'This decision *is* by the decree of the watchers,
And the sentence by the word of the holy ones,
In order that the living may know
That the Most High rules in the kingdom of men,
Gives it to whomever He will,
And sets over it the lowest of men.'

18 "This dream I, King Nebuchadnezzar, have seen. Now you, Belteshazzar, declare its interpretation, since all the wise *men* of my kingdom are not able to make known to

---

4:16 [a]Possibly *seven years,* and so in verses 23, 25, and 32

me the interpretation; but you *are* able, for the Spirit of the Holy God *is* in you."

Daniel Explains the Second Dream

19 Then Daniel, whose name was Belteshazzar, was astonished for a time, and his thoughts troubled him. *So* the king spoke, and said, "Belteshazzar, do not let the dream or its interpretation trouble you."

Belteshazzar answered and said, "My lord, *may* the dream concern those who hate you, and its interpretation concern your enemies!

20 "The tree that you saw, which grew and became strong, whose height reached to the heavens and which *could be seen* by all the earth, 21whose leaves *were* lovely and its fruit abundant, in which *was* food for all, under which the beasts of the field dwelt, and in whose branches the birds of the heaven had their home— 22it *is* you, O king, who have grown and become strong; for your greatness has grown and reaches to the heavens, and your dominion to the end of the earth.

23 "And inasmuch as the king saw a watcher, a holy one, coming down from heaven and saying, 'Chop down the tree and destroy it, but leave its stump and roots in the earth, *bound* with a band of iron and bronze in the tender grass of the field; let it be wet with the dew of heaven, and let him graze with the beasts of the field, till seven times pass over him'; 24this is the interpretation, O king, and this is the decree of the Most High, which has come upon my lord the king: 25They shall drive you from men, your dwelling shall be with the beasts of the field, and they shall make you eat grass like oxen. They shall wet you with the dew of heaven, and seven times shall pass over you, till you know that the Most High rules in the kingdom of men, and gives it to whomever He chooses.

26 "And inasmuch as they gave the command to leave the stump *and* roots of the tree, your kingdom shall be assured to you, after you come to know that Heaven rules. 27Therefore, O king, let my advice be acceptable to you; break off your sins by *being* righteous, and your iniquities by showing mercy to *the* poor. Perhaps there may be a lengthening of your prosperity."

Nebuchadnezzar's Humiliation

28 All *this* came upon King Nebuchadnezzar. 29At the end of the twelve months he was walking about the royal palace of Babylon. 30The king spoke, saying, "Is not this great Babylon, that I have built for a royal dwelling by my mighty power and for the honor of my majesty?"

31 While the word *was still* in the king's mouth, a voice fell from heaven: "King Nebuchadnezzar, to you it is spoken: the kingdom has departed from you! 32And they shall drive you from men, and your dwelling *shall be* with the beasts of the field. They shall make you eat grass like oxen; and seven times shall pass over you, until you know that the Most High rules in the kingdom of men, and gives it to whomever He chooses."

33 That very hour the word was fulfilled concerning Nebuchadnezzar; he was driven from men and ate grass like oxen; his body was wet with the dew of heaven till his hair had grown like eagles' *feathers* and his nails like birds' *claws*.

Nebuchadnezzar Praises God

34 And at the end of the time[a] I, Nebuchadnezzar, lifted my eyes to heaven, and my understanding returned to me; and I blessed the Most High and praised and honored Him who lives forever:

For His dominion *is* an everlasting dominion,
And His kingdom *is* from generation to generation.
35 All the inhabitants of the earth *are* reputed as nothing;
He does according to His will in the army of heaven
And *among* the inhabitants of the earth.
No one can restrain His hand
Or say to Him, "What have You done?"

36 At the same time my reason returned to me, and for the glory of my kingdom, my honor and splendor returned to me. My counselors and nobles resorted to me, I was restored to my kingdom, and excellent majesty was

4:34 [a]Literally *days*

TEACHABILITY

The King Is Slow to Learn
(Daniel 4:1–37)

King Nebuchadnezzar proved himself to be one of the most arrogant leaders in history, so self-centered and prideful that God dealt with him in a most unusual way.

God gave the king a vision of a huge tree, chopped down by an angel. The tree represented *him*. God removed him from his position and drove him into the wilderness to live like an animal. His hair and fingernails grew long; he ate the same diet as the beasts of the field; he dwelt in caves and dirt shelters. And he stayed out there until he fully recognized God as the supreme Ruler of the world. He had to learn submission, relinquish control and power, and become teachable.

Fortunately, God's discipline worked. Once the king returned to the palace, he became a different man. He no longer laid claim to sovereignty or wisdom. He perceived his greatness as God-given (Dan. 4:36). He sought to honor God rather than himself as the source of every good thing (4:37). Notice how Nebuchadnezzar developed a teachable spirit:

1. Grateful Words
The king expressed appreciation and blessing for God's grace and mercy.

2. Hungry Mind
The king possessed a passion and hunger for personal growth.

3. Big-picture Perspective
The king saw things from a new, larger viewpoint.

4. Dissatisfaction with the Present
The king did not feel content with the status quo or mediocrity.

5. Humble Heart
The king expressed humility regarding his own importance and power.

6. Magnetic Spirit
The king began once more to attract nobles and counselors.

How about you? Are you a teachable leader? Do you want to dictate the people or circumstances from whom you will learn, or will you learn from anyone? Consider a few steps to improve your teachability:

1. *Don't believe your own press.* The greatest enemy of tomorrow's success is today's. Don't get distracted by your achievements.

2. *Observe how you react to mistakes.* Do you admit them when you make them? Do you apologize or get defensive? Get honest about your needs.

3. *Try something new.* When was the last time you did something for the first time? Challenges change us for the better and keep us learning.

4. *Grow in the area of your strength.* Read books on leadership and in your area of giftedness. Don't be satisfied with where you are today. Keep stretching.

For a positive example of teachability, see p. 1351.

added to me. ³⁷Now I, Nebuchadnezzar, praise and extol and honor the King of heaven, all of whose works *are* truth, and His ways justice. And those who walk in pride He is able to put down.

Belshazzar's Feast

5 Belshazzar the king made a great feast for a thousand of his lords, and drank wine in the presence of the thousand. ²While he tasted the wine, Belshazzar gave the command to bring the gold and silver vessels which his father Nebuchadnezzar had taken from the temple which *had been* in Jerusalem, that the king and his lords, his wives, and his concubines might drink from them. ³Then they brought the gold vessels that had been taken from the temple of the house of God which *had been* in Jerusalem; and the king and his lords, his wives, and his concubines drank from them. ⁴They drank wine, and praised the gods of gold and silver, bronze and iron, wood and stone.

⁵In the same hour the fingers of a man's hand appeared and wrote opposite the lampstand on the plaster of the wall of the king's palace; and the king saw the part of the hand that wrote. ⁶Then the king's countenance changed, and his thoughts troubled him, so that the joints of his hips were loosened and his knees knocked against each other. ⁷The king cried aloud to bring in the astrologers, the Chaldeans, and the soothsayers. The king spoke, saying to the wise *men* of Babylon, "Whoever reads this writing, and tells me its interpretation, shall be clothed with purple and *have* a chain of gold around your neck; and he shall be the third ruler in the kingdom." ⁸Now all the king's wise *men* came, but they could not read the writing, or make known to the king its interpretation. ⁹Then King Belshazzar was greatly troubled, his countenance was changed, and his lords were astonished.

¹⁰The queen, because of the words of the king and his lords, came to the banquet hall. The queen spoke, saying, "O king, live forever! Do not let your thoughts trouble you, nor let your countenance change. ¹¹There is a man in your kingdom in whom *is* the Spirit of the Holy God. And in the days of your father, light and understanding and wisdom, like the wisdom of the gods, were found in him; and King Nebuchadnezzar your father—your father the king—made him chief of the magicians, astrologers, Chaldeans, *and* soothsayers. ¹²Inasmuch as an excellent spirit, knowledge, understanding, interpreting dreams, solving riddles, and explaining enigmasᵃ were found in this Daniel, whom the king

named Belteshazzar, now let Daniel be called, and he will give the interpretation."

The Writing on the Wall Explained

¹³Then Daniel was brought in before the king. The king spoke, and said to Daniel, "*Are* you that Daniel who is one of the captivesᵃ from Judah, whom my father the king brought from Judah? ¹⁴I have heard of you, that the Spirit of God *is* in you, and *that* light and understanding and excellent wisdom are found in you. ¹⁵Now the wise *men,* the astrologers, have been brought in before me, that they should read this writing and make known to me its interpretation, but they could not give the interpretation of the thing. ¹⁶And I have heard of you, that you can give interpretations and explain enigmas. Now if you can read the writing and make known to me its interpretation, you shall be clothed with purple and *have* a chain of gold around your neck, and shall be the third ruler in the kingdom."

¹⁷Then Daniel answered, and said before the king, "Let your gifts be for yourself, and give your rewards to another; yet I will read the writing to the king, and make known to him the interpretation. ¹⁸O king, the Most High God gave Nebuchadnezzar your father a kingdom and majesty, glory and honor. ¹⁹And because of the majesty that He gave him, all peoples, nations, and languages trembled and feared before him. Whomever he wished, he executed; whomever he wished, he kept alive; whomever he wished, he set up; and whomever he wished, he put down. ²⁰But when his heart was lifted up, and his spirit was hardened in pride, he was deposed from his kingly throne, and they took his glory from him. ²¹Then he was driven from the sons of men, his heart was made like the beasts, and his dwelling *was* with the wild donkeys. They fed him with grass like oxen, and his body was wet with the dew of heaven, till he knew that the Most High God rules in the kingdom of men, and appoints over it whomever He chooses.

²²"But you his son, Belshazzar, have not humbled your heart, although you knew all this. ²³And you have lifted yourself up against the Lord of heaven. They have brought the vessels of His house before you, and you and your lords, your wives and your concubines, have drunk wine from them. And you have praised the gods of silver and gold, bronze and iron, wood and stone, which do not see or hear or know; and the God who *holds* your breath in His hand and

---

5:12 ᵃLiterally *untying knots,* and so in verse 16
5:13 ᵃLiterally *of the sons of the captivity*

The Law of E. F. Hutton:
When Daniel Speaks, People Listen
(Daniel 5:13, 14)

When Daniel spoke, everyone listened. Why? People listened to Daniel for the following reasons:

1. **Relationships:** People listen to us because of who we know.
   Daniel had a reputation for knowing the God of Israel.
2. **Sacrifice:** People listen to us because of what we have suffered.
   Daniel gave up his right to eat the king's food.
3. **Character:** People listen to us because of our integrity.
   Daniel remained blameless and trustworthy even when he had to rebuke kings.
4. **Relevance:** People listen to us because we identify with their needs.
   Daniel lived with the Babylonians and identified with their struggles and lifestyle.
5. **Insight:** People listen to us because of what we know.
   Daniel could interpret dreams and visions that confused everyone else.
6. **Vulnerability:** People listen to us because we are genuinely transparent.
   Daniel's life was an open book.
7. **Experience:** People listen to us because we've succeeded in the past.
   Daniel's credibility came from years of living well.
8. **Humility:** People listen to us when we incarnate meekness.
   Daniel served and submitted to authorities, unless they broke a higher law.
9. **Competence:** People listen to us because of our abilities and expertise.
   Daniel did many things better than anyone else.
10. **Courage:** People listen to us because we demonstrate conviction.
    Daniel was no one's puppet and showed he would die for his convictions.

owns all your ways, you have not glorified. [24]Then the fingers[a] of the hand were sent from Him, and this writing was written. [25]"And this is the inscription that was written:

MENE,[a] MENE, TEKEL,[b] UPHARSIN.[c]

[26]This *is* the interpretation of *each* word. MENE: God has numbered your kingdom, and finished it; [27]TEKEL: You have been weighed in the balances, and found wanting; [28]PERES: Your kingdom has been divided, and given to the Medes and Persians."[a] [29]Then Belshazzar gave the command, and they clothed Daniel with purple and *put* a chain of gold around his neck, and made a proclamation concerning him that he should be the third ruler in the kingdom.

Belshazzar's Fall

[30]That very night Belshazzar, king of the Chaldeans, was slain. [31]And Darius the Mede received the kingdom, *being* about sixty-two years old.

The Plot Against Daniel

6 It pleased Darius to set over the kingdom one hundred and twenty satraps, to be over the whole kingdom; [2]and over these, three governors, of whom Daniel *was* one, that the satraps might give account to them, so that the king would suffer no loss. [3]Then this Daniel distinguished himself above the governors and satraps, because an excellent spirit *was* in him; and the king gave thought to setting him over the whole realm. [4]So the governors and satraps sought to find *some* charge against Daniel concerning the kingdom; but they could find no charge or fault, because he *was* faithful; nor was there any error or fault found in him. [5]Then these men said, "We shall not find any charge

5:24 [a]Literally *palm* 5:25 [a]Literally *a mina* (50 shekels) from the verb "to number" [b]Literally *a shekel* from the verb "to weigh" [c]Literally *and half-shekels* from the verb "to divide" 5:28 [a]Aramaic *Paras,* consonant with *Peres* against this Daniel unless we find *it* against him concerning the law of his God."

⁶So these governors and satraps thronged before the king, and said thus to him: "King Darius, live forever! ⁷All the governors of the kingdom, the administrators and satraps, the counselors and advisors, have consulted together to establish a royal statute and to make a firm decree, that whoever petitions any god or man for thirty days, except you, O king, shall be cast into the den of lions. ⁸Now, O king, establish the decree and sign the writing, so that it cannot be changed, according to the law of the Medes and Persians, which does not alter." ⁹Therefore King Darius signed the written decree.

Decision Making: Choices Confirm or Compromise Values

(Daniel 6:1–10)

One day Daniel had to decide whether he would submit to an ungodly law, or stick with his convictions. He chose his life principles. He likely followed in the footsteps of other strong leaders of the Old Testament:

1. Weigh out the options in front of you.
2. Ask if those choices force you to compromise personal values.
3. Seek wise counsel.
4. Count the cost.
5. Decide based on principles.
6. Act on your decision swiftly and firmly.

Someone once said, "If you take so much time making a decision that it is too late to act, then you might as well have whittled a stick." This happens too often among contemporary leaders. They desire to do right, but by waiting to survey the pulse of their people, they paralyze the organization. Some leaders are so indecisive, their favorite color is plaid. Daniel maintained a set of values and principles that enabled him to make decisions quickly and confidently.

Daniel in the Lions' Den

¹⁰Now when Daniel knew that the writing was signed, he went home. And in his upper room, with his windows open toward Jerusalem, he knelt down on his knees three times that day,

and prayed and gave thanks before his God, as was his custom since early days.

¹¹Then these men assembled and found Daniel praying and making supplication before his God. ¹²And they went before the king, and spoke concerning the king's decree: "Have you not signed a decree that every man who petitions any god or man within thirty days, except you, O king, shall be cast into the den of lions?"

The king answered and said, "The thing *is* true, according to the law of the Medes and Persians, which does not alter."

¹³So they answered and said before the king, "That Daniel, who is one of the captives[a] from Judah, does not show due regard for you, O king, or for the decree that you have signed, but makes his petition three times a day."

¹⁴And the king, when he heard *these* words, was greatly displeased with himself, and set *his* heart on Daniel to deliver him; and he labored till the going down of the sun to deliver him. ¹⁵Then these men approached the king, and said to the king, "Know, O king, that *it is* the law of the Medes and Persians that no decree or statute which the king establishes may be changed."

¹⁶So the king gave the command, and they brought Daniel and cast *him* into the den of lions. *But* the king spoke, saying to Daniel, "Your God, whom you serve continually, He will deliver you." ¹⁷Then a stone was brought and laid on the mouth of the den, and the king sealed it with his own signet ring and with the signets of his lords, that the purpose concerning Daniel might not be changed.

Daniel Saved from the Lions

¹⁸Now the king went to his palace and spent the night fasting; and no musicians[a] were brought before him. Also his sleep went from him. ¹⁹Then the king arose very early in the morning and went in haste to the den of lions. ²⁰And when he came to the den, he cried out with a lamenting voice to Daniel. The king spoke, saying to Daniel, "Daniel, servant of the living God, has your God, whom you serve continually, been able to deliver you from the lions?"

²¹Then Daniel said to the king, "O king, live forever! ²²My God sent His angel and shut the lions' mouths, so that they have not hurt me, because I was found innocent before Him; and also, O king, I have done no wrong before you."

²³Now the king was exceedingly glad for him, and commanded that they should take

---

6:13 [a]Literally *of the sons of the captivity* **6:18** [a]Exact meaning unknown

Daniel up out of the den. So Daniel was taken up out of the den, and no injury whatever was found on him, because he believed in his God.

Darius Honors God

[24]And the king gave the command, and they brought those men who had accused Daniel, and they cast *them* into the den of lions—them, their children, and their wives; and the lions overpowered them, and broke all their bones in pieces before they ever came to the bottom of the den.

[25]Then King Darius wrote:

To all peoples, nations, and languages that dwell in all the earth:

Peace be multiplied to you.

[26]   I make a decree that in every dominion of my kingdom *men must* tremble and fear before the God of Daniel.

For He *is* the living God,
And steadfast forever;
His kingdom *is the one* which shall not be destroyed,
And His dominion *shall endure* to the end.
[27]   He delivers and rescues,
And He works signs and wonders
In heaven and on earth,
Who has delivered Daniel from the power of the lions.

[28]So this Daniel prospered in the reign of Darius and in the reign of Cyrus the Persian.

Vision of the Four Beasts

7 In the first year of Belshazzar king of Babylon, Daniel had a dream and visions of his head *while* on his bed. Then he wrote down the dream, telling the main facts.[a]

[2]Daniel spoke, saying, "I saw in my vision by night, and behold, the four winds of heaven were stirring up the Great Sea. [3]And four great beasts came up from the sea, each different from the other. [4]The first *was* like a lion, and had eagle's wings. I watched till its wings were plucked off; and it was lifted up from the earth and made to stand on two feet like a man, and a man's heart was given to it.

[5]"And suddenly another beast, a second, like a bear. It was raised up on one side, and *had* three ribs in its mouth between its teeth. And they said thus to it: 'Arise, devour much flesh!'

[6]"After this I looked, and there was another, like a leopard, which had on its back four wings of a bird. The beast also had four heads, and dominion was given to it.

[7]"After this I saw in the night visions, and behold, a fourth beast, dreadful and terrible, exceedingly strong. It had huge iron teeth; it was devouring, breaking in pieces, and trampling the residue with its feet. It *was* different from all the beasts that *were* before it, and it had ten horns. [8]I was considering the horns, and there was another horn, a little one, coming up among them, before whom three of the first horns were plucked out by the roots. And there, in this horn, *were* eyes like the eyes of a man, and a mouth speaking pompous words.

The Role of Praying and Planning in Leadership
(Daniel 7:1—12:13)

God controls the future. Therefore, we should never plan without praying. If God isn't in our plans, we waste our time. At the same time, we should respond to the guidance God gives us. Once we get confirmation and peace from God, we should act accordingly. Obedience is a reflection of faith.

Vision of the Ancient of Days

[9]   "I watched till thrones were put in place,
And the Ancient of Days was seated;
His garment *was* white as snow,
And the hair of His head *was* like pure wool.
His throne *was* a fiery flame,
Its wheels a burning fire;
[10]   A fiery stream issued
And came forth from before Him.
A thousand thousands ministered to Him;
Ten thousand times ten thousand stood before Him.
The court[a] was seated,
And the books were opened.

[11]"I watched then because of the sound of the pompous words which the horn was speaking; I watched till the beast was slain, and its body destroyed and given to the burning flame. [12]As for the rest of the beasts, they had their

---

7:1 [a]Literally *the head* (or *chief*) *of the words*
7:10 [a]Or *judgment*

dominion taken away, yet their lives were prolonged for a season and a time.

13 "I was watching in the night visions,
And behold, *One* like the Son of Man,
Coming with the clouds of heaven!
He came to the Ancient of Days,
And they brought Him near before Him.
14 Then to Him was given dominion and
glory and a kingdom,
That all peoples, nations, and languages
should serve Him.
His dominion *is* an everlasting dominion,
Which shall not pass away,
And His kingdom *the one*
Which shall not be destroyed.

Daniel's Visions Interpreted

15"I, Daniel, was grieved in my spirit within *my* body, and the visions of my head troubled me. 16I came near to one of those who stood by, and asked him the truth of all this. So he told me and made known to me the interpretation of these things: 17'Those great beasts, which are four, *are* four kings[a] *which* arise out of the earth. 18But the saints of the Most High shall receive the kingdom, and possess the kingdom forever, even forever and ever.'

19"Then I wished to know the truth about the fourth beast, which was different from all the others, exceedingly dreadful, *with* its teeth of iron and its nails of bronze, *which* devoured, broke in pieces, and trampled the residue with its feet; 20and the ten horns that *were* on its head, and the other *horn* which came up, before which three fell, namely, that horn which had eyes and a mouth which spoke pompous words, whose appearance *was* greater than his fellows. 21"I was watching; and the same horn was making war against the saints, and prevailing against them, 22until the Ancient of Days came, and a judgment was made *in favor* of the saints of the Most High, and the time came for the saints to possess the kingdom.

23"Thus he said:

'The fourth beast shall be
A fourth kingdom on earth,
Which shall be different from all *other*
kingdoms,
And shall devour the whole earth,
Trample it and break it in pieces.
24 The ten horns *are* ten kings
Who shall arise from this kingdom.
And another shall rise after them;
He shall be different from the first *ones,*

And shall subdue three kings.
25 He shall speak *pompous* words against the
Most High,
Shall persecute[a] the saints of the Most
High,
And shall intend to change times and law.
Then *the saints* shall be given into his hand
For a time and times and half a time.

26 'But the court shall be seated,
And they shall take away his dominion,
To consume and destroy *it* forever.
27 Then the kingdom and dominion,
And the greatness of the kingdoms under
the whole heaven,
Shall be given to the people, the saints of
the Most High.
His kingdom *is* an everlasting kingdom,
And all dominions shall serve and obey
Him.'

28"This *is* the end of the account.[a] As for me, Daniel, my thoughts greatly troubled me, and my countenance changed; but I kept the matter in my heart."

Vision of a Ram and a Goat

8 In the third year of the reign of King Belshazzar a vision appeared *to* me—to me, Daniel—after the one that appeared to me the first time. 2I saw in the vision, and it so happened while I was looking, that I *was* in Shushan, the citadel, which *is* in the province of Elam; and I saw in the vision that I was by the River Ulai. 3Then I lifted my eyes and saw, and there, standing beside the river, was a ram which had two horns, and the two horns *were* high; but one *was* higher than the other, and the higher *one* came up last. 4I saw the ram pushing westward, northward, and southward, so that no animal could withstand him; nor *was there any* that could deliver from his hand, but he did according to his will and became great.

5And as I was considering, suddenly a male goat came from the west, across the surface of the whole earth, without touching the ground; and the goat *had* a notable horn between his eyes. 6Then he came to the ram that had two horns, which I had seen standing beside the river, and ran at him with furious power. 7And I saw him confronting the ram; he was moved with rage against him, attacked the ram, and broke his two horns. There was no power in the

---

7:17 [a]Representing their kingdoms (compare verse 23) **7:25** [a]Literally *wear out* **7:28** [a]Literally *the word*

ram to withstand him, but he cast him down to the ground and trampled him; and there was no one that could deliver the ram from his hand.

[8]Therefore the male goat grew very great; but when he became strong, the large horn was broken, and in place of it four notable ones came up toward the four winds of heaven. [9]And out of one of them came a little horn which grew exceedingly great toward the south, toward the east, and toward the Glorious *Land*. [10]And it grew up to the host of heaven; and it cast down *some* of the host and *some* of the stars to the ground, and trampled them. [11]He even exalted *himself* as high as the Prince of the host; and by him the daily *sacrifices* were taken away, and the place of His sanctuary was cast down. [12]Because of transgression, an army was given over *to the horn* to oppose the daily *sacrifices;* and he cast truth down to the ground. He did *all this* and prospered.

[13]Then I heard a holy one speaking; and *another* holy one said to that certain *one* who was speaking, "How long *will* the vision *be, concerning* the daily *sacrifices* and the transgression of desolation, the giving of both the sanctuary and the host to be trampled underfoot?"

[14]And he said to me, "For two thousand three hundred days;[a] then the sanctuary shall be cleansed."

Gabriel Interprets the Vision

[15]Then it happened, when I, Daniel, had seen the vision and was seeking the meaning, that suddenly there stood before me one having the appearance of a man. [16]And I heard a man's voice between *the banks of* the Ulai, who called, and said, "Gabriel, make this *man* understand the vision." [17]So he came near where I stood, and when he came I was afraid and fell on my face; but he said to me, "Understand, son of man, that the vision *refers* to the time of the end."

[18]Now, as he was speaking with me, I was in a deep sleep with my face to the ground; but he touched me, and stood me upright. [19]And he said, "Look, I am making known to you what shall happen in the latter time of the indignation; for at the appointed time the end *shall be*. [20]The ram which you saw, having the two horns—*they are* the kings of Media and Persia. [21]And the male goat *is* the kingdom[a] of Greece. The large horn that *is* between its eyes *is* the first king. [22]As for

8:14 [a]Literally *evening-mornings* **8:21** [a]Literally *king,* representing his kingdom (compare 7:17, 23)

the broken *horn* and the four that stood up in its place, four kingdoms shall arise out of that nation, but not with its power.

23 "And in the latter time of their kingdom,
When the transgressors have reached their fullness,
A king shall arise,
Having fierce features,
Who understands sinister schemes.

24 His power shall be mighty, but not by his own power;
He shall destroy fearfully,
And shall prosper and thrive;
He shall destroy the mighty, and *also* the holy people.

25 "Through his cunning
He shall cause deceit to prosper under his rule;[a]
And he shall exalt *himself* in his heart.
He shall destroy many in *their* prosperity.
He shall even rise against the Prince of princes;
But he shall be broken without *human* means.[b]

26 "And the vision of the evenings and mornings
Which was told is true;
Therefore seal up the vision,
For *it refers* to many days *in the future.*"

27And I, Daniel, fainted and was sick for days; afterward I arose and went about the king's business. I was astonished by the vision, but no one understood it.

Daniel's Prayer for the People

9 In the first year of Darius the son of Ahasuerus, of the lineage of the Medes, who was made king over the realm of the Chaldeans— 2in the first year of his reign I, Daniel, understood by the books the number of the years *specified* by the word of the LORD through Jeremiah the prophet, that He would accomplish seventy years in the desolations of Jerusalem.

3Then I set my face toward the Lord God to make request by prayer and supplications, with fasting, sackcloth, and ashes. 4And I prayed to the LORD my God, and made confession, and said, "O Lord, great and awesome God, who keeps His covenant and mercy with those who love Him, and with those who keep His commandments, 5we have sinned and committed iniquity, we have done wickedly and rebelled, even by

departing from Your precepts and Your judgments. 6Neither have we heeded Your servants the prophets, who spoke in Your name to our kings and our princes, to our fathers and all the people of the land. 7O Lord, righteousness *belongs* to You, but to us shame of face, as *it is* this day— to the men of Judah, to the inhabitants of Jerusalem and all Israel, those near and those far off in all the countries to which You have driven them, because of the unfaithfulness which they have committed against You.

8"O Lord, to us *belongs* shame of face, to our kings, our princes, and our fathers, because we have sinned against You. 9To the Lord our God *belong* mercy and forgiveness, though we have rebelled against Him. 10We have not obeyed the voice of the LORD our God, to walk in His laws, which He set before us by His servants the prophets. 11Yes, all Israel has transgressed Your law, and has departed so as not to obey Your voice; therefore the curse and the oath written in the Law of Moses the servant of God have been poured out on us, because we have sinned against Him. 12And He has confirmed His words, which He spoke against us and against our judges who judged us, by bringing upon us a great disaster; for under the whole heaven such has never been done as what has been done to Jerusalem.

13"As *it is* written in the Law of Moses, all this disaster has come upon us; yet we have not made our prayer before the LORD our God, that we might turn from our iniquities and understand Your truth. 14Therefore the LORD has kept the disaster in mind, and brought it upon us; for LORD our God *is* righteous in all the works which He does, though we have not obeyed His voice. 15And now, O Lord our God, who brought Your people out of the land of Egypt with a mighty hand, and made Yourself a name, as *it is* this day— we have sinned, we have done wickedly! 16"O Lord, according to all Your righteousness, I pray, let Your anger and Your fury be turned away from Your city Jerusalem, Your holy mountain; because for our sins, and for the iniquities of our fathers, Jerusalem and Your people *are* a reproach to all *those* around us. 17Now therefore, our God, hear the prayer of Your servant, and his supplications, and for the Lord's sake cause Your face to shine on Your sanctuary, which is desolate. 18O my God, incline Your ear and hear; open Your eyes and see our desolations, and the city which is called by Your name; for we do not present our supplications before You because of our righteous deeds, but because of

8:25 [a]Literally *hand* [b]Literally *hand*

Your great mercies. [19]O Lord, hear! O Lord, forgive! O Lord, listen and act! Do not delay for Your own sake, my God, for Your city and Your people are called by Your name."

The Seventy-Weeks Prophecy

[20]Now while I *was* speaking, praying, and confessing my sin and the sin of my people Israel, and presenting my supplication before the LORD my God for the holy mountain of my God, [21]yes, while I *was* speaking in prayer, the man Gabriel, whom I had seen in the vision at the beginning, being caused to fly swiftly, reached me about the time of the evening offering. [22]And he informed *me,* and talked with me, and said, "O Daniel, I have now come forth to give you skill to understand. [23]At the beginning of your supplications the command went out, and I have come to tell *you,* for you *are* greatly beloved; therefore consider the matter, and understand the vision:

[24] "Seventy weeks[a] are determined
   For your people and for your holy city,
   To finish the transgression,
   To make an end of[b] sins,
   To make reconciliation for iniquity,
   To bring in everlasting righteousness,
   To seal up vision and prophecy,
   And to anoint the Most Holy.

[25] "Know therefore and understand,
   That from the going forth of the
     command
   To restore and build Jerusalem
   Until Messiah the Prince,
   There shall be seven weeks and sixty-two
     weeks;
   The street[a] shall be built again, and the
     wall,[b]
   Even in troublesome times.

[26] "And after the sixty-two weeks
   Messiah shall be cut off, but not for
     Himself;
   And the people of the prince who is to
     come
   Shall destroy the city and the sanctuary.
   The end of it *shall be* with a flood,
   And till the end of the war desolations are
     determined.
[27] Then he shall confirm a covenant with
     many for one week;
   But in the middle of the week
   He shall bring an end to sacrifice and
     offering.

And on the wing of abominations shall be
   one who makes desolate,
Even until the consummation, which is
   determined,
Is poured out on the desolate."

Vision of the Glorious Man

10 In the third year of Cyrus king of Persia a message was revealed to Daniel, whose name was called Belteshazzar. The message *was* true, but the appointed time *was* long;[a] and he understood the message, and had understanding of the vision. [2]In those days I, Daniel, was mourning three full weeks. [3]I ate no pleasant food, no meat or wine came into my mouth, nor did I anoint myself at all, till three whole weeks were fulfilled.

[4]Now on the twenty-fourth day of the first month, as I was by the side of the great river, that *is,* the Tigris,[a] [5]I lifted my eyes and looked, and behold, a certain man clothed in linen, whose waist *was* girded with gold of Uphaz! [6]His body *was* like beryl, his face like the appearance of lightning, his eyes like torches of fire, his arms and feet like burnished bronze in color, and the sound of his words like the voice of a multitude.

[7]And I, Daniel, alone saw the vision, for the men who were with me did not see the vision; but a great terror fell upon them, so that they fled to hide themselves. [8]Therefore I was left alone when I saw this great vision, and no strength remained in me; for my vigor was turned to frailty in me, and I retained no strength. [9]Yet I heard the sound of his words; and while I heard the sound of his words I was in a deep sleep on my face, with my face to the ground.

Prophecies Concerning Persia and Greece

[10]Suddenly, a hand touched me, which made me tremble on my knees and *on* the palms of my hands. [11]And he said to me, "O Daniel, man greatly beloved, understand the words that I speak to you, and stand upright, for I have now been sent to you." While he was speaking this word to me, I stood trembling. [12]Then he said to me, "Do not fear, Daniel, for from the first day that you set your heart to understand, and to humble yourself before your

---

9:24 [a]Literally *sevens,* and so throughout the chapter [b]Following Qere, Septuagint, Syriac, and Vulgate; Kethib and Theodotion read *To seal up.* **9:25** [a]Or *open square* [b]Or *moat* **10:1** [a]Or *and of great conflict* **10:4** [a]Hebrew *Hiddekel*

God, your words were heard; and I have come because of your words. [13]But the prince of the kingdom of Persia withstood me twenty-one days; and behold, Michael, one of the chief princes, came to help me, for I had been left alone there with the kings of Persia. [14]Now I have come to make you understand what will happen to your people in the latter days, for the vision *refers* to *many* days yet *to come.*"

Spiritual Leaders Lead God's Family and God's Army

(Daniel 10:1–21)

The vision Daniel receives in chapter 10 presents him with a deeper challenge than any in his past. He now learns he is engaged in spiritual warfare. In his dialogue with an angel, Daniel learns some important lessons every leader ought to master:

1. Spiritual leaders lead not only God's family, but God's army (vv. 10–21).
2. Prayer ignites spiritual warfare invisible to us (vv. 10–12).
3. Both spiritual kingdoms seem to have princes (v. 13).
4. Spiritual warfare can delay victories (vv. 13, 14).
5. We must not fear spiritual warfare (vv. 18, 19).
6. Understanding warfare enables us to co-operate with God's purposes (vv. 20, 21).

As you seek to lead in a more strategic way, recognize that you will encounter struggles beyond mere human opposition. You must wisely face an invisible, spiritual world around you. You need both prayer and persistence.

---

[15]When he had spoken such words to me, I turned my face toward the ground and became speechless. [16]And suddenly, *one* having the likeness of the sons[a] of men touched my lips; then I opened my mouth and spoke, saying to him who stood before me, "My lord, because of the vision my sorrows have overwhelmed me, and I have retained no strength. [17]For how can this servant of my lord talk with you, my lord? As for me, no strength remains in me now, nor is any breath left in me."

[18]Then again, *the one* having the likeness of a man touched me and strengthened me. [19]And he said, "O man greatly beloved, fear not! Peace *be* to you; be strong, yes, be strong!"

So when he spoke to me I was strengthened, and said, "Let my lord speak, for you have strengthened me."

[20]Then he said, "Do you know why I have come to you? And now I must return to fight with the prince of Persia; and when I have gone forth, indeed the prince of Greece will come. [21]But I will tell you what is noted in the Scripture of Truth. (No one upholds me against these, except Michael your prince.

11 "Also in the first year of Darius the Mede, I, *even* I, stood up to confirm and strengthen him.) [2]And now I will tell you the truth: Behold, three more kings will arise in Persia, and the fourth shall be far richer than *them* all; by his strength, through his riches, he shall stir up all against the realm of Greece. [3]Then a mighty king shall arise, who shall rule with great dominion, and do according to his will. [4]And when he has arisen, his kingdom shall be broken up and divided toward the four winds of heaven, but not among his posterity nor according to his dominion with which he ruled; for his kingdom shall be uprooted, even for others besides these.

Warring Kings of North and South

[5]"Also the king of the South shall become strong, as well as *one* of his princes; and he shall gain power over him and have dominion. His dominion *shall be* a great dominion. [6]And at the end of *some* years they shall join forces, for the daughter of the king of the South shall go to the king of the North to make an agreement; but she shall not retain the power of her authority,[a] and neither he nor his authority[b] shall stand; but she shall be given up, with those who brought her, and with him who begot her, and with him who strengthened her in *those* times. [7]But from a branch of her roots *one* shall arise in his place, who shall come with an army, enter the fortress of the king of the North, and deal with them and prevail. [8]And he shall also carry their gods captive to Egypt, with their princes[a] *and* their precious articles of silver and gold; and he shall continue *more* years than the king of the North.

[9]"Also *the king of the North* shall come to the kingdom of the king of the South, but shall re-

---

10:16 [a]Theodotion and Vulgate read *the son;* Septuagint reads *a hand.* **11:6** [a]Literally *arm* [b]Literally *arm* **11:8** [a]Or *molded images* turn to his own land. [10]However his sons shall stir up strife, and assemble a multitude of great forces; and *one* shall certainly come and overwhelm and pass through; then he shall return to his fortress and stir up strife.

[11]"And the king of the South shall be moved with rage, and go out and fight with him, with the king of the North, who shall muster a great multitude; but the multitude shall be given into the hand of his *enemy.* [12]When he has taken away the multitude, his heart will be lifted up; and he will cast down tens of thousands, but he will not prevail. [13]For the king of the North will return and muster a multitude greater than the former, and shall certainly come at the end of some years with a great army and much equipment.

[14]"Now in those times many shall rise up against the king of the South. Also, violent men[a] of your people shall exalt themselves in fulfillment of the vision, but they shall fall. [15]So the king of the North shall come and build a siege mound, and take a fortified city; and the forces[a] of the South shall not withstand *him.* Even his choice troops *shall have* no strength to resist. [16]But he who comes against him shall do according to his own will, and no one shall stand against him. He shall stand in the Glorious Land with destruction in his power.[a]

[17]"He shall also set his face to enter with the strength of his whole kingdom, and upright ones[a] with him; thus shall he do. And he shall give him the daughter of women to destroy it; but she shall not stand *with him,* or be for him. [18]After this he shall turn his face to the coastlands, and shall take many. But a ruler shall bring the reproach against them to an end; and with the reproach removed, he shall turn back on him. [19]Then he shall turn his face toward the fortress of his own land; but he shall stumble and fall, and not be found.

[20]"There shall arise in his place one who imposes taxes *on* the glorious kingdom; but within a few days he shall be destroyed, but not in anger or in battle. [21]And in his place shall arise a vile person, to whom they will not give the honor of royalty; but he shall come in peaceably, and seize the kingdom by intrigue. [22]With the force[a] of a flood they shall be swept away from before him and be broken, and also the prince of the covenant. [23]And after the league *is made* with him he shall act deceitfully, for he shall come up and become strong with a small *number* of people. [24]He shall enter peaceably, even into the richest places of the province; and he shall do *what* his fathers have not done, nor his forefathers: he shall disperse among them the plunder, spoil, and riches;

and he shall devise his plans against the strongholds, but *only* for a time.

[25]"He shall stir up his power and his courage against the king of the South with a great army. And the king of the South shall be stirred up to battle with a very great and mighty army; but he shall not stand, for they shall devise plans against him. [26]Yes, those who eat of the portion of his delicacies shall destroy him; his army shall be swept away, and many shall fall down slain. [27]Both these kings' hearts *shall be* bent on evil, and they shall speak lies at the same table; but it shall not prosper, for the end *will* still *be* at the appointed time. [28]While returning to his land with great riches, his heart shall be *moved* against the holy covenant; so he shall do *damage* and return to his own land.

The Northern King's Blasphemies

[29]"At the appointed time he shall return and go toward the south; but it shall not be like the former or the latter. [30]For ships from Cyprus[a] shall come against him; therefore he shall be grieved, and return in rage against the holy covenant, and do *damage.*

"So he shall return and show regard for those who forsake the holy covenant. [31]And forces[a] shall be mustered by him, and they shall defile the sanctuary fortress; then they shall take away the daily *sacrifices,* and place *there* the abomination of desolation. [32]Those who do wickedly against the covenant he shall corrupt with flattery; but the people who know their God shall be strong, and carry out *great exploits.* [33]And those of the people who understand shall instruct many; yet *for many* days they shall fall by sword and flame, by captivity and plundering. [34]Now when they fall, they shall be aided with a little help; but many shall join with them by intrigue. [35]And *some* of those of understanding shall fall, to refine them, purify *them,* and make *them* white, *until* the time of the end; because *it is* still for the appointed time.

[36]"Then the king shall do according to his own will: he shall exalt and magnify himself above every god, shall speak blasphemies against the God of gods, and shall prosper till the wrath has been accomplished; for what has been determined shall be done. [37]He shall regard neither the God[a] of his fathers nor the desire of women, nor

---

11:14 [a]Or *robbers,* literally *sons of breakage*
11:15 [a]Literally *arms* **11:16** [a]Literally *hand*
11:17 [a]Or *bring equitable terms* **11:22** [a]Literally *arms*
11:30 [a]Hebrew *Kittim,* western lands, especially Cyprus **11:31** [a]Literally *arms* **11:37** [a]Or *gods*

regard any god; for he shall exalt himself above *them* all. ³⁸But in their place he shall honor a god of fortresses; and a god which his fathers did not know he shall honor with gold and silver, with precious stones and pleasant things. ³⁹Thus he shall act against the strongest fortresses with a foreign god, which he shall acknowledge, *and* advance *its* glory; and he shall cause them to rule over many, and divide the land for gain.

The Northern King's Conquests

⁴⁰"At the time of the end the king of the South shall attack him; and the king of the North shall come against him like a whirlwind, with chariots, horsemen, and with many ships; and he shall enter the countries, overwhelm *them,* and pass through. ⁴¹He shall also enter the Glorious Land, and many *countries* shall be overthrown; but these shall escape from his hand: Edom, Moab, and the prominent people of Ammon. ⁴²He shall stretch out his hand against the countries, and the land of Egypt shall not escape. ⁴³He shall have power over the treasures of gold and silver, and over all the precious things of Egypt; also the Libyans and Ethiopians *shall follow* at his heels. ⁴⁴But news from the east and the north shall trouble him; therefore he shall go out with great fury to destroy and annihilate many. ⁴⁵And he shall plant the tents of his palace between the seas and the glorious holy mountain; yet he shall come to his end, and no one will help him.

Prophecy of the End Time

12 "At that time Michael shall stand up,
The great prince who stands *watch*
over the sons of your people;
And there shall be a time of trouble,
Such as never was since there was a nation,
Even to that time.
And at that time your people shall be
delivered,
Every one who is found written in the
book.

²　And many of those who sleep in the dust
of the earth shall awake,
Some to everlasting life,
Some to shame *and* everlasting contempt.
³　Those who are wise shall shine
Like the brightness of the firmament,
And those who turn many to
righteousness
Like the stars forever and ever.

⁴"But you, Daniel, shut up the words, and seal the book until the time of the end; many shall run to and fro, and knowledge shall increase."

⁵Then I, Daniel, looked; and there stood two others, one on this riverbank and the other on that riverbank. ⁶And *one* said to the man clothed in linen, who *was* above the waters of the river, "How long shall the fulfillment of these wonders *be?*"

⁷Then I heard the man clothed in linen, who *was* above the waters of the river, when he held up his right hand and his left hand to heaven, and swore by Him who lives forever, that *it shall be* for a time, times, and half *a time;* and when the power of the holy people has been completely shattered, all these *things* shall be finished.

⁸Although I heard, I did not understand. Then I said, "My lord, what *shall be* the end of these *things?*"

⁹And he said, "Go *your way,* Daniel, for the words *are* closed up and sealed till the time of the end. ¹⁰Many shall be purified, made white, and refined, but the wicked shall do wickedly; and none of the wicked shall understand, but the wise shall understand.

¹¹"And from the time *that* the daily *sacrifice* is taken away, and the abomination of desolation is set up, *there shall be* one thousand two hundred and ninety days. ¹²Blessed *is* he who waits, and comes to the one thousand three hundred and thirty-five days.

¹³"But you, go *your way* till the end; for you shall rest, and will arise to your inheritance at the end of the days."

HOSEA

A Visual Demonstration of Israel's Unfaithfulness to God

SUMMARY

Hosea, the first of the "minor prophets," led and prophesied in Israel during a season of material wealth but spiritual poverty. Because of this, God called him to do something very costly. In order to send a memorable message to the people of Israel, Hosea was to marry a harlot—thus giving the people a visual demonstration of their unfaithfulness to Yahweh. Hosea's words were to help the people feel the grief of God, who responded to their rebellion like a husband with an adulterous wife. In the same way Gomer had betrayed Hosea, Israel had betrayed God.

Hosea vividly illustrates the Law of Sacrifice. In order to fulfill his divine calling, he had to pay a huge price. At his own expense, he married Gomer and watched her drift from her marriage time and again. We can only imagine his pain, called to live with her lies and deception, having to explain to his children that their mother would not be home that night, then watching her public humiliation as evil men auctioned off her body for the carnal delight of strangers. Certainly, when Hosea spoke to the Israelites about their spiritual state, he could do it with empathy and passion. He knew firsthand how God felt about the spiritual adultery of His chosen people.

Leadership really is about sacrifice. Many of us want the perks of leadership without the price of leadership. Yet becoming a leader isn't about gaining rights; it's about giving them up. Leaders in the business world often err in thinking that becoming a C.E.O. means more liberties with the budget, more options with their time, and more freedom with their lifestyle. From God's perspective, leadership means quite the opposite. Leaders relinquish options and remain careful to do all things for the sake of the gospel (1 Cor. 9:19–23).

Leading people is also about more than words; it really is a lifestyle. We cannot separate our communication from our conduct. To speak with the kind of credibility and emotion he did, Hosea had to live what God was living. Hollow leadership results when we do not incarnate the values we want others to embrace. Hypocrisy replaces integrity. No one wants to follow this kind of leader. The way we talk, the way we lead, and the way we live should mesh. Just ask Hosea.

God's Role in Hosea

God reveals Himself in this book as both a forgiving Lord and a holy Judge who requires repentance on the part of His erring people. Because He endured an adulterous bride in Israel, He called Hosea to imitate His situation—then to speak to the people about His forgiveness and judgment. God led His leader, Hosea, in an experience he would never forget. Hosea got to step into God's shoes for a season and feel what He felt. Through Hosea, God communicated both His unconditional love and His unchanging law.

Leaders in Hosea

Hosea

Other People of Influence in Hosea

Gomer

Lessons in Leadership

- Leaders must maintain poise even in the midst of unfair demands.
- The simple game plan is the best when restoring or rebuilding.
- Followers in volatile situations need consistency from leaders.
- Leaders must lead from established values and standards.
- Regardless of what the people do, leaders must model what is right.
- Effective leaders never lose sight of the big picture.

1 The word of the LORD that came to Hosea the son of Beeri, in the days of Uzziah, Jotham, Ahaz, *and* Hezekiah, kings of Judah, and in the days of Jeroboam the son of Joash, king of Israel.

The Family of Hosea

[2]When the LORD began to speak by Hosea, the LORD said to Hosea:

> "Go, take yourself a wife of harlotry
> And children of harlotry,
> For the land has committed great harlotry
> *By departing* from the LORD."

[3]So he went and took Gomer the daughter of Diblaim, and she conceived and bore him a son. [4]Then the LORD said to him:

> "Call his name Jezreel,
> For in a little *while*
> I will avenge the bloodshed of Jezreel on the house of Jehu,
> And bring an end to the kingdom of the house of Israel.
> [5] It shall come to pass in that day
> That I will break the bow of Israel in the Valley of Jezreel."

[6]And she conceived again and bore a daughter. Then *God* said to him:

> "Call her name Lo-Ruhamah,[a]
> For I will no longer have mercy on the house of Israel,
> But I will utterly take them away.[b]
> [7] Yet I will have mercy on the house of Judah,
> Will save them by the LORD their God,
> And will not save them by bow,
> Nor by sword or battle,
> By horses or horsemen."

[8]Now when she had weaned Lo-Ruhamah, she conceived and bore a son. [9]Then *God* said:

> "Call his name Lo-Ammi,[a]
> For you *are* not My people,
> And I will not be your *God*.

The Restoration of Israel

[10] "Yet the number of the children of Israel
> Shall be as the sand of the sea,

1:6 [a]Literally *No-Mercy* [b]Or *That I may forgive them at all* **1:9** [a]Literally *Not-My-People*

HOSEA

THE COST OF LEADERSHIP
(Hosea 1:1—3:5)

PROFILE IN LEADERSHIP

It can be painful to read the story of Hosea. Out of obedience to God, the prophet marries the prostitute Gomer, who refuses to change her ways for her husband or for their children. Still, Hosea tries to bring his wife back, to redeem her from the sordid life to which she so stubbornly clings.

From the human perspective, it is easy to wonder why Hosea continues to punish himself this way. Why would a man subject himself to the kind of heartache he must have felt in trying to make a faithful wife out of a prostitute? Why wouldn't he just "cut his losses" and rid himself of this wicked woman?

The quick answer is that Hosea's life did not belong to him alone. Like us, he had given his heart and soul to God. In Paul's words, "You are not your own . . . you were bought at a price" (1 Cor. 6:19, 20). Hosea realized that God had called him to become a living metaphor of the love of God for His people—and he obeyed, regardless of the personal cost.

Hosea illustrates the heartaches that may come from following the call of God. As leaders, we continue to pray for and minister to those who have strayed from the Lord—even when it hurts—knowing that God did the same for us.

The Law of Sacrifice:
Hosea Marries a Harlot to Teach the Truth
(Hosea 1:2)

Can you imagine what Hosea must have felt when God asked him to propose to a prostitute? The Lord instructed him to marry Gomer, a harlot, in order to illustrate the spiritual adultery Israel had committed against God. The Hebrews had been unfaithful to God and pursued other gods, just as a harlot joins herself to several men. What a request!

Leadership is about sacrifice. It means giving up personal options in order to guide the people to where they need to go. Hosea made several sacrifices in his leadership:

1. He was asked to marry a prostitute.
2. He was asked to lead in a time of rebellion.
3. He was given a very unpopular message.
4. He was told to have children despite an absentee wife.
5. He was committed to remain poised under harsh demands.
6. He was instructed to live faithfully and consistently in a volatile situation.

Leaders lose their right to selfishness. They must take into account the lives of others when making decisions. They must say what the people *need* to hear, not merely what they *want* to hear. They must guide the people to where they *ought* to go, not necessarily where they *desire* to go. Could this explain why we have so few good leaders?

Which cannot be measured or numbered.
And it shall come to pass
In the place where it was said to them,
'You *are* not My people,'[a]
There it shall be said to them,
'*You are* sons of the living God.'
11 Then the children of Judah and the
    children of Israel
Shall be gathered together,
And appoint for themselves one head;
And they shall come up out of the land,
For great *will be* the day of Jezreel!

2 Say to your brethren, 'My people,'[a]
And to your sisters, 'Mercy[b] *is*
    shown.'

God's Unfaithful People
2 "Bring charges against your mother, bring
    charges;
For she *is* not My wife, nor *am* I her
    Husband!
Let her put away her harlotries from her
    sight,
And her adulteries from between her
    breasts;
3 Lest I strip her naked
And expose her, as in the day she was
    born,
And make her like a wilderness,

And set her like a dry land,
And slay her with thirst.

4 "I will not have mercy on her children,
For they *are* the children of harlotry.
5 For their mother has played the harlot;
She who conceived them has behaved
    shamefully.
For she said, 'I will go after my lovers,
Who give *me* my bread and my water,
My wool and my linen,
My oil and my drink.'

6 "Therefore, behold,
I will hedge up your way with thorns,
And wall her in,
So that she cannot find her paths.
7 She will chase her lovers,
But not overtake them;
Yes, she will seek them, but not find *them*.
Then she will say,
'I will go and return to my first husband,
For then *it was* better for me than now.'
8 For she did not know
That I gave her grain, new wine, and oil,

1:10 [a]Hebrew *lo-ammi* (compare verse 9)
2:1 [a]Hebrew *Ammi* (compare 1:9, 10) [b]Hebrew *Ruhamah* (compare 1:6)

And multiplied her silver and gold—
Which they prepared for Baal.

9 "Therefore I will return and take away
My grain in its time
And My new wine in its season,
And will take back My wool and My
linen,
Given to cover her nakedness.
10 Now I will uncover her lewdness in the
sight of her lovers,
And no one shall deliver her from My
hand.
11 I will also cause all her mirth to cease,
Her feast days,
Her New Moons,
Her Sabbaths—
All her appointed feasts.

12 "And I will destroy her vines and her fig
trees,
Of which she has said,
'These *are* my wages that my lovers have
given me.'
So I will make them a forest,
And the beasts of the field shall eat them.
13 I will punish her
For the days of the Baals to which she
burned incense.
She decked herself with her earrings and
jewelry,
And went after her lovers;
But Me she forgot," says the LORD.

God's Mercy on His People

14 "Therefore, behold, I will allure her,
Will bring her into the wilderness,
And speak comfort to her.
15 I will give her her vineyards from there,
And the Valley of Achor as a door of hope;
She shall sing there,
As in the days of her youth,
As in the day when she came up from the
land of Egypt.

16 "And it shall be, in that day,"
Says the LORD,
"*That* you will call Me 'My Husband,'[a]
And no longer call Me 'My Master,'[b]
17 For I will take from her mouth the names
of the Baals,
And they shall be remembered by their
name no more.
18 In that day I will make a covenant for
them

With the beasts of the field,
With the birds of the air,
And *with* the creeping things of the
ground.
Bow and sword of battle I will shatter
from the earth,
To make them lie down safely.

19 "I will betroth you to Me forever;
Yes, I will betroth you to Me
In righteousness and justice,
In lovingkindness and mercy;
20 I will betroth you to Me in faithfulness,
And you shall know the LORD.

21 "It shall come to pass in that day
That I will answer," says the LORD;
"I will answer the heavens,
And they shall answer the earth.
22 The earth shall answer
With grain,
With new wine,
And with oil;
They shall answer Jezreel.[a]
23 Then I will sow her for Myself in the
earth,
And I will have mercy on *her who had* not
obtained mercy;[a]
Then I will say to *those who were* not My
people,[b]
'You *are* My people!'
And they shall say, '*You are* my God!'"

Israel Will Return to God

3 Then the LORD said to me, "Go again, love
a woman *who is* loved by a lover[a] and is
committing adultery, just like the love of
the LORD for the children of Israel, who look to
other gods and love *the* raisin cakes *of the pagans.*"

2So I bought her for myself for fifteen *shekels*
of silver, and one and one-half homers of barley.
3And I said to her, "You shall stay with me many
days; you shall not play the harlot, nor shall you
have a man—so, too, *will* I *be* toward you."

4For the children of Israel shall abide many
days without king or prince, without sacrifice or
sacred pillar, without ephod or teraphim. 5Afterward the children of Israel shall return and seek
the LORD their God and David their king. They
shall fear the LORD and His goodness in the latter days.

2:16 [a]Hebrew *Ishi* [b]Hebrew *Baali* 2:22 [a]Literally
God Will Sow 2:23 [a]Hebrew *lo-ruhamah* [b]Hebrew
lo-ammi 3:1 [a]Literally *friend* or *husband*

The Law of Empowerment: Hosea Loves by Decision, Not Reaction

(Hosea 3:1)

In Hosea 3 the prophet receives one profound command. He is told to go and reconcile with his wife, who remains in an adulterous relationship. He is told to act, not react. He is to love Gomer rather than take revenge.

God calls leaders to live on a higher level than followers. We are called to respond as God did to Israel. Although Israel had committed falsehood (Hos. 4:1), harlotry (4:11), murder (5:2), robbery (7:1), and oppression (12:7), along with repeated spiritual adultery, God continued to guide and empower His people.

In the final chapter, the prophet pleas with Israel to return to the Lord (14:1), that they might be graciously received, restored, and healed (14:2–4). Leaders can do this only when they live and lead from principle rather than from reaction.

God's Charge Against Israel

4 Hear the word of the LORD,
You children of Israel,
For the LORD *brings* a charge against the
inhabitants of the land:

"There is no truth or mercy
Or knowledge of God in the land.
2 *By* swearing and lying,
Killing and stealing and committing
adultery,
They break all restraint,
With bloodshed upon bloodshed.
3 Therefore the land will mourn;
And everyone who dwells there will waste
away
With the beasts of the field
And the birds of the air;
Even the fish of the sea will be taken away.

4 "Now let no man contend, or rebuke
another;

For your people *are* like those who
contend with the priest.
5 Therefore you shall stumble in the day;
The prophet also shall stumble with you in
the night;
And I will destroy your mother.
6 My people are destroyed for lack of
knowledge.
Because you have rejected knowledge,
I also will reject you from being priest for
Me;
Because you have forgotten the law of
your God,
I also will forget your children.

7 "The more they increased,
The more they sinned against Me;
I will change[a] their glory[b] into shame.
8 They eat up the sin of My people;
They set their heart on their iniquity.
9 And it shall be: like people, like priest.
So I will punish them for their ways,
And reward them for their deeds.
10 For they shall eat, but not have enough;
They shall commit harlotry, but not
increase;
Because they have ceased obeying the
LORD.

The Idolatry of Israel

11 "Harlotry, wine, and new wine enslave the
heart.
12 My people ask counsel from their wooden
idols,
And their staff informs them.
For the spirit of harlotry has caused *them*
to stray,
And they have played the harlot against
their God.
13 They offer sacrifices on the mountaintops,
And burn incense on the hills,
Under oaks, poplars, and terebinths,
Because their shade *is* good.
Therefore your daughters commit harlotry,
And your brides commit adultery.

14 "I will not punish your daughters when
they commit harlotry,
Nor your brides when they commit
adultery;

4:7 [a]Following Masoretic Text, Septuagint, and
Vulgate; scribal tradition, Syriac, and Targum read
They will change. [b]Following Masoretic Text,
Septuagint, Syriac, Targum, and Vulgate; scribal
tradition reads *My glory*.

For *the* men themselves go apart with
harlots,
And offer sacrifices with a ritual harlot.[a]
Therefore people *who* do not understand
will be trampled.

15 "Though you, Israel, play the harlot,
Let not Judah offend.
Do not come up to Gilgal,
Nor go up to Beth Aven,
Nor swear an oath, *saying,* 'As the LORD
lives'—

16 "For Israel is stubborn
Like a stubborn calf;
Now the LORD will let them forage
Like a lamb in open country.

17 "Ephraim *is* joined to idols,
Let him alone.

18 Their drink is rebellion,
They commit harlotry continually.
Her rulers dearly[a] love dishonor.

19 The wind has wrapped her up in its wings,
And they shall be ashamed because of their
sacrifices.

Impending Judgment on Israel and Judah

5 "Hear this, O priests!
Take heed, O house of Israel!
Give ear, O house of the king!
For yours *is* the judgment,
Because you have been a snare to Mizpah
And a net spread on Tabor.

2 The revolters are deeply involved in
slaughter,
Though I rebuke them all.

3 I know Ephraim,
And Israel is not hidden from Me;
For now, O Ephraim, you commit
harlotry;
Israel is defiled.

4 "They do not direct their deeds
Toward turning to their God,
For the spirit of harlotry is in their midst,
And they do not know the LORD.

5 The pride of Israel testifies to his face;
Therefore Israel and Ephraim stumble in
their iniquity;
Judah also stumbles with them.

6 "With their flocks and herds
They shall go to seek the LORD,
But they will not find *Him;*

He has withdrawn Himself from them.

7 They have dealt treacherously with the
LORD,
For they have begotten pagan children.
Now a New Moon shall devour them and
their heritage.

8 "Blow the ram's horn in Gibeah,
The trumpet in Ramah!
Cry aloud *at* Beth Aven,
'*Look* behind you, O Benjamin!'

9 Ephraim shall be desolate in the day of
rebuke;
Among the tribes of Israel I make known
what is sure.

10 "The princes of Judah are like those who
remove a landmark;
I will pour out My wrath on them like
water.

11 Ephraim is oppressed *and* broken in
judgment,
Because he willingly walked by *human*
precept.

12 Therefore I *will be* to Ephraim like a moth,
And to the house of Judah like rottenness.

The Law of Solid Ground: Leaders Who Move Boundaries

(Hosea 5:10)

Boundary stones were to be fixed and so bring definition to a plot of land. Israel's leaders moved what never should have been moved; they compromised values. Leaders who cannot be trusted with basic integrity will surely suffer God's anger. Every organization needs boundary stones. Leaders must establish and keep them.

---

13 "When Ephraim saw his sickness,
And Judah *saw* his wound,
Then Ephraim went to Assyria
And sent to King Jareb;
Yet he cannot cure you,

4:14 [a]Compare Deuteronomy 23:18 **4:18** [a]Hebrew
is difficult; a Jewish tradition reads *Her rulers
shamefully love,* 'Give!'

14 Nor heal you of your wound.
For I *will be* like a lion to Ephraim,
And like a young lion to the house of
Judah.
I, *even* I, will tear *them* and go away;
I will take *them* away, and no one shall
rescue.

15 I will return again to My place
Till they acknowledge their offense.
Then they will seek My face;
In their affliction they will earnestly seek
Me."

A Call to Repentance

6 Come, and let us return to the LORD;
For He has torn, but He will heal us;
He has stricken, but He will bind us up.

2 After two days He will revive us;
On the third day He will raise us up,
That we may live in His sight.

3 Let us know,
Let us pursue the knowledge of the LORD.
His going forth is established as the
morning;
He will come to us like the rain,
Like the latter *and* former rain to the
earth.

Impenitence of Israel and Judah

4 "O Ephraim, what shall I do to you?
O Judah, what shall I do to you?
For your faithfulness is like a morning
cloud,
And like the early dew it goes away.

5 Therefore I have hewn *them* by the
prophets,
I have slain them by the words of My
mouth;
And your judgments *are like* light *that* goes
forth.

6 For I desire mercy and not sacrifice,
And the knowledge of God more than
burnt offerings.

7 "But like men[a] they transgressed the
covenant;
There they dealt treacherously with Me.

8 Gilead *is* a city of evildoers
And defiled with blood.

9 As bands of robbers lie in wait for a man,
So the company of priests murder on the
way to Shechem;
Surely they commit lewdness.

10 I have seen a horrible thing in the house
of Israel:
There *is* the harlotry of Ephraim;

Israel is defiled.

11 Also, O Judah, a harvest is appointed for
you,
When I return the captives of My people.

The Art of Confrontation

(Hosea 6:1—7:16)

Hosea is not above speaking words of confrontation. He uses vivid imagery and colorful images to describe the evil behavior of his people. Look at his train of thought:

1. He clarifies the desired relationship he wishes to have (6:1–3).
2. He defines the unacceptable behavior (6:4, 5).
3. He highlights his values and priorities (6:6).
4. He lists the conduct that illustrates his point (7:1–14).
5. He reminds the people of their training (7:15).
6. He declares the consequences (7:16).

For six more chapters Hosea continues to detail the people's unacceptable conduct. Then, in chapter 14, he offers words of restoration. All good confrontation ends in the hope of restoration. The goal is always reconciliation, not excommunication.

When team members drift from goals, leaders owe it to them and to the organization to confront or clarify the situation. This is the only way to stay on track and to maintain respect from the team. Hosea has written the book on it!

7 "When I would have healed Israel,
Then the iniquity of Ephraim was
uncovered,
And the wickedness of Samaria.
For they have committed fraud;
A thief comes in;
A band of robbers takes spoil outside.

2 They do not consider in their hearts
That I remember all their wickedness;
Now their own deeds have surrounded
them;
They are before My face.

6:7 [a]Or *like Adam*

3 They make a king glad with their
    wickedness,
And princes with their lies.

4 "They *are* all adulterers.
Like an oven heated by a baker—
He ceases stirring *the fire* after kneading
    the dough,
Until it is leavened.

5 In the day of our king
Princes have made *him* sick, inflamed with
    wine;
He stretched out his hand with scoffers.

6 They prepare their heart like an oven,
While they lie in wait;
Their baker[a] sleeps all night;
In the morning it burns like a flaming fire.

7 They are all hot, like an oven,
And have devoured their judges;
All their kings have fallen.
None among them calls upon Me.

8 "Ephraim has mixed himself among the
    peoples;
Ephraim is a cake unturned.

9 Aliens have devoured his strength,
But he does not know *it;*
Yes, gray hairs are here and there on him,
Yet he does not know *it.*

10 And the pride of Israel testifies to his
    face,
But they do not return to the LORD their
    God,
Nor seek Him for all this.

Futile Reliance on the Nations

11 "Ephraim also is like a silly dove, without
    sense—
They call to Egypt,
They go to Assyria.

12 Wherever they go, I will spread My net on
    them;
I will bring them down like birds of the
    air;
I will chastise them
According to what their congregation has
    heard.

13 "Woe to them, for they have fled from Me!
Destruction to them,
Because they have transgressed against Me!
Though I redeemed them,
Yet they have spoken lies against Me.

14 They did not cry out to Me with their
    heart
When they wailed upon their beds.

"They assemble together for[a] grain and new
    wine,
They rebel against Me;[b]

15 Though I disciplined *and* strengthened
    their arms,
Yet they devise evil against Me;

16 They return, *but* not to the Most High;[a]
They are like a treacherous bow.
Their princes shall fall by the sword
For the cursings of their tongue.
This *shall be* their derision in the land of
    Egypt.

The Apostasy of Israel

8 "*Set* the trumpet[a] to your mouth!
He shall come like an eagle against the
    house of the LORD,
Because they have transgressed My
    covenant
And rebelled against My law.

2 Israel will cry to Me,
'My God, we know You!'

3 Israel has rejected the good;
The enemy will pursue him.

4 "They set up kings, but not by Me;
They made princes, but I did not
    acknowledge *them.*
From their silver and gold
They made idols for themselves—
That they might be cut off.

5 Your calf is rejected, O Samaria!
My anger is aroused against them—
How long until they attain to innocence?

6 For from Israel *is* even this:
A workman made it, and it *is* not God;
But the calf of Samaria shall be broken to
    pieces.

7 "They sow the wind,
And reap the whirlwind.
The stalk has no bud;
It shall never produce meal.
If it should produce,
Aliens would swallow it up.

8 Israel is swallowed up;

7:6 [a]Following Masoretic Text and Vulgate; Syriac
and Targum read *Their anger;* Septuagint reads
Ephraim. 7:14 [a]Following Masoretic Text and
Targum; Vulgate reads *thought upon;* Septuagint reads
slashed themselves for (compare 1 Kings 18:28).
[b]Following Masoretic Text, Syriac, and Targum;
Septuagint omits *They rebel against Me;* Vulgate reads
They departed from Me. 7:16 [a]Or *upward*
8:1 [a]Hebrew *shophar,* ram's horn

Now they are among the Gentiles
Like a vessel in which *is* no pleasure.
9 For they have gone up to Assyria,
Like a wild donkey alone by itself;
Ephraim has hired lovers.
10 Yes, though they have hired among the
nations,
Now I will gather them;
And they shall sorrow a little,[a]
Because of the burden[b] of the king of
princes.

11 "Because Ephraim has made many altars for
sin,
They have become for him altars for
sinning.
12 I have written for him the great things of
My law,
But they were considered a strange thing.
13 *For* the sacrifices of My offerings they
sacrifice flesh and eat *it,*
But the LORD does not accept them.
Now He will remember their iniquity and
punish their sins.
They shall return to Egypt.

14 "For Israel has forgotten his Maker,
And has built temples;[a]
Judah also has multiplied fortified cities;
But I will send fire upon his cities,
And it shall devour his palaces."

Judgment of Israel's Sin

9 Do not rejoice, O Israel, with joy like
other peoples,
For you have played the harlot against
your God.
You have made love *for* hire on every
threshing floor.
2 The threshing floor and the winepress
Shall not feed them,
And the new wine shall fail in her.

3 They shall not dwell in the LORD's land,
But Ephraim shall return to Egypt,
And shall eat unclean *things* in Assyria.
4 They shall not offer wine *offerings* to the
LORD,
Nor shall their sacrifices be pleasing to
Him.
It shall be like bread of mourners to
them;
All who eat it shall be defiled.
For their bread *shall be* for their *own* life;
It shall not come into the house of the
LORD.

5 What will you do in the appointed day,
And in the day of the feast of the LORD?
6 For indeed they are gone because of
destruction.
Egypt shall gather them up;
Memphis shall bury them.
Nettles shall possess their valuables of
silver;
Thorns *shall be* in their tents.

7 The days of punishment have come;
The days of recompense have come.
Israel knows!
The prophet *is* a fool,
The spiritual man *is* insane,
Because of the greatness of your iniquity
and great enmity.
8 The watchman of Ephraim *is* with my
God;
But the prophet *is* a fowler's[a] snare in all
his ways—
Enmity in the house of his God.
9 They are deeply corrupted,
As in the days of Gibeah.
He will remember their iniquity;
He will punish their sins.

10 "I found Israel
Like grapes in the wilderness;
I saw your fathers
As the firstfruits on the fig tree in its first
season.
But they went to Baal Peor,
And separated themselves *to that* shame;
They became an abomination like the
thing they loved.
11 *As for* Ephraim, their glory shall fly away
like a bird—
No birth, no pregnancy, and no conception!
12 Though they bring up their children,
Yet I will bereave them to the last man.
Yes, woe to them when I depart from
them!
13 Just as I saw Ephraim like Tyre, planted in
a pleasant place,
So Ephraim will bring out his children to
the murderer."

14 Give them, O LORD—
What will You give?
Give them a miscarrying womb
And dry breasts!

8:10 [a]Or *begin to diminish* [b]Or *oracle* **8:14** [a]Or
palaces **9:8** [a]That is, one who catches birds in a trap
or snare

15 "All their wickedness *is* in Gilgal,
   For there I hated them.
   Because of the evil of their deeds
   I will drive them from My house;
   I will love them no more.
   All their princes *are* rebellious.
16 Ephraim is stricken,
   Their root is dried up;
   They shall bear no fruit.
   Yes, were they to bear children,
   I would kill the darlings of their womb."

17 My God will cast them away,
   Because they did not obey Him;
   And they shall be wanderers among the
      nations.

Israel's Sin and Captivity

10 Israel empties *his* vine;
   He brings forth fruit for himself.
   According to the multitude of his
      fruit
   He has increased the altars;
   According to the bounty of his land
   They have embellished *his sacred* pillars.
2 Their heart is divided;
   Now they are held guilty.
   He will break down their altars;
   He will ruin their *sacred* pillars.

3 For now they say,
   "We have no king,
   Because we did not fear the LORD.
   And as for a king, what would he do for us?"
4 They have spoken words,
   Swearing falsely in making a covenant.
   Thus judgment springs up like hemlock in
      the furrows of the field.

Israel's Leaders Broke the Law of Solid Ground

(Hosea 10:3, 4)

How had Israel drifted into such serious sin? Hosea's answer: Israel had no real leadership. False promises had eroded the people's confidence in their leaders. They concluded: "We have no king. . . . They have spoken words, swearing falsely in making a covenant" (Hos. 10:3, 4). People follow only in proportion to their trust in the leader.

---

5 The inhabitants of Samaria fear
   Because of the calf[a] of Beth Aven.
   For its people mourn for it,
   And its priests shriek for it—
   Because its glory has departed from it.
6 *The idol* also shall be carried to Assyria
   As a present for King Jareb.
   Ephraim shall receive shame,
   And Israel shall be ashamed of his own
      counsel.

7 *As for* Samaria, her king is cut off
   Like a twig on the water.
8 Also the high places of Aven, the sin of
      Israel,
   Shall be destroyed.
   The thorn and thistle shall grow on their
      altars;
   They shall say to the mountains, "Cover
      us!"
   And to the hills, "Fall on us!"

9 "O Israel, you have sinned from the days of
      Gibeah;
   There they stood.
   The battle in Gibeah against the children
      of iniquity[a]
   Did not overtake them.
10 When *it is* My desire, I will chasten them.
   Peoples shall be gathered against them
   When I bind them for their two
      transgressions.[a]
11 Ephraim *is* a trained heifer
   That loves to thresh *grain;*
   But I harnessed her fair neck,
   I will make Ephraim pull *a plow.*
   Judah shall plow;
   Jacob shall break his clods."

12 Sow for yourselves righteousness;
   Reap in mercy;
   Break up your fallow ground,
   For *it is* time to seek the LORD,
   Till He comes and rains righteousness on
      you.

13 You have plowed wickedness;
   You have reaped iniquity.
   You have eaten the fruit of lies,
   Because you trusted in your own way,
   In the multitude of your mighty men.

10:5 [a]Literally *calves* **10:9** [a]So read many Hebrew manuscripts, Septuagint, and Vulgate; Masoretic Text reads *unruliness.* **10:10** [a]Or *in their two habitations*

14 Therefore tumult shall arise among your
people,
And all your fortresses shall be plundered
As Shalman plundered Beth Arbel in the
day of battle—
A mother dashed in pieces upon *her*
children.

15 Thus it shall be done to you, O Bethel,
Because of your great wickedness.
At dawn the king of Israel
Shall be cut off utterly.

God's Continuing Love for Israel

11 "When Israel *was* a child, I loved
him,
And out of Egypt I called My son.

2 *As* they called them,[a]
So they went from them;[b]
They sacrificed to the Baals,
And burned incense to carved images.

3 "I taught Ephraim to walk,
Taking them by their arms;[a]
But they did not know that I healed them.

4 I drew them with gentle cords,[a]
With bands of love,
And I was to them as those who take the
yoke from their neck.[b]
I stooped *and* fed them.

5 "He shall not return to the land of Egypt;
But the Assyrian shall be his king,
Because they refused to repent.

6 And the sword shall slash in his cities,
Devour his districts,
And consume *them,*
Because of their own counsels.

7 My people are bent on backsliding from Me.
Though they call to the Most High,[a]
None at all exalt *Him.*

8 "How can I give you up, Ephraim?
How can I hand you over, Israel?
How can I make you like Admah?
How can I set you like Zeboiim?
My heart churns within Me;
My sympathy is stirred.

9 I will not execute the fierceness of My
anger;
I will not again destroy Ephraim.
For I *am* God, and not man,
The Holy One in your midst;
And I will not come with terror.[a]

10 "They shall walk after the LORD.
He will roar like a lion.

When He roars,
Then *His* sons shall come trembling from
the west;

11 They shall come trembling like a bird from
Egypt,
Like a dove from the land of Assyria.
And I will let them dwell in their houses,"
Says the LORD.

God's Charge Against Ephraim

12 "Ephraim has encircled Me with lies,
And the house of Israel with deceit;
But Judah still walks with God,
Even with the Holy One[a] *who is* faithful.

12 "Ephraim feeds on the wind,
And pursues the east wind;
He daily increases lies and desolation.
Also they make a covenant with the
Assyrians,
And oil is carried to Egypt.

2 "The LORD also *brings* a charge against
Judah,
And will punish Jacob according to his
ways;
According to his deeds He will
recompense him.

3 He took his brother by the heel in the
womb,
And in his strength he struggled with God.[a]

4 Yes, he struggled with the Angel and
prevailed;
He wept, and sought favor from Him.
He found Him *in* Bethel,
And there He spoke to us—

5 That is, the LORD God of hosts.
The LORD *is* His memorable name.

6 So you, by *the help of* your God, return;
Observe mercy and justice,
And wait on your God continually.

7 "A cunning Canaanite!
Deceitful scales *are* in his hand;
He loves to oppress.

8 And Ephraim said,

11:2 [a]Following Masoretic Text and Vulgate;
Septuagint reads *Just as I called them;* Targum
interprets as *I sent prophets to a thousand of them.*
[b]Following Masoretic Text, Targum, and Vulgate;
Septuagint reads *from My face.* **11:3** [a]Some Hebrew
manuscripts, Septuagint, Syriac, and Vulgate read
My arms. **11:4** [a]Literally *cords of a man* [b]Literally
jaws **11:7** [a]Or *upward* **11:9** [a]Or *I will not enter a city*
11:12 [a]Or *holy ones* **12:3** [a]Compare Genesis 32:28

'Surely I have become rich,
I have found wealth for myself;
In all my labors
They shall find in me no iniquity that *is* sin.'

9 "But I *am* the LORD your God,
Ever since the land of Egypt;
I will again make you dwell in tents,
As in the days of the appointed feast.
10 I have also spoken by the prophets,
And have multiplied visions;
I have given symbols through the witness
of the prophets."

11 Though Gilead *has* idols—
Surely they are vanity—
Though they sacrifice bulls in Gilgal,
Indeed their altars *shall be* heaps in the
furrows of the field.

12 Jacob fled to the country of Syria;
Israel served for a spouse,
And for a wife he tended *sheep.*
13 By a prophet the LORD brought Israel out
of Egypt,
And by a prophet he was preserved.
14 Ephraim provoked *Him* to anger most
bitterly;
Therefore his Lord will leave the guilt of
his bloodshed upon him,
And return his reproach upon him.

Relentless Judgment on Israel

13 When Ephraim spoke, trembling,
He exalted *himself* in Israel;
But when he offended through Baal
worship, he died.
2 Now they sin more and more,
And have made for themselves molded
images,
Idols of their silver, according to their skill;
All of it *is* the work of craftsmen.
They say of them,
"Let the men who sacrifice[a] kiss the calves!"
3 Therefore they shall be like the morning
cloud
And like the early dew that passes away,
Like chaff blown off from a threshing floor
And like smoke from a chimney.

4 "Yet I *am* the LORD your God
Ever since the land of Egypt,
And you shall know no God but Me;
For *there is* no savior besides Me.
5 I knew you in the wilderness,
In the land of great drought.

6 When they had pasture, they were filled;
They were filled and their heart was exalted;
Therefore they forgot Me.

7 "So I will be to them like a lion;
Like a leopard by the road I will lurk;
8 I will meet them like a bear deprived *of
her cubs;*
I will tear open their rib cage,
And there I will devour them like a lion.
The wild beast shall tear them.

9 "O Israel, you are destroyed,[a]
But your help[b] *is* from Me.
10 I will be your King;[a]
Where *is any other,*
That he may save you in all your cities?

13:2 [a]Or *those who offer human sacrifice*
13:9 [a]Literally *it* or *he destroyed you* [b]Literally *in your help* **13:10** [a]Septuagint, Syriac, Targum, and Vulgate read *Where is your king?*

Humility: No Matter Who the Leader Is— God Still Rules!

(Hosea 14:1–7)

One of the missing pieces in Israel's leadership was humility. They had forgotten who created their prosperity and good fortune. Hosea 11:1–4 and 12:7–9 remind the nation that God taught them and provided for them.

Leaders err when they assume they are the source of blessing. Wise leaders seek to make good decisions, but realize the outcome remains in God's hands. Leaders merely manage what God owns. Leaders are in charge, but God is in control.

Hosea 14:1–7 gives a prescription to help leaders recapture humility:

1. **Return:** Do a turnaround and pursue the Lord (v. 1).
2. **Repent:** Confess specifically your self-sufficiency (v. 2).
3. **Remember:** Remind yourself that only God is in control (v. 3).
4. **Result:** Only then will God respond with blessing and restoration (vv. 4–7).

And your judges to whom you said,
'Give me a king and princes'?
11 I gave you a king in My anger,
And took *him* away in My wrath.

12 "The iniquity of Ephraim *is* bound up;
His sin *is* stored up.
13 The sorrows of a woman in childbirth
shall come upon him.
He *is* an unwise son,
For he should not stay long where
children are born.

14 "I will ransom them from the power of the
grave;[a]
I will redeem them from death.
O Death, I will be your plagues![b]
O Grave,[c] I will be your destruction![d]
Pity is hidden from My eyes."

15 Though he is fruitful among *his* brethren,
An east wind shall come;
The wind of the LORD shall come up
from the wilderness.
Then his spring shall become dry,
And his fountain shall be dried up.
He shall plunder the treasury of every
desirable prize.
16 Samaria is held guilty,[a]
For she has rebelled against her God.
They shall fall by the sword,
Their infants shall be dashed in pieces,

And their women with child ripped
open.

Israel Restored at Last

14 O Israel, return to the LORD your
God,
For you have stumbled because of
your iniquity;
2 Take words with you,
And return to the LORD.
Say to Him,
"Take away all iniquity;
Receive *us* graciously,
For we will offer the sacrifices[a] of our lips.
3 Assyria shall not save us,
We will not ride on horses,
Nor will we say anymore to the work of
our hands, '*You are* our gods.'
For in You the fatherless finds mercy."

4 "I will heal their backsliding,
I will love them freely,
For My anger has turned away from him.
5 I will be like the dew to Israel;
He shall grow like the lily,
And lengthen his roots like Lebanon.
6 His branches shall spread;

13:14 [a]Or *Sheol* [b]Septuagint reads *where is your
punishment?* [c]Or *Sheol* [d]Septuagint reads *where is
your sting?* 13:16 [a]Septuagint reads *shall be disfigured*
14:2 [a]Literally *bull calves;* Septuagint reads *fruit.*

Leaders Love Everyone,
but Don't Drop Their Convictions

(Hosea 14:9)

D o leaders always love and care for people, regardless of who they are? Certainly, both God
and Hosea modeled unconditional love. But does a time come when showing compassion for
someone ends, or otherwise a leader violates a bedrock principle?

This is where leaders draw a line in the sand. While they are to love and care for anyone they
contact, this doesn't mean they chuck their convictions. They respond with grace, but never
drift from their guiding priorities and principles. We cling to convictions even in our lowest moment.

Both God and Hosea continued to act from principle. Leaders practice the Law of Empowerment by living out priorities:

Leaders are to . . .
1. Act from their principles.
2. Empower others even when it's difficult.
3. Live off of character.

Followers often . . .
1. React from their feelings.
2. Withdraw in difficult times.
3. Live off of emotions.

His beauty shall be like an olive tree,
And his fragrance like Lebanon.
7 Those who dwell under his shadow shall
   return;
They shall be revived *like* grain,
And grow like a vine.
Their scent[a] *shall be* like the wine of
   Lebanon.

8 "Ephraim *shall say,* 'What have I to do
   anymore with idols?'
I have heard and observed him.

I *am* like a green cypress tree;
Your fruit is found in Me."

9 Who *is* wise?
Let him understand these things.
Who is prudent?
Let him know them.
For the ways of the LORD *are* right;
The righteous walk in them,
But transgressors stumble in them.

14:7 [a]Literally *remembrance*

JOEL

A God-Given Message to Judah

SUMMARY

The prophet Joel directed his message to Judah and, more specifically, to the city of Jerusalem. Joel was an educated, well-read leader who knew not only the writings of the other prophets, but also the current events of his day. He used them all to illustrate the message God had given him.

Joel effectively used an invasion of locusts that occurred during his day as his primary word picture. He utilized this natural catastrophe to underscore his message of repentance. He spoke of the "day of the LORD" which would come much like the locusts—surprising and terrifying. He attempted to awaken the people of Judah from their spiritual apathy and disobedience and provoke them to return to the Lord.

Joel teaches us that leaders must see the future clearly and project what steps must be taken to thrive in it. Joel called the leaders of his day to sound a warning of repentance to successive generations he would never meet—a futurist in the truest sense of the word.

Second, leaders must read and interpret current events. Joel saw and explained the locusts of his day in a way that made his message vivid and memorable. He took a physical reality and capitalized on it to illustrate a spiritual reality. His mind focused on both current events and eternal outcomes.

Third, corporate or community repentance begins with the leader. People usually act *en masse* when a leader sounds the trumpet and provides an example of what must be done. This proved true in Joel's case. Joel called the priests to model repentance with sackcloth and mourning. People do what people see.

Fourth, leaders must never cry out for change without providing some solutions. It does little good to merely complain. Leaders must sound the alarm, but then say, "And here are some steps we can take to improve." Along with his warning of judgment, Joel talks about the promise of the Holy Spirit and the need for His filling. He spoke of the coming day of the Lord and the need to call on God for deliverance. He listed the steps of repentance the people of Judah needed to take if they were to renew themselves and find restoration in the grace of God.

God's Role in Joel

God is the Ultimate Leader in control, the One who sends the locusts and the One who will come on the day of the Lord—a day far more terrifying than mere locusts. God sometimes uses the natural realm to direct us to truths in the spiritual realm. God uses the disastrous locust plague to illustrate a far greater spiritual catastrophe to come if His people refuse to return to Him.

Leaders in Joel

Joel

Other People of Influence in Joel

Leaders in Jerusalem and Judah

Lessons in Leadership

- Leaders are realistic futurists—they define reality and distribute hope.
- Great leaders communicate in relevant ways, connecting the known to the unknown.
- If leaders project a problem to the people, they must propose a plan for the people.

LEADERSHIP HIGHLIGHTS IN JOEL

THE LAW OF INTUITION: Joel Interprets the Disaster of the Locusts (1:6, 7)	*page 1060*
THE LAW OF CONNECTION: Joel Uses the Times to Say the Timeless (2:1–32)	*page 1061*
THE LAW OF NAVIGATION: Joel Declares Hope if Judah Will Respond (3:1–21)	*page 1063*

1

The word of the LORD that came to Joel the son of Pethuel.

The Land Laid Waste

2   Hear this, you elders,
    And give ear, all you inhabitants of the
        land!
    Has *anything like* this happened in your
        days,
    Or even in the days of your fathers?
3   Tell your children about it,
    Let your children *tell* their children,
    And their children another generation.

4   What the chewing locust[a] left, the
        swarming locust has eaten;
    What the swarming locust left, the
        crawling locust has eaten;
    And what the crawling locust left, the
        consuming locust has eaten.

5   Awake, you drunkards, and weep;
    And wail, all you drinkers of wine,
    Because of the new wine,
    For it has been cut off from your mouth.
6   For a nation has come up against My
        land,
    Strong, and without number;
    His teeth *are* the teeth of a lion,
    And he has the fangs of a fierce lion.
7   He has laid waste My vine,
    And ruined My fig tree;
    He has stripped it bare and thrown *it* away;
    Its branches are made white.

8   Lament like a virgin girded with sackcloth
    For the husband of her youth.
9   The grain offering and the drink offering
    Have been cut off from the house of the
        LORD;
    The priests mourn, who minister to the
        LORD.
10 The field is wasted,
    The land mourns;
    For the grain is ruined,
    The new wine is dried up,
    The oil fails.

11 Be ashamed, you farmers,
    Wail, you vinedressers,
    For the wheat and the barley;
    Because the harvest of the field has
        perished.
12 The vine has dried up,
    And the fig tree has withered;
    The pomegranate tree,

The Law of Intuition: Joel Interprets the Disaster of the Locusts

(Joel 1:6, 7)

Joel provides us with an example of a leader who rightly reads his times and culture and interprets them for the masses. His divine intuition enables him to stay ahead of the times and lead in a wise and discerning manner.

Intuition is like a head start in a race; you can beat the fastest runner in the world with a big enough head start. Joel provides this head start to the Hebrews, then gives them a plan to respond to the coming disaster. "Consecrate a fast, call a sacred assembly; gather the elders and all the inhabitants of the land into the house of the LORD your God, and cry out to the LORD," he advises them (Joel 1:14). He helps us see that God sometimes uses the natural realm to illustrate realities in the spiritual realm.

The palm tree also,
And the apple tree—
All the trees of the field are withered;
Surely joy has withered away from the sons
    of men.

Mourning for the Land

13 Gird yourselves and lament, you priests;
    Wail, you who minister before the altar;
    Come, lie all night in sackcloth,
    You who minister to my God;
    For the grain offering and the drink
        offering
    Are withheld from the house of your God.
14 Consecrate a fast,
    Call a sacred assembly;
    Gather the elders
    And all the inhabitants of the land
    Into the house of the LORD your God,
    And cry out to the LORD.

15 Alas for the day!
    For the day of the LORD *is* at hand;
    It shall come as destruction from the
        Almighty.

1:4 [a]Exact identity of these locusts is unknown.

16 Is not the food cut off before our eyes,
   Joy and gladness from the house of our
   God?
17 The seed shrivels under the clods,
   Storehouses are in shambles;
   Barns are broken down,
   For the grain has withered.
18 How the animals groan!
   The herds of cattle are restless,
   Because they have no pasture;
   Even the flocks of sheep suffer
   punishment.[a]

19 O LORD, to You I cry out;
   For fire has devoured the open pastures,
   And a flame has burned all the trees of the
   field.
20 The beasts of the field also cry out to You,
   For the water brooks are dried up,
   And fire has devoured the open pastures.

The Day of the LORD

2 Blow the trumpet in Zion,
   And sound an alarm in My holy
   mountain!
   Let all the inhabitants of the land tremble;
   For the day of the LORD is coming,
   For it is at hand:
2 A day of darkness and gloominess,
   A day of clouds and thick darkness,
   Like the morning *clouds* spread over the
   mountains.
   A people *come*, great and strong,
   The like of whom has never been;
   Nor will there ever be any *such* after them,
   Even for many successive generations.

3 A fire devours before them,
   And behind them a flame burns;
   The land *is* like the Garden of Eden before
   them,
   And behind them a desolate wilderness;
   Surely nothing shall escape them.
4 Their appearance is like the appearance of
   horses;
   And like swift steeds, so they run.
5 With a noise like chariots
   Over mountaintops they leap,
   Like the noise of a flaming fire that
   devours the stubble,
   Like a strong people set in battle array.

6 Before them the people writhe in pain;
   All faces are drained of color.[a]
7 They run like mighty men,
   They climb the wall like men of war;

Every one marches in formation,
And they do not break ranks.
8 They do not push one another;
   Every one marches in his own column.[a]
   Though they lunge between the weapons,
   They are not cut down.[b]
9 They run to and fro in the city,
   They run on the wall;
   They climb into the houses,
   They enter at the windows like a thief.

10 The earth quakes before them;
   The heavens tremble;
   The sun and moon grow dark,
   And the stars diminish their brightness.
11 The LORD gives voice before His army,
   For His camp is very great;
   For strong *is the One* who executes His
   word.
   For the day of the LORD *is* great and very
   terrible;
   Who can endure it?

1:18 [a]Septuagint and Vulgate read *are made desolate.*
2:6 [a]Septuagint, Targum, and Vulgate read *gather
blackness.* 2:8 [a]Literally *his own highway* [b]That is,
they are not halted by losses

The Law of Connection: Joel Uses the Times to Say the Timeless

(Joel 2:1–32)

Leaders understand how to be relevant.
Relevance means using temporal events to
say what is timeless.

The prophet uses the current events of his
time to share timeless truth. Every Hebrew
knew of the plague of locusts. When that subject came up, everyone paid attention. Joel
grabbed their attention with a current event
and used it to illustrate God's coming judgment. He and God communicated in these
ways:

1. *Creatively:* They used word pictures and
   current events.
2. *Constantly:* They continued to speak until
   the people understood.
3. *Consistently:* Their messages didn't contradict each other.

A Call to Repentance

12 "Now, therefore," says the LORD,
    "Turn to Me with all your heart,
        With fasting, with weeping, and with
            mourning."
13   So rend your heart, and not your
            garments;
        Return to the LORD your God,
        For He *is* gracious and merciful,
        Slow to anger, and of great kindness;
        And He relents from doing harm.
14   Who knows *if* He will turn and relent,
        And leave a blessing behind Him—
        A grain offering and a drink offering
        For the LORD your God?

15   Blow the trumpet in Zion,
        Consecrate a fast,
        Call a sacred assembly;
16   Gather the people,
        Sanctify the congregation,
        Assemble the elders,
        Gather the children and nursing babes;
        Let the bridegroom go out from his
            chamber,
        And the bride from her dressing room.
17   Let the priests, who minister to the LORD,
        Weep between the porch and the altar;
        Let them say, "Spare Your people, O LORD,
        And do not give Your heritage to
            reproach,
        That the nations should rule over them.
        Why should they say among the peoples,
        'Where *is* their God?'"

The Land Refreshed

18   Then the LORD will be zealous for His
            land,
        And pity His people.
19   The LORD will answer and say to His
            people,
        "Behold, I will send you grain and new
            wine and oil,
        And you will be satisfied by them;
        I will no longer make you a reproach
            among the nations.

20   "But I will remove far from you the
            northern *army,*
        And will drive him away into a barren and
            desolate land,
        With his face toward the eastern sea
        And his back toward the western sea;
        His stench will come up,
        And his foul odor will rise,
        Because he has done monstrous things."

21   Fear not, O land;
        Be glad and rejoice,
        For the LORD has done marvelous things!
22   Do not be afraid, you beasts of the field;
        For the open pastures are springing up,
        And the tree bears its fruit;
        The fig tree and the vine yield their
            strength.
23   Be glad then, you children of Zion,
        And rejoice in the LORD your God;
        For He has given you the former rain
            faithfully,[a]
        And He will cause the rain to come down
            for you—
        The former rain,
        And the latter rain in the first *month.*
24   The threshing floors shall be full of wheat,
        And the vats shall overflow with new wine
            and oil.

25   "So I will restore to you the years that the
            swarming locust has eaten,
        The crawling locust,
        The consuming locust,
        And the chewing locust,[a]
        My great army which I sent among you.
26   You shall eat in plenty and be satisfied,
        And praise the name of the LORD your
            God,
        Who has dealt wondrously with you;
        And My people shall never be put to
            shame.
27   Then you shall know that I *am* in the
            midst of Israel:
        I *am* the LORD your God
        And there is no other.
        My people shall never be put to shame.

God's Spirit Poured Out

28   "And it shall come to pass afterward
        That I will pour out My Spirit on all
            flesh;
        Your sons and your daughters shall
            prophesy,
        Your old men shall dream dreams,
        Your young men shall see visions.
29   And also on *My* menservants and on *My*
            maidservants
        I will pour out My Spirit in those days.

30   "And I will show wonders in the heavens
            and in the earth:
        Blood and fire and pillars of smoke.

2:23 [a]Or *the teacher of righteousness* **2:25** [a]Compare
1:4

31 The sun shall be turned into darkness,
And the moon into blood,
Before the coming of the great and
awesome day of the LORD.
32 And it shall come to pass
That whoever calls on the name of the
LORD
Shall be saved.
For in Mount Zion and in Jerusalem there
shall be deliverance,
As the LORD has said,
Among the remnant whom the LORD
calls.

God Judges the Nations

3 "For behold, in those days and at that
time,
When I bring back the captives of Judah
and Jerusalem,
2 I will also gather all nations,
And bring them down to the Valley of
Jehoshaphat;
And I will enter into judgment with them
there
On account of My people, My heritage
Israel,
Whom they have scattered among the
nations;
They have also divided up My land.
3 They have cast lots for My people,
Have given a boy *as payment* for a harlot,
And sold a girl for wine, that they may
drink.

4 "Indeed, what have you to do with Me,
O Tyre and Sidon, and all the coasts of
Philistia?
Will you retaliate against Me?
But if you retaliate against Me,
Swiftly and speedily I will return your
retaliation upon your own head;
5 Because you have taken My silver and My
gold,
And have carried into your temples My
prized possessions.
6 Also the people of Judah and the people of
Jerusalem
You have sold to the Greeks,
That you may remove them far from their
borders.

7 "Behold, I will raise them
Out of the place to which you have sold
them,
And will return your retaliation upon your
own head.

8 I will sell your sons and your daughters
Into the hand of the people of Judah,
And they will sell them to the Sabeans,[a]
To a people far off;
For the LORD has spoken."

The Law of Navigation: Joel Declares Hope if Judah Will Respond

(Joel 3:1–21)

In the last chapter of his short book, Joel pronounces judgment on the nations. The nation of Israel could look forward to a future full of hope—if they would respond with obedience. Joel predicts that God will use them to judge the nations. The day of the Lord will bring terror to the rebellious and hope to the trusting.

The Law of Navigation forces leaders to become students of three facets of leadership: discernment, strategy, and the future. They must interpret the times, see the future, and plan the steps. Joel paints pictures for the people to help them see what he sees.

9 Proclaim this among the nations:
"Prepare for war!
Wake up the mighty men,
Let all the men of war draw near,
Let them come up.
10 Beat your plowshares into swords
And your pruning hooks into spears;
Let the weak say, 'I *am* strong.'"
11 Assemble and come, all you nations,
And gather together all around.
Cause Your mighty ones to go down
there, O LORD.

12 "Let the nations be wakened, and come up
to the Valley of Jehoshaphat;
For there I will sit to judge all the
surrounding nations.
13 Put in the sickle, for the harvest is
ripe.
Come, go down;
For the winepress is full,

3:8 [a]Literally *Shebaites* (compare Isaiah 60:6 and Ezekiel 27:22)

The vats overflow—
For their wickedness *is* great."

14 Multitudes, multitudes in the valley of
   decision!
   For the day of the LORD *is* near in the
   valley of decision.

15 The sun and moon will grow dark,
   And the stars will diminish their
   brightness.

16 The LORD also will roar from Zion,
   And utter His voice from Jerusalem;
   The heavens and earth will shake;
   But the LORD will be a shelter for His
   people,
   And the strength of the children of Israel.

17 "So you shall know that I *am* the LORD
   your God,
   Dwelling in Zion My holy mountain.
   Then Jerusalem shall be holy,
   And no aliens shall ever pass through her
   again."

God Blesses His People

18 And it will come to pass in that day
   That the mountains shall drip with new
   wine,
   The hills shall flow with milk,
   And all the brooks of Judah shall be
   flooded with water;
   A fountain shall flow from the house of
   the LORD
   And water the Valley of Acacias.

19 "Egypt shall be a desolation,
   And Edom a desolate wilderness,
   Because of violence *against* the people of
   Judah,
   For they have shed innocent blood in their
   land.

20 But Judah shall abide forever,
   And Jerusalem from generation to
   generation.

21 For I will acquit them of the guilt of
   bloodshed, whom I had not acquitted;
   For the LORD dwells in Zion."

AMOS
A Spiritual Plumb Line Raised

SUMMARY

God called the fiery prophet Amos to correct the injustice of the leaders of his day in Israel, Judah, and the surrounding nations. He seems an unlikely leader, called as a shepherd in the desert of Judah. As a shepherd, he supplemented his income by taking care of sycamore "fig trees" (1:1; 7:14, 15). He brought no known credentials to his prophetic work except for his divine call.

Amos first challenged the sins of the surrounding nations—something the Israelites liked. But when he turned to correct his own people, his popularity plummeted. The writings of this clear thinker show that he possessed a thorough knowledge of history and the problems of his day. He uses language rich in symbols and figures, with close attention to detail. He tries to compel the people to see the immorality and injustice of their generation and to make it right.

In Amos's day, marketplace exploitation had grown so bad that God used him to threaten the people with "fire": war, economic depression, and destruction. God gives power to leaders for the provision, protection, and progress of followers. Whenever leaders abuse that power, God shows His displeasure with their stewardship.

Amos also shows us that God hates injustice. While it may look as if He doesn't do anything about the outrage, He is watching and disapproves of leaders who tolerate it. Amos accused leaders of a spiritual deterioration that paralleled their material prosperity (5:12, 21). They still "went to church," yet didn't see their own hypocrisy. Amos castigated the leaders for their corruption (2:7, 8) and pointed out their disregard for human rights (2:6). For about a decade, Amos became God's eyes, heart, and mouthpiece to the people of Israel.

Amos taught that leaders must lead from moral absolutes, not from convenience and expediency. Amos used a plumb line to illustrate that God's people had drifted from the revealed standard. A plumb line helped builders detect the straightness of a wall, the equivalent of a level today. Builders attached a weight to a string, then let gravity use the string to draw a straight vertical line. Amos attempted to raise a spiritual plumb line against the corruption and crookedness of his day.

God's Role in Amos

Amos did not base his plea on the nature of man or the innate goodness of human nature. *God* was the standard—and He remains the same at all times and in every place. Self-interest always distorts man's perspective. Amos based his plea on the nature and righteousness of God, the "plumb line" from which every person is measured. Despite the shifting values of mankind, God never changes, nor does He grade on a curve. He is the absolute leader and controller of history and challenges leaders when they drift from His absolutes.

Leaders in Amos

Amos, Jeroboam II, Uzziah

Other People of Influence in Amos

Amaziah, the sellers in the marketplace

Lessons in Leadership

- It's easiest for leaders to drift when there is economic security.

- God gives power to leaders to help followers, not themselves.

- When an organization goes bad, leaders must own the responsibility.

- The foundation for all leadership is trust, integrity, and justice.

- Leaders must raise the standard; as the leader goes, so goes the organization.

LEADERSHIP HIGHLIGHTS IN AMOS

1 The words of Amos, who was among the sheepbreeders[a] of Tekoa, which he saw concerning Israel in the days of Uzziah king of Judah, and in the days of Jeroboam the son of Joash, king of Israel, two years before the earthquake.

2 And he said:

"The LORD roars from Zion,
And utters His voice from Jerusalem;
The pastures of the shepherds mourn,
And the top of Carmel withers."

Efficiency Minus Ethics Equals Emptiness

(Amos 1:1—2:16)

Leaders who fail morally do not lead anyone to a better place. The higher the leader goes, the deeper his character must develop. The larger the outward privilege, the larger the inward character must be. Character represents the inner life of a leader. God judged ancient leaders because of missing character:

1. *Damascus, Syria*—because they ruthlessly butchered Gilead without just cause.
2. *Gaza*—because they made captives of free people and sold them into slavery.
3. *Tyre*—because they ignored a covenant of peace and brotherhood.
4. *Edom*—because they attacked their own family tribes and showed no compassion.
5. *Ammon*—because they murdered women in order to expand their territory.
6. *Moab*—because they displayed no respect for leadership in neighboring nations.

Judgment on the Nations

3 Thus says the LORD:

"For three transgressions of Damascus, and for four,
I will not turn away its *punishment,*
Because they have threshed Gilead with implements of iron.
4 But I will send a fire into the house of Hazael,
Which shall devour the palaces of Ben-Hadad.
5 I will also break the *gate* bar of Damascus,
And cut off the inhabitant from the Valley of Aven,
And the one who holds the scepter from Beth Eden.
The people of Syria shall go captive to Kir,"
Says the LORD.

6 Thus says the LORD:

"For three transgressions of Gaza, and for four,
I will not turn away its *punishment,*
Because they took captive the whole captivity
To deliver *them* up to Edom.
7 But I will send a fire upon the wall of Gaza,
Which shall devour its palaces.
8 I will cut off the inhabitant from Ashdod,
And the one who holds the scepter from Ashkelon;
I will turn My hand against Ekron,
And the remnant of the Philistines shall perish,"
Says the Lord GOD.

9 Thus says the LORD:

"For three transgressions of Tyre, and for four,
I will not turn away its *punishment,*
Because they delivered up the whole captivity to Edom,
And did not remember the covenant of brotherhood.
10 But I will send a fire upon the wall of Tyre,
Which shall devour its palaces."

11 Thus says the LORD:

"For three transgressions of Edom, and for four,
I will not turn away its *punishment,*
Because he pursued his brother with the sword,
And cast off all pity;
His anger tore perpetually,
And he kept his wrath forever.
12 But I will send a fire upon Teman,
Which shall devour the palaces of Bozrah."

1:1 [a] Compare 2 Kings 3:4.

¹³Thus says the LORD:

"For three transgressions of the people of
　　Ammon, and for four,
　I will not turn away its *punishment*,
　Because they ripped open the women
　　with child in Gilead,
　That they might enlarge their territory.
¹⁴　But I will kindle a fire in the wall of
　　Rabbah,
　And it shall devour its palaces,
　Amid shouting in the day of battle,
　And a tempest in the day of the
　　whirlwind.
¹⁵　Their king shall go into captivity,
　He and his princes together,"
　Says the LORD.

2 Thus says the LORD:

"For three transgressions of Moab, and for
　　four,
　I will not turn away its *punishment*,
　Because he burned the bones of the king
　　of Edom to lime.
²　But I will send a fire upon Moab,
　And it shall devour the palaces of Kerioth;
　Moab shall die with tumult,
　With shouting *and* trumpet sound.
³　And I will cut off the judge from its midst,

And slay all its princes with him,"
　Says the LORD.

Judgment on Judah
⁴Thus says the LORD:

"For three transgressions of Judah, and for
　　four,
　I will not turn away its *punishment*,
　Because they have despised the law of the
　　LORD,
　And have not kept His commandments.
　Their lies lead them astray,
　Lies which their fathers followed.
⁵　But I will send a fire upon Judah,
　And it shall devour the palaces of
　　Jerusalem."

Judgment on Israel
⁶Thus says the LORD:

"For three transgressions of Israel, and for
　　four,
　I will not turn away its *punishment*,
　Because they sell the righteous for silver,
　And the poor for a pair of sandals.
⁷　They pant after[a] the dust of the earth *which
　is* on the head of the poor,

2:7 [a]Or *trample on*

The Law of Solid Ground:
Good Leaders Remove the Planks from Their Eyes
(Amos 2:4–16)

The entire first chapter of Amos and part of the second details God's judgment on Israel's
neighbors. No doubt Israel enjoyed these words. They likely cheered Amos on, yelling, "Preach
it, brother! Those heathen nations really need to get their act together!"

Once Amos finished with Damascus, Gaza, Tyre, Edom, Ammon, and Moab, however, he directed
his words closer to home—to Judah. Now his listeners probably squirmed. Finally, Amos dropped
the bomb and declared judgment on Israel. Everyone grew quiet. How dare Amos lump *them* into
God's judgment!

Quality leaders remain objective. They can be trusted because they see the "plank in their own
eye" before trying to remove the speck from their brother's (Matt. 7:3–5). When leaders fail to be
objective, people begin to question whether their perspective is skewed by self-interest. Trust
wanes. People trust leaders who practice the Law of Solid Ground. Such leaders fulfill three primary objectives:

1. Protection: To make sure the people are defended from harm.
2. Provision: To make sure the people are resourced to do their work.
3. Progress: To make sure the enterprise reaches the desired destination.

And pervert the way of the humble.
A man and his father go in to the *same*
  girl,
To defile My holy name.
8 They lie down by every altar on clothes
  taken in pledge,
And drink the wine of the condemned *in*
  the house of their god.

9 "Yet *it was* I *who* destroyed the Amorite
  before them,
Whose height *was* like the height of the
  cedars,
And he *was* as strong as the oaks;
Yet I destroyed his fruit above
And his roots beneath.
10 Also *it was* I *who* brought you up from the
  land of Egypt,
And led you forty years through the
  wilderness,
To possess the land of the Amorite.
11 I raised up some of your sons as prophets,
And some of your young men as
  Nazirites.
Is it not so, O you children of Israel?"
Says the LORD.
12 "But you gave the Nazirites wine to
  drink,
And commanded the prophets saying,
'Do not prophesy!'

13 "Behold, I am weighed down by you,
As a cart full of sheaves is weighed down.
14 Therefore flight shall perish from the
  swift,
The strong shall not strengthen his
  power,
Nor shall the mighty deliver himself;
15 He shall not stand who handles the bow,
The swift of foot shall not escape,
Nor shall he who rides a horse deliver
  himself.
16 The most courageous men of might
  Shall flee naked in that day,"
Says the LORD.

Authority of the Prophet's Message

3 Hear this word that the LORD has spoken
against you, O children of Israel, against
the whole family which I brought up from
the land of Egypt, saying:

2 "You only have I known of all the families
  of the earth;
Therefore I will punish you for all your
  iniquities."

God Holds His People Accountable to Lead the World

(Amos 3:1, 2)

God's people failed to realize that he held them to a higher standard than other nations. God intended to guide them Himself, making them a nation of leaders who could become a model for the world. His heavy judgment fell because He held His people accountable to lead the world to Himself.

---

3 Can two walk together, unless they are
  agreed?
4 Will a lion roar in the forest, when he has
  no prey?
  Will a young lion cry out of his den, if he
  has caught nothing?
5 Will a bird fall into a snare on the earth,
  where there is no trap for it?
  Will a snare spring up from the earth, if it
  has caught nothing at all?
6 If a trumpet is blown in a city, will not the
  people be afraid?
  If there is calamity in a city, will not the
  LORD have done *it?*

7 Surely the Lord GOD does nothing,
  Unless He reveals His secret to His
  servants the prophets.
8 A lion has roared!
  Who will not fear?
  The Lord GOD has spoken!
  Who can but prophesy?

Punishment of Israel's Sins

9 "Proclaim in the palaces at Ashdod,[a]
  And in the palaces in the land of Egypt,
  and say:
  'Assemble on the mountains of Samaria;
  See great tumults in her midst,
  And the oppressed within her.
10 For they do not know to do right,'
  Says the LORD,
  'Who store up violence and robbery in
  their palaces.'"

3:9 [a]Following Masoretic Text; Septuagint reads
Assyria.

[11]Therefore thus says the Lord GOD:

"An adversary *shall be* all around the land;
  He shall sap your strength from you,
  And your palaces shall be plundered."

[12]Thus says the LORD:

"As a shepherd takes from the mouth of a
    lion
  Two legs or a piece of an ear,
  So shall the children of Israel be taken out
  Who dwell in Samaria—
  In the corner of a bed and on the edge[a] of
    a couch!

[13] Hear and testify against the house of
    Jacob,"
  Says the Lord GOD, the God of hosts,

[14] "That in the day I punish Israel for their
    transgressions,
  I will also visit *destruction* on the altars of
    Bethel;
  And the horns of the altar shall be cut off
  And fall to the ground.

[15] I will destroy the winter house along with
    the summer house;
  The houses of ivory shall perish,

And the great houses shall have an end,"
  Says the LORD.

4 Hear this word, you cows of Bashan, who
  are on the mountain of Samaria,
  Who oppress the poor,
  Who crush the needy,
  Who say to your husbands,[a] "Bring *wine,*
    let us drink!"

[2] The Lord GOD has sworn by His holiness:
  "Behold, the days shall come upon you
  When He will take you away with
    fishhooks,
  And your posterity with fishhooks.

[3] You will go out *through* broken *walls,*
  Each one straight ahead of her,
  And you will be cast into Harmon,"
  Says the LORD.

[4] "Come to Bethel and transgress,
  At Gilgal multiply transgression;
  Bring your sacrifices every morning,
  Your tithes every three days.[a]

3:12 [a]The Hebrew is uncertain. **4:1** [a]Literally *their lords* or *their masters* **4:4** [a]Or *years* (compare Deuteronomy 14:28)

AMOS · A PROPHET OF WRATH AND MERCY
(Amos 4:1–12)

PROFILE IN LEADERSHIP

Sometimes it's easy to forget that the God who showers grace upon His people is the same God who warns of impending judgment and who exercises His wrath.

Amos teaches us that leaders must present God as He presents Himself: as the God of love and mercy *and* the God of holiness and wrath. As the apostle Paul says in Romans 11:22, "Therefore consider the goodness and severity of God."

Can you imagine calling the women of your church or organization, "cows of Bashan"? Yet that is the very name Amos uses to address the women of Israel (Amos 4:1). The prophet speaks harsh words to His people, warning them finally to "prepare to meet your God, O Israel!" (4:12). This was no promise of a pleasant encounter, but a pronouncement of wrath on those who refused to return to and bow to the God who had faithfully guided, protected, and provided for them.

But Amos also speaks words of hope. Through the prophet, God tells the people that they can still humble themselves and return to Him and receive mercy (9:8–15).

This is the picture of God that today's leaders must present. God's people must see that He is a God of grace and mercy *and* a God of wrath and judgment. Any presentation that falls short of that standard is at best incomplete.

5 Offer a sacrifice of thanksgiving with
        leaven,
    Proclaim *and* announce the freewill
        offerings;
    For this you love,
    You children of Israel!"
    Says the Lord GOD.

Israel Did Not Accept Correction

6 "Also I gave you cleanness of teeth in all
        your cities.
    And lack of bread in all your places;
    Yet you have not returned to Me,"
    Says the LORD.

7 "I also withheld rain from you,
    When *there were* still three months to the
        harvest.
    I made it rain on one city,
    I withheld rain from another city.
    One part was rained upon,
    And where it did not rain the part withered.

8 So two *or* three cities wandered to another
        city to drink water,
    But they were not satisfied;
    Yet you have not returned to Me,"
    Says the LORD.

9 "I blasted you with blight and mildew.
    When your gardens increased,
    Your vineyards,
    Your fig trees,
    And your olive trees,
    The locust devoured *them;*
    Yet you have not returned to Me,"
    Says the LORD.

10 "I sent among you a plague after the
        manner of Egypt;
    Your young men I killed with a sword,
    Along with your captive horses;
    I made the stench of your camps come up
        into your nostrils;
    Yet you have not returned to Me,"
    Says the LORD.

11 "I overthrew *some* of you,
    As God overthrew Sodom and Gomorrah,
    And you were like a firebrand plucked
        from the burning;
    Yet you have not returned to Me,"
    Says the LORD.

12 "Therefore thus will I do to you, O Israel;
    Because I will do this to you,
    Prepare to meet your God, O Israel!"

13 For behold,
    He who forms mountains,
    And creates the wind,
    Who declares to man what his[a] thought *is,*
    And makes the morning darkness,
    Who treads the high places of the earth—
    The LORD God of hosts *is* His name.

A Lament for Israel

5 Hear this word which I take up against
    you, a lamentation, O house of Israel:

2 The virgin of Israel has fallen;
    She will rise no more.
    She lies forsaken on her land;
    There is no one to raise her up.

3 For thus says the Lord GOD:

"The city that goes out by a thousand
    Shall have a hundred left,
    And that which goes out by a hundred
    Shall have ten left to the house of Israel."

A Call to Repentance

4 For thus says the LORD to the house of
Israel:

"Seek Me and live;
5 But do not seek Bethel,
    Nor enter Gilgal,
    Nor pass over to Beersheba;
    For Gilgal shall surely go into captivity,
    And Bethel shall come to nothing.
6 Seek the LORD and live,
    Lest He break out like fire *in* the house of
        Joseph,
    And devour *it,*
    With no one to quench *it* in Bethel—
7 You who turn justice to wormwood,
    And lay righteousness to rest in the
        earth!"

8 He made the Pleiades and Orion;
    He turns the shadow of death into
        morning
    And makes the day dark as night;
    He calls for the waters of the sea
    And pours them out on the face of the
        earth;
    The LORD *is* His name.
9 He rains ruin upon the strong,
    So that fury comes upon the fortress.

4:13 [a]Or *His*

10 They hate the one who rebukes in the
gate,
And they abhor the one who speaks
uprightly.

11 Therefore, because you tread down the poor
And take grain taxes from him,
Though you have built houses of hewn
stone,
Yet you shall not dwell in them;
You have planted pleasant vineyards,
But you shall not drink wine from them.

12 For I know your manifold transgressions
And your mighty sins:
Afflicting the just and taking bribes;
Diverting the poor from justice at the gate.

13 Therefore the prudent keep silent at that
time,
For it is an evil time.

The Law of Influence: Amos Judges Leaders for Abusing Their Positions

(Amos 5:7–17)

Amos is sometimes called the angry prophet. Most of his words express heated emotion. He condemns leaders who fail to provide justice for their people. Amos 5:7–17 contains his lamentation and call for repentance to those who turn justice into bitterness.

When leaders act unjustly, their influence creates a ripple effect. God hates injustice, but especially among leaders whose crooked influence infects an entire nation! Note the leadership abuses in Amos's day:

1. They abandoned morality (v. 7).
2. They confused values (v. 10).
3. They taxed the poor for selfish gain (v. 11).
4. They were corrupt and oppressed citizens (v. 12).
5. They took bribes (v. 12).
6. They deprived people of justice in court (v. 12).

The scary part of this sad story is that these leaders could not see their own corruption. Amos 5:18 warns against longing for the day of the Lord, for it will be a dreadful day of judgment, not a joyful celebration.

---

14 Seek good and not evil,
That you may live;
So the LORD God of hosts will be with
you,
As you have spoken.

15 Hate evil, love good;
Establish justice in the gate.
It may be that the LORD God of hosts
Will be gracious to the remnant of
Joseph.

The Day of the LORD

16 Therefore the LORD God of hosts, the
Lord, says this:

" There shall be wailing in all streets,
And they shall say in all the highways,
'Alas! Alas!'
They shall call the farmer to mourning,
And skillful lamenters to wailing.

17 In all vineyards there shall be wailing,
For I will pass through you,"
Says the LORD.

18 Woe to you who desire the day of the
LORD!
For what good is the day of the LORD to
you?
It will be darkness, and not light.

19 It will be as though a man fled from a lion,
And a bear met him!
Or as though he went into the house,
Leaned his hand on the wall,
And a serpent bit him!

20 Is not the day of the LORD darkness, and
not light?
Is it not very dark, with no brightness in it?

21 "I hate, I despise your feast days,
And I do not savor your sacred
assemblies.

22 Though you offer Me burnt offerings and
your grain offerings,
I will not accept them,
Nor will I regard your fattened peace
offerings.

23 Take away from Me the noise of your
songs,
For I will not hear the melody of your
stringed instruments.

24 But let justice run down like water,
And righteousness like a mighty stream.

25 "Did you offer Me sacrifices and offerings
In the wilderness forty years, O house of
Israel?

26 You also carried Sikkuth[a] your king[b]
And Chiun,[c] your idols,
The star of your gods,
Which you made for yourselves.
27 Therefore I will send you into captivity
    beyond Damascus,"
Says the LORD, whose name *is* the God of
    hosts.

Warnings to Zion and Samaria

6 Woe to you *who are* at ease in Zion,
    And trust in Mount Samaria,
    Notable persons in the chief nation,
    To whom the house of Israel comes!
2 Go over to Calneh and see;
And from there go to Hamath the great;
Then go down to Gath of the Philistines.
Are you better than these kingdoms?
Or is their territory greater than your
    territory?
3 *Woe to* you who put far off the day of
    doom,
Who cause the seat of violence to come
    near;
4 Who lie on beds of ivory,
Stretch out on your couches,
Eat lambs from the flock
And calves from the midst of the stall;
5 Who sing idly to the sound of stringed
    instruments,
And invent for yourselves musical
    instruments like David;
6 Who drink wine from bowls,
And anoint yourselves with the best
    ointments,
But are not grieved for the affliction of
    Joseph.
7 Therefore they shall now go captive as the
    first of the captives,
And those who recline at banquets shall be
    removed.

8 The Lord GOD has sworn by Himself,
The LORD God of hosts says:
"I abhor the pride of Jacob,
And hate his palaces;
Therefore I will deliver up *the* city
And all that is in it."

9Then it shall come to pass, that if ten men remain in one house, they shall die. 10And when a relative *of the dead*, with one who will burn *the bodies*, picks up the bodies[a] to take them out of the house, he will say to one inside the house, "*Are there* any more with you?"

Then someone will say, "None."
And he will say, "Hold your tongue! For we dare not mention the name of the LORD."

11 For behold, the LORD gives a command:
He will break the great house into bits,
And the little house into pieces.

12 Do horses run on rocks?
Does *one* plow *there* with oxen?
Yet you have turned justice into gall,
And the fruit of righteousness into
    wormwood,
13 You who rejoice over Lo Debar,[a]
Who say, "Have we not taken Karnaim[b]
    for ourselves
By our own strength?"

14 "But, behold, I will raise up a nation against
    you,
    O house of Israel,"
Says the LORD God of hosts;
"And they will afflict you from the entrance
    of Hamath
To the Valley of the Arabah."

Vision of the Locusts

7 Thus the Lord GOD showed me: Behold, He formed locust swarms at the beginning of the late crop; indeed *it was* the late crop after the king's mowings. 2And so it was, when they had finished eating the grass of the land, that I said:

"O Lord GOD, forgive, I pray!
Oh, that Jacob may stand,
For he *is* small!"
3 *So* the LORD relented concerning this.
"It shall not be," said the LORD.

Vision of the Fire

4Thus the Lord GOD showed me: Behold, the Lord GOD called for conflict by fire, and it consumed the great deep and devoured the territory. 5Then I said:

"O Lord GOD, cease, I pray!
Oh, that Jacob may stand,
For he *is* small!"
6 *So* the LORD relented concerning this.
"This also shall not be," said the Lord GOD.

5:26 [a]A pagan deity [b]Septuagint and Vulgate read *tabernacle of Moloch.* [c]A pagan deity 6:10 [a]Literally *bones* 6:13 [a]Literally *Nothing* [b]Literally *Horns,* symbol of strength

Leaders Influence in the Prayer Closet

(Amos 7:1–6)

Amos must have felt overwhelmed: God had threatened to annihilate Israel! The prophet already had warned the people of judgment; now it had arrived. What could he do?

The only thing he could do was to beg God to forgive. Amos prayed for his people with compassion and honesty. Tiny Israel, he said, would not survive the judgment. Twice he interceded and twice God withdrew His judgment. Amos stepped in between the people and God, and negotiated their survival.

Prayer changes things. Amos shows us what to do with impossible problems. Of course, prayer doesn't take the place of solid leadership; Amos continued to perform his job of truth telling (Amos 7:10–17). Yet he reminds leaders how powerful their prayers can be in the face of trouble. Sometimes we have no idea what kind of changes we orchestrate or what kind of pain we spare others by what we do in our prayer closet!

Vision of the Plumb Line

7Thus He showed me: Behold, the Lord stood on a wall *made* with a plumb line, with a plumb line in His hand. 8And the LORD said to me, "Amos, what do you see?"

And I said, "A plumb line."

Then the Lord said:

> "Behold, I am setting a plumb line
> In the midst of My people Israel;
> I will not pass by them anymore.
> 9 The high places of Isaac shall be desolate,
> And the sanctuaries of Israel shall be laid waste.
> I will rise with the sword against the house of Jeroboam."

Amaziah's Complaint

10Then Amaziah the priest of Bethel sent to Jeroboam king of Israel, saying, "Amos has conspired against you in the midst of the house of Israel. The land is not able to bear all his words. 11For thus Amos has said:

> 'Jeroboam shall die by the sword,
> And Israel shall surely be led away captive
> From their own land.'"

12Then Amaziah said to Amos:

> "Go, you seer!
> Flee to the land of Judah.
> There eat bread,
> And there prophesy.
> 13 But never again prophesy at Bethel,
> For it *is* the king's sanctuary,
> And it *is* the royal residence."

14Then Amos answered, and said to Amaziah:

> "I *was* no prophet,
> Nor *was* I a son of a prophet,
> But I *was* a sheepbreeder[a]
> And a tender of sycamore fruit.
> 15 Then the LORD took me as I followed the flock,
> And the LORD said to me,
> 'Go, prophesy to My people Israel.'
> 16 Now therefore, hear the word of the LORD:
> You say, 'Do not prophesy against Israel,
> And do not spout against the house of Isaac.'

17"Therefore thus says the LORD:

> 'Your wife shall be a harlot in the city;
> Your sons and daughters shall fall by the sword;
> Your land shall be divided by *survey* line;
> You shall die in a defiled land;
> And Israel shall surely be led away captive
> From his own land.'"

Vision of the Summer Fruit

8Thus the Lord GOD showed me: Behold, a basket of summer fruit. 2And He said, "Amos, what do you see?"

So I said, "A basket of summer fruit."

Then the LORD said to me:

> "The end has come upon My people Israel;
> I will not pass by them anymore.
> 3 And the songs of the temple
> Shall be wailing in that day,"
> Says the Lord GOD—
> "Many dead bodies everywhere,
> They shall be thrown out in silence."

7:14 aCompare 2 Kings 3:4

⁴ Hear this, you who swallow up^a the needy,
And make the poor of the land fail,

⁵Saying:

"When will the New Moon be past,
That we may sell grain?
And the Sabbath,
That we may trade wheat?
Making the ephah small and the shekel
large,
Falsifying the scales by deceit,
⁶ That we may buy the poor for silver,
And the needy for a pair of sandals—
Even sell the bad wheat?"

⁷ The LORD has sworn by the pride of
Jacob:
"Surely I will never forget any of their
works.
⁸ Shall the land not tremble for this,
And everyone mourn who dwells in it?
All of it shall swell like the River,ᵃ
Heave and subside
Like the River of Egypt.

⁹ "And it shall come to pass in that day," says
the Lord GOD,
"That I will make the sun go down at
noon,
And I will darken the earth in broad
daylight;
¹⁰ I will turn your feasts into mourning,
And all your songs into lamentation;
I will bring sackcloth on every waist,
And baldness on every head;
I will make it like mourning for an only
son,
And its end like a bitter day.

¹¹ "Behold, the days are coming," says the
Lord GOD,
"That I will send a famine on the land,
Not a famine of bread,
Nor a thirst for water,
But of hearing the words of the LORD.
¹² They shall wander from sea to sea,
And from north to east;
They shall run to and fro, seeking the
word of the LORD,
But shall not find it.

¹³ "In that day the fair virgins
And strong young men
Shall faint from thirst.
¹⁴ Those who swear by the sinᵃ of Samaria,

Who say,
'As your god lives, O Dan!'
And, 'As the way of Beersheba lives!'
They shall fall and never rise again."

The Destruction of Israel

9 I saw the Lord standing by the altar, and
He said:

"Strike the doorposts, that the thresholds
may shake,
And break them on the heads of them all.
I will slay the last of them with the sword.
He who flees from them shall not get
away,
And he who escapes from them shall not
be delivered.

² "Though they dig into hell,ᵃ
From there My hand shall take them;
Though they climb up to heaven,
From there I will bring them down;
³ And though they hide themselves on top
of Carmel,
From there I will search and take them;
Though they hide from My sight at the
bottom of the sea,
From there I will command the serpent,
and it shall bite them;
⁴ Though they go into captivity before their
enemies,
From there I will command the sword,
And it shall slay them.
I will set My eyes on them for harm and
not for good."

⁵ The Lord GOD of hosts,
He who touches the earth and it melts,
And all who dwell there mourn;
All of it shall swell like the River,ᵃ
And subside like the River of Egypt.
⁶ He who builds His layers in the sky,
And has founded His strata in the earth;
Who calls for the waters of the sea,
And pours them out on the face of the
earth—
The LORD is His name.

⁷ "Are you not like the people of Ethiopia to
Me,

8:4 ᵃOr *trample on* (compare 2:7) **8:8** ᵃThat is, the
Nile; some Hebrew manuscripts, Septuagint, Syriac,
Targum, and Vulgate read *River*; Masoretic Text
reads *the light.* **8:14** ᵃOr *Ashima,* a Syrian goddess
9:2 ᵃOr *Sheol* **9:5** ᵃThat is, the Nile

O children of Israel?" says the LORD.
"Did I not bring up Israel from the land of
  Egypt,
The Philistines from Caphtor,
And the Syrians from Kir?

8 "Behold, the eyes of the Lord GOD *are* on
    the sinful kingdom,
   And I will destroy it from the face of the
    earth;
   Yet I will not utterly destroy the house of
    Jacob,"
   Says the LORD.

9 "For surely I will command,
   And will sift the house of Israel among all
    nations,
   As *grain* is sifted in a sieve;
   Yet not the smallest grain shall fall to the
    ground.
10 All the sinners of My people shall die by
    the sword,
   Who say, 'The calamity shall not overtake
    nor confront us.'

Israel Will Be Restored

11 "On that day I will raise up
   The tabernacle[a] of David, which has fallen
    down,
   And repair its damages;
   I will raise up its ruins,
   And rebuild it as in the days of old;
12 That they may possess the remnant of
    Edom,[a]
   And all the Gentiles who are called by My
    name,"
   Says the LORD who does this thing.

13 "Behold, the days are coming," says the
    LORD,
   "When the plowman shall overtake the
    reaper,
   And the treader of grapes him who sows
    seed;
   The mountains shall drip with sweet wine,
   And all the hills shall flow *with it.*
14 I will bring back the captives of My
    people Israel;
   They shall build the waste cities and
    inhabit *them;*

They shall plant vineyards and drink wine
  from them;
They shall also make gardens and eat fruit
  from them.
15 I will plant them in their land,
   And no longer shall they be pulled up
   From the land I have given them,"
   Says the LORD your God.

9:11 [a]Literally *booth,* figure of a deposed dynasty
9:12 [a]Septuagint reads *mankind.*

Vision: Amos Finishes with a Hopeful Vision of the Future

(Amos 9:11–15)

The prophet followed his warnings of judgment with words of encouragement. The book concludes with Amos's vision for the future—full of hope, healing, and positive change. It illustrates once again how much people need both admonishment and affirmation.

The prophets nearly always followed the same pattern to address the erring population. They pronounced judgment, then painted a picture of a preferred future in which people would repent and realign themselves with the vision. In Amos 9:11–15, Amos spoke of this better tomorrow. Look at how he put it:

1. Leadership would be restored (v. 11).
2. Broken places would be repaired (v. 11).
3. Lost land would be replaced (v. 12).
4. Hope for prosperity would be renewed (vv. 13–15).

Proverbs 29:18 reminds us that without a vision, the people perish. Men and women become depressed when they hear only words of judgment. We all need some picture of how we can cooperate with God to redeem our situation.

OBADIAH
A Message to the People of Edom

SUMMARY

No more obscure Old Testament prophet exists than Obadiah. He wrote the shortest book in the Old Testament, with just 21 verses. We know very little about the dating of the book or the author, except for his name, which means, "servant of the Lord."

We do know, however, his message. Obadiah wrote about the people of Edom, the descendants of Esau. Esau was Jacob's twin brother, an outdoorsman and a hunter whom God scolded after he succumbed to his lust for immediate gratification (Gen. 25:27–34; Heb. 12:16). Esau neglected his priorities and lost sight of God's eternal perspective. This inclination led to self-centered descendants, angry and arrogant people who desired vengeance over Jacob's descendants (Israel). For centuries the Edomites gloated over the misfortunes of the Jews. Obadiah targeted their selfish pride.

The prophet's timeless lesson applies to leaders universally. Obadiah declares that pride and treachery earn the reward of destruction, but humility and loyalty to God gain the Lord's blessing.

We learn from Obadiah that destructive rivalry, comparison, and competition provide a horrible motivation for leadership. Those incentives so moved the Edomites that they lost perspective and sabotaged their own activities. How often does this happen to leaders today?

Second, God hates pride. He promised to humble the Edomites for their arrogant attitudes and their self-centered worldview. They thought they had achieved the success they enjoyed, but God exposed their faulty thinking. Leaders must never buy into the notion that they "did it all" themselves. The higher leaders go and the deeper they grow, the more they become aware that God has promoted them. Their success does not deceive them. Leaders blinded by pride should be pitied. God will raise up an Obadiah to humble them and clear up the issue.

God's Role in Obadiah

God sees what goes on worldwide and stands ready to move with irresistible power. He used Obadiah to confront the pride of the Edomites as an example to leaders and nations everywhere. He will not allow arrogance to continue indefinitely. Generally, He grants a warning to leaders through a word from another leader, a failure, a broken relationship, a personal weakness, or a plan that falls through. If the leader fails to take heed, God sets the wheels of justice in motion. And He will execute His sentence through whatever means He wishes.

Leaders in Obadiah

Obadiah, Edom's leaders

Other People of Influence in Obadiah

Esau and his descendants

Lessons in Leadership

- Leaders must not violate a primary reason they have power: to protect the powerless.
- Pride clouds a leader's perspective and causes him or her to act illogically.
- One can gain power in any of three fundamental ways: intimidation, exchange, or honor.
- God judges leaders who abuse their power.

LEADERSHIP HIGHLIGHTS IN OBADIAH

GOD IS THE SOURCE for a Leader's Success (2–4)	*page 1079*
POWER ABUSE: Edom Used Its Power for Unjust Causes (8–14)	*page 1079*
THE PRINCIPLE OF THE HARVEST: Leaders Reap What They Sow (15–18)	*page 1080*

The Coming Judgment on Edom

The vision of Obadiah.

Thus says the Lord GOD concerning
Edom
(We have heard a report from the LORD,
And a messenger has been sent among the
nations, *saying,*
"Arise, and let us rise up against her for
battle"):

2 "Behold, I will make you small among the
nations;
You shall be greatly despised.
3 The pride of your heart has deceived you,
You who dwell in the clefts of the rock,
Whose habitation is high;
You who say in your heart, 'Who will
bring me down to the ground?'
4 Though you ascend *as* high as the eagle,
And though you set your nest among the
stars,
From there I will bring you down," says
the LORD.

God Is the Source for a Leader's Success

(Obadiah 2–4)

We humans tend toward self-centeredness, self-promotion, self-sufficiency, self-reliance, and self-righteousness. When leaders succumb to this tendency, they adversely affect their followers. While leaders may determine the course of their success, God remains the source of their success. God is the source of any gains we make.

5 "If thieves had come to you,
If robbers by night—
Oh, how you will be cut off!—
Would they not have stolen till they had
enough?
If grape-gatherers had come to you,
Would they not have left *some* gleanings?

6 "Oh, how Esau shall be searched out!
How his hidden treasures shall be sought
after!
7 All the men in your confederacy
Shall force you to the border;
The men at peace with you
Shall deceive you *and* prevail against you.
Those who eat your bread shall lay a trap[a]
for you.
No one is aware of it.

8 "Will I not in that day," says the LORD,
"Even destroy the wise *men* from Edom,
And understanding from the mountains of
Esau?
9 Then your mighty men, O Teman, shall be
dismayed,
To the end that everyone from the
mountains of Esau
May be cut off by slaughter.

Power Abuse: Edom Used Its Power for Unjust Causes

(Obadiah 8–14)

The Edomites violated an important use of power: to protect the powerless. Even though the Edomites did not directly violate the Jews, they did stand idly by when another country abused them. When leaders have the power to do good and don't use it, God holds them equally guilty (James 4:17).

Edom Mistreated His Brother

10 "For violence against your brother Jacob,
Shame shall cover you,
And you shall be cut off forever.
11 In the day that you stood on the other
side—
In the day that strangers carried captive his
forces,
When foreigners entered his gates
And cast lots for Jerusalem—
Even you *were* as one of them.

12 "But you should not have gazed on the day
of your brother
In the day of his captivity;[a]
Nor should you have rejoiced over the
children of Judah
In the day of their destruction;

---

7 [a]Or *wound,* or *plot* **12** [a]Literally *on the day he became a foreigner*

Nor should you have spoken proudly
In the day of distress.
13 You should not have entered the gate of
My people
In the day of their calamity.
Indeed, you should not have gazed on
their affliction
In the day of their calamity,
Nor laid *hands* on their substance
In the day of their calamity.
14 You should not have stood at the crossroads
To cut off those among them who
escaped;
Nor should you have delivered up those
among them who remained
In the day of distress.

15 "For the day of the LORD upon all the
nations *is* near;
As you have done, it shall be done to you;
Your reprisal shall return upon your own
head.

The Principle of the Harvest: Leaders Reap What They Sow

(Obadiah 15–18)

Every leader reaps what he sows. The self-preoccupation that kept the Edomites from helping neighboring nations came back to haunt them in the day of their need. Power can be used to achieve or to intimidate; it can help others or haunt others. Edom misused its power and reaped terror and destruction.

---

16 For as you drank on My holy mountain,
So shall all the nations drink continually;
Yes, they shall drink, and swallow,
And they shall be as though they had
never been.

Israel's Final Triumph
17 "But on Mount Zion there shall be
deliverance,
And there shall be holiness;
The house of Jacob shall possess their
possessions.
18 The house of Jacob shall be a fire,
And the house of Joseph a flame;
But the house of Esau *shall be* stubble;
They shall kindle them and devour them,
And no survivor shall *remain* of the house
of Esau,"
For the LORD has spoken.

19 The South[a] shall possess the mountains of
Esau,
And the Lowland shall possess Philistia.
They shall possess the fields of Ephraim
And the fields of Samaria.
Benjamin *shall possess* Gilead.
20 And the captives of this host of the
children of Israel
Shall possess the land of the Canaanites
As far as Zarephath.
The captives of Jerusalem who are in
Sepharad
Shall possess the cities of the South.[a]
21 Then saviors[a] shall come to Mount Zion
To judge the mountains of Esau,
And the kingdom shall be the LORD's.

19 [a]Hebrew *Negev* 20 [a]Hebrew *Negev* 21 [a]Or
deliverers

JONAH
The Perfect Portrait of a Reluctant Leader

SUMMARY

We should feel grateful that God included Jonah in the canon of Scripture. If ever God provided a picture of our human nature—our inclination to run from duty in favor of serving self—He did it through Jonah. He furnishes the perfect portrait of a reluctant leader in a needy time.

Yet he is not alone! God has called many reluctant leaders. Consider Moses who, in Egypt, thought he could do more than he really could. God called him only after 40 years of preparation, when he thought he could do less than he really could. He expressed total reluctance as he stood before a burning bush, trying to excuse himself from leadership. Or consider Gideon, whom God called to lead an attack against the Midianites. He argued with an angel, explaining why he couldn't do it. Or consider King Saul, who stood head and shoulders above everyone else. Yet he hid among the luggage when Samuel came to anoint him king of Israel. Or consider Jeremiah, whom God called to be a prophet to the nations. This young man debated with God on the basis of his tender age, as though God had forgotten how old he was. God basically responded, "I have been preparing you since before you took shape in your mother's womb."

Jonah's reluctance didn't take the form of a debate; he simply ran in the other direction. He didn't object to his call on the basis of his inabilities, but upon the seeming irrationality of calling Nineveh to repent. Jonah saw this as an evil culture that didn't deserve a warning of impending doom. So he ran. Days later he discovered that called leaders can't outrun God. Some frightened sailors threw him overboard (at his direction) and a huge fish swallowed the sputtering prophet. Over the next three days he regained perspective while in the belly of the fish, and when God ordered the beast to spit him up on shore, the chastened prophet at last fulfilled the task God had given him.

It is interesting to note that every major player in the story—the storm, the sailors, the fish, the king, the Ninevites, the vine, the worm, and the east wind—all obey God . . . except for Jonah, the leader God chose. Sometimes the leader must repent before he can call the people to do so.

Despite Jonah's disobedience, his lack of perspective, his cultural prejudice, his self-righteousness, his wrong motives, and his bad attitude, God never gave up on him. The central lesson? Sometimes God uses us, in spite of us. He even uses reluctant leaders to accomplish His gracious mission.

God's Role in Jonah

God once again takes the initiative in this book. The leader He chooses refuses at first to obey. God chases Him down, calls upon a huge fish (perhaps a whale) to swallow him, enables him to live for three days in the belly of that creature, then orders him spit up on shore. Only then does Jonah go to Nineveh to speak. Yet even after he delivers his message, God has to take the initiative once more when Jonah reacts angrily to their repentance. God raises up a vine to give him shade, then teaches him a lesson about mercy and grace. God must work harder at getting His chosen leader into an obedient posture than He has to for the Ninevites!

Leaders in Jonah

Jonah, the king of Nineveh

Other People of Influence in Jonah

The sailors

Lessons in Leadership

- Motives are key: Why a leader does something ultimately determines what he does.

- Leaders must model what they demand from the people.

- God's mercy overcomes our reluctance, prejudice, and small thinking.

- We can still lead if our impulse for obedience grows stronger than our reluctance.

- Leaders lose their right to be selfish.

LEADERSHIP

HIGHLIGHTS IN JONAH

Jonah's Disobedience

1 Now the word of the LORD came to Jonah the son of Amittai, saying, [2]"Arise, go to Nineveh, that great city, and cry out against it; for their wickedness has come up before Me." [3]But Jonah arose to flee to Tarshish from the presence of the LORD. He went down to Joppa, and found a ship going to Tarshish; so he paid the fare, and went down into it, to go with them to Tarshish from the presence of the LORD.

Character: Jonah Runs from Commitment

(Jonah 1:1–10)

When God told Jonah to warn the people of Nineveh to repent, the prophet turned the other direction and fled. Spot someone who runs from commitment, and you'll find a person who lacks character.

Many times a leader must ask his followers to make a commitment. Usually God first asks the leader to commit. At this point, the leader discovers how much he's embraced the cause. Is he cautious, curious, or committed? Jonah teaches us the consequences of avoiding God's call to commitment:

1. We miss the privilege of partnership with God (vv. 1–3).
2. Our choice damages more people than we know (v. 4).
3. We become hardened and desensitized to the tragedies we cause (vv. 5–8).
4. We lose both integrity and trust (vv. 9, 10).

The Storm at Sea

[4]But the LORD sent out a great wind on the sea, and there was a mighty tempest on the sea, so that the ship was about to be broken up. [5]Then the mariners were afraid; and every man cried out to his god, and threw the cargo that *was* in the ship into the sea, to lighten the load.[a] But Jonah had gone down into the lowest parts of the ship, had lain down, and was fast asleep. [6]So the captain came to him, and said to him, "What do you mean, sleeper? Arise, call on your God; perhaps your God will consider us, so that we may not perish."

[7]And they said to one another, "Come, let us cast lots, that we may know for whose cause this trouble *has come* upon us." So they cast lots, and the lot fell on Jonah. [8]Then they said to him, "Please tell us! For whose cause *is* this trouble upon us? What is your occupation? And where do you come from? What is your country? And of what people are you?"

[9]So he said to them, "I *am* a Hebrew; and I fear the LORD, the God of heaven, who made the sea and the dry *land*."

Jonah Thrown into the Sea

[10]Then the men were exceedingly afraid, and said to him, "Why have you done this?" For the men knew that he fled from the presence of the LORD, because he had told them. [11]Then they said to him, "What shall we do to you that the sea may be calm for us?"—for the sea was growing more tempestuous. [12]And he said to them, "Pick me up and throw me into the sea; then the sea will become calm for you. For I know that this great tempest *is* because of me." [13]Nevertheless the men rowed hard to return to land, but they could not, for the sea continued to grow more tempestuous against them. [14]Therefore they cried out to the LORD and said, "We pray, O LORD, please do not let us perish for this man's life, and do not charge us with innocent blood; for You, O LORD, have done as it pleased You." [15]So they picked up Jonah and threw him into the sea, and the sea ceased from its raging. [16]Then the men feared the LORD exceedingly, and offered a sacrifice to the LORD and took vows.

Jonah's Prayer and Deliverance

[17]Now the LORD had prepared a great fish to swallow Jonah. And Jonah was in the belly of the fish three days and three nights.

2 Then Jonah prayed to the LORD his God from the fish's belly. [2]And he said:

"I cried out to the LORD because of my affliction,
  And He answered me.

"Out of the belly of Sheol I cried,
  And You heard my voice.
[3] For You cast me into the deep,
  Into the heart of the seas,
  And the floods surrounded me;

1:5 [a]Literally *from upon them*

All Your billows and Your waves passed
over me.
4 Then I said, 'I have been cast out of Your
sight;
Yet I will look again toward Your holy
temple.'
5 The waters surrounded me, *even* to my
soul;
The deep closed around me;
Weeds were wrapped around my head.
6 I went down to the moorings of the
mountains;
The earth with its bars *closed* behind me
forever;
Yet You have brought up my life from the
pit,
O LORD, my God.

7 "When my soul fainted within me,
I remembered the LORD;
And my prayer went *up* to You,
Into Your holy temple.

8 "Those who regard worthless idols
Forsake their own Mercy.
9 But I will sacrifice to You
With the voice of thanksgiving;
I will pay what I have vowed.
Salvation *is* of the LORD."

The Principle of Incarnation: Leaders Must Model What They Request

(Jonah 2:7–9)

God humbled Jonah and gave him perspective in the belly of the fish, where the prophet got his heart right through a profound worship experience. God knew that the leader must first incarnate the life he calls the people to live. Once Jonah repented, he was ready to call others to repent.

10 So the LORD spoke to the fish, and it vomited Jonah onto dry *land*.

Jonah Preaches at Nineveh

3 Now the word of the LORD came to Jonah the second time, saying, 2"Arise, go to Nineveh, that great city, and preach to it the message that I tell you." 3So Jonah arose and went to Nineveh, according to the word of the

JONAH

THE PROPHET WHO RAN *DOWN*
(Jonah 1:1–17)

PROFILE IN LEADERSHIP

Who among us hasn't heard God telling us to do something we *really* didn't want to do? Sometimes it's easy to convince ourselves that we know better than God what needs to be done.

Jonah was a godly prophet, yet when God commanded him to preach repentance to the Ninevites, Jonah ran in the opposite direction. As he ran, he went nowhere but *down—down* to the seashore, *down* to the bottom of the ship, *down* to the water, and *down* into the belly of the fish. Jonah learned what can happen to the man or woman who is called to lead but who shrinks from that role of leadership.

One can only imagine the wretched conditions inside the creature God had prepared to temporarily house Jonah. But was it any worse than the situations into which we put ourselves when we run from God? Eventually the Lord will bring us to a place where we have little choice but to stop, listen, and obey.

But why wait for such an unpleasant place?

Leaders may not always understand why God wants them to do certain things, but He doesn't ask us to depend upon our own understanding or logic. Rather, He calls us to walk in obedience to His instruction. Don't make it necessary for God to introduce you to the inside of a fish!

INITIATIVE

One Earmark of a True Leader
(Jonah 2:10—3:10)

One earmark of a true leader is the display of initiative. By definition, leaders cannot wait for someone else to move; if they do, they are really followers, not leaders. Initiative requires an element of risk, faith, and foresight. When did you last initiate something significant? If you haven't pushed yourself lately and left your comfort zone, you may need a jump start in initiative.

Why Do We Fail to Initiate?

It seems easier to run from a challenge than to step out and take a risk. When we initiate, we commit ourselves to a direction. We may feel uncertain about what the future holds. What if we change our minds? What if no one follows? What if we fail in front of our followers? We run from commitment and initiative for a variety of reasons.

Reason	Issue
1. We are afraid we'll be unable to keep the commitment.	1. Low sense of security
2. We suspect we might find "greener grass" somewhere else.	2. Paralyzed will
3. We expend time and energy only for personal gain.	3. No surrender
4. Our past makes trust difficult.	4. Emotional baggage
5. We are lazy and unmotivated.	5. Apathy and neutrality
6. We fear the risk of being rejected.	6. Poor self-esteem
7. We fear the unknown and the unfamiliar.	7. Low confidence
8. We don't want to lose our freedom.	8. Entitlement philosophy
9. We fear being different from others.	9. Politically correct
10. We don't really know who we are.	10. Gifts and calling

Jonah had to learn initiative. It started with learning submission to God. Once we surrender to His call on our life and leadership, we can step out to follow Him. We can take risks because our future lies in His hands. Once Jonah submitted to God's call, he saw all kinds of results. What happens when *we* accept God's call to initiate and commit?

1. We assume healthy personal responsibility (1:12).
2. We'll likely see many come to faith in God (1:13–16).
3. We receive a God-given time and place to gain perspective (1:17).
4. We deepen our experience of worship and prayer (2:1–9).
5. We progress toward a new level of personal freedom (2:10).
6. We enjoy partnership with God (3:1–9).
7. We gain the satisfaction of seeing changed lives (3:10).

For a positive example of initiative, see p. 579.

God Can Use Even a Reluctant Leader

(Jonah 3:1–3)

We often get caught up in the story of "the big fish" and miss the story of "the big God!" The miracle of Nineveh's redemption is a story of God's pursuit of a leader who ran from a commitment. God wanted a divine partnership in which both parties committed themselves to the cause with reckless abandon.

What might have happened had Jonah failed to go? What if he had rejected God's call to commitment? What if he avoided it and God never pursued him? History might be different . . . at least for one ancient people.

Fortunately, God comes for us when we run from commitment. Most of the time He gives us a second opportunity, just as He did with Jonah. Note the stages leading up to that second chance:

1. Recognition of failure or inability
2. A crisis of honest reflection
3. Drawing near to God for empowerment
4. The opportunity to recommit ourselves

LORD. Now Nineveh was an exceedingly great city, a three-day journey[a] *in extent.* [4]And Jonah began to enter the city on the first day's walk. Then he cried out and said, "Yet forty days, and Nineveh shall be overthrown!"

The People of Nineveh Believe

[5]So the people of Nineveh believed God, proclaimed a fast, and put on sackcloth, from the greatest to the least of them. [6]Then word came to the king of Nineveh; and he arose from his throne and laid aside his robe, covered *himself* with sackcloth and sat in ashes. [7]And he caused *it* to be proclaimed and published throughout Nineveh by the decree of the king and his nobles, saying,

Let neither man nor beast, herd nor flock, taste anything; do not let them eat, or drink water. [8]But let man and beast be covered with sackcloth, and cry mightily to God; yes, let every one turn from his evil way and from the violence that is in his hands. [9]Who

can tell *if* God will turn and relent, and turn away from His fierce anger, so that we may not perish?

[10]Then God saw their works, that they turned from their evil way; and God relented from the disaster that He had said He would bring upon them, and He did not do it.

Jonah's Anger and God's Kindness

4 But it displeased Jonah exceedingly, and he became angry. [2]So he prayed to the LORD, and said, "Ah, LORD, was not this what I said when I was still in my country? Therefore I fled previously to Tarshish; for I know that You *are* a gracious and merciful God, slow to anger and abundant in lovingkindness, One who relents from doing harm. [3]Therefore now, O LORD, please take my life from me, for *it is* better for me to die than to live!"

3:3 [a]Exact meaning unknown

The Law of Influence: The King Leads in Delivering Nineveh

(Jonah 3:6–9)

When the news of Jonah's message of judgment reached the king of Nineveh, he immediately repented. He took off his royal robe, covered himself with sackcloth, and sat down in the dust. He repented for his own sin. Then he used his influence to bring about city-wide revival. He issued a decree that every citizen follow his lead. When God saw his response, He had compassion on the Ninevites and did not destroy them.

In this case, the leader influenced the fate of an entire population. He did so by providing the three fundamentals every follower needs:

1. **A clear model:** He repented first, setting an example (v. 6).
2. **A clear message:** He called his people to a specific action (vv. 7, 8).
3. **A clear motivation:** He gave the people a reason for taking action (v. 9).

Motive Check: Why We Act Determines How We React

(Jonah 4:1, 2)

Jonah felt great delight when God planned to destroy the wicked people of Nineveh, but he grew angry when they repented and God showed them compassion. He suspected God might do something just like that, and that made him even angrier. He would have preferred to see God remove the threat of Nineveh. His selfish motives led him astray.

Consequently, God gave him an object lesson. When the Lord sent a worm to eat the plant that gave Jonah shade, the prophet grew angry. God reminded him that he had no right to his anger, since he had done nothing to create the plant. Would he be angry at the death of a mere vine, but unmoved at the destruction of more than 120,000 people? Didn't the Creator have a right to restore them? Of course He did.

God gave Jonah a motive check—and us a reminder. Leaders must determine to be motivated only by what motivates God.

⁴Then the LORD said, "*Is it* right for you to be angry?"

⁵So Jonah went out of the city and sat on the east side of the city. There he made himself a shelter and sat under it in the shade, till he might see what would become of the city. ⁶And the LORD God prepared a plantᵃ and made it come up over Jonah, that it might be shade for his head to deliver him from his misery. So Jonah was very grateful for the plant. ⁷But as morning dawned the next day God prepared a worm, and it *so* damaged the plant that it withered. ⁸And it happened, when the sun arose, that God prepared a vehement east wind; and the sun beat on Jonah's head, so that he grew faint. Then he wished death for himself, and said, "*It is* better for me to die than to live."

⁹Then God said to Jonah, "*Is it* right for you to be angry about the plant?"

And he said, "*It is* right for me to be angry, even to death!"

¹⁰But the LORD said, "You have had pity on the plant for which you have not labored, nor made it grow, which came up in a night and perished in a night. ¹¹And should I not pity Nineveh, that great city, in which are more than one hundred and twenty thousand persons who cannot discern between their right hand and their left—and much livestock?"

4:6 ᵃHebrew *kikayon*, exact identity unknown

MICAH

What Does the Lord Require of You?

SUMMARY

Micah's name means, "Who is like the LORD?" This is precisely the question he posed in his prophetic ministry in the middle of the eighth century B.C. His life modeled one who is "like the Lord," and he called the people of Judah to this same lifestyle of divine imitation. His leadership challenged false prophets, corrupt political leaders, and wayward residents of Judah to live their faith authentically.

The summary verse of his book, Micah 6:8, asks: "He has shown you, O man, what is good; and what does the LORD require of you but to do justly, to love mercy, and to walk humbly with your God?"

Micah deeply suspected the wickedness and corruption of the cities of Judah. This country prophet intuitively perceived the greed that lay behind the decisions of the priestly and political leaders of his day. He championed the cause of the poor and the oppressed and rebuked those in charge for their exploitation of others.

Micah warns leaders today about leading for personal gain rather than organizational gain. When leaders benefit from the system apart from followers—something is wrong with the leader or the system, and maybe both.

Micah also cautions leaders about doing what's right on the surface to hide a corrupt heart. Leadership cannot merely be an "outside" job; it must be an "inside" job as well. Healthy, effective leadership stems from who we are, not just what we do. Leaders can masquerade only for a while . . . before reality becomes obvious.

Finally, Micah teaches us that a leader's spiritual life must transform his or her social ethics and approach to leadership. Integrity means "oneness," the opposite of hypocrisy. One compartment of our life cannot contradict another.

God's Role in Micah

The Book of Micah pictures God as the Ruler of all things. The Lord used the prophet Micah to spell out what He wanted from the Hebrews—but He also used ungodly neighbors like Assyria to punish the corrupt leaders of Israel and Judah. Micah began to connect the wickedness of Judah and the lightning raids of the Assyrians. As evil rose in Judah, military power rose in Assyria. God would sovereignly use even this to accomplish His purposes. He will use even unjust instruments to correct His own unjust people.

In addition, God assumed the role of watching over the peasants of Judah. Passing armies would often invade villages and make slaves of the residents while Judah's leaders looked the other way. God chose to use Micah to speak out against the selfishness of the nation's leaders.

Leaders in Micah

Micah, King Jotham, King Ahaz, King Hezekiah

Other People of Influence in Micah

The Assyrians, the corrupt vendors, the false prophets

Lessons in Leadership

- Healthy leadership enables everyone to win: the leader, the follower, and the organization.
- God expects leaders to guard the poor and oppressed, those without an advocate.
- Leadership is a life we live, not a show we perform.
- Values absent from the leader cannot be exported.
- Leadership plus hypocrisy equals leadership minus credibility.

LEADERSHIP

HIGHLIGHTS IN MICAH

VALUES: Leaders Know What to Cry About (1:1–9)	*page 1090*
CHARACTER: Leaders Can't Give What They Don't Have (2:1–13)	*page 1091*
THE LAW OF INFLUENCE: Woe to Leaders Who Abuse Power (3:1–12)	*page 1092*
VISION: Leaders See It, Say It, and Show It Before They Seize It (4:1, 2)	*page 1093*
LEADERS Who Fail to Practice Servant Leadership Become Self-Serving (7:3, 4)	*page 1097*

1 The word of the LORD that came to Micah of Moresheth in the days of Jotham, Ahaz, *and* Hezekiah, kings of Judah, which he saw concerning Samaria and Jerusalem.

Values: Leaders Know What to Cry About

(Micah 1:1–9)

Micah provides us with an example of a leader who knows what to cry about. While he could declare the Lord's judgment against Samaria and Jerusalem, he also wept over the punishment their citizens were to endure. They would always be the people he loved.

The more leaders mature, the more value they place on people. When all is said and done, leadership isn't about strategy, marketing, organization, efficiency, or high-quality products, but about people. Micah hurt when others hurt, even though they were in the wrong. The high value he placed on people teaches us . . .

1. People are an organization's most appreciable asset.
2. People skills are a leader's most important asset.
3. If you are good with people, you can lead in a variety of contexts.
4. You can have people skills and not be a good leader, but you cannot be a good leader without people skills.

The Coming Judgment on Israel

2 Hear, all you peoples!
  Listen, O earth, and all that is in it!
  Let the Lord GOD be a witness against you,
  The Lord from His holy temple.

3 For behold, the LORD is coming out of His place;
  He will come down
  And tread on the high places of the earth.
4 The mountains will melt under Him,
  And the valleys will split
  Like wax before the fire,
  Like waters poured down a steep place.
5 All this is for the transgression of Jacob
  And for the sins of the house of Israel.
  What *is* the transgression of Jacob?
  Is it not Samaria?
  And what *are* the high places of Judah?
  Are they not Jerusalem?

6 "Therefore I will make Samaria a heap of ruins in the field,
  Places for planting a vineyard;
  I will pour down her stones into the valley,
  And I will uncover her foundations.
7 All her carved images shall be beaten to pieces,
  And all her pay as a harlot shall be burned with the fire;
  All her idols I will lay desolate,
  For she gathered *it* from the pay of a harlot,
  And they shall return to the pay of a harlot."

Mourning for Israel and Judah

8 Therefore I will wail and howl,
  I will go stripped and naked;
  I will make a wailing like the jackals
  And a mourning like the ostriches,
9 For her wounds *are* incurable.
  For it has come to Judah;
  It has come to the gate of My people—
  To Jerusalem.

10 Tell *it* not in Gath,
  Weep not at all;
  In Beth Aphrah[a]
  Roll yourself in the dust.
11 Pass by in naked shame, you inhabitant of Shaphir;
  The inhabitant of Zaanan[a] does not go out.
  Beth Ezel mourns;
  Its place to stand is taken away from you.
12 For the inhabitant of Maroth pined[a] for good,
  But disaster came down from the LORD
  To the gate of Jerusalem.
13 O inhabitant of Lachish,
  Harness the chariot to the swift steeds
  (She *was* the beginning of sin to the daughter of Zion),
  For the transgressions of Israel were found in you.

1:10 [a]Literally *House of Dust* **1:11** [a]Literally *Going Out* **1:12** [a]Literally *was sick*

14 Therefore you shall give presents to
    Moresheth Gath;[a]
The houses of Achzib[b] *shall be* a lie to the
    kings of Israel.
15 I will yet bring an heir to you, O
    inhabitant of Mareshah;[a]
The glory of Israel shall come to
    Adullam.
16 Make yourself bald and cut off your hair,
    Because of your precious children;
Enlarge your baldness like an eagle,
    For they shall go from you into captivity.

Woe to Evildoers

2 Woe to those who devise iniquity,
    And work out evil on their beds!
At morning light they practice it,
    Because it is in the power of their hand.
2 They covet fields and take *them* by
    violence,
Also houses, and seize *them*.
So they oppress a man and his house,
    A man and his inheritance.

3 Therefore thus says the LORD:

"Behold, against this family I am devising
    disaster,
From which you cannot remove your
    necks;
Nor shall you walk haughtily,
    For this *is* an evil time.
4 In that day *one* shall take up a proverb
    against you,
And lament with a bitter lamentation,
    saying:
'We are utterly destroyed!
He has changed the heritage of my
    people;
How He has removed *it* from me!
To a turncoat He has divided our fields.'"

5 Therefore you will have no one to
    determine boundaries[a] by lot
In the assembly of the LORD.

Lying Prophets

6 "Do not prattle," *you say to those* who
    prophesy.
So they shall not prophesy to you;[a]
    They shall not return insult for insult.[b]
7 *You who are* named the house of Jacob:
"Is the Spirit of the LORD restricted?
Are these His doings?
Do not My words do good
    To him who walks uprightly?

Character: Leaders Can't Give What They Don't Have

(Micah 2:1–13)

The wicked leaders of Micah's day led out of convenience and expediency. They did what was right by *them*.

The Greek word for character is often translated "image." It means a notch, indentation, a sharpening, scratching, or writing on a stone or a coin. Consequently, character historically meant a distinctive mark impressed or formed on the inside of a person by an outside force. To better understand character, take a look at some common misconceptions about it:

1. Character is not merely how a person acts; some can masquerade poor character.
2. Character isn't just what a person will ideally be in the future; that's called hope.
3. Character is not only what others see on the outside; it begins on the inside.
4. Character isn't limited to wisdom in evaluating others' behavior; that's judgment.
5. Character isn't only about discipline; I may be disciplined in one area and not in another.

---

8 "Lately My people have risen up as an
    enemy—
You pull off the robe with the garment
From those who trust *you,* as they
    pass by,
Like men returned from war.
9 The women of My people you cast out
From their pleasant houses;
From their children
    You have taken away My glory forever.

10 "Arise and depart,
    For this *is* not *your* rest;

1:14 [a]Literally *Possession of Gath* [b]Literally *Lie*
1:15 [a]Literally *Inheritance* **2:5** [a]Literally *one casting a surveyor's line* **2:6** [a]Literally *to these* [b]Vulgate reads *He shall not take shame.*

Because it is defiled, it shall destroy,
Yes, with utter destruction.
11 If a man should walk in a false spirit
And speak a lie, *saying,*
'I will prophesy to you of wine and
drink,'
Even he would be the prattler of this
people.

Israel Restored
12 "I will surely assemble all of you, O
Jacob,
I will surely gather the remnant of
Israel;
I will put them together like sheep of the
fold,[a]
Like a flock in the midst of their pasture;
They shall make a loud noise because of *so
many* people.
13 The one who breaks open will come up
before them;
They will break out,
Pass through the gate,
And go out by it;
Their king will pass before them,
With the LORD at their head."

Leaders Must Motivate, Not Manipulate
(Micah 2:12, 13)

God pronounces judgment on the win-lose
proposition of manipulation. Manipulation
means moving together for my advantage;
motivation means moving together for mutual
advantage. God warns that plans should be
laid for the benefit of the people, not the
leader. And He promises to deliver His people
from selfish, wicked leaders.

Wicked Rulers and Prophets
3 And I said:

"Hear now, O heads of Jacob,
And you rulers of the house of Israel:
Is it not for you to know justice?
2 You who hate good and love evil;
Who strip the skin from My people,[a]
And the flesh from their bones;
3 Who also eat the flesh of My people,
Flay their skin from them,

The Law of Influence: Woe to Leaders Who Abuse Power
(Micah 3:1–12)

God pronounces a dark future for leaders
who practice injustice and abuse their
power to take advantage of others. God rebukes poor leaders and false prophets for
their sins that impacted the entire land. God
notes that these leaders had power and influence, but that they used it for their own purposes. Study the chapter to see what God
hated so much about these abusive leaders:

1. They destroyed people instead of developing them (vv. 1–3).
2. They misled people into confusion, instead of leading them in a cause (vv. 5–7).
3. They distorted justice instead of upholding justice for the common man
(vv. 9, 10).
4. They took bribes for themselves instead
of taking responsibility for the people
(vv. 11, 12).

Break their bones,
And chop *them* in pieces
Like *meat* for the pot,
Like flesh in the caldron."

4 Then they will cry to the LORD,
But He will not hear them;
He will even hide His face from them at
that time,
Because they have been evil in their
deeds.

5 Thus says the LORD concerning the
prophets
Who make my people stray;
Who chant "Peace"
While they chew with their teeth,
But who prepare war against him
Who puts nothing into their mouths:
6 "Therefore you shall have night without
vision,
And you shall have darkness without
divination;

2:12 [a]Hebrew *Bozrah* 3:2 [a]Literally *them*

The sun shall go down on the prophets,
And the day shall be dark for them.

7 So the seers shall be ashamed,
And the diviners abashed;
Indeed they shall all cover their lips;
For *there is* no answer from God."

8 But truly I am full of power by the Spirit
of the LORD,
And of justice and might,
To declare to Jacob his transgression
And to Israel his sin.

9 Now hear this,
You heads of the house of Jacob
And rulers of the house of Israel,
Who abhor justice
And pervert all equity,

10 Who build up Zion with bloodshed
And Jerusalem with iniquity:

11 Her heads judge for a bribe,
Her priests teach for pay,
And her prophets divine for money.
Yet they lean on the LORD, and say,
"Is not the LORD among us?
No harm can come upon us."

12 Therefore because of you
Zion shall be plowed *like* a field,
Jerusalem shall become heaps of ruins,
And the mountain of the temple[a]
Like the bare hills of the forest.

The LORD's Reign in Zion

4 Now it shall come to pass in the latter days
That the mountain of the LORD's house
Shall be established on the top of the
mountains,
And shall be exalted above the hills;
And peoples shall flow to it.

2 Many nations shall come and say,
"Come, and let us go up to the mountain
of the LORD,
To the house of the God of Jacob;
He will teach us His ways,
And we shall walk in His paths."
For out of Zion the law shall go forth,
And the word of the LORD from
Jerusalem.

3 He shall judge between many peoples,
And rebuke strong nations afar off;
They shall beat their swords into
plowshares,
And their spears into pruning hooks;
Nation shall not lift up sword against
nation,
Neither shall they learn war anymore.[a]

4 But everyone shall sit under his vine and
under his fig tree,

3:12 [a]Literally *house*   **4:3** [a]Compare Isaiah 2:2–4

Vision: Leaders See It, Say It, and Show It Before They Seize It

(Micah 4:1, 2)

All great leaders begin their journey with a vision. People have to buy in to both the leader and the vision before they take the journey.

The prophet paints a picture of what life will be like in the future, during the last days—a glorious vision anyone could get excited about!

The "house of the LORD" was to be a strategic place (Mic. 4:1), an influential place (4:2), and an equipping place (4:2). In order for Micah to succeed, he had to possess and persuade the people concerning God's vision for them. Then, he had to wait. Visions usually work like the birth of a baby; they take a long time in coming.

For any leader to successfully communicate a vision, they should know the vital signs of a successful vision:

1. A clear picture—the ability to see the vision.
2. A committed people—the ability to transmit the vision.
3. A consistent prayer—the ability to intercede for the vision.
4. A constructive passion—the ability to work toward the vision.
5. A calm persistence—The ability to patiently wait for the vision.

And no one shall make *them* afraid;
For the mouth of the LORD of hosts has
spoken.
5 For all people walk each in the name of
his god,
But we will walk in the name of the
LORD our God
Forever and ever.

Zion's Future Triumph

6 "In that day," says the LORD,
"I will assemble the lame,
I will gather the outcast
And those whom I have afflicted;
7 I will make the lame a remnant,
And the outcast a strong nation;
So the LORD will reign over them in
Mount Zion
From now on, even forever.
8 And you, O tower of the flock,
The stronghold of the daughter of Zion,
To you shall it come,
Even the former dominion shall come,
The kingdom of the daughter of
Jerusalem."

9 Now why do you cry aloud?
Is there no king in your midst?
Has your counselor perished?
For pangs have seized you like a woman in
labor.
10 Be in pain, and labor to bring forth,
O daughter of Zion,
Like a woman in birth pangs.
For now you shall go forth from the city,
You shall dwell in the field,
And to Babylon you shall go.
There you shall be delivered;
There the LORD will redeem you
From the hand of your enemies.

11 Now also many nations have gathered
against you,
Who say, "Let her be defiled,
And let our eye look upon Zion."
12 But they do not know the thoughts of the
LORD,
Nor do they understand His counsel;
For He will gather them like sheaves to
the threshing floor.

13 "Arise and thresh, O daughter of Zion;
For I will make your horn iron,
And I will make your hooves bronze;
You shall beat in pieces many peoples;
I will consecrate their gain to the LORD,

And their substance to the Lord of the
whole earth."

5 Now gather yourself in troops,
O daughter of troops;
He has laid siege against us;
They will strike the judge of Israel with a
rod on the cheek.

The Coming Messiah

2 "But you, Bethlehem Ephrathah,
Though you are little among the thousands
of Judah,
Yet out of you shall come forth to Me
The One to be Ruler in Israel,
Whose goings forth *are* from of old,
From everlasting."

3 Therefore He shall give them up,
Until the time *that* she who is in labor has
given birth;
Then the remnant of His brethren
Shall return to the children of Israel.
4 And He shall stand and feed *His flock*
In the strength of the LORD,
In the majesty of the name of the LORD
His God;
And they shall abide,
For now He shall be great
To the ends of the earth;
5 And this *One* shall be peace.

Judgment on Israel's Enemies

When the Assyrian comes into our land,
And when he treads in our palaces,
Then we will raise against him
Seven shepherds and eight princely men.
6 They shall waste with the sword the land
of Assyria,
And the land of Nimrod at its entrances;
Thus He shall deliver *us* from the Assyrian,
When he comes into our land
And when he treads within our borders.

7 Then the remnant of Jacob
Shall be in the midst of many peoples,
Like dew from the LORD,
Like showers on the grass,
That tarry for no man
Nor wait for the sons of men.
8 And the remnant of Jacob
Shall be among the Gentiles,
In the midst of many peoples,
Like a lion among the beasts of the forest,
Like a young lion among flocks of sheep,
Who, if he passes through,
Both treads down and tears in pieces,

And none can deliver.
9 Your hand shall be lifted against your
    adversaries,
And all your enemies shall be cut off.

10 "And it shall be in that day," says the LORD,
    "That I will cut off your horses from your
    midst
And destroy your chariots.
11 I will cut off the cities of your land
And throw down all your strongholds.
12 I will cut off sorceries from your hand,
And you shall have no soothsayers.
13 Your carved images I will also cut off,
And your *sacred* pillars from your midst;
You shall no more worship the work of
    your hands;
14 I will pluck your wooden images[a] from
    your midst;
Thus I will destroy your cities.
15 And I will execute vengeance in anger and
    fury
On the nations that have not heard."[a]

God Pleads with Israel

6 Hear now what the LORD says:

"Arise, plead your case before the
    mountains,
And let the hills hear your voice.
2 Hear, O you mountains, the LORD's
    complaint,
And you strong foundations of the earth;
For the LORD has a complaint against His
    people,
And He will contend with Israel.

3 "O My people, what have I done to you?
And how have I wearied you?
Testify against Me.
4 For I brought you up from the land of
    Egypt,
I redeemed you from the house of
    bondage;
And I sent before you Moses, Aaron, and
    Miriam.
5 O My people, remember now
What Balak king of Moab counseled,
And what Balaam the son of Beor
    answered him,
From Acacia Grove[a] to Gilgal,
That you may know the righteousness of
    the LORD."

6 With what shall I come before the LORD,
And bow myself before the High God?

Shall I come before Him with burnt
    offerings,
With calves a year old?
7 Will the LORD be pleased with thousands
    of rams,
Ten thousand rivers of oil?
Shall I give my firstborn *for* my
    transgression,
The fruit of my body *for* the sin of my
    soul?

8 He has shown you, O man, what *is*
    good;
And what does the LORD require of you
But to do justly,
To love mercy,
And to walk humbly with your God?

God Holds Leaders Responsible for Creating an Environment of Justice

(Micah 6:8)

Micah 6:8 declares what God expects of every one of His people, a lesson especially crucial for leaders. Why? Because God holds leaders responsible for creating healthy environments. The people learn to love justice and show mercy when their leader creates an environment for both.

The three items listed in this text define the values and character of a godly leader:

1. **Act justly:** Justice and integrity rule their decisions regarding policy and program.
2. **Love mercy:** A love for people and relationship skills remain a high priority.
3. **Walk humbly with God:** A respectful relationship with God governs their strategy and lifestyle.

Punishment of Israel's Injustice

9 The LORD's voice cries to the city—
Wisdom shall see Your name:

5:14 [a]Hebrew *Asherim,* Canaanite deities **5:15** [a]Or *obeyed* **6:5** [a]Hebrew *Shittim* (compare Numbers 25:1; Joshua 2:1; 3:1)

"Hear the rod!
Who has appointed it?
10 Are there yet the treasures of wickedness
In the house of the wicked,
And the short measure *that is an
abomination?*
11 Shall I count pure *those* with the wicked
scales,
And with the bag of deceitful weights?
12 For her rich men are full of violence,
Her inhabitants have spoken lies,
And their tongue is deceitful in their
mouth.

13 "Therefore I will also make *you* sick by
striking you,
By making *you* desolate because of your
sins.
14 You shall eat, but not be satisfied;
Hunger[a] *shall be* in your midst.
You may carry *some* away,[b] but shall not
save *them;*
And what you do rescue I will give over
to the sword.

15 "You shall sow, but not reap;
You shall tread the olives, but not anoint
yourselves with oil;
And *make* sweet wine, but not drink wine.
16 For the statutes of Omri are kept;
All the works of Ahab's house *are done;*
And you walk in their counsels,
That I may make you a desolation,
And your inhabitants a hissing.
Therefore you shall bear the reproach of
My people."[a]

Sorrow for Israel's Sins

7 Woe is me!
For I am like those who gather summer
fruits,
Like those who glean vintage grapes;
There is no cluster to eat
Of the first-ripe fruit *which* my soul
desires.
2 The faithful *man* has perished from the
earth,
And *there is* no one upright among men.
They all lie in wait for blood;
Every man hunts his brother with a net.

3 That they may successfully do evil with
both hands—
The prince asks *for gifts,*
The judge *seeks* a bribe,
And the great *man* utters his evil desire;

So they scheme together.
4 The best of them *is* like a brier;
The most upright *is sharper* than a thorn
hedge;
The day of your watchman and your
punishment comes;
Now shall be their perplexity.

5 Do not trust in a friend;
Do not put your confidence in a
companion;
Guard the doors of your mouth
From her who lies in your bosom.
6 For son dishonors father,
Daughter rises against her mother,
Daughter-in-law against her mother-in-
law;
A man's enemies *are* the men of his own
household.
7 Therefore I will look to the LORD;
I will wait for the God of my salvation;
My God will hear me.

Israel's Confession and Comfort

8 Do not rejoice over me, my enemy;
When I fall, I will arise;
When I sit in darkness,
The LORD *will be* a light to me.
9 I will bear the indignation of the LORD,
Because I have sinned against Him,
Until He pleads my case
And executes justice for me.
He will bring me forth to the light;
I will see His righteousness.
10 Then *she who is* my enemy will see,
And shame will cover her who said to me,
"Where is the LORD your God?"
My eyes will see her;
Now she will be trampled down
Like mud in the streets.

11 *In* the day when your walls are to be built,
In that day the decree shall go far and
wide.[a]
12 *In* that day they[a] shall come to you
From Assyria and the fortified cities,[b]
From the fortress[c] to the River,[d]
From sea to sea,

6:14 [a]Or *Emptiness* or *Humiliation* [b]Targum and
Vulgate read *You shall take hold.* **6:16** [a]Following
Masoretic Text, Targum, and Vulgate; Septuagint
reads *of nations.* **7:11** [a]Or *the boundary shall be
extended* **7:12** [a]Literally *he,* collective of the captives
[b]Hebrew *arey mazor,* possibly *cities of Egypt* [c]Hebrew
mazor, possibly *Egypt* [d]That is, the Euphrates

And mountain *to* mountain.
13 Yet the land shall be desolate
Because of those who dwell in it,
And for the fruit of their deeds.

God Will Forgive Israel
14 Shepherd Your people with Your staff,
The flock of Your heritage,
Who dwell solitarily *in* a woodland,
In the midst of Carmel;
Let them feed *in* Bashan and Gilead,
As in days of old.

15 "As in the days when you came out of the
land of Egypt,
I will show them[a] wonders."

16 The nations shall see and be ashamed of all
their might;
They shall put *their* hand over *their*
mouth;
Their ears shall be deaf.
17 They shall lick the dust like a serpent;

They shall crawl from their holes like
snakes of the earth.
They shall be afraid of the LORD our God,
And shall fear because of You.
18 Who *is* a God like You,
Pardoning iniquity
And passing over the transgression of the
remnant of His heritage?

He does not retain His anger forever,
Because He delights *in* mercy.
19 He will again have compassion on us,
And will subdue our iniquities.

You will cast all our[a] sins
Into the depths of the sea.
20 You will give truth to Jacob
And mercy to Abraham,
Which You have sworn to our fathers
From days of old.

7:15 [a]Literally *him,* collective for the captives
7:19 [a]Literally *their*

Leaders Who Fail to Practice Servant Leadership Become Self-Serving

(Micah 7:3, 4)

The final chapter of Micah paints a dim picture of Israel. The people couldn't be trusted, but lied in wait to use, abuse, and destroy each other.

Micah 7:3, 4 tells us why this happened: poor leadership at the top. The rulers, princes, and judges worked for kickbacks and bribes. They schemed how they could beat the system and better their own status. They expected the people to serve them instead of them serving the people.

When leaders fail to practice servant leadership, inevitably they become self-serving. Without a compelling cause to better mankind, all leaders find a cause to serve their own interests. This self-service eventually becomes a thorn in their leadership. Consider these other case studies in Scripture:

1. With a cause, Samson won many battles; without one, he couldn't beat the temptation posed by Delilah.
2. With a cause, Saul conquered the kingdom; without one, he could not conquer even his own jealousy.
3. With a cause, David conquered Goliath; without one, he could not conquer his own lust.
4. With a cause, Elijah prayed down fire from heaven and beat 450 prophets of Baal; without one, he ran in fear from a solitary woman, Jezebel.
5. With a cause, Simon Peter preached at Pentecost and 3,000 people were saved; without one, he denied he even belonged to the crowd that followed Jesus.

NAHUM
God's Fundamental Message for Every Erring Leader

SUMMARY

The little-known prophet Nahum witnessed to the people of Judah, just as did the prophets Jeremiah, Habakkuk, and Zephaniah. God instructed him to announce His judgment on the wicked city of Nineveh.

More than a century before, God had commissioned Jonah to call the people of Nineveh to repent—and they did. That generation failed to leave any legacy of humility or repentance, however, and by the seventh century B.C., the nation had fallen into pitiful shape, both morally and spiritually.

Nahum sounds the alarm. In chapter one, he clearly communicates God's anger against the city of Nineveh—a declaration of judgment against wicked government and public immorality. In chapter two, he predicts Nineveh's impending doom. He prophesies it will be attacked and will fall. In chapter three, he describes in detail what this downfall will look like.

This little book packs a wallop. It contains God's fundamental message for every erring leader: No matter how much power you accumulate, it can never compensate for failure with God.

The Ninevites had it all—or so it seemed. They wielded power over many nations and arrogantly flaunted their might. But leadership success without spiritual success equals failure. Jesus asked, "What will it profit a man if he gains the whole world, and loses his own soul?" (Mark 8:36). Put another way, professional wealth minus personal health yields bankruptcy. Organizational power is only temporary; personal power with God lasts. When leaders are right spiritually, they are able to lead *with* their soul rather than in spite of it.

In the final chapter of this book, Nahum notices a fatal flaw in the king of Nineveh. He had failed to reproduce leaders to shepherd the people. Even if he had been a moral man, by himself he lacked the influence to save his nation. He didn't develop healthy governmental leaders and the nation collapsed morally (3:18).

God's Role in Nahum

God confronts and disciplines in this book. He is the divine Judge who must serve papers on Nineveh and execute justice. He used Nahum to lay out the charges against the Assyrians. God indicted them not only for the crimes they committed within their own borders, but for the cruelty they inflicted on other nations they victimized, including Israel.

God once again demonstrates that He is the ultimate power broker in the world. He builds up and tears down. He is not only the King of kings and the Lord of lords, but the Leader of leaders.

Leaders in Nahum

Nahum, the king of Nineveh

Other People of Influence in Nahum

Leaders and public officers of Nineveh

Lessons in Leadership

- Every generation must respond to God for themselves; you can't inherit salvation.
- Wicked leaders ultimately reap what they sow.
- Self-sufficiency can blind leaders from their own infirmities and weaknesses.

LEADERSHIP HIGHLIGHTS IN NAHUM

GOD'S LEADERSHIP Is Like a Judge and a Father (1:2–13)	*page 1100*
THE LAW OF REPRODUCTION: Assyria's King Failed and Paid for It (3:18, 19)	*page 1102*

1 The burden[a] against Nineveh. The book of the vision of Nahum the Elkoshite.

God's Wrath on His Enemies

2 God *is* jealous, and the LORD avenges;
 The LORD avenges and *is* furious.
 The LORD will take vengeance on His adversaries,
 And He reserves *wrath* for His enemies;
3 The LORD *is* slow to anger and great in power,
 And will not at all acquit *the wicked*.

 The LORD has His way
 In the whirlwind and in the storm,
 And the clouds *are* the dust of His feet.
4 He rebukes the sea and makes it dry,
 And dries up all the rivers.
 Bashan and Carmel wither,
 And the flower of Lebanon wilts.
5 The mountains quake before Him,
 The hills melt,
 And the earth heaves[a] at His presence,
 Yes, the world and all who dwell in it.

6 Who can stand before His indignation?
 And who can endure the fierceness of His anger?
 His fury is poured out like fire,
 And the rocks are thrown down by Him.

7 The LORD *is* good,
 A stronghold in the day of trouble;
 And He knows those who trust in Him.
8 But with an overflowing flood

He will make an utter end of its place,
 And darkness will pursue His enemies.

9 What do you conspire against the LORD?
 He will make an utter end *of it*.
 Affliction will not rise up a second time.
10 For while tangled *like* thorns,
 And while drunken *like* drunkards,
 They shall be devoured like stubble fully dried.
11 From you comes forth *one*
 Who plots evil against the LORD,
 A wicked counselor.

12 Thus says the LORD:

 "Though *they are* safe, and likewise many,
 Yet in this manner they will be cut down
 When he passes through.
 Though I have afflicted you,
 I will afflict you no more;
13 For now I will break off his yoke from you,
 And burst your bonds apart."

14 The LORD has given a command concerning you:
 "Your name shall be perpetuated no longer.
 Out of the house of your gods
 I will cut off the carved image and the molded image.
 I will dig your grave,
 For you are vile."

1:1 [a]Or *oracle*   1:5 [a]Targum reads *burns.*

God's Leadership Is Like a Judge and a Father

(Nahum 1:2–13)

Although their ancestors had repented, the generation to which Nahum spoke failed miserably. The Ninevites that Jonah confronted returned to God, while those Nahum confronted never did. Yet in both cases, God led appropriately.

God modeled situational leadership for leaders everywhere, showing when to act as Judge and when to act as Father. These two images demonstrate a wonderful balance every leader must strike. Examine what God did in each situation:

The Leader as a Judge
1. God is jealous (v. 2).
2. God is an avenger (v. 2).
3. God is furious (v. 2).
4. God is great in power (v. 3).
5. God punishes the guilty (v. 3).

The Leader as a Father
1. God is slow to anger (v. 3).
2. God is good (v. 7).
3. God is a stronghold (v. 7).
4. God is a refuge (v. 7).
5. God is a liberator (v. 13).

15 Behold, on the mountains
The feet of him who brings good tidings,
Who proclaims peace!
O Judah, keep your appointed feasts,
Perform your vows.
For the wicked one shall no more pass
    through you;
He is utterly cut off.

The Destruction of Nineveh

2 He who scatters[a] has come up before
    your face.
Man the fort!
Watch the road!
Strengthen *your* flanks!
Fortify *your* power mightily.

2 For the LORD will restore the excellence
    of Jacob
Like the excellence of Israel,
For the emptiers have emptied them out
And ruined their vine branches.

3 The shields of his mighty men *are* made red,
The valiant men *are* in scarlet.
The chariots *come* with flaming torches
In the day of his preparation,
And the spears are brandished.[a]

4 The chariots rage in the streets,
They jostle one another in the broad
    roads;
They seem like torches,
They run like lightning.

5 He remembers his nobles;
They stumble in their walk;
They make haste to her walls,
And the defense is prepared.

6 The gates of the rivers are opened,
And the palace is dissolved.

7 It is decreed:[a]
She shall be led away captive,
She shall be brought up;
And her maidservants shall lead *her* as with
    the voice of doves,
Beating their breasts.

8 Though Nineveh of old *was* like a pool of
    water,
Now they flee away.
"Halt! Halt!" *they cry;*
But no one turns back.

9 Take spoil of silver!
Take spoil of gold!
There is no end of treasure,
Or wealth of every desirable prize.

10 She is empty, desolate, and waste!
The heart melts, and the knees shake;
Much pain *is* in every side,
And all their faces are drained of color.[a]

11 Where *is* the dwelling of the lions,
And the feeding place of the young lions,
Where the lion walked, the lioness *and*
    lion's cub,
And no one made *them* afraid?

12 The lion tore in pieces enough for his
    cubs,
Killed for his lionesses,
Filled his caves with prey,
And his dens with flesh.

13 "Behold, I *am* against you," says the LORD of
hosts, "I will burn your[a] chariots in smoke, and
the sword shall devour your young lions; I will
cut off your prey from the earth, and the voice
of your messengers shall be heard no more."

God's Method of Discipline

(Nahum 2:13)

God uses many methods to discipline His
erring people—even pagan nations like
Assyria. This means, first, that no sin is more
acceptable than another. Second, God desires
to humble as well as discipline. Third, He is
sovereign and will correct His people in whatever manner He sees fit.

The Woe of Nineveh

3 Woe to the bloody city!
It *is* all full of lies *and* robbery.
Its victim never departs.

2 The noise of a whip
And the noise of rattling wheels,
Of galloping horses,
Of clattering chariots!

3 Horsemen charge with bright sword and
    glittering spear.
There is a multitude of slain,

2:1 [a]Vulgate reads *He who destroys.* **2:3** [a]Literally *the
cypresses are shaken;* Septuagint and Syriac read *the
horses rush about;* Vulgate reads *the drivers are stupefied.*
2:7 [a]Hebrew *Huzzab* **2:10** [a]Compare Joel 2:6
2:13 [a]Literally *her*

A great number of bodies,
Countless corpses—
They stumble over the corpses—

4 Because of the multitude of harlotries of
    the seductive harlot,
The mistress of sorceries,
Who sells nations through her harlotries,
And families through her sorceries.

5 "Behold, I *am* against you," says the LORD
    of hosts;
"I will lift your skirts over your face,
I will show the nations your nakedness,
And the kingdoms your shame.

6 I will cast abominable filth upon you,
Make you vile,
And make you a spectacle.

7 It shall come to pass *that* all who look
    upon you
Will flee from you, and say,
'Nineveh is laid waste!
Who will bemoan her?'
Where shall I seek comforters for you?"

8 Are you better than No Amon[a]
That was situated by the River,[b]

That had the waters around her,
Whose rampart *was* the sea,
Whose wall *was* the sea?

9 Ethiopia and Egypt *were* her strength,
And *it was* boundless;
Put and Lubim were your[a] helpers.

10 Yet she *was* carried away,
She went into captivity;
Her young children also were dashed to
    pieces
At the head of every street;
They cast lots for her honorable men,
And all her great men were bound in
    chains.

11 You also will be drunk;
You will be hidden;
You also will seek refuge from the enemy.

12 All your strongholds *are* fig trees with
    ripened figs:
If they are shaken,

3:8 [a]That is, ancient Thebes; Targum and Vulgate read *populous Alexandria*. [b]Literally *rivers,* that is, the Nile and the surrounding canals **3:9** [a]Septuagint reads *her*.

The Law of Reproduction:
Assyria's King Failed and Paid for It
(Nahum 3:18, 19)

Through Nahum, God offers some insight as to why Nineveh failed so deeply. The prophet declared, "Your shepherds slumber, O king of Assyria; your nobles rest in the dust. Your people are scattered on the mountains, and no one gathers them" (Nah. 3:18). Since the king had failed to reproduce other leaders, his people lay scattered like sheep without a shepherd. When we fail to develop other leaders, our leadership is limited to:

- Whatever leadership abilities we can offer
- The generation we live in
- The finite volume of gifts we possess
- The boundaries of our own wisdom
- The scope of our own influence

Because the King of Assyria had failed to develop other leaders, he had no way to change what was happening to the people of Nineveh. The population had grown too large for one man to perform a turnaround; one leader could not prevent the calamity the city had earned. Consider what happened when the king failed to practice the Law of Reproduction:

1. The local leaders grew blind and failed at their duties (v. 18).
2. The people had scattered and no one could organize them (v. 18).
3. The people had no relief or healing for their wounds (v. 19).
4. Everyone who heard of Nineveh's chaos would clap their hands and cheer (v. 19).

They fall into the mouth of the eater.

13 Surely, your people in your midst *are* women!
The gates of your land are wide open for your enemies;
Fire shall devour the bars of your *gates*.

14 Draw your water for the siege!
Fortify your strongholds!
Go into the clay and tread the mortar!
Make strong the brick kiln!

15 There the fire will devour you,
The sword will cut you off;
It will eat you up like a locust.

Make yourself many—like the locust!
Make yourself many— like the *swarming* locusts!

16 You have multiplied your merchants more than the stars of heaven.

The locust plunders and flies away.

17 Your commanders *are* like *swarming* locusts,
And your generals like great grasshoppers,
Which camp in the hedges on a cold day;
When the sun rises they flee away,
And the place where they *are* is not known.

18 Your shepherds slumber, O king of Assyria;
Your nobles rest *in the dust*.
Your people are scattered on the mountains,
And no one gathers them.

19 Your injury *has* no healing,
Your wound is severe.
All who hear news of you
Will clap *their* hands over you,
For upon whom has not your wickedness passed continually?

HABAKKUK
Leadership with No Easy Answers

SUMMARY

God commissioned Habakkuk, a contemporary of Jeremiah and Ezekiel, to lead in troubled times. His name means "to embrace," and he earned the title by wrestling with God in the beginning of his book and by developing deep intimacy with God by the book's end.

Habakkuk could have titled his book, *Leadership with No Easy Answers*. This prophet struggled with why God allowed the people of Judah to get by with their immoral and sinful ways. He cried out to God and at first got no answer. God seemed far too tolerant for Habakkuk's tastes. Finally, God gave him a vision about His plan to rectify the situation by raising up Babylon to plunder and capture Judah in war. At this point, Habakkuk faced a whole new dilemma. Would God really use a nation even *more* wicked than Judah to correct Judah? This seemed preposterous to him. So he presented God with an integrity check: *Do You really know what You are doing here?* When God answered his question, he learned to trust, and ended the book with a beautiful psalm of faith.

Habakkuk teaches us to be praying leaders. The entire book is a dialogue between God and him, the only book in the Bible laid out in this way. As a prophet, Habakkuk had to *feed* the people and *lead* the people—but first, *intercede* for the people. Far too often, those of us who assume leadership positions are "doers" who forget this key role. In the New Testament, Peter said he would give himself to two priorities: the Word of God and prayer. This is the first job of a spiritual leader.

Habakkuk also teaches us that it's OK to ask God questions. We should enjoy such intimacy with God that we can candidly express our questions, concerns, or confusion over God's ways. When we lack answers, we ought to run to God, seeking His wisdom. Habakkuk asked detailed and specific questions. Leaders must feel secure enough to admit they don't know it all and seek insight from God.

Finally, the greatest leadership principle we learn from Habakkuk is trust. He knew he wasn't in control, any more than we are today. He waited on God. When God finally spoke, Habakkuk had to trust Him; he certainly didn't understand. In essence, his closing psalm says, "Although I don't understand what is happening, and nothing is working out the way I would like it—I'll still rejoice and trust God's wisdom."

God's Role in Habakkuk

Habakkuk has to learn to follow God as the Leader. The Lord remains silent in the beginning and teaches His leader to wait. He eventually responds to Habakkuk's complaint in an unexpected fashion and teaches His leader to trust. He later confirms His sovereign control over all things and teaches His leader to rejoice, regardless of the circumstances. Habakkuk rises to a whole new level of leadership by the way God deals with him. May God do the same for each of us.

Leaders in Habakkuk

Habakkuk, the leaders of Judah, King Jehoahaz

Other People of Influence in Habakkuk

The Babylonian army

Lessons in Leadership

- Leaders must learn to wait on the Lord before they act on His Word.

- Wise leaders acknowledge their limitations and seek wise counsel from God.

- Godly leaders are not ashamed or afraid to ask detailed questions of the Lord.

- Good leaders discipline themselves to listen to the voice of God and thereby develop an intimate relationship with Him.

- Mature leaders rejoice in each circumstance, knowing who controls all things.

LEADERSHIP

HIGHLIGHTS IN HABAKKUK

LISTENING: Leaders Earn Their Right to Be Heard (1:1–11) *page 1106*
WAITING: The Act Most Leaders Hate (2:1–20) *page 1107*
VISION: The Blueprint for Building a Bridge to the Future (2:2, 3) *page 1108*
GOD'S LEADERSHIP in the World (3:1–16) *page 1109*
RESOURCES, Wisdom, and People Follow Commitment (3:17–19) *page 1110*

1

The burden[a] which the prophet Habakkuk saw.

The Prophet's Question

2   O Lord, how long shall I cry,
And You will not hear?
Even cry out to You, "Violence!"
And You will not save.

3   Why do You show me iniquity,
And cause *me* to see trouble?
For plundering and violence *are* before me;
There is strife, and contention arises.

4   Therefore the law is powerless,
And justice never goes forth.
For the wicked surround the righteous;
Therefore perverse judgment proceeds.

The Lord's Reply

5   "Look among the nations and watch—
Be utterly astounded!
For *I will* work a work in your days
Which you would not believe, though it were told *you*.

6   For indeed I am raising up the Chaldeans,
A bitter and hasty nation

Which marches through the breadth of the earth,
To possess dwelling places *that are* not theirs.

7   They are terrible and dreadful;
Their judgment and their dignity proceed from themselves.

8   Their horses also are swifter than leopards,
And more fierce than evening wolves.
Their chargers charge ahead;
Their cavalry comes from afar;
They fly as the eagle *that* hastens to eat.

9   "They all come for violence;
Their faces are set *like* the east wind.
They gather captives like sand.

10   They scoff at kings,
And princes are scorned by them.
They deride every stronghold,
For they heap up earthen *mounds* and seize it.

11   Then *his* mind[a] changes, and he transgresses;
He commits offense,
Ascribing this power to his god."

1:1 [a]Or *oracle*   1:11 [a]Literally *spirit* or *wind*

Listening: Leaders Earn Their Right to Be Heard

(Habakkuk 1:1–11)

Habakkuk teaches us that leaders must first be listeners. In the first four verses of his book, the prophet cries out for God to answer his questions. He begs God to respond to the injustice, the violence, and the perversion of his nation. He knew God was infinitely just, and he could not understand why God didn't seem interested in doing something about Judah's rebellion.

When God finally did respond, He gave Habakkuk a distasteful answer. God declared that He planned to use the Babylonians to punish Judah. He intended to use a nation more unjust than Judah to correct injustice among the Jews. That just didn't make sense to Habakkuk!

Even so, the prophet continued to listen. He wrestled with God but knew that leaders earn their right to speak by listening. When they listen, they gain something more precious than the privilege to speak:

1. They gain insight about people.
2. They connect with the speaker.
3. They earn their right to speak.
4. They become relevant.
5. They understand the keys to the speaker's heart.
6. They identify.
7. They gain authority.
8. They learn.

Remember: When you speak, nothing you say will teach you anything. Only when you listen—to God and to others—will you gain understanding.

The Prophet's Second Question

12 Are You not from everlasting,
O LORD my God, my Holy One?
We shall not die.
O LORD, You have appointed them for
judgment;
O Rock, You have marked them for
correction.

13 *You are* of purer eyes than to behold evil,
And cannot look on wickedness.
Why do You look on those who deal
treacherously,
And hold Your tongue when the wicked
devours
A *person* more righteous than he?

14 *Why* do You make men like fish of the sea,
Like creeping things *that have* no ruler over
them?

15 They take up all of them with a hook,
They catch them in their net,
And gather them in their dragnet.
Therefore they rejoice and are glad.

16 Therefore they sacrifice to their net,
And burn incense to their dragnet;
Because by them their share *is* sumptuous
And their food plentiful.

17 Shall they therefore empty their net,
And continue to slay nations without pity?

2 I will stand my watch
And set myself on the rampart,
And watch to see what He will say to me,
And what I will answer when I am
corrected.

The Just Live by Faith

2 Then the LORD answered me and said:

"Write the vision
And make *it* plain on tablets,
That he may run who reads it.

3 For the vision *is* yet for an appointed time;
But at the end it will speak, and it will not
lie.
Though it tarries, wait for it;
Because it will surely come,
It will not tarry.

4 "Behold the proud,
His soul is not upright in him;
But the just shall live by his faith.

Woe to the Wicked

5 "Indeed, because he transgresses by wine,
He is a proud man,

And he does not stay at home.
Because he enlarges his desire as hell,[a]
And he *is* like death, and cannot be
satisfied,
He gathers to himself all nations
And heaps up for himself all peoples.

Waiting: The Act Most Leaders Hate

(Habakkuk 2:1–20)

Habakkuk teaches us that leaders must learn to cherish the waiting time before they get their answers. In chapter one, the prophet is positioned to watch and see. In chapter two, he is positioned to stand and see. In chapter three, he is positioned to kneel and see.

God declares five "woes" to Habakkuk in the second chapter of his book, describing His intense displeasure with His people. Yet if God is sovereign, reigning over everything, then why doesn't He use His leader to bring about justice *immediately?* The answer appears to be this: While Habakkuk waited, God did a wonderful work in his heart. Before God leads the world, He first wants to lead His leaders. Habakkuk learned at least four lessons about God's leadership in the world:

1. Not everything that happens conforms to God's will and wishes.
2. Nothing that happens gets overlooked by God.
3. Everything that happens will ultimately be addressed with justice.
4. Nothing that happens should distract us from continuing to respond faithfully.

6 "Will not all these take up a proverb against
him,
And a taunting riddle against him, and
say,
'Woe to him who increases
What is not his—how long?
And to him who loads himself with many
pledges'?[a]

2:5 [a]Or *Sheol* 2:6 [a]Syriac and Vulgate read *thick clay.*

Vision: The Blueprint for Building a Bridge to the Future

(Habakkuk 2:2, 3)

Leaders and vision go together like fire and heat; you can't separate them without destroying their essence. Through Habakkuk, God furnishes some instruction on vision for all of us. A divine vision . . .

- should be written down (v. 2).
- should be distributed to people (v. 2).
- should be acted on (v. 2).
- is for a select time in the future (v. 3).
- motivates us toward the goal (v. 3).
- should not be discarded (v. 3).
- will not fail (v. 3).

7 Will not your creditors[a] rise up suddenly?
Will they not awaken who oppress you?
And you will become their booty.
8 Because you have plundered many nations,
All the remnant of the people shall plunder you,
Because of men's blood
And the violence of the land *and* the city,
And of all who dwell in it.

9 "Woe to him who covets evil gain for his house,
That he may set his nest on high,
That he may be delivered from the power of disaster!
10 You give shameful counsel to your house,
Cutting off many peoples,
And sin *against* your soul.
11 For the stone will cry out from the wall,
And the beam from the timbers will answer it.

12 "Woe to him who builds a town with bloodshed,
Who establishes a city by iniquity!
13 Behold, *is it* not of the LORD of hosts
That the peoples labor to feed the fire,[a]
And nations weary themselves in vain?
14 For the earth will be filled
With the knowledge of the glory of the LORD,
As the waters cover the sea.

15 "Woe to him who gives drink to his neighbor,
Pressing[a] *him to* your bottle,
Even to make *him* drunk,
That you may look on his nakedness!
16 You are filled with shame instead of glory.
You also—drink!
And be exposed as uncircumcised![a]
The cup of the LORD's right hand *will be* turned against you,
And utter shame will be on your glory.
17 For the violence *done to* Lebanon will cover you,
And the plunder of beasts *which* made them afraid,
Because of men's blood
And the violence of the land *and* the city,
And of all who dwell in it.

18 "What profit is the image, that its maker should carve it,
The molded image, a teacher of lies,
That the maker of its mold should trust in it,
To make mute idols?
19 Woe to him who says to wood, 'Awake!'
To silent stone, 'Arise! It shall teach!'
Behold, it is overlaid with gold and silver,
Yet in it there is no breath at all.

20 "But the LORD is in His holy temple.
Let all the earth keep silence before Him."

The Prophet's Prayer

3 A prayer of Habakkuk the prophet, on Shigionoth.[a]

2 O LORD, I have heard Your speech *and* was afraid;
O LORD, revive Your work in the midst of the years!
In the midst of the years make *it* known;
In wrath remember mercy.

3 God came from Teman,
The Holy One from Mount Paran.
　　　　　　　　　　　Selah

2:7 [a]Literally *those who bite you* **2:13** [a]Literally *for what satisfies fire,* that is, for what is of no lasting value **2:15** [a]Literally *Attaching* or *Joining* **2:16** [a]Dead Sea Scrolls and Septuagint read *And reel!;* Syriac and Vulgate read *And fall fast asleep!* **3:1** [a]Exact meaning unknown

God's Leadership in the World

(Habakkuk 3:1–16)

Who can fully grasp God's method of dealing with the world around us? He truly is the Ultimate Leader who governs the affairs of mankind. Habakkuk shows how God influences the nations to perform His will. Consider His methods of influence:

1. *He sometimes exerts a restraining influence.*
   Through this, He prevents people from doing what they feel naturally inclined to do.
2. *He sometimes exerts a softening influence.*
   Through this, He causes them to move contrary to natural inclinations and to promote His cause.
3. *He sometimes exerts a directing influence.*
   Through this, He causes good to result from the evil that others intend.

His glory covered the heavens,
And the earth was full of His praise.
4 *His* brightness was like the light;
He had rays *flashing* from His hand,
And there His power *was* hidden.
5 Before Him went pestilence,
And fever followed at His feet.

6 He stood and measured the earth;
He looked and startled the nations.
And the everlasting mountains were scattered,
The perpetual hills bowed.
His ways *are* everlasting.
7 I saw the tents of Cushan in affliction;
The curtains of the land of Midian trembled.

8 O LORD, were *You* displeased with the rivers,
Was Your anger against the rivers,
Was Your wrath against the sea,
That You rode on Your horses,
Your chariots of salvation?

9 Your bow was made quite ready;
Oaths were sworn over *Your* arrows.[a]

Selah

You divided the earth with rivers.
10 The mountains saw You *and* trembled;
The overflowing of the water passed by.
The deep uttered its voice,
And lifted its hands on high.
11 The sun and moon stood still in their habitation;
At the light of Your arrows they went,
At the shining of Your glittering spear.

12 You marched through the land in indignation;
You trampled the nations in anger.
13 You went forth for the salvation of Your people,
For salvation with Your Anointed.
You struck the head from the house of the wicked,
By laying bare from foundation to neck.

Selah

14 You thrust through with his own arrows
The head of his villages.
They came out like a whirlwind to scatter me;
Their rejoicing was like feasting on the poor in secret.

3:9 [a]Literally *rods* or *tribes* (compare verse 14)

The Difference Between Leaders and Followers Is Perspective

(Habakkuk 3:17–19)

Once Habakkuk grasps God's leadership of the world, he can lead with confidence and poise. He once felt perplexed; now he has peace. He once felt confused; now he has contentment. He once felt fearful; now he has faith in the future God has planned. The only thing that changed? His perspective!

Resources, Wisdom, and People Follow Commitment

(Habakkuk 3:17–19)

The prophet concludes his book with a ringing declaration of his commitment. He recommits himself to God, to His vision, and to the destiny of his nation. Regardless of what happened, he would trust the process in which God had placed him.

This is the kind of attitude that enables leaders to "make it." Once we make this kind of commitment, all sorts of resources, wisdom, and people follow. When leaders commit in this way, followers rise to the occasion despite adverse circumstances. Habakkuk teaches us the steps to this kind of commitment:

1. **Request:** Go ahead and ask for God's wisdom and will to be done.
2. **Relax:** Rest in His control; trust His power and providence.
3. **Receive:** Listen and wait for His instruction; remain open to change.
4. **Respond:** Obey whatever He commands.
5. **Rejoice:** Worship Him regardless of your present circumstances.

15 You walked through the sea with Your
　horses,
　Through the heap of great waters.

16 When I heard, my body trembled;
　My lips quivered at *the* voice;
　Rottenness entered my bones;
　And I trembled in myself,
　That I might rest in the day of trouble.
　When he comes up to the people,
　He will invade them with his troops.

A Hymn of Faith

17 Though the fig tree may not blossom,
　Nor fruit be on the vines;
　Though the labor of the olive may fail,
　And the fields yield no food;
　Though the flock may be cut off from the
　　fold,
　And there be no herd in the stalls—
18 Yet I will rejoice in the LORD,
　I will joy in the God of my salvation.

19 The LORD God[a] is my strength;
　He will make my feet like deer's *feet,*
　And He will make me walk on my high
　　hills.

To the Chief Musician. With my stringed instruments.

3:19 [a]Hebrew *YHWH Adonai*

ZEPHANIAH
Repentance Goes Deeper Than Outward Behavior

SUMMARY

Zephaniah, a contemporary of Judah's King Josiah, represents a type of leader that every organization needs. Josiah was the godly king who, as a 20-year-old monarch, began to initiate much-needed national reforms. He restored the worship practices of old, ordered the Book of the Law to be read aloud, and required everyone to bow down and repent for their sin and spiritual drifting.

Merely external reforms, however, remain incomplete. You cannot perfume a skunk and expect to transform him. Many in Josiah's day performed the repentance rituals but continued in their secret sins. Many never acknowledged their private sinfulness, nor did they inwardly repent of their personal wickedness.

Zephaniah decided that repentance needed to go deeper than outward behavior. You might say that he practiced the Law of Intuition. He intuitively knew that real change requires more than what the leader can legislate. He sought more than external reformation—he wanted internal transformation. He knew that mere respect for the king could not produce the needed metamorphosis. The people didn't need to turn over a new leaf; they needed a new life. So the prophet took a risk and acted. He began to call the Hebrews to look at their hearts, their motives, their desires, their private lives. He meddled—but touched a chord. He spoke to issues that needed to be addressed, issues that most leaders fear to bring up.

The people of Judah respected the prophet Zephaniah. Many scholars believe that royal blood coursed through his veins, giving him direct access to the king. As such, he could have enjoyed his favored position and let well enough alone. But he refused to sit still. He wouldn't allow his power and position to water down his convictions. Instead, he leveraged his influence with King Josiah to create needed civil and religious reforms. He called a spade, a spade.

Early in Josiah's reign, Zephaniah began challenging the wicked patterns initiated under the kings Manasseh and Amon. He warned the people of impending judgment and likely played an influential role in Josiah's determination to initiate national change. Nevertheless, even though the king joined Zephaniah in the reform movement, the evil tide rolled on. This led the prophet to predict that God would use an outsider (namely Nebuchadnezzar) as the rod of His discipline.

Despite this, the book ends on a note of hope as Zephaniah points to a time when all people will call on the name of the Lord.

God's Role in Zephaniah

In Zephaniah's day, God played a key role as the broker of talents. God used King Josiah to bring about necessary legislative reforms. He called the people to corporate reform. But to transform the people, He also used Zephaniah's gift to call the people to personal reflection and repentance. If the nation were to benefit from the new legislation, each individual needed to repent of specific private sins. Change always begins in the heart of an individual. So, God raised up both a Josiah and a Zephaniah. The nation needed their complementary gifts.

Leaders in Zephaniah

Zephaniah, King Josiah

Other People of Influence in Zephaniah

Wicked people of Judah, Nebuchadnezzar

Lessons in Leadership

- God brings about change from the inside out.

- Leadership is often best exercised in teams, where complementary gifts are used.

- Leaders cannot let their safe positions keep them from risking radical obedience.

- Leaders must never shift their focus from doing their job to keeping their job.

- Leaders who confront tough issues will enjoy the respect of others and the joy of corporate purity.

LEADERSHIP

HIGHLIGHTS IN ZEPHANIAH

1

The word of the LORD which came to Zephaniah the son of Cushi, the son of Gedaliah, the son of Amariah, the son of Hezekiah, in the days of Josiah the son of Amon, king of Judah.

The Great Day of the LORD

2 "I will utterly consume everything
   From the face of the land,"
   Says the LORD;
3 "I will consume man and beast;
   I will consume the birds of the heavens,
   The fish of the sea,
   And the stumbling blocks[a] along with the
      wicked.
   I will cut off man from the face of the
      land,"
   Says the LORD.

4 "I will stretch out My hand against Judah,
   And against all the inhabitants of
      Jerusalem.
   I will cut off every trace of Baal from this
      place,
   The names of the idolatrous priests[a] with
      the *pagan* priests—
5 Those who worship the host of heaven on
      the housetops;

Those who worship and swear *oaths* by the
   LORD,
But who *also* swear by Milcom;[a]
6 Those who have turned back from
      following the LORD,
   And have not sought the LORD, nor
      inquired of Him."

7 Be silent in the presence of the Lord GOD;
   For the day of the LORD *is* at hand,
   For the LORD has prepared a sacrifice;
   He has invited[a] His guests.

8 "And it shall be,
   In the day of the LORD's sacrifice,
   That I will punish the princes and the
      king's children,
   And all such as are clothed with foreign
      apparel.
9 In the same day I will punish
   All those who leap over the threshold,[a]
   Who fill their masters' houses with
      violence and deceit.

1:3 [a]Figurative of idols   **1:4** [a]Hebrew *chemarim*   **1:5** [a]Or *Malcam*, an Ammonite god, also called *Molech* (compare Leviticus 18:21)   **1:7** [a]Literally *set apart, consecrated*   **1:9** [a]Compare 1 Samuel 5:5

Communication: Zephaniah Spoke with Divine Authority
(Zephaniah 1:1–18)

Zephaniah spoke for God, just as other Old Testament prophets had done. This divine message required Zephaniah to possess unique qualifications, for God called him to deliver a message his audience didn't want to hear. The message wasn't fun to preach and contained difficult and even disgusting metaphors.

Nevertheless, Zephaniah communicated judgment upon the house of Judah with great authority. How could he stand strong and deliver his message with passion in the face of entrenched opposition? And how can we follow his example? Make sure you follow the pattern Zephaniah did:

1. **Believe in your God.**
   Zephaniah had to trust in God to protect and empower him to communicate the message.
2. **Believe in your message.**
   Zephaniah had to be convinced that this hard word was exactly what the people needed to hear.
3. **Believe in your cause.**
   Zephaniah had to embrace his ultimate cause.
4. **Believe in your people.**
   Zephaniah had to have hope that the people would change and buy into his message.
5. **Believe in yourself.**
   Zephaniah had to be convinced that he was the man to deliver this message.

10 "And there shall be on that day," says the
     LORD,
"The sound of a mournful cry from the
     Fish Gate,
A wailing from the Second Quarter,
And a loud crashing from the hills.
11 Wail, you inhabitants of Maktesh!ᵃ
For all the merchant people are cut down;
All those who handle money are cut off.

12 "And it shall come to pass at that time
     That I will search Jerusalem with lamps,
And punish the men
Who are settled in complacency,ᵃ
Who say in their heart,
'The LORD will not do good,
Nor will He do evil.'
13 Therefore their goods shall become booty,
And their houses a desolation;
They shall build houses, but not inhabit them;
They shall plant vineyards, but not drink
     their wine."

14 The great day of the LORD is near;
It is near and hastens quickly.
The noise of the day of the LORD is bitter;
There the mighty men shall cry out.
15 That day is a day of wrath,
A day of trouble and distress,
A day of devastation and desolation,
A day of darkness and gloominess,
A day of clouds and thick darkness,
16 A day of trumpet and alarm
Against the fortified cities
And against the high towers.

17 "I will bring distress upon men,
And they shall walk like blind men,
Because they have sinned against the LORD;
Their blood shall be poured out like dust,
And their flesh like refuse."

18 Neither their silver nor their gold
Shall be able to deliver them
In the day of the LORD's wrath;
But the whole land shall be devoured
By the fire of His jealousy,
For He will make speedy riddance
Of all those who dwell in the land.

A Call to Repentance

2 Gather yourselves together, yes, gather
     together,
O undesirableᵃ nation,
2 Before the decree is issued,
Or the day passes like chaff,

Before the LORD's fierce anger comes
     upon you,
Before the day of the LORD's anger comes
     upon you!
3 Seek the LORD, all you meek of the
     earth,
Who have upheld His justice.
Seek righteousness, seek humility.
It may be that you will be hidden
In the day of the LORD's anger.

1:11 ᵃLiterally *Mortar,* a market district of Jerusalem
1:12 ᵃLiterally *on their lees,* that is, settled like the
dregs of wine **2:1** ᵃOr *shameless*

The Law of Intuition: The Prophet Knows Change Begins Inside

(Zephaniah 2:1–3)

The prophet intuitively knows what needs to
happen to change the people of Judah.
Zephaniah lived during the reform of King
Josiah. Even with the external reforms in worship the king initiated, Zephaniah knew more
changes were required. He knew change begins with the heart. Transformation happens
from the inside out.

To enhance your own leadership intuition,
practice the following activities:

1. **Work in the areas of your strength.**
   We are most intuitive in the areas of our
   gifts and interests.
2. **Explore the opportunities in front
   of you.**
   Our intuition comes most alive when we
   size up the options near us.
3. **Discern root causes for the issues
   you face.**
   Work to get past superficial answers and
   solve root issues.
4. **Analyze past successes.**
   Study your victories and see if you find a
   pattern that reveals how you won them.
5. **Listen to your gut.**
   Effective leaders lead from their soul.
   Both your heart and your head have
   answers.

Judgment on Nations

4 For Gaza shall be forsaken,
And Ashkelon desolate;
They shall drive out Ashdod at noonday,
And Ekron shall be uprooted.

5 Woe to the inhabitants of the seacoast,
The nation of the Cherethites!
The word of the LORD *is* against you,
O Canaan, land of the Philistines:
"I will destroy you;
So there shall be no inhabitant."

6 The seacoast shall be pastures,
With shelters[a] for shepherds and folds for
flocks.

7 The coast shall be for the remnant of the
house of Judah;
They shall feed *their* flocks there;
In the houses of Ashkelon they shall lie
down at evening.
For the LORD their God will intervene for
them,
And return their captives.

8 "I have heard the reproach of Moab,
And the insults of the people of Ammon,
With which they have reproached My
people,
And made arrogant threats against their
borders.

9 Therefore, as I live,"
Says the LORD of hosts, the God of
Israel,
"Surely Moab shall be like Sodom,
And the people of Ammon like
Gomorrah—
Overrun with weeds and saltpits,
And a perpetual desolation.
The residue of My people shall plunder
them,
And the remnant of My people shall
possess them."

10 This they shall have for their pride,
Because they have reproached and made
arrogant threats
Against the people of the LORD of hosts.

11 The LORD *will be* awesome to them,
For He will reduce to nothing all the gods
of the earth;
People shall worship Him,
Each one from his place,
Indeed all the shores of the nations.

12 "You Ethiopians also,
You shall be slain by My sword."

13 And He will stretch out His hand against
the north,
Destroy Assyria,
And make Nineveh a desolation,
As dry as the wilderness.

14 The herds shall lie down in her midst,
Every beast of the nation.
Both the pelican and the bittern
Shall lodge on the capitals *of her* *pillars;*
Their voice shall sing in the windows;
Desolation *shall be* at the threshold;
For He will lay bare the cedar work.

15 This is the rejoicing city
That dwelt securely,
That said in her heart,
"I *am it,* and *there is* none besides me."
How has she become a desolation,
A place for beasts to lie down!
Everyone who passes by her
Shall hiss and shake his fist.

Confrontation: Zephaniah Does It and Gains Credibility

(Zephaniah 2:4–15)

While not everyone agreed with Zephaniah's judgment on Judah, he gained widespread credibility due to his ability to confront tough issues. He called out specific groups of people to be judged for their sins, then named their specific sins. When leaders are willing to confront difficult issues, they win the respect of others.

The Wickedness of Jerusalem

3 Woe to her who is rebellious and
polluted,
To the oppressing city!

2 She has not obeyed *His* voice,
She has not received correction;
She has not trusted in the LORD,
She has not drawn near to her God.

3 Her princes in her midst *are* roaring
lions;
Her judges *are* evening wolves
That leave not a bone till morning.

2:6 [a]Literally *excavations,* either underground huts or
cisterns

4 Her prophets are insolent, treacherous
   people;
   Her priests have polluted the sanctuary,
   They have done violence to the law.
5 The LORD *is* righteous in her midst,
   He will do no unrighteousness.
   Every morning He brings His justice to
     light;
   He never fails,
   But the unjust knows no shame.

6 "I have cut off nations,
   Their fortresses are devastated;
   I have made their streets desolate,
   With none passing by.
   Their cities are destroyed;
   There is no one, no inhabitant.
7 I said, 'Surely you will fear Me,
   You will receive instruction'—
   So that her dwelling would not be cut off,
   Despite everything for which I punished
     her.
   But they rose early and corrupted all their
     deeds.

A Faithful Remnant

8 "Therefore wait for Me," says the LORD,
   "Until the day I rise up for plunder;[a]
   My determination *is* to gather the nations
   To My assembly of kingdoms,
   To pour on them My indignation,
   All My fierce anger;
   All the earth shall be devoured
   With the fire of My jealousy.

9 "For then I will restore to the peoples a
     pure language,
   That they all may call on the name of the
     LORD,
   To serve Him with one accord.
10 From beyond the rivers of Ethiopia
   My worshipers,
   The daughter of My dispersed ones,
   Shall bring My offering.
11 In that day you shall not be shamed for
     any of your deeds
   In which you transgress against Me;
   For then I will take away from your
     midst
   Those who rejoice in your pride,
   And you shall no longer be haughty
   In My holy mountain.
12 I will leave in your midst
   A meek and humble people,
   And they shall trust in the name of the
     LORD.

The Law of Navigation: Zephaniah Gives Hope and a Plan

(Zephaniah 3:8–20)

Regardless of the hopeless situation they had to judge, the Old Testament prophets almost always closed their writings with words of hope. Zephaniah even offers a plan for repentance and invites the people to walk in it. He navigates the path back to God, outlining it this way:

1. Wait for God to *remove* the cancerous population (vv. 8–11).
2. Trust God to *restore* a remnant of humble, obedient men and women (vv. 12, 13).
3. Look to God and *rejoice* that he has taken away your guilt (vv. 14, 15).
4. Hope in God to *renew* your peace and strength (vv. 16, 17).
5. Allow God to *recover* the appointed feasts and the lost people (vv. 18–20).

13 The remnant of Israel shall do no
     unrighteousness
   And speak no lies,
   Nor shall a deceitful tongue be found in
     their mouth;
   For they shall feed *their* flocks and lie
     down,
   And no one shall make *them* afraid."

Joy in God's Faithfulness

14 Sing, O daughter of Zion!
   Shout, O Israel!
   Be glad and rejoice with all *your* heart,
   O daughter of Jerusalem!
15 The LORD has taken away your
     judgments,
   He has cast out your enemy.
   The King of Israel, the LORD, *is* in your
     midst;
   You shall see[a] disaster no more.

3:8 [a]Septuagint and Syriac read *for witness;* Targum reads *for the day of My revelation for judgment;* Vulgate reads *for the day of My resurrection that is to come.*
3:15 [a]Some Hebrew manuscripts, Septuagint, and Bomberg read *see;* Masoretic Text and Vulgate read *fear.*

16 In that day it shall be said to Jerusalem:
"Do not fear;
Zion, let not your hands be weak.
17 The LORD your God in your midst,
The Mighty One, will save;
He will rejoice over you with gladness,
He will quiet *you* with His love,
He will rejoice over you with singing."
18 "I will gather those who sorrow over the
appointed assembly,
Who are among you,
To *whom* its reproach *is* a burden.
19 Behold, at that time

I will deal with all who afflict you;
I will save the lame,
And gather those who were driven out;
I will appoint them for praise and
fame
In every land where they were put to
shame.
20 At that time I will bring you back,
Even at the time I gather you;
For I will give you fame and praise
Among all the peoples of the earth,
When I return your captives before your
eyes,"
Says the LORD.

HAGGAI
Calling God's People Back to Their Faith and Values

SUMMARY

The prophet Haggai teaches us about the Law of Priorities. God raised him up to address the misplaced priorities of the Hebrews under the Persian reign of Cyrus. Haggai insisted on doing the right things at the right time, for the right reasons.

Haggai became the first prophet to serve God's people when the Jews returned to their homeland after the Babylonian exile. King Cyrus conquered the Babylonians 70 years after they had taken the Jews into captivity. Cyrus allowed the Jews to return to their homeland, just as the prophets Jeremiah and Daniel had foretold. He sent them back to Israel in order to rebuild the Jerusalem temple.

Upon their arrival, they laid the foundation for the sanctuary and the work began. But soon hostile neighbors tried to stop the work. (There is a spiritual lesson in there somewhere!) Slowly, the building project ground to a halt—but outward opposition accounted for only part of the problem. An inward enemy called "indifference" posed the major threat.

Most of the workers became apathetic, even though the rebuilding project supplied the very reason for their return to Jerusalem. Before long, many began constructing their own homes and businesses and all but lost the divine vision for their presence in Zion. By the time King Darius took the throne of Persia, the temple had lain untouched for 16 years. God sent Haggai, and later Zechariah, to call the people back to their priorities. He called them back to their vision ("this is why we are here") and back to their faith and values ("we exist to glorify the Lord and make Him famous").

Haggai was more than just a building supervisor; his leadership addressed priorities in general. He began his message by talking about finishing the building, but then focused on the presence of God. He teaches us how our calendars and behavior reflect what is really important to us. He longed to see not only Israel, but all nations, turn to God and live out proper priorities.

God's Role in Haggai

Haggai served as a mouthpiece for God, like the other prophets in the Old Testament. God was the One who called the people to recover their misplaced priorities. He found a man named Haggai who shared this passion and who would eagerly voice it. God had to deal with a people who had become spiritually lethargic, discouraged about paying a price to rebuild the temple, and disinterested in their own walk with God. God inspired Haggai to write this book as a wake-up call to draw the people back to the original purpose for their homecoming. Through this book God continues to remind leaders everywhere that we should never feel satisfied until we incarnate His priorities.

Leaders in Haggai

Haggai, Joshua, Darius, Cyrus, Zerubbabel

Other People of Influence in Haggai

Shealtiel, the priests

Lessons in Leadership

- If you forget the ultimate, you will become a slave to the immediate.

- Activity does not always mean accomplishment.

- The issue is not, "Will my calendar be full?" but, "What will fill my calendar?"

- If I don't evaluate, I will stagnate.

- Priorities are a matter of both perception and practice; I must know and do them.

LEADERSHIP

HIGHLIGHTS IN HAGGAI

PRIORITIES: If I Forget the Ultimate, I'll Be Enslaved to the Immediate (1:3–9)	*page 1120*
LEADERSHIP PERSPECTIVE: Keeping Your Eye on the Big Picture (2:6–9)	*page 1121*

The Command to Build God's House

1 In the second year of King Darius, in the sixth month, on the first day of the month, the word of the LORD came by Haggai the prophet to Zerubbabel the son of Shealtiel, governor of Judah, and to Joshua the son of Jehozadak, the high priest, saying, ²"Thus speaks the LORD of hosts, saying: 'This people says, "The time has not come, the time that the LORD's house should be built."'"

³Then the word of the LORD came by Haggai the prophet, saying, ⁴"'Is it time for you yourselves to dwell in your paneled houses, and this temple^a to lie in ruins?" ⁵Now therefore, thus says the LORD of hosts: "Consider your ways!

6 "You have sown much, and bring in little;
　You eat, but do not have enough;
　You drink, but you are not filled with
　　drink;
　You clothe yourselves, but no one is
　　warm;
　And he who earns wages,
　Earns wages *to put* into a bag with holes."

⁷Thus says the LORD of hosts: "Consider your ways! ⁸Go up to the mountains and bring wood and build the temple, that I may take pleasure in it and be glorified," says the LORD. ⁹"*You* looked for much, but indeed *it came to* little; and when you brought it home, I blew it away. Why?" says the LORD of hosts. "Because of My house that *is in* ruins, while every one of you runs to his own house. ¹⁰Therefore the heavens above you withhold the dew, and the earth withholds its fruit. ¹¹For I called for a drought on the land and the mountains, on the grain and the new wine and the oil, on whatever the ground brings forth, on men and livestock, and on all the labor of *your* hands."

The People's Obedience

¹²Then Zerubbabel the son of Shealtiel, and Joshua the son of Jehozadak, the high priest, with all the remnant of the people, obeyed the voice of the LORD their God, and the words of Haggai the prophet, as the LORD their God had sent him; and the people feared the presence of the LORD. ¹³Then Haggai, the LORD's messenger, spoke the LORD's message to the people, saying, "I *am* with you, says the LORD." ¹⁴So the LORD stirred up the spirit of Zerubbabel the son of Shealtiel, governor of Judah, and the spirit of Joshua the son of Jehozadak, the high priest, and the spirit of all the remnant of the people; and

---

Priorities: If I Forget the Ultimate, I'll Be Enslaved to the Immediate
(Haggai 1:3–9)

Leadership means you lose your right to be selfish. The builders in Haggai's day had left their original purpose to construct the temple and instead went to work on their own houses and businesses. It took a leader like Haggai to call them back to their purpose. Chapter one outlines what happened when they abandoned their highest priority:

1. They failed to consider how their actions contradicted their faith (vv. 3–5).
2. They worked hard but saw few results (v. 6).
3. They spent much but received little in return (v. 6).
4. They felt dissatisfied in their production (vv. 7–9).

When leaders and people fail to maintain proper priorities, disappointment always results. Remember the 80/20 Principle: With the right priorities, 20% of your effort will get you 80% of the desired results. But with the wrong priorities, 80% of your effort will get you 20% of the desired results. It is not about working harder, but smarter.

---

they came and worked on the house of the LORD of hosts, their God, ¹⁵on the twenty-fourth day of the sixth month, in the second year of King Darius.

The Coming Glory of God's House

2 In the seventh *month,* on the twenty-first of the month, the word of the LORD came by Haggai the prophet, saying: ²"Speak now to Zerubbabel the son of Shealtiel, governor of Judah, and to Joshua the son of Jehozadak, the high priest, and to the remnant of the people, saying: ³"Who is left among you who saw this temple^a in its former glory? And how do you see

---

1:4 ^aLiterally *house,* and so in verse 8 **2:3** ^aLiterally *house,* and so in verses 7 and 9

it now? In comparison with it, *is this* not in your eyes as nothing? ⁴'Yet now be strong, Zerubbabel,' says the LORD; 'and be strong, Joshua, son of Jehozadak, the high priest; and be strong, all you people of the land,' says the LORD, 'and work; for I *am* with you,' says the LORD of hosts. ⁵*According to* the word that I covenanted with you when you came out of Egypt, so My Spirit remains among you; do not fear!'

⁶"For thus says the LORD of hosts: 'Once more (it *is* a little while) I will shake heaven and earth, the sea and dry land; ⁷and I will shake all nations, and they shall come to the Desire of All Nations,ᵃ and I will fill this temple with glory,' says the LORD of hosts. ⁸'The silver *is* Mine, and the gold *is* Mine,' says the LORD of hosts. ⁹'The glory of this latter temple shall be greater than the former,' says the LORD of hosts. 'And in this place I will give peace,' says the LORD of hosts.'

The People Are Defiled

¹⁰On the twenty-fourth *day* of the ninth *month,* in the second year of Darius, the word of the LORD came by Haggai the prophet, saying, ¹¹"Thus says the LORD of hosts: 'Now, ask the priests *concerning the* law, saying, ¹²"If one carries holy meat in the fold of his garment, and with the edge he touches bread or stew, wine or oil, or any food, will it become holy?"'"

Then the priests answered and said, "No."

¹³And Haggai said, "If *one who is* unclean be-cause of a dead body touches any of these, will it be unclean?"

So the priests answered and said, "It shall be unclean."

¹⁴Then Haggai answered and said, "'So is this people, and so is this nation before Me,' says the LORD, 'and so is every work of their hands; and what they offer there is unclean.

Promised Blessing

¹⁵"And now, carefully consider from this day forward: from before stone was laid upon stone in the temple of the LORD— ¹⁶since those *days,* when *one* came to a heap of twenty ephahs, there were *but* ten; when *one* came to the wine vat to draw out fifty baths from the press, there were *but* twenty. ¹⁷I struck you with blight and mildew and hail in all the labors of your hands; yet you did not *turn* to Me,' says the LORD. ¹⁸Consider now from this day forward, from the twenty-fourth day of the ninth month, from the day that the foundation of the LORD's temple was laid— consider it: ¹⁹Is the seed still in the barn? As yet the vine, the fig tree, the pomegranate, and the olive tree have not yielded *fruit.* But from this day I will bless *you.*'"

Zerubbabel Chosen as a Signet

²⁰And again the word of the LORD came to Haggai on the twenty-fourth day of the month,

---

2:7 ᵃOr *the desire of all nations*

Leadership Perspective:
Keeping Your Eye on the Big Picture

(Haggai 2:6–9)

Leaders must understand their priorities before they can implement them. Once they perceive what is most important, their work is half finished. It's all about perspective.

Haggai had big-picture perspective. He didn't focus on personal interests—on immediate gratification, on easy results, or on pleasing people. Instead, he put first things first.

In the second chapter of his book, the prophet addresses the complaints of the nation simply and in a straightforward manner. Haggai spoke for God and gave his countrymen the divine perspective on the challenge before them:

The People's Complaint (Haggai 1)

1. The job is too big.
2. The resources are too small.
3. What we build will not be as great as the past.

God's Response (Haggai 2)

1. The job is Mine; let's work together.
2. I am your Source; I own all the resources.
3. What you build, I will fill with My glory. That's good enough!

saying, [21]"Speak to Zerubbabel, governor of Judah, saying:

'I will shake heaven and earth.
[22] I will overthrow the throne of kingdoms;
I will destroy the strength of the Gentile kingdoms.
I will overthrow the chariots
And those who ride in them;

The horses and their riders shall come down,
Every one by the sword of his brother.

[23]"In that day,' says the LORD of hosts, 'I will take you, Zerubbabel My servant, the son of Shealtiel,' says the LORD, 'and will make you like a signet *ring;* for I have chosen you,' says the LORD of hosts.'"

ZECHARIAH
Leadership Equals Vision and Purpose

SUMMARY

Two leadership words come to mind in reading the book of Zechariah: *vision* and *purpose*. This prophet, whose name means "the LORD remembers," reminds the people of Israel that God does indeed remember His covenant with them and will fulfill His part of it—if the people will only perform their part.

Like Haggai, his older contemporary, Zechariah calls the people to finish the work of rebuilding the temple. He saw their lethargy as Haggai did, but instead of an angry chastisement, he encourages them by painting a mental picture of how it will impact their future. For about a dozen years the temple had lain half finished. God commissioned Zechariah to encourage its completion through use of a metaphor. The rising of the temple pictured their lives. One day the Messiah would dwell in this temple and eventually in them. So, both the temple and their lives must be given top priority. As they worked on both, they built their future.

Vision is a key word in this book. Zechariah sees eight visions between chapters one and six. But while he was a man of many visions, he kept to only one priority. All these visions call the people to repent and turn to God. Like any great leader, Zechariah knows he must cast a compelling vision for the people to act on. These pictures rock the people and serve to ignite them to finish what they had started.

Purpose is yet another key word in Zechariah. The prophet feels the need to remind the people of the higher purpose to which they had been called. Again, like all great leaders, he reminds them of the big picture. They aren't merely constructing a building; they are building their legacy. Zechariah delivers four messages in response to questions about fasting. First, he rebukes the people for performing empty rituals. Next, he reminds them of past disobedience. Third, he speaks of the restoration of Israel. Finally, he points to the recovery of joy within the reign of God. In the last six chapters, he sheds light on the first and second comings of Christ—definitely a big-picture, long-term purpose. Although Zechariah lived during tough times, he kept alive an undying vision of a greater vision and purpose.

God's Role in Zechariah

God has a two-fold role in this book. First, He uses Zechariah to speak for Him about needed change. The prophet calls the people to repent and obey. He challenges and encourages them to fulfill the covenant they had entered into and expected God to fulfill. Second, God uses Zechariah to forecast the coming Messiah as the Righteous Branch, the King-Priest, the humble King, the Cornerstone, the Good Shepherd, and the pierced One. By book's end, God promises to return to His people and dwell in the midst of Zion.

Leaders in Zechariah

Zechariah, Zerubbabel, Joshua, Darius

Other People of Influence in Zechariah

Heldai, Tobijah, Jedaiah

Lessons in Leadership

- A vision should include a principle for the "head" and a picture for the "heart."

- Encouragement is vital; you catch more bees with honey than with vinegar.

- Where there is no hope in the future, there is no power in the present.

- If you stop learning today, you stop leading tomorrow.

- A big vision without core values is like a winding road without guard rails.

- When communicating vision, always give the people something to act upon.

LEADERSHIP

HIGHLIGHTS IN ZECHARIAH

TEACHABILITY: If We Don't Learn from History, We Will
Repeat It (1:4–6) — *page 1125*

VISION: People Are Energized by a Picture of a Better
Tomorrow (3:1–10) — *page 1127*

THE POWER OF A PICTURE: We Do on the Outside What
We Picture Inside (5:1–11) — *page 1129*

COMMUNICATION: Without It, the Leader Travels Alone (8:1–8) — *page 1131*

A Call to Repentance

1 In the eighth month of the second year of Darius, the word of the LORD came to Zechariah the son of Berechiah, the son of Iddo the prophet, saying, ²"The LORD has been very angry with your fathers. ³Therefore say to them, 'Thus says the LORD of hosts: "Return to Me," says the LORD of hosts, "and I will return to you," says the LORD of hosts. ⁴"Do not be like your fathers, to whom the former prophets preached, saying, 'Thus says the LORD of hosts: "Turn now from your evil ways and your evil deeds."' But they did not hear nor heed Me," says the LORD.

Teachability: If We Don't Learn from History, We Will Repeat It

(Zechariah 1:4–6)

Good leaders are continual learners. We must keep learning or we will stop leading. We cannot afford to stagnate, for our world and our people are changing too quickly. New insights and new opportunities appear all the time.

Zechariah needed to learn from the past. His Hebrew forefathers had failed to follow Yahweh. God warned Zechariah to take heed and not follow in their footsteps. God told him to learn from . . .

1. **The past**—Israel's previous years were to warn future generations.
2. **The prophets**—These men of God spoke God's word and cautioned Israel to listen.
3. **The people**—The people repeatedly failed to repent, and felt miserable.
4. **The problems**—Trials served to punish the people for disobedience.
5. **The present**—Zechariah found himself in a similar predicament.
6. **The principles of God**—God's truth cried out to Zechariah's generation.

---

5   "Your fathers, where *are* they?
      And the prophets, do they live forever?
6   Yet surely My words and My statutes,
      Which I commanded My servants the prophets,
      Did they not overtake your fathers?

"So they returned and said:

'Just as the LORD of hosts determined to
    do to us,
According to our ways and according to
    our deeds,
So He has dealt with us."'"

Vision of the Horses

⁷On the twenty-fourth day of the eleventh month, which is the month Shebat, in the second year of Darius, the word of the LORD came to Zechariah the son of Berechiah, the son of Iddo the prophet: ⁸I saw by night, and behold, a man riding on a red horse, and it stood among the myrtle trees in the hollow; and behind him *were* horses: red, sorrel, and white. ⁹Then I said, "My lord, what *are* these?" So the angel who talked with me said to me, "I will show you what they *are*."

¹⁰And the man who stood among the myrtle trees answered and said, "These *are the ones* whom the LORD has sent to walk to and fro throughout the earth."

¹¹So they answered the Angel of the LORD, who stood among the myrtle trees, and said, "We have walked to and fro throughout the earth, and behold, all the earth is resting quietly."

The LORD Will Comfort Zion

¹²Then the Angel of the LORD answered and said, "O LORD of hosts, how long will You not have mercy on Jerusalem and on the cities of Judah, against which You were angry these seventy years?"

¹³And the LORD answered the angel who talked to me, *with* good *and* comforting words. ¹⁴So the angel who spoke with me said to me, "Proclaim, saying, 'Thus says the LORD of hosts:

"I am zealous for Jerusalem
    And for Zion with great zeal.
15   I am exceedingly angry with the nations at
        ease;
      For I was a little angry,
      And they helped—*but* with evil *intent*."

16'Therefore thus says the LORD:

"I am returning to Jerusalem with mercy;
    My house shall be built in it," says the
        LORD of hosts,
"And a *surveyor's* line shall be stretched out
    over Jerusalem."'

¹⁷"Again proclaim, saying, 'Thus says the LORD of hosts:

"My cities shall again spread out through
   prosperity;
The LORD will again comfort Zion,
And will again choose Jerusalem.'''"

Vision of the Horns

[18]Then I raised my eyes and looked, and there
were four horns. [19]And I said to the angel who
talked with me, "What *are* these?"

So he answered me, "These *are* the horns that
have scattered Judah, Israel, and Jerusalem."

[20]Then the LORD showed me four craftsmen.
[21]And I said, "What are these coming to do?"

So he said, "These *are* the horns that scattered
Judah, so that no one could lift up his head; but
the craftsmen[a] are coming to terrify them, to cast
out the horns of the nations that lifted up *their*
horn against the land of Judah to scatter it."

Vision of the Measuring Line

2 Then I raised my eyes and looked, and
   behold, a man with a measuring line in his
   hand. [2]So I said, "Where are you going?"

And he said to me, "To measure Jerusalem, to
see what *is* its width and what *is* its length."

[3]And there *was* the angel who talked with
me, going out; and another angel was coming
out to meet him, [4]who said to him, "Run, speak
to this young man, saying: 'Jerusalem shall be inhabited *as* towns without walls, because of the
multitude of men and livestock in it. [5]For I,' says
the LORD, 'will be a wall of fire all around her,
and I will be the glory in her midst.'"

Future Joy of Zion and Many Nations

[6]"Up, up! Flee from the land of the north,"
says the LORD; "for I have spread you abroad like
the four winds of heaven," says the LORD. [7]"Up,
Zion! Escape, you who dwell with the daughter
of Babylon."

[8]For thus says the LORD of hosts: "He sent
Me after glory, to the nations which plunder
you; for he who touches you touches the apple
of His eye. [9]For surely I will shake My hand
against them, and they shall become spoil for
their servants. Then you will know that the
LORD of hosts has sent Me.

[10]"Sing and rejoice, O daughter of Zion! For
behold, I am coming and I will dwell in your
midst," says the LORD. [11]"Many nations shall be
joined to the LORD in that day, and they shall become My people. And I will dwell in your midst.
Then you will know that the LORD of hosts has
sent Me to you. [12]And the LORD will take possession of Judah as His inheritance in the Holy

Land, and will again choose Jerusalem. [13]Be
silent, all flesh, before the LORD, for He is
aroused from His holy habitation!"

The Law of Connection: Encouragement Is the Oxygen of the Soul
(Zechariah 2:3–13)

Through a vision, Zechariah tries to encourage the people concerning their future. God plans to gather them again and
expand their population. God promises to
bless His people in the following areas:

1. More people (v. 4)
2. More livestock (v. 4)
3. Divine protection (v. 5)
4. Deliverance from enemies (v. 9)
5. Conversions of other ethnic groups (v. 11)
6. The return of the favor of God on His
   people (v. 12)

Leaders know that encouragement is the
oxygen of the soul. Notice that Zechariah's
encouragement was: 1. specific; 2. personal;
3. public; 4. detailed; 5. hopeful; 6. sincere; and
7. centered around results only God could pull
off. Leaders who encourage always draw more
from their people than those who don't.

Vision of the High Priest

3 Then he showed me Joshua the high priest
   standing before the Angel of the LORD,
   and Satan standing at his right hand to oppose him. [2]And the LORD said to Satan, "The
LORD rebuke you, Satan! The LORD who has
chosen Jerusalem rebuke you! *Is* this not a brand
plucked from the fire?"

[3]Now Joshua was clothed with filthy garments, and was standing before the Angel.

[4]Then He answered and spoke to those who
stood before Him, saying, "Take away the filthy
garments from him." And to him He said, "See,
I have removed your iniquity from you, and I
will clothe you with rich robes."

[5]And I said, "Let them put a clean turban on
his head."

So they put a clean turban on his head, and

1:21 [a]Literally *these*

they put the clothes on him. And the Angel of the LORD stood by.

Vision: People Are Energized by a Picture of a Better Tomorrow

(Zechariah 3:1–10)

Vision is an essential part of healthy leadership. Good leaders feel moved by God-given dreams and visions regarding the future. Zechariah illustrates the power of vision by describing eight visions in the first six chapters of his book:

1. The vision of the horses (1:7–17)
2. The vision of the horns and craftsmen (1:18–21)
3. The vision of the measure (2:1–13)
4. The vision of Joshua (3:1–10)
5. The vision of the lampstand and olive trees (4:1–14)
6. The vision of the flying scroll (5:1–4)
7. The vision of the basket (5:5–11)
8. The vision of the chariots and horses (6:1–8)

When was the last time you were moved by a God-given vision? Is your leadership driven by the power of a vision? How have you communicated your vision to others?

The Coming Branch

⁶Then the Angel of the LORD admonished Joshua, saying, ⁷"Thus says the LORD of hosts:

'If you will walk in My ways,
   And if you will keep My command,
Then you shall also judge My house,
   And likewise have charge of My courts;
I will give you places to walk
   Among these who stand here.

⁸ 'Hear, O Joshua, the high priest,
   You and your companions who sit before you,
For they are a wondrous sign;
   For behold, I am bringing forth My Servant the BRANCH.
⁹ For behold, the stone
   That I have laid before Joshua:

Upon the stone *are* seven eyes.
   Behold, I will engrave its inscription,'
   Says the LORD of hosts,
'And I will remove the iniquity of that land
   in one day.
¹⁰ In that day,' says the LORD of hosts,
'Everyone will invite his neighbor
   Under his vine and under his fig tree.'"

Vision of the Lampstand and Olive Trees

4 Now the angel who talked with me came back and wakened me, as a man who is wakened out of his sleep. ²And he said to me, "What do you see?"

So I said, "I am looking, and there *is* a lampstand of solid gold with a bowl on top of it, and on the *stand* seven lamps with seven pipes to the seven lamps. ³Two olive trees *are* by it, one at the right of the bowl and the other at its left." ⁴So I answered and spoke to the angel who talked with me, saying, "What *are* these, my lord?"

⁵Then the angel who talked with me answered and said to me, "Do you not know what these are?"

And I said, "No, my lord."

⁶So he answered and said to me:

"This *is* the word of the LORD to
      Zerubbabel:
'Not by might nor by power, but by My
      Spirit,'
   Says the LORD of hosts.
⁷ 'Who *are* you, O great mountain?
   Before Zerubbabel *you shall become* a plain!
And he shall bring forth the capstone
   With shouts of "Grace, grace to it!"'"

⁸Moreover the word of the LORD came to me, saying:

⁹ "The hands of Zerubbabel
      Have laid the foundation of this temple;ᵃ
   His hands shall also finish *it*.
   Then you will know
      That the LORD of hosts has sent Me to you.
¹⁰ For who has despised the day of small
      things?
   For these seven rejoice to see
The plumb line in the hand of
      Zerubbabel.
   They are the eyes of the LORD,
Which scan to and fro throughout the
      whole earth."

4:9 ᵃLiterally *house*

The God Factor: Leaders Must Lean on Someone Bigger

(Zechariah 4:6–9)

God reminds the people through Zechariah that they would succeed, not because of their own might and power, but because of His Spirit. *He* would be the Source of their victory.

Secure leaders do not feel put off by this truth; they aren't interested in monopolizing the credit. They welcome God's intervention and direct their followers to seek it. Every great leader yearns for God's partnership. We are wise when, from the beginning, we welcome God's direction and strength as we enter a new project. Consider what Zechariah wants to teach us:

1. Great works are done by God's divine hands (v. 6).
2. The foundation of these works are human; the Lord works through people (v. 9).
3. Great works are done by God's Spirit, through us, to glorify Him (v. 9).

¹¹Then I answered and said to him, "What *are* these two olive trees—at the right of the lampstand and at its left?" ¹²And I further answered and said to him, "What *are these* two olive branches that *drip* into the receptaclesᵃ of the two gold pipes from which the golden *oil drains?*"

¹³Then he answered me and said, "Do you not know what these *are?*"

And I said, "No, my lord."

¹⁴So he said, "These *are* the two anointed ones, who stand beside the Lord of the whole earth."

Vision of the Flying Scroll

5 Then I turned and raised my eyes, and saw there a flying scroll.

²And he said to me, "What do you see?"

So I answered, "I see a flying scroll. Its length *is* twenty cubits and its width ten cubits."

³Then he said to me, "This *is* the curse that goes out over the face of the whole earth: 'Every thief shall be expelled,' according *to* this side of *the scroll;* and, 'Every perjurer shall be expelled,' according *to* that side of it."

⁴ "I will send out *the curse,*" says the Lord of hosts;

"It shall enter the house of the thief
And the house of the one who swears
falsely by My name.
It shall remain in the midst of his house
And consume it, with its timber and
stones."

Vision of the Woman in a Basket

⁵Then the angel who talked with me came out and said to me, "Lift your eyes now, and see what this *is* that goes forth."

⁶So I asked, "What *is* it?" And he said, "It *is* a basketᵃ that is going forth."

He also said, "This *is* their resemblance throughout the earth: ⁷Here *is* a lead disc lifted up, and this *is* a woman sitting inside the basket"; ⁸then he said, "This *is* Wickedness!" And he thrust her down into the basket, and threw the lead coverᵃ over its mouth. ⁹Then I raised my eyes and looked, and there *were* two women, coming with the wind in their wings; for they had wings like the wings of a stork, and they lifted up the basket between earth and heaven.

¹⁰So I said to the angel who talked with me, "Where are they carrying the basket?"

¹¹And he said to me, "To build a house for it in the land of Shinar;ᵃ when it is ready, *the basket* will be set there on its base."

Vision of the Four Chariots

6 Then I turned and raised my eyes and looked, and behold, four chariots *were* coming from between two mountains, and the mountains *were* mountains of bronze. ²With the first chariot *were* red horses, with the second chariot black horses, ³with the third chariot white horses, and with the fourth chariot dappled horses—strong *steeds.* ⁴Then I answered and said to the angel who talked with me, "What *are* these, my lord?"

⁵And the angel answered and said to me, "These *are* four spirits of heaven, who go out from *their* station before the Lord of all the earth. ⁶The one with the black horses is going to the north country, the white are going after them, and the dappled are going toward the south country." ⁷Then the strong *steeds* went out, eager to go, that they might walk to and fro throughout the earth. And He said, "Go, walk to and fro throughout the earth." So they walked to and fro

---

4:12 ᵃLiterally *into the hands of* 5:6 ᵃHebrew *ephah,* a measuring container, and so elsewhere 5:8 ᵃLiterally *stone* 5:11 ᵃThat is, Babylon throughout the earth. [8]And He called to me, and spoke to me, saying, "See, those who go toward the north country have given rest to My Spirit in the north country."

The Command to Crown Joshua

[9]Then the word of the LORD came to me, saying: [10]"Receive *the gift* from the captives—from Heldai, Tobijah, and Jedaiah, who have come from Babylon—and go the same day and enter the house of Josiah the son of Zephaniah. [11]Take the silver and gold, make an elaborate crown, and set *it* on the head of Joshua the son of Jehozadak, the high priest. [12]Then speak to him, saying, 'Thus says the LORD of hosts, saying:

> "Behold, the Man whose name *is* the BRANCH!
> From His place He shall branch out,
> And He shall build the temple of the LORD;
> [13]   Yes, He shall build the temple of the LORD.
> He shall bear the glory,
> And shall sit and rule on His throne;
> So He shall be a priest on His throne,
> And the counsel of peace shall be between them both."'

[14]"Now the elaborate crown shall be for a memorial in the temple of the LORD for Helem,[a] Tobijah, Jedaiah, and Hen the son of Zephaniah. [15]Even those from afar shall come and build the temple of the LORD. Then you shall know that the LORD of hosts has sent Me to you. And *this* shall come to pass if you diligently obey the voice of the LORD your God."

Obedience Better than Fasting

7 Now in the fourth year of King Darius it came to pass *that* the word of the LORD came to Zechariah, on the fourth day of the ninth month, Chislev, [2]when *the people*[a] sent Sherezer,[b] with Regem-Melech and his men, *to* the house of God,[c] to pray before the LORD, [3]*and* to ask the priests who *were* in the house of the LORD of hosts, and the prophets, saying, "Should I weep in the fifth month and fast as I have done for so many years?"

[4]Then the word of the LORD of hosts came to me, saying, [5]"Say to all the people of the land,

---

6:14 [a]Following Masoretic Text, Targum, and Vulgate; Syriac reads *for Heldai* (compare verse 10); Septuagint reads *for the patient ones.* **7:2** [a]Literally *they* (compare verse 5) [b]Or *Sar-Ezer* [c]Hebrew *Bethel*

The Power of a Picture:
We Do on the Outside What We Picture Inside
(Zechariah 5:1–11)

Zechariah knew how to paint vivid pictures in the minds of his people. He did so because he knew people think in images. In chapter five, he describes a vision of a flying scroll declaring a curse on everyone who steals or swears. Then he tells of another vision concerning a basket. Two women flew, carrying it through the air to Shinar, where a "house" would be built for it.

These kinds of portraits capture our imaginations and make God's thoughts memorable. Because the prophet's chief concern was to prepare the land for the coming Messiah, he relayed several images about Christ. Zechariah foretold of Christ more than any other Old Testament prophet. Consider how he did it:

Christ Is Seen As:

1. Servant and Branch (3:8)
2. Priest (6:13)
3. Just and Lowly King (9:9)
4. Shepherd (9:16; 13:7)
5. Firstborn Son (12:10)
6. Fountain (13:1)

How do you communicate vision? Do people remember your words? Do you paint pictures inside of them?

and to the priests: 'When you fasted and mourned in the fifth and seventh *months* during those seventy years, did you really fast for Me—for Me? ⁶When you eat and when you drink, do you not eat and drink *for yourselves?* ⁷*Should you not have obeyed* the words which the LORD proclaimed through the former prophets when Jerusalem and the cities around it were inhabited and prosperous, and the South[a] and the Lowland were inhabited?'"

Discernment: Zechariah Knew the Issue Was Justice, Not Fasting

(Zechariah 7:1–10)

God questions the motives behind our behavior. While the Jews had fasted and feasted at appropriate times, Zechariah declared their spiritual rituals meant little unless accompanied by justice. When leaders discern people and relationships, they get a head start in providing relevant help to those who need it.

Disobedience Resulted in Captivity

⁸Then the word of the LORD came to Zechariah, saying, ⁹"Thus says the LORD of hosts:

'Execute true justice,
　Show mercy and compassion
　Everyone to his brother.
¹⁰ Do not oppress the widow or the
　　fatherless,
　The alien or the poor.
　Let none of you plan evil in his heart
　Against his brother.'

¹¹"But they refused to heed, shrugged their shoulders, and stopped their ears so that they could not hear. ¹²Yes, they made their hearts like flint, refusing to hear the law and the words which the LORD of hosts had sent by His Spirit through the former prophets. Thus great wrath came from the LORD of hosts. ¹³Therefore it happened, *that* just as He proclaimed and they would not hear, so they called out and I would not listen," says the LORD of hosts. ¹⁴"But I scattered them with a whirlwind among all the nations which they had not known. Thus the land became desolate after them, so that no one passed

through or returned; for they made the pleasant land desolate."

Jerusalem, Holy City of the Future

8 Again the word of the LORD of hosts came, saying, ²"Thus says the LORD of hosts:

'I am zealous for Zion with great zeal;
　With great fervor I am zealous for her.'

³"Thus says the LORD:

'I will return to Zion,
　And dwell in the midst of Jerusalem.
　Jerusalem shall be called the City of Truth,
　The Mountain of the LORD of hosts,
　The Holy Mountain.'

⁴"Thus says the LORD of hosts:

'Old men and old women shall again sit
　In the streets of Jerusalem,
　Each one with his staff in his hand
　Because of great age.
⁵ The streets of the city
　Shall be full of boys and girls
　Playing in its streets.'

⁶"Thus says the LORD of hosts:

'If it is marvelous in the eyes of the
　　remnant of this people in these days,
　Will it also be marvelous in My eyes?'
　Says the LORD of hosts.

⁷"Thus says the LORD of hosts:

'Behold, I will save My people from the
　　land of the east
　And from the land of the west;
⁸ I will bring them *back,*
　And they shall dwell in the midst of
　　Jerusalem.
　They shall be My people
　And I will be their God,
　In truth and righteousness.'

⁹"Thus says the LORD of hosts:

'Let your hands be strong,
　You who have been hearing in these days
　These words by the mouth of the
　　prophets,

7:7 [a]Hebrew *Negev*

Communication: Without It, the Leader Travels Alone

(Zechariah 8:1–8)

Israel struggled morally and needed immediate discipline during the dark days of Zechariah's ministry. Yet before the end of his prophecy, Zechariah offers the hope of a better tomorrow, even if in the distant future. He gives the people a specific hope, just as in Zechariah 3:4, 5, where he promises Joshua would be cleansed, clothed, and crowned.

Successful leaders know how to empower their people through effective communication. They also know what to communicate that will encourage their people. Note the clear distinctions:

Poor Communicators Offer:

1. *Hoops*
   People grow discouraged by all they must do to "make progress."

2. *Hype*
   People may get excited, but they have nothing tangible to grasp and apply when it's over.

Good Communicators Offer:

1. *Hope*
   People are encouraged by a picture of a better and brighter tomorrow.

2. *Help*
   People receive practical help as the leader offers steps to take.

Who *spoke* in the day the foundation was laid
For the house of the LORD of hosts,
That the temple might be built.

10 For before these days
There were no wages for man nor any hire for beast;
There was no peace from the enemy for whoever went out or came in;
For I set all men, everyone, against his neighbor.

11 But now I *will* not *treat* the remnant of this people as in the former days,' says the LORD of hosts.

12 'For the seed *shall be* prosperous,
The vine shall give its fruit,
The ground shall give her increase,
And the heavens shall give their dew—
I will cause the remnant of this people
To possess all these.

13 And it shall come to pass
That just as you were a curse among the nations,
O house of Judah and house of Israel,
So I will save you, and you shall be a blessing.
Do not fear,
Let your hands be strong.'

14 "For thus says the LORD of hosts:

'Just as I determined to punish you
When your fathers provoked Me to wrath,'

Says the LORD of hosts,
'And I would not relent,
15 So again in these days
I am determined to do good
To Jerusalem and to the house of Judah.
Do not fear.
16 These *are* the things you shall do:
Speak each man the truth to his neighbor;
Give judgment in your gates for truth, justice, and peace;
17 Let none of you think evil in your[a] heart against your neighbor;
And do not love a false oath.
For all these *are things* that I hate,'
Says the LORD."

18 Then the word of the LORD of hosts came to me, saying, 19 "Thus says the LORD of hosts:

'The fast of the fourth *month,*
The fast of the fifth,
The fast of the seventh,
And the fast of the tenth,
Shall be joy and gladness and cheerful feasts
For the house of Judah.
Therefore love truth and peace.'

20 "Thus says the LORD of hosts:

8:17 [a]Literally *his*

'Peoples shall yet come,
Inhabitants of many cities;

21 The inhabitants of one *city* shall go to
another, saying,
"Let us continue to go and pray before the
LORD,
And seek the LORD of hosts.
I myself will go also."

22 Yes, many peoples and strong nations
Shall come to seek the LORD of hosts in
Jerusalem,
And to pray before the LORD.'

23 "Thus says the LORD of hosts: 'In those days
ten men from every language of the nations shall
grasp the sleeve of a Jewish man, saying, "Let us
go with you, for we have heard *that* God *is* with
you."'"

Israel Defended Against Enemies

9 The burden[a] of the word of the LORD
Against the land of Hadrach,
And Damascus its resting place
(For the eyes of men
And all the tribes of Israel
Are on the LORD);

2 Also *against* Hamath, *which* borders on it,
And *against* Tyre and Sidon, though they
are very wise.

3 For Tyre built herself a tower,
Heaped up silver like the dust,
And gold like the mire of the streets.

4 Behold, the LORD will cast her out;
He will destroy her power in the sea,
And she will be devoured by fire.

5 Ashkelon shall see *it* and fear;
Gaza also shall be very sorrowful;
And Ekron, for He dried up her
expectation.
The king shall perish from Gaza,
And Ashkelon shall not be inhabited.

6 "A mixed race shall settle in Ashdod,
And I will cut off the pride of the
Philistines.

7 I will take away the blood from his mouth,
And the abominations from between his
teeth.
But he who remains, even he *shall be* for
our God,
And shall be like a leader in Judah,
And Ekron like a Jebusite.

8 I will camp around My house
Because of the army,
Because of him who passes by and him
who returns.
No more shall an oppressor pass through
them,
For now I have seen with My eyes.

The Coming King

9 "Rejoice greatly, O daughter of Zion!
Shout, O daughter of Jerusalem!
Behold, your King is coming to you;
He *is* just and having salvation,
Lowly and riding on a donkey,
A colt, the foal of a donkey.

10 I will cut off the chariot from Ephraim
And the horse from Jerusalem;
The battle bow shall be cut off.
He shall speak peace to the nations;
His dominion *shall be* 'from sea to sea,
And from the River to the ends of the
earth.'[a]

God Will Save His People

11 "As for you also,
Because of the blood of your covenant,
I will set your prisoners free from the
waterless pit.

12 Return to the stronghold,
You prisoners of hope.
Even today I declare
That I will restore double to you.

13 For I have bent Judah, My *bow,*
Fitted the bow with Ephraim,
And raised up your sons, O Zion,
Against your sons, O Greece,
And made you like the sword of a mighty
man."

14 Then the LORD will be seen over them,
And His arrow will go forth like lightning.
The Lord GOD will blow the trumpet,
And go with whirlwinds from the south.

15 The LORD of hosts will defend them;
They shall devour and subdue with
slingstones.
They shall drink *and* roar as if with wine;
They shall be filled *with blood* like basins,
Like the corners of the altar.

16 The LORD their God will save them in
that day,
As the flock of His people.
For they *shall be* like the jewels of a
crown,
Lifted like a banner over His land—

9:1 [a]Or *oracle*   **9:10** [a]Psalm 72:8

17 For how great is its[a] goodness
And how great its[b] beauty!
Grain shall make the young men thrive,
And new wine the young women.

Restoration of Judah and Israel

10 Ask the LORD for rain
In the time of the latter rain.[a]
The LORD will make flashing
    clouds;
He will give them showers of rain,
Grass in the field for everyone.

Commitment: It Comes Before Authority and Responsibility

(Zechariah 10:1–3)

Few things present more danger than an uncommitted leader. While followers may often remain uncommitted, they usually wield limited influence. Leaders, however, impact everyone who follows. When *they* remain uncommitted, they not only fail their organizations and God, but they model failure for others.

---

2 For the idols[a] speak delusion;
The diviners envision lies,
And tell false dreams;
They comfort in vain.
Therefore *the people* wend their way like
    sheep;
They are in trouble because *there is* no
    shepherd.

3 "My anger is kindled against the shepherds,
And I will punish the goatherds.
For the LORD of hosts will visit His flock,
The house of Judah,
And will make them as His royal horse in
    the battle.
4 From him comes the cornerstone,
From him the tent peg,
From him the battle bow,
From him every ruler[a] together.
5 They shall be like mighty men,
Who tread down *their enemies*
In the mire of the streets in the battle.
They shall fight because the LORD is with
    them,

And the riders on horses shall be put to
    shame.

6 "I will strengthen the house of Judah,
And I will save the house of Joseph.
I will bring them back,
Because I have mercy on them.
They shall be as though I had not cast
    them aside;
For I *am* the LORD their God,
And I will hear them.
7 *Those of* Ephraim shall be like a mighty
    man,
And their heart shall rejoice as if with wine.
Yes, their children shall see *it* and be glad;
Their heart shall rejoice in the LORD.
8 I will whistle for them and gather them,
For I will redeem them;
And they shall increase as they once
    increased.

9 "I will sow them among the peoples,
And they shall remember Me in far
    countries;
They shall live, together with their
    children,
And they shall return.
10 I will also bring them back from the land
    of Egypt,
And gather them from Assyria.
I will bring them into the land of Gilead
    and Lebanon,
Until no *more room* is found for them.
11 He shall pass through the sea with
    affliction,
And strike the waves of the sea:
All the depths of the River[a] shall dry up.
Then the pride of Assyria shall be brought
    down,
And the scepter of Egypt shall depart.

12 "So I will strengthen them in the LORD,
And they shall walk up and down in His
    name,"
Says the LORD.

Desolation of Israel

11 Open your doors, O Lebanon,
That fire may devour your cedars.
2 Wail, O cypress, for the cedar
    has fallen,
Because the mighty *trees* are ruined.

9:17 [a]Or *His* [b]Or *His* **10:1** [a]That is, spring rain
10:2 [a]Hebrew *teraphim* **10:4** [a]Or *despot*
10:11 [a]That is, the Nile

Wail, O oaks of Bashan,
For the thick forest has come down.
³ *There is* the sound of wailing shepherds!
For their glory is in ruins.
There is the sound of roaring lions!
For the pride[a] of the Jordan is in ruins.

Prophecy of the Shepherds

⁴Thus says the LORD my God, "Feed the flock for slaughter, ⁵whose owners slaughter them and feel no guilt; those who sell them say, 'Blessed be the LORD, for I am rich'; and their shepherds do not pity them. ⁶For I will no longer pity the inhabitants of the land," says the LORD. "But indeed I will give everyone into his neighbor's hand and into the hand of his king. They shall attack the land, and I will not deliver *them* from their hand."

⁷So I fed the flock for slaughter, in particular the poor of the flock.[a] I took for myself two staffs: the one I called Beauty,[b] and the other I called Bonds;[c] and I fed the flock. ⁸I dismissed the three shepherds in one month. My soul loathed them, and their soul also abhorred me. ⁹Then I said, "I will not feed you. Let what is dying die, and what is perishing perish. Let those that are left eat each other's flesh." ¹⁰And I took my staff, Beauty, and cut it in two, that I might break the covenant which I had made with all the peoples. ¹¹So it was broken on that day. Thus the poor[a] of the flock, who were watching me, knew that it *was* the word of the LORD. ¹²Then I said to them, "If it is agreeable to you, give *me* my wages; and if not, refrain." So they weighed out for my wages thirty *pieces* of silver.

¹³And the LORD said to me, "Throw it to the potter"—that princely price they set on me. So I took the thirty *pieces* of silver and threw them into the house of the LORD for the potter. ¹⁴Then I cut in two my other staff, Bonds, that I might break the brotherhood between Judah and Israel.

¹⁵And the LORD said to me, "Next, take for yourself the implements of a foolish shepherd. ¹⁶For indeed I will raise up a shepherd in the land *who* will not care for those who are cut off, nor seek the young, nor heal those that are broken, nor feed those that still stand. But he will eat the flesh of the fat and tear their hooves in pieces.

¹⁷ "Woe to the worthless shepherd,
Who leaves the flock!
A sword *shall be* against his arm
And against his right eye;
His arm shall completely wither,
And his right eye shall be totally blinded."

The Coming Deliverance of Judah

12 The burden[a] of the word of the LORD against Israel. Thus says the LORD, who stretches out the heavens, lays the foundation of the earth, and forms the spirit of man within him: ²"Behold, I will make Jerusalem a cup of drunkenness to all the surrounding peoples, when they lay siege against Judah and Jerusalem. ³And it shall happen in that day that I will make Jerusalem a very heavy stone for all peoples; all who would heave it away will surely be cut in pieces, though all nations of the earth are gathered against it. ⁴In that day," says the LORD, "I will strike every horse with confusion, and its rider with madness; I will open My eyes on the house of Judah, and will strike every horse of the peoples with blindness. ⁵And the governors of Judah shall say in their heart, 'The inhabitants of Jerusalem *are* my strength in the LORD of hosts, their God.' ⁶In that day I will make the governors of Judah like a firepan in the woodpile, and like a fiery torch in the sheaves; they shall devour all the surrounding peoples on the right hand and on the left, but Jerusalem shall be inhabited again in her own place—Jerusalem.

⁷"The LORD will save the tents of Judah first, so that the glory of the house of David and the glory of the inhabitants of Jerusalem shall not become greater than that of Judah. ⁸In that day the LORD will defend the inhabitants of Jerusalem; the one who is feeble among them in that day shall be like David, and the house of David *shall be* like God, like the Angel of the LORD before them. ⁹It shall be in that day *that* I will seek to destroy all the nations that come against Jerusalem.

Mourning for the Pierced One

¹⁰"And I will pour on the house of David and on the inhabitants of Jerusalem the Spirit of grace and supplication; then they will look on Me whom they pierced. Yes, they will mourn for Him as one mourns for *his* only *son,* and grieve for Him as one grieves for a firstborn. ¹¹In that day there shall be a great mourning in Jerusalem, like the mourning at Hadad Rimmon in the plain of Megiddo.[a] ¹²And the land shall mourn, every family by itself: the family of the house of

---

11:3 [a]Or *floodplain, thicket* **11:7** [a]Following Masoretic Text, Targum, and Vulgate; Septuagint reads *for the Canaanites.* [b]Or *Grace,* and so in verse 10 [c]Or *Unity,* and so in verse 14 **11:11** [a]Following Masoretic Text, Targum, and Vulgate; Septuagint reads *the Canaanites.* **12:1** [a]Or *oracle* **12:11** [a]Hebrew *Megiddon*

David by itself, and their wives by themselves; the family of the house of Nathan by itself, and their wives by themselves; [13]the family of the house of Levi by itself, and their wives by themselves; the family of Shimei by itself, and their wives by themselves; [14]all the families that remain, every family by itself, and their wives by themselves.

Idolatry Cut Off

13 "In that day a fountain shall be opened for the house of David and for the inhabitants of Jerusalem, for sin and for uncleanness.

[2]"It shall be in that day," says the LORD of hosts, "that I will cut off the names of the idols from the land, and they shall no longer be remembered. I will also cause the prophets and the unclean spirit to depart from the land. [3]It shall come to pass that if anyone still prophesies, then his father and mother who begot him will say to him, 'You shall not live, because you have spoken lies in the name of the LORD.' And his father and mother who begot him shall thrust him through when he prophesies.

[4]"And it shall be in that day that every prophet will be ashamed of his vision when he prophesies; they will not wear a robe of coarse hair to deceive. [5]But he will say, 'I am no prophet, I am a farmer; for a man taught me to keep cattle from my youth.' [6]And one will say to him, 'What are these wounds between your arms?'[a] Then he will answer, 'Those with which I was wounded in the house of my friends.'

The Shepherd Savior

[7]   "Awake, O sword, against My Shepherd,
    Against the Man who is My Companion,"
    Says the LORD of hosts.
    "Strike the Shepherd,
    And the sheep will be scattered;
    Then I will turn My hand against the little
        ones.
[8]   And it shall come to pass in all the land,"
    Says the LORD,
    "That two-thirds in it shall be cut off and
        die,
    But one-third shall be left in it:
[9]   I will bring the one-third through the fire,
    Will refine them as silver is refined,
    And test them as gold is tested.
    They will call on My name,
    And I will answer them.
    I will say, 'This is My people';
    And each one will say, 'The LORD is my
        God.'"

The Day of the LORD

14 Behold, the day of the LORD is
        coming,
    And your spoil will be divided in
        your midst.
[2]   For I will gather all the nations to battle
        against Jerusalem;
    The city shall be taken,
    The houses rifled,
    And the women ravished.
    Half of the city shall go into captivity,
    But the remnant of the people shall not be
        cut off from the city.

[3]   Then the LORD will go forth
    And fight against those nations,
    As He fights in the day of battle.
[4]   And in that day His feet will stand on the
        Mount of Olives,
    Which faces Jerusalem on the east.
    And the Mount of Olives shall be split in
        two,
    From east to west,
    Making a very large valley;
    Half of the mountain shall move toward
        the north
    And half of it toward the south.

[5]   Then you shall flee through My mountain
        valley,
    For the mountain valley shall reach to
        Azal.
    Yes, you shall flee
    As you fled from the earthquake
    In the days of Uzziah king of Judah.

    Thus the LORD my God will come,
    And all the saints with You.[a]

[6]   It shall come to pass in that day
    That there will be no light;
    The lights will diminish.
[7]   It shall be one day
    Which is known to the LORD—
    Neither day nor night.
    But at evening time it shall happen
    That it will be light.

[8]   And in that day it shall be
    That living waters shall flow from
        Jerusalem,
    Half of them toward the eastern sea
    And half of them toward the western sea;

13:6 [a]Or hands **14:5** [a]Or you; Septuagint, Targum, and Vulgate read Him.

In both summer and winter it shall occur.

9 And the LORD shall be King over all the
earth.
In that day it shall be—
"The LORD is one,"[a]
And His name one.

[10] All the land shall be turned into a plain from
Geba to Rimmon south of Jerusalem. Jerusalem[a]
shall be raised up and inhabited in her place from
Benjamin's Gate to the place of the First Gate
and the Corner Gate, and from the Tower of
Hananel to the king's winepresses.

11 The people shall dwell in it;
And no longer shall there be utter
destruction,
But Jerusalem shall be safely inhabited.

[12] And this shall be the plague with which the
LORD will strike all the people who fought
against Jerusalem:

Their flesh shall dissolve while they stand
on their feet,
Their eyes shall dissolve in their sockets,
And their tongues shall dissolve in their
mouths.

13 It shall come to pass in that day
That a great panic from the LORD will be
among them.
Everyone will seize the hand of his
neighbor,
And raise his hand against his neighbor's
hand;

14 Judah also will fight at Jerusalem.
And the wealth of all the surrounding
nations
Shall be gathered together:
Gold, silver, and apparel in great
abundance.

15 Such also shall be the plague
On the horse and the mule,
On the camel and the donkey,
And on all the cattle that will be in those
camps.
So shall this plague be.

The Nations Worship the King

[16] And it shall come to pass that everyone
who is left of all the nations which came against
Jerusalem shall go up from year to year to worship the King, the LORD of hosts, and to keep
the Feast of Tabernacles. [17] And it shall be that
whichever of the families of the earth do not
come up to Jerusalem to worship the King, the
LORD of hosts, on them there will be no rain.
[18] If the family of Egypt will not come up and
enter in, they shall have no rain; they shall receive the plague with which the LORD strikes
the nations who do not come up to keep the
Feast of Tabernacles. [19] This shall be the punishment of Egypt and the punishment of all the
nations that do not come up to keep the Feast
of Tabernacles.

[20] In that day "HOLINESS TO THE
LORD" shall be engraved on the bells of the
horses. The pots in the LORD's house shall be like
the bowls before the altar. [21] Yes, every pot in Jerusalem and Judah shall be holiness to the LORD
of hosts.[a] Everyone who sacrifices shall come
and take them and cook in them. In that day
there shall no longer be a Canaanite in the house
of the LORD of hosts.

14:9 [a] Compare Deuteronomy 6:4 14:10 [a] Literally
She 14:21 [a] Or on every pot . . . shall be (engraved)
"HOLINESS TO THE LORD OF HOSTS"

The Law of Victory:
Leaders Know What It
Takes to Win in the End
(Zechariah 14:16–21)

It is appropriate that the final chapter of
Zechariah declares God's ultimate victory.
No one practices the Law of Victory quite like
the Lord Himself! In this case, God predicts
victory and gives the people direction on how
to live, motivation to persist, and hope for a
better tomorrow.

MALACHI
Calling God's People to Authenticity

SUMMARY

Malachi, the final book of the Old Testament, was written by a prophet who served during Nehemiah's day—a period of corrupt priests, wicked practices, compromising leaders, and a false sense of security in their status with God. Malachi calls God's people to authenticity. More than that, however, he calls God's leaders to lead from relationship rather than mere position.

The name Malachi means "Messenger of Yahweh"—and no further messenger from God came until John the Baptizer arrived centuries later in the New Testament era. Malachi uses an easy-to-follow question and answer format to address specific issues such as divorce, infidelity, mixed marriages, hypocrisy, tithing, false worship, complacency, and arrogance. This divine dialogue contrasts God's perspective with the people's perspective. It illustrates not only the difference between the eternal God and finite man, but serves as a metaphor for the gap between the perspective of a leader and a follower. The spiritual leader maintains the eternal and ultimate viewpoint, while the follower may see only the immediate and the temporal.

The book supplies leaders with a wonderful case study in communication. Without communication, we travel alone. Malachi uses a heartfelt appeal featuring not only passion for repentance, but also compassion and understanding for the people's point of view. Six times Malachi does the "point-counterpoint" debate, where he speaks for the listener and identifies their apathetic attitude. He can hear them arguing, "Oh, come now—it's not that bad!" In response he lays out an explicit, persuasive argument for why it really *is* that bad!

Four hundred years of divine silence follow the Book of Malachi, as God refuses to speak to His people through a prophet. Malachi becomes His last word until the New Covenant arrives, calling for authentic faith and genuine leadership integrity from priests and governors alike.

God's Role in Malachi

God uses the Book of Malachi to communicate that while He understands their vantage point, He does not change His own or grade on a curve. God uses Malachi's series of questions and answers to expose the people's underlying motives, their negative attitudes, and their selfish ways. The book concerns itself with the heart of God's followers. These people had become consumed with outward appearances rather than inward purity and submission. God wants obedience from our hearts, not just our hands. His leadership raises the bar once again on what it means to follow with our whole heart.

Leaders in Malachi

Malachi, Persian governors

Other People of Influence in Malachi

The priests and religious leaders

Lessons in Leadership

- Effective leaders seek to understand before they seek to be understood.

- Great leaders are great communicators.

- Complete obedience involves inward submission, not mere outward service.

- Strong leaders raise the bar and challenge people to reach it.

- Effective leaders know what they stand for and what they won't stand for.

- Healthy leaders compromise on methods but never on principles.

LEADERSHIP

HIGHLIGHTS IN MALACHI

THE LAW OF CONNECTION: Malachi Touches the Heart First (1:2–14)	*page 1139*
LEADERS KNOW That Demonstration Must Precede Imitation (2:7–9)	*page 1141*
THE LAW OF TIMING: God Knows When and How to Move (4:5)	*page 1143*

1 The burden[a] of the word of the LORD to Israel by Malachi.

Israel Beloved of God

2 "I have loved you," says the LORD.
"Yet you say, 'In what way have You loved us?'
Was not Esau Jacob's brother?"
Says the LORD.
"Yet Jacob I have loved;
3 But Esau I have hated,
And laid waste his mountains and his heritage
For the jackals of the wilderness."

4 Even though Edom has said,
"We have been impoverished,
But we will return and build the desolate places,"

Thus says the LORD of hosts:

"They may build, but I will throw down;
They shall be called the Territory of Wickedness,
And the people against whom the LORD will have indignation forever.
5 Your eyes shall see,
And you shall say,
'The LORD is magnified beyond the border of Israel.'

Polluted Offerings

6 "A son honors *his* father,
And a servant *his* master.
If then I am the Father,
Where *is* My honor?
And if I *am* a Master,
Where *is* My reverence?
Says the LORD of hosts
To you priests who despise My name.
Yet you say, 'In what way have we despised Your name?'

7 "You offer defiled food on My altar,
But say,
'In what way have we defiled You?'

1:1 [a]Or *oracle*

The Law of Connection: Malachi Touches the Heart First

(Malachi 1:2–14)

Malachi begins his book by practicing the Law of Connection. Prior to any declarations of judgment, Malachi speaks words of compassion, straight from the heart of God (Mal. 1:2–5). The Lord reviews how much He loves the people, how He has chosen them and privileged them above the Edomites. Only then does He begin to address their need for improvement (1:6–14). He makes both His love and His correction very specific:

Affirmation
1. I have loved you (v. 2).
2. I have chosen you (v. 2).
3. I will defeat your enemies (vv. 3, 4).
4. I will be magnified worldwide (v. 5).

Admonishment
1. Where is My honor? (v. 6).
2. You defiled My altar (vv. 7, 8).
3. You act like My enemy (v. 10).
4. You've profaned My name (v. 12).

Effective leaders connect before they correct. They earn their right to change the life of their followers by first affirming their identity and relationship to the leader. How do we do this? Consider the following simple process:

1. Look for the good first.
2. Identify what you can affirm.
3. Be specific about your encouragement.
4. Note what needs to be changed.
5. Challenge the person to grow through change.
6. Tell them why the change is important.
7. Express confidence that they can do it.

By saying,
'The table of the LORD is contemptible.'
8 And when you offer the blind as a
  sacrifice,
Is it not evil?
And when you offer the lame and sick,
Is it not evil?
Offer it then to your governor!
Would he be pleased with you?
Would he accept you favorably?"
Says the LORD of hosts.

Excellence: Leaders Don't Just Set Goals, They Set Standards

(Malachi 1:7, 8)

If we give our best for our people, how much more should we pursue excellence with God! Good leaders don't settle for less than excellence. They don't merely set goals, they set standards that raise the bar for everyone. Malachi insists that these standards begin with our spiritual life.

---

9 "But now entreat God's favor,
  That He may be gracious to us.
  While this is being *done* by your hands,
  Will He accept you favorably?"
  Says the LORD of hosts.
10 "Who *is there* even among you who would
  shut the doors,
  So that you would not kindle fire *on* My
  altar in vain?
  I have no pleasure in you,"
  Says the LORD of hosts,
  "Nor will I accept an offering from your
  hands.
11 For from the rising of the sun, even to its
  going down,
  My name *shall be* great among the Gentiles;
  In every place incense *shall be* offered to
  My name,
  And a pure offering;
  For My name shall be great among the
  nations,"
  Says the LORD of hosts.

12 "But you profane it,
  In that you say,

'The table of the LORD[a] is defiled;
And its fruit, its food, *is* contemptible.'
13 You also say,
'Oh, what a weariness!'
And you sneer at it,"
Says the LORD of hosts.
"And you bring the stolen, the lame, and
  the sick;
Thus you bring an offering!
Should I accept this from your hand?"
Says the LORD.
14 "But cursed *be* the deceiver
Who has in his flock a male,
And takes a vow,
But sacrifices to the Lord what is
  blemished—
For I *am* a great King,"
Says the LORD of hosts,
"And My name *is to be* feared among the
  nations.

Corrupt Priests

2 "And now, O priests, this commandment
  is for you.
2   If you will not hear,
And if you will not take *it* to heart,
To give glory to My name,"
Says the LORD of hosts,
"I will send a curse upon you,
And I will curse your blessings.
Yes, I have cursed them already,
Because you do not take *it* to heart.
3 "Behold, I will rebuke your descendants
And spread refuse on your faces,
The refuse of your solemn feasts;
And *one* will take you away with it.
4 Then you shall know that I have sent this
  commandment to you,
That My covenant with Levi may
  continue,"
Says the LORD of hosts.
5 "My covenant was with him, *one* of life and
  peace,
And I gave them to him *that he might* fear
  Me;
So he feared Me
And was reverent before My name.
6 The law of truth[a] was in his mouth,
And injustice was not found on his lips.
He walked with Me in peace and equity,
And turned many away from iniquity.

1:12 [a]Following Bomberg; Masoretic Text reads
Lord. **2:6** [a]Or *true instruction*

7 "For the lips of a priest should keep
    knowledge,
   And *people* should seek the law from his
    mouth;
   For he is the messenger of the LORD of
    hosts.
8 But you have departed from the way;
   You have caused many to stumble at the
    law.
   You have corrupted the covenant of Levi,"
   Says the LORD of hosts.
9 "Therefore I also have made you
    contemptible and base
   Before all the people,
   Because you have not kept My ways
   But have shown partiality in the law."

Leaders Know That Demonstration Must Precede Imitation

(Malachi 2:7–9)

The priests and other leaders of Malachi's day failed to walk their talk. The second chapter of Malachi brims with accusations against their hypocrisy: treachery in the home, profanity in the sanctuary, mixed marriages, rampant divorce, and false teaching (Mal. 2:10–17).

God expects leaders to incarnate the life their followers should live. Successful leaders know they must first demonstrate the desired lifestyle. People do what people see. Leaders are models before they are ministers, mentors, or managers.

Notice what happened when Israel's leaders failed to live model lives:

1. They failed to preserve truth for the people (v. 7).
2. They diluted the people's appetite for growth and instruction (v. 7).
3. They caused many to stumble due to their poor example (v. 8).
4. They corrupted the covenant God made with them (v. 8).
5. They lost their credibility (v. 9).

Treachery of Infidelity

10 Have we not all one Father?
   Has not one God created us?
   Why do we deal treacherously with one
    another
   By profaning the covenant of the fathers?
11 Judah has dealt treacherously,
   And an abomination has been committed
    in Israel and in Jerusalem,
   For Judah has profaned
   The LORD's holy *institution* which He
    loves:
   He has married the daughter of a foreign
    god.
12 May the LORD cut off from the tents of
    Jacob
   The man who does this, being awake and
    aware,[a]
   Yet who brings an offering to the LORD of
    hosts!

13 And this is the second thing you do:
   You cover the altar of the LORD with
    tears,
   With weeping and crying;
   So He does not regard the offering
    anymore,
   Nor receive *it* with goodwill from your
    hands.
14 Yet you say, "For what reason?"
   Because the LORD has been witness
   Between you and the wife of your youth,
   With whom you have dealt treacherously;
   Yet she is your companion
   And your wife by covenant.
15 But did He not make *them* one,
   Having a remnant of the Spirit?
   And why one?
   He seeks godly offspring.
   Therefore take heed to your spirit,
   And let none deal treacherously with the
    wife of his youth.

16 "For the LORD God of Israel says
   That He hates divorce,
   For it covers one's garment with violence,"
   Says the LORD of hosts.
   "Therefore take heed to your spirit,
   That you do not deal treacherously."

17 You have wearied the LORD with your
    words;
   Yet you say,
   "In what way have we wearied *Him?*"
   In that you say,
   "Everyone who does evil
   Is good in the sight of the LORD,

2:12 [a]Talmud and Vulgate read *teacher and student.*

And He delights in them,"
Or, "Where *is* the God of justice?"

The Coming Messenger

3 "Behold, I send My messenger,
And he will prepare the way before Me.
And the Lord, whom you seek,
Will suddenly come to His temple,
Even the Messenger of the covenant,
In whom you delight.
Behold, He is coming,"
Says the LORD of hosts.

2 "But who can endure the day of His coming?
And who can stand when He appears?
For He *is* like a refiner's fire
And like launderers' soap.
3 He will sit as a refiner and a purifier of silver;
He will purify the sons of Levi,
And purge them as gold and silver,
That they may offer to the LORD
An offering in righteousness.

4 "Then the offering of Judah and Jerusalem
Will be pleasant to the LORD,
As in the days of old,
As in former years.
5 And I will come near you for judgment;
I will be a swift witness
Against sorcerers,
Against adulterers,
Against perjurers,
Against those who exploit wage earners
and widows and orphans,
And against those who turn away an alien—
Because they do not fear Me,"
Says the LORD of hosts.

6 "For I *am* the LORD, I do not change;
Therefore you are not consumed, O sons of Jacob.
7 Yet from the days of your fathers
You have gone away from My ordinances
And have not kept *them*.
Return to Me, and I will return to you,"
Says the LORD of hosts.
"But you said,
'In what way shall we return?'

Do Not Rob God

8 "Will a man rob God?
Yet you have robbed Me!
But you say,

'In what way have we robbed You?'
In tithes and offerings.
9 You are cursed with a curse,
For you have robbed Me,
Even this whole nation.
10 Bring all the tithes into the storehouse,
That there may be food in My house,
And try Me now in this,"
Says the LORD of hosts,
"If I will not open for you the windows of heaven
And pour out for you *such* blessing
That *there will* not *be room* enough *to receive it.*

11 "And I will rebuke the devourer for your sakes,
So that he will not destroy the fruit of your ground,
Nor shall the vine fail to bear fruit for you in the field,"
Says the LORD of hosts;
12 And all nations will call you blessed,
For you will be a delightful land,"
Says the LORD of hosts.

Stewardship: Leaders Are Only Stewards of What God Owns

(Malachi 3:8–12)

We are stewards of what God owns, nothing more. God promises that if we practice good stewardship, He will bless us greatly. But if we disobey, He will allow the devourer to destroy what we produce. Leaders especially must remember that we do not own anything; we only manage God's resources.

The People Complain Harshly

13 "Your words have been harsh against Me,"
Says the LORD,
"Yet you say,
'What have we spoken against You?'
14 You have said,
'It is useless to serve God;
What profit *is it* that we have kept His ordinance,
And that we have walked as mourners
Before the LORD of hosts?
15 So now we call the proud blessed,

For those who do wickedness are raised up;
They even tempt God and go free.'"

A Book of Remembrance

16 Then those who feared the LORD spoke to
one another,
And the LORD listened and heard *them;*
So a book of remembrance was written
before Him
For those who fear the LORD
And who meditate on His name.

17 "They shall be Mine," says the LORD of hosts,
"On the day that I make them My jewels.[a]
And I will spare them
As a man spares his own son who serves
him."

18 Then you shall again discern
Between the righteous and the wicked,
Between one who serves God
And one who does not serve Him.

The Great Day of God

4 "For behold, the day is coming,
Burning like an oven,
And all the proud, yes, all who do
wickedly will be stubble.
And the day which is coming shall burn
them up,"
Says the LORD of hosts,
"That will leave them neither root nor
branch.

2 But to you who fear My name
The Sun of Righteousness shall arise
With healing in His wings;
And you shall go out
And grow fat like stall-fed calves.

3 You shall trample the wicked,
For they shall be ashes under the soles of
your feet
On the day that I do *this,*"
Says the LORD of hosts.

4 "Remember the Law of Moses, My servant,
Which I commanded him in Horeb for all
Israel,

With the statutes and judgments.

5 Behold, I will send you Elijah the
prophet
Before the coming of the great and
dreadful day of the LORD.

6 And he will turn
The hearts of the fathers to the children,
And the hearts of the children to their
fathers,
Lest I come and strike the earth with a
curse."

3:17 [a]Literally *special treasure*

The Law of Timing: God Knows When and How to Move
(Malachi 4:5)

God is a master at timing. Like any good leader, He knows when to move and how to prepare the people for His moves.

Malachi predicts a day when God will bring justice to everyone and burn away the evil, like chaff burning away from the wheat. God promises to send Elijah the prophet before this terrible day of the Lord. Like so many prophecies, this scripture has two fulfillments. The first came after Jesus was born in Bethlehem; as the Elijah figure, John the Baptizer prepared the way. The ultimate fulfillment of this passage will occur in the last days, when God will send another Elijah figure to prepare the way for His second coming.

God practices the Law of Timing, making sure everything is in order when He makes His move. This word from Malachi is the last word God gave before coming in the Person of Jesus.

THE
NEW TESTAMENT

MATTHEW

Jesus as the Long-Awaited Messiah

SUMMARY

Matthew is the first of four books in the New Testament that depict the Ultimate Leader, Jesus Christ. Matthew describes Jesus as the long-awaited Messiah for the Jews, the fulfillment of so much Old Testament prophecy. Every Jew knew that when the Messiah came, He would right the wrongs in Israel and somehow restore the nation to her rightful place.

Of course, Jesus fulfilled these expectations in a far different manner than what most people expected. He *did* fulfill Old Testament prophecy, but most Jews missed the part about the suffering Messiah (Is. 53). He *did* make things right, but He worked on the spiritual dimension of the nation's life rather than the political aspect. He concerned Himself more with cleansing them and making them whole than with helping them gain economic freedom from Rome. He brought about change from the inside out, rather than by some legislative act or military revolution.

Jesus' leadership differs from all others. He doesn't merely reform—He transforms. He knew that if He got the people's spirit right, the rest would follow. Jesus was a uniquely different leader, an "upside-down" leader who reversed the values and conduct of nearly every other leader of His day.

Matthew shows Jesus practicing every one of the 21 Laws of Leadership, incarnating everything that makes for successful, transformational leadership. And this was only the beginning!

Try to read Matthew's stories with fresh eyes. See Jesus not only as a wonderful Savior and Redeemer, but as the greatest Leader who ever walked the earth. When you have begun to see Him this way, jot down how He led others. Note His unusual style, His unorthodox methods and strategy, His unshakable commitment to His mission and values. What a Leader!

God's Role in Matthew

This book assumes a unique role among the four Gospels. Matthew wrote to the Jews, who needed to be convinced from Scripture that Jesus was who He claimed to be. Jesus worked not only to ensure that He did indeed fulfill Old Testament prophecies, but that He performed sufficient miracles to demonstrate His compassion and credibility as Messiah. Once God confirmed His word with signs following, the writing came easy.

God guided Matthew to include dozens of Old Testament scriptures, confirming each with an act or statement from Jesus. We see God acting well in advance to map out details and fulfill future prophetic statements.

Leaders in Matthew
Jesus, John the Baptizer, Pilate, Herod, the centurion

Other People of Influence in Matthew
The zealots, the twelve disciples, the scribes and Pharisees

Lessons in Leadership

- The fastest way to gain leadership is to solve problems.

- Leaders go where the people are.

- Leaders first instill new values into their team.

- Leaders never misrepresent their product or service.

- Leaders don't allow rejection to change their opinion of themselves.

- Leaders know they have something the people need.

- Leaders are motivated by a love for people and a desire to serve.

- Leaders are on a mission and never drift from it.

LEADERSHIP HIGHLIGHTS IN MATTHEW

SECURITY: Herod Felt the Threat of Competition (2:1–18)	*page 1150*
THE LAW OF SACRIFICE: Quality Leaders Are Prepared in the Wilderness (4:1–11)	*page 1153*
FOLLOWERS OF GOD Are to Be Leaders of Men and Live at a Higher Level (5:1–48)	*page 1155*
THE LAW OF EMPOWERMENT: Jesus Gave Power Away . . . and Multiplied His Influence (10:1–15)	*page 1163*
JESUS: An Unwavering Commitment to Speak the Truth (12:22—13:53)	*page 1168*
SERVANTHOOD: Jesus Teaches That We Lead by Serving and Serve by Leading (20:25–28)	*page 1179*
RESPONSIBILITY: Pontius Pilate Failed to Lead (27:11–31)	*page 1190*
JESUS AND THE LAW OF LEGACY: A Leader's Lasting Value Is Measured by Succession (28:16–20)	*pages 1192, 1193*

The Genealogy of Jesus Christ

1 The book of the genealogy of Jesus Christ, the Son of David, the Son of Abraham:

²Abraham begot Isaac, Isaac begot Jacob, and Jacob begot Judah and his brothers. ³Judah begot Perez and Zerah by Tamar, Perez begot Hezron, and Hezron begot Ram. ⁴Ram begot Amminadab, Amminadab begot Nahshon, and Nahshon begot Salmon. ⁵Salmon begot Boaz by Rahab, Boaz begot Obed by Ruth, Obed begot Jesse, ⁶and Jesse begot David the king.

David the king begot Solomon by her *who had been the wife*ᵃ of Uriah. ⁷Solomon begot Rehoboam, Rehoboam begot Abijah, and Abijah begot Asa.ᵃ ⁸Asa begot Jehoshaphat, Jehoshaphat begot Joram, and Joram begot Uzziah. ⁹Uzziah begot Jotham, Jotham begot Ahaz, and Ahaz begot Hezekiah. ¹⁰Hezekiah begot Manasseh, Manasseh begot Amon,ᵃ and Amon begot Josiah. ¹¹Josiah begot Jeconiah and his brothers about the time they were carried away to Babylon.

¹²And after they were brought to Babylon, Jeconiah begot Shealtiel, and Shealtiel begot Zerubbabel. ¹³Zerubbabel begot Abiud, Abiud begot Eliakim, and Eliakim begot Azor. ¹⁴Azor begot Zadok, Zadok begot Achim, and Achim begot Eliud. ¹⁵Eliud begot Eleazar, Eleazar begot Matthan, and Matthan begot Jacob. ¹⁶And Jacob begot Joseph the husband of Mary, of whom was born Jesus who is called Christ.

¹⁷So all the generations from Abraham to David *are* fourteen generations, from David until the captivity in Babylon *are* fourteen generations, and from the captivity in Babylon until the Christ *are* fourteen generations.

Christ Born of Mary

¹⁸Now the birth of Jesus Christ was as follows: After His mother Mary was betrothed to Joseph, before they came together, she was found with child of the Holy Spirit. ¹⁹Then Joseph her husband, being a just *man,* and not wanting to make her a public example, was minded to put her away secretly. ²⁰But while he thought about these things, behold, an angel of the Lord appeared to him in a dream, saying, "Joseph, son of David, do not be afraid to take to you Mary your wife, for that which is conceived in her is of the Holy Spirit. ²¹And she will bring forth a Son, and you shall call His name JESUS, for He will save His people from their sins."

²²So all this was done that it might be fulfilled which was spoken by the Lord through the prophet, saying: ²³*"Behold, the virgin shall be with child, and bear a Son, and they shall call His name Immanuel,"*ᵃ which is translated, "God with us."

²⁴Then Joseph, being aroused from sleep, did as the angel of the Lord commanded him and took to him his wife, ²⁵and did not know her till she had brought forth her firstborn Son.ᵃ And he called His name JESUS.

Wise Men from the East

2 Now after Jesus was born in Bethlehem of Judea in the days of Herod the king, behold, wise men from the East came to Jerusalem, ²saying, "Where is He who has been born King of the Jews? For we have seen His star in the East and have come to worship Him."

³When Herod the king heard *this,* he was troubled, and all Jerusalem with him. ⁴And when he had gathered all the chief priests and scribes of the people together, he inquired of them where the Christ was to be born.

⁵So they said to him, "In Bethlehem of Judea, for thus it is written by the prophet:

⁶ 'But you, Bethlehem, *in the land of Judah,*
    Are not the least among the rulers of Judah;
    For out of you shall come a Ruler
    Who will shepherd My people Israel.' "ᵃ

⁷Then Herod, when he had secretly called the wise men, determined from them what time

---

Planning: God Uses Long-Range Planning to Prepare the World

(Matthew 1:1–17)

Matthew provides an exhaustive list of Jesus' ancestors, beginning with Abraham. This genealogy demonstrates God's long-range plan to save the human race. He made sure to cover every step and prepare every person to participate in the line of Christ. Effective leaders lay plans with the end in mind.

1:6 ᵃWords in italic type have been added for clarity. They are not found in the original Greek. **1:7** ᵃNU-Text reads *Asaph.* **1:10** ᵃNU-Text reads *Amos.* **1:23** ᵃIsaiah 7:14. Words in oblique type in the New Testament are quoted from the Old Testament. **1:25** ᵃNU-Text reads *a Son.* **2:6** ᵃMicah 5:2

21 QUALITIES

SECURITY

Herod Felt the Threat of Competition

(Matthew 2:1–18)

The tremendous insecurity of King Herod became apparent when strangers announced Jesus' birth. Upon hearing the news, Herod grew angry, impatient, self-consumed, and disturbed—all signs of an insecure leader. Insecure leaders share several common traits:

1. They don't provide security for others.
2. They take more than they give.
3. They continually limit their best people.
4. They continually limit or sabotage their organization's success.
5. They spend more energy trying to keep their job than to do their job.

Effective leadership begins with an emotionally and spiritually healthy leader. Why is this true? Why must we focus on our personal security? Consider several reasons:

1. Leadership must flow out of "being," not merely "doing."
2. Strong character is necessary to sustain strong conduct.
3. Insecure leaders cause their organizations to plateau.
4. Personal security provides the infrastructure to support leaders in adversity.
5. Insecure leaders will never empower and develop secure followers.
6. Inward strength provides the only hope of finishing well.

Most of us struggle with feelings of insecurity. Leadership roles, however, work like a magnifying glass on our personal insecurity, blowing everything out of proportion because we know everyone is watching. We tend to react by trying to cover up our flaws, rather than being honest. This is yet another reason why leaders must commit to laying a foundation of strong personal security.

None of us ever grow beyond four fundamental human needs:

1. *A Sense of Worth*—if missing, we feel inferior.
2. *A Sense of Belonging*—if missing, we feel insecure.
3. *A Sense of Purpose*—if missing, we feel illegitimate.
4. *A Sense of Competence*–if missing, we feel inadequate.

How, then, should we respond to these crucial issues?

1. Leaders should settle this issue with God before they reach positions of influence.
2. Our personal worth and security must come from our "secret history" with God.
3. We should never place our emotional health in the hands of another.
4. We must release people from the expectation that they will meet our basic needs.

We become healthy leaders only when we don't expect others to meet the needs that only God can meet.

For a positive example of security, see p. 381.

the star appeared. ⁸And he sent them to Bethlehem and said, "Go and search carefully for the young Child, and when you have found *Him*, bring back word to me, that I may come and worship Him also."

⁹When they heard the king, they departed; and behold, the star which they had seen in the East went before them, till it came and stood over where the young Child was. ¹⁰When they saw the star, they rejoiced with exceedingly great joy. ¹¹And when they had come into the house, they saw the young Child with Mary His mother, and fell down and worshiped Him. And when they had opened their treasures, they presented gifts to Him: gold, frankincense, and myrrh.

¹²Then, being divinely warned in a dream that they should not return to Herod, they departed for their own country another way.

The Law of Empowerment: Herod Abused Power Instead of Sharing It

(Matthew 2:3–18)

King Herod failed to empower anyone; in fact, he drained power from people in a continual grab for power. Check out the ugly symptoms we see in his leadership that every one of us should avoid:

1. He felt disturbed and threatened when he learned of a coming king (v. 3).
2. He leveraged his power against any possible competitor (v. 4).
3. He used people to serve his own purposes (vv. 7, 8).
4. He lied in order to project the right image (v. 8).
5. He reacted with fury when he didn't get his way (v. 16).
6. He concerned himself only with his own benefit (v. 16).
7. He sought to destroy any potential threat to his leadership (vv. 16–18).

The Flight into Egypt

¹³Now when they had departed, behold, an angel of the Lord appeared to Joseph in a dream, saying, "Arise, take the young Child and His mother, flee to Egypt, and stay there until I bring you word; for Herod will seek the young Child to destroy Him."

¹⁴When he arose, he took the young Child and His mother by night and departed for Egypt, ¹⁵and was there until the death of Herod, that it might be fulfilled which was spoken by the Lord through the prophet, saying, *"Out of Egypt I called My Son."*ᵃ

Massacre of the Innocents

¹⁶Then Herod, when he saw that he was deceived by the wise men, was exceedingly angry; and he sent forth and put to death all the male children who were in Bethlehem and in all its districts, from two years old and under, according to the time which he had determined from the wise men. ¹⁷Then was fulfilled what was spoken by Jeremiah the prophet, saying:

18   *"A voice was heard in Ramah,*
    Lamentation, weeping, and great mourning,
    Rachel weeping for her children,
    Refusing to be comforted,
    *Because they are no more."*ᵃ

The Home in Nazareth

¹⁹Now when Herod was dead, behold, an angel of the Lord appeared in a dream to Joseph in Egypt, ²⁰saying, "Arise, take the young Child and His mother, and go to the land of Israel, for those who sought the young Child's life are dead." ²¹Then he arose, took the young Child and His mother, and came into the land of Israel. ²²But when he heard that Archelaus was reigning over Judea instead of his father Herod, he was afraid to go there. And being warned by God in a dream, he turned aside into the region of Galilee. ²³And he came and dwelt in a city called Nazareth, that it might be fulfilled which was spoken by the prophets, "He shall be called a Nazarene."

John the Baptist Prepares the Way

3 In those days John the Baptist came preaching in the wilderness of Judea, ²and saying, "Repent, for the kingdom of heaven is at hand!" ³For this is he who was spoken of by the prophet Isaiah, saying:

    "The voice of one crying in the wilderness:
    'Prepare the way of the LORD;
    *Make His paths straight.'"*ᵃ

2:15 ᵃHosea 11:1   **2:18** ᵃJeremiah 31:15   **3:3** ᵃIsaiah 40:3

Courage: John Demonstrates Courageous Leadership

(Matthew 3:1–10)

John the Baptizer, the cousin of Jesus, paved the way for Christ. John prepared the people for Jesus' ministry with a unique ministry of his own, courageously calling people to repent and live out what they claimed to believe.

John confronted Pharisees, common people who lived hypocritically, and even King Herod himself. Note how his courageous leadership demonstrated itself:

1. John preached a clear message; the Pharisees, a complex one (vv. 1–3).
2. John cared more about his integrity than about his image (vv. 4–6).
3. John had stronger convictions than his critics (vv. 7–10).

How did John become so courageous? What helped him build his courage?

1. *His mission was deliberate:* His job was to prepare for the coming of the Lord.
2. *His message was decisive:* He said, "Repent, for the kingdom of heaven is at hand" (Matt. 3:2).
3. *His motive was direct:* He had Elijah's voice, crying in the wilderness.
4. *His manner was different:* His clothes came from camel hair; he ate locusts.
5. *His principles were deep:* He believed people must exhibit the fruit of repentance.
6. *His method was daring:* He directed people to confess their sins and be baptized.
7. *His mind was discerning:* He perceived the pretenses of the Pharisees.
8. *His ministry was developing:* He drew people from all over Judea.

⁴Now John himself was clothed in camel's hair, with a leather belt around his waist; and his food was locusts and wild honey. ⁵Then Jerusalem, all Judea, and all the region around the Jordan went out to him ⁶and were baptized by him in the Jordan, confessing their sins.

⁷But when he saw many of the Pharisees and Sadducees coming to his baptism, he said to them, "Brood of vipers! Who warned you to flee from the wrath to come? ⁸Therefore bear fruits worthy of repentance, ⁹and do not think to say to yourselves, 'We have Abraham as *our* father.' For I say to you that God is able to raise up children to Abraham from these stones. ¹⁰And even now the ax is laid to the root of the trees. Therefore every tree which does not bear good fruit is cut down and thrown into the fire. ¹¹I indeed baptize you with water unto repentance, but He who is coming after me is mightier than I, whose sandals I am not worthy to carry. He will baptize you with the Holy Spirit and fire.[a] ¹²His winnowing fan *is* in His hand, and He will thoroughly clean out His threshing floor, and gather His wheat into the barn; but He will burn up the chaff with unquenchable fire."

John Baptizes Jesus

¹³Then Jesus came from Galilee to John at the Jordan to be baptized by him. ¹⁴And John *tried to*

The Law of Respect: John Submits to Jesus' Leadership

(Matthew 3:11–14)

Even though John the Baptizer possessed the strongest voice of his day, when Jesus stepped forward, he willingly submitted to His authority. He even predicted Christ's coming. He knew his role was to prepare everyone for the Messiah. He laid his ego aside and humbly fulfilled his calling. He acknowledged the One who was greater than he and publicly said to Jesus: "I need to be baptized by You" (Matt. 3:14).

Healthy leaders remain in touch with their own influence and wield it without reservation. Yet they never allow ego to drive them. They yield to stronger leaders when they appear, because the cause is more important than personal popularity.

3:11 [a]M-Text omits *and fire.*

prevent Him, saying, "I need to be baptized by You, and are You coming to me?"

[15]But Jesus answered and said to him, "Permit *it to be so* now, for thus it is fitting for us to fulfill all righteousness." Then he allowed Him.

[16]When He had been baptized, Jesus came up immediately from the water; and behold, the heavens were opened to Him, and He[a] saw the Spirit of God descending like a dove and alighting upon Him. [17]And suddenly a voice *came* from heaven, saying, "This is My beloved Son, in whom I am well pleased."

Satan Tempts Jesus

4 Then Jesus was led up by the Spirit into the wilderness to be tempted by the devil. [2]And when He had fasted forty days and forty nights, afterward He was hungry. [3]Now when the tempter came to Him, he said, "If You are the Son of God, command that these stones become bread."

[4]But He answered and said, "It is written, *'Man shall not live by bread alone, but by every word that proceeds from the mouth of God.'*"[a]

[5]Then the devil took Him up into the holy city, set Him on the pinnacle of the temple, [6]and said to Him, "If You are the Son of God, throw Yourself down. For it is written:

'He shall give His angels charge over you,'

and,

'In their hands they shall bear you up,
Lest you dash your foot against a stone.'"[a]

[7]Jesus said to him, "It is written again, *'You shall not tempt the LORD your God.'*"[a]

[8]Again, the devil took Him up on an exceedingly high mountain, and showed Him all the kingdoms of the world and their glory. [9]And he said to Him, "All these things I will give You if You will fall down and worship me."

[10]Then Jesus said to him, "Away with you,[a] Satan! For it is written, *'You shall worship the LORD your God, and Him only you shall serve.'*"[b]

[11]Then the devil left Him, and behold, angels came and ministered to Him.

3:16 [a]Or *he* **4:4** [a]Deuteronomy 8:3 **4:6** [a]Psalm 91:11, 12 **4:7** [a]Deuteronomy 6:16 **4:10** [a]M-Text reads *Get behind Me.* [b]Deuteronomy 6:13

The Law of Sacrifice:
Quality Leaders Are Prepared in the Wilderness
(Matthew 4:1–11)

The Holy Spirit led Jesus out into the wilderness right after His baptism by John, reminding us that at least part of His preparation for ministry came from a wilderness experience.

Does this sound familiar? Quality leaders can almost always point to a wilderness experience as part of their leadership preparation. During this time, our motives get purified, our backbone solidifies, and our calling gets clarified.

The devil tempted Jesus for 40 days in the wilderness—a screening process to see what Jesus would give up and how He would trust God to provide. In his book, *In the Name of Jesus,* Henry Nouwen reminds us that the three temptations of Jesus correspond to three temptations leaders face today:

1. *The temptation to be self-sufficient* (vv. 2–4)
   Jesus didn't become controlling, even with His legitimate needs. He trusted God.
2. *The temptation to be spectacular* (vv. 5–7)
   Jesus refused to become a stunt man. He didn't perform in order to become a celebrity.
3. *The temptation to be powerful* (vv. 8–10)
   Jesus wouldn't take a shortcut to gain power or worship.

How do you deal with the temptations of leadership? Study Jesus' method for combating these familiar temptations of legitimate needs, gifting, and fame. Jesus provides our standard for defeating temptation. He never lost.

The Law of Reproduction and Legacy: Jesus Raised Up Leaders

(Matthew 4:12–25)

As Jesus began His public ministry, He preached (Matt. 4:12–17), then passed yet another test of leadership: He called other leaders to join Him (4:18–22). These twelve men He called disciples. Immediately He began developing them into future leaders for the church.

Jesus passed the acid test of leadership: *Could He reproduce His leadership in someone else?* At the same time He chose three fishermen, He cast vision for spiritual reproduction: "Follow Me," He said, "and I will make you fishers of men" (4:19). Clearly, He called these men to become leaders as well.

What do we learn about Jesus' selection and development of leaders?

1. *He found them in the course of His everyday world* (v. 18).
   Jesus was walking by the Sea of Galilee and spotted men close to Him.
2. *He handpicked them* (v. 19).
   Jesus didn't hold a popularity vote; He chose the ones He knew were right.
3. *He called them to become leaders* (v. 19).
   Jesus called them not only to follow Him, but to influence others.
4. *He used language they understood* (v. 19).
   Jesus plainly challenged them to catch men instead of fish.
5. *He took them on a journey and demonstrated leadership* (vv. 23–25).
   Jesus modeled leadership as he traveled through Judea.

Jesus Begins His Galilean Ministry

[12]Now when Jesus heard that John had been put in prison, He departed to Galilee. [13]And leaving Nazareth, He came and dwelt in Capernaum, which is by the sea, in the regions of Zebulun and Naphtali, [14]that it might be fulfilled which was spoken by Isaiah the prophet, saying:

[15] "*The land of Zebulun and the land of Naphtali,*
By the way of the sea, beyond the Jordan,
Galilee of the Gentiles:
[16] *The people who sat in darkness have seen a great light,*
And upon those who sat in the region and shadow of death
Light has dawned."[a]

[17]From that time Jesus began to preach and to say, "Repent, for the kingdom of heaven is at hand."

Four Fishermen Called as Disciples

[18]And Jesus, walking by the Sea of Galilee, saw two brothers, Simon called Peter, and Andrew his brother, casting a net into the sea; for they were fishermen. [19]Then He said to them, "Follow Me, and I will make you fishers of men." [20]They immediately left *their* nets and followed Him.

[21]Going on from there, He saw two other brothers, James *the son* of Zebedee, and John his brother, in the boat with Zebedee their father, mending their nets. He called them, [22]and immediately they left the boat and their father, and followed Him.

Jesus Heals a Great Multitude

[23]And Jesus went about all Galilee, teaching in their synagogues, preaching the gospel of the kingdom, and healing all kinds of sickness and all kinds of disease among the people. [24]Then His fame went throughout all Syria; and they brought to Him all sick people who were afflicted with various diseases and torments, and those who were demon-possessed, epileptics, and paralytics; and He healed them. [25]Great multitudes followed Him—from Galilee, and *from* Decapolis, Jerusalem, Judea, and beyond the Jordan.

4:16 [a]Isaiah 9:1, 2

The Beatitudes

5 And seeing the multitudes, He went up on a mountain, and when He was seated His disciples came to Him. [2]Then He opened His mouth and taught them, saying:

[3] "Blessed *are* the poor in spirit,
For theirs is the kingdom of heaven.
[4] Blessed *are* those who mourn,
For they shall be comforted.
[5] Blessed *are* the meek,
For they shall inherit the earth.
[6] Blessed *are* those who hunger and thirst for righteousness,
For they shall be filled.
[7] Blessed *are* the merciful,
For they shall obtain mercy.
[8] Blessed *are* the pure in heart,
For they shall see God.
[9] Blessed *are* the peacemakers,
For they shall be called sons of God.
[10] Blessed *are* those who are persecuted for righteousness' sake,
For theirs is the kingdom of heaven.

[11]"Blessed are you when they revile and persecute you, and say all kinds of evil against you falsely for My sake. [12]Rejoice and be exceedingly glad, for great *is* your reward in heaven, for so they persecuted the prophets who were before you.

Believers Are Salt and Light

[13]"You are the salt of the earth; but if the salt loses its flavor, how shall it be seasoned? It is then good for nothing but to be thrown out and trampled underfoot by men.

[14]"You are the light of the world. A city that is set on a hill cannot be hidden. [15]Nor do they light a lamp and put it under a basket, but on a lampstand, and it gives light to all *who are* in the house. [16]Let your light so shine before men, that they may see your good works and glorify your Father in heaven.

Christ Fulfills the Law

[17]"Do not think that I came to destroy the Law or the Prophets. I did not come to destroy but to fulfill. [18]For assuredly, I say to you, till heaven and earth pass away, one jot or one tittle will by no means pass from the law till all is fulfilled. [19]Whoever therefore breaks one of the least of these commandments, and teaches men so, shall be called least in the kingdom of heaven; but whoever does and teaches *them,* he shall be called great in the kingdom of heaven. [20]For I say to you, that unless your righteousness exceeds *the righteousness* of the scribes and Pharisees, you will by no means enter the kingdom of heaven.

Followers of God Are to Be Leaders of Men and Live at a Higher Level

(Matthew 5:1–48)

Between the "seed" of leadership planted in the early stages and the fruit of leadership that comes with maturity, every leader goes through two major phases: the call and the preparation.

During the preparation season, all leaders get tested to live at a higher level than others. No one responded better than Jesus.

Jesus calls His people to live at a higher level than the rest of the world. His call brings many other tests along the way, for tests always follow the call in order to prepare leaders for the role they are to play.

The Call		The Preparation	
The Seed of Leadership	The Beginning of Leadership	The Tests of Leadership	The Fulfillment of Leadership

During the middle two stages, emerging leaders experiment to discover their strengths and weaknesses. To reach their potential, however, leaders must pass many tests. Ask yourself: Do I measure up to living at a higher level?

Leadership Development Begins with an Attitude Adjustment

(Matthew 5:1—7:29)

Jesus' most famous message, the Sermon on the Mount, focused on the hearts of His listeners. He targeted His disciples as the audience (Matt. 5:1, 2) and proceeded to preach what we now call the "Beatitudes." He called His men to be different, to see the world from God's perspective, to relate to people in a supernatural fashion.

Jesus demonstrated that leadership development begins with shaping the perspective of the listener. Jesus challenged the normal human perspective on . . .

- spiritual poverty and success
- sadness and mourning
- meekness and gentleness
- passion and hunger
- mercy and compassion
- purity and integrity
- peacemaking and revenge
- persecution and adversity

Murder Begins in the Heart

[21]"You have heard that it was said to those of old, '*You shall not murder*,[a] and whoever murders will be in danger of the judgment.' [22]But I say to you that whoever is angry with his brother without a cause[a] shall be in danger of the judgment. And whoever says to his brother, 'Raca!' shall be in danger of the council. But whoever says, 'You fool!' shall be in danger of hell fire. [23]Therefore if you bring your gift to the altar, and there remember that your brother has something against you, [24]leave your gift there before the altar, and go your way. First be reconciled to your brother, and then come and offer your gift. [25]Agree with your adversary quickly, while you are on the way with him, lest your adversary deliver you to the judge, the judge hand you over to the officer, and you be thrown into prison. [26]Assuredly, I say to you, you will by no means get out of there till you have paid the last penny.

Adultery in the Heart

[27]"You have heard that it was said to those of old,[a] '*You shall not commit adultery*.'[b] [28]But I say to you that whoever looks at a woman to lust for her has already committed adultery with her in his heart. [29]If your right eye causes you to sin, pluck it out and cast *it* from you; for it is more profitable for you that one of your members perish, than for your whole body to be cast into hell. [30]And if your right hand causes you to sin, cut it off and cast *it* from you; for it is more profitable for you that one of your members perish, than for your whole body to be cast into hell.

Marriage Is Sacred and Binding

[31]"Furthermore it has been said, 'Whoever divorces his wife, let him give her a certificate of divorce.' [32]But I say to you that whoever divorces his wife for any reason except sexual immorality[a] causes her to commit adultery; and whoever marries a woman who is divorced commits adultery.

Jesus Forbids Oaths

[33]"Again you have heard that it was said to those of old, 'You shall not swear falsely, but shall perform your oaths to the Lord.' [34]But I say to you, do not swear at all: neither by heaven, for it is God's throne; [35]nor by the earth, for it is His footstool; nor by Jerusalem, for it is the city of the great King. [36]Nor shall you swear by your head, because you cannot make one hair white or black. [37]But let your 'Yes' be 'Yes,' and your 'No,' 'No.' For whatever is more than these is from the evil one.

Go the Second Mile

[38]"You have heard that it was said, '*An eye for an eye and a tooth for a tooth*.'[a] [39]But I tell you not to resist an evil person. But whoever slaps you on your right cheek, turn the other to him also. [40]If anyone wants to sue you and take away your tunic, let him have *your* cloak also. [41]And whoever compels you to go one mile, go with him two. [42]Give to him who asks you, and from him who wants to borrow from you do not turn away.

Love Your Enemies

[43]"You have heard that it was said, '*You shall love your neighbor*[a] and hate your enemy.' [44]But

5:21 [a]Exodus 20:13; Deuteronomy 5:17
5:22 [a]NU-Text omits *without a cause*. 5:27 [a]NU-Text and M-Text omit *to those of old*. [b]Exodus 20:14; Deuteronomy 5:18 5:32 [a]Or *fornication*
5:38 [a]Exodus 21:24; Leviticus 24:20; Deuteronomy 19:21 5:43 [a]Compare Leviticus 19:18

I say to you, love your enemies, bless those who curse you, do good to those who hate you, and pray for those who spitefully use you and persecute you,[a] [45]that you may be sons of your Father in heaven; for He makes His sun rise on the evil and on the good, and sends rain on the just and on the unjust. [46]For if you love those who love you, what reward have you? Do not even the tax collectors do the same? [47]And if you greet your brethren[a] only, what do you do more *than others?* Do not even the tax collectors[b] do so? [48]Therefore you shall be perfect, just as your Father in heaven is perfect.

Do Good to Please God

6 "Take heed that you do not do your charitable deeds before men, to be seen by them. Otherwise you have no reward from your Father in heaven. [2]Therefore, when you do a charitable deed, do not sound a trumpet before you as the hypocrites do in the synagogues and in the streets, that they may have glory from men. Assuredly, I say to you, they have their reward. [3]But when you do a charitable deed, do not let your left hand know what your right hand is doing, [4]that your charitable deed may be in secret; and your Father who sees in secret will Himself reward you openly.[a]

The Model Prayer

[5]"And when you pray, you shall not be like the hypocrites. For they love to pray standing in the synagogues and on the corners of the streets, that they may be seen by men. Assuredly, I say to you, they have their reward. [6]But you, when you pray, go into your room, and when you have shut your door, pray to your Father who *is* in the secret *place;* and your Father who sees in secret will reward you openly.[a] [7]And when you pray, do not use vain repetitions as the heathen *do.* For they think that they will be heard for their many words.

[8]"Therefore do not be like them. For your Father knows the things you have need of before you ask Him. [9]In this manner, therefore, pray:

Our Father in heaven,
Hallowed be Your name.
[10] Your kingdom come.
Your will be done
On earth as *it is* in heaven.
[11] Give us this day our daily bread.
[12] And forgive us our debts,
As we forgive our debtors.
[13] And do not lead us into temptation,
But deliver us from the evil one.

For Yours is the kingdom and the power and the glory forever. Amen.[a]

[14]"For if you forgive men their trespasses, your heavenly Father will also forgive you. [15]But if you do not forgive men their trespasses, neither will your Father forgive your trespasses.

Fasting to Be Seen Only by God

[16]"Moreover, when you fast, do not be like the hypocrites, with a sad countenance. For they disfigure their faces that they may appear to men to be fasting. Assuredly, I say to you, they have their reward. [17]But you, when you fast, anoint your head and wash your face, [18]so that you do not appear to men to be fasting, but to your Father who *is* in the secret *place;* and your Father who sees in secret will reward you openly.[a]

5:44 [a]NU-Text omits three clauses from this verse, leaving, *"But I say to you, love your enemies and pray for those who persecute you."* **5:47** [a]M-Text reads *friends.* [b]NU-Text reads *Gentiles.* **6:4** [a]NU-Text omits *openly.* **6:6** [a]NU-Text omits *openly.* **6:13** [a]NU-Text omits *For Yours* through *Amen.* **6:18** [a]NU-Text and M-Text omit *openly.*

Motive Check: Leaders Must Do the Right Thing for the Right Reason
(Matthew 6:1–34)

Leaders can so easily get caught up in doing things for image sake—after all, so many people are watching.

Jesus warns us about facades and hypocrisy. He means this text for everyone, with crucial application to leaders. Our Lord speaks about doing things to be seen by men rather than to please God (Matt. 6:1). Jesus wants to build strong convictions in His followers. He wants to produce God-pleasers (1 Thess. 4:1), not people-pleasers (Col. 3:22). In this text, Jesus covers our motives for:

- doing good (v. 1)
- giving to charity (vv. 2–4)
- prayer (vv. 5–15)
- fasting (vv. 16–18)
- priorities and values (vv. 19–24)
- work and worry (vv. 25–34)

The First Task of a Leader Is to Define Core Values

(Matthew 6:1—7:27)

In the first sermon recorded in his Gospel, Matthew spotlights Jesus' major emphasis on values. Jesus knew His first task was to provide a set of core values for His men. Note Jesus' list of core values:

1. Do the right things for the right reasons (6:1–8, 16–18).
2. Pray God's agenda, not your own (6:9–13).
3. Relationships will make or break you (6:14, 15).
4. Prioritize eternal things, not temporal things (6:19–24).
5. Don't sweat the small stuff (6:25–31, 34).
6. God's kingdom is paramount; seek it first (6:32, 33).
7. Judge yourself before you judge others (7:1–6).
8. If you need something, ask; if you have something, give it (7:7–12).
9. Stay true to your convictions; don't wander from the narrow path (7:13–20).
10. Obedience to God is the only sure foundation for life (7:21–27).

If you're still not convinced that Jesus gives a list of core values here, look at Matthew 7:12, where He summarizes the Law in a single statement.

Lay Up Treasures in Heaven

19"Do not lay up for yourselves treasures on earth, where moth and rust destroy and where thieves break in and steal; 20but lay up for yourselves treasures in heaven, where neither moth nor rust destroys and where thieves do not break in and steal. 21For where your treasure is, there your heart will be also.

The Lamp of the Body

22"The lamp of the body is the eye. If therefore your eye is good, your whole body will be full of light. 23But if your eye is bad, your whole body will be full of darkness. If therefore the light that is in you is darkness, how great is that darkness!

You Cannot Serve God and Riches

24"No one can serve two masters; for either he will hate the one and love the other, or else he will be loyal to the one and despise the other. You cannot serve God and mammon.

Do Not Worry

25"Therefore I say to you, do not worry about your life, what you will eat or what you will drink; nor about your body, what you will put on. Is not life more than food and the body more than clothing? 26Look at the birds of the air, for they neither sow nor reap nor gather into barns; yet your heavenly Father feeds them. Are you not of more value than they? 27Which of you by worrying can add one cubit to his stature?

28"So why do you worry about clothing? Consider the lilies of the field, how they grow: they neither toil nor spin; 29and yet I say to you that even Solomon in all his glory was not arrayed like one of these. 30Now if God so clothes the grass of the field, which today is, and tomorrow is thrown into the oven, *will He* not much more *clothe* you, O you of little faith?

31"Therefore do not worry, saying, 'What shall we eat?' or 'What shall we drink?' or 'What shall we wear?' 32For after all these things the Gentiles seek. For your heavenly Father knows that you need all these things. 33But seek first the kingdom of God and His righteousness, and all these things shall be added to you. 34Therefore do not worry about tomorrow, for tomorrow will worry about its own things. Sufficient for the day *is* its own trouble.

Do Not Judge

7 "Judge not, that you be not judged. 2For with what judgment you judge, you will be judged; and with the measure you use, it will be measured back to you. 3And why do you look at the speck in your brother's eye, but do not consider the plank in your own eye? 4Or how can you say to your brother, 'Let me remove the speck from your eye'; and look, a plank *is* in your own eye? 5Hypocrite! First remove the plank from your own eye, and then you will see clearly to remove the speck from your brother's eye.

6"Do not give what is holy to the dogs; nor cast your pearls before swine, lest they trample them under their feet, and turn and tear you in pieces.

Keep Asking, Seeking, Knocking

7"Ask, and it will be given to you; seek, and you will find; knock, and it will be opened to you. [8]For everyone who asks receives, and he who seeks finds, and to him who knocks it will be opened. [9]Or what man is there among you who, if his son asks for bread, will give him a stone? [10]Or if he asks for a fish, will he give him a serpent? [11]If you then, being evil, know how to give good gifts to your children, how much more will your Father who is in heaven give good things to those who ask Him! [12]Therefore, whatever you want men to do to you, do also to them, for this is the Law and the Prophets.

The Narrow Way

[13]"Enter by the narrow gate; for wide *is* the gate and broad *is* the way that leads to destruction, and there are many who go in by it. [14]Because[a] narrow *is* the gate and difficult *is* the way which leads to life, and there are few who find it.

You Will Know Them by Their Fruits

[15]"Beware of false prophets, who come to you in sheep's clothing, but inwardly they are ravenous wolves. [16]You will know them by their fruits. Do men gather grapes from thornbushes or figs from thistles? [17]Even so, every good tree bears good fruit, but a bad tree bears bad fruit. [18]A good tree cannot bear bad fruit, nor *can* a bad tree bear good fruit. [19]Every tree that does not bear good fruit is cut down and thrown into the fire. [20]Therefore by their fruits you will know them.

I Never Knew You

[21]"Not everyone who says to Me, 'Lord, Lord,' shall enter the kingdom of heaven, but he who does the will of My Father in heaven. [22]Many will say to Me in that day, 'Lord, Lord, have we not prophesied in Your name, cast out demons in Your name, and done many wonders in Your name?' [23]And then I will declare to them, 'I never knew you; depart from Me, you who practice lawlessness!'

Build on the Rock

[24]"Therefore whoever hears these sayings of Mine, and does them, I will liken him to a wise man who built his house on the rock: [25]and the rain descended, the floods came, and the winds blew and beat on that house; and it did not fall, for it was founded on the rock.

[26]"But everyone who hears these sayings of Mine, and does not do them, will be like a foolish man who built his house on the sand: [27]and the rain descended, the floods came, and the winds blew and beat on that house; and it fell. And great was its fall."

[28]And so it was, when Jesus had ended these sayings, that the people were astonished at His teaching, [29]for He taught them as one having authority, and not as the scribes.

Jesus Cleanses a Leper

8 When He had come down from the mountain, great multitudes followed Him. [2]And behold, a leper came and worshiped Him, saying, "Lord, if You are willing, You can make me clean."

[3]Then Jesus put out *His* hand and touched him, saying, "I am willing; be cleansed." Immediately his leprosy was cleansed.

[4]And Jesus said to him, "See that you tell no one; but go your way, show yourself to the priest, and offer the gift that Moses commanded, as a testimony to them."

Jesus Heals a Centurion's Servant

[5]Now when Jesus had entered Capernaum, a centurion came to Him, pleading with Him, [6]saying, "Lord, my servant is lying at home paralyzed, dreadfully tormented."

The Centurion Teaches a Lesson on Authority

(Matthew 8:5–13)

The centurion who asked Jesus to heal his servant clearly understood authority. In the same way that he commanded soldiers under his charge, he knew Jesus could command diseases. When leaders possess authority, their words carry weight. How much weight do your words carry? Who listens to you?

---

[7]And Jesus said to him, "I will come and heal him."

[8]The centurion answered and said, "Lord, I am not worthy that You should come under my roof. But only speak a word, and my servant will be healed. [9]For I also am a man under authority, having soldiers under me. And I say to this *one,* 'Go,' and he goes; and to another, 'Come,' and he comes; and to my servant, 'Do this,' and he does *it.*"

[10]When Jesus heard *it,* He marveled, and said

7:14 [a]NU-Text and M-Text read *How . . . !*

to those who followed, "Assuredly, I say to you, I have not found such great faith, not even in Israel! ¹¹And I say to you that many will come from east and west, and sit down with Abraham, Isaac, and Jacob in the kingdom of heaven. ¹²But the sons of the kingdom will be cast out into outer darkness. There will be weeping and gnashing of teeth." ¹³Then Jesus said to the centurion, "Go your way; and as you have believed, *so* let it be done for you." And his servant was healed that same hour.

Peter's Mother-in-Law Healed

¹⁴Now when Jesus had come into Peter's house, He saw his wife's mother lying sick with a fever. ¹⁵So He touched her hand, and the fever left her. And she arose and served them.ᵃ

Many Healed in the Evening

¹⁶When evening had come, they brought to Him many who were demon-possessed. And He cast out the spirits with a word, and healed all who were sick, ¹⁷that it might be fulfilled which was spoken by Isaiah the prophet, saying:

"*He Himself took our infirmities*
And bore our sicknesses."ᵃ

The Cost of Discipleship

¹⁸And when Jesus saw great multitudes about Him, He gave a command to depart to the other side. ¹⁹Then a certain scribe came and said to Him, "Teacher, I will follow You wherever You go."

²⁰And Jesus said to him, "Foxes have holes and birds of the air *have* nests, but the Son of Man has nowhere to lay *His* head."

²¹Then another of His disciples said to Him, "Lord, let me first go and bury my father."

²²But Jesus said to him, "Follow Me, and let the dead bury their own dead."

Wind and Wave Obey Jesus

²³Now when He got into a boat, His disciples followed Him. ²⁴And suddenly a great tempest arose on the sea, so that the boat was covered with the waves. But He was asleep. ²⁵Then His disciples came to *Him* and awoke Him, saying, "Lord, save us! We are perishing!"

²⁶But He said to them, "Why are you fearful, O you of little faith?" Then He arose and rebuked the winds and the sea, and there was a great calm. ²⁷So the men marveled, saying, "Who can this be, that even the winds and the sea obey Him?"

Commitment: What All Leaders Must Demonstrate and Draw

(Matthew 8:18–34)

Jesus issues tough challenges to potential followers about what it means to follow Him. He questions His disciples' wavering faith when they fear a storm. It is as if He were screening His audience and testing their level of commitment to Him and to the kingdom.

Jesus never begged anyone to follow Him. In fact, He often sifted through His followers to see what they were made of and where they stood. No good leader is afraid to do this. Look at how Jesus did it:

1. Jesus' **clarification** of our commitment (vv. 18–22)
   When He saw the crowd, He knew it was time to clarify the cost of following Him.
2. Jesus' **credibility** for our commitment (vv. 23–27)
   After the clarification, He demonstrated good reason to follow Him by His miracles.
3. Jesus' **challenge** for our commitment (vv. 28–34)
   In Gadara, He divided the cautious, the curious, and the committed.

Two Demon-Possessed Men Healed

²⁸When He had come to the other side, to the country of the Gergesenes,ᵃ there met Him two demon-possessed *men,* coming out of the tombs, exceedingly fierce, so that no one could pass that way. ²⁹And suddenly they cried out, saying, "What have we to do with You, Jesus, You Son of God? Have You come here to torment us before the time?"

³⁰Now a good way off from them there was a herd of many swine feeding. ³¹So the demons begged Him, saying, "If You cast us out, permit us to go awayᵃ into the herd of swine."

³²And He said to them, "Go." So when they had come out, they went into the herd of swine. And suddenly the whole herd of swine ran vio-

---

8:15 ᵃNU-Text and M-Text read *Him.* **8:17** ᵃIsaiah 53:4 **8:28** ᵃNU-Text reads *Gadarenes.* **8:31** ᵃNU-Text reads *send us.*

lently down the steep place into the sea, and perished in the water.

[33]Then those who kept *them* fled; and they went away into the city and told everything, including what *had happened* to the demon-possessed *men*. [34]And behold, the whole city came out to meet Jesus. And when they saw Him, they begged *Him* to depart from their region.

Jesus Forgives and Heals a Paralytic

9 So He got into a boat, crossed over, and came to His own city. [2]Then behold, they brought to Him a paralytic lying on a bed. When Jesus saw their faith, He said to the paralytic, "Son, be of good cheer; your sins are forgiven you."

[3]And at once some of the scribes said within themselves, "This Man blasphemes!"

[4]But Jesus, knowing their thoughts, said, "Why do you think evil in your hearts? [5]For which is easier, to say, *'Your* sins are forgiven you,' or to say, 'Arise and walk'? [6]But that you may know that the Son of Man has power on earth to forgive sins"—then He said to the paralytic, "Arise, take up your bed, and go to your house." [7]And he arose and departed to his house.

[8]Now when the multitudes saw *it,* they marveled[a] and glorified God, who had given such power to men.

Matthew the Tax Collector

[9]As Jesus passed on from there, He saw a man named Matthew sitting at the tax office. And He said to him, "Follow Me." So he arose and followed Him.

[10]Now it happened, as Jesus sat at the table in the house, *that* behold, many tax collectors and sinners came and sat down with Him and His disciples. [11]And when the Pharisees saw *it,* they said to His disciples, "Why does your Teacher eat with tax collectors and sinners?"

[12]When Jesus heard *that,* He said to them, "Those who are well have no need of a physician, but those who are sick. [13]But go and learn what *this* means: *'I desire mercy and not sacrifice.'*[a] For I did not come to call the righteous, but sinners, to repentance."[b]

Jesus Is Questioned About Fasting

[14]Then the disciples of John came to Him, saying, "Why do we and the Pharisees fast often,[a] but Your disciples do not fast?"

[15]And Jesus said to them, "Can the friends of the bridegroom mourn as long as the bridegroom is with them? But the days will come when the bridegroom will be taken away from them, and then they will fast. [16]No one puts a piece of unshrunk cloth on an old garment; for the patch pulls away from the garment, and the tear is made worse. [17]Nor do they put new wine into old wineskins, or else the wineskins break, the wine is spilled, and the wineskins are ruined. But they put new wine into new wineskins, and both are preserved."

A Girl Restored to Life and a Woman Healed

[18]While He spoke these things to them, behold, a ruler came and worshiped Him, saying, "My daughter has just died, but come and lay Your hand on her and she will live." [19]So Jesus arose and followed him, and so *did* His disciples.

[20]And suddenly, a woman who had a flow of blood for twelve years came from behind and touched the hem of His garment. [21]For she said to herself, "If only I may touch His garment, I shall be made well." [22]But Jesus turned around,

---

9:8 [a]NU-Text reads *were afraid.* **9:13** [a]Hosea 6:6
[b]NU-Text omits *to repentance.* **9:14** [a]NU-Text brackets *often* as disputed.

The Law of Intuition: Jesus' Diagnosis and Prescription

(Matthew 9:35–38)

The Ultimate Leader teaches us about the divine order of capturing and casting a vision. Leaders often err by flitting from vision to vision. Why? Because they fail to take the time to become burdened over a need. Burden always comes first; then vision. Consider the order we see in Jesus' leadership:

1. *He sought a need:* As Jesus traveled the villages, He saw their needs (vv. 35, 36).
2. *He bought a burden:* He diagnosed the problem: "I need more workers" (v. 37).
3. *He caught a vision:* He gave a prescription for the burden (v. 38).

Leaders remain relevant only as they meet real needs. Consequently, we must pause long enough to observe needs, then feel the tug of a burden. Finally, we must catch a vision that will address the burden.

and when He saw her He said, "Be of good cheer, daughter; your faith has made you well." And the woman was made well from that hour.

²³When Jesus came into the ruler's house, and saw the flute players and the noisy crowd wailing, ²⁴He said to them, "Make room, for the girl is not dead, but sleeping." And they ridiculed Him. ²⁵But when the crowd was put outside, He went in and took her by the hand, and the girl arose. ²⁶And the report of this went out into all that land.

Two Blind Men Healed

²⁷When Jesus departed from there, two blind men followed Him, crying out and saying, "Son of David, have mercy on us!"

²⁸And when He had come into the house, the blind men came to Him. And Jesus said to them, "Do you believe that I am able to do this?"

They said to Him, "Yes, Lord."

²⁹Then He touched their eyes, saying, "According to your faith let it be to you." ³⁰And their eyes were opened. And Jesus sternly warned them, saying, "See *that* no one knows *it*." ³¹But when they had departed, they spread the news about Him in all that country.

A Mute Man Speaks

³²As they went out, behold, they brought to Him a man, mute and demon-possessed. ³³And when the demon was cast out, the mute spoke. And the multitudes marveled, saying, "It was never seen like this in Israel!"

³⁴But the Pharisees said, "He casts out demons by the ruler of the demons."

The Compassion of Jesus

³⁵Then Jesus went about all the cities and villages, teaching in their synagogues, preaching the gospel of the kingdom, and healing every sickness and every disease among the people.ª ³⁶But when He saw the multitudes, He was moved with compassion for them, because they were wearyª and scattered, like sheep having no shepherd. ³⁷Then He said to His disciples, "The harvest truly *is* plentiful, but the laborers *are* few. ³⁸Therefore pray the Lord of the harvest to send out laborers into His harvest."

9:35 ªNU-Text omits *among the people.* **9:36** ªNU-Text and M-Text read *harassed.*

Vision: The Process Toward Fulfilling a God-Given Vision

(Matthew 9:35—10:5)

Jesus teaches us the process of fulfilling a God-given vision. Study this passage and watch for these steps:

1. *Take initiative to obey.* Get active in service.
   "Jesus went about all the cities and villages . . ." (9:35).
2. *Communicate the truth you have already.*
   ". . . teaching in their synagogues [and] preaching the gospel of the kingdom" (9:35).
3. *Observe and understand the reality of human conditions.*
   "But when He saw the multitudes . . ." (9:36).
4. *Allow God to burden you with a specific need.*
   "He was moved with compassion for them, because they were . . . like sheep having no shepherd" (9:36).
5. *See a divine diagnosis.* What is the issue to be resolved?
   "The harvest truly is plentiful, but the laborers are few" (9:37).
6. *Pray to determine what action could meet that need.*
   "Therefore pray the Lord of the harvest to send out laborers into His harvest" (9:38).
7. *Choose a team and empower them for partnership.*
   "And when He had called His twelve disciples to Him, He gave them power . . ." (10:1).
8. *Take immediate action toward the fulfillment of the vision.*
   "These twelve Jesus sent out . . ." (10:5).

The Twelve Apostles

10 And when He had called His twelve disciples to *Him,* He gave them power *over* unclean spirits, to cast them out, and to heal all kinds of sickness and all kinds of disease. ²Now the names of the twelve apostles are these: first, Simon, who is called Peter, and Andrew his brother; James the *son* of Zebedee, and John his brother; ³Philip and Bartholomew; Thomas and Matthew the tax collector; James the *son* of Alphaeus, and Lebbaeus, whose surname was^a Thaddaeus; ⁴Simon the Cananite,^a and Judas Iscariot, who also betrayed Him.

Sending Out the Twelve

⁵These twelve Jesus sent out and commanded them, saying: "Do not go into the way of the Gentiles, and do not enter a city of the Samaritans. ⁶But go rather to the lost sheep of the house of Israel. ⁷And as you go, preach, saying, 'The kingdom of heaven is at hand.' ⁸Heal the sick, cleanse the lepers, raise the dead,^a cast out demons. Freely you have received, freely give. ⁹Provide neither gold nor silver nor copper in your money belts, ¹⁰nor bag for *your* journey, nor two tunics, nor sandals, nor staffs; for a worker is worthy of his food.

¹¹"Now whatever city or town you enter, inquire who in it is worthy, and stay there till you go out. ¹²And when you go into a household, greet it. ¹³If the household is worthy, let your peace come upon it. But if it is not worthy, let your peace return to you. ¹⁴And whoever will not receive you nor hear your words, when you depart from that house or city, shake off the dust from your feet. ¹⁵Assuredly, I say to you, it will be more tolerable for the land of Sodom and Gomorrah in the day of judgment than for that city!

Persecutions Are Coming

¹⁶"Behold, I send you out as sheep in the midst of wolves. Therefore be wise as serpents and harmless as doves. ¹⁷But beware of men, for they will deliver you up to councils and scourge

---

10:3 ^aNU-Text omits *Lebbaeus, whose surname was.* **10:4** ^aNU-Text reads *Cananaean.* **10:8** ^aNU-Text reads *raise the dead, cleanse the lepers;* M-Text omits *raise the dead.*

The Law of Empowerment: Jesus Gave Power Away . . . and Multiplied His Influence
(Matthew 10:1–15)

Effective leadership attracts and brokers the talents of others. Leaders must develop others to reach their potential. No one did this better than Jesus.

In Matthew 10 we see the results of Jesus' vision for more workers (9:37, 38). Even though He has not finished training His disciples, He sent them out to exercise their gifts.

So it is with our people. At some point we need to end the lecture and send them out to try what they have learned. Consider how Jesus empowered His twelve-man staff:

1. *A personal call* (vv. 1–4)
   Jesus selected them and called them by name.
2. *A direct commission* (v. 5)
   After instructing them, He sent them out.
3. *A central objective* (vv. 5, 6)
   He told them to go to the Hebrews, not the Gentiles.
4. *A clear message* (v. 7)
   He gave them the specific message.
5. *Practical credentials* (v. 8)
   He equipped them to gain credibility by giving them tools to confirm their message.
6. *Confidence for provision* (vv. 9, 10)
   He instilled confidence and gave them a plan to acquire needed resources.
7. *Solid convictions* (vv. 11–15)
   He furnished convictions on how they were to act with both friends and critics.

you in their synagogues. [18]You will be brought before governors and kings for My sake, as a testimony to them and to the Gentiles. [19]But when they deliver you up, do not worry about how or what you should speak. For it will be given to you in that hour what you should speak; [20]for it is not you who speak, but the Spirit of your Father who speaks in you.

[21]"Now brother will deliver up brother to death, and a father *his* child; and children will rise up against parents and cause them to be put to death. [22]And you will be hated by all for My name's sake. But he who endures to the end will be saved. [23]When they persecute you in this city, flee to another. For assuredly, I say to you, you will not have gone through the cities of Israel before the Son of Man comes.

[24]"A disciple is not above *his* teacher, nor a servant above his master. [25]It is enough for a disciple that he be like his teacher, and a servant like his master. If they have called the master of the house Beelzebub,[a] how much more *will they call* those of his household! [26]Therefore do not fear them. For there is nothing covered that will not be revealed, and hidden that will not be known.

Jesus Teaches the Fear of God

[27]"Whatever I tell you in the dark, speak in the light; and what you hear in the ear, preach on the housetops. [28]And do not fear those who kill the body but cannot kill the soul. But rather fear Him who is able to destroy both soul and body in hell. [29]Are not two sparrows sold for a copper coin? And not one of them falls to the ground apart from your Father's will. [30]But the very hairs of your head are all numbered. [31]Do not fear therefore; you are of more value than many sparrows.

Confess Christ Before Men

[32]"Therefore whoever confesses Me before men, him I will also confess before My Father who is in heaven. [33]But whoever denies Me before men, him I will also deny before My Father who is in heaven.

Christ Brings Division

[34]"Do not think that I came to bring peace on earth. I did not come to bring peace but a sword. [35]For I have come to '*set a man against his father, a daughter against her mother, and a daughter-in-law against her mother-in-law*'; [36]and '*a man's enemies will be those of his own household.*'[a] [37]He who loves father or mother more than Me is not worthy of Me. And he who

10:25 [a]NU-Text and M-Text read *Beelzebul.*
10:36 [a]Micah 7:6

The Law of Reproduction: Jesus Prepared Leaders for the Future

(Matthew 10:16–33)

Jesus not only sends out His twelve disciples to serve, but He reminds them that He intends to reproduce His own leadership in them. As part of the preparation process, He instructs them on what is coming:

1. He challenges them to be wise, but innocent (v. 16).
2. He warns them about future hardships (vv. 17, 18).
3. He instructs them on how to handle these hardships (vv. 19, 20).
4. He predicts their personal anguish (vv. 21, 22).
5. He gives them hope and assurance of ultimate victory (v. 23).

Jesus also clarifies the meaning of discipleship. He continues to prepare His men for any contingency. From the perspective of an equipper, consider what Jesus teaches trainers and trainees about leadership development:

1. Trainees should submit to the authority of the trainer (v. 24).
2. Trainees must recognize that trainers can reproduce only what they are (v. 25).
3. Trainees are to emulate their master (v. 25).
4. Trainees must trust God to care for their needs (vv. 26–31).
5. Trainees are to be loyal (vv. 32, 33).

loves son or daughter more than Me is not worthy of Me. [38]And he who does not take his cross and follow after Me is not worthy of Me. [39]He who finds his life will lose it, and he who loses his life for My sake will find it.

A Cup of Cold Water

[40]"He who receives you receives Me, and he who receives Me receives Him who sent Me. [41]He who receives a prophet in the name of a prophet shall receive a prophet's reward. And he who receives a righteous man in the name of a righteous man shall receive a righteous man's reward. [42]And whoever gives one of these little ones only a cup of cold water in the name of a disciple, assuredly, I say to you, he shall by no means lose his reward."

John the Baptist Sends Messengers to Jesus

11 Now it came to pass, when Jesus finished commanding His twelve disciples, that He departed from there to teach and to preach in their cities.

[2]And when John had heard in prison about the works of Christ, he sent two of[a] his disciples [3]and said to Him, "Are You the Coming One, or do we look for another?"

The Law of the Inner Circle: John Feels the Vacuum of Isolation

(Matthew 11:2, 3)

When John loses his inner circle of disciples, his empty emotional tank prompts him to question Jesus' identity and credentials. Leaders need a close team of associates who allow the leader to vent, and who lend support through speaking words of truth. Do you have an inner circle?

---

[4]Jesus answered and said to them, "Go and tell John the things which you hear and see: [5]The blind see and the lame walk; the lepers are cleansed and the deaf hear; the dead are raised up and the poor have the gospel preached to them. [6]And blessed is he who is not offended because of Me."

[7]As they departed, Jesus began to say to the multitudes concerning John: "What did you go out into the wilderness to see? A reed shaken by the wind? [8]But what did you go out to see? A man clothed in soft garments? Indeed, those who wear soft clothing are in kings' houses. [9]But what did you go out to see? A prophet? Yes, I say to you, and more than a prophet. [10]For this is he of whom it is written:

'Behold, I send My messenger before Your face,
    Who will prepare Your way before You.'[a]

[11]"Assuredly, I say to you, among those born of women there has not risen one greater than John the Baptist; but he who is least in the kingdom of heaven is greater than he. [12]And from the days of John the Baptist until now the kingdom of heaven suffers violence, and the violent take it by force. [13]For all the prophets and the law prophesied until John. [14]And if you are willing to receive it, he is Elijah who is to come. [15]He who has ears to hear, let him hear!

[16]"But to what shall I liken this generation? It is like children sitting in the marketplaces and calling to their companions, [17]and saying:

'We played the flute for you,
    And you did not dance;
We mourned to you,
    And you did not lament.'

[18]For John came neither eating nor drinking, and they say, 'He has a demon.' [19]The Son of Man came eating and drinking, and they say, 'Look, a glutton and a winebibber, a friend of tax collectors and sinners!' But wisdom is justified by her children."[a]

Woe to the Impenitent Cities

[20]Then He began to rebuke the cities in which most of His mighty works had been done, because they did not repent: [21]"Woe to you, Chorazin! Woe to you, Bethsaida! For if the mighty works which were done in you had been done in Tyre and Sidon, they would have repented long ago in sackcloth and ashes. [22]But I say to you, it will be more tolerable for Tyre and Sidon in the day of judgment than for you. [23]And you, Capernaum, who are exalted to heaven, will be[a] brought down to Hades; for if the mighty works which were done in you had been done in Sodom, it would have remained until this day. [24]But I say to you that it shall be more tolerable for the land of Sodom in the day of judgment than for you."

11:2 [a]NU-Text reads by for two of. **11:10** [a]Malachi 3:1 **11:19** [a]NU-Text reads works. **11:23** [a]NU-Text reads will you be exalted to heaven? No, you will be.

Jesus Gives True Rest

[25]At that time Jesus answered and said, "I thank You, Father, Lord of heaven and earth, that You have hidden these things from *the* wise and prudent and have revealed them to babes. [26]Even so, Father, for so it seemed good in Your sight. [27]All things have been delivered to Me by My Father, and no one knows the Son except the Father. Nor does anyone know the Father except the Son, and *the one* to whom the Son wills to reveal *Him.* [28]Come to Me, all *you* who labor and are heavy laden, and I will give you rest. [29]Take My yoke upon you and learn from Me, for I am gentle and lowly in heart, and you will find rest for your souls. [30]For My yoke *is* easy and My burden is light."

The Law of Empowerment: Jesus Touches Hearts First

(Matthew 11:28–30)

Although Jesus puts His early disciples to work, He knows He has to touch their hearts before He asks for their hands. So He promises to give them rest.

The word "rest" refers to an inward holiday—not a cessation of activity, but a whole new energy and motive. Many of us are more active on vacation than at work; what changes is our reason for activity. We feel energized on vacation because we *want* to do certain things. Jesus describes a new relationship that changes us on the inside. Note what He promises to give us:

1. *Rest:* an inward rest, free from anxieties (v. 28)
2. *Framework:* a yoke, by which we are guided by a stronger partner (v. 29)
3. *Gentle and humble leadership:* an understanding leader who meets our needs (v. 29)
4. *A manageable load:* a system and workload that fits who we are (v. 30)

Jesus Is Lord of the Sabbath

12 At that time Jesus went through the grainfields on the Sabbath. And His disciples were hungry, and began to pluck heads of grain and to eat. [2]And when the Pharisees saw *it,* they said to Him, "Look, Your disciples are doing what is not lawful to do on the Sabbath!"

[3]But He said to them, "Have you not read what David did when he was hungry, he and those who were with him: [4]how he entered the house of God and ate the showbread which was not lawful for him to eat, nor for those who were with him, but only for the priests? [5]Or have you not read in the law that on the Sabbath the priests in the temple profane the Sabbath, and are blameless? [6]Yet I say to you that in this place there is *One* greater than the temple. [7]But if you had known what *this* means, '*I desire mercy and not sacrifice,*'[a] you would not have condemned the guiltless. [8]For the Son of Man is Lord even[a] of the Sabbath."

Healing on the Sabbath

[9]Now when He had departed from there, He went into their synagogue. [10]And behold, there was a man who had a withered hand. And they asked Him, saying, "Is it lawful to heal on the Sabbath?"—that they might accuse Him.

[11]Then He said to them, "What man is there among you who has one sheep, and if it falls into a pit on the Sabbath, will not lay hold of it and lift *it* out? [12]Of how much more value then is a man than a sheep? Therefore it is lawful to do good on the Sabbath." [13]Then He said to the man, "Stretch out your hand." And he stretched *it* out, and it was restored as whole as the other. [14]Then the Pharisees went out and plotted against Him, how they might destroy Him.

Behold, My Servant

[15]But when Jesus knew *it,* He withdrew from there. And great multitudes[a] followed Him, and He healed them all. [16]Yet He warned them not to make Him known, [17]that it might be fulfilled which was spoken by Isaiah the prophet, saying:

[18] "*Behold! My Servant whom I have chosen,*
　　My Beloved in whom My soul is well
　　　pleased!
　I will put My Spirit upon Him,
　And He will declare justice to the Gentiles.
[19] *He will not quarrel nor cry out,*
　Nor will anyone hear His voice in the streets.
[20] *A bruised reed He will not break,*
　And smoking flax He will not quench,
　Till He sends forth justice to victory;
[21] *And in His name Gentiles will trust.*"[a]

12:7 [a]Hosea 6:6 **12:8** [a]NU-Text and M-Text omit *even.* **12:15** [a]NU-Text brackets *multitudes* as disputed. **12:21** [a]Isaiah 42:1–4

A House Divided Cannot Stand

22Then one was brought to Him who was demon-possessed, blind and mute; and He healed him, so that the blind anda mute man both spoke and saw. 23And all the multitudes were amazed and said, "Could this be the Son of David?"

24Now when the Pharisees heard *it* they said, "This *fellow* does not cast out demons except by Beelzebub,a the ruler of the demons."

25But Jesus knew their thoughts, and said to them: "Every kingdom divided against itself is brought to desolation, and every city or house divided against itself will not stand. 26If Satan casts out Satan, he is divided against himself. How then will his kingdom stand? 27And if I cast out demons by Beelzebub, by whom do your sons cast *them* out? Therefore they shall be your judges. 28But if I cast out demons by the Spirit of God, surely the kingdom of God has come upon you. 29Or how can one enter a strong man's house and plunder his goods, unless he first binds the strong man? And then he will plunder his house. 30He who is not with Me is against Me, and he who does not gather with Me scatters abroad.

The Unpardonable Sin

31"Therefore I say to you, every sin and blasphemy will be forgiven men, but the blasphemy *against* the Spirit will not be forgiven men. 32Anyone who speaks a word against the Son of Man, it will be forgiven him; but whoever speaks against the Holy Spirit, it will not be forgiven him, either in this age or in the *age* to come.

A Tree Known by Its Fruit

33"Either make the tree good and its fruit good, or else make the tree bad and its fruit bad; for a tree is known by *its* fruit. 34Brood of vipers! How can you, being evil, speak good things? For out of the abundance of the heart the mouth speaks. 35A good man out of the good treasure of his hearta brings forth good things, and an evil man out of the evil treasure brings forth evil things. 36But I say to you that for every idle word men may speak, they will give account of it in the day of judgment. 37For by your words you will be justified, and by your words you will be condemned."

The Scribes and Pharisees Ask for a Sign

38Then some of the scribes and Pharisees answered, saying, "Teacher, we want to see a sign from You."

Communication: Words Carry a Thought and Shape a Destiny

(Matthew 12:33–37)

Jesus teaches us the centrality of communication. Like an echo of Proverbs 18:21, the Ultimate Leader helps us see that words carry the power of life and death:

1. Words transmit power (vv. 33–37).
2. Words reveal our character (vv. 33–35).
3. Words determine our reward and judgment (vv. 36, 37).
4. Words produce fruit (vv. 33, 35, 36).
5. Words shape our destiny (v. 37).

Leaders must never forget the power of their words. God shaped the universe with His words (Gen. 1; 2). He sustains His creation with His Word (Heb. 1:3). He even performs miracles through the use of words (Rom. 4:17). What's more, God designed us to accomplish things by the wise use of our words.

39But He answered and said to them, "An evil and adulterous generation seeks after a sign, and no sign will be given to it except the sign of the prophet Jonah. 40For as Jonah was three days and three nights in the belly of the great fish, so will the Son of Man be three days and three nights in the heart of the earth. 41The men of Nineveh will rise up in the judgment with this generation and condemn it, because they repented at the preaching of Jonah; and indeed a greater than Jonah *is* here. 42The queen of the South will rise up in the judgment with this generation and condemn it, for she came from the ends of the earth to hear the wisdom of Solomon; and indeed a greater than Solomon *is* here.

An Unclean Spirit Returns

43"When an unclean spirit goes out of a man, he goes through dry places, seeking rest, and finds none. 44Then he says, 'I will return to my house from which I came.' And when he comes, he finds *it* empty, swept, and put in order. 45Then

---

12:22 aNU-Text omits *blind and.* **12:24** aNU-Text and M-Text read *Beelzebul.* **12:35** aNU-Text and M-Text omit *of his heart.*

he goes and takes with him seven other spirits more wicked than himself, and they enter and dwell there; and the last *state* of that man is worse than the first. So shall it also be with this wicked generation."

Jesus' Mother and Brothers Send for Him

⁴⁶While He was still talking to the multitudes, behold, His mother and brothers stood outside, seeking to speak with Him. ⁴⁷Then one said to Him, "Look, Your mother and Your brothers are standing outside, seeking to speak with You."

⁴⁸But He answered and said to the one who told Him, "Who is My mother and who are My brothers?" ⁴⁹And He stretched out His hand toward His disciples and said, "Here are My mother and My brothers! ⁵⁰For whoever does the will of My Father in heaven is My brother and sister and mother."

The Parable of the Sower

13 On the same day Jesus went out of the house and sat by the sea. ²And great multitudes were gathered together to Him, so that He got into a boat and sat; and the whole multitude stood on the shore.

³Then He spoke many things to them in parables, saying: "Behold, a sower went out to sow. ⁴And as he sowed, some *seed* fell by the wayside; and the birds came and devoured them. ⁵Some fell on stony places, where they did not have much earth; and they immediately sprang up because they had no depth of earth. ⁶But when the sun was up they were scorched, and because they had no root they withered away. ⁷And some fell among thorns, and the thorns sprang up and choked them. ⁸But others fell on good ground and yielded a crop: some a hundredfold, some sixty, some thirty. ⁹He who has ears to hear, let him hear!"

The Purpose of Parables

¹⁰And the disciples came and said to Him, "Why do You speak to them in parables?"

¹¹He answered and said to them, "Because it has been given to you to know the mysteries of the kingdom of heaven, but to them it has not been given. ¹²For whoever has, to him more will be given, and he will have abundance; but whoever does not have, even what he has will be taken away from him. ¹³Therefore I speak to them in parables, because seeing they do not see, and hearing they do not hear, nor do they

---

JESUS

An Unwavering Commitment to Speak the Truth

(Matthew 12:22—13:53)

PROFILE IN LEADERSHIP

The apostle Matthew knew Jesus—after all, he had accepted Christ's invitation to leave his life as a tax collector to follow Him. But the Savior's commitment to speaking truth must have amazed even Matthew.

In a single day, Jesus chided the religious leaders for their insistence on seeing signs; He told His own mother that His true family consisted of all those who obey God; then He told a great crowd of people some revolutionary ideas about the kingdom of God.

This tax-collector-turned-disciple recognized Jesus as the kind of leader who spoke the Word of God with great conviction and authority, but who also spoke in such a way that only those who truly desired to know the truth could discern His meaning. He recognized Christ as the kind of leader who didn't necessarily say what the people *wanted* to hear, but one who always said what they *needed* to hear.

Not everyone who heard Jesus' words understood and applied them. Some eagerly received His truth, while the hearts of others had grown too hard to hear Him.

As it was then, so it is today. Nevertheless, it is not the leader's job to prepare human hearts to receive God's truth. Rather, it is his or her responsibility to speak that same truth with all the authority He has given His servants.

understand. [14]And in them the prophecy of Isaiah is fulfilled, which says:

> 'Hearing you will hear and shall not
>   understand,
> And seeing you will see and not perceive;
> [15] For the hearts of this people have grown
>   dull.
> Their ears are hard of hearing,
> And their eyes they have closed,
> Lest they should see with their eyes and
>   hear with their ears,
> Lest they should understand with their
>   hearts and turn,
> So that I should[a] heal them.'[b]

[16]But blessed *are* your eyes for they see, and your ears for they hear; [17]for assuredly, I say to you that many prophets and righteous *men* desired to see what you see, and did not see *it,* and to hear what you hear, and did not hear *it.*

The Parable of the Sower Explained

[18]"Therefore hear the parable of the sower: [19]When anyone hears the word of the kingdom, and does not understand *it,* then the wicked *one* comes and snatches away what was sown in his heart. This is he who received seed by the wayside. [20]But he who received the seed on stony places, this is he who hears the word and immediately receives it with joy; [21]yet he has no root in himself, but endures only for a while. For when tribulation or persecution arises because of the word, immediately he stumbles. [22]Now he who received seed among the thorns is he who hears the word, and the cares of this world and the deceitfulness of riches choke the word, and he becomes unfruitful. [23]But he who received seed on the good ground is he who hears the word and understands *it,* who indeed bears fruit and produces: some a hundredfold, some sixty, some thirty."

The Parable of the Wheat and the Tares

[24]Another parable He put forth to them, saying: "The kingdom of heaven is like a man who sowed good seed in his field; [25]but while men slept, his enemy came and sowed tares among the wheat and went his way. [26]But when the grain had sprouted and produced a crop, then the tares also appeared. [27]So the servants of the owner came and said to him, 'Sir, did you not sow good seed in your field? How then does it have tares?' [28]He said to them, 'An enemy has done this.' The servants said to him, 'Do you want us then to go and gather them up?' [29]But he said, 'No, lest while you gather up the tares you also uproot the wheat with them. [30]Let both grow together until the harvest, and at the time of harvest I will say to the reapers, "First gather together the tares and bind them in bundles to burn them, but gather the wheat into my barn."'"

Communicating Vision: Jesus Defined a Mission Larger Than Life

(Matthew 13:3–58)

Matthew 13 contains some of Jesus' simplest but most profound parables in the Bible. Jesus is a Master at communicating vision. His simple stories illustrate the kingdom of heaven. Jesus teaches us some fundamentals about communicating a vision:

1. *Simplify the message* (vv. 3, 10–13). Make it clear, repeat it often, focus on the familiar.
2. *See the person* (vv. 1, 2, 9). Know the audience and its needs; don't try to impress.
3. *Seize the moment* (vv. 2, 14–17). Recognize teachable moments and receptivity.
4. *Show the truth* (v. 54). Be sure your life lends credibility to your words.
5. *See the response* (v. 51). Evaluate to ensure the audience understands and can respond to you.

The Parable of the Mustard Seed

[31]Another parable He put forth to them, saying: "The kingdom of heaven is like a mustard seed, which a man took and sowed in his field, [32]which indeed is the least of all the seeds; but when it is grown it is greater than the herbs and becomes a tree, so that the birds of the air come and nest in its branches."

The Parable of the Leaven

[33]Another parable He spoke to them: "The kingdom of heaven is like leaven, which a woman took and hid in three measures[a] of meal till it was all leavened."

13:15 [a]NU-Text and M-Text read *would.* [b]Isaiah 6:9, 10 **13:33** [a]Greek *sata,* approximately two pecks in all

Prophecy and the Parables

³⁴All these things Jesus spoke to the multitude in parables; and without a parable He did not speak to them, ³⁵that it might be fulfilled which was spoken by the prophet, saying:

> *"I will open My mouth in parables;*
> *I will utter things kept secret from the*
> *foundation of the world."*ᵃ

The Parable of the Tares Explained

³⁶Then Jesus sent the multitude away and went into the house. And His disciples came to Him, saying, "Explain to us the parable of the tares of the field."

³⁷He answered and said to them: "He who sows the good seed is the Son of Man. ³⁸The field is the world, the good seeds are the sons of the kingdom, but the tares are the sons of the wicked *one*. ³⁹The enemy who sowed them is the devil, the harvest is the end of the age, and the reapers are the angels. ⁴⁰Therefore as the tares are gathered and burned in the fire, so it will be at the end of this age. ⁴¹The Son of Man will send out His angels, and they will gather out of His kingdom all things that offend, and those who practice lawlessness, ⁴²and will cast them into the furnace of fire. There will be wailing and gnashing of teeth. ⁴³Then the righteous will shine forth as the sun in the kingdom of their Father. He who has ears to hear, let him hear!

The Parable of the Hidden Treasure

⁴⁴"Again, the kingdom of heaven is like treasure hidden in a field, which a man found and hid; and for joy over it he goes and sells all that he has and buys that field.

The Parable of the Pearl of Great Price

⁴⁵"Again, the kingdom of heaven is like a merchant seeking beautiful pearls, ⁴⁶who, when he had found one pearl of great price, went and sold all that he had and bought it.

The Parable of the Dragnet

⁴⁷"Again, the kingdom of heaven is like a dragnet that was cast into the sea and gathered some of every kind, ⁴⁸which, when it was full, they drew to shore; and they sat down and gathered the good into vessels, but threw the bad away. ⁴⁹So it will be at the end of the age. The angels will come forth, separate the wicked from among the just, ⁵⁰and cast them into the furnace of fire. There will be wailing and gnashing of teeth."

⁵¹Jesus said to them,ᵃ "Have you understood all these things?"

They said to Him, "Yes, Lord."ᵇ

⁵²Then He said to them, "Therefore every scribe instructed concerningᵃ the kingdom of heaven is like a householder who brings out of his treasure *things* new and old."

Jesus Rejected at Nazareth

⁵³Now it came to pass, when Jesus had finished these parables, that He departed from there. ⁵⁴When He had come to His own country, He taught them in their synagogue, so that they were astonished and said, "Where did this *Man* get this wisdom and *these* mighty works? ⁵⁵Is this not the carpenter's son? Is not His mother called Mary? And His brothers James, Joses,ᵃ Simon, and Judas? ⁵⁶And His sisters, are they not all with us? Where then did this *Man* get all these things?" ⁵⁷So they were offended at Him.

But Jesus said to them, "A prophet is not without honor except in his own country and in his own house." ⁵⁸Now He did not do many mighty works there because of their unbelief.

John the Baptist Beheaded

14 At that time Herod the tetrarch heard the report about Jesus ²and said to his servants, "This is John the Baptist; he is risen from the dead, and therefore these powers are at work in him." ³For Herod had laid hold of John and bound him, and put *him* in prison for the sake of Herodias, his brother Philip's wife. ⁴Because John had said to him, "It is not lawful for you to have her." ⁵And although he wanted to put him to death, he feared the multitude, because they counted him as a prophet.

⁶But when Herod's birthday was celebrated, the daughter of Herodias danced before them and pleased Herod. ⁷Therefore he promised with an oath to give her whatever she might ask.

⁸So she, having been prompted by her mother, said, "Give me John the Baptist's head here on a platter."

⁹And the king was sorry; nevertheless, because of the oaths and because of those who sat with him, he commanded *it* to be given to *her*. ¹⁰So he sent and had John beheaded in prison. ¹¹And his head was brought on a platter and given to the girl, and she brought *it* to her mother. ¹²Then his disciples came and took away the body and buried it, and went and told Jesus.

13:35 ᵃPsalm 78:2 **13:51** ᵃNU-Text omits *Jesus said to them.* ᵇNU-Text omits *Lord.* **13:52** ᵃOr *for* **13:55** ᵃNU-Text reads *Joseph.*

Servanthood: Jesus Faced Difficulty by Putting Others First

(Matthew 14:1–14)

When Jesus hears about John's execution, He withdraws to be alone. John is His cousin and the only one who seems to understand Jesus' mission. Now he is gone. Jesus wants some quiet time to grieve and gain perspective. But does He get it? Not a chance. When the multitudes learn of His presence, they seek Him out, thinking only of their own needs.

This is often the lot of the leader. Jesus would have been justified in saying: "Can't you see I need some time away from all of you?" But He didn't. Instead, He responded by focusing on the needs of others. He felt compassion for the crowds and began to heal their sick.

One of the greatest remedies for our own suffering is serving others. Servant-leadership becomes a solution for both the one serving and the one being served.

Feeding the Five Thousand

[13]When Jesus heard *it,* He departed from there by boat to a deserted place by Himself. But when the multitudes heard it, they followed Him on foot from the cities. [14]And when Jesus went out He saw a great multitude; and He was moved with compassion for them, and healed their sick. [15]When it was evening, His disciples came to Him, saying, "This is a deserted place, and the hour is already late. Send the multitudes away, that they may go into the villages and buy themselves food."

[16]But Jesus said to them, "They do not need to go away. You give them something to eat."

[17]And they said to Him, "We have here only five loaves and two fish."

[18]He said, "Bring them here to Me." [19]Then He commanded the multitudes to sit down on the grass. And He took the five loaves and the two fish, and looking up to heaven, He blessed and broke and gave the loaves to the disciples; and the disciples gave to the multitudes. [20]So they all ate and were filled, and they took up twelve baskets full of the fragments that remained. [21]Now those who had eaten were about five thousand men, besides women and children.

Jesus Walks on the Sea

[22]Immediately Jesus made His disciples get into the boat and go before Him to the other side, while He sent the multitudes away. [23]And when He had sent the multitudes away, He went up on the mountain by Himself to pray. Now when evening came, He was alone there. [24]But the boat was now in the middle of the sea,[a] tossed by the waves, for the wind was contrary.

[25]Now in the fourth watch of the night Jesus went to them, walking on the sea. [26]And when the disciples saw Him walking on the sea, they were troubled, saying, "It is a ghost!" And they cried out for fear.

[27]But immediately Jesus spoke to them, saying, "Be of good cheer! It is I; do not be afraid."

[28]And Peter answered Him and said, "Lord, if it is You, command me to come to You on the water."

[29]So He said, "Come." And when Peter had come down out of the boat, he walked on the water to go to Jesus. [30]But when he saw that the wind *was* boisterous,[a] he was afraid; and beginning to sink he cried out, saying, "Lord, save me!"

[31]And immediately Jesus stretched out *His* hand and caught him, and said to him, "O you of little faith, why did you doubt?" [32]And when they got into the boat, the wind ceased.

[33]Then those who were in the boat came and[a] worshiped Him, saying, "Truly You are the Son of God."

Many Touch Him and Are Made Well

[34]When they had crossed over, they came to the land of[a] Gennesaret. [35]And when the men of that place recognized Him, they sent out into all that surrounding region, brought to Him all who were sick, [36]and begged Him that they might only touch the hem of His garment. And as many as touched *it* were made perfectly well.

Defilement Comes from Within

15 Then the scribes and Pharisees who were from Jerusalem came to Jesus, saying, [2]"Why do Your disciples transgress the tradition of the elders? For they do not wash their hands when they eat bread."

[3]He answered and said to them, "Why do you also transgress the commandment of God because of your tradition? [4]For God commanded,

---

14:24 [a]NU-Text reads *many furlongs away from the land.* **14:30** [a]NU-Text brackets *that* and *boisterous* as disputed. **14:33** [a]NU-Text omits *came and.* **14:34** [a]NU-Text reads *came to land at.*

saying, *'Honor your father and your mother'*;[a] and, *'He who curses father or mother, let him be put to death.'*[b] 5But you say, 'Whoever says to his father or mother, "Whatever profit you might have received from me *is* a gift *to God*"— 6then he need not honor his father or mother.'[a] Thus you have made the commandment[b] of God of no effect by your tradition. 7Hypocrites! Well did Isaiah prophesy about you, saying:

8   *'These people draw near to Me with their*
     mouth,
    And[a] *honor Me with their lips,*
    But their heart is far from Me.
9   *And in vain they worship Me,*
    Teaching as doctrines the commandments
    of men.' "[a]

10When He had called the multitude to *Himself*, He said to them, "Hear and understand: 11Not what goes into the mouth defiles a man; but what comes out of the mouth, this defiles a man."

12Then His disciples came and said to Him, "Do You know that the Pharisees were offended when they heard this saying?"

13But He answered and said, "Every plant which My heavenly Father has not planted will be uprooted. 14Let them alone. They are blind leaders of the blind. And if the blind leads the blind, both will fall into a ditch."

15Then Peter answered and said to Him, "Explain this parable to us."

16So Jesus said, "Are you also still without understanding? 17Do you not yet understand that whatever enters the mouth goes into the stomach and is eliminated? 18But those things which proceed out of the mouth come from the heart, and they defile a man. 19For out of the heart proceed evil thoughts, murders, adulteries, fornications, thefts, false witness, blasphemies. 20These are *the things* which defile a man, but to eat with unwashed hands does not defile a man."

A Gentile Shows Her Faith

21Then Jesus went out from there and departed to the region of Tyre and Sidon. 22And behold, a woman of Canaan came from that region and cried out to Him, saying, "Have mercy on me, O Lord, Son of David! My daughter is severely demon-possessed."

23But He answered her not a word.

And His disciples came and urged Him, saying, "Send her away, for she cries out after us."

24But He answered and said, "I was not sent except to the lost sheep of the house of Israel."

25Then she came and worshiped Him, saying, "Lord, help me!"

26But He answered and said, "It is not good to take the children's bread and throw *it* to the little dogs."

27And she said, "Yes, Lord, yet even the little dogs eat the crumbs which fall from their masters' table."

28Then Jesus answered and said to her, "O woman, great *is* your faith! Let it be to you as you desire." And her daughter was healed from that very hour.

Jesus Heals Great Multitudes

29Jesus departed from there, skirted the Sea of Galilee, and went up on the mountain and sat down there. 30Then great multitudes came to Him, having with them the lame, blind, mute, maimed, and many others; and they laid them down at Jesus' feet, and He healed them. 31So the multitude marveled when they saw *the* mute speaking, *the* maimed made whole, *the* lame walking, and *the* blind seeing; and they glorified the God of Israel.

Problem Solving: The Fastest Way to Gain Leadership

(Matthew 15:29–39)

Jesus deepened His credibility by solving the problem of a hungry crowd:

1. He identified the problem and informed His team (v. 32).
2. He instructed them to brainstorm the solution (vv. 33, 34).
3. He invited them into the problem-solving process (vv. 35, 36).
4. He included them in the solution (vv. 35–38).

Feeding the Four Thousand

32Now Jesus called His disciples to *Himself* and said, "I have compassion on the multitude, because they have now continued with Me three days and have nothing to eat. And I do not want

---

15:4 [a]Exodus 20:12; Deuteronomy 5:16 [b]Exodus 21:17 **15:6** [a]NU-Text omits *or mother.* [b]NU-Text reads *word.* **15:8** [a]NU-Text omits *draw near to Me with their mouth, And.* **15:9** [a]Isaiah 29:13

to send them away hungry, lest they faint on the way."

³³Then His disciples said to Him, "Where could we get enough bread in the wilderness to fill such a great multitude?"

³⁴Jesus said to them, "How many loaves do you have?"

And they said, "Seven, and a few little fish."

³⁵So He commanded the multitude to sit down on the ground. ³⁶And He took the seven loaves and the fish and gave thanks, broke *them* and gave *them* to His disciples; and the disciples *gave* to the multitude. ³⁷So they all ate and were filled, and they took up seven large baskets full of the fragments that were left. ³⁸Now those who ate were four thousand men, besides women and children. ³⁹And He sent away the multitude, got into the boat, and came to the region of Magdala.ᵃ

The Pharisees and Sadducees Seek a Sign

16 Then the Pharisees and Sadducees came, and testing Him asked that He would show them a sign from heaven. ²He answered and said to them, "When it is evening you say, '*It will be* fair weather, for the sky is red'; ³and in the morning, '*It will be* foul weather today, for the sky is red and threatening.' Hypocrites!ᵃ You know how to discern the face of the sky, but you cannot *discern* the signs of the times. ⁴A wicked and adulterous generation seeks after a sign, and no sign shall be given to it except the sign of the prophetᵃ Jonah." And He left them and departed.

The Leaven of the Pharisees and Sadducees

⁵Now when His disciples had come to the other side, they had forgotten to take bread. ⁶Then Jesus said to them, "Take heed and beware of the leaven of the Pharisees and the Sadducees."

⁷And they reasoned among themselves, saying, "*It is* because we have taken no bread."

⁸But Jesus, being aware of *it,* said to them, "O you of little faith, why do you reason among yourselves because you have brought no bread?ᵃ ⁹Do you not yet understand, or remember the five loaves of the five thousand and how many baskets you took up? ¹⁰Nor the seven loaves of the four thousand and how many large baskets you took up? ¹¹How is it you do not understand that I did not speak to you concerning bread?—*but* to beware of the leaven of the Pharisees and Sadducees." ¹²Then they understood that He did not tell *them* to beware of the leaven of bread, but of the doctrine of the Pharisees and Sadducees.

Peter Confesses Jesus as the Christ

¹³When Jesus came into the region of Caesarea Philippi, He asked His disciples, saying, "Who do men say that I, the Son of Man, am?"

¹⁴So they said, "Some *say* John the Baptist, some Elijah, and others Jeremiah or one of the prophets."

¹⁵He said to them, "But who do you say that I am?"

¹⁶Simon Peter answered and said, "You are the Christ, the Son of the living God."

¹⁷Jesus answered and said to him, "Blessed are you, Simon Bar-Jonah, for flesh and blood has not revealed *this* to you, but My Father who is in heaven. ¹⁸And I also say to you that you are Peter, and on this rock I will build My church, and the gates of Hades shall not prevail against it. ¹⁹And I will give you the keys of the kingdom of heaven, and whatever you bind on earth will be bound in heaven, and whatever you loose on earth will be loosedᵃ in heaven."

²⁰Then He commanded His disciples that they should tell no one that He was Jesus the Christ.

Jesus Predicts His Death and Resurrection

²¹From that time Jesus began to show to His disciples that He must go to Jerusalem, and suffer many things from the elders and chief priests and scribes, and be killed, and be raised the third day.

²²Then Peter took Him aside and began to rebuke Him, saying, "Far be it from You, Lord; this shall not happen to You!"

²³But He turned and said to Peter, "Get behind Me, Satan! You are an offense to Me, for you are not mindful of the things of God, but the things of men."

Take Up the Cross and Follow Him

²⁴Then Jesus said to His disciples, "If anyone desires to come after Me, let him deny himself, and take up his cross, and follow Me. ²⁵For whoever desires to save his life will lose it, but whoever loses his life for My sake will find it. ²⁶For what profit is it to a man if he gains the whole world, and loses his own soul? Or what will a

---

15:39 ᵃNU-Text reads *Magadan.* **16:3** ᵃNU-Text omits *Hypocrites.* **16:4** ᵃNU-Text omits *the prophet.* **16:8** ᵃNU-Text reads *you have no bread.* **16:19** ᵃOr *will have been bound . . . will have been loosed*

Peter's Charisma Compels Others to Affirm His Lead
(Matthew 16:13–20)

In a decisive conversation, Jesus asks Simon Peter about His identity: "But who do you say that I am?" (Matt. 16:15). Peter doesn't hesitate; He confesses Christ as Lord. Jesus then affirms his confession and declares that on the rock of that confession He will build His church (16:18). Jesus promises divine authority to Peter (16:19)—and during the infancy of the church, Peter did indeed lead in Jerusalem.

Peter was loaded with charisma and attracted others to follow him. As a disciple, he became a leader among leaders. What gave Peter this charisma that sparked others to affirm his leadership? From the four Gospels, we can surmise the answer:

1. *His Personality*
   Peter seemed to possess a sanguine/choleric temperament. Usually he was the first to speak.
2. *His Purpose*
   Peter embraced His mission as quickly as any of the twelve. He was the first to act.
3. *His People Skills*
   Peter was drawn to people. He acted like a magnet that either attracted or repelled others.
4. *His Passion*
   Peter had a fire inside. He wanted to please God and make a difference.

man give in exchange for his soul? ²⁷For the Son of Man will come in the glory of His Father with His angels, and then He will reward each according to his works.

Jesus Transfigured on the Mount
²⁸Assuredly, I say to you, there are some standing here who shall not taste death till they see the Son of Man coming in His kingdom."

17 Now after six days Jesus took Peter, James, and John his brother, led them up on a high mountain by themselves; ²and He was transfigured before them. His face shone like the sun, and His clothes became as white as the light. ³And behold, Moses and Elijah appeared to them, talking with Him. ⁴Then Peter answered and said to Jesus, "Lord, it is good for us to be here; if You wish, let us^a make here three tabernacles: one for You, one for Moses, and one for Elijah."

⁵While he was still speaking, behold, a bright cloud overshadowed them; and suddenly a voice came out of the cloud, saying, "This is My beloved Son, in whom I am well pleased. Hear Him!" ⁶And when the disciples heard *it,* they fell on their faces and were greatly afraid. ⁷But Jesus came and touched them and said, "Arise, and do not be afraid." ⁸When they had lifted up their eyes, they saw no one but Jesus only.

⁹Now as they came down from the mountain, Jesus commanded them, saying, "Tell the vision to no one until the Son of Man is risen from the dead."

¹⁰And His disciples asked Him, saying, "Why then do the scribes say that Elijah must come first?"

¹¹Jesus answered and said to them, "Indeed, Elijah is coming first^a and will restore all things. ¹²But I say to you that Elijah has come already, and they did not know him but did to him whatever they wished. Likewise the Son of Man is also about to suffer at their hands." ¹³Then the disciples understood that He spoke to them of John the Baptist.

A Boy Is Healed
¹⁴And when they had come to the multitude, a man came to Him, kneeling down to Him and saying, ¹⁵"Lord, have mercy on my son, for he is an epileptic^a and suffers severely; for he often falls into the fire and often into the water. ¹⁶So I brought him to Your disciples, but they could not cure him."

¹⁷Then Jesus answered and said, "O faithless and perverse generation, how long shall I be

---

17:4 ^aNU-Text reads *I will.* **17:11** ^aNU-Text omits *first.* **17:15** ^aLiterally *moonstruck* with you? How long shall I bear with you? Bring him here to Me." [18]And Jesus rebuked the demon, and it came out of him; and the child was cured from that very hour.

[19]Then the disciples came to Jesus privately and said, "Why could we not cast it out?"

[20]So Jesus said to them, "Because of your unbelief;[a] for assuredly, I say to you, if you have faith as a mustard seed, you will say to this mountain, 'Move from here to there,' and it will move; and nothing will be impossible for you. [21]However, this kind does not go out except by prayer and fasting."[a]

Mentoring: Jesus Assesses and Holds His Disciples Accountable

(Matthew 17:14–21)

Following Jesus' transfiguration, He comes down from the mountain to find nine of His disciples attempting to cast a demon out of a boy. At that moment, He again becomes a mentor for His men. He commits Himself to the training of the Twelve, believing every exposure they get becomes an opportunity to learn. Review the story and see what we learn from Jesus, the leadership Mentor:

1. He feels angry that His disciples can't do the job (v. 17).
2. He assumes responsibility to model for them what they should do (v. 18).
3. He evaluates their performance and assesses why they failed (vv. 19–21).
4. He affirms the truth and holds them accountable to embrace it (v. 20, 21).

Jesus' methods include four elements: instruction; demonstration; experience; and assessment. He teaches them, shows them, allows them to try it themselves, and then processes what happened. Jesus is the master Mentor in developing leaders.

Jesus Again Predicts His Death and Resurrection

[22]Now while they were staying[a] in Galilee, Jesus said to them, "The Son of Man is about to be betrayed into the hands of men, [23]and they will kill Him, and the third day He will be raised up." And they were exceedingly sorrowful.

Peter and His Master Pay Their Taxes

[24]When they had come to Capernaum,[a] those who received the *temple* tax came to Peter and said, "Does your Teacher not pay the *temple* tax?"

[25]He said, "Yes."

And when he had come into the house, Jesus anticipated him, saying, "What do you think, Simon? From whom do the kings of the earth take customs or taxes, from their sons or from strangers?"

[26]Peter said to Him, "From strangers."

Jesus said to him, "Then the sons are free. [27]Nevertheless, lest we offend them, go to the sea, cast in a hook, and take the fish that comes up first. And when you have opened its mouth, you will find a piece of money;[a] take that and give it to them for Me and you."

Who Is the Greatest?

18 At that time the disciples came to Jesus, saying, "Who then is greatest in the kingdom of heaven?"

[2]Then Jesus called a little child to Him, set him in the midst of them, [3]and said, "Assuredly, I say to you, unless you are converted and become as little children, you will by no means enter the kingdom of heaven. [4]Therefore whoever humbles himself as this little child is the greatest in the kingdom of heaven. [5]Whoever receives one little child like this in My name receives Me.

Jesus Warns of Offenses

[6]"Whoever causes one of these little ones who believe in Me to sin, it would be better for him if a millstone were hung around his neck, and he were drowned in the depth of the sea. [7]Woe to the world because of offenses! For offenses must come, but woe to that man by whom the offense comes!

[8]"If your hand or foot causes you to sin, cut it off and cast *it* from you. It is better for you to enter into life lame or maimed, rather than having two hands or two feet, to be cast into the everlasting fire. [9]And if your eye causes you to sin, pluck it out and cast *it* from you. It is better for you to enter into life with one eye, rather than having two eyes, to be cast into hell fire.

17:20 [a]NU-Text reads *little faith.* **17:21** [a]NU-Text omits this verse. **17:22** [a]NU-Text reads *gathering together.* **17:24** [a]NU-Text reads *Capharnaum* (here and elsewhere). **17:27** [a]Greek *stater,* the exact amount to pay the temple tax (didrachma) for two

The Parable of the Lost Sheep

10"Take heed that you do not despise one of these little ones, for I say to you that in heaven their angels always see the face of My Father who is in heaven. 11For the Son of Man has come to save that which was lost.ᵃ

12"What do you think? If a man has a hundred sheep, and one of them goes astray, does he not leave the ninety-nine and go to the mountains to seek the one that is straying? 13And if he should find it, assuredly, I say to you, he rejoices more over that *sheep* than over the ninety-nine that did not go astray. 14Even so it is not the will of your Father who is in heaven that one of these little ones should perish.

Dealing with a Sinning Brother

15"Moreover if your brother sins against you, go and tell him his fault between you and him alone. If he hears you, you have gained your brother. 16But if he will not hear, take with you one or two more, that *'by the mouth of two or three witnesses every word may be established.'*ᵃ 17And if he refuses to hear them, tell *it* to the church. But if he refuses even to hear the church, let him be to you like a heathen and a tax collector.

18"Assuredly, I say to you, whatever you bind on earth will be bound in heaven, and whatever you loose on earth will be loosed in heaven.

19"Again I sayᵃ to you that if two of you agree on earth concerning anything that they ask, it will be done for them by My Father in heaven. 20For where two or three are gathered together in My name, I am there in the midst of them."

The Parable of the Unforgiving Servant

21Then Peter came to Him and said, "Lord, how often shall my brother sin against me, and I forgive him? Up to seven times?"

22Jesus said to him, "I do not say to you, up to seven times, but up to seventy times seven. 23Therefore the kingdom of heaven is like a certain king who wanted to settle accounts with his servants. 24And when he had begun to settle accounts, one was brought to him who owed him ten thousand talents. 25But as he was not able to pay, his master commanded that he be sold, with his wife and children and all that he had, and that payment be made. 26The servant therefore fell down before him, saying, 'Master, have patience

18:11 ᵃNU-Text omits this verse.
18:16 ᵃDeuteronomy 19:15 18:19 ᵃNU-Text and M-Text read *Again, assuredly, I say.*

Conflict Resolution:
Jesus Taught How to Manage Conflict
(Matthew 18:15–20)

There may be no clearer passage in the Gospels on conflict resolution than Matthew 18. While Jesus spoke about addressing sin in the church, His words suggest broader principles. According to Jesus, addressing conflict and healing offenses should be a priority for us. He even instructs us to postpone our worship if we remember an unresolved offense (Matt. 5:23, 24).

Conflicts *will* arise in any organization. Humans disagree because they are wired differently and have different agendas. Note what Jesus taught about organizational conflict when someone has clearly done wrong:

1. Initiate the contact (v. 15).
2. Confront the person in private (v. 15).
3. If no resolution comes, meet again with one or two more people (v. 16).
4. Confirm the facts in the meeting and work toward a solution (v. 16).
5. If no resolution comes, bring the issue before the church or organization (v. 17).
6. Agree upon the truth and the appropriate options for the offender (v. 17).
7. If no resolution comes, release the offender from the church or organization (v. 17).

Behind this process lies the authority Jesus has given to church leaders (Matt. 18:18–20). We must act wisely, because we have God-given authority (18:18), because God will confirm and support the decisions made in harmony (18:19), and because He is present when we gather in His name (18:20).

with me, and I will pay you all.' ²⁷Then the master of that servant was moved with compassion, released him, and forgave him the debt.

²⁸"But that servant went out and found one of his fellow servants who owed him a hundred denarii; and he laid hands on him and took *him* by the throat, saying, 'Pay me what you owe!'²⁹So his fellow servant fell down at his feet[a] and begged him, saying, 'Have patience with me, and I will pay you all.'[b] ³⁰And he would not, but went and threw him into prison till he should pay the debt. ³¹So when his fellow servants saw what had been done, they were very grieved, and came and told their master all that had been done. ³²Then his master, after he had called him, said to him, 'You wicked servant! I forgave you all that debt because you begged me. ³³Should you not also have had compassion on your fellow servant, just as I had pity on you?' ³⁴And his master was angry, and delivered him to the torturers until he should pay all that was due to him.

³⁵"So My heavenly Father also will do to you if each of you, from his heart, does not forgive his brother his trespasses."[a]

Marriage and Divorce

19 Now it came to pass, when Jesus had finished these sayings, *that* He departed from Galilee and came to the region of Judea beyond the Jordan. ²And great multitudes followed Him, and He healed them there.

³The Pharisees also came to Him, testing Him, and saying to Him, "Is it lawful for a man to divorce his wife for *just* any reason?"

⁴And He answered and said to them, "Have you not read that He who made[a] *them* at the beginning 'made them male and female,'[b] ⁵and said, 'For this reason a man shall leave his father and mother and be joined to his wife, and the two shall become one flesh'?[a] ⁶So then, they are no longer two but one flesh. Therefore what God has joined together, let not man separate."

⁷They said to Him, "Why then did Moses command to give a certificate of divorce, and to put her away?"

⁸He said to them, "Moses, because of the hardness of your hearts, permitted you to divorce your wives, but from the beginning it was not so. ⁹And I say to you, whoever divorces his wife, except for sexual immorality,[a] and marries another, commits adultery; and whoever marries her who is divorced commits adultery."

¹⁰His disciples said to Him, "If such is the case of the man with *his* wife, it is better not to marry."

Jesus Teaches on Celibacy

¹¹But He said to them, "All cannot accept this saying, but only *those* to whom it has been given: ¹²For there are eunuchs who were born thus from *their* mother's womb, and there are eunuchs who were made eunuchs by men, and there are eunuchs who have made themselves eunuchs for the kingdom of heaven's sake. He who is able to accept *it,* let him accept *it."*

Jesus Blesses Little Children

¹³Then little children were brought to Him that He might put *His* hands on them and pray, but the disciples rebuked them. ¹⁴But Jesus said, "Let the little children come to Me, and do not forbid them; for of such is the kingdom of heaven." ¹⁵And He laid *His* hands on them and departed from there.

Jesus Counsels the Rich Young Ruler

¹⁶Now behold, one came and said to Him, "Good[a] Teacher, what good thing shall I do that I may have eternal life?"

¹⁷So He said to him, "Why do you call Me good?[a] No one *is* good but One, *that is,* God.[b] But if you want to enter into life, keep the commandments."

¹⁸He said to Him, "Which ones?"

Jesus said, " 'You shall not murder,' 'You shall not commit adultery,' 'You shall not steal,' 'You shall not bear false witness,' ¹⁹'Honor your father and your mother,'[a] and, 'You shall love your neighbor as yourself.' "[b]

²⁰The young man said to Him, "All these things I have kept from my youth.[a] What do I still lack?"

²¹Jesus said to him, "If you want to be perfect, go, sell what you have and give to the poor, and you will have treasure in heaven; and come, follow Me."

²²But when the young man heard that saying, he went away sorrowful, for he had great possessions.

With God All Things Are Possible

²³Then Jesus said to His disciples, "Assuredly, I say to you that it is hard for a rich man to enter

---

18:29 [a]NU-Text omits *at his feet.* [b]NU-Text and M-Text omit *all.* **18:35** [a]NU-Text omits *his trespasses.* **19:4** [a]NU-Text reads *created.* [b]Genesis 1:27; 5:2 **19:5** [a]Genesis 2:24 **19:9** [a]Or *fornication* **19:16** [a]NU-Text omits *Good.* **19:17** [a]NU-Text reads *Why do you ask Me about what is good?* [b]NU-Text reads *There is One who is good.* **19:19** [a]Exodus 20:12–16; Deuteronomy 5:16–20 [b]Leviticus 19:18 **19:20** [a]NU-Text omits *from my youth.*

the kingdom of heaven. ²⁴And again I say to you, it is easier for a camel to go through the eye of a needle than for a rich man to enter the kingdom of God."

²⁵When His disciples heard *it*, they were greatly astonished, saying, "Who then can be saved?"

²⁶But Jesus looked at *them* and said to them, "With men this is impossible, but with God all things are possible."

Discernment: Jesus and the Rich Young Ruler

(Matthew 19:16–26)

Jesus cut through the periphery to get to the real issues. Discerning that a young man had failed to "have no other gods before [him]" (Ex. 20:3), Jesus tells him to sell everything, give it to the poor, and follow Him. The man walks away, unable to take the step that would free him from bondage.

---

²⁷Then Peter answered and said to Him, "See, we have left all and followed You. Therefore what shall we have?"

²⁸So Jesus said to them, "Assuredly I say to you, that in the regeneration, when the Son of Man sits on the throne of His glory, you who have followed Me will also sit on twelve thrones, judging the twelve tribes of Israel. ²⁹And everyone who has left houses or brothers or sisters or father or mother or wife[a] or children or lands, for My name's sake, shall receive a hundredfold, and inherit eternal life. ³⁰But many *who are* first will be last, and the last first.

The Parable of the Workers in the Vineyard

20 "For the kingdom of heaven is like a landowner who went out early in the morning to hire laborers for his vineyard. ²Now when he had agreed with the laborers for a denarius a day, he sent them into his vineyard. ³And he went out about the third hour and saw others standing idle in the marketplace, ⁴and said to them, 'You also go into the vineyard, and whatever is right I will give you.' So they went. ⁵Again he went out about the sixth and the ninth hour, and did likewise. ⁶And about the eleventh hour he went out and found others standing idle,[a] and said to them, 'Why have you been standing here idle all day?' ⁷They said to

him, 'Because no one hired us.' He said to them, 'You also go into the vineyard, and whatever is right you will receive.'[a]

⁸"So when evening had come, the owner of the vineyard said to his steward, 'Call the laborers and give them *their* wages, beginning with the last to the first.' ⁹And when those came who *were hired* about the eleventh hour, they each received a denarius. ¹⁰But when the first came, they supposed that they would receive more; and they likewise received each a denarius. ¹¹And when they had received *it*, they complained against the landowner, ¹²saying, 'These last *men* have worked *only* one hour, and you made them equal to us who have borne the burden and the heat of the day.' ¹³But he answered one of them and said, 'Friend, I am

---

19:29 ᵃNU-Text omits *or wife.* **20:6** ᵃNU-Text omits *idle.* **20:7** ᵃNU-Text omits the last clause of this verse.

Attitude: Leaders Must Focus on God's Ability, Not Their Own

(Matthew 20:1–16)

Leaders should often read this story. It describes God's grace, illustrated by a landowner and his vineyard workers. The workers show us how leaders look when they take their eyes off God and focus on themselves. Through this parable Jesus attempts to correct wrong attitudes. He is trying to address:

1. *Self-absorption*
   We grumble and complain about inequities. We focus more on our work than God's.

2. *Comparison*
   We ignore God's grace, remaining preoccupied with the status of others.

3. *Presumption*
   We assume too much when it comes to rewards, forgetting that every blessing is a gift.

4. *Distortion*
   When we judge others as unworthy, we misunderstand that the entire kingdom is built on grace.

doing you no wrong. Did you not agree with me for a denarius? [14]Take *what is* yours and go your way. I wish to give to this last man *the same* as to you. [15]Is it not lawful for me to do what I wish with my own things? Or is your eye evil because I am good?' [16]So the last will be first, and the first last. For many are called, but few chosen."[a]

Jesus a Third Time Predicts His Death and Resurrection

[17]Now Jesus, going up to Jerusalem, took the twelve disciples aside on the road and said to them, [18]"Behold, we are going up to Jerusalem, and the Son of Man will be betrayed to the chief priests and to the scribes; and they will condemn Him to death, [19]and deliver Him to the Gentiles to mock and to scourge and to crucify. And the third day He will rise again."

Greatness Is Serving

[20]Then the mother of Zebedee's sons came to Him with her sons, kneeling down and asking something from Him.

[21]And He said to her, "What do you wish?"

She said to Him, "Grant that these two sons of mine may sit, one on Your right hand and the other on the left, in Your kingdom."

[22]But Jesus answered and said, "You do not know what you ask. Are you able to drink the cup that I am about to drink, and be baptized with the baptism that I am baptized with?"[a]

They said to Him, "We are able."

[23]So He said to them, "You will indeed drink My cup, and be baptized with the baptism that I am baptized with;[a] but to sit on My right hand and on My left is not Mine to give, but *it is for those* for whom it is prepared by My Father."

[24]And when the ten heard *it,* they were greatly displeased with the two brothers. [25]But Jesus called them to *Himself* and said, "You know

---

20:16 [a]NU-Text omits the last sentence of this verse. **20:22** [a]NU-Text omits *and be baptized with the baptism that I am baptized with.* **20:23** [a]NU-Text omits *and be baptized with the baptism that I am baptized with.*

Servanthood: Jesus Teaches That We Lead by Serving and Serve by Leading

(Matthew 20:25–28)

As Jesus makes His way toward Jerusalem to be executed, the mother of James and John request that her sons be given a preferred seat, next to Jesus, in the kingdom of heaven. Both the disciples and their families have become preoccupied with status rather than serving. They have missed the whole point of Jesus' leadership.

Jesus tells them plainly that His style of leadership stands in stark contrast to the world's. He teaches that the greatest must be the servant. As responsibilities increase, rights decrease. Consider a "leadership pyramid" based on this principle:

Opportunities and Responsibilities

RIGHTS

RESPONSIBILITIES

Rights DECREASE as you climb toward leadership in the church

Responsibilities INCREASE as you climb toward leadership in the church

Options and Rights

If this pyramid represents your life and the base represents the beginning of your leadership journey, your range of options is widest at the beginning. The younger you are, the more liberties you have with your time, vocabulary, money, etc. But as you grow into leadership, you deliberately surrender those rights and options. Servants push for no options and assume no rights.

that the rulers of the Gentiles lord it over them, and those who are great exercise authority over them. ²⁶Yet it shall not be so among you; but whoever desires to become great among you, let him be your servant. ²⁷And whoever desires to be first among you, let him be your slave— ²⁸just as the Son of Man did not come to be served, but to serve, and to give His life a ransom for many."

Two Blind Men Receive Their Sight

²⁹Now as they went out of Jericho, a great multitude followed Him. ³⁰And behold, two blind men sitting by the road, when they heard that Jesus was passing by, cried out, saying, "Have mercy on us, O Lord, Son of David!"

³¹Then the multitude warned them that they should be quiet; but they cried out all the more, saying, "Have mercy on us, O Lord, Son of David!"

³²So Jesus stood still and called them, and said, "What do you want Me to do for you?"

³³They said to Him, "Lord, that our eyes may be opened." ³⁴So Jesus had compassion and touched their eyes. And immediately their eyes received sight, and they followed Him.

The Triumphal Entry

21 Now when they drew near Jerusalem, and came to Bethphage,^a at the Mount of Olives, then Jesus sent two disciples, ²saying to them, "Go into the village opposite you, and immediately you will find a donkey tied, and a colt with her. Loose *them* and bring *them* to Me. ³And if anyone says anything to you, you shall say, 'The Lord has need of them,' and immediately he will send them."

⁴All^a this was done that it might be fulfilled which was spoken by the prophet, saying:

⁵ "*Tell the daughter of Zion,*
  '*Behold, your King is coming to you,*
  Lowly, and sitting on a donkey,
  A colt, the foal of a donkey.'"^a

⁶So the disciples went and did as Jesus commanded them. ⁷They brought the donkey and the colt, laid their clothes on them, and set *Him*^a on them. ⁸And a very great multitude spread their clothes on the road; others cut down branches from the trees and spread *them* on the road. ⁹Then the multitudes who went before and those who followed cried out, saying:

"Hosanna to the Son of David!
'*Blessed is He who comes in the name of the LORD!*'^a
Hosanna in the highest!"

¹⁰And when He had come into Jerusalem, all the city was moved, saying, "Who is this?"

¹¹So the multitudes said, "This is Jesus, the prophet from Nazareth of Galilee."

Jesus Cleanses the Temple

¹²Then Jesus went into the temple of God^a and drove out all those who bought and sold in the temple, and overturned the tables of the money changers and the seats of those who sold doves. ¹³And He said to them, "It is written, '*My house shall be called a house of prayer,*'^a but you have made it a '*den of thieves.*'"^b

¹⁴Then *the* blind and *the* lame came to Him in the temple, and He healed them. ¹⁵But when the chief priests and scribes saw the wonderful things that He did, and the children crying out in the temple and saying, "Hosanna to the Son of David!" they were indignant ¹⁶and said to Him, "Do You hear what these are saying?"

And Jesus said to them, "Yes. Have you never read,

'*Out of the mouth of babes and nursing infants*
    You have perfected praise'?"^a

¹⁷Then He left them and went out of the city to Bethany, and He lodged there.

The Fig Tree Withered

¹⁸Now in the morning, as He returned to the city, He was hungry. ¹⁹And seeing a fig tree by the road, He came to it and found nothing on it but leaves, and said to it, "Let no fruit grow on you ever again." Immediately the fig tree withered away.

The Lesson of the Withered Fig Tree

²⁰And when the disciples saw *it,* they marveled, saying, "How did the fig tree wither away so soon?"

²¹So Jesus answered and said to them, "Assuredly, I say to you, if you have faith and do not doubt, you will not only do what was done to the fig tree, but also if you say to this mountain, 'Be removed and be cast into the sea,' it will be done. ²²And whatever things you ask in prayer, believing, you will receive."

21:1 ^aM-Text reads *Bethsphage.* **21:4** ^aNU-Text omits *All.* **21:5** ^aZechariah 9:9 **21:7** ^aNU-Text reads *and He sat.* **21:9** ^aPsalm 118:26 **21:12** ^aNU-Text omits *of God.* **21:13** ^aIsaiah 56:7 ^bJeremiah 7:11 **21:16** ^aPsalm 8:2

Jesus' Authority Questioned

²³Now when He came into the temple, the chief priests and the elders of the people confronted Him as He was teaching, and said, "By what authority are You doing these things? And who gave You this authority?"

²⁴But Jesus answered and said to them, "I also will ask you one thing, which if you tell Me, I likewise will tell you by what authority I do these things: ²⁵The baptism of John—where was it from? From heaven or from men?"

And they reasoned among themselves, saying, "If we say, 'From heaven,' He will say to us, 'Why then did you not believe him?' ²⁶But if we say, 'From men,' we fear the multitude, for all count John as a prophet." ²⁷So they answered Jesus and said, "We do not know."

And He said to them, "Neither will I tell you by what authority I do these things.

Communication: The Test of a Hostile Crowd

(Matthew 21:23–27)

The religious leaders challenged Jesus' authority when He entered the temple. He responded by using the best tool a leader has when facing such antagonism: He answered their question with a question. Handling people who don't want to travel with you is the acid test of a leader's poise.

The Parable of the Two Sons

²⁸"But what do you think? A man had two sons, and he came to the first and said, 'Son, go, work today in my vineyard.' ²⁹He answered and said, 'I will not,' but afterward he regretted it and went. ³⁰Then he came to the second and said likewise. And he answered and said, 'I go, sir,' but he did not go. ³¹Which of the two did the will of his father?"

They said to Him, "The first."

Jesus said to them, "Assuredly, I say to you that tax collectors and harlots enter the kingdom of God before you. ³²For John came to you in the way of righteousness, and you did not believe him; but tax collectors and harlots believed him; and when you saw it, you did not afterward relent and believe him.

The Parable of the Wicked Vinedressers

³³"Hear another parable: There was a certain landowner who planted a vineyard and set a hedge around it, dug a winepress in it and built a tower. And he leased it to vinedressers and went into a far country. ³⁴Now when vintage-time drew near, he sent his servants to the vinedressers, that they might receive its fruit. ³⁵And the vinedressers took his servants, beat one, killed one, and stoned another. ³⁶Again he sent other servants, more than the first, and they did likewise to them. ³⁷Then last of all he sent his son to them, saying, 'They will respect my son.' ³⁸But when the vinedressers saw the son, they said among themselves, 'This is the heir. Come, let us kill him and seize his inheritance.' ³⁹So they took him and cast *him* out of the vineyard and killed *him*.

⁴⁰"Therefore, when the owner of the vineyard comes, what will he do to those vinedressers?"

⁴¹They said to Him, "He will destroy those wicked men miserably, and lease *his* vineyard to other vinedressers who will render to him the fruits in their seasons."

⁴²Jesus said to them, "Have you never read in the Scriptures:

'The stone which the builders rejected
Has become the chief cornerstone.
This was the LORD's doing,
And it is marvelous in our eyes'?[a]

⁴³"Therefore I say to you, the kingdom of God will be taken from you and given to a nation bearing the fruits of it. ⁴⁴And whoever falls on this stone will be broken; but on whomever it falls, it will grind him to powder."

⁴⁵Now when the chief priests and Pharisees heard His parables, they perceived that He was speaking of them. ⁴⁶But when they sought to lay hands on Him, they feared the multitudes, because they took Him for a prophet.

The Parable of the Wedding Feast

22 And Jesus answered and spoke to them again by parables and said: ²"The kingdom of heaven is like a certain king who arranged a marriage for his son, ³and sent out his servants to call those who were invited to the wedding; and they were not willing to come. ⁴Again, he sent out other servants, saying, 'Tell those who are invited, "See, I have prepared my dinner; my oxen and fatted

21:42 [a]Psalm 118:22, 23

cattle *are* killed, and all things *are* ready. Come to the wedding."' [5]But they made light of it and went their ways, one to his own farm, another to his business. [6]And the rest seized his servants, treated *them* spitefully, and killed *them*. [7]But when the king heard *about it*, he was furious. And he sent out his armies, destroyed those murderers, and burned up their city. [8]Then he said to his servants, 'The wedding is ready, but those who were invited were not worthy. [9]Therefore go into the highways, and as many as you find, invite to the wedding.' [10]So those servants went out into the highways and gathered together all whom they found, both bad and good. And the wedding *hall* was filled with guests.

[11]"But when the king came in to see the guests, he saw a man there who did not have on a wedding garment. [12]So he said to him, 'Friend, how did you come in here without a wedding garment?' And he was speechless. [13]Then the king said to the servants, 'Bind him hand and foot, take him away, and[a] cast *him* into outer darkness; there will be weeping and gnashing of teeth.'

[14]"For many are called, but few *are* chosen."

The Pharisees: Is It Lawful to Pay Taxes to Caesar?

[15]Then the Pharisees went and plotted how they might entangle Him in *His* talk. [16]And they sent to Him their disciples with the Herodians, saying, "Teacher, we know that You are true, and teach the way of God in truth; nor do You care about anyone, for You do not regard the person of men. [17]Tell us, therefore, what do You think? Is it lawful to pay taxes to Caesar, or not?"

[18]But Jesus perceived their wickedness, and said, "Why do you test Me, *you* hypocrites? [19]Show Me the tax money."

So they brought Him a denarius.

[20]And He said to them, "Whose image and inscription *is* this?"

[21]They said to Him, "Caesar's."

And He said to them, "Render therefore to Caesar the things that are Caesar's, and to God the things that are God's." [22]When they had heard *these words,* they marveled, and left Him and went their way.

The Sadducees: What About the Resurrection?

[23]The same day the Sadducees, who say there is no resurrection, came to Him and asked Him, [24]saying: "Teacher, Moses said that if a man dies, having no children, his brother shall marry his wife and raise up offspring for his brother. [25]Now there were with us seven brothers. The first died

---

22:13 [a]NU-Text omits *take him away, and.*

The Law of Solid Ground: Jesus' Character

(Matthew 22:15–46)

Each time Jesus faces some leadership tests, He proves His integrity by handling the situation expertly:

1. *The Pharisees attempt to trap Him with the tax issue* (vv. 15–22).

   Should the Jews pay taxes to Caesar? Either expected answer would get Jesus in trouble, either with the Romans or the Jews. So Jesus answers the question with a question. He asks for a coin, then says: "Whose image and inscription is this?" (Matt. 22:20). The coin carried Caesar's image—so it should be surrendered to him. But the people were made in God's image—so they should surrender themselves to Him.

2. *The Sadducees attempt to trap Him with the marriage issue* (vv. 23–33).

   If a woman lost several husbands to premature death, whose wife would she be in heaven? Jesus explains there is no marriage in heaven, so it is a moot point. But then He poses his own question, proving from their own scriptures the existence of both a resurrection and a heaven.

3. *The Pharisees attempt to ask Him an unanswerable question* (vv. 34–40).

   What was the greatest commandment? Surely Jesus wouldn't want to leave out any. Jesus summarizes the Law with a single command: Love God and your neighbor. Then He poses an unanswerable question of His own, proving He knew the scriptures better than they did (vv. 41–46).

after he had married, and having no offspring, left his wife to his brother. ²⁶Likewise the second also, and the third, even to the seventh. ²⁷Last of all the woman died also. ²⁸Therefore, in the resurrection, whose wife of the seven will she be? For they all had her."

²⁹Jesus answered and said to them, "You are mistaken, not knowing the Scriptures nor the power of God. ³⁰For in the resurrection they neither marry nor are given in marriage, but are like angels of God[a] in heaven. ³¹But concerning the resurrection of the dead, have you not read what was spoken to you by God, saying, ³²'I am the God of Abraham, the God of Isaac, and the God of Jacob'?[a] God is not the God of the dead, but of the living." ³³And when the multitudes heard this, they were astonished at His teaching.

The Scribes: Which Is the First Commandment of All?

³⁴But when the Pharisees heard that He had silenced the Sadducees, they gathered together. ³⁵Then one of them, a lawyer, asked Him a question, testing Him, and saying, ³⁶"Teacher, which is the great commandment in the law?"

³⁷Jesus said to him, "'You shall love the LORD your God with all your heart, with all your soul, and with all your mind.'[a] ³⁸This is the first and great commandment. ³⁹And the second is like it: 'You shall love your neighbor as yourself.'[a] ⁴⁰On these two commandments hang all the Law and the Prophets."

Jesus: How Can David Call His Descendant Lord?

⁴¹While the Pharisees were gathered together, Jesus asked them, ⁴²saying, "What do you think about the Christ? Whose Son is He?"

They said to Him, "The Son of David."

⁴³He said to them, "How then does David in the Spirit call Him 'Lord,' saying:

⁴⁴ 'The LORD said to my Lord,
"Sit at My right hand,
Till I make Your enemies Your footstool"'?[a]

⁴⁵If David then calls Him 'Lord,' how is He his Son?" ⁴⁶And no one was able to answer Him a word, nor from that day on did anyone dare question Him anymore.

Woe to the Scribes and Pharisees

23 Then Jesus spoke to the multitudes and to His disciples, ²saying: "The scribes and the Pharisees sit in Moses' seat. ³Therefore whatever they tell you to observe,[a] that observe and do, but do not do ac-

cording to their works; for they say, and do not do. ⁴For they bind heavy burdens, hard to bear, and lay them on men's shoulders; but they themselves will not move them with one of their fingers. ⁵But all their works they do to be seen by men. They make their phylacteries broad and enlarge the borders of their garments. ⁶They love the best places at feasts, the best seats in the synagogues, ⁷greetings in the marketplaces, and to be called by men, 'Rabbi, Rabbi.' ⁸But you, do not be called 'Rabbi'; for One is your Teacher, the Christ,[a] and you are all brethren. ⁹Do not call anyone on earth your father; for One is your Father, He who is in heaven. ¹⁰And do not be called teachers; for One is your Teacher, the Christ. ¹¹But he who is greatest among you shall be your servant. ¹²And whoever exalts himself will be humbled, and he who humbles himself will be exalted.

¹³"But woe to you, scribes and Pharisees, hypocrites! For you shut up the kingdom of heaven against men; for you neither go in yourselves, nor do you allow those who are entering to go in. ¹⁴Woe to you, scribes and Pharisees, hypocrites! For you devour widows' houses, and for a pretense make long prayers. Therefore you will receive greater condemnation.[a]

¹⁵"Woe to you, scribes and Pharisees, hypocrites! For you travel land and sea to win one proselyte, and when he is won, you make him twice as much a son of hell as yourselves.

22:30 [a]NU-Text omits of God. **22:32** [a]Exodus 3:6, 15 **22:37** [a]Deuteronomy 6:5 **22:39** [a]Leviticus 19:18 **22:44** [a]Psalm 110:1 **23:3** [a]NU-Text omits to observe. **23:8** [a]NU-Text omits the Christ. **23:14** [a]NU-Text omits this verse.

The Law of Solid Ground: The Pharisees' Contrast

(Matthew 23:13–32)

Jesus instructed others to follow the Pharisees' words, but not their actions. Their confused priorities, two-faced behavior, impure motives, and damaging leadership had lost them the trust of many common folk. Leaders must never forget: If people can't trust you, neither will they travel with you.

[16]"Woe to you, blind guides, who say, 'Whoever swears by the temple, it is nothing; but whoever swears by the gold of the temple, he is obliged *to perform it*.' [17]Fools and blind! For which is greater, the gold or the temple that sanctifies[a] the gold? [18]And, 'Whoever swears by the altar, it is nothing; but whoever swears by the gift that is on it, he is obliged *to perform it*.' [19]Fools and blind! For which is greater, the gift or the altar that sanctifies the gift? [20]Therefore he who swears by the altar, swears by it and by all things on it. [21]He who swears by the temple, swears by it and by Him who dwells[a] in it. [22]And he who swears by heaven, swears by the throne of God and by Him who sits on it.

[23]"Woe to you, scribes and Pharisees, hypocrites! For you pay tithe of mint and anise and cummin, and have neglected the weightier *matters* of the law: justice and mercy and faith. These you ought to have done, without leaving the others undone. [24]Blind guides, who strain out a gnat and swallow a camel!

[25]"Woe to you, scribes and Pharisees, hypocrites! For you cleanse the outside of the cup and dish, but inside they are full of extortion and self-indulgence.[a] [26]Blind Pharisee, first cleanse the inside of the cup and dish, that the outside of them may be clean also.

[27]"Woe to you, scribes and Pharisees, hypocrites! For you are like whitewashed tombs which indeed appear beautiful outwardly, but inside are full of dead *men's* bones and all uncleanness. [28]Even so you also outwardly appear righteous to men, but inside you are full of hypocrisy and lawlessness.

[29]"Woe to you, scribes and Pharisees, hypocrites! Because you build the tombs of the prophets and adorn the monuments of the righteous, [30]and say, 'If we had lived in the days of our fathers, we would not have been partakers with them in the blood of the prophets.'

[31]"Therefore you are witnesses against yourselves that you are sons of those who murdered the prophets. [32]Fill up, then, the measure of your fathers' *guilt*. [33]Serpents, brood of vipers! How can you escape the condemnation of hell? [34]Therefore, indeed, I send you prophets, wise men, and scribes: *some* of them you will kill and crucify, and *some* of them you will scourge in your synagogues and persecute from city to city, [35]that on you may come all the righteous blood shed on the earth, from the blood of righteous Abel to the blood of Zechariah, son of Berechiah, whom you murdered between the temple and the altar. [36]Assuredly, I say to you, all these things will come upon this generation.

Jesus Laments over Jerusalem

[37]"O Jerusalem, Jerusalem, the one who kills the prophets and stones those who are sent to her! How often I wanted to gather your children together, as a hen gathers her chicks under *her* wings, but you were not willing! [38]See! Your house is left to you desolate; [39]for I say to you, you shall see Me no more till you say, '*Blessed is He who comes in the name of the* LORD!'"[a]

Jesus Predicts the Destruction of the Temple

24 Then Jesus went out and departed from the temple, and His disciples came up to show Him the buildings of the temple. [2]And Jesus said to them, "Do you not see all these things? Assuredly, I say to you, not *one* stone shall be left here upon another, that shall not be thrown down."

The Law of Navigation: Jesus Knew the Steps to Take into the Future

(Matthew 24:1–44)

Jesus instructed His disciples on how to prepare for the future and what they could expect to endure. The Master gained credibility by charting their course into the future. Few things help us more than leaders who can mentally walk their people into the future, providing both direction and hope.

The Signs of the Times and the End of the Age

[3]Now as He sat on the Mount of Olives, the disciples came to Him privately, saying, "Tell us, when will these things be? And what *will be* the sign of Your coming, and of the end of the age?"

[4]And Jesus answered and said to them: "Take heed that no one deceives you. [5]For many will come in My name, saying, 'I am the Christ,' and will deceive many. [6]And you will hear of wars and rumors of wars. See that you are not troubled; for all[a] *these things* must come to pass, but the end is not yet. [7]For nation will rise against nation, and kingdom against kingdom. And there

---

23:17 [a]NU-Text reads *sanctified*. **23:21** [a]M-Text reads *dwelt*. **23:25** [a]M-Text reads *unrighteousness*. **23:39** [a]Psalm 118:26 **24:6** [a]NU-Text omits *all*.

will be famines, pestilences,[a] and earthquakes in various places. [8]All these *are* the beginning of sorrows.

[9]"Then they will deliver you up to tribulation and kill you, and you will be hated by all nations for My name's sake. [10]And then many will be offended, will betray one another, and will hate one another. [11]Then many false prophets will rise up and deceive many. [12]And because lawlessness will abound, the love of many will grow cold. [13]But he who endures to the end shall be saved. [14]And this gospel of the kingdom will be preached in all the world as a witness to all the nations, and then the end will come.

The Great Tribulation

[15]"Therefore when you see the '*abomination of desolation*,'[a] spoken of by Daniel the prophet, standing in the holy place" (whoever reads, let him understand), [16]"then let those who are in Judea flee to the mountains. [17]Let him who is on the housetop not go down to take anything out of his house. [18]And let him who is in the field not go back to get his clothes. [19]But woe to those who are pregnant and to those who are nursing babies in those days! [20]And pray that your flight may not be in winter or on the Sabbath. [21]For then there will be great tribulation, such as has not been since the beginning of the world until this time, no, nor ever shall be. [22]And unless those days were shortened, no flesh would be saved; but for the elect's sake those days will be shortened.

[23]"Then if anyone says to you, 'Look, here *is* the Christ!' or 'There!' do not believe *it*. [24]For false christs and false prophets will rise and show great signs and wonders to deceive, if possible, even the elect. [25]See, I have told you beforehand. [26]"Therefore if they say to you, 'Look, He is in the desert!' do not go out; *or* 'Look, *He is* in the inner rooms!' do not believe *it*. [27]For as the lightning comes from the east and flashes to the west, so also will the coming of the Son of Man be. [28]For wherever the carcass is, there the eagles will be gathered together.

The Coming of the Son of Man

[29]"Immediately after the tribulation of those days the sun will be darkened, and the moon will not give its light; the stars will fall from heaven, and the powers of the heavens will be shaken. [30]Then the sign of the Son of Man will appear in heaven, and then all the tribes of the earth will mourn, and they will see the Son of Man coming on the clouds of heaven with power and great glory. [31]And He will send His angels with a great sound of a trumpet, and they will gather together His elect from the four winds, from one end of heaven to the other.

The Parable of the Fig Tree

[32]"Now learn this parable from the fig tree: When its branch has already become tender and puts forth leaves, you know that summer *is* near. [33]So you also, when you see all these things, know that it[a] is near—at the doors! [34]Assuredly, I say to you, this generation will by no means pass away till all these things take place. [35]Heaven and earth will pass away, but My words will by no means pass away.

No One Knows the Day or Hour

[36]"But of that day and hour no one knows, not even the angels of heaven,[a] but My Father only. [37]But as the days of Noah *were,* so also will the coming of the Son of Man be. [38]For as in the days before the flood, they were eating and drinking, marrying and giving in marriage, until the day that Noah entered the ark, [39]and did not know until the flood came and took them all away, so also will the coming of the Son of Man be. [40]Then two *men* will be in the field: one will be taken and the other left. [41]Two *women will be* grinding at the mill: one will be taken and the other left. [42]Watch therefore, for you do not know what hour[a] your Lord is coming. [43]But know this, that if the master of the house had known what hour the thief would come, he would have watched and not allowed his house to be broken into. [44]Therefore you also be ready, for the Son of Man is coming at an hour you do not expect.

The Faithful Servant and the Evil Servant

[45]"Who then is a faithful and wise servant, whom his master made ruler over his household, to give them food in due season? [46]Blessed *is* that servant whom his master, when he comes, will find so doing. [47]Assuredly, I say to you that he will make him ruler over all his goods. [48]But if that evil servant says in his heart, 'My master is delaying his coming,'[a] [49]and begins to beat *his* fellow servants, and to eat and drink with the drunkards, [50]the master of that servant will come on a day when he is not looking for *him* and at an hour that he is not aware of, [51]and will cut

---

24:7 [a]NU-Text omits *pestilences*. **24:15** [a]Daniel 11:31; 12:11 **24:33** [a]Or *He* **24:36** [a]NU-Text adds *nor the Son.* **24:42** [a]NU-Text reads *day.* **24:48** [a]NU-Text omits *his coming.*

him in two and appoint *him* his portion with the hypocrites. There shall be weeping and gnashing of teeth.

The Parable of the Wise and Foolish Virgins

25 "Then the kingdom of heaven shall be likened to ten virgins who took their lamps and went out to meet the bridegroom. ²Now five of them were wise, and five *were* foolish. ³Those who *were* foolish took their lamps and took no oil with them, ⁴but the wise took oil in their vessels with their lamps. ⁵But while the bridegroom was delayed, they all slumbered and slept.

⁶"And at midnight a cry was *heard:* 'Behold, the bridegroom is coming;ᵃ go out to meet him!' ⁷Then all those virgins arose and trimmed their lamps. ⁸And the foolish said to the wise, 'Give us *some* of your oil, for our lamps are going out.' ⁹But the wise answered, saying, '*No,* lest there should not be enough for us and you; but go rather to those who sell, and buy for yourselves.' ¹⁰And while they went to buy, the bridegroom came, and those who were ready went in with him to the wedding; and the door was shut.

¹¹"Afterward the other virgins came also, saying, 'Lord, Lord, open to us!' ¹²But he answered and said, 'Assuredly, I say to you, I do not know you.'

¹³"Watch therefore, for you know neither the day nor the hourᵃ in which the Son of Man is coming.

The Parable of the Talents

¹⁴"For *the kingdom of heaven is* like a man traveling to a far country, *who* called his own servants and delivered his goods to them. ¹⁵And to one he gave five talents, to another two, and to another one, to each according to his own ability; and immediately he went on a journey. ¹⁶Then he who had received the five talents went and traded with them, and made another five talents. ¹⁷And likewise he who *had received* two gained two more also. ¹⁸But he who had received one went and dug in the ground, and hid his lord's money. ¹⁹After a long time the lord of those servants came and settled accounts with them.

²⁰"So he who had received five talents came and brought five other talents, saying, 'Lord, you delivered to me five talents; look, I have gained five more talents besides them.' ²¹His lord said to him, 'Well *done,* good and faithful servant; you were faithful over a few things, I will make you ruler over many things. Enter into the joy of your lord.' ²²He also who had received two talents came and said, 'Lord, you delivered to me two talents; look, I have gained two more talents besides them.' ²³His lord said to him, 'Well *done,* good and faithful servant; you have been faithful over a few things, I will make you ruler over many things. Enter into the joy of your lord.'

²⁴"Then he who had received the one talent came and said, 'Lord, I knew you to be a hard man, reaping where you have not sown, and gathering where you have not scattered seed. ²⁵And I was afraid, and went and hid your talent in the ground. Look, *there* you have *what is* yours.'

²⁶"But his lord answered and said to him, 'You wicked and lazy servant, you knew that I reap where I have not sown, and gather where I have not scattered seed. ²⁷So you ought to have deposited my money with the bankers, and at my coming I would have received back my own with interest. ²⁸So take the talent from him, and give *it* to him who has ten talents.

²⁹"For to everyone who has, more will be given, and he will have abundance; but from him who does not have, even what he has will be taken away. ³⁰And cast the unprofitable servant into the outer darkness. There will be weeping and gnashing of teeth.'

Preparation: The Man with the Plan Is the Man with the Power

(Matthew 25:1–30)

Charles de Gaulle once said, "History does not teach fatalism. . . . People get the history they deserve." Jesus taught two parables which illustrate this truth, both about people who diligently pursued a goal. Prepared leaders stand ready to meet the future. They don't react and are not easily surprised. This gives them power when it's time to move.

The Son of Man Will Judge the Nations

³¹"When the Son of Man comes in His glory, and all the holyᵃ angels with Him, then He will sit on the throne of His glory. ³²All the nations will be gathered before Him, and He will sepa-

25:6 ᵃNU-Text omits *is coming.* 25:13 ᵃNU-Text omits the rest of this verse. 25:31 ᵃNU-Text omits *holy.*

rate them one from another, as a shepherd divides *his* sheep from the goats. ³³And He will set the sheep on His right hand, but the goats on the left. ³⁴Then the King will say to those on His right hand, 'Come, you blessed of My Father, inherit the kingdom prepared for you from the foundation of the world: ³⁵for I was hungry and you gave Me food; I was thirsty and you gave Me drink; I was a stranger and you took Me in; ³⁶I *was* naked and you clothed Me; I was sick and you visited Me; I was in prison and you came to Me.'

³⁷"Then the righteous will answer Him, saying, 'Lord, when did we see You hungry and feed *You,* or thirsty and give *You* drink? ³⁸When did we see You a stranger and take *You* in, or naked and clothe *You?* ³⁹Or when did we see You sick, or in prison, and come to You?' ⁴⁰And the King will answer and say to them, 'Assuredly, I say to you, inasmuch as you did *it* to one of the least of these My brethren, you did *it* to Me.'

⁴¹"Then He will also say to those on the left hand, 'Depart from Me, you cursed, into the everlasting fire prepared for the devil and his angels: ⁴²for I was hungry and you gave Me no food; I was thirsty and you gave Me no drink; ⁴³I was a stranger and you did not take Me in, naked and you did not clothe Me, sick and in prison and you did not visit Me.'

⁴⁴"Then they also will answer Him,ᵃ saying, 'Lord, when did we see You hungry or thirsty or a stranger or naked or sick or in prison, and did not minister to You?' ⁴⁵Then He will answer them, saying, 'Assuredly, I say to you, inasmuch as you did not do *it* to one of the least of these, you did not do *it* to Me.' ⁴⁶And these will go away into everlasting punishment, but the righteous into eternal life."

The Plot to Kill Jesus

26 Now it came to pass, when Jesus had finished all these sayings, *that* He said to His disciples, ²"You know that after two days is the Passover, and the Son of Man will be delivered up to be crucified."

³Then the chief priests, the scribes,ᵃ and the elders of the people assembled at the palace of the high priest, who was called Caiaphas, ⁴and plotted to take Jesus by trickery and kill *Him.* ⁵But they said, "Not during the feast, lest there be an uproar among the people."

The Anointing at Bethany

⁶And when Jesus was in Bethany at the house of Simon the leper, ⁷a woman came to Him having an alabaster flask of very costly fragrant oil, and she poured *it* on His head as He sat *at the table.* ⁸But when His disciples saw *it,* they were indignant, saying, "Why this waste? ⁹For this fragrant oil might have been sold for much and given to *the* poor."

¹⁰But when Jesus was aware of *it,* He said to them, "Why do you trouble the woman? For she has done a good work for Me. ¹¹For you have the poor with you always, but Me you do not have always. ¹²For in pouring this fragrant oil on My body, she did *it* for My burial. ¹³Assuredly, I say to you, wherever this gospel is preached in the whole world, what this woman has done will also be told as a memorial to her."

Judas Agrees to Betray Jesus

¹⁴Then one of the twelve, called Judas Iscariot, went to the chief priests ¹⁵and said, "What are you willing to give me if I deliver Him to you?" And they counted out to him thirty pieces of silver. ¹⁶So from that time he sought opportunity to betray Him.

Jesus Celebrates Passover with His Disciples

¹⁷Now on the first *day of the Feast* of the Unleavened Bread the disciples came to Jesus, saying to Him, "Where do You want us to prepare for You to eat the Passover?"

25:44 ᵃNU-Text and M-Text omit *Him.*
26:3 ᵃNU-Text omits *the scribes.*

The Law of Legacy: Jesus Left a Memorial to His Followers
(Matthew 26:17–30)

Leaders solidify their legacy when they add the following components:

1. *Tangible Elements*
Jesus left the bread and the cup as symbols of His body and blood.
2. *Memorable Words*
Jesus spoke simple words and phrases to be restated, year after year.
3. *Regular Events*
Jesus instituted an event to be periodically celebrated.

[18]And He said, "Go into the city to a certain man, and say to him, 'The Teacher says, "My time is at hand; I will keep the Passover at your house with My disciples."'"

[19]So the disciples did as Jesus had directed them; and they prepared the Passover.

[20]When evening had come, He sat down with the twelve. [21]Now as they were eating, He said, "Assuredly, I say to you, one of you will betray Me."

[22]And they were exceedingly sorrowful, and each of them began to say to Him, "Lord, is it I?"

[23]He answered and said, "He who dipped *his* hand with Me in the dish will betray Me. [24]The Son of Man indeed goes just as it is written of Him, but woe to that man by whom the Son of Man is betrayed! It would have been good for that man if he had not been born."

[25]Then Judas, who was betraying Him, answered and said, "Rabbi, is it I?"

He said to him, "You have said it."

Jesus Institutes the Lord's Supper

[26]And as they were eating, Jesus took bread, blessed[a] and broke *it,* and gave *it* to the disciples and said, "Take, eat; this is My body."

[27]Then He took the cup, and gave thanks, and gave *it* to them, saying, "Drink from it, all of you. [28]For this is My blood of the new[a] covenant, which is shed for many for the remission of sins. [29]But I say to you, I will not drink of this fruit of the vine from now on until that day when I drink it new with you in My Father's kingdom."

[30]And when they had sung a hymn, they went out to the Mount of Olives.

Jesus Predicts Peter's Denial

[31]Then Jesus said to them, "All of you will be made to stumble because of Me this night, for it is written:

'I will strike the Shepherd,
 And the sheep of the flock will be
   scattered.'[a]

[32]But after I have been raised, I will go before you to Galilee."

[33]Peter answered and said to Him, "Even if all are made to stumble because of You, I will never be made to stumble."

[34]Jesus said to him, "Assuredly, I say to you that this night, before the rooster crows, you will deny Me three times."

[35]Peter said to Him, "Even if I have to die with You, I will not deny You!"

And so said all the disciples.

The Prayer in the Garden

[36]Then Jesus came with them to a place called Gethsemane, and said to the disciples, "Sit here while I go and pray over there." [37]And He took with Him Peter and the two sons of Zebedee, and He began to be sorrowful and deeply distressed. [38]Then He said to them, "My soul is exceedingly sorrowful, even to death. Stay here and watch with Me."

[39]He went a little farther and fell on His face, and prayed, saying, "O My Father, if it is possible, let this cup pass from Me; nevertheless, not as I will, but as You *will.*"

[40]Then He came to the disciples and found them sleeping, and said to Peter, "What! Could you not watch with Me one hour? [41]Watch and pray, lest you enter into temptation. The spirit indeed *is* willing, but the flesh *is* weak."

[42]Again, a second time, He went away and prayed, saying, "O My Father, if this cup cannot pass away from Me unless[a] I drink it, Your will be done." [43]And He came and found them asleep again, for their eyes were heavy.

[44]So He left them, went away again, and prayed the third time, saying the same words. [45]Then He came to His disciples and said to them, "Are *you* still sleeping and resting? Behold, the hour is at hand, and the Son of Man is being betrayed into the hands of sinners. [46]Rise, let us be going. See, My betrayer is at hand."

Betrayal and Arrest in Gethsemane

[47]And while He was still speaking, behold, Judas, one of the twelve, with a great multitude with swords and clubs, came from the chief priests and elders of the people.

[48]Now His betrayer had given them a sign, saying, "Whomever I kiss, He is the One; seize Him." [49]Immediately he went up to Jesus and said, "Greetings, Rabbi!" and kissed Him.

[50]But Jesus said to him, "Friend, why have you come?"

Then they came and laid hands on Jesus and took Him. [51]And suddenly, one of those *who were* with Jesus stretched out *his* hand and drew his sword, struck the servant of the high priest, and cut off his ear.

[52]But Jesus said to him, "Put your sword in its place, for all who take the sword will perish[a] by the sword. [53]Or do you think that I cannot now pray to My Father, and He will provide Me with

---

26:26 [a]M-Text reads *gave thanks for.*
26:28 [a]NU-Text omits *new.* 26:31 [a]Zechariah 13:7
26:42 [a]NU-Text reads *if this may not pass away unless.* 26:52 [a]M-Text reads *die.*

more than twelve legions of angels? [54]How then could the Scriptures be fulfilled, that it must happen thus?"

The Law of Sacrifice: Jesus Gave Up His Life

(Matthew 26:47—27:54)

Jesus gave up His life so we could have ours back. He died like us so we could live like Him. He not only pleased His Father, but received us as a bounty. This is the mark of a true leader. Leaders pay any price to get the job done.

[55]In that hour Jesus said to the multitudes, "Have you come out, as against a robber, with swords and clubs to take Me? I sat daily with you, teaching in the temple, and you did not seize Me. [56]But all this was done that the Scriptures of the prophets might be fulfilled."

Then all the disciples forsook Him and fled.

Jesus Faces the Sanhedrin

[57]And those who had laid hold of Jesus led *Him* away to Caiaphas the high priest, where the scribes and the elders were assembled. [58]But Peter followed Him at a distance to the high priest's courtyard. And he went in and sat with the servants to see the end.

[59]Now the chief priests, the elders,[a] and all the council sought false testimony against Jesus to put Him to death, [60]but found none. Even though many false witnesses came forward, they found none.[a] But at last two false witnesses[b] came forward [61]and said, "This *fellow* said, 'I am able to destroy the temple of God and to build it in three days.'"

[62]And the high priest arose and said to Him, "Do You answer nothing? What *is it* these men testify against You?" [63]But Jesus kept silent. And the high priest answered and said to Him, "I put You under oath by the living God: Tell us if You are the Christ, the Son of God!"

[64]Jesus said to him, "*It is as* you said. Nevertheless, I say to you, hereafter you will see the Son of Man sitting at the right hand of the Power, and coming on the clouds of heaven."

[65]Then the high priest tore his clothes, saying, "He has spoken blasphemy! What further need do we have of witnesses? Look, now you have heard His blasphemy! [66]What do you think?"

They answered and said, "He is deserving of death."

[67]Then they spat in His face and beat Him; and others struck *Him* with the palms of their hands, [68]saying, "Prophesy to us, Christ! Who is the one who struck You?"

Peter Denies Jesus, and Weeps Bitterly

[69]Now Peter sat outside in the courtyard. And a servant girl came to him, saying, "You also were with Jesus of Galilee."

[70]But he denied it before *them* all, saying, "I do not know what you are saying."

[71]And when he had gone out to the gateway, another *girl* saw him and said to those *who were* there, "This *fellow* also was with Jesus of Nazareth."

[72]But again he denied with an oath, "I do not know the Man!"

[73]And a little later those who stood by came up and said to Peter, "Surely you also are *one* of them, for your speech betrays you."

[74]Then he began to curse and swear, *saying,* "I do not know the Man!"

Immediately a rooster crowed. [75]And Peter remembered the word of Jesus who had said to him, "Before the rooster crows, you will deny Me three times." So he went out and wept bitterly.

Jesus Handed Over to Pontius Pilate

27 When morning came, all the chief priests and elders of the people plotted against Jesus to put Him to death. [2]And when they had bound Him, they led Him away and delivered Him to Pontius[a] Pilate the governor.

Judas Hangs Himself

[3]Then Judas, His betrayer, seeing that He had been condemned, was remorseful and brought back the thirty pieces of silver to the chief priests and elders, [4]saying, "I have sinned by betraying innocent blood."

And they said, "What *is that* to us? You see *to it!*"

[5]Then he threw down the pieces of silver in the temple and departed, and went and hanged himself.

26:59 [a]NU-Text omits *the elders*. **26:60** [a]NU-Text puts a comma after *but found none,* does not capitalize *Even,* and omits *they found none.* [b]NU-Text omits *false witnesses*. **27:2** [a]NU-Text omits *Pontius*.

21 QUALITIES

RESPONSIBILITY

Pontius Pilate Failed to Lead
(Matthew 27:11–31)

President Harry Truman was right when he said, "The buck stops here." Leaders cannot pass the buck. We cannot lead without taking responsibility. It comes with the territory.

Pontius Pilate, the Roman governor of Israel, gives us a sad example of a leader who failed to take responsibility. When Jesus appeared before him for judgment, he could find nothing wrong with Him. Yet instead of judging Him as innocent, he succumbed to the pressure of the crowd. Sensing they wanted to punish an innocent man, he gave them a choice: Barabbas or Jesus? When they wrongly chose Jesus as the more guilty man, Pilate walked over to a basin of water and tried to wash his hands of any responsibility for his decision. He pretended he could evade ownership of the consequences. Pilate committed the sin of omission and tried to get off on a legal technicality.

None of this surprised the Jews, since Pilate had a history of such behavior. He tended to withdraw whenever things heated up. Once he put the Roman eagle in the temple, prompting 5,000 Jews to march to his vacation home to demand he remove it. He called in the army and demanded they leave. When they refused, he threatened to cut off their heads. The Jews got down on their knees, in essence saying, "Go ahead!" Shocked by their moral conviction, he backed down. From that point on, the Jews knew this man lacked a backbone and would run from responsibility. He illustrates moral and political compromise.

Just why did Pilate "wash his hands" of responsibility?

1. *He had a problem with foundations* (v. 22).
   Pilate never forged the character to withstand adversity. Conflict paralyzed him.
2. *He had a problem with futility* (vv. 23, 24).
   He perceived that no good would come from a right decision, so why waste time? Apathy proliferates when we sense that action seems useless.
3. *He had a problem with fear* (v. 24).
   Pilate felt preoccupied with survival. If he fought the Jews, he feared the loss of control, image, or position. His wife's warning added fuel to his fear.
4. *He had a problem with failure* (v. 24).
   Pilate knew a riot was brewing. The last time it happened, he failed to rise to the occasion and the Jews called his bluff. They knew he worried more about failure than they did.
5. *He had a problem with focus* (v. 24).
   Leaders cannot be neutral or passive over crucial decisions. Pilate picked up a basin and tried to wash his hands of the whole mess. No good leader does this.

For a positive example of responsibility, see p. 536.

⁶But the chief priests took the silver pieces and said, "It is not lawful to put them into the treasury, because they are the price of blood." ⁷And they consulted together and bought with them the potter's field, to bury strangers in. ⁸Therefore that field has been called the Field of Blood to this day.

⁹Then was fulfilled what was spoken by Jeremiah the prophet, saying, *"And they took the thirty pieces of silver, the value of Him who was priced, whom they of the children of Israel priced, ¹⁰and gave them for the potter's field, as the* LORD *directed me."*ᵃ

Jesus Faces Pilate

¹¹Now Jesus stood before the governor. And the governor asked Him, saying, "Are You the King of the Jews?"

Jesus said to him, *"It is as* you say." ¹²And while He was being accused by the chief priests and elders, He answered nothing.

¹³Then Pilate said to Him, "Do You not hear how many things they testify against You?" ¹⁴But He answered him not one word, so that the governor marveled greatly.

Taking the Place of Barabbas

¹⁵Now at the feast the governor was accustomed to releasing to the multitude one prisoner whom they wished. ¹⁶And at that time they had a notorious prisoner called Barabbas.ᵃ ¹⁷Therefore, when they had gathered together, Pilate said to them, "Whom do you want me to release to you? Barabbas, or Jesus who is called Christ?" ¹⁸For he knew that they had handed Him over because of envy.

¹⁹While he was sitting on the judgment seat, his wife sent to him, saying, "Have nothing to do with that just Man, for I have suffered many things today in a dream because of Him."

²⁰But the chief priests and elders persuaded the multitudes that they should ask for Barabbas and destroy Jesus. ²¹The governor answered and said to them, "Which of the two do you want me to release to you?"

They said, "Barabbas!"

²²Pilate said to them, "What then shall I do with Jesus who is called Christ?"

They all said to him, "Let Him be crucified!"

²³Then the governor said, "Why, what evil has He done?"

But they cried out all the more, saying, "Let Him be crucified!"

²⁴When Pilate saw that he could not prevail at all, but rather *that* a tumult was rising, he took water and washed *his* hands before the multitude, saying, "I am innocent of the blood of this just Person.ᵃ You see *to it.*"

²⁵And all the people answered and said, "His blood *be* on us and on our children."

²⁶Then he released Barabbas to them; and when he had scourged Jesus, he delivered *Him* to be crucified.

The Soldiers Mock Jesus

²⁷Then the soldiers of the governor took Jesus into the Praetorium and gathered the whole garrison around Him. ²⁸And they stripped Him and put a scarlet robe on Him. ²⁹When they had twisted a crown of thorns, they put *it* on His head, and a reed in His right hand. And they bowed the knee before Him and mocked Him, saying, "Hail, King of the Jews!" ³⁰Then they spat on Him, and took the reed and struck Him on the head. ³¹And when they had mocked Him, they took the robe off Him, put His *own* clothes on Him, and led Him away to be crucified.

The King on a Cross

³²Now as they came out, they found a man of Cyrene, Simon by name. Him they compelled to bear His cross. ³³And when they had come to a place called Golgotha, that is to say, Place of a Skull, ³⁴they gave Him sourᵃ wine mingled with gall to drink. But when He had tasted *it,* He would not drink.

³⁵Then they crucified Him, and divided His garments, casting lots,ᵃ that it might be fulfilled which was spoken by the prophet:

" *They divided My garments among them,
And for My clothing they cast lots."*ᵇ

³⁶Sitting down, they kept watch over Him there. ³⁷And they put up over His head the accusation written against Him:

THIS IS JESUS THE KING
OF THE JEWS.

³⁸Then two robbers were crucified with Him, one on the right and another on the left.

³⁹And those who passed by blasphemed Him, wagging their heads ⁴⁰and saying, "You who destroy the temple and build *it* in three days, save Yourself! If You are the Son of God, come down from the cross."

⁴¹Likewise the chief priests also, mocking

27:10 ᵃJeremiah 32:6–9 27:16 ᵃNU-Text reads *Jesus Barabbas.* 27:24 ᵃNU-Text omits *just.* 27:34 ᵃNU-Text omits *sour.* 27:35 ᵃNU-Text and M-Text omit the rest of this verse. ᵇPsalm 22:18

21 LAWS

JESUS AND THE LAW OF LEGACY

A Leader's Lasting Value Is Measured by Succession
(Matthew 28:16–20)

Just about anybody can make an organization look good for a moment—by launching a flashy new program or product, drawing crowds to a big event, or slashing the budget to boost the bottom line. But leaders who leave a legacy take a different approach. They lead with tomorrow as well as today in mind.

When all is said and done, your ability as a leader will be judged by how well your people and your organization did after you were gone. Your lasting value will be measured by succession.

To create a legacy, you need to be strategic and intentional. The following guidelines can help you get started:

1. *Decide ahead of time what you are willing to give up.*

Being a leader has a price; being a leader who leaves a legacy has an even greater price. When you work to create a legacy, your life is no longer your own. That's why it's so important to *know* what you are willing to give up so that others can go up.

What are you willing to give up? How much of your time? How much of your money? How many opportunities will you forgo? How many of your dreams are you willing to set aside to ensure that one or maybe two survive in the lives of others?

2. *Take the initiative to start the process.*

If you want to create a legacy, you have to initiate the process—and there will be times when you'll have to fight for it. Jesus' followers had various agendas. Some, like Simon the Zealot, wanted Him to lead a revolt against Rome. Others, like James and John, wanted positions of power (Mark 10:37). Even Peter tried to dissuade Jesus from the very act that would release the other disciples to follow in Jesus' footsteps (Matt. 16:22).

3. *Know your goals with each person.*

The process of creating a legacy relies primarily on people. It requires the selection of the right people and the right development process for each individual. Jesus carefully chose His legacy carriers. Scripture says He intentionally picked the twelve He wanted; He didn't take the first guys who showed up. And He didn't treat all of them the same. He had a specific development process for each person.

4. *Prepare to pass the baton well.*

Once you have prepared your people, you need to prepare for the transition. There's a real art to preparing a successor, and it doesn't always go smoothly. Jesus had trouble handing the baton to His followers. He appeared to them after His resurrection and gave them the Great Commission because some of them still didn't get it. Peter, James, and John all returned to fishing *after they saw Jesus resurrected!* As you prepare to hand off to a successor, do everything you can to make for a smooth transition. And even then, plan to offer additional assistance without getting in the way.

Jesus' IDEA for Leaving a Legacy

Jesus faced the task of changing the lives of people thousands of years after Him—and He succeeded. He did it without writing any books, building any schools, or founding any institutions. So if Jesus chose to deposit His legacy in people, we should learn His method and practice it as best we can. Consider Jesus' IDEA for working in the lives of people:

Instruction

Jesus constantly taught, most often with parables. More than half of the Gospels' content presents Jesus' teaching. The parable of the sower gives us insight into how Jesus worked. When the disciples asked Him about the meaning of the parable, He explained it, revealing insightful truth cloaked in the story.

Demonstration

Educational philosophy today relies too heavily on instruction. If Jesus had taught the disciples and done nothing more, they never would have carried on His legacy. But Jesus shared His life with them.

Jesus' disciples went through three phases in their training:

- *Come and see.* Jesus invited them to observe Him and His priorities. He invited them to evaluate Him (and themselves in light of what He was doing).
- *Come and follow Me.* Jesus asked for a greater level of commitment. The disciples were to do more than observe; they were to associate with Him.
- *Come and be with Me.* This phase occupied most of Jesus' three years of ministry. He required the disciples' commitment and companionship. The Twelve were present with Him as He taught, traveled, prayed, ate with "sinners," healed the sick, and raised the dead. They saw consistency between His teaching and His actions, and they learned the *how* and *why* of all He did.

Experience

After Jesus had modeled good leadership and taught spiritual truths, He didn't turn His men loose and move on. He gradually worked them into positions of independent leadership by giving them valuable experience. Jesus gave His followers an opportunity to practice what He had taught and to practice leadership.

Assessment

Jesus repeatedly evaluated the progress of His disciples. After the return of the seventy, He debriefed them, gave them instruction concerning priorities, and celebrated with them (Luke 10:17–24). Jesus also gave individual assessment to His disciples, including specific feedback concerning their character and their capabilities.

If you want to leave a legacy, you must look to people to carry it for you. Find the right people, and use the right preparation process for each of them. Only as you pour yourself into them will they be able to pour out themselves for others. No one can give what he does not have.

with the scribes and elders,[a] said, [42]"He saved others; Himself He cannot save. If He is the King of Israel,[a] let Him now come down from the cross, and we will believe Him.[b] [43]He trusted in God; let Him deliver Him now if He will have Him; for He said, 'I am the Son of God.'"

[44]Even the robbers who were crucified with Him reviled Him with the same thing.

Jesus Dies on the Cross

[45]Now from the sixth hour until the ninth hour there was darkness over all the land. [46]And about the ninth hour Jesus cried out with a loud voice, saying, "Eli, Eli, lama sabachthani?" that is, *"My God, My God, why have You forsaken Me?"*[a]

[47]Some of those who stood there, when they heard *that,* said, "This Man is calling for Elijah!" [48]Immediately one of them ran and took a sponge, filled *it* with sour wine and put *it* on a reed, and offered it to Him to drink.

[49]The rest said, "Let Him alone; let us see if Elijah will come to save Him."

[50]And Jesus cried out again with a loud voice, and yielded up His spirit.

[51]Then, behold, the veil of the temple was torn in two from top to bottom; and the earth quaked, and the rocks were split, [52]and the graves were opened; and many bodies of the saints who had fallen asleep were raised; [53]and coming out of the graves after His resurrection, they went into the holy city and appeared to many.

[54]So when the centurion and those with him, who were guarding Jesus, saw the earthquake and the things that had happened, they feared greatly, saying, "Truly this was the Son of God!"

[55]And many women who followed Jesus from Galilee, ministering to Him, were there looking on from afar, [56]among whom were Mary Magdalene, Mary the mother of James and Joses,[a] and the mother of Zebedee's sons.

Jesus Buried in Joseph's Tomb

[57]Now when evening had come, there came a rich man from Arimathea, named Joseph, who himself had also become a disciple of Jesus. [58]This man went to Pilate and asked for the body of Jesus. Then Pilate commanded the body to be given to him. [59]When Joseph had taken the body, he wrapped it in a clean linen cloth, [60]and laid it in his new tomb which he had hewn out of the rock; and he rolled a large stone against the door of the tomb, and departed. [61]And Mary Magdalene was there, and the other Mary, sitting opposite the tomb.

Pilate Sets a Guard

[62]On the next day, which followed the Day of Preparation, the chief priests and Pharisees gathered together to Pilate, [63]saying, "Sir, we remember, while He was still alive, how that deceiver said, 'After three days I will rise.' [64]Therefore command that the tomb be made secure until the third day, lest His disciples come by night[a] and steal Him *away,* and say to the people, 'He has risen from the dead.' So the last deception will be worse than the first."

[65]Pilate said to them, "You have a guard; go your way, make *it* as secure as you know how." [66]So they went and made the tomb secure, sealing the stone and setting the guard.

He Is Risen

28 Now after the Sabbath, as the first *day* of the week began to dawn, Mary Magdalene and the other Mary came to see the tomb. [2]And behold, there was a great earthquake; for an angel of the Lord descended from heaven, and came and rolled back the stone from the door,[a] and sat on it. [3]His countenance was like lightning, and his clothing as white as snow. [4]And the guards shook for fear of him, and became like dead *men.*

[5]But the angel answered and said to the women, "Do not be afraid, for I know that you seek Jesus who was crucified. [6]He is not here; for He is risen, as He said. Come, see the place where the Lord lay. [7]And go quickly and tell His disciples that He is risen from the dead, and indeed He is going before you into Galilee; there you will see Him. Behold, I have told you."

[8]So they went out quickly from the tomb with fear and great joy, and ran to bring His disciples word.

The Women Worship the Risen Lord

[9]And as they went to tell His disciples,[a] behold, Jesus met them, saying, "Rejoice!" So they came and held Him by the feet and worshiped Him. [10]Then Jesus said to them, "Do not be afraid. Go *and* tell My brethren to go to Galilee, and there they will see Me."

The Soldiers Are Bribed

[11]Now while they were going, behold, some of the guard came into the city and reported to

---

27:41 [a]M-Text reads *with the scribes, the Pharisees, and the elders.* **27:42** [a]NU-Text reads *He is the King of Israel!* [b]NU-Text and M-Text read *we will believe in Him.* **27:46** [a]Psalm 22:1 **27:56** [a]NU-Text reads *Joseph.* **27:64** [a]NU-Text omits *by night.* **28:2** [a]NU-Text omits *from the door.* **28:9** [a]NU-Text omits the first clause of this verse.

The Law of Victory: Jesus Defeated Our Greatest Enemy

(Matthew 28:1–20)

Jesus raised several people from the dead, but each case differed from His own resurrection. Those people would eventually die again. But Jesus rose from the dead, never to die again. He defeated mankind's greatest enemy: death. All other problems *are* problems because they kill us. Once Jesus defeated death, His followers could operate in total security.

No struggle is too big for God. No question is unanswerable. No problem is too difficult. The resurrection of Christ trumpeted good news from the graveyard! In spite of the black prospects, in spite of the big problems, in spite of the bad predictions—Jesus practiced the Law of Victory, decisively defeating even death itself.

the chief priests all the things that had happened. [12]When they had assembled with the elders and consulted together, they gave a large sum of money to the soldiers, [13]saying, "Tell them, 'His disciples came at night and stole Him *away* while we slept.' [14]And if this comes to the governor's ears, we will appease him and make you secure." [15]So they took the money and did as they were instructed; and this saying is commonly reported among the Jews until this day.

The Great Commission

[16]Then the eleven disciples went away into Galilee, to the mountain which Jesus had appointed for them. [17]When they saw Him, they worshiped Him; but some doubted.

[18]And Jesus came and spoke to them, saying, "All authority has been given to Me in heaven and on earth. [19]Go therefore[a] and make disciples of all the nations, baptizing them in the name of the Father and of the Son and of the Holy Spirit, [20]teaching them to observe all things that I have commanded you; and lo, I am with you always, *even* to the end of the age." Amen.[a]

28:19 [a]M-Text omits *therefore*. **28:20** [a]NU-Text omits *Amen*.

MARK
Jesus as a Servant-Leader

SUMMARY

The Book of Mark is the shortest of the four Gospels. Written during a time of acute persecution, it cuts straight to the point, discussing Jesus' identity, the role of suffering, and the necessity of faith.

Mark, the author, was a disciple of Peter; therefore Peter's perspective appears repeatedly in the book. Mark paints a picture of Jesus as a Servant-leader. He clearly and concisely portrays Christ as a compassionate model to follow. His fast-paced narrative describes the suffering Servant who engaged in consistent ministry to others through healing, teaching, feeding, encouraging, and restoring the broken.

It makes sense that Mark might maintain such a focus, since he needed such encouragement himself. He traveled with Paul and Barnabas across Asia Minor on their first missionary journey, but sometime during their ministry, Mark grew frightened and left the team to return home. Later, when he wanted to try it again, Paul considered him young and cowardly and rejected his participation. Barnabas, however, took Mark under his wing and mentored this young, emerging leader. Years afterward, Paul wrote from prison and asked that Mark be sent to him, since "he is useful to me for ministry" (2 Tim. 4:11). Paul changed his opinion because Mark had grown into a responsible leader.

Mark sees Jesus as the Ultimate Leader, just as did Matthew. Mark's picture, however, portrays Him not so much as the Messiah but as the model for all people. Jesus gave Himself to others. He spent Himself meeting physical needs (3:1–11); He spent time with His twelve staff members (3:13, 14); He empowered those twelve for ministry (3:14–19); and He spent time teaching the people (3:23–29). More than anything, Mark teaches us that the Master considers relationships to be paramount. In this book we see Jesus incarnating the Laws of Empowerment, Sacrifice, Connection, Priorities, Timing, Reproduction, and Legacy.

God's Role in Mark

God's role is best seen in Jesus, the incarnation of God, and in the Holy Spirit, the inspiration of God. Jesus demonstrated what God looks like as a human. Through Him we have a model to follow for our attitudes, our lifestyles, our conversations, our worldview, and our relationships. Through the Holy Spirit, we have a divinely inspired biography of this incarnated God. Through their work, we have a picture of the authority God exercises over both the spiritual and the physical realms.

Leaders in Mark

Jesus, John the Baptizer, Herod, Pontius Pilate, the chief priests in the Sanhedrin

Other People of Influence in Mark

The twelve disciples, the women who followed Jesus, the Pharisees

Lessons in Leadership

- Effective leadership requires no worldly credentials.

- Leaders who are change agents always transform the traditional paradigm.

- Healthy leaders are first servants.

- Effective leaders balance the need for solitude and socializing.

- Good leaders provide security and confidence for their followers.

- The greater the leader, the greater the humility and sacrifice required.

- Principles serve effective leaders so leaders can effectively serve the people.

LEADERSHIP HIGHLIGHTS IN MARK

John the Baptist Prepares the Way

1 The beginning of the gospel of Jesus Christ, the Son of God. [2]As it is written in the Prophets:[a]

> "Behold, I send My messenger before Your face,
> Who will prepare Your way before You."[b]
>
> [3] "The voice of one crying in the wilderness:
> 'Prepare the way of the LORD;
> Make His paths straight.'"[a]

[4]John came baptizing in the wilderness and preaching a baptism of repentance for the remission of sins. [5]Then all the land of Judea, and those from Jerusalem, went out to him and were all baptized by him in the Jordan River, confessing their sins.

[6]Now John was clothed with camel's hair and with a leather belt around his waist, and he ate locusts and wild honey. [7]And he preached, saying, "There comes One after me who is mightier than I, whose sandal strap I am not worthy to stoop down and loose. [8]I indeed baptized you with water, but He will baptize you with the Holy Spirit."

John Baptizes Jesus

[9]It came to pass in those days that Jesus came from Nazareth of Galilee, and was baptized by John in the Jordan. [10]And immediately, coming up from[a] the water, He saw the heavens parting and the Spirit descending upon Him like a dove. [11]Then a voice came from heaven, "You are My beloved Son, in whom I am well pleased."

Satan Tempts Jesus

[12]Immediately the Spirit drove Him into the wilderness. [13]And He was there in the wilderness forty days, tempted by Satan, and was with the wild beasts; and the angels ministered to Him.

Jesus Begins His Galilean Ministry

[14]Now after John was put in prison, Jesus came to Galilee, preaching the gospel of the kingdom[a] of God, [15]and saying, "The time is fulfilled, and the kingdom of God is at hand. Repent, and believe in the gospel."

1:2 [a]NU-Text reads *Isaiah the prophet.* [b]Malachi 3:1
1:3 [a]Isaiah 40:3 **1:10** [a]NU-Text reads *out of.*
1:14 [a]NU-Text omits *of the kingdom.*

JOHN THE BAPTIZER

GOOD LEADERS PREPARE THE WAY FOR CHANGE
(Mark 1:1–8)

PROFILE IN LEADERSHIP

One of the marks of an excellent leader is how he or she brings about transformation in people and organizations. John the Baptizer performed this role well as he prepared the Jewish people for Jesus. Since this Messiah would be very different from what everyone expected, John had to get the people ready for this radical shift.

A great word picture for the kind of person necessary to lead change comes from the airline industry. When people take their seats, airline flight attendants always look for leaders. As they announce the requirements for sitting in the exit row, they concisely explain the role of a leader:

1. You must be able to understand the instructions concerning the exit door.
2. You must be able to open the door.
3. You must be able to verbally guide others through the door.

Have you ever stopped to think that this is what is required when you lead others? You need to know what must happen. You must be able to pull it off. And you need to be able to take others with you.

Four Fishermen Called as Disciples

[16]And as He walked by the Sea of Galilee, He saw Simon and Andrew his brother casting a net into the sea; for they were fishermen. [17]Then Jesus said to them, "Follow Me, and I will make you become fishers of men." [18]They immediately left their nets and followed Him.

[19]When He had gone a little farther from there, He saw James the *son* of Zebedee, and John his brother, who also *were* in the boat mending their nets. [20]And immediately He called them, and they left their father Zebedee in the boat with the hired servants, and went after Him.

Marks of Leadership in Jesus' Ministry

(Mark 1:16–35)

Jesus clearly was a different sort of leader from the scribes and Pharisees of His day. Mark 1 reveals the following qualities in Him:

1. *Competence:* He took responsibility to "make" them fishers of men (v. 17).
2. *Comprehension:* He had a thorough understanding of the scriptures (v. 22).
3. *Command:* He had authority and command of every situation (vv. 25–27).
4. *Compassion:* He served and healed the pain of others (vv. 30, 31).
5. *Control:* He maintained organization and control in messy situations (v. 34).
6. *Communion:* He stayed renewed by connecting to the Source of His power (v. 35).

Jesus Casts Out an Unclean Spirit

[21]Then they went into Capernaum, and immediately on the Sabbath He entered the synagogue and taught. [22]And they were astonished at His teaching, for He taught them as one having authority, and not as the scribes.

[23]Now there was a man in their synagogue with an unclean spirit. And he cried out, [24]saying, "Let *us* alone! What have we to do with You, Jesus of Nazareth? Did You come to destroy us? I know who You are—the Holy One of God!"

[25]But Jesus rebuked him, saying, "Be quiet, and come out of him!" [26]And when the unclean spirit had convulsed him and cried out with a loud voice, he came out of him. [27]Then they were all amazed, so that they questioned among themselves, saying, "What is this? What new doctrine *is* this? For with authority[a] He commands even the unclean spirits, and they obey Him." [28]And immediately His fame spread throughout all the region around Galilee.

Peter's Mother-in-Law Healed

[29]Now as soon as they had come out of the synagogue, they entered the house of Simon and Andrew, with James and John. [30]But Simon's wife's mother lay sick with a fever, and they told Him about her at once. [31]So He came and took her by the hand and lifted her up, and immediately the fever left her. And she served them.

Many Healed After Sabbath Sunset

[32]At evening, when the sun had set, they brought to Him all who were sick and those who were demon-possessed. [33]And the whole city was gathered together at the door. [34]Then He healed many who were sick with various diseases, and cast out many demons; and He did not allow the demons to speak, because they knew Him.

Preaching in Galilee

[35]Now in the morning, having risen a long while before daylight, He went out and departed to a solitary place; and there He prayed. [36]And Simon and those *who were* with Him searched for Him. [37]When they found Him, they said to Him, "Everyone is looking for You."

[38]But He said to them, "Let us go into the next towns, that I may preach there also, because for this purpose I have come forth." [39]And He was preaching in their synagogues throughout all Galilee, and casting out demons.

Jesus Cleanses a Leper

[40]Now a leper came to Him, imploring Him, kneeling down to Him and saying to Him, "If You are willing, You can make me clean."

[41]Then Jesus, moved with compassion, stretched out *His* hand and touched him, and said to him, "I am willing; be cleansed." [42]As soon as He had spoken, immediately the leprosy left him, and he was cleansed. [43]And He strictly warned him and sent him away at once, [44]and said to him, "See that you say nothing to anyone; but go your way, show yourself to the priest, and offer for your cleansing those things which Moses commanded, as a testimony to them."

[45]However, he went out and began to proclaim *it* freely, and to spread the matter, so that

---

1:27 [a]NU-Text reads *What is this? A new doctrine with authority.*

The Law of Priorities:
Jesus Didn't Let Others Dictate His Agenda
(Mark 1:32–38)

Jesus often left the demands of His work to come apart and pray. He used this solitude to regain perspective and once more see the big picture. Watch the sequence of events detailed in this passage:

1. *The pressure is on.* The day is over, but the crowds have just begun to make demands (vv. 32–34).
2. *The paradox is obvious.* Jesus left in the middle of ministry time, with needs unmet (v. 35).
3. *The point is clear.* Jesus had to pause, leave the people, and replenish His own life (v. 35).
4. *The people are demanding.* Followers hunted for Jesus, reminding Him how much they needed Him (vv. 36, 37).
5. *The purpose is declared.* His Father renewed His perspective and given direction (v. 38).

Jesus' priorities came from His heavenly Father, not from people. He always used the priorities He established to serve the people. So, how do you determine your own daily priorities?

Jesus could no longer openly enter the city, but was outside in deserted places; and they came to Him from every direction.

Jesus Forgives and Heals a Paralytic

2 And again He entered Capernaum after *some* days, and it was heard that He was in the house. ²Immediately[a] many gathered together, so that there was no longer room to receive *them,* not even near the door. And He preached the word to them. ³Then they came to Him, bringing a paralytic who was carried by four *men.* ⁴And when they could not come near Him because of the crowd, they uncovered the roof where He was. So when they had broken through, they let down the bed on which the paralytic was lying.

⁵When Jesus saw their faith, He said to the paralytic, "Son, your sins are forgiven you."

⁶And some of the scribes were sitting there and reasoning in their hearts, ⁷"Why does this *Man* speak blasphemies like this? Who can forgive sins but God alone?"

⁸But immediately, when Jesus perceived in His spirit that they reasoned thus within themselves, He said to them, "Why do you reason about these things in your hearts? ⁹Which is easier, to say to the paralytic, '*Your* sins are forgiven you,' or to say, 'Arise, take up your bed and walk'? ¹⁰But that you may know that the Son of Man has power on earth to forgive sins"—He said to the paralytic, ¹¹"I say to you, arise, take up your bed, and go to your house." ¹²Immediately he arose,

took up the bed, and went out in the presence of them all, so that all were amazed and glorified God, saying, "We never saw *anything* like this!"

2:2 ªNU-Text omits *Immediately.*

The Law of Victory: The Four Men Got Their Friend to Jesus
(Mark 2:1–12)

Four men collected their paralyzed friend and attempted to take him to Jesus to be healed, but because of the large crowd, they could not reach Christ. So did that stop them? Absolutely not. They cut a hole in the roof and used a rope to let their paralyzed friend down through the opening.

Leaders who practice the Law of Victory don't allow obstacles to stop their progress. They determine to find a way to reach their goal and help their team win. Fulfilling a dream often does not come easy or within the realm of the conventional. In this case, practicing the Law of Victory forced the men to dare to do the difficult, the unorthodox, and the costly thing.

Team Building: Jesus Assembled a Team to Own a Vision

(Mark 2:14–17)

One could argue that Jesus constructed the most important team ever assembled. He chose specific individuals for specific roles. He chose the unlikely and developed them to reach their potential. And He chose an odd player—Matthew—to add to the mix.

Matthew was a hated tax collector, despised because he and his ilk seized money for the Roman government—traitors in the eyes of most Israelites. Jesus had the spiritual insight to choose those who were unloved and showed little promise. He saw Matthew's potential to become an apostle and a writer. Jesus never felt bound by human opinion or approval. He didn't judge by externals. He treated individuals based on their future potential, not present status.

In the same way, we must free ourselves from the boundaries that keep us from building a balanced team. Consider some questions we might learn from Jesus:

1. What positive qualities exist that may be seen as negative behavior?
2. Do the individuals show initiative, even if it has been misdirected?
3. Would these people add positive chemistry and unique value if placed on the team?
4. Are they hungry to become something more than what they are now?
5. Do they demonstrate passion that could be redirected?
6. Could they play a needed role on the team?

Matthew the Tax Collector

¹³Then He went out again by the sea; and all the multitude came to Him, and He taught them. ¹⁴As He passed by, He saw Levi the *son* of Alphaeus sitting at the tax office. And He said to him, "Follow Me." So he arose and followed Him.

¹⁵Now it happened, as He was dining in *Levi's* house, that many tax collectors and sinners also sat together with Jesus and His disciples; for there were many, and they followed Him. ¹⁶And when the scribes and[a] Pharisees saw Him eating with the tax collectors and sinners, they said to His disciples, "How *is it* that He eats and drinks with tax collectors and sinners?"

¹⁷When Jesus heard *it,* He said to them, "Those who are well have no need of a physician, but those who are sick. I did not come to call *the* righteous, but sinners, to repentance."[a]

Jesus Is Questioned About Fasting

¹⁸The disciples of John and of the Pharisees were fasting. Then they came and said to Him, "Why do the disciples of John and of the Pharisees fast, but Your disciples do not fast?"

¹⁹And Jesus said to them, "Can the friends of the bridegroom fast while the bridegroom is with them? As long as they have the bridegroom with them they cannot fast. ²⁰But the days will come when the bridegroom will be taken away from them, and then they will fast in those days. ²¹No one sews a piece of unshrunk cloth on an old garment; or else the new piece pulls away from the old, and the tear is made worse. ²²And no one puts new wine into old wineskins; or else the new wine bursts the wineskins, the wine is spilled, and the wineskins are ruined. But new wine must be put into new wineskins."

Jesus Is Lord of the Sabbath

²³Now it happened that He went through the grainfields on the Sabbath; and as they went His disciples began to pluck the heads of grain. ²⁴And the Pharisees said to Him, "Look, why do they do what is not lawful on the Sabbath?"

²⁵But He said to them, "Have you never read what David did when he was in need and hungry, he and those with him: ²⁶how he went into the house of God *in the days of* Abiathar the high priest, and ate the showbread, which is not lawful to eat except for the priests, and also gave some to those who were with him?"

²⁷And He said to them, "The Sabbath was made for man, and not man for the Sabbath. ²⁸Therefore the Son of Man is also Lord of the Sabbath."

2:16 [a]NU-Text reads *of the.* **2:17** [a]NU-Text omits *to repentance.*

Healing on the Sabbath

3 And He entered the synagogue again, and a man was there who had a withered hand. [2]So they watched Him closely, whether He would heal him on the Sabbath, so that they might accuse Him. [3]And He said to the man who had the withered hand, "Step forward." [4]Then He said to them, "Is it lawful on the Sabbath to do good or to do evil, to save life or to kill?" But they kept silent. [5]And when He had looked around at them with anger, being grieved by the hardness of their hearts, He said to the man, "Stretch out your hand." And he stretched *it* out, and his hand was restored as whole as the other.[a] [6]Then the Pharisees went out and immediately plotted with the Herodians against Him, how they might destroy Him.

A Great Multitude Follows Jesus

[7]But Jesus withdrew with His disciples to the sea. And a great multitude from Galilee followed Him, and from Judea [8]and Jerusalem and Idumea and beyond the Jordan; and those from Tyre and Sidon, a great multitude, when they heard how many things He was doing, came to Him. [9]So He told His disciples that a small boat should be kept ready for Him because of the multitude, lest they should crush Him. [10]For He healed many, so that as many as had afflictions pressed about Him to touch Him. [11]And the unclean spirits, whenever they saw Him, fell down before Him and cried out, saying, "You are the Son of God." [12]But He sternly warned them that they should not make Him known.

The Twelve Apostles

[13]And He went up on the mountain and called to *Him* those He Himself wanted. And they came to Him. [14]Then He appointed twelve,[a] that they might be with Him and that He might send them out to preach, [15]and to have power to heal sicknesses and[a] to cast out demons: [16]Simon,[a] to whom He gave the name Peter; [17]James the *son* of Zebedee and John the brother of James, to whom He gave the name Boanerges, that is, "Sons of Thunder"; [18]Andrew, Philip, Bartholomew, Matthew, Thomas, James the *son* of Alphaeus, Thaddaeus, Simon the Cananite; [19]and Judas Iscariot, who also betrayed Him. And they went into a house.

A House Divided Cannot Stand

[20]Then the multitude came together again, so that they could not so much as eat bread. [21]But when His own people heard *about this,* they went out to lay hold of Him, for they said, "He is out of His mind."

[22]And the scribes who came down from Jerusalem said, "He has Beelzebub," and, "By the ruler of the demons He casts out demons."

[23]So He called them to *Himself* and said to them in parables: "How can Satan cast out Satan? [24]If a kingdom is divided against itself, that kingdom cannot stand. [25]And if a house is divided against itself, that house cannot stand. [26]And if Satan has risen up against himself, and is divided, he cannot stand, but has an end. [27]No one can enter a strong man's house and plunder his goods, unless he first binds the strong man. And then he will plunder his house.

The Unpardonable Sin

[28]"Assuredly, I say to you, all sins will be forgiven the sons of men, and whatever blasphemies they may utter; [29]but he who blasphemes against the Holy Spirit never has forgiveness, but is sub-

---

The Law of Empowerment: Jesus Gave Authority to His Team

(Mark 3:13–19)

Leadership teams must be chosen. Jesus deliberately chose all twelve members of His staff. He didn't call for a vote; He made the personnel decisions Himself. Note what we learn about team building from Jesus' selection of the Twelve:

1. *Selection:* He handpicked them. He prayed all night about it (Luke 6:12).
2. *Motivation:* He selected the ones He personally wanted. There was chemistry.
3. *Connection:* He chose them to be with Him. He modeled life in close proximity.
4. *Permission:* He released them and gave them specific assignments.
5. *Commission:* He empowered them and gave them authority to do their job.

3:5 [a]NU-Text omits *as whole as the other.*
3:14 [a]NU-Text adds *whom He also named apostles.*
3:15 [a]NU-Text omits *to heal sicknesses and.*
3:16 [a]NU-Text reads *and He appointed the twelve:* Simon. . . .

ject to eternal condemnation"— [30]because they said, "He has an unclean spirit."

Jesus' Mother and Brothers Send for Him

[31]Then His brothers and His mother came, and standing outside they sent to Him, calling Him. [32]And a multitude was sitting around Him; and they said to Him, "Look, Your mother and Your brothers[a] are outside seeking You."

[33]But He answered them, saying, "Who is My mother, or My brothers?" [34]And He looked around in a circle at those who sat about Him, and said, "Here are My mother and My brothers! [35]For whoever does the will of God is My brother and My sister and mother."

The Parable of the Sower

4 And again He began to teach by the sea. And a great multitude was gathered to Him, so that He got into a boat and sat *in it* on the sea; and the whole multitude was on the land facing the sea. [2]Then He taught them many things by parables, and said to them in His teaching:

[3]"Listen! Behold, a sower went out to sow. [4]And it happened, as he sowed, *that* some *seed* fell by the wayside; and the birds of the air[a] came and devoured it. [5]Some fell on stony ground, where it did not have much earth; and immediately it sprang up because it had no depth of earth. [6]But when the sun was up it was scorched, and because it had no root it withered away. [7]And some *seed* fell among thorns; and the thorns grew up and choked it, and it yielded no crop. [8]But other *seed* fell on good ground and yielded a crop that sprang up, increased and produced: some thirtyfold, some sixty, and some a hundred."

[9]And He said to them,[a] "He who has ears to hear, let him hear!"

The Purpose of Parables

[10]But when He was alone, those around Him with the twelve asked Him about the parable. [11]And He said to them, "To you it has been given to know the mystery of the kingdom of God; but to those who are outside, all things come in parables, [12]so that

> 'Seeing they may see and not perceive,
> And hearing they may hear and not
>   understand;
> Lest they should turn,
> And their sins be forgiven them.' "[a]

The Principle of the Seed
(Mark 4:2–20)

Who is the sower in Jesus' parable? The sower is a person of influence, a leader, anyone who declares God's Word. The sower scatters a lot of seed, and only later determines the character of the soil. Note a few principles all leaders need to know about sowing seed:

1. A lot of seed must be scattered to produce a crop.
2. Not all soils produce, but we cannot reap if we do not sow.
3. We must continue sowing, because one day we will reap a harvest.
4. The soil that produces will multiply; we will reap more than we sow.
5. We will reap in proportion to what we have sown.
6. We cannot do anything about last year's harvest, but we can about this year's.
7. We must believe in the seed we sow, knowing that some will produce fruit.
8. Once we see fruit, all our effort seems worthwhile.

The Parable of the Sower Explained

[13]And He said to them, "Do you not understand this parable? How then will you understand all the parables? [14]The sower sows the word. [15]And these are the ones by the wayside where the word is sown. When they hear, Satan comes immediately and takes away the word that was sown in their hearts. [16]These likewise are the ones sown on stony ground who, when they hear the word, immediately receive it with gladness; [17]and they have no root in themselves, and so endure only for a time. Afterward, when tribulation or persecution arises for the word's sake, immediately they stumble. [18]Now these are the ones sown among thorns; *they are* the ones who hear the word, [19]and the cares of this world, the deceitfulness of riches, and the desires for

---

3:32 [a]NU-Text and M-Text add *and Your sisters.*
4:4 [a]NU-Text and M-Text omit *of the air.*
4:9 [a]NU-Text and M-Text omit *to them.*
4:12 [a]Isaiah 6:9, 10

other things entering in choke the word, and it becomes unfruitful. [20]But these are the ones sown on good ground, those who hear the word, accept *it,* and bear fruit: some thirtyfold, some sixty, and some a hundred."

Light Under a Basket

[21]Also He said to them, "Is a lamp brought to be put under a basket or under a bed? Is it not to be set on a lampstand? [22]For there is nothing hidden which will not be revealed, nor has anything been kept secret but that it should come to light. [23]If anyone has ears to hear, let him hear."

[24]Then He said to them, "Take heed what you hear. With the same measure you use, it will be measured to you; and to you who hear, more will be given. [25]For whoever has, to him more will be given; but whoever does not have, even what he has will be taken away from him."

The Parable of the Growing Seed

[26]And He said, "The kingdom of God is as if a man should scatter seed on the ground, [27]and should sleep by night and rise by day, and the seed should sprout and grow, he himself does not know how. [28]For the earth yields crops by itself: first the blade, then the head, after that the full grain in the head. [29]But when the grain ripens, immediately he puts in the sickle, because the harvest has come."

The Parable of the Mustard Seed

[30]Then He said, "To what shall we liken the kingdom of God? Or with what parable shall we picture it? [31]*It is* like a mustard seed which, when it is sown on the ground, is smaller than all the seeds on earth; [32]but when it is sown, it grows up and becomes greater than all herbs, and shoots out large branches, so that the birds of the air may nest under its shade."

Jesus' Use of Parables

[33]And with many such parables He spoke the word to them as they were able to hear *it.* [34]But without a parable He did not speak to them. And when they were alone, He explained all things to His disciples.

Wind and Wave Obey Jesus

[35]On the same day, when evening had come, He said to them, "Let us cross over to the other side." [36]Now when they had left the multitude, they took Him along in the boat as He was. And other little boats were also with Him. [37]And a great windstorm arose, and the waves beat into the boat, so that it was already filling. [38]But He was in the stern, asleep on a pillow. And they awoke Him and said to Him, "Teacher, do You not care that we are perishing?"

[39]Then He arose and rebuked the wind, and said to the sea, "Peace, be still!" And the wind ceased and there was a great calm. [40]But He said to them, "Why are you so fearful? How *is it* that you have no faith?"[a] [41]And they feared exceedingly, and said to one another, "Who can this be, that even the wind and the sea obey Him!"

The Principle of Resting and Caring

(Mark 4:35–41)

When a terrifying storm convinced the disciples they were about to die, they forgot one important factor: Jesus was in the boat and had told them they were going to the other side of the lake (Mark 4:35). His word always comes to pass.

When they finally awakened Jesus, He got up, rebuked the wind and the sea, and everything became completely calm. So long as the disciples assumed control of their situation, Jesus rested. But when they cast their care on Him and released control to Him, He cared for everything and they could rest.

This remains true for every leader today. While we must take responsibility, we are never to take control. Only God is big enough to take control. The principle works this way:

1. *We care . . . He rests.* God will allow us to mess up our situation.
2. *He cares . . . we rest.* When we release control to Him, we find peace.

A Demon-Possessed Man Healed

5 Then they came to the other side of the sea, to the country of the Gadarenes.[a] [2]And when He had come out of the boat, immediately there met Him out of the tombs a man with an unclean spirit, [3]who had *his* dwelling among the tombs; and no one could bind him,[a] not even with chains, [4]because he had often been bound with shackles and chains. And

---

4:40 [a]NU-Text reads *Have you still no faith?*
5:1 [a]NU-Text reads *Gerasenes.* **5:3** [a]NU-Text adds *anymore.*

the chains had been pulled apart by him, and the shackles broken in pieces; neither could anyone tame him. ⁵And always, night and day, he was in the mountains and in the tombs, crying out and cutting himself with stones.

⁶When he saw Jesus from afar, he ran and worshiped Him. ⁷And he cried out with a loud voice and said, "What have I to do with You, Jesus, Son of the Most High God? I implore You by God that You do not torment me."

⁸For He said to him, "Come out of the man, unclean spirit!" ⁹Then He asked him, "What *is* your name?"

And he answered, saying, "My name *is* Legion; for we are many." ¹⁰Also he begged Him earnestly that He would not send them out of the country.

¹¹Now a large herd of swine was feeding there near the mountains. ¹²So all the demons begged Him, saying, "Send us to the swine, that we may enter them." ¹³And at once Jesus^a gave them permission. Then the unclean spirits went out and entered the swine (there were about two thousand); and the herd ran violently down the steep place into the sea, and drowned in the sea.

¹⁴So those who fed the swine fled, and they told *it* in the city and in the country. And they went out to see what it was that had happened. ¹⁵Then they came to Jesus, and saw the one *who had been* demon-possessed and had the legion, sitting and clothed and in his right mind. And they were afraid. ¹⁶And those who saw it told them how it happened to him *who had been* demon-possessed, and about the swine. ¹⁷Then they began to plead with Him to depart from their region.

¹⁸And when He got into the boat, he who had been demon-possessed begged Him that he might be with Him. ¹⁹However, Jesus did not permit him, but said to him, "Go home to your friends, and tell them what great things the Lord has done for you, and how He has had compassion on you." ²⁰And he departed and began to proclaim in Decapolis all that Jesus had done for him; and all marveled.

A Girl Restored to Life and a Woman Healed

²¹Now when Jesus had crossed over again by boat to the other side, a great multitude gathered to Him; and He was by the sea. ²²And behold,

5:13 ^aNU-Text reads *And He gave.*

SIMON PETER

PRIVILEGED TO SEE WHAT MOST OTHERS COULDN'T
(Mark 5:35–43)

PROFILE IN LEADERSHIP

As one of Jesus' most beloved and privileged leaders, the apostle Peter saw some astonishing things, things that others—not even most of the other twelve—ever had a chance to witness.

Mark records how Jesus allowed no one to follow Him to the home of Jairus, a synagogue ruler whose daughter had just died from an illness, except Peter and the brothers James and John. For a reason not clearly spelled out in the Scripture, Jesus wanted only these three leaders with Him when He performed one of His most amazing miracles.

No one could see what Peter saw that day without coming away profoundly changed and inspired. Peter had witnessed Jesus cast out demons and perform miracles of healing, and he had heard Him teach with God-given authority. But on this remarkable day, Jesus gave Peter the privilege of seeing how He held power over life and death itself.

All who believe in the Lord Jesus Christ for their salvation have access to Him at any time. But at special times, Jesus specifically calls His leaders—those with a unique call of service in ministry—to see and hear special things, things they alone have the privilege to witness. It is a special trust with unique responsibilities.

one of the rulers of the synagogue came, Jairus by name. And when he saw Him, he fell at His feet [23]and begged Him earnestly, saying, "My little daughter lies at the point of death. Come and lay Your hands on her, that she may be healed, and she will live." [24]So *Jesus* went with him, and a great multitude followed Him and thronged Him.

[25]Now a certain woman had a flow of blood for twelve years, [26]and had suffered many things from many physicians. She had spent all that she had and was no better, but rather grew worse. [27]When she heard about Jesus, she came behind *Him* in the crowd and touched His garment. [28]For she said, "If only I may touch His clothes, I shall be made well."

[29]Immediately the fountain of her blood was dried up, and she felt in *her* body that she was healed of the affliction. [30]And Jesus, immediately knowing in Himself that power had gone out of Him, turned around in the crowd and said, "Who touched My clothes?"

[31]But His disciples said to Him, "You see the multitude thronging You, and You say, 'Who touched Me?'"

[32]And He looked around to see her who had done this thing. [33]But the woman, fearing and trembling, knowing what had happened to her, came and fell down before Him and told Him the whole truth. [34]And He said to her, "Daughter, your faith has made you well. Go in peace, and be healed of your affliction."

[35]While He was still speaking, *some* came from the ruler of the synagogue's *house* who said, "Your daughter is dead. Why trouble the Teacher any further?"

[36]As soon as Jesus heard the word that was spoken, He said to the ruler of the synagogue, "Do not be afraid; only believe." [37]And He permitted no one to follow Him except Peter, James, and John the brother of James. [38]Then He came to the house of the ruler of the synagogue, and saw a tumult and those who wept and wailed loudly. [39]When He came in, He said to them, "Why make this commotion and weep? The child is not dead, but sleeping."

[40]And they ridiculed Him. But when He had put them all outside, He took the father and the mother of the child, and those *who were* with Him, and entered where the child was lying. [41]Then He took the child by the hand, and said to her, "Talitha, cumi," which is translated, "Little girl, I say to you, arise." [42]Immediately the girl arose and walked, for she was twelve years *of age.* And they were overcome with great amazement. [43]But He commanded them strictly that no one

should know it, and said that *something* should be given her to eat.

Jesus Rejected at Nazareth

6 Then He went out from there and came to His own country, and His disciples followed Him. [2]And when the Sabbath had come, He began to teach in the synagogue. And many hearing *Him* were astonished, saying, "Where *did* this Man *get* these things? And what wisdom *is* this which is given to Him, that such mighty works are performed by His hands! [3]Is this not the carpenter, the Son of Mary, and brother of James, Joses, Judas, and Simon? And are not His sisters here with us?" So they were offended at Him.

[4]But Jesus said to them, "A prophet is not without honor except in his own country, among his own relatives, and in his own house." [5]Now He could do no mighty work there, except that He laid His hands on a few sick people and healed *them.* [6]And He marveled because of their unbelief. Then He went about the villages in a circuit, teaching.

Sending Out the Twelve

[7]And He called the twelve to *Himself,* and began to send them out two *by* two, and gave them power over unclean spirits. [8]He commanded them to take nothing for the journey except a staff—no bag, no bread, no copper in *their* money belts— [9]but to wear sandals, and not to put on two tunics.

[10]Also He said to them, "In whatever place you enter a house, stay there till you depart from that place. [11]And whoever[a] will not receive you nor hear you, when you depart from there, shake off the dust under your feet as a testimony against them.[b] Assuredly, I say to you, it will be more tolerable for Sodom and Gomorrah in the day of judgment than for that city!"

[12]So they went out and preached that *people* should repent. [13]And they cast out many demons, and anointed with oil many who were sick, and healed *them.*

John the Baptist Beheaded

[14]Now King Herod heard *of Him,* for His name had become well known. And he said, "John the Baptist is risen from the dead, and therefore these powers are at work in him."

[15]Others said, "It is Elijah."

6:11 [a]NU-Text reads *whatever place.* [b]NU-Text omits the rest of this verse.

And others said, "It is the Prophet, or[a] like one of the prophets."

[16]But when Herod heard, he said, "This is John, whom I beheaded; he has been raised from the dead!" [17]For Herod himself had sent and laid hold of John, and bound him in prison for the sake of Herodias, his brother Philip's wife; for he had married her. [18]Because John had said to Herod, "It is not lawful for you to have your brother's wife."

[19]Therefore Herodias held it against him and wanted to kill him, but she could not; [20]for Herod feared John, knowing that he *was* a just and holy man, and he protected him. And when he heard him, he did many things, and heard him gladly.

[21]Then an opportune day came when Herod on his birthday gave a feast for his nobles, the high officers, and the chief *men* of Galilee. [22]And when Herodias' daughter herself came in and danced, and pleased Herod and those who sat with him, the king said to the girl, "Ask me whatever you want, and I will give *it* to you." [23]He also swore to her, "Whatever you ask me, I will give you, up to half my kingdom."

[24]So she went out and said to her mother, "What shall I ask?"

And she said, "The head of John the Baptist!"

[25]Immediately she came in with haste to the king and asked, saying, "I want you to give me at once the head of John the Baptist on a platter."

[26]And the king was exceedingly sorry; *yet,* because of the oaths and because of those who sat with him, he did not want to refuse her. [27]Immediately the king sent an executioner and commanded his head to be brought. And he went and beheaded him in prison, [28]brought his head on a platter, and gave it to the girl; and the girl gave it to her mother. [29]When his disciples heard *of it,* they came and took away his corpse and laid it in a tomb.

Feeding the Five Thousand

[30]Then the apostles gathered to Jesus and told Him all things, both what they had done and what they had taught. [31]And He said to them, "Come aside by yourselves to a deserted place and rest a while." For there were many coming and going, and they did not even have time to eat. [32]So they departed to a deserted place in the boat by themselves.

[33]But the multitudes[a] saw them departing, and many knew Him and ran there on foot from all the cities. They arrived before them and came together to Him. [34]And Jesus, when He came out, saw a great multitude and was moved with compassion for them, because they were like sheep not having a shepherd. So He began to teach them many things. [35]When the day was now far spent, His disciples came to Him and said, "This is a deserted place, and already the hour *is* late. [36]Send them away, that they may go into the surrounding country and villages and buy themselves bread;[a] for they have nothing to eat."

Compassion: Love for People Moves Jesus to Lead

(Mark 6:34)

Jesus' leadership was empowered not by a sense of duty or obligation, or by a desire to build an image, but by compassion. Great leaders, like Jesus, build a deep love for people that moves them to do far more than obligation could ever induce. Do you deeply love those you lead?

---

[37]But He answered and said to them, "You give them something to eat."

And they said to Him, "Shall we go and buy two hundred denarii worth of bread and give them *something* to eat?"

[38]But He said to them, "How many loaves do you have? Go and see."

And when they found out they said, "Five, and two fish."

[39]Then He commanded them to make them all sit down in groups on the green grass. [40]So they sat down in ranks, in hundreds and in fifties. [41]And when He had taken the five loaves and the two fish, He looked up to heaven, blessed and broke the loaves, and gave *them* to His disciples to set before them; and the two fish He divided among *them* all. [42]So they all ate and were filled. [43]And they took up twelve baskets full of fragments and of the fish. [44]Now those who had eaten the loaves were about[a] five thousand men.

6:15 [a]NU-Text and M-Text omit *or.*
6:33 [a]NU-Text and M-Text read *they.*
6:36 [a]NU-Text reads *something to eat* and omits the rest of this verse. **6:44** [a]NU-Text and M-Text omit *about.*

Jesus Walks on the Sea

[45] Immediately He made His disciples get into the boat and go before Him to the other side, to Bethsaida, while He sent the multitude away. [46] And when He had sent them away, He departed to the mountain to pray. [47] Now when evening came, the boat was in the middle of the sea; and He *was* alone on the land. [48] Then He saw them straining at rowing, for the wind was against them. Now about the fourth watch of the night He came to them, walking on the sea, and would have passed them by. [49] And when they saw Him walking on the sea, they supposed it was a ghost, and cried out; [50] for they all saw Him and were troubled. But immediately He talked with them and said to them, "Be of good cheer! It is I; do not be afraid." [51] Then He went up into the boat to them, and the wind ceased. And they were greatly amazed in themselves beyond measure, and marveled. [52] For they had not understood about the loaves, because their heart was hardened.

Many Touch Him and Are Made Well

[53] When they had crossed over, they came to the land of Gennesaret and anchored there. [54] And when they came out of the boat, immediately the people recognized Him, [55] ran through that whole surrounding region, and began to carry about on beds those who were sick to wherever they heard He was. [56] Wherever He entered, into villages, cities, or the country, they laid the sick in the marketplaces, and begged Him that they might just touch the hem of His garment. And as many as touched Him were made well.

Defilement Comes from Within

7 Then the Pharisees and some of the scribes came together to Him, having come from Jerusalem. [2] Now when[a] they saw some of His disciples eat bread with defiled, that is, with unwashed hands, they found fault. [3] For the Pharisees and all the Jews do not eat unless they wash *their* hands in a special way, holding the tradition of the elders. [4] *When they come* from the marketplace, they do not eat unless they wash. And there are many other things which they have received and hold, *like* the washing of cups, pitchers, copper vessels, and couches.

[5] Then the Pharisees and scribes asked Him, "Why do Your disciples not walk according to the tradition of the elders, but eat bread with unwashed hands?"

[6] He answered and said to them, "Well did Isaiah prophesy of you hypocrites, as it is written:

'This people honors Me with *their* lips,
   But their heart is far from Me.
[7] And in vain they worship Me,
   Teaching as doctrines the commandments
   of men.'[a]

[8] For laying aside the commandment of God, you hold the tradition of men[a]—the washing of pitchers and cups, and many other such things you do."

[9] He said to them, "*All too* well you reject the commandment of God, that you may keep your tradition. [10] For Moses said, 'Honor your father and your mother';[a] and, 'He who curses father or mother, let him be put to death.'[b] [11] But you say, 'If a man says to his father or mother, "Whatever profit you might have received from me is Corban"—' (that is, a gift *to God*), [12] then you no longer let him do anything for his father or his mother, [13] making the word of God of no effect through your tradition which you have handed down. And many such things you do."

[14] When He had called all the multitude to *Himself,* He said to them, "Hear Me, everyone, and understand: [15] There is nothing that enters a man from outside which can defile him; but the things which come out of him, those are the things that defile a man. [16] If anyone has ears to hear, let him hear!"[a]

[17] When He had entered a house away from the crowd, His disciples asked Him concerning the parable. [18] So He said to them, "Are you thus without understanding also? Do you not perceive that whatever enters a man from outside cannot defile him, [19] because it does not enter his heart but his stomach, and is eliminated, *thus* purifying all foods?"[a] [20] And He said, "What comes out of a man, that defiles a man. [21] For from within, out of the heart of men, proceed evil thoughts, adulteries, fornications, murders, [22] thefts, covetousness, wickedness, deceit, lewdness, an evil eye, blasphemy, pride, foolishness. [23] All these evil things come from within and defile a man."

A Gentile Shows Her Faith

[24] From there He arose and went to the region of Tyre and Sidon.[a] And He entered a house and

---

7:2 [a]NU-Text omits *when* and *they found fault.*
7:7 [a]Isaiah 29:13 **7:8** [a]NU-Text omits the rest of this verse. **7:10** [a]Exodus 20:12; Deuteronomy 5:16 [b]Exodus 21:17 **7:16** [a]NU-Text omits this verse.
7:19 [a]NU-Text ends quotation with *eliminated,* setting off the final clause as Mark's comment that Jesus has declared all foods clean. **7:24** [a]NU-Text omits *and Sidon.*

wanted no one to know *it,* but He could not be hidden. [25]For a woman whose young daughter had an unclean spirit heard about Him, and she came and fell at His feet. [26]The woman was a Greek, a Syro-Phoenician by birth, and she kept asking Him to cast the demon out of her daughter. [27]But Jesus said to her, "Let the children be filled first, for it is not good to take the children's bread and throw *it* to the little dogs."

[28]And she answered and said to Him, "Yes, Lord, yet even the little dogs under the table eat from the children's crumbs."

[29]Then He said to her, "For this saying go your way; the demon has gone out of your daughter."

[30]And when she had come to her house, she found the demon gone out, and her daughter lying on the bed.

Jesus Heals a Deaf-Mute

[31]Again, departing from the region of Tyre and Sidon, He came through the midst of the region of Decapolis to the Sea of Galilee. [32]Then they brought to Him one who was deaf and had an impediment in his speech, and they begged Him to put His hand on him. [33]And He took him aside from the multitude, and put His fingers in his ears, and He spat and touched his tongue. [34]Then, looking up to heaven, He sighed, and said to him, "Ephphatha," that is, "Be opened."

[35]Immediately his ears were opened, and the impediment of his tongue was loosed, and he spoke plainly. [36]Then He commanded them that they should tell no one; but the more He commanded them, the more widely they proclaimed *it.* [37]And they were astonished beyond measure, saying, "He has done all things well. He makes both the deaf to hear and the mute to speak."

Feeding the Four Thousand

8 In those days, the multitude being very great and having nothing to eat, Jesus called His disciples *to Him* and said to them, [2]"I have compassion on the multitude, because they have now continued with Me three days and have nothing to eat. [3]And if I send them away hungry to their own houses, they will faint on the way; for some of them have come from afar."

[4]Then His disciples answered Him, "How can one satisfy these people with bread here in the wilderness?"

[5]He asked them, "How many loaves do you have?"

And they said, "Seven."

Commitment: Moving from Displaying Care to Drawing Commitment

(Mark 8:1–21)

Leadership development always begins with showing concern for the emerging leader, then securing a foundation, and finally drawing commitment.

Jesus models this process in Mark 8: For the second time, Jesus fed thousands in a miraculous way (vv. 1–9), teaching the disciples that God can provide food. A deeper lesson came later when they recognized Jesus had performed the miracle to show them God would meet all their needs (vv. 17–21). Jesus also warned them about the "leaven of the Pharisees" and to guard against their attitude and perspective (vv. 14, 15).

Jesus slowly moved His men from consumers to contributors. Jesus wanted to get emerging leaders to think about issues beyond themselves. Note the stages of His developmental process:

1. *Shepherd:* He met their immediate needs; He provided security.
2. *Equipper:* He trained them to serve; He provided opportunities.
3. *Developer:* He mentored them to lead others; He provided personal challenge.

---

[6]So He commanded the multitude to sit down on the ground. And He took the seven loaves and gave thanks, broke *them* and gave *them* to His disciples to set before *them;* and they set *them* before the multitude. [7]They also had a few small fish; and having blessed them, He said to set them also before *them.* [8]So they ate and were filled, and they took up seven large baskets of leftover fragments. [9]Now those who had eaten were about four thousand. And He sent them away, [10]immediately got into the boat with His disciples, and came to the region of Dalmanutha.

The Pharisees Seek a Sign

[11]Then the Pharisees came out and began to dispute with Him, seeking from Him a sign from heaven, testing Him. [12]But He sighed deeply in His spirit, and said, "Why does this generation

seek a sign? Assuredly, I say to you, no sign shall be given to this generation."

Beware of the Leaven of the Pharisees and Herod

[13]And He left them, and getting into the boat again, departed to the other side. [14]Now the disciples[a] had forgotten to take bread, and they did not have more than one loaf with them in the boat. [15]Then He charged them, saying, "Take heed, beware of the leaven of the Pharisees and the leaven of Herod."

[16]And they reasoned among themselves, saying, "It is because we have no bread."

[17]But Jesus, being aware of it, said to them, "Why do you reason because you have no bread? Do you not yet perceive nor understand? Is your heart still[a] hardened? [18]Having eyes, do you not see? And having ears, do you not hear? And do you not remember? [19]When I broke the five loaves for the five thousand, how many baskets full of fragments did you take up?"

They said to Him, "Twelve."

[20]"Also, when I broke the seven for the four thousand, how many large baskets full of fragments did you take up?"

And they said, "Seven."

[21]So He said to them, "How is it you do not understand?"

A Blind Man Healed at Bethsaida

[22]Then He came to Bethsaida; and they brought a blind man to Him, and begged Him to touch him. [23]So He took the blind man by the hand and led him out of the town. And when He had spit on his eyes and put His hands on him, He asked him if he saw anything.

[24]And he looked up and said, "I see men like trees, walking."

[25]Then He put His hands on his eyes again and made him look up. And he was restored and saw everyone clearly. [26]Then He sent him away to his house, saying, "Neither go into the town, nor tell anyone in the town."[a]

Peter Confesses Jesus as the Christ

[27]Now Jesus and His disciples went out to the towns of Caesarea Philippi; and on the road He asked His disciples, saying to them, "Who do men say that I am?"

[28]So they answered, "John the Baptist; but some say, Elijah; and others, one of the prophets."

[29]He said to them, "But who do you say that I am?"

Peter answered and said to Him, "You are the Christ."

[30]Then He strictly warned them that they should tell no one about Him.

Jesus Predicts His Death and Resurrection

[31]And He began to teach them that the Son of Man must suffer many things, and be rejected by the elders and chief priests and scribes, and be killed, and after three days rise again. [32]He spoke this word openly. Then Peter took Him aside and began to rebuke Him. [33]But when He had turned around and looked at His disciples, He rebuked Peter, saying, "Get behind Me, Satan! For you are not mindful of the things of God, but the things of men."

Vision: Jesus Based His Vision on His Values

(Mark 8:31–33)

While Peter sought comfort for his King, Jesus sought conquest for the kingdom. This teaches us that leaders must:

- build a vision off of their values
- correct others who drift from the vision
- help the team lay aside personal agendas to reach their vision
- pay the price to achieve their vision

Take Up the Cross and Follow Him

[34]When He had called the people to Himself, with His disciples also, He said to them, "Whoever desires to come after Me, let him deny himself, and take up his cross, and follow Me. [35]For whoever desires to save his life will lose it, but whoever loses his life for My sake and the gospel's will save it. [36]For what will it profit a man if he gains the whole world, and loses his own soul? [37]Or what will a man give in exchange for his soul? [38]For whoever is ashamed of Me and My words in this adulterous and sinful generation, of him the Son of Man also will be ashamed when He comes in the glory of His Father with the holy angels."

8:14 [a]NU-Text and M-Text read they.
8:17 [a]NU-Text omits still. **8:26** [a]NU-Text reads "Do not even go into the town."

The Top Ten Leadership Principles of Jesus

(Mark 8:34–38)

The Gospels demonstrate beyond all doubt that Jesus really is the Ultimate leader. No one has influenced people more than He. Although He never wrote a book or taught in a seminary, His movement continues to grow over two thousand years after He departed the earth. Consider ten leadership principles we see in His life, as recorded in the four Gospels:

1. Leadership is servanthood (Matt. 20:25–28; Mark 8:35).
2. Let your purpose prioritize your life (Matt. 6:33; Luke 19:10; John 17:4).
3. Live the life before you lead others (Luke 7:22, 23; John 14:11).
4. Impact comes from relationships, not positions (Luke 9:6; John 4:5–30).
5. Leaders must replenish themselves (Mark 1:35–38; 6:31).
6. Great leaders call for great commitment (Matt. 10:17; Mark 8:34–38).
7. Show security when handling tough issues (Mark 11:27–33; Luke 20:19–26).
8. Credibility comes by meeting needs and solving problems (Luke 5:12–15; 8:38, 39).
9. Leaders must choose and develop their key people (Mark 3:14; Luke 10:1).
10. There is no success without a successor (Matt. 28:20; Acts 1:8).

Jesus Transfigured on the Mount

9 And He said to them, "Assuredly, I say to you that there are some standing here who will not taste death till they see the kingdom of God present with power."

²Now after six days Jesus took Peter, James, and John, and led them up on a high mountain apart by themselves; and He was transfigured before them. ³His clothes became shining, exceedingly white, like snow, such as no launderer on earth can whiten them. ⁴And Elijah appeared to them with Moses, and they were talking with Jesus. ⁵Then Peter answered and said to Jesus, "Rabbi, it is good for us to be here; and let us make three tabernacles: one for You, one for Moses, and one for Elijah"— ⁶because he did not know what to say, for they were greatly afraid.

⁷And a cloud came and overshadowed them; and a voice came out of the cloud, saying, "This is My beloved Son. Hear Him!" ⁸Suddenly, when they had looked around, they saw no one anymore, but only Jesus with themselves.

⁹Now as they came down from the mountain, He commanded them that they should tell no one the things they had seen, till the Son of Man had risen from the dead. ¹⁰So they kept this word to themselves, questioning what the rising from the dead meant.

¹¹And they asked Him, saying, "Why do the scribes say that Elijah must come first?"

¹²Then He answered and told them, "Indeed, Elijah is coming first and restores all things. And how is it written concerning the Son of Man, that He must suffer many things and be treated with contempt? ¹³But I say to you that Elijah has also come, and they did to him whatever they wished, as it is written of him."

A Boy Is Healed

¹⁴And when He came to the disciples, He saw a great multitude around them, and scribes disputing with them. ¹⁵Immediately, when they saw Him, all the people were greatly amazed, and running to *Him,* greeted Him. ¹⁶And He asked the scribes, "What are you discussing with them?"

¹⁷Then one of the crowd answered and said, "Teacher, I brought You my son, who has a mute spirit. ¹⁸And wherever it seizes him, it throws him down; he foams at the mouth, gnashes his teeth, and becomes rigid. So I spoke to Your disciples, that they should cast it out, but they could not."

¹⁹He answered him and said, "O faithless generation, how long shall I be with you? How long shall I bear with you? Bring him to Me." ²⁰Then they brought him to Him. And when he saw Him, immediately the spirit convulsed him, and he fell on the ground and wallowed, foaming at the mouth.

²¹So He asked his father, "How long has this been happening to him?"

And he said, "From childhood. ²²And often he has thrown him both into the fire and into the water to destroy him. But if You can do anything, have compassion on us and help us."

[23]Jesus said to him, "If you can believe,[a] all things *are* possible to him who believes."

[24]Immediately the father of the child cried out and said with tears, "Lord, I believe; help my unbelief!"

[25]When Jesus saw that the people came running together, He rebuked the unclean spirit, saying to it, "Deaf and dumb spirit, I command you, come out of him and enter him no more!" [26]Then *the spirit* cried out, convulsed him greatly, and came out of him. And he became as one dead, so that many said, "He is dead." [27]But Jesus took him by the hand and lifted him up, and he arose.

[28]And when He had come into the house, His disciples asked Him privately, "Why could we not cast it out?"

[29]So He said to them, "This kind can come out by nothing but prayer and fasting."[a]

Jesus Again Predicts His Death and Resurrection

[30]Then they departed from there and passed through Galilee, and He did not want anyone to know *it.* [31]For He taught His disciples and said to them, "The Son of Man is being betrayed into the hands of men, and they will kill Him. And after He is killed, He will rise the third day." [32]But they did not understand this saying, and were afraid to ask Him.

Who Is the Greatest?

[33]Then He came to Capernaum. And when He was in the house He asked them, "What was it you disputed among yourselves on the road?" [34]But they kept silent, for on the road they had disputed among themselves who *would be the greatest.* [35]And He sat down, called the twelve, and said to them, "If anyone desires to be first, he shall be last of all and servant of all." [36]Then He took a little child and set him in the midst of them. And when He had taken him in His arms, He said to them, [37]"Whoever receives one of these little children in My name receives Me; and whoever receives Me, receives not Me but Him who sent Me."

Jesus Forbids Sectarianism

[38]Now John answered Him, saying, "Teacher, we saw someone who does not follow us casting out demons in Your name, and we forbade him because he does not follow us."

[39]But Jesus said, "Do not forbid him, for no one who works a miracle in My name can soon afterward speak evil of Me. [40]For he who is not against us is on our[a] side. [41]For whoever gives you

---

Servant Leadership: The Way Up Is Down
(Mark 9:33—10:16)

When Jesus caught His disciples arguing about who among them was the greatest, they felt embarrassed—but Jesus didn't rebuke them for wanting to be great. He simply gave them an unexpected formula: Be a servant.

Later, when the disciples asked about those who cast out demons in His name, Jesus said, "He who is not against us is on our side" (Mark 9:40, 41). A short time later, His disciples angered Him again when they became more concerned with crowd control than with humility and service (10:13–16).

For Jesus, children presented the best example of the required attitude for servant leaders. Children exhibit humility, wonder, honesty, innocence, trust, and dependence. Note four leadership lessons we glean from Mark 9; 10:

1. The greater the leader, the greater the servant (9:35).
2. Leaders include others when they serve (9:40).
3. Any service rendered will be rewarded (9:41).
4. Servant leaders must become childlike (10:13–16).

---

a cup of water to drink in My name, because you belong to Christ, assuredly, I say to you, he will by no means lose his reward.

Jesus Warns of Offenses

[42]"But whoever causes one of these little ones who believe in Me to stumble, it would be better for him if a millstone were hung around his neck, and he were thrown into the sea. [43]If your hand causes you to sin, cut it off. It is better for you to enter into life maimed, rather than having two hands, to go to hell, into the fire that shall never be quenched— [44]where

---

9:23 [a]NU-Text reads " *'If You can!' All things. . . .*"
9:29 [a]NU-Text omits *and fasting.* **9:40** [a]M-Text reads *against you is on your side.*

'*Their worm does not die*
And the fire is not quenched.'[a]

[45]And if your foot causes you to sin, cut it off. It is better for you to enter life lame, rather than having two feet, to be cast into hell, into the fire that shall never be quenched— [46]where

'*Their worm does not die*
And the fire is not quenched.'[a]

[47]And if your eye causes you to sin, pluck it out. It is better for you to enter the kingdom of God with one eye, rather than having two eyes, to be cast into hell fire— [48]where

'*Their worm does not die*
And the fire is not quenched.'[a]

Tasteless Salt Is Worthless

[49]"For everyone will be seasoned with fire,[a] and every sacrifice will be seasoned with salt. [50]Salt *is* good, but if the salt loses its flavor, how will you season it? Have salt in yourselves, and have peace with one another."

Marriage and Divorce

10 Then He arose from there and came to the region of Judea by the other side of the Jordan. And multitudes gathered to Him again, and as He was accustomed, He taught them again.

[2]The Pharisees came and asked Him, "Is it lawful for a man to divorce *his* wife?" testing Him.

[3]And He answered and said to them, "What did Moses command you?"

[4]They said, "Moses permitted *a man* to write a certificate of divorce, and to dismiss *her.*"

[5]And Jesus answered and said to them, "Because of the hardness of your heart he wrote you this precept. [6]But from the beginning of the creation, God '*made them male and female.*'[a] [7]'*For this reason a man shall leave his father and mother and be joined to his wife,* [8]*and the two shall become one flesh*';[a] so then they are no longer two, but one flesh. [9]Therefore what God has joined together, let not man separate."

[10]In the house His disciples also asked Him again about the same *matter.* [11]So He said to them, "Whoever divorces his wife and marries another commits adultery against her. [12]And if a woman divorces her husband and marries another, she commits adultery."

Jesus Blesses Little Children

[13]Then they brought little children to Him, that He might touch them; but the disciples rebuked those who brought *them.* [14]But when Jesus saw *it,* He was greatly displeased and said to them, "Let the little children come to Me, and do not forbid them; for of such is the kingdom of God. [15]Assuredly, I say to you, whoever does not receive the kingdom of God as a little child will by no means enter it." [16]And He took them up in His arms, laid *His* hands on them, and blessed them.

Jesus Counsels the Rich Young Ruler

[17]Now as He was going out on the road, one came running, knelt before Him, and asked Him, "Good Teacher, what shall I do that I may inherit eternal life?"

[18]So Jesus said to him, "Why do you call Me good? No one *is* good but One, *that is,* God. [19]You know the commandments: '*Do not commit adultery,*' '*Do not murder,*' '*Do not steal,*' '*Do not bear false witness,*' '*Do not defraud,*' '*Honor your father and your mother.*'"[a]

[20]And he answered and said to Him, "Teacher, all these things I have kept from my youth."

[21]Then Jesus, looking at him, loved him, and said to him, "One thing you lack: Go your way, sell whatever you have and give to the poor, and you will have treasure in heaven; and come, take up the cross, and follow Me."

[22]But he was sad at this word, and went away sorrowful, for he had great possessions.

With God All Things Are Possible

[23]Then Jesus looked around and said to His disciples, "How hard it is for those who have riches to enter the kingdom of God!" [24]And the disciples were astonished at His words. But Jesus answered again and said to them, "Children, how hard it is for those who trust in riches[a] to enter the kingdom of God! [25]It is easier for a camel to go through the eye of a needle than for a rich man to enter the kingdom of God."

[26]And they were greatly astonished, saying among themselves, "Who then can be saved?"

[27]But Jesus looked at them and said, "With men *it is* impossible, but not with God; for with God all things are possible."

[28]Then Peter began to say to Him, "See, we have left all and followed You."

9:44 [a]NU-Text omits this verse. **9:46** [a]NU-Text omits the last clause of verse 45 and all of verse 46. **9:48** [a]Isaiah 66:24 **9:49** [a]NU-Text omits the rest of this verse. **10:6** [a]Genesis 1:27; 5:2 **10:8** [a]Genesis 2:24 **10:19** [a]Exodus 20:12–16; Deuteronomy 5:16–20 **10:24** [a]NU-Text omits *for those who trust in riches.*

²⁹So Jesus answered and said, "Assuredly, I say to you, there is no one who has left house or brothers or sisters or father or mother or wife[a] or children or lands, for My sake and the gospel's, ³⁰who shall not receive a hundredfold now in this time—houses and brothers and sisters and mothers and children and lands, with persecutions—and in the age to come, eternal life. ³¹But many *who are* first will be last, and the last first."

Jesus a Third Time Predicts His Death and Resurrection

³²Now they were on the road, going up to Jerusalem, and Jesus was going before them; and they were amazed. And as they followed they were afraid. Then He took the twelve aside again and began to tell them the things that would happen to Him: ³³"Behold, we are going up to Jerusalem, and the Son of Man will be betrayed to the chief priests and to the scribes; and they will condemn Him to death and deliver Him to the Gentiles; ³⁴and they will mock Him, and scourge Him, and spit on Him, and kill Him. And the third day He will rise again."

Greatness Is Serving

³⁵Then James and John, the sons of Zebedee, came to Him, saying, "Teacher, we want You to do for us whatever we ask."

³⁶And He said to them, "What do you want Me to do for you?"

³⁷They said to Him, "Grant us that we may sit, one on Your right hand and the other on Your left, in Your glory."

³⁸But Jesus said to them, "You do not know what you ask. Are you able to drink the cup that I drink, and be baptized with the baptism that I am baptized with?"

³⁹They said to Him, "We are able."

So Jesus said to them, "You will indeed drink the cup that I drink, and with the baptism I am baptized with you will be baptized; ⁴⁰but to sit on My right hand and on My left is not Mine to give, but *it is for those* for whom it is prepared."

⁴¹And when the ten heard *it,* they began to be greatly displeased with James and John. ⁴²But Jesus called them to *Himself* and said to them, "You know that those who are considered rulers over the Gentiles lord it over them, and their great ones exercise authority over them. ⁴³Yet it shall not be so among you; but whoever desires to become great among you shall be your servant. ⁴⁴And whoever of you desires to be first shall be slave of all. ⁴⁵For even the Son of Man did not come to be served, but to serve, and to give His life a ransom for many."

Jesus Heals Blind Bartimaeus

⁴⁶Now they came to Jericho. As He went out of Jericho with His disciples and a great multitude, blind Bartimaeus, the son of Timaeus, sat by the road begging. ⁴⁷And when he heard that it was Jesus of Nazareth, he began to cry out and say, "Jesus, Son of David, have mercy on me!"

⁴⁸Then many warned him to be quiet; but he cried out all the more, "Son of David, have mercy on me!"

⁴⁹So Jesus stood still and commanded him to be called.

Then they called the blind man, saying to him, "Be of good cheer. Rise, He is calling you."

⁵⁰And throwing aside his garment, he rose and came to Jesus.

⁵¹So Jesus answered and said to him, "What do you want Me to do for you?"

The blind man said to Him, "Rabboni, that I may receive my sight."

⁵²Then Jesus said to him, "Go your way; your faith has made you well." And immediately he received his sight and followed Jesus on the road.

The Triumphal Entry

11 Now when they drew near Jerusalem, to Bethphage[a] and Bethany, at the Mount of Olives, He sent two of His disciples; ²and He said to them, "Go into the village opposite you; and as soon as you have entered it you will find a colt tied, on which no one has sat. Loose it and bring *it.* ³And if anyone says to you, 'Why are you doing this?' say, 'The Lord has need of it,' and immediately he will send it here."

⁴So they went their way, and found the[a] colt tied by the door outside on the street, and they loosed it. ⁵But some of those who stood there said to them, "What are you doing, loosing the colt?"

⁶And they spoke to them just as Jesus had commanded. So they let them go. ⁷Then they brought the colt to Jesus and threw their clothes on it, and He sat on it. ⁸And many spread their clothes on the road, and others cut down leafy branches from the trees and spread *them* on the road. ⁹Then those who went before and those who followed cried out, saying:

"Hosanna!
'Blessed is He who comes in the name of the LORD!'[a]

10:29 [a]NU-Text omits *or wife.* **11:1** [a]M-Text reads *Bethsphage.* **11:4** [a]NU-Text and M-Text read *a.* **11:9** [a]Psalm 118:26

¹⁰ Blessed *is* the kingdom of our father David
That comes in the name of the Lord!ᵃ
Hosanna in the highest!"

¹¹And Jesus went into Jerusalem and into the temple. So when He had looked around at all things, as the hour was already late, He went out to Bethany with the twelve.

The Fig Tree Withered

¹²Now the next day, when they had come out from Bethany, He was hungry. ¹³And seeing from afar a fig tree having leaves, He went to see if perhaps He would find something on it. When He came to it, He found nothing but leaves, for it was not the season for figs. ¹⁴In response Jesus said to it, "Let no one eat fruit from you ever again."

And His disciples heard *it.*

Jesus Cleanses the Temple

¹⁵So they came to Jerusalem. Then Jesus went into the temple and began to drive out those who bought and sold in the temple, and overturned the tables of the money changers and the seats of those who sold doves. ¹⁶And He would not allow anyone to carry wares through the temple. ¹⁷Then He taught, saying to them, "Is it not written, '*My house shall be called a house of prayer for all nations*'?ᵃ But you have made it a '*den of thieves.*'"ᵇ

¹⁸And the scribes and chief priests heard it and sought how they might destroy Him; for they feared Him, because all the people were astonished at His teaching. ¹⁹When evening had come, He went out of the city.

Security: Jesus Could Do the Unpopular

(Mark 11:15–17)

How could Jesus, so full of love, drive the money changers out of the temple? He felt secure in His identity and mission; He did not need consensus. Margaret Thatcher once rightly asked, "What great cause would have been fought and won under the banner, 'I stand for consensus'?"

The Lesson of the Withered Fig Tree

²⁰Now in the morning, as they passed by, they saw the fig tree dried up from the roots. ²¹And Pe-

ter, remembering, said to Him, "Rabbi, look! The fig tree which You cursed has withered away."

²²So Jesus answered and said to them, "Have faith in God. ²³For assuredly, I say to you, whoever says to this mountain, 'Be removed and be cast into the sea,' and does not doubt in his heart, but believes that those things he says will be done, he will have whatever he says. ²⁴Therefore I say to you, whatever things you ask when you pray, believe that you receive *them,* and you will have *them.*

Forgiveness and Prayer

²⁵"And whenever you stand praying, if you have anything against anyone, forgive him, that your Father in heaven may also forgive you your trespasses. ²⁶But if you do not forgive, neither will your Father in heaven forgive your trespasses."ᵃ

Jesus' Authority Questioned

²⁷Then they came again to Jerusalem. And as He was walking in the temple, the chief priests, the scribes, and the elders came to Him. ²⁸And they said to Him, "By what authority are You doing these things? And who gave You this authority to do these things?"

²⁹But Jesus answered and said to them, "I also will ask you one question; then answer Me, and I will tell you by what authority I do these things: ³⁰The baptism of John—was it from heaven or from men? Answer Me."

³¹And they reasoned among themselves, saying, "If we say, 'From heaven,' He will say, 'Why then did you not believe him?' ³²But if we say, 'From men'"—they feared the people, for all counted John to have been a prophet indeed. ³³So they answered and said to Jesus, "We do not know."

And Jesus answered and said to them, "Neither will I tell you by what authority I do these things."

The Parable of the Wicked Vinedressers

12 Then He began to speak to them in parables: "A man planted a vineyard and set a hedge around *it,* dug *a place for* the wine vat and built a tower. And he leased it to vinedressers and went into a far country. ²Now at vintage-time he sent a servant to the vinedressers, that he might receive some of the fruit of the vineyard from the vinedressers. ³And they took *him* and beat him and sent *him* away empty-handed. ⁴Again he sent them another

---

11:10 ᵃNU-Text omits *in the name of the Lord.*
11:17 ᵃIsaiah 56:7 ᵇJeremiah 7:11 **11:26** ᵃNU-Text omits this verse.

servant, and at him they threw stones,[a] wounded *him* in the head, and sent *him* away shamefully treated. [5]And again he sent another, and him they killed; and many others, beating some and killing some. [6]Therefore still having one son, his beloved, he also sent him to them last, saying, 'They will respect my son.' [7]But those vine-dressers said among themselves, 'This is the heir. Come, let us kill him, and the inheritance will be ours.' [8]So they took him and killed *him* and cast *him* out of the vineyard.

[9]"Therefore what will the owner of the vineyard do? He will come and destroy the vine-dressers, and give the vineyard to others. [10]Have you not even read this Scripture:

'*The stone which the builders rejected
    Has become the chief cornerstone.*
[11]   *This was the LORD's doing,
    And it is marvelous in our eyes*'?"[a]

[12]And they sought to lay hands on Him, but feared the multitude, for they knew He had spoken the parable against them. So they left Him and went away.

The Pharisees: Is It Lawful to Pay Taxes to Caesar?

[13]Then they sent to Him some of the Pharisees and the Herodians, to catch Him in *His* words. [14]When they had come, they said to Him, "Teacher, we know that You are true, and care about no one; for You do not regard the person of men, but teach the way of God in truth. Is it lawful to pay taxes to Caesar, or not? [15]Shall we pay, or shall we not pay?"

But He, knowing their hypocrisy, said to them, "Why do you test Me? Bring Me a denarius that I may see *it.*" [16]So they brought *it.*

And He said to them, "Whose image and inscription *is* this?" They said to Him, "Caesar's."

[17]And Jesus answered and said to them, "Render to Caesar the things that are Caesar's, and to God the things that are God's."

And they marveled at Him.

The Sadducees: What About the Resurrection?

[18]Then *some* Sadducees, who say there is no resurrection, came to Him; and they asked Him, saying: [19]"Teacher, Moses wrote to us that if a man's brother dies, and leaves *his* wife behind, and leaves no children, his brother should take his wife and raise up offspring for his brother. [20]Now there were seven brothers. The first took a wife; and dying, he left no offspring. [21]And the second took her, and he died; nor did he leave

any offspring. And the third likewise. [22]So the seven had her and left no offspring. Last of all the woman died also. [23]Therefore, in the resurrection, when they rise, whose wife will she be? For all seven had her as wife."

[24]Jesus answered and said to them, "Are you not therefore mistaken, because you do not know the Scriptures nor the power of God? [25]For when they rise from the dead, they neither marry nor are given in marriage, but are like angels in heaven. [26]But concerning the dead, that they rise, have you not read in the book of Moses, in the *burning* bush *passage,* how God spoke to him, saying, '*I am the God of Abraham, the God of Isaac, and the God of Jacob*'?[a] [27]He is not the God of the dead, but the God of the living. You are therefore greatly mistaken."

The Scribes: Which Is the First Commandment of All?

[28]Then one of the scribes came, and having heard them reasoning together, perceiving[a] that He had answered them well, asked Him, "Which is the first commandment of all?"

[29]Jesus answered him, "The first of all the commandments *is:* '*Hear, O Israel, the LORD our God, the LORD is one.* [30]*And you shall love the LORD your God with all your heart, with all your soul, with all your mind, and with all your strength.*'[a] This *is* the first commandment.[b] [31]And the second, like *it, is* this: '*You shall love your neighbor as yourself.*'[a] There is no other commandment greater than these."

12:4 [a]NU-Text omits *and at him they threw stones.*
12:11 [a]Psalm 118:22, 23 **12:26** [a]Exodus 3:6, 15
12:28 [a]NU-Text reads *seeing.* **12:30** [a]Deuteronomy 6:4, 5 [b]NU-Text omits this sentence.
12:31 [a]Leviticus 19:18

Jesus Reduces His Core Values to Two

(Mark 12:28–34)

Jesus declared that the entire Law could be reduced to loving God with all our hearts and loving our neighbor as we love ourselves. This is the genius behind core values. Jesus summarized His vast kingdom using two simple phrases. Can you do that with your life and work?

³²So the scribe said to Him, "Well *said*, Teacher. You have spoken the truth, for there is one God, and there is no other but He. ³³And to love Him with all the heart, with all the understanding, with all the soul,ᵃ and with all the strength, and to love one's neighbor as oneself, is more than all the whole burnt offerings and sacrifices."

³⁴Now when Jesus saw that he answered wisely, He said to him, "You are not far from the kingdom of God."

But after that no one dared question Him.

Jesus: How Can David Call His Descendant Lord?

³⁵Then Jesus answered and said, while He taught in the temple, "How *is it* that the scribes say that the Christ is the Son of David? ³⁶For David himself said by the Holy Spirit:

'The LORD said to my Lord,
"Sit at My right hand,
Till I make Your enemies Your footstool."'ᵃ

³⁷Therefore David himself calls Him '*Lord*'; how is He *then* his Son?"

And the common people heard Him gladly.

Beware of the Scribes

³⁸Then He said to them in His teaching, "Beware of the scribes, who desire to go around in long robes, *love* greetings in the marketplaces, ³⁹the best seats in the synagogues, and the best places at feasts, ⁴⁰who devour widows' houses, and for a pretense make long prayers. These will receive greater condemnation."

The Widow's Two Mites

⁴¹Now Jesus sat opposite the treasury and saw how the people put money into the treasury. And many *who were* rich put in much. ⁴²Then one poor widow came and threw in two mites,ᵃ which make a quadrans. ⁴³So He called His disciples to *Himself* and said to them, "Assuredly, I say to you that this poor widow has put in more than all those who have given to the treasury; ⁴⁴for they all put in out of their abundance, but she out of her poverty put in all that she had, her whole livelihood."

Jesus Predicts the Destruction of the Temple

13 Then as He went out of the temple, one of His disciples said to Him, "Teacher, see what manner of stones and what buildings *are here!*"

²And Jesus answered and said to him, "Do you

Bell Sheep: Jesus Found a Model to Affirm

(Mark 12:41–44)

Once in a while, Jesus would use someone as a public example. For example, He affirmed the centurion for his faith, admonished the Pharisees for their pride, and commended a poor widow for her generosity.

One day Jesus spotted a destitute woman in the temple. Although she had almost nothing, she put two small coins into the treasury. Jesus singled her out and lauded her example. He even favorably compared her to the rich who gave out of their surplus. God considered Her gift more noble than theirs!

Jesus used a strategy called "bell sheep." When you want to encourage certain behavior, find someone who is doing what you want, and call attention to it. Affirm it. Like a shepherd hanging a bell around the neck of the sheep he wants the flock to follow, encourage others to watch the example of the one doing right. Visual sermons yield far better results than verbal ones.

---

see these great buildings? Not *one* stone shall be left upon another, that shall not be thrown down."

The Signs of the Times and the End of the Age

³Now as He sat on the Mount of Olives opposite the temple, Peter, James, John, and Andrew asked Him privately, "'Tell us, when will these things be? And what *will be* the sign when all these things will be fulfilled?"

⁵And Jesus, answering them, began to say: "Take heed that no one deceives you. ⁶For many will come in My name, saying, 'I am *He*,' and will deceive many. ⁷But when you hear of wars and rumors of wars, do not be troubled; for *such things* must happen, but the end *is* not yet. ⁸For nation will rise against nation, and kingdom against kingdom. And there will be earthquakes in various places, and there will be famines and troubles.ᵃ These *are* the beginnings of sorrows.

12:33 ᵃNU-Text omits *with all the soul*.
12:36 ᵃPsalm 110:1 **12:42** ᵃGreek *lepta*, very small copper coins worth a fraction of a penny
13:8 ᵃNU-Text omits *and troubles*.

Vision: Jesus Called His Followers Back to the Original Goal

(Mark 13:1–37)

In His discourse on the end of time, Jesus paused to remind His men why He bothered to reveal such prophetic information. He declared that the gospel must be preached to the whole world—then the end would come. Jesus regularly called attention to the vision of God.

9"But watch out for yourselves, for they will deliver you up to councils, and you will be beaten in the synagogues. You will be brought[a] before rulers and kings for My sake, for a testimony to them. 10And the gospel must first be preached to all the nations. 11But when they arrest *you* and deliver you up, do not worry beforehand, or premeditate[a] what you will speak. But whatever is given you in that hour, speak that; for it is not you who speak, but the Holy Spirit. 12Now brother will betray brother to death, and a father *his* child; and children will rise up against parents and cause them to be put to death. 13And you will be hated by all for My name's sake. But he who endures to the end shall be saved.

The Great Tribulation

14"So when you see the *'abomination of desolation,'*[a] spoken of by Daniel the prophet,[b] standing where it ought not" (let the reader understand), "then let those who are in Judea flee to the mountains. 15Let him who is on the housetop not go down into the house, nor enter to take anything out of his house. 16And let him who is in the field not go back to get his clothes. 17But woe to those who are pregnant and to those who are nursing babies in those days! 18And pray that your flight may not be in winter. 19For *in* those days there will be tribulation, such as has not been since the beginning of the creation which God created until this time, nor ever shall be. 20And unless the Lord had shortened those days, no flesh would be saved; but for the elect's sake, whom He chose, He shortened the days. 21"Then if anyone says to you, 'Look, here *is* the Christ!' or, 'Look, *He is* there!' do not believe

it. 22For false christs and false prophets will rise and show signs and wonders to deceive, if possible, even the elect. 23But take heed; see, I have told you all things beforehand.

The Coming of the Son of Man

24"But in those days, after that tribulation, the sun will be darkened, and the moon will not give its light; 25the stars of heaven will fall, and the powers in the heavens will be shaken. 26Then they will see the Son of Man coming in the clouds with great power and glory. 27And then He will send His angels, and gather together His elect from the four winds, from the farthest part of earth to the farthest part of heaven.

The Parable of the Fig Tree

28"Now learn this parable from the fig tree: When its branch has already become tender, and puts forth leaves, you know that summer is near. 29So you also, when you see these things happening, know that it[a] is near—at the doors! 30Assuredly, I say to you, this generation will by no means pass away till all these things take place. 31Heaven and earth will pass away, but My words will by no means pass away.

No One Knows the Day or Hour

32"But of that day and hour no one knows, not even the angels in heaven, nor the Son, but only the Father. 33Take heed, watch and pray; for you do not know when the time is. 34*It is* like a man going to a far country, who left his house and gave authority to his servants, and to each his work, and commanded the doorkeeper to watch. 35Watch therefore, for you do not know when the master of the house is coming—in the evening, at midnight, at the crowing of the rooster, or in the morning— 36lest, coming suddenly, he find you sleeping. 37And what I say to you, I say to all: Watch!"

The Plot to Kill Jesus

14 After two days it was the Passover and *the Feast* of Unleavened Bread. And the chief priests and the scribes sought how they might take Him by trickery and put *Him* to death. 2But they said, "Not during the feast, lest there be an uproar of the people."

13:9 [a]NU-Text and M-Text read *will stand*.
13:11 [a]NU-Text omits *or premeditate*. **13:14** [a]Daniel 11:31; 12:11 [b]NU-Text omits *spoken of by Daniel the prophet*. **13:29** [a]Or *He*

The Anointing at Bethany

³And being in Bethany at the house of Simon the leper, as He sat at the table, a woman came having an alabaster flask of very costly oil of spikenard. Then she broke the flask and poured *it* on His head. ⁴But there were some who were indignant among themselves, and said, "Why was this fragrant oil wasted? ⁵For it might have been sold for more than three hundred denarii and given to the poor." And they criticized her sharply.

⁶But Jesus said, "Let her alone. Why do you trouble her? She has done a good work for Me. ⁷For you have the poor with you always, and whenever you wish you may do them good; but Me you do not have always. ⁸She has done what she could. She has come beforehand to anoint My body for burial. ⁹Assuredly, I say to you, wherever this gospel is preached in the whole world, what this woman has done will also be told as a memorial to her."

Judas Agrees to Betray Jesus

¹⁰Then Judas Iscariot, one of the twelve, went to the chief priests to betray Him to them. ¹¹And when they heard *it,* they were glad, and promised to give him money. So he sought how he might conveniently betray Him.

Jesus Celebrates the Passover with His Disciples

¹²Now on the first day of Unleavened Bread, when they killed the Passover *lamb,* His disciples said to Him, "Where do You want us to go and prepare, that You may eat the Passover?"

¹³And He sent out two of His disciples and said to them, "Go into the city, and a man will meet you carrying a pitcher of water; follow him. ¹⁴Wherever he goes in, say to the master of the house, 'The Teacher says, "Where is the guest room in which I may eat the Passover with My disciples?"' ¹⁵Then he will show you a large upper room, furnished *and* prepared; there make ready for us."

¹⁶So His disciples went out, and came into the city, and found it just as He had said to them; and they prepared the Passover.

¹⁷In the evening He came with the twelve. ¹⁸Now as they sat and ate, Jesus said, "Assuredly, I say to you, one of you who eats with Me will betray Me."

¹⁹And they began to be sorrowful, and to say to Him one by one, "*Is it* I?" And another *said,* "*Is it* I?"^a

²⁰He answered and said to them, "*It is* one of the twelve, who dips with Me in the dish. ²¹The Son of Man indeed goes just as it is written of Him, but woe to that man by whom the Son of Man is betrayed! It would have been good for that man if he had never been born."

Jesus Institutes the Lord's Supper

²²And as they were eating, Jesus took bread, blessed and broke *it,* and gave *it* to them and said, "Take, eat;^a this is My body."

²³Then He took the cup, and when He had given thanks He gave *it* to them, and they all drank from it. ²⁴And He said to them, "This is My blood of the new^a covenant, which is shed for many. ²⁵Assuredly, I say to you, I will no longer drink of the fruit of the vine until that day when I drink it new in the kingdom of God."

²⁶And when they had sung a hymn, they went out to the Mount of Olives.

Jesus Predicts Peter's Denial

²⁷Then Jesus said to them, "All of you will be made to stumble because of Me this night,^a for it is written:

'I will strike the Shepherd,
And the sheep will be scattered.'^b

²⁸"But after I have been raised, I will go before you to Galilee."

²⁹Peter said to Him, "Even if all are made to stumble, yet I *will* not *be.*"

³⁰Jesus said to him, "Assuredly, I say to you that today, *even* this night, before the rooster crows twice, you will deny Me three times."

³¹But he spoke more vehemently, "If I have to die with You, I will not deny You!"

And they all said likewise.

The Prayer in the Garden

³²Then they came to a place which was named Gethsemane; and He said to His disciples, "Sit here while I pray." ³³And He took Peter, James, and John with Him, and He began to be troubled and deeply distressed. ³⁴Then He said to them, "My soul is exceedingly sorrowful, *even* to death. Stay here and watch."

³⁵He went a little farther, and fell on the ground, and prayed that if it were possible, the hour might pass from Him. ³⁶And He said, "Abba, Father, all things *are* possible for You.

14:19 ^aNU-Text omits this sentence.
14:22 ^aNU-Text omits *eat.* **14:24** ^aNU-Text omits *new.* **14:27** ^aNU-Text omits *because of Me this night.*
^bZechariah 13:7

Take this cup away from Me; nevertheless, not what I will, but what You *will*."

³⁷Then He came and found them sleeping, and said to Peter, "Simon, are you sleeping? Could you not watch one hour? ³⁸Watch and pray, lest you enter into temptation. The spirit indeed *is* willing, but the flesh *is* weak."

³⁹Again He went away and prayed, and spoke the same words. ⁴⁰And when He returned, He found them asleep again, for their eyes were heavy; and they did not know what to answer Him.

⁴¹Then He came the third time and said to them, "Are you still sleeping and resting? It is enough! The hour has come; behold, the Son of Man is being betrayed into the hands of sinners. ⁴²Rise, let us be going. See, My betrayer is at hand."

Responsibility: Caring in the Midst of Crisis

(Mark 14:32–42)

J esus must have endured His most difficult moments in the Garden of Gethsemane, just prior to His arrest, trial, and crucifixion. The Gospels tell us He felt deeply distressed and troubled (Mark 14:33). He cried out and His sweat became like blood (Luke 22:44). In His time of dire need, however, His twelve followers drifted off to sleep. Twice He found them snoring. They had no idea how critical this night would be.

Instead of screaming at them in anguish, however, He encouraged them to pray for themselves (Mark 14:38). Even though He had every right to demand better performance, He felt compassion for them and gave them direction. He wanted them to stay protected from temptation. His sense of responsibility and concern overcame His preoccupation with the Cross. His date with destiny did not overshadow His love and concern for His weak and sleepy staff. In the garden He provided us with the ultimate display of a leader's responsibility.

Betrayal and Arrest in Gethsemane

⁴³And immediately, while He was still speaking, Judas, one of the twelve, with a great multi-tude with swords and clubs, came from the chief priests and the scribes and the elders. ⁴⁴Now His betrayer had given them a signal, saying, "Whomever I kiss, He is the One; seize Him and lead *Him* away safely."

⁴⁵As soon as he had come, immediately he went up to Him and said to Him, "Rabbi, Rabbi!" and kissed Him.

⁴⁶Then they laid their hands on Him and took Him. ⁴⁷And one of those who stood by drew his sword and struck the servant of the high priest, and cut off his ear.

⁴⁸Then Jesus answered and said to them, "Have you come out, as against a robber, with swords and clubs to take Me? ⁴⁹I was daily with you in the temple teaching, and you did not seize Me. But the Scriptures must be fulfilled."

⁵⁰Then they all forsook Him and fled.

A Young Man Flees Naked

⁵¹Now a certain young man followed Him, having a linen cloth thrown around *his* naked *body*. And the young men laid hold of him, ⁵²and he left the linen cloth and fled from them naked.

Jesus Faces the Sanhedrin

⁵³And they led Jesus away to the high priest; and with him were assembled all the chief priests, the elders, and the scribes. ⁵⁴But Peter followed Him at a distance, right into the courtyard of the high priest. And he sat with the servants and warmed himself at the fire.

⁵⁵Now the chief priests and all the council sought testimony against Jesus to put Him to death, but found none. ⁵⁶For many bore false witness against Him, but their testimonies did not agree.

⁵⁷Then some rose up and bore false witness against Him, saying, ⁵⁸"We heard Him say, 'I will destroy this temple made with hands, and within three days I will build another made without hands.'" ⁵⁹But not even then did their testimony agree.

⁶⁰And the high priest stood up in the midst and asked Jesus, saying, "Do You answer nothing? What *is it* these men testify against You?" ⁶¹But He kept silent and answered nothing.

Again the high priest asked Him, saying to Him, "Are You the Christ, the Son of the Blessed?"

⁶²Jesus said, "I am. And you will see the Son of Man sitting at the right hand of the Power, and coming with the clouds of heaven."

⁶³Then the high priest tore his clothes and

said, "What further need do we have of witnesses? [64]You have heard the blasphemy! What do you think?"

And they all condemned Him to be deserving of death.

[65]Then some began to spit on Him, and to blindfold Him, and to beat Him, and to say to Him, "Prophesy!" And the officers struck Him with the palms of their hands.[a]

Peter Denies Jesus, and Weeps

[66]Now as Peter was below in the courtyard, one of the servant girls of the high priest came. [67]And when she saw Peter warming himself, she looked at him and said, "You also were with Jesus of Nazareth."

[68]But he denied it, saying, "I neither know nor understand what you are saying." And he went out on the porch, and a rooster crowed.

[69]And the servant girl saw him again, and began to say to those who stood by, "This is one of them." [70]But he denied it again.

And a little later those who stood by said to Peter again, "Surely you are one of them; for you are a Galilean, and your speech shows it."[a]

[71]Then he began to curse and swear, "I do not know this Man of whom you speak!"

[72]A second time the rooster crowed. Then Peter called to mind the word that Jesus had said to him, "Before the rooster crows twice, you will deny Me three times." And when he thought about it, he wept.

Jesus Faces Pilate

15 Immediately, in the morning, the chief priests held a consultation with the elders and scribes and the whole council; and they bound Jesus, led Him away, and delivered Him to Pilate. [2]Then Pilate asked Him, "Are You the King of the Jews?"

He answered and said to him, "It is as you say."

[3]And the chief priests accused Him of many things, but He answered nothing. [4]Then Pilate asked Him again, saying, "Do You answer nothing? See how many things they testify against You!"[a] [5]But Jesus still answered nothing, so that Pilate marveled.

14:65 [a]NU-Text reads received Him with slaps.
14:70 [a]NU-Text omits and your speech shows it.
15:4 [a]NU-Text reads of which they accuse You.

PONTIUS PILATE

A LEADER WHO REFUSED TO TAKE RESPONSIBILITY
(Mark 15:1–15)

PROFILE IN LEADERSHIP

Pontius Pilate, the governor of Judea, stood at a crossroads. The fate of the very Son of God rested in his hands. This same Jesus, who only a week before had performed miracles of healing and provision, now faced a mob demanding his death.

Pilate interrogated Jesus and found He had done nothing worthy of crucifixion. But instead of leading—instead of taking an unpopular stand and allowing this innocent man to go free—Pilate gave in to the outrage of an unruly crowd. He released a notorious criminal and sentenced this guiltless man to die an agonizing death on a cross. Pilate recognized the injustice. But with the mob looking on, Pilate "washed his hands" of Jesus' blood (Matt. 27:24) and allowed Him to be executed.

In a moment of supreme paradox, God used Pilate's refusal to lead and do what was right to carry out His own plan of salvation. In His providence, God saw into the heart of Pilate and knew that when push came to shove, this man would give in to the demands of the crowd.

When God calls His people to lead, when He calls us to make unpopular stands, we cannot "wash our hands" of the responsibility. Leaders will face moments when they have no choice but to stand up to the crowd and do what is right.

Taking the Place of Barabbas

[6]Now at the feast he was accustomed to releasing one prisoner to them, whomever they requested. [7]And there was one named Barabbas, *who was* chained with his fellow rebels; they had committed murder in the rebellion. [8]Then the multitude, crying aloud,[a] began to ask *him to do* just as he had always done for them. [9]But Pilate answered them, saying, "Do you want me to release to you the King of the Jews?" [10]For he knew that the chief priests had handed Him over because of envy.

[11]But the chief priests stirred up the crowd, so that he should rather release Barabbas to them. [12]Pilate answered and said to them again, "What then do you want me to do *with Him* whom you call the King of the Jews?"

[13]So they cried out again, "Crucify Him!"

[14]Then Pilate said to them, "Why, what evil has He done?"

But they cried out all the more, "Crucify Him!"

[15]So Pilate, wanting to gratify the crowd, released Barabbas to them; and he delivered Jesus, after he had scourged *Him,* to be crucified.

The Law of Sacrifice: Jesus Gave Up His Life to Gain the World

(Mark 15:15–24)

Anywhere worth going carries a price tag. Jesus chose to endure torture, mocking, humiliation, and an excruciating death, even though He could have stopped it at any moment (Matt. 26:53). The Leader of humankind, the Last Adam (1 Cor. 15:45), decided that gaining the world was worth the pain of the Cross.

The Soldiers Mock Jesus

[16]Then the soldiers led Him away into the hall called Praetorium, and they called together the whole garrison. [17]And they clothed Him with purple; and they twisted a crown of thorns, put it on His *head,* [18]and began to salute Him, "Hail, King of the Jews!" [19]Then they struck Him on the head with a reed and spat on Him; and bowing the knee, they worshiped Him. [20]And when they had mocked Him, they took the purple off Him, put His own clothes on Him, and led Him out to crucify Him.

The King on a Cross

[21]Then they compelled a certain man, Simon a Cyrenian, the father of Alexander and Rufus, as he was coming out of the country and passing by, to bear His cross. [22]And they brought Him to the place Golgotha, which is translated, Place of a Skull. [23]Then they gave Him wine mingled with myrrh to drink, but He did not take *it*. [24]And when they crucified Him, they divided His garments, casting lots for them to determine what every man should take.

[25]Now it was the third hour, and they crucified Him. [26]And the inscription of His accusation was written above:

THE KING OF THE JEWS.

[27]With Him they also crucified two robbers, one on His right and the other on His left. [28]So the Scripture was fulfilled[a] which says, *"And He was numbered with the transgressors."*[b]

[29]And those who passed by blasphemed Him, wagging their heads and saying, "Aha! *You* who destroy the temple and build *it* in three days, [30]save Yourself, and come down from the cross!" [31]Likewise the chief priests also, mocking among themselves with the scribes, said, "He saved others; Himself He cannot save. [32]Let the Christ, the King of Israel, descend now from the cross, that we may see and believe."[a]

Even those who were crucified with Him reviled Him.

Jesus Dies on the Cross

[33]Now when the sixth hour had come, there was darkness over the whole land until the ninth hour. [34]And at the ninth hour Jesus cried out with a loud voice, saying, "Eloi, Eloi, lama sabachthani?" which is translated, *"My God, My God, why have You forsaken Me?"*[a] [35]Some of those who stood by, when they heard *that,* said, "Look, He is calling for Elijah!" [36]Then someone ran and filled a sponge full of sour wine, put *it* on a reed, and offered *it* to Him to drink, saying, "Let Him alone; let us see if Elijah will come to take Him down."

[37]And Jesus cried out with a loud voice, and breathed His last.

[38]Then the veil of the temple was torn in two from top to bottom. [39]So when the centurion, who stood opposite Him, saw that He cried out

---

15:8 [a]NU-Text reads *going up.* **15:28** [a]Isaiah 53:12 [b]NU-Text omits this verse. **15:32** [a]M-Text reads *believe Him.* **15:34** [a]Psalm 22:1

like this and breathed His last,[a] he said, "Truly this Man was the Son of God!"

[40]There were also women looking on from afar, among whom were Mary Magdalene, Mary the mother of James the Less and of Joses, and Salome, [41]who also followed Him and ministered to Him when He was in Galilee, and many other women who came up with Him to Jerusalem.

Jesus Buried in Joseph's Tomb

[42]Now when evening had come, because it was the Preparation Day, that is, the day before the Sabbath, [43]Joseph of Arimathea, a prominent council member, who was himself waiting for the kingdom of God, coming and taking courage, went in to Pilate and asked for the body of Jesus. [44]Pilate marveled that He was already dead; and summoning the centurion, he asked him if He had been dead for some time. [45]So when he found out from the centurion, he granted the body to Joseph. [46]Then he bought fine linen, took Him down, and wrapped Him in the linen. And he laid Him in a tomb which had been hewn out of the rock, and rolled a stone against the door of the tomb. [47]And Mary Magdalene and Mary the mother of Joses observed where He was laid.

He Is Risen

16 Now when the Sabbath was past, Mary Magdalene, Mary the mother of James, and Salome bought spices, that they might come and anoint Him. [2]Very early in the morning, on the first day of the week, they came to the tomb when the sun had risen. [3]And they said among themselves, "Who will roll away the stone from the door of the tomb for us?" [4]But when they looked up, they saw that the stone had been rolled away— for it was very large. [5]And entering the tomb, they saw a young man clothed in a long white robe sitting on the right side; and they were alarmed.

[6]But he said to them, "Do not be alarmed. You seek Jesus of Nazareth, who was crucified. He is risen! He is not here. See the place where they laid Him. [7]But go, tell His disciples—and Peter—that He is going before you into Galilee; there you will see Him, as He said to you."

[8]So they went out quickly[a] and fled from the tomb, for they trembled and were amazed. And they said nothing to anyone, for they were afraid.

Mary Magdalene Sees the Risen Lord

[9]Now when He rose early on the first day of the week, He appeared first to Mary Magdalene,

---

The Law of Victory: Jesus' Resurrection Surprised Everyone

(Mark 16:1–7)

Every Easter in churches around the world, Christians retell the story of Jesus' resurrection from the dead. From a leadership perspective, this event is the paramount illustration of the Law of Victory.

The disciples had lost their Teacher and Lord. The Jewish leaders had quieted their opposition. The common people had lost their hope of a revolution against Rome. Even the devil thought he had finally stopped this divine Leader and forced Him to abort His mission (1 Cor. 2:8).

What a surprise awaited that first Resurrection Sunday morning!

When Jesus rose from the dead, He gave His followers a potent hope to end every doubt about His kingdom. Jesus practiced the Law of Victory—and at least part of every leader's credibility comes from practicing this law (although no one can do it quite the way He did!).

---

out of whom He had cast seven demons. [10]She went and told those who had been with Him, as they mourned and wept. [11]And when they heard that He was alive and had been seen by her, they did not believe.

Jesus Appears to Two Disciples

[12]After that, He appeared in another form to two of them as they walked and went into the country. [13]And they went and told it to the rest, but they did not believe them either.

The Great Commission

[14]Later He appeared to the eleven as they sat at the table; and He rebuked their unbelief and hardness of heart, because they did not believe those who had seen Him after He had risen. [15]And He said to them, "Go into all the world and preach the gospel to every creature. [16]He who believes and is baptized will be saved; but he

---

15:39 [a]NU-Text reads *that He thus breathed His last.*
16:8 [a]NU-Text and M-Text omit *quickly.*

The Law of Legacy: Jesus Turned His Ministry Over to His Disciples

(Mark 16:15, 16)

Before Jesus departed this world, He gathered His disciples and issued a final command. We call it the Great Commission. He told them to go and preach the gospel to every creature on earth. Just as He came to seek and save the lost, they were to continue His ministry and fulfill it.

Jesus' legacy remains to this day because He carefully laid a foundation. He trained twelve men to reproduce His ministry. He passed on transferable concepts that anyone could learn after He had gone. If He had failed to multiply Himself in others, Christianity would have died long ago.

If we step back and look at Jesus' three-and-a-half-year ministry outlined in Mark, we can see Him preparing to leave His legacy from the beginning:

1. He chose twelve potential leaders to mentor (3:13–19).
2. He spent the majority of His time with them (3:14).
3. He told them from the start that they, too, would be doing this (1:17).
4. He reproduced both His burden and His vision for people (6:7–13).
5. He allowed them to witness and even participate in His miracles (8:1–9).
6. He issued an imperative for them to go and do what He did (16:15, 16).
7. He promised the credibility and provision they would need (16:17, 18).
8. He worked with them, confirming their work and words (16:19, 20).

who does not believe will be condemned. [17]And these signs will follow those who believe: In My name they will cast out demons; they will speak with new tongues; [18]they[a] will take up serpents; and if they drink anything deadly, it will by no means hurt them; they will lay hands on the sick, and they will recover."

Christ Ascends to God's Right Hand

[19]So then, after the Lord had spoken to them, He was received up into heaven, and sat down at the right hand of God. [20]And they went out and preached everywhere, the Lord working with *them* and confirming the word through the accompanying signs. Amen.[a]

16:18 [a]NU-Text reads *and in their hands they will.*
16:20 [a]Verses 9–20 are bracketed in NU-Text as not original. They are lacking in Codex Sinaiticus and Codex Vaticanus, although nearly all other manuscripts of Mark contain them.

LUKE
Jesus as the Perfect Man

SUMMARY

Luke is the only Gospel writer to record the events of Jesus' life in chronological order. Experts consider him to be one of the most accurate historians of his day, although by trade, he was a medical doctor. Rather than beginning his Gospel traditionally, he assures his readers that he founded his account on historically verifiable information and evidence—he wants to establish credibility for his message.

Luke portrays Jesus as the perfect Man. He recognizes Jesus' divinity, but wants to give his readers a picture of what a human life might look like if a man were to walk with God consistently. Jesus, once again, becomes the Ultimate Leader.

From Luke's vantage point, Jesus lives the perfect life of leadership and authority. He is the Man who, because He never sins, truly does take dominion over the earth and subdue it (Gen. 1:26–28). The animals and fish obey Him; the wind and the sea obey Him; sick bodies obey Him; fig trees obey Him—even the dead obey Him. Everywhere Jesus goes, He leads. Everywhere Jesus goes, He serves.

Luke also portrays Jesus as an equipping Leader. He focuses on the teaching ministry of Jesus, that He equips and empowers every hungry person who comes to Him. Those who come to Him already full and satisfied get nothing. Those who come to Him starving receive everything needed. That's how Jesus leads. He compels no one to do anything, yet followers flock to Him by the thousands. As you read through Luke, look especially for examples of the Laws of Empowerment, Navigation, Influence, Connection, Intuition, and Reproduction.

God's Role in Luke

God reveals to us in Luke what a perfect leader looks like; he looks like Jesus. Instead of forcing others to follow or submit to His power, Jesus loves them into a desire to follow. He sets the standard for us in His exercise of authority over people, over the elements of nature, and even over the powers of His day. His serene and authoritative response to adverse circumstances shows us how we are to respond to our own difficult circumstances. His fulfillment of a divine purpose challenges us to pursue our own.

Jesus teaches us that a leader cannot pursue love and power simultaneously.

Instead of pursuing power, Jesus pursues love—and in the end, He gets both. Today He holds more power and elicits more love than anyone in history.

Leaders in Luke

Jesus, John the Baptizer, the Pharisees, Pilate, Herod

Other People of Influence in Luke

Mary, the centurion, the twelve disciples, the 72 followers, Zacchaeus

Lessons in Leadership

- Healthy leaders have nothing to prove, nothing to lose, and nothing to hide.

- Wise leaders speak the truth, whatever the cost.

- Effective leaders provide incentives to their followers.

- Successful leaders discern, then develop, then delegate.

- Great leaders feel secure enough to express emotions and be vulnerable.

- The best leaders love the world, serve the many, but train the few.

- Good leaders practice repetition until others embrace the vision.

- The most powerful force in a leader's life is love for people.

LEADERSHIP HIGHLIGHTS IN LUKE

Dedication to Theophilus

1 Inasmuch as many have taken in hand to set in order a narrative of those things which have been fulfilled[a] among us, [2]just as those who from the beginning were eyewitnesses and ministers of the word delivered them to us, [3]it seemed good to me also, having had perfect understanding of all things from the very first, to write to you an orderly account, most excellent Theophilus, [4]that you may know the certainty of those things in which you were instructed.

Credibility: Luke's Authority to Write About Jesus

(Luke 1:1–4)

Luke felt the need to establish his credibility as a biographer for Jesus. He wasn't one of the twelve disciples, an eyewitness of Christ, or even a theologian. So he opens his book by explaining why he chose to write Jesus' story. Good leaders recognize the need to establish their credibility.

John's Birth Announced to Zacharias

[5]There was in the days of Herod, the king of Judea, a certain priest named Zacharias, of the division of Abijah. His wife *was* of the daughters of Aaron, and her name *was* Elizabeth. [6]And they were both righteous before God, walking in all the commandments and ordinances of the Lord blameless. [7]But they had no child, because Elizabeth was barren, and they were both well advanced in years.

[8]So it was, that while he was serving as priest before God in the order of his division, [9]according to the custom of the priesthood, his lot fell to burn incense when he went into the temple of the Lord. [10]And the whole multitude of the people was praying outside at the hour of incense. [11]Then an angel of the Lord appeared to him, standing on the right side of the altar of incense. [12]And when Zacharias saw *him,* he was troubled, and fear fell upon him.

[13]But the angel said to him, "Do not be afraid, Zacharias, for your prayer is heard; and your wife Elizabeth will bear you a son, and you shall call his name John. [14]And you will have joy and gladness, and many will rejoice at his birth. [15]For he will be great in the sight of the Lord, and shall drink neither wine nor strong drink. He will also be filled with the Holy Spirit, even from his mother's womb. [16]And he will turn many of the children of Israel to the Lord their God. [17]He will also go before Him in the spirit and power of Elijah, '*to turn the hearts of the fathers to the children,*'[a] and the disobedient to the wisdom of the just, to make ready a people prepared for the Lord."

[18]And Zacharias said to the angel, "How shall I know this? For I am an old man, and my wife is well advanced in years."

[19]And the angel answered and said to him, "I am Gabriel, who stands in the presence of God, and was sent to speak to you and bring you these glad tidings. [20]But behold, you will be mute and not able to speak until the day these things take place, because you did not believe my words which will be fulfilled in their own time."

[21]And the people waited for Zacharias, and marveled that he lingered so long in the temple. [22]But when he came out, he could not speak to them; and they perceived that he had seen a vision in the temple, for he beckoned to them and remained speechless.

[23]So it was, as soon as the days of his service were completed, that he departed to his own house. [24]Now after those days his wife Elizabeth conceived; and she hid herself five months, saying, [25]"Thus the Lord has dealt with me, in the days when He looked on *me,* to take away my reproach among people."

Christ's Birth Announced to Mary

[26]Now in the sixth month the angel Gabriel was sent by God to a city of Galilee named Nazareth, [27]to a virgin betrothed to a man whose name was Joseph, of the house of David. The virgin's name *was* Mary. [28]And having come in, the angel said to her, "Rejoice, highly favored *one,* the Lord *is* with you; blessed *are* you among women!"[a]

[29]But when she saw *him,*[a] she was troubled at his saying, and considered what manner of greeting this was. [30]Then the angel said to her, "Do not be afraid, Mary, for you have found favor with God. [31]And behold, you will conceive in your womb and bring forth a Son, and shall call His name JESUS. [32]He will be great, and will be called the Son of the Highest; and the Lord God

---

1:1 [a]Or *are most surely believed*   **1:17** [a]Malachi 4:5, 6
1:28 [a]NU-Text omits *blessed are you among women.*
1:29 [a]NU-Text omits *when she saw him.*

will give Him the throne of His father David. ³³And He will reign over the house of Jacob forever, and of His kingdom there will be no end."

³⁴Then Mary said to the angel, "How can this be, since I do not know a man?"

³⁵And the angel answered and said to her, "*The* Holy Spirit will come upon you, and the power of the Highest will overshadow you; therefore, also, that Holy One who is to be born will be called the Son of God. ³⁶Now indeed, Elizabeth your relative has also conceived a son in her old age; and this is now the sixth month for her who was called barren. ³⁷For with God nothing will be impossible."

³⁸Then Mary said, "Behold the maidservant of the Lord! Let it be to me according to your word." And the angel departed from her.

Mary Visits Elizabeth

³⁹Now Mary arose in those days and went into the hill country with haste, to a city of Judah, ⁴⁰and entered the house of Zacharias and greeted Elizabeth. ⁴¹And it happened, when Elizabeth heard the greeting of Mary, that the babe leaped in her womb; and Elizabeth was filled with the Holy Spirit. ⁴²Then she spoke out with a loud voice and said, "Blessed *are* you among women, and blessed *is* the fruit of your womb! ⁴³But why *is* this *granted* to me, that the mother of my Lord should come to me? ⁴⁴For indeed, as soon as the voice of your greeting sounded in my ears, the babe leaped in my womb for joy. ⁴⁵Blessed *is* she who believed, for there will be a fulfillment of those things which were told her from the Lord."

The Song of Mary

⁴⁶And Mary said:

" My soul magnifies the Lord,
⁴⁷ And my spirit has rejoiced in God my Savior.
⁴⁸ For He has regarded the lowly state of His maidservant;
For behold, henceforth all generations will call me blessed.
⁴⁹ For He who is mighty has done great things for me,
And holy *is* His name.
⁵⁰ And His mercy *is* on those who fear Him From generation to generation.
⁵¹ He has shown strength with His arm;
He has scattered *the* proud in the imagination of their hearts.

52 He has put down the mighty from *their* thrones,
And exalted *the* lowly.
53 He has filled *the* hungry with good things,
And *the* rich He has sent away empty.
54 He has helped His servant Israel,
In remembrance of *His* mercy,
55 As He spoke to our fathers,
To Abraham and to his seed forever."

56And Mary remained with her about three months, and returned to her house.

Birth of John the Baptist

57Now Elizabeth's full time came for her to be delivered, and she brought forth a son. 58When her neighbors and relatives heard how the Lord had shown great mercy to her, they rejoiced with her.

Circumcision of John the Baptist

59So it was, on the eighth day, that they came to circumcise the child; and they would have called him by the name of his father, Zacharias. 60His mother answered and said, "No; he shall be called John."

61But they said to her, "There is no one among your relatives who is called by this name." 62So they made signs to his father—what he would have him called.

63And he asked for a writing tablet, and wrote, saying, "His name is John." So they all marveled. 64Immediately his mouth was opened and his tongue *loosed,* and he spoke, praising God. 65Then fear came on all who dwelt around them; and all these sayings were discussed throughout all the hill country of Judea. 66And all those who heard *them* kept *them* in their hearts, saying, "What kind of child will this be?" And the hand of the Lord was with him.

Zacharias' Prophecy

67Now his father Zacharias was filled with the Holy Spirit, and prophesied, saying:

68 "Blessed *is* the Lord God of Israel,
For He has visited and redeemed His people,
69 And has raised up a horn of salvation for us
In the house of His servant David,
70 As He spoke by the mouth of His holy prophets,
Who *have been* since the world began,
71 That we should be saved from our enemies
And from the hand of all who hate us,

72 To perform the mercy *promised* to our fathers
And to remember His holy covenant,
73 The oath which He swore to our father Abraham:
74 To grant us that we,
Being delivered from the hand of our enemies,
Might serve Him without fear,
75 In holiness and righteousness before Him all the days of our life.

76 "And you, child, will be called the prophet of the Highest;
For you will go before the face of the Lord to prepare His ways,
77 To give knowledge of salvation to His people
By the remission of their sins,
78 Through the tender mercy of our God,
With which the Dayspring from on high has visited[a] us;
79 To give light to those who sit in darkness and the shadow of death,
To guide our feet into the way of peace."

80So the child grew and became strong in spirit, and was in the deserts till the day of his manifestation to Israel.

Christ Born of Mary

2 And it came to pass in those days *that* a decree went out from Caesar Augustus that all the world should be registered. 2This census first took place while Quirinius was governing Syria. 3So all went to be registered, everyone to his own city.

4Joseph also went up from Galilee, out of the city of Nazareth, into Judea, to the city of David, which is called Bethlehem, because he was of the house and lineage of David, 5to be registered with Mary, his betrothed wife,[a] who was with child. 6So it was, that while they were there, the days were completed for her to be delivered. 7And she brought forth her firstborn Son, and wrapped Him in swaddling cloths, and laid Him in a manger, because there was no room for them in the inn.

Glory in the Highest

8Now there were in the same country shepherds living out in the fields, keeping watch over

---

1:78 [a]NU-Text reads *shall visit.* **2:5** [a]NU-Text omits *wife.*

their flock by night. [9]And behold,[a] an angel of the Lord stood before them, and the glory of the Lord shone around them, and they were greatly afraid. [10]Then the angel said to them, "Do not be afraid, for behold, I bring you good tidings of great joy which will be to all people. [11]For there is born to you this day in the city of David a Savior, who is Christ the Lord. [12]And this *will be* the sign to you: You will find a Babe wrapped in swaddling cloths, lying in a manger."

[13]And suddenly there was with the angel a multitude of the heavenly host praising God and saying:

[14]   "Glory to God in the highest,
       And on earth peace, goodwill toward men!"[a]

[15]So it was, when the angels had gone away from them into heaven, that the shepherds said to one another, "Let us now go to Bethlehem and see this thing that has come to pass, which the Lord has made known to us." [16]And they came with haste and found Mary and Joseph, and the Babe lying in a manger. [17]Now when they had seen *Him,* they made widely[a] known the saying which was told them concerning this Child. [18]And all those who heard *it* marveled at those things which were told them by the shepherds. [19]But Mary kept all these things and pondered *them* in her heart. [20]Then the shepherds returned, glorifying and praising God for all the things that they had heard and seen, as it was told them.

Circumcision of Jesus

[21]And when eight days were completed for the circumcision of the Child,[a] His name was called JESUS, the name given by the angel before He was conceived in the womb.

Jesus Presented in the Temple

[22]Now when the days of her purification according to the law of Moses were completed, they brought Him to Jerusalem to present *Him* to the Lord [23](as it is written in the law of the Lord, *"Every male who opens the womb shall be called holy to the LORD"*),[a] [24]and to offer a sacrifice according to what is said in the law of the Lord, *"A pair of turtledoves or two young pigeons."*[a]

Simeon Sees God's Salvation

[25]And behold, there was a man in Jerusalem whose name was Simeon, and this man was just and devout, waiting for the Consolation of Israel, and the Holy Spirit was upon him. [26]And it had been revealed to him by the Holy Spirit that he would not see death before he had seen the Lord's Christ. [27]So he came by the Spirit into the temple. And when the parents brought in the Child Jesus, to do for Him according to the custom of the law, [28]he took Him up in his arms and blessed God and said:

[29]   "Lord, now You are letting Your servant
         depart in peace,
       According to Your word;
[30]   For my eyes have seen Your salvation
[31]   Which You have prepared before the face
         of all peoples,
[32]   A light to *bring* revelation to the Gentiles,
       And the glory of Your people Israel."

[33]And Joseph and His mother[a] marveled at those things which were spoken of Him. [34]Then Simeon blessed them, and said to Mary His mother, "Behold, this *Child* is destined for the fall and rising of many in Israel, and for a sign which will be spoken against [35](yes, a sword will pierce through your own soul also), that the thoughts of many hearts may be revealed."

Anna Bears Witness to the Redeemer

[36]Now there was one, Anna, a prophetess, the daughter of Phanuel, of the tribe of Asher. She was of a great age, and had lived with a husband seven years from her virginity; [37]and this woman *was* a widow of about eighty-four years,[a] who did not depart from the temple, but served *God* with fastings and prayers night and day. [38]And coming in that instant she gave thanks to the Lord,[a] and spoke of Him to all those who looked for redemption in Jerusalem.

The Family Returns to Nazareth

[39]So when they had performed all things according to the law of the Lord, they returned to Galilee, to their *own* city, Nazareth. [40]And the Child grew and became strong in spirit,[a] filled with wisdom; and the grace of God was upon Him.

The Boy Jesus Amazes the Scholars

[41]His parents went to Jerusalem every year at the Feast of the Passover. [42]And when He was

---

2:9 [a]NU-Text omits *behold.* **2:14** [a]NU-Text reads *toward men of goodwill.* **2:17** [a]NU-Text omits *widely.* **2:21** [a]NU-Text reads *for His circumcision.* **2:23** [a]Exodus 13:2, 12, 15 **2:24** [a]Leviticus 12:8 **2:33** [a]NU-Text reads *And His father and mother.* **2:37** [a]NU-Text reads *a widow until she was eighty-four.* **2:38** [a]NU-Text reads *to God.* **2:40** [a]NU-Text omits *in spirit.*

twelve years old, they went up to Jerusalem according to the custom of the feast. [43]When they had finished the days, as they returned, the Boy Jesus lingered behind in Jerusalem. And Joseph and His mother[a] did not know *it;* [44]but supposing Him to have been in the company, they went a day's journey, and sought Him among *their* relatives and acquaintances. [45]So when they did not find Him, they returned to Jerusalem, seeking Him. [46]Now so it was *that* after three days they found Him in the temple, sitting in the midst of the teachers, both listening to them and asking them questions. [47]And all who heard Him were astonished at His understanding and answers. [48]So when they saw Him, they were amazed; and His mother said to Him, "Son, why have You done this to us? Look, Your father and I have sought You anxiously."

[49]And He said to them, "Why did you seek Me? Did you not know that I must be about My Father's business?" [50]But they did not understand the statement which He spoke to them.

Jesus Advances in Wisdom and Favor

[51]Then He went down with them and came to Nazareth, and was subject to them, but His mother kept all these things in her heart. [52]And Jesus increased in wisdom and stature, and in favor with God and men.

Listening: Jesus Did This to Connect with People

(Luke 2:42–52)

Even at 12 years of age, Jesus was listening and asking questions. He never grew out of the habit. Before ministering to needy people or telling them about the kingdom, He took the time to listen. He knew that to connect with people's hearts, He had to use His ears.

John the Baptist Prepares the Way

3 Now in the fifteenth year of the reign of Tiberius Caesar, Pontius Pilate being governor of Judea, Herod being tetrarch of Galilee, his brother Philip tetrarch of Iturea and the region of Trachonitis, and Lysanias tetrarch of Abilene, [2]while Annas and Caiaphas were high priests,[a] the word of God came to John the son of Zacharias in the wilderness. [3]And he went into all the region around the Jordan, preaching a baptism of repentance for the remission of sins, [4]as it is written in the book of the words of Isaiah the prophet, saying:

> " *The voice of one crying in the wilderness:*
> '*Prepare the way of the LORD;*
> *Make His paths straight.*
> [5]   *Every valley shall be filled*
> *And every mountain and hill brought low;*
> *The crooked places shall be made straight*
> *And the rough ways smooth;*
> [6]   *And all flesh shall see the salvation of God.*'"[a]

John Preaches to the People

[7]Then he said to the multitudes that came out to be baptized by him, "Brood of vipers! Who warned you to flee from the wrath to come? [8]Therefore bear fruits worthy of repentance, and do not begin to say to yourselves, 'We have Abraham as *our* father.' For I say to you that God is able to raise up children to Abraham from these stones. [9]And even now the ax is laid to the root of the trees. Therefore every tree which does not bear good fruit is cut down and thrown into the fire."

[10]So the people asked him, saying, "What shall we do then?"

[11]He answered and said to them, "He who has two tunics, let him give to him who has none; and he who has food, let him do likewise."

[12]Then tax collectors also came to be baptized, and said to him, "Teacher, what shall we do?"

[13]And he said to them, "Collect no more than what is appointed for you."

[14]Likewise the soldiers asked him, saying, "And what shall we do?"

So he said to them, "Do not intimidate anyone or accuse falsely, and be content with your wages."

[15]Now as the people were in expectation, and all reasoned in their hearts about John, whether he was the Christ *or* not, [16]John answered, saying to all, "I indeed baptize you with water; but One mightier than I is coming, whose sandal strap I am not worthy to loose. He will baptize you with the Holy Spirit and fire. [17]His winnowing fan *is* in His hand, and He will thoroughly clean out His threshing floor, and gather the wheat into His barn; but the chaff He will burn with unquenchable fire."

[18]And with many other exhortations he preached to the people. [19]But Herod the tetrarch,

---

2:43 [a]NU-Text reads *And His parents.*
3:2 [a]NU-Text and M-Text read *in the high priesthood of Annas and Caiaphas.* **3:6** [a]Isaiah 40:3–5

21 QUALITIES

PASSION

John Served God with Gusto
(Luke 3:2–22)

The best single word to describe John the Baptizer might be the word "passion." John's passion began even before he was born. He leaped in his mother's womb when Mary spoke of her pregnancy (Luke 1:41). His passion for God grew so great, that before he began his public ministry, he lived alone in the desert, wearing camel's hair and a leather belt and eating locusts and wild honey (Matt. 3:4). He was a radical and unafraid to let anyone know it.

John needed passion to fulfill his God-given calling. Every pioneer needs passion. Pioneers cannot be satisfied with mere maintenance, for they have nothing yet to maintain. They create from nothing. The common folk often view them as eccentric—but their passion attracts other pioneers.

What gave John *his* passion?

1. *He spent time in solitude.*
   Before John began his public ministry, he lived in the wilderness and spent much time with God. He boiled with the presence of God and could hardly stay quiet.
2. *He felt consumed with his mission.*
   John knew of Jesus' identity and His soon advent. John urgently tried to prepare the way for Him.
3. *He possessed a magnetic temperament and wiring.*
   John is described as a voice crying out (Luke 3:4) and as an exhorter (3:18). Like a magnet, he repelled some and attracted others.
4. *He possessed a strong sense of justice.*
   When people asked John what they should do, he told them to do justice (3:10–14). This hunger for justice drove him. He wouldn't sit still until he saw results.
5. *He saw things as black and white.*
   Like others with prophetic gifts, John saw most issues as either black or white. While this sounds narrow to most pastors or businesspersons, this is part of what gave John his passion.
6. *He felt dissatisfied with anything but action.*
   John was a doer. He didn't want people to merely talk about repentance and faith. He told the Pharisees they should bring forth fruit to prove their repentance.

Passion makes for an effective ministry. So how can you increase your passion?

1. *Take your temperature.* Get an honest assessment from coworkers: Are you passionate about what you do? You can't start a fire in your organization unless it first burns in you.
2. *Return to your first love.* Many leaders allow life to push them off track. Think back to when you first started your career. What drove you? What made you enthusiastic?
3. *Associate with people of passion.* Birds of a feather flock together. Hot coals stay hot when they remain in the fire. Find passionate people and let them rub off on you.

For a negative example of passion, see p. 385.

being rebuked by him concerning Herodias, his brother Philip's wife,[a] and for all the evils which Herod had done, [20]also added this, above all, that he shut John up in prison.

John Baptizes Jesus

[21]When all the people were baptized, it came to pass that Jesus also was baptized; and while He prayed, the heaven was opened. [22]And the Holy Spirit descended in bodily form like a dove upon Him, and a voice came from heaven which said, "You are My beloved Son; in You I am well pleased."

The Genealogy of Jesus Christ

[23]Now Jesus Himself began *His ministry at* about thirty years of age, being (as was supposed) *the* son of Joseph, *the son* of Heli, [24]*the son* of Matthat,[a] *the son* of Levi, *the son* of Melchi, *the son* of Janna, *the son* of Joseph, [25]*the son* of Mattathiah, *the son* of Amos, *the son* of Nahum, *the son* of Esli, *the son* of Naggai, [26]*the son* of Maath, *the son* of Mattathiah, *the son* of Semei, *the son* of Joseph, *the son* of Judah, [27]*the son* of Joannas, *the son* of Rhesa, *the son* of Zerubbabel, *the son* of Shealtiel, *the son* of Neri, [28]*the son* of Melchi, *the son* of Addi, *the son* of Cosam, *the son* of Elmodam, *the son* of Er, [29]*the son* of Jose, *the son* of Eliezer, *the son* of Jorim, *the son* of Matthat, *the son* of Levi, [30]*the son* of Simeon, *the son* of Judah, *the son* of Joseph, *the son* of Jonan, *the son* of Eliakim, [31]*the son* of Melea, *the son* of Menan, *the son* of Mattathah, *the son* of Nathan, *the son* of David, [32]*the son* of Jesse, *the son* of Obed, *the son* of Boaz, *the son* of Salmon, *the son* of Nahshon, [33]*the son* of Amminadab, *the son* of Ram, *the son* of Hezron, *the son* of Perez, *the son* of Judah, [34]*the son* of Jacob, *the son* of Isaac, *the son* of Abraham, *the son* of Terah, *the son* of Nahor, [35]*the son* of Serug, *the son* of Reu, *the son* of Peleg, *the son* of Eber, *the son* of Shelah, [36]*the son* of Cainan, *the son* of Arphaxad, *the son* of Shem, *the son* of Noah, *the son* of Lamech, [37]*the son* of Methuselah, *the son* of Enoch, *the son* of Jared, *the son* of Mahalalel, *the son* of Cainan, [38]*the son* of Enosh, *the son* of Seth, *the son* of Adam, *the son* of God.

Satan Tempts Jesus

4 Then Jesus, being filled with the Holy Spirit, returned from the Jordan and was led by the Spirit into[a] the wilderness, [2]being tempted for forty days by the devil. And in those days He ate nothing, and afterward, when they had ended, He was hungry.

[3]And the devil said to Him, "If You are the

The Role of the Wilderness

(Luke 4:1–13)

The role of the wilderness in the preparation of a leader cannot be overemphasized. Both Luke and Matthew record Jesus' time in the wilderness at the beginning of His ministry. Jesus spent 40 days alone, in a desert, abstaining from food and noise and distraction. Both Gospel writers tell us this was a time ordained by the Holy Spirit.

So what happens to leaders in this wilderness season? Luke gives us a hint:

1. We recognize that God will lead us into seasons of growth, not gratification.
2. We fight battles and overcome temptations to take shortcuts.
3. We learn discipline and the art of depending on God.
4. We are broken of self-sufficiency and self-promotion.
5. We solidify our sense of mission.
6. We gain perspective.
7. We are prepared to enter our vocation.

Son of God, command this stone to become bread."

[4]But Jesus answered him, saying,[a] "It is written, '*Man shall not live by bread alone, but by every word of God.*'"[b]

[5]Then the devil, taking Him up on a high mountain, showed Him[a] all the kingdoms of the world in a moment of time. [6]And the devil said to Him, "All this authority I will give You, and their glory; for *this* has been delivered to me, and I give it to whomever I wish. [7]Therefore, if You will worship before me, all will be Yours."

[8]And Jesus answered and said to him, "Get

3:19 [a]NU-Text reads *his brother's wife.* **3:24** [a]This and several other names in the genealogy are spelled somewhat differently in the NU-Text. Since the New King James Version uses the Old Testament spelling for persons mentioned in the New Testament, these variations, which come from the Greek, have not been footnoted. **4:1** [a]NU-Text reads *in.* **4:4** [a]Deuteronomy 8:3 [b]NU-Text omits *but by every word of God.* **4:5** [a]NU-Text reads *And taking Him up, he showed Him.*

Self-Discipline: Jesus Teaches That the First Person You Lead Is You

(Luke 4:3–10)

Jesus faced three major temptations during His 40 days in the desert. The enemy approached Him and tried to entice Him through the following temptations:

1. *Legitimate needs* (v. 3): He tried to get Jesus to act apart from God in order to meet His legitimate needs.
2. *Spiritual gifting* (vv. 6, 7): He tried to urge Jesus to use His giftedness for self-profit or to draw a crowd.
3. *Personal worship* (vv. 9, 10): He tried to convince Jesus to get ahead by linking up with a power other than God.

Jesus teaches every leader that the first person you lead is *you*. We earn the right to lead others when they see us lead well in our own lives.

behind Me, Satan![a] For[b] it is written, '*You shall worship the LORD your God, and Him only you shall serve.*'[c]

[9]Then he brought Him to Jerusalem, set Him on the pinnacle of the temple, and said to Him, "If You are the Son of God, throw Yourself down from here. [10]For it is written:

'*He shall give His angels charge over you,
To keep you,*'

[11]and,

'*In their hands they shall bear you up,
Lest you dash your foot against a stone.*'[a]

[12]And Jesus answered and said to him, "It has been said, '*You shall not tempt the LORD your God.*'"[a]

[13]Now when the devil had ended every temptation, he departed from Him until an opportune time.

Jesus Begins His Galilean Ministry

[14]Then Jesus returned in the power of the Spirit to Galilee, and news of Him went out through all the surrounding region. [15]And He taught in their synagogues, being glorified by all.

Jesus Rejected at Nazareth

[16]So He came to Nazareth, where He had been brought up. And as His custom was, He went into the synagogue on the Sabbath day, and stood up to read. [17]And He was handed the book of the prophet Isaiah. And when He had opened the book, He found the place where it was written:

[18] "*The Spirit of the LORD is upon Me,
Because He has anointed Me
To preach the gospel to the poor;
He has sent Me to heal the brokenhearted,*[a]
*To proclaim liberty to the captives
And recovery of sight to the blind,
To set at liberty those who are oppressed;*
[19] *To proclaim the acceptable year of the
LORD.*"[a]

[20]Then He closed the book, and gave *it* back to the attendant and sat down. And the eyes of all who were in the synagogue were fixed on Him. [21]And He began to say to them, "Today this Scripture is fulfilled in your hearing." [22]So all bore witness to Him, and marveled at the gracious words which proceeded out of His mouth. And they said, "Is this not Joseph's son?"

[23]He said to them, "You will surely say this proverb to Me, 'Physician, heal yourself! Whatever we have heard done in Capernaum,[a] do also here in Your country.'" [24]Then He said, "Assuredly, I say to you, no prophet is accepted in his own country. [25]But I tell you truly, many widows

---

4:8 [a]NU-Text omits *Get behind Me, Satan.* [b]NU-Text and M-Text omit *For.* [c]Deuteronomy 6:13 **4:11** [a]Psalm 91:11, 12 **4:12** [a]Deuteronomy 6:16 **4:18** [a]NU-Text omits *to heal the brokenhearted.* **4:19** [a]Isaiah 61:1, 2 **4:23** [a]Here and elsewhere the NU-Text spelling is *Capharnaum.*

Focus: Jesus Won't Be Distracted from His Mission or Anointing

(Luke 4:18–29)

Jesus spoke from Isaiah 61 about His anointing (Luke 4:18). Even when His audience didn't like what He had to say (4:28, 29), He moved on to the next town to continue His work. He would not let anything drain His anointing or distract Him from His mission.

were in Israel in the days of Elijah, when the heaven was shut up three years and six months, and there was a great famine throughout all the land; [26]but to none of them was Elijah sent except to Zarephath,[a] *in the region* of Sidon, to a woman *who was* a widow. [27]And many lepers were in Israel in the time of Elisha the prophet, and none of them was cleansed except Naaman the Syrian."

[28]So all those in the synagogue, when they heard these things, were filled with wrath, [29]and rose up and thrust Him out of the city; and they led Him to the brow of the hill on which their city was built, that they might throw Him down over the cliff. [30]Then passing through the midst of them, He went His way.

Jesus Casts Out an Unclean Spirit

[31]Then He went down to Capernaum, a city of Galilee, and was teaching them on the Sabbaths. [32]And they were astonished at His teaching, for His word was with authority. [33]Now in the synagogue there was a man who had a spirit of an unclean demon. And he cried out with a loud voice, [34]saying, "Let *us* alone! What have we to do with You, Jesus of Nazareth? Did You come to destroy us? I know who You are—the Holy One of God!"

[35]But Jesus rebuked him, saying, "Be quiet, and come out of him!" And when the demon had thrown him in *their* midst, it came out of him and did not hurt him. [36]Then they were all amazed and spoke among themselves, saying, "What a word this *is!* For with authority and power He commands the unclean spirits, and they come out." [37]And the report about Him went out into every place in the surrounding region.

Peter's Mother-in-Law Healed

[38]Now He arose from the synagogue and entered Simon's house. But Simon's wife's mother was sick with a high fever, and they made request of Him concerning her. [39]So He stood over her and rebuked the fever, and it left her. And immediately she arose and served them.

Many Healed After Sabbath Sunset

[40]When the sun was setting, all those who had any that were sick with various diseases brought them to Him; and He laid His hands on every one of them and healed them. [41]And demons also came out of many, crying out and saying, "You are the Christ,[a] the Son of God!"

And He, rebuking *them,* did not allow them to speak, for they knew that He was the Christ.

Jesus Preaches in Galilee

[42]Now when it was day, He departed and went into a deserted place. And the crowd sought Him and came to Him, and tried to keep Him from leaving them; [43]but He said to them, "I must preach the kingdom of God to the other cities also, because for this purpose I have been sent." [44]And He was preaching in the synagogues of Galilee.[a]

Four Fishermen Called as Disciples

5 So it was, as the multitude pressed about Him to hear the word of God, that He stood by the Lake of Gennesaret, [2]and saw two boats standing by the lake; but the fishermen had gone from them and were washing *their* nets. [3]Then He got into one of the boats, which was Simon's, and asked him to put out a little from the land. And He sat down and taught the multitudes from the boat.

[4]When He had stopped speaking, He said to

4:26 [a]Greek *Sarepta* 4:41 [a]NU-Text omits *the Christ.* 4:44 [a]NU-Text reads *Judea.*

The Law of Buy-In: Jesus Builds a Team Before His Men Understand It All

(Luke 5:1–11)

The Law of Buy-In reminds us that people buy in to the leader before they buy in to the vision of that leader. Jesus directed three seasoned fishermen to let down their nets in a certain part of the lake in order to get a catch. Peter responded that they had fished hard all night, without catching anything. Yet he gave Jesus' word higher authority than his own experience.

This is crucial. Jesus' leadership drew a buy-in from professionals who felt certain they knew the fishing business better than He did. When Jesus' directions proved fruitful, they became willing to follow Him anywhere. Even before they understood all the places they would be going, they left everything to follow Him.

Simon, "Launch out into the deep and let down your nets for a catch."

[5]But Simon answered and said to Him, "Master, we have toiled all night and caught nothing; nevertheless at Your word I will let down the net." [6]And when they had done this, they caught a great number of fish, and their net was breaking. [7]So they signaled to *their* partners in the other boat to come and help them. And they came and filled both the boats, so that they began to sink. [8]When Simon Peter saw *it,* he fell down at Jesus' knees, saying, "Depart from me, for I am a sinful man, O Lord!"

[9]For he and all who were with him were astonished at the catch of fish which they had taken; [10]and so also *were* James and John, the sons of Zebedee, who were partners with Simon. And Jesus said to Simon, "Do not be afraid. From now on you will catch men." [11]So when they had brought their boats to land, they forsook all and followed Him.

Communicating Vision: Jesus Shared a Compelling Vision

(Luke 5:10)

Jesus presented a compelling vision, using assuring terms ("Do not be afraid"), familiar pictures ("you will catch"), and a challenging goal ("men"). He cast His vision in one sentence of 11 words! A vision that is short, sharp, and shaped to fit the people enables leaders to succeed.

Jesus Cleanses a Leper

[12]And it happened when He was in a certain city, that behold, a man who was full of leprosy saw Jesus; and he fell on *his* face and implored Him, saying, "Lord, if You are willing, You can make me clean."

[13]Then He put out *His* hand and touched him, saying, "I am willing; be cleansed." Immediately the leprosy left him. [14]And He charged him to tell no one, "But go and show yourself to the priest, and make an offering for your cleansing, as a testimony to them, just as Moses commanded."

[15]However, the report went around concerning Him all the more; and great multitudes came together to hear, and to be healed by Him of

The Law of Intuition: Jesus Saw Potential in Simon and Matthew

(Luke 5:10, 11, 27, 28)

Would any of us have picked Simon the fisherman or Matthew the tax collector to be on our team? The former spoke more than he thought; the latter took more than he gave. But Jesus saw them both as diamonds in the rough.

Jesus could see beyond the imperfections, and He put a "ten" on their foreheads instead of the "three" or "four" they deserved. Unstable Peter became a solid leader of the church at Jerusalem, while Matthew became one of the most generous people in the Gospels.

The Law of Intuition enables leaders to spot potential. Consider the biblical record . . .

1. Who would have chosen a stammering Moses to be a spokesman for God?
2. Who would have chosen a shepherd boy like David to be King of Israel?
3. Who would have chosen an uncouth John the Baptizer to prepare the way for Jesus?
4. Who would have chosen a converted prostitute, Mary, to herald the resurrection?

their infirmities. [16]So He Himself *often* withdrew into the wilderness and prayed.

Jesus Forgives and Heals a Paralytic

[17]Now it happened on a certain day, as He was teaching, that there were Pharisees and teachers of the law sitting by, who had come out of every town of Galilee, Judea, and Jerusalem. And the power of the Lord was *present* to heal them.[a] [18]Then behold, men brought on a bed a man who was paralyzed, whom they sought to bring in and lay before Him. [19]And when they could not find how they might bring him in, because of the crowd, they went up on the housetop and let him down with *his* bed through the tiling into the midst before Jesus.

[20]When He saw their faith, He said to him, "Man, your sins are forgiven you."

5:17 [a]NU-Text reads *present with Him to heal.*

²¹And the scribes and the Pharisees began to reason, saying, "Who is this who speaks blasphemies? Who can forgive sins but God alone?" ²²But when Jesus perceived their thoughts, He answered and said to them, "Why are you reasoning in your hearts? ²³Which is easier, to say, 'Your sins are forgiven you,' or to say, 'Rise up and walk'? ²⁴But that you may know that the Son of Man has power on earth to forgive sins"—He said to the man who was paralyzed, "I say to you, arise, take up your bed, and go to your house."

²⁵Immediately he rose up before them, took up what he had been lying on, and departed to his own house, glorifying God. ²⁶And they were all amazed, and they glorified God and were filled with fear, saying, "We have seen strange things today!"

Matthew the Tax Collector

²⁷After these things He went out and saw a tax collector named Levi, sitting at the tax office. And He said to him, "Follow Me." ²⁸So he left all, rose up, and followed Him.

²⁹Then Levi gave Him a great feast in his own house. And there were a great number of tax collectors and others who sat down with them. ³⁰And their scribes and the Pharisees[a] complained against His disciples, saying, "Why do You eat and drink with tax collectors and sinners?"

³¹Jesus answered and said to them, "Those who are well have no need of a physician, but those who are sick. ³²I have not come to call the righteous, but sinners, to repentance."

Jesus Is Questioned About Fasting

³³Then they said to Him, "Why do[a] the disciples of John fast often and make prayers, and likewise those of the Pharisees, but Yours eat and drink?"

³⁴And He said to them, "Can you make the friends of the bridegroom fast while the bridegroom is with them? ³⁵But the days will come when the bridegroom will be taken away from them; then they will fast in those days."

³⁶Then He spoke a parable to them: "No one puts a piece from a new garment on an old one;[a] otherwise the new makes a tear, and also the piece that was taken out of the new does not match the old. ³⁷And no one puts new wine into old wineskins; or else the new wine will burst the wineskins and be spilled, and the wineskins will be ruined. ³⁸But new wine must be put into new wineskins, and both are preserved.[a] ³⁹And no one, having drunk old wine, immediately[a] desires new; for he says, 'The old is better.'"[b]

Jesus Is Lord of the Sabbath

6 Now it happened on the second Sabbath after the first[a] that He went through the grainfields. And His disciples plucked the heads of grain and ate them, rubbing them in their hands. ²And some of the Pharisees said to them, "Why are you doing what is not lawful to do on the Sabbath?"

³But Jesus answering them said, "Have you not even read this, what David did when he was hungry, he and those who were with him: ⁴how he went into the house of God, took and ate the showbread, and also gave some to those with him, which is not lawful for any but the priests to eat?" ⁵And He said to them, "The Son of Man is also Lord of the Sabbath."

Healing on the Sabbath

⁶Now it happened on another Sabbath, also, that He entered the synagogue and taught. And a man was there whose right hand was withered. ⁷So the scribes and Pharisees watched Him closely, whether He would heal on the Sabbath, that they might find an accusation against Him. ⁸But He knew their thoughts, and said to the man who had the withered hand, "Arise and stand here." And he arose and stood. ⁹Then Jesus said to them, "I will ask you one thing: Is it lawful on the Sabbath to do good or to do evil, to save life or to destroy?"[a] ¹⁰And when He had looked around at them all, He said to the man,[a] "Stretch out your hand." And he did so, and his hand was restored as whole as the other.[b] ¹¹But they were filled with rage, and discussed with one another what they might do to Jesus.

The Twelve Apostles

¹²Now it came to pass in those days that He went out to the mountain to pray, and continued all night in prayer to God. ¹³And when it was day, He called His disciples to Himself; and from them He chose twelve whom He also named apostles: ¹⁴Simon, whom He also named Peter, and Andrew his brother; James and John; Philip and Bartholomew; ¹⁵Matthew and Thomas; James the

---

5:30 [a]NU-Text reads But the Pharisees and their scribes. **5:33** [a]NU-Text omits Why do, making the verse a statement. **5:36** [a]NU-Text reads No one tears a piece from a new garment and puts it on an old one. **5:38** [a]NU-Text omits and both are preserved. **5:39** [a]NU-Text omits immediately. [b]NU-Text reads good. **6:1** [a]NU-Text reads on a Sabbath. **6:9** [a]M-Text reads to kill. **6:10** [a]NU-Text and M-Text read to him. [b]NU-Text omits as whole as the other.

son of Alphaeus, and Simon called the Zealot; [16]Judas *the son* of James, and Judas Iscariot who also became a traitor.

Jesus Heals a Great Multitude

[17]And He came down with them and stood on a level place with a crowd of His disciples and a great multitude of people from all Judea and Jerusalem, and from the seacoast of Tyre and Sidon, who came to hear Him and be healed of their diseases, [18]as well as those who were tormented with unclean spirits. And they were healed. [19]And the whole multitude sought to touch Him, for power went out from Him and healed *them* all.

The Beatitudes

[20]Then He lifted up His eyes toward His disciples, and said:

"Blessed *are you* poor,
For yours is the kingdom of God.
[21] Blessed *are you* who hunger now,
For you shall be filled.
Blessed *are you* who weep now,
For you shall laugh.

[22] Blessed are you when men hate you,
And when they exclude you,
And revile *you,* and cast out your name
as evil,
For the Son of Man's sake.
[23] Rejoice in that day and leap for joy!
For indeed your reward *is* great in
heaven,
For in like manner their fathers did to
the prophets.

Jesus Pronounces Woes

[24] "But woe to you who are rich,
For you have received your consolation.
[25] Woe to you who are full,
For you shall hunger.
Woe to you who laugh now,
For you shall mourn and weep.
[26] Woe to you[a] when all[b] men speak well of
you,
For so did their fathers to the false
prophets.

6:26 [a]NU-Text and M-Text omit *to you.* [b]M-Text omits *all.*

Mentoring: Jesus Spent the Majority of His Time with Twelve, Not Twelve Hundred

(Luke 6:12–19)

In less than one generation, the disciples of Jesus progressed from ignorant laborers to bold spiritual leaders in what is now the largest organization in the world. How could this transformation occur?

It happened because Jesus spent the bulk of His time with them. The Son of God invested the vast majority of His time with twelve, not twelve hundred. Jesus practiced the axiom: More time with less people equals greater kingdom impact.

Like all good mentors, Jesus provided:

1. *Handles:* He simplified truth into something his men could grasp, practice, and pass on to others. He took complex theology and made it usable.
2. *Roadmaps:* Roadmaps give you the big picture; they reveal where you are; they show you what roads to take; and they tell you what roads to avoid. Jesus did this consistently with the Twelve.
3. *Laboratories:* Labs are safe places for experimentation. Jesus didn't just lecture, He provided labs for His disciples to practice what they learned.
4. *Roots:* Jesus gave His followers a firm foundation and a sense of heritage. They sunk their roots into solid ground and were willing to die for Him and His teaching.
5. *Wings:* Jesus empowered His men to soar beyond where He went Himself (John 14:12). He pushed them and cheered them on in their victories.

Positive Attitude: Jesus' First Job Was to Change Their Perspective

(Luke 6:20–23)

What did Jesus do first when training His leaders? He transformed their perspective and attitude. He talked about the blessing of being poor, hungry, hated, insulted, or persecuted. Talk about a change of attitude! Effective training always begins with attitude and perspective, changing individuals from the inside out.

Love Your Enemies

27"But I say to you who hear: Love your enemies, do good to those who hate you, 28bless those who curse you, and pray for those who spitefully use you. 29To him who strikes you on the *one* cheek, offer the other also. And from him who takes away your cloak, do not withhold *your* tunic either. 30Give to everyone who asks of you. And from him who takes away your goods do not ask *them* back. 31And just as you want men to do to you, you also do to them likewise.

32"But if you love those who love you, what credit is that to you? For even sinners love those who love them. 33And if you do good to those who do good to you, what credit is that to you? For even sinners do the same. 34And if you lend *to those* from whom you hope to receive back, what credit is that to you? For even sinners lend to sinners to receive as much back. 35But love your enemies, do good, and lend, hoping for nothing in return; and your reward will be great, and you will be sons of the Most High. For He is kind to the unthankful and evil. 36Therefore be merciful, just as your Father also is merciful.

Do Not Judge

37"Judge not, and you shall not be judged. Condemn not, and you shall not be condemned. Forgive, and you will be forgiven. 38Give, and it will be given to you: good measure, pressed down, shaken together, and running over will be put into your bosom. For with the same measure that you use, it will be measured back to you."

39And He spoke a parable to them: "Can the blind lead the blind? Will they not both fall into the ditch? 40A disciple is not above his teacher, but everyone who is perfectly trained will be like his teacher. 41And why do you look at the speck in your brother's eye, but do not perceive the plank in your own eye? 42Or how can you say to your brother, 'Brother, let me remove the speck that *is* in your eye,' when you yourself do not see the plank that *is* in your own eye? Hypocrite! First remove the plank from your own eye, and then you will see clearly to remove the speck that is in your brother's eye.

A Tree Is Known by Its Fruit

43"For a good tree does not bear bad fruit, nor does a bad tree bear good fruit. 44For every tree is known by its own fruit. For *men* do not gather figs from thorns, nor do they gather grapes from a bramble bush. 45A good man out of the good treasure of his heart brings forth good; and an evil man out of the evil treasure of his heart[a] brings forth evil. For out of the abundance of the heart his mouth speaks.

Build on the Rock

46"But why do you call Me 'Lord, Lord,' and not do the things which I say? 47Whoever comes to Me, and hears My sayings and does them, I will show you whom he is like: 48He is like a man building a house, who dug deep and laid the foundation on the rock. And when the flood arose, the stream beat vehemently against that house, and could not shake it, for it was founded on the rock.[a] 49But he who heard and did nothing is like a man who built a house on the earth without a foundation, against which the stream beat vehemently; and immediately it fell.[a] And the ruin of that house was great."

Jesus Heals a Centurion's Servant

7 Now when He concluded all His sayings in the hearing of the people, He entered Capernaum. 2And a certain centurion's servant, who was dear to him, was sick and ready to die. 3So when he heard about Jesus, he sent elders of the Jews to Him, pleading with Him to come and heal his servant. 4And when they came to Jesus, they begged Him earnestly, saying that the one for whom He should do this was deserving, 5"for he loves our nation, and has built us a synagogue."

6Then Jesus went with them. And when He was already not far from the house, the centurion sent friends to Him, saying to Him, "Lord, do not trouble Yourself, for I am not worthy that

6:45 [a]NU-Text omits *treasure of his heart.*
6:48 [a]NU-Text reads *for it was well built.*
6:49 [a]NU-Text reads *collapsed.*

You should enter under my roof. [7]Therefore I did not even think myself worthy to come to You. But say the word, and my servant will be healed. [8]For I also am a man placed under authority, having soldiers under me. And I say to one, 'Go,' and he goes; and to another, 'Come,' and he comes; and to my servant, 'Do this,' and he does *it*."

[9]When Jesus heard these things, He marveled at him, and turned around and said to the crowd that followed Him, "I say to you, I have not found such great faith, not even in Israel!" [10]And those who were sent, returning to the house, found the servant well who had been sick.[a]

Jesus Raises the Son of the Widow of Nain

[11]Now it happened, the day after, *that* He went into a city called Nain; and many of His disciples went with Him, and a large crowd. [12]And when He came near the gate of the city, behold, a dead man was being carried out, the only son of his mother; and she was a widow. And a large crowd from the city was with her. [13]When the Lord saw her, He had compassion on her and said to her, "Do not weep." [14]Then He came and touched the open coffin, and those who carried *him* stood still. And He said, "Young man, I say to you, arise." [15]So he who was dead sat up and began to speak. And He presented him to his mother.

[16]Then fear came upon all, and they glorified God, saying, "A great prophet has risen up among us"; and, "God has visited His people." [17]And this report about Him went throughout all Judea and all the surrounding region.

John the Baptist Sends Messengers to Jesus

[18]Then the disciples of John reported to him concerning all these things. [19]And John, calling two of his disciples to *him,* sent *them* to Jesus,[a] saying, "Are You the Coming One, or do we look for another?"

[20]When the men had come to Him, they said, "John the Baptist has sent us to You, saying, 'Are You the Coming One, or do we look for another?'" [21]And that very hour He cured many of infirmities, afflictions, and evil spirits; and to many blind He gave sight.

[22]Jesus answered and said to them, "Go and tell John the things you have seen and heard: that *the* blind see, *the* lame walk, *the* lepers are

---

7:10 [a]NU-Text omits *who had been sick.*
7:19 [a]NU-Text reads *the Lord.*

JESUS

THE PERFECT MAN
(Luke 7:1–17)

PROFILE IN LEADERSHIP

There exists no better example of a godly leader than the Lord Jesus Christ. Every word He spoke, everything He did, served to model what godly leadership looks like.

We see Jesus spending a day ministering, not to those who seemed by human standards to be most worthy, but to those who needed Him most. He healed the sick and lame, cast out evil spirits, even raised the dead. And when He entered the home of one of the religious leaders of the day, He spent His time ministering to a lowly sinner.

All of those to whom Jesus ministered had one thing in common: They knew of their own need. They came to Him with empty, outstretched hands, hoping He would show them compassion. And He did not disappoint their hope, for when the people saw Jesus' loving power in action, they glorified God and said, "A great prophet has risen up among us," and "God has visited His people" (Luke 7:16).

Our world is full of needy people, overflowing with men and women who know they're missing out on something, bursting with hurting individuals who come to us with hands outstretched. As leaders for Christ, it is our job to reach out to the whole world so that those who admit their need have a chance to come to Him.

cleansed, *the* deaf hear, *the* dead are raised, *the* poor have the gospel preached to them. ²³And blessed is *he* who is not offended because of Me."

²⁴When the messengers of John had departed, He began to speak to the multitudes concerning John: "What did you go out into the wilderness to see? A reed shaken by the wind? ²⁵But what did you go out to see? A man clothed in soft garments? Indeed those who are gorgeously appareled and live in luxury are in kings' courts. ²⁶But what did you go out to see? A prophet? Yes, I say to you, and more than a prophet. ²⁷This is *he* of whom it is written:

'Behold, I send My messenger before Your face,
Who will prepare Your way before You.'ᵃ

²⁸For I say to you, among those born of women there is not a greater prophet than John the Baptist;ᵃ but he who is least in the kingdom of God is greater than he."

²⁹And when all the people heard *Him,* even the tax collectors justified God, having been baptized with the baptism of John. ³⁰But the Pharisees and lawyers rejected the will of God for themselves, not having been baptized by him.

³¹And the Lord said,ᵃ "To what then shall I liken the men of this generation, and what are they like? ³²They are like children sitting in the marketplace and calling to one another, saying:

'We played the flute for you,
And you did not dance;
We mourned to you,
And you did not weep.'

³³For John the Baptist came neither eating bread nor drinking wine, and you say, 'He has a demon.' ³⁴The Son of Man has come eating and drinking, and you say, 'Look, a glutton and a winebibber, a friend of tax collectors and sinners!' ³⁵But wisdom is justified by all her children."

A Sinful Woman Forgiven

³⁶Then one of the Pharisees asked Him to eat with him. And He went to the Pharisee's house, and sat down to eat. ³⁷And behold, a woman in the city who was a sinner, when she knew that *Jesus* sat at the table in the Pharisee's house, brought an alabaster flask of fragrant oil, ³⁸and stood at His feet behind *Him* weeping; and she began to wash His feet with her tears, and wiped *them* with the hair of her head; and she kissed His feet and anointed *them* with the fragrant oil. ³⁹Now when the Pharisee who had invited Him saw *this,* he spoke to himself, saying, "This Man, if He were a prophet, would know who and what manner of woman *this is* who is touching Him, for she is a sinner."

⁴⁰And Jesus answered and said to him, "Simon, I have something to say to you."

So he said, "Teacher, say it."

⁴¹"There was a certain creditor who had two debtors. One owed five hundred denarii, and the other fifty. ⁴²And when they had nothing with which to repay, he freely forgave them both. Tell Me, therefore, which of them will love him more?"

⁴³Simon answered and said, "I suppose the *one* whom he forgave more."

And He said to him, "You have rightly judged." ⁴⁴Then He turned to the woman and said to Simon, "Do you see this woman? I entered your house; you gave Me no water for My feet, but she has washed My feet with her tears and wiped *them* with the hair of her head. ⁴⁵You gave Me no kiss, but this woman has not ceased to kiss My feet since the time I came in. ⁴⁶You did not anoint My head with oil, but this woman has anointed My feet with fragrant oil. ⁴⁷Therefore I say to you, her sins, *which are* many, are forgiven, for she loved much. But to whom little is forgiven, *the same* loves little."

⁴⁸Then He said to her, "Your sins are forgiven."

⁴⁹And those who sat at the table with Him began to say to themselves, "Who is this who even forgives sins?"

⁵⁰Then He said to the woman, "Your faith has saved you. Go in peace."

Many Women Minister to Jesus

8 Now it came to pass, afterward, that He went through every city and village, preaching and bringing the glad tidings of the kingdom of God. And the twelve *were* with Him, ²and certain women who had been healed of evil spirits and infirmities—Mary called Magdalene, out of whom had come seven demons, ³and Joanna the wife of Chuza, Herod's steward, and Susanna, and many others who provided for Himᵃ from their substance.

The Parable of the Sower

⁴And when a great multitude had gathered, and they had come to Him from every city, He spoke by a parable: ⁵"A sower went out to sow

---

7:27 ᵃMalachi 3:1 7:28 ᵃNU-Text reads *there is none greater than John.* 7:31 ᵃNU-Text and M-Text omit *And the Lord said.* 8:3 ᵃNU-Text and M-Text read *them.*

his seed. And as he sowed, some fell by the way-side; and it was trampled down, and the birds of the air devoured it. ⁶Some fell on rock; and as soon as it sprang up, it withered away because it lacked moisture. ⁷And some fell among thorns, and the thorns sprang up with it and choked it. ⁸But others fell on good ground, sprang up, and yielded a crop a hundredfold." When He had said these things He cried, "He who has ears to hear, let him hear!"

The Purpose of Parables

⁹Then His disciples asked Him, saying, "What does this parable mean?"

¹⁰And He said, "To you it has been given to know the mysteries of the kingdom of God, but to the rest it is given in parables, that

'Seeing they may not see,
   And hearing they may not understand.'ᵃ

The Parable of the Sower Explained

¹¹"Now the parable is this: The seed is the word of God. ¹²Those by the wayside are the ones who hear; then the devil comes and takes away the word out of their hearts, lest they should believe and be saved. ¹³But the ones on the rock are those who, when they hear, receive the word with joy; and these have no root, who believe for a while and in time of temptation fall away. ¹⁴Now the ones that fell among thorns are those who, when they have heard, go out and are choked with cares, riches, and pleasures of life, and bring no fruit to maturity. ¹⁵But the ones that fell on the good ground are those who, having

heard the word with a noble and good heart, keep it and bear fruit with patience.

The Parable of the Revealed Light

¹⁶"No one, when he has lit a lamp, covers it with a vessel or puts it under a bed, but sets it on a lampstand, that those who enter may see the light. ¹⁷For nothing is secret that will not be revealed, nor anything hidden that will not be known and come to light. ¹⁸Therefore take heed how you hear. For whoever has, to him more will be given; and whoever does not have, even what he seems to have will be taken from him."

Jesus' Mother and Brothers Come to Him

¹⁹Then His mother and brothers came to Him, and could not approach Him because of the crowd. ²⁰And it was told Him by some, who said, "Your mother and Your brothers are standing outside, desiring to see You."

²¹But He answered and said to them, "My mother and My brothers are these who hear the word of God and do it."

Wind and Wave Obey Jesus

²²Now it happened, on a certain day, that He got into a boat with His disciples. And He said to them, "Let us cross over to the other side of the lake." And they launched out. ²³But as they sailed He fell asleep. And a windstorm came down on the lake, and they were filling with water, and were in jeopardy. ²⁴And they came to Him and

8:10 ᵃIsaiah 6:9

The Law of Connection: Jesus Always Met Needs First

(Luke 8:24—9:6)

Jesus always approached people to meet their needs before He asked them to follow or obey Him. After He delivered the demonized man in Gadara, the man wanted to do something in return. Jesus told him to return to his hometown and spread the news of God's kingdom. The man acted as he did in response to a leader who practiced the Law of Connection. Gratitude nearly always follows grace. Look at the connection and response in these verses alone:

The Leader Connects
1. Jesus calmed the sea for His disciples (8:24).
2. Jesus delivered the demonized man (8:33).
3. Jesus healed the woman's blood disease (8:47).
4. Jesus raised Jairus's daughter from the dead (8:54).

The People's Response
1. They were sent out (9:1–6).
2. He was to preach at home (8:39).
3. She was to exhibit peace (8:48).
4. He was to feed and minister (8:55).

awoke Him, saying, "Master, Master, we are perishing!"

Then He arose and rebuked the wind and the raging of the water. And they ceased, and there was a calm. [25]But He said to them, "Where is your faith?"

And they were afraid, and marveled, saying to one another, "Who can this be? For He commands even the winds and water, and they obey Him!"

A Demon-Possessed Man Healed

[26]Then they sailed to the country of the Gadarenes,[a] which is opposite Galilee. [27]And when He stepped out on the land, there met Him a certain man from the city who had demons for a long time. And he wore no clothes,[a] nor did he live in a house but in the tombs. [28]When he saw Jesus, he cried out, fell down before Him, and with a loud voice said, "What have I to do with You, Jesus, Son of the Most High God? I beg You, do not torment me!" [29]For He had commanded the unclean spirit to come out of the man. For it had often seized him, and he was kept under guard, bound with chains and shackles; and he broke the bonds and was driven by the demon into the wilderness.

[30]Jesus asked him, saying, "What is your name?"

And he said, "Legion," because many demons had entered him. [31]And they begged Him that He would not command them to go out into the abyss.

[32]Now a herd of many swine was feeding there on the mountain. So they begged Him that He would permit them to enter them. And He permitted them. [33]Then the demons went out of the man and entered the swine, and the herd ran violently down the steep place into the lake and drowned.

[34]When those who fed *them* saw what had happened, they fled and told *it* in the city and in the country. [35]Then they went out to see what had happened, and came to Jesus, and found the man from whom the demons had departed, sitting at the feet of Jesus, clothed and in his right mind. And they were afraid. [36]They also who had seen *it* told them by what means he who had been demon-possessed was healed. [37]Then the whole multitude of the surrounding region of the Gadarenes[a] asked Him to depart from them,

---

8:26 [a]NU-Text reads *Gerasenes.* 8:27 [a]NU-Text reads *who had demons and for a long time wore no clothes.* 8:37 [a]NU-Text reads *Gerasenes.*

Commitment: Solve Our Problems but Save Our Pigs

(Luke 8:26–37)

Jesus once met a man controlled by a legion of demons. The poor man had lost control and had to be chained and kept under guard. When Jesus cast the offending demons into some nearby pigs, the man instantly grew calm and whole.

Ironically, when the area's residents took one look at the man, they asked Jesus to depart. No doubt they felt pleased to see this man healed—but not at the expense of their livestock! They feared the demon-possessed man, but they feared even more a Jesus who took complete control over the situation. It's important to remember in any conflict: Jesus doesn't want to take sides; He wants to take over!

Often we resemble the Gadarenes, those who wanted Jesus to solve their problems but save their pigs. "We don't want to upset things or get radical," we say. "We want change . . . as long as it doesn't change *us*." But this is not Jesus' way.

Note several lessons this passage teaches us about leadership:

1. *Leadership means discomfort.*
   If you're going to be an effective leader, you must live outside of your comfort zone.
2. *Leadership means dissatisfaction.*
   God uses dissatisfaction as a tool to move us to greater things and higher ground.
3. *Leadership means disruption.*
   The status quo is never the goal of a leader. Disruption is our constant companion.

for they were seized with great fear. And He got into the boat and returned.

38Now the man from whom the demons had departed begged Him that he might be with Him. But Jesus sent him away, saying, 39"Return to your own house, and tell what great things God has done for you." And he went his way and proclaimed throughout the whole city what great things Jesus had done for him.

A Girl Restored to Life and a Woman Healed

40So it was, when Jesus returned, that the multitude welcomed Him, for they were all waiting for Him. 41And behold, there came a man named Jairus, and he was a ruler of the synagogue. And he fell down at Jesus' feet and begged Him to come to his house, 42for he had an only daughter about twelve years of age, and she was dying.

But as He went, the multitudes thronged Him. 43Now a woman, having a flow of blood for twelve years, who had spent all her livelihood on physicians and could not be healed by any, 44came from behind and touched the border of His garment. And immediately her flow of blood stopped.

45And Jesus said, "Who touched Me?"

When all denied it, Peter and those with him[a] said, "Master, the multitudes throng and press You, and You say, 'Who touched Me?'"[b]

46But Jesus said, "Somebody touched Me, for I perceived power going out from Me." 47Now when the woman saw that she was not hidden, she came trembling; and falling down before Him, she declared to Him in the presence of all the people the reason she had touched Him and how she was healed immediately.

48And He said to her, "Daughter, be of good cheer;[a] your faith has made you well. Go in peace."

49While He was still speaking, someone came from the ruler of the synagogue's house, saying to him, "Your daughter is dead. Do not trouble the Teacher."[a]

50But when Jesus heard it, He answered him, saying, "Do not be afraid; only believe, and she will be made well." 51When He came into the house, He permitted no one to go in[a] except Peter, James, and John,[b] and the father and mother of the girl. 52Now all wept and mourned for her; but He said, "Do not weep; she is not dead, but sleeping." 53And they ridiculed Him, knowing that she was dead.

54But He put them all outside,[a] took her by the hand and called, saying, "Little girl, arise." 55Then her spirit returned, and she arose imme-

diately. And He commanded that she be given something to eat. 56And her parents were astonished, but He charged them to tell no one what had happened.

Sending Out the Twelve

9 Then He called His twelve disciples together and gave them power and authority over all demons, and to cure diseases. 2He sent them to preach the kingdom of God and to heal the sick. 3And He said to them, "Take nothing for the journey, neither staffs nor bag nor bread nor money; and do not have two tunics apiece.

4"Whatever house you enter, stay there, and from there depart. 5And whoever will not receive you, when you go out of that city, shake off the very dust from your feet as a testimony against them."

6So they departed and went through the towns, preaching the gospel and healing everywhere.

Herod Seeks to See Jesus

7Now Herod the tetrarch heard of all that was done by Him; and he was perplexed, because it was said by some that John had risen from the dead, 8and by some that Elijah had appeared, and by others that one of the old prophets had risen again. 9Herod said, "John I have beheaded, but who is this of whom I hear such things?" So he sought to see Him.

Feeding the Five Thousand

10And the apostles, when they had returned, told Him all that they had done. Then He took them and went aside privately into a deserted place belonging to the city called Bethsaida. 11But when the multitudes knew it, they followed Him; and He received them and spoke to them about the kingdom of God, and healed those who had need of healing. 12When the day began to wear away, the twelve came and said to Him, "Send the multitude away, that they may go into the surrounding towns and country, and lodge and get provisions; for we are in a deserted place here."

13But He said to them, "You give them something to eat."

8:45 [a]NU-Text omits and those with him.
[b]NU-Text omits and You say, 'Who touched Me?'
8:48 [a]NU-Text omits be of good cheer.
8:49 [a]NU-Text adds anymore. **8:51** [a]NU-Text adds with Him. [b]NU-Text and M-Text read Peter, John, and James. **8:54** [a]NU-Text omits put them all outside.

Delegation: Jesus Shared Both Responsibility and Authority

(Luke 9:1–10)

Jesus sent out His disciples, two by two, for some on-the-job training. Note how He got them ready for this ministry experience:

1. *Motivation:* He called them together (v. 1).
2. *Impartation:* He empowered them and gave them authority (v. 1).
3. *Delegation:* He sent them out to do a job (v. 2).
4. *Communication:* He gave them specific direction (vv. 3–5).
5. *Evaluation:* He held them accountable when they finished (v. 10).

If we are going to succeed in our mission (and live to tell about it), we must share the work-load with a team. Jesus aimed to develop people as He shared the work. Consider three methods of distributing tasks among a team:

1. *Dumping:* Leaders unload a task, happy to relieve themselves of the burden. There is little to no preparation; the leaders focus on getting rid of a task. Major damage can be done to the people who receive the work.
2. *Delegating:* Leaders prepare ahead of time, then plan how to best give work away to the right people. Less damage results, but the leaders still focus on eliminating the task, not building the people.
3. *Developing:* This is the ultimate way to share work. Leaders prepare the people and the work, then focus on the training of the people. Both the leaders and the workers benefit.

And they said, "We have no more than five loaves and two fish, unless we go and buy food for all these people." [14]For there were about five thousand men.

Then He said to His disciples, "Make them sit down in groups of fifty." [15]And they did so, and made them all sit down.

Generosity: A Candle Loses Nothing by Lighting Another

(Luke 9:12–17)

God likes win/win situations. We see this in the account of the feeding of the five thousand. Jesus took one basket of fish and bread, blessed it, and fed multitudes. Whoever gave up his lunch basket in the beginning, received *12 times* more at the end of the day. This is how generosity works.

[16]Then He took the five loaves and the two fish, and looking up to heaven, He blessed and broke *them,* and gave *them* to the disciples to set before the multitude. [17]So they all ate and were filled, and twelve baskets of the leftover fragments were taken up by them.

Peter Confesses Jesus as the Christ

[18]And it happened, as He was alone praying, *that* His disciples joined Him, and He asked them, saying, "Who do the crowds say that I am?"

[19]So they answered and said, "John the Baptist, but some *say* Elijah; and others *say* that one of the old prophets has risen again."

[20]He said to them, "But who do you say that I am?"

Peter answered and said, "The Christ of God."

Jesus Predicts His Death and Resurrection

[21]And He strictly warned and commanded them to tell this to no one, [22]saying, "The Son of Man must suffer many things, and be rejected by the elders and chief priests and scribes, and be killed, and be raised the third day."

Take Up the Cross and Follow Him

²³Then He said to *them* all, "If anyone desires to come after Me, let him deny himself, and take up his cross daily,ᵃ and follow Me. ²⁴For whoever desires to save his life will lose it, but whoever loses his life for My sake will save it. ²⁵For what profit is it to a man if he gains the whole world, and is himself destroyed or lost? ²⁶For whoever is ashamed of Me and My words, of him the Son of Man will be ashamed when He comes in His *own* glory, and *in His* Father's, and of the holy angels. ²⁷But I tell you truly, there are some standing here who shall not taste death till they see the kingdom of God."

Jesus Transfigured on the Mount

²⁸Now it came to pass, about eight days after these sayings, that He took Peter, John, and James and went up on the mountain to pray. ²⁹As He prayed, the appearance of His face was altered, and His robe *became* white *and* glistening. ³⁰And behold, two men talked with Him, who were Moses and Elijah, ³¹who appeared in glory and spoke of His decease which He was about to accomplish at Jerusalem. ³²But Peter and those with him were heavy with sleep; and when they were fully awake, they saw His glory and the two men who stood with Him. ³³Then it happened, as they were parting from Him, *that* Peter said to Jesus, "Master, it is good for us to be here; and let us make three tabernacles: one for You, one for Moses, and one for Elijah"—not knowing what he said.

³⁴While he was saying this, a cloud came and overshadowed them; and they were fearful as they entered the cloud. ³⁵And a voice came out of the cloud, saying, "This is My beloved Son.ᵃ Hear Him!" ³⁶When the voice had ceased, Jesus was found alone. But they kept quiet, and told no one in those days any of the things they had seen.

A Boy Is Healed

³⁷Now it happened on the next day, when they had come down from the mountain, that a great multitude met Him. ³⁸Suddenly a man from the multitude cried out, saying, "Teacher, I implore You, look on my son, for he is my only child. ³⁹And behold, a spirit seizes him, and he suddenly cries out; it convulses him so that he foams *at the mouth;* and it departs from him with great difficulty, bruising him. ⁴⁰So I implored Your disciples to cast it out, but they could not."

⁴¹Then Jesus answered and said, "O faithless and perverse generation, how long shall I be

---

The Law of the Inner Circle: Jesus Prepared Men to Represent Him

(Luke 9:28–36)

Three of Jesus' key men saw Him transfigured on a mountain. He had specifically chosen these three to share the experience with Him, one of several special times He arranged for Peter, James, and John. While the other nine disciples waited at the foot of the mountain for their comrades to return, this "inner circle" witnessed a miracle.

Jesus, the ultimate Trainer and Mentor, did things this way to prepare some key players for future leadership. Watch how He did it. Jesus . . .

- selected a group of key men (v. 28)
- took them to a special place (v. 28)
- spent time praying with them (vv. 28, 29)
- shared an unusual experience with them (vv. 30, 31)
- provided a lasting memory for them (vv. 32, 33)
- invested special time speaking with them (vv. 34, 35)
- gave them a secret history with Him that prepared them for the future (v. 36)

---

with you and bear with you? Bring your son here." ⁴²And as he was still coming, the demon threw him down and convulsed *him.* Then Jesus rebuked the unclean spirit, healed the child, and gave him back to his father.

Jesus Again Predicts His Death

⁴³And they were all amazed at the majesty of God.

But while everyone marveled at all the things which Jesus did, He said to His disciples, ⁴⁴"Let these words sink down into your ears, for the Son of Man is about to be betrayed into the hands of men." ⁴⁵But they did not understand this saying, and it was hidden from them so that they did not perceive it; and they were afraid to ask Him about this saying.

9:23 ᵃM-Text omits *daily.* **9:35** ᵃNU-Text reads *This is My Son, the Chosen One.*

The Law of Explosive Growth: Jesus Expands His Training to Seventy

(Luke 9:1—10:24)

Some time after Jesus sent out His twelve, handpicked disciples for on-the-job training (Luke 9), He expanded His training to include 70 unnamed disciples who followed Him (Luke 10). We have reason to believe both men and women made up this group of 70 trainees, and what they accomplished greatly multiplied Jesus' ministry in Judah.

Before they left, however, many felt apprehensive about being sent out—just look at the long briefing Jesus gave them. Also, after they returned, note their surprise at how well things went. Jesus expected a lot from them, but He also gave them a lot. This valuable team prepared each city for Jesus' coming and in return received valuable training from the experience.

The Law of Explosive Growth teaches that success is determined by *who* and *what* the leader teaches. To multiply his or her influence, the leader must teach other leaders and equip them with skills and principles to enable them to influence others. When a leader does this, he or she moves from addition to multiplication.

Who Is the Greatest?

⁴⁶Then a dispute arose among them as to which of them would be greatest. ⁴⁷And Jesus, perceiving the thought of their heart, took a little child and set him by Him, ⁴⁸and said to them, "Whoever receives this little child in My name receives Me; and whoever receives Me receives Him who sent Me. For he who is least among you all will be great."

Jesus Forbids Sectarianism

⁴⁹Now John answered and said, "Master, we saw someone casting out demons in Your name, and we forbade him because he does not follow with us."

⁵⁰But Jesus said to him, "Do not forbid *him*, for he who is not against us[a] is on our[b] side."

A Samaritan Village Rejects the Savior

⁵¹Now it came to pass, when the time had come for Him to be received up, that He steadfastly set His face to go to Jerusalem, ⁵²and sent messengers before His face. And as they went, they entered a village of the Samaritans, to prepare for Him. ⁵³But they did not receive Him, because His face was *set* for the journey to Jerusalem. ⁵⁴And when His disciples James and John saw *this*, they said, "Lord, do You want us to command fire to come down from heaven and consume them, just as Elijah did?"[a]

⁵⁵But He turned and rebuked them,[a] and said, "You do not know what manner of spirit you are of. ⁵⁶For the Son of Man did not come to destroy men's lives but to save *them*."[a] And they went to another village.

Focus: Jesus Resolved to Move Toward a Difficult Climax

(Luke 9:51–56)

Although Jesus saw the end coming, "He steadfastly set His face to go to Jerusalem" (Luke 9:51). His focus could be seen in His face (9:51–53) and in the arrangements to expedite His journey (9:52). Yet He never lost sight of the big picture (9:54–56). Jesus determined to reach His ultimate destination.

The Cost of Discipleship

⁵⁷Now it happened as they journeyed on the road, *that* someone said to Him, "Lord, I will follow You wherever You go."

⁵⁸And Jesus said to him, "Foxes have holes and birds of the air *have* nests, but the Son of Man has nowhere to lay *His* head."

⁵⁹Then He said to another, "Follow Me."

But he said, "Lord, let me first go and bury my father."

⁶⁰Jesus said to him, "Let the dead bury their own dead, but you go and preach the kingdom of God."

9:50 [a]NU-Text reads *you*. [b]NU-Text reads *your*.
9:54 [a]NU-Text omits *just as Elijah did*.
9:55 [a]NU-Text omits the rest of this verse.
9:56 [a]NU-Text omits the first sentence of this verse.

⁶¹And another also said, "Lord, I will follow You, but let me first go *and* bid them farewell who are at my house."

⁶²But Jesus said to him, "No one, having put his hand to the plow, and looking back, is fit for the kingdom of God."

The Seventy Sent Out

10 After these things the Lord appointed seventy others also,ᵃ and sent them two by two before His face into every city and place where He Himself was about to go. ²Then He said to them, "The harvest truly *is* great, but the laborers *are* few; therefore pray the Lord of the harvest to send out laborers into His harvest. ³Go your way; behold, I send you out as lambs among wolves. ⁴Carry neither money bag, knapsack, nor sandals; and greet no one along the road. ⁵But whatever house you enter, first say, 'Peace to this house.' ⁶And if a son of peace is there, your peace will rest on it; if not, it will return to you. ⁷And remain in the same house, eating and drinking such things as they give, for the laborer is worthy of his wages. Do not go from house to house. ⁸Whatever city you enter, and they receive you, eat such things as are set before you. ⁹And heal the sick there, and say to them, 'The kingdom of God has come near to you.' ¹⁰But whatever city you enter, and they do not receive you, go out into its streets and say, ¹¹'The very dust of your city which clings to usᵃ we wipe off against you. Nevertheless know this, that the kingdom of God has come near you.' ¹²Butᵃ I say to you that it will be more tolerable in that Day for Sodom than for that city.

Woe to the Impenitent Cities

¹³"Woe to you, Chorazin! Woe to you, Bethsaida! For if the mighty works which were done in you had been done in Tyre and Sidon, they would have repented long ago, sitting in sackcloth and ashes. ¹⁴But it will be more tolerable for Tyre and Sidon at the judgment than for you. ¹⁵And you, Capernaum, who are exalted to heaven, will be brought down to Hades.ᵃ ¹⁶He who hears you hears Me, he who rejects you rejects Me, and he who rejects Me rejects Him who sent Me."

The Seventy Return with Joy

¹⁷Then the seventyᵃ returned with joy, saying, "Lord, even the demons are subject to us in Your name."

¹⁸And He said to them, "I saw Satan fall like lightning from heaven. ¹⁹Behold, I give you the authority to trample on serpents and scorpions,

---

The Law of Empowerment: Jesus Empowered His Team to Work

(Luke 10:1–24)

Jesus gave away His power to a team of 70 leaders and sent them out. Although they felt apprehensive about this first ministry tour, Jesus gave them everything they needed to succeed. Note how He equipped these leaders:

1. He appointed them and sent them out (v. 1).
2. He gave them a meaningful task to prepare cities for His arrival (v. 1).
3. He told them why their mission was so important (v. 2).
4. He calmed their fears with a long preparation speech (vv. 2–16).
5. He cautioned them about possible hardship (v. 3).
6. He issued explicit instructions about potential scenarios (vv. 4–11).
7. He imparted His convictions about their work (vv. 12–15).
8. He rejoiced with them as they returned (vv. 17, 18).
9. He evaluated and debriefed them on their experience (vv. 19, 20).
10. He prayed with them and affirmed their gifts and their future (vv. 21–24).

---

and over all the power of the enemy, and nothing shall by any means hurt you. ²⁰Nevertheless do not rejoice in this, that the spirits are subject to you, but ratherᵃ rejoice because your names are written in heaven."

Jesus Rejoices in the Spirit

²¹In that hour Jesus rejoiced in the Spirit and said, "I thank You, Father, Lord of heaven and

---

10:1 ᵃNU-Text reads *seventy-two others.*
10:11 ᵃNU-Text reads *our feet.* 10:12 ᵃNU-Text and M-Text omit *But.* 10:15 ᵃNU-Text reads *will you be exalted to heaven? You will be thrust down to Hades!* 10:17 ᵃNU-Text reads *seventy-two.*
10:20 ᵃNU-Text and M-Text omit *rather.*

Evaluation and Debriefing: Jesus Helps His Team Interpret Results

(Luke 10:17–20)

When the 70 workers returned from their ministry trip, they reported to Jesus what had happened to them. They felt elated at the power that flowed through them and with the fruit they bore (Luke 10:17).

Jesus helped them to reflect on the results. He rejoiced with them and affirmed their authority over the enemy. He didn't stop there, however. He reminded them of the big picture and about what is really worth celebrating (10:20).

Practice doesn't make perfect; practice *with evaluation* makes perfect. In this passage, we see a master Mentor who evaluated what happened, guided the learning of His learners, and helped them assess the takeaway value of their experience.

earth, that You have hidden these things from *the* wise and prudent and revealed them to babes. Even so, Father, for so it seemed good in Your sight. [22]All[a] things have been delivered to Me by My Father, and no one knows who the Son is except the Father, and who the Father is except the Son, and *the one* to whom the Son wills to reveal *Him*."

[23]Then He turned to *His* disciples and said privately, "Blessed *are* the eyes which see the things you see; [24]for I tell you that many prophets and kings have desired to see what you see, and have not seen *it,* and to hear what you hear, and have not heard *it.*"

The Parable of the Good Samaritan

[25]And behold, a certain lawyer stood up and tested Him, saying, "Teacher, what shall I do to inherit eternal life?"

[26]He said to him, "What is written in the law? What is your reading *of it?*"

[27]So he answered and said, " '*You shall love the* LORD *your God with all your heart, with all your soul, with all your strength, and with all your mind,*'[a] and '*your neighbor as yourself.*'"[b]

[28]And He said to him, "You have answered rightly; do this and you will live."

[29]But he, wanting to justify himself, said to Jesus, "And who is my neighbor?"

[30]Then Jesus answered and said: "A certain *man* went down from Jerusalem to Jericho, and fell among thieves, who stripped him of his clothing, wounded *him,* and departed, leaving *him* half dead. [31]Now by chance a certain priest came down that road. And when he saw him, he passed by on the other side. [32]Likewise a Levite, when he arrived at the place, came and looked, and passed by on the other side. [33]But a certain Samaritan, as he journeyed, came where he was. And when he saw him, he had compassion. [34]So he went to *him* and bandaged his wounds, pouring on oil and wine; and he set him on his own animal, brought him to an inn, and took care of him. [35]On the next day, when he departed,[a] he took out two denarii, gave *them* to the innkeeper, and said to him, 'Take care of him; and whatever more you spend, when I come again, I will repay you.' [36]So which of these three do you think was neighbor to him who fell among the thieves?"

[37]And he said, "He who showed mercy on him."

Then Jesus said to him, "Go and do likewise."

Mary and Martha Worship and Serve

[38]Now it happened as they went that He entered a certain village; and a certain woman named Martha welcomed Him into her house. [39]And she had a sister called Mary, who also sat at

---

10:22 [a]M-Text reads *And turning to the disciples He said, "All.... * **10:27** [a]Deuteronomy 6:5 [b]Leviticus 19:18 **10:35** [a]NU-Text omits *when he departed.*

The Law of Priorities: Jesus Clarifies Priority One for Martha

(Luke 10:38–42)

When Martha became preoccupied with impressing her guests, Jesus clarified for her the most important activity. Jesus revealed to her that only "one thing is needed" (Luke 10:42). All through His ministry, Jesus helped people get clarity on the important things. It's the job of the leader.

Jesus'ᵃ feet and heard His word. ⁴⁰But Martha was distracted with much serving, and she approached Him and said, "Lord, do You not care that my sister has left me to serve alone? Therefore tell her to help me."

⁴¹And Jesusᵃ answered and said to her, "Martha, Martha, you are worried and troubled about many things. ⁴²But one thing is needed, and Mary has chosen that good part, which will not be taken away from her."

The Model Prayer

11 Now it came to pass, as He was praying in a certain place, when He ceased, *that* one of His disciples said to Him, "Lord, teach us to pray, as John also taught his disciples."

²So He said to them, "When you pray, say:

Jesus Teaches Paternal Leadership and the Priority of Prayer

(Luke 11:1–13)

Jesus answered His disciples' request for instruction on prayer by giving them a model we call "the Lord's Prayer." In it, Jesus refers to God as "Father." On the heels of that prayer, He teaches about paternal leadership (Luke 11:5–13).

The wonderful father image suggests the strength and respect of a leader as well as the love and concern of a leader. Consider the ingredients of a healthy paternal leader in the home:

1. *His pattern for the family*
   He is to set an example for everyone else, to be a model.
2. *His provision for the family*
   He is to provide for others, insuring they have the resources they need.
3. *His protection for the family*
   He is to keep them from harm's way and make sure they are safe and secure.
4. *His prayer for the family*
   He is to pray for them to reach their potential and become all God intends them to be.

Our Father in heaven,ᵃ
Hallowed be Your name.
Your kingdom come.ᵇ
Your will be done
On earth as *it is* in heaven.
³ Give us day by day our daily bread.
⁴ And forgive us our sins,
For we also forgive everyone who is indebted to us.
And do not lead us into temptation,
But deliver us from the evil one." ᵃ

A Friend Comes at Midnight

⁵And He said to them, "Which of you shall have a friend, and go to him at midnight and say to him, 'Friend, lend me three loaves; ⁶for a friend of mine has come to me on his journey, and I have nothing to set before him'; ⁷and he will answer from within and say, 'Do not trouble me; the door is now shut, and my children are with me in bed; I cannot rise and give to you'? ⁸I say to you, though he will not rise and give to him because he is his friend, yet because of his persistence he will rise and give him as many as he needs.

Keep Asking, Seeking, Knocking

⁹"So I say to you, ask, and it will be given to you; seek, and you will find; knock, and it will be opened to you. ¹⁰For everyone who asks receives, and he who seeks finds, and to him who knocks it will be opened. ¹¹If a son asks for breadᵃ from any father among you, will he give him a stone? Or if *he asks* for a fish, will he give him a serpent instead of a fish? ¹²Or if he asks for an egg, will he offer him a scorpion? ¹³If you then, being evil, know how to give good gifts to your children, how much more will *your* heavenly Father give the Holy Spirit to those who ask Him!"

A House Divided Cannot Stand

¹⁴And He was casting out a demon, and it was mute. So it was, when the demon had gone out, that the mute spoke; and the multitudes marveled. ¹⁵But some of them said, "He casts out demons by Beelzebub,ᵃ the ruler of the demons." ¹⁶Others, testing *Him,* sought from Him a sign from heaven. ¹⁷But He, knowing their thoughts,

---

10:39 ᵃNU-Text reads *the Lord's.* **10:41** ᵃNU-Text reads *the Lord.* **11:2** ᵃNU-Text omits *Our* and *in heaven.* ᵇNU-Text omits the rest of this verse. **11:4** ᵃNU-Text omits *But deliver us from the evil one.* **11:11** ᵃNU-Text omits the words from *bread* through *for* in the next sentence. **11:15** ᵃNU-Text and M-Text read *Beelzebul.*

said to them: "Every kingdom divided against itself is brought to desolation, and a house *divided* against a house falls. ¹⁸If Satan also is divided against himself, how will his kingdom stand? Because you say I cast out demons by Beelzebub. ¹⁹And if I cast out demons by Beelzebub, by whom do your sons cast *them* out? Therefore they will be your judges. ²⁰But if I cast out demons with the finger of God, surely the kingdom of God has come upon you. ²¹When a strong man, fully armed, guards his own palace, his goods are in peace. ²²But when a stronger than he comes upon him and overcomes him, he takes from him all his armor in which he trusted, and divides his spoils. ²³He who is not with Me is against Me, and he who does not gather with Me scatters.

An Unclean Spirit Returns

²⁴"When an unclean spirit goes out of a man, he goes through dry places, seeking rest; and finding none, he says, 'I will return to my house from which I came.' ²⁵And when he comes, he finds *it* swept and put in order. ²⁶Then he goes and takes with *him* seven other spirits more wicked than himself, and they enter and dwell there; and the last *state* of that man is worse than the first."

Keeping the Word

²⁷And it happened, as He spoke these things, that a certain woman from the crowd raised her voice and said to Him, "Blessed *is* the womb that bore You, and *the* breasts which nursed You!"

²⁸But He said, "More than that, blessed *are* those who hear the word of God and keep it!"

Seeking a Sign

²⁹And while the crowds were thickly gathered together, He began to say, "This is an evil generation. It seeks a sign, and no sign will be given to it except the sign of Jonah the prophet.ᵃ ³⁰For as Jonah became a sign to the Ninevites, so also the Son of Man will be to this generation. ³¹The queen of the South will rise up in the judgment with the men of this generation and condemn them, for she came from the ends of the earth to hear the wisdom of Solomon; and indeed a greater than Solomon *is* here. ³²The men of Nineveh will rise up in the judgment with this generation and condemn it, for they repented at the preaching of Jonah; and indeed a greater than Jonah *is* here.

The Lamp of the Body

³³"No one, when he has lit a lamp, puts *it* in a secret place or under a basket, but on a lampstand, that those who come in may see the light. ³⁴The lamp of the body is the eye. Therefore, when your eye is good, your whole body also is full of light. But when *your eye* is bad, your body also *is* full of darkness. ³⁵Therefore take heed that the light which is in you is not darkness. ³⁶If then your whole body *is* full of light, having no part dark, *the* whole *body* will be full of light, as when the bright shining of a lamp gives you light."

Woe to the Pharisees and Lawyers

³⁷And as He spoke, a certain Pharisee asked Him to dine with him. So He went in and sat down to eat. ³⁸When the Pharisee saw *it,* he marveled that He had not first washed before dinner. ³⁹Then the Lord said to him, "Now you Pharisees make the outside of the cup and dish clean, but your inward part is full of greed and wickedness. ⁴⁰Foolish ones! Did not He who made the outside make the inside also? ⁴¹But rather give alms of such things as you have; then indeed all things are clean to you.

⁴²"But woe to you Pharisees! For you tithe mint and rue and all manner of herbs, and pass by justice and the love of God. These you ought to have done, without leaving the others undone. ⁴³Woe to you Pharisees! For you love the best seats in the synagogues and greetings in the marketplaces. ⁴⁴Woe to you, scribes and Pharisees, hypocrites!ᵃ For you are like graves which are not seen, and the men who walk over *them* are not aware *of them.*"

⁴⁵Then one of the lawyers answered and said to Him, "Teacher, by saying these things You reproach us also."

⁴⁶And He said, "Woe to you also, lawyers! For you load men with burdens hard to bear, and you yourselves do not touch the burdens with one of your fingers. ⁴⁷Woe to you! For you build the tombs of the prophets, and your fathers killed them. ⁴⁸In fact, you bear witness that you approve the deeds of your fathers; for they indeed killed them, and you build their tombs. ⁴⁹Therefore the wisdom of God also said, 'I will send them prophets and apostles, and *some* of them they will kill and persecute,' ⁵⁰that the blood of all the prophets which was shed from the foundation of the world may be required of this generation, ⁵¹from the blood of Abel to the blood of Zechariah who perished between the altar and the temple. Yes, I say to you, it shall be required of this generation.

⁵²"Woe to you lawyers! For you have taken away the key of knowledge. You did not enter in

---

11:29 ᵃNU-Text omits *the prophet.*
11:44 ᵃNU-Text omits *scribes and Pharisees, hypocrites.*

yourselves, and those who were entering in you hindered."

⁵³And as He said these things to them,ᵃ the scribes and the Pharisees began to assail *Him* vehemently, and to cross-examine Him about many things, ⁵⁴lying in wait for Him, and seeking to catch Him in something He might say, that they might accuse Him.ᵃ

Beware of Hypocrisy

12 In the meantime, when an innumerable multitude of people had gathered together, so that they trampled one another, He began to say to His disciples first *of all*, "Beware of the leaven of the Pharisees, which is hypocrisy. ²For there is nothing covered that will not be revealed, nor hidden that will not be known. ³Therefore whatever you have spoken in the dark will be heard in the light, and what you have spoken in the ear in inner rooms will be proclaimed on the housetops.

Jesus Teaches the Fear of God

⁴"And I say to you, My friends, do not be afraid of those who kill the body, and after that have no more that they can do. ⁵But I will show you whom you should fear: Fear Him who, after He has killed, has power to cast into hell; yes, I say to you, fear Him! ⁶"Are not five sparrows sold for two copper coins?ᵃ And not one of them is forgotten before God. ⁷But the very hairs of your head are all numbered. Do not fear therefore; you are of more value than many sparrows.

Confess Christ Before Men

⁸"Also I say to you, whoever confesses Me before men, him the Son of Man also will confess before the angels of God. ⁹But he who denies Me before men will be denied before the angels of God.

¹⁰"And anyone who speaks a word against the Son of Man, it will be forgiven him; but to him who blasphemes against the Holy Spirit, it will not be forgiven.

¹¹"Now when they bring you to the synagogues and magistrates and authorities, do not worry about how or what you should answer, or what you should say. ¹²For the Holy Spirit will teach you in that very hour what you ought to say."

The Parable of the Rich Fool

¹³Then one from the crowd said to Him, "Teacher, tell my brother to divide the inheritance with me."

¹⁴But He said to him, "Man, who made Me a judge or an arbitrator over you?" ¹⁵And He said to them, "Take heed and beware of covetousness,ᵃ for one's life does not consist in the abundance of the things he possesses."

¹⁶Then He spoke a parable to them, saying: "The ground of a certain rich man yielded plentifully. ¹⁷And he thought within himself, saying, 'What shall I do, since I have no room to store my crops?' ¹⁸So he said, 'I will do this: I will pull down my barns and build greater, and there I will store all my crops and my goods. ¹⁹And I will say to my soul, "Soul, you have many goods laid

---

11:53 ᵃNU-Text reads *And when He left there.* **11:54** ᵃNU-Text omits *and seeking* and *that they might accuse Him.* **12:6** ᵃGreek *assarion,* a coin of very small value **12:15** ᵃNU-Text reads *all covetousness.*

The Law of Navigation: Jesus Charts the Course for His Disciples

(Luke 12:1–59)

Jesus provided good instruction for His disciples on issues such as integrity, anxiety, convictions, problem solving, greed, jealousy, priorities, and trusting God. Why these topics? Because Jesus intended to navigate life for His followers, to teach them how to live successfully.

If we were to condense the Lord's perspective on success in life, we might say that success involves:

- *Decisions:* We must know the truth and accept it.
- *Servanthood:* We must find a need and fill it.
- *Determination:* We must face a challenge and meet it.
- *Sacrifice:* We must lose our life to find it.
- *Preparation:* We must develop a plan and follow it.
- *Action:* We must discover God's will and obey it.
- *A gift:* We must find our talent and share it.
- *Durability:* We must be tenacious and finish well.

up for many years; take your ease; eat, drink, *and* be merry."' [20]But God said to him, 'Fool! This night your soul will be required of you; then whose will those things be which you have provided?'

[21]"So *is* he who lays up treasure for himself, and is not rich toward God."

Do Not Worry

[22]Then He said to His disciples, "Therefore I say to you, do not worry about your life, what you will eat; nor about the body, what you will put on. [23]Life is more than food, and the body *is more* than clothing. [24]Consider the ravens, for they neither sow nor reap, which have neither storehouse nor barn; and God feeds them. Of how much more value are you than the birds? [25]And which of you by worrying can add one cubit to his stature? [26]If you then are not able to do *the* least, why are you anxious for the rest? [27]Consider the lilies, how they grow: they neither toil nor spin; and yet I say to you, even Solomon in all his glory was not arrayed like one of these. [28]If then God so clothes the grass, which today is in the field and tomorrow is thrown into the oven, how much more *will He clothe* you, O *you* of little faith?

[29]"And do not seek what you should eat or what you should drink, nor have an anxious mind. [30]For all these things the nations of the world seek after, and your Father knows that you need these things. [31]But seek the kingdom of God, and all these things[a] shall be added to you.

[32]"Do not fear, little flock, for it is your Father's good pleasure to give you the kingdom. [33]Sell what you have and give alms; provide yourselves money bags which do not grow old, a treasure in the heavens that does not fail, where no thief approaches nor moth destroys. [34]For where your treasure is, there your heart will be also.

The Faithful Servant and the Evil Servant

[35]"Let your waist be girded and *your* lamps burning; [36]and you yourselves be like men who wait for their master, when he will return from the wedding, that when he comes and knocks they may open to him immediately. [37]Blessed *are* those servants whom the master, when he comes, will find watching. Assuredly, I say to you that he will gird himself and have them sit down *to eat,* and will come and serve them. [38]And if he should come in the second watch, or come in the third watch, and find *them* so, blessed are those servants. [39]But know this, that if the master of the house had known what hour the thief would come, he would have watched and[a] not allowed his house to be broken into. [40]Therefore you also be ready, for the Son of Man is coming at an hour you do not expect."

[41]Then Peter said to Him, "Lord, do You speak this parable *only* to us, or to all *people?*"

[42]And the Lord said, "Who then is that faithful and wise steward, whom *his* master will make ruler over his household, to give *them their* portion of food in due season? [43]Blessed *is* that servant whom his master will find so doing when he comes. [44]Truly, I say to you that he will make him ruler over all that he has. [45]But if that servant says in his heart, 'My master is delaying his coming,' and begins to beat the male and female servants, and to eat and drink and be drunk, [46]the master of that servant will come on a day when he is not looking for *him,* and at an hour when he is not aware, and will cut him in two and appoint *him* his portion with the unbelievers. [47]And that servant who knew his master's will, and did not prepare *himself* or do according to his will, shall be beaten with many *stripes.* [48]But he who did not know, yet committed things deserving of stripes, shall be beaten with few. For everyone to whom much is given, from him much will be required; and to whom much has been committed, of him they will ask the more.

12:31 [a]NU-Text reads *His kingdom, and these things.*
12:39 [a]NU-Text reads *he would not have allowed.*

The Law of Navigation: Jesus Helps Listeners Interpret the Times

(Luke 12:35–59)

Like all good leaders, Jesus left His followers with a plan for the future and gave them some key tools, including:

1. *Lenses:* He modeled the right attitude to approach the future.
2. *A road map:* He warned them about rough roads ahead.
3. *A barometer:* He helped them interpret future conditions.

Christ Brings Division

[49]"I came to send fire on the earth, and how I wish it were already kindled! [50]But I have a baptism to be baptized with, and how distressed I am till it is accomplished! [51]Do *you* suppose that I came to give peace on earth? I tell you, not at all, but rather division. [52]For from now on five in one house will be divided: three against two, and two against three. [53]Father will be divided against son and son against father, mother against daughter and daughter against mother, mother-in-law against her daughter-in-law and daughter-in-law against her mother-in-law."

Discern the Time

[54]Then He also said to the multitudes, "Whenever you see a cloud rising out of the west, immediately you say, 'A shower is coming'; and so it is. [55]And when *you see* the south wind blow, you say, 'There will be hot weather'; and there is. [56]Hypocrites! You can discern the face of the sky and of the earth, but how *is it* you do not discern this time?

Make Peace with Your Adversary

[57]"Yes, and why, even of yourselves, do you not judge what is right? [58]When you go with your adversary to the magistrate, make every effort along the way to settle with him, lest he drag you to the judge, the judge deliver you to the officer, and the officer throw you into prison. [59]I tell you, you shall not depart from there till you have paid the very last mite."

Repent or Perish

13 There were present at that season some who told Him about the Galileans whose blood Pilate had mingled with their sacrifices. [2]And Jesus answered and said to them, "Do you suppose that these Galileans were worse sinners than all *other* Galileans, because they suffered such things? [3]I tell you, no; but unless you repent you will all likewise perish. [4]Or those eighteen on whom the tower in Siloam fell and killed them, do you think that they were worse sinners than all *other* men who dwelt in Jerusalem? [5]I tell you, no; but unless you repent you will all likewise perish."

The Parable of the Barren Fig Tree

[6]He also spoke this parable: "A certain *man* had a fig tree planted in his vineyard, and he came seeking fruit on it and found none. [7]Then he said to the keeper of his vineyard, 'Look, for three years I have come seeking fruit on this fig tree and find none. Cut it down; why does it use up the ground?' [8]But he answered and said to him, 'Sir, let it alone this year also, until I dig around it and fertilize *it*. [9]And if it bears fruit, *well*. But if not, after that[a] you can cut it down.'"

A Spirit of Infirmity

[10]Now He was teaching in one of the synagogues on the Sabbath. [11]And behold, there was a woman who had a spirit of infirmity eighteen years, and was bent over and could in no way raise *herself* up. [12]But when Jesus saw her, He called *her* to *Him* and said to her, "Woman, you are loosed from your infirmity." [13]And He laid *His* hands on her, and immediately she was made straight, and glorified God.

[14]But the ruler of the synagogue answered with indignation, because Jesus had healed on the Sabbath; and he said to the crowd, "There are six days on which men ought to work; therefore come and be healed on them, and not on the Sabbath day."

[15]The Lord then answered him and said, "Hypocrite![a] Does not each one of you on the Sabbath loose his ox or donkey from the stall, and lead *it* away to water it? [16]So ought not this woman, being a daughter of Abraham, whom Satan has bound—think of it—for eighteen years, be loosed from this bond on the Sabbath?" [17]And when He said these things, all His adversaries were put to shame; and all the multitude rejoiced for all the glorious things that were done by Him.

The Parable of the Mustard Seed

[18]Then He said, "What is the kingdom of God like? And to what shall I compare it? [19]It is like a mustard seed, which a man took and put in his garden; and it grew and became a large[a] tree, and the birds of the air nested in its branches."

The Parable of the Leaven

[20]And again He said, "To what shall I liken the kingdom of God? [21]It is like leaven, which a woman took and hid in three measures[a] of meal till it was all leavened."

The Narrow Way

[22]And He went through the cities and villages, teaching, and journeying toward Jerusalem. [23]Then one said to Him, "Lord, are there few who are saved?"

13:9 [a]NU-Text reads *And if it bears fruit after that, well. But if not, you can cut it down.* **13:15** [a]NU-Text and M-Text read *Hypocrites.* **13:19** [a]NU-Text omits *large.* **13:21** [a]Greek *sata,* approximately two pecks in all

And He said to them, [24]"Strive to enter through the narrow gate, for many, I say to you, will seek to enter and will not be able. [25]When once the Master of the house has risen up and shut the door, and you begin to stand outside and knock at the door, saying, 'Lord, Lord, open for us,' and He will answer and say to you, 'I do not know you, where you are from,' [26]then you will begin to say, 'We ate and drank in Your presence, and You taught in our streets.' [27]But He will say, 'I tell you I do not know you, where you are from. Depart from Me, all you workers of iniquity.' [28]There will be weeping and gnashing of teeth, when you see Abraham and Isaac and Jacob and all the prophets in the kingdom of God, and yourselves thrust out. [29]They will come from the east and the west, from the north and the south, and sit down in the kingdom of God. [30]And indeed there are last who will be first, and there are first who will be last."

[31]On that very day[a] some Pharisees came, saying to Him, "Get out and depart from here, for Herod wants to kill You."

[32]And He said to them, "Go, tell that fox, 'Behold, I cast out demons and perform cures today and tomorrow, and the third *day* I shall be perfected.' [33]Nevertheless I must journey today, tomorrow, and the *day* following; for it cannot be that a prophet should perish outside of Jerusalem.

Jesus Laments over Jerusalem

[34]"O Jerusalem, Jerusalem, the one who kills the prophets and stones those who are sent to her! How often I wanted to gather your children together, as a hen *gathers* her brood under *her* wings, but you were not willing! [35]See! Your house is left to you desolate; and assuredly,[a] I say to you, you shall not see Me until *the time* comes when you say, '*Blessed is He who comes in the name of the* LORD!' "[b]

A Man with Dropsy Healed on the Sabbath

[14] Now it happened, as He went into the house of one of the rulers of the Pharisees to eat bread on the Sabbath, that they watched Him closely. [2]And behold, there was a certain man before Him who had dropsy. [3]And Jesus, answering, spoke to the lawyers and Pharisees, saying, "Is it lawful to heal on the Sabbath?"[a]

[4]But they kept silent. And He took *him* and healed him, and let him go. [5]Then He answered them, saying, "Which of you, having a donkey[a] or an ox that has fallen into a pit, will not immediately pull him out on the Sabbath day?"

[6]And they could not answer Him regarding these things.

Take the Lowly Place

[7]So He told a parable to those who were invited, when He noted how they chose the best places, saying to them: [8]"When you are invited by anyone to a wedding feast, do not sit down in the best place, lest one more honorable than you be invited by him; [9]and he who invited you and him come and say to you, 'Give place to this man,' and then you begin with shame to take the lowest place. [10]But when you are invited, go and sit down in the lowest place, so that when he who invited you comes he may say to you, 'Friend, go up higher.' Then you will have glory in the presence of those who sit at the table with you. [11]For whoever exalts himself will be humbled, and he who humbles himself will be exalted."

[12]Then He also said to him who invited Him, "When you give a dinner or a supper, do not ask your friends, your brothers, your relatives, nor rich neighbors, lest they also invite you back, and you be repaid. [13]But when you give a feast, invite *the* poor, *the* maimed, *the* lame, *the* blind. [14]And you will be blessed, because they cannot repay you; for you shall be repaid at the resurrection of the just."

The Parable of the Great Supper

[15]Now when one of those who sat at the table with Him heard these things, he said to Him, "Blessed *is* he who shall eat bread[a] in the kingdom of God!"

[16]Then He said to him, "A certain man gave a great supper and invited many, [17]and sent his servant at supper time to say to those who were invited, 'Come, for all things are now ready.' [18]But they all with one *accord* began to make excuses. The first said to him, 'I have bought a piece of ground, and I must go and see it. I ask you to have me excused.' [19]And another said, 'I have bought five yoke of oxen, and I am going to test them. I ask you to have me excused.' [20]Still another said, 'I have married a wife, and therefore I cannot come.' [21]So that servant came and reported these things to his master. Then the master of the house, being angry, said to his servant, 'Go out quickly into the streets and lanes of the city, and bring in here *the* poor and *the*

13:31 [a]NU-Text reads *In that very hour.*
13:35 [a]NU-Text and M-Text omit *assuredly.* [b]Psalm 118:26 **14:3** [a]NU-Text adds *or not.* **14:5** [a]NU-Text and M-Text read *son.* **14:15** [a]M-Text reads *dinner.*

maimed and *the* lame and *the* blind.' ²²And the servant said, 'Master, it is done as you commanded, and still there is room.' ²³Then the master said to the servant, 'Go out into the highways and hedges, and compel *them* to come in, that my house may be filled. ²⁴For I say to you that none of those men who were invited shall taste my supper.'"

Leaving All to Follow Christ

²⁵Now great multitudes went with Him. And He turned and said to them, ²⁶"If anyone comes to Me and does not hate his father and mother, wife and children, brothers and sisters, yes, and his own life also, he cannot be My disciple. ²⁷And whoever does not bear his cross and come after Me cannot be My disciple. ²⁸For which of you, intending to build a tower, does not sit down first and count the cost, whether he has *enough* to finish *it*— ²⁹lest, after he has laid the foundation, and is not able to finish, all who see *it* begin to mock him, ³⁰saying, 'This man began to build and was not able to finish.' ³¹Or what king, going to make war against another king, does not sit down first and consider whether he is able with ten thousand to meet him who comes against him with twenty thousand? ³²Or else, while the other is still a great way off, he sends a delegation and asks conditions of peace. ³³So likewise, whoever of you does not forsake all that he has cannot be My disciple.

Tasteless Salt Is Worthless

³⁴"Salt *is* good; but if the salt has lost its flavor, how shall it be seasoned? ³⁵It is neither fit for the land nor for the dunghill, *but* men throw it out. He who has ears to hear, let him hear!"

Commitment: The Best Leaders Vote with Their Lives
(Luke 14:26, 27)

Jesus gave Himself wholly to His cause and to His men. Consequently, He could ask them to do the same. When leaders vote with their lives, their followers gain all kinds of security. Jesus' call for commitment both screened the uncommitted and attracted the committed.

The Law of Navigation: Count the Cost, Then Determine the Direction
(Luke 14:28–32)

In two small but wonderful parables, Jesus speaks about planning and preparation. He teaches listeners to count the cost before taking action, applauds evaluation before taking action, and encourages damage prevention through preparation and negotiation. To calculate in this way is not a lack of faith, but foresight based on insight and hindsight.

The Parable of the Lost Sheep

15 Then all the tax collectors and the sinners drew near to Him to hear Him. ²And the Pharisees and scribes complained, saying, "This Man receives sinners and eats with them." ³So He spoke this parable to them, saying:

⁴"What man of you, having a hundred sheep, if he loses one of them, does not leave the ninety-nine in the wilderness, and go after the one which is lost until he finds it? ⁵And when he has found *it,* he lays *it* on his shoulders, rejoicing. ⁶And when he comes home, he calls together *his* friends and neighbors, saying to them, 'Rejoice with me, for I have found my sheep which was lost!' ⁷I say to you that likewise there will be more joy in heaven over one sinner who repents than over ninety-nine just persons who need no repentance.

The Parable of the Lost Coin

⁸"Or what woman, having ten silver coins,[a] if she loses one coin, does not light a lamp, sweep the house, and search carefully until she finds *it?* ⁹And when she has found *it,* she calls *her* friends and neighbors together, saying, 'Rejoice with me, for I have found the piece which I lost!' ¹⁰Likewise, I say to you, there is joy in the presence of the angels of God over one sinner who repents."

The Parable of the Lost Son

¹¹Then He said: "A certain man had two sons. ¹²And the younger of them said to *his* father,

---

15:8 ªGreek *drachma,* a valuable coin often worn in a ten-piece garland by married women

COMPETENCE

A Necessary Step on the Road to Excellence
(Luke 14:28–32)

Labeling someone competent or incompetent may seem judgmental and narrow, yet all leaders must possess a level of competence that enables them to get the job done. The kingdom of God cannot do without competence.

Everyone knows that leaders must demonstrate a level of competence in order to gain the trust and respect of followers. No one chooses to follow an incompetent leader over a competent one, regardless of personality. Friendship is not synonymous with leadership; people can like you as a friend but not follow you as a leader. To the degree they feel you are incompetent to lead, they will distance themselves from your leadership.

Competence goes beyond words. It's the leader's ability to *say* it, *plan* it, and *do* it in such a way that others know you know your business—and know that they want to follow you. Competence must be sought at every organizational level. Incompetence can be tolerated nowhere. John Gardner once wrote, "The society which scorns excellence in plumbing because plumbing is a humble activity and tolerates shoddiness in philosophy because it is an exalted activity will have neither good plumbing nor good philosophy. Neither its pipes nor its theories will hold water."

Jesus highlights the issue of competence in the two stories recounted in Luke 14. In both stories, what is missing is *competence*. The builder and the king in these stories lacked what it took to get the job done. Therefore the tower never got built and the war never was won. According to Jesus, competence requires three ingredients:

1. *Commitment*
   Jesus said our commitment to Him must look like disdain for everyone else. We must pick up our cross and follow Him.

2. *Resources*
   Jesus spoke about a builder calculating whether he had enough to finish a tower. Determine whether your resources, gifts, talents, and abilities are available to do the job.

3. *Intelligence*
   Jesus spoke about a king seeking counsel to know whether he should go to battle. Part of competence is the insight to know what to do, when to do it, and how to do it.

The combination of these three components spells not only competence, but excellence. It's what makes people follow a leader. So—in what area are you most competent? Where do you excel? What makes others follow you?

For a positive example of competence, see p. 257.

'Father, give me the portion of goods that falls *to me.*' So he divided to them *his* livelihood. [13]And not many days after, the younger son gathered all together, journeyed to a far country, and there wasted his possessions with prodigal living. [14]But when he had spent all, there arose a severe famine in that land, and he began to be in want. [15]Then he went and joined himself to a citizen of that country, and he sent him into his fields to feed swine. [16]And he would gladly have filled his stomach with the pods that the swine ate, and no one gave him *anything.*

[17]"But when he came to himself, he said, 'How many of my father's hired servants have bread enough and to spare, and I perish with hunger! [18]I will arise and go to my father, and will say to him, "Father, I have sinned against heaven and before you, [19]and I am no longer worthy to be called your son. Make me like one of your hired servants."'

[20]"And he arose and came to his father. But when he was still a great way off, his father saw him and had compassion, and ran and fell on his neck and kissed him. [21]And the son said to him, 'Father, I have sinned against heaven and in your sight, and am no longer worthy to be called your son.'

[22]"But the father said to his servants, 'Bring[a] out the best robe and put *it* on him, and put a ring on his hand and sandals on *his* feet. [23]And bring the fatted calf here and kill *it,* and let us eat and be merry; [24]for this my son was dead and is alive again; he was lost and is found.' And they began to be merry.

[25]"Now his older son was in the field. And as he came and drew near to the house, he heard music and dancing. [26]So he called one of the servants and asked what these things meant. [27]And he said to him, 'Your brother has come, and because he has received him safe and sound, your father has killed the fatted calf.'

[28]"But he was angry and would not go in. Therefore his father came out and pleaded with him. [29]So he answered and said to *his* father, 'Lo, these many years I have been serving you; I never transgressed your commandment at any time; and yet you never gave me a young goat, that I might make merry with my friends. [30]But as soon as this son of yours came, who has devoured your livelihood with harlots, you killed the fatted calf for him.'

[31]"And he said to him, 'Son, you are always with me, and all that I have is yours. [32]It was right that we should make merry and be glad, for your brother was dead and is alive again, and was lost and is found.'"

The Law of Priorities: Jesus Focused On the Lost

(Luke 15:1–32)

Luke 15 is often called the "lost chapter." In this passage, Jesus talks about the lost sheep, the lost coin, and the lost son. The sheep got lost naturally; the coin got lost accidentally; and the son got lost willfully. In every case, someone went out to look for what got lost (Luke 15:4, 8, 20).

Jesus attempted to underscore God's passion to seek and save the lost. He would not be diverted from this paramount activity. Jesus believed He needed to underscore this priority because the scribes and Pharisees grumbled about how much time He spent with tax collectors and sinners. Instead of retreating and appeasing the wishes of the religious leaders, He reminded everyone of priority one. Jesus communicated His top priorities using these tools:

1. *Narrative*
   He told memorable stories illustrating His priorities.
2. *Repetition*
   He repeated three accounts that all underscored the priority.
3. *Familiarity*
   He spoke about familiar people and situations.

The Parable of the Unjust Steward

16 He also said to His disciples: "There was a certain rich man who had a steward, and an accusation was brought to him that this man was wasting his goods. [2]So he called him and said to him, 'What is this I hear about you? Give an account of your stewardship, for you can no longer be steward.'

[3]"Then the steward said within himself, 'What shall I do? For my master is taking the stewardship away from me. I cannot dig; I am ashamed to beg. [4]I have resolved what to do, that when I am put out of the stewardship, they may receive me into their houses.'

15:22 [a]NU-Text reads *Quickly bring.*

⁵"So he called every one of his master's debtors to *him,* and said to the first, 'How much do you owe my master?' ⁶And he said, 'A hundred measures^a of oil.' So he said to him, 'Take your bill, and sit down quickly and write fifty.' ⁷Then he said to another, 'And how much do you owe?' So he said, 'A hundred measures^a of wheat.' And he said to him, 'Take your bill, and write eighty.' ⁸So the master commended the unjust steward because he had dealt shrewdly. For the sons of this world are more shrewd in their generation than the sons of light.

⁹"And I say to you, make friends for yourselves by unrighteous mammon, that when you fail,^a they may receive you into an everlasting home. ¹⁰He who *is* faithful in *what is* least is faithful also in much; and he who is unjust in *what is* least is unjust also in much. ¹¹Therefore if you have not been faithful in the unrighteous mammon, who will commit to your trust the true *riches?* ¹²And if you have not been faithful in what is another man's, who will give you what is your own?

¹³"No servant can serve two masters; for either he will hate the one and love the other, or else he will be loyal to the one and despise the other. You cannot serve God and mammon."

The Law, the Prophets, and the Kingdom

¹⁴Now the Pharisees, who were lovers of money, also heard all these things, and they derided Him. ¹⁵And He said to them, "You are those who justify yourselves before men, but God knows your hearts. For what is highly esteemed among men is an abomination in the sight of God.

¹⁶"The law and the prophets *were* until John. Since that time the kingdom of God has been preached, and everyone is pressing into it. ¹⁷And it is easier for heaven and earth to pass away than for one tittle of the law to fail.

¹⁸"Whoever divorces his wife and marries another commits adultery; and whoever marries her who is divorced from *her* husband commits adultery.

The Rich Man and Lazarus

¹⁹"There was a certain rich man who was clothed in purple and fine linen and fared

16:6 ^aGreek *batos,* eight or nine gallons each (Old Testament *bath*) **16:7** ^aGreek *koros,* ten or twelve bushels each (Old Testament *kor*) **16:9** ^aNU-Text reads *it fails.*

Lessons from a Lousy Leader

(Luke 16:1–13)

Jesus' story of an unrighteous manager teaches us lessons about shrewd business and a few subtle truths about leadership. This lousy leader . . .

1. *Violated rule number one: Leadership is not to be used for personal benefit* (v. 1).
   He forgot that leadership is about giving, not getting. Leaders lose the right to be selfish.
2. *Learned that a leader cannot hide his heart* (vv. 1, 2).
   Leadership rises or falls to the level of the leader's integrity. Leaders are vulnerable.
3. *Was proactive in facing problems* (v. 3).
   He surmised how he could address the problem. Good leaders aren't afraid to face reality.
4. *Understood the value of relationships* (v. 4).
   He utilized the relationships he had developed already. He received a return on his investment.
5. *Understood the nature of his influence* (vv. 4, 5).
   Since leadership is influence, leaders know with whom they have influence—and they go there.
6. *Learned the keys to motivating others* (vv. 5–7).
   Everyone is motivated in different ways. He found ways to make friends and get results.
7. *Reminds us of the value of godly leadership* (vv. 8–10).
   In the end, his master praised his shrewdness; but Jesus has a deeper lesson for us.

sumptuously every day. [20]But there was a certain beggar named Lazarus, full of sores, who was laid at his gate, [21]desiring to be fed with the crumbs which fell[a] from the rich man's table. Moreover the dogs came and licked his sores. [22]So it was that the beggar died, and was carried by the angels to Abraham's bosom. The rich man also died and was buried. [23]And being in torments in Hades, he lifted up his eyes and saw Abraham afar off, and Lazarus in his bosom.

[24]"Then he cried and said, 'Father Abraham, have mercy on me, and send Lazarus that he may dip the tip of his finger in water and cool my tongue; for I am tormented in this flame.' [25]But Abraham said, 'Son, remember that in your lifetime you received your good things, and likewise Lazarus evil things; but now he is comforted and you are tormented. [26]And besides all this, between us and you there is a great gulf fixed, so that those who want to pass from here to you cannot, nor can those from there pass to us.'

[27]"Then he said, 'I beg you therefore, father, that you would send him to my father's house, [28]for I have five brothers, that he may testify to them, lest they also come to this place of torment.' [29]Abraham said to him, 'They have Moses and the prophets; let them hear them.' [30]And he said, 'No, father Abraham; but if one goes to them from the dead, they will repent.' [31]But he said to him, 'If they do not hear Moses and the prophets, neither will they be persuaded though one rise from the dead.'"

Jesus Warns of Offenses

17 Then He said to the disciples, "It is impossible that no offenses should come, but woe to him through whom they do come! [2]It would be better for him if a millstone were hung around his neck, and he were thrown into the sea, than that he should offend one of these little ones. [3]Take heed to yourselves. If your brother sins against you,[a] rebuke him; and if he repents, forgive him. [4]And if he sins against you seven times in a day, and seven times in a day returns to you,[a] saying, 'I repent,' you shall forgive him."

Faith and Duty

[5]And the apostles said to the Lord, "Increase our faith."

[6]So the Lord said, "If you have faith as a mustard seed, you can say to this mulberry tree, 'Be pulled up by the roots and be planted in the sea,' and it would obey you. [7]And which of you, having a servant plowing or tending sheep, will say to him when he has come in from the field,

'Come at once and sit down to eat'? [8]But will he not rather say to him, 'Prepare something for my supper, and gird yourself and serve me till I have eaten and drunk, and afterward you will eat and drink'? [9]Does he thank that servant because he did the things that were commanded him? I think not.[a] [10]So likewise you, when you have done all those things which you are commanded, say, 'We are unprofitable servants. We have done what was our duty to do.'"

Ten Lepers Cleansed

[11]Now it happened as He went to Jerusalem that He passed through the midst of Samaria and Galilee. [12]Then as He entered a certain village, there met Him ten men who were lepers, who stood afar off. [13]And they lifted up their voices and said, "Jesus, Master, have mercy on us!"

[14]So when He saw them, He said to them, "Go, show yourselves to the priests." And so it was that as they went, they were cleansed.

[15]And one of them, when he saw that he was healed, returned, and with a loud voice glorified God, [16]and fell down on his face at His feet, giving Him thanks. And he was a Samaritan.

[17]So Jesus answered and said, "Were there not ten cleansed? But where are the nine? [18]Were there not any found who returned to give glory to God except this foreigner?" [19]And He said to him, "Arise, go your way. Your faith has made you well."

The Coming of the Kingdom

[20]Now when He was asked by the Pharisees when the kingdom of God would come, He answered them and said, "The kingdom of God does not come with observation; [21]nor will they say, 'See here!' or 'See there!'[a] For indeed, the kingdom of God is within you."

[22]Then He said to the disciples, "The days will come when you will desire to see one of the days of the Son of Man, and you will not see it. [23]And they will say to you, 'Look here!' or 'Look there!'[a] Do not go after them or follow them. [24]For as the lightning that flashes out of one part under heaven shines to the other part under heaven, so also the Son of Man will be in His day. [25]But first He must suffer many things and be rejected by this generation. [26]And as it was in the days of Noah, so it will be also in the days of the

---

16:21 [a]NU-Text reads with what fell.   **17:3** [a]NU-Text omits against you.   **17:4** [a]M-Text omits to you.   **17:9** [a]NU-Text ends verse with commanded; M-Text omits him.   **17:21** [a]NU-Text reverses here and there.   **17:23** [a]NU-Text reverses here and there.

Son of Man: [27]They ate, they drank, they married wives, they were given in marriage, until the day that Noah entered the ark, and the flood came and destroyed them all. [28]Likewise as it was also in the days of Lot: They ate, they drank, they bought, they sold, they planted, they built; [29]but on the day that Lot went out of Sodom it rained fire and brimstone from heaven and destroyed *them* all. [30]Even so will it be in the day when the Son of Man is revealed.

[31]"In that day, he who is on the housetop, and his goods *are* in the house, let him not come down to take them away. And likewise the one who is in the field, let him not turn back. [32]Remember Lot's wife. [33]Whoever seeks to save his life will lose it, and whoever loses his life will preserve it. [34]I tell you, in that night there will be two *men* in one bed: the one will be taken and the other will be left. [35]Two *women* will be grinding together: the one will be taken and the other left. [36]Two *men* will be in the field: the one will be taken and the other left."[a]

[37]And they answered and said to Him, "Where, Lord?"

So He said to them, "Wherever the body is, there the eagles will be gathered together."

The Parable of the Persistent Widow

18 Then He spoke a parable to them, that men always ought to pray and not lose heart, [2]saying: "There was in a certain city a judge who did not fear God nor regard man. [3]Now there was a widow in that city; and she came to him, saying, 'Get justice for me from my adversary.' [4]And he would not for a while; but afterward he said within himself, 'Though I do not fear God nor regard man, [5]yet because this widow troubles me I will avenge her, lest by her continual coming she weary me.'"

[6]Then the Lord said, "Hear what the unjust judge said. [7]And shall God not avenge His own elect who cry out day and night to Him, though He bears long with them? [8]I tell you that He will avenge them speedily. Nevertheless, when the Son of Man comes, will He really find faith on the earth?"

The Parable of the Pharisee and the Tax Collector

[9]Also He spoke this parable to some who trusted in themselves that they were righteous, and despised others: [10]"Two men went up to the temple to pray, one a Pharisee and the other a tax collector. [11]The Pharisee stood and prayed thus with himself, 'God, I thank You that I am not like other men—extortioners, unjust, adulterers, or even as this tax collector. [12]I fast twice a week; I give tithes of all that I possess.' [13]And the tax collector, standing afar off, would not so much as raise *his* eyes to heaven, but beat his breast, saying, 'God, be merciful to me a sinner!' [14]I tell you, this man went down to his house justified *rather* than the other; for everyone who exalts himself will be humbled, and he who humbles himself will be exalted."

Jesus Blesses Little Children

[15]Then they also brought infants to Him that He might touch them; but when the disciples saw *it,* they rebuked them. [16]But Jesus called them to *Him* and said, "Let the little children come to Me, and do not forbid them; for of such is the kingdom of God. [17]Assuredly, I say to you, whoever does not receive the kingdom of God as a little child will by no means enter it."

Jesus Counsels the Rich Young Ruler

[18]Now a certain ruler asked Him, saying, "Good Teacher, what shall I do to inherit eternal life?"

[19]So Jesus said to him, "Why do you call Me good? No one *is* good but One, *that is,* God. [20]You know the commandments: 'Do not commit adultery,' 'Do not murder,' 'Do not steal,' 'Do not bear false witness,' 'Honor your father and your mother.'"[a]

[21]And he said, "All these things I have kept from my youth."

[22]So when Jesus heard these things, He said to him, "You still lack one thing. Sell all that you have and distribute to the poor, and you will have treasure in heaven; and come, follow Me."

[23]But when he heard this, he became very sorrowful, for he was very rich.

With God All Things Are Possible

[24]And when Jesus saw that he became very sorrowful, He said, "How hard it is for those who have riches to enter the kingdom of God! [25]For it is easier for a camel to go through the eye of a needle than for a rich man to enter the kingdom of God."

[26]And those who heard it said, "Who then can be saved?"

[27]But He said, "The things which are impossible with men are possible with God."

[28]Then Peter said, "See, we have left all[a] and followed You."

17:36 [a]NU-Text and M-Text omit verse 36.
18:20 [a]Exodus 20:12–16; Deuteronomy 5:16–20
18:28 [a]NU-Text reads *our own.*

Commitment: The Rich Young Ruler Fails the Test

(Luke 18:18–23)

When a rich young man approached Jesus to ask about eternal life, the Lord gave him a radical imperative: Sell all you possess and give it to the poor, then come and follow Me.

Jesus didn't say this to everyone. In fact, He said it only to His disciples. He knew this man needed the challenge, even though he refused to accept it. Only greed held him back from freedom. Even though he claimed to obey all the commands, he miserably failed at the first one: "You shall have no other gods before Me" (Ex. 20:3).

Jesus went straight to the central issue, preventing him from making a commitment he desperately needed to make. The man walked away, full of sadness. He clung to what he had instead of committing to what he could obtain.

²⁹So He said to them, "Assuredly, I say to you, there is no one who has left house or parents or brothers or wife or children, for the sake of the kingdom of God, ³⁰who shall not receive many times more in this present time, and in the age to come eternal life."

Jesus a Third Time Predicts His Death and Resurrection

³¹Then He took the twelve aside and said to them, "Behold, we are going up to Jerusalem, and all things that are written by the prophets concerning the Son of Man will be accomplished. ³²For He will be delivered to the Gentiles and will be mocked and insulted and spit upon. ³³They will scourge *Him* and kill Him. And the third day He will rise again."

³⁴But they understood none of these things; this saying was hidden from them, and they did not know the things which were spoken.

A Blind Man Receives His Sight

³⁵Then it happened, as He was coming near Jericho, that a certain blind man sat by the road begging. ³⁶And hearing a multitude passing by, he asked what it meant. ³⁷So they told him that Jesus of Nazareth was passing by. ³⁸And he cried out, saying, "Jesus, Son of David, have mercy on me!"

³⁹Then those who went before warned him that he should be quiet; but he cried out all the more, "Son of David, have mercy on me!"

⁴⁰So Jesus stood still and commanded him to be brought to Him. And when he had come near, He asked him, ⁴¹saying, "What do you want Me to do for you?"

He said, "Lord, that I may receive my sight."

⁴²Then Jesus said to him, "Receive your sight; your faith has made you well." ⁴³And immediately he received his sight, and followed Him, glorifying God. And all the people, when they saw *it,* gave praise to God.

Jesus Comes to Zacchaeus' House

19 Then *Jesus* entered and passed through Jericho. ²Now behold, *there was* a man named Zacchaeus who was a chief tax collector, and he was rich. ³And he sought to see who Jesus was, but could not because of the crowd, for he was of short stature. ⁴So he ran ahead and climbed up into a sycamore tree to see Him, for He was going to pass that *way.* ⁵And when Jesus came to the place, He looked up and saw him,ᵃ and said to him, "Zacchaeus, make haste and come down, for today I must stay at your house." ⁶So he made haste and came down, and received Him joyfully. ⁷But when they saw *it,* they all complained, saying, "He has gone to be a guest with a man who is a sinner."

⁸Then Zacchaeus stood and said to the Lord, "Look, Lord, I give half of my goods to the poor; and if I have taken anything from anyone by false accusation, I restore fourfold."

19:5 ᵃNU-Text omits *and saw him.*

The Law of Influence: Jesus Knew Influence Had a Ripple Effect

(Luke 19:1–27)

During his time with Jesus, Zacchaeus pledged to give half of his possessions to the poor and to repay those he had defrauded *four times* what he had taken. Immediately afterwards, Jesus declared that good stewards will be rewarded. God rewards good stewardship, multiplying the influence of godly leaders.

[9]And Jesus said to him, "Today salvation has come to this house, because he also is a son of Abraham; [10]for the Son of Man has come to seek and to save that which was lost."

The Parable of the Minas

[11]Now as they heard these things, He spoke another parable, because He was near Jerusalem and because they thought the kingdom of God would appear immediately. [12]Therefore He said: "A certain nobleman went into a far country to receive for himself a kingdom and to return. [13]So he called ten of his servants, delivered to them ten minas,[a] and said to them, 'Do business till I come.' [14]But his citizens hated him, and sent a delegation after him, saying, 'We will not have this *man* to reign over us.'

[15]"And so it was that when he returned, having received the kingdom, he then commanded these servants, to whom he had given the money, to be called to him, that he might know how much every man had gained by trading. [16]Then came the first, saying, 'Master, your mina has earned ten minas.' [17]And he said to him, 'Well *done,* good servant; because you were faithful in a very little, have authority over ten cities.' [18]And the second came, saying, 'Master, your mina has earned five minas.' [19]Likewise he said to him, 'You also be over five cities.'

[20]"Then another came, saying, 'Master, here is your mina, which I have kept put away in a handkerchief. [21]For I feared you, because you are an austere man. You collect what you did not deposit, and reap what you did not sow.' [22]And he said to him, 'Out of your own mouth I will judge you, *you* wicked servant. You knew that I was an austere man, collecting what I did not deposit and reaping what I did not sow. [23]Why then did you not put my money in the bank, that at my coming I might have collected it with interest?'

[24]"And he said to those who stood by, 'Take the mina from him, and give *it* to him who has ten minas.' [25](But they said to him, 'Master, he has ten minas.') [26]For I say to you, that to everyone who has will be given; and from him who does not have, even what he has will be taken away from him. [27]But bring here those enemies of mine, who did not want me to reign over them, and slay *them* before me.'"

The Triumphal Entry

[28]When He had said this, He went on ahead, going up to Jerusalem. [29]And it came to pass, when He drew near to Bethphage[a] and Bethany, at the mountain called Olivet, *that* He sent two of His disciples, [30]saying, "Go into the village opposite *you,* where as you enter you will find a colt tied, on which no one has ever sat. Loose it and bring *it* here. [31]And if anyone asks you, 'Why are you loosing *it?*' thus you shall say to him, 'Because the Lord has need of it.'"

[32]So those who were sent went their way and found *it* just as He had said to them. [33]But as they were loosing the colt, the owners of it said to them, "Why are you loosing the colt?"

[34]And they said, "The Lord has need of him." [35]Then they brought him to Jesus. And they threw their own clothes on the colt, and they set Jesus on him. [36]And as He went, *many* spread their clothes on the road.

[37]Then, as He was now drawing near the descent of the Mount of Olives, the whole multitude of the disciples began to rejoice and praise God with a loud voice for all the mighty works they had seen, [38]saying:

Stewardship: Leaders Are Brokers of Resources

(Luke 19:11–26)

Jesus told a story about a landowner who gave three men some funds to spend, save, or invest. Each did as he saw fit, and when the owner returned, he rewarded them according to how wisely they used their resources. Those who multiplied what had been entrusted to them received even more to use. The one who failed had even his little money taken away.

Our Lord wants us to remember that leaders are brokers of the resources they have been given. Those resources may include people, budget, time, wisdom, and talents. When leaders broker those resources well, God rewards them and gives them even more to invest. When they fail, they lose what little they have.

This is a sobering truth, but one that leaders would do well to remember. Do you want more resources? If so, what are you doing with what you already have?

19:13 [a]The *mina* (Greek *mna,* Hebrew *minah*) was worth about three months' salary. **19:29** [a]M-Text reads *Bethsphage.*

"'*Blessed is the King who comes in the name of the LORD!*'[a]

Peace in heaven and glory in the highest!"

[39]And some of the Pharisees called to Him from the crowd, "Teacher, rebuke Your disciples."

[40]But He answered and said to them, "I tell you that if these should keep silent, the stones would immediately cry out."

Jesus Weeps over Jerusalem

[41]Now as He drew near, He saw the city and wept over it, [42]saying, "If you had known, even you, especially in this your day, the things *that make* for your peace! But now they are hidden from your eyes. [43]For days will come upon you when your enemies will build an embankment around you, surround you and close you in on every side, [44]and level you, and your children within you, to the ground; and they will not leave in you one stone upon another, because you did not know the time of your visitation."

Jesus Cleanses the Temple

[45]Then He went into the temple and began to drive out those who bought and sold in it,[a] [46]saying to them, "It is written, '*My house is*[a] *a house of prayer,*'[b] but you have made it a '*den of thieves.*'"[c]

[47]And He was teaching daily in the temple. But the chief priests, the scribes, and the leaders of the people sought to destroy Him, [48]and were unable to do anything; for all the people were very attentive to hear Him.

Jesus' Authority Questioned

20 Now it happened on one of those days, as He taught the people in the temple and preached the gospel, *that* the chief priests and the scribes, together with the elders, confronted *Him* [2]and spoke to Him, saying, "Tell us, by what authority are You doing these things? Or who is he who gave You this authority?"

[3]But He answered and said to them, "I also will ask you one thing, and answer Me: [4]The baptism of John—was it from heaven or from men?"

[5]And they reasoned among themselves, saying, "If we say, 'From heaven,' He will say, 'Why then[a] did you not believe him?' [6]But if we say, 'From men,' all the people will stone us, for they are persuaded that John was a prophet." [7]So they answered that they did not know where *it was* from.

[8]And Jesus said to them, "Neither will I tell you by what authority I do these things."

The Parable of the Wicked Vinedressers

[9]Then He began to tell the people this parable: "A certain man planted a vineyard, leased it to vinedressers, and went into a far country for a long time. [10]Now at vintage-time he sent a servant to the vinedressers, that they might give him some of the fruit of the vineyard. But the vinedressers beat him and sent *him* away empty-handed. [11]Again he sent another servant; and they beat him also, treated *him* shamefully, and sent *him* away empty-handed. [12]And again he sent a third; and they wounded him also and cast *him* out.

[13]"Then the owner of the vineyard said, 'What shall I do? I will send my beloved son. Probably they will respect *him* when they see him.' [14]But when the vinedressers saw him, they reasoned among themselves, saying, 'This is the heir. Come, let us kill him, that the inheritance may be ours.' [15]So they cast him out of the vineyard and killed *him*. Therefore what will the owner of the vineyard do to them? [16]He will come and destroy those vinedressers and give the vineyard to others."

And when they heard *it* they said, "Certainly not!"

[17]Then He looked at them and said, "What then is this that is written:

'*The stone which the builders rejected Has become the chief cornerstone*'?[a]

[18]Whoever falls on that stone will be broken; but on whomever it falls, it will grind him to powder."

[19]And the chief priests and the scribes that very hour sought to lay hands on Him, but they feared the people[a]—for they knew He had spoken this parable against them.

The Pharisees: Is It Lawful to Pay Taxes to Caesar?

[20]So they watched *Him*, and sent spies who pretended to be righteous, that they might seize on His words, in order to deliver Him to the power and the authority of the governor. [21]Then they asked Him, saying, "Teacher, we

---

19:38 [a]Psalm 118:26 **19:45** [a]NU-Text reads *those who were selling.* **19:46** [a]NU-Text reads *shall be.* [b]Isaiah 56:7 [c]Jeremiah 7:11 **20:5** [a]NU-Text and M-Text omit *then.* **20:17** [a]Psalm 118:22 **20:19** [a]M-Text reads *but they were afraid.*

The Law of Intuition:
Jesus Discerned the Real Issue Was Surrender

(Luke 20:19–26)

One day the scribes sent spies to trap Jesus, asking about whether it was right to pay taxes to Caesar. They knew that if He said yes, they could label him a traitor. If He said no, they could report him to the Roman authorities. They thought they had a perfect plan to silence this radical leader.

In a classic reversal, Jesus turned the tables on them. Because He practiced the Law of Intuition, He was able to see past the facade they had erected. Taxes weren't the issue; surrender was the issue. So Jesus answered their question with another question. Whose image was on the coin they showed Him? He meant that any object stamped with a person's image belongs to the individual pictured. This coin carried Caesar's image, so they were to surrender that coin to Caesar. On the other hand, God had stamped His image on *them*! They had been made in His image and should therefore surrender themselves to God.

What a memorable lesson! No wonder they became silent. This intuitive Leader answered their question by quickly getting to the real issue.

know that You say and teach rightly, and You do not show personal favoritism, but teach the way of God in truth: ²²Is it lawful for us to pay taxes to Caesar or not?"

²³But He perceived their craftiness, and said to them, "Why do you test Me?[a] ²⁴Show Me a denarius. Whose image and inscription does it have?"

They answered and said, "Caesar's."

²⁵And He said to them, "Render therefore to Caesar the things that are Caesar's, and to God the things that are God's."

²⁶But they could not catch Him in His words in the presence of the people. And they marveled at His answer and kept silent.

The Sadducees: What About the Resurrection?

²⁷Then some of the Sadducees, who deny that there is a resurrection, came to *Him* and asked Him, ²⁸saying: "Teacher, Moses wrote to us *that* if a man's brother dies, having a wife, and he dies without children, his brother should take his wife and raise up offspring for his brother. ²⁹Now there were seven brothers. And the first took a wife, and died without children. ³⁰And the second[a] took her as wife, and he died childless. ³¹Then the third took her, and in like manner the seven also; and they left no children,[a] and died. ³²Last of all the woman died also. ³³Therefore, in the resurrection, whose wife does she become? For all seven had her as wife."

³⁴Jesus answered and said to them, "The sons of this age marry and are given in marriage. ³⁵But those who are counted worthy to attain that age, and the resurrection from the dead, neither marry nor are given in marriage; ³⁶nor can they die anymore, for they are equal to the angels and are sons of God, being sons of the resurrection. ³⁷But even Moses showed in the *burning* bush *passage* that the dead are raised, when he called the Lord '*the God of Abraham, the God of Isaac, and the God of Jacob.*'[a] ³⁸For He is not the God of the dead but of the living, for all live to Him."

³⁹Then some of the scribes answered and said, "Teacher, You have spoken well." ⁴⁰But after that they dared not question Him anymore.

Jesus: How Can David Call His Descendant Lord?

⁴¹And He said to them, "How can they say that the Christ is the Son of David? ⁴²Now David himself said in the Book of Psalms:

'*The LORD said to my Lord,
"Sit at My right hand,
⁴³   Till I make Your enemies Your footstool.*"'[a]

20:23 [a]NU-Text omits *Why do you test Me?*
20:30 [a]NU-Text ends verse 30 here.
20:31 [a]NU-Text and M-Text read *the seven also left no children.* **20:37** [a]Exodus 3:6, 15 **20:43** [a]Psalm 110:1

[44]Therefore David calls Him '*Lord*'; how is He then his Son?"

Beware of the Scribes

[45]Then, in the hearing of all the people, He said to His disciples, [46]"Beware of the scribes, who desire to go around in long robes, love greetings in the marketplaces, the best seats in the synagogues, and the best places at feasts, [47]who devour widows' houses, and for a pretense make long prayers. These will receive greater condemnation."

The Widow's Two Mites

21 And He looked up and saw the rich putting their gifts into the treasury, [2]and He saw also a certain poor widow putting in two mites. [3]So He said, "Truly I say to you that this poor widow has put in more than all; [4]for all these out of their abundance have put in offerings for God,[a] but she out of her poverty put in all the livelihood that she had."

Jesus Predicts the Destruction of the Temple

[5]Then, as some spoke of the temple, how it was adorned with beautiful stones and donations, He said, [6]"These things which you see— the days will come in which not *one* stone shall be left upon another that shall not be thrown down."

The Signs of the Times and the End of the Age

[7]So they asked Him, saying, "Teacher, but when will these things be? And what sign *will there be* when these things are about to take place?"

[8]And He said: "Take heed that you not be deceived. For many will come in My name, saying, 'I am *He*,' and, 'The time has drawn near.' Therefore[a] do not go after them. [9]But when you hear of wars and commotions, do not be terrified; for these things must come to pass first, but the end *will not come* immediately."

[10]Then He said to them, "Nation will rise against nation, and kingdom against kingdom. [11]And there will be great earthquakes in various places, and famines and pestilences; and there will be fearful sights and great signs from heaven. [12]But before all these things, they will lay their hands on you and persecute *you,* delivering *you* up to the synagogues and prisons. You will be brought before kings and rulers for My name's sake. [13]But it will turn out for you as an occasion for testimony. [14]Therefore settle *it* in your hearts not to meditate beforehand on what you will answer; [15]for I will give you a mouth and wisdom which all your adversaries will not be able to contradict or resist. [16]You will be betrayed even by parents and brothers, relatives and friends; and they will put *some* of you to death. [17]And you will be hated by all for My name's sake. [18]But not a hair of your head shall be lost. [19]By your patience possess your souls.

The Destruction of Jerusalem

[20]"But when you see Jerusalem surrounded by armies, then know that its desolation is near. [21]Then let those who are in Judea flee to the mountains, let those who are in the midst of her depart, and let not those who are in the country enter her. [22]For these are the days of vengeance, that all things which are written may be fulfilled. [23]But woe to those who are pregnant and to those who are nursing babies in those days! For there will be great distress in the land and wrath upon this people. [24]And they will fall by the edge of the sword, and be led away captive into all nations. And Jerusalem will be trampled by Gentiles until the times of the Gentiles are fulfilled.

The Coming of the Son of Man

[25]"And there will be signs in the sun, in the moon, and in the stars; and on the earth distress of nations, with perplexity, the sea and the waves roaring; [26]men's hearts failing them from fear and the expectation of those things which are coming on the earth, for the powers of the heavens will be shaken. [27]Then they will see the Son of Man coming in a cloud with power and great glory. [28]Now when these things begin to happen, look up and lift up your heads, because your redemption draws near."

The Parable of the Fig Tree

[29]Then He spoke to them a parable: "Look at the fig tree, and all the trees. [30]When they are already budding, you see and know for yourselves that summer is now near. [31]So you also, when you see these things happening, know that the kingdom of God is near. [32]Assuredly, I say to you, this generation will by no means pass away till all things take place. [33]Heaven and earth will pass away, but My words will by no means pass away.

21:4 [a]NU-Text omits *for God.* **21:8** [a]NU-Text omits *Therefore.*

The Importance of Watching

[34]"But take heed to yourselves, lest your hearts be weighed down with carousing, drunkenness, and cares of this life, and that Day come on you unexpectedly. [35]For it will come as a snare on all those who dwell on the face of the whole earth. [36]Watch therefore, and pray always that you may be counted worthy[a] to escape all these things that will come to pass, and to stand before the Son of Man."

[37]And in the daytime He was teaching in the temple, but at night He went out and stayed on the mountain called Olivet. [38]Then early in the morning all the people came to Him in the temple to hear Him.

The Plot to Kill Jesus

22 Now the Feast of Unleavened Bread drew near, which is called Passover. [2]And the chief priests and the scribes sought how they might kill Him, for they feared the people.

[3]Then Satan entered Judas, surnamed Iscariot, who was numbered among the twelve. [4]So he went his way and conferred with the chief priests and captains, how he might betray Him to them. [5]And they were glad, and agreed to give him money. [6]So he promised and sought opportunity to betray Him to them in the absence of the multitude.

Servanthood: Judas Fails the Test of Leadership
(Luke 22:1–23)

While Judas had accompanied Jesus for three-and-a-half years, enjoying the mentoring of Christ, he never learned the fundamentals of leadership. Luke 22 records Judas's betrayal of Jesus on the night of the Passover feast. Even though Jesus had served Judas supper, and even washed his feet (John 13:1–7), Judas missed the lesson on servanthood. He joined the others in a discussion on who was the greatest (Luke 22:24), then left to betray Jesus, turning Him over to the Jewish authorities.

That night Judas led the entire team of disciples in failing the test of Jesus' style of leadership: servanthood.

Jesus and His Disciples Prepare the Passover

[7]Then came the Day of Unleavened Bread, when the Passover must be killed. [8]And He sent Peter and John, saying, "Go and prepare the Passover for us, that we may eat."

[9]So they said to Him, "Where do You want us to prepare?"

[10]And He said to them, "Behold, when you have entered the city, a man will meet you carrying a pitcher of water; follow him into the house which he enters. [11]Then you shall say to the master of the house, 'The Teacher says to you, "Where is the guest room where I may eat the Passover with My disciples?"' [12]Then he will show you a large, furnished upper room; there make ready."

[13]So they went and found it just as He had said to them, and they prepared the Passover.

Jesus Institutes the Lord's Supper

[14]When the hour had come, He sat down, and the twelve[a] apostles with Him. [15]Then He said to them, "With *fervent* desire I have desired to eat this Passover with you before I suffer; [16]for I say to you, I will no longer eat of it until it is fulfilled in the kingdom of God."

[17]Then He took the cup, and gave thanks, and said, "Take this and divide *it* among yourselves; [18]for I say to you,[a] I will not drink of the fruit of the vine until the kingdom of God comes."

[19]And He took bread, gave thanks and broke *it,* and gave *it* to them, saying, "This is My body which is given for you; do this in remembrance of Me."

[20]Likewise He also *took* the cup after supper, saying, "This cup *is* the new covenant in My blood, which is shed for you. [21]But behold, the hand of My betrayer *is* with Me on the table. [22]And truly the Son of Man goes as it has been determined, but woe to that man by whom He is betrayed!"

[23]Then they began to question among themselves, which of them it was who would do this thing.

The Disciples Argue About Greatness

[24]Now there was also a dispute among them, as to which of them should be considered the greatest. [25]And He said to them, "The kings of the Gentiles exercise lordship over them, and those who exercise authority over them are called

---

21:36 [a]NU-Text reads *may have strength.*
22:14 [a]NU-Text omits *twelve.* **22:18** [a]NU-Text adds *from now on.*

'benefactors.' [26]But not so *among* you; on the contrary, he who is greatest among you, let him be as the younger, and he who governs as he who serves. [27]For who *is* greater, he who sits at the table, or he who serves? *Is* it not he who sits at the table? Yet I am among you as the One who serves.

[28]"But you are those who have continued with Me in My trials. [29]And I bestow upon you a kingdom, just as My Father bestowed *one* upon Me, [30]that you may eat and drink at My table in My kingdom, and sit on thrones judging the twelve tribes of Israel."

Jesus Predicts Peter's Denial

[31]And the Lord said,[a] "Simon, Simon! Indeed, Satan has asked for you, that he may sift *you* as wheat. [32]But I have prayed for you, that your faith should not fail; and when you have returned to *Me,* strengthen your brethren."

[33]But he said to Him, "Lord, I am ready to go with You, both to prison and to death."

[34]Then He said, "I tell you, Peter, the rooster shall not crow this day before you will deny three times that you know Me."

Supplies for the Road

[35]And He said to them, "When I sent you without money bag, knapsack, and sandals, did you lack anything?"

So they said, "Nothing."

[36]Then He said to them, "But now, he who has a money bag, let him take *it,* and likewise a knapsack; and he who has no sword, let him sell his garment and buy one. [37]For I say to you that this which is written must still be accomplished in Me: '*And He was numbered with the transgressors.*'[a] For the things concerning Me have an end."

[38]So they said, "Lord, look, here *are* two swords."

And He said to them, "It is enough."

The Prayer in the Garden

[39]Coming out, He went to the Mount of Olives, as He was accustomed, and His disciples also followed Him. [40]When He came to the place, He said to them, "Pray that you may not enter into temptation."

[41]And He was withdrawn from them about a stone's throw, and He knelt down and prayed, [42]saying, "Father, if it is Your will, take this cup away from Me; nevertheless not My will, but Yours, be done." [43]Then an angel appeared to Him from heaven, strengthening Him. [44]And being in agony, He prayed more earnestly. Then His sweat became like great drops of blood falling down to the ground.[a]

Leaders and Their Gethsemanes

(Luke 22:39–46)

At times all leaders feel alone, as when they pioneer new territory. Jesus endured one of His loneliest times in the Garden of Gethsemane. Just hours before He would be tried, tortured, and crucified, every one of His team deserted Him. His story in the garden provides us with one of the greatest examples in history of a leader's commitment.

Every leader who does something significant for God experiences a Gethsemane. What can we learn about this lonely season? Gethsemane is the place where . . .

1. spiritual battles occur (vv. 40–44).
2. loneliness is felt (v. 41).
3. honesty is expressed (vv. 41, 42).
4. submission is required (v. 42).
5. strength is received (v. 43).

---

[45]When He rose up from prayer, and had come to His disciples, He found them sleeping from sorrow. [46]Then He said to them, "Why do you sleep? Rise and pray, lest you enter into temptation."

Betrayal and Arrest in Gethsemane

[47]And while He was still speaking, behold, a multitude; and he who was called Judas, one of the twelve, went before them and drew near to Jesus to kiss Him. [48]But Jesus said to him, "Judas, are you betraying the Son of Man with a kiss?"

[49]When those around Him saw what was going to happen, they said to Him, "Lord, shall we strike with the sword?" [50]And one of them struck the servant of the high priest and cut off his right ear.

[51]But Jesus answered and said, "Permit even this." And He touched his ear and healed him.

[52]Then Jesus said to the chief priests, captains of the temple, and the elders who had come to Him, "Have you come out, as against a robber,

---

22:31 [a]NU-Text omits *And the Lord said.*
22:37 [a]Isaiah 53:12 **22:44** [a]NU-Text brackets verses 43 and 44 as not in the original text.

21 QUALITIES

COMMITMENT

Jesus Christ vs. Simon Peter
(Luke 22:54–62)

Luke records a stark contrast between the commitment of two leaders, Jesus Christ and Simon Peter. While Jesus remained resolutely committed to His cause and His people in the face of betrayal and rejection, Simon Peter ran away. Although the big fisherman claimed he would never deny his Master, he did so three times before the night ended.

While Peter emphatically denied Christ around a little courtyard fire, that moment merely expressed the condition of his heart. His commitment level had already drained away in the Garden of Gethsemane. There he felt helpless, powerless to maintain the promise he had made (Matt. 26:35).

When our commitment drains away, we follow the same progression as Peter:

Stage 1: His following became distant.
"Peter followed at a distance" (Luke 22:54). This is not what Jesus had in mind in Matthew 16:24. Peter is still following Christ, but incognito. He's no longer ready to die.
Stage 2: His fellowship became divided.
"Peter sat among them" (22:55). Now the guilty disciple is mixing with an uncommitted crowd. He's a man without a country. He's torn between the apathetic and the committed.
Stage 3: His faith became deluded.
"But he denied Him saying, 'Woman, I do not know Him' " (22:57). His words now reveal his weakness, even among men and women who pose no immediate threat to him.
Stage 4: His fervor became denial.
"But Peter said, 'Man, I do not know what you are saying!' " (22:60). Peter rejects any association with Jesus. His words no longer display apathy, but rejection.

Levels of Commitment

Jesus always related to people at the level of commitment they were ready to make. Note four levels of commitment in Jesus' disciples:

Level One: Come and See
This is the curiosity level (see John 1:35–51). At this stage Jesus' interaction is light and easy. When people are here, look for chemistry and faithfulness.
Level Two: Come and Follow
This is the commitment level (see Luke 5:1–11). Jesus' words now call for some commitment. The person is ready to be challenged. Look for hunger and teachability.
Level Three: Come and Surrender
This is the conviction level (see Mark 8:34, 35). This step is appropriate only after deep relationship and mutual trust have developed. Look for initiative and determination.
Level Four: Come and Multiply
This is the commissioned level (see Matt. 28:19, 20). Here, Jesus calls His men to reproduce what He did with them. Look for leadership and people skills.

For a positive example of commitment, see p. 1329.

with swords and clubs? ⁵³When I was with you daily in the temple, you did not try to seize Me. But this is your hour, and the power of darkness."

Peter Denies Jesus, and Weeps Bitterly

⁵⁴Having arrested Him, they led *Him* and brought Him into the high priest's house. But Peter followed at a distance. ⁵⁵Now when they had kindled a fire in the midst of the courtyard and sat down together, Peter sat among them. ⁵⁶And a certain servant girl, seeing him as he sat by the fire, looked intently at him and said, "This man was also with Him."

⁵⁷But he denied Him,ª saying, "Woman, I do not know Him."

⁵⁸And after a little while another saw him and said, "You also are of them."

But Peter said, "Man, I am not!"

⁵⁹Then after about an hour had passed, another confidently affirmed, saying, "Surely this *fellow* also was with Him, for he is a Galilean."

⁶⁰But Peter said, "Man, I do not know what you are saying!"

Immediately, while he was still speaking, the roosterª crowed. ⁶¹And the Lord turned and looked at Peter. Then Peter remembered the word of the Lord, how He had said to him, "Before the rooster crows,ª you will deny Me three times." ⁶²So Peter went out and wept bitterly.

Jesus Mocked and Beaten

⁶³Now the men who held Jesus mocked Him and beat Him. ⁶⁴And having blindfolded Him, they struck Him on the face and asked Him,ª saying, "Prophesy! Who is the one who struck You?" ⁶⁵And many other things they blasphemously spoke against Him.

Jesus Faces the Sanhedrin

⁶⁶As soon as it was day, the elders of the people, both chief priests and scribes, came together and led Him into their council, saying, ⁶⁷"If You are the Christ, tell us."

But He said to them, "If I tell you, you will by no means believe. ⁶⁸And if I also ask *you,* you will by no means answer Me or let *Me* go.ª ⁶⁹Hereafter the Son of Man will sit on the right hand of the power of God."

⁷⁰Then they all said, "Are You then the Son of God?"

So He said to them, "You *rightly* say that I am."

⁷¹And they said, "What further testimony do we need? For we have heard it ourselves from His own mouth."

Jesus Handed Over to Pontius Pilate

23 Then the whole multitude of them arose and led Him to Pilate. ²And they began to accuse Him, saying, "We found this *fellow* perverting theª nation, and forbidding to pay taxes to Caesar, saying that He Himself is Christ, a King."

³Then Pilate asked Him, saying, "Are You the King of the Jews?"

He answered him and said, "*It is as* you say."

⁴So Pilate said to the chief priests and the crowd, "I find no fault in this Man."

⁵But they were the more fierce, saying, "He stirs up the people, teaching throughout all Judea, beginning from Galilee to this place."

The Law of Sacrifice: Jesus Gave It All Up to Gain It All Back

(Luke 23:1–47)

Jesus stayed so committed to His mission that He allowed weaker men to seize Him, arrest Him, and crucify Him. Jesus laid down His life, practicing the Law of Sacrifice. Leaders must give up to go up. Jesus paid the ultimate price because He knew what was coming.

Jesus Faces Herod

⁶When Pilate heard of Galilee,ª he asked if the Man were a Galilean. ⁷And as soon as he knew that He belonged to Herod's jurisdiction, he sent Him to Herod, who was also in Jerusalem at that time. ⁸Now when Herod saw Jesus, he was exceedingly glad; for he had desired for a long *time* to see Him, because he had heard many things about Him, and he hoped to see some miracle done by Him. ⁹Then he questioned Him with many words, but He answered him nothing. ¹⁰And the chief priests and scribes stood and vehemently accused Him. ¹¹Then Herod, with his men of war, treated Him with contempt and mocked *Him,* arrayed Him in a gorgeous robe,

---

22:57 ªNU-Text reads *denied it.* 22:60 ªNU-Text and M-Text read *a rooster.* 22:61 ªNU-Text adds *today.* 22:64 ªNU-Text reads *And having blindfolded Him, they asked Him.* 22:68 ªNU-Text omits *also* and *Me or let Me go.* 23:2 ªNU-Text reads *our.* 23:6 ªNU-Text omits *of Galilee.*

and sent Him back to Pilate. ¹²That very day Pilate and Herod became friends with each other, for previously they had been at enmity with each other.

Taking the Place of Barabbas

¹³Then Pilate, when he had called together the chief priests, the rulers, and the people, ¹⁴said to them, "You have brought this Man to me, as one who misleads the people. And indeed, having examined *Him* in your presence, I have found no fault in this Man concerning those things of which you accuse Him; ¹⁵no, neither did Herod, for I sent you back to him;ª and indeed nothing deserving of death has been done by Him. ¹⁶I will therefore chastise Him and release *Him*" ¹⁷(for it was necessary for him to release one to them at the feast).ª

¹⁸And they all cried out at once, saying, "Away with this *Man,* and release to us Barabbas"— ¹⁹who had been thrown into prison for a certain rebellion made in the city, and for murder.

²⁰Pilate, therefore, wishing to release Jesus, again called out to them. ²¹But they shouted, saying, "Crucify *Him,* crucify Him!"

²²Then he said to them the third time, "Why, what evil has He done? I have found no reason for death in Him. I will therefore chastise Him and let *Him* go."

²³But they were insistent, demanding with loud voices that He be crucified. And the voices of these men and of the chief priests prevailed.ª ²⁴So Pilate gave sentence that it should be as they requested. ²⁵And he released to themª the one they requested, who for rebellion and murder had been thrown into prison; but he delivered Jesus to their will.

The King on a Cross

²⁶Now as they led Him away, they laid hold of a certain man, Simon a Cyrenian, who was coming from the country, and on him they laid the cross that he might bear *it* after Jesus.

²⁷And a great multitude of the people followed Him, and women who also mourned and lamented Him. ²⁸But Jesus, turning to them, said, "Daughters of Jerusalem, do not weep for Me, but weep for yourselves and for your children. ²⁹For indeed the days are coming in which they will say, 'Blessed *are* the barren, wombs that never bore, and breasts

---

23:15 ªNU-Text reads *for he sent Him back to us.*
23:17 ªNU-Text omits verse 17. **23:23** ªNU-Text omits *and of the chief priests.* **23:25** ªNU-Text and M-Text omit *to them.*

PROFILE IN LEADERSHIP

HEROD

PICTURE OF AN EGO-DRIVEN LEADER
(Luke 23:6–12)

Herod Antipas—ruler of Galilee and Nazareth, where Christ had grown up—eagerly looked forward to seeing Jesus. The king had heard a great deal about Jesus and the miracles He had performed. He had waited a long time to meet this intriguing man.

Finally, with this reputed "miracle worker" standing before him, Herod had a chance to see for himself what Jesus was all about. Herod questioned Jesus at length, challenging Him to perform a miracle—any miracle. All during the interrogation, the religious leaders hurled their accusations at Jesus. A single miracle would have silenced His accusers—but Jesus remained mute. Instead of defending Himself, He allowed this "trial" to move forward.

Herod no doubt felt disappointed that Jesus didn't come through with a miracle, and he and his guards greatly abused Jesus that day. They insulted Him and physically assaulted Him. Then, to directly mock His title, "King of the Jews," they dressed Him in a royal robe and sent Him back to Pilate . . . and a sure date with a cross of death.

Herod resembled a lot of leaders in Jesus' day: As long as He performed miracles, they were fine with Him. But when He refused, they not only lost interest in Him, but they committed the gravest injustice in history. That's what can happen when any leader habitually focuses on self.

which never nursed!' [30]Then they will begin 'to say to the mountains, "Fall on us!" and to the hills, "Cover us!"'[a] [31]For if they do these things in the green wood, what will be done in the dry?"

[32]There were also two others, criminals, led with Him to be put to death. [33]And when they had come to the place called Calvary, there they crucified Him, and the criminals, one on the right hand and the other on the left. [34]Then Jesus said, "Father, forgive them, for they do not know what they do."[a]

And they divided His garments and cast lots. [35]And the people stood looking on. But even the rulers with them sneered, saying, "He saved others; let Him save Himself if He is the Christ, the chosen of God."

[36]The soldiers also mocked Him, coming and offering Him sour wine, [37]and saying, "If You are the King of the Jews, save Yourself."

[38]And an inscription also was written over Him in letters of Greek, Latin, and Hebrew:[a]

THIS IS THE KING OF THE JEWS.

[39]Then one of the criminals who were hanged blasphemed Him, saying, "If You are the Christ,[a] save Yourself and us."

[40]But the other, answering, rebuked him, saying, "Do you not even fear God, seeing you are under the same condemnation? [41]And we indeed justly, for we receive the due reward of our deeds; but this Man has done nothing wrong." [42]Then he said to Jesus, "Lord,[a] remember me when You come into Your kingdom."

[43]And Jesus said to him, "Assuredly, I say to you, today you will be with Me in Paradise."

Jesus Dies on the Cross

[44]Now it was[a] about the sixth hour, and there was darkness over all the earth until the ninth hour. [45]Then the sun was darkened,[a] and the veil of the temple was torn in two. [46]And when Jesus had cried out with a loud voice, He said, "Father, 'into Your hands I commit My spirit.'"[a] Having said this, He breathed His last.

[47]So when the centurion saw what had happened, he glorified God, saying, "Certainly this was a righteous Man!"

[48]And the whole crowd who came together to that sight, seeing what had been done, beat their breasts and returned. [49]But all His acquaintances, and the women who followed Him from Galilee, stood at a distance, watching these things.

Jesus Buried in Joseph's Tomb

[50]Now behold, there was a man named Joseph, a council member, a good and just man. [51]He had not consented to their decision and deed. He was from Arimathea, a city of the Jews, who himself was also waiting[a] for the kingdom of God. [52]This man went to Pilate and asked for the body of Jesus. [53]Then he took it down, wrapped it in linen, and laid it in a tomb that was hewn out of the rock, where no one had ever lain before. [54]That day was the Preparation, and the Sabbath drew near.

[55]And the women who had come with Him from Galilee followed after, and they observed the tomb and how His body was laid. [56]Then they returned and prepared spices and fragrant oils. And they rested on the Sabbath according to the commandment.

He Is Risen

24 Now on the first day of the week, very early in the morning, they, and certain other women with them,[a] came to the tomb bringing the spices which they had prepared. [2]But they found the stone rolled away from the tomb. [3]Then they went in and did not find the body of the Lord Jesus. [4]And it happened, as they were greatly[a] perplexed about this, that behold, two men stood by them in shining garments. [5]Then, as they were afraid and bowed their faces to the earth, they said to them, "Why do you seek the living among the dead? [6]He is not here, but is risen! Remember how He spoke to you when He was still in Galilee, [7]saying, 'The Son of Man must be delivered into the hands of sinful men, and be crucified, and the third day rise again.'"

[8]And they remembered His words. [9]Then they returned from the tomb and told all these things to the eleven and to all the rest. [10]It was Mary Magdalene, Joanna, Mary the mother of James, and the other women with them, who told these things to the apostles. [11]And their words seemed to them like idle tales, and they did not believe them. [12]But Peter arose and ran to the tomb; and stooping down, he saw the linen cloths lying[a] by themselves; and he departed, marveling to himself at what had happened.

23:30 [a]Hosea 10:8 **23:34** [a]NU-Text brackets the first sentence as a later addition. **23:38** [a]NU-Text omits written and in letters of Greek, Latin, and Hebrew. **23:39** [a]NU-Text reads Are You not the Christ? **23:42** [a]NU-Text reads And he said, "Jesus, remember me. **23:44** [a]NU-Text adds already. **23:45** [a]NU-Text reads obscured. **23:46** [a]Psalm 31:5 **23:51** [a]NU-Text reads who was waiting. **24:1** [a]NU-Text omits and certain other women with them. **24:4** [a]NU-Text omits greatly. **24:12** [a]NU-Text omits lying.

The Road to Emmaus

¹³Now behold, two of them were traveling that same day to a village called Emmaus, which was seven milesª from Jerusalem. ¹⁴And they talked together of all these things which had happened. ¹⁵So it was, while they conversed and reasoned, that Jesus Himself drew near and went with them. ¹⁶But their eyes were restrained, so that they did not know Him.

¹⁷And He said to them, "What kind of conversation *is* this that you have with one another as you walk and are sad?"ª

¹⁸Then the one whose name was Cleopas answered and said to Him, "Are You the only stranger in Jerusalem, and have You not known the things which happened there in these days?"

¹⁹And He said to them, "What things?"

So they said to Him, "The things concerning Jesus of Nazareth, who was a Prophet mighty in deed and word before God and all the people, ²⁰and how the chief priests and our rulers delivered Him to be condemned to death, and crucified Him. ²¹But we were hoping that it was He who was going to redeem Israel. Indeed, besides all this, today is the third day since these things happened. ²²Yes, and certain women of our company, who arrived at the tomb early, astonished us. ²³When they did not find His body, they came saying that they had also seen a vision of angels who said He was alive. ²⁴And certain of those *who were* with us went to the tomb and found *it* just as the women had said; but Him they did not see."

²⁵Then He said to them, "O foolish ones, and slow of heart to believe in all that the prophets have spoken! ²⁶Ought not the Christ to have suffered these things and to enter into His glory?" ²⁷And beginning at Moses and all the Prophets, He expounded to them in all the Scriptures the things concerning Himself.

The Disciples' Eyes Opened

²⁸Then they drew near to the village where they were going, and He indicated that He would have gone farther. ²⁹But they constrained Him, saying, "Abide with us, for it is toward evening, and the day is far spent." And He went in to stay with them.

³⁰Now it came to pass, as He sat at the table with them, that He took bread, blessed and broke *it,* and gave it to them. ³¹Then their eyes were opened and they knew Him; and He vanished from their sight.

³²And they said to one another, "Did not our heart burn within us while He talked with us on the road, and while He opened the Scriptures to

---

The Law of Intuition: Jesus Interprets Current Events

(Luke 24:13–31)

As two grieving men conversed about Jesus' crucifixion, they struggled to understand what it all meant. Jesus saw their confusion and could tell they needed someone to guide them. So He joined them and began to explain His resurrection in light of Scripture (Luke 24:27, 45). By the end of their time together, it all made sense.

Leaders interpret reality for their people. They see a bigger picture and have a leadership bias. They offer clear perspective to those who need it. They understand current events and how they fit into the overall scheme of things. Remember: Who you are dictates what you see.

---

us?" ³³So they rose up that very hour and returned to Jerusalem, and found the eleven and those *who were* with them gathered together, ³⁴saying, "The Lord is risen indeed, and has appeared to Simon!" ³⁵And they told about the things *that had happened* on the road, and how He was known to them in the breaking of bread.

Jesus Appears to His Disciples

³⁶Now as they said these things, Jesus Himself stood in the midst of them, and said to them, "Peace to you." ³⁷But they were terrified and frightened, and supposed they had seen a spirit. ³⁸And He said to them, "Why are you troubled? And why do doubts arise in your hearts? ³⁹Behold My hands and My feet, that it is I Myself. Handle Me and see, for a spirit does not have flesh and bones as you see I have."

⁴⁰When He had said this, He showed them His hands and His feet.ª ⁴¹But while they still did not believe for joy, and marveled, He said to them, "Have you any food here?" ⁴²So they gave Him a piece of a broiled fish and some honeycomb.ª ⁴³And He took *it* and ate in their presence.

24:13 ªLiterally *sixty stadia* **24:17** ªNU-Text reads *as you walk? And they stood still, looking sad.*
24:40 ªSome printed New Testaments omit this verse. It is found in nearly all Greek manuscripts.
24:42 ªNU-Text omits *and some honeycomb.*

The Scriptures Opened

⁴⁴Then He said to them, "These *are* the words which I spoke to you while I was still with you, that all things must be fulfilled which were written in the Law of Moses and *the* Prophets and *the* Psalms concerning Me." ⁴⁵And He opened their understanding, that they might comprehend the Scriptures.

⁴⁶Then He said to them, "Thus it is written, and thus it was necessary for the Christ to suffer and to rise^a from the dead the third day, ⁴⁷and that repentance and remission of sins should be preached in His name to all nations, beginning at Jerusalem. ⁴⁸And you are witnesses of these things. ⁴⁹Behold, I send the Promise of My Father upon you; but tarry in the city of Jerusalem^a until you are endued with power from on high."

The Ascension

⁵⁰And He led them out as far as Bethany, and He lifted up His hands and blessed them. ⁵¹Now it came to pass, while He blessed them, that He was parted from them and carried up into heaven. ⁵²And they worshiped Him, and returned to Jerusalem with great joy, ⁵³and were continually in the temple praising and^a blessing God. Amen.^b

24:46 ^aNU-Text reads *written, that the Christ should suffer and rise.* **24:49** ^aNU-Text omits *of Jerusalem.* **24:53** ^aNU-Text omits *praising and.* ^bNU-Text omits *Amen.*

The Law of Reproduction: Jesus Turns His Work Over to His Trainees

(Luke 24:46–49)

Last words should always get our attention. Luke 24 records some of Jesus' last words to His disciples. He had trained them for more than three years. Now they were ready to go out as leaders and trainers themselves.

Jesus' work would have failed unless His followers had taken what He gave them and reproduced it in others. After His earthly ministry, Jesus trusted the future of His organization, the church, to former fishermen and tax collectors. Jesus employed at least 12 factors in reproducing His leadership:

1. *Vision* (Matt. 4:19; John 4:35)
2. *Trust* (Matt. 10:8)
3. *Commitment* (Matt. 16:24; John 13:1)
4. *Launch* (Matt. 28:18–20)
5. *Proximity* (Mark 3:14; Luke 8:1)
6. *Responsibility* (Mark 6:7)
7. *Initiative* (Luke 6:12, 13)
8. *Knowledge* (Luke 8:9, 10)
9. *Evaluation* (Luke 10:17–24)
10. *Example* (John 13:15)
11. *Friendship* (John 15:15)
12. *Power* (John 20:22; Acts 1:8)

The Law of Victory: Jesus' Resurrection Brings Victory to the Hopeless

(Luke 24:50–53)

What a difference in the behavior of Jesus' disciples before the resurrection and after it! Just before, all they had was an executed Leader. They ran from everyone, hoping to save their own necks. Afterward, they became invincible. Leaders find a way for the team to win—something reflected in the team's morale.

JOHN
Jesus as the Son of God

SUMMARY

John's Gospel provides a wealth of material on Jesus' life and ministry not found in the Gospels of Matthew, Mark, or Luke. His work is considered the simplest yet most profound of the four Gospels. Only John is written from a divine perspective, in which Jesus is portrayed as the Son of God. "In the beginning was the Word," John writes, "and the Word was with God, and the Word was God. . . . And the Word became flesh and dwelt among us" (1:1, 2, 14).

John writes as a leader attempting to persuade his readers to believe in Jesus. He writes "that you may believe that Jesus is the Christ, the Son of God, and that believing you may have life in His name" (20:31). He tells certain stories from Jesus' life for a particular purpose and details many of Jesus' teachings concerning His identity.

Like the other Gospels, much of this book focuses on the final week of Jesus' life; in fact, almost half of it does so. We can learn much from this concentration.

For one thing, we see that the strength of one's leadership is magnified during one's most difficult times. Almost anyone can lead with momentum on his or her side, but it takes a true leader to lead with death staring you in the face. As John focuses on Jesus' critical climax, we see what a great leader does under pressure. We catch a glimpse of a Leader in the most stressful situation imaginable, yet one who displays more peace than ever before. He communicates vision more vividly than ever before. He assures His staff of His love and belief in them more than ever before. He speaks of the future and lays a track for His men to run on more clearly than ever before. And He prays more intensely than He ever has before.

Read this Gospel and see Jesus, not only as the King of kings, but as the Leader of leaders, who led under pressure better than anyone ever did before . . . or since.

God's Role in John

If we had to distill this book and pull out just one divine message for leaders, it would be this: God grafts leaders into Jesus so that they might draw their strength and nourishment from Christ Himself. In John 15, Jesus even describes Himself as the "Vine" and us as the "branches."

No leader is an island. If we are to accomplish a divine mission, we must draw upon a divine power. God sustains and directs us as we lead. We must stay connected to Him if we are to be competent for Him. Because we see Jesus from God's perspective in this book, we can also see leadership from God's perspective. Jesus, the Ultimate Leader, labors to stay connected to the Father. He even says that He speaks only what He hears the Father speaking, and does only what He sees the Father doing (5:19, 20). From a horizontal perspective, leadership is about initiating with people. But from a vertical perspective, it is about responding to God.

Leaders in John

Jesus, John the Baptizer, chief priests, Pharisees, Pilate

Other People of Influence in John

The twelve disciples, Samaritan woman at the well, Mary Magdalene

Lessons in Leadership

- Godly leaders first submit to God, then serve the people.
- Great leaders call for great commitment.
- Spiritual leaders prioritize building relationships with those they lead.
- Leaders have the courage to let go of the familiar.
- Effective leaders see people development as their greatest accomplishment.
- Wise leaders never judge by outward appearance.
- Good leaders move where their cause is celebrated instead of merely tolerated.

LEADERSHIP

HIGHLIGHTS IN JOHN

The Eternal Word

1 In the beginning was the Word, and the Word was with God, and the Word was God. [2]He was in the beginning with God. [3]All things were made through Him, and without Him nothing was made that was made. [4]In Him was life, and the life was the light of men. [5]And the light shines in the darkness, and the darkness did not comprehend[a] it.

Leadership Begins with Identity: Jesus Led from Who He Was

(John 1:1, 14)

The best leadership simply expresses who we are. Jesus led from who He was: God incarnate, the perfect expression of the Father. As He pursued His divine mission, He influenced others. Similarly, as we pursue who God called us to be, our leadership will be most natural and effective.

John's Witness: The True Light

[6]There was a man sent from God, whose name *was* John. [7]This man came for a witness, to bear witness of the Light, that all through him might believe. [8]He was not that Light, but *was* sent to bear witness of that Light. [9]That was the true Light which gives light to every man coming into the world.[a]

[10]He was in the world, and the world was made through Him, and the world did not know Him. [11]He came to His own,[a] and His own[b] did not receive Him. [12]But as many as received Him, to them He gave the right to become children of God, to those who believe in His name: [13]who were born, not of blood, nor of the will of the flesh, nor of the will of man, but of God.

The Word Becomes Flesh

[14]And the Word became flesh and dwelt among us, and we beheld His glory, the glory as of the only begotten of the Father, full of grace and truth.

[15]John bore witness of Him and cried out, saying, "This was He of whom I said, 'He who comes after me is preferred before me, for He was before me.'"

[16]And[a] of His fullness we have all received, and grace for grace. [17]For the law was given

through Moses, *but* grace and truth came through Jesus Christ. [18]No one has seen God at any time. The only begotten Son,[a] who is in the bosom of the Father, He has declared *Him.*

A Voice in the Wilderness

[19]Now this is the testimony of John, when the Jews sent priests and Levites from Jerusalem to ask him, "Who are you?"

[20]He confessed, and did not deny, but confessed, "I am not the Christ."

[21]And they asked him, "What then? Are you Elijah?"

He said, "I am not."

"Are you the Prophet?"

And he answered, "No."

[22]Then they said to him, "Who are you, that we may give an answer to those who sent us? What do you say about yourself?"

[23]He said: "I *am*

'*The voice of one crying in the wilderness:*
"*Make straight the way of the LORD,*"'[a]

as the prophet Isaiah said."

[24]Now those who were sent were from the Pharisees. [25]And they asked him, saying, "Why then do you baptize if you are not the Christ, nor Elijah, nor the Prophet?"

[26]John answered them, saying, "I baptize with water, but there stands One among you whom you do not know. [27]It is He who, coming after me, is preferred before me, whose sandal strap I am not worthy to loose."

[28]These things were done in Bethabara[a] beyond the Jordan, where John was baptizing.

The Lamb of God

[29]The next day John saw Jesus coming toward him, and said, "Behold! The Lamb of God who takes away the sin of the world! [30]This is He of whom I said, 'After me comes a Man who is preferred before me, for He was before me.' [31]I did not know Him; but that He should be revealed to Israel, therefore I came baptizing with water."

[32]And John bore witness, saying, "I saw the Spirit descending from heaven like a dove, and He remained upon Him. [33]I did not know Him, but He who sent me to baptize with water said

---

1:5 [a]Or *overcome* **1:9** [a]Or *That was the true Light which, coming into the world, gives light to every man.* **1:11** [a]That is, His own things or domain [b]That is, His own people **1:16** [a]NU-Text reads *For.* **1:18** [a]NU-Text reads *only begotten God.* **1:23** [a]Isaiah 40:3 **1:28** [a]NU-Text and M-Text read *Bethany.*

to me, 'Upon whom you see the Spirit descending, and remaining on Him, this is He who baptizes with the Holy Spirit.' [34]And I have seen and testified that this is the Son of God."

The First Disciples

[35]Again, the next day, John stood with two of his disciples. [36]And looking at Jesus as He walked, he said, "Behold the Lamb of God!"

[37]The two disciples heard him speak, and they followed Jesus. [38]Then Jesus turned, and seeing them following, said to them, "What do you seek?"

They said to Him, "Rabbi" (which is to say, when translated, Teacher), "where are You staying?"

[39]He said to them, "Come and see." They came and saw where He was staying, and remained with Him that day (now it was about the tenth hour).

[40]One of the two who heard John *speak,* and followed Him, was Andrew, Simon Peter's brother. [41]He first found his own brother Simon, and said to him, "We have found the Messiah" (which is translated, the Christ). [42]And he brought him to Jesus.

Now when Jesus looked at him, He said, "You are Simon the son of Jonah.[a] You shall be called Cephas" (which is translated, A Stone).

Philip and Nathanael

[43]The following day Jesus wanted to go to Galilee, and He found Philip and said to him, "Follow Me." [44]Now Philip was from Bethsaida, the city of Andrew and Peter. [45]Philip found Nathanael and said to him, "We have found Him of whom Moses in the law, and also the prophets, wrote—Jesus of Nazareth, the son of Joseph."

[46]And Nathanael said to him, "Can anything good come out of Nazareth?"

Philip said to him, "Come and see."

[47]Jesus saw Nathanael coming toward Him, and said of him, "Behold, an Israelite indeed, in whom is no deceit!"

[48]Nathanael said to Him, "How do You know me?"

Jesus answered and said to him, "Before Philip called you, when you were under the fig tree, I saw you."

[49]Nathanael answered and said to Him, "Rabbi, You are the Son of God! You are the King of Israel!"

[50]Jesus answered and said to him, "Because I said to you, 'I saw you under the fig tree,' do you believe? You will see greater things than these." [51]And He said to him, "Most assuredly, I say to you, hereafter[a] you shall see heaven open, and the angels of God ascending and descending upon the Son of Man."

Water Turned to Wine

2 On the third day there was a wedding in Cana of Galilee, and the mother of Jesus was there. [2]Now both Jesus and His disciples were invited to the wedding. [3]And when they ran out of wine, the mother of Jesus said to Him, "They have no wine."

[4]Jesus said to her, "Woman, what does your concern have to do with Me? My hour has not yet come."

[5]His mother said to the servants, "Whatever He says to you, do *it.*"

[6]Now there were set there six waterpots of stone, according to the manner of purification of the Jews, containing twenty or thirty gallons apiece. [7]Jesus said to them, "Fill the waterpots with water." And they filled them up to the brim. [8]And He said to them, "Draw *some* out now, and take *it* to the master of the feast." And they took *it.* [9]When the master of the feast had tasted the water that was made wine, and did not know where it came from (but the servants who had drawn the water knew), the master of the feast called the bridegroom. [10]And he said to him, "Every man at the beginning sets out the good wine, and when the *guests* have well drunk, then the inferior. You have kept the good wine until now!"

[11]This beginning of signs Jesus did in Cana of Galilee, and manifested His glory; and His disciples believed in Him.

[12]After this He went down to Capernaum, He, His mother, His brothers, and His disciples; and they did not stay there many days.

Jesus Cleanses the Temple

[13]Now the Passover of the Jews was at hand, and Jesus went up to Jerusalem. [14]And He found in the temple those who sold oxen and sheep and doves, and the money changers doing business. [15]When He had made a whip of cords, He drove them all out of the temple, with the sheep and the oxen, and poured out the changers' money and overturned the tables. [16]And He said to those who sold doves, "Take these things away! Do not make My Father's house a house of merchandise!" [17]Then His disciples remembered that it was written, *Zeal for Your house has eaten[a] Me up."*[b]

1:42 [a]NU-Text reads *John.* **1:51** [a]NU-Text omits *hereafter.* **2:17** [a]NU-Text and M-Text read *will eat.* [b]Psalm 69:9

The Law of Buy-In: The Disciples Embrace Jesus' Vision

(John 2:11)

The apostle John gives Jesus eight titles in his first chapter alone:

- the Word (v. 1)
- God (v. 1)
- Life (v. 4)
- Light (v. 7)
- Fullness (v. 16)
- Christ (v. 17)
- LORD (v. 23)
- Lamb of God (v. 29)

John 2 tells how Jesus' disciples embrace who He is after He performs His first miracle at the wedding in Cana (v. 11). They bought in to His identity before they bought in to His cause.

This is how the Law of Buy-In works. People buy in to the leader before they accept the vision. Once they believe in the leader, they generally go with the vision. Once the disciples recognized Jesus' identity, they felt ready to do whatever He called them to do. The leader's credibility precedes the leader's plan.

Courage: Jesus Did the Unpopular to Accomplish the Unforgettable

(John 2:13–21)

When Jesus threw the money changers out of the temple, everyone understood this loving "Shepherd" was dead serious about justice and righteousness. He could *lead* people because He didn't *need* people. His courage came from His sufficiency in His Father, which allowed Him to carry out unpopular tasks and leave His unforgettable mark.

---

¹⁸So the Jews answered and said to Him, "What sign do You show to us, since You do these things?"

¹⁹Jesus answered and said to them, "Destroy this temple, and in three days I will raise it up."

²⁰Then the Jews said, "It has taken forty-six years to build this temple, and will You raise it up in three days?"

²¹But He was speaking of the temple of His body. ²²Therefore, when He had risen from the dead, His disciples remembered that He had said this to them;ᵃ and they believed the Scripture and the word which Jesus had said.

The Discerner of Hearts

²³Now when He was in Jerusalem at the Passover, during the feast, many believed in His name when they saw the signs which He did. ²⁴But Jesus did not commit Himself to them, because He knew all *men,* ²⁵and had no need that anyone should testify of man, for He knew what was in man.

The New Birth

3 There was a man of the Pharisees named Nicodemus, a ruler of the Jews. ²This man came to Jesus by night and said to Him, "Rabbi, we know that You are a teacher come from God; for no one can do these signs that You do unless God is with him."

³Jesus answered and said to him, "Most assuredly, I say to you, unless one is born again, he cannot see the kingdom of God."

⁴Nicodemus said to Him, "How can a man be born when he is old? Can he enter a second time into his mother's womb and be born?"

⁵Jesus answered, "Most assuredly, I say to you, unless one is born of water and the Spirit, he cannot enter the kingdom of God. ⁶That which is born of the flesh is flesh, and that which is born of the Spirit is spirit. ⁷Do not marvel that I said to you, 'You must be born again.' ⁸The wind blows where it wishes, and you hear the sound of it, but cannot tell where it comes from and where it goes. So is everyone who is born of the Spirit."

⁹Nicodemus answered and said to Him, "How can these things be?"

¹⁰Jesus answered and said to him, "Are you the teacher of Israel, and do not know these things? ¹¹Most assuredly, I say to you, We speak what We know and testify what We have seen, and you do not receive Our witness. ¹²If I have told you earthly things and you do not believe, how will you believe if I tell you heavenly things? ¹³No one has ascended to heaven but He who came down from heaven, *that is,* the Son of

---

2:22 ᵃNU-Text and M-Text omit *to them.*

New Testament Pictures of a Leader

(John 2:13–22)

While at times Jesus could act in ways that seemed harsh—as when He drove out the money changers and confronted the Jews—His short ministry also provides us with some crucial relational pictures of a leader. By looking at the entire record, we see both the tough and tender sides of Christ's leadership. Consider several of the New Testament's greatest pictures of leadership:

1. *Father and Child:* This is a warm and loving relationship in which the leader nurtures and respects his or her followers. "You know how we exhorted, and comforted, and charged every one of you, as a father does his own children," says the apostle Paul (1 Thess. 2:11).

2. *Husband and Wife:* This is a supportive, covenant relationship in which the leader shows love and commitment. "I am jealous for you with godly jealousy. For I have betrothed you to one husband . . . to Christ," says Paul to the Corinthians (2 Cor. 11:2).

3. *Head and Body:* This is a picture of the governing, protecting relationship in which the leader gives direction. "Speaking the truth in love," writes Paul, "may [we] grow up in all things into Him who is the head—Christ—from whom the whole body, joined and knit together by what every joint supplies, according to the effective working by which every part does its share" (Eph. 4:15, 16).

4. *Vine and Branches:* This is a picture of the leader as a source of nourishment. The leader offers provision. "I am the vine, you are the branches," says Jesus. "He who abides in Me, and I in him, bears much fruit" (John 15:5).

5. *King and Citizens:* This is a picture of wisdom and influence. The leader guides the people. "You are no longer strangers and foreigners, but fellow citizens with the saints and members of the household of God" (Eph. 2:19).

6. *Potter and Clay:* This is a picture of responsibility and surrender. The leader develops the people. "Does not the potter have power over the clay, from the same lump to make one vessel for honor and another for dishonor?" (Rom. 9:21).

7. *Vinedresser and Vineyard:* This is a picture of a farmer who prunes and cares for his own. The leader disciplines the people. "Every branch that bears fruit He prunes, that it may bear more fruit" (John 15:2).

8. *Captain and Army:* This is a picture of authority and training. The leader prepares the troops for battle. "You therefore must endure hardship as a good soldier of Jesus Christ. No one engaged in warfare entangles himself with the affairs of this life" (2 Tim. 2:3, 4).

9. *Creator and Creature:* This is a picture of power and submission. The leader reproduces himself in others. "Put on the new man who is renewed in knowledge according to the image of Him who created him" (Col. 3:10).

10. *Prophet and People:* This is a picture of anointing and spiritual power. The leader corrects and envisions. "A certain prophet named Agabus came down from Judea. When he had come to us, he . . . said, 'Thus says the Holy Spirit . . .' " (Acts 21:10).

11. *Shepherd and Sheep:* This is a picture of warmth and beauty. The leader guides and protects his sheep. "I am the good shepherd. The good shepherd gives His life for the sheep" (John 10:11).

12. *Priest and Worshipers:* This is a picture of godliness and spiritual intimacy. The leader connects people with God. "You are a chosen generation, a royal priesthood, a holy nation, His own special people, that you may proclaim the praises of Him who called you out of darkness into His marvelous light" (1 Pet. 2:9).

As you read through Jesus' life and the rest of the New Testament, watch for these metaphors. They provide wonderful pictures of the kind of leadership roles God wants us to fulfill.

Man who is in heaven.[a] [14]And as Moses lifted up the serpent in the wilderness, even so must the Son of Man be lifted up, [15]that whoever believes in Him should not perish but[a] have eternal life. [16]For God so loved the world that He gave His only begotten Son, that whoever believes in Him should not perish but have everlasting life. [17]For God did not send His Son into the world to condemn the world, but that the world through Him might be saved.

[18]"He who believes in Him is not condemned; but he who does not believe is condemned already, because he has not believed in the name of the only begotten Son of God. [19]And this is the condemnation, that the light has come into the world, and men loved darkness rather than light, because their deeds were evil. [20]For everyone practicing evil hates the light and does not come to the light, lest his deeds should be exposed. [21]But he who does the truth comes to the light, that his deeds may be clearly seen, that they have been done in God."

John the Baptist Exalts Christ

[22]After these things Jesus and His disciples came into the land of Judea, and there He remained with them and baptized. [23]Now John also was baptizing in Aenon near Salim, because there

---

Communication: Jesus Reduced His Message to One Memorable Phrase
(John 3:16)

In one verse of 25 words, Jesus explained the essence of His mission. Effective leaders know the importance of compressing their complex activities into an easily memorized sentence. This is a secret of good communication. Make it short! Make it simple! Make it significant! Make it sizzle!

---

was much water there. And they came and were baptized. [24]For John had not yet been thrown into prison.

[25]Then there arose a dispute between *some* of John's disciples and the Jews about purification. [26]And they came to John and said to him, "Rabbi, He who was with you beyond the

---

3:13 [a]NU-Text omits *who is in heaven.*
3:15 [a]NU-Text omits *not perish but.*

JESUS   GOD'S SON, GOD'S LEADER
(John 3:1–21)

PROFILE IN LEADERSHIP

A Pharisee named Nicodemus recognized something special about Jesus, something that set Him apart from the many other religious types he had met. Jesus seemed to possess a unique authority in everything He did or said. So this zealous leader rightly confessed to Jesus, "No one can do these signs that You do unless God is with him" (John 3:2). With that statement, Nicodemus showed how close he had come to understanding the true identity of Jesus Christ.

In His conversation with Nicodemus—and in the encounter with the Samaritan woman at the well and in a series of miracles and teachings that followed (John 4—6)—Jesus established Himself in word and in deed as the One God had sent to be the Savior of the world.

While Nicodemus recognized that God had sent Jesus, there was much more to it than that. Christ wasn't just sent *of* God; He *was* God in the flesh, the Son of the true and living God.

Since none of us can claim Jesus' lofty heritage, none of us can exactly match the kind of leadership expressed by the Lord Jesus Christ when He walked the earth. But we *can* look to Him as our model and example of perfect leadership, and rely on the Holy Spirit (as He did) to empower our leadership.

Jordan, to whom you have testified—behold, He is baptizing, and all are coming to Him!"

[27]John answered and said, "A man can receive nothing unless it has been given to him from heaven. [28]You yourselves bear me witness, that I said, 'I am not the Christ,' but, 'I have been sent before Him.' [29]He who has the bride is the bridegroom; but the friend of the bridegroom, who stands and hears him, rejoices greatly because of the bridegroom's voice. Therefore this joy of mine is fulfilled. [30]He must increase, but I *must* decrease. [31]He who comes from above is above all; he who is of the earth is earthly and speaks of the earth. He who comes from heaven is above all. [32]And what He has seen and heard, that He testifies; and no one receives His testimony. [33]He who has received His testimony has certified that God is true. [34]For He whom God has sent speaks the words of God, for God does not give the Spirit by measure. [35]The Father loves the Son, and has given all things into His hand. [36]He who believes in the Son has everlasting life; and he who does not believe the Son shall not see life, but the wrath of God abides on him."

A Samaritan Woman Meets Her Messiah

4 Therefore, when the Lord knew that the Pharisees had heard that Jesus made and baptized more disciples than John [2](though Jesus Himself did not baptize, but His disciples), [3]He left Judea and departed again to Galilee. [4]But He needed to go through Samaria.

[5]So He came to a city of Samaria which is called Sychar, near the plot of ground that Jacob gave to his son Joseph. [6]Now Jacob's well was there. Jesus therefore, being wearied from *His* journey, sat thus by the well. It was about the sixth hour.

[7]A woman of Samaria came to draw water. Jesus said to her, "Give Me a drink." [8]For His disciples had gone away into the city to buy food.

[9]Then the woman of Samaria said to Him, "How is it that You, being a Jew, ask a drink from me, a Samaritan woman?" For Jews have no dealings with Samaritans.

[10]Jesus answered and said to her, "If you knew the gift of God, and who it is who says to you, 'Give Me a drink,' you would have asked Him, and He would have given you living water."

The Law of Connection:
Jesus Connects with a Woman, Changes a City

(John 4:1–26)

We don't even know her name. Other Jews wouldn't even speak with her. Yet because Jesus was different, He spoke with this Samaritan woman—a snubbed gender within a despised race. Through this personal connection, God reached an entire city. We learn at least seven principles from Jesus' leadership in John 4:

1. *Leaders initiate the contact* (vv. 1–7).
   Jesus spoke first. He didn't isolate Himself even from "undesirables."

2. *Leaders establish common ground* (vv. 7, 8).
   He connected with her about a familiar interest: water.

3. *Leaders listen and allow others to speak* (v. 9).
   He knew people like to hear their own voices most of all.

4. *Leaders arouse interest* (vv. 10–15).
   Jesus built a verbal bridge by making her thirsty for something more than water.

5. *Leaders take others only so far as they are ready to go* (vv. 16–19).
   Jesus knew He mustn't go too far. He said enough to make her hungry for more.

6. *Leaders accept others where they are* (vv. 17, 18).
   Jesus knew her lifestyle, but never condemned her for it.

7. *Leaders stick with the key issues* (vv. 20–24).
   He didn't allow her to get distracted. He wouldn't divert the focus from the real issue.

8. *Leaders communicate issues directly and simply* (vv. 25, 26).
   Jesus revealed His identity in clear and simple terms.

[11]The woman said to Him, "Sir, You have nothing to draw with, and the well is deep. Where then do You get that living water? [12]Are You greater than our father Jacob, who gave us the well, and drank from it himself, as well as his sons and his livestock?"

[13]Jesus answered and said to her, "Whoever drinks of this water will thirst again, [14]but whoever drinks of the water that I shall give him will never thirst. But the water that I shall give him will become in him a fountain of water springing up into everlasting life."

[15]The woman said to Him, "Sir, give me this water, that I may not thirst, nor come here to draw."

[16]Jesus said to her, "Go, call your husband, and come here."

[17]The woman answered and said, "I have no husband."

Jesus said to her, "You have well said, 'I have no husband,' [18]for you have had five husbands, and the one whom you now have is not your husband; in that you spoke truly."

[19]The woman said to Him, "Sir, I perceive that You are a prophet. [20]Our fathers worshiped on this mountain, and you *Jews* say that in Jerusalem is the place where one ought to worship."

[21]Jesus said to her, "Woman, believe Me, the hour is coming when you will neither on this mountain, nor in Jerusalem, worship the Father. [22]You worship what you do not know; we know what we worship, for salvation is of the Jews. [23]But the hour is coming, and now is, when the true worshipers will worship the Father in spirit and truth; for the Father is seeking such to worship Him. [24]God *is* Spirit, and those who worship Him must worship in spirit and truth."

[25]The woman said to Him, "I know that Messiah is coming" (who is called Christ). "When He comes, He will tell us all things."

[26]Jesus said to her, "I who speak to you am *He.*"

The Whitened Harvest

[27]And at this *point* His disciples came, and they marveled that He talked with a woman; yet no one said, "What do You seek?" or, "Why are You talking with her?"

[28]The woman then left her waterpot, went her way into the city, and said to the men, [29]"Come, see a Man who told me all things that I ever did. Could this be the Christ?" [30]Then they went out of the city and came to Him.

[31]In the meantime His disciples urged Him, saying, "Rabbi, eat."

[32]But He said to them, "I have food to eat of which you do not know."

[33]Therefore the disciples said to one another, "Has anyone brought Him *anything* to eat?"

[34]Jesus said to them, "My food is to do the will of Him who sent Me, and to finish His work. [35]Do you not say, 'There are still four months and *then* comes the harvest'? Behold, I say to you, lift up your eyes and look at the fields, for they are already white for harvest! [36]And he who reaps receives wages, and gathers fruit for eternal life, that both he who sows and he who reaps may rejoice together. [37]For in this the saying is true: 'One sows and another reaps.' [38]I sent you to reap that for which you have not labored; others have labored, and you have entered into their labors."

The Savior of the World

[39]And many of the Samaritans of that city believed in Him because of the word of the woman who testified, "He told me all that I *ever* did." [40]So when the Samaritans had come to Him, they urged Him to stay with them; and He stayed there two days. [41]And many more believed because of His own word.

[42]Then they said to the woman, "Now we believe, not because of what you said, for we ourselves have heard *Him* and we know that this is indeed the Christ,[a] the Savior of the world."

Welcome at Galilee

[43]Now after the two days He departed from there and went to Galilee. [44]For Jesus Himself testified that a prophet has no honor in his own country. [45]So when He came to Galilee, the Galileans received Him, having seen all the things He did in Jerusalem at the feast; for they also had gone to the feast.

A Nobleman's Son Healed

[46]So Jesus came again to Cana of Galilee where He had made the water wine. And there was a certain nobleman whose son was sick at Capernaum. [47]When he heard that Jesus had come out of Judea into Galilee, he went to Him and implored Him to come down and heal his son, for he was at the point of death. [48]Then Jesus said to him, "Unless you *people* see signs and wonders, you will by no means believe."

[49]The nobleman said to Him, "Sir, come down before my child dies!"

[50]Jesus said to him, "Go your way; your son lives." So the man believed the word that Jesus

---

4:42 [a]NU-Text omits *the Christ.*

spoke to him, and he went his way. [51]And as he was now going down, his servants met him and told *him,* saying, "Your son lives!"

[52]Then he inquired of them the hour when he got better. And they said to him, "Yesterday at the seventh hour the fever left him." [53]So the father knew that *it was* at the same hour in which Jesus said to him, "Your son lives." And he himself believed, and his whole household.

[54]This again *is* the second sign Jesus did when He had come out of Judea into Galilee.

A Man Healed at the Pool of Bethesda

5 After this there was a feast of the Jews, and Jesus went up to Jerusalem. [2]Now there is in Jerusalem by the Sheep *Gate* a pool, which is called in Hebrew, Bethesda,[a] having five porches. [3]In these lay a great multitude of sick people, blind, lame, paralyzed, waiting for the moving of the water. [4]For an angel went down at a certain time into the pool and stirred up the water; then whoever stepped in first, after the stirring of the water, was made well of whatever disease he had.[a] [5]Now a certain man was there who had an infirmity thirty-eight years. [6]When Jesus saw him lying there, and knew that he already had been *in that condition* a long time, He said to him, "Do you want to be made well?"

[7]The sick man answered Him, "Sir, I have no man to put me into the pool when the water is stirred up; but while I am coming, another steps down before me."

[8]Jesus said to him, "Rise, take up your bed and walk." [9]And immediately the man was made well, took up his bed, and walked.

The Law of Solid Ground: Jesus' Credibility Came from Results

(John 5:1–14)

When the Jews confronted Jesus after He healed a man on the Sabbath, He replied that He was working only because His Father was working. In other words, Jesus' credibility came from results, not rhetoric. Leaders practice the Law of Solid Ground when their lives back up their words.

And that day was the Sabbath. [10]The Jews therefore said to him who was cured, "It is the Sabbath; it is not lawful for you to carry your bed."

[11]He answered them, "He who made me well said to me, 'Take up your bed and walk.'"

[12]Then they asked him, "Who is the Man who said to you, 'Take up your bed and walk'?" [13]But the one who was healed did not know who it was, for Jesus had withdrawn, a multitude being in *that* place. [14]Afterward Jesus found him in the temple, and said to him, "See, you have been made well. Sin no more, lest a worse thing come upon you."

[15]The man departed and told the Jews that it was Jesus who had made him well.

Honor the Father and the Son

[16]For this reason the Jews persecuted Jesus, and sought to kill Him,[a] because He had done these things on the Sabbath. [17]But Jesus answered them, "My Father has been working until now, and I have been working."

[18]Therefore the Jews sought all the more to kill Him, because He not only broke the Sabbath, but also said that God was His Father, making Himself equal with God. [19]Then Jesus answered and said to them, "Most assuredly, I say to you, the Son can do nothing of Himself, but what He sees the Father do; for whatever He does, the Son also does in like manner. [20]For the Father loves the Son, and shows Him all things that He Himself does; and He will show Him greater works than these, that you may marvel. [21]For as the Father raises the dead and gives life to *them,* even so the Son gives life to whom He will. [22]For the Father judges no one, but has committed all judgment to the Son, [23]that all should honor the Son just as they honor the Father. He who does not honor the Son does not honor the Father who sent Him.

Life and Judgment Are Through the Son

[24]"Most assuredly, I say to you, he who hears My word and believes in Him who sent Me has everlasting life, and shall not come into judgment, but has passed from death into life. [25]Most assuredly, I say to you, the hour is coming, and now is, when the dead will hear the voice of the Son of God; and those who hear will live. [26]For as the Father has life in Himself, so He has

---

5:2 [a]NU-Text reads *Bethzatha.* **5:4** [a]NU-Text omits *waiting for the moving of the water* at the end of verse 3, and all of verse 4. **5:16** [a]NU-Text omits *and sought to kill Him.*

granted the Son to have life in Himself, [27]and has given Him authority to execute judgment also, because He is the Son of Man. [28]Do not marvel at this; for the hour is coming in which all who are in the graves will hear His voice [29]and come forth—those who have done good, to the resurrection of life, and those who have done evil, to the resurrection of condemnation. [30]I can of Myself do nothing. As I hear, I judge; and My judgment is righteous, because I do not seek My own will but the will of the Father who sent Me.

The Fourfold Witness

[31]"If I bear witness of Myself, My witness is not true. [32]There is another who bears witness of Me, and I know that the witness which He witnesses of Me is true. [33]You have sent to John, and he has borne witness to the truth. [34]Yet I do not receive testimony from man, but I say these things that you may be saved. [35]He was the burning and shining lamp, and you were willing for a time to rejoice in his light. [36]But I have a greater witness than John's; for the works which the Father has given Me to finish—the very works that I do—bear witness of Me, that the Father has sent Me. [37]And the Father Himself, who sent Me, has testified of Me. You have neither heard His voice at any time, nor seen His form. [38]But you do not have His word abiding in you, because whom He sent, Him you do not believe. [39]You search the Scriptures, for in them you think you have eternal life; and these are they which testify of Me. [40]But you are not willing to come to Me that you may have life.

[41]"I do not receive honor from men. [42]But I know you, that you do not have the love of God in you. [43]I have come in My Father's name, and you do not receive Me; if another comes in his own name, him you will receive. [44]How can you believe, who receive honor from one another, and do not seek the honor that *comes* from the only God? [45]Do not think that I shall accuse you to the Father; there is *one* who accuses you—Moses, in whom you trust. [46]For if you believed Moses, you would believe Me; for he wrote about Me. [47]But if you do not believe his writings, how will you believe My words?"

Feeding the Five Thousand

6 After these things Jesus went over the Sea of Galilee, which is *the Sea* of Tiberias. [2]Then a great multitude followed Him, because they saw His signs which He performed on those who were diseased. [3]And Jesus went up on the mountain, and there He sat with His disciples. [4]Now the Passover, a feast of the Jews, was

near. [5]Then Jesus lifted up *His* eyes, and seeing a great multitude coming toward Him, He said to Philip, "Where shall we buy bread, that these may eat?" [6]But this He said to test him, for He Himself knew what He would do.

[7]Philip answered Him, "Two hundred denarii worth of bread is not sufficient for them, that every one of them may have a little."

[8]One of His disciples, Andrew, Simon Peter's brother, said to Him, [9]"There is a lad here who has five barley loaves and two small fish, but what are they among so many?"

[10]Then Jesus said, "Make the people sit down." Now there was much grass in the place. So the men sat down, in number about five thousand. [11]And Jesus took the loaves, and when He had given thanks He distributed *them* to the disciples, and the disciples[a] to those sitting down; and likewise of the fish, as much as they wanted. [12]So when they were filled, He said to His disciples, "Gather up the fragments that remain, so that nothing is lost." [13]Therefore they gathered *them* up, and filled twelve baskets with the fragments of the five barley loaves which were left over by those who had eaten. [14]Then those men, when they had seen the sign that Jesus did, said, "This is truly the Prophet who is to come into the world."

Jesus Walks on the Sea

[15]Therefore when Jesus perceived that they were about to come and take Him by force to make Him king, He departed again to the mountain by Himself alone.

[16]Now when evening came, His disciples went down to the sea, [17]got into the boat, and went over the sea toward Capernaum. And it was already dark, and Jesus had not come to them. [18]Then the sea arose because a great wind was blowing. [19]So when they had rowed about three or four miles,[a] they saw Jesus walking on the sea and drawing near the boat; and they were afraid. [20]But He said to them, "It is I; do not be afraid." [21]Then they willingly received Him into the boat, and immediately the boat was at the land where they were going.

The Bread from Heaven

[22]On the following day, when the people who were standing on the other side of the sea saw that there was no other boat there, except that one which His disciples had entered,[a] and

---

6:11 [a]NU-Text omits *to the disciples, and the disciples.*
6:19 [a]Literally *twenty-five or thirty stadia* **6:22** [a]NU-Text omits *that* and *which His disciples had entered.*

The Law of Reproduction: A Lesson in Servanthood

(John 6:3–14)

As Jesus fed five thousand people with one small basket of food, the disciples learned another lesson in serving others. Jesus allowed the disciples to participate in this miracle; they served the food as it multiplied.

Through this experience, Jesus was beginning to reproduce His ministry in His followers. He taught that a pupil becomes like his teacher (Luke 6:40). Author Frank Damazio notes how reproduction occurs from Father, to Son, to leader:

From the Father	To the Son	To the Leader
My Father is working (John 5:17–19).	I myself am working (John 5:17; 9:4).	Leaders are to do the work (Acts 6:4; Eph. 4:12).
The Father judges (John 8:16).	I judge (John 8:16).	Leaders must judge (1 Cor. 6:1–6).
God is light (1 John 1:5).	I am the light of the world (John 8:12; 12:46).	Leaders are light and are to walk in the light (Matt. 5:14; 1 John 1:7).
The Father teaches (John 8:28).	The Son teaches (John 8:28; Acts 1:1).	Leaders are teachers (Acts 5:42; 1 Tim. 3:2; 4:11).
The Father gave His Son (John 3:16).	The Son gave His life (John 10:11).	Leaders lay down their lives (1 John 3:16).
The Father is perfect.	The Son is perfect.	Leaders are to be perfect and set the example (Matt. 5:48; 1 Cor. 3:18; Col. 3:10).

that Jesus had not entered the boat with His disciples, but His disciples had gone away alone— [23]however, other boats came from Tiberias, near the place where they ate bread after the Lord had given thanks— [24]when the people therefore saw that Jesus was not there, nor His disciples, they also got into boats and came to Capernaum, seeking Jesus. [25]And when they found Him on the other side of the sea, they said to Him, "Rabbi, when did You come here?"

[26]Jesus answered them and said, "Most assuredly, I say to you, you seek Me, not because you saw the signs, but because you ate of the loaves and were filled. [27]Do not labor for the food which perishes, but for the food which endures to everlasting life, which the Son of Man will give you, because God the Father has set His seal on Him."

[28]Then they said to Him, "What shall we do, that we may work the works of God?"

[29]Jesus answered and said to them, "This is the work of God, that you believe in Him whom He sent."

[30]Therefore they said to Him, "What sign will You perform then, that we may see it and believe

You? What work will You do? [31]Our fathers ate the manna in the desert; as it is written, *'He gave them bread from heaven to eat.'*[a]

[32]Then Jesus said to them, "Most assuredly, I say to you, Moses did not give you the bread from heaven, but My Father gives you the true bread from heaven. [33]For the bread of God is He who comes down from heaven and gives life to the world."

[34]Then they said to Him, "Lord, give us this bread always."

[35]And Jesus said to them, "I am the bread of life. He who comes to Me shall never hunger, and he who believes in Me shall never thirst. [36]But I said to you that you have seen Me and yet do not believe. [37]All that the Father gives Me will come to Me, and the one who comes to Me I will by no means cast out. [38]For I have come down from heaven, not to do My own will, but the will of Him who sent Me. [39]This is the will of the Father who sent Me, that of all He has given Me I should lose nothing, but should raise it up at the last day. [40]And this is the will of Him

6:31 [a]Exodus 16:4; Nehemiah 9:15; Psalm 78:24

who sent Me, that everyone who sees the Son and believes in Him may have everlasting life; and I will raise him up at the last day."

Rejected by His Own

[41]The Jews then complained about Him, because He said, "I am the bread which came down from heaven." [42]And they said, "Is not this Jesus, the son of Joseph, whose father and mother we know? How is it then that He says, 'I have come down from heaven'?"

Commitment: Jesus Clarified and Purified

(John 6:41–65)

Jesus never pursued huge crowds. In fact, He often had to find ways to escape them! To do so, Jesus clarified the level of commitment He expected from followers. Two things always happen when a leader calls for commitment: He clarifies where people stand, and he purifies the organization.

---

[43]Jesus therefore answered and said to them, "Do not murmur among yourselves. [44]No one can come to Me unless the Father who sent Me draws him; and I will raise him up at the last day. [45]It is written in the prophets, '*And they shall all be taught by God.*'[a] Therefore everyone who has heard and learned[b] from the Father comes to Me. [46]Not that anyone has seen the Father, except He who is from God; He has seen the Father. [47]Most assuredly, I say to you, he who believes in Me[a] has everlasting life. [48]I am the bread of life. [49]Your fathers ate the manna in the wilderness, and are dead. [50]This is the bread which comes down from heaven, that one may eat of it and not die. [51]I am the living bread which came down from heaven. If anyone eats of this bread, he will live forever; and the bread that I shall give is My flesh, which I shall give for the life of the world."

[52]The Jews therefore quarreled among themselves, saying, "How can this Man give us *His* flesh to eat?"

[53]Then Jesus said to them, "Most assuredly, I say to you, unless you eat the flesh of the Son of Man and drink His blood, you have no life in you. [54]Whoever eats My flesh and drinks My blood has eternal life, and I will raise him up at the last day. [55]For My flesh is food indeed,[a] and

My blood is drink indeed. [56]He who eats My flesh and drinks My blood abides in Me, and I in him. [57]As the living Father sent Me, and I live because of the Father, so he who feeds on Me will live because of Me. [58]This is the bread which came down from heaven—not as your fathers ate the manna, and are dead. He who eats this bread will live forever."

[59]These things He said in the synagogue as He taught in Capernaum.

Many Disciples Turn Away

[60]Therefore many of His disciples, when they heard *this,* said, "This is a hard saying; who can understand it?"

[61]When Jesus knew in Himself that His disciples complained about this, He said to them, "Does this offend you? [62]*What* then if you should see the Son of Man ascend where He was before? [63]It is the Spirit who gives life; the flesh profits nothing. The words that I speak to you are spirit, and *they* are life. [64]But there are some of you who do not believe." For Jesus knew from the beginning who they were who did not believe, and who would betray Him. [65]And He said, "Therefore I have said to you that no one can come to Me unless it has been granted to him by My Father."

[66]From that *time* many of His disciples went back and walked with Him no more. [67]Then Jesus said to the twelve, "Do you also want to go away?"

[68]But Simon Peter answered Him, "Lord, to whom shall we go? You have the words of eternal life. [69]Also we have come to believe and know that You are the Christ, the Son of the living God."[a]

[70]Jesus answered them, "Did I not choose you, the twelve, and one of you is a devil?" [71]He spoke of Judas Iscariot, *the son* of Simon, for it was he who would betray Him, being one of the twelve.

Jesus' Brothers Disbelieve

7 After these things Jesus walked in Galilee; for He did not want to walk in Judea, because the Jews[a] sought to kill Him. [2]Now the Jews' Feast of Tabernacles was at hand. [3]His brothers therefore said to Him, "Depart from here and go into Judea, that Your disciples also

---

6:45 [a]Isaiah 54:13 [b]M-Text reads *hears and has learned.* **6:47** [a]NU-Text omits *in Me.*
6:55 [a]NU-Text reads *true food* and *true drink.*
6:69 [a]NU-Text reads *You are the Holy One of God.*
7:1 [a]That is, the ruling authorities

may see the works that You are doing. [4]For no one does anything in secret while he himself seeks to be known openly. If You do these things, show Yourself to the world." [5]For even His brothers did not believe in Him.

[6]Then Jesus said to them, "My time has not yet come, but your time is always ready. [7]The world cannot hate you, but it hates Me because I testify of it that its works are evil. [8]You go up to this feast. I am not yet[a] going up to this feast, for My time has not yet fully come." [9]When He had said these things to them, He remained in Galilee.

The Heavenly Scholar

[10]But when His brothers had gone up, then He also went up to the feast, not openly, but as it were in secret. [11]Then the Jews sought Him at the feast, and said, "Where is He?" [12]And there was much complaining among the people concerning Him. Some said, "He is good"; others said, "No, on the contrary, He deceives the people." [13]However, no one spoke openly of Him for fear of the Jews.

[14]Now about the middle of the feast Jesus went up into the temple and taught. [15]And the Jews marveled, saying, "How does this Man know letters, having never studied?"

[16]Jesus[a] answered them and said, "My doctrine is not Mine, but His who sent Me. [17]If anyone wills to do His will, he shall know concerning the doctrine, whether it is from God or whether I speak on My own authority. [18]He who speaks from himself seeks his own glory; but He who seeks the glory of the One who sent Him is true, and no unrighteousness is in Him. [19]Did not Moses give you the law, yet none of you keeps the law? Why do you seek to kill Me?"

[20]The people answered and said, "You have a demon. Who is seeking to kill You?"

[21]Jesus answered and said to them, "I did one work, and you all marvel. [22]Moses therefore gave you circumcision (not that it is from Moses, but from the fathers), and you circumcise a man on the Sabbath. [23]If a man receives circumcision on the Sabbath, so that the law of Moses should not be broken, are you angry with Me because I made a man completely well on the Sabbath? [24]Do not judge according to appearance, but judge with righteous judgment."

Could This Be the Christ?

[25]Now some of them from Jerusalem said, "Is this not He whom they seek to kill? [26]But look! He speaks boldly, and they say nothing to Him. Do the rulers know indeed that this is truly[a] the Christ? [27]However, we know where this Man is from; but when the Christ comes, no one knows where He is from."

[28]Then Jesus cried out, as He taught in the temple, saying, "You both know Me, and you know where I am from; and I have not come of Myself, but He who sent Me is true, whom you do not know. [29]But[a] I know Him, for I am from Him, and He sent Me."

[30]Therefore they sought to take Him; but no one laid a hand on Him, because His hour had not yet come. [31]And many of the people believed in Him, and said, "When the Christ comes, will He do more signs than these which this Man has done?"

Jesus and the Religious Leaders

[32]The Pharisees heard the crowd murmuring these things concerning Him, and the Pharisees and the chief priests sent officers to take Him. [33]Then Jesus said to them,[a] "I shall be with you a little while longer, and then I go to Him who sent Me. [34]You will seek Me and not find Me, and where I am you cannot come."

[35]Then the Jews said among themselves, "Where does He intend to go that we shall not find Him? Does He intend to go to the Dispersion among the Greeks and teach the Greeks? [36]What is this thing that He said, 'You will seek Me and not find Me, and where I am you cannot come'?"

The Promise of the Holy Spirit

[37]On the last day, that great day of the feast, Jesus stood and cried out, saying, "If anyone thirsts, let him come to Me and drink. [38]He who believes in Me, as the Scripture has said, out of his heart will flow rivers of living water." [39]But this He spoke concerning the Spirit, whom those believing[a] in Him would receive; for the Holy[b] Spirit was not yet given, because Jesus was not yet glorified.

Who Is He?

[40]Therefore many[a] from the crowd, when they heard this saying, said, "Truly this is the Prophet." [41]Others said, "This is the Christ."

But some said, "Will the Christ come out of

7:8 [a]NU-Text omits yet. **7:16** [a]NU-Text and M-Text read So Jesus. **7:26** [a]NU-Text omits truly. **7:29** [a]NU-Text and M-Text omit But. **7:33** [a]NU-Text and M-Text omit to them. **7:39** [a]NU-Text reads who believed. [b]NU-Text omits Holy. **7:40** [a]NU-Text reads some.

Galilee? [42]Has not the Scripture said that the Christ comes from the seed of David and from the town of Bethlehem, where David was?" [43]So there was a division among the people because of Him. [44]Now some of them wanted to take Him, but no one laid hands on Him.

Rejected by the Authorities

[45]Then the officers came to the chief priests and Pharisees, who said to them, "Why have you not brought Him?"

[46]The officers answered, "No man ever spoke like this Man!"

[47]Then the Pharisees answered them, "Are you also deceived? [48]Have any of the rulers or the Pharisees believed in Him? [49]But this crowd that does not know the law is accursed."

[50]Nicodemus (he who came to Jesus by night,[a] being one of them) said to them, [51]"Does our law judge a man before it hears him and knows what he is doing?"

[52]They answered and said to him, "Are you also from Galilee? Search and look, for no prophet has arisen[a] out of Galilee."

An Adulteress Faces the Light of the World

[53]And everyone went to his *own* house.[a]

8 But Jesus went to the Mount of Olives. [2]Now early[a] in the morning He came again into the temple, and all the people came to Him; and He sat down and taught them. [3]Then the scribes and Pharisees brought to Him a woman caught in adultery. And when they had set her in the midst, [4]they said to Him, "Teacher, this woman was caught[a] in adultery, in the very act. [5]Now Moses, in the law, commanded[a] us that such should be stoned.[b] But what do You say?"[c] [6]This they said, testing Him, that they might have *something* of which to accuse Him. But Jesus stooped down and wrote on the ground with *His* finger, as though He did not hear.[a]

[7]So when they continued asking Him, He raised Himself up[a] and said to them, "He who is without sin among you, let him throw a stone at her first." [8]And again He stooped down and wrote on the ground. [9]Then those who heard *it,* being convicted by *their* conscience,[a] went out one by one, beginning with the oldest *even* to the last. And Jesus was left alone, and the woman standing in the midst. [10]When Jesus had raised Himself up and saw no one but the woman, He said to her,[a] "Woman, where are those accusers of yours?[b] Has no one condemned you?"

[11]She said, "No one, Lord."

And Jesus said to her, "Neither do I condemn you; go and[a] sin no more."

[12]Then Jesus spoke to them again, saying, "I am the light of the world. He who follows Me shall not walk in darkness, but have the light of life."

Jesus Defends His Self-Witness

[13]The Pharisees therefore said to Him, "You bear witness of Yourself; Your witness is not true."

[14]Jesus answered and said to them, "Even if I bear witness of Myself, My witness is true, for I know where I came from and where I am going; but you do not know where I come from and where I am going. [15]You judge according to the flesh; I judge no one. [16]And yet if I do judge, My judgment is true; for I am not alone, but I *am* with the Father who sent Me. [17]It is also written in your law that the testimony of two men is true. [18]I am One who bears witness of Myself, and the Father who sent Me bears witness of Me."

[19]Then they said to Him, "Where is Your Father?"

Jesus answered, "You know neither Me nor My Father. If you had known Me, you would have known My Father also."

[20]These words Jesus spoke in the treasury, as He taught in the temple; and no one laid hands on Him, for His hour had not yet come.

Jesus Predicts His Departure

[21]Then Jesus said to them again, "I am going away, and you will seek Me, and will die in your sin. Where I go you cannot come."

[22]So the Jews said, "Will He kill Himself, because He says, 'Where I go you cannot come'?"

[23]And He said to them, "You are from beneath; I am from above. You are of this world; I

7:50 [a]NU-Text reads *before.* **7:52** [a]NU-Text reads *is to rise.* **7:53** [a]The words *And everyone* through *sin no more* (8:11) are bracketed by NU-Text as not original. They are present in over 900 manuscripts. **8:2** [a]M-Text reads *very early.* **8:4** [a]M-Text reads *we found this woman.* **8:5** [a]M-Text reads *in our law Moses commanded.* [b]NU-Text and M-Text read *to stone such.* [c]M-Text adds *about her.* **8:6** [a]NU-Text and M-Text omit *as though He did not hear.* **8:7** [a]M-Text reads *He looked up.* **8:9** [a]NU-Text and M-Text omit *being convicted by their conscience.* **8:10** [a]NU-Text omits *and saw no one but the woman;* M-Text reads *He saw her and said.* [b]NU-Text and M-Text omit *of yours.* **8:11** [a]NU-Text and M-Text add *from now on.*

21 QUALITIES

SERVANTHOOD

A Conflict Between Two Worldviews
(John 8:1–59)

John 8 depicts one long showdown between two conflicting worldviews. It begins with the woman caught committing adultery (vv. 1–11), then moves to an argument between Jesus and the Pharisees about their fleshly judgment (vv. 12–30). Next, the Lord explains what it means to truly be born of Abraham (vv. 31–47). Finally, He debates the synagogue leaders about His identity (vv. 48–59).

The flawed worldview of the Jewish leaders contributed greatly to their continuing inability to understand Jesus. They sat in a place of power and feared being displaced. Jesus taught that leadership meant serving others; they sought titles and positions of honor. Jesus taught that leadership meant giving up rights; they took pride in their heritage as sons of Abraham. Jesus told them that their actions revealed their true father—and that's when they had had enough. This Jesus simply was too radical for them.

Still, they couldn't win a debate with Him. He seemed to know the Scriptures better than they did! He was different from them—but much to their disappointment, He was right.

The Pharisees sought power and already competed with the Roman Empire for control of the masses. Not only did they have to deal with their own king, Herod, but they also needed to consider a Roman governor named Pontius Pilate. Consequently, they protected every bit of turf they could.

Does this sound like any leader you know? Someone who fights to maintain manmade traditions and rules? Someone blind to the needs of others and preoccupied with himself or herself? Such leaders stand in contrast to the servant leadership Jesus modeled.

Secular Leadership vs. Spiritual Leadership

Take a moment to contrast the world's leadership model with Jesus' model.

Issue	Secular Leadership	Spiritual Leadership
How to gain influence	Leverage power	Love people (Phil. 2:3–11)
How to possess confidence	Compete and win	Depend on God (2 Cor. 3:4–6)
How to acquire authority	Claim your rights and position	Servanthood (Matt. 20:20–28)
How to grow an organization	Demand of people	Develop people (Acts 19:8–10)
What vision drives you	Temporal gain	Eternal gain (Matt. 6:31–33)
What is success	Overcoming the competition	Obeying the Lord (1 Cor. 4:1–5)
The heart of leadership	A boss	A Father (1 Cor. 4:15)

What does your leadership look like? Are you a Pharisee or servant?

For a positive example of servanthood, see p. 1299.

am not of this world. ²⁴Therefore I said to you that you will die in your sins; for if you do not believe that I am *He,* you will die in your sins."

²⁵Then they said to Him, "Who are You?"

And Jesus said to them, "Just what I have been saying to you from the beginning. ²⁶I have many things to say and to judge concerning you, but He who sent Me is true; and I speak to the world those things which I heard from Him."

²⁷They did not understand that He spoke to them of the Father.

²⁸Then Jesus said to them, "When you lift up the Son of Man, then you will know that I am *He,* and *that* I do nothing of Myself; but as My Father taught Me, I speak these things. ²⁹And He who sent Me is with Me. The Father has not left Me alone, for I always do those things that please Him." ³⁰As He spoke these words, many believed in Him.

The Truth Shall Make You Free

³¹Then Jesus said to those Jews who believed Him, "If you abide in My word, you are My disciples indeed. ³²And you shall know the truth, and the truth shall make you free."

³³They answered Him, "We are Abraham's descendants, and have never been in bondage to anyone. How *can* You say, 'You will be made free'?"

³⁴Jesus answered them, "Most assuredly, I say to you, whoever commits sin is a slave of sin. ³⁵And a slave does not abide in the house forever, *but* a son abides forever. ³⁶Therefore if the Son makes you free, you shall be free indeed.

Abraham's Seed and Satan's

³⁷"I know that you are Abraham's descendants, but you seek to kill Me, because My word has no place in you. ³⁸I speak what I have seen with My Father, and you do what you have seen with ͣ your father."

³⁹They answered and said to Him, "Abraham is our father."

Jesus said to them, "If you were Abraham's children, you would do the works of Abraham. ⁴⁰But now you seek to kill Me, a Man who has told you the truth which I heard from God. Abraham did not do this. ⁴¹You do the deeds of your father."

Then they said to Him, "We were not born of fornication; we have one Father—God."

⁴²Jesus said to them, "If God were your Father, you would love Me, for I proceeded forth and came from God; nor have I come of Myself, but He sent Me. ⁴³Why do you not understand My speech? Because you are not able to listen to My word. ⁴⁴You are of *your* father the devil, and the desires of your father you want to do. He was a murderer from the beginning, and does not stand in the truth, because there is no truth in him. When he speaks a lie, he speaks from his own *resources,* for he is a liar and the father of it. ⁴⁵But because I tell the truth, you do not believe Me. ⁴⁶Which of you convicts Me of sin? And if I tell the truth, why do you not believe Me? ⁴⁷He who is of God hears God's words; therefore you do not hear, because you are not of God."

Before Abraham Was, I AM

⁴⁸Then the Jews answered and said to Him, "Do we not say rightly that You are a Samaritan and have a demon?"

⁴⁹Jesus answered, "I do not have a demon; but I honor My Father, and you dishonor Me. ⁵⁰And I do not seek My *own* glory; there is One who seeks and judges. ⁵¹Most assuredly, I say to you, if anyone keeps My word he shall never see death."

8:38 ͣNU-Text reads *heard from.*

Conflict Management: Confrontation Is the Way to Resolution

(John 8:48–59)

Many times Jesus had to confront opposition among the Pharisees, scribes, and other Jewish leaders. Although Old Testament prophecies called Him the "Prince of Peace," He decided on this day that there could be no peaceful agreement. Jesus stood toe-to-toe with His opponents and tackled the issue head-on—and things quickly got heated.

Sometimes, confrontation is the only way to resolution. What do we learn from Jesus about confrontation? Consider four steps to reach the heart of an issue:

1. Be clear and direct (vv. 48, 49).
2. Don't draw attention to yourself (vv. 49, 50).
3. Lay out the issue and ask for a decision (v. 51).
4. Trust God to justify and reveal the truth (vv. 52–54).

⁵²Then the Jews said to Him, "Now we know that You have a demon! Abraham is dead, and the prophets; and You say, 'If anyone keeps My word he shall never taste death.' ⁵³Are You greater than our father Abraham, who is dead? And the prophets are dead. Who do You make Yourself out to be?"

⁵⁴Jesus answered, "If I honor Myself, My honor is nothing. It is My Father who honors Me, of whom you say that He is yourᵃ God. ⁵⁵Yet you have not known Him, but I know Him. And if I say, 'I do not know Him,' I shall be a liar like you; but I do know Him and keep His word. ⁵⁶Your father Abraham rejoiced to see My day, and he saw *it* and was glad."

⁵⁷Then the Jews said to Him, "You are not yet fifty years old, and have You seen Abraham?"

⁵⁸Jesus said to them, "Most assuredly, I say to you, before Abraham was, I AM."

⁵⁹Then they took up stones to throw at Him; but Jesus hid Himself and went out of the temple,ᵃ going through the midst of them, and so passed by.

A Man Born Blind Receives Sight

9 Now as *Jesus* passed by, He saw a man who was blind from birth. ²And His disciples asked Him, saying, "Rabbi, who sinned, this man or his parents, that he was born blind?"

³Jesus answered, "Neither this man nor his parents sinned, but that the works of God should be revealed in him. ⁴Iᵃ must work the works of Him who sent Me while it is day; *the night is coming when no one can work.* ⁵As long as I am in the world, I am the light of the world."

⁶When He had said these things, He spat on the ground and made clay with the saliva; and He anointed the eyes of the blind man with the clay. ⁷And He said to him, "Go, wash in the pool of Siloam" (which is translated, Sent). So he went and washed, and came back seeing.

⁸Therefore the neighbors and those who previously had seen that he was blindᵃ said, "Is not this he who sat and begged?"

⁹Some said, "This is he." Others *said,* "He is like him."ᵃ

He said, "I am *he.*"

¹⁰Therefore they said to him, "How were your eyes opened?"

¹¹He answered and said, "A Man called Jesus made clay and anointed my eyes and said to me, 'Go to the pool ofᵃ Siloam and wash.' So I went and washed, and I received sight."

¹²Then they said to him, "Where is He?" He said, "I do not know."

The Law of Victory: Jesus Heals a Blind Man and No One Can Deny It

(John 9:1–34)

B y healing the blind man, Jesus silenced His opposition. When they questioned the man who was healed, he could only declare the result: "Whether He is a sinner or not I do not know. One thing I know: that though I was blind, now I see" (John 9:25). Jesus practiced the Law of Victory.

The Pharisees Excommunicate the Healed Man

¹³They brought him who formerly was blind to the Pharisees. ¹⁴Now it was a Sabbath when Jesus made the clay and opened his eyes. ¹⁵Then the Pharisees also asked him again how he had received his sight. He said to them, "He put clay on my eyes, and I washed, and I see."

¹⁶Therefore some of the Pharisees said, "This Man is not from God, because He does not keep the Sabbath."

Others said, "How can a man who is a sinner do such signs?" And there was a division among them.

¹⁷They said to the blind man again, "What do you say about Him because He opened your eyes?"

He said, "He is a prophet."

¹⁸But the Jews did not believe concerning him, that he had been blind and received his sight, until they called the parents of him who had received his sight. ¹⁹And they asked them, saying, "Is this your son, who you say was born blind? How then does he now see?"

²⁰His parents answered them and said, "We know that this is our son, and that he was born blind; ²¹but by what means he now sees we do not know, or who opened his eyes we do not know. He is of age; ask him. He will speak for himself." ²²His parents said these *things* because they feared the Jews, for the Jews had agreed already that if anyone confessed *that* He *was* Christ,

8:54 ᵃNU-Text and M-Text read *our.*
8:59 ᵃNU-Text omits the rest of this verse.
9:4 ᵃNU-Text reads *We.* 9:8 ᵃNU-Text reads *a beggar.* 9:9 ᵃNU-Text reads *"No, but he is like him."*
9:11 ᵃNU-Text omits *the pool of.*

he would be put out of the synagogue. ²³Therefore his parents said, "He is of age; ask him."

²⁴So they again called the man who was blind, and said to him, "Give God the glory! We know that this Man is a sinner."

²⁵He answered and said, "Whether He is a sinner *or not* I do not know. One thing I know: that though I was blind, now I see."

²⁶Then they said to him again, "What did He do to you? How did He open your eyes?"

²⁷He answered them, "I told you already, and you did not listen. Why do you want to hear *it* again? Do you also want to become His disciples?"

²⁸Then they reviled him and said, "You are His disciple, but we are Moses' disciples. ²⁹We know that God spoke to Moses; *as for this fellow,* we do not know where He is from."

³⁰The man answered and said to them, "Why, this is a marvelous thing, that you do not know where He is from; yet He has opened my eyes! ³¹Now we know that God does not hear sinners; but if anyone is a worshiper of God and does His will, He hears him. ³²Since the world began it has been unheard of that anyone opened the eyes of one who was born blind. ³³If this Man were not from God, He could do nothing."

³⁴They answered and said to him, "You were completely born in sins, and are you teaching us?" And they cast him out.

True Vision and True Blindness

³⁵Jesus heard that they had cast him out; and when He had found him, He said to him, "Do you believe in the Son of God?"[a]

³⁶He answered and said, "Who is He, Lord, that I may believe in Him?"

³⁷And Jesus said to him, "You have both seen Him and it is He who is talking with you."

³⁸Then he said, "Lord, I believe!" And he worshiped Him.

³⁹And Jesus said, "For judgment I have come into this world, that those who do not see may see, and that those who see may be made blind."

⁴⁰Then *some* of the Pharisees who were with Him heard these words, and said to Him, "Are we blind also?"

⁴¹Jesus said to them, "If you were blind, you would have no sin; but now you say, 'We see.' Therefore your sin remains.

Jesus the True Shepherd

10 "Most assuredly, I say to you, he who does not enter the sheepfold by the door, but climbs up some other way, the same is a thief and a robber. ²But he who enters by the door is the shepherd of the sheep. ³To him the doorkeeper opens, and the sheep hear

---

9:35 [a]NU-Text reads *Son of Man.*

The Law of Connection: Jesus Relates Like a Shepherd to Sheep

(John 10:1–16)

Jesus describes Himself as the Good Shepherd, a Leader who guides His people as a shepherd leads his sheep. The Old Testament prophets used this metaphor many times, from Moses (Num. 27:15–17) all the way to Ezekiel (Ezek. 34:1–10).

Everyone who wants to lead in the kingdom of God must develop certain heart qualifications. The image of the shepherd best captures the heart of a godly leader: Shepherds are tender, sincere, intimate, loving. They guide, correct, protect, and feed. John contrasts the good shepherd with the hireling. A hireling receives pay for his job, but has no heart for it. He watches out for the sheep until he no longer benefits.

The Hireling	The Shepherd
1. Labors only for money (Matt. 20:7)	1. Labors out of love
2. Has no heart for the sheep (John 10:13)	2. Has a heart for the sheep
3. Leaves when trouble comes (Jer. 46:21)	3. Gives his life for sheep
4. Is unfaithful to his master (John 10:12)	4. Faithfully serves his master
5. Feeds himself, not the sheep (Ezek. 34:3)	5. Feeds the sheep
6. Neglects the sheep (Ezek. 34:3)	6. Tenderly cares for the sheep
7. Drives sheep hard and lacks mercy (Jer. 23:2)	7. Leads the sheep wisely

his voice; and he calls his own sheep by name and leads them out. ⁴And when he brings out his own sheep, he goes before them; and the sheep follow him, for they know his voice. ⁵Yet they will by no means follow a stranger, but will flee from him, for they do not know the voice of strangers." ⁶Jesus used this illustration, but they did not understand the things which He spoke to them.

Jesus the Good Shepherd

⁷Then Jesus said to them again, "Most assuredly, I say to you, I am the door of the sheep. ⁸All who *ever* came before Me[a] are thieves and robbers, but the sheep did not hear them. ⁹I am the door. If anyone enters by Me, he will be saved, and will go in and out and find pasture. ¹⁰The thief does not come except to steal, and to kill, and to destroy. I have come that they may have life, and that they may have *it* more abundantly.

¹¹"I am the good shepherd. The good shepherd gives His life for the sheep. ¹²But a hireling, *he who is* not the shepherd, one who does not own the sheep, sees the wolf coming and leaves the sheep and flees; and the wolf catches the sheep and scatters them. ¹³The hireling flees because he is a hireling and does not care about the sheep. ¹⁴I am the good shepherd; and I know My *sheep,* and am known by My own. ¹⁵As the Father knows Me, even so I know the Father; and I lay down My life for the sheep. ¹⁶And other sheep I have which are not of this fold; them also I must bring, and they will hear My voice; and there will be one flock *and* one shepherd.

¹⁷"Therefore My Father loves Me, because I lay down My life that I may take it again. ¹⁸No one takes it from Me, but I lay it down of Myself. I have power to lay it down, and I have power to take it again. This command I have received from My Father."

¹⁹Therefore there was a division again among the Jews because of these sayings. ²⁰And many of them said, "He has a demon and is mad. Why do you listen to Him?"

²¹Others said, "These are not the words of one who has a demon. Can a demon open the eyes of the blind?"

The Shepherd Knows His Sheep

²²Now it was the Feast of Dedication in Jerusalem, and it was winter. ²³And Jesus walked in the temple, in Solomon's porch. ²⁴Then the Jews surrounded Him and said to Him, "How long do You keep us in doubt? If You are the Christ, tell us plainly."

²⁵Jesus answered them, "I told you, and you do not believe. The works that I do in My Father's name, they bear witness of Me. ²⁶But you do not believe, because you are not of My sheep, as I said to you.[a] ²⁷My sheep hear My voice, and I know them, and they follow Me. ²⁸And I give them eternal life, and they shall never perish; neither shall anyone snatch them out of My hand. ²⁹My Father, who has given *them* to Me, is greater than all; and no one is able to snatch *them* out of My Father's hand. ³⁰I and *My* Father are one."

Renewed Efforts to Stone Jesus

³¹Then the Jews took up stones again to stone Him. ³²Jesus answered them, "Many good works I have shown you from My Father. For which of those works do you stone Me?"

³³The Jews answered Him, saying, "For a good work we do not stone You, but for blasphemy, and because You, being a Man, make Yourself God."

³⁴Jesus answered them, "Is it not written in your law, *'I said, "You are gods"'*?[a] ³⁵If He called them gods, to whom the word of God came (and the Scripture cannot be broken), ³⁶do you say of Him whom the Father sanctified and sent into the world, 'You are blaspheming,' because I said, 'I am the Son of God'? ³⁷If I do not do the works of My Father, do not believe Me; ³⁸but if I do, though you do not believe Me, believe the works, that you may know and believe[a] that the Father *is* in Me, and I in Him." ³⁹Therefore they sought again to seize Him, but He escaped out of their hand.

The Believers Beyond Jordan

⁴⁰And He went away again beyond the Jordan to the place where John was baptizing at first, and there He stayed. ⁴¹Then many came to Him and said, "John performed no sign, but all the things that John spoke about this Man were true." ⁴²And many believed in Him there.

The Death of Lazarus

11 Now a certain *man* was sick, Lazarus of Bethany, the town of Mary and her sister Martha. ²It was *that* Mary who anointed the Lord with fragrant oil and wiped His feet with her hair, whose brother Lazarus was sick. ³Therefore the sisters sent to Him, saying, "Lord, behold, he whom You love is sick."

10:8 [a]M-Text omits *before Me.* **10:26** [a]NU-Text omits *as I said to you.* **10:34** [a]Psalm 82:6 **10:38** [a]NU-Text reads *understand.*

The Law of Timing: Jesus Timed His Visit to Lazarus and Won Big

(John 11:1–6)

When Jesus got word that one of His closest friends was near death, He waited two days before leaving to visit Him. Why? Jesus knew the Law of Timing and waited until Lazarus died, then left for Bethany. When He raised his friend back to life, it got the attention of everyone in Jerusalem.

⁴When Jesus heard *that,* He said, "This sickness is not unto death, but for the glory of God, that the Son of God may be glorified through it." ⁵Now Jesus loved Martha and her sister and Lazarus. ⁶So, when He heard that he was sick, He stayed two more days in the place where He was. ⁷Then after this He said to *the* disciples, "Let us go to Judea again."

⁸*The* disciples said to Him, "Rabbi, lately the Jews sought to stone You, and are You going there again?"

⁹Jesus answered, "Are there not twelve hours in the day? If anyone walks in the day, he does not stumble, because he sees the light of this world. ¹⁰But if one walks in the night, he stumbles, because the light is not in him." ¹¹These things He said, and after that He said to them, "Our friend Lazarus sleeps, but I go that I may wake him up."

¹²Then His disciples said, "Lord, if he sleeps he will get well." ¹³However, Jesus spoke of his death, but they thought that He was speaking about taking rest in sleep.

¹⁴Then Jesus said to them plainly, "Lazarus is dead. ¹⁵And I am glad for your sakes that I was not there, that you may believe. Nevertheless let us go to him."

¹⁶Then Thomas, who is called the Twin, said to his fellow disciples, "Let us also go, that we may die with Him."

I Am the Resurrection and the Life

¹⁷So when Jesus came, He found that he had already been in the tomb four days. ¹⁸Now Bethany was near Jerusalem, about two milesᵃ away. ¹⁹And many of the Jews had joined the women around Martha and Mary, to comfort them concerning their brother.

²⁰Now Martha, as soon as she heard that Jesus was coming, went and met Him, but Mary was sitting in the house. ²¹Now Martha said to Jesus, "Lord, if You had been here, my brother would not have died. ²²But even now I know that whatever You ask of God, God will give You."

²³Jesus said to her, "Your brother will rise again."

²⁴Martha said to Him, "I know that he will rise again in the resurrection at the last day."

²⁵Jesus said to her, "I am the resurrection and the life. He who believes in Me, though he may die, he shall live. ²⁶And whoever lives and believes in Me shall never die. Do you believe this?"

²⁷She said to Him, "Yes, Lord, I believe that You are the Christ, the Son of God, who is to come into the world."

Jesus and Death, the Last Enemy

²⁸And when she had said these things, she went her way and secretly called Mary her sister, saying, "The Teacher has come and is calling for you." ²⁹As soon as she heard *that,* she arose quickly and came to Him. ³⁰Now Jesus had not yet come into the town, but wasᵃ in the place where Martha met Him. ³¹Then the Jews who were with her in the house, and comforting her, when they saw that Mary rose up quickly and went out, followed her, saying, "She is going to the tomb to weep there."ᵃ

³²Then, when Mary came where Jesus was, and saw Him, she fell down at His feet, saying to Him, "Lord, if You had been here, my brother would not have died."

³³Therefore, when Jesus saw her weeping, and the Jews who came with her weeping, He groaned in the spirit and was troubled. ³⁴And He said, "Where have you laid him?"

They said to Him, "Lord, come and see."

³⁵Jesus wept. ³⁶Then the Jews said, "See how He loved him!"

³⁷And some of them said, "Could not this Man, who opened the eyes of the blind, also have kept this man from dying?"

Lazarus Raised from the Dead

³⁸Then Jesus, again groaning in Himself, came to the tomb. It was a cave, and a stone lay against it. ³⁹Jesus said, "Take away the stone."

Martha, the sister of him who was dead, said

11:18 ᵃLiterally *fifteen stadia* **11:30** ᵃNU-Text adds *still.* **11:31** ᵃNU-Text reads *supposing that she was going to the tomb to weep there.*

to Him, "Lord, by this time there is a stench, for he has been *dead* four days."

[40]Jesus said to her, "Did I not say to you that if you would believe you would see the glory of God?" [41]Then they took away the stone *from the place* where the dead man was lying.[a] And Jesus lifted up *His* eyes and said, "Father, I thank You that You have heard Me. [42]And I know that You always hear Me, but because of the people who are standing by I said *this,* that they may believe that You sent Me." [43]Now when He had said these things, He cried with a loud voice, "Lazarus, come forth!" [44]And he who had died came out bound hand and foot with graveclothes, and his face was wrapped with a cloth. Jesus said to them, "Loose him, and let him go."

The Plot to Kill Jesus

[45]Then many of the Jews who had come to Mary, and had seen the things Jesus did, believed in Him. [46]But some of them went away to the Pharisees and told them the things Jesus did. [47]Then the chief priests and the Pharisees gathered a council and said, "What shall we do? For this Man works many signs. [48]If we let Him alone like this, everyone will believe in Him, and the Romans will come and take away both our place and nation."

[49]And one of them, Caiaphas, being high priest that year, said to them, "You know nothing at all, [50]nor do you consider that it is expedient for us[a] that one man should die for the people, and not that the whole nation should perish." [51]Now this he did not say on his own *authority;* but being high priest that year he prophesied that Jesus would die for the nation, [52]and not for that nation only, but also that He would gather together in one the children of God who were scattered abroad.

[53]Then, from that day on, they plotted to put Him to death. [54]Therefore Jesus no longer walked openly among the Jews, but went from there into the country near the wilderness, to a city called Ephraim, and there remained with His disciples.

[55]And the Passover of the Jews was near, and many went from the country up to Jerusalem before the Passover, to purify themselves. [56]Then they sought Jesus, and spoke among themselves as they stood in the temple, "What do you think—that He will not come to the feast?" [57]Now both the chief priests and the Pharisees had given a command, that if anyone knew where He was, he should report *it,* that they might seize Him.

The Anointing at Bethany

12 Then, six days before the Passover, Jesus came to Bethany, where Lazarus was who had been dead,[a] whom He had raised from the dead. [2]There they made Him a supper; and Martha served, but Lazarus was one of those who sat at the table with Him. [3]Then Mary took a pound of very costly oil of spikenard, anointed the feet of Jesus, and wiped His feet with her hair. And the house was filled with the fragrance of the oil.

[4]But one of His disciples, Judas Iscariot, Simon's *son,* who would betray Him, said, [5]"Why was this fragrant oil not sold for three hundred denarii[a] and given to the poor?" [6]This he said, not that he cared for the poor, but because he was a thief, and had the money box; and he used to take what was put in it.

[7]But Jesus said, "Let her alone; she has kept[a] this for the day of My burial. [8]For the poor you have with you always, but Me you do not have always."

The Plot to Kill Lazarus

[9]Now a great many of the Jews knew that He was there; and they came, not for Jesus' sake only, but that they might also see Lazarus, whom He had raised from the dead. [10]But the chief priests plotted to put Lazarus to death also, [11]because on account of him many of the Jews went away and believed in Jesus.

The Triumphal Entry

[12]The next day a great multitude that had come to the feast, when they heard that Jesus was coming to Jerusalem, [13]took branches of palm trees and went out to meet Him, and cried out:

"Hosanna!

'Blessed is He who comes in the name of the LORD!'[a]

The King of Israel!"

[14]Then Jesus, when He had found a young donkey, sat on it; as it is written:

[15] "Fear not, daughter of Zion;
Behold, your King is coming,
Sitting on a donkey's colt.'"[a]

11:41 [a]NU-Text omits *from the place where the dead man was lying.* **11:50** [a]NU-Text reads *you.*
12:1 [a]NU-Text omits *who had been dead.*
12:5 [a]About one year's wages for a worker
12:7 [a]NU-Text reads *that she may keep.*
12:13 [a]Psalm 118:26 **12:15** [a]Zechariah 9:9

[16]His disciples did not understand these things at first; but when Jesus was glorified, then they remembered that these things were written about Him and *that* they had done these things to Him. [17]Therefore the people, who were with Him when He called Lazarus out of his tomb and raised him from the dead, bore witness. [18]For this reason the people also met Him, because they heard that He had done this sign. [19]The Pharisees therefore said among themselves, "You see that you are accomplishing nothing. Look, the world has gone after Him!"

The Fruitful Grain of Wheat

[20]Now there were certain Greeks among those who came up to worship at the feast. [21]Then they came to Philip, who was from Bethsaida of Galilee, and asked him, saying, "Sir, we wish to see Jesus."

[22]Philip came and told Andrew, and in turn Andrew and Philip told Jesus.

[23]But Jesus answered them, saying, "The hour has come that the Son of Man should be glorified. [24]Most assuredly, I say to you, unless a grain of wheat falls into the ground and dies, it remains alone; but if it dies, it produces much grain. [25]He who loves his life will lose it, and he who hates his life in this world will keep it for eternal life. [26]If anyone serves Me, let him follow Me; and where I am, there My servant will be also. If anyone serves Me, him *My* Father will honor.

The Law of Sacrifice: Jesus Gave Up to Go Up Permanently

(John 12:24–33)

Jesus compared His own death to a grain of wheat, falling to the earth, dying, and bearing much fruit (John 12:24). He then applied this law to us (12:25). Only when we give up our self-life and die can we really live. The greatest leaders willingly give up their lives for others.

Jesus Predicts His Death on the Cross

[27]"Now My soul is troubled, and what shall I say? 'Father, save Me from this hour'? But for this purpose I came to this hour. [28]Father, glorify Your name."

Then a voice came from heaven, *saying,* "I have both glorified *it* and will glorify *it* again."

[29]Therefore the people who stood by and heard *it* said that it had thundered. Others said, "An angel has spoken to Him."

[30]Jesus answered and said, "This voice did not come because of Me, but for your sake. [31]Now is the judgment of this world; now the ruler of this world will be cast out. [32]And I, if I am lifted up from the earth, will draw all *peoples* to Myself." [33]This He said, signifying by what death He would die.

[34]The people answered Him, "We have heard from the law that the Christ remains forever; and how *can* You say, 'The Son of Man must be lifted up'? Who is this Son of Man?"

[35]Then Jesus said to them, "A little while longer the light is with you. Walk while you have the light, lest darkness overtake you; he who walks in darkness does not know where he is going. [36]While you have the light, believe in the light, that you may become sons of light." These things Jesus spoke, and departed, and was hidden from them.

Who Has Believed Our Report?

[37]But although He had done so many signs before them, they did not believe in Him, [38]that the word of Isaiah the prophet might be fulfilled, which he spoke:

> "Lord, who has believed our report?
>   And to whom has the arm of the LORD
>   been revealed?"[a]

[39]Therefore they could not believe, because Isaiah said again:

[40] " He has blinded their eyes and hardened
>   their hearts,
>   Lest they should see with *their* eyes,
>   Lest they should understand with *their*
>   hearts and turn,
>   So that I should heal them.'"[a]

[41]These things Isaiah said when[a] he saw His glory and spoke of Him.

Walk in the Light

[42]Nevertheless even among the rulers many believed in Him, but because of the Pharisees they did not confess *Him,* lest they should be put out of the synagogue; [43]for they loved the praise of men more than the praise of God.

12:38 [a]Isaiah 53:1 **12:40** [a]Isaiah 6:10
12:41 [a]NU-Text reads *because.*

[44]Then Jesus cried out and said, "He who believes in Me, believes not in Me but in Him who sent Me. [45]And he who sees Me sees Him who sent Me. [46]I have come *as* a light into the world, that whoever believes in Me should not abide in darkness. [47]And if anyone hears My words and does not believe,[a] I do not judge him; for I did not come to judge the world but to save the world. [48]He who rejects Me, and does not receive My words, has that which judges him—the word that I have spoken will judge him in the last day. [49]For I have not spoken on My own *authority;* but the Father who sent Me gave Me a command, what I should say and what I should speak. [50]And I know that His command is everlasting life. Therefore, whatever I speak, just as the Father has told Me, so I speak."

Jesus Washes the Disciples' Feet

13 Now before the Feast of the Passover, when Jesus knew that His hour had come that He should depart from this world to the Father, having loved His own who were in the world, He loved them to the end. [2]And supper being ended,[a] the devil having already put it into the heart of Judas Iscariot, Simon's *son,* to betray Him, [3]Jesus, knowing that the Father had given all things into His hands, and that He had come from God and was going to God, [4]rose from supper and laid aside His garments, took a towel and girded Himself. [5]After that, He poured water into a basin and began to wash the disciples' feet, and to wipe *them* with the towel with which He was girded. [6]Then He came to Simon Peter. And *Peter* said to Him, "Lord, are You washing my feet?"

[7]Jesus answered and said to him, "What I am doing you do not understand now, but you will know after this."

[8]Peter said to Him, "You shall never wash my feet!"

Jesus answered him, "If I do not wash you, you have no part with Me."

[9]Simon Peter said to Him, "Lord, not my feet only, but also *my* hands and *my* head!"

[10]Jesus said to him, "He who is bathed needs only to wash *his* feet, but is completely clean; and you are clean, but not all of you." [11]For He knew who would betray Him; therefore He said, "You are not all clean."

[12]So when He had washed their feet, taken His garments, and sat down again, He said to them, "Do you know what I have done to you? [13]You call Me Teacher and Lord, and you say well, for *so* I am. [14]If I then, *your* Lord and Teacher, have washed your feet, you also ought to wash one another's feet. [15]For I have given you an example, that you should do as I have done to you. [16]Most assuredly, I say to you, a servant is not greater than his master; nor is he who is sent greater than he who sent him. [17]If you know these things, blessed are you if you do them.

Jesus Identifies His Betrayer

[18]"I do not speak concerning all of you. I know whom I have chosen; but that the Scripture may be fulfilled, 'He who eats bread with Me[a] has lifted up his heel against Me.'[b] [19]Now I tell you before it comes, that when it does come to pass, you may believe that I am *He.* [20]Most assuredly, I say to you, he who receives whomever I send receives Me; and he who receives Me receives Him who sent Me."

[21]When Jesus had said these things, He was troubled in spirit, and testified and said, "Most assuredly, I say to you, one of you will betray Me." [22]Then the disciples looked at one another, perplexed about whom He spoke.

[23]Now there was leaning on Jesus' bosom one of His disciples, whom Jesus loved. [24]Simon Peter therefore motioned to him to ask who it was of whom He spoke.

[25]Then, leaning back[a] on Jesus' breast, he said to Him, "Lord, who is it?"

[26]Jesus answered, "It is he to whom I shall give a piece of bread when I have dipped *it.*" And having dipped the bread, He gave *it* to Judas Iscariot, *the son* of Simon. [27]Now after the piece of bread, Satan entered him. Then Jesus said to him, "What you do, do quickly." [28]But no one at the table knew for what reason He said this to him. [29]For some thought, because Judas had the money box, that Jesus had said to him, "Buy *those things* we need for the feast," or that he should give something to the poor.

[30]Having received the piece of bread, he then went out immediately. And it was night.

The New Commandment

[31]So, when he had gone out, Jesus said, "Now the Son of Man is glorified, and God is glorified in Him. [32]If God is glorified in Him, God will also glorify Him in Himself, and glorify Him immediately. [33]Little children, I shall be with you

---

12:47 [a]NU-Text reads *keep them.* **13:2** [a]NU-Text reads *And during supper.* **13:18** [a]NU-Text reads *My bread.* [b]Psalm 41:9 **13:25** [a]NU-Text and M-Text add *thus.*

21 QUALITIES

SERVANTHOOD

Jesus Provides a Visual Aid
(John 13:1–17)

The Savior of the world proved Himself to be the greatest Servant of all time. The story is familiar to many. When the disciples booked an upper room for their supper, they forgot to book a servant to wash dirty feet at the door, as per custom. Yet when the disciples realized the servant was missing, none of them volunteered for the job. Instead, they argued over who was the greatest. When Jesus saw this, He decided to use the opportunity to present an object lesson. After supper, Jesus stripped down to a small piece of cloth around his waist, even looking the part of the servant. Then He took a basin of water and a towel and began washing the feet of His men. As He interacted with them, several lessons about servanthood became clear.

Christlike Servant Leaders . . .

1. *Are motivated by love to serve others* (vv. 1, 2).
   Jesus' love was undeserved, unending, unconditional and unselfish. Love made Him serve.
2. *Possess a security that allows them to serve others* (v. 3).
   The insecure are into titles; the secure are into towels. Jesus' security enabled Him to both stoop and stretch.
3. *Initiate servant ministry to others* (vv. 4, 5).
   Jesus didn't wait for someone to clarify protocol. He saw a need and met it.
4. *Receive servant ministry from others* (vv. 6, 7).
   A servant's heart exposes pride in others. Peter had a hard time letting Jesus serve him.
5. *Want nothing to hinder their relationship with God* (vv. 8, 9).
   Peter moved from one extreme to the other. If Jesus offered to wash him, he didn't want to miss anything else He might do.
6. *Teach servanthood by their example* (vv. 12–15).
   Jesus let them know that if the Master washed their feet, they ought to imitate Him.
7. *Live a blessed life* (vv. 16, 17).
   Jesus reminded His men that they were blessed if they obeyed Him.

What ought we to do to imitate Jesus' servant leadership?

1. Put others ahead of your agenda.
2. Develop the confidence and security to take risks.
3. Look for a need and take initiative.
4. Perform small acts anonymously.
5. Learn to walk slowly through the crowd.
6. Begin your day by reflecting on your love for others.
7. Develop a bias for action.

For a negative example of servanthood, see p. 1290.

a little while longer. You will seek Me; and as I said to the Jews, 'Where I am going, you cannot come,' so now I say to you. ³⁴A new commandment I give to you, that you love one another; as I have loved you, that you also love one another. ³⁵By this all will know that you are My disciples, if you have love for one another."

Jesus Predicts Peter's Denial

³⁶Simon Peter said to Him, "Lord, where are You going?"

Jesus answered him, "Where I am going you cannot follow Me now, but you shall follow Me afterward."

³⁷Peter said to Him, "Lord, why can I not follow You now? I will lay down my life for Your sake."

³⁸Jesus answered him, "Will you lay down your life for My sake? Most assuredly, I say to you, the rooster shall not crow till you have denied Me three times.

The Way, the Truth, and the Life

14 "Let not your heart be troubled; you believe in God, believe also in Me. ²In My Father's house are many mansions;ᵃ if *it were* not *so,* I would have told you. I go to prepare a place for you.ᵇ ³And if I go and prepare a place for you, I will come again and receive you to Myself; that where I am, *there* you may be also. ⁴And where I go you know, and the way you know."

⁵Thomas said to Him, "Lord, we do not know where You are going, and how can we know the way?"

⁶Jesus said to him, "I am the way, the truth, and the life. No one comes to the Father except through Me.

The Father Revealed

⁷"If you had known Me, you would have known My Father also; and from now on you know Him and have seen Him."

⁸Philip said to Him, "Lord, show us the Father, and it is sufficient for us."

⁹Jesus said to him, "Have I been with you so long, and yet you have not known Me, Philip? He who has seen Me has seen the Father; so how can you say, 'Show us the Father'? ¹⁰Do you not believe that I am in the Father, and the Father in Me? The words that I speak to you I do not speak on My own *authority;* but the Father who dwells in Me does the works. ¹¹Believe Me that I *am* in the Father and the Father in Me, or else believe Me for the sake of the works themselves.

The Law of Navigation: Jesus Laid a Plan for the Future

(John 14:1–31)

Jesus practiced the Law of Navigation by looking to the future. He reminded His men that He would prepare a place for them (John 14:1–4) and that He was preparing them for a place (14:16–29). He laid plans for the Holy Spirit to finish the work He had begun.

The Answered Prayer

¹²"Most assuredly, I say to you, he who believes in Me, the works that I do he will do also; and greater *works* than these he will do, because I go to My Father. ¹³And whatever you ask in My name, that I will do, that the Father may be glorified in the Son. ¹⁴If you askᵃ anything in My name, I will do *it.*

Jesus Promises Another Helper

¹⁵"If you love Me, keepᵃ My commandments. ¹⁶And I will pray the Father, and He will give you another Helper, that He may abide with you forever— ¹⁷the Spirit of truth, whom the world cannot receive, because it neither sees Him nor knows Him; but you know Him, for He dwells with you and will be in you. ¹⁸I will not leave you orphans; I will come to you.

Indwelling of the Father and the Son

¹⁹"A little while longer and the world will see Me no more, but you will see Me. Because I live, you will live also. ²⁰At that day you will know that I *am* in My Father, and you in Me, and I in you. ²¹He who has My commandments and keeps them, it is he who loves Me. And he who loves Me will be loved by My Father, and I will love him and manifest Myself to him."

²²Judas (not Iscariot) said to Him, "Lord, how is it that You will manifest Yourself to us, and not to the world?"

²³Jesus answered and said to him, "If anyone

14:2 ᵃLiterally *dwellings* ᵇNU-Text adds a word which would cause the text to read either *if it were not so, would I have told you that I go to prepare a place for you?* or *if it were not so I would have told you; for I go to prepare a place for you.* **14:14** ᵃNU-Text adds *Me.* **14:15** ᵃNU-Text reads *you will keep.*

The Law of Reproduction: Jesus Had a Great IDEA to Equip Others

(John 14:12)

Jesus told His men that they would do greater works than He had done. How would this be possible?

First, He would send the Holy Spirit to live in each of them. Second, He had already given so much of Himself to equip them; He had prepared them to reproduce their leadership in the lives of others. Talk about being ready to change the world!

How did Jesus mentor and reproduce His leadership in His disciples? Consider Jesus' IDEA of how to reproduce leadership in someone else:

I *nstruction*
He verbally taught them. He constantly used daily routines to instruct them in leadership.

D *emonstration*
He modeled truth and let His men observe His life. He provided show-and-tell.

E *xperience*
He let the disciples participate and apply the truths themselves. They got to practice.

A *ssessment*
He debriefed their shared experience. He assessed their growth and gave them direction.

---

loves Me, he will keep My word; and My Father will love him, and We will come to him and make Our home with him. ²⁴He who does not love Me does not keep My words; and the word which you hear is not Mine but the Father's who sent Me.

The Gift of His Peace

²⁵"These things I have spoken to you while being present with you. ²⁶But the Helper, the Holy Spirit, whom the Father will send in My name, He will teach you all things, and bring to your remembrance all things that I said to you. ²⁷Peace I leave with you, My peace I give to you; not as the world gives do I give to you. Let not your heart be troubled, neither let it be afraid. ²⁸You have heard Me say to you, 'I am going away and coming *back* to you.' If you loved Me, you would rejoice because I said,[a] 'I am going to the Father,' for My Father is greater than I.

²⁹"And now I have told you before it comes, that when it does come to pass, you may believe. ³⁰I will no longer talk much with you, for the ruler of this world is coming, and he has nothing in Me. ³¹But that the world may know that I love the Father, and as the Father gave Me commandment, so I do. Arise, let us go from here.

The True Vine

15 "I am the true vine, and My Father is the vinedresser. ²Every branch in Me that does not bear fruit He takes away;[a] and every *branch* that bears fruit He prunes, that it may bear more fruit. ³You are already clean because of the word which I have spoken to you. ⁴Abide in Me, and I in you. As the branch cannot bear fruit of itself, unless it abides in the vine, neither can you, unless you abide in Me.

⁵"I am the vine, you *are* the branches. He who abides in Me, and I in him, bears much fruit; for without Me you can do nothing. ⁶If anyone does not abide in Me, he is cast out as a branch and is withered; and they gather them and throw *them* into the fire, and they are burned. ⁷If you abide in Me, and My words abide in you, you will[a] ask what you desire, and it shall be done for you. ⁸By this My Father is glorified, that you bear much fruit; so you will be My disciples.

Love and Joy Perfected

⁹"As the Father loved Me, I also have loved you; abide in My love. ¹⁰If you keep My com-

---

14:28 [a]NU-Text omits *I said*. **15:2** [a]Or *lifts up*
15:7 [a]NU-Text omits *you will*.

Fruitfulness Is Fun!

(John 15:1–16)

Jesus taught His staff how to be fruitful so that their joy might be full (John 15:11). In other words, fruitfulness is fun! There is great joy in gaining the results God desires.

Jesus said that He chose us and appointed us in order to go and bear fruit (15:16). As leaders, our goal is not only to bear fruit, but to help others do the same. We must be more than faithful; we must be fruitful.

We have great potential for fruitful leadership because of our . . .

1. *Source* (v. 1)
   Jesus is the true Vine. If we stay connected to Him, we naturally bear fruit.
2. *Care* (v. 1)
   Our Heavenly Father is the Vinedresser. He owns us and cares for us.
3. *Pruning* (v. 2)
   God removes anything that hinders our usefulness. He trims our weaknesses.
4. *Partnership* (v. 4)
   Our job isn't to artificially push fruit out, but to stay connected to the Vine.
5. *Promise* (v. 7)
   If we let His word abide in us, He promises He will do what we ask.
6. *Purpose* (v. 8)
   God created us to glorify Him by bearing much fruit.
7. *Obedience* (v. 10)
   Jesus gives only one condition to all this: We must obey God. We are to remain *in* Him, receive *from* Him, and reproduce *for* Him.

---

mandments, you will abide in My love, just as I have kept My Father's commandments and abide in His love.

[11]"These things I have spoken to you, that My joy may remain in you, and *that* your joy may be full. [12]This is My commandment, that you love one another as I have loved you. [13]Greater love has no one than this, than to lay down one's life for his friends. [14]You are My friends if you do whatever I command you. [15]No longer do I call you servants, for a servant does not know what his master is doing; but I have called you friends, for all things that I heard from My Father I have made known to you. [16]You did not choose Me, but I chose you and appointed you that you should go and bear fruit, and *that* your fruit should remain, that whatever you ask the Father in My name He may give you. [17]These things I command you, that you love one another.

The World's Hatred

[18]"If the world hates you, you know that it hated Me before *it hated* you. [19]If you were of the world, the world would love its own. Yet because you are not of the world, but I chose you out of the world, therefore the world hates you. [20]Remember the word that I said to you, 'A servant is not greater than his master.' If they persecuted Me, they will also persecute you. If they kept My word, they will keep yours also. [21]But all these things they will do to you for My name's sake, because they do not know Him who sent Me. [22]If I had not come and spoken to them, they would have no sin, but now they have no excuse for their sin. [23]He who hates Me hates My Father also. [24]If I had not done among them the works which no one else did, they would have no sin; but now they have seen and also hated both Me and My Father. [25]But *this happened* that the word might be fulfilled which is written in their law, 'They hated Me without a cause.'[a]

The Coming Rejection

[26]"But when the Helper comes, whom I shall send to you from the Father, the Spirit of truth who proceeds from the Father, He will testify of Me. [27]And you also will bear witness, because you have been with Me from the beginning.

15:25 [a]Psalm 69:4

16

"These things I have spoken to you, that you should not be made to stumble. [2]They will put you out of the synagogues; yes, the time is coming that whoever kills you will think that he offers God service. [3]And these things they will do to you[a] because they have not known the Father nor Me. [4]But these things I have told you, that when the[a] time comes, you may remember that I told you of them.

"And these things I did not say to you at the beginning, because I was with you.

The Work of the Holy Spirit

[5]"But now I go away to Him who sent Me, and none of you asks Me, 'Where are You going?' [6]But because I have said these things to you, sorrow has filled your heart. [7]Nevertheless I tell you the truth. It is to your advantage that I go away; for if I do not go away, the Helper will not come to you; but if I depart, I will send Him to you. [8]And when He has come, He will convict the world of sin, and of righteousness, and of judgment: [9]of sin, because they do not believe in Me; [10]of righteousness, because I go to My Father and you see Me no more; [11]of judgment, because the ruler of this world is judged.

[12]"I still have many things to say to you, but you cannot bear *them* now. [13]However, when He, the Spirit of truth, has come, He will guide you into all truth; for He will not speak on His own *authority,* but whatever He hears He will speak; and He will tell you things to come. [14]He will glorify Me, for He will take of what is Mine and declare *it* to you. [15]All things that the Father has are Mine. Therefore I said that He will take of Mine and declare *it* to you.[a]

Sorrow Will Turn to Joy

[16]"A little while, and you will not see Me; and again a little while, and you will see Me, because I go to the Father."

[17]Then *some* of His disciples said among themselves, "What is this that He says to us, 'A little while, and you will not see Me; and again a little while, and you will see Me'; and, 'because I go to the Father'?" [18]They said therefore, "What is this that He says, 'A little while'? We do not know what He is saying."

[19]Now Jesus knew that they desired to ask Him, and He said to them, "Are you inquiring among yourselves about what I said, 'A little while, and you will not see Me; and again a little while, and you will see Me'? [20]Most assuredly, I say to you that you will weep and lament, but the world will rejoice; and you will be sorrowful, but your sorrow will be turned into joy. [21]A woman, when she is in labor, has sorrow because her hour has come; but as soon as she has given birth to the child, she no longer remembers the anguish, for joy that a human being has been born into the world. [22]Therefore you now have sorrow; but I will see you again and your heart will rejoice, and your joy no one will take from you.

[23]"And in that day you will ask Me nothing. Most assuredly, I say to you, whatever you ask the Father in My name He will give you. [24]Until now you have asked nothing in My name. Ask, and you will receive, that your joy may be full.

Jesus Christ Has Overcome the World

[25]"These things I have spoken to you in figurative language; but the time is coming when I will no longer speak to you in figurative language, but I will tell you plainly about the Father. [26]In that day you will ask in My name, and I do not say to you that I shall pray the Father for you; [27]for the Father Himself loves you, because you have loved Me, and have believed that I came forth from God. [28]I came forth from the Father and have come into the world. Again, I leave the world and go to the Father."

[29]His disciples said to Him, "See, now You are speaking plainly, and using no figure of speech! [30]Now we are sure that You know all things, and have no need that anyone should question You. By this we believe that You came forth from God."

[31]Jesus answered them, "Do you now believe? [32]Indeed the hour is coming, yes, has now come, that you will be scattered, each to his own, and will leave Me alone. And yet I am not alone, because the Father is with Me. [33]These things I have spoken to you, that in Me you may have peace. In the world you will[a] have tribulation; but be of good cheer, I have overcome the world."

Jesus Prays for Himself

17

Jesus spoke these words, lifted up His eyes to heaven, and said: "Father, the hour has come. Glorify Your Son, that Your Son also may glorify You, [2]as You have given Him authority over all flesh, that He should[a] give eternal life to as many as You have given Him. [3]And this is eternal life, that they may know You, the only true God, and Jesus Christ

---

16:3 [a]NU-Text and M-Text omit *to you.*
16:4 [a]NU-Text reads *their.* 16:15 [a]NU-Text and M-Text read *He takes of Mine and will declare it to you.* 16:33 [a]NU-Text and M-Text omit *will.*
17:2 [a]M-Text reads *shall.*

whom You have sent. [4]I have glorified You on the earth. I have finished the work which You have given Me to do. [5]And now, O Father, glorify Me together with Yourself, with the glory which I had with You before the world was.

Jesus Prays for His Disciples

[6]"I have manifested Your name to the men whom You have given Me out of the world. They were Yours, You gave them to Me, and they have kept Your word. [7]Now they have known that all things which You have given Me are from You. [8]For I have given to them the words which You have given Me; and they have received *them,* and have known surely that I came forth from You; and they have believed that You sent Me.

[9]"I pray for them. I do not pray for the world but for those whom You have given Me, for they are Yours. [10]And all Mine are Yours, and Yours are Mine, and I am glorified in them. [11]Now I am no longer in the world, but these are in the world, and I come to You. Holy Father, keep through Your name those whom You have given Me,[a] that they may be one as We *are.* [12]While I was with them in the world,[a] I kept them in Your name. Those whom You gave Me I have kept;[b]

and none of them is lost except the son of perdition, that the Scripture might be fulfilled. [13]But now I come to You, and these things I speak in the world, that they may have My joy fulfilled in themselves. [14]I have given them Your word; and the world has hated them because they are not of the world, just as I am not of the world. [15]I do not pray that You should take them out of the world, but that You should keep them from the evil one. [16]They are not of the world, just as I am not of the world. [17]Sanctify them by Your truth. Your word is truth. [18]As You sent Me into the world, I also have sent them into the world. [19]And for their sakes I sanctify Myself, that they also may be sanctified by the truth.

Jesus Prays for All Believers

[20]"I do not pray for these alone, but also for those who will[a] believe in Me through their word; [21]that they all may be one, as You, Father, *are* in Me, and I in You; that they also may be one

---

17:11 [a]NU-Text and M-Text read *keep them through Your name which You have given Me.* **17:12** [a]NU-Text omits *in the world.* [b]NU-Text reads *in Your name which You gave Me. And I guarded them;* (or *it;*). **17:20** [a]NU-Text and M-Text omit *will.*

The Law of the Inner Circle: Leading When No One Sees

(John 17:11–26)

The majority of what we call Jesus' "high priestly prayer" concerns His inner circle. At the end of His life, He felt acutely aware that the success of His work depended chiefly on the twelve disciples He had trained. Observe what He prayed for:

1. Their faith (vv. 11, 12)
2. Their fulfillment (v. 13)
3. Their future (vv. 14, 15)
4. Their faithfulness (vv. 16, 17)
5. Their fruitfulness (vv. 18–20)
6. Their fellowship (vv. 21–23)
7. Their sense of family (vv. 24–26)

When Jesus knew He had but twelve hours left to live, He didn't start big campaigns. He didn't try to change laws. He didn't even do any more public ministry. He spent the time *praying.*

Prayer is a chief task of the leader (Acts 6:4). The leadership we provide which no one sees may be more important than what we do in public. Followers think of leadership in terms of the visible. In reality, leadership is like an iceberg; most of it lies unseen.

A leader's prayer tells you a lot about the leader. It reveals his or her commitment and concerns. Prayer keeps the leader focused. It keeps a leader dependent on God. It sustains the leader's heart for people. If we are to lead people, we must pray for them.

in Us, that the world may believe that You sent Me. ²²And the glory which You gave Me I have given them, that they may be one just as We are one: ²³I in them, and You in Me; that they may be made perfect in one, and that the world may know that You have sent Me, and have loved them as You have loved Me.

²⁴"Father, I desire that they also whom You gave Me may be with Me where I am, that they may behold My glory which You have given Me; for You loved Me before the foundation of the world. ²⁵O righteous Father! The world has not known You, but I have known You; and these have known that You sent Me. ²⁶And I have declared to them Your name, and will declare *it,* that the love with which You loved Me may be in them, and I in them."

Betrayal and Arrest in Gethsemane

18 When Jesus had spoken these words, He went out with His disciples over the Brook Kidron, where there was a garden, which He and His disciples entered. ²And Judas, who betrayed Him, also knew the place; for Jesus often met there with His disciples. ³Then Judas, having received a detachment *of troops,* and officers from the chief priests and Pharisees, came there with lanterns, torches, and weapons. ⁴Jesus therefore, knowing all things that would come upon Him, went forward and said to them, "Whom are you seeking?"

⁵They answered Him, "Jesus of Nazareth."

Jesus said to them, "I am *He.*" And Judas, who betrayed Him, also stood with them. ⁶Now when He said to them, "I am *He,*" they drew back and fell to the ground.

⁷Then He asked them again, "Whom are you seeking?"

And they said, "Jesus of Nazareth."

⁸Jesus answered, "I have told you that I am *He.* Therefore, if you seek Me, let these go their way," ⁹that the saying might be fulfilled which He spoke, "Of those whom You gave Me I have lost none."

¹⁰Then Simon Peter, having a sword, drew it and struck the high priest's servant, and cut off his right ear. The servant's name was Malchus.

¹¹So Jesus said to Peter, "Put your sword into the sheath. Shall I not drink the cup which My Father has given Me?"

Before the High Priest

¹²Then the detachment *of troops* and the captain and the officers of the Jews arrested Jesus and bound Him. ¹³And they led Him away to Annas first, for he was the father-in-law of Caiaphas who was high priest that year. ¹⁴Now it was Caiaphas who advised the Jews that it was expedient that one man should die for the people.

Peter Denies Jesus

¹⁵And Simon Peter followed Jesus, and so *did* another[a] disciple. Now that disciple was known to the high priest, and went with Jesus into the courtyard of the high priest. ¹⁶But Peter stood at the door outside. Then the other disciple, who was known to the high priest, went out and spoke to her who kept the door, and brought Peter in. ¹⁷Then the servant girl who kept the door said to Peter, "You are not also *one* of this Man's disciples, are you?"

He said, "I am not."

¹⁸Now the servants and officers who had made a fire of coals stood there, for it was cold, and they warmed themselves. And Peter stood with them and warmed himself.

Jesus Questioned by the High Priest

¹⁹The high priest then asked Jesus about His disciples and His doctrine.

²⁰Jesus answered him, "I spoke openly to the world. I always taught in synagogues and in the temple, where the Jews always meet,[a] and in secret I have said nothing. ²¹Why do you ask Me? Ask those who have heard Me what I said to them. Indeed they know what I said."

²²And when He had said these things, one of the officers who stood by struck Jesus with the palm of his hand, saying, "Do You answer the high priest like that?"

²³Jesus answered him, "If I have spoken evil, bear witness of the evil; but if well, why do you strike Me?"

²⁴Then Annas sent Him bound to Caiaphas the high priest.

Peter Denies Twice More

²⁵Now Simon Peter stood and warmed himself. Therefore they said to him, "You are not also *one* of His disciples, are you?"

He denied *it* and said, "I am not!"

²⁶One of the servants of the high priest, a relative *of him* whose ear Peter cut off, said, "Did I not see you in the garden with Him?" ²⁷Peter then denied again; and immediately a rooster crowed.

In Pilate's Court

²⁸Then they led Jesus from Caiaphas to the Praetorium, and it was early morning. But they

---

18:15 [a]M-Text reads *the other.* **18:20** [a]NU-Text reads *where all the Jews meet.*

themselves did not go into the Praetorium, lest they should be defiled, but that they might eat the Passover. [29]Pilate then went out to them and said, "What accusation do you bring against this Man?"

[30]They answered and said to him, "If He were not an evildoer, we would not have delivered Him up to you."

[31]Then Pilate said to them, "You take Him and judge Him according to your law."

Therefore the Jews said to him, "It is not lawful for us to put anyone to death," [32]that the saying of Jesus might be fulfilled which He spoke, signifying by what death He would die.

[33]Then Pilate entered the Praetorium again, called Jesus, and said to Him, "Are You the King of the Jews?"

[34]Jesus answered him, "Are you speaking for yourself about this, or did others tell you this concerning Me?"

[35]Pilate answered, "Am I a Jew? Your own nation and the chief priests have delivered You to me. What have You done?"

[36]Jesus answered, "My kingdom is not of this world. If My kingdom were of this world, My servants would fight, so that I should not be delivered to the Jews; but now My kingdom is not from here."

[37]Pilate therefore said to Him, "Are You a king then?"

Jesus answered, "You say *rightly* that I am a king. For this cause I was born, and for this cause I have come into the world, that I should bear witness to the truth. Everyone who is of the truth hears My voice."

[38]Pilate said to Him, "What is truth?" And when he had said this, he went out again to the Jews, and said to them, "I find no fault in Him at all.

Taking the Place of Barabbas

[39]"But you have a custom that I should release someone to you at the Passover. Do you therefore want me to release to you the King of the Jews?"

[40]Then they all cried again, saying, "Not this Man, but Barabbas!" Now Barabbas was a robber.

The Soldiers Mock Jesus

19 So then Pilate took Jesus and scourged *Him.* [2]And the soldiers twisted a crown of thorns and put *it* on His head, and they put on Him a purple robe. [3]Then they said,[a] "Hail, King of the Jews!" And they struck Him with their hands.

[4]Pilate then went out again, and said to them,

"Behold, I am bringing Him out to you, that you may know that I find no fault in Him."

Pilate's Decision

[5]Then Jesus came out, wearing the crown of thorns and the purple robe. And *Pilate* said to them, "Behold the Man!"

[6]Therefore, when the chief priests and officers saw Him, they cried out, saying, "Crucify *Him,* crucify *Him!*"

Pilate said to them, "You take Him and crucify *Him,* for I find no fault in Him."

[7]The Jews answered him, "We have a law, and according to our[a] law He ought to die, because He made Himself the Son of God."

[8]Therefore, when Pilate heard that saying, he was the more afraid, [9]and went again into the Praetorium, and said to Jesus, "Where are You from?" But Jesus gave him no answer.

[10]Then Pilate said to Him, "Are You not speaking to me? Do You not know that I have power to crucify You, and power to release You?"

[11]Jesus answered, "You could have no power at all against Me unless it had been given you from above. Therefore the one who delivered Me to you has the greater sin."

[12]From then on Pilate sought to release Him, but the Jews cried out, saying, "If you let this Man go, you are not Caesar's friend. Whoever makes himself a king speaks against Caesar."

[13]When Pilate therefore heard that saying, he brought Jesus out and sat down in the judgment seat in a place that is called *The* Pavement, but in Hebrew, Gabbatha. [14]Now it was the Preparation Day of the Passover, and about the sixth hour. And he said to the Jews, "Behold your King!"

[15]But they cried out, "Away with *Him,* away with *Him!* Crucify Him!"

Pilate said to them, "Shall I crucify your King?"

The chief priests answered, "We have no king but Caesar!"

[16]Then he delivered Him to them to be crucified. Then they took Jesus and led *Him* away.[a]

The King on a Cross

[17]And He, bearing His cross, went out to a place called *the Place* of a Skull, which is called in Hebrew, Golgotha, [18]where they crucified Him, and two others with Him, one on either side,

---

19:3 [a]NU-Text reads *And they came up to Him and said.* **19:7** [a]NU-Text reads *the law.* **19:16** [a]NU-Text omits *and led Him away.*

and Jesus in the center. [19]Now Pilate wrote a title and put *it* on the cross. And the writing was:

JESUS OF NAZARETH,
THE KING OF THE JEWS.

[20]Then many of the Jews read this title, for the place where Jesus was crucified was near the city; and it was written in Hebrew, Greek, *and* Latin. [21]Therefore the chief priests of the Jews said to Pilate, "Do not write, 'The King of the Jews,' but, 'He said, "I am the King of the Jews."'" [22]Pilate answered, "What I have written, I have written."

[23]Then the soldiers, when they had crucified Jesus, took His garments and made four parts, to each soldier a part, and also the tunic. Now the tunic was without seam, woven from the top in one piece. [24]They said therefore among themselves, "Let us not tear it, but cast lots for it, whose it shall be," that the Scripture might be fulfilled which says:

"*They divided My garments among them,
And for My clothing they cast lots.*"[a]

Therefore the soldiers did these things.

Behold Your Mother

[25]Now there stood by the cross of Jesus His mother, and His mother's sister, Mary the *wife of* Clopas, and Mary Magdalene. [26]When Jesus therefore saw His mother, and the disciple whom He loved standing by, He said to His mother, "Woman, behold your son!" [27]Then He said to the disciple, "Behold your mother!" And from that hour that disciple took her to his own *home.*

It Is Finished

[28]After this, Jesus, knowing[a] that all things were now accomplished, that the Scripture might be fulfilled, said, "I thirst!" [29]Now a vessel full of sour wine was sitting there; and they filled a sponge with sour wine, put *it* on hyssop, and put *it* to His mouth. [30]So when Jesus had received the sour wine, He said, "It is finished!" And bowing His head, He gave up His spirit.

Jesus' Side Is Pierced

[31]Therefore, because it was the Preparation *Day,* that the bodies should not remain on the cross on the Sabbath (for that Sabbath was a high day), the Jews asked Pilate that their legs might be broken, and *that* they might be taken away. [32]Then the soldiers came and broke the legs of the first and of the other who was crucified with Him. [33]But when they came to Jesus and saw that

Jesus: The Ultimate Radical Leader
(John 19:30)

Jesus showed He was the Ultimate Radical Leader by willingly giving up His life to accomplish His purpose. It was not easy for Him; He felt pain just like you and I. But His kind of abandonment to His earthly body challenges us to take notice and choose sides.

He was already dead, they did not break His legs. [34]But one of the soldiers pierced His side with a spear, and immediately blood and water came out. [35]And he who has seen has testified, and his testimony is true; and he knows that he is telling the truth, so that you may believe. [36]For these things were done that the Scripture should be fulfilled, "*Not one of His bones shall be broken.*"[a] [37]And again another Scripture says, "*They shall look on Him whom they pierced.*"[a]

Jesus Buried in Joseph's Tomb

[38]After this, Joseph of Arimathea, being a disciple of Jesus, but secretly, for fear of the Jews, asked Pilate that he might take away the body of Jesus; and Pilate gave *him* permission. So he came and took the body of Jesus. [39]And Nicodemus, who at first came to Jesus by night, also came, bringing a mixture of myrrh and aloes, about a hundred pounds. [40]Then they took the body of Jesus, and bound it in strips of linen with the spices, as the custom of the Jews is to bury. [41]Now in the place where He was crucified there was a garden, and in the garden a new tomb in which no one had yet been laid. [42]So there they laid Jesus, because of the Jews' Preparation *Day,* for the tomb was nearby.

The Empty Tomb

20 Now the first *day* of the week Mary Magdalene went to the tomb early, while it was still dark, and saw *that* the stone had been taken away from the tomb. [2]Then she ran and came to Simon Peter, and to the other disciple, whom Jesus loved, and said to them, "They have taken away the Lord out of the tomb, and we do not know where they have laid Him."

19:24 [a]Psalm 22:18 **19:28** [a]M-Text reads *seeing.*
19:36 [a]Exodus 12:46; Numbers 9:12; Psalm 34:20
19:37 [a]Zechariah 12:10

³Peter therefore went out, and the other disciple, and were going to the tomb. ⁴So they both ran together, and the other disciple outran Peter and came to the tomb first. ⁵And he, stooping down and looking in, saw the linen cloths lying *there;* yet he did not go in. ⁶Then Simon Peter came, following him, and went into the tomb; and he saw the linen cloths lying *there,* ⁷and the handkerchief that had been around His head, not lying with the linen cloths, but folded together in a place by itself. ⁸Then the other disciple, who came to the tomb first, went in also; and he saw and believed. ⁹For as yet they did not know the Scripture, that He must rise again from the dead. ¹⁰Then the disciples went away again to their own homes.

Mary Magdalene Sees the Risen Lord

¹¹But Mary stood outside by the tomb weeping, and as she wept she stooped down *and looked* into the tomb. ¹²And she saw two angels in white sitting, one at the head and the other at the feet, where the body of Jesus had lain. ¹³Then they said to her, "Woman, why are you weeping?"

She said to them, "Because they have taken away my Lord, and I do not know where they have laid Him."

¹⁴Now when she had said this, she turned around and saw Jesus standing *there,* and did not know that it was Jesus. ¹⁵Jesus said to her, "Woman, why are you weeping? Whom are you seeking?"

She, supposing Him to be the gardener, said to Him, "Sir, if You have carried Him away, tell me where You have laid Him, and I will take Him away."

¹⁶Jesus said to her, "Mary!"

She turned and said to Him,ᵃ "Rabboni!" (which is to say, Teacher).

¹⁷Jesus said to her, "Do not cling to Me, for I have not yet ascended to My Father; but go to My brethren and say to them, 'I am ascending to My Father and your Father, and *to* My God and your God.'"

¹⁸Mary Magdalene came and told the disciples that she had seen the Lord,ᵃ and *that* He had spoken these things to her.

20:16 ᵃNU-Text adds *in Hebrew.* 20:18 ᵃNU-Text reads *disciples, "I have seen the Lord," . . .*

The Law of Empowerment:
Jesus Gave His Ministry Away

(John 20:21, 22)

Many leaders say they intend to work themselves out of a job. That is exactly what Jesus did. In John 20 Jesus puts His final touches on the empowerment of His twelve, then turns them loose. He gives them His peace (v. 21) and breathes on them to receive the power of the Holy Spirit (v. 22). This peace and power would enable them to serve supernaturally. Those men He mentored were now ready to be change agents.

How can we do the same? What steps can we take to mentor and empower others? Note some practical applications of the process Jesus modeled:

1. Pray for conviction and vision.
2. Select a person or group from your sphere of influence to mentor.
3. Spend two initial meetings together to discuss expectations and goals.
4. Cast vision to them for spiritual reproduction.
5. Ask for commitment.
6. Determine what tools or resources you will use together.
7. Prepare yourself and set goals for each meeting.
8. Meet regularly for a set time.
9. Discuss and apply the truths you learn together.
10. Invest yourself in the person, the process, and the purpose.
11. Help them find a potential person to mentor.
12. Evaluate and launch them to try the process themselves.

The Apostles Commissioned

[19]Then, the same day at evening, being the first *day* of the week, when the doors were shut where the disciples were assembled,[a] for fear of the Jews, Jesus came and stood in the midst, and said to them, "Peace *be* with you." [20]When He had said this, He showed them *His* hands and His side. Then the disciples were glad when they saw the Lord.

[21]So Jesus said to them again, "Peace to you! As the Father has sent Me, I also send you." [22]And when He had said this, He breathed on *them,* and said to them, "Receive the Holy Spirit. [23]If you forgive the sins of any, they are forgiven them; if you retain the *sins* of any, they are retained."

Seeing and Believing

[24]Now Thomas, called the Twin, one of the twelve, was not with them when Jesus came. [25]The other disciples therefore said to him, "We have seen the Lord."

So he said to them, "Unless I see in His hands the print of the nails, and put my finger into the print of the nails, and put my hand into His side, I will not believe."

[26]And after eight days His disciples were again inside, and Thomas with them. Jesus came, the doors being shut, and stood in the midst, and said, "Peace to you!" [27]Then He said to Thomas, "Reach your finger here, and look at My hands; and reach your hand *here,* and put *it* into My side. Do not be unbelieving, but believing."

[28]And Thomas answered and said to Him, "My Lord and my God!"

[29]Jesus said to him, "Thomas,[a] because you have seen Me, you have believed. Blessed *are* those who have not seen and *yet* have believed."

That You May Believe

[30]And truly Jesus did many other signs in the presence of His disciples, which are not written in this book; [31]but these are written that you may believe that Jesus is the Christ, the Son of God, and that believing you may have life in His name.

Breakfast by the Sea

21 After these things Jesus showed Himself again to the disciples at the Sea of Tiberias, and in this way He showed *Himself:* [2]Simon Peter, Thomas called the Twin, Nathanael of Cana in Galilee, the *sons* of Zebedee, and two others of His disciples were together. [3]Simon Peter said to them, "I am going fishing."

They said to him, "We are going with you also." They went out and immediately[a] got into the boat, and that night they caught nothing. [4]But when the morning had now come, Jesus stood on the shore; yet the disciples did not know that it was Jesus. [5]Then Jesus said to them, "Children, have you any food?"

They answered Him, "No."

[6]And He said to them, "Cast the net on the right side of the boat, and you will find *some.*" So they cast, and now they were not able to draw it in because of the multitude of fish.

[7]Therefore that disciple whom Jesus loved said to Peter, "It is the Lord!" Now when Simon Peter heard that it was the Lord, he put on *his* outer garment (for he had removed it), and plunged into the sea. [8]But the other disciples came in the little boat (for they were not far from land, but about two hundred cubits), dragging the net with fish. [9]Then, as soon as they had come to land, they saw a fire of coals there, and fish laid on it, and bread. [10]Jesus said to them, "Bring some of the fish which you have just caught."

[11]Simon Peter went up and dragged the net to land, full of large fish, one hundred and fifty-three; and although there were so many, the net was not broken. [12]Jesus said to them, "Come *and* eat breakfast." Yet none of the disciples dared ask Him, "Who are You?"—knowing that it was the Lord. [13]Jesus then came and took the bread and gave it to them, and likewise the fish.

[14]This *is* now the third time Jesus showed Himself to His disciples after He was raised from the dead.

Jesus Restores Peter

[15]So when they had eaten breakfast, Jesus said to Simon Peter, "Simon, *son* of Jonah,[a] do you love Me more than these?"

He said to Him, "Yes, Lord; You know that I love You."

He said to him, "Feed My lambs."

[16]He said to him again a second time, "Simon, *son* of Jonah,[a] do you love Me?"

He said to Him, "Yes, Lord; You know that I love You."

He said to him, "Tend My sheep."

[17]He said to him the third time, "Simon, *son* of Jonah,[a] do you love Me?" Peter was grieved because He said to him the third time, "Do you love Me?"

20:29 [a]NU-Text and M-Text omit *Thomas.*
21:3 [a]NU-Text omits *immediately.* 21:15 [a]NU-Text reads *John.* 21:16 [a]NU-Text reads *John.*
21:17 [a]NU-Text reads *John.*

Jesus and the 21 Irrefutable Laws of Leadership

(John 20:30, 31)

The Gospels demonstrate that Jesus embodied each of the 21 Irrefutable Laws of Leadership:

1. The Law of the Lid: *Leadership ability determines a person's level of effectiveness.*
- John 1:35–37—John the Baptizer knew Jesus could lead his disciples further than he could.
- John 6:66–68—Peter confessed the disciples had no better leader to whom to turn.

2. The Law of Influence: *The true measure of leadership is influence—nothing more, nothing less.*
- Matthew 4:18–20—Jesus called His disciples, who left everything to follow Him.
- John 11:47, 48—The Pharisees feared that if Jesus continued, everyone would follow Him.

3. The Law of Process: *Leadership develops daily, not in a day.*
- Luke 2:52—Jesus continued to grow in wisdom, stature, and favor with God and men.
- Hebrews 5:7–9—Although He was God's Son, Jesus grew and learned through suffering.

4. The Law of Navigation: *Anyone can steer the ship, but it takes a leader to chart the course.*
- Matthew 10:1–23—Jesus gave specific direction in sending out His disciples.
- Luke 14:25–35—Jesus taught the value of planning and calculating one's resources.

5. The Law of E. F. Hutton: *When the real leader speaks, people listen.*
- Mark 1:21–28—Jesus' teaching amazed people and His word spread.
- Mark 11:15–23—Jesus spoke to money changers, leaders, and fig trees; they all obeyed.

6. The Law of Solid Ground: *Trust is the foundation of leadership.*
- Matthew 17:24–27—To prevent offending anyone, Jesus paid even the smallest tax.
- Matthew 22:15–46—Jesus debated enemies and answered questions with integrity.

7. The Law of Respect: *People naturally follow leaders stronger than themselves.*
- Matthew 3:11–15—John the Baptizer acknowledged Jesus' superiority over his ministry.
- Matthew 8:5–10—A centurion sought out Jesus, knowing His authority over all things.

8. The Law of Intuition: *Leaders evaluate everything with a leadership bias.*
- Matthew 9:35–38—Jesus saw the masses and discerned how to reach them.
- Luke 5:1–11—Jesus saw Simon's leadership potential when he didn't see it himself.

9. The Law of Magnetism: *Who you are is who you attract.*
- Mark 10:28–31—Peter reminded Jesus that he left everything, just as Christ did.
- John 17:13–21—Jesus confessed the similarities and unity of the men God gave Him.

10. The Law of Connection: *Leaders touch a heart before they ask for a hand.*
- Luke 8:22–9:1—Jesus met the needs of His disciples, a demoniac, and Jairus—then sent them out.
- John 4:7–26—Jesus connected with a Samaritan woman right where she lived.

11. **The Law of the Inner Circle:** *A leader's potential is determined by those closest to him.*
- Luke 9:1—10:42—Jesus sent out the Twelve and the 70, who multiplied His impact.
- John 17:1–26—Jesus spent a night praying for the success of His inner circle.

12. **The Law of Empowerment:** *Only secure leaders give power to others.*
- John 13:1–20—Jesus felt secure enough to wash feet and send men out to do the same.
- Luke 10:1–24—Jesus gave His power away to the 70 so they could serve others.

13. **The Law of Reproduction:** *It takes a leader to raise up a leader.*
- Matthew 28:18–20—Jesus finished training His twelve, then told them to train others.
- John 15:1–20—Jesus trained the Twelve so that they would be like Him.

14. **The Law of Buy-In:** *People buy in to the leader, then the vision.*
- Luke 5:3–11—Jesus built His team before they understood the details of His vision.
- Luke 9:57–62—Jesus confronted men who followed Him before they knew His vision.

15. **The Law of Victory:** *Leaders find a way for the team to win.*
- Matthew 14:13–33—Jesus found a way to feed the masses and saved His disciples on the ship.
- Mark 16:1–20—Jesus' resurrection surprised everyone and restored their hope.

16. **The Law of the Big Mo:** *Momentum is a leader's best friend.*
- Mark 1:40–45—Jesus' fame spread until He couldn't even enter a public place.
- John 12:9–19—After Lazarus's resuscitation, it seemed the whole world sought Jesus.

17. **The Law of Priorities:** *Leaders understand that activity is not necessarily accomplishment.*
- Mark 1:32–38—Jesus ministered all night, then got alone and decided to move on.
- Luke 10:38–42—Jesus narrowed Martha's to-do list to one key priority.

18. **The Law of Sacrifice:** *A leader must give up to go up.*
- Matthew 20:20–28—Jesus demonstrated that if you want to be great, you have to serve.
- John 10:10–18—Jesus willingly laid down His life for His sheep.

19. **The Law of Timing:** *When to lead is as important as what to do and where to go.*
- John 7:6–8—Jesus knew when His time had come to reveal the kingdom.
- John 11:1–6—When Lazarus got sick, Jesus waited to visit him until after he had died.

20. **The Law of Explosive Growth:** *To add growth, lead followers; to multiply, lead leaders.*
- Mark 16:15–20—Jesus trained and sent leaders, expecting them to reach the world.
- John 14:12—Jesus prepared the Twelve to do greater works than He did.

21. **The Law of Legacy:** *A leader's lasting value is measured by succession.*
- Acts 1:6–8—Jesus' most important words were His last ones to the next generation.
- Acts 17:1–6—The apostles' reputation spread: They turned the world upside down.

The Law of Legacy: Success Without a Successor Is a Failure

(John 21:15–17)

Just before He left earth for heaven, Jesus invested significant time in Simon Peter. He wanted to help him recover from his sin the night he denied Jesus three times. Christ intended to call Peter to minister and lead.

Jesus knew that His time was short. Yet He asked Peter three times if he loved Him. When Peter assured his Lord of his love, Christ called him to the natural response: "Feed My lambs" (John 21:15).

Love should motivate us to serve. In the same way the Father sent Jesus to save the lost sheep of Israel, Jesus called Peter to feed His lambs. Jesus made His legacy dependent on Peter and the other disciples who picked up the baton and ran with it.

And he said to Him, "Lord, You know all things; You know that I love You."

Jesus said to him, "Feed My sheep. [18]Most as– suredly, I say to you, when you were younger, you girded yourself and walked where you wished; but when you are old, you will stretch out your hands, and another will gird you and carry *you* where you do not wish." [19]This He spoke, signifying by what death he would glorify God. And when He had spoken this, He said to him, "Follow Me."

The Beloved Disciple and His Book

[20]Then Peter, turning around, saw the disciple whom Jesus loved following, who also had leaned on His breast at the supper, and said, "Lord, who is the one who betrays You?" [21]Peter, seeing him, said to Jesus, "But Lord, what *about* this man?"

[22]Jesus said to him, "If I will that he remain till I come, what *is that* to you? You follow Me."

[23]Then this saying went out among the brethren that this disciple would not die. Yet Jesus did not say to him that he would not die, but, "If I will that he remain till I come, what *is that* to you?"

[24]This is the disciple who testifies of these things, and wrote these things; and we know that his testimony is true.

[25]And there are also many other things that Jesus did, which if they were written one by one, I suppose that even the world itself could not contain the books that would be written. Amen.

ACTS
Followers of Jesus Transition into Leaders

SUMMARY

Acts is a book of action! Notice, it's called "Acts," not "*Reacts*." It is about the initiative and action of the Holy Spirit in the lives of disciples who formerly were cowardly, unsure, and ignorant. Those men, who had learned to follow Jesus for three years, were now learning to lead!

In this sequel to his Gospel, Luke reports that those early disciples mobilized the church so effectively that they reached entire cities (9:35) and saturated whole countries with the gospel (19:10).

The action described in this book shows God empowering men and women who decide to stand for God with the Holy Spirit. They determine to be influencers. Despite their lack of human qualifications, they begin to penetrate their society. God accomplished this primarily through ordinary people with little in the way of education, political clout, or prestige (1 Cor. 1:26).

The fisherman, Peter, becomes the leader of the church in Jerusalem. Philip becomes the first evangelist and missionary to cross-cultural groups. Stephen takes a stand against the false religious leaders of his day and becomes the first martyr. Barnabas and Paul establish the first equipping/sending church in Antioch, then lead the first mission team.

These leaders accomplish so much because they are governed by the priorities of God, incarnate the power of God, are motivated by the purposes of God, stay dependent on the provisions of God, and equip the people of God. Everyone gets involved in the task. Leaders equip followers and cheer on the church as she marches into the culture. Miracles break out. The community takes care of outstanding personal needs.

As you read through the book, note how many leaders emerge from within the church. Many are not apostles; we would consider most lay people. Yet everyone seems committed to the vision of impacting the world for Christ.

God's Role in Acts

God filled these ordinary people with His Spirit and bid them to influence the world. Miracles occurred as God confirmed His Word with signs following (Mark 16:17, 18). Jesus personally appeared to Saul of Tarsus in order to call him to be an apostle (9:1–9). The Holy Spirit established this early church in purity so that He could empower it without limits. God entrusts His power to the pure. Note the sequence: first purity; then power; then proclamation; and finally, penetration.

Leaders in Acts

Peter and the original apostles, Gamaliel and the Sanhedrin, Stephen, Philip, Aquila and Priscilla, Paul, Barnabas, Herod, Agrippa, Festus, Apollos, Silas

Other People of Influence in Acts

The core of believers in the Upper Room, Lydia, Luke, Timothy, the Ephesian businessmen, the Antioch church family

Lessons in Leadership

- Holy Spirit power plus obedient leadership equals church growth.

- God raises up leaders in order to bring all people to Himself.

- Leaders break down barriers and connect the familiar to the unfamiliar.

- When the church adds more leaders, it adds more followers.

- There is no success without sacrifice.

- Momentum comes as a result of unity.

- Leaders start to thrive when they don't have to survive.

LEADERSHIP HIGHLIGHTS IN ACTS

Prologue

1 The former account I made, O Theophilus, of all that Jesus began both to do and teach, ²until the day in which He was taken up, after He through the Holy Spirit had given commandments to the apostles whom He had chosen, ³to whom He also presented Himself alive after His suffering by many infallible proofs, being seen by them during forty days and speaking of the things pertaining to the kingdom of God.

The Holy Spirit Promised

⁴And being assembled together with *them,* He commanded them not to depart from Jerusalem, but to wait for the Promise of the Father, "which," *He said,* "you have heard from Me; ⁵for John truly baptized with water, but you shall be baptized with the Holy Spirit not many days from now." ⁶Therefore, when they had come together, they asked Him, saying, "Lord, will You at this time restore the kingdom to Israel?" ⁷And He said to them, "It is not for you to know times or seasons which the Father has put in His own authority. ⁸But you shall receive power when the Holy Spirit has come upon you; and you shall be witnesses to Meª in Jerusalem, and in all Judea and Samaria, and to the end of the earth."

Jesus Ascends to Heaven

⁹Now when He had spoken these things, while they watched, He was taken up, and a cloud received Him out of their sight. ¹⁰And while they looked steadfastly toward heaven as He went up, behold, two men stood by them in white apparel, ¹¹who also said, "Men of Galilee, why do you stand gazing up into heaven? This *same* Jesus, who was taken up from you into heaven, will so come in like manner as you saw Him go into heaven."

The Upper Room Prayer Meeting

¹²Then they returned to Jerusalem from the mount called Olivet, which is near Jerusalem, a Sabbath day's journey. ¹³And when they had entered, they went up into the upper room where they were staying: Peter, James, John, and Andrew; Philip and Thomas; Bartholomew and Matthew; James *the son* of Alphaeus and Simon the Zealot; and Judas *the son* of James. ¹⁴These all continued with one accord in prayer and supplication,ª with the women and Mary the mother of Jesus, and with His brothers.

1:8 ªNU-Text reads *My witnesses.* **1:14** ªNU-Text omits *and supplication.*

Vision: Leaders Communicate Vision to Empower and Direct

(Acts 1:4–8)

The Book of Acts begins with a bang. Jesus speaks His final words to His men before ascending to heaven. Even though they are now leaders, not merely followers, they ask Jesus when His kingdom would come (Acts 1:6). Jesus doesn't tell them, but instead communicates a vision about reaching the world (1:8). His men thought *defense;* Jesus wanted them to think *offense.*

Christ instructed them to stay in Jerusalem until they received the power they needed, then they were to go out, expanding little by little. They were to start with Jerusalem, then move to the rest of Judea, then expand to Samaria, and ultimately to the ends of the earth. This was no man-made vision, but a God-given vision. Note the differences:

Man-Made Vision	God-Given Vision
1. Created based on human gifts and skills	1. Received as a revelation
2. Fulfilled by staying ahead of others	2. Fulfilled through obedience
3. Sees similar organizations as competitors	3. Sees similar organizations as complementary
4. Aims to grow the organization and generate revenue	4. Aims to serve people and advance God's rule
5. Stress may emerge both inwardly and outwardly	5. Accompanied by inward peace and outward opposition
6. May be dropped for something better	6. Compelling and captivating until fulfilled

Matthias Chosen

[15]And in those days Peter stood up in the midst of the disciples[a] (altogether the number of names was about a hundred and twenty), and said, [16]"Men *and* brethren, this Scripture had to be fulfilled, which the Holy Spirit spoke before by the mouth of David concerning Judas, who became a guide to those who arrested Jesus; [17]for he was numbered with us and obtained a part in this ministry."

[18](Now this man purchased a field with the wages of iniquity; and falling headlong, he burst open in the middle and all his entrails gushed out. [19]And it became known to all those dwelling in Jerusalem; so that field is called in their own language, Akel Dama, that is, Field of Blood.)

[20]"For it is written in the Book of Psalms:

'Let his dwelling place be desolate,
And let no one live in it';[a]

and,

'Let[b] another take his office.'[c]

[21]"Therefore, of these men who have accompanied us all the time that the Lord Jesus went in and out among us, [22]beginning from the baptism of John to that day when He was taken up from us, one of these must become a witness with us of His resurrection."

[23]And they proposed two: Joseph called Barsabas, who was surnamed Justus, and Matthias. [24]And they prayed and said, "You, O Lord, who know the hearts of all, show which of these two You have chosen [25]to take part in this ministry and apostleship from which Judas by transgression fell, that he might go to his own place." [26]And they cast their lots, and the lot fell on Matthias. And he was numbered with the eleven apostles.

Coming of the Holy Spirit

2 When the Day of Pentecost had fully come, they were all with one accord[a] in one place. [2]And suddenly there came a sound from heaven, as of a rushing mighty wind, and it filled the whole house where they were sitting. [3]Then there appeared to them divided tongues, as of fire, and *one* sat upon each of them. [4]And they were all filled with the Holy Spirit and began to speak with other tongues, as the Spirit gave them utterance.

Qualified Leaders Must Be Selected

(Acts 1:20–26)

The apostles chose Matthias to replace Judas, who betrayed Jesus and committed suicide soon afterward. Notice two things.

First, they didn't hold an election. Church eldership is never determined through a democracy in the New Testament. Leaders were chosen, not voted on.

Second, the apostles cast lots to discover God's choice for the position—a common method in biblical times to receive direction from the Lord. Today, Christians receive direction from the New Testament (2 Tim. 3:16; Titus 1:5–9) and from the witness of the Holy Spirit (Rom. 8:14–16). Elders are leaders chosen by God and confirmed by the church.

The Book of Acts makes 18 references to elders, ten relating directly to the ministry of a church elder. The various Greek words used to discuss leadership are most often translated by the terms "elder," "bishop," or "deacon." They all concern responsibility, spiritual oversight, inspection, service, and ministry.

Empowerment: Leaders Must Be Empowered Before They Empower

(Acts 2:1–4)

Leaders can never empower anyone else until they are first supernaturally empowered themselves. The term "filled with the Holy Spirit" is used five times in Acts (2:4; 4:8, 31; 9:17; 13:9). Whenever someone is filled with the Holy Spirit, something *happens*. Empowered leaders express God's power, then empower others.

The Crowd's Response

[5]And there were dwelling in Jerusalem Jews, devout men, from every nation under heaven. [6]And when this sound occurred, the multitude came together, and were confused, because

---

1:15 [a]NU-Text reads *brethren.* **1:20** [a]Psalm 69:25
[b]Psalm 109:8 [c]Greek *episkopen, position of overseer*
2:1 [a]NU-Text reads *together.*

21 QUALITIES

CHARISMA

Peter Was a Magnet
(Acts 2:1–41)

Acts 2 marks a pivotal point in the New Testament. One hundred and twenty men and women become charter members of the church when it is born in an upper room somewhere in Jerusalem. Yet by end of the chapter, it explodes into a body of more than three thousand members.

After the Holy Spirit falls on the believers (Acts 2:1–4), those visiting Jerusalem begin to wonder how these disciples of Jesus could speak so many languages (2:5–13). While some think the disciples are drunk, most just feel confused. Chaos seems to rule.

That's when Peter stands up and begins to speak. This same Peter, who ran in fear on the night of Jesus' trial, now speaks boldly. Within minutes, he has captivated everyone with his compelling words. The crowd gladly accepts his message. Why? He has charisma. Through a combination of God-given wiring and the gift of the Holy Spirit, this leader captures and motivates three thousand people to follow Christ.

What Are the Traits of a Charismatic Leader?

Most people think of charisma as something mystical, almost undefinable. They think it comes at birth or not at all. But that's not true. Charisma is the ability to draw people to you or your cause. Some people possess more of it naturally. Like other character traits, however, it can be learned. Notice what made Peter so charismatic (2:14–40):

1. *Confidence*
   Peter displayed poise and optimism as a buoyant communicator.
2. *Conviction*
   He knew where he was going and what he had to say. He spoke straight from his heart.
3. *Connection*
   He focused not on himself, but on others. He magnetically connected with his audience.
4. *Compassion*
   He exuded warmth and love. He gave the people practical answers to their needs.

By the end of his message, everyone asked, "What shall we do?" (2:37). They felt motivated and ready to act. God used Peter's charisma like a magnet.

How Can We Build Charisma?

How about you? Do you demonstrate charisma? To make yourself the kind of person who attracts others, build the following into your life:

1. *Love life.* Celebrate; don't complain. Enjoy the journey.
2. *Put a "10" on everyone's forehead.* Expect the best of people and treat them well.
3. *Give people hope.* Everyone looks for hope; leaders deal it out.
4. *Share yourself.* Be vulnerable and real. Share your heart, wisdom, and resources.

For a negative example of charisma, see p. 437.

everyone heard them speak in his own language. [7]Then they were all amazed and marveled, saying to one another, "Look, are not all these who speak Galileans? [8]And how *is it that* we hear, each in our own language in which we were born? [9]Parthians and Medes and Elamites, those dwelling in Mesopotamia, Judea and Cappadocia, Pontus and Asia, [10]Phrygia and Pamphylia, Egypt and the parts of Libya adjoining Cyrene, visitors from Rome, both Jews and proselytes, [11]Cretans and Arabs—we hear them speaking in our own tongues the wonderful works of God." [12]So they were all amazed and perplexed, saying to one another, "Whatever could this mean?"

[13]Others mocking said, "They are full of new wine."

The Law of Magnetism: Passionate Leaders Are Magnetic for Others

(Acts 2:7–21)

When Peter stood up to preach, no doubt the crowd saw God-given power and purpose—but first they saw God-given passion. Passion made up for Peter's lack of natural gifts or education. When Peter became a magnet for others, three thousand people joined the church that day. Passion draws passion.

Peter's Sermon

[14]But Peter, standing up with the eleven, raised his voice and said to them, "Men of Judea and all who dwell in Jerusalem, let this be known to you, and heed my words. [15]For these are not drunk, as you suppose, since it is *only* the third hour of the day. [16]But this is what was spoken by the prophet Joel:

[17]   'And it shall come to pass in the last days,
          says God,
          That I will pour out of My Spirit on all
          flesh;
          Your sons and your daughters shall
          prophesy,
          Your young men shall see visions,
          Your old men shall dream dreams.
[18]   And on My menservants and on My
          maidservants
          I will pour out My Spirit in those days;

          And they shall prophesy.
[19]   I will show wonders in heaven above
          And signs in the earth beneath:
          Blood and fire and vapor of smoke.
[20]   The sun shall be turned into darkness,
          And the moon into blood,
          Before the coming of the great and
          awesome day of the LORD.
[21]   And it shall come to pass
          That whoever calls on the name of the
          LORD
          Shall be saved.'[a]

[22]"Men of Israel, hear these words: Jesus of Nazareth, a Man attested by God to you by miracles, wonders, and signs which God did through Him in your midst, as you yourselves also know— [23]Him, being delivered by the determined purpose and foreknowledge of God, you have taken[a] by lawless hands, have crucified, and put to death; [24]whom God raised up, having loosed the pains of death, because it was not possible that He should be held by it. [25]For David says concerning Him:

     'I foresaw the LORD always before my face,
          For He is at my right hand, that I may not
          be shaken.
[26]   Therefore my heart rejoiced, and my
          tongue was glad;
          Moreover my flesh also will rest in hope.
[27]   For You will not leave my soul in Hades,
          Nor will You allow Your Holy One to see
          corruption.
[28]   You have made known to me the ways of
          life;
          You will make me full of joy in Your
          presence.'[a]

[29]"Men *and* brethren, let *me* speak freely to you of the patriarch David, that he is both dead and buried, and his tomb is with us to this day. [30]Therefore, being a prophet, and knowing that God had sworn with an oath to him that of the fruit of his body, according to the flesh, He would raise up the Christ to sit on his throne,[a] [31]he, foreseeing this, spoke concerning the resurrection of the Christ, that His soul was not left in Hades, nor did His flesh see corruption. [32]This Jesus God has raised up, of which we are all witnesses. [33]Therefore being exalted to the right hand of God, and having received from the Fa-

---

2:21 [a]Joel 2:28–32 **2:23** [a]NU-Text omits *have taken.* **2:28** [a]Psalm 16:8–11 **2:30** [a]NU-Text omits *according to the flesh, He would raise up the Christ* and completes the verse with *He would seat one on his throne.*

ther the promise of the Holy Spirit, He poured out this which you now see and hear.

³⁴"For David did not ascend into the heavens, but he says himself:

> 'The LORD said to my Lord,
> "Sit at My right hand,
> ³⁵ Till I make Your enemies Your
> footstool." 'ᵃ

³⁶"Therefore let all the house of Israel know assuredly that God has made this Jesus, whom you crucified, both Lord and Christ."

³⁷Now when they heard this, they were cut to the heart, and said to Peter and the rest of the apostles, "Men and brethren, what shall we do?"

³⁸Then Peter said to them, "Repent, and let every one of you be baptized in the name of Jesus Christ for the remission of sins; and you shall receive the gift of the Holy Spirit. ³⁹For the promise is to you and to your children, and to all who are afar off, as many as the Lord our God will call."

A Vital Church Grows

⁴⁰And with many other words he testified and exhorted them, saying, "Be saved from this per-verse generation." ⁴¹Then those who gladlyᵃ received his word were baptized; and that day about three thousand souls were added to them. ⁴²And they continued steadfastly in the apostles' doctrine and fellowship, in the breaking of bread, and in prayers. ⁴³Then fear came upon every soul, and many wonders and signs were done through the apostles. ⁴⁴Now all who believed were together, and had all things in common, ⁴⁵and sold their possessions and goods, and divided them among all, as anyone had need.

⁴⁶So continuing daily with one accord in the temple, and breaking bread from house to house, they ate their food with gladness and simplicity of heart, ⁴⁷praising God and having favor with all the people. And the Lord added to the churchᵃ daily those who were being saved.

A Lame Man Healed

3 Now Peter and John went up together to the temple at the hour of prayer, the ninth hour. ²And a certain man lame from his mother's womb was carried, whom they laid daily at the gate of the temple which is called

---

2:35 ᵃPsalm 110:1 2:41 ᵃNU-Text omits gladly.
2:47 ᵃNU-Text omits to the church.

PROFILE IN LEADERSHIP

PETER

MOST IMPROVED PLAYER AND TURNAROUND LEADER
(Acts 3:1–26)

The apostle Peter may be the greatest turnaround leader in the New Testament.

Peter—the same man who had promised to follow Jesus even if it meant death, but who cowered in fear when a mere servant girl identified him as one of the Lord's followers (Luke 22:56, 57)—spoke the name of Christ with great power and authority and without fear of the consequences.

Peter knew the danger of preaching Jesus. He knew the hostility it could elicit. He knew that by doing the will of God and preaching he would be taking his life in his hands. Still, he had no choice. He had to preach. He had to speak the name of Jesus. As he told the authorities, he could do nothing else. After the things he had seen and heard—after the powerful touch he had received from the Holy Spirit of God—he felt compelled to preach the gospel (Acts 4:19, 20).

So Peter preached . . . and the whole world turned upside down!

This is the kind of turnaround that occurs in the life of one touched by the Holy Spirit of God. When we have a genuine encounter with Jesus, when He transforms our hearts and minds and empowers us and emboldens us, we have no choice—we must preach the gospel, we must speak the Word of God.

Demonstration + Proclamation = Credibility

(Acts 3:1–26)

Immediately following Pentecost, the Christian movement picked up steam. Two leaders, Peter and John, encountered a lame man on their way to the temple. When the name of Jesus healed the man, they immediately gained credibility to share the gospel. In other words, once they walked the walk, they attracted an audience when they talked. Note how Acts 3 describes these early church leaders:

1. They faithfully did what they knew to do (v. 1).
2. They stopped and sensitively addressed needs (v. 3).
3. They had the courage to face problems (v. 4).
4. Others anticipated receiving solutions from them (v. 5).
5. They realistically admitted their lack of material resources (v. 6).
6. They fearlessly used their God-given authority (v. 6).
7. They generously gave away their spiritual resources (v. 6).
8. They solved practical problems (vv. 7, 8).
9. They gained credibility through demonstration, not just proclamation (vv. 9, 10).
10. Peter's demonstration gave him a platform and a convincing argument (vv. 11–26).

Beautiful, to ask alms from those who entered the temple; ³who, seeing Peter and John about to go into the temple, asked for alms. ⁴And fixing his eyes on him, with John, Peter said, "Look at us." ⁵So he gave them his attention, expecting to receive something from them. ⁶Then Peter said, "Silver and gold I do not have, but what I do have I give you: In the name of Jesus Christ of Nazareth, rise up and walk." ⁷And he took him by the right hand and lifted *him* up, and immediately his feet and ankle bones received strength. ⁸So he, leaping up, stood and walked and entered the temple with them—walking, leaping, and praising God. ⁹And all the people saw him walking and praising God. ¹⁰Then they knew that it was he who sat begging alms at the Beautiful Gate of the temple; and they were filled with wonder and amazement at what had happened to him.

Preaching in Solomon's Portico

¹¹Now as the lame man who was healed held on to Peter and John, all the people ran together to them in the porch which is called Solomon's, greatly amazed. ¹²So when Peter saw *it*, he responded to the people: "Men of Israel, why do you marvel at this? Or why look so intently at us, as though by our own power or godliness we had made this man walk? ¹³The God of Abraham, Isaac, and Jacob, the God of our fathers, glorified His Servant Jesus, whom you delivered up and denied in the presence of Pilate, when he was determined to let *Him* go. ¹⁴But you denied the

Holy One and the Just, and asked for a murderer to be granted to you, ¹⁵and killed the Prince of life, whom God raised from the dead, of which we are witnesses. ¹⁶And His name, through faith in His name, has made this man strong, whom you see and know. Yes, the faith which *comes* through Him has given him this perfect soundness in the presence of you all.

¹⁷"Yet now, brethren, I know that you did *it* in ignorance, as *did* also your rulers. ¹⁸But those things which God foretold by the mouth of all His prophets, that the Christ would suffer, He has thus fulfilled. ¹⁹Repent therefore and be converted, that your sins may be blotted out, so that times of refreshing may come from the presence of the Lord, ²⁰and that He may send Jesus Christ, who was preached to you before,ᵃ ²¹whom heaven must receive until the times of restoration of all things, which God has spoken by the mouth of all His holy prophets since the world began. ²²For Moses truly said to the fathers, '*The LORD your God will raise up for you a Prophet like me from your brethren. Him you shall hear in all things, whatever He says to you.* ²³*And it shall be that every soul who will not hear that Prophet shall be utterly destroyed from among the people.*'ᵃ ²⁴Yes, and all the prophets, from Samuel and those who follow, as many as have

3:20 ᵃNU-Text and M-Text read *Christ Jesus, who was ordained for you before.* **3:23** ᵃDeuteronomy 18:15, 18, 19

spoken, have also foretold[a] these days. [25]You are sons of the prophets, and of the covenant which God made with our fathers, saying to Abraham, *'And in your seed all the families of the earth shall be blessed.'*[a] [26]To you first, God, having raised up His Servant Jesus, sent Him to bless you, in turning away every one *of you* from your iniquities."

Peter and John Arrested

4 Now as they spoke to the people, the priests, the captain of the temple, and the Sadducees came upon them, [2]being greatly disturbed that they taught the people and preached in Jesus the resurrection from the dead. [3]And they laid hands on them, and put *them* in custody until the next day, for it was already evening. [4]However, many of those who heard the word believed; and the number of the men came to be about five thousand.

Addressing the Sanhedrin

[5]And it came to pass, on the next day, that their rulers, elders, and scribes, [6]as well as Annas the high priest, Caiaphas, John, and Alexander, and as many as were of the family of the high

priest, were gathered together at Jerusalem. [7]And when they had set them in the midst, they asked, "By what power or by what name have you done this?"

[8]Then Peter, filled with the Holy Spirit, said to them, "Rulers of the people and elders of Israel: [9]If we this day are judged for a good deed *done* to a helpless man, by what means he has been made well, [10]let it be known to you all, and to all the people of Israel, that by the name of Jesus Christ of Nazareth, whom you crucified, whom God raised from the dead, by Him this man stands here before you whole. [11]This is the *'stone which was rejected by you builders, which has become the chief cornerstone.'*[a] [12]Nor is there salvation in any other, for there is no other name under heaven given among men by which we must be saved."

The Name of Jesus Forbidden

[13]Now when they saw the boldness of Peter and John, and perceived that they were uneducated and untrained men, they marveled. And

---

3:24 [a]NU-Text and M-Text read *proclaimed.*
3:25 [a]Genesis 22:18; 26:4; 28:14 **4:11** [a]Psalm 118:22

Courage: One Person with Courage Is a Majority

(Acts 4:10–13)

In Acts 4 we see courage on display in the life of Peter and John. These two leaders were thrown in jail for preaching and for performing a miracle (vv. 1–4). When their captors ask about their ministry, Peter boldly asserts that the name of Jesus, not their own talent, had healed the man (v. 10). He also explains that salvation comes through no other name (v. 12). What accounted for his boldness? Not his education, but his experience with Jesus (v. 13).

Leadership requires courage. All leaders need courage to:

1. *Seek the truth*
   You never find yourself until you face the truth.

2. *Change*
   Courage is the power to let go of the familiar.

3. *Express convictions*
   Convictions help us to stand alone. The test of courage comes when we're in the minority.

4. *Overcome obstacles*
   Whatever you do, someone will think you're wrong. Expect trouble. Project courage.

5. *Learn and grow*
   You haven't learned until you step out, take a risk, and do something new.

6. *Take the high road*
   There is no traffic jam on the second mile.

7. *Lead others*
   Leadership is the expression of courage that compels others to do the right thing.

they realized that they had been with Jesus. [14]And seeing the man who had been healed standing with them, they could say nothing against it. [15]But when they had commanded them to go aside out of the council, they conferred among themselves, [16]saying, "What shall we do to these men? For, indeed, that a notable miracle has been done through them *is* evident to all who dwell in Jerusalem, and we cannot deny *it.* [17]But so that it spreads no further among the people, let us severely threaten them, that from now on they speak to no man in this name."

[18]So they called them and commanded them not to speak at all nor teach in the name of Jesus. [19]But Peter and John answered and said to them, "Whether it is right in the sight of God to listen to you more than to God, you judge. [20]For we cannot but speak the things which we have seen and heard." [21]So when they had further threatened them, they let them go, finding no way of punishing them, because of the people, since they all glorified God for what had been done. [22]For the man was over forty years old on whom this miracle of healing had been performed.

Prayer for Boldness

[23]And being let go, they went to their own *companions* and reported all that the chief priests and elders had said to them. [24]So when they heard that, they raised their voice to God with one accord and said: "Lord, You *are* God, who made heaven and earth and the sea, and all that is in them, [25]who by the mouth of Your servant David[a] have said:

> ' *Why did the nations rage,*
> *And the people plot vain things?*
> [26]   *The kings of the earth took their stand,*
> *And the rulers were gathered together*
> *Against the LORD and against His Christ.'*[a]

[27]"For truly against Your holy Servant Jesus, whom You anointed, both Herod and Pontius Pilate, with the Gentiles and the people of Israel, were gathered together [28]to do whatever Your hand and Your purpose determined before to be done. [29]Now, Lord, look on their threats, and grant to Your servants that with all boldness they may speak Your word, [30]by stretching out Your hand to heal, and that signs and wonders may be done through the name of Your holy Servant Jesus."

[31]And when they had prayed, the place where they were assembled together was shaken; and they were all filled with the Holy Spirit, and they spoke the word of God with boldness.

Sharing in All Things

[32]Now the multitude of those who believed were of one heart and one soul; neither did anyone say that any of the things he possessed was his own, but they had all things in common. [33]And with great power the apostles gave witness to the resurrection of the Lord Jesus. And great grace was upon them all. [34]Nor was there anyone among them who lacked; for all who were possessors of lands or houses sold them, and brought the proceeds of the things that were sold, [35]and laid *them* at the apostles' feet; and they distributed to each as anyone had need.

[36]And Joses,[a] who was also named Barnabas by the apostles (which is translated Son of Encouragement), a Levite of the country of Cyprus, [37]having land, sold *it,* and brought the money and laid *it* at the apostles' feet.

Lying to the Holy Spirit

5 But a certain man named Ananias, with Sapphira his wife, sold a possession. [2]And he kept back *part* of the proceeds, his wife also being aware *of it,* and brought a certain part and laid *it* at the apostles' feet. [3]But Peter said, "Ananias, why has Satan filled your heart to lie to the Holy Spirit and keep back *part* of the price of the land for yourself? [4]While it remained, was it not your own? And after it was sold, was it not in your own control? Why have you conceived this thing in your heart? You have not lied to men but to God."

[5]Then Ananias, hearing these words, fell down and breathed his last. So great fear came upon all those who heard these things. [6]And the young men arose and wrapped him up, carried *him* out, and buried *him.*

[7]Now it was about three hours later when his wife came in, not knowing what had happened. [8]And Peter answered her, "Tell me whether you sold the land for so much?"

She said, "Yes, for so much."

[9]Then Peter said to her, "How is it that you have agreed together to test the Spirit of the Lord? Look, the feet of those who have buried your husband *are* at the door, and they will carry you out." [10]Then immediately she fell down at his feet and breathed her last. And the young men came in and found her dead, and, carrying *her* out, buried *her* by her husband. [11]So great fear came upon all the church and upon all who heard these things.

4:25 [a]NU-Text reads *who through the Holy Spirit, by the mouth of our father, Your servant David.*
4:26 [a]Psalm 2:1, 2 **4:36** [a]NU-Text reads *Joseph.*

GENEROSITY

Ananias and Sapphira Only Pretended
(Acts 5:1–11)

Leaders give of themselves liberally—at least, they did in the New Testament.

The whole church enjoyed unity and generosity, and it all started at the top. The example of the apostles spread a spirit of generosity throughout the whole church. Unfortunately, a couple of pretenders, Ananias and Sapphira, sold some land and gave part of the proceeds to the apostles, reporting that they had given *all* the money to the church. God revealed their deception to Peter and he called them on it. Their sin was not lack of generosity, but lack of honesty. They lied about what they had done. They wanted to be thought of as generous without paying the price.

God would have nothing to do with it. He surgically removed the spiritual cancer from the church by taking their lives. "So great fear came upon all the church and upon all who heard these things," Luke says (Acts 5:11).

Let's look more closely at the problem and itemize it. Ananias and Sapphira . . .

1. Clung to their possessions.
2. Agreed to lie about their giving.
3. Pretended to be someone they were not.
4. Thought they could get by with appearing to be generous.
5. Felt more concerned with their image than their relationship to God.

Many leaders struggle with the same issues. Not only do we live in a materialistic world, but we buy into the world's economy. We think that if we grasp and cling to our possessions through our own cleverness, we will eventually "make it." God's economy is radically different. He is an extravagant Lord who gives generously to everyone with a need. He enjoys meeting the needs of His followers, directly or indirectly. He doesn't merely give of His resources, but of Himself.

Building Generosity into Your Life

Nothing speaks to others more loudly or serves them better than a leader's generosity. Effective leaders gather for others, then give it away. Consider several ways to cultivate generosity in your own life:

1. Be grateful for whatever you have.
2. Put people first.
3. Don't allow greed to control you.
4. Regard money as a resource.
5. Develop the habit of giving.

Sometimes we hold on to our possessions because we fear we might run out—life seems scarce. But when we believe that giving is the way to live, we will produce more in the future—life seems abundant. This is the life Jesus had in mind for us (John 10:10).

For a positive example of generosity, see p. 312.

Growth: Seven Signs of Leadership in the Early Church

(Acts 5:1–42)

The leadership of the early church produced growth naturally. The leaders didn't pursue growth, but practiced obedience, commitment, healthy relationships, and faith. Growth was the natural result.

This is a sign of healthy leadership. In Acts 5 we see the leadership ingredients that enable the church to grow:

1. *Purity* (vv. 1–11)
   The leaders didn't settle for anything less than integrity.
2. *Power* (vv. 12–16)
   The leaders modeled an attractive, supernatural power that met human needs.
3. *Persecution* (vv. 17, 18)
   Opposition served to strengthen the leaders and their convictions.
4. *Proclamation* (vv. 19–28)
   The leaders eagerly communicated their message.
5. *Priorities* (vv. 29–32)
   The leaders clearly laid out their top priority, which made decisions easier.
6. *Praise* (v. 41)
   In the midst of adversity, leaders maintained an attitude of gratitude and praised God for everything.
7. *Perseverance* (v. 42)
   The leaders kept right on influencing others, living a life of conviction, not caution..

Continuing Power in the Church

[12]And through the hands of the apostles many signs and wonders were done among the people. And they were all with one accord in Solomon's Porch. [13]Yet none of the rest dared join them, but the people esteemed them highly. [14]And believers were increasingly added to the Lord, multitudes of both men and women, [15]so that they brought the sick out into the streets and laid *them* on beds and couches, that at least the shadow of Peter passing by might fall on some of them. [16]Also a multitude gathered from the surrounding cities to Jerusalem, bringing sick people and those who were tormented by unclean spirits, and they were all healed.

Imprisoned Apostles Freed

[17]Then the high priest rose up, and all those who *were* with him (which is the sect of the Sadducees), and they were filled with indignation, [18]and laid their hands on the apostles and put them in the common prison. [19]But at night an angel of the Lord opened the prison doors and brought them out, and said, [20]"Go, stand in the temple and speak to the people all the words of this life."

[21]And when they heard *that*, they entered the temple early in the morning and taught. But the high priest and those with him came and called the council together, with all the elders of the children of Israel, and sent to the prison to have them brought.

Apostles on Trial Again

[22]But when the officers came and did not find them in the prison, they returned and reported, [23]saying, "Indeed we found the prison shut securely, and the guards standing outside[a] before the doors; but when we opened them, we found no one inside!" [24]Now when the high priest,[a] the captain of the temple, and the chief priests heard these things, they wondered what the outcome would be. [25]So one came and told them, saying,[a] "Look, the men whom you put in prison are standing in the temple and teaching the people!"

[26]Then the captain went with the officers and brought them without violence, for they feared the people, lest they should be stoned. [27]And when they had brought them, they set *them* before the council. And the high priest asked them, [28]saying, "Did we not strictly command you not

5:23 [a]NU-Text and M-Text omit *outside*.
5:24 [a]NU-Text omits *the high priest*.
5:25 [a]NU-Text and M-Text omit *saying*.

to teach in this name? And look, you have filled Jerusalem with your doctrine, and intend to bring this Man's blood on us!"

²⁹But Peter and the *other* apostles answered and said: "We ought to obey God rather than men. ³⁰The God of our fathers raised up Jesus whom you murdered by hanging on a tree. ³¹Him God has exalted to His right hand *to be* Prince and Savior, to give repentance to Israel and forgiveness of sins. ³²And we are His witnesses to these things, and *so* also *is* the Holy Spirit whom God has given to those who obey Him."

Gamaliel's Advice

³³When they heard *this,* they were furious and plotted to kill them. ³⁴Then one in the council stood up, a Pharisee named Gamaliel, a teacher of the law held in respect by all the people, and commanded them to put the apostles outside for a little while. ³⁵And he said to them: "Men of Israel, take heed to yourselves what you intend to do regarding these men. ³⁶For some time ago Theudas rose up, claiming to be somebody. A number of men, about four hundred, joined him. He was slain, and all who obeyed him were scattered and came to nothing. ³⁷After this man, Judas of Galilee rose up in the days of the census, and drew away many people after him. He also perished, and all who obeyed him were dispersed. ³⁸And now I say to you, keep away from these men and let them alone; for if this plan or this work is of men, it will come to nothing; ³⁹but if it is of God, you cannot overthrow it— lest you even be found to fight against God."

⁴⁰And they agreed with him, and when they had called for the apostles and beaten *them,* they commanded that they should not speak in the name of Jesus, and let them go. ⁴¹So they departed from the presence of the council, rejoicing that they were counted worthy to suffer shame for His[a] name. ⁴²And daily in the temple, and in every house, they did not cease teaching and preaching Jesus *as* the Christ.

Seven Chosen to Serve

6 Now in those days, when *the number of* the disciples was multiplying, there arose a complaint against the Hebrews by the Hellenists,[a] because their widows were neglected in the daily distribution. ²Then the twelve summoned the multitude of the disciples and said, "It is not desirable that we should leave the word of God and serve tables. ³Therefore, brethren, seek out from among you seven men of *good* reputation, full of the Holy Spirit and wisdom, whom we may appoint over this business; ⁴but we will

---

Leaders Must Be Determined and Developed

(Acts 6:3)

G ood leadership responds effectively to the need for more leaders and workers. In the early church, no one took a vote to determine the identify of these people. The apostles had specific qualifications in mind for the leaders they wanted, and chose men who were . . .

1. *Known from their sphere of influence*— "seek out from among you."
2. *People who could serve on a team*— "seven men."
3. *Trusted among the people*—"of good reputation."
4. *Empowered for the task*—"full of the Holy Spirit."
5. *Competent and intelligent*—"full of . . . wisdom."
6. *Responsible*—"whom we may appoint over this business."

---

give ourselves continually to prayer and to the ministry of the word."

⁵And the saying pleased the whole multitude. And they chose Stephen, a man full of faith and the Holy Spirit, and Philip, Prochorus, Nicanor, Timon, Parmenas, and Nicolas, a proselyte from Antioch, ⁶whom they set before the apostles; and when they had prayed, they laid hands on them.

⁷Then the word of God spread, and the number of the disciples multiplied greatly in Jerusalem, and a great many of the priests were obedient to the faith.

Stephen Accused of Blasphemy

⁸And Stephen, full of faith[a] and power, did great wonders and signs among the people. ⁹Then there arose some from what is called the Synagogue of the Freedmen (Cyrenians, Alexandrians, and those from Cilicia and Asia), disputing with Stephen. ¹⁰And they were not able to

---

5:41 [a]NU-Text reads *the name;* M-Text reads *the name of Jesus.* 6:1 [a]That is, Greek-speaking Jews 6:8 [a]NU-Text reads *grace.*

PETER AND THE LAW OF PRIORITIES

Leaders Understand That Activity Is Not Necessarily Accomplishment

(Acts 6:1–7)

Leaders never grow to the point where they no longer need to prioritize. Good leaders keep prioritizing, whether they're leading a small group, pastoring a church, running a small business, or leading a billion-dollar corporation.

The things that bring the greatest personal reward light the fires in a leader's life. Nothing energizes a person the way passion does. Tim Redmond admitted, "There are many things that will catch my eye, but there are only a few things that will catch my heart."

Take some time to reassess your leadership priorities. Are you spread out all over the place? Or are you focused on the few things that bring the highest reward? The greatest success comes only when you focus your people on what really matters.

Sharpening Your Focus by Expanding Your View

Maybe you're similar to Peter—he began full of passion, but lacking direction. The good news is that you already have half of the equation. The bad news is that if you don't know where you're going, you'll end up spinning your wheels—or worse, you could spend years heading in the wrong direction.

When you know where you should be headed, your priorities become clearer and your actions take on significance. The equation looks something like this:

$$\text{Great Passion} + \text{Clear Mission} = \text{Focused Action}$$

When the Grecian Jews came to Peter to voice their complaints, Peter recognized that he could further his mission by meeting their felt need. But he also understood that God had called *him* to focus on the people's *deepest* need—to hear the truth of God's Word. Instead of trying to do it all, he delegated the task of addressing the people's complaint to seven men competent to follow through. As a result, the church met both needs.

By examining Peter's situation, we learn a lot about remaining focused on priorities while still seeing the big picture. Peter demonstrated that when a need arises, focused leaders . . .

1. *Determine the validity of the need.*

Strong leaders quickly recognize when a course of action needs to be taken, and they promptly consider how to get the job done. Peter knew that the church could lose momentum if it didn't meet the Grecian Jews' request. Rather than trying to meet the need by himself (as many leaders do), he figured out another way to meet it.

How do you react when your people bring a genuine need before you? Do you stop what you're doing and immediately try to take care of it? Do you nod your head as if you're interested, then push it to the side and forget about it? Or, like Peter, do you step back, look at the big picture, and determine appropriate action according to your priorities?

2. *Look for a leadership opportunity.*

Even when a valid need doesn't fit *your* priorities, it may provide a learning opportunity for one of your people. Peter quickly recognized that he and the other disciples needed to continue teaching rather than hand out food. But he also recognized an opportunity to develop some emerging leaders.

Are your people one of your top priorities? Before you put something on a back burner, evaluate whether it fits the responsibilities of one or more of your people. The most effective leaders focus on only a few things; they trust their people to do the rest.

3. *Delegate the task to competent people.*

Leaders use delegation as a basic tool. Used the right way, it can take your efficiency to a whole new level. Peter and the disciples carefully chose a team of seven whom they deemed mature and capable to carry out the task.

It's always your responsibility to delegate to the right people. There's nothing worse than having to revisit a need because you assigned an incompetent person to the job. That decreases your efficiency and can damage your credibility. Before you delegate a task, make sure you know your people's skills and abilities.

4. *Publicly confirm and commission their people.*

Peter and the disciples set up their team for success. They not only made sure the seven men could meet the need, but also presented them to the people as worthy leaders. In doing so, they built trust and confidence in the men.

Is it more important to you to get things done or to get things done *right*? Many leaders hurriedly delegate a task just to check it off their to-do list. They falsely perceive delegation as a way of decreasing distractions instead of increasing effectiveness. But great leaders understand that their effectiveness depends on their people's success. Therefore they make it a priority to help them succeed.

Like all effective leaders, Peter understood the difference between activity and accomplishment. He viewed a need through the biggest lens first—his overall mission. Then he zoomed in on what needed to be done—first by him, then by others. As a result, Scripture says the number of Christians continually increased under his leadership.

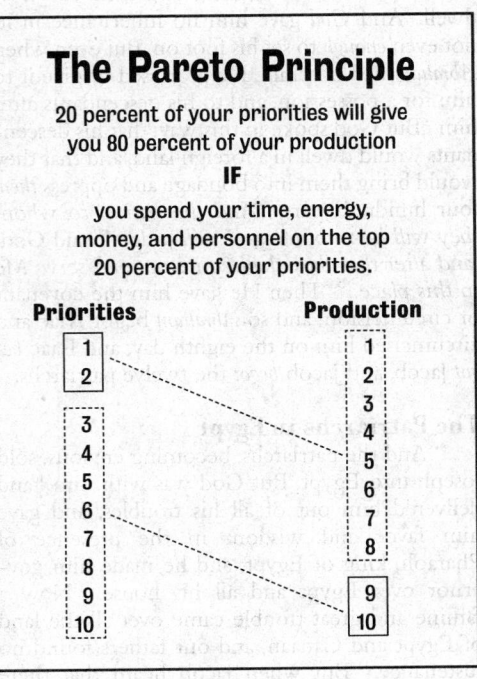

The Pareto Principle

20 percent of your priorities will give
you 80 percent of your production

IF

you spend your time, energy,
money, and personnel on the top
20 percent of your priorities.

Priorities   Production

resist the wisdom and the Spirit by which he spoke. [11]Then they secretly induced men to say, "We have heard him speak blasphemous words against Moses and God." [12]And they stirred up the people, the elders, and the scribes; and they came upon *him,* seized him, and brought *him* to the council. [13]They also set up false witnesses who said, "This man does not cease to speak blasphemous[a] words against this holy place and the law; [14]for we have heard him say that this Jesus of Nazareth will destroy this place and change the customs which Moses delivered to us." [15]And all who sat in the council, looking steadfastly at him, saw his face as the face of an angel.

Stephen's Address: The Call of Abraham

7 Then the high priest said, "Are these things so?"

[2]And he said, "Brethren and fathers, listen: The God of glory appeared to our father Abraham when he was in Mesopotamia, before he dwelt in Haran, [3]and said to him, *'Get out of your country and from your relatives, and come to a land that I will show you.'*[a] [4]Then he came out of the land of the Chaldeans and dwelt in Haran. And from there, when his father was dead, He moved him to this land in which you now dwell. [5]And *God* gave him no inheritance in it, not even *enough* to set his foot on. But even when *Abraham* had no child, He promised to give it to him for a possession, and to his descendants after him. [6]But God spoke in this way: that his descendants would dwell in a foreign land, and that they would bring them into bondage and oppress *them* four hundred years. [7]*'And the nation to whom they will be in bondage I will judge,'*[a] said God, *'and after that they shall come out and serve Me in this place.'*[b] [8]Then He gave him the covenant of circumcision; and so *Abraham* begot Isaac and circumcised him on the eighth day; and Isaac *begot* Jacob, and Jacob *begot* the twelve patriarchs.

The Patriarchs in Egypt

[9]"And the patriarchs, becoming envious, sold Joseph into Egypt. But God was with him [10]and delivered him out of all his troubles, and gave him favor and wisdom in the presence of Pharaoh, king of Egypt; and he made him governor over Egypt and all his house. [11]Now a famine and great trouble came over all the land of Egypt and Canaan, and our fathers found no sustenance. [12]But when Jacob heard that there was grain in Egypt, he sent out our fathers first. [13]And the second *time* Joseph was made known to his brothers, and Joseph's family became known to the Pharaoh. [14]Then Joseph sent and called his father Jacob and all his relatives to *him,* seventy-five[a] people. [15]So Jacob went down to Egypt; and he died, he and our fathers. [16]And they were carried back to Shechem and laid in the tomb that Abraham bought for a sum of money from the sons of Hamor, *the father* of Shechem.

God Delivers Israel by Moses

[17]"But when the time of the promise drew near which God had sworn to Abraham, the people grew and multiplied in Egypt [18]till another king arose who did not know Joseph. [19]This man dealt treacherously with our people, and oppressed our forefathers, making them expose their babies, so that they might not live. [20]At this time Moses was born, and was well pleasing to God; and he was brought up in his father's house for three months. [21]But when he was set out, Pharaoh's daughter took him away and brought him up as her own son. [22]And Moses was learned in all the wisdom of the Egyptians, and was mighty in words and deeds.

[23]"Now when he was forty years old, it came into his heart to visit his brethren, the children of Israel. [24]And seeing one of *them* suffer wrong, he defended and avenged him who was oppressed, and struck down the Egyptian. [25]For he supposed that his brethren would have understood that God would deliver them by his hand, but they did not understand. [26]And the next day he appeared to two of them as they were fighting, and *tried to* reconcile them, saying, 'Men, you are brethren; why do you wrong one another?' [27]But he who did his neighbor wrong pushed him away, saying, *'Who made you a ruler and a judge over us? [28]Do you want to kill me as you did the Egyptian yesterday?'*[a] [29]Then, at this saying, Moses fled and became a dweller in the land of Midian, where he had two sons.

[30]"And when forty years had passed, an Angel of the Lord[a] appeared to him in a flame of fire in a bush, in the wilderness of Mount Sinai. [31]When Moses saw *it,* he marveled at the sight; and as he drew near to observe, the voice of the Lord came to him, [32]*saying, 'I am the God of your fathers—the God of Abraham, the God of Isaac, and the God of Jacob.'*[a] And Moses trembled and dared not look. [33]*Then the LORD said to him, "Take your sandals off your feet, for the place where you stand is holy ground.* [34]*I have surely seen the*

6:13 [a]NU-Text omits *blasphemous.* **7:3** [a]Genesis 12:1 **7:7** [a]Genesis 15:14 [b]Exodus 3:12 **7:14** [a]Or *seventy* (compare Exodus 1:5) **7:28** [a]Exodus 2:14 **7:30** [a]NU-Text omits *of the Lord.* **7:32** [a]Exodus 3:6, 15

21 QUALITIES

COMMITMENT

Stephen Knew What to Stand For and Not Stand For
(Acts 7:2–60)

Stephen, the first Christian martyr, had earned great influence among the people (Acts 6:8). Fearing the loss of their own influence, Jewish religious leaders seize this leader and bring him before the council.

In his defense, Stephen displays an unwavering commitment to his convictions. In the face of authorities with the power to execute him, he stands and expresses what he knows to be true, both about Christ and the religious leaders' stubborn hearts. This leads to his stoning (7:58–60). His straightforward manner leaves the religious leaders with no argument; they can only throw rocks. Yet even this doesn't shake him. He dies, gazing into heaven, asking God to forgive his murderers.

Where Did the Commitment Come From?

See the source of Stephen's commitment by considering his words and sensing his attitude:

1. He had the presence of God in his life (6:8, 15).
2. He based his commitment on a biblical foundation (7:2–38).
3. He saw the error of past thinking (7:39–41).
4. He spotted the resistance of the religious leaders (7:51–53).
5. He kept his eyes on Jesus, the truth (7:55).
6. He maintained his perspective (7:60).

Commitment moves past the mind and emotions and goes straight to the will. The ancient Chinese said that the will of a man is like a cart pulled by two horses: the mind and the emotions. You must get both horses moving in the same direction to move the cart. Commitment results when your mind and emotions move forward, whatever the cost.

Leaders cannot expect followers to make commitments deeper than the ones they make. To develop commitment we must understand the following truths:

1. *Commitment starts in the heart.*
   Commitment precedes achievement. Look inside: where is your heart committed?
2. *Commitment is tested by action.*
   The only real measure of commitment is action. Talk is cheap; action is expensive.
3. *Commitment opens the door for accomplishment.*
   Once you commit yourself, all kinds of resources come your way to help you succeed.
4. *Commitment can be measured.*
   Leaders must evaluate their calendars and checkbooks to measure their commitment.
5. *Commitment enables a leader to make decisions.*
   Leaders must determine what's worth dying for, then make that the basis for decisions.
6. *Commitment flourishes with public accountability.*
   Go public with your commitments; then you'll have incentive to follow through.

For a negative example of commitment, see p. 1269.

oppression of My people who are in Egypt; I have heard their groaning and have come down to deliver them. And now come, I will send you to Egypt."[a]

[35]"This Moses whom they rejected, saying, 'Who made you a ruler and a judge?'[a] is the one God sent to be a ruler and a deliverer by the hand of the Angel who appeared to him in the bush. [36]He brought them out, after he had shown wonders and signs in the land of Egypt, and in the Red Sea, and in the wilderness forty years.

Israel Rebels Against God

[37]"This is that Moses who said to the children of Israel,[a] 'The LORD your God will raise up for you a Prophet like me from your brethren. Him you shall hear.'[b]

[38]"This is he who was in the congregation in the wilderness with the Angel who spoke to him on Mount Sinai, and with our fathers, the one who received the living oracles to give to us, [39]whom our fathers would not obey, but rejected. And in their hearts they turned back to Egypt, [40]saying to Aaron, 'Make us gods to go before us; as for this Moses who brought us out of the land of Egypt, we do not know what has become of him.'[a] [41]And they made a calf in those days, offered sacrifices to the idol, and rejoiced in the works of their own hands. [42]Then God turned and gave them up to worship the host of heaven, as it is written in the book of the Prophets:

'Did you offer Me slaughtered animals and sacrifices during forty years in the wilderness,
O house of Israel?
[43]   You also took up the tabernacle of Moloch,
And the star of your god Remphan,
Images which you made to worship;
And I will carry you away beyond Babylon.'[a]

God's True Tabernacle

[44]"Our fathers had the tabernacle of witness in the wilderness, as He appointed, instructing Moses to make it according to the pattern that he had seen, [45]which our fathers, having received it in turn, also brought with Joshua into the land possessed by the Gentiles, whom God drove out before the face of our fathers until the days of David, [46]who found favor before God and asked to find a dwelling for the God of Jacob. [47]But Solomon built Him a house.

[48]"However, the Most High does not dwell in temples made with hands, as the prophet says:

[49]   'Heaven is My throne,
And earth is My footstool.

What house will you build for Me? says
the LORD,
Or what is the place of My rest?
[50]   Has My hand not made all these things?'[a]

Israel Resists the Holy Spirit

[51]"You stiff-necked and uncircumcised in heart and ears! You always resist the Holy Spirit; as your fathers did, so do you. [52]Which of the prophets did your fathers not persecute? And they killed those who foretold the coming of the Just One, of whom you now have become the betrayers and murderers, [53]who have received the law by the direction of angels and have not kept it."

Stephen the Martyr

[54]When they heard these things they were cut to the heart, and they gnashed at him with their teeth. [55]But he, being full of the Holy Spirit, gazed into heaven and saw the glory of God, and Jesus standing at the right hand of God, [56]and said, "Look! I see the heavens opened and the Son of Man standing at the right hand of God!"

[57]Then they cried out with a loud voice, stopped their ears, and ran at him with one accord; [58]and they cast him out of the city and stoned him. And the witnesses laid down their clothes at the feet of a young man named Saul. [59]And they stoned Stephen as he was calling on God and saying, "Lord Jesus, receive my spirit." [60]Then he knelt down and cried out with a loud voice, "Lord, do not charge them with this sin." And when he had said this, he fell asleep.

Saul Persecutes the Church

8 Now Saul was consenting to his death.
At that time a great persecution arose against the church which was at Jerusalem; and they were all scattered throughout the regions of Judea and Samaria, except the apostles. [2]And devout men carried Stephen to his burial, and made great lamentation over him.

[3]As for Saul, he made havoc of the church, entering every house, and dragging off men and women, committing them to prison.

Christ Is Preached in Samaria

[4]Therefore those who were scattered went everywhere preaching the word. [5]Then Philip went down to the[a] city of Samaria and preached Christ to them. [6]And the multitudes with one

7:34 [a]Exodus 3:5, 7, 8, 10 **7:35** [a]Exodus 2:14
7:37 [a]Deuteronomy 18:15 [b]NU-Text and M-Text omit Him you shall hear. **7:40** [a]Exodus 32:1, 23
7:43 [a]Amos 5:25–27 **7:50** [a]Isaiah 66:1, 2 **8:5** [a]Or a

accord heeded the things spoken by Philip, hearing and seeing the miracles which he did. [7]For unclean spirits, crying with a loud voice, came out of many who were possessed; and many who were paralyzed and lame were healed. [8]And there was great joy in that city.

The Sorcerer's Profession of Faith

[9]But there was a certain man called Simon, who previously practiced sorcery in the city and astonished the people of Samaria, claiming that he was someone great, [10]to whom they all gave heed, from the least to the greatest, saying, "This man is the great power of God." [11]And they heeded him because he had astonished them with his sorceries for a long time. [12]But when they believed Philip as he preached the things concerning the kingdom of God and the name of Jesus Christ, both men and women were baptized. [13]Then Simon himself also believed; and when he was baptized he continued with Philip, and was amazed, seeing the miracles and signs which were done.

The Sorcerer's Sin

[14]Now when the apostles who were at Jerusalem heard that Samaria had received the word of God, they sent Peter and John to them, [15]who, when they had come down, prayed for them that they might receive the Holy Spirit. [16]For as yet He had fallen upon none of them. They had only been baptized in the name of the Lord Jesus. [17]Then they laid hands on them, and they received the Holy Spirit.

[18]And when Simon saw that through the laying on of the apostles' hands the Holy Spirit was given, he offered them money, [19]saying, "Give me this power also, that anyone on whom I lay hands may receive the Holy Spirit."

[20]But Peter said to him, "Your money perish with you, because you thought that the gift of God could be purchased with money! [21]You have neither part nor portion in this matter, for your heart is not right in the sight of God. [22]Repent therefore of this your wickedness, and pray God if perhaps the thought of your heart may be forgiven you. [23]For I see that you are poisoned by bitterness and bound by iniquity."

[24]Then Simon answered and said, "Pray to the Lord for me, that none of the things which you have spoken may come upon me."

[25]So when they had testified and preached the word of the Lord, they returned to Jerusalem, preaching the gospel in many villages of the Samaritans.

PHILIP

ORDINARY MAN, EXTRAORDINARY RESULTS
(Acts 8:5–8)

PROFILE IN LEADERSHIP

It's amazing what can happen to and through an ordinary man when God pours a little hardship and the power of the Holy Spirit into the mix.

The believers of the Jerusalem church began fleeing the city in droves due to the waves of persecution they faced because of their testimony for Jesus Christ. But what the enemies of the faith meant for evil, God used for good, as the scattering believers carried with them the message of salvation through the Lord Jesus Christ.

Philip fled Jerusalem and headed toward Samaria, where his commitment to preaching the gospel led to the salvation of multitudes. When Philip performed miracles—casting out evil spirits and healing many—the people listened to Philip's words about the Messiah, who empowered him to perform these astonishing deeds.

One ordinary man, a little persecution, and a touch from the Spirit of God led to massive conversions in the city of Samaria. As Jesus had predicted, the gospel message made its way from Jerusalem into the outlying world (Acts 1:8).

Philip illustrates what one leader, with the empowerment of the Spirit of God and with the authority of Jesus Christ, can do to change the world.

Discernment: Leaders Read the Situation Before They Lead

(Acts 8:26–40)

Philip illustrates the importance of a leader who can adapt to a new situation and meet the need. Flexibility is the name of the game.

Philip had been preaching and praying for the sick in Samaria. While in the middle of revival, an angel spoke to him and told him to go south, to the Gaza road. Philip had to adjust his sails and redirect his course. On the road to Gaza, he read the situation. A significant official, the treasurer of Ethiopia, had stopped to read the Scriptures. Philip seized the opportunity to introduce the man to Christ.

How do leaders read similar situations? Spirit-filled leadership involves . . .

1. *Seeing your responsibilities* (v. 25).
   Philip was already doing what he knew to do.
2. *Surrendering your rights* (vv. 26–28).
   Philip didn't demand his own way, but remained flexible. He left a revival to go to a desert.
3. *Sensing your revelation* (vv. 29, 30).
   Philip listened to the Spirit. God may speak through people, Scripture, or spiritual intuition.
4. *Sharing your relationship* (vv. 31–34).
   Philip approached the need from a relational perspective, not just a result perspective.
5. *Showing your relevance* (v. 35).
   Philip started where the Ethiopian eunuch was and connected with him there.
6. *Securing your response* (vv. 36–39).
   Philip led the man to a point of decision and saw results.

Christ Is Preached to an Ethiopian

²⁶Now an angel of the Lord spoke to Philip, saying, "Arise and go toward the south along the road which goes down from Jerusalem to Gaza." This is desert. ²⁷So he arose and went. And behold, a man of Ethiopia, a eunuch of great authority under Candace the queen of the Ethiopians, who had charge of all her treasury, and had come to Jerusalem to worship, ²⁸was returning. And sitting in his chariot, he was reading Isaiah the prophet. ²⁹Then the Spirit said to Philip, "Go near and overtake this chariot."

³⁰So Philip ran to him, and heard him reading the prophet Isaiah, and said, "Do you understand what you are reading?"

³¹And he said, "How can I, unless someone guides me?" And he asked Philip to come up and sit with him. ³²The place in the Scripture which he read was this:

"*He was led as a sheep to the slaughter;*
And as a lamb before its shearer is silent,
So He opened not His mouth.
³³ *In His humiliation His justice was taken*
away,

And who will declare His generation?
For His life is taken from the earth."ᵃ

³⁴So the eunuch answered Philip and said, "I ask you, of whom does the prophet say this, of himself or of some other man?" ³⁵Then Philip opened his mouth, and beginning at this Scripture, preached Jesus to him. ³⁶Now as they went down the road, they came to some water. And the eunuch said, "See, *here is* water. What hinders me from being baptized?"

³⁷Then Philip said, "If you believe with all your heart, you may."

And he answered and said, "I believe that Jesus Christ is the Son of God."ᵃ

³⁸So he commanded the chariot to stand still. And both Philip and the eunuch went down into the water, and he baptized him. ³⁹Now when they came up out of the water, the Spirit of the Lord caught Philip away, so that the eunuch saw

8:33 ᵃIsaiah 53:7, 8　**8:37** ᵃNU-Text and M-Text omit this verse. It is found in Western texts, including the Latin tradition.

him no more; and he went on his way rejoicing. [40]But Philip was found at Azotus. And passing through, he preached in all the cities till he came to Caesarea.

The Damascus Road: Saul Converted

9 Then Saul, still breathing threats and murder against the disciples of the Lord, went to the high priest [2]and asked letters from him to the synagogues of Damascus, so that if he found any who were of the Way, whether men or women, he might bring them bound to Jerusalem.

[3]As he journeyed he came near Damascus, and suddenly a light shone around him from heaven. [4]Then he fell to the ground, and heard a voice saying to him, "Saul, Saul, why are you persecuting Me?"

[5]And he said, "Who are You, Lord?"

Then the Lord said, "I am Jesus, whom you are persecuting.[a] It *is* hard for you to kick against the goads."

[6]So he, trembling and astonished, said, "Lord, what do You want me to do?"

Then the Lord *said* to him, "Arise and go into the city, and you will be told what you must do."

[7]And the men who journeyed with him stood speechless, hearing a voice but seeing no one. [8]Then Saul arose from the ground, and when his eyes were opened he saw no one. But they led him by the hand and brought *him* into Damascus. [9]And he was three days without sight, and neither ate nor drank.

Ananias Baptizes Saul

[10]Now there was a certain disciple at Damascus named Ananias; and to him the Lord said in a vision, "Ananias."

And he said, "Here I am, Lord."

[11]So the Lord *said* to him, "Arise and go to the street called Straight, and inquire at the house of Judas for *one* called Saul of Tarsus, for behold, he is praying. [12]And in a vision he has seen a man named Ananias coming in and putting *his* hand on him, so that he might receive his sight."

[13]Then Ananias answered, "Lord, I have heard from many about this man, how much harm he has done to Your saints in Jerusalem. [14]And here he has authority from the chief priests to bind all who call on Your name."

[15]But the Lord said to him, "Go, for he is a chosen vessel of Mine to bear My name before Gentiles, kings, and the children of Israel. [16]For I will show him how many things he must suffer for My name's sake."

Leadership: Deliberate Selection vs. Democratic Election

(Acts 9:1–20)

Saul of Tarsus began his journey to becoming Paul the apostle on the road to Damascus. God knew Saul was perfectly suited for the task.

First, Paul was a Hebrew and a Pharisee. No one could accuse him of indifference or failure to set a standard. He had studied under Gamaliel, so no Jew would consider him ignorant of the Scriptures. He grew up in Tarsus, which gave him his Roman citizenship and acquainted him with the ways of the world. He was an articulate communicator, which made him perfect to write nearly two thirds of the New Testament. He hotly pursued righteousness, a passion that helped him reach Asia Minor.

God appoints specific leaders to fulfill a mission; He doesn't hold a popular vote. If He had, no ancient believer would have voted for Saul. Instead, God saw Saul's qualities and called him to both follow Jesus and lead men.

---

[17]And Ananias went his way and entered the house; and laying his hands on him he said, "Brother Saul, the Lord Jesus,[a] who appeared to you on the road as you came, has sent me that you may receive your sight and be filled with the Holy Spirit." [18]Immediately there fell from his eyes *something* like scales, and he received his sight at once; and he arose and was baptized. [19]So when he had received food, he was strengthened. Then Saul spent some days with the disciples at Damascus.

Saul Preaches Christ

[20]Immediately he preached the Christ[a] in the synagogues, that He is the Son of God.

[21]Then all who heard were amazed, and said, "Is this not he who destroyed those who called on this name in Jerusalem, and has come here for

---

9:5 [a]NU-Text and M-Text omit the last sentence of verse 5 and begin verse 6 with *But arise and go.*
9:17 [a]M-Text omits *Jesus.* **9:20** [a]NU-Text reads *Jesus.*

BARNABAS AND THE LAW OF EMPOWERMENT

Only Secure Leaders Give Power to Others

(Acts 9:27)

Only empowered people can reach their potential. When a leader can't or won't empower others, he creates barriers within the organization that people cannot overcome. If the barriers remain long enough, the people give up, or they move to another organization where they can maximize their potential.

If you want to be a successful leader, you have to become an empowerer. Theodore Roosevelt realized that "the best executive is one who has the sense enough to pick good men to do what he wants done, and the self-restraint enough to keep from meddling with them while they do it."

The truth is that the only way to make yourself indispensable is to make yourself dispensable. In other words, if you are able to continually empower others and help them develop so that they become capable of taking over your job, you will become so valuable to the organization that you become indispensable.

Can I Get a Lift?

Barnabas was definitely a lifter of people. It seems as though he let no opportunity escape to add value to others. And his greatest single contribution in terms of empowerment can be seen in his interaction with Paul.

1. *He believed in Paul before anyone else did.*

It's easy to give an opinion about a controversial person or subject after other leaders have given their support. It's something else to step up and speak before *anyone* else does. That's what Barnabas did. He didn't wait until the apostles endorsed Paul before believing in him. In fact, he believed in Paul while Peter and the others feared him.

To be an encouraging leader, you have to be willing to take chances on people. You have to look for the potential in them and encourage them to believe in themselves. And that can be risky, because they may not come through. But if they do, the payoff can be huge. You may be responsible for inspiring a new leader to achieve things he never thought possible. And leaders never forget the first person who believed in them.

2. *He endorsed Paul's leadership to other leaders.*

Scripture says that Barnabas took Paul "and brought him to the apostles. And he declared to them how he had seen the Lord on the road, and that He had spoken to him, and how he had preached boldly at Damascus in the name of Jesus" (Acts 9:27).

Can you imagine how things might have gone in Jerusalem in those days? Once Paul arrived in the city, word reached the apostles that he was claiming to be a supporter of Christ. They must have thought it was a trick. Here was the same man who had stood by and approved the stoning of Stephen, the first Christian martyr!

Barnabas must have shown up at one of the apostles' gatherings with Paul in tow. An uncomfortable silence no doubt fell over the gathering as people realized the identity of Barnabas's companion. And then Barnabas told Paul's story. Paul didn't have to say a word. All the believers knew Barnabas. They knew his reputation, his integrity. That was all it took. Scripture records, "So he was with them at Jerusalem, coming in and going out" (Acts 9:28). The church had accepted Paul.

One of the best things you can do as an empowering leader is to sing your people's praises to others. When they're doing a good job, tell everyone. Be especially intentional about praising them to their friends and families. But also bring them before other leaders. Help them to make a connection on the strength of your credibility.

3. *He empowered Paul to reach his potential.*

The connection between Barnabas and Paul didn't end in Jerusalem. After Barnabas's endorsement enabled Paul to move freely throughout Jerusalem, teaching the people and debating the truth of Scripture, it wasn't long before Paul became an enemy of nonbelievers. The apostles wisely sent him back to Tarsus for his own safety.

But later, when Barnabas was assigned to help the church in Antioch, he found Paul and made him his companion. That action empowered Paul to take his first "assignment" as a leader, and it led to Paul's partnership with Barnabas as a missionary—the role for which God had destined him.

To be an empowering leader, you must do more than believe in emerging leaders. You need to take steps to help them *become* the leaders they have the potential to be. You must invest in them if you want to empower them to become their best.

Empowering people takes a personal investment. It requires energy and time. But it's worth the price. If you do it right, you will have the privilege of seeing someone move up to a higher level. And as an added bonus, when you empower others you create power in your organization.

that purpose, so that he might bring them bound to the chief priests?"

²²But Saul increased all the more in strength, and confounded the Jews who dwelt in Damascus, proving that this *Jesus* is the Christ.

Saul Escapes Death

²³Now after many days were past, the Jews plotted to kill him. ²⁴But their plot became known to Saul. And they watched the gates day and night, to kill him. ²⁵Then the disciples took him by night and let *him* down through the wall in a large basket.

Saul at Jerusalem

²⁶And when Saul had come to Jerusalem, he tried to join the disciples; but they were all afraid of him, and did not believe that he was a disciple. ²⁷But Barnabas took him and brought *him* to the apostles. And he declared to them how he had seen the Lord on the road, and that He had spoken to him, and how he had preached boldly at Damascus in the name of Jesus. ²⁸So he was with them at Jerusalem, coming in and going out. ²⁹And he spoke boldly in the name of the Lord Jesus and disputed against the Hellenists, but they attempted to kill him. ³⁰When the brethren found out, they brought him down to Caesarea and sent him out to Tarsus.

The Church Prospers

³¹Then the churches[a] throughout all Judea, Galilee, and Samaria had peace and were edified. And walking in the fear of the Lord and in the comfort of the Holy Spirit, they were multiplied.

Aeneas Healed

³²Now it came to pass, as Peter went through all *parts of the country,* that he also came down to the saints who dwelt in Lydda. ³³There he found a certain man named Aeneas, who had been bedridden eight years and was paralyzed. ³⁴And Peter said to him, "Aeneas, Jesus the Christ heals you. Arise and make your bed." Then he arose immediately. ³⁵So all who dwelt at Lydda and Sharon saw him and turned to the Lord.

Dorcas Restored to Life

³⁶At Joppa there was a certain disciple named Tabitha, which is translated Dorcas. This woman was full of good works and charitable deeds which she did. ³⁷But it happened in those days that she became sick and died. When they had washed her, they laid *her* in an upper room. ³⁸And since Lydda was near Joppa, and the disciples had heard that Peter was there, they sent two men to him, imploring *him* not to delay in coming to them. ³⁹Then Peter arose and went with them. When he had come, they brought *him* to the upper room. And all the widows stood by him weeping, showing the tunics and garments which Dorcas had made while she was with them. ⁴⁰But Peter put them all out, and knelt down and prayed. And turning to the body he said, "Tabitha, arise." And she opened her eyes, and when she saw Peter she sat up. ⁴¹Then he gave her *his* hand and lifted her up; and when he had called the saints and widows, he presented her alive. ⁴²And it became known throughout all Joppa, and many believed on the Lord. ⁴³So it was that he stayed many days in Joppa with Simon, a tanner.

Cornelius Sends a Delegation

10 There was a certain man in Caesarea called Cornelius, a centurion of what was called the Italian Regiment, ²a devout *man* and one who feared God with all his household, who gave alms generously to the people, and prayed to God always. ³About the ninth hour of the day he saw clearly in a vision an angel of God coming in and saying to him, "Cornelius!"

⁴And when he observed him, he was afraid, and said, "What is it, lord?"

So he said to him, "Your prayers and your alms have come up for a memorial before God. ⁵Now send men to Joppa, and send for Simon whose surname is Peter. ⁶He is lodging with Simon, a tanner, whose house is by the sea.[a] He will tell you what you must do." ⁷And when the angel who spoke to him had departed, Cornelius called two of his household servants and a devout soldier from among those who waited on him continually. ⁸So when he had explained all *these* things to them, he sent them to Joppa.

Peter's Vision

⁹The next day, as they went on their journey and drew near the city, Peter went up on the housetop to pray, about the sixth hour. ¹⁰Then he became very hungry and wanted to eat; but while they made ready, he fell into a trance ¹¹and saw heaven opened and an object like a great sheet bound at the four corners, descending to him and let down to the earth. ¹²In it were all kinds of four-footed animals of the earth, wild

---

9:31 [a]NU-Text reads *church . . . was edified.*
10:6 [a]NU-Text and M-Text omit the last sentence of this verse.

Cornelius: Peter's Paradigm Expands

(Acts 10:1–35)

Missiologists would have called him ethnocentric. While the apostle Peter knew that Jesus told him to go into all the world and preach the gospel, he still had trouble speaking with a Roman centurion named Cornelius. So God provided fresh vision for him. Author Steve Moore notes the sequence of God's vision-building work:

1. *Supernatural Revelation* (vv. 9–16)
   God expands Peter's horizons and helps him out of the box—education that led to new conviction.
2. *Supernatural Invitation* (vv. 17–23)
   God sends associates of Cornelius to invite Peter to enter a new scope of ministry to Gentiles—exposure that led to a new compassion.
3. *Supernatural Confirmation* (vv. 24–35)
   God confirmed this enlarged vision with a receptive Cornelius and signs following his conversion—an experience that led to new commitment.

When God wants to draw new obedience from His servants, He almost always communicates fresh vision. This is exactly what Peter got.

beasts, creeping things, and birds of the air. [13]And a voice came to him, "Rise, Peter; kill and eat."

[14]But Peter said, "Not so, Lord! For I have never eaten anything common or unclean."

[15]And a voice *spoke* to him again the second time, "What God has cleansed you must not call common." [16]This was done three times. And the object was taken up into heaven again.

Summoned to Caesarea

[17]Now while Peter wondered within himself what this vision which he had seen meant, behold, the men who had been sent from Cornelius had made inquiry for Simon's house, and stood before the gate. [18]And they called and asked whether Simon, whose surname was Peter, was lodging there.

[19]While Peter thought about the vision, the Spirit said to him, "Behold, three men are seek-

ing you. [20]Arise therefore, go down and go with them, doubting nothing; for I have sent them."

[21]Then Peter went down to the men who had been sent to him from Cornelius,[a] and said, "Yes, I am he whom you seek. For what reason have you come?"

[22]And they said, "Cornelius *the* centurion, a just man, one who fears God and has a good reputation among all the nation of the Jews, was divinely instructed by a holy angel to summon you to his house, and to hear words from you." [23]Then he invited them in and lodged *them*.

On the next day Peter went away with them, and some brethren from Joppa accompanied him.

Peter Meets Cornelius

[24]And the following day they entered Caesarea. Now Cornelius was waiting for them, and had called together his relatives and close friends. [25]As Peter was coming in, Cornelius met him and fell down at his feet and worshiped *him*. [26]But Peter lifted him up, saying, "Stand up; I myself am also a man." [27]And as he talked with him, he went in and found many who had come together. [28]Then he said to them, "You know how unlawful it is for a Jewish man to keep company with or go to one of another nation. But God has shown me that I should not call any man common or unclean. [29]Therefore I came without objection as soon as I was sent for. I ask, then, for what reason have you sent for me?"

[30]So Cornelius said, "Four days ago I was fasting until this hour; and at the ninth hour[a] I prayed in my house, and behold, a man stood before me in bright clothing, [31]and said, 'Cornelius, your prayer has been heard, and your alms are remembered in the sight of God. [32]Send therefore to Joppa and call Simon here, whose surname is Peter. He is lodging in the house of Simon, a tanner, by the sea.[a] When he comes, he will speak to you.' [33]So I sent to you immediately, and you have done well to come. Now therefore, we are all present before God, to hear all the things commanded you by God."

Preaching to Cornelius' Household

[34]Then Peter opened *his* mouth and said: "In truth I perceive that God shows no partiality. [35]But in every nation whoever fears Him and works righteousness is accepted by Him. [36]The word which *God* sent to the children of Israel,

---

10:21 [a]NU-Text and M-Text omit *who had been sent to him from Cornelius.* **10:30** [a]NU-Text reads *Four days ago to this hour, at the ninth hour.* **10:32** [a]NU-Text omits the last sentence of this verse.

preaching peace through Jesus Christ—He is Lord of all— [37]that word you know, which was proclaimed throughout all Judea, and began from Galilee after the baptism which John preached: [38]how God anointed Jesus of Nazareth with the Holy Spirit and with power, who went about doing good and healing all who were oppressed by the devil, for God was with Him. [39]And we are witnesses of all things which He did both in the land of the Jews and in Jerusalem, whom they[a] killed by hanging on a tree. [40]Him God raised up on the third day, and showed Him openly, [41]not to all the people, but to witnesses chosen before by God, *even* to us who ate and drank with Him after He arose from the dead. [42]And He commanded us to preach to the people, and to testify that it is He who was ordained by God *to be* Judge of the living and the dead. [43]To Him all the prophets witness that, through His name, whoever believes in Him will receive remission of sins."

The Holy Spirit Falls on the Gentiles

[44]While Peter was still speaking these words, the Holy Spirit fell upon all those who heard the word. [45]And those of the circumcision who believed were astonished, as many as came with Peter, because the gift of the Holy Spirit had been poured out on the Gentiles also. [46]For they heard them speak with tongues and magnify God.

Then Peter answered, [47]"Can anyone forbid water, that these should not be baptized who have received the Holy Spirit just as we *have?*" [48]And he commanded them to be baptized in the name of the Lord. Then they asked him to stay a few days.

Peter Defends God's Grace

11 Now the apostles and brethren who were in Judea heard that the Gentiles had also received the word of God. [2]And when Peter came up to Jerusalem, those of the circumcision contended with him, [3]saying, "You went in to uncircumcised men and ate with them!"

[4]But Peter explained *it* to them in order from the beginning, saying: [5]"I was in the city of Joppa praying; and in a trance I saw a vision, an object descending like a great sheet, let down from heaven by four corners; and it came to me. [6]When I observed it intently and considered, I saw four-footed animals of the earth, wild beasts, creeping things, and birds of the air. [7]And I heard a voice saying to me, 'Rise, Peter; kill and eat.' [8]But I said, 'Not so, Lord! For nothing common or unclean has at any time entered my mouth.' [9]But the voice answered me again from heaven,

'What God has cleansed you must not call common.' [10]Now this was done three times, and all were drawn up again into heaven. [11]At that very moment, three men stood before the house where I was, having been sent to me from Caesarea. [12]Then the Spirit told me to go with them, doubting nothing. Moreover these six brethren accompanied me, and we entered the man's house. [13]And he told us how he had seen an angel standing in his house, who said to him, 'Send men to Joppa, and call for Simon whose surname is Peter, [14]who will tell you words by which you and all your household will be saved.' [15]And as I began to speak, the Holy Spirit fell upon them, as upon us at the beginning. [16]Then I remembered the word of the Lord, how He said, 'John indeed baptized with water, but you shall be baptized with the Holy Spirit.' [17]If therefore God gave them the same gift as *He gave* us when we believed on the Lord Jesus Christ, who was I that I could withstand God?"

[18]When they heard these things they became silent; and they glorified God, saying, "Then God has also granted to the Gentiles repentance to life."

Teachability: Peter's New Market Accepted by Church Leaders

(Acts 11:1–18)

Jesus must have been serious when He told the church to go to the Gentiles! Peter reported to his peers how God had led him to a whole new audience. By the time they heard the story, they glorified God for the new ministry. They remained teachable. The moment you stop learning, you stop leading.

Barnabas and Saul at Antioch

[19]Now those who were scattered after the persecution that arose over Stephen traveled as far as Phoenicia, Cyprus, and Antioch, preaching the word to no one but the Jews only. [20]But some of them were men from Cyprus and Cyrene, who, when they had come to Antioch, spoke to the Hellenists, preaching the Lord Jesus. [21]And the hand of the Lord was with them, and a great number believed and turned to the Lord.

10:39 [a]NU-Text and M-Text add *also.*

²²Then news of these things came to the ears of the church in Jerusalem, and they sent out Barnabas to go as far as Antioch. ²³When he came and had seen the grace of God, he was glad, and encouraged them all that with purpose of heart they should continue with the Lord. ²⁴For he was a good man, full of the Holy Spirit and of faith. And a great many people were added to the Lord.

²⁵Then Barnabas departed for Tarsus to seek Saul. ²⁶And when he had found him, he brought him to Antioch. So it was that for a whole year they assembled with the church and taught a great many people. And the disciples were first called Christians in Antioch.

Relief to Judea

²⁷And in these days prophets came from Jerusalem to Antioch. ²⁸Then one of them, named Agabus, stood up and showed by the Spirit that there was going to be a great famine throughout all the world, which also happened in the days of Claudius Caesar. ²⁹Then the disciples, each according to his ability, determined to send relief to the brethren dwelling in Judea. ³⁰This they also did, and sent it to the elders by the hands of Barnabas and Saul.

Herod's Violence to the Church

12 Now about that time Herod the king stretched out *his* hand to harass some from the church. ²Then he killed James the brother of John with the sword. ³And because he saw that it pleased the Jews, he proceeded further to seize Peter also. Now it was *during* the Days of Unleavened Bread. ⁴So when he had arrested him, he put *him* in prison, and delivered *him* to four squads of soldiers to keep him, intending to bring him before the people after Passover.

Peter Freed from Prison

⁵Peter was therefore kept in prison, but constant[a] prayer was offered to God for him by the church. ⁶And when Herod was about to bring him out, that night Peter was sleeping, bound with two chains between two soldiers; and the guards before the door were keeping the prison. ⁷Now behold, an angel of the Lord stood by *him,* and a light shone in the prison; and he struck Peter on the side and raised him up, saying, "Arise quickly!" And his chains fell off *his* hands. ⁸Then the angel said to him, "Gird yourself

12:5 ᵃNU-Text reads *constantly* (or *earnestly*).

Servanthood: No Task Too Small

(Acts 11:22–24)

If any early church leader could be called a servant, it is Barnabas. He took initiative and did whatever it took to raise morale, men, or money. He led with clarity and example by becoming a servant. He considered no task too small. What allowed Barnabas to demonstrate such a lifestyle? He had . . .

1. *Nothing to prove.*
   Barnabas didn't have to play games. He never sought the limelight. When he mentored Paul, he happily let the emerging apostle rise above him. Barnabas didn't feel the need to project his self-worth or prove himself to anyone.

2. *Nothing to lose.*
   Barnabas didn't have to guard his reputation or fear that he would lose popularity. He came to serve, not to be served. This enabled him to focus on giving, not getting. As a servant, he had no rights to lose.

3. *Nothing to hide.*
   Barnabas didn't maintain a façade or image. He remained authentic, vulnerable, and transparent. He could rejoice with other's victories (Acts 11:23) and never wondered about his own fame.

If God called you to be another Barnabas to another Paul—if you knew that this new, emerging leader would soon overshadow you—would you accept the call? In other words, are you a servant? You must love your people more than your position.

21 QUALITIES

CHARACTER

Herod Lacked It and Lost Everything
(Acts 12:1–23)

Ego drove King Herod of Paul's day, just as it had driven his father and grandfather. They all desperately lacked character.

Herod was the surname of a family of rulers who held power by permission of the Roman Empire. Herod the Great ruled at the time of Jesus' birth; he's the one who killed all the male babies in Bethlehem. Herod Antipas ordered the beheading of John the Baptizer. The Herod in Acts 12 is Herod Agrippa I, the grandson of Herod the Great.

Herod's lack of character provides us with many examples of what *not* to do as a leader:

1. *He mistreated his own citizens* (v. 1).
   He unjustly ordered the arrests of Jewish believers in order to harass them.
2. *He executed innocent people* (v. 2).
   He had James killed by the sword, although he had committed no crime.
3. *He made decisions based on popularity* (v. 3).
   When he saw it pleased the Jews to kill James, he had Peter arrested, too.
4. *He acted irrationally in difficult times* (v. 19).
   He killed the 16 guards who had been on duty at the time of Peter's prison escape.
5. *He harbored anger toward others* (v. 20).
   He remained angry toward outside ethnic groups and looked for ways to get even.
6. *He sought power out of insecurity* (v. 20).
   He enjoyed controlling others and especially loved having people at his mercy.
7. *He projected an infallible image* (vv. 21, 22).
   He loved wearing his royal garb and being worshiped.
8. *He was blinded by his ego* (v. 23).
   He lived in an unreal world and couldn't see how his ego sabotaged his leadership.

How Do We Avoid Herod's Trap?

To improve your character and build a solid foundation for your own leadership, you must:

1. *Search for the cracks.*
   Look at the major areas of your life. Identify where you're weak or have taken shortcuts.
2. *Look for patterns.*
   Do any weaknesses remain? Patterns can help you diagnose character flaws.
3. *Face the music.*
   Character repair begins when you face your flaws and apologize to those you've wronged.
4. *Stay teachable and rebuild.*
   Once you face your past, create a plan to build inward strength.

For a positive example of character, see p. 1025.

and tie on your sandals"; and so he did. And he said to him, "Put on your garment and follow me." ⁹So he went out and followed him, and did not know that what was done by the angel was real, but thought he was seeing a vision. ¹⁰When they were past the first and the second guard posts, they came to the iron gate that leads to the city, which opened to them of its own accord; and they went out and went down one street, and immediately the angel departed from him.

¹¹And when Peter had come to himself, he said, "Now I know for certain that the Lord has sent His angel, and has delivered me from the hand of Herod and *from* all the expectation of the Jewish people."

¹²So, when he had considered *this,* he came to the house of Mary, the mother of John whose surname was Mark, where many were gathered together praying. ¹³And as Peter knocked at the door of the gate, a girl named Rhoda came to answer. ¹⁴When she recognized Peter's voice, because of *her* gladness she did not open the gate, but ran in and announced that Peter stood before the gate. ¹⁵But they said to her, "You are beside yourself!" Yet she kept insisting that it was so. So they said, "It is his angel."

¹⁶Now Peter continued knocking; and when they opened *the door* and saw him, they were astonished. ¹⁷But motioning to them with his hand to keep silent, he declared to them how the Lord had brought him out of the prison. And he said, "Go, tell these things to James and to the brethren." And he departed and went to another place.

¹⁸Then, as soon as it was day, there was no small stir among the soldiers about what had become of Peter. ¹⁹But when Herod had searched for him and not found him, he examined the guards and commanded that *they* should be put to death.

And he went down from Judea to Caesarea, and stayed *there.*

Herod's Violent Death

²⁰Now Herod had been very angry with the people of Tyre and Sidon; but they came to him with one accord, and having made Blastus the king's personal aide their friend, they asked for peace, because their country was supplied with food by the king's *country.*

²¹So on a set day Herod, arrayed in royal apparel, sat on his throne and gave an oration to them. ²²And the people kept shouting, "The voice of a god and not of a man!" ²³Then immediately an angel of the Lord struck him, because

he did not give glory to God. And he was eaten by worms and died.

²⁴But the word of God grew and multiplied.

Barnabas and Saul Appointed

²⁵And Barnabas and Saul returned from[a] Jerusalem when they had fulfilled *their* ministry, and they also took with them John whose surname was Mark.

13 Now in the church that was at Antioch there were certain prophets and teachers: Barnabas, Simeon who was called Niger, Lucius of Cyrene, Manaen who had been brought up with Herod the tetrarch, and Saul. ²As they ministered to the Lord and fasted, the Holy Spirit said, "Now separate to Me Barnabas and Saul for the work to which I have called them." ³Then, having fasted and prayed, and laid hands on them, they sent *them* away.

Preaching in Cyprus

⁴So, being sent out by the Holy Spirit, they went down to Seleucia, and from there they sailed to Cyprus. ⁵And when they arrived in Salamis, they preached the word of God in the synagogues of the Jews. They also had John as *their* assistant.

⁶Now when they had gone through the island[a] to Paphos, they found a certain sorcerer, a false prophet, a Jew whose name *was* Bar-Jesus, ⁷who was with the proconsul, Sergius Paulus, an intelligent man. This man called for Barnabas and Saul and sought to hear the word of God. ⁸But Elymas the sorcerer (for so his name is translated) withstood them, seeking to turn the proconsul away from the faith. ⁹Then Saul, who also *is called* Paul, filled with the Holy Spirit, looked intently at him ¹⁰and said, "O full of all deceit and all fraud, *you* son of the devil, *you* enemy of all righteousness, will you not cease perverting the straight ways of the Lord? ¹¹And now, indeed, the hand of the Lord *is* upon you, and you shall be blind, not seeing the sun for a time."

And immediately a dark mist fell on him, and he went around seeking someone to lead him by the hand. ¹²Then the proconsul believed, when he saw what had been done, being astonished at the teaching of the Lord.

At Antioch in Pisidia

¹³Now when Paul and his party set sail from Paphos, they came to Perga in Pamphylia; and John, departing from them, returned to Jerusalem.

12:25 [a]NU-Text and M-Text read *to.*
13:6 [a]NU-Text reads *the whole island.*

The Law of Explosive Growth: Antioch Sends Out Leaders

(Acts 13:1–3)

By the middle of the Book of Acts, three churches have sent out leaders: Cyprus, Cyrene, and Jerusalem. Unfortunately, those endeavors seem to be isolated events. By Acts 13, God's attention shifts to the church in Antioch. Why? Because it remains committed to global impact, busy about raising up leaders to become international change agents. Jerusalem ceases to be the center of God's activity. In fact, it becomes a needy church, requiring the help of churches in Asia and Greece.

Antioch thrives because of its vision to send out leaders. It sends out its leaders as a team, members with complementary gifts and shared vision. This enables them to connect with people and produce results almost everywhere they go.

God does His work by sending out teams of leaders. Jesus sent out His team of twelve (Luke 9:1–6), and the pattern continued in Acts. Most of these leadership teams came from the church in Antioch:

1. Peter and John (Acts 3)
2. Philip, Peter, John (Acts 8)
3. Peter and certain brethren (Acts 10)
4. Men from Cyprus and Cyrene (Acts 11)
5. Paul and Barnabas (Acts 13; 14)
6. Judas, Silas, Paul (Acts 15)
7. Barnabas and Mark (Acts 15)
8. Timothy, Paul, Silas (Acts 16)
9. Paul, Aquila, Priscilla (Acts 18)
10. Timothy and Erastus (Acts 19)

¹⁴But when they departed from Perga, they came to Antioch in Pisidia, and went into the synagogue on the Sabbath day and sat down. ¹⁵And after the reading of the Law and the Prophets, the rulers of the synagogue sent to them, saying, "Men *and* brethren, if you have any word of exhortation for the people, say on."

¹⁶Then Paul stood up, and motioning with *his* hand said, "Men of Israel, and you who fear God, listen: ¹⁷The God of this people Israel[a] chose our fathers, and exalted the people when they dwelt as strangers in the land of Egypt, and with an uplifted arm He brought them out of it. ¹⁸Now for a time of about forty years He put up with their ways in the wilderness. ¹⁹And when He had destroyed seven nations in the land of Canaan, He distributed their land to them by allotment.

²⁰"After that He gave *them* judges for about four hundred and fifty years, until Samuel the prophet. ²¹And afterward they asked for a king; so God gave them Saul the son of Kish, a man of the tribe of Benjamin, for forty years. ²²And when He had removed him, He raised up for them David as king, to whom also He gave testimony and said, 'I have found David[a] the son of Jesse, *a man after My own heart,* who will do all My will.'[b] ²³From this man's seed, according to *the* promise, God raised up for Israel a Savior—Jesus—[a] ²⁴after John had first preached, before His coming, the baptism of repentance to all the people of Israel. ²⁵And as John was finishing his course, he said, 'Who do you think I am? I am not *He.* But behold, there comes One after me, the sandals of whose feet I am not worthy to loose.'

²⁶"Men *and* brethren, sons of the family of Abraham, and those among you who fear God, to you the word of this salvation has been sent. ²⁷For those who dwell in Jerusalem, and their

---

13:17 [a]M-Text omits *Israel.* **13:22** [a]Psalm 89:20 [b]1 Samuel 13:14 **13:23** [a]M-Text reads *for Israel salvation.*

rulers, because they did not know Him, nor even the voices of the Prophets which are read every Sabbath, have fulfilled *them* in condemning *Him.* [28]And though they found no cause for death *in Him,* they asked Pilate that He should be put to death. [29]Now when they had fulfilled all that was written concerning Him, they took *Him* down from the tree and laid *Him* in a tomb. [30]But God raised Him from the dead. [31]He was seen for many days by those who came up with Him from Galilee to Jerusalem, who are His witnesses to the people. [32]And we declare to you glad tidings—that promise which was made to the fathers. [33]God has fulfilled this for us their children, in that He has raised up Jesus. As it is also written in the second Psalm:

' You are My Son,
    Today I have begotten You.'[a]

[34]And that He raised Him from the dead, no more to return to corruption, He has spoken thus:

' I will give you the sure mercies of David.'[a]

[35]Therefore He also says in another *Psalm:*

' You will not allow Your Holy One to see
    corruption.'[a]

[36]"For David, after he had served his own generation by the will of God, fell asleep, was buried with his fathers, and saw corruption; [37]but He whom God raised up saw no corruption. [38]Therefore let it be known to you, brethren, that through this Man is preached to you the forgiveness of sins; [39]and by Him everyone who believes is justified from all things from which you could not be justified by the law of Moses. [40]Beware therefore, lest what has been spoken in the prophets come upon you:

[41] ' Behold, you despisers,
    Marvel and perish!
    For I work a work in your days,
    A work which you will by no means believe,
    Though one were to declare it to you.' "[a]

Blessing and Conflict at Antioch

[42]So when the Jews went out of the synagogue,[a] the Gentiles begged that these words might be preached to them the next Sabbath. [43]Now when the congregation had broken up, many of the Jews and devout proselytes followed Paul and Barnabas, who, speaking to them, persuaded them to continue in the grace of God.

[44]On the next Sabbath almost the whole city came together to hear the word of God. [45]But when the Jews saw the multitudes, they were filled with envy; and contradicting and blaspheming, they opposed the things spoken by Paul. [46]Then Paul and Barnabas grew bold and said, "It was necessary that the word of God should be spoken to you first; but since you reject it, and judge yourselves unworthy of everlasting life, behold, we turn to the Gentiles. [47]For so the Lord has commanded us:

' I have set you as a light to the Gentiles,
    That you should be for salvation to the
        ends of the earth.' "[a]

[48]Now when the Gentiles heard this, they were glad and glorified the word of the Lord. And as many as had been appointed to eternal life believed. [49]And the word of the Lord was being spread throughout all the region. [50]But the Jews stirred up the devout and prominent women and the chief men of the city, raised up persecution against Paul and Barnabas, and expelled them from their region. [51]But they shook off the dust from their feet against them, and came to Iconium. [52]And the disciples were filled with joy and with the Holy Spirit.

At Iconium

14 Now it happened in Iconium that they went together to the synagogue of the Jews, and so spoke that a great multitude both of the Jews and of the Greeks believed. [2]But the unbelieving Jews stirred up the Gentiles and poisoned their minds against the brethren. [3]Therefore they stayed there a long time, speaking boldly in the Lord, who was bearing witness to the word of His grace, granting signs and wonders to be done by their hands.

[4]But the multitude of the city was divided: part sided with the Jews, and part with the apostles. [5]And when a violent attempt was made by both the Gentiles and Jews, with their rulers, to abuse and stone them, [6]they became aware of it and fled to Lystra and Derbe, cities of Lycaonia, and to the surrounding region. [7]And they were preaching the gospel there.

13:33 [a]Psalm 2:7 **13:34** [a]Isaiah 55:3 **13:35** [a]Psalm 16:10 **13:41** [a]Habakkuk 1:5 **13:42** [a]Or *And when they went out of the synagogue of the Jews;* NU-Text reads *And when they went out of the synagogue, they begged.* **13:47** [a]Isaiah 49:6

Idolatry at Lystra

⁸And in Lystra a certain man without strength in his feet was sitting, a cripple from his mother's womb, who had never walked. ⁹This man heard Paul speaking. Paul, observing him intently and seeing that he had faith to be healed, ¹⁰said with a loud voice, "Stand up straight on your feet!" And he leaped and walked. ¹¹Now when the people saw what Paul had done, they raised their voices, saying in the Lycaonian *language,* "The gods have come down to us in the likeness of men!" ¹²And Barnabas they called Zeus, and Paul, Hermes, because he was the chief speaker. ¹³Then the priest of Zeus, whose temple was in front of their city, brought oxen and garlands to the gates, intending to sacrifice with the multitudes.

¹⁴But when the apostles Barnabas and Paul heard this, they tore their clothes and ran in among the multitude, crying out ¹⁵and saying, "Men, why are you doing these things? We also are men with the same nature as you, and preach to you that you should turn from these useless things to the living God, who made the heaven, the earth, the sea, and all things that are in them, ¹⁶who in bygone generations allowed all nations to walk in their own ways. ¹⁷Nevertheless He did not leave Himself without witness, in that He did good, gave us rain from heaven and fruitful seasons, filling our hearts with food and gladness." ¹⁸And with these sayings they could scarcely restrain the multitudes from sacrificing to them.

Stoning, Escape to Derbe

¹⁹Then Jews from Antioch and Iconium came there; and having persuaded the multitudes, they stoned Paul *and* dragged *him* out of the city, supposing him to be dead. ²⁰However, when the disciples gathered around him, he rose up and went into the city. And the next day he departed with Barnabas to Derbe.

Strengthening the Converts

²¹And when they had preached the gospel to that city and made many disciples, they returned to Lystra, Iconium, and Antioch, ²²strengthening the souls of the disciples, exhorting *them* to continue in the faith, and *saying,* "We must through many tribulations enter the kingdom of God." ²³So when they had appointed elders in every church, and prayed with fasting, they commended them to the Lord in whom they had believed. ²⁴And after they had passed through Pisidia, they came to Pamphylia. ²⁵Now when they had preached the word in Perga, they went down to Attalia. ²⁶From there they sailed to Antioch, where

they had been commended to the grace of God for the work which they had completed.

²⁷Now when they had come and gathered the church together, they reported all that God had done with them, and that He had opened the door of faith to the Gentiles. ²⁸So they stayed there a long time with the disciples.

Accountability: The Team Remains Accountable to the Church

(Acts 14:26–28)

Although leaders do not require a formal position to make a difference, God rarely calls them to act alone. He usually calls them to be a part of a team to be sent out by an organization, such as a local church. Some leaders send; others go. Both are to support the other.

Conflict over Circumcision

15 And certain *men* came down from Judea and taught the brethren, "Unless you are circumcised according to the custom of Moses, you cannot be saved." ²Therefore, when Paul and Barnabas had no small dissension and dispute with them, they determined that Paul and Barnabas and certain others of them should go up to Jerusalem, to the apostles and elders, about this question.

³So, being sent on their way by the church, they passed through Phoenicia and Samaria, describing the conversion of the Gentiles; and they caused great joy to all the brethren. ⁴And when they had come to Jerusalem, they were received by the church and the apostles and the elders; and they reported all things that God had done with them. ⁵But some of the sect of the Pharisees who believed rose up, saying, "It is necessary to circumcise them, and to command *them* to keep the law of Moses."

The Jerusalem Council

⁶Now the apostles and elders came together to consider this matter. ⁷And when there had been much dispute, Peter rose up and said to them: "Men and brethren, you know that a good while ago God chose among us, that by my mouth the Gentiles should hear the word of the gospel and believe. ⁸So God, who knows the

The Law of Intuition: Peter Proposes a Major Shift from the Old

(Acts 15:7–11)

Peter's suggested change to the way the church does things amounts to a paradigm shift in both thought and belief. He persuades leaders to change by convincingly communicating what God is doing. Peter sees the need for change before others do. His perception, coupled with his credibility, keeps the church moving forward.

heart, acknowledged them by giving them the Holy Spirit, just as *He did* to us, ⁹and made no distinction between us and them, purifying their hearts by faith. ¹⁰Now therefore, why do you test God by putting a yoke on the neck of the disciples which neither our fathers nor we were able to bear? ¹¹But we believe that through the grace of the Lord Jesus Christ[a] we shall be saved in the same manner as they."

¹²Then all the multitude kept silent and listened to Barnabas and Paul declaring how many miracles and wonders God had worked through them among the Gentiles. ¹³And after they had become silent, James answered, saying, "Men *and* brethren, listen to me: ¹⁴Simon has declared how God at the first visited the Gentiles to take out of them a people for His name. ¹⁵And with this the words of the prophets agree, just as it is written:

¹⁶ 'After this I will return
And will rebuild the tabernacle of David,
which has fallen down;
I will rebuild its ruins,
And I will set it up;
¹⁷ So that the rest of mankind may seek the
LORD,
Even all the Gentiles who are called by My
name,
Says the LORD who does all these things.'[a]

¹⁸"Known to God from eternity are all His works.[a] ¹⁹Therefore I judge that we should not trouble those from among the Gentiles who are turning to God, ²⁰but that we write to them to abstain from things polluted by idols, *from* sexual immorality,[a] *from* things strangled, and *from* blood. ²¹For Moses has had throughout many

generations those who preach him in every city, being read in the synagogues every Sabbath."

The Jerusalem Decree

²²Then it pleased the apostles and elders, with the whole church, to send chosen men of their own company to Antioch with Paul and Barnabas, *namely,* Judas who was also named Barsabas,[a] and Silas, leading men among the brethren. ²³They wrote this, *letter* by them:

The apostles, the elders, and the brethren,

To the brethren who are of the Gentiles in Antioch, Syria, and Cilicia:

Greetings.

²⁴ Since we have heard that some who went out from us have troubled you with words, unsettling your souls, saying, "You must be circumcised and keep the law"[a]—to whom we gave no *such* commandment—²⁵it seemed good to us, being assembled with one accord, to send chosen men to you with our beloved Barnabas and Paul, ²⁶men who have risked their lives for the name of our Lord Jesus Christ. ²⁷We have therefore sent Judas and Silas, who will also report the

---

15:11 [a]NU-Text and M-Text omit *Christ*.
15:17 [a]Amos 9:11, 12 **15:18** [a]NU-Text (combining with verse 17) reads *Says the Lord, who makes these things known from eternity (of old)*.
15:20 [a]Or *fornication* **15:22** [a]NU-Text and M-Text read *Barsabbas*. **15:24** [a]NU-Text omits *saying, "You must be circumcised and keep the law."*

The Law of Influence: The Council Impacts the Gentiles

(Acts 15:22–29)

Through one document the Jerusalem church liberated Christians everywhere of terrible burdens and potential guilt laid on them by Jewish law. They exercised their influence and changed the course of church history. Power isn't always evil. The Jerusalem Council exercised positive influence on its generation; so can we.

Recruiting Volunteers

(Acts 15:32–35)

Organizations staffed by volunteers require the most leadership of any group. Such organizations must have good leaders, because their volunteers' only incentive comes through the vision of the leadership. The organization gives no salary, no retirement benefits, no perks.

The fact is, only a small percentage of volunteers do the work. In most churches, about 20 percent of the members do 80 percent of the ministry. Why is this? Why don't more people serve?

1. *No one has asked them.*
   Hesitant to infringe on someone else's territory, they wait to serve until they're asked.
2. *They have a fear of responsibility.*
   Afraid that duties may force them to become over-committed, they hesitate to do anything.
3. *They suffer from past burnout.*
   Having gone from "pillars" to "pew-sitters," they feel the need to rest and be fed.
4. *They're intimidated by present workers.*
   "Pillars" unwilling to exchange power for fresh ideas keep others idle.
5. *They are ignorant of the biblical paradigm for ministry.*
   Many churches don't model the priesthood of the believer or the truth of Ephesians 4:11, 12.
6. *They have a preoccupation with their personal agenda and busyness.*
   Most people play defense with their calendar and the ultimate loses to the immediate.
7. *They feel untrained, ill-equipped, and ungifted.*
   Many people mistakenly believe that only trained or gifted people can serve and, since they have no training or special gifts, they don't qualify.
8. *They're unaware of the options available.*
   Most leaders wrongly assume that people know the vast opportunities that exist.
9. *They don't "own" the cause.*
   Many would sign up for a ministry if they could only catch a vision for the big picture.
10. *They are selfish, lazy, and indifferent.*
    Some don't get involved simply because they don't care for anything but themselves.

So what can be done to mobilize volunteers? Try the following:

1. Schedule ministry interviews with new people to explain the opportunities.
2. Offer training for every position. Model servanthood.
3. Match ministry opportunities with spiritual gifts.
4. Constantly publicize available ministry options.
5. Make ministry involvement part of membership.
6. Create several entry-level positions for the new, apprehensive person.
7. Teach and cast vision on the priesthood of the believer—everyone has a gift to use.
8. Develop realistic commitment blocks for people to share the load.
9. Rotate as many ministry positions as possible to make room for new people.
10. Constantly applaud ordinary servants who make a difference.

same things by word of mouth. [28]For it seemed good to the Holy Spirit, and to us, to lay upon you no greater burden than these necessary things:[29]that you abstain from things offered to idols, from blood, from things strangled, and from sexual immorality.[a] If you keep yourselves from these, you will do well.

Farewell.

15:29 [a]Or *fornication*

Continuing Ministry in Syria

³⁰So when they were sent off, they came to Antioch; and when they had gathered the multitude together, they delivered the letter. ³¹When they had read it, they rejoiced over its encouragement. ³²Now Judas and Silas, themselves being prophets also, exhorted and strengthened the brethren with many words. ³³And after they had stayed *there* for a time, they were sent back with greetings from the brethren to the apostles.ᵃ

³⁴However, it seemed good to Silas to remain there.ᵃ ³⁵Paul and Barnabas also remained in Antioch, teaching and preaching the word of the Lord, with many others also.

Division over John Mark

³⁶Then after some days Paul said to Barnabas, "Let us now go back and visit our brethren in every city where we have preached the word of the Lord, *and see* how they are doing." ³⁷Now Barnabas was determined to take with them John called Mark. ³⁸But Paul insisted that they should not take with them the one who had departed from them in Pamphylia, and had not gone with them to the work. ³⁹Then the contention became so sharp that they parted from one another. And so Barnabas took Mark and sailed to Cyprus; ⁴⁰but Paul chose Silas and departed, being commended by the brethren to the grace of God. ⁴¹And he went through Syria and Cilicia, strengthening the churches.

Timothy Joins Paul and Silas

16 Then he came to Derbe and Lystra. And behold, a certain disciple was there, named Timothy, *the* son of a certain Jewish woman who believed, but his father *was* Greek. ²He was well spoken of by the brethren who were at Lystra and Iconium. ³Paul wanted to have him go on with him. And he took *him* and circumcised him because of the Jews who were in that region, for they all knew that his father was Greek. ⁴And as they went through the cities, they delivered to them the decrees to keep, which were determined by the apostles and elders at Jerusalem. ⁵So the churches were strengthened in the faith, and increased in number daily.

The Macedonian Call

⁶Now when they had gone through Phrygia and the region of Galatia, they were forbidden by the Holy Spirit to preach the word in Asia. ⁷After they had come to Mysia, they tried to go into Bithynia, but the Spiritᵃ did not permit them. ⁸So passing by Mysia, they came down to

---

Discernment: Paul Changed His Plans As He Discerned the Needs
(Acts 16:1–13)

All leaders need discernment. Paul had it and he used it to select new leaders, to size up what to say in a courtroom, and to know where to go next on his missionary trips.

As Paul's team traveled through Asia, he must have been listening to the Holy Spirit in his quiet times. God prevented him from speaking any more in Asia and compelled him to move on. Next, the Spirit forbade Paul to minister in Mysia and Bithynia. In Troas, he had a vision in which a man begged him to visit Macedonia.

Such was the dynamic leadership of God. Discerning leaders usually share some common traits. They are:

- good listeners
- intuitive or perceptive
- well-networked
- flexible
- optimistic

Troas. ⁹And a vision appeared to Paul in the night. A man of Macedonia stood and pleaded with him, saying, "Come over to Macedonia and help us." ¹⁰Now after he had seen the vision, immediately we sought to go to Macedonia, concluding that the Lord had called us to preach the gospel to them.

Lydia Baptized at Philippi

¹¹Therefore, sailing from Troas, we ran a straight course to Samothrace, and the next *day* came to Neapolis, ¹²and from there to Philippi, which is the foremost city of that part of Macedonia, a colony. And we were staying in that city for some days. ¹³And on the Sabbath day we went out of the city to the riverside, where prayer was customarily made; and we sat down and spoke to the women who met *there*. ¹⁴Now a certain woman named Lydia heard *us*. She was a seller of purple from the city of Thyatira, who worshiped

---

15:33 ᵃNU-Text reads *to those who had sent them.*
15:34 ᵃNU-Text and M-Text omit this verse.
16:7 ᵃNU-Text adds *of Jesus.*

God. The Lord opened her heart to heed the things spoken by Paul. [15]And when she and her household were baptized, she begged *us,* saying, "If you have judged me to be faithful to the Lord, come to my house and stay." So she persuaded us.

Paul and Silas Imprisoned

[16]Now it happened, as we went to prayer, that a certain slave girl possessed with a spirit of divination met us, who brought her masters much profit by fortune-telling. [17]This girl followed Paul and us, and cried out, saying, "These men are the servants of the Most High God, who proclaim to us the way of salvation." [18]And this she did for many days.

But Paul, greatly annoyed, turned and said to the spirit, "I command you in the name of Jesus Christ to come out of her." And he came out that very hour. [19]But when her masters saw that their hope of profit was gone, they seized Paul and Silas and dragged *them* into the marketplace to the authorities.

[20]And they brought them to the magistrates, and said, "These men, being Jews, exceedingly trouble our city; [21]and they teach customs which are not lawful for us, being Romans, to receive or observe." [22]Then the multitude rose up together against them; and the magistrates tore off their clothes and commanded *them* to be beaten with rods. [23]And when they had laid many stripes on them, they threw *them* into prison, commanding the jailer to keep them securely. [24]Having received such a charge, he put them into the inner prison and fastened their feet in the stocks.

The Philippian Jailer Saved

[25]But at midnight Paul and Silas were praying and singing hymns to God, and the prisoners were listening to them. [26]Suddenly there was a great earthquake, so that the foundations of the prison were shaken; and immediately all the doors were opened and everyone's chains were loosed. [27]And the keeper of the prison, awaking from sleep and seeing the prison doors open, supposing the prisoners had fled, drew his sword and was about to kill himself. [28]But Paul called with a loud voice, saying, "Do yourself no harm, for we are all here."

[29]Then he called for a light, ran in, and fell down trembling before Paul and Silas. [30]And he brought them out and said, "Sirs, what must I do to be saved?"

[31]So they said, "Believe on the Lord Jesus Christ, and you will be saved, you and your household." [32]Then they spoke the word of the Lord to him and to all who were in his house. [33]And he took them the same hour of the night and washed *their* stripes. And immediately he and all his family were baptized. [34]Now when he had brought them into his house, he set food before them; and he rejoiced, having believed in God with all his household.

Paul Refuses to Depart Secretly

[35]And when it was day, the magistrates sent the officers, saying, "Let those men go."

[36]So the keeper of the prison reported these words to Paul, saying, "The magistrates have sent to let you go. Now therefore depart, and go in peace."

[37]But Paul said to them, "They have beaten us openly, uncondemned Romans, *and* have thrown *us* into prison. And now do they put us out secretly? No indeed! Let them come themselves and get us out."

[38]And the officers told these words to the magistrates, and they were afraid when they heard that they were Romans. [39]Then they came and pleaded with them and brought *them* out, and asked *them* to depart from the city. [40]So they went out of the prison and entered *the house of* Lydia; and when they had seen the brethren, they encouraged them and departed.

Preaching Christ at Thessalonica

17 Now when they had passed through Amphipolis and Apollonia, they came to Thessalonica, where there was a synagogue of the Jews. [2]Then Paul, as his custom was, went in to them, and for three Sabbaths reasoned with them from the Scriptures, [3]explaining and demonstrating that the Christ had to suffer and rise again from the dead, and *saying,* "This Jesus whom I preach to you is the Christ." [4]And some of them were persuaded; and a great multitude of the devout Greeks, and not a few of the leading women, joined Paul and Silas.

Assault on Jason's House

[5]But the Jews who were not persuaded, becoming envious,[a] took some of the evil men from the marketplace, and gathering a mob, set all the city in an uproar and attacked the house of Jason, and sought to bring them out to the people. [6]But when they did not find them, they dragged Jason and some brethren to the rulers of the city, crying out, "These who have turned the

---

17:5 [a]NU-Text omits *who were not persuaded;* M-Text omits *becoming envious.*

world upside down have come here too. [7]Jason has harbored them, and these are all acting contrary to the decrees of Caesar, saying there is another king—Jesus." [8]And they troubled the crowd and the rulers of the city when they heard these things. [9]So when they had taken security from Jason and the rest, they let them go.

Ministering at Berea

[10]Then the brethren immediately sent Paul and Silas away by night to Berea. When they arrived, they went into the synagogue of the Jews. [11]These were more fair-minded than those in Thessalonica, in that they received the word with all readiness, and searched the Scriptures daily *to find out* whether these things were so. [12]Therefore many of them believed, and also not a few of the Greeks, prominent women as well as men. [13]But when the Jews from Thessalonica learned that the word of God was preached by Paul at Berea, they came there also and stirred up the crowds. [14]Then immediately the brethren sent Paul away, to go to the sea; but both Silas and Timothy remained there. [15]So those who conducted Paul brought him to Athens; and receiving a command for Silas and Timothy to come to him with all speed, they departed.

The Philosophers at Athens

[16]Now while Paul waited for them at Athens, his spirit was provoked within him when he saw that the city was given over to idols. [17]Therefore

he reasoned in the synagogue with the Jews and with the *Gentile* worshipers, and in the marketplace daily with those who happened to be there. [18]Then[a] certain Epicurean and Stoic philosophers encountered him. And some said, "What does this babbler want to say?"

Others said, "He seems to be a proclaimer of foreign gods," because he preached to them Jesus and the resurrection.

[19]And they took him and brought him to the Areopagus, saying, "May we know what this new doctrine *is* of which you speak? [20]For you are bringing some strange things to our ears. Therefore we want to know what these things mean." [21]For all the Athenians and the foreigners who were there spent their time in nothing else but either to tell or to hear some new thing.

Addressing the Areopagus

[22]Then Paul stood in the midst of the Areopagus and said, "Men of Athens, I perceive that in all things you are very religious; [23]for as I was passing through and considering the objects of your worship, I even found an altar with this inscription:

TO THE UNKNOWN GOD.

Therefore, the One whom you worship without knowing, Him I proclaim to you: [24]God, who made the world and everything in it, since He is

17:18 [a]NU-Text and M-Text add *also*.

The Law of Connection: Paul Was Effective in Athens
(Acts 17:22–34)

Peter, Stephen, and Paul all practiced the Law of Connection in the four sermons that Luke records (Acts 2:14–36; 7:2–53; 13:16–41; 17:22–31). The one Paul delivered in Acts 17 is a masterpiece. He connected brilliantly with people from a different culture, showing he understood both Greek society and human needs. Read his message and watch a master communicator in action:

1. He began with affirmation (v. 22).
2. He bridged his subject with the familiar (v. 23).
3. He enlarged their vision of God (vv. 24, 25).
4. He used inclusive language (v. 26).
5. He gave them encouragement and hope (v. 27).
6. He identified with some of their own poets (v. 28).
7. He gave them specific action steps (vv. 29–31).

Effective leaders *connect* before they *expect.* Only when Paul had built relational bridges with the people, did he issue a clear call to repent. Connection precedes decision. And what happened? According to the text, everyone acted. Some sneered at Paul; others said they wanted to hear more; and others followed immediately (vv. 32–34).

Lord of heaven and earth, does not dwell in temples made with hands. [25]Nor is He worshiped with men's hands, as though He needed anything, since He gives to all life, breath, and all things. [26]And He has made from one blood[a] every nation of men to dwell on all the face of the earth, and has determined their preappointed times and the boundaries of their dwellings, [27]so that they should seek the Lord, in the hope that they might grope for Him and find Him, though He is not far from each one of us; [28]for in Him we live and move and have our being, as also some of your own poets have said, 'For we are also His offspring.' [29]Therefore, since we are the offspring of God, we ought not to think that the Divine Nature is like gold or silver or stone, something shaped by art and man's devising. [30]Truly, these times of ignorance God overlooked, but now commands all men everywhere to repent, [31]because He has appointed a day on which He will judge the world in righteousness by the Man whom He has ordained. He has given assurance of this to all by raising Him from the dead."

[32]And when they heard of the resurrection of the dead, some mocked, while others said, "We will hear you again on this *matter.*" [33]So Paul departed from among them. [34]However, some men joined him and believed, among them Dionysius the Areopagite, a woman named Damaris, and others with them.

Ministering at Corinth

18 After these things Paul departed from Athens and went to Corinth. [2]And he found a certain Jew named Aquila, born in Pontus, who had recently come from Italy with his wife Priscilla (because Claudius had commanded all the Jews to depart from Rome); and he came to them. [3]So, because he was of the same trade, he stayed with them and worked; for by occupation they were tentmakers. [4]And he reasoned in the synagogue every Sabbath, and persuaded both Jews and Greeks.

[5]When Silas and Timothy had come from Macedonia, Paul was compelled by the Spirit, and testified to the Jews *that* Jesus *is* the Christ. [6]But when they opposed him and blasphemed, he shook *his* garments and said to them, "Your blood *be* upon your *own* heads; I *am* clean. From now on I will go to the Gentiles." [7]And he departed from there and entered the house of a

---

17:26 [a]NU-Text omits *blood.*

AQUILA AND PRISCILLA

LEADERS WHO TRAINED MORE LEADERS
(Acts 18:24–28)

PROFILE IN LEADERSHIP

Leadership doesn't mean just getting others to follow; it also means equipping and preparing leaders to guide God's people. The account of Aquila, his wife Priscilla, the apostle Paul, and Apollos illustrates this principle.

Aquila and Priscilla—who, like Paul, were Jewish believers and tentmakers—had fled to Corinth from Rome when the Emperor Claudius ordered all Jews to leave the city. When Paul arrived in Corinth, he stayed with this couple and evidently taught them a great deal about the things of God. They took the teaching seriously, for when they traveled to Ephesus, they instructed a minister named Apollos about the gospel of Jesus Christ.

Apollos had heard and believed a portion of the Christian message and with great eloquence was vigorously teaching what he knew. But when Aquila and Priscilla heard him preach, they realized he hadn't heard the complete message, so they took him aside and explained the gospel more fully. After that, Apollos could preach with even greater effectiveness.

When we come to Christ for salvation, God calls us to "go . . . and make disciples" (Matt. 28:19). Similarly, when God calls us to leadership, He directs us to help equip others to lead more effectively.

21 QUALITIES

TEACHABILITY

Apollos Learned and Grew
(Acts 18:24–28)

The Book of Acts portrays Apollos as an excellent teacher. God greatly used him in a number of cultures, and he became known as the apostle's right-hand man.

What most impresses about Apollos, however, is his teachability. He never thought he had learned so much that he couldn't improve his game. Luke points out several facts about this man:

1. He came from a cultured city (v. 24).
2. He was an educated man (v. 24).
3. He knew the Scriptures well (v. 24).
4. He'd been taught the Christian faith (v. 25).
5. He had an obvious gift (v. 25).
6. He taught truth accurately (v. 25).
7. He taught truth passionately (v. 26).

Church history tells us that Apollos was such a good teacher that most people would rather have listened to him than to the apostle Paul. That's quite a feather in his cap! This might cause us to assume he had everything together. Yet Apollos "knew only the baptism of John" (18:25). He understood repentance. He understood what it meant to surrender to God. But he wasn't familiar with the deeper truths of discipleship or the Spirit-filled life. So Aquila and Priscilla mentored him by taking the time to listen, evaluate, relate, and explain "the way of God" (18:26).

Leaders face the danger of contentment with the status quo. After all, if a leader already possesses influence and has achieved a level of respect, why should he or she keep growing?

1. Your growth determines who you are.
2. Who you are determines who you attract.
3. Who you attract determines the success of your organization.

Leaders must remain teachable. Consider five guidelines to cultivate a teachable attitude:

1. *Cure your destination disease.*
   Lack of teachability is rooted in achievement. If you stop growing, you stop leading.
2. *Overcome your success.*
   Success often hinders teachability. Look not at past trophies, but future goals.
3. *Swear off shortcuts.*
   Everything valuable has a price. The longest distance between two points is a shortcut.
4. *Trade in your pride.*
   Admit you don't know everything, even though you do know some things.
5. *Never pay the price twice for the same mistake*
   Growth means you'll make mistakes, but you must learn from each of them.

For a negative example of teachability, see p. 1031.

certain *man* named Justus,[a] *one* who worshiped God, whose house was next door to the synagogue. [8]Then Crispus, the ruler of the synagogue, believed on the Lord with all his household. And many of the Corinthians, hearing, believed and were baptized.

[9]Now the Lord spoke to Paul in the night by a vision, "Do not be afraid, but speak, and do not keep silent; [10]for I am with you, and no one will attack you to hurt you; for I have many people in this city." [11]And he continued *there* a year and six months, teaching the word of God among them.

[12]When Gallio was proconsul of Achaia, the Jews with one accord rose up against Paul and brought him to the judgment seat, [13]saying, "This *fellow* persuades men to worship God contrary to the law."

[14]And when Paul was about to open *his* mouth, Gallio said to the Jews, "If it were a matter of wrongdoing or wicked crimes, O Jews, there would be reason why I should bear with you. [15]But if it is a question of words and names and your own law, look *to it* yourselves; for I do not want to be a judge of such *matters.*" [16]And he drove them from the judgment seat. [17]Then all the Greeks[a] took Sosthenes, the ruler of the synagogue, and beat *him* before the judgment seat. But Gallio took no notice of these things.

Paul Returns to Antioch

[18]So Paul still remained a good while. Then he took leave of the brethren and sailed for Syria, and Priscilla and Aquila *were* with him. He had *his* hair cut off at Cenchrea, for he had taken a vow. [19]And he came to Ephesus, and left them there; but he himself entered the synagogue and reasoned with the Jews. [20]When they asked *him* to stay a longer time with them, he did not consent, [21]but took leave of them, saying, "I must by all means keep this coming feast in Jerusalem;[a] but I will return again to you, God willing." And he sailed from Ephesus.

[22]And when he had landed at Caesarea, and gone up and greeted the church, he went down to Antioch. [23]After he had spent some time *there*, he departed and went over the region of Galatia and Phrygia in order, strengthening all the disciples.

Ministry of Apollos

[24]Now a certain Jew named Apollos, born at Alexandria, an eloquent man *and* mighty in the Scriptures, came to Ephesus. [25]This man had been instructed in the way of the Lord; and being fervent in spirit, he spoke and taught accurately the things of the Lord, though he knew only the baptism of John. [26]So he began to speak boldly in the synagogue. When Aquila and Priscilla heard him, they took him aside and explained to him the way of God more accurately. [27]And when he desired to cross to Achaia, the brethren wrote, exhorting the disciples to receive him; and when he arrived, he greatly helped those who had believed through grace; [28]for he vigorously refuted the Jews publicly, showing from the Scriptures that Jesus is the Christ.

Paul at Ephesus

19 And it happened, while Apollos was at Corinth, that Paul, having passed through the upper regions, came to Ephesus. And finding some disciples [2]he said to them, "Did you receive the Holy Spirit when you believed?"

So they said to him, "We have not so much as heard whether there is a Holy Spirit."

[3]And he said to them, "Into what then were you baptized?"

So they said, "Into John's baptism."

[4]Then Paul said, "John indeed baptized with a baptism of repentance, saying to the people that they should believe on Him who would come after him, that is, on Christ Jesus." [5]When they heard *this,* they were baptized in the name of the Lord Jesus. [6]And when Paul had laid hands on them, the Holy Spirit came upon them, and they spoke with tongues and prophesied. [7]Now the men were about twelve in all.

[8]And he went into the synagogue and spoke boldly for three months, reasoning and persuading concerning the things of the kingdom of God. [9]But when some were hardened and did not believe, but spoke evil of the Way before the multitude, he departed from them and withdrew the disciples, reasoning daily in the school of Tyrannus. [10]And this continued for two years, so that all who dwelt in Asia heard the word of the Lord Jesus, both Jews and Greeks.

Miracles Glorify Christ

[11]Now God worked unusual miracles by the hands of Paul, [12]so that even handkerchiefs or aprons were brought from his body to the sick, and the diseases left them and the evil spirits went out of them. [13]Then some of the itinerant Jewish exorcists took it upon themselves to call the name of the Lord Jesus over those who had

---

18:7 [a]NU-Text reads *Titius Justus.* **18:17** [a]NU-Text reads *they all.* **18:21** [a]NU-Text omits *I must* through *Jerusalem.*

The Law of Explosive Growth: Paul's Mini Seminary Reaches Asia

(Acts 19:8–10)

Paul began a miniature seminary in Ephesus to teach students the ins and outs of the gospel. For two years he rounded up young men and trained them in the lecture hall of Tyrannus. No doubt the education included practical application—with plenty of hands-on experience—for Luke says that everyone in Asia Minor heard the word of the Lord during those two years (Acts 19:10)!

As he mentored students, Paul remained committed to the people, to the process, and to the purpose. His training always resulted in Great Commission activities. Paul committed himself to developing leaders. Consider how we can do the same as we develop others:

1. Know yourself; be familiar with your strengths and weaknesses.
2. Know the person you wish to develop.
3. Clearly define the goals and assignments.
4. Teach the "why" behind the assignments.
5. Discuss their growth process as you go.
6. Spend relational time with them.
7. Allow them to watch you serve and lead.
8. Give them the resources you need.
9. Encourage them to journal during the process.
10. Hold them accountable for their work.
11. Give them the freedom to fail.
12. Evaluate and affirm regularly.

evil spirits, saying, "We[a] exorcise you by the Jesus whom Paul preaches." [14]Also there were seven sons of Sceva, a Jewish chief priest, who did so.

[15]And the evil spirit answered and said, "Jesus I know, and Paul I know; but who are you?"

[16]Then the man in whom the evil spirit was leaped on them, overpowered[a] them, and prevailed against them,[b] so that they fled out of that house naked and wounded. [17]This became known both to all Jews and Greeks dwelling in Ephesus; and fear fell on them all, and the name of the Lord Jesus was magnified. [18]And many who had believed came confessing and telling their deeds. [19]Also, many of those who had practiced magic brought their books together and burned *them* in the sight of all. And they counted up the value of them, and *it* totaled fifty thousand *pieces* of silver. [20]So the word of the Lord grew mightily and prevailed.

The Riot at Ephesus

[21]When these things were accomplished, Paul purposed in the Spirit, when he had passed through Macedonia and Achaia, to go to Jerusalem, saying, "After I have been there, I must also see Rome." [22]So he sent into Macedonia two of those who ministered to him, Timothy and Erastus, but he himself stayed in Asia for a time.

[23]And about that time there arose a great commotion about the Way. [24]For a certain man named Demetrius, a silversmith, who made silver shrines of Diana,[a] brought no small profit to the craftsmen. [25]He called them together with the workers of similar occupation, and said: "Men, you know that we have our prosperity by this trade. [26]Moreover you see and hear that not only at Ephesus, but throughout almost all Asia, this Paul has persuaded and turned away many people, saying that they are not gods which are made with hands. [27]So not only is this trade of ours in danger of falling into disrepute, but also the temple of the great goddess Diana may be despised and her magnificence destroyed,[a] whom all Asia and the world worship."

[28]Now when they heard *this,* they were full of

19:13 [a]NU-Text reads *I*. **19:16** [a]M-Text reads *and they overpowered.* [b]NU-Text reads *both of them.* **19:24** [a]Greek *Artemis* **19:27** [a]NU-Text reads *she be deposed from her magnificence.*

wrath and cried out, saying, "Great *is* Diana of the Ephesians!" 29So the whole city was filled with confusion, and rushed into the theater with one accord, having seized Gaius and Aristarchus, Macedonians, Paul's travel companions. 30And when Paul wanted to go in to the people, the disciples would not allow him. 31Then some of the officials of Asia, who were his friends, sent to him pleading that he would not venture into the theater. 32Some therefore cried one thing and some another, for the assembly was confused, and most of them did not know why they had come together. 33And they drew Alexander out of the multitude, the Jews putting him forward. And Alexander motioned with his hand, and wanted to make his defense to the people. 34But when they found out that he was a Jew, all with one voice cried out for about two hours, "Great *is* Diana of the Ephesians!"

35And when the city clerk had quieted the crowd, he said: "Men of Ephesus, what man is there who does not know that the city of the Ephesians is temple guardian of the great goddess Diana, and of the *image* which fell down from Zeus? 36Therefore, since these things cannot be denied, you ought to be quiet and do nothing rashly. 37For you have brought these men here who are neither robbers of temples nor blasphemers of youra goddess. 38Therefore, if Demetrius and his fellow craftsmen have a case against anyone, the courts are open and there are proconsuls. Let them bring charges against one another. 39But if you have any other inquiry to make, it shall be determined in the lawful assembly. 40For we are in danger of being called in question for today's uproar, there being no reason which we may give to account for this disorderly gathering." 41And when he had said these things, he dismissed the assembly.

Journeys in Greece

20 After the uproar had ceased, Paul called the disciples to *himself,* embraced *them,* and departed to go to Macedonia. 2Now when he had gone over that region and encouraged them with many words, he came to Greece 3and stayed three months. And when the Jews plotted against him as he was about to sail to Syria, he decided to return through Macedonia. 4And Sopater of Berea accompanied him to Asia—also Aristarchus and Secundus of the Thessalonians, and Gaius of Derbe, and Timothy, and Tychicus and Trophimus of Asia. 5These men, going ahead, waited for us at Troas. 6But we sailed away from Philippi after the Days of Unleavened Bread, and

in five days joined them at Troas, where we stayed seven days.

Ministering at Troas

7Now on the first *day* of the week, when the disciples came together to break bread, Paul, ready to depart the next day, spoke to them and continued his message until midnight. 8There were many lamps in the upper room where theya were gathered together. 9And in a window sat a certain young man named Eutychus, who was sinking into a deep sleep. He was overcome by sleep; and as Paul continued speaking, he fell down from the third story and was taken up dead. 10But Paul went down, fell on him, and embracing *him* said, "Do not trouble yourselves, for his life is in him." 11Now when he had come up, had broken bread and eaten, and talked a long while, even till daybreak, he departed. 12And they brought the young man in alive, and they were not a little comforted.

From Troas to Miletus

13Then we went ahead to the ship and sailed to Assos, there intending to take Paul on board; for so he had given orders, intending himself to go on foot. 14And when he met us at Assos, we took him on board and came to Mitylene. 15We sailed from there, and the next *day* came opposite Chios. The following *day* we arrived at Samos and stayed at Trogyllium. The next *day* we came to Miletus. 16For Paul had decided to sail past Ephesus, so that he would not have to spend time in Asia; for he was hurrying to be at Jerusalem, if possible, on the Day of Pentecost.

The Ephesian Elders Exhorted

17From Miletus he sent to Ephesus and called for the elders of the church. 18And when they had come to him, he said to them: "You know, from the first day that I came to Asia, in what manner I always lived among you, 19serving the Lord with all humility, with many tears and trials which happened to me by the plotting of the Jews; 20how I kept back nothing that was helpful, but proclaimed it to you, and taught you publicly and from house to house, 21testifying to Jews, and also to Greeks, repentance toward God and faith toward our Lord Jesus Christ. 22And see, now I go bound in the spirit to Jerusalem, not knowing the things that will happen to me there, 23except that the Holy Spirit testifies in every city, saying that chains and tribulations await me. 24But none

---

19:37 aNU-Text reads *our.* **20:8** aNU-Text and M-Text read *we.*

Paul: The Heart of an Effective Leader

(Acts 20:18–24)

Who you are comes before what you do. Leadership is "being" before "doing."
As Paul spoke to the Ephesians, he described the ingredients of an effective leader. Paul led from his soul. He made tough calls, yet shed tears in front of his people. One thing is sure: Leadership begins with the heart. Paul had a heart that was . . .

1. *Consistent*—he lived steadily while moving among them (v. 18).
2. *Contrite*—he acted humbly and willingly showed his weakness (v. 19).
3. *Courageous*—he didn't shrink from doing the right thing (v. 20).
4. *Convictional*—he communicated his convictions boldly (v. 21).
5. *Committed*—he left for Jerusalem, willing to die for Jesus (vv. 22, 23).
6. *Captivated*—he showed that a surrendered man doesn't have to survive (v. 24).

of these things move me; nor do I count my life dear to myself,[a] so that I may finish my race with joy, and the ministry which I received from the Lord Jesus, to testify to the gospel of the grace of God.

[25]"And indeed, now I know that you all, among whom I have gone preaching the kingdom of God, will see my face no more. [26]Therefore I testify to you this day that I *am* innocent of the blood of all *men*. [27]For I have not shunned to declare to you the whole counsel of God. [28]Therefore take heed to yourselves and to all the flock, among which the Holy Spirit has made you overseers, to shepherd the church of God[a] which He purchased with His own blood. [29]For I know this, that after my departure savage wolves will come in among you, not sparing the flock. [30]Also from among yourselves men will rise up, speaking perverse things, to draw away the disciples after themselves. [31]Therefore watch, and remember that for three years I did not cease to warn everyone night and day with tears.

[32]"So now, brethren, I commend you to God and to the word of His grace, which is able to build you up and give you an inheritance among all those who are sanctified. [33]I have coveted no one's silver or gold or apparel. [34]Yes,[a] you yourselves know that these hands have provided for my necessities, and for those who were with me. [35]I have shown you in every way, by laboring like this, that you must support the weak. And remember the words of the Lord Jesus, that He said, 'It is more blessed to give than to receive.'"

[36]And when he had said these things, he knelt down and prayed with them all. [37]Then they all wept freely, and fell on Paul's neck and kissed him, [38]sorrowing most of all for the words which he spoke, that they would see his face no more. And they accompanied him to the ship.

Warnings on the Journey to Jerusalem

21 Now it came to pass, that when we had departed from them and set sail, running a straight course we came to Cos, the following *day* to Rhodes, and from there to Patara. [2]And finding a ship sailing over to Phoenicia, we went aboard and set sail. [3]When we had sighted Cyprus, we passed it on the left, sailed to Syria, and landed at Tyre; for there the ship was to unload her cargo. [4]And finding disciples,[a] we stayed there seven days. They told Paul through the Spirit not to go up to Jerusalem. [5]When we had come to the end of those days, we departed and went on our way; and they all accompanied us, with wives and children, till *we were* out of the city. And we knelt down on the shore and prayed. [6]When we had taken our leave of one another, we boarded the ship, and they returned home.

[7]And when we had finished *our* voyage from Tyre, we came to Ptolemais, greeted the brethren, and stayed with them one day. [8]On the next *day* we who were Paul's companions[a] departed and came to Caesarea, and entered the house of Philip the evangelist, who was *one* of the seven, and stayed with him. [9]Now this man had four

---

20:24 [a]NU-Text reads *But I do not count my life of any value or dear to myself.* **20:28** [a]M-Text reads *of the Lord and God.* **20:34** [a]NU-Text and M-Text omit *Yes.* **21:4** [a]NU-Text reads *the disciples.* **21:8** [a]NU-Text omits *who were Paul's companions.*

virgin daughters who prophesied. [10]And as we stayed many days, a certain prophet named Agabus came down from Judea. [11]When he had come to us, he took Paul's belt, bound his *own* hands and feet, and said, "Thus says the Holy Spirit, 'So shall the Jews at Jerusalem bind the man who owns this belt, and deliver *him* into the hands of the Gentiles.'"

[12]Now when we heard these things, both we and those from that place pleaded with him not to go up to Jerusalem. [13]Then Paul answered, "What do you mean by weeping and breaking my heart? For I am ready not only to be bound, but also to die at Jerusalem for the name of the Lord Jesus."

[14]So when he would not be persuaded, we ceased, saying, "The will of the Lord be done."

Paul Urged to Make Peace

[15]And after those days we packed and went up to Jerusalem. [16]Also some of the disciples from Caesarea went with us and brought with them a certain Mnason of Cyprus, an early disciple, with whom we were to lodge.

[17]And when we had come to Jerusalem, the brethren received us gladly. [18]On the following *day* Paul went in with us to James, and all the elders were present. [19]When he had greeted them, he told in detail those things which God had done among the Gentiles through his ministry. [20]And when they heard *it,* they glorified the Lord. And they said to him, "You see, brother, how many myriads of Jews there are who have believed, and they are all zealous for the law; [21]but they have been informed about you that you teach all the Jews who are among the Gentiles to forsake Moses, saying that they ought not to circumcise *their* children nor to walk according to the customs. [22]What then? The assembly must certainly meet, for they will[a] hear that you have come. [23]Therefore do what we tell you: We have four men who have taken a vow. [24]Take them and be purified with them, and pay their expenses so that they may shave *their* heads, and that all may know that those things of which they were informed concerning you are nothing, but *that* you yourself also walk orderly and keep the law. [25]But concerning the Gentiles who believe, we have written *and* decided that they should observe no such thing, except[a] that they should keep themselves from *things* offered to idols, from blood, from things strangled, and from sexual immorality."

Arrested in the Temple

[26]Then Paul took the men, and the next day, having been purified with them, entered the temple to announce the expiration of the days of purification, at which time an offering should be made for each one of them.

[27]Now when the seven days were almost ended, the Jews from Asia, seeing him in the temple, stirred up the whole crowd and laid hands on him, [28]crying out, "Men of Israel, help! This is the man who teaches all *men* everywhere against the people, the law, and this place; and furthermore he also brought Greeks into the temple and has defiled this holy place." [29](For they had previously[a] seen Trophimus the Ephesian with him in the city, whom they supposed that Paul had brought into the temple.)

[30]And all the city was disturbed; and the people ran together, seized Paul, and dragged him out of the temple; and immediately the doors were shut. [31]Now as they were seeking to kill him, news came to the commander of the garrison that all Jerusalem was in an uproar. [32]He immediately took soldiers and centurions, and ran down to them. And when they saw the commander and the soldiers, they stopped beating Paul. [33]Then the commander came near and took him, and commanded *him* to be bound with two chains; and he asked who he was and what he had done. [34]And some among the multitude cried one thing and some another.

So when he could not ascertain the truth because of the tumult, he commanded him to be taken into the barracks. [35]When he reached the stairs, he had to be carried by the soldiers because of the violence of the mob. [36]For the multitude of the people followed after, crying out, "Away with him!"

Addressing the Jerusalem Mob

[37]Then as Paul was about to be led into the barracks, he said to the commander, "May I speak to you?"

He replied, "Can you speak Greek? [38]Are you not the Egyptian who some time ago stirred up a rebellion and led the four thousand assassins out into the wilderness?"

[39]But Paul said, "I am a Jew from Tarsus, in Cilicia, a citizen of no mean city; and I implore you, permit me to speak to the people."

[40]So when he had given him permission, Paul stood on the stairs and motioned with his hand to the people. And when there was a great si-

---

21:22 [a]NU-Text reads *What then is to be done? They will certainly.* **21:25** [a]NU-Text omits *that they should observe no such thing, except.* **21:29** [a]M-Text omits *previously.*

lence, he spoke to *them* in the Hebrew language, saying,

22

"Brethren and fathers, hear my defense before you now." [2]And when they heard that he spoke to them in the Hebrew language, they kept all the more silent.

Then he said: [3]"I am indeed a Jew, born in Tarsus of Cilicia, but brought up in this city at the feet of Gamaliel, taught according to the strictness of our fathers' law, and was zealous toward God as you all are today. [4]I persecuted this Way to the death, binding and delivering into prisons both men and women, [5]as also the high priest bears me witness, and all the council of the elders, from whom I also received letters to the brethren, and went to Damascus to bring in chains even those who were there to Jerusalem to be punished.

[6]"Now it happened, as I journeyed and came near Damascus at about noon, suddenly a great light from heaven shone around me. [7]And I fell to the ground and heard a voice saying to me, 'Saul, Saul, why are you persecuting Me?' [8]So I answered, 'Who are You, Lord?' And He said to me, 'I am Jesus of Nazareth, whom you are persecuting.'

[9]"And those who were with me indeed saw the light and were afraid,[a] but they did not hear the voice of Him who spoke to me. [10]So I said, 'What shall I do, Lord?' And the Lord said to me, 'Arise and go into Damascus, and there you will be told all things which are appointed for you to do.' [11]And since I could not see for the glory of that light, being led by the hand of those who were with me, I came into Damascus.

[12]"Then a certain Ananias, a devout man according to the law, having a good testimony with all the Jews who dwelt *there*, [13]came to me; and he stood and said to me, 'Brother Saul, receive your sight.' And at that same hour I looked up at him. [14]Then he said, 'The God of our fathers has chosen you that you should know His will, and see the Just One, and hear the voice of His mouth. [15]For you will be His witness to all men of what you have seen and heard. [16]And now why are you waiting? Arise and be baptized, and wash away your sins, calling on the name of the Lord.'

[17]"Now it happened, when I returned to Jerusalem and was praying in the temple, that I was in a trance [18]and saw Him saying to me, 'Make haste and get out of Jerusalem quickly, for they will not receive your testimony concerning Me.' [19]So I said, 'Lord, they know that in every synagogue I imprisoned and beat those who believe

Communication: Paul Adapts, Shares His Story to Persuade
(Acts 22:1–21; 26:4–23)

Three times the Book of Acts recounts Paul's conversion. Twice he tells his story before government rulers. In both settings he adapts his story and emphasizes a facet that meets the needs of his audience.

Effective leaders know not only *what* to say, but *how* to say it in order to most powerfully impact their listeners. When they speak, they take into account impact, not image. They evaluate their audience and communicate in a way that best connects with their listeners, then they help them to make practical applications to their message.

Try a little exercise. Read Paul's testimony in Acts 22 and 26, with an eye toward comparing and contrasting his accounts. What differences do you note? What similarities? Why would he emphasize one thing to one audience and another to a second audience? What do you learn from Paul about effectively shaping your message to different groups?

on You. [20]And when the blood of Your martyr Stephen was shed, I also was standing by consenting to his death,[a] and guarding the clothes of those who were killing him.' [21]Then He said to me, 'Depart, for I will send you far from here to the Gentiles.'"

Paul's Roman Citizenship

[22]And they listened to him until this word, and *then* they raised their voices and said, "Away with such a *fellow* from the earth, for he is not fit to live!" [23]Then, as they cried out and tore off *their* clothes and threw dust into the air, [24]the commander ordered him to be brought into the barracks, and said that he should be examined under scourging, so that he might know why they shouted so against him. [25]And as they bound him with thongs, Paul said to the centurion who stood by, "Is it lawful for you to scourge a man who is a Roman, and uncondemned?"

22:9 [a]NU-Text omits *and were afraid.*
22:20 [a]NU-Text omits *to his death.*

[26]When the centurion heard *that,* he went and told the commander, saying, "Take care what you do, for this man is a Roman."

[27]Then the commander came and said to him, "Tell me, are you a Roman?"

He said, "Yes."

[28]The commander answered, "With a large sum I obtained this citizenship."

And Paul said, "But I was born *a citizen.*"

[29]Then immediately those who were about to examine him withdrew from him; and the commander was also afraid after he found out that he was a Roman, and because he had bound him.

The Sanhedrin Divided

[30]The next day, because he wanted to know for certain why he was accused by the Jews, he released him from *his* bonds, and commanded the chief priests and all their council to appear, and brought Paul down and set him before them.

23 Then Paul, looking earnestly at the council, said, "Men *and* brethren, I have lived in all good conscience before God until this day." [2]And the high priest Ananias commanded those who stood by him to strike him on the mouth. [3]Then Paul said to him, "God will strike you, *you* whitewashed wall! For you sit to judge me according to the law, and do you command me to be struck contrary to the law?"

[4]And those who stood by said, "Do you revile God's high priest?"

[5]Then Paul said, "I did not know, brethren, that he was the high priest; for it is written, '*You shall not speak evil of a ruler of your people.*'"[a]

[6]But when Paul perceived that one part were Sadducees and the other Pharisees, he cried out in the council, "Men *and* brethren, I am a Pharisee, the son of a Pharisee; concerning the hope and resurrection of the dead I am being judged!"

[7]And when he had said this, a dissension arose between the Pharisees and the Sadducees; and the assembly was divided. [8]For Sadducees say that there is no resurrection—and no angel or spirit; but the Pharisees confess both. [9]Then there arose a loud outcry. And the scribes of the Pharisees' party arose and protested, saying, "We find no evil in this man; but if a spirit or an angel has spoken to him, let us not fight against God."[a]

[10]Now when there arose a great dissension,

23:5 [a]Exodus 22:28 **23:9** [a]NU-Text omits last clause and reads *what if a spirit or an angel has spoken to him?*

the commander, fearing lest Paul might be pulled to pieces by them, commanded the soldiers to go down and take him by force from among them, and bring *him* into the barracks.

The Plot Against Paul

[11]But the following night the Lord stood by him and said, "Be of good cheer, Paul; for as you have testified for Me in Jerusalem, so you must also bear witness at Rome."

[12]And when it was day, some of the Jews banded together and bound themselves under an oath, saying that they would neither eat nor drink till they had killed Paul. [13]Now there were more than forty who had formed this conspiracy. [14]They came to the chief priests and elders, and said, "We have bound ourselves under a great oath that we will eat nothing until we have killed Paul. [15]Now you, therefore, together with the council, suggest to the commander that he be brought down to you tomorrow,[a] as though you were going to make further inquiries concerning him; but we are ready to kill him before he comes near."

[16]So when Paul's sister's son heard of their ambush, he went and entered the barracks and told Paul. [17]Then Paul called one of the centurions to *him* and said, "Take this young man to the commander, for he has something to tell him." [18]So he took him and brought *him* to the commander and said, "Paul the prisoner called me to *him* and asked *me* to bring this young man to you. He has something to say to you."

[19]Then the commander took him by the hand, went aside, and asked privately, "What is it that you have to tell me?"

[20]And he said, "The Jews have agreed to ask that you bring Paul down to the council tomorrow, as though they were going to inquire more fully about him. [21]But do not yield to them, for more than forty of them lie in wait for him, men who have bound themselves by an oath that they will neither eat nor drink till they have killed him; and now they are ready, waiting for the promise from you."

[22]So the commander let the young man depart, and commanded *him,* "Tell no one that you have revealed these things to me."

Sent to Felix

[23]And he called for two centurions, saying, "Prepare two hundred soldiers, seventy horsemen, and two hundred spearmen to go to Caesarea at the third hour of the night; [24]and provide mounts to set Paul on, and bring *him* safely to Felix the governor." [25]He wrote a letter in the following manner:

[26]Claudius Lysias,

To the most excellent governor Felix:

Greetings.

[27]This man was seized by the Jews and was about to be killed by them. Coming with the troops I rescued him, having learned that he was a Roman. [28]And when I wanted to know the reason they accused him, I brought him before their council. [29]I found out that he was accused concerning questions of their law, but had nothing charged against him deserving of death or chains. [30]And when it was told me that the Jews lay in wait for the man,[a] I sent him immediately to you, and also commanded his accusers to state before you the charges against him.

Farewell.

[31]Then the soldiers, as they were commanded, took Paul and brought *him* by night to Antipatris. [32]The next day they left the horsemen to go on with him, and returned to the barracks. [33]When they came to Caesarea and had delivered the letter to the governor, they also presented Paul to him. [34]And when the governor had read *it,* he asked what province he was from. And when he understood that *he was* from Cilicia, [35]he said, "I will hear you when your accusers also have come." And he commanded him to be kept in Herod's Praetorium.

Accused of Sedition

24 Now after five days Ananias the high priest came down with the elders and a certain orator *named* Tertullus. These gave evidence to the governor against Paul. [2]And when he was called upon, Tertullus began his accusation, saying: "Seeing that through you we enjoy great peace, and prosperity is being brought to this nation by your foresight, [3]we accept *it* always and in all places, most noble Felix, with all thankfulness. [4]Nevertheless, not to be tedious to you any further, I beg you to hear, by your courtesy, a few words from us. [5]For we have found this man a plague, a creator of dissension among all the Jews throughout the world, and a ringleader of the sect of the Nazarenes. [6]He even tried to profane the temple,

---

23:15 [a]NU-Text omits *tomorrow.* **23:30** [a]NU-Text reads *there would be a plot against the man.*

and we seized him,[a] and wanted to judge him according to our law. [7]But the commander Lysias came by and with great violence took *him* out of our hands, [8]commanding his accusers to come to you. By examining him yourself you may ascertain all these things of which we accuse him." [9]And the Jews also assented,[a] maintaining that these things were so.

The Defense Before Felix

[10]Then Paul, after the governor had nodded to him to speak, answered: "Inasmuch as I know that you have been for many years a judge of this nation, I do the more cheerfully answer for myself, [11]because you may ascertain that it is no more than twelve days since I went up to Jerusalem to worship. [12]And they neither found me in the temple disputing with anyone nor inciting the crowd, either in the synagogues or in the city. [13]Nor can they prove the things of which they now accuse me. [14]But this I confess to you, that according to the Way which they call a sect, so I worship the God of my fathers, believing all things which are written in the Law and in the Prophets. [15]I have hope in God, which they themselves also accept, that there will be a resurrection of *the* dead,[a] both of *the* just and *the* unjust. [16]This *being* so, I myself always strive to have a conscience without offense toward God and men.

[17]"Now after many years I came to bring alms and offerings to my nation, [18]in the midst of which some Jews from Asia found me purified in the temple, neither with a mob nor with tumult. [19]They ought to have been here before you to object if they had anything against me. [20]Or else let those who are *here* themselves say if they found any wrongdoing[a] in me while I stood before the council, [21]unless *it is* for this one statement which I cried out, standing among them, 'Concerning the resurrection of the dead I am being judged by you this day.' "

Felix Procrastinates

[22]But when Felix heard these things, having more accurate knowledge of *the* Way, he adjourned the proceedings and said, "When Lysias the commander comes down, I will make a decision on your case." [23]So he commanded the centurion to keep Paul and to let *him* have liberty, and told him not to forbid any of his friends to provide for or visit him.

[24]And after some days, when Felix came with his wife Drusilla, who was Jewish, he sent for Paul and heard him concerning the faith in Christ. [25]Now as he reasoned about righteousness, self-control, and the judgment to come, Felix was afraid and answered, "Go away for now; when I have a convenient time I will call for you." [26]Meanwhile he also hoped that money would be given him by Paul, that he might release him.[a] Therefore he sent for him more often and conversed with him.

[27]But after two years Porcius Festus succeeded Felix; and Felix, wanting to do the Jews a favor, left Paul bound.

Paul Appeals to Caesar

25 Now when Festus had come to the province, after three days he went up from Caesarea to Jerusalem. [2]Then the high priest[a] and the chief men of the Jews informed him against Paul; and they petitioned him, [3]asking a favor against him, that he would summon him to Jerusalem—while *they* lay in ambush along the road to kill him. [4]But Festus answered that Paul should be kept at Caesarea, and that he himself was going *there* shortly. [5]"Therefore," he said, "let those who have authority among you go down with *me* and accuse this man, to see if there is any fault in him."

[6]And when he had remained among them more than ten days, he went down to Caesarea. And the next day, sitting on the judgment seat, he commanded Paul to be brought. [7]When he had come, the Jews who had come down from Jerusalem stood about and laid many serious complaints against Paul, which they could not prove, [8]while he answered for himself, "Neither against the law of the Jews, nor against the temple, nor against Caesar have I offended in anything at all."

[9]But Festus, wanting to do the Jews a favor, answered Paul and said, "Are you willing to go up to Jerusalem and there be judged before me concerning these things?"

[10]So Paul said, "I stand at Caesar's judgment seat, where I ought to be judged. To the Jews I have done no wrong, as you very well know. [11]For if I am an offender, or have committed anything deserving of death, I do not object to dying; but if there is nothing in these things of

---

24:6 [a]NU-Text ends the sentence here and omits the rest of verse 6, all of verse 7, and the first clause of verse 8. **24:9** [a]NU-Text and M-Text read *joined the attack.* **24:15** [a]NU-Text omits *of the dead.* **24:20** [a]NU-Text and M-Text read *say what wrongdoing they found.* **24:26** [a]NU-Text omits *that he might release him.* **25:2** [a]NU-Text reads *chief priests.*

which these men accuse me, no one can deliver me to them. I appeal to Caesar."

[12]Then Festus, when he had conferred with the council, answered, "You have appealed to Caesar? To Caesar you shall go!"

Paul Before Agrippa

[13]And after some days King Agrippa and Bernice came to Caesarea to greet Festus. [14]When they had been there many days, Festus laid Paul's case before the king, saying: "There is a certain man left a prisoner by Felix, [15]about whom the chief priests and the elders of the Jews informed me, when I was in Jerusalem, asking for a judgment against him. [16]To them I answered, 'It is not the custom of the Romans to deliver any man to destruction[a] before the accused meets the accusers face to face, and has opportunity to answer for himself concerning the charge against him.' [17]Therefore when they had come together, without any delay, the next day I sat on the judgment seat and commanded the man to be brought in. [18]When the accusers stood up, they brought no accusation against him of such things as I supposed, [19]but had some questions against him about their own religion and about a certain Jesus, who had died, whom Paul affirmed to be alive. [20]And because I was uncertain of such questions, I asked whether he was willing to go to Jerusalem and there be judged concerning these matters. [21]But when Paul appealed to be reserved for the decision of Augustus, I commanded him to be kept till I could send him to Caesar."

[22]Then Agrippa said to Festus, "I also would like to hear the man myself."

"Tomorrow," he said, "you shall hear him."

[23]So the next day, when Agrippa and Bernice had come with great pomp, and had entered the auditorium with the commanders and the prominent men of the city, at Festus' command Paul was brought in. [24]And Festus said: "King Agrippa and all the men who are here present with us, you see this man about whom the whole assembly of the Jews petitioned me, both at Jerusalem and here, crying out that he was not fit to live any longer. [25]But when I found that he had committed nothing deserving of death, and that he himself had appealed to Augustus, I decided to send him. [26]I have nothing certain to write to my lord concerning him. Therefore I have brought him out before you, and especially

25:16 [a]NU-Text omits *to destruction,* although it is implied.

PAUL

THE MOST INFLUENTIAL LEADER OF THE EARLY CHURCH

(Acts 26:1–23)

From the very beginning, the apostle Paul's life in Christ greatly influenced everyone around him.

This persecutor-turned-apostle stood before kings, governors, and the religious power structures of the day. His enemies accused him, imprisoned him, beat him, and threatened him with death. He traveled untold thousands of miles and even survived a shipwreck. Through all of this, Paul never failed to vigorously and courageously defend and preach the gospel of Jesus Christ.

Paul didn't become an influential leader because of his eloquence or because he possessed some special talent withheld from everyone else. Paul gained influence because, regardless of his circumstances—whether he sat in shackles during another interrogation, whether he lay in a cold prison cell, or whether he roamed free to do his work—he stayed committed to one thing: preaching the name of Jesus.

Without question, Paul became the most influential leader of the early church. We continue to feel his influence to this day.

By the world's standards—then *and* today—Paul must have appeared a fanatic. But all he did was obey God's call to influence the world around him. Wise leaders today would do well to follow Paul's example by purposefully taking the Word of God both to the body of Christ and to the unbelieving world.

before you, King Agrippa, so that after the examination has taken place I may have something to write. ²⁷For it seems to me unreasonable to send a prisoner and not to specify the charges against him."

Paul's Early Life

26 Then Agrippa said to Paul, "You are permitted to speak for yourself."

So Paul stretched out his hand and answered for himself: ²"I think myself happy, King Agrippa, because today I shall answer for myself before you concerning all the things of which I am accused by the Jews, ³especially because you are expert in all customs and questions which have to do with the Jews. Therefore I beg you to hear me patiently.

⁴"My manner of life from my youth, which was spent from the beginning among my own nation at Jerusalem, all the Jews know. ⁵They knew me from the first, if they were willing to testify, that according to the strictest sect of our religion I lived a Pharisee. ⁶And now I stand and am judged for the hope of the promise made by God to our fathers. ⁷To this *promise* our twelve tribes, earnestly serving *God* night and day, hope

to attain. For this hope's sake, King Agrippa, I am accused by the Jews. ⁸Why should it be thought incredible by you that God raises the dead?

⁹"Indeed, I myself thought I must do many things contrary to the name of Jesus of Nazareth. ¹⁰This I also did in Jerusalem, and many of the saints I shut up in prison, having received authority from the chief priests; and when they were put to death, I cast my vote against *them.* ¹¹And I punished them often in every synagogue and compelled *them* to blaspheme; and being exceedingly enraged against them, I persecuted *them* even to foreign cities.

Paul Recounts His Conversion

¹²"While thus occupied, as I journeyed to Damascus with authority and commission from the chief priests, ¹³at midday, O king, along the road I saw a light from heaven, brighter than the sun, shining around me and those who journeyed with me. ¹⁴And when we all had fallen to the ground, I heard a voice speaking to me and saying in the Hebrew language, 'Saul, Saul, why are you persecuting Me? *It is* hard for you to kick against the goads.' ¹⁵So I said, 'Who are You, Lord?' And He said, 'I am Jesus, whom you are

---

Persuasion: Leaders Speak to Transform, Not Merely Inform

(Acts 26:1–29)

In one of his most compelling court speeches, Paul addressed King Agrippa. As you read this chapter, try to sense Paul's strategy. Paul believed the best defense is a good offense and nearly converted King Agrippa. Observe how this leader attempted to persuade his audience:

1. He appeared relaxed, yet used animated gestures (v. 1).
2. He humbly thanked the king for allowing him to speak (v. 2).
3. He affirmed the king's knowledge and expertise (v. 3).
4. He admitted his life was an open book (v. 4).
5. He reminded them of his strict past (vv. 5–8).
6. He identified with their opposition to the life he now embraced (vv. 9–11).
7. He used a narrative to defend his changed life (vv. 12–18).
8. He described his motives as pure and constructive (v. 18).
9. He conceded that he was obeying a divine vision (vv. 19, 20).
10. He explained that his obedience to God caused his trouble (v. 21).
11. He illustrated God's favor on his life (v. 22).
12. He affirmed that he preached the Scripture (vv. 22, 23).
13. He challenged them with reasonable and verifiable facts (v. 25).
14. He admitted the king knew these facts (v. 26).
15. He confronted the king directly with a question (v. 27).
16. He pled with them to obey God (v. 29).

would come— [23]that the Christ would suffer, that He would be the first to rise from the dead, and would proclaim light to the *Jewish* people and to the Gentiles."

Agrippa Parries Paul's Challenge

[24]Now as he thus made his defense, Festus said with a loud voice, "Paul, you are beside yourself! Much learning is driving you mad!"

[25]But he said, "I am not mad, most noble Festus, but speak the words of truth and reason. [26]For the king, before whom I also speak freely, knows these things; for I am convinced that none of these things escapes his attention, since this thing was not done in a corner. [27]King Agrippa, do you believe the prophets? I know that you do believe."

[28]Then Agrippa said to Paul, "You almost persuade me to become a Christian."

[29]And Paul said, "I would to God that not only you, but also all who hear me today, might become both almost and altogether such as I am, except for these chains."

[30]When he had said these things, the king stood up, as well as the governor and Bernice and those who sat with them; [31]and when they had gone aside, they talked among themselves, saying, "This man is doing nothing deserving of death or chains."

[32]Then Agrippa said to Festus, "This man might have been set free if he had not appealed to Caesar."

The Voyage to Rome Begins

27 And when it was decided that we should sail to Italy, they delivered Paul and some other prisoners to *one* named Julius, a centurion of the Augustan Regiment. [2]So, entering a ship of Adramyttium, we put to sea, meaning to sail along the coasts of Asia. Aristarchus, a Macedonian of Thessalonica, was with us. [3]And the next *day* we landed at Sidon. And Julius treated Paul kindly and gave *him* liberty to go to his friends and receive care. [4]When we had put to sea from there, we sailed under *the shelter* of Cyprus, because the winds were contrary. [5]And when we had sailed over the sea which is off Cilicia and Pamphylia, we came to Myra, *a city* of Lycia. [6]There the centurion found an Alexandrian ship sailing to Italy, and he put us on board.

[7]When we had sailed slowly many days, and arrived with difficulty off Cnidus, the wind not permitting us to proceed, we sailed under *the shelter* of Crete off Salmone. [8]Passing it with

---

Vision: Paul's Vision Led to His Victory

(Acts 26:12–29)

Paul's vision on the road to Damascus became the captivating force behind his success. The apostle teaches us the power of a vision. God's vision for Paul accomplished a number of things:

1. *It stopped him* (vv. 12–15).
   Vision allows us to see ourselves. We see things not as *they* are, but as *we* are.
2. *It sent him* (vv. 16–18).
   Vision allows us to see others. We feel compelled to act.
3. *It strengthened him* (vv. 20–23).
   Vision enables us to continue despite struggle and lack of resources.
4. *It stretched him* (vv. 24–29).
   Vision gave him conviction to stand, confidence to speak, and compassion to share.
5. *It satisfied him* (v. 19).
   Obedience to this vision motivated Paul to act. It fulfilled him.

---

persecuting. [16]But rise and stand on your feet; for I have appeared to you for this purpose, to make you a minister and a witness both of the things which you have seen and of the things which I will yet reveal to you. [17]I will deliver you from the *Jewish* people, as well as *from* the Gentiles, to whom I now[a] send you, [18]to open their eyes, *in order* to turn *them* from darkness to light, and *from* the power of Satan to God, that they may receive forgiveness of sins and an inheritance among those who are sanctified by faith in Me.'

Paul's Post-Conversion Life

[19]"Therefore, King Agrippa, I was not disobedient to the heavenly vision, [20]but declared first to those in Damascus and in Jerusalem, and throughout all the region of Judea, and *then* to the Gentiles, that they should repent, turn to God, and do works befitting repentance. [21]For these reasons the Jews seized me in the temple and tried to kill *me*. [22]Therefore, having obtained help from God, to this day I stand, witnessing both to small and great, saying no other things than those which the prophets and Moses said

---

26:17 [a]NU-Text and M-Text omit *now*.

The Law of E. F. Hutton: An Inmate Takes Command

(Acts 27:1–44)

As an inmate on a virtual prison ship, Paul began with no influence (Acts 27:11). By the end of the voyage, however, everyone was listening to him, including the centurion. Note how this leader gained his influence:

1. *He built trust* (v. 3).
   Julius allowed Paul special privileges, noting his trustworthiness.
2. *He took initiative* (vv. 9, 10).
   With no position or permission, Paul stepped in and took action.
3. *He possessed good judgment* (v. 10).
   Paul's speech revealed wisdom and experience.
4. *He spoke with authority and credibility* (v. 21).
   Paul unashamedly reminded the crew he had been right earlier.
5. *He was optimistic and confident* (vv. 22–24).
   Paul spoke boldly.
6. *He gave encouragement* (v. 25).
   Paul gave hope for survival and rescue.
7. *He was honest* (v. 26).
   Paul candidly told the crew they would face problems.
8. *He didn't compromise on absolutes* (vv. 27–32).
   Paul wouldn't drift from God-given instructions.
9. *He stayed focused* (vv. 33, 34).
   Paul focused on objectives, not obstacles.
10. *He led by example* (vv. 35–38).
    Paul led by modeling the right attitude.
11. *He ultimately succeeded* (vv. 39–44).
    Paul eventually accomplished what he set out to do.

difficulty, we came to a place called Fair Havens, near the city *of* Lasea.

Paul's Warning Ignored

[9]Now when much time had been spent, and sailing was now dangerous because the Fast was already over, Paul advised them, [10]saying, "Men, I perceive that this voyage will end with disaster and much loss, not only of the cargo and ship, but also our lives." [11]Nevertheless the centurion was more persuaded by the helmsman and the owner of the ship than by the things spoken by Paul. [12]And because the harbor was not suitable to winter in, the majority advised to set sail from there also, if by any means they could reach Phoenix, a harbor of Crete opening toward the southwest and northwest, *and* winter *there.*

In the Tempest

[13]When the south wind blew softly, supposing that they had obtained *their* desire, putting out to sea, they sailed close by Crete. [14]But not long after, a tempestuous head wind arose, called Euroclydon.[a] [15]So when the ship was caught, and could not head into the wind, we let *her* drive. [16]And running under *the shelter of* an island called Clauda,[a] we secured the skiff with difficulty. [17]When they had taken it on board, they used cables to undergird the ship; and fearing lest they should run aground on the Syrtis[a] *Sands,* they struck sail and so were driven. [18]And because we were exceedingly tempest-tossed, the next *day* they lightened the ship. [19]On the third *day* we threw the ship's tackle overboard with our own hands. [20]Now when neither sun nor stars appeared for many days, and no small tempest beat on *us,* all hope that we would be saved was finally given up.

[21]But after long abstinence from food, then

27:14 [a]NU-Text reads *Euraquilon.* 27:16 [a]NU-Text reads *Cauda.* 27:17 [a]M-Text reads *Syrtes.*

Paul stood in the midst of them and said, "Men, you should have listened to me, and not have sailed from Crete and incurred this disaster and loss. [22]And now I urge you to take heart, for there will be no loss of life among you, but only of the ship. [23]For there stood by me this night an angel of the God to whom I belong and whom I serve, [24]saying, 'Do not be afraid, Paul; you must be brought before Caesar; and indeed God has granted you all those who sail with you.' [25]Therefore take heart, men, for I believe God that it will be just as it was told me. [26]However, we must run aground on a certain island."

[27]Now when the fourteenth night had come, as we were driven up and down in the Adriatic *Sea,* about midnight the sailors sensed that they were drawing near some land. [28]And they took soundings and found *it* to be twenty fathoms; and when they had gone a little farther, they took soundings again and found *it* to be fifteen fathoms. [29]Then, fearing lest we should run aground on the rocks, they dropped four anchors from the stern, and prayed for day to come. [30]And as the sailors were seeking to escape from the ship, when they had let down the skiff into the sea, under pretense of putting out anchors from the prow, [31]Paul said to the centurion and the soldiers, "Unless these men stay in the ship, you cannot be saved." [32]Then the soldiers cut away the ropes of the skiff and let it fall off.

[33]And as day was about to dawn, Paul implored *them* all to take food, saying, "Today is the fourteenth day you have waited and continued without food, and eaten nothing. [34]Therefore I urge you to take nourishment, for this is for your survival, since not a hair will fall from the head of any of you." [35]And when he had said these things, he took bread and gave thanks to God in the presence of them all; and when he had broken *it* he began to eat. [36]Then they were all encouraged, and also took food themselves. [37]And in all we were two hundred and seventy-six persons on the ship. [38]So when they had eaten enough, they lightened the ship and threw out the wheat into the sea.

Shipwrecked on Malta

[39]When it was day, they did not recognize the land; but they observed a bay with a beach, onto which they planned to run the ship if possible. [40]And they let go the anchors and left *them* in the sea, meanwhile loosing the rudder ropes; and they hoisted the mainsail to the wind and made for shore. [41]But striking a place where two seas met, they ran the ship aground; and the prow stuck fast and remained immovable, but the stern was being broken up by the violence of the waves.

[42]And the soldiers' plan was to kill the prisoners, lest any of them should swim away and escape. [43]But the centurion, wanting to save Paul, kept them from *their* purpose, and commanded that those who could swim should jump *overboard* first and get to land, [44]and the rest, some on boards and some on *parts* of the ship. And so it was that they all escaped safely to land.

Paul's Ministry on Malta

28 Now when they had escaped, they then found out that the island was called Malta. [2]And the natives showed us unusual kindness; for they kindled a fire and made us all welcome, because of the rain that was falling and because of the cold. [3]But when Paul had gathered a bundle of sticks and laid *them* on the fire, a viper came out because of the heat, and fastened on his hand. [4]So when the natives saw the creature hanging from his hand, they said to one another, "No doubt this man is a murderer, whom, though he has escaped the sea, yet justice does not allow to live." [5]But he shook off the creature into the fire and suffered no harm. [6]However, they were expecting that he would swell up or suddenly fall down dead. But after they had looked for a long time and saw no harm come to him, they changed their minds and said that he was a god.

[7]In that region there was an estate of the leading citizen of the island, whose name was Publius, who received us and entertained us courteously for three days. [8]And it happened that the father of Publius lay sick of a fever and dysentery. Paul went in to him and prayed, and he laid his hands on him and healed him. [9]So

---

The Law of Solid Ground: Paul Earned the Right to Be Heard

(Acts 28:3–6)

When Paul continued living after a snake bit him, the locals proclaimed him a god (Acts 28:6). Credibility comes in one of two ways: Someone can loan you theirs, or you can get it from the life you live. People attach credibility to leaders who get the job done.

when this was done, the rest of those on the island who had diseases also came and were healed. [10]They also honored us in many ways; and when we departed, they provided such things as were necessary.

Arrival at Rome

[11]After three months we sailed in an Alexandrian ship whose figurehead was the Twin Brothers, which had wintered at the island. [12]And landing at Syracuse, we stayed three days. [13]From there we circled round and reached Rhegium. And after one day the south wind blew; and the next day we came to Puteoli, [14]where we found brethren, and were invited to stay with them seven days. And so we went toward Rome. [15]And from there, when the brethren heard about us, they came to meet us as far as Appii Forum and Three Inns. When Paul saw them, he thanked God and took courage.

[16]Now when we came to Rome, the centurion delivered the prisoners to the captain of the guard; but Paul was permitted to dwell by himself with the soldier who guarded him.

Paul's Ministry at Rome

[17]And it came to pass after three days that Paul called the leaders of the Jews together. So when they had come together, he said to them: "Men *and* brethren, though I have done nothing against our people or the customs of our fathers, yet I was delivered as a prisoner from Jerusalem into the hands of the Romans, [18]who, when they had examined me, wanted to let *me* go, because there was no cause for putting me to death. [19]But when the Jews[a] spoke against *it,* I was compelled to appeal to Caesar, not that I had anything of which to accuse my nation. [20]For this reason therefore I have called for you, to see *you* and speak with *you,* because for the hope of Israel I am bound with this chain."

[21]Then they said to him, "We neither received letters from Judea concerning you, nor have any of the brethren who came reported or spoken any evil of you. [22]But we desire to hear from you what you think; for concerning this sect, we know that it is spoken against everywhere."

[23]So when they had appointed him a day, many came to him at *his* lodging, to whom he explained and solemnly testified of the kingdom of God, persuading them concerning Jesus from both the Law of Moses and the Prophets, from morning till evening. [24]And some were persuaded by the things which were spoken, and some disbelieved. [25]So when they did not agree among themselves, they departed after Paul had said one word: "The Holy Spirit spoke rightly through Isaiah the prophet to our[a] fathers, [26]saying,

'Go to this people and say:
"Hearing you will hear, and shall not
   understand;
And seeing you will see, and not perceive;
[27]   For the hearts of this people have grown
   dull.
Their ears are hard of hearing,
And their eyes they have closed,
Lest they should see with their eyes and
   hear with their ears,
Lest they should understand with their
   hearts and turn,
So that I should heal them." '[a]

[28]"Therefore let it be known to you that the salvation of God has been sent to the Gentiles, and they will hear it!" [29]And when he had said these words, the Jews departed and had a great dispute among themselves.[a]

[30]Then Paul dwelt two whole years in his own rented house, and received all who came to him, [31]preaching the kingdom of God and teaching the things which concern the Lord Jesus Christ with all confidence, no one forbidding him.

28:19 [a]That is, the ruling authorities
28:25 [a]NU-Text reads *your.* **28:27** [a]Isaiah 6:9, 10
28:29 [a]NU-Text omits this verse.

ROMANS
God's Solution for the Human Dilemma

SUMMARY

The Book of Romans offers the most systematic teaching in the Bible about the human dilemma and God's solution for it. Written by the apostle Paul about A.D. 57, Romans lays out the major themes of sin, salvation, redemption, justification, grace, and reconciliation.

Because Paul is such an outstanding teaching-leader, he communicates with purpose. No one could miss his objectives. He doesn't attempt merely to *inform,* but to *transform* this church (12:1, 2), even though he had never visited it. With his words he endeavored to influence the believers in the most influential city in the world. Consider his classic methods for doing so.

First, Paul influences by building rapport. The first 17 verses of chapter one prepare the reader for all the apostle intends to write. He affirms and tells his readers how much he looks forward to meeting them, since he's heard so much about them.

Second, Paul influences by creating a dilemma relevant to everyone. He reminds the people how God spoke through creation and the human conscience. He discusses the predicament of sin and its universal impact on mankind. He then moves to God's gift of righteousness that we receive by faith. He contrasts how man tries to make everything right on his own, but never succeeds.

Third, Paul influences by proposing potential questions and objections, then by responding to them. He often brings up a question as though the reader had thought of it—then he rationally answers the question.

Fourth, Paul influences by providing feasible steps for the reader to take toward God. Everyone can do what Paul suggests. His plan is manageable and understandable.

In the final five chapters of this book, Paul supplies practical applications of all he has taught. Chapters 1—11 concern doctrine, while chapters 12—16 highlight duty.

Finally, Paul influences by affirming his love for the people and thanks many of them by name. He encourages the church to follow those he names as models of the life he has challenged them to live.

God's Role in Romans

Because Paul is so convinced that real change happens from the inside out, God plays a huge role in this book. Paul argues that if we want to think like God, we must renew our minds and present our bodies to Him as living sacrifices. We must trust Him to revolutionize our lives and transform them as only He can.

God orchestrates the metamorphosis inside the believer. In that sense, spiritual leadership is about leading others to Christ to allow Him to do the necessary work inside of them. Hence, Christian leadership cooperates with God's initiative to transform men and women, one life at a time.

Leaders in Romans

Paul, Phoebe, Aquila, Priscilla, the host of others listed in Romans 16

Other People of Influence in Romans

Tertius, Erastus, the host of others listed in Romans 16

Lessons in Leadership

- Leaders increase their effectiveness when they improve their ability to communicate.
- The most consistent leaders are led by their own values, beliefs, and convictions.
- Great leaders communicate both passion and substance.
- Great leaders connect with both the head and heart.
- Lasting leaders motivate through grace and relationship, not guilt and religious ritual.
- People want to follow leaders who offer hope and direction.
- Spiritual leaders work to change people from the inside out, not the outside in.

LEADERSHIP

HIGHLIGHTS IN ROMANS

Greeting

1 Paul, a bondservant of Jesus Christ, called *to be* an apostle, separated to the gospel of God ²which He promised before through His prophets in the Holy Scriptures, ³concerning His Son Jesus Christ our Lord, who was born of the seed of David according to the flesh, ⁴*and* declared *to be* the Son of God with power according to the Spirit of holiness, by the resurrection from the dead. ⁵Through Him we have received grace and apostleship for obedience to the faith among all nations for His name, ⁶among whom you also are the called of Jesus Christ;

⁷To all who are in Rome, beloved of God, called *to be* saints:

Grace to you and peace from God our Father and the Lord Jesus Christ.

Desire to Visit Rome

⁸First, I thank my God through Jesus Christ for you all, that your faith is spoken of throughout the whole world. ⁹For God is my witness, whom I serve with my spirit in the gospel of His Son, that without ceasing I make mention of you always in my prayers, ¹⁰making request if, by some means, now at last I may find a way in the will of God to come to you. ¹¹For I long to see you, that I may impart to you some spiritual gift, so that you may be established— ¹²that is, that I may be encouraged together with you by the mutual faith both of you and me.

¹³Now I do not want you to be unaware, brethren, that I often planned to come to you (but was hindered until now), that I might have some fruit among you also, just as among the other Gentiles. ¹⁴I am a debtor both to Greeks and to barbarians, both to wise and to unwise. ¹⁵So, as much as is in me, *I am* ready to preach the gospel to you who are in Rome also.

The Just Live by Faith

¹⁶For I am not ashamed of the gospel of Christ,ᵃ for it is the power of God to salvation for everyone who believes, for the Jew first and also for the Greek. ¹⁷For in it the righteousness of God is revealed from faith to faith; as it is written, *"The just shall live by faith."*ᵃ

God's Wrath on Unrighteousness

¹⁸For the wrath of God is revealed from heaven against all ungodliness and unrighteousness

---

1:16 ᵃNU-Text omits *of Christ*. **1:17** ᵃHabakkuk 2:4

PAUL

GENIUS WITH A PEN
(Romans 1:1–7)

PROFILE IN LEADERSHIP

A nyone writing a set of instructions ought to communicate the steps for completing a certain task with simplicity, clarity, and power. That is exactly what the apostle Paul has done in his letter to the Romans.

The book systematically presents the Good News of salvation through Christ. It starts by explaining God's wrath on humankind for its sinfulness, then works its way through the grace of God as demonstrated through the atoning sacrifice of the Lord Jesus, and finishes by describing the kind of life those whom God has made "not guilty" should live. Along the way it anticipates and answers objections, provides vital encouragement and hope, and offers enough theological meat to keep thoughtful believers chewing for centuries.

Paul communicates with clarity and power what all leaders in the body of Christ need to keep on declaring to the world. All of us—from the greatest to the least—are sinners who deserve God's eternal judgment. But God has lavished His grace on every one of us through the person of His Son, Jesus Christ—and the key to accessing that grace is faith.

Paul left us a great many gifts of the faith, but none is greater than the message of Romans. We should rather have no bread than have no Romans.

The Attitude of a Leader

(Romans 1:1, 14–16)

Paul begins Romans by profiling himself as a servant of the Lord Jesus. Before he is an apostle or a preacher of the gospel, he is a servant. This is the most comprehensive picture of leadership in the New Testament. Paul uses the Greek word *doulos*, which most often signifies a servant who has willingly and legally bonded himself to a master (Rom. 1:1; Phil. 1:1; Titus 1:1).

The Old Testament gives the Hebrew background for this concept (Deut. 15:1–23). When it came time for a master to release a slave, that slave had two options: Accept his freedom, or remain and serve the master by choice. To stay as a love-slave made him far more useful, since he served willingly. Note how Paul describes this servant attitude:

1. "I am a debtor" (v. 14).
   This literally meant he had a debt to pay. Notice it wasn't a debt he had to the Lord, but to people! He owed those who hadn't heard the gospel.
2. "I am ready" (v. 15).
   The word literally means he was burning inside. He passionately gave himself to the cause by choice. His enthusiasm came in response to God's grace.
3. "I am not ashamed" (v. 16).
   Why not? Because although he was a despised minority within a despised minority, his message brought God's power to save everyone.

of men, who suppress the truth in unrighteousness, [19]because what may be known of God is manifest in them, for God has shown *it* to them. [20]For since the creation of the world His invisible *attributes* are clearly seen, being understood by the things that are made, *even* His eternal power and Godhead, so that they are without excuse, [21]because, although they knew God, they did not glorify *Him* as God, nor were thankful, but became futile in their thoughts, and their foolish hearts were darkened. [22]Professing to be wise, they became fools, [23]and changed the glory of the incorruptible God into an image made like corruptible man—and birds and four-footed animals and creeping things.

[24]Therefore God also gave them up to uncleanness, in the lusts of their hearts, to dishonor their bodies among themselves, [25]who exchanged the truth of God for the lie, and worshiped and served the creature rather than the Creator, who is blessed forever. Amen.

[26]For this reason God gave them up to vile passions. For even their women exchanged the natural use for what is against nature. [27]Likewise also the men, leaving the natural use of the woman, burned in their lust for one another, men with men committing what is shameful, and receiving in themselves the penalty of their error which was due.

[28]And even as they did not like to retain God in *their* knowledge, God gave them over to a debased mind, to do those things which are not fitting; [29]being filled with all unrighteousness, sexual immorality,[a] wickedness, covetousness, maliciousness; full of envy, murder, strife, deceit, evil-mindedness; *they are* whisperers, [30]backbiters, haters of God, violent, proud, boasters, inventors of evil things, disobedient to parents, [31]undiscerning, untrustworthy, unloving, unforgiving,[a] unmerciful; [32]who, knowing the righteous judgment of God, that those who practice such things are deserving of death, not only do the same but also approve of those who practice them.

God's Righteous Judgment

2 Therefore you are inexcusable, O man, whoever you are who judge, for in whatever you judge another you condemn yourself; for you who judge practice the same things. [2]But we know that the judgment of God is according to truth against those who practice such things. [3]And do you think this, O man, you who judge those practicing such things, and doing the same, that you will escape the judg-

1:29 [a]NU-Text omits *sexual immorality*.
1:31 [a]NU-Text omits *unforgiving*.

Problem Solving: Paul Addresses Man's Number One Dilemma

(Romans 1:17—2:29)

Alfter Paul addresses mankind's ultimate problem—God's judgment for our sinful, imperfect condition—he masterfully offers the remedy for it. He knows that leaders gain an audience when they solve problems. Problem solving is the fastest way to gain leadership.

ment of God? ⁴Or do you despise the riches of His goodness, forbearance, and longsuffering, not knowing that the goodness of God leads you to repentance? ⁵But in accordance with your hardness and your impenitent heart you are treasuring up for yourself wrath in the day of wrath and revelation of the righteous judgment of God, ⁶who *"will render to each one according to his deeds"*:ᵃ ⁷eternal life to those who by patient continuance in doing good seek for glory, honor, and immortality; ⁸but to those who are self-seeking and do not obey the truth, but obey unrighteousness—indignation and wrath, ⁹tribulation and anguish, on every soul of man who does evil, of the Jew first and also of the Greek; ¹⁰but glory, honor, and peace to everyone who works what is good, to the Jew first and also to the Greek. ¹¹For there is no partiality with God.

¹²For as many as have sinned without law will also perish without law, and as many as have sinned in the law will be judged by the law ¹³(for not the hearers of the law *are* just in the sight of God, but the doers of the law will be justified; ¹⁴for when Gentiles, who do not have the law, by nature do the things in the law, these, although not having the law, are a law to themselves, ¹⁵who show the work of the law written in their hearts, their conscience also bearing witness, and between themselves *their* thoughts accusing or else excusing *them*) ¹⁶in the day when God will judge the secrets of men by Jesus Christ, according to my gospel.

The Jews Guilty as the Gentiles

¹⁷Indeedᵃ you are called a Jew, and rest on the law, and make your boast in God, ¹⁸and know *His* will, and approve the things that are excellent, being instructed out of the law, ¹⁹and are confident that you yourself are a guide to the blind, a light to those who are in darkness, ²⁰an instructor

of the foolish, a teacher of babes, having the form of knowledge and truth in the law. ²¹You, therefore, who teach another, do you not teach yourself? You who preach that a man should not steal, do you steal? ²²You who say, "Do not commit adultery," do you commit adultery? You who abhor idols, do you rob temples? ²³You who make your boast in the law, do you dishonor God through breaking the law? ²⁴For *"the name of God is blasphemed among the Gentiles because of you,"*ᵃ as it is written.

Circumcision of No Avail

²⁵For circumcision is indeed profitable if you keep the law; but if you are a breaker of the law, your circumcision has become uncircumcision. ²⁶Therefore, if an uncircumcised man keeps the righteous requirements of the law, will not his uncircumcision be counted as circumcision? ²⁷And will not the physically uncircumcised, if he fulfills the law, judge you who, *even* with *your* written *code* and circumcision, *are* a transgressor of the law? ²⁸For he is not a Jew who *is one* outwardly, nor *is* circumcision that which *is* outward in the flesh; ²⁹but *he is* a Jew who *is one* inwardly; and circumcision *is that* of the heart, in the Spirit, not in the letter; whose praise *is* not from men but from God.

God's Judgment Defended

3 What advantage then has the Jew, or what *is* the profit of circumcision? ²Much in every way! Chiefly because to them were committed the oracles of God. ³For what if some did not believe? Will their unbelief make the faithfulness of God without effect? ⁴Certainly not! Indeed, let God be true but every man a liar. As it is written:

> *"That You may be justified in Your words,*
> *And may overcome when You are judged."*ᵃ

⁵But if our unrighteousness demonstrates the righteousness of God, what shall we say? *Is* God unjust who inflicts wrath? (I speak as a man.) ⁶Certainly not! For then how will God judge the world?

⁷For if the truth of God has increased through my lie to His glory, why am I also still judged as a sinner? ⁸And *why* not *say*, "Let us do evil that good may come"?—as we are slanderously reported and as some affirm that we say. Their condemnation is just.

2:6 ᵃPsalm 62:12; Proverbs 24:12 **2:17** ᵃNU-Text reads *But if.* **2:24** ᵃIsaiah 52:5; Ezekiel 36:22 **3:4** ᵃPsalm 51:4

All Have Sinned

[9]What then? Are we better *than they?* Not at all. For we have previously charged both Jews and Greeks that they are all under sin.

[10]As it is written:

" *There is none righteous, no, not one;*
[11]   *There is none who understands;*
    There is none who seeks after God.
[12]   *They have all turned aside;*
    They have together become unprofitable;
    There is none who does good, no, not one."[a]
[13]   " *Their throat is an open tomb;*
    With their tongues they have practiced deceit";[a]
    " *The poison of asps is under their lips*";[b]
[14]   " *Whose mouth is full of cursing and bitterness.*"[a]
[15]   " *Their feet are swift to shed blood;*
[16]   *Destruction and misery are in their ways;*
[17]   *And the way of peace they have not known.*"[a]
[18]   " *There is no fear of God before their eyes.*"[a]

[19]Now we know that whatever the law says, it says to those who are under the law, that every mouth may be stopped, and all the world may become guilty before God. [20]Therefore by the deeds of the law no flesh will be justified in His sight, for by the law *is* the knowledge of sin.

God's Righteousness Through Faith

[21]But now the righteousness of God apart from the law is revealed, being witnessed by the Law and the Prophets, [22]even the righteousness of God, through faith in Jesus Christ, to all and on all[a] who believe. For there is no difference; [23]for all have sinned and fall short of the glory of God, [24]being justified freely by His grace through the redemption that is in Christ Jesus, [25]whom God set forth *as* a propitiation by His blood, through faith, to demonstrate His righteousness, because in His forbearance God had passed over the sins that were previously committed, [26]to demonstrate at the present time His righteousness, that He might be just and the justifier of the one who has faith in Jesus.

Boasting Excluded

[27]Where *is* boasting then? It is excluded. By what law? Of works? No, but by the law of faith. [28]Therefore we conclude that a man is justified by faith apart from the deeds of the law. [29]Or *is* He the God of the Jews only? *Is He* not also the God of the Gentiles? Yes, of the Gentiles also, [30]since *there is* one God who will justify the cir-

---

Discernment: The Leader as a Doctor

(Romans 3:21–26)

Paul gives us a new picture of leadership: the leader as spiritual doctor. Leaders must match problems with solutions. Their understanding must be broad and general, but also deep and personal. Although doctors have graduated from medical school, to be relevant they must examine their patients. Only then can they suggest prescriptions.

---

cumcised by faith and the uncircumcised through faith. [31]Do we then make void the law through faith? Certainly not! On the contrary, we establish the law.

Abraham Justified by Faith

4 What then shall we say that Abraham our father has found according to the flesh?[a] [2]For if Abraham was justified by works, he has *something* to boast about, but not before God. [3]For what does the Scripture say? *"Abraham believed God, and it was accounted to him for righteousness."*[a] [4]Now to him who works, the wages are not counted as grace but as debt.

David Celebrates the Same Truth

[5]But to him who does not work but believes on Him who justifies the ungodly, his faith is accounted for righteousness, [6]just as David also describes the blessedness of the man to whom God imputes righteousness apart from works:

[7]   *"Blessed are those whose lawless deeds are forgiven,*
    And whose sins are covered;
[8]   *Blessed is the man to whom the* LORD *shall not impute sin."*[a]

Abraham Justified Before Circumcision

[9]*Does* this blessedness then *come* upon the circumcised *only,* or upon the uncircumcised also?

3:12 [a]Psalms 14:1–3; 53:1–3; Ecclesiastes 7:20
3:13 [a]Psalm 5:9 [b]Psalm 140:3 **3:14** [a]Psalm 10:7
3:17 [a]Isaiah 59:7, 8 **3:18** [a]Psalm 36:1
3:22 [a]NU-Text omits *and on all.* **4:1** [a]Or *Abraham our (fore)father according to the flesh has found?*
4:3 [a]Genesis 15:6 **4:8** [a]Psalm 32:1, 2

For we say that faith was accounted to Abraham for righteousness. [10]How then was it accounted? While he was circumcised, or uncircumcised? Not while circumcised, but while uncircumcised. [11]And he received the sign of circumcision, a seal of the righteousness of the faith which *he had while still* uncircumcised, that he might be the father of all those who believe, though they are uncircumcised, that righteousness might be imputed to them also, [12]and the father of circumcision to those who not only *are* of the circumcision, but who also walk in the steps of the faith which our father Abraham *had while still* uncircumcised.

Vision: The Leader as an Artist

(Romans 4:1–22)

Communicators know the value of pictures. Paul paints a picture of the life he promotes, illustrating the life of faith using individuals such as Abraham, Sarah, and David. People need a point for their heads and a picture for their hearts.

The Promise Granted Through Faith

[13]For the promise that he would be the heir of the world *was* not to Abraham or to his seed through the law, but through the righteousness of faith. [14]For if those who are of the law *are* heirs, faith is made void and the promise made of no effect, [15]because the law brings about wrath; for where there is no law *there is* no transgression.

[16]Therefore *it is* of faith that *it might be* according to grace, so that the promise might be sure to all the seed, not only to those who are of the law, but also to those who are of the faith of Abraham, who is the father of us all [17](as it is written, *"I have made you a father of many nations"*[a]) in the presence of Him whom he believed—God, who gives life to the dead and calls those things which do not exist as though they did; [18]who, contrary to hope, in hope believed, so that he became the father of many nations, according to what was spoken, *"So shall your descendants be."*[a] [19]And not being weak in faith, he did not consider his own body, already dead (since he was about a hundred years old), and the deadness of Sarah's womb. [20]He did not waver at the promise of God through unbelief, but was strengthened in faith, giving glory to God, [21]and being fully convinced that what He had promised He was also able to perform. [22]And therefore *"it was accounted to him for righteousness."*[a]

[23]Now it was not written for his sake alone that it was imputed to him, [24]but also for us. It shall be imputed to us who believe in Him who raised up Jesus our Lord from the dead, [25]who was delivered up because of our offenses, and was raised because of our justification.

Faith Triumphs in Trouble

5 Therefore, having been justified by faith, we have[a] peace with God through our Lord Jesus Christ, [2]through whom also we have access by faith into this grace in which we stand, and rejoice in hope of the glory of God. [3]And not only *that,* but we also glory in tribulations, knowing that tribulation produces perseverance; [4]and perseverance, character; and character, hope. [5]Now hope does not disappoint, because the love of God has been poured out in our hearts by the Holy Spirit who was given to us.

Christ in Our Place

[6]For when we were still without strength, in due time Christ died for the ungodly. [7]For scarcely for a righteous man will one die; yet perhaps for a good man someone would even dare to die. [8]But God demonstrates His own love toward us, in that while we were still sinners, Christ died for us. [9]Much more then, having now been justified by His blood, we shall be saved from wrath through Him. [10]For if when we were enemies we were reconciled to God through the death of His Son, much more, having been reconciled, we shall be saved by His life. [11]And not only *that,* but we also rejoice in God through our Lord Jesus Christ, through whom we have now received the reconciliation.

Death in Adam, Life in Christ

[12]Therefore, just as through one man sin entered the world, and death through sin, and thus death spread to all men, because all sinned— [13](For until the law sin was in the world, but sin is not imputed when there is no law. [14]Nevertheless death reigned from Adam to Moses, even over those who had not sinned according to the likeness of the transgression of Adam, who is a type of Him who was to come. [15]But the free gift *is* not like the offense. For if by the one man's

---

4:17 [a]Genesis 17:5 **4:18** [a]Genesis 15:5
4:22 [a]Genesis 15:6 **5:1** [a]Another ancient reading is, *let us have peace.*

offense many died, much more the grace of God and the gift by the grace of the one Man, Jesus Christ, abounded to many. [16]And the gift *is* not like *that which came* through the one who sinned. For the judgment *which came* from one *offense* resulted in condemnation, but the free gift *which came* from many offenses *resulted* in justification. [17]For if by the one man's offense death reigned through the one, much more those who receive abundance of grace and of the gift of righteousness will reign in life through the One, Jesus Christ.)

[18]Therefore, as through one man's offense *judgment* came to all men, resulting in condemnation, even so through one Man's righteous act *the free gift came* to all men, resulting in justification of life. [19]For as by one man's disobedience many were made sinners, so also by one Man's obedience many will be made righteous.

[20]Moreover the law entered that the offense might abound. But where sin abounded, grace abounded much more, [21]so that as sin reigned in death, even so grace might reign through righteousness to eternal life through Jesus Christ our Lord.

Dead to Sin, Alive to God

6 What shall we say then? Shall we continue in sin that grace may abound? [2]Certainly not! How shall we who died to sin live any longer in it? [3]Or do you not know that as many of us as were baptized into Christ Jesus were baptized into His death? [4]Therefore we were buried with Him through baptism into death, that just as Christ was raised from the dead by the glory of the Father, even so we also should walk in newness of life.

[5]For if we have been united together in the likeness of His death, certainly we also shall be *in the likeness* of *His* resurrection, [6]knowing this, that our old man was crucified with *Him,* that the body of sin might be done away with, that we should no longer be slaves of sin. [7]For he who has died has been freed from sin. [8]Now if we died with Christ, we believe that we shall also live with Him, [9]knowing that Christ, having been raised from the dead, dies no more. Death no longer has dominion over Him. [10]For *the death* that He died, He died to sin once for all; but *the life* that He lives, He lives to God. [11]Likewise you

---

The Law of Empowerment:
God Changes Us from the Inside Out
(Romans 5:12–21)

God's leadership is transformational. Paul carefully compares and contrasts Adam's work with Christ's and shows the fundamental changes God makes in us. He radically and permanently changes His people from the inside out.

God never demands conduct that He doesn't first empower His followers to achieve. Romans provides a virtual survey of New Testament theology and of God's empowering leadership:

1. *He liberates.*
   He frees us from the chains, stains, and pains of the past.
2. *He elevates.*
   He embraces us and lifts us up to reign with Him.
3. *He educates.*
   He gives us wise counsel and future direction.
4. *He compensates.*
   He fills areas where we are weak or lack competence.
5. *He motivates.*
   He is our source of vision, hope, and purpose.
6. *He regenerates.*
   He transforms us to live on a higher level by His supernatural resources.
7. *He activates.*
   He commissions us to obey and move forward in His cause.

Communicating Vision: Paul Delivers a Clear Image of Our Need

(Romans 6:1—7:6)

Knowing that his readers would need pictures to catch the revolutionary truth of the gospel, Paul uses the vivid images of water baptism, dead bodies, and slavery to explain God's message.

Paul sums up his point in Romans 6:23 and in Romans 7 moves to a marriage analogy. The first six verses remind us that the dead are no longer bound to sin. Although none of us started well, we can all finish well, thanks to God. He remains committed to our welfare.

These chapters are the final ones dedicated to helping us see humankind's need. Because of our fallen human state, everybody has three fundamental needs:

1. *To believe:* All human hearts need to have faith in something or Someone.
2. *To belong:* All human hearts need to experience community and family.
3. *To become:* All human hearts need to grow, stretch, and reach their potential.

also, reckon yourselves to be dead indeed to sin, but alive to God in Christ Jesus our Lord.

[12]Therefore do not let sin reign in your mortal body, that you should obey it in its lusts. [13]And do not present your members *as* instruments of unrighteousness to sin, but present yourselves to God as being alive from the dead, and your members *as* instruments of righteousness to God. [14]For sin shall not have dominion over you, for you are not under law but under grace.

From Slaves of Sin to Slaves of God

[15]What then? Shall we sin because we are not under law but under grace? Certainly not! [16]Do you not know that to whom you present yourselves slaves to obey, you are that one's slaves whom you obey, whether of sin *leading* to death, or of obedience *leading* to righteousness? [17]But God be thanked that *though* you were slaves of sin, yet you obeyed from the heart that form of doctrine to which you were delivered. [18]And having been set free from sin, you became slaves of righteousness. [19]I speak in human *terms* be-

cause of the weakness of your flesh. For just as you presented your members *as* slaves of uncleanness, and of lawlessness *leading* to *more* lawlessness, so now present your members *as* slaves *of* righteousness for holiness.

[20]For when you were slaves of sin, you were free in regard to righteousness. [21]What fruit did you have then in the things of which you are now ashamed? For the end of those things *is* death. [22]But now having been set free from sin, and having become slaves of God, you have your fruit to holiness, and the end, everlasting life. [23]For the wages of sin *is* death, but the gift of God *is* eternal life in Christ Jesus our Lord.

Freed from the Law

7 Or do you not know, brethren (for I speak to those who know the law), that the law has dominion over a man as long as he lives? [2]For the woman who has a husband is bound by the law to *her* husband as long as he lives. But if the husband dies, she is released from the law of *her* husband. [3]So then if, while *her* husband lives, she marries another man, she will be called an adulteress; but if her husband dies, she is free from that law, so that she is no adulteress, though she has married another man. [4]Therefore, my brethren, you also have become dead to the law through the body of Christ, that you may be married to another—to Him who was raised from the dead, that we should bear fruit to God. [5]For when we were in the flesh, the sinful passions which were aroused by the law were at work in our members to bear fruit to death. [6]But now we have been delivered from the law, having died to what we were held by, so that we should serve in the newness of the Spirit and not *in* the oldness of the letter.

Sin's Advantage in the Law

[7]What shall we say then? *Is* the law sin? Certainly not! On the contrary, I would not have known sin except through the law. For I would not have known covetousness unless the law had said, *"You shall not covet."*[a] [8]But sin, taking opportunity by the commandment, produced in me all *manner of* evil desire. For apart from the law sin *was* dead. [9]I was alive once without the law, but when the commandment came, sin revived and I died. [10]And the commandment, which *was* to *bring* life, I found to *bring* death. [11]For sin, taking occasion by the commandment, deceived me, and by it killed *me*. [12]Therefore the law *is* holy, and the commandment holy and just and good.

7:7 [a]Exodus 20:17; Deuteronomy 5:21

Law Cannot Save from Sin

[13]Has then what is good become death to me? Certainly not! But sin, that it might appear sin, was producing death in me through what is good, so that sin through the commandment might become exceedingly sinful. [14]For we know that the law is spiritual, but I am carnal, sold under sin. [15]For what I am doing, I do not understand. For what I will to do, that I do not practice; but what I hate, that I do. [16]If, then, I do what I will not to do, I agree with the law that *it is* good. [17]But now, *it is* no longer I who do it, but sin that dwells in me. [18]For I know that in me (that is, in my flesh) nothing good dwells; for to will is present with me, but *how* to perform what is good I do not find. [19]For the good that I will *to do,* I do not do; but the evil I will not *to do,* that I practice. [20]Now if I do what I will not *to do,* it is no longer I who do it, but sin that dwells in me.

[21]I find then a law, that evil is present with me, the one who wills to do good. [22]For I delight in the law of God according to the inward man. [23]But I see another law in my members, warring against the law of my mind, and bringing me into captivity to the law of sin which is in my members. [24]O wretched man that I am! Who will deliver me from this body of death? [25]I thank God—through Jesus Christ our Lord!

So then, with the mind I myself serve the law of God, but with the flesh the law of sin.

Free from Indwelling Sin

8 *There* is therefore now no condemnation to those who are in Christ Jesus,[a] who do not walk according to the flesh, but according to the Spirit. [2]For the law of the Spirit of life in Christ Jesus has made me free from the law of sin and death. [3]For what the law could not do in that it was weak through the flesh, God *did* by sending His own Son in the likeness of sinful flesh, on account of sin: He condemned sin in the flesh, [4]that the righteous requirement of the law might be fulfilled in us who do not walk according to the flesh but according to the Spirit. [5]For those who live according to the flesh set their minds on the things of the flesh, but those *who live* according to the Spirit, the things of the Spirit. [6]For to be carnally minded *is* death, but to be spiritually minded *is* life and peace. [7]Because the carnal mind *is* enmity against God; for it is not subject to the law of God, nor indeed can be. [8]So then, those who are in the flesh cannot please God.

[9]But you are not in the flesh but in the Spirit, if indeed the Spirit of God dwells in you. Now if anyone does not have the Spirit of Christ, he

---

Identification: Paul Identifies with the Struggles of His Listeners

(Romans 7:14–25)

Paul identifies with the struggles of common men and women. He knows we all can feel trapped (Rom. 7:14); confused (7:15); eager to do what is right (7:18); unable to follow through (7:18); an inward war (7:21–23); and frustration (7:24). Good leaders do not seek to impress, but to identify.

---

is not His. [10]And if Christ *is* in you, the body *is* dead because of sin, but the Spirit *is* life because of righteousness. [11]But if the Spirit of Him who raised Jesus from the dead dwells in you, He who raised Christ from the dead will also give life to your mortal bodies through His Spirit who dwells in you.

Sonship Through the Spirit

[12]Therefore, brethren, we are debtors—not to the flesh, to live according to the flesh. [13]For if you live according to the flesh you will die; but if by the Spirit you put to death the deeds of the body, you will live. [14]For as many as are led by the Spirit of God, these are sons of God. [15]For you did not receive the spirit of bondage again to fear, but you received the Spirit of adoption by whom we cry out, "Abba, Father." [16]The Spirit Himself bears witness with our spirit that we are children of God, [17]and if children, then heirs—heirs of God and joint heirs with Christ, if indeed we suffer with *Him,* that we may also be glorified together.

From Suffering to Glory

[18]For I consider that the sufferings of this present time are not worthy *to be compared* with the glory which shall be revealed in us. [19]For the earnest expectation of the creation eagerly waits for the revealing of the sons of God. [20]For the creation was subjected to futility, not willingly, but because of Him who subjected *it* in hope; [21]because the creation itself also will be delivered

---

8:1 [a]NU-Text omits the rest of this verse.

The Law of Navigation: Paul Describes the Spirit-Filled Life

(Romans 8:1–39)

After declaring that the law of the Spirit of life has set us free from the law of sin and death, Paul navigates the Spirit-filled life. He is the under-navigator, directing us to the Holy Spirit, the ultimate navigator.

This reveals the difference between Christian mentoring and the world's mentoring. Christian mentors do not build a reliance on themselves, but point their protégés to God. The life Paul navigates is a life of liberty (Rom. 8:1–8), hope (8:9–15), and power (8:26–39). Observe how the Holy Spirit navigates life for us:

1. *He intercedes and groans for us* (Rom. 8:22, 23, 26, 27).
2. *He directs and testifies to us* (John 16:13; Acts 20:22, 23; Rom. 8:14).
3. *He empowers and anoints for service* (Acts 1:8; Rom. 8:28–37; 1 John 2:27).
4. *He searches and enables us to discern* (Rom. 8:26, 27; 1 Cor. 2:9–15).
5. *He confirms and bears witness with us* (Rom. 8:14–16; 1 John 5:5–9).

from the bondage of corruption into the glorious liberty of the children of God. ²²For we know that the whole creation groans and labors with birth pangs together until now. ²³Not only *that*, but we also who have the firstfruits of the Spirit, even we ourselves groan within ourselves, eagerly waiting for the adoption, the redemption of our body. ²⁴For we were saved in this hope, but hope that is seen is not hope; for why does one still hope for what he sees? ²⁵But if we hope for what we do not see, we eagerly wait for *it* with perseverance.

²⁶Likewise the Spirit also helps in our weaknesses. For we do not know what we should pray for as we ought, but the Spirit Himself makes intercession for us[a] with groanings which cannot be uttered. ²⁷Now He who searches the hearts knows what the mind of the Spirit *is,* because He makes intercession for the saints according to *the will of* God.

²⁸And we know that all things work together for good to those who love God, to those who are the called according to *His* purpose. ²⁹For whom He foreknew, He also predestined *to be* conformed to the image of His Son, that He might be the firstborn among many brethren. ³⁰Moreover whom He predestined, these He also called; whom He called, these He also justified; and whom He justified, these He also glorified.

God's Everlasting Love

³¹What then shall we say to these things? If God *is* for us, who *can be* against us? ³²He who did not spare His own Son, but delivered Him up for us all, how shall He not with Him also freely give us all things? ³³Who shall bring a charge against God's elect? *It is* God who justifies. ³⁴Who *is* he who condemns? *It is* Christ who died, and furthermore is also risen, who is even at the right hand of God, who also makes intercession for us. ³⁵Who shall separate us from the love of Christ? *Shall* tribulation, or distress, or persecution, or famine, or nakedness, or peril, or sword? ³⁶As it is written:

> "For Your sake we are killed all day long;
> We are accounted as sheep for the
>   slaughter."[a]

³⁷Yet in all these things we are more than conquerors through Him who loved us. ³⁸For I am persuaded that neither death nor life, nor angels nor principalities nor powers, nor things present nor things to come, ³⁹nor height nor depth, nor any other created thing, shall be able to separate us from the love of God which is in Christ Jesus our Lord.

8:26 [a]NU-Text omits *for us.* **8:36** [a]Psalm 44:22

The Law of Intuition: Paul Intuitively Knew the Remedy

(Romans 8:12–39)

Paul intuitively knew both man's fundamental sickness and the cure. He explained the proof (Rom. 8:14), the problems (8:18–25), the privilege (8:26–30), and the promise (8:31–39) of the Spirit-filled lifestyle. When leaders face problems, they automatically measure them and begin solving them using the Law of Intuition.

Israel's Rejection of Christ

9 I tell the truth in Christ, I am not lying, my conscience also bearing me witness in the Holy Spirit, ²that I have great sorrow and continual grief in my heart. ³For I could wish that I myself were accursed from Christ for my brethren, my countrymenᵃ according to the flesh, ⁴who are Israelites, to whom *pertain* the adoption, the glory, the covenants, the giving of the law, the service *of God,* and the promises; ⁵of whom *are* the fathers and from whom, according to the flesh, Christ *came,* who is over all, *the* eternally blessed God. Amen.

Israel's Rejection and God's Purpose

⁶But it is not that the word of God has taken no effect. For they *are* not all Israel who *are* of Israel, ⁷nor *are they* all children because they are the seed of Abraham; but, *"In Isaac your seed shall be called."*ᵃ ⁸That is, those who *are* the children of the flesh, these *are* not the children of God; but the children of the promise are counted as the seed. ⁹For this *is* the word of promise: *"At this time I will come and Sarah shall have a son."*ᵃ

¹⁰And not only *this,* but when Rebecca also had conceived by one man, *even* by our father Isaac ¹¹(for *the children* not yet being born, nor having done any good or evil, that the purpose of God according to election might stand, not of works but of Him who calls), ¹²it was said to her, *"The older shall serve the younger."*ᵃ ¹³As it is written, *"Jacob I have loved, but Esau I have hated."*ᵃ

Israel's Rejection and God's Justice

¹⁴What shall we say then? *Is there* unrighteousness with God? Certainly not! ¹⁵For He says to Moses, *"I will have mercy on whomever I will have mercy, and I will have compassion on whomever I will have compassion."*ᵃ ¹⁶So then *it is* not of him who wills, nor of him who runs, but of God who shows mercy. ¹⁷For the Scripture says to the Pharaoh, *"For this very purpose I have raised you up, that I may show My power in you, and that My name may be declared in all the earth."*ᵃ ¹⁸Therefore He has mercy on whom He wills, and whom He wills He hardens.

¹⁹You will say to me then, "Why does He still find fault? For who has resisted His will?" ²⁰But indeed, O man, who are you to reply against God? Will the thing formed say to him who formed *it,* "Why have you made me like this?" ²¹Does not the potter have power over the clay, from the same lump to make one vessel for honor and another for dishonor? ²²*What* if God, wanting to show *His* wrath

and to make His power known, endured with much longsuffering the vessels of wrath prepared for destruction, ²³and that He might make known the riches of His glory on the vessels of mercy, which He had prepared beforehand for glory, ²⁴*even* us whom He called, not of the Jews only, but also of the Gentiles?

²⁵As He says also in Hosea:

> "I will call them My people, who were not
>   My people,
>   And her beloved, who was not beloved."ᵃ
> ²⁶ "And it shall come to pass in the place
>   where it was said to them,
>   'You are not My people,'
>   There they shall be called sons of the living
>   God."ᵃ

²⁷Isaiah also cries out concerning Israel:ᵃ

> "Though the number of the children of
>   Israel be as the sand of the sea,
>   The remnant will be saved.
> ²⁸ For He will finish the work and cut it
>   short in righteousness,
>   Because the LORD will make a short work
>   upon the earth."ᵃ

²⁹And as Isaiah said before:

> "Unless the LORD of Sabaothᵃ had left us a
>   seed,
>   We would have become like Sodom,
>   And we would have been made like
>   Gomorrah."ᵇ

Present Condition of Israel

³⁰What shall we say then? That Gentiles, who did not pursue righteousness, have attained to righteousness, even the righteousness of faith; ³¹but Israel, pursuing the law of righteousness, has not attained to the law of righteousness.ᵃ ³²Why? Because *they did* not *seek it* by faith, but as it were, by the works of the law.ᵃ For they stumbled at that stumbling stone. ³³As it is written:

9:3 ᵃOr *relatives* **9:7** ᵃGenesis 21:12 **9:9** ᵃGenesis 18:10, 14 **9:12** ᵃGenesis 25:23 **9:13** ᵃMalachi 1:2, 3 **9:15** ᵃExodus 33:19 **9:17** ᵃExodus 9:16 **9:25** ᵃHosea 2:23 **9:26** ᵃHosea 1:10 **9:27** ᵃIsaiah 10:22, 23 **9:28** ᵃNU-Text reads *For the LORD will finish the work and cut it short upon the earth.* **9:29** ᵃLiterally, in Hebrew, *Hosts* ᵇIsaiah 1:9 **9:31** ᵃNU-Text omits *of righteousness.* **9:32** ᵃNU-Text reads *by works.*

"Behold, I lay in Zion a stumbling stone
and rock of offense,
And whoever believes on Him will not be
put to shame.""ᵃ

Israel Needs the Gospel

10 Brethren, my heart's desire and prayer to God for Israelᵃ is that they may be saved. ²For I bear them witness that they have a zeal for God, but not according to knowledge. ³For they being ignorant of God's righteousness, and seeking to establish their own righteousness, have not submitted to the righteousness of God. ⁴For Christ *is* the end of the law for righteousness to everyone who believes.

⁵For Moses writes about the righteousness which is of the law, *"The man who does those things shall live by them.""ᵃ* ⁶But the righteousness of faith speaks in this way, *"Do not say in your heart, 'Who will ascend into heaven?'""ᵃ* (that is, to bring Christ down *from above*) ⁷or, *"'Who will descend into the abyss?'""ᵃ* (that is, to bring Christ up from the dead). ⁸But what does it say? *"The word is near you, in your mouth and in your heart""ᵃ* (that is, the word of faith which we preach): ⁹that if you confess with your mouth the Lord Jesus and believe in your heart that God has raised Him from the dead, you will be saved. ¹⁰For with the heart one believes unto righteousness, and with the mouth confession is made unto salvation. ¹¹For the Scripture says, *"Whoever believes on Him will not be put to shame.""ᵃ* ¹²For there is no distinction between Jew and Greek, for the same Lord over all is rich to all who call upon Him. ¹³For *"whoever calls on the name of the LORD shall be saved.""ᵃ*

Israel Rejects the Gospel

¹⁴How then shall they call on Him in whom they have not believed? And how shall they believe in Him of whom they have not heard? And how shall they hear without a preacher? ¹⁵And how shall they preach unless they are sent? As it is written:

"How beautiful are the feet of those who
preach the gospel of peace,ᵃ
Who bring glad tidings of good things!""ᵇ

¹⁶But they have not all obeyed the gospel. For Isaiah says, *"LORD, who has believed our report?""ᵃ* ¹⁷So then faith *comes* by hearing, and hearing by the word of God.

¹⁸But I say, have they not heard? Yes indeed:

The Law of Victory: Paul Communicates What to Do to Be Saved

(Romans 10:8–17)

In his earlier days, Paul believed personal victory came through self-righteousness. By the time he wrote to the Romans, he understood that the only way to gain victory came through God's righteousness.

How can one be saved from God's just condemnation? Paul explains his answer in Romans 10: "that if you confess with your mouth the Lord Jesus and believe in your heart that God has raised Him from the dead, you will be saved," he says (v. 9).

In a sense, this chapter provides the climax to the dilemma building through the book's first nine chapters. Only after thoroughly explaining the problem does the apostle lay out the plan to find and experience victory. Leaders always progress toward solutions.

"Their sound has gone out to all the earth,
And their words to the ends of the world.""ᵃ

¹⁹But I say, did Israel not know? First Moses says:

"I will provoke you to jealousy by those who
are not a nation,
I will move you to anger by a foolish
nation.""ᵃ

²⁰But Isaiah is very bold and says:

"I was found by those who did not seek Me;
I was made manifest to those who did not
ask for Me.""ᵃ

²¹But to Israel he says:

9:33 ᵃIsaiah 8:14; 28:16 **10:1** ᵃNU-Text reads *them.*
10:5 ᵃLeviticus 18:5 **10:6** ᵃDeuteronomy 30:12
10:7 ᵃDeuteronomy 30:13 **10:8** ᵃDeuteronomy
30:14 **10:11** ᵃIsaiah 28:16 **10:13** ᵃJoel 2:32
10:15 ᵃNU-Text omits *preach the gospel of peace, Who.* ᵇIsaiah 52:7; Nahum 1:15 **10:16** ᵃIsaiah 53:1
10:18 ᵃPsalm 19:4 **10:19** ᵃDeuteronomy 32:21
10:20 ᵃIsaiah 65:1

*"All day long I have stretched out My hands
To a disobedient and contrary people."*[a]

Israel's Rejection Not Total

11 I say then, has God cast away His people? Certainly not! For I also am an Israelite, of the seed of Abraham, *of the tribe of Benjamin.* [2]God has not cast away His people whom He foreknew. Or do you not know what the Scripture says of Elijah, how he pleads with God against Israel, saying, [3]*"LORD, they have killed Your prophets and torn down Your altars, and I alone am left, and they seek my life"?*[a] [4]But what does the divine response say to him? *"I have reserved for Myself seven thousand men who have not bowed the knee to Baal."*[a] [5]Even so then, at this present time there is a remnant according to the election of grace. [6]And if by grace, then *it is* no longer of works; otherwise grace is no longer grace.[a] But if *it is* of works, it is no longer grace; otherwise work is no longer work.

[7]What then? Israel has not obtained what it seeks; but the elect have obtained it, and the rest were blinded. [8]Just as it is written:

*"God has given them a spirit of stupor,
Eyes that they should not see
And ears that they should not hear,
To this very day."*[a]

[9]And David says:

*"Let their table become a snare and a trap,
A stumbling block and a recompense to
   them.*
[10] *Let their eyes be darkened, so that they do
   not see,
And bow down their back always."*[a]

Israel's Rejection Not Final

[11]I say then, have they stumbled that they should fall? Certainly not! But through their fall, to provoke them to jealousy, salvation *has come* to the Gentiles. [12]Now if their fall *is* riches for the world, and their failure riches for the Gentiles, how much more their fullness!

[13]For I speak to you Gentiles; inasmuch as I am an apostle to the Gentiles, I magnify my ministry, [14]if by any means I may provoke to jealousy *those who are* my flesh and save some of them. [15]For if their being cast away *is* the reconciling of the world, what *will* their acceptance *be* but life from the dead?

[16]For if the firstfruit *is* holy, the lump *is* also *holy;* and if the root *is* holy, so *are* the branches. [17]And if some of the branches were broken off,

and you, being a wild olive tree, were grafted in among them, and with them became a partaker of the root and fatness of the olive tree, [18]do not boast against the branches. But if you do boast, *remember that* you do not support the root, but the root supports you.

[19]You will say then, "Branches were broken off that I might be grafted in." [20]Well *said.* Because of unbelief they were broken off, and you stand by faith. Do not be haughty, but fear. [21]For if God did not spare the natural branches, He may not spare you either. [22]Therefore consider the goodness and severity of God: on those who

---

10:21 [a]Isaiah 65:2 **11:3** [a]1 Kings 19:10, 14 **11:4** [a]1 Kings 19:18 **11:6** [a]NU-Text omits the rest of this verse. **11:8** [a]Deuteronomy 29:4; Isaiah 29:10 **11:10** [a]Psalm 69:22, 23

The Law of Connection: Paul Touches Hearts, Then Asks for Response
(Romans 12:1, 2)

After climbing an enormous theological hill, Paul shifts gears in Romans 12. The first eleven chapters provide a basis for our belief, but from chapter twelve to the end of the book, the apostle supplies a basis for our behavior. First doctrine; then duty. This is how Paul always attempted to connect with his listeners.

Paul pleads with his friends, based on God's mercy, to lovingly surrender themselves to the Lord. He urges them to respond in four ways:

1. *Presentation:* We are to present our bodies to God as living sacrifices (v. 1).
2. *Separation:* We are to avoid conforming to the world's ways (v. 2).
3. *Transformation:* We are to renew our minds and thus change our lives (v. 2).
4. *Demonstration:* We are to prove we belong to God by doing His will (v. 2).

Paul argues that these four acts provide the logical response to God's grace. He knew this was a tall request, but he spent 11 chapters building a foundation for the "big ask." Leaders who connect touch hearts in a big way, then ask for a big response.

Leaders Are Brokers of Gifts

(Romans 12:6–8)

Paul describes seven spiritual gifts, distributed to different members in the body of Christ. Like any good leader, he recognizes his role as a broker of gifts, talents, and resources. He urges everyone to discover, develop, and distribute his or her gift.

Every resource God provides should be in use. Every believer is a steward of the abilities he or she has been given. Every leader is a manager whose goal should be to maximize everyone's gift.

The list of gifts in Romans 12 is not exhaustive. They are commonly called "motivational gifts," which means they are central to our lives, the hub of the wheel around which our particular set of gifts revolve. Paul's list includes:

1. *Gift of Prophecy:* to challenge others by declaring God's truth and calling for action.
2. *Gift of Service or Ministry:* to serve others and meet their needs.
3. *Gift of Teaching:* to explain truth so that others can understand and apply it.
4. *Gift of Exhortation:* to encourage, strengthen, and inspire others to be their best.
5. *Gift of Giving:* to generously share what God has given.
6. *Gift of Leadership:* to govern and oversee others so that the group moves forward.
7. *Gift of Mercy:* to empathize with, cheer, and show compassion to those who hurt.

fell, severity; but toward you, goodness,ᵃ if you continue in *His* goodness. Otherwise you also will be cut off. ²³And they also, if they do not continue in unbelief, will be grafted in, for God is able to graft them in again. ²⁴For if you were cut out of the olive tree which is wild by nature, and were grafted contrary to nature into a cultivated olive tree, how much more will these, who *are* natural *branches,* be grafted into their own olive tree?

²⁵For I do not desire, brethren, that you should be ignorant of this mystery, lest you should be wise in your own opinion, that blindness in part has happened to Israel until the fullness of the Gentiles has come in. ²⁶And so all Israel will be saved,ᵃ as it is written:

"The Deliverer will come out of Zion,
And He will turn away ungodliness from
        Jacob;
²⁷   For this is My covenant with them,
        When I take away their sins."ᵃ

²⁸Concerning the gospel *they are* enemies for your sake, but concerning the election *they are* beloved for the sake of the fathers. ²⁹For the gifts and the calling of God *are* irrevocable. ³⁰For as you were once disobedient to God, yet have now obtained mercy through their disobedience, ³¹even so these also have now been disobedient, that through the mercy shown you they also may

obtain mercy. ³²For God has committed them all to disobedience, that He might have mercy on all.

³³Oh, the depth of the riches both of the wisdom and knowledge of God! How unsearchable *are* His judgments and His ways past finding out!

³⁴   "For who has known the mind of the LORD?
        Or who has become His counselor?"ᵃ
³⁵   "Or who has first given to Him
        And it shall be repaid to him?"ᵃ

³⁶For of Him and through Him and to Him *are* all things, to whom *be* glory forever. Amen.

Living Sacrifices to God

12 I beseech you therefore, brethren, by the mercies of God, that you present your bodies a living sacrifice, holy, acceptable to God, *which is* your reasonable service. ²And do not be conformed to this world, but be transformed by the renewing of your mind, that you may prove what *is* that good and acceptable and perfect will of God.

Serve God with Spiritual Gifts

³For I say, through the grace given to me, to everyone who is among you, not to think of

---

11:22 ᵃNU-Text adds *of God.* **11:26** ᵃOr *delivered* **11:27** ᵃIsaiah 59:20, 21 **11:34** ᵃIsaiah 40:13; Jeremiah 23:18 **11:35** ᵃJob 41:11

Relationships: If You Get Along, They Will Go Along

(Romans 12:9–21)

Many leaders commit the error of separating leadership from relationships. This happens when a person steps into a position of leadership and assumes that everyone will follow his or her ideas because of his or her position. Some leaders wrongly believe that their knowledge alone qualifies them to lead others.

People don't care how much you know until they know how much you care. We cannot separate leadership from relationships. Leaders help themselves by developing good relational skills. Paul instructs us how to lead through relationships:

1. *Avoid hypocrisy*—be sincere and genuine (v. 9).
2. *Be loyal to colleagues*—treat others like brothers or sisters (v. 10).
3. *Give preference to others*—honor the desires of others above your own (v. 10).
4. *Be hospitable*—look for ways to meet the needs of others (v. 13).
5. *Return good for evil*—act, don't react, when others hurt you (v. 14).
6. *Identify with others*—treat others' needs or victories as your own (v. 15).
7. *Be open-minded toward others*—seek to connect with anyone you speak to (v. 16).
8. *Treat everyone with respect*—this is a compliment to any person (v. 17).
9. *Do everything possible to keep peace*—choose wisely which hills to die on (v. 18).
10. *Remove revenge from your life*—let God judge others; you love them (vv. 19–21).

himself more highly than he ought to think, but to think soberly, as God has dealt to each one a measure of faith. [4]For as we have many members in one body, but all the members do not have the same function, [5]so we, *being* many, are one body in Christ, and individually members of one another. [6]Having then gifts differing according to the grace that is given to us, *let us use them:* if prophecy, *let us prophesy* in proportion to our faith; [7]or ministry, *let us use it* in *our* ministering; he who teaches, in teaching; [8]he who exhorts, in exhortation; he who gives, with liberality; he who leads, with diligence; he who shows mercy, with cheerfulness.

Behave Like a Christian

[9]*Let* love *be* without hypocrisy. Abhor what is evil. Cling to what is good. [10]*Be* kindly affectionate to one another with brotherly love, in honor giving preference to one another; [11]not lagging in diligence, fervent in spirit, serving the Lord; [12]rejoicing in hope, patient in tribulation, continuing steadfastly in prayer; [13]distributing to the needs of the saints, given to hospitality.

[14]Bless those who persecute you; bless and do not curse. [15]Rejoice with those who rejoice, and weep with those who weep. [16]Be of the same mind toward one another. Do not set your mind on high things, but associate with the humble. Do not be wise in your own opinion.

[17]Repay no one evil for evil. Have regard for good things in the sight of all men. [18]If it is possible, as much as depends on you, live peaceably with all men. [19]Beloved, do not avenge yourselves, but *rather* give place to wrath; for it is written, *"Vengeance is Mine, I will repay,"*[a] says the Lord. [20]Therefore

> *"If your enemy is hungry, feed him;*
> *If he is thirsty, give him a drink;*
> *For in so doing you will heap coals of fire*
> *on his head."*[a]

[21]Do not be overcome by evil, but overcome evil with good.

Submit to Government

13 Let every soul be subject to the governing authorities. For there is no authority except from God, and the authorities that exist are appointed by God. [2]Therefore whoever resists the authority resists the ordinance of God, and those who resist will bring judgment on themselves. [3]For rulers are

12:19 [a]Deuteronomy 32:35 **12:20** [a]Proverbs 25:21, 22

not a terror to good works, but to evil. Do you want to be unafraid of the authority? Do what is good, and you will have praise from the same. [4]For he is God's minister to you for good. But if you do evil, be afraid; for he does not bear the sword in vain; for he is God's minister, an avenger to *execute* wrath on him who practices evil. [5]Therefore *you* must be subject, not only because of wrath but also for conscience' sake. [6]For because of this you also pay taxes, for they are God's ministers attending continually to this very thing. [7]Render therefore to all their due: taxes to whom taxes *are due,* customs to whom customs, fear to whom fear, honor to whom honor.

Love Your Neighbor

[8]Owe no one anything except to love one another, for he who loves another has fulfilled the law. [9]For the commandments, *"You shall not commit adultery," "You shall not murder," "You shall not steal," "You shall not bear false witness,"*[a] *"You shall not covet,"*[b] and if *there is* any other commandment, are *all* summed up in this saying, namely, *"You shall love your neighbor as yourself."*[c] [10]Love does no harm to a neighbor; therefore love *is* the fulfillment of the law.

The Authority Test: Submitting to God-Given Authority

(Romans 13:1–7)

Paul gets very practical in how to apply our beliefs to our lives by challenging us to submit to God-given authorities. For children, this means parents; for adults, this means leaders in government, the workplace, and the church.

Why should we so submit? Is it because these leaders are the smartest, most reliable individuals on earth? No. God simply provides us with an authority test. Before we will ever become leaders of integrity, we must learn to follow other leaders, regardless of differences. In fact, the acid test of character comes when we disagree with legitimate authorities. When we refuse to demand our own way and instead submit to others, our hearts are right. This is when God can trust us to lead others.

Put on Christ

[11]And *do* this, knowing the time, that now *it is* high time to awake out of sleep; for now our salvation *is* nearer than when we *first* believed. [12]The night is far spent, the day is at hand. Therefore let us cast off the works of darkness, and let us put on the armor of light. [13]Let us walk properly, as in the day, not in revelry and drunkenness, not in lewdness and lust, not in strife and envy. [14]But put on the Lord Jesus Christ, and make no provision for the flesh, to *fulfill its* lusts.

The Law of Liberty

14 Receive one who is weak in the faith, *but* not to disputes over doubtful things. [2]For one believes he may eat all things, but he who is weak eats *only* vegetables. [3]Let not him who eats despise him who does not eat, and let not him who does not eat judge him who eats; for God has received him. [4]Who are you to judge another's servant? To his own master he stands or falls. Indeed, he will be made to stand, for God is able to make him stand.

[5]One person esteems *one* day above another; another esteems every day *alike.* Let each be fully convinced in his own mind. [6]He who observes the day, observes *it* to the Lord;[a] and he who does not observe the day, to the Lord he does not observe *it.* He who eats, eats to the Lord, for he gives God thanks; and he who does not eat, to the Lord he does not eat, and gives God thanks. [7]For none of us lives to himself, and no one dies to himself. [8]For if we live, we live to the Lord; and if we die, we die to the Lord. Therefore, whether we live or die, we are the Lord's. [9]For to this end Christ died and rose[a] and lived again, that He might be Lord of both the dead and the living. [10]But why do you judge your brother? Or why do you show contempt for your brother? For we shall all stand before the judgment seat of Christ.[a] [11]For it is written:

> *"As I live, says the LORD,*
> *Every knee shall bow to Me,*
> *And every tongue shall confess to God."*[a]

13:9 [a]NU-Text omits *"You shall not bear false witness."* [b]Exodus 20:13–15, 17; Deuteronomy 5:17–19, 21 [c]Leviticus 19:18 **14:6** [a]NU-Text omits the rest of this sentence. **14:9** [a]NU-Text omits *and rose.* **14:10** [a]NU-Text reads *of God.* **14:11** [a]Isaiah 45:23

The Values and Conscience of a Leader

(Romans 14:1–23)

How are we to respond to others who hold values different from our own? That's the issue of Romans 14.

Paul speaks in this passage not of eternal issues or absolute truths, but about "gray areas"— subjects that are questionable and maybe even fuzzy. Christians can differ on these issues and still be part of the same organization. On these issues, no scripture declares an unequivocal right or wrong. Note Paul's counsel for situations like this:

1. Be open, not condescending (vv. 1–3).
2. Remember that everyone answers to the Lord, not to you (v. 4).
3. Cling to your own convictions (v. 5).
4. Whatever your values, your motive should be to please God (vv. 6–9).
5. You are ultimately accountable to the Lord (vv. 10–12).
6. Do not cause anyone to stumble (v. 13).
7. Don't let others impose their values on you, and vice versa (v. 14).
8. Make love your highest aim (v. 15).
9. Major on the majors and minor on the minors (vv. 16–18).
10. Pursue peace and adding value to people (v. 19).
11. Don't destroy anyone by imposing your values on them (vv. 20–22).
12. Anything is wrong that is not done out of personal faith (v. 23).

¹²So then each of us shall give account of himself to God. ¹³Therefore let us not judge one another anymore, but rather resolve this, not to put a stumbling block or a cause to fall in *our* brother's way.

The Law of Love

¹⁴I know and am convinced by the Lord Jesus that *there is* nothing unclean of itself; but to him who considers anything to be unclean, to him *it is* unclean. ¹⁵Yet if your brother is grieved because of *your* food, you are no longer walking in love. Do not destroy with your food the one for whom Christ died. ¹⁶Therefore do not let your good be spoken of as evil; ¹⁷for the kingdom of God is not eating and drinking, but righteousness and peace and joy in the Holy Spirit. ¹⁸For he who serves Christ in these things[a] *is* acceptable to God and approved by men.

¹⁹Therefore let us pursue the things *which make* for peace and the things by which one may edify another. ²⁰Do not destroy the work of God for the sake of food. All things indeed *are* pure, but *it is* evil for the man who eats with offense. ²¹*It is* good neither to eat meat nor drink wine nor *do anything* by which your brother stumbles or is offended or is made weak.[a] ²²Do you have

faith?[a] Have *it* to yourself before God. Happy *is* he who does not condemn himself in what he approves. ²³But he who doubts is condemned if he eats, because *he does* not *eat* from faith; for whatever *is* not from faith is sin.[a]

Bearing Others' Burdens

15 We then who are strong ought to bear with the scruples of the weak, and not to please ourselves. ²Let each of us please *his* neighbor for *his* good, leading to edification. ³For even Christ did not please Himself; but as it is written, *"The reproaches of those who reproached You fell on Me."*[a] ⁴For whatever things were written before were written for our learning, that we through the patience and comfort of the Scriptures might have hope. ⁵Now may the God of patience and comfort grant you to be like-minded toward one another, according to Christ Jesus, ⁶that you may with one mind *and* one mouth glorify the God and Father of our Lord Jesus Christ.

14:18 [a]NU-Text reads *this.* **14:21** [a]NU-Text omits *or is offended or is made weak.* **14:22** [a]NU-Text reads *The faith which you have—have.* **14:23** [a]M-Text puts Romans 16:25–27 here. **15:3** [a]Psalm 69:9

Servanthood: Leaders Lose the Right to Be Selfish

(Romans 15:1–6)

How can leaders increasingly gain a servant's heart? This passage serves as another reminder that leadership is about serving others, not wielding power. Notice how Paul describes a servant:

1. *Denies self*—we are to please others, not ourselves (v. 1).
2. *Develops others*—we are to add value to others (v. 2).
3. *Accepts mistreatment*—we are to forgive wrongs (v. 3).
4. *Imitates Christ*—we are to look to Jesus as our model (v. 3).
5. *Takes the attitude of a student*—we are to remain teachable (v. 4).
6. *Pursues the harmony of relationships*—we are to pursue unity and peace (vv. 5, 6).

Glorify God Together

7 Therefore receive one another, just as Christ also received us,[a] to the glory of God. 8 Now I say that Jesus Christ has become a servant to the circumcision for the truth of God, to confirm the promises *made* to the fathers, 9 and that the Gentiles might glorify God for *His* mercy, as it is written:

> "For this reason I will confess to You
> among the Gentiles,
> And sing to Your name."[a]

10 And again he says:

> "Rejoice, O Gentiles, with His people!"[a]

11 And again:

> "Praise the LORD, all you Gentiles!
> Laud Him, all you peoples!"[a]

12 And again, Isaiah says:

> "There shall be a root of Jesse;
> And He who shall rise to reign over the
> Gentiles,
> In Him the Gentiles shall hope."[a]

13 Now may the God of hope fill you with all joy and peace in believing, that you may abound in hope by the power of the Holy Spirit.

From Jerusalem to Illyricum

14 Now I myself am confident concerning you, my brethren, that you also are full of goodness, filled with all knowledge, able also to admonish one another.[a] 15 Nevertheless, brethren, I have written more boldly to you on *some* points, as reminding you, because of the grace given to me by God, 16 that I might be a minister of Jesus Christ to the Gentiles, ministering the gospel of God, that the offering of the Gentiles might be acceptable, sanctified by the Holy Spirit. 17 Therefore I have reason to glory in Christ Jesus in the things *which pertain* to God. 18 For I will not dare to speak of any of those things which Christ has not accomplished through me, in word and deed, to make the Gentiles obedient— 19 in mighty signs and wonders, by the power of the Spirit of God, so that from Jerusalem and round about to Illyricum I have fully preached the gospel of Christ. 20 And so I have made it my aim to preach the gospel, not where Christ was named, lest I should build on another man's foundation, 21 but as it is written:

> "To whom He was not announced, they
> shall see;
> And those who have not heard shall
> understand."[a]

Plan to Visit Rome

22 For this reason I also have been much hindered from coming to you. 23 But now no longer having a place in these parts, and having a great desire these many years to come to you, 24 whenever I journey to Spain, I shall come to you.[a] For I hope to see you on my journey, and to be helped on my way there by you, if first I may enjoy your *company* for a while. 25 But now I am going to Jerusalem to minister to the saints. 26 For it pleased those from Macedonia and Achaia to make a certain contribution for the poor among the saints who are in Jerusalem. 27 It pleased them indeed, and they are their debtors. For if the Gentiles have been partakers of their spiritual things, their duty is also to minister to

---

15:7 [a]NU-Text and M-Text read *you*.
15:9 [a]2 Samuel 22:50; Psalm 18:49
15:10 [a]Deuteronomy 32:43 **15:11** [a]Psalm 117:1
15:12 [a]Isaiah 11:10 **15:14** [a]M-Text reads *others*.
15:21 [a]Isaiah 52:15 **15:24** [a]NU-Text omits *I shall come to you* (and joins *Spain* with the next sentence).

them in material things. [28]Therefore, when I have performed this and have sealed to them this fruit, I shall go by way of you to Spain. [29]But I know that when I come to you, I shall come in the fullness of the blessing of the gospel[a] of Christ.

[30]Now I beg you, brethren, through the Lord Jesus Christ, and through the love of the Spirit, that you strive together with me in prayers to God for me, [31]that I may be delivered from those in Judea who do not believe, and that my service for Jerusalem may be acceptable to the saints, [32]that I may come to you with joy by the will of God, and may be refreshed together with you. [33]Now the God of peace be with you all. Amen.

Sister Phoebe Commended

16 I commend to you Phoebe our sister, who is a servant of the church in Cenchrea, [2]that you may receive her in the Lord in a manner worthy of the saints, and assist her in whatever business she has need of you; for indeed she has been a helper of many and of myself also.

Greeting Roman Saints

[3]Greet Priscilla and Aquila, my fellow workers in Christ Jesus, [4]who risked their own necks for my life, to whom not only I give thanks, but also all the churches of the Gentiles. [5]Likewise greet the church that is in his house.

Greet my beloved Epaenetus, who is the firstfruits of Achaia[a] to Christ. [6]Greet Mary, who labored much for us. [7]Greet Andronicus and Junia, my countrymen and my fellow prisoners, who are of note among the apostles, who also were in Christ before me.

[8]Greet Amplias, my beloved in the Lord. [9]Greet Urbanus, our fellow worker in Christ, and Stachys, my beloved. [10]Greet Apelles, approved in Christ. Greet those who are of the household of Aristobulus. [11]Greet Herodion, my countryman.[a] Greet those who are of the household of Narcissus who are in the Lord.

[12]Greet Tryphena and Tryphosa, who have labored in the Lord. Greet the beloved Persis, who labored much in the Lord. [13]Greet Rufus, chosen in the Lord, and his mother and mine. [14]Greet Asyncritus, Phlegon, Hermas, Patrobas, Hermes, and the brethren who are with them. [15]Greet Philologus and Julia, Nereus and his sister, and Olympas, and all the saints who are with them.

[16]Greet one another with a holy kiss. The[a] churches of Christ greet you.

Avoid Divisive Persons

[17]Now I urge you, brethren, note those who cause divisions and offenses, contrary to the doc-

15:29 [a]NU-Text omits of the gospel.
16:5 [a]NU-Text reads Asia. **16:11** [a]Or relative
16:16 [a]NU-Text reads All the churches.

Relationships: Paul Affirms His Colleagues by Name

(Romans 16:1–21)

Paul sent his personal greetings to a variety of individuals in Rome. Perhaps this was Paul's way of establishing credibility with his readers, since he had never visited Rome. In any case, we see the warm, relational approach this tough leader practiced.

Note that the first few people Paul greets are women: Phoebe, Priscilla, Mary. Many pillars of the early church were faithful ladies who ministered and gave strong leadership. Jesus' life began with a woman named Mary and ended at His resurrection with a woman at the tomb. Recall several significant women in the New Testament:

1. Anna (Luke 2:36–38)
2. Bernice (Acts 25:13)
3. Candace (Acts 8:27)
4. Chloe (1 Cor. 1:11)
5. Claudia (2 Tim. 4:21)
6. Damaris (Acts 17:34)
7. Dorcas (Acts 9:36–41)
8. Drusilla (Acts 24:24)
9. Elizabeth (Luke 1:5, 13)
10. Eunice (2 Tim. 1:5)
11. Herodias (Matt. 14:3–10)
12. Joanna (Luke 8:3)
13. Lois (2 Tim. 1:5)
14. Lydia (Acts 16:14)
15. Martha, Mary (Luke 10:38–42)
16. Mary, the mother of Jesus (Luke 1:26–56)
17. Mary Magdalene (Matt. 27:61)
18. Phoebe (Rom. 16:1, 2)
19. Priscilla (Acts 18:2, 18)
20. Salome (Matt. 20:20–26)
21. Sapphira (Acts 5:1)
22. Susanna (Luke 8:3)

trine which you learned, and avoid them. [18]For those who are such do not serve our Lord Jesus[a] Christ, but their own belly, and by smooth words and flattering speech deceive the hearts of the simple. [19]For your obedience has become known to all. Therefore I am glad on your behalf; but I want you to be wise in what is good, and simple concerning evil. [20]And the God of peace will crush Satan under your feet shortly.

The grace of our Lord Jesus Christ *be* with you. Amen.

Greetings from Paul's Friends

[21]Timothy, my fellow worker, and Lucius, Jason, and Sosipater, my countrymen, greet you.

[22]I, Tertius, who wrote *this* epistle, greet you in the Lord.

[23]Gaius, my host and *the host* of the whole church, greets you. Erastus, the treasurer of the city, greets you, and Quartus, a brother. [24]The grace of our Lord Jesus Christ *be* with you all. Amen.[a]

Benediction

[25]Now to Him who is able to establish you according to my gospel and the preaching of Jesus Christ, according to the revelation of the mystery kept secret since the world began [26]but now made manifest, and by the prophetic Scriptures made known to all nations, according to the commandment of the everlasting God, for obedience to the faith— [27]to God, alone wise, *be* glory through Jesus Christ forever. Amen.[a]

16:18 [a]NU-Text and M-Text omit *Jesus.*
16:24 [a]NU-Text omits this verse. **16:27** [a]M-Text puts Romans 16:25–27 after Romans 14:23.

1 CORINTHIANS

Leaders Must Take Risks and Overcome Fear

SUMMARY

The two books to the Corinthian church teach us much about leadership. Various scholars agree that Paul actually wrote four letters to Corinth; our Bibles have letters two and four. While Paul appointed leaders for this church, he also led this body through his letters. He provided wise direction and needed confrontation, without ignoring their need for ministry to the heart.

The city of Corinth became a strategic center for Paul and even influenced his missionary endeavors. In order to impact this key, wealthy, commercial port, he planted the church with the help of Aquilla and Priscilla (Acts 18:1–17).

First Corinthians teaches us that leaders must take risks and overcome fear. By definition, leaders initiate. They take risks. Paul stood for his convictions even when he stood alone. He confronted sin without help from others. He attempted new methods and strategies no one else was using. When rejected in his attempt to preach Christ in the synagogue, he began to equip others in the house of Titus Justus next door. Imagine the fear! He taught right next to where the Jewish religious leaders could arrest him. The Lord appeared to him in a vision and encouraged him to "not be afraid" and to continue teaching, for God had "many people in this city" (Acts 18:9, 10).

Second, we learn that the best leaders invest time in building other leaders. While in Corinth, Paul started one of the first underground seminaries. So far as we can tell, he taught leaders in the afternoon when they were on a "siesta" from their workplace, just as he did in Ephesus. Most would go home to rest each afternoon, but Paul equipped leaders willing to give up their personal time to gain some tools to plant a church or evangelize the lost.

Third, leaders must be both tough and tender. Paul waded through several difficult issues in the Corinthian letters, beautifully balancing love and discipline. Call him a "velvet-covered brick!" In the end, his gentle wisdom helped resolve the sticky issues.

God's Role in 1 Corinthians

God used the words and personality of the apostle Paul to both encourage and correct the Corinthian church. God used Paul's educated mind to confound the wise and educated, the apostle's Jewish background to identify and convince the Hebrews, and his Roman political and social background to reach the Gentiles. First Corinthians 9 tells us that Paul became all things to all people for the purpose of reaching as many as possible.

Leaders in 1 Corinthians

Paul, Apollos, Aquila, Priscilla, Timothy, Crispus, Sosthenes

Other People of Influence in 1 Corinthians

Stephanas, the church members who abused their spiritual gifts and caused division

Lessons in Leadership

- Leaders must find their identity in Christ, not in people.
- Confrontation and criticism go with the leader's territory.
- Corporate purity and security result when a leader courageously deals with problems.
- Good leaders create a unified corporate atmosphere.
- Effective leaders find a place for every member to serve effectively.
- It is a leader's job to keep the main thing the main thing.

HIGHLIGHTS IN 1 CORINTHIANS

Greeting

1 Paul, called *to be* an apostle of Jesus Christ through the will of God, and Sosthenes *our* brother,

²To the church of God which is at Corinth, to those who are sanctified in Christ Jesus, called *to be* saints, with all who in every place call on the name of Jesus Christ our Lord, both theirs and ours:

³Grace to you and peace from God our Father and the Lord Jesus Christ.

Spiritual Gifts at Corinth

⁴I thank my God always concerning you for the grace of God which was given to you by Christ Jesus, ⁵that you were enriched in everything by Him in all utterance and all knowledge, ⁶even as the testimony of Christ was confirmed in you, ⁷so that you come short in no gift, eagerly waiting for the revelation of our Lord Jesus Christ, ⁸who will also confirm you to the end, *that you may be* blameless in the day of our Lord Jesus Christ. ⁹God *is* faithful, by whom you were called into the fellowship of His Son, Jesus Christ our Lord.

Sectarianism Is Sin

¹⁰Now I plead with you, brethren, by the name of our Lord Jesus Christ, that you all speak the same thing, and *that* there be no divisions among you, but *that* you be perfectly joined together in the same mind and in the same judgment. ¹¹For it has been declared to me concerning you, my brethren, by those of Chloe's *household,* that there are contentions among you. ¹²Now I say this, that each of you says, "I am of Paul," or "I am of Apollos," or "I am of Cephas," or "I am of Christ." ¹³Is Christ divided? Was Paul crucified for you? Or were you baptized in the name of Paul? ¹⁴I thank God that I baptized none of you except Crispus and Gaius, ¹⁵lest anyone should say that I had baptized in my own name. ¹⁶Yes, I also baptized the household of Stephanas. Besides, I do not know whether I baptized any other. ¹⁷For Christ did not send me to baptize, but to preach the gospel, not with wisdom of words, lest the cross of Christ should be made of no effect.

Christ the Power and Wisdom of God

¹⁸For the message of the cross is foolishness to those who are perishing, but to us who are being saved it is the power of God. ¹⁹For it is written:

PAUL — THE VELVET-COVERED BRICK
(1 Corinthians 1:1, 2)

PROFILE IN LEADERSHIP

As the human founder of the Corinthian church (Acts 18:1–17), Paul had a *really* big task before him.

Paul loved his Corinthian brothers and sisters in Christ. But when he received reports that divisions, immorality, and pride had crept their way into the church, he knew he had to speak up and confront the sin that some members of the church had grown proud of.

Paul felt grieved—perhaps even angered—over the reports he received about his Corinthian colleagues. We can see in his letter the anguish he felt over what had been going on in the church, but we also read of an overriding sense of love and concern for these dear friends, the ones he had referred to as "those who are sanctified in Christ Jesus, called to be saints" (1 Cor. 1:2).

It was as if Paul were hitting the Corinthian church on the head with a velvet-covered brick—the brick being his condemnation of their sin, the velvet being his love for those whom God had set apart for good works.

It isn't always easy to speak correction to those we know are clearly in the wrong. But the Lord uses strong leaders to correct His people, courageous leaders who can speak the truth in love. May each of us whom God has called be that kind of leader.

The 101% Principle
(1 Corinthians 1:4–10)

The church at Corinth provided Paul with one of his greatest challenges. In this letter, he was forced to confront several problems. This was a *defiled* church—some members had committed sexual immorality and drunkenness. It was a *divided* church—at least four groups competed for leadership. It was a *disgraced* church—its problems became known throughout the community. Paul's letter could have become one long, verbal spanking.

Instead, Paul saw this church's potential, despite its problems. He practiced "The 101% Principle"—find the 1 percent you can affirm, and give it 100 percent of your attention. As the old saying goes, you catch more bees with honey than with vinegar.

While Paul knew he must confront the issues, he began his letter with words of appreciation (1 Cor. 1:1–9). Leadership rule #1 is this: Affirmation comes before confrontation. Although Corinth had some problem people, Paul still saw the good in them:

1. They were enriched by God (vv. 4–8).
2. They had fellowship with God (v. 9).
3. They could make positive, right decisions (v. 10).

Good leaders look for the good in people and affirm it. Only then do they address the problem.

"I will destroy the wisdom of the wise,
And bring to nothing the understanding of
the prudent.'"[a]

[20]Where *is* the wise? Where *is* the scribe? Where *is* the disputer of this age? Has not God made foolish the wisdom of this world? [21]For since, in the wisdom of God, the world through wisdom did not know God, it pleased God through the foolishness of the message preached to save those who believe. [22]For Jews request a sign, and Greeks seek after wisdom; [23]but we preach Christ crucified, to the Jews a stumbling block and to the Greeks[a] foolishness, [24]but to those who are called, both Jews and Greeks, Christ the power of God and the wisdom of God. [25]Because the foolishness of God is wiser than men, and the weakness of God is stronger than men.

Glory Only in the Lord
[26]For you see your calling, brethren, that not many wise according to the flesh, not many mighty, not many noble, *are called*. [27]But God has chosen the foolish things of the world to put to shame the wise, and God has chosen the weak things of the world to put to shame the things which are mighty; [28]and the base things of the world and the things which are despised God has chosen, and the things which are not, to bring to nothing the things that are, [29]that no flesh should glory in His presence. [30]But of Him you are in Christ Jesus, who became for us wisdom from God—and righteousness and sanctification and redemption— [31]that, as it is written, *"He who glories, let him glory in the LORD."*[a]

Responsibility: Leaders Assume Responsibility to Build Community
(1 Corinthians 1:10)

Good things happen when leaders take responsibility for creating an organization's atmosphere and culture. They create:

1. *A sense of destiny:* We are here by God's design to do His work.
2. *A sense of family:* We are in this together.
3. *A militant spirit:* We must get the job done at any cost.

1:19 [a]Isaiah 29:14 **1:23** [a]NU-Text reads *Gentiles*.
1:31 [a]Jeremiah 9:24

The Glory Factor
(1 Corinthians 1:18—2:5)

It is natural for leaders to want a bit of glory. Most leaders enjoy the limelight and feel it is only human to want their ego stroked from time to time. Paul resisted this tendency to pursue the glory that only God deserves. He focused on the superiority of God's wisdom and teaches leaders some valuable truths about:

1. *The perception of God's wisdom*—it seems to be foolishness (1:18).
2. *The permanence of God's wisdom*—it is infinite (1:19, 20).
3. *The power of God's wisdom*—it can do what ours cannot (1:21–25).
4. *The paradox of God's wisdom*—it is backwards (1:26–28).
5. *The purpose of God's wisdom*—it ensures He gets the glory (1:29–31).

Paul concludes that leaders must respond in humility, seek dependence on God, and not seek the glory He alone deserves. He draws three conclusions about his leadership:

1. *I renounce human values*—I will think the way God thinks (2:1, 2).
2. *I renounce human strength*—I'll be weak and seek His strength (2:3).
3. *I renounce human wisdom*—I'll ask for God's wisdom and favor (2:4, 5).

Christ Crucified

And I, brethren, when I came to you, did not come with excellence of speech or of wisdom declaring to you the testimony[a] of God. [2]For I determined not to know anything among you except Jesus Christ and Him crucified. [3]I was with you in weakness, in fear, and in much trembling. [4]And my speech and my preaching *were* not with persuasive words of human[a] wisdom, but in demonstration of the Spirit and of power, [5]that your faith should not be in the wisdom of men but in the power of God.

Spiritual Wisdom

[6]However, we speak wisdom among those who are mature, yet not the wisdom of this age, nor of the rulers of this age, who are coming to nothing. [7]But we speak the wisdom of God in a mystery, the hidden *wisdom* which God ordained before the ages for our glory, [8]which none of the rulers of this age knew; for had they known, they would not have crucified the Lord of glory. [9]But as it is written:

"Eye has not seen, nor ear heard,
 Nor have entered into the heart of man
The things which God has prepared for
 those who love Him."[a]

[10]But God has revealed *them* to us through His Spirit. For the Spirit searches all things, yes, the deep things of God. [11]For what man knows the things of a man except the spirit of the man which is in him? Even so no one knows the things of God except the Spirit of God. [12]Now we have received, not the spirit of the world, but the Spirit who is from God, that we might know the things that have been freely given to us by God.

[13]These things we also speak, not in words which man's wisdom teaches but which the Holy[a] Spirit teaches, comparing spiritual things with spiritual. [14]But the natural man does not receive the things of the Spirit of God, for they are foolishness to him; nor can he know *them*, because they are spiritually discerned. [15]But he who is spiritual judges all things, yet he himself is *rightly* judged by no one. [16]For *"who has known the mind of the LORD that he may instruct Him?"*[a] But we have the mind of Christ.

Sectarianism Is Carnal

And I, brethren, could not speak to you as to spiritual *people* but as to carnal, as to babes in Christ. [2]I fed you with milk and not with solid food; for until now you were not able *to receive it*, and even now you are still not able; [3]for you are still carnal. For where *there are* envy, strife, and divisions among you, are you not carnal and behaving like *mere* men? [4]For when

---

2:1 [a]NU-Text reads *mystery*. **2:4** [a]NU-Text omits *human*. **2:9** [a]Isaiah 64:4 **2:13** [a]NU-Text omits *Holy*. **2:16** [a]Isaiah 40:13

The Law of Process: Three Pictures of Growth

(1 Corinthians 3:1–23)

Paul, the pioneer and leader of the Corinthian church, had trouble hiding his disappointment. The members of this church were acting like babies rather than adults (1 Cor. 3:1–3). No doubt he had to remind himself that leadership development is a process, not an event.

Paul desperately wanted competent leaders to rise up within the church, leaders who were healthy, strong, and able to make decisions without his help. Paul gave them three pictures to illustrate how God wanted them to grow:

1. *The church is a family*—the goal is maturity (vv. 1–4).

   It is natural for children to grow physically as they age. This should also be true spiritually. The marks of maturity are what you eat (vv. 1, 2), what you do (v. 3), and what you say (v. 4).

2. *The church is a field*—the goal is fruitfulness (vv. 5–9).

   It doesn't matter who planted or who watered; the point is, are the plants growing? Fruit includes the results of your work, the response of your people, and the reward of your fulfillment.

3. *The church is a building*—the goal is quality (vv. 9–23).

   We are like a building. The measure of a good structure is quality. This includes the right foundation (vv. 9–11), the right materials (vv. 12–17), and the right motives (vv. 18–23).

---

one says, "I am of Paul," and another, "I *am* of Apollos," are you not carnal?

Watering, Working, Warning

[5]Who then is Paul, and who *is* Apollos, but ministers through whom you believed, as the Lord gave to each one? [6]I planted, Apollos watered, but God gave the increase. [7]So then neither he who plants is anything, nor he who waters, but God who gives the increase. [8]Now he who plants and he who waters are one, and each one will receive his own reward according to his own labor.

[9]For we are God's fellow workers; you are God's field, *you are* God's building. [10]According to the grace of God which was given to me, as a wise master builder I have laid the foundation, and another builds on it. But let each one take heed how he builds on it. [11]For no other foundation can anyone lay than that which is laid, which is Jesus Christ. [12]Now if anyone builds on this foundation *with* gold, silver, precious stones, wood, hay, straw, [13]each one's work will become clear; for the Day will declare it, because it will be revealed by fire; and the fire will test each one's work, of what sort it is. [14]If anyone's work which he has built on *it* endures, he will receive a reward. [15]If anyone's work is burned, he will suffer loss; but he himself will be saved, yet so as through fire.

[16]Do you not know that you are the temple

of God and *that* the Spirit of God dwells in you? [17]If anyone defiles the temple of God, God will destroy him. For the temple of God is holy, which *temple* you are.

Avoid Worldly Wisdom

[18]Let no one deceive himself. If anyone among you seems to be wise in this age, let him become a fool that he may become wise. [19]For the wisdom of this world is foolishness with God. For it is written, *"He catches the wise in their own craftiness"*;[a] [20]and again, *"The LORD knows the thoughts of the wise, that they are futile."*[a] [21]Therefore let no one boast in men. For all things are yours: [22]whether Paul or Apollos or Cephas, or the world or life or death, or things present or things to come—all are yours. [23]And you *are* Christ's, and Christ *is* God's.

Stewards of the Mysteries of God

4 Let a man so consider us, as servants of Christ and stewards of the mysteries of God. [2]Moreover it is required in stewards that one be found faithful. [3]But with me it is a very small thing that I should be judged by you or by a human court.[a] In fact, I do not even judge myself. [4]For I know of nothing against myself, yet I am not justified by this; but He who judges me is the Lord. [5]Therefore judge nothing

3:19 [a]Job 5:13   **3:20** [a]Psalm 94:11   **4:3** [a]Literally *day*

Accountability: Leaders Are Servants with a Sacred Trust

(1 Corinthians 4:1–5)

Paul viewed himself as a servant-leader with a sacred trust (1 Cor. 4:1) to which he needed to stay faithful (4:2). Neither the opinions of others or his own would sway him (4:3). Leaders are to serve people, but obey God, proving faithful to their sacred trust.

before the time, until the Lord comes, who will both bring to light the hidden things of darkness and reveal the counsels of the hearts. Then each one's praise will come from God.

Fools for Christ's Sake

⁶Now these things, brethren, I have figuratively transferred to myself and Apollos for your sakes, that you may learn in us not to think beyond what is written, that none of you may be puffed up on behalf of one against the other. ⁷For who makes you differ *from another?* And what do you have that you did not receive? Now if you did indeed receive *it,* why do you boast as if you had not received *it?*

⁸You are already full! You are already rich! You have reigned as kings without us—and indeed I could wish you did reign, that we also might reign with you! ⁹For I think that God has displayed us, the apostles, last, as men condemned to death; for we have been made a spectacle to the world, both to angels and to men. ¹⁰We *are* fools for Christ's sake, but you *are* wise in Christ! We *are* weak, but you *are* strong! You *are* distinguished, but we *are* dishonored! ¹¹To the present hour we both hunger and thirst, and we are poorly clothed, and beaten, and homeless. ¹²And we labor, working with our own hands. Being reviled, we bless; being persecuted, we endure; ¹³being defamed, we entreat. We have been made as the filth of the world, the offscouring of all things until now.

Paul's Paternal Care

¹⁴I do not write these things to shame you, but as my beloved children I warn *you.* ¹⁵For though you might have ten thousand instructors in Christ, yet *you do* not *have* many fathers; for in Christ Jesus I have begotten you through the gospel. ¹⁶Therefore I urge you, imitate me. ¹⁷For this reason I have sent Timothy to you, who is my beloved and faithful son in the Lord, who will remind you of my ways in Christ, as I teach everywhere in every church.

Modeling: Leadership Is Caught More Than Taught

(1 Corinthians 4:9–21)

The greatest missing ingredient in Christian leaders today is credibility. Paul tests his level of credibility with his Corinthian followers by reminding them of how he had modeled what was right. Now he pleads with them to imitate him as a father in the Lord.

Leaders add infinite weight to their words by incarnating the principles they teach. Paul was able to scold the erring people and sternly correct them because he never asked them to do something he hadn't already done. Listen to him:

1. His leadership was on display and open for ridicule (v. 9).
2. He was willing to play the fool in order to model a surrendered life (v. 10).
3. He endured mocking from others, but didn't waver (v. 10).
4. He sacrificed luxuries that others enjoyed (v. 11).
5. He worked hard and didn't retaliate against opposition (vv. 12, 13).
6. He saw his role as a father, living an exemplary life for his children (vv. 14, 15).
7. He urged his followers to imitate his life (v. 16).
8. He sent Timothy to help them live up to godly standards (vv. 17, 18).
9. He warned them of his own coming (v. 19).
10. He reminded them that God's kingdom was not about talk, but power (v. 20).

How Do Leaders Confront?

(1 Corinthians 5:1, 2)

Once Paul had identified the sin that plagued the church, as well as what should be done about it, he encouraged the leaders to confront this erring man. Most of us avoid confrontation; only a sadistic person *likes* it. So, how do we confront in a healthy and effective manner? Try to follow these steps:

1. Address the issue immediately and personally.
2. Confront with the right spirit.
3. Start on a positive note.
4. Outline the problem.
5. Encourage a response.
6. Show that you understand the other person's position.
7. Explain why the action is damaging.
8. Indicate the desired action.
9. Reiterate the positive strengths of the person.
10. Put the issue in the past.

[18]Now some are puffed up, as though I were not coming to you. [19]But I will come to you shortly, if the Lord wills, and I will know, not the word of those who are puffed up, but the power. [20]For the kingdom of God *is* not in word but in power. [21]What do you want? Shall I come to you with a rod, or in love and a spirit of gentleness?

Immorality Defiles the Church

5 It is actually reported *that there is* sexual immorality among you, and such sexual immorality as is not even named[a] among the Gentiles—that a man has his father's wife! [2]And you are puffed up, and have not rather mourned, that he who has done this deed might be taken away from among you. [3]For I indeed, as absent in body but present in spirit, have already judged (as though I were present) him who has so done this deed. [4]In the name of our Lord Jesus Christ, when you are gathered together, along with my spirit, with the power of our Lord Jesus Christ, [5]deliver such a one to Satan for the destruction of the flesh, that his spirit may be saved in the day of the Lord Jesus.[a]

[6]Your glorying *is* not good. Do you not know that a little leaven leavens the whole lump? [7]Therefore purge out the old leaven, that you

5:1 [a]NU-Text omits *named.* **5:5** [a]NU-Text omits *Jesus.*

Confrontation Results in Purity and Security

(1 Corinthians 5:1–13)

Paul had to confront the problems the Corinthians faced, the first one over the issue of incest in the church (1 Cor. 5:1). Unfortunately, the leaders failed to deal with this sin; many felt proud of what they should be ashamed of, and vice versa (5:2). Paul therefore instructs leaders in how to deal with a member who deliberately rebels against a life of obedience to the Lord (5:2–13). This standard does not apply to outsiders, but to those who call themselves brothers (5:9–11). We learn from 2 Corinthians that the leaders followed Paul's instruction, bringing both purity and security to the church.

Why is confrontation so difficult? We often misunderstand its purpose. Our goal should not be to punish or excommunicate, but to restore. Confrontation is a redemptive act of leadership. So what are the goals of healthy confrontation?

1. *Clarification:* I will get a better understanding of the person and what happened.
2. *Change:* I hope to get improvement from it (and it may be me!).
3. *Relationship:* I will likely deepen my relationship with this person.
4. *Purity:* As word gets out, the organization will be purified and sobered.
5. *Respect:* The organization will likely raise the members' level of respect for the leadership.
6. *Security:* People feel safe knowing leaders are strong enough to take a stand.

may be a new lump, since you truly are unleavened. For indeed Christ, our Passover, was sacrificed for us.[a] [8]Therefore let us keep the feast, not with old leaven, nor with the leaven of malice and wickedness, but with the unleavened *bread* of sincerity and truth.

Immorality Must Be Judged

[9]I wrote to you in my epistle not to keep company with sexually immoral people. [10]Yet *I* certainly *did* not *mean* with the sexually immoral people of this world, or with the covetous, or extortioners, or idolaters, since then you would need to go out of the world. [11]But now I have written to you not to keep company with anyone named a brother, who is sexually immoral, or covetous, or an idolater, or a reviler, or a drunkard, or an extortioner—not even to eat with such a person.

[12]For what *have* I *to do* with judging those also who are outside? Do you not judge those who are inside? [13]But those who are outside God judges. Therefore *"put away from yourselves the evil person."*[a]

Do Not Sue the Brethren

6 Dare any of you, having a matter against another, go to law before the unrighteous, and not before the saints? [2]Do you not know that the saints will judge the world? And if the world will be judged by you, are you unworthy to judge the smallest matters? [3]Do you not know that we shall judge angels? How much more, things that pertain to this life? [4]If then you have judgments concerning things pertaining to this life, do you appoint those who are least esteemed by the church to judge? [5]I say this to your shame. Is it so, that there is not a wise man among you, not even one, who will be able to judge between his brethren? [6]But brother goes to law against brother, and that before unbelievers!

[7]Now therefore, it is already an utter failure for you that you go to law against one another. Why do you not rather accept wrong? Why do you not rather *let yourselves* be cheated? [8]No, you yourselves do wrong and cheat, and *you do* these things *to your* brethren! [9]Do you not know that the unrighteous will not inherit the kingdom of God? Do not be deceived. Neither fornicators, nor idolaters, nor adulterers, nor homosexuals,[a] nor sodomites, [10]nor thieves, nor covetous, nor drunkards, nor revilers, nor extortioners will inherit the kingdom of God. [11]And such were some of you. But you were washed, but you were sanctified, but you were justified in the name of the Lord Jesus and by the Spirit of our God.

Self-Discipline: Leaders Remove Stumbling Blocks

(1 Corinthians 6:1–20)

Paul believed all things were lawful for the obedient Christian. Yet while he remained free of legalism and bondage, he had the self-discipline to refuse anything that would hinder him from fulfilling his call. Paul knew that the first person a leader must lead is himself.

Glorify God in Body and Spirit

[12]All things are lawful for me, but all things are not helpful. All things are lawful for me, but I will not be brought under the power of any. [13]Foods for the stomach and the stomach for foods, but God will destroy both it and them. Now the body *is* not for sexual immorality but for the Lord, and the Lord for the body. [14]And God both raised up the Lord and will also raise us up by His power.

[15]Do you not know that your bodies are members of Christ? Shall I then take the members of Christ and make *them* members of a harlot? Certainly not! [16]Or do you not know that he who is joined to a harlot is one body *with her?* For *"the two,"* He says, *"shall become one flesh."*[a] [17]But he who is joined to the Lord is one spirit *with Him.*

[18]Flee sexual immorality. Every sin that a man does is outside the body, but he who commits sexual immorality sins against his own body. [19]Or do you not know that your body is the temple of the Holy Spirit *who is* in you, whom you have from God, and you are not your own? [20]For you were bought at a price; therefore glorify God in your body[a] and in your spirit, which are God's.

Principles of Marriage

7 Now concerning the things of which you wrote to me:

It is good for a man not to touch a woman. [2]Nevertheless, because of sexual immorality, let each man have his own wife, and let each woman have her own husband. [3]Let the

---

5:7 [a]NU-Text omits *for us.* **5:13** [a]Deuteronomy 17:7; 19:19; 22:21, 24; 24:7 **6:9** [a]That is, catamites **6:16** [a]Genesis 2:24 **6:20** [a]NU-Text ends the verse at *body.*

husband render to his wife the affection due her, and likewise also the wife to her husband. [4]The wife does not have authority over her own body, but the husband *does*. And likewise the husband does not have authority over his own body, but the wife *does*. [5]Do not deprive one another except with consent for a time, that you may give yourselves to fasting and prayer; and come together again so that Satan does not tempt you because of your lack of self-control. [6]But I say this as a concession, not as a commandment. [7]For I wish that all men were even as I myself. But each one has his own gift from God, one in this manner and another in that.

[8]But I say to the unmarried and to the widows: It is good for them if they remain even as I am; [9]but if they cannot exercise self-control, let them marry. For it is better to marry than to burn *with passion*.

Keep Your Marriage Vows

[10]Now to the married I command, *yet* not I but the Lord: A wife is not to depart from *her* husband. [11]But even if she does depart, let her remain unmarried or be reconciled to *her* husband. And a husband is not to divorce *his* wife.

[12]But to the rest I, not the Lord, say: If any brother has a wife who does not believe, and she is willing to live with him, let him not divorce her. [13]And a woman who has a husband who does not believe, if he is willing to live with her, let her not divorce him. [14]For the unbelieving husband is sanctified by the wife, and the unbelieving wife is sanctified by the husband; otherwise your children would be unclean, but now they are holy. [15]But if the unbeliever departs, let him depart; a brother or a sister is not under bondage in such *cases*. But God has called us to peace. [16]For how do you know, O wife, whether you will save *your* husband? Or how do you know, O husband, whether you will save *your* wife?

Live as You Are Called

[17]But as God has distributed to each one, as the Lord has called each one, so let him walk. And so I ordain in all the churches. [18]Was anyone called while circumcised? Let him not become uncircumcised. Was anyone called while uncircumcised? Let him not be circumcised. [19]Circumcision is nothing and uncircumcision is nothing, but keeping the commandments of God *is what matters*. [20]Let each one remain in the same calling in which he was called. [21]Were you called *while* a slave? Do not be concerned about it; but if you can be made free, rather use *it*. [22]For he who is called in the Lord *while* a slave is the Lord's freedman. Likewise he who is called *while* free is Christ's slave. [23]You were bought at a price; do not become slaves of men. [24]Brethren, let each one remain with God in that *state* in which he was called.

To the Unmarried and Widows

[25]Now concerning virgins: I have no commandment from the Lord; yet I give judgment as one whom the Lord in His mercy *has made* trustworthy. [26]I suppose therefore that this is good because of the present distress—that *it is* good for a man to remain as he is: [27]Are you bound to a wife? Do not seek to be loosed. Are you loosed from a wife? Do not seek a wife. [28]But even if you do marry, you have not sinned; and if a virgin marries, she has not sinned. Nevertheless such will have trouble in the flesh, but I would spare you.

[29]But this I say, brethren, the time *is* short, so that from now on even those who have wives should be as though they had none, [30]those who weep as though they did not weep, those who rejoice as though they did not rejoice, those who buy as though they did not possess, [31]and those who use this world as not misusing *it*. For the form of this world is passing away.

[32]But I want you to be without care. He who is unmarried cares for the things of the Lord—how he may please the Lord. [33]But he who is married cares about the things of the world—how he may please *his* wife. [34]There is[a] a difference between a wife and a virgin. The unmarried woman cares about the things of the Lord, that she may be holy both in body and in spirit. But she who is married cares about the things of the world—how she may please *her* husband. [35]And this I say for your own profit, not that I may put a leash on you, but for what is proper, and that you may serve the Lord without distraction.

[36]But if any man thinks he is behaving improperly toward his virgin, if she is past the flower of youth, and thus it must be, let him do what he wishes. He does not sin; let them marry. [37]Nevertheless he who stands steadfast in his heart, having no necessity, but has power over his own will, and has so determined in his heart that he will keep his virgin,[a] does well. [38]So then he who gives *her*[a] in marriage does well, but he who does not give *her* in marriage does better.

[39]A wife is bound by law as long as her husband lives; but if her husband dies, she is at liberty to be married to whom she wishes, only in the Lord. [40]But she is happier if she remains as

---

7:34 [a]M-Text adds *also*. **7:37** [a]Or *virgin daughter*
7:38 [a]NU-Text reads *his own virgin*.

she is, according to my judgment—and I think I also have the Spirit of God.

Be Sensitive to Conscience

8 Now concerning things offered to idols: We know that we all have knowledge. Knowledge puffs up, but love edifies. ²And if anyone thinks that he knows anything, he knows nothing yet as he ought to know. ³But if anyone loves God, this one is known by Him.

⁴Therefore concerning the eating of things offered to idols, we know that an idol *is* nothing in the world, and that *there is* no other God but one. ⁵For even if there are so-called gods, whether in heaven or on earth (as there are many gods and many lords), ⁶yet for us *there is* one God, the Father, of whom *are* all things, and we for Him; and one Lord Jesus Christ, through whom *are* all things, and through whom we *live.*

⁷However, *there is* not in everyone that knowledge; for some, with consciousness of the idol, until now eat *it* as a thing offered to an idol; and their conscience, being weak, is defiled. ⁸But food does not commend us to God; for neither if we eat are we the better, nor if we do not eat are we the worse.

⁹But beware lest somehow this liberty of yours become a stumbling block to those who are weak. ¹⁰For if anyone sees you who have knowledge eating in an idol's temple, will not the conscience of him who is weak be emboldened to eat those things offered to idols? ¹¹And because of your knowledge shall the weak brother perish, for whom Christ died? ¹²But when you thus sin against the brethren, and wound their weak conscience, you sin against Christ. ¹³Therefore, if food makes my brother stumble, I will never again eat meat, lest I make my brother stumble.

A Pattern of Self-Denial

9 Am I not an apostle? Am I not free? Have I not seen Jesus Christ our Lord? Are you not my work in the Lord? ²If I am not an apostle to others, yet doubtless I am to you. For you are the seal of my apostleship in the Lord.

³My defense to those who examine me is this: ⁴Do we have no right to eat and drink? ⁵Do

---

The Law of Sacrifice: What Paul Gave Up

(1 Corinthians 9:5–15)

P aul was a leader who surrendered the rights he could have legally held on to—and this is what made him effective. Consider what this leader gave up:

1. He was a man who gave up his right to a wife (v. 5).
2. He was a soldier who gave up his right to a salary (v. 7).
3. He was a vineyard worker who gave up his right to eat his grapes (v. 7).
4. He was a shepherd who gave up his right to drink the sheep's milk (v. 7).
5. He was an ox who gave up his right to eat grain (vv. 9, 10).
6. He was a plowman who gave up his right to the harvest (v. 10).
7. He was a temple worker who gave up his right to its food (vv. 13, 14).
8. He was a preacher who gave up his right to an offering (vv. 14, 15).

THE LEADERSHIP TRIANGLE

This pyramid diagrams how biblical leadership works. As leaders grow up, they give up options. Contrary to the world's thinking, they willingly surrender their rights when they reach the top.

The Law of Sacrifice: Freedom Plus Responsibility

(1 Corinthians 8:9–13)

T he hot issue in Paul's day was meat sacrificed to idols. Today, it may be personal freedoms such as drinking, clothing fashions, or topics of conversation. Spiritual leaders live free from legalism, but also set aside personal preferences when dealing with a sensitive conscience. Leaders always put others first.

The Law of Intuition: Leaders Read Accurately, Lead Accordingly

(1 Corinthians 9:19–23)

Leaders always read their situation, then lead their situation. Paul refused to cling to his past as a Pharisee or to his rights as an apostle (1 Cor. 9:7–18), but he laid both aside because they often got in the way of leading Gentiles. The goal is always more important than the role.

we have no right to take along a believing wife, as *do* also the other apostles, the brothers of the Lord, and Cephas? ⁶Or *is it* only Barnabas and I *who* have no right to refrain from working? ⁷Who ever goes to war at his own expense? Who plants a vineyard and does not eat of its fruit? Or who tends a flock and does not drink of the milk of the flock?

⁸Do I say these things as a *mere* man? Or does not the law say the same also? ⁹For it is written in the law of Moses, *"You shall not muzzle an ox while it treads out the grain."*ᵃ Is it oxen God is concerned about? ¹⁰Or does He say *it* altogether for our sakes? For our sakes, no doubt, *this* is written, that he who plows should plow in hope, and he who threshes in hope should be partaker of his hope. ¹¹If we have sown spiritual things for you, *is it* a great thing if we reap your material things? ¹²If others are partakers of *this* right over you, *are* we not even more?

Nevertheless we have not used this right, but endure all things lest we hinder the gospel of Christ. ¹³Do you not know that those who minister the holy things eat *of the things* of the temple, and those who serve at the altar partake of *the offerings of* the altar? ¹⁴Even so the Lord has commanded that those who preach the gospel should live from the gospel.

¹⁵But I have used none of these things, nor have I written these things that it should be done so to me; for it *would be* better for me to die than that anyone should make my boasting void. ¹⁶For if I preach the gospel, I have nothing to boast of, for necessity is laid upon me; yes, woe is me if I do not preach the gospel! ¹⁷For if I do this willingly, I have a reward; but if against my will, I have been entrusted with a stewardship. ¹⁸What is my reward then? That when I preach the gospel, I may present the gospel of Christᵃ without charge, that I may not abuse my authority in the gospel.

Serving All Men

¹⁹For though I am free from all *men*, I have made myself a servant to all, that I might win the more; ²⁰and to the Jews I became as a Jew, that I might win Jews; to those *who are* under the law, as under the law,ᵃ that I might win those *who are* under the law; ²¹to those *who are* without law, as without law (not being without law toward God,ᵃ but under law toward Christᵇ), that I might win those *who are* without law; ²²to the weak I became asᵃ weak, that I might win the

9:9 ᵃDeuteronomy 25:4 9:18 ᵃNU-Text omits *of Christ.* 9:20 ᵃNU-Text adds *though not being myself under the law.* 9:21 ᵃNU-Text reads *God's law.* ᵇNU-Text reads *Christ's law.* 9:22 ᵃNU-Text omits *as.*

Passion: Paul's Energy for Serving Others

(1 Corinthians 9:19–27)

Paul was a leader who possessed both passion (1 Cor. 9:19–23) and discipline (9:24–27). The reason? He felt consumed with his mission. Note some truths about his leadership:

1. *Paul's passion exceeded his position* (v. 19).
   His position: I am free from all men. His passion: I have become a slave to all men.
2. *Paul's passion exceeded his personal preferences* (vv. 20–22).
   He insists on fulfilling his mission. Compassion drove him, not compromise.
3. *Paul was high on people, low on procedure* (v. 22).
   Paul knew what was worth dying for and what wasn't. He valued people over procedure.
4. *Paul remained fixed on his mission and flexible in his methods* (v. 23).
   Paul remained flexible because he kept his mission in sharp focus. He committed himself to God and his goal.

weak. I have become all things to all *men*, that I might by all means save some. ²³Now this I do for the gospel's sake, that I may be partaker of it with *you*.

Striving for a Crown

²⁴Do you not know that those who run in a race all run, but one receives the prize? Run in such a way that you may obtain *it*. ²⁵And everyone who competes *for the prize* is temperate in all things. Now they *do it* to obtain a perishable crown, but we *for* an imperishable *crown*. ²⁶Therefore I run thus: not with uncertainty. Thus I fight: not as *one who* beats the air. ²⁷But I discipline my body and bring *it* into subjection, lest, when I have preached to others, I myself should become disqualified.

Self-Discipline: Running for Eternal Rewards

(1 Corinthians 9:24–27)

Paul, the leader, challenges his readers to run the Christian life with focus (1 Cor. 9:24), train (9:25), compete with passion (9:26), fight with purpose (9:26) and master their flesh (9:27). Paul asks, If athletes work to get a trophy, why not we who receive eternal rewards?

Old Testament Examples

10 Moreover, brethren, I do not want you to be unaware that all our fathers were under the cloud, all passed through the sea, ²all were baptized into Moses in the cloud and in the sea, ³all ate the same spiritual food, ⁴and all drank the same spiritual drink. For they drank of that spiritual Rock that followed them, and that Rock was Christ. ⁵But with most of them God was not well pleased, for *their bodies* were scattered in the wilderness.

⁶Now these things became our examples, to the intent that we should not lust after evil things as they also lusted. ⁷And do not become idolaters *as were* some of them. As it is written, "The people sat down to eat and drink, and rose up to play."ᵃ ⁸Nor let us commit sexual immorality, as some of them did, and in one day twenty-three thousand fell; ⁹nor let us tempt Christ, as some of them also tempted, and were

destroyed by serpents; ¹⁰nor complain, as some of them also complained, and were destroyed by the destroyer. ¹¹Now allᵃ these things happened to them as examples, and they were written for our admonition, upon whom the ends of the ages have come.

¹²Therefore let him who thinks he stands take heed lest he fall. ¹³No temptation has overtaken you except such as is common to man; but God *is* faithful, who will not allow you to be tempted beyond what you are able, but with the temptation will also make the way of escape, that you may be able to bear *it*.

Teachability: Leaders Learn from the Past

(1 Corinthians 10:1–13)

Paul reminds us of Israel's patriarchs, whose disobedience forced them to wander through the wilderness for 40 years. The first generation had the opportunity to enter the Promised Land (1 Cor. 10:1–5), but never made it. These things were recorded as examples for us! We are to remain teachable and learn from the past.

Flee from Idolatry

¹⁴Therefore, my beloved, flee from idolatry. ¹⁵I speak as to wise men; judge for yourselves what I say. ¹⁶The cup of blessing which we bless, is it not the communion of the blood of Christ? The bread which we break, is it not the communion of the body of Christ? ¹⁷For we, *though* many, are one bread *and* one body; for we all partake of that one bread.

¹⁸Observe Israel after the flesh: Are not those who eat of the sacrifices partakers of the altar? ¹⁹What am I saying then? That an idol is anything, or what is offered to idols is anything? ²⁰Rather, that the things which the Gentiles sacrifice they sacrifice to demons and not to God, and I do not want you to have fellowship with demons. ²¹You cannot drink the cup of the Lord and the cup of demons; you cannot partake of the Lord's table and of the table of demons. ²²Or do we provoke the Lord to jealousy? Are we stronger than He?

10:7 ᵃExodus 32:6 **10:11** ᵃNU-Text omits *all*.

All to the Glory of God

[23]All things are lawful for me,[a] but not all things are helpful; all things are lawful for me,[b] but not all things edify. [24]Let no one seek his own, but each one the other's *well-being.*

[25]Eat whatever is sold in the meat market, asking no questions for conscience' sake; [26]for *"the earth is the LORD's, and all its fullness."*[a]

[27]If any of those who do not believe invites you *to dinner,* and you desire to go, eat whatever is set before you, asking no question for conscience' sake. [28]But if anyone says to you, "This was offered to idols," do not eat it for the sake of the one who told you, and for conscience' sake;[a] for *"the earth is the LORD's, and all its fullness."*[b] [29]"Conscience," I say, not your own, but that of the other. For why is my liberty judged by another *man's* conscience? [30]But if I partake with thanks, why am I evil spoken of for *the food* over which I give thanks?

[31]Therefore, whether you eat or drink, or whatever you do, do all to the glory of God. [32]Give no offense, either to the Jews or to the Greeks or to the church of God, [33]just as I also please all *men* in all *things,* not seeking my own profit, but the *profit* of many, that they may be saved.

11

Imitate me, just as I also *imitate* Christ.

Head Coverings

[2]Now I praise you, brethren, that you remember me in all things and keep the traditions just as I delivered *them* to you. [3]But I want you to know that the head of every man is Christ, the head of woman *is* man, and the head of Christ *is* God. [4]Every man praying or prophesying, having *his* head covered, dishonors his head. [5]But every woman who prays or prophesies with *her* head uncovered dishonors her head, for that is one and the same as if her head were shaved. [6]For if a woman is not covered, let her also be shorn. But if it is shameful for a woman to be shorn or shaved, let her be covered. [7]For a man indeed ought not to cover *his* head, since he is the image and glory of God; but woman is the glory of man. [8]For man is not from woman, but woman from man. [9]Nor was man created for the woman, but woman for the man. [10]For this reason the woman ought to have *a symbol of* authority on *her* head, because of the angels. [11]Nevertheless, neither *is* man independent of woman, nor woman independent of man, in the Lord. [12]For as woman *came* from man, even so man also *comes* through woman; but all things are from God.

[13]Judge among yourselves. Is it proper for a woman to pray to God with her head uncovered? [14]Does not even nature itself teach you that if a man has long hair, it is a dishonor to him? [15]But if a woman has long hair, it is a glory to

10:23 [a]NU-Text omits *for me.* [b]NU-Text omits *for me.* **10:26** [a]Psalm 24:1 **10:28** [a]NU-Text omits the rest of this verse. [b]Psalm 24:1

Decision Making in the Gray Areas

(1 Corinthians 10:24–33)

Leaders regularly face choices that affect not only their own lives, but many others. What's more, many of these decisions have no clear answer; they do not appear black and white, but gray. So how does a leader make good decisions in the gray areas? Paul describes a system for making tough decisions:

1. *Prioritize God's people (vv. 24–30).*

   Put others first. The term *others* describes a person unlike you, one with whom you are likely to disagree. Leaders must choose what is best for others, not what appeals to their own tastes. Ask yourself: Who will benefit most from this decision, me or others?

2. *Pursue God's glory (v. 31).*

   Does the decision glorify God or someone else? Paul would agree with the shorter catechism: The chief end of man is to glorify God and to enjoy Him forever. Ask yourself: Does this decision give people a better picture of who God is?

3. *Perceive God's purpose (vv. 32, 33).*

   The ultimate purpose for our being on earth is to bring others to Christ. We must always move toward fulfilling this mission. Ask yourself: Will this decision please God and fulfill His purposes?

her; for *her* hair is given to her[a] for a covering. [16]But if anyone seems to be contentious, we have no such custom, nor *do* the churches of God.

Conduct at the Lord's Supper

[17]Now in giving these instructions I do not praise *you,* since you come together not for the better but for the worse. [18]For first of all, when you come together as a church, I hear that there are divisions among you, and in part I believe it. [19]For there must also be factions among you, that those who are approved may be recognized among you. [20]Therefore when you come together in one place, it is not to eat the Lord's Supper. [21]For in eating, each one takes his own supper ahead of *others;* and one is hungry and another is drunk. [22]What! Do you not have houses to eat and drink in? Or do you despise the church of God and shame those who have nothing? What shall I say to you? Shall I praise you in this? I do not praise *you.*

Institution of the Lord's Supper

[23]For I received from the Lord that which I also delivered to you: that the Lord Jesus on the *same* night in which He was betrayed took bread; [24]and when He had given thanks, He broke *it* and said, "Take, eat;[a] this is My body which is broken[b] for you; do this in remembrance of Me." [25]In the same manner *He* also *took* the cup after supper, saying, "This cup is the new covenant in My blood. This do, as often as you drink *it,* in remembrance of Me."

[26]For as often as you eat this bread and drink this cup, you proclaim the Lord's death till He comes.

Examine Yourself

[27]Therefore whoever eats this bread or drinks *this* cup of the Lord in an unworthy manner will be guilty of the body and blood[a] of the Lord. [28]But let a man examine himself, and so let him eat of the bread and drink of the cup. [29]For he who eats and drinks in an unworthy manner[a] eats and drinks judgment to himself, not discerning the Lord's[b] body. [30]For this reason many *are* weak and sick among you, and many sleep. [31]For if we would judge ourselves, we would not be judged. [32]But when we are judged, we are chastened by the Lord, that we may not be condemned with the world.

[33]Therefore, my brethren, when you come together to eat, wait for one another. [34]But if anyone is hungry, let him eat at home, lest you come together for judgment. And the rest I will set in order when I come.

Spiritual Gifts: Unity in Diversity

12 Now concerning spiritual *gifts,* brethren, I do not want you to be ignorant: [2]You know that[a] you were Gentiles, carried away to these dumb idols, however you were led. [3]Therefore I make known to you that no one speaking by the Spirit of God calls Jesus accursed, and no one can say that Jesus is Lord except by the Holy Spirit.

[4]There are diversities of gifts, but the same Spirit. [5]There are differences of ministries, but the same Lord. [6]And there are diversities of activities, but it is the same God who works all in all. [7]But the manifestation of the Spirit is given to each one for the profit *of all:* [8]for to one is given the word of wisdom through the Spirit, to another the word of knowledge through the same Spirit, [9]to another faith by the same Spirit, to another gifts of healings by the same[a] Spirit, [10]to another the working of miracles, to another prophecy, to another discerning of spirits, to another *different* kinds of tongues, to another the interpretation of tongues. [11]But one and the same Spirit works all these things, distributing to each one individually as He wills.

Unity and Diversity in One Body

[12]For as the body is one and has many members, but all the members of that one body, being many, are one body, so also *is* Christ. [13]For by one Spirit we were all baptized into one body—whether Jews or Greeks, whether slaves or free—and have all been made to drink into[a] one Spirit. [14]For in fact the body is not one member but many.

[15]If the foot should say, "Because I am not a hand, I am not of the body," is it therefore not of the body? [16]And if the ear should say, "Because I am not an eye, I am not of the body," is it therefore not of the body? [17]If the whole body *were* an eye, where *would be* the hearing? If the whole *were* hearing, where *would be* the smelling? [18]But now God has set the members, each one of them, in the body just as He pleased. [19]And if they *were* all one member, where *would* the body *be?*

[20]But now indeed *there are* many members, yet one body. [21]And the eye cannot say to the

---

11:15 [a]M-Text omits *to her.* **11:24** [a]NU-Text omits *Take, eat.* [b]NU-Text omits *broken.* **11:27** [a]NU-Text and M-Text read *the blood.* **11:29** [a]NU-Text omits *in an unworthy manner.* [b]NU-Text omits *Lord's.*
12:2 [a]NU-Text and M-Text add *when.*
12:9 [a]NU-Text reads *one.* **12:13** [a]NU-Text omits *into.*

Team Building: Leaders Are Brokers of Gifts

(1 Corinthians 12:4–31)

Leaders aren't supposed to do all the work of the church, but are to effectively broker the talent on their team. Good teams use every gift and enjoy both unity and diversity. Consider Paul's philosophy of team building:

1. The team possesses a variety of gifts or positions, but pursues the same goal and God (vv. 4–6).
2. Everyone has a contribution to make which benefits the team (v. 7).
3. God is the source of each gift, so He deserves the glory (vv. 8–10).
4. God chooses who has what gifts, so we must not compete or compare (v. 11).
5. Team members are to function like the organs and muscles in a body (vv. 12–14).
6. No team member is less important than another; all are necessary (vv. 15–21).
7. Sometimes, the players who seem less important are actually more important (vv. 22–24).
8. God's goal is team harmony and mutual care (vv. 25, 26).
9. Although members are equally important, they are meant to be diverse (vv. 27, 28).
10. We should not compete with each other, but complete each other (vv. 29–31).

hand, "I have no need of you"; nor again the head to the feet, "I have no need of you." ²²No, much rather, those members of the body which seem to be weaker are necessary. ²³And those *members* of the body which we think to be less honorable, on these we bestow greater honor; and our unpresentable *parts* have greater modesty, ²⁴but our presentable *parts* have no need. But God composed the body, having given greater honor to that *part* which lacks it, ²⁵that there should be no schism in the body, but *that* the members should have the same care for one another. ²⁶And if one member suffers, all the members suffer with *it;* or if one member is honored, all the members rejoice with *it.*

²⁷Now you are the body of Christ, and members individually. ²⁸And God has appointed these in the church: first apostles, second prophets, third teachers, after that miracles, then gifts of healings, helps, administrations, varieties of tongues. ²⁹*Are* all apostles? *Are* all prophets? *Are* all teachers? *Are* all workers of miracles? ³⁰Do all have gifts of healings? Do all speak with tongues? Do all interpret? ³¹But earnestly desire the best[a] gifts. And yet I show you a more excellent way.

The Greatest Gift

13 Though I speak with the tongues of men and of angels, but have not love, I have become sounding brass or a clanging cymbal. ²And though I have *the gift of* prophecy, and understand all mysteries and all knowledge, and though I have all faith, so that I could remove mountains, but have not love, I am nothing. ³And though I bestow all my goods to feed *the poor,* and though I give my body to be burned,[a] but have not love, it profits me nothing.

⁴Love suffers long *and* is kind; love does not envy; love does not parade itself, is not puffed up; ⁵does not behave rudely, does not seek its own, is not provoked, thinks no evil; ⁶does not rejoice in iniquity, but rejoices in the truth; ⁷bears all

Leaders Who Celebrate Diversity Accomplish More

(1 Corinthians 12:14–31)

Leaders must build a team spirit that celebrates diversity. Teams must share a common goal, but not the same gifts. Teams mature when the leader insists on diversity and celebrates what everyone does together. Former UCLA basketball coach John Wooden said, "Individuals win trophies, but teams win championships."

12:31 [a]NU-Text reads *greater.* **13:3** [a]NU-Text reads *so I may boast.*

Love: The Foundation for Every Act of a Leader

(1 Corinthians 13:4–7)

Have you ever pondered why Paul took an entire chapter of the Bible to discuss the supremacy of love?

In the early church, leaders modeled love to their churches. In turn, the churches modeled it to the rest of the world. They lived by the watchwords in 1 Corinthians 13:4–7. Love was the foundation and motive for the leaders' actions. They were first love-slaves and served the people. While leaders indeed possessed great gifts, their gifts took second place to serving others out of love. Consider how the early leaders lived out this passage:

1. Timothy and Erastus served the church and Paul (Acts 19:22).
2. Phoebe served the church in Cenchrea (Rom. 16:1).
3. Aquila and Priscilla risked death to serve Paul and the Gentiles (Rom. 16:3, 4).
4. Stephanas's family devoted themselves to serving the saints (1 Cor. 16:15).
5. The apostles served the Corinthian church (2 Cor. 3:3).
6. Titus served the church in Corinth (2 Cor. 8:16, 17).
7. Paul ministered to the needs of the saints at Jerusalem (2 Cor. 8:18, 19).
8. Epaphroditus served Paul in prison (Phil. 2:25–30).
9. Epaphras served the Colossian church (Col. 1:7).
10. Onesiphorus served Paul in Ephesus (2 Tim. 1:16–18).

things, believes all things, hopes all things, endures all things.

[8]Love never fails. But whether *there are* prophecies, they will fail; whether *there are* tongues, they will cease; whether *there is* knowledge, it will vanish away. [9]For we know in part and we prophesy in part. [10]But when that which is perfect has come, then that which is in part will be done away.

[11]When I was a child, I spoke as a child, I understood as a child, I thought as a child; but when I became a man, I put away childish things. [12]For now we see in a mirror, dimly, but then face to face. Now I know in part, but then I shall know just as I also am known.

[13]And now abide faith, hope, love, these three; but the greatest of these *is* love.

Prophecy and Tongues

14 Pursue love, and desire spiritual *gifts,* but especially that you may prophesy. [2]For he who speaks in a tongue does not speak to men but to God, for no one understands *him;* however, in the spirit he speaks mysteries. [3]But he who prophesies speaks edification and exhortation and comfort to men. [4]He who speaks in a tongue edifies himself, but he who prophesies edifies the church. [5]I wish you all spoke with tongues, but even more that you

prophesied; for[a] he who prophesies *is* greater than he who speaks with tongues, unless indeed he interprets, that the church may receive edification.

Tongues Must Be Interpreted

[6]But now, brethren, if I come to you speaking with tongues, what shall I profit you unless I speak to you either by revelation, by knowledge, by prophesying, or by teaching? [7]Even things without life, whether flute or harp, when they make a sound, unless they make a distinction in the sounds, how will it be known what is piped or played? [8]For if the trumpet makes an uncertain sound, who will prepare for battle? [9]So likewise you, unless you utter by the tongue words easy to understand, how will it be known what is spoken? For you will be speaking into the air. [10]There are, it may be, so many kinds of languages in the world, and none of them *is* without significance. [11]Therefore, if I do not know the meaning of the language, I shall be a foreigner to him who speaks, and he who speaks *will be* a foreigner to me. [12]Even so you, since you are zealous for spiritual *gifts, let it be* for the edification of the church *that* you seek to excel.

[13]Therefore let him who speaks in a tongue pray that he may interpret. [14]For if I pray in a

14:5 [a]NU-Text reads *and.*

tongue, my spirit prays, but my understanding is unfruitful. [15]What is *the conclusion* then? I will pray with the spirit, and I will also pray with the understanding. I will sing with the spirit, and I will also sing with the understanding. [16]Otherwise, if you bless with the spirit, how will he who occupies the place of the uninformed say "Amen" at your giving of thanks, since he does not understand what you say? [17]For you indeed give thanks well, but the other is not edified.

[18]I thank my God I speak with tongues more than you all; [19]yet in the church I would rather speak five words with my understanding, that I may teach others also, than ten thousand words in a tongue.

Tongues a Sign to Unbelievers

[20]Brethren, do not be children in understanding; however, in malice be babes, but in understanding be mature. [21]In the law it is written:

> "With men of other tongues and other lips
> I will speak to this people;
> And yet, for all that, they will not hear Me,"[a]

says the Lord.

[22]Therefore tongues are for a sign, not to those who believe but to unbelievers; but prophesying is not for unbelievers but for those who believe. [23]Therefore if the whole church comes together in one place, and all speak with tongues, and there come in *those who are* uninformed or unbelievers, will they not say that you are out of your mind? [24]But if all prophesy, and an unbeliever or an uninformed person comes in, he is convinced by all, he is convicted by all. [25]And thus[a] the secrets of his heart are revealed; and so, falling down on *his* face, he will worship God and report that God is truly among you.

Order in Church Meetings

[26]How is it then, brethren? Whenever you come together, each of you has a psalm, has a teaching, has a tongue, has a revelation, has an interpretation. Let all things be done for edification. [27]If anyone speaks in a tongue, *let there be* two or at the most three, *each* in turn, and let one interpret. [28]But if there is no interpreter, let him keep silent in church, and let him speak to himself and to God. [29]Let two or three prophets speak, and let the others judge. [30]But if *anything* is revealed to another who sits by, let the first keep silent. [31]For you can all prophesy one by one, that all may learn and all may be encouraged. [32]And the spirits of the prophets are subject to the

---

Organization: Leaders Organize So They Don't Have to Agonize

(1 Corinthians 14:1–40)

Paul wrote to bring order to a church in chaos. The Corinthians were abusing their gifts and calling attention to themselves rather than to Christ. As a leader, Paul had to change this. In fact, 1 Corinthians 14:40 urges them to do everything "decently and in order." What can we learn about organization from this chapter?

1. Identify and pursue your top priorities (v. 1).
2. Seek to practice what will benefit the most people (vv. 2–12).
3. Communicate clearly (vv. 7, 8).
4. See things through the eyes of the outsider (vv. 23–25).
5. Order activities simply for the purpose of adding value to others (vv. 26–33).
6. Make sure everything is done in an appropriate manner (v. 40).

---

prophets. [33]For God is not *the author* of confusion but of peace, as in all the churches of the saints.

[34]Let your[a] women keep silent in the churches, for they are not permitted to speak; but *they are* to be submissive, as the law also says. [35]And if they want to learn something, let them ask their own husbands at home; for it is shameful for women to speak in church.

[36]Or did the word of God come *originally* from you? Or *was it* you only that it reached? [37]If anyone thinks himself to be a prophet or spiritual, let him acknowledge that the things which I write to you are the commandments of the Lord. [38]But if anyone is ignorant, let him be ignorant.[a]

[39]Therefore, brethren, desire earnestly to prophesy, and do not forbid to speak with tongues. [40]Let all things be done decently and in order.

14:21 [a]Isaiah 28:11, 12　**14:25** [a]NU-Text omits *And thus.*　**14:34** [a]NU-Text omits *your.*　**14:38** [a]NU-Text reads *if anyone does not recognize this, he is not recognized.*

The Risen Christ, Faith's Reality

15 Moreover, brethren, I declare to you the gospel which I preached to you, which also you received and in which you stand, [2]by which also you are saved, if you hold fast that word which I preached to you—unless you believed in vain.

[3]For I delivered to you first of all that which I also received: that Christ died for our sins according to the Scriptures, [4]and that He was buried, and that He rose again the third day according to the Scriptures, [5]and that He was seen by Cephas, then by the twelve. [6]After that He was seen by over five hundred brethren at once, of whom the greater part remain to the present, but some have fallen asleep. [7]After that He was seen by James, then by all the apostles. [8]Then last of all He was seen by me also, as by one born out of due time.

[9]For I am the least of the apostles, who am not worthy to be called an apostle, because I persecuted the church of God. [10]But by the grace of God I am what I am, and His grace toward me was not in vain; but I labored more abundantly than they all, yet not I, but the grace of God *which was* with me. [11]Therefore, whether *it was* I or they, so we preach and so you believed.

The Law of Victory: Paul Closes with Hope and Victory

(1 Corinthians 15:1–9, 57, 58)

Like any good leader, Paul closes his letter by reminding his friends of the absolute victory of their cause. Paul fuels their convictions to stay the course and fulfill their mission (1 Cor. 15:57, 58). Leaders find a way for the team to win, then use past victories to build future ones.

The Risen Christ, Our Hope

[12]Now if Christ is preached that He has been raised from the dead, how do some among you say that there is no resurrection of the dead? [13]But if there is no resurrection of the dead, then Christ is not risen. [14]And if Christ is not risen, then our preaching *is* empty and your faith *is* also empty. [15]Yes, and we are found false witnesses of God, because we have testified of God that He raised up Christ, whom He did not raise up—if in fact the dead do not rise. [16]For if *the* dead do not rise, then Christ is not risen. [17]And if Christ is not risen, your faith *is* futile; you are still in your sins! [18]Then also those who have fallen asleep in Christ have perished. [19]If in this life only we have hope in Christ, we are of all men the most pitiable.

The Last Enemy Destroyed

[20]But now Christ is risen from the dead, *and* has become the firstfruits of those who have fallen asleep. [21]For since by man *came* death, by Man also *came* the resurrection of the dead. [22]For as in Adam all die, even so in Christ all shall be made alive. [23]But each one in his own order: Christ the firstfruits, afterward those *who are* Christ's at His coming. [24]Then *comes* the end, when He delivers the kingdom to God the Father, when He puts an end to all rule and all authority and power. [25]For He must reign till He has put all enemies under His feet. [26]The last enemy *that* will be destroyed *is* death. [27]For *"He has put all things under His feet."*[a] But when He says "all things are put under *Him*," *it is* evident that He who put all things under Him is excepted. [28]Now when all things are made subject to Him, then the Son Himself will also be subject to Him who put all things under Him, that God may be all in all.

Effects of Denying the Resurrection

[29]Otherwise, what will they do who are baptized for the dead, if the dead do not rise at all? Why then are they baptized for the dead? [30]And why do we stand in jeopardy every hour? [31]I affirm, by the boasting in you which I have in Christ Jesus our Lord, I die daily. [32]If, in the manner of men, I have fought with beasts at Ephesus, what advantage *is it* to me? If *the* dead do not rise, *"Let us eat and drink, for tomorrow we die!"*[a]

[33]Do not be deceived: "Evil company corrupts good habits." [34]Awake to righteousness, and do not sin; for some do not have the knowledge of God. I speak *this* to your shame.

A Glorious Body

[35]But someone will say, "How are the dead raised up? And with what body do they come?" [36]Foolish one, what you sow is not made alive unless it dies. [37]And what you sow, you do not sow that body that shall be, but mere grain—perhaps wheat or some other *grain*. [38]But God gives

---

15:27 [a]Psalm 8:6 **15:32** [a]Isaiah 22:13

it a body as He pleases, and to each seed its own body.

[39]All flesh *is* not the same flesh, but *there is* one *kind of* flesh[a] of men, another flesh of animals, another of fish, *and* another of birds.

[40]*There are* also celestial bodies and terrestrial bodies; but the glory of the celestial *is* one, and the *glory* of the terrestrial *is* another. [41]*There is* one glory of the sun, another glory of the moon, and another glory of the stars; for *one* star differs from *another* star in glory.

[42]So also *is* the resurrection of the dead. *The body* is sown in corruption, it is raised in incorruption. [43]It is sown in dishonor, it is raised in glory. It is sown in weakness, it is raised in power. [44]It is sown a natural body, it is raised a spiritual body. There is a natural body, and there is a spiritual body. [45]And so it is written, *"The first man Adam became a living being."*[a] The last Adam *became* a life-giving spirit.

[46]However, the spiritual is not first, but the natural, and afterward the spiritual. [47]The first man *was* of the earth, *made* of dust; the second Man *is* the Lord[a] from heaven. [48]As *was* the *man* of dust, so also *are* those *who are made* of dust; and as *is* the heavenly *Man,* so also *are* those *who are* heavenly. [49]And as we have borne the image of the *man* of dust, we shall also bear[a] the image of the heavenly *Man.*

Our Final Victory

[50]Now this I say, brethren, that flesh and blood cannot inherit the kingdom of God; nor does corruption inherit incorruption. [51]Behold, I tell you a mystery: We shall not all sleep, but we shall all be changed— [52]in a moment, in the twinkling of an eye, at the last trumpet. For the trumpet will sound, and the dead will be raised incorruptible, and we shall be changed. [53]For this corruptible must put on incorruption, and this mortal *must* put on immortality. [54]So when this corruptible has put on incorruption, and this mortal has put on immortality, then shall be brought to pass the saying that is written: *"Death is swallowed up in victory."*[a]

[55]   *"O Death, where is your sting?*[a]
        O Hades, where is your victory?"[b]

[56]The sting of death *is* sin, and the strength of sin *is* the law. [57]But thanks *be* to God, who gives us the victory through our Lord Jesus Christ.

[58]Therefore, my beloved brethren, be steadfast, immovable, always abounding in the work of the Lord, knowing that your labor is not in vain in the Lord.

Collection for the Saints

16 Now concerning the collection for the saints, as I have given orders to the churches of Galatia, so you must do also: [2]On the first *day* of the week let each one of you lay something aside, storing up as he may prosper, that there be no collections when I come. [3]And when I come, whomever you approve by *your* letters I will send to bear your gift to Jerusalem. [4]But if it is fitting that I go also, they will go with me.

Personal Plans

[5]Now I will come to you when I pass through Macedonia (for I am passing through Macedonia). [6]And it may be that I will remain, or even spend the winter with you, that you may send me on my journey, wherever I go. [7]For I do

---

15:39 [a]NU-Text and M-Text omit *of flesh.*
15:45 [a]Genesis 2:7 **15:47** [a]NU-Text omits *the Lord.*
15:49 [a]M-Text reads *let us also bear.* **15:54** [a]Isaiah 25:8 **15:55** [a]Hosea 13:14 [b]NU-Text reads *O Death, where is your victory? O Death, where is your sting?*

The Law of Navigation: The Strategy to Reach Asia Minor

(1 Corinthians 16:5–9)

Paul had a plan to reach the major cities of his day. In a conversational manner, he describes his plan to start in Macedonia, then move south to Corinth, and finally visit Asia Minor and the major port city of Ephesus, where "a great and effective door [was] opened" to him (1 Cor. 16:9).

Effective leaders don't drift from one place to another. Paul had a divine plan to impact major cities that would in turn influence those who visited these cities. He focused on the large metropolitan areas, knowing that well-trained followers would bring God's message to the smaller towns and villages in the region.

Leaders can do anything, but they can't do everything. Paul did not spend his energies haphazardly, but charted the course to reach the Roman Empire in his lifetime.

What kind of plan do you have?

not wish to see you now on the way; but I hope to stay a while with you, if the Lord permits.

[8]But I will tarry in Ephesus until Pentecost. [9]For a great and effective door has opened to me, and *there are* many adversaries.

[10]And if Timothy comes, see that he may be with you without fear; for he does the work of the Lord, as I also *do.* [11]Therefore let no one despise him. But send him on his journey in peace, that he may come to me; for I am waiting for him with the brethren.

[12]Now concerning *our* brother Apollos, I strongly urged him to come to you with the brethren, but he was quite unwilling to come at this time; however, he will come when he has a convenient time.

Final Exhortations

[13]Watch, stand fast in the faith, be brave, be strong. [14]Let all *that* you *do* be done with love.

[15]I urge you, brethren—you know the household of Stephanas, that it is the firstfruits of Achaia, and *that* they have devoted themselves to the ministry of the saints— [16]that you also submit to such, and to everyone who works and labors with *us.*

[17]I am glad about the coming of Stephanas, Fortunatus, and Achaicus, for what was lacking on your part they supplied. [18]For they refreshed my spirit and yours. Therefore acknowledge such men.

Greetings and a Solemn Farewell

[19]The churches of Asia greet you. Aquila and Priscilla greet you heartily in the Lord, with the church that is in their house. [20]All the brethren greet you.

Greet one another with a holy kiss.

[21]The salutation with my own hand—Paul's.

[22]If anyone does not love the Lord Jesus Christ, let him be accursed.[a] O Lord, come![b]

[23]The grace of our Lord Jesus Christ *be* with you. [24]My love *be* with you all in Christ Jesus. Amen.

16:22 [a]Greek *anathema* [b]Aramaic *Maranatha*

2 CORINTHIANS
Leadership Amidst a Difficult Situation

SUMMARY

Like its counterpart, 1 Corinthians, this letter was written by the apostle Paul to the believers in Corinth, a strategic port city with great influence and exposure to the rest of the Roman Empire. The fact that Paul selected Corinth as a site for a church plant shows his leadership intuition. Cities like Corinth, Ephesus, Athens, and Rome all provided great exposure for a new movement.

Scholars believe the Book of 2 Corinthians was actually Paul's fourth letter to the church. The letter provides a marvelous case study of leadership amidst a difficult situation. For a moment, step into Paul's sandals and try to feel what he faced.

First, he had to defend his leadership and authority in the face of false teachers who undermined his leadership. If you've led anything, you know this is a tough call to make. How much should you defend yourself? When does it become too much so that people think you're simply projecting your self-worth?

Second, the church was fragmenting and dividing over personalities and theological issues. The church in Corinth gave Paul one of his greatest challenges. Its members were spiritually immature and carnal (3:1–3). Paul made a valiant effort to bring the people together and produce a culture of cooperation. In the process, he teaches us how leaders must take responsibility to foster an environment of teamwork and unity.

Third, the Corinthians struggled with moral compromise and upholding basic behavioral standards. Even the leaders looked out for themselves and failed to catch any vision for leadership. Paul had to correct immorality, idolatry, and carnality. He wanted to receive an offering for the church in Jerusalem, but he realized he first had to offer a theological discourse on the benefits of giving.

Second Corinthians is the most personal of all of Paul's church letters. Like an outraged father, he pleads, rebukes, and weeps with the people, sharing his heart and vision for their future.

God's Role in 2 Corinthians

God must have approved of Paul's defense of his leadership and his argument that he did not receive his power from man, but from the Lord. God gave Paul the strength and the language to articulate some of the most difficult claims any leader will have to communicate. God furnishes Paul with the power to argue and defend himself; the power to correct laxity among the Corinthians; and the power to persuade the people to repent of their selfishness.

Leaders in 2 Corinthians

Paul, the Corinthian church leaders, Titus

Other People of Influence in 2 Corinthians

False apostles (teachers)

Lessons in Leadership

- When defending your leadership, check your motives; pure motives are essential.

- When followers doubt your authority and direction, always go back to the basics.

- If you lead with a clear conscience, you can defend your actions with deep passion.

- There is no success without sacrifice.

- It is easier to follow a leader who acknowledges he/she is following God.

- When all else fails, remember the original vision God gave you.

- Leaders should invest in people like a farmer plants seed—with expectancy.

LEADERSHIP

HIGHLIGHTS IN 2 CORINTHIANS

Greeting

1 Paul, an apostle of Jesus Christ by the will of God, and Timothy *our* brother,

To the church of God which is at Corinth, with all the saints who are in all Achaia:

[2]Grace to you and peace from God our Father and the Lord Jesus Christ.

Comfort in Suffering

[3]Blessed *be* the God and Father of our Lord Jesus Christ, the Father of mercies and God of all comfort, [4]who comforts us in all our tribulation, that we may be able to comfort those who are in any trouble, with the comfort with which we ourselves are comforted by God. [5]For as the sufferings of Christ abound in us, so our consolation also abounds through Christ. [6]Now if we are afflicted, *it is* for your consolation and salvation, which is effective for enduring the same sufferings which we also suffer. Or if we are comforted, *it is* for your consolation and salvation. [7]And our hope for you *is* steadfast, because we know that as you are partakers of the sufferings, so also *you will partake* of the consolation.

Delivered from Suffering

[8]For we do not want you to be ignorant, brethren, of our trouble which came to us in Asia: that we were burdened beyond measure, above strength, so that we despaired even of life. [9]Yes, we had the sentence of death in ourselves, that we should not trust in ourselves but in God who raises the dead, [10]who delivered us from so great a death, and does[a] deliver us; in whom we trust that He will still deliver *us,* [11]you also helping together in prayer for us, that thanks may be given by many persons on our[a] behalf for the gift *granted* to us through many.

Paul's Sincerity

[12]For our boasting is this: the testimony of our conscience that we conducted ourselves in the world in simplicity and godly sincerity, not

---

1:10 [a]NU-Text reads *shall.* **1:11** [a]M-Text reads *your behalf.*

The Law of Empowerment:
Our Comfort Allows Us to Comfort Others
(2 Corinthians 1:2–4)

God promises to comfort us in our troubles, then asks us to share that comfort with others. Remember, we can't give away what we don't possess. We are to pass on what God gives to us. We don't receive as an end in itself, but as a means to an end. We are to empower others with the power God gives us. Leaders who empower others offer these gifts:

1. *Accountability*
   They help others keep their commitments to God.
2. *Affirmation*
   They speak words of support and encouragement.
3. *Assessment*
   They evaluate others' progress, offering an objective perspective.
4. *Advice*
   They offer words of wise counsel and direction.
5. *Admonishment*
   They lend words of caution, rebuke, or correction.
6. *Assets*
   They give tangible resources to help their people reach their goals.
7. *Acceptance*
   They provide unconditional love, regardless of the recipients' identity.
8. *Application*
   They help others find places to apply and practice what they learn.

Communication: When Plans Change, Leaders Overcommunicate

(2 Corinthians 1:12–17)

When Paul had to change his travel plans, some of the Corinthians used it against him, accusing him of indecision and weakness. This would not have bothered Paul, except that it affected people's view of his message; they considered it fickle, as well. To explain his position, Paul openly communicated with the church, explaining his change of plans.

Paul knew leaders must be flexible, not fickle. Yet when plans change, people need more communication. Leaders maintain integrity when they overcommunicate and calmly assure their people that they are still making progress.

with fleshly wisdom but by the grace of God, and more abundantly toward you. ¹³For we are not writing any other things to you than what you read or understand. Now I trust you will understand, even to the end ¹⁴(as also you have understood us in part), that we are your boast as you also *are* ours, in the day of the Lord Jesus.

Sparing the Church

¹⁵And in this confidence I intended to come to you before, that you might have a second benefit— ¹⁶to pass by way of you to Macedonia, to come again from Macedonia to you, and be helped by you on my way to Judea. ¹⁷Therefore, when I was planning this, did I do it lightly? Or the things I plan, do I plan according to the flesh, that with me there should be Yes, Yes, and No, No? ¹⁸But *as* God *is* faithful, our word to you was not Yes and No. ¹⁹For the Son of God, Jesus Christ, who was preached among you by us—by me, Silvanus, and Timothy—was not Yes and No, but in Him was Yes. ²⁰For all the promises of God in Him *are* Yes, and in Him Amen, to the glory of God through us. ²¹Now He who establishes us with you in Christ and has anointed us *is* God, ²²who also has sealed us and given us the Spirit in our hearts as a guarantee.

²³Moreover I call God as witness against my soul, that to spare you I came no more to Corinth. ²⁴Not that we have dominion over your faith, but are fellow workers for your joy; for by faith you stand.

2 But I determined this within myself, that I would not come again to you in sorrow. ²For if I make you sorrowful, then who is he who makes me glad but the one who is made sorrowful by me?

Forgive the Offender

³And I wrote this very thing to you, lest, when I came, I should have sorrow over those from whom I ought to have joy, having confi-

Follow-Up and Confrontation

(2 Corinthians 2:6–8)

It has been said that 2 Corinthians was written with a pen dipped in tears. In chapter 2, Paul has to follow up on the confrontation he first brought up in 1 Corinthians 5. The church had responded well to his advice, and now Paul encourages them to reaffirm their love for their erring brother (2 Cor. 2:6–8).

Paul knew that follow-up has to take place after confrontation. The organization and leadership must live up to their values. When the confrontation is done well, the follow-up can be especially warm and personal. Compare the differences between Paul's two letters to the Corinthians:

1 Corinthians	2 Corinthians
1. Very objective content and character	1. Very subjective character
2. Practical in its approach	2. Personal in its approach
3. Deliberate church instruction	3. Personal life and experience
4. Gives insight into the church ministry	4. Gives insight into Paul's life

dence in you all that my joy is *the joy* of you all. ⁴For out of much affliction and anguish of heart I wrote to you, with many tears, not that you should be grieved, but that you might know the love which I have so abundantly for you.

⁵But if anyone has caused grief, he has not grieved me, but all of you to some extent—not to be too severe. ⁶This punishment which *was inflicted* by the majority *is* sufficient for such a man, ⁷so that, on the contrary, you *ought* rather to forgive and comfort *him,* lest perhaps such a one be swallowed up with too much sorrow. ⁸Therefore I urge you to reaffirm *your* love to him. ⁹For to this end I also wrote, that I might put you to the test, whether you are obedient in all things. ¹⁰Now whom you forgive anything, I also *forgive.* For if indeed I have forgiven anything, I have forgiven that oneᵃ for your sakes in the presence of Christ, ¹¹lest Satan should take advantage of us; for we are not ignorant of his devices.

Triumph in Christ

¹²Furthermore, when I came to Troas to *preach* Christ's gospel, and a door was opened to me by the Lord, ¹³I had no rest in my spirit, because I did not find Titus my brother; but taking my leave of them, I departed for Macedonia.

¹⁴Now thanks *be* to God who always leads us in triumph in Christ, and through us diffuses the fragrance of His knowledge in every place. ¹⁵For we are to God the fragrance of Christ among those who are being saved and among those who are perishing. ¹⁶To the one *we are* the aroma of death *leading* to death, and to the other the aroma of life *leading* to life. And who *is* sufficient for these things? ¹⁷For we are not, as so many,ᵃ peddling the word of God; but as of sincerity, but as from God, we speak in the sight of God in Christ.

Christ's Epistle

3 Do we begin again to commend ourselves? Or do we need, as some *others,* epistles of commendation to you or *letters* of commendation from you? ²You are our epistle written in our hearts, known and read by all men; ³clearly *you are* an epistle of Christ, ministered by us, written not with ink but by the Spirit of the living God, not on tablets of stone but on tablets of flesh, *that is,* of the heart.

2:10 ᵃNU-Text reads *For indeed, what I have forgiven, if I have forgiven anything, I did it.* **2:17** ᵃM-Text reads *the rest.*

The Spirit, Not the Letter

[4]And we have such trust through Christ toward God. [5]Not that we are sufficient of ourselves to think of anything as *being* from ourselves, but our sufficiency *is* from God, [6]who also made us sufficient as ministers of the new covenant, not of the letter but of the Spirit;[a] for the letter kills, but the Spirit gives life.

Humility: It Is Easier to Follow a Leader Who Follows God

(2 Corinthians 3:4–6)

Paul could have taken great pride in his accomplishments, but instead threw away his trophies (Phil. 3:4–7). He explained that his competency came from God, not himself. Let your people notice your achievements on their own. They will follow a leader more easily who humbly follows God.

Glory of the New Covenant

[7]But if the ministry of death, written *and* engraved on stones, was glorious, so that the children of Israel could not look steadily at the face of Moses because of the glory of his countenance, which *glory* was passing away, [8]how will the ministry of the Spirit not be more glorious? [9]For if the ministry of condemnation *had* glory, the ministry of righteousness exceeds much more in glory. [10]For even what was made glorious had no glory in this respect, because of the glory that excels. [11]For if what is passing away *was* glorious, what remains *is* much more glorious.

[12]Therefore, since we have such hope, we use great boldness of speech— [13]unlike Moses, *who* put a veil over his face so that the children of Israel could not look steadily at the end of what was passing away. [14]But their minds were blinded. For until this day the same veil remains unlifted in the reading of the Old Testament, because the *veil* is taken away in Christ. [15]But even to this day, when Moses is read, a veil lies on their heart. [16]Nevertheless when one turns to the Lord, the veil is taken away. [17]Now the Lord is the Spirit; and where the Spirit of the Lord *is,* there *is* liberty. [18]But we all, with unveiled face, beholding as in a mirror the glory of the Lord, are being transformed into the same image from glory to glory, just as by the Spirit of the Lord.

The Light of Christ's Gospel

4 Therefore, since we have this ministry, as we have received mercy, we do not lose heart. [2]But we have renounced the hidden things of shame, not walking in craftiness nor handling the word of God deceitfully, but by manifestation of the truth commending ourselves to every man's conscience in the sight of God. [3]But even if our gospel is veiled, it is veiled to those who are perishing, [4]whose minds the god of this age has blinded, who do not believe, lest the light of the gospel of the glory of Christ, who is the image of God, should shine on them. [5]For we do not preach ourselves, but Christ Jesus the Lord, and ourselves your bondservants for Jesus' sake. [6]For it is the God who commanded light to shine out of darkness, who has shone in our hearts to *give* the light of the knowledge of the glory of God in the face of Jesus Christ.

Cast Down but Unconquered

[7]But we have this treasure in earthen vessels, that the excellence of the power may be of God and not of us. [8]*We are* hard-pressed on every side, yet not crushed; *we are* perplexed, but not in despair; [9]persecuted, but not forsaken; struck down, but not destroyed— [10]always carrying about in the body the dying of the Lord Jesus, that the life of Jesus also may be manifested in our body. [11]For we who live are always delivered to death for Jesus' sake, that the life of Jesus also may be manifested in our mortal flesh. [12]So then death is working in us, but life in you.

[13]And since we have the same spirit of faith, according to what is written, *"I believed and therefore I spoke,"*[a] we also believe and therefore

---

3:6 [a]Or *spirit*　**4:13** [a]Psalm 116:10

Perspective: Leaders Paint the Big Picture for Others

(2 Corinthians 4:16–18)

Success has less to do with gifts than with perspective. Paul tells us: Never lose heart (2 Cor. 4:16); progress isn't always visible (4:16); our struggles develop us (4:17); we must fix our eyes on the invisible (4:18); the importance of the eternal realm far exceeds the visible one (4:18).

The Law of Sacrifice:
Leaders Surrender to Stick with the Mission

(2 Corinthians 4:7–12)

aul regularly had to give up to go up. In fact, Paul said, "I die daily" (1 Cor. 15:31). The apostle made all kinds of sacrifices so he could stick with his God-given mission. Each time Paul gave up something, he moved forward and honored God.

Note how Paul gave up to go up:

What Paul Gave Up:	**How Paul Went Up:**
1. Health and comfort. He felt hard-pressed (v. 8).	1. He was never crushed (v. 8).
2. Calm and certainty. He felt perplexed (v. 8).	2. He never fell into despair (v. 8).
3. Peace and acceptance. He was persecuted (v. 9).	3. He was never forsaken (v. 9).
4. Strength and poise. He was struck down (v. 9).	4. He was never destroyed (v. 9).
5. His own life. He bore the marks of Christ's death (v. 10).	5. He received the life of Jesus (v. 10).

---

speak, [14]knowing that He who raised up the Lord Jesus will also raise us up with Jesus, and will present *us* with you. [15]For all things *are* for your sakes, that grace, having spread through the many, may cause thanksgiving to abound to the glory of God.

Seeing the Invisible

[16]Therefore we do not lose heart. Even though our outward man is perishing, yet the inward *man* is being renewed day by day. [17]For our light affliction, which is but for a moment, is working for us a far more exceeding *and* eternal weight of glory, [18]while we do not look at the things which are seen, but at the things which are not seen. For the things which are seen *are* temporary, but the things which are not seen *are* eternal.

Assurance of the Resurrection

For we know that if our earthly house, *this* tent, is destroyed, we have a building from God, a house not made with hands, eternal in the heavens. [2]For in this we groan, earnestly desiring to be clothed with our habitation which is from heaven, [3]if indeed, having been clothed, we shall not be found naked. [4]For we who are in *this* tent groan, being burdened, not because we want to be unclothed, but further clothed, that mortality may be swallowed up by life. [5]Now He who has prepared us for this very thing *is* God, who also has given us the Spirit as a guarantee.

[6]So *we are* always confident, knowing that while we are at home in the body we are absent from the Lord. [7]For we walk by faith, not by sight. [8]We are confident, yes, well pleased rather to be absent from the body and to be present with the Lord.

The Judgment Seat of Christ

[9]Therefore we make it our aim, whether present or absent, to be well pleasing to Him. [10]For we must all appear before the judgment seat of Christ, that each one may receive the things *done* in the body, according to what he has done, whether good or bad. [11]Knowing, therefore, the terror of the Lord, we persuade men; but we are well known to God, and I also trust are well known in your consciences.

Be Reconciled to God

[12]For we do not commend ourselves again to you, but give you opportunity to boast on our behalf, that you may have *an answer* for those who boast in appearance and not in heart. [13]For if we are beside ourselves, *it is* for God; or if we are of sound mind, *it is* for you. [14]For the love of Christ compels us, because we judge thus: that One died for all, then all died; [15]and He died for all, that those who live should live no longer for themselves, but for Him who died for them and rose again.

[16]Therefore, from now on, we regard no one

Reward vs. Inheritance:
What a Leader Can Expect from His Labor

(2 Corinthians 5:10)

Every spiritual leader needs to remember that we will all face the judgment seat of Christ. This event is not the Great White Throne judgment, mentioned in the Book of Revelation, for that judgment concerns sin, and every Christian already has passed through that judgment based on Jesus' work on the Cross. At the judgment seat of Christ, we will be rewarded or admonished for the labor we give after our conversion. Paul mentions the testing of our work (1 Cor. 3:12–15; Eph. 6:8). Note the difference between inheritance and rewards:

Inheritance	Reward
1. Based on Jesus' merits	1. Based on our service
2. Given freely by God's grace	2. Given in proportion to our work
3. The condition: being a son or daughter	3. The condition: being a laborer
4. Salvation based on birthright	4. Blessing based on obedience
5. We must have faith in Christ	5. We must be faithful to Him
6. Secure	6. Pending

Faithful leaders can expect their inheritance to include both the gift of salvation and the blessing of a reward for their spiritual leadership. The Bible teaches that rewards in heaven will be handed out justly, but not equally. Our degree of faithfulness determines our heavenly reward and responsibility (Luke 19:11–26).

---

according to the flesh. Even though we have known Christ according to the flesh, yet now we know *Him thus* no longer. [17]Therefore, if anyone *is* in Christ, *he is* a new creation; old things have passed away; behold, all things have become new. [18]Now all things *are* of God, who has reconciled us to Himself through Jesus Christ, and has given us the ministry of reconciliation, [19]that is, that God was in Christ reconciling the world to Himself, not imputing their trespasses to them, and has committed to us the word of reconciliation.

[20]Now then, we are ambassadors for Christ, as though God were pleading through us: we implore *you* on Christ's behalf, be reconciled to God. [21]For He made Him who knew no sin *to be* sin for us, that we might become the righteousness of God in Him.

Marks of the Ministry

6 We then, *as* workers together *with Him* also plead with *you* not to receive the grace of God in vain. [2]For He says:

"In an acceptable time I have heard you,
    And in the day of salvation I have helped
    you."[a]

Behold, now *is* the accepted time; behold, now *is* the day of salvation.

[3]We give no offense in anything, that our ministry may not be blamed. [4]But in all *things we* commend ourselves as ministers of God: in much patience, in tribulations, in needs, in distresses, [5]in stripes, in imprisonments, in tumults, in labors, in sleeplessness, in fastings; [6]by purity, by knowledge, by longsuffering, by kindness, by the Holy Spirit, by sincere love, [7]by the word of truth, by the power of God, by the armor of righteousness on the right hand and on the left, [8]by honor and dishonor, by evil report and good report; as deceivers, and *yet* true; [9]as unknown, and *yet* well known; as dying, and behold we live; as chastened, and *yet* not killed; [10]as sorrowful, yet always rejoicing; as poor, yet making many rich; as having nothing, and *yet* possessing all things.

Be Holy

[11]O Corinthians! We have spoken openly to you, our heart is wide open. [12]You are not restricted by us, but you are restricted by your *own* affections. [13]Now in return for the same (I speak as to children), you also be open.

6:2 [a]Isaiah 49:8

Partnerships: They Make or Break the Leader

(2 Corinthians 6:14–18)

Healthy leaders often partner with others to reach their goals. In fact, we live in an age of partnerships, both in the corporate world and in the church. Paul reminds us that there is nothing more dangerous to a leader than an unhealthy or destructive partnership. Note several signs of a bad partnership:

1. The parties don't share the same values.
2. The parties don't agree on the goal.
3. One or both parties must compromise their convictions.
4. One party selfishly demands that the other surrender.
5. One party benefits and the other loses.

Good partnerships do not foster codependence or independence, but interdependence. Every party feels secure, is stretched, and enjoys synergy. The partnership multiplies the productivity of both parties.

---

¹⁴Do not be unequally yoked together with unbelievers. For what fellowship has righteousness with lawlessness? And what communion has light with darkness? ¹⁵And what accord has Christ with Belial? Or what part has a believer with an unbeliever? ¹⁶And what agreement has the temple of God with idols? For you[a] are the temple of the living God. As God has said:

> "I will dwell in them
> And walk among them.
> I will be their God,
> And they shall be My people."[b]

¹⁷Therefore

> "Come out from among them
> And be separate, says the Lord.
> Do not touch what is unclean,
> And I will receive you."[a]

¹⁸ "I will be a Father to you,
> And you shall be My sons and daughters,
> Says the LORD Almighty."[a]

6:16 [a]NU-Text reads *we.* [b]Leviticus 26:12; Jeremiah 32:38; Ezekiel 37:27 **6:17** [a]Isaiah 52:11; Ezekiel 20:34, 41 **6:18** [a]2 Samuel 7:14

TITUS — TROUBLESHOOTER IN CORINTH

(2 Corinthians 7:2–16)

PROFILE IN LEADERSHIP

The Corinthian church had a big problem, and the apostle Paul had the right man to deal with it. Paul sent a young gentile by the name of Titus to visit the Corinthians. Titus was, in effect, the apostle's "troubleshooter."

When Titus arrived in Corinth, he found a church that had, by and large, rejected the teaching and authority of Paul. His previous letter to them had contained some honest, accurate, and hard words concerning divisions, pride, and sexual immorality among them, and it didn't receive a warm welcome. Although Paul had written from a heart of love and concern, false teachers undermined his authority by portraying him as arrogant, unqualified to teach, and dishonest.

Young Titus traveled to Corinth, dealt with the problem, and returned to Paul with news that many of the Corinthian Christians had repented and accepted Paul's authority as their leader sent from God. The Bible doesn't describe exactly what Titus did to correct the situation in Corinth, but it is clear that he returned to Paul with good news.

The body of Christ needs leaders who have the patience and perceptivity to look into a troubled situation, discern the problem, then do what it takes to correct the difficulty. In short, the church needs "troubleshooters" in order to grow and maintain its spiritual health.

7 Therefore, having these promises, beloved, let us cleanse ourselves from all filthiness of the flesh and spirit, perfecting holiness in the fear of God.

The Corinthians' Repentance

2Open *your hearts* to us. We have wronged no one, we have corrupted no one, we have cheated no one. 3I do not say *this* to condemn; for I have said before that you are in our hearts, to die together and to live together. 4Great *is* my boldness of speech toward you, great *is* my boasting on your behalf. I am filled with comfort. I am exceedingly joyful in all our tribulation.

5For indeed, when we came to Macedonia, our bodies had no rest, but we were troubled on every side. Outside *were* conflicts, inside *were* fears. 6Nevertheless God, who comforts the downcast, comforted us by the coming of Titus, 7and not only by his coming, but also by the consolation with which he was comforted in you, when he told us of your earnest desire, your mourning, your zeal for me, so that I rejoiced even more.

8For even if I made you sorry with my letter, I do not regret it; though I did regret it. For I perceive that the same epistle made you sorry, though only for a while. 9Now I rejoice, not that you were made sorry, but that your sorrow led to repentance. For you were made sorry in a godly manner, that you might suffer loss from us in nothing. 10For godly sorrow produces repentance *leading* to salvation, not to be regretted; but the sorrow of the world produces death. 11For observe this very thing, that you sorrowed in a godly manner: What diligence it produced in you, *what* clearing *of yourselves, what* indignation, *what* fear, *what* vehement desire, *what* zeal, *what* vindication! In all *things* you proved yourselves to be clear in this matter. 12Therefore, although I wrote to you, *I did* not *do it* for the sake of him who had done the wrong, nor for the sake of him who suffered wrong, but that our care for you in the sight of God might appear to you.

The Joy of Titus

13Therefore we have been comforted in your comfort. And we rejoiced exceedingly more for the joy of Titus, because his spirit has been refreshed by you all. 14For if in anything I have boasted to him about you, I am not ashamed. But as we spoke all things to you in truth, even so our boasting to Titus was found true. 15And his affections are greater for you as he remembers the obedience of you all, how with fear and trembling you received him. 16Therefore I rejoice that I have confidence in you in everything.

Excel in Giving

8 Moreover, brethren, we make known to you the grace of God bestowed on the churches of Macedonia: 2that in a great trial of affliction the abundance of their joy and their deep poverty abounded in the riches of their liberality. 3For I bear witness that according to *their* ability, yes, and beyond *their* ability, *they were* freely willing, 4imploring us with much urgency that

---

The Tough and Tender Leader

(2 Corinthians 7:8–13)

In his previous letter to the church, Paul played the role of the tough leader. He instigated conflict. In this letter, he speaks more from a personal viewpoint, more from his heart. He exudes tenderness.

In this passage, the apostle discusses how he caused the Corinthians sorrow, but distinguishes between good sorrow and bad sorrow. Every leader will find this distinction profitable to understand. Consider the differences:

Bad Sorrow	Good Sorrow
1. Pain goes on indefinitely	1. Pain is temporary
2. Example: Judas (Matt. 27:3–5)	2. Example: Peter (Luke 22:54–62)
3. Leads to regret and death	3. Leads to repentance and life
4. Suffering based on selfishness	4. Suffering based on God's will

Leaders should never seek revenge or desire to hurt someone just to vindicate their action. The pain they bring should have the constructive purpose of repentance and recovery.

we would receive[a] the gift and the fellowship of the ministering to the saints. [5]And not *only* as we had hoped, but they first gave themselves to the Lord, and *then* to us by the will of God. [6]So we urged Titus, that as he had begun, so he would also complete this grace in you as well. [7]But as you abound in everything—in faith, in speech, in knowledge, in all diligence, and in your love for us—*see* that you abound in this grace also.

Generosity: Leaders Can't Love Without Giving

(2 Corinthians 8:2–5)

Paul encouraged generosity among the Corinthians by bragging on the poverty-stricken church in Macedonia, proving that liberality has nothing to do with feeling comfortable (2 Cor. 8:2), having abundance (8:2), calculating what one can afford (8:3), or being coerced (8:4). Effective leaders are generous with themselves.

Christ Our Pattern

[8]I speak not by commandment, but I am testing the sincerity of your love by the diligence of others. [9]For you know the grace of our Lord Jesus Christ, that though He was rich, yet for your sakes He became poor, that you through His poverty might become rich.

[10]And in this I give advice: It is to your advantage not only to be doing what you began and were desiring to do a year ago; [11]but now you also must complete the doing *of it;* that as *there was* a readiness to desire *it,* so *there* also *may be* a completion out of what *you* have. [12]For if there is first a willing mind, *it is* accepted according to what one has, *and* not according to what he does not have.

[13]For *I do* not *mean* that others should be eased and you burdened; [14]but by an equality, *that* now at this time your abundance *may supply* their lack, that their abundance also may supply your lack—that there may be equality. [15]As it is written, *"He who gathered much had nothing left over, and he who gathered little had no lack."*[a]

Collection for the Judean Saints

[16]But thanks *be* to God who puts[a] the same earnest care for you into the heart of Titus. [17]For

he not only accepted the exhortation, but being more diligent, he went to you of his own accord. [18]And we have sent with him the brother whose praise *is* in the gospel throughout all the churches, [19]and not only *that,* but who was also chosen by the churches to travel with us with this gift, which is administered by us to the glory of the Lord Himself and *to show* your ready mind, [20]avoiding this: that anyone should blame us in this lavish gift which is administered by us— [21]providing honorable things, not only in the sight of the Lord, but also in the sight of men.

[22]And we have sent with them our brother whom we have often proved diligent in many things, but now much more diligent, because of the great confidence which *we have* in you. [23]If *anyone inquires* about Titus, *he is* my partner and fellow worker concerning you. Or if our brethren *are inquired about, they are* messengers of the churches, the glory of Christ. [24]Therefore show to them, and[a] before the churches, the proof of your love and of our boasting on your behalf.

Administering the Gift

9 Now concerning the ministering to the saints, it is superfluous for me to write to you; [2]for I know your willingness, about which I boast of you to the Macedonians, that Achaia was ready a year ago; and your zeal has stirred up the majority. [3]Yet I have sent the brethren, lest our boasting of you should be in vain in this respect, that, as I said, you may be ready; [4]lest if *some* Macedonians come with me and find you unprepared, we (not to mention you!) should be ashamed of this confident boasting.[a] [5]Therefore I thought it necessary to exhort the brethren to go to you ahead of time, and prepare your generous gift beforehand, which *you had* previously promised, that it may be ready as *a matter of* generosity and not as a grudging obligation.

The Cheerful Giver

[6]But this *I* say: He who sows sparingly will also reap sparingly, and he who sows bountifully will also reap bountifully. [7]So let each one *give* as he purposes in his heart, not grudgingly or of necessity; for God loves a cheerful giver. [8]And

---

8:4 [a]NU-Text and M-Text omit *that we would receive,* thus changing text to *urgency for the favor and fellowship* .... **8:15** [a]Exodus 16:18 **8:16** [a]NU-Text reads *has put.* **8:24** [a]NU-Text and M-Text omit *and.* **9:4** [a]NU-Text reads *this confidence.*

Stewardship: Leaders Invest Resources Like Farmers Sow Seed
(2 Corinthians 9:6–11)

Paul uses dozens of metaphors throughout this book. In this passage, he compares steward-ship to farming. In trying to encourage the Corinthian church to give generously to their brothers and sisters in Jerusalem, he instructs the church to view its resources as a farmer views sowing seed. A good farmer liberally sows seed, trying to ensure a good fall harvest. The more he sows, the more he reaps. You can't harvest if you haven't planted.

Some leaders, like the Corinthians, find it hard to invest resources because they seem so defi-cient—feeling their commodities are about to run out. Good leaders see the same resources as sufficient seed to be sown—knowing the harvest will come and more will be created. We must guard life against poverty; we should give our life because it is plentiful. Consider the differences:

Deficiency Perspective	Sufficiency Perspective
1. Defense	1. Offense
2. Maintain	2. Create
3. Escape loss	3. Pursue vision
4. Gifts contained	4. Gifts released
5. Reactive	5. Proactive
6. Guard and protect	6. Risk and seize opportunity
7. Stagnation	7. Multiplication
8. Paralyzed: Hold on!	8. Dynamic: Let go!
9. Narrow and closed	9. Wide and open
10. Thinks win/lose	10. Thinks win/win

God *is* able to make all grace abound toward you, that you, always having all sufficiency in all *things*, may have an abundance for every good work. [9]As it is written:

"He has dispersed abroad,
He has given to the poor;
His righteousness endures forever."[a]

[10]Now may[a] He who supplies seed to the sower, and bread for food, supply and multiply the seed you have *sown* and increase the fruits of your righteousness, [11]while *you are* enriched in everything for all liberality, which causes thanksgiving through us to God. [12]For the ad-ministration of this service not only supplies the needs of the saints, but also is abounding through many thanksgivings to God, [13]while, through the proof of this ministry, they glorify God for the obedience of your confession to the gospel of Christ, and for *your* liberal sharing with them and all *men*, [14]and by their prayer for you, who long for you because of the exceeding grace of God in you. [15]Thanks *be* to God for His inde-scribable gift!

The Spiritual War

10 Now I, Paul, myself am pleading with you by the meekness and gen-tleness of Christ—who in presence *am* lowly among you, but being absent am bold toward you. [2]But I beg *you* that when I am pres-ent I may not be bold with that confidence by which I intend to be bold against some, who think of us as if we walked according to the flesh. [3]For though we walk in the flesh, we do not war according to the flesh. [4]For the weapons of our warfare *are* not carnal but mighty in God for pulling down strongholds, [5]casting down ar-guments and every high thing that exalts itself against the knowledge of God, bringing every thought into captivity to the obedience of Christ, [6]and being ready to punish all disobedi-ence when your obedience is fulfilled.

Reality of Paul's Authority

[7]Do you look at things according to the outward appearance? If anyone is convinced in

9:9 [a]Psalm 112:9 **9:10** [a]NU-Text reads *Now He who supplies . . . will supply . . . .*

The Law of Solid Ground: Paul Answers His Critics

(2 Corinthians 10:1—11:33)

Paul felt embarrassed to defend his ministry and leadership, but he believed he had to do so. He had lost his credibility in the eyes of many Corinthians, and good leaders know that is the one thing they *cannot* lose. When leaders surrender their credibility, they lose the right to lead.

Still, the price of leadership is criticism. Aristotle said, "Criticism is something you can avoid easily—by saying nothing, doing nothing, and being nothing." Paul handled his criticism by reviewing his track record and reminding the people of his commitment to them. Paul attacked the problem head-on. Sometimes this is right, while at other times it's best to wait. Ponder the following list of ten ways to handle criticism successfully:

1. Understand the difference between constructive and destructive criticism.
2. Don't take yourself too seriously.
3. Look beyond the criticism and see the critic. Do *you* constantly criticize?
4. Watch your own attitude toward the critic.
5. Recognize that good people (even Jesus!) get criticized.
6. Stay in shape—physically, emotionally, and spiritually.
7. Don't just see the critic; see the crowd: Are many criticizing you?
8. Don't get defensive. Wait for a time to prove them wrong.
9. Try to learn a principle. Thank the critic for what you learn.
10. Concentrate on your mission; change your mistake.

himself that he is Christ's, let him again consider this in himself, that just as he *is* Christ's, even so we *are* Christ's.[a] [8]For even if I should boast somewhat more about our authority, which the Lord gave us[a] for edification and not for your destruction, I shall not be ashamed— [9]lest I seem to terrify you by letters. [10]"For *his* letters," they say, "*are* weighty and powerful, but *his* bodily presence *is* weak, and *his* speech contemptible." [11]Let such a person consider this, that what we are in word by letters when we are absent, such *we will* also *be* in deed when we are present.

Limits of Paul's Authority

[12]For we dare not class ourselves or compare ourselves with those who commend themselves. But they, measuring themselves by themselves, and comparing themselves among themselves, are not wise. [13]We, however, will not boast beyond measure, but within the limits of the sphere which God appointed us—a sphere which especially includes you. [14]For we are not overextending ourselves (as though *our authority* did not extend to you), for it was to you that we came with the gospel of Christ; [15]not boasting of things beyond measure, *that is,* in other men's labors, but having hope, *that* as your faith is increased, we shall be greatly enlarged by you in our sphere, [16]to preach

the gospel in the *regions* beyond you, *and* not to boast in another man's sphere of accomplishment. [17]But *"he who glories, let him glory in the* LORD."[a] [18]For not he who commends himself is approved, but whom the Lord commends.

Concern for Their Faithfulness

11 Oh, that you would bear with me in a little folly—and indeed you do bear with me. [2]For I am jealous for you with godly jealousy. For I have betrothed you to one husband, that I may present *you as* a chaste virgin to Christ. [3]But I fear, lest somehow, as the serpent deceived Eve by his craftiness, so your minds may be corrupted from the simplicity[a] that is in Christ. [4]For if he who comes preaches another Jesus whom we have not preached, or *if* you receive a different spirit which you have not received, or a different gospel which you have not accepted—you may well put up with it!

Paul and False Apostles

[5]For I consider that I am not at all inferior to the most eminent apostles. [6]Even though *I am*

10:7 [a]NU-Text reads *even as we are.* **10:8** [a]NU-Text omits *us.* **10:17** [a]Jeremiah 9:24 **11:3** [a]NU-Text adds *and purity.*

untrained in speech, yet *I am* not in knowledge. But we have been thoroughly manifested[a] among you in all things.

[7]Did I commit sin in humbling myself that you might be exalted, because I preached the gospel of God to you free of charge? [8]I robbed other churches, taking wages *from them* to minister to you. [9]And when I was present with you, and in need, I was a burden to no one, for what I lacked the brethren who came from Macedonia supplied. And in everything I kept myself from being burdensome to you, and so I will keep *myself.* [10]As the truth of Christ is in me, no one shall stop me from this boasting in the regions of Achaia. [11]Why? Because I do not love you? God knows!

[12]But what I do, I will also continue to do, that I may cut off the opportunity from those who desire an opportunity to be regarded just as we are in the things of which they boast. [13]For such *are* false apostles, deceitful workers, transforming themselves into apostles of Christ. [14]And no wonder! For Satan himself transforms himself into an angel of light. [15]Therefore *it is* no great thing if his ministers also transform themselves into ministers of righteousness, whose end will be according to their works.

Reluctant Boasting

[16]I say again, let no one think me a fool. If otherwise, at least receive me as a fool, that I also may boast a little. [17]What I speak, I speak not according to the Lord, but as it were, foolishly, in this confidence of boasting. [18]Seeing that many boast according to the flesh, I also will boast. [19]For you put up with fools gladly, since you *yourselves* are wise! [20]For you put up with it if one brings you into bondage, if one devours *you,* if one takes *from you,* if one exalts himself, if one strikes you on the face. [21]To *our* shame I say that we were too weak for that! But in whatever anyone is bold—I speak foolishly—I am bold also.

Suffering for Christ

[22]Are they Hebrews? So *am* I. Are they Israelites? So *am* I. Are they the seed of Abraham? So *am* I. [23]Are they ministers of Christ?—I speak as a fool—I *am* more: in labors more abundant, in stripes above measure, in prisons more frequently, in deaths often. [24]From the Jews five times I received forty *stripes* minus one. [25]Three times I was beaten with rods; once I was stoned; three times I was shipwrecked; a night and a day I have been in the deep; [26]*in* journeys often, *in* perils of waters, *in* perils of robbers, *in* perils of *my own* countrymen, *in* perils of the Gentiles, *in* perils in the

city, *in* perils in the wilderness, *in* perils in the sea, *in* perils among false brethren; [27]in weariness and toil, in sleeplessness often, in hunger and thirst, in fastings often, in cold and nakedness— [28]besides the other things, what comes upon me daily: my deep concern for all the churches. [29]Who is weak, and I am not weak? Who is made to stumble, and I do not burn *with indignation?*

[30]If I must boast, I will boast in the things which concern my infirmity. [31]The God and Father of our Lord Jesus Christ, who is blessed forever, knows that I am not lying. [32]In Damascus the governor, under Aretas the king, was guarding the city of the Damascenes with a garrison, desiring to arrest me; [33]but I was let down in a basket through a window in the wall, and escaped from his hands.

The Vision of Paradise

12 It is doubtless[a] not profitable for me to boast. I will come to visions and revelations of the Lord: [2]I know a man in Christ who fourteen years ago—whether in the body I do not know, or whether out of the body I do not know, God knows—such a one was caught up to the third heaven. [3]And I know such a man—whether in the body or out of the body I do not know, God knows— [4]how he was caught up into Paradise and heard inexpressible words, which it is not lawful for a man to utter. [5]Of such a one I will boast; yet of myself I will not boast, except in my infirmities. [6]For though I might desire to boast, I will not be a fool; for I will speak the truth. But I refrain, lest anyone should think of me above what he sees me *to be* or hears from me.

The Thorn in the Flesh

[7]And lest I should be exalted above measure by the abundance of the revelations, a thorn in the flesh was given to me, a messenger of Satan to buffet me, lest I be exalted above measure. [8]Concerning this thing I pleaded with the Lord three times that it might depart from me. [9]And He said to me, "My grace is sufficient for you, for My strength is made perfect in weakness." Therefore most gladly I will rather boast in my infirmities, that the power of Christ may rest upon me. [10]Therefore I take pleasure in infirmities, in reproaches, in needs, in persecutions, in distresses, for Christ's sake. For when I am weak, then I am strong.

11:6 [a]NU-Text omits *been.* **12:1** [a]NU-Text reads *necessary, though not profitable, to boast.*

Vision: Paul's Vision and Thorn
(2 Corinthians 12:7–9)

Paul linked an extraordinary vision with an exasperating thorn. God gave Paul a motivating vista of heaven, but also some opposition to keep him humble. God gave him the grace and power to overcome the thorn, but didn't take it away. Visions make leaders passionate; thorns keep them authentic.

The Law of Intuition: Paul Relished His Weaknesses
(2 Corinthians 12:7–10)

Instead of getting angry at his thorn and the way it slowed him down, Paul relished how weak it made him. Why? It kept him in close dependence on the power of God (2 Cor. 12:10).

Paul understood that the weaker he was, the stronger God became within him. When there is less of you as *a* leader, there is more of God as *the* Leader. Only a wise leader can understand this paradox.

Paul practiced the Law of Intuition. What did Paul's leadership intuition enable him to understand? He recognized that . . .

1. The opposition was not from God (v. 7).
2. He must seek God's answer to this problem (v. 8).
3. God's answer was grace (v. 9).
4. Grace is perfected in his imperfections (v. 9).
5. He should boast about his weaknesses, not brag on his strength (v. 9).
6. The tougher his problems, the greater the grace (v. 10).

Signs of an Apostle

[11] I have become a fool in boasting;[a] you have compelled me. For I ought to have been commended by you; for in nothing was I behind the most eminent apostles, though I am nothing. [12] Truly the signs of an apostle were accomplished among you with all perseverance, in signs and wonders and mighty deeds. [13] For what is it in which you were inferior to other churches, except that I myself was not burdensome to you? Forgive me this wrong!

Love for the Church

[14] Now *for* the third time I am ready to come to you. And I will not be burdensome to you; for I do not seek yours, but you. For the children ought not to lay up for the parents, but the parents for the children. [15] And I will very gladly spend and be spent for your souls; though the more abundantly I love you, the less I am loved.

[16] But be that *as it may,* I did not burden you. Nevertheless, being crafty, I caught you by cunning! [17] Did I take advantage of you by any of those whom I sent to you? [18] I urged Titus, and sent our brother with *him.* Did Titus take advantage of you? Did we not walk in the same spirit? Did *we* not *walk* in the same steps?

[19] Again, do you think[a] that we excuse ourselves to you? We speak before God in Christ. But *we do* all things, beloved, for your edification. [20] For I fear lest, when I come, I shall not find you such as I wish, and *that* I shall be found by you such as you do not wish; lest *there be* contentions, jealousies, outbursts of wrath, selfish ambitions, backbitings, whisperings, conceits, tumults; [21] lest, when I come again, my God will humble me among you, and I shall mourn for many who have sinned before and have not repented of the uncleanness, fornication, and lewdness which they have practiced.

Coming with Authority

13 This *will be* the third *time* I am coming to you. *"By the mouth of two or three witnesses every word shall be established."*[a] [2] I have told you before, and foretell as if I were present the second time, and now being absent I write[a] to those who have sinned before, and to all the rest, that if I come again I will not spare— [3] since you seek a proof of Christ speaking in me, who is not weak toward you, but mighty in you. [4] For though He was crucified in weakness, yet He lives by the power of God. For we also are weak in Him, but we shall live with Him by the power of God toward you.

[5] Examine yourselves *as to* whether you are in

12:11 [a]NU-Text omits *in boasting.* **12:19** [a]NU-Text reads *You have been thinking for a long time. . . .* **13:1** [a]Deuteronomy 19:15 **13:2** [a]NU-Text omits *I write.*

the faith. Test yourselves. Do you not know yourselves, that Jesus Christ is in you?—unless indeed you are disqualified. [6]But I trust that you will know that we are not disqualified.

Paul Prefers Gentleness

[7]Now I[a] pray to God that you do no evil, not that we should appear approved, but that you should do what is honorable, though we may seem disqualified. [8]For we can do nothing against the truth, but for the truth. [9]For we are glad when we are weak and you are strong. And this also we pray, that you may be made complete. [10]Therefore I write these things being absent, lest being present I should use sharpness, according to the authority which the Lord has given me for edification and not for destruction.

Greetings and Benediction

[11]Finally, brethren, farewell. Become complete. Be of good comfort, be of one mind, live in peace; and the God of love and peace will be with you.

[12]Greet one another with a holy kiss.

[13]All the saints greet you.

[14]The grace of the Lord Jesus Christ, and the love of God, and the communion of the Holy Spirit be with you all. Amen.

13:7 [a]NU-Text reads we.

GALATIANS
How God Saves Mankind

SUMMARY

Only in the Book of Galatians does Paul fail to affirm anything or anyone as he begins his letter. After a brief salutation, the apostle jumps right in and contends with the erring Galatian believers.

This letter contains the most emphatic statement of salvation apart from the Law to be found in Scripture. It is the only letter in which Paul develops a lengthy allegory to explain how God saves mankind. It provides us with a tremendous case study of a leader who must lead an erring group of followers back to God's original plan and purpose.

First, it teaches us that leaders worth their salt will confront those who drift from the vision. A drifting team member dilutes the organization, the vision, the momentum, and the resources. Effective leaders always seek to maintain focus on their organization's primary mission. Paul defends both his own leadership and the original mission he declared. He takes a stand. He determines to help the Galatians walk by faith.

Second, healthy leaders motivate rather than manipulate. Paul argues against the idea that people must work to earn their salvation. He wants the Galatians to live free. How much more mercenary it would have been to push them toward a "works theology!" Paul could have benefited from this as the leader who won them to Christ. Instead, he calls them to grace, where they cannot be manipulated by anyone. He has enough integrity to keep a clear conscience and to build trust with others.

Third, we learn that leaders communicate best when they speak the truth in love. Paul addresses these hard issues out of his love for the Galatians. He will not compromise his message, but neither does he burn any relational bridges. No one can question his deep compassion for those he corrects. He never minces words, either in his admonition or his affirmation. As you read through this book, observe how Paul incarnates each of these lessons. Allow him to mentor you.

God's Role in Galatians

God speaks through Paul and calls the Galatians back to the original gospel. Like the words of an Old Testament prophet, Paul's words cut deep with truth at the very point of his readers' need. People naturally tend to think they must earn God's approval. Something inside of us feels drawn to achieve. We like to merit what we possess, like a trophy.

But God knows the downside of that empty theology. First, no one is good enough to merit heaven. Second, our own labor and leadership grows stronger when we cannot earn it, because grace, not guilt, is our motivation; love, not law, drives us to act. Leaders who lead in an environment of grace always obtain superior results.

Leaders in Galatians

Paul, Abraham, Sarah, the false teachers

Other People of Influence in Galatians

The members of the Galatian church, Hagar, Ishmael, Isaac

Lessons in Leadership

- Integrity builds trust and trust builds relationships.
- Leaders know what they'll stand for and won't stand for.
- Effective leaders aren't afraid to confront when necessary.
- Spiritual leaders lead from the inside out.

LEADERSHIP

HIGHLIGHTS IN GALATIANS

CONFRONTATION: Paul Exhibits Integrity with Peter (2:11–21)	*page 1428*
THE LAW OF CONNECTION: Paul Illustrates and Invites (3:6—4:31)	*page 1429*
PAUL: Navigator and Corrector (4:8–20)	*page 1431*
LEADERSHIP QUALITIES and the Fruit of the Spirit (5:22, 23)	*page 1432*
ACCOUNTABILITY: Leaders Need Alarm Bells (6:7–10)	*page 1433*

Greeting

1 Paul, an apostle (not from men nor through man, but through Jesus Christ and God the Father who raised Him from the dead), [2]and all the brethren who are with me,

To the churches of Galatia:

[3]Grace to you and peace from God the Father and our Lord Jesus Christ, [4]who gave Himself for our sins, that He might deliver us from this present evil age, according to the will of our God and Father, [5]to whom *be* glory forever and ever. Amen.

Only One Gospel

[6]I marvel that you are turning away so soon from Him who called you in the grace of Christ, to a different gospel, [7]which is not another; but there are some who trouble you and want to pervert the gospel of Christ. [8]But even if we, or an angel from heaven, preach any other gospel to you than what we have preached to you, let him be accursed. [9]As we have said before, so now I say again, if anyone preaches any other gospel to you than what you have received, let him be accursed.

[10]For do I now persuade men, or God? Or do I seek to please men? For if I still pleased men, I would not be a bondservant of Christ.

The Law of Influence: Paul Exercises Emotional Authority

(Galatians 1:6–10)

Paul challenges the direction of the Galatian church, accusing it of embracing a different gospel. The apostle risks his leadership by exercising his emotional authority. This is the acid test of the Law of Influence. A leader discovers his or her level of influence when he or she must confront an erring group's direction.

Call to Apostleship

[11]But I make known to you, brethren, that the gospel which was preached by me is not according to man. [12]For I neither received it from man, nor was I taught *it,* but *it came* through the revelation of Jesus Christ.

[13]For you have heard of my former conduct in Judaism, how I persecuted the church of God beyond measure and *tried to* destroy it. [14]And I advanced in Judaism beyond many of my contemporaries in my own nation, being more exceedingly zealous for the traditions of my fathers.

[15]But when it pleased God, who separated me from my mother's womb and called *me* through His grace, [16]to reveal His Son in me, that I might preach Him among the Gentiles, I did not immediately confer with flesh and blood, [17]nor did I go up to Jerusalem to those *who were* apostles before me; but I went to Arabia, and returned again to Damascus.

Contacts at Jerusalem

[18]Then after three years I went up to Jerusalem to see Peter,[a] and remained with him fifteen days. [19]But I saw none of the other apostles except James, the Lord's brother. [20](Now *concerning* the things which I write to you, indeed, before God, I do not lie.)

[21]Afterward I went into the regions of Syria and Cilicia. [22]And I was unknown by face to the churches of Judea which *were* in Christ. [23]But they were hearing only, "He who formerly persecuted us now preaches the faith which he once *tried to* destroy." [24]And they glorified God in me.

Defending the Gospel

2 Then after fourteen years I went up again to Jerusalem with Barnabas, and also took Titus with *me.* [2]And I went up by revelation, and communicated to them that gospel which I preach among the Gentiles, but privately to those who were of reputation, lest by any means I might run, or had run, in vain. [3]Yet not even Titus who *was* with me, being a Greek, was compelled to be circumcised. [4]And *this occurred* because of false brethren secretly brought in (who came in by stealth to spy out our liberty which we have in Christ Jesus, that they might bring us into bondage), [5]to whom we did not yield submission even for an hour, that the truth of the gospel might continue with you.

[6]But from those who seemed to be something—whatever they were, it makes no difference to me; God shows personal favoritism to no man—for those who seemed *to be something* added nothing to me. [7]But on the contrary, when they saw that the gospel for the uncircumcised had been committed to me, as *the gospel* for the circumcised *was* to Peter [8](for He who worked

---

1:18 [a]NU-Text reads *Cephas.*

The Law of Solid Ground: How Leaders Gain Trust

(Galatians 2:1–10)

It seems Paul constantly had to defend his leadership with some churches. He felt compelled to proclaim his trustworthiness with the churches in both Corinth and Galatia. He earned their trust by . . .

1. Investing his time in learning from God (v. 1).
2. Associating with a trusted leader (v. 1).
3. Submitting to respected leaders and sharing his journey (v. 2).
4. Asserting that even the leaders didn't correct his team (vv. 3, 6).
5. Standing up to those who opposed God's truth (vv. 4, 5).
6. Putting no confidence in people's infallibility, but trusting in God (v. 6).
7. Affirming that even the leaders fully endorse him (vv. 7–9).
8. Cooperating with the present leaders and honoring their requests (v. 10).

effectively in Peter for the apostleship to the circumcised also worked effectively in me toward the Gentiles), [9]and when James, Cephas, and John, who seemed to be pillars, perceived the grace that had been given to me, they gave me and Barnabas the right hand of fellowship, that we *should go* to the Gentiles and they to the circumcised. [10]*They desired* only that we should remember the poor, the very thing which I also was eager to do.

No Return to the Law

[11]Now when Peter[a] had come to Antioch, I withstood him to his face, because he was to be blamed; [12]for before certain men came from James, he would eat with the Gentiles; but when they came, he withdrew and separated himself, fearing those who were of the circumcision. [13]And the rest of the Jews also played the hypocrite with him, so that even Barnabas was carried away with their hypocrisy.

[14]But when I saw that they were not straightforward about the truth of the gospel, I said to Peter before *them* all, "If you, being a Jew, live in the manner of Gentiles and not as the Jews, why do you[a] compel Gentiles to live as Jews?[b] [15]We *who are* Jews by nature, and not sin-

---

2:11 [a]NU-Text reads *Cephas.* **2:14** [a]NU-Text reads *how can you.* [b]Some interpreters stop the quotation here.

Confrontation: Paul Exhibits Integrity with Peter

(Galatians 2:11–21)

Paul's integrity drove him to stand up to Peter, his fellow leader, in front of several Jewish and Gentile believers. He criticized Peter's hypocrisy and demanded that all Christian leaders remain consistent, regardless of the company they keep.

Paul teaches us how to critique someone. Consider his checklist:

1. *Check your motive.* Your goal should be to help, not humiliate.
2. *Make sure the issue is worthy of criticism.* Does it really matter?
3. *Be specific.* Don't drop hints, but clearly name the problem.
4. *Don't undermine the person's self-confidence or identity.* Make it obvious that you value the person.
5. *Don't compare people.* Use realistic standards to measure conduct.
6. *Be creative or don't criticize.* Find ways to reach a solution.
7. *Don't attack the person.* Critique the problem, not the person.
8. *Do not postpone needed criticism.* If the issue is big, act now.
9. *Look at yourself looking at others.* Take the log out of your own eye.
10. *End criticism with encouragement.* Finish on a positive note.

ners of the Gentiles, [16]knowing that a man is not justified by the works of the law but by faith in Jesus Christ, even we have believed in Christ Jesus, that we might be justified by faith in Christ and not by the works of the law; for by the works of the law no flesh shall be justified.

[17]"But if, while we seek to be justified by Christ, we ourselves also are found sinners, *is* Christ therefore a minister of sin? Certainly not! [18]For if I build again those things which I destroyed, I make myself a transgressor. [19]For I through the law died to the law that I might live to God. [20]I have been crucified with Christ; it is no longer I who live, but Christ lives in me; and the *life* which I now live in the flesh I live by faith in the Son of God, who loved me and gave Himself for me. [21]I do not set aside the grace of God; for if righteousness *comes* through the law, then Christ died in vain."

Justification by Faith

3 O foolish Galatians! Who has bewitched you that you should not obey the truth,[a] before whose eyes Jesus Christ was clearly portrayed among you[b] as crucified? [2]This only I want to learn from you: Did you receive the Spirit by the works of the law, or by the hearing of faith? [3]Are you so foolish? Having begun in the Spirit, are you now being made perfect by the flesh? [4]Have you suffered so many things in vain—if indeed *it was* in vain?

[5]Therefore He who supplies the Spirit to you and works miracles among you, *does He do it* by the works of the law, or by the hearing of faith?— [6]just as Abraham *"believed God, and it was accounted to him for righteousness."*[a] [7]Therefore know that *only* those who are of faith are sons of Abraham. [8]And the Scripture, foreseeing that God would justify the Gentiles by faith, preached the gospel to Abraham beforehand, *saying, "In you all the nations shall be blessed."*[a] [9]So then those who *are* of faith are blessed with believing Abraham.

The Law Brings a Curse

[10]For as many as are of the works of the law are under the curse; for it is written, *"Cursed is everyone who does not continue in all things*

3:1 [a]NU-Text omits *that you should not obey the truth.* [b]NU-Text omits *among you.* **3:6** [a]Genesis 15:6 **3:8** [a]Genesis 12:3; 18:18; 22:18; 26:4; 28:14

The Law of Connection: Paul Illustrates and Invites
(Galatians 3:6—4:31)

To make plain his teaching on grace, Paul uses stories and allegories. To drive home the truth, he uses an illustration of Abraham (Gal. 3:6–29); an Old Testament scripture (3:10–14); an illustration of a son and a slave (4:1–7); and an allegory of Sarah and Hagar (4:21–31). Paul knew just how to connect with his audience. He painted familiar pictures to connect them with unfamiliar truths.

Paul also knew how to connect with a difficult group of people. Although they are living in error and it might feel tempting to focus on their foolishness (3:1), instead the apostle invites them into the experience of discovery.

Consider the "Ten Commandments of Handling Difficult People":

1. *Use the 101% Principle.* Find the 1 percent you agree on and give it 100 percent of your attention.
2. *Love people more than policies, but love truth more than people.*
3. *Give others the benefit of the doubt.*
4. *Learn to be flexible where you can.*
5. *Check your own attitude.*
6. *Don't overreact to conflict and disagreement.*
7. *Welcome the conflict.* Make it a learning experience.
8. *Provide an escape for the person in conflict.* Let them maintain their dignity.
9. *Take a risk.* Give people a second chance.
10. *Take the high road.* Be generous and believe the best about others.

which are written in the book of the law, to do them."[a] [11]But that no one is justified by the law in the sight of God *is* evident, for *"the just shall live by faith."*[a] [12]Yet the law is not of faith, but *"the man who does them shall live by them."*[a]

[13]Christ has redeemed us from the curse of the law, having become a curse for us (for it is written, *"Cursed is everyone who hangs on a tree"*[a]), [14]that the blessing of Abraham might come upon the Gentiles in Christ Jesus, that we might receive the promise of the Spirit through faith.

The Changeless Promise

[15]Brethren, I speak in the manner of men: Though *it is* only a man's covenant, yet *if it is* confirmed, no one annuls or adds to it. [16]Now to Abraham and his Seed were the promises made. He does not say, "And to seeds," as of many, but as of one, *"And to your Seed,"*[a] who is Christ. [17]And this I say, *that* the law, which was four hundred and thirty years later, cannot annul the covenant that was confirmed before by God in Christ,[a] that it should make the promise of no effect. [18]For if the inheritance *is* of the law, *it is* no longer of promise; but God gave *it* to Abraham by promise.

Purpose of the Law

[19]What purpose then *does* the law *serve?* It was added because of transgressions, till the Seed should come to whom the promise was made; *and it was* appointed through angels by the hand of a mediator. [20]Now a mediator does not *mediate* for one *only,* but God is one.

[21]*Is* the law then against the promises of God? Certainly not! For if there had been a law given which could have given life, truly righteousness would have been by the law. [22]But the Scripture has confined all under sin, that the promise by faith in Jesus Christ might be given to those who believe. [23]But before faith came, we were kept under guard by the law, kept for the faith which would afterward be revealed. [24]Therefore the law was our tutor *to bring us* to Christ, that we might be justified by faith. [25]But after faith has come, we are no longer under a tutor.

Sons and Heirs

[26]For you are all sons of God through faith in Christ Jesus. [27]For as many of you as were baptized into Christ have put on Christ. [28]There is neither Jew nor Greek, there is neither slave nor free, there is neither male nor female; for you are all one in Christ Jesus. [29]And if you *are* Christ's, then you are Abraham's seed, and heirs according to the promise.

[4]Now I say *that* the heir, as long as he is a child, does not differ at all from a slave, though he is master of all, [2]but is under guardians and stewards until the time appointed by the father. [3]Even so we, when we were children, were in bondage under the elements of the world. [4]But when the fullness of the time had come, God sent forth His Son, born[a] of a woman, born under the law, [5]to redeem those who were under the law, that we might receive the adoption as sons.

[6]And because you are sons, God has sent forth the Spirit of His Son into your hearts, crying out, "Abba, Father!" [7]Therefore you are no longer a slave but a son, and if a son, then an heir of[a] God through Christ.

Fears for the Church

[8]But then, indeed, when you did not know God, you served those which by nature are not gods. [9]But now after you have known God, or rather are known by God, how *is it that* you turn again to the weak and beggarly elements, to which you desire again to be in bondage? [10]You observe days and months and seasons and years. [11]I am afraid for you, lest I have labored for you in vain.

[12]Brethren, I urge you to become like me, for I *became* like you. You have not injured me at all. [13]You know that because of physical infirmity I preached the gospel to you at the first. [14]And my trial which was in my flesh you did not despise or reject, but you received me as an angel of God, *even* as Christ Jesus. [15]What[a] then was the blessing you *enjoyed?* For I bear you witness that, if possible, you would have plucked out your own eyes and given them to me. [16]Have I therefore become your enemy because I tell you the truth?

[17]They zealously court you, *but* for no good; yes, they want to exclude you, that you may be zealous for them. [18]But it is good to be zealous in a good thing always, and not only when I am present with you. [19]My little children, for whom I labor in birth again until Christ is formed in you, [20]I would like to be present with you now and to change my tone; for I have doubts about you.

3:10 [a]Deuteronomy 27:26 **3:11** [a]Habakkuk 2:4
3:12 [a]Leviticus 18:5 **3:13** [a]Deuteronomy 21:23
3:16 [a]Genesis 12:7; 13:15; 24:7 **3:17** [a]NU-Text
omits *in Christ.* **4:4** [a]Or *made* **4:7** [a]NU-Text reads
through God and omits *through Christ.*
4:15 [a]NU-Text reads *Where.*

Two Covenants

[21]Tell me, you who desire to be under the law, do you not hear the law? [22]For it is written that Abraham had two sons: the one by a bondwoman, the other by a freewoman. [23]But he *who was* of the bondwoman was born according to the flesh, and he of the freewoman through promise, [24]which things are symbolic. For these are the[a] two covenants: the one from Mount Sinai which gives birth to bondage, which is Hagar— [25]for this Hagar is Mount Sinai in Arabia, and corresponds to Jerusalem which now is, and is in bondage with her children— [26]but the Jerusalem above is free, which is the mother of us all. [27]For it is written:

"Rejoice, O barren,
You who do not bear!
Break forth and shout,
You who are not in labor!
For the desolate has many more children
Than she who has a husband."[a]

[28]Now we, brethren, as Isaac *was,* are children of promise. [29]But, as he who was born according to the flesh then persecuted him *who was born* according to the Spirit, even so *it is* now. [30]Nevertheless what does the Scripture say? "Cast out the bondwoman and her son, for the son of the bondwoman shall not be heir with the son of the freewoman."[a] [31]So then, brethren, we are not children of the bondwoman but of the free.

Christian Liberty

5 Stand fast therefore in the liberty by which Christ has made us free,[a] and do not be entangled again with a yoke of bondage. [2]Indeed I, Paul, say to you that if you become circumcised, Christ will profit you nothing. [3]And I testify again to every man who becomes circumcised that he is a debtor to keep the whole law. [4]You have become estranged from Christ, you who *attempt to* be justified by law; you have fallen from grace. [5]For we through the Spirit eagerly wait for the hope of righteousness by faith. [6]For in Christ Jesus neither circumcision nor uncircumcision avails anything, but faith working through love.

Love Fulfills the Law

[7]You ran well. Who hindered you from obeying the truth? [8]This persuasion does not *come*

4:24 [a]NU-Text and M-Text omit *the.* 4:27 [a]Isaiah 54:1 4:30 [a]Genesis 21:10 5:1 [a]NU-Text reads *For freedom Christ has made us free; stand fast therefore.*

PAUL — NAVIGATOR AND CORRECTOR
(Galatians 4:8–20)

PROFILE IN LEADERSHIP

The apostle Paul knew that, in his role as a leader of the Galatian Christians, God had called him to navigate the church. But more than that, Paul knew what to navigate his fellow Christians *toward.*

False teachers were trying to convince the Galatians to rely on their own works for salvation instead of the grace God had poured out on them in the person of Jesus. This Paul could not ignore.

Something within each of us tempts us to believe that we need to add *something* to God's perfect plan of salvation—to believe that, without our own efforts, we just aren't going to make it into the kingdom of heaven. This remains just as true today as it was in the days of the first-century church.

Paul attempted to correct the errant course the Galatians had chosen by pointing out that no one can add anything to what Jesus already has accomplished on the Cross. No one can do a single thing to make themselves "more acceptable" to God.

To navigate means to make course corrections, to steer *toward* something. Godly leaders know they are to navigate their people to one thing only: the Lord Jesus Christ who died for their sins on the Cross.

from Him who calls you. ⁹A little leaven leavens the whole lump. ¹⁰I have confidence in you, in the Lord, that you will have no other mind; but he who troubles you shall bear his judgment, whoever he is.

¹¹And I, brethren, if I still preach circumcision, why do I still suffer persecution? Then the offense of the cross has ceased. ¹²I could wish that those who trouble you would even cut themselves off!

¹³For you, brethren, have been called to liberty; only do not *use* liberty as an opportunity for the flesh, but through love serve one another. ¹⁴For all the law is fulfilled in one word, *even in* this: *"You shall love your neighbor as yourself."*ᵃ ¹⁵But if you bite and devour one another, beware lest you be consumed by one another!

The Law of Empowerment: Paul Gives Power to Act

(Galatians 5:13–15)

When leaders empower their followers, they give them the freedom to act—and trust that they will do so responsibly. Paul released the Galatians to become all God intended them to be. They felt free and empowered by God's Spirit and Paul's leadership. As a secure leader, Paul freely gave power to others.

Walking in the Spirit

¹⁶I say then: Walk in the Spirit, and you shall not fulfill the lust of the flesh. ¹⁷For the flesh lusts against the Spirit, and the Spirit against the flesh; and these are contrary to one another, so that you do not do the things that you wish. ¹⁸But if you are led by the Spirit, you are not under the law.

¹⁹Now the works of the flesh are evident, which are: adultery,ᵃ fornication, uncleanness, lewdness, ²⁰idolatry, sorcery, hatred, contentions, jealousies, outbursts of wrath, selfish ambitions, dissensions, heresies, ²¹envy, murders,ᵃ drunkenness, revelries, and the like; of which I tell you beforehand, just as I also told *you* in time past, that those who practice such things will not inherit the kingdom of God.

²²But the fruit of the Spirit is love, joy, peace, longsuffering, kindness, goodness, faithfulness,

Leadership Qualities and the Fruit of the Spirit

(Galatians 5:22, 23)

Probably the most memorable verses in this book are those that list the "fruit of the Spirit." Fruit results from planted seeds. When seeds grow, they bear fruit. Fruit represents outward, visible behavior. Every leader should embrace this marvelous list of inward qualities. Evaluate yourself against them:

1. *Love:* Is my leadership motivated by love for people?
2. *Joy:* Do I exhibit an unshakable joy, regardless of circumstances?
3. *Peace:* Do people see my inward peace and take courage?
4. *Longsuffering:* Do I wait patiently for results as I develop people or goals?
5. *Kindness:* Am I caring and understanding toward everyone I meet?
6. *Goodness:* Do I want the best for others and the organization?
7. *Faithfulness:* Have I kept my commitments to the mission?
8. *Gentleness:* Is my strength under control? Can I be both tough and tender?
9. *Self-Control:* Am I disciplined to make progress toward my goals?

²³gentleness, self-control. Against such there is no law. ²⁴And those *who are* Christ's have crucified the flesh with its passions and desires. ²⁵If we live in the Spirit, let us also walk in the Spirit. ²⁶Let us not become conceited, provoking one another, envying one another.

Bear and Share the Burdens

6 Brethren, if a man is overtaken in any trespass, you who *are* spiritual restore such a one in a spirit of gentleness, considering yourself lest you also be tempted. ²Bear one another's burdens, and so fulfill the law of Christ. ³For if anyone thinks himself to be something, when he is nothing, he deceives himself. ⁴But let each one examine his own work, and then he will have rejoicing in himself alone, and not

---

5:14 ᵃLeviticus 19:18 **5:19** ᵃNU-Text omits *adultery.* **5:21** ᵃNU-Text omits *murders.*

Responsibility: If You Won't Carry the Ball, You Can't Lead the Team

(Galatians 6:1–6)

Responsibility must start at the top. Leaders are to restore those who've failed, guard against their own sin, help bear others' burdens, and stay humble (Gal. 6:1–3). This attitude should then bleed down through the ranks (6:4–6). Shoulders that bear responsibility leave no room for chips.

Accountability: Leaders Need Alarm Bells

(Galatians 6:7–10)

We can't pull a fast one on God. He sees all and cannot be deceived. He notices our shortcuts and also our efforts when we do well. To ensure that we live by this truth, seek others to hold you accountable and act as your "alarm bells." Invite others to ask you tough questions, such as the following:

1. Is my personal walk with God up-to-date?
2. Am I keeping my priorities straight?
3. Am I asking myself the hard questions?
4. Am I accountable to someone in authority?
5. Am I sensitive to what God is saying to the whole body of Christ?
6. Am I over-concerned with building my image?
7. Do I put more stock in "events" rather than "process"?
8. Am I a loner in my leadership and personal life?
9. Am I aware and honest about my weaknesses?
10. Is my calling constantly before me?

---

in another. ⁵For each one shall bear his own load.

Be Generous and Do Good

⁶Let him who is taught the word share in all good things with him who teaches.

⁷Do not be deceived, God is not mocked; for whatever a man sows, that he will also reap. ⁸For he who sows to his flesh will of the flesh reap corruption, but he who sows to the Spirit will of the Spirit reap everlasting life. ⁹And let us not grow weary while doing good, for in due season we shall reap if we do not lose heart. ¹⁰Therefore, as we have opportunity, let us do good to all, especially to those who are of the household of faith.

Glory Only in the Cross

¹¹See with what large letters I have written to you with my own hand! ¹²As many as desire to make a good showing in the flesh, these *would* compel you to be circumcised, only that they may not suffer persecution for the cross of Christ. ¹³For not even those who are circumcised keep the law, but they desire to have you circumcised that they may boast in your flesh. ¹⁴But God forbid that I should boast except in the cross of our Lord Jesus Christ, by whomᵃ the world has been crucified to me, and I to the world. ¹⁵For in Christ Jesus neither circumcision

nor uncircumcision avails anything, but a new creation.

Blessing and a Plea

¹⁶And as many as walk according to this rule, peace and mercy *be* upon them, and upon the Israel of God.

¹⁷From now on let no one trouble me, for I bear in my body the marks of the Lord Jesus.

¹⁸Brethren, the grace of our Lord Jesus Christ *be* with your spirit. Amen.

6:14 ᵃOr *by which* (the cross)

EPHESIANS
The Whole Panorama of God's Redemptive Work

SUMMARY

Some consider this epistle to be the most profound work in the Bible. The apostle Paul wrote Ephesians while in prison. In it he covers the whole panorama of God's redemptive work—from before the foundation of the world to its consummation in the fullness of Christ. Clearly, Paul casts a huge vision for followers of Jesus.

Paul describes his vision in the first half of the letter, paving the way for application in the second half. Once someone catches Paul's vision, the only logical response is to "walk worthy of the calling with which you were called" (4:1).

What can we learn about leadership from this grand work?

First, Ephesians classically illustrates a leader who first casts a vision for the big picture before he calls the people to act. Paul knew that his readers would better obey when they simply responded to a huge initiative from God.

Second, Paul uses the metaphor of a human body to help leaders and followers better understand the church. He calls Christ the "head," while he calls followers the "body." What a wonderful picture of leadership! Just as a "head" cannot accomplish anything apart from the hands, feet, eyes, ears, etc., so a leader cannot accomplish any goal without each part of the team contributing to the whole. In the same way that Jesus enables us to act on His vision for the world, so the leader enables the followers to act on the organizational vision.

Third, Paul recognizes the diversity of the body of Christ and calls for unity in the midst of variety. Good leaders always do this. There may be one goal or vision, but a variety of gifts must be tapped to accomplish it. Paul attempts to build a team out of disparate believers: pastors, teachers, apostles, prophets, and evangelists. Any good coach wants every player to flourish. This can happen only when tasks match abilities. Players must find their correct positions.

Finally, Paul warns of hardship. He doesn't want to scare his readers, but to prepare them for battle. He soberly tells them what to expect in the coming spiritual warfare. This, too, is good leadership.

God's Role in Ephesians

Paul and God work hand in hand; both play a leadership role. God is the Head Coach who furnishes church members with a position of authority, then provides them with gifts and positions. Paul follows God's leadership as an assistant coach, equipping the people to use their gifts in service. He instructs the people to find their calling and pursue it. Finally, both God and Paul equip the reader to engage in battle. God provides the armor, Paul the instructions to use it.

Leaders in Ephesians

Paul, Timothy, the apostles, prophets, evangelists, pastor-teachers

Other People of Influence in Ephesians

Tychicus

Lessons in Leadership

- Leaders touch a heart before they ask for a hand.

- The primary role of the leader is to equip people to use their gifts.

- Authority must always accompany responsibility.

- Leaders raise the bar and call followers to a high standard.

- Leaders celebrate diversity while they work for unity.

- Leaders understand that belief precedes behavior.

- A person's influence must flow from his or her identity.

- Leaders avoid living in denial, but define reality.

LEADERSHIP HIGHLIGHTS IN EPHESIANS

COMMUNICATING VISION: Paul Remembers Who They Were and Are (2:1–10)	*page 1437*
PAUL AND TIMOTHY: A Model for Equipping (3:1–7)	*page 1438*
TEAM BUILDING: Paul Builds Unity Amidst Diversity (4:1–8)	*page 1439*
FIVE LEADERSHIP ROLES in the Church (4:11–16)	*page 1440*
LEADERSHIP in the Home (5:21–33)	*page 1442*

Greeting

1 Paul, an apostle of Jesus Christ by the will of God,

To the saints who are in Ephesus, and faithful in Christ Jesus:

[2]Grace to you and peace from God our Father and the Lord Jesus Christ.

Redemption in Christ

[3]Blessed *be* the God and Father of our Lord Jesus Christ, who has blessed us with every spiritual blessing in the heavenly *places* in Christ, [4]just as He chose us in Him before the foundation of the world, that we should be holy and without blame before Him in love, [5]having predestined us to adoption as sons by Jesus Christ to Himself, according to the good pleasure of His will, [6]to the praise of the glory of His grace, by which He made us accepted in the Beloved.

[7]In Him we have redemption through His blood, the forgiveness of sins, according to the riches of His grace [8]which He made to abound toward us in all wisdom and prudence, [9]having made known to us the mystery of His will, according to His good pleasure which He purposed in Himself, [10]that in the dispensation of the fullness of the times He might gather together in one all things in Christ, both[a] which are in heaven and which are on earth—in Him. [11]In Him also we have obtained an inheritance, being predestined according to the purpose of Him who works all things according to the counsel of His will, [12]that we who first trusted in Christ should be to the praise of His glory.

[13]In Him you also *trusted,* after you heard the word of truth, the gospel of your salvation; in whom also, having believed, you were sealed with the Holy Spirit of promise, [14]who[a] is the guarantee of our inheritance until the redemption of the purchased possession, to the praise of His glory.

The Law of Connection: Empowerment Precedes Imperative

(Ephesians 1:1–14)

Because Paul believes he needs to give before he asks, he reminds us of our choice position in Christ: chosen (Eph. 1:4); predestined (1:5); accepted (1:6); redeemed (1:7); informed (1:9); heirs (1:11); and sealed (1:13). He declares what God has done for us before demanding we do anything for Him.

The Law of Empowerment: Influence Flows from Identity

(Ephesians 1:15–23)

Paul prays that God will reveal to his readers the riches of their inheritance (hope, calling, glory, and power). Then he reminds them they are Christ's body. Power, influence, and confidence all come from a strong sense of identity. Are you secure in your identity? Does your influence reflect this strength?

Prayer for Spiritual Wisdom

[15]Therefore I also, after I heard of your faith in the Lord Jesus and your love for all the saints, [16]do not cease to give thanks for you, making mention of you in my prayers: [17]that the God of our Lord Jesus Christ, the Father of glory, may give to you the spirit of wisdom and revelation in the knowledge of Him, [18]the eyes of your understanding[a] being enlightened; that you may know what is the hope of His calling, what are the riches of the glory of His inheritance in the saints, [19]and what *is* the exceeding greatness of His power toward us who believe, according to the working of His mighty power [20]which He worked in Christ when He raised Him from the dead and seated *Him* at His right hand in the heavenly *places,* [21]far above all principality and power and might and dominion, and every name that is named, not only in this age but also in that which is to come.

[22]And He put all *things* under His feet, and gave Him *to be* head over all *things* to the church, [23]which is His body, the fullness of Him who fills all in all.

1:10 [a]NU-Text and M-Text omit *both.*
1:14 [a]NU-Text reads *which.* **1:18** [a]NU-Text and M-Text read *hearts.*

Communicating Vision:
Paul Remembers Who They Were and Are

(Ephesians 2:1–10)

Paul took time to reflect on our past failures and God's present redemption. He insists that God not only raised Jesus up and sat Him in heavenly places above all authority (Eph. 2:20, 21), but He did the same for us (2:4–6). We must identify with Christ in His life, death, resurrection, and *ascension*. We have been *raised* with Christ. No wonder Paul could lead with such boldness! He lived and led off of this paramount truth.

What must we do to experience the same kind of authority in Christ? Paul gives his answer:

1. *Renew your perspective* (Col. 3:1–3).
   We must think like God thinks. We must see ourselves as He does and fix our minds on Him. We must base our life on this position rather than our experience.
2. *Release your past* (Gal. 2:20).
   We must let go of old patterns. We will never lead in an empowering way if we hold on to our old self, our old baggage, our old citizenship. We must die to the past.
3. *Remember your purpose* (Eph. 1:3–12).
   We drift when we lose sight of why God left us on earth. Our goal is to participate in God's redemptive plan for the world. If we embrace purpose, we gain power.

By Grace Through Faith

2 And you *He made alive,* who were dead in trespasses and sins, ²in which you once walked according to the course of this world, according to the prince of the power of the air, the spirit who now works in the sons of disobedience, ³among whom also we all once conducted ourselves in the lusts of our flesh, fulfilling the desires of the flesh and of the mind, and were by nature children of wrath, just as the others.

⁴But God, who is rich in mercy, because of His great love with which He loved us, ⁵even when we were dead in trespasses, made us alive together with Christ (by grace you have been saved), ⁶and raised *us* up together, and made *us* sit together in the heavenly *places* in Christ Jesus, ⁷that in the ages to come He might show the exceeding riches of His grace in *His* kindness toward us in Christ Jesus. ⁸For by grace you have been saved through faith, and that not of yourselves; *it is* the gift of God, ⁹not of works, lest anyone should boast. ¹⁰For we are His workmanship, created in Christ Jesus for good works, which God prepared beforehand that we should walk in them.

Brought Near by His Blood

¹¹Therefore remember that you, once Gentiles in the flesh—who are called Uncircumcision by what is called the Circumcision made in the flesh by hands— ¹²that at that time you were

Equipping: Paul Gives
the Tools to Do the Job

(Ephesians 2:8–22)

Paul provides some tools for his readers to live in the way God intends for them to live. He informs them they are saved by grace (Eph. 2:8, 9) and created to do good works (2:10). Then he equips them for these good works with divine tools, explaining how they have been delivered from darkness and transformed into new persons (2:14–16) and a new building (2:19–22).

Paul labored hard to unleash the church and prepare its members for service. If we pursue the same goal, we must embrace the following assumptions:

1. Everyone wants to feel worthwhile.
2. Everyone needs and responds to encouragement.
3. People buy into the leader before they buy into the plan.
4. Most people don't know how to be successful.
5. People are naturally motivated.
6. Most people will move once they receive permission and equipping.

without Christ, being aliens from the common-wealth of Israel and strangers from the covenants of promise, having no hope and without God in the world. [13]But now in Christ Jesus you who once were far off have been brought near by the blood of Christ.

Christ Our Peace

[14]For He Himself is our peace, who has made both one, and has broken down the middle wall of separation, [15]having abolished in His flesh the enmity, *that is,* the law of commandments *contained* in ordinances, so as to create in Himself one new man *from* the two, *thus* making peace, [16]and that He might reconcile them both to God in one body through the cross, thereby putting to death the enmity. [17]And He came and preached peace to you who were afar off and to those who were near. [18]For through Him we both have access by one Spirit to the Father.

Christ Our Cornerstone

[19]Now, therefore, you are no longer strangers and foreigners, but fellow citizens with the saints and members of the household of God, [20]having been built on the foundation of the apostles and prophets, Jesus Christ Himself being the chief cornerstone, [21]in whom the whole building, being fitted together, grows into a holy temple in the Lord, [22]in whom you also are being built together for a dwelling place of God in the Spirit.

The Mystery Revealed

3 For this reason I, Paul, the prisoner of Christ Jesus for you Gentiles— [2]if indeed you have heard of the dispensation of the grace of God which was given to me for you, [3]how that by revelation He made known to me the mystery (as I have briefly written already, [4]by which, when you read, you may understand my knowledge in the mystery of Christ), [5]which in other ages was not made known to the sons of men, as it has now been revealed by the Spirit to His holy apostles and prophets: [6]that the Gentiles should be fellow heirs, of the same body, and partakers of His promise in Christ through the gospel, [7]of which I became a minister according to the gift of the grace of God given to me by the effective working of His power.

Purpose of the Mystery

[8]To me, who am less than the least of all the saints, this grace was given, that I should preach among the Gentiles the unsearchable riches of

---

PAUL AND TIMOTHY

A MODEL FOR EQUIPPING
(Ephesians 3:1–7)

PROFILE IN LEADERSHIP

By themselves, not even the best accountants or financial advisers can create wealth for their clients. All they can do is give advice concerning the accumulation of financial reserves. The rest is up to the recipients of that advice.

The same is true for leaders who wish to see others access the riches of heaven. The lives and ministries of the apostle Paul and Timothy—the young leader of the church at Ephesus—demonstrate this principle.

On their own, neither Paul nor Timothy could equip the Ephesians to please God. But they knew how to direct their charges to the ultimate source of ultimate power: the Holy Spirit and the Word of God.

Paul exhorts the Ephesian Christians to take full advantage of all the resources and power God has made available to them. The apostle knows that all believers have at their disposal immeasurable wealth and power, infinite resources sufficient to equip every believer for the spiritual fight ahead.

Godly leaders have at their disposal the same kind of power Paul describes here. Leaders are responsible to direct other believers to the place where they can be enriched and equipped so they can serve God and do battle for the kingdom.

Passion: Paul Teaches Them to Take This Life and Love It

(Ephesians 3:14–21)

Paul prays passionately that his readers comprehend the love of God (Eph. 3:14, 18), experience the love of Christ (3:19), and be filled with God (3:19). Then he declares God is able to do exceedingly, abundantly, above all we ask or think (3:20)! Passion is the first step to achievement.

Christ, [9]and to make all see what *is* the fellowship[a] of the mystery, which from the beginning of the ages has been hidden in God who created all things through Jesus Christ;[b] [10]to the intent that now the manifold wisdom of God might be made known by the church to the principalities and powers in the heavenly *places,* [11]according to the eternal purpose which He accomplished in Christ Jesus our Lord, [12]in whom we have boldness and access with confidence through faith in Him. [13]Therefore I ask that you do not lose heart at my tribulations for you, which is your glory.

Appreciation of the Mystery

[14]For this reason I bow my knees to the Father of our Lord Jesus Christ,[a] [15]from whom the whole family in heaven and earth is named, [16]that He would grant you, according to the riches of His glory, to be strengthened with might through His Spirit in the inner man, [17]that Christ may dwell in your hearts through faith; that you, being rooted and grounded in love, [18]may be able to comprehend with all the saints what *is* the width and length and depth and height— [19]to know the love of Christ which passes knowledge; that you may be filled with all the fullness of God.

[20]Now to Him who is able to do exceedingly abundantly above all that we ask or think, according to the power that works in us, [21]to Him *be* glory in the church by Christ Jesus to all generations, forever and ever. Amen.

Walk in Unity

4 I, therefore, the prisoner of the Lord, beseech you to walk worthy of the calling with which you were called, [2]with all lowliness and gentleness, with longsuffering, bearing with one another in love, [3]endeavoring to keep

3:9 [a]NU-Text and M-Text read *stewardship* (dispensation). [b]NU-Text omits *through Jesus Christ.* 3:14 [a]NU-Text omits *of our Lord Jesus Christ.*

Team Building: Paul Builds Unity Amidst Diversity

(Ephesians 4:1–8)

The apostle Paul labored to foster unity amidst a diverse population—in other words, he worked at team building.

He reminds the Ephesians of the attitude of the individual players (Eph. 4:1–3), then discusses the attitude of the corporate body (3:4–6). Paul insists there is one body, one Spirit, one hope, one Lord, one faith, one baptism, and one God and Father. He says each player has been given some grace and some gifts. He calls the church a temple, a bride, a mystery, an army, and a body.

Think of Paul as a coach, building his team. How do we build a diverse group into a unified team? Ask the following questions:

1. Am I building people, or building my kingdom and using people?
2. Do I care enough to confront people when it will make a difference?
3. Am I listening with more than my ears?
4. Am I asking the right questions to develop the right relationships?
5. What are the major strengths of each individual?
6. Have I placed a high priority on their jobs?
7. Have I shown the value they will receive from this work?
8. Are their goals compatible with mine?

Five Leadership Roles in the Church

(Ephesians 4:11–16)

God gave at least five types of leaders to the church: apostles, prophets, evangelists, pastors, and teachers. They exist to complete the members' growth and to equip them to serve (Eph. 4:12–16). Their roles vary:

1. *Apostle:* One sent forth to pioneer and establish new works and new leaders.
2. *Prophet:* One who speaks forth God's Word to inspire, correct, and motivate.
3. *Evangelist:* One who shares Christ with outsiders and trains others to do so.
4. *Pastor:* One who shepherds, guides, and guards God's people as they serve.
5. *Teacher:* One who trains God's people in the truth and teaches others to do so.

When the church fills these five offices, ordinary people get equipped for ministry. Ask yourself the following questions:

1. What eternally significant growth occurs in the lives of those I lead (vv. 11–13)?
2. Do our people understand that my role is to equip them to serve (v. 12)?
3. How are our followers serving and ministering (v. 12)?
4. Do our people know that involvement in service is essential to growth (v. 12)?
5. Do our people grow spiritually mature as a result of their ministry involvement (v. 13)?
6. Do our people's lifestyles reflect Christ's character (v. 13)?
7. What percentage of our people's faith and involvement is easily shaken (v. 14)?
8. Do our people build up one another (vv. 15, 16)?

the unity of the Spirit in the bond of peace. ⁴*There is* one body and one Spirit, just as you were called in one hope of your calling; ⁵one Lord, one faith, one baptism; ⁶one God and Father of all, who *is* above all, and through all, and in you[a] all.

Spiritual Gifts

⁷But to each one of us grace was given according to the measure of Christ's gift. ⁸Therefore He says:

> "When He ascended on high,
> He led captivity captive,
> And gave gifts to men."[a]

⁹(Now this, *"He ascended"*—what does it mean but that He also first[a] descended into the lower parts of the earth? ¹⁰He who descended is also the One who ascended far above all the heavens, that He might fill all things.)

¹¹And He Himself gave some *to be* apostles, some prophets, some evangelists, and some pastors and teachers, ¹²for the equipping of the saints for the work of ministry, for the edifying of the body of Christ, ¹³till we all come to the unity of the faith and of the knowledge of the Son of God, to a perfect man, to the measure of the

stature of the fullness of Christ; ¹⁴that we should no longer be children, tossed to and fro and carried about with every wind of doctrine, by the trickery of men, in the cunning craftiness of deceitful plotting, ¹⁵but, speaking the truth in love, may grow up in all things into Him who is the head—Christ— ¹⁶from whom the whole body, joined and knit together by what every joint supplies, according to the effective working by which every part does its share, causes growth of the body for the edifying of itself in love.

The New Man

¹⁷This I say, therefore, and testify in the Lord, that you should no longer walk as the rest of[a] the Gentiles walk, in the futility of their mind, ¹⁸having their understanding darkened, being alienated from the life of God, because of the ignorance that is in them, because of the blindness of their heart; ¹⁹who, being past feeling, have given themselves over to lewdness, to work all uncleanness with greediness.

²⁰But you have not so learned Christ, ²¹if indeed you have heard Him and have been taught

4:6 [a]NU-Text omits *you;* M-Text reads *us.*
4:8 [a]Psalm 68:18 4:9 [a]NU-Text omits *first.*
4:17 [a]NU-Text omits *the rest of.*

Equipping: The Leader's Job

(Ephesians 4:12–16)

Equipping is a tough job, much harder than shepherding. The leader is to equip others for ministry. Paul explains the goal for the shepherd (Eph. 4:12) and the goal of the sheep (4:13), then describes the result (4:14–16).

If leaders wish to equip their people, they *must* give them certain gifts:

1. I must CARE for them (Communication, Affirmation, Recognition, and Example).
2. I must work *on* their weaknesses, but work *out* their strengths.
3. I must give them myself (time, energy, and focus).
4. I must give them ownership of the ministry.
5. I must become a resource person (atmosphere, training, support, tools).
6. I must make expectations clear.
7. I must eliminate unnecessary burdens.
8. I must catch them doing something good, then reward them.

by Him, as the truth is in Jesus: [22]that you put off, concerning your former conduct, the old man which grows corrupt according to the deceitful lusts, [23]and be renewed in the spirit of your mind, [24]and that you put on the new man which was created according to God, in true righteousness and holiness.

Do Not Grieve the Spirit

[25]Therefore, putting away lying, *"Let each one of you speak truth with his neighbor,"*[a] for we are members of one another. [26]*"Be angry, and do not sin"*:[a] do not let the sun go down on your wrath, [27]nor give place to the devil. [28]Let him who stole steal no longer, but rather let him labor, working with *his* hands what is good, that he may have something to give him who has need. [29]Let no corrupt word proceed out of your mouth, but what is good for necessary edification, that it may impart grace to the hearers. [30]And do not grieve the Holy Spirit of God, by whom you were sealed for the day of redemption. [31]Let all bitterness, wrath, anger, clamor, and evil speaking be put away from you, with all malice. [32]And be kind to one another, tenderhearted, forgiving one another, even as God in Christ forgave you.

Walk in Love

5 Therefore be imitators of God as dear children. [2]And walk in love, as Christ also has loved us and given Himself for us, an offering and a sacrifice to God for a sweet-smelling aroma.

[3]But fornication and all uncleanness or covetousness, let it not even be named among you,

as is fitting for saints; [4]neither filthiness, nor foolish talking, nor coarse jesting, which are not fitting, but rather giving of thanks. [5]For this you know,[a] that no fornicator, unclean person, nor covetous man, who is an idolater, has any inheritance in the kingdom of Christ and God. [6]Let no one deceive you with empty words, for because of these things the wrath of God comes upon the sons of disobedience. [7]Therefore do not be partakers with them.

Walk in Light

[8]For you were once darkness, but now *you are* light in the Lord. Walk as children of light [9](for the fruit of the Spirit[a] *is* in all goodness, righteousness, and truth), [10]finding out what is acceptable to the Lord. [11]And have no fellowship with the unfruitful works of darkness, but rather expose *them*. [12]For it is shameful even to speak of those things which are done by them in secret. [13]But all things that are exposed are made manifest by the light, for whatever makes manifest is light, [14]Therefore He says:

> "Awake, you who sleep,
> Arise from the dead,
> And Christ will give you light."

Walk in Wisdom

[15]See then that you walk circumspectly, not as fools but as wise, [16]redeeming the time, because the days are evil.

4:25 [a]Zechariah 8:16 **4:26** [a]Psalm 4:4 **5:5** [a]NU-Text reads *For know this.* **5:9** [a]NU-Text reads *light.*

The Law of Priorities: Redeem Your Time

(Ephesians 5:15–17)

Because activity is not necessarily accomplishment, Paul advises us to: analyze our lifestyles (Eph. 5:15); utilize the present (5:16); and prioritize what is important (5:17). While every leader, every day, gets the same amount of time, not every leader gets the same results.

[17]Therefore do not be unwise, but understand what the will of the Lord *is.* [18]And do not be drunk with wine, in which is dissipation; but be filled with the Spirit, [19]speaking to one another in psalms and hymns and spiritual songs, singing and making melody in your heart to the Lord, [20]giving thanks always for all things to God the Father in the name of our Lord Jesus Christ, [21]submitting to one another in the fear of God.[a]

Marriage—Christ and the Church

[22]Wives, submit to your own husbands, as to the Lord. [23]For the husband is head of the wife, as also Christ is head of the church; and He is the Savior of the body. [24]Therefore, just as the church is subject to Christ, so *let* the wives *be* to their own husbands in everything.

[25]Husbands, love your wives, just as Christ also loved the church and gave Himself for her, [26]that He might sanctify and cleanse her with the washing of water by the word, [27]that He might present her to Himself a glorious church, not having spot or wrinkle or any such thing, but that she should be holy and without blemish. [28]So husbands ought to love their own wives as their own bodies; he who loves his wife loves himself. [29]For no one ever hated his own flesh, but nourishes and cherishes it, just as the Lord *does* the church. [30]For we are members of His body,[a] of His flesh and of His bones. [31]*"For this reason a man shall leave his father and mother and be joined to his wife, and the two shall become one flesh."*[a] [32]This is a great mystery, but I speak concerning Christ and the church. [33]Nevertheless let each one of you in particular so love his own wife as himself, and let the wife *see* that she respects *her* husband.

5:21 [a]NU-Text reads *Christ.* **5:30** [a]NU-Text omits the rest of this verse. **5:31** [a]Genesis 2:24

Leadership in the Home

(Ephesians 5:21–33)

Contrary to what many teach, leadership in the home is not about power or control. Paul asks for mutual submission (Eph. 5:21) and calls husbands to be Christ-figures (5:23–25). And how did Christ lead the church? He provided, taught, wept, healed, and died on a cross. Spiritual leadership means giving up yourself for someone else (5:25). It means assuming responsibility for the health and development of your relationships. Evaluate your home leadership in each of the following categories:

1. *Initiative*
   Do I give direction and take responsibility for my primary relationships?
2. *Intimacy*
   Do I experience intimacy with God and others through open conversation?
3. *Influence*
   Do I exercise biblical influence by encouraging and developing others?
4. *Integrity*
   Do I lead an honest life, unashamed of who I am when no one is looking?
5. *Identity*
   Am I secure in who I am in Christ? Or am I defensive?
6. *Inner Character*
   Do I exhibit the fruit of the Spirit in my life, including self-discipline?

Children and Parents

6 Children, obey your parents in the Lord, for this is right. [2]*"Honor your father and mother,"* which is the first commandment with promise: [3]*"that it may be well with you and you may live long on the earth."*[a]

[4]And you, fathers, do not provoke your children to wrath, but bring them up in the training and admonition of the Lord.

Bondservants and Masters

[5]Bondservants, be obedient to those who are your masters according to the flesh, with fear and trembling, in sincerity of heart, as to Christ; [6]not with eyeservice, as men-pleasers, but as bondservants of Christ, doing the will of God from the heart, [7]with goodwill doing service, as to the Lord, and not to men, [8]knowing that whatever good anyone does, he will receive the same from the Lord, whether *he is* a slave or free.

[9]And you, masters, do the same things to them, giving up threatening, knowing that your own Master also[a] is in heaven, and there is no partiality with Him.

The Whole Armor of God

[10]Finally, my brethren, be strong in the Lord and in the power of His might. [11]Put on the whole armor of God, that you may be able to stand against the wiles of the devil. [12]For we do not wrestle against flesh and blood, but against principalities, against powers, against the rulers of

6:3 [a]Deuteronomy 5:16 **6:9** [a]NU-Text reads *He who is both their Master and yours.*

Work Ethic: You're Not Working for People
(Ephesians 6:5–9)

The principles Paul taught to owners and slaves apply today to employees and employers. He twice states the important principle: We are not to be people pleasers (Eph. 6:6). We aren't to work while others watch, then slack off when alone. We are to render service as though we are working for God, who watches at all times (6:7). Not only does God watch, but He rewards anything good we do (6:8).

People may forget how fast you did your last job, but they will remember how well you did it. Ultimately, we all work for ourselves and for God.

The Law of Intuition: Paul Understood How to Defeat the Enemy
(Ephesians 6:10–20)

Like any good leader, Paul issues a warning at the end of his letter about the tough times his people will face. They are up against Satan himself (Eph. 6:12), an enemy who will do everything to stop their progress.

Instead of moping about the situation, however, Paul lays out a specific plan for his Ephesian friends. They are not to approach this fight in their own strength, but remember that only God can defeat the enemy (6:10). As a Warrior, God fills a role His people desperately need. He serves as their Protector, Defender, Deliverer, Provider, and Guide. God gives His army every supply needed to win.

Paul then instructs his readers to put on the whole armor of God, in order to stand and prevail (6:11–17). Serving as an officer under God, Paul issues the orders for the troops. When leaders practice the Law of Intuition, they provide their people with . . .

1. A strategy to win (vv. 11, 12).
2. Knowledge of the opposition (v. 12).
3. The resources they need (v. 13).
4. A plan for how to use them (vv. 14–17).
5. Detailed communication (vv. 14–20).

the darkness of this age,[a] against spiritual *hosts* of wickedness in the heavenly *places.* [13]Therefore take up the whole armor of God, that you may be able to withstand in the evil day, and having done all, to stand.

[14]Stand therefore, having girded your waist with truth, having put on the breastplate of righteousness, [15]and having shod your feet with the preparation of the gospel of peace; [16]above all, taking the shield of faith with which you will be able to quench all the fiery darts of the wicked one. [17]And take the helmet of salvation, and the sword of the Spirit, which is the word of God; [18]praying always with all prayer and supplication in the Spirit, being watchful to this end with all perseverance and supplication for all the saints— [19]and for me, that utterance may be given to me, that I may open my mouth boldly

to make known the mystery of the gospel, [20]for which I am an ambassador in chains; that in it I may speak boldly, as I ought to speak.

A Gracious Greeting

[21]But that you also may know my affairs *and* how I am doing, Tychicus, a beloved brother and faithful minister in the Lord, will make all things known to you; [22]whom I have sent to you for this very purpose, that you may know our affairs, and *that* he may comfort your hearts.

[23]Peace to the brethren, and love with faith, from God the Father and the Lord Jesus Christ. [24]Grace *be* with all those who love our Lord Jesus Christ in sincerity. Amen.

6:12 [a]NU-Text reads *rulers of this darkness.*

PHILIPPIANS

For the Progress of the Gospel

SUMMARY

This letter proves that even while the apostle Paul sat in a foul Roman prison, he never lost his passion, his sense of mission, his sense of direction, or his command of the situation. While Paul remained an inmate of Rome, he couldn't plant new churches as he felt called to do. Instead, he sat in chains, attached to a Praetorian guard, awaiting a trial that he thought could end his life (1:21). Yet even in the midst of all of this, he never abandoned his role of leadership.

In chapter one, he speaks of his unchanging mission. He remains on track, even in prison. He insists that his circumstances have actually turned out for the progress of the gospel. No matter where he ends up, Paul uses his location as a platform to accomplish the mission.

The apostle also models for us an incredible attitude toward adversity. He mentions that he can't choose between life or death; to him, both seem positive options. Finally, he decides he will continue to live, knowing he can be more useful to the cause while alive.

In chapter two, he discusses the servant's heart of a leader, illustrating with the humility Christ displayed in coming to earth. Jesus didn't insist on the prerogatives of deity, but instead emptied Himself and assumed the position of a man, taking the form of a bondservant, becoming mortal and dying—even a terrible kind of death: crucifixion. Paul claims that all effective leaders must live such a selfless life.

In chapter three, Paul discusses priorities, goal setting, and perseverance. He reminds the reader of his trophies. Then he discards them, treating them like trash compared to the priority of knowing Christ and fulfilling His priorities. He speaks of the "one thing" he's set his mind to do, forgetting what lies behind him and looking forward to what lies ahead. He persists, pressing on toward the goal until he has obtained it.

In his final chapter, Paul concludes with words of rejoicing. He urges his readers to maintain tough minds, fixing on what is right and profitable. Discipline, contentment, and focus are all key. Paul thanks the members of the Philippian church for their partnership and affirms his love for them—a fitting close to a warm, personal exhortation from a model leader.

God's Role in Philippians

God's heart shows up vividly in this book. God can be seen in people who, although they find themselves in positions of adversity, nevertheless display attitudes of conquest, joy, peace, and ministry. This is the supernatural leader, empowered by God to live out His values and vision in a fallen world.

God is the source of Paul's joy, his peace, his conquering spirit, and his heart for ministry, even when he is an inmate and in need of someone to minister to him. God enables us to remain leaders who are "on mission" no matter where we find ourselves.

Leaders in Philippians

Paul, Epaphroditus, Timothy, the Philippian church elders

Other People of Influence in Philippians

Euodia, Syntyche

Lessons in Leadership

- Leaders either surrender to a cause or they surrender to their circumstances.

- Only secure leaders will stoop and stretch.

- A leader's attitude at the beginning of a task will affect its outcome more than anything else.

- Leaders can do anything, but they can't do everything.

- One cannot be a great leader without being a great servant.

LEADERSHIP HIGHLIGHTS IN PHILIPPIANS

THE LAW OF SACRIFICE: Jesus' Six Steps of Servanthood (2:2–11)	*page 1448*
EPAPHRODITUS: A Leader Who Didn't Make a Name for Himself (2:25–30)	*page 1449*
FOCUS: Letting Go of Nice Things That Don't Matter (3:5–9)	*page 1450*
THE LAW OF PRIORITIES: Paul Narrowed His Activities (3:7–14)	*page 1451*
PAUL: A Leader Who Couldn't Be Stopped (4:4–13)	*page 1453*

Greeting

1 Paul and Timothy, bondservants of Jesus Christ,

To all the saints in Christ Jesus who are in Philippi, with the bishops[a] and deacons:

[2]Grace to you and peace from God our Father and the Lord Jesus Christ.

Thankfulness and Prayer

[3]I thank my God upon every remembrance of you, [4]always in every prayer of mine making request for you all with joy, [5]for your fellowship in the gospel from the first day until now, [6]being confident of this very thing, that He who has begun a good work in you will complete *it* until the day of Jesus Christ; [7]just as it is right for me to think this of you all, because I have you in my heart, inasmuch as both in my chains and in the defense and confirmation of the gospel, you all are partakers with me of grace. [8]For God is my witness, how greatly I long for you all with the affection of Jesus Christ.

[9]And this I pray, that your love may abound still more and more in knowledge and all discernment, [10]that you may approve the things that are excellent, that you may be sincere and without offense till the day of Christ, [11]being filled with the fruits of righteousness which *are* by Jesus Christ, to the glory and praise of God.

Encouragement: Leaders Connect When They Encourage

(Philippians 1:3–11)

Paul never issues some worn-out, generic brand of encouragement. His words speak to specific needs, express specific love for particular people, and communicate a specific hope for their future. Encouragement ought to be given sincerely, personally, specifically, publicly, and frequently.

Christ Is Preached

[12]But I want you to know, brethren, that the things *which happened* to me have actually turned out for the furtherance of the gospel, [13]so that it has become evident to the whole palace guard, and to all the rest, that my chains are in Christ;

Purpose: Paul Stayed on Mission, Even in Prison

(Philippians 1:12–18)

Paul might have been forgiven had he chosen to take a little sabbatical as he sat in prison, awaiting his trial. Yet he used even this opportunity to advance the gospel (Phil. 1:12).

Paul was a leader who never drifted from his mission. He determined to leave his mark wherever he went. George Washington Carver wrote, "No individual has any right to come into the world and go out of it without leaving behind him distinct and legitimate reasons for having passed through it."

How did Paul's sense of purpose keep him in the battle as he sat in prison? What did he learn behind bars? Consider the following:

1. A purpose will motivate you.
2. A purpose will keep your priorities straight.
3. A purpose will develop your potential.
4. A purpose will give you power to live in the present.
5. A purpose will help you evaluate your progress.

---

[14]and most of the brethren in the Lord, having become confident by my chains, are much more bold to speak the word without fear.

[15]Some indeed preach Christ even from envy and strife, and some also from goodwill: [16]The former[a] preach Christ from selfish ambition, not sincerely, supposing to add affliction to my chains; [17]but the latter out of love, knowing that I am appointed for the defense of the gospel. [18]What then? Only *that* in every way, whether in pretense or in truth, Christ is preached; and in this I rejoice, yes, and will rejoice.

To Live Is Christ

[19]For I know that this will turn out for my deliverance through your prayer and the supply of the Spirit of Jesus Christ, [20]according to my earnest expectation and hope that in nothing I shall be ashamed, but with all boldness, as always, so now also Christ will be magnified in my

---

1:1 [a]Literally *overseers* **1:16** [a]NU-Text reverses the contents of verses 16 and 17.

Positive Attitude: Paul's Attitude Determined His Altitude

(Philippians 1:12–18)

A personal sense of purpose works in two ways. First, we work on it. Then, it works on us.

Once Paul had determined his life mission, that purpose daily improved his attitude. In prisons, shipwrecks, beatings, through trials and debates, Paul kept on smiling because of his strong sense of purpose. He understood that leaders can either surrender to their circumstances, or they can surrender to a cause that is so great, their circumstances won't matter.

When we surrender to our circumstances, we have good days and bad days. We are at the mercy of what happens to us. When we surrender to a cause or purpose, we have good days wherever we go; the purpose never dies. Paul's attitude helped his purpose go forward, then his purpose helped his attitude go forward! His attitude helped him conclude that it didn't matter what happened to him or others—so long as the mission continued.

body, whether by life or by death. [21]For to me, to live *is* Christ, and to die *is* gain. [22]But if *I* live on in the flesh, this *will mean* fruit from *my* labor; yet what I shall choose I cannot tell. [23]For[a] I am hard-pressed between the two, having a desire to depart and be with Christ, *which is* far better. [24]Nevertheless to remain in the flesh *is* more needful for you. [25]And being confident of this, I know that I shall remain and continue with you all for your progress and joy of faith, [26]that your rejoicing for me may be more abundant in Jesus Christ by my coming to you again.

Striving and Suffering for Christ

[27]Only let your conduct be worthy of the gospel of Christ, so that whether I come and see you or am absent, I may hear of your affairs, that you stand fast in one spirit, with one mind striving together for the faith of the gospel, [28]and not in any way terrified by your adversaries, which is to them a proof of perdition, but to you of sal-

vation,[a] and that from God. [29]For to you it has been granted on behalf of Christ, not only to believe in Him, but also to suffer for His sake, [30]having the same conflict which you saw in me and now hear *is* in me.

Unity Through Humility

2 Therefore if *there is* any consolation in Christ, if any comfort of love, if any fellowship of the Spirit, if any affection and mercy, [2]fulfill my joy by being like-minded, having the same love, *being* of one accord, of one mind. [3]*Let* nothing *be done* through selfish ambition or conceit, but in lowliness of mind let each esteem others better than himself. [4]Let each of you look out not only for his own interests, but also for the interests of others.

1:23 [a]NU-Text and M-Text read *But*.
1:28 [a]NU-Text reads *of your salvation*.

The Law of Sacrifice: Jesus' Six Steps of Servanthood

(Philippians 2:2–11)

P aul used Jesus as the ultimate example of servant leadership. After urging his audience to humble themselves and live selflessly (Phil. 2:2–4), he reminds them of Christ's incarnation. Here the Ultimate Leader made the ultimate sacrifice. He left the glories of heaven and the highest position in heaven, not only to join His creation, but to take on the lowest form of the creation.

Jesus stepped through six levels as He moved downward toward us. In His leadership He practiced the Law of Sacrifice:

Level One: He gave up His divine form (v. 6).

Level Two: He emptied Himself of any rights (v. 7).

Level Three: He became a man (v. 7).

Level Four: He became a servant (v. 7).

Level Five: He was obedient to the point of death (v. 8).

Level Six: He died a terrible kind of death (v. 8).

The Humbled and Exalted Christ

[5]Let this mind be in you which was also in Christ Jesus, [6]who, being in the form of God, did not consider it robbery to be equal with God, [7]but made Himself of no reputation, taking the form of a bondservant, *and* coming in the likeness of men. [8]And being found in appearance as a man, He humbled Himself and became obedient to *the point of* death, even the death of the cross. [9]Therefore God also has highly exalted Him and given Him the name which is above every name, [10]that at the name of Jesus every knee should bow, of those in heaven, and of those on earth, and of those under the earth, [11]and *that* every tongue should confess that Jesus Christ *is* Lord, to the glory of God the Father.

Light Bearers

[12]Therefore, my beloved, as you have always obeyed, not as in my presence only, but now much more in my absence, work out your own salvation with fear and trembling; [13]for it is God who works in you both to will and to do for *His* good pleasure.

[14]Do all things without complaining and disputing, [15]that you may become blameless and harmless, children of God without fault in the midst of a crooked and perverse generation, among whom you shine as lights in the world, [16]holding fast the word of life, so that I may rejoice in the day of Christ that I have not run in vain or labored in vain.

[17]Yes, and if I am being poured out *as a drink offering* on the sacrifice and service of your faith, I am glad and rejoice with you all. [18]For the same reason you also be glad and rejoice with me.

Timothy Commended

[19]But I trust in the Lord Jesus to send Timothy to you shortly, that I also may be encouraged when I know your state. [20]For I have no one likeminded, who will sincerely care for your state. [21]For all seek their own, not the things which are of Christ Jesus. [22]But you know his proven character, that as a son with *his* father he served with me in the gospel. [23]Therefore I hope to send him at once, as soon as I see how it goes with me. [24]But I trust in the Lord that I myself shall also come shortly.

EPAPHRODITUS

A LEADER WHO DIDN'T MAKE A NAME FOR HIMSELF
(Philippians 2:25–30)

Several leaders in the Bible qualify as "nobodies." They never became famous, like Moses or David or Paul, but remained obscure, even though they played a vital role in the kingdom. Epaphroditus was such a man.

Epaphroditus is mentioned only in Philippians. No books were ever written about him, to him, or by him. We know of no statues or memorials erected to him. He was a "nobody" who became a "somebody" to Paul. He ran all the way from Philippi to Rome to join Paul in prison and minister to him. He also carried this letter back home to the Philippians. Note how Paul describes him:

1. *A People Lover*
   Paul calls him a minister. He feels distressed that the Philippians might worry about him when he became sick (vv. 25, 26).

2. *A Risk Taker*
   Paul calls him a fellow soldier. He keeps on risking his life when most would have pampered themselves (vv. 25, 30).

3. *A Tireless Worker*
   Paul calls him a fellow worker. We know little about his illness, except that it was tied to his hard work (vv. 25, 27).

4. *A Servant-Leader*
   Paul calls him a messenger. Paul tells the church to give him a hero's welcome (vv. 25, 29). He both led and served as he became a spokesman for the church.

21 QUALITIES

FOCUS

Letting Go of Nice Things That Don't Matter
(Philippians 3:5–9)

Paul's absolute focus gave him an absolute willingness to let go of nice things that didn't matter. Note some items that he discarded:

1. *His heritage:* a Hebrew of the Hebrews (v. 5)
2. *His pure lineage:* from the tribe of Benjamin (v. 5)
3. *His former legalism:* a strict Pharisee (v. 5)
4. *His past zeal:* a persecutor of the church (v. 6)
5. *His self-righteousness:* a blameless life (v. 6)

Paul so narrowed his focus that he discarded not only the things he once counted as gain, but he counted *everything* as garbage for the sake of obtaining Christ! He would lose it all if that allowed him to gain intimacy with Christ (Phil. 3:8, 9).

Leaders who change the world have this kind of sharp focus. Think about the leaders of the Bible and the focus they had to bring about revolutionary change:

1. Abraham left his homeland, wealth, and friends for a new land because he focused on an unseen kingdom.
2. Joseph had strength to endure hardship and prisons because his dream focused on the greatness of God.
3. Moses could turn his back on Egypt because he focused on God's plan.
4. Stephen preached an unpopular message and died a martyr because of his focus.
5. Paul gave everything up and said, "This one thing I do."
6. Jesus told Martha, "Only one thing is necessary."

What does it take to gain the focus required to become a truly effective leader? The keys are *priorities* and *concentration*. A leader who knows his priorities but lacks concentration knows what to do, but never gets it done. A leader with concentration but no priorities has excellence without progress. But when leaders harness both, they gain the potential to achieve great things.

People base their decisions on a variety of things:

1. *The Ultimate:* first things first.
2. *The Urgent:* loud things first.
3. *The Unpleasant:* hard things first.
4. *The Unfinished:* last things first.
5. *The Unfulfilling:* dull things first.

Paul exemplifies a leader who focused on the ultimate every day. How about you? To get back on track with your focus, work on these items:

1. *Work on yourself.* You are your greatest asset or worst liability.
2. *Work on your priorities.* Fight for the important ones.
3. *Work in your strengths.* You can reach your potential if you do.
4. *Work with your colleagues.* You can't be effective alone.

For a negative example of focus, see p. 787.

Epaphroditus Praised

[25]Yet I considered it necessary to send to you Epaphroditus, my brother, fellow worker, and fellow soldier, but your messenger and the one who ministered to my need; [26]since he was longing for you all, and was distressed because you had heard that he was sick. [27]For indeed he was sick almost unto death; but God had mercy on him, and not only on him but on me also, lest I should have sorrow upon sorrow. [28]Therefore I sent him the more eagerly, that when you see him again you may rejoice, and I may be less sorrowful. [29]Receive him therefore in the Lord with all gladness, and hold such men in esteem; [30]because for the work of Christ he came close to death, not regarding his life, to supply what was lacking in your service toward me.

All for Christ

3 Finally, my brethren, rejoice in the Lord. For me to write the same things to you *is* not tedious, but for you *it is* safe.

[2]Beware of dogs, beware of evil workers, beware of the mutilation! [3]For we are the circumcision, who worship God in the Spirit,[a] rejoice in Christ Jesus, and have no confidence in the flesh, [4]though I also might have confidence in the flesh. If anyone else thinks he may have confidence in the flesh, I more so: [5]circumcised the eighth day, of the stock of Israel, *of* the tribe of Benjamin, a Hebrew of the Hebrews; concerning the law, a Pharisee; [6]concerning zeal, persecuting the church; concerning the righteousness which is in the law, blameless.

[7]But what things were gain to me, these I have counted loss for Christ. [8]Yet indeed I also count all things loss for the excellence of the knowledge of Christ Jesus my Lord, for whom I have suffered the loss of all things, and count them as rubbish, that I may gain Christ [9]and be found in Him, not having my own righteousness, which *is* from the law, but that which *is* through faith in Christ, the righteousness which is from God by faith; [10]that I may know Him and the power of His resurrection, and the fellowship of His sufferings, being conformed to His death, [11]if, by any means, I may attain to the resurrection from the dead.

Pressing Toward the Goal

[12]Not that I have already attained, or am already perfected; but I press on, that I may lay hold of that for which Christ Jesus has also laid hold of me. [13]Brethren, I do not count myself to have apprehended; but one thing *I do,* forgetting those things which are behind and reaching forward to those things which are ahead, [14]I press toward the goal for the prize of the upward call of God in Christ Jesus.

3:3 [a]NU-Text and M-Text read *who worship in the Spirit of God.*

The Law of Priorities: Paul Narrowed His Activities

(Philippians 3:7–14)

Paul openly communicated his priorities. All the trophies and culture of his past he counted as rubbish, in order to gain Christ. He wanted to know Christ, experience His power, share in and complete His sufferings, and ultimately be conformed to His death (Phil. 3:10, 11). He did all of this for the purpose of attaining the resurrection.

Here is a man on a mission. Paul narrowed his wedge and his focus to the essentials. What was his secret?

1. *He discerned what hindered him* (vv. 7, 8).
   Paul had to let go of all the things he once cherished, considering them distractions to grace.
2. *He discovered what he wanted* (vv. 9–11).
   Paul wanted God's righteousness, not his own. Christ became his solitary pursuit.
3. *He determined how to get it* (vv. 12–14).
   With single-minded passion, Paul forgot the past and pursued the prize of his call.

How about you? Have you narrowed your focus? What is your "one thing"? Can you list your priorities on one hand? What are you pursuing?

[15]Therefore let us, as many as are mature, have this mind; and if in anything you think otherwise, God will reveal even this to you. [16]Nevertheless, to *the degree* that we have already attained, let us walk by the same rule,[a] let us be of the same mind.

Our Citizenship in Heaven

[17]Brethren, join in following my example, and note those who so walk, as you have us for a pattern. [18]For many walk, of whom I have told you often, and now tell you even weeping, *that they are* the enemies of the cross of Christ: [19]whose end *is* destruction, whose god *is their* belly, and *whose* glory *is* in their shame—who set their mind on earthly things. [20]For our citizenship is in heaven, from which we also eagerly wait for the Savior, the Lord Jesus Christ, [21]who will transform our lowly body that it may be conformed to His glorious body, according to the working by which He is able even to subdue all things to Himself.

4 Therefore, my beloved and longed-for brethren, my joy and crown, so stand fast in the Lord, beloved.

Be United, Joyful, and in Prayer

[2]I implore Euodia and I implore Syntyche to be of the same mind in the Lord. [3]And[a] I urge you also, true companion, help these women

---

Self-Discipline: Paul Mastered What Would Help Him

(Philippians 4:1–19)

Philippians 4 provides a call to discipline. Paul declares that the goal of peace and fulfillment runs through the path of self-discipline. The apostle elaborates on three disciplines that help leaders stay aligned with their mission:

1. *Govern your actions* (vv. 1–5).
   Paul pleads with his friends to stand firm. Live in harmony. Display self-control.
2. *Guard your attitudes* (vv. 6–9).
   He says to replace worry with prayer and to think on the positive things that edify.
3. *Give your assets* (vv. 10–19).
   Nothing purifies more than sharing resources and trusting God to meet your needs.

Teamwork: Petty Differences Can Prevent Victory

(Philippians 4:2, 3)

Paul knows the importance of teamwork, so he encourages two women who have been quarreling to make peace.

Euodia and Syntyche, members of the Philippian church, had by their disharmony created some division. Paul uses them as examples to launch into an entire chapter on peace. He doesn't ask these women to act uniformly, but rather to be of the same mind. The word he uses connotes harmony. Singing in harmony doesn't mean singing in unison. Players *should* play different positions on a team. Harmony means their efforts complement the efforts of others, rather than conflict with them.

---

who labored with me in the gospel, with Clement also, and the rest of my fellow workers, whose names *are* in the Book of Life.

[4]Rejoice in the Lord always. Again I will say, rejoice!

[5]Let your gentleness be known to all men. The Lord *is* at hand.

[6]Be anxious for nothing, but in everything by prayer and supplication, with thanksgiving, let your requests be made known to God; [7]and the peace of God, which surpasses all understanding, will guard your hearts and minds through Christ Jesus.

Meditate on These Things

[8]Finally, brethren, whatever things are true, whatever things *are* noble, whatever things *are* just, whatever things *are* pure, whatever things *are* lovely, whatever things *are* of good report, if *there is* any virtue and if *there is* anything praiseworthy—meditate on these things. [9]The things which you learned and received and heard and saw in me, these do, and the God of peace will be with you.

Philippian Generosity

[10]But I rejoiced in the Lord greatly that now at last your care for me has flourished again;

4:3 [a]NU-Text and M-Text read *Yes.*

though you surely did care, but you lacked opportunity. [11]Not that I speak in regard to need, for I have learned in whatever state I am, to be content: [12]I know how to be abased, and I know how to abound. Everywhere and in all things I have learned both to be full and to be hungry, both to abound and to suffer need. [13]I can do all things through Christ[a] who strengthens me.

[14]Nevertheless you have done well that you shared in my distress. [15]Now you Philippians know also that in the beginning of the gospel, when I departed from Macedonia, no church shared with me concerning giving and receiving but you only. [16]For even in Thessalonica you sent *aid* once and again for my necessities. [17]Not that I seek the gift, but I seek the fruit that abounds to your account. [18]Indeed I have all and abound. I am full, having received from Epaphroditus the things *sent* from you, a sweet-smelling aroma, an acceptable sacrifice, well pleasing to God. [19]And my God shall supply all your need according to His riches in glory by Christ Jesus. [20]Now to our God and Father *be* glory forever and ever. Amen.

Greeting and Blessing

[21]Greet every saint in Christ Jesus. The brethren who are with me greet you. [22]All the saints

greet you, but especially those who are of Caesar's household.

[23]The grace of our Lord Jesus Christ be with you all.[a] Amen.

4:13 [a]NU-Text reads *Him who.* **4:23** [a]NU-Text reads *your spirit.*

Positive Attitude: Paul Had the Mind to Make It

(Philippians 4:11–13)

Paul maintained a positive attitude even on rotten days. He teaches us that:

1. Attitude has little to do with circumstances (v. 11).
2. Attitudes can change, just like circumstances (v. 12).
3. Attitudes can be improved, if we learn the secret (v. 12).
4. Attitudes have a source for their strength (v. 13).

PAUL   A LEADER WHO COULDN'T BE STOPPED

(Philippians 4:4–13)

PROFILE IN LEADERSHIP

The apostle Paul was a man who truly practiced what he preached.

Paul challenged the Philippian believers to rejoice because of their relationship with Jesus Christ, to cast aside all worry because He cared about them, and to focus their minds on the things of God (Phil. 4:4–8). He encouraged them to put into practice the things he had taught them, and he reminded them that the true and living God would be with them to empower them to do those things.

Paul was the kind of leader who could say such things with great conviction and authority—even while sitting in prison—because he practiced them daily. He depended upon and felt grateful to the God he served, and he focused his heart on serving God by making the preaching of the gospel of Jesus Christ his prime activity.

With a mind and heart like that, Paul truly became an unstoppable leader. As he so rightly stated, "I can do *all* things through Christ who strengthens me" (4:13, emphasis added).

Paul, the man who willingly endured incredible suffering, persecution, and want during the course of his missionary journeys, demonstrated a state of heart and mind that made him God's kind of leader. *Anyone* who adopts a similar attitude and heart can become a similar unstoppable kind of leader.

COLOSSIANS
Knowing God and Making Him Known

SUMMARY

The apostle Paul wrote the Book of Colossians from prison to a group of believers in Colosse. It may well remind you of Ephesians, since about a quarter of the message of Ephesians is found in Colossians. Paul clearly believed that everyone needed to embrace a few fundamental building blocks.

What makes this book unique, however, and especially helpful to leaders, is that Paul wrote it in response to heresy. Some false teachers were making their way through the church, indoctrinating believers with a combination of Jewish and Hellenistic beliefs that troubled and confused these new Christians. Paul stepped in to rescue the church from cultic doctrine and restore believers to the business of knowing God and making Him known.

Paul's leadership training course begins with courage. He does not shrink from addressing trouble and making the tough call. His love for people doesn't cause him to become a people-pleaser. Quite the opposite, it prompts him to want the best for them, even if it means speaking corrective words.

It follows, then, that Paul teaches a second leadership lesson. He sets a standard for excellence and articulates it repeatedly. He raises the bar, teaching that Jesus is not only a wonderful Savior, but the preeminent Lord, Creator, and Master of everything. He is, in fact, our "all in all" (1:15–17). "Excellence" is Paul's description of Jesus and what he calls for from fellow believers.

Finally, in order to prevent the Colossians from feeling overwhelmed by this high calling, Paul teaches them the Law of Process. In the second chapter, he urges them to continue growing in Christ, just as they have been rooted in Him. Maturity is a process, not an event.

In the final two chapters, the apostle lays out a game plan for growth which addresses the Christian's thought life, relationships, solitude, work ethic, and family. Colossians remains a basic training manual for us today.

God's Role in Colossians

God appears in this book as the cosmic Christ, superior to every other deity and armed with truths greater than any doctrine or philosophy in the world. Colossians 2 teaches that "in Him dwells all the fullness of the Godhead bodily" (v. 9), and we are made "complete in Him, who is the head of all principality and power" (v. 10). Consequently, God not only is our Leader, but He also is our source of power, our wisdom for decision making, our peace in the midst of stress, and our love for those who seem unlovable. His supernatural leadership resources us with every tool we need to imitate Jesus.

Leaders in Colossians

Paul, Barnabas, Aristarchus

Other People of Influence in Colossians

Justus, the gnostic (heretical) teachers in Colosse

Lessons in Leadership

- Christ is the center of all complete leadership.

- To be a lifelong leader, you must be a lifelong learner.

- Leaders can't simultaneously pursue pleasing God and pleasing people.

- Excellence is not an accident; it happens when leaders call for it.

- Leadership begins on the inside; it starts with "being," not "doing."

LEADERSHIP
HIGHLIGHTS IN COLOSSIANS

EQUIPPING: Paul Was a Provider (1:28, 29)	*page 1457*
THE LAW OF PROCESS: Growth Is Not an Event (2:1–7)	*page 1458*
SELF-DISCIPLINE: The Battle Begins in the Mind (3:1–14)	*page 1459*
YOU CAN'T DIVORCE Leadership from Relationships (3:18—4:6)	*page 1460*

Greeting

1 Paul, an apostle of Jesus Christ by the will of God, and Timothy our brother,

²To the saints and faithful brethren in Christ *who are* in Colosse:

Grace to you and peace from God our Father and the Lord Jesus Christ.ᵃ

Their Faith in Christ

³We give thanks to the God and Father of our Lord Jesus Christ, praying always for you, ⁴since we heard of your faith in Christ Jesus and of your love for all the saints; ⁵because of the hope which is laid up for you in heaven, of which you heard before in the word of the truth of the gospel, ⁶which has come to you, as *it has* also in all the world, and is bringing forth fruit,ᵃ as *it is* also among you since the day you heard and knew the grace of God in truth; ⁷as you also learned from Epaphras, our dear fellow servant, who is a faithful minister of Christ on your behalf, ⁸who also declared to us your love in the Spirit.

Teachability: Paul Encouraged Readers to Be Lifelong Learners

(Colossians 1:4–10)

A lthough the Colossians already understood saving knowledge (Col. 1:4–7), their leader wanted them to know how to apply that knowledge. These are two different things. Teachability begins with knowledge (1:9), moves to understanding (1:9), then results in application (1:10). You are teachable if you're changing.

Preeminence of Christ

⁹For this reason we also, since the day we heard it, do not cease to pray for you, and to ask that you may be filled with the knowledge of His will in all wisdom and spiritual understanding; ¹⁰that you may walk worthy of the Lord, fully pleasing *Him,* being fruitful in every good work and increasing in the knowledge of God; ¹¹strengthened with all might, according to His glorious power, for all patience and longsuffering with joy; ¹²giving thanks to the Father who has qualified us to be partakers of the inheritance of

---

The Law of Respect: Jesus Is Superior to Everyone

(Colossians 1:13–20)

A lthough Paul clearly was a strong leader, he constantly declared his submission to the leadership of Christ.

At the very beginning of his letter to the Colossians, Paul paints a picture of Jesus' supremacy over every authority on earth. Our Lord rescues, redeems, and transforms. He is the image of the invisible God, who created everything, including other leaders and authorities. Christ takes priority among every created thing as the "firstborn from the dead" (Col. 1:18). Paul argues Jesus' supremacy based on the Law of Respect.

---

the saints in the light. ¹³He has delivered us from the power of darkness and conveyed *us* into the kingdom of the Son of His love, ¹⁴in whom we have redemption through His blood,ᵃ the forgiveness of sins.

¹⁵He is the image of the invisible God, the firstborn over all creation. ¹⁶For by Him all things were created that are in heaven and that are on earth, visible and invisible, whether thrones or dominions or principalities or powers. All things were created through Him and for Him. ¹⁷And He is before all things, and in Him all things consist. ¹⁸And He is the head of the body, the church, who is the beginning, the firstborn from the dead, that in all things He may have the preeminence.

Reconciled in Christ

¹⁹For it pleased *the Father that* in Him all the fullness should dwell, ²⁰and by Him to reconcile all things to Himself, by Him, whether things on earth or things in heaven, having made peace through the blood of His cross.

²¹And you, who once were alienated and enemies in your mind by wicked works, yet now He has reconciled ²²in the body of His flesh through death, to present you holy, and blame-

---

1:2 ᵃNU-Text omits *and the Lord Jesus Christ.*
1:6 ᵃNU-Text and M-Text add *and growing.*
1:14 ᵃNU-Text and M-Text omit *through His blood.*

less, and above reproach in His sight— [23]if indeed you continue in the faith, grounded and steadfast, and are not moved away from the hope of the gospel which you heard, which was preached to every creature under heaven, of which I, Paul, became a minister.

Sacrificial Service for Christ

[24]I now rejoice in my sufferings for you, and fill up in my flesh what is lacking in the afflictions of Christ, for the sake of His body, which is the church, [25]of which I became a minister according to the stewardship from God which was given to me for you, to fulfill the word of God, [26]the mystery which has been hidden from ages and from generations, but now has been revealed to His saints. [27]To them God willed to make known what are the riches of the glory of this mystery among the Gentiles: which[a] is Christ in you, the hope of glory. [28]Him we preach, warning every man and teaching every man in all wisdom, that we may present every man perfect in Christ Jesus. [29]To this *end* I also labor, striving according to His working which works in me mightily.

Not Philosophy but Christ

2 For I want you to know what a great conflict I have for you and those in Laodicea, and *for* as many as have not seen my face in the flesh, [2]that their hearts may be encouraged, being knit together in love, and *attaining* to all riches of the full assurance of understanding, to the knowledge of the mystery of God, both of the Father and[a] of Christ, [3]in whom are hidden all the treasures of wisdom and knowledge.

[4]Now this I say lest anyone should deceive you with persuasive words. [5]For though I am absent in the flesh, yet I am with you in spirit, rejoicing to see your *good* order and the steadfastness of your faith in Christ.

[6]As you therefore have received Christ Jesus the Lord, so walk in Him, [7]rooted and built up in Him and established in the faith, as you have been taught, abounding in it[a] with thanksgiving.

[8]Beware lest anyone cheat you through philosophy and empty deceit, according to the tradition of men, according to the basic principles of the world, and not according to Christ. [9]For in Him dwells all the fullness of the Godhead bodily; [10]and you are complete in Him, who is the head of all principality and power.

Not Legalism but Christ

[11]In Him you were also circumcised with the circumcision made without hands, by putting off the body of the sins[a] of the flesh, by the circumcision of Christ, [12]buried with Him in baptism, in which you also were raised with *Him* through

---

1:27 [a]M-Text reads *who*. **2:2** [a]NU-Text omits *both of the Father and*. **2:7** [a]NU-Text omits *in it*. **2:11** [a]NU-Text omits *of the sins*.

Equipping: Paul Was a Provider

(Colossians 1:28, 29)

Paul longed to present everyone complete in Christ. In Colossians 1:28, 29 he speaks not of adding anything to Christ's redemptive work, but rather he declares his intention to equip others to realize their God-given potential. He did part of his equipping through letters like this one.

The apostle says his goal is to preach, warn, and teach, so that listeners become complete in Christ. What does this mean? Part of it, no doubt, means that those he taught could reproduce themselves in others. Paul was an equipping leader with a heart to develop others. He was a *provider* for the people in his life. Providers are:

P urposeful: They approach others with a purpose: to add value.

R elational: They are warm and inviting and work at relationships.

O bjective: They assess strengths and weaknesses objectively.

V ulnerable: They model self-disclosure and honesty.

I ncarnational: They are examples of what they teach.

D ependable: They are consistent and responsible for their promises.

E mpowering: They give power away and facilitate growth in others.

R esourceful: They use every tool they have to grow people.

The Law of Process: Growth Is Not an Event

(Colossians 2:1–7)

Spiritual growth doesn't "just happen," any more than climbing a mountain "just happens." You don't wander up a mountain and surprise yourself when you reach the top. Growth results from hard work.

Paul compares maturing a person to growing a plant (Col. 2:6, 7). When you take seed, soil, sunshine, and water and put them together, you don't get a plant overnight. You need time. Paul knows that the Colossians' roots won't grow deep overnight. So he reminds them of what must happen for growth to occur:

1. *Labor* (v. 1)—Someone has to work.
2. *Stretching* (v. 2)—You have to stretch for more.
3. *Learning* (vv. 2, 3)—Knowledge must be consumed.
4. *Focus* (v. 4)—You cannot drift or get distracted.
5. *Accountability* (v. 5)—Growth accelerates when someone watches.
6. *Building on the past* (v. 6)—Growth always uses past truth.
7. *Application* (v. 6)—Growth solidifies when you practice what you know.
8. *Gratitude* (v. 7)—Give joyful thanksgiving for past blessings.

The Law of Victory: Jesus Defeats Death, Provides Weapons

(Colossians 2:10–15)

Jesus not only provides us the weapons we need for victory (Col. 2:10–14), but He also disarms the enemy, thus assuring our success (2:15). Christ ensures us of victory by providing the resources we need, by removing hindrances, by stripping the enemy of his own devices, and by publicly declaring victory.

things which he has not[a] seen, vainly puffed up by his fleshly mind, [19]and not holding fast to the Head, from whom all the body, nourished and knit together by joints and ligaments, grows with the increase *that is* from God.

[20]Therefore,[a] if you died with Christ from the basic principles of the world, why, as *though* living in the world, do you subject yourselves to regulations— [21]"Do not touch, do not taste, do not handle," [22]which all concern things which perish with the using—according to the commandments and doctrines of men? [23]These things indeed have an appearance of wisdom in self-imposed religion, *false* humility, and neglect of the body, *but are* of no value against the indulgence of the flesh.

Not Carnality but Christ

3 If then you were raised with Christ, seek those things which are above, where Christ is, sitting at the right hand of God. [2]Set your mind on things above, not on things on the earth. [3]For you died, and your life is hidden with Christ in God. [4]When Christ *who is* our life appears, then you also will appear with Him in glory.

[5]Therefore put to death your members which are on the earth: fornication, uncleanness, passion, evil desire, and covetousness, which is idolatry. [6]Because of these things the wrath of God is coming upon the sons of disobedience, [7]in which you yourselves once walked when you lived in them.

[8]But now you yourselves are to put off all

faith in the working of God, who raised Him from the dead. [13]And you, being dead in your trespasses and the uncircumcision of your flesh, He has made alive together with Him, having forgiven you all trespasses, [14]having wiped out the handwriting of requirements that was against us, which was contrary to us. And He has taken it out of the way, having nailed it to the cross. [15]Having disarmed principalities and powers, He made a public spectacle of them, triumphing over them in it.

[16]So let no one judge you in food or in drink, or regarding a festival or a new moon or sabbaths, [17]which are a shadow of things to come, but the substance is of Christ. [18]Let no one cheat you of your reward, taking delight in *false* humility and worship of angels, intruding into those

---

2:18 [a]NU-Text omits *not*. **2:20** [a]NU-Text and M-Text omit *Therefore*.

Self-Discipline: The Battle Begins in the Mind

(Colossians 3:1–14)

The battle begins in the mind. Paul argues that since we have a new position, we need to get a new perspective (Col. 3:1). Permanent change and improvement always happen from the inside out. Consider Paul's prescription for self-discipline:

1. *Remember your identity* (v. 1).
   We must focus first on our position in Christ. It all starts there.
2. *Renew your thought life* (v. 2).
   We must focus our minds on things above. We must raise new internal standards.
3. *Recognize your old life is dead* (vv. 3–7).
   Change doesn't happen if we maintain any way to return to old patterns.
4. *Release past habits* (vv. 8–11).
   We must put off the old, like taking off a worn-out set of clothes.
5. *Replace them with new ones* (vv. 12–14).
   We get rid of old habits only when we substitute new habits for them.

these: anger, wrath, malice, blasphemy, filthy language out of your mouth. 9Do not lie to one another, since you have put off the old man with his deeds, 10and have put on the new *man* who is renewed in knowledge according to the image of Him who created him, 11where there is neither Greek nor Jew, circumcised nor uncircumcised, barbarian, Scythian, slave *nor* free, but Christ *is* all and in all.

Character of the New Man

12Therefore, as *the* elect of God, holy and beloved, put on tender mercies, kindness, humility, meekness, longsuffering; 13bearing with one another, and forgiving one another, if anyone has a complaint against another; even as Christ forgave you, so you also *must do*. 14But above all these things put on love, which is the bond of perfection. 15And let the peace of God rule in your hearts, to which also you were called in one body; and be thankful. 16Let the word of Christ dwell in you richly in all wisdom, teaching and admonishing one another in psalms and hymns and spiritual songs, singing with grace in

your hearts to the Lord. 17And *whatever* you do in word or deed, *do* all in the name of the Lord Jesus, giving thanks to God the Father through Him.

The Christian Home

18Wives, submit to your own husbands, as is fitting in the Lord.

19Husbands, love your wives and do not be bitter toward them.

20Children, obey your parents in all things, for this is well pleasing to the Lord.

21Fathers, do not provoke your children, lest they become discouraged.

22Bondservants, obey in all things your masters according to the flesh, not with eyeservice, as men-pleasers, but in sincerity of heart, fearing God. 23And whatever you do, do it heartily, as to the Lord and not to men, 24knowing that from the Lord you will receive the reward of the inheritance; for[a] you serve the Lord Christ. 25But he who does wrong will be repaid for what he has done, and there is no partiality.

4 Masters, give your bondservants what is just and fair, knowing that you also have a Master in heaven.

Christian Graces

2Continue earnestly in prayer, being vigilant in it with thanksgiving; 3meanwhile praying also for us, that God would open to us a door for the word, to speak the mystery of Christ, for which I am also in chains, 4that I may make it manifest, as I ought to speak.

5Walk in wisdom toward those *who are* outside, redeeming the time. 6*Let* your speech always *be* with grace, seasoned with salt, that you may know how you ought to answer each one.

Final Greetings

7Tychicus, a beloved brother, faithful minister, and fellow servant in the Lord, will tell you all the news about me. 8I am sending him to you for this very purpose, that he[a] may know your circumstances and comfort your hearts, 9with Onesimus, a faithful and beloved brother, who is *one* of you. They will make known to you all things which *are happening* here.

10Aristarchus my fellow prisoner greets you, with Mark the cousin of Barnabas (about whom you received instructions: if he comes to you, welcome him), 11and Jesus who is called Justus.

3:24 [a]NU-Text omits *for*. **4:8** [a]NU-Text reads *you may know our circumstances and he may.*

You Can't Divorce Leadership from Relationships

(Colossians 3:18—4:6)

Paul spends a lot of time in Colossians discussing relationships, a paramount concern for leaders. Leadership is about relationships. Consider three levels of leadership:

1. Leaders can *impress* others from a distance.
   This requires the will of the leader. The leader must determine to perform excellently.
2. Leaders can *influence* others if they get a bit closer.
   This requires the will of the followers. They must choose to emulate the leader.
3. Leaders can *impact* others only in close relationship.
   This requires both the will of the leader and the follower. It occurs when intimacy and trust develop.

Paul begins his instruction on relationships with the home (Col. 3:18–21). Then he moves outward to colleagues, to masters and slaves (3:22—4:4). Finally, he addresses relationships with outsiders (4:5, 6).

God has placed everyone within a chain of care. Leaders are to connect with followers, from parenting, to supervising, to evangelizing. These circles of relationship serve as proving grounds, each giving credibility to the next. When we lead well in the home, we gain credibility to be heard in the marketplace. If it doesn't work at home, don't export it! Success is gaining the respect of those who know us best.

These *are my* only fellow workers for the kingdom of God who are of the circumcision; they have proved to be a comfort to me.

[12]Epaphras, who is *one* of you, a bondservant of Christ, greets you, always laboring fervently for you in prayers, that you may stand perfect and complete[a] in all the will of God. [13]For I bear him witness that he has a great zeal[a] for you, and those who are in Laodicea, and those in Hierapolis. [14]Luke the beloved physician and Demas greet you. [15]Greet the brethren who are in Laodicea, and Nymphas and the church that *is* in his[a] house.

Closing Exhortations and Blessing

[16]Now when this epistle is read among you, see that it is read also in the church of the Laodiceans, and that you likewise read the epistle from Laodicea. [17]And say to Archippus, "Take heed to the ministry which you have received in the Lord, that you may fulfill it."

[18]This salutation by my own hand—Paul. Remember my chains. Grace *be* with you. Amen.

4:12 [a]NU-Text reads *fully assured.* **4:13** [a]NU-Text reads *concern.* **4:15** [a]NU-Text reads *Nympha . . . her house.*

1 THESSALONIANS

The Basics of the Christian Life

SUMMARY

The apostle Paul planted the church of Thessalonica during his second missionary journey. Thessalonica was yet another of those key, port cities where multitudes interacted and engaged in commerce. Unfortunately, the Jews harassed Paul and ran him out of town shortly after he started this infant church. He wrote the letters we call 1 and 2 Thessalonians almost immediately after leaving town in order to equip those young believers in the basics of the Christian life. In these letters he assumes his rightful role as leader of the church family and answers questions, solves problems, and casts vision for the ultimate plan of God on earth.

Paul demonstrates that you must lead differently based on who your followers are and the context in which they live. The spiritually young Thessalonians needed to hear things that Paul didn't have to say to others. They had caught only a glimpse of Paul's message, so he had to teach them big-picture perspectives on Christ's return and the end of the age. Paul discerned how this people needed to be led. He customized his leadership to the needs of Thessalonica.

Paul also demonstrated a leader's follow-through. Since he had to leave town prematurely, he sent Timothy (one of his team members) back to Thessalonica to check on the church's growth and spiritual health. Paul consistently developed a plan to continue making progress in his church planting efforts, but he also determined to finish what he started. He dispatched team members to follow up; identified and equipped local leaders; and wrote letters and corresponded with his young churches to answer specific questions.

Paul understood the necessity of mentoring leaders. He selected key leaders in Thessalonica and encouraged them all to "follow" him, to observe and remember his lifestyle (1:5, 6). In chapter 2 he even takes it a step further when his mentoring becomes parental. "We were gentle among you, just as a nursing mother cherishes her own children," he writes. "So, affectionately longing for you, we were well pleased to impart to you not only the gospel of God, but also our own lives. . . . You know how we exhorted, and comforted, and charged every one of you, as a father does his own children" (vv. 7, 8, 11). He gave his "children" more than mere lectures. He mentored like a parent.

God's Role in 1 Thessalonians

God used Paul as a church pioneer, but He also took on a greater role to the young believers, safeguarding them while few or no experienced shepherds existed to lead them. Paul had to trust God to do what the apostle could not, given the little time he had in town. God worked on the people's hearts and used Paul's brief letters to disciple them and ready them for what lay ahead.

Leaders in 1 Thessalonians

Paul, church leaders in Thessalonica

Other People of Influence in 1 Thessalonians

Silas, Silvanus, Timothy

Lessons in Leadership

- The more a leader loves the people, the easier it is to lead the people.

- A bright and promising future motivates faster than a fond and memorable past.

- Leaders must tailor their approach to the needs of the people.

- Leaders who last mentor a second generation of leaders.

- People can live with a tough today if they believe a terrific tomorrow is coming.

LEADERSHIP HIGHLIGHTS IN 1 THESSALONIANS

THE LAW OF REPRODUCTION: Paul Trains Leaders (1:5–8)	*page 1463*
THE LAW OF CONNECTION: Paul Mentors His Children (2:7–12)	*page 1464*
THE LAW OF THE INNER CIRCLE: Paul's Team Represented Him (3:2–10)	*page 1465*
VISION: Paul Was a Futurist (4:13—5:11)	*page 1466*

Greeting

1 Paul, Silvanus, and Timothy,

To the church of the Thessalonians in God the Father and the Lord Jesus Christ:

Grace to you and peace from God our Father and the Lord Jesus Christ.[a]

Their Good Example

[2]We give thanks to God always for you all, making mention of you in our prayers, [3]remembering without ceasing your work of faith, labor of love, and patience of hope in our Lord Jesus Christ in the sight of our God and Father, [4]knowing, beloved brethren, your election by God. [5]For our gospel did not come to you in word only, but also in power, and in the Holy Spirit and in much assurance, as you know what kind of men we were among you for your sake.

[6]And you became followers of us and of the Lord, having received the word in much affliction, with joy of the Holy Spirit, [7]so that you became examples to all in Macedonia and Achaia who believe. [8]For from you the word of the Lord has sounded forth, not only in Macedonia and Achaia, but also in every place. Your faith toward God has gone out, so that we do not need to say anything. [9]For they themselves declare concerning us what manner of entry we had to you, and how you turned to God from idols to serve the living and true God, [10]and to wait for His Son from heaven, whom He raised from the dead, *even* Jesus who delivers us from the wrath to come.

Paul's Conduct

2 For you yourselves know, brethren, that our coming to you was not in vain. [2]But even[a] after we had suffered before and were spitefully treated at Philippi, as you know, we were bold in our God to speak to you the gospel of God in much conflict. [3]For our exhortation *did* not *come* from error or uncleanness, nor *was it* in deceit.

[4]But as we have been approved by God to be entrusted with the gospel, even so we speak, not as pleasing men, but God who tests our hearts. [5]For neither at any time did we use flattering words, as you know, nor a cloak for covetousness—God *is* witness. [6]Nor did we seek glory from men, either from you or from others, when we might have made demands as apostles of Christ. [7]But we were gentle among you, just as a nursing *mother* cherishes her own children. [8]So, affectionately longing for you, we were well pleased to impart to you not only the gospel of God, but also our own lives, because you had become dear to us. [9]For you remember, brethren, our labor and toil; for laboring night and day, that we might not be a burden to any of you, we preached to you the gospel of God.

[10]You *are* witnesses, and God *also,* how devoutly and justly and blamelessly we behaved ourselves among you who believe; [11]as you

---

1:1 [a]NU-Text omits *from God our Father and the Lord Jesus Christ.* **2:2** [a]NU-Text and M-Text omit *even.*

The Law of Reproduction: Paul Trains Leaders

(1 Thessalonians 1:5–8)

B ecause Paul was forced to leave Thessalonica shortly after he planted a church there, he developed many of its leaders through the mail. The apostle wrote 1 and 2 Thessalonians to disciple and train those who had recently chosen to follow Christ. Paul tried to work himself out of a job through this training. The apostle reminds us how good training works:

1. Training involves not only words, but also demonstration (v. 5).
2. Training transforms others when done with conviction (v. 5).
3. Training is remembered when the life of the trainer supports the message (v. 5).
4. Training is incarnated when the follower imitates the teacher (v. 6).
5. Training is relevant when done in the midst of problems (v. 6).
6. Training is complete when the trainee becomes a trainer (vv. 7, 8).
7. Training has been reproduced when the original trainer has no need to say more (v. 8).

The Law of Connection: Paul Mentors His Children

(1 Thessalonians 2:7–12)

Although Paul had met with this young church only on three Sabbaths, he longed for them like a parent longs for a child. As Paul mentored his "children," he developed a parental, coaching relationship with them. Note how he describes this relationship:

1. We were like a gentle, nurturing mother to you (v. 7).
2. We shared not only the good news, but also our very lives (v. 8).
3. We worked hard not to burden you with our needs (v. 9).
4. We strove to be an example while among you (v. 10).
5. We dealt with you as a father deals with his children (v. 11).
6. We encouraged you to live up to your potential as God's children (v. 12).

Relationships grow strong when those involved share common experiences (vv. 17–20); continual encouragement (vv. 2, 6, 7, 9); concerned expressions (vv. 1, 3–5); and challenging expectations (vv. 8, 10–13). Good relationships both comfort and stretch.

know how we exhorted, and comforted, and charged[a] every one of you, as a father *does* his own children, [12]that you would walk worthy of God who calls you into His own kingdom and glory.

Their Conversion

[13]For this reason we also thank God without ceasing, because when you received the word of God which you heard from us, you welcomed *it* not *as* the word of men, but as it is in truth, the word of God, which also effectively works in you who believe. [14]For you, brethren, became imitators of the churches of God which are in Judea in Christ Jesus. For you also suffered the same things from your own countrymen, just as they *did* from the Judeans, [15]who killed both the Lord Jesus and their own prophets, and have persecuted us; and they do not please God and are contrary to all men, [16]forbidding us to speak to the Gentiles that they may be saved, so as always to fill up *the measure of* their sins; but wrath has come upon them to the uttermost.

Longing to See Them

[17]But we, brethren, having been taken away from you for a short time in presence, not in heart, endeavored more eagerly to see your face with great desire. [18]Therefore we wanted to come to you—even I, Paul, time and again—but Satan hindered us. [19]For what *is* our hope, or joy, or crown of rejoicing? *Is it* not even you in the presence of our Lord Jesus Christ at His coming? [20]For you are our glory and joy.

Concern for Their Faith

3 Therefore, when we could no longer endure it, we thought it good to be left in Athens alone, [2]and sent Timothy, our brother and minister of God, and our fellow laborer in the gospel of Christ, to establish you and encourage you concerning your faith, [3]that no one should be shaken by these afflictions; for you yourselves know that we are appointed to this. [4]For, in fact, we told you before when we were with you that we would suffer tribulation, just as it happened, and you know. [5]For this reason,

2:11 [a]NU-Text and M-Text read *implored*.

Accountability: Paul Sent Timothy to Support and Report

(1 Thessalonians 3:1–10)

Leaders understand the power of accountability for the purposes of support and challenge. Accountability provides a *cure* for situations like the one Paul encountered in Thessalonica, where the Jews ran him out of town after only three weeks of work. CURE stands for the four gifts of accountability: **C**orrection, **U**pdates, **R**eminders, and **E**ncouragement.

The Law of the Inner Circle: Paul's Team Represented Him

(1 Thessalonians 3:2–10)

Paul found it difficult to send Timothy to Thessalonica; he would rather have returned himself. If he had, however, he might have been killed. The religious leaders remained on the lookout for him, ever since they ran him out of town. So Paul sent one of his key players, Timothy, a member of Paul's inner circle.

Paul's potential multiplied because of individuals like Timothy. Timothy did just what Paul would have done had he been present:

1. *Provide*—He gave them strength and encouragement (v. 2).
2. *Protect*—He worked to rescue those who might fall away (v. 3).
3. *Preserve*—He fought to ensure their work had not been in vain (vv. 4, 5).
4. *Promote*—He motivated them and cheered them on to grow (vv. 6, 7).
5. *Present*—He reported to Paul how their faith had flourished (vv. 6–8).
6. *Pray*—He led the way in praying for what they still lacked (vv. 9, 10).

when I could no longer endure it, I sent to know your faith, lest by some means the tempter had tempted you, and our labor might be in vain.

Encouraged by Timothy

[6]But now that Timothy has come to us from you, and brought us good news of your faith and love, and that you always have good remembrance of us, greatly desiring to see us, as we also *to see* you— [7]therefore, brethren, in all our affliction and distress we were comforted concerning you by your faith. [8]For now we live, if you stand fast in the Lord.

[9]For what thanks can we render to God for you, for all the joy with which we rejoice for your sake before our God, [10]night and day praying exceedingly that we may see your face and perfect what is lacking in your faith?

Prayer for the Church

[11]Now may our God and Father Himself, and our Lord Jesus Christ, direct our way to you.

[12]And may the Lord make you increase and abound in love to one another and to all, just as we *do* to you, [13]so that He may establish your hearts blameless in holiness before our God and Father at the coming of our Lord Jesus Christ with all His saints.

Plea for Purity

4 Finally then, brethren, we urge and exhort in the Lord Jesus that you should abound more and more, just as you received from us how you ought to walk and to please God; [2]for you know what commandments we gave you through the Lord Jesus.

[3]For this is the will of God, your sanctification: that you should abstain from sexual immorality; [4]that each of you should know how to possess his own vessel in sanctification and honor, [5]not in passion of lust, like the Gentiles who do not know God; [6]that no one should take advantage of and defraud his brother in this matter, because the Lord *is* the avenger of all such, as we also forewarned you and testified. [7]For God did not call us to uncleanness, but in holiness. [8]Therefore he who rejects *this* does not reject man, but God, who has also given[a] us His Holy Spirit.

A Brotherly and Orderly Life

[9]But concerning brotherly love you have no need that I should write to you, for you yourselves are taught by God to love one another; [10]and indeed you do so toward all the brethren who are in all Macedonia. But we urge you, brethren, that you increase more and more; [11]that you also aspire to lead a quiet life, to mind your own business, and to work with your own hands, as we commanded you, [12]that you may walk properly toward those who are outside, and *that* you may lack nothing.

The Comfort of Christ's Coming

[13]But I do not want you to be ignorant, brethren, concerning those who have fallen asleep, lest you sorrow as others who have no hope. [14]For if we believe that Jesus died and rose again, even so God will bring with Him those who sleep in Jesus.[a]

[15]For this we say to you by the word of the Lord, that we who are alive *and* remain until the coming of the Lord will by no means precede those who are asleep. [16]For the Lord Himself will descend from heaven with a shout, with the voice of an archangel, and with the trumpet of

---

4:8 [a]NU-Text reads *who also gives.* **4:14** [a]Or *those who through Jesus sleep*

The Law of Solid Ground: Paul Built Respect

(1 Thessalonians 4:11, 12)

If the Thessalonians were to win their city for Christ, they would have to commit themselves to excellence. They needed to lead a peaceful life, pay their bills, and work with integrity. When we gain the respect of others by leading our own lives well, we gain the opportunity to lead others.

Vision: Paul Was a Futurist

(1 Thessalonians 4:13—5:11)

As he closes his letter, Paul turns his attention to the future and the day of the Lord. Every leader can count on Christ's return as the one certain future event. Because of this, Paul casts vision for the future and communicates his convictions about this great event.

Like all good leaders, Paul understood the power of vision. He purposely closed this letter with encouraging words that would motivate his readers for years to come. He knew that when there is no hope for the future, there is no power in the present. By communicating his vision, Paul accomplished the following:

1. Comfort for those who had lost loved ones (4:13–15).
2. Assurance for those who believe (4:16–18).
3. Warning for those who might forget (5:1–5).
4. Direction for those who needed it (5:6–11).

God. And the dead in Christ will rise first. ¹⁷Then we who are alive *and* remain shall be caught up together with them in the clouds to meet the Lord in the air. And thus we shall always be with the Lord. ¹⁸Therefore comfort one another with these words.

The Day of the Lord

5 But concerning the times and the seasons, brethren, you have no need that I should write to you. ²For you yourselves know perfectly that the day of the Lord so comes as a thief in the night. ³For when they say, "Peace and safety!" then sudden destruction comes upon them, as labor pains upon a pregnant woman. And they shall not escape. ⁴But you, brethren, are not in darkness, so that this Day should overtake you as a thief. ⁵You are all sons of light and sons of the day. We are not of the night nor of darkness. ⁶Therefore let us not sleep, as others *do,* but let us watch and be sober. ⁷For those who sleep, sleep at night, and those who get drunk are drunk at night. ⁸But let us who are of the day be sober, putting on the breastplate of faith and love, and *as* a helmet the hope of salvation. ⁹For God did not appoint us to wrath, but to obtain salvation through our Lord Jesus Christ, ¹⁰who died for us, that whether we wake or sleep, we should live together with Him.

¹¹Therefore comfort each other and edify one another, just as you also are doing.

Various Exhortations

¹²And we urge you, brethren, to recognize those who labor among you, and are over you in the Lord and admonish you, ¹³and to esteem them very highly in love for their work's sake. Be at peace among yourselves.

¹⁴Now we exhort you, brethren, warn those who are unruly, comfort the fainthearted, uphold the weak, be patient with all. ¹⁵See that no one renders evil for evil to anyone, but always pursue what is good both for yourselves and for all.

¹⁶Rejoice always, ¹⁷pray without ceasing, ¹⁸in everything give thanks; for this is the will of God in Christ Jesus for you.

¹⁹Do not quench the Spirit. ²⁰Do not despise prophecies. ²¹Test all things; hold fast what is good. ²²Abstain from every form of evil.

Blessing and Admonition

²³Now may the God of peace Himself sanctify you completely; and may your whole spirit, soul, and body be preserved blameless at the coming of our Lord Jesus Christ. ²⁴He who calls you *is* faithful, who also will do *it.*

²⁵Brethren, pray for us.

²⁶Greet all the brethren with a holy kiss.

²⁷I charge you by the Lord that this epistle be read to all the holy[a] brethren.

²⁸The grace of our Lord Jesus Christ *be* with you. Amen.

5:27 [a]NU-Text omits *holy.*

2 THESSALONIANS
Develop a Life of Integrity

SUMMARY

Do the basics well and you can build your life from that foundation. In short, that was Paul's message in his second letter to the Thessalonians. The apostle wanted his friends to develop a life of integrity and trustworthiness for others to see, and he didn't much care if they lacked "razzle-dazzle" or polish. He just wanted to know: Were you faithful to the commitments you made? Did you keep your word? Are you loving and warm when you interact with others? Can you refrain from gossip and sarcasm? Do others trust you? Is your work ethic solid?

Such questions deserved high priority among the young church members of Thessalonica, for they had become preoccupied that they might be living in the last days. Christ could return at any moment! Consequently, they began to wonder, *Why even bother working? Why bother paying off debts? Why try to invest in relationships for the long haul? We probably won't be around long anyway!* Paul recognized this unhealthy perspective and, while he agreed they should get ready for Christ's return, they also must prepare for a marathon, not a sprint. Paul challenged them to think about the future and to anticipate serving and influencing others for years to come.

To put it succinctly, some of the Thessalonians had grown lazy. They didn't prepare for tomorrow, nor did they care much about who or what they might leave behind when they left. Jesus was coming back and they simply wanted to *go*. Paul argued, "You don't get ready for Christ's return by packing suitcases and waiting on a hillside, but by staying busy obeying God and serving your fellowman. When Jesus comes back, He wants to find His people working, not idle."

God still has a message here for leaders today. First, we can never allow ourselves to slip into ruts where we become physically or mentally idle. Second, we should always strive for excellence in everything we do. We honor God when we excel above mediocrity. Leadership really is about excelling beyond the crowd. Otherwise, are we really leading anyone?

As you read this book, allow the Lord to train and admonish you to push for improvement and excellence. Press beyond "good enough" and go the "second mile" (Matt. 5:41).

God's Role in 2 Thessalonians

God uses this book to spank and chastise His people. It is parental in nature and, while it does encourage the reader, it also corrects wrong patterns of thought and behavior. God uses Paul to speak as a father and mother, just as he did in his first letter to the Thessalonians (2:7–11). This time, the letter challenges believers to build some discipline into their lives: find work, avoid gossip, refrain from being a busybody. God used this letter to "disciple" the young Thessalonians, even though Paul lived miles away.

Leaders in 2 Thessalonians

Paul, the man of sin

Other People of Influence in 2 Thessalonians

Undisciplined believers in the church

Lessons in Leadership

- Even followers who catch your vision need midcourse corrections and reminders.

- Leaders must communicate confidence and assurance.

- Good leaders practice reverse gossip: They applaud/affirm individuals behind their backs.

- Leaders who show the way succeed faster than ones who simply share the way.

HIGHLIGHTS IN 2 THESSALONIANS

ENCOURAGEMENT: Paul Knew How to Boast About His People (1:3–6)	*page 1469*
THE MAN of Sin (2:1–11)	*page 1470*
PAUL: A Different Kind of Leader (2:13–17)	*page 1470*
THE LAW OF BUY-IN: Examples Beat Exhortation (3:6–13)	*page 1471*

Greeting

1 Paul, Silvanus, and Timothy,

To the church of the Thessalonians in God our Father and the Lord Jesus Christ:

²Grace to you and peace from God our Father and the Lord Jesus Christ.

God's Final Judgment and Glory

³We are bound to thank God always for you, brethren, as it is fitting, because your faith grows exceedingly, and the love of every one of you all abounds toward each other, ⁴so that we ourselves boast of you among the churches of God for your patience and faith in all your persecutions and tribulations that you endure, ⁵*which is* manifest evidence of the righteous judgment of God, that you may be counted worthy of the kingdom of God, for which you also suffer; ⁶since *it is a* righteous thing with God to repay with tribulation those who trouble you, ⁷and to *give* you who are troubled rest with us when the Lord Jesus is revealed from heaven with His mighty angels, ⁸in flaming fire taking vengeance on those who do not know God, and on those who do not obey the gospel of our Lord Jesus Christ. ⁹These shall be punished with everlasting destruction from the presence of the Lord and from the glory of His power, ¹⁰when He comes, in that Day, to be glorified in His saints and to be admired among all those who believe,ᵃ because our testimony among you was believed.

¹¹Therefore we also pray always for you that our God would count you worthy of *this* calling, and fulfill all the good pleasure of *His* goodness and the work of faith with power, ¹²that the name of our Lord Jesus Christ may be glorified in you, and you in Him, according to the grace of our God and the Lord Jesus Christ.

The Great Apostasy

2 Now, brethren, concerning the coming of our Lord Jesus Christ and our gathering together to Him, we ask you, ²not to be soon shaken in mind or troubled, either by spirit or by word or by letter, as if from us, as though the day of Christᵃ had come. ³Let no one deceive you by any means; for *that Day will not come* unless the falling away comes first, and the man of sinᵃ is revealed, the son of perdition, ⁴who opposes and exalts himself above all that is called God or that is worshiped, so that he sits as Godᵃ in the temple of God, showing himself that he is God.

⁵Do you not remember that when I was still with you I told you these things? ⁶And now you know what is restraining, that he may be revealed in his own time. ⁷For the mystery of lawlessness is already at work; only Heᵃ who now restrains *will do so* until Heᵇ is taken out of the way. ⁸And then the lawless one will be revealed, whom the Lord will consume with the breath of His mouth and destroy with the brightness of His coming. ⁹The coming of the *lawless one* is according to the working of Satan, with all power, signs, and lying wonders, ¹⁰and with all unrighteous deception among those who perish, because they did not receive the love of the truth, that they might be saved. ¹¹And for this reason God will send them strong delusion, that they should believe the lie, ¹²that they all may be condemned who did not

---

Encouragement: Paul Knew How to Boast About His People

(2 Thessalonians 1:3–6)

Encouragement is the oxygen of the soul; everyone needs it and they perform better when they get it. Paul understood this fact, so in this letter he tells his friends how much he boasts about them all over Asia.

Good leaders liberally hand out encouragement. It costs little to affirm others, yet pays great dividends. In this text Paul capitalizes on the power of encouragement and teaches us a few things along way. Encouragement should be . . .

1. *Personal* (v. 3).
   He told them personally how much he believed in them.
2. *Pointed* (v. 4).
   He told them specifically what he appreciated about them.
3. *Public* (v. 4).
   He told all his other churches how much he thought of the Thessalonians.
4. *Purposeful* (vv. 5, 6).
   He had a goal he was shooting for in their lives—their motivation and vindication.

1:10 ᵃNU-Text and M-Text read *have believed.*
2:2 ᵃNU-Text reads *the Lord.* 2:3 ᵃNU-Text reads *lawlessness.* 2:4 ᵃNU-Text omits *as God.* 2:7 ᵃOr *he* ᵇOr *he*

The Man of Sin

(2 Thessalonians 2:1–11)

The "man of sin" (or the "son of perdition," 2 Thess. 2:3) will be an extremely influential leader with international fame. He will be powerful and prideful, and will usurp a divine place in the world. Other biblical texts call him the "Antichrist" or the "Beast."

This evil leader reminds us that it is possible to be a great leader, but not a good one. God calls his leaders to be both great and good. Note why both great and good leadership is necessary:

Great Leadership
1. Has to do with our competence
2. Makes us effective in our work
3. Enables our cause to progress
4. Means we have good heads
5. Ensures our skills will influence

Good Leadership
1. Has to do with our character
2. Makes our work constructive
3. Enables us to choose the right cause
4. Means we have good hearts
5. Ensures our service will impact

believe the truth but had pleasure in unrighteousness.

Stand Fast

¹³But we are bound to give thanks to God always for you, brethren beloved by the Lord, because God from the beginning chose you for salvation through sanctification by the Spirit and belief in the truth, ¹⁴to which He called you by our gospel, for the obtaining of the glory of our Lord Jesus Christ. ¹⁵Therefore, brethren, stand fast and hold the traditions which you were taught, whether by word or our epistle.

¹⁶Now may our Lord Jesus Christ Himself, and our God and Father, who has loved us and given *us* everlasting consolation and good hope

---

PAUL — A DIFFERENT KIND OF LEADER
(2 Thessalonians 2:13–17)

PROFILE IN LEADERSHIP

Godly leaders tend to have a strong passion and a deep optimism about the future. This attitude springs from their sense of purpose and from the assurance of their ultimate destination.

The apostle Paul was just such a leader.

Paul led a Thessalonian church full of young believers who expected the soon and imminent return of Christ. Add to this expectation the persecution and hardship the church faced, and you might expect to find great confusion and anxiety. It got to the point where many of the Thessalonians not only stopped working, but also attempted to thwart others from doing so.

Paul knew he needed to speak some sense to these erring brothers and correct some misperceptions about the second coming of Jesus. He told them that Christ wouldn't return until certain things had taken place, events that had not yet transpired. He also instructed them to continue working as though Christ would not return for a very long time.

Effective leaders have reason for Paul's kind of passion and optimism. They know that if Jesus returns tomorrow, all believers will share in the joy of being with Him in person. On the other hand, they know that if He tarries, believers have all the more time to work to bring others to Him. Who could ask for a better no-lose situation?

by grace, [17]comfort your hearts and establish you in every good word and work.

Pray for Us

3 Finally, brethren, pray for us, that the word of the Lord may run *swiftly* and be glorified, just as *it is* with you, [2]and that we may be delivered from unreasonable and wicked men; for not all have faith.

[3]But the Lord is faithful, who will establish you and guard *you* from the evil one. [4]And we have confidence in the Lord concerning you, both that you do and will do the things we command you.

[5]Now may the Lord direct your hearts into the love of God and into the patience of Christ.

Warning Against Idleness

[6]But we command you, brethren, in the name of our Lord Jesus Christ, that you withdraw from every brother who walks disorderly and not according to the tradition which he[a] received from us. [7]For you yourselves know how you ought to follow us, for we were not disorderly among you; [8]nor did we eat anyone's bread free of charge, but worked with labor and toil night and day, that we might not be a burden to any of you, [9]not because we do not have author-

ity, but to make ourselves an example of how you should follow us.

[10]For even when we were with you, we commanded you this: If anyone will not work, neither shall he eat. [11]For we hear that there are some who walk among you in a disorderly manner, not working at all, but are busybodies. [12]Now those who are such we command and exhort through our Lord Jesus Christ that they work in quietness and eat their own bread.

[13]But *as for* you, brethren, do not grow weary *in* doing good. [14]And if anyone does not obey our word in this epistle, note that person and do not keep company with him, that he may be ashamed. [15]Yet do not count *him* as an enemy, but admonish *him* as a brother.

Benediction

[16]Now may the Lord of peace Himself give you peace always in every way. The Lord *be* with you all.

[17]The salutation of Paul with my own hand, which is a sign in every epistle; so I write.

[18]The grace of our Lord Jesus Christ *be* with you all. Amen.

3:6 [a]NU-Text and M-Text read *they.*

The Law of Buy-In: Examples Beat Exhortation

(2 Thessalonians 3:6–13)

Paul wanted desperately to challenge the Thessalonians regarding their lifestyle. He instinctively knew the Law of Buy-In—that people buy in to the leader before they buy in to his words. Consequently, he reminds them of the model that he and Silas left them. He knows that example is always stronger than exhortation. So, before he exhorts them to work hard, he reminds them of how hard his team had worked while among them (2 Thess. 3:7, 8). Consider Paul's argument:

The Issue	Paul's Example	Paul's Exhortation
1. Discipline	1. We're not undisciplined (v. 7)	1. Some are undisciplined (vv. 11, 12)
2. Work	2. We worked hard (v. 8)	2. No work, no food (v. 10)
3. Burdens	3. We weren't a burden (vv. 8, 9)	3. Don't be a burden (vv. 11–13)

1 TIMOTHY
A Leadership Training Manual

SUMMARY

The Book of 1 Timothy amounts to a leadership training manual. Written by the apostle Paul to his young apprentice, Timothy, it contains not only good instruction for emerging leaders, but also lists the qualifications of a leader.

Paul and Timothy provide the clearest mentoring relationship in Scripture of any since Elijah and Elisha. Their story begins in Acts 16:1–3, when Timothy joined Paul in Lystra. Paul invested in him for a long time, taking him on short-term mission trips, letting him preach, leaving him to pastor a young church, and writing instructional letters to him while apart. Paul would do anything for his young protégé. Note how Paul developed Timothy as a leader.

First, we spot the *Principle of Purposeful Pursuit*. Paul proactively identified a young leader he could develop. He had been to Lystra and seen Timothy. His antennas were up. He insisted his team go back to challenge and invite the young man to join them.

Second, we see the *Principle of Proven Potential*. Paul did his homework on Timothy. He recognized him as a diamond in the rough. He watched Timothy prove himself in his hometown while growing up, and he knew Timothy's family and the spiritual stock he came from.

Third, Paul demonstrated the *Principle of Practical Patience*. Paul patiently selected and mentored Timothy. He was careful not to act prematurely and even advised his student not to "lay hands on anyone hastily" (5:22). He believed his team had acted too quickly in letting John Mark travel with them (Acts 12:25), and he didn't want to pick fruit too early.

Fourth, notice the *Principle of the Participatory Process*. Paul recognized that he was but one participant in a long line of contributors in Timothy's life. In his second letter, Paul reminds Timothy of his other mentors, including his mother and grandmother. Timothy had a strong heritage before Paul came along; Paul simply played his role in the process.

Finally, we see the *Principle of Passion and Pricetags*. Paul made clear the price of leadership in both of his letters to Timothy. After Paul found Timothy in Lystra, a mob dragged the apostle out of the city, stoned him, and left him for dead. When he recovered, he returned, grabbed Timothy, and finished his work there. This kind of passion for leadership drove Paul to reproduce leaders like Timothy.

God's Role in 1 Timothy

God plays out His role in 1 Timothy as the One who develops leaders who develop other leaders. Our Lord is the Master Developer who raised up Paul the apostle to equip Timothy to equip His church in Ephesus. God revealed to Timothy the fundamental principles and guidelines for church leadership, and the qualifications for overseers and their code of conduct. Through this book God speaks very personally to Timothy and every spiritual leader.

Leaders in 1 Timothy

Paul, Timothy, elders

Other People of Influence in 1 Timothy

Hymenaeus, Alexander, deacons

Lessons in Leadership

- Leaders must live by a higher standard than followers.

- Leaders are not mass produced, but must be mentored one at a time.

- Leaders must celebrate diversity, but confront deviancy.

- The greatest contribution a leader can make is to develop more leaders.

- Young leaders can influence by their example, if nothing else.

- A leader's integrity will directly affect his/her influence.

LEADERSHIP

HIGHLIGHTS IN 1 TIMOTHY

LEADERSHIP by Objective (1:1, 2)	*page 1474*
QUALIFICATIONS of Spiritual Leaders (3:1–13)	*page 1475*
THE QUALITIES of a Spiritual Leader (3:2–13)	*page 1476*
TIMOTHY: An Unlikely Leader (4:12)	*page 1477*
MOTIVE CHECK: Why You Do Something Determines What You Do (6:3–10, 17–19)	*page 1480*

Greeting

1 Paul, an apostle of Jesus Christ, by the commandment of God our Savior and the Lord Jesus Christ, our hope,

[2]To Timothy, a true son in the faith:

Grace, mercy, *and* peace from God our Father and Jesus Christ our Lord.

No Other Doctrine

[3]As I urged you when I went into Macedonia—remain in Ephesus that you may charge some that they teach no other doctrine, [4]nor give heed to fables and endless genealogies, which cause disputes rather than godly edification which is in faith. [5]Now the purpose of the commandment is love from a pure heart, *from* a good conscience, and *from* sincere faith, [6]from which some, having strayed, have turned aside to idle talk, [7]desiring to be teachers of the law, understanding neither what they say nor the things which they affirm.

[8]But we know that the law *is* good if one uses it lawfully, [9]knowing this: that the law is not made for a righteous person, but for *the* lawless and insubordinate, for *the* ungodly and for sinners, for *the* unholy and profane, for murderers of fathers and murderers of mothers, for manslayers, [10]for fornicators, for sodomites, for kidnappers, for liars, for perjurers, and if there is any other thing that is contrary to sound doctrine, [11]according to the glorious gospel of the blessed God which was committed to my trust.

Glory to God for His Grace

[12]And I thank Christ Jesus our Lord who has enabled me, because He counted me faithful, putting *me* into the ministry, [13]although I was formerly a blasphemer, a persecutor, and an insolent man; but I obtained mercy because I did *it* ignorantly in unbelief. [14]And the grace of our Lord was exceedingly abundant, with faith and love which are in Christ Jesus. [15]This *is* a faithful saying and worthy of all acceptance, that Christ Jesus came into the world to save sinners, of whom I am chief. [16]However, for this reason I obtained mercy, that in me first Jesus Christ might show all longsuffering, as a pattern to those who are going to believe on Him for everlasting life. [17]Now to the King eternal, immortal, invisible, to God who alone is wise,[a] *be* honor and glory forever and ever. Amen.

1:17 [a]NU-Text reads *to the only God.*

Leadership by Objective

(1 Timothy 1:1, 2)

Paul wrote this book as a training manual for young Timothy and sent it to the young leader as he attempted to pastor an intimidating church in Ephesus. Paul issues five charges for Timothy:

1. *First charge:* Wage the good warfare (1:18–20).
2. *Second charge:* Conduct yourself worthy of God's house (3:14, 15).
3. *Third charge:* Do not neglect your gift (4:11–16).
4. *Fourth charge:* Observe these things without prejudice (5:21).
5. *Fifth charge:* Guard what is committed to you (6:20, 21).

Paul communicates his purpose on several occasions. He declares it in 1 Timothy 1:5. Paul believed in management by objective. He was quick to share his bottom line goals with his team and encouraged them to meet those objectives in the manner that suited them best. He considered the mission, not the methods, sacred. He teaches us that:

1. *Leaders manage goals.* They let people choose their own methods.
2. *Leaders create atmosphere.* They let people own their style.
3. *Leaders determine budget.* They give ownership of how money is spent.
4. *Leaders choose priorities.* They share activities with gifted people.
5. *Leaders train the team.* They freely give away the credit for victories.

Humility: Paul Never Forgot Where He Came From

(1 Timothy 1:12–17)

While we know Paul as the greatest evangelist in history, he knew that, left to himself, he was the worst sinner (1 Tim. 1:15). God chose him because of his weakness, so that the Lord could display His great patience and grace in him. The more leaders mature, the more humble they become.

Fight the Good Fight

[18]This charge I commit to you, son Timothy, according to the prophecies previously made concerning you, that by them you may wage the good warfare, [19]having faith and a good conscience, which some having rejected, concerning the faith have suffered shipwreck, [20]of whom are Hymenaeus and Alexander, whom I delivered to Satan that they may learn not to blaspheme.

Pray for All Men

2 Therefore I exhort first of all that supplications, prayers, intercessions, *and* giving of thanks be made for all men, [2]for kings and all who are in authority, that we may lead a quiet and peaceable life in all godliness and reverence. [3]For this *is* good and acceptable in the sight of

Leaders Need Prayer Partners

(1 Timothy 2:1–4)

When we pray for God to change leaders, we affect them and everyone who follows them. Praying for our leaders results in an atmosphere conducive to the spreading of the gospel. Every leader ought to be proactive, recruiting and equipping a team of prayer partners, who will pray for their protection, wisdom, and strength.

God our Savior, [4]who desires all men to be saved and to come to the knowledge of the truth. [5]For *there is* one God and one Mediator between God and men, *the* Man Christ Jesus, [6]who gave Himself a ransom for all, to be testified in due time, [7]for which I was appointed a preacher and an apostle—I am speaking the truth in Christ[a] *and* not lying—a teacher of the Gentiles in faith and truth.

Men and Women in the Church

[8]I desire therefore that the men pray everywhere, lifting up holy hands, without wrath and doubting; [9]in like manner also, that the women adorn themselves in modest apparel, with propriety and moderation, not with braided hair or

2:7 [a]NU-Text omits *in Christ.*

Qualifications of Spiritual Leaders

(1 Timothy 3:1–13)

In Paul's list of qualifications for church leaders, 1 Timothy 3:10 is key: "But let these also first be tested." Every leader should be tested before given an official position. The preparation of a leader is crucial to their success. Frank Damazio outlines Paul's logic concerning leadership:

Leader's Salvation	Leader's Call	Leader's Preparation	Leader's Position
Leadership is planted as a seed.	Leadership begins to sprout.	Leadership is tested as a plant.	Leadership matures and bears fruit.

Paul gave this list of qualifications for two reasons: first, to provide guidelines for churches to select leaders; second, to give church leaders a checkpoint for their own spiritual lives. Paul reminds us that if anyone aspires to be a leader, he aspires to a noble task. To have the gifts and qualities and not take on leadership positions may be disobedience. The desire, however, must be accompanied by discipline.

gold or pearls or costly clothing, [10]but, which is proper for women professing godliness, with good works. [11]Let a woman learn in silence with all submission. [12]And I do not permit a woman to teach or to have authority over a man, but to be in silence. [13]For Adam was formed first, then Eve. [14]And Adam was not deceived, but the woman being deceived, fell into transgression. [15]Nevertheless she will be saved in childbearing if they continue in faith, love, and holiness, with self-control.

Qualifications of Overseers

3 This *is* a faithful saying: If a man desires the position of a bishop,[a] he desires a good work. [2]A bishop then must be blameless, the husband of one wife, temperate, sober-minded, of good behavior, hospitable, able to teach; [3]not given to wine, not violent, not greedy for money,[a] but gentle, not quarrelsome, not covetous; [4]one who rules his own house well, having *his* children in submission with all reverence [5](for if a man does not know how to rule his own house, how will he take care of the church of God?); [6]not a novice, lest being puffed up with pride he fall into the *same* condemnation as the devil. [7]Moreover he must have a

good testimony among those who are outside, lest he fall into reproach and the snare of the devil.

Qualifications of Deacons

[8]Likewise deacons *must be* reverent, not double-tongued, not given to much wine, not greedy for money, [9]holding the mystery of the faith with a pure conscience. [10]But let these also first be tested; then let them serve as deacons, being *found* blameless. [11]Likewise, *their* wives *must be* reverent, not slanderers, temperate, faithful in all things. [12]Let deacons be the husbands of one wife, ruling *their* children and their own houses well. [13]For those who have served well as deacons obtain for themselves a good standing and great boldness in the faith which is in Christ Jesus.

The Great Mystery

[14]These things I write to you, though I hope to come to you shortly; [15]but if I am delayed, *I write* so that you may know how you ought to conduct yourself in the house of God, which is

---

3:1 [a]Literally *overseer* **3:3** [a]NU-Text omits *not greedy for money.*

The Qualities of a Spiritual Leader

(1 Timothy 3:2–13)

What sort of qualifications must church leaders possess? Paul lists the following traits:

1. *Blameless* (v. 2)—Question: Am I quick to improve those areas that can damage my integrity?
2. *Husband of one wife* (v. 2)—Question: Am I loving my wife as Christ loved the church?
3. *Temperate, sober-minded, of good behavior* (v. 2)—Question: Am I master of myself, that I may be a servant to many?
4. *Hospitable* (v. 2)—Question: Do I exhibit a warm and welcoming spirit?
5. *Able to teach* (v. 2)—Question: Do I consistently help others learn and become better disciples?
6. *Not given to wine* (v. 3)—Question: Am I sober, watchful, and diligent, so that I do not damage those who watch me?
7. *Not violent, not quarrelsome* (v. 3)—Question: Do I have an approachable disposition that brings peace and healing?
8. *Not greedy, not covetous* (v. 3)—Question: Am I allowing my leadership to be controlled by the rich?
9. *Rules his own house well* (vv. 4, 5)—Question: Do I manage my own family before I try to manage the church?
10. *Not a novice* (v. 6)—Question: Am I a seasoned, solid example for both insiders and outsiders?

the church of the living God, the pillar and ground of the truth. ¹⁶And without controversy great is the mystery of godliness:

> God[a] was manifested in the flesh,
> Justified in the Spirit,
> Seen by angels,
> Preached among the Gentiles,
> Believed on in the world,
> Received up in glory.

The Great Apostasy

4 Now the Spirit expressly says that in latter times some will depart from the faith, giving heed to deceiving spirits and doctrines of demons, ²speaking lies in hypocrisy, having their own conscience seared with a hot iron, ³forbidding to marry, *and commanding* to abstain from foods which God created to be received with thanksgiving by those who believe and know the truth. ⁴For every creature of God *is* good, and nothing is to be refused if it is received with thanksgiving; ⁵for it is sanctified by the word of God and prayer.

A Good Servant of Jesus Christ

⁶If you instruct the brethren in these things, you will be a good minister of Jesus Christ,

---

The Law of Solid Ground: Timothy Must Earn Trust

(1 Timothy 4:1–16)

E very spiritual leader faces at least two important duties. First, they must confront those who fall away from the faith (1 Tim. 4:1–6). Second, they must discipline themselves for godliness (4:7–16). When leaders fulfill these two duties, they practice the Law of Solid Ground and earn the trust of others.

---

nourished in the words of faith and of the good doctrine which you have carefully followed. ⁷But reject profane and old wives' fables, and exercise yourself toward godliness. ⁸For bodily exercise profits a little, but godliness is profitable for all things, having promise of the life that now is and of that which is to come. ⁹This *is* a faithful saying and worthy of all acceptance. ¹⁰For to this *end*

3:16 [a]NU-Text reads *Who.*

TIMOTHY

AN UNLIKELY LEADER

(1 Timothy 4:12)

PROFILE IN LEADERSHIP

N othing can make someone more unlikely—even unwilling—to lead than feelings of inadequacy.

Timothy, the young protégé of the apostle Paul, must have felt much as Moses did when God called him to lead Israel out of Egyptian captivity. Moses felt inadequate for the task, and likely so did Timothy.

We can identify any number of reasons that Timothy might have felt unfit to accept his assignment as pastor of the Ephesian church. He was too young and too inexperienced, and the church seemed too large for a first pastoral assignment. Besides, how could he take over for the church's founder, Paul? Would anyone take him seriously?

"Never mind all that," Paul tells him in his letter. "If you follow my instructions, you will be more than able to do the job. Don't let anyone look down on you because of your relative youth and inexperience. Rather, be the kind of example of godliness that won't allow anyone to treat you with anything but respect."

God doesn't necessarily choose leaders based on their natural talent or ability. Neither does He always choose them based on their age and experience. As Paul tells Timothy, God chooses leaders based on their availability, not their ability; on their willingness to walk in obedience to Him, not their experience.

The Law of E. F. Hutton: The Most Important Lesson About Influence

(1 Timothy 4:12–16)

How can Timothy prevent anyone looking down on him because of his youth? By being an example; this will ensure his influence (1 Tim. 4:15, 16). The more you walk, the less you have to talk. Our leadership is more caught than taught. People would rather see a sermon than hear one.

we both labor and suffer reproach,[a] because we trust in the living God, who is *the* Savior of all men, especially of those who believe. [11]These things command and teach.

Take Heed to Your Ministry

[12]Let no one despise your youth, but be an example to the believers in word, in conduct, in love, in spirit,[a] in faith, in purity. [13]Till I come, give attention to reading, to exhortation, to doctrine. [14]Do not neglect the gift that is in you, which was given to you by prophecy with the laying on of the hands of the eldership. [15]Meditate on these things; give yourself entirely to them, that your progress may be evident to all. [16]Take heed to yourself and to the doctrine. Continue in them, for in doing this you will save both yourself and those who hear you.

Treatment of Church Members

5 Do not rebuke an older man, but exhort *him* as a father, younger men as brothers, [2]older women as mothers, younger women as sisters, with all purity.

Honor True Widows

[3]Honor widows who are really widows. [4]But if any widow has children or grandchildren, let them first learn to show piety at home and to repay their parents; for this is good and[a] acceptable before God. [5]Now she who is really a widow, and left alone, trusts in God and continues in supplications and prayers night and day. [6]But she who lives in pleasure is dead while she lives. [7]And these things command, that they may be blameless. [8]But if anyone does not provide for his own, and especially for those of his household, he has denied the faith and is worse than an unbeliever.

[9]Do not let a widow under sixty years old be taken into the number, *and not unless* she has been the wife of one man, [10]well reported for good works: if she has brought up children, if she has lodged strangers, if she has washed the saints' feet, if she has relieved the afflicted, if she has diligently followed every good work.

[11]But refuse *the* younger widows; for when they have begun to grow wanton against Christ, they desire to marry, [12]having condemnation because they have cast off their first faith. [13]And besides they learn *to be* idle, wandering about from house to house, and not only idle but also gossips and busybodies, saying things which they ought not. [14]Therefore I desire that *the* younger *widows* marry, bear children, manage the house, give no opportunity to the adversary to speak reproachfully. [15]For some have already turned aside after Satan. [16]If any believing man or[a] woman has widows, let them relieve them, and do not let the

---

4:10 [a]NU-Text reads *we labor and strive.*
4:12 [a]NU-Text omits *in spirit.* **5:4** [a]NU-Text and M-Text omit *good and.* **5:16** [a]NU-Text omits *man or.*

The Law of Priorities: Leadership Begins at Home, Then Goes Public

(1 Timothy 5:8)

In the midst of all his teaching about how believers are to relate to one another in the church, Paul prioritizes Timothy's leadership as a pastor. If anyone doesn't provide for his own home, the apostle declares, he cannot expect to provide for the church with any integrity (1 Tim. 5:8).

Leadership starts at home. If it doesn't work at home, don't export it. Pastors, especially, must heed this warning. Leadership works best when it is prioritized as follows:

1. I am first a *person*. I must prioritize my own relationship with God.
2. Second, I am a *partner*. I must prioritize my relationship with my spouse.
3. Third, I am a *parent*. I must prioritize my relationship with my children.
4. Fourth, I am a *pastor*. I must prioritize my relationship with my ministry.

The Law of Reproduction: Timothy Was to Equip Elders

(1 Timothy 5:17–22)

Leaders are crucial to any organization. Mistakes made at the leadership level impact everyone. As the senior pastor, Timothy was to identify, prepare, and affirm his church leaders. He was to honor those who served well (1 Tim. 5:17, 18), correct those in error (5:19–21), and prepare those who were called, patiently and carefully (5:22). Nothing should be done in haste.

Consider the steps Paul endorsed concerning the establishment of leaders in the church:

1. *Identification:* Identify those with character, gifts, and influence.
2. *Separation:* Set them apart for the work of their calling.
3. *Preparation:* Equip them with the tools and experiences they need.
4. *Recognition:* Allow the church to affirm their calling.
5. *Ordination:* Lay hands on them and ordain them for the work.

---

church be burdened, that it may relieve those who are really widows.

Honor the Elders

[17]Let the elders who rule well be counted worthy of double honor, especially those who labor in the word and doctrine. [18]For the Scripture says, *"You shall not muzzle an ox while it treads out the grain,"*[a] and, *"The laborer is worthy of his wages."*[b] [19]Do not receive an accusation against an elder except from two or three witnesses. [20]Those who are sinning rebuke in the presence of all, that the rest also may fear.

[21]I charge *you* before God and the Lord Jesus Christ and the elect angels that you observe these things without prejudice, doing nothing with partiality. [22]Do not lay hands on anyone hastily, nor share in other people's sins; keep yourself pure.

[23]No longer drink only water, but use a little wine for your stomach's sake and your frequent infirmities.

[24]Some men's sins are clearly evident, preced-

ing *them* to judgment, but those of some *men* follow later. [25]Likewise, the good works *of some* are clearly evident, and those that are otherwise cannot be hidden.

Honor Masters

6 Let as many bondservants as are under the yoke count their own masters worthy of all honor, so that the name of God and *His* doctrine may not be blasphemed. [2]And those who have believing masters, let them not despise *them* because they are brethren, but rather serve *them* because those who are benefited are believers and beloved. Teach and exhort these things.

Error and Greed

[3]If anyone teaches otherwise and does not consent to wholesome words, *even* the words of our Lord Jesus Christ, and to the doctrine which accords with godliness, [4]he is proud, knowing nothing, but is obsessed with disputes and arguments over words, from which come envy, strife, reviling, evil suspicions, [5]useless wranglings[a] of men of corrupt minds and destitute of the truth, who suppose that godliness is a *means of* gain. From such withdraw yourself.[b]

[6]Now godliness with contentment is great gain. [7]For we brought nothing into *this* world, *and it is* certain[a] we can carry nothing out. [8]And having food and clothing, with these we shall be content. [9]But those who desire to be rich fall into temptation and a snare, and *into* many foolish and harmful lusts which drown men in destruction and perdition. [10]For the love of money is a root of all *kinds of* evil, for which some have strayed from the faith in their greediness, and pierced themselves through with many sorrows.

The Good Confession

[11]But you, O man of God, flee these things and pursue righteousness, godliness, faith, love, patience, gentleness. [12]Fight the good fight of faith, lay hold on eternal life, to which you were also called and have confessed the good confession in the presence of many witnesses. [13]I urge you in the sight of God who gives life to all things, and *before* Christ Jesus who witnessed the good confession before Pontius Pilate, [14]that you keep *this* commandment without spot, blameless until our Lord Jesus Christ's appearing, [15]which

---

5:18 [a]Deuteronomy 25:4 [b]Luke 10:7
6:5 [a]NU-Text and M-Text read *constant friction*.
[b]NU-Text omits this sentence. **6:7** [a]NU-Text omits *and it is certain*.

Motive Check: Why You Do Something Determines What You Do

(1 Timothy 6:3–10, 17–19)

Because our motives eventually determine our direction, Paul taught that right motives were even more important for the leader than right moves. Note Paul's teaching on motives:

1. *The evidence of wrong motives* (v. 3)
   The leader's doctrine drifts and the teaching does not produce godliness.
2. *The nature of wrong motives* (vv. 4, 5)
   The proud leader stirs division and pursues personal gain.
3. *The results of wrong motives* (vv. 9, 10)
   The leader falls into temptation, wanders from the faith, and destroys himself or herself.

So how are we to watch our motives? What key principles should we keep in mind?

1. Trouble comes when leadership performs for the wrong reasons.
2. Spiritual leadership brings rewards, so long as the rewards don't control us.
3. Prosperity is everything God gives you above food and covering.
4. We must be content with God's provision and placement.
5. We must remain dissatisfied with our own fruitfulness and pursuit of God.
6. Wrong motives can lead to wrong moves, and even disqualify us for leadership.

He will manifest in His own time, *He who is* the blessed and only Potentate, the King of kings and Lord of lords, [16]who alone has immortality, dwelling in unapproachable light, whom no man has seen or can see, to whom *be* honor and everlasting power. Amen.

Instructions to the Rich

[17]Command those who are rich in this present age not to be haughty, nor to trust in uncertain riches but in the living God, who gives us richly all things to enjoy. [18]Let them do good, that they be rich in good works, ready to give, willing to share, [19]storing up for themselves a good foundation for the time to come, that they may lay hold on eternal life.

Guard the Faith

[20]O Timothy! Guard what was committed to your trust, avoiding the profane *and* idle babblings and contradictions of what is falsely called knowledge— [21]by professing it some have strayed concerning the faith.

Grace *be* with you. Amen.

2 TIMOTHY

Final Lessons for a Protégé

SUMMARY

You can often tell what is important to a man by listening to his last words. Deathbed statements and confessions have furnished the themes of movies and books for decades. David Livingston uttered his last words in prayer for the tribes he tried to reach in Africa. Jesus' last words make up the Great Commission. And we read the apostle Paul's last words in 2 Timothy.

This epistle is the last extant book written by the great first-century leader. In it he communicates several crucial issues with his spiritual son Timothy, the young pastor of the church in Ephesus. Paul had been his mentor and discipler. This letter contains the apostle's final lessons for his protégé.

Paul exhorts Timothy to stir up his leadership gifts. Timothy, young and timid, at times felt overwhelmed by his leadership role. Paul reminds Timothy of the day he laid his hands on him and commissioned him for ministry. Now Timothy needs to fan into flame those God-given gifts and use them without fear or shame.

Paul also motivates Timothy with word pictures. In chapter two alone the apostle uses seven leadership metaphors: teacher, soldier, athlete, farmer, worker, vessel, and servant. These pictures portray a leader who is generous, disciplined, patient, rugged, tenacious, pure, hardworking, and sacrificial.

Paul also mentors his young leader in how to face difficult times. He reviews with him the culture around him and warns him of coming opposition. He describes the gospel as a trust to be preserved, a tool to be proven, and a treasure to be prized. Timothy is to advance this gospel beyond where Paul has taken it.

Finally, Paul challenges Timothy to carry on his legacy. He speaks as a mentor, particularly at the end of his book, and charges him to lead with conviction, to preach the gospel just as he had received it, and to reproduce other leaders to be as faithful as he has been. This kind of labor will bring a heavenly crown of reward.

God's Role in 2 Timothy

God made sure that Paul spoke to the heart of a leader, not merely to the head. While the book contains practical instructions for the mind and challenging exhortations for the will, God delivers through Paul's pen words that fly straight to the heart and the emotions of Timothy.

Any leader can receive valuable encouragement from this letter. It calls leaders to lead out of their souls and their convictions, to stand for what is right even when no one else does, to finish well, regardless of the moral failure of the world. God speaks very personally and mentors us to be His kind of leaders—good ones and not evil, great ones instead of miserable.

Leaders in 2 Timothy

Paul, Timothy

Other People of Influence in 2 Timothy

Demas, Crescens, Carpus, Titus, Luke, John Mark, Alexander

Lessons in Leadership

- We are most effective when we lead in the area of our gifts.

- Leaders are to equip and develop other leaders who will do the same.

- Leaders set the standard for excellence, morality, productivity, and atmosphere.

- The pathway to effective leadership is uphill with lots of hurdles along the way.

- Leaders must consciously work to finish well.

- Spiritual leaders who finish well will be rewarded richly.

LEADERSHIP
HIGHLIGHTS IN 2 TIMOTHY

THE LAW OF EMPOWERMENT: God Gives Us What We Need to Lead (1:7, 8)	*page 1483*
PAUL AND THE LAW OF EXPLOSIVE GROWTH: To Add Growth, Lead Followers—To Multiply, Lead Leaders (2:1)	*pages 1484, 1485*
THE LAW OF REPRODUCTION: Leaders Who Lead Followers vs. Leaders Who Lead Leaders (2:2)	*page 1486*
COURAGE: The Process of Taking a Stand (2:22—3:17)	*page 1487*
THE LAW OF PRIORITIES: Timothy's Three Priorities (4:1–8)	*page 1489*

Greeting

1 Paul, an apostle of Jesus Christ[a] by the will of God, according to the promise of life which is in Christ Jesus,

[2]To Timothy, a beloved son:

Grace, mercy, *and* peace from God the Father and Christ Jesus our Lord.

Timothy's Faith and Heritage

[3]I thank God, whom I serve with a pure conscience, as *my* forefathers *did,* as without ceasing I remember you in my prayers night and day, [4]greatly desiring to see you, being mindful of your tears, that I may be filled with joy, [5]when I call to remembrance the genuine faith that is in you, which dwelt first in your grandmother Lois and your mother Eunice, and I am persuaded is in you also. [6]Therefore I remind you to stir up the gift of God which is in you through the laying on of my hands. [7]For God has not given us a spirit of fear, but of power and of love and of a sound mind.

Not Ashamed of the Gospel

[8]Therefore do not be ashamed of the testimony of our Lord, nor of me His prisoner, but

---

Gifts: We Are Most Effective When We Lead from Our Gifts

(2 Timothy 1:5–7)

Our leadership will always be most natural, most effective, and most influential when we lead from our gifts and strengths. Then it won't be forced, feel awkward, seem artificial, or copy someone else. Effective leadership occurs when we lead from our own identity. Paul believed Timothy's leadership would grow strong when he remembered three truths:

1. *His secure heritage* (v. 5)
   Paul reminded Timothy of the spiritual foundation his family gave him.
2. *His spiritual gift* (v. 6)
   Paul reminded Timothy to stir up the gifts inside him and lead from those gifts.
3. *His solid conviction* (v. 7)
   Paul reminded Timothy that God didn't give him fear, but the tools to do the job.

The Law of Empowerment: God Gives Us What We Need to Lead

(2 Timothy 1:7, 8)

God always gives us what we need to lead. Paul reminded Timothy that God didn't give him the timidity he felt; that came either from Timothy's own baggage or from the pit of hell itself. Instead, God equipped him with love, power, and a sound mind. All leaders need these three fundamental tools:

Love: The relational ingredient that enables us to attract and connect with others.
Power: The courage and competence to get the job done.
Sound mind: The perspective and wisdom to grasp a vision and take the right steps.

Because God has so equipped us, He instructs us to "not be ashamed . . . but share . . . in the sufferings" (2 Tim. 1:8). God gave Timothy (and us!) everything needed to accomplish the job. He empowers us before He ever expects from us. He gives before He demands. We receive His competence before we receive His commands.

---

share with me in the sufferings for the gospel according to the power of God, [9]who has saved us and called *us* with a holy calling, not according to our works, but according to His own purpose and grace which was given to us in Christ Jesus before time began, [10]but has now been revealed by the appearing of our Savior Jesus Christ, *who* has abolished death and brought life and immortality to light through the gospel, [11]to which I was appointed a preacher, an apostle, and a teacher of the Gentiles.[a] [12]For this reason I also suffer these things; nevertheless I am not ashamed, for I know whom I have believed and am persuaded that He is able to keep what I have committed to Him until that Day.

Be Loyal to the Faith

[13]Hold fast the pattern of sound words which you have heard from me, in faith and love which

---

1:1 [a]NU-Text and M-Text read *Christ Jesus.*
1:11 [a]NU-Text omits *of the Gentiles.*

PAUL AND THE LAW OF EXPLOSIVE GROWTH

To Add Growth, Lead Followers— To Multiply, Lead Leaders

(2 Timothy 2:1)

Leaders who develop followers grow their organization only one person at a time. But leaders who develop leaders multiply their growth, because for every leader they develop, they also receive all of that leader's followers. Add ten followers to your organization, and you have the power of ten people. Add ten leaders to your organization, and you have the power of ten leaders times all the followers and leaders *they* influence. That's the difference between addition and multiplication. It's like growing your organization by teams instead of by individuals.

Paul was a master of explosive growth. He dedicated himself to people and activities that would impact the world. His strategy remains as effective today as it was two thousand years ago. To promote explosive growth . . .

1. *Attract and equip people.*

Everywhere Paul went, he gathered listeners and taught them. Paul would enter a town and begin teaching—for days, months, and sometimes years. No matter where he went, he continually equipped as many people as possible.

2. *Find and mentor emerging leaders.*

Paul mentored too many leaders to count. Some of them, such as Silas, came to him already possessing influence and leadership skills (Acts 15:22). Others were home-grown, such as Timothy (1 Tim. 1:2). But no matter their background, Paul took them with him as he worked, preached, and led. Then he turned them loose, giving them responsibility and authority.

3. *Create new organizations.*

Paul didn't hoard the leaders he developed. He raised up leaders to multiply and extend his influence. And he did it with a strategy—he planted churches. Wherever he traveled, he left a church with leaders to carry on the ministry.

4. *Engage in the ongoing development of leaders.*

Paul visited the leaders in his churches to follow up with them, encourage them, and give them direction. Paul's second missionary journey began with the following suggestion: "Let us now go back and visit our brethren in every city where we have preached the word of the Lord, and see how they are doing" (Acts 15:36).

You can achieve a large vision only through explosive growth. Anything less will leave you far short of your dreams. But becoming an explosive-growth leader requires more than a change in the way you work; it requires a change in the way you think.

Leaders Who Gather Followers vs. Leaders Who Develop Leaders

Consider seven major differences between leaders who gather followers and leaders who develop other leaders:

1. *Leaders who gather followers need to be needed; leaders who develop leaders want to be succeeded.*

Many who desire to lead followers do so because followers stroke their egos. They feel indispensable. But leaders who develop leaders work to make themselves dispensable. They don't want a following, but a legacy.

2. *Leaders who gather followers focus on people's weaknesses; leaders who develop leaders focus on their strengths.*

Ineffective leaders focus on their followers' weaknesses, sometimes out of misunderstanding the way development and encouragement work, other times because of insecurity—they want to keep their followers off-balance. But strong leaders focus on their people's strengths because they know that is the key to developing people.

3. *Leaders who gather followers focus on the bottom 20 percent; leaders who develop leaders focus on the top 20 percent.*

Explosive-growth leaders focus on the best in their leaders; they also focus on the best potential leaders. In contrast, leaders of followers usually give their attention to the loudest and most difficult people, the ones who take and take, giving nothing in return.

4. *Leaders who gather followers treat everyone the same; leaders who develop leaders treat people as individuals.*

When Paul went on his missionary journeys, he didn't try to take everybody with him. Nor did he give everyone an equal chance to oversee the churches he started. He treated each person he encountered according to his gifts, calling, and willingness to grow.

5. *Leaders who gather followers spend their time; leaders who develop leaders invest their time.*

Everywhere Paul went, he took companions. He considered the time he spent with them an investment. And if he didn't see a return—as in the case of John Mark (Acts 13:13)—Paul felt reluctant to keep investing in them (15:37–40). Think of your work with emerging leaders as an opportunity to invest in them.

6. *Leaders who gather followers ask for little commitment; leaders who develop leaders ask for great commitment.*

Following a leader takes commitment. But it's nothing compared to the commitment of a follower who is asked to lead others. As you ask people to step up to leadership, don't treat your request lightly. Let them know to what you are asking them to commit. Acquaint them with the sacrifice and the service that come with leadership.

7. *Leaders who gather followers impact this generation; leaders who develop leaders impact future generations.*

People who lead followers impact only the individuals whose lives they touch personally. But people who develop and lead leaders extend their reach.

It takes a good leader to gather a group of followers and lead them to achieve a worthy goal. But it takes a great leader to lead other leaders—and that's the only kind of leader who can take an organization to the highest level and achieve explosive growth.

The Law of Reproduction: Leaders Who Lead Followers vs. Leaders Who Lead Leaders

(2 Timothy 2:2)

God challenges us to lead leaders, not merely followers. Paul lists four generations of leaders: *Paul* trained *Timothy* who trained *faithful men* who trained *others* also. Leaders who lead followers add to the organization; leaders who lead leaders multiply. Consider the chief differences between the two:

Leaders Who Lead Followers
1. Love to be needed
2. Focus on the weaknesses of people
3. Devote attention to the bottom 20 percent priorities
4. Have good influence
5. Lift up themselves
6. Spend time with people
7. Ask for little commitment
8. Lead everyone the same way
9. See immediate needs clearly
10. Impact this generation

Leaders Who Lead Leaders
1. Want to be succeeded
2. Focus on the strengths of people
3. Devote attention to the top 20 percent priorities
4. Have great influence
5. Lift up others
6. Invest time with people
7. Ask for much commitment
8. Lead everyone differently
9. See ultimate needs clearly
10. Impact the next generation

are in Christ Jesus. [14]That good thing which was committed to you, keep by the Holy Spirit who dwells in us.

[15]This you know, that all those in Asia have turned away from me, among whom are Phygellus and Hermogenes. [16]The Lord grant mercy to the household of Onesiphorus, for he often refreshed me, and was not ashamed of my chain; [17]but when he arrived in Rome, he sought me out very zealously and found *me.* [18]The Lord grant to him that he may find mercy from the Lord in that Day—and you know very well how many ways he ministered *to me*[a] at Ephesus.

Be Strong in Grace

2 You therefore, my son, be strong in the grace that is in Christ Jesus. [2]And the things that you have heard from me among many witnesses, commit these to faithful men who will be able to teach others also. [3]You therefore must endure[a] hardship as a good soldier of Jesus Christ. [4]No one engaged in warfare entangles himself with the affairs of *this* life, that he may please him who enlisted him as a soldier. [5]And also if anyone competes in athletics, he is not crowned unless he competes according to the rules. [6]The hardworking farmer must be first to partake of the crops. [7]Consider what I say, and may[a] the Lord give you understanding in all things.

[8]Remember that Jesus Christ, of the seed of David, was raised from the dead according to my gospel, [9]for which I suffer trouble as an evildoer, *even* to the point of chains; but the word of God is not chained. [10]Therefore I endure all things for the sake of the elect, that they also may obtain the salvation which is in Christ Jesus with eternal glory.

[11]*This is* a faithful saying:

For if we died with *Him,*
    We shall also live with *Him.*
[12]   If we endure,
    We shall also reign with *Him.*
If we deny *Him,*
    He also will deny us.
[13]   If we are faithless,
    He remains faithful;
    He cannot deny Himself.

Approved and Disapproved Workers

[14]Remind *them* of these things, charging *them* before the Lord not to strive about words to no profit, to the ruin of the hearers. [15]Be diligent to present yourself approved to God, a worker who

---

1:18 [a]*To me* is from the Vulgate and a few Greek manuscripts. **2:3** [a]NU-Text reads *You must share.* **2:7** [a]NU-Text reads *the Lord will give you.*

Portraits of a Leader

(2 Timothy 2:2–26)

Paul was a master at using metaphors to illustrate what a leader should look like. Right after he encourages Timothy to be strong (2 Tim. 2:1), he gives him seven snapshots of what he meant:

1. *A teacher* (v. 2)
   A leader is to be reproductive.
2. *A soldier* (vv. 3, 4)
   A leader is to be loyal.
3. *An athlete* (v. 5)
   A leader is to be disciplined.
4. *A farmer* (vv. 6, 7)
   A leader is to be a hard worker.
5. *A worker* (vv. 15–19)
   A leader is to be diligent.
6. *A vessel* (vv. 20–22)
   A leader is to be pure.
7. *A servant* (vv. 23–26)
   A leader is to be submissive.

does not need to be ashamed, rightly dividing the word of truth. [16]But shun profane *and* idle babblings, for they will increase to more ungodliness. [17]And their message will spread like cancer. Hymenaeus and Philetus are of this sort, [18]who have strayed concerning the truth, saying that the resurrection is already past; and they overthrow the faith of some. [19]Nevertheless the solid foundation of God stands, having this seal: "The Lord knows those who are His," and, "Let everyone who names the name of Christ[a] depart from iniquity."

[20]But in a great house there are not only vessels of gold and silver, but also of wood and clay, some for honor and some for dishonor. [21]Therefore if anyone cleanses himself from the latter, he will be a vessel for honor, sanctified and useful for the Master, prepared for every good work. [22]Flee also youthful lusts; but pursue righteousness, faith, love, peace with those who call on the Lord out of a pure heart. [23]But avoid foolish and ignorant disputes, knowing that they generate strife. [24]And a servant of the Lord must not quarrel but be gentle to all, able to teach, patient, [25]in humility correcting those who are in opposition, if God perhaps will grant them repentance, so that they may know the truth, [26]and *that* they may come to their senses *and escape* the snare of the devil, having been taken captive by him to *do* his will.

2:19 [a]NU-Text and M-Text read *the Lord.*

Courage: The Process of Taking a Stand

(2 Timothy 2:22—3:17)

Paul knew how important it was to encourage Timothy, for the young leader would have to take a stand in many tough situations. So he charged him to take courage and do what was right in difficult times.

Courage is the first essential quality for effective leadership. Leaders initiate and take a stand even when no one else travels with them. Paul prepares Timothy for this act with his words:

1. *There is something to prevent* (2:22, 23).
   Leaders must flee temptations, such as pleasure and power, that ruin their personal lives.
2. *There are some things to pursue* (2:22).
   Leaders must chase after qualities that will build their character and integrity.
3. *There are some things to portray* (2:24–26).
   Leaders must model right attitudes so that others will want to submit to God.
4. *There are some things to perceive* (3:1–9).
   Leaders must read the times and take responsibility to hold firm to what is right.
5. *There is something to pronounce* (3:10–17).
   Leaders must hold forth God's Word and use it as a standard for training.

Perilous Times and Perilous Men

3 But know this, that in the last days perilous times will come: [2]For men will be lovers of themselves, lovers of money, boasters, proud, blasphemers, disobedient to parents, unthankful, unholy, [3]unloving, unforgiving, slanderers, without self-control, brutal, despisers of good, [4]traitors, headstrong, haughty, lovers of pleasure rather than lovers of God, [5]having a form of godliness but denying its power. And from such people turn away! [6]For of this sort are those who creep into households and make captives of gullible women loaded down with sins, led away by various lusts, [7]always learning and never able to come to the knowledge of the truth. [8]Now as Jannes and Jambres resisted Moses, so do these also resist the truth: men of corrupt minds, disapproved concerning the faith; [9]but they will progress no further, for their folly will be manifest to all, as theirs also was.

The Man of God and the Word of God

[10]But you have carefully followed my doctrine, manner of life, purpose, faith, longsuffering, love, perseverance, [11]persecutions, afflictions, which happened to me at Antioch, at Iconium, at Lystra—what persecutions I endured. And out of them all the Lord delivered me. [12]Yes, and all who desire to live godly in Christ Jesus will suffer persecution. [13]But evil men and impostors will grow worse and worse, deceiving and being deceived. [14]But you must continue in the things which you have learned and been assured of, knowing from whom you have learned them, [15]and that from childhood you have known the Holy Scriptures, which are able to make you wise for salvation through faith which is in Christ Jesus.

[16]All Scripture is given by inspiration of God, and is profitable for doctrine, for reproof, for correction, for instruction in righteousness, [17]that the man of God may be complete, thoroughly equipped for every good work.

The Word of God: An Equipping Tool

(2 Timothy 3:16, 17)

The Scripture is a thorough equipping tool, providing doctrine, reproof, correction, and instruction, so that everyone may be equipped for every good work (2 Tim. 3:16, 17). Using Scripture, the leader is to lay the foundation, provide direction, confront others when they err, correct their behavior, and help them progress again.

Preach the Word

4 I charge you therefore before God and the Lord Jesus Christ, who will judge the living and the dead at[a] His appearing and His kingdom: [2]Preach the word! Be ready in season and out of season. Convince, rebuke, exhort, with all longsuffering and teaching. [3]For the time will come when they will not endure sound doctrine, but according to their own desires, because they have itching ears, they will heap up for themselves teachers; [4]and they will turn their ears away from the truth, and be turned aside to fables. [5]But you be watchful in all things, endure afflictions, do the work of an evangelist, fulfill your ministry.

Paul's Valedictory

[6]For I am already being poured out as a drink offering, and the time of my departure is at hand. [7]I have fought the good fight, I have finished the race, I have kept the faith. [8]Finally, there is laid up for me the crown of righteousness, which the Lord, the righteous Judge, will give to me on that Day, and not to me only but also to all who have loved His appearing.

The Abandoned Apostle

[9]Be diligent to come to me quickly; [10]for Demas has forsaken me, having loved this present world, and has departed for Thessalonica—Crescens for Galatia, Titus for Dalmatia. [11]Only

---

The Law of Sacrifice: Timothy Must Give Up to Go Up

(2 Timothy 3:10–17)

Paul called Timothy to surrender many of the comforts he could have enjoyed as a pastor. Paul teaches us how to handle sacrifices by addressing our example as a leader (2 Tim. 3:10–13), our experience as a leader (3:14, 15), and our equipping as a leader (3:16, 17).

4:1 [a]NU-Text omits therefore and reads and by for at.

The Law of Priorities: Timothy's Three Priorities

(2 Timothy 4:1–8)

Paul's last written communication reveals a sense of urgency. He wastes no words; every one of them counts. More than any other passage, this text tells us what is most important to Paul, the leader. He challenges Timothy with three priorities:

1. *Preach the Word* (vv. 1, 2).
   Timothy must keep the message alive, teaching urgently, persistently, and with conviction.
2. *Do the work* (vv. 3–5).
   Timothy was to do the work of an evangelist, fulfilling his call, reaching his potential.
3. *Run the race* (vv. 6–8).
   Timothy was to emulate Paul, who finished his course and won the prize.

Luke is with me. Get Mark and bring him with you, for he is useful to me for ministry. [12]And Tychicus I have sent to Ephesus. [13]Bring the cloak that I left with Carpus at Troas when you come—and the books, especially the parchments.

The Law of Legacy

(2 Timothy 4:6–8)

Paul's deathbed was no place of sorrow. He had planted churches, mentored leaders, established doctrine, and written epistles. The only thing left was his homecoming. Paul saw life as a race to be won, a battle to be fought, and a trust to be kept (2 Tim. 4:7). His crown awaited him.

[14]Alexander the coppersmith did me much harm. May the Lord repay him according to his works. [15]You also must beware of him, for he has greatly resisted our words.

[16]At my first defense no one stood with me, but all forsook me. May it not be charged against them.

The Lord Is Faithful

[17]But the Lord stood with me and strengthened me, so that the message might be preached fully through me, and *that* all the Gentiles might hear. Also I was delivered out of the mouth of the lion. [18]And the Lord will deliver me from every evil work and preserve *me* for His heavenly kingdom. To Him *be* glory forever and ever. Amen!

Mentoring: Paul and Timothy Both Fulfill the Call

(2 Timothy 4:9–21)

From many of the leaders in whom Paul invested, he also needed an investment in return. He acknowledges he needs Timothy (2 Tim. 4:9), Mark (4:11), and the books of Carpus (4:13). Paul poured his life into every one of them and received from every one of them.

Come Before Winter

[19]Greet Prisca and Aquila, and the household of Onesiphorus. [20]Erastus stayed in Corinth, but Trophimus I have left in Miletus sick.

[21]Do your utmost to come before winter. Eubulus greets you, as well as Pudens, Linus, Claudia, and all the brethren.

Farewell

[22]The Lord Jesus Christ[a] be with your spirit. Grace be with you. Amen.

4:22 [a]NU-Text omits *Jesus Christ*.

TITUS
Instruction on Leadership Qualifications

SUMMARY

The epistle of Titus is the third book in a row written by Paul the apostle to a young leader he was mentoring. Titus joined Paul's ministry team and traveled with him through Asia Minor. Paul believed in Titus and called him a "true son" in the faith (1:4). The apostle trusted him with the toughest of assignments, often sending him to troubled churches so that he could iron out problems and correct leadership errors.

Paul's mentoring relationship to Titus often gets lost in the shadow of Timothy or other team members in the Book of Acts. Titus's name never appears in Acts and shows up in only three of Paul's other letters. The little information we have indicates that Titus became one of Paul's closest and most trusted apprentices and colleagues. The apostle describes Titus as having the same "earnest care" for the Corinthian church that he does (2 Cor. 8:16, 17), and the young man even goes to Corinth to appeal to the church *on his own initiative*. Clearly, Paul and Titus seem cut from the same cloth. Paul chose his men well.

Many apt descriptions come to mind for Titus. First, he was a *trusted son*. When Paul traveled to Jerusalem to fight for salvation by grace through faith alone, he took Titus with him. This young man became Paul's prime exhibit of a Gentile convert worthy of full acceptance by the church, apart from the ritual of circumcision.

Second, Titus was a *troubleshooter*. Like Paul, Titus was a tough, bottom-line decision maker. In fact, Paul wrote this letter to Titus while the young leader completed a special assignment in Crete. He had been sent there to resolve some problems and prepare a set of leaders in the church (1:5), like a secretary of state dispatched to troubled nations on missions of diplomacy.

Third, Titus was a *task-oriented specialist*. Paul sent him on a number of special assignments that required a specialist. The apostle sent Titus to Corinth to collect an offering for the needy in Jerusalem. On another occasion, Paul sent him back to Corinth to confront some messy situations and opponents of Paul's teaching. In Crete he needed to organize and establish church leaders in each city.

Finally, Titus was a *teachable servant*. He demonstrated himself to be a meek and willing learner under Paul's tutelage. He remained subordinate to Paul; we have no record of him questioning Paul's judgment or demands. This servant-leader proved valuable in reaching Asia Minor, since he was a Gentile himself.

God's Role in Titus

God has used this book in the lives of many leaders throughout history. Through it He has provided instruction on leadership qualifications, the mentoring roles of older saints to younger ones, principles for dealing with false teachers, and the relationship between sound doctrine and lifestyle. God teaches us it is possible for a strong leader to reproduce himself in another strong leader and thereby extend his accomplishments. Titus provides a terrific example of the Law of the Inner Circle. Paul accomplished more and was able to follow up on work he'd started because he could send Titus as an extension of himself.

Leaders in Titus

Paul, Titus, elders

Other People of Influence in Titus

Zenas, Apollos, older saints of the church in Crete

Lessons in Leadership

- The quickest way to gain leadership is to solve problems.
- Leaders must be both tough and tender, knowing how to confront and resolve conflict.
- Leaders must not only prepare other leaders, but also furnish guiding principles by which to lead.
- Elders are to assume the role of mentors to the younger generation.
- Positions of authority require leaders to model an appropriate lifestyle.

LEADERSHIP HIGHLIGHTS IN TITUS

Greeting

1 Paul, a bondservant of God and an apostle of Jesus Christ, according to the faith of God's elect and the acknowledgment of the truth which accords with godliness, ²in hope of eternal life which God, who cannot lie, promised before time began, ³but has in due time manifested His word through preaching, which was committed to me according to the commandment of God our Savior;

⁴To Titus, a true son in *our* common faith:

Grace, mercy, *and* peace from God the Father and the Lord Jesus Christ[a] our Savior.

Qualified Elders

⁵For this reason I left you in Crete, that you should set in order the things that are lacking, and appoint elders in every city as I commanded you— ⁶if a man is blameless, the husband of one wife, having faithful children not accused of dissipation or insubordination. ⁷For a bishop[a] must be blameless, as a steward of God, not self-willed, not quick-tempered, not given to wine, not violent, not greedy for money, ⁸but hospitable, a lover of what is good, sober-minded, just, holy, self-controlled, ⁹holding fast the faithful word as he has been taught, that he may be able, by sound doctrine, both to exhort and convict those who contradict.

The Elders' Task

¹⁰For there are many insubordinate, both idle talkers and deceivers, especially those of the circumcision, ¹¹whose mouths must be stopped, who subvert whole households, teaching things which they ought not, for the sake of dishonest gain. ¹²One of them, a prophet of their own, said, "Cretans *are* always liars, evil beasts, lazy gluttons." ¹³This testimony is true. Therefore rebuke them sharply, that they may be sound in the faith, ¹⁴not giving heed to Jewish fables and commandments of men who turn from the truth. ¹⁵To the pure all things are pure, but to those who are defiled and unbelieving nothing is pure; but even their mind and conscience are defiled. ¹⁶They profess to know God, but in works they

---

1:4 [a]NU-Text reads *and Christ Jesus.* **1:7** [a]Literally *overseer*

The Law of Reproduction:
Titus's Job Was to Prepare Leaders

(Titus 1:5)

Paul left Titus in Crete to do two things: organize the people and appoint leaders. The new converts in Crete had experienced the power of God. Now they needed strong leadership to preserve what God had done.

Titus was a leader of leaders whom Paul trusted to solve problems in the most difficult of places. Paul knew that every church needs a leader to establish order and to develop a team of elders. This was Titus's job, and it remains the job of leaders today. Consider the following method of accomplishing this important task:

1. *Choose the men.*
   How creative am I at finding new people to invest in?
2. *Cultivate the models.*
   How am I doing at turning my people into examples?
3. *Create the ministries.*
   How am I at creating ministry opportunities for these leaders?
4. *Construct the management.*
   How am I at monitoring them along the way?
5. *Communicate the mindset.*
   How am I at constantly keeping the vision alive?
6. *Celebrate the mentoring.*
   How do I encourage and celebrate growth?

21 QUALITIES

While Timothy had a shepherd's heart and a tendency toward timidity, Titus was the man to call upon when a church had a problem. The apostle Paul sent Titus to both Corinth and Crete to organize the chaos and establish leaders. Titus later returned to Corinth to organize the offering Paul wanted to collect for the church in Jerusalem. Still later, when conflict arose between the Corinthian church and Paul, Titus took the initiative and negotiated with the church until he achieved peace. Paul trusted him more than anyone else to solve problems and make peace among the people.

Problem solving is the fastest way to gain leadership. Left alone, things go awry. Left alone, people go astray. Left alone, plans go amiss. When someone steps forward with solutions, he or she catches the attention of others. The man with the plan is the man with the power. Consider the characteristics of good problem solvers:

1. *They anticipate problems.*
   Titus anticipated problems in Corinth and prevented a possible church split.
2. *They accept the truth.*
   Titus was always honest with Paul and the troubled churches he led. He faced reality.
3. *They see the big picture.*
   Titus knew how to deal with the church in Crete, due to his larger perspective.
4. *They handle one thing at a time.*
   Titus took the initiative and dealt with one major conflict at a time.
5. *They don't give up a major goal when they're down.*
   Titus tenaciously addressed the conflicts in Corinth until he solved them.

When you face a problem, how do you react? Do you ignore it and hope it will go away? Do you feel paralyzed or powerless? Do you tend to give up after one attempt at a solution? The ability to solve problems comes from experience in facing and overcoming obstacles. If you never try, fail, and try again, you'll never master the difficulty. To improve your problem-solving skills, do the following:

1. *Look for trouble.*
   Don't avoid problems; attack them. Use caution, but find them and take them to someone with experience in that area. We learn to solve problems by pursuing them.
2. *Develop a method.*
   Come up with a system. Take time to discover the real issue; find out what others have done; have your team study options; prioritize solutions and try one.
3. *Surround yourself with problem solvers.*
   Find others who complement your weaknesses, especially if you aren't a good problem solver. Diverse thinking allows you to solve a variety of problems.

For a negative example of problem solving, see p. 20.

Character: Qualifications for Church Leadership

(Titus 1:5–9)

What qualities should church leaders possess? Paul outlines for Titus a list similar to the one he gave Timothy. Note that most of the traits he mentions deal with personal character, not techniques, gifts, or skills. Note what Paul considered most important:

1. *Personal life:* blameless, not self-willed, not quick-tempered, not violent, sober-minded, holy, self-controlled.
2. *Family life:* husband of one wife, with faithful children.
3. *Social life:* hospitable, not accused of dissipation, not given to wine.
4. *Financial life:* a steward of God, not greedy for money.
5. *Professional life:* not accused of insubordination, a lover of what is good, just, holding fast the faithful word, able to exhort and convict those who contradict.

The Law of Empowerment: Elders Are to Mentor and Model for Young Leaders

(Titus 2:1–7)

Paul helps us to see four levels of leadership development. He himself represented the first level. He charged Titus as the second level. Titus was to teach older men and women, representing the third level. Finally, Titus was also to teach the young men and women, representing the fourth level. Each level was to model leadership and mentor others in leadership. This is the pattern throughout Scripture:

1. Abraham and Lot
2. Jacob and Joseph
3. Jethro and Moses
4. Moses and Joshua
5. Naomi and Ruth
6. Eli and Samuel
7. Jonathan and David
8. David and Mephibosheth
9. Nathan and David
10. Elijah and Elisha
11. Elijah and the prophets
12. Elizabeth and Mary
13. John the Baptizer and disciples
14. Barnabas and Saul
15. Barnabas and Mark
16. Paul and Silas
17. Paul and Timothy
18. Paul and Philemon
19. Paul and Aquila
20. Paul and Julius
21. Jesus and the Twelve

deny Him, being abominable, disobedient, and disqualified for every good work.

Qualities of a Sound Church

2 But as for you, speak the things which are proper for sound doctrine: ²that the older men be sober, reverent, temperate, sound in faith, in love, in patience; ³the older women likewise, that they be reverent in behavior, not slanderers, not given to much wine, teachers of good things— ⁴that they admonish the young women to love their husbands, to love their children, ⁵to be discreet, chaste, homemakers, good, obedient to their own husbands, that the word of God may not be blasphemed.

⁶Likewise, exhort the young men to be sober-minded, ⁷in all things showing yourself *to be* a pattern of good works; in doctrine *showing* integrity, reverence, incorruptibility,ᵃ ⁸sound speech that cannot be condemned, that one who is an opponent may be ashamed, having nothing evil to say of you.ᵃ

⁹*Exhort* bondservants to be obedient to their own masters, to be well pleasing in all *things,* not answering back, ¹⁰not pilfering, but showing all good fidelity, that they may adorn the doctrine of God our Savior in all things.

Trained by Saving Grace

¹¹For the grace of God that brings salvation has appeared to all men, ¹²teaching us that, denying ungodliness and worldly lusts, we should live soberly, righteously, and godly in the present age, ¹³looking for the blessed hope and glorious ap-

2:7 ᵃNU-Text omits *incorruptibility.* **2:8** ᵃNU-Text and M-Text read *us.*

The Law of Reproduction: From Shepherding to Developing

(Titus 2:15)

Paul modeled more than mere nurturing of his young disciple, Titus; the apostle developed him as a leader. He focused not merely on meeting immediate needs, but on producing a leader who could go on meeting needs without Paul's help.

Paul had a passion for developing leaders such as Timothy and Titus. Consider the necessary progression for growing beyond mere shepherding, to equipping and developing:

Shepherding	Equipping	Developing
1. Care	1. Train for ministry	1. Train for personal growth
2. Immediate-need focus	2. Task focus	2. Person focus
3. Need-oriented	3. Skill-oriented	3. Character-oriented
4. Masses	4. Many	4. Few
5. Maintenance	5. Addition	5. Multiplication
6. Feel better	6. Unleashing	6. Empowering
7. Immediate	7. Short-term	7. Long-term
8. Nurture	8. Teaching	8. Mentoring
9. What is the problem?	9. What do I need?	9. What do they need?
10. They begin to walk	10. They walk the first mile	10. They walk the second mile

pearing of our great God and Savior Jesus Christ, [14]who gave Himself for us, that He might redeem us from every lawless deed and purify for Himself *His* own special people, zealous for good works.

[15]Speak these things, exhort, and rebuke with all authority. Let no one despise you.

Graces of the Heirs of Grace

3 Remind them to be subject to rulers and authorities, to obey, to be ready for every good work, [2]to speak evil of no one, to be peaceable, gentle, showing all humility to all men. [3]For we ourselves were also once foolish, disobedient, deceived, serving various lusts and pleasures, living in malice and envy, hateful and hating one another. [4]But when the kindness and the love of God our Savior toward man appeared, [5]not by works of righteousness which we have done, but according to His mercy He saved us, through the washing of regeneration and renewing of the Holy Spirit, [6]whom He poured out on us abundantly through Jesus Christ our Savior, [7]that having been justified by His grace we should become heirs according to the hope of eternal life.

[8]This is a faithful saying, and these things I want you to affirm constantly, that those who have believed in God should be careful to main-

tain good works. These things are good and profitable to men.

Avoid Dissension

[9]But avoid foolish disputes, genealogies, contentions, and strivings about the law; for they are unprofitable and useless. [10]Reject a divisive man after the first and second admonition, [11]knowing that such a person is warped and sinning, being self-condemned.

Authority and Submission: Everyone Is Responsible to Someone

(Titus 3:1, 2)

Everyone and everything exists in submission to someone else. Even in the home, God has called parents to assume responsibility for the health and growth of the family. Those in authority do not necessarily have greater intelligence or gifts, but they do have greater responsibility.

Final Messages

¹²When I send Artemas to you, or Tychicus, be diligent to come to me at Nicopolis, for I have decided to spend the winter there. ¹³Send Zenas the lawyer and Apollos on their journey with haste, that they may lack nothing. ¹⁴And let our *people* also learn to maintain good works, to *meet* urgent needs, that they may not be unfruitful.

Farewell

¹⁵All who *are* with me greet you. Greet those who love us in the faith.

Grace *be* with you all. Amen.

PHILEMON
A Case Study in Healthy Confrontation

SUMMARY

The letter from Paul to his friend Philemon reveals a warm, touching side to the apostle's personality and leadership style. Philemon was a friend of Paul's who helped start the Colossian church in his own home. Some time after Paul left, one of Philemon's slaves, Onesimus, ran away. Interestingly, Paul does not deliver a discourse against slavery, but instead teaches on how we are to relate to each other in Christ. He suggests that a completely new frame of reference, brotherhood, should transform all earthly relationships. Consequently, Paul leads Philemon as a brother, avoiding compulsion. Paul leads Onesimus not as a slave, but as a brother who has learned to want to do what is right. In this letter we see Paul act as a mentor to Philemon and to Onesimus in their relationship to one another.

Yet what a heavy issue to discuss through the mail! Philemon had a legal right to punish Onesimus for running away. However, as God would have it, Onesimus found Paul in prison and joined him there to talk. During those discussions, no doubt, Paul led him to the Lord. At this point, the issue got sticky, for Onesimus was not merely a runaway slave, but a brother in Christ. Paul challenged Philemon to receive Onesimus back as a brother—clearly, a lot to ask. Philemon must have felt confused, angry, and perhaps even thought about ignoring the request and giving Paul the silent treatment.

Paul made this option nearly impossible, however. The apostle wrote with such heart and grace that Philemon couldn't help but respond in kind. This letter stands as a case study in healthy confrontation, the act every leader must master. All leaders *will* face conflict. Difficult people and circumstances *will* arise. Leaders must recognize that conflict is *natural:* It occurs simply because of human differences. Conflict is also *neutral:* In itself, it is neither destructive nor constructive. And conflict is *normal:* It happens to all of us.

Paul seemed to understand all this. He addressed the problem through this letter written from prison, then sent it with great confidence to Philemon through a messenger—none other than Onesimus himself.

God's Role in Philemon

Some have wondered why the Lord included this personal letter in Scripture. After all, it doesn't address general issues facing everyone. Yet a number of reasons suggest why God wanted this letter in the Bible.

First, it teaches us about healthy leadership and relationships within the church. Second, at the time Paul wrote, the master-slave relationship posed a problem for the whole church. Even today in employer-employee relationships, we are to relate to believers in a way distinct from the unbelieving world. Finally, God provides a snapshot of the personal side of a leader practicing healthy confrontation.

Leaders in Philemon

Paul, Timothy, Philemon

Other People of Influence in Philemon

Onesimus, Apphia, Archippus

Lessons in Leadership

- Good leaders always initiate confrontation.
- Managing conflict goes with the leader's territory.
- Leadership is relationships.
- Spiritual leaders motivate others as brothers and sisters, not through compulsion.

LEADERSHIP

HIGHLIGHTS IN PHILEMON

THE LAW OF CONNECTION: Paul Connects, Then Asks for Help (4–22)	*page 1499*
PROBLEM SOLVING: Healthy Confrontation and Resolution (8–10)	*page 1500*

Greeting

Paul, a prisoner of Christ Jesus, and Timothy *our* brother,

To Philemon our beloved *friend* and fellow laborer, [2]to the beloved[a] Apphia, Archippus our fellow soldier, and to the church in your house:

[3]Grace to you and peace from God our Father and the Lord Jesus Christ.

Philemon's Love and Faith

[4]I thank my God, making mention of you always in my prayers, [5]hearing of your love and faith which you have toward the Lord Jesus and toward all the saints, [6]that the sharing of your faith may become effective by the acknowledgment of every good thing which is in you[a] in Christ Jesus. [7]For we have[a] great joy[b] and consolation in your love, because the hearts of the saints have been refreshed by you, brother.

The Plea for Onesimus

[8]Therefore, though I might be very bold in Christ to command you what is fitting, [9]yet for love's sake I rather appeal *to you*—being such a one as Paul, the aged, and now also a prisoner of Jesus Christ— [10]I appeal to you for my son Onesimus, whom I have begotten *while* in my chains, [11]who once was unprofitable to you, but now is profitable to you and to me.

[12]I am sending him back.[a] You therefore receive him, that is, my own heart, [13]whom I wished to keep with me, that on your behalf he might minister to me in my chains for the gospel. [14]But without your consent I wanted to do nothing, that your good deed might not be by compulsion, as it were, but voluntary.

[15]For perhaps he departed for a while for this *purpose,* that you might receive him forever, [16]no longer as a slave but more than a slave—a beloved brother, especially to me but how much more to you, both in the flesh and in the Lord.

Philemon's Obedience Encouraged

[17]If then you count me as a partner, receive him as *you would* me. [18]But if he has wronged you

---

2 [a]NU-Text reads *to our sister Apphia.* **6** [a]NU-Text and M-Text read *us.* **7** [a]NU-Text reads *had.* [b]M-Text reads *thanksgiving.* **12** [a]NU-Text reads *back to you in person, that is, my own heart.*

The Law of Connection:
Paul Connects, Then Asks for Help

(Philemon 4–22)

In the very personal letter of Philemon, Paul asks his friend to do something very difficult: graciously receive back a runaway slave. Before he confronts Philemon, Paul connects by walking through the following stages of conflict management:

1. *The compliment stage* (vv. 4–7)
   Paul affirmed Philemon and reminded him of his love. Good leaders begin confrontation with affirmation. They focus on positive qualities.
2. *The compromise stage* (vv. 8–13)
   Before his appeal, Paul concedes the present status of the slave, Onesimus. Good leaders own some responsibility for the conflict and recognize their differences.
3. *The choice stage* (v. 14)
   Paul sought the consent of Philemon to send back Onesimus. He laid out the challenge to receive him. In this stage, leaders clearly articulate the decision in front of both parties.
4. *The challenge stage* (vv. 15–20)
   Paul challenged Philemon to do what was right. He committed to steps he'd take to make things right, but issued a challenge to Philemon to respond and take the high road.
5. *The confidence stage* (vv. 21, 22)
   Paul expressed confidence in Philemon that he would, indeed, do what was right in the sight of God. Paul believed the best about his friend and communicated his love for him.

Problem Solving: Healthy Confrontation and Resolution

(Philemon 8–10)

The best way to solve many problems is to confront them. Sometimes those problems are people. Paul took great pains to confront Philemon about Onesimus. Consider these steps for confronting someone:

1. *Pray through your own anger.* Don't let emotion lead you. Wait until you can be objective.
2. *Initiate the contact.* Don't wait for the other person. God calls *us* to make things right.
3. *Begin with affirmation.* Encourage first, then receive permission to talk candidly.
4. *Admit you have a problem.* Don't say it's the other person's problem; admit you are struggling.
5. *Bring up the issue and explain you don't understand what's happened.* Aim to clarify.
6. *Let the person respond.* After you lay out the issue, let the individual speak from his or her angle.
7. *Narrow the focus.* Identify and prioritize the issues. Go after one change at a time.
8. *Establish forgiveness and repentance, if needed.* Don't stop until change occurs.
9. *Compromise on opinions, not on principles.* Be flexible with everything except truth.
10. *Pray and affirm your love as you close.* Never let the person doubt God's love or yours.

or owes anything, put that on my account. ¹⁹I, Paul, am writing with my own hand. I will repay—not to mention to you that you owe me even your own self besides. ²⁰Yes, brother, let me have joy from you in the Lord; refresh my heart in the Lord.

²¹Having confidence in your obedience, I write to you, knowing that you will do even more than I say. ²²But, meanwhile, also prepare a guest room for me, for I trust that through your prayers I shall be granted to you.

Farewell

²³Epaphras, my fellow prisoner in Christ Jesus, greets you, ²⁴as do Mark, Aristarchus, Demas, Luke, my fellow laborers.

²⁵The grace of our Lord Jesus Christ *be* with your spirit. Amen.

When Leaders Are Challenged to Do the Difficult

(Philemon 21)

Would Philemon forgive or erect emotional walls against Paul? He had done nothing wrong; in fact, *he* had been wronged. Fortunately, Philemon acted instead of reacting. Church history tells us Philemon responded with grace, received Onesimus back, and enabled him not only to participate in the church, but later to become a bishop!

HEBREWS
A Solid Foundation for Faith in Christ

SUMMARY

Like Romans, the Book of Hebrews addresses both doctrine and duty in the Christian's life. An unnamed author wrote the book to Jewish believers who needed a solid foundation for their faith in Jesus as the Messiah. They needed to learn that their new lifestyle didn't require circumcision, sacrifices, or other Old Testament traditions. This book provides a radical apologetic on Christianity.

Three profound leadership truths jump off the pages of this great book. First, the writer is not merely a teacher, but a leader attempting to convince Jewish believers to shift to new paradigms and to live in the freedom of grace. Every leader is a teacher in one sense, helping others to learn the ways of the organization and prepare for their job. But not every teacher is a leader! While no one can positively identify the author, one thing is clear: It was written by a strong, compelling leader determined to help his people change the way they thought and acted. New paradigms had to be embraced and fresh vision had to be cast to explain the superiority of the new paradigms.

Second, the book portrays Jesus not only as a wonderful Savior, but also as a superior Leader. Several times the book speaks of the superiority of Christ as compared to other Old Covenant leaders (Moses, Joshua, angels). The book can be divided into three sections. The first section talks about the superiority of Christ's Person (1:1—4:13); the second talks about the superiority of Christ's work (4:14—10:18); the third discusses the superiority of the Christian lifestyle (10:19—13:25). Hence, the book proclaims Jesus to be a superior Leader with a superior life.

Third, the book clearly develops the power of vision. Effective leadership always operates off of a compelling vision. Throughout the 13 chapters of Hebrews, the writer paints pictures of a better life, contrasting it with the old one. In the famous "Hall of Faith" (11:1–40), we see a number of patriarchs living by faith and energized by a vision: "These all died in faith, not having received the promises, *but having seen them afar off* were assured of them, embraced them . . ." (11:13, emphasis added). The entire book communicates a huge vision and a preferred future.

God's Role in Hebrews

God uses the Book of Hebrews to build a bridge between the Old and New Testaments. Hebrews quotes a wide variety of Old Testament passages to present a strong case for Jesus' superiority over everything that came before Him. God speaks clearly of the Person and work of Christ, and in this book provides us with a clear discourse on the need for a New Covenant and why faith is so central to His kingdom. God acts as both an Apologist and a Visionary, convincing readers to change and move with Him as He ushers in an age of grace.

Leaders in Hebrews

The writer, Moses, Joshua, Melchizedek, Hebrew patriarchs, Jesus

Other People of Influence in Hebrews

The Old Testament Israelites, the high priests

Lessons in Leadership

- As both God and man, Jesus had authority to lead.
- Leaders gain credibility when they suffer with those they lead.
- Good leaders build a sense of urgency, destiny, and family.
- Leaders earn their right to be heard by serving others.
- Effective leaders build a convincing case for why their people should change.
- Productive leaders communicate the superiority and the benefits of their ideas.
- Faith and vision are not options to good leadership, but necessities.
- Christ's leadership and covenant are superior to any before or since.

LEADERSHIP

HIGHLIGHTS IN HEBREWS

THE LAW OF SACRIFICE: Jesus Became Like Us So We Could Be Like Him (2:1–18)	page 1504
THE LAW OF RESPECT: Jesus Is Superior to Moses (3:2–5)	page 1505
COMMUNICATION: Melchizedek Is a Metaphor for Christ (7:1–22)	page 1508
VISION: Seeing the Invisible Future (11:1–32)	page 1512
THE LAW OF SACRIFICE: Moses Gave Up the Riches of Egypt (11:23–29)	page 1513
PASSION: Run with Passion, Purpose, and Perspective (12:1–3)	page 1514

God's Supreme Revelation

1 God, who at various times and in various ways spoke in time past to the fathers by the prophets, [2]has in these last days spoken to us by *His* Son, whom He has appointed heir of all things, through whom also He made the worlds; [3]who being the brightness of *His* glory and the express image of His person, and upholding all things by the word of His power, when He had by Himself[a] purged our[b] sins, sat down at the right hand of the Majesty on high, [4]having become so much better than the angels, as He has by inheritance obtained a more excellent name than they.

The Law of Respect: Jesus Is the Superior Leader

(Hebrews 1:3–12)

H ebrews paints Jesus as the ultimate revelation of God, superior to the prophets or the angels. Jesus is the exact representation of God (Heb. 1:3) and has a position above everyone (1:5–12). Jesus displayed His strength in creation and salvation. He is the strongest Leader and even the angels follow Him.

The Son Exalted Above Angels

[5]For to which of the angels did He ever say:

" You are My Son,
Today I have begotten You"?[a]

And again:

" I will be to Him a Father,
And He shall be to Me a Son"?[b]

[6]But when He again brings the firstborn into the world, He says:

" Let all the angels of God worship Him."[a]

[7]And of the angels He says:

" Who makes His angels spirits
And His ministers a flame of fire."[a]

[8]But to the Son He says:

" Your throne, O God, is forever and ever;
A scepter of righteousness is the scepter of Your kingdom.
[9]You have loved righteousness and hated lawlessness;
Therefore God, Your God, has anointed You
With the oil of gladness more than Your companions."[a]

[10]And:

" You, LORD, in the beginning laid the foundation of the earth,
And the heavens are the work of Your hands.
[11]They will perish, but You remain;
And they will all grow old like a garment;
[12]Like a cloak You will fold them up,
And they will be changed.
But You are the same,
And Your years will not fail."[a]

[13]But to which of the angels has He ever said:

" Sit at My right hand,
Till I make Your enemies Your footstool"?[a]

[14]Are they not all ministering spirits sent forth to minister for those who will inherit salvation?

Do Not Neglect Salvation

2 Therefore we must give the more earnest heed to the things we have heard, lest we drift away. [2]For if the word spoken through angels proved steadfast, and every transgression and disobedience received a just reward, [3]how shall we escape if we neglect so great a salvation, which at the first began to be spoken by the Lord, and was confirmed to us by those who heard *Him,* [4]God also bearing witness both with signs and wonders, with various miracles, and gifts of the Holy Spirit, according to His own will?

The Son Made Lower than Angels

[5]For He has not put the world to come, of which we speak, in subjection to angels. [6]But one testified in a certain place, saying:

1:3 [a]NU-Text omits *by Himself.* [b]NU-Text omits *our.* **1:5** [a]Psalm 2:7 [b]2 Samuel 7:14
1:6 [a]Deuteronomy 32:43 (Septuagint, Dead Sea Scrolls); Psalm 97:7 **1:7** [a]Psalm 104:4 **1:9** [a]Psalm 45:6, 7 **1:12** [a]Psalm 102:25–27 **1:13** [a]Psalm 110:1

The Law of Sacrifice: Jesus Became Like Us So We Could Be Like Him

(Hebrews 2:1–18)

Jesus is the ultimate example of a leader who paid the price to get the job done. Consider how Christ practiced the Law of Sacrifice:

1. He was made lower than the angels, even though they worshiped Him (v. 9).
2. He tasted death for everyone, even though He is the immortal God (v. 9).
3. He suffered for us, even though He is the omnipotent Savior (v. 10).
4. He calls us brothers, even though He is the Creator of us all (vv. 11–13).
5. He shared our humanity, even though He is the unlimited, perfect Spirit (v. 14).

Why did Jesus go through all this sacrifice? Verses 17 and 18 give the answer:

1. That He could be merciful to us in our humanity.
2. That He could empathize with our temptations.
3. That He could deliver us from our sufferings.

"What is man that You are mindful of him,
　Or the son of man that You take care of him?
7　You have made him a little lower than the angels;
　You have crowned him with glory and honor,[a]
　And set him over the works of Your hands.
8　You have put all things in subjection under his feet."[a]

For in that He put all in subjection under him, He left nothing *that is* not put under him. But now we do not yet see all things put under him. [9]But we see Jesus, who was made a little lower than the angels, for the suffering of death crowned with glory and honor, that He, by the grace of God, might taste death for everyone.

Bringing Many Sons to Glory

[10]For it was fitting for Him, for whom *are* all things and by whom *are* all things, in bringing many sons to glory, to make the captain of their salvation perfect through sufferings. [11]For both He who sanctifies and those who are being sanctified *are* all of one, for which reason He is not ashamed to call them brethren, [12]saying:

"I will declare Your name to My brethren;
　In the midst of the assembly I will sing praise to You."[a]

[13]And again:

"I will put My trust in Him."[a]

And again:

"Here am I and the children whom God has given Me."[b]

[14]Inasmuch then as the children have partaken of flesh and blood, He Himself likewise shared in the same, that through death He might destroy him who had the power of death, that is, the devil, [15]and release those who through fear of death were all their lifetime subject to bondage. [16]For indeed He does not give aid to angels, but He does give aid to the seed of Abraham. [17]Therefore, in all things He had to be made like *His* brethren, that He might be a merciful and faithful High Priest in things *pertaining* to God, to make propitiation for the sins of the people. [18]For in that He Himself has suffered, being tempted, He is able to aid those who are tempted.

The Son Was Faithful

3 Therefore, holy brethren, partakers of the heavenly calling, consider the Apostle and High Priest of our confession, Christ Jesus, [2]who was faithful to Him who appointed Him, as Moses also *was faithful* in all His house. [3]For this One has been counted worthy of more glory than Moses, inasmuch as He who built the house has more honor than the house. [4]For every house is built by someone, but He who built all things *is* God. [5]And Moses indeed *was* faithful in all His house as a servant, for a testimony of those things which would be spoken *afterward,* [6]but Christ as a Son over His own house, whose house we are

---

2:7 [a]NU-Text and M-Text omit the rest of verse 7.
2:8 [a]Psalm 8:4–6 **2:12** [a]Psalm 22:22
2:13 [a]2 Samuel 22:3; Isaiah 8:17 [b]Isaiah 8:18

The Law of Respect: Jesus Is Superior to Moses

(Hebrews 3:2–5)

By comparing Jesus' priesthood to Moses and the Old Covenant, once again the writer attempts to demonstrate Christ's superiority to Moses, knowing that people naturally follow the strongest leader. They followed Moses, but if Jesus is measurably superior to Moses, then perhaps He deserves a look. Consider the unequaled leadership of Jesus:

Moses' Priesthood	Jesus' Priesthood
1. Faithful to God (v. 2)	1. Faithful to God (v. 2)
2. Honor and glory (v. 3)	2. More honor and glory (v. 3)
3. The house (vv. 3, 4)	3. The builder of the house (vv. 3, 4)
4. A servant (v. 5)	4. A Son (v. 5)
5. Testimony to truth (v. 5)	5. The Truth (v. 5)

if we hold fast the confidence and the rejoicing of the hope firm to the end.[a]

Be Faithful

[7]Therefore, as the Holy Spirit says:

" *Today, if you will hear His voice,*
[8] *Do not harden your hearts as in the rebellion,*
In the day of trial in the wilderness,
[9] *Where your fathers tested Me, tried Me,*
And saw My works forty years.
[10] *Therefore I was angry with that generation,*
And said, 'They always go astray in their heart,
And they have not known My ways.'
[11] *So I swore in My wrath,*
'They shall not enter My rest.'"[a]

[12]Beware, brethren, lest there be in any of you an evil heart of unbelief in departing from the living God; [13]but exhort one another daily, while it is called "Today," lest any of you be hardened through the deceitfulness of sin. [14]For we have become partakers of Christ if we hold the beginning of our confidence steadfast to the end, [15]while it is said:

" *Today, if you will hear His voice,*
Do not harden your hearts as in the rebellion."[a]

Failure of the Wilderness Wanderers

[16]For who, having heard, rebelled? Indeed, *was it* not all who came out of Egypt, *led* by Moses? [17]Now with whom was He angry forty years? *Was it* not with those who sinned, whose corpses fell in the wilderness? [18]And to whom did He swear that they would not enter His rest, but to those who did not obey? [19]So we see that they could not enter in because of unbelief.

The Promise of Rest

4 Therefore, since a promise remains of entering His rest, let us fear lest any of you seem to have come short of it. [2]For indeed the gospel was preached to us as well as to them; but the word which they heard did not profit them,[a] not being mixed with faith in those who heard *it.* [3]For we who have believed do enter that rest, as He has said:

" *So I swore in My wrath,*
'They shall not enter My rest,'"[a]

although the works were finished from the foundation of the world. [4]For He has spoken in a certain place of the seventh *day* in this way: "*And God rested on the seventh day from all His works*";[a] [5]and again in this *place:* "*They shall not enter My rest.*"[a]

[6]Since therefore it remains that some *must* enter it, and those to whom it was first preached did not enter because of disobedience, [7]again He designates a certain day, saying in David, "*Today,*" after such a long time, as it has been said:

3:6 [a]NU-Text omits *firm to the end.* **3:11** [a]Psalm 95:7–11 **3:15** [a]Psalm 95:7, 8 **4:2** [a]NU-Text and M-Text read *profit them, since they were not united by faith with those who heeded it.* **4:3** [a]Psalm 95:11 **4:4** [a]Genesis 2:2 **4:5** [a]Psalm 95:11

Servanthood: Jesus Earns His Right to Be Followed

(Hebrews 4:1–16)

We face no temptation that Jesus did not face. He earned His right to be followed by enduring every temptation, without succumbing to any of them. He worked to identify with us, but didn't stop there. We can put our confidence in Him because He serves us with His sympathy and His salvation.

"*Today, if you will hear His voice,*
Do not harden your hearts."[a]

[8]For if Joshua had given them rest, then He would not afterward have spoken of another day. [9]There remains therefore a rest for the people of God. [10]For he who has entered His rest has himself also ceased from his works as God *did* from His.

The Word Discovers Our Condition

[11]Let us therefore be diligent to enter that rest, lest anyone fall according to the same example of disobedience. [12]For the word of God *is* living and powerful, and sharper than any two-edged sword, piercing even to the division of soul and spirit, and of joints and marrow, and is a discerner of the thoughts and intents of the heart. [13]And there is no creature hidden from His sight, but all things *are* naked and open to the eyes of Him to whom we *must give* account.

Our Compassionate High Priest

[14]Seeing then that we have a great High Priest who has passed through the heavens, Jesus the Son of God, let us hold fast *our* confession. [15]For we do not have a High Priest who cannot sympathize with our weaknesses, but was in all *points* tempted as *we are,* yet without sin. [16]Let us therefore come boldly to the throne of grace, that we may obtain mercy and find grace to help in time of need.

Qualifications for High Priesthood

5 For every high priest taken from among men is appointed for men in things *pertaining* to God, that he may offer both gifts and sacrifices for sins. [2]He can have compassion on those who are ignorant and going astray, since he himself is also subject to weakness. [3]Because of this he is required as for the people, so also for himself, to offer *sacrifices* for sins. [4]And no man takes this honor to himself, but he who is called by God, just as Aaron *was.*

A Priest Forever

[5]So also Christ did not glorify Himself to become High Priest, *but it* was He who said to Him:

"*You are My Son,*
Today I have begotten You."[a]

[6]As *He* also *says* in another *place:*

"*You are a priest forever*
According to the order of Melchizedek";[a]

4:7 [a]Psalm 95:7, 8 **5:5** [a]Psalm 2:7 **5:6** [a]Psalm 110:4

The Law of Navigation: Jesus Is Our Forerunner

(Hebrews 4:14–16; 6:19, 20)

A forerunner was a small boat that navigated its way through dark waters, connecting a rope from the mother ship to the shore so the ship could dock without damage. Jesus is our forerunner, navigating unsafe waters ahead of us. He makes it possible for all His followers to make it home safely.

Teachability: Even Jesus Learned Obedience

(Hebrews 5:8)

Although Hebrews describes Jesus as the superior Leader and perfect High Priest, He learned obedience through the things He suffered. Luke 2:52 tells us Jesus increased in wisdom, stature, and favor with God and man. This growth didn't stop at age 12. All good leaders learn from their experiences, especially suffering.

[7]who, in the days of His flesh, when He had offered up prayers and supplications, with vehement cries and tears to Him who was able to save Him from death, and was heard because of His godly fear, [8]though He was a Son, *yet* He learned obedience by the things which He suffered. [9]And having been perfected, He became the author of eternal salvation to all who obey Him, [10]called by God as High Priest *"according to the order of Melchizedek,"* [11]of whom we have much to say, and hard to explain, since you have become dull of hearing.

Spiritual Immaturity

[12]For though by this time you ought to be teachers, you need *someone* to teach you again the first principles of the oracles of God; and you have come to need milk and not solid food. [13]For everyone who partakes *only* of milk *is* unskilled in the word of righteousness, for he is a babe. [14]But solid food belongs to those who are of full age, *that is,* those who by reason of use have their senses exercised to discern both good and evil.

The Peril of Not Progressing

6 Therefore, leaving the discussion of the elementary *principles* of Christ, let us go on to perfection, not laying again the foundation of repentance from dead works and of faith toward God, [2]of the doctrine of baptisms, of laying on of hands, of resurrection of the dead, and of eternal judgment. [3]And this we will[a] do if God permits.

[4]For *it is* impossible for those who were once enlightened, and have tasted the heavenly gift, and have become partakers of the Holy Spirit, [5]and have tasted the good word of God and the powers of the age to come, [6]if they fall away,[a] to renew them again to repentance, since they crucify again for themselves the Son of God, and put *Him* to an open shame.

[7]For the earth which drinks in the rain that often comes upon it, and bears herbs useful for those by whom it is cultivated, receives blessing from God; [8]but if it bears thorns and briers, *it is* rejected and near to being cursed, whose end *is* to be burned.

A Better Estimate

[9]But, beloved, we are confident of better things concerning you, yes, things that accompany salvation, though we speak in this manner. [10]For God *is* not unjust to forget your work and labor of[a] love which you have shown toward His name, *in that* you have ministered to the saints, and do minister. [11]And we desire that each one of

---

The Law of Solid Ground: God Swore by Himself

(Hebrews 6:13–18)

When God made a promise to Abraham, both took an oath. God not only kept His promise, but could find no better way to communicate His good faith than to use His own name. Leaders whose word is as good as a bond personify both integrity and trustworthiness.

---

you show the same diligence to the full assurance of hope until the end, [12]that you do not become sluggish, but imitate those who through faith and patience inherit the promises.

God's Infallible Purpose in Christ

[13]For when God made a promise to Abraham, because He could swear by no one greater, He swore by Himself, [14]saying, *"Surely blessing I will bless you, and multiplying I will multiply you."*[a] [15]And so, after he had patiently endured, he obtained the promise. [16]For men indeed swear by the greater, and an oath for confirmation *is* for them an end of all dispute. [17]Thus God, determining to show more abundantly to the heirs of promise the immutability of His counsel, confirmed *it* by an oath, [18]that by two immutable things, in which it *is* impossible for God to lie, we might[a] have strong consolation, who have fled for refuge to lay hold of the hope set before *us*.

[19]This *hope* we have as an anchor of the soul, both sure and steadfast, and which enters the *Presence* behind the veil, [20]where the forerunner has entered for us, *even* Jesus, having become High Priest forever according to the order of Melchizedek.

The King of Righteousness

7 For this Melchizedek, king of Salem, priest of the Most High God, who met Abraham returning from the slaughter of the kings and blessed him, [2]to whom also Abraham gave a tenth part of all, first being translated "king of righteousness," and then also king of Salem,

---

6:3 [a]M-Text reads *let us do.* **6:6** [a]Or *and have fallen away* **6:10** [a]NU-Text omits *labor of.* **6:14** [a]Genesis 22:17 **6:18** [a]M-Text omits *might.*

receives *them*, of whom it is witnessed that he lives. [9]Even Levi, who receives tithes, paid tithes through Abraham, so to speak, [10]for he was still in the loins of his father when Melchizedek met him.

Need for a New Priesthood

[11]Therefore, if perfection were through the Levitical priesthood (for under it the people received the law), what further need *was there* that another priest should rise according to the order of Melchizedek, and not be called according to the order of Aaron? [12]For the priesthood being changed, of necessity there is also a change of the law. [13]For He of whom these things are spoken belongs to another tribe, from which no man has officiated at the altar.

[14]For *it is* evident that our Lord arose from Judah, of which tribe Moses spoke nothing concerning priesthood.[a] [15]And it is yet far more evident if, in the likeness of Melchizedek, there arises another priest [16]who has come, not according to the law of a fleshly commandment, but according to the power of an endless life. [17]For He testifies:[a]

> "*You are a priest forever*
> *According to the order of Melchizedek.*"[b]

[18]For on the one hand there is an annulling of the former commandment because of its weakness and unprofitableness, [19]for the law made nothing perfect; on the other hand, *there is the* bringing in of a better hope, through which we draw near to God.

Greatness of the New Priest

[20]And inasmuch as He was not *made priest* without an oath [21](for they have become priests without an oath, but He with an oath by Him who said to Him:

> "*The LORD has sworn*
> *And will not relent,*
> '*You are a priest forever*[a]
> *According to the order of Melchizedek*'"),[b]

[22]by so much more Jesus has become a surety of a better covenant.

[23]Also there were many priests, because they were prevented by death from continuing. [24]But He, because He continues forever, has an un-

---

Communication: Melchizedek Is a Metaphor for Christ

(Hebrews 7:1–22)

If leaders fail to communicate with others, they travel alone. The writer to the Hebrews provides a picture of Christ's superiority by comparing Jesus to Melchizedek. Good communicators give a picture of something familiar to explain something unfamiliar. Melchizedek supplied a powerful metaphor because, like Christ . . .

1. *His leadership was universal, not national.*
   He wasn't limited to a priesthood in a single country.
2. *His leadership was superior, not mediocre.*
   He is pictured as a superior and respected leader to whom even Abraham gave a tithe.
3. *His leadership was based on righteousness, not selfishness.*
   This king's name meant "righteousness over Salem (peace)."
4. *His leadership was personal, not hereditary.*
   He didn't lead because he was born into the right family or had the right genes.
5. *His leadership is eternal, not temporary.*
   He abides as a priest perpetually, just like Christ.

---

meaning "king of peace," [3]without father, without mother, without genealogy, having neither beginning of days nor end of life, but made like the Son of God, remains a priest continually.

[4]Now consider how great this man *was*, to whom even the patriarch Abraham gave a tenth of the spoils. [5]And indeed those who are of the sons of Levi, who receive the priesthood, have a commandment to receive tithes from the people according to the law, that is, from their brethren, though they have come from the loins of Abraham; [6]but he whose genealogy is not derived from them received tithes from Abraham and blessed him who had the promises. [7]Now beyond all contradiction the lesser is blessed by the better. [8]Here mortal men receive tithes, but there he

---

7:14 [a]NU-Text reads *priests.* **7:17** [a]NU-Text reads *it is testified.* [b]Psalm 110:4 **7:21** [a]NU-Text ends the quotation here. [b]Psalm 110:4

changeable priesthood. ²⁵Therefore He is also able to save to the uttermost those who come to God through Him, since He always lives to make intercession for them.

²⁶For such a High Priest was fitting for us, *who is* holy, harmless, undefiled, separate from sinners, and has become higher than the heavens; ²⁷who does not need daily, as those high priests, to offer up sacrifices, first for His own sins and then for the people's, for this He did once for all when He offered up Himself. ²⁸For the law appoints as high priests men who have weakness, but the word of the oath, which came after the law, *appoints* the Son who has been perfected forever.

The New Priestly Service

8 Now *this is* the main point of the things we are saying: We have such a High Priest, who is seated at the right hand of the throne of the Majesty in the heavens, ²a Minister of the sanctuary and of the true tabernacle which the Lord erected, and not man.

³For every high priest is appointed to offer both gifts and sacrifices. Therefore *it is* necessary that this One also have something to offer. ⁴For if He were on earth, He would not be a priest, since there are priests who offer the gifts according to the law; ⁵who serve the copy and shadow of the heavenly things, as Moses was divinely instructed when he was about to make the tabernacle. For He said, *"See that you make all things according to the pattern shown you on the mountain."*[a] ⁶But now He has obtained a more excellent ministry, inasmuch as He is also Mediator of a better covenant, which was established on better promises.

A New Covenant

⁷For if that first *covenant* had been faultless, then no place would have been sought for a second. ⁸Because finding fault with them, He says: *"Behold, the days are coming, says the* LORD, *when I will make a new covenant with the house of Israel and with the house of Judah—* ⁹*not according to the covenant that I made with their fathers in the day when I took them by the hand to lead them out of the land of Egypt; because they did not continue in My covenant, and I disregarded them, says the* LORD. ¹⁰*For this is the covenant that I will make with the house of Israel after those days, says the* LORD: *I will put My laws in their mind and write them on their hearts; and I will be their God, and they shall be My people.* ¹¹*None of them shall teach his neighbor, and none his brother, saying, 'Know the* LORD,'

for all shall know Me, from the least of them to the greatest of them. ¹²*For I will be merciful to their unrighteousness, and their sins and their lawless deeds*[a] *I will remember no more."*[b]

¹³In that He says, *"A new covenant,"* He has made the first obsolete. Now what is becoming obsolete and growing old is ready to vanish away.

The Earthly Sanctuary

9 Then indeed, even the first *covenant* had ordinances of divine service and the earthly sanctuary. ²For a tabernacle was prepared: the first *part,* in which *was* the lampstand, the table, and the showbread, which is called the sanctuary; ³and behind the second veil, the part of the tabernacle which is called the Holiest of All, ⁴which had the golden censer and the ark of the covenant overlaid on all sides with gold, in which *were* the golden pot that had the manna, Aaron's rod that budded, and the tablets of the covenant; ⁵and above it were the cherubim of glory overshadowing the mercy seat. Of these things we cannot now speak in detail.

Limitations of the Earthly Service

⁶Now when these things had been thus prepared, the priests always went into the first part of the tabernacle, performing the services. ⁷But into the second part the high priest *went* alone once a year, not without blood, which he offered for himself and *for* the people's sins *committed* in ignorance; ⁸the Holy Spirit indicating this, that the way into the Holiest of All was not yet made manifest while the first tabernacle was still

---

> ## The Law of Connection: God Connects with the Head and Heart
> *(Hebrews 8:1—9:28)*
>
> T he New Covenant is a better ministry, established by a better Mediator, and established on better promises (Heb. 8:6). God will write His law on the heart, not just on a stone tablet. By this point, the writer has convinced readers at both the head and the heart level—thus making the connection.

8:5 ^aExodus 25:40 **8:12** ^aNU-Text omits *and their lawless deeds.* ^bJeremiah 31:31–34 standing. [9]It *was* symbolic for the present time in which both gifts and sacrifices are offered which cannot make him who performed the service perfect in regard to the conscience— [10]*concerned* only with foods and drinks, various washings, and fleshly ordinances imposed until the time of reformation.

The Heavenly Sanctuary

[11]But Christ came *as* High Priest of the good things to come,[a] with the greater and more perfect tabernacle not made with hands, that is, not of this creation. [12]Not with the blood of goats and calves, but with His own blood He entered the Most Holy Place once for all, having obtained eternal redemption. [13]For if the blood of bulls and goats and the ashes of a heifer, sprinkling the unclean, sanctifies for the purifying of the flesh, [14]how much more shall the blood of Christ, who through the eternal Spirit offered Himself without spot to God, cleanse your conscience from dead works to serve the living God? [15]And for this reason He is the Mediator of the new covenant, by means of death, for the redemption of the transgressions under the first covenant, that those who are called may receive the promise of the eternal inheritance.

The Mediator's Death Necessary

[16]For where there *is* a testament, there must also of necessity be the death of the testator. [17]For a testament *is* in force after men are dead, since it has no power at all while the testator lives. [18]Therefore not even the first *covenant* was dedicated without blood. [19]For when Moses had spoken every precept to all the people according to the law, he took the blood of calves and goats, with water, scarlet wool, and hyssop, and sprinkled both the book itself and all the people, [20]saying, "This is the blood of the covenant which God has commanded you."[a] [21]Then likewise he sprinkled with blood both the tabernacle and all the vessels of the ministry. [22]And according to the law almost all things are purified with blood, and without shedding of blood there is no remission.

Greatness of Christ's Sacrifice

[23]Therefore *it was* necessary that the copies of the things in the heavens should be purified with these, but the heavenly things themselves with better sacrifices than these. [24]For Christ has not entered the holy places made with hands, *which are* copies of the true, but into heaven itself, now to appear in the presence of God for us; [25]not that He should offer Himself often, as the high priest enters the Most Holy Place every year

with blood of another— [26]He then would have had to suffer often since the foundation of the world; but now, once at the end of the ages, He has appeared to put away sin by the sacrifice of Himself. [27]And as it is appointed for men to die once, but after this the judgment, [28]so Christ was offered once to bear the sins of many. To those who eagerly wait for Him He will appear a second time, apart from sin, for salvation.

Animal Sacrifices Insufficient

10 For the law, having a shadow of the good things to come, *and* not the very image of the things, can never with these same sacrifices, which they offer continually year by year, make those who approach perfect. [2]For then would they not have ceased to be offered? For the worshipers, once purified, would have had no more consciousness of sins. [3]But in those *sacrifices there is* a reminder of sins every year. [4]For *it is* not possible that the blood of bulls and goats could take away sins.

Christ's Death Fulfills God's Will

[5]Therefore, when He came into the world, He said:

> "Sacrifice and offering You did not desire,
> But a body You have prepared for Me.
> [6] In burnt offerings and sacrifices for sin
> You had no pleasure.
> [7] Then I said, 'Behold, I have come—
> In the volume of the book it is written of
>   Me—
> To do Your will, O God.'"[a]

[8]Previously saying, "Sacrifice and offering, burnt offerings, and offerings for sin You did not desire, nor had pleasure in them" (which are offered according to the law), [9]then He said, "Behold, I have come to do Your will, O God."[a] He takes away the first that He may establish the second. [10]By that will we have been sanctified through the offering of the body of Jesus Christ once *for all.*

Christ's Death Perfects the Sanctified

[11]And every priest stands ministering daily and offering repeatedly the same sacrifices, which can never take away sins. [12]But this Man, after He had offered one sacrifice for sins forever, sat down at the right hand of God, [13]from that

---

9:11 [a]NU-Text reads *that have come.* **9:20** [a]Exodus 24:8 **10:7** [a]Psalm 40:6–8 **10:9** [a]NU-Text and M-Text omit *O God.*

time waiting till His enemies are made His footstool. [14]For by one offering He has perfected forever those who are being sanctified.

[15]But the Holy Spirit also witnesses to us; for after He had said before,

[16]*"This is the covenant that I will make with them after those days, says the LORD: I will put My laws into their hearts, and in their minds I will write them,"*[a] [17]*then He adds, "Their sins and their lawless deeds I will remember no more."*[a] [18]Now where there is remission of these, *there is* no longer an offering for sin.

Hold Fast Your Confession

[19]Therefore, brethren, having boldness to enter the Holiest by the blood of Jesus, [20]by a new and living way which He consecrated for us, through the veil, that is, His flesh, [21]and *having* a High Priest over the house of God, [22]let us draw near with a true heart in full assurance of faith, having our hearts sprinkled from an evil conscience and our bodies washed with pure water. [23]Let us hold fast the confession of *our* hope without wavering, for He who promised *is* faithful. [24]And let us consider one another in order to stir up love and good works, [25]not forsaking the assembling of ourselves together, as *is* the manner of some, but exhorting *one another,* and so much the more as you see the Day approaching.

The Just Live by Faith

[26]For if we sin willfully after we have received the knowledge of the truth, there no longer remains a sacrifice for sins, [27]but a certain fearful expectation of judgment, and fiery indignation which will devour the adversaries. [28]Anyone who has rejected Moses' law dies without mercy on the testimony of two or three witnesses. [29]Of how much worse punishment, do you suppose, will he be thought worthy who has trampled the Son of God underfoot, counted the blood of the covenant by which he was sanctified a common thing, and insulted the Spirit of grace? [30]For we know Him who said, *"Vengeance is Mine, I will repay,"*[a] says the Lord.[b] And again, *"The LORD will judge His people."*[c] [31]It is a fearful thing to fall into the hands of the living God.

[32]But recall the former days in which, after you were illuminated, you endured a great struggle with sufferings: [33]partly while you were made a spectacle both by reproaches and tribulations, and partly while you became companions of those who were so treated; [34]for you had compassion on me[a] in my chains, and joyfully accepted the plundering of your goods, knowing that you have a better and an enduring possession for yourselves in heaven.[b] [35]Therefore do not cast away your confidence, which has great reward. [36]For you have need of endurance, so that after you have done the will of God, you may receive the promise:

[37]   "For yet a little while,
        And He[a] who is coming will come and
            will not tarry.
[38]   Now the[a] just shall live by faith;
        But if anyone draws back,
        My soul has no pleasure in him."[b]

[39]But we are not of those who draw back to perdition, but of those who believe to the saving of the soul.

By Faith We Understand

11 Now faith is the substance of things hoped for, the evidence of things not seen. [2]For by it the elders obtained a *good* testimony.

[3]By faith we understand that the worlds were framed by the word of God, so that the things which are seen were not made of things which are visible.

Faith at the Dawn of History

[4]By faith Abel offered to God a more excellent sacrifice than Cain, through which he

---

The Law of Process: Perseverance Is Essential to Finish Well

(Hebrews 10:19–39)

Every leader should aim to finish well. We need to persevere because confidence will be rewarded; obedience will be recognized; shrinking back will be regretted; and Christ's return will be celebrated. Our journey is not a sprint, but a marathon. We must pace ourselves and endure to the end.

10:16 [a]Jeremiah 31:33 **10:17** [a]Jeremiah 31:34
10:30 [a]Deuteronomy 32:35 [b]NU-Text omits *says the Lord.* [c]Deuteronomy 32:36 **10:34** [a]NU-Text reads *the prisoners* instead of *me in my chains.* [b]NU-Text omits *in heaven.* **10:37** [a]Or *that which* **10:38** [a]NU-Text reads *My just one.* [b]Habakkuk 2:3, 4

Vision: Seeing the Invisible Future

(Hebrews 11:1–32)

Hebrews 11 is often called the "Hall of Faith" because it enshrines men and women of faith who triumphed in their own lifetimes. The passage summarizes an initial list of heroes with a word about vision (Heb. 11:13).

It is almost impossible to separate faith and vision. These leaders died in faith, and although they didn't receive the tangible fulfillment of God's promises, they did see them from a distance. Their journey was all about vision, about seeing the invisible future. Leaders live by vision. These ancient men and women of faith continue to lead the way because of their:

1. *Vision:* They saw the promises afar off. These leaders had power for today because they had a vision for tomorrow.
2. *Confidence:* They were assured of the promises. They remained optimistic because they wanted to make a legacy more than a living.
3. *Hunger:* They embraced the promises. They had ownership of what only their descendants would enjoy.
4. *Resolve:* They confessed they were strangers and pilgrims. They made up their minds. Their dreams, not their memories, consumed them.

obtained witness that he was righteous, God testifying of his gifts; and through it he being dead still speaks.

[5] By faith Enoch was taken away so that he did not see death, *"and was not found, because God had taken him";*[a] for before he was taken he had this testimony, that he pleased God. [6] But without faith *it is* impossible to please *Him,* for he who comes to God must believe that He is, and *that* He is a rewarder of those who diligently seek Him.

[7] By faith Noah, being divinely warned of things not yet seen, moved with godly fear, prepared an ark for the saving of his household, by which he condemned the world and became heir of the righteousness which is according to faith.

Faithful Abraham

[8] By faith Abraham obeyed when he was called to go out to the place which he would receive as an inheritance. And he went out, not knowing where he was going. [9] By faith he dwelt in the land of promise as *in* a foreign country, dwelling in tents with Isaac and Jacob, the heirs with him of the same promise; [10] for he waited for the city which has foundations, whose builder and maker *is* God.

[11] By faith Sarah herself also received strength to conceive seed, and she bore a child[a] when she was past the age, because she judged Him faithful who had promised. [12] Therefore from one man, and him as good as dead, were born *as many* as the stars of the sky in multitude—innumerable as the sand which is by the seashore.

The Heavenly Hope

[13] These all died in faith, not having received the promises, but having seen them afar off were assured of them,[a] embraced *them* and confessed that they were strangers and pilgrims on the earth. [14] For those who say such things declare plainly that they seek a homeland. [15] And truly if they had called to mind that *country* from which they had come out, they would have had opportunity to return. [16] But now they desire a better, that is, a heavenly *country.* Therefore God is not ashamed to be called their God, for He has prepared a city for them.

The Faith of the Patriarchs

[17] By faith Abraham, when he was tested, offered up Isaac, and he who had received the promises offered up his only begotten *son,* [18] of whom it was said, *"In Isaac your seed shall be called,"*[a] [19] concluding that God *was* able to raise *him* up, even from the dead, from which he also received him in a figurative sense.

11:5 [a]Genesis 5:24 **11:11** [a]NU-Text omits *she bore a child.* **11:13** [a]NU-Text and M-Text omit *were assured of them.* **11:18** [a]Genesis 21:12

The Law of Sacrifice:
Moses Gave Up the Riches of Egypt

(Hebrews 11:23–29)

Moses exemplified the Law of Sacrifice as well as any leader. Moses understood that life is full of tradeoffs. He made some tradeoffs that looked ridiculous to the Egyptians—but his choices later paid great dividends. He became one of the greatest leaders in Israel's history because he settled his priorities and willingly gave up pleasure for purpose.

Consider what Moses gave up and received in return. Notice that the first four all appear negative, but the last four confirm he made the right decision. The payoff came *after* the sacrifice.

Gave Up	Received
1. Being called son of Pharoah's daughter	1. Called a Hebrew
2. Pleasures of sin	2. Ill treatment of God's people
3. Treasures of Egypt	3. Reproach of Christ
4. Life in Egypt	4. Life in the wilderness
5. Losing his firstborn son	5. Keeping his firstborn son
6. Divine plagues	6. Divine protection
7. Drowning in the Red Sea	7. Walking through the Red Sea
8. A life outside of God's purposes	8. Fulfilling God's purpose for his life

[20]By faith Isaac blessed Jacob and Esau concerning things to come. [21]By faith Jacob, when he was dying, blessed each of the sons of Joseph, and worshiped, *leaning* on the top of his staff. [22]By faith Joseph, when he was dying, made mention of the departure of the children of Israel, and gave instructions concerning his bones.

The Faith of Moses

[23]By faith Moses, when he was born, was hidden three months by his parents, because they saw *he was* a beautiful child; and they were not afraid of the king's command. [24]By faith Moses, when he became of age, refused to be called the son of Pharoah's daughter, [25]choosing rather to suffer affliction with the people of God than to enjoy the passing pleasures of sin, [26]esteeming the reproach of Christ greater riches than the treasures in[a] Egypt; for he looked to the reward. [27]By faith he forsook Egypt, not fearing the wrath of the king; for he endured as seeing Him who is invisible. [28]By faith he kept the Passover and the sprinkling of blood, lest he who destroyed the firstborn should touch them.

[29]By faith they passed through the Red Sea as by dry *land, whereas* the Egyptians, attempting *to do* so, were drowned.

By Faith They Overcame

[30]By faith the walls of Jericho fell down after they were encircled for seven days. [31]By faith the harlot Rahab did not perish with those who did not believe, when she had received the spies with peace.

[32]And what more shall I say? For the time would fail me to tell of Gideon and Barak and Samson and Jephthah, also *of* David and Samuel and the prophets: [33]who through faith subdued kingdoms, worked righteousness, obtained promises, stopped the mouths of lions, [34]quenched the violence of fire, escaped the edge of the sword, out of weakness were made strong, became valiant in battle, turned to flight the armies of the aliens. [35]Women received their dead raised to life again.

Others were tortured, not accepting deliverance, that they might obtain a better resurrection. [36]Still others had trial of mockings and scourgings, yes, and of chains and imprisonment. [37]They were stoned, they were sawn in two, were tempted,[a] were slain with the sword. They wandered about in sheepskins and goatskins, being destitute, afflicted, tormented— [38]of whom the world was not worthy. They wandered in deserts and mountains, *in* dens and caves of the earth.

11:26 [a]NU-Text and M-Text read *of.*
11:37 [a]NU-Text omits *were tempted.*

Passion: Run with Passion, Purpose, and Perspective

(Hebrews 12:1–3)

Hebrews 12 develops the theme of endurance. The first three verses teach us that the key to persistence is passion.

All the men and women of faith in Hebrews 11 "made it" because they felt passionate about their cause. The writer compares our lives to a race and tries to convince us that we must run with endurance if we plan to finish well.

The text also suggests that if the key to persistence is passion, then the key to passion is purpose. We must run with purpose, not aimlessly.

And the key to purpose? Perspective. The writer of Hebrews admonishes us to consider three things that will help us to finish well:

1. *Consider them* (v. 1).
   Since a great cloud of witnesses has gone before us, we must get serious about finishing well.
2. *Consider ourselves* (v. 1).
   It is now our turn to run the race and watch for pitfalls. We must lay aside every encumbrance that would prevent us from finishing well.
3. *Consider Jesus* (vv. 2, 3).
   Jesus ran His own race and endured hardship by fixing His eyes on the rewards; we must follow His example.

---

³⁹And all these, having obtained a good testimony through faith, did not receive the promise, ⁴⁰God having provided something better for us, that they should not be made perfect apart from us.

The Race of Faith

12 Therefore we also, since we are surrounded by so great a cloud of witnesses, let us lay aside every weight, and the sin which so easily ensnares *us,* and let us run with endurance the race that is set before us, ²looking unto Jesus, the author and finisher of *our* faith, who for the joy that was set before Him endured the cross, despising the shame, and has sat down at the right hand of the throne of God.

The Discipline of God

³For consider Him who endured such hostility from sinners against Himself, lest you become weary and discouraged in your souls. ⁴You have not yet resisted to bloodshed, striving against sin. ⁵And you have forgotten the exhortation which speaks to you as to sons:

"*My son, do not despise the chastening of
   the LORD,*

*Nor be discouraged when you are rebuked
   by Him;*
⁶ *For whom the LORD loves He chastens,
   And scourges every son whom He
   receives.*"ᵃ

⁷Ifᵃ you endure chastening, God deals with you as with sons; for what son is there whom a father does not chasten? ⁸But if you are without chastening, of which all have become partakers, then you are illegitimate and not sons. ⁹Furthermore, we have had human fathers who corrected *us,* and we paid *them* respect. Shall we not much more readily be in subjection to the Father of spirits and live? ¹⁰For they indeed for a few days chastened *us* as seemed *best* to them, but He for *our* profit, that *we* may be partakers of His holiness. ¹¹Now no chastening seems to be joyful for the present, but painful; nevertheless, afterward it yields the peaceable fruit of righteousness to those who have been trained by it.

Renew Your Spiritual Vitality

¹²Therefore strengthen the hands which hang down, and the feeble knees, ¹³and make straight

---

12:6 ᵃProverbs 3:11, 12 **12:7** ᵃNU-Text and M-Text read *It is for discipline that you endure; God . . . .*

Self-Discipline: You Must Lead Yourself Before You Can Lead Others

(Hebrews 12:5–13)

People follow leaders primarily because they see a life they believe they can trust and one they want to emulate. We are to welcome God's discipline and respond with self-discipline. Once we yield both to God's discipline (Heb. 12:5–11) and our own (12:12, 13), we produce a life worth following.

paths for your feet, so that what is lame may not be dislocated, but rather be healed.

[14]Pursue peace with all *people,* and holiness, without which no one will see the Lord: [15]looking carefully lest anyone fall short of the grace of God; lest any root of bitterness springing up cause trouble, and by this many become defiled; [16]lest there *be* any fornicator or profane person like Esau, who for one morsel of food sold his birthright. [17]For you know that afterward, when he wanted to inherit the blessing, he was rejected, for he found no place for repentance, though he sought it diligently with tears.

The Glorious Company

[18]For you have not come to the mountain that[a] may be touched and that burned with fire, and to blackness and darkness[b] and tempest, [19]and the sound of a trumpet and the voice of words, so that those who heard *it* begged that the word should not be spoken to them anymore. [20](For they could not endure what was commanded: *"And if so much as a beast touches the mountain, it shall be stoned[a] or shot with an arrow."*[b] [21]And so terrifying was the sight *that* Moses said, *"I am exceedingly afraid* and trembling."[a])

[22]But you have come to Mount Zion and to the city of the living God, the heavenly Jerusalem, to an innumerable company of angels, [23]to the general assembly and church of the firstborn *who are* registered in heaven, to God the Judge of all, to the spirits of just men made perfect, [24]to Jesus the Mediator of the new covenant, and to the blood of sprinkling that speaks better things than *that of* Abel.

Hear the Heavenly Voice

[25]See that you do not refuse Him who speaks. For if they did not escape who refused Him who spoke on earth, much more *shall we not escape* if we turn away from Him who *speaks* from heaven, [26]whose voice then shook the earth; but now He has promised, saying, *"Yet once more I shake[a] not only the earth, but also heaven."*[b] [27]Now this, *"Yet once more,"* indicates the removal of those things that are being shaken, as of things that are made, that the things which cannot be shaken may remain.

[28]Therefore, since we are receiving a kingdom which cannot be shaken, let us have grace, by which we may[a] serve God acceptably with reverence and godly fear. [29]For our God *is* a consuming fire.

Concluding Moral Directions

13 Let brotherly love continue. [2]Do not forget to entertain strangers, for by so *doing* some have unwittingly entertained angels. [3]Remember the prisoners as if chained with them—those who are mistreated—since you yourselves are in the body also.

[4]Marriage *is* honorable among all, and the bed undefiled; but fornicators and adulterers God will judge.

[5]*Let your* conduct *be* without covetousness; *be* content with such things as you have. For He Himself has said, *"I will never leave you nor forsake you."*[a] [6]So we may boldly say:

> *"The LORD is my helper;*
> *I will not fear.*
> *What can man do to me?"*[a]

Concluding Religious Directions

[7]Remember those who rule over you, who have spoken the word of God to you, whose faith follow, considering the outcome of *their* conduct. [8]Jesus Christ *is* the same yesterday, today, and forever. [9]Do not be carried about[a] with various and strange doctrines. For *it is* good that the heart be established by grace, not with foods which have not profited those who have been occupied with them.

[10]We have an altar from which those who serve the tabernacle have no right to eat. [11]For the bodies of those animals, whose blood is brought into the sanctuary by the high priest for

---

12:18 [a]NU-Text reads *to that which.* [b]NU-Text reads *gloom.* **12:20** [a]NU-Text and M-Text omit the rest of this verse. [b]Exodus 19:12, 13 **12:21** [a]Deuteronomy 9:19 **12:26** [a]NU-Text reads *will shake.* [b]Haggai 2:6 **12:28** [a]M-Text omits *may.* **13:5** [a]Deuteronomy 31:6, 8; Joshua 1:5 **13:6** [a]Psalm 118:6 **13:9** [a]NU-Text and M-Text read *away.*

Leadership Models: God Can Do for You What He Did for Them

(Hebrews 13:7, 8)

Although verses 7 and 8 of Hebrews 13 are rarely tied together, they should be, for verse 7 furnishes the context for the truth of verse 8.

The writer of Hebrews tells us to remember the leaders from yesterday, think about their lives, and imitate their faith. Then he reminds us that Jesus Christ is the same yesterday, today, and forever. In other words, what God did for those leaders in years gone by, He can do for you and me! The same great things He accomplished through their leadership—like liberating a nation or building a temple or equipping other leaders—He would like to do through us today.

When you read of any great leader in the Bible, just remember it was God who worked through them. And the same God who led through them wants to lead through you! God is in the business of not only saving lives, but also leading leaders.

---

sin, are burned outside the camp. [12]Therefore Jesus also, that He might sanctify the people with His own blood, suffered outside the gate. [13]Therefore let us go forth to Him, outside the camp, bearing His reproach. [14]For here we have no continuing city, but we seek the one to come. [15]Therefore by Him let us continually offer the sacrifice of praise to God, that is, the fruit of *our* lips, giving thanks to His name. [16]But do not forget to do good and to share, for with such sacrifices God is well pleased.

[17]Obey those who rule over you, and be submissive, for they watch out for your souls, as those who must give account. Let them do so with joy and not with grief, for that would be unprofitable for you.

Prayer Requested

[18]Pray for us; for we are confident that we have a good conscience, in all things desiring to live honorably. [19]But I especially urge *you* to do this, that I may be restored to you the sooner.

Benediction, Final Exhortation, Farewell

[20]Now may the God of peace who brought up our Lord Jesus from the dead, that great Shepherd of the sheep, through the blood of the everlasting covenant, [21]make you complete in every good work to do His will, working in you[a] what is well pleasing in His sight, through Jesus Christ, to whom *be* glory forever and ever. Amen.

[22]And I appeal to you, brethren, bear with the word of exhortation, for I have written to you in few words. [23]Know that *our* brother Timothy has been set free, with whom I shall see you if he comes shortly.

[24]Greet all those who rule over you, and all the saints. Those from Italy greet you.

[25]Grace *be* with you all. Amen.

13:21 [a]NU-Text and M-Text read *us.*

Accountability: Leaders Are Stewards of Their Resources

(Hebrews 13:17)

Why should believers obey their leaders? Because their leaders watch out for their souls and must give account to God. Leaders are stewards of everyone who follows them. God has placed leaders in "middle management" under His leadership. When their life ends, they will answer for how responsibly they tended to His divine vision and values.

JAMES
Translating Faith into Obedience

SUMMARY

James is the kind of book you ought to read standing up. It contains a ringing call for action, a plea for vital Christianity and a faith that demonstrates itself not in mere words, but in lifestyle. James is one of the most practical books of the Bible, teaching that faith without corresponding action is dead.

If James were leading an organization and you were his employee, you would feel the heat of this leader. He would motivate you with words like:

"Don't tell me about your accomplishments; show me!"

"The more you walk the walk, the less you have to talk!"

"Let's put some shoe leather on our core values!"

In this short book of five chapters, James addresses temptation, hypocrisy, prejudice, how to deal with problems, deception, discipline, controlling the tongue, recognizing godly wisdom, conflict, humility, priorities, patience, and faith. In essence, we have a transcribed sermon delivered to Jewish Christians all over the Roman Empire.

James models a leadership weary of sterile mission statements framed on a wall. He cares nothing for the set of core values the subcommittee wrote down last year if they were only words on paper that got filed away. He is an activist who labels as "self-deceived" those who say they are committed to do something but never do it.

James also models a leadership that errs on the side of pragmatism. Because he doesn't want anyone to miss "practicing what they preach," he suggests several ideas on how to flesh out the mission of Christ—from feeding and clothing the poor, to providing good seating at church services for the poor, to controlling your speech, to praying for the sick and those in need. He intuitively knows that leadership integrity exists only when our words and actions meet.

James also furnishes us with the best common-sense wisdom regarding life on earth. He strongly advocates humility in the sight of God and encourages us to pray when we don't know what to do next. He possesses a divine perspective that enables a follower to trust him more easily. James maintains a big-picture view of eternity while incarnating his beliefs in a pair of overalls.

God's Role in James

God speaks to leaders in this book about real-life situations. This book especially helps the leader who gets caught up in an idealistic vision and never gets to his to-do list. God calls us to translate our faith into obedience.

Every leader should read this brief book with the goal of personal faithfulness to God and to his or her leadership position. After reading this book, you will sense a leader's passion and conviction about justice. You will also observe a wise leader communicating perspective to erring followers. And you will be challenged to pay the price to practice what you preach.

Leaders in James

James, teachers, church elders

Other People of Influence in James

Rich people, Old Testament prophets, Job

Lessons in Leadership

- The more you walk, the less you have to talk.
- Integrity occurs when words and actions match.
- Leaders will be judged more strictly than followers.
- If you can bridle your tongue, you can discipline any part of your life.
- Leadership motives must be pure; mercy and justice are healthy motivators.
- Leaders are to humble themselves and let God exalt them in due time.

LEADERSHIP HIGHLIGHTS IN JAMES

Greeting to the Twelve Tribes

1 James, a bondservant of God and of the Lord Jesus Christ,

To the twelve tribes which are scattered abroad:

Greetings.

Profiting from Trials

²My brethren, count it all joy when you fall into various trials, ³knowing that the testing of your faith produces patience. ⁴But let patience have *its* perfect work, that you may be perfect and complete, lacking nothing. ⁵If any of you lacks wisdom, let him ask of God, who gives to all liberally and without reproach, and it will be given to him. ⁶But let him ask in faith, with no doubting, for he who doubts is like a wave of the sea driven and tossed by the wind. ⁷For let not that man suppose that he will receive anything from the Lord; ⁸*he is* a double-minded man, unstable in all his ways.

The Perspective of Rich and Poor

⁹Let the lowly brother glory in his exaltation, ¹⁰but the rich in his humiliation, because as a flower of the field he will pass away. ¹¹For no sooner has the sun risen with a burning heat than it withers the grass; its flower falls, and its beautiful appearance perishes. So the rich man also will fade away in his pursuits.

Loving God Under Trials

¹²Blessed *is* the man who endures temptation; for when he has been approved, he will receive the crown of life which the Lord has promised to those who love Him. ¹³Let no one say when he is tempted, "I am tempted by God"; for God cannot be tempted by evil, nor does He Himself tempt anyone. ¹⁴But each one is tempted when he is drawn away by his own desires and enticed. ¹⁵Then, when desire has conceived, it gives birth to sin; and sin, when it is full-grown, brings forth death.

¹⁶Do not be deceived, my beloved brethren. ¹⁷Every good gift and every perfect gift is from above, and comes down from the Father of lights, with whom there is no variation or shadow of turning. ¹⁸Of His own will He brought us forth by the word of truth, that we might be a kind of firstfruits of His creatures.

Qualities Needed in Trials

¹⁹So then,ᵃ my beloved brethren, let every man be swift to hear, slow to speak, slow to wrath; ²⁰for the wrath of man does not produce the righteousness of God.

1:19 ᵃNU-Text reads *Know this* or *This you know.*

Problem Solving: Leaders Must Maintain Perspective with Problems

(James 1:1–8)

James is vitally concerned with big-picture living. After his brief greeting, he jumps into how to handle problems. Because leadership depends to a large degree on problem solving, James remains relevant to every leader. He teaches us to approach problems with:

1. *Contemplation* (vv. 2–4)
   We can find joy in the midst of problems only when we recognize their purpose and results. The key is perspective. Leaders must think correctly about problems and see that their followers grow stronger through them.

2. *Supplication* (v. 5)
   God gives us trials in such a way that we lack nothing in the end. James says, however, that if we do lack wisdom, we should ask God for it. It is no sign of weakness for a leader to pray for wisdom when facing problems.

3. *Expectation* (vv. 6–8)
   If we do ask God for wisdom, we must ask in faith, expecting His answer. Once leaders gain perspective and trust God for wisdom, the only thing left to do is to anticipate solutions and exude optimism.

Listening: To Connect with Hearts, Use Your Ears

(James 1:19)

Good leaders motivate others by their listening skills. We are to: avoid prejudicial first impressions; become less self-centered; withhold initial criticism; stay calm; listen with empathy; be active listeners; clarify what we hear; and recognize the healing power of listening. Then we are to act on what we hear (James 1:22)!

Doers—Not Hearers Only

²¹Therefore lay aside all filthiness and overflow of wickedness, and receive with meekness the implanted word, which is able to save your souls.

²²But be doers of the word, and not hearers only, deceiving yourselves. ²³For if anyone is a hearer of the word and not a doer, he is like a man observing his natural face in a mirror; ²⁴for he observes himself, goes away, and immediately forgets what kind of man he was. ²⁵But he who looks into the perfect law of liberty and continues *in it,* and is not a forgetful hearer but a doer

The Law of Solid Ground: Hypocritical Leaders Sabotage Themselves

(James 1:22–26)

If a man thinks himself to be religious, but doesn't bridle his tongue, he deceives himself. His religion is worthless. Why? Because when he thinks one way, but talks another way, he becomes double-minded.

The Greek word translated "doubt" is taken from the same root as the word "double." A leader who thinks one way, but whose words stand in contrast to his mindset, will fail. The power of his mind and the power of his words neutralize each other. Such a leader fails to practice the Law of Solid Ground and will eventually sabotage himself.

of the work, this one will be blessed in what he does.

²⁶If anyone among you[a] thinks he is religious, and does not bridle his tongue but deceives his

1:26 [a]NU-Text omits *among you.*

Relationships: Leaders Must Love out of a Decision, Not a Reaction

(James 2:1–9)

Relationships and leadership cannot be divorced. Further, leaders must learn to relate to people based on a decision, not a reaction. We must love people regardless of what they can give in return.

James 2 begins by talking about the sin of partiality. Leaders must not treat a rich man well and a poor man poorly. Love must be given unconditionally. Does this mean we treat everyone the same? Not at all. We must relate to each individual based on his or her inward gifts, not outward gifts. Leaders must identify talents and gifts in others, then place the individuals in suitable positions to encourage the use of their gifts. Note the diagram below.

The Issue	My Response
1. Loving people	1. I love them based on an unconditional decision.
2. Positions and tasks	2. I place them according to their giftedness.
3. Recognition	3. I recognize everyone's value and contribution.
4. Affirmation	4. I base it on the need of the person.

own heart, this one's religion *is* useless. [27]Pure and undefiled religion before God and the Father is this: to visit orphans and widows in their trouble, *and* to keep oneself unspotted from the world.

Beware of Personal Favoritism

2 My brethren, do not hold the faith of our Lord Jesus Christ, *the Lord* of glory, with partiality. [2]For if there should come into your assembly a man with gold rings, in fine apparel, and there should also come in a poor man in filthy clothes, [3]and you pay attention to the one wearing the fine clothes and say to him, "You sit here in a good place," and say to the poor man, "You stand there," or, "Sit here at my footstool," [4]have you not shown partiality among yourselves, and become judges with evil thoughts?

[5]Listen, my beloved brethren: Has God not chosen the poor of this world *to be* rich in faith and heirs of the kingdom which He promised to those who love Him? [6]But you have dishonored the poor man. Do not the rich oppress you and drag you into the courts? [7]Do they not blaspheme that noble name by which you are called?

[8]If you really fulfill *the* royal law according to the Scripture, *"You shall love your neighbor as yourself,"*[a] you do well; [9]but if you show partiality, you commit sin, and are convicted by the law as transgressors. [10]For whoever shall keep the whole law, and yet stumble in one *point,* he is guilty of all. [11]For He who said, *"Do not commit adultery,"*[a] also said, *"Do not murder."*[b] Now if you do not commit adultery, but you do murder, you have become a transgressor of the law. [12]So speak and so do as those who will be judged by the law of liberty. [13]For judgment is without mercy to the one who has shown no mercy. Mercy triumphs over judgment.

Faith Without Works Is Dead

[14]What *does it* profit, my brethren, if someone says he has faith but does not have works? Can faith save him? [15]If a brother or sister is naked and destitute of daily food, [16]and one of you says to them, "Depart in peace, be warmed and filled," but you do not give them the things which are needed for the body, what *does it* profit? [17]Thus also faith by itself, if it does not have works, is dead.

2:8 [a]Leviticus 19:18 **2:11** [a]Exodus 20:14; Deuteronomy 5:18 [b]Exodus 20:13; Deuteronomy 5:17

Servanthood: The Measure of Our Commitment Is Action

(James 2:1–26)

James reminds us that we are called to serve others. The measuring stick of our commitment is not our lip service, but our life. Leaders must act on their values; action is the gauge, not mere words or thoughts.

James proceeds to give us six pictures and six principles to back up his teaching:

Picture One: The rich and the poor (vv. 1–4)
   Selfish motives prevent a servant's ministry.
Picture Two: The legalist (vv. 9–13)
   Following rules cannot save us, but following Jesus can.
Picture Three: The hypocrite (vv. 14–17)
   A lifestyle that costs nothing is worth nothing.
Picture Four: The foolish man (vv. 18, 19)
   A faith that's only in my head is dead.
Picture Five: Abraham (vv. 21–23)
   Faith justifies the leader; works justify the faith.
Picture Six: Rahab (vv. 25, 26)
   A worthless past is resolved by a present that works.

[18]But someone will say, "You have faith, and I have works." Show me your faith without your[a] works, and I will show you my faith by my[b] works. [19]You believe that there is one God. You do well. Even the demons believe—and tremble! [20]But do you want to know, O foolish man, that faith without works is dead?[a] [21]Was not Abraham our father justified by works when he offered Isaac his son on the altar? [22]Do you see that faith was working together with his works, and by works faith was made perfect? [23]And the Scripture was fulfilled which says, *"Abraham believed God, and it was accounted to him for righteousness."*[a] And he was called the friend of God. [24]You see then that a man is justified by works, and not by faith only.

[25]Likewise, was not Rahab the harlot also justified by works when she received the messengers and sent *them* out another way?

[26]For as the body without the spirit is dead, so faith without works is dead also.

The Untamable Tongue

3 My brethren, let not many of you become teachers, knowing that we shall receive a stricter judgment. [2]For we all stumble in many things. If anyone does not stumble in word, he *is* a perfect man, able also to bridle the whole body. [3]Indeed,[a] we put bits in horses' mouths that they may obey us, and we turn their whole body. [4]Look also at ships: although they are so large and are driven by fierce winds, they are turned by a very small rudder wherever the pilot desires. [5]Even so the tongue is a little member and boasts great things.

See how great a forest a little fire kindles! [6]And the tongue *is* a fire, a world of iniquity. The tongue is so set among our members that it defiles the whole body, and sets on fire the course of nature; and it is set on fire by hell. [7]For every kind of beast and bird, of reptile and creature of the sea, is tamed and has been tamed by mankind. [8]But no man can tame the tongue. *It is* an unruly evil, full of deadly poison. [9]With it we bless our God and Father, and with it we curse men, who have been made in the similitude of God. [10]Out of the same mouth proceed blessing and cursing. My brethren, these things ought not to be so. [11]Does a spring send forth fresh *water* and bitter from the same opening? [12]Can a fig

2:18 [a]NU-Text omits *your.* [b]NU-Text omits *my.*
2:20 [a]NU-Text reads *useless.* **2:23** [a]Genesis 15:6
3:3 [a]NU-Text reads *Now if.*

JAMES — BROTHER OF JESUS, LEADER OF MEN
(James 2:24, 26)

PROFILE IN LEADERSHIP

If you were trying to find an apple tree, you would look for a tall, woody plant with a fairly sturdy trunk, beautiful green foliage, and, of course, apples. Certain kinds of trees produce certain kinds of fruit.

It's like that with faith in God. James tells us that if we are looking for someone with saving faith, we should look for a person who voices belief in the works of Jesus Christ *and* whose actions back up his or her words. That is the governing principle of James's epistle, which describes religion that is practical, that produces change, and that works. Without those works, James tells us, such a person's faith isn't the genuine article.

James doesn't mean that our good works save us. He knew there is nothing we can do or say to add to what Christ has already done on the Cross. Rather, he means that we recognize genuine, saving faith by the works it produces in the life of the believer.

Godly leaders challenge us to embrace a faith beyond mere mental assent, more than emotionalism, more than words. They challenge us to examine our faith and determine if it is producing the kind of fruit James tells us it should.

Accountability: Leaders Will Endure a Stricter Judgment

(James 3:1)

James informs us that leaders and teachers will receive a stricter judgment than other believers when they stand before God. Why? Because of their greater influence.

When a follower makes a mistake, he affects only himself and perhaps his family. When a leader makes a mistake, he affects the many who follow.

The Law of E. F. Hutton reminds us that when the real leader speaks, people listen. This can be both good news and bad news, depending on whether the leader's words are worth listening to! God promises that those in positions of influence will give account for how they use that influence.

In one sense, God will be a spiritual accountant, the heavenly C.P.A., calling leaders to answer for how they used the resources He gave them. At the judgment seat of Christ we will be required to give an account for what we did with our lives and our influence.

tree, my brethren, bear olives, or a grapevine bear figs? Thus no spring yields both salt water and fresh.[a]

Heavenly Versus Demonic Wisdom

[13]Who *is* wise and understanding among you? Let him show by good conduct *that* his works *are done* in the meekness of wisdom. [14]But if you have bitter envy and self-seeking in your hearts, do not boast and lie against the truth. [15]This wisdom does not descend from above, but is earthly, sensual, demonic. [16]For where envy and self-seeking *exist,* confusion and every evil thing *are* there. [17]But the wisdom that is from above is first pure, then peaceable, gentle, willing to yield, full of mercy and good fruits, without partiality and without hypocrisy. [18]Now the fruit of righteousness is sown in peace by those who make peace.

Pride Promotes Strife

4 Where do wars and fights *come* from among you? Do *they* not *come* from your *desires for* pleasure that war in your members? [2]You lust and do not have. You murder and covet and cannot obtain. You fight and war. Yet[a] you do not have because you do not ask. [3]You ask and do not receive, because you ask amiss, that you may spend *it* on your pleasures. [4]Adulterers

3:12 [a]NU-Text reads *Neither can a salty spring produce fresh water.* **4:2** [a]NU-Text and M-Text omit *Yet.*

The Law of Intuition: Godly Wisdom vs. Worldly Wisdom

(James 3:13–18)

James speaks of two kinds of wisdom: the wisdom from above and the wisdom from below. Good leadership intuition always springs from the wisdom from above. Notice the following differences.

Wisdom from Above	Wisdom from Below
1. Gentle and generous	1. Selfishly ambitious and jealous
2. Speaks the truth	2. Speaks lies and deceives
3. Pure and organized	3. Disorderly and demonic
4. Results in peace	4. Results in disharmony
5. Reasonable	5. Self-centered
6. The fruit of love and mercy	6. The fruit of strife and competition

Self-Discipline: If You Can Tame the Tongue, You Can Tame Anything

(James 3:1–18)

What power our words contain! James focuses on the little muscle inside our mouths, called the tongue, a little thing that dispenses both blessing and cursing. Leaders must pay close attention, for they communicate often and carry great influence when they speak. James lists four functions of the tongue:

1. *Function One: to gauge* (vv. 1, 2)
   The tongue is a spiritual meter. If we can bridle it, we can bridle the whole body. It becomes the gauge for our maturity. Our faith will never register higher than our words.
2. *Function Two: to guide* (vv. 3–5)
   The tongue is like a horse's bit, a ship's rudder, or kindling wood. It starts things in motion. If we can control it, we can guide our lives, just as a bit directs a horse or a rudder steers a ship.
3. *Function Three: to gird* (vv. 6–8)
   The tongue is powerful. Like a huge fire, it can ruin or bless our entire lives. This power was meant to send us down the right path, not to kill us.
4. *Function Four: to guard* (vv. 9–18)
   The tongue can reveal what sort of wisdom we harbor inside. A good tongue protects our integrity. James asks: Is yours a good guard or a bad one? Does it create peace or reveal hypocrisy?

and[a] adulteresses! Do you not know that friendship with the world is enmity with God? Whoever therefore wants to be a friend of the world makes himself an enemy of God. ⁵Or do you think that the Scripture says in vain, "The Spirit who dwells in us yearns jealously"?

⁶But He gives more grace. Therefore He says:

"God resists the proud,
But gives grace to the humble."[a]

Humility Cures Worldliness

⁷Therefore submit to God. Resist the devil and he will flee from you. ⁸Draw near to God and He will draw near to you. Cleanse *your* hands, *you* sinners; and purify *your* hearts, *you* double-minded. ⁹Lament and mourn and weep! Let your laughter be turned to mourning and *your* joy to gloom. ¹⁰Humble yourselves in the sight of the Lord, and He will lift you up.

Do Not Judge a Brother

¹¹Do not speak evil of one another, brethren. He who speaks evil of a brother and judges his brother, speaks evil of the law and judges the law. But if you judge the law, you are not a doer of the law but a judge. ¹²There is one Lawgiver,[a]

who is able to save and to destroy. Who[b] are you to judge another?[c]

Do Not Boast About Tomorrow

¹³Come now, you who say, "Today or tomorrow we will[a] go to such and such a city, spend a year there, buy and sell, and make a profit"; ¹⁴whereas you do not know what *will happen* tomorrow. For what *is* your life? It is even a vapor that appears for a little time and then vanishes away. ¹⁵Instead you *ought* to say, "If the Lord wills, we shall live and do this or that." ¹⁶But now you boast in your arrogance. All such boasting is evil. ¹⁷Therefore, to him who knows to do good and does not do *it,* to him it is sin.

Rich Oppressors Will Be Judged

5 Come now, *you* rich, weep and howl for your miseries that are coming upon *you!* ²Your riches are corrupted, and your garments are moth-eaten. ³Your gold and silver are corroded, and their corrosion will be a witness

---

4:4 [a]NU-Text omits *Adulterers and.* 4:6 [a]Proverbs 3:34 4:12 [a]NU-Text adds *and Judge.* [b]NU-Text and M-Text read *But who.* [c]NU-Text reads *a neighbor.* 4:13 [a]M-Text reads *let us.*

Problem Solving:
The Reason, Results, and Remedy for Problems
(James 4:1–10)

James gives a lot of attention to problem solving. He begins by asking a question: What is the source of conflict among his readers? On their own they could not resolve their divisions and quarrels. When James steps in, he cuts through the fat and spells out the reason and the remedy for their problems.

Good leaders discern the root of problems quickly and offer practical solutions. Most of the time they find people problems:

1. *The reason for our problems: Hedonism* (vv. 1–3)
   James offers the answer to his own question. The source of their problems? Their own self-centered search for pleasure. The Greek term he uses is the root word for "hedonism." Like symptoms of a disease, their emotions revealed selfish goals: lust, envy, quarreling, and fighting.

2. *The results of our problems: Hostility* (vv. 4–6)
   Hedonism always leads to hostility. Because the people got so caught up in their own pursuits, they became hostile toward others and God. They were like adulterers who so badly wanted self-fulfillment, they forgot their marriage.

3. *The remedy to our problems: Humility* (vv. 7–10)
   Since God opposes the proud but helps the humble, the solution lies in asking humbly for God's grace. These people hadn't asked for anyone's help (v. 2). Most of the time humility brings both peace and solutions.

The Law of Process: We Mature Like a Seed Awaiting Harvest
(James 5:7, 8)

James calls us to be patient, just like a farmer who patiently waits for his harvest. The farmer knows that if he picks the corn too early, he will miss out on some of the grain.

So it is with us. The Law of Process reminds us that our leadership development is a process, not an event. We grow daily, not in a day. Not only do we wait on Jesus to return, but He waits on us to grow! He is not only preparing a place for us, but us for a place.

If the metaphor of the farmer doesn't do the trick for us, James supplies two more images. He reminds us of two further examples of patience: the prophets and Job (James 5:11, 12). Regardless of the image, the key is to focus on the fruit or the result that will surely come in the end.

against you and will eat your flesh like fire. You have heaped up treasure in the last days. ⁴Indeed the wages of the laborers who mowed your fields, which you kept back by fraud, cry out; and the cries of the reapers have reached the ears of the Lord of Sabaoth.ᵃ ⁵You have lived on the earth in pleasure and luxury; you have fattened your hearts asᵃ in a day of slaughter. ⁶You have condemned, you have murdered the just; he does not resist you.

Be Patient and Persevering

⁷Therefore be patient, brethren, until the coming of the Lord. See *how* the farmer waits for the precious fruit of the earth, waiting patiently for it until it receives the early and latter rain. ⁸You also be patient. Establish your hearts, for the coming of the Lord is at hand.

⁹Do not grumble against one another, brethren, lest you be condemned.ᵃ Behold, the Judge is standing at the door! ¹⁰My brethren, take the prophets, who spoke in the name of the Lord, as an example of suffering and patience. ¹¹Indeed we count them blessed who endure. You have

---

5:4 ᵃLiterally, in Hebrew, *Hosts* **5:5** ᵃNU-Text omits *as.* **5:9** ᵃNU-Text and M-Text read *judged.*

Prayer Partners: The Leader as an Intercessor

(James 5:13–20)

Not only do leaders need prayer partners, but leaders *are* prayer partners for the needy. James calls us to identify the problem, intercede for others, and intervene in the process.

James 5:14, in particular, speaks to leaders. Prayer is a significant function that leaders are to perform. (Peter echoes this instruction in Acts 6:4.)

Consider what James calls leaders to do:

1. *Identify*
   Leaders are to identify the problems, then identify *with* the problems. They are to come to the aid of those in need, whether they suffer from sickness, suffering, or sin.
2. *Intercede*
   Leaders are to pray for those in need. This involves anointing the person with oil, laying hands on him or her, and praying for restoration.
3. *Intervene*
   Leaders are to throw themselves in the direction of their prayers. In addition to prayer, they should do anything they can to aid in the restoration for which they so earnestly pray.

---

heard of the perseverance of Job and seen the end *intended by* the Lord—that the Lord is very compassionate and merciful.

[12]But above all, my brethren, do not swear, either by heaven or by earth or with any other oath. But let your "Yes" be "Yes," and *your* "No," "No," lest you fall into judgment.[a]

Meeting Specific Needs

[13]Is anyone among you suffering? Let him pray. Is anyone cheerful? Let him sing psalms. [14]Is anyone among you sick? Let him call for the elders of the church, and let them pray over him, anointing him with oil in the name of the Lord. [15]And the prayer of faith will save the sick, and the Lord will raise him up. And if he has committed sins, he will be forgiven. [16]Confess *your* trespasses[a] to one another, and pray for one another, that you may be healed. The effective, fervent prayer of a righteous man avails much. [17]Elijah was a man with a nature like ours, and he prayed earnestly that it would not rain; and it did not rain on the land for three years and six months. [18]And he prayed again, and the heaven gave rain, and the earth produced its fruit.

Bring Back the Erring One

[19]Brethren, if anyone among you wanders from the truth, and someone turns him back, [20]let him know that he who turns a sinner from the error of his way will save a soul[a] from death and cover a multitude of sins.

5:12 [a]M-Text reads *hypocrisy.* **5:16** [a]NU-Text reads *Therefore confess your sins.* **5:20** [a]NU-Text reads *his soul.*

1 PETER
Lessons and Principles for Leaders

SUMMARY

Simon Peter, one of Jesus' own disciples, wrote 1 and 2 Peter to encourage believers who had fallen prey to the persecution of the Roman Empire. He sent his letter to all five provinces of Asia Minor.

As a recipient of persecution for taking a stand himself, Peter could speak with credibility and conviction. Acts 5 describes how he suffered for his faith; Acts 12 reports his imprisonment. Eventually, the Romans crucified Peter upside down. Tradition says he told his executors that he felt unworthy to die in the same manner as His Lord, so they hung him upside down instead of right side up.

Peter filled his letter with lessons and principles for leaders; Jesus had groomed him to be a leader. Peter began his journey as a crude, brash, outspoken, but influential individual. By the time Jesus sent the Holy Spirit upon His church as reported in Acts 2, Peter had become wise, winsome, convictional, and even more influential. Consider some of the lessons he learned along the way.

First, *find your security in the Lord*. Peter didn't embrace this lesson at first. He consistently projected his self-worth and drew his value from the attention others gave him. He teaches that those "who once were not a people but are now the people of God." He drives home that God chose us to be a royal priesthood (2:9, 10).

Second, *leaders must recognize that suffering and opposition come with the territory*. Peter writes to Christians who have begun to suffer opposition for their convictions. By the time he wrote, Peter had suffered opposition for many years. He knew what it meant to be rebuked, beaten, arrested, imprisoned, and mocked. Yet in a classic response to the authorities, Peter said, "We ought to obey God rather than men" (Acts 5:29).

Third, *your highest call is to use your gifts to serve and shepherd others*. In 1 Peter 4, Peter tells us to identify our spiritual gifts and use them to serve others. As we do this, we glorify God. In chapter five, he challenges leaders to "shepherd the flock of God which is among you" (v. 2). To Peter, it doesn't get any better than this.

Finally, *strive for holiness and humility*. Peter addresses both the holy lifestyle (chs. 1; 2) and the humble lifestyle (chs. 3—5). These are high but elusive aims for leaders who battle with ego. Peter's own struggle and victory in these two areas drove him to call others to the same standard.

God's Role in 1 Peter

God plays the role of encourager. Leaders can come away from this book knowing that they are not alone in their sacrifice and suffering. Their cause has not gone unnoticed, so long as it lies within the boundaries of the kingdom of God.

God exhorts leaders to be holy and humble; to be patient and persistent; and to be servants and shepherds. The book unflinchingly depicts the harsh realities of life. Leadership can be a thankless job. But any leader can receive hope and strength from the insights and instructions God provides. When we humble ourselves, we receive God's power.

Leaders in 1 Peter

Peter, elders and under-shepherds, government authorities

Other People of Influence in 1 Peter

Husbands and wives

Lessons in Leadership

- If leaders will humble themselves, God will exalt them.

- A leader's identity must be found in Christ, not in the corporate ladder.

- Opposition and struggle are part of the leadership territory.

- Leaders who practice holiness and humility receive God's hope and help.

- Spiritual leaders are to be models, ministers, mentors, and managers.

LEADERSHIP

HIGHLIGHTS IN 1 PETER

Greeting to the Elect Pilgrims

1 Peter, an apostle of Jesus Christ,

To the pilgrims of the Dispersion in Pontus, Galatia, Cappadocia, Asia, and Bithynia, ²elect according to the foreknowledge of God the Father, in sanctification of the Spirit, for obedience and sprinkling of the blood of Jesus Christ:

Grace to you and peace be multiplied.

A Heavenly Inheritance

³Blessed *be* the God and Father of our Lord Jesus Christ, who according to His abundant mercy has begotten us again to a living hope through the resurrection of Jesus Christ from the dead, ⁴to an inheritance incorruptible and undefiled and that does not fade away, reserved in heaven for you, ⁵who are kept by the power of God through faith for salvation ready to be revealed in the last time.

⁶In this you greatly rejoice, though now for a little while, if need be, you have been grieved by various trials, ⁷that the genuineness of your faith, *being* much more precious than gold that perishes, though it is tested by fire, may be found to praise, honor, and glory at the revelation of Jesus Christ, ⁸whom having not seen[a] you love. Though now you do not see *Him,* yet believing, you rejoice with joy inexpressible and full of glory, ⁹receiving the end of your faith—the salvation of *your* souls.

¹⁰Of this salvation the prophets have inquired and searched carefully, who prophesied of the grace *that would come* to you, ¹¹searching what, or what manner of time, the Spirit of Christ who was in them was indicating when He testified beforehand the sufferings of Christ and the glories that would follow. ¹²To them it was revealed that, not to themselves, but to us[a] they were ministering the things which now have been reported to you through those who have preached the gospel to you by the Holy Spirit sent from heaven—things which angels desire to look into.

Living Before God Our Father

¹³Therefore gird up the loins of your mind, be sober, and rest *your* hope fully upon the grace that is to be brought to you at the revelation of Jesus Christ; ¹⁴as obedient children, not

---

1:8 [a]M-Text reads *known.* **1:12** [a]NU-Text and M-Text read *you.*

PETER

A LEADER WHO LEARNED FROM HIS FAILURE
(1 Peter 1:1–5)

PROFILE *IN LEADERSHIP*

No New Testament leader realized more deeply his own fallibility than the apostle Peter.

At the moment of truth, Peter—the same one who stepped out of a boat to walk on water when Jesus called him (Matt. 14:27–30); the same one who identified Jesus as the Christ (Matt. 16:13–20); the same one who witnessed the transfiguration (Matt. 17:1–8)—miserably failed his Lord, denying Him three times on the night of His arrest.

Yet this man, in the face of incredible persecution and opposition, got up off the ground to do incredible things for Christ's church. Now he writes to Jewish Christians enduring intense persecution for their faith, encouraging them to persevere through their suffering by remembering that their reward awaits them.

This is not the brash, impetuous, emotional Peter who traveled with Jesus during His earthly ministry. This is a Peter who has matured in his faith, a man who has learned from his failures—and who, most of all, has been filled with the Holy Spirit of God.

Effective leaders walk by the power of the Holy Spirit. They realize that all of us—even those with the best of intentions—are prone to fail when we walk in our own strength and not in the empowerment of the Spirit.

Leadership Is Built on the Foundation of Focus and Self-Discipline

(1 Peter 1:13–16)

Focus and self-discipline provide the foundation for solid leadership. Peter learned this lesson the hard way. Over three and a half tough years, God transformed Peter from an impetuous, loud influence to a thoughtful, humble leader. Consider the marching orders Peter gives leaders:

1. *Gird your minds* (v. 13).

   Just as men would gird their loins so their robes wouldn't get caught on obstructions as they walked, so we are to gird the loins of our minds. We must remain focused and sober.

2. *Guard your hearts* (v. 14).

   Leaders must prevent old patterns from penetrating their hearts. Peter specifically warns against former lusts, which would not only distract them, but might also destroy their leadership.

3. *Guide your lifestyle* (vv. 15, 16).

   Leaders must pursue holiness—and the only way to attain it is to embrace the model Christ gave. Since God is holy, we must copy what we see Him doing.

---

conforming yourselves to the former lusts, *as in* your ignorance; [15]but as He who called you *is* holy, you also be holy in all *your* conduct, [16]because it is written, *"Be holy, for I am holy."*[a]

[17]And if you call on the Father, who without partiality judges according to each one's work, conduct yourselves throughout the time of your stay *here* in fear; [18]knowing that you were not redeemed with corruptible things, *like* silver or gold, from your aimless conduct *received* by tradition from your fathers, [19]but with the precious blood of Christ, as of a lamb without blemish and without spot. [20]He indeed was foreordained before the foundation of the world, but was manifest in these last times for you [21]who through Him believe in God, who raised Him from the dead and gave Him glory, so that your faith and hope are in God.

The Enduring Word

[22]Since you have purified your souls in obeying the truth through the Spirit[a] in sincere love of the brethren, love one another fervently with a pure heart, [23]having been born again, not of corruptible seed but incorruptible, through the word of God which lives and abides forever,[a] [24]because

"*All flesh is as grass,*
And all the glory of man[a] *as the flower of the grass.*
The grass withers,

And its flower falls away,
[25] *But the word of the LORD endures forever."*[a]

Now this is the word which by the gospel was preached to you.

Therefore, laying aside all malice, all deceit, hypocrisy, envy, and all evil speaking, [2]as newborn babes, desire the pure milk of the word, that you may grow thereby,[a] [3]if indeed you have tasted that the Lord *is* gracious.

The Chosen Stone and His Chosen People

[4]Coming to Him *as to* a living stone, rejected indeed by men, but chosen by God *and* precious, [5]you also, as living stones, are being built up a spiritual house, a holy priesthood, to offer up spiritual sacrifices acceptable to God through Jesus Christ. [6]Therefore it is also contained in the Scripture,

"*Behold, I lay in Zion*
A chief cornerstone, elect, precious,
And he who believes on Him will by no means be put to shame."[a]

1:16 [a]Leviticus 11:44, 45; 19:2; 20:7
1:22 [a]NU-Text omits *through the Spirit.*
1:23 [a]NU-Text omits *forever.* **1:24** [a]NU-Text reads *all its glory.* **1:25** [a]Isaiah 40:6–8 **2:2** [a]NU-Text adds *up to salvation.* **2:6** [a]Isaiah 28:16

God's Twofold Call

(1 Peter 2:9, 10)

Every leader in the body of Christ is to serve in response to a divine calling. Five times Peter brings up the issue of calling (1 Pet. 1:15; 2:9, 21; 3:9; 5:10).

God's call is twofold and is confirmed in two ways. There is a *general* calling He offers to everyone; anyone who responds to Him is considered the "called" (Is. 6:8). But a second call is more specific. This call is given to individuals who are meant to serve in a particular role (Acts 9:3–6). This calling is confirmed both by an inward witness of the heart and an outward recognition by the body of Christ.

What is your calling? How is your call recognized by others?

7Therefore, to you who believe, *He is* precious; but to those who are disobedient,[a]

> "The stone which the builders rejected
> Has become the chief cornerstone,"[b]

8and

> "A stone of stumbling
> And a rock of offense."[a]

They stumble, being disobedient to the word, to which they also were appointed.

9But you *are* a chosen generation, a royal priesthood, a holy nation, His own special people, that you may proclaim the praises of Him who called you out of darkness into His marvelous light; 10who once *were* not a people but *are* now the people of God, who had not obtained mercy but now have obtained mercy.

Living Before the World

11Beloved, I beg *you* as sojourners and pilgrims, abstain from fleshly lusts which war against the soul, 12having your conduct honorable among the Gentiles, that when they speak against you as evildoers, they may, by *your* good works which they observe, glorify God in the day of visitation.

Submission to Government

13Therefore submit yourselves to every ordinance of man for the Lord's sake, whether to the king as supreme, 14or to governors, as to those who are sent by him for the punishment of evildoers and *for the* praise of those who do good. 15For this is the will of God, that by doing good you may put to silence the ignorance of foolish men— 16as free, yet not using liberty as a cloak for vice, but as bondservants of God. 17Honor all *people.* Love the brotherhood. Fear God. Honor the king.

2:7 [a]NU-Text reads *to those who disbelieve.* [b]Psalm 118:22 **2:8** [a]Isaiah 8:14

The Law of Sacrifice: Christ Is Our Model for Leadership

(1 Peter 2:13–18)

Peter calls everyone to respect and submit to authorities, regardless of how the authorities might treat their subjects. He reminds us that no one occupies a leadership position without God's sanction.

To illustrate his point, he brings up Christ's leadership (1 Pet. 2:21–23). Jesus suffered unjustly and endured it without complaint. Just as our Lord sacrificed so much in heading toward the Cross, we are to practice the Law of Sacrifice, giving up the pleasures and comforts we might normally enjoy. Consider how Jesus practiced this law:

What Happened to Him
1. Insults and mockery
2. Suffered through beating
3. Accused falsely
4. Carried our sin

His Sacrificial Response
1. Didn't retaliate, but kept silent
2. Made no threats
3. No deceit was in His mouth
4. Entrusted Himself to the Father

Submission to Masters

[18]Servants, *be* submissive to *your* masters with all fear, not only to the good and gentle, but also to the harsh. [19]For this *is* commendable, if because of conscience toward God one endures grief, suffering wrongfully. [20]For what credit *is it* if, when you are beaten for your faults, you take it patiently? But when you do good and suffer, if you take it patiently, this *is* commendable before God. [21]For to this you were called, because Christ also suffered for us,[a] leaving us[b] an example, that you should follow His steps:

[22] "*Who committed no sin,*
    Nor was deceit found in His mouth";[a]

[23]who, when He was reviled, did not revile in return; when He suffered, He did not threaten, but committed *Himself* to Him who judges righteously; [24]who Himself bore our sins in His own body on the tree, that we, having died to sins, might live for righteousness—by whose stripes you were healed. [25]For you were like sheep going astray, but have now returned to the Shepherd and Overseer[a] of your souls.

Submission to Husbands

3 Wives, likewise, *be* submissive to your own husbands, that even if some do not obey the word, they, without a word, may be won by the conduct of their wives, [2]when they observe your chaste conduct *accompanied* by fear. [3]Do not let your adornment be *merely* outward—arranging the hair, wearing gold, or putting on *fine* apparel— [4]rather *let it be* the hidden person of the heart, with the incorruptible *beauty* of a gentle and quiet spirit, which is very precious in the sight of God. [5]For in this manner, in former times, the holy women who trusted in God also adorned themselves, being submissive to their own husbands, [6]as Sarah obeyed Abraham, calling him lord, whose daughters you are if you do good and are not afraid with any terror.

A Word to Husbands

[7]Husbands, likewise, dwell with *them* with understanding, giving honor to the wife, as to the weaker vessel, and as *being* heirs together of the grace of life, that your prayers may not be hindered.

Called to Blessing

[8]Finally, all *of you be* of one mind, having compassion for one another; love as brothers, *be* tenderhearted, *be* courteous;[a] [9]not returning evil for evil or reviling for reviling, but on the con-

---

Leadership in the Home
(1 Peter 3:1–7)

No home can thrive without functioning according to sound leadership principles. Peter first challenges wives to submit to their husbands, even those who do not submit to Christ. This is the principle of authority and submission. It shows up most pointedly when you disagree with the leader. When the wife submits even though she opposes her husband's decision, she gives a powerful witness to Christ and brings a special honor to Him.

Husbands are called to live with their wives in an understanding way. They are to honor their wives and model submission and service. They are to initiate blessing, rather than retaliate when things go wrong.

Spiritual leaders assume responsibility for the health of their relationships. This means they set the tone. They must initiate what they want others to do.

---

trary blessing, knowing that you were called to this, that you may inherit a blessing. [10]For

"*He who would love life*
    And see good days,
    Let him refrain his tongue from evil,
    And his lips from speaking deceit.
[11]   *Let him turn away from evil and do good;*
    Let him seek peace and pursue it.
[12]   *For the eyes of the LORD are on the*
        righteous,
    And His ears are open to their prayers;
    But the face of the LORD is against those
        who do evil."[a]

Suffering for Right and Wrong

[13]And who *is* he who will harm you if you become followers of what is good? [14]But even if you should suffer for righteousness' sake, *you are* blessed. "*And do not be afraid of their threats, nor be troubled.*"[a] [15]But sanctify the Lord God[a] in your hearts, and always *be* ready to *give* a defense to everyone who asks you a reason for the

---

2:21 [a]NU-Text reads *you.* [b]NU-Text and M-Text read *you.* **2:22** [a]Isaiah 53:9 **2:25** [a]Greek *Episkopos* **3:8** [a]NU-Text reads *humble.* **3:12** [a]Psalm 34:12–16 **3:14** [a]Isaiah 8:12 **3:15** [a]NU-Text reads *Christ as Lord.*

hope that is in you, with meekness and fear; [16]having a good conscience, that when they defame you as evildoers, those who revile your good conduct in Christ may be ashamed. [17]For *it is* better, if it is the will of God, to suffer for doing good than for doing evil.

Christ's Suffering and Ours

[18]For Christ also suffered once for sins, the just for the unjust, that He might bring us[a] to God, being put to death in the flesh but made alive by the Spirit, [19]by whom also He went and preached to the spirits in prison, [20]who formerly were disobedient, when once the Divine longsuffering waited[a] in the days of Noah, while *the* ark was being prepared, in which a few, that is, eight souls, were saved through water. [21]There is also an antitype which now saves us—baptism (not the removal of the filth of the flesh, but the answer of a good conscience toward God), through the resurrection of Jesus Christ, [22]who has gone into heaven and is at the right hand of God, angels and authorities and powers having been made subject to Him.

Therefore, since Christ suffered for us[a] in the flesh, arm yourselves also with the same mind, for he who has suffered in the flesh has ceased from sin, [2]that he no longer should live the rest of *his* time in the flesh for the lusts of men, but for the will of God. [3]For we *have spent* enough of our past lifetime[a] in doing the will of the Gentiles—when we walked in lewdness, lusts, drunkenness, revelries, drinking parties, and abominable idolatries. [4]In regard to these, they think it strange that you do not run with *them* in the same flood of dissipation, speaking evil of *you.* [5]They will give an account to Him who is ready to judge the living and the dead. [6]For this reason the gospel was preached also to those who are dead, that they might be judged according to men in the flesh, but live according to God in the spirit.

Serving for God's Glory

[7]But the end of all things is at hand; therefore be serious and watchful in your prayers. [8]And above all things have fervent love for one another, for *"love will cover a multitude of sins."*[a] [9]*Be* hospitable to one another without grumbling. [10]As each one has received a gift, minister it to one another, as good stewards of the manifold grace of God. [11]If anyone speaks, *let him speak* as the oracles of God. If anyone ministers, *let him do it* as with the ability which God supplies, that in all things God may be glorified through Jesus Christ, to whom belong

---

Spiritual Gifts: We Lead Best When We Lead from Our Gifts

(1 Peter 4:10, 11)

In this passage, Peter encourages us to make five observations about our spiritual gifts:

1. Every one of us has at least one spiritual gift (v. 10).
2. Spiritual gifts are intended to serve people, not bolster our reputations (v. 10).
3. We use our gifts as stewards, not owners (v. 10).
4. God is the source and the sustainer of every gift (v. 11).
5. We are to employ our gifts as though we were serving the Lord (v. 11).

Three disappointments result when we fail to use our gifts properly:

1. We are disobedient.
2. The Body of Christ suffers.
3. God is not glorified.

---

the glory and the dominion forever and ever. Amen.

Suffering for God's Glory

[12]Beloved, do not think it strange concerning the fiery trial which is to try you, as though some strange thing happened to you; [13]but rejoice to the extent that you partake of Christ's sufferings, that when His glory is revealed, you may also be glad with exceeding joy. [14]If you are reproached for the name of Christ, blessed *are you,* for the Spirit of glory and of God rests upon you.[a] On their part He is blasphemed, but on your part He is glorified. [15]But let none of you suffer as a murderer, a thief, an evildoer, or as a busybody in other people's matters. [16]Yet if *anyone suffers* as a Christian, let him not be ashamed, but let him glorify God in this matter.[a]

[17]For the time *has come* for judgment to begin

3:18 [a]NU-Text and M-Text read *you.* 3:20 [a]NU-Text and M-Text read *when the longsuffering of God waited patiently.* 4:1 [a]NU-Text omits *for us.*
4:3 [a]NU-Text reads *time.* 4:8 [a]Proverbs 10:12
4:14 [a]NU-Text omits the rest of this verse.
4:16 [a]NU-Text reads *name.*

The Role of Spiritual Leaders

(1 Peter 5:1–4)

Peter closes his book by addressing the church elders and encouraging them to lead well, according to a whole new paradigm of leadership. He urges them to follow Christ, not only as their suffering Savior, but as their example of leadership. A leader is called to be . . .

1. *A minister to the people* (v. 2).
   Peter exhorts them to shepherd their flock, serving them before being served.
2. *A mentor of the people* (vv. 2, 3).
   Peter asks them to eagerly invest in the flock, not as lords, but as examples.
3. *A manager of the people* (vv. 2, 3).
   Peter calls them to exercise oversight over those entrusted to their care.
4. *A model for the people* (v. 3).
   Peter tells them to be examples to the flock, demonstrating how to live.

at the house of God; and if *it begins* with us first, what will *be* the end of those who do not obey the gospel of God? [18]Now

> "If the righteous one is scarcely saved,
> Where will the ungodly and the sinner
> appear?"[a]

[19]Therefore let those who suffer according to the will of God commit their souls *to Him* in doing good, as to a faithful Creator.

Shepherd the Flock

5 The elders who are among you I exhort, I who am a fellow elder and a witness of the sufferings of Christ, and also a partaker of the glory that will be revealed: [2]Shepherd the flock of God which is among you, serving as overseers, not by compulsion but willingly,[a] not for dishonest gain but eagerly; [3]nor as being lords over those entrusted to you, but being examples to the flock; [4]and when the Chief Shepherd appears, you will receive the crown of glory that does not fade away.

Submit to God, Resist the Devil

[5]Likewise you younger people, submit yourselves to *your* elders. Yes, all of *you* be submissive to one another, and be clothed with humility, for

> "God resists the proud,
> But gives grace to the humble."[a]

[6]Therefore humble yourselves under the mighty hand of God, that He may exalt you in due time,

[7]casting all your care upon Him, for He cares for you.

[8]Be sober, be vigilant; because[a] your adver-

4:18 [a]Proverbs 11:31 **5:2** [a]NU-Text adds *according to God.* **5:5** [a]Proverbs 3:34 **5:8** [a]NU-Text and M-Text omit *because.*

Leadership Motive Check

(1 Peter 5:1–4)

At the end of his first letter, Peter furnishes a motive check for leaders. Note that he calls us to: lead and serve voluntarily, not for selfish gain; eagerly do God's will, not to get ahead; serve as an example, not as a lord. Take the following motive check:

1. When you lead, do you remember the example of Christ's sufferings? (v. 1).
2. When you shepherd, do you do it out of a sense of obligation, or privilege? (v. 2).
3. When you serve, are you motivated by the will of God, or men? (v. 2).
4. When you minister, are you driven by personal gain, or godly passion? (v. 2).
5. When influencing others, does your life example speak clearly? (v. 3).
6. When sacrificing, can you wait for the ultimate reward, or must you see an immediate payback? (v. 3).

The Law of Sacrifice: Leaders Humble Themselves to Be Exalted

(1 Peter 5:5–7)

To the degree that we display pride, God removes His grace from us. The leader is to humble himself by casting all his cares on God (1 Pet. 5:7). Only then does God promise to exalt the leader. What do you find yourself doing these days—humbling yourself, or feeding your pride?

sary the devil walks about like a roaring lion, seeking whom he may devour. ⁹Resist him,

steadfast in the faith, knowing that the same sufferings are experienced by your brotherhood in the world. ¹⁰But mayᵃ the God of all grace, who called usᵇ to His eternal glory by Christ Jesus, after you have suffered a while, perfect, establish, strengthen, and settle *you*. ¹¹To Him *be* the glory and the dominion forever and ever. Amen.

Farewell and Peace

¹²By Silvanus, our faithful brother as I consider him, I have written to you briefly, exhorting and testifying that this is the true grace of God in which you stand.

¹³She who is in Babylon, elect together with *you*, greets you; and *so does* Mark my son. ¹⁴Greet one another with a kiss of love.

Peace to you all who are in Christ Jesus. Amen.

5:10 ᵃNU-Text reads *But the God of all grace . . . will perfect, establish, strengthen, and settle you.*
ᵇNU-Text and M-Text read *you.*

2 PETER

Confronting Problems of Opposition

SUMMARY

Knowledge of Simon Peter's personal biography helps us understand why his words carry so much weight. Peter was Christ's most outspoken disciple, a natural leader who frequently erred on the side of impulsiveness and presumption. More than once during Jesus' days on earth, Peter stuck his foot in his mouth.

Despite this, God greatly used him. Peter maintained his personality while the Holy Spirit groomed him as a leader. From the crucifixion of Jesus until the day of Pentecost, Peter went through some radical changes. Later, he deepened as a trustworthy apostle and church leader in Jerusalem.

Peter's writings come out of his own life failures. He provides an example of how God must break leaders in the area of their strengths. Peter took great pride in his courage. He boasted that although the other disciples might deny Jesus, he never would. Christ had to declare to him that he would fail in his commitment three times before the rooster crowed. Peter wept bitterly after his failure, but God was working on him, building him into a leader others could trust. Peter wrote of the leadership lessons he learned and the qualities he developed along the way. Note some of the lessons and qualities he addresses in this book:

1. *Character in the midst of low morals.* Peter strongly advocated living out of character. For years, he had lived off of impulse and emotion. Later, he discovered the importance of demonstrating character, especially in his day of moral laxity. In chapter one he lists the ingredients leaders must possess in this area.

2. *Initiative in the midst of poor models.* Peter never lacked initiative, but he had to learn how to curb his enthusiasm. He was a "ready, fire, aim" sort of leader who learned to take better aim before firing. Religious leaders in Peter's day were slow to believe in Jesus, so he confronted them about their lethargic ways. He also lived in a day filled with false teachers quick to mislead Christians. In chapters one and two, Peter confronts them both.

3. *Risk in the midst of increasing martyrdom.* When Peter erred, he did so on the side of risk. In his day, torture and executions multiplied. Over the years, he identified which issues were worth dying for and which weren't. When he determined

his priorities, he risked his life for them. He calls for this kind of conviction in chapters two and three.

4. *Faith in the midst of fearful masses.* After failing in his own faith during Jesus' trial, Peter came back strong and began calling others to an unshakable faith. In the final chapter, Peter speaks of Christ's return and our need to trust Him completely until that day. The Romans martyred Peter for his faith in the late 60s A.D.

God's Role in 2 Peter

God uses this book to confront the problems of internal opposition to the gospel. Peter raises his trusted voice to address the issues church leaders must face. His humanity makes him believable, and his humility makes him approachable.

God dealt with spiritual counterfeits through Peter, who understood the necessity of taking a stand for what is right. Leaders can take comfort in this book, written by a man who wasn't afraid to get back up after he had fallen.

Leaders in 2 Peter

Peter, prophets

Other People of Influence in 2 Peter

False teachers, lawless men

Lessons in Leadership

- Leadership is built on the foundation of character, not gifts or charisma.
- A leader's motive will determine his movement and mindset.
- If you don't stand for something, you will fall for anything.
- Effective leaders see both the big picture and the little process.

HIGHLIGHTS IN 2 PETER

Greeting the Faithful

1 Simon Peter, a bondservant and apostle of Jesus Christ,

To those who have obtained like precious faith with us by the righteousness of our God and Savior Jesus Christ:

[2]Grace and peace be multiplied to you in the knowledge of God and of Jesus our Lord, [3]as His divine power has given to us all things that *pertain* to life and godliness, through the knowledge of Him who called us by glory and virtue, [4]by which have been given to us exceedingly great and precious promises, that through these you may be partakers of the divine nature, having escaped the corruption *that is* in the world through lust.

Fruitful Growth in the Faith

[5]But also for this very reason, giving all diligence, add to your faith virtue, to virtue knowledge, [6]to knowledge self-control, to self-control perseverance, to perseverance godliness, [7]to godliness brotherly kindness, and to brotherly kindness love. [8]For if these things are yours and abound, *you will be* neither barren nor unfruitful in the knowledge of our Lord Jesus Christ. [9]For he who lacks these things is shortsighted, even to blindness, and has forgotten that he was cleansed from his old sins.

[10]Therefore, brethren, be even more diligent to make your call and election sure, for if you do these things you will never stumble; [11]for so an entrance will be supplied to you abundantly into the everlasting kingdom of our Lord and Savior Jesus Christ.

Peter's Approaching Death

[12]For this reason I will not be negligent to remind you always of these things, though you know and are established in the present truth. [13]Yes, I think it is right, as long as I am in this tent, to stir you up by reminding *you,* [14]knowing that shortly I *must* put off my tent, just as our Lord Jesus Christ showed me. [15]Moreover I will be careful to ensure that you always have a reminder of these things after my decease.

The Trustworthy Prophetic Word

[16]For we did not follow cunningly devised fables when we made known to you the power and coming of our Lord Jesus Christ, but were eyewitnesses of His majesty. [17]For He received from God the Father honor and glory when such a voice came to Him from the Excellent Glory: "This is My beloved Son, in whom I am well pleased." [18]And we heard this voice which came from heaven when we were with Him on the holy mountain.

[19]And so we have the prophetic word confirmed,[a] which you do well to heed as a light that shines in a dark place, until the day dawns

---

1:19 [a]Or *We also have the more sure prophetic word.*

The Law of Empowerment:
God Gave Us All We Need in a Seed

(2 Peter 1:1–8)

Second Peter emphasizes God's empowerment of His people. Like all good leaders, God equips us with everything we need to do what He calls us to do.

Peter tells us that God granted to us "all things that pertain to life and godliness" (2 Pet. 1:3). God's divine power has granted us His divine nature (1:3), and we participate in this divine nature by laying hold of His divine promises (1:4). We cooperate with Him by developing ourselves. We exercise our new nature by being diligent. We are to add virtue to our faith, then knowledge, self-control, perseverance, godliness, brotherly kindness, and finally love. When we have gone through this sequence of character development, the divine nature has matured in us (1:2–8).

Jesus said the process works like a seed (Matt. 13:31, 32). The seed is planted and, although it is entirely present, it is very small. As it grows, it becomes large and helpful. Seeds are complete, but undeveloped.

In the same way, God has planted within us all we need, but these resources require time and growth before they become visible to others.

men of God[a] spoke *as they were* moved by the Holy Spirit.

Destructive Doctrines

2 But there were also false prophets among the people, even as there will be false teachers among you, who will secretly bring in destructive heresies, even denying the Lord who bought them, *and* bring on themselves swift destruction. [2]And many will follow their destructive ways, because of whom the way of truth will be blasphemed. [3]By covetousness they will exploit you with deceptive words; for a long time their judgment has not been idle, and their destruction does[a] not slumber.

Doom of False Teachers

[4]For if God did not spare the angels who sinned, but cast *them* down to hell and delivered *them* into chains of darkness, to be reserved for judgment; [5]and did not spare the ancient world, but saved Noah, *one of* eight *people,* a preacher of righteousness, bringing in the flood on the world of the ungodly; [6]and turning the cities of Sodom and Gomorrah into ashes, condemned *them* to destruction, making *them* an example to those who afterward would live ungodly; [7]and delivered righteous Lot, *who was* oppressed by the filthy conduct of the wicked [8](for that righteous man, dwelling among them, tormented *his* righteous soul from day to day by seeing and hearing *their* lawless deeds)— [9]then the Lord knows how to deliver the godly out of temptations and to reserve the unjust under punishment for the day of judgment, [10]and especially those who walk according to the flesh in the lust of uncleanness and despise authority. *They are* presumptuous, self-willed. They are not afraid to speak evil of dignitaries, [11]whereas angels, who are greater in power and might, do not bring a reviling accusation against them before the Lord.

Depravity of False Teachers

[12]But these, like natural brute beasts made to be caught and destroyed, speak evil of the things they do not understand, and will utterly perish in their own corruption, [13]and will receive the wages of unrighteousness, *as those who count it* pleasure to carouse in the daytime. *They are* spots and blemishes, carousing in their own deceptions while they feast with you, [14]having eyes full of adultery and that cannot cease from sin, enticing

---

The Law of Process: Leadership Begins with Eight Characteristics

(2 Peter 1:5–11)

Peter gives us a ladder to climb that leads to maturity, demonstrating that he believed in the Law of Process. Spiritual leadership happens daily, not in a day. Peter selects choice words to describe the sequence of our process. We are to diligently add . . .

1. *Faith:* the foundation on which we grow spiritually.
2. *Virtue:* a life of strong character and discipline.
3. *Knowledge:* an understanding of what God thinks and values.
4. *Self-control:* the ability to lead oneself before leading others.
5. *Perseverance:* the ability to patiently stick to what is right.
6. *Godliness:* a Spirit-filled, Spirit-led lifestyle that reflects the Lord.
7. *Brotherly kindness:* a lifestyle that is warm, relational, and caring.
8. *Love:* the highest quality that enables a leader to sacrificially give to others.

---

and the morning star rises in your hearts; [20]knowing this first, that no prophecy of Scripture is of any private interpretation,[a] [21]for prophecy never came by the will of man, but holy

---

The Law of Solid Ground: Peter's Credible Leadership

(2 Peter 1:16–18)

Every leader must remember that people subconsciously ask the question: *Why should I listen to you?* Peter reminds his audience that he was an eyewitness of the power and life of Jesus. He saw Christ on the Mount of Transfiguration and heard the voice of God. This gives his words more weight.

1:20 [a]Or *origin* **1:21** [a]NU-Text reads *but men spoke from God.* **2:3** [a]M-Text reads *will not.*

Courage: Leaders Stand for What Is True

(2 Peter 2:1–6)

Peter earnestly warns his readers about false teachers. He describes in detail their destructive beliefs, their lust for power, their denial of Christ's deity, their greed, and their perverted sensuality. These false leaders exploit God's people. Therefore, God has chosen to punish them and rescue those who stand for what is right.

Peter illustrates his point by contrasting self-appointed leaders with godly leaders:

1. *The fall of the angels:* God cast them into prison to preserve the godly (v. 4).
2. *The days of Noah:* God sent the flood, but rescued Noah (v. 5).
3. *The destruction of Sodom:* God destroyed the city, but spared Lot (v. 6).

It is never easy to take a courageous stand; there is always a price. It always seems cheaper to . . .

1. *Stand for what is easy:* Some leaders look for the easy road and take it.
2. *Stand for what is popular:* Some leaders check the pulse of the majority.
3. *Stand for what is comfortable:* Some leaders choose what fits them best.
4. *Stand for what is convenient:* Some leaders do what fits their calendar.
5. *Stand for what is beneficial:* Some leaders stand for what profits them.
6. *Stand for what is wrong:* Some leaders simply stand for the wrong issues.

---

unstable souls. *They have* a heart trained in covetous practices, *and are* accursed children. [15]They have forsaken the right way and gone astray, following the way of Balaam the *son* of Beor, who loved the wages of unrighteousness; [16]but he was rebuked for his iniquity: a dumb donkey speaking with a man's voice restrained the madness of the prophet.

[17]These are wells without water, clouds[a] carried by a tempest, for whom is reserved the blackness of darkness forever.[b]

Deceptions of False Teachers

[18]For when they speak great swelling *words* of emptiness, they allure through the lusts of the flesh, through lewdness, the ones who have actually escaped[a] from those who live in error. [19]While they promise them liberty, they themselves are slaves of corruption; for by whom a person is overcome, by him also he is brought into bondage. [20]For if, after they have escaped the pollutions of the world through the knowledge of the Lord and Savior Jesus Christ, they are again entangled in them and overcome, the latter end is worse for them than the beginning. [21]For it would have been better for them not to have known the way of righteousness, than having known *it*, to turn from the holy commandment delivered to them. [22]But it has happened to them according to the true proverb: "A dog returns to his own vomit,"[a] and, "a sow, having washed, to her wallowing in the mire."

God's Promise Is Not Slack

3 Beloved, I now write to you this second epistle (in *both* of which I stir up your pure minds by way of reminder), [2]that you may be mindful of the words which were spoken before by the holy prophets, and of the commandment of us,[a] the apostles of the Lord and Savior, [3]knowing this first: that scoffers will come in the last days, walking according to their own lusts, [4]and saying, "Where is the promise of His coming? For since the fathers fell asleep, all things continue as *they were* from the beginning of creation." [5]For this they willfully forget: that by the word of God the heavens were of old, and the earth standing out of water and in the water, [6]by which the world *that* then existed perished, being flooded with water. [7]But the heavens and the earth *which* are now preserved by the same word, are reserved for fire until the day of judgment and perdition of ungodly men.

2:17 [a]NU-Text reads *and mists.* [b]NU-Text omits *forever.* **2:18** [a]NU-Text reads *are barely escaping.* **2:22** [a]Proverbs 26:11 **3:2** [a]NU-Text and M-Text read *commandment of the apostles of your Lord and Savior* or *commandment of your apostles of the Lord and Savior.*

The Law of Timing: Peter Calls Leaders to See the Big Picture
(2 Peter 3:8, 9)

God looks at time differently than we do. Jesus waits patiently to return because He wants to harvest every soul He can (2 Pet. 3:9). Leaders must combine the ability to wait for results with the ability to seize the day. Leaders must both wait and watch.

The Law of Priorities: Leaders Recognize How to Steward Resources
(2 Peter 3:8–13)

Peter teaches us five lessons about our stewardship of resources:
1. God sees the big picture (v. 8).
2. God patiently and actively waits for the results He desires (v. 9).
3. Because God could end this world at any time, we should live wisely (vv. 10, 11).
4. We should prioritize the things that will hasten His return (v. 12).
5. We should seek to align our priorities with His priorities (v. 13).

⁸But, beloved, do not forget this one thing, that with the Lord one day *is* as a thousand years, and a thousand years as one day. ⁹The Lord is not slack concerning *His* promise, as some count slackness, but is longsuffering toward us,ᵃ not willing that any should perish but that all should come to repentance.

The Day of the Lord

¹⁰But the day of the Lord will come as a thief in the night, in which the heavens will pass away with a great noise, and the elements will melt with fervent heat; both the earth and the works that are in it will be burned up.ᵃ ¹¹Therefore, since all these things will be dissolved, what manner *of persons* ought you to be in holy conduct and godliness, ¹²looking for and hastening the coming of the day of God, because of which the heavens will be dissolved, being on fire, and the elements will melt with fervent heat? ¹³Nevertheless we, according to His promise, look for new heavens and a new earth in which righteousness dwells.

Be Steadfast

¹⁴Therefore, beloved, looking forward to these things, be diligent to be found by Him in peace, without spot and blameless; ¹⁵and consider *that* the longsuffering of our Lord *is* salvation—as also our beloved brother Paul, according to the wisdom given to him, has written to you, ¹⁶as also in all his epistles, speaking in them of these things, in which are some things hard to understand, which untaught and unstable *people* twist to their own destruction, as *they do* also the rest of the Scriptures.

¹⁷You therefore, beloved, since you know *this* beforehand, beware lest you also fall from your own steadfastness, being led away with the error of the wicked; ¹⁸but grow in the grace and knowledge of our Lord and Savior Jesus Christ.

To Him *be* the glory both now and forever. Amen.

3:9 ᵃNU-Text reads *you.* **3:10** ᵃNU-Text reads *laid bare* (literally *found*).

THE EPISTLES OF JOHN

Life . . . Light . . . Love

SUMMARY

John was the youngest of the twelve disciples whom Jesus chose to follow Him, one of the "sons of thunder," along with his brother, James. In the beginning, he displayed a lot of selfishness and anger, constantly looking for ways to get ahead or gain a favored position. But soon, Jesus began to mold him as a leader.

Jesus' transforming ministry and model eventually turned John into the disciple "whom Jesus loved" (John 13:23). John slowly learned to trust Jesus, while earning Jesus' trust. For example, John leaned his head on Jesus' lap during the last supper; he couldn't get close enough to Him. Even at the Cross, John was the only one of the Twelve to remain near the Master. While he stood at the foot of Jesus' cross, he risked crucifixion himself. He knelt right next to Mary, the mother of Jesus. In fact, Jesus spoke one of His last words to John as He hung from the cross: "Behold your mother!" (John 19:27). In doing this, Jesus fulfilled a Jewish custom. As the firstborn son, it was His responsibility to make sure His parents were cared for. His mother needed someone to care for her needs—and Jesus chose John for this crucial job.

Church history tells us that John stuck to that commission. While all the other apostles fanned out to preach the gospel, John remained with Mary until her death. Why? Trust. Jesus had commanded John to watch His mother. John had become a trusted leader, full of integrity.

John wrote three small letters to the early church, touching upon several fundamental themes: maintaining honesty and integrity; living by our authority as children of God; relating to others with love and compassion; internalizing and applying the truth we say we believe; and holding fast the values we first embraced as disciples.

Three key words appear throughout the letters: life, light, and love. These are the qualities that Jesus Christ, the Leader of leaders, embodies for His people. They are also the qualities a good leader breathes into his or her organization. Effective leaders *love* their people and relate to them well. They shed *light* on issues and the decisions that need to be made. And they push *life* into the organization by their presence, their skills, and their character.

God's Role in the Epistles of John

John describes God, the original Leader, as the source of life, light, and love. God takes the initiative on each one. "We love Him because He first loved us" (1 John 4:19). "God is light and in Him is no darkness at all. . . . If we walk in the light as He is in the light, we have fellowship with one another" (1:5, 7). "He who has the Son has life; he who does not have the Son of God does not have life" (5:12). God models each of the characteristics He desires for us to develop, just as any good leader does.

Leaders in the Epistles of John

John

Other People of Influence in the Epistles of John

The elect lady (2 John), deceivers, Gaius (3 John), Diotrephes (3 John)

Lessons in Leadership

- Leaders need not attempt great things, but good things done with great love.

- There must be no disparity between our words and our actions.

- The power of any leader comes from the authority God gives him or her.

- Godly leaders must be sources of love, light, and life.

HIGHLIGHTS IN THE EPISTLES OF JOHN

What Was Heard, Seen, and Touched

1 That which was from the beginning, which we have heard, which we have seen with our eyes, which we have looked upon, and our hands have handled, concerning the Word of life— [2]the life was manifested, and we have seen, and bear witness, and declare to you that eternal life which was with the Father and was manifested to us— [3]that which we have seen and heard we declare to you, that you also may have fellowship with us; and truly our fellowship *is* with the Father and with His Son Jesus Christ. [4]And these things we write to you that your[a] joy may be full.

Fellowship with Him and One Another

[5]This is the message which we have heard from Him and declare to you, that God is light and in Him is no darkness at all. [6]If we say that we have fellowship with Him, and walk in darkness, we lie and do not practice the truth. [7]But if we walk in the light as He is in the light, we have fellowship with one another, and the blood of Jesus Christ His Son cleanses us from all sin.

[8]If we say that we have no sin, we deceive ourselves, and the truth is not in us. [9]If we confess our sins, He is faithful and just to forgive us *our* sins and to cleanse us from all unrighteousness. [10]If we say that we have not sinned, we make Him a liar, and His word is not in us.

2 My little children, these things I write to you, so that you may not sin. And if anyone sins, we have an Advocate with the Father, Jesus Christ the righteous. [2]And He Himself is the propitiation for our sins, and not for ours only but also for the whole world.

The Test of Knowing Him

[3]Now by this we know that we know Him, if we keep His commandments. [4]He who says, "I know Him," and does not keep His commandments, is a liar, and the truth is not in him. [5]But whoever keeps His word, truly the love of God is perfected in him. By this we know that we are in Him. [6]He who says he abides in Him ought himself also to walk just as He walked.

[7]Brethren,[a] I write no new commandment to you, but an old commandment which you have had from the beginning. The old commandment is the word which you heard from the beginning.[b]

1:4 [a]NU-Text and M-Text read *our.* **2:7** [a]NU-Text reads *Beloved.* [b]NU-Text omits *from the beginning.*

The Law of Solid Ground: Our Words and Actions Must Align

(1 John 1:6, 8; 2:4, 9)

L eaders must value the truth more than anything else. John describes four lies we often tell ourselves:

1. We say we have fellowship with Him, but walk in darkness (1:6).
2. We say we have no sin and deceive ourselves (1:8).
3. We say we know Him, but do not keep His commandments (2:4).
4. We say we are in the light, but hate our brothers/sisters in Christ (2:9).

When we lie to ourselves, our words and lives don't line up, and people lose confidence in our leadership. Only when we tell the truth do people trust us.

The Law of Connection: Love Is the Gauge for Spiritual Leaders

(1 John 2:7–11)

J ohn's greatest theme is love. Church history tells us that as a very old and mature believer, he had to be carried in on a stretcher to give his last public message—an encouragement for believers to love each other. John knew how to connect with people by letting them know how much he cared for them.

Love is the highest motivation for a leader to connect with people. If you don't love them, don't try to lead them. For John, love and relationship provided the gauge for spiritual leadership. A spiritual leader assumes responsibility for the health and development of his or her relationships. John calls leaders back to the basics:

- We must love the Lord.
- We must love the truth.
- We must love our calling.
- We must love the people.

[8]Again, a new commandment I write to you, which thing is true in Him and in you, because the darkness is passing away, and the true light is already shining.

[9]He who says he is in the light, and hates his brother, is in darkness until now. [10]He who loves his brother abides in the light, and there is no cause for stumbling in him. [11]But he who hates his brother is in darkness and walks in darkness, and does not know where he is going, because the darkness has blinded his eyes.

Their Spiritual State

[12] I write to you, little children,
    Because your sins are forgiven you for
        His name's sake.
[13] I write to you, fathers,
    Because you have known Him *who is*
        from the beginning.
    I write to you, young men,
    Because you have overcome the wicked
        one.
    I write to you, little children,
    Because you have known the Father.
[14] I have written to you, fathers,
    Because you have known Him *who is*
        from the beginning.
    I have written to you, young men,
    Because you are strong, and the word of
        God abides in you,
    And you have overcome the wicked
        one.

Do Not Love the World

[15]Do not love the world or the things in the world. If anyone loves the world, the love of the Father is not in him. [16]For all that *is* in the world—the lust of the flesh, the lust of the eyes, and the pride of life—is not of the Father but is of the world. [17]And the world is passing away, and the lust of it; but he who does the will of God abides forever.

Deceptions of the Last Hour

[18]Little children, it is the last hour; and as you have heard that the[a] Antichrist is coming, even now many antichrists have come, by which we know that it is the last hour. [19]They went out from us, but they were not of us; for if they had been of us, they would have continued with us; but *they went out* that they might be made manifest, that none of them were of us.

[20]But you have an anointing from the Holy One, and you know all things.[a] [21]I have not written to you because you do not know the truth, but because you know it, and that no lie is of the truth.

[22]Who is a liar but he who denies that Jesus is the Christ? He is antichrist who denies the Father and the Son. [23]Whoever denies the Son does not have the Father either; he who acknowledges the Son has the Father also.

Let Truth Abide in You

[24]Therefore let that abide in you which you heard from the beginning. If what you heard from the beginning abides in you, you also will abide in the Son and in the Father. [25]And this is the promise that He has promised us—eternal life.

2:18 [a]NU-Text omits *the.* **2:20** [a]NU-Text reads *you all know.*

The Law of Process: Three Stages of Maturity
(1 John 2:12–14)

John illustrates the Law of Process by speaking to three different groups: children, young men, and fathers. He does not write to believers at differing chronological stages, however, but to those in differing spiritual stages. Each stage faces fundamentally different issues. So says the Law of Process.

As we grow toward mature leadership and influence, we will pass through various phases and have to settle various issues along the way. Remember, leadership development doesn't happen in a day, but daily. Consider the issues in each of the stages:

Stage	Issue
1. Little children	1. Getting right with God and forgiven of sins
2. Young men	2. Waging spiritual warfare and defeating opposition
3. Fathers	3. Intimacy with God

[26]These things I have written to you concerning those who *try to* deceive you. [27]But the anointing which you have received from Him abides in you, and you do not need that anyone teach you; but as the same anointing teaches you concerning all things, and is true, and is not a lie, and just as it has taught you, you will[a] abide in Him.

The Children of God

[28]And now, little children, abide in Him, that when[a] He appears, we may have confidence and not be ashamed before Him at His coming. [29]If you know that He is righteous, you know that everyone who practices righteousness is born of Him.

3 Behold what manner of love the Father has bestowed on us, that we should be called children of God![a] Therefore the world does not know us,[b] because it did not know Him. [2]Beloved, now we are children of God; and it has not yet been revealed what we shall be, but we know that when He is revealed, we shall be like Him, for we shall see Him as He is. [3]And everyone who has this hope in Him purifies himself, just as He is pure.

Sin and the Child of God

[4]Whoever commits sin also commits lawlessness, and sin is lawlessness. [5]And you know that He was manifested to take away our sins, and in Him there is no sin. [6]Whoever abides in Him does not sin. Whoever sins has neither seen Him nor known Him.

[7]Little children, let no one deceive you. He who practices righteousness is righteous, just as He is righteous. [8]He who sins is of the devil, for the devil has sinned from the beginning. For this purpose the Son of God was manifested, that He might destroy the works of the devil. [9]Whoever has been born of God does not sin, for His seed remains in him; and he cannot sin, because he has been born of God.

The Imperative of Love

[10]In this the children of God and the children of the devil are manifest: Whoever does not practice righteousness is not of God, nor *is* he who does not love his brother. [11]For this is the message that you heard from the beginning, that we should love one another, [12]not as Cain *who* was of the wicked one and murdered his brother. And why did he murder him? Because his works were evil and his brother's righteous.

[13]Do not marvel, my brethren, if the world hates you. [14]We know that we have passed from death to life, because we love the brethren. He who does not love *his* brother[a] abides in death. [15]Whoever hates his brother is a murderer, and you know that no murderer has eternal life abiding in him.

The Outworking of Love

[16]By this we know love, because He laid down His life for us. And we also ought to lay down *our* lives for the brethren. [17]But whoever has this world's goods, and sees his brother in need, and shuts up his heart from him, how does the love of God abide in him?

[18]My little children, let us not love in word or in tongue, but in deed and in truth. [19]And by this we know[a] that we are of the truth, and shall assure our hearts before Him. [20]For if our heart condemns us, God is greater than our heart, and knows all things. [21]Beloved, if our heart does not condemn us, we have confidence toward God. [22]And whatever we ask we receive from Him, because we keep His commandments and do those things that are pleasing in His sight. [23]And this is His commandment: that we should believe on the name of His Son Jesus Christ and love one another, as He gave us[a] commandment.

The Spirit of Truth and the Spirit of Error

[24]Now he who keeps His commandments abides in Him, and He in him. And by this we know that He abides in us, by the Spirit whom He has given us.

4 Beloved, do not believe every spirit, but test the spirits, whether they are of God; because many false prophets have gone out into the world. [2]By this you know the Spirit of God: Every spirit that confesses that Jesus Christ has come in the flesh is of God, [3]and every spirit that does not confess that[a] Jesus Christ has come in the flesh is not of God. And this is the *spirit* of the Antichrist, which you have heard was coming, and is now already in the world.

[4]You are of God, little children, and have overcome them, because He who is in you is greater than he who is in the world. [5]They are of the world. Therefore they speak *as* of the world, and the world hears them. [6]We are of God. He

---

2:27 [a]NU-Text reads *you abide.* **2:28** [a]NU-Text reads *if.* **3:1** [a]NU-Text adds *And we are.* [b]M-Text reads *you.* **3:14** [a]NU-Text omits *his brother.* **3:19** [a]NU-Text reads *we shall know.* **3:23** [a]M-Text omits *us.* **4:3** [a]NU-Text omits *that* and *Christ has come in the flesh.*

The Law of Intuition: Leaders Must Discern the Spirit of Behavior

(1 John 4:1–8)

Leaders are to read the spirit behind a person's behavior to sense how ready he or she may be to contribute to the team. Leaders look for a spirit that: confesses Christ as Lord (1 John 4:1–3); agrees with and believes the truth (4:5, 6); and loves others (4:7, 8).

who knows God hears us; he who is not of God does not hear us. By this we know the spirit of truth and the spirit of error.

Knowing God Through Love

[7]Beloved, let us love one another, for love is of God; and everyone who loves is born of God and knows God. [8]He who does not love does not know God, for God is love. [9]In this the love of God was manifested toward us, that God has sent His only begotten Son into the world, that we might live through Him. [10]In this is love, not that we loved God, but that He loved us and sent His Son *to be* the propitiation for our sins. [11]Beloved, if God so loved us, we also ought to love one another.

Seeing God Through Love

[12]No one has seen God at any time. If we love one another, God abides in us, and His love has been perfected in us. [13]By this we know that we abide in Him, and He in us, because He has given us of His Spirit. [14]And we have seen and testify that the Father has sent the Son *as* Savior of the world. [15]Whoever confesses that Jesus is the Son of God, God abides in him, and he in God. [16]And we have known and believed the love that God has for us. God is love, and he who abides in love abides in God, and God in him.

The Consummation of Love

[17]Love has been perfected among us in this: that we may have boldness in the day of judgment; because as He is, so are we in this world.

JOHN   A LEADER MOTIVATED BY LOVE

(1 John 3:16–18)

PROFILE IN LEADERSHIP

The apostle John reveled in God's love for him personally. In his own Gospel, John gleefully refers to himself as the disciple "whom Jesus loved" (John 13:23).

John knew that Jesus' love for the Father motivated Him to do and say everything He did for His disciples and for those around Him. John personalized that love. He knew that Jesus, the Son of God, loved *him,* and he recognized it was his calling as a leader chosen by God to pass that love on to others.

Central to the Book of 1 John is the theme of love for God and love for one another. The apostle tells us that love is not merely a sign of Christ's ownership of us, but that it actually provides proof of our salvation. John insists this is the kind of love we must demonstrate in our actions, not just in our words (1 John 3:18).

God loves us infinitely beyond what we can understand, and we His children are to love Him—and one another—in return. All believers, John suggests—and in particular those who are called to lead—are to be conduits through whom God demonstrates His amazing and undying love.

Leaders need to constantly remind themselves that God is love, and that He requires His people to share His love with one another and with the outside world.

[18]There is no fear in love; but perfect love casts out fear, because fear involves torment. But he who fears has not been made perfect in love. [19]We love Him[a] because He first loved us.

Obedience by Faith

[20]If someone says, "I love God," and hates his brother, he is a liar; for he who does not love his brother whom he has seen, how can[a] he love God whom he has not seen? [21]And this commandment we have from Him: that he who loves God *must* love his brother also.

5 Whoever believes that Jesus is the Christ is born of God, and everyone who loves Him who begot also loves him who is begotten of Him. [2]By this we know that we love the children of God, when we love God and keep His commandments. [3]For this is the love of God, that we keep His commandments. And His commandments are not burdensome. [4]For whatever is born of God overcomes the world. And this is the victory that has overcome the world—our[a] faith. [5]Who is he who overcomes the world, but he who believes that Jesus is the Son of God?

The Certainty of God's Witness

[6]This is He who came by water and blood—Jesus Christ; not only by water, but by water and blood. And it is the Spirit who bears witness, because the Spirit is truth. [7]For there are three that bear witness in heaven: the Father, the Word, and the Holy Spirit; and these three are one. [8]And there are three that bear witness on earth:[a] the Spirit, the water, and the blood; and these three agree as one.

[9]If we receive the witness of men, the witness of God is greater; for this is the witness of God which[a] He has testified of His Son. [10]He who believes in the Son of God has the witness in himself; he who does not believe God has made Him a liar, because he has not believed the testimony that God has given of His Son. [11]And this is the testimony: that God has given us eternal life, and this life is in His Son. [12]He who has the Son has life; he who does not have the Son of God does not have life. [13]These things I have written to you who believe in the name of the Son of God, that you may know that you have eternal life,[a] and that you may *continue to* believe in the name of the Son of God.

Confidence and Compassion in Prayer

[14]Now this is the confidence that we have in Him, that if we ask anything according to His will, He hears us. [15]And if we know that He hears

4:19 [a]NU-Text omits *Him.* **4:20** [a]NU-Text reads *he cannot.* **5:4** [a]M-Text reads *your.* **5:8** [a]NU-Text and M-Text omit the words from *in heaven* (verse 7) through *on earth* (verse 8). Only four or five very late manuscripts contain these words in Greek. **5:9** [a]NU-Text reads *God, that.* **5:13** [a]NU-Text omits the rest of this verse.

The Law of Empowerment: Love Casts Out Fear

(1 John 4:17–21)

When God perfects His love in us, we need not fear or feel insecure. We remain secure in His grace. We don't fear punishment or judgment. We are free to love others (1 John 4:19).

Only these sorts of leaders empower others. The Law of Empowerment reminds us that only secure leaders give power away. Insecure leaders focus on themselves and feel consumed with how they look and whether people like them. The love of God is the only source of absolute security—and all of us can have it. Consider what John teaches us about living secure in Christ:

1. Embracing God's love gives confidence (v. 17).
2. Leaders can incarnate God's security and peace even in this life (v. 17).
3. Enjoying God's love eliminates fear and insecurity (v. 18).
4. We can love others only because God has given us His love (v. 19).
5. Leaders must allow God to empower them with His love before leading others (v. 19).
6. Our love for others is a sign that we love God (v. 20).
7. If I can't get along with people, I can't get along with God (vv. 20, 21).

The Law of Victory: God Provides Victory to All of Us

(1 John 5:1–21)

As the Ultimate Leader, God practices the Law of Victory and allows each of His people to share in His victory. He found a way for the team to win! Consider how God practices this law and takes us to a new level:

1. His people receive a new birth (v. 1).
2. His people receive a lighter load (v. 3).
3. His people overcome the world (v. 4).
4. His people gain a victorious faith (vv. 4, 5).
5. His people receive an inward confirmation (vv. 10, 11).
6. His people receive a new life (v. 12).
7. His people gain answers to prayer (vv. 14, 15).
8. His people receive protection (v. 18).
9. His people gain wisdom and understanding (v. 20).
10. His people receive a new position (v. 20).

us, whatever we ask, we know that we have the petitions that we have asked of Him.

[16]If anyone sees his brother sinning a sin *which does* not *lead* to death, he will ask, and He will give him life for those who commit sin not *leading* to death. There is sin *leading* to death. I do not say that he should pray about that. [17]All unrighteousness is sin, and there is sin not *leading* to death.

Knowing the True—Rejecting the False

[18]We know that whoever is born of God does not sin; but he who has been born of God keeps himself,[a] and the wicked one does not touch him.

[19]We know that we are of God, and the whole world lies *under the sway of* the wicked one.

[20]And we know that the Son of God has come and has given us an understanding, that we may know Him who is true; and we are in Him who is true, in His Son Jesus Christ. This is the true God and eternal life.

[21]Little children, keep yourselves from idols. Amen.

5:18 [a]NU-Text reads *him.*

Greeting the Elect Lady

The Elder,

[1]To the elect lady and her children, whom I love in truth, and not only I, but also all those who have known the truth, [2]because of the truth which abides in us and will be with us forever:

[3]Grace, mercy, *and* peace will be with you[a] from God the Father and from the Lord Jesus Christ, the Son of the Father, in truth and love.

Walk in Christ's Commandments

[4]I rejoiced greatly that I have found *some* of your children walking in truth, as we received commandment from the Father. [5]And now I plead with you, lady, not as though I wrote a new commandment to you, but that which we have had from the beginning: that we love one another. [6]This is love, that we walk according to His commandments. This is the commandment, that as you have heard from the beginning, you should walk in it.

Beware of Antichrist Deceivers

[7]For many deceivers have gone out into the world who do not confess Jesus Christ *as* coming in the flesh. This is a deceiver and an antichrist. [8]Look to yourselves, that we[a] do not lose those things we worked for, but *that* we[b] may receive a full reward.

[9]Whoever transgresses[a] and does not abide in the doctrine of Christ does not have God. He who abides in the doctrine of Christ has both the Father and the Son. [10]If anyone comes to you and does not bring this doctrine, do not receive him into your house nor greet him; [11]for he who greets him shares in his evil deeds.

John's Farewell Greeting

[12]Having many things to write to you, I did not wish *to do so* with paper and ink; but I hope to come to you and speak face to face, that our joy may be full.

[13]The children of your elect sister greet you. Amen.

---

3 [a]NU-Text and M-Text read *us.* **8** [a]NU-Text reads *you.* [b]NU-Text reads *you.* **9** [a]NU-Text reads *goes ahead.*

Values: Leaders Must Cherish Truth More Than Anything
(2 John 1–4)

Leaders need to examine their professional relationships in light of their organization's vision. Energy follows when the leader's personal beliefs align with the organization's values. When leaders eliminate hypocrisy and deception from their organizations, liberty and power prevail. John uses the word "truth" five times in this short letter to underscore the necessity of integrity.

Leaders must value truth more than anything else. When truth presides in an organization, several benefits result:

1. Trust is evident among staff.
2. The leader has less mental clutter.
3. People feel the freedom to be transparent.
4. The leader has credibility when he or she speaks.

3 JOHN
The Third Epistle

Greeting to Gaius

The Elder,

[1]To the beloved Gaius, whom I love in truth:

[2]Beloved, I pray that you may prosper in all things and be in health, just as your soul prospers. [3]For I rejoiced greatly when brethren came and testified of the truth *that is* in you, just as you walk in the truth. [4]I have no greater joy than to hear that my children walk in truth.[a]

Gaius Commended for Generosity

[5]Beloved, you do faithfully whatever you do for the brethren and[a] for strangers, [6]who have borne witness of your love before the church. If you send them forward on their journey in a manner worthy of God, you will do well, [7]because they went forth for His name's sake, taking nothing from the Gentiles. [8]We therefore ought to receive[a] such, that we may become fellow workers for the truth.

Diotrephes and Demetrius

[9]I wrote to the church, but Diotrephes, who loves to have the preeminence among them, does not receive us. [10]Therefore, if I come, I will call to mind his deeds which he does, prating against us with malicious words. And not content with that, he himself does not receive the brethren, and forbids those who wish to, putting *them* out of the church.

[11]Beloved, do not imitate what is evil, but what is good. He who does good is of God, but[a] he who does evil has not seen God.

[12]Demetrius has a *good* testimony from all, and from the truth itself. And we also bear witness, and you know that our testimony is true.

Farewell Greeting

[13]I had many things to write, but I do not wish to write to you with pen and ink; [14]but I hope to see you shortly, and we shall speak face to face.

Peace to you. Our friends greet you. Greet the friends by name.

---

4 [a]NU-Text reads *the truth.* **5** [a]NU-Text adds *especially.* **8** [a]NU-Text reads *support.* **11** [a]NU-Text and M-Text omit *but.*

Initiative: Leaders Are to Host the People in Their Lives
(3 John 3–12)

While 1 John is about God's life and 2 John is about God's truth, 3 John is about God's way. Jesus said, "I am the way, the truth, and the life" (John 14:6).

In his last letter, John uses the picture of a host. Hosts take initiative with their guests. They do what is right by others, make them feel comfortable, give direction to conversation, and provide for others. Leaders, like hosts, don't react; they act. They go first and risk whether the other person will respond positively. It is part of being a leader.

Interestingly, John distinguishes between *going* first and *wanting to be* first. He brings up Diotrephes, "who loves to have the preeminence among them" (3 John 9). Diotrephes wanted to be first, but not necessarily go first in serving others. Here we see the difference between a "guest" and a "host." Consider what this letter teaches us about the leader as "host." Leaders take initiative . . .

- In their lifestyle (vv. 3, 4)
- With others, especially strangers (vv. 5, 6)
- In owning responsibility (vv. 7, 8)
- In doing good, by acting and not reacting (v. 11)
- In modeling for others (v. 12)

JUDE
Correcting Error in the Church

SUMMARY

Like James, Jude was the half brother of Jesus. He struggled early on with Jesus' ministry, but after the Lord's resurrection he became a radical spokesman for the kingdom of God. This brief letter exhibits his commitment to radical faith and obedience.

Jude wrote his letter to correct error in the early church. An early form of gnosticism had begun to trouble God's people, and many unstable believers had drifted from their original faith in Jesus Christ. Jude confronts the issue head-on and uses no fewer than three powerful illustrations to remind the people that God cannot put up with those who depart from their original mission and adopt some alien lifestyle.

Jude teaches leaders how to confront those who meander from the vision. He is direct, yet rational. He is convictional, yet compassionate. He reminds his readers of past incidents and the outcome of such drifting. He mentions the journey from Egypt into the Promised Land, the fallen angels who failed to believe, and the citizens of Sodom and Gomorrah who indulged in self-serving lifestyles. Jude has backbone!

Jude also teaches leaders how to communicate values. Every organization has values, whether they talk about them or not. Jude urges his readers to "contend earnestly for the faith" (v. 3). He communicates simply and with great humility, making an example of Michael, the archangel, who contended with Satan, but who spoke only in the authority and power of Jesus' name.

At the end of the book, Jude teaches leaders how to motivate others to act. He creates a sense of urgency and a sense of destiny in his readers with the examples he chooses. In closing his epistle, he speaks of Enoch, the man who walked with God until God took him home. He persuasively reminds his readers of God's promise to execute justice for all. He inspires and instructs us by listing six action steps that, if followed, will please the Lord, then prays a benediction of victory.

God's Role in Jude

God plays the role of the Chief Executive Officer, for whom Jude is speaking. Jude sees God as the righteous Judge who will execute justice; as the One who saved the Hebrews out of Egypt; and as the Protector who is able to keep us from stumbling en route to heaven.

Jude speaks on behalf of God with prophetic boldness. He clearly represents God, who is both merciful and just and who gives to all what they deserve. Jude acts and talks like an Old Testament prophet, calling the Lord's people back to the changeless God who is victorious in the end, the God who will include His people in His victory if they choose to remain true to His vision and values.

Leaders in Jude

Jude, Enoch

Other People of Influence in Jude

False teachers (proto-gnostics)

Lessons in Leadership

- Leaders must use pictures to capture the hearts of their people.

- Leaders must express certainty when possible, but clarity at all times.

- Effective leaders don't demand, but exhort, appeal, and urge others to act.

- People need both negative and positive reinforcement.

LEADERSHIP

HIGHLIGHTS IN JUDE

VISION: Jude Uses Three Powerful Pictures (5–7)	*page 1554*
EMPOWERMENT: People Need Positive and Negative Reinforcement (14–16)	*page 1555*

Greeting to the Called

[1]Jude, a bondservant of Jesus Christ, and brother of James,

To those who are called, sanctified[a] by God the Father, and preserved in Jesus Christ:

[2]Mercy, peace, and love be multiplied to you.

Contend for the Faith

[3]Beloved, while I was very diligent to write to you concerning our common salvation, I found it necessary to write to you exhorting you to contend earnestly for the faith which was once for all delivered to the saints. [4]For certain men have crept in unnoticed, who long ago were marked out for this condemnation, ungodly men, who turn the grace of our God into lewdness and deny the only Lord God[a] and our Lord Jesus Christ.

Confrontation: Jude Admonishes People to Do Right

(Jude 3–4)

Confrontation is a necessary evil. No one enjoys it, but it must be done in order to rectify, purify, and unify the organization. When leaders refuse to confront wrongs, the atmosphere can become lethargic and unfocused. When leaders don't stand for something, their people will fall for anything.

Old and New Apostates

[5]But I want to remind you, though you once knew this, that the Lord, having saved the people out of the land of Egypt, afterward destroyed those who did not believe. [6]And the angels who did not keep their proper domain, but left their own abode, He has reserved in everlasting chains under darkness for the judgment of the great day; [7]as Sodom and Gomorrah, and the cities around them in a similar manner to these, having given themselves over to sexual immorality and gone after strange flesh, are set forth as an example, suffering the vengeance of eternal fire.

[8]Likewise also these dreamers defile the flesh, reject authority, and speak evil of dignitaries. [9]Yet Michael the archangel, in contending with the

---

Vision: Jude Uses Three Powerful Pictures

(Jude 5–7)

Jude uses three powerful pictures to illustrate the importance of staying true to God's vision. He knew people could seize only what they could see. Therefore, Jude gives his readers a *point* for their head and some *pictures* for their heart.

He makes his point in verse 4: We must remain true to the message we have been given; we must keep the faith. Then he furnishes pictures to illustrate this point:

1. The Jews in the wilderness were destroyed due to unbelief (v. 5).
2. The fallen angels were imprisoned due to disobedience (v. 6).
3. Sodom and Gomorrah were burned due to immorality and rebellion (v. 7).

This repetition proved to be a powerful tool to drive home his point. Effective leaders are good communicators who know how to illustrate their point to make it both memorable and transformational.

---

devil, when he disputed about the body of Moses, dared not bring against him a reviling accusation, but said, "The Lord rebuke you!" [10]But

---

1 [a]NU-Text reads *beloved.* **4** [a]NU-Text omits *God.*

Humility: Leaders Know Authority Comes from God, Not from Within

(Jude 9)

Even Michael the archangel did not combat the enemy on his own authority, but spoke in the name of the Lord. Mature leaders swallow their egos and recognize God as their power source. They walk confidently in His authority, but never assume credit for it. Faith enables them to stretch, while humility enables them to stoop.

these speak evil of whatever they do not know; and whatever they know naturally, like brute beasts, in these things they corrupt themselves. [11]Woe to them! For they have gone in the way of Cain, have run greedily in the error of Balaam for profit, and perished in the rebellion of Korah.

Apostates Depraved and Doomed

[12]These are spots in your love feasts, while they feast with you without fear, serving *only* themselves. *They are* clouds without water, carried about[a] by the winds; late autumn trees without fruit, twice dead, pulled up by the roots; [13]raging waves of the sea, foaming up their own shame; wandering stars for whom is reserved the blackness of darkness forever.

[14]Now Enoch, the seventh from Adam, prophesied about these men also, saying, "Behold, the Lord comes with ten thousands of His saints, [15]to execute judgment on all, to convict all who are ungodly among them of all their ungodly deeds which they have committed in an ungodly way, and of all the harsh things which ungodly sinners have spoken against Him."

Apostates Predicted

[16]These are grumblers, complainers, walking according to their own lusts; and they mouth great swelling *words,* flattering people to gain advantage. [17]But you, beloved, remember the words which were spoken before by the apostles of our Lord Jesus Christ: [18]how they told you that there would be mockers in the last time who would walk according to their own ungodly lusts. [19]These are sensual persons, who cause divisions, not having the Spirit.

Communication: Good Leaders Provide Action Steps

(Jude 17–23)

Jude doesn't close his message with mere information, but offers points of application. Jude challenges his readers to pray in the Spirit (v. 20), remain in the love of God (v. 21), have compassion on doubters (v. 22), and snatch others out of their sin (v. 23). Effective leaders give both information and application.

Maintain Your Life with God

[20]But you, beloved, building yourselves up on your most holy faith, praying in the Holy Spirit, [21]keep yourselves in the love of God, looking for the mercy of our Lord Jesus Christ unto eternal life.

[22]And on some have compassion, making a distinction;[a] [23]but others save with fear, pulling *them* out of the fire,[a] hating even the garment defiled by the flesh.

---

12 [a]NU-Text and M-Text read *along.* **22** [a]NU-Text reads *who are doubting* (or *making distinctions*).
23 [a]NU-Text adds *and on some have mercy with fear* and omits *with fear* in first clause.

Empowerment: People Need Positive and Negative Reinforcement

(Jude 14–16)

Four times Jude uses the word "ungodly" to guide his readers into a lifestyle pleasing to God. Like all good leaders, Jude understands the need for both positive and negative reinforcement. He empowers his readers to do what is right by sharing the rewards of righteous living and the consequences of unrighteous living. Note both sides of this motivational coin:

Positive Reinforcement
1. Enoch's prophecy of the Lord's return
2. The apostle's writings about Christ
3. God's judgment will bless the godly

Negative Reinforcement
1. The Lord's judgment against the ungodly
2. The last days will produce selfish people
3. God's judgment will punish the wicked

Glory to God

24 Now to Him who is able to keep you[a]
   from stumbling,
   And to present *you* faultless
   Before the presence of His glory with
   exceeding joy,
25 To God our Savior,[a]
   Who alone is wise,[b]
   Be glory and majesty,
   Dominion and power,[c]
   Both now and forever.
   Amen.

---

24 [a]M-Text reads *them*. **25** [a]NU-Text reads *To the only God our Savior*. [b]NU-Text omits *Who . . . is wise* and adds *Through Jesus Christ our Lord*. [c]NU-Text adds *Before all time*.

REVELATION

The Revealing of Jesus to the World

SUMMARY

The Book of Revelation differs from every other New Testament book. It contains not only a message for the first century church, to whom it was written, but also to the church through the ages, particularly those living in the "end times" who will see Christ return to earth.

The apostle John, the author of this unique book, wrote five books in the New Testament. This was his last, written just before his death. The name "Revelation" comes from the main event of the book: the revealing of Jesus to the world's inhabitants in the final days. So what does this prophetic book have to say about leadership?

First, it is a book about *vision*. God gave John a vision about the final events of world history. In the midst of this grand vision John teaches us how to live and perceive life in light of the revelation. Vision drives all good leaders; throughout the book we see its power to change lives.

Second, it is a book about *virtue*. The book revolves around the final conflict between good and evil, God and Satan. Consequently, we see the centrality of God's character and virtue, as He ensures that right makes might and that virtue triumphs. Good leaders continue to stand for what is right, despite occasionally losing battles.

Third, it is a book about a *verdict*. Leaders must draw tough conclusions somewhere along the way. They can research, hold focus groups, and survey the needs of a culture—but sooner or later, they must issue a verdict about what they perceive to be true. Leaders make decisions. This book is about the verdict God and His people make, a verdict that influences the whole world.

Fourth, it is a book about *vigor*. John and the saints throughout history display passion, energy, and deep convictions. This book teaches leaders that logic alone accomplishes little. Success comes with passionate commitment and radical obedience.

Finally, it is a book about *victory*. Revelation vividly portrays the imminent showdown between God and Satan. God is the Ultimate Leader while Satan is the temporary influence—the "god of this age," as Paul put it (2 Cor. 4:4). Although Satan's influence is real, he has no chance in the final struggle. The Ultimate Leader practices the Law of Victory.

God's Role in Revelation

God is the Ultimate Leader, the One who provides the vision to John and the One who implements the vision, defeating His enemies as the Captain of heaven's army. God is also the coming Judge who will sit before the world's population, assessing what each individual has done with his or her life. Finally, God is the King of kings, the Sovereign Lord who gives a clear picture of His ultimate control and dominion.

Leaders in Revelation

John, Jesus—the Lamb of God, the dragon, the angels (or messengers) of the seven churches in Asia

Other People of Influence in Revelation

The two witnesses, the remnant of Israel (144,000 individuals)

Lessons in Leadership

- A leader can be seen in four pictures: a shepherd, a seer, a soldier, and a servant.
- Effective leaders assess their people and furnish them with a plan for improvement.
- Vision is the driving force behind all of heaven's activities.
- Leaders find a way to bring victory to their people.
- Leadership is about transformation, not mere information.
- A leader's victory always comes at a high cost.
- In the end, great leaders give God all the glory.

LEADERSHIP

HIGHLIGHTS IN REVELATION

Introduction and Benediction

1 The Revelation of Jesus Christ, which God gave Him to show His servants—things which must shortly take place. And He sent and signified *it* by His angel to His servant John, [2]who bore witness to the word of God, and to the testimony of Jesus Christ, to all things that he saw. [3]Blessed *is* he who reads and those who hear the words of this prophecy, and keep those things which are written in it; for the time *is* near.

Greeting the Seven Churches

[4]John, to the seven churches which are in Asia:

Grace to you and peace from Him who is and who was and who is to come, and from the seven Spirits who are before His throne, [5]and from Jesus Christ, the faithful witness, the first-born from the dead, and the ruler over the kings of the earth.

To Him who loved us and washed[a] us from our sins in His own blood, [6]and has made us kings[a] and priests to His God and Father, to Him *be* glory and dominion forever and ever. Amen.

[7]Behold, He is coming with clouds, and every eye will see Him, even they who pierced Him. And all the tribes of the earth will mourn because of Him. Even so, Amen.

[8]"I am the Alpha and the Omega, *the* Beginning and *the* End,"[a] says the Lord,[b] "who is and who was and who is to come, the Almighty."

Vision of the Son of Man

[9]I, John, both[a] your brother and companion in the tribulation and kingdom and patience of Jesus Christ, was on the island that is called Patmos for the word of God and for the testimony of Jesus Christ. [10]I was in the Spirit on the Lord's Day, and I heard behind me a loud voice, as of a trumpet, [11]saying, "I am the Alpha and the Omega, the First and the Last," and,[a] "What you see, write in a book and send *it* to the seven churches which are in Asia:[b] to Ephesus, to

---

1:5 [a]NU-Text reads *loves us and freed;* M-Text reads *loves us and washed.* **1:6** [a]NU-Text and M-Text read *a kingdom.* **1:8** [a]NU-Text and M-Text omit *the Beginning and the End.* [b]NU-Text and M-Text add *God.* **1:9** [a]NU-Text and M-Text omit *both.* **1:11** [a]NU-Text and M-Text omit *I am* through third *and.* [b]NU-Text and M-Text omit *which are in Asia.*

JOHN

A VISIONARY LEADER WHO REFUSED TO DIE UNTIL DONE
(Revelation 1:1, 2)

PROFILE IN LEADERSHIP

The apostle John lived an amazing life of service to Christ. Not only was he numbered among the original twelve apostles, but Jesus included him in His "inner circle" during His earthly ministry. John walked closely with the Lord and even witnessed Jesus' transfiguration (Luke 9:28–36). Later—following Jesus' death, resurrection, and ascension—John became a respected leader in the church at Jerusalem (Acts 4:1–12). He also wrote the Gospel and three New Testament epistles that bear his name.

John enjoyed a life full of service to Christ, but before he died, God would give him one more assignment: prophet. During the latter part of John's life, as he sat in exile on the rocky and remote island of Patmos, he penned the Book of Revelation, a prophecy detailing the final conflict between good and evil.

John adopted the attitude and mindset of a truly godly leader. He devoted himself to doing what God had assigned to him, right up to the very end of his life. John knew that God had called him to a lifetime of service. And he saw his own life—his own body—as expendable for the purpose of serving the Lord Jesus Christ.

Wise leaders keep in mind that each day God gives them is to be used for His glory and the benefit of His people.

Vision: What You See Is What You Get

(Revelation 1:9–20)

While John worships God on the island of Patmos, Jesus speaks to him; but when he turns to hear the voice, he "sees" a vision (Rev. 1:12). For the remainder of the book, John describes the vision that drove him to write and encourage others.

Vision always drives leaders, especially when they believe God is its source. Note the qualities of a divine vision:

1. It is not discovered or created, but revealed.
2. It doesn't compete with others, but completes others.
3. It is captivating, not optional. I cannot get it out of my mind.
4. Its goal is not to make money, but to meet needs.
5. Its success depends not on staying ahead of others, but on serving others.
6. It stops me before it drives me to act.
7. Its fulfillment doesn't rest on staying ahead of others, but on simple obedience.
8. Its purpose is not to feed my ego, but to glorify God.

Smyrna, to Pergamos, to Thyatira, to Sardis, to Philadelphia, and to Laodicea."

[12]Then I turned to see the voice that spoke with me. And having turned I saw seven golden lampstands, [13]and in the midst of the seven lampstands *One* like the Son of Man, clothed with a garment down to the feet and girded about the chest with a golden band. [14]His head and hair *were* white like wool, as white as snow, and His eyes like a flame of fire; [15]His feet *were* like fine brass, as if refined in a furnace, and His voice as the sound of many waters; [16]He had in His right hand seven stars, out of His mouth went a sharp two-edged sword, and His countenance *was* like the sun shining in its strength. [17]And when I saw Him, I fell at His feet as dead. But He laid His right hand on me, saying to me,[a] "Do not be afraid; I am the First and the Last. [18]I *am* He who lives, and was dead, and behold, I am alive forevermore. Amen. And I have the keys of Hades and of Death. [19]Write[a] the things which you have seen, and the things which are, and the things which will take place after this. [20]The mystery of the seven stars which you saw in My right hand, and the seven golden lampstands: The seven stars are the angels of the seven churches, and the seven lampstands which you saw[a] are the seven churches.

The Loveless Church

2 "To the angel of the church of Ephesus write,

'These things says He who holds the seven stars in His right hand, who walks in the midst of the seven golden lampstands: [2]"I know

your works, your labor, your patience, and that you cannot bear those who are evil. And you have tested those who say they are apostles and are not, and have found them liars; [3]and you have persevered and have patience, and have labored for My name's sake and have not become weary. [4]Nevertheless I have *this* against you, that you have left your first love. [5]Remember therefore from where you have fallen; repent and do the first works, or else I will come to you quickly and remove your lampstand from its place—unless you repent. [6]But this you have, that you hate the deeds of the Nicolaitans, which I also hate.

[7]"He who has an ear, let him hear what the Spirit says to the churches. To him who overcomes I will give to eat from the tree of life, which is in the midst of the Paradise of God."'

The Persecuted Church

[8]"And to the angel of the church in Smyrna write,

'These things says the First and the Last, who was dead, and came to life: [9]"I know your works, tribulation, and poverty (but you are rich); and *I know* the blasphemy of those who say they are Jews and are not, but *are* a synagogue of Satan. [10]Do not fear any of those things which you are about to suffer. Indeed, the devil is about to throw *some* of you into prison, that you may be

1:17 [a]NU-Text and M-Text omit *to me.*
1:19 [a]NU-Text and M-Text read *Therefore, write.*
1:20 [a]NU-Text and M-Text omit *which you saw.*

Priorities: Church Leaders Left Their First Love

(Revelation 2:1–7)

The church at Ephesus provides a classic illustration of leaders who failed to practice the Law of Priorities. Leaders can't merely stay busy; they must stay busy with the right activities. They don't just do things right; they do the right things.

The Ephesian leaders kept their people busy (Rev. 2:2, 3) and the Lord commends them for their labor, but somehow they had left their first priority, which was to love God. Their work *for* God had actually distracted them *from* God! They had busy hands, crowded calendars, full heads—but empty hearts.

What does God say about the remedy for their situation? In one sentence it is this: Remember and repent, or I will return and remove your light (2:5). This is good advice for any leader who has drifted from the top priorities:

1. *Reflect:* Think back and remember the original vision and goals.
2. *Repent:* Decide to change. List what you must discard and prioritize.
3. *Restore:* Begin to restore one top priority at a time, each week.
4. *Recognize:* Remember that God holds us accountable. He rewards fruit, not activity.

---

tested, and you will have tribulation ten days. Be faithful until death, and I will give you the crown of life.

¹¹"He who has an ear, let him hear what the Spirit says to the churches. He who overcomes shall not be hurt by the second death."'

The Compromising Church

¹²"And to the angel of the church in Pergamos write,

'These things says He who has the sharp two-edged sword: ¹³"I know your works, and where you dwell, where Satan's throne *is*. And you hold fast to My name, and did not deny My faith even in the days in which Antipas *was* My faithful martyr, who was killed among you, where Satan dwells. ¹⁴But I have a few things against you, because you have there those who hold the doctrine of Balaam, who taught Balak to put a stumbling block before the children of Israel, to eat things sacrificed to idols, and to commit sexual immorality. ¹⁵Thus you also have those who hold the doctrine of the Nicolaitans, which thing I hate.^a ¹⁶Repent, or else I will come

2:15 ^aNU-Text and M-Text read *likewise* for *which thing I hate.*

The Law of Connection: Jesus Puts Compassion Before Correction

(Revelation 2:1–29)

Jesus lets each church know He understands their situation. He affirms their positive qualities—He touches their hearts—then voices concern over an area that needs attention. Finally, He beseeches them to listen. He consistently shows compassion before He corrects. Leaders touch a heart before they ask for a hand.

Encouragement: Jesus Affirms the Church at Smyrna

(Revelation 2:8–11)

Jesus encourages the hard-pressed church at Smyrna to stand firm and to keep doing what its members know to be right. He reminds them of the reward that awaits them and that their trouble will be temporary. People get emotionally low, they grow weary, and they become doubtful and insecure. They need a leader's encouragement.

to you quickly and will fight against them with the sword of My mouth.

[17]"He who has an ear, let him hear what the Spirit says to the churches. To him who overcomes I will give some of the hidden manna to eat. And I will give him a white stone, and on the stone a new name written which no one knows except him who receives *it*.''

The Corrupt Church

[18]"And to the angel of the church in Thyatira write,

'These things says the Son of God, who has eyes like a flame of fire, and His feet like fine brass: [19]"I know your works, love, service, faith,[a] and your patience; and *as* for your works, the last *are* more than the first. [20]Nevertheless I have a few things against you, because you allow[a] that woman[b] Jezebel, who calls herself a prophetess, to teach and seduce[c] My servants to commit sexual immorality and eat things sacrificed to idols. [21]And I gave her time to repent of her sexual immorality, and she did not repent.[a] [22]Indeed I will cast her into a sickbed, and those who commit adultery with her into great tribulation, unless they repent of their[a] deeds. [23]I will kill her children with death, and all the churches shall know that I am He who searches the minds and hearts. And I will give to each one of you according to your works.

[24]"Now to you I say, and[a] to the rest in Thyatira, as many as do not have this doctrine, who have not known the depths of Satan, as they say, I will[b] put on you no other burden. [25]But hold fast what you have till I come. [26]And he who overcomes, and keeps My works until the end, to him I will give power over the nations—

[27] 'He shall rule them with a rod of iron;
They shall be dashed to pieces like the potter's vessels'[a]—

as I also have received from My Father; [28]and I will give him the morning star.

[29]"He who has an ear, let him hear what the Spirit says to the churches.''

The Dead Church

3 "And to the angel of the church in Sardis write,

'These things says He who has the seven Spirits of God and the seven stars: "I know your works, that you have a name that you are alive, but you are dead. [2]Be watchful, and strengthen the things which remain, that are ready to die, for I have not found your works perfect before God.[a]

2:19 [a]NU-Text and M-Text read *faith, service.*
2:20 [a]NU-Text and M-Text read *I have against you that you tolerate.* [b]M-Text reads *your wife Jezebel.* [c]NU-Text and M-Text read *and teaches and seduces.*
2:21 [a]NU-Text and M-Text read *time to repent, and she does not want to repent of her sexual immorality.*
2:22 [a]NU-Text and M-Text read *her.* **2:24** [a]NU-Text and M-Text omit *and.* [b]NU-Text and M-Text omit *will.* **2:27** [a]Psalm 2:9 **3:2** [a]NU-Text and M-Text read *My God.*

Perspective: The Leader Must Define Reality

(Revelation 3:1–22)

John, writing for Jesus, sends a message to the churches of Sardis, Philadelphia, and Laodicea. In each case, He calls attention to something that has escaped their attention.

Call these words midcourse corrections. Call them healthy accountability. Or just call them sound wisdom. In any case, these three churches illustrate the truth that a leader must define reality. See how Jesus does this:

Church	Reality Check	Action Step
1. Sardis	1. Fell asleep on the job	1. Wake up and repent
2. Philadelphia	2. Little power but big opportunity	2. Don't give up
3. Laodicea	3. Deceived; blind to their condition	3. Change your priorities

Leaders must stay on top of what is happening in their organization. They must discern what keeps their people from moving to the next level. They must confront mediocrity and give steps to correct it. They must never feel satisfied with the status quo.

[3]Remember therefore how you have received and heard; hold fast and repent. Therefore if you will not watch, I will come upon you as a thief, and you will not know what hour I will come upon you. [4]You[a] have a few names even in Sardis who have not defiled their garments; and they shall walk with Me in white, for they are worthy. [5]He who overcomes shall be clothed in white garments, and I will not blot out his name from the Book of Life; but I will confess his name before My Father and before His angels.

[6]"He who has an ear, let him hear what the Spirit says to the churches."'

The Faithful Church

[7]"And to the angel of the church in Philadelphia write,

'These things says He who is holy, He who is true, *"He who has the key of David, He who opens and no one shuts, and shuts and no one opens"*:[a] [8]"I know your works. See, I have set before you an open door, and no one can shut it;[a] for you have a little strength, have kept My word, and have not denied My name. [9]Indeed I will make *those* of the synagogue of Satan, who say they are Jews and are not, but lie—indeed I will make them come and worship before your feet, and to know that I have loved you. [10]Because you have kept My command to persevere, I also will keep you from the hour of trial which shall come upon the whole world, to test those who dwell on the earth. [11]Behold,[a] I am coming quickly! Hold fast what you have, that no one may take your crown. [12]He who overcomes, I will make him a pillar in the temple of My God, and he shall go out no more. I will write on him the name of My God and the name of the city of My God, the New Jerusalem, which comes down out of heaven from My God. And *I will write on him* My new name.

[13]"He who has an ear, let him hear what the Spirit says to the churches."'

The Lukewarm Church

[14]"And to the angel of the church of the Laodiceans[a] write,

'These things says the Amen, the Faithful and True Witness, the Beginning of the creation of God: [15]"I know your works, that you are neither cold nor hot. I could wish you were cold or hot. [16]So then, because you are lukewarm, and neither cold nor hot,[a] I will vomit you out of My mouth. [17]Because you say, 'I am rich, have become wealthy, and have need of nothing'— and do not know that you are wretched, miserable, poor, blind, and naked— [18]I counsel you to buy from Me gold refined in the fire, that you may be rich; and white garments, that you may be clothed, *that* the shame of your nakedness may not be revealed; and anoint your eyes with eye salve, that you may see. [19]As many as I love, I rebuke and chasten. Therefore be zealous and repent. [20]Behold, I stand at the door and knock. If anyone hears My voice and opens the door, I will come in to him and dine with him, and he with Me. [21]To him who overcomes I will grant to sit with Me on My throne, as I also overcame and sat down with My Father on His throne.

[22]"He who has an ear, let him hear what the Spirit says to the churches."'"

The Throne Room of Heaven

4 After these things I looked, and behold, a door *standing* open in heaven. And the first voice which I heard *was* like a trumpet speaking with me, saying, "Come up here, and I will show you things which must take place after this."

[2]Immediately I was in the Spirit; and behold, a throne set in heaven, and *One* sat on the throne. [3]And He who sat there was[a] like a jasper and a sardius stone in appearance; and *there was* a rainbow around the throne, in appearance like an emerald. [4]Around the throne *were* twenty-four thrones, and on the thrones I saw twenty-four elders sitting, clothed in white robes; and they had

---

3:4 [a]NU-Text and M-Text read *Nevertheless you have a few names in Sardis.* **3:7** [a]Isaiah 22:22
3:8 [a]NU-Text and M-Text read *which no one can shut.* **3:11** [a]NU-Text and M-Text omit *Behold.*
3:14 [a]NU-Text and M-Text read *in Laodicea.*
3:16 [a]NU-Text and M-Text read *hot nor cold.*
4:3 [a]M-Text omits *And He who sat there was* (which makes the description in verse 3 modify the throne rather than God).

God's Nature Is Organization, Not Chaos

(Revelation 4:1–11)

John's description of heaven reminds us that we serve a God of order and harmony, not of chaos or anarchy. John paints a portrait of form, structure, harmony, precision, and dignity. God's acts never result in disarray. "God is not the author of confusion but of peace" (1 Cor. 14:33).

crowns[a] of gold on their heads. [5]And from the throne proceeded lightnings, thunderings, and voices.[a] Seven lamps of fire *were* burning before the throne, which are the[b] seven Spirits of God.

[6]Before the throne *there was*[a] a sea of glass, like crystal. And in the midst of the throne, and around the throne, *were* four living creatures full of eyes in front and in back. [7]The first living creature *was* like a lion, the second living creature like a calf, the third living creature had a face like a man, and the fourth living creature *was* like a flying eagle. [8]*The* four living creatures, each having six wings, were full of eyes around and within. And they do not rest day or night, saying:

"Holy, holy, holy,[a]
Lord God Almighty,
Who was and is and is to come!"

[9]Whenever the living creatures give glory and honor and thanks to Him who sits on the throne, who lives forever and ever, [10]the twenty-four elders fall down before Him who sits on the throne and worship Him who lives forever and ever, and cast their crowns before the throne, saying:

[11] "You are worthy, O Lord,[a]
To receive glory and honor and power;

For You created all things,
And by Your will they exist[b] and were created."

The Lamb Takes the Scroll

5 And I saw in the right *hand* of Him who sat on the throne a scroll written inside and on the back, sealed with seven seals. [2]Then I saw a strong angel proclaiming with a loud voice, "Who is worthy to open the scroll and to loose its seals?" [3]And no one in heaven or on the earth or under the earth was able to open the scroll, or to look at it.

[4]So I wept much, because no one was found worthy to open and read[a] the scroll, or to look at it. [5]But one of the elders said to me, "Do not weep. Behold, the Lion of the tribe of Judah, the Root of David, has prevailed to open the scroll and to loose[a] its seven seals."

4:4 [a]NU-Text and M-Text read *robes, with crowns.* **4:5** [a]NU-Text and M-Text read *voices, and thunderings.* [b]M-Text omits *the.* **4:6** [a]NU-Text and M-Text add *something like.* **4:8** [a]M-Text has *holy* nine times. **4:11** [a]NU-Text and M-Text read *our Lord and God.* [b]NU-Text and M-Text read *existed.* **5:4** [a]NU-Text and M-Text omit *and read.* **5:5** [a]NU-Text and M-Text omit *to loose.*

The Law of Sacrifice:
Jesus Served First, Now Is Exalted

(Revelation 5:11–14)

The leader's job is to sacrifice; God's job is to promote. If we will stoop down, He will raise up. This message is given in other New Testament books (James 4:10; 1 Pet. 5:6), but is never clearer than here.

The Lamb of God, who came to be slaughtered, now sits on a throne far above every other leader (Rev. 5:11–14). Paul predicted this in Philippians 2:9.

The rule of thumb seems to be: The lower you go, the higher you grow. We lower; God lifts. Jesus is the ultimate example of this leadership law. Yet many others in history have also obeyed this law. Reflect for a moment on a few biblical illustrations:

Leader	His Sacrifice	The Result
1. Abraham	1. Security, rich land, success	1. Became father of nations
2. Moses	2. Royal position in Egypt	2. Became deliverer of Israel
3. Jesus' disciples	3. Everything they had	3. Leaders of the church
4. Apostle Paul	4. Leader among Pharisees	4. Greatest apostle in history
5. Jesus Christ	5. His divine rights and His life	5. Ruler of the universe

Question: What have you given up to go up?

[6]And I looked, and behold,[a] in the midst of the throne and of the four living creatures, and in the midst of the elders, stood a Lamb as though it had been slain, having seven horns and seven eyes, which are the seven Spirits of God sent out into all the earth. [7]Then He came and took the scroll out of the right hand of Him who sat on the throne.

Worthy Is the Lamb

[8]Now when He had taken the scroll, the four living creatures and the twenty-four elders fell down before the Lamb, each having a harp, and golden bowls full of incense, which are the prayers of the saints. [9]And they sang a new song, saying:

"You are worthy to take the scroll,
And to open its seals;
For You were slain,
And have redeemed us to God by Your blood
Out of every tribe and tongue and people and nation,
[10] And have made us[a] kings[b] and priests to our God;
And we[c] shall reign on the earth."

[11]Then I looked, and I heard the voice of many angels around the throne, the living creatures, and the elders; and the number of them was ten thousand times ten thousand, and thousands of thousands, [12]saying with a loud voice:

"Worthy is the Lamb who was slain
To receive power and riches and wisdom,
And strength and honor and glory and blessing!"

[13]And every creature which is in heaven and on the earth and under the earth and such as are in the sea, and all that are in them, I heard saying:

"Blessing and honor and glory and power
Be to Him who sits on the throne,
And to the Lamb, forever and ever!"[a]

[14]Then the four living creatures said, "Amen!" And the twenty-four[a] elders fell down and worshiped Him who lives forever and ever.[b]

First Seal: The Conqueror

6 Now I saw when the Lamb opened one of the seals;[a] and I heard one of the four living creatures saying with a voice like thunder, "Come and see." [2]And I looked, and behold, a white horse. He who sat on it had a bow; and a crown was given to him, and he went out conquering and to conquer.

Second Seal: Conflict on Earth

[3]When He opened the second seal, I heard the second living creature saying, "Come and see."[a] [4]Another horse, fiery red, went out. And it was granted to the one who sat on it to take peace from the earth, and that *people* should kill one another; and there was given to him a great sword.

Third Seal: Scarcity on Earth

[5]When He opened the third seal, I heard the third living creature say, "Come and see." So I looked, and behold, a black horse, and he who sat on it had a pair of scales in his hand. [6]And I heard a voice in the midst of the four living creatures saying, "A quart[a] of wheat for a denarius,[b] and three quarts of barley for a denarius; and do not harm the oil and the wine."

Fourth Seal: Widespread Death on Earth

[7]When He opened the fourth seal, I heard the voice of the fourth living creature saying, "Come and see." [8]So I looked, and behold, a pale horse. And the name of him who sat on it was Death, and Hades followed with him. And power was given to them over a fourth of the earth, to kill with sword, with hunger, with death, and by the beasts of the earth.

Fifth Seal: The Cry of the Martyrs

[9]When He opened the fifth seal, I saw under the altar the souls of those who had been slain for the word of God and for the testimony which they held. [10]And they cried with a loud voice, saying, "How long, O Lord, holy and true, until You judge and avenge our blood on those who dwell on the earth?" [11]Then a white robe was given to each of them; and it was said to them that they should rest a little while longer, until both *the number of* their fellow servants and

---

5:6 [a]NU-Text and M-Text read *I saw in the midst . . . a Lamb standing.* **5:10** [a]NU-Text and M-Text read *them.* [b]NU-Text reads *a kingdom.* [c]NU-Text and M-Text read *they.* **5:13** [a]M-Text adds *Amen.* **5:14** [a]NU-Text and M-Text omit *twenty-four.* [b]NU-Text and M-Text omit *Him who lives forever and ever.* **6:1** [a]NU-Text and M-Text read *seven seals.* **6:3** [a]NU-Text and M-Text omit *and see.* **6:6** [a]Greek *choinix;* that is, approximately one quart [b]This was approximately one day's wage for a worker.

their brethren, who would be killed as they *were,* was completed.

Sixth Seal: Cosmic Disturbances

[12]I looked when He opened the sixth seal, and behold,[a] there was a great earthquake; and the sun became black as sackcloth of hair, and the moon[b] became like blood. [13]And the stars of heaven fell to the earth, as a fig tree drops its late figs when it is shaken by a mighty wind. [14]Then the sky receded as a scroll when it is rolled up, and every mountain and island was moved out of its place. [15]And the kings of the earth, the great men, the rich men, the commanders,[a] the mighty men, every slave and every free man, hid themselves in the caves and in the rocks of the mountains, [16]and said to the mountains and rocks, "Fall on us and hide us from the face of Him who sits on the throne and from the wrath of the Lamb! [17]For the great day of His wrath has come, and who is able to stand?"

The Sealed of Israel

7 After these things I saw four angels standing at the four corners of the earth, holding the four winds of the earth, that the wind should not blow on the earth, on the sea, or on any tree. [2]Then I saw another angel ascending from the east, having the seal of the living God. And he cried with a loud voice to the four angels to whom it was granted to harm the earth and the sea, [3]saying, "Do not harm the earth, the sea, or the trees till we have sealed the servants of our God on their foreheads." [4]And I heard the number of those who were sealed. One hundred *and* forty-four thousand of all the tribes of the children of Israel *were* sealed:

[5]   of the tribe of Judah twelve thousand *were*
        sealed;[a]
    of the tribe of Reuben twelve thousand
        were sealed;
    of the tribe of Gad twelve thousand *were*
        sealed;
[6]   of the tribe of Asher twelve thousand *were*
        sealed;
    of the tribe of Naphtali twelve thousand
        were sealed;
    of the tribe of Manasseh twelve thousand
        were sealed;
[7]   of the tribe of Simeon twelve thousand
        were sealed;
    of the tribe of Levi twelve thousand *were*
        sealed;
    of the tribe of Issachar twelve thousand
        were sealed;

Commitment: When Leaders Are Tested, Commitment Is Revealed

(Revelation 7:4–17)

Tribulation always tests a leader's commitment level. Trouble doesn't always make a leader become committed, but it does reveal his or her commitment. Unless leaders remain committed, they will be tempted to hesitate or withdraw in tough times. This is why leaders must begin with commitment, before they are tested.

---

[8]   of the tribe of Zebulun twelve thousand
        were sealed;
    of the tribe of Joseph twelve thousand *were*
        sealed;
    of the tribe of Benjamin twelve thousand
        were sealed.

A Multitude from the Great Tribulation

[9]After these things I looked, and behold, a great multitude which no one could number, of all nations, tribes, peoples, and tongues, standing before the throne and before the Lamb, clothed with white robes, with palm branches in their hands, [10]and crying out with a loud voice, saying, "Salvation *belongs* to our God who sits on the throne, and to the Lamb!" [11]All the angels stood around the throne and the elders and the four living creatures, and fell on their faces before the throne and worshiped God, [12]saying:

"Amen! Blessing and glory and wisdom,
    Thanksgiving and honor and power and
        might,
Be to our God forever and ever.
    Amen."

[13]Then one of the elders answered, saying to me, "Who are these arrayed in white robes, and where did they come from?"

6:12 [a]NU-Text and M-Text omit *behold.*
[b]NU-Text and M-Text read *the whole moon.*
6:15 [a]NU-Text and M-Text read *the commanders, the rich men.* **7:5** [a]In NU-Text and M-Text *were sealed* is stated only in verses 5a and 8c; the words are understood in the remainder of the passage.

[14]And I said to him, "Sir,[a] you know."

So he said to me, "These are the ones who come out of the great tribulation, and washed their robes and made them white in the blood of the Lamb. [15]Therefore they are before the throne of God, and serve Him day and night in His temple. And He who sits on the throne will dwell among them. [16]They shall neither hunger anymore nor thirst anymore; the sun shall not strike them, nor any heat; [17]for the Lamb who is in the midst of the throne will shepherd them and lead them to living fountains of waters.[a] And God will wipe away every tear from their eyes."

Seventh Seal: Prelude to the Seven Trumpets

8 When He opened the seventh seal, there was silence in heaven for about half an hour. [2]And I saw the seven angels who stand before God, and to them were given seven trumpets. [3]Then another angel, having a golden censer, came and stood at the altar. He was given much incense, that he should offer *it* with the prayers of all the saints upon the golden altar which was before the throne. [4]And the smoke of the incense, with the prayers of the saints, ascended before God from the angel's hand. [5]Then the angel took the censer, filled it with fire from the altar, and threw *it* to the earth. And there were noises, thunderings, lightnings, and an earthquake.

[6]So the seven angels who had the seven trumpets prepared themselves to sound.

First Trumpet: Vegetation Struck

[7]The first angel sounded: And hail and fire followed, mingled with blood, and they were thrown to the earth.[a] And a third of the trees were burned up, and all green grass was burned up.

Second Trumpet: The Seas Struck

[8]Then the second angel sounded: And *something* like a great mountain burning with fire was thrown into the sea, and a third of the sea became blood. [9]And a third of the living creatures in the sea died, and a third of the ships were destroyed.

Third Trumpet: The Waters Struck

[10]Then the third angel sounded: And a great star fell from heaven, burning like a torch, and it fell on a third of the rivers and on the springs of water. [11]The name of the star is Wormwood. A third of the waters became wormwood, and many men died from the water, because it was made bitter.

Fourth Trumpet: The Heavens Struck

[12]Then the fourth angel sounded: And a third of the sun was struck, a third of the moon, and a third of the stars, so that a third of them were darkened. A third of the day did not shine, and likewise the night.

[13]And I looked, and I heard an angel[a] flying through the midst of heaven, saying with a loud voice, "Woe, woe, woe to the inhabitants of the earth, because of the remaining blasts of the trumpet of the three angels who are about to sound!"

Fifth Trumpet: The Locusts from the Bottomless Pit

9 Then the fifth angel sounded: And I saw a star fallen from heaven to the earth. To him was given the key to the bottomless pit. [2]And he opened the bottomless pit, and smoke arose out of the pit like the smoke of a great furnace. So the sun and the air were darkened because of the smoke of the pit. [3]Then out of the smoke locusts came upon the earth. And to them was given power, as the scorpions of the earth have power. [4]They were commanded not to harm the grass of the earth, or any green thing, or any tree, but only those men who do not have the seal of God on their foreheads. [5]And they were not given *authority* to kill them, but to torment them *for* five months. Their torment *was* like the torment of a scorpion when it strikes a man. [6]In those days men will seek death and will not find it; they will desire to die, and death will flee from them.

[7]The shape of the locusts was like horses prepared for battle. On their heads were crowns of something like gold, and their faces *were* like the faces of men. [8]They had hair like women's hair, and their teeth were like lions' *teeth*. [9]And they had breastplates like breastplates of iron, and the sound of their wings *was* like the sound of chariots with many horses running into battle. [10]They had tails like scorpions, and there were stings in their tails. Their power *was* to hurt men five months. [11]And they had as king over them the angel of the bottomless pit, whose name in Hebrew *is* Abaddon, but in Greek he has the name Apollyon.

[12]One woe is past. Behold, still two more woes are coming after these things.

7:14 [a]NU-Text and M-Text read *My lord.*
7:17 [a]NU-Text and M-Text read *to fountains of the waters of life.* **8:7** [a]NU-Text and M-Text add *and a third of the earth was burned up.* **8:13** [a]NU-Text and M-Text read *eagle.*

Sixth Trumpet: The Angels from the Euphrates

[13]Then the sixth angel sounded: And I heard a voice from the four horns of the golden altar which is before God, [14]saying to the sixth angel who had the trumpet, "Release the four angels who are bound at the great river Euphrates." [15]So the four angels, who had been prepared for the hour and day and month and year, were released to kill a third of mankind. [16]Now the number of the army of the horsemen *was* two hundred million; I heard the number of them. [17]And thus I saw the horses in the vision: those who sat on them had breastplates of fiery red, hyacinth blue, and sulfur yellow; and the heads of the horses *were* like the heads of lions; and out of their mouths came fire, smoke, and brimstone. [18]By these three *plagues* a third of mankind was killed—by the fire and the smoke and the brimstone which came out of their mouths. [19]For their power[a] is in their mouth and in their tails; for their tails *are* like serpents, having heads; and with them they do harm.

[20]But the rest of mankind, who were not killed by these plagues, did not repent of the works of their hands, that they should not worship demons, and idols of gold, silver, brass, stone, and wood, which can neither see nor hear nor walk. [21]And they did not repent of their murders or their sorceries[a] or their sexual immorality or their thefts.

The Mighty Angel with the Little Book

10 I saw still another mighty angel coming down from heaven, clothed with a cloud. And a rainbow *was* on his head, his face *was* like the sun, and his feet like pillars of fire. [2]He had a little book open in his hand. And he set his right foot on the sea and *his* left *foot* on the land, [3]and cried with a loud voice, as *when* a lion roars. When he cried out, seven thunders uttered their voices. [4]Now when the seven thunders uttered their voices,[a] I was about to write; but I heard a voice from heaven saying to me,[b] "Seal up the things which the seven thunders uttered, and do not write them."

[5]The angel whom I saw standing on the sea and on the land raised up his hand[a] to heaven [6]and swore by Him who lives forever and ever, who created heaven and the things that are in it, the earth and the things that are in it, and the sea and the things that are in it, that there should be delay no longer, [7]but in the days of the sounding of the seventh angel, when he is about to sound, the mystery of God would be finished, as He declared to His servants the prophets.

John Eats the Little Book

[8]Then the voice which I heard from heaven spoke to me again and said, "Go, take the little book which is open in the hand of the angel who stands on the sea and on the earth."

[9]So I went to the angel and said to him, "Give me the little book."

And he said to me, "Take and eat it; and it will make your stomach bitter, but it will be as sweet as honey in your mouth."

[10]Then I took the little book out of the angel's hand and ate it, and it was as sweet as honey in my mouth. But when I had eaten it, my stomach became bitter. [11]And he[a] said to me, "You must prophesy again about many peoples, nations, tongues, and kings."

The Two Witnesses

11 Then I was given a reed like a measuring rod. And the angel stood,[a] saying, "Rise and measure the temple of God, the altar, and those who worship there. [2]But leave out the court which is outside the temple, and do not measure it, for it has been given to the Gentiles. And they will tread the holy city underfoot *for* forty-two months. [3]And I will give *power* to my two witnesses, and they will prophesy one thousand two hundred and sixty days, clothed in sackcloth."

[4]These are the two olive trees and the two lampstands standing before the God[a] of the earth. [5]And if anyone wants to harm them, fire proceeds from their mouth and devours their enemies. And if anyone wants to harm them, he must be killed in this manner. [6]These have power to shut heaven, so that no rain falls in the days of their prophecy; and they have power over waters to turn them to blood, and to strike the earth with all plagues, as often as they desire.

The Witnesses Killed

[7]When they finish their testimony, the beast that ascends out of the bottomless pit will make war against them, overcome them, and kill

---

9:19 [a]NU-Text and M-Text read *the power of the horses.* **9:21** [a]NU-Text and M-Text read *drugs.* **10:4** [a]NU-Text and M-Text read *sounded.* [b]NU-Text and M-Text omit *to me.* **10:5** [a]NU-Text and M-Text read *right hand.* **10:11** [a]NU-Text and M-Text read *they.* **11:1** [a]NU-Text and M-Text omit *And the angel stood.* **11:4** [a]NU-Text and M-Text read *Lord.*

The Law of Navigation: God Raises Up Leaders to Correct and Direct

(Revelation 11:3–13)

John describes two remarkable "witnesses" whom God will raise up as leaders during the Great Tribulation. Notice how John portrays these two end-times leaders:

1. They are given power over people and nature (vv. 3, 6).
2. They speak for the cause of righteousness (v. 3).
3. They are burdened for the world's condition (v. 3).
4. They are a source of light and hope (v. 4).
5. They are given divine protection (v. 5).
6. They eventually die for their cause (v. 7).
7. They and their cause ultimately succeed (vv. 11, 12).

Why will God raise up these leaders? Because the world will always need someone to practice the Law of Navigation. The spiritual vacuum in the world will call for leaders to correct and direct the people back to God. God will raise up these two leaders to chart the course for everyone. How does your leadership stack up to theirs?

---

them. ⁸And their dead bodies *will lie* in the street of the great city which spiritually is called Sodom and Egypt, where also our[a] Lord was crucified. ⁹Then *those* from the peoples, tribes, tongues, and nations will see their dead bodies three-and-a-half days, and not allow[a] their dead bodies to be put into graves. ¹⁰And those who dwell on the earth will rejoice over them, make merry, and send gifts to one another, because these two prophets tormented those who dwell on the earth.

The Witnesses Resurrected

¹¹Now after the three-and-a-half days the breath of life from God entered them, and they stood on their feet, and great fear fell on those who saw them. ¹²And they[a] heard a loud voice from heaven saying to them, "Come up here." And they ascended to heaven in a cloud, and their enemies saw them. ¹³In the same hour there

was a great earthquake, and a tenth of the city fell. In the earthquake seven thousand people were killed, and the rest were afraid and gave glory to the God of heaven.

¹⁴The second woe is past. Behold, the third woe is coming quickly.

Seventh Trumpet: The Kingdom Proclaimed

¹⁵Then the seventh angel sounded: And there were loud voices in heaven, saying, "The kingdoms[a] of this world have become *the kingdoms* of our Lord and of His Christ, and He shall reign forever and ever!" ¹⁶And the twenty-four elders who sat before God on their thrones fell on their faces and worshiped God, ¹⁷saying:

"We give You thanks, O Lord God Almighty,
The One who is and who was and who is to come,[a]
Because You have taken Your great power and reigned.
¹⁸ The nations were angry, and Your wrath has come,
And the time of the dead, that they should be judged,
And that You should reward Your servants the prophets and the saints,
And those who fear Your name, small and great,
And should destroy those who destroy the earth."

¹⁹Then the temple of God was opened in heaven, and the ark of His covenant[a] was seen in His temple. And there were lightnings, noises, thunderings, an earthquake, and great hail.

The Woman, the Child, and the Dragon

12 Now a great sign appeared in heaven: a woman clothed with the sun, with the moon under her feet, and on her head a garland of twelve stars. ²Then being with child, she cried out in labor and in pain to give birth.

³And another sign appeared in heaven: behold, a great, fiery red dragon having seven heads

---

11:8 [a]NU-Text and M-Text read *their*. **11:9** [a]NU-Text and M-Text read *nations see . . . and will not allow.* **11:12** [a]M-Text reads *I.* **11:15** [a]NU-Text and M-Text read *kingdom . . . has become.* **11:17** [a]NU-Text and M-Text omit *and who is to come.* **11:19** [a]M-Text reads *the covenant of the Lord.*

and ten horns, and seven diadems on his heads. [4]His tail drew a third of the stars of heaven and threw them to the earth. And the dragon stood before the woman who was ready to give birth, to devour her Child as soon as it was born. [5]She bore a male Child who was to rule all nations with a rod of iron. And her Child was caught up to God and His throne. [6]Then the woman fled into the wilderness, where she has a place prepared by God, that they should feed her there one thousand two hundred and sixty days.

Satan Thrown Out of Heaven

[7]And war broke out in heaven: Michael and his angels fought with the dragon; and the dragon and his angels fought, [8]but they did not prevail, nor was a place found for them[a] in heaven any longer. [9]So the great dragon was cast out, that serpent of old, called the Devil and Satan, who deceives the whole world; he was cast to the earth, and his angels were cast out with him.

[10]Then I heard a loud voice saying in heaven,

The Law of Victory: Godly Leadership Won't Succeed Without a Fight

(Revelation 12:7–12)

In order for leaders to find a way for the team to win, there must be a contest. In Revelation 12, we read about the ultimate contest between the forces of good and the forces of evil. The hosts of heaven take on the dragon and his angels. Good eventually wins out through the blood of Christ and the testimony of the believers (Rev. 12:11).

The truth for leaders? First, victory rarely comes without a fight. There is no success without sacrifice; there is a cost to every crown. The good news is, anything worth achieving is worth the battle. Second, victory rarely comes without a team effort. Michael didn't fight alone (12:7). The saints didn't overcome the enemy alone (12:11). God designed us to win in community. Third, victory should never come without a celebration. The heavens rejoice at the victory of the Lamb (12:12). The greater the victory, the bigger the celebration!

"Now salvation, and strength, and the kingdom of our God, and the power of His Christ have come, for the accuser of our brethren, who accused them before our God day and night, has been cast down. [11]And they overcame him by the blood of the Lamb and by the word of their testimony, and they did not love their lives to the death. [12]Therefore rejoice, O heavens, and you who dwell in them! Woe to the inhabitants of the earth and the sea! For the devil has come down to you, having great wrath, because he knows that he has a short time."

The Woman Persecuted

[13]Now when the dragon saw that he had been cast to the earth, he persecuted the woman who gave birth to the male *Child*. [14]But the woman was given two wings of a great eagle, that she might fly into the wilderness to her place, where she is nourished for a time and times and half a time, from the presence of the serpent. [15]So the serpent spewed water out of his mouth like a flood after the woman, that he might cause her to be carried away by the flood. [16]But the earth helped the woman, and the earth opened its mouth and swallowed up the flood which the dragon had spewed out of his mouth. [17]And the dragon was enraged with the woman, and he went to make war with the rest of her offspring, who keep the commandments of God and have the testimony of Jesus Christ.[a]

The Beast from the Sea

13 Then I[a] stood on the sand of the sea. And I saw a beast rising up out of the sea, having seven heads and ten horns,[b] and on his horns ten crowns, and on his heads a blasphemous name. [2]Now the beast which I saw was like a leopard, his feet were like *the feet of* a bear, and his mouth like the mouth of a lion. The dragon gave him his power, his throne, and great authority. [3]And *I saw* one of his heads as if it had been mortally wounded, and his deadly wound was healed. And all the world marveled and followed the beast. [4]So they worshiped the dragon who gave authority to the beast; and they worshiped the beast, saying, "Who *is* like the beast? Who is able to make war with him?"

[5]And he was given a mouth speaking great things and blasphemies, and he was given au-

---

12:8 [a]M-Text reads *him*. **12:17** [a]NU-Text and M-Text omit *Christ*. **13:1** [a]NU-Text reads *he*. [b]NU-Text and M-Text read *ten horns and seven heads*.

The Law of Buy-In: Passion Draws People, Even to the Wrong Causes

(Revelation 13:1–18)

The Beast demonstrates that leaders can have a passion for evil. This man builds a large following despite his immoral vision. This illustrates the awesome power of passion. People flock to passionate leaders, even when their cause is wrong. When people are attracted to the leader, they buy in to his vision.

thority to continue[a] for forty-two months. [6]Then he opened his mouth in blasphemy against God, to blaspheme His name, His tabernacle, and those who dwell in heaven. [7]It was granted to him to make war with the saints and to overcome them. And authority was given him over every tribe,[a] tongue, and nation. [8]All who dwell on the earth will worship him, whose names have not been written in the Book of Life of the Lamb slain from the foundation of the world.

[9]If anyone has an ear, let him hear. [10]He who leads into captivity shall go into captivity; he who kills with the sword must be killed with the sword. Here is the patience and the faith of the saints.

The Beast from the Earth

[11]Then I saw another beast coming up out of the earth, and he had two horns like a lamb and spoke like a dragon. [12]And he exercises all the authority of the first beast in his presence, and causes the earth and those who dwell in it to worship the first beast, whose deadly wound was healed. [13]He performs great signs, so that he even makes fire come down from heaven on the earth in the sight of men. [14]And he deceives those[a] who dwell on the earth by those signs which he was granted to do in the sight of the beast, telling those who dwell on the earth to make an image to the beast who was wounded by the sword and lived. [15]He was granted *power* to give breath to the image of the beast, that the image of the beast should both speak and cause as many as would not worship the image of the beast to be killed. [16]He causes all, both small and great, rich and poor, free and slave, to receive a mark on

their right hand or on their foreheads, [17]and that no one may buy or sell except one who has the mark or[a] the name of the beast, or the number of his name.

[18]Here is wisdom. Let him who has understanding calculate the number of the beast, for it is the number of a man: His number *is* 666.

The Lamb and the 144,000

14 Then I looked, and behold, a[a] Lamb standing on Mount Zion, and with Him one hundred *and* forty-four thousand, having[b] His Father's name written on their foreheads. [2]And I heard a voice from heaven, like the voice of many waters, and like the voice of loud thunder. And I heard the sound of harpists playing their harps. [3]They sang as it were a new song before the throne, before the four living creatures, and the elders; and no one could learn that song except the hundred *and* forty-four thousand who were redeemed from the earth. [4]These are the ones who were not defiled with women, for they are virgins. These are the ones who follow the Lamb wherever He goes. These were redeemed[a] from *among* men, *being* firstfruits to God and to the Lamb. [5]And in their mouth was found no deceit,[a] for they are without fault before the throne of God.[b]

The Proclamations of Three Angels

[6]Then I saw another angel flying in the midst of heaven, having the everlasting gospel to preach to those who dwell on the earth—to every nation, tribe, tongue, and people— [7]saying with a loud voice, "Fear God and give glory to Him, for the hour of His judgment has come; and worship Him who made heaven and earth, the sea and springs of water."

[8]And another angel followed, saying, "Babylon[a] is fallen, is fallen, that great city, because she has made all nations drink of the wine of the wrath of her fornication."

[9]Then a third angel followed them, saying with a loud voice, "If anyone worships the beast and his image, and receives *his* mark on his fore-

---

13:5 [a]M-Text reads *make war*. **13:7** [a]NU-Text and M-Text add *and people*. **13:14** [a]M-Text reads *my own people*. **13:17** [a]NU-Text and M-Text omit *or*. **14:1** [a]NU-Text and M-Text read *the*. [b]NU-Text and M-Text add *His name and*. **14:4** [a]M-Text adds *by Jesus*. **14:5** [a]NU-Text and M-Text read *falsehood*. [b]NU-Text and M-Text omit *before the throne of God*. **14:8** [a]NU-Text reads *Babylon the great is fallen, is fallen, which has made;* M-Text reads *Babylon the great is fallen. She has made.*

Justice: The Ultimate Leader Executes Justice for All

(Revelation 14:1—16:21)

Healthy leaders hunger for justice, not only in their organizations, but in the public arena. Here we see Jesus executing justice on the earth. As the Ultimate Leader, Christ feels motivated to provide justice to everyone. How about you? Are you doing anything to influence your world for the cause of justice?

head or on his hand, [10]he himself shall also drink of the wine of the wrath of God, which is poured out full strength into the cup of His indignation. He shall be tormented with fire and brimstone in the presence of the holy angels and in the presence of the Lamb. [11]And the smoke of their torment ascends forever and ever; and they have no rest day or night, who worship the beast and his image, and whoever receives the mark of his name."

[12]Here is the patience of the saints; here *are* those[a] who keep the commandments of God and the faith of Jesus.

[13]Then I heard a voice from heaven saying to me,[a] "Write: 'Blessed *are* the dead who die in the Lord from now on.'"

"Yes," says the Spirit, "that they may rest from their labors, and their works follow them."

Reaping the Earth's Harvest

[14]Then I looked, and behold, a white cloud, and on the cloud sat *One* like the Son of Man, having on His head a golden crown, and in His hand a sharp sickle. [15]And another angel came out of the temple, crying with a loud voice to Him who sat on the cloud, "Thrust in Your sickle and reap, for the time has come for You[a] to reap, for the harvest of the earth is ripe." [16]So He who sat on the cloud thrust in His sickle on the earth, and the earth was reaped.

Reaping the Grapes of Wrath

[17]Then another angel came out of the temple which is in heaven, he also having a sharp sickle. [18]And another angel came out from the altar, who had power over fire, and he cried with a loud cry to him who had the sharp sickle, saying,

"Thrust in your sharp sickle and gather the clusters of the vine of the earth, for her grapes are fully ripe." [19]So the angel thrust his sickle into the earth and gathered the vine of the earth, and threw *it* into the great winepress of the wrath of God. [20]And the winepress was trampled outside the city, and blood came out of the winepress, up to the horses' bridles, for one thousand six hundred furlongs.

Prelude to the Bowl Judgments

15 Then I saw another sign in heaven, great and marvelous: seven angels having the seven last plagues, for in them the wrath of God is complete.

[2]And I saw *something* like a sea of glass mingled with fire, and those who have the victory over the beast, over his image and over his mark[a] *and* over the number of his name, standing on the sea of glass, having harps of God. [3]They sing the song of Moses, the servant of God, and the song of the Lamb, saying:

"Great and marvelous *are* Your works,
   Lord God Almighty!
Just and true *are* Your ways,
   O King of the saints![a]
[4] Who shall not fear You, O Lord, and
   glorify Your name?
For *You* alone *are* holy.
For all nations shall come and worship
   before You,
For Your judgments have been
   manifested."

[5]After these things I looked, and behold,[a] the temple of the tabernacle of the testimony in heaven was opened. [6]And out of the temple came the seven angels having the seven plagues, clothed in pure bright linen, and having their chests girded with golden bands. [7]Then one of the four living creatures gave to the seven angels seven golden bowls full of the wrath of God who lives forever and ever. [8]The temple was filled with smoke from the glory of God and from His power, and no one was able to enter the temple till the seven plagues of the seven angels were completed.

14:12 [a]NU-Text and M-Text omit *here are those.*
14:13 [a]NU-Text and M-Text omit *to me.*
14:15 [a]NU-Text and M-Text omit *for You.*
15:2 [a]NU-Text and M-Text omit *over his mark.*
15:3 [a]NU-Text and M-Text read *nations.*
15:5 [a]NU-Text and M-Text omit *behold.*

16

Then I heard a loud voice from the temple saying to the seven angels, "Go and pour out the bowls[a] of the wrath of God on the earth."

First Bowl: Loathsome Sores

[2]So the first went and poured out his bowl upon the earth, and a foul and loathsome sore came upon the men who had the mark of the beast and those who worshiped his image.

Second Bowl: The Sea Turns to Blood

[3]Then the second angel poured out his bowl on the sea, and it became blood as of a dead *man;* and every living creature in the sea died.

Third Bowl: The Waters Turn to Blood

[4]Then the third angel poured out his bowl on the rivers and springs of water, and they became blood. [5]And I heard the angel of the waters saying:

" You are righteous, O Lord,[a]
    The One who is and who was and who is
        to be,[b]
    Because You have judged these things.
[6]   For they have shed the blood of saints and
        prophets,
    And You have given them blood to drink.
    For[a] it is their just due."

[7]And I heard another from[a] the altar saying, "Even so, Lord God Almighty, true and righteous *are* Your judgments."

Fourth Bowl: Men Are Scorched

[8]Then the fourth angel poured out his bowl on the sun, and power was given to him to scorch men with fire. [9]And men were scorched with great heat, and they blasphemed the name of God who has power over these plagues; and they did not repent and give Him glory.

Fifth Bowl: Darkness and Pain

[10]Then the fifth angel poured out his bowl on the throne of the beast, and his kingdom became full of darkness; and they gnawed their tongues because of the pain. [11]They blasphemed the God of heaven because of their pains and their sores, and did not repent of their deeds.

Sixth Bowl: Euphrates Dried Up

[12]Then the sixth angel poured out his bowl on the great river Euphrates, and its water was dried up, so that the way of the kings from the east might be prepared. [13]And I saw three unclean spirits like frogs *coming* out of the mouth of the dragon, out of the mouth of the beast, and out of the mouth of the false prophet. [14]For they are spirits of demons, performing signs, *which* go out to the kings of the earth and[a] of the whole world, to gather them to the battle of that great day of God Almighty.

[15]"Behold, I am coming as a thief. Blessed *is* he who watches, and keeps his garments, lest he walk naked and they see his shame."

[16]And they gathered them together to the place called in Hebrew, Armageddon.[a]

Seventh Bowl: The Earth Utterly Shaken

[17]Then the seventh angel poured out his bowl into the air, and a loud voice came out of the temple of heaven, from the throne, saying, "It is done!" [18]And there were noises and thunderings and lightnings; and there was a great earthquake, such a mighty and great earthquake as had not occurred since men were on the earth. [19]Now the great city was divided into three parts, and the cities of the nations fell. And great Babylon was remembered before God, to give her the cup of the wine of the fierceness of His wrath. [20]Then every island fled away, and the mountains were not found. [21]And great hail from heaven fell upon men, *each hailstone* about the weight of a talent. Men blasphemed God because of the plague of the hail, since that plague was exceedingly great.

The Scarlet Woman and the Scarlet Beast

17

Then one of the seven angels who had the seven bowls came and talked with me, saying to me,[a] "Come, I will show you the judgment of the great harlot who sits on many waters, [2]with whom the kings of the earth committed fornication, and the inhabitants of the earth were made drunk with the wine of her fornication."

[3]So he carried me away in the Spirit into the wilderness. And I saw a woman sitting on a scarlet beast *which was* full of names of blasphemy, having seven heads and ten horns. [4]The woman

16:1 [a]NU-Text and M-Text read *seven bowls.*
16:5 [a]NU-Text and M-Text omit *O Lord.*
[b]NU-Text and M-Text read *who was, the Holy One.*
16:6 [a]NU-Text and M-Text omit *For.*
16:7 [a]NU-Text and M-Text omit *another from.*
16:14 [a]NU-Text and M-Text omit *of the earth and.*
16:16 [a]M-Text reads *Megiddo.* **17:1** [a]NU-Text and M-Text omit *to me.*

was arrayed in purple and scarlet, and adorned with gold and precious stones and pearls, having in her hand a golden cup full of abominations and the filthiness of her fornication.[a] 5And on her forehead a name *was* written:

MYSTERY, BABYLON THE GREAT,
THE MOTHER OF HARLOTS AND
OF THE ABOMINATIONS OF
THE EARTH.

6I saw the woman, drunk with the blood of the saints and with the blood of the martyrs of Jesus. And when I saw her, I marveled with great amazement.

The Meaning of the Woman and the Beast

7But the angel said to me, "Why did you marvel? I will tell you the mystery of the woman and of the beast that carries her, which has the seven heads and the ten horns. 8The beast that you saw was, and is not, and will ascend out of the bottomless pit and go to perdition. And those who dwell on the earth will marvel, whose names are not written in the Book of Life from the foundation of the world, when they see the beast that was, and is not, and yet is.[a]

9"Here *is* the mind which has wisdom: The seven heads are seven mountains on which the woman sits. 10There are also seven kings. Five have fallen, one is, *and* the other has not yet come. And when he comes, he must continue a short time. 11The beast that was, and is not, is himself also the eighth, and is of the seven, and is going to perdition.

12"The ten horns which you saw are ten kings who have received no kingdom as yet, but they receive authority for one hour as kings with the beast. 13These are of one mind, and they will give their power and authority to the beast. 14These will make war with the Lamb, and the Lamb will overcome them, for He is Lord of lords and King of kings; and those *who are* with Him *are* called, chosen, and faithful."

15Then he said to me, "The waters which you saw, where the harlot sits, are peoples, multitudes, nations, and tongues. 16And the ten horns which you saw on[a] the beast, these will hate the harlot, make her desolate and naked, eat her flesh and burn her with fire. 17For God has put it into their hearts to fulfill His purpose, to be of one mind, and to give their kingdom to the beast, until the words of God are fulfilled. 18And the woman whom you saw is that great city which reigns over the kings of the earth."

The Fall of Babylon the Great

18 After these things I saw another angel coming down from heaven, having great authority, and the earth was illuminated with his glory. 2And he cried mightily[a] with a loud voice, saying, "Babylon the great is fallen, is fallen, and has become a dwelling place of demons, a prison for every foul spirit, and a cage for every unclean and hated bird! 3For all the nations have drunk of the wine of the wrath of her fornication, the kings of the earth have committed fornication with her, and the merchants of the earth have become rich through the abundance of her luxury."

4And I heard another voice from heaven saying, "Come out of her, my people, lest you share in her sins, and lest you receive of her plagues. 5For her sins have reached[a] to heaven, and God has remembered her iniquities. 6Render to her just as she rendered to you,[a] and repay her double according to her works; in the cup which she has mixed, mix double for her. 7In the measure that she glorified herself and lived luxuriously, in the same measure give her torment and sorrow; for she says in her heart, 'I sit *as* queen, and am no widow, and will not see sorrow.' 8Therefore her plagues will come in one day—death and mourning and famine. And she will be utterly burned with fire, for strong *is* the Lord God who judges[a] her.

The World Mourns Babylon's Fall

9"The kings of the earth who committed fornication and lived luxuriously with her will weep and lament for her, when they see the smoke of her burning, 10standing at a distance for fear of her torment, saying, 'Alas, alas, that great city Babylon, that mighty city! For in one hour your judgment has come.'

11"And the merchants of the earth will weep and mourn over her, for no one buys their merchandise anymore: 12merchandise of gold and silver, precious stones and pearls, fine linen and purple, silk and scarlet, every kind of citron wood, every kind of object of ivory, every kind of object of most precious wood, bronze, iron, and marble; 13and cinnamon and incense, fragrant oil and frankincense, wine and oil, fine flour and wheat, cattle and sheep, horses and chariots, and

---

17:4 [a]M-Text reads *the filthiness of the fornication of the earth.* **17:8** [a]NU-Text and M-Text read *and shall be present.* **17:16** [a]NU-Text and M-Text read *saw, and the beast.* **18:2** [a]NU-Text and M-Text omit *mightily.* **18:5** [a]NU-Text and M-Text read *have been heaped up.* **18:6** [a]NU-Text and M-Text omit *to you.* **18:8** [a]NU-Text and M-Text read *has judged.*

bodies and souls of men. [14]The fruit that your soul longed for has gone from you, and all the things which are rich and splendid have gone from you,[a] and you shall find them no more at all. [15]The merchants of these things, who became rich by her, will stand at a distance for fear of her torment, weeping and wailing, [16]and saying, 'Alas, alas, that great city that was clothed in fine linen, purple, and scarlet, and adorned with gold and precious stones and pearls! [17]For in one hour such great riches came to nothing.' Every shipmaster, all who travel by ship, sailors, and as many as trade on the sea, stood at a distance [18]and cried out when they saw the smoke of her burning, saying, 'What is like this great city?'

[19]"They threw dust on their heads and cried out, weeping and wailing, and saying, 'Alas, alas, that great city, in which all who had ships on the sea became rich by her wealth! For in one hour she is made desolate.'

[20]"Rejoice over her, O heaven, and you holy apostles[a] and prophets, for God has avenged you on her!"

Finality of Babylon's Fall

[21]Then a mighty angel took up a stone like a great millstone and threw it into the sea, saying, "Thus with violence the great city Babylon shall be thrown down, and shall not be found anymore. [22]The sound of harpists, musicians, flutists, and trumpeters shall not be heard in you anymore. No craftsman of any craft shall be found in you anymore, and the sound of a millstone shall not be heard in you anymore. [23]The light of a lamp shall not shine in you anymore, and the voice of bridegroom and bride shall not be heard in you anymore. For your merchants were the great men of the earth, for by your sorcery all the nations were deceived. [24]And in her was found the blood of prophets and saints, and of all who were slain on the earth."

Heaven Exults over Babylon

19 After these things I heard[a] a loud voice of a great multitude in heaven, saying, "Alleluia! Salvation and glory and honor and power belong to the Lord[b] our God! [2]For true and righteous are His judgments, because He has judged the great harlot who corrupted the earth with her fornication; and He has avenged on her the blood of His servants shed by her." [3]Again they said, "Alleluia! Her smoke rises up forever and ever!" [4]And the twenty-four elders and the four living creatures fell down and worshiped God who sat on the throne, saying, "Amen! Alleluia!" [5]Then a voice came from the throne, saying, "Praise our God, all you His servants and those who fear Him, both[a] small and great!"

[6]And I heard, as it were, the voice of a great multitude, as the sound of many waters and as the sound of mighty thunderings, saying, "Alleluia!

18:14 [a]NU-Text and M-Text read been lost to you.
18:20 [a]NU-Text and M-Text read saints and apostles.
19:1 [a]NU-Text and M-Text add something like.
[b]NU-Text and M-Text omit the Lord.
19:5 [a]NU-Text and M-Text omit both.

Problem Solving:
Jesus Resolves Earth's Conflict at Its Root
(Revelation 19:1–21)

Jesus will take decisive action to resolve the world conflict raging during the Great Tribulation. Four times heavenly voices shout "Alleluia!" to celebrate the end of the problems that prevailed on the earth for seven long years.

Like any effective leader, Jesus didn't merely put a bandage on the problem; He solved it permanently. Take note of how efficiently the King of kings has and will take care of man's root problems:

Our Greatest Problem	Why?	How Christ Solved It
1. Our greatest flaw: sin.	1. It leads to death.	1. He died for our sin.
2. Our greatest defeat: death.	2. It severs us from God.	2. He eliminated death.
3. Our greatest emotion: fear.	3. We fear dying.	3. He rose from the dead.
4. Our greatest enemy: Satan.	4. He destroys us.	4. He will cast him into hell.

For the[a] Lord God Omnipotent reigns! [7]Let us be glad and rejoice and give Him glory, for the marriage of the Lamb has come, and His wife has made herself ready." [8]And to her it was granted to be arrayed in fine linen, clean and bright, for the fine linen is the righteous acts of the saints.

[9]Then he said to me, "Write: 'Blessed *are* those who are called to the marriage supper of the Lamb!' " And he said to me, "These are the true sayings of God." [10]And I fell at his feet to worship him. But he said to me, "See *that you do not do that!* I am your fellow servant, and of your brethren who have the testimony of Jesus. Worship God! For the testimony of Jesus is the spirit of prophecy."

Christ on a White Horse

[11]Now I saw heaven opened, and behold, a white horse. And He who sat on him *was* called Faithful and True, and in righteousness He judges and makes war. [12]His eyes *were* like a flame of fire, and on His head *were* many crowns. He had[a] a name written that no one knew except Himself. [13]He *was* clothed with a robe dipped in blood, and His name is called The Word of God. [14]And the armies in heaven, clothed in fine linen, white and clean,[a] followed Him on white horses. [15]Now out of His mouth goes a sharp[a] sword, that with it He should strike the nations. And He Himself will rule them with a rod of iron. He Himself treads the winepress of the fierceness and wrath of Almighty God. [16]And He has on *His* robe and on His thigh a name written:

KING OF KINGS AND
LORD OF LORDS.

The Beast and His Armies Defeated

[17]Then I saw an angel standing in the sun; and he cried with a loud voice, saying to all the birds that fly in the midst of heaven, "Come and gather together for the supper of the great God,[a] [18]that you may eat the flesh of kings, the flesh of captains, the flesh of mighty men, the flesh of horses and of those who sit on them, and the flesh of all *people,* free[a] and slave, both small and great."

[19]And I saw the beast, the kings of the earth, and their armies, gathered together to make war against Him who sat on the horse and against His army. [20]Then the beast was captured, and with him the false prophet who worked signs in his presence, by which he deceived those who received the mark of the beast and those who worshiped his image. These two were cast alive into the lake of fire burning with brimstone.

[21]And the rest were killed with the sword which proceeded from the mouth of Him who sat on the horse. And all the birds were filled with their flesh.

Satan Bound 1000 Years

20 Then I saw an angel coming down from heaven, having the key to the bottomless pit and a great chain in his hand. [2]He laid hold of the dragon, that serpent of old, who is *the* Devil and Satan, and bound him for a thousand years; [3]and he cast him into the bottomless pit, and shut him up, and set a seal on him, so that he should deceive the nations no more till the thousand years were finished. But after these things he must be released for a little while.

The Saints Reign with Christ 1000 Years

[4]And I saw thrones, and they sat on them, and judgment was committed to them. Then *I saw* the souls of those who had been beheaded for their witness to Jesus and for the word of God, who had not worshiped the beast or his image, and had not received *his* mark on their foreheads or on their hands. And they lived and reigned with Christ for a[a] thousand years. [5]But the rest of the dead did not live again until the thousand years were finished. This *is* the first resurrection. [6]Blessed and holy *is* he who has part in the first resurrection. Over such the second death has no power, but they shall be priests of God and of Christ, and shall reign with Him a thousand years.

Satanic Rebellion Crushed

[7]Now when the thousand years have expired, Satan will be released from his prison [8]and will go out to deceive the nations which are in the four corners of the earth, Gog and Magog, to gather them together to battle, whose number *is* as the sand of the sea. [9]They went up on the breadth of the earth and surrounded the camp of the saints and the beloved city. And fire came down from God out of heaven and devoured them. [10]The devil, who deceived them, was cast into the lake of fire and brimstone where[a] the

19:6 [a]NU-Text and M-Text read *our.*
19:12 [a]M-Text adds *names written, and.*
19:14 [a]NU-Text and M-Text read *pure white linen.*
19:15 [a]M-Text adds *two-edged.* **19:17** [a]NU-Text and M-Text read *the great supper of God.*
19:18 [a]NU-Text and M-Text read *both free.*
20:4 [a]M-Text reads *the.* **20:10** [a]NU-Text and M-Text add *also.*

beast and the false prophet *are*. And they will be tormented day and night forever and ever.

The Great White Throne Judgment

[11]Then I saw a great white throne and Him who sat on it, from whose face the earth and the heaven fled away. And there was found no place for them. [12]And I saw the dead, small and great, standing before God,[a] and books were opened. And another book was opened, which is *the Book of Life*. And the dead were judged according to their works, by the things which were written in the books. [13]The sea gave up the dead who were in it, and Death and Hades delivered up the dead who were in them. And they were judged, each one according to his works. [14]Then Death and Hades were cast into the lake of fire. This is the second death.[a] [15]And anyone not found written in the Book of Life was cast into the lake of fire.

All Things Made New

21 Now I saw a new heaven and a new earth, for the first heaven and the first earth had passed away. Also there was no more sea. [2]Then I, John,[a] saw the holy city, New Jerusalem, coming down out of heaven from God, prepared as a bride adorned for her husband. [3]And I heard a loud voice from heaven saying, "Behold, the tabernacle of God *is* with men, and He will dwell with them, and they shall be His people. God Himself will be with them *and be* their God. [4]And God will wipe away every tear from their eyes; there shall be no more death, nor sorrow, nor crying. There shall be no more pain, for the former things have passed away."

[5]Then He who sat on the throne said, "Behold, I make all things new." And He said to me,[a]

"Write, for these words are true and faithful."

[6]And He said to me, "It is done![a] I am the Alpha and the Omega, the Beginning and the End. I will give of the fountain of the water of life freely to him who thirsts. [7]He who overcomes shall inherit all things,[a] and I will be his God and he shall be My son. [8]But the cowardly, unbelieving,[a] abominable, murderers, sexually immoral, sorcerers, idolaters, and all liars shall have their part in the lake which burns with fire and brimstone, which is the second death."

The New Jerusalem

[9]Then one of the seven angels who had the seven bowls filled with the seven last plagues came to me[a] and talked with me, saying, "Come, I will show you the bride, the Lamb's wife."[b] [10]And he carried me away in the Spirit to a great and high mountain, and showed me the great city, the holy[a] Jerusalem, descending out of heaven from God, [11]having the glory of God. Her light *was* like a most precious stone, like a jasper stone, clear as crystal. [12]Also she had a great and high wall with twelve gates, and twelve angels at the gates, and names written on them, which are *the names* of the twelve tribes of the children of Israel: [13]three gates on the east, three gates on the north, three gates on the south, and three gates on the west.

[14]Now the wall of the city had twelve foundations, and on them were the names[a] of the twelve apostles of the Lamb. [15]And he who talked with me had a gold reed to measure the city, its gates, and its wall. [16]The city is laid out as a square; its length is as great as its breadth. And he measured the city with the reed: twelve thousand furlongs. Its length, breadth, and height are equal. [17]Then he measured its wall: one hundred *and* forty-four cubits, *according* to the measure of a man, that is, of an angel. [18]The construction of its wall was *of* jasper; and the city *was* pure gold, like clear glass. [19]The foundations of the wall of the city *were* adorned with all kinds of precious stones: the first foundation *was* jasper, the second

---

Vision: The Ultimate Leader Reveals His Person and Plan

(Revelation 21:1–7)

The vision of Christ for a new heaven and earth is creative (Rev. 21:1, 2), an improvement on the present (21:3), meets needs (21:4), and offers a permanent solution (21:6). Vision is an informed bridge to a better tomorrow. Jesus restores what we lost in the Garden of Eden.

20:12 [a]NU-Text and M-Text read *the throne*.
20:14 [a]NU-Text and M-Text add *the lake of fire*.
21:2 [a]NU-Text and M-Text omit *John*.
21:5 [a]NU-Text and M-Text omit *to me*.
21:6 [a]M-Text omits *It is done*. **21:7** [a]M-Text reads *overcomes, I shall give him these things*. **21:8** [a]M-Text adds *and sinners*. **21:9** [a]NU-Text and M-Text omit *to me*. [b]M-Text reads *I will show you the woman, the Lamb's bride*. **21:10** [a]NU-Text and M-Text omit *the great* and read *the holy city, Jerusalem*. **21:14** [a]NU-Text and M-Text read *twelve names*.

sapphire, the third chalcedony, the fourth emerald, [20]the fifth sardonyx, the sixth sardius, the seventh chrysolite, the eighth beryl, the ninth topaz, the tenth chrysoprase, the eleventh jacinth, and the twelfth amethyst. [21]The twelve gates *were* twelve pearls: each individual gate was of one pearl. And the street of the city *was* pure gold, like transparent glass.

The Glory of the New Jerusalem

[22]But I saw no temple in it, for the Lord God Almighty and the Lamb are its temple. [23]The city had no need of the sun or of the moon to shine in it,[a] for the glory[b] of God illuminated it. The Lamb *is* its light. [24]And the nations of those who are saved[a] shall walk in its light, and the kings of the earth bring their glory and honor into it.[b] [25]Its gates shall not be shut at all by day (there shall be no night there). [26]And they shall bring the glory and the honor of the nations into it.[a] [27]But there shall by no means enter it anything that defiles, or causes[a] an abomination or a lie, but only those who are written in the Lamb's Book of Life.

The River of Life

22 And he showed me a pure[a] river of water of life, clear as crystal, proceeding from the throne of God and of the Lamb. [2]In the middle of its street, and on either side of the river, *was* the tree of life, which bore twelve fruits, each *tree* yielding its fruit every month. The leaves of the tree *were* for the healing of the nations. [3]And there shall be no more curse, but the throne of God and of the Lamb shall be in it, and His servants shall serve Him. [4]They shall see His face, and His name *shall be* on their foreheads. [5]There shall be no night there: They need no lamp nor light of the sun, for the Lord God gives them light. And they shall reign forever and ever.

The Time Is Near

[6]Then he said to me, "These words *are* faithful and true." And the Lord God of the holy[a] prophets sent His angel to show His servants the things which must shortly take place.

[7]"Behold, I am coming quickly! Blessed *is* he who keeps the words of the prophecy of this book."

[8]Now I, John, saw and heard[a] these things. And when I heard and saw, I fell down to worship before the feet of the angel who showed me these things.

[9]Then he said to me, "See *that you do* not *do that.* For[a] I am your fellow servant, and of your brethren the prophets, and of those who keep the words of this book. Worship God." [10]And he said to me, "Do not seal the words of the prophecy of this book, for the time is at hand. [11]He who is unjust, let him be unjust still; he who is filthy, let him be filthy still; he who is righ-

21:23 [a]NU-Text and M-Text omit *in it.* [b]M-Text reads *the very glory.* **21:24** [a]NU-Text and M-Text omit *of those who are saved.* [b]M-Text reads *the glory and honor of the nations to Him.* **21:26** [a]M-Text adds *that they may enter in.* **21:27** [a]NU-Text and M-Text read *anything profane, nor one who causes.* **22:1** [a]NU-Text and M-Text omit *pure.* **22:6** [a]NU-Text and M-Text read *spirits of the prophets.* **22:8** [a]NU-Text and M-Text read *am the one who heard and saw.* **22:9** [a]NU-Text and M-Text omit *For.*

The Law of Victory: Jesus Reigns After Defeating the Enemy for Good

(Revelation 22:12–16)

You can almost hear John gasp as he describes the conditions of the Holy City, with its crystal clear river, its streets of transparent gold, and its splendid trees.

Christ has practiced the Law of Victory for the final time, finding a way for His people to win. He shares His victory, like a rich man shares his inheritance with his family. There is great *consolation,* great *celebration,* and great *confirmation* in this victory, as the Ultimate Leader keeps the promise of victory He made through the Old Testament prophets. The final book of the Bible refers to this victorious Leader by several names:

1. Faithful witness (1:5)
2. Firstborn from the dead (1:5)
3. Ruler of the kings (1:5)
4. Alpha and Omega (1:8)
5. Lion of the tribe of Judah (5:5)
6. The root of David (5:5)
7. The Lamb (17:14)
8. The Word of God (19:13)
9. King of kings (19:16)
10. Lord of lords (19:16)

teous, let him be righteous[a] still; he who is holy, let him be holy still."

Jesus Testifies to the Churches

[12]"And behold, I am coming quickly, and My reward *is* with Me, to give to every one according to his work. [13]I am the Alpha and the Omega, *the* Beginning and *the* End, the First and the Last."[a]

[14]Blessed *are* those who do His commandments,[a] that they may have the right to the tree of life, and may enter through the gates into the city. [15]But[a] outside *are* dogs and sorcerers and sexually immoral and murderers and idolaters, and whoever loves and practices a lie.

[16]"I, Jesus, have sent My angel to testify to you these things in the churches. I am the Root and the Offspring of David, the Bright and Morning Star."

[17]And the Spirit and the bride say, "Come!" And let him who hears say, "Come!" And let him who thirsts come. Whoever desires, let him take the water of life freely.

A Warning

[18]For[a] I testify to everyone who hears the words of the prophecy of this book: If anyone adds to these things, God will add[b] to him the plagues that are written in this book; [19]and if anyone takes away from the words of the book of this prophecy, God shall take away[a] his part from the Book[b] of Life, from the holy city, and *from* the things which are written in this book.

I Am Coming Quickly

[20]He who testifies to these things says, "Surely I am coming quickly."

Amen. Even so, come, Lord Jesus!

[21]The grace of our Lord Jesus Christ *be* with you all.[a] Amen.

22:11 [a]NU-Text and M-Text read *do right.*
22:13 [a]NU-Text and M-Text read *the First and the Last, the Beginning and the End.* **22:14** [a]NU-Text reads *wash their robes.* **22:15** [a]NU-Text and M-Text omit *But.* **22:18** [a]NU-Text and M-Text omit *For.* [b]M-Text reads *may God add.* **22:19** [a]M-Text reads *may God take away.* [b]NU-Text and M-Text read *tree of life.* **22:21** [a]NU-Text reads *with all;* M-Text reads *with all the saints.*

LEADERSHIP LAWS

The main article for each of the 21 Laws of Leadership is set in boldface color type.

The Law of the Lid

Saul and David's Success
  1 Samuel 17:24-40
Saul vs. David
  2 Samuel 5:1-4
As the Leader, So the Nation
  1 Kings 14:1—15:34

The Law of Influence

Jacob and Rebekah Deceive
  Genesis 25:29-34; 27:1-30
Joshua Expands Reach
  Numbers 14:6-9
God Uses Rahab
  Joshua 2:1-21
Tola and Jair's Influence
  Judges 10:1-6
Short-Lived Influence
  Judges 12:8-15
Samuel's Influence
  1 Samuel 7:1-17
David Led Before Saul Left
  1 Chronicles 11:1-3
Esther's Influence
  Esther 1:12
Measuring Leadership
  Psalm 82:1-8
People Thrive or Groan
  Proverbs 29:2-18
A Woman of Influence
  Proverbs 31:10-31
Can't Force Action
  Ezekiel 14:12-14
Amos Judges Leaders
  Amos 5:7-17

King Leads Nineveh
  Jonah 3:6-9
Woe to Abusive Leaders
  Micah 3:1-12
Ripple Effect
  Luke 19:1-27
Council Impacts Gentiles
  Acts 15:22-29
Emotional Authority
  Galatians 1:6-10

The Law of Process

Joseph's Leadership
  Genesis 37:1—50:22
Moses' Test of Time
  Exodus 2:1—4:31
Pictures of Growth
  1 Corinthians 3:1-23
Growth Not an Event
  Colossians 2:1-7
Perseverance Essential
  Hebrews 10:19-39
Like a Seed
  James 5:7, 8
Eight Characteristics
  2 Peter 1:5-11
Three Stages of Maturity
  1 John 2:12-14

The Law of Navigation

Plan Ahead
  Exodus 5:1
Planning and Structure
  Numbers 2:1-34

The Law of E. F. Hutton

The Law of Solid Ground

The Law of Respect

The Law of Intuition

Jesus Changes a City
John 4:1–26

Jesus a Shepherd
John 10:1–16

Paul Effective in Athens
Acts 17:22-34

Paul Touches Hearts
Romans 12:1, 2

Paul Illustrates and Invites
Galatians 3:6—4:31

Empowerment Precedes Imperative
Ephesians 1:1-14

Paul Mentors
1 Thessalonians 2:7-12

Paul Connects
Philemon 4–22

God Connects with Head and Heart
Hebrews 8:1—9:28

Love Is Gauge
1 John 2:7-11

Compassion Before Correction
Revelation 2:1-29

The Law of the Inner Circle

Moses Needed Aaron
Exodus 6:26—7:20

Moses Needed Help
Exodus 17:8-13

Moses Implemented Plan
Deuteronomy 1:6-18

Nathan Confronts David
2 Samuel 12:1-15

Loyalty Through Modeling
2 Samuel 23:14-17

Solomon Ensures Loyalty
1 Kings 2:1-46

Development Beats Discouragement
1 Kings 19:4-10

David and Those Closest to Him
1 Chronicles 11:10—12:40

Rehoboam
2 Chronicles 10:6-8

Where You Get Counsel
Psalm 1:1-3

Advisors Make or Break
Proverbs 11:14

John Feels Isolation
Matthew 11:2, 3

Jesus Prepared Men
Luke 9:28-36

When No One Sees
John 17:11-26

Paul's Team
1 Thessalonians 3:2-10

The Law of Empowerment

Joseph and His Brothers
Genesis 45:4–7

Pharaoh Violates Law
Exodus 1:8-22

Potential Leaders Need
Numbers 11:16-30

Saul Couldn't Give Power Away
1 Samuel 18:7-29

Hosea Loves by Decision
Hosea 3:1

Herod Abused Power
Matthew 2:3-18

Jesus Gave Power Away
Matthew 10:1-15

Jesus Touches Hearts
Matthew 11:28-30

Jesus Gave Authority
Mark 3:13-19

Jesus Empowered His Team
Luke 10:1-24

Jesus Gave Ministry Away
John 20:21, 22

Leaders Must Be Empowered
Acts 2:1-4

Barnabas Gives Power to Others
Acts 9:27

God Changes from Inside
Romans 5:12-21

Comfort Others
2 Corinthians 1:2-4

Paul Gives Power
Galatians 5:13-15

Influence from Identity
Ephesians 1:15-23

God Gives What We Need
2 Timothy 1:7, 8

Elders Mentor and Model
Titus 2:1-7

God Gave Us All
2 Peter 1:1-8

Love Casts Out Fear
1 John 4:17-21

Positive and Negative Reinforcement
Jude 14-16

The Law of Reproduction

Moses Became Leader
Exodus 18:19-26

Moses and Joshua
Numbers 27:18-23

Joshua Fails to Practice
Joshua 24:29

David Raised Up Leaders
1 Chronicles 12:1-38

Giant Killers
1 Chronicles 20:4-8

Nehemiah Develops Others
Nehemiah 2:5—6:14

Assyria's King Failed
Nahum 3:18, 19

Jesus Raised Up Leaders
Matthew 4:12-25

Jesus Prepared Leaders
Matthew 10:16-33

Jesus Turns Work Over
Luke 24:46-49

Lesson in Servanthood
John 6:3-14

Jesus' Great IDEA
John 14:12

Paul Trains Leaders
1 Thessalonians 1:5-8

Timothy to Equip Elders
1 Timothy 5:17-22

Lead Followers, Lead Leaders
2 Timothy 2:2

Titus to Prepare Leaders
Titus 1:5

Shepherding to Developing
Titus 2:15

The Law of Buy-In

Moses Gains Credibility
Exodus 14:1-28

Leading Change
Exodus 24:1-7

Balaam Fails to Observe
Numbers 22:5—24:25

Gideon: People Buy In
Judges 6:11—8:35

David Draws Loyal Renegades
1 Samuel 22:1—23:29

Why Before *What*
Nehemiah 2:5-17

Jesus Builds Team
Luke 5:1-11

Things Don't Make Leader
Ecclesiastes 2:1–26

What's Really Valuable
Jeremiah 9:23, 24

Jesus Didn't Let Others Dictate
Mark 1:32–38

Jesus Clarifies for Martha
Luke 10:38–42

Jesus Focused on Lost
Luke 15:1–32

Peter: Activity and Accomplishment
Acts 6:1–7

Redeem Your Time
Ephesians 5:15–17

Paul Narrowed Activities
Philippians 3:7–14

Leadership Begins at Home
1 Timothy 5:8

Timothy's Three Priorities
2 Timothy 4:1–8

How to Steward Resources
2 Peter 3:8–13

The Law of Sacrifice

God and Noah
Genesis 6:17, 18; 8:21, 22

Abraham Pays a Price
Genesis 22:1–18

Moses: Leader Must Give Up
Exodus 3:1—4:13

Give Up to Get It Right
Leviticus 1:1—6:30

Nazirites Give Up to Go Up
Numbers 6:1–21

Stop Sacrificing, Stop Succeeding
2 Samuel 11:1—12:31

Esther Gives Her Life
Esther 4:11–16

Things Don't Make Leader
Ecclesiastes 2:1–26

God Practices
Isaiah 43:1–7

Gave Up Loads to Lead
Jeremiah 1:18, 19

Hosea Marries Harlot
Hosea 1:2

Prepared in Wilderness
Matthew 4:1–11

Jesus Gave Up His Life
Matthew 26:47—27:54

Jesus Gave Up to Gain
Mark 15:15–24

Jesus Gave All Up
Luke 23:1–47

Jesus Gave Up to Go Up
John 12:24–33

Freedom Plus Responsibility
1 Corinthians 8:9–13

What Paul Gave Up
1 Corinthians 9:5–15

Leaders Stick with Mission
2 Corinthians 4:7–12

Steps of Servanthood
Philippians 2:2–11

Timothy Must Give Up
2 Timothy 3:10–17

Jesus Became Like Us
Hebrews 2:1–18

Moses Gave Up Riches
Hebrews 11:23–29

Christ Our Model
1 Peter 2:13–18

Leaders Humble Themselves
1 Peter 5:5–7

Jesus Served First
Revelation 5:11–14

The Law of Timing

God's Dynamic Leadership
Numbers 9:15-23

Divine Call and Charge
Joshua 1:1-9

Nehemiah Chose the Moment
Nehemiah 2:1-5

Esther: When to Lead
Esther 4:6-17

Leaders Value Time
Psalm 39:4, 5

A Season for Everything
Ecclesiastes 3:1-8

God Knows When and How
Malachi 4:5

Jesus' Visit to Lazarus
John 11:1-6

See Big Picture
2 Peter 3:8, 9

The Law of Explosive Growth

Solomon Impacted Others
1 Kings 10:24, 25

Vision and Values
Isaiah 1:10-17

Jesus Expands Training
Luke 9:1—10:24

Antioch Sends Leaders
Acts 13:1-3

Paul's Mini Seminary
Acts 19:8-10

Paul: Master of Growth
2 Timothy 2:1

The Law of Legacy

Success Without Successor
Deuteronomy 31:1-13

Tola and Jair's Influence
Judges 10:1-6

David and Solomon
1 Kings 1:28-40

David Sets Up Solomon
1 Chronicles 29:1-5

No Success Without Successor
Nehemiah 13:1-31

Jesus Raised Up Leaders
Matthew 4:12-25

Jesus Left Memorial
Matthew 26:17-30

Jesus: Leader's Lasting Value
Matthew 28:16-20

Jesus Turned Ministry Over
Mark 16:15, 16

Success Without Successor
John 21:15-17

Paul's Crown
2 Timothy 4:6-8

LEADERSHIP QUALITIES

Both positive and negative examples for each of the 21 Indispensable Qualities of a Leader are set in boldface color type.

Character

Breeds Perspective
> Genesis 50:15-21

Take It Seriously
> Leviticus 10:1—12:8

Foundational for Leaders
> Deuteronomy 5:1-22

Joshua and the Gibeonites
> Joshua 10:1-15

Boaz and Ruth Exhibit
> Ruth 4:1-6

Job Challenges Friends
> Job 6:1—7:21

Consistency
> Job 31:1-40

Moral Failure
> Proverbs 5:3-23

Sustain God's Conquest
> Lamentations 1:7, 8

Daniel Had What It Took
> **Daniel 2:48 (positive)**

Efficiency - Ethics = Emptiness
> Amos 1:1—2:16

Jonah Runs from Commitment
> Jonah 1:1-10

Can't Give What They Don't Have
> Micah 2:1-13

God Holds Leaders Responsible
> Micah 6:8

Herod Lacked It
> **Acts 12:1-23 (negative)**

Qualifications for Church Leadership
> Titus 1:5-9

Charisma

Ahab and Jezebel
> **1 Kings 19:1—22:40 (negative)**

Peter Compels Others
> Matthew 16:13-20

Peter a Magnet
> **Acts 2:1-41 (positive)**

Commitment

Esau Releases Jacob
> Genesis 33:1-4

Of a Leader
> Deuteronomy 7:7-9

Picture of Faithful Leader
> Joshua 24:29-31

Precedes Resources
> Ruth 1:1-22

Hezekiah Had It
> 2 Chronicles 31:20, 21

How to Beat Problems
> Nehemiah 4:1—5:13

Four Characteristics
> Nehemiah 6:15, 16

Steady at All Costs
> Job 13:15

Comes Before Provision
> Psalm 145:8-20

Resources Follow Resolve
> Daniel 3:1-18

Resources, Wisdom, People Follow
> Habakkuk 3:17-19

Before Authority, Responsibility
> Zechariah 10:1-3

All Leaders Must Demonstrate
    Matthew 8:18–34
From Care to Commitment
    Mark 8:1–21
Solve Problems
    Luke 8:26–37
Leaders Vote with Their Lives
    Luke 14:26, 27
Rich Young Ruler
    Luke 18:18–23
Leaders' Gethsemanes
    Luke 22:39–46
Jesus vs. Simon Peter
    Luke 22:54–62 (negative)
Jesus Clarified
    John 6:41–65
Stephen Knew What to Stand For
    Acts 7:2–60 (positive)
When Leaders Are Tested
    Revelation 7:4–17

Communication

Adam Failed to Connect
    Genesis 2:15–17; 3:1–6 (negative)
God Instructs
    Exodus 12:3–23
Joshua Gives Handles
    Joshua 4:1–9
Clear Communication
    1 Samuel 10:3—12:25 (positive)
Don't Go Until You Know
    2 Samuel 5:19, 23; 7:3–16
Leaders Communicate
    Psalm 19:1–14
Master Communication, Manage Conflict
    Proverbs 15:1–7

Communicate Until Results
    Isaiah 55:1–11
Use Memorable Imagery
    Jeremiah 2:1–16
Word Pictures
    Jeremiah 43:8–13
Communicating Vision
    Ezekiel 1:1–3
Zephaniah Spoke with Authority
    Zephaniah 1:1–18
Without It, Leader Travels Alone
    Zechariah 8:1–8
Words Shape Destiny
    Matthew 12:33–37
Test of Hostile Crowd
    Matthew 21:23–27
One Memorable Phrase
    John 3:16
Paul Adapts, Shares Story
    Acts 22:1–21; 26:4–23
When Plans Change
    2 Corinthians 1:12–17
Melchizedek
    Hebrews 7:1–22
Provide Action Steps
    Jude 17–23

Competence

Joshua Got the Job Done
    Joshua 11:16–23 (positive)
David's Royal Administration
    1 Chronicles 26:1—27:34
Eleven Keys to Excellence
    Psalm 78:72
A Gift in Action
    Daniel 4:8
Necessary Step to Excellence
    Luke 14:28–32 (negative)

Courage

Ruth Takes a Risk
Ruth 3:1-6

Samuel's Influence
1 Samuel 7:1-17

One Item Saul Forgot
1 Samuel 10:17—13:14 (negative)

Elijah's Fire and Passion
1 Kings 18:1-40 (positive)

Permission to Take Risks
Ezra 3:7

One Person Standing with God
Jeremiah 15:15-21

Ezekiel Speaks with Courage
Ezekiel 28:1-19

John Demonstrates
Matthew 3:1-10

Jesus Did the Unpopular
John 2:13-21

One Person a Majority
Acts 4:10-13

Taking a Stand
2 Timothy 2:22—3:17

Stand for Truth
2 Peter 2:1-6

Discernment

Balaam Didn't Get It
Numbers 22:21-35 (negative)

Nathan Saw Below Surface
2 Samuel 12:1-15 (positive)

Before Decision
1 Chronicles 12:32

Zerubbabel Reads People
Ezra 4:1-3

Leaders Assess, Then Respond
Ezekiel 18:1-32

Issue Was Justice, Not Fasting
Zechariah 7:1-10

Rich Young Ruler
Matthew 19:16-26

Leaders Read Situation
Acts 8:25-40

Paul Changed Plans
Acts 16:1-13

Leader as Doctor
Romans 3:21-26

Focus

Distraction
1 Kings 11:1-43

Too Many Pursuits
Ecclesiastes 2:1-11 (negative)

Jesus Not Distracted
Luke 4:18-29

Jesus Resolved
Luke 9:51-56

Letting Go
Philippians 3:5-9 (positive)

Leadership Built On
1 Peter 1:13-16

Generosity

Candle Loses Nothing
Deuteronomy 14:27—15:18

Boaz Doesn't Keep Score
Ruth 2:8—4:10 (positive)

Leaders Give First
Ecclesiastes 11:1-9

Leaders Bless People
Song of Solomon 4:1-16

Candle Loses Nothing
Luke 9:12-17

Ananias and Sapphira Pretended
Acts 5:1-11 (negative)

Can't Love Without Giving
2 Corinthians 8:2-5

Initiative

The Ultimate Leader
Genesis 1:1—2:25
Nehemiah Takes Lead
Nehemiah 1:4—2:8 (positive)
Lessons from the Ant
Proverbs 6:6-8
Earmark of True Leader
Jonah 2:10—3:10 (negative)
Leaders Host People
3 John 3-12

Listening

Samuel Learns to Listen
1 Samuel 3:1-3
David's Conflict Resolution
1 Samuel 26:1-25 (positive)
Rehoboam Fails to Listen
2 Chronicles 10:15 (negative)
Job's Friends Listen
Job 2:11-13
Earn Right to Be Heard
Habakkuk 1:1-11
Jesus Did This to Connect
Luke 2:42-52
Connect with Hearts
James 1:19

Passion

Purpose and Passion
Deuteronomy 4:32-40
Absalom Ruins Own Cause
2 Samuel 13:22—18:9 (negative)

Three Questions
Psalm 137:1-6
Consuming Love of God
Song of Solomon 1:1
John Served with Gusto
Luke 3:2-22 (positive)
Paul's Energy
1 Corinthians 9:19-27
Take Life and Love It
Ephesians 3:14-21
Run with Passion
Hebrews 12:1-3

Positive Attitude

Ten Spies vs. Two
Numbers 13:1—14:10
(positive and negative)
Leadership Development Begins
Matthew 5:1—7:29
Focus on God's Ability
Matthew 20:1-16
Jesus' First Job
Luke 6:20-23
Attitude of a Leader
Romans 1:1, 14-16
Determined Altitude
Philippians 1:12-18
The Mind to Make It
Philippians 4:11-13

Problem Solving

Sarah Has It Her Way
Genesis 16:1-16 (negative)
Moses: God's Problem Solver
Leviticus 15:1-33
Fastest Way to Leadership
Matthew 15:29-39

Man's Dilemma
Romans 1:17—2:29
101% Principle
1 Corinthians 1:4-10
Titus, the Man to Look For
Titus 1:10-14 (positive)
Healthy Confrontation
Philemon 8-10
Maintain Perspective
James 1:1-8
Reason, Results, Remedy
James 4:1-10
Jesus Resolves Earth's Conflicts
Revelation 19:1-21

Relationships

Abigail vs. Nabal
1 Samuel 25:1-42
(positive and negative)
Difficult People
2 Samuel 21:1-14
Job Takes High Road
Job 42:10
Partnerships
Proverbs 13:20
When People Are Esteemed
Proverbs 27:1-21
Leaders as Shepherds
Ezekiel 34:11-24
Get Along to Go Along
Romans 12:9-21
Paul Affirms by Name
Romans 16:1-21
Tough and Tender
2 Corinthians 7:8-13
Can't Divorce Leadership From
Colossians 3:18—4:6

Love out of Decision
James 2:1-9

Responsibility

Carry the Ball
2 Samuel 13:1-39
David Assumes Blame
1 Chronicles 21:1-17
Cannot Give Away
2 Chronicles 20:1-25 (positive)
Buck Stops with Leader
Jeremiah 38:1-6
Qualifications Are Prerequisite
Daniel 1:4-19
Pilate Failed to Lead
Matthew 27:11-31 (negative)
Caring in Crisis
Mark 14:32-42
Build Community
1 Corinthians 1:10
Carry the Ball
Galatians 6:1-6

Security

Nathan Feared No One
2 Samuel 12:1-14 (positive)
Found in the Lord
Psalm 127:1
Herod Felt Threat
Matthew 2:1-18 (negative)
Jesus Could Do Unpopular
Mark 11:15-17

Self-Discipline

Travel on Inside First
Numbers 33:1-49 (positive)

Samson Lost It
   Judges 16:1-20 (negative)
Job Maintains Perspective
   Job 1:1-22
If Leader Can't Rule Self
   Ezekiel 19:1-14
First Person You Lead
   Luke 4:3-10
Remove Stumbling Blocks
   1 Corinthians 6:1-20
Eternal Rewards
   1 Corinthians 9:24-27
Paul Mastered
   Philippians 4:1-19
Begins in the Mind
   Colossians 3:1-14
Lead Yourself Before Others
   Hebrews 12:5-13
Tame the Tongue
   James 3:1-18
Leadership Built On
   1 Peter 1:13-16

Servanthood

Leader as Servant
   Deuteronomy 15:12-18
Leaders Serve People
   2 Chronicles 22:1-9
Leader Who Lasts
   Ecclesiastes 8:1-9
Modeled by the Messiah
   Isaiah 52:13—53:12
Leaders Who Fail to Practice
   Micah 7:3, 4
Jesus Put Others First
   Matthew 14:1-14
Lead by Serving
   Matthew 20:25-28

Way Up Is Down
   Mark 9:33—10:16
Judas Fails Test
   Luke 22:1-23
Conflict Between Two Worldviews
   John 8:1-59 (negative)
Jesus Provides Visual Aid
   John 13:1-17 (positive)
Ultimate Radical Leader
   John 19:30
No Task Too Small
   Acts 11:22-24
Lose Right to Be Selfish
   Romans 15:1-6
Love Is Foundation
   1 Corinthians 13:4-7
Steps of Servanthood
   Philippians 2:2-11
Jesus Earns Right
   Hebrews 4:1-16
Measure of Commitment
   James 2:1-26

Teachability

Naaman Learned Lesson
   2 Kings 5:1-14
Leaders Must Be Teachable
   1 Chronicles 13:5-12
Keep Learning
   Jeremiah 18:18
King Is Slow to Learn
   Daniel 4:1-37 (negative)
Learn from History
   Zechariah 1:4-6
Peter's New Market
   Acts 11:1-18
Apollos Learned
   Acts 18:24-28 (positive)

Learn from Past
1 Corinthians 10:1-13

Lifelong Learners
Colossians 1:4-10

Jesus Learned Obedience
Hebrews 5:8

Vision

Abraham Seizes What He Sees
Genesis 12:1—22:4 (positive)

Esau Fails to See Big Picture
Genesis 25:29-34; 32:3-23; 33:1-20
(negative)

Leader's Motivation
Exodus 6:2, 3

Double Vision: Moses
Deuteronomy 27:1—28:68

Value of Vision
2 Samuel 5:1-12

Elisha's Divine Perspective
2 Kings 6:8-17

David Sees Bigger Picture
1 Chronicles 22:1-19

Abijah Gets Results
2 Chronicles 13:1-18

Followers and Leaders
Psalm 73:1-17

Hope for a Future
Proverbs 23:7-19

No Meaning, No Mission
Ecclesiastes 1:3-11

Value of Vision
Isaiah 4:2-6

Never Lose Big Picture
Isaiah 25:1-12

God-Given or Man-Made
Jeremiah 23:13-40

Communicating
Ezekiel 1:1-3

Seize Only What You See
Ezekiel 1:4-28

Revelation Without Action
Ezekiel 12:1-28

Hopeful Vision of Future
Amos 9:11-15

See It, Say It, Show It
Micah 4:1, 2

Blueprint for Building
Habakkuk 2:2, 3

People Energized
Zechariah 3:1-10

Power of a Picture
Zechariah 5:1-11

Process to Fulfilling
Matthew 9:35—10:5

Jesus Defined Mission
Matthew 13:3-58

Based on Values
Mark 8:31-33

Original Goal
Mark 13:1-37

Jesus' Compelling Vision
Luke 5:10

Communicate to Empower
and Direct
Acts 1:4-8

Peter's Paradigm Expands
Acts 10:1-35

Paul's Vision Led to Victory
Acts 26:12-29

Leader as Artist
Romans 4:1-22

Clear Image of Need
Romans 6:1—7:6

Paul's Thorn
2 Corinthians 12:7-9

LEADERSHIP ISSUES

Accountability

Gehazi Got from Elisha
  2 Kings 5:15-17
God Holds People Accountable
  Amos 3:1, 2
Team Accountable to Church
  Acts 14:26-28
Servants with Sacred Trust
  1 Corinthians 4:1-5
Alarm Bells
  Galatians 6:7-10
Paul Sent Timothy
  1 Thessalonians 3:1-10
Stewards of Resources
  Hebrews 13:17
Stricter Judgment
  James 3:1

Adaptability

Effective Leaders Adapt
  Ezekiel 3:8, 9

Anointing

Moses Leads From
  Exodus 34:5-7
Requirements and Results
  Deuteronomy 7:11-13
Fruit from God's
  Psalm 89:19-29
Purpose of God's
  Isaiah 61:1-3

Authority

Rod of God
  Exodus 17:3-7

Test: David Submits
  2 Samuel 1:17-27
Centurion Teaches
  Matthew 8:5-13
Submitting to God-Given
  Romans 13:1-7
Everyone Is Responsible
  Titus 3:1, 2

Brokenness

Jacob Made Usable
  Genesis 25:26—32:32
Breaking Before Blessing
  Genesis 32:24-32
Maturity Comes
  2 Samuel 18:19-33

Calling

When God Chooses
  Exodus 2:11—4:20
Aaron's Cost of Leadership
  Leviticus 7:33-35
God's Call, People's Confirmation
  Leviticus 8:1-36
Call of a Leader
  Isaiah 6:1-8
Responding to Divine Call
  Isaiah 6:1-8
God's Call and Empowerment
  Jeremiah 1:4-10
Necessity in Tough Times
  Ezekiel 2:1-10
Followers of God
  Matthew 5:1-48
Selection vs. Election
  Acts 9:1-20

Know Way to Show Way
Psalm 119:1-176

Discipline

Moral Failure
Proverbs 5:3-23
God Punishes, Rewards
Jeremiah 30:10-22
God's Method
Nahum 2:13

Emotions

Burnout
1 Kings 19:1-3
Leader and Stress
Psalm 23:1-6

Encouragement

Affirm Qualities in Others
Song of Solomon 1:10-15
Leaders Connect
Philippians 1:3-11
Paul Knew How
2 Thessalonians 1:3-6
Jesus Affirms Smyrna
Revelation 2:8-11

Equipping

Aaron Equips Moses
Exodus 5:1—12:37
Fruitfulness Is Fun
John 15:1-6
Tools to Do Job
Ephesians 2:8-22
The Leader's Job
Ephesians 4:12-16

Paul Was Provider
Colossians 1:28, 29
The Word of God
2 Timothy 3:16, 17

Ethics

Absolute Leader in Relative World
Psalm 18:1-34
Reflect God's Values
Isaiah 58:1-14
Efficiency - Ethics = Emptiness
Amos 1:1—2:16
Not Working for People
Ephesians 6:5-9

Evaluation

Round Two of Census
Numbers 26:1-63
God Looks at Heart
Ezekiel 11:1-13
What God Looks For
Ezekiel 22:30
Evaluation and Debriefing
Luke 10:17-20

Excellence

Leaders Set Standards
Malachi 1:7, 8

Excuses

Moses' Five Big Excuses
Exodus 3:11—4:14

False/Corrupt Leaders

Judah's Lousy Leaders
Isaiah 3:1-4

Mislead and Damage Others
Jeremiah 14:14-16
Measure of a Man
Jeremiah 22:6-30
Changing of the Guard
Jeremiah 23:1-16
Unrighteous Prunes Righteous
Jeremiah 27:1-8
Lessons from Lousy Leader
Luke 16:1-13
Man of Sin
2 Thessalonians 2:1-11

Family

Eli's Leadership
1 Samuel 2:12-17, 22-36
Genealogies
1 Chronicles 1:1—9:44
Leading Our Children
Proverbs 22:6
Woman of Influence
Proverbs 31:10-31
Leadership in the Home
Ephesians 5:21-33
Leadership in the Home
1 Peter 3:1-7

God-Appointed Leadership

Human Promotion
1 Samuel 8:4, 5
God Is Source of Success
Obadiah 2-4
Reluctant Leader
Jonah 3:1-3
See also Calling

Gratitude

David Returns Favor
2 Samuel 9:1-13

Growth

Learn from History
Zechariah 1:4-6
Role of the Wilderness
Luke 4:1-13
Seven Signs
Acts 5:1-42

Humanity

Don't Hide It
Psalm 6:1-10
Celebrate Diversity
1 Corinthians 12:14-31

Humility

Pharaoh Leads With
Genesis 41:1-55
Receive God's Grace
Deuteronomy 8:1-20
Mark of a Leader
1 Chronicles 17:1-27
Job Acknowledges Weakness
Job 40:3-5; 42:1-6
Benefits
Isaiah 10:1-6
Contrast in Pride and Humility
Daniel 2:1-28
God Still Rules
Hosea 14:1-7
Leader Who Follows God
2 Corinthians 3:4-6
Paul Never Forgot
1 Timothy 1:12-17

Long-Range Planning
   Matthew 1:1-17
Man with the Plan
   Matthew 25:1-30

Power

Jotham's Parable
   Judges 9:7-15
Difficulty of Handling
   1 Kings 6:1-38
Measure of a Man
   2 Kings 1:1-17
Never Underestimate God's
   2 Kings 20:1-7
Power Abuse: Edom
   Obadiah 8-14
Principle of Harvest
   Obadiah 15-18

Practicality

Practical Leader
   Nehemiah 8:8

Prayer

Nehemiah Prays First
   Nehemiah 1:4
Role of Praying and Planning
   Daniel 7:1—12:13
Influence in Prayer Closet
   Amos 7:1-6
Priority
   Luke 11:1-13
Leaders Need Partners
   1 Timothy 2:1-4
Leader as Intercessor
   James 5:13-20

Pride

Obsessed with Image
   2 Samuel 6:20
Riches to Rags
   Isaiah 14:3-23
Contrast in Pride and Humility
   Daniel 2:1-28
The Glory Factor
   1 Corinthians 1:18—2:5

Principle

Solomon Forgot Wisdom
   1 Kings 4:29-34
70-25-5 Principle
   1 Kings 10:1-9
Number One Principle
   Ezra 9:1—10:44
Principle-Centered Leadership
   Proverbs 4:20-27
Of Rewards
   Lamentations 4:6-8
Of Harvest
   Obadiah 15-18
Of Incarnation
   Jonah 2:7-9
Of the Seed
   Mark 4:2-20
Of Resting and Caring
   Mark 4:35-41
Jesus' Top Ten Principles
   Mark 8:34-38
101% Principle
   1 Corinthians 1:4-10

Priorities

Being Before *Doing*
   Ezra 7:10

Spirituality

Four Spiritual Flaws
    Numbers 20:10–12
Intimacy with God
    2 Samuel 6:1–23
Jabez
    1 Chronicles 4:9, 10
Natural vs. Spiritual
    Psalm 103:13–18
Balancing Childlike and Childish
    Psalm 131:1–3
Lead God's Family and Army
    Daniel 10:1–21
Qualifications of Leader
    1 Timothy 3:1–13
Qualities of Spiritual Leader
    1 Timothy 3:2–13
Role of Spiritual Leaders
    1 Peter 5:1–4

Standards

Raising Higher Standard
    Leviticus 18:1—21:24

Stewardship

Stewards Not Owners
    Psalm 104:1–5
Watchmen
    Ezekiel 33:1–6
What God Owns
    Malachi 3:8–12
Brokers of Resources
    Luke 19:11–26
Brokers of Gifts
    Romans 12:6–8
Invest Resources
    2 Corinthians 9:6–11

Strength

70-25-5 Principle
    1 Kings 10:1–9

Submission

Give God Credit
    1 Kings 8:12–61
God Raises Up and Removes
    Ezekiel 30:20–26
Everyone Is Responsible
    Titus 3:1, 2

Teamwork

Leaders Honor Teams
    Song of Solomon 4:1–16
Jesus Assembled Team
    Mark 2:14–17
Brokers of Gifts
    1 Corinthians 12:4–31
Paul Builds Unity
    Ephesians 4:1–8
Petty Differences
    Philippians 4:2, 3

Time

Do More with Less
    Psalm 90:12, 17
Waiting
    Habakkuk 2:1–20

Tolerance

Compromise: No Room For
    2 Chronicles 18:1–31

PROFILES IN LEADERSHIP

Aaron

Cost of Leadership
Leviticus 7:33-35

Abed-Nego

Courage Fueled by Faith
Daniel 3:16-18

Abigail

Law of Connection
1 Samuel 25:1-42

Abimelech

Self-Promotion
Judges 9:1-57

Abraham

Went the Distance
Genesis 12:1—25:11

Absalom

Tragic Case
2 Samuel 16:1—18:18

Achan

Ripple Effect of Sin
Joshua 7:1-25

Adam

Drops the Ball
Genesis 3:6-19

Agrippa

Power Trip
Acts 23:23—26:32

Amnon

No Self-Discipline
1 Chronicles 3:1

Amos

Prophet of Wrath and Mercy
Amos 4:1-12

Aquila

Trained More Leaders
Acts 18:24-28

Asa

Difficulty of Finishing Well
2 Chronicles 15:1—16:13

Athalia

Pursuing Power
2 Chronicles 22:10—23:15

Bad Leaders

Refuse Warnings
Jeremiah 36:1—40:16

Balaam

Good but Not Godly
Numbers 22:5—24:25

Boaz

Model of Kindness
Ruth 2:4–17

Caleb

Brave Heart
Joshua 14:10–12

Daniel

Sought Understanding
Daniel 8:15, 17, 27

David

Leader After God's Heart
1 Samuel 16:1–13
Partnership with Jonathan
1 Samuel 19:1—23:18
Heart of Great King
2 Samuel 4:5–12
Assumes Blame
1 Chronicles 21:1–17
Trusting in God
Psalm 40:1–17

Elijah

Standing Alone
1 Kings 17:1—18:40

Elisha

Prophet with Heart
2 Kings 4:1–44

Epaphroditus

Didn't Make a Name
Philippians 2:25–30

Esther

Protected Messianic Line
Esther 2:1–17

Eve

Learned from Failure
Genesis 4:1—5:5

Ezekiel

Zealous for the Lord
Ezekiel 6:7, 10, 13, 14

Ezra

Doing the Right Thing
Ezra 7:6–10

Felix

Power Trip
Acts 23:23—26:32

Festus

Power Trip
Acts 23:23—26:32

Hannah

Power of Persistence
1 Samuel 1:1–28

Hebrew Midwives

People of Influence
Exodus 1:15–20

Herod

Ego-Driven
Luke 23:6–12

Hezekiah

Art of Thanksgiving
Isaiah 38:9-20

Hosea

Cost of Leadership
Hosea 1:1—3:5

Isaiah

Love for the Unlovely
Isaiah 15:5; 16:9, 11

Jacob

Usable through Brokenness
Genesis 25:26—32:32

James

Leader of Men
James 2:24, 26

Jehoshaphat

Destructive Alliances
2 Chronicles 20:1-37

Jehu

Compromise
2 Kings 10:1-36

Jephthah

Makes Poor Choice
Judges 11:1-31

Jeremiah

Truth Without Compromise
Jeremiah 8:1-13

Hope in Calamity
Lamentations 3:1-66

Jesus

Commits to Speak Truth
Matthew 12:22—13:53
Perfect Man
Luke 7:1-17
God's Leader
John 3:1-21

Joab

Forgot Real Boss
2 Samuel 3:6-39

Job

Puzzled, Not Unbelieving
Job 13:20—14:22

Job's Friends

Misguided Companions
Job 24:25

John

Motivated by Love
1 John 3:16-18
Visionary Leader
Revelation 1:1, 2

John the Baptizer

Prepares the Way
Mark 1:1-8

Jonah

Prophet Who Ran *Down*
Jonah 1:1-17

Jonathan

Partnership with David
1 Samuel 19:1—23:18

Joshua

Obedience Sets Pace
Joshua 5:13-15

Josiah

Could Do No Wrong
2 Kings 22:1—23:30
Personal Repentance
2 Chronicles 34:3-33

Korah

Illegitimate Desire for More
Numbers 16:1-11

Mary

Chosen Vessel
Luke 1:26-38

Meshach

Courage Fueled by Faith
Daniel 3:16-18

Mordecai

Refusing Compromise
Esther 3:1-6

Moses

Unexpected Leader
Exodus 11:3
God's Problem Solver
Leviticus 15:1-33

Confidence of God's Presence
Deuteronomy 20:1-20

Naaman

New Lesson Learned
2 Kings 5:1-14

Naomi

Ruth Willingly Follows
Ruth 1:8-18

Nebuchadnezzar

Face-to-Face with God
Daniel 3:1-30

Nehemiah

Committed to God
Nehemiah 10:1-29

Noah

Man of Righteousness
Genesis 6:8-18

Paul

Most Influential
Acts 26:1-23
Genius with a Pen
Romans 1:1-7
Velvet-Covered Brick
1 Corinthians 1:1, 2
Follow-Up Friend
2 Corinthians 3:1-6
Navigator and Corrector
Galatians 4:8-20
Model for Equipping
Ephesians 3:1-7

Couldn't Be Stopped
Philippians 4:4–13
Different Kind of Leader
2 Thessalonians 2:13–17

Peter

Privileged to See
Mark 5:35–43
Most Improved
Acts 3:1–26
Learned from Failure
1 Peter 1:1–5

Pharaoh

Leading with Humility
Genesis 41:1–55
My Way or Highway
Exodus 10:1–29

Philip

Extraordinary Results
Acts 8:5–8

Pontius Pilate

Refused Responsibility
Mark 15:1–15

Priscilla

Trained More Leaders
Acts 18:24–28

Rahab

Unusual Woman of Faith
Joshua 2:1–21; 6:22–25

Ruth

Willingly Follows Naomi
Ruth 1:8–18

Samuel

Learned to Listen
1 Samuel 3:1–21

Sanballat

Great Distracter
Nehemiah 4:1–23; 6:1–19

Sarah

God Had Last Laugh
Genesis 18:9–15; 21:1–7

Saul

Served Own Interests
1 Samuel 15:1–26

Seventy Elders

Sharing the Burden
Numbers 11:11–17

Shadrach

Courage Fueled by Faith
Daniel 3:16–18

Sluggard

Worthless to the Kingdom
Proverbs 6:6, 9–11

Solomon

Forgot Principle of Wisdom
1 Kings 4:29–34